The Original

THOROUGHBRED TIMES
RACING
ALMANAC™
2003

THOROUGHBRED TIMES BOOKS

The Original

THOROUGHBRED TIMES

RACING ALMANAC™

2003
A Thoroughbred Times Book™

Editor in Chief:	Mark Simon
Almanac Editor:	Don Clippinger
Director of Research:	John Sparkman
Editors:	Amy Owens, Michele MacDonald, Tom Law, Myra Lewyn
Director Information Technology:	Alan Johnson
Editorial Research:	Bill Heller, John Harrell, Steve Schuelein, Victor Ryan, Liane Crossley, Frank Angst, Jeff Lowe
Statistical Research:	Gail Allensworth, Bonnie Holder, Melissa Humphrey, Aylett Melton, Billy Huntington Jr., Vicky Van Camp, Kathleen Donovan
Editorial Assistants:	Laura Tucker, Deanna Lyons, Katie Hostetter, Denise Steffanus
Production Director:	Jeanette Vance
Production Staff:	Betty Gee, Erica Ellerbusch, Tami Helmreich-Zigo, Laura Lacy, Nicole Elliott
Cover Design:	Tami Helmreich-Zigo
Cover Photo:	Enzina Mastrippolito

Thoroughbred Times Company Inc.

Publisher:	Norman Ridker
Vice President Editorial:	Mark Simon
Editorial Office:	496 Southland Dr., Lexington, KY 40503

THOROUGHBRED TIMES RACING ALMANAC welcomes comments and suggestions from readers.
Every communication is read by the editors and receives consideration and attention.
THOROUGHBRED TIMES RACING ALMANAC does not decide wagers.

THOROUGHBRED TIMES RACING ALMANAC™ and THOROUGHBRED TIMES ®
are registered trademarks of Thoroughbred Times Company Inc.
International Standard Serial Number (ISSN) 1540-5486
ISBN Number 1-889540-94-3

THOROUGHBRED TIMES RACING ALMANAC ™
A Thoroughbred Times Books™
An imprint of BowTie Press™
www.thoroughbredtimes.com
e-mail: letters@thoroughbredtimes.com

Foreword

An almanac, especially its first edition, is a huge undertaking, and publication of the *Thoroughbred Times Racing Almanac* is a credit to the staff and correspondents of THOROUGHBRED TIMES, the award-winning weekly publication based in Lexington, Kentucky. This project was launched in 2000 by Norman Ridker, publisher of Thoroughbred Times Co. Inc., who perceived the need for a new publication that provides essential information about Thoroughbred racing and breeding. Along with his vision, he brought more than 30 years of publishing experience, including the start-up of BowTie Press, the books division of his Fancy Publications.

Mark Simon, editor of THOROUGHBRED TIMES, took the vision and gave it a solid and comprehensive foundation. From the first days, he had a mental image of what the *Racing Almanac* would look like and what information and features its pages would contain. He exhibited faultless judgment and a keen eye for fact, figure, and typography.

John P. Sparkman, bloodstock/sales editor of THOROUGHBRED TIMES, made inestimable contributions to this work. His knowledge of the Thoroughbred industry's worldwide history is boundless, and he made significant contributions to all sections of this volume. In the breeding and statistical sections, his technological expertise helped to set the parameters for the information presented in these pages. Assisting him in turning concepts into tables and charts were members of the Research Department: Gail Allensworth, Melissa Humphrey, Billy Huntington, Bonnie Holder, Aylett Melton, and Vicky Van Camp. They worked through some of the thornier problems of developing statistical presentations that are truly unique in the Thoroughbred industry.

Also deserving special mention is Alan Johnson, THOROUGHBRED TIMES's information-technology guru who wrote all the programs to extract data. When the editorial staff was stumped or stumbling, he always came through with an elegant and workable solution to a problem.

Week in and week out, THOROUGHBRED TIMES depends upon its far-flung correspondents to help gather news and features for the weekly magazine, and they also made invaluable contributions to the *Racing Almanac*. Mary Simon provided a condensation of her Eclipse Award-winning history of the sport through the 19th and 20th centuries. She also is responsible for the biographies of all American leading sires, a unique resource found in no other publication. Bill Heller, another Eclipse Award winner, researched and wrote several sections of this publication, including the Belmont Stakes history and the section on how to handicap a race. John Harrell, a former THOROUGHBRED TIMES staff writer and now a Louisville-based correspondent, contributed his voluminous knowledge of the Kentucky Derby and, with Bill Heller, wrote most of the profiles of North American racetracks. Other correspondents contributing to the *Racing Almanac* were Steve Schuelein, based in California, and London-based Alan Smith.

The mountainous task of checking all the facts and figures in this volume fell to copy editor Laura Tucker and editorial assistants Deanna Lyons and Katie Hostetter. Putting together the mass of information into a comprehensible volume was THOROUGHBRED TIMES's Art Department and its director, Jeanette Vance, who was confronted with publishing problems never encountered in a weekly magazine. With hard work and perseverance, she solved them all. She was assisted by her staff, most notably Betty Gee, who served as the traffic cop for all the text and tables flowing into the *Racing Almanac*.

Also deserving mention is Amy Owens, managing editor, to whom fell the task of serving as the liaison between a telecommuting almanac editor and the Art Department.

Without all the Herculean efforts of so many people, this premiere edition of the *Thoroughbred Times Racing Almanac* never would have been possible.

Don Clippinger
Almanac Editor
Lexington, Kentucky
June 14, 2002

Table of Contents

General Index

STATE OF THE INDUSTRY
2001 in Review: Turmoil, Tragedy, Triumph
Mare Reproductive Loss Syndrome Top Story

The Thoroughbred industry sustained three devastating blows in 2001, two of which it shared with the nation. The National Bureau of Economic Research declared the United States economy in recession beginning in April 2001, ending a business expansion that lasted exactly ten years. The bloodstock markets, which had begun to shake as the technology stock bubble burst in 2000, headed sharply downward in '01 after an eight-year advance. Total revenues declined more than 20% at major bloodstock sales, and all segments posted declines in average prices, with broodmare prices falling more than 20% on sharply reduced volume. (See Auctions section.)

Along with all of America and much of the world, the Thoroughbred industry was stunned by the September 11 attacks in which terrorists hijacked commercial airliners and crashed them into the twin towers of the World Trade Center in lower Manhattan and the Pentagon near Washington, D.C. A fourth airliner crashed near Johnstown, Pennsylvania, when its passengers overpowered the terrorists, who were believed to be part of the al-Qaeda network. In all, more than 3,000 people died in the attacks. Both World Trade Center towers were destroyed, and the Pentagon sustained heavy damage. Keeneland stopped in the midst of its September sale for one day in memory of the victims, and Belmont Park on Long Island did not race for one week. Industry members donated generously to funds set up to benefit the families of the victims.

The commercial breeding industry in Kentucky also sustained a devastating and mystifying blow from late April until early July when hundreds of late-term fetuses were aborted or frail foals died shortly after birth, and thousands of mares suffered early-term abortions. The occurrence, for which no definitive cause was determined in 2001, became known as mare reproductive loss syndrome, or MRLS.

The abnormally high numbers of late-term and early-term abortions were first noticed in April and exploded in the first days of May. On Kentucky Derby (G1) day, May 5, vans carrying 73 stillborn and aborted foals were lined up for a quarter-mile at the University of Kentucky's Livestock Disease Diagnostic Center near Lexington. By the end of the breeding season, 516 Thoroughbred foals were lost in the 2001 crop due to MRLS, and 2,998 Thoroughbred mares lost their early-term fetuses. In addition to the early-term and late-term fetal losses, MRLS was associated with heart (pericarditis) and eye (uveitis) problems in living foals.

The outbreak became public knowledge on Derby weekend, and the University of Kentucky's Maxwell H. Gluck Equine Research Center soon focused its resources on the mysterious killer. In a detailed farm survey, University of Kentucky researchers found that the largest numbers of fetal deaths were found on farms that had black cherry trees around its pastures and heavy infestations of Eastern tent caterpillars. A working theory was developed that the caterpillars had transported a poison related to cyanide from the wild black cherry trees, but further studies linked the caterpillars themselves to early abortions.

Another theory was that unusual weather patterns had contributed to creating toxins in the pastures. March 2001 was unusually cold, while April was significantly warmer than normal and created an explosion of plant growth. A freeze occurred in the third week of April, followed by more abnormally warm weather in Central Kentucky. Higher than normal early fetal losses had occurred in 1980 and to a lesser extent in '81, and both years had weather conditions strikingly similar to those in 2001. But the losses in those years nowhere approached the devastation of 2001. Large numbers of waterfowl also were noted near the farms struck most heavily by MRLS, and another theory linked the deaths to poisonous hemlock at the edge of pastures.

The economic damage to Kentucky's commercial breeding industry was immediate, significant, and widespread. Moreover, the heaviest economic losses were not expected until 2002. Kentucky Governor Paul Patton commissioned a study of the economic loss, and the investigation was conducted on a fast-track schedule by Richard Thalheimer, Ph.D., and Robert G. Lawrence, Ph.D., of the University of Louisville's Department of Equine Business. Based on a survey of 1,024 breeders and breeding farm operations, they calculated the loss to the Thoroughbred industry at $300.5-million, with a statewide loss of $335.9-million for all breeds. Basing their calculations on Thoroughbred registrations in 1999, they found the loss from the 2001 crop to be 5.3%, and the reduction of the '02 Kentucky crop to be a devastating 30.5%.

While the loss to Kentucky's Thoroughbred industry was calculated at $109.4-million in 2001, the damage increased to $124.8-million in '02. The loss in 2003, when the lost fetuses presumably would have gone to auction as yearlings, was set at $51.1-million. But 2002 also would have been the year in which the yearlings generated cash from their sales to pay for the upkeep of

their dams as well as depreciation expenses.

With Kentucky's agricultural resources focused on solving the mystery, the state's lawmakers, the American Horse Council, and the National Thoroughbred Racing Association sought legislative relief for the state's breeders and breeding farms. Legislation passed by the United States Senate and House of Representatives authorized emergency, last-resort loans to breeders and farm owners who lost at least 30% of their potential offspring to MRLS. President Bush signed the legislation in November. As the 2002 breeding season progressed, researchers were no closer to finding the cause of MRLS, though they were increasingly sure the problem was caused by Eastern tent caterpillars. Farm owners took steps to prevent another outbreak by cutting down cherry trees near pastures and instituting other pasture-management measures, but they did so with no assurance that the mysterious killer was a one-time occurrence. Indeed, a significantly smaller outbreak of MRLS occurred in May of 2002.

Each year, THOROUGHBRED TIMES editors and writers collectively determine the leading stories. MRLS was 2001's top story, and here in order are the year's other major stories.

2. Point Given's championship season. The Thoroughbred Corp.'s homebred missed a juvenile championship by a nose to Macho Uno in the 2000 Breeders' Cup Juvenile (G1), but the hulking Thunder Gulch colt would not be denied in '01. He won everything but the one race that everyone watches, the Kentucky Derby (G1), finishing fifth, 11½ lengths behind winner Monarchos on a rock-hard Churchill Downs track, but he sailed through the remainder of the Triple Crown. He won the Preakness Stakes (G1) by an easy 2¼ lengths and then took the Belmont Stakes (G1) by 12¼ lengths, the seventh-largest winning margin in the race's 133-year history. He subsequently won the Haskell Invitational Handicap (G1) and Travers Stakes (G1), becoming the first horse ever to win four races worth $1-million or more in a single season, before a tendon injury forced his retirement. He was syndicated for approximately $50-million to stand at Three Chimneys Farm at Midway, Kentucky.

3. Medication in racing. Racing turned its attention to the persistently difficult question of medication for racehorses in 2001. The American Association of Equine Practitioners convened a two-day, closed-door medication summit in Tucson, Arizona, in December to present the widely varying opinions on the role of medication in the industry. Although the summit ended with calls for uniform rules across the nation, the regulatory process remained fragmented because state racing commissions determine the rules for their jurisdictions, and changes in some cases require legislative action.

4. Proposed sale of New York City Off-Track Betting Corp. A group led by Magna Entertainment Corp. on August 4 won the bidding battle for the nation's largest OTB system, with outgoing New York Mayor Rudolph Giuliani rebuffing the New York Racing Association, operator of the state's three major tracks. Before legislative hearings could be held, however, terrorists slammed commercial jetliners into the World Trade Center towers, postponing any action. NYRA Chairman Barry Schwartz asserted that the complicated Magna proposal undervalued New York OTB and vowed to fight any proposed sale in the Legislature.

5. Bobby Frankel's amazing year. The Brooklyn-born trainer finally won a Breeders' Cup race, the 2001 Sprint (G1) with Squirtle Squirt, after a long drought, but his '01 season was most notable for 17 other Grade 1 victories from New York to California, where he has been based since 1972. His top horses were fillies Flute and You, older males Skimming and Aptitude, and grass horses Timboroa (GB) and Senure. Elected to the Racing Hall of Fame in 1995, Frankel trains principally for Juddmonte Farms and was voted Eclipse Awards as outstanding trainer in 1993, 2000, and 2001.

6. Racing's contributions after terrorist attacks. The Thoroughbred industry as a whole stepped forward to assist the victims of the September 11 terrorist attacks. Two of the sport's most prominent Arab members, Sheikh Mohammed bin Rashid al Maktoum and Prince Ahmed bin Salman, condemned the attacks by Islamic radicals and contributed generously to relief efforts. Both chose not to attend the Breeders' Cup World Thoroughbred Championships at Belmont Park on October 27 because of international tensions. The National Thoroughbred Racing Association's NTRA Charities-New York Heroes Fund raised $5-million, including $2-million from Sheikh Mohammed, who pledged net earnings from Godolphin Stable's runners in the Breeders' Cup races. Breeder Harry T. Mangurian Jr. pledged $1-million, and Ernie Paragallo pledged $1-million to be donated over several years.

7. Tiznow's repeat victory in the Breeders' Cup Classic. Tiznow became the first horse ever to win the Breeders' Cup Classic (G1) twice with his courageous, second-effort victory over Sakhee, but the California-bred's back-to-back victories were by no means easy. After narrowly defeating Giant's Causeway in the 2000 Classic at Churchill Downs, Tiznow was voted Horse of the Year and champion three-year-old male. He appeared to be reaching his best form when he won the 2001 Santa Anita Handicap (G1) in

March, but a mysterious back injury kept him from the races until September. He finished third in his two starts before the Classic and sometimes refused to train, but he was all business at Belmont, coming back after Sakhee passed him in the stretch to win by a nose. Retired to stud at WinStar Farm in Kentucky, he was voted an Eclipse Award as champion older male.

8. Upheaval in the Jockeys' Guild. In a coup reportedly engineered by Racing Hall of Fame jockey Chris McCarron, Jockeys' Guild national manager John Giovanni was ousted in June, and within weeks Guild President Pat Day, past President Jerry Bailey, and Treasurer Anthony S. Black had resigned from the organization. With its Lexington staff fired, the Guild was operated by McCarron associate Wayne Gertmenian, an economics professor at Pepperdine University. In September, Giovanni filed suit seeking payment of his salary through the end of 2002 and damages for allegedly slanderous statements made by two jockeys.

9. Triumph of Seabiscuit. Laura Hillenbrand, author of the bestselling *Seabiscuit: An American Legend*, continued to pile up honors for her acclaimed story of the unlikely cham-pion. *Seabiscuit* ranked atop the New York *Times*'s nonfiction bestseller list for six weeks and remained on the list for seven months altogether. Universal Pictures has purchased the film rights, and *Seabiscuit* was British book-maker William Hill's selection as sports book of the year. Hillenbrand was selected as the Turf Publicists of America's 2001 Big Sport of Turfdom, and at year's end she was voted second Eclipse Award for her writings on the 1938 Horse of the Year.

10. Aidan O'Brien's record-setting year. Aidan O'Brien, youthful trainer of the powerful stable based at Ballydoyle Stud in Ireland, won a record 23 Group 1 or Grade 1 races in 2001. His only Grade 1 victory of the year came in the Breeders' Cup Juvenile with Johannesburg, who was voted champion juvenile male. At Ballydoyle, the trainer succeeded Vincent O'Brien, who is no relation. The younger O'Brien trains for Susan and John Magnier, the elder O'Brien's daughter and son-in-law, and Michael Tabor, a principal client of the Coolmore Stud operation headed by John Magnier. O'Brien trained Galileo (Ire) to victories in the Epsom Derby (Eng-G1) and the Irish Derby (Ire-G1).—*Don Clippinger*

Triple Crown Winner Seattle Slew Dies in 2002

When 1977 Triple Crown winner Seattle Slew died on May 7, 2002, Thoroughbred racing found itself without a living Triple Crown winner for the first time since June 11, 1919. From Sir Barton's victory in the 1919 Belmont until that day in 2002, Thoroughbred racing had always had a living Triple Crown winner.

In the minds of many, Seattle Slew ranked second only to Secretariat among American racing heroes in the 1970s, and he was the first ever to complete the sweep of the series undefeated. Bred in Kentucky by Lexington restaurateur Ben S. Castleman, he was purchased as a yearling for $17,500 by Washington lumberman Mickey Taylor and his wife, Karen, on the recommendation of veterinarian Jim Hill. Hill and his wife Sally later became partners in the son of Bold Reasoning out of My Charmer, by Poker, but he raced in the name of Karen Taylor.

Seattle Slew won all three of his starts at two, culminating with a stakes-record triumph in the Champagne Stakes (G1) that clinched the juvenile championship. He continued unbeaten with a series of scintillating victories through the Triple Crown, memorably barging his way to the front after starting slowly in the Kentucky Derby (G1). Beaten for the first time in an ill-conceived run in Hollywood Park's Swaps Stakes (G1) less than a month after his Belmont triumph, Seattle Slew was transferred from Billy Turner, who had trained him from the start of his career, to young horseman Doug Peterson that fall. Slew was voted Horse of the Year and champion three-year-old male of 1977.

After surviving a near-fatal bout with colitis the following winter, he was better than ever at four, trouncing 1978 Triple Crown winner Affirmed in the Marlboro Cup Handicap (G1), winning the Woodward Stakes (G1), and adding to his legend in defeat with a courageous nose second to Exceller in the Jockey Club Gold Cup (G1).

Syndicated for a $12-million value to stand at Spendthrift Farm, Slew made the best possible start at stud, siring champions Slew o' Gold and Landaluce in his first crop. He moved to Three Chimneys Farm in 1985 and subsequent crops included champions A.P. Indy, Swale, Surfside, Capote, and Digression. At his death, Seattle Slew had sired 102 stakes winners, 56 group or graded winners, and earners of $75,926,135.

Leading sire in 1984, he led the broodmare sire list in 1995-'96.

After surviving spinal-fusion surgery in 2000 and 2002, Seattle Slew died peacefully at age 28 on the 25th anniversary of his Derby win and was buried at Hill 'n' Dale Farms near Lexington.—*John P. Sparkman*

Chronology 2001

January 6—Tampa Bay and its horsemen agree on a contract extending through the 2002-'03 race meet.

January 7—Racing Hall of Fame jockey Russell Baze receives National Turf Writers Association's Isaac Murphy Award for the highest winning percentage, 27.2%, in 2000. Baze, the only person to receive the award, repeats in 2001.

January 9—Bernice L. Givens Sykes defaults on more than $700,000 of purchases at the Keeneland November and Fasig-Tipton Midlantic December sales.

January 10—Breeders' Cup Ltd. reported an eighth consecutive record for foal nominations, 15,760 foals of 2000, to the series. The nominations generated a record $7,880,000.

January 10—Tracy Hebert, who has a long history of drug and alcohol violations, agrees not to ride in Kentucky for five years but may seek a license elsewhere.

January 10—J. Terrence Lanni, Thoroughbred owner and chairman of MGM Mirage, awarded Lifetime Achievement Award at American Gaming Summit.

January 11—Los Angeles County coroner rules that jockey Chris Antley's death on December 2, 2000, was due to an overdose of multiple drugs.

January 12—Kent Desormeaux receives ESPY Award.

January 13—Keeneland January horses of all ages sale concludes with 1,207 horses sold for $39,657,700, a drop of 34.9% from 2000.

January 14—Kent Desormeaux rides 4,000th winner of his career at Santa Anita Park.

January 14—Frank Stronach hosts a controversial forum on horse racing's future for industry leaders at Gulfstream Park.

January 16—Jockey Felix Pinero is acquitted on charges that he fixed races at Penn National Race Course.

January 17—Magna Entertainment Corp.'s racetracks rejoin National Thoroughbred Racing Association, and Magna Chairman Frank Stronach agrees to join the NTRA board if his demands for stakeholder representation are honored.

January 22—Marjorie Clayton Cordero, trainer and former jockey married to Racing Hall of Fame member Angel Cordero Jr., is killed when struck by a hit-and-run driver in Greenvale, New York.

January 24—Leonard C. Hale resigns as vice president of racing of the Maryland Jockey Club.

January 30—Jim McKay receives Eclipse Award of Merit for his five decades of television racing coverage. John Hettinger receives Special Eclipse Award for his efforts involving racehorse retirement programs. Laffit Pincay Jr. honored with Big Sport of Turfdom Award.

January 30—Tiznow is crowned as 2000 Horse of the Year at annual Eclipse Awards dinner.

January 30—The NTRA board is expanded from 11 to 15 members, with increased representation for racetracks, as demanded by Frank Stronach.

January 31—Illinois Gaming Board rejects a planned riverboat casino in the Chicago suburb of Rosemont, citing a lack of full disclosure by its investors and concerns over organized crime ties.

February 2—Martin Pedroza scores his 2,000th career victory at Santa Anita Park.

February 2—Cliff Berry wins 1,000th race aboard Lightspeedtoendor at Remington Park.

February 4—Victor Espinoza rides his 1,000th career winner at Santa Anita.

February 12—Leading sire Seattle Slew returns to breeding shed after successful neck surgery.

February 14—Ten Mid-Atlantic tracks and Hawthorne Race Course vote not to rejoin NTRA. Earlier, Fair Grounds, Yavapai Downs, and Sunland Park had rejoined the organization.

February 19—Adalberto Lopez notches his 2,000th career victory aboard Aswhatilldois (Ire) in the California Oaks Handicap at Golden Gate Fields.

February 20—Foot-and-mouth disease outbreak spreads in England to neighboring countries and closes racetracks in England and Ireland.

February 21—J. T. Lundy begins serving a 4½-year prison sentence for fraud, bribery, and conspiracy related to the 1991 collapse of Calumet Farm when he was its president.

February 27—Average declines 4% to $207,250 at the Fasig-Tipton Calder sale of two-year-olds in training.

March 1—Racing Hall of Fame jockey Pat Day inducted into Colorado Sports Hall of Fame.

March 5—William S. Farish, owner of Lane's End near Versailles, Kentucky, is nominated to be United States ambassador to Great Britain and Northern Ireland.

March 7—Dean Kutz, who twice returned to riding after serious illnesses, is named as the recipient of 52nd George Woolf Memorial Jockey Award. Off-course betting tax in Great Britain abolished.

March 11—Average price declines 21.1% at Barretts March two-year-olds in training sale.

March 16—Terry Thompson wins 1,000th career race aboard Really Sumptin at Oaklawn Park.

March 19—Jay Hickey, president of the American Horse Council, is honored as Kentucky HBPA's Man of the Year.

March 19—Louisiana Downs is granted gaming license but extended approval process delays opening of slots at Bossier City track into 2003.

March 20-21—Total receipts at Ocala Breeders' Sales Co.'s two-year-olds in training sale decline 13.4%.

March 24—Captain Steve wins Dubai World Cup (UAE-G1).

March 30—Maryland Jockey Club, operator of Pimlico Race Course and Laurel Park, rejoins National Thoroughbred Racing Association.

April 5—*Seabiscuit: An American Legend* reaches number one on the New York *Times* bestseller list for nonfiction and remains in the top ten for 26 weeks.

April 6—Magna Entertainment Corp. completes purchase of Ladbroke Racing Corp. account-wagering system based at the Meadows in Western Pennsylvania and an 18.3% interest in the Racing Network.

April 9—Body of John Tammaro Jr., trainer of champion Deputy Minister, is found in his car in a South Florida canal. He had been missing since February.

April 10—Manor Downs in Texas cancels inaugural Thoroughbred meeting.

April 16—Robert E. Brennan, former head of Garden State Park, is convicted of bankruptcy fraud and subsequently is sentenced to nine years in prison.

April 17—Total receipts at Keeneland April two-year-olds in training sale decline 19.5%.

April 22—John Velazquez wins 2,000th race of his career aboard Tom's Thunder at Aqueduct.

April 23—Racing Hall of Fame jockey Angel Cordero Jr. inducted in Nassau County, NY, Hall of Fame.

April 23-26—Ocala Breeders' Sales Co.'s April two-year-olds in training sale's receipts increase 4.2%.

April 26—Delta Downs in Vinton, Louisiana, sold to

Boyd Gaming Group for $130-million.

April 28—Chris McCarron wins 7,000th race of his career aboard Spinelessjellyfish.

April 29—Dubai Millennium, winner of the 2000 Dubai World Cup, dies of grass sickness in England.

April 30—Ramon Pena, Lazaro Vives, Luis Morales, and Andres Reyes are sentenced for race fixing at Penn National Race Course.

May 1—Holy Bull, Earlie Fires, Richard Mandella, Paseana (Arg), and Maskette are announced as National Museum of Racing Hall of Fame inductees.

May 3—Garden State Park, rebuilt in 1985 at a cost of $180-million, closes; site is to become a commercial and business development.

May 5—Monarchos wins Kentucky Derby (G1) in 1:59.97, second-fastest Derby ever behind Secretariat's 1:59⅖. Effects of mare reproductive loss syndrome (MLRS) crest in Central Kentucky.

May 7—Racing Hall of Fame trainer D. Wayne Lukas wins 4,000th race in his Thoroughbred career with Added Spice at Delaware Park.

May 19—Point Given wins Preakness Stakes (G1).

May 21—Television Games Network and Youbet.com Inc. agree to cooperate on marketing and promotion.

May 22—Hialeah closes and will not reopen in 2002.

May 25—Mike Luzzi named recipient of Mike Venezia Memorial Award.

May 25—Thoroughbred owner and breeder John W. Kluge donates his 7,300-acre Morven Farm to University of Virginia.

May 26—Yavapai Downs, a new racetrack that replaces Prescott Downs, opens in Arizona.

May 30—Indiana Racing Commission votes 4-0 to grant license to Indianapolis Downs, which is scheduled to open by September 2002.

May 31—Pat Day rides the 8,000th winner in his career aboard Camden Park, becoming only the third rider in history to reach that milestone, after Bill Shoemaker and Laffit Pincay Jr.

June 1—Lasix, the diuretic furosemide, is renamed Salix for veterinary applications.

June 9—Chris Loseth named as recipient of Avelino Gomez Memorial Award.

June 9—Michael Rowland wins 3,500th victory of his career aboard Providence Pete at Thistledown.

June 9—Point Given wins the Belmont Stakes by a dominant 12¼ lengths and becomes the 45th horse to win two legs of the Triple Crown.

June 11—Jockey Club registers first foal using DNA typing, a Florida-bred filly by Eskimo out of the Homebuilder mare Home Together. Gemstar-TV Guide International Inc., owner of the Television Games Network, reaches a 20-year agreement with cable provider Adelphia Communications Corp. for carrying TVG's programming on Adelphia's system.

June 16—John Giovanni is ousted as national manager of the Jockeys' Guild as Matrix Capital Associates Inc. is hired to manage Guild operations.

June 19—Bill to reduce pari-mutuel takeout unanimously passes New York Legislature.

June 22—Canadian Hall of Fame inductees are Awesome Again, Runaway Groom, Larry Attard, and Jack Hardy. Jerry Bailey wins the NTRA All-Star Championship at Lone Star Park.

June 22—Television Games Network to take over operation of wagering hub in Oregon from NTRA Services, beginning on July 1.

June 23—THOROUGHBRED TIMES wins General Excellence award for tabloid/newspaper publications at the American Horse Publication's annual awards.

June 26—Breeders' Cup changes the name of its championship event to the Breeders' Cup World Thoroughbred Championships.

June 28—New Jersey Senate and Assembly approves legislation that will permit off-track and telephone account wagering.

July 1—Galileo (Ire) wins Irish Derby (Ire-G1), becoming only the 14th horse in history to win both the Irish and Epsom Derbys.

July 8—Takemi Sasaki, all-time leading jockey in Japan by wins, retires.

July 15—Former racetrack executive Lonny Powell becomes president of the Association of Racing Commissioners International, succeeding Tony Chamblin.

July 16-17—With smallest catalog ever, average price at Keeneland July sale of selected yearlings increases 14.4% to record $710,247.

July 18-19—Fasig-Tipton July yearling sale posts increase of 25.7% in average to $97,671, highest since 1984, but total receipts drop 11.6%.

July 19—Four New York Racing Association mutuel clerks are indicted on money-laundering charges. California Horse Racing Board approves advertising on silks, jockeys' attire, and track saddlecloths.

July 24—Carl Pollard elected chairman of Churchill Downs Inc., succeeding William S. Farish, who becomes United States ambassador to Great Britain and Northern Ireland.

July 30—Racing Network, based at Philadelphia Park, ceases operations after three years. Satellite-based network attracted only 2,500 subscribers.

July 31—Sunline named Australian Horse of the Year for the second consecutive year.

August 1—Padua Stables removes its horses from trainer D. Wayne Lukas.

August 2—Magna Entertainment Corp.-led group is awarded right to buy a majority interest in the New York City Off-Track Betting Corp. for up to $260-million and annual payments based on wagering levels. Hearings are postponed into 2002.

August 7-9—Total receipts at Fasig-Tipton Saratoga sale of selected yearlings soar 49% to $62.4-million, and average price surges 26% to record $385,259.

August 8—Tomey Jean Swan elected acting chairman of the Jockeys' Guild.

August 11—Remi Bellocq, a former racetrack marketing executive, becomes executive director of the National Horsemen's Benevolent and Protective Association.

August 12—Trainer Donnie Von Hemel posts his 100th stakes win.

August 13—California Governor Gray Davis signs legislation authorizing telephone-account wagering.

August 19—Jockey Isiah Sala, 23, is killed in a race at Marquis Downs in Saskatoon, Saskatchewan.

August 20—New Jersey Racing Commission approves sale of Atlantic City Race Course to Greenwood Racing for $13-million.

August 24—California Horse Racing Board medication committee approves regulatory amendment to legalize threshold levels of clenbuterol, a bronchodilator that resulted in several positive findings after its use was legalized in the late 1990s.

August 31—Point Given is found to have a strained tendon in his left front leg and is retired. He will stand at Three Chimneys Farm for a $125,000 fee.

September 1—Tim Moccasin sets North American record of 14 consecutive wins at Marquis Downs.

September 2—Horace Allyn "Jimmy" Jones, Racing Hall of Fame trainer of Citation, dies.

September 7—Arlington Park is tentatively confirmed

as the site for the Breeders' Cup World Thoroughbred Championships on October 26, 2002. Planned renovations prevent Santa Anita from hosting the event in 2002, but it is to be the host track in '03. Churchill Downs is announced as the 2004 site, and Lone Star Park in Texas will be the host track in '05.

September 11—Terrorists crash airliners into World Trade Center towers in lower Manhattan and Pentagon outside Washington, D.C., killing more than 3,000 people. As a result of the attack, second day of Keeneland September sale of yearlings is postponed by one day. Donations to relief fund created by Keeneland Association total more than $5.7-million.

September 13—Churchill Downs seeks state assistance for a $127-million renovation to track, but Kentucky Governor Paul Patton cautions that economic downturn and its effect on state revenues might limit assistance. Churchill plans to bear the bulk of the cost, approximately $100-million.

September 14—In-depth study associates high concentrations of cherry trees and Eastern tent caterpillars with mare reproductive loss syndrome.

September 15—Russell Baze wins his 7,500th race aboard Valid Double at Bay Meadows Race Course.

September 19—Racing resumes at Belmont Park for the first time since September 11 terrorist attacks.

September 20—John Giovanni sues Jockeys' Guild, contending he was wrongfully discharged.

September 21—Emirates Airlines ends sponsorship of the World Series Thoroughbred Championships.

September 23—Keeneland September yearling sale concludes with total receipts down 12.9% to $254.2-million, but average remains virtually unchanged at $87,803.

October 1—Sheikh Mohammed bin Rashid al Maktoum completes purchase of Jonabell Farm and plans to turn Lexington property into a station for Darley stallions.

October 1—Arizona Department of Racing orders Jerry Simms to sell Turf Paradise, citing the majority owner's alleged ties to organized crime and his involvement in a California bribery scandal.

October 5—Keeneland Race Course's 17-date fall meet opens with experimental reduction in takeout on exotic wagers to 16% from 19%.

October 6—Tax-free, off-course betting returns to Great Britain for the first time since 1966.

October 8—Ramon Dominguez has 1,000th career victory aboard Carnie's Secret at Pimlico.

October 9—NTRA creates "Great State Challenge," which will feature six races worth a total of $1.5-million. The event will be held at Sam Houston Race Park in December 2002.

October 10—Surgical sponges are found in the nostrils of three horses at Santa Anita Park.

October 12—Scott Stevens rides his 3,000th winner, Lynne Louise, at Turf Paradise.

October 13—Slow Down becomes 100th stakes winner for Seattle Slew.

October 13—Brazilian jockey Jorge Ricardo becomes fourth rider in racing history to reach 8,000 wins aboard Thoroughbreds.

October 17—James E. "Ted" Bassett III steps down as chairman of Keeneland Association, ending a 33-year career at the Lexington institution.

October 18—Unbridled, champion and leading sire, is euthanized after two surgeries to repair an intestinal problem.

October 27—Tiznow wins the Breeders' Cup Classic

(G1) for the second straight year as the Breeders' Cup World Thoroughbred Championships are held at Belmont Park in New York.

October 29—Nureyev, champion and leading sire, dies.

October 30—Boyd Gaming Corp. receives Louisiana Gaming Control Board approval for gaming license to operate slot machines at Delta Downs Racetrack and Casino.

October 30—Ground is broken by Magna Entertainment Corp. officials for Palm Meadows, a training track near Boynton Beach, Florida.

October 31—New York Governor George Pataki signs into law legislation authorizing slots at Aqueduct, Finger Lakes, and three Standardbred tracks.

November 4, 8—Fasig-Tipton Kentucky mixed sale shows 42.4% decline in total receipts.

November 5-15—Keeneland November breeding stock sale's total receipts fall 41% to $179.6-million as prices decline across the board.

November 7—Massachusetts Legislature approves racing legislation intended to increase purses at Suffolk Downs. Later in month, Governor Jane Swift signs bill expected to raise purses by $3-million a year.

November 13—Ballydoyle-based trainer Aidan O'Brien sets a world record with his 23rd Group 1 or Grade 1 stakes victory of 2001.

November 14—Fantastic Light, winner of the Breeders' Cup Turf (G1), named Cartier European Horse of the Year.

November 15—Farm bill that includes a relief package for breeders hard hit by mare reproductive loss syndrome is approved by the U.S. Senate and subsequently signed by President George W. Bush.

November 16—Tiznow retired from racing and will stand the 2002 season at WinStar Farm near Versailles, Kentucky, for a $30,000 fee.

November 26—Laura Hillenbrand is selected as recipient of William Hill Sports Book of the Year Award for her *Seabiscuit: An American Legend*.

November 29—Louisiana Downs to be sold to a group of seven investors headed by lawyer Jim Davis.

December 2—Ramon Dominguez scored 400th victory of 2001 aboard Native Two Stepper at Laurel.

December 4—Agreement reached at the University of Arizona Race Track Industry Program's Symposium to seek uniform national medication policies.

December 6—Trainer Robert Camac and his wife, Maryann, are shot to death at their New Jersey farm; Camac's stepson is charged with murder.

December 9—Gerard Melancon scores his 2,000th career victory aboard Racing for Riches at Fair Grounds.

December 10—Pam Blatz-Murff, Breeders' Cup Ltd.'s senior VP of operations, is first woman to receive Derby Award for Services to International Racing

December 14—Jockey Patrick Valenzuela, out of racing for nearly two years because of drug violations, is granted a one-year conditional license by the California Horse Racing Board.

December 14—Boyd Gaming clears way to complete purchase of Delta Downs for $130.1-million by making $5.1-million payment to former owner.

December 20—Eugene Melnyk agrees to purchase Mockingbird Farm from Harry T. Mangurian Jr

December 22—Arnold Ruiz, 33, dies of injuries sustained in a three-horse spill at Beulah Park in Grove City, Ohio. He is the 144th North American jockey to die in a race-related accident since 1940.

2001 Obituaries

Paul T. Adwell, 86, trainer of 1976 Preakness Stakes (G1) winner Elocutionist and a veteran on the Chicago-Hot Springs circuit; on October 22 in Hot Springs, Arkansas.

Doug Atkins, 76, founder of public relations firm Horsemen's International, whose clients included jockeys Bill Shoemaker, Eddie Arcaro, owner Liz (Whitney) Tippett, trainer Charlie Whittingham, and Northern California racetracks Bay Meadows and Golden Gate Fields; chief operating officer of the Horsemen's Benevolent and Protective Association from 1967 until his retirement in '87; campaigned Monarm, winner of the 1976 Lady Morvich Handicap at Bay Meadows; on November 29 in Solana Beach, California.

Joe Attard, 68, one of four training brothers with Tino, Sid, and Larry; veteran of the Ontario racing circuit since 1976; son Steve is a trainer at Woodbine racecourse, daughter Josie DePaulo is an assistant trainer to her husband, Mike DePaulo; campaigned several stakes winners, including My Imperial Slew and Parisianprospector; on November 20 in Toronto.

Les Berwick, 79, founded Delta Downs in Vinton, Louisiana, in 1973 and served as track president until '97; on April 26 in Vinton.

Jerome "Jerry" Brody, 78, New York restaurateur and owner of Gallagher's Farm near Ghent, New York; with wife, Marlene, campaigned homebreds 1986 German champion three-year-old Allez Milord and Grade 3 winner Adorable Micol; owner of Gallagher's Steak House and the Oyster Bar in Grand Central Station; president of Restaurant Associates, which created The Four Seasons; on May 15 in New York.

Heywood Hale Broun, 83, whose colorful commentaries on the Kentucky Derby enlivened CBS television broadcasts of the American classic; on September 5 in Kingston, New York.

Gary W. Burke, 61, chairman of Thoroughbred Owners of California; longtime horse owner and a founding member of TOC; raced 1996 Morvich Handicap winner Comininalittlehot; on August 7 in Del Mar, California.

Tom Caldwell, 72, longtime Keeneland auctioneer; succeeded George Swinebroad as director of auctions in 1975; auctioned the most-expensive horse ever, Seattle Dancer, for $13.1-million in 1985; on February 23 in Eagle Point, Oregon.

Robert Camac, 60, saddled more than 1,800 winners in his 40-year training career; longtime trainer for Arthur Appleton, for whom he trained multiple stakes winners Jolie's Halo and Fire Plug; on December 6 of gunshot wounds with his wife, Maryann, 55, at the couple's Camac Thoroughbred Horse Farm in Oldmans Township, New Jersey.

Lord Harry Carnarvon, 77, racing manager for Queen Elizabeth II; managing director of Highclere Stud; served as chairman of the Flat Pattern committee and chairman of the National Stud's stallions advisory committee; owner of Group 1 winner Lyric Fantasy (Ire), highweighted filly at two on the 1992 English Free Handicap; on September 11 of a heart attack in England.

William Francis "Jelly" Caulder, 86, member of the International Horseshoeing Hall of Fame who shod horses at Calumet Farm, Spendthrift Farm, and Hamburg Place during his 45 years as a farrier; on August 15 in Lexington.

George "Jay" Chadwick, 89, former legal counsel for the National Horsemen's Benevolent and Protective Association; inducted into HBPA Hall of Fame in 1976; on July 20 in Adamstown, Maryland.

Melville Church III, 62, longtime Virginia breeder; operated North Cliff Farm in Rixeyville; bred Peacefully, dam of 1982 Kentucky Derby (G1) winner Gato Del Sol, and 1988 French champion two-year-old filly Tersa; former vice president of National Steeplechase Association; on January 1 near Tappahannock, Virginia, after saving a beloved hunting dog from an icy pond.

Dale Harrison Clark, 53, owner of Starview Farm near Ocala; on March 25 in Jacksonville, Florida.

John Clark, 48, jockey at Thistledown for more than two decades; won more than 900 races with purses in excess of $5-million; died in May after suffering a heart attack in jockeys' room shower at the Cleveland-area track.

Jim Coleman, 89, veteran Canadian sportswriter and former member of the Ontario Racing Commission; inducted into Canada's Sports Hall of Fame in 1985; Canadian horse racing's 1984 Man of the Year; on January 14 of heart failure in Canada.

Marjorie Cordero, 41, jockey's agent, former jockey and trainer; wife of Racing Hall of Fame jockey Angel Cordero Jr.; rode 71 winners from 907 mounts from 1982 to '85; saddled 42 winners from 400 starters from 1985 to '99; on January 22 of injuries suffered in a hit-and-run accident in Greenvale, New York.

Jack Diamond, 91, instrumental in forming the British Columbia Jockey Club in 1961; inducted into Canadian Thoroughbred Racing Hall of Fame in 1977; Austrian immigrant purchased butcher shops to build his Pacific Meats chain; bought first horse in 1936 and became a co-owner of Exhibition Park in 1961; former chancellor of Simon Frasier University; on March 25 in Vancouver, British Columbia.

Dale Evans, 88, who with husband, Roy Rogers, bred and owned Thoroughbreds, many with names similar to famed Palomino trick horse Trigger, including homebred 1975 El Encino Handicap winner Triggairo, Run Trigger Run, and Lady Trigger; on February 6 in Apple Valley, California.

Dave Feldman, 85, Turf writer and handicapper, track announcer at Sportman's Park for 32 years; served as president of the Illinois Horsemen's and Benevolent and Protective Association; co-owned and trained Old Frankfort, winner of 1978 Stars and Stripes Handicap (G2) at Arlington Park; on April 30 in Chicago.

James Fitzsimmons, 71, Canadian jockey won the Queen's Plate Stakes with Canadian champion three-year-old filly Flaming Page in 1962 and Jammed Lovely in 1967; inducted into the Canadian Horse Racing Hall of Fame; on March 18 in Calgary, Alberta.

Bobby "Cotton" Gallimore, 62, jockey whose mounts included 1964 and '65 champion handicap mare Old Hat; on December 21 in Hot Springs, Arkansas.

George Getz, 69, veteran Illinois trainer who saddled Flag Officer to win the 1977 Illinois Derby (G3); in late May.

Theodore "Ted" Gregory, 78, known for his love of gambling and his Cincinnati-area ribs restaurants; dubbed the "Ribs King" by clients at his internationally known Montgomery Inn; was a well-known figure at Turfway Park and River Downs; campaigned both Thoroughbreds and Standardbreds; on December 2 in suburban Cincinnati.

Robert Griffin, 50, director of Goffs auction company in Ireland; chairman of Goffs France; graduates of his Loughbrown Stud on the Curragh included Leggera (Ire), dual highweight on 1998 and '99 European Free Handicap; Millenary, winner of 2000 St. Leger (Eng-G1); and Preseli (Ire), highweighted filly on 1999 and 2000 Irish Free Handicap; on March 6 in Ireland.

Larry Hammer, 63, who served on the Oklahoma Racing Commission for six years; in July while vacationing in Saskatchewan.

Mark Hardin, 70, owned and operated Rockburn and Meadowville Farms near Middleburg, Virginia; son of Newstead Farm proprietor Taylor Hardin; operated Newstead as one of three trustees until the Newstead Farm Trust dispersal in 1985 by Fasig-Tipton, which established several world records, including broodmare Miss Oceana for $7-million, a $2.5-million weanling by Seattle Slew eventually named Magic of Life, who became a Group 1 winner in England; and $4-million for the barren broodmare Larida; on September 5 near Omaha, Nebraska.

Harold Harrison, 81, longtime breeder who donated the proceeds from the sale of $3.9-million Kris S. colt who topped the 1999 Keeneland September yearling sale to build a church in his native Georgia; on April 18 in Atlanta.

Dr. Lyle Hartrick, 82, a Michigan veterinarian; three-term president of the Michigan United Thoroughbred Breeders and Owners Association; on August 29 in Troy, Michigan.

Peter Hayes, 52, son of late trainer Colin Hayes and one of Australia's leading trainers; trainer of 13 Group 1 winners, including 1999 Victoria Derby (Aus-G1) winner Blackfriars; on March 12 in a plane crash in Victoria.

Bonnie Heath, 85, prominent Florida horseman who co-owned 1956 Kentucky Derby winner Needles; from the 1950s to the late '90s, owned and operated Bonnie Heath Farm, where dual classic winner and champion Silver Charm, Horse of the Year Holy Bull, Grade 1 winner Tsunami Slew, and Grade 2 winner Candi's Gold were raised; was instrumental in founding of Florida Breeders' Sales Co., which merged with the Ocala Breeders' Sales Co. in 1984; on November 4 in Ocala.

Bart Heller, 63, one of Northern California's leading Thoroughbred owners and breeders; raced multiple graded stakes winner and millionaire Dixie Dot Com in a partnership that included his wife, Ronelle; on August 10 in Stanford, California.

Chris Hummel, 38, a regular rider on the Northern California circuit who rode Minutes Away to victory in the 1985 Bay Meadows Derby (G3); of pancreatic cancer on April 2 in Burbank, California.

Ethel Jacobs, 91, widow of Racing Hall of Fame trainer Hirsch Jacobs; owned majority of horses trained by her husband during the 1930s and '40s; in 1936, '37,

and '43 ranked as nation's leading owner; campaigned Racing Hall of Fame members Stymie, Searching, and Affectionately; son John Jacobs trained classic winners Personality and High Echelon for her; raced a handful of horses through Harbor View Farm, owned by her daughter, Patrice, and Louis Wolfson, who bred and campaigned two-time Horse of the Year and 1978 Triple Crown winner Affirmed; on October 9 in Miami Beach, Florida.

Job Dean Jessop, 74, retired jockey who led the nation by victories in 1945 and who finished third in the Kentucky Derby with Hampden in 1946 and Ruhe in 1951; on January 29 in Texas.

Jeff Jacobs, 40, trainer of stakes winners Sister Act, Humble Eight, and Hot Jaws; on February 11 in Hot Springs, Arkansas.

Horace A. "Jimmy" Jones, 94, Racing Hall of Fame trainer who, along with his father, Ben, trained for Calumet Farm during its glory days in the 1940s and '50s; won the Kentucky Derby with Iron Liege in 1957 and Tim Tam in '58; saddled Citation to win the 1948 Preakness and Belmont Stakes; also trained Calumet stars Armed, Coaltown, Bewitch, and Two Lea before retiring in 1964 to become director of racing at Monmouth Park, a position he held until 1976; inducted into the Racing Hall of Fame in 1959; on September 2 in Maryville, Missouri.

Harry Katz, 82, owner of Mabar Farm near Ocala and a shareholder of the Ocala Breeders' Sales Co.; with Norman Casse bred multiple stakes winner Isitingood; raced stakes winner Hold Your Tricks; on January 2 in Chicago.

Howard Koch, 84, Hollywood producer and director whose horses included graded stakes winner Telly's Pop, whom he co-owned with actor Telly Savalas; served on Hollywood Park board of directors until 1999; co-owned Bel-Air Productions; produced "The Odd Couple" and "The Manchurian Candidate," among others; on February 16 in California.

Cawood Ledford, 75, broadcaster and race announcer who was a three-time Eclipse Award winner for local television achievement; known throughout Kentucky as the "Voice of the Wildcats," for his long association with the University of Kentucky men's basketball team; member of the National Basketball Hall of Fame; on September 5 in Lexington.

John J. Lenzini Sr., 80, veteran East Coast trainer for six decades and father of the late classic-winning trainer John Lenzini Jr.; best horses were 1997 Maryland Million Sprint Handicap winner Aberfoyle and stakes winner Admiral's Image; on June 30 in Baltimore.

Jane duPont Lunger, 87, prominent owner and breeder who campaigned champion Go for Wand and other top-class runners under the Christiana Stables banner, including multiple Grade 1 winner Broom Dance (who produced graded stakes winner and eventual record-setting freshman sire End Sweep), Tingle Stone, Linkage, and Croquis; on September 18 in Wilmington, Delaware.

Thomas Jefferson "Tommy" Luther, 92, played role in formation of Jockeys' Guild; in 1928 won on Crystal Pennant in $92,700 Coffroth Handicap at Tijuana, Mexico; also won races aboard Time Supply, Lycedes, Spooky, Top Row, and War Relic; on January 27 in Saratoga Springs, New York.

Pat Lynch, 84, former New York Racing Association vice president of public relations; stationed in Europe in World War II, was awarded Silver Star, Bronze Star, and three Purple Hearts; received battlefield commission as second lieutenant; also a longtime sports columnist for Hearst Newspapers, on January 25 in New York.

Sam Maple, 48, retired jockey, younger brother of retired New York rider Eddie Maple; rode top runners Smarten, Jatski, Heatherten, and Joachim; was the regular rider of Smart Angle during her 1979 champion two-year-old filly season; on November 13 in Wilmore, Kentucky.

Ted Martin, 65, former general manager of Portland Meadows and Playfair Race Course; on June 19 near Spokane, Washington.

Edward J. McGrath, 75, insurance executive whose E. J. McGrath Insurance Co. covered some of Thoroughbred racing's most prominent horses, including Affirmed and Genuine Risk; served on the Kentucky Racing Commission; on December 1 in Louisville.

Paddy McGrath, 74, chairman of Goffs Bloodstock sales, the Irish Racing Board, Irish Hospital Sweepstakes, and Leopardstown racecourse; former master of Ballymaglassan Stud in County Meath; also served in Irish Senate. Older brothers Joe and Seamus also were heavily involved in Irish racing; in October in Ireland.

James Sheldon "Shelly" Meredith Jr., 67, owner of multiple stakes winner Hawkster; had been in medical technology business in California; on April 17 in Lexington.

Jim Powell, 50, a Phoenix native who led the Turf Paradise jockey standings eight times and rode for years on the Chicago circuit; on March 13 in Phoenix.

J. R. Preston, veteran owner-breeder who along with younger brothers Art and Jack campaigned champion and 1998 Belmont Stakes (G1) winner Victory Gallop; Groovy, champion sprinter in 1987; and two-time Breeders' Cup Mile (G1) winner Da Hoss; operated Prestonwood Farm in Versailles, Kentucky, before its sale to Bill Casner and Kenny Troutt in January 2000; on March 21 in San Angelo, Texas.

Eileen Barrett Quigley, 48, a former racetrack official and wife of former racetrack executive Robert J. Quigley; served as executive secretary at the Meadowlands where she helped establish horsemen relations programs; also held executive positions at Garden State Park and Retama Park; on August 9 in Marlton, New Jersey.

Robert Resoff, 85, Thoroughbred owner and Emerald Downs co-owner; headed seafood processing company American Freezerships; his Snipledo won the 1990 Longacres Mile Handicap (G3); on December 23 in Seattle.

Ben Rochelle, 91, a well-known vaudevillian in the 1940s; in partnership with Carl Grinstead campaigned 1986 champion three-year-old colt and Preakness Stakes (G1) winner Snow Chief; also raced 1987 Breeders' Cup Sprint (G1) winner Very Subtle, graded stakes winner Sari's Heroine, and stakes winner Rare Starlet; on May 11 in Beverly Hills, California.

Graham Rock, 56, founder of the British racing newspaper *Racing Post*; campaigned steeplechaser Pasternak, who earned $267,533; jockey's agent for Michael Roberts in 1992 when he ranked as England's champion rider; on October 13 in England.

Van Rose, 81, owner of Van Mar Farms near Galt, California, and breeder of multiple Grade 1 winner Southern Truce; on February 24 in California.

Louis Roussel Jr., 95, father of Louis Roussel III, who campaigned 1988 champion and dual classic winner Risen Star with Ronnie Lamarque; a former streetcar conductor who became president of Fair Grounds in New Orleans in the 1980s, a position he held until the track was sold in 1990; on October 20 in New Orleans.

Lewis Rudin, 74, New York Racing Association trustee and a real estate executive in New York; was instrumental in keeping the United States Open tennis tournament in New York; on September 20 in New York.

Fahd bin Salman al Saud, 46, leading international owner and brother of Ahmed bin Salman of The Thoroughbred Corp.; nephew of Saudi Arabian King Saud; campaigned 1998 champion grass female Fiji (GB) in the name of his Newgate Stud; also raced Generous, winner of the 1991 Epsom Derby (Eng-G1) and Irish Derby (Ire-G1); 1999 Epsom Oaks (Eng-G1) winner Ramruma; and Group 1 winners Bint Pasha, Ibn Bey (GB), and Zoman; on July 24 of a heart attack in Riyadh, Saudi Arabia.

Bob Savage, 70, talented big-band musician in 1930s and '40s who turned his attention to Thoroughbred racing and became track announcer at Calder Race Course and Hialeah Park; on May 8 in Chicago.

Arthur Seeligson Jr., 80, previously part-owner of Hialeah Park; bred and raced 1975 Belmont Stakes (G1) winner Avatar; served on National Museum of Racing Hall of Fame board and was co-chairperson of campaign to legalize pari-mutuel wagering in Texas in 1967; on April 17.

Bob Slater, 90, handicapper for the Miami *Herald* for 30 years, founded the Florida Turf Writers Association in 1958; on November 2 in Miami.

George Sloan, 62, champion amateur steeplechase jockey; founder of the International Steeplechasing Group and its Sport of Kings Challenge, a series for novice steeplechasers on both sides of the Atlantic; instrumental in creating the steeplechase triple crown, a series for novices that coincides with flat racing's Triple Crown; on October 11 of an accidental gunshot wound on his Panorama Farm in Franklin, Tennessee.

Bruce Stearns, 58, former publicity director at Rockingham Park who served as executive director of the New Jersey Sire Stakes program since 1985; on July 27 of a heart attack at his vacation home in Wolfesboro, New Hampshire.

Robert F. Stewart, 65, owner of leading Montana sire Black Mackee; on January 26 at his Skylark Ranch near Arlee, Montana.

Chuck Swain, 81, former jockey and racing official at Oaklawn Park; rode Modest Lad in 1943 Kentucky Derby; clerk of scales at Oaklawn from 1980 until his retirement in 2000; on July 2 in Hot Springs, Arkansas.

Raymond Tackett, 97, who with son Paul bred a number of prominent horses, including Belle de Jour, dam of 1985 Kentucky Derby (G1) winner Spend a Buck; on April 25 in Stamping Ground, Kentucky.

John Tammaro, 75, trainer of several Canadian champions, including Deputy Minister, 1981 Canadian Horse of the Year and North American two-year-old

champion of 1981; on February 25 when his car went into a canal in Miramar, Florida.

William Garrard Talbot II, 91, owner of Mt. Lebanon Farm near Paris, Kentucky; bred several stakes winners, including Joanne's Joy, with his wife, Elizabeth Hinton Talbot; on January 5 in Lexington.

Billy Vessels, 70, breeder who served on the Florida Pari-Mutuel Commission from 1976 to '83 and became its executive director; president of the National Association of State Racing Commissions in 1984 and director of the Florida Division of Pari-Mutuel Wagering from 1987-'89; won Heisman Award as a University of Oklahoma halfback in 1952; member of the College Football Hall of Fame; on November 17 in South Florida.

Glenn Webster, 43, lead Churchill Downs outrider; on May 6 of heart attack after Kentucky Oaks (G1) in Louisville.

Truman C. Welling, 92, founding member of the Pennsylvania Horse Breeders Association who served as a director and treasurer; bred Dam I'm Gorgeous, 1998 Pennsylvania-bred juvenile filly champion, and $417,585-earner B Flat Major, the 1997 Pennsylvania

Futurity winner; on December 18 at his Scarlett Thicket Farm near Kennett Square, Pennsylvania.

Jerry West, 70, former jockey; leading rider at Churchill Downs 1949 spring meeting; father of Dallas *Morning News* Turf writer Gary West; on April 13 in New Orleans.

Daniel Wildenstein, 84, one of Europe's most influential owners-breeders; campaigned 1983 Horse of the Year and French champion older mare All Along (Fr), 1974 French Horse of the Year Allez France, 1977 French champion three-year-old filly Madelia (Fr), 1985 French champion older horse Sagace (Fr), 1976 English Horse of the Year Pawneese, 1992 European highweight Pistolet Bleu (Ire), 1997 French highweight Peintre Celebre, and 1993 Breeders' Cup Classic (G1) winner Arcangues; on October 24 in Paris.

David Yunich, 84, New York Racing Association trustee emeritus, former vice chairman of R. H. Macy and Co.; served as chairman of the Metropolitan Transit Authority; was a professional baseball player for the Cincinnati Reds farm team; on September 19 in Scarsdale, New York.

2001 Horse Deaths

Aferd, 1976 b. h., Hoist the Flag—Secret Retreat, by Clandestine. Unraced. Sire of at least 22 stakes winners, including 1998 Oaklawn H. (G1) winner Precocity; leading sire in North Dakota 1991-2001; pensioned in 1999; died on April 12 at Verdine Boschee Farm near Wishek, North Dakota.

Affirmed, 1975 ch. h., Exclusive Native—Won't Tell You, by Crafty Admiral. 29-22-5-1, $2,393,818. 1978, '79 Horse of the Year, 1977 champion two-year-old male, won 1978 Triple Crown; best known for his legendary duels with Alydar; his Belmont S. (G1) victory is considered one of the best races of all time; sire of at least nine champions, including 1992-'93 champion grass mare Flawlessly, 2000 Canadian Horse of the Year Quiet Resolve, 1993 Canadian Horse of the Year Peteski; died on January 12 at Jonabell Farm near Lexington due to infirmities of old age.

Alcovy, 1990 dk. b. or br. m., Salutely—Forever Cup, by Raise a Cup. 29-14-3-7, $897,590. Won 1996 Sixty Sails H. (G3), etc.; died on May 21.

Ali'lbito'reality, 1991 b. h., Proper Reality—Saratoga Fleet, by Sir Gaylord. 62-7-5-6, $231,421. Won 1996 Lago Mar H., etc.; died on November 7.

Ali-Royal, 1993 b. h., Royal Academy—Alidiva, by Chief Singer. 16-7-3-3, $328,409. Won 1997 Sussex S. (Eng-G1), etc.; highweighted on 1997 English Free Handicap, 7 to 9½ furlongs; sire of at least two stakes winners, including 2002 Gold Sovereign S. winner Fracas; euthanized on January 19 in an equine hospital in Randwick, Australia, due to the onset of chronic laminitis.

Altibr, 1995 ch. h., Diesis (GB)—Love's Reward (Ire), by Nonoalco. 16-5-5-1, $758,650. Won 2000 Shadwell Keeneland Turf Mile S. (G2), 1999 Dubai Duty Free (UAE-G3), etc.; euthanized on March 13 after developing laminitis nearly one month after shattering a bone in his right hind leg while at a California veterinary clinic where he had been sent for minor knee surgery.

Alydar's Promise, 1983 ch. m., Alydar—Summertime

Promise, by Nijinsky II. Unplaced in one start; dam of at least four winners, including 1991 Volante H. (G3) winner General Meeting; died on October 24.

American Dance, 1985 b. m., Seattle Slew—Expressive Dance, by Riva Ridge. 3-1-1-1, $25,380. Dam of at least two stakes winners, including 1992 Jersey Derby (G2) winner American Chance; died on September 14.

Anne Campbell, 1973 b. m., Never Bend—Repercussion, by *Tatan. 14-3-3-1, $37,386. Broodmare of the Year in 1999; dam of Grade 1 winners Desert Wine and Menifee; won 1976 Old Hat S.; died on May 10 of heart failure at Arthur Hancock III's Stone Farm near Paris, Kentucky.

Asher, 1997 gr. or ro. m., Mountain Cat—Magic Snow, by Silent Dignity. 27-7-3-5, $392,243. Won 2001 Gardenia H. (G3), etc.; euthanized on December 11 at Rood and Riddle Equine Hospital in Lexington after suffering from colic.

Auto Dial, 1988 ch. m., Phone Trick—Here and Gone, by Royal Ski. 32-10-6-2, $383,220. Won 1992 Queen's H. (G3); dam of Grade 3 winner Connected; died on April 8.

Banshee Breeze, 1995 b. m., Unbridled—Banshee Winds, by Known Fact. 18-10-5-2, $2,784,798. 1998 champion three-year-old filly; won 1998 Coaching Club American Oaks (G1), etc.; euthanized on April 11 at Hagyard-Davidson-McGee Equine Clinic in Lexington due to foaling complications.

Barbakoa, 1989 b. m., Ribot Blanquiar—Si Si Ine, by No No Billy. 60-15-19-9. 1992 champion three-year-old filly in Puerto Rico; died on November 3.

Barberstown, 1980 dk. b. or br. h., Gummo—Available Miss, by Bolinas Boy. 12-6-0-2, $336,570. Won 1985 Del Mar Invitational H. (G2), third in 1983 Belmont Stakes (G1); sire of at least two stakes winners, including 1999 Hutcheson S. (G2) winner Bet Me Best; died on September 5.

Batonnier, 1975 b. h., His Majesty—Mira Femme, by *Dumpty Humpty. 18-7-5-2, $232,105. Won 1978 Illi-

nois Derby (G3); sire of at least 20 stakes winners, including 1996 Santa Anita Derby (G1) winner Cavonnier, 1987 Remsen S. (G1) winner Batty; died on July 15 at Ellen Jackson's Victory Rose Thoroughbreds near Vacaville, California, of a heart attack.

Bet On Red, 1997 ch. g., Prospectors Gamble—Red Mistress, by Deputy Minister. 21-4-3-5, $318,290. Won 2000 California Derby.

Bevo, 1997 ch. h., Prospectors Gamble—Wheatly Way, by Wheatly Hall. 13-6-2-1, $410,328. Won 1999 Futurity S. (G1), etc.; died on July 1 at New Jersey Equine Clinic in Clarksburg, New Jersey, after developing laminitis from a quarter crack.

Big Jag, 1993 dk. b. or br. g., Kleven—In Hopes, by Affirmed. 30-13-5-3, $1,800,329. Won 1999 Palos Verdes H. (G2), 2000 Dubai Golden Shaheen, etc.; euthanized in September in Dubai because of complications of laminitis nearly seven months after suffering from a severely fractured sesamoid in his left front leg on February 28 at Nad al Sheba, where he was preparing to defend his Dubai Golden Shaheen victory.

Bivvy, 1984 ch. m., Sassafras (Fr)—Campfire Gal, by Angle Light. 70-16-8-18. Dam of at least three winners, including 1998 Coney Island S. winner Coed Ruth E.; first horse to ship to and gallop at Birmingham Turf Club prior to its 1987 inaugural season; died on January 18.

Blissful Union, 1987 dk. b. or br. m., John's Choice—Alta's Lady, by Traffic Mark. 43-12-12-5, $473,410. Won 1990 Southland S., etc.; dam of stakes winner Blissful Kiss; died on March 27.

Blue Ensign, 1977 gr. h., Hoist the Flag—Laughter, by Bold Ruler. 28-9-5-2, $243,065. Won 1980 Woodlawn S. (G3); sire of at least 22 stakes winners, including 1994 Panamanian champion two-year-old male El Andarin, 1990 Saratoga Special S. (G2) winner To Freedom, etc.; euthanized on June 24 at a Marion County, Florida, equine clinic after undergoing surgery to remove a noncancerous, fatty tumor from an area near his small intestines.

Bo Knows to Pass, 1990 dk. b. or br. m., South Pass—Little Bo Fleet, by Fleet Allard. 42-14-7-11, $176,433. Won 1995 Peony S. at Hoosier Park, where she set a track record for six furlongs in 1:10; died on June 29.

Bold Badgett, 1985 b. h., Damascus—Anne Campbell, by Never Bend. Unraced. Sire of at least 80 winners, including 1996 Courtship S. winner Takes Two to Mango; died on August 26 of complications from knee surgery.

Bold Laddie, 1973 b. h., Boldnesian—Santiago Lassie, by Vertex. 22-8-5-0, $125,052. Won 1976 Hibiscus S., etc.; sire of at least 33 stakes winners, including 1996 Juvenile Breeders' Cup S. winner Knave; euthanized on August 7 at Salishan Meadows Farm near Surrey, British Columbia, due to infirmities of old age.

Bonne Ile (GB), 1981 dk. b. or br. m., Ile de Bourbon—Good Lass, by Reform. 24-7-5-6, $534,241. Won 1986 Yellow Ribbon Invitational S. (G1), etc.; dam of 2000 champion steeplechaser All Gong (GB); died on May 31.

Bonnie Scot, 1998 dk. b. or br. g., Lord Avie—Crystal Woods, by Woodman. 9-4-1-1, $136,997. Won 2001 John Battaglia Memorial S.; euthanized on April 21 after suffering fatal breakdown in Coolmore Lexington S. (G2).

Boys Nite Out, 1978 b. h., Cutlass—Baqueta, by Bolinas Boy. 41-14-10-5, $310,719. Won 1982 and '83 Pel-

leteri H.; sire of at least seven stakes winners, including 1997 Cajun S. winner Boys Revenge; died on March 2.

Cad, 1978 b. h., Timeless Moment—Verna M, by Three Bagger. 39-10-7-6, $242,903. Won 1983 Fayette H. (G3), etc.; sire of at least 20 winners, including stakes-placed Hudson Hornet.

Canadian Factor, 1980 dk. b. or br. h., Sinister Purpose—Tico's Donna, by Bosun. 31-8-5-6, $657,975. 1984 Canadian champion older male horse; set Aqueduct track record in winning 1984 Excelsior H. (G2); sire of at least one stakes winner, 2000 Saskatchewan Derby victor Max Factor; died on July 1.

Catherine's Bet, 1975 ch. m., *Grey Dawn II—Betsy Be Good, by *Pretendre. 35-12-5-7, $247,512. Won 1979 Firenze H. (G2); dam of 1989 Canadian champion three-year-old filly Blushing Katy; died on February 15.

Chain Store, 1972 b. m., Nodouble—General Store, by To Market. 36-8-3-0, $83,612. Won 1977 Rare Treat H.; dam of 1985 Irish One Thousand Guineas (Ire-G1) winner Al Bahathri, 1983 Diana H. (G2) winner Geraldine's Store, etc.; died on May 23.

Charming Lassie, 1987 dk. b. or br. m., Seattle Slew—Lassie Dear, by Buckpasser. 1-1-0-0, $16,500. Dam of 2000 champion older male and 1999 Belmont S. (G1) winner Lemon Drop Kid; died on March 12 at Lane's End near Versailles, Kentucky, of foaling complications.

Chris Evert, 1971 ch. m., Swoon's Son—Miss Carmie, by T. V. Lark. 15-10-2-2, $679,475. 1974 champion three-year-old filly, won 1974 filly triple crown, etc.; inducted into Racing Hall of Fame in 1988; dam of stakes winners Six Crowns and Wimbledon Star; grandam of 1984 champion two-year-old male Chief's Crown; euthanized on January 8 at Three Chimneys Farm near Midway, Kentucky, due to infirmities of old age.

Classy Cathy, 1983 dk. b. or br. m., Private Account—Trestle, by Tom Rolfe. 15-7-1-2, $537,970. Won 1986 Alabama S. (G1), Ashland S. (G1), etc.; dam of 1993 Prince of Wales's S. (Eng-G2) winner Placerville.; died on June 13 at Claiborne Farm near Paris, Kentucky, of complications from colic.

Colonial Waters, 1985 dk. b. or br. m., Pleasant Colony—Water Cress, by Hail to Reason. 32-6-12-3, $1,112,847. Won John A. Morris H. (G1), etc.; dam of 1998 Next Move H. (G3) winner Panama Canal; died on June 8.

Con Game, 1974 dk. b. or br. m., Buckpasser—Broadway, by Hasty Road. 12-2-3-2, $24,080. Dam of 1988 Super Derby (G1) winner Seeking the Gold, 1988 Remsen S. (G1) winner Fast Play, 1987 Jamaica H. (G3) winner Stacked Pack; euthanized on March 30 at Claiborne Farm near Paris, Kentucky, due to infirmities of old age.

Coral Dance (Fr), 1978 b. m., Green Dancer—Carvinia, by *Diatome. 13-3-1-3, $76,822. Dam of 2001 Irish Two Thousand Guineas (Ire-G1) winner Black Minnaloushe, 1995 Two Thousand Guineas (Eng-G1) winner Pennekamp, 1989 Charles H. Strub S. (G1) winner Nasr El Arab; died on December 14.

Crimson Saint, 1969 ch. m., Crimson Satan—Bolero Rose, by Bolero. 11-7-0-2. $91,770. Won 1973 Hollywood Express H. (G3), etc.; dam of 1990 Breeders' Cup Mile (G1) winner Royal Academy, 1978 Hollywood Juvenile Championship S. (G2) winner Terlingua, 1985 Bay Shore S. (G2) winner Pancho Villa;

grandam of leading sire Storm Cat; euthanized on May 12 at Offutt-Cole Farm near Midway, Kentucky, due to infirmities of old age.

Dahlia, 1970 ch. m., *Vaguely Noble—Charming Alibi, by Honeys Alibi. 48-15-3-7, $1,489,105. 1974 and '75 Horse of the Year in England, 1973 champion three-year-old in Ireland and England, 1974 champion grass horse in U.S., 1974 and '75 champion older mare in England, 1973 and '74 King George VI and Queen Elizabeth S. (Eng-G1), 1973 Washington D.C. International (G1), etc.; dam of 1986 San Juan Capistrano Invitational H. (G1) winner Dahar, 1987 Hollywood Invitational H. (G1) winner Rivlia, 1990 San Juan Capistrano Invitational H. (G1) winner Delegant, 1994 Flower Bowl Invitational H. (G1) winner Dahlia's Dreamer, 1991 Grand Prix d'Evry (Fr-G2) winner Wajd, 1993 Jersey Derby (G2) winner Landaff; euthanized on April 6 at Diamond A Farm in Versailles, Kentucky, due to infirmities of old age.

Darshaan, 1981 br. h., Shirley Heights—Delsey, by Abdos. 8-5-0-1, $226,979. 1984 French champion three-year-old; 1999 English leading broodmare sire; sire of at least 71 stakes winners, including 1993 Horse of the Year and champion grass male Kotashaan (Fr); euthanized on May 22 at Troytown Hospital in County Kildare, Ireland, of a ruptured aorta.

De La Rose, 1978 b. m., Nijinsky II—Rosetta Stone, by Round Table. 26-11-6-0, $544,647. 1981 champion grass female; Hollywood Derby (G1), etc.; dam of 1986 Young America S. (G1) winner Conquistarose, 1989 Golden Rod S. (G3) winner De La Devil; euthanized on March 1 at Calumet Farm in Lexington due to infirmities of old age.

Demons Begone, 1984 b. h., Elocutionist—Rowdy Angel, by Halo. 14-7-2-1, $609,944. Won 1987 Arkansas Derby (G1), etc.; sire of at least 14 stakes winners, including 1997 Venezuelan champion stayer Demons Cloak (Ven), 1995 National Museum of Racing Hall of Fame S. (G2) winner Flitch; died on July 4 at El Dorado Farms near Enumclaw, Washington, of a ruptured aorta.

Detroit (Fr), 1977 dk. b. or br. m., Riverman—Derna, by Sunny Boy. 13-8-0-1, $494,202. 1980 French Horse of the Year and champion three-year-old filly, won 1980 Prix de l'Arc de Triomphe (Fr-G1), etc.; dam of 1994 Prix de l'Arc de Triomphe winner Carnegie (Ire), 1987 St. Simon S. (Eng-G3) winner Lake Erie, 1990 Prix Guillaume d'Ornano (Fr-G2) winner Antisaar; died on May 20 at Swettenham Stud in England of foaling complications.

Din's Dancer, 1985 dk. b. or br. h., Sovereign Dancer—Din's Times, by Olden Times. 50-11-13-5, $537,979. Won 1990 Fast Hilarious H., etc.; sire of at least four stakes winners, including 2000 Eddie Read H. (G1) winner Ladies Din; euthanized on October 12 at Gary and Merlene Howard's Hideaway Farm near San Jacinto, California, after suffering a fractured pastern bone in his left front leg in a paddock accident.

Doc's Leader, 1986 ch. h., Mr. Leader—With Patience, by Nodouble. 38-9-8-5, $494,325. Won 1989 West Virginia Derby, etc.; sire of at least seven stakes winners, including 1999 Saranac H. (G3) winner Phi Beta Doc; euthanized on October 14 at Alfred Nuckols Jr.'s Hurstland Farm near Midway, Kentucky, of complications from a neurological disorder.

Do It Again Dan, 1982 b. h., Mr. Leader—Bimbo Sue, by Our Michael. 30-8-5-9, $383,044. Won 1986 New

Hampshire Sweepstakes H. (G3), etc.; sire of at least five stakes winners, including 2000 Queen of the Green H. winner Sunnie Do It; died on May 4.

Drouilly (Fr), 1976 ch. h., Mill Reef—Provide for Me, by Gun Shot. 40-11-5-7, $423,980. Won 1983 Pomona Invitational H.; sire of at least nine stakes winners, including 1989 Joe Gottstein Futurity winner T. D. Passer; euthanized on March 17 at Harris Farms near Coalinga, California, due to infirmities of old age.

Dubai Millennium, 1996 b. h., Seeking the Gold—Colorado Dancer (Ire), by Shareef Dancer. 10-9-0-0, $4,470,404. Cartier European 2000 Horse of the Year; highweighted on 1999 and 2000 English Free Handicaps at 7 to 9½ furlongs and 9½ to 11 furlongs; won 2000 Dubai World Cup (UAE-G1), etc.; died on April 29 at Newmarket, England, of grass sickness after undergoing three surgeries in one week for colic.

Eleven Stitches, 1977 b. h., Windy Sands—O'L Clementine, by My Host. 16-8-3-0, $684,500. Won 1981 Hollywood Gold Cup (G1), etc.; sire of at least six stakes winners, including 1987 British Columbia Oaks winner Stitch an a Half; died on January 23.

Empire Glory, 1981 dk. b. or br. h., Nijinsky II—Spearfish, by Fleet Nasrullah. 6-2-2-2, $35,420. Set a world record when purchased by Robert Sangster for $4.25-million at the 1982 Keeneland July selected yearling sale; won 1984 Royal Whip S. (Ire-G3); sire of at least four stakes winners, including 1991 California Breeders' Champion S. winner Simple Surprise; died on August 1 after rupturing a major artery above his kidneys during a pasture breeding at the University of California at Davis.

Endearingly, 1988 b. m., Lyphard—So Endearing, by Raise a Native. Unraced. Dam of 1999 Jaipur H. (G3) winner Notoriety; died on April 10.

Exemplary Leader, 1986 dk. b. or br. h., Vigors—Paradigmatic, by Aristocratic. 50-12-5-11, $541,243. Won 1993 San Simeon H. (G3), etc.; sire of at least two stakes winners, including 2001 Hill Rise H. winner Jamaican Rum; died on March 9 at Ron and Vicky Kellum's V R Ranch near Pilot Point, Texas, of a heart attack.

First Albert, 1977 b. h., *Tudor Grey—Sumba, by Groton. 21-5-6-3, $443,076. Won 1980 Swaps S. (G1), etc.; sire of at least five stakes winners, including 1988 Barksdale H. winner Albert's First.

First Patriot, 1984 b. h., Salutely—Social Duty, by Road At Sea. 47-6-8-8, $298,165. Won 1988 Louisville H., etc.; sire of at least 23 winners; died on November 26.

Flag Waver, 1979, b. m., Hoist the Flag—Bcboppcr, by Tom Fool. 14-4-2-1, $102,051. Won 1983 Rampart H.; dam of eight winners, including Grade 1-placed Bunting; died on May 10.

Flying Heat, 1982, dk. b. or br. m., Private Account—Turn Down the Heat, by Key to the Mint. 34-9-11-8, $372,842. Won 1986 Rumson H., etc.; dam of 2001 Personal Ensign H. (G1) winner Pompeii, 2002 Stymie H. (G3) winner Ground Storm, and 1997 Arlington Matron H. (G3) winner Omi; died on April 1.

Formulate, 1976, ch. m., Reform—Tabulator, by Never Say Die. 7-4-0-0, $44,877. 1978 champion two-year-old filly in England; dam of at least 11 winners, including 1998 Epsom Oaks (Eng-G1) winner Shahtoush and 1990 Epsom Oaks runner-up Game Plan; died on January 24

Forty One Carats, 1996 ch. h., Tactical Advantage—Aly's Jewel, by Alysheba. 22-7-3-1, $828,843. Won

1999 Pegasus H. (G2), etc.; set track record at Calder Race Course, six furlongs in 1:08.95, on October 7, 2000; died on July 2.

Frosty Tail, 1980 ch. m., It's Freezing—Me Challenge, by Challenge All, 28-11-6-4, $361,078. Won 1982 Santa Fe Futurity, etc; dam of at least eight winners; died on March 8.

Fuzzbuster, 1976 ch. h., No Robbery—Clear Road, by Hasty Road. 23-5-5-4, $106,787. Won 1978 Sanford S. (G2); sire of at least three stakes winners, including 1988 Columbus Classic H. winner Fuzzy Jack; died on October 8.

Gdynia, 1978 ch. m., Sir Ivor—Classicist, by *Princequillo. 22-2-3-4, $48,600; dam of 1986 Belmont S. (G1) winner Danzig Connection and 1989 Dwyer S. (G2) winner Roi Danzig.

Ghaza, 1982 b. h., Damascus—Queen's Bid, by Hoist the Flag. 13-1-1-1, $18,145. Sire of at least eight winners, including 2001 Canada S. victor Roll the Stage.

Globe, 1977 dk. b. or br. h., Secretariat—Hippodamia, by Hail to Reason. 20-6-5-3, $212,533. Won 1982 Excelsior H. (G2), etc.; sire of at least five stakes winners, including 1988 Pippin S. winner Bestofbothworlds; died on June 11.

Gray Slewpy, 1988 gr. h., Slewpy—Beau Gris, by *Grey Dawn II. 15-8-3-0, $399,197. Won 1993 Potrero Grande H. (G3), etc.; sire of at least two stakes winners, including 1999 Khaled S. winner Del Mar Gray; euthanized on March 29 at J Z Stock Farm near Temecula, California, from complications of colic.

***Green Valley II**, 1967 dk. b. or br. m.,*Val de Loir— Sly Pola, by Spy Song. Unraced. Dam of 13 winners, including 1975 Poule d'Essai des Poulains (Fr-G1) (French Two Thousand Guineas) winner and 1991 French leading sire Green Dancer and 1998 Golden Gate H. (G2) winner Val Danseur; died on July 22 at Haras de Saint-Leonard in France.

Grosvenor, 1979 b. h., *Sir Tristram—My Tricia, by Hermes. 18-7-6-5 in Australia. Won 1982 Sires' Produce S. (Aus-G1), etc.; sire of at least 50 stakes winners, including 1996 New Zealand champion three-year-old filly Alacrity; died on June 26.

***Habitony**, 1974 b. h., Habitat—Courteous Lady, by *Gallant Man. 12-5-4-2, $304,190. Won 1977 Santa Anita Derby (G1), etc.; sire of at least 27 stakes winners, including 1992 Santa Anita H. (G1) winner and $5.7-million-earner Best Pal and 2000 Frank J. De Francis Memorial Dash S. (G1) winner Richter Scale; died on January 30 at John and Betty Mabee's Golden Eagle Farm near Ramona, California, due to infirmities of old age.

Hoedown's Day, 1978 b. h., Bargain Day—Miss Hoedown, by Dance Lesson. 40-11-10-5, $336,929. Set world record, 1¹⁄₁₆ miles in 1:38⅘, in winning 1983 San Joaquin Invitational H. at Bay Meadows Race Course; sire of at least ten stakes winners, including 1994 Tiburon H. winner B. Hoedown; died on November 3.

Hurricane Bertie, 1995 ch. m., Storm Boot—Clever Bertie, by Timeless Native. 35-14-7-5, $940,041. Won 1998 Prioress S. (G2), etc.; died in early January of complications of laminitis.

I Am the Game, 1982 b. h., Lord Gaylord—Kitchen Window, by Dead Ahead. 24-5-5-1, $369,051. Won 1986 Roseben H. (G3), etc.; sire of at least two stakes winners, including 1996 Park Heights S. winner Oops I Am; died on April 1.

Illusioned, 1998 ch. c., Woodman—Undeniably, by In

Reality. 9-5-2-1, $335,726. Won 2001 Ack Ack H. (G3) in a track record 1:28.63 for 7½ furlongs at Churchill Downs; euthanized on November 24 after sustaining a fractured sesamoid and other injuries in the Cigar Mile H. (G1) at Aqueduct.

Intrepid Lady, 1970 dk. b. or br. m., Bold Ruler—Stepping Stone, by *Princequillo. 3-1-1-1, $8,654. Dam of eight winners, including 1993 European champion three-year-old filly Intrepidity (GB), 1980 Pretty Polly S. (Ire-G2) winner Calandra, and 1987 Irish highweighted older mare Acushla (Ire); died on January 4.

Jadana (Ire), 1979 b. m., Pharly—Janina, by *Match II. 6-3-1-1, $19,680. Won division of 1982 Marigold S.; dam of at least six winners, including 1988 Gulfstream Park H. (G1) winner and sire Jade Hunter; died on October 18.

Jewell Ridge, 1985 b. m., Melyno (Ire)—Say What You Mean, by Judger. 5-1-0-0, $2,830. Dam of at least five winners, including 1996 champion older female Jewel Princess; died on August 1 at Franks Farm Southland Division in Ocala of heart failure.

Joachim, 1973 dk. b. or br. h., Proud Clarion—Whirl for Joy, by Johns Joy. 68-9-6-8, $274,160. Won 1976 Secretariat S. (G2), etc.; sire of at least three stakes winners, including 1989 Michigan Breeders Governor's Cup H. winner Run the Light.

Kapalua Butterfly, 1981 ch. m., Stage Door Johnny— Aces Swinging, by Native Dancer. 30-6-4-2, $177,929. Won 1985 Modesty S. (G3), etc.; dam of at least four winners, including 1991 Martha Washington H. (G3) winner Polish Holiday; died on July 6.

Kenmare, 1975 gr. h., Kalamoun—Belle of Ireland, by Milesian. 11-6-0-1, $146,100. Won 1978 Prix Jacques le Marois (Fr-G1), etc.; leading sire in France twice; sire of at least 64 stakes winners, including 1988 French champion two-year-old Kendor, 1991 Hungarian champion three-year-old Jeremy, and 1998 South African champion three-year-old filly Joie de Grise; died on February 7 at Arrowfield Stud near Scone, New South Wales, Australia, of a heart attack.

Kerosene, 1986 b. h., Devil's Bag—Issues n' Answers, by Jacinto. 4-2-1-0, $41,600. Second in 1989 Everglades S. (G3); sire of at least five stakes winners, including 1999 Dominican Republic champion imported three-year-old filly Palas Atenea and 1997 Dixieland S. winner Power Flame; euthanized on November 23 at Spendthrift Farm near Lexington after developing encephalitis that caused paralysis.

License Fee, 1995 ch. m., Black Tie Affair (Ire)—Star Deputy, by Deputy Minister. 43-16-7-6, $1,200,416. Won 2001 Sixty Sails H. (G3), etc.; euthanized on June 30 after fracturing her right front leg in the Molly Pitcher Breeders' Cup H. (G2) at Monmouth Park.

Lost Code, 1984 dk. b. or br. h., Codex—Loss Or Gain, by Ack Ack. 27-15-5-2, $2,085,396. Won 1988 Oaklawn H. (G1), etc.; sire of at least 47 stakes winners, including 1999 Canadian champion older female Magic Code and 2002 Santa Monica H. (G1) winner Kalookan Queen; died on February 10 at Legacy Farm near Bluemont, Virginia, of an apparent heart attack.

Loudrangle, 1974 ch. m., Quadrangle—Lady Known as Lou, by Nearctic. 22-9-2-2, $105,804. Won 1978 Mountain Laurel H., etc.; 1986 Canadian Broodmare of the Year; dam of seven winners, including 1986 Canadian Horse of the Year Ruling Angel and 1988 Canadian champion three-year-old filly Tilt My Halo; died on December 11 at Sam-Son Farm in Ontario.

Lucky Lady Lauren, 1987 b. m., Carnivalay—War Exchange, by Wise Exchange. 32-10-4-2, $307,673. Won 1991 Arlington Matron H. (G3), etc.; dam of at least three winners; euthanized on March 29 at Hickstead Farm near Ocala after sustaining injuries in a severe thunderstorm and tornado.

Make Change, 1985 ch. m., Roberto—Equal Change, by Arts and Letters. 23-5-6-5, $506,338. Won 1988 Miss Liberty S.; dam of at least four winners, including 1998 Prix Isola Bella winner Time Changes.

Marfa, 1980 gr. h., Foolish Pleasure—Gray Matter, by Stratmat. 15-3-4-1, $407,944. Won 1983 Santa Anita Derby (G1), etc.; sire of at least 24 stakes winners, including 1991 Santa Anita H. (G1) winner Farma Way, 1989 Santa Anita Oaks (G1) winner Imaginary Lady, 1999 Dominican Republic champion imported two-year-old male Evil Wind; died in March after being pensioned at Valor Farm near Pilot Point, Texas.

Meadow Flight, 1991 b. h., Meadowlake—Cassowary, by Cormorant. 24-5-4-1, $526,936. Won 1994 Pennsylvania Derby (G2), etc.; sire of at least two stakes winners, including 2001 Duchess S. (Can-G3) winner Meadow Gem; died on July 2 at Irish Acres Farm in Ocala after suffering a head injury in his stall.

Millencolin, 1997 ch. c., Dehere—Imaglee, by *Grey Dawn II. 16-3-1-5, $260,000. Won 1999 Kentucky Cup Juvenile S. (G3), etc.; euthanized on January 15 after breaking down in a Santa Anita Park allowance race.

My Darling One, 1981 ch. m., Exclusive Native—Princess Marshua, by Prince John. 8-5-0-2, $343,780. Won 1984 Fantasy S. (G1), etc.; dam of at least six winners, including 1994 Coolmore Stud Concorde S. (Ire-G3) winner Heart Lake; died on May 21.

Mystical Mood, 1979 b. m., Roberto—Mystery Mood, by Night Invader. 20-3-4-3, $139,067. Won 1981 Schuylerville S. (G3), etc.; dam of at least nine winners, including 1989 Citation H. (G2) winner Fair Judgment, etc.; died on November 26.

Nafees, 1979 b. m., Raja Baba—Summer Legend, by Raise a Native. 22-3-4-2, $96,196. Won 1982 Rare Perfume S.; dam of at least ten winners, including 1988 Premio Alberto de Obarrio (Pan-G3) winner Persistence; died on February 5.

Never Knock, 1979 dk. b. or br. m., Stage Door Johnny—Never Hula, by Never Bend. 16-2-2-0, $29,035. Dam of at least five winners, including 1992 champion older male Pleasant Tap and '94 Kentucky Derby (G1) winner Go for Gin; died in early March of foaling complications at Pillar Stud near Lexington.

Nureyev, 1977 b. h., Northern Dancer—Special, by *Forli. 3-2-0-0, $42,522. 1980 French champion miler; twice leading sire in France; as a $1.3-million sale yearling, he was considered one of the world's most influential stallions; sire of at least 132 stakes winners, including 1987 champion turf male Theatrical (Ire), multiple champion Miesque, 1997 European Horse of the Year Peintre Celebre; was given a 10% chance of survival when he suffered a fractured right hind leg in May 1987; returned to breeding shed in April 1988; euthanized on October 29 at Walmac International near Lexington due to complications of cancer in his right front foot.

Oh So Sharp (Ire), 1982 ch. m., Kris—Oh So Fair, by Graustark. 9-7-2-0, $505,280. 1985 English champion three-year-old filly; won '85 English filly triple crown, etc.; dam of at least seven winners, including 1992 Prix Saint-Alary (Fr-G1) winner Rosefinch and 1991

Long Island H. (G2) winner Shaima; euthanized due to laminitis complications in October at Dalham Stud Farms in Newmarket, England.

Our Native, 1970 b. h., Exclusive Native—Our Jackie, by Crafty Admiral. 37-14-4-7, $426,969. Won 1973 Flamingo S. (G1), etc.; third in Secretariat's Kentucky Derby (G1); sire of at least 49 stakes winners, including 1979 champion two-year-old male Rockhill Native, 1985 Hollywood Turf Cup (G1) winner Zoffany; euthanized on August 26 at High Point Farm near Lexington due to complications of arthritis.

Percy Hope, 1998 b. c., Ide—Ridinghood, by Red Ransom. 14-4-2-2, $428,397. Won 2001 Lone Star Derby, etc., finished ninth in 2001 Preakness S. (G1); euthanized on July 5 after suffering from complications of a bacterial infection.

Peteski, 1990 ch. h., Affirmed—Vive, by Nureyev. 11-7-2-1, $1,287,866. 1993 Canadian Horse of the Year, won 1993 Canadian Triple Crown; sire of at least 11 stakes winners, including 2000 Panamanian Horse of the Year Viva Pancho, 1999 Regret S. (G3) winner Nani Rose; euthanized on April 3 at the New Bolton Center of the University of Pennsylvania's School of Veterinary Medicine due to complications from colic.

Polar Falcon, 1987 dk. b. or br. h., Nureyev—Marie d'Argonne (Fr), by Jefferson. 14-5-2-1, $376,096. Highweighted older horse on 1991 European Free Handicap at 5 to 7 furlongs, won '91 Ladbroke Sprint Cup S. (Eng-G1), etc.; sire of at least 23 stakes winners, including 1996 Nunthorpe Stakes (Eng-G1) winner Pivotal, 2001 Czech champion sprinter and 1999 Slovakian champion miler Sammetsman, 2001 Premio Roma (Ity-G1) winner Shibuni's Falcon; euthanized on September 5 due to complications of a lung tumor in Newmarket, England.

Polemic, 1988 ch. m., Roberto—Solartic, by Briartic. 18-4-2-3, $323,228. Won 1992 California Jockey Club H. (G3); dam of at least three winners, including 1998 Prix Casimir Delamarre winner Cyrillic; died on April 30.

Pookette, 1986 b. m., Miswaki—Pensioner, by Irish Stronghold. 9-2-3-0, $93,340. Won 1989 Ontario Damsel S.; dam of at least four winners, including 1994 Canadian champion two-year-old male and 1995 Wood Memorial S. (G2) winner Talkin Man; died on June 10.

Powis Castle, 1991 b. h., Rare Brick—Castle Eight, by Key to the Kingdom. 27-7-4-4, $569,518. Won 1994 Malibu S. (G2), etc.; died in early January at Killion Farms near Palestine, Texas, a few days after suffering a severe chest injury when he crashed into a paddock fence during a thunderstorm.

Prime Directive, 1996 dk. b. or br. h., Tactical Advantage—Primedex, by Deputy Minister. 28-5-6-2, $429,359. Won 1998 Saratoga Special S. (G2), etc.; died after being pulled up in distress in a Philadelphia Park allowance race on January 6.

Prospectors Delite, 1989 ch. m., Mr. Prospector—Up the Flagpole, by Hoist the Flag. 9-6-1-1, $432,953. Won 1992 Ashland S. (G1), etc.; dam of at least four winners, including 1998 Personal Ensign H. (G1) winner Tomisue's Delight and 2000 Tetrarch S. (Ire-G3) winner Monashee Mountain; euthanized on June 21 at Lane's End near Versailles, Kentucky, after suffering from laminitis.

Quarrel, 1973 ch. m., Raise a Native—Rhubarb, by Barbizon. 33-5-2-7, $68,847. Dam of at least eight winners, including 1981 Arlington-Washington Futurity (G1) winner Lets Dont Fight, 1985 Aqueduct H. (G3)

winner Fight Over, and 1984 Kentucky Jockey Club S. (G3) winner Fuzzy; died on March 6 due to infirmities of old age at Hurstland Farm near Midway, Kentucky.

Red Anchor, 1981 ch. h., Sea Anchor—Decoy Girl, by Decoy Boy. 10-7-3-0. 1984-'85 Australian Horse of the Year, won 1984 W. S. Cox Plate (Aus-G1), etc.; sire of at least 85 winners, including 1994 Epsom H. (Aus-G1) winner Navy Seal; euthanized on April 9 at River Oak Lodge near Tambourine, Queensland, Australia, after fracturing his left front leg.

Rexson's Hope, 1981 dk. b. or br. h., Rexson—Abe's Miss, by Abe's Hope. 58-8-11-11, 379,379. Won 1983 In Reality S. (div. 2) Florida Stallion series, etc.; sire of at least four stakes winners, including 1995 Bonnie Miss S. (G2) winner Mia's Hope, dam of 2000 Florida Derby (G1) winner Hal's Hope.

Rollin With Nolan, 1997 ch. h., Summer Squall—Pi Phi Hi D, by Sauce Boat. 15-5-0-3, $241,194. Won 2001 Eillo S.; euthanized on May 25 at Ramsey Farm near Nicholasville, Kentucky, because of complications of two fractured sesamoid bones in his left front leg suffered on May 5 during the Lane's End Churchill Downs H. (G2).

Rose's Cantina, 1984 gr. m., Naskra—Soft as Satin, by Promised Land. 38-9-6-6, $723,139. Won 1989 Hempstead H. (G1), etc.; dam of two winners; died on January 15.

Royal Pennant, 1983, ch. h., Raja Baba—French Flag, by Hoist the Flag. 26-9-6-3, $283,271. Won 1988 Gulfstream Sprint Championship H., etc.; sire of at least two stakes winners, including 1997 Longhorn Sprint S. winner Stroke; died on April 1.

Ruling Angel, 1984 ch. m., Vice Regent—Loudrangle, by Quadrangle. 26-12-6-2, $785,707. 1986 Canadian Horse of the Year, champion two-year-old filly; dam of at least three winners, including 1992 Natalma S. winner All An Angel; died on May 25 at Tsa-La-Gi Farm near Midway, Kentucky, of foaling complications.

Ryafan, 1994 b. m., Lear Fan—Carya, by Northern Dancer. 10-7-1-0, $1,342,142. 1997 North American champion grass female and European champion three-year-old filly; won 1996 Prix Marcel Boussac Criterium des Pouliches (Fr-G1) (French One Thousand Guineas), 1997 Matriarch S. (G1), etc.; dam of three foals; died on April 12 at Juddmonte Farms of a ruptured uterine artery shortly after foaling.

Salse, 1985 b. h., Topsider—Carnival Princess, by Prince John. 13-8-4-1, $438,342. 1988 French champion three-year-old male; won 1988 Prix de la Foret (Fr-G1); sire of at least 18 stakes winners, including 1993 European champion two-year-old filly Lemon Souffle (GB) and 1997 Hong Kong International Vase (HK-G2) winner Luso; euthanized on May 25 in Newmarket, England, after contracting an infection in his left front foot.

Saros (GB), 1974 dk. b. or br. h., Sassafras (Fr)—Rose Copse, by Floribunda, 29-6-5-0, $90,024. Won 1978 City and Suburban H. at Epsom Downs; sire of at least 16 stakes winners, including 1985 Kentucky Oaks (G1) winner Fran's Valentine; euthanized on November 19 at Circle H Ranch near Murrieta, California, due to infirmities of old age.

Serheed, 1980 b. h., Nijinsky II—Native Partner, by Raise a Native. 18-5-2-1, $29,109. Leading Western Australian sire five times; sire of at least 20 stakes

winners, including 2001 Cox Plate (Aus-G1) winner Northerly; euthanized on December 5 in Australia due to complications from an injured hoof.

Set Free, 1980 b. h., Majestic Prince—Marianna Trench, by *Pago Pago. 46-6-12-7, $138,952. Won 1985 Flying Cloud H.; sired at least one stakes winner, 1993 Plymouth S. winner Set's Free Spirit; died on December 9.

Shaamit, 1993 b. h., Mtoto—Shomoose, by Habitat. 6-2-0-1, $900,797. Won 1996 Epsom Derby (Eng-G1), highweighted on 1996 English Free Handicap at 11 to 14 furlongs; sire of at least 14 winners; died on April 7 at a veterinary clinic near Scarvagh House Stud, Scarvagh, County Down, Northern Ireland, of an intestinal rupture.

Sheer Ice, 1982 gr. m., Cutlass—Hey Dolly A., by Ambehaving. 43-17-13-5, $432,425. Won 1988 Pembroke Lakes H., etc.; dam of at least two stakes winners, including 2001 Ancient Title Breeders' Cup H. (G1) winner Swept Overboard; died on February 23.

Shoot a Line (GB), 1977 b. m., High Line—Death Ray, by Tamerlane. 17-7-2-0, $374,607. 1980 English and Irish champion three-year-old filly; won Yorkshire Oaks (Eng-G1), Irish Oaks (Ire-G1), etc.; dam of at least three winners, including Grade 1-placed Line of Thunder, who is the dam of 1995 champion three-year-old male and Kentucky Derby (G1) winner Thunder Gulch; died on January 5.

Sillery, 1988 b. h., Blushing Groom (Fr)—Silvermine (Fr), by Bellypha (Ire). 18-7-6-0, $712,571. Won 1991 Prix Jean Prat (Fr-G1), etc.; sire of at least ten stakes winners, including 1999 Breeders' Cup Mile (G1) winner Silic (Fr); died at Haras du Quesnay near Deauville, France.

Sing Sing, 1978 b. h., Stop the Music—Fuchsia Filch, by No Robbery. 38-8-7-6, $520,642. Won 1981 Secretariat S. (G2), etc.; sire of at least one stakes winner, 1990 Jim Foti Memorial H. winner Blairwood; died on December 4.

Slewpy, 1980 dk. b. or br. h., Seattle Slew—Rare Bouquet, by Prince John. 21-8-2-1, $710,248. Won 1983 Meadowlands Cup H. (G1), etc.; sire of at least 26 stakes winners, including 1992 Breeders' Cup Sprint (G1) winner Thirty Slews; died on December 19 at Flag Is Up Farms near Solvang, California, of complications from a jaw fracture suffered in a paddock accident.

Smart Angle, 1977 b. m., Quadrangle—Smartaire, by *Quibu. 17-7-4-1, $414,217. 1979 champion two-year-old filly; dam of at least 12 winners, including 1989 Bay Shore S. (G2) winner Houston; died on December 17.

Song of Syria, 1985 b. m., Damascus—Passerine, by Dr. Fager. 7-2-2-0, $12,920. Dam of at least five winners, including 1999 champion two-year-old filly Chilukki; died on June 11.

Spanish Drums, 1979 gr. h., Top Command—La Tamborera, by Drone. 32-9-1-5, $386,825. Won 1982 Ohio Derby (G2), etc.; sire of at least 14 stakes winners, including 1992 Roseben H. (G3) winner Drummond Lane.

Spook Express (SAf), 1994 b. m., Comic Blush—Park Walk (GB), by Green Dancer. 22-11-2-3, $1,016,744. 1998 South African champion three-year-old filly; won 2001 WinStar Galaxy S. (G2), etc.; third in 2001 Breeders' Cup Filly and Mare Turf (G1); euthanized on November 25 at Hollywood Park after suffering a compound displacement of her left fetlock joint in the

Matriarch S. (G1).

Squander, 1974 b. m., Buckpasser—Discipline, by *Princequillo. 14-3-4-2, $129,855. Won 1976 Sorority S. (G1), etc.; dam of at least three stakes winners, including 1994 Gallant Fox H. (G3) winner Serious Spender; died on October 31.

Stacie's Toy, 1987 dk. b. or br. m., Baldski—Butter Fat, by *Prince Taj. 23-6-6-3, $450,753. Won 1990 Pimlico Oaks; dam of at least two winners, including Stacie's Halo; died on March 2.

State Dinner, 1975 b. m., Buckpasser—Silver Bright, by Barbizon. 23-8-5-4, $537,859. Won 1979 Suburban H. (G1), etc.; sire of at least 17 stakes winners, including 1985 champion two-year-old filly Family Style; died on April 8 at Frazier Farm near Bonnerdale, Arkansas, of a heart attack.

Steinlen (GB), 1983 b. h., Habitat—Southern Seas (GB), by Jim French. 45-20-10-7, $3,297,169. 1989 champion grass male; won 1989 Breeders' Cup Mile (G1) and Arlington Million S. (G1), etc.; sire of at least two stakes winners, including 1994 Young America S. (G3) winner Miss Union Avenue; euthanized on June 9 at Harris Farms near Coalinga, California, after fracturing a hind leg in a paddock accident.

Sun Princess, 1980 b. m., English Prince—Sunny Valley, by *Val de Loir. 10-3-2-1, $584,071. English and French champion three-year-old filly in 1983; won 1983 Epsom Oaks (Eng-G1), St. Leger (Eng-G1), etc.; dam of at least seven winners, including 1988 Three Chimneys Dewhurst S. (Eng-G1) winner Prince of Dance; euthanized on December 19 at Ballymacoll Stud Farm in Ireland after developing an incurable sinus tumor.

Ten Toes, 1983 b. m., Our Native—Calculator, by Golden Ruler. Unraced. Dam of at least five winners, including 1990 Arch Ward S. winner Tentacular; died on June 4.

Timebank, 1987 ch. h., Water Bank—Countless Times, by Timeless Moment. 9-4-3-0, $155,150. Second in 1991 Bel Air H. (G2); sire of at least three stakes winners, including 1997 Redbud H. winner Natomas Bank.

Timely Times, 1984 b. m., Hostage—Trying Times, by He's a Pistol. 8-1-3-1, $18,310. Dam of at least five winners, including 1999 Sabin H. (G3) winner Timely Broad; died on May 15.

Toga Toga Toga, 1992 ch. m., Saratoga Six—Northern Neck, by Northern Baby. 18-7-4-4, $374,490. Won 1997 Santa Monica H. (G1); was nearly hit by a gym bag thrown by a man who ran onto Del Mar's track during a 1995 allowance race; euthanized on November 21 after fracturing her left front leg in a paddock accident at Greenfield Farm near Lexington.

Transworld, 1974 ch. h., Prince John—*Hornpipe II, by Hornbeam. 5-3-1-0, $38,610. Won 1977 Irish St. Leger (Ire-G1); leading Colorado stallion; sire of at least 19 stakes winners, including five-time steeplechase champion Lonesome Glory, 1986 Venezuelan Horse of the Year Winton, and 1986 Pan American H. (G1) winner Powder Break; died on June 24 at Alexander Farm near Byers, Colorado.

Truly Bound, 1978 b. m., In Reality—Natashka, by Dedicate. 12-9-1-0, $382,449. Won 1981 Ashland S. (G2), etc.; dam of at least six winners, including 1996 Killavullan S. (Ire-G3) winner Shell Ginger (Ire); died on May 14.

Tweak, 1976 dk. b. or br. m., Secretariat—Ta Wee, by

Intentionally. 28-7-4-3, $148,597. Won 1979 Fair Lawn S.; dam of at least 13 winners; died on February 7.

Unbridled, 1987 b. h., Fappiano—Gana Facil, by *Le Fabuleux. 24-8-6-6, $4,489,475. 1990 champion three-year-old male; won 1990 Kentucky Derby (G1) and Breeders' Cup Classic (G1), etc.; sire of at least 28 stakes winners, including 1998 champion three-year-old filly Banshee Breeze and 1999 champion two-year-old male Anees; euthanized on October 18 at Hagyard-Davidson-McGee equine clinic near Lexington due to complications of colic surgery.

Vivid Imagination, 1989 ch. m., Raise a Man—Imagining, by Northfields. 21-4-1-6, $194,237. Won 1991 Golden Rod S. (G3), etc.; dam of at least two winners; died on May 1.

Vodika Collins, 1978 ch. h., Vodika—Ruthie G., by Royal Saxon. 56-18-12-12, $581,171. Won 1982 Michigan Mile and One-Eighth H. (G2), etc.; sire of at least 51 winners, including stakes-placed Rosa O Collins.

Wajima, 1972 b. h., Bold Ruler—* Iskra, by Le Haar. 16-9-5-0, $537,837. 1975 champion three-year-old male; won Travers S. (G1), Marlboro Cup Invitational H. (G1), etc.; record-priced yearling, $600,000, when bought by Japanese breeder Zenya Yoshida, at the 1973 Keeneland July selected yearling sale; sire of at least 26 stakes winners, including 1984 Canadian champion three-year-old male Key to the Moon; euthanized on August 27 at Stone Farm near Paris, Kentucky, due to infirmities of old age.

Waya (Fr), 1974 b. m., Faraway Son—War Path III, by Blue Prince. 29-14-6-4, $822,948. 1979 champion older female, won Beldame S. (G1), Man o' War S. (G1), etc.; dam of at least eight winners, including 1994 Tremont Breeders' Cup S. (G3) winner De Niro and 1983 Criterium Femminile (Ity-G3) winner Vidalia; euthanized on December 12 at Derry Meeting Farm near Cochranville, Pennsylvania, due to complications of laminitis.

Weekend Surprise, 1980 b. m., Secretariat—Lassie Dear, by Buckpasser. 31-7-5-10, $402,892. Won 1982 Golden Rod S. (G3), etc.; 1992 Broodmare of the Year; dam of at least eight winners, including 1992 Horse of the Year A.P. Indy and 1990 Preakness S. (G1) winner Summer Squall; died on March 13 at Lane's End near Versailles, Kentucky, of foaling complications.

Wind Flyer, 1981 b. h., Full Pocket—Demure Miss, by Cyane. 41-3-11-6, $212,926. Won 1983 Freshman S., etc.; sire of at least eight stakes winners, including 1997 Iowa Derby winner Fleet Flyer; died on May 10.

Winglet, 1988 b. m., Alydar—Highest Trump, by Bold Bidder. 9-2-1-4, $155,975. Won 1991 Princess S. (G2); dam of at least two graded stakes winners, 1997 champion three-year-old filly Ajina and 2000 Lexington S. (G3) winner Rob's Spirit; died on May 23.

Zaizafon, 1982 ch. m., The Minstrel—Mofida (GB), by Right Tack. 14-2-0-3, $50,196. Won 1984 Seaton Delaval S. (Eng-G3); dam of at least three stakes winners, including 1992 English and French highweighted juvenile European champion two-year-old male and sire Zafonic; died on February 16.

Zignew, 1990 b. h., Danzig—Newfoundland, by Prince John. 13-5-2-2, $285,025. Won 1994 San Fernando S. (G2); sire of at least 15 winners, including 2001 Lady Razorback Futurity winner Humble Danzig; died on June 18.

All About Purses 2001

by Mark Simon

The big picture for racehorse owners continued to improve in 2001. Race purses in North America rose to a record $1.15-billion, a 4.8% increase over total purses distributed in 2000. The 2001 increase marked the eighth consecutive annual rise in total North American purses, which grew 48.7% from 1992 to 2001.

Average purse in 2001 increased to a record, as did average earnings per runner and median earnings per runner. When adjusted for inflation, all those barometers also increased. Despite the higher average and total purses distributed, owning a racehorse remains a risky proposition; the number of racehorses actually paying their way is just a small fraction of the total number of runners.

Highlights of the data in this review of 2001 purses and runners in North America are:

• A record $1,146,337,367 in purses was distributed in 60,538 races, the second-lowest number of races held in North America since 1972.

• Average purse climbed to $18,936, a one-year rise of 4.9% and an increase of 89.6% since 1992.

• The total number of runners rose for the third straight year, the first such increase since the 1980s, when total runners grew every year.

• Average earnings per runner increased to a record $16,159, a 34.4% rise since 1996.

• Median earnings per runner in current dollars continued to increase dramatically, rising 3.7% in 2001 and 120.1% over the last decade.

• Inflation-adjusted average earnings per runner remained basically unchanged from 2000, and inflation-adjusted median earnings tipped upward by a modest 1.4%.

• A total of 6,703 runners—9.4% of all starters—failed to earn any part of a purse.

• More than half of all starters—51.2%—failed to win a race in 2001.

• Winners earned an average of $29,585, while nonwinners earned an average of $3,361.

• Horses that won a stakes race earned an average of $144,643.

• Winners collectively earned 89.4% of all purse money.

• 17.6% of all runners earned $25,000 or more and collectively won 68.5% of all purse money.

• 71.3% of all runners earned less than $15,000.

• Races at 1¼ miles accounted for just 0.4% of the total number of races but distributed 2.8% of all purse money, an average of $143,765.

• Stakes races constituted 4.3% of all races and offered 23% of all purses.

• 44% of all races offered a purse of less than $10,000.

• Claiming races—straight claiming and maiden claiming—accounted for 65.5% of all races.

• Almost half of all races were carded at six furlongs or less.

• The average number of starts per horse continued its long decline, falling to 7.0 in 2001, the fewest ever.

• Average field size moved up marginally to 8.2.

The data reflect all Thoroughbred purses distributed to racehorses in North America in 2001, excluding Mexico and Puerto Rico, and were obtained from the Jockey Club Information Systems Inc. Steeplechase races are excluded.

Table 1
Selected Racing Statistics, North American Thoroughbred Racing, 1992-2001

Year	No. of runners	No. of races	Total purses	Average purse	Earnings per runner Average	Earnings per runner Median
1992	83,468	77,711	$ 771,136,296	$ 9,989	$ 9,238	$2,731
1993	78,763	72,224	748,415,925	10,362	9,502	2,850
1994	74,939	70,617	770,426,193	10,910	10,280	3,314
1995	72,316	68,197	815,987,125	11,965	11,283	3,702
1996	70,371	64,263	845,916,706	13,163	12,021	3,937
1997	69,067	63,491	888,667,752	13,997	12,867	4,425
1998	68,419	61,141	968,366,929	15,838	14,153	4,939
1999	68,435	60,118	1,008,162,608	16,770	14,732	5,310
2000	69,230	60,579	1,093,661,241	18,053	15,798	5,796
2001	70,942	60,538	1,146,337,367	18,936	16,159	6,010
Percent Change:						
1992-2001	−15.0%	−22.1%	48.7%	89.6%	74.9%	120.1%
2000-2001	2.5%	−0.1%	4.8%	4.9%	2.3%	3.7%
Average Percent Change:						
19921-2001	−1.5%	−2.2%	4.9%	9.0%	7.5%	12.0%

Table 2
Distribution of Earnings of Runners for 2001

Earnings range	No. of runners	Percent of runners	Earnings	Percent of earnings	Average earnings
$300,000 or more	173	0.2%	$100,886,590	8.8%	$583,159
$200,000 - 299,999	174	0.2%	41,007,424	3.6%	235,675
$100,000 - 199,999	1,030	1.5%	136,272,397	11.9%	132,303
$75,000 - 99,999	1,037	1.5%	89,208,911	7.8%	86,026
$50,000 - 74,999	2,542	3.6%	154,433,432	13.5%	60,753
$25,000 - 49,999	7,541	10.6%	262,782,889	22.9%	34,847
$20,000 - 24,999	3,299	4.7%	73,839,604	6.4%	22,382
$15,000 - 19,999	4,646	6.5%	80,325,151	7.0%	17,289
$10,000 - 14,999	6,941	9.8%	85,393,176	7.4%	12,303
$5,000 - 9,999	10,717	15.1%	78,210,933	6.8%	7,298
$1,000 - 4,999	14,376	20.4%	39,306,164	3.4%	2,734
$1 - 999	11,763	16.6%	4,670,696	0.4%	397
None	6,703	9.4%	0	0.0%	0
Totals	**70,942**	**100.0%**	**$1,146,337,367**	**100.0%**	**$ 16,159**

Averages up

From 1991 through 2000, average purse and average earnings per runner increased every year. In that period, average purse increased 86.5% and average earnings per runner 79.4%; those were large increases when total purses increased a significantly smaller percentage, 43.6%, during that time period.

Generally responsible for the higher averages were declines in the number of races and a decline in the number of runners. From 1999 to 2001, however, the number of runners in North America has risen, the first increases in successive years since 1989. This has put a damper on percentage growth in the averages. While average purse increased by an annualized 8.64% from 1991 to 2000, the increase was a significantly smaller 4.9% in '01. Similarly, average earnings per runner increased an annualized 7.9% from 1991 to 2000, but in '01 the increase was a modest 2.3%.

The number of runners has been increasing because breeders have put more mares into production as the economics on the racetrack improved over the past ten years. However, the loss of foals from mare reproductive loss syndrome most likely will reduce the number of runners in 2003 and for several years thereafter.

Rising purses have come from several sources, not entirely from increases in pari-mutuel handle. A significant amount of purse money now comes from slot machines (video lottery terminals) at racetracks, as well as from state taxes on other forms of gambling and, in some years, state grants to purses. While pari-mutuel handle in the United States and Canada in 2001 rose 2% to $15.1-billion, according to Equibase, in this time period total purses increased 4.8%.

Still, median earnings per runner were a relatively paltry $6,010 in 2001—meaning half

Table 3
Earnings as a Function of Number of Starts for 2001

Starts	No. of runners	Percent of runners	Earnings	Percent of earnings	Average earnings	Earnings per start
More than 10	16,345	23.0%	$426,534,026	37.2%	$26,096	$1,869
More than 21	305	0.4%	7,019,739	0.6%	23,016	975
19 - 21	984	1.4%	25,462,063	2.2%	25,876	1,310
16 - 18	2,769	3.9%	71,472,273	6.2%	25,812	1,536
13 - 15	6,000	8.5%	158,218,419	13.8%	26,370	1,906
11 - 12	6,287	8.9%	164,361,532	14.3%	26,143	2,280
10	3,761	5.3%	91,057,196	7.9%	24,211	2,421
9	4,120	5.8%	105,236,160	9.2%	25,543	2,838
8	4,416	6.2%	102,941,360	9.0%	23,311	2,914
7	4,790	6.8%	100,384,112	8.8%	20,957	2,994
6	5,130	7.2%	96,427,697	8.4%	18,797	3,133
5	5,504	7.8%	76,554,615	6.7%	13,909	2,782
4	5,930	8.4%	61,546,856	5.4%	10,379	2,595
3	6,593	9.3%	41,709,840	3.6%	6,326	2,109
2	7,206	10.2%	28,657,060	2.5%	3,977	1,988
1	7,147	10.1%	15,288,445	1.3%	2,139	2,139
Totals	**70,942**	**100.0%**	**$1,146,337,367**	**100.0%**	**16,159**	**$2,315**

Table 4
Distribution of Races and Purses by Age and Sex for 2001

Sex	No. of races	Percent of races	Purses	Percent of purses	Avg. purse per race
		Two-Year-Olds			
Females	2,182	3.6%	$ 57,595,790	5.0%	$26,396
Males	92	0.2%	4,753,118	0.4%	51,664
Either sex	2,457	4.1%	60,834,720	5.3%	24,760
Overall	4,731	7.8%	123,183,628	10.7%	26,038
		Three-Year-Olds			
Females	3,084	5.1%	82,648,529	7.2%	26,799
Males	89	0.1%	2,687,908	0.2%	30,201
Either sex	3,528	5.8%	108,355,033	9.5%	30,713
Overall	6,701	11.1%	193,691,470	16.9%	28,905
		Three-Year-Olds and Up			
Females	15,670	25.9%	271,043,451	23.6%	17,297
Males	75	0.1%	1,887,282	0.2%	25,164
Either sex	23,843	39.4%	393,252,362	34.3%	16,493
Overall	39,588	65.4%	666,183,095	58.1%	16,828
		Four-Year-Olds and Up			
Females	3,573	5.9%	63,482,158	5.5%	17,767
Males	10	0.0%	446,880	0.0%	44,688
Either sex	5,936	9.8%	99,356,836	8.7%	16,738
Overall	9,519	15.7%	163,285,874	14.3%	17,154
		Totals			
Females	**24,508**	**40.5%**	**474,769,928**	**41.4%**	**19,371**
Males	**266**	**0.4%**	**9,775,188**	**0.9%**	**36,749**
Either sex	**35,764**	**59.1%**	**661,798,951**	**57.7%**	**18,505**
Overall	**60,539**	**100.0%**	**1,146,344,067**	**100.0%**	**18,936**

earned more than $6,010 and half earned less than that amount. Granted, that figure is 120.1% higher than in 1992, but an owner whose runner earns $6,010 is not covering training costs, let alone the cost of the horse. Median earnings per runner increased 3.7% from 2000, but that gain barely kept pace with inflation.

Total purses adjusted for inflation made some gains, rising 2.5%. Total deflated purses in 2000 exceeded $1-billion for the first time, and in '01 it inched up further to $1,048,319,494. With the number of races declining slightly from 2000, deflated average purse also increased 2.6% to $17,317, which is 60% higher than in 1992. Average purse in the 1981-'90 decade actually declined 2.5% when adjusted for inflation.

Average deflated earnings per runner in 2001 remained flat, rising just $2 to $14,777. But that was an all-time record and up from a low of $9,820 in 1991. Median deflated earnings per runner, like current-dollar median earnings per runner, continued to show nice gains, rising 84.6% in the past ten years to $5,496 in 2001.

While Table 1 looks at the big picture of 2001 purses in current dollars, Table 2 examines how those purses were distributed. While the average runner earned $16,159 in 2001, the distribution of earnings varied widely. Of the 70,942 runners in 2001, only 1,377 earned $100,000 or more. Those 1.9% of all runners earned 24.3% of all purses, and their average earnings were $202,009. At the other end of the spectrum, 6,703 runners, 9.4% of the total, earned nothing. And another 11,763 starters, 16.6% of the total, earned less than $1,000 each. That means slightly more than one-quarter of all runners earned less than $1,000.

Everyone in racing wants to have a stakes winner, and for good reasons. The 1,779 stakes winners in 2001 earned an average of $144,643, or almost nine times more than the average runner. While just 2.5% of all runners won stakes, these stakes winners collected 22.4% of all purses, earning $257.3-million. Though average earnings of stakes winners in '01 climbed 4.2% from '00, the percentage of purses flowing into stakes races declined, an indication that more money was put into overnight races than in stakes in '01. In 2000, 23.4% of all money was paid in stakes, while in '01 it dropped to 23%.

Starts and wins

Table 3 breaks down earnings as a function of number of starts in 2001, and clearly the horses that start the most generally earn the most. Horses that started fewer than six times earned

Table 5
Distribution of Runners and Earnings by Age and Sex for 2001

Sex	No. of runners	Percent of runners	Earnings	Percent of earnings	Average earnings
			Two-Year-Olds		
Females	5,760	8.1%	$ 59,796,004	5.2%	$10,381
Males	5,767	8.1%	63,487,515	5.5%	11,009
Overall	11,527	16.2%	123,283,519	10.8%	10,695
			Three-Year-Olds		
Females	9,951	14.0%	181,873,427	15.9%	18,277
Males	10,449	14.7%	208,343,418	18.2%	19,939
Overall	20,400	28.8%	390,216,845	34.0%	19,128
			Four-Year-Olds		
Females	7,441	10.5%	133,122,718	11.6%	17,890
Males	8,750	12.3%	164,542,280	14.4%	18,805
Overall	16,192	22.8%	297,785,268	26.0%	18,391
			Five-Year-Olds and Up		
Females	7,787	11.0%	106,593,738	9.3%	13,689
Males	15,035	21.2%	228,457,149	19.9%	15,195
Overall	22,823	32.2%	335,051,735	29.2%	14,680
			Totals		
Females	**30,939**	**43.6%**	**481,385,887**	**42.0%**	**15,559**
Males	**40,001**	**56.4%**	**664,830,362**	**58.0%**	**16,620**
Overall	**70,942**	**100.0%**	**1,146,337,367**	**100.0%**	**16,159**

less on average than the overall average for all runners, $16,159. Horses that started six times earned an average of $18,797, and average earnings per runner increased in lockstep with number of starts. Horses that started more than ten times accounted for $426.5-million in purse earnings. Those 16,345 runners earned 37.2% of all purses. Average earnings per start in 2001 was $2,315.

While starting is important, winning is everything. In 2001, the 36,321 horses that failed to win earned an average of $3,361. Horses able to win one race earned an average of $17,350, roughly five times more than the horses that failed to win. Each additional win dramatically increased average earnings. Horses that won twice earned almost twice as much as those that won once, and horses that won three times earned three times as much as those that could win but once. Horses that won six races earned an average of $93,064, and those winning nine races (just 14 horses) earning an average of $175,838. Winners collectively earned 89.4% of all purse money.

Table 4 takes a closer look at how purses are distributed by age and sex, and it reveals a significant difference in opportunity by both measures. In terms of age, three-year-olds have the best opportunity to earn money. The average purse for races exclusively for three-year-olds is $28,905, 34.5% higher than the overall average purse of $18,936. While just 11.1% of all races are for three-year-olds, those 6,701 races distributed 16.9% of all purses in 2001.

Two-year-olds are offered the fewest races, 7.8% of the total, accounting for 10.7% of all purse money. Of course, opportunities for two-year-olds are concentrated in the second half of each year. The category with the most races was three-year-olds and up, with 65.4% of the races and 58.1% of the purses. The average purse of $16,828 for three-year-olds and up was less than the overall average.

In terms of sex, races open to either sex were far more abundant than races exclusively for females, with 59.1% of all races open to either sex and 40.5% restricted to females. Races restricted to fillies and mares featured purses higher on average than those open to either sex. Average purse for races restricted to females was $19,371, while the average for either sex was $18,505.

However, Table 5 makes clear that fillies and mares have less earnings potential than males. Overall, females in 2001 earned an average of $15,559, 6.4% less than the male average of $16,620. Moreover, females accounted for 43.6% of all runners but earned 42% of all purses. In every age bracket, males earned more than females. In the three-year-old category, males earned an average of $19,939 per runner compared with $18,277 for fillies.

Claiming most prevalent

Claiming races are the staple of any race card, and Table 6 illustrates their dominance on the American scene. In 2001, claiming races accounted for nearly two-thirds of all races. The percentage

Table 6
Distribution of Races by Class for 2001

	No. of races	Percent of races	Average starters	Purses	Percent of purses	Avg. purse per race
Maiden Claiming	9,586	15.8%	8.8	$100,317,848	8.8%	$ 10,465
Claiming	30,069	49.7%	8.1	328,582,274	28.7%	10,928
$0 to 999	0	0.0%	0.0	0	0.0%	0
$1,000 to 4,999	9,292	15.3%	8.4	52,620,516	4.6%	5,663
$5,000 to 9,999	9,796	16.2%	8.2	78,827,842	6.9%	8,047
$10,000 to 19,999	6,919	11.4%	7.9	90,429,803	7.9%	13,070
$20,000 and up	4,062	6.7%	7.6	106,704,113	9.3%	26,269
Total Claiming	39,655	65.5%	8.3	428,900,122	37.4%	10,816
Optional Claiming	545	0.9%	7.2	17,577,364	1.5%	32,252
Starter Allowance	1,307	2.2%	7.4	20,138,794	1.8%	15,408
Starter Handicap	88	0.1%	7.8	1,726,844	0.2%	19,623
Maiden	6,292	10.4%	8.9	142,846,140	12.5%	22,703
Allowance	8,554	14.1%	7.7	224,406,601	19.6%	26,234
Handicap	54	0.1%	7.1	1,522,606	0.1%	28,196
Stakes	2,622	4.3%	7.7	263,117,963	23.0%	100,350
Total Nonclaiming	19,462	32.1%	8.1	671,336,312	58.6%	34,495
Total all races	**60,538**	**100.0%**	**8.2**	**$1,146,337,367**	**100.0%**	**$18,936**

of claiming races has declined markedly in the past decade. In 1991, before whole-card simulcasting took off across this country, claiming races composed 74.3% of all races. In 2001, claiming races actually increased as a percentage of all races, climbing from 64.5% in 2000 to 65.5%. While plentiful, claiming races distributed just 37.4% of all 2001 purse money. Allowance races are the second-most common races and featured an average purse of $26,234, distributing 19.6% of all purses. The third-most common race was straight maiden races, amounting to 10.4% of all

Table 7
Distribution of all North American
Races by Purse for 2001

Range of purses	No. of races	Total purses
$999 or less	19	$ 15,623
$1,000-9,999	26,647	165,288,933
$10,000-19,999	17,209	238,170,978
$20,000-29,999	6,778	164,731,927
$30,000-49,999	6,698	257,156,554
$50,000-74,999	2,029	114,030,094
$75,000-99,999	303	24,336,119
$100,000-199,999	585	71,946,407
$200,000-299,999	145	32,954,952
$300,000-399,999	30	9,602,975
$400,000-499,999	19	7,980,575
$500,000-749,999	42	22,069,750
$750,000-999,999	15	11,829,000
$1,000,000 and up	19	26,223,480
Totals	**60,538**	**$1,146,337,367**

races and distributing 12.5% of all purses.

Largest fields on average came in maiden races. Straight maiden races featured average fields of 8.9 starters, while maiden claiming events averaged 8.8 starters per race. As has been the case for the past three decades, average number of starts per horse per year is still declining. In 2001, the number dropped to an all-time low of 7.0. In 1960, horses were averaging slightly more than 11 starts per year.

The most common distance of races in 2001 was six furlongs, with 18,118 races, approaching one in every three races held in North America for horses older than age two. Though six-furlong races were the most common, they offered below-average purses of $15,032. The most lucrative race distance was 1½ miles, featuring an average purse of $150,863, though there were just 90 races at that distance. The second-highest average was for the American classic distance of 1¼ miles, which featured an average purse of $143,765. In that category are rich races like the Breeders' Cup Classic (G1) and Kentucky Derby (G1).

As seen in Table 7, just 76 races, or 0.01% of the 2001 total, offered a purse of $500,000 or more. Another 779 races, or 1.3% of the total, offered purses of $100,000 to $499,999. Those 855 races distributed $182.6-million, or 15.9% of all purse money.

Mark Simon is editor of THOROUGHBRED TIMES.

Racetrack Purses by Region in 2001

While racetrack purses increased in 2001, the gains were not spread uniformly across the continent. Some racing circuits increased payments to their horsemen by attracting more wagering on their full-card simulcasting signals, and a few racetracks managed to increase wagering within their facilities. Other tracks lost ground, both on track and in total wagering.

Some of the largest gains in purses were recorded by tracks that offered alternate forms of gambling. Slot machines or their equivalents have resurrected racing in Delaware, West Virginia, Iowa, and New Mexico, and they promise sizable increases at some Louisiana tracks. Ontario's two Thoroughbred tracks have raised purses significantly since slot machines were installed in their facilities. In addition, a card club has helped the once-shuttered Canterbury Park in Minnesota to become a profitable racing operation.

The 2001 economic downturn pinched budgets of state and local governments, and some racetrack purses were affected. Purse supplements in New Jersey and Maryland were reduced for 2002, and a new contract with the association operating Prairie Meadows Racetrack in Iowa led to a sizable purse reduction for 2002 and beyond. In the following sections, purses are reviewed by racetrack by region.

Northeast

Racetrack ownership has been consolidating over the last five years, and the major players are two publicly traded companies, Frank Stronach-led Magna Entertainment Corp. and Churchill Downs Inc. However, another major player exists and, although it cannot venture outside its New York borders, the New York Racing Association has been a major force in the sport since being founded as a not-for-profit entity in the 1950s.

Long before full-card simulcasting became widespread in the 1990s, NYRA was sending its major stakes races to markets large and small. New York racing has a grand tradition, and it also has had one of the best purse structures in the country. Purses at NYRA's metropolitan New York tracks—Aqueduct and Belmont Park—and its upstate Saratoga Race Course remain among the best in the country, and purses might improve if slot machines, approved in late 2001, become operational at Aqueduct. Saratoga had a 2001 daily purse distribution second only to Keeneland Race Course in Kentucky.

New Jersey's shrinking Thoroughbred racing schedule—Garden State Park closed in 2001 and Atlantic City Race Course races only a few days each year—has left two strong players, Monmouth Park and the Meadowlands. Both tracks are owned by the New Jersey Sports and Exposition Authority and pay purses well above the national average.

However, a tightening state budget cut their purses somewhat in 2002.

All other tracks in the Northeast region paid purses that were below the 2001 national average of $18,936 per race. The purses range from Philadelphia Park's average of more than $15,000 per race to Penn National Race Course's average, which is approaching $8,000 per race.

Mid-Atlantic

The Eastern Seaboard is loaded with racetracks, and the sport's changing economics forced Delaware Park to close in 1982. With that closure, Maryland entered an era of year-round racing. Under the ownership of William Rickman Sr., however, Delaware reopened in 1984. Despite its blue-blooded roots—it was built by William duPont Jr.—Delaware became a scrappy, creative competitor. But the game changed in late 1995 when slot machines made their debut at Delaware Park. Soon, horsemen from all over the country were relocating to Delaware to run for its rich purses. In 2001, Delaware Park paid an average purse of more than $29,000.

While continuing to lobby for slots, Maryland has been able to increase purses through full-card simulcasting. Still, average purses at Pimlico Race Course and Laurel Park are below those offered in Delaware.

Virginia's Colonial Downs, which opened in 1997, has been beset by unrealistic expectations for a new racing market in the Richmond area, a dysfunctional relationship between the track's principal owner and the track's regulators, and a virtual freeze on the number of off-track betting parlors it operates at four. But the track, whose racing operations are handled by the Maryland Jockey Club, pays respectable purses for its short, live Thoroughbred meet.

Although average purses at West Virginia's Mountaineer Race Track and Charles Town Races are still slightly below the national average, the transformation has been remarkable as first full-card simulcasting then video lottery terminals and finally coin-drop slot machines poured money into the purse accounts. Mountaineer's average daily distribution in 2001 rose 23% from 2000 levels, and Charles Town's advance was 32%.

Southeast

Hialeah Park once was the queen of winter racetracks, but by the 1980s such feisty and innovative competitors as Gulfstream Park and Calder Race Course came on the scene and took a bite out of the Miami-area track's business. Blessed with a superior location in fast-growing Broward County, Gulfstream successfully challenged Hialeah's hegemony over the prime midwinter dates and eventually took those dates as its own. Through the 1990s, Hialeah flirted with extinction, and after Florida's

racing dates were deregulated in 2001, the track did not open in 2002. Horsemen mourned the closing of Hialeah but gained purse money in the process. Both Gulfstream and Calder pay higher purses than Hialeah did in 2001. While South Florida's remaining tracks and horsemen have explored innovative new methods to promote their product, Tampa Bay Downs's continuing disputes with its horsemen have been an anchor on prospects for Florida's gulf coast track. Purses at its 2001-'02 meet rose a modest 2% from year-earlier levels.

Midwest

While Churchill Downs, home of the Kentucky Derby (G1), advertises itself as the world's best-known racetrack, the king of purses in both Kentucky and North America is its highly traditional neighbor some 80 miles away in Lexington, Keeneland, where the average purse per race exceeded $70,000 in 2001. Keeneland's spring meeting always has had healthy purses, but the fall meeting did not have such generous allocations to purses in the past. The combination of full-card wagering revenues and an improving Thoroughbred commercial market has allowed Keeneland to substantially boost purses at its fall meeting.

Full-card simulcasting also has benefited Churchill Downs, which has fortified its fall meeting as well, and Churchill Downs Inc.-owned Ellis Park has outgrown its image as a small-time pea patch—long being known for the soybeans growing in its infield. Churchill Downs also is the operator and part-owner of Hoosier Park in Indiana.

Turfway Park, now co-owned by Keeneland and two gaming companies, led Kentucky into the new world of full-card simulcasting, and it continues to benefit from the interstate action. But the Cincinnati-area track's gains have been eroded by Ohio's full-card programs—River Downs is less than 20 miles away—and the presence of nearby Indiana riverboat casinos has hurt on-track attendance and handle.

After a two-year hiatus, Arlington Park resumed operations in 2000, and Illinois regained a sizable piece of purse money. Now a Churchill Downs-owned track, Arlington paid the third-highest average purse in the Midwest, and in 2001 total purse distribution rose 2% from Arlington's comeback year.

Located within blocks of each other in Chicago's near southwest suburbs, Hawthorne Park and Sportsman's Park each paid average purses that were higher than the national average.

Slot machines pulled Prairie Meadows away from the edge of extinction and created a healthy racing operation in Iowa—but new contracts with the track's municipal owner, Polk County, and horsemen will mean that the plant's operators will be paying more rent and smaller purses in the future. The average purse in 2001 exceeded $20,000, but the average purse will fall below the national average

in 2002. All other racetracks in the region pay purses below the national average.

Southwest

Racing in America's Southwest is in transition. New Mexico has slots, one Louisiana track has already added them, and Magna Entertainment Inc. was on course to purchase Lone Star Park, Texas's most successful operation, in 2002. Many of the changes—especially the addition of slots—affect purses in the Southwest, the last significant growth area for American racing.

The region's best purses are found at Fair Grounds, the New Orleans dowager that literally has risen from the ashes of a devastating fire in late 1993 to take the leadership spot from Oaklawn Park in Arkansas. The 2001-'02 season certainly will not stand out as one of Fair Grounds's best in recent years, with a 6.9% decline in total wagering and daily average attendance down more than 11%. But since the track opened its $27.5-million grandstand and clubhouse in November 1997, the facility owned by the Krantz family has risen to greater prominence in the region and nationally. For now, Fair Grounds is barred from installing slots at the track, but the machines are in place or on their way at other Louisiana tracks. Already, they have made a huge difference at Delta Downs in Vinton, a short distance from the Texas border, where slots money led to a 48% increase in purses for the 2001-'02 season. Purses at Louisiana Downs slipped 17% in 2001, but track officials, in anticipation of getting slots, vowed to raise purses substantially in 2002.

Sam Houston Race Park opened in 1994 with poor immediate results, but sound management and full-card simulcasting raised the average purse above $11,000 for its 2001-'02 season. Lone Star Park, the first significant successful opening for a new racetrack since the Meadowlands in 1976, pays the region's second-best purses. In the San Antonio area, Retama Park pays purses that are the lowest of the state's three Class I tracks.

The Fair Grounds program has in particular eroded the numbers at Oaklawn Park in historic Hot Springs, Arkansas. Since 1993, horsemen at Oaklawn have seen only a small increase in average purse. Without its Instant Racing game, purses at Oaklawn would have fallen below '93 levels.

Slot machines have turned racing around in New Mexico, where substantial increases in purse payments have occurred in the past several years. Still, purses remain below the national average there and at Oklahoma's Remington Park, which is owned by Magna Entertainment.

West Coast

From just about any perspective, Southern California is a great place to race. The weather is temperate, the competition is high quality, and the purses are among the best in the country. Southern California also is the principal battleground

for Magna, owner of Santa Anita Park, and Churchill Downs Inc., which owns Hollywood Park. A not-for-profit entity, Del Mar racetrack tops the Golden State with the country's third-highest average purse per race, behind only Keeneland and Saratoga. Not far behind Del Mar was the main Santa Anita meet, from late December through mid-April. Santa Anita also is host to the Oak Tree Racing Association meeting each October. Hollywood has a spring-summer meeting and a late fall season.

All Southern California tracks pay purses that are more than double the national average. Santa Anita, however, has advanced little in inflation-adjusted average purse since 1993. The two Northern California tracks, Golden Gate Fields and Bay Meadows Race Course, may be California's junior circuit but are major league by national standards. Both tracks offer purses roughly equal to the national average per race.

Purses at Emerald Downs, the Pacific North-west's newest track, slipped in 2001, the average purse per race declining 3.9% and falling below $10,000. Turf Paradise in Arizona, which has been seeking slots, lost ground in its 2001-'02 season. Colorado's Arapahoe Park scored a substantial gain in 2001, up 9.4%.

Canada

In 2001, the Ontario Jockey Club changed its name to Woodbine Entertainment Group after slot machines arrived at the Toronto-area track. Indeed, slots have turned around the fortunes of Ontario's two Thoroughbred tracks, Woodbine and Fort Erie. As the tracks' finances improve, so too do their purses. Even without slot machines, race purses generally are climbing in the provinces from Ontario to British Columbia. Alberta's two largest Thoroughbred tracks, Northlands and Stampede Park, in particular have posted double-digit gains over the last several years with help from slot machines.—*Don Clippinger*

Purse Distribution by Track for 2001

Northeast

Track, state	No. racing days	Average daily purse distribution (% change from prev. year)		Average purse	Average stakes purses (% total purse)	
Aqueduct, NY	134	$368,272		$40,583	$125,548	(16%)
Atlantic City Race Course, NJ	10	$116,061	(–26%)	$14,508	$30,000	(3%)
Belmont Park, NY	87	$526,268	(–1%)	$57,447	$220,402	(40%)
Finger Lakes, NY	165	$78,302	(–3%)	$8,694	$51,589	(6%)
Garden State Park, NJ	15	$137,767	(39%)	$16,532	$0	(0%)
Monmouth Park, NJ	72	$361,354	(20%)	$36,904	$113,835	(26%)
Penn National Race Course, PA	205	$70,221	(–9%)	$7,802	$37,499	(3%)
Philadelphia Park, PA	220	$149,248	(13%)	$15,394	$72,120	(9%)
Rockingham Park, NH	73	$90,870	(10%)	$9,642	$46,304	(10%)
Saratoga Race Course, NY	37	$590,608		$63,896	$262,428	(43%)
Suffolk Downs, MA	143	$83,617	(–4%)	$9,558	$41,000	(13%)
The Meadowlands, NJ	44	$418,557	(41%)	$40,036	$104,500	(26%)

Mid-Atlantic

Track, state	No. racing days	Average daily purse distribution (% change from prev. year)		Average purse	Average stakes purses (% total purse)	
Charles Town, WV	233	$142,154	(32%)	$14,283	$51,468	(7%)
Colonial Downs, VA	26	$188,479	(32%)	$19,068	$58,908	(16%)
Delaware Park, DE	139	$255,018	(4%)	$29,515	$87,725	(19%)
Laurel Park, MD	112	$189,197	(–12%)	$20,734	$72,377	(16%)
Mountaineer Park, WV	228	$145,463	(23%)	$16,100	$75,500	(6%)
Pimlico, MD	107	$236,098	(–14%)	$25,087	$104,991	(28%)
Timonium, MD	8	$140,298		$14,965	$40,000	(7%)

Southeast

Track, state	No. racing days	Average daily purse distribution (% change from prev. year)		Average purse	Average stakes purses (% total purse)	
Calder Race Course, FL	171	$220,319	(8%)	$20,965	$78,980	(24%)
Gulfstream Park, FL	63	$369,683	(31%)	$35,449	$140,132	(24%)
Hialeah Park, FL	61	$158,196		$17,450	$72,321	(25%)
Ocala Training Center, FL	1	$380,000	(1%)	$54,286	$61,667	(97%)
Tampa Bay Downs, FL	93	$104,556	(7%)	$10,246	$69,747	(13%)

Midwest

Track, state	No. racing days	Average daily purse distribution (% change from prev. year)		Average purse	Average stakes purses (% total purse)	
Anthony Downs, KS	6	$8,967	(9%)	$2,445	$5,875	(44%)
Arlington Park, IL	101	$310,159	(2%)	$33,326	$133,008	(22%)
Atokad Park, NE	1	$125,600		$15,700	$0	(0%)
Beulah Park, OH	141	$59,246	(6%)	$7,445	$49,167	(11%)
Canterbury Park, MN	61	$110,090	(10%)	$12,552	$51,287	(24%)
Chippewa Downs, ND	6	$12,444		$2,409	$4,750	(6%)
Churchill Downs, KY	76	$416,613	(–3%)	$41,993	$227,518	(28%)
Columbus, NE	25	$34,133	(9%)	$4,103	$9,971	(9%)

Track	No. racing days	Average daily purse distribution (% change from prev. year)		Average purse	Average stakes purses (% total purse)	
Ellis Park, KY	41	$191,109	(3%)	$19,018	$83,868	(12%)
Eureka Downs, KS	19	$8,609	(35%)	$2,638	$7,465	(18%)
Fairmount Park, IL	125	$52,396	(−24%)	$5,377	$35,840	(3%)
Fonner Park, NE	38	$52,099	(−11%)	$5,308	$26,753	(23%)
Great Lakes Downs, MI	128	$84,027	(−1%)	$10,204	$64,604	(20%)
Hawthorne Race Course, IL	77	$206,407	(−4%)	$22,105	$86,347	(15%)
Hoosier Park, IN	70	$165,296	(−1%)	$15,700	$67,460	(15%)
Horsemen's Park, NE	3	$129,983	(19%)	$32,496	$41,590	(53%)
Keeneland, KY	32	$641,141	(2%)	$71,736	$208,149	(45%)
Kentucky Downs, KY	7	$261,857	(8%)	$41,659	$119,286	(46%)
Lincoln State Fair, NE	34	$45,037	(−1%)	$5,335	$13,839	(14%)
Mt. Pleasant Meadows, MI	19	$5,358	(−7%)	$4,242	$0	(0%)
Prairie Meadows, IA	97	$160,447	(9%)	$20,108	$85,563	(22%)
River Downs, OH	122	$61,366	(−5%)	$8,059	$63,581	(14%)
Sportsman's Park, IL	43	$245,290	(12%)	$26,238	$123,351	(20%)
The Woodlands, KS	26	$50,107	(2%)	$7,198	$20,909	(18%)
Thistledown, OH	187	$73,454	(−2%)	$9,783	$61,316	(8%)
Turfway Park, KY	112	$168,965	(−6%)	$17,188	$99,308	(16%)

Southwest

Track, state	No. racing days	Average daily purse distribution (% change from prev. year)		Average purse	Average stakes purses (% total purse)	
Blue Ribbon Downs, OK	78	$9,380	(27%)	$3,074	$10,903	(12%)
Delta Downs, LA	85	$49,404	(−4%)	$5,999	$43,412	(4%)
Evangeline Downs, LA	82	$75,848	(−4%)	$7,697	$50,143	(6%)
Fair Grounds, LA	89	$271,595	(2%)	$27,190	$118,015	(27%)
Fair Meadows at Tulsa, OK	32	$46,981	(−4%)	$9,112	$31,594	(15%)
Gillespie County Downs, TX	7	$4,857	(−14%)	$3,400	$15,500	(46%)
Lone Star Park, TX	74	$231,393	(−1%)	$24,185	$132,462	(24%)
Louisiana Downs, LA	89	$124,801	(−17%)	$13,129	$59,578	(24%)
Oaklawn Park, AR	52	$211,267	(−2%)	$20,965	$124,768	(32%)
Remington Park, OK	81	$88,230	(−3%)	$10,342	$48,157	(24%)
Retama Park, TX	54	$90,717	(32%)	$9,402	$43,632	(20%)
Ruidoso Downs, NM	57	$41,615	(7%)	$8,323	$36,614	(29%)
Sam Houston Race Park, TX	81	$101,999	(3%)	$10,661	$49,153	(20%)
Sunland Park, NM	79	$78,144	(22%)	$12,650	$56,211	(21%)
SunRay Park, NM	46	$46,621	(12%)	$9,324	$45,696	(26%)
The Downs at Albuquerque, NM	63	$52,892	(14%)	$10,680	$37,377	(30%)
Will Rogers Downs, OK	10	$26,130	(−9%)	$3,579	$0	(0%)

West

Track, state	No. racing days	Average daily purse distribution (% change from prev. year)		Average purse	Average stakes purses (% total purse)	
Arapahoe Park, CO	37	$71,772	(11%)	$9,002	$32,450	(23%)
Bay Meadows, CA	107	$168,216	(6%)	$19,671	$84,499	(15%)
Bay Meadows Fair, CA	12	$141,206	(−1%)	$16,451	$48,333	(9%)
Del Mar, CA	43	$469,449	(1%)	$54,558	$164,950	(37%
Emerald Downs, WA	91	$90,873	(−3%)	$9,683	$52,999	(24%)
Fairplex Park, CA	17	$241,828		$23,627	$63,181	(28%)
Golden Gate Fields, CA	103	$162,357	(−5%)	$19,112	$86,541	(16%)
Grants Pass, OR	9	$10,043	(−17%)	$1,772	$3,583	(12%)
Great Falls, MT	11	$11,182	(−10%)	$1,836	$5,700	(5%)
Hollywood Park, CA	97	$400,746		$46,222	$162,085	(37%)
Les Bois Park, ID	46	$19,096	(−9%)	$3,126	$14,812	(37%)
Los Alamitos, CA	161	$10,598	(16%)	$5,706	$0	(0%)
Portland Meadows, OR	80	$29,797	(10%)	$3,748	$10,245	(16%)
Rillito Park, AZ	12	$10,944	(−6%)	$2,052	$3,383	(15%)
Santa Anita Park, CA	115	$432,851	(−1%)	$50,434	$168,549	(37%)
Sun Downs, WA	10	$8,930	(5%)	$1,822	$3,550	(8%)
Turf Paradise, AZ	168	$81,488	(7%)	$8,198	$36,358	(19%)
Yavapai Downs, AZ	55	$31,369		$4,846	$12,392	(9%)
Wyoming Downs, WY	15	$4,678	(−9%)	$2,193	$4,525	(45%)
Yellowstone Downs, MT	8	$14,873	(16%)	$2,428	$16,535	(14%)

Canada

Track, province	No. racing days	Average daily purse distribution (% change from prev. year)		Average purse	Average stakes purses (% total purse)	
Assiniboia Downs, MB	75	$60,443		$7,543	$30,034	(23%)
Fort Erie, ON	116	$170,315	(34%)	$16,871	$90,846	(8%)
Grand Prairie, AB	15	$5,186	(27%)	$1,995	$2,507	(16%)
Hastings Park Racecourse, BC	93	$118,488	(5%)	$14,518	$55,981	(24%)
Kamloops, BC	10	$10,500	(−1%)	$2,442	$5,459	(21%)
Kin Park, BC	5	$10,009	(−5%)	$2,275	$0	(0%)
Lethbridge, AB	40	$17,102	(33%)	$3,321	$7,458	(28%)
Marquis Downs, SK	45	$16,247	(−21%)	$2,547	$8,417	(33%)
Millarville, AB	1	$16,450	(44%)	$2,742	$3,850	(23%)
Northlands Park, AB	68	$105,657	(27%)	$12,452	$46,152	(20%)
Stampede Park, AB	42	$88,239	(37%)	$11,063	$41,997	(14%)
Woodbine, ON	165	$494,595	(2%)	$52,380	$179,750	(25%)

HISTORY OF RACING

by Mary Simon

Horse racing officially appeared in the annals of history in approximately 1000 B.C. when Greeks started racing horses with chariots drawn behind them, a dangerous game that subsequently was adopted by the Romans and Egyptians. For the 33rd Olympiad in 644 B.C., formal competition began with riders astride the horses. The Romans, who conquered England in A.D. 43 under Emperor Claudius and ruled it until A.D. 410, carried their horses and their sport to the island nation, where a millennium later it would blossom into the sport known as Thoroughbred racing.

By the late 1500s, racing had become a favorite pastime of English noblemen. King Henry VIII and his daughter Queen Elizabeth I both maintained racing stables, and Elizabeth's cousin King James I established Newmarket racecourse early in the 17th century. His son Charles I also was a racing enthusiast, but he was overthrown and beheaded in 1649, and Lord Protector Oliver Cromwell banned horse racing. After the restoration of the monarchy in 1660, racing flourished under its ardent devotee King Charles II.

Because of Charles II's love for the sport, racing became known as the sport of kings, and during his rule three imported Arabian stallions began the genetic progression toward the Thoroughbred of today. In 1688, Capt. Robert Byerly returned from Hungary with a captured stallion who became known as the Byerly Turk. Sixteen years later, British consul Thomas Darley smuggled an Arabian stallion out of Syria and transplanted him to Yorkshire; he became known as the Darley Arabian. In approximately 1730, an Arabian stallion of unknown lineage appeared in the stable of the Earl of Godolphin. These three stallions would become the foundation sires of the Thoroughbred. The Darley Arabian sired Flying Childers, generally regarded as the first great Thoroughbred, in 1714. (For more on the development of the Thoroughbred, see Evolution of the Breed.)

In the late 18th century, racing began to assume a formal structure. Racecourses were established, and the first of the English classics, the St. Leger Stakes, was run in 1776. The Epsom Derby followed four years later, and the Two Thousand Guineas had its first running in 1809. As racing developed in England, it found its way to the American colonies. In 1665, New York Governor Richard Nicholls gave the name Newmarket to America's first racetrack. Although the first track was located in New York, horse racing tended to be frowned upon by religious leaders and communities in the North, but the sport flourished in the South. The first known Thoroughbred sire imported to North America from England was *Bulle Rock, an aged son of the Darley Arabian. Although *Bulle Rock had no lasting influence, pre-Revolution imports such as *Fearnought, pint-sized *Janus, and the *Cub mare influenced the breed's development.

19th Century

Early American presidents, particularly those from the South, were racing fans. Thomas Jefferson approved the Senate's practice of adjourning early to attend local meets. Senators of the day might have marveled at the fabled 28-foot stride of the great colt Florizel or witnessed the unbeatable brilliance of First Consul during his 21-race winning streak.

It was an era of often unrecorded and disputed genealogies, and races were crudely timed, if at all. The 1823 victory of American Eclipse over Henry in the North-South match at Long Island's Union Course proved a milestone in post-Colonial racing. The $20,000-a-side event drew a significant portion of the New York populace and helped American Eclipse stake his claim as the first American earnings champion, with $56,700. At the same time, *Leviathan was standing for America's highest known fee—$75—but he was not the most notable stallion of the period. That honor went to *Diomed, a British castoff after the Revolutionary War. The inaugural Epsom Derby winner in 1780, he arrived on American shores in 1798, acquired for a meager $220. *Diomed proceeded over 11 seasons to reshape the American Thoroughbred in his own remarkable image, getting runners that were uniformly taller, heavier of bone, stouter, stronger, and faster than their contemporaries.

Unlike England, where the Epsom Derby and St. Leger heralded a trend toward shorter races, America maintained its long heat races for the first half of the century. While the style of racing evolved over time, change of another kind arrived on March 17, 1850, when *Diomed's great-great grandson Lexington was born on a Central Kentucky farm. Brilliant on the racecourse and even more accomplished at stud, Lexington would reign 16 times—including 14 in succession—as the country's leading sire.

As the century progressed, races became shorter, purses rose, and racing began to become organized. Saratoga Race Course, Pimlico Race Course, Churchill Downs, and Fair Grounds opened for business. The Travers Stakes had its first running in 1864, and the Belmont Stakes was run for the first time in 1867. The Preakness Stakes followed in 1873, and the Kentucky Derby was staged for the first time in 1875. Later in the

century, the Jockey Club was established to oversee the growing sport, and it soon assumed control of the *American Stud Book*. In 1889, Miss Woodford became the first American Thoroughbred to top $100,000 in career earnings. Two-year-old racing gained popularity with the inaugural 1888 Futurity, worth $40,000 to the winner; five years later, a juvenile named Domino set a single-season earnings record of $170,790 that would stand for decades. Kingston—last of the great iron horses of a dying era—retired in 1894 with 89 victories, a record to this day. By the end of the 19th century, Kentucky had become the heart of America's Thoroughbred business, with more professional horsemen than any other region. America and its Thoroughbred industry were thus poised to enter a modern era of even greater change.

1901-'10

The American century's first decade was one of promise and turmoil for the Thoroughbred racing industry. Trouble brewed even as financier James R. Keene's great Commando blistered the track at the dawn of the century and as Commando's unbeatable son Colin carried the Keene colors to victory after brilliant victory a few years later. Even as Keene's stable racked up unprecedented earnings, as record purses were dispensed, and as Belmont Park opened its glorious gates, a dark cloud was settling ominously on racing's horizon.

Racing may have been the sport of kings, but it was also part of a larger gambling industry. Increasingly, the taint of corruption eroded public confidence in the sport as high-profile incidents were exposed. Keene's Sysonby, one of the sport's all-time greats, suffered his only loss in the 1904 Futurity after being drugged by a groom. Delhi, the 1904 Belmont Stakes winner, later ran sluggishly and was found to have sponges inserted far up into his nostrils. Electric prods, dopings, ringers, crooked jockeys, and diverse gambling scams involving track bookmakers were daily journalistic fodder.

By 1907, anti-racetrack wagering laws had been simmering for some time on legislative back burners across America. In June 1908, New York passed the Agnew-Hart bill with the ardent blessing of Governor Charles Evans Hughes, who used the legislation as a weapon against the Tammany Hall political machine, a major beneficiary of racing in the New York metropolitan area. Without revenues from legalized gambling, racing soon found it impossible to support itself. In 1910, historic Saratoga was among the racetracks that ceased operation, and E. J. "Lucky" Baldwin's original Santa Anita Park was forced to close.

A domino effect occurred as other states rushed to pass similar legislation. The national purse structure collapsed, declining from a 1907 average of $949 per race to $643 in '09. Top stables, including Keene's, shipped overseas in a European invasion so successful that it would pave the way for the next great blow to the American Thoroughbred industry—England's 1913 passage of the "Jersey Act." In 1908, Churchill Downs's energetic general manager, Col. Matt Winn, pulled some old pari-mutuel machines out of storage, dusted them off, and put them back into use. When racing resumed in the next decade, the pari-mutuel wagering system quickly would become dominant.

Despite all, several great competitors appeared on racing's stage to illuminate the decade. Colin was one of nine future Racing Hall of Fame members who campaigned during the decade. Man o' War's fiery sire, Fair Play, was another, along with Commando, Sysonby, Artful, Beldame, Roseben, Broomstick, and Peter Pan.

1911-'20

As indignation among the American populace swelled over puritan campaigners' assault on gambling and alcohol consumption, a group of wealthy horsemen began to stockpile a fund with which to hold future race meets. The future came quickly. Although the Agnew-Hart legislation moldered on the books until 1934, the penalties associated with it were stripped away by May 30, 1913, when Belmont Park opened for the first time since 1910. Between 1908 and '13, however, American breeders had sent overseas more than 1,500 horses, among them at least 24 champions. Some eventually came back, but many did not. Leading sires *Rock Sand and *Meddler, also part of the exodus, were lost forever to American breeding.

The British responded with the Jersey Act in 1913, which effectively barred many old American lines from England's *General Stud Book*, but the first shots of World War I one year later quickly changed the United States from an exporter of bloodstock into an aggressive importer. Between 1916-'20, numerous English-breds and French-breds became American champions, including *Short Grass, *Sun Briar, *Hourless, *Omar Khayyam, *Johren, *Sunbonnet, *Enfilade, and *Constancy.

Even in the shadow of war, the decade was memorable for its outstanding runners, including future Racing Hall of Fame geldings Roamer, Old Rosebud, and Exterminator. Together, they won 129 races and set or equaled 29 records from five furlongs to 2¼ miles at 14 different racetracks. Iron Mask set a North American record for 5½ furlongs that would stand for 30 years, and the mare Pan Zareta took a back seat to no male in the realm of blazing speed. H. P. Whit-

ney's Regret routinely whipped the boys and in 1915 became the first filly to win the Kentucky Derby. The Triple Crown was won for the first time in 1919 by Sir Barton, although the sweep did not take on its popular name until the 1930s.

Sir Barton won the Belmont on June 11, five days after the decade's finest specimen made his first career start at Belmont Park. Man o' War, considered the greatest American horse of all time, was ineligible for admission to the *General Stud Book*, but in 16 months of competition redefined greatness. He lost one race at two that he should have won, failing to overcome a bad start in the Sanford Stakes at Saratoga Race Course, losing to Upset, but he never lost again. In 1920, "Big Red" established five American and two track records in 11 starts and won his races by a combined 164 lengths. Man o' War capped his extraordinary career on October 12, 1920, by galloping away from Sir Barton in a winner-take-all race at Kenilworth Park in Canada. The $80,000 purse sent him to stud as the richest American Thoroughbred in history with $249,465.

1921-'30

On the surface at least, the Roaring Twenties were a time of outrageous fun—flappers and the fox trot are indelible images of the era—and horse racing rode the crest of this postwar celebration. Elaborate new racetracks were the overt symbol of this prosperity—at least 15 of note were constructed in the United States during the 1920s, including Arlington and Washington Parks in Chicago and Hialeah Park in Florida. Purses went through the roof. In 1923, Zev became the first American racehorse to bank $200,000 in a season and, by 1930, Gallant Fox— the second Triple Crown winner and the first to be recognized for sweeping the three American classics—had raised that bar to $300,000. Jockey Earle Sande, trainer James Fitzsimmons, breeder Harry Payne Whitney, and owner Harry Sinclair each established earnings records that would stand for years. Bloodstock prices also went into orbit, with a yearling commanding a record $75,000 in 1928.

Because the Jersey Act remained in force, horses mostly migrated to the west. Future leading sires *St. Germans, *Sickle, and *Challenger II were among the importees, as was the great matron *La Troienne. In late 1925, *Sir Gallahad III arrived at Claiborne Farm, where he would reign four times as America's premier sire and 12 times as its leading broodmare sire. *Sir Gallahad III's American-bred counterpart was Man o' War, a private stallion who had seven of his eight champions in his first four crops and in 1926—with only three crops racing—set a progeny earnings record of $409,927.

No single racehorse towered above all others

in the 1920s as Man o' War and Colin had before, but the decade nonetheless yielded 15 Racing Hall of Fame members. Foremost among them was Exterminator, the wonderful gelding who scored a 20th-century record 34 stakes victories and retired as America's richest Thoroughbred. Grey Lag flirted with greatness, as did champions Sarazen, Blue Larkspur, Reigh Count, and Gallant Fox. Zev, Crusader, and Sun Beau were big money winners. Princess Doreen won 34 races and broke Miss Woodford's 40-year female earnings record with $174,745. Other notable fillies included 1924 Preakness winner Nellie Morse; multiple champions Black Maria and Bateau; and Rose of Sharon, considered best of either sex at three in 1929. For a time, it appeared the good times would go on forever, but the stock market crashed in October 1929, which led to events that caused the Great Depression.

1931-'40

As the Depression shrunk race purses 40%, the average yearling price slumped to $570 in 1932. But, as the Depression eased, the Thoroughbred industry entered one of its healthiest eras. Purses rose by decade's end to record heights, and yearling sales gained strength. Racing also had some wealthy, influential leaders. Joseph E. Widener, vice chairman of the New York Jockey Club, crusaded tirelessly to return the sport in the Empire State to its former glory. Jockey Club Chairman William Woodward campaigned 1935 Triple Crown winner Omaha, but more importantly that year he fired some of the angriest, most articulate words at England's discriminatory Jersey Act. During the decade, increasingly sophisticated stall starting gates were developed, photo-finish cameras were installed, and saliva testing for drugs gained widespread use. Keeneland Race Course, Del Mar Thoroughbred Club, Santa Anita Park, and Hollywood Park opened for business.

Although the 1930s featured many standout racehorses, including 17 future Racing Hall of Fame members and two Triple Crown winners, three in particular captured the hearts of America—C. V. Whitney's Equipoise, Australasian wonder *Phar Lap, and claimer-turned-champion Seabiscuit. Although bred in the purple and owned by one of America's wealthiest bluebloods, there was nothing pretentious about Equipoise, a son of Pennant who was a champion at two in 1930, a three-time handicap champion, and a world-record miler. Seabiscuit, an undersized Wheatley Stable reject, developed into a megastar, reigning as 1938 Horse of the Year and twice as America's handicap champion. In one of the decade's greatest moments, Seabiscuit defeated 1937 Triple Crown winner War Admiral in the two-horse 1938 Pimlico Special Stakes. *Phar

Lap illuminated the Depression's darkest hour by winning the 1932 Agua Caliente Handicap in record time, but the huge New Zealander died just 17 days later under suspicious circumstances.

The 1930s launched a feminine revolution of sorts. Top Flight defeated males in the 1931 Futurity to become the first $200,000 juvenile earner and richest American female. Mrs. Payne Whitney's Twenty Grand won that year's Kentucky Derby, and Isabel Dodge Sloane became America's leading owner in 1934. As war in Europe approached, America imported several top stallions. In 1936, Hancock organized a syndicate to purchase *Blenheim II, for $250,000; four years later, Whitney acquired the stallion's classic-winning son, *Mahmoud.

1941-'50

Despite a world at war for half the decade, the 1940s very well may have been racing's finest hour, with four Triple Crown winners crowning the decade. The war years were grim for the sport, however. California's tracks were shut down—Santa Anita was an internment camp for Japanese-Americans, Hollywood was an army storage unit, and Del Mar was used for assembling aircraft wings. Travel restrictions crippled the Saratoga yearling sale and led to the creation of the Breeders' Sales Co., precursor of the Keeneland July sale. In late 1944, the government banned racing, and only victory in Europe saved the 1945 Triple Crown.

Leavening the somber news from overseas were the exploits of Whirlaway, Calumet's "Mr. Longtail," winner of the 1941 Triple Crown. Then there was Alsab, a $700 yearling of peasant lineage who outgamed Whirlaway by a nose in a famous 1942 match race at Narragansett Park. Mrs. John D. Hertz's 1943 Triple Crown winner, Count Fleet, habitually crushed his opposition and romped to a 25-length Belmont Stakes victory, despite a career-ending injury. High-headed, flame-coated Stymie was not the best, but he was nevertheless beloved by fans who made him the people's horse. Claimed for $1,500 from King Ranch by trainer Hirsch Jacobs, Stymie became the first Thoroughbred to surpass $900,000 in career earnings. King Ranch had Assault, who overcame a deformed right fore foot to win the 1946 Triple Crown. The 1940s also produced several top fillies, including Racing Hall of Fame members Twilight Tear, Busher, Gallorette, Bewitch, Two Lea, and Bed o' Roses. Argentine-bred *Miss Grillo set a 2½-mile world record in the 1948 Pimlico Cup Handicap.

The decade virtually belonged to Warren Wright's magnificent Calumet Stable, whose champions were trained by Ben and Jimmy Jones and in many cases ridden by Eddie Arcaro—all Racing Hall of Fame members. Calumet reigned as America's top owner seven times during the decade, edged only by a trio of prominent women—Mrs. Payne Whitney (1942), Elizabeth Graham ('45), and Isabel Dodge Sloane ('50). Runners who carried the feared devil's red and blue silks during the 1940s included Racing Hall of Fame members Whirlaway, Twilight Tear, Armed, Citation, Bewitch, Coaltown, and Two Lea, and father-son Kentucky Derby winners Pensive and Ponder. Citation was not only Calumet's best but also one of the century's most talented runners. Champion at two and three, American Triple Crown hero, and winner of 16 consecutive races, Citation would become the sport's first millionaire in 1951.

Late in the decade, Claiborne acquired *Nasrullah, a rogue stallion who would transform the American bloodstock industry. Also in 1949, England's Jockey Club backed down after 36 years and rescinded the despised Jersey Act, by now long outdated and hindering rather than helping the British breeding industry. America thus regained its former stature as a respected source of international bloodstock.

1951-'60

As it entered the second half of the 20th century, the U.S. confronted a rapidly changing world. It was at war in Korea, the threat of Nazism had been replaced by the peril of nuclear cataclysm, television was helping to create a truly national society, and polio had been conquered. America's appetite for racing seemed utterly insatiable; attendance and handle records were established almost annually. Perhaps it was too successful. In this decade, racing failed to build a lasting partnership with television—an arrogant decision that the industry would regret into the 21st century.

The 1950s were a time of rising incomes and rising expectations. In 1956, Nashua became the first million-dollar stallion syndication. Also that year, jockey Bill Hartack became the first to ride winners of $2-million in a single season; he topped $3-million the following year. The 1950s witnessed a growing interest in early competition—particularly after the spectacular 1953 debut of the world's richest race, the $270,000 Garden State Stakes for two-year-olds at Garden State Park in New Jersey. Soundness also became an issue in the 1950s with the high-profile breakdowns of such stars as Hail to Reason and Swaps. In 1960, phenylbutazone—an anti-inflammatory drug popularly known as Bute—came into wide use to ease the aches and pains of racing.

Racing in the 1950s had several stars but no Triple Crown winner. (Eddie Arcaro blamed himself for Nashua's loss to Swaps in the 1955 Derby. Nashua subsequently won the Preakness and Belmont.) The first equine superhero of the TV

age was Native Dancer—the "Gray Ghost of Sagamore," whose only loss in 22 starts was by a head in the 1953 Kentucky Derby. Also racing at that time was Tom Fool, who carried heavy imposts to ten straight victories. As Native Dancer and Tom Fool exited the stage, the prodigiously talented pair of Nashua and Swaps took their place. They met twice, with Swaps winning the 1955 Derby and Nashua the 1955 $100,000 Washington Park match race. The foal crop of 1954 contained Bold Ruler, Round Table, and *Gallant Man, all Racing Hall of Fame members. Round Table lasted the longest, 66 races, and was America's first great grass horse. Talent was so widespread that no one noticed an ordinary-looking bay gelding who won only a maiden race in 1959. But Kelso went on to become one of the major heroes of the 1960s.

1961-'70

The 1960s were a watershed for America and American racing. Inaugurated in January 1961 was John F. Kennedy, the first President born in the 20th century. Racial segregation was overthrown in the South, but lives were lost in the battle. Kennedy's assassination in 1963 shook America to its core, and soon the collective conformism of the 1950s crumbled. As men walked on the moon, young soldiers were dying in an unpopular Vietnam war.

Racing increasingly became a game of haves and have-nots. In 1967, Damascus banked a single-season record $817,941. That same year, North America's earnings per runner averaged $3,359, or about half of training costs for a year. Medication also became an issue, especially when Dancer's Image was disqualified from his 1968 Kentucky Derby victory over a Bute positive.

State legislators looked to racing to plug budget gaps; at the end of the decade, proposed federal tax changes led to the creation of the American Horse Council to help lobby on behalf of horse racing and breeding interests. Simultaneously, racing was losing some of its audience as other professional sports and entertainment forms gained popularity. National attendance declined in 1967 for the first time since World War II, despite nearly 100 added racing days. During the 1960s, total racing days increased 35% while average daily attendance declined 3%. At decade's end, off-track betting was approved in New York, which would lead to even larger attendance declines.

Against this chaotic and disquieting backdrop, Kelso—and others like him—redeemed this troubled era and made it one of the most remarkable in 200 years. Allaire duPont's Kelso tore through the handicap ranks, ruling as Horse of the Year from 1960 through '64. Carry Back emerged from Florida to win the 1961 Kentucky Derby and Preakness Stakes. Other outstanding performers of the era were Arts and Letters, Majestic Prince, Nodouble, Northern Dancer, and Fort Marcy, but the second half of the decade belonged to Buckpasser, Damascus, and Dr. Fager. Together, they started 85 times and compiled a 64-13-5 record.

Fillies of the 1960s deserve special mention. Cicada, Old Hat, Affectionately, Straight Deal, Tosmah, Politely, Gamely, and Shuvee averaged 56 career starts. Cicada set an earnings record; Moccasin became the first juvenile filly to take Horse of the Year honors in the 1965 Thoroughbred Racing Associations poll; Dark Mirage was first to sweep New York's filly triple crown in 1968; Dr. Fager's younger half sister, Ta Wee, toted an average of 136 pounds in 1970. Women gained the right to ride in races in 1969, and trailblazer Diane Crump rode in the 1970 Derby. Bloodstock prices were heating up, and Nijinsky II was syndicated for a record $5.44-million in 1970.

1971-'80

In some respects, the decade between 1971 and '80 was one of the century's most satisfying periods for American Thoroughbred racing. Great runners and big money energized the era, but they also disguised some troubling problems, such as race fixing, increasingly lenient medication rules, and a declining audience. The 1970s were racing's best years since the '40s, with three Triple Crown winners within five years. The bloodstock markets were supercharged as well, with the beginning of the Northern Dancer era and the speculative buying that eventually wrecked the markets in the 1980s.

Secretariat, Seattle Slew, and Affirmed, the three Triple Crown winners, attracted most of the attention, and they shared the limelight with Forego, Ruffian, and Spectacular Bid, among others. It has been said that Secretariat appeared at the precise moment when America and racing needed him most. A transcendent, larger-than-life figure bursting with almost supernatural vitality, he streaked across racing's stage in 1972 and '73, leaving behind an impression of pure greatness unrivaled since Man o' War. After he won the 1973 Kentucky Derby (G1) in record time (1:59⅖, a mark that still stands) and the Preakness Stakes (G1) with consummate ease (also probably a record even though the timing was botched), Secretariat quieted every skeptic with his 31-length triumph in the Belmont Stakes (G1) in 2:24, 2⅕ seconds—11 lengths—faster than the existing world record. Seattle Slew blazed through the Triple Crown, becoming the first to complete the sweep with an unbeaten record, and one year later Affirmed won the Triple Crown over his nemesis Alydar, who was second in all three races.

The Triple Crown winners did not stand alone

in the spotlight. Twenty-two future Racing Hall of Fame members campaigned during this decade, including six from a remarkable 1970 foal crop. Among them were the first distaff millionaire, Dahlia, 12-for-12 juvenile La Prevoyante, and Forego, who was Horse of the Year three times. Ruffian cruised unbeaten through ten starts until the ill-fated 1975 match race with Kentucky Derby winner Foolish Pleasure that took her life. The era closed with yet another performer for the ages. The Triple Crown eluded Spectacular Bid, but not much else did between 1978 and '80. The compact gray colt set nine track, American, and world standards. In 1980, Genuine Risk became only the second filly in 106 years to wear the blanket of roses.

The 1970s signaled the dramatic rise of top Hispanic jockeys, with none more prominent than Laffit Pincay Jr. Among trainers, the torch passed to Charlie Whittingham and Laz Barrera, whose West Coast-based stables also hailed the arrival of California as a centerpiece of American racing. The industry was changing in other ways, due in part to the 1971 introduction of off-track betting in New York. By 1977, OTB wagers finally exceeded money wagered on track in New York, and the gap would widen thereafter.

1981-'90

The breeding industry follows the fortunes of the racetrack, but for a few years in the 1980s that relationship became temporarily detached, or so it seemed, as rich foreign buyers pursued yearlings by Northern Dancer and his sons. In 1985, a Nijinsky II colt sold for a record $13.1-million at the Keeneland July sale of selected yearlings, but by then the bloodstock markets had entered a slide that would last into the 1990s. Stud fees climbed to unsupportable levels on the fantasy, and everything came crashing down. On the track, attendance was falling while wagering and purses stagnated.

In 1982, at the peak of the bloodstock boom, horseman John Gaines worried over the industry's fundamentals and came up with an idea to market it. One year earlier, the Arlington Million had been inaugurated in Chicago as the world's first $1-million race. Enthusiastically received, it had drawn a field of international grass stars and was won by all-American hero John Henry. Gaines envisioned a single championship day of racing, offering millions of dollars in purse money, paid for by stallion and foal nomination fees. In November 1984 at Hollywood Park, his dream became reality at the first Breeders' Cup championship day, arguably the sport's greatest innovation since the Triple Crown.

Although he missed the first Breeders' Cup and never raced again, Dotsam Stable's John Henry proved once again that the American Dream was alive and well. He was a gelded son of an obscure sire, and he earned more than $6.5-million. In the 1980s, fillies shined brightest. Eight of the decade's 13 Racing Hall of Fame performers thus far have been members of the distaff set, including Horses of the Year All Along (Fr) and Lady's Secret, 1988 Kentucky Derby winner Winning Colors, undefeated champions Personal Ensign (13-for-13) and Landaluce (5-for-5 before her death), and two-time champion Go for Wand, who died on the track in the 1990 Breeders' Cup Distaff (G1). Also notable were two-time champions Bayakoa (Arg) and Miesque.

Although males of the 1980s lacked the brilliance of their female counterparts, they did provide memorable moments. Ferdinand gave Whittingham his first Kentucky Derby victory at age 73 in 1986, and in '87 he fought to the bitter end under Hall of Fame member Bill Shoemaker to edge Derby winner Alysheba in the Breeders' Cup Classic (G1). The fierce 1989 rivalry between Sunday Silence and Easy Goer ranks among the sport's best, and also memorable was Conquistador Cielo's 14-length triumph in the 1982 Belmont Stakes (G1), the first of trainer Woody Stephens's historic five straight wins in that classic. One of the decade's most poignant moments was trainer Carl Nafzger's spontaneous televised description of Unbridled's 1990 Kentucky Derby stretch run for 92-year-old owner Frances Genter. Trainer D. Wayne Lukas rewrote the record books repeatedly during these years, setting and breaking his own earnings standards.

1991-2000

The century's final decade was a breakthrough for America's racetracks, which built a solid foundation first on intrastate intertrack wagering and then on the true bonanza, interstate full-card wagering. The full-card explosion forever altered the sport. By mid-decade, off-site wagering accounted for 74% of racing's handle, a figure that jumped to 82% by 1999. Some tracks added slot machines to boost both purses and profits without putting any new patrons in the stands. The bloodstock markets recovered from a prolonged recession and rose to new heights as the decade ended.

Lexington ad executive Fred Pope, with counsel from John Gaines, in 1996 proposed an industry alliance to revitalize the sport and create a "major league of racing." Their National Thoroughbred Association, an owner-driven organization, soon was swallowed up by the National Thoroughbred Racing Association (NTRA), which was launched in April 1998 and reached into every corner of the sport. Racing series added hours of television coverage, and in 1999 Television Games Network (TVG) debuted on satel-

lite and a few cable stations.

In the bloodstock market, stallion owners began breeding their stars to large books of mares and sent them to the Southern Hemisphere for double duty. A record for a stallion syndication was set in 2000 when Fusaichi Pegasus commanded a record $60-million to $70-million price tag.

A trio of sensational grays—Holy Bull, Silver Charm, and Skip Away—and Allen Paulson's marvelous bay Cigar captured the imagination of the racing public in the 1990s. Together they won classics, championships, and $30-million, but they were sired by stallions with average stud fees of just $7,800. Among females, Serena's Song and Dance Smartly were the decade's standouts.

It was an exciting classics decade, with the Triple Crown on the line each year between 1997 and '99, with Silver Charm, Real Quiet, and Charismatic winning the Derby and Preakness before coming up short in the Belmont. Silver Charm and Real Quiet were trained by Bob Baffert, but the classics of the 1990s virtually belonged to Lukas, who won six consecutive classic races with five different horses and also trained Charismatic for Robert and Beverly Lewis, Californians who owned Silver Charm and Serena's Song. Cigar, a two-time Horse of the Year, won 16 consecutive races but proved sterile.

Class I racing returned to Texas, but the first two tracks to open, Sam Houston Race Park and Retama Park, struggled initially. Lone Star Park in the populous Dallas-Fort Worth area was a success from its opening in April 1997. An important trend that began toward the end of the decade was the consolidation of racetrack ownership under Magna Entertainment Corp. and Churchill Downs Inc. That consolidation would continue into the 21st century.

Condensed from "Racing Through the Century," for which Mary Simon was awarded the 2000 Eclipse Award for outstanding features-enterprise writing.

History of Racing Silks

Worn by each jockey to represent a horse's owner, racing silks have been associated with horse racing for nearly two millennia. *Kennets Roman Antiquities* (1696) cites colors worn at chariot races: "At these races, the Romans rode in different colours, particularly the companies of Charioteers, to distinguish themselves." Nero was so fond of his green colors that he often wore a green toga when he attended the races during the first century.

The records of England's King Henry VIII mention jockeys' attire in the first half of the 16th century. His 1530 purse accounts show payments for "doublets (shirts) of Bruges Satin for the boys that runne the gueldings" and for "ryding cappes of Black Satin lyned with black vellute (velvet)." Silk, though expensive, was used for jockeys' jackets and caps because of its light weight and soft, smooth texture. Velvet also was used through the first half of the 19th century.

On October 4, 1762, 19 members of the English Jockey Club registered their colors at Newmarket "for the greater convenience of distinguishing the horses in running." Across the Atlantic Ocean just four years later, Philadelphia horsemen registered their silks with the Philadelphia Jockey Club. Registering yellow silks was Lewis Morris Jr., a signer of the Declaration of Independence.

One of the longest-used silks in America belonged to Howell E. Jackson, a relative of President Andrew Jackson who chose all-maroon colors first used in the early 1820s. The all-scarlet silks of Francis Morris (no relation to Lewis) were first worn in 1862 at the Union Course on Long Island. The Morris family used those colors for four generations through John A. Morris.

Rules published for the October 17-19, 1826, race meeting in Lexington required jockeys to wear a silk jacket and cap. The American Jockey Club, founded in 1894, registered silks for $1 annually or $25 lifetime. The most famous silks in American racing have been those of prominent, private stables—the devil's red and blue of Calumet Farm, the plain black jacket with cherry cap of the late Ogden Phipps, and the all-orange silks of Claiborne Farm.

Sporadically, racetracks have experimented with color-coded silks and jockeys' caps. In 1947, Portland Meadows assigned silks colors by post positions, an idea that was copied at Sportsman's Park and Prescott Downs. Narragansett Park matched the colors of jockeys' caps with post positions. Neither experiment caught on nationally.

In the evolution of Thoroughbred racing in the United States, silk has mostly yielded to nylon or Lycra as the preferred fabric for jockeys' colors. Aerodynamic silks have become commonplace in American racing. First unveiled in 1988 when trainer D. Wayne Lukas used them on all 12 of his horses in the Breeders' Cup, aerodynamic silks, though more costly, are widely available today.

Approximately 28,000 sets of silks are registered with the Jockey Club. Owners pay an annual fee of $15 or $60 every five years. The Jockey Club ceased registering lifetime silks in 1964 while perpetually reserving 3,500 designs.

The Jockey Club has registered silks with various punctuation marks, geometric figures, riding equipment, racetracks, vegetables, musical notes, instruments, birds, dogs, horses, foxes, and even an elephant. Though silks can vary from state to state, roughly 95% of all silks designs are registered with the Jockey Club.—*Bill Heller*

Great Horses in Racing

Racing Hall of Fame members are listed in italics

The name of each great horse is followed by year of birth and year of death, if known. Color and sex (colt, filly, or gelding) are followed by sire, dam, and broodmare sire. The horse's race record is detailed by number of starts, wins, seconds, thirds, and earnings, followed by championship honors and most important wins. Records from the 18th and 19th centuries may be incomplete, or earnings may be impossible to determine. If the horse sired or produced significant stakes winners, that information follows the race record. A sire's or dam's place in important male or female lines is also noted. Namesakes of current graded stakes races are included in this listing.

ACK ACK, 1966-1990. B. c., Battle Joined—Fast Turn, by *Turn-to. 27-19-6-0, $636,641, Horse of the Year in 1971, champion sprinter, champion older male, Santa Anita H., Hollywood Gold Cup H., etc. Sire of 54 stakes winners, including Youth, Broad Brush, Ack's Secret, Rascal Lass, Caline. Broodmare sire of Sharp Cat, Royal Anthem, Benny the Dip, North Sider, Lost Code.

AFFECTIONATELY, 1960-1979. Dk. b. or br. f., Swaps—Searching, by War Admiral. 52-28-8-6, $546,659, champion two-year-old filly, champion sprinter, champion older mare, Top Flight H., Spinaway S., etc. Dam of Personality.

AFFIRMED, 1975-2001. Ch. c., Exclusive Native—Won't Tell You, by Crafty Admiral. 29-22-5-1, $2,393,818, Horse of the Year in 1978-'79, champion two- and three-year-old colt, champion older male, Triple Crown, Jockey Club Gold Cup (G1), etc. Sire of more than 75 stakes winners, including Flawlessly, Quiet Resolve, Affirmed Success, Peteski, Zoman, Charlie Barley, Bint Pasha. Broodmare sire of Chelsey Flower, Harlan's Holiday, Stinger, Balanchine.

A GLEAM, 1949-1974. B. f., *Blenheim II—Twilight Tear, by Bull Lea. 30-12-8-7, $251,395, Hollywood Oaks, Milady H. twice, etc. Dam of A Glitter, Gleaming; grandam of Before Dawn.

ALARM, 1869-1895. B. c., *Eclipse—*Maud, by Stockwell. 9-6-2-1, $12,500, match race with Inverary. Sire of Himyar, Panique, Danger, Ann Fief, Fidele.

ALCIBIADES, 1927-1957. Ch. f., Supremus—*Regal Roman, by Roi Herode. 23-7-2-4, $47,860, champion two-year-old filly, Kentucky Oaks, etc. Dam of Menow, Lithe, Salaminia. Foundation mare of family that includes Sir Ivor, Firm Policy, Rash Statement, Twice the Vice, Shine Again, Halo America.

ALL ALONG (Fr), 1979-. B. f., Targowice—Agujita (Fr), by Vieux Manoir. 21-9-4-2, $2,125,809, Horse of the Year in 1983, champion older female, champion older horse in France, Prix de l'Arc de Triomphe (Fr-G1), Turf Classic S. (G1), etc. Dam of Along All, Arnaqueur.

ALLEGED, 1974-2000. B. c., Hoist the Flag—Princess Pout, by Prince John. 10-9-1-0, $623,187, champion three-year-old in England and France, champion older horse in Europe, Prix de l'Arc de Triomphe (Fr-G1) twice, etc. One of only five horses to win consecutive runnings of the Prix de l'Arc de Triomphe. Sire of more than 100 stakes winners, including Miss Alleged, Law Society, Midway Lady, Shantou, Muhtarram, Romanette. Broodmare sire of Suave Dancer, Dr. Devious (Ire), Dream Well (Fr), Go and Go (Ire), Sulamani.

ALMAHMOUD, 1947-1971. Ch. f., *Mahmoud—Arbitrator, by Peace Chance. 11-4-0-1, $32,760, Vineland H., etc. Dam of Cosmah, Natalma. Foundation mare of family that includes Northern Dancer, Halo, Danehill, Tosmah, Flawlessly, Arctic Tern, Machiavellian, Coup de Genie, L'Emigrant, Cannonade, La Prevoyante.

ALSAB, 1939-1963. B. c., Good Goods—Winds Chant, by Wildair. 51-25-11-5, $350,015, champion two- and three-year-old colt, Preakness S., American Derby, etc. Sire of 17 stakes winners, including Myrtle Charm, Armageddon, Sabette. Defeated Triple Crown winner Whirlaway in match race. Tail-male ancestor of line that leads to Broad Brush.

ALYDAR, 1975-1990. Ch. c., Raise a Native—Sweet Tooth, by On-and-On. 26-14-9-1, $957,195, Travers S. (G1), Florida Derby (G1), etc. Leading sire in 1990. Sire of 77 stakes winners, including Alysheba, Easy Goer, Criminal Type, Turkoman, Althea, Alydaress, Strike the Gold, Miss Oceana, Endear, Peinture Bleue, Winglet. Broodmare sire of Ajina, Amilynx, Anees, Cat Thief, General Meeting, Lakeway, Lure, Peintre Celebre.

ALYSHEBA, 1984-. B. c., Alydar—Bel Sheba, by Lt. Stevens. 26-11-8-2, $6,679,242, Horse of the Year in 1988, champion three-year-old colt, champion older male, Kentucky Derby (G1), Preakness S. (G1), Breeders' Cup Classic (G1), etc. Sire of more than 15 stakes winners, including Alywow, Bright Moon, Moonlight Dance.

AMERICAN ECLIPSE, 1814-1847. Ch. c., Duroc—Millers Damsel, by *Messenger. 8-8-0-0, $56,700, North-South Match Race with (Sir) Henry. Sire of Black Maria, Ariel, Medoc, Fanny, Lance. First great American champion.

AMERICAN FLAG, 1922-1942. Ch. c., Man o' War—*Lady Comfey, by Roi Herode. 17-8-1-1, $82,725, champion three-year-old colt, Belmont S., Withers S., etc. Sire of stakes winners Nellie Flag, Gusto. Broodmare sire of Raise You, Mar-Kell.

ANCIENT TITLE, 1970-1981. Dk. b. or br. g., Gummo—Hi Little Gal, by Bar Le Duc. 57-24-11-9, $1,252,791, Hollywood Gold Cup Invitational H. (G1), Charles H. Strub S. (G1), etc. Won 20 stakes. Leading California-bred money earner at the time of his death.

A.P. INDY, 1989-. Dk. b. or br. c., Seattle Slew—Weekend Surprise, by Secretariat. 11-8-0-1, $2,979,815, Horse of the Year in 1992, champion three-year-old colt, Belmont S. (G1), Breeders' Cup Classic (G1), etc. Sire of more than 30 stakes winners, including Tempera, Golden Missile, Aptitude, Lu Ravi, Secret Status, A P Valentine, Old Trieste.

ARIEL, 1822-1843. Gr. f., American Eclipse—Young Empress, by Financier. 57-42-14-1, about $25,000. Ran four-mile heats 28 times, winning 18. Dam of three foals, no winners.

ARISTIDES, 1872-1893. Ch. c., *Leamington—Sarong, by Lexington. 21-9-5-1, $18,325, Kentucky Derby, Withers S., Jerome S., etc. First winner of Kentucky Derby in 1875.

ARMED, 1941-1964. Br. g., Bull Lea—Armful, by Chance Shot. 81-41-20-10, $817,475, Horse of the Year in 1947, champion handicap horse twice, Suburban H., Widener H. twice, Gulfstream Park H., etc.

ARTFUL, 1902-1927. B. f., Hamburg—Martha II, by Dandie Dinmont. 8-6-2-0, $81,125, Futurity S., Brighton H., etc. Tail-female ancestor of family that includes Education, Runaway Groom.

ARTS AND LETTERS, 1966-1998. Ch. c., *Ribot—All Beautiful, by Battlefield. 23-11-6-1, $632,404, Horse of the Year in 1969, champion three-year-old colt, champion handicap horse, Belmont S., Jockey Club Gold Cup, etc. Sire of 30 stakes winners, including Codex, Winter's Tale, Illiterate.

ASSAULT, 1943-1971. Ch. c., Bold Venture—Igual, by Equipoise. 42-18-6-7, $675,470, Horse of the year in 1946, champion three-year-old colt, Triple Crown, Suburban H., Brooklyn H. twice, etc. Sterile at stud.

ASTEROID, 1861-1886. B. c., Lexington—Nebula, by *Glencoe. 12-12-0-0, $12,800, Woodlawn Vase, etc. One of three sons of Lexington, along with Kentucky and Norfolk, to be considered the best racehorses of the 1860s, called the "great triumvirate." Sire of Creedmoor, Ballankeel.

***AUSTRALIAN**, 1858-1879. Ch. c. West Australian—*Emilia, by Young Emilius. 10-3-3-3, $12,150, Doswell S., Galt House S. Sire of Spendthrift, Wildidle, Baden Baden, Fellowcraft, Joe Daniels, Springbok. American founder of male line that includes Man o' War, War Admiral, In Reality, Tiznow.

BALD EAGLE, 1955-1977. B. c., *Nasrullah—Siama, by Tiger. 29-12-5-4, $692,946, champion older horse, Metropolitan H., Suburban H., etc. Sire of 12 stakes winners, including Too Bald, San San.

BALLOT, 1904-1937. Ch. c., *Voter—*Cerito, by Lowland Chief. 38-20-6-6, $154,545, Suburban H., etc. Sire of Midway, Chilhowee, Star Voter. Broodmare sire of Bull Lea.

BATTLEFIELD, 1948-1964. Ch. c., War Relic—Dark Display, by Display. 44-22-14-2, $474,727, champion two-year-old colt, Futurity S., Hopeful S., Travers S., etc. Sire of Yorktown. Broodmare sire of Arts and Letters, Steeple Jill.

BATTLESHIP, 1927-1958. Ch. c., Man o' War—*Quarantaine, by Sea Sick. 55-24-6-4, $71,641, Grand National Steeplechase in England and U.S., etc. Sire of Shipboard, War Battle. First American-bred to win England's Grand National Steeplechase.

BAYAKOA (Arg), 1984-1997. B. f., Consultant's Bid—Arlucea (Arg), by Good Manners. 39-21-9-0, $2,861,701, champion older female twice, Breeders' Cup Distaff (G1) twice, Spinster S. (G1) twice, etc.

BEAUGAY, 1943-unknown. B. f., Stimulus—Risk, by *Sir Gallahad III. 18-9-3-0, $148,070, champion two-year-old filly, Matron S., Fashion S., etc.

BED O' ROSES, 1947-1953. B. f., Rosemont—Good Thing, by Discovery. 46-18-8-6, $383,925, champion two-year-old filly, champion handicap mare, Santa Margarita H., Matron S., etc.

BELDAME, 1901-1923. Ch. f., Octagon—*Bella Donna, by Hermit. 31-17-6-4, $102,135, Suburban H., Alabama S., Ladies H., etc. Dam of Belvale. Tail-female ancestor of family that includes Revoked, Insouciant.

BEN ALI, 1883-unknown. Br. c., Virgil—Ulrica, by Lexington. 40-12-3-5, $25,090, Kentucky Derby, Hopeful S., etc.

BEN BRUSH, 1893-1918. B. c., Bramble—Roseville, by Reform. 40-25-5-5, $65,208, Kentucky Derby, Suburban H., etc. Leading sire in 1909. Sire of Broomstick, Sweep, Delhi, Meridian, Pebbles, Theo Cook, Von Tromp.

BEND OR, 1877-1903. Ch. c., Doncaster—Rouge Rose, by Thormanby. 14-10-2-0, $90,304, Epsom Derby, Champion S., etc. Sire of *Ormonde, Bona Vista, Kendal, Orvieto. Tail-male ancestor of Phalaris, *Teddy lines.

BEST PAL, 1988-1998. B. g., *Habitony—Ubetshedid, by King Pellinore. 47-18-11-4, $5,668,245, Santa Anita H. (G1), Hollywood Gold Cup H. (G1), etc. Leading California-bred money earner at retirement.

BEWITCH, 1945-1959. Br. f., Bull Lea—Potheen, by Wildair. 55-20-10-11, $462,605, champion two-year-old filly, champion handicap mare, Arlington Lassie S., Vanity H., etc. Defeated stablemate Citation in 1947 Washington Park Futurity.

BIMELECH, 1937-1966. B. c., Black Toney—*La Troienne, by *Teddy. 15-11-2-1, $248,745, champion two- and three-year-old colt, Preakness S., Belmont S., etc. Sire of 30 stakes winners, including Better Self, Be Faithful, Guillotine, Hilarious, Brookfield. Full brother to Black Helen.

BLACK GOLD, 1921-1928. Bl. c. Black Toney—Useeit, by Bonnie Joe. 35-18-5-4, $110,553, champion three-year-old colt, Kentucky Derby, Ohio Derby, etc. Broke down and euthanized at seven and buried in the infield at Fair Grounds.

BLACK HELEN, 1932-1957. B. f., Black Toney—*La Troienne, by *Teddy. 22-15-0-2, $61,800, champion three-year-old filly, Coaching Club American Oaks, Florida Derby, etc. Tail-female ancestor of family that includes Pleasant Tap, Go for Gin, But Why Not, Princess Rooney. Full sister to Bimelech.

BLACK MARIA, 1826-unknown. Bl. f., American Eclipse—Lady Lightfoot, by Sir Archy. 26-13-(placings unknown), $14,900, Jockey Club Purse, etc. Ran 17 times in four-mile heats. Won a five-heat, four-mile heat race that caused death of one opponent from exhaustion.

BLACK MARIA, 1923-1932. Bl. f., Black Toney—*Bird Loose, by Sardanapale. 52-18-14-6, $110,350, champion three-year-old filly, champion older mare twice, Kentucky Oaks, Metropolitan H., Ladies H. twice, etc. Tail-female ancestor of family that includes Polynesian, Air Forbes Won.

BLANDFORD, 1919-1935. Br. c., Swynford—Blanche, by White Eagle. 4-3-1-0, $16,041, Princess of Wales's S., etc. Leading sire three times in Europe. Sire of *Blenheim II, *Bahram, Brantome, Windsor Lad, Campanula, Trigo, Dalmary, Mistress Ford, Pasch, Udaipur, Umidwar. Tail-male ancestor of line leading to The Axe II, Quadrangle, Crepello, Mtoto.

***BLENHEIM II**, 1927-1958. Br. c., Blandford—Malva, by Charles O'Malley. 10-5-3-0, $73,060, Epsom Derby, etc. Leading sire in 1941. Sire of 47 stakes winners, including Whirlaway, *Mahmoud, Donatello II, Mar-Kell, Fervent, A Gleam, Jet Pilot. Broodmare sire of A Glitter, Coaltown, Hill Gail, Kauai King, Le Paillon, *Nasrullah, Wistful. Tail-male ancestor of line leading to The Axe II, Quadrangle, Crepello, Mtoto.

BLUE LARKSPUR, 1926-1947. B. c., Black Servant—Blossom Time, by *North Star III. 16-10-3-1, $272,070, Horse of the Year in 1929, champion three-year-old colt, champion handicap horse, Belmont S., Classic S., etc. Sire of 44 stakes winners, including

But Why Not, Myrtlewood, Painted Veil, Blue Swords, Alablue, Revoked, Blue Delight, Bee Ann Mac. Broodmare sire of Alanesian, Be Faithful, Busanda, By Jimminy, Cohoes, Durazna, Real Delight, Twilight Tear.

BLUSHING GROOM (Fr), 1974-1992. Ch. c., Red God—Runaway Bride (GB), by Wild Risk. 10-7-1-2, $407,153, champion two-year-old in France, champion miler in France, Grand Criterium (Fr-G1), Poule d'Essai des Poulains (French Two Thousand Guineas) (Fr-G1), etc. Leading sire in England in 1989. Sire of 92 stakes winners, including Nashwan, Rainbow Quest, Arazi, Sky Beauty, Rahy, Blushing John, Runaway Groom, Al Bahathri, Blush With Pride, Mt. Livermore. Broodmare sire of Awesome Again, Flute, Kahyasi, Lammtarra, Macho Uno, Stravinsky, T.M. Opera O.

BOLD FORBES, 1973-2000. Dk. b. or br. c., Irish Castle—Comely Nell, by Commodore M. 18-13-1-4, $546,536, champion three-year-old colt, champion two-year-old in Puerto Rico, Kentucky Derby (G1), Belmont S. (G1), etc. Sire of 29 stakes winners, including Tiffany Lass, Air Forbes Won.

BOLD 'N DETERMINED, 1977-1997. B. f., Bold and Brave—Pidi, by Determine. 20-16-2-0, $949,599. Winner of six Grade 1 races at three in 1980, including the Coaching Club American Oaks and the Kentucky Oaks, she had the misfortune of being in the same crop as Kentucky Derby (G1) winner and champion three-year-old filly Genuine Risk. Owned by Corbin Robertson's Saron Stable and trained by Neil Drysdale, she defeated Genuine Risk in the 1980 Maskette Stakes (G2).

BOLD RULER, 1954-1971. Dk. b. or br. c., *Nasrullah—Miss Disco, by Discovery. 33-23-4-2, $764,204, Horse of the Year in 1957, champion three-year-old colt, champion sprinter, Preakness S., Futurity S., Suburban H., etc. Leading sire eight times, seven in succession (1963-'69). Sire of 82 stakes winners, including Secretariat, Gamely, Lamb Chop, Bold Lad (out of Misty Morn), Bold Lad (out of Barn Pride), Bold Bidder, Wajima, Queen Empress, Queen of the Stage, Boldnesian, Chieftain, Dewan, Reviewer. Broodmare sire of Autobiography, Christmas Past, Private Terms, Quick as Lightning, Sensational. Tail-male ancestor of Seattle Slew line.

BOLD VENTURE, 1933-1958. Ch. c., *St. Germans—Possible, by Ultimus. 11-6-2-0, $68,300, champion three-year-old colt, Kentucky Derby, Preakness S. Sire of 12 stakes winners, including Assault, Middleground. Broodmare sire of Miss Cavandish, Prove Out.

BON NOUVEL, 1960-unknown. B. g., Duc de Fer—Good News, by *Happy Argo. 51-16-11-7, $176,148, champion steeplechaser three times, Temple Gwathmey Stp. H., Brook Stp. H. twice, etc.

BORROW, 1908-unknown. Ch. g., Hamburg—Forget, by Exile. 91-24-20-12. $87,275, Middle Park Plate (in England), Brooklyn H., etc. Defeated three Kentucky Derby winners in 1917 Brooklyn H.

BOSTON, 1833-1850. Ch. c., Timoleon—Sister to Tuckahoe, by Ball's Florizel. 45-40-2-1, $51,700, champion of his era. Leading sire three times. Sire of Lexington, Lecompte, Commodore, Madeline, Nina, Ringgold, Red Eye. Won 70 of 81 heats, 47 at 4 miles. Lost famous match race with Fashion.

BOWL OF FLOWERS, 1958-unknown. Ch. f., Sailor—Flower Bowl, by *Alibhai. 16-10-3-3, $398,504, champion two- and three-year-old filly, Coaching Club American Oaks, Spinster S., etc. Dam of sires Whiskey

Road, Big Burn.

BROAD BRUSH, 1983- . B. c., Ack Ack—Hay Patcher, by Hoist the Flag. 27-14-5-5, $2,656,793, Santa Anita H. (G1), Suburban H. (G1), etc. Leading sire in 1994. Sire of more than 65 stakes winners, including Concern, Include, Broad Appeal, Pompeii.

BROOMSTICK, 1901-1931. B. c., Ben Brush—*Elf, by Galliard. 39-14-11-5, $74,730, Travers S., Brighton H., etc. Leading sire 1913-'15; leading broodmare sire 1932-'33. Sire of 69 stakes winners, including Regret, Whisk Broom II, Bostonian, Broomspun, Cudgel, Halcyon, Sweeper, Traffic, Transmute, Wildair, Escoba, Flying Witch, Remembrance, Rowes Bud. Broodmare sire of Equipoise, Mother Goose, Whichone.

BROWN BESS, 1982- . Dk. b. or br. f., *Petrone—Chickadee, by Windy Sands. 36-16-8-6, $1,300,920, champion grass female, Santa Barbara H. (G1), Ramona H. (G1), Yellow Ribbon Inv. S. (G1), etc.

BUCKPASSER, 1963-1978. B. c., Tom Fool—Busanda, by War Admiral. 31-25-4-1, $1,462,014, Horse of the Year in 1966, champion two- and three-year-old colt, champion handicap horse twice, Jockey Club Gold Cup, Metropolitan H., etc. Leading broodmare sire 1983-'84, '88-'89. Sire of 35 stakes winners, including Numbered Account, Relaxing, La Prevoyante, L'Enjoleur, Norcliffe, State Dinner, Silver Buck, Buckaroo, Quick as Lightning, Lassie Dear, Passing Mood. Broodmare sire of Slew o'Gold, Seeking the Gold, Coastal, Woodman, Private Account, Easy Goer, El Gran Senor, Miswaki, Touch Gold.

BULL DOG, 1927-1954. Dk. b. or br. c., *Teddy—Plucky Liege, by Spearmint. 8-2-1-0, $7,802 Prix Daphnis, etc. Leading sire in 1943; leading broodmare sire in 1953, '54, '56. Sire of 52 stakes winners, including Bull Lea, Occupy, Our Boots, Occupation, Johns Joy, The Doge, Canina, Miss Dogwood, Miss Mommy, Tiger. Broodmare sire of Tom Fool, Decathlon, Dark Star, Rough'n Tumble. Full brother to *Sir Gallahad III; half brother to Bois Roussel, Admiral Drake.

BULLE ROCK, 1709-unknown. C., Darley Arabian—Byerley Turk mare, by Byerley Turk. Earliest Thoroughbred recorded as imported (in 1730) to the United States in the *American Stud Book*. No horse matching his description and pedigree appears in the *General Stud Book*, but he is generally accepted as America's first Thoroughbred.

BULL LEA, 1935-1964. Br. c., *Bull Dog—Rose Leaves, by Ballot. 27-10-7-3, $94,825, Widener H., Blue Grass S., etc. Leading sire in 1947, '48, '49, '52, '53; leading broodmare sire 1958-'61. Sire of 58 stakes winners, ten champions, including Citation, Coaltown, Hill Gail, Two Lea, Twilight Tear, Bewitch, Real Delight, Iron Liege, Armed, Durazna, Next Move. Broodmare sire of Barbizon, Bramalea, Gate Dancer, Idun, Leallah, Pucker Up, Quadrangle, Tim Tam.

BUSHER, 1942-1955. Ch. f., War Admiral—Baby League, by Bubbling Over. 21-15-3-1, $334,035, Horse of the Year in 1945, champion two- and three-year-old filly, champion handicap mare, Hollywood Derby, Santa Margarita H., etc. Dam of Jet Action. Tail-female ancestor of family that includes Beau's Eagle, Play On.

BUSHRANGER, 1930-1937. Ch. g., *Stefan the Great—War Path, by Man o' War. 21-11-3-1, $20,635, champion steeplechaser, Grand National Stp. H., Broad Hollow Stp. H. twice, etc.

BYERLEY TURK, ca. 1680. Bl. c. of unknown parentage. Sire of Jigg, Basto, Black Hearty. One of

three Thoroughbred male-line foundation sires. Tail-male ancestor of the Herod line leading to *Ambiorix, The Tetrarch, Dr Devious (Ire), Indian Ridge.

CAFE PRINCE, 1970-unknown. B. g., Creme dela Creme—Princess Blair, by Blue Prince. 52-18-5-4, $228,238, champion steeplechaser twice, Colonial Cup International Stp. twice, etc.

CAPOT, 1946-1974. Br. c., Menow—Piquet, by *St. Germans. 28-12-4-7, $347,260, Horse of the Year in 1949, champion three-year-old colt, Preakness S., Belmont S., etc. Sired 13 foals, no stakes winners.

CARRY BACK, 1958-1983. Br. c., Saggy—Joppy, by Star Blen. 62-21-11-11, $1,241,165, champion three-year-old colt, Kentucky Derby, Preakness S., etc. Sire of ten stakes winners, including Taken Aback, Sharp Gary, Back in Paris.

CAVALCADE, 1931-1940. Br. c., *Lancegaye—*Hastily, by Hurry On. 22-8-5-3, $127,165, Horse of the Year in 1934, champion two- and three-year-old colt, Kentucky Derby, American Derby, etc. Sire of three stakes winners.

CHALLEDON, 1936-1958. B. c., *Challenger II—Laura Gal, by *Sir Gallahad III. 44-20-7-6, $334,660, Horse of the Year in 1939 and '40, champion three-year-old colt, champion handicap horse, Preakness S., Whitney S., etc. Sire of 13 stakes winners, including Ancestor, Tenacious, Donor.

CHAPOSA SPRINGS, 1992- . B. f., Baldski—La Chaposa (Per), by Ups. 23-14-5-0, $762,115, Test S. (G1), Ballerina H. (G1), etc.

CHIEF'S CROWN, 1982-1997. B. c., Danzig—Six Crowns, by Secretariat. 21-12-3-3, $2,191,168, champion two-year-old colt, Breeders' Cup Juvenile (G1), Travers S. (G1), etc. Sire of more than 50 stakes winners, including Erhaab, Grand Lodge, Chief Bearhart, Concerto, Chief Honcho.

CHRIS EVERT, 1971-2001. Ch. f., Swoon's Son—Miss Carmie, by T. V. Lark. 15-10-2-2, $679,475, champion three-year-old filly, filly triple crown, Coaching Club American Oaks (G1), Hollywood Special S. (match race with Miss Musket), etc. Dam of Six Crowns, Wimbledon Star. Second dam of Chief's Crown.

CICADA, 1959-1981. B. f., Bryan G.—Satsuma, by Bossuet. 42-23-8-6, $783,674, champion two- and three-year-old filly, champion older mare, Kentucky Oaks, Beldame S., etc. Dam of Cicada's Pride. Retired as world's leading money-winning female.

CIGAR, 1990-. B. c., Palace Music—Solar Slew, by Seattle Slew. 33-19-4-5, $9,999,815, Horse of the Year in 1995 and '96, champion older male twice, Breeders' Cup Classic (G1), Dubai World Cup, etc. Leading earner all-time in North America. Sterile at stud. Resides at Kentucky Horse Park.

CITATION, 1945-1970. B. c., Bull Lea—*Hydroplane II, by Hyperion. 45-32-10-2, $1,085,760, Horse of the Year in 1948, champion two- and three-year-old colt, champion handicap horse twice, Triple Crown, Jockey Club Gold Cup, Hollywood Gold Cup, etc. First $1-million earner. Sire of 12 stakes winners, including Silver Spoon, Fabius.

CLEOPATRA, 1917-unknown. Ch. f., Corcyra—*Gallice, by Gallinule. 26-8-10-4, $55,937, champion three-year-old filly, Coaching Club American Oaks, Alabama S., etc. Dam of Pompey, Laughing Queen; third dam of Tom Fool. Tail-female ancestor of family that includes Ambiopoise, Dust Commander.

CLIFFORD, 1890-1917. B. c., Bramble—Duchess, by Kingfisher. 63-42-14-5, $59,757 Second Special

S., Flight S. twice, Phoenix S., etc. Defeated three Racing Hall of Fame members. Regarded as one of the worst gate horses in history, a trait that cost him several races he should have won.

COALTOWN, 1945-1965. B. c., Bull Lea—Easy Lass, by *Blenheim II. 39-23-6-3, $415,675, Horse of the Year in 1949, champion sprinter, champion handicap horse, Jerome H., Blue Grass S., etc. Never sired a stakes winner.

COLIN, 1905-1932. Br. c., Commando—*Pastorella, by Springfield. 15-15-0-0, $178,110, champion two- and three-year-old colt, Belmont S., Futurity S., etc. Sire of Jock, Neddie, On Watch. Shy breeder.

COMELY, 1912-unknown. Br. f., Disguise—Pretty Maiden, by Kingston. 22-7-8-3, $17,355, Keene Memorial S., Laureate S., etc. Bred and owned by James Butler, owner of Empire City Racecourse, who named a stakes race in honor of his favorite filly.

COMMANDO, 1898-1905. B. c., Domino—Emma C., by *Darebin. 9-7-2-0, $58,196, champion two- and three-year-old colt, Belmont S., Junior Champion S., etc. Leading sire in 1907. Sire of ten stakes winners from 27 foals, including Colin, Peter Pan, Celt, Hippodrome, Superman, Transvaal, and of Ultimus. Tail-male ancestor of line that leads to Broad Brush.

CORRECTION, 1888-unknown. B. f., Himyar—Mannie Gray, by Enquirer. 122-38-35-22, $45,600, Toboggan Slide H., etc. Dam of Yankee, Miss Malaprop, Nature. Tail-female ancestor of family that includes Affirmed, Royal Native, Haste. Full sister to Domino.

COSMAH, 1953-1979. B. f., Cosmic Bomb—Almahmoud, by *Mahmoud. 30-9-5-2, $86,525, Astarita S., etc. Broodmare of the year in 1974. Dam of Tosmah, Halo, Fathers Image, Maribeau. Foundation mare of family that includes Flawlessly, L'Emigrant, Cannonade, Stephan's Odyssey.

***COUGAR II**, 1966-1989. Dk b. or br. c., Tale of Two Cities—*Cindy Lou II, by Madara. 50-20-7-17, $1,172,625, champion grass horse, Santa Anita H. (G1), Sunset H. (G1), etc. Sire of 24 stakes winners, including Gato Del Sol, Exploded.

COUNTERPOINT, 1948-1970. Ch. c., Count Fleet—Jabot, by *Sickle. 21-10-3-1, $284,575, Horse of the Year in 1951, champion three-year-old colt, Belmont S., Jockey Club Gold Cup, etc. Sire of 11 stakes winners, including Dotted Swiss, Harmonizing, Honey Dear, Snow White.

COUNT FLEET, 1940-1973. Br. c., Reigh Count—Quickly, by Haste. 21-16-4-1, $250,300, Horse of the Year in 1943, champion two- and three-year-old colt, Triple Crown, Champagne S., Withers S., etc. Leading sire in 1951; leading broodmare sire in 1963. Sire of 39 stakes winners, including Counterpoint, One Count, Kiss Me Kate, Count Turf, Straight Face, Count of Honor, Countess Fleet, County Delight, Juliets Nurse. Broodmare sire of Kelso, Prince John, Quill, Fleet Nasrullah, Gallant Romeo, Lamb Chop.

CREME FRAICHE, 1982- . B. g., Rich Cream—Likely Exchange, by Terrible Tiger. 64-17-12-13, $4,024,727, Belmont S. (G1), Jockey Club Gold Cup (G1) twice, Super Derby (G1), etc.

CRIMSON SATAN, 1959-1982. Ch. c., Spy Song—*Papila, by Requiebro. 58-18-9-9, $796,077, champion two-year-old colt, Garden State S., Charles H. Strub S., etc. Sire of 33 stakes winners, including Crimson Saint, Krislin, Whitesburg.

CRUSADER, 1923-1940. Ch. c., Man o' War—Star Fancy, by *Star Shoot. 42-18-8-4, $203,261, Horse of

the Year in 1926, champion three-year-old colt, Belmont S., Jockey Club Gold Cup, Suburban H. twice, etc. Sire of six stakes winners, including *Crossbow II.

DAHLIA, 1970-2001. Ch. f., *Vaguely Noble—Charming Alibi, by Honeys Alibi. 48-15-3-7, $1,489,105, Horse of the Year in England in 1974 and '75, champion three-year-old in Ireland, champion three-year-old in England, champion grass horse in U.S., champion older mare twice in England, King George VI and Queen Elizabeth S. (Eng-G1) twice, Washington, D. C., International (G1), etc. Dam of Dahar, Rivlia, Delegant, Dahlia's Dreamer, Wajd, Llandaff.

DAMASCUS, 1964-1995. B. c., Sword Dancer—Kerala, by *My Babu. 32-21-7-3, $1,176,781, Horse of the Year in 1967, champion three-year-old colt, champion handicap horse, Preakness S., Belmont S., Jockey Club Gold Cup S., etc. Sire of 71 stakes winners, including Private Account, Desert Wine, Highland Blade, Ogygian, Honorable Miss, Time for a Change, Judger, Bailjumper, Timeless Moment, Cutlass. Broodmare sire of Boundary, Chilukki, Coronado's Quest, Shadeed.

DANCE SMARTLY, 1988-. Dk. b. or br. f., Danzig—Classy 'n Smart, by Smarten. 17-12-2-3, $3,263,835, champion three-year-old filly in U.S., Canadian Horse of the Year, champion two- and three-year-old filly in Canada, Canadian Triple Crown, Breeders' Cup Distaff (G1), Queen's Plate S., etc. Dam of Queen's Plate winners Scatter the Gold, Dancethruthedawn.

DANZIG, 1977-. B. c., Northern Dancer—Pas de Nom, by Admiral's Voyage. 3-3-0-0, $32,400. Leading sire 1991-'93. Sire of more than 165 stakes winners, including Chief's Crown, Polish Precedent, Dayjur, Danehill, Dance Smartly, Langfuhr, Anabaa, Green Desert, Pine Bluff. Broodmare sire of Caller One, Dancethruthedawn, Fusaichi Pegasus.

DARK MIRAGE, 1965-1969. Dk. b. or br. f., *Persian Road II—Home by Dark, by Hill Prince. 27-12-3-2, $362,788, champion three-year-old filly, first winner of the filly triple crown in New York, Kentucky Oaks, Delaware Oaks, etc. Won nine consecutive stakes and broke down trying for tenth. Died at four.

DARK STAR, 1950-1972. Br. c., *Royal Gem II—Isolde, by *Bull Dog. 13-6-2-2, $131,337, Kentucky Derby, Derby Trial, etc. Only horse to defeat Native Dancer. Sire of 26 stakes winners, including *Gazala II, My Dad George, Hidden Treasure.

DARLEY ARABIAN, 1700. B. c. of unknown parentage. Leading sire in England in 1722. Sire of Flying Childers, Aleppo, Almanzor, Bartlett's Childers. One of three male line foundation sires. Tail-male ancestor of the Eclipse male line leading to Phalaris, Blandford, Hyperion lines.

DAVONA DALE, 1976- . B. f., Best Turn—Royal Entrance, by Tim Tam. 18-11-2-1, $641,612, champion three-year-old filly, filly triple crown, Kentucky Oaks (G1), etc.

DECATHLON, 1953-1972. B. c., Olympia—Dog Blessed, by *Bull Dog. 42-25-8-1, $269,530, champion sprinter twice, Oceanport H. twice, Hutcheson S., etc. Sire of 12 stakes winners, including Juanita, Slipped Disc.

DELANCEY'S CUB MARE, 1762. F., Cub—Second mare (dam of Amaranthus), by Second. One of first great imported American foundation mares. Dam of (Maria) Slamerkin. Tail-female ancestor of family that includes Nearco, Neckar, Golden Trail, Parole, Imp, Black Gold, Mad Hatter, Sun Beau, Flirtilla,

Sumpter, Artful, Delhi, Falsetto, Halma.

DEPUTY MINISTER, 1979- . Dk. b. or br. c., Vice Regent—Mint Copy, by Bunty's Flight. 22-12-2-2, $696,964, champion two-year-old colt in U.S., Horse of the Year in Canada in 1981, champion two-year-old colt in Canada, Laurel Futurity (G1), Donn H. (G2), etc. Leading sire in 1997 and '98. Sire of more than 65 stakes winners, including Go for Wand, Open Mind, Awesome Again, Dehere, Touch Gold, Deputy Commander, Keeper Hill, Victory Speech, Clear Mandate, Salt Lake, French Deputy.

DESERT STORMER, 1990- . B. f., Storm Cat—Breezy Stories, by Damascus. 17-7-3-4, $862,950, Breeders' Cup Sprint (G1), etc. Dam of Sahara Gold.

DESERT VIXEN, 1970-1982. Dk. b. or br. f., In Reality—Desert Trial, by Moslem Chief. 28-13-6-3, $421,538, champion three-year-old filly, champion older female, Alabama S. (G1), Beldame S. (G1) twice, etc. Dam of Real Shadai; full sister to Valid Appeal.

DETERMINE, 1951-1972. Gr. c., *Alibhai—Koubis, by *Mahmoud. 44-18-7-9, $573,360, Kentucky Derby, Santa Anita Derby, etc. First gray winner of the Kentucky Derby. Sire of 21 stakes winners, including Decidedly, Warfare, Donut King. Broodmare sire of Bold 'n Determined, Gummo, Princess Pout.

DEVIL DIVER, 1939-1961. B. c., *St. Germans—Dabchick, by *Royal Minstrel. 47-22-12-3, $261,064, champion handicap horse twice, Metropolitan H. twice, Suburban H., Whitney S., etc. Sire of 17 stakes winners, including Beau Diable, Call Over, Ruddy.

***DIOMED**, 1777-1808. Ch. c., Florizel—Spectator mare (sister to Juno), by Spectator. 20-11-5-3, $38,200, champion three-year-old in England, Epsom Derby, etc. First winner of the Epsom Derby. Sire of Sir Archy, Haynie's Maria, Ball's Florizel, Duroc, Fanny, Young Giantess, Potomac, Virginius. Imported to U.S. in 1798. Tail-male ancestor of Boston, Lexington.

DISCOVERY, 1931-1958. Ch. c., Display—Ariadne, by *Light Brigade. 63-27-10-10, $195,287, Horse of the Year in 1935, champion handicap horse twice, Whitney S. three times, Brooklyn H. three times, etc. Sire of 25 stakes winners, including Conniver, Miss Disco, Find, Loser Weeper, Traffic Court. Broodmare sire of Bold Ruler, Native Dancer, Intentionally, Hasty Road, Traffic Judge, Bed o' Roses. Famed as a weight carrier.

DISGUISE, 1897-1927. B. c., Domino—*Bonnie Gal, by Galopin. 8-3-0-4, $40,275, Jockey Club S., 3rd Epsom Derby, etc. Sire of Maskette, Court Dress, Harmonicon, Helmet, Miss Puzzle, Wonder, Comely.

DISPLAY, 1923-1944. B. c., Fair Play—*Cicuta, by *Nassovian. 103-23-25-27, $256,326, Preakness S., Hawthorne Gold Cup, etc. Sire of 11 stakes winners, including Discovery, Parade Girl.

DOMINO, 1891-1897. Br. c., Himyar—Mannie Gray, by Enquirer. 25-19-2-1, $193,550, Champion two-year-old, Futurity S., Withers S., etc. Sire of Commando, Cap and Bells, Disguise, Noonday, Running Stream, Pink Domino. Sired only 20 foals in two crops, eight stakes winners, two classic winners.

DR. FAGER, 1964-1976. B. c., Rough'n Tumble—Aspidistra, by Better Self. 22-18-2-1, $1,002,642, Horse of the Year in 1968, champion older horse, champion sprinter twice, champion grass horse, Whitney S., Vosburgh H. twice, etc. Leading sire in 1977. Sire of 35 stakes winners, including Dr. Patches, Dearly Precious, L'Alezane, Dr. Blum, Tree of Knowledge, Lie Low, Lady Love. Broodmare sire of Cure

the Blues, Equalize, Fappiano, Quiet American, Sewickley. Won every championship for which he was eligible in 1968.

EASY GOER, 1986-1994. Ch. c., Alydar—Relaxing, by Buckpasser. 20-14-5-1, $4,873,770, champion two-year-old colt, Belmont S. (G1), Jockey Club Gold Cup (G1), etc. Sire of nine stakes winners, including Will's Way, My Flag, Furlough.

ECLIPSE, 1764-1789. Ch. c., Marske—Spiletta, by Regulus. 18-18-0-0, undefeated champion in England, won 11 King's Plates. Never leading sire but runner-up 11 times. Sire of Pot-8o's, King Fergus, Serjeant, Dungannon, Alexander, Joe Andrews, Mercury, Meteor, Saltram, Volunteer. Tail-male line ancestor of more than 95% of modern Thoroughbreds, including Phalaris, Hyperion, Blandford lines.

*ECLIPSE, 1855-1878. B. c., Orlando—Gaze, by Bay Middleton. 9-4-0-1, $9,015, Newmarket S., Clearwell S. Sire of Alarm, Ruthless, Scathelock. Tail-male line ancestor of Domino, Plaudit, Dr. Fager, Holy Bull, Broad Brush.

EIGHT THIRTY, 1936-1965. Ch. c., Pilate—Dinner Time, by High Time. 27-16-3-5, $155,475, Travers S., Whitney S., Metropolitan H., etc. Sire of 45 stakes winners, including Sailor, Bolero, Royal Coinage, Rare Perfume, Sunday Evening, Make Tracks, Anyoldtime. Broodmare sire of Cornish Prince, Evening Out, Hold Your Peace, Jaipur, Rare Treat.

ELKRIDGE, 1938-1961. B. g., Mate—Best by Test, by Black Toney. 123-31-18-15, $230,680, champion steeplechaser twice, North American Stp. H. four times, Indian River Stp. H. four times, etc.

EMPEROR OF NORFOLK, 1885-1907. B. c., Norfolk—Marian, by Malcolm. 29-21-2-4, $72,400, American Derby, Brooklyn Derby, etc. Sire of Americus (Rey del Carreras), Cruzados. Buried at Santa Anita Park.

ENDINE, 1954-unknown. Ch. f., *Rico Monte—Sea Snack, by Hard Tack. 45-10-6-7, $306,547, Delaware H. twice, Ladies H., etc.

ENDURANCE BY RIGHT, 1899-1908. B. f., Inspector B.—*Early Morn, by Silvester. 18-16-0-2, $27,645, champion two-year-old filly, Champagne S., Clipsetta S., etc. Dam of Stamina. Tail-female ancestor of family that includes Plucky Play, Windjammer, Racing Room, Porter's Cap.

ENQUIRER, 1867-1895. B. c., *Leamington—Lida, by Lexington. 11-7-0-0, $17,550, champion three-year-old, Kenner S., Phoenix S., etc. Sire of Falsetto, Inspector B., Blue Eyes, Mannie Gray.

*EPINARD, 1920-unknown. Ch. c., Badajoz—Epine Blanche, by *Rock Sand. 20-12-6-0, $46,688, champion two-year-old in France, Grand Criterium, Prix d'Ispahan, etc. Great French champion who ran second in each of three international races in U.S. in 1925. Sire of Rodosto, Marica, Epithet.

EQUIPOISE, 1928-1938. Ch. c., Pennant—Swinging, by Broomstick. 51-29-10-4, $338,610, Horse of the Year in 1932 and '33, champion handicap horse three times, champion two-year-old colt, Metropolitan H. twice, Whitney S., etc. Leading sire in 1942. Sire of nine stakes winners, including Shut Out, Level Best, Bolingbroke, Attention, Swing and Sway. Broodmare sire of Assault, Myrtle Charm.

EXCELLER, 1973-1997. B. c., *Vaguely Noble—Too Bald, by Bald Eagle. 33-15-5-6, $1,674,587, Jockey Club Gold Cup (G1), Grand Prix de Paris (Fr-G1), etc. Sire of 19 stakes winners, including Slew's Exceller, Squan Song.

EXPLOSIVE BID, 1978-1990. Ch. c., Explodent—Golden Way, by Diplomat Way. 59-17-14-6, $488,147, Pennsylvania Governor's Cup (G3), Louisiana H., etc.

EXTERMINATOR, 1915-1945. Ch. g., *McGee—Fair Empress, by Jim Gore. 100-50-17-17, $252,996, Kentucky Derby, Saratoga Cup twice, etc. Won record 33 stakes races. Won 19 times carrying 130 pounds or more.

FAIRMOUNT, 1921-unknown. Ch. g., Fair Play—Sunflower, by *Rock Sand. 22-12-5-0, $74,075, Temple Gwathmey Memorial Stp. H. three times, Manley Memorial Stp. H., etc.

FAIR PLAY, 1905-1929. Ch. c., Hastings—*Fairy Gold, by Bend Or. 32-10-11-3, $86,950, Flash S., Coney Island Jockey Club S., etc. Leading sire in 1920, '24, '27; leading broodmare sire in 1931, '34, '38. Sire of Man o' War, Chance Play, Mad Hatter, Display, Chance Shot, Mad Play, Ladkin, Chatterton, Olambala, Stagecraft, Masda, Native Wit, Oval. Broodmare sire of Fair Story, High Quest, Jamestown, Stagehand, Sun Beau. Tail-male ancestor of line that leads to In Reality, Valid Appeal, Tiznow.

FAIRWAY, 1925-1948. B. c., Phalaris—Scapa Flow, by Chaucer. 15-12-1-0, $194,685, champion three-year-old in England, St. Leger S., Champion S. twice, etc. Leading sire in England four times; leading broodmare sire in England in 1946 and '47. Sire of Blue Peter, Fair Copy, Fair Trial, Full Sail, Garden Path, Honeyway, Ribbon, Tide-Way, *Watling Street. Founder of sire line that leads to Shergar, Troy, Ela-Mana-Mou, Brigadier Gerard, Lord At War (Arg).

FALL ASPEN, 1976-1998. Ch. f., Pretense—Change Water, by Swaps. 20-8-3-0, $198,037, Matron S. (G1), Prioress S., etc. Broodmare of the Year in 1994. Dam of nine stakes winners, including Timber Country, Northern Aspen, Hamas (Ire), Elle Seule, Colorado Dancer (Ire), Fort Wood. Tail-female ancestor of family that includes Dubai Millennium, Charnwood Forest (Ire), Elnadim, Mehthaaf, Occupandiste.

FASHION, 1837-1860. Ch. f., *Trustee—Bonnets o' Blue, by Sir Charles. 36-32-0-0, $41,500, won Match race with Boston, etc. Dam of A la Mode. Greatest of four-mile heat fillies.

FASTNESS (Ire), 1990-. Gr. or ro. c., Rousillon—City Fortress, by Troy. 24-9-6-1, $1,581,165, Eddie Read H. (G1) twice, Citation H. (G2), etc.

*FEARNOUGHT, 1755-1776. B. c., Regulus—Silvertail, by Heneage's Whitenose. Five wins in England, won three King's Plates. Early American foundation sire. Sire of Symme's Wildair, Fitzhugh's Regulus, Spotswood's Apollo, Eden's Whynot, Gallant, Othello, Harris's Eclipse, Goldfinder.

FERDINAND, 1983- . Ch. c., Nijinsky II—Banja Luka, by Double Jay. 29-8-9-6, $3,777,978, Horse of the Year in 1987, champion older male, Kentucky Derby (G1), Breeders' Cup Classic (G1), etc. Sire of Bull Inthe Heather.

FIRENZE (FIRENZI), 1884-1902. B. f., Glenelg—Florida, by Virgil. 82-47-21-9, $112,471, Gazelle S., Monmouth H., Jerome S. (beating Hanover), etc. Tail-female ancestor of family that includes Carry Back, Paul Jones, Petrify.

FIRST FLIGHT, 1944-1975. B. f., *Mahmoud—Fly Swatter, by *Dis Donc. 24-11-3-3, $197,965, champion two-year-old filly, Matron S., Monmouth Oaks, etc. Defeated Jet Pilot in Futurity S.

FIRST LANDING, 1956-1987. B. c., *Turn-to—Hildene, by Bubbling Over. 37-19-9-2, $779,577, champion two-year-old colt, Champagne S., Hopeful S., etc. Sire of 27 stakes winners, including Riva Ridge, First Family, Gladwin.

FLATTERER, 1979-. Dk. b. or br. g., Mo Bay—Horizontal, by Nade. 51-24-7-5, $534,854, four-time champion steeplechaser 1983-'86, Marion duPont Scott Colonial Cup International Stp. three times, Temple Gwathmey Stp. H. twice, etc.

FLAWLESSLY, 1988-. B. f., Affirmed—La Confidence, by Nijinsky II. 28-16-4-3, $2,572,536, champion grass female twice, Beverly D. S. (G1), Matriarch S. (G1) 3 times, etc.

FLOWER BOWL, 1952-1968. B. f., *Alibhai—Flower Bed, by *Beau Pere. 32-7-4-3, $174,625, Ladies H., Delaware H., etc. Dam of Bowl of Flowers, Graustark, His Majesty.

FOOLISH PLEASURE, 1972-1994. B. c., What a Pleasure—Fool-Me-Not, by Tom Fool. 26-16-4-3, $1,216,705, champion two-year-old colt, Kentucky Derby (G1), Suburban H. (G1), Great Match S. (with Ruffian), etc. Sire of 43 stakes winners, including Baiser Vole, Marfa, Kiri's Clown, Maudlin, Prayers'n Promises.

FOREGO, 1970-1997. B. g., *Forli—Lady Golconda, by Hasty Road. 57-34-9-7, $1,938,957, three-time Horse of the Year 1974-'76, champion older male 1974-'77, champion sprinter, Marlboro Cup H. (G1), Metropolitan H. (G1) twice, Woodward H. (G1) 3 times, etc. Last of the great weight carriers. Retired to Kentucky Horse Park.

FORT MARCY, 1964-1991. B. g., *Amerigo—Key Bridge, by *Princequillo. 75-21-18-14, $1,109,791, Horse of the Year in 1970, champion grass horse twice, champion handicap horse, Washington, D. C., International S. twice, Man o' War S., etc.

FORWARD GAL, 1968-1984. Ch. f., Native Charger—Forward Thrust, by Jet Action. 26-12-4-6, $438,933, champion two-year-old filly, Frizette S., Monmouth Oaks, etc. Third dam of Freedom Cry (GB).

FOURSTARDAVE, 1985-. Ch. g., Compliance—Broadway Joan, by Bold Arian. 100-21-18-16, $1,636,737, St. Paul Derby (G2), Daryl's Joy S. (G3) twice, etc. Won a race at Saratoga Race Course for eight consecutive years. Full brother to Irish classic winner Fourstars Allstar.

FREE FOR ALL, 1942-1964. Br. c., Questionnaire—Panay, by *Chicle. 7-6-0-0, $111,225, Arlington Futurity, Washington Park Futurity, etc. Sire of Rough'n Tumble. Tail-male ancestor of Dr. Fager, Holy Bull.

FRIAR ROCK, 1913-1928. Ch. c., *Rock Sand—*Fairy Gold, by Bend Or. 21-9-1-3, $20,365, champion three-year-old, Belmont S., Suburban H., Brooklyn H., etc. Sire of Pilate, Friar's Carse, Apprehension, Inchcape, Black Curl, Emotion, Heloise, Tenez.

FRIZETTE, 1905-unknown. B. f., Hamburg—*Ondulee, by St. Simon. 36-12-8-7, $16,135, Rosedale S., Laureate S., etc. Dam of Banshee, Durzetta, *Lespedeza II. Foundation mare of family that includes Myrtlewood, Seattle Slew, Mr. Prospector, Tourbillon, Sinndar, Cordova, Darshaan, Corejada, *Apollonia, Akiyda, Acamas, Akarad, *Priam II, *Djeddah, Sing Sing, Jet Pilot, Shecky Greene, Typecast, Bahri, Forestry, Chief Bearhart, Escena, Dahlia, Vitriolic, Vagrancy, Anees, Truly Bound, Baldric, Honorable Miss.

FUSAICHI PEGASUS, 1997-. B. c., Mr. Prospector—Angel Fever, by Danzig. 9-6-2-0, $1,994,400, Kentucky Derby (G1), Wood Memorial S. (G2), etc. Syndicated for a world record $60-million to $70-million in 2000.

GALLANT BLOOM, 1966-1991. B. f., *Gallant Man—Multiflora, by Beau Max. 22-16-1-1, $535,739, champion two- and three-year-old filly, champion handicap mare, Santa Margarita Invitational H., Spinster S., Monmouth Oaks, etc.

GALLANT FOX, 1927-1954. B. c., *Sir Gallahad III—Marguerite, by Celt. 17-11-3-2, $328,165, Horse of the Year in 1930, champion three-year-old colt, Triple Crown, Jockey Club Gold Cup, etc. Sire of 18 stakes winners, including Omaha, Granville, Flares.

GALLANT MAN, 1954-1988. B. c., *Migoli—*Majideh, by *Mahmoud. 26-14-4-1, $510,355, Belmont S., Jockey Club Gold Cup, etc. Sire of 51 stakes winners, including Gallant Bloom, Gallant Romeo, War Censor, Spicy Living, Ring Twice. Broodmare sire of Genuine Risk, *Habitony, Lord Avie.

GALLORETTE, 1942-1959. Ch. f., *Challenger II—Gallette, by *Sir Gallahad III. 72-21-20-13, $445,535, champion handicap mare, Metropolitan H., Whitney S., Beldame H., etc. Dam of Mlle. Lorette, Courbette. Foundation mare of family that includes Minstrella, Misty Gallore, Silver Ghost, White Gloves, Greenwood Lake, Dancing Moss.

GAMELY, 1964-1975. B. f., Bold Ruler—Gambetta, by *My Babu. 41-16-9-6, $574,961, champion three-year-old filly, champion older mare twice, Alabama S., Beldame S. twice, etc. Dam of Cellini.

GENUINE RISK, 1977-. Ch. f., Exclusive Native—Virtuous, by *Gallant Man. 15-10-3-2, $646,587, champion three-year-old filly, Kentucky Derby (G1), Ruffian H. (G1), etc. Second filly to win Kentucky Derby.

GLENCOE, 1831-1858. Ch. c., Sultan—Trampoline, by Tramp. 10-8-1-1, $33,459, Two Thousand Guineas, Ascot Gold Cup, etc. Sire of Pocahontas, Peytona, Reel, Pryor, Star Davis, Vandal. Male-line ancestor of Hanover, Hamburg.

GODOLPHIN ARABIAN, 1724-1753. Br. c. of unknown parentage. Leading sire in England three times. Sire of Cade, Lath, Dismal, Regulus, Babraham, Blank. One of three male line foundation sires. Tail-male ancestor of Matchem line leading to Man o' War, In Reality, Tiznow.

GO FOR WAND, 1987-1990. B. f., Deputy Minister—Obeah, by Cyane. 13-10-2-0, $1,373,338, champion two- and three-year-old filly, Alabama S. (G1), Breeders' Cup Juvenile Fillies (G1), etc. Died in Breeders' Cup Distaff (G1). Buried in infield at Saratoga Race Course.

GOOD AND PLENTY, 1900-1907. B. g., Rossington—Famine, by Jils Johnson. 21-14-4-1, $45,815, Grand National Stp. H., Westbury Stp. H., etc.

GRANVILLE, 1933-1951. B. c., Gallant Fox—Gravita, by *Sarmatian. 18-8-4-3, $111,820, Horse of the Year in 1936, champion three-year-old colt, Belmont S., Travers S., etc. Sired only two stakes winners.

GREY LAG, 1918-1942. Ch. c., *Star Shoot—Miss Minnie, by *Meddler. 47-25-9-3, $136,715, Horse of the Year in 1921, champion three-year-old colt, champion handicap horse twice, Belmont S., Metropolitan H., Suburban H., etc. Shy breeder, sired only one stakes winner from 17 foals.

GUN BOW, 1960-unknown. B. c., Gun Shot—Ribbons and Bows, by War Admiral. 42-17-8-4, $798,722,

Metropolitan H., Whitney S., etc. Sire of six stakes winners, including Pistol Packer.

HAIL TO REASON, 1958-1976. Br. c., *Turn-to—Nothirdchance, by Blue Swords. 18-9-2-2, $328,434, champion two-year-old colt, Hopeful S., Sanford S., etc. Broke down and retired at end of two-year-old season. Leading sire in 1970. Sire of 43 stakes winners, including Roberto, Halo, Stop the Music, Mr. Leader, Bold Reason, Trillion, Priceless Gem, Straight Deal, Hail to All, Regal Gleam, Personality, Proud Clarion, Admiring. Broodmare sire of Allez France, Escaline (Fr), Royal Glint, Silver Buck, Triptych. Tail-male ancestor of line that includes Saint Ballado, Sunday Silence, Red Ransom, Brian's Time.

HALO, 1969-2000. Dk. b. or br. c., Hail to Reason—Cosmah, by Cosmic Bomb. 31-9-8-5, $259,553, United Nations H. (G1), Tidal H. (G2), etc. Leading sire in 1983 and '89. Sire of 63 stakes winners, including Sunday Silence, Sunny's Halo, Glorious Song, Devil's Bag, Saint Ballado, Rainbow Connection, Goodbye Halo, Lively One, Jolie's Halo, Coup de Folie. Broodmare sire of Halo America, Machiavellian, Pine Bluff, Singspiel (Ire).

HAMBURG, 1895-1915. B. c., Hanover—Lady Reel, by Fellowcraft. 21-16-3-2, $60,380, champion three-year-old colt, Lawrence Realization, Brighton Cup, etc. Leading sire in 1905. Sire of Artful, Borrow, Burgomaster, Frizette, Prince Eugene, Lady Hamburg II, Biturica, Jersey Lightning, Rosie O'Grady.

HANOVER, 1884-1899. Ch. c., Hindoo—Bourbon Belle, by *Bonnie Scotland. 50-32-14-2, $118,887, champion three-year-old colt, Belmont S., Lawrence Realization, etc. Won 17 consecutive races. Leading sire 1895-'98. Sire of Hamburg, Abe Frank, Blackstock, David Garrick, Halma, Handspun, Rhoda B., Tea's Over, The Commoner, Urania, Yankee.

HARRY BASSETT, 1868-1878. Ch. c., Lexington—Canary Bird, by *Albion. 36-23-6-3 $59,450, champion three-year-old colt, Belmont S., Travers S., etc.

HASTINGS, 1893-1917. Br. c., Spendthrift—*Cinderella, by Tomahawk or Blue Ruin. 21-10-8-0, $16,340, Belmont S., Toboggan H., etc. Leading sire 1902, '08. Sire of Fair Play, Gunfire, Don Enrique, Flittergold, Masterman. Notorious for his savage temperament.

HAYNIE'S MARIA, 1808-unknown. Ch. f., *Diomed—Bellair mare, by Bellair. 9-8-1-0. Won at distances from four furlongs to four-mile heats. Famed as the nemesis of the stable of Andrew Jackson who said, "I could not beat her."

***HELIOPOLIS**, 1936-1959. B. c., Hyperion—Drift, by Swynford. 15 5 2 1, $71,216, Prince of Wales's S., Imperial Produce S., etc. Leading sire in 1950, '54. Sire of 53 stakes winners, including High Gun, Olympia, Helioscope, Grecian Queen, Parlo, Berlo, Aunt Jinny, Summer Tan, Princess Turia, Camargo. Broodmare sire of Riva Ridge, Summer Guest.

HENRY (SIR HENRY), 1819-1837. Ch. c., Sir Archy—Diomed mare, by *Diomed. Southern representative in first great North-South four-mile heat match race against American Eclipse at the Union Course, New York, in 1823. Won first heat, but beaten in second and third. Won four-mile and three-mile heat races, including 1823 Jockey Club Purse at Petersburg, Virginia. Sire of Post Boy, Decatur, Alice Grey.

HENRY OF NAVARRE, 1891-1917. Ch. c., Knight of Ellerslie—Moss Rose, by *The Ill-Used. 42-29-8-3, $68,985, champion three-year-old colt, Belmont

S., Travers S., etc. Sire of Grave and Gay, Orienta.

HERECOMESTHEBRIDE, 1974-. Ro. f., Al Hattab—Like a Charm, by Pied d'Or. 16-12-2-0, $174,368, Columbiana H. (G3), Bonnie Miss S., etc.

HEROD, 1758-1780. B. c., Tartar—Cypron, by Blaze. 10-6-3-0, Match against Antinous, etc. Leading sire in England eight times. Sire of Highflyer, Florizel, Woodpecker, Bridget, Bagot, Maid Of The Oaks, Phenomenom. Tail-male line ancestor of The Tetrarch, Tourbillon, *Ambiorix, Ahonoora, Dr Devious (Ire), Indian Ridge.

HIGHFLYER, 1774-1793. B. c., Herod—Rachel, by Blank. 12-12-0-0, Grosvenor S., Great Subscription Race, etc. Leading sire in England a record 13 times, record 12 in succession. Sire of Sir Peter Teazle, Delpini, Huncamunca, Noble, Rockingham, Skyscraper, Maid Of All Work, Prunella.

HIGH GUN, 1951-1962. Br. c., *Heliopolis—Rocket Gun, by Brazado. 24-11-5-4, $486,025, champion three-year-old colt, champion handicap horse, Belmont S., Jockey Club Gold Cup, etc. Virtually sterile; sired only four foals.

HILL PRINCE, 1947-1970. B. c., *Princequillo—Hildene, by Bubbling Over. 30-17-5-4, $422,140, Horse of the Year in 1950, champion two- and three-year-old colt, champion handicap horse, Preakness S., Jockey Club Gold Cup, etc. Sire of 23 stakes winners, including Bayou, Levee, Royal Living, Middle Brother. Broodmare sire of Dark Mirage, Shuvee.

HILLSDALE, 1955-1972. B. c., Take Away—Johann, by Johnstown. 41-23-6-4, $646,935, Hollywood Gold Cup H., Californian S., etc. Sire of nine stakes winners, including Bravery II, Hi Q., and of Acroterion.

***HINDOO**, 1878-1901. B. c., Virgil—Florence, by Lexington. 35-30-3-2, $71,875, champion two- and three-year-old colt, Kentucky Derby, Travers S., etc. Won 18 consecutive races at two and three. Sire of Hanover, Buddhist, Hindoo Rose, Jim Gore, Sallie McClelland.

***HOLY BULL**, 1991-. Gr. c., Great Above—Sharon Brown, by Al Hattab. 16-13-0-0, $2,481,760, Horse of the Year in 1994, champion three-year-old colt, Travers S. (G1), Metropolitan H. (G1), etc. Sire of more than 15 stakes winners, including Macho Uno, Confessional, Thunder Blitz.

HONEY FOX, 1977. B. f., Minnesota Mac—War Sparkler, by Fort Salonga. 27-13-5-3, $582,256, Ramona H. (G2), Black Helen H. (G2), etc.

HONEYMOON, 1943-unknown. B. f., *Beau Pere—Panoramic, by Chance Shot. 78-20-14-9, $387,760, Top Flight H., Hollywood Oaks, etc. Dam of Honeys Gem, Honeys Alibi from only three foals.

HONORABLE MISS, 1970-1987. B. f., Damascus—Court Circuit, by *Royal Vale. 62-19-12-9, $437,973, Fall Highweight H. (G2) twice, Vagrancy H. (G3), etc.

HYPERION, 1930-1960. Ch. c., Gainsborough—Selene, by Chaucer. 13-9-1-2, $124,386, champion three-year-old in England, Epsom Derby, St. Leger S., etc. Leading sire in England six times; leading broodmare sire in England four times. Sire of *Alibhai, Aristophanes, Aureole, Godiva, Gulf Stream, *Heliopolis, High Hat, *Khaled, Owen Tudor, Pensive, Sun Chariot. Broodmare sire of Alycidon, *Aunt Edith II, *Carrozza, Citation, Nearctic, Pretense. Foundation sire of sire line that leads to *Forli, Star Kingdom, *Vaguely Noble, Marscay, Nodouble, Efisio.

IDLEWILD, 1859-1883. B. f., Lexington—Florine, by *Glencoe. 25-18-1-1, $9,700, Post S., etc. Dam of Wildidle. Full sister to Aerolite, dam of Spendthrift.

IMP, 1894-1909. Br. f., Wagner—Fondling, by Fonso. 171-62-35-29, $70,069, champion older mare twice, Suburban H., etc. Immortalized in verse as "My Coal Black Lady."

IRISH LAD, 1900-unknown. Dk. b or br. c., *Candlemas—Arrowgrass, by Enquirer. 23-12-5-2, $98,210, champion older horse, Metropolitan H., Brooklyn H., etc. Sire in France of Banshee, Blarney.

IROQUOIS, 1878-1899. B. c., *Leamington—Maggie B.B., by *Australian. 26-12-4-3, $99,707, champion three-year-old in England, Epsom Derby, St. Leger S., etc. First American-bred winner of the Epsom Derby in 1881. Leading sire in 1892. Sire of Tammany, Huron.

JAIPUR, 1959-1987. Dk. b. or br. c., *Nasrullah—Rare Perfume, by Eight Thirty. 19-10-6-0, $618,926, champion three-year-old colt, Belmont S., Travers S., etc. Sire of Amber Rama, Mansingh, Pontifex.

***JANUS (LITTLE JANUS)**, 1746-1780. Ch. c., Janus—Fox mare, by Fox. Won twice in England and once in the U.S. at four-mile heats. Sire of Meade's Celer, Clodius, Goode's Old Twigg. Early Colonial Thoroughbred foundation sire and foundation sire of the original Virginia Quarter Horse.

JAY TRUMP, 1957-1988. Dk. b. or br. g., Tonga Prince—Be Trump, by *Bernborough. 29-13-5-2, Grand National Stp. H. in England, etc. Also won three Maryland Hunt Cups.

JIM DANDY, 1927-unknown. Ch. g., Jim Gaffney—Thunderbird, by *Star Shoot. 141-7-6-8, $49,570, Travers S., Grand Union Hotel S., etc. Upset Gallant Fox and Whichone in 1930 Travers S. at 100-to-1.

JOHN HENRY, 1975-. B. g., Ole Bob Bowers—Once Double, by Double Jay. 83-39-15-9, $6,591,860, Horse of the Year 1981, '84, champion grass male four times, Santa Anita H. (G1) twice, Jockey Club Gold Cup (G1), Oak Tree Invitational (G1) three times, Hollywood Invitational H. (G1) three times, etc. Resides at Kentucky Horse Park.

JOHN P. GRIER, 1917-1943. Ch. c., Whisk Broom II—Wonder, by Disguise. 17-10-4-2, $37,006, Queens County H., Aqueduct H., etc. Sire of 27 stakes winners, including Boojum, El Chico, Jack High, Miyako, White Lies. Pressed Man o' War to narrowest victory in 1920 Dwyer H.

JOHNSTOWN, 1936-1950. B. c., Jamestown—La France, by *Sir Gallahad III. 21-14-0-3, $169,315, Kentucky Derby, Belmont S., etc. Sire of Flood Town, Acoma. Broodmare sire of Nashua.

JOLLY ROGER, 1922-1948. Ch. g., Pennant—Lethe, by *All Gold. 49-18-9-9, $143,240, Grand National Stp. H. twice, Brook Stp. H., etc.

JUST A GAME (Ire), 1976-1993. Dk. b. or br. f., Tarboosh—Hobby (Ire), by Falcon. 28-14-4-3, $416,265, champion grass female, Flower Bowl H. (G2), Diana H. (G2), etc.

***KAYAK II**, 1935-1946. Dk. br. or c., Congreve—Mosquita, by Your Majesty. 26-14-8-1, $213,205, champion handicap horse, Santa Anita H., Hollywood Gold Cup, etc. Shy breeder.

KELSO, 1957-1983. Dk. b. or br. g., Your Host—Maid of Flight, by Count Fleet. 63-39-12-2, $1,977,896, Horse of the Year 1960-'64, champion three-year-old colt, champion older horse four times, handicap triple crown, Jockey Club Gold Cup five times, Woodward S. three times, etc. Only five-time Horse of the Year.

KENTUCKY, 1861-1875. B. c., Lexington—Magnolia, by *Glencoe. 23-21-0-0, $33,700, Travers S., Saratoga Cup twice, etc. Won 20 consecutive races; first winner of the Travers S. Sire of Nina, Woodbine. Along with Norfolk and Asteroid, one of three dominant sons of Lexington called the "great triumvirate."

***KHALED**, 1943-1968. Dk. b. or br. c., Hyperion—Eclair, by Ethnarch. 12-6-1-1, $38,860, Middle Park S., Coventry S., etc. Sire of 61 stakes winners, including Swaps, Terrang, Going Abroad, New Policy, Correspondent, A Glitter, Bushel-n-Peck. Broodmare sire of Candy Spots, Outing Class, Prove It.

KING'S BISHOP, 1969-1981. B. c., Round Table—Spearfish, by Fleet Nasrullah. 28-11-4-3, $308,079, Carter H. (G2), Fall Highweight H. (G3), etc. Sire of 30 stakes winners, including King's Swan, Possible Mate, Queen to Conquer, Queen Lib, Bishop's Ring.

KINGSTON, 1884-1912. Br. c., Spendthrift—*Kapanga, by Victorious. 138-89-33-12, $140,195, First Special S., etc. Leading sire in 1900, '10. Sire of Novelty, Wild Mint, Lida B. Holds American record for most races won at 89.

LADY LIGHTFOOT, 1812-1834. Br. f., Sir Archy—Black Maria, by *Shark. Won at least 23 races, 15 at four-mile heats. Dam of Black Maria, Terror.

LADY'S SECRET, 1982-. Gr. f., Secretariat—Great Lady M., by Icecapade. 45-25-9-3, $3,021,325, Horse of the Year in 1986, champion older female, Breeders' Cup Distaff (G1), Whitney H. (G1), etc. All-time distaff leading earner at time of retirement.

LAMPLIGHTER, 1889-unknown. Br. c., Spendthrift—*Torchlight, by Speculum. 67-30-13-11, $86,228, Choice S., First Special S. twice, etc.

LANDALUCE, 1980-1982. Dk. b. or br. f., Seattle Slew—Strip Poker, by Bold Bidder. 5-5-0-0, $372,365, champion two-year-old filly, Oak Leaf S. (G1), Del Mar Debutante S. (G2), etc. Died at two.

LA PREVOYANTE, 1970-1974. B. f., Buckpasser—Arctic Dancer, by Nearctic. 39-25-5-3, $572,417, champion two-year-old filly in U.S., Horse of the Year in Canada in 1972, champion two-year-old filly in Canada, champion older female in Canada, Frizette S., Spinaway S., etc. Died at four.

***LA TROIENNE**, 1926-1954. B. f., *Teddy—Helene de Troie, by Helicon. 7-0-1-1, $146. Greatest American foundation mare of the 20th century. Dam of Bimelech, Black Helen. Foundation mare of family that includes Buckpasser, Easy Goer, Allez France, Affectionately, Busher, Glamour, Numbered Account, Private Account, Woodman, Bee Ann Mac, Autobiography, Cohoes, The Axe II, Big Hurry, Searching, Relaxing, Bridal Flower, Caerleon, Straight Deal, Glowing Tribute, Sea Hero, Lite Light, Go for Gin, Pleasant Tap, Princess Rooney, Prairie Bayou.

LECOMPTE, 1850-1856. Ch. c., Boston—Reel, by *Glencoe. 16-11-5-0, $12,630, Jockey Club Purse, etc. Only horse to defeat Lexington. Sire of Umpire, Sherrod.

***L'ESCARGOT**, 1963-1984. Ch. g., Escart III—What a Daisy, by Grand Inquisitor. 63-14-15-8, $237,572, champion steeplechaser, Cheltenham Gold Cup Stp. H. twice, Meadow Brook Stp. H., etc.

LEXINGTON, 1850-1875. B. c., Boston—Alice Carneal, by *Sarpedon. 7-6-1-0, $56,600, Great State Post S., etc. Leading sire 1861-'74, '76, '78. Sire of Asteroid, Norfolk, Kentucky, Tom Ochiltree, Duke of Magenta, Tom Bowling, Harry Bassett, Sultana,

Maiden, Florence, General Duke, Hira, Idlewild, Lida, Preakness, Salina, Ulrica, War Dance. Leading sire record 16 times, 14 in succession.

LONESOME GLORY, 1988-2002. Ch. g., Transworld—Stronghold (Fr) by Green Dancer. 44-24-5-6, $1,325,868, champion steeplechaser five times, Carolina Cup Hurdle S. twice, Colonial Cup Stp. S. twice, etc. First steeplechase millionaire.

LONGFELLOW, 1867-1893. Br. c., *Leamington—Nantura, by Brawner's Eclipse. 16-13-2-0, $11,200, Monmouth Cup twice, Saratoga Cup, etc. Leading sire in 1891. Sire of Freeland, The Bard, Thora, Longstreet, Leonatus, Riley.

LUKE BLACKBURN, 1877-1904. B. c., *Bonnie Scotland—Nevada, by Lexington. 39-25-6-2, $49,460, Champion S., Kenner S., etc. Won 22 of 24 races at three. Sire of Proctor Knott.

LYPHARD, 1969-. B. c., Northern Dancer—Goofed, by *Court Martial. 12-6-1-0, $195,427, Prix Jacques le Marois, Prix de la Foret, etc. Leading sire in U.S. in 1986, leading sire in France 1978 and '79; leading broodmare sire in France in 1985 and '86. Sire of 115 stakes winners, including Dancing Brave, Manila, Three Troikas (Fr), Reine de Saba (Fr), Jolypha, Dancing Maid (Fr), Pharly, Bellypha (Ire), Sangue (Ire), Sabin, Al Nasr (Fr), Elliodor, Featherhill (Fr), Lypheor (GB), Skimble. Broodmare Sire of Bering (GB), Groom Dancer, Hatoof, Skimming.

MAD HATTER, 1916-1935. Dk. b. or br. c., Fair Play—Madcap, by *Rock Sand. 98-32-22-15, $194,525, champion handicap horse, Jockey Club Gold Cup twice, Toboggan H., etc. Sire of 22 stakes winners, including Snowflake, The Nut.

MAGGIE B.B., 1867-1889. B. f., *Australian—Madeline, by Boston. 7-3-4-0, $2,950, Sequel S. Greatest American broodmare of 19th century. Dam of Iroquois, Harold, Jaconet, Pera, Panique, Red and Blue. Tail-female ancestor of family that includes Alanesian, Boldnesian, Lawrin, Idun, Top Flight, Whisk Broom II, Life's Magic, Bald Eagle, Dubai Millennium.

MAHMOUD, 1933-1962. Gr. c., *Blenheim II—Mah Mahal, by Gainsborough. 11-4-2-3, $85,413, champion three-year-old in England, Epsom Derby, Champagne S., etc. Leading sire in 1946; leading broodmare sire in 1957. Sire of 66 stakes winners, including The Axe II, Oil Capitol, Cohoes, First Flight, Vulcan's Forge, Mount Marcy, Aldie, Snow Goose, Almahmoud, Happy Mood, Mahmoudess. Broodmare sire of Cosmah, Determine, *Gallant Man, *Grey Dawn II, Misty Morn, Silver Spoon, Your Host.

MAIDEN, 1862-1880. B. f., Lexington—Kitty Clark, by *Glencoe. 15-5-8-3, $5,500, Travers S., Produce S., etc. Second Travers S. winner. Dam of Parole, sixth dam of Nearco.

MAJESTIC PRINCE, 1966-1981. Ch. c., Raise a Native—Gay Hostess, by *Royal Charger. 10-9-1-0, $414,200, Kentucky Derby, Preakness S., etc. Sire of 33 stakes winners, including Majestic Light, Coastal, Sensitive Prince, Eternal Prince.

MAN O' WAR, 1917-1947. Ch. c., Fair Play—Mahubah, by *Rock Sand. 21-20-1-0, $249,465, champion two- and three-year-old colt, Belmont S., Travers S., etc. Leading sire in 1926. Sire of 62 stakes winners, including War Admiral, Crusader, American Flag, War Relic, Bateau, Scapa Flow, Edith Cavell, Maid at Arms, Florence Nightingale, Battleship, Clyde Van Dusen, Hard Tack. Broodmare sire of Blue Swords, Helioscope, Mata Hari, Pavot, Vagrancy. Tail-male

ancestor of line that leads to In Reality, Tiznow.

MASKETTE, 1906-c.1930. B. f., Disguise—Biturica, by Hamburg. 17-12-3-0, $77,090, champion two- and three-year-old filly, Futurity S., Alabama S., Matron S., Spinaway S., etc.

MATA HARI, 1931-1957. Br. f., Peter Hastings—War Woman, by Man o' War. 16-7-0-2, $66,699, champion two- and three-year-old filly, Breeders' Futurity, Kentucky Jockey Club S., Illinois Derby, etc. Dam of Spy Song, Mr. Music.

MATCHEM, 1748-1781. B. c., Cade—Partner mare, by Partner. 8 wins, The Whip, etc. Leading sire three times in England. Sire of Conductor, Pantaloon, Alfred, Hollandaise, Tetotum. Male-line ancestor of Man o' War, In Reality, Tiznow, Hurry On, Sassafras (Fr).

MATE, 1928-1953. Ch. c., Prince Pal—Killashandra, by *Ambassador IV. 75-20-14-19, $301,810, Preakness S., American Derby, etc. Great rival of Equipoise, Twenty Grand. Sire of five stakes winners, including two-time champion steeplechaser Elkridge.

MEDLEY, 1776-1792. Gr. c., Gimcrack—Arminda, by Snap. 13 wins. Sire of Bellair, Calypso, Grey Diomed, Grey Medley, Lamplighter. Early American foundation sire.

MESSENGER, 1780-1808. Gr. c., Mambrino—Turf mare, by Turf. 10 wins, $7,365. Sire of Miller's Damsel, Tippoo Saib, Potomac, Bright Phoebus, Mambrino. Early American foundation sire; also foundation sire of the American Standardbred breed.

MIDDLEGROUND, 1947-1972. Ch. c., Bold Venture—Verguenza, by Chicaro. 15-6-6-2, $237,725, Kentucky Derby, Belmont S., Hopeful S., etc. Sire of seven stakes winners, including Resaca, Here and There, Disperse. Shy breeder.

MIESQUE, 1984-. B. f., Nureyev—Pasadoble, by Prove Out. 16-12-3-1, $2,070,163, champion grass female twice in U.S., champion two-year-old in France, champion miler in England, champion older female in France, Breeders' Cup Mile (G1) twice, One Thousand Guineas (Eng-G1), etc. Dam of Kingmambo, East of the Moon, Miesque's Son, Moon Is Up.

MISS WOODFORD, 1880-1899. Br. f., *Billet—Fancy Jane, by Neil Robinson. 48-37-7-2, $118,270, Alabama S., Spinaway S., Pimlico S., etc. First American horse to earn $100,000.

MOCCASIN, 1963-1986. Ch. f., Nantallah—*Rough Shod II, by Gold Bridge. 21-11-2-4, $388,075, Horse of the Year in 1965, champion two-year-old filly, Gardenia S., Test S., etc. Dam of Apalachee, Scuff, Flippers.

MODESTY, 1881-unknown. Ch. f., War Dance—Ballet, by Planet. 82-35-8-11, $49,135, Kentucky Oaks, American Derby, etc. First filly winner of the American Derby. Tail-female ancestor of family that includes Regret, Thunderer, First Fiddle.

MOLLIE McCARTHY, 1873-unknown. B. f., Monday—Hennie Farrow, by Shamrock. 17-15-0-0, $18,750, Winter S., Garden City Cup, etc. One of the last great four-mile heat fillies.

MONSIEUR TONSON, 1822-unknown. B. c., Pacolet—Madame Tonson, by Top Gallant. 12-11-0-0. Leading sire in 1834. Sire of Argyle. First horse bred west of the Appalachians to win in East.

MORVICH, 1919-unknown. Bl. c., Runnymede—Hymir, by Dr. Leggo. 16-12-2-1, $172,909, Kentucky Derby, Hopeful S., etc. First California-bred winner of the Kentucky Derby in 1922, won first 12 starts. Sire of 12 stakes winners.

MOTHER GOOSE, 1922-unknown. Br. f., *Chicle—Flying Witch, by Broomstick. 10-3-1-3, $72,755, champion two-year-old filly, Futurity S. (defeated 28 others in a record field), Fashion S., etc. Dam of Arbitrator. Full sister to Whichone. Tail-female ancestor of family that includes Northern Dancer, Halo, Arctic Tern, Machiavellian, La Prevoyante, Tosmah, Danehill.

MR. PROSPECTOR, 1970-1999. B. c., Raise a Native—Gold Digger, by Nashua. 14-7-4-2, $112,171, Gravesend H., Whirlaway S., etc. Leading sire in 1987-'88; leading broodmare sire in 1997-2001. Sire of more than 175 stakes winners, including Forty Niner, Fusaichi Pegasus, Seeking the Gold, It's in the Air, Fappiano, Woodman, Gulch, Carson City, Conquistador Cielo, Gone West, Gold Beauty, Kingmambo, Machiavellian, Miswaki. Broodmare sire of Dayjur, Fasliyev, Hollywood Wildcat, Pulpit.

MRS. REVERE, 1981- . B. f., Silver Series—Gudewife, by Hard Work. 28-12-7-2, $429,545, Dogwood S., Furl Sail H., etc.

MY CHARMER, 1969-1993. B. f., Poker—Fair Charmer, by Jet Action. 32-6-4-2, $34,133, Fair Grounds Oaks. Dam of Seattle Slew, Lomond, Seattle Dancer (record $13.1-million yearling).

MYRTLEWOOD, 1932-1950. B. f., Blue Larkspur—*Frizeur, by *Sweeper. 22-15-4-2, $40,620, champion sprinter, champion handicap female, Ashland S., Hawthorne Sprint H., etc. Equaled three and set five track records. Dam of Durazna, Miss Dogwood. Foundation mare of family that includes Seattle Slew, Mr. Prospector, Myrtle Charm, Lomond, Typecast, Siberian Express, Highest Trump, Bahri, Ajina, Escena, Sewickley, Forestry, Chief Bearhart.

NASHUA, 1952-1982. B. c., *Nasrullah—Segula, by Johnstown. 30-22-4-1, $1,288,565, Horse of the Year in 1955, champion two- and three-year-old colt, Preakness S., Belmont S., Jockey Club Gold Cup twice, etc. Sire of 77 stakes winners, including Shuvee, Noble Nashua, Diplomat Way, Producer, Marshua, Bramalea, Bombay Duck, Good Manners, Nalee. Broodmare sire of Mr. Prospector, Roberto. First $1-million syndicated stallion.

*NASRULLAH, 1940-1959. B. c., Nearco—Mumtaz Begum, by *Blenheim II. 10-5-1-2, $15,259, champion two-year-old colt in England, Champion S., Coventry S., etc. Leading sire in 1955-'56, '59-'60, '62 in U.S.; leading sire in England. Sire of 93 stakes winners, including Bold Ruler, Nashua, Never Bend, Nearula, *Musidora, Never Say Die, Jaipur, Bald Eagle, Red God, Delta, Grey Sovereign. Broodmare sire of Drumtop, Natashka, *Sovereign II, Talking Picture, Turkish Trousers. Tail-male ancestor of Bold Ruler, Never Bend, Blushing Groom (Fr), Caro (Ire) lines.

NATIVE DANCER, 1950-1967. Gr. c., Polynesian—Geisha, by Discovery. 22-21-1-0, $785,240, Horse of the Year in 1952, '54, champion two- and three-year-old colt, champion handicap horse, Belmont S., Preakness S., Travers S., Futurity S., etc. Sire of 44 stakes winners, including Raise a Native, Hula Dancer, Dan Cupid, Secret Step, Kauai King, Dancer's Image, Native Charger, Native Street, Exclusive Dancer. Broodmare sire of General Assembly, Icecapade, Northern Dancer, Ruffian. Founder of male line that includes Mr. Prospector, Alydar, *Sea-Bird, Forty Niner, Seeking the Gold, Woodman, Thunder Gulch.

NATIVE DIVER, 1959-1967. Br. g., Imbros—Fleet Diver, by Devil Diver. 81-37-7-12, $1,026,500, Hollywood Gold Cup three times, San Carlos H. twice, etc. Won 33 stakes.

NEARCO, 1935-1957. B. c., Pharos—Nogara, by Havresac II. 14-14-0-0, $5,974, champion two- and three-year-old in Italy, Grand Prix de Paris, Derby Italiano, etc. Leading sire three times in England; leading broodmare sire three times in England. Sire of *Nasrullah, Dante, *Masaka, *Amerigo, Mossborough, Narrator, Nimbus, *Royal Charger, Sayajirao, Felucca, Infatuation, *Malindi, Neasham Belle, Netherton Maid, Noorani, Neocracy, Noble Lassie, *Rivaz. Broodmare sire of *Arctic Prince, Charlottesville, Saint Crespin III, Sheshoon, *Tulyar, *Vaguely Noble. Tail-male ancestor of Northern Dancer, Bold Ruler, Blushing Groom (Fr), Never Bend, Caro (Ire) male lines.

NEARCTIC, 1954-1973. Br. c., Nearco—*Lady Angela, by Hyperion. 47-21-5-3, $152,384, Horse of the Year in Canada in 1958, Michigan Mile, Saratoga Special S., Canadian Maturity, etc. Sire of 49 stakes winners, including Northern Dancer, Icecapade, Nonoalco, Briartic, Cool Reception, Cold Comfort, Cool Moon, Arctic Dancer, Christmas Wind. Broodmare sire of Kennedy Road, La Prevoyante.

NEEDLES, 1953-1984. B. c., Ponder—Noodle Soup, by Jack High. 21-11-3-3, $600,355, champion two- and three-year-old colt, Kentucky Derby, Belmont S., etc. Sire of 21 stakes winners, including Irish Rebellion, Needles n Pens. First Florida-bred winner of the Kentucky Derby.

NEJI, 1950-1982. Ch. g., *Hunters Moon IV—Accra, by Annapolis. 46-17-11-8, $270,694, champion steeplechaser three times, Temple Gwathmey Stp. H. twice, Grand National Stp. H. twice, etc.

NELLIE FLAG, 1932-1953. Ch. f., American Flag—Nellie Morse, by Luke McLuke. 22-6-5-1, $59,665, champion two-year-old filly, Kentucky Jockey Club S., Matron S., etc. Dam of Mar-Kell, Sunshine Nell, Nellie L. Foundation mare of family that includes Forego, Bold Forbes, Bet Twice, Lakeway, Mark-Ye-Well, Dewan, Saratoga Six.

NELLIE MORSE, 1921-1941. B. f., Luke McLuke—La Venganza, by Abercorn. 34-7-9-3, $73,565, champion three-year-old filly, Preakness S., Fashion S. etc. Dam of Nellie Flag, Count Morse.

NEXT MOVE, 1947-1968. Br. f., Bull Lea—Now What, by Chance Play. 46-17-11-3, $398,550, champion three-year-old filly, champion older mare, Coaching Club American Oaks, Beldame H. twice, etc. Dam of Good Move, Restless Native.

NIJINSKY II, 1967-1992. B. c., Northern Dancer—Flaming Page, by Bull Page. 13-11-2-0, $667,220, Horse of the Year in Europe in 1970, champion two- and three-year-old in England and Ireland, English Triple Crown, King George VI and Queen Elizabeth S., etc. Leading sire in England in 1986; leading broodmare sire in U.S. in 1993-'94. Sire of 155 stakes winners, including Caerleon, Lammtarra, Ferdinand, Ile de Bourbon, Sky Classic, Golden Fleece, Royal Academy, Green Dancer, Number, Javamine, Maplejinsky. Broodmare sire of Fantastic Light, Flawlessly, Forest Flower, Heavenly Prize, Java Gold, Rubiano, Sky Beauty. Last winner of the English Triple Crown.

NOBLE DAMSEL, 1978-. Ch. f., *Vaguely Noble—*Tender Camilla, by Prince Tenderfoot. 26-6-4-8, $212,575, New York H. (G3), etc.

NODOUBLE, 1965-1990. Ch. c., *Noholme II—AblaJay, by Double Jay. 42-13-11-5, $846,749, champion handicap horse twice, Santa Anita H., Metropolitan H., etc. Leading sire in 1981. Sire of 91 stakes winners, including Overskate, Mairzy Doates, Coolawin, Chain Store.

NOOR, 1945-1974. Br. c., *Nasrullah—Queen of Baghdad, by *Bahram. 31-12-5-3, $356,940, champion handicap horse, Santa Anita H., Hollywood Gold Cup H., etc. Sire of Yours, Flutterby, Noureddin. Broodmare sire of Dancer's Image, Delta Judge. Defeated Citation four times at five.

NORFOLK, 1861-1890. B. c., Lexington—Novice, by *Glencoe. 5-5-0-0, $10,550, Jersey Derby, etc. Sire of Emperor of Norfolk, El Rio Rey, Flood, Ralston. Member of sire Lexington's "great triumvirate" with Asteroid and Kentucky.

NORTHERN DANCER, 1961-1990. B. c. Nearctic—Natalma, by Native Dancer. 18-14-2-2, $580,647, champion three-year-old colt, Horse of the Year in 1964 in Canada, champion two-year-old colt in Canada, Kentucky Derby, Preakness S., etc. Leading sire in U.S. in 1971, leading broodmare sire in U.S. in 1991; leading sire in England four times. Sire of 146 stakes winners, including Nijinsky II, Sadler's Wells, Nureyev, The Minstrel, El Gran Senor, Storm Bird, Lyphard, Northern Taste, Northfields, Unfuwain, Northernette, Fanfreluche, Shareef Dancer, Try My Best, Be My Guest, Cool Mood, Dixieland Band. Broodmare sire of Arazi, Eillo, L'Alezane, L'Enjoleur, Narita Brian, Noverre, Rhythm, Ryafan, Southern Halo.

NUREYEV, 1977-2001. B. c., Northern Dancer—Special, by *Forli. 3-2-0-0, $42,522, champion miler in France, Prix Thomas Bryon (Fr-G3), Prix Djebel. Disqualified from victory in 1980 Two Thousand Guineas (Eng-G1). Leading sire twice in France. Sire of more than 130 stakes winners, including Miesque, Peintre Celebre, Theatrical (Ire), Soviet Star, Sonic Lady, Fasliyev, Polar Falcon, Reams of Verse, Stravinsky, Zilzal, Skimming. Broodmare sire of Desert King, East of the Moon, Kingmambo, Peteski, Zabeel.

OEDIPUS, 1946-1978. Br. g., Blue Larkspur—Be Like Mom, by *Sickle. 58-14-12-9, $132,405, champion steeplechaser three times, Grand National Stp. H., Brook Stp. H. twice, etc.

OLD ROSEBUD, 1911-1922. B. g., Uncle—Ivory Bells, by Himyar. 80-40-13-8, $74,729, Kentucky Derby, Carter H., Flash S., etc.

OMAHA, 1932-1959. Ch. c., Gallant Fox—Flambino, by *Wrack. 22-9-7-2, $154,705, champion three-year-old colt, Triple Crown, Dwyer S., Classic S., etc. Sire of seven stakes winners, including Prevaricator. Broodmare sire of Summer Tan.

ONE COUNT, 1949-1966. Dk. br. or br. c., Count Fleet—Ace Card, by Case Ace. 23-9-3-3, $245,625, Horse of the Year in 1952, champion three-year-old colt, Belmont S., Travers S., etc. Sire of 12 stakes winners, including Airmans Guide.

ORMONDE, 1883-1904. B. c., Bend Or—Lily Agnes, by Macaroni. 16-16-0-0, $138,340, Champion at two, three, and four in England, English Triple Crown. Sire of Orme, Ormondale, *Gold Finch, Ossary. Progressively sterile. Tail-male ancestor of *Teddy line. Greatest English racehorse of 19th century; he was a roarer.

PAN ZARETA, 1910-1918. Ch. f., Abe Frank—Caddie Griffith, by Rancocas. 151-76-31-21, $39,082, Juarez H., Rio Grande H., etc. Won carrying 140

pounds or more five times. Died at eight and is buried in infield at Fair Grounds.

PAPYRUS, 1920-1941. Br. c., Tracery—Miss Matty, by Marcovil. 18-9-5-1, $110,068, Epsom Derby, Chester Vase, etc. First Epsom Derby winner to race in the U.S. in international match race against Zev in 1923. Sire of Barbara Burrini, *Cosquilla, *Osiris II, Honey Buzzard.

PARLO, 1951-1978. Ch. f., *Heliopolis—Fairy Palace, by Pilate. 34-8-6-3, $309,240, champion three-year-old filly, champion handicap mare twice, Alabama S., Beldame H., etc. Tail-female ancestor of Arts and Letters, Silverbulletday, Saudi Poetry, Zaccio, Waquoit.

PAROLE, 1873-1903. Br. g., *Leamington—Maiden, by Lexington. 127-59-22-16, $82,111, Saratoga Cup, Epsom Gold Cup (in England), etc.

PASEANA (Arg), 1987-. B. f., Ahmad—Pasiflin (Arg), by Flintham. 36-19-10-2, $3,317,427, champion older female twice, Breeders' Cup Distaff (G1), Milady H. (G1) twice, Apple Blossom H. (G1) twice, etc.

PAVOT, 1942-1975. Dk. b. or br. c., Case Ace—Coquelicot, by Man o' War. 32-14-6-2, $373,365, undefeated champion two-year-old colt, Belmont S., Futurity S., etc. Sire of 14 stakes winners, including Andre, Cigar Maid.

PERSONAL ENSIGN, 1984- . B. f., Private Account—Grecian Banner, by Hoist the Flag. 13-13-0-0, $1,679,880, champion older female, Breeders' Cup Distaff (G1), Beldame S. (G1) twice, etc. Broodmare of the Year in 1996. Dam of My Flag, Miner's Mark, Traditionally, Our Emblem.

PETER PAN, 1904-1933. B. c., Commando—*Cinderella, by Hermit. 17-10-3-1, $115,450, Belmont S., Hopeful S., etc. Sire of Black Toney, Pennant, Peter Hastings, Tryster, Prudery, Vexatious, Panoply, Wendy.

PEYTONA, 1839-1858. Ch. f., *Glencoe—Giantess, by *Leviathan. 8-6-1-0, $62,400, Peyton S., North-South Match, etc. One-time leading American money earner; defeated Fashion in last great North-South match race.

PHALARIS, 1913-1931. B. c., Polymelus—Bromus, by Sainfoin. 24-16-2-1, $26,376, Challenge S. twice, Stud Produce S., etc. Leading sire twice in England. Sire of 65 stakes winners, including Pharos, Fairway, Colorado, Manna, Fair Isle, *Sickle, *Pharamond II, Chatelaine. Broodmare sire of *Easton, Godiva, Mid-day Sun, Picture Play. Tail-male ancestor of *Nasrullah, Northern Dancer, Native Dancer, Buckpasser sire lines.

PHAR LAP, 1926-1932. Ch. g., Night Raid—Entroaty, by Winkie. 51-37-3-2, $305,921, AJC Derby, Victoria Derby, W. S. Cox Plate (twice); won Agua Caliente H. in only start in North America; died shortly after under mysterious circumstances. Considered Australia's greatest racehorse.

PLANET, 1855-1875. Ch. c., Revenue—Nina, by Boston. 31-27-4-0, $69,700, Great Post S. twice, etc. Sire of Katy Pease, Hubbard, Ballet. Replaced Peytona as America's leading money earner.

PLAUDIT, 1895-1919 B. c., Himyar—*Cinderella, by Tomahawk or Blue Ruin. 20-8-5-0, $32,715, Kentucky Derby, Champagne S., etc. Sire of King James, Casuarina, Rosa Mundi, Spoonful. Tail-male ancestor of Dr. Fager, Holy Bull.

POCAHONTAS, 1837-1870. B. f., *Glencoe—Marpessa, by Muley. 9-0-3-0, $0. Greatest English broodmare of 19th century, dam of Stockwell, King Tom, Rataplan. Ancestress of modern families that in-

clude foundation mares Rosy Legend, Kizil-Kourgan, Traverse, Traffic Court, Segula as well as racehorses and sires Dante, Sayajirao, *Ksar, *Kantar, Traffic Judge, Hasty Road, Nashua, Louis Quatorze.

POKER, 1963-1986. B. c., Round Table—Glamour, by *Nasrullah. 36-7-4-4, $111,097, Bowling Green H., etc. Sire of 19 stakes winners, including Poker Night, Silver Badge, My Charmer. Broodmare sire of Seattle Slew, Silver Charm.

POT8O'S, 1773-unknown. Ch. c., Eclipse—Sportsmistress, by Sportsman. 30 wins in England, Craven S., Jockey Club Plate three times, etc. Sire of Champion, Coriander, Mandane, Waxy. Tail-male line ancestor of Phalaris, Hyperion, Blandford, Domino lines.

PREAKNESS, 1867-1881. B. c., Lexington—Bayleaf, by *Yorkshire. 39-18-11-5, $43,679, Dinner Party S., Saratoga Cup, etc. Sire in England of Fiddler, Piccadilly.

PRECISIONIST, 1981-. Ch. c., Crozier—Excellently, by *Forli. 46-20-10-4, $3,485,398, champion sprinter, Breeders' Cup Sprint (G1), Woodward S. (G1), etc. Virtually sterile.

PRIMONETTA, 1958-1993. Ch. f., Swaps—Banquet Bell, by Polynesian. 25-17-2-2, $306,690, champion older mare, Alabama S., Spinster S. twice, etc. Broodmare of the Year in 1978; dam of Prince Thou Art, Maud Muller, Cum Laude Laurie, Grenfall. Sister to Chateaugay.

***PRINCEQUILLO**, 1940-1964. B. c., Prince Rose—*Cosquilla, by *Papyrus. 33-12-5-7, $96,550, Jockey Club Gold Cup, Saratoga Cup, etc. Leading sire 1957-'58; leading broodmare sire 1966-'70, '72, '73, '76. Sire of 65 stakes winners, including Round Table, Dedicate, Prince John, How, Quill, Hill Prince, Misty Morn, Princessnesian, Cherokee Rose, Discipline. Broodmare sire of Bold Lad, *Comtesse de Loir, Fort Marcy, Key to the Mint, Kris S., Mill Reef, Secretariat, Sham, Sir Gaylord.

PRINCESS DOREEN, 1921-1952. B. f., *Spanish Prince II—Lady Doreen, by Ogden. 94-34-15-17, $174,754, Coaching Club American Oaks, Saratoga H., etc. Dam of Miss Doreen. Tail-female ancestor of Brown Bess, Caller I. D.

PRINCESS ROONEY, 1980-. Gr. f., Verbatim—Parrish Princess, by Drone. 21-17-2-1, $1,343,339, champion older female, Breeders' Cup Distaff (G1), Spinster S. (G1), etc.

PRIORESS, 1853-1868. B. f., *Sovereign—Reel, by *Glencoe. 24-10-1-3, $22,637, Cesarewitch H., two Queen's Plates, etc. First American-bred to win in England, victorious in a runoff after a dead heat in the 1857 Cesarewitch H.

PRUDERY, 1918-1930. B. f., Peter Pan—Polly Flinders, by Burgomaster. 22-7-6-5, $47,625, champion two-year-old filly, Alabama S., Spinaway S., etc. Dam of Whiskery, Victorian, Halcyon. Tail-female ancestor of Taylor's Special.

PUCKER UP, 1953-1975. B. f., Olympia—Lou Lea, by Bull Lea. 32-16-8-4, $304,585, champion older mare, Beldame H., Washington Park H., etc. Dam of Plucky Pan.

QUESTIONNAIRE, 1927-1950. B. c., Sting—Miss Puzzle, by Disguise. 45-19-8-4, $89,611, Metropolitan H., Brooklyn H., etc. Sire of 24 stakes winners, including Requested, Free For All, Carolyn A., Hash, Stefanita, Third Degree. Tail-male line ancestor of Dr. Fager, Holy Bull.

RAISE A NATIVE, 1961-1988. Ch. c., Native Dancer—Raise You, by Case Ace. 4-4-0-0, $45,955, champion two-year-old colt, Juvenile S., Great American S. Sire of 78 stakes winners, including Alydar, Mr. Prospector, Exclusive Native, Majestic Prince, Laomedonte, Crowned Prince, Native Royalty, Marshua's Dancer, Native Partner, Where You Lead. Broodmare sire of Ajdal, Meadowlake, Slightly Dangerous.

RARE TREAT, 1952-1975. Ch. f., Stymie—Rare Perfume, by Eight Thirty. 101-16-20-14, $273,227, Firenze H., Ladies H., etc. Dam of What a Treat, Ring Twice; grandam of Golden Fleece.

REAL DELIGHT, 1949-1969. B. f., Bull Lea—Blue Delight, by Blue Larkspur. 15-12-1-0, $261,822, champion three-year-old filly, champion handicap mare, Coaching Club American Oaks, Kentucky Oaks, etc. Dam of Plum Cake, No Fooling, Spring Sunshine. Foundation mare of family that includes Alydar, Our Mims, Codex, Rich Cream, Christmas Bonus, Grand Slam, Sugar and Spice, Christmas Past.

REEL, 1838-unknown. Gr. f., *Glencoe—*Gallopade, by Catton. 8-7-1-0. Dam of Lecompte, Prioress, Starke, War Dance. Tail-female ancestor of modern family that includes Two Lea, Tim Tam, Miz Clementine, Best Turn, Chris Evert, Chief's Crown, Winning Colors.

REGRET, 1912-1934. Ch. f., Broomstick—Jersey Lightning, by Hamburg. 11-9-1-0, $35,093, Kentucky Derby, Hopeful S., etc. First filly to win the Kentucky Derby. Tail-female ancestor of family that includes First Fiddle, Divine Comedy.

REIGH COUNT, 1925-1948. Ch. c., *Sunreigh—*Contessina, by Count Schomberg. 27-12-4-0, $178,170, champion two- and three-year-old colt, Kentucky Derby, Jockey Club Gold Cup S., Coronation Cup (in England), etc. Sire of 22 stakes winners, including Count Fleet, Triplicate, Count Arthur. Broodmare sire of Gallahadion.

REVENUE, 1843-unknown. B. c., *Trustee—Rosalie Somers, by Sir Charles. 21-16-5-0. Jockey Club Purse, Proprietor's Purse, etc. Leading sire in 1860. Sire of Planet, Fanny Washington, Revolver.

***RIBOT**, 1952-1972. B. c., Tenerani—Romanella, by El Greco. 16-16-0-0, $288,648, champion at two, three, and four in Italy, champion at four in England and France, Prix de l'Arc de Triomphe twice, King George VI and Queen Elizabeth S., etc. Leading sire three times in England. Sire of 65 stakes winners, including Arts and Letters, Tom Rolfe, Graustark, His Majesty, Ragusa, Molvedo, Romulus, Boucher, Long Look, *Prince Royal II, Regal Exception, Arkadina. Broodmare sire of Bireme, Cannonade, Cascapedia, Majestic Light, Treizieme.

RIVA RIDGE, 1969-1985. B. c., First Landing—Iberia, by *Heliopolis. 30-17-3-1, $1,111,497, champion two-year-old colt, champion handicap male, Kentucky Derby, Belmont S., etc. Sire of 29 stakes winners, including Tap Shoes, Rivalero, Blitey.

RIVERMAN, 1969-1999. B. c., Never Bend—River Lady, by Prince John. 8-5-2-1, $223,960, Poule d'Essai des Poulains (French Two Thousand Guineas), etc. Leading sire in France in 1980-'81. Sire of 128 stakes winners, including Irish River (Fr), Triptych, Bahri, Gold River (Fr), Detroit (Fr), Imperfect Circle, Korveya. Broodmare sire of Bosra Sham, Carnegie (Ire), Erhaab, Hector Protector, Highest Honor (Fr), Saint Cyrien, Spinning World.

ROAMER, 1911-1919. B. g., *Knight Errant—*Rose Tree II, by Bona Vista. 98-39-26-9, $98,828, Travers S., Carter H., Saratoga H. 3 times, etc.

ROBERTO, 1969-1988. B. c., Hail to Reason—Bramalea, by Nashua. 14-7-4-0, $332,272, champion three-year-old in England in 1972, champion two-year-old in Ireland in 1971, Epsom Derby, etc. Sire of 85 stakes winners, including Sunshine Forever, Brian's Time, Plenty of Grace, Dynaformer, and of Red Ransom. Broodmare sire of Blushing K.D., Commander in Chief, Warning (GB).

ROSEBEN, 1901-1918. B. g., *Ben Strome—Rose Leaf, by Duke of Montrose. 111-52-25-12, $75,110, Carter H., Manhattan H. twice, etc. Great sprinter who won 14 races under 140 pounds or more, known as "the big train."

ROUGH'N TUMBLE, 1948-1968. B. c., Free For All—Roused, by *Bull Dog. 16-4-5-4, $126,980, Santa Anita Derby, Primer S., etc. Sire of 24 stakes winners, including Dr. Fager, My Dear Girl, Flag Raiser, Ruffled Feathers, Minnesota Mac, Treasure Chest. Florida foundation sire.

ROUGH SHOD II, 1944-unknown. B. f., Gold Bridge—Dalmary, by Blandford. 7-1-1-1, $1,306. Dam of Moccasin, Ridan, Lt. Stevens, Gambetta, Thong. Foundation mare of family that includes Sadler's Wells, Nureyev, Thatch, Gamely, Drumtop, Fairy King, King Pellinore, El Condor Pasa, Number, Bienamado.

ROUND TABLE, 1954-1987. B. c., *Princequillo—*Knight's Daughter, by Sir Cosmo. 66-43-8-5, $1,749,869, Horse of the Year in 1958, champion grass horse three times, champion handicap horse twice, Santa Anita H., Hollywood Gold Cup H., etc. Leading sire in 1972. Sire of 83 stakes winners, including Baldric, Apalachee, Flirting Around, Targowice, Royal Glint, King Pellinore, Drumtop, Knightly Manner, Advocator, King's Bishop, Artaius, Dancealot, Foreseer, Poker, Tell. Broodmare sire of Bowl Game, Caerleon, Hidden Lake, Outstandingly, Topsider.

ROYAL CHARGER, 1942-1961. Ch. c., Nearco—Sun Princess by Solario. 20-6-7-2, $20,291, Queen Anne S., Ayr Gold Cup, etc. Sire of 54 stakes winners, including *Turn-to, Mongo, *Royal Serenade, Royal Native, Idun, Royal Orbit, Gilles de Retz, Happy Laughter, Royal Palm, *Banri an Oir. Broodmare sire of Majestic Prince, Tudor Queen. Tail-male ancestor of Roberto, Halo lines.

ROYAL HEROINE (Ire), 1980-. Dk. b. or br. f., Lypheor (GB)—My Sierra Leone, by Relko. 21-10-4-2, $1,229,449, champion grass female, Breeders' Cup Mile (G1), Matriarch S. (G1), etc.

RUFFIAN, 1972-1975. Dk. b. or br. f., Reviewer—Shenanigans, by Native Dancer. 11-10-0-0, $313,428, champion two- and three-year-old filly, filly triple crown, Spinaway S. (G1), etc. Broke down in match race with Foolish Pleasure and euthanized when she reinjured leg after surgery. Buried in infield at Belmont Park.

RUTHLESS, 1864-1876. B. f., *Eclipse—Barbarity, by *Simoom. 11-7-4-0, $11,000, Belmont S., Travers S., etc. Won first Belmont S. Best of five high-class sisters out of Barbarity nicknamed "the barbarous battalion."

SABIN, 1980-. Ch. f., Lyphard—Beaconaire, by *Vaguely Noble. 25-18-0-2, $1,098,341, Yellow Ribbon Invitational S. (G1), etc. Dam of Sabina, Al Sabin.

SADLER'S WELLS, 1981- . B. c., Northern Dancer—Fairy Bridge, by Bold Reason. 11-6-3-0, $713,690, Irish Two Thousand Guineas (Ire-G1),

Eclipse S. (Eng-G1), etc. Leading sire in England 11 times. Sire of more than 195 stakes winners (world record), including Galileo (Ire), In the Wings (GB), Salsabil (Ire), Old Vic, Northern Spur (Ire), El Prado (Ire), Montjeu (Ire), Carnegie (Ire), Barathea (Ire), Imagine, King of Kings (Ire), Fort Wood.

SAFELY KEPT, 1986-. B. f., Horatius—Safely Home, by Winning Hit. 31-24-2-3, $2,194,206, champion sprinter, Breeders' Cup Sprint (G1), Test S. (G1), etc.

SALVATOR, 1886-1909. Ch. c., *Prince Charlie—Salina, by Lexington. 19-16-1-1, $113,240, champion three-year-old, Suburban H., Lawrence Realization, etc. Sire of Salvation.

SARAZEN, 1921-1940. Ch. g., High Time—Rush Box, by Box. 55-27-2-6, $225,000, Champagne S., Carter H., Dixie H. twice, etc. Defeated *Epinard in third installment of the International Series of 1924.

*SEA-BIRD, 1962-1973. Ch. c., Dan Cupid—Sicalade, by Sicambre. 8-7-1-0, $645,283, Horse of the Year in France and England, Epsom Derby, Prix de l'Arc de Triomphe, etc. Sire of 33 stakes winners, including Allez France, Little Current, Gyr, Arctic Tern, Kittiwake. Broodmare sire of Alydar's Best, Assert (Ire), Bikala, Miss Oceana.

SEABISCUIT, 1933-1947. B. c., Hard Tack—Swing On, by Whisk Broom II. 89-33-15-13, $437,730, Horse of the Year in 1938, champion handicap male twice, Pimlico Special, Santa Anita H., etc. Sire of four stakes winners, including Sea Swallow.

SEARCHING, 1952-1973. B. f., War Admiral—Big Hurry, by Black Toney. 89-25-14-16, $327,381, Maskette H., Diana H. twice, etc. Dam of Affectionately, Priceless Gem, Admiring. Foundation mare of family that includes Allez France, Sea Hero, Lite Light, Personality, Al Mamoon.

SEATTLE SLEW, 1974-2002. Dk. b. or br. c., Bold Reasoning—My Charmer, by Poker. 17-14-2-0, $1,208,726, Horse of the Year in 1977, champion two- and three-year-old colt, champion older male, Triple Crown, Woodward S. (G1), etc. Leading sire in 1984; leading broodmare sire 1995-'96. Sire of more than 100 stakes winners, including A.P. Indy, Swale, Slew o' Gold, Surfside, Capote, Landaluce, Slew City Slew, Taiki Blizzard, Lakeway, Honest Lady, General Meeting, Avenue of Flags, Slewvescent, Slewacide. Broodmare sire of Cigar, Agnes World, Escena, Golden Attraction, Seeking the Pearl. Only horse to win Triple Crown while undefeated.

SECRETARIAT, 1970-1989. Ch. c., Bold Ruler—Somethingroyal, by *Princequillo. 21-16-3-1, $1,316,808, Horse of the Year in 1972-'73, champion two- and three-year-old colt, champion grass male, Triple Crown, Marlboro Cup H., etc. Leading broodmare sire in 1992. Sire of 56 stakes winners, including Lady's Secret, Risen Star, Medaille d'Or, Terlingua, General Assembly, Tinners Way, Weekend Surprise, Secrettame, Six Crowns. Broodmare sire of A.P. Indy, Chief's Crown, Dehere, Gone West, Secreto, Storm Cat, Summer Squall.

*SELIMA, 1745-1766. B. f., Godolphin Arabian—Shireborn mare, by Hobgoblin. 2-2-0-0, $10,200, Great Intercolonial Match Race with Tryal. Dam of Ariel, Selim, Ebony, Bellair, Lightfoot's Partner. Tail-female ancestor of family that includes Hanover, Inspector B., Peytona, Foxhall, The Vid.

SENSATION, 1877-1899. Br. c., *Leamington—Susan Beane, by Lexington. 8-8-0-0, $20,250, champion two-year-old colt, Flash S., Nursery S., etc. Sire

of Democrat.

SERENA'S SONG, 1992-. B. f., Rahy—Imagining, by Northfields. 38-18-11-3, $3,283,388, champion three-year-old filly, Mother Goose S. (G1), Beldame S. (G1), etc. Leading North American money-earning female at time of retirement. Dam of Serena's Tune, Sophisticat.

SHIRLEY JONES, 1956-1978. B. f., Double Jay—L'Omelette, by *Alibhai. 49-18-9-5, $282,313, Test S., Maskette H., etc.

SHUVEE, 1966-1986. Ch. f., Nashua—Levee, by Hill Prince. 44-16-10-6, $890,445, champion handicap mare, champion older female, filly triple crown, Jockey Club Gold Cup twice, etc. Dam of Tom Swift, Shukey, Benefice.

***SICKLE**, 1924-1943. Br. c., Phalaris—Selene, by Chaucer. 10-3-4-2, $23,629, Prince of Wales's S., etc. Leading sire in 1936, '38. Sire of 41 stakes winners, including Stagehand, Brevity, Unbreakable, Star Pilot, Cravat, Reaping Reward, Misty Isle, Jabot. Broodmare sire of Bornastar, Counterpoint, Dan Cupid, How, Social Outcast. Tail-male ancestor of Native Dancer sire line.

SILVERBULLETDAY, 1996-. B. f., Silver Deputy—Rokeby Rose, by Tom Rolfe. 23-15-3-1, $3,093,207, champion two- and three-year-old filly, Breeders' Cup Juvenile Fillies (G1), Kentucky Oaks (G1), etc.

SILVER CHARM, 1994-. Gr. or ro. c., Silver Buck—Bonnie's Poker, by Poker. 24-12-7-2, $6,944,369, champion three-year-old colt, Kentucky Derby (G1), Preakness S. (G1), Dubai World Cup (UAE-G1), etc.

SILVER SPOON, 1956-1978. Ch. f., Citation—Silver Fog, by *Mahmoud. 27-13-3-4, $313,930, champion three-year-old filly, Santa Anita Derby, Milady H., etc. Dam of Inca Queen. Tail-female ancestor of family that includes Catinca, Metfield.

SIR ARCHY, 1805-1833. Ch. c., *Diomed—*Castianira, by Rockingham. 7-4-1-0, Post S. Leading Colonial sire. Sire of Sir Charles, Timoleon, Flirtilla, Bertrand, Henry, Kosciusko, Lady Lightfoot, Sumpter, Reality. Oldest member of the Racing Hall of Fame.

SIR BARTON, 1916-1937. Ch. c., *Star Shoot—Lady Sterling, by Hanover. 31-13-6-5, $116,857, champion three-year-old colt, Triple Crown, Saratoga H., etc. First winner of the American Triple Crown. Sire of seven stakes winners, including Easter Stockings.

***SIR GALLAHAD III**, 1920-1949. B. c., *Teddy—Plucky Liege, by Spearmint. 24-11-3-3, $17,009, Poule d'Essai des Poulains (French Two Thousand Guineas), Prix Jacques le Marois, Match race with *Epinard, etc. Leading sire 1930, '33-'34, '40; leading broodmare sire '39, '43-'52, '55. Sire of 56 stakes winners, including Gallant Fox, Gallahadion, High Quest, Vagrancy, Foxborough, Fighting Fox, Hoop, Jr., Roman. Broodmare sire of Beaugay, Challedon, *Galatea II, Gallorette, Johnstown, Royal Native. Greatest American broodmare sire of the 20th century.

SIXTY SAILS, 1970-1990. Dk. b. or br. f., Creme dela Creme—Bunch of Daisies, by Sir Gaylord. 49-12-13-7, $220,131, Matron H. (G2) twice, Louisiana Gold Cup H., etc.

SKIP AWAY, 1993-. Gr. or ro. c., Skip Trial—Ingot Way, by Diplomat Way. 38-18-10-6, $9,616,360, Horse of the Year in 1998, champion three-year-old colt, champion older male twice, Breeders' Cup Classic (G1), Jockey Club Gold Cup (G1) twice, etc.

SKY BEAUTY, 1990-. B. f., Blushing Groom (Fr)—Maplejinsky, by Nijinsky II. 21-15-2-2, $1,336,000,

champion older female, filly triple crown, Alabama S. (G1), etc.

SLEW O' GOLD, 1980- . B. c., Seattle Slew—Alluvial, by Buckpasser. 21-12-5-1, $3,533,534, champion three-year-old colt, champion older male, Jockey Club Gold Cup (G1) twice, Woodward S. (G1) twice, etc. Sire of Golden Opinion, Gorgeous, Dramatic Gold, Thirty Six Red, Awe Inspiring.

SOMETHINGROYAL, 1952-1983. B. f., *Princequillo—Imperatrice, by Caruso. 1-0-0-0, $0. Broodmare of the Year in 1973. Dam of Secretariat, Sir Gaylord, First Family, Syrian Sea, Somethingfabulous. Foundation mare of family that includes Saratoga Dew, Alada, John Cherry, Personal Business.

SPECTACULAR BID, 1976-. Gr. or ro. c., Bold Bidder—Spectacular, by Promised Land. 30-26-2-1, $2,781,608, Horse of the Year in 1980, champion two- and three-year-old colt, champion older male, Kentucky Derby (G1), Preakness S. (G1), etc. Sire of more than 40 stakes winners, including Lotus Pool, Double Feint, Spectacular Love.

SPENDTHRIFT, 1876-1900. Ch. c., *Australian—Aerolite, by Lexington. 13-10-5-0, $27,250, Belmont S., Jersey Derby, etc. Sire of Kingston, Hastings, Lamplighter, Bankrupt. Tail-male ancestor of line that leads to Fair Play, Man o' War, War Admiral, In Reality, Tiznow.

SPINAWAY, 1878-unknown. Ch. f., *Leamington—Megara, by *Eclipse. 9-7-2-0, $16,225, champion two-year-old filly, Hopeful S., Juvenile S., etc. Dam of Lazzarone. Tail-female ancestor of family that includes Giant's Causeway, Tanya, Floradora, Star Pilot, By Land By Sea, Gummo, Spearfish, Gaily, King's Bishop.

SPORT PAGE, 1946-1972. Ch. c., Our Boots—Our Page, by Blue Larkspur. 15-4-4-2, $79,175, East View S., etc.

***STAR SHOOT**, 1898-1919. B. c., Isinglass—Astrology, by Hermit. 10-3-1-1, $34,747 in England, National Breeders' Produce S., etc. Leading sire 1911-'12, '16-'17, '19; leading broodmare sire 1924-'26, '28-'29. Sire of Sir Barton, Grey Lag, Uncle, Wistful, Daylight Saving, Mindful, Priscilla. Broodmare sire of Blazes, Crusader, Gusto, Jack High.

STOCKWELL, 1849-1870. Ch. c., The Baron—Pocahontas, by *Glencoe. 16-11-3-0, $48,457, champion three-year-old in England, Two Thousand Guineas, St. Leger S., etc. Leading sire in England seven times. Sire of Doncaster, Achievement, Caller Ou, Cantiniere, Chevisaunce, Lord Lyon, Regalia, St. Albans, The Marquis. Known as the "Emperor of Stallions." Tail-male ancestor of Phalaris male line.

STRAIGHT DEAL, 1962-1982. B. f., Hail to Reason—No Fiddling, by King Cole. 99-21-21-9, $733,020, champion handicap mare, Delaware H., Santa Margarita H., etc. Dam of Desiree, Reminiscing.

ST. SIMON, 1881-1908. Br. c., Galopin—St. Angela, by King Tom. 9-9-0-0, $23,121, Ascot Gold Cup, Epsom Gold Cup, Goodwood Cup, etc. Leading sire in England nine times. Sire of Persimmon, Diamond Jubilee, St. Frusquin, Rabelais, Chaucer, Memoir, La Fleche. Tail-male ancestor of *Ribot, *Princequillo male lines.

STYMIE, 1941-1962. Ch. c., Equestrian—Stop Watch, by On Watch. 131-35-33-28, $918,485, champion handicap horse, Metropolitan H. twice, Whitney S., etc. Sire of 12 stakes winners, including Rare

Treat, Joe Jones, Paper Tiger. Broodmare sire of Regal Gleam, What a Treat. Retired as world's leading money earner in 1950.

SUN BEAU, 1925-1944. B. c., *Sun Briar—Beautiful Lady, by Fair Play. 74-33-12-10, $376,744, champion handicap horse three times, Hawthorne Gold Cup three times, Aqueduct H., etc. Sire of six stakes winners, including Sun Lover. Leading money earner at his retirement in 1931.

***SUN BRIAR**, 1915-1943. B. c., Sundridge—*Sweet Briar II, by St. Frusquin. 22-8-4-5, $74,355, champion two-year-old colt, Travers S., Hopeful S., etc. Sire of more than 30 stakes winners, including Sun Beau, Pompey, Firethorn.

SUNDAY SILENCE, 1986- . Dk. b. or br. c., Halo—Wishing Well, by Understanding. 14-9-5-0, $4,968,554, Horse of the Year in 1989, champion three-year-old colt, Kentucky Derby (G1), Preakness S. (G1), Breeders' Cup Classic (G1), etc. Leading sire in Japan 1995-2001. Sire of more than 70 stakes winners, including Air Shakur, Dance Partner, Marvelous Sunday, Dance in the Dark, Bubble Gum Fellow, Fuji Kiseki, Special Week, Stay Gold, Genuine, Tayasu Tsuyoshi.

SUSAN'S GIRL, 1969-1988. B. f., Quadrangle—Quaze, by *Quibu. 63-29-14-11, $1,251,668, champion three-year-old filly, champion older female twice, Spinster S. (G1) twice, Delaware H. (G1) twice, etc. First filly to become a millionaire. Dam of Copelan, Paramount Jet.

SWALE, 1981-1984. Dk. b. or br. c., Seattle Slew—Tuerta, by *Forli. 14-9-2-2, $1,583,660, champion three-year-old colt, Kentucky Derby (G1), Belmont S. (G1), etc. Died at three.

SWAPS, 1952-1972. Ch. c., *Khaled—Iron Reward, by *Beau Pere. 25-19-2-2, $848,900, Horse of the Year in 1956, champion handicap horse, Kentucky Derby, Hollywood Gold Cup H., etc. Sire of 35 stakes winners, including Affectionately, Chateaugay, Primonetta, No Robbery. Broodmare sire of Best Turn, Fall Aspen, Numbered Account, Personality.

SWOON'S SON, 1953-1977. B. c., The Doge—Swoon, by Sweep Like. 51-30-10-3, $970,605, American Derby, Arlington Classic, etc. Sire of 22 stakes winners, including Chris Evert, Loom, Mr. Washington. Won 22 stakes.

SWORD DANCER, 1956-1984. Ch. c., Sunglow—Highland Fling, by By Jimminy. 39-15-7-4, $829,610, Horse of the Year in 1959, champion three-year-old colt, champion handicap horse, Belmont S., Jockey Club Gold Cup, etc. Sire of 15 stakes winners, including Damascus, Lady Pitt.

SYSONBY, 1902-1906. B. c., *Melton—*Optime, by Orme. 15-14-0-1, $184,438, champion two- and three-year-old colt, Metropolitan H., Saratoga Special, etc. Died at four.

TA WEE, 1966-1980. Dk. b. or br. f., Intentionally—Aspidistra, by Better Self. 21-15-2-1, $284,941, champion sprinter twice, Vosburgh H., Fall Highweight H. twice, etc. Dam of Great Above, Tax Holiday, Entropy, Tweak.

***TEDDY**, 1913-1936. B. c., Ajax—Rondeau, by Bay Ronald. 8-5-1-2, Grand Premio de San Sebastian, Prix des Trois Ans, etc. Leading sire in France twice. Sire of *Sir Gallahad III, *Bull Dog, *La Troienne, *Ortello, Aethelstan, Asterus, Rose of England, Brumeux, Case Ace, Sun Teddy, Anne de Bretagne, Anna Bolena, Assignation, Boxeuse, Coeur

a Coeur, La Moqueuse. Tail-male ancestor of male line leading to Damascus, Private Account, Captain Steve.

TEMPTED, 1955-unknown. Ch. f., *Half Crown—Enchanted Eve, by Lovely Night. 45-18-4-9, $330,760, champion handicap mare, Alabama S., Ladies H., etc. Dam of Lead Me On.

TEN BROECK, 1872-1887. B. c., *Phaeton—Fanny Holton, by Lexington. 30-23-3-1, $27,550, Phoenix Hotel S., Louisville Cup, etc. Sire of Jim Gray.

THAD STEVENS, 1865-unknown. Ch. g., Langford—Mary Chilton, by *Glencoe. 21-13-5-2, $36,675. Great California four-miler.

THE VERY ONE, 1975-1992. B. f., One for All—*Veruschka, by Venture. 71-22-12-9, $1,104,623, Santa Barbara H. (G1), Black Helen H. (G2), etc.

THUNDER GULCH, 1992-. Ch. c., Gulch—Line of Thunder, by Storm Bird. 16-9-2-2, $2,915,086, champion three-year-old colt, Kentucky Derby (G1), Belmont S. (G1), etc. Sire of Point Given, Spain.

TIMOLEON, 1813-1836. Ch. c., Sir Archy—Saltram mare, by *Saltram. 16-14-0-0. Sire of Boston, Hotspur, Sally Walker, Saluda, Omega, Washington.

TIM TAM, 1955-1982. Dk. b. or br. c., Tom Fool—Two Lea, by Bull Lea. 14-10-1-2, $467,475, champion three-year-old colt, Kentucky Derby, Preakness S., etc. Sire of 14 stakes winners, including Tosmah, Timmy Lad, Nancy Jr. Broodmare sire of Before Dawn, Davona Dale, Known Fact, Mac Diarmida, Tentam.

TIPPITY WITCHET, 1915-unknown. B. g., Broomstick—*Lady Frivoles, by St. Simon. 266-78-52-42, $88,241. Raced to age 14, beginning his career in stakes but descending to the claiming ranks.

TOM BOWLING, 1870-unknown. B. c., Lexington—Lucy Fowler, by *Albion. 17-14-3-0, $35,000, champion three-year-old colt, Travers S., Jersey Derby, Jerome S., Monmouth Cup, etc. Sire of General Monroe.

TOM FOOL, 1949-1976. B. c., Menow—Gaga, by *Bull Dog. 30-21-7-1, $570,165, Horse of the Year in 1953, champion two-year-old colt, champion handicap horse, champion sprinter, handicap triple crown, Futurity S., etc. Leading broodmare sire in England in 1965. Sire of 36 stakes winners, including Buckpasser, Tim Tam, Silly Season, Tompion, Dunce, Jester, Funloving, Sweet Folly, Dinner Partner, Dunce Cap II. Broodmare sire of Foolish Pleasure, Hatchet Man, Late Bloomer, *Meadow Court, Stop the Music.

TOP FLIGHT, 1929-1949. Dk. br. or br. f., *Dis Donc—Flyatit, by Peter Pan. 16-12-0-0, $275,900, champion two- and three-year-old filly, Coaching Club American Oaks, Futurity S., etc. Dam of Flight Command. Tail-female ancestor of family that includes Watch Fob, Sikeston. World's leading money-winning female at time of retirement.

TOSMAH, 1961-1992. B. f., Tim Tam—Cosmah, by Cosmic Bomb. 39-23-6-2, $612,588, champion two- and three-year-old filly, champion handicap mare, Frizette S., Beldame S., etc. Dam of La Guidecca.

TREMONT, 1884-1901. Bl. c., Virgil—Ann Fief, by Alarm. 13-13-0-0, $39,135, champion two-year-old colt, Great American S., etc.

TURNBACK THE ALARM, 1989-. Gr. or ro. f., Darn That Alarm—Boomie's Girl E., by *Figonero. 22-8-6-4, $960,504, Coaching Club American Oaks (G1), Mother Goose S. (G1), etc.

***TURN-TO**, 1951-1973. B. c., *Royal Charger—*Source Sucree, by Admiral Drake. 8-6-1-1, $280,032,

Garden State S., Flamingo S., etc. Sire of 25 stakes winners, including First Landing, Hail to Reason, Sir Gaylord, Best Turn, Cyane, Turn to Talent. Broodmare sire of Ack Ack.

T. V. LARK, 1957-1975. B. c., *Indian Hemp—Miss Larksfly, by Heelfly. 72-19-13-6, $902,194, champion grass horse, Washington, D. C., International S., United Nations H., etc. Leading sire in 1974. Sire of 53 stakes winners, including Quack, T. V. Commercial, Pink Pigeon, Buffalo Lark, Golden Don, T. V. Vixen, Romeo, Became a Lark, Tumble Lark. Broodmare sire of Bates Motel, Chris Evert

TWENTY GRAND, 1928-1948. B. c., *St. Germans—Bonus, by *All Gold. 23-14-4-3, $261,790, Horse of the Year in 1931, champion three-year-old colt, Kentucky Derby, Belmont S., etc. Sterile at stud.

TWILIGHT TEAR, 1941-1954. B. f., Bull Lea—Lady Lark, by Blue Larkspur. 24-18-2-2, $202,165, Horse of the Year in 1944, champion two- and three-year-old filly, champion handicap mare, Coaching Club American Oaks, Pimlico Special, etc. Dam of A Gleam, Bardstown, Coiner. Tail-female ancestor of family that includes Before Dawn, Gleaming, A Glitter.

TWO LEA, 1946-1973. B. f., Bull Lea—Two Bob, by The Porter. 26-15-6-3, $309,250, champion three-year-old filly, champion handicap mare, Hollywood Gold Cup H., Santa Margarita H., etc. Dam of Tim Tam, On-and-On, Pied d'Or.

UNBRIDLED, 1987-2001. B. c., Fappiano—Gana Facil, by *Le Fabuleux. 24-8-6-6, $4,489,475, champion three-year-old colt, Kentucky Derby (G1), Breeders' Cup Classic (G1), etc. Sire of Banshee Breeze, Anees, Unbridled's Song, Manistique.

UPSET, 1917-1941. Ch. c., Whisk Broom II—Pankhurst, by *Voter. 17-5-7-1, $37,504, Sanford S., etc. Only horse to defeat Man o' War. Sire of 11 stakes winners, including Misstep.

VAGRANCY, 1939-1964. Dk. b. or br. f., *Sir Gallahad III—Valkyr, by Man o' War. 42-15-8-8, $102,480, champion three-year-old filly, champion handicap mare, Coaching Club American Oaks, Alabama S., etc. Dam of Black Tarquin, Vulcania. Tail-female ancestor of family that includes Ferdinand, Fiddle Isle, Natashka, Tallahto, Hidden Light, Truly Bound, Anees.

VANDAL, 1850-unknown. B. c., *Glencoe—Tranby Mare, by *Tranby. 6-4-1-1. Sire of Vandalite, Survivor, Virgil, Capitola, Vicksburg, Mollie Jackson, Ella D.

VERTEX, 1954-1981. Ch c., The Rhymer—Kanace, by Case Ace. 25-17-3-1, $453,424, Pimlico Special, Gulfstream Park H., etc. Sire of 25 stakes winners, including Lucky Debonair, Top Knight, Vertee.

VICTORIA PARK, 1957-1985. B. c., Chop Chop—Victoriana, by Windfields. 19-10-4-2, $250,076, Horse of the Year in Canada, Queen's Plate, Remsen S., etc. Sire of 25 stakes winners, including Kennedy Road, Solometeor, Victorian Era, Floral Victory. Broodmare sire of Northern Taste, The Minstrel.

VOLANTE, 1882-unknown. B. c., Grinstead—Sister Anne, by Glenelg. 84-35-28-12, $72,099, American Derby, Saratoga Cup, etc.

*VOTER, 1894-unknown. Ch. c., Friar's Balsam—*Mavourneen, by Barcaldine. 49-26-6-7, $34,217, Metropolitan H., Toboggan H., etc. Sire of Ballot, Runnymede, Curiosity, Electioneer, Inaugural, Pankhurst.

WAGNER, 1834-1862. Ch. c., Sir Charles—Maria West, by Marion. 18-12-6-0, $34,150, Jockey Club Purse, etc. Sire of Imp, Starke, Lavender, Rhyno-

dyne, Neil Robinson, Endorser.

WANDA, 1882-1905. Ch. f., *Mortemer—Minnie Minor, by Lexington. 24-12-8-0, $58,160, Monmouth Oaks, Champion Stallion S., etc. Tail-female ancestor of family that includes Swaps, Iron Liege, Flying Ebony, Creme dela Creme, Cascapedia, Althea, Green Desert, *Durbar II, Kauai King.

WAR ADMIRAL, 1934-1959. Br. c., Man o' War—Brushup, by Sweep. 26-21-3-1, $273,240, Horse of the Year in 1937, champion three-year-old colt, Triple Crown, Jockey Club Gold Cup, Whitney S., etc. Leading sire in 1945; leading broodmare sire '62, '64. Sire of 40 stakes winners, including Busher, Blue Peter, Searching, Admiral Vee, Busanda, War Date, Blue Banner, Mr. Busher, Bee Mac, Striking. Broodmare sire of Affectionately, Better Self, Buckpasser, Crafty Admiral, Gun Bow, Hoist the Flag, Iron Liege, Never Say Die, Priceless Gem.

WAR RELIC, 1938-1963. Ch. c., Man o' War—Friar's Carse, by Friar Rock. 20-9-4-2, $89,495, Massachusetts H., Kenner S., etc. Sire of Battlefield, Intent, Relic, Missile. Broodmare sire of Hail to All, My Dear Girl. Tail-male ancestor of male line that includes Tiznow, In Reality, Relaunch.

WEEKEND SURPRISE, 1980-2001. B. f., Secretariat—Lassie Dear, by Buckpasser. 31-7-5-10, $402,892, Golden Rod S. (G3), Schuylerville S. (G3), etc. Broodmare of the Year in 1992. Dam of A.P. Indy, Summer Squall, Welcome Surprise, Honor Grades.

WHICHONE, 1927-1944. Br. c., *Chicle—Flying Witch, by Broomstick. 14-10-2-1, $192,705, champion two-year-old colt, Futurity S., Champagne S., etc. Sire of ten stakes winners, including Handcuff, Today. Rival of Gallant Fox; first winner of $100,000 first-prize purse. Full brother to Mother Goose.

WHIRLAWAY, 1938-1953. Ch. c., *Blenheim II—Dustwhirl, by Sweep. 60-32-15-9, $561,161, Horse of the Year in 1941-'42, champion two- and three-year-old colt, champion handicap horse, Triple Crown, Jockey Club Gold Cup, Travers S., etc. Sire of 18 stakes winners, including Scattered, Kurun, Whirl Some, Duchess Peg, Rock Drill.

WHISK BROOM II, 1907-1928. Ch. c., Broomstick—Audience, by Sir Dixon. 26-10-8-0, $38,776, handicap triple crown, Victoria Cup (in England), etc. Sire of Whiskery, Diavolo, Victorian, Whiskaway, John P. Grier, Broomshot, Swing On, Upset, Weno.

WINNING COLORS, 1985-. Ro. f., Caro (Ire)—All Rainbows, by Bold Hour. 19-8-3-1, $1,526,837, champion three-year-old filly, Kentucky Derby (G1), Santa Anita Derby (G1), etc.

YO TAMBIEN, 1889-1896. Ch. f., Joe Hooker—Marian, by Malcolm. 73-44-11-9, $89,480, Garfield Park Derby, etc. Half sister to Emperor of Norfolk, El Rio Rey.

YOUR HOST, 1947-1961. Ch. c., *Alibhai—*Boudoir II, by *Mahmoud. 23-13-5-2, $384,795, Santa Anita Derby, Del Mar Futurity, etc. Sire of 16 stakes winners, including Kelso, Social Climber, Windy Sands.

ZACCIO, 1976-. Ch. g., *Lorenzaccio—Delray Dancer, by Chateaugay. 42-22-7-3, $288,124, champion steeplechaser three times, Colonial Cup International Stp. twice, Temple Gwathmey Stp. H., etc.

ZEV, 1920-1943. Br. c., The Finn—Miss Kearney, by *Planudes. 43-23-8-5, $313,639, champion two- and three-year-old colt, Kentucky Derby, Belmont S., International Race S., etc. Sire of two stakes winners. Defeated *Papyrus in first international race in U.S. Retired as world's leading money earner.

History of the Eclipse Awards

Thoroughbred racing's first official champions were recognized for the 1936 racing season by *Daily Racing Form*, which named Granville as Horse of the Year and selected champions in six other divisions.

Beginning in the 1950 racing season, Thoroughbred Racing Associations, formed nine years earlier, announced its own set of champions. Usually the *Form*'s and TRA's separate lists of champions coincided, but sometimes they did not. For example, Horse of the Year titles went to both One Count and Native Dancer in 1952, Bold Ruler and Dedicate in '57, Roman Brother and Moccasin in '65, and Fort Marcy and Personality in '70.

In 1971, J. B. Faulconer was president of the Turf Publicists of America, an organization of marketing and public-relations representatives from racetrack and industry organizations. Monmouth Park executive Philip H. Iselin selected him to head a special committee to consolidate the year-end championship honors. Faulconer helped to bring together the *Form*, TRA, and the National Turf Writers Association, an organization of racing's print journalists, to select one set of champions.

Faulconer is credited with the naming of the Eclipse Award, which honors Eclipse, the great 18th-century English racehorse and sire from whom many modern-day Thoroughbreds descend. He also selected Lexington artist Adalin Wichman to design the award statuette of a lone Thoroughbred tacked in preparation for a race, and he served as master of ceremonies at the inaugural awards dinner held on January 26, 1972, at New York's Waldorf Astoria. Faulconer was the ceremony's host through 1976.

Today, the National Thoroughbred Racing Association has replaced the TRA in the three voting groups. Members of the three eligible organizations vote on winners of the ten divisional categories and then select the Horse of the Year. In addition, the groups vote on the outstanding breeder, owner, trainer, jockey, and apprentice jockey. In the equine categories, each voting group's first choice counts ten points, with five points for second and one point for third, for a maximum of 30 points. In balloting for Horse of the Year and outstanding owner, breeder, trainer, jockey, and apprentice jockey, each voting group receives one vote counting one point for a maximum of three points.

Additionally, an Award of Merit and a Special Award are given on occasion to individuals, racetracks, and organizations for noteworthy contributions to Thoroughbred racing.

Eclipse Awards generally are presented shortly after the conclusion of the previous year's racing season. Since the awards were founded, a few notable events have occurred. In 1978, a tie in the voting for the leading two-year-old filly resulted in It's in the Air and Candy Eclair being named co-champions, while Dr. Patches and J. O. Tobin were voted co-champion sprinters. Voting procedures were changed to eliminate ties, and there has not been a tie since in the horse categories. In 1979, the champion turf horse division was divided into male and female categories.

In Eclipse history, two-year-olds have been voted Horse of the Year just twice: Secretariat (1972) and Favorite Trick ('97). The honor remains one of the most elusive in the sport.

While horses and horsemen are honored with Eclipse Awards, so too are members of the media. Selected committees vote on the outstanding submission in the categories of news and commentary writing, feature and enterprise writing, national television, local television, radio, and photography.

Eclipse Award-Winning Horses

Horse of the Year

2001	Point Given
2000	Tiznow
1999	Charismatic
1998	Skip Away
1997	Favorite Trick
1996	Cigar
1995	Cigar
1994	Holy Bull
1993	Kotashaan (Fr)
1992	A.P. Indy
1991	Black Tie Affair (Ire)
1990	Criminal Type
1989	Sunday Silence
1988	Alysheba
1987	Ferdinand
1986	Lady's Secret
1985	Spend a Buck
1984	John Henry
1983	All Along (Fr)
1982	Conquistador Cielo
1981	John Henry
1980	Spectacular Bid
1979	Affirmed
1978	Affirmed
1977	Seattle Slew
1976	Forego
1975	Forego
1974	Forego
1973	Secretariat
1972	Secretariat
1971	Ack Ack

Two-Year-Old Male

2001	Johannesburg
2000	Macho Uno
1999	Anees
1998	Answer Lively
1997	Favorite Trick
1996	Boston Harbor
1995	Maria's Mon
1994	Timber Country
1993	Dehere
1992	Gilded Time
1991	Arazi
1990	Fly So Free
1989	Rhythm
1988	Easy Goer
1987	Forty Niner
1986	Capote
1985	Tasso
1984	Chief's Crown
1983	Devil's Bag
1982	Roving Boy
1981	Deputy Minister
1980	Lord Avie
1979	Rockhill Native
1978	Spectacular Bid
1977	Affirmed
1976	Seattle Slew
1975	Honest Pleasure
1974	Foolish Pleasure
1973	Protagonist
1972	Secretariat
1971	Riva Ridge

Two-Year-Old Filly

2001	Tempera
2000	Caressing
1999	Chilukki
1998	Silverbulletday
1997	Countess Diana
1996	Storm Song
1995	Golden Attraction
1994	Flanders
1993	Phone Chatter

1992 Eliza
1991 Pleasant Stage
1990 Meadow Star
1989 Go for Wand
1988 Open Mind
1987 Epitome
1986 Brave Raj
1985 Family Style
1984 Outstandingly
1983 Althea
1982 Landaluce
1981 Before Dawn
1980 Heavenly Cause
1979 Smart Angle
1978 †It's in the Air
    †Candy Eclair
1977 Lakeville Miss
1976 Sensational
1975 Dearly Precious
1974 Ruffian
1973 Talking Picture
1972 La Prevoyante
1971 Numbered Account

†Tied in voting, named co-champions

Three-Year-Old Male
2001 Point Given
2000 Tiznow
1999 Charismatic
1998 Real Quiet
1997 Silver Charm
1996 Skip Away
1995 Thunder Gulch
1994 Holy Bull
1993 Prairie Bayou
1992 A.P. Indy
1991 Hansel
1990 Unbridled
1989 Sunday Silence
1988 Risen Star
1987 Alysheba
1986 Snow Chief
1985 Spend a Buck
1984 Swale
1983 Slew o' Gold
1982 Conquistador Cielo
1981 Pleasant Colony
1980 Temperence Hill
1979 Spectacular Bid
1978 Affirmed
1977 Seattle Slew
1976 Bold Forbes
1975 Wajima
1974 Little Current
1973 Secretariat
1972 Key to the Mint
1971 Canonero II

Three-Year-Old Filly
2001 Xtra Heat
2000 Surfside
1999 Silverbulletday
1998 Banshee Breeze
1997 Ajina
1996 Yanks Music
1995 Serena's Song

1994 Heavenly Prize
1993 Hollywood Wildcat
1992 Saratoga Dew
1991 Dance Smartly
1990 Go for Wand
1989 Open Mind
1988 Winning Colors
1987 Sacahuista
1986 Tiffany Lass
1985 Mom's Command
1984 Life's Magic
1983 Heartlight No. One
1982 Christmas Past
1981 Wayward Lass
1980 Genuine Risk
1979 Davona Dale
1978 Tempest Queen
1977 Our Mims
1976 Revidere
1975 Ruffian
1974 Chris Evert
1973 Desert Vixen
1972 Susan's Girl
1971 Turkish Trousers

Older Male
2001 Tiznow
2000 Lemon Drop Kid
1999 Victory Gallop
1998 Skip Away
1997 Skip Away
1996 Cigar
1995 Cigar
1994 The Wicked North
1993 Bertrando
1992 Pleasant Tap
1991 Black Tie Affair (Ire)
1990 Criminal Type
1989 Blushing John
1988 Alysheba
1987 Ferdinand
1986 Turkoman
1985 Vanlandingham
1984 Slew o' Gold
1983 Bates Motel
1982 Lemhi Gold
1981 John Henry
1980 Spectacular Bid
1979 Affirmed
1978 Seattle Slew
1977 Forego
1976 Forego
1975 Forego
1974 Forego
1973 Riva Ridge
1972 Autobiography
1971 Ack Ack

Older Female
2001 Gourmet Girl
2000 Riboletta (Brz)
1999 Beautiful Pleasure
1998 Escena
1997 Hidden Lake
1996 Jewel Princess
1995 Inside Information
1994 Sky Beauty
1993 Paseana (Arg)

1992 Paseana (Arg)
1991 Queena
1990 Bayakoa (Arg)
1989 Bayakoa (Arg)
1988 Personal Ensign
1987 North Sider
1986 Lady's Secret
1985 Life's Magic
1984 Princess Rooney
1983 Ambassador of Luck
1982 Track Robbery
1981 Relaxing
1980 Glorious Song
1979 Waya (Fr)
1978 Late Bloomer
1977 Cascapedia
1976 Proud Delta
1975 Susan's Girl
1974 Desert Vixen
1973 Susan's Girl
1972 Typecast
1971 Shuvee

Turf Male[1]
2001 Fantastic Light
2000 Kalanisi (Ire)
1999 Daylami (Ire)
1998 Buck's Boy
1997 Chief Bearhart
1996 Singspiel (Ire)
1995 Northern Spur (Ire)
1994 Paradise Creek
1993 Kotashaan (Fr)
1992 Sky Classic
1991 Tight Spot
1990 Itsallgreektome
1989 Steinlen (GB)
1988 Sunshine Forever
1987 Theatrical (Ire)
1986 Manila
1985 Cozzene
1984 John Henry
1983 John Henry
1982 Perrault (GB)
1981 John Henry
1980 John Henry
1979 Bowl Game

Turf female[1]
2001 Banks Hill (GB)
2000 Perfect Sting
1999 Soaring Softly
1998 Fiji (GB)
1997 Ryafan
1996 Wandesta (GB)
1995 Possibly Perfect
1994 Hatoof
1993 Flawlessly
1992 Flawlessly
1991 Miss Alleged
1990 Laugh and Be Merry
1989 Brown Bess
1988 Miesque
1987 Miesque
1986 Estrapade
1985 Pebbles (GB)
1984 Royal Heroine (Ire)
1983 All Along (Fr)

1982 April Run (Ire)
1981 De La Rose
1980 Just a Game (Ire)
1979 Trillion

Turf Horse[1]
1978 Mac Diarmida
1977 Johnny D.
1976 Youth
1975 *Snow Knight
1974 Dahlia (female)
1973 Secretariat
1972 *Cougar II
1971 Run the Gantlet

[1]One turf category prior to 1979

Sprinter
2001 Squirtle Squirt
2000 Kona Gold
1999 Artax
1998 Reraise
1997 Smoke Glacken
1996 Lit de Justice
1995 Not Surprising
1994 Cherokee Run
1993 Cardmania
1992 Rubiano
1991 Housebuster
1990 Housebuster
1989 Safely Kept
1988 Gulch
1987 Groovy
1986 Smile
1985 Precisionist
1984 Eillo
1983 Chinook Pass
1982 Gold Beauty
1981 Guilty Conscience
1980 Plugged Nickle
1979 Star de Naskra
1978 †Dr. Patches
    †J. O. Tobin
1977 What a Summer
1976 My Juliet
1975 Gallant Bob
1974 Forego
1973 Shecky Greene
1972 Chou Croute
1971 Ack Ack

†Tied in voting, named co-champions

Steeplechaser
2001 Pompeyo (Chi)
2000 All Gong (GB)
1999 Lonesome Glory
1998 Flat Top
1997 Lonesome Glory
1996 Correggio (Ire)
1995 Lonesome Glory
1994 Warm Spell
1993 Lonesome Glory
1992 Lonesome Glory
1991 Morley Street (Ire)
1990 Morley Street (Ire)
1989 Highland Bud
1988 Jimmy Lorenzo (GB)

1987	Inlander (GB)	1982	Zaccio	1977	Cafe Prince	1972	Soothsayer
1986	Flatterer	1981	Zaccio	1976	Straight and True	1971	Shadow Brook
1985	Flatterer	1980	Zaccio	1975	Life's Illusion		
1984	Flatterer	1979	Martie's Anger	1974	*Gran Kan		
1983	Flatterer	1978	Cafe Prince	1973	Athenian Idol		

Eclipse Award-Winning Individuals

Owner

2001	Richard Englander
2000	Frank Stronach
1999	Frank Stronach
1998	Frank Stronach
1997	Carolyn Hine
1996	Allen E. Paulson
1995	Allen E. Paulson
1994	John Franks
1993	John Franks
1992	Juddmonte Farms
1991	Sam-Son Farm
1990	Mrs. Frances Genter
1989	Ogden Phipps
1988	Ogden Phipps
1987	Mr. and Mrs. Eugene Klein
1986	Mr. and Mrs. Eugene Klein
1985	Mr. and Mrs. Eugene Klein
1984	John Franks
1983	John Franks
1982	Viola Sommer
1981	Dotsam Stable
1980	Mr. and Mrs. Bertram Firestone
1979	Harbor View Farm
1978	Harbor View Farm
1977	Maxwell Gluck
1976	Dan Lasater
1975	Dan Lasater
1974	Dan Lasater
1973	Not awarded
1972	Not awarded
1971	Mr. and Mrs. E. E. Fogelson

Breeder

2001	Juddmonte Farms
2000	Frank Stronach
1999	William S. Farish & Partners
1998	John and Betty Mabee
1997	John and Betty Mabee
1996	Farnsworth Farms
1995	Juddmonte Farms
1994	William I. Young
1993	Allen E. Paulson
1992	William S. Farish III
1991	John and Betty Mabee
1990	Calumet Farm
1989	North Ridge Farm
1988	Ogden Phipps
1987	Nelson Bunker Hunt
1986	Paul Mellon
1985	Nelson Bunker Hunt
1984	Claiborne Farm
1983	E. P. Taylor
1982	Fred W. Hooper
1981	Golden Chance Farm
1980	Adele Paxson
1979	Claiborne Farm
1978	Harbor View Farm

1977	E. P. Taylor
1976	Nelson Bunker Hunt
1975	Fred W. Hooper
1974	John W. Galbreath
1973	Not awarded
1972	Not awarded
1971	Not awarded

Owner-Breeder

1973	Meadow Stable-Meadow Stud (C. T. Chenery)
1972	Meadow Stable-Meadow Stud (C. T. Chenery)
1971	Paul Mellon

Trainer

2001	Bobby Frankel
2000	Bobby Frankel
1999	Bob Baffert
1998	Bob Baffert
1997	Bob Baffert
1996	Bill Mott
1995	Bill Mott
1994	D. Wayne Lukas
1993	Robert Frankel
1992	Ron McAnally
1991	Ron McAnally
1990	Carl A. Nafzger
1989	Charles Whittingham
1988	C. R. McGaughey
1987	D. Wayne Lukas
1986	D. Wayne Lukas
1985	D. Wayne Lukas
1984	Jack Van Berg
1983	Woody Stephens
1982	Charles Whittingham
1981	Ron McAnally
1980	Grover G. "Buddy" Delp
1979	Lazaro Barrera
1978	Lazaro Barrera
1977	Lazaro Barrera
1976	Lazaro Barrera
1975	Steve DiMauro
1974	Sherrill Ward
1973	H. Allen Jerkens
1972	Lucien Laurin
1971	Charles Whittingham

Jockey

2001	Jerry Bailey
2000	Jerry Bailey
1999	Jorge Chavez
1998	Gary Stevens
1997	Jerry Bailey
1996	Jerry Bailey
1995	Jerry Bailey
1994	Mike Smith
1993	Mike Smith
1992	Kent Desormeaux

1991	Pat Day
1990	Craig Perret
1989	Kent Desormeaux
1988	Jose Santos
1987	Pat Day
1986	Pat Day
1985	Laffit Pincay Jr.
1984	Pat Day
1983	Angel Cordero Jr.
1982	Angel Cordero Jr.
1981	William Shoemaker
1980	Chris McCarron
1979	Laffit Pincay Jr.
1978	Darrel McHargue
1977	Steve Cauthen
1976	Sandy Hawley
1975	Braulio Baeza
1974	Laffit Pincay Jr.
1973	Laffit Pincay Jr.
1972	Braulio Baeza
1971	Laffit Pincay Jr.

Apprentice jockey

2001	Jeremy Rose
2000	Tyler Baze
1999	Ariel Smith
1998	Shaun Bridgmohan
1997	Roberto Rosado, Philip Teator (tie)
1996	Neil Poznansky
1995	Ramon Perez
1994	Dale Beckner
1993	Juan L. Umana
1992	†Rosemary Homeister Jr.
1991	Mickey Walls
1990	Mark Johnston
1989	Michael Luzzi
1988	Steve Capanas
1987	Kent Desormeaux
1986	Allen Stacy
1985	Art Madrid Jr.
1984	Wesley Ward
1983	Declan Murphy
1982	Alberto Delgado
1981	Richard Migliore
1980	Frank Lovato Jr.
1979	Cash Asmussen
1978	Ron Franklin
1977	Steve Cauthen
1976	George Martens
1975	Jimmy Edwards
1974	Chris McCarron
1973	Steve Valdez
1972	Thomas Wallis
1971	Gene St. Leon

†Jesus Bracho was originally awarded the title but relinquished it in 1994.

Eclipse Award of Merit
2001 Harry T. Mangurian Jr.
2000 Jim McKay
1999 Not awarded
1998 D. G. Van Clief Jr.
1997 Bob and Beverly Lewis
1996 Allen E. Paulson
1995 James E. "Ted" Bassett III
1994 Alfred G. Vanderbilt
1993 Paul Mellon
1992 Robert P. Strub, Joe Hirsch
1991 Fred W. Hooper
1990 Warner L. Jones
1989 Michael Sandler
1988 John Forsythe
1987 J. B. Faulconer
1986 Herman Cohen
1985 Keene Daingerfield
1984 John Gaines
1983 Not awarded
1982 Not awarded
1981 William Shoemaker
1980 John D. Schapiro
1979 Frank E. "Jimmy" Kilroe

1978 Ogden Mills "Dinny" Phipps
1977 Steve Cauthen
1976 Jack J. Dreyfus Jr.

Special Award
2001 Sheikh Mohammed bin Rashid al Maktoum
2000 John Hettinger
1999 Laffit Pincay Jr.
1998 Oak Tree Racing Association
1997 Not awarded
1996 Not awarded
1995 Russell Baze
1994 Eddie Arcaro, John Longden
1993 Not awarded
1992 Not awarded
1991 Not awarded
1990 Not awarded
1989 Richard L. Duchossois
1988 Edward J. DeBartolo Sr.
1987 Anheuser-Busch
1986 Not awarded
1985 Arlington Park
1984 C. V. Whitney

1983 Not awarded
1982 Not awarded
1981 Not awarded
1980 John T. Landry, Pierre E. Bellocq
1979 Not awarded
1978 Not awarded
1977 Not awarded
1976 William Shoemaker
1975 Not awarded
1974 Charles Hatton
1973 Not awarded
1972 Not awarded
1971 Robert J. Kleberg

Man of the Year
1975 John A. Morris
1974 William L. McKnight
1973 Edward P. Taylor
1972 John W. Galbreath

Outstanding Achievement
1972 Arthur B. Hancock (posthumously)
1971 Charles Engelhard (posthumously)

Eclipse Award Media Winners

Outstanding Newspaper Writing
1999 Maryjean Wall, Lexington *Herald-Leader*
1998 Tom Keyser, Baltimore *Sun*
1997 Maryjean Wall, Lexington *Herald-Leader*
1996 Tom Keyser, Baltimore *Sun*
1995 Stephanie Diaz, Riverside *Press-Enterprise*
1994 Mike Downey, Los Angeles *Times*
1993 Jennie Rees, Louisville *Courier-Journal*
1992 James Wallace, Seattle *Post Intelligencer*
1990 Paul Moran, *Newsday*
1989 Ronnie Virgets, *Gambit*
1988 Billy Reed, Lexington *Herald-Leader*
1987 Tim Layden, Capital Newspapers
1986 Edwin Pope, Miami *Herald*
1985 Paul Moran, *Newsday*
1984 Bill Christine, Los Angeles *Times*
Eddie Donnally, Dallas *Morning News*
1983 Dave Koemer, Louisville *Times*
1982 Edwin Pope, Miami *Herald*
1981 Dave Kindred, Washington *Post*
1980 Maryjean Wall, Lexington *Herald*
1979 Billy Reed, Louisville *Courier-Journal*
1978 Joe Hirsch, *Daily Racing Form*
1977 Skip Bayless, Los Angeles *Times*
1976 Edwin Pope, Miami *Herald*
1975 Bob Harding, Newark *Star-Ledger*
1974 William H. Rudy, New York *Post*
1973 Red Smith, New York *Times*
1972 Phil Ranallo, Buffalo *Courier Express*
1971 Scott Young, Toronto *Telegram*

Outstanding Magazine Writing
1999 Tom Keyser, Baltimore *Sun*
1998 Laura Hillenbrand, *American Heritage*
1997 Bill Heller, *The Backstretch*
1996 Don Clippinger, *Mid-Atlantic Thoroughbred*
1995 Not awarded
1994 Jay Hovdey, *The Blood-Horse*
1993 Stephanie Diaz, *The Backstretch*
1992 Joseph P. Pons Jr., *The Blood-Horse*

1990 Bill Nack, *Sports Illustrated*
1989 Bill Nack, *Sports Illustrated*
1988 Jennie Rees, Lexington *Courier-Journal* (Sunday Magazine)
1987 Jack Mann, *Spur*
1986 Bill Nack, *Sports Illustrated*
1985 Bill Mooney, *The Thoroughbred Record*
1984 Frank Deford, *Sports Illustrated*
1983 Arnold Kirkpatrick, *Keeneland*
1982 Jay Hovdey, *Horsemen's Journal*
1981 Joseph P. Pons Jr., *The Blood-Horse*
1980 Clive Gammon, *Sports Illustrated*
1979 William Leggett, *Sports Illustrated*
1978 Bill Nack, *Sports Illustrated*
1977 Whitney Tower, *Classic*
1976 Whitney Tower, *Classic*
1975 Frank Deford, *Sports Illustrated*
1974 Chet Hagan, *Spur*
1973 Pete Axthelm, *Newsweek*
1972 Edward L. Bowen, *The Blood-Horse*
1971 Bill Surface, *Reader's Digest*

Outstanding Feature and Enterprise Writing
2001 Laura Hillenbrand, *EQUUS*
2000 Mary Simon, THOROUGHBRED TIMES

Outstanding Feature Writing
1991 Bill Nack, *Sports Illustrated*

Outstanding News Writing
1991 Bill Nack, *Sports Illustrated*

Outstanding News and Commentary Writing
2001 Janet Patton, Lexington *Herald-Leader*
2000 Jay Hovdey, *Daily Racing Form*

Local Television Achievement
2001 WTVI, Charlotte, NC
2000 WMAR-TV, Baltimore
1999 Amy Zimmerman and Michael Ewing, Fox-TV Sports West2

1998	Jeff Lifson, WHAS-TV, Louisville
1997	Brian Blessing, Ontario Jockey Club
1996	Kenny Rice, WTVQ-TV, Lexington
1995	JCM Productions, New York
1994	Ronnie Virgets, WNXO, New Orleans
1993	Stephen Sadis, KBTC, Tacoma
1992	Rick Cushing, WKPC-TV, Louisville
1991	WABC-TV, New York
1990	Philip Von Borries, WKPC-TV, Louisville
1989	Chris Thomas, WFLA-TV, Tampa
1988	Joseph Kwong, KCET-TV, Los Angeles
1987	Arlington Park
1986	Louisiana Downs
1985	Oak Tree Racing Association
1984	NYRA/Cinema Mistral
1983	Cawood Ledford Productions
1982	ON-TV, Los Angeles
1981	WHAS, Louisville
1980	WCAU, Philadelphia
1979	Dave Johnson, ON-TV
1978	Cawood Ledford, WHAS, Louisville
1977	Jane Chastain, KABC, Los Angeles
1976	NYRA-OTB Race of the Week
1975	Cawood Ledford, WHAS, Louisville

National Television Achievement

1999	Mark Shapiro and William Rapaport, ESPN-TV
1998	E. S. Lamoreaux III, *CBS News Sunday Morning*
1997	E. S. Lamoreaux III, *CBS News Sunday Morning*
1996	NBC Sports
1995	ABC's Wide World of Sports
1994	ABC's Wide World of Sports
1993	E. S. Lamoreaux III, CBS News, *Sunday Morning with Charles Kuralt*
1992	ABC Sports
1991	CBS News, *Sunday Morning with Charles Kuralt*
1990	ABC Sports
1989	ABC Sports
1988	Thoroughbred Sports, *Racing Across America*
1987	ABC
1986	ABC
1985	CBS
1984	NBC
1983	CBS
1982	ESPN
1981	Canadian Broadcasting Corp.
1980	ABC
1979	Don Ohlmeyer, NBC
1978	Roger Murphy, Public Broadcasting System
1977	Jack Whitaker, CBS
1976	CBS
1975	CBS
1974	Pen Densham, John Watson, Insight Productions
1973	Chuck Milton, Tony Verna, CBS
1972	Chuck Milton, Tony Verna, CBS
1971	Burt Bacharach, CBS

National Television— Live Racing Programming

2001	NBC
2000	ABC Sports
1999	Curt Gowdy Jr., Craig Janoff, Howard Katz, and John Filippelli, ABC Sports

National Television Features

2001	ESPN Classic

Radio Achievement

2001	WBAL, Baltimore
2000	Shelby Whitfield, Premiere Radio
1999	Tom Leach, WVLK-AM, Lexington
1998	Not awarded
1997	John Patti, WBAL, Baltimore
1996	Robin Dawson, CJCL, Toronto
1995	Vic Stauffer, KKAR, Omaha
1994	John Asher, WHAS, Louisville
1993	Tom Leach, WVLK, Lexington
1992	John Asher, WHAS, Louisville
1991	Julia McEvoy, National Public Radio
1990	John Asher, WHAS, Louisville
1989	John Asher, WAVG, Louisville
1988	John Asher, WAVG, Louisville
1987	Bob Lauder, WHAS, Louisville
1986	ABC Radio Network
1985	Bob Lauder, WHAS, Louisville
1984	WBAL, Baltimore
1983	Tom Davis, WCBM, Baltimore
1982	ABC Radio Network
1981	WBAL, Baltimore
1980	Not awarded
1979	Dick Woolley, WITH, Baltimore
1978	Ted Patterson, WBAL, Baltimore
1977	Not awarded
1976	Win Elliot, CBS
1975	Not awarded
1974	Not awarded
1973	Not awarded
1972	Not awarded
1971	Win Elliot, CBS

Film Achievement

1972	Joseph Burnham

Photography Achievement

2001	Barbara Livingston, *The Thoroughbred Chronicle*
2000	Dave Landry, *Canadian Thoroughbred*
1999	Michael Marten, *Daily Racing Form*
1998	Ryan Haynes, Northlands Park
1997	Jean Raftery, Calder Race Course
1996	Skip Dickstein, *The Blood-Horse*
1995	Michael J. Marten, *Daily Racing Form*
1994	Tony Leonard, THOROUGHBRED TIMES
1993	Michael Burns, Ontario Jockey Club
1992	Barbara Livingston, *The Blood-Horse*
1991	Rayetta Burr, Benoit and Associates
1990	Michael Cartee, *Thoroughbred of California*
1989	Ron Cortes, Philadelphia *Inquirer*
1988	Ben Van Hook, Louisville *Courier-Journal*
1987	Dan Farrell, New York *Daily News*
1986	Janice Wilkman, Los Angeles *Times*
1985	Kim Pratt, Garden State Park
1984	Bill Straus, *The Thoroughbred Record*
1983	Rayetta Burr, *Paddock*
1982	Kay Coyte, *Horsemen's Journal*
1981	Tom Baker, River Downs
1980	Bob Coglianese, New York Racing Association
1979	Skip Ball, *Maryland Horse*
1978	Douglas Lees, Fauquier *Democrat*
1977	John Walther, Miami *Herald*
1976	John J. Vasile, Covina (California) *Sentinel*
1975	John Pineda, Miami *Herald*
1974	Michael Burns, Ontario Jockey Club
1973	Harry Leder, United Press International
1972	Bob Coglianese, New York Racing Association
1971	Art Rogers, Los Angeles *Times*

Owners of Eclipse Award Winners

Aga Khan—Kalanisi (Ire).

Aykroyd, David, Helen Alexander, and Helen Groves—Althea.

Alexander, Helen, David Aykroyd, and Helen Groves—Althea.

Allbritton, Joseph—Hansel.

Anderson, Frank, Verne H. Winchell, and Rick Carradini—Tight Spot.

Arnemann, Jurgen and Calumet Farm—Criminal Type.

Augustin Stables—Cafe Prince (1977-'78), Pompeyo (Chi).

Bacharach, Burt C.—Heartlight No. One.

Bailey, Richard E.—Dearly Precious.

Beal, Barry, L. R. French, and Eugene Klein—Capote.

Bell III, John A.—Epitome.

Blue Vista—Possibly Perfect.

Brant, Peter M.—Gulch, Just a Game (Ire), Waya (Fr).

Bray Jr., Dana S.—Johnny D.

Buckland Farm—Pleasant Colony, Pleasant Stage, Pleasant Tap.

Caibett, Edgar—Canonero II.

Calbourne Farm—Brown Bess.

Calumet Farm—Before Dawn, Davona Dale, Our Mims.

Calumet Farm and Jurgen Arnemann—Criminal Type.

Carradini, Rick, Verne H. Winchell, and Frank Anderson—Tight Spot.

Cee's Stable—Tiznow (2001).

Cella, Charles—Northern Spur (Ire).

Centennial Farms—Rubiano.

Christiana Stables—Go for Wand (1989-'90).

Claiborne Farm—Swale, Forty Niner.

Clark Jr., Mrs. F. Ambrose—*Gran Kan.

Clark Jr., Stephen C.—Shadow Brook.

Class Racing Stable, Barry Fey, Moon Han, Larry Opas, Frank Sinatra, and Craig Dollase—Reraise.

Clay, Robert and Tracy Farmer—Hidden Lake.

Cooper, Audrey H. and Michael Fennessy—Yanks Music.

Cooper, Michael and Cecilia Straub-Rubens—Tiznow (2000).

Couvercelle, Jean—Cardmania.

Cowan, Irving and Marjorie—Hollywood Wildcat.

Craig, Sidney and Jenny—Paseana (Arg) (1992-'93).

Croll Jr., Warren A.—Holy Bull.

Crown Stable—Eillo.

Darby Dan Farm—Little Current, Sunshine Forever, Tempest Queen.

Davison, Mrs. Richard—Guilty Conscience.

De Kwiatkowski, Henryk—Conquistador Cielo, De La Rose.

Dogwood Stable—Inlander (GB), Storm Song.

Dollase, Craig, Barry Fey, Moon Han,

Class Racing Stable, Larry Opas, and Frank Sinatra—Reraise.

Dotsam Stable—John Henry (1980-'81, 1983-'84).

Due Process Stables—Dehere.

East-West Stable—Wajima.

Elmendorf Farm—Protagonist, Talking Picture.

Engel, Charles F.—Saratoga Dew.

Envoy Stable—Ambassador of Luck.

Equusequity Stable—Slew o' Gold (1983-'84).

Evergreen Farm—Lit de Justice.

Fares, Issam M.—Miss Alleged.

Farish, Will, William Kilroy, Harold Goodman, and Tomonori Tsuru-maki—A.P. Indy.

Farmer, Tracy and Robert Clay—Hidden Lake.

Fennessy, Michael and Audrey H. Cooper—Yanks Music.

Fey, Barry, Moon Han, Class Racing Stable, Larry Opas, Frank Sinatra, and Craig Dollase—Reraise.

Firestone, Mr. and Mrs. Bertram R.—April Run (Ire), Genuine Risk, Honest Pleasure, Jimmy Lorenzo (GB), What a Summer.

Firestone, Bertram R., and Allen E. Paulson—Theatrical (Ire).

505 Farms and Ed Nahem—Bertrando.

Flying Zee Stables—Wayward Lass.

Folsom Farm and J. Merrick Jones Jr.—Chou Croute.

Forked Lightning Ranch—Ack Ack.

Fradkoff, Serge and Baron Thierry Van Zuylen de Nyevelt—Perrault (GB).

Franks, John—Answer Lively.

French, L. R. and Barry Beal—Landaluce, Sacahuista.

French, L. R., Barry Beal, and Eugene Klein—Capote.

Fuller, Peter—Mom's Command.

Gaillard, Dr. Ernest, Arthur Hancock III, and Charlie Whittingham—Sunday Silence.

Gainesway Farm, Robert and Beverly Lewis, and Overbrook Farm—Timber Country.

Genter, Frances A. Stable—Smile, Unbridled.

Gerry, Nancy—Flat Top.

Godolphin Racing—Daylami (Ire), Fantastic Light, Tempera.

Goodman, Harold, William Kilroy, Will Farish, and Tomonori Tsuru-maki—A.P. Indy.

Green, Dolly—Brave Raj.

Grinstead, Carl and Ben Rochelle—Snow Chief.

Greentree Stable—Bowl Game, Late Bloomer.

Greer, John L.—Foolish Pleasure.

Griggs, John K.—Warm Spell.

Groves, Helen, Helen Alexander, and

Leading owners
Wholly or in partnership, by number of titles won

9—Allen E. Paulson
7—Harbor View Farm
7—Eugene V. Klein
6—Mr. and Mrs. Bertram Firestone
6—William L. Pape
5—Overbrook Farm
5—Ogden Phipps
5—Mrs. Walter M. Jeffords Jr.
4—Calumet Farm
4—Dotsam Stable
4—George Harris
4—Fred W. Hooper Jr.
4—Nelson Bunker Hunt
4—Lazy F Ranch
4—Robert and Beverly Lewis
4—Jonathan Sheppard
3—Augustin Stables
3—Barry Beal
3—Peter M. Brant
3—Buckland Farm
3—Darby Dan Farm
3—L. R. French
3—Godolphin Racing
3—Hawksworth Farm
3—Carolyn Hine
3—Aaron Jones
3—Juddmonte Farms
3—Robert P. Levy
3—Loblolly Stable
3—Sheikh Mohammed bin Rashid al Maktoum
3—Meadow Stable
3—Mrs. Lewis C. Murdock
3—Mike Pegram
3—Sam-Son Farm
3—The Thoroughbred Corp.

David Aykroyd—Althea.

Guest, Virginia—Life's Illusion.

Hamilton, Emory Alexander—Queena.

Han, Moon, Barry Fey, Class Racing Stable, Larry Opas, Frank Sinatra, and Craig Dollase—Reraise.

Hancock III, Arthur, Charlie Whittingham, and Dr. Ernest Gaillard—Sunday Silence.

Harbor View Farm—Affirmed (1977-'79), Flawlessly (1992-'93), It's in the Air, Outstandingly.

Harris, George, William L. Pape, and Jonathan Sheppard—Flatterer (1983-'86).

Hatley, Melvin E. and Eugene V. Klein—Life's Magic.

Hawksworth Farm—Spectacular Bid (1978-'80).

Headley, Bruce, Irwin and Andrew Molasky, and High Tech Stable (Michael Singh)—Kona Gold.

Silverman, Marc and Jack, and David Milch—Gilded Time.

Sinatra, Frank, Barry Fey, Moon Han, Class Racing Stable, Larry Opas, and Craig Dollase—Reraise.

SKS Stable—Lord Avie.

Sommer, Sigmund—Autobiography.

Star Crown Stable—Chief's Crown.

Stephen, Martha and Richard and The Thoroughbred Corp.—Jewel Princess.

Stephenson, Edward L. and Nelson Bunker Hunt—Trillion.

Stone, Mrs. Whitney—Shuvee.

Stonerside Stable—Chilukki.

Straub-Rubens, Cecilia, and Michael Cooper—Tiznow (2000).

Stronach, Frank and Nelson Bunker Hunt—Glorious Song.

Stronach Stable—Macho Uno, Perfect Sting.

Sullivan, Jeffrey—Black Tie Affair (Ire).

Summa Stable—Track Robbery.

Tabor, Michael—Thunder Gulch.

Tabor, Michael and Mrs. John Magnier—Johannesburg.

Tafel, James, Richard Santulli, and Jayeff B Stables—Banshee Breeze.

Tanaka, Gary—Gourmet Girl.

Tartan Stable—Dr. Patches.

Tayhill Stable—Seattle Slew (1978).

Taylor, Mrs. Karen L.—Seattle Slew (1976-'77).

The Thoroughbred Corp.—Anees, Point Given.

The Thoroughbred Corp. and Martha and Richard Stephen—Jewel Princess.

Tizol, E. Rodriguez—Bold Forbes.

Torsney, Dr. Jerome M.—Mac Diarmida.

Tsurumaki, Tomonori, Will Farish, William Kilroy, and Harold Goodman—A.P. Indy.

Tucker, Paula—Princess Rooney.

Valando, Thomas—Fly So Free.

Vance, Jeanne—Lemon Drop Kid.

Van Worp, Robert—Not Surprising.

Van Zuylen de Nyevelt, Baron Thierry, and Serge Frådkoff—Perrault (GB).

Weasel Jr., George—My Juliet.

Weinsier, Randolph—Lakeville Miss.

Weisbord, Barry and Jayeff B Stables—Safely Kept.

Westerly Stud—Typecast.

Whitham, Mr. and Mrs. Frank E.—Bayakoa (Arg) (1989-'90).

Whittingham, Charlie, Arthur Hancock III, and Dr. Ernest Gaillard—Sunday Silence.

Wildenstein, Daniel—All Along (Fr).

Wildenstein Stable—Steinlen (GB).

Willmot, Donald and David, and Morton and Marjoh Levy—Deputy Minister.

Winchell, Verne H., Frank Anderson, and Rick Carradini—Tight Spot.

Windfields Farm and Neil Phillips—*Snow Knight.

Breeders of Eclipse Award Winners

Adams, Mrs. Vanderbilt—Desert Vixen.

Adena Springs—Macho Uno, Perfect Sting.

Aga Khan—Daylami (Ire), Kalanisi (Ire).

Alexander, Emory—Queena.

Alexander, Helen, David Aykroyd, and Helen Groves—Althea.

Allez France Stables—Steinlen (GB).

Augustus, Peggy—Johnny D.

Aykroyd, David, Helen Alexander, and Helen Groves—Althea.

Baker, Dr. Howard—Serena's Song.

Ballydoyle Stud—Correggio (Ire).

Barnhart, Anna Marie—Skip Away (1996-'98).

Bell, H. Bennett, and Jessica Bell Nicholson—Epitome.

Benjamin, Edward Bernard—Canonero II.

Benjamin, E. V. III, and William G. Clark—Chou Croute.

Bettersworth, J. R.—My Juliet.

Blue Bear Stud—Zaccio (1980-'82).

Blue Diamond Ranch—Snow Chief.

Blue Seas Music Inc.—Heartlight No. One.

Brant, Peter M.—Gulch, Thunder Gulch.

Calbourne Farm—Brown Bess.

Calumet Farm—Before Dawn, Criminal Type, Davona Dale, Our Mims.

Cannata, Carl and Olivia—Gourmet Girl.

Carolaine Farm and Dr. E. W. Thomas—Rockhill Native.

Carondelet Farm and Vinery—Artax.

Carrion, Jaime S.—Meadow Star.

Castleman, Ben S.—Seattle Slew (1976-'78).

Centurion Farms—Deputy Minister.

Chenery, Helen B.—Saratoga Dew.

Christiana Stables—Go for Wand (1989-'90).

Cisley Stable and Robert P. Levy—North Sider.

Claiborne Farm—Wajima, Revidere, Slew o' Gold (1983-'84), Swale, Forty Niner.

Clark, William G., and E. V. Benjamin III—Chou Croute.

Cleaboy Farms Co.—Inlander (GB).

Clear Creek and Highclere Inc.—Silverbulletday (1998-'99).

Cohen, Ollie A.—Eillo.

Cojuangco, Edwardo M. Jr.—Manila.

Cowan, Irving and Marjorie—Hollywood Wildcat.

Danada Farm—Proud Delta.

Darley Stud Management—Tempera.

Davison, Mrs. Richard—Guilty Conscience.

Dayton Ltd.—All Along (Fr), Waya (Fr).

Delta Thoroughbreds Inc.—Cardmania.

De Mestre, J. W.—Jimmy Lorenzo (GB).

Due Process Stables—Dehere, Open Mind (1988-'89).

Eaton Farms Inc. and Red Bull Stable—Bold Forbes.

Echo Valley Horse Farm Inc.—Chris Evert, Winning Colors.

Elmendorf Farm—Protagonist, Shadow Brook, Talking Picture.

Evans, Thomas Mellon—Pleasant Colony, Pleasant Tap.

Evans, Mrs. Thomas Mellon—Pleasant Stage.

Leading breeders
By number of titles won

7—Harbor View Farm
6—Claiborne Farm
5—William S. Farish and Partners
5—William L. Pape
5—Allen E. Paulson
5—Ogden Phipps
5—Jonathan Sheppard
5—Walter M. Jefffords Jr.
4—Calumet Farm
4—Golden Chance Farm
4—Nelson Bunker Hunt
4—Lazy F Ranch
4—Overbrook Farm
3—Anna Marie Barnhart
3—Blue Bear Stud
3—Ben Castleman
3—Due Process Stables
3—Elmendorf Farm
3—Mr. & Mrs. Thomas Mellon Evans
3—Mr. and Mrs. John W. Galbreath
3—Mrs. William Gilmore
3—Fred W. Hooper Jr.
3—Mrs. William M. Jason
3—Juddmonte Farms
3—Meadow Stud
3—Ogden Mills Phipps
3—Verne H. Winchell

Farfellow Farms Ltd.—Anees.

Farish, William S., and G. Watts Humphrey Jr.—Sacahuista.

Farish, William S., and W. S. Kilroy—A.P. Indy, Lemon Drop Kid.

Farish, William S., and Ogden Mills Phipps—Storm Song.

Farish, William S., and Parrish Hill Farm—Charismatic.

Farnsworth Farms—Beautiful Pleasure, Jewel Princess.

Feeney, F.—April Run (Ire).

Financiera, Mimika, and Warren Hill Stud—Pebbles (GB).

Firestone, Mr. and Mrs. Bertram R.—Paradise Creek, Theatrical (Ire).

Flaxman Holdings Ltd.—Miesque (1987-'88).

Floyd, William—Highland Bud.

Franks, John—Answer Lively.

Freeman, Carl M.—Miss Alleged.

Fuller, C. T.—Ambassador of Luck.

Fuller, Peter—Mom's Command.

Gainsborough Farm—Fantastic Light, Hatoof.

Galbreath, John W.—Little Current, Sunshine Forever.

Galbreath, Mrs. John W.—Tempest Queen.

Galbreath/Phillips Racing Partnership—Soaring Softly.

Garrison, Wayne and Bruce Hundley—Fly So Free.

Genter Stable Inc., Frances A.—Smile.

Gilmore, Mrs. William, and Mrs. William M. Jason—Spectacular Bid (1978-'80).

Golden Chance Farm Inc.—John Henry (1980-'81, 1983-'84).

Greentree Stud Inc.—Bowl Game, Late Bloomer.

Groves, Helen, Helen Alexander, and David Aykroyd—Althea.

Guest, Raymond R.—Cascapedia.

Guest, Virginia D.—Life's Illusion.

Guggenheim, Harry F.—Ack Ack.

Hancock, Arthur B. III, and Leone J. Peters—Risen Star.

Happy Valley Farm—It's in the Air.

Haras El Huerton—*Gran Kan.

Haras General Cruz—*Cougar II.

Haras Principal—Bayakoa (Arg) (1989-'90).

Haras Santa Ana do Rio Grande—Riboletta (Brz).

Haras Santa Amelia—Pompeyo (Chi).

Haras Vacacion—Pascana (Arg) (1992-'93).

Harbor View Farm—Affirmed (1977-'79), Athenian Idol, Outstandingly, Flawlessly (1992-'93).

Harper, Rowe W., and Irish Hill Farm—Spend a Buck.

Hartigan, John H.—Mac Diarmida.

Hayden, Mr. and Mrs. David—Safely Kept.

Hibbert, Robert E.—Roving Boy.

Hickey, P. Noel—Buck's Boy.

Highclere Inc. and Clear Creek—Silverbulletday (1998-'99).

Hi Yu Stables—Chinook Pass.

Hofmann, Mr. and Mrs. Philip B.—Gold Beauty.

Homan, J. L.—Gallant Bob.

Hooper Jr., Fred W.—Susan's Girl (1972-'73, 1975).

Hooper Sr., Fred W.—Precisionist.

Humphrey, G. Watts Jr., and William S. Farish III—Sacahusta.

Humphrey, Mrs. G. Watts Jr.—Genuine Risk.

Hundley, Bruce, and Wayne Garrison—Fly So Free.

Hunt, Nelson Bunker—Dahlia, Estrapade, Trillion, Youth.

Iandoli, Lewis E.—Conquistador Cielo.

Irish American Bloodstock Agency Ltd.—Yanks Music.

Irish Hill Farm and Rowe W. Harper—Spend a Buck.

Janney, Mr. and Mrs. Stuart S. Jr.—Ruffian (1974-'75).

Jason, Mrs. William M., and Mrs. William Gilmore—Spectacular Bid (1978-'80).

Jayeff B Stables and W. G. Lyster III—Johannesburg.

Jeffords, Walter M. Jr.—Lonesome Glory (1992-'93, '95, '97, '99).

Jones, Aaron U.—Lemhi Gold, Tiffany Lass.

Jones, Brereton C.—Caressing.

Juddmonte Farms—Banks Hill (GB), Ryafan, Wandesta (GB).

Karutz, Dr. Wallace—Brave Raj.

Kaster, Richard S.—Countess Diana.

Keck, Howard B.—Ferdinand, Turkish Trousers.

Kellman, Joseph—Shecky Greene.

Kernan, Francis, and Spendthrift Farm—Landaluce.

Kilroy, W. S., and William S. Farish III—A.P. Indy, Lemon Drop Kid.

Kirtlington Stud Ltd. and the Kris syndicate—All Gong (GB).

Kitchen, Edgar—Track Robbery.

Kluener, Robert G.—Warm Spell.

Knight, Landon—Flat Top.

Kris syndicate, the, and Kirtlington Stud Ltd.—All Gong (GB).

Lancaster, Carlyle J.—Star de Naskra.

Lazy F Ranch—Forego (1974-'77).

Levesque, Jean-Louis—La Prevoyante.

Levy, Blanche P., and Murphy Stable—Housebuster (1990-'91).

Levy, Robert P., and Cisley Stable—North Sider.

Lilley, J. A. C.—*Snow Knight.

Little Hill Farm—Real Quiet.

Little, Marvin A. Jr.—Hansel.

Loblolly Stable—Prairie Bayou, Vanlandingham.

Lowquest Ltd.—Timber Country.

Luro, Horatio A.—Wayward Lass.

Lyster III, W. G. and Jayeff B Stables—Johannesburg.

Madden, Preston—Alysheba (1987-'88).

Maktoum, Sheikh Mohammed bin Rashid al—Singspiel (Ire).

Mangurian, Mr. and Mrs. Harry T.

Jr.—Gilded Time.

Maynard, Richard D.—Chief Bearhart.

Meadow Stud—Riva Ridge, Secretariat (1972-'73).

Mellon, Paul—Key to the Mint, Run the Gantlet.

Mill House—Sensational.

Miller, MacKenzie, and Dr. and Mrs. R. Smiser West—De La Rose.

Miller, Mr. and Mrs. MacKenzie, and Dr. and Mrs. R. Smiser West—Chilukki.

Murphy Stable and Blanche P. Levy—Housebuster (1990-'91).

Nahem, Ed—Bertrando.

Narducci, M.D., Audrey—Squirtle Squirt.

Nerud, John A.—Cozzene.

Newgate Stud Company—Fiji (GB).

Nicholson, Jessica Bell, and H. Bennett Bell—Epitome.

North Ridge Farm—Blushing John, Capote.

Nuckols Brothers—Typecast.

Nuckols, Charles Jr. and Sons—Hidden Lake.

Oak Cliff Thoroughbreds Ltd.—Sunday Silence.

Onett, George C.—Cherokee Run.

Overbrook Farm—Boston Harbor, Flanders, Golden Attraction, Surfside.

Pancoast, Mrs. Jean R.—Dearly Precious.

Pape, William L., and Jonathan Sheppard—Flatterer (1983-'86), Martie's Anger.

Parkhill, Marshall—Morley Street (Ire) (1990-'91).

Parrish, Dr. David C. III, Estate of Emma Haggin Parrish, and Douglas Parrish—Life's Magic.

Parrish, Douglas, Estate of Emma Haggin Parrish, and Dr. David C. Parrish III—Life's Magic.

Parrish, Estate of Emma Haggin, Douglas Parrish, and Dr. David C. Parrish III—Life's Magic.

Parrish Hill Farm and William S. Farish—Charismatic.

Paulson, Allen E.—Ajina, Cigar (1995-'96), Eliza, Escena.

Paxson, Adele—Candy Eclair.

Pelican Stable—Holy Bull.

Perez, Carlos—Kona Gold.

Peskoff, Stephen D.—Black Tie Affair (Ire).

Peters, Leone J., and Arthur B. Hancock III—Risen Star.

Phillips, Mrs. Jacqueline Getty—Bates Motel.

Phillips Racing Partnership/Galbreath—Soaring Softly.

Phipps, Cynthia—Christmas Past.

Phipps, Mrs. Ogden—Straight and True.

Phipps, Ogden—Easy Goer, Heavenly

Prize, Numbered Account, Personal Ensign, Relaxing.

Phipps, Ogden Mills—Inside Information, Rhythm.

Phipps, Ogden Mills, and William S. Farish—Storm Song.

Pin Oak Farm—Laugh and Be Merry.

Polinger, Milton—What a Summer.

Polk, Dr. Albert F. Jr.—Temperence Hill.

Pope, George A. Jr.—J. O. Tobin.

Ravenbrook Farm Inc.—Not Surprising.

Rathvale Stud—Just a Game (Ire).

Red Bull Stable and Eaton Farms Inc.—Bold Forbes.

Roach, Dr. Ben, and Tom Roach—Princess Rooney.

Roach, Tom, and Dr. Ben Roach—Princess Rooney.

Robertson, Corbin—Turkoman.

Robins, Gerald W. and Timothy H. Sams—Tasso.

Robinson, Marshall T.—Groovy.

Rosebrock, Perry M.—Smoke Glacken.

Rosen, Carl—Chief's Crown.

Rosenthal, Morton—Maria's Mon.

Ryan, B. L.—Royal Heroine (Ire).

Ryehill Farm—Heavenly Cause, Smart Angle.

Sam-Son Farm—Dance Smartly, Sky Classic.

Sams, Timothy H. and Gerald W. Robins—Tasso.

Sarkowsky, Herman—Phone Chatter.

Sasse, F. H. and A. D. Shead—Perrault (GB).

Schiff, John M.—Plugged Nickle.

Scott, Mrs. Marion duPont—Soothsayer.

Selective Seasons—Family Style.

Sergent, Willard—Reraise.

Shead, A. D. and F. H. Sasse—Perrault (GB).

Sheppard, Jonathan, and William L. Pape—Flatterer (1983-'86), Martie's Anger.

Spendthrift Farm and Francis Kernan—Landaluce.

Spreen, Robert H.—Lady's Secret.

Stone, Whitney—Shuvee.

Straub-Rubens, Cecilia—Tiznow (2000-'01).

Sugar Maple Farm—Itsallgreektome, Sky Beauty.

Swettenham Stud—Lit de Justice.

Swettenham Stud and Partners—Northern Spur (Ire).

Tafel, James B.—Banshee Breeze.

Tall Oaks Farm—Victory Gallop.

Tartan Farms Corp.—Dr. Patches, Unbridled.

Taylor, E. P.—Devil's Bag, Glorious Song.

The Thoroughbred Corp.—Point Given.

Third Kirsmith Racing Associates—Rubiano.

Thomas, Dr. E. W., and Carolaine Farm—Rockhill Native.

Viking Farms Ltd.—Lord Avie.

Vinery and Carondelet Farm—Artax.

Waldemar Farms Inc.—Foolish Pleasure, Honest Pleasure.

Warren Hill Stud and Mimika Financiera—Pebbles (GB).

Weinsier, Randolph—Lakeville Miss.

Wertheimer and Brother—Kotashaan (Fr.).

West, Dr. and Mrs. R. Smiser, and MacKenzie Miller—De La Rose.

West, Dr. and Mrs. R. Smiser and Mr. and Mrs. MacKenzie Miller—Chilukki.

Wheatley Stable—Autobiography.

Wilson, Ralph C. Jr.—Arazi.

Winchell, Verne H.—Cafe Prince (1977-'78), Tight Spot.

Witt, Mr. and Mrs. Robert—Possibly Perfect.

Wood, Mr. and Mrs. M. L.—Favorite Trick.

Wootton, Mary Lou—Silver Charm.

Zurek, Edward N.—The Wicked North.

Trainers of Eclipse Award Winners

Albertrani, Louis—Artax.

Alexander, Frank—Cherokee Run.

Allard, Edward T.—Mom's Command.

Anderson, Laurie—Chinook Pass.

Arias, Juan—Canonero II.

Badgett Jr., William—Go for Wand (1989-'90).

Baffert, Robert—Chilukki, Point Given, Real Quiet, Silverbulletday (1998-'99), Silver Charm.

Balding, Gerald B. "Toby"—Morley Street (Ire) (1990-'91).

Barnett, Robert—Answer Lively.

Barrera, Lazaro S.—Affirmed (1977-'79), Bold Forbes, It's in the Air, J. O. Tobin, Lemhi Gold, Tiffany Lass.

Bary, Pascal—Miss Alleged (with Charles Whittingham).

Belanger Jr., Gerald W.—Glorious Song.

Bernstein, David—The Wicked North.

Biancone, Patrick L.—All Along (Fr).

Bin Suroor, Saeed—Daylami (Ire), Fantastic Light.

Bohannan, Thomas—Prairie Bayou.

Boutin, Francois—April Run (Ire), Arazi, Miesque (1987-'88).

Brittain, Clive E.—Pebbles (GB).

Brothers, Frank—Hansel.

Burch, J. Elliot—Key to the Mint, Run the Gantlet.

Byrne, Patrick—Countess Diana, Favorite Trick.

Campbell, Gordon C.—Cascapedia.

Campo, John P.—Pleasant Colony, Protagonist, Talking Picture.

Cantey, Joseph B.—Temperence Hill.

Carroll, Henry—Smoke Glacken.

Cocks, W. Burling—Zaccio (1980-'82).

Croll Jr., Warren A.—Holy Bull, Housebuster (1990-'91).

Curtis Jr., William—Gold Beauty.

Day, Jim—Dance Smartly, Sky Classic.

Delp, Grover G.—Spectacular Bid (1978-'80).

DiMauro, Steve—Dearly Precious, Wajima.

Dollase, Craig—Reraise.

Dollase, Wallace—Itsallgreektome, Jewel Princess.

Doyle, A. T.—Typecast.

Drysdale, Neil—A.P. Indy, Fiji (GB), Hollywood Wildcat, Princess Rooney, Tasso.

Dunham, Robert G.—Chou Croute.

Elliot, Janet E.—Correggio (Ire), Flat Top.

Euster, Eugene—My Juliet.

Fabre, Andre—Banks Hill (GB).

Fensternmaker, L. Ross—Precisionist, Susan's Girl (1975).

Fenwick, Charles—Inlander (GB).

Ferris, Richard D.—Star de Naskra.

Fout, Paul R.—Life's Illusion.

Frankel, Robert—Bertrando, Possib-

ly Perfect, Ryafan, Squirtle Squirt, Wandesta (GB).

Freeman, W. C.—Shuvee.

Furr, C.—*Gran Kan.

Frostad, Mark—Chief Bearhart.

Gambolati, Cam—Spend a Buck.

Gaver, John M.—Late Bloomer.

Gaver Jr., John M..—Bowl Game.

Goldberg, Alan E.—Safely Kept.

Goldfine, Lou M.—Shecky Greene.

Gosden, John H. M.—Bates Motel, Royal Heroine (Ire).

Griggs, John K.—Warm Spell.

Harty, Eoin—Tempera.

Hassinger Jr., Alex—Anees, Eliza.

Hauswald, Phil—Epitome.

Head, Christiane—Hatoof.

Headley, Bruce—Kona Gold.

Hertler, John O.—Slew o' Gold (1983-'84).

Hickey, P. Noel—Buck's Boy.

Hine, Hubert—Guilty Conscience, Skip Away (1996-'98).

Howe, Peter M.—Proud Delta, Soothsayer.

Inda, Eduardo—Riboletta (Brz).

Jenda, Charles J.—Brown Bess.

Jerkens, H. Allen—Sky Beauty.

Jolley, LeRoy—Foolish Pleasure, Genuine Risk, Honest Pleasure, Manila, Meadow Star, What a Summer.

Jones, Gary—Turkoman.

Kay, Michael—Johnny D.

Kelly, Thomas J.—Plugged Nickle.

Kimmel, John—Hidden Lake.

King Jr., S. Allen—Candy Eclair.

Laurin, Lucien—Riva Ridge, Secretariat (1972-'73).

Laurin, Roger—Chief's Crown, Numbered Account.

Lepman, Budd—Eillo.

Lukas, D. Wayne—Althea, Boston Harbor, Capote, Charismatic, Criminal Type, Family Style, Flanders, Golden Attraction, Gulch, Lady's Secret, Landaluce, Life's Magic (1984-'85), North Sider, Open Mind (1988-'89), Sacahuista, Serena's Song, Steinlen (GB), Surfside, Thunder Gulch, Timber Country, Winning Colors.

Lundy, Richard J.—Blushing John.

Mandella, Richard—Kotashaan (Fr),

Phone Chatter.

Manzi, Joseph—Roving Boy.

Marquette, Joseph D.—Gallant Bob.

Marti, Pedro—Heartlight No. One.

Martin, Frank—Autobiography, Outstandingly.

Martin, Jose—Groovy, Lakeville Miss, Wayward Lass.

McAnally, Ronald—Bayakoa (Arg) (1989-'90), John Henry (1980, 1983-'84), Northern Spur (Ire), Paseana (Arg) (1992-'93), Tight Spot.

McAnally, Ronald and Victor J. Nickerson—John Henry (1981).

McGaughey III, Claude R.—Easy Goer, Heavenly Prize, Inside Information, Personal Ensign, Queena, Rhythm, Vanlandingham.

Meredith, Derek—Cardmania.

Miller, F. Bruce—All Gong (GB), Lonesome Glory (1992-'93, '95, '97, '99).

Miller, MacKenzie—*Snow Knight.

Mott, Bill—Ajina, Cigar (1995-'96), Escena, Paradise Creek, Theatrical (Ire).

Neilson, Sanna—Pompeyo (Chi).

Nafzger, Carl A.—Banshee Breeze, Unbridled.

Nerud, Jan H.—Cozzene.

Nerud, John A.—Dr. Patches.

Nobles, Reynaldo—Dehere.

O'Brien, Aidan—Johannesburg.

O'Brien, Leo—Yanks Music.

Orseno, Joseph F.—Macho Uno, Perfect Sting.

Penna, Angel—Relaxing.

Penna Jr., Angel—Christmas Past, Laugh and Be Merry.

Perlsweig, Daniel—Lord Avie.

Perdomo, Pico—Gourmet Girl.

Peterson, Douglas—Seattle Slew (1978).

Poulos, Ernie—Black Tie Affair (Ire).

Preger, Mitchell C.—Ambassador of Luck.

Robbins, Jay—Tiznow (2000-'01).

Rondinello, Thomas L.—Little Current, Tempest Queen.

Root Sr., T. F.—Desert Vixen.

Roussel III, Louis J.—Risen Star.

Russell, John W.—Susan's Girl (1972-'73).

Sahadi, Jenine—Lit de Justice.

Schosberg, Richard—Maria's Mon.

Schulhofer, Flint S.—Fly So Free, Lemon Drop Kid, Mac Diarmida, Rubiano, Smile.

Sciacca, Gary—Saratoga Dew.

Sheppard, Jonathan E.—Athenian Idol, Cafe Prince (1977-'78), Flatterer (1983-'86), Highland Bud, Jimmy Lorenzo (GB), Martie's Anger.

Smithwick, D. Michael—Straight and True.

Speckert, Chris—Pleasant Colony, Pleasant Tap.

Starr, John—La Prevoyante.

Stephens, Woodford C.—Conquistador Cielo, De La Rose, Devil's Bag, Forty Niner, Heavenly Cause, Sensational, Smart Angle, Swale.

Stevens, Herbert—Rockhill Native.

Stoute, Sir Michael—Kalanisi (Ire), Singspiel (Ire).

Stute, Mel—Brave Raj, Snow Chief.

Tammaro, John—Deputy Minister.

Toner, James J.—Soaring Softly.

Trovato, Joseph A.—Chris Evert.

Turner Jr., William H.—Seattle Slew (1976-'77).

Van Berg, Jack—Alysheba (1987-'88).

Vance, David R.—Caressing.

Van Worp, Judson—Not Surprising.

Veitch, John M.—Before Dawn, Davona Dale, Our Mims, Sunshine Forever.

Vienna, Darrell—Gilded Time.

Walden, W. Elliott—Victory Gallop.

Ward, John T.—Beautiful Pleasure.

Ward, Sherrill W.—Forego (1974-'75).

Watters Jr., Sidney—Shadow Brook, Slew o' Gold (1983-'84).

Wheeler, Robert L. and John W. Russell—Track Robbery.

Whiteley, David A.—Just a Game (Ire), Revidere, Waya (Fr).

Whiteley Jr., Frank Y.—Forego (1976-'77), Ruffian (1974-'75).

Whittingham, Charles—Ack Ack, *Cougar II, Estrapade, Ferdinand, Flawlessly (1992-'93), Miss Alleged (with Pascal Bary), Perrault (GB), Sunday Silence, Turkish Trousers.

Zilber, Maurice—Youth, Dahlia, Trillion.

Zito, Nicholas P.—Storm Song.

Sires of Eclipse Award Winners

Ack Ack—Youth.

Affirmed—Flawlessly (1992-'93).

Ahmad—Paseana (Arg) (1992-'93).

Air Forbes Won—Yanks Music.

*Alcibiades II—Athenian Idol.

Alleged—Flat Top, Miss Alleged.

Alydar—Althea, Alysheba (1987-'88), Criminal Type, Easy Goer, Turkoman.

A.P. Indy—Tempera.

Bagdad—Turkish Trousers.

Battle Joined—Ack Ack.

Best Turn—Davona Dale.

Blushing Groom (Fr)—Arazi, Blushing John, Sky Beauty.

Bold Bidder—Spectacular Bid (1978-'80).

Bold Forbes—Tiffany Lass.

Bold Reasoning—Seattle Slew (1976-'78).

Bold Ruler—Secretariat (1972-'73), Wajima.

Buckaroo—Spend a Buck.

Buckpasser—La Prevoyante, Numbered Account, Relaxing.

Bucksplasher—Buck's Boy.

Capote—Boston Harbor.

Caro (Ire)—Cozzene, Winning Colors.

Cee's Tizzy—Gourmet Girl, Tiznow (2000-'01).

Cherokee Run—Chilukki.

Chief's Crown—Chief Bearhart.

Chieftain—Cascapedia.

Cohoes—Shadow Brook.

Consultant's Bid—Bayakoa (Arg) (1989-'90).

Cormorant—Saratoga Dew.

Court Ruling—Guilty Conscience.

Cox's Ridge—Cardmania, Life's Magic 1984-'85), Vanlandingham.

Creme dela Creme—Cafe Prince (1977-'78).

Crozier—Precisionist.

Cryptoclearance—Victory Gallop.

Danehill—Banks Hill (GB).

Danzaro—Reraise.

Danzig—Chief's Crown, Dance Smartly.

Darshaan—Kotashaan (Fr).

Deep Run—Morley Street (Ire) (1990-'91).

Deerhound—Countess Diana.

Delta Judge—Proud Delta.

Deputy Minister—Dehere, Go for Wand (1989-'90), Open Mind (1988-'89).

Djakao—Perrault (GB).

Doyoun—Daylami (Ire), Kalanisi (Ire).

Dr. Fager—Dearly Precious, Dr. Patches.

El Gran Senor—Lit de Justice.

Erins Isle (Ire)—Laugh and Be Merry.

Exclusive Native—Affirmed (1977-'79), Genuine Risk, Outstandingly.

Fappiano—Tasso, Unbridled, Rubiano.

Faraway Son—Waya (Fr).

Far North—The Wicked North.

Firestreak—*Snow Knight.

First Landing—Riva Ridge.

*Forli—Forego (1974-'77).

Gallant Romeo—Gallant Bob, My Juliet.

Graustark—Key to the Mint, Tempest Queen.

Great Above—Holy Bull.

*Grey Dawn II—Christmas Past, Heavenly Cause.

Gulch—Thunder Gulch.

Habitat—Steinlen (GB).

Hail the Pirates—Wayward Lass.

Hail to Reason—Trillion.

Halo—Devil's Bag, Glorious Song, Sunday Silence.

Hennessy—Johannesburg.

*Herbager—Our Mims.

His Majesty—Pleasant Colony, Tight Spot.

Hoist the Flag—Sensational.

Holy Bull—Macho Uno.

Honour and Glory—Caressing.

Horatius—Safely Kept.

Ile de Bourbon—Inlander (GB).

In Reality—Desert Vixen, Smile.

In the Wings (GB)—Singspiel (Ire).

Irish Castle—Bold Forbes.

Irish River (Fr)—Hatoof, Paradise Creek.

Java Gold—Kona Gold.

Key to the Mint—Jewel Princess, Plugged Nickle.

Kingmambo—Lemon Drop Kid.

Kris—All Gong (GB).

Kris S.—Hollywood Wildcat, Soaring Softly.

Lear Fan—Ryafan.

Licencioso—*Gran Kan.

Little Missouri—Prairie Bayou.

Lively One—Answer Lively.

Lord Gaylord—Lord Avie.

*Lorenzaccio—Zaccio (1980-'82).

Lt. Stevens—Chou Croute.

Lyphard—Manila.

Lypheor (GB)—Royal Heroine (Ire).

Marquetry—Artax, Squirtle Squirt.

Maudlin—Beautiful Pleasure.

Meadowlake—Meadow Star.

Medieval Man—Not Surprising.

Minnesota Mac—Mac Diarmida.

Miswaki—Black Tie Affair (Ire).

Mo Bay—Flatterer (1983-'86).

Mr. Prospector—Conquistador Cielo, Eillo, Forty Niner, Gold Beauty, Golden Attraction, Gulch, It's in the Air, Queena, Rhythm.

Mt. Livermore—Housebuster (1990-'91), Eliza.

Mystic II—Life's Illusion, Soothsayer.

Nashua—Shuvee.

Nashwan—Wandesta (GB).

Naskra—Star de Naskra.

Native Born—Chinook Pass.

Never Bend—J. O. Tobin, Straight and True.

Nijinsky II—De La Rose, Ferdinand, Sky Classic.

*Noholme II—Shecky Greene.

Norcliffe—Groovy.

No Robbery—Track Robbery.

Northern Baby—Highland Bud, Possibly Perfect, Warm Spell.

Northern Jove—Candy Eclair.

Nureyev—Miesque (1987-'88), Theatrical (Ire).

Nureyev Dancer—Pompeyo (Chi).

Olden Times—Roving Boy.

Ole Bob Bowers—John Henry (1980-'81, 1983-'84).

Our Jimmy—Jimmy Lorenzo (GB).

Our Native—Rockhill Native.

Palace Music—Cigar (1995-'96).

*Petrone—Brown Bess.

Phone Trick—Favorite Trick, Phone Chatter.

Pleasant Colony—Pleasant Stage, Pleasant Tap.

*Pretendre—Canonero II.

Prince John—Protagonist, Typecast.

Private Account—Inside Information, Personal Ensign.

Quadrangle—Smart Angle, Susan's Girl (1972-'73, 1975).

Quiet American—Hidden Lake, Real Quiet.

Rahy—Fantastic Light, Serena's Song.

Rainbow Quest—Fiji (GB).

Rainy Lake—Lakeville Miss.

Raise a Cup—Before Dawn.

Rajab—Brave Raj.

Raja Baba—Sacahuista.

Red Ransom—Perfect Sting.

Reflected Glory—Snow Chief.

Reviewer—Revidere, Ruffian (1974-'75).

Roberto—Sunshine Forever.

Rock Talk—Heartlight No. One.

Leading sires
By number of titles won

9—Mr. Prospector
7—Seattle Slew
6—Alydar
5—Deputy Minister
5—Exclusive Native
5—Transworld
4—Cox's Ridge
4—*Forli
4—Mo Bay
4—Ole Bob Bowers
4—Quadrangle
3—Blushing Groom (Fr)
3—Bold Bidder
3—Bold Reasoning
3—Bold Ruler
3—Buckpasser
3—Cee's Tizzy
3—Fappiano
3—Halo
3—*Lorenzaccio
3—Mt. Livermore
3—Nijinsky II
3—Northern Baby
3—Nureyev
3—Reviewer
3—Skip Trial
3—*Vaguely Noble

Roi Normand—Riboletta (Brz).

Runaway Groom—Cherokee Run.

Run the Gantlet—April Run (Ire).

Sadler's Wells—Correggio (Ire), Northern Spur (Ire).

*Sea-Bird—Little Current.

Seattle Slew—A.P. Indy, Capote, Landaluce, Slew o' Gold (1983-'84), Surfside, Swale.

Secretariat—Lady's Secret, Risen Star.

Seeking the Gold—Flanders, Heavenly Prize.

Sharpen Up (GB)—Pebbles (GB).

Silver Buck—Silver Charm.

Silver Deputy—Silverbulletday (1998-'99).

Sir Ivor—Bates Motel.

Skip Trial—Skip Away (1996-'98).

*Sky High II—Autobiography.

Skywalker—Bertrando.

Sovereign Dancer—Itsallgreektome.

Speak John—Talking Picture.

Spring Double—Martie's Anger.

Stage Door Johnny—Johnny D., Late Bloomer.

State Dinner—Family Style.

Stop the Music—Temperence Hill.

Strawberry Road (Aus)—Ajina, Escena.

Summer Squall—Charismatic, Storm Song.

Summing—Epitome.

Swoon's Son—Chris Evert.

Tale of Two Cities—*Cougar II.

Tarboosh—Just a Game (Ire).

Targowice—All Along (Fr).

Thunder Gulch—Point Given.
Time for a Change—Fly So Free.
Timeless Moment—Gilded Time.
Tom Rolfe—Bowl Game, Run the Gantlet.
Top Command—Mom's Command.
Topsider—North Sider.

Transworld—Lonesome Glory (1992-'93, '95, '97, '99).
Two Punch—Smoke Glacken.
Unbridled—Anees, Banshee Breeze.
*Vaguely Noble—Dahlia, Estrapade, Lemhi Gold.
Verbatim—Princess Rooney.

Vice Regent—Deputy Minister.
Wavering Monarch—Maria's Mon.
What a Pleasure—Foolish Pleasure, Honest Pleasure.
What Luck—What a Summer, Ambassador of Luck.
Woodman—Hansel, Timber Country.

2001 Eclipse Award Winners

POINT GIVEN
Horse of the Year
Three-year-old male
Ch. c., 1998, Thunder Gulch—Turko's Turn, by Turkoman
Owner-breeder: The Thoroughbred Corp. (Ky.)
Trainer: Bob Baffert
2001 record: 7-6-0-0, $3,350,000
Career record: 13-9-3-0, $3,968,500
2001 stakes victories: Preakness S. (G1), Belmont S. (G1), Santa Anita Derby (G1), Travers S. (G1), Haskell Invitational H. (G1), San Felipe S. (G2)

After missing the 2000 juvenile male championship by a nose in the Breeders' Cup Juvenile (G1) on a hard, speed-favoring Churchill Downs track, Point Given was crowned 2001 Horse of the Year and champion three-year-old male with only one blemish on his record for the year, a fifth-place finish in the Kentucky Derby (G1) on another hard, speed-favoring Churchill track. The tall, willful colt, known in trainer Bob Baffert's barn as "T. Rex" and "Big Red Train," dominated his opponents outside Churchill Downs, winning the Santa Anita Derby (G1) by 5½ lengths and the Belmont Stakes (G1) by 12¼ lengths. After a minor scare in his half-length Haskell Invitational Handicap (G1) victory, Point Given captured Saratoga Race Course's Travers Stakes (G1) by 3½ lengths, becoming the first horse ever to win four consecutive races with a purse of $1-million or more each. A tendon injury discovered after the Travers ended his racing career, and he was retired to Three Chimneys Farm near Midway, Kentucky, with a $125,000 stud fee for 2002.

JOHANNESBURG
Two-year-old male
B. c., 1999, Hennessy—Myth, by Ogygian
Breeders: Wayne G. Lyster III and Jayeff B Stables (Ky.)
Owners: Michael Tabor and Susan Magnier
Trainer: Aidan O'Brien
2001 record: 7-7-0-0, $1,002,893
Career record through 2001: 7-7-0-0, $1,002,893
2001 stakes victories: Breeders' Cup Juvenile (G1), Prix Morny (Fr-G1), Phoenix S. (Ire-G1), Middle Park S. (Eng-G1), Anglesey S. (Ire-G3), Norfolk S. (Eng-G3)

A $200,000 Keeneland September purchase by Coolmore Stud talent-spotter Demi O'Byrne, Johannesburg capped a perfect, globe-trotting juvenile season with a surprisingly easy, 1¼-length victory in the Breeders' Cup Juvenile (G1) at Belmont Park. Distance and surface posed no problems for the Hennessy colt, who made his first dirt start and his first attempt beyond six furlongs in the 1¹⁄₁₆-mile Breeders' Cup Juvenile. Favored in every start before the Breeders' Cup race—at Belmont he was the 7.20-to-1 third betting choice behind the spectacularly disappointing Officer, at 0.75-to-1—Johannesburg handled ground rated as good to soft in the Middle Park Stakes (Eng-G1) at Newmarket before his New York trip. Ridden in all his starts by Michael Kinane, Johannesburg contributed four Grade 1 or Group 1 victories—in four countries—to the record 23 attained by trainer Aidan O'Brien.

TEMPERA
Two-year-old filly
Dk. b. or br. f., 1999, A.P. Indy—Colour Chart, by Mr. Prospector
Breeder: Darley Stud Management (Ky.)
Owner: Godolphin Racing
Trainer: Eoin Harty
2001 record: 5-3-0-2, $670,240
Career record through 2001: 5-3-0-2, $670,240
2001 stakes victories: Breeders' Cup Juvenile Fillies (G1), Sorrento S. (G2)

Tempera represented the first significant success of Godolphin Racing's strategy of preparing its young horses in Dubai before sending them to the United States for their juvenile seasons. Raised at Raceland Farm in Paris, Kentucky—a facility now owned by Sheikh Mohammed bin Rashid al Maktoum's Darley Stud Management—Tempera was slightly underdeveloped when trainer Eoin Harty first saw her in late 2000. But she matured well through the spring and won her maiden victory in her second career start at Hollywood Park. She attracted attention with a nine-length win in Del Mar's Sorrento Stakes (G1), but a third-place finish in the Del Mar Debutante (G1), for which she was wound up too tight, led Harty to back off of her and prepare her for the Breeders' Cup Juvenile Fillies (G1) on workouts alone. Sent off at 11.90-to-1, Tempera made a sweeping move under David Flores to gain the lead inside Belmont's furlong pole and won by 1½ lengths over stablemate Imperial Gesture.

XTRA HEAT
Three-year-old filly
B. f., 1998, Dixieland Heat—Begin, by Hatchet Man
Breeders: Pope McLean Sr., Pope McLean Jr., Marc McLean, Scott Rion, and Peter Feringa Jr. (Ky.)
Owners: Kenneth Taylor, Harry Deitchman, and John E. Salzman Sr.
Trainer: John E. Salzman Sr.
2001 record: 13-9-3-1, $1,012,040
Career record through 2001: 24-19-3-1, $1,443,305
2001 stakes victories: Prioress S. (G1), Stonerside Beaumont S. (G2), Endine S. (G3), Cicada S. (G3), Straight Deal Breeders' Cup H., Sweet and Sassy S., Ruthless S., Arctic Cloud S.

The Eclipse Award for champion three-year-old filly usually goes to winners of such races as the Breeders' Cup Distaff (G1) or weight-for-age contests such as the Beldame Stakes (G1). But in a highly competitive and confusing 2001 season for the division, the filly who emerged from the pack had started in neither of those races and never raced beyond seven furlongs. But at sprint distances, Xtra Heat was extra special, and her nine victories in 13 starts earned her the 2001 title. The Dixieland Heat filly, a $5,000 bargain as a two-year-old in training, notched her first and only Grade 1 victory in Belmont Park's Prioress Stakes, but she also ran a courageous second to Squirtle Squirt in the Breeders' Cup Sprint (G1), finishing a half-length back under Jorge Chavez, who took over the mount from injured jockey Rick Wilson, the filly's regular rider.

TIZNOW
Older male
B. c., 1997, Cee's Tizzy—Cee's Song, by Seattle Song
Breeder: Cecilia Straub-Rubens (Cal.)
Owners: Cee's Stable (Michael Cooper, Pamela Ziebarth, and Kevin Cochrane)
Trainer: Jay Robbins
2001 record: 6-3-1-2, $2,981,880
Career record: 15-8-4-2, $6,427,830
2001 stakes victories: Breeders' Cup Classic (G1), Santa Anita H. (G1), San Fernando Breeders' Cup H. (G2)

Horse of the Year in 2000 after a storybook victory in the Breeders' Cup Classic (G1), Tiznow became the first horse to

win the Breeders' Cup Classic twice when he overcame all odds and came back in Belmont Park's stretch to nip Sakhee at the finish. Tiznow's season had started out on a championship path, with victories in the San Fernando Breeders' Cup Handicap (G1) and Santa Anita Handicap (G1), but a mysterious back problem and willful behavior threatened to tarnish his 2001 season. Trainer Jay Robbins sent him out for third-place finishes in the Woodward Stakes (G1) and Goodwood Breeders' Cup Handicap (G2) before Tiznow decided to train seriously prior to his Breeders' Cup Classic triumph. With Chris McCarron in the saddle, Tiznow was passed by Sakhee but fought back in the final 30 yards to secure his second win in the $4-million race. He was retired to stud at WinStar Farm near Versailles, Kentucky, for the 2002 season with a stud fee of $30,000.

GOURMET GIRL
Older female
Dk. b. or br. m., 1995, Cee's Tizzy—Rhondaling (GB), by Welsh Pageant (Fr)
Breeders: Carl and Olivia Cannata (Cal.)
Owner: Gary A. Tanaka
Trainer: A. Pico Perdomo
2001 record: 6-3-1-0, $554,950
Career record: 33-9-7-10, $1,255,373
2001 stakes victories: Vanity H. (G1), Apple Blossom H. (G1), Sacramento H.

Gourmet Girl, a mare who made only one start in the second half of the year, emerged from an inscrutable pack of older fillies and mares to claim the 2001 Eclipse Award. Gary Tanaka, who purchased her early in 1999, had considered retiring Gourmet Girl at the beginning of 2001, but trainer A. Pico Perdomo persuaded him to give her one more racing season. After a fifth-place finish in the Santa Margarita Invitational Handicap (G1), Perdomo shipped her to Arkansas, where she won the Apple Blossom Handicap (G1) while equipped with blinkers for the first time. Back in California, she led at every point of call to win the Vanity Handicap (G1) by five lengths. In her final start of the year, she finished second in Del Mar's Clement L. Hirsch Handicap (G2). With the Eclipse Award in hand, Tanaka again followed Perdomo's advice and retired Gourmet Girl in late February.

FANTASTIC LIGHT
Turf male
B. h., 1996, Rahy—Jood, by Nijinsky II
Breeder: Gainsborough Farm (Ky.)
Owner: Godolphin Racing
Trainer: Saeed bin Suroor
2001 record: 6-4-2-0, $3,634,859
Career record: 25-12-5-3, $8,486,957
2001 stakes victories: Breeders' Cup Turf (G1), Irish Champion S. (Ire-G1), Prince of Wales's S. (Eng-G1), Tattersalls Gold Cup S. (Ire-G1)

Fantastic Light was crowned North America's champion turf male, but he just as easily could be regarded as a world champion. His feats in Europe earned him the Cartier Horse of the Year designation, and the 6,500-member Racehorse Owners Association voted him European Horse of the Year. In addition, the Rahy horse won the World Series Racing Championship title for the second straight year. He won four Grade 1 or Group 1 races in three countries, and, prior to the Breeders' Cup, won a thrilling battle with Galileo (Ire) in the Irish Champion Stakes (Ire-G1). He won the Breeders' Cup Turf by three-quarters of a length over Milan (GB) after opening a large advantage in midstretch. At season's end, Fantastic Light was retired to stud at Sheikh Mohammed bin Rashid al Maktoum's Dalham Hall Stud near Newmarket, England.

BANKS HILL (GB)
Turf female
B. f., 1998, Danehill—Hasili, by Kahyasi
Breeder-owner: Juddmonte Farms (GB)
Trainer: Andre Fabre
2001 record: 7-3-3-0, $1,145,276
Career record through 2001: 8-4-3-0, $1,156,931
2001 stakes victories: Breeders' Cup Filly and Mare Turf (G1), Coronation S. (Eng-G1), Prix de Sandringham (Fr-G2)

Like Fantastic Light and Johannesburg, Banks Hill (GB) earned her 2001 Eclipse Award with a single North American start, and an impressive one it was. She burst away from her competitors impressively in the Breeders' Cup Filly and Mare Turf (G1) under jockey Olivier Peslier and won by 5½ lengths on the firm ground that she prefers. Banks Hill also broke the Breeders' Cup drought of Juddmonte Farms, her owner and breeder. Second in the Poule d'Essai des Pouliches (Fr-G1), the French equivalent of the One Thousand Guineas (Eng-G1), Banks Hill won the Prix de Sandringham (Fr-G2) at Chantilly and Ascot's Coronation Stakes (Eng-G1) within three weeks of each other in June. After the Danehill filly placed in two Group 1 mile stakes for older horses, Fabre considered running her in the Prix de l'Opera (Fr-G1) in early October but decided against that start when the ground at Longchamp came up soft, and instead trained her up to the Breeders' Cup.

SQUIRTLE SQUIRT
Sprinter
Dk. b. or br. c., 1998, Marquetry—Lost the Code, by Lost Code
Breeder: Audrey Narducci, M.D. (Ky.)
Owner: David J. Lanzman Racing Stable
Trainer: Robert J. Frankel
2001 record: 6-3-3-0, $817,720
Career record through 2001: 15-8-4-0. $1,097,220
2001 stakes wins: Breeders' Cup Sprint (G1), King's Bishop S. (G1)

Even with a chip in his knee, Squirtle Squirt turned out to be a great bargain for David Lanzman, who named the Marquetry colt for his son's favorite Pokemon character. Of course, Lanzman did not know that the colt had the chip when he paid $25,000 for him at the 2000 Barretts March selected sale of two-year-olds in training, and Squirtle Squirt won four stakes races with the problem. After surgery, Squirtle Squirt was turned over to Racing Hall of Fame trainer Bobby Frankel, who quickly recognized that the colt wanted to sprint. After an allowance victory at Hollywood Park in June, Frankel kept Squirtle Squirt at seven furlongs, including a victory in the King's Bishop Stakes (G1) at Saratoga Race Course, on the theory that the added distance would help provide him with the stamina to carry his speed at six furlongs. The strategy worked, with Squirtle Squirt tracking Xtra Heat throughout the Breeders' Cup Sprint (G1) before getting up late to win by a half-length.

POMPEYO (Chi)
Steeplechaser
Dk. b. or br. g., 1994, Nureyev Dancer—Pouliche (Chi), by Domineau
Breeder: Haras Santa Amelia (Chi.)
Owner: Augustin Stables
Trainer: Sanna Neilson
2001 record: 2-2-0-0, $141,525
Career record: 33-11-6-5, $528,325
2001 stakes victories: Woodward-Kirkover Cup Novice Hurdle S., Royal Chase for the Sport of Kings Hurdle S.

In 2001, a steeplechase horse with the ability to climb to the top of the sport emerged, and just as quickly was taken away as a result of a freak training accident. Pompeyo (Chi), a classic winner in his native country, never achieved his potential on the flat in the United States because of his headstrong personality. But he loved to jump, and in the hands of trainer Sanna Neilson, he rose to the head of an evenly balanced class of jumpers in 2001, scoring in his only two starts to secure the Eclipse Award as champion steeplechase horse. His season began at Camden, South Carolina, where he won a stakes race limited to novices, and he surged away to a three-length victory in the Royal Chase for the Sport of Kings at Keeneland Race Course in late April. He sustained a fractured left elbow when kicked by another horse in September. A plate was inserted and removed after the fracture healed, but the joint became infected, and Pompeyo was euthanized on January 19, 2002.

Champions Before Eclipse Awards

Daily Racing Form (DRF) began naming champions in 1936. Beginning in 1950, the Thoroughbred Racing Associations (TRA) began naming its own champions. The following tables reflect the horses named champions by those two organizations. Where neither the letter (D) or (T) follow the name of the horse, both the DRF and the TRA named that horse champion.

When there were different champions named in any category, the DRF champion is noted with the letter (D) and the TRA with the letter (T). The DRF and the TRA poll were consolidated with that of the National Turf Writers Association in 1971 to create the Eclipse Awards, which now recognize the champions of racing in North America.

†-filly, *-imported horse; (D) *Daily Racing Form*; (T) Thoroughbred Racing Associations

Horse of the Year

1970	Fort Marcy (D)
	Personality (T)
1969	Arts and Letters
1968	Dr. Fager
1967	Damascus
1966	Buckpasser
1965	Roman Brother (D)
	†Moccasin (T)
1964	Kelso
1963	Kelso
1962	Kelso
1961	Kelso
1960	Kelso
1959	Sword Dancer
1958	Round Table
1957	Bold Ruler (D)
	Dedicate (T)
1956	Swaps
1955	Nashua
1954	Native Dancer
1953	Tom Fool
1952	One Count (D)
	Native Dancer (T)
1951	Counterpoint
1950	Hill Prince
1949	Capot
1948	Citation
1947	Armed
1946	Assault
1945	†Busher
1944	†Twilight Tear
1943	Count Fleet
1942	Whirlaway
1941	Whirlaway
1940	Challedon
1939	Challedon
1938	Seabiscuit
1937	War Admiral
1936	Granville

Two-Year-Old Male

1970	Hoist the Flag
1969	Silent Screen
1968	Top Knight
1967	Vitriolic
1966	Successor
1965	Buckpasser
1964	Bold Lad
1963	Hurry to Market
1962	Never Bend
1961	Crimson Satan
1960	Hail to Reason
1959	Warfare
1958	First Landing
1957	Nadir (D)
	Jewel's Reward (T)

1956	Barbizon
1955	Needles
1954	Nashua
1953	Porterhouse
1952	Native Dancer
1951	Tom Fool
1950	Battlefield
1949	Hill Prince
1948	Blue Peter
1947	Citation
1946	Double Jay
1945	Star Pilot
1944	Pavot
1943	Platter
1942	Count Fleet
1941	Alsab
1940	Our Boots
1939	Bimelech
1938	El Chico
1937	Menow
1936	Pompoon

Two-Year-Old Filly

1970	Forward Gal
1969	Fast Attack (D)
	Tudor Queen (T)
1968	Gallant Bloom (D)
	Process Shot (T)
1967	Queen of the Stage
1966	Regal Gleam
1965	Moccasin
1964	Queen Empress
1963	Tosmah (D)
	Castle Forbes (T)
1962	Smart Deb
1961	Cicada
1960	Bowl of Flowers
1959	My Dear Girl
1958	Quill
1957	Idun
1956	Leallah (D)
	Romanita (T)
1955	Doubledogdare (D)
	Nasrina (T)
1954	High Voltage
1953	Evening Out
1952	Sweet Patootie
1951	Rose Jet
1950	Aunt Jinny
1949	Bed o' Roses
1948	Myrtle Charm
1947	Bewitch
1946	First Flight
1945	Beaugay
1944	Busher
1943	Durazna
1942	Askmenow

1941	Petrify
1940	Level Best
1939	Now What
1938	Incoselda
1937	Jacola
1936	Apogee

Three-Year-Old Male

1970	Personality
1969	Arts and Letters
1968	Stage Door Johnny
1967	Damascus
1966	Buckpasser
1965	Tom Rolfe
1964	Northern Dancer
1963	Chateaugay
1962	Jaipur
1961	Carry Back
1960	Kelso
1959	Sword Dancer
1958	Tim Tam
1957	Bold Ruler
1956	Needles
1955	Nashua
1954	High Gun
1953	Native Dancer
1952	One Count
1951	Counterpoint
1950	Hill Prince
1949	Capot
1948	Citation
1947	Phalanx
1946	Assault
1945	Fighting Step
1944	By Jimminy
1943	Count Fleet
1942	Alsab
1941	Whirlaway
1940	Bimelech
1939	Challedon
1938	Stagehand
1937	War Admiral
1936	Granville

Three-Year-Old Filly

1970	Office Queen (D)
	Fanfreluche (T)
1969	Gallant Bloom
1968	Dark Mirage
1967	Furl Sail (D)
	Gamely (T)
1966	Lady Pitt
1965	What a Treat
1964	Tosmah
1963	Lamb Chop
1962	Cicada
1961	Bowl of Flowers

1960 Berlo
1959 Royal Native (D)
Silver Spoon (T)
1958 Idun
1957 Bayou
1956 Doubledogdare
1955 Misty Morn
1954 Parlo
1953 Grecian Queen
1952 Real Delight
1951 Kiss Me Kate
1950 Next Move
1949 ‡Two Lea
‡Wistful
1948 Miss Request
1947 But Why Not
1946 Bridal Flower
1945 Busher
1944 Twilight Tear
1943 Stefanita
1942 Vagrancy
1941 Painted Veil
1940 Not awarded
1939 Unerring
1938 Not awarded
1937 Not awarded
1936 Not awarded

‡ (D) co-champions

Older Male (Handicap Div.)

1970 Fort Marcy (D)
Nodouble (T)
1969 Arts and Letters (D)
Nodouble (T)
1968 Dr. Fager
1967 Damascus (D)
Buckpasser (T)
1966 Buckpasser (D)
Bold Bidder (T)
1965 Roman Brother
1964 Kelso
1963 Kelso
1962 Kelso
1961 Kelso
1960 Bald Eagle
1959 Sword Dancer (D)
Round Table (T)
1958 Round Table
1957 Dedicate
1956 Swaps
1955 High Gun
1954 Native Dancer
1953 Tom Fool
1952 Crafty Admiral
1951 Hill Prince
1950 *Noor
1949 Coaltown
1948 Citation
1947 Armed
1946 Armed
1945 Stymie
1944 Devil Diver
1943 Market Wise
Devil Diver
1942 Whirlaway
1941 Mioland
1940 Challedon
1939 *Kayak II
1938 Seabiscuit
1937 Seabiscuit
1936 Discovery

Older Female (Handicap Div.)

1970 Shuvee
1969 Gallant Bloom (D)
Gamely (T)
1968 Gamely
1967 Straight Deal
1966 Open Fire (D)
Summer Scandal (T)
1965 Old Hat
1964 Tosmah (D)
Old Hat (T)
1963 Cicada
1962 Primonetta
1961 Airmans Guide
1960 Royal Native
1959 Tempted
1958 Bornastar
1957 Pucker Up
1956 Blue Sparkler
1955 Misty Morn (D)
Parlo (T)
1954 Parlo (D)
Lavender Hill (T)
1953 Sickle's Image
1952 Real Delight (D)
Next Move (T)
1951 Bed o' Roses
1950 Two Lea
1949 Bewitch
1948 Conniver
1947 But Why Not
1946 Gallorette
1945 Busher
1944 Twilight Tear
1943 Mar-Kell
1942 Vagrancy
1941 Fairy Chant
1940 War Plumage
1939 Lady Maryland
1938 Marica
1937 Not awarded
1936 Myrtlewood

Sprinter

1970 †Ta Wee
1969 †Ta Wee
1968 Dr. Fager
1967 Dr. Fager
1966 Impressive
1965 †Affectionately
1964 Ahoy
1963 Not awarded
1962 Not awarded
1961 Not awarded
1960 Not awarded
1959 Intentionally
1958 Bold Ruler
1957 Decathlon
1956 Decathlon
1955 Berseem
1954 White Skies
1953 Tom Fool
1952 Tea-Maker
1951 Sheilas Reward
1950 Sheilas Reward
1949 Delegate
Royal Governor
1948 Coaltown
1947 Polynesian

1947: first year category included

Turf Horse

1970 Fort Marcy
1969 *Hawaii
1968 Dr. Fager (D)
Fort Marcy (T)
1967 Fort Marcy
1966 Assagai
1965 Parka
1964 *Turbo Jet II
1963 Mongo
1962 Not awarded
1961 T. V. Lark
1960 Not awarded
1959 Round Table
1958 Round Table
1957 Round Table
1956 Career Boy
1955 *St. Vincent
1954 *Stan
1953 *Iceberg II

1953: first year category included

Steeplechase

1970 Top Bid
1969 *L'Escargot
1968 Bon Nouvel
1967 Quick Pitch
1966 Mako (D)
Tuscalee (T)
1965 Bon Nouvel
1964 Bon Nouvel
1963 Amber Diver
1962 Barnabys Bluff
1961 Peal
1960 Benguala
1959 Ancestor
1958 Neji
1957 Neji
1956 Shipboard
1955 Neji
1954 King Commander
1953 The Mast
1952 Jam (D)
Oedipus (T)
1951 Oedipus
1950 Oedipus
1949 Trough Hill
1948 American Way
1947 War Battle
1946 Elkridge
1945 Mercator
1944 Rouge Dragon
1943 Brother Jones
1942 Elkridge
1941 Speculate
1940 Not awarded
1939 Not awarded
1938 Not awarded
1937 Jungle King
1936 Bushranger

Racing Hall of Fame

The Racing Hall of Fame was founded in 1955 to honor the all-time greats of the sport, though it is limited to horses, jockeys, and trainers. Housed in the National Museum of Racing in Saratoga Springs, New York, the Racing Hall of Fame contains plaques that summarize the accomplishments of each inductee.

In addition to the horses, jockeys, and trainers, the Hall of Fame has a special category, Exemplar of Racing, reserved for a handful of people who have made a lasting impact on the sport as owners, breeders, or racing executives. Otherwise, the Hall of Fame does not individually recognize the accomplishments of owners, breeders, Turf writers, racing secretaries, racetrack owners, or other industry participants.

Each spring, a panel votes on the horses and people nominated for induction into the Hall of Fame. The results are usually announced the first week of May. The induction ceremonies usually take place the second Monday of August in Saratoga Springs.

Categories under consideration each year are Contemporary Male, Contemporary Female, Horse of Yesteryear, Jockey, and Trainer.

Nominees for induction into the Hall of Fame are first obtained from the 125 members of the Hall of Fame voting panel. The suggestions then go before a Nomination Committee, which narrows the names down to three for each category for that year's ballots. Names of the three finalists in each division then go before the entire voting panel. The top vote-getter in each category is selected as that year's inductee.

From time to time, additional selections to the Hall of Fame are made by the Historical Review Committee and the Steeplechase Committee. Candidates in these categories must meet the General Eligibility Criteria for consideration. The Historical Review Committee meets to consider if a jockey, trainer, or horse merits consideration for induction into the Hall of Fame but otherwise would remain unrecognized. The Steeplechase Committee meets to consider if a steeplechase jockey, trainer, or horse merits consideration for induction into the Hall of Fame.

Hall of Fame Eligibility Criteria:

To earn a place on the annual ballot, nominees must meet the following criteria:

1. Thoroughbreds become eligible when five calendar years have elapsed between their final racing year and their year of nomination.

2. Eligible Thoroughbreds are classified as Contemporary Male or Female if they have been retired between five and 25 years ago. Horses that have been retired for more than 25 years are classified as Horses of Yesteryear.

3. Active jockeys become eligible after riding Thoroughbreds for 15 years (any interruptions in their careers for injury are not counted against them).

4. Active trainers become eligible after 25 years as licensed Thoroughbred trainers.

5. The 15- and 25-year requirements may be waived for retired jockeys and trainers, but a five-year waiting period is then observed before they become eligible. In cases of fragile health, the Hall of Fame Committee may request that the five-year waiting period be waived at the discretion of the Executive Committee.

Members of the National Museum of Racing Hall of Fame

Jockeys (Year elected)

Frank D. "Dooley" Adams (1970)
John Adams (1965)
Joe Aitcheson Jr. (1978)
Edward Arcaro (1958)
Ted Atkinson (1957)
Braulio Baeza (1976)
Jerry Bailey (1995)
George Barbee (1996)
Carroll K. Bassett (1972)
Russell Baze (1999)
Walter Blum (1987)
George "Pete" Bostwick (1968)
Sam Boulmetis Sr. (1973)
Steve Brooks (1963)
Don Brumfield (1996)
Thomas H. Burns (1983)
James H. Butwell (1984)
J. Dallett "Dilly" Byers (1967)
Steve Cauthen (1994)
Frank Coltiletti (1970)

Angel Cordero Jr. (1988)
Robert H. "Specs" Crawford (1973)
Pat Day (1991)
Eddie Delahoussaye (1993)
Lavelle "Buddy" Ensor (1962)
Laverne Fator (1955)
Earlie Fires (2001)
Jerry Fishback (1992)
Andrew "Mack" Garner (1969)
Edward "Snapper" Garrison (1955)
Avelino Gomez (1982)
Henry F. Griffin (1956)
Eric Guerin (1972)
William J. Hartack (1959)
Sandy Hawley (1992)
Albert Johnson (1971)
William J. Knapp (1969)
Julie Krone (2000)
Clarence Kummer (1972)

Charles Kurtsinger (1967)
John P. Loftus (1959)
John Longden (1958)
Daniel A. Maher (1955)
J. Linus McAtee (1956)
Chris McCarron (1989)
Conn McCreary (1975)
Rigan McKinney (1968)
James McLaughlin (1955)
Walter Miller (1955)
Isaac B. Murphy (1955)
Ralph Neves (1960)
Joe Notter (1963)
George M. Odom (1955)
Winfield "Winnie" O'Connor (1956)
Frank O'Neill (1956)
Ivan H. Parke (1978)
Gilbert W. Patrick (1970)
Laffit Pincay Jr. (1975)
Samuel Purdy (1970)
John Reiff (1956)

Alfred Robertson (1971)
John L. Rotz (1983)
Earl Sande (1955)
Carroll H. Schilling (1970)
William Shoemaker (1958)
Willie Simms (1977)
James "Tod" Sloan (1955)
Alfred P. "Paddy" Smithwick (1973)
Gary Stevens (1997)
James Stout (1968)
Fred Taral (1955)
Bayard Tuckerman Jr. (1973)
Ron Turcotte (1979)
Nash Turner (1955)
Robert N. Ussery (1980)
Jacinto Vasquez (1998)
Jorge Velasquez (1990)
Jack Westrope (2002)
George M. Woolfe (1955)
Raymond Workman (1956)
Manuel Ycaza (1977)

Trainers (Year elected)

Lazaro S. Barrera (1979)
H. Guy Bedwell (1971)
Edward D. Brown (1984)
J. Elliott Burch (1980)
Preston M. Burch (1963)
William P. Burch (1955)
Fred Burlew (1973)
Frank E. Childs (1968)
Henry S. Clark (1982)
W. Burling Cocks (1985)
James P. Conway (1996)
Warren A. "Jimmy" Croll Jr. (1994)
Grover G. "Buddy" Delp (2002)
Neil Drysdale (2000)
William Duke (1956)
Louis Feustel (1964)
James Fitzsimmons (1958)
Robert Frankel (1995)
John M. Gaver Sr. (1966)
Thomas J. Healey (1955)

Samuel C. Hildreth (1955)
Maximilian Hirsch (1959)
William J. "Buddy" Hirsch (1982)
Thomas Hitchcock Sr. (1973)
Hollie Hughes (1973)
John J. Hyland (1956)
Hirsch Jacobs (1958)
H. Allen Jerkens (1975)
Philip G. "Phil" Johnson (1997)
William R. Johnson (1986)
LeRoy Jolley (1987)
Ben A. Jones (1958)
Horace A. "Jimmy" Jones (1959)
Andrew Jackson Joyner (1955)
Thomas J. Kelly (1993)
Lucien Laurin (1977)
J. Howard Lewis (1969)
D. Wayne Lukas (1999)

Horatio Luro (1980)
John E. Madden (1983)
James W. Maloney (1989)
Richard Mandella (2001)
Frank "Pancho" Martin (1981)
Ron McAnally (1990)
Henry McDaniel (1956)
MacKenzie "Mack" Miller (1987)
William Molter Jr. (1960)
William I. Mott (1998)
Winbert Mulholland (1967)
Edward A. Neloy (1983)
John A. Nerud (1972)
Burley Parke (1986)
Angel Penna Sr. (1988)
Jacob Pincus (1988)
John W. Rogers (1955)
James G. Rowe Sr. (1955)
Flint S. "Scotty" Schulhofer (1992)
Jonathan Sheppard (1990)

Robert A. Smith (1976)
Tom Smith (2001)
D. M. "Mike" Smithwick (1971)
Woodford C. "Woody" Stephens (1976)
Meshach "Mesh" Tenney (1991)
Henry J. Thompson (1969)
Harry Trotsek (1984)
Jack C. Van Berg (1985)
Marion H. Van Berg (1970)
Sylvester Veitch (1977)
Robert W. Walden (1970)
Sherrill Ward (1978)
Frank Whiteley Jr. (1978)
Charles Whittingham (1974)
Ansel Williamson (1998)
G. Carey Winfrey (1975)
William C. Winfrey (1971)

Horses (Year elected, year foaled)

Ack Ack (1986, 1966)
Affectionately (1989, 1960)
Affirmed (1980, 1975)
All Along (Fr) (1990, 1979)
Alsab (1976, 1939)
Alydar (1989, 1975)
Alysheba (1993, 1984)
American Eclipse (1970, 1814)
A.P. Indy (2000, 1989)
Armed (1963, 1941)
Artful (1956, 1902)
Arts and Letters (1994, 1966)
Assault (1964, 1943)
Battleship (1969, 1927)
Bayakoa (Arg) (1998, 1984)
Bed o' Roses (1976, 1947)
Beldame (1956, 1901)
Ben Brush (1955, 1893)
Bewitch (1977, 1945)
Bimelech (1990, 1937)
Black Gold (1989, 1921)
Black Helen (1991, 1932)
Blue Larkspur (1957, 1926)
Bold 'n Determined (1997, 1977)
Bold Ruler (1973, 1954)
Bon Nouvel (1976, 1960)
Boston (1955, 1833)
Broomstick (1956, 1901)
Buckpasser (1970, 1963)
Busher (1964, 1942)
Bushranger (1967, 1930)
Cafe Prince (1985, 1970)
Carry Back (1975, 1958)
Cavalcade (1993, 1931)
Challedon (1977, 1936)
Chris Evert (1988, 1971)
Cicada (1967, 1959)
Cigar (2002, 1990)
Citation (1959, 1945)
Coaltown (1983, 1945)
Colin (1956, 1905)
Commando (1956, 1898)

Count Fleet (1961, 1940)
Crusader (1995, 1923)
Dahlia (1981, 1970)
Damascus (1974, 1964)
Dark Mirage (1974, 1965)
Davona Dale (1985, 1976)
Desert Vixen (1979, 1970)
Devil Diver (1980, 1939)
Discovery (1969, 1931)
Domino (1955, 1891)
Dr. Fager (1971, 1964)
Easy Goer (1997, 1986)
Eight Thirty (1994, 1936)
Elkridge (1966, 1938)
Emperor of Norfolk (1988, 1885)
Equipoise (1957, 1928)
Exceller (1999, 1973)
Exterminator (1957, 1915)
Fairmount (1985, 1921)
Fair Play (1956, 1905)
Fashion (1980, 1837)
Firenze (1981, 1884)
Flatterer (1994, 1979)
Foolish Pleasure (1995, 1972)
Forego (1979, 1970)
Fort Marcy (1998, 1964)
Gallant Bloom (1977, 1966)
Gallant Fox (1957, 1927)
*Gallant Man (1987, 1954)
Gallorette (1962, 1942)
Gamely (1980, 1964)
Genuine Risk (1986, 1977)
Go for Wand (1996, 1987)
Good and Plenty (1956, 1900)
Granville (1997, 1933)
Grey Lag (1957, 1918)
Gun Bow (1999, 1960)
Hamburg (1986, 1895)
Hanover (1955, 1884)
Henry of Navarre (1985, 1891)

Hill Prince (1991, 1947)
Hindoo (1955, 1878)
Holy Bull (2001, 1991)
Imp (1965, 1894)
Jay Trump (1971, 1957)
John Henry (1990, 1975)
Johnstown (1992, 1936)
Jolly Roger (1965, 1922)
Kelso (1967, 1957)
Kentucky (1983, 1861)
Kingston (1955, 1884)
Lady's Secret (1992, 1982)
La Prevoyante (1995, 1970)
*L'Escargot (1977, 1963)
Lexington (1955, 1850)
Longfellow (1971, 1867)
Luke Blackburn (1955, 1877)
Majestic Prince (1988, 1966)
Man o' War (1957, 1917)
Maskette (2001, 1906)
Miesque (1999, 1984)
Miss Woodford (1967, 1880)
Myrtlewood (1979, 1932)
Nashua (1965, 1952)
Native Dancer (1963, 1950)
Native Diver (1978, 1959)
Needles (2000, 1953)
Neji (1966, 1950)
*Noor (2002, 1945)
Northern Dancer (1976, 1961)
Oedipus (1978, 1946)
Old Rosebud (1968, 1911)
Omaha (1965, 1932)
Pan Zareta (1972, 1910)
Parole (1984, 1873)
Paseana (Arg) (2001, 1987)
Personal Ensign (1993, 1984)
Peter Pan (1956, 1904)
Princess Doreen (1982, 1921)
Princess Rooney (1991, 1980)

Real Delight (1987, 1949)
Regret (1957, 1912)
Reigh Count (1978, 1925)
Riva Ridge (1998, 1969)
Roamer (1981, 1911)
Roseben (1956, 1901)
Round Table (1972, 1954)
Ruffian (1976, 1972)
Ruthless (1975, 1864)
Salvator (1955, 1886)
Sarazen (1957, 1921)
Seabiscuit (1958, 1933)
Searching (1978, 1952)
Seattle Slew (1981, 1974)
Secretariat (1974, 1970)
Serena's Song (2002, 1992)
Shuvee (1975, 1966)
Silver Spoon (1978, 1956)
Sir Archy (1955, 1805)
Sir Barton (1957, 1916)
Slew o' Gold (1992, 1980)
Spectacular Bid (1982, 1976)
Stymie (1975, 1941)
Sun Beau (1996, 1925)
Sunday Silence (1996, 1986)
Susan's Girl (1976, 1969)
Swaps (1966, 1952)
Sword Dancer (1977, 1956)
Sysonby (1956, 1902)
Ta Wee (1994, 1966)
Ten Broeck (1982, 1872)
Tim Tam (1985, 1955)
Tom Fool (1960, 1949)
Top Flight (1966, 1929)
Tosmah (1984, 1961)
Twenty Grand (1957, 1928)
Twilight Tear (1963, 1941)
Two Lea (1982, 1946)
War Admiral (1958, 1934)
Whirlaway (1959, 1938)
Whisk Broom II (1979, 1907)
Winning Colors (2000, 1985)
Zaccio (1990, 1976)
Zev (1983, 1920)

TRIPLE CROWN
History of the Triple Crown

As with other great sporting events such as the Olympics and the World Series, the Triple Crown has a rich tradition and history. While modern memory places the Triple Crown in a fixed format—the Kentucky Derby (G1) on the first Saturday in May, the Preakness Stakes (G1) two weeks later, and the Belmont Stakes (G1) three weeks after the Preakness—the series has undergone changes ranging from subtle to seismic in its history.

Origins

The Triple Crown did not start with the inauguration of the three races—the Belmont in 1867, the Preakness six years later, and the Derby in 1875. Of the three races, only the Derby has been run continuously, with gaps in the history of the Preakness (1891-'93) and the Belmont (1911 and '12, when antigambling legislation shut down New York racing). In some years, the Derby and Preakness were run within days of each other, and in two years (1917 and '22) they were run on the same day. In some years, the Preakness was run before the Derby.

Far from being one of the three most-prestigious races for American three-year-olds, the Derby in the early 20th century was a struggling regional race. Only the marketing and showmanship genius of Churchill track executive Col. Matt J. Winn elevated the race to national and international prominence during the first quarter of the century.

When Sir Barton became the first Triple Crown winner in 1919, he was not recognized as a Triple Crown winner, just as a fast-developing three-year-old who went from maiden to multiple major stakes winner within two months.

In fact, the origin of the term "Triple Crown" (which had been in use in England for decades) has been disputed for many years. For decades, credit for coining the expression generally was accorded to legendary *Daily Racing Form* columnist Charlie Hatton. While Hatton's stature and repeated use of the term closely associated him with the Triple Crown, the phrase arguably was first put in print by New York *Times* writer Bryan Field, who used the expression in 1930 after Gallant Fox won the Belmont.

The Triple Crown has been characterized by clusters of winners, especially in the 1930s, '40s, and '70s, and long droughts in between. After Gallant Fox won the 1930 Triple Crown for owner-breeder Belair Stud, only five years passed before Gallant Fox's son Omaha won for Belair. Two

Triple Crown television ratings and share

Year	Kentucky Derby Rating	Kentucky Derby Share	Preakness Stakes Rating	Preakness Stakes Share	Belmont Stakes Rating	Belmont Stakes Share
2002	7.1	18	5.7	14	7.6	21
2001	8.1	21	5.6	16	4.5	13
2000	5.8	17	3.6	10	2.8	9
1999	6.3	19	3.4	10	6.0	17
1998	6.1	18	3.6	11	5.9	18
1997	7.1	19	4.8	14	5.3	16
1996	7.4	21	3.7	11	2.9	9
1995	6.0	17	3.2	10	3.5	11
1994	7.5	21	4.4	14	3.9	12
1993	7.3	22	4.7	15	4.2	11

Each rating point represents approximately one-million homes; share is the percentage of televisions tuned to that program.

years later in 1937, Man o' War's son War Admiral took the Triple Crown for Samuel D. Riddle's Glen Riddle Farm.

The Triple Crown sweep was achieved four times in the 1940s. First, Calumet Farm and jockey Eddie Arcaro won in 1941 with Whirlaway, and Mrs. John D. Hertz's Count Fleet rolled to victory two years later with Johnny Longden in the saddle. In 1946, King Ranch's homebred Assault scored the triple, and two years later Arcaro and Calumet collected their second Triple Crown sweep with Citation.

In 1950, the Thoroughbred Racing Associations formally recognized the three-race series as the Triple Crown and commissioned Cartier to craft a three-sided trophy, one side for each race. The trophy would be in storage many years before Secretariat breezed to a Triple Crown victory in 1973, the first sweep in a quarter-century. Four years later, the brilliant Seattle Slew became the first to win the series without a defeat on his record. In 1978, the first back-to-back Triple Crown sweep occurred when Affirmed defeated Alydar in three classic battles. Harbor View Farm's Affirmed would be the last Triple Crown winner of the 20th century as another long drought took hold.

Modern Triple Crown

The perception that the Triple Crown's prestige made it an irresistible goal for the connections of leading three-year-olds was shaken twice in the 1980s. Gato Del Sol won the 1982 Derby, but trainer Edwin Gregson, speaking for owners-breeders Arthur Hancock III and Leone J. Peters,

declined to run in the Preakness. Well aware that Gato Del Sol was unsuited to a speed-favoring Pimlico Race Course track for the Preakness, Gregson and his owners awaited the Belmont, in which Gato Del Sol finished a distant second to Conquistador Cielo.

Dennis Diaz's speedy Spend a Buck crushed his competition in the 1985 Derby, but Diaz turned his back on the Preakness and Belmont, opting for the $1-million Jersey Derby (G3) at newly rebuilt Garden State Park. Spend a Buck had won two Derby prep races at the New Jersey track, making him eligible for a $2-million bonus if he swept the track's three races for three-year-olds and the Kentucky Derby. Diaz was courted by Garden State officials, and two factors led to Spend a Buck running in the Jersey Derby. First, a serious question arose over Spend a Buck's ability to stay the Belmont's 1½ miles after a rigorous spring campaign. The money also was a factor. Spend a Buck ran for (and collected) $2.6-million in purse and bonus in the Jersey Derby. The winner's purses for that year's Triple Crown raced totaled $1,137,740.

The Spend a Buck affair, wrought with acrimony and recrimination, led to a positive event—the creation of Triple Crown Productions late in 1985 to market the three races as a single, unified entity and to offer $5-million to a Triple Crown winner. Triple Crown Productions began operations in early 1986.

Through the remainder of the 20th century, five horses came within one race of winning the Triple Crown but none collected the $5-million—first offered as purse and bonus and exclusively as a bonus beginning in 1998. Alysheba won the first two legs in 1987 but was a distant fourth to Bet Twice in the Belmont. Sunday Silence won two spirited battles with Easy Goer in 1989 and finished a well-beaten second to his nemesis in the Belmont. The Triple Crown bids of the 1990s occurred in three consecutive years, 1997-'99. In 1997, Derby and Preakness winner Silver Charm could not repel the late charge of Touch Gold in the Belmont. The following year, Real Quiet appeared to have the Belmont won but fell by a nose in the last stride to Victory Gallop. Charismatic, the 1999 Derby and Preakness winner, finished third by less than two lengths despite sustaining a leg fracture in the Belmont's late stages. And, the start of the 21st century brought another reminder of how tough it is to win the Triple Crown. War Emblem won the first two legs in 2002, only to finish a well-beaten eighth in the Belmont.—*John Harrell*

Triple Crown Productions

Charged with marketing the Kentucky Derby (G1), Preakness Stakes (G1), and Belmont Stakes (G1), Triple Crown Productions was created at a time of turmoil within the industry and especially at the three tracks that stage the races. Threatened with a hostile takeover, Churchill Downs Inc. reorganized in 1984 and hired Thomas Meeker, a lawyer, as its president. The following year, Garden State Park opened and lured the Derby winner, Spend a Buck, off the Triple Crown trail to the Jersey Derby (G3) with a $2-million bonus. Robert E. Brennan, then Garden State's chairman, spoke of the Jersey Derby taking the place of the Preakness at Pimlico Race Course in the Triple Crown. The New York Racing Association also was mired in internal turmoil.

Incorporated in September 1985, Triple Crown Productions opened its office at Churchill Downs in January '86 with Audrey R. Korotkin as its first executive director. In addition to its marketing function, Triple Crown Productions inaugurated a common nomination form and fees for the races, with early nominations of $600 each closing in mid-January and late nominations, originally $3,000 and now $6,000, closing three weeks before the Derby. Previously, each track obtained nominations for its own races. Supplemental entries ($150,000 for the Derby and $100,000 for the Preakness and Belmont) were permitted beginning in 1990.

In 1987, the company offered the first Triple Crown Challenge—$5-million in purse money and bonuses to a Triple Crown winner and a $1-million bonus to the horse with the best overall performances in all three races. Triple Crown Productions financed the first bonus year (Bet Twice collected $1-million after he finished second

Nominations Since Unified Under Triple Crown Productions

Year	Early	Late	Total	Total Fees	Each Track's Share
2002	405	12	417	$315,000	$105,000
2001	440	7	447	306,000	102,000
2000	387	13	400	310,200	103,400
1999	396	11	407	303,600	101,200
1998	384	6	390	266,800	88,933
1997	375	13	388	303,000	101,000
1996	354	7	361	254,800	84,800
1995	317	7	324	232,400	77,400
1994	354	9	363	266,400	88,800
1993	342	25	367	317,700	105,900
1992	389	18	407	314,400	104,800
1991	369	8	377	257,400	85,800
1990	315	33	348	282,000	94,000
1989	381	13	394	267,600	89,200
1988	381	20	401	288,600	96,200
1987	398	24	422	310,800	103,600
1986	422	30	452	343,200	144,400

Early nomination fee has been $600 since 1986; late nomination fee: 1986-'90, $3,000; 1991-'93, $4,500; 1994-present, $6,000.

to Alysheba in the Derby and Preakness and won the Belmont). In September 1987, the company announced that Chrysler Corp. would become the sponsor of the bonus beginning in '88.

Meeker, chairman of Triple Crown Productions, eliminated the executive director position in August 1989, but media attention the following winter led to the hiring of Edward Seigenfeld, a former NYRA marketing vice president, as the organization's executive director. Seigenfeld was given the title of executive vice president in 1996. In 1993, the $1-million bonus for the best overall finish was eliminated.

Chrysler bowed out as the Triple Crown Challenge sponsor after 1995 and was replaced by Visa USA, the credit-card marketing company. Beginning in 1998, a Triple Crown sweep would earn a $5-million bonus in addition to purse earnings from the three races. In 1999, Visa extended its sponsorship through 2005.

Triple Crown Productions board of directors (on June 1, 2002): Representing Churchill Downs, Thomas H. Meeker (TCP president), Arthur B. Modell; representing the Maryland Jockey Club, Joseph A. De Francis (TCP vice president-treasurer), Martin Jacobs; representing the New York Racing Association, Barry K. Schwartz, Terence J. Meyocks (TCP vice president-secretary).

The $5-Million Visa Triple Crown Challenge

Triple Crown Productions LLC will pay a bonus of $5-million to the owner of any horse that is declared the official winner of all three races in 2002. The bonus will be paid in accordance with the rules of the Visa Triple Crown Challenge Bonus.

Triple Crown Productions will present the Triple Crown trophy to the owner of any horse that sweeps the Kentucky Derby, Preakness Stakes, and Belmont Stakes.

No horse has won the Triple Crown since the bonus has been offered.

From 1987 through '93, a $1-million bonus was offered to the horse that compiled the most points who raced in all three Triple Crown events.

Points were assigned on the following basis for finishing each Triple Crown race: 10 for first, 5 for second, 3 for third, and 1 for fourth.

A $1-million bonus has been awarded to horses who compiled the most points in the Triple Crown races.

The bonus winners were:

1987—Bet Twice, second in the Kentucky Derby and Preakness Stakes, first in Belmont Stakes, with earnings of $1,499,160.

1988—Risen Star, third in the Kentucky Derby and first in the Preakness and Belmont, with earnings of $1,767,420.

1989—Sunday Silence, first in the Kentucky Derby and Preakness and second in the Belmont, with earnings of $2,164,054.

1990—Unbridled, first in the Kentucky Derby, second in the Preakness, and fourth in the Belmont, with earnings of $1,759,360.

1991—Hansel, tenth in the Kentucky Derby and first in the Preakness and Belmont, with earnings of $1,850,250.

1992—Pine Bluff, fifth in the Kentucky Derby, first in the Preakness, and third in the Belmont, with earnings of $1,575,896.

1993—Sea Hero, first in the Kentucky Derby, fifth in the Preakness, and seventh in the Belmont, with earnings of $1,000,000.

Triple Crown Race Conditions

(Note: All conditions below are based on 2002 conditions and are subject to change.)

First deadline: January 18, 2003, $600
Second closing: March 29, 2003, $6,000

Nominations to each and all of the Triple Crown races, the Kentucky Derby, the Preakness Stakes, and the Belmont Stakes (the "races"), may be made by payment of a single nomination fee to Triple Crown Productions LLC as agent for Churchill Downs Inc., the Maryland Jockey Club of Baltimore City Inc., and the New York Racing Association Inc. (the "association" or "associations" as the case may be). The nomination fee for nominations postmarked or hand delivered by January 18, 2003, is $600 and for nominations postmarked or hand delivered from January 19 through March 29, 2003, is $6,000. Horses nominated on or before March 29, 2003, shall be considered original nominees ("original nominees").

At any time prior to the closing for the Kentucky Derby, as defined below, additional nominations to all three races may be made and the nominee will be eligible for the Visa Triple Crown Challenge Bonus upon payment of a supplementary fee of $150,000 to Churchill Downs Inc.

Following the running of the Kentucky Derby, horses may be nominated at any time prior to closing for the Preakness Stakes or the Belmont Stakes (time of closing being defined below) but will not be eligible for the Visa Triple Crown Challenge Bonus. The supplementary fee payable for such nomination shall be $100,000 payable to the Maryland Jockey Club of Baltimore City Inc. for supplemental nomination to the Preakness Stakes and the Belmont Stakes or $100,000 payable to New York Racing Association Inc. for supplemental nomination to the Belmont Stakes only.

All supplemental fees will be included in the purse distribution for the race run by the association to which the supplemental nomination is paid, unless otherwise specified in the specific race rules below.

The ability of horses nominated by payment of the foregoing supplementary fees ("supplemental nominees") to enter any race will be determined in accordance with the conditions of that race. All nominees, original, supplemental, or otherwise, will be required to pay entry and starting fees for the race or races in which they participate before they may start.

Triple Crown Productions LLC will pay a bonus of $5-million to the owner of any horse that is declared the official winner of all the races in 2003. The bonus will be paid in accordance with the official rules of the Visa Triple Crown Challenge Bonus, which are incorporated herein by reference.

129th running of Kentucky Derby (G1)
$1-million guaranteed minimum gross
to be run on Saturday, May 3, 2003
One mile and a quarter

For three-year-olds with an entry fee of $15,000 each and a starting fee of $15,000 each. Supplemental nominations may be made upon payment of $150,000 and in accordance with the rules set forth.

All fees, including supplemental nominations in excess of $500,000 in the aggregate, shall be paid to the winner. Churchill Downs Inc. shall guarantee a minimum gross purse of $1-million (the "guaranteed purse").

The winner shall receive $700,000, second place shall receive $170,000, third place shall receive $85,000, and fourth place shall receive $45,000 from the guaranteed purse (the guaranteed purse to each place to be divided equally in the event of a dead heat).

Starters shall be named through the entry box on Wednesday, April 30, 2003, at 10 a.m. EDT (the "closing"). The maximum number of starters shall be limited to 20. Colts and geldings shall each carry a weight of 126 pounds; fillies shall each carry 121 pounds. Supplemental nominees will be allowed to enter but will not have preference over any original nominee and will not be allowed to start the race if the maximum number of starters has otherwise been reached by original nominees prior to the closing.

If the number of nominees exceeds the number of available starting positions at the closing, these conditions shall be applied to determine which nominees will be allowed to start. In the event that more than 20 entries pass through the entry box at the closing, the starters shall be determined at the closing from original nominees first, then supplemental nominees if starting positions are still available with preference given to those horses that have accumulated the highest earnings in graded stakes races, including all money actually paid for performance in such graded stakes races. For purposes of this preference, the graded status of each race shall be the graded status assigned to the race by the International Cataloguing Standards Committee in Part I of the International Cataloguing Standards as published by the Jockey Club Information Systems Inc. each year.

Should additional starters be needed to bring the field to 20, the remaining starters shall be determined at the closing with preference given to those horses that have accumulated the highest earnings in nonrestricted sweepstakes. For purposes of this preference, a "nonrestricted sweepstakes" shall mean those sweepstakes whose conditions contain no restrictions other than that of age or sex.

In the case of ties resulting from preferences or otherwise, the additional starter(s) shall be determined by lot.

Any horse excluded from running because of the aforementioned preference(s) shall be refunded the $15,000 entry fee and the $150,000 fee, if applicable. An "also-eligible" list will not be maintained and in no event will starters be added or allowed to run in the race, which are not determined to be starters at the closing.

Post position shall be determined as follows: A nontransferable lot number shall be drawn for each horse named as a starter at the closing. The lot number drawn for each starter shall determine the numerical order for selection of post position. Selection of post position shall be made by each owner of a horse (or, if more than one, the owners collectively) or the authorized agent of the horse's owner(s).

Horses having common ties through ownership or training shall each be treated separately for purposes of selecting post position.

Detailed rules governing the post position draw process are available from the racing secretary's office and will be distributed prior to the closing. These rules shall control.

The owner of the winner of the race shall receive a gold trophy.

128th running of Preakness Stakes (G1)
$1-million guaranteed minimum gross
to be run on Saturday, May 17, 2003
One mile and three-sixteenths

For three-year-olds, $10,000 to pass the entry box, starters to pay $10,000 additional. Supplemental nominations may be made in accordance with the rules, upon payment of $100,000, 65% of the purse to the winner, 20% to second, 10% to third, and 5% to fourth. Weight is 126 pounds for colts and geldings, 121 pounds for fillies.

Starters to be named through the entry box on Wednesday, May 14, 2003, three days before the race by the usual time of closing (the "closing").

The Preakness field will be limited to 14 entries and shall be determined on the Wednesday immediately preceding the day of the race.

In the event that more than 14 horses are properly nominated and pass through the entry box by the usual time of closing, the starters will be determined at the closing with 50% of the field (seven starters) given preference by accumulating the highest earnings in graded stakes (lifetime), including all money paid for performance in such graded stakes.

The next four starters (approximately 30%) will be determined by accumulating the highest earnings (lifetime) in all races except restricted stakes (i.e., any stakes containing eligibility conditions other than sex and age).

The remaining three starters (approximately 20%) shall be determined by accumulating the highest earnings (lifetime) in all races.

Should this preference produce any ties, the additional starter(s) shall be determined by lot.

For purposes of this preference, the graded status of each race shall be the graded status assigned to the race by the International Cataloguing Standards Committee in Part I of the International Cataloguing Standards as published by the Jockey Club Information Systems Inc. each year.

In application of the above described rule, each horse will be separately considered without regard to identity of its owner.

If the rules described in this paragraph result in the exclusion of any horse, the $10,000 entry fee previously paid will be refunded to the owner of said horse. The above conditions notwithstanding, no horse that earns purse money in the Kentucky Derby shall be denied the opportunity to enter and start in the Preakness Stakes.

Post position shall be determined as follows: A nontransferable lot number shall be drawn for each horse named as a starter at the closing. The lot number drawn for each starter shall determine the numerical order for selection of post position. Selection of post position shall be made by each owner of a horse (or, if more than one, the owners collectively) or the authorized agent of the horse's owner(s).

Horses having common ties through ownership or training shall each be treated separately for purposes of selecting post position.

Detailed rules governing the post position draw process will be distributed prior to the closing. These rules shall control.

A replica of the Woodlawn Vase will be presented to the winning owner to remain his or her personal property.

135th running of Belmont Stakes (G1)
$1-million gross
to be run on Saturday, June 7, 2003
One mile and a half

For three-year-olds with an entry fee of $10,000 to pass the entry box and $10,000 additional to start. Supplemental nominations may be made in accordance with the rules set forth above, upon payment of $100,000. The purse to be divided 60% to the winner, 20% to second, 11% to third, 6% to fourth, and 3% to fifth. Colts and geldings, 126 pounds;

fillies, 121 pounds.

Starters to be named through the entry box on Wednesday, June 4, 2003, three days before the race by the usual time of closing (the "closing"). The Belmont field will be limited to 16 starters.

In the event that more than 16 entries pass through the entry box on Wednesday, June 4, 2003, at the closing (the "closing"), the starters will be determined at the closing with 50% of the field (eight starters) given preference by accumulating the highest earnings in graded stakes (lifetime), including all money paid for performance in such graded stakes.

The next five starters (approximately 30%) will be determined by accumulating the highest earnings (lifetime) in all races except restricted stakes (i.e., any stakes containing eligibility conditions others than sex and age).

The remaining three starters (approximately 20%) shall be determined by accumulating the highest earnings (lifetime) in all races.

Should this preference produce any ties, the additional starter(s) shall be determined by lot. If the rules described result in the exclusion of any horse, the $10,000 entry fee will be refunded to the owner of said horse.

The above conditions notwithstanding, any horse that earns purse money in either the Kentucky Derby or the Preakness Stakes shall be included in the initial eight starters in the Belmont Stakes. These rules shall control.

The winning owner will be presented with the August Belmont Memorial Cup, to be retained for one year, as well as a trophy for permanent possession and trophies will be presented to the winning trainer and jockey.

Road to the Triple Crown

The following races are traditionally used as preps for the Triple Crown races. The table includes the dates and winners of the races in 2002.

Date	Race	Track	Distance	Time	First Three Finishers
1/1	Tropical Park Derby-G3	Crc	1⅛m	1:51.71	**POLITICAL ATTACK**, The Judge Sez Who, **Deeliteful Guy**
1/3	Spectacular Bid S.-G3	GP	6f	1:12.19	**MAYBRY'S BOY**, **Showmeitall**, Harmony Hall
1/5	Count Fleet S.	Aqu	1m70yd	1:41.67	POTOSI, **D' Coach**, No Parole
1/12	Golden Gate Derby-G3	GG	1 1/16m	1:43.87	**DANTHEBLUEGRASSMAN**, **Cappuchino**, U S S Tinosa
1/13	San Miguel S.-G3	SA	6f	1:09.00	**POPULAR**, Roman Dancer, **Royal Moro**
1/19	Holy Bull S.-G3	GP	1 1/16m	1:46.16	**BOOKLET**, **Harlan's Holiday**, Thiscannonsloaded
1/19	Santa Catalina S.-G2	SA	1 1/16m	1:42.50	**LABAMTA BABE**, **Siphonic**, Cascade Cowboy
1/26	Lecomte H.	FG	1m	1:37.98	**EASYFROMTHEGITGO**, Sky Terrace, **It'sallinthechase**
2/2	Hutcheson S.-G2	GP	7f	1:26.07	**SHOWMEITALL**, **Monthir**, Royal Lad
2/2	San Vicente S.-G2	SA	7f	1:21.92	**CAME HOME**, **Jack's Silver**, **Werblin**
2/9	Whirlaway S.	Aqu	1 1/16m	1:44.93	**SARATOGA BLUES**, **Smoked Em**, **D' Coach**
2/10	Golden State Mile S.	GG	1m	1:35.57	**CAPPUCHINO**, Yougottawanna, **Arsen**
2/16	Fountain of Youth S.-G1	GP	1 1/16m	1:44.49	**BOOKLET**, **Harlan's Holiday**, **Blue Burner**
2/17	Risen Star S.-G3	FG	1 1/16m	1:43.17	**REPENT**, **Bob's Image**, **Easyfromthegitgo**
2/22	Palm Beach S.-G3	GP	1⅛mT	1:49.80	ORCHARD PARK, Lord Juban, Red's Top Gun
2/23	Best Turn S.	Aqu	6f	1:10.76	**SMOOTH JAZZ**, **Tank's Expectation**, President Butler
2/24	Baldwin S.-G3	SA	abt6½fT	1:13.30	SHUFFLING KID (GB), Red Briar (Ire), Dark Sorceror (GB)
3/2	San Rafael S.-G2	SA	1m	1:36.24	**CAME HOME**, **Easy Grades**, **Werblin**
3/2	Southwest S. (Div. 1)	OP	1m	1:40.29	**PRIVATE EMBLEM**, Dusty Spike, **Clergy**
3/2	Southwest S. (Div. 2)	OP	1m	1:41.70	PALOMA PARILLA, Cope With an Image, **Windward Passage**
3/2	John Battaglia Memorial S.	TP	1 1/16m	1:43.08	**REQUEST FOR PAROLE**, **Perfect Drift**, Thunder On Land
3/9	El Camino Real Derby-G3	GG	1 1/16m	1:43.48	**YOUGOTTAWANNA**, **Danthebluegrassman**, **Lusty Latin**
3/10	Louisiana Derby-G2	FG	1 1/16m	1:43.86	**REPENT**, **Easyfromthegitgo**, **It'sallinthechase**
3/16	Florida Derby-G1	GP	1⅛m	1:48.80	**HARLAN'S HOLIDAY**, **Blue Burner**, **Peekskill**
3/16	Swale S.-G3	GP	7f	1:22.29	**ETHAN MAN**, **Listen Here**, **Governor Hickel**
3/17	San Felipe S.-G2	SA	1 1/16m	1:41.95	**MEDAGLIA D'ORO**, U S S Tinosa, **Siphonic**
3/17	Gotham S.-G3	Aqu	1m	1:34.90	**MAYAKOVSKY**, **Saarland**, Parade of Music
3/17	Tampa Bay Derby	Tam	1 1/16m	1:43.66	**EQUALITY**, **Tails of the Crypt**, **Political Attack**
3/23	Lane's End Spiral S.-G2	TP	1⅛m	1:36.66	**PERFECT DRIFT**, **Azillion (Ire)**, **Request for Parole**
3/23	Rebel S.-G3	OP	1 1/16m	1:45.06	**WINDWARD PASSAGE**, **Ocean Sound (Ire)**, Dusty Spike
3/23	San Pedro S.	SA	6½f	1:16.36	ROMAN DANCER, **Werblin**, **Saturday Hero**
4/6	Santa Anita Derby-G1	SA	1⅛m	1:50.02	**CAME HOME**, **Easy Grades**, **Lusty Latin**
4/6	Illinois Derby-G2	Spt	1⅛m	1:49.92	**WAR EMBLEM**, **Repent**, **Fonz's**
4/7	Lafayette S.-G3	Kee	7f	1:24.47	**CASHEL CASTLE**, **Governor Hickel**, Sky Terrace
4/13	Blue Grass S.-G1	Kee	1⅛m	1:51.51	**HARLAN'S HOLIDAY**, **Booklet**, **Ocean Sound (Ire)**
4/13	Arkansas Derby-G2	OP	1⅛m	1:50.20	**PRIVATE EMBLEM**, **Wild Horses**, **Windward Passage** (DH), Bay Monster (DH)
4/13	Wood Memorial S.-G1	Aqu	1⅛m	1:48.61	**BUDDHA**, **Medgalia d'Oro**, **Sunday Break (Jpn)**
4/13	Bay Shore S.-G3	Aqu	7f	1:22.21	ROMAN DANCER, **Warners**, **Monthir**
4/17	Forerunner S.	Kee	1⅛mT	1:49.15	**RED MASQUE**, No More Chads, **Royal Gem**
4/20	Coolmore Lexington S.-G2	Kee	1 1/16m	1:44.58	**PROUD CITIZEN**, **Crimson Hero**, **Easyfromthegitgo**
4/20	Federico Tesio S.	Pim	1⅛m	1:50.33	**SMOKED EM**, **Magic Weisner**, Heir D' Twine
4/27	Derby Trial-G3	CD	1m	1:36.87	**SKY TERRACE**, **Cashel Castle**, Ide Be Spencers
5/4	Kentucky Derby-G1	CD	1¼m	2:01.13	**WAR EMBLEM**, **Proud Citizen**, **Perfect Drift**
5/11	Lone Star Derby-G3	LS	1⅛m	1:49.92	**WISEMAN'S FERRY**, **Tracemark**, **Peekskill**
5/18	Preakness S.-G1	Pim	1 3/16m	1:56.36	**WAR EMBLEM**, **Magic Weisner**, **Proud Citizen**
6/8	Belmont S.-G1	Bel	1½m	2:29.21	**SARAVA**, **Medaglia d'Oro**, **Sunday Break (Jpn)**

Horses in bold face were Triple Crown nominees

Triple Crown Winners

America's Triple Crown Winners

Year	Horse	Owner	Trainer	Jockey
1919	Sir Barton	J. K. L. Ross	H. Guy Bedwell	John Loftus
1930	Gallant Fox	Belair Stud	James Fitzsimmons	Earle Sande
1935	Omaha	Belair Stud	James Fitzsimmons	William Saunders
1937	War Admiral	Samuel D. Riddle	George Conway	Charles Kurtsinger
1941	Whirlaway	Calumet Farm	Ben A. Jones	Eddie Arcaro
1943	Count Fleet	Mrs. John D. Hertz	Don Cameron	John Longden
1946	Assault	King Ranch	Max Hirsch	Warren Mehrtens
1948	Citation	Calumet Farm	H. A. (Jimmy) Jones	Eddie Arcaro
1973	Secretariat	Meadow Stable	Lucien Laurin	Ron Turcotte
1977	Seattle Slew	Karen L. Taylor	William Turner Jr.	Jean Cruguet
1978	Affirmed	Harbor View Farm	Lazaro Barrera	Steve Cauthen

Triple Crown Trophy

The Triple Crown trophy was commissioned in 1950 by the Thoroughbred Racing Associations, which copyrighted the term Triple Crown, and has three sides to symbolize the three races in the series. The trophy was presented retroactively to the eight previous winners of the three races.

The first three-year-old with a chance to claim the silver Triple Crown trophy was Tim Tam, who won the 1958 Kentucky Derby and Preakness Stakes but finished second to *Cavan in the Belmont Stakes. Secretariat in 1973 was the first horse to be presented the trophy after sweeping the three races.

Sir Barton

At the start of 1919, Sir Barton was far down the pecking order in trainer H. Guy Bedwell's stable. Commander J. K. L. Ross had purchased the *Star Shoot colt at Saratoga for $10,000 in 1918, but Sir Barton was winless in his six starts as a two-year-old and made his three-year-old debut in the '19 Kentucky Derby. His role in the Derby on May 10, 1919, was to serve as a pacemaker for his highly fancied stablemate, Billy Kelly. They went off at 2.60-to-1, second choice behind the 2.10-to-1 entry of Sailor and Eternal. Ridden by Johnny Loftus, Sir Barton bucked the odds, leading all the way and winning the Derby by five lengths over his stablemate. He immediately shipped to Baltimore and won the Preakness Stakes on May 14 (a Wednesday) by four lengths over Eternal as the 7-to-5 favorite. In the Belmont Stakes on June 11, Sir Barton was 2-to-5 against the entry of Sweep On, third in the Preakness, and Natural Bridge. Sir Barton allowed Natural Bridge to set the pace for three-quarters of a mile before taking the lead and winning by five lengths. Between his Preakness and Belmont victories, Sir Barton won the Withers Stakes.

Sir Barton's achievement was unprecedented, but he was overshadowed by the appearance of Man o' War, who sustained the only defeat of his career in that year's Sanford Memorial Stakes at Saratoga Race Course.

Ch. c., 1916, by *Star Shoot— Lady Sterling, by Hanover

Owner: Commander J. K. L. Ross
Breeders: Madden and Gooch (Ky.)
Trainer: H. Guy Bedwell
Jockey: Johnny Loftus

		Race record			
Year	Starts	1st	2nd	3rd	Earnings
1918	6	0	1 (1)	0	$ 4,113
1919	13	8 (8)	3 (2)	2 (1)	88,250
1920	12	5 (5)	2 (2)	3 (3)	24,494
	31	13 (13)	6 (5)	5 (4)	$116,857

1919—1st Kentucky Derby, Preakness Stakes, Belmont Stakes, Withers Stakes, Potomac Handicap, etc.
1920—1st Saratoga Handicap, Merchants' and Citizens' Handicap, Dominion Handicap, etc.

As a four-year-old in 1920, Sir Barton alternated between the brilliant and the ordinary, winning five of 12 starts but finishing off the board twice. Because of his chronically sore feet and difficult temperament, he lost several races that he should have won against overmatched opponents.

After losing a match race to Man o' War, Sir Barton faded from view. Retired to stud at the end of the 1920 season, he enjoyed only moderate success, was sold to the United States Cavalry Remount Station, and lived on a Wyoming ranch until his death in 1937.

Gallant Fox

Bred and owned by Belair Stud of William Woodward, Gallant Fox marked a shift in the standards of American breeding. The introduction of *Sir Gallahad III to the United States from France in the late 1920s represented an important step forward for the American breeding industry. For the next several decades, American breeders went to Europe for proven stallions or prospects, particularly in England. The result was a significant increase in the quality of American racehorses. Woodward was one of the syndicate members involved in the purchase of *Sir Gallahad III, who stood at Claiborne Farm.

Gallant Fox was a good but not outstanding two-year-old, winning the Flash and Junior Champion Stakes and placing in two other stakes in his seven starts in 1929. In the care of trainer James "Sunny Jim" Fitzsimmons, Gallant Fox developed into an imposing physical specimen at three.

A four-length winner in Aqueduct's 1930 Wood Memorial Stakes, Gallant Fox hurtled through the Triple Crown, winning the Preakness on May 9 by three-quarters of a length, the Kentucky Derby eight days later by two lengths, and the Belmont on June 7 by three lengths over Whichone, his leading rival.

B. c., 1927, by *Sir Gallahad III— Marguerite, by Celt

Owner-breeder: Belair Stud (Ky.)
Trainer: James Fitzsimmons
Jockey: Earl Sande

Year	Starts	Race record			Earnings
		1st	2nd	3rd	
1929	7	2 (2)	2 (1)	2 (2)	$ 19,890
1930	10	9 (9)	1 (1)	0	308,275
	17	11 (11)	3 (2)	2 (2)	$328,165

1929—1st Flash Stakes, Junior Champion Stakes
1930—1st Kentucky Derby, Preakness Stakes, Belmont Stakes, Classic Stakes, Saratoga Cup, etc.

Three weeks later, Gallant Fox added the Dwyer Stakes to his list of triumphs.

His only loss of the year occurred in the Travers Stakes at Saratoga, where he ran second to 100-to-1 longshot Jim Dandy.

At the end of the year, Gallant Fox was retired to stud at Claiborne, where he sired 1935 Triple Crown winner Omaha and '36 Belmont Stakes winner Granville. Gallant Fox died on November 13, 1954, and was buried at Claiborne alongside his sire and dam.

Omaha

Five years after his Gallant Fox became the second Triple Crown winner, William Woodward saw his decision to participate in the syndication of French runner *Sir Gallahad III for stud duties in the United States pay off with a second Triple Crown winner. Omaha, a son of Gallant Fox and grandson of *Sir Gallahad III, won nine of 22 starts, but his career did not measure up to that of his sire. At two, he won only once in nine starts, although he finished second in the Sanford and Champagne Stakes.

Once again, trainer James "Sunny Jim" Fitzsimmons's patient hand allowed the chestnut colt to fill out nicely over the winter between his two- and three-year-old years. On May 4, 1935, Omaha stepped onto an off track at Churchill Downs as the 4-to-1 second choice for the Kentucky Derby (favored at 3.80-to-1 was the filly Nellie Flag). Omaha made his move for the lead on the far turn, led by two lengths at the top of the stretch, and won by a relatively easy 1½ lengths over Roman Soldier.

One week later, Omaha was a runaway, six-length winner of the Preakness Stakes over Firethorn, who had skipped the Derby. Despite losing two weeks later in the Withers Stakes, Omaha won the Belmont Stakes by 1½ lengths

---

Ch. c., 1932, by Gallant Fox— Flambino, by *Wrack

Owner-breeder: Belair Stud (Ky.)
Trainer: James Fitzsimmons
Jockey: Willie Saunders

Year	Starts	Race record			Earnings
		1st	2nd	3rd	
1934 (U.S.)	9	1	4 (3)	0	$ 3,850
1935 (U.S.)	9	6 (5)	1 (1)	2 (2)	142,255
1936 (Eng.)	4	2	2 (2)	0	8,650
	22	9 (5)	7 (6)	2 (2)	$154,705

1935—1st Kentucky Derby, Preakness Stakes, Belmont Stakes, Dwyer Stakes, Classic Stakes

---

on June 8. Omaha finished third in the Brooklyn Handicap in his next start but won his next two starts, the Dwyer Stakes and the Arlington Classic, before an injury ended his season.

As a four-year-old, Omaha was shipped to England and finished second in the Ascot Gold Cup. Omaha failed at stud, and Claiborne in 1943 sent him to a New York farm. Moved to a farm in Nebraska in 1950, Omaha died in 1959 and was buried at Ak-Sar-Ben racetrack in Omaha.

War Admiral

Glen Riddle Farms owner Samuel Riddle owned War Admiral's famous father, Man o' War, but chose to skip the Kentucky Derby with him in 1920. In Riddle's estimation, Churchill Downs was too far west, and the Derby was too early in the year for his comfort.

War Admiral, a striking brown colt out of the Sweep mare Brushup, had won three of six starts as a two-year-old, and his one stakes victory was in the minor Eastern Shore Handicap at Havre de Grace in Maryland. He returned to Havre de Grace for his first start of 1937 and won the Chesapeake Stakes. Riddle then decided to give War Admiral a shot at the Kentucky Derby.

Sent off as the 8-to-5 favorite in a Derby field of 20, War Admiral led at every point of call and easily held off two-year-old champion Pompoon in the final furlong to win by 1¾ lengths.

One week later, War Admiral was put to a much sterner test in the Preakness Stakes by Pompoon, who battled the Derby winner from the top of Pimlico Race Course's stretch. War Admiral won by a head. In the Belmont Stakes on June 5, War Admiral stumbled at the start, injuring his right foreleg, but the diminutive colt cruised to an easy, three-length victory over Sceneshifter.

Whirlaway

Prone to wild trips around the racetrack, Whirlaway could be a danger to himself and those around him, but he was worth the risk to train and run. In his three- and four-year-old seasons, he made 42 starts, won 25 times, finished second 13 times, and was third in his other four starts. Handled patiently by Racing Hall of Fame trainer Ben Jones, Whirlaway became the first of eight Kentucky Derby winners and two Triple Crown winners for Calumet Farm.

For the Derby on May 3, 1941, Jones fashioned a new blinker for Whirlaway, cutting away the left cup but leaving the right cup intact. He also made a riding change, with Eddie Arcaro replacing Wendall Eads. On Derby day, Whirlaway displayed his customary tendency to run near the back of the pack early. With a quarter-mile left, Whirlaway had moved up to fourth place and was flying. He exploded through a final quarter-mile, running it in :24, and won by eight lengths.

Despite walking out of the gate and trailing by more than nine lengths after a half-mile of the Preakness on May 10, Whirlaway again came on late and won by 5½ lengths. Nearly one month later in the Belmont Stakes, Whirlaway stunned his three rivals by taking off after a half-mile and opening up a seven-length lead

Br. c., 1934, by Man o' War—Brushup, by Sweep

Owner: Glen Riddle Farms
Breeder: Samuel Riddle (Ky.)
Trainer: George Conway
Jockey: Charles Kurtsinger

		Race record			
Year	Starts	1st	2nd	3rd	Earnings
1936	6	3 (1)	2 (2)	1 (1)	$ 14,800
1937	8	8 (6)	0	0	166,500
1938	11	9 (8)	1 (1)	0	90,840
1939	1	1	0	0	1,100
	26	21 (15)	3 (3)	1 (1)	$273,240

1936—1st Eastern Shore Handicap
1937—1st Kentucky Derby, Preakness Stakes, Belmont Stakes, Chesapeake Stakes, Pimlico Special, Washington Handicap
1938—1st Whitney Stakes, Jockey Club Gold Cup, Saratoga Handicap, etc.

Voted Horse of the Year and champion three-year-old, War Admiral lost a 1938 match race to Seabiscuit in the Pimlico Special.

At stud, War Admiral got 40 stakes winners and two champions in 320 starters, 12.5% of starters, in his 20-year stud career. He died in 1959.

Ch. c., 1938, by *Blenheim II—Dustwhirl, by Sweep

Owner-breeder: Calumet Farm (Ky.)
Trainer: Ben A. Jones
Jockey: Eddie Arcaro

		Race record			
Year	Starts	1st	2nd	3rd	Earnings
1940	16	7 (4)	2 (2)	4 (3)	$77,275
1941	20	13 (8)	5 (5)	2	272,386
1942	22	12 (10)	8 (6)	2 (2)	211,250
1943	2	0	0	1	250
	60	32 (22)	15 (13)	9 (5)	$561,161

1940—1st Saratoga Special, Hopeful Stakes, Breeders' Futurity
1941—1st Kentucky Derby, Preakness Stakes, Belmont Stakes, Travers Stakes, Lawrence Realization, etc.
1942—1st Brooklyn Handicap, Jockey Club Gold Cup, Massachusetts Handicap, etc.

after six furlongs. Despite entering the stretch a bit wide, he won by 2½ lengths to become the fifth Triple Crown winner.

The colt maintained his brilliance through 1942, when he was named Horse of the Year a second time.

Sold to French interests, Whirlaway died in southern Normandy on April 6, 1953.

Count Fleet

In 1927, Yellow Cab founder John D. Hertz watched a two-year-old race in which one of the runners reached out and bit another horse dueling with him for the lead. It was a remarkable display of aggression and a single-minded will to win. Hertz was sufficiently impressed to buy the colt, Reigh Count, who won the 1928 Kentucky Derby. Hertz never had much faith in Reigh Count as a stallion and bred him to only a few mares each year, including Quickly, who on March 24, 1940, gave birth to a gangly brown package named Count Fleet. The youngster was so clumsy and awkward that Hertz considered selling him as a yearling and again early in his two-year-old campaign. At two, Count Fleet won ten of 15 starts, was voted champion two-year-old male, and on the Experimental Free Handicap was accorded highweight of 132 pounds, still the highest weight ever assigned.

As a three-year-old, Count Fleet had no equal. He usually went to the lead early, discouraged his competition by the stretch, and won as he pleased.

In the Kentucky Derby on May 1, Count Fleet went off as the 2-to-5 favorite in the field of ten. He broke sharply under John Longden, went immediately to the lead, opened two lengths after

Br. c., 1940, by Reigh Count—Quickly, by Haste				
Owner-breeder: Mrs. John D. Hertz (Ky.)				
Trainer: Don Cameron				
Jockey: John Longden				

		Race record			
Year	Starts	1st	2nd	3rd	Earnings
1942	15	10 (4)	4 (2)	1 (1)	$ 76,245
1943	6	6 (5)	0	0	174,055
	21	16 (9)	4 (2)	1 (1)	$250,300

1942—1st Champagne Stakes, Pimlico Futurity, Walden Stakes, Wakefield Stakes
1943—1st Kentucky Derby, Preakness Stakes, Belmont Stakes, Wood Memorial Stakes, Withers Stakes

six furlongs, and won by an easy three lengths over Blue Swords. One week later, Count Fleet won the Preakness by eight lengths. In the Belmont Stakes on June 5, Count Fleet, 1-to-20, won by 25 lengths in 2:28⅕.

A seemingly minor injury to Count Fleet's left fore ankle refused to respond to treatment and ended his career. At stud, he sired champions Counterpoint and Kiss Me Kate as well as Count Turf, upset winner of the 1951 Kentucky Derby. Count Fleet died on December 3, 1973.

Assault

As a foal, Assault stepped on a surveyor's stake at King Ranch, which left him with a malformed right fore hoof. As a result, he was called the club-footed comet.

Trainer Max Hirsch initially was unsure that Assault could withstand training because of the foot injury, but the Bold Venture colt won two of nine starts at two in 1945. He went off at 8.20-to-1 in the Kentucky Derby on May 4, 1946. Assault, with jockey Warren Mehrtens up, blew past Spy Song and Knockdown early in the stretch and won by eight lengths.

One week later in the Preakness Stakes, Assault's Triple Crown dreams nearly ended. Mehrtens decided to go for the knockout punch and sent Assault after the leaders going into the far turn. Assault tired and staggered home, winning by a fast-diminishing neck over Lord Boswell.

When the Belmont Stakes came around on June 1, many racing fans believed the 1½ miles would expose Assault. Lord Boswell was sent off the 1.35-to-1 favorite, with Assault the second choice at 7-to-5. Mehrtens allowed Assault to reach contention gradually. Trailing Natchez by two lengths in midstretch, Assault exploded past him in the final 200 yards and won by three lengths.

Ch. c., 1943, by Bold Venture—Igual, by Equipoise				
Owner-breeder: King Ranch (Tx.)				
Trainer: Max Hirsch				
Jockey: Warren Mehrtens				

		Race record			
Year	Starts	1st	2nd	3rd	Earnings
1945	9	2 (1)	2	1 (1)	$ 17,250
1946	15	8 (8)	2 (2)	3 (3)	424,195
1947	7	5 (5)	1	1 (1)	181,925
1948	2	1	0	0	3,250
1949	6	1 (1)	1	1 (1)	45,900
1950	3	1	0	1	2,950
	42	18 (15)	6 (2)	7 (6)	$675,470

1945—1st Flash Stakes
1946—1st Kentucky Derby, Preakness Stakes, Belmont Stakes, Wood Memorial Stakes, Dwyer Stakes, etc.
1947—1st Suburban Handicap, Brooklyn Handicap, etc.
1949—1st Brooklyn Handicap

Horse of the Year in 1946, Assault won five of seven starts in '47 and spent much of the year battling fellow handicappers Stymie and Armed for the all-time earnings crown.

Assault was retired in early 1948 but proved to be sterile at stud. Returned to the racetrack, he ran until he was seven. Pensioned at King Ranch, he was euthanized in 1971 after fracturing a leg.

Citation

Citation resulted from a mating of Calumet Farm's premier sire, Bull Lea, with *Hydroplane II, whom Warren Wright purchased from Lord Derby in the spring of 1941. Citation was foaled on April 11, 1945, and joined trainer Jimmy Jones's Maryland division in the spring of '47 to begin his racing career.

At two his only loss was in the Washington Park Futurity to stablemate Bewitch.

Citation began his three-year-old season with two victories over older horses at Hialeah Park before winning the Everglades and Flamingo Stakes. His jockey, Al Snider, died in a boating accident after the Flamingo, and Jimmy Jones induced Eddie Arcaro to take the mount.

In the Kentucky Derby against only five opponents on May 1, Citation spotted stablemate Coaltown six lengths in the opening half-mile and ran him down to win by 3½ lengths.

In the Preakness two weeks later, Citation set all the pace and won by 5½ lengths as the 1-to-10 favorite. With four weeks between the Preakness and Belmont, Jones sent out Citation for an 11-length victory in the Jersey Derby. On June 12 in the Belmont Stakes, Citation, at 1-to-5 odds, scored an eight-length triumph over Better Self.

Citation won nine more times in 1948, including

B. c., 1945, by Bull Lea—*Hydroplane II, by Hyperion

Owner-breeder: Calumet Farm (Ky.)
Trainers: Ben A. Jones and H. A. "Jimmy" Jones
Jockey: Eddie Arcaro

Year	Starts	Race record 1st	2nd	3rd	Earnings
1947	9	8 (3)	1 (1)	0	$ 155,680
1948	20	19 (16)	1 (1)	0	709,470
1949	—	—	—	—	—
1950	9	2 (1)	7 (5)	0	73,480
1951	7	3 (2)	1 (1)	2	147,130
	45	32 (22)	10 (8)	2	$1,085,760

1947—1st Futurity Stakes, Pimlico Futurity
1948—1st Kentucky Derby, Preakness Stakes, Belmont Stakes, Jockey Club Gold Cup, Pimlico Special, etc.
1950—1st Golden Gate Mile Handicap
1951—1st American Handicap, Hollywood Gold Cup

a walkover in the Pimlico Special. At the end of his three-year-old season, Citation had 27 victories and two seconds in 29 starts, with earnings of $865,150.

In 1951, Citation won the Hollywood Gold Cup, becoming racing's first $1-million earner. Immediately retired to Calumet, he was an undistinguished sire. He died on August 8, 1970.

Secretariat

Like Man o' War, Secretariat was known as Big Red, and both were big in accomplishments. Secretariat, by leading sire Bold Ruler and out of the *Princequillo mare Somethingroyal, made his career debut on July 4, 1972, in a 5½-furlong maiden race at Aqueduct and finished fourth with a late surge. Secretariat subsequently won five stakes races impressively and was voted Horse of the Year.

In February 1973, as Secretariat was being prepared for the Triple Crown campaign, he was syndicated by Claiborne Farm for a record $6.08-million. Secretariat easily won his first two starts of the year, the Bay Shore (G3) and Gotham (G2) Stakes, but the colt ran third in the Wood Memorial Stakes (G1) on April 20, most likely due to a lip abscess. His Kentucky Derby (G1) was one that will forever be remembered. After breaking near the back of the pack, Secretariat began picking up horses on the first turn, collared Sham at the top of the lane, and drew away to a 2½-length victory in a Derby record 1:59⅖ for 1¼ miles.

In the Preakness Stakes (G1), jockey Ron Turcotte sensed a slow early pace and allowed Secretariat to surge to the lead as the six-horse field entered the backstretch. Secretariat dominated the rest of the race and again won by 2½ lengths over Sham. A timer malfunction effectively nullified

Ch. c., 1970, by Bold Ruler—Somethingroyal, by *Princequillo

Owner: Meadow Stable
Breeder: Meadow Stud (Va.)
Trainer: Lucien Laurin
Jockey: Ron Turcotte

Year	Starts	Race record 1st	2nd	3rd	Earnings
1972	9	7 (5)	1 (1)	0	$ 456,404
1973	12	9 (9)	2 (2)	1 (1)	860,404
	21	16 (14)	3 (3)	1 (1)	$1,316,808

1972—1st Hopeful Stakes, Futurity Stakes, Garden State Stakes, etc.
1973—1st Kentucky Derby (G1), Preakness Stakes (G1), Belmont Stakes (G1), Man o' War Stakes (G1), Canadian International Championship Stakes (G2), Marlboro Cup H., etc.

what should have been a track record.

Only Sham and three others showed up to oppose Secretariat in the Belmont Stakes (G1) on June 9. Secretariat and Sham dueled through the first six furlongs in 1:09⅘ before Sham surrendered. Secretariat steadily pulled away to win by 31 lengths while running 1½ miles in 2:24, an American record.

Retired to Claiborne, Secretariat was a good but not great sire. He died of complications from laminitis on October 4, 1989.

Seattle Slew

A son of Bold Reasoning out of My Charmer, by Poker, Seattle Slew was brought along patiently by his young trainer, William H. Turner Jr. He was voted champion two-year-old male after a stunning Champagne Stakes (G1) win.

At three, Seattle Slew won Hialeah's Flamingo Stakes (G1) by four lengths on March 26, and took Aqueduct's Wood Memorial Stakes (G1) by 3¼ lengths on April 23.

For the Derby on May 7, Seattle Slew went off as the 1-to-2 favorite. Disaster nearly struck at the start when he swerved out and was sharply taken up by jockey Jean Cruguet. At the top of the stretch, Seattle Slew put away For The Moment and then cruised home by 1¾ lengths over Run Dusty Run.

Two weeks later in the Preakness Stakes (G1), 2-to-5 Seattle Slew took command leaving the backstretch and won by 1½ lengths over Iron Constitution. Seattle Slew then dominated the Belmont Stakes (G1), winning by four lengths over Run Dusty Run. In addition to becoming the tenth Triple Crown winner, Seattle Slew was the first to complete the series without a defeat. Turner suggested a rest, but owners Karen and Mickey Taylor and Sally and Jim Hill insisted on running in Hollywood Park's Swaps Stakes (G1). Slew finished fourth and did not race again in 1977.

**Dk. b. or br. c., 1974, by Bold Reasoning—
My Charmer, by Poker**

Owners: Mickey and Karen L. Taylor, Dr. Jim and Sally Hill
Breeder: Ben S. Castleman (Ky.)
Trainers: William H. Turner Jr. (1976-'77); Doug Peterson (1978)
Jockey: Jean Cruguet

		Race record			
Year	Starts	1st	2nd	3rd	Earnings
1976	3	3 (1)	0	0	$ 94,350
1977	7	6 (5)	0	0	641,370
1978	7	5 (3)	2 (2)	0	473,006
	17	14 (9)	2 (2)	0	$1,208,726

1976—1st Champagne Stakes (G1)
1977—1st Kentucky Derby (G1), Preakness Stakes (G1), Belmont Stakes (G1), Wood Memorial Stakes (G1), Flamingo Stakes (G1)
1978—1st Marlboro Cup Invitational Handicap (G1), Woodward Stakes (G1), Stuyvesant Stakes (G3)

Seattle Slew made seven starts as a four-year-old, and his five victories included an epic win over Affirmed in the Marlboro Cup Invitational Handicap (G1). Standing first at Spendthrift Farm and then at Three Chimneys Farm, he sired A.P. Indy, 1992 Horse of the Year, and more than 100 stakes winners. He died May 7, 2002.

Affirmed

The 1978 Triple Crown, the first ever won in back-to-back years, belonged to Affirmed, but his name will forever be linked with Alydar, the first horse to finish second in all three races to a Triple Crown winner.

Both colts dominated their arenas at three, and the Kentucky Derby (G1), in which Alydar went off as the 6-to-5 favorite with Affirmed at 9-to-5, was a clash of the titans. Third early under jockey Steve Cauthen, Affirmed surged past Believe It early in the stretch and opened a two-length lead in midstretch. Alydar made a late charge but finished second by 1½ lengths.

Two weeks later on May 20, the two would stage an epic duel in the Preakness Stakes (G1). Affirmed, 1-to-2, once again stalked the early pace and inherited the lead after a half-mile. Jorge Velasquez asked Alydar for speed on the backstretch, and the Raise a Native colt reached Affirmed's side leaving the turn. They fought to the wire, with Affirmed winning by a neck.

In the Belmont Stakes (G1) three weeks later, 3-to-5 Affirmed was the only speed in the field of five, and 1.10-to-1 Alydar shadowed him practically from the start. After a half-mile, Affirmed led by one length, and by the top of Belmont's stretch they were a head apart. Alydar

---

**Ch. c., 1975, by Exclusive Native—
Won't Tell You, by Crafty Admiral**

Owner-breeder: Harbor View Farm (Fl.)
Trainer: Lazaro Barrera
Jockey: Steve Cauthen

		Race record			
Year	Starts	1st	2nd	3rd	Earnings
1977	9	7 (6)	2 (2)	0	$ 343,477
1978	11	8 (7)	2 (2)	0	901,541
1979	9	7 (6)	1 (1)	1 (1)	1,148,800
	29	22 (19)	5 (5)	1 (1)	$2,393,818

1977—1st Hopeful Stakes (G1), Futurity Stakes (G1), Laurel Futurity (G1), etc.
1978—1st Kentucky Derby (G1), Preakness Stakes (G1), Belmont Stakes (G1), Santa Anita Derby (G1), Hollywood Derby (G1), etc.
1979—1st Jockey Club Gold Cup (G1), Hollywood Gold Cup (G1), Santa Anita Handicap (G1), etc.

---

appeared to take a narrow lead inside the furlong pole, but Affirmed fought back and won by a head. He was voted Horse of the Year and repeated in 1979 with six consecutive Grade 1 victories. The sport's first $2-million earner, he was a moderately successful sire before his death on January 12, 2001, at Jonabell Farm.

Near Triple Crown Winners

While the Triple Crown has been swept on 11 occasions, in 46 other years three-year-olds have won two legs of the Triple Crown. Among the 46 near successes are 18 horses who won the Kentucky Derby and Preakness Stakes but not the Belmont Stakes.

Of those 18, injury felled several in the Belmont (including Tim Tam and Charismatic), several have come agonizingly close (Silver Charm, Real Quiet), and two did not run in the Belmont (Burgoo King, Bold Venture) because of injuries before the race.

Following are the 46 horses who won two of the three races. Winner of the race the Triple Crown hopeful lost is in parentheses.

Year	Horse	Kentucky Derby	Preakness	Belmont
2002	War Emblem	Won	Won	8th (Sarava)
2001	Point Given	5th (Monarchos)	Won	Won
1999	Charismatic	Won	Won	3rd (Lemon Drop Kid)
1998	Real Quiet	Won	Won	2nd (Victory Gallop)
1997	Silver Charm	Won	Won	2nd (Touch Gold)
1995	Thunder Gulch	Won	3rd (Timber Country)	Won
1994	Tabasco Cat	6th (Go for Gin)	Won	Won
1991	Hansel	10th (Strike the Gold)	Won	Won
1989	Sunday Silence	Won	Won	2nd (Easy Goer)
1988	Risen Star	3rd (Winning Colors)	Won	Won
1987	Alysheba	Won	Won	4th (Bet Twice)
1984	Swale	Won	7th (Gate Dancer)	Won
1981	Pleasant Colony	Won	Won	3rd (Summing)
1979	Spectacular Bid	Won	Won	3rd (Coastal)
1976	Bold Forbes	Won	3rd (Elocutionist)	Won
1974	Little Current	5th (Cannonade)	Won	Won
1972	Riva Ridge	Won	4th (Bee Bee Bee)	Won
1971	Canonero II	Won	Won	4th (Pass Catcher)
1969	Majestic Prince	Won	Won	2nd (Arts and Letters)
1968	Forward Pass	Won†	Won	2nd (Stage Door Johnny)
1967	Damascus	3rd (Proud Clarion)	Won	Won
1966	Kauai King	Won	Won	4th (Amberoid)
1964	Northern Dancer	Won	Won	3rd (Quadrangle)
1963	Chateaugay	Won	2nd (Candy Spots)	Won
1961	Carry Back	Won	Won	7th (Sherluck)
1958	Tim Tam	Won	Won	2nd (*Cavan)
1956	Needles	Won	2nd (Fabius)	Won
1955	Nashua	2nd (Swaps)	Won	Won
1953	Native Dancer	2nd (Dark Star)	Won	Won
1950	Middleground	Won	2nd (Hill Prince)	Won
1949	Capot	2nd (Ponder)	Won	Won
1944	Pensive	Won	Won	2nd (Bounding Home)
1942	Shut Out	Won	5th (Alsab)	Won
1940	Bimelech	2nd (Gallahadion)	Won	Won
1939	Johnstown	Won	5th (Challedon)	Won
1936	Bold Venture	Won	Won	Did not start
1932	Burgoo King	Won	Won	Did not start
1931	Twenty Grand	Won	2nd (Mate)	Won
1923	Zev	Won	12th (Vigil)	Won
1922	Pillory	Did not start	Won	Won
1920	Man o' War	Did not start	Won	Won
1895	Belmar	Did not start	Won	Won
1881	Saunterer	Did not start	Won	Won
1880	Grenada	Did not start	Won	Won
1878	Duke of Magenta	Did not start	Won	Won
1877	Cloverbrook	Did not start	Won	Won

†Won on disqualification of Dancer's Image

Leading Breeders of Triple Crown Race Winners

18 Calumet Farm: Kentucky Derby: Whirlaway (1941), Pensive ('44), Citation ('48), Ponder ('49), Hill Gail ('52), Iron Liege ('57), Tim Tam ('58), Forward Pass ('68), Strike the Gold ('91); Preakness: Whirlaway ('41), Pensive ('44), Faultless ('47), Citation ('48), Fabius ('56), Tim Tam ('58), Forward Pass ('68); Belmont: Whirlaway ('41), Citation ('48)

15 A. J. Alexander: Kentucky Derby: Baden-Baden (1877), Fonso ('80), Joe Cotton ('85), Chant ('94); Preakness: Tom Ochiltree ('75), Shirley ('76), Grenada ('80), Duke of Magenta ('90); Belmont: Harry Bassett ('71), Joe Daniels ('72), Springbok ('73), Duke of Magenta ('78), Spendthrift ('79), Grenada ('80), Burlington ('90)

12 Harry P. Whitney: Kentucky Derby: Regret (1915), Whiskery ('27); Preakness: Royal Tourist ('08), Buskin ('13), Holiday ('14), Broomspun ('21), Bostonian ('27), Victorian ('28); Belmont: Tanya ('05), Burgomaster ('06), Prince Eugene ('13), *Johren ('18)

11 John E. Madden
8—John E. Madden: Kentucky Derby: Old Rosebud (1914), Paul Jones ('20), Zev ('23), Flying Ebony ('25); Belmont: Joe Madden ('09), The Finn ('15), Grey Lag ('21), Zev ('23)
3—John E. Madden and Vivian A. Gooch: Kentucky Derby: Sir Barton (1919); Preakness: Sir Barton ('19); Belmont: Sir Barton ('19)

10 Belair Stud: Kentucky Derby: Gallant Fox (1930), Omaha ('35); Preakness: Gallant Fox ('30), Omaha ('35), Nashua ('55); Belmont: Gallant Fox ('30), Faireno ('32), Omaha ('35), Granville ('36), Nashua ('55)
August Belmont II: Preakness: Margrave (1896), Don Enrique (1907), Watervale ('11), Damrosch ('16), Man o' War ('20); Belmont: Masterman ('02), Friar Rock ('16), *Hourless ('17), Man o' War ('20), Chance Shot ('27)

8 E. R. Bradley (Idle Hour Stock Farm): Kentucky Derby: Behave Yourself (1921), Bubbling Over ('26), Burgoo King ('32), Brokers Tip ('33); Preakness: Burgoo King ('32), Bimelech ('40); Belmont: Blue Larkspur ('29), Bimelech ('40)

7 Greentree Stud: Kentucky Derby: Twenty Grand (1931), Shut Out ('42); Preakness: Capot ('49); Belmont: Twenty Grand ('31), Shut Out ('42), Capot ('49), Stage Door Johnny ('68)

6 William S. Farish
3—William S. Farish and William S. Kilroy: Preakness: Summer Squall (1990); Belmont: A.P. Indy ('90), Lemon Drop Kid ('99)
2—Parrish Hill Farm and William S. Farish: Kentucky Derby: Charismatic (1999); Preakness: Charismatic ('99)
1—William S. Farish and E. J. Hudson: Belmont: Bet Twice (1987)
J. B. A. Haggin: Kentucky Derby: Stone Street (1908); Preakness: Old England ('02), Cairngorm ('05), Rhine Maiden ('15); Belmont: Commanche (1893), Africander (1903)

Meadow Stud (C. T. Chenery): Kentucky Derby: Riva Ridge (1972), Secretariat ('73); Preakness: Hill Prince ('50), Secretariat ('73); Belmont: Riva Ridge ('72), Secretariat ('73)

5 Ezekiel F. Clay
4—Clay and Woodford: Kentucky Derby: Ben Brush (1896); Preakness: Buddhist ('89); Belmont: Hanover ('87), Sir Dixon ('88)
1—Ezekiel F. Clay: Kentucky Derby: Agile (1905)
John W. Galbreath: Kentucky Derby: Chateaugay (1963), Proud Clarion ('67); Preakness: Little Current ('74); Belmont: Chateaugay ('63), Little Current ('74)
James R. Keene: Belmont: Commando (1901), Delhi ('04), Peter Pan ('07), Colin ('08), Sweep ('10)
King Ranch: Kentucky Derby: Assault (1946), Middleground ('50); Preakness: Assault ('46); Belmont: Assault ('46), Middleground ('50)
Samuel D. Riddle: Kentucky Derby: War Admiral (1937); Preakness: War Admiral ('37); Belmont: American Flag ('25), Crusader ('26), War Admiral ('37)

4 Arthur B. Hancock III
3—Arthur B. Hancock III and Leone J. Peters: Kentucky Derby: Gato Del Sol (1982); Preakness: Risen Star ('88); Belmont: Risen Star ('88)
1—Arthur B. Hancock III and Stonerside Ltd.: Kentucky Derby: Fusaichi Pegasus (2000)
Arthur B. Hancock Sr.
3—Arthur B. Hancock: Kentucky Derby: Johnstown (1939); Preakness: Vigil ('23); Belmont: Johnstown ('39)
1—Arthur B. Hancock and Mrs. R. A. Van Clief: Kentucky Derby: Jet Pilot (1947)
Aristides Welch: Preakness: Harold (1879), Saunterer ('81); Belmont: Saunterer ('81), Panique ('84)

3 August Belmont I: Preakness: Jacobus (1883); Belmont: Fenian ('69), Forester ('82)
A. J. Cassatt: Preakness: Montague (1890); Belmont: Foxford ('91), Patron ('92)
Ben S. Castleman: Kentucky Derby: Seattle Slew (1977), Preakness: Seattle Slew ('77); Belmont: Seattle Slew ('77)
Claiborne Farm: Kentucky Derby: Swale (1984); Belmont: Coastal ('79), Swale ('84)
Harbor View Farm: Kentucky Derby: Affirmed (1978); Preakness: Affirmed ('78); Belmont: Affirmed ('78)
Mrs. John D. Hertz: Kentucky Derby: Count Fleet (1943); Preakness: Count Fleet ('43); Belmont: Count Fleet ('43)
George J. Long: Kentucky Derby: Azra (1892), Manuel (1899), Sir Huon (1906)
H. Price McGrath (McGrathiana Stud): Kentucky Derby: Aristides (1875); Preakness: Paul Kauvar ('97); Belmont: Calvin ('75)
Paul Mellon: Kentucky Derby: Sea Hero (1993); Belmont: Quadrangle ('64), Arts and Letters ('69)
Overbrook Farm
2—Overbrook Farm and David Reynolds:

Preakness: Tabasco Cat (1994); Belmont: Tabasco Cat ('94)

1—Overbrook Farm: Kentucky Derby: Grindstone (1996)

3 Daniel Swigert: Kentucky Derby: Hindoo (1881), Apollo ('82), Ben Ali ('86)

2 Mrs. Thomas Bancroft: Preakness: Damascus (1967); Belmont: Damascus ('67)

E. B. Benjamin: Kentucky Derby: Canonero II (1971); Preakness: Canonero II ('71)

Bieber-Jacobs Stable: Preakness: Personality (1970); Belmont: High Echelon ('70).

Peter M. Brant: Kentucky Derby: Thunder Gulch (1995); Belmont: Thunder Gulch ('95)

Brookmeade Stable: Preakness: Bold (1951); Belmont: Sword Dancer ('59)

E. A. Clabaugh: Preakness: Cloverbrook (1877); Belmont: Cloverbrook ('77)

John M. Clay: Kentucky Derby: Day Star (1878); Preakness: Survivor ('73)

Leslie B. Combs II: Kentucky Derby: Majestic Prince (1969), Preakness: Majestic Prince ('69)

Eaton and Red Bull Stable: Kentucky Derby: Bold Forbes (1976); Belmont: Bold Forbes ('76)

Rex C. Ellsworth: Kentucky Derby: Swaps (1955); Preakness: Candy Spots ('63)

Thomas Mellon Evans: Kentucky Derby: Pleasant Colony (1981); Preakness: Pleasant Colony ('81)

R. A. Fairbairn: Kentucky Derby: Gallahadion (1940), Hoop, Jr. ('45)

James Galway (Preakness Stable): Preakness: Belmar (1895); Belmont: Belmar ('95)

Mrs. William Jason and Mrs. William Gilmore: Kentucky Derby: Spectacular Bid (1979); Preakness: Spectacular Bid ('79)

W. G. Harding: Belmont: Tyrant (1885), Inspector B. ('86)

Walter M. Jeffords: Belmont: Pavot (1945), One Count ('52)

W. E. Leach: Kentucky Derby: Needles (1956); Belmont: Needles ('56)

Little Hill Farm: Kentucky Derby: Real Quiet (1998); Preakness: Real Quiet ('98)

Marvin Little Jr.: Preakness: Hansel (1991); Belmont: Hansel ('91)

Loblolly Stable: Preakness: Pine Bluff (1992), Prairie Bayou ('93)

Preston Madden: Kentucky Derby: Alysheba (1987); Preakness: Alysheba ('87)

Dr. J. D. Neet: Kentucky Derby: Plaudit (1898); Belmont: Hastings ('96)

Oak Cliff Thoroughbred Breeders Ltd.: Kentucky Derby: Sunday Silence (1989); Preakness: Sunday Silence ('89)

Jack A. Price: Kentucky Derby: Carry Back (1961); Preakness: Carry Back ('61)

Pine Brook Farm: Kentucky Derby: Kauai King (1966); Preakness: Kauai King ('66)

Walter J. Salmon: Preakness: Display (1926), Dr. Freeland ('29)

M. H. Sanford: Kentucky Derby: Vagrant (1876); Preakness: Vanguard ('82)

Morton L. Schwartz: Kentucky Derby: Bold Venture (1936); Preakness: Bold Venture ('36)

Tartan Farms Corp.: Kentucky Derby: Unbridled (1990); Preakness: Codex ('80)

E. P. Taylor: Kentucky Derby: Northern Dancer (1964); Preakness: Northern Dancer ('64)

The Thoroughbred Corp.: Preakness: Point Given (2001); Belmont: Point Given ('01)

Alfred G. Vanderbilt: Preakness: Native Dancer (1953); Belmont: Native Dancer ('53)

C. V. Whitney: Preakness: Dauber (1938); Belmont: Counterpoint ('51)

Joseph E. Widener: Belmont: Hurryoff (1933), Peace Chance ('34)

Mary Lou Wooton: Kentucky Derby: Silver Charm (1997); Preakness: Silver Charm ('97)

Milton Young: Kentucky Derby: Montrose (1887), Donau (1910)

Leading Owners of Triple Crown Race Winners

17 Calumet Farm: Kentucky Derby: Whirlaway (1941), Pensive ('44), Citation ('48), Ponder ('49), Hill Gail ('52), Iron Liege ('57), Tim Tam ('58), Forward Pass ('68); Preakness: Whirlaway ('41), Pensive ('44), Faultless ('47), Citation ('48), Fabius ('56), Tim Tam ('58), Forward Pass ('68); Belmont: Whirlaway ('41), Citation ('48)

12 Belair Stud: Kentucky Derby: Gallant Fox (1930), Omaha ('35), Johnstown ('39); Preakness: Gallant Fox ('30), Omaha ('35), Nashua ('55); Belmont: Gallant Fox ('30), Faireno ('32), Omaha ('35), Granville ('36), Johnstown ('39), Nashua ('55)

10 Harry P. Whitney: Kentucky Derby: Regret (1915), Whiskery ('27); Preakness: Royal Tourist ('08), Broomspun ('21), Bostonian ('27), Victorian ('28); Belmont: Tanya ('05), Burgomaster ('06), Prince Eugene ('13), *Johren ('18)

9   E. R. Bradley (Idle Hour Stock Farm): Kentucky Derby: Behave Yourself (1921), Bubbling Over ('26), Burgoo King ('32), Brokers Tip ('33); Preakness: Kalitan ('17), Burgoo King ('32), Bimelech ('40); Belmont: Blue Larkspur ('29), Bimelech ('40)

8   Dwyer Brothers:

6—Dwyer Brothers (M. F. and Phil J.): Kentucky Derby: Hindoo (1881); Belmont: George Kinney ('83), Panique ('84), Inspector B. ('86), Hanover ('87), Sir Dixon ('88)

1—M. F. Dwyer: Kentucky Derby: Ben Brush (1896)

1—Phil J. Dwyer: Preakness: Half Time (1899)

George L. Lorillard: Preakness: Duke of Magenta (1878), Harold ('79), Grenada ('80), Saunterer ('81), Vanguard ('82); Belmont: Duke of Magenta ('78), Grenada ('80), Saunterer ('81)

7   August Belmont II: Preakness: Margrave (1896), Don Enrique (1907), Watervale ('11); Belmont: Hastings (1896), Masterman (1902), Friar Rock ('16), *Hourless ('17)

7   Glen Riddle Farms: Kentucky Derby: War Admiral (1937); Preakness: Man o' War ('20), War Admiral ('37); Belmont: Man o' War ('20), American Flag ('25), Crusader (1926), War Admiral ('37)

Greentree Stable: Kentucky Derby: Twenty Grand (1931), Shut Out ('42); Preakness: Capot ('49); Belmont: Twenty Grand ('31), Shut Out ('42), Capot ('49), Stage Door Johnny ('68)

James R. Keene:
6—James R. Keene: Belmont: Spendthrift (1879), Commando (1901), Delhi ('04), Peter Pan ('07), Colin ('08), Sweep ('10)
1—James R. Keene and Foxhall P. Keene: Preakness: Assignee (1894)

6   Robert and Beverly Lewis:
5—Robert and Beverly Lewis: Kentucky Derby: Silver Charm (1997), Charismatic ('99); Preakness: Silver Charm ('97), Charismatic ('99); Belmont: Commendable (2000)
1—Gainesway Farm, Robert and Beverly Lewis, and Overbrook Farm: Preakness: Timber Country (1995)

Meadow Stable (C. T. and Penny Chenery): Kentucky Derby: Riva Ridge (1972), Secretariat ('73); Preakness: Hill Prince ('50), Secretariat ('73); Belmont: Riva Ridge ('72), Secretariat ('73)

5   Overbrook Farm (W. T. Young):
2—Overbrook Farm: Kentucky Derby: Grindstone (1996); Belmont: Editor's Note ('96)
2—Overbrook Farm and David Reynolds: Preakness: Tabasco Cat (1994); Belmont: Tabasco Cat ('94)
1—Gainesway Farm, Robert and Beverly Lewis, and Overbrook Farm: Preakness: Timber Country (1995)

King Ranch: Kentucky Derby: Assault (1946), Middleground ('50); Preakness: Assault ('46); Belmont: Assault ('46), Middleground ('50), High Gun ('54)

Darby Dan Farm: Kentucky Derby: Chateaugay (1963), Proud Clarion ('67); Preakness: Little Current ('74); Belmont: Chateaugay ('63), Little Current ('74)

4   Brookmeade Stable: Kentucky Derby: Cavalcade (1934); Preakness: High Quest ('34), Bold ('51); Belmont: Sword Dancer ('59)

Mrs. John D. Hertz: Kentucky Derby: Reigh Count (1928), Count Fleet ('43); Preakness: Count Fleet ('43); Belmont: Count Fleet ('43)

J.K.L. Ross: Kentucky Derby: Sir Barton (1919); Preakness: Damrosch ('16), Sir Barton ('19); Belmont: Sir Barton ('19)

The Thoroughbred Corp: Kentucky Derby: War Emblem (2002); Preakness: Point Given ('01), War Emblem ('02); Belmont: Point Given ('01)

3   William Condren:
1—B. Giles Brophy, William Condren, and Joseph Cornacchia: Kentucky Derby: Strike the Gold (1991)
1—William Condren and Joseph Cornacchia: Kentucky Derby: Go for Gin (1994)
1—William Condren, Georgia Hofmann, and Joseph Cornacchia: Preakness: Louis Quatorze (1996)

Joseph Cornacchia:
1—B. Giles Brophy, William Condren, and Joseph Cornacchia: Kentucky Derby: Strike the Gold (1991)
1—William Condren and Joseph Cornacchia: Kentucky Derby: Go for Gin (1994)
1—William Condren, Georgia Hofmann, and Joseph Cornacchia: Preakness: Louis Quatorze (1996)

Arthur B. Hancock III:
1—Arthur B. Hancock III and Leone J. Peters: Kentucky Derby: Gato Del Sol (1982)
2—Arthur B. Hancock III, Ernest Gaillard, and Charlie Whittingham: Kentucky Derby: Sunday Silence (1989); Preakness: Sunday Silence ('89)

Harbor View Farm: Kentucky Derby: Affirmed (1978); Preakness: Affirmed ('78); Belmont: Affirmed ('78)

Loblolly Stable: Preakness: Pine Bluff (1992), Prairie Bayou ('93); Belmont: Temperence Hill ('80)

David McDaniel: Belmont: Harry Bassett (1871), Joe Daniels ('72), Springbok ('73)

Preakness Stable (James Galway): Preakness: Montague (1890), Belmar ('95); Belmont: Belmar ('95)

Rokeby Stable: Kentucky Derby: Sea Hero (1993); Belmont: Quadrangle ('64), Arts and Letters ('69)

Walter J. Salmon: Preakness: Vigil (1923), Display ('26), Dr. Freeland ('29)

H. F. Sinclair: Belmont: Grey Lag (1921), Zev ('23), Mad Play ('24)

Karen and Mickey Taylor and Sally and James Hill: Kentucky Derby: Seattle Slew (1977); Preakness: Seattle Slew ('77); Belmont: Seattle Slew ('77)

Joseph E. Widener: Belmont: Chance Shot (1927), Hurryoff ('33), Peace Chance ('34)

Richard T. Wilson Jr.: Preakness: The Parader (1901), Pillory ('22); Belmont: Pillory ('22)

Leading Trainers of Triple Crown Race Winners

13   James "Sunny Jim" Fitzsimmons: Kentucky Derby: Gallant Fox (1930), Omaha ('35), Johnstown ('39); Preakness: Gallant Fox ('30), Omaha ('35), Nashua ('55), Bold Ruler ('57); Belmont: Gallant Fox ('30), Fareino ('32), Omaha ('35), Granville ('36), Johnstown ('39), Nashua ('55)

D. Wayne Lukas: Kentucky Derby: Winning Colors (1988), Thunder Gulch ('95), Grindstone ('96), Charismatic ('99); Preakness: Codex ('80), Tank's Prospect ('85), Tabasco Cat ('94), Timber Country ('95), Charismatic ('99); Belmont: Tabasco Cat ('94), Thunder Gulch ('95), Editor's Note ('96), Commendable (2000)

11   James Rowe Sr.: Kentucky Derby: Hindoo (1881), Regret (1915); Preakness: Broomspun

(1921); Belmont: George Kinney (1883), Panique (1884), Commando (1901), Delhi ('04), Peter Pan ('07), Colin ('08), Sweep ('10), Prince Eugene ('13)

R. Wyndham Walden: Preakness: Tom Ochiltree (1875), Duke of Magenta ('78), Harold ('79), Grenada ('80), Saunterer ('81), Vanguard ('82), Refund ('88); Belmont: Duke of Magenta ('78), Grenada ('80), Saunterer ('81), *Bowling Brook ('98)

9   **Max Hirsch**: Kentucky Derby: Bold Venture (1936), Assault ('46), Middleground ('50); Preakness: Bold Venture ('36), Assault ('46); Belmont: Vito ('28), Assault ('46), Middleground ('50), High Gun ('54)

B. A. "Ben" Jones: Kentucky Derby: Lawrin (1938), Whirlaway ('41), Pensive ('44), Citation ('48), Ponder ('49), Hill Gail ('52); Preakness: Whirlaway ('41), Pensive ('44); Belmont: Whirlaway ('41)

8   **Bob Baffert**: Kentucky Derby: Silver Charm (1997), Real Quiet ('98), War Emblem (2002); Preakness: Silver Charm ('97), Real Quiet ('98), Point Given (2001), War Emblem ('02); Belmont: Point Given ('01)

Woodford C. "Woody" Stephens: Kentucky Derby: Cannonade (1974), Swale ('84); Preakness: Blue Man ('52); Belmont: Conquistador Cielo ('82), Caveat ('83), Swale ('84), Creme Fraiche ('85), Danzig Connection ('86)

7   **H. A. "Jimmy" Jones**: Kentucky Derby: Iron Liege (1957), Tim Tam ('58); Preakness: Faultless ('47), Citation ('48), Fabius ('56), Tim Tam ('58); Belmont: Citation ('48)

Sam Hildreth: Belmont: Jean Bereaud (1899), Joe Madden (1909), Friar Rock ('16), *Hourless ('17), Grey Lag ('21), Zev ('23), Mad Play ('24)

6   **Thomas J. Healy**: Preakness: The Parader (1901), Pillory ('22), Vigil ('23), Display ('26), Dr. Freeland ('29); Belmont: Pillory ('22)

Lucien Laurin: Kentucky Derby: Riva Ridge (1972), Secretariat ('73); Preakness: Secretariat ('73); Belmont: Amberoid ('66), Riva Ridge ('72), Secretariat ('73)

5   **John M. Gaver**: Kentucky Derby: Shut Out (1942); Preakness: Capot ('49); Belmont: Shut Out ('42), Capot ('49), Stage Door Johnny ('68)

Lazaro Barrera: Kentucky Derby: Bold Forbes (1976), Affirmed ('78); Preakness: Affirmed ('78); Belmont: Bold Forbes ('76), Affirmed ('78)

H. J. "Dick" Thompson: Kentucky Derby: Behave Yourself (1921), Bubbling Over ('26), Burgoo King ('32), Brokers Tip ('33); Preakness: Burgoo King ('32)

4   **Henry Forrest**: Kentucky Derby: Kauai King (1966), Forward Pass ('68); Preakness: Kauai King ('66), Forward Pass ('68)

George Conway: Kentucky Derby: War Admiral (1937); Preakness: War Admiral ('37); Belmont: Crusader ('26), War Admiral ('37)

Frank McCabe: Preakness: Half Time (1899); Belmont: Inspector B. ('86), Hanover ('87), Sir Dixon ('88)

3   **H. Guy Bedwell**: Kentucky Derby: Sir Barton (1919); Preakness: Sir Barton ('19); Belmont: Sir Barton ('19)

J. Elliott Burch: Belmont: Sword Dancer (1959), Quadrangle ('64), Arts and Letters ('69)

G. D. Cameron: Kentucky Derby: Count Fleet (1943); Preakness: Count Fleet ('43); Belmont: Count Fleet ('43)

Peter Coyne: Kentucky Derby: Sir Huon (1906); Belmont: Chance Shot ('27), Peace Chance ('34)

Edward Feakes: Preakness: Montague (1890), Belmar ('95); Belmont: Belmar ('95)

Thomas P. Hayes: Kentucky Derby: Donerail (1913); Preakness: Paul Kauvar (1897), Head Play (1933)

William Hurley: Preakness: Kalitan (1917), Bimelech ('40); Belmont: Bimelech ('40)

Horatio Luro: Kentucky Derby: Decidedly (1962), Northern Dancer ('64); Preakness: Northern Dancer ('64)

David McDaniel: Belmont: Harry Bassett (1871), Joe Daniels ('72), Springbok ('73)

James Rowe Jr.: Kentucky Derby: Twenty Grand (1931); Preakness: Victorian ('28), Belmont: Twenty Grand ('31)

William H. Turner Jr.: Kentucky Derby: Seattle Slew (1977); Preakness: Seattle Slew ('77); Belmont: ('77)

James Whalen: Preakness: Don Enrique (1907), Watervale ('11), Buskin ('13)

Frank Y. Whiteley Jr.: Preakness: Tom Rolfe (1965), Damascus ('67); Belmont: Damascus ('67)

Charles Whittingham: Kentucky Derby: Ferdinand (1986), Sunday Silence ('89); Preakness: Sunday Silence ('89)

Nicholas P. Zito: Kentucky Derby: Strike the Gold (1991), Go for Gin ('94); Preakness: Louis Quatorze ('96)

Leading Jockeys of Triple Crown Race Winners

17 **Eddie Arcaro**: Kentucky Derby: Lawrin (1938), Whirlaway ('41), Hoop, Jr. ('45), Citation ('48), Hill Gail ('52); Preakness: Whirlaway ('41), Citation ('48), Hill Prince ('50), Bold ('51), Nashua ('55), Bold Ruler ('57); Belmont: Whirlaway ('41), Shut Out ('42), Pavot ('45), Citation ('48), One Count ('52), Nashua ('55)

11 **William Shoemaker**: Kentucky Derby: Swaps (1955), *Tomy Lee ('59), Lucky Debonair ('65),

Ferdinand ('86); Preakness: Candy Spots ('63), Damascus ('67); Belmont: *Gallant Man ('57), Sword Dancer ('59), Jaipur ('62), Damascus ('67), Avatar ('75)

9   **Pat Day**: Kentucky Derby: Lil E. Tee (1992); Preakness: Tank's Prospect ('85), Summer Squall ('90), Tabasco Cat ('94), Timber Country ('95), Louis Quatorze ('96); Belmont: Easy Goer ('89), Tabasco Cat ('94), Commendable (2000)

William J. Hartack: Kentucky Derby: Iron Liege (1957), Venetian Way ('60), Decidedly ('62), Northern Dancer ('64), Majestic Prince ('69); Preakness: Fabius ('56), Northern Dancer ('64), Majestic Prince ('69); Belmont: *Celtic Ash ('60)

Earl Sande: Kentucky Derby: Zev (1923), Flying Ebony ('25), Gallant Fox ('30); Preakness: Gallant Fox ('30); Belmont: Grey Lag ('21), Zev ('23), Mad Play ('24), Chance Shot ('27), Gallant Fox ('30)

8   James McLaughlin: Kentucky Derby: Hindoo (1881); Preakness: Tecumseh ('85); Belmont: Forester ('82), George Kinney ('83), Panique ('84), Inspector B. ('86), Hanover ('87), Sir Dixon ('88)

Gary Stevens: Kentucky Derby: Winning Colors (1988), Thunder Gulch ('95), Silver Charm ('97); Preakness: Silver Charm ('97), Point Given (2001); Belmont: Thunder Gulch (1995), Victory Gallop ('98), Point Given (2001)

6   Angel Cordero Jr.: Kentucky Derby: Cannonade (1974), Bold Forbes ('76), Spend a Buck ('85); Preakness: Codex ('80), Gate Dancer ('84); Belmont: Bold Forbes ('76)

Charles Kurtsinger: Kentucky Derby: Twenty Grand (1931), War Admiral ('37); Preakness: Head Play ('33), War Admiral ('37); Belmont: Twenty Grand ('31), War Admiral ('37)

Chris McCarron: Kentucky Derby: Alysheba (1987), Go for Gin ('94); Preakness: Alysheba ('87), Pine Bluff ('92), Belmont: Danzig Connection ('86), Touch Gold ('97)

Ron Turcotte: Kentucky Derby: Riva Ridge (1972), Secretariat ('73); Preakness: Tom Rolfe ('65), Secretariat ('73); Belmont: Riva Ridge ('72), Secretariat ('73)

5   Jerry Bailey: Kentucky Derby: Sea Hero (1993), Grindstone ('96); Preakness: Hansel ('91), Red Bullet ('00); Belmont: Hansel (1991)

Eddie Delahoussaye: Kentucky Derby: Gato Del Sol (1982), Sunny's Halo ('83); Preakness: Risen Star ('88); Belmont: Risen Star ('88), A.P. Indy ('92)

Lloyd Hughes: Preakness: Tom Ochiltree (1875), Harold ('79), Grenada ('80); Belmont: Duke of Magenta ('78), Grenada ('80)

John Loftus: Kentucky Derby: George Smith (1916), Sir Barton ('19); Preakness: *War Cloud ('18), Sir Barton ('19); Belmont: Sir Barton ('19)

Willie Simms: Kentucky Derby: Ben Brush (1898), Plaudit ('98); Preakness: Sly Fox ('98); Belmont: Comanche ('93), Henry Of Navarre ('94)

4   Braulio Baeza: Kentucky Derby: Chateaugay (1963); Belmont: Sherluck ('61), Chateaugay ('63), Arts and Letters ('69)

George Barbee: Preakness: Survivor (1873), Shirley ('76), Jacobus ('83); Belmont: Saxon ('74)

William "Billy" Donohue: Kentucky Derby: Leonatus (1883); Preakness: Culpepper ('74), Dunboyne ('87); Belmont: Algerine ('76)

Eric Guerin: Kentucky Derby: Jet Pilot (1947); Preakness: Native Dancer ('53); Belmont: Native Dancer ('53), High Gun ('54)

Albert Johnson: Kentucky Derby: Morvich (1922), Bubbling Over ('26); Belmont: American Flag ('25), Crusader ('26)

Clarence Kummer: Preakness: Man o' War (1920), Coventry ('25); Belmont: Man o' War ('20), Vito ('28)

Conn McCreary: Kentucky Derby: Pensive (1944), Count Turf ('51); Preakness: Pensive ('44), Blue Man ('52)

Laffit Pincay Jr.: Kentucky Derby: Swale (1984); Belmont: Conquistador Cielo ('82), Caveat ('83), Swale ('84)

James Stout: Kentucky Derby: Johnstown (1939); Belmont: Granville ('36), Pasteurized ('38), Johnstown ('39)

Fred Taral: Kentucky Derby: Manuel (1899); Preakness: Assignee ('94), Belmar ('95); Belmont: Belmar ('95)

Ismael "Milo" Valenzuela: Kentucky Derby: Tim Tam (1958), Forward Pass ('68); Preakness: Tim Tam ('58), Forward Pass ('68)

3   Chris Antley: Kentucky Derby: Strike the Gold (1991), Charismatic ('99); Preakness: Charismatic ('99)

William Boland: Kentucky Derby: Middleground (1950); Belmont: Middleground ('50), Amberoid ('66)

James H. "Jimmy" Butwell: Preakness: Buskin (1913); Belmont: Sweep ('10), *Hourless ('17)

Steve Cauthen: Kentucky Derby: Affirmed (1978); Preakness: Affirmed ('78); Belmont: Affirmed ('78)

T. Costello: Preakness: Saunterer (1881), Vanguard ('82); Belmont: Saunterer ('81)

Jean Cruguet: Kentucky Derby: Seattle Slew (1977), Preakness: Seattle Slew ('77); Belmont: Seattle Slew ('77)

Kent Desormeaux: Kentucky Derby: Real Quiet (1998), Fusaichi Pegasus (2000); Preakness: Real Quiet (1998)

Eddie Dugan: Preakness: Royal Tourist (1908), Watervale ('11); Belmont: Joe Madden ('09)

Mack Garner: Kentucky Derby: Cavalcade (1934); Belmont: Blue Larkspur ('29), Hurryoff ('33)

C. Holloway: Preakness: Cloverbrook (1877), Duke of Magenta ('78); Belmont: Cloverbrook ('77)

John Longden: Kentucky Derby: Count Fleet (1943); Preakness: Count Fleet ('43); Belmont: Count Fleet ('43)

J. Linus "Pony" McAtee: Kentucky Derby: Whiskery (1927), Clyde Van Dusen ('29); Preakness: Damrosch ('16)

Warren Mehrtens: Kentucky Derby: Assault (1946); Preakness: Assault ('46), Belmont: Assault ('46)

Isaac Murphy: Kentucky Derby: Buchanan (1884), Riley ('90), Kingman ('91)

William "Smokey" Saunders: Kentucky Derby: Omaha (1935); Preakness: Omaha ('35); Belmont: Omaha ('35)

John Sellers: Kentucky Derby: Carry Back (1961); Preakness: Carry Back ('61); Belmont: Hail to All ('65)

Bobby Swim: Kentucky Derby: Vagrant (1876); Belmont: General Duke ('68), Calvin ('75)

Wayne D. Wright: Kentucky Derby: Shut Out (1942); Preakness: Polynesian ('45); Belmont: Peace Chance ('34)

Kentucky Derby History

The Kentucky Derby was the dream of Col. Meriwether Lewis Clark Jr., grandson of William Clark of Lewis and Clark Expedition fame. Just 29 when the first Derby was run in 1875, Meriwether Clark had the family's sense of adventure and ambition but devoted his energies to equine pursuits.

Racing in Louisville was essentially dead in the early 1870s following the closure in 1870 of Woodlawn Course, located east of the city. In 1872, Clark traveled to England to observe the racing scene there.

He returned with grand ambitions of creating a racing palace in Louisville with races modeled on such leading events in England as the Epsom Derby, Epsom Oaks, and St. Leger Stakes. With $32,000 in investment capital, Clark set about building Louisville's new racetrack in 1874. The facility, built on 80 acres of land leased from Clark's uncles, John and Henry Churchill, was called the Louisville Jockey Club.

The Louisville Jockey Club opened on Monday, May 17, 1875, with four races. It was a sunny day with a crisp breeze, according to an account in the *Kentucky Live Stock Record* (precursor of *The Thoroughbred Record* and THOROUGHBRED TIMES), and the "course was in splendid order, and all the appurtenances requisite for the comfort and convenience of racing was ready to hand."

All 42 nominees for the inaugural Derby were listed in the program and 15 started, with H. P. McGrath's nobly named Aristides becoming the first Derby winner.

One week after the first meet ended, the *Kentucky Live Stock Record*'s editor, B. G. Bruce, noted that, while he had attended the inaugural meet at Jerome Park and had visited Saratoga and Long Branch, "never have we seen such a grand success, taking it from its beginning to its close, as the late inaugural meeting of the Louisville Jockey Club."

While the first race meet was an artistic success, at least in Bruce's view, the financial situation of the Louisville Jockey Club was perilous almost from its start. For most of its first 40 years, the Derby would be regarded as a strong regional race at best and an embarrassing farce at worst. There were many reasons for the race's decline. Louisville was still considered western territory to many leading Eastern stables, and the situation grew worse when a track official insulted leading owner James Ben Ali Haggin in 1886. The race's initial 1½-mile distance was considered too taxing for three-year-olds in the spring.

The revival of the track and its signature race began in 1902. Matt Winn, a Louisville tailor with no racetrack management experience but an undying love for the track—he attended every Kentucky Derby from 1875 to 1949—recruited a

Kentucky Derby Attendance, 1970-2002

Year	Attendance	Year	Attendance
2002	145,033	1985	108,573
2001	154,210	1984	126,453
2000	153,204	1983	134,444
1999	151,051	1982	141,009
1998	143,215	1981	139,195
1997	141,981	1980	131,859
1996	142,668	1979	128,488
1995	144,110	1978	131,004
1994	130,594	1977	124,038
1993	136,817	1976	115,387
1992	132,543	1975	113,324
1991	135,554	1974	163,628
1990	128,257	1973	134,476
1989	122,653	1972	130,564
1988	137,694	1971	123,284
1987	130,532	1970	105,087
1986	123,819		

group of Louisvillians to purchase the track for $40,000. Winn spent a decade straightening out the financial mess at the track, which by then was known as Churchill Downs. Then, he set out to revive the Kentucky Derby.

The years 1913-'15 would establish the race's credentials from both a romantic and qualitative standpoint. The 1913 running was won by 91.45-to-1 longshot Donerail, who remains the race's longest-priced winner. The race also picked up an unofficial ambassador in winning rider Roscoe Goose, who lived for a half-century mere blocks from the track, dispensing wisdom and schooling such prospective jockeys as two-time Derby winner Charlie Kurtsinger.

The next year, the gallant gelding Old Rosebud won, enhancing the race's reputation. And, in 1915, New York owner Harry Payne Whitney shipped his marvelous, unbeaten filly Regret to Louisville, where she became the first filly to win the Derby. While some Eastern stables still shied away from shipping west for the Derby—most notably Samuel Riddle's decision not to run Man o' War in 1920—the Derby's reputation was set after 1915.

Matt Winn was a showman who combined a promoter's instincts with a passion for the Derby. The Kentucky Derby benefited from Winn's skill until he died on October 6, 1949. At the time of his death, the Derby had become a national racing institution, traditionally run on the first Saturday in May and part of the Triple Crown, a three-race series for three-year-olds considered as the ultimate test for young horses. The track's Twin Spires, constructed in 1895 when the physical plant was rebuilt on what had been the backstretch side of the original track, were transformed from a unique architectural feature to an iconic symbol.

Before he died, however, Winn witnessed some amazing Derbys. Longshot Exterminator won the 1918 Derby in his three-year-old debut after he was purchased to help train another horse who did not make the race. There were two famous victories by maidens: Sir Barton's 1919 victory launched the first successful Triple Crown campaign, while Brokers Tip won in 1933 after his jockey, Don Meade, fought with Head Play's rider, Herb Fisher, down the stretch.

Winn also had to adjust to the circumstances of World War II. Travel restrictions in 1943 gave that Derby a distinctly local flavor and became known as the "Street Car Derby." Further war restrictions shut down the sport in early 1945; when the restrictions were lifted after V-E Day, the Derby was scheduled for June 9, the only time the race has been run in June. Three years later, Citation won the Triple Crown—the eighth during Winn's tenure at Churchill.

History flows easily through the Kentucky Derby. Each year seems to bring an amazing, astounding, or simply amusing story. From the sublime (Bill Shoemaker standing up at the sixteenth pole and possibly costing *Gallant Man the 1957 Derby) to the ridiculous (the antics of unraced Nevada gelding One Eyed Tom, who failed to make it to the starting gate in 1972), the Derby has something to offer every racing fan.

Over the past 30 years, the Derby's story has been about the growth of the event as a local and international event. Attendance rose from the 120,000-to-130,000 level in the late 1980s to more than 150,000 starting in 1999. (Security restrictions following the September 11, 2001, terrorist attacks held the 2002 crowd to 145,033.) Unsuccessful Triple Crown bids by Silver Charm, Real Quiet, and Charismatic from 1997-'99 created a heightened level of awareness in the Triple Crown races. The efforts of Godolphin Racing (Dubai), The Thoroughbred Corp. (Saudi Arabia and successful with War Emblem in 2002), and Michael Tabor and John Magnier (Monaco and Ireland, respectively) to win the race in the late 1990s and early 2000s have given the race an international flavor.

—John Harrell

Presidents at the Derby

Since World War II, attending the Kentucky Derby has become a pastime of United States Presidents. Getting them to attend while they are actually in office, however, has proved to be a challenge.

Eight U.S. Presidents have been seen under the twin spires on the first Saturday in May, but Richard Nixon is the only one to attend the race while in office. He attended the event in 1968 while he was running for his first term and then fulfilled a promise when he returned the next year, his first in the Oval Office.

Also attending the Derby in 1969 were two future Presidents, Gerald Ford and Ronald Reagan. Ford returned in 1983, along with Jimmy Carter, who defeated him in the 1976 presidential race, and future President George Bush. Bush returned in 2000, along with his son and future President, George W. Bush.

Other Presidents who have attended the race—though not in the Oval Office at the time—are Harry Truman and Lyndon B. Johnson.

Kentucky Derby Trophy

The Kentucky Derby trophy, featuring a simple but classic design with a horse and garland of roses on top, was first presented in 1924, when Black Gold won the 50th running of the Derby.

The trophy had been commissioned for the golden anniversary Derby by Churchill Downs President Matt Winn, who wanted a standard trophy for the connections of each Derby winner. The original design remains to this day except for one change, when the horseshoe on the trophy was inverted upward starting with the 1999 Derby. The horseshoe had been pointed down for 75 years, according to ancient belief that an upside-down shoe afforded protection. But since racing superstition maintains that luck runs out when horseshoes are pointed down, the shoe was inverted.

The only other changes made to the Derby trophy were for the 75th (1949), 100th ('74), and 125th ('99) runnings, when additional jewels were added to the trophy. Several Derby trophies are on display at the Kentucky Derby Museum; the oldest is Flying Ebony's trophy from the 1925 Derby.

Kentucky Derby Handle

Year	On-track	Off-track	Total
2002	$8,630,408	$70,464,398	$79,094,806
2001	8,360,273	59,192,483	67,552,756
2000	8,737,659	53,059,793	61,797,452
1999	8,025,318	46,171,266	54,196,586
1998	7,890,907	44,586,385	52,477,292
1997	7,401,141	41,891,506	49,292,647
1996	7,488,725	37,734,438	45,223,163
1995	7,207,060	37,618,438	44,815,488
1994	7,449,744	37,289,274	44,739,018
1993	6,811,130	33,458,735	40,269,865
1992	6,690,746	28,250,209	34,940,955
1991	6,744,979	27,499,222	34,244,201
1990	6,948,762	27,452,177	34,400,939
1989	6,751,067	23,089,515	29,840,582
1988	7,346,411	25,525,312	32,871,723
1987	6,362,673	20,829,236	27,191,909
1986	6,165,119	19,932,231	26,097,350
1985	5,770,074	14,474,555	20,244,629
1984	5,420,787	13,521,146	18,941,933
1983	5,546,977	—	5,546,977
1982	5,011,575	—	5,011,575
1981	4,566,179	455,163	5,021,342

Kentucky Derby simulcast wagering began in 1981, as three tracks (Longacres, Yakima Meadows, and Centennial) wagered a total of $455,163. Simulcast wagering was shelved for two years and resumed in 1984. Off-track wagering includes interstate and intrastate wagering.

Derby Glasses and Mint Julep Cups

The popularity of the mint julep as the official Kentucky Derby drink grew in proportion with the introduction of Derby glasses and sterling silver julep cups as Derby souvenirs in the middle years of the 20th century.

The Derby glass made its introduction in 1938 after Churchill officials noted that patrons took water glasses from their tables on Derby day as souvenirs. In 1939, glass manufacturers were encouraged to add color to the glasses, making them attractive as mint julep glasses. Sales of mint juleps increased threefold, according to track officials, and the glasses have gone on to become the most prominent of Derby souvenirs.

The sterling silver cups were introduced in 1951 as part of the legacy of Col. Matt Winn, who had died two years earlier. Winn wished to make the cups an official Derby souvenir, and they have been part of Derby lore now for a half-century. The cups, which hold 12 fluid ounces, were unchanged in design until 1984, when noted owner-breeder Leslie Combs II pointed out that the horseshoe on the glass was pointed down, a sign of bad luck in racing superstition although an upside-down shoe was regarded in folklore as affording protection. The horseshoe was turned upright and remains so to this day.

Leading Derby Owners by Wins

8 **Calumet Farm:** Whirlaway, 1941; Pensive, 1944; Citation, 1948; Ponder, 1949; Hill Gail, 1952; Iron Liege, 1957; Tim Tam, 1958; Forward Pass, 1968.

4 **Col. E. R. Bradley:** Behave Yourself, 1921; Bubbling Over, 1926; Burgoo King, 1932; Brokers Tip, 1933.

3 **Belair Stud:** Gallant Fox, 1930; Omaha, 1935; Johnstown, 1939.

2 **Bashford Manor Stable:** Azra, 1892; Sir Huon, 1906.

Harry Payne Whitney: Regret, 1915; Whiskery, 1927.

Mrs. John D. Hertz: Reigh Count, 1928; Count Fleet, 1943.

Greentree Stable: Twenty Grand, 1931; Shut Out, 1942.

King Ranch: Assault, 1946; Middleground, 1950.

Darby Dan Farm: Chateaugay, 1963; Proud Clarion, 1967.

Meadow Stable: Riva Ridge, 1972; Secretariat, 1973.

William Condren and Joseph Cornacchia: Strike the Gold, 1991; Go for Gin, 1994.

Robert and Beverly Lewis: Silver Charm, 1997; Charismatic, 1999.

Leading Derby Trainers by Wins

6 **Ben A. Jones:** Lawrin, 1938; Whirlaway, 1941; Pensive, 1944; Citation, 1948; Ponder, 1949; Hill Gail, 1952.

4 **H. J. "Dick" Thompson:** Behave Yourself, 1921; Bubbling Over, 1926; Burgoo King, 1932; Brokers Tip, 1933.

D. Wayne Lukas: Winning Colors, 1988; Thunder Gulch, 1995; Grindstone, 1996; Charismatic, 1999.

3 **Bob Baffert:** Silver Charm, 1997; Real Quiet, 1998; War Emblem 2002.

James "Sunny Jim" Fitzsimmons: Gallant Fox, 1930; Omaha, 1935; Johnstown, 1939.

Max Hirsch: Bold Venture, 1936; Assault, 1946; Middleground, 1950.

2 **John McGinty:** Leonatus, 1883; Montrose, 1887.

James Rowe Sr.: Hindoo, 1881; Regret, 1915.

H. A. "Jimmy" Jones: Iron Liege, 1957; Tim Tam, 1958.

Horatio Luro: Decidedly, 1962; Northern Dancer, 1964.

Henry Forrest: Kauai King, 1966; Forward Pass, 1968.

Lucien Laurin: Riva Ridge, 1972; Secretariat, 1973.

W. C. "Woody" Stephens: Cannonade, 1974; Swale, 1984.

LeRoy Jolley: Foolish Pleasure, 1975; Genuine Risk, 1980.

Lazaro Barrera: Bold Forbes, 1976; Affirmed, 1978.

Charlie Whittingham: Ferdinand, 1986; Sunday Silence, 1989.

Nicholas P. Zito: Strike the Gold, 1991; Go for Gin, 1994.

Trainers With Most Derby Starters

Trainer	Strs.	Wins	2nd	3rd	Unplaced
D. Wayne Lukas	39	4	1	5	29
H. J. Thompson	24	4	2	1	17
James Rowe Sr.*	18	2	1	1	14
Max Hirsch	14	3	0	2	9
W. C. Stephens	14	2	3	3	6
LeRoy Jolley	13	2	2	1	8
Bob Baffert	12	3	1	2	6
Nicholas P. Zito	12	2	0	0	10
James Fitzsimmons	11	3	1	0	7
Ben A. Jones	11	6	2	1	2

*Information on James Rowe Sr. is incomplete

Leading Derby Jockeys by Wins

5 **Eddie Arcaro:** Lawrin, 1938; Whirlaway, 1941; Hoop, Jr., 1945; Citation, 1948; Hill Gail, 1952.

Bill Hartack: Iron Liege, 1957; Venetian Way, 1960; Decidedly, 1962; Northern Dancer, 1964; Majestic Prince, 1969.

4 **Bill Shoemaker:** Swaps, 1955; *Tomy Lee, 1959; Lucky Debonair, 1965; Ferdinand, 1986.

3 **Isaac Murphy:** Buchanan, 1884; Riley, 1890; Kingman, 1891.

Earl Sande: Zev, 1923; Flying Ebony, 1925; Gallant Fox, 1930.

Angel Cordero Jr.: Cannonade, 1974; Bold Forbes, 1976; Spend a Buck, 1985.

Gary Stevens: Winning Colors, 1988; Thunder Gulch, 1995; Silver Charm, 1997.

Jockeys With Most Derby Starters

Jockey	Strs.	Wins	2nd	3rd	Unplaced
Bill Shoemaker	26	4	3	4	15
Eddie Arcaro	21	5	3	2	11
Laffit Pincay Jr.	21	1	4	2	14
Pat Day	20	1	4	2	13
Angel Cordero Jr.	17	3	1	0	13
Chris McCarron	19	2	3	0	14
Gary Stevens	16	3	2	0	11
Jerry Bailey	15	2	1	1	11
Jorge Velasquez	14	1	1	2	10
Mack Garner	14	1	0	1	12
Don Brumfield	13	1	0	1	11
Johnny Adams	13	0	2	0	11

Female Jockeys and Trainers in the Derby

A woman has yet to win the Kentucky Derby (G1) as either a jockey or a trainer, but several female trainers have come close to landing one of racing's biggest prizes.

Northern California-based trainer Shelley Riley came closest in 1992, when 29.90-to-1 longshot Casual Lies finished second to Lil E. Tee. Riley, who also

owned the colt, sent Casual Lies out in all three Triple Crown races.

The first female trainer to send a horse to the Derby was Mary Hirsch, daughter of Racing Hall of Fame trainer Max Hirsch. Her No Sir finished 13th in the 1937 Derby. The most recent woman to train a Derby starter was Jenine Sahadi, who sent out The Deputy (Ire), who finished 14th in 2000.

Female trainers in the Derby:

Trainer	Horse	Year	Finish
Jenine Sahadi	The Deputy (Ire)	2000	14th
Akiko Gothard	K One King	1999	8th
Kathy Walsh	Hanuman Highway	1998	8th
Cynthia Reese	In Contention	1996	15th
Shelley Riley	Casual Lies	1992	2nd
Dianne Carpenter	Kingpost	1988	14th
	Biloxi Indian	1984	12th
Patti Johnson	Fast Account	1985	4th
Mary Keim	Mr. Pak	1965	6th
Mrs. Albert Roth	Senecas Coin	1949	DNF
Mary Hirsch	No Sir	1937	13th

The first female jockey in the Derby was Diane Crump, who rode Fathom to a 15th-place finish in 1970. Three other female riders have since participated in the Derby—Patricia Cooksey, Andrea Seefeldt, and Julie Krone—but none finished better than 11th.

Female jockeys in the Derby:

Jockey	Mount	Year	Finish
Julie Krone	Suave Prospect	1995	11th
	Ecstatic Ride	1992	14th
Andrea Seefeldt	Forty Something	1991	16th
Patricia Cooksey	So Vague	1984	11th
Diane Crump	Fathom	1970	15th

African-American Jockeys in the Derby

African-American jockeys dominated the Kentucky Derby during the race's first quarter-century. Between 1875 and 1902, 11 African-American riders won 15 runnings of the Derby. The most famous were Isaac Murphy, the first jockey to win the Derby three times, and Jimmy Winkfield, who won the Derby in 1901 and '02.

Marlon St. Julien became the first African-American rider in the Derby in 79 years when he finished seventh aboard Curule in the 2000 renewal.

African-American riders who have won the Derby:

Jockey	Year	Mount
Jimmy Winkfield	1902	Alan-a-Dale
	1901	His Eminence
Willie Simms	1898	Plaudit
	1896	Ben Brush
James "Soup" Perkins	1895	Halma
Alonzo "Lonnie" Clayton	1892	Azra
Oliver Lewis	1875	Aristides
Isaac Murphy	1891	Kingman
	1890	Riley
	1884	Buchanan
Isaac Lewis	1887	Montrose
Erskine Henderson	1885	Joe Cotton
Babe Hurd	1882	Apollo
George Garret Lewis	1880	Fonso
William Walker	1877	Baden-Baden

Leading Sires of Derby Winners

3　Virgil: Vagrant, 1876; Hindoo, 1881; Ben Ali, 1886.
Falsetto: Chant, 1894; His Eminence, 1901; Sir Huon, 1906.
*Sir Gallahad III: Gallant Fox, 1930; Gallahadion,

1940; Hoop, Jr., 1945.
Bull Lea: Citation, 1948; Hill Gail, 1952; Iron Liege, 1957.
2　King Alfonso: Fonso, 1880; Joe Cotton, 1885.
Longfellow: Leonatus, 1883; Riley, 1890.
Broomstick: Meridian, 1911; Regret, 1915.
*McGee: Donerail, 1913; Exterminator, 1918.
The Finn: Zev, 1923; Flying Ebony, 1925.
Black Toney: Black Gold, 1924; Brokers Tip, 1933.
Man o' War: Clyde Van Dusen, 1929; War Admiral, 1937.
*St. Germans: Twenty Grand, 1931; Bold Venture, 1936.
*Blenheim II: Whirlaway, 1941; Jet Pilot, 1947.
Bold Venture: Assault, 1946; Middleground, 1950.
Bold Bidder: Cannonade, 1974; Spectacular Bid, 1979.
Exclusive Native: Affirmed, 1978; Genuine Risk, 1980.
Halo: Sunny's Halo, 1983; Sunday Silence, 1989.
Alydar: Alysheba, 1987; Strike the Gold, 1991.

Derby Winners Who Sired Winners

2　Bold Venture (1936) (2): Assault, 1946; Middleground, 1950.
1　Halma (1895): Alan-a-Dale, 1902.
Bubbling Over (1926): Burgoo King (1932)
Reigh Count (1928): Count Fleet, 1943.
Gallant Fox (1930): Omaha, 1935.
Count Fleet (1943): Count Turf (1951)
Pensive (1944): Ponder, 1949.
Ponder (1949): Needles, 1956.
Determine (1954): Decidedly, 1962.
Swaps (1955): Chateaugay, 1963.
Seattle Slew (1977): Swale, 1984.
Unbridled (1990): Grindstone, 1996.

Fastest Derby Winning Times
1¼ miles

Year	Winner	Time	Cond.
1973	Secretariat	1:59⅖	Fast
2001	Monarchos	1:59.97	Fast
1964	Northern Dancer	2:00	Fast
1985	Spend a Buck	2:00⅕	Fast
1962	Decidedly	2:00⅖	Fast
1967	Proud Clarion	2:00⅗	Fast
1996	Grindstone	2:01.06	Fast
2000	Fusaichi Pegasus	2:01.12	Fast
2002	War Emblem	2:01.13	Fast
1978	Affirmed	2:01⅕	Fast
1965	Lucky Debonair	2:01⅕	Fast
1995	Thunder Gulch	2:01.27	Fast

1½ miles

Year	Winner	Time	Cond.
1889	Spokane	2:34½	Fast
1886	Ben Ali	2:36½	Fast
1879	Lord Murphy	2:37	Fast
1878	Day Star	2:37¼	Dusty
1885	Joe Cotton	2:37¼	Good

Times recorded in hundredths of a second beginning in 1991

Slowest Derby Winning Times
1¼ miles

Year	Winner	Time	Cond.
1908	Stone Street	2:15⅕	Heavy
1907	Pink Star	2:12⅗	Heavy
1897	Typhoon II	2:12½	Heavy

1899	Manuel	2:12	Fast
1918	Exterminator	2:10$\frac{4}{5}$	Muddy
1929	Clyde Van Dusen	2:10$\frac{4}{5}$	Muddy
1905	Agile	2:10$\frac{3}{4}$	Heavy
1928	Reigh Count	2:10$\frac{2}{5}$	Heavy
1919	Sir Barton	2:09$\frac{4}{5}$	Heavy
1912	Worth	2:09$\frac{2}{5}$	Muddy

1$\frac{1}{2}$ miles

Year	Winner	Time	Cond.
1891	Kingman	2:52$\frac{1}{4}$	Slow
1890	Riley	2:45	Muddy
1883	Leonatus	2:43	Heavy
1892	Azra	2:41$\frac{1}{2}$	Heavy
1894	Chant	2:41	Fast

Fastest Derby fractions

Quarter-mile: :21$\frac{1}{5}$, Top Avenger (1981)
Half-mile: 44.86, Songandaprayer (2001)
Six furlongs: 1:09.25, Songandaprayer (2001)
One mile: 1:34$\frac{4}{5}$, Spend a Buck (1985)

Evolution of Derby Stakes Record at 1$\frac{1}{4}$ miles

Year	Winner	Time
1896	Ben Brush	2:07$\frac{3}{4}$
1900	Lieut. Gibson	2:06$\frac{1}{4}$
1911	Meridian	2:05
1913	Donerail	2:04$\frac{4}{5}$
1914	Old Rosebud	2:03$\frac{2}{5}$
1931	Twenty Grand	2:01$\frac{4}{5}$
1941	Whirlaway	2:01$\frac{2}{5}$
1962	Decidedly	2:00$\frac{2}{5}$
1964	Northern Dancer	2:00
1973	Secretariat	1:59$\frac{2}{5}$

Shortest-Priced Derby Beaten Favorites

Year	Horse	Odds	Finish
1976	Honest Pleasure	.40-to-1	2nd
1940	Bimelech	.40-to-1	2nd
1953	Native Dancer	.70-to-1	2nd
1989	Easy Goer	.80-to-1	2nd
1949	Olympia	.80-to-1	6th
1936	Brevity	.80-to-1	2nd
1992	Arazi	.90-to-1	8th
1911	Governor Gray	1-to-1	2nd
1916	Thunderer	1.05-to-1	5th
1960	Tompion	1.10-to-1	4th
1962	Ridan	1.10-to-1	3rd
1946	Lord Boswell	1.10-to-1	4th
1921	Prudery	1.10-to-1	3rd

Shortest-Priced Winning Favorites

Year	Winner	Odds
1948	Citation	.40-to-1
1943	Count Fleet	.40-to-1
1977	Seattle Slew	.50-to-1
1979	Spectacular Bid	.60-to-1
1939	Johnstown	.60-to-1
1912	Worth	.80-to-1
1914	Old Rosebud	.85-to-1
1931	Twenty Grand	.88-to-1
1952	Hill Gail	1.10-to-1
1906	Sir Huon	1.10-to-1
1930	Gallant Fox	1.19-to-1

Largest Winning Margins

Year	Winner	Lengths
1946	Assault	8
1941	Whirlaway	8
1939	Johnstown	8
1914	Old Rosebud	8
1880	Fonso	7
1945	Hoop, Jr.	6
1894	Chant	6
1985	Spend a Buck	5$\frac{3}{4}$
1970	Dust Commander	5
1932	Burgoo King	5
1926	Bubbling Over	5
1919	Sir Barton	5
1895	Halma	5

Smallest Winning Margins

Year	Winner	Lengths
1996	Grindstone	nose
1959	*Tomy Lee	nose
1957	Iron Liege	nose
1933	Brokers Tip	nose
1902	Alan-a-Dale	nose
1898	Plaudit	nose
1896	Ben Brush	nose
1892	Azra	nose
1889	Spokane	nose
1997	Silver Charm	head
1953	Dark Star	head
1947	Jet Pilot	head
1936	Bold Venture	head
1927	Whiskery	head
1921	Behave Yourself	head
1920	Paul Jones	head

Birthplace of Derby Winners

State	Winners
Kentucky	97
Florida	6
Virginia	4
California	3
Tennessee	3
New Jersey	2
Texas	2
Canada	2
Great Britain	2
Illinois	1
Kansas	1
Maryland	1
Missouri	1
Montana	1
Ohio	1
Pennsylvania	1

Fillies Who Have Won the Derby

In the Kentucky Derby's long history, only three fillies have won—Regret in 1915, Genuine Risk in '80, and Winning Colors in '88. Although fillies commonly ran in the Derby until the 1930s, only ten fillies have started since 1945. They are:

Year	Filly	Finish
1999	Excellent Meeting	5th
	Three Ring	19th
1995	Serena's Song	16th
1988	**Winning Colors**	**1st**
1984	Life's Magic	8th
	Althea	19th
1982	Cupecoy's Joy	10th
1980	**Genuine Risk**	**1st**
1959	Silver Spoon	5th
1945	Misweet	12th
****		
1915	**Regret**	**1st**

Maiden Starters Since 1950

Only three maidens have won the Kentucky Derby—Buchanan (1884), Sir Barton (1919), and Brokers Tip (1933)—but maidens in the Derby were a common occurrence until the mid-1930s.

Since 1950, only seven maidens have run in the Derby, and none came close to winning. The connections of several runners, most notably Great Redeemer in 1979, were harshly criticized for running.

Of the recent group, the most accomplished runner may have been Nationalore, who finished third in the 1997 Breeders' Cup Juvenile (G1) and Hollywood Futurity (G1). Despite his credentials, Nationalore never won and was euthanized after breaking down in his 26th start, a maiden race at Hollywood Park on July 12, 2000.

Year	Horse	Finish
1998	Nationalore	9th
1990	Pendleton Ridge	13th
1979	Great Redeemer	10th
1971	Fourulla	19th
1959	The Chosen One	14th
1958	Flamingo	13th
1950	On the Mark	8th

Geldings in the Derby

Without doubt, the longest losing streak in the Derby is for geldings, winless since Clyde Van Dusen in 1929. In the 1990s, three geldings finished second. They were Best Pal (1991), Prairie Bayou (1993), and Cavonnier (1996), who lost by a nose to Grindstone. The winning geldings:

Year	Gelding
1929	Clyde Van Dusen
1920	Paul Jones
1918	Exterminator
1914	Old Rosebud
1888	Macbeth II
1882	Apollo
1876	Vagrant

Front-Running Derby Winners

The following Kentucky Derby winners were on the lead at all points of call.

Year	Winner	Winning margin
2002	War Emblem	4
1988	Winning Colors	neck
1985	Spend a Buck	5¼
1976	Bold Forbes	1
1972	Riva Ridge	3¼
1966	Kauai King	½
1955	Swaps	1½
1953	Dark Star	head
1947	Jet Pilot	head
1945	Hoop, Jr.	6
1943	Count Fleet	3
1939	Johnstown	8
1937	War Admiral	1¾
1929	Clyde Van Dusen	2
1926	Bubbling Over	5
1923	Zev	1½
1922	Morvich	1½
1920	Paul Jones	head
1919	Sir Barton	5
1915	Regret	2
1914	Old Rosebud	8
1912	Worth	neck
1911	Meridian	3/4
1910	Donau	1/2
1909	Wintergreen	4
1905	Agile	3

1902	Alan-a-Dale	nose
1901	His Eminence	1½
1900	Lieut. Gibson	3
1897	Typhoon II	neck
1895	Halma	5
1894	Chant	6
1893	Lookout	4
1887	Montrose	2
1883	Leonatus	3
1881	Hindoo	4
1880	Fonso	1
1878	Day Star	1
1875	Aristides	2

Winning Derby Post Positions

Winning Derby post positions since 1900:

Post	Winners	Post	Winners
1	12	11	3
2	9	12	3
3	8	13	3
4	10	14	2
5	10	15	3
6	6	16	3
7	7	17	0
8	8	18	1
9	4	19	0
10	9	20	1

Longest Winning Odds

Year	Horse	Odds
1913	Donerail	91.45-to-1
1940	Gallahadion	35.20-to-1
1999	Charismatic	31.30-to-1
1967	Proud Clarion	30.10-to-1
1918	Exterminator	29.60-to-1
1953	Dark Star	24.90-to-1
1995	Thunder Gulch	24.50-to-1
1908	Stone Street	23.72-to-1
1982	Gato Del Sol	21.20-to-1
2002	War Emblem	20.50-to-1
1936	Bold Venture	20.50-to-1
1923	Zev	19.20-to-1
1986	Ferdinand	17.70-to-1

Undefeated Starters

Seattle Slew, the 1977 Triple Crown winner, was only the fourth undefeated horse to win the Derby. The other three were Regret in 1915, Morvich in 1922, and Majestic Prince in 1969.

The undefeated Derby starters since Regret in 1915:

Year	Horse	Pre-Derby starts	Derby finish
2000	China Visit	2	6th
	Trippi	4	11th
1998	Indian Charlie	4	3rd
1990	Mister Frisky	16	8th
1988	Private Terms	7	9th
1982	Air Forbes Won	4	7th
1978	Sensitive Prince	6	6th
1977	**Seattle Slew**	6	**1st**
1969	**Majestic Prince**	7	**1st**
1963	Candy Spots	6	3rd
	No Robbery	5	5th
1953	Native Dancer	11	2nd
1948	Coaltown	4	2nd
1940	Bimelech	8	2nd
1922	**Morvich**	11	**1st**
1916	Thunderer	3	5th
1915	**Regret**	3	**1st**

Derby Trivia

Largest field: 23 in 1974.

Smallest field: Three in 1892 and 1905.

Longest-priced runner since 1908: A Dragon Killer, seventh in 1958 at 294.40-to-1.

Most maidens in one race: Six in 1882 (Highflyer, seventh; Pat Malloy colt, ninth; Wallensee, tenth; Newsboy, 11th; Mistral, 12th; Robert Bruce, 14th).

Most lifetime starts going into Derby: 66, Florizar, 1900 (second).

Fewest lifetime starts going into Derby: Zero, 11 times, most recently by Col. Hogan, 1911 (seventh).

Mutuel field horses who won the Derby: Canonero II, 1971; Count Turf, 1951; Flying Ebony, 1925.

Derby winners who never started again: Grindstone, 1996; Bubbling Over, 1926.

Derby winner as both jockey and trainer: Johnny Longden, rider of Count Fleet in 1943 and trainer of Majestic Prince in 1969.

Longest-priced Derby favorite: Harlan's Holiday, 6-to-1, in 2002.

Kentucky Derby

Grade 1, Churchill Downs, three-year-olds, 1¼ miles, dirt. Held on May 4, 2002, with gross value of $2,175,000 (includes $1-million bonus awarded by Sportsman's Park to War Emblem for winning Illinois Derby and a Triple Crown race). First run in 1875. Weights: colts and geldings, 126 pounds; fillies, 121 pounds.

Year	Winner	Jockey	Second	Third	Strs	Time	Track	1st purse
2002	**War Emblem**	V. Espinoza	Proud Citizen	Perfect Drift	18	2:01.13	ft	**$1,875,000**
2001	**Monarchos**	J. Chavez	Invisible Ink	Congaree	17	1:59.97	ft	$812,000
2000	**Fusaichi Pegasus**	K. Desormeaux	Aptitude	Impeachment	19	2:01.12	ft	$888,400
1999	**Charismatic**	C. Antley	Menifee	Cat Thief	19	2:03.29	ft	$886,200
1998	**Real Quiet**	K. Desormeaux	Victory Gallop	Indian Charlie	15	2:02.38	ft	$738,800
1997	**Silver Charm**	G. Stevens	Captain Bodgit	Free House	13	2:02.44	ft	$700,000
1996	**Grindstone**	J. Bailey	‡Cavonnier	Prince of Thieves	19	2:01.06	ft	$869,800
1995	**Thunder Gulch**	G. Stevens	Tejano Run	Timber Country	19	2:01.27	ft	$707,400
1994	**Go for Gin**	C. McCarron	Strodes Creek	Blumin Affair	14	2:03.72	sy	$628,800
1993	**Sea Hero**	J. Bailey	‡Prairie Bayou	Wild Gale	19	2:02.42	ft	$735,900
1992	**Lil E. Tee**	P. Day	Casual Lies	Dance Floor	18	2:03.04	ft	$724,800
1991	**Strike the Gold**	C. Antley	‡Best Pal	Mane Minister	16	2:03.08	ft	$655,800
1990	**Unbridled**	C. Perret	Summer Squall	Pleasant Tap	15	2:02	gd	$581,000
1989	**Sunday Silence**	P. Valenzuela	Easy Goer	Awe Inspiring	15	2:05	my	$574,200
1988	**†Winning Colors**	G. Stevens	Forty Niner	Risen Star	17	2:02⅕	ft	$611,200
1987	**Alysheba**	C. McCarron	Bet Twice	Avies Copy	17	2:03⅖	ft	$618,600
1986	**Ferdinand**	W. Shoemaker	Bold Arrangement (GB)	Broad Brush	16	2:02⅘	ft	$609,400
1985	**Spend a Buck**	A. Cordero Jr.	Stephan's Odyssey	Chief's Crown	13	2:00⅕	ft	$406,800
1984	**Swale**	L. Pincay Jr.	Coax Me Chad	At the Threshold	20	2:02⅖	ft	$537,400
1983	**Sunny's Halo**	E. Delahoussaye	Desert Wine	Caveat	20	2:02⅕	ft	$426,000
1982	**Gato Del Sol**	E. Delahoussaye	Laser Light	Reinvested	19	2:02⅖	ft	$428,850
1981	**Pleasant Colony**	J. Velasquez	Woodchopper	Partez	21	2:02	ft	$317,200
1980	**†Genuine Risk**	J. Vasquez	Rumbo	Jaklin Klugman	13	2:02	ft	$250,550
1979	**Spectacular Bid**	R. Franklin	General Assembly	Golden Act	10	2:02⅖	ft	$228,650
1978	**AFFIRMED**	S. Cauthen	Alydar	Believe It	11	2:01⅕	ft	$186,900
1977	**SEATTLE SLEW**	J. Cruguet	Run Dusty Run	Sanhedrin	15	2:02⅕	ft	$214,700
1976	**Bold Forbes**	A. Cordero Jr.	Honest Pleasure	Elocutionist	9	2:01⅗	ft	$165,200
1975	**Foolish Pleasure**	J. Vasquez	Avatar	Diabolo	15	2:02	ft	$209,600
1974	**Cannonade**	A. Cordero Jr.	Hudson County	Agitate	**23**	2:04	ft	$274,000
1973	**SECRETARIAT**	R. Turcotte	Sham	Our Native	13	**1:59⅖**	ft	$155,050
1972	**Riva Ridge**	R. Turcotte	No Le Hace	Hold Your Peace	16	2:01⅘	ft	$140,300
1971	**Canonero II**	G. Avila	Jim French	Bold Reason	20	2:03⅕	ft	$145,500
1970	**Dust Commander**	M. Manganello	My Dad George	High Echelon	17	2:03⅖	gd	$127,800
1969	**Majestic Prince**	W. Hartack	Arts and Letters	Dike	8	2:01⅘	ft	$113,200
1968	**Forward Pass**	I. Valenzuela	Francie's Hat	T. V. Commercial	14	2:02⅕	ft	$122,600
1967	**Proud Clarion**	R. Ussery	Barbs Delight	Damascus	14	2:00⅗	ft	$119,700
1966	**Kauai King**	D. Brumfield	Advocator	Blue Skyer	15	2:02	ft	$120,500
1965	**Lucky Debonair**	W. Shoemaker	Dapper Dan	Tom Rolfe	11	2:01⅕	ft	$112,000
1964	**Northern Dancer**	W. Hartack	Hill Rise	The Scoundrel	12	2:00	ft	$114,300
1963	**Chateaugay**	B. Baeza	Never Bend	Candy Spots	9	2:01⅘	ft	$108,900
1962	**Decidedly**	W. Hartack	Roman Line	Ridan	15	2:00⅖	ft	$119,650
1961	**Carry Back**	J. Sellers	Crozier	Bass Clef	15	2:04	gd	$120,500
1960	**Venetian Way**	W. Hartack	Bally Ache	Victoria Park	13	2:02⅖	gd	$114,850
1959	***Tomy Lee**	W. Shoemaker	Sword Dancer	First Landing	17	2:02⅕	ft	$119,650
1958	**Tim Tam**	I. Valenzuela	Lincoln Road	Noureddin	14	2:05	my	$116,400
1957	**Iron Liege**	W. Hartack	*Gallant Man	Round Table	9	2:02⅕	ft	$107,950
1956	**Needles**	D. Erb	Fabius	Come On Red	17	2:03⅖	ft	$123,450
1955	**Swaps**	W. Shoemaker	Nashua	Summer Tan	10	2:01⅘	ft	$108,400
1954	**Determine**	R. York	Hasty Road	Hasseyampa	17	2:03	ft	$102,050
1953	**Dark Star**	H. Moreno	Native Dancer	Invigorator	11	2:02	ft	$90,050
1952	**Hill Gail**	E. Arcaro	Sub Fleet	Blue Man	16	2:01⅗	ft	$96,300
1951	**Count Turf**	C. McCreary	Royal Mustang	‡Ruhe	20	2:02⅗	ft	$98,050
1950	**Middleground**	W. Boland	Hill Prince	Mr. Trouble	14	2:01⅗	ft	$92,650
1949	**Ponder**	S. Brooks	Capot	Palestinian	14	2:04⅕	ft	$91,600
1948	**CITATION**	E. Arcaro	Coaltown	My Request	6	2:05⅖	sy	$83,400
1947	**Jet Pilot**	E. Guerin	Phalanx	Faultless	13	2:06⅘	sl	$92,160
1946	**ASSAULT**	W. Mehrtens	Spy Song	Hampden	17	2:06⅗	sl	$96,400

Year	Winner	Jockey	Second	Third	Strs	Time	Track	1st purse
1945	**Hoop, Jr.**	E. Arcaro	Pot o'Luck	‡Darby Dieppe	16	2:07	my	$64,850
1944	**Pensive**	C. McCreary	Broadcloth	‡Stir Up	16	2:04⅕	gd	$64,675
1943	**COUNT FLEET**	J. Longden	Blue Swords	Slide Rule	10	2:04	ft	$60,725
1942	**Shut Out**	W. Wright	Alsab	Valdina Orphan	15	2:04⅖	ft	$64,225
1941	**WHIRLAWAY**	E. Arcaro	Staretor	Market Wise	11	2:01⅖	ft	$61,275
1940	**Gallahadion**	C. Bierman	Bimelech	‡Dit	8	2:05	ft	$60,150
1939	**Johnstown**	J. Stout	Challedon	Heather Broom	8	2:03⅖	ft	$46,350
1938	**Lawrin**	E. Arcaro	Dauber	Can't Wait	10	2:04⅘	ft	$47,050
1937	**WAR ADMIRAL**	C. Kurtsinger	Pompoon	Reaping Reward	20	2:03⅕	ft	$52,050
1936	**Bold Venture**	I. Hanford	Brevity	Indian Broom	14	2:03⅗	ft	$37,725
1935	**OMAHA**	W. Saunders	Roman Soldier	Whiskolo	18	2:05	gd	$39,525
1934	**Cavalcade**	M. Garner	Discovery	Agrarian	13	2:04	ft	$28,175
1933	**Brokers Tip**	D. Meade	Head Play	Charley O.	13	2:06⅘	gd	$48,925
1932	**Burgoo King**	E. James	Economic	Stepenfetchit	20	2:05⅕	ft	$52,350
1931	**Twenty Grand**	C. Kurtsinger	Sweep All	Mate	12	2:01⅘	ft	$48,725
1930	**GALLANT FOX**	E. Sande	Gallant Knight	Ned O.	15	2:07⅗	gd	$50,725
1929	**‡Clyde Van Dusen**	L. McAtee	Naishapur	Panchio	21	2:10⅘	my	$53,950
1928	**Reigh Count**	C. Lang	Misstep	Toro	22	2:10⅖	hy	$55,375
1927	**Whiskery**	L. McAtee	‡Osmand	Jock	15	2:06	sl	$51,000
1926	**Bubbling Over**	A. Johnson	Bagenbaggage	Rock Man	13	2:03⅘	ft	$50,075
1925	**Flying Ebony**	E. Sande	Captain Hal	Son of John	20	2:07⅗	sy	$52,950
1924	**Black Gold**	J. Mooney	Chilhowee	Beau Butler	19	2:05⅕	ft	$52,775
1923	**Zev**	E. Sande	Martingale	Vigil	21	2:05⅖	ft	$53,600
1922	**Morvich**	A. Johnson	Bet Mosie	John Finn	10	2:04⅗	ft	$53,775
1921	**Behave Yourself**	C. Thompson	Black Servant	†Prudery	12	2:04⅕	ft	$38,450
1920	**‡Paul Jones**	T. Rice	Upset	On Watch	17	2:09	sl	$30,375
1919	**SIR BARTON**	J. Loftus	‡Billy Kelly	*Under Fire	12	2:09⅘	hy	$20,825
1918	**‡Exterminator**	W. Knapp	Escoba	†Viva America	8	2:10⅘	my	$14,700
1917	***Omar Khayyam**	C. Borel	Ticket	Midway	15	2:04⅗	ft	$16,600
1916	**George Smith**	J. Loftus	Star Hawk	Franklin	9	2:04	ft	$9,750
1915	**†Regret**	J. Notter	Pebbles	‡Sharpshooter	16	2:05⅖	ft	$11,450
1914	**‡Old Rosebud**	J. McCabe	‡Hodge	†Bronzewing	7	2:03⅖	ft	$9,125
1913	**Donerail**	R. Goose	Ten Point	†Gowell	8	2:04⅘	ft	$5,475
1912	**Worth**	C. Schilling	Duval	†Flamma	7	2:09⅖	my	$4,850
1911	**Meridian**	G. Archibald	‡Governor Gray	Colston	7	2:05	ft	$4,850
1910	**Donau**	F. Herbert	Joe Morris	Fighting Bob	7	2:06⅖	ft	$4,850
1909	**Wintergreen**	V. Powers	‡Miami	Dr. Barkley	10	2:08⅕	sl	$4,850
1908	**Stone Street**	A. Pickens	‡Sir Cleges	Dunvegan	8	2:15⅕	hy	$4,850
1907	**Pink Star**	A. Minder	Zal	Ovelando	6	2:12⅗	hy	$4,850
1906	**Sir Huon**	R. Troxler	†Lady Navarre	James Reddick	6	2:08⅘	ft	$4,850
1905	**Agile**	J. Martin	Ram's Horn	Layson	3	2:10¾	hy	$4,850
1904	**Elwood**	F. Prior	Ed Tierney	Brancas	5	2:08½	ft	$4,850
1903	**Judge Himes**	H. Booker	Early	Bourbon	6	2:09	ft	$4,850
1902	**Alan-a-Dale**	J. Winkfield	Inventor	The Rival	4	2:08¾	ft	$4,850
1901	**His Eminence**	J. Winkfield	Sannazarro	Driscoll	5	2:07¾	ft	$4,850
1900	**Lieut. Gibson**	J. Boland	Florizar	Thrive	7	2:06¼	ft	$4,850
1899	**Manuel**	F. Taral	‡Corsine	Mazo	5	2:12	ft	$4,850
1898	**Plaudit**	W. Simms	Lieber Karl	Isabey	4	2:09	gd	$4,850
1897	**Typhoon II**	F. Garner	Ornament	Dr. Catlett	6	2:12½	hy	$4,850
1896	**Ben Brush**	W. Simms	Ben Eder	Semper Ego	8	2:07¾	dy	$4,850
1895	**Halma**	J. Perkins	Basso	Laureate	4	2:37½	ft	$2,970
1894	**Chant**	F. Goodale	Pearl Song	Sigurd	5	2:41	ft	$4,020
1893	**Lookout**	E. Kunze	Plutus	Boundless	6	2:39¼	ft	$3,840
1892	**Azra**	A. Clayton	Huron	Phil Dwyer	3	2:41½	hy	$4,230
1891	**Kingman**	I. Murphy	Balgowan	High Tariff	4	2:52¼	sl	$4,550
1890	**Riley**	I. Murphy	Bill Letcher	Robespierre	6	2:45	my	$5,460
1889	**Spokane**	T. Kiley	‡Proctor Knott	Once Again	8	2:34½	ft	$4,880
1888	**‡Macbeth II**	G. Covington	Gallifet	White	7	2:38¼	ft	$4,740
1887	**Montrose**	I. Lewis	Jim Gore	‡Jacobin	7	2:39¼	ft	$4,200
1886	**Ben Ali**	P. Duffy	Blue Wing	Free Knight	10	2:36½	ft	$4,890
1885	**Joe Cotton**	E. Henderson	Bersan	‡Ten Booker	10	2:37¼	gd	$4,630
1884	**Buchanan**	I. Murphy	Loftin	Audrain	9	2:40¼	gd	$3,990
1883	**Leonatus**	W. Donohue	‡Drake Carter	Lord Raglan	7	2:43	hy	$3,760
1882	**‡Apollo**	B. Hurd	Runnymede	Bengal	14	2:40¼	gd	$4,560
1881	**Hindoo**	J. McLaughlin	‡Lelex	Alfambra	6	2:40	ft	$4,410
1880	**Fonso**	G. Lewis	Kimball	‡Bancroft	5	2:37½	dy	$3,800
1879	**Lord Murphy**	C. Shauer	Falsetto	Strathmore	9	2:37	ft	$3,550
1878	**Day Star**	J. Carter	Himyar	Leveller	9	2:37¼	dy	$4,050
1877	**Baden-Baden**	W. Walker	Leonard	King William	11	2:38	ft	$3,300
1876	**‡Vagrant**	B. Swim	Creedmore	Harry Hill	11	2:38¼	ft	$2,950
1875	**Aristides**	O. Lewis	Volcano	Verdigris	15	2:37¾	ft	$2,850

†—filly, ‡—gelding, *—imported horse

1875-'95: 1½ miles; 1973-present: Grade 1; 1968: Dancer's Image finished first but was disqualified from purse money; bold indicates records set in number of starters, time, and winning purse; Triple Crown winners are in all capitalized letters.

History of the Preakness Stakes

Born out of a party boast and named for a horse who met an unfortunate end, the Preakness Stakes (G1) is the second jewel of the American Triple Crown and the second-oldest American classic.

Both the Preakness Stakes and Pimlico Race Course, the track where the classic race is staged annually on the third Saturday of May, trace their roots to a party hosted by Milton H. Sanford in Saratoga Springs, New York, in 1868. At the party, Maryland Governor Oden Bowie promised that a new racetrack would open in Baltimore to play host to the Dinner Party Stakes, to which he pledged a hefty purse.

A 70-acre track site, which had been known as Pimlico since the 1850s and had been used for racing since then, was purchased by the Maryland Agricultural Society from Robert Wylie in 1866. The organization held a fair meet at the site in 1869 but failed to raise enough money to complete the track.

Bowie, a horse owner and sportsman, helped another group, the Maryland Jockey Club, to negotiate a lease of the property—$1,000 annual rent for ten years. Gen. John Elliott designed the track, and Pimlico opened on October 25, 1870. Among the amenities was the Pimlico Clubhouse, a Baltimore landmark until destroyed by fire in 1966.

Sanford, a New York horseman who made a portion of his fortune by selling blankets to the army in the Civil War, sent his three-year-old colt Preakness to make his only start of that year in the new Dinner Party Stakes. Bred in Kentucky by A. J. Alexander, Sanford bought the Kentucky-bred colt by Lexington out of Bay Leaf, by *Yorkshire, as a yearling for $2,000. He named the colt after his farms in New Jersey and Kentucky, which also bore the name Preakness. The name is derived from the language of the Minisi Indians in northern New Jersey; in their language, "pra-qua-les" meant "quail woods."

Under English jockey Billy Hayward, Preakness won the first Dinner Party Stakes, which today is known as the Dixie Stakes (G2) and is run on grass. Three years later, in 1873, the Maryland Jockey Club staged its first spring meeting and honored the winner of the first Dinner Party Stakes by naming the 1½-mile race for three-year-olds the Preakness Stakes.

Second race on a three-race program on Tuesday, May 23, 1873, the first Preakness Stakes attracted a field of seven to compete for the $2,050 total purse. A crowd estimated at 12,000 made Bowie's Catesby the favorite, but John Chamberlin's Survivor won by ten lengths, which remains the race's largest winning margin.

Preakness, the horse for whom the race was named, continued to race until age eight, winning the 1875 Baltimore Cup and finishing in a dead heat with Springbok in that year's Saratoga Cup. Sold to England for stud, Preakness became difficult to handle in his later years and was shot to death by his owner, the Duke of Hamilton.

Pimlico staged the first 17 runnings of the Preakness, but the Maryland Jockey Club encountered financial difficulties in 1889 and the race was run the following year at Morris Park in New York. It was not run in 1891, '92, and '93—thus, though two years older than the Kentucky Derby, the Preakness has had one fewer running—and reappeared in 1894 at Gravesend Race Course in Brooklyn, where it would be renewed for 15 years.

Pimlico regained its financial health early in the new century, but the Preakness did not return to Baltimore until May 12, 1909, when Effendi set the pace and won by one length over Fashion Plate while running a mile in 1:39⅖. Unlike the Belmont Stakes, which was not run in 1911 and '12 because of New York antigambling legislation, the Preakness was run with betting through those years.

The race proved so popular that in 1918 the Preakness—now at 1⅛ miles—was run in two divisions, the only American classic race to be split. On May 14 of the following year, J.K.L. Ross's Sir Barton won the Preakness, only four days after scoring his maiden victory in the Kentucky Derby. On June 11, 1919, the *Star Shoot colt defeated two opponents in the Belmont Stakes to become the first Triple Crown winner. The feat was noted after the fact when *Daily Racing Form* columnist Charles Hatton popularized the designation for the three races in 1930.

The Preakness's reputation was sealed in 1920

Preakness Attendance 1970-2002

Year	On-track	Total	Year	On-track	Total
2002	101,138	117,055	1985		81,235
2001	104,454	118,926	1984		80,566
2000	98,304	111,821	1983		71,768
1999	100,311	116,526	1982		80,724
1998	91,122	103,269	1981		84,133
1997	88,594	102,118	1980		83,455
1996	85,122	97,751	1979		72,607
1995	87,707	100,818	1978		81,261
1994	86,343	99,834	1977		77,346
1993	85,495	97,641	1976		62,256
1992	85,294	96,865	1975		75,216
1991	87,245	96,695	1974		54,911
1990	86,531	96,106	1973		61,657
1989	90,145	98,896	1972		48,721
1988	81,282	88,654	1971		47,221
1987		87,945	1970		42,474
1986		87,652			

Attendance figures from 1988 include combined intertrack sites (Laurel, Rosecroft, Delmarva Downs) and exclude Maryland off-track betting sites.

when the great Man o' War opened his three-year-old season with a 1½-length victory over Upset, the only horse ever to defeat him. The Preakness remained at 1⅛ miles until 1925, when it was changed to its present 1³⁄₁₆ miles.

In 1930, the Preakness was the first leg of Gallant Fox's Triple Crown, but after '31 the race took its place as the second leg in the series. In 1945, after victory in Europe led to the lifting of a voluntary ban on racing, the Preakness was run one week after the Derby and one week before the Belmont.

Pimlico was the scene of three memorable Triple Crown efforts in the 1970s: Secretariat's sweeping move to the lead on the clubhouse turn in 1973, Seattle Slew's brilliance in '77, and the stretch-long battle of Affirmed and Alydar in '78.

The race has had its share of controversy as well. In 1962, Greek Money won by a nose over Ridan, whose rider, Manuel Ycaza, claimed foul. A head-on photo, however, disclosed that Ycaza was in fact using his hands and elbows to restrain Greek Money. In 1980, Kentucky Derby winner Genuine Risk was herded wide at the top of the stretch by winner Codex, ridden by Angel Cordero Jr. An objection by Genuine Risk's jockey, Jacinto Vasquez, was disallowed, and Bertram Firestone, the filly's co-owner, forced a long Maryland Racing Commission hearing into the result. The original order of finish was upheld.

The Preakness in the 1980s and '90s was notable for two close finishes: Sunday Silence's 1989 nose victory over Easy Goer and the '97 race, in which Silver Charm won by a head over Free House, with third-place finisher Captain Bodgit another head farther back.—*Don Clippinger*

Preakness in the Pedigree

The Preakness winners and the Preakness winners they sired are:

Man o' War (1920): War Admiral (1937)
Gallant Fox (1930): Omaha (1935)
Bold Venture (1936): Assault (1946).
Polynesian (1945): Native Dancer (1953)
Citation (1948): Fabius (1956)
Native Dancer (1953): Kauai King (1966)
Bold Ruler (1957): Secretariat (1973)
Secretariat (1973): Risen Star (1988)
Summer Squall (1990): Charismatic (1999)

Fillies in the Preakness

Four fillies have won the Preakness Stakes, but the females' most recent triumph was in 1924, when Nellie Morse conquered Transmute by 1½ lengths on a sloppy Pimlico track. Prior filly winners were Flocarline in 1903, Whimsical in '06, and Rhine Maiden in '15, the year in which Regret became the first filly to win the Kentucky Derby.

Through 2001, 52 fillies have competed in the Preakness, although their participation has been relatively rare in recent decades. A span of 41 years

stood between Ciencia's sixth-place finish in 1939 and Genuine Risk's controversial second-place finish to Codex in '80.

Only two fillies started in the next two decades. The start of Winning Colors, also a Derby winner and the next filly to start in the Preakness, sparked controversy, too. Gary Stevens, rider of Winning Colors, complained after the 1988 race that Forty Niner had purposely pushed his filly through fast early fractions and bumped with her repeatedly, thus costing her all chance of winning. Risen Star won, with Winning Colors checking in third and Forty Niner seventh.

Woodlawn Vase

The Woodlawn Vase, which is said to be the most valuable trophy in sports, is presented annually to the owner of the Preakness Stakes winner. The trophy, standing 34 inches tall and weighing almost 30 pounds, was created in 1860 by Tiffany and Co. for the Woodlawn Racing Association in Louisville.

After being buried during the Civil War to prevent it from being melted down, the trophy was unearthed and remained in Louisville until 1878, when the Dwyer brothers won it. They presented it to the Coney Island Jockey Club, and it was subsequently presented at two other New York tracks, Jerome Park and Morris Park.

Thomas C. Clyde won the trophy in 1904 and gave it to the Maryland Jockey Club, of which he was a director, in 1917. That year, E. R. Bradley's Kalitan was the first horse to win the Woodlawn Vase at Pimlico.

A Preakness Tradition

A Preakness Stakes tradition observed each year is the painting of the winner's silks on a weather vane atop the Preakness presentation stand. The practice dates to 1909, when lightning destroyed a weather vane atop the Members' Clubhouse, which dated to 1870. The track's directors commissioned a new weather vane depicting a horse and rider, and the weather vane was adorned with the colors of Effendi that year.

The clubhouse structure, an ornate Victorian building that contained dining rooms, sleeping rooms, and a library, burned to the ground in June 1966. Since then, winner's colors have been painted on a weather vane atop an infield replica of the old clubhouse's cupola.

Leading Preakness Jockeys

Eddie Arcaro, known as "The Master," held sway over the Preakness Stakes in his storied career, winning the race six times in 15 starts. His closest challenger is Pat Day, who won the race three consecutive times, 1994-'96, and has five victories with 15 Preakness starters.

Here are the leading Preakness jockeys with two or more victories:

6   **Eddie Arcaro**: Whirlaway, 1941; Citation, 1948; Hill Prince, 1950; Bold, 1951; Nashua, 1955; Bold Ruler, 1957.

5   **Pat Day**: Tank's Prospect, 1985; Summer Squall, 1990; Tabasco Cat, 1994; Timber Country, 1995; Louis Quatorze, 1996.

3 **George Barbee**: Survivor, 1873; Shirley, 1876; Jacobus, 1883.

William Hartack: Fabius, 1956; Northern Dancer, 1964; Majestic Prince, 1969.

L. Hughes: Tom Ochiltree, 1875; Harold, 1879; Grenada, 1880.

2 **Jerry Bailey**: Hansel, 1991; Red Bullet, 2000.

Angel Cordero Jr.: Codex, 1980; Gate Dancer, 1984.

Costello: Saunterer, 1881; Vanguard, 1882.

Fisher: Knight of Ellersie, 1884; The Bard, 1886.

C. Holloway: Cloverbrook, 1877; Duke of Magenta, 1878.

Clarence Kummer: Man o' War, 1920; Coventry, 1925.

Charles Kurtsinger: Head Play, 1933; War Admiral, 1937.

John Loftus: War Cloud, 1918; Sir Barton, 1919.

Chris McCarron: Alysheba, 1987; Pine Bluff, 1992.

Conn McCreary: Pensive, 1944; Blue Man, 1952.

Bill Shoemaker: Candy Spots, 1963; Damascus, 1967.

Gary Stevens: Silver Charm, 1997; Point Given, 2001.

Fred Taral: Assignee, 1894; Belmar, 1895.

Ismael Valenzuela: Tim Tam, 1958; Forward Pass, 1968.

Most Preakness Mounts

Pat Day has the most Preakness starts with 16. Following are the Preakness jockeys with ten or more starters and their number of victories:

Jockey	Starts	Wins
Pat Day	16	5
Eddie Arcaro	15	6
Angel Cordero Jr.	13	2
Chris McCarron	13	2
Gary Stevens	13	2
Bill Shoemaker	12	2
Jerry Bailey	12	2
William Hartack	11	3
Jorge Velasquez	11	1
Braulio Baeza	10	0
Linus McAtee	10	1

Leading Preakness Trainers

7 **Robert W. Walden**: Tom Ochiltree, 1875; Duke of Magenta, 1878; Harold, 1879; Grenada, 1880; Saunterer, 1881; Vanguard, 1882; Refund, 1888.

5 **Thomas J. Healey**: The Parader, 1901; Pillory, 1922; Vigil, 1923; Display, 1926; Dr. Freeland, 1929.

D. Wayne Lukas: Codex, 1980; Tank's Prospect, 1985; Tabasco Cat, 1994; Timber Country, 1995; Charismatic, 1999.

4 **Bob Baffert**: Silver Charm, 1997; Real Quiet, 1998; Point Given, 2001; War Emblem, 2002.

James E. "Sunny Jim" Fitzsimmons: Gallant Fox, 1930; Omaha, 1935; Nashua, 1955; Bold Ruler, 1957.

H. A. "Jimmy" Jones: Faultless, 1947; Citation, 1948; Fabius, 1956; Tim Tam, 1958.

3 **James Whalen**: Don Enrique, 1907; Watervale, 1911; Buskin, 1913.

2 **Thomas Bohannan**: Pine Bluff, 1992; Prairie Bayou, 1993.

Edward Feakes: Montague, 1890; Belmar, 1895.

Henry Forrest: Kauai King, 1966; Forward Pass, 1968.

T. P. Hayes: Paul Kauvar, 1897; Head Play, 1933.

J. S. Healey: Layminster, 1910; Holiday, 1914.

Max Hirsch: Bold Venture, 1936; Assault, 1946.

William Hurley: Kalitan, 1917; Bimelech, 1940.

B. A. "Ben" Jones: Whirlaway, 1941; Pensive, 1944.

Andrew W. Joyner: Cairngorm, 1905; Royal Tourist, 1908.

Jack Van Berg: Gate Dancer, 1984; Alysheba, 1987.

Frank Y. Whiteley Jr.: Tom Rolfe, 1965; Damascus, 1967.

Trainers with Most Starters

Trainer	Starters	Wins
D. Wayne Lukas	28	5
Max Hirsch	19	2
James E. Fitzsimmons	18	4
James Rowe Sr.	14	1
Nicholas Zito	12	1
Woody Stephens	9	1
Preston Burch	8	1
John P. Campo	8	1

Leading Preakness Owners

7 **Calumet Farm:** Whirlaway, 1941; Pensive, 1944; Faultless, 1947; Citation, 1948; Fabius, 1956; Tim Tam, 1958; Forward Pass, 1968.

5 **George L. Lorillard:** Duke of Magenta, 1878; Harold, 1879; Grenada, 1880; Saunterer, 1881; Vanguard, 1882.

4 **Harry Payne Whitney:** Royal Tourist, 1908; Broomspun, 1921; Bostonian, 1927; Victorian, 1928.

3 **Belair Stud**: Gallant Fox, 1930; Omaha, 1935; Nashua, 1955.

E. R. Bradley: Kalitan, 1917; Burgoo King, 1932; Bimelech, 1940.

Robert and Beverly Lewis: Timber Country (co-owners), 1995; Silver Charm, 1997; Charismatic, 1999.

Walter J. Salmon: Vigil, 1923; Display, 1926; Dr. Freeland, 1929.

2 **August Belmont II:** Don Enrique, 1907; Watervale, 1911.

Brookmeade Stable: High Quest, 1934; Bold, 1951.

J. F. Chamberlin: Survivor, 1873; Tom Ochiltree, 1875.

Glen Riddle Farm: Man o' War, 1920; War Admiral, 1937.

Loblolly Stable: Pine Bluff, 1992; Prairie Bayou, 1993.

Overbrook Farm: Tabasco Cat (co-owner), 1994; Timber Country (co-owner), 1995.

Preakness Stable: Montague, 1890; Belmar, 1895.

J. K. L. Ross: Damrosch, 1916; Sir Barton, 1919.

The Thoroughbred Corp.: Point Given, 2001; War Emblem 2002.

Owners with Most Starters

Owner	Starters	Wins
Greentree Stable	20	1
Harry Payne Whitney	15	4
Calumet Farm	14	7
August Belmont II	11	2
George L. Lorillard	11	5
Overbrook Farm	11	2
Brookmeade Stable	9	2
King Ranch	8	1
Pierre Lorillard	8	1
Wheatley Stable	7	1
Rancocas Stable	6	0
Mrs. Ethel D. Jacobs	6	1

Leading Preakness Breeders

7   **Calumet Farm:** Whirlaway, 1941; Pensive, 1944; Faultless, 1947; Citation, 1948; Fabius, 1956; Tim Tam, 1958; Forward Pass, 1968.

6   **Harry Payne Whitney:** Royal Tourist, 1908; Buskin, 1913; Holiday, 1914; Broomspun, 1921; Bostonian, 1927; Victorian, 1928.

     August Belmont II: Jacobus, 1883; Margrave, 1896; Don Enrique, 1907; Watervale, 1911; Damrosch, 1916; Man o' War, 1920.

4   **A. J. Alexander:** Tom Ochiltree, 1875; Shirley, 1876; Duke of Magenta, 1878; Grenada, 1880.

3   **Belair Stud:** Gallant Fox, 1930; Omaha, 1935; Nashua, 1955.

     James Ben Ali Haggin: Old England, 1902; Cairngorm, 1905; Rhine Maiden, 1915.

2   **William S. Farish:** Summer Squall (co-breeder), 1990; Charismatic (co-breeder), 1999.

     Idle Hour Stock Farm: Burgoo King (co-breeder), 1932; Bimelech, 1940.

     Loblolly Stable: Pine Bluff, 1992; Prairie Bayou, 1993.

     Raceland Stud: Whimsical, 1906; Colonel Holloway, 1912.

     Walter J. Salmon: Display, 1926; Dr. Freeland, 1929.

     R. W. Walden: Vanguard, 1882; Refund, 1882.

     Aristides Welch: Harold, 1879; Saunterer, 1881.

Leading Preakness Sires

3   **Lexington:** Tom Ochiltree, 1875; Shirley, 1876; Duck of Magenta, 1878.

     Broomstick: Holiday, 1914; Broomspun, 1921; Bostonian, 1927.

2   ***Leamington:** Harold, 1879; Saunterer, 1881.

     *Watercress: Watervale, 1911; Rhine Maiden, 1915.

     Fair Play: Man o' War, 1920; Display, 1926.

     *Sir Gallahad III: Gallant Fox, 1930; High Quest, 1934.

     Bull Lea: Faultless, 1947; Citation, 1948.

     *Nasrullah: Nashua, 1955; Bold Ruler, 1957.

     Sovereign Dancer: Gate Dancer, 1984; Louis Quatorze, 1996.

     Woodman: Hansel, 1991; Timber Country, 1995.

Preakness Trivia

• The shortest-priced winners of the Preakness were Citation (1948) and Spectacular Bid (1979), both at 1-to-10. The shortest-priced beaten favorites were Riva Ridge (1972) and Fusaichi Pegasus (2000) at 3-to-10.

• Derby winners in recent years were not necessarily favored in the Preakness. Since 1986, the following Derby winners did not go off as the Preakness favorites: Ferdinand, 1986, second; Sunday Silence, 1989, won; Lil E. Tee, 1992, fifth; Sea Hero, 1993, fifth; Silver Charm, 1997, won; Real Quiet, 1998, won; Charismatic, 1999, won.

• Two individuals have won the Preakness both as jockeys and trainers. Louis Schaefer rode Dr. Freeland to victory in 1929 and one decade later trained Challedon to a Preakness win. Johnny Longden rode Count Fleet in 1943 and trained Majestic Prince in '69.

• A starting gate was first used for the Preakness in 1930.

• The Preakness has been run at seven different distances since 1873. The race was as short as one mile in 1909 and '10, as long as 1¾ miles in 1889, and at 1³⁄₁₆ miles since 1925.

• Two African-American jockeys have won the Preakness: George B. "Spider" Anderson aboard Buddhist in 1889 and Willie Simms on Sly Fox in '98. The only black jockey to ride in the Preakness in modern times was Wayne Barnett, who finished eighth aboard Sparrowvon in 1985.

• Only two female jockeys have ridden in the Preakness: Patricia Cooksey, sixth on Tajawa in 1985, and Andrea Seefeldt, seventh on Looming in '94.

• The Preakness preceded the Kentucky Derby on the racing calendar 11 times between 1888 and 1931.

• In 1890, the Preakness and the Belmont Stakes were run on the same card at Morris Park. The race was not run from 1891 to '93.

• From 1910 through '16, the Preakness was run as a handicap. From 1895 through 1907, the race was under money allowance conditions, limiting it to horses that had not won a race worth a certain amount.

• The Preakness was run in divisions in 1918, when War Cloud and Jack Hare Jr. won.

Fastest Preakness Fractions

First quarter-mile: :22⅖ Flag Raiser (1965), Fight Over (1984), Eternal Prince (1985), Vicar (1999).

First half-mile: :45, Bold Forbes (1976).

First six furlongs: 1:09, Bold Forbes (1976).

Fastest first mile: 1:34⅕, Chief's Crown (1985), Sunday Silence (1989).

Fastest final three-sixteenths: :18, Summer Squall, 1990.

Evolution of Preakness Stakes Record

Year	Winner	Time
1925	Coventry	1:59
1934	High Quest	1:58⅕
1942	Alsab	1:57
1949	Capot	1:56
1955	Nashua	1:54⅗

1971	Canonero II	1:54
1984	Gate Dancer	1:53$\frac{3}{5}$
1985	Tank's Prospect	1:53$\frac{2}{5}$
1996	Louis Quatorze	1:53$\frac{2}{5}$ (1:53.43)

Fastest in the Preakness

Tank's Prospect and Louis Quatorze share the record for the fastest running of the Preakness Stakes, 1:53$\frac{2}{5}$. Louis Quatorze, the 1996 winner, was timed in 1:53.43, but Tank's Prospect in 1985 was timed in one-fifths of a second, the standard at that time.

Unofficially, Secretariat ran the Preakness's 1$\frac{3}{16}$ miles in the same time. He was caught in 1:53$\frac{2}{5}$ by *Daily Racing Form* clockers who were hand-timing the race. A malfunctioning official timer recorded a time of 1:55, but that was subsequently adjusted to 1:54$\frac{2}{5}$.

The fastest official runnings of the Preakness:

Year	Winner	Time	Cond.
1996	Louis Quatorze	1:53.43	Fast
1985	Tank's Prospect	1:53$\frac{2}{5}$	Fast
1984	Gate Dancer	1:53$\frac{3}{5}$	Fast
1990	Summer Squall	1:53$\frac{4}{5}$	Fast
1971	Canonero II	1:54	Fast
1979	Spectacular Bid	1:54$\frac{1}{5}$	Fast
1995	Timber Country	1:54.45	Fast
1980	Codex	1:54$\frac{1}{5}$	Fast
1973	Secretariat	1:54$\frac{2}{5}$	Fast
1977	Seattle Slew	1:54$\frac{2}{5}$	Fast
1978	Affirmed	1:54$\frac{2}{5}$	Fast

Slowest Preakness Times

Citation, a Triple Crown winner and regarded as one of the greatest Thoroughbreds of the 20th century, ran the slowest Preakness Stakes ever, 2:02$\frac{2}{5}$. But the *Daily Racing Form* chart characterized the track as heavy, which would have been considerably slower than today's speed-tuned racing surfaces.

Following are the slowest Preakness runnings since 1925, when the race's distance became 1$\frac{3}{16}$ miles.

Year	Winner	Time	Cond.
1948	Citation	2:02$\frac{2}{5}$	Heavy
1933	Head Play	2:02	Slow
1927	Bostonian	2:01$\frac{3}{5}$	Good
1929	Dr. Freeland	2:01$\frac{3}{5}$	Fast
1946	Assault	2:01$\frac{2}{5}$	Fast
1930	Gallant Fox	2:00$\frac{3}{5}$	Fast
1928	Victorian	2:00$\frac{1}{5}$	Fast
1932	Burgoo King	1:59$\frac{4}{5}$	Fast
1938	Dauber	1:59$\frac{4}{5}$	Sloppy
1939	Challedon	1:59$\frac{4}{5}$	Muddy
1926	Display	1:59$\frac{4}{5}$	Fast
1950	Hill Prince	1:59$\frac{1}{5}$	Slow
1944	Pensive	1:59$\frac{1}{5}$	Fast

Largest Winning Margins

Year	Winner	Lengths
1873	Survivor	10
1943	Count Fleet	8
1889	Buddhist	8
1991	Hansel	7
1974	Little Current	7
1951	Bold	7
1938	Dauber	7
1968	Forward Pass	6
1935	Omaha	6
1878	Duke of Magenta	6
1979	Spectacular Bid	5$\frac{1}{2}$
1948	Citation	5$\frac{1}{2}$
1941	Whirlaway	5$\frac{1}{2}$
1950	Hill Prince	5
1912	Colonel Holloway	5

Smallest Winning Margins

Year	Winner	Margin
1989	Sunday Silence	nose
1962	Greek Money	nose
1936	Bold Venture	nose
1934	High Quest	nose
1928	Victorian	nose
1902	Old England	nose
1997	Silver Charm	head
1985	Tank's Prospect	head
1969	Majestic Prince	head
1949	Capot	head
1937	War Admiral	head
1932	Burgoo King	head
1926	Display	head
1922	Pillory	head
1905	Cairngorm	head
1900	Hindus	head

Preakness Odds-On Beaten Favorites

The shortest-priced beaten favorites in the Preakness Stakes were Riva Ridge in 1972 and Fusaichi Pegasus in 2000. Both entered the Preakness off Derby victories and both went off at 3-to-10. Riva Ridge fell to Bee Bee Bee on a sloppy track, and Fusaichi Pegasus finished second to Red Bullet.

Here are the odds-on beaten favorites in the Preakness:

Year	Horse	Odds	Finish
2000	Fusaichi Pegasus	.30-to-1	2nd
1972	Riva Ridge	.30-to-1	4th
1939	Gilded Knight- Johnstown entry	.45-to-1	2nd 5th
1982	Linkage	.50-to-1	2nd
1989	Easy Goer	.60-to-1	2nd
1956	Needles	.60-to-1	2nd
1984	Swale	.80-to-1	7th
1964	Hill Rise	.80-to-1	3rd
1976	Honest Pleasure	.90-to-1	5th
1954	Correlation	.90-to-1	2nd

Winning Preakness Favorites

Since pari-mutuel wagering began at Pimlico Race Course in 1911, 65 favorites have won the Preakness Stakes. Unlike the Kentucky Derby, which went 21 years without a winning favorite (Spectacular Bid in 1979 to Fusaichi Pegasus in 2000), the Preakness had several winning favorites in the latter years of the 20th century.

Point Given kicked off the 21st century by winning

the 2001 Preakness as the 2.30-to-1 favorite.

In the span during which a Derby favorite did not win the Louisville classic, the Preakness was won by the following favorites:

Year	Winner	Odds
1994	Timber Country	1.90-to-1
1993	Prairie Bayou	2.20-to-1
1992	Pine Bluff	7-to-2
1987	Alysheba	2-to-1
1981	Pleasant Colony	3-to-2

Shortest-Priced Preakness Winners

Year	Winner	Odds
1979	Spectacular Bid	.10-to-1
1948	Citation	.10-to-1
1943	Count Fleet	.15-to-1
1953	Native Dancer	.20-to-1
1973	Secretariat	.30-to-1
1955	Nashua	.30-to-1
1937	War Admiral	.35-to-1
1977	Seattle Slew	.40-to-1
1934	High Quest	.45-to-1
1978	Affirmed	.50-to-1

Longest-Priced Preakness Winners

Year	Winner	Odds
1975	Master Derby	23.40-to-1
1925	Coventry	21.80-to-1
1926	Display	19.35-to-1
1972	Bee Bee Bee	18.70-to-1
1983	Deputed Testamony	14.50-to-1
1974	Little Current	13.10-to-1
1924	Nellie Morse	12.10-to-1
1945	Polynesian	12-to-1
1922	Pillory	11.15-to-1
1962	Greek Money	10.90-to-1
1976	Elocutionist	10.10-to-1

Preakness Front-Runners

The following Preakness winners were on the lead at all points of call, beginning at a quarter-mile (approaching the clubhouse turn). Regarded as speed horses, neither Seattle Slew nor Affirmed led the opening quarter-mile in the Preakness.

Year	Winner	Winning margin
1996	Louis Quatorze	3¼
1982	Aloma's Ruler	½
1972	Bee Bee Bee	1½
1960	Bally Ache	4
1957	Bold Ruler	2
1954	Hasty Road	neck
1951	Bold	7
1948	Citation	5½
1945	Polynesian	2½
1943	Count Fleet	8
1940	Bimelech	3
1937	War Admiral	head
1934	High Quest	nose
1933	Head Play	4
1920	Man o' War	1½
1919	Sir Barton	4

1918	Jack Hare Jr.	2
1915	Rhine Maiden	1½
1914	Holiday	¾
1911	Watervale	1
1909	Effendi	1
1902	Old England	nose
1899	Half Time	1
1896	Margrave	1
1889	Buddhist	8
1882	Vanguard	neck

Preakness Post Positions

Since 1909, Preakness Stakes winners have come out of the sixth post position 14 times. Only two Preakness winners, Display in 1926 and Point Given in 2001, have come out of the 11th starting position.

Twelve winners have come out of the fourth hole, and 11 each have broken from the second, third, and seventh slots.

Here are the winning post positions since 1909:

Post position	Winners
1	9
2	11
3	11
4	12
5	10
6	14
7	11
8	9
9	2
10	2
11	2
12	2

Women in Preakness

Although women have made their mark in racing over the last quarter-century, relatively few women have participated in the Preakness Stakes. Only two female jockeys have ridden in the Preakness, and nine female trainers have saddled Preakness starters. The closest to the winner's circle was owner-breeder Nancy Alberts, who saddled Magic Weisner for a second-place finish in 2002. Shelley L. Riley saddled Casual Lies for a third-place finish in 1992.

Following are how women have fared in the Preakness:

Jockeys

Jockey	Year	Horse	Finish
Andrea Seefeldt	1994	Looming	7th
Patricia Cooksey	1985	Tajawa	6th

Trainers

Trainer	Year	Horse	Finish
Nancy Alberts	2002	Magic Weisner	2nd
Jean L. Rolfe	1998	Silver's Prospect	10th
Cynthia Reese	1996	In Contention	6th
Penny Lewis	1993	Hegar	9th
Dean Gaudet	1992	Speakerphone	14th
Shelley L. Riley	1992	Casual Lies	3rd
Nancy Heil	1990	Fighting Notion	5th
Judith Zouck	1980	Samoyed	6th
Judy Johnson	1968	Sir Beau	7th

Preakness Stakes

Grade 1, Pimlico Race Course, three-year-olds, 1 3/16 miles, dirt. Held on May 18, 2002, with gross value of $1,000,000. First run in 1873. Weights: colts and geldings, 126 pounds; fillies, 121 pounds.

Year	Winner	Jockey	Second	Third	Strs	Time	Track	1st purse
2002	**War Emblem**	V. Espinoza	Magic Weisner	Proud Citizen	13	1:56.36	ft	$650,000
2001	**Point Given**	G. Stevens	A P Valentine	Congaree	11	1:55.51	ft	$650,000
2000	**Red Bullet**	J. Bailey	Fusaichi Pegasus	Impeachment	8	1:56.04	gd	$650,000
1999	**Charismatic**	C. Antley	Menifee	Badge	13	1:55.32	ft	$650,000
1998	**Real Quiet**	K. Desormeaux	Victory Gallop	Classic Cat	10	1:54.75	ft	**$650,000**
1997	**Silver Charm**	G. Stevens	Free House	Captain Bodgit	10	1:54.84	ft	$488,150
1996	**Louis Quatorze**	P. Day	Skip Away	Editor's Note	12	**1:53.43**	ft	$458,120
1995	**Timber Country**	P. Day	Oliver's Twist	Thunder Gulch	11	1:54.45	ft	$446,810
1994	**Tabasco Cat**	P. Day	Go for Gin	Concern	10	1:56.47	ft	$447,720
1993	**‡Prairie Bayou**	M. Smith	Cherokee Run	‡El Bakan	12	1:56.61	ft	$471,835
1992	**Pine Bluff**	C. McCarron	Alydeed	Casual Lies	14	1:55.60	gd	$484,120
1991	**Hansel**	J. Bailey	Corporate Report	Mane Minister	8	1:54	ft	$432,770
1990	**Summer Squall**	P. Day	Unbridled	Mister Frisky	9	1:53⅗	ft	$445,900
1989	**Sunday Silence**	P. Valenzuela	Easy Goer	Rock Point	8	1:53⅘	ft	$438,230
1988	**Risen Star**	E. Delahoussaye	Brian's Time	†Winning Colors	9	1:56⅕	gd	$413,700
1987	**Alysheba**	C. McCarron	Bet Twice	Cryptoclearance	9	1:55⅘	ft	$421,100
1986	**Snow Chief**	A. Solis	Ferdinand	Broad Brush	7	1:54⅘	ft	$411,900
1985	**Tank's Prospect**	P. Day	Chief's Crown	Eternal Prince	11	**1:53⅖**	ft	$423,200
1984	**Gate Dancer**	A. Cordero Jr.	Play On	Fight Over	10	1:53⅗	ft	$243,600
1983	**Deputed Testamony**	D. A. Miller Jr.	Desert Wine	High Honors	12	1:55⅖	sy	$251,200
1982	**Aloma's Ruler**	J. Kaenel	Linkage	Cut Away	7	1:55⅖	ft	$209,900
1981	**Pleasant Colony**	J. Velasquez	Bold Ego	Paristo	13	1:54⅗	ft	$200,800
1980	**Codex**	A. Cordero Jr.	†Genuine Risk	Colonel Moran	8	1:54⅕	ft	$180,600
1979	**Spectacular Bid**	R. Franklin	Golden Act	Screen King	5	1:54⅕	gd	$165,300
1978	**AFFIRMED**	S. Cauthen	Alydar	Believe It	7	1:54⅖	ft	$136,200
1977	**SEATTLE SLEW**	J. Cruguet	Iron Constitution	Run Dusty Run	9	1:54⅖	ft	$138,600
1976	**Elocutionist**	J. Lively	Play the Red	Bold Forbes	6	1:55	ft	$129,700
1975	**Master Derby**	D. G. McHargue	Foolish Pleasure	Diabolo	10	1:56⅖	ft	$158,100
1974	**Little Current**	M. A. Rivera	‡Neapolitan Way	Cannonade	13	1:54⅗	gd	$156,500
1973	**SECRETARIAT**	R. Turcotte	Sham	Our Native	6	1:55	ft	$129,900
1972	**Bee Bee Bee**	E. Nelson	No Le Hace	Key to the Mint	7	1:55⅗	sy	$135,300
1971	**Canonero II**	G. Avila	Eastern Fleet	Jim French	11	1:54	ft	$137,400
1970	**Personality**	E. Belmonte	My Dad George	Silent Screen	14	1:56⅕	ft	$151,300
1969	**Majestic Prince**	W. Hartack	Arts and Letters	Jay Ray	8	1:55⅗	ft	$129,500
1968	**Forward Pass**	I. Valenzuela	Out of the Way	Nodouble	10	1:56⅘	ft	$142,700
1967	**Damascus**	W. Shoemaker	In Reality	Proud Clarion	10	1:55⅕	ft	$151,500
1966	**Kauai King**	D. Brumfield	Stupendous	Amberoid	9	1:55⅖	ft	$129,000
1965	**Tom Rolfe**	R. Turcotte	Dapper Dan	Hail to All	9	1:56⅕	ft	$128,100
1964	**Northern Dancer**	W. Hartack	The Scoundrel	Hill Rise	6	1:56⅘	ft	$124,200
1963	**Candy Spots**	W. Shoemaker	Chateaugay	Never Bend	8	1:56⅕	ft	$127,500
1962	**Greek Money**	J. L. Rotz	Ridan	Roman Line	11	1:56⅕	ft	$135,800
1961	**Carry Back**	J. Sellers	Globemaster	Crozier	9	1:57⅗	ft	$126,200
1960	**Bally Ache**	R. Ussery	Victoria Park	*Celtic Ash	6	1:57⅗	ft	$121,000
1959	**Royal Orbit**	W. Harmatz	Sword Dancer	Dunce	11	1:57	ft	$136,200
1958	**Tim Tam**	I. Valenzuela	Lincoln Road	Gone Fishin'	12	1:57⅕	ft	$97,900
1957	**Bold Ruler**	E. Arcaro	Iron Liege	Inside Tract	7	1:56⅕	ft	$66,300
1956	**Fabius**	W. Hartack	Needles	No Regrets	9	1:58⅖	ft	$84,250
1955	**Nashua**	E. Arcaro	Saratoga	Traffic Judge	8	1:54⅗	ft	$67,550
1954	**Hasty Road**	J. Adams	Correlation	Hasseyampa	11	1:57⅖	ft	$91,600
1953	**Native Dancer**	E. Guerin	Jamie K.	Royal Bay Gem	7	1:57⅘	ft	$65,200
1952	**Blue Man**	C. McCreary	‡Jampol	One Count	10	1:57⅖	ft	$86,135
1951	**Bold**	E. Arcaro	Counterpoint	Alerted	8	1:56⅖	ft	$83,110
1950	**Hill Prince**	E. Arcaro	Middleground	Dooly	6	1:59⅕	sl	$56,115
1949	**Capot**	T. Atkinson	Palestinian	Noble Impulse	9	1:56	ft	$79,985
1948	**CITATION**	E. Arcaro	Vulcan's Forge	Bovard	4	2:02⅖	hy	$91,870
1947	**Faultless**	D. Dodson	On Trust	Phalanx	11	1:59	ft	$98,005
1946	**ASSAULT**	W. Mehrtens	Lord Boswell	Hampden	10	2:01⅖	ft	$96,620
1945	**Polynesian**	W. D. Wright	Hoop, Jr.	‡Darby Dieppe	9	1:58⅘	ft	$66,170
1944	**Pensive**	C. McCreary	Platter	‡Stir Up	7	1:59⅕	ft	$60,075
1943	**COUNT FLEET**	J. Longden	Blue Swords	Vincentive	4	1:57⅖	gd	$43,190
1942	**Alsab**	B. James	dh-Requested	dh-Sun Again	10	1:57	ft	$58,175
1941	**WHIRLAWAY**	E. Arcaro	King Cole	Our Boots	8	1:58⅘	gd	$49,365
1940	**Bimelech**	F. A. Smith	Mioland	Gallahadion	9	1:58⅗	ft	$53,230
1939	**Challedon**	G. Seabo	Gilded Knight	Volitant	6	1:59⅘	my	$53,710
1938	**Dauber**	M. Peters	Cravat	Menow	9	1:59⅘	sy	$51,875
1937	**WAR ADMIRAL**	C. Kurtsinger	Pompoon	Flying Scot	8	1:58⅖	gd	$45,600

Year	Winner	Jockey	Second	Third	Strs	Time	Track	1st purse
1936	**Bold Venture**	G. Woolf	Granville	Jean Bart	11	1:59	ft	$27,325
1935	**OMAHA**	W. Saunders	Firethorn	Psychic Bid	8	1:58⅖	ft	$25,325
1934	**High Quest**	R. Jones	Cavalcade	Discovery	7	1:58⅕	ft	$25,175
1933	**Head Play**	C. Kurtsinger	Ladysman	Utopian	10	2:02	sl	$26,850
1932	**Burgoo King**	E. James	Tick On	Boatswain	9	1:59⅘	ft	$50,375
1931	**Mate**	G. Ellis	Twenty Grand	Ladder	7	1:59	ft	$48,225
1930	**GALLANT FOX**	E. Sande	Crack Brigade	†Snowflake	11	2:00⅗	ft	$51,925
1929	**Dr. Freeland**	L. Schaefer	Minotaur	African	11	2:01⅗	ft	$52,325
1928	**Victorian**	R. Workman	Toro	Solace	**18**	2:00⅕	ft	$60,000
1927	**Bostonian**	A. Abel	Sir Harry	Whiskery	12	2:01⅗	gd	$53,100
1926	**Display**	J. Malben	Blondin	Mars	13	1:59⅘	ft	$53,625
1925	**Coventry**	C. Kummer	‡Backbone	Almadel	12	1:59	ft	$52,700
1924	**†Nellie Morse**	J. Merimee	Transmute	Mad Play	15	1:57⅕	sy	$54,000
1923	**Vigil**	B. Marinelli	Gen. Thatcher	‡Rialto	13	1:53⅗	ft	$52,000
1922	**Pillory**	L. Morris	Hea	June Grass	12	1:51⅗	ft	$51,000
1921	**Broomspun**	F. Coltiletti	†Polly Ann	Jeg	14	1:54⅕	sl	$43,000
1920	**Man o' War**	C. Kummer	Upset	Wildair	9	1:51⅗	ft	$23,000
1919	**SIR BARTON**	J. Loftus	Eternal	Sweep On	12	1:53	ft	$24,500
1918	***War Cloud**	J. Loftus	Sunny Slope	*Lanius	10	1:53⅗	gd	$12,250
	Jack Hare, Jr.	C. Peak	The Porter	†Kate Bright	6	1:53⅖	gd	$11,250
1917	**Kalitan**	E. Haynes	Al. M. Dick	‡Kentucky Boy	14	1:54⅖	ft	$4,800
1916	**Damrosch**	L. McAtee	Greenwood	Achievement	9	1:54⅘	ft	$1,380
1915	**†Rhine Maiden**	D. Hoffman	Half Rock	Runes	6	1:58	my	$1,275
1914	**‡Holiday**	A. Schuttinger	Brave Cunarder	Defendum	6	1:53⅘	ft	$1,355
1913	**‡Buskin**	J. Butwell	Kleburne	‡Barnegat	8	1:53⅖	ft	$1,670
1912	**Col. Holloway**	C. Turner	Bwana Tumbo	Tipsand	7	1:56⅗	sl	$1,450
1911	**Watervale**	E. Dugan	Zeus	‡The Nigger	7	1:51	ft	$2,700
1910	**‡Layminster**	R. Estep	Dalhousie	Sager	12	1:40⅕	ft	$2,800
1909	**Effendi**	W. Doyle	Fashion Plate	†Hill Top	10	1:39⅘	ft	$2,725
1908	**Royal Tourist**	E. Dugan	Live Wire	‡Robert Cooper	4	1:46⅖	ft	$2,455
1907	**‡Don Enrique**	G. Mountain	Ethon	Zambesi	7	1:45⅖	hy	$2,260
1906	**†Whimsical**	W. Miller	†Content	Larabie	10	1:45	ft	$2,355
1905	**Cairngorm**	W. Davis	†Kiamesha	†Coy Maid	10	1:45⅘	ft	$2,145
1904	**Bryn Mawr**	E. Hildebrand	Wotan	‡Dolly Spanker	10	1:44⅕	ft	$2,355
1903	**†Flocarline**	W. Gannon	Mackey Dwyer	Rightful	6	1:44⅘	ft	$1,875
1902	**Old England**	L. Jackson	Major Daingerfield	Namtor	7	1:45⅘	hy	$2,240
1901	**The Parader**	F. Landry	†Sadie S.	Dr. Barlow	5	1:47⅕	hy	$1,605
1900	**Hindus**	H. Spencer	*Sarmatian	Ten Candles	10	1:48⅖	ft	$1,900
1899	**Half Time**	R. Clawson	Filigrane	Lackland	3	1:47	ft	$1,580
1898	**Sly Fox**	W. Simms	The Huguenot	Nuto	4	1:49¾	gd	$1,450
1897	**Paul Kauvar**	C. Thorpe	Elkin	On Deck	7	1:51¼	sy	$1,420
1896	**Margrave**	H. Griffin	Hamilton II	*Intermission	4	1:51	ft	$1,350
1895	**Belmar**	F. Taral	‡April Fool	†Sue Kittie	7	1:50½	ft	$1,350
1894	**Assignee**	F. Taral	Potentate	‡Ed Kearney	14	1:49¼	ft	$1,830
1890	**Montague**	J. Martin	Philosophy	Barrister	4	2:36¾	ft	$1,215
1889	**Buddhist**	G. Anderson	Japhet	———	2	2:17½	ft	$1,130
1888	**Refund**	F. Littlefield	Judge Murray	Glendale	4	2:49	hy	$1,185
1887	**Dunboyne**	W. Donohue	Mahony	Raymond	4	2:39½	ft	$1,675
1886	**The Bard**	S. Fisher	Eurus	Elkwood	5	2:45	gd	$2,050
1885	**Tecumseh**	J. McLaughlin	Wickham	‡John C.	4	2:49	hy	$2,160
1884	**Knight of Ellerslie**	S. Fisher	Welcher	———	2	2:39½	ft	$1,905
1883	**Jacobus**	G. Barbee	Parnell	———	2	2:42½	gd	$1,635
1882	**Vanguard**	T. Costello	Heck	‡Col. Watson	3	2:44½	gd	$1,250
1881	**Saunterer**	T. Costello	‡Compensation	Baltic	6	2:40½	gd	$1,950
1880	**Grenada**	L. Hughes	Oden	†Emily F.	5	2:40½	ft	$2,000
1879	**Harold**	L. Hughes	Jerico	‡Rochester	6	2:40½	ft	$2,550
1878	**Duke of Magenta**	C. Holloway	Bayard	‡Albert	3	2:41¾	gd	$2,100
1877	**Cloverbrook**	C. Holloway	Bombast	Lucifer	4	2:45½	sl	$1,600
1876	**‡Shirley**	G. Barbee	Rappahannock	Compliments	8	2:44¾	gd	$1,950
1875	**Tom Ochiltree**	L. Hughes	Viator	†Bay Final	9	2:43½	sl	$1,900
1874	**Culpepper**	W. Donohue	*King Amadeus	Scratch	6	2:56½	my	$1,900
1873	**Survivor**	G. Barbee	John Boulger	Artist	7	2:43	sl	$1,800

†—filly; ‡—gelding; *—imported horse; dh-dead heat; bold indicates records set in starters, time, and 1st purse; Triple Crown winners are in all capitalized letters.

1894, 1½ miles; 1889, 1¼ miles; 1894-1900,1908, 1 1/16 miles; 1901-'07, 1 mile and 70 yards; 1909,1910, 1 mile; 1911-'24 1⅛ miles. 1891-'93, not run. 1890 held at Morris Park, New York; 1894-1908 Gravesend, New York. Run in two divisions in 1918. 1973-present, Grade 1. Dancer's Image disqualified from third to eighth in 1968. Secretariat's time in 1973 originally reported as 1:55; hand-timed by *Daily Racing Form* clockers in 1:53⅖

Belmont Stakes History

Unforgettable horses, jockeys, and trainers punctuate the glorious history of the Belmont Stakes, a compelling race if only because two three-year-olds carrying equal weights of 126 pounds can battle its testing 1½-mile distance and be separated at the finish line by inches. It has happened more than once in the final leg of the Triple Crown.

First run in 1867, the Belmont Stakes is named for August Belmont I, a prominent investment banker and Thoroughbred owner who was president of the American Jockey Club. The Belmont Stakes preceded the Preakness by six years and the Kentucky Derby by eight. Francis Morris's filly Ruthless won the first Belmont Stakes, which was contested at Jerome Park in the Bronx on a Thursday afternoon at 1⅝ miles, "cleverly by a head" over De Coursey. The purse was $2,500.

The first 23 runnings of the Belmont Stakes were held on a ribbon-like course at Jerome Park. In 1890, the Belmont Stakes moved to Morris Park, a 1⅜-mile track a few miles east of what is now Van Cortland Park in the Bronx.

Fifteen years later, in 1905, the Belmont Stakes had a new home, Belmont Park, but the race was not run in 1911 and '12 because antigambling legislation shut down racing in New York in those years. Unlike the Belmont's current counterclockwise path, the race was run clockwise—like many English and European races—until 1921. By then, two great champions with a unique link had won the race known as the Test of Champions in strikingly different styles.

Colin is one of only two undefeated American champions with more than five starts in the past 93 years (the other is Personal Ensign). Colin nearly lost his unbeaten record because of a mistake by Joe Notter, his jockey in the 1908 Belmont Stakes. In a driving rainstorm so intense that no final time was taken, Notter misjudged the finish line on Colin, and his five-length lead was shaved to a head by a fast closing Fair Play.

Colin continued to a perfect 15-for-15 record. Fair Play sired Man o' War, the once-beaten champion who won the Belmont by 20 lengths over his only challenger, Donnacona, at odds of 0.04-to-1.

Gallant Fox is one of only two Triple Crown winners who was not the favorite in the Belmont Stakes. The previous year, Whichone had beaten Gallant Fox in the 1929 Futurity and had also won the Champagne and Saratoga Special Stakes. Whichone missed the Kentucky Derby and Preakness Stakes the following spring because of knee problems, but he returned to win the Withers Stakes and went off the 0.70-to-1 favorite in the 1930 Belmont Stakes.

Gallant Fox had won the Wood Memorial Stakes, Preakness, and Kentucky Derby (in that order)

Belmont Attendance 1970-2002			
Year	Attendance	Year	Attendance
2002	103,222	1985	43,446
2001	73,857	1984	46,430
2000	67,810	1983	56,677
1999	85,818	1982	46,050
1998	80,162	1981	61,200
1997	70,682	1980	58,883
1996	40,797	1979	59,073
1995	37,171	1978	65,417
1994	42,695	1977	71,026
1993	45,037	1976	58,788
1992	50,204	1975	60,611
1991	51,766	1974	52,153
1990	50,123	1973	67,605
1989	64,959	1972	54,635
1988	56,223	1971	82,694
1987	64,772	1970	54,299
1986	42,555		

yet went off at 8-to-5 in the field of just four in the Belmont. Gallant Fox uncharacteristically took the lead immediately and scampered to a surprisingly easy three-length victory in a stakes record of 2:31⅗ for 1½ miles.

Gallant Fox's winning Belmont Stakes margin paled next to the 25-length romp of Count Fleet, who completed his 1943 Triple Crown at odds of 1-to-20 "galloping," according to his chart. Three years later, Assault went off the 7-to-5 second choice in the Belmont Stakes but, like Gallant Fox, he completed his Triple Crown with a three-length victory. Favored Lord Boswell finished fifth in the field of seven at 1.35-to-1.

In 1948, Citation cruised to an eight-length win in the Belmont to become the fourth Triple Crown winner in eight years. There would not be another for a quarter-century.

Plenty of upsets occurred in those 25 years from Citation to Secretariat, and none was more shocking than Sherluck's 1961 victory over 2-to-5 favorite Carry Back at odds of 65.05-to-1, resulting in a then-record Belmont Stakes win payout of $132.10.

Carry Back, who finished seventh, joined Pensive (1944) and Tim Tam ('58) as Kentucky Derby and Preakness winners who lost in the Belmont Stakes. Five more followed Carry Back in the next ten years: Northern Dancer (1964), Kauai King ('66), Forward Pass ('68), Majestic Prince ('69), and Canonero II, who attracted 82,694, then the largest crowd in Belmont Park history, on June 5, 1971, only to finish fourth to Pass Catcher, a 34.50-to-1 longshot.

Just when everybody thought there might not ever be another Triple Crown winner—the tremendous growth in the number of foals was frequently cited as a reason—along came Secretariat. To provide a perspective on his 31-length

1973 Belmont Stakes victory in a world record 2:24, consider that the next fastest winners, Easy Goer in '89 and A.P. Indy in '92, went in 2:26, the equivalent of ten lengths slower.

Secretariat's 1973 Triple Crown was followed by two more in the ensuing six years: Seattle Slew, who became the only undefeated Triple Crown winner in 1977, and Affirmed one year later.

The Triple Crowns of 1977 and '78 were starkly different. Seattle Slew dominated his generation, while Affirmed was pushed to the limit by his nemesis, Alydar. The final sixteenth of a mile of the 1978 Belmont Stakes, with Affirmed on the inside under Steve Cauthen and Alydar at his throat under Jorge Velasquez, was a dramatic test of will in which Affirmed prevailed by a head. That was not the closest Belmont Stakes finish. Colin had won by the same margin, and Granville in 1936 and Jaipur in '62 by a nose.

Spectacular Bid had a shot at becoming the third consecutive Triple Crown winner in 1979 but checked in third at 3-to-10 to Coastal in the Belmont after reportedly stepping on a safety pin that morning. Two years later, Derby and Preakness winner Pleasant Colony also failed to sweep the series, finishing third to Summing.

Then, Woody Stephens took over. People questioned the Racing Hall of Fame trainer's judgment when he announced that Conquistador Cielo, who had just routed older horses by 7¼ lengths in the one-mile Metropolitan Handicap (G1), would start in the Belmont Stakes five days later. Stephens knew his horse, and the colt won the Belmont by 14 lengths under Laffit Pincay Jr.

Stephens-trained Caveat won the 1983 Belmont, and ill-fated Swale won in '84. Then Stephens ran first and second with Creme Fraiche and Stephan's Odyssey in 1985. In 1986, Stephens won his fifth consecutive Belmont Stakes with Danzig Connection, at odds of 8-to-1.

Three consecutive blowouts occurred in the late 1980s, with Bet Twice winning by 14 lengths over Derby and Preakness winner Alysheba in '87, Risen Star adding to his Preakness triumph with a 14¾-length Belmont romp the following June, and Easy Goer avenging his Derby and Preakness losses to Sunday Silence by winning the '89 Belmont Stakes by eight lengths.

The middle years of the 1990s were dominated by Racing Hall of Fame trainer D. Wayne Lukas, who secured consecutive victories with Tabasco Cat (1994), Thunder Gulch ('95), and Editor's Note ('96).

Julie Krone became the first female rider to win a Triple Crown race when she guided Colonial Affair to a 2¼-length win in the 1993 Belmont Stakes for trainer Flint S. "Scotty" Schulhofer. The Racing Hall of Fame trainer collected his second Belmont victory in 1989 when Lemon Drop Kid denied Lukas-trained Charismatic a Triple Crown before a record crowd of 85,818.

Charismatic's loss marked the third straight year that a Triple Crown was on the line. In 1997, Silver Charm, trained by Bob Baffert, led 100 yards before the finish but was passed by Touch Gold, who won by three-quarters of a length. One year later, Baffert-trained Real Quiet looked home free in the Belmont before weakening late and losing by a nose in the final stride to Victory Gallop.

Two years later, Baffert recorded his first Belmont victory with Point Given's 2001 victory before 73,857, the largest Belmont Stakes crowd ever without a Triple Crown on the line.

In 2002, a record crowd of 103,222 witnessed War Emblem's loss in his attempt to sweep the Triple Crown.—*Bill Heller*

Leading Belmont Jockeys

6   **James McLaughlin:** Forester, 1882; George Kinney, 1883; Panique, 1884; Inspector B., 1886; Hanover, 1887; Sir Dixon, 1888.

Eddie Arcaro: Whirlaway, 1941; Shut Out, 1942; Pavot, 1945; Citation, 1948; One Count, 1952; Nashua, 1955.

5   **Earle Sande:** Grey Lag, 1921; Zev, 1923; Mad Play, 1924; Chance Shot, 1927; Gallant Fox, 1930.

Bill Shoemaker: Gallant Man, 1957; Sword Dancer, 1959; Jaipur, 1962; Damascus, 1967; Avatar, 1975.

3   **Braulio Baeza:** Sherluck, 1961; Chateaugay, 1963; Arts and Letters, 1969.

Pat Day: Easy Goer, 1989; Tabasco Cat, 1994; Commendable, 2000.

Laffit Pincay Jr.: Conquistador Cielo, 1982; Caveat, 1983; Swale, 1984.

James Stout: Granville, 1936; Pasteurized, 1938; Johnstown, 1939.

Leading Belmont Trainers

8   **James Rowe:** George Kinney, 1883; Panique, 1884; Commando, 1901; Delhi, 1904; Peter Pan, 1907; Colin, 1908; Sweep, 1910; Prince Eugene, 1913.

7   **Sam Hildreth:** Jean Bereaud, 1899; Joe Madden, 1909; Friar Rock, 1916; Hourless, 1917; Grey Lag, 1921; Zev, 1923; Mad Play, 1924.

6   **James "Sunny Jim" Fitzsimmons:** Gallant Fox, 1930; Faireno, 1932; Omaha, 1935; Granville, 1936; Johnstown, 1939; Nashua, 1955.

5   **W. C. "Woody" Stephens:** Conquistador Cielo, 1982; Caveat, 1983; Swale, 1984; Creme Fraiche, 1985; Danzig Connection, 1986.

4   **Max Hirsch:** Vito, 1928; Assault, 1946; Middleground, 1950; High Gun, 1954.

D. Wayne Lukas: Tabasco Cat, 1994; Thunder Gulch, 1995; Editor's Note, 1996; Commendable, 2000.

R. W. Walden: Duke of Magenta, 1878; Grenada, 1880; Saunterer, 1881; *Bowling Brook, 1898.

3   **Elliott Burch:** Sword Dancer, 1959; Quadrangle, 1964; Arts and Letters, 1969.

John M. Gaver: Shut Out, 1942; Capot, 1949; Stage Door Johnny, 1968.

Lucien Laurin: Amberoid, 1966; Riva Ridge, 1972; Secretariat, 1973.

Frank McCabe: Inspector B., 1886; Hanover, 1887; Sir Dixon, 1888.

David McDaniel: Harry Bassett, 1871; Joe Daniels, 1872; Springbok, 1873.

2 **Tom Barry:** *Cavan, 1958; *Celtic Ash, 1960.
Flint S. "Scotty" Schulhofer: Colonial Affair, 1993; Lemon Drop Kid, 1999.
Sylvester Veitch: Phalanx, 1947; Counterpoint, 1951.
Oscar White: Pavot, 1945; One Count, 1952.

Leading Belmont Owners

6 **James R. Keene: (6):** Spendthrift, 1879; Commando, 1901; Delhi, 1904; Peter Pan, 1907; Colin 1908; Sweep, 1910.
Belair Stud: Gallant Fox, 1930; Faireno, 1932; Omaha, 1935; Granville, 1936; Johnstown, 1939; Nashua, 1955.
5 **Mike and Phil Dwyer:** George Kinney, 1883; Panique, 1884; Inspector B., 1886; Hanover, 1887; Sir Dixon, 1888.
4 **Glen Riddle Farms:** Man o' War, 1920; American Flag, 1925; Crusader, 1926; War Admiral, 1937.
Greentree Stable: Twenty Grand, 1931; Shut Out, 1942; Capot, 1949; Stage Door Johnny, 1968.
3 **August Belmont II:** Masterman, 1902; Friar Rock, 1916; *Hourless, 1917.
King Ranch: Assault, 1946; Middleground, 1950; High Gun, 1954.

Leading Belmont Breeders

7 **A. J. Alexander:** Harry Bassett, 1871; Joe Daniels, 1872; Springbok, 1873; Duke of Magenta, 1878; Spendthrift, 1879; Grenada, 1880; Burlington, 1890.
5 **Belair Stud:** Gallant Fox, 1930; Faireno, 1932; Omaha, 1935; Granville, 1936; Nashua, 1955.
J. R. Keene: Commando, 1901; Delhi, 1904; Peter Pan, 1907; Colin, 1908; Sweep, 1910.
John E. Madden: Joe Madden, 1909; The Finn, 1915; Sir Barton, 1919; Grey Lag, 1921; Zev, 1923.
4 **August Belmont II:** Masterman, 1902; Friar Rock, 1916; *Hourless, 1917; Man o' War, 1920.
Greentree: Twenty Grand, 1931; Shut Out, 1942; Capot, 1949; Stage Door Johnny, 1968.
H. P. Whitney: Tanya, 1905; Burgomaster, 1906; Prince Eugene, 1913; *Johren, 1918.
3 **W. S. Farish:** Bet Twice, 1987; A.P. Indy, 1991; Lemon Drop Kid, 1999.
Sam Riddle: American Flag, 1925; Crusader, 1926; War Admiral, 1937.

Derby-Preakness Winners Not Favored in the Belmont

A total of 29 three-year-olds swept the Kentucky Derby and Preakness to earn a chance at the Triple Crown. Ironically, the only two who were not the betting favorites in the Belmont Stakes became Triple Crown champions.

Gallant Fox in 1930 was the 8-to-5 second choice to 4-to-5 Whichone, who finished second. Assault in 1946 was the 7-to-5 second choice to 1.35-to-1 Lord Boswell, who finished fifth.

Fastest Belmont Times

Year	Winner	Time	Cond.
1973	Secretariat	2:24	Fast
1989	Easy Goer	2:26	Fast
1992	A.P. Indy	2:26	Good
1988	Risen Star	2:26⅖	Fast
2001	Point Given	2:26.56	Fast
1957	Gallant Man	2:26⅗	Fast
1978	Affirmed	2:26⅘	Fast
1994	Tabasco Cat	2:26.82	Fast

Fastest Fractions

Quarter-mile	:23	Another Review, 1991
Half-mile	:46⅕	Secretariat, 1973
Six furlongs	1:09⅘	Secretariat, 1973
One mile	1:34⅕	Secretariat, 1973
1¼ miles	1:59	Secretariat, 1973

Evolution of Belmont Stakes Record at 1½ Miles

Year	Winner	Time	Cond.
1874	Saxon	2:39½	Fast
1926	Crusader	2:32⅕	Sloppy
1930	Gallant Fox	2:31⅗	Good
1931	Twenty Grand	2:29⅗	Fast
1934	Peace Chance	2:29⅕	Fast
1937	War Admiral	2:28⅗	Fast
1943	Count Fleet	2:28⅕	Fast
1957	Gallant Man	2:26⅗	Fast
1973	Secretariat	2:24	Fast

Slowest Winning Times

Year	Winner	Time	Cond.
1970	High Echelon	2:34	Sloppy
1928	Vito	2:33⅕	Fast
1932	Faireno	2:32⅘	Fast
1929	Blue Larkspur	2:32⅘	Sloppy
1933	Hurryoff	2:32⅗	Fast
1927	Chance Shot	2:32⅖	Fast
1944	Bounding Home	2:32⅕	Fast
1926	Crusader	2:32⅕	Fast
1995	Thunder Gulch	2:32.02	Good
1930	Gallant Fox	2:31⅗	Fast
2000	Commendable	2:31.19	Fast
1941	Whirlaway	2:31	Fast

Leading Sires of Belmont Winners

5 **Lexington:** General Duke, 1868; Kingfisher, 1870; Harry Bassett, 1871; Duke of Magenta, 1878; Saunterer, 1881.
3 ***Australian :** Joe Daniels, 1872; Springbok, 1873; Spendthrift, 1879.
Fair Play: Man o' War, 1920; Mad Play, 1924; Chance Shot, 1927.
Man o' War: American Flag, 1925; Crusader, 1926; War Admiral, 1937.
2 **Commando:** Peter Pan, 1907; Colin, 1908.
Count Fleet: Counterpoint, 1951; One Count, 1952.
Gallant Fox: Omaha, 1935; Granville, 1936.
Hamburg: Burgomaster, 1906; Prince Eugene, 1913.
***Nasrullah:** Nashua, 1955; Jaipur, 1962.
***Negofol:** *Hourless, 1917; Vito, 1928.
Seattle Slew: Swale, 1984; A.P. Indy, 1992.
***Star Shoot:** Sir Barton, 1919; Grey Lag, 1921.

Belmont Winners Who Sired Belmont Winners

3 **Man o' War (1920):** American Flag, 1925; Crusader, 1926; War Admiral, 1937.
2 **Commando (1901):** Peter Pan, 1907; Colin, 1908.
Gallant Fox (1930): Omaha, 1935; Granville, 1936.
Count Fleet (1943): Counterpoint, 1951; One Count, 1952.
Seattle Slew (1977): Swale, 1984; A.P. Indy, 1992.
1 **Duke of Magenta (1878):** Eric, 1889.
Spendthrift (1879): Hastings, 1896.
Hastings (1896): Masterman, 1902.
The Finn (1915): Zev, 1923.
Sword Dancer (1959): Damascus, 1967.
Secretariat (1973): Risen Star, 1988.

Shortest-Priced Winning Favorites

Winner	Year	Odds
Man o' War	1920	.04-to-1
Hanover	1887	.05-to-1
Count Fleet	1943	.05-to-1
George Kinney	1883	.08-to-1
Sweep	1910	.10-to-1
Secretariat	1973	.10-to-1
Johnstown	1939	.12-to-1
Nashua	1955	.15-to-1
Tim Tam	1958	.15-to-1
Forester	1882	.20-to-1
Citation	1948	.20-to-1
*Hourless	1917	.25-to-1
Whirlaway	1941	.25-to-1
Chance Shot	1927	.29-to-1
Sir Dixon	1888	.36-to-1
Burgomaster	1906	.40-to-1
Seattle Slew	1977	.40-to-1
American Flag	1925	.45-to-1
Native Dancer	1953	.45-to-1
Grenada	1880	.50-to-1
Jean Bereaud	1899	.50-to-1
Colin	1908	.50-to-1

Longest Winning Odds

Year	Horse	Odds
2002	Sarava	70.25-to-1
1961	Sherluck	65.05-to-1
1980	Temperence Hill	53.40-to-1
1971	Pass Catcher	34.50-to-1
1999	Lemon Drop Kid	29.75-to-1
2000	Commendable	18.80-to-1
1944	Bounding Home	16.35-to-1

Odds-On Beaten Favorites

Year	Horse	Odds	Finish
1958	Tim Tam	.15-to-1	2nd
1979	Spectacular Bid	.30-to-1	3rd
1922	*Snob II	.33-to-1	2nd
1938	Dauber	.33-to-1	2nd
1942	Alsab	.40-to-1	2nd
1928	Victorian	.45-to-1	5th
1961	Carry Back	.45-to-1	7th
1900	Missionary	.50-to-1	3rd
1944	Pensive	.50-to-1	2nd
1952	Blue Man	.50-to-1	2nd
1963	Candy Spots	.50-to-1	2nd
1915	Pebbles	.60-to-1	3rd
1966	Kauai King	.60-to-1	4th
1913	Rock View	.70-to-1	2nd
1930	Whichone	.70-to-1	2nd
1971	Canonero II	.70-to-1	4th
1947	Faultless	.75-to-1	5th
1889	Diablo	.80-to-1	2nd
1891	Montana	.80-to-1	2nd
1895	Counter Tenor	.80-to-1	2nd
1936	Brevity	.80-to-1	5th
1949	Ponder	.80-to-1	2nd
1964	Northern Dancer	.80-to-1	3rd
1981	Pleasant Colony	.80-to-1	3rd
1987	Alysheba	.80-to-1	4th
1998	Real Quiet	.80-to-1	2nd
1950	Hill Prince	.85-to-1	7th
1960	Tompion	.85-to-1	4th
1957	Bold Ruler	.85-to-1	3rd
1989	Sunday Silence	.90-to-1	2nd

Belmont Front Runners

Since Capot in 1949, only six horses have won the Belmont while leading at every point of call, and none since Swale in '84. The following Belmont Stakes winners were on the lead at all points of call.

Year	Winner	Winning margin
1898	*Bowling Brook	8
1901	Commando	½
1902	Masterman	2
1904	Delhi	3½
1905	Tanya	½
1906	Burgomaster	4
1907	Peter Pan	1
1908	Colin	Head
1910	Sweep	6
1915	The Finn	4
1916	Friar Rock	3
1917	*Hourless	10
1920	Man o' War	20
1923	Zev	1½
1927	Chance Shot	1½
1930	Gallant Fox	3
1932	Faireno	1½
1937	War Admiral	3
1939	Johnstown	5
1943	Count Fleet	25
1948	Citation	8
1949	Capot	½
1972	Riva Ridge	7
1973	Secretariat	31
1976	Bold Forbes	Neck
1977	Seattle Slew	4
1978	Affirmed	Head
1984	Swale	4

Winning Belmont Post Positions

Post	Winners	Post	Winners
1	22	7	11
2	11	8	5
3	13	9	3
4	8	10	2
5	13	11	2
6	7		

Female Jockeys and Trainers in the Belmont

Julie Krone, the only female jockey ever to ride in the Belmont Stakes (G1), made Triple Crown history on June 5, 1993, when she won the Belmont aboard Colonial Affair for trainer Flint S. "Scotty" Schulhofer. Krone, who retired in 1999, had four other Belmont Stakes mounts. She finished ninth aboard Subordinated Debt in 1991, sixth on Colony Light in '92, second on Star Standard in '95, and eased South Salem in '96 when her mount lost contact with the field.

No woman trainer has ever won the Belmont. The best finish by a female trainer was Dianne Carpenter, who trained Kingpost to a second-place finish, 14¾ lengths behind Risen Star, in 1988. Previously, Sarah Lundy finished 11th with Minstrel Star in 1984, while Patricia Johnson's Fast Account finished fourth in '85. Following Carpenter, Shelley Riley's Casual Lies was fifth in 1992, Cynthia Reese had ninth-place finisher In Contention in '96, and owner-breeder-trainer Nancy Alberts sent out fouth-finisher Magic Weisner in 2002.

Fillies in the Belmont

Ruthless left a tough act to follow when she won the inaugural Belmont Stakes in 1867. Only 20 other fillies have raced in the Belmont Stakes, and just one other won, Tanya, in 1905. Kentucky Derby winner and Preakness runner-up Genuine Risk was a brave second to Temperence Hill in 1980, and six other fillies have finished third, most recently My Flag in '96.

Year	Filly	Finish
1867	Ruthless	1st
1868	Fanny Ludlow	3rd
1869	Invercauld	3rd
	Viola	7th
1870	Midday	3rd
	Nellie James	4th
	Stamps	6th
1871	Nellie Gray	4th
	Mary Clark	9th
1885	Miss Palmer	9th
1905	Tanya	1st
	Funders	7th
1913	Flying Fairy	3rd
1923	Miss Smith	8th
1927	Flambino	3rd
1932	Laughing Queen	10th
1954	Riverina	7th
1980	Genuine Risk	2nd
1988	Winning Colors	6th
1996	My Flag	3rd
1999	Silverbulletday	7th

Belmont Trophy and Other Traditions

The Belmont Stakes trophy is a solid silver bowl originally crafted by Tiffany's, and it was the trophy that August Belmont I's Fenian won in 1869 after taking the third running of the race. The Belmont family presented it as a perpetual trophy for the Belmont Stakes in 1926, and each winning owner is given the option of keeping the trophy for the year his horse wins. Atop the cover of the trophy is a silver figure of Fenian. The bowl is supported by three horses representing foundation sires Eclipse, Herod, and Matchem. The winning owner also receives a permanent large silver tray with the names of previous Belmont Stakes winners engraved on it. Trays also are presented to the winning trainer, jockey, exercise rider, and groom.

The white carnation is the traditional flower of the Belmont Stakes, and the blanket of carnations presented to the winning horse consists of 300 to 400 flowers glued onto a green velveteen spread. The flowers are shipped in from either California or Bogota, Colombia.

Until 1997, "Sidewalks of New York" was played as horses came onto the track for the Belmont Stakes. In 1997, "New York, New York" became the song of the Belmont. Written by John Kander and Fred Ebb, "New York, New York" was a huge hit for Frank Sinatra.

Largest Winning Margins

Year	Horse	Margin in lengths
1973	Secretariat	31
1943	Count Fleet	25
1920	Man o' War	20
1988	Risen Star	14¾
1987	Bet Twice	14
1982	Conquistador Cielo	14
2001	Point Given	12¼
1888	Sir Dixon	12
1931	Twenty Grand	10
1917	*Hourless	10

Smallest Winning Margins

Year	Horse	Margin
1998	Victory Gallop	nose
1962	Jaipur	nose
1936	Granville	nose
1999	Lemon Drop Kid	head
1991	Hansel	head
1978	Affirmed	head
1908	Colin	head
1900	Ildrim	head
1899	Jean Bereaud	head
1895	Belmar	head
1893	Commanche	head
1889	Eric	head
1876	Algerine	head
1867	Ruthless	head
1981	Summing	neck
1976	Bold Forbes	neck
1975	Avatar	neck
1965	Hail to All	neck
1956	Needles	neck
1954	High Gun	neck
1953	Native Dancer	neck
1938	Pasteurized	neck
1936	Granville	neck
1896	Hastings	neck
1891	Foxford	neck
1881	Saunterer	neck
1874	Saxon	neck

Belmont Trivia

- The Belmont Stakes has not always been contested at 1½ miles. Prior to 1874, the race was run at 1⅝ miles. The Belmont was held at 1¼ miles from 1890 through '92, and in '95, 1904, and 1905. It was 1⅛ miles in 1893 and '94; at 1⅜ miles 1896 through 1903 and from 1906 through 1925. The Belmont was run at 1½ miles from 1874 through '89 and from 1926 to the present.
- The Belmont Stakes was run at Aqueduct from 1963 through '67 while Belmont Park was being rebuilt.
- The smallest Belmont Stakes field was two. It happened in 1887, '88, '92, 1910 and '20. The largest Belmont Stakes field was 15 in 1983.
- Point Given was the 50th chestnut to win the Belmont Stakes. Fifty-two winners have been bay, 27 dark bay or brown, three black, two gray, and one roan.
- Thirty-five of the 134 runnings of the Belmont Stakes have been run on off tracks, the last in 1993 when Colonial Affair won.
- Creme Fraiche, who won the 1985 Belmont Stakes, is the only gelding to win the final leg of the Triple Crown. Geldings were barred from the Belmont Stakes from 1919 to '56.
- The 2001 Belmont Stakes drew a crowd of 73,857, the largest ever for the race without a horse going for the Triple Crown and fifth highest ever behind 103,222 in 2002, 85,818 in 1999, 82,694 in 1971, and 80,162 in 1998.
- Sarava became the 86th Belmont Stakes winner who was bred in Kentucky. Virginia is a distant second with 11 winners, followed by New Jersey (7), England (6), and Florida (5). New York, Pennsylvania and Tennessee each have three.
- Sarava was the 17th Belmont winner whose name began with the letter 'S'. Twenty Belmont Stakes winners had names beginning with 'C'.

Belmont Stakes

Grade 1, Belmont Park, three-year-olds, 1½ miles, dirt. Held on June 8, 2002, with gross value of $1,000,000. First run in 1867. Weights: colts and geldings, 126 pounds; fillies, 121 pounds.

Year	Winner	Jockey	Second	Third	Strs	Time	Track	1st purse
2002	**Sarava**	E. Prado	Medaglia d'Oro	Sunday Break (Jpn)	11	2:29.71	ft	$600,000
2001	**Point Given**	G. Stevens	A P Valentine	Monarchos	9	2:26.56	ft	$600,000
2000	**Commendable**	P. Day	Aptitude	‡Unshaded	11	2:31.19	ft	$600,000
1999	**Lemon Drop Kid**	J. Santos	Vision and Verse	Charismatic	12	2:27.88	ft	$600,000
1998	**Victory Gallop**	G. Stevens	Real Quiet	‡Thomas Jo	11	2:29.16	ft	**$600,000**
1997	**Touch Gold**	C. McCarron	Silver Charm	Free House	7	2:28.82	ft	$432,600
1996	**Editor's Note**	R. Douglas	Skip Away	†My Flag	14	2:28.96	ft	$437,880
1995	**Thunder Gulch**	G. Stevens	Star Standard	‡Citadeed	11	2:32.02	ft	$415,440
1994	**Tabasco Cat**	P. Day	Go for Gin	Strodes Creek	6	2:26.82	ft	$392,280
1993	**Colonial Affair**	J. Krone	Kissin Kris	Wild Gale	13	2:29.97	gd	$444,540
1992	**A.P. Indy**	E. Delahoussaye	My Memoirs (GB)	Pine Bluff	11	2:26.13	gd	$458,880
1991	**Hansel**	J. Bailey	Strike the Gold	Mane Minister	11	2:28.10	ft	$417,480
1990	**Go and Go (Ire)**	M. Kinane	Thirty Six Red	Baron de Vaux	9	2:27⅕	gd	$411,600
1989	**Easy Goer**	P. Day	Sunday Silence	Le Voyageur	10	2:26	ft	$413,520
1988	**Risen Star**	E. Delahoussaye	‡Kingpost	Brian's Time	6	2:26⅖	ft	$303,720
1987	**Bet Twice**	C. Perret	Cryptoclearance	Gulch	9	2:28⅕	ft	$329,160
1986	**Danzig Connection**	C. McCarron	Johns Treasure	Ferdinand	10	2:29⅘	sy	$338,640
1985	**‡Creme Fraiche**	E. Maple	Stephan's Odyssey	Chief's Crown	11	2:27	my	$307,740
1984	**Swale**	L. Pincay Jr.	Pine Circle	Morning Bob	11	2:27⅕	ft	$310,020
1983	**Caveat**	L. Pincay Jr.	Slew o' Gold	Barberstown	**15**	2:27⅘	ft	$215,100
1982	**Conquistador Cielo**	L. Pincay Jr.	Gato Del Sol	Illuminate	11	2:28⅕	sy	$159,720
1981	**Summing**	G. Martens	Highland Blade	Pleasant Colony	11	2:29	ft	$170,580
1980	**Temperence Hill**	E. Maple	†Genuine Risk	Rockhill Native	10	2:29⅘	my	$176,228
1979	**Coastal**	R. Hernandez	Golden Act	Spectacular Bid	8	2:29⅗	ft	$161,400
1978	**AFFIRMED**	S. Cauthen	Alydar	Darby Creek Road	5	2:26⅘	ft	$110,580
1977	**SEATTLE SLEW**	J. Cruguet	Run Dusty Run	Sanhedrin	8	2:29⅗	my	$109,080
1976	**Bold Forbes**	A. Cordero Jr.	McKenzie Bridge	Great Contractor	10	2:29	ft	$117,000
1975	**Avatar**	W. Shoemaker	Foolish Pleasure	Master Derby	9	2:28⅕	ft	$116,160
1974	**Little Current**	M. Rivera	Jolly Johu	Cannonade	9	2:29⅕	ft	$101,970
1973	**SECRETARIAT**	R. Turcotte	Twice a Prince	My Gallant	5	**2:24**	ft	$90,120
1972	**Riva Ridge**	R. Turcotte	Ruritania	Cloudy Dawn	10	2:28	ft	$83,540
1971	**Pass Catcher**	W. Blum	Jim French	Bold Reason	13	2:30⅗	ft	$97,710
1970	**High Echelon**	J. Rotz	Needles n Pens	Naskra	10	2:34	sy	$115,000
1969	**Arts and Letters**	B. Baeza	Majestic Prince	Dike	6	2:28⅘	ft	$104,050
1968	**Stage Door Johnny**	H. Gustines	Forward Pass	Call Me Prince	9	2:27⅕	ft	$117,700
1967	**Damascus**	W. Shoemaker	Cool Reception	Gentleman James	9	2:28⅘	ft	$104,950
1966	**Amberoid**	W. Boland	Buffle	Advocator	11	2:29⅗	ft	$117,700
1965	**Hail to All**	J. Sellers	Tom Rolfe	First Family	8	2:28⅖	ft	$104,150
1964	**Quadrangle**	M. Ycaza	Roman Brother	Northern Dancer	8	2:28⅖	ft	$110,850
1963	**Chateaugay**	B. Baeza	Candy Spots	Choker	7	2:30⅕	gd	$101,700
1962	**Jaipur**	W. Shoemaker	Admiral's Voyage	Crimson Satan	8	2:28⅘	ft	$109,550
1961	**Sherluck**	B. Baeza	Globemaster	Guadalcanal	9	2:29⅕	ft	$104,900
1960	***Celtic Ash**	W. Hartack	Venetian Way	Disperse	7	2:29⅗	ft	$96,785
1959	**Sword Dancer**	W. Shoemaker	Bagdad	Royal Orbit	9	2:28⅗	sy	$93,525
1958	***Cavan**	P. Anderson	Tim Tam	‡Flamingo	8	2:30⅕	ft	$73,440
1957	***Gallant Man**	W. Shoemaker	Inside Tract	Bold Ruler	6	2:26⅗	ft	$78,350
1956	**Needles**	D. Erb	Career Boy	Fabius	8	2:29⅘	ft	$83,600
1955	**Nashua**	E. Arcaro	Blazing Count	Portersville	8	2:29	ft	$83,700
1954	**High Gun**	E. Guerin	Fisherman	*Limelight	13	2:30⅘	ft	$89,000
1953	**Native Dancer**	E. Guerin	Jamie K.	Royal Bay Gem	6	2:28⅗	ft	$82,500
1952	**One Count**	E. Arcaro	Blue Man	Armageddon	6	2:30⅕	ft	$82,400
1951	**Counterpoint**	D. Gorman	Battlefield	Battle Morn	9	2:29	ft	$82,000
1950	**Middleground**	W. Boland	Lights Up	Mr. Trouble	9	2:28⅗	ft	$61,350
1949	**Capot**	T. Atkinson	Ponder	Palestinian	8	2:30⅕	ft	$60,900
1948	**CITATION**	E. Arcaro	Better Self	Escadru	8	2:28⅕	ft	$77,700
1947	**Phalanx**	R. Donoso	Tide Rips	Tailspin	9	2:29⅗	ft	$78,900
1946	**ASSAULT**	W. Mehrtens	Natchez	Cable	7	2:30⅘	ft	$75,400
1945	**Pavot**	E. Arcaro	Wildlife	Jeep	8	2:30⅕	ft	$52,675
1944	**Bounding Home**	G. L. Smith	Pensive	Bull Dandy	7	2:32⅕	ft	$55,000
1943	**COUNT FLEET**	J. Longden	Fairy Manhurst	‡Deseronto	3	2:28⅕	ft	$35,340
1942	**Shut Out**	E. Arcaro	Alsab	Lochinvar	7	2:29⅕	ft	$44,520
1941	**WHIRLAWAY**	E. Arcaro	Robert Morris	‡Yankee Chance	4	2:31	ft	$39,770
1940	**Bimelech**	F. Smith	Your Chance	Andy K.	6	2:29⅗	ft	$35,030
1939	**Johnstown**	J. Stout	Belay	Gilded Knight	6	2:29⅗	ft	$37,020
1938	**Pasteurized**	J. Stout	Dauber	Cravat	6	2:29⅖	ft	$34,530
1937	**WAR ADMIRAL**	C. Kurtsinger	Sceneshifter	Vamoose	7	2:28⅗	ft	$38,020
1936	**Granville**	J. Stout	Mr. Bones	Hollyrood	10	2:30	ft	$29,800
1935	**OMAHA**	W. Saunders	Firethorn	Rosemont	5	2:30⅗	sy	$35,480

Year	Winner	Jockey	Second	Third	Strs	Time	Track	1st purse
1934	**Peace Chance**	W. Wright	High Quest	Good Goods	8	2:29⅕	ft	$43,410
1933	**Hurryoff**	M. Garner	Nimbus	Union	9	2:32⅗	ft	$49,490
1932	**Faireno**	T. Malley	Osculator	Flag Pole	11	2:32⅘	ft	$55,120
1931	**Twenty Grand**	C. Kurtsinger	Sun Meadow	Jamestown	3	2:29⅗	ft	$58,770
1930	**GALLANT FOX**	E. Sande	Whichone	Questionnaire	4	2:31⅗	gd	$66,040
1929	**Blue Larkspur**	M. Garner	African	Jack High	8	2:32⅘	sy	$59,650
1928	**Vito**	C. Kummer	Genie	Diavolo	6	2:33⅕	ft	$63,430
1927	**Chance Shot**	E. Sande	Bois de Rose	†Flambino	6	2:32⅖	ft	$60,910
1926	**Crusader**	A. Johnson	Espino	Haste	9	2:32⅕	sy	$48,550
1925	**American Flag**	A. Johnson	Dangerous	Swope	7	2:16⅘	ft	$38,500
1924	**Mad Play**	E. Sande	Mr. Mutt	Modest	11	2:18⅘	gd	$42,880
1923	**Zev**	E. Sande	Chickvale	‡Rialto	8	2:19	gd	$38,000
1922	**Pillory**	C. H. Miller	*Snob II	Hea	4	2:18⅘	ft	$39,200
1921	**Grey Lag**	E. Sande	Sporting Blood	Leonardo II	4	2:16⅘	ft	$8,650
1920	**Man o' War**	C. Kummer	*Donnacona	———	2	2:14⅕	ft	$7,950
1919	**SIR BARTON**	J. Loftus	Sweep On	Natural Bridge	3	2:17⅖	ft	$11,950
1918	***Johren**	F. Robinson	*War Cloud	‡Cum Sah	4	2:20⅖	ft	$8,950
1917	***Hourless**	J. Butwell	Skeptic	Wonderful	3	2:17⅘	gd	$5,800
1916	**Friar Rock**	E. Haynes	Spur	Churchill	4	2:22	my	$4,100
1915	**The Finn**	G. Byrne	Half Rock	Pebbles	3	2:18⅖	ft	$1,825
1914	**Luke McLuke**	M. Buxton	‡Gainer	‡Charlestonian	3	2:20	ft	$3,275
1913	**Prince Eugene**	R. Troxler	Rock View	†Flying Fairy	4	2:18	ft	$3,075
1910	**Sweep**	J. Butwell	Duke of Ormonde	———	2	2:22	ft	$9,700
1909	**Joe Madden**	E. Dugan	Wise Mason	‡Donald Macdonald	5	2:21⅗	ft	$24,550
1908	**Colin**	J. Notter	Fair Play	King James	4	n/a	sy	$22,765
1907	**Peter Pan**	G. Mountain	Superman	Frank Gill	5	n/a	ft	$22,765
1906	**Burgomaster**	L. Lyne	The Quail	Accountant	6	2:20	gd	$22,700
1905	**†Tanya**	E. Hildebrand	Blandy	Hot Shot	7	2:08	ft	$17,240
1904	**Delhi**	G. Odom	Graziallo	Rapid Water	8	2:06⅗	ft	$14,685
1903	**Africander**	J. Bullman	Whorler	Red Knight	4	2:21¾	ft	$12,285
1902	**Masterman**	J. Bullman	Ranald	King Hanover	6	2:22⅗	ft	$12,020
1901	**Commando**	H. Spencer	The Parader	All Green	3	2:21	ft	$11,595
1900	**Ildrim**	N. Turner	‡Petruchio	Missionary	7	2:21¼	ft	$14,790
1899	**Jean Bereaud**	R. Clawson	Half Time	Glengar	4	2:23	ft	$10,680
1898	***Bowling Brook**	F. Littlefield	Previous	Hamburg	4	2:32	hy	$7,810
1897	**Scottish Chieftain**	J. Scherrer	On Deck	Octagon	6	2:23¼	ft	$3,350
1896	**Hastings**	H. Griffin	Handspring	Hamilton II	4	2:24½	gd	$3,025
1895	**Belmar**	F. Taral	Counter Tenor	Nanki Pooh	5	2:11½	hy	$2,700
1894	**Henry of Navarre**	W. Simms	Prig	Assignee	3	1:56½	ft	$6,680
1893	**Commanche**	W. Simms	Dr. Rice	Rainbow	5	1:53¼	ft	$5,310
1892	**Patron**	W. Hayward	Shellbark	———	2	2:12	my	$6,610
1891	**Foxford**	E. Garrison	Montana	Laurestan	6	2:08¾	gd	$5,070
1890	**Burlington**	S. Barnes	Devotee	Padishah	9	2:07¾	ft	$8,560
1889	**Eric**	W. Hayward	Diablo	Zephyrus	3	2:47¼	gd	$4,960
1888	**Sir Dixon**	J. McLaughlin	Prince Royal	———	2	2:40¼	ft	$3,440
1887	**Hanover**	J. McLaughlin	Oneko	———	2	2:43½	hy	$2,900
1886	**Inspector B.**	J. McLaughlin	The Bard	Linden	5	2:41	ft	$2,720
1885	**Tyrant**	P. Duffy	‡St. Augustine	Tecumseh	6	2:43	gd	$2,710
1884	**Panique**	J. McLaughlin	Knight of Ellerslie	Himalaya	4	2:42	gd	$3,150
1883	**George Kinney**	J. McLaughlin	‡Trombone	Renegade	4	2:42½	ft	$3,070
1882	**Forester**	J. McLaughlin	Babcock	‡Wyoming	3	2:43	ft	$2,600
1881	**Saunterer**	T. Costello	Eole	Baltic	6	2:47	hy	$3,000
1880	**Grenada**	W. Hughes	Ferncliffe	Turenne	4	2:47	gd	$2,800
1879	**Spendthrift**	G. Evans	‡Monitor	Jericho	6	2:24¾	sy	$4,250
1878	**Duke of Magenta**	W. Hughes	Bramble	Sparta	6	2:43½	my	$3,850
1877	**Cloverbrook**	C. Holloway	‡Loiterer	Baden-Baden	13	2:46	hy	$5,200
1876	**Algerine**	W. Donohue	Fiddlesticks	Barricade	5	2:40½	ft	$3,700
1875	**Calvin**	R. Swim	Aristides	Milner	14	2:42¼	ft	$4,450
1874	**Saxon**	G. Barbee	Grinstead	Aaron Pennington	9	2:39½	ft	$4,200
1873	**Springbok**	J. Rowe	Count d'Orsay	Strachino	10	3:01¾	fr	$5,200
1872	**Joe Daniels**	J. Rowe	‡Meteor	Shylock	9	2:58¼	fr	$4,500
1871	**Harry Bassett**	W. Miller	Stockwood	By the Sea	11	2:56	ft	$5,450
1870	**Kingfisher**	Dick	Foster	†Midday	7	2:59½	ft	$3,750
1869	**Fenian**	C. Miller	Glenelg	†Invercauld	8	3:04¼	hy	$3,350
1868	**General Duke**	R. Swim	Northumberland	†Fanny Ludlow	6	3:02	ft	$2,800
1867	**†Ruthless**	J. Gilpatrick	DeCourcey	Rivoli	4	3:05	hy	$1,850

†—filly, ‡—gelding, *—imported horse

1867-'73, 1⅝ miles; 1890-'92, 1895, 1904-'05, 1¼ miles; 1893-'94, 1⅛ miles; 1896-1903, 1906-'25, 1⅜ miles. 1867-'89, held at Jerome Park; 1890-1904, Morris Park; 1963-'67, Aqueduct. Not run 1911 and '12. 1973-present, Grade 1. Hansel (1991), Risen Star (1988), and Bet Twice (1987) earned $1-million bonus from Triple Crown Productions. 1907-'08 no official time recorded; bold-faced type shows records in starters, time, and purse earnings.

2002 Kentucky Derby: Baffert's third

With only four weeks left before the 2002 Kentucky Derby (G1), Bob Baffert was in the unfamiliar position of not having a live contender for the first time since 1995. The Derby is the focal point of Baffert's year, and the days leading up to the race are a time for the often-wisecracking trainer to show off not only his new quips and shtick but also the deft horsemanship that had already landed him two victories in the race.

Baffert appeared resigned to watch the race as a spectator. All that changed on April 10 when he and Richard Mulhall, racing manager for owner Ahmed bin Salman's The Thoroughbred Corp., purchased War Emblem, a son of Our Emblem who romped to victory in the the Illinois Derby (G2) on April 6 but was on course to skip the Derby and await the Preakness Stakes (G1). The purchase price was $900,000 plus commissions, with the colt's previous owner, Russell Reineman, retaining a 10% interest.

This was the same War Emblem who failed to pass the scrutiny of veterinarians and picky horsemen when offered for sale earlier in his career, and, yes, the same War Emblem who on May 4 made those who doubted Baffert pay dearly.

War Emblem would become Baffert's 12th career Derby starter and third winner in six years with a powerful, front-running victory under jockey Victor Espinoza. Left alone on the lead around the first turn and down the long Churchill backstretch, War Emblem destroyed the field in the 128th Derby, which had been disparaged by the press and public as below average, slow, and uninspiring.

The winning margin was four lengths over D.

Matt Goins photo

War Emblem leads all the way
Overlooked Illinois Derby victor wins by four lengths

Wayne Lukas-trained Proud Citizen. Perfect Drift, who was kept away from the bustle of Churchill's stable area and who was trained at the nearby Trackside training center by Australian-born Murray Johnson, was another three-quarters of a length back in third. Bobby Frankel-trained Medaglia d'Oro finished a troubled fourth in the field of 18 three-year-olds, which was reduced from its original 20 after Wood Memorial Stakes (G1) winner Buddha and Danthebluegrassman were scratched.

Harlan's Holiday, the longest-priced favorite in Derby history at 6-to-1, checked in seventh, just ahead of champion and Breeders' Cup Juvenile (G1) winner Johannesburg, and three spots ahead of 6.90-to-1 co-second choice Saarland. Dismissed at 20.50-to-1 by the announced crowd of 145,033, War Emblem completed the 1¼ miles in 2:01.13 on a fast track. The time was nowhere near as quick as one year earlier when Monarchos won in 1:59.97, but it still was the eighth-fastest in Derby history.

Baffert and Mulhall became intrigued with War Emblem after watching the Illinois Derby and after hearing about the speed figure he earned in that race. Salman watched the race by satellite from his home in Saudi Arabia, and from there he set the wheels in motion to have a Derby starter after his disappointment one year earlier when his Point Given finished fifth as the 9-to-5 favorite, his only loss at age three.

"We took a couple of days, stayed quiet," Baffert said of the early negotiations. "I told Richard, and we told the prince, and the prince says, 'Go get him.' I said he's not going to vet, he's got chips or whatever. He says, 'Go get him.' Richard calls me up and says, 'We're going to go look at him.'" And, they bought him.

Rival horsemen found out how good War

Emblem could be if left alone in front after Espinoza loped along on an uncontested lead through early fractions of :23.25, :47.04, and 1:11.75 for the first six furlongs. Mike Smith tried to keep Proud Citizen close, and on the far turn Chris McCarron and Came Home inched slightly closer to War Emblem, Proud Citizen, and Perfect Drift.

Espinoza was still waiting midway around the turn. Following Baffert's orders to be patient until midstretch, he was waiting for a challenge and waiting to turn his colt loose. The challenge never really came as they flew through the lane to win going away.

War Emblem earned a $1-million bonus from Sportsman's Park for winning both the Illinois Derby and the Kentucky Derby.—*Tom Law*

NINTH RACE 1¼ MILES (1:59⅖). 128th running of the Kentucky Derby. Grade 1. 3-year-olds. Purse $1,000,000. Plus, $1-million bonus from Sportsman's Park to any horse that wins Illinois Derby and a Triple Crown race.

Churchill

May 4, 2002

Value of race $2,175,000; Winner $1,875,000; second $170,000; third $85,000; fourth $45,000. Mutuel WPS Pool $34,083,706. Exacta Pool $16,069,772. Trifecta Pool $16,910,173. Superfecta Pool $3,965,135.

Horse	M/Eqt.	Wt.	PP	¼	½	¾	1 mi.	Str.	Fin.	Jockey	Odds $1
War Emblem	L	126	5	$1^{1/2}$	$1^{1\,1/2}$	$1^{1\,1/2}$	$1^{1\,1/2}$	$1^{1\,1/2}$	1^{4}	V. Espinoza	20.50
Proud Citizen	L	126	12	2^{1}	$2^{1/2}$	$2^{1/2}$	3^{1}	2^{hd}	$2^{3/4}$	M. Smith	23.30
Perfect Drift	L	126	3	4^{hd}	3^{1}	$3^{1/2}$	2^{hd}	$3^{3\,1/2}$	$3^{3\,1/4}$	E. Delahoussaye	7.90
Medaglia d'Oro	L	126	9	10^{1}	9^{1}	$7^{1/2}$	8^{3}	6^{1}	$4^{1\,1/2}$	L. Pincay Jr.	6.90
Request for Parole	L	126	7	6^{hd}	$5^{1/2}$	5^{hd}	5^{hd}	$5^{1/2}$	$5^{3/4}$	R. Albarado	29.80
Came Home	L	126	14	$3^{1/2}$	$4^{1/2}$	$4^{1/2}$	4^{2}	$4^{1/2}$	6^{2}	C. McCarron	8.20
Harlan's Holiday	L	126	13	$9^{1/2}$	$11^{1\,1/2}$	8^{hd}	6^{hd}	7^{1}	$7^{3/4}$	E. Prado	*6.00
Johannesburg	L	126	1	$11^{1/2}$	10^{1}	$10^{1/2}$	$9^{1/2}$	8^{1}	8no	G. Stevens	8.10
Essence of Dubai	Lb	126	8	13^{2}	12^{hd}	12^{hd}	$7^{1/2}$	9^{3}	9^{1}	D. Flores	10.00
Saarland	L	126	15	17^{2}	17^{2}	$14^{1/2}$	16^{hd}	$13^{1/2}$	$10^{2\,1/2}$	J. Velazquez	6.90
Blue Burner	Lb	126	18	5^{hd}	$8^{1/2}$	$9^{1\,1/2}$	$10^{1/2}$	11^{hd}	$11^{1/2}$	P. Day	24.20
Castle Gandolfo	L	126	11	15^{hd}	15^{1}	$15^{1/2}$	14^{1}	$12^{2\,1/2}$	$12^{4\,1/4}$	J. Bailey	14.50
Easy Grades	L	126	17	12^{1}	14^{hd}	16^{hd}	11^{hd}	14^{2}	13^{nk}	J. Chavez	43.80
Private Emblem	L	126	10	7^{1}	7^{hd}	$11^{1\,1/2}$	12^{hd}	10^{1}	$14^{4\,1/2}$	D. Meche	22.40
Lusty Latin	Lb	126	4	18	18	18	18	18	$15^{2\,1/4}$	G. Corbett	22.10
It'sallinthechase	L	126	16	$16^{2\,1/2}$	16^{hd}	17^{2}	$13^{1\,1/2}$	15^{3}	$16^{2\,3/4}$	E. Martin Jr.	94.50
Ocean Sound (Ire)	L	126	6	14^{hd}	$13^{1\,1/2}$	13^{1}	17^{2}	17^{2}	$17^{2\,1/4}$	A. Solis	48.70
Wild Horses	L	126	2	$8^{1/2}$	6^{1}	6^{hd}	15^{hd}	$16^{1/2}$	18	R. Douglas	58.50

Scratched—Buddha and Danthebluegrassman.

OFF AT 6:12. Times: :23.25, :47.04, 1:11.75, 1:36.70, 2:01.13.
Start: Good. Winner: Pace, three wide, hand urging. Track: Fast. Weather: Clear.

$2 Mutuel Prices:				
	5—WAR EMBLEM	43.00	22.80	13.60
	13—PROUD CITIZEN		24.60	13.40
	3—PERFECT DRIFT			6.40

$2 EXACTA 5-13 PAID $1,300.80 **$2 TRIFECTA 5-13-3 PAID $18,373.20**
$2 PICK THREE 12-3-5 PAID $1,411.40 **$2 SUPERFECTA 5-13-3-9 PAID $183,529.00**

Dkbbr. c., by Our Emblem out of Sweetest Lady, by Lord At War (Arg). Trainer: Bob Baffert. Breeder: Charles Nuckols Jr. and Sons (Ky.)

WAR EMBLEM gained lead early, raced three wide, drew off late, strong hand urging. PROUD CITIZEN stalked winner, four or five wide, in hand early, loomed, no match late. PERFECT DRIFT reserved inside, well placed, checked at three-sixteenths, angled out, empty. MEDAGLIA D'ORO bobbled start, bumped, swung out lane, bumped foe, no final bid. REQUEST FOR PAROLE well placed, between foes, held position, no late threat. CAME HOME stalked pace, edged in, five or six wide, asked, flattened out. HARLAN'S HOLIDAY moved near inside, between, bid five wide at second turn, empty in drive. JOHANNESBURG within striking distance, near inside throughout, no closing bid. ESSENCE OF DUBAI came out bump start, near inside, angled out lane, bumped, empty. SAARLAND outrun into stretch, failed to threaten, improved position. BLUE BURNER worked way inward, forwardly five or six wide, weakened gradually. CASTLE GANDOLFO between foes much of trip, failed to menace. EASY GRADES leaned in bumped start, nine or ten wide early, moved, failed to threaten. PRIVATE EMBLEM within striking distance, between foes, weakened, far turn. LUSTY LATIN near inside early, moved out eight or ten wide backstretch, passed tired ones. IT'SALLINTHECHASE never close, outrun. OCEAN SOUND (Ire) never prominent, outrun. WILD HORSES forwardly inside to end of backstretch, faded.

Preakness Stakes: Espinoza's Victory

Victor Espinoza and The Thoroughbred Corp.'s War Emblem are a lot alike. Both are young, impulsive, aggressive, and hugely talented. Both won surprisingly few believers inside Thoroughbred racing circles with their complete dominance of the 2002 Kentucky Derby (G1) on May 4.

That all changed in the 1:56.36 that War Emblem and Espinoza required to cover the 1³⁄₁₆ miles of the 127th Preakness Stakes (G1) on May 18 at Pimlico Race Course.

It was up to Espinoza to control that upstart impulsiveness and channel the natural aggression, both his own and his mount's. He did so brilliantly, tugging War Emblem just off the early pace of Menacing Dennis, turning back the challenge of Proud Citizen in midstretch, and then comfortably holding off the late charge of longshot Magic Weisner by three-quarters of a length.

Proud Citizen finished third, another three-quarters of a length behind Magic Weisner and 1½ lengths ahead of Harlan's Holiday. Easyfromthegitgo finished stoutly in fifth place, a neck behind Harlan's Holiday, but the rest of the 13-strong field was badly outclassed.

War Emblem's fourth straight victory and sixth in nine career starts earned him $650,000 from the $1-million Preakness purse, increasing his total earnings to $2,891,000.

"I thought Medaglia d'Oro would be the one to get out and go, but I was worried about Menacing Dennis before the race," said trainer Bob Baffert. "I knew he had a lot of speed, and Victor [who had ridden Menacing Dennis twice] said he had a lot of speed if they used it.

"They went :46 and change," Baffert added. "They were really cooking. That's when you find out how good these horses really are. If they're going to win this Triple Crown, they've got to earn it."

"When the other horse take the lead, he [War Emblem] get really aggressive," Espinoza said. "He didn't want nobody to take his place. He wants to be the man; he wants to be in control

Photo by Z

Courageous victory
War Emblem wins the Preakness, withstanding the late charge by Magic Weisner

of everybody else."

It was a record-tying fourth straight Triple Crown race win for owner Ahmed bin Salman's The Thoroughbred Corp., which purchased 90% of War Emblem from Russell Reineman 3½ weeks before the Kentucky Derby.

War Emblem broke alertly but toward the outside, bumping mildly with Table Limit. When 51.20-to-1 outsider Menacing Dennis sprinted for the lead from the outside under local rider Mario Pino, Espinoza grabbed a firm hold on the reins, not jerking hard on War Emblem's mouth. In the run by the stands, the colt twice leaped toward the leader, his body language screaming, "Let me run," but Espinoza deftly controlled his boiling energy just enough to keep War Emblem a head off the leader the first time under the wire.

As the field moved into the first turn, the rider made the move that sealed the victory. With expected pace-presser Booklet on his right flank and stalker Proud Citizen just outside him, Espinoza allowed War Emblem to corner slightly wide, entering the turn in the two path and exiting in the five.

That clever move accomplished two objectives. It moved the all-too-eager War Emblem away from an eye-to-eye duel with Menacing Dennis, encouraging him to relax back into Espinoza's anaconda grip. Also, it floated Booklet and Proud Citizen even wider, costing them irretrievable ground.

The field reached the half-mile point in :46.10, nearly one second faster than the much-criticized slower pace in the Derby, and completed six furlongs in 1:10.60, 1.15 seconds faster than at the same point at Churchill Downs.

It did not matter. When Espinoza finally agreed to War Emblem's demands to let him run at the three-eighths pole, the colt bounded away from the tiring Menacing Dennis in two strides. Proud Citizen went after him, but second-choice

Medaglia d'Oro, given a perfect, ground-saving ride by Jerry Bailey, backpedaled. Only the game Harlan's Holiday, Magic Weisner, and Easyfromthegitgo emerged from the pack.

Proud Citizen reached War Emblem's saddle-cloth above the eighth pole but, as at Churchill Downs, his stamina gave out in the final sixteenth, and War Emblem's steady, floating rhythm inexorably extended his lead. Magic Weisner, who never changed leads in the stretch, kept coming, but War Emblem appeared to be idling in front, never allowed the second finisher to pass him, and was drawing away again as he galloped out while still tugging at the reins.

"I tell you, I still have plenty of horse [at the finish]," Espinoza said. "If anybody come after me, they're never going to go by me. That other horse was coming from behind, but when any horse get close to him, he kicked on."

—*John P. Sparkman*

12TH RACE
PIMLICO
May 18, 2002

1³⁄₁₆ MILES. Purse $1,000,000. 127th running of the Preakness Stakes. 3-year-olds. Grade 1.

Value of race $1,000,000; Winner $650,000; second $200,000; third $100,000; fourth $50,000. Mutuel WPS Pool $17,104,079. Exacta Pool $10,399,293. Trifecta Pool $11,588,399. Superfecta Pool $2,951,397.

Horse	M/Eqt.	Wt.	PP	St	¼	½	¾	Str.	Fin.	Jockey	Odds $1
War Emblem	L	126	8	5	2¹	2¹	2½	1¹½	1¾	V. Espinoza	*2.80
Magic Weisner	LA	126	2	10	11²	10¹½	7¹½	4¹½	2¾	R. Migliore	45.70
Proud Citizen	L	126	12	8	6½	5¹½	3½	2⁴½	3¹½	M. Smith	7.40
Harlan's Holiday	LA	126	6	9	10ʰᵈ	9ʰᵈ	6¹½	3½	4ⁿᵏ	E. Prado	5.20
Easyfromthegitgo	LA	126	7	4	7½	7¹½	9½	5⁵	5⁷	D. Meche	23.40
U S S Tinosa	LAb	126	1	3	5ʰᵈ	6²	4ʰᵈ	6¹½	6⁶½	K. Desormeaux	10.20
Crimson Hero	L	126	4	13	13	13	13	10³	7½	C. McCarron	14.80
Medaglia d'Oro	LA	126	5	7	3ʰᵈ	3ʰᵈ	5¹	7³	8¾	J. Bailey	3.00
Straight Gin	L	126	3	12	12⁷	11ʰᵈ	11³	12½	9³	R. Albarado	28.00
Menacing Dennis	LAb	126	11	1	1ʰᵈ	1ʰᵈ	1ʰᵈ	9½	10⁶¾	M. Pino	51.20
Table Limit	Lb	126	9	6	8¹	8ʰᵈ	10ʰᵈ	11⁴	11ʰᵈ	G. Stevens	23.10
Booklet	L	126	10	2	4¹	4ʰᵈ	8ʰᵈ	8¹½	12½	P. Day	9.90
Equality	Lb	126	13	11	9¹	12⁶	12²	13	13	R. Dominguez	27.50

L=Lasix   LA=Lasix and adjunct bleeder medication   b=blinkers

OFF AT: 6:12. Weather: Cloudy. Track: Fast. Start: Good.
Time :22.87, :46.10, 1:10.60, 1:36.22, 1:56.36. Winner: Rated three-wide, stiff drive.

	8—WAR EMBLEM	7.60	6.00	4.40
$2 Mutuel Prices:	2—MAGIC WEISNER		33.00	14.00
	12—PROUD CITIZEN			5.00

$2 PICK THREE 3/6/8-2-8 PAID $133.00 $2 PICK FOUR 4/7/10-3/6/8-2-8 PAID $398.00
DAILY DOUBLE 2-8 PAID $49.20 $2 EXACTA 8-2 PAID $327.00
$2 TRIFECTA 8-2-12 PAID $2,311.00 $2 SUPERFECTA 8-2-12-6 PAID $13,403.00

Dkbbr. c., by Our Emblem out of Sweetest Lady, by Lord At War (Arg). Trainer: Bob Baffert. Breeder: Charles Nuckols Jr. and Sons (Ky.)

WAR EMBLEM prompted the pace outside of MENACING DENNIS under stout rating, raced four wide into the backstretch, took over nearing the three-furlong marker, drew clear midway on the final turn then was fully extended to hold off MAGIC WEISNER. MAGIC WEISNER saved ground while unhurried, angled out midway on the final turn, swung outside of HARLAN'S HOLIDAY in upper stretch, and closed gamely while racing on his left lead. PROUD CITIZEN lost ground while racing five wide for a good portion of the opening six furlongs, made a run outside of the winner to loom boldly in midstretch but could not sustain his bid. HARLAN'S HOLIDAY lost ground four wide most of the trip, advanced into contention nearing the stretch but lacked a strong closing response. EASYFROMTHEGITGO settled in the two path in the early stages, angled out five wide approaching the stretch, altered course back to the inside in midstretch and finished evenly. U S S TINOSA was hustled along inside trying to keep the early pace, steadied briefly behind the leaders entering the stretch, then drifted out while fading in the final furlong. CRIMSON HERO broke a bit awkwardly, trailed for nearly a mile, raced wide in the drive, and passed tiring rivals. MEDAGLIA D'ORO raced in close pursuit between rivals under some rating, continued within striking distance to the quarter pole then tired. STRAIGHT GIN lacked speed while saving ground, swung six wide for the drive, failed to respond, then pulled up in apparent distress and was vanned off. MENACING DENNIS angled to the inside after sprinting clear in the opening furlong, set a pressured pace inside of the winner to the far turn then gave way steadily thereafter. TABLE LIMIT steadied on the heels of rivals entering the first turn, raced very wide down the backstretch, and tired. BOOKLET raced wide between rivals while just off the pace for six furlongs, faltered leaving the far turn, and was not abused late. EQUALITY steadied briefly nearing the clubhouse turn, raced wide, and failed to threaten.

Belmont Stakes: A Historic Upset

A record crowd of 103,222 turned out at Belmont Park on June 8 for a chance to witness history as War Emblem, conqueror of the Kentucky Derby (G1) and Preakness Stakes (G1) in the preceding five weeks, sought to become the 12th Triple Crown winner in the Belmont Stakes (G1). Indeed, the media hype gave the impression that his coronation was all but assured, although a nation of cautious and grizzled bettors made him the 1.25-to-1 favorite, which is something less than a certainty.

Racing is a game of breaks—good breaks and bad breaks—and a bad break at the start perhaps robbed War Emblem of his chance at immortality. As War Emblem faded on Belmont's sweeping far turn, Sarava seized control of the Belmont from a game Medaglia d'Oro down the stretch and won by a half-length at 70.25-to-1, the longest odds for a Belmont winner in the race's 134-year history.

"It was lost at the start," said dejected trainer Bob Baffert, whose bid for a Triple Crown triumph was foiled for an unprecedented third time in six years. "When he stumbled like that, I knew that it was just way too much for this poor guy to overcome."

In the days leading up to the race, trainer Ken McPeek had just been hoping his luck would change. Four days before the Belmont, he had

Little horse, big win
Surprising Sarava defeats Medaglia d'Oro

Photo by Z

been notified by Starlight Stable principal Jack Wolf that Harlan's Holiday, whom McPeek saddled for victories in the Florida Derby (G1) and Blue Grass Stakes (G1), would be transferred to trainer Todd Pletcher after finishing unplaced in the Kentucky Derby and Preakness.

McPeek took the potentially devastating blow philosophically. "I don't think I should have lost the horse, but I did. Let's not look backward, let's look forward. Life is a zero game," McPeek said. "You start with zero and you end with zero. When you have a big negative, you're going to get a big positive."

To be sure, McPeek has plenty of positives. His wife, Sue, is cancer-free after a scare while she was pregnant with their only child, Jenna, 18 months earlier. And, he had Sarava, a fast-developing Wild Again colt who had scored an impressive victory in the Sir Barton Stakes on the Preakness undercard.

The expected pace scenario for the Belmont fell apart at the break when War Emblem stumbled and nearly went to his knees, bumped into Magic Weisner, and then almost went to his knees again.

As expected, jockey Jorge Chavez sent Wiseman's Ferry to the lead, with Medaglia d'Oro and Kent Desormeaux tracking them, about 1½ lengths back, through fractions of :24.11 and :48.09 for the first-half mile on a drying out track that was labeled as fast. Proud Citizen also was in contention as Edgar Prado rated Sarava in midpack after breaking from the outside post position in the field of 11 starters after Puzzlement was scratched.

Meanwhile, Espinoza was left with few options. Instead of rushing his mount immediately to the lead, he tried to get him to settle, but War Emblem became rank and ran down part of the backstretch with his head in the air, fighting the jockey while

Owners

Gary Drake, principal owner of New Phoenix Stable, and Paul and Susan Roy, also owners of Sarava, never met in person before the colt's stunning Belmont Stakes (G1) victory. Drake is the president of Phoenix Process Equipment Co. in Louisville and previously had raced several stakes winners. The Roys reside in Surrey, England, south of London; Paul Roy is a Merrill Lynch executive. The Roys, who became involved in the sport in the late 1990s, purchased Sarava for $250,000 at the 2001 Fasig-Tipton Florida sale of two-year-olds in training; after three disappointing starts in England, Drake bought half-interest for $250,000.

Breeder

Timber Bay Farm is the racing and breeding operation of William Entenmann, a resident of Islip, New York, approximately 30 miles east of Belmont Park. An avid participant in steeplechase racing for the last two decades, Entenmann is a retired executive of the baking company that bears his family's name. He acquired Sarava's dam, Rhythm of Life, at the 1998 Keeneland sale of breeding stock when she was carrying the 2002 Belmont winner. Acting through agent Jeffry Morris, Entenmann bought the half sister of 1992 Canadian champion older mare Wilderness Song for $180,000. Sarava was sold at the 2000 Fasig-Tipton Midlantic Eastern fall yearling sale for $190,000.

quickly ranging up to third. "I was thinking about where I could save him," Espinoza said. "I had to wait as much as I could. I didn't want to use my horse too early."

Although the crowd roared with approval when War Emblem spurted up to gain a short lead, he did not maintain it for long. Medaglia d'Oro pushed his head in front after a mile in 1:37.01. Proud Citizen appeared ready to rally from third, only a half-length behind the tiring War Emblem, and Sunday Break (Jpn) had reached a threatening position around the far turn. All but unnoticed,

Sarava moved fluidly up the rail behind Medaglia d'Oro until Prado saw his chance. Steering outside Medaglia d'Oro and inside Proud Citizen while swinging out of the far turn, Prado urged Sarava to take on Medaglia d'Oro. With that move, the Belmont was transformed into a match race down the stretch. Medaglia d'Oro battled on, but Sarava—named for the hit song in a Brazilian musical—surged to the front with one furlong remaining and hit the wire with a half-length advantage in 2:29.71 for the Belmont's 1½ miles.

—Michele MacDonald

TENTH RACE	1½ MILES (2:24). 134th running of the Belmont Stakes. Purse $1,000,000. Grade 1. 3-year-olds.									

Belmont
June 8, 2002

Value of race: $916,000. Value to winner: $520,000; second: $200,000; third: $120,000; fourth: $56,000; fifth, $20,000. Mutuel Pool $4,200,733.

Horse	Wgt.	M/Eqt	PP	St.	¼	½	¾	Str.	Fin.	Jockey	Odds $1
Sarava	L	126	11	5hd	6½	4hd	3hd	1½	1½	E. Prado	70.25
Medaglia d'Oro	L	126	7	2½	2½	1hd	1½	25½	29½	K. Desormeaux	16.00
Sunday Break (Jpn)	Lf	126	5	7½	7½	64½	41½	33½	31	G. Stevens	8.10
Magic Weisner	L	126	10	62½	54½	7½	62½	5½	41¼	R. Migliore	7.30
Proud Citizen	L	126	8	41½	3½	31	2hd	42	51¼	M. Smith	7.00
Essence of Dubai	Lb	126	4	102½	10½	108	85	6½	64¼	J. Bailey	20.60
Like a Hero	L	126	2	11	11	9½	73½	822	71¾	P. Day	25.50
War Emblem	L	126	9	3hd	42½	2½	52½	75	830¾	V. Espinoza	*1.25
Wiseman's Ferry	L	126	3	11½	1½	5½	1012	9hd	91	J. Chavez	18.80
Perfect Drift	L	126	6	92	96	86	9hd	1024	1024¾	E. Delahoussaye	5.60
Artax Too	Lb	126	1	8hd	8½	11	11	11	11	J. Santos	71.75

Scratched—Puzzlement.
L=Lasix   b=blinkers   f=front bandages

OFF AT 6:15 p.m. Start: Good for all but Artax Too, War Emblem.
Weather: Clear. Track: Fast. Winner: Driving.
Time: :24.11, :48.09, 1:12.38, 1:37.01, 2:03.50, 2:29.71.

$2 Mutuel Prices:	12—SARAVA	142.50	50.00	22.40
	8—MEDAGLIA D'ORO		16.00	10.60
	5—SUNDAY BREAK (Jpn)			7.10

EXACTA 12-8 PAID $2,454.00   TRIFECTA 12-8-5 PAID $25,209.00
SUPERFECTA 12-8-5-11 PAID $145,334.00   DAILY DOUBLE 2-12 PAID $348.50

Dk. b. or br. c., by Wild Again—Rhythm of Life, by Deputy Minister. Trainer: Kenneth McPeek. Breeder: Timber Bay Farm (Ky.)

SARAVA settled just off the early pace, was rated behind Medaglia d'Oro along the backstretch, angled to the inside nearing the far turn, waited patiently while edging closer on the turn, split rivals to challenge leaving the quarter pole, battled heads apart from outside in upper stretch, surged to the front nearing the furlong marker, then turned back Medaglia d'Oro under steady right hand encouragement. MEDAGLIA D'ORO rushed up from outside to contest the early pace; stalked three wide along the backstretch, surged to the front nearing the half-mile pole, maintained a slim advantage along the inside on the turn, fought heads apart inside the winner through the stretch, and yielded grudgingly. SUNDAY BREAK (Jpn) bumped with Perfect Drift at the start, was unhurried for six furlongs, gradually worked his way forward while five wide leaving the backstretch, made a run while continuing wide to threaten at the top of the stretch but couldn't sustain his bid. MAGIC WEISNER bumped with the favorite at the start, raced in the middle of the pack along the backstretch, swung six wide for clear sailing while gaining a bit on the turn, then lacked a strong finishing response. PROUD CITIZEN moved up from outside going into the first turn, stalked the leaders while five wide along the backstretch, raced in close contention while just outside the winner approaching the quarter pole, then steadily tired thereafter. Proud Citizen pulled up in distress after the finish and was vanned off. ESSENCE OF DUBAI never reached contention while being outrun for a mile and a quarter, then passed only tiring horses. LIKE A HERO was bumped offstride at the start and was never close thereafter. WAR EMBLEM stumbled badly then bumped with Magic Weisner at the start, rushed up between horses, was under a snug hold while rank for three-quarters of a mile, moved through along the rail to gain a brief lead nearing the half-mile pole, remained a factor to the turn, then gave way. WISEMAN'S FERRY rushed up along the inside after being bumped at the start, set the pace under pressure for six furlongs, relinquished the lead approaching the far turn and steadily tired thereafter. PERFECT DRIFT was bumped at the start, steadied in tight between horses on the first turn, raced well back for a mile, swung wide on the turn, and lacked a further response. ARTAX TOO stumbled, then broke outward, causing crowding at the start, steading along the inside on the first turn, and was never close thereafter.

BREEDERS' CUP
Breeders' Cup History

John R. Gaines, one of the central figures in the North American commercial breeding industry in the last quarter of the 20th century, is renowned for his creativity and his powers of persuasion. In the early 1980s, Gaines needed all his considerable talents to get a fractious industry lined up behind his concept, which he believed would help define the Thoroughbred industry and give it a centerpiece.

Gaines's creation was the Breeders' Cup. From the perspective of the 21st century, the Breeders' Cup stands as the most successful initiative of the Thoroughbred industry in the last half of the 20th century. Creation of the Breeders' Cup allowed the sport to hold a championship day of racing in late fall for the majority of age and sex divisions, an important element missing from a sport that had its major fall championship races scattered across the nation at a number of tracks.

Gaines conceived the idea in part out of anger and frustration. He was angered by a television program in the early 1980s that had depicted Thoroughbred racing as a haven of drug abuse. Indeed, permissive medication policies at racetracks had eroded confidence in the sport's integrity, and racing had continued a long, slow slide in popularity—a decline that began shortly after World War II. Even as the commercial bloodstock markets boomed in the early 1980s, race purses were shrinking in real terms.

The highly successful owner of Gainesway Farm in Lexington and an innovator in the stallion-station concept, Gaines developed the idea for a championship day of racing with multimillion-dollar purses to attract the world's best runners, with the races being broadcast nationally on one of the major networks. The day of racing, as important as it was, would not be an end in itself. The event would be used to build racing's popularity, with the organization running the event becoming a leader in marketing the sport.

Given the sport's propensity for self-destructive infighting, however, it is surprising that the Breeders' Cup came into being in very much the form that Gaines first envisioned Thoroughbred racing's championship day. But it was not easy.

Gaines had to sell the concept to a skeptical industry in 1982, and he had to do it one person at a time. His first target was John W. Galbreath, owner of Darby Dan Farm and an influential sportsman in the United States and England. (At the time, Galbreath was the only person to have raced both a Kentucky Derby winner [Chateaugay] and an Epsom Derby victor [Roberto].) Gaines flew to Columbus, Ohio, to meet with Galbreath, who initially thought little of the idea. But, as Gaines sketched out his idea in detail, Galbreath came on board. Moving quickly, Gaines lined up other supporters, including Spendthrift Farm's Leslie Combs II, Nelson Bunker Hunt, Windfields Farms' Charles Taylor, Will Farish, Racing Hall of Fame trainer John Nerud, Brereton C. Jones, John T. L. Jones Jr., and Seth Hancock, who a decade earlier had taken over management of his family's Claiborne Farm.

All great ideas have their moments, and Gaines's idea came at just the right time for the Thoroughbred industry. Commercial breeders, who would pay a big part of the program's cost by nominating their stallions and foals, were enjoying unprecedented prosperity as bloodstock prices rose to record levels and stallion fees climbed.

At the same time, racing was perceived as a sport in trouble, and relatively low purse levels dissuaded some prospective owners from buying horses. Although overseas interests had sent the bloodstock markets skyrocketing, many breeders realized that the prices they received for their sale offerings and the stallion fees they charged were directly related to purses on the racetrack, which determined how much a sale purchase potentially could earn.

Gaines chose the sport's most prestigious event, the Kentucky Derby (G1), to announce his idea. He was honored at the Kentucky Derby Festival's "They're Off" luncheon on April 23, 1982, and there he outlined his idea, a $13-million afternoon featuring the world's best racehorses. Gaines named it the Breeders' Cup.

He moved quickly to name a board of directors and girded for the inevitable naysayers. New York racing interests were opposed because Gaines's proposal would diminish the importance of the New York Racing Association's fall races, which frequently decided year-end titles.

Smaller-scale breeders also voiced their opposition. Gaines had said that breeders could breed one more mare to a stallion to cover the cost of the stallion nomination fee each year. Such a strategy certainly would work for a breeder with barns filled with desirable stallions and whose books were filled, and Gaines was one of those breeders. But, for a small-scale breeder trying to fill the book of a less commercial stallion, the stallion nomination most likely would be paid out of the stallion owner's pocket.

Other breeders raised concerns that Gaines was putting all the money into one event, arguing that the money should be spread throughout the year to supplement purses of existing stakes

races. On that point, a compromise was reached, with $10-million earmarked for the championship day and an equal portion going into Breeders' Cup-sponsored races around the country.

By fall of 1982, the Breeders' Cup was beset with infighting, and Seth Hancock delivered an unexpected blow when he did not nominate Claiborne's stallions on grounds that the organization had not developed a clear game plan. Gaines realized he had become a lightning rod for opponents and resigned the presidency on October 22, becoming chairman. C. Gibson Downing, a Lexington lawyer with a modest-sized stud farm and a reputation for consensus building, became Breeders' Cup president. Hancock signed up after a rules book was written on how the money would be spent, and smaller breeders followed his lead. D. G. Van Clief Jr. came on board that fall as executive director.

For several months, Gaines and Nerud traveled the country, selling breeders and racetrack operators on the concept. By April 15, 1983, 1,083 stallions had been nominated to the program, and the Breeders' Cup was up and running. Nerud said in 1985 that a decision was made early to hold the first Breeders' Cup in a warm climate so television viewers would see racing in a pleasant setting. Marjorie Everett, chief executive of Hollywood Park, lobbied heavily for the first event, and on February 24, 1983, the Inglewood, California, track was named to host the first Breeders' Cup, to be held on November 10, 1984. In a bow to New York interests, Aqueduct was host of the second Breeders' Cup in 1985.

At Nerud's suggestion, marketers Mike Letis and Mike Trager of Sports Marketing and Television International were brought in to negotiate a television deal, and a contract with NBC was signed on September 13, 1983. The show would run for four hours on a Saturday afternoon and include all seven of the Breeders' Cup championship races. In January 1984, all seven races were granted Grade 1 status.

From the first race, won by Chief's Crown in the $1-million Breeders' Cup Juvenile (G1), the Breeders' Cup was an unprecedented success. The afternoon's races attracted a crowd of 64,254, and the day concluded with a breathtaking $3-million Breeders' Cup Classic (G1), in which supplemental entry Wild Again edged Gate Dancer and Slew o' Gold for the biggest race purse ever offered.

An even larger crowd, 69,155, attended the third Breeders' Cup at Santa Anita Park in suburban Los Angeles, but that record lasted only two years until Churchill Downs hosted the fifth Breeders' Cup in 1988 before a crowd of 71,237. On a dreary, rainy, chilly day in Louisville, they were treated to one of the event's most exciting races when undefeated Personal Ensign closed relentlessly in the final yards and caught Kentucky Derby winner Winning Colors at the finish line to win the Breeders' Cup Distaff (G1) by a nose. With that victory, Personal Ensign retired unbeaten in 13 starts.

The Breeders' Cup traveled to Florida for the first time in 1989, and Gulfstream Park was the scene for another monumental struggle in which Sunday Silence fought off the challenge of Easy Goer to win the Breeders' Cup Classic. The event reached its nadir the following year at Belmont Park when Go for Wand sustained a fatal breakdown near the finish line of the Breeders' Cup Distaff and was humanely destroyed. Earlier on the card, a spill in the Sprint (G1) led to the deaths of Mr. Nickerson and Shaker Knit. Subsequently, Breeders' Cup Ltd. instituted prerace examinations to limit breakdowns.

Through the late 1980s and '90s, the Breeders' Cup grew in importance both to the racing industry, which began to regain its footing in that period, and to the sport's participants. The Breeders' Cup races often determine end-of-year titles, and such popular champions as Cigar sealed Horse of the Year honors with victories in the Breeders' Cup Classic.

As rich races became more common, especially internationally, Breeders' Cup Ltd. increased its championship day purses, raising the Classic to $4-million in 1996 and the Distaff to $2-million in '98. In 1999, a new race, the $1-million Filly and Mare Turf (G1), was added, raising the afternoon's total purses to $13-million. In 2001, the championship day was renamed the Breeders' Cup World Thoroughbred Championships. By 2002, the Breeders' Cup Stakes program had grown to 95 stakes races, with purses exceeding $17-million.—*Don Clippinger*

Television Ratings for Breeders' Cup

Date	Racetrack	Rating/share
2001	Belmont Park	1.7/5
2000	Churchill Downs	1.8/5
1999	Gulfstream Park	1.9/5
1998	Churchill Downs	2.2/6
1997	Hollywood Park	2.2/6
1996	Woodbine	2.5/8
1995	Belmont Park	2.8/9
1994	Churchill Downs	2.7/8
1993	Santa Anita Park	3.4/9
1992	Gulfstream Park	3.0/8
1991	Churchill Downs	3.0/9
1990	Belmont Park	2.7/9
1989	Gulfstream Park	3.7/11
1988	Churchill Downs	4.0/11
1987	Hollywood Park	2.9/7
1986	Santa Anita Park	4.4/12
1985	Aqueduct	4.0/11
1984	Hollywood Park	5.1/13

Breeders' Cup Leaders

Leading Jockeys by Wins

12 Pat Day (Unbridled Elaine, 2001 Distaff; Cat Thief, 1999 Classic; Awesome Again, 1998 Classic; Favorite Trick, 1997 Juvenile; Timber Country, 1994 Juvenile; Flanders, 1994 Juvenile Fillies; Dance Smartly, 1991 Distaff; Unbridled, 1990 Classic; Theatrical (Ire), 1987 Turf; Epitome, 1987 Juvenile Fillies; Lady's Secret, 1986 Distaff; Wild Again, 1984 Classic)

Jerry Bailey (Squirtle Squirt, 2001 Sprint; Macho Uno, 2000 Juvenile; Perfect Sting, 2000 Filly and Mare Turf; Soaring Softly, 1999 Filly and Mare Turf; Cash Run, 1999 Juvenile Fillies; Answer Lively, 1998 Juvenile; Boston Harbor, 1996 Juvenile; Cigar, 1995 Classic; My Flag, 1995 Juvenile Fillies; Concern, 1994 Classic; Arcangues, 1993 Classic; Black Tie Affair [Ire], 1991 Classic)

9 Chris McCarron (Tiznow [twice], 2000, '01 Classic; Alphabet Soup, 1996 Classic; Northern Spur [Ire], 1995 Turf; Paseana [Arg], 1992 Distaff; Gilded Time, 1992 Juvenile; Sunday Silence, 1989 Classic; Alysheba, 1988 Classic; Precisionist, 1985 Sprint)

8 Gary Stevens (War Chant, 2000 Mile; Anees, 1999 Juvenile; Escena, 1998 Distaff; Silverbulletday, 1998 Juvenile Fillies; Da Hoss, 1996 Mile; One Dreamer, 1994 Distaff; Brocco, 1993 Juvenile; In the Wings [GB], 1990 Turf)

Mike Smith (Skip Away, 1997 Classic; Ajina, 1997 Distaff; Unbridled's Song, 1995 Juvenile; Inside Information, 1995 Distaff; Tikkanen, 1994 Turf; Cherokee Run, 1994 Sprint; Lure [twice], 1992, '93 Mile)

7 Eddie Delahoussaye (Hollywood Wildcat, 1993 Distaff; Cardmania, 1993 Sprint; A.P. Indy, 1992 Classic; Thirty Slews, 1992 Sprint; Pleasant Stage, 1991 Juvenile Fillies; Prized, 1989 Turf; Princess Rooney, 1984 Distaff)

Laffit Pincay Jr. (Phone Chatter, 1993 Juvenile Fillies; Bayakoa [Arg], [twice], 1989, '90 Distaff; Is It True, 1988 Juvenile; Skywalker, 1986 Classic; Capote, 1986 Juvenile; Tasso, 1985 Juvenile)

6 Jose Santos (Chief Bearhart, 1997 Turf; Fly So Free, 1990 Juvenile; Meadow Star, 1990 Juvenile Fillies; Steinlen [GB], 1989 Mile; Success Express, 1987 Juvenile; Manila, 1986 Turf)

Patrick Valenzuela (Fraise, 1992 Turf; Eliza, 1992 Juvenile Fillies; Arazi, 1991 Juvenile; Opening Verse, 1991 Mile; Very Subtle, 1987 Sprint; Brave Raj, 1986 Juvenile Fillies)

5 Corey Nakatani (Silic [Fr], 1999 Mile; Reraise, 1998 Sprint; Elmhurst, 1997 Sprint; Jewel Princess, 1996 Distaff; Lit de Justice, 1996 Sprint)

4 Angel Cordero (Dancing Spree, 1989 Sprint; Gulch, 1988 Sprint; Open Mind, 1988 Juvenile Fillies; Life's Magic, 1985 Distaff)

Craig Perret (Storm Song, 1996 Juvenile Fillies; Safely Kept, 1990 Sprint; Rhythm, 1989 Juvenile; Eillo, 1984 Sprint)

3 Lanfranco Dettori (Fantastic Light, 2001 Turf; Daylami [Ire], 1999 Turf; Barathea [Ire], 1994 Mile)

Randy Romero (Go for Wand, 1989 Juvenile Fillies; Personal Ensign, 1988 Distaff; Sacahuista, 1987 Distaff)

Leading Trainers by Wins

16 D. Wayne Lukas (Spain, 2000 Distaff; Cat Thief, 1999 Classic; Cash Run, 1999 Juvenile Fillies; Boston Harbor, 1996 Juvenile; Timber Country, 1994 Juvenile; Flanders, 1994 Juvenile Fillies; Steinlen [GB], 1989 Mile; Is It True, 1988 Juvenile; Gulch, 1988 Sprint; Open Mind, 1988 Juvenile Fillies; Success Express, 1987 Juvenile; Sacahuista, 1987 Distaff; Capote, 1986 Juvenile; Lady's Secret, 1986 Distaff; Twilight Ridge, 1985 Juvenile Fillies)

7 Claude R. "Shug" McGaughey III (Inside Information, 1995 Distaff; My Flag, 1995 Juvenile Fillies; Lure [twice], 1992, '93 Mile; Rhythm, 1989 Juvenile; Dancing Spree, 1989 Sprint; Personal Ensign, 1988 Distaff)

6 Neil Drysdale (War Chant, 2000 Mile; Hollywood Wildcat, 1993 Distaff; A.P. Indy, 1992 Classic; Prized, 1989 Turf; Tasso, 1985 Juvenile; Princess Rooney, 1984 Distaff)

5 William I. Mott (Escena, 1998 Distaff; Ajina, 1997 Distaff; Cigar, 1995 Classic; Fraise, 1992 Turf; Theatrical [Ire], 1987 Turf)

4 Ron McAnally (Northern Spur [Ire], 1995 Turf; Paseana [Arg], 1992 Distaff; Bayakoa [Arg] [twice], 1989, '90 Distaff)

3 Francois Boutin (Arazi, 1991 Juvenile; Miesque [twice], 1987, '88 Mile)

Patrick Byrne (Awesome Again, 1998 Classic; Favorite Trick, 1997 Juvenile; Countess Diana, 1997 Juvenile Fillies)

Leading Owners by Wins

6 Allen E. Paulson (Escena, 1998 Distaff; Ajina, 1997 Distaff; Cigar, 1995 Classic; Eliza, 1992 Juvenile Fillies; Opening Verse, 1991 Mile; Theatrical [Ire], 1987 Turf)

4 Eugene V. Klein (Is It True, 1988 Juvenile; Open Mind, 1988 Juvenile Fillies; Success Express, 1987 Juvenile; Twilight Ridge, 1985 Juvenile Fillies)

3 Flaxman Holdings (Spinning World, 1997 Mile; Miesque [twice], 1987, '88 Mile)

Godolphin Racing (Fantastic Light, 2001 Turf; Tempera, 2001 Juvenile Fillies; Daylami [Ire], 1999 Turf)

Overbrook Farm (Cat Thief, 1999 Classic; Boston Harbor, 1996 Juvenile; Flanders, 1994 Juvenile Fillies)

Ogden Phipps (My Flag, 1995 Juvenile Fillies; Dancing Spree, 1989 Sprint; Personal Ensign, 1988 Distaff)

Frank Stronach (Macho Uno, 2000 Juvenile; Perfect Sting, 2000 Filly and Mare Turf; Awesome Again, 1998 Classic)

Leading Breeders by Wins

5 Allen E. Paulson (Escena, 1998 Distaff; Ajina, 1997 Distaff; Cigar, 1995 Classic; Fraise, 1992 Turf; Eliza, 1992 Juvenile Fillies)

3 Aga Khan (Kalanisi [Ire], 2000 Turf; Daylami [Ire], 1999 Turf; Lashkari [GB], 1984 Turf)

Flaxman Holdings (Spinning World, 1997 Mile; Miesque [twice], 1987, '88 Mile)

Overbrook Farm (Cat Thief, 1999 Classic; Boston Harbor, 1996 Juvenile; Flanders, 1994 Juvenile Fillies)

Ogden Phipps (My Flag, 1995 Juvenile Fillies; Dancing Spree, 1989 Sprint; Personal Ensign, 1988 Distaff)

Frank Stronach (Macho Uno, 2000 Juvenile; Perfect Sting, 2000 Filly and Mare Turf; Awesome Again, 1998 Classic)

Leading Sires by Wins

5 **Danzig** (War Chant, 2000 Mile; Lure [twice], 1992, 1993 Mile; Dance Smartly, 1991 Distaff; Chief's Crown, 1984 Juvenile)

4 **Nureyev** (Spinning World, 1997 Mile; Miesque [twice], 1987, 1988 Mile; Theatrical [Ire], 1987 Turf)

Kris S. (Soaring Softly, 1999 Filly and Mare Turf; Brocco, 1993 Juvenile; Hollywood Wildcat, 1993 Distaff; Prized, 1989 Turf)

3 **Cox's Ridge** (Cardmania, 1993 Sprint; Twilight Ridge, 1985 Juvenile Fillies; Life's Magic, 1985 Distaff)

Deputy Minister (Awesome Again, 1999 Classic; Go for Wand, 1989 Juvenile Fillies; Open Mind, 1988 Juvenile Fillies)

Mr. Prospector (Rhythm, 1989 Juvenile; Gulch, 1988 Sprint; Eillo, 1984 Sprint)

Nijinsky II (Royal Academy, 1990 Mile; Dancing Spree, 1989 Sprint; Ferdinand, 1987 Classic)

Sadler's Wells (Northern Spur [Ire], 1995 Turf; Barathea [Ire], 1994 Mile; In the Wings [GB], 1990 Turf)

Strawberry Road (Aus) (Escena, 1998 Distaff; Ajina, 1997 Distaff; Fraise, 1992 Turf)

Leading Jockeys by Purses Won

Jockey	Mounts	Wins	Earnings
Pat Day	101	12	$21,717,800
Chris McCarron	100	9	17,669,520
Jerry Bailey	75	12	13,691,000
Gary Stevens	85	8	13,324,720
Mike Smith	42	8	8,194,200
Eddie Delahoussaye	68	7	7,775,000
Laffit Pincay Jr.	61	7	6,811,000
Angel Cordero Jr.	48	4	6,020,000
Corey Nakatani	43	5	6,441,120
Jose Santos	53	6	5,828,800
Lanfranco Dettori	27	3	5,115,560
Kent Desormeaux	43	2	4,263,200
Patrick Valenzuela	32	6	4,202,000
Shane Sellers	29	2	3,960,600
Pat Eddery	30	2	3,570,000

Leading Trainers by Purses Won

Trainer	Starts	Wins	Earnings
D. Wayne Lukas	136	16	$18,007,200
William I. Mott	39	5	8,492,560
Claude R. McGaughey III	45	7	6,733,560
Andre Fabre	33	3	6,435,400
Neil Drysdale	26	6	5,795,840

Jay Robbins	2	2	4,938,400
Bobby Frankel	42	1	4,311,800
Charles Whittingham	24	2	4,298,000
Bob Baffert	29	2	3,771,480
Patrick Byrne	6	3	3,718,000
Jack Van Berg	14	1	3,600,000
Ron McAnally	27	4	3,518,000
Sir Michael Stoute	22	2	2,981,800

Leading Owners by Purses Won

Owner	Starts	Wins	Earnings
Allen E. Paulson	32	6	$7,570,000
Frank Stronach	19	3	4,897,600
Godolphin Racing	26	3	4,700,600
Overbrook Farm	26	3	4,387,000
Daniel Wildenstein	19	2	3,917,000
Ogden Phipps	19	3	3,611,000
Sheikh Mohammed bin Rashid al Maktoum	21	2	3,564,160
Prince Ahmed bin Salman	20	2	3,220,600
Juddmonte Farms	32	1	3,013,200
Sam-Son Farms	16	2	2,878,000
Frances A. Genter	8	2	2,835,000
Eugene V. Klein	17	4	2,593,000
Aga Khan	7	2	2,489,600
Cooper & Straub-Rubens	1	1	2,480,400
Carolyn Hine	2	1	2,288,000

Leading Breeders of Purses Won

Breeder	Starts	Wins	Earnings
Allen E. Paulson	24	5	$6,652,000
Overbrook Farm	23	3	4,618,000
Cecilia Straub-Rubens	2	2	4,560,400
Frank Stronach	8	3	4,072,000
Ogden Phipps	17	3	3,611,000
Aga Khan	10	3	3,529,600
Juddmonte Farms	31	1	2,962,800
Oak Cliff Thoroughbreds	3	2	2,700,000
Sheikh Mohammed bin Rashid al Maktoum	14	1	2,506,800
Allez France Stables	9	2	2,305,000
Anna Marie Barnhart	2	1	2,288,000
Bertram & Diana Firestone	13	1	2,240,000
Preston Madden	3	1	2,133,000
W. S. Farish & W. S. Kilroy	8	1	2,085,400

Leading Sires by Purses Won

Sire	Starts	Wins	Earnings
Deputy Minister	24	3	$5,487,560
Cee's Tizzy	3	2	5,360,400
Storm Cat	24	2	5,297,200
Alydar	19	1	4,495,000
Danzig	39	5	4,495,000
Seattle Slew	23	2	4,085,000
Cozzene	5	2	3,468,000
Sadler's Wells	23	3	3,424,000
Mr. Prospector	39	3	3,421,680
Fappiano	15	2	3,316,000
Nijinsky II	12	3	3,283,000
Nureyev	19	4	3,280,000
Sovereign Dancer	11	0	3,053,000
Kris S.	11	4	2,856,400

Winners by Country and State Bred

Country	Starters	Winners
Ireland	107	9
Great Britain	93	7
Argentina	12	3
Canada	63	3
France	35	3
Kentucky	846	75
Florida	166	18
Maryland	23	3
Pennsylvania	17	3
California	53	2
Illinois	7	1
New Jersey	10	1
Oklahoma	3	1

Where Championship Days Were Held

Churchill Downs (5): 1988, 1991, 1994, 1998, 2000
Hollywood Park (3): 1984, 1987, 1997
Belmont Park (3): 1990, 1995, 2001
Gulfstream Park (3): 1989, 1992, 1999
Santa Anita Park (2): 1986, 1993
Aqueduct (1): 1985
Woodbine (1) 1996

Breeders' Cup Trophy

The Breeders' Cup trophy is an authentic reproduction of the Torrie horse, created by Giovanni da Bologna in Florence, Italy, mostly likely in the late 1580s. The sculpture is known as an ecorche or flayed horse and shows the horse's muscles in great detail.

Although its original commission is not known, the sculpture may have been a study made for an equestrian statue of Duke Cosimo I, which was completed in 1591 and stands today in the Piazza della Signoria in Florence.

The sculptor's original ecorche in bronze was acquired by Sir James Erskine of Torrie in the early 1800s. It was bequeathed to the University of Edinburgh in 1836 and today is housed in the university's Museum of Fine Arts in Scotland.

The Breeders' Cup trophy was cast from the original under supervision of University of Edinburgh curators, and the replica is owned by Breeders' Cup Ltd. Smaller replicas are presented to winners of each Breeders' Cup race, and winning breeders, trainers, and jockeys also are presented with replicas.

Breeders' Cup Purses

When John Gaines first proposed the Breeders' Cup in 1982, he envisioned a purse structure of $13-million for the championship day. As the concept was put into final form for the first championship day in 1984, purses and nominator fees totaled $10-million. Five of seven races had $1-million purses (Juvenile, Juvenile Fillies, Sprint, Distaff, Mile); the Turf had a $2-million purse, and the Classic was $3-million.

In 1996, the Classic was increased to $4-million, and the Distaff was raised to $2-million two years later. The addition of the Filly and Mare Turf in 1999 raised the day's total purse structure to $13-million.

A 1997 change in the rules for supplemental nominations has resulted in higher purses. Beginning in 1998, supplemental-nomination money is added to the total purse. Thus, the 1998 Breeders' Cup Classic, which contained supplemental nominees Gentlemen (Arg),

Silver Charm, and Skip Away, raised the total purse ($4,689,920) and nominator fees above $5-million, then the biggest race purse ever.

In addition to purse money paid to the horse's owner or owners, the Breeders' Cup purse structure contains 5% awards for both the stallion nominator and the foal nominator. Here is the 2001 distribution for a $1-million race:

Finish	% Purse	Owner	Stallion nominator	Foal nominator
1st	57.2%	$520,000	$26,000	$26,000
2nd	22.0%	200,000	10,000	10,000
3rd	13.2%	120,000	6,000	6,000
4th	5.6%	56,000		
5th	2.0%	20,000		
Total	100.0%	$916,000	$42,000	$42,000

Largest Breeders' Cup Purses

(Not including stallion and foal nominator fees)

Year	Race	Purse	Winner	Value to winner
1998	Classic	$4,689,920	Awesome Again	$2,662,400
2000	Classic	4,369,320	Tiznow	2,480,400
1997	Classic	4,030,400	Skip Away	2,288,000
2001	Classic	3,664,000	Tiznow	2,080,000
1999	Classic	3,664,000	Cat Thief	2,080,000
1996	Classic	3,664,000	Alphabet Soup	2,080,000
1995	Classic	2,798,000	Cigar	1,560,000
1994	Classic	2,748,000	Concern	1,560,000
1993	Classic	2,748,000	Arcangues	1,560,000
1992	Classic	2,748,000	A.P. Indy	1,560,000
1991	Classic	2,748,000	Black Tie Affair (Ire)	1,560,000

From 1984 through 1990, the Breeders' Cup Classic had a race purse of $2,739,000 and a winner's share of $1,350,000. The next highest purse was $2,271,680 in the 2000 Breeders' Cup Turf, won by Kalanisi (Ire).

Nominations, Pre-entries, Entries and Starters by Year

Year	Foal nominations	Pre-entries	Entries	Starters
2001	15,020	109	98	94
2000	15,760	135	105	103
1999	15,191	128	102	101
1998	14,081	117	85	82
1997	12,751	94	77	76
1996	11,971	90	85	82
1995	10,543	101	84	81
1994	9,738	126	94	91
1993	9,564	103	82	81
1992	9,392	112	92	91
1991	10,056	116	91	90
1990	11,003	110	91	83
1989	11,734	101	89	80
1988	11,276	87	79	76
1987	12,183	106	91	84
1986	11,494	90	79	76
1985	10,907	110	90	82
1984	10,034	77	69	68
1983	7,839			
1982	9,260			

Pre-entries are number of individual horses made eligible. Owners may pre-enter a horse in up to two races.

Breeders' Cup Attendance and Betting Handle by Year

Year	Site	On-track attendance	On-track wagering*	Total wagering*
2001	Belmont	52,987	$12,067,995	$98,008,747
2000	Churchill	76,043	13,579,798	101,283,427
1999	Gulfstream	45,124	11,065,973	96,485,255
1998	Churchill	80,452	13,544,859	91,338,477
1997	Hollywood	51,161	8,191,459	71,639,333
1996	Woodbine	42,243	5,925,469	67,738,890
1995	Belmont	37,246	7,590,332	64,075,207
1994	Churchill	71,671	10,146,524	78,224,530
1993	Santa Anita	55,130	12,142,750	79,744,742
1992	Gulfstream	45,415	9,915,542	76,876,726
1991	Churchill	66,204	11,945,562	67,588,113
1990	Belmont	51,236	9,107,270	55,328,195
1989	Gulfstream	51,342	10,216,258	55,345,677
1988	Churchill	71,237	9,219,083	42,932,379
1987	Hollywood	57,734	10,202,252	31,864,457
1986	Santa Anita	69,155	12,510,109	31,984,490
1985	Aqueduct	42,568	7,200,175	26,941,288
1984	Hollywood	64,254	8,443,070	16,452,179

*Breeders' Cup races only.

Average Field Sizes

Race	Average field	Most starters	Fewest starters
Distaff	8.7	14	6
Juvenile Fillies	11.3	14	8
Mile	13.2	14	10
Sprint	13.0	14	9
Filly and Mare Turf	13.3	14	12
Juvenile	12.0	14	8
Turf	12.4	14	10
Classic	11.4	14	8

Most Pre-Entries for a Breeders' Cup Race

Year	Race	Pre-entries
2000	Mile	29
1998	Mile	27
1999	Mile	25
1994	Sprint	25
1994	Turf	24
1995	Mile	24
1998	Sprint	24
1994	Mile	23
1999	Sprint	23
1993	Sprint	23
1998	Juvenile	21
1997	Sprint	21
1995	Sprint	21
1994	Classic	20

Breeders' Cup Race Winners by Total Earnings

Horse	Breeders' Cup victory	Total earnings
Cigar	1995 Classic	$9,999,815
Skip Away	1997 Classic	9,616,360
Fantastic Light	2001 Turf	7,486,957
Alysheba	1988 Classic	6,679,242
Tiznow	2000, '01 Classic	6,427,830
Sunday Silence	1989 Classic	4,968,554
Daylami (Ire)	1999 Turf	4,614,762
Unbridled	1990 Classic	4,489,475

Awesome Again	1998 Classic	4,374,590
Pilsudski (Ire)	1996 Turf	4,080,297
Cat Thief	1999 Classic	3,951,012
Ferdinand	1987 Classic	3,777,978
Precisionist	1985 Sprint	3,485,398
Chief Bearhart	1997 Turf	3,462,014
Black Tie Affair (Ire)	1991 Classic	3,381,557

Largest Winning Margins

Year	Winner	Race	Margin
1995	Inside Information	Distaff	13½
1997	Countess Diana	Juvenile Fillies	8½
1984	Princess Rooney	Distaff	7
1990	Bayakoa (Arg)	Distaff	6¾
1985	Life's Magic	Distaff	6¼
1997	Skip Away	Classic	6
2001	Banks Hill (GB)	Filly and Mare Turf	5½
1997	Favorite Trick	Juvenile	5½
1986	Brave Raj	Juvenile Fillies	5½

Smallest Winning Margins

Year	Winner	Race	Margin
2001	Tiznow	Classic	nose
2000	Macho Uno	Juvenile	nose
1998	Escena	Distaff	nose
1996	Alphabet Soup	Classic	nose
1993	Hollywood Wildcat	Distaff	nose
1992	Fraise	Turf	nose
1988	Personal Ensign	Distaff	nose
1987	Ferdinand	Classic	nose
1987	Epitome	Juvenile Fillies	nose
1985	Tasso	Juvenile	nose
1984	Eillo	Sprint	nose

Jockeys With Most Starts

Jockey	Starts	Wins	Earnings
Pat Day	101	12	$21,717,800
Chris McCarron	100	9	17,669,520
Gary Stevens	86	8	13,324,720
Jerry Bailey	74	12	13,691,000
Eddie Delahoussaye	68	7	7,775,000
Laffit Pincay Jr.	61	7	6,811,000
Jose Santos	53	6	5,828,800
Angel Cordero Jr.	48	4	6,020,000
Corey Nakatani	43	5	6,441,160
Kent Desormeaux	43	2	4,263,200

Trainers With Most Starts

Trainer	Starts	Wins	Earnings
D. Wayne Lukas	136	16	$18,007,200
Claude R. McGaughey III	45	7	6,733,560
Bobby Frankel	42	1	4,311,800
William I. Mott	39	5	8,492,560
Andre Fabre	33	3	6,435,400
Bob Baffert	29	2	3,771,400
Ron McAnally	27	4	3,518,000
Neil Drysdale	26	6	5,795,840
Flint S. Schulhofer	26	2	2,841,400

Owners With Most Starts

Owner	Starts	Wins	Earnings
Allen E. Paulson	32	6	$7,570,000
Juddmonte Farms	32	1	3,013,200
Godolphin Racing	26	3	4,700,600
Overbrook Farm	26	3	4,387,000

Owners with most starts, continued

Sheikh Mohammed			
bin Rashid al Maktoum	21	2	3,564,160
Prince Ahmed bin Salman	20	2	3,220,600
Frank Stronach	19	3	4,897,600
Daniel Wildenstein	19	2	3,917,000
Ogden Phipps	19	3	3,611,000
Eugene V. Klein	17	4	2,593,000
Sam-Son Farms	16	2	2,878,000
Golden Eagle Farm	15	0	1,443,800
Peter M. Brant	14	2	1,198,000

Most Starters on a Program
Owners

Starters	Owner	Year
8	Godolphin Racing	2001
7	Eugene V. Klein	1988
	Eugene V. Klein	1987
5	Allen E. Paulson	1997
	The Thoroughbred Corp.	1997
4	Susan Magnier & Michael Tabor	2001
	Stronach Stables	2000
	The Thoroughbred Corp.	2000
	Godolphin	1996
	Overbrook Farm	1996
	Juddmonte Farms	1994
	Juddmonte Farms	1992
	Peter Brant	1986

Trainers

Starters	Trainer	Year
14	D. Wayne Lukas	1987
12	D. Wayne Lukas	1988
11	D. Wayne Lukas	1989
10	D. Wayne Lukas	1996
	D. Wayne Lukas	1985

Jockeys

Starters	Jockey	Year
8	Jerry Bailey	2001
	Jerry Bailey	2000
	Jerry Bailey	1999

Largest Breeders' Cup On-Track Attendance

Year	Site	On-Track Attendance
1998	Churchill Downs	80,452
2000	Churchill Downs	76,043
1994	Churchill Downs	71,671
1988	Churchill Downs	71,237
1986	Santa Anita Park	69,155
1991	Churchill Downs	66,204
1984	Hollywood Park	64,254
1987	Hollywood Park	57,734

Smallest Breeders' Cup On-Track Attendance

Year	Site	On-Track Attendance
1995	Belmont Park	37,246
1996	Woodbine	42,243
1985	Aqueduct	42,568
1999	Gulfstream Park	45,124
1992	Gulfstream Park	45,415
1997	Hollywood Park	51,161
1990	Belmont Park	51,236
1989	Gulfstream Park	51,342

Largest Breeders' Cup On-Track Betting

Year	Site	On-Track Wagering
2000	Churchill Downs	$13,579,798
1998	Churchill Downs	13,544,859
1986	Santa Anita Park	12,510,109
1993	Santa Anita Park	12,142,750
2001	Belmont Park	12,067,995
1991	Churchill Downs	11,945,562

Lowest Breeders' Cup On-Track Betting

Year	Site	On-Track Wagering
1996	Woodbine	$5,925,469
1985	Aqueduct	7,200,175
1995	Belmont Park	7,590,332
1997	Hollywood Park	8,191,459
1984	Hollywood Park	8,443,070
1990	Belmont Park	9,107,270

Average Pari-Mutuel Payout by Year

Year	Track	Average Payout ($2 bet)
1993	Santa Anita Park	$44.37
2000	Churchill Downs	35.30
1984	Hollywood Park	33.97
1991	Churchill Downs	32.71
1999	Gulfstream Park	27.40
1994	Churchill Downs	26.91
1986	Santa Anita Park	22.77
1987	Hollywood Park	19.20
1996	Woodbine	16.97
1992	Gulfstream Park	15.17
2001	Belmont Park	15.15
1989	Gulfstream Park	12.00
1988	Churchill Downs	11.17
1995	Belmont Park	10.79
1997	Hollywood Park	10.69
1998	Churchill Downs	10.63
1990	Belmont Park	9.49
1985	Aqueduct	8.63

Shortest-Priced Winners

Year	Horse	Race	Odds
1990	Meadow Star	Juvenile Fillies	.20-to-1
1985	Life's Magic	Distaff	.40-to-1*
1994	Flanders	Juvenile Fillies	.40-to-1*
1986	Lady's Secret	Distaff	.50-to-1*
1988	Personal Ensign	Distaff	.50-to-1
1991	Dance Smartly	Distaff	.50-to-1*
1985	Twilight Ridge	Juvenile Fillies	.60-to-1*
1984	Chief's Crown	Juvenile	.70-to-1
1984	Princess Rooney	Distaff	.70-to-1
1988	Open Mind	Juvenile Fillies	.70-to-1*
1989	Bayakoa (Arg)	Distaff	.70-to-1
1995	Cigar	Classic	.70-to-1

*Part of entry.

Longest-Priced Winners

Year	Horse	Race	Odds
1993	Arcangues	Classic	133.60-to-1
2000	Spain	Distaff	55.90-to-1
1984	Lashkari (GB)	Turf	53.40-to-1
1994	One Dreamer	Distaff	47.10-to-1
2000	Caressing	Juvenile Fillies	47.00-to-1
1986	Last Tycoon	Mile	35.90-to-1
1999	Cash Run	Juvenile Fillies	32.50-to-1
1984	Wild Again	Classic	31.30-to-1
1987	Epitome	Juvenile Fillies	30.40-to-1
1999	Anees	Juvenile	30.30-to-1

History of Breeders' Cup Races
Breeders' Cup Classic

America's classic distance is 1¼ miles on dirt, and the Breeders' Cup Classic (G1) has offered up some classic, spine-tingling contests. The race has been the kingmaker among the eight Breeders' Cup races, producing nine Horses of the Year in its first 18 runnings.

Although the year's best horse does not always win the Breeders' Cup Classic, the race has been extremely well matched, with more than half the races decided by less than one length. The only runaway was Skip Trial's six-length victory at Hollywood Park in 1997. The eventual champion older horse that year, Skip Away won in 1:59.16, the fastest time ever for the Classic's 1¼ miles.

The series began with a classic finish in the 1984 Breeders' Cup at Hollywood Park, with three horses charging together through the final furlong. Longshot Wild Again set all the pace and prevailed by a neck on the inside. Gate Dancer bore in on favorite Slew o' Gold nearing the wire, and jockey Angel Cordero Jr. restrained Slew o' Gold through the final yards to protect the eventual champion older male. Gate Dancer finished second, but Hollywood's stewards advanced Slew o' Gold to the second spot.

The race did not yield its first Horse of the Year until 1987, when the Breeders' Cup returned to Hollywood Park and '86 Kentucky Derby (G1) winner Ferdinand met '87 Derby victor Alysheba. They hooked up inside Hollywood's sixteenth pole and fought to the wire, with even-money favorite Ferdinand prevailing by a nose under jockey Bill Shoemaker. Ferdinand was voted Horse of the Year and champion older male, while Alysheba was honored as champion three-year-old male. The following year, Alysheba won the Classic in near darkness at Churchill Downs's first Breeders' Cup and was voted Horse of the Year and champion older male.

The 1989 Breeders' Cup Classic reunited Triple Crown rivals Sunday Silence and Easy Goer, and they battled through deep stretch as they had in the Derby and Preakness Stakes (G1) that year. Sunday Silence, who had won both the Derby and Preakness, proved best and won by a neck over Belmont Stakes (G1) victor Easy Goer. Sunday Silence was voted champion three-year-old male and Horse of the Year. After a truncated four-year-old campaign, Sunday Silence was sold for stud duty in Japan, where he has become that country's all-time leading sire.

Tiznow, the race's only two-time winner, provided two scintillating finishes, holding off Giant's Causeway in 2000 by a neck at Churchill Downs and then coming back courageously to best Sakhee by a nose in '01 at Belmont Park.

Three-year-olds have done well in the Classic, winning seven of the first 18 Classics, and two three-year-old winners have become successful sires. The 1990 Classic winner, Derby victor Unbridled, sired winners of the Kentucky Derby and Preakness as well as two Breeders' Cup Juvenile (G1) victors. A.P. Indy, the 1992

Breeders' Cup Classic

Grade 1, $4-million, three-year-olds and up, 1¼ miles, dirt. Run October 27, 2001, at Belmont Park with gross value of $3,664,000. First run in 1984. Weights: Northern Hemisphere three-year-olds, 122 pounds, older, 126 pounds; Southern Hemisphere three-year-olds, 117 pounds, older, 126 pounds; fillies and mares allowed three pounds.

Year	Winner	Jockey	Second	Third	Site	Time	Track	1st purse
2001	Tiznow, 4	C. McCarron	Sakhee	Albert the Great	Bel	2:00.62	ft	$2,080,000
2000	Tiznow, 3	C. McCarron	Giant's Causeway	Captain Steve	CD	2:00.75	ft	$2,480,400
1999	Cat Thief, 3	P. Day	Budroyale	Golden Missile	GP	1:59.52	ft	$2,080,000
1998	Awesome Again, 4	P. Day	Silver Charm	Swain (Ire)	CD	2:02.16	ft	$2,662,400
1997	Skip Away, 4	M. Smith	Deputy Commander	Dowty	Hol	1:59.16	ft	$2,288,000
1996	Alphabet Soup, 5	C. McCarron	Louis Quatorze	Cigar	WO	2:01.00	ft	$2,080,000
1995	Cigar, 5	J. Bailey	L'Carriere	Unaccounted For	Bel	1:59.58	my	$1,560,000
1994	Concern, 3	J. Bailey	Tabasco Cat	Dramatic Gold	CD	2:02.41	ft	$1,560,000
1993	Arcangues, 5	J. Bailey	Bertrando	Kissin Kris	SA	2:00.83	ft	$1,560,000
1992	A.P. Indy, 3	E. Delahoussaye	Pleasant Tap	Jolypha	GP	2:00.20	ft	$1,560,000
1991	Black Tie Affair (Ire), 5	J. Bailey	Twilight Agenda	Unbridled	CD	2:02.95	ft	$1,560,000
1990	Unbridled, 3	P. Day	Ibn Bey (GB)	Thirty Six Red	Bel	2:02 1/5	ft	$1,350,000
1989	Sunday Silence, 3	C. McCarron	Easy Goer	Blushing John	GP	2:00 1/5	ft	$1,350,000
1988	Alysheba, 4	C. McCarron	Seeking the Gold	Waquoit	CD	2:04 4/5	my	$1,350,000
1987	Ferdinand, 4	W. Shoemaker	Alysheba	Judge Angelucci	Hol	2:01 2/5	ft	$1,350,000
1986	Skywalker, 4	L. Pincay Jr.	Turkoman	Precisionist	SA	2:00 2/5	ft	$1,350,000
1985	Proud Truth, 3	J. Velasquez	Gate Dancer	Turkoman	Aqu	2:00 4/5	ft	$1,350,000
1984	Wild Again, 4	P. Day	Slew o' Gold	Gate Dancer	Hol	2:03 2/5	ft	$1,350,000

1997: Skip Away supplemental entry; Whiskey Wisdom disqualified from third to fourth; 1984: Gate Dancer disqualified from second to third

winner and Horse of the Year, regularly ranks among North America's leading sires and sired 2001 Juvenile Fillies (G1) winner Tempera. Tiznow was a three-year-old when he won in 2000 and was voted Horse of the Year.

While the Classic has yielded some classic contests, it also has produced its share of puzzles and one especially bizarre finish. Arcangues won in 1993 at 133.60-to-1, the longest price for any Breeders' Cup winner. The unusual finish came in the 1998 Classic, which featured the best field ever assembled for a Breeders' Cup race. Silver Charm took the lead in the stretch but began to bear out in the final furlong. Swain (Ire), a leading European contender, followed Silver Charm to the far outside under left-handed whipping by his jockey, Frankie Dettori. Awesome Again dashed through the hole they created and won by three-quarters of a length over Silver Charm. Skip Away, the 1.90-to-1 favorite who finished sixth, was voted champion older male and Horse of the Year.

Jockeys by Wins

5   **Chris McCarron** (Alphabet Soup, Alysheba, Sunday Silence, Tiznow [twice])
4   **Jerry Bailey** (Arcangues, Black Tie Affair [Ire], Cigar, Concern), **Pat Day** (Awesome Again, Cat Thief, Unbridled, Wild Again)
1   **Eddie Delahoussaye** (A.P. Indy), **Laffit Pincay Jr.** (Skywalker), **Bill Shoemaker** (Ferdinand), **Mike Smith** (Skip Away), **Jorge Velasquez** (Proud Truth)

Trainers by Wins

2   **Jay Robbins** (Tiznow [twice]), **Charlie Whittingham** (Ferdinand, Sunday Silence)
1   **Patrick Byrne** (Awesome Again), **Neil Drysdale** (A.P. Indy), **Andre Fabre** (Arcangues), **Hubert "Sonny" Hine** (Skip Away), **David Hofmans** (Alphabet Soup), **D. Wayne Lukas** (Cat Thief), **William Mott** (Cigar), **Carl Nafzger** (Unbridled), **Ernie Poulos** (Black Tie Affair [Ire]), **Richard Small** (Concern), **Vincent Timphony** (Wild Again), **Jack Van Berg** (Alysheba), **John Veitch** (Proud Truth), **Mike Whittingham** (Skywalker)

Owners by Wins

1   **Black Chip Stable** (Wild Again), **Cee's Stable** (Tiznow), **Michael Cooper and Cecilia Straub-Rubens** (Tiznow), **Darby Dan Farm** (Proud Truth), **William S. Farish, Harold Goodman, William S. Kilroy, and Tomonori Tsurumaki** (A.P. Indy), **Frances Genter** (Unbridled), **Arthur Hancock III, Ernest Gaillard, and Charlie Whittingham** (Sunday Silence), **Carolyn Hine** (Skip Away), **Elizabeth Keck** (Ferdinand), **Robert Meyerhoff** (Concern), **Oak Cliff Stable** (Skywalker), **Overbrook Farm** (Cat Thief), **Allen E. Paulson** (Cigar), **Ridder Thoroughbred Stable** (Alphabet Soup), **Dorothy and Pamela Scharbauer** (Alysheba), **Stronach Stables** (Awesome Again), **Jeffrey Sullivan** (Black Tie Affair [Ire]), **Daniel Wildenstein** (Arcangues)

Breeders of Winners

2   **Oak Cliff Thoroughbreds** (Skywalker, Sunday Silence), **Cecilia Straub-Rubens** (Tiznow [twice])
1   **Allez France Stables** (Arcangues), **Anna Marie Barnhart** (Skip Away), **William S. Farish and William S. Kilroy** (A.P. Indy), **Mrs. John W. Galbreath** (Proud Truth), **Howard B. Keck** (Ferdinand), **W. Paul Little** (Wild Again), **Preston Madden** (Alysheba), **Robert Meyerhoff** (Concern), **Overbrook Farm** (Cat Thief), **Allen E. Paulson** (Cigar), **Stephen Peskoff** (Black Tie Affair [Ire]), **Southeast Associates** (Alphabet Soup), **Frank L. Stronach** (Awesome Again), **Tartan Farms** (Unbridled)

Sires of Winners

2   **Cee's Tizzy** (Tiznow [twice])
1   **Alydar** (Alysheba), **Broad Brush** (Concern), **Cozzene** (Alphabet Soup), **Deputy Minister** (Awesome Again), **Fappiano** (Unbridled), **Graustark** (Proud Truth), **Halo** (Sunday Silence), **Icecapade** (Wild Again), **Miswaki** (Black Tie Affair [Ire]), **Nijinsky II** (Ferdinand), **Palace Music** (Cigar), **Relaunch** (Skywalker), **Sagace** (Arcangues), **Seattle Slew** (A.P. Indy), **Skip Trial** (Skip Away), **Storm Cat** (Cat Thief)

Winners by Place Where Bred

Locality	Winners	Locality	Winners
Kentucky	9	Pennsylvania	1
Maryland	2	Canada	1
California	2	Ireland	1
Florida	2		

Supplemental Entries

Year	Runner	Fee	Finish	Earnings
2001	**Tiznow**	$360,000	1	$2,080,000
	Gander	360,000	9	0
2000	**Tiznow**	360,000	1	2,480,400
	Captain Steve	360,000	3	562,800
	Gander	360,000	9	0
1998	Silver Charm	480,000	2	1,024,000
	Skip Away	480,000	6	0
	Gentlemen (Arg)	800,000	10	0
1997	**Skip Away**	480,000	1	2,121,600
1994	Best Pal	360,000	5	60,000
	Bertrando	360,000	6	0
1993	Bertrando	360,000	2	600,000
	Best Pal	360,000	10	0
1988	Waquoit	360,000	3	324,000
	Cutlass Reality	360,000	7	0
1985	Vanlandingham	360,000	7	0
1984	**Wild Again**	360,000	1	1,350,000

Champions from Race

Year	Runner	Finish	Title
2001	**Tiznow**	1	Older male
2000	**Tiznow**	1	HOY, 3yo male
	Lemon Drop Kid	5	Older male
1998	Skip Away	6	HOY, older male
1997	**Skip Away**	1	Older male
1996	Cigar	3	HOY, older male
1995	**Cigar**	1	HOY, older male
1993	Bertrando	2	Older male

1992	**A.P. Indy**	1	HOY, 3yo male	
1991	**Black Tie Affair (Ire)**	1	HOY, older male	
1990	**Unbridled**	1	3yo male	
1989	**Sunday Silence**	1	HOY, 3yo male	
1988	**Alysheba**	1	HOY, older male	
1987	**Ferdinand**	1	HOY, older male	
	Alysheba	2	3yo male	
1986	Turkoman	2	Older male	
1985	Vanlandingham	7	Older male	
1984	Slew o' Gold	2	Older male	

HOY = Horse of the Year

Largest Winning Margins

Year	Winner	Margin
1997	Skip Away	6
1995	Cigar	2½
1993	Arcangues	2
1992	A.P. Indy	2

Smallest Winning Margins

Year	Winner	Margin
2001	Tiznow	nose
1996	Alphabet Soup	nose
1987	Ferdinand	nose
1985	Proud Truth	head
1984	Wild Again	head
2000	Tiznow	neck
1994	Concern	neck
1989	Sunday Silence	neck

Shortest-Priced Winners

Year	Horse	Odds
1995	Cigar	0.70-to-1
1987	Ferdinand	1.00-to-1
1988	Alysheba	1.50-to-1
1997	Skip Away	1.80-to-1

Longest-Priced Winners

Year	Horse	Odds
1993	Arcangues	133.60-to-1
1984	Wild Again	31.30-to-1
1996	Alphabet Soup	19.85-to-1
1999	Cat Thief	19.60-to-1

Fastest Winners

Year	Horse	Track	Time	Cond.
1997	Skip Away	Hol	1:59.16	fast
1999	Cat Thief	GP	1:59.52	fast
1995	Cigar	Bel	1:59.58	muddy

1992	A.P. Indy	GP	2:00.20	fast
1989	Sunday Silence	GP	2:00⅕	fast

Slowest Winners

Year	Horse	Track	Time	Cond.
1988	Alysheba	CD	2:04⅕	muddy
1984	Wild Again	Hol	2:03⅗	fast
1991	Black Tie Affair (Ire)	CD	2:02.95	fast
1994	Concern	CD	2:02.41	fast

Most Starters

Year	Track	Starters
1999	Gulfstream Park	14
1994	Churchill Downs	14
1992	Gulfstream Park	14
1990	Belmont Park	14

Fewest Starters

Year	Track	Starters
1989	Gulfstream Park	8
1985	Aqueduct	8
1984	Hollywood Park	8
1997	Gulfstream Park	9
1988	Churchill Downs	9

Winning Post Positions

Post	Starters	Winners	Percent
1	18	1	5.6%
2	18	1	5.6%
3	18	2	11.1%
4	18	1	5.6%
5	18	1	5.6%
6	18	3	16.7%
7	18	0	0.0%
8	18	2	11.1%
9	15	0	0.0%
10	15	2	13.3%
11	13	1	7.8%
12	9	3	33.3%
13	8	0	0.0%
14	4	1	25.0%

Changes in Classic

The only change in the Breeders' Cup Classic was an increase in the purse from $3-million to $4-million beginning in 1996.

Breeders' Cup Turf

The race conditions of the Breeders' Cup Turf (G1), 1½ miles on grass at weight for age, constitute the classic standard of European racing, and as a result, overseas runners have won a plurality of the $2-million contests. But they have not been dominant, probably because running in late October or early November—sometimes in tropical conditions—is not part of the European schedule, which traditionally culminates for top horses in early October with the running of the Prix de l'Arc de Triomphe (Fr-G1).

In fact, American owners and trainers have fielded some outstanding grass runners, and they have defeated top-level European competitors over the years. In other years, lesser American runners have prevailed because the Europeans were past their best form or did not adapt well to warm weather in the Florida or Southern California Breeders' Cup sites.

Because of its importance on the world racing calendar, the Breeders' Cup Turf has become the definitive North American championship

race. In every year except 1984 (John Henry's last championship season) and '89 (when the male title went to Breeders' Cup Mile [G1] winner Steinlen [GB]), a North American turf champion has come out of the Turf.

In 1993, American-trained Kotashaan (Fr) dominated grass racing in Southern California and scored a half-length victory over fellow Californian Bien Bien in the Turf. With a weak handicap division that year and no dominant three-year-old coming out of the Triple Crown series, Kotashaan was voted both champion turf male and Horse of the Year. He remains the only Turf winner to earn the top North American honor.

Early in the Turf's history, European runners gave indications they would dominate the race. Unheralded Lashkari (GB) won the inaugural running at Hollywood Park in 1984 at 53.40-to-1, the longest winning odds in the race's history. Lashkari, who never duplicated that effort, was bred and owned by the Aga Khan, who also bred back-to-back Turf winners Daylami (Ire), who was leased to Godolphin Racing, and Kalanisi (Ire), also owned by the Aga Khan. In 2001, Godolphin's Fantastic Light won at 7-to-5, the shortest odds in the Turf's history.

Pebbles (GB) was supplemented to the race in 1985 and scored a hard-fought victory over Strawberry Road (Aus). The Turf in the following year at Santa Anita Park was expected to showcase Dancing Brave, the Arc winner whose only career defeat was a second-place finish in the Epsom Derby (Eng-G1). But Dancing Brave was clearly over the top and tired to finish fourth as Manila stormed over a neck victory over Theatrical (Ire), who would win the Turf the following year.

California-based runners Great Communicator and Prized won in 1988 and '89, respectively, and the American home-court advantage appeared to be an important factor in the Turf. But European runners won in the following two years and subsequently have performed well. In 1996, overseas interests swept the top four spots as Pilsudski (Ire) finished ahead of Singspiel (Ire), Swain (Ire), and Shantou, and the top three spots in 2001 were swept by European invaders Fantastic Light, Milan (GB), and Timboroa (GB).

Canada's only victory came in 1997 with Chief Bearhart. Europe failed to field a strong team the following year, and front-running Buck's Boy, an Illinois-bred, won. The pattern changed in 1999, when Daylami bounced back from a poor Arc effort to win the Turf. In a race that usually is decided by a half-length or less, Daylami's 2½-length triumph remains the Turf's largest winning margin.

Jockeys by Wins

2   **Lanfranco Dettori** (Daylami [Ire], Fantastic Light), **Jose Santos** (Chief Bearhart, Manila)

1   **Pat Day** (Theatrical [Ire]), **Eddie Delahoussaye** (Prized), **Kent Desormeaux** (Kotashaan [Fr]), **Pat Eddery** (Pebbles [GB]), **Eric Legrix** (Miss Alleged), **Chris McCarron** (Northern Spur [Ire]), **John Murtagh** (Kalanisi [Ire]), **Yves Saint-Martin** (Lashkari [GB]), **Shane Sellers** (Buck's Boy), **Ray Sibille** (Great Communicator), **Mike Smith** (Tikkanen), **Gary Stevens** (In the Wings [GB]), **Walter Swinburn** (Pilsudski [GB]), **Patrick Valenzuela** (Fraise)

Trainers by Wins

2   **William Mott** (Fraise, Theatrical [Ire]), **Sir Michael Stoute** (Kalanisi [Ire], Pilsudski [Ire]), **Saeed bin Suroor** (Daylami [Ire], Fantastic Light)

1   **Thad Ackel** (Great Communicator), **Pascal Bary** (Miss Alleged), **Clive Brittain** (Pebbles [GB]), **Neil Drysdale** (Prized), **Andre Fabre** (In the Wings

---

Breeders' Cup Turf

Grade 1, $2-million, three-year-olds and up, 1½ miles, turf. Run October 27, 2001, at Belmont Park with gross value of $1,960,240. First run in 1984. Weights: Northern Hemisphere three-year-olds, 122 pounds; older, 126 pounds; Southern Hemisphere three-year-olds, 117 pounds; older, 126 pounds; fillies and mares allowed three pounds.

Year	Winner	Jockey	Second	Third	Site	Time	Track	1st purse
2001	Fantastic Light, 5	L. Dettori	Milan (GB)	Timboroa (GB)	Bel	2:24.36	fm	$1,112,800
2000	Kalinisi (Ire), 4	J. Murtagh	Quiet Resolve	John's Call	CD	2:26.96	fm	$1,289,600
1999	Daylami (Ire), 5	L. Dettori	Royal Anthem	Buck's Boy	GP	2:24.73	gd	$1,040,000
1998	Buck's Boy, 5	S. Sellers	Yagli	Dushyantor	CD	2:28.74	fm	$1,040,000
1997	Chief Bearhart, 4	J. Santos	Borgia (Ger)	Flag Down	Hol	2:23.92	fm	$1,040,000
1996	Pilsudski (Ire), 4	W. Swinburn	Singspiel (Ire)	Swain (Ire)	WO	2:30.20	gd	$1,040,000
1995	Northern Spur (Ire), 4	C. McCarron	Freedom Cry (GB)	Carnegie (Ire)	Bel	2:42.07	sf	$1,040,000
1994	Tikkanen, 3	M. Smith	Hatoof	Paradise Creek	CD	2:26.50	fm	$1,040,000
1993	Kotashaan (Fr), 5	K. Desormeaux	Bien Bien	Luazur (Fr)	SA	2:25.16	fm	$1,040,000
1992	Fraise, 4	P. Valenzuela	Sky Classic	Quest for Fame (GB)	GP	2:24.08	fm	$1,040,000
1991	Miss Alleged, f, 4	E. Legrix	Itsallgreektome	Quest for Fame (GB)	CD	2:30.95	fm	$1,040,000
1990	In the Wings (GB), 4	G. Stevens	With Approval	El Senor	Bel	2:29⅗	gd	$900,000
1989	Prized, 3	E. Delahoussaye	Sierra Roberta (Fr)	Star Lift (GB)	GP	2:28	gd	$900,000
1988	Great Communicator, 5	R. Sibille	Sunshine Forever	Indian Skimmer	CD	2:35⅕	gd	$900,000
1987	Theatrical (Ire), 5	P. Day	Trempolino	Village Star (Fr)	Hol	2:24⅖	fm	$900,000
1986	Manila, 3	J. Santos	Theatrical (Ire)	Estrapade	SA	2:25⅖	fm	$900,000
1985	Pebbles (GB), f, 4	P. Eddery	Strawberry Road (Aus)	Mourjane (Ire)	Aqu	2:27	fm	$900,000
1984	Lashkari (GB), 3	Y. Saint-Martin	All Along (Fr)	Raami (GB)	Hol	2:25⅕	fm	$900,000

1985—Pebbles (GB) supplementary entry.

[GB]), **Mark Frostad** (Chief Bearhart), **P. Noel Hickey** (Buck's Boy), **LeRoy Jolley** (Manila), **Richard Mandella** (Kotashaan [Fr]), **Ron McAnally** (Northern Spur [Ire]), **Jonathan Pease** (Tikkanen), **Alain de Royer-Dupre** (Lashkari [GB])

Owners by Wins

2 **Aga Khan** (Kalanisi [Ire], Lashkari [GB]), **Godolphin Racing** (Daylami [Ire], Fantastic Light), **Sheikh Mohammed bin Rashid al Maktoum** (In the Wings [GB], Pebbles [GB])

1 **Augustin Stables** (Tikkanen), **Charles Cella** (Northern Spur [Ire]), **Class Act Stable** (Great Communicator), **Clover Racing Stable and Meadowbrook Farm** (Prized), **Fares Farm** (Miss Alleged), **La Presle Farm** (Kotashaan [Fr]), **Allen Paulson** (Theatrical [Ire]), **Madeleine Paulson** (Fraise), **Quarter B Farm** (Buck's Boy), **Sam-Son Farm** (Chief Bearhart), **Bradley M. "Mike" Shannon** (Manila), **Lord Arnold Weinstock and executors of Simon Weinstock** (Pilsudski [Ire])

Breeders of Winners

3 **Aga Khan** (Daylami [Ire], Kalanisi [Ire], Lashkari [GB])

1 **Ballymacoll Stud** (Pilsudski [Ire]), **Eduardo Cojuangco Jr.** (Manila), **Bertram and Diana Firestone** (Theatrical [Ire]), **Carl M. Freeman** (Miss Alleged), **Gainsborough Farm** (Fantastic Light), **Irish Acres Farm** (Buck's Boy), **Sheikh Mohammed bin Rashid al Maktoum** (In the Wings [GB]), **Richard Maynard** (Chief Bearhart), **Meadowbrook Farm** (Prized), **Allen E. Paulson** (Fraise), **George M. Strawbridge Jr.** (Tikkanen), **Swettenham Stud & Partners** (Northern Spur [Ire]), **Warren Hill Stud** (Pebbles [GB]), **James B. Watriss** (Great Communicator), **Wertheimer & Frere** (Kotashaan [Fr])

Sires of Winners

2 **Doyoun** (Daylami [Ire], Kalanisi [Ire]), **Sadler's Wells** (In the Wings [GB], Northern Spur [Ire])

1 **Alleged** (Miss Alleged), **Bucksplasher** (Buck's Boy), **Chief's Crown** (Chief Bearhart), **Cozzene** (Tikkanen), **Darshaan** (Kotashaan [Fr]), **Key to the Kingdom** (Great Communicator), **Kris S.** (Prized), **Lyphard** (Manila), **Mill Reef** (Lashkari [GB]), **Nureyev** (Theatrical [Ire]), **Polish Precedent** (Pilsudski [Ire]), **Rahy** (Fantastic Light), **Sharpen Up (GB)** (Pebbles [GB]), **Strawberry Road (Aus)** (Fraise)

Winners by Place Where Bred

Locality	Winners	Locality	Winners
Ireland	5	Florida	1
Kentucky	5	France	1
Great Britain	3	Illinois	1
Canada	1	Pennsylvania	1

Supplemental Entries

Year	Runner	Fee	Finish	Earnings
2001	Timboroa (GB)	$180,000	3	$256,800
2000	John's Call	240,000	3	297,600
	Montjeu (Ire)	180,000	7	0
	Subtle Power (Ire)	180,000	10	0
1986	Estrapade	240,000	3	216,000
1985	**Pebbles (GB)**	240,000	1	900,000
	Greinton (GB)	240,000	7	0

Champions from Race

Year	Runner	Finish	Title
2001	**Fantastic Light**	1	Turf male
2000	**Kalanisi (Ire)**	1	Turf male
1999	**Daylami (Ire)**	1	Turf male
1998	**Buck's Boy**	1	Turf male
1997	**Chief Bearhart**	1	Turf male
1996	Singspiel (Ire)	2	Turf male
1995	**Northern Spur (Ire)**	1	Turf male
1994	Paradise Creek	3	Turf male
1993	**Kotashaan (Fr)**	1	Turf male, HOY
1992	Sky Classic	2	Turf male
1991	**Miss Alleged**	1	Turf female
1988	Sunshine Forever	2	Turf male
1987	**Theatrical (Ire)**	1	Turf male
1986	Manila	1	Turf male
1985	**Pebbles (GB)**	1	Turf female

HOY = Horse of the Year

Largest Winning Margins

Year	Winner	Margin
1999	Daylami (Ire)	2½
1994	Tikkanen	1½
1999	Buck's Boy	1¼
1996	Pilsudski (Ire)	1¼

Smallest Winning Margins

Year	Winner	Margin
1992	Fraise	nose
1989	Prized	head
1995	Northern Spur (Ire)	neck
1986	Manila	neck
1985	Pebbles (GB)	neck
1984	Lashkari (GB)	neck

Shortest-Priced Winners

Year	Horse	Odds
2001	Fantastic Light	1.40-to-1
1993	Kotashaan (Fr)	1.50-to-1
1999	Daylami (Ire)	1.60-to-1
1987	Theatrical (Ire)	1.80-to-1
1997	Chief Bearhart	1.90-to-1
1990	In the Wings (GB)	1.90-to-1

Longest-Priced Winners

Year	Horse	Odds
1984	Lashkari (GB)	53.40-to-1
1991	Miss Alleged	42.10-to-1
1994	Tikkanen	16.60-to-1
1992	Fraise	14.00-to-1

Fastest Winners

Year	Horse	Track	Time	Cond.
1997	Chief Bearhart	Hol	2:23.92	firm
1992	Fraise	GP	2:24.08	firm
2001	Fantastic Light	Bel	2:24.36	firm
1987	Theatrical (Ire)	Hol	2:24⅖	firm
1999	Daylami (Ire)	GP	2:24.73	good

Slowest Winners

Year	Horse	Track	Time	Cond.
1995	Northern Spur (Ire)	Bel	2:42.07	soft
1988	Great Communicator	CD	2:35⅕	good
1991	Miss Alleged	CD	2:30.95	firm
1996	Pilsudski (Ire)	WO	2:30.20	good

Most Starters

Year	Track	Starters
1999	Gulfstream Park	14
1996	Woodbine	14
1994	Churchill Downs	14
1993	Santa Anita Park	14
1989	Gulfstream Park	14
1987	Hollywood Park	14
1985	Aqueduct	14

Fewest Starters

Year	Track	Starters
1986	Santa Anita Park	9
1992	Gulfstream Park	10
1988	Churchill Downs	10
2001	Belmont Park	11
1997	Hollywood Park	11
1990	Belmont Park	11
1984	Hollywood Park	11

Winning Post Positions

Post	Starters	Winners	Percent
1	18	2	11.1%
2	18	5	27.8%
3	18	1	5.6%
4	18	0	0.0%
5	18	1	5.6%
6	18	0	0.0%
7	18	1	5.6%
8	18	1	5.6%
9	18	2	11.1%
10	17	0	0.0%
11	15	0	0.0%
12	11	3	27.3%
13	10	2	20.0%
14	7	0	0.0%

Changes in Turf

No changes have been made in the 1½-mile distance or $2-million purse of the Breeders' Cup Turf since its inaugural running in 1984.

Breeders' Cup Juvenile

Until a winner of the Breeders' Cup Juvenile (G1) delivers a Kentucky Derby (G1) victory, the 1 1/16-mile race will be regarded as a measure of two-year-old form—which it obviously is—rather than a reliable yardstick of classic potential.

The race has gone 18 years without fielding a Derby winner, and only one classic winner, 1995 Preakness Stakes (G1) victor Timber Country, has won the Juvenile.

With regularity, however, the Derby winner and other classic winners have been in the beaten Juvenile field, implying that classic winners were either not sufficiently precocious to win the Juvenile or found its distance to be too short for their best efforts.

The first Breeders' Cup Juvenile was won by Chief's Crown, who finished third in all of the following year's classics, won the Travers Stakes (G1) against three-year-olds, and took the Marlboro Cup Handicap (G1) against older horses. He had the three-year-old title and Horse of the Year honors in his sights until finishing fourth as the favorite in the 1985 Breeders' Cup Classic (G1).

Second to Chief's Crown in the 1984 Juvenile was Tank's Prospect, who won the following year's Preakness. Tiring to finish third, beaten only 1½ lengths, was Spend a Buck, the 1985 Derby winner as well as three-year-old male champion and Horse of the Year.

The pattern would be repeated in subsequent editions of the Juvenile. Alysheba, third in 1986, won the following year's Derby and Preakness and was voted three-year-old male champion. Bet Twice, who conquered him in the Belmont

Stakes (G1), finished fourth in the '86 Juvenile. Pine Bluff was not competitive in the 1991 Juvenile but won the Preakness the following year. Sea Hero, equally outclassed in the 1992 Breeders' Cup race, won the following year's Derby. Finishing third to Brocco in the 1993 Juvenile was Tabasco Cat, who would become a dual classics winner in '94 for D. Wayne Lukas, the leading trainer of Juvenile winners. Seven years later, Point Given came off a close second-place finish in the Juvenile to win the 2001 Preakness, Belmont, and Travers. Retired with an injury after the Travers, he was voted 2001 Horse of the Year and champion three-year-old male.

Losing an equally close decision was the best sire of the late 1990s, Storm Cat, who just failed to last the one-mile distance of the Juvenile at Aqueduct in 1985. Capote, winner of the 1986 Juvenile, did not train on at three but became a successful sire, getting '96 Juvenile winner Boston Harbor.

Perhaps the most memorable running of the Juvenile occurred at Churchill Downs in 1991, when French-trained Arazi broke from the outside post position, blew by the field on Churchill's final turn, and romped to a five-length victory. Voted two-year-old male champion off that one North American start, Arazi was regarded as the next superhorse. But he was hampered by knee problems early in his three-year-old season and was not in peak fitness when shipped back to the United States for the 1992 Derby, finishing eighth.

Another disappointment was Favorite Trick, who was voted 1997 Horse of the Year after an overwhelming victory in the Juvenile. His con-

temporaries caught up to him at age three and he finished eighth in the Derby.

Michael Tabor and Susan Magnier (Johannesburg), **The Thoroughbred Corp.** (Anees), **Thomas Valando** (Fly So Free)

Jockeys by Wins

3 **Jerry Bailey** (Macho Uno, Answer Lively, Boston Harbor), **Laffit Pincay Jr.** (Is It True, Capote, Tasso)

2 **Pat Day** (Favorite Trick, Timber Country), **Jose Santos** (Fly So Free, Success Express), **Gary Stevens** (Anees, Brocco)

1 **Michael Kinane** (Johannesburg), **Donald MacBeth** (Chief's Crown), **Chris McCarron** (Gilded Time), **Craig Perret** (Rhythm), **Mike Smith** (Unbridled's Song), **Patrick Valenzuela** (Arazi)

Trainers by Wins

5 **D. Wayne Lukas** (Boston Harbor, Timber Country, Is It True, Success Express, Capote)

1 **Bobby Barnett** (Answer Lively), **Francois Boutin** (Arazi), **Patrick Byrne** (Favorite Trick), **Neil Drysdale** (Tasso), **Alex Hassinger Jr.** (Anees), **Roger Laurin** (Chief's Crown), **Claude R. "Shug" McGaughey III** (Rhythm), **Aidan O'Brien** (Johannesburg), **Joseph Orseno** (Macho Uno), **James Ryerson** (Unbridled's Song), Flint S. "Scotty" Schulhofer (Fly So Free), **Darrell Vienna** (Gilded Time), **Randy Winick** (Brocco)

Owners by Wins

1 **Barry A. Beal, Lloyd R. "Bob" French Jr., Eugene V. Klein** (Capote), **Mr. and Mrs. Albert Broccoli** (Brocco), **John Franks** (Answer Lively), **Gainesway Stable, Overbrook Farm, Robert and Beverly Lewis** (Timber Country), **Eugene V. Klein** (Success Express), **Joseph LaCombe** (Favorite Trick), **David Milch, Jack and Mark Silverman** (Gilded Time), **Paraneck Stable** (Unbridled's Song), **Allen E. Paulson, Sheikh Mohammed bin Rashid al Maktoum** (Arazi), **Ogden Mills Phipps** (Rhythm), **Gerald Robins** (Tasso), **Star Crown Stable** (Chief's Crown),

Breeders of Winners

1 **Adena Springs Farm** (Macho Uno), **Farfellow Farms** (Anees), **John Franks** (Answer Lively), **Bruce Hundley and Wayne Garrison** (Fly So Free), **Warner L. Jones** (Is It True), **Wayne G. Lyster III and Jayeff B Stables** (Johannesburg), **Lowquest Ltd.** (Timber Country), **Mandysland Farm** (Unbridled's Song), **Mr. and Mrs. Harry T. Mangurian Jr.** (Gilded Time), **Meadowbrook Farms** (Brocco), **North Ridge Farm** (Capote), **Overbrook Farm** (Boston Harbor), **Ogden Mills Phipps** (Rhythm), **Gerald L. Robins and Timothy H. Sams** (Tasso), **Carl Rosen** (Chief's Crown), **Tri Star Stable** (Success Express), **Ralph Wilson Jr.** (Arazi), **Mr. and Mrs. M. L. Wood** (Favorite Trick)

Sires of Winners

2 **Unbridled** (Anees, Unbridled's Song)

1 **Blushing Groom (Fr)** (Arazi), **Capote** (Boston Harbor), **Danzig** (Chief's Crown), **Fappiano** (Tasso), **Hennessy** (Johannesburg), **Hold Your Peace** (Success Express), **Holy Bull** (Macho Uno), **Kris S.** (Brocco), **Lively One** (Answer Lively), **Mr. Prospector** (Rhythm), **Phone Trick** (Favorite Trick), **Raja Baba** (Is It True), **Seattle Slew** (Capote), **Time for a Change** (Fly So Free), **Timeless Moment** (Gilded Time), **Woodman** (Timber Country)

Winners by Place Where Bred

Locality	Winners
Kentucky	15
Florida	3

Supplemental Entries

Year	Runner	Fee	Finish	Earnings
2001	Ibn Al Haitham (GB)	$90,000	9	$0
2000	Arabian Night	90,000	5	21,400

Breeders' Cup Juvenile

Grade 1, $1-million, two-year-old colts and geldings, 1 1/16 miles, dirt. Run October 27, 2001, at Belmont Park with gross value of $1-million. First run in 1984. Weights: 122 pounds.

Year	Winner	Jockey	Second	Third	Site	Time	Track	1st purse
2001	Johannesburg	M. Kinane	Repent	Siphonic	Bel	1:42.27	ft	$520,000
2000	Macho Uno	J. Bailey	Point Given	Street Cry (Ire)	CD	1:42.05	ft	$556,400
1999	Anees	G. Stevens	Chief Seattle	High Yield	GP	1:42.29	ft	$556,400
1998	Answer Lively	J. Bailey	Aly's Alley	Cat Thief	CD	1:44	ft	$520,000
1997	Favorite Trick	P. Day	Dawson's Legacy	Nationalore	Hol	1:41.47	ft	$520,000
1996	Boston Harbor	J. Bailey	Acceptable	Ordway	WO	1:43.40	ft	$520,000
1995	Unbridled's Song	M. Smith	Hennessy	Editor's Note	Bel	1:41.60	my	$520,000
1994	Timber Country	P. Day	Eltish	Tejano Run	CD	1:44.55	ft	$520,000
1993	Brocco	G. Stevens	Blumin Affair	Tabasco Cat	SA	1:42.99	ft	$520,000
1992	Gilded Time	C. McCarron	It'sali'lknownfact	River Special	GP	1:43.43	ft	$520,000
1991	Arazi	P. Valenzuela	Bertrando	Snappy Landing	CD	1:44.78	ft	$520,000
1990	Fly So Free	J. Santos	Take Me Out	Lost Mountain	Bel	1:43 3/5	ft	$450,000
1989	Rhythm	C. Perret	Grand Canyon	Slavic	GP	1:43 3/5	ft	$450,000
1988	Is It True	L. Pincay Jr.	Easy Goer	Tagel	CD	1:46 3/5	my	$450,000
1987	Success Express	J. Santos	Regal Classic	Tejano	Hol	1:35 1/5	ft	$450,000
1986	Capote	L. Pincay Jr.	Qualify	Alysheba	SA	1:43 3/5	ft	$450,000
1985	Tasso	L. Pincay Jr.	Storm Cat	Scat Dancer	Aqu	1:36 1/5	ft	$450,000
1984	Chief's Crown	D. MacBeth	Tank's Prospect	Spend a Buck	Hol	1:36 1/5	ft	$450,000

1984-'85, 1987—run at one mile; 1985—Tasso supplementary entry.

1999	Captain Steve	90,000	11	0
1992	Caponostro	120,000	6	0
1991	Bertrando	120,000	2	200,000
	Agincourt	120,000	5	20,000
1990	Best Pal	120,000	6	10,000
1985	**Tasso**	120,000	1	450,000
1984	Spend a Buck	120,000	3	108,000

Champions from Race

Year	Runner	Finish	Title
2001	**Johannesburg**	1	Juvenile male
2000	**Macho Uno**	1	Juvenile male
1999	**Anees**	1	Juvenile male
1998	**Answer Lively**	1	Juvenile male
1997	**Favorite Trick**	1	Horse of the Year, Juvenile male
1996	**Boston Harbor**	1	Juvenile male
1994	**Timber Country**	1	Juvenile male
1993	Dehere	8	Juvenile male
1992	**Gilded Time**	1	Juvenile male
1991	**Arazi**	1	Juvenile male
1990	**Fly So Free**	1	Juvenile male
1989	**Rhythm**	1	Juvenile male
1988	Easy Goer	2	Juvenile male
1986	**Capote**	1	Juvenile male
1985	**Tasso**	1	Juvenile male
1984	**Chief's Crown**	1	Juvenile male

Largest Winning Margins

Year	Winner	Margin
1997	Favorite Trick	5½
1993	Brocco	5
1991	Arazi	5
1994	Fly So Free	3

Smallest Winning Margins

Year	Winner	Margin
2000	Macho Uno	nose
1985	Tasso	nose
1998	Answer Lively	head
1996	Boston Harbor	neck
1995	Unbridled's Song	neck

Shortest-Priced Winners

Year	Horse	Odds
1984	Chief's Crown	0.70-to-1
1997	Favorite Trick	1.20-to-1
1990	Fly So Free	1.40-to-1
1992	Gilded Time	2.00-to-1

Longest-Priced Winners

Year	Horse	Odds
1999	Anees	30.30-to-1
1988	Is It True	9.20-to-1
2001	Johannesburg	7.20-to-1

2000	Macho Uno	6.30-to-1
1985	Tasso	5.60-to-1

Fastest Winners

Year	Horse	Track	Time	Cond.
1997	Favorite Trick	Hol	1:41.47	fast
1995	Unbridled's Song	Bel	1:41.60	muddy
2000	Macho Uno	CD	1:42.05	fast
2001	Johannesburg	Bel	1:42:27	fast
1999	Anees	GP	1:42.29	fast

Slowest Winners

Year	Horse	Track	Time	Cond.
1988	Is It True	CD	1:46⅗	muddy
1991	Arazi	CD	1:44.78	fast
1994	Timber Country	CD	1:44.55	fast
1998	Answer Lively	CD	1:44.00	

Most Starters

Year	Track	Starters
2000	Churchill Downs	14
1999	Gulfstream Park	14
1991	Churchill Downs	14

Fewest Starters

Year	Track	Starters
1997	Hollywood Park	8
1996	Woodbine	10
1988	Churchill Downs	10
1984	Hollywood Park	10

Winning Post Positions

Post	Starters	Winners	Percent
1	18	1	5.6%
2	18	1	5.6%
3	18	6	33.3%
4	18	2	11.1%
5	18	2	11.1%
6	18	0	0.0%
7	18	2	11.1%
8	18	1	5.6%
9	17	0	0.0%
10	17	0	0.0%
11	14	1	7.1%
12	12	1	8.3%
13	10	0	0.0%
14	3	1	33.3%

Changes in Juvenile

Originally contested at one mile, the Breeders' Cup Juvenile was run at 1¹⁄₁₆ miles at Santa Anita Park in 1986 to accommodate the track's layout. The distance was changed permanently to 1¹⁄₁₆ miles in 1988.

Breeders' Cup Filly and Mare Turf

In July 1998, the Breeders' Cup board of directors voted to fill an obvious gap in its championship lineup by creating the $1-million Breeders' Cup Filly and Mare Turf. Until the first Filly and Mare Turf at Gulfstream Park in 1999, the female turf division had no definitive

championship race, and distaffers were forced to race in open company in either the Breeders' Cup Turf (G1) at 1½ miles or the Breeders' Cup Mile (G1) at a flat mile.

The new race for fillies and mares, first run at 1⅜ miles because of Gulfstream's turf course

configuration, fulfilled its intended function. Phillips Racing Partnership's Soaring Softly locked up an Eclipse Award as champion turf female with a three-quarter-length victory over Coretta (Ire) at Gulfstream in 1999. The following year, Stronach Stable's Perfect Sting won by the same margin over Tout Charmant at Churchill Downs. Perfect Sting was subsequently voted an Eclipse Award as champion turf female. European interests finally broke through in 2001 when Juddmonte Farms' French-based Banks Hill (GB) won by 5½ lengths at Belmont Park. For the first time in 2001, the Filly and Mare Turf was run at 1¼ miles, its prescribed distance when turf-course configurations permit.

Jockeys by Wins

2 Jerry Bailey (Soaring Softly, Perfect Sting)
1 Olivier Peslier (Banks Hill [GB])

Trainers by Wins

1 Andre Fabre (Banks Hill [GB]), **Joseph Orseno** (Perfect Sting), **James J. Toner** (Soaring Softly)

Owners by Wins

1 Juddmonte Farms (Banks Hill [GB]), **Phillips Racing Partnership** (Soaring Softly), **Stronach Stables** (Perfect Sting)

Breeders of Winners

1 Juddmonte Farms (Banks Hill [GB]), **Frank Stronach** (Perfect Sting), **Galbreath-Phillips Racing Partnership** (Soaring Softly)

Sires of Winners

1 Danehill (Banks Hill [GB]), **Kris S.** (Soaring Softly), **Red Ransom** (Perfect Sting)

Winners by Place Where Bred

Locality	Winners
Kentucky	2
Great Britain	1

Supplemental Entries

Year	Runner	Fee	Finish	Earnings
2001	Spook Express (SAf)	$200,000	2	$278,000
	Kalypso Katie (Ire)	200,000	6	0
	Starine (Fr)	90,000	10	0
	England's Legend (Fr)	90,000	11	0

Year				
2000	Caffe Latte (Ire)	0	9	0
	Catella (Ger)	90,000	3	145,200
	Colstar	90,000	7	0
	Petrushka (Ire)	90,000	5	24,200
1999	Caffe Latte (Ire)	90,000	4	59,920

Champions from Race

Year	Runner	Finish	Title
2001	**Banks Hill (GB)**	1	Turf female
2000	**Perfect Sting**	1	Turf female
1999	**Soaring Softly**	1	Turf female

Odds of Winners

Year	Horse	Odds
2001	Banks Hill (GB)	6.00-to-1
2000	Perfect Sting	5.00-to-1
1999	Soaring Softly	3.60-to-1

Winning Times

Year	Horse	Track	Time	Cond.
2001	Banks Hill (GB)	Bel	2:00.36	Firm
2000	Perfect Sting	CD	2:13.07	Firm
1999	Soaring Softly	GP	2:13.89	Good

Number of Starters

Year	Track	Starters
2001	Belmont Park	12
2000	Churchill Downs	14
1999	Gulfstream Park	14

Winning Post Positions

Post	Starters	Winners	Percent
1	3	0	0.0%
2	3	0	0.0%
3	3	0	0.0%
4	3	0	0.0%
5	3	1	33.3%
6	3	0	0.0%
7	3	0	0.0%
8	3	1	33.3%
9	3	0	0.0%
10	3	0	0.0%
11	3	0	0.0%
12	3	1	33.3%
13	2	0	0.0%
14	2	0	0.0%

Changes in Filly and Mare Turf

No changes in conditions or purse other than the distance have been made since the Breeders' Cup Filly and Mare Turf was inaugurated in 1999.

Breeders' Cup Filly and Mare Turf

Grade 1, $1-million, fillies and mares, three-year-olds and up, 1¼ miles, turf. Run October 27, 2001, at Belmont Park with gross value of $1-million. First run in 1999. Weights: Northern Hemisphere three-year-olds, 119 pounds; older, 123 pounds; Southern Hemisphere three-year-olds, 114 pounds; older, 123 pounds.

Year	Winner	Jockey	Second	Third	Site	Time	Track	1st purse
2001	Banks Hill (GB), 3	O. Peslier	Spook Express (SAf)	Spring Oak (GB)	Bel	**2:00.36**	fm	**$722,800**
2000	Perfect Sting, 4	J. Bailey	Tout Charmant	Catella (Ger)	CD	**2:13.07**	fm	$629,200
1999	Soaring Softly, 4	J. Bailey	Coretta (Ire)	Zomaradah (GB)	GP	2:13.89	gd	$556,400

1999-2000, 1⅜ miles; 2001, 1¼ miles

Breeders' Cup Sprint

Roughly half of all North American races are run at six furlongs, and thus the $1-million Breeders' Cup Sprint (G1) is the prototypical American race. The six-furlong dash has proved to be a competitive contest, principally among North American runners, and in many years it has been a nightmare for handicappers.

As a championship event, the Breeders' Cup Sprint has been especially decisive in years when no horse clearly dominated the division. In 11 of the 18 runnings of the Sprint, the Eclipse Award for champion sprinter has gone to the winner.

The first Breeders' Cup Sprint in 1984 set the tone for the series, with Eillo desperately holding off Commemorate to win by a nose. Seven runnings of the Breeders' Cup Sprint have been decided by a neck or less. Eillo was favored at 1.30-to-1, and no favorite would again win the Sprint for ten years, until Cherokee Run (2.80-to-1) in 1994. Lit de Justice was a lukewarm 4-to-1 favorite in 1997, and Kona Gold won at 1.70-to-1 in 2000.

Between Eillo and Cherokee Run, the Sprint was won by two champions, Precisionist (1985) and Gulch ('88), who could not be characterized as pure sprinters. Fred Hooper's homebred Precisionist won the 1¼-mile Charles H. Strub Stakes (G1) the same year he was sprint champion, and Gulch was really best at one mile, winning the Metropolitan Handicap (G1) twice, 1987 and '88, the latter his championship year.

The Sprint in 1990 remains one of the most memorable in Breeders' Cup history. Safely Kept, the prior year's champion sprinter, fought a spirited, head-to-head battle with English invader Dayjur, the 2.40-to-1 favorite. Inside the furlong

pole, Dayjur appeared to take command, but 40 yards from the wire he jumped the shadow of Belmont Park's grandstand on the racetrack and briefly lost his action. Those missteps proved sufficient for 12.20-to-1 Safely Kept to regain the lead and hold on for a neck victory.

Although Dayjur failed to become the first overseas horse to win the Sprint, the European contingent broke through the following year when Sheikh Albadou (GB) won at Churchill Downs. At 26.30-to-1, Sheikh Albadou remains the longest-priced winner of the Sprint. Average odds of Sprint winners over the first 18 years were a healthy 9.12-to-1.

Kona Gold, the 2000 winner, proved that top-quality sprinters could be durable as well as fast. Carefully managed by co-owner and trainer Bruce Headley, the Java Gold gelding ran third in 1998, second in '99, and finally won at age six. In winning at Churchill Downs, Kona Gold set a track record, 1:07.77, the fastest time ever for the Sprint. Kona Gold was the 7-to-2 favorite when seeking a second straight win in 2001 but finished seventh behind winner Squirtle Squirt.

Jockeys by Wins

3 **Corey Nakatani** (Reraise, Elmhurst, Lit de Justice)

2 **Angel Cordero Jr.** (Dancing Spree, Gulch), **Eddie Delahoussaye** (Cardmania, Thirty Slews), **Craig Perret** (Safely Kept, Eillo)

1 **Jerry Bailey** (Squirtle Squirt), **Jorge Chavez** (Artax), **Kent Desormeaux** (Desert Stormer), **Pat Eddery** (Sheikh Albadou [GB]), **Chris McCarron** (Precisionist), **Mike Smith** (Cherokee Run), **Alex Solis** (Kona Gold), **Patrick Valenzuela** (Very Subtle), **Jacinto Vasquez** (Smile)

Breeders' Cup Sprint

Grade 1, $1-million, three-year-olds and up, 6 furlongs. Held on October 27, 2001, at Belmont Park with gross value of $1-million. First run in 1984. Weights: Northern Hemisphere three-year-olds, 124 pounds; older, 126 pounds; Southern Hemisphere three-year-olds, 122 pounds; older, 126 pounds; fillies and mares allowed three pounds.

Year	Winner	Jockey	Second	Third	Site	Time	Track	1st purse
2001	Squirtle Squirt, 3	J. Bailey	Xtra Heat	Caller One	Bel	1:08.41	ft	$520,000
2000	Kona Gold, 6	A. Solis	Honest Lady	Bet On Sunshine	CD	**1:07.77**	ft	$520,000
1999	Artax, 4	J. Chavez	Kona Gold	Big Jag	GP	1:07.89	ft	$624,000
1998	Reraise, 3	C. Nakatani	Grand Slam	Kona Gold	CD	1:09.07	ft	$572,000
1997	Elmhurst, 7	C. Nakatani	Hesabull	Bet On Sunshine	Hol	1:08.01	ft	$613,600
1996	Lit de Justice, 6	C. Nakatani	Paying Dues	Honour and Glory	WO	1:08.60	ft	$520,000
1995	Desert Stormer, f, 5	K. Desormeaux	Mr. Greeley	Lit de Justice	Bel	1:09.14	my	$520,000
1994	Cherokee Run, 4	M. Smith	Soviet Problem	Cardmania	CD	1:09.54	ft	$520,000
1993	Cardmania, 7	E. Delahoussaye	Meafara	Gilded Time	SA	1:08.76	ft	$520,000
1992	Thirty Slews, 5	E. Delahoussaye	Meafara	Rubiano	GP	1:08.21	ft	$520,000
1991	Sheikh Albadou (GB), 3	P. Eddery	Pleasant Tap	Robyn Dancer	CD	1:09.36	ft	$520,000
1990	Safely Kept, f, 4	C. Perret	Dayjur	Black Tie Affair (Ire)	Bel	1:09 3/5	ft	$450,000
1989	Dancing Spree, 4	A. Cordero Jr.	Safely Kept	Dispersal	GP	1:09	ft	$450,000
1988	Gulch, 4	A. Cordero Jr.	Play the King	Afleet	CD	1:10 2/5	sy	$450,000
1987	Very Subtle, f, 3	P. Valenzuela	Groovy	Exclusive Enough	Hol	1:08 4/5	ft	$450,000
1986	Smile, 4	J. Vasquez	Pine Tree Lane	Beside Promise	SA	1:08 2/5	ft	$450,000
1985	Precisionist, 4	C. McCarron	Smile	Mt. Livermore	Aqu	1:08 2/5	ft	$450,000
1984	Eillo, 4	C. Perret	Commemorate	Fighting Fit	Hol	1:10 1/5	ft	$450,000

Trainers by Wins

2 Jenine Sahadi (Elmhurst, Lit de Justice)

1 Louis Albertrani (Artax), Frank Alexander (Cherokee Run), Bob Baffert (Thirty Slews), Craig Dollase (Reraise), Robert Frankel (Squirtle Squirt), Ross Fenstermaker (Precisionist), Alan Goldberg (Safely Kept), Bruce Headley (Kona Gold), Budd Lepman (Eillo), D. Wayne Lukas (Gulch), Frank Lyons (Desert Stormer), Claude R. "Shug" McGaughey III (Dancing Spree), Derek Meredith (Cardmania), Flint S. "Scotty" Schulhofer (Smile), Alexander Scott (Sheikh Albadou [GB]), Mel Stute (Very Subtle)

Owners by Wins

1 Peter M. Brant (Gulch), Jean Couvercelle (Cardmania), Crown Stable (Eillo), Mitch Degroot, Dutch Masters III, and Mike Pegram (Thirty Slews), Craig Dollase, Barry Fey, Moon Han, and Frank Sinatra (Reraise), Evergreen Farm (Lit de Justice), Evergreen Farm and Jenine Sahadi (Elmhurst), Frances Genter Stable (Smile), Fred Hooper (Precisionist), Bruce Headley, Irwin and Andrew Molasky, and High Tech Stable (Kona Gold), Jayeff B Stables and Barry Weisbord (Safely Kept), David J. Lanzman (Squirtle Squirt), Joanne Nor (Desert Stormer), Paraneck Stable (Artax), Ogden Phipps (Dancing Spree), Jill Robinson (Cherokee Run), Ben Rochelle (Very Subtle), Hilal Salem (Sheikh Albadou [GB])

Breeders of Winners

1 Peter M. Brant (Gulch), Calumet Farm (Elmhurst), Carondelet Farm and Vinery (Artax), Ollie A. Cohen (Eillo), Delta Thoroughbreds (Cardmania), Frances Genter Stable (Smile), Grousemont Farm (Thirty Slews), Mr. and Mrs. David Hayden (Safely Kept), Highclere Stud (Sheikh Albadou [GB]) Fred Hooper (Precisionist), John Howard King (Very Subtle), Audrey Narducci, M.D., (Squirtle Squirt), Joanne Nor (Desert Stormer), George Onett (Cherokee Run), Carlos Perez (Kona Gold), Ogden Phipps (Dancing Spree), Swettenham Stud (Lit de Justice), Willard Sergent (Reraise)

Sires of Winners

2 Marquetry (Artax, Squirtle Squirt), Mr. Prospector (Eillo, Gulch)

1 Cox's Ridge (Cardmania), Crozier (Precisionist), Danzatore (Reraise), El Gran Senor (Lit de Justice), Green Desert (Sheikh Albadou [GB]), Hoist the Silver (Very Subtle), Horatius (Safely Kept), In Reality (Smile), Java Gold (Kona Gold), Nijinsky II (Dancing Spree), Runaway Groom (Cherokee Run), Slewpy (Thirty Slews), Storm Cat (Desert Stormer), Wild Again (Elmhurst)

Winners by place where bred

Locality	Winners
Kentucky	12
Florida	4
Maryland	1
Great Britain	1

Supplemental Entries

Year	Runner	Fee	Finish	Earnings
1999	Son of a Pistol	$120,000	13	$0
	Enjoy the Moment	120,000	14	0
1998	Reraise	120,000	1	572,000
1997	Men's Exclusive	200,000	6	0
1996	Criollito	200,000	12	0
1994	Cherokee Run	120,000	1	520,000
	Soviet Problem	120,000	2	200,000
	Exclusive Praline	120,000	9	0
1989	Sewickley	120,000	5	50,000
1987	Zabaleta	120,000	4	70,000
	Zany Tactics	120,000	9	0
1985	Committed	200,000	7	0
1984	Pac Mania	200,000	9	0

Champions from Race

Year	Runner	Finish	Title
2001	Squirtle Squirt	1	Sprinter
2000	Kona Gold	1	Sprinter
1999	Artax	1	Sprinter
1998	Reraise	1	Sprinter
1996	Lit de Justice	1	Sprinter
1995	Not Surprising	4	Sprinter
1994	Cherokee Run	1	Sprinter
1993	Cardmania	1	Sprinter
1992	Rubiano	3	Sprinter
1991	Housebuster	9	Sprinter
1989	Safely Kept	2	Sprinter
1988	Gulch	1	Sprinter
1987	Groovy	2	Sprinter
1986	Smile	1	Sprinter
1985	Precisionist	1	Sprinter
1984	Eillo	1	Sprinter

Largest Winning Margins

Year	Winner	Margin
1987	Very Subtle	4
1991	Sheikh Albadou (GB)	3
1998	Reraise	2
1988	Gulch	1¾
1985	Precisionist	1¾

Smallest Winning Margins

Year	Winner	Margin
1984	Eillo	nose
1994	Cherokee Run	head
1995	Desert Stormer	neck
1993	Cardmania	neck
1992	Thirty Slews	neck
1990	Safely Kept	neck
1989	Dancing Spree	neck

Shortest-Priced Winners

Year	Horse	Odds
1984	Eillo	1.30-to-1
2000	Kona Gold	1.70-to-1
1994	Cherokee Run	2.80-to-1
1985	Precisionist	3.40-to-1
1999	Artax	3.70-to-1
1998	Reraise	3.80-to-1

Longest-Priced Winners

Year	Horse	Odds
1991	Sheikh Albadou (GB)	26.30-to-1
1992	Thirty Slews	18.70-to-1
1997	Elmhurst	16.60-to-1
1989	Dancing Spree	16.60-to-1
1987	Very Subtle	16.40-to-1
1995	Desert Stormer	14.50-to-1**
1990	Safely Kept	12.20-to-1
1986	Smile	11.00-to-1

** pari-mutuel field

Fastest Winners

Year	Horse	Track	Time	Cond.
2000	Kona Gold	CD	1:07.77	Fast
1999	Artax	GP	1:07.89	Fast
1997	Elmhurst	Hol	1:08.01	Fast
1992	Thirty Slews	GP	1:08.21	Firm
1986	Smile	SA	1:08⅖	Fast
1985	Precisionist	Aqu	1:08⅖	Fast

Slowest Winners

Year	Horse	Track	Time	Cond.
1988	Gulch	CD	1:10⅖	Sloppy
1984	Eillo	Hol	1:10⅕	Fast
1990	Safely Kept	Bel	1:09⅗	Fast
1994	Cherokee Run	CD	1:09.54	Fast

Most Starters

Year	Track	Starters
2001	Belmont Park	14
2000	Churchill	14
1999	Gulfstream Park	14
1998	Churchill Downs	14
1997	Hollywood Park	14
1994	Churchill Downs	14
1993	Santa Anita Park	14
1992	Gulfstream Park	14
1990	Belmont Park	14
1985	Aqueduct	14

Fewest Starters

Year	Track	Starters
1986	Santa Anita Park	9
1991	Churchill Downs	11
1984	Hollywood Park	11

Winning Post Positions

Post	Starters	Winners	Percent
1	18	1	5.6%
2	18	2	11.1%
3	18	2	11.1%
4	18	2	11.1%
5	18	5	27.8%
6	18	0	0.0%
7	18	0	0.0%
8	18	1	5.6%
9	18	1	5.6%
10	17	2	11.8%
11	17	2	11.8%
12	15	0	0.0%
13	15	0	0.0%
14	10	0	0.0%

Changes in Sprint

No changes have been made in the conditions or purse of the Breeders' Cup Sprint since its first running in 1984.

Breeders' Cup Mile

In the Breeders' Cup Mile, good things have come in twos. Only three Breeders' Cup races have had repeat winners, and the Breeders' Cup Mile has had three horses who have posted two victories each. (Bayakoa [Arg] won the Breeders' Cup Distaff in 1989 and '90, and Tiznow won the Classic in 2000 and '01.)

Miesque, bred by owner Stavros Niarchos's Flaxman Holdings Ltd., sparkled in the Mile on turf at Hollywood Park in 1987 and conquered a significantly slower surface at Churchill Downs the following year. The remarkable Francois Boutin-trained filly won by 3½ lengths in California and by four lengths in Kentucky—the largest winning margins in the race's history. On the strength of her single North American victories, Miesque was voted champion grass female in 1987 and '88.

Claiborne Farm's homebred Lure, arguably one of the most accomplished horses never to win an end-of-year championship, also scored two daylight victories, winning by three lengths at Gulfstream Park in 1992 and by 2¼ lengths the following year at Santa Anita Park for trainer Claude R. "Shug" McGaughey III.

Although not necessarily possessing talent to equal Miesque or Lure, Da Hoss became a two-time Mile winner by virtue of his courage and the innovative training regimen of Michael Dickinson. In 1996, Dickinson had his assistant, Joan Wakefield, test the Woodbine turf course in high heels to determine the best path for the Gone West gelding, who won by 1½ lengths. Da Hoss missed the entire following season due to injury and came back to run in the 1998 Mile with only one start in two years. Da Hoss rallied on a firm Churchill turf course to overtake Hawksley Hill (Ire) and win by a head.

European-based horses have had consistent success in the Mile. Seven of the first 18 winners were based with European trainers prior to their win.

Most remarkable about the Mile has been the domination of the Northern Dancer sire line. Although the great Windfields Farm stallion did not sire a winner himself, five of his sons and three of his grandsons have sired winners, accounting for 13 victories in the first 18 years. His sons Danzig and Nureyev have each sired three winners.

Jockeys by Wins

2 **Freddie Head** (Miesque, 1987 and '88), **Mike Smith** (Lure, 1992 and '93), **Gary Stevens** (Da Hoss, War Chant)

1 **Cash Asmussen** (Spinning World), **Lanfranco Dettori** (Barathea [Ire]), **Walter Guerra** (Cozzene), **John Murtagh** (Ridgewood Pearl [GB]), **Corey Nakatani** (Silic [Fr]), **Lester Piggott** (Royal Academy), **Yves Saint-Martin** (Last Tycoon [Ire]), **Jose Santos** (Steinlen [GB]), **Fernando Toro** (Royal Heroine [Ire]), **Jose Valdivia Jr.** (Val Royal [Fr]), **John Velazquez** (Da Hoss), **Patrick Valenzuela** (Opening Verse)

Trainers by Wins

2 **Francois Boutin** (Miesque, 1987 and '88), **Julio Canani** (Silic [Fr], Val Royal [Fr]), **Michael Dickinson** (Da Hoss, 1996 and '98), **Claude R. "Shug" McGaughey III** (Lure, 1992 and '93)

1 **Robert Collet** (Last Tycoon [Ire]), **Luca Cumani** (Barathea [Ire]), **Neil Drysdale** (War Chant), **John Gosden** (Royal Heroine [Ire]), **D. Wayne Lukas** (Steinlen [GB]), **Richard Lundy** (Opening Verse), **Jan Nerud** (Cozzene), **Vincent O'Brien** (Royal Academy), **John Oxx** (Ridgewood Pearl [GB]), **Jonathan Pease** (Spinning World)

Owners by Wins

2 **Claiborne Farm** (Lure, 1992 and '93), **Stavros Niarchos** (Miesque, 1987 and '88), **Prestonwood Farm and Wall Street Stable** (Da Hoss, 1996 and '98)

1 **Classic Thoroughbreds PLC** (Royal Academy), **Anne Coughlan** (Ridgewood Pearl [GB]), **Marjorie and Irving Cowan** (War Chant), **Flaxman Holdings Ltd.** (Spinning World), **J. Terrence Lanni, Bernard Schiappa, Kenneth Poslosky, et al.** (Silic [Fr]), **David S. Milch** (Val Royal [Fr]), **Sheikh Mohammed bin Rashid al Maktoum and Gerald Leigh** (Barathea [Ire]), **John Nerud** (Cozzene), **Allen E. Paulson** (Opening Verse), **Richard C. Strauss** (Last Tycoon [Ire]), **Robert Sangster** (Royal Heroine [Ire]), **Wildenstein Stable** (Steinlen [GB])

Breeders of Winners

3 **Flaxman Holdings Ltd.** (Miesque, 1987 and '88, Spinning World)

2 **Claiborne Farm and Gamely Corp.** (Lure, 1992 and '93), **Fares Farm** (Da Hoss, 1996 and '98)

1 **Allez France Stables Ltd.** (Steinlen [GB]), **Tom Gentry** (Royal Academy), **Sean Coughlan** (Ridgewood Pearl [GB]), **Marjorie and Irving Cowan** (War Chant), **M. Armenio Simoes de Almeida** (Silic [Fr]), **Jean-Luc Lagardere** (Val Royal [Fr]), **Gerald Leigh** (Barathea [Ire]), **John Nerud** (Cozzene), **Jacques D. Wimpfheimer** (Opening Verse), **Kilfrush Stud Ltd.** (Last Tycoon [Ire]), **B. L. Ryan** (Royal Heroine [Ire])

Sires of Winners

3 **Danzig** (Lure, 1992 and '93, War Chant), **Nureyev** (Miesque, 1987 and '88, Spinning World)

2 **Gone West** (Da Hoss, 1996 and '98)

1 **Caro (Ire)** (Cozzene), **Habitat** (Steinlen [GB]), **Indian Ridge** (Ridgewood Pearl [GB]), **Lypheor (GB)** (Royal Heroine [Ire]), **Nijinsky II** (Royal Academy), **Royal Academy** (Val Royal [Fr]), **Sadler's Wells** (Barathea [Ire]), **Sillery** (Silic [Fr]), **The Minstrel** (Opening Verse), **Try My Best** (Last Tycoon [Ire])

Winners by Place Where Bred

Locality	Winners
Kentucky	10
Ireland	3
France	2
Great Britain	2
Florida	1

Breeders' Cup Mile

Grade 1, $1-million, three-year-olds and up, 1 mile, turf. Run October 27, 2001, at Belmont Park with gross value of $1-million. First run in 1984. Weights: Northern Hemisphere three-year-olds, 123 pounds; older, 126 pounds; Southern Hemisphere three-year-olds, 120 pounds; older, 126 pounds; fillies and mares allowed three pounds.

Year	Winner	Jockey	Second	Third	Site	Time	Track	1st purse
2001	**Val Royal (Fr)**, 5	J. Valdivia Jr.	Forbidden Apple	Bach (Ire)	Bel	**1:32.05**	fm	$592,800
2000	**War Chant**, 3	G. Stevens	North East Bound	Dansili (GB)	CD	1:34.67	fm	$608,400
1999	**Silic (Fr)**, 4	C. Nakatani	Tuzla (Fr)	Docksider	GP	1:34.26	gd	$520,000
1998	**Da Hoss**, 6	J. Velazquez	Hawksley Hill (Ire)	Labeeb (GB)	CD	1:35.27	fm	$520,000
1997	**Spinning World**, 4	C. Asmussen	Geri	Decorated Hero (GB)	Hol	1:32.77	fm	$572,000
1996	**Da Hoss**, 4	G. Stevens	Spinning World	Same Old Wish	WO	1:35.80	gd	$520,000
1995	**Ridgewood Pearl (GB)**, f, 3	J. Murtagh	Fastness (Ire)	Sayyedati (GB)	Bel	1:43.65	sf	$520,000
1994	**Barathea (Ire)**, 4	L. Dettori	Johann Quatz (Fr)	Unfinished Symph	CD	1:34.50	fm	$520,000
1993	**Lure**, 4	M. Smith	Ski Paradise	Fourstars Allstar	SA	1:33.58	fm	$520,000
1992	**Lure**, 3	M. Smith	Paradise Creek	Brief Truce	GP	1:32.90	fm	$520,000
1991	**Opening Verse**, 5	P. Valenzuela	Val des Bois (Fr)	Star of Cozzene	CD	1:37.59	fm	$520,000
1990	**Royal Academy**, 3	L. Piggott	Itsallgreektome	Priolo	Bel	1:35⅕	gd	$450,000
1989	**Steinlen (GB)**, 6	J. Santos	Sabona	Most Welcome (GB)	GP	1:37⅕	gd	$450,000
1988	**Miesque**, f, 4	F. Head	Steinlen (GB)	Simply Majestic	CD	1:38⅗	gd	$450,000
1987	**Miesque**, f, 3	F. Head	Show Dancer	Sonic Lady	Hol	1:32⅘	fm	$450,000
1986	**Last Tycoon (Ire)**, 3	Y. Saint-Martin	Palace Music	Fred Astaire	SA	1:35⅕	fm	$450,000
1985	**Cozzene**, 5	W. Guerra	Al Mamoon	Shadeed	Aqu	1:35	fm	$450,000
1984	**Royal Heroine (Ire)**, f, 4	F. Toro	Star Choice	Cozzene	Hol	1:32⅗	fm	$450,000

1985—Palace Music disqualified from second to ninth.

Supplemental Entries

Year	Runner	Fee	Finish	Earnings
2001	**Val Royal (Fr)**	$90,000	1	$592,800
	Express Tour	90,000	10	0
2000	Ladies Din	120,000	8	0
	Indian Lodge (Ire)	90,000	13	0
1997	Lucky Coin	120,000	4	61,600
1992	Bistro Garden	120,000	14	0
1991	Star of Cozzene	120,000	3	120,000
1986	Hatim	120,000	13	0
	Truce Maker	120,000	14	0
1985	Rousillon	120,000	9	0
1984	Night Mover	120,000	8	0

Champions from Race

Year	Runner	Finish	Title
1993	Flawlessly	9	Turf female
1991	Tight Spot	9	Turf male
1990	Itsallgreektome	2	Turf male
1989	**Steinlen (GB)**	1	Turf male
1988	**Miesque**	1	Turf female
1987	**Miesque**	1	Turf female
1985	**Cozzene**	1	Turf male
1984	**Royal Heroine (Ire)**	1	Turf female

Largest Winning Margins

Year	Winner	Margin
1988	Miesque	4
1987	Miesque	3½
1994	Baratthea (Ire)	3
1992	Lure	3

Smallest Winning Margins

Year	Winner	Margin
1998	Da Hoss	head
1986	Last Tycoon (Ire)	head
2000	War Chant	neck
1999	Silic (Fr)	neck
1990	Royal Academy	neck

Shortest-Priced Winners

Year	Horse	Odds
1993	Lure	1.30-to-1
1984	Royal Heroine (Ire)	1.70-to-1*
1989	Steinlen (GB)	1.80-to-1
1988	Miesque	2.00-to-1*

*Part of entry

Longest-Priced Winners

Year	Horse	Odds
1986	Last Tycoon (Ire)	35.90-to-1
1991	Opening Verse	26.70-to-1
1998	Da Hoss	11.60-to-1
1994	Baratthea (Ire)	10.40-to-1

Fastest Winners

Year	Horse	Track	Time	Cond.
2001	Val Royal (Fr)	Bel	1:32.05	Firm
1984	Royal Heroine (Ire)	Hol	1:32⅗	Firm
1997	Spinning World	CD	1:32.77	Firm
1987	Miesque	Hol	1:32⅘	Firm
1992	Lure	GP	1:32.90	Firm

Slowest Winners

Year	Horse	Track	Time	Cond.
1995	Ridgewood Pearl (GB)	Bel	1:43.65	Soft
1988	Miesque	CD	1:38⅗	Good
1991	Opening Verse	CD	1:37.59	Firm
1989	Steinlen (GB)	GP	1:37⅕	Good

Most Starters

Year	Track	Starters
2000	Churchill Downs`	14
1999	Gulfstream Park	14
1998	Churchill Downs	14
1996	Woodbine	14
1994	Churchill Downs	14
1992	Gulfstream Park	14
1991	Churchill Downs	14
1987	Hollywood Park	14
1986	Santa Anita	14
1985	Aqueduct	14

Fewest Starters

Year	Track	Starters
1984	Hollywood Park	10
1989	Gulfstream Park	11
2001	Belmont Park	12
1997	Hollywood Park	12
1988	Churchill Downs	12

Winning Post Positions

Post	Starters	Winners	Percent
1	18	3	16.7%
2	18	3	16.7%
3	18	1	5.6%
4	18	2	11.1%
5	18	0	0.0%
6	18	2	11.1%
7	18	1	5.6%
8	18	1	5.6%
9	18	0	0.0%
10	18	1	5.6%
11	17	2	11.8%
12	16	2	12.5%
13	13	0	0.0%
14	10	0	0.0%

Changes in Mile

No changes have been made in the conditions or purse of the Breeders' Cup Mile since its inauguration.

Breeders' Cup Juvenile Fillies

One of the most all-American of the Breeders' Cup races, the Breeders' Cup Juvenile Fillies has produced the most champions in year-end Eclipse Award balloting among Breeders' Cup races. Fifteen of the first 18 winners were subsequently voted year-end champions.

The first Breeders' Cup Juvenile Fillies, the second race on the inaugural card in 1984, pro-

duced the afternoon's first bit of controversy. In making a winning move at the top of the stretch, Fran's Valentine knocked Pirate's Glow off stride and pushed her into Canadian star Bessarabian. Fran's Valentine held off Outstandingly to reach the finish line first, but stewards disqualified Fran's Valentine to tenth for causing interference. After Outstandingly followed with a win in the Hollywood Starlet Stakes, she was voted an Eclipse Award as champion two-year-old filly, a title that would be earned by all but three of the succeeding Juvenile Fillies winners.

The Juvenile Fillies at Aqueduct in 1985 launched a dominating run by D. Wayne Lukas, who took the first two spots that year with Twilight Ridge and Family Style. Lukas saddled the top three finishers in 1988, with Open Mind the winner. In 1994, he sent out Flanders and Serena's Song to finish one-two. Flanders pulled up lame after the race and subsequently was retired. Serena's Song, second by a head, was champion three-year-old filly the following year and retired as North America's then-leading female earner with $3,283,388. Lukas also won in 1999 with longshot Cash Run.

In addition to Open Mind, who was voted champion at two and three, Juvenile Fillies winners who earned two championship titles were Go for Wand and Silverbulletday. Go for Wand took the two-year-old title with a triumph at Gulfstream Park in 1989 and was voted an Eclipse Award as champion three-year-old filly posthumously after a fatal breakdown in the 1990 Breeders' Cup Distaff. Silverbulletday scored a half-length victory over stablemate Excellent Meeting in the 1998 Juvenile Fillies and won four Grade 1 races the following year to wrap up the three-year-old filly title.

Through 2001, only 11 overseas-based fillies have competed in the Fillies, with their best finishes a pair of fourths in 1993 and '94. Godolphin Racing won in 2001 with Tempera, who was trained in the United States by Eoin Harty.

Jockeys by Wins

2 **Jerry Bailey** (My Flag, Cash Run); **Pat Day** (Epitome, Flanders); **Patrick Valenzuela** (Brave Raj, Eliza)

1 **Angel Cordero Jr.** (Open Mind); **Eddie Delahoussaye** (Pleasant Stage); **David Flores** (Tempera), **Walter Guerra** (Outstandingly); **Laffit Pincay Jr.** (Phone Chatter); **Craig Perret** (Storm Song); **Randy Romero** (Go for Wand); **Jose Santos** (Meadow Star); **Shane Sellers** (Countess Diana); **Gary Stevens** (Silverbulletday); **Jorge Velasquez** (Twilight Ridge); **John Velazquez** (Caressing)

Trainers by Wins

4 **D. Wayne Lukas** (Twilight Ridge, Open Mind, Flanders, Cash Run)

1 **William Badgett** (Go for Wand), **Bob Baffert** (Silverbulletday), **Patrick Byrne** (Countess Diana), **Eoin Harty** (Tempera), **Alex Hassinger Jr.** (Eliza), **Philip Hauswald** (Epitome), **LeRoy Jolley** (Meadow Star), **Richard Mandella** (Phone Chatter), **Frank Martin** (Outstandingly), **Claude R. "Shug" McGaughey III** (My Flag), **Christopher Speckert** (Pleasant Stage), **Mel Stute** (Brave Raj), **David Vance** (Caressing), **Nick P. Zito** (Storm Song)

Owners by Wins

2 **Eugene V. Klein** (Twilight Ridge, Open Mind)

1 **John A. Bell III** (Epitome), **Buckland Farm** (Pleasant Stage), **Christiana Stable** (Go for Wand), **Dogwood Stable** (Storm Song), **Dolly Green**

Breeders' Cup Juvenile Fillies

Grade 1, $1-million, two-year-old fillies, 1$\frac{1}{16}$ miles, dirt. Run October 27, 2001, at Belmont Park with gross value of $1-million. First run in 1984. Weights: 119 pounds.

Year	Winner	Jockey	Second	Third	Site	Time	Track	1st purse
2001	**Tempera**	D. Flores	Imperial Gesture	Bella Bellucci	Bel	1:41.49	ft	$520,000
2000	**Caressing**	J. Velazquez	Platinum Tiara	She's a Devil Due	CD	1:42.77	ft	**$592,800**
1999	**Cash Run**	J. Bailey	Chilukki	Surfside	GP	1:43.31	ft	$520,000
1998	**Silverbulletday**	G. Stevens	Excellent Meeting	Three Ring	CD	1:43.68	ft	$520,000
1997	**Countess Diana**	S. Sellers	Career Collection	Primaly	Hol	**1:42.11**	ft	$535,600
1996	**Storm Song**	C. Perret	Love That Jazz	Critical Factor	WO	1:43.60	ft	$520,000
1995	**My Flag**	J. Bailey	Cara Rafaela	Golden Attraction	Bel	1:42.55	my	$520,000
1994	**Flanders**	P. Day	Serena's Song	Stormy Blues	CD	1:45.28	ft	$520,000
1993	**Phone Chatter**	L. Pincay	Sardula	Heavenly Prize	SA	1:43.08	ft	$520,000
1992	**Eliza**	P. Valenzuela	Educated Risk	Boots 'n Jackie	GP	1:42.93	ft	$520,000
1991	**Pleasant Stage**	E. Delahoussaye	La Spia	Cadillac Women	CD	1:46.48	ft	$520,000
1990	**Meadow Star**	J. Santos	Private Treasure	Dance Smartly	Bel	1:44	ft	$450,000
1989	**Go for Wand**	R. Romero	Sweet Roberta	Stella Madrid	GP	1:44$\frac{1}{5}$	ft	$450,000
1988	**Open Mind**	A. Cordero Jr.	Darby Shuffle	Lea Lucinda	CD	1:46$\frac{3}{5}$	my	$450,000
1987	**Epitome**	P. Day	Jeanne Jones	Dream Team	Hol	1:36$\frac{2}{5}$	ft	$450,000
1986	**Brave Raj**	P. Valenzuela	Tappiano	Saros Brig	SA	1:43$\frac{1}{5}$	ft	$450,000
1985	**Twilight Ridge**	J. Velasquez	Family Style	Steal a Kiss	Aqu	1:35$\frac{4}{5}$	ft	$450,000
1984	**Outstandingly**	W. Guerra	Dusty Heart	Fine Spirit	Hol	1:37$\frac{4}{5}$	ft	$450,000

1984-'85, '87—run at one mile; 1984—Fran's Valentine disqualified from first to tenth.

(Brave Raj), **Godolphin Racing** (Tempera), **Harbor View Farm** (Outstandingly), **Richard A. Kaster, Nancy R. Kaster, Nancy A. Kaster, and Donald Propson** (Countess Diana), **Carl Icahn** (Meadow Star), **Overbrook Farm** (Flanders), **Padua Stables** (Cash Run), **Allen E. Paulson** (Eliza), **Mike Pegram** (Silverbulletday), **Ogden Phipps** (My Flag), **Carl F. Pollard** (Caressing), **Herman Sarkowsky** (Phone Chatter)

Breeders of Winners

1   **Thomas E. Burrow** (Twilight Ridge), **Jaime S. Carrion** (Meadow Star), **Christiana Stable** (Go for Wand), **Darley Stud Management** (Tempera), **Due Process Stable** (Open Mind), **Robert S. Evans** (Cash Run), **Mrs. Thomas M. Evans** (Pleasant Stage), **William S. Farish and Ogden Mills Phipps** (Storm Song), **Harbor View Farm** (Outstandingly), **Highclere Inc. and Clear Creek** (Silverbulletday), **Brereton C. Jones** (Caressing), **Richard A. and Nancy R. Kaster** (Countess Diana), **Wallace S. Karutz** (Brave Raj), **Jessica Bell Nicholson and H. Bennett Bell** (Epitome), **Overbrook Farm** (Flanders), **Ogden Phipps** (My Flag), **Allen E. Paulson** (Eliza), **Herman Sarkowsky** (Phone Chatter)

Sires of Winners

2   **Deputy Minister** (Open Mind, Go for Wand), **Seeking the Gold** (Flanders, Cash Run)
1   **A.P. Indy** (Tempera), **Cox's Ridge** (Twilight Ridge), **Deerhound** (Countess Diana), **Easy Goer** (My Flag), **Exclusive Native** (Outstandingly), **Honour and Glory** (Caressing), **Meadowlake** (Meadow Star), **Mt. Livermore** (Eliza), **Phone Trick** (Phone Chatter), **Pleasant Colony** (Pleasant Stage), **Rajab** (Brave Raj), **Silver Deputy** (Silverbulletday), **Summer Squall** (Storm Song), **Summing** (Epitome)

Winners by Place Where Bred

Locality	Winners
Kentucky	13
Florida	3
New Jersey	1
Pennsylvania	1

Supplemental Entries

Year	Runner	Fee	Finish	Earnings
2000	Cindy's Hero	$90,000	4	$63,840
	Out of Sync	90,000	9	0
1995	Tipically Irish	120,000	6	0
1994	Post It	120,000	6	0

Champions from Race

Year	Runner	Finish	Title
2001	**Tempera**	1	Juvenile filly
2000	**Caressing**	1	Juvenile filly
1999	Chilukki	2	Juvenile filly
1998	**Silverbulletday**	1	Juvenile filly
1997	**Countess Diana**	1	Juvenile filly
1996	**Storm Song**	1	Juvenile filly
1995	Golden Attraction	3	Juvenile filly
1994	**Flanders**	1	Juvenile filly
1993	**Phone Chatter**	1	Juvenile filly
1992	**Eliza**	1	Juvenile filly
1991	**Pleasant Stage**	1	Juvenile filly
1990	**Meadow Star**	1	Juvenile filly
1989	**Go for Wand**	1	Juvenile filly
1988	**Open Mind**	1	Juvenile filly
1987	**Epitome**	1	Juvenile filly
1986	**Brave Raj**	1	Juvenile filly
1985	Family Style	2	Juvenile filly
1984	**Outstandingly**	1	Juvenile filly

Largest Winning Margins

Year	Winner	Margin
1997	Countess Diana	8½
1986	Brave Raj	5½
1990	Meadow Star	5
1996	Storm Song	4½

Smallest Winning Margins

Year	Winner	Margin
1987	Epitome	nose
1994	Flanders	head
1993	Phone Chatter	head
1991	Pleasant Stage	head

Shortest-Priced Winners

Year	Horse	Odds
1990	Meadow Star	.20-to-1
1994	Flanders	.40-to-1*
1985	Twilight Ridge	.60-to-1*
1988	Open Mind	.70-to-1*
1998	Silverbulletday	.80-to-1

*Part of entry

Longest-Priced Winners

Year	Horse	Odds
2000	Caressing	47.00-to-1
1999	Cash Run	32.50-to-1
1987	Epitome	30.40-to-1
1984	Outstandingly	22.80-to-1

Odds-On Beaten Favorites

Year	Horse	Odds
2001	You	0.95-to-1

Fastest Winners at 1¹/₁₆ Miles

Year	Horse	Track	Time	Cond.
2001	Tempera	Bel	1:41.49	Fast
1997	Countess Diana	Hol	1:42.11	Fast
1995	My Flag	Bel	1:42.55	Muddy
2000	Caressing	CD	1:42.77	Fast
1992	Eliza	GP	1:42.93	Fast

Slowest Winners at 1¹/₁₆ Miles

Year	Horse	Track	Time	Cond.
1988	Open Mind	CD	1:46⅗	Muddy
1991	Pleasant Stage	CD	1:46.48	Fast
1994	Flanders	CD	1:45.28	Fast
1989	Go for Wand	GP	1:44⅕	Fast

Most Starters

Year	Track	Starters
1997	Hollywood Park	14
1991	Churchill Downs	14
1994	Churchill Downs	13
1990	Belmont Park	13

Fewest Starters

Year	Track	Starters
1995	Belmont Park	8
1993	Santa Anita Park	8
2001	Belmont Park	9
1999	Gulfstream Park	9

8	18	4	22.2%
9	16	3	16.7%
10	14	0	0.0%
11	13	1	7.7%
12	12	0	0.0%
13	4	0	0.0%
14	2	1	50.0%

Winning Post Positions

Post	Starters	Winners	Percent
1	18	1	5.6%
2	18	1	5.6%
3	18	0	0.0%
4	18	3	16.7%
5	18	1	5.6%
6	18	3	16.7%
7	18	0	0.0%

Changes in Juvenile Fillies

Only change to the Juvenile Fillies over the years has been the distance. Originally at one mile for the 1984 and '85 runnings, the distance was changed to 1 1/16 miles for 1986 to accommodate the Santa Anita Park track configuration. The distance returned to one mile for the 1987 edition at Hollywood Park but returned to 1 1/16 miles for '88 and thereafter.

Breeders' Cup Distaff

Although the Breeders' Cup Distaff (G1) has produced two of the four highest-priced winners in the history's series, the race for fillies and mares has in fact been one of the most consistent and predictable of the original seven races.

That record of consistency began with the inaugural Breeders' Cup Distaff at Hollywood Park in 1984. Princess Rooney, winner of the Vanity Handicap (G1) and Spinster Stakes (G1) in prior starts, went off as the 7-to-10 favorite and rolled to a seven-length victory.

In subsequent editions, the Distaff generally would be characterized by dominant winners scoring by open lengths. In fact, Inside Information's 13½-length win in 1995 remains the series' largest winning margin. Lady's Secret, the only Horse of the Year to emerge from the Distaff, won by 2½ lengths in 1986 to seal her title. Odds-on favorites have won the race seven times.

In 1988, Breeders' Cup Ltd. shortened the Distaff's distance from 1¼ miles to 1⅛ miles with no effect on the quality of the race. Indeed, the 1988 running remains one of the most memorable of all Breeders' Cup races. Undefeated Personal Ensign, seemingly beaten at the sixteenth pole, closed relentlessly on Winning Colors, that year's Kentucky Derby winner, and put her nose in front at the wire to close out her career with 13 victories.

At year's end, Personal Ensign was voted an Eclipse Award as champion older female and Winning Colors received an Eclipse as champion three-year-old filly. Dance Smartly, the 1991 Distaff winner, was voted an Eclipse Award as champion three-year-old filly and Canada's Horse of the Year after sweeping the Canadian Triple Crown. In 14 of 18 years, both the champion three-year-old filly and older female have competed in the Distaff.

Supplemental entries, principally top-quality mares from South America, have had excellent success in the Distaff. Bayakoa (Arg), supplemented at a $200,000 cost in 1989 and '90, won both years. The latter year was the darkest day in Breeders' Cup history, when Go for Wand broke down fatally while battling Bayakoa for the lead deep in Belmont Park's stretch. Paseana (Arg), supplemented in 1992 and '93, won in her first try and finished second by a nose to Hollywood Wildcat in '93.

The biggest upset in Distaff history occurred in 2000, when dominant West Coast mare Riboletta (Brz) went off as the 2-to-5 favorite but did not handle the hard Churchill Downs track and finished seventh. Spain, at 55.90-to-1, won the race, becoming the second-longest-priced winner in Breeders' Cup history.

Racing Hall of Fame members who have contested the race are Princess Rooney, Lady's Secret, Personal Ensign, Winning Colors, Bayakoa, Go for Wand, and Paseana.

Jockeys by Wins

3 **Pat Day** (Dance Smartly, Lady's Secret, Unbridled Elaine)

2 **Eddie Delahoussaye** (Hollywood Wildcat, Princess Rooney), **Laffit Pincay Jr.** (Bayakoa [Arg], twice), **Randy Romero** (Personal Ensign, Sacahuista), **Mike Smith** (Ajina, Inside Information), **Gary Stevens** (Escena, One Dreamer)

1 **Jorge Chavez** (Beautiful Pleasure), **Angel Cordero** (Life's Magic), **Victor Espinoza** (Spain), **Chris McCarron** (Paseana [Arg]), **Corey Nakatani** (Jewel Princess)

Trainers by Wins

4 **D. Wayne Lukas** (Lady's Secret, Life's Magic, Sacahuista, Spain)

3 **Ron McAnally (**Bayakoa [Arg], twice, Paseana [Arg])

2 **Neil Drysdale** (Hollywood Wildcat, Princess Rooney), **Claude R. "Shug" McGaughey III** (Inside Information, Personal Ensign), **William I. Mott** (Ajina, Escena)

1 **James Day** (Dance Smartly), **Wallace Dollase** (Jewel Princess), **Tom Proctor** (One Dreamer), **Dallas Stewart** (Unbridled Elaine), **John T. Ward Jr.** (Beautiful Pleasure)

Owners by Wins

2 **Allen E. Paulson** (Ajina, Escena), **Frank and Janis Whitham** (Bayakoa [Arg], twice)

1 **Barry A. Beal and L. R. French Jr.** (Sacahuista), **Irving and Margorie Cowan** (Hollywood Wildcat), **Sidney Craig** (Paseana [Arg]), **Roger J. Devenport** (Unbridled Elaine), **Glen Hill Farm** (One Dreamer), **Mel Hatley and Eugene V. Klein** (Life's Magic), **Mr. and Mrs. Eugene V. Klein** (Lady's Secret), **John Oxley** (Beautiful Pleasure), **Ogden Phipps** (Personal Ensign), **Ogden Mills Phipps** (Inside Information), **Sam-Son Farms** (Dance Smartly), **The Thoroughbred Corp. and Martha and Richard Stephen** (Jewel Princess), **The Thoroughbred Corp.** (Spain), **Paula Tucker** (Princess Rooney)

Breeders of Winners

2 **Farnsworth Farms** (Beautiful Pleasure, Jewel Princess), **Haras Principal** (Bayakoa [Arg], twice), **Allen E. Paulson** (Ajina, Escena)

1 **Irving and Margorie Cowan** (Hollywood Wildcat), **Glen Hill Farm** (One Dreamer), **Golden Orb Farm and K. David Schwartz** (Unbridled Elaine), **Haras Vacacion** (Paseana [Arg]), **G. Watts Humphrey and William S. Farish** (Sacahuista), **Mr. and Mrs. Douglas Parrish and David Parrish III** (Life's Magic), **Ogden Phipps** (Personal Ensign), **Ogden Mills Phipps** (Inside Information), **Ben and Tom Roach** (Princess Rooney), **Sam-Son Farms** (Dance Smartly), **Robert H. Spreen** (Lady's Secret), **The Thoroughbred Corp.** (Spain)

Sires of Winners

2 **Consultant's Bid** (Bayakoa [Arg], twice), **Private Account** (Inside Information, Personal Ensign), **Strawberry Road (Aus)** (Ajina, Escena)

1 **Ahmad** (Paseana [Arg]), **Cox's Ridge** (Life's Magic), **Danzig** (Dance Smartly), **Key to the Mint** (Jewel Princess), **Kris S.** (Hollywood Wildcat), **Maudlin** (Beautiful Pleasure), **Raja Baba** (Sacahuista), **Relaunch** (One Dreamer), **Secretariat** (Lady's Secret), **Thunder Gulch** (Spain), **Unbridled's Song** (Unbridled Elaine), **Verbatim** (Princess Rooney)

Winners by Place Where Bred

Locality	Winners
Kentucky	9
Florida	4
Argentina	3
Oklahoma	1
Ontario	1

Supplemental Entries

Year	Runner	Fee	Finish	Earnings
2001	Miss Linda (Arg)	$400,000	6	$0
2000	Riboletta (Brz)	400,000	7	0
1996	Different (Arg)	200,000	3	120,000
1993	Paseana (Arg)	200,000	2	200,000
1992	**Paseana (Arg)**	200,000	1	520,000
1990	**Bayakoa (Arg)**	200,000	1	450,000
1989	**Bayakoa (Arg)**	200,000	1	450,000
1986	Classy Cathy	120,000	4	70,000
1985	Dontstop Themusic	120,000	3	108,000
	Isayso	120,000	6	10,000

Champions from Race

Year	Runner	Finish	Title
2000	Surfside	2	3yo filly
	Riboletta (Brz)	7	Older female
1999	**Beautiful Pleasure**	1	Older female
	Silverbulletday	6	3yo filly
1998	**Escena**	1	Older female
	Banshee Breeze	2	3yo filly

Breeders' Cup Distaff

Grade 1, $2-million, fillies and mares, three-year-olds and up, 1⅛ miles. Run October 27, 2001, at Belmont Park with gross value of $2-million. First run in 1984. Weights: Northern Hemisphere three-year-olds, 120 pounds; older, 123 pounds; Southern Hemisphere three-year-olds, 115 pounds; older, 123 pounds.

Year	Winner	Jockey	Second	Third	Site	Time	Track	1st purse
2001	**Unbridled Elaine**, 3	P. Day	Spain	Two Item Limit	Bel	1:49.21	ft	$1,227,200
2000	**Spain**, 3	V. Espinoza	Surfside	Heritage of Gold	CD	1:47.66	ft	**$1,227,200**
1999	**Beautiful Pleasure**, 4	J. Chavez	Banshee Breeze	Heritage of Gold	GP	1:47.56	ft	$1,040,000
1998	**Escena**, 5	G. Stevens	Banshee Breeze	Keeper Hill	CD	1:49.89	ft	$1,040,000
1997	**Ajina**, 3	M. Smith	Sharp Cat	Escena	Hol	1:47.20	ft	$520,000
1996	**Jewel Princess**, 4	C. Nakatani	Serena's Song	Different (Arg)	WO	1:48.40	ft	$520,000
1995	**Inside Information**, 4	M. Smith	Heavenly Prize	Lakeway	Bel	**1:46.15**	my	$520,000
1994	**One Dreamer**, 6	G. Stevens	Heavenly Prize	Miss Dominique	CD	1:50.70	ft	$520,000
1993	**Hollywood Wildcat**, 3	E. Delahoussaye	Paseana (Arg)	Re Toss (Arg)	SA	1:48.35	ft	$520,000
1992	**Paseana (Arg)**, 5	C. McCarron	Versailles Treaty	Magical Maiden	GP	1:48.17	ft	$520,000
1991	**Dance Smartly**, 3	P. Day	Versailles Treaty	Brought to Mind	CD	1:50.95	ft	$520,000
1990	**Bayakoa (Arg)**, 6	L. Pincay Jr.	Colonial Waters	Valay Maid	Bel	1:49⅕	ft	$450,000
1989	**Bayakoa (Arg)**, 5	L. Pincay Jr.	Gorgeous	Open Mind	GP	1:47⅖	ft	$450,000
1988	**Personal Ensign**, 4	R. Romero	Winning Colors	Goodbye Halo	CD	1:52	my	$450,000
1987	**Sacahuista**, 3	R. Romero	Clabber Girl	Oueee Bebe	Hol	2:02⅘	ft	$450,000
1986	**Lady's Secret**, 4	P. Day	Fran's Valentine	Outstandingly	SA	**2:01⅕**	ft	$450,000
1985	**Life's Magic**, 4	A. Cordero Jr.	Lady's Secret	Dontstop Themusic	Aqu	2:02	ft	$450,000
1984	**Princess Rooney**, 4	E. Delahoussaye	Life's Magic	Adored	Hol	2:02⅖	ft	$450,000

1984-'87—run at 1¼ miles; 1989 and '90—Bayakoa (Arg) supplementary entry; 1992—Paseana (Arg) supplemental entry.

Champions from race, continued

1997	**Ajina**	1	3yo filly
	Hidden Lake	7	Older female
1996	**Jewel Princess**	1	Older female
1995	**Inside Information**	1	Older female
	Serena's Song	5	3yo filly
1994	Heavenly Prize	2	3yo filly
	Sky Beauty	9	Older female
1993	**Hollywood Wildcat**	1	3yo filly
	Paseana (Arg)	2	Older female
1992	**Paseana (Arg)**	1	Older female
	Saratoga Dew	12	3yo filly
1991	**Dance Smartly**	1	3yo filly
	Queena	5	Older female
1990	**Bayakoa (Arg)**	1	Older female
	Go for Wand	DNF	3yo filly
1989	**Bayakoa (Arg)**	1	Older female
	Open Mind	3	3yo female
1988	**Personal Ensign**	1	Older female
	Winning Colors	2	3yo filly
1987	**Sacahuista**	1	3yo filly
	North Sider	6	Older female
1986	**Lady's Secret**	1	Horse of the Year, Older female
1985	**Life's Magic**	1	Older female
1984	**Princess Rooney**	1	Older female
	Life's Magic	2	3yo filly

Largest Winning Margins

Year	Winner	Margin
1995	Inside Information	13½
1984	Princess Rooney	7
1990	Bayakoa (Arg)	6¾
1985	Life's Magic	6¼
1992	Paseana (Arg)	4

Smallest Winning Margins

Year	Winner	Margin
1998	Escena	nose
1993	Hollywood Wildcat	nose
1988	Personal Ensign	nose
1994	One Dreamer	neck

Shortest-Priced Winners

Year	Horse	Odds
1985	Life's Magic	.40-to-1*
1991	Dance Smartly	.50-to-1*
1988	Personal Ensign	.50-to-1
1986	Lady's Secret	.50-to-1*
1989	Bayakoa (Arg)	.70-to-1
1984	Princess Rooney	.70-to-1
1995	Inside Information	.80-to-1*

*Part of entry

Longest-Priced Winners

Year	Horse	Odds
2000	Spain	55.90-to-1
1994	One Dreamer	47.10-to-1
2001	Unbridled Elaine	12.30-to-1
1997	Ajina	4.80-to-1*
1999	Beautiful Pleasure	3-to-1
1998	Escena	3-to-1

*Part of entry

Odds-On Beaten Favorites

Year	Horse	Odds	Finish
2000	Riboletta (Brz)	.40-to-1	7
1998	Banshee Breeze	.80-to-1	2
1990	Go for Wand	.70-to-1	DNF
1987	Infinidad (Arg)	.70-to-1	4

Fastest Winners at 1⅛ Miles

Year	Horse	Track	Time	Cond.
1995	Inside Information	Bel	1:46.15	Muddy
1997	Ajina	Hol	1:47.20	Fast
1989	Bayakoa (Arg)	GP	1:47⅖	Fast
1999	Beautiful Pleasure	GP	1:47.56	Fast
2000	Spain	CD	1:47.66	Fast

Slowest Winners at 1⅛ Miles

Year	Horse	Track	Time	Cond.
1988	Personal Ensign	CD	1:52	Muddy
1991	Dance Smartly	CD	1:50.95	Fast
1994	One Dreamer	CD	1:50.70	Fast
1998	Escena	CD	1:49.89	Fast
1990	Bayakoa (Arg)	Bel	1:49⅕	Fast
2001	Unbridled Elaine	Bel	1:49.21	Fast

Most Starters

Year	Track	Starters
1992	Gulfstream Park	14
1991	Churchill Downs	13
2001	Belmont Park	11
1995	Belmont Park	10
1989	Gulfstream Park	10

Fewest Starters

Year	Track	Starters
1996	Woodbine	6
1987	Hollywood Park	6
1990	Belmont Park	7
1985	Aqueduct	7
1984	Hollywood Park	7

Winning Post Positions

Post	Starters	Winners	Percent
1	18	4	22.2%
2	18	0	0.0%
3	18	0	0.0%
4	18	4	22.2%
5	18	4	22.2%
6	18	3	16.7%
7	16	1	6.25%
8	13	0	0.0%
9	8	0	0.0%
10	5	1	20.0%
11	3	0	0.0%
12	2	0	0.0%
13	2	0	0.0%
14	1	1	100.0%

Changes in Distaff

Two significant changes have occurred in the conditions of the Breeders' Cup Distaff. For the 1988 running, the distance was shortened to 1⅛ miles from 1¼ miles, and in 1998 the purse was increased to $2-million from $1-million.

2001 Classic: Tiznow Again

Almost from the start of the 2001 season, soft-spoken California trainer Jay Robbins was perplexed by reigning Horse of the Year Tiznow. From Tiznow's boredom to balky rebellion to mystery back ailments and lameness, Robbins said he felt at times overwhelmed by the quirks and ailments of the four-year-old Cee's Tizzy colt. On some days, it seemed that retirement might be the only answer. But Robbins's patient determination to quell the demons in Tiznow's mind and body was rewarded on October 27 when he saddled the colt for a defense of his victory in the 2000 Breeders' Cup Classic (G1).

After tracking the early pace of Orientate and Albert the Great, Tiznow was intent on overtaking Albert the Great when Godolphin Racing's European star Sakhee swooped by them and gained a half-length advantage at the furlong pole. Summoning all his reserves and powering through on pure courage, Tiznow refused to surrender in the shadowy stretch of Belmont Park. Even though jockey Chris McCarron said he felt he was riding for second place, Tiznow battled back nearing the wire.

In the final strides, in a show of sheer will even more resolute than his repelling of Giant's Causeway one year earlier, Tiznow thrust his nose ahead of Sakhee as a roar from the crowd of 52,987 reverberated through the cavernous grandstand. Both horses earned the respect due runners who engage in epic duels destined to be remembered for years, but only Tiznow would wear the victor's blanket of yellow, white, and purple flowers on his

Photo by Z

Tiznow fights back for second victory
California-bred defeats European hope Sakhee

withers.

The first California-bred to win a Breeders' Cup race a year earlier, Tiznow won another line in the record books as the first Classic winner to repeat his victory in the $4-million race. "I don't have a good enough vocabulary to describe his resolve," McCarron said. "He's absolutely awesome."

Jockey Frankie Dettori, who steered Sakhee past Tiznow with ease in the upper stretch, could barely believe the outcome. "How did [Tiznow] come back?" Dettori shouted as he jogged his gallant colt—who was making his first career start on dirt less than three weeks after winning the Prix de l'Arc de Triomphe (Fr-G1) over soft turf at Longchamp—back to be unsaddled.

Robbins seemed almost stunned as he led Tiznow into the winner's circle. "It hasn't sunk in yet," he said. "He's been, at times, the most trying horse I've ever trained, but he has certainly given me the most pleasure." Tiznow's 2001 record reflected Robbins's travails. After beginning the year with a victory in Santa Anita Park's San Fernando Breeders' Cup Stakes (G2), Tiznow finished second in Santa Anita's Strub Stakes (G2). The colt bounced back to win the Santa Anita Handicap (G1) on March 3, but then physical problems kept him away from the racetrack until late summer. He ran third in his two starts before the Breeders' Cup, in Belmont's Woodward Stakes (G1) and Santa Anita's Goodwood Breeders' Cup Handicap (G2). Although his physical problems seemed to have abated, Tiznow appeared to be determined to train himself, refusing to gallop on some days. But all was well when the starting gate opened for the 2001 Classic.

Although the second victory was sweeter in some ways than the first, co-owner Michael Cooper said he keenly missed his late business

---

Owner

Cee's Stable is a partnership of Michael Cooper of Coto de Caza, California, and the children of the late Cecilia Straub-Rubens, Pamela Ziebarth and Kevin Cochrane. Cooper, the longtime racing partner of Straub-Rubens who also helped her with her financial assets, manages the stable interests. Cooper advised Straub-Rubens to purchase Cee's Tizzy and Cee's Song, the sire and dam of Tiznow. He plans to acquire his own broodmares eventually.

Breeder

Cecilia Straub-Rubens. A devotee of racing from 1962 until her death three days after she witnessed Tiznow win the 2000 Breeders' Cup Classic at Churchill Downs, Straub-Rubens raced Australian champion Brewery Boy with her first husband, Arthur Straub, who ran an Anheuser-Busch distributing company in Orange County, California. Many of her horses carried her nickname, "Cee," in their names.

partner, Tiznow's breeder Cecilia Straub-Rubens, who died at age 83 three days after witnessing her colt's 2000 Classic victory at Churchill Downs. Retired in mid-November by Cooper and Straub-Rubens's two children, Tiznow stood his first stud season at WinStar Farm near Versailles, Kentucky.

Although he finished second, Sakhee earned the respect of the racing world and particularly American journalists who believed he should have been pointed toward the Breeders' Cup Turf (G1) rather than the Classic. In their pre-Breeders' Cup workouts, Godolphin's Fantastic Light appeared to handle Belmont's dirt track well, but Sakhee seemed uncomfortable on the surface. But Godolphin head Sheikh Mohammed bin Rashid al Maktoum, trainer Saeed bin Suroor, and the rest of the Godolphin brain trust chose to send Fantastic Light into the Turf, which he won in course-record time, and Sakhee into the Classic. Sakhee, a son of Bahri, performed admirably, but his inability to put away Tiznow early in the stretch cost him the race. In the 2001 International Classifications, Sakhee was rated as the 133-pound highweight, four pounds more than Fantastic Light.—*Michele MacDonald*

TENTH RACE
Belmont Park
October 27, 2001

1¼ miles. 18th running of the Breeders' Cup Classic (G1). Purse $4,000,000. 3-year-olds and up. Weights (Northern Hemisphere): 3-year-olds, 122 lbs. Older, 126 lbs. (Southern Hemisphere): 3-year-olds, 117 lbs. Older, 126 lbs. Fillies and mares allowed 3 lbs.

Value of race: $3,664,000. Value to winner: $2,080,000; second: $800,000; third: $480,000; fourth: $224,000; fifth: $80,000. Mutuel Pool: $6,459,980.

Horse	Wt	M/Eqt	PP	¼	½	¾	1	Str.	Fin.	Jockey	Odds $1
Tiznow	126	L	10	3¹	3ʰᵈ	3½	2¹½	3²½	1ⁿᵒ	C. McCarron	6.90
Sakhee	126	L	6	6¹½	6¹	5¹	4ʰᵈ	1½	2¹¾	L. Dettori	4.80
Albert the Great	126	L	9	2¹	2¹	1¹	1¹	2ʰᵈ	3²¾	J. Chavez	13.00
Macho Uno	122	Lbf	7	8½	9½	9½	6½	4ʰᵈ	4¹¼	G. Stevens	19.50
Guided Tour	126	Lb	2	4¹	4¹	2½	3¹	5²	5²	L. Melancon	18.20
Galileo (Ire)	122	L	5	5¹	5¹	6ʰᵈ	8½	6ʰᵈ	6½	M. Kinane	3.35
Include	126	Lb	4	9ʰᵈ	8ʰᵈ	10¹	9²½	7¹½	7¹½	J. Velazquez	10.50
Aptitude	126	Lbf	12	7ʰᵈ	7ʰᵈ	7ʰᵈ	7½	8½	8ⁿᵏ	J. Bailey	2.35*
Gander	126	Lb	8	12⁴	11¹½	8½	5ʰᵈ	10¹	9ⁿᵏ	V. Espinoza	80.75
Black Minnaloushe	122	L	3	10¹½	10¹	11¹½	10²½	9½	10¹	J. Murtagh	51.00
A Fleets Dancer	126	Lb	11	13	13	13	11²	11¹²	11¹⁸½	R. Landry	146.00
Orientate	122	L	1	1¹	1½	4ʰᵈ	13	13	12³¼	P. Day	34.25
Freedom Crest	126	L	13	11ʰᵈ	12²	12²	12²	12½	13	K. Desormeaux	68.50

OFF AT 5:41. Start: Good for all. Winner: Prevailed, gamely. Weather: Cloudy. Track: Fast.
Time: :23.27, 47.04, 1:11.32, 1:35.87, 2:00.62.

$2 Mutuel Prices:

10—TIZNOW	15.80	7.20	5.60
6—SAKHEE		7.80	4.40
9—ALBERT THE GREAT			7.80

PICK THREE 3-2-10 PAID $359.50   PICK FOUR 5-3-2-10 PAID $1,627.00
PICK SIX 12-3-5-3-2-10 (5 CORRECT) PAID $1,475.00, (6 CORRECT) PAID $262,442.00
DAILY DOUBLE 2-10 PAID $39.20   EXACTA 10-6 PAID $140.50
SUPERFECTA 10-6-9-7 PAID $24,496.00   TRIFECTA 10-6-9 PAID $1,341.00

B. c., by Cee's Tizzy—Cee's Song, by Seattle Song. Trainer Jay M. Robbins. Bred by Cecilia Straub-Rubens (Ca.).

TIZNOW tracked the leaders from outside along the backstretch, raced just off the pace between horses while five wide leaving the turn, dropped back slightly in upper stretch, dug in gamely while between horses leaving the furlong marker, battled heads apart inside Sahkee into deep stretch, and prevailed in a long drive. SAHKEE bobbled a few strides away from the gate, raced in the middle of the pack while well off the rail along the backstretch, ranged up seven wide to threaten on the turn, accelerated to the front in upper stretch, continued on the lead into deep stretch but could not hold the winner safe. ALBERT THE GREAT forced the early pace while four wide, surged to the front nearing the far turn, extended his lead on the turn, maintained a slim advantage into upper stretch, relinquished the lead to Sahkee in midstretch, then held well to gain a share. MACHO UNO was unhurried early, raced well back for a half, closed the gap between horses to reach contention on the turn but could not sustain his rally. GUIDED TOUR settled in good position while saving ground, angled between horses while launching his bid near the far turn, remained a factor to the top of the stretch, then weakened in the drive. GALILEO (Ire) was well placed just behind the early leaders, raced within striking distance between horses to the turn, then lacked a strong closing bid. INCLUDE reserved early, gained some ground along the rail midway on the turn, then flattened out. APTITUDE was strung out seven wide along the backstretch, continued very wide while lodging a mild rally on the turn, then lacked a further response. GANDER steadied while being pinched back at the start, moved up while wide along the backstretch, angled out on the far turn, rallied just inside Aptitude nearing the stretch, then tired. BLACK MINNALOUSHE steadied in traffic between horses on the far turn but failed to threaten thereafter. A FLEETS DANCER never reached contention after being shuffled back in the early stages. ORIENTATE dueled along the rail to the far turn, then gave way and was not abused in the late stages. FREEDOM CREST was never a factor while racing wide.

2001 Turf: Fantastic Choice

Godolphin Racing, the enterprise led by Dubai Crown Prince Sheikh Mohammed bin Rashid al Maktoum, has always kept its own counsel, and it has never lacked doubters. With some success, the operation has prepared its horses in Dubai for the European racing season despite the sneers of traditionalists who said the strategy would never work.

Godolphin's collective judgment was questioned again in the days leading up to the 2001 Breeders' Cup World Thoroughbred Championships. American journalists in particular were all over the Godolphin Racing brain trust—the Maktoum brothers, racing manager Simon Crisford, senior adviser John Ferguson, and trainer Saeed bin Suroor—over their strategy in the Breeders' Cup Turf (G1) and Breeders' Cup Classic (G1). Questions arose not so much for choosing to run Fantastic Light in the Breeders' Cup Turf. After all, the five-year-old Rahy horse was at worst one of the three best 1½-mile horses in Europe and a certain favorite in the Turf.

No, what seemed really crazy to American pundits was the decision to run his stablemate Sakhee in the Breeders' Cup Classic instead of the Turf after he appeared to work uncomfortably over Belmont Park's main track on October 23. Godolphin's judgments were vindicated when Fantastic Light set a Belmont Park course record for 1½ miles on a firm Widener Turf Course, holding off the late charge of Michael Tabor's and Susan Magnier's Milan (GB) by three-quarters of a length in 2:24.36. Timboroa (GB) finished third, another 5¾ lengths farther back. Sakhee, the Prix de l'Arc de Triomphe (Fr-G1) victor, then

Adam Coglianese/NYRA photo

Fantastic Light triumphs for Godolphin
European champion holds off Milan's late bid

finished a courageous second to Tiznow in the Classic.

"Everybody say, 'Godolphin, they are crazy,' but I think we are not really," Suroor said at the close of Breeders' Cup day on October 27. "Sometimes really [we are], but other times we are okay."

Fantastic Light has always been a good horse, but as a five-year-old he became something fantastic. Bred in Kentucky by Sheikh Maktoum bin Rashid al Maktoum's Gainsborough Farm out of Jood, by Nijinsky II, the Turf winner began his racing career in England under the care of Sir Michael Stoute. Winner of two of three starts at two, he improved at three, when his three wins in seven starts included the Great Voltigeur Stakes (Eng-G2). Transferred to Godolphin and trainer Suroor as a four-year-old, Fantastic Light collected his first Grade 1 in the Man o' War Stakes at Belmont but finished fifth in the 2000 Turf at Churchill Downs.

Fantastic Light began his final year of racing with a nose loss to the Japanese mare Stay Gold in the Dubai Sheema Classic (UAE-G2) but then won Ireland's Tattersalls Gold Cup Stakes (Ire-G1) in May and the Prince of Wales's Stakes (Eng-G1) in June. The Godolphin horse finished second in the 2001 King George VI and Queen Elizabeth Stakes (Eng-G1), beaten by the brilliant three-year-old Galileo (Ire). He earned his 7-to-5 favoritism in the Turf through a thrilling conquest of Galileo in the Irish Champion Stakes (Ire-G1) on September 8.

In the Turf, rider Frankie Dettori positioned Fantastic Light in fifth early as With Anticipation and then Timboroa set the pace. Fantastic Light moved into second on the bit around the final turn and then burst past Timboroa at the head of the stretch. In trouble on the turn, Milan

---

Owner

Godolphin Stable is a partnership that includes certain horses owned by the four Maktoum brothers: Sheikhs Maktoum, Hamdan, Mohammed, and Ahmed bin Rashid al Maktoum, and managed by Sheikh Mohammed. The stable is trained by Saeed bin Suroor and winters annually in Dubai. The Turf was Godolphin's third Breeders' Cup victory following Daylami (Ire)'s Turf win in 1999 and Tempera's Juvenile Fillies (G1) win in 2001.

Breeder

Gainsborough Farm is the American arm (located near Versailles, Kentucky) of Sheikh Maktoum bin Rashid al Maktoum's Gainsborough Stud Management. Sheikh Maktoum is the ruler of the Emirate of Dubai in the United Arab Emirates. Fantastic Light is Gainsborough's first Breeders' Cup winner.

closed a lot of ground in the stretch but never threatened the winner.

In November, Fantastic Light was voted recipient of Cartier Awards as Europe's Horse of the Year and champion older male. Godolphin announced he would begin his stud career at Sheikh Mohammed's Dalham Hall Stud in Newmarket, England.

"I was always in control, and he has got a good turn of foot," Dettori said. "He did lose a bit of concentration in front, and he was looking at everything, but I was never in danger of getting caught. Like good wine, he gets better with age."

Michael Kinane, on 7.50-to-1 fourth choice Milan, was a bit less fortunate but had no real excuses. "He was a little bit unlucky," Kinane said, "because I got a little bit tangled up on the turn as Muta-

mam (GB) tightened up on us. He [Fantastic Light] got four or five lengths on me, and that made it tough. I thought I just had too much to do. Milan is a very high-class colt. He's probably been a little overshadowed by Galileo (Ire), but he's come into his own."

Winner of the classic St. Leger Stakes (Eng-G1), Milan closed brilliantly from impossibly far back to finish fifth to Sakhee in the Prix de l'Arc de Triomphe (Fr-G1) in his previous start. "He ran a great race," said Irish bloodstock agent Demi O'Byrne, who purchased Milan for Tabor and Magnier for $1,122,440 at the 1999 Tattersalls Ltd. Houghton yearling sale. Third choice (5.60-to-1) Hap, the best American hope, failed to stay the trip and finished fifth. With Anticipation, 3.95-to-1, wilted under early pressure and finished seventh.—*John P. Sparkman*

NINTH RACE
Belmont Park
October 27, 2001

1½ miles on turf. 18th running of the Breeders' Cup Turf (G1). Purse $2-million. 3-year-olds and up. Weights (Northern Hemisphere): 3-year-olds, 122 lbs. Older, 126 lbs. (Southern Hemisphere): 3-year-olds, 117 lbs. Older, 126 lbs. Fillies and mares allowed 3 lbs.

Value of race $1,960,240; Winner $1,112,800; second $428,000; third $256,800; fourth $119,840; fifth $42,800. Mutuel Pool $3,816,494.

Horse	Wt	M/Eqt	PP	¼	½	1m	1¼	Str.	Fin.	Jockey	Odds $1
Fantastic Light	126	L	2	5¹½	5½	4½	2²	12½	1¾	L. Dettori	1.40*
Milan (GB)	121	L	11	9²½	9¹	9¹	5hd	3³	2⁵¾	M. Kinane	7.50
Timboroa (GB)	126	L	7	3¹	1hd	1¹	1²	2¹	3¾	E. Prado	8.30
Blazing Fury	121	Lb	3	10½	10³	10½	8²½	54½	43¼	C. Nakatani	51.50
Hap	126	L	10	6hd	6½	6½	3²	4hd	5²	J. Bailey	5.60
Chorwon	126	L	4	11	11	11	9¹½	7½	6½	J. Court	58.50
With Anticipation	126	Lb	1	1hd	2hd	3hd	6hd	6½	7¹	P. Day	3.95
Lodge Hill	126	L	5	8¹½	8²	7½	7½	83½	85½	J. Velazquez	57.25
Slew the Red	126		6	7hd	7hd	8½	11	9⁴	94¾	O. Peslier	58.00
Quiet Resolve	126	L	8	2hd	3hd	2hd	4hd	10⁹	1018¼	R. Albarado	38.50
Mutamam (GB)	126	L	9	4½	4¹½	5hd	10hd	11	11	R. Hills	11.30

Scratched: Slew Valley

OFF AT 5:01. Start: Good for all. Weather: Cloudy. Track: Firm. Won: Driving.
Time: :24.40, :48.02, 1:12.34, 1:36.66, 2:01.15, 2:24.36.

	2—FANTASTIC LIGHT	4.80	4.20	3.10
$2 Mutuel Prices:	12—MILAN (GB)		7.10	4.50
	8—TIMBOROA (GB)			4.60

PICK THREE 5-3-2 PAID $291.50   EXACTA 2-12 PAID $33.60
SUPERFECTA 2-12-8-3 PAID $3,965.00   TRIFECTA 2-12-8 PAID $211.00

B. h., by Rahy—Jood, by Nijinsky II. Trainer Saeed bin Suroor. Bred by Gainsborough Farm, Inc. (Ky.).

FANTASTIC LIGHT settled in good position along the backstretch, launched a rally between horses midway on the turn, closed the gap in upper stretch, charged to the front nearing the furlong marker, then held off MILAN under steady right hand urging. MILAN (GB) was reserved for six furlongs, moved out along the backstretch, circled five wide rallying into the stretch, then finished well along the inside, but could not overtake the winner. TIMBOROA (GB) rushed up to contest the early pace, took the lead along the backstretch, shook loose on the turn, relinquished the lead to the winner nearing the furlong marker, then weakened from his early efforts. BLAZING FURY was outrun for a mile while saving ground, swung five wide on the turn, then improved his position with a mild late rally. HAP was strung out four wide on the first turn, raced in the middle of the pack while wide along the backstretch, gained a bit on the turn, but could not sustain his rally. CHORWON failed to mount a serious rally while six wide on the turn. WITH ANTICIPATION took the lead soon after the start, set or forced the pace along the rail for a little more than a mile, and steadily tired thereafter. LODGE HILL raced within striking distance along the inside to the far turn, steadied sharply midway on the turn, and failed to threaten thereafter. SLEW THE RED was shuffled back between horses on the far turn, then lacked a further response. QUIET RESOLVE forced the pace three wide to the far turn and faltered. MUTAMAM (GB) chased the leaders four wide for a mile and gave way.

2001 Juvenile: Questions Answered

In the days leading up to the Breeders' Cup World Thoroughbred Championships on October 27, questions lingered over whether the leading European contenders could adapt to a switch from turf to the sandy loam of Belmont Park's expansive main track.

Aidan O'Brien, in the midst of the best season in European racing history as head conditioner for Coolmore Stud, was eager to see if Johannesburg could make the adjustment effectively enough to compete in the Breeders' Cup Juvenile (G1).

There were no doubts about the class of the two-year-old son of Hennessy, who was undefeated in six starts. Another unknown was his lack of experience beyond six furlongs and if the 1 1/16-mile trip was within Johannesburg's scope.

Despite the tough obstacles, which included a trans-Atlantic flight just four days before the race, both questions were answered with an emphatic yes.

Michael Tabor's and Susan Magnier's Johannesburg answered the call, handled the dirt and distance, and toyed with the best field of American juveniles assembled in 2001 when he posted a 1 1/4-length win over Repent in the $916,000 Breeders' Cup Juvenile on October 27. Siphonic, winner of the Lane's End Breeders' Futurity Stakes (G2) in his previous start on October 6, finished 1 1/4 lengths farther back in third, while the heaviest favorite on the program, 0.75-to-1 Officer, checked in a disappointing fifth. Michael Kinane

Photo by Z

Johannesburg shines brilliantly
Draws away to an easy victory in his first dirt start

rode the winner, who was dismissed as the 7.20-to-1 third choice in the field of 12. Johannesburg ran the 1 1/16 miles in 1:42.27 on a fast track.

"This horse was six-for-six, and I think the Americans overlooked him a little bit," Kinane said. "He's the general, and the other one is the Officer."

Johannesburg's victory over Repent was his fourth consecutive Group 1 or Grade 1 win in as many countries, and the $200,000 Keeneland September yearling purchase gave O'Brien his first Breeders' Cup win.

Johannesburg came into the Juvenile from victories in the Phoenix Stakes at Leopardstown in Ireland, the Prix Morny at Deauville in France, and the Middle Park Stakes at Newmarket in England. All three races were at six furlongs, and the only other distance at which Johannesburg had competed was five furlongs when he won the Norfolk Stakes (Eng-G3) at Royal Ascot.

Kinane assured O'Brien that seven furlongs would be easily within Johannesburg's scope, but doubts still lingered. "We had a lot of concerns," O'Brien said. "Obviously, he's raced only on turf and soft turf. But he handled that so well."

"He's been a champion every step of the way," Kinane said. "We always thought he was made for the dirt, and he proved it."

Aside from the runners in the Breeders' Cup Classic (G1), the Bob Baffert-trained Officer attracted the most attention during the week leading up to the Breeders' Cup. The California-bred son of Bertrando had won his five career starts with devastating ease, including a 3 3/4-length tally in the Champagne Stakes (G1) at Belmont.

Officer finished 5 1/4 lengths behind Johannesburg after breaking from the inside and getting into a protracted speed duel with Hopeful Stakes (G1) winner Came Home. Siphonic gained the lead in midstretch but had no answer for Johannesburg's winning charge.

Owners

Michael Tabor and **Susan Magnier**. Tabor made a fortune through the ownership of a string of betting shops in England, which he sold to the Coral bookmaking firm for a reported $15-million to $35-million. He started to increase his Thoroughbred holdings in 1994 and today is one of the most active buyers at European and American public auctions. Magnier is the wife of Coolmore Stud master John Magnier and the daughter of legendary European trainer Vincent O'Brien.

Breeder

Wayne G. Lyster III and **Jayeff B Stables**. A resident of Versailles, Kentucky, Lyster owns the 250-acre Ashview Farm, which he started with just nine acres in 1978. Lyster's history in the industry dates back to 1967, and his current breeding operation includes 15 mares owned in partnership and another 25 mares boarded for clients. Jayeff B Stables, a partnership between Brooklyn, New York, natives Richard Santulli and George Prussin, bred and raced Grade 1 winner Ciro, and campaigned champion and Breeders' Cup Sprint (G1) winner Safely Kept.

onTrack

"Johannesburg had the perfect style," Baffert said. "We need that style if we're going to be effective. You can't do it on the front end like that, especially going one turn. You can do that on two turns, but not one turn."

Johannesburg's European season and his Breeders' Cup Juvenile victory earned him a Cartier Award as Europe's champion two-year-old male.

"He's a wonderful horse," O'Brien said. "He's a natural in everything he does. He has such speed, which we knew was his forte. The way he travels is something beautiful. Obviously, he can go anywhere."

The Juvenile also provided further vindication for the investment strategy of Coolmore, headed by John Magnier, co-owner Susan Magnier's husband. Demi O'Byrne serves as the chief talent-spotter and buyer for the Coolmore combine. O'Byrne purchased the colt for $200,000 at the 2000 Keeneland September yearling sale.

Kentucky Cup Juvenile Stakes (G3) winner Repent, sent out by trainer Ken McPeek and dismissed at 42.25-to-1, rallied strongly in the stretch under rookie Breeders' Cup rider Tony D'Amico to earn the place spot. McPeek, who trained Tejano Run to a second-place finish in the 1995 Kentucky Derby, was pleased with the race and the prospects for Select Stable's Louis Quatorze colt. "He's every bit as good as Tejano Run, maybe better. He'll be formidable," McPeek said.

Trainer David Hofmans said he was pleased with the effort turned in by Siphonic, a son of freshman sire Siphon (Brz) who broke from the rail and was making just his third start for owners John and Jerry Amerman.—*Tom Law*

EIGHTH RACE
Belmont Park
October 27, 2001

1¹⁄₁₆ miles. 18th running of the Breeders' Cup Juvenile (G1). Purse $1-million. Colts and geldings, 2-year-olds. Weight: 122 lbs.

Value of race: $916,000. Value to winner: $520,000; second: $200,000; third: $120,000; fourth: $56,000; fifth, $20,000. Mutuel Pool $4,200,733.

Horse	Wgt.	M/Eqt	PP	St.	¼	½	¾	Str.	Fin.	Jockey	Odds $1
Johannesburg	122	L	3	11	5hd	5hd	5²½	4²	1¹¼	M. Kinane	7.20
Repent	122	Lb	10	8	9²½	8½	7¹½	6²½	2¹¼	A. D'Amico	42.25
Siphonic	122	L	1	6	3hd	4hd	4hd	1hd	3¾	J. Bailey	9.30
Publication	122	Lb	6	10	12	12	11²½	7²½	4²	M. Smith	103.25
Officer	122	Lb	2	12	2¹½	1hd	1hd	2hd	5hd	V. Espinoza	0.75*
French Assault	122	L	7	4	6½	6²½	3½	5hd	6hd	K. Desormeaux	61.50
Came Home	122	L	11	2	1hd	2¹½	2½	3hd	7nk	C. McCarron	5.00
Saarland	122	L	9	9	10½	10¹½	9hd	8²½	8⁶½	J. Velazquez	21.60
Ibn Al Haitham (GB)	122	L	8	3	7¹½	7²½	6²½	9³½	9²¼	D. Flores	94.25
It'sallinthechase	122	L	12	1	11¹½	11²	12	10½	10¹¾	R. Williams	147.25
Jump Start	122	Lb	5	5	8½	9²½	10½	11½	11⁴	P. Day	12.30
Essence of Dubai	122	Lb	4	7	4hd	3hd	8¹½	12	12	A. Solis	33.25

OFF AT 4:28. Start: Good for all. Weather: Cloudy. Track: Fast. Won: Driving.
Time: :23.61, :46.85, 1:11.01, 1:36.01, 1:42.27.

$2 Mutuel Prices:	3—JOHANNESBURG	16.40	8.60	6.00
	10—REPENT		25.00	13.40
	1—SIPHONIC			7.90

PICK THREE 3-5-3 PAID $1,609.00 EXACTA 3-10 PAID $530.00
SUPERFECTA 3-10-1-6 PAID $56,927.00 TRIFECTA 3-10-1 PAID $3,665.00

B. c., by Hennessy—Myth, by Ogygian. Trainer Aidan O'Brien. Bred by W. G. Lyster III and Jayeff "B" Stables (Ky.).

JOHANNESBURG raced close up between rivals while under wraps, waited patiently while surrounded by rivals approaching the stretch, angled out in upper stretch, found room between rivals nearing the eighth pole, burst through when set down, and drew clear under a drive. REPENT was outrun early, raced three wide, responded when asked for run, and finished gamely outside to earn the place award. SIPHONIC raced close up inside while in hand, got through on the rail to earn a short lead approaching the eighth pole, and stayed on gamely inside. PUBLICATION was outrun early, swung wide into the stretch, and was going well from the far outside late. OFFICER was hustled up inside, contested the pace, and tired in the final furlong. FRENCH ASSAULT raced close up outside, put in a four wide run on the turn, and tired in the stretch. CAME HOME contested the pace from the outside and gave way leaving the eighth pole. SAARLAND was outrun early, raced wide, and had no response when roused. IBN AL HAITHAM (GB) was hustled along outside, chased the pace while four wide, and tired in the stretch. IT'SALLINTHECHASE stumbled after the start, dropped back, and tired. JUMP START had no reponse when roused, tired, and was vanned off after the finish. ESSENCE OF DUBAI chased the pace while three wide and tired after three quarters.

2001 Filly and Mare Turf: Money in Banks

Juddmonte Farms, the racing and breeding operation of Saudi Arabian Prince Khalid Abdullah, has accounted for most of the world's best races, but until 2001 Juddmonte had been blanked repeatedly in the Breeders' Cup. In a year when European interests enjoyed their best overall performance in the World Thoroughbred Championships series, Juddmonte collected its first Breeders' Cup win in 32 attempts with Banks Hill (GB) in the third running of the $1-million Filly and Mare Turf (G1). By leading dual-hemisphere sire Danehill, three-year-old Banks Hill is trained in France by Andre Fabre.

A filly who prefers firm ground, Banks Hill found the type of surface she savors at Belmont Park, whose inner turf course was rated as firm for the Filly and Mare Turf. She had finished second in the Poule d'Essai des Pouliches (Fr-G1) (French One Thousand Guineas) and had won the Coronation Stakes (Eng-G1) against other three-year-old fillies at Ascot in June. "Soft is not her turf," said jockey Olivier Peslier, who rode her in the Breeders' Cup. "On the firm ground, she runs better. Ascot is very hard."

In her two starts prior to the Breeders' Cup on October 27, Banks Hill had run well against older horses without winning, finishing second

Patricia McQueen photo

Banks Hill breaks losing skein for Juddmonte
French-trained filly dominates her opponents

in both the Prix du Haras de Fresnay-le-Buffard-Jacques le Marois (Fr-G1) and the Prix du Moulin de Longchamp (Fr-G1) in early September. Juddmonte racing manager Teddy Beckett said the plan had been to run her in the Prix de l'Opera (Fr-G1) on October 7 but, when the Longchamp course came up soggy, he and Fabre decided to train Banks Hill up to the Breeders' Cup.

Banks Hill went off at 6-to-1, the fourth betting choice, because of her starts preceding the long layoff and because she had never raced beyond one mile in her seven career races. But both Beckett and Fabre were confident she would stay the Filly and Mare Turf's distance, at 1¼ miles for the first time. "We were really confident she was going to get a mile and a quarter," Beckett said. "Her sire, Danehill, had a lot of speed, and her dam, Hasili, was a staying mare."

Favored at 2.65-to-1 was England's Legend (Fr), runaway winner of Arlington Park's Beverly D. Stakes (G1) in August. The 2.75-to-1 second pick was Lailani (GB), who had defeated England's Legend in Belmont's Flower Bowl Invitational Stakes (G1) in late September. Third choice at 5.40-to-1 was Starine (Fr), owned and trained by Juddmonte's principal American trainer, Bobby Frankel. Winner of Saratoga Race Course's Diana Handicap (G2) in early September, Starine had finished third in the Flower Bowl. As it turned out, none of the three favorites would finish anywhere close to Banks Hill.

Banks Hill's lack of competition surprised Peslier. "I started to think there was one more turn because I didn't hear anyone coming," he said. Banks Hill reached the finish with a 5½-length advantage over Spook Express (SAf), a 20% sup-

Owner-Breeder

Juddmonte Farms is the international breeding operation of Prince Khalid Abdullah of Saudi Arabia. Abdullah is one of the most successful owners-breeders in the world, annually producing runners of the highest class that compete in both Europe and North America. He has won an Eclipse Award as outstanding owner in 1992 and as outstanding breeder in '95. His Juddmonte Farm near Lexington is 2,500 acres, and he owns four farms in England, including Banstead Manor, and two in Ireland, including Ferrans Stud. His best runners in Europe include Known Fact, Dancing Brave, Quest for Fame (GB), Zafonic, and Commander in Chief, and in North America he has been represented by Tinners Way, Skimming, Senure, Marquetry, Chester House, Defensive Play, Wandesta (GB), Ryafan, and Exbourne. In the 2001 Breeders' Cup, he was represented by homebreds Aptitude in the Classic (G1) and Flute in the Distaff (G1). Prior to 2001, he was represented by 30 Breeders' Cup starters as an owner or breeder. A first cousin and brother-in-law of King Faud and father-in-law of the late Fahd Salman, Abdullah is a semi-retired businessman whose international operation under the Mawared Inc. banner is involved in catering, electronics, cement, and insurance.

plemental entry, in 2:00.36. Spring Oak (GB) finished third, 1¾ lengths farther back. Lailani finished eighth, the best showing among the favorites. Starine was tenth, and England's Legend faded to 11th in the field of 12.

After having to check shortly after the start, Banks Hill was taken to the inside by Peslier and assumed a good position early in the race. Moving along the rail in the backstretch, Banks Hill stayed coiled in a contending position. By the time she reached the quarter pole, she had advanced into second, a head behind England's Legend, who had recorded moderate fractions of :24.21, :48.65, 1:13.55, and 1:37.69 for the first mile.

Peslier, who was shooting for his first career Breeders' Cup victory, was exactly where he wanted to be. "She had a good draw [fifth post position], and I just wanted to stay behind England's Legend," he said. Leaving the turn for home, Banks Hill bade farewell to the fast-fading England's Legend, who bumped Crystal Music off stride and effectively knocked her out of the race as she was advancing on the leaders. In that instant, the 12-horse contest was transformed into a one-horse race. —*Neil Milbert*

SEVENTH RACE
Belmont Park
October 27, 2001

1¼ miles on turf. 3rd running of the Breeders' Cup Filly and Mare Turf (G1). Purse $1-million. Fillies and mares 3-year-olds and up. Weights (Northern Hemisphere): 3-year-olds, 119 lbs. Older, 123 lbs. (Southern Hemisphere): 3-year-olds, 114 lbs. Older, 123 lbs.

Value of race: $1,273,240. Value to winner: $722,800; second: $278,000; third: $166,800; fourth: $77,840; fifth, $27,800. Mutuel Pool $3,730,972.

Horse	Wt	M/Eqt	PP	¼	½	¾	1	Str.	Fin.	Jockey	Odds $1
Banks Hill (GB)	119		5	3hd	4½	3hd	2¹	1⁵	1⁵½	O. Peslier	6.00
Spook Express (SAf)	123	L	1	10¹	8½	9½	9½	4½	2¹¾	M. Smith	13.70
Spring Oak (GB)	119		11	8½	7½	8½	5½	3½	3nk	L. Dettori	36.75
Solvig	123	Lf	8	7¹	10²½	7½	7½	2½	4nk	P. Day	34.25
Volga (Ire)	119	L	6	12	12	12	12	10½	5¹	J. Santos	13.20
Kalypso Katie (Ire)	123	L	7	11²½	11²	11²½	10²	8hd	6nk	G. Stevens	18.80
Crystal Music	119	L	9	5hd	6½	6hd	4½	7½	7¼	C. McCarron	35.00
Lailani (GB)	119	L	12	6¹	5½	5¹	6½	9²	8nk	J. Bailey	2.75
Chaste	123	L	4	9½	9hd	10½	11¹½	11¹	9²¾	E. Prado	79.00
Starine (Fr)	123	Lb	10	4½	3¹	2hd	3½	6hd	10²	J. Velazquez	5.40
England's Legend (Fr)	123	L	2	1¹	1¹	1½	1hd	5hd	11⁷	C. Nakatani	2.65*
Mot Juste (GB)	119	L	3	2½	2hd	4½	8¹	12	12	M. Kinane	21.20

OFF AT 3:52. Start: Good for all. Winner: Driving. Weather: Clear. Track: Firm.
Time: :24.21, :48.65, 1:13.55, 1:37.69, 2:00.36.

	$2 Mutuel Prices:			
	5—BANKS HILL (GB)	14.00	9.20	6.10
	1—SPOOK EXPRESS (SAf)		11.40	7.70
	11—SPRING OAK (GB)			11.60

PICK THREE 12-3-5 PAID $1,641.00   EXACTA 5-1 PAID $229.00
TRIFECTA 5-1-11 PAID $5,166.00 $2 SUPERFECTA 5-1-11-8 PAID $44,331.00

B. f., by Danehill—=Hasili (Ire), by =Kahyasi. Trainer Andre Fabre. Bred by Juddmonte Farms (GB).

BANKS HILL (GB) checked slightly then angled to the inside in the early stages, settled in good position along the backstretch, rallied along the rail to take the lead leaving the turn, opened a clear advantage in upper stretch, then drew off with authority under a vigorous hand ride. SPOOK EXPRESS (SAf) was taken in hand while behind horses along the inside going into the first turn, raced in the two path while well back for five furlongs, waited patiently for room behind horses on the turn, angled to the outside in upper stretch, then finished well in the middle of the track to clearly best the others. SPRING OAK (GB) was unhurried for five furlongs, ranged up while in hand on the turn, made a run six wide to threaten at the top of the stretch, then hung a bit in the final sixteenth. SOLVIG was outrun while saving ground along the backstretch, closed the gap a bit along the rail leaving the turn, was bumped slightly while rallying in upper stretch, then flattened out in the final eighth. VOLGA (Ire) trailed to the turn, angled to the middle of the track in upper stretch, then failed to threaten while improving her position. KALYPSO KATIE (Ire) was outrun for six furlongs, circled seven wide into the stretch, drifted in nearing the furlong marker, then lacked a strong closing response. CRYSTAL MUSIC was reserved early, gained between horses on the turn, steadied between horses while being bumped by England's Legend in upper stretch, and failed to threaten thereafter. LAILANI (GB) was hung five wide on the first turn, continued wide while just off the pace along the backstretch, dropped back slightly on the turn, then steadied in tight between horses while tiring in midstretch. CHASTE checked slightly on the far turn, failed to mount a serious rally while saving ground. STARINE (Fr) chased the leaders while three wide for a half, lodged a brief bid from outside on the turn, then faded in the stretch. ENGLAND'S LEGEND (Fr) set the pace while racing out from the rail to the turn, came in to bump with Crystal Music in upper stretch, then gave way. MOT JUSTE (GB) forced the pace from outside on the turn and tired.

2001 Sprint: Drought Ends

The $1-million Breeders' Cup Sprint (G1) was the fourth of eight World Thoroughbred Championship races on October 27, and by then the longest, most notable shutout in Breeders' Cup history had extended to 38 defeats. Bobby Frankel, a Racing Hall of Fame and Eclipse Award-winning trainer, had lost with Flute in the Breeders' Cup Distaff (G1) (seventh as the 1.15-to-1 favorite) and You in the Breeders' Cup Juvenile Fillies (G1) (fourth as the 0.95-to-1 favorite). He had no starter in the Breeders' Cup Mile (G1) and figured that Squirtle Squirt, a three-year-old owned by David J. Lanzman, was his fourth-best chance of getting a Breeders' Cup victory.

But Squirtle Squirt got the job done for Frankel and Lanzman, then 44, a former rock 'n' roll band member who owns a real estate mortgage company in Los Angeles. Ridden by Jerry Bailey, Squirtle Squirt allowed speedsters Xtra Heat and Caller One to soften each other up on the front end before surging from just off the pace in the final furlong to win by a half-length in 1:08.41 for six furlongs. Xtra Heat finished second, with Caller One a neck farther back in third. Swept Overboard finished fourth, while defending sprint champion and 3.50-to-1 favorite Kona Gold showed little rally and finished seventh.

Frankel, who in recent years has had his greatest success with handicap horses that race over longer distances, took over the training of Squirtle Squirt in the spring of the colt's three-year-old season. Lanzman, who began sneaking into Hollywood Park at age 13 and betting money he earned from scalping tickets at the nearby Forum in Inglewood, California, said he sought out Frankel because he had trained Marquetry, Squir-

Adam Coglianese/NYRA photo

Squirtle Squirt wins for Frankel
Three-year-old overtakes game filly Xtra Heat

tle Squirt's sire. He said he also chose Frankel because "I figured he was the only one on the planet who wanted a Breeders' Cup win more than I did."

Lanzman, whose 20 horses included eight in training, acquired the colt at the 2000 Barretts March sale of two-year-olds in training for $25,000. Lanzman thought the colt would sell for between $80,000 and $150,000 and was unaware that he had a substantial bone chip in his knee.

Named after the favorite Pokemon character of one of Lanzman's sons, Squirtle Squirt won the 2000 Hollywood Juvenile Championship Stakes (G3) but was off the board in the Best Pal Stakes (G3) and Del Mar Futurity (G2) while trained by Joe Garcia Jr. Lanzman learned of the knee chip only after the colt had won Fairplex Park's Barretts Juvenile Stakes in September 2000. The chip was successfully removed and the colt came back to win an allowance race in May, eight months later.

Frankel, who took over the colt's training early in 2001, immediately recognized that Squirtle Squirt was meant to sprint and sent him out for second-place finishes in two seven-furlong California stakes, the Lazaro Barrera Memorial Stakes (G3) and the Triple Bend Breeders' Cup Invitational Handicap (G2). Frankel then shipped the colt to Saratoga Race Course for the King's Bishop Stakes (G1) in August and obtained the services of Bailey, the sport's leading jockey in 2001. Favored at 3-to-2, Squirtle Squirt won the seven-furlong King's Bishop by 3¼ lengths but then finished second to four-year-old Left Bank in Belmont Park's Vosburgh Stakes (G1), also at seven furlongs, on September 22.

The question in the Sprint was whether Squirtle Squirt would be part of the pace with Xtra Heat, a $5,000 yearling with a ten-for-ten record at six furlongs, and Caller One, who had been

---

Owner

David Lanzman, owner of a real estate mortgage company, spent more than a decade singing for various California rock 'n' roll bands. He still plays "serious" softball in the highest-rated league in Los Angeles. He bought his first horse in 1991 and now owns 20, including stakes-placed Ima Mile High Guy.

Breeder

Audrey Narducci, M.D., is a board-certified surgeon and a member of the Society of Laparo-endoscopic (abdominal wall) Surgeons in Jasper, Indiana. She is a member of the United States Dressage Federation, in which she competes former racehorse Dangerous Double. She is also a part of the horse adoption programs Crossed Sabers Stables and Second Wind Adoption.

on the lead in 14 of 15 starts. Bailey, who chose to ride Squirtle Squirt over Delaware Township, was well aware how important the pace would be for his horse. "Ideally, I'd like for him to relax about a length or so off the leaders," Bailey said two days before the Sprint, "but I don't know if he'll do that. It's a tough race."

Indeed it was, and 17.50-to-1 Xtra Heat answered the pace question immediately by going to the lead on the rail under Jorge Chavez, riding the three-year-old filly for injured jockey Rick Wilson. Caller One was outside her, and 9.60-to-1 Squirtle Squirt was right behind them. The first quarter-mile went in an honest but unspectacular :22.45. Caller One and Corey Nakatani pressed Xtra Heat, but she still led by

one length after a half-mile in :44.75. Squirtle Squirt was exactly where Bailey wanted him, a little bit more than one length off the lead. "I was hoping he'd relax if they outran him, and he did," Bailey said. Caller One surged again in the middle of the track, but Xtra Heat was not wilting despite racing on a rail that was dead the entire day. Bailey, meanwhile, sent Squirtle Squirt between them, and he wore the filly down in the final yards to secure the victory.

The race yielded two champions and certainly contributed to Bobby Frankel's third Eclipse Award as outstanding trainer. Squirtle Squirt was voted champion sprinter, and Xtra Heat was honored as champion three-year-old filly.

— Bill Heller

SIXTH RACE
Belmont Park
October 27, 2001

6 furlongs. 18th running of the Breeders' Cup Sprint (G1). Purse $1-million. 3-year-olds and up. Weights (Northern Hemisphere): 3-year-olds, 124 lbs. Older, 126 lbs. (Southern Hemisphere): 3-year-olds, 122 lbs. Older, 126 lbs. Fillies and mares allowed 3 lbs.

Value of race $916,000; Winner $520,000; second $200,000; third $120,000; fourth $56,000; fifth $20,000. Mutuel Pool $4,409,177.

Horse	Wgt.	M/Eqt	PP	St.	¼	½	Str.	Fin.	Jockey	Odds $1
Squirtle Squirt	124	L	3	2	3hd	3hd	32	1½	J. Bailey	9.60
Xtra Heat	121	L	1	1	1hd	11	11	2nk	J. Chavez	17.50
Caller One	126	Lbf	6	3	2½	2½	2hd	3nk	C. Nakatani	11.20
Swept Overboard	126	L	12	14	12hd	10½	4½	41½	E. Delahoussaye	4.90
Left Bank	126	Lbf	8	10	51½	61	61½	5nk	J. Velazquez	8.90
Delaware Township	126	L	7	8	81½	7hd	7½	61¼	E. Coa	10.50
Kona Gold	126	L	4	5	11hd	136	82½	71	A. Solis	*3.50
Five Star Day	126	L	9	6	4½	4½	5½	81¾	G. Garrett	48.50
Peeping Tom	126	Lb	13	12	134	121	11½	92½	S. Bridgmohan	73.75
Alannan	126	Lf	5	9	9½	9½	91½	10½	E. Prado	102.25
Mozart (Ire)	124	L	11	11	101	11hd	121	113	M. Kinane	11.20
El Corredor	126	L	10	4	7½	82	10½	122¾	V. Espinoza	4.40
Bet On Sunshine	126	Lf	2	13	14	14	14	132¾	C. Borel	24.50
Hook and Ladder	126	Lb	14	7	6½	5hd	132½	14	R. Migliore	92.25

OFF AT 3:18. Start: Good for all. Weather: Clear. Track: Fast. Won: Driving.
Time: :22.45, :44.75, :56.30, 1:08.41.

$2 Mutuel Prices:	3—SQUIRTLE SQUIRT	21.20	10.60	9.20
	1—XTRA HEAT		16.20	13.20
	6—CALLER ONE			10.00

PICK THREE 9-12-3 PAID $2,396.00   EXACTA 3-1 PAID $290.00
SUPERFECTA 3-1-6-12 PAID $27,799.00   TRIFECTA 3-1-6 PAID $2,162.00

Dkbbr. c., by Marquetry—Lost the Code, by Lost Code. Trainer Robert Frankel. Bred by Dr. Audrey Narducci (Ky.).

SQUIRTLE SQUIRT raced close up inside, responded when roused nearing the stretch, split rivals in midstretch, dug in gamely, and prevailed under a drive. XTRA HEAT quickly showed in front, set the pace along the inside, dug in when roused in upper stretch, and fought it out gamely to the wire. CALLER ONE raced with the pace while in hand and dug in gamely through the stretch. SWEPT OVERBOARD was taken to the inside soon after the start, raced on the rail, and was going well along the inside late. LEFT BANK was urged along early, chased the pace while three wide, and finished well. DELAWARE TOWNSHIP was hustled along early, rallied five wide approaching the stretch, and finished well outside. KONA GOLD was hard ridden inside and lacked a rally. FIVE STAR DAY showed speed from the outside, chased the pace while four wide, and tired in the stretch. PEEPING TOM was outrun early, raced five wide, and had no response when roused. ALANNAN was hustled along inside, raced on the rail, and tired after a half-mile. MOZART (Ire) broke sluggishly, was hard ridden while four wide, and tired in the stretch. EL CORREDOR raced six wide and had no response when roused. BET ON SUNSHINE dropped back early, raced inside, and tired. HOOK AND LADDER chased the pace while four wide and tired after a half–mile.

2001 Mile: Made for TV

The Val Royal (Fr) story had all the plot elements of a successful made-for-television movie: a media-savvy owner, a horse who has overcome adversity repeatedly, a trainer who has returned to the track after personal difficulties, and a jockey rising from relative obscurity.

David Milch, Val Royal's owner, certainly could write such a script about his Breeders' Cup Mile (G1) winner if he were not occupied with "NYPD Blue," his long-running hit TV series.

Making only his fourth start in 25 months, Val Royal closed powerfully from the back of the 12-horse field to win by 1¾ lengths over Forbidden Apple. Bach (Ire) finished third, another three-quarters of a length farther back. Godolphin Racing's Sussex Stakes (Eng-G1) victor Noverre, a lukewarm 4.10-to-1 favorite, ran poorly on the firm Belmont Park main turf course on October 27 and finished seventh.

Val Royal ran the mile in 1:32.05, a Belmont course record and the fastest time ever in the Breeders' Cup Mile, surpassing the 1:32⅖ mark of Royal Heroine (Ire) at Hollywood Park in 1984. Val Royal was the second Breeders' Cup victor in three years for trainer Julio Canani, who won with Silic (Fr) in 1999. Both Silic and Val Royal took the Mile after victories in the Oak Tree Breeders' Cup Mile Stakes (G2), as did 2000 winner War Chant.

Val Royal certainly had a long and difficult road to his Breeders' Cup victory. Bred by eight-time leading French breeder Jean-Luc Lagardere, the son of 1990 Mile winner Royal Academy had won the '99 Prix Guillaume d'Ornano (Fr-G2) and Prix de Guiche (Fr-G3) before his sale to Milch for $1-million.

Adam Coglianese/NYRA photo

Val Royal scripts a win for David Milch
Trainer Canani's patience pays off with decisive score

Transferred to Canani, who had withdrawn from the racetrack for four years from 1993 to '97 to resolve personal issues, Val Royal immediately won the Del Mar Derby (G2) in early September '99. But he came out of that race with heat in a tendon, and treatment kept Val Royal out of action for more than 18 months. In the meantime, Canani picked up the services of Jose Valdivia Jr. to ride Val Royal. "He gets along with the horse," Canani said.

Val Royal finally returned to the races on March 3, 2001, and finished second in Santa Anita Park's Frank E. Kilroe Mile Handicap (G2). But he sustained a deep quarter crack that took months to heal, and the horse made his next start in the Oak Tree Mile, which he won by two lengths.

Val Royal prepared well for the Breeders' Cup Mile over the Belmont main track, and Canani was jubilant when the horse drew the 12th starting assignment, the same as Silic two years earlier. Canadian hope Numerous Times's withdrawal reduced the field to 12, and Val Royal started as the 5.10-to-1 third betting choice in post position 11. City Zip and Balto Star, both three-year-old stakes winners on dirt, set a swift early pace, and as they weakened on the turn Arthur Appleton's Forbidden Apple grabbed the lead early in the stretch. Valdivia put Val Royal into the game on the turn, and they flew into the stretch on the far outside. "I didn't want to be cute and weave my way through traffic," Valdivia said. Although 11th after six furlongs in 1:08.65, Val Royal was third by two lengths and eating up ground at the furlong pole. He took command and was moving away from 8.20-to-1 Forbidden Apple at the finish. In the winner's circle, Peruvian native Canani waved an American flag, and he later used an automotive metaphor to describe Val Royal's victory. "He ran like a Mercedes," the trainer said.

Owner

David S. Milch is an Emmy Award- winning writer-producer of television shows "Hill Street Blues" and "NYPD Blue." He once co-authored college textbooks on literature and taught at Yale University. He bought his first horse with earnings from "Hill Street Blues." His first notable horse was Gilded Time, winner of the 1992 Breeders' Cup Juvenile.

Breeder

Jean-Luc Lagardere is chairman of the Lagardere Group, which owns a bank and 93.3% of the technology and communications company Matra Hachette, which makes missiles, electronics, and transport equipment. Lagardere bought his first racehorse more than 30 years ago. He was France's leading breeder for the first time in 1988, and the 2001 title marked his eighth in a row. He owns about 60 broodmares and has about 50 horses in training.

"Julio [Canani] said to ride your horse, not to worry about any kind of bias. If he comes running, he would be very tough," Valdivia said. "When I turned him for home, I had all the confidence in the world. He gave me such a powerful kick, I knew that I would get there and knew that if anybody was going around me, they would have to be flying—literally."

Valdivia sported a huge grin as he crossed the finish line, a smile that did not stop as he guided the bay horse back to the winner's circle. Plucking an orchid from the blanket of flowers draped across Val Royal's shoulders, he brought it to his nose and then gestured skyward. Canani had the same giddy expression.

Val Royal earned $592,800 to more than double his lifetime earnings to $1,108,687 and more than earn back the 9% supplemental fee of $70,000 paid by owner Milch. Canani said Milch, who was a co-owner of 1992 Breeders' Cup Juvenile (G1) winner Gilded Time, was nursing a cold and decided not to leave his California home to attend the Breeders' Cup.

Canani, who now has two victories from his seven Breeders' Cup starters, said of Val Royal: "He has so much ability. He has an amazing stride. He breezes on the dirt like he could be a champion on the dirt, but I have experience with horses. Run grass horses on the dirt and they won't run the same." —*Jenny Kellner*

TENTH RACE
Belmont Park
October 27, 2001

1 mile on turf. 18th running of the Breeders' Cup Mile (G1). Purse $1-million. 3-year-olds and up. Weights (Northern Hemisphere): 3-year-olds, 123 lbs. Older, 126 lbs. (Southern Hemisphere): 3-year-olds, 120 lbs. Older, 126 lbs. Fillies and mares allowed 3 lbs.

Value of race: $1,044,240. Value to winner: $592,800; second: $228,800; third: $136,800; fourth: $63,840; fifth, $22,800. Mutuel Pool: $3,696,908.

Horse	Wgt.	M/Eqt	PP	St.	¼	½	¾	Str.	Fin.	Jockey	Odds $1
Val Royal (Fr)	126	L	11	11	$11^{2\frac{1}{2}}$	11^2	$11^{\frac{1}{2}}$	3^{hd}	$1^{1\frac{3}{4}}$	J. Valdivia Jr.	5.10
Forbidden Apple	126	L	1	2	$4^{\frac{1}{2}}$	$4^{\frac{1}{2}}$	2^1	$11^{\frac{1}{2}}$	$2^{\frac{3}{4}}$	C. Nakatani	8.20
Bach (Ire)	126	L	4	6	6^1	6^{hd}	5^{hd}	$4^{1\frac{1}{2}}$	$3^{1\frac{1}{2}}$	M. Kinane	33.50
Irish Prize	126	L	12	10	$10^{2\frac{1}{2}}$	$10^{1\frac{1}{2}}$	$9^{\frac{1}{2}}$	5^{hd}	4^{nk}	G. Stevens	5.00
Navesink	123	L	2	7	$7^{\frac{1}{2}}$	8^2	$8^{\frac{1}{2}}$	7^{hd}	5^{nk}	E. Prado	17.00
Brahms	126	Lb	10	9	9^1	$9^{\frac{1}{2}}$	$10^{\frac{1}{2}}$	11^{hd}	6^{nk}	A. Solis	12.40
Noverre	123	L	3	8	$8^{2\frac{1}{2}}$	7^{hd}	7^{hd}	$8^{\frac{1}{2}}$	7^1	L. Dettori	4.10*
Sarafan	126	Lb	9	12	12	12	12	10^1	8^{nk}	V. Espinoza	26.75
City Zip	123	Lb	6	1	$1^{\frac{1}{2}}$	1^{hd}	$1^{\frac{1}{2}}$	$2^{\frac{1}{2}}$	$9^{2\frac{1}{4}}$	J. Chavez	32.25
Express Tour	123	L	7	4	3^1	3^{hd}	$3^{1\frac{1}{2}}$	6^{hd}	$10^{2\frac{1}{4}}$	J. Velazquez	21.40
Affirmed Success	126	L	8	5	$5^{\frac{1}{2}}$	$5^{1\frac{1}{2}}$	$6^{1\frac{1}{2}}$	12	$11^{1\frac{3}{4}}$	J. Bailey	5.40
Balto Star	123	L	5	3	2^1	$2^{1\frac{1}{2}}$	4^{hd}	$9^{1\frac{1}{2}}$	12	P. Day	8.10

Scratched: Numerous Times

OFF AT 2:43. Start Good for all. Weather: Clear. Track: Firm. Won: Driving.
Time, :22.79, :45.49, 1:08.65, 1:32.05.

	12—VAL ROYAL (Fr)	12.20	6.40	5.10
$2 Mutuel Prices:	1—FORBIDDEN APPLE		8.60	6.20
	4—BACH (Ire)			12.40

PICK THREE 6-9-12 PAID $1,671.00
EXACTA 12-1 PAID $105.50   TRIFECTA 12-1-4 PAID $2,445.00

B. h., by Royal Academy—=Vadlava, by =Bikala. Trainer Julio Canani. Bred by J. L. Lagardere (Fr.).

VAL ROYAL (Fr) checked slightly when IRISH PRIZE angled to the inside in the early stages, moved out along the backstretch, raced well back for five furlongs, rapidly gained between horses while eight wide entering the stretch, then unleashed a strong late run in the middle of the track to win going away. FORBIDDEN APPLE settled just behind the dueling leaders while saving ground, closed the gap on the turn, angled out to challenge at the top of the stretch, surged to the front in upper stretch, continued on the lead into deep stretch, then yielded to the winner in the final fifty yards. BACH (Ire) raced in the middle of the pack along the backstretch, launched a rally between horses on the turn, then finished willingly to gain a share. IRISH PRIZE angled to the inside in the early stages, was unhurried for five furlongs while saving ground, waited patiently on the turn, launched a bid along the rail at the top of the stretch, then failed to threaten while improving his position with a mild late rally. NAVESINK rushed up along the rail after breaking a bit slowly, raced within striking distance while saving ground on the turn, angled out in upper stretch, then rallied mildly. BRAHMS raced well back for five furlongs, advanced seven wide on the turn, then finished evenly. NOVERRE raced in the middle of the pack while five wide for six furlongs, then lacked the needed response when called upon. SARAFAN checked while being pinched back at the start, raced just outside the winner while nine wide on the turn, then lacked a strong closing response. CITY ZIP sprinted to the front soon after the start, set the pace under pressure for five furlongs, shook off BALTO STAR to gain a clear advantage on the turn, then tired in the drive. EXPRESS TOUR chased the leaders while three wide for six furlongs and gave way in the stretch. AFFIRMED SUCCESS raced in good position while four wide to the turn, then lacked a further response. BALTO STAR forced the pace along the rail to the turn and gave way.

2001 Juvenile Fillies: Harty's Girls

The American-based juvenile program of Godolphin Racing, the global powerhouse headed by Sheikh Mohammed bin Rashid al Maktoum, scored its most significant victory to date when Tempera won the $916,000 Breeders' Cup Juvenile Fillies (G1) on October 27 at Belmont Park. Tempera, who defeated stablemate Imperial Gesture by 1½ lengths, won the 1¹⁄₁₆-mile race in a stakes-record time of 1:41.49 and took sole control of the two-year-old filly division.

By 1992 Horse of the Year and Breeders' Cup Classic (G1) winner A.P. Indy and out of the Mr. Prospector mare Colour Chart, Tempera was bred by Sheikh Mohammed's Darley Stud Management and foaled in Kentucky. She is trained by Eoin Harty, a fifth-generation Irish horseman who was an assistant to trainer Bob Baffert before joining Godolphin in early 2000 to handle the juveniles racing in the United States.

Harty first saw Tempera in January 2001 when he was in Dubai to inspect the Godolphin juveniles that soon would join him in the U.S. "I didn't think much of her when I first saw her," Harty said. "She was slight, narrow, very highly strung, carrying very little condition. But that didn't last long. Within a month of being here, she matured

Adam Coglianese/NYRA photo

Tempera matures into a champion
A.P. Indy filly scores over stablemate Imperial Gesture

quite a bit, and she showed tremendous talent early on."

In her third start, on August 4, 2001, Tempera won Del Mar's Sorrento Stakes (G2) by nine lengths. But, after a taxing performance in the Del Mar Debutante Stakes (G1) later that month, Harty gave her time off and trained her up to the Breeders' Cup.

"Two-year-olds change every day," said Harty, then 38, whose first Breeders' Cup starter, Street Cry (Ire), finished third in the 2000 Breeders' Cup Juvenile (G1). "[Tempera] just got better and better once she got to New York."

Meanwhile, Imperial Gesture was convincing Harty that she also belonged in the Juvenile Fillies. Godolphin purchased the Langfuhr filly for $350,000 as a weanling at the 1999 Keeneland November breeding stock sale. Fifth to Habibti in her first start at Del Mar on July 29, Imperial Gesture won a maiden special weight race at Saratoga Race Course on August 24 by 10¾ lengths. She then returned to California, where she ran second to Tali'sluckybusride in the Oak Leaf Stakes (G1) at Santa Anita Park on September 30. Harty considered starting Imperial Gesture in Belmont's Tempted Stakes (G3) the day after the Breeders' Cup but, because she too had been training so well, he left her in the Juvenile Fillies.

At 11.90-to-1, Tempera was the sixth choice in the Juvenile Fillies behind Frizette Stakes (G1) winner and 0.95-to-1 favorite You, Astarita Stakes (G2) winner Bella Bellucci, Del Mar Debutante winner Habibti, Walmac Int'l Alcibiades Stakes (G2) winner Take Charge Lady, and New York Breeders' Futurity winner Shesastonecoldfox.

Shesastonecoldfox, the first Breeders' Cup starter to have raced at Finger Lakes in western New York, stumbled at the start of the Juvenile Fillies but quickly took the early lead. She and Take Charge Lady led the other seven starters into a head wind down the backstretch in fractions of :23.50, :46.89, and 1:10.96.

Owners

Godolphin Racing is a partnership that includes certain horses owned by the four Maktoum brothers—Sheikhs Maktoum, Hamdan, Mohammed, and Ahmed bin Rashid al Maktoum—and managed by Sheikh Mohammed. At this year's Breeders' Cup World Thoroughbred Championships, Godolphin's Tempera and Imperial Gesture ran one-two in the Juvenile Fillies (G1); Fantastic Light won the Turf (G1); Sakhee finished second in the Classic (G1); Noverre and Express Tour were seventh and tenth, respectively, in the Mile (G1); and Ibn al Haitham (GB) and Essence of Dubai were ninth and 12th, respectively, in the Juvenile (G1). Godolphin's first Breeders' Cup winner was Daylami (Ire), who won the Turf in 1999.

Breeder

Darley Stud Management is owned by Sheikh Mohammed bin Rashid al Maktoum, crown prince of Dubai and minister of defense of the United Arab Emirates. Sheikh Mohammed purchased his first Thoroughbred in 1976 and now ranks as one of the world's largest and most successful breeders and owners. Darley bred other Breeders' Cup starters Catienus (13th in the Classic in 1999), Noverre (11th in the Juvenile in 2000 and seventh in the Mile in '01), Shantou (fourth in the Turf in '96), and Wall Street (eighth in the Turf in '96).

Jockey David Flores sat in midpack with Tempera as Bella Bellucci stole through an opening on the inside. As the field turned for home, Bella Bellucci snatched the lead while Tempera and Imperial Gesture, the 53.75-to-1 longshot, appeared to be within perfect striking position to her outside. Imperial Gesture surged to the front briefly before Tempera took command inside the final furlong and charged ahead to win.

Bella Bellucci was third. Completing the order of finish were You, Sophisticat, Take Charge Lady, Habibti, Jealous Forum, and Shesastonecoldfox.

"The whole idea was to get her relaxed the first part and then let her run," said Flores, who gave Tempera two quick taps with his whip as she took the lead. Flores earned his first Breeders' Cup victory after going winless with 13 previous starters but scoring two seconds with Chilukki in the 1999 Juvenile Fillies and on Tuzla (Fr) in the '99 Mile (G1).

Bella Bellucci, who pulled jockey Gary Stevens to the lead at the quarter pole, finished five lengths back in third. She was a half-length in front of You, who finished one-half length in front of European invader Sophisticat, a Storm Cat filly out of leading North American distaff earner Serena's Song who was sold as a yearling for $3.4-million. Take Charge Lady finished sixth and was followed by Habibti, who had struggled while racing from the inside post; Woodbine stakes winner Jealous Forum; and Shesastonecoldfox, who tired badly and was eased in the stretch.

While Harty was heading to the winner's circle, Frankel was staring at the television monitor in the Belmont racing secretary's office, where he watched each Breeders' Cup race. "She had no kick today," said You's rider, Edgar Prado. "She just ran even the whole way. She'd had dirt kicked in her face before so she was used to that, but she didn't have any kick." You developed a fever the following day.

Tempera provided Harty with his first graded stakes winner and his first champion when she was voted champion two-year-old filly. She became ill and died shortly after her return to the United States in April 2002.—*Amy Owens*

FOURTH RACE
Belmont Park
October 27, 2001

1¹/₁₆ miles. 18th running of the Breeders' Cup Juvenile Fillies (G1). Purse $1-million. Fillies, 2-year-olds. Weight: 119 lbs.

Value of race, $916,000. Value to winner: $520,000; second: $200,000; third: $120,000; fourth: $56,000; fifth: $20,000. Mutuel Pool: $3,334,729.

Horse	Wgt.	M/Eqt	PP	St	¼	½	¾	Str.	Fin.	Jockey	Odds $1
Tempera	119	L	9	2	4hd	5½	3½	2½	1¹½	D. Flores	11.90
Imperial Gesture	119	Lf	7	4	3½	4hd	2¹	1hd	2³½	L. Dettori	53.75
Bella Bellucci	119		2	9	7¹½	3hd	3²½	3½	3¹	G. Stevens	3.90
You	119	L	5	5	5½	6½	5hd	4hd	4½	E. Prado	0.95*
Sophisticat	119	L	4	7	6hd	7²	6¹	5½	54¼	M. Kinane	15.30
Take Charge Lady	119	L	8	3	2½	2½	4hd	6¹	6nk	A. D'Amico	11.00
Habibti	119	Lb	1	8	9	9	7³½	7⁷	7⁶	V. Espinoza	6.90
Jealous Forum	119	L	3	6	8½	8¹½	8³	8²⁰	8	P. Husbands	77.00
Shesastonecoldfox	119	L	6	1	1hd	1hd	9	9	—	J. Bailey	11.80

OFF AT 2:05. Start Good for all. Winner: Driving. Weather: Clear. Track: Fast.
Time, :23.50, :46.89, 1:10.96, 1:35.34, 1:41.49.

	9—TEMPERA	25.80	11.80	7.50
$2 Mutuel Prices:	7—IMPERIAL GESTURE		41.80	14.80
	2—BELLA BELLUCCI			5.30

PICK THREE 7-6-9 PAID $650.00   CONSOLATION PICK 7-3-9 THREE PAID $60
DAILY DOUBLE 6-9 PAID $260.50   EXACTA 9-7 PAID $768.00
TRIFECTA 9-7-2 PAID $3,823.00

Dkbbr. f., by A.P. Indy out of Colour Chart, by Mr. Prospector. Trainer Eoin Harty. Bred by Darley Stud Management LLC (Ky.)

TEMPERA raced with the pace from the outside while well in hand, was five deep around the turn, responded when set down in upper stretch, and drew clear from stablemate Imperial Gesture in the final yards under a drive. IMPERIAL GESTURE contested the pace while four wide, earned a short lead in midstretch, and dug in gamely but could not stay with the winner in the final sixteenth while clearly best of the others. BELLA BELLUCCI was bumped at the start and was rated along early, advanced inside nearing the turn, reached the front midway on the turn, and weakened along the inside in the final furlong. YOU was close up while in hand between rivals, angled out and came wide nearing the stretch, and had no response when roused. SOPHISTICAT was urged along outside, raced four wide, and had no response when roused. TAKE CHARGE LADY contested the pace while between rivals and tired after the opening three-quarters. JEALOUS FORUM dropped back after the start, raced inside, and tired. SHESASTONECOLDFOX stumbled at the start but quickly showed in front, set the pace for a half-mile, tired badly, and was eased in the stretch.

2001 Distaff: New Arrival

Trainer Dallas Stewart stood in the winner's circle at Belmont Park after the $2,161,760 Breeders' Cup Distaff (G1) wearing a great big grin and looking like he was the luckiest guy in the world. And who could blame him? Eight days before the Breeders' Cup, Stewart was one of a hundred or so trainers at Churchill Downs who figured to be watching the October 27 championship races on television. Then he received a phone call from Roger Devenport.

"I looked at the number on the display, and I knew it was Roger," Stewart said. "We talked about a few things, made some jokes, and I asked about his health. He wanted me to take his horses again. I told him I would pray and think about it."

Stewart had trained all of Devenport's horses until June, when they were abruptly taken away from him and sent to David Vance. Then, eight days before the Breeders' Cup, Devenport asked him to take back his horses, including Unbridled Elaine, who had been re-entered in the Distaff. Stewart took the horses, and the rest, as they say, is history.

Unbridled Elaine delivered a powerful closing kick under jockey Pat Day to win the Distaff by a head over Spain, who was trying to become the second filly in the race's history to repeat, after Bayakoa (Arg) in 1989 and '90. It was the pupil beating the teacher; Stewart came up as an assistant to D. Wayne Lukas, trainer of Spain. For Day, it was his 12th win in a Breeders' Cup race, and he edged ahead of Jerry Bailey's.

The Distaff, however, was a tragedy for owner-breeder Centaur Farm and trainer Flint S. "Scotty" Schulhofer, the connections of Exogenous. Winner of the Beldame Stakes (G1), Exogenous became spooked when walking onto the track for the post parade, reared, fell, and ensnared her leg between uprights in an iron fence. She hit her

Photo by Z

Unbridled Elaine overtakes Spain
Last-minute addition to Dallas Stewart's stable

head hard on the ground when she flipped over backward. After 15 minutes, she was freed and taken by track ambulance to her barn. Despite an optimistic prognosis immediately afterward, Exogenous was euthanized five days later, on November 2.

For trainer Bobby Frankel, the Distaff extended his futility in Breeders' Cup races to zero for 37 when Juddmonte Farms' 1.15-to-1 favorite Flute finished seventh.

Unlike the other seven Breeders' Cup races, the Distaff did not have a foreign-based starter. One starter, Miss Linda (Arg), was supplemented at a cost of $400,000 by her owner, Ackerley Brothers, and finished sixth.

At the start, Tranquility Lake went to the lead, and the six-year-old West Coast-based mare was pressed by Queenie Belle as the field raced into a strong head wind, with the opening quarter-mile in :23.62 and the half in :46.94. Flute was fourth early, but down along the inside, the worst part of the track. By the time Bailey moved her off the rail, it was too late. Her early exertions and the dead surface took too much out of her.

The Thoroughbred Corp.'s Spain looped the leaders on the turn and quickly took charge of the race. By midstretch, with her lead increasing to two lengths, she appeared to be home free. But Day and Unbridled Elaine rallied hard on the outside, and they got up to win by a head. Spain finished 1¼ lengths in front of longshot Two Item Limit, third by a nose over Alelier.

Unbridled Elaine, the 12.30-to-1 sixth betting choice, completed the Distaff's 1⅛ miles in 1:49.21 on a fast track. With the $1,227,200 winner's share of the purse, the three-year-old Unbridled's Song filly increased her earnings to $1,743,390 in her tenth career start.

"I was pretty comfortably placed in the middle of the field," Day said, "and on the turn she was moving nicely. Inside the three-sixteenths pole, I had to alter course as [Miss Linda] came

Owner

Roger Devenport owns 75-acre Six D Ranch near Lexington. He formerly owned a butter business in West Bend, Wisconsin, and owned and bred Quarter Horses in that state for about 40 years. Devenport has owned and bred Thoroughbreds for about ten years. Unbridled Elaine is his first Thoroughbred stakes winner.

Breeders

K. David Schwartz and **Golden Orb Farm**. A Miami resident, Schwartz owns 110-acre Golden Orb Farm north of Ocala. He has been in racing about 25 years and also bred multiple graded stakes winner Glitter Woman, a half sister to Unbridled Elaine, plus stakes winners Country Day and Pilgrim's Pleasure. He privately sold Carols Folly, dam of Unbridled Elaine, to Summer Wind Farm of Jane and Frank Lyon Jr. in 2000.

across my horse's heels. I turned up my stick and got after her. She responded beautifully. I didn't know if I was going to get there in time."

Though Stewart developed Unbridled Elaine into a stakes winner at two, taking the Pocahontas Stakes at Churchill the day before the 2000 Breeders' Cup, owner Devenport was displeased after the filly lost the Acorn Stakes (G1) in her second start of 2001. After he sent her to Vance, she won the Iowa Oaks and Monmouth Breeders' Cup Oaks (G2), finished second to Macho Uno in the Pennsylvania Derby (G3), and then fourth in the Overbrook Spinster Stakes (G1) after a wide trip on a speed-favoring oval. Devenport was unhappy that Vance did not ship Unbridled Elaine to Belmont several weeks in advance to prepare for the Distaff, however, so he made the change back to Stewart.

The day after Stewart took Unbridled Elaine back, he worked her five furlongs at Churchill. "I had been watching her train. You can't miss her. She really takes control when she's out on the racetrack. She was training really well," Stewart said. "It was a maintenance work. I didn't want to get fancy or cute. I thought she was capable."

Devenport, then 81, did not attend the Breeders' Cup because he was undergoing radiation therapy for cancer. He watched the Distaff at Keeneland Race Course. His daughter, Elaine Averill, for whom the horse is named, represented him at Belmont. For only the third time in 18 years, the Distaff did not produce a champion. Gourmet Girl, champion older female of 2001, did not start in the race, and eventual champion three-year-old filly Xtra Heat ran second in the Breeders' Cup Sprint (G1).—*Mark Simon*

THIRD RACE Belmont Park October 27, 2001	1 1/8 miles. 18th running of the Breeders' Cup Distaff (G1). Purse $2-million. Fillies and mares 3-year-olds and upward. Weights (Northern Hemisphere): 3-year-olds, 120 lbs. Older, 123 lbs. (Southern Hemisphere): 3-year-olds, 115 lbs. Older, 123 lbs.

Value of race: $2,161,760. Value to winner: $1,227,200; second: $472,000; third: $283,200; fourth: $132,160; fifth, $47,200. Mutuel Pool $3,151,445.

Horse	Wgt.	M/Eqt	PP	St.	1/4	1/2	3/4	Str.	Fin.	Jockey	Odds $1
Unbridled Elaine	120	L	5	9	$8^{1/2}$	9^1	10^3	$5^{1^{1/2}}$	1^{hd}	P. Day	12.30
Spain	123	L	11	1	3^{hd}	6^1	2^1	1^2	$2^{1^{1/4}}$	V. Espinoza	4.90
Two Item Limit	120	Lb	4	11	$10^{1/2}$	$10^{1^{1/2}}$	8^1	3^{hd}	3no	A. Solis	32.00
Atelier	123	L	9	10	$9^{1/2}$	$8^{1/2}$	5^1	$2^{1/2}$	$4^{1^{1/4}}$	E. Prado	53.25
Starrer	120	L	8	4	$7^{1^{1/2}}$	7^{hd}	7^{hd}	4^{hd}	$5^{1^{1/2}}$	C. McCarron	17.50
Miss Linda (Arg)	123	L	3	7	6^1	5^{hd}	6^1	$6^{1^{1/2}}$	$6^{3^{1/4}}$	R. Migliore	6.00
Flute	120	L	2	8	5^1	4^1	$4^{1/2}$	7^3	$7^{1/2}$	J. Bailey	1.15*
Critical Eye	123	L	10	3	11	11	11	$8^{2^{1/2}}$	8^9	J. Chavez	36.50
Tranquility Lake	123	L	1	6	$1^{1/2}$	1^{hd}	3^{hd}	9^2	$9^{2^{1/2}}$	E. Delahoussaye	7.90
Queenie Belle	123	L	6	5	$2^{1/2}$	2^1	$9^{1/2}$	10^4	10^8	B. Blanc	79.25
Pompeii	123	L	7	2	4^{hd}	$3^{1/2}$	1^{hd}	11	11	G. Stevens	12.10

Scratched—Exogenous and Fleet Renee.

OFF AT 1:30. Start: Good for all. Winner: Driving. Weather: Clear. Track: Fast.
Time: :23.62, :46.94, 1:11.87, 1:36.51, 1:49.21.

$2 Mutuel Prices:	6—UNBRIDLED ELAINE................	26.60	11.00 8.40
	12—SPAIN..		6.40 4.90
	5—TWO ITEM LIMIT.........................		10.20

PICK THREE 3-7-6 PAID $159.50 CONSOLATION PICK THREE 3-7-3 PAID $8.80
EXACTA 6-12 PAID $133.50 TRIFECTA 6-12-5 PAID $2,551.00

Gr. or ro. f., by Unbridled's Song—Carols Folly, by Taylor's Falls. Trainer Dallas Stewart. Bred by Golden Orb Farm and K. David Schwartz (Ky.).

UNBRIDLED ELAINE broke in the air at the start, was unhurried along the backstretch, gained along the inside on the far turn, checked behind a wall of horses midway on the turn, steadied then altered course to the outside in upper stretch, then closed strongly in the middle of the track to get up in the final strides. SPAIN stalked the leaders from outside along the backstretch, closed the gap while four wide on the turn, surged to the front leaving the five-sixteenths pole, drifted out while opening a clear advantage at midstretch, continued on the front into deep stretch but could not hold the winner safe. TWO ITEM LIMIT was pinched back soon after the start, raced well back for a half, circled seven wide while launching her bid on the turn, then rallied belatedly in the middle of the track. ATELIER was unhurried early, moved into contention while five wide on the turn, made a run to threaten in midstretch but could not sustain her bid. STARRER raced in the middle of the pack along the backstretch, gained between horses while six wide on the turn, made a run to reach contention with the rider losing the whip at the top of the stretch, then lacked a strong closing bid. MISS LINDA (Arg) in hand early, was rated just behind the leaders while between horses to the turn, then lacked the needed response when called upon. FLUTE checked behind Tranquility Lake in the early stages, was rated along the inside for five furlongs, attempted to move out leaving the turn, then came up empty in the stretch. CRITICAL EYE failed to mount a serious rally while wide throughout. TRANQUILITY LAKE drifted out soon after the start, rushed up to gain a slim early advantage, dueled heads apart for five furlongs, then gave way on the turn. QUEENIE BELLE battled heads apart from outside to the turn and steadily tired thereafter. POMPEII chased the leaders while three wide for five furlongs, then lacked a further response. EXOGENOUS flipped just before entering the track and was scratched. As a result, post time was delayed ten minutes.

RACING
Review of 2001 Racing Season

In some years, the Horse of the Year title is determined in one-on-one combat on the racetrack. Ferdinand and Alysheba engaged in one of those down-to-the-wire battles in the 1987 Breeders' Cup Classic (G1). Two years later, the epic slugfests of Sunday Silence and Easy Goer, which had begun on a chilly afternoon in Kentucky, concluded in the Florida sun in the Breeders' Cup Classic at Gulfstream Park.

Although the 2001 racing season had its charms, the road to the sport's top title did not include any head-to-head duels. Point Given, the year's best three-year-old male and Horse of the Year, competed only in his age group—although he did so spectacularly, with one exception—and never met the defending champion, Tiznow, whose quirky season led to an unprecedented second consecutive victory in the Breeders' Cup Classic.

The season also led to the inescapable conclusion that the racing world is getting smaller by the year. European-based stables came within two inches of winning a majority of the eight Breeders' Cup World Thoroughbred Championship races at Belmont Park on October 27, when European champion Sakhee finished a nose behind Tiznow in the Breeders' Cup Classic.

Among the divisional champions, only three—Xtra Heat, Squirtle Squirt, and Tiznow—had no overseas ties through breeding or ownership. Dubai-based Godolphin Racing, which is becoming a significant force in American as well as European racing, won titles with two horses whom it bred in the United States, Fantastic Light and Tempera. Point Given was bred and owned by The Thoroughbred Corp. of Ahmed bin Salman, a Saudi Arabian prince.

Following are reviews of each North American racing division along with a recap of European racing in 2001.

Three-year-old male

The road to the American classics began with champion juvenile male Macho Uno on the shelf while Point Given, the hulking colt who nearly defeated Macho Uno in the 2000 Breeders' Cup Juvenile (G1), was making a shambles of the West Coast three-year-old races. But the road to the Kentucky Derby (G1) and the Triple Crown is always filled with turns and potholes as well as new challengers.

Point Given, the thunderous Thunder Gulch colt, easily polished off his West Coast opponents in the San Felipe Stakes (G2) and Santa Anita Derby (G1) before heading to Churchill Downs and a chance to become trainer Bob Baffert's third Derby winner. The East Coast picture was less clear, however. Among a large group of fast-developing three-year-old colts, the most notable was John C. Oxley's Monarchos, who ripped through victories in a maiden race, an allowance race, and the Florida Derby (G1) to establish himself as Florida's best. But trainer John T. Ward Jr. shipped the Maria's Mon colt to New York for the Wood Memorial Stakes (G2), where he was beaten by a fast-developing Congaree. Meanwhile, the gelding Balto Star marked himself as a horse to watch by winning the Turfway Spiral Stakes (G2) and Arkansas Derby (G2), while Millennium Wind roared to a 5¼-length victory in the Blue Grass Stakes (G1).

Towering above the contenders, though, was Point Given, and he went off as the 9-to-5 favorite in the Kentucky Derby. The day belonged to Monarchos, however, who had trained well after the Wood and won by 4¾ lengths in 1:59.97, second only to Secretariat's 1:59⅖ in 1973, on a Churchill track that was very hard and very fast. Point Given finished fifth, beaten by 11½ lengths. Richard Mulhall, manager of The Thoroughbred Corp., said a tactical error had been made in trying to keep Point Given close to the pace. While the track may have been a factor in the Derby, Monarchos clearly was the best three-year-old on May 5.

But no horse would beat Point Given for the rest of the year. He took the Preakness Stakes (G1) with surprising ease and ran away from his Belmont Stakes (G1) opponents to win by 12¼ lengths. He had a slight scare in Monmouth Park's Haskell Invitational Handicap (G1), prevailing by a half-length over Touch Tone, but he took no prisoners in Saratoga Race Course's Travers Stakes (G1), winning by 3½ lengths. He became the first horse to win four consecutive races with a purse of $1-million or more each. A tendon injury was discovered after the Travers, and Point Given was retired to Three Chimneys Farm, where he stood the 2002 season for a $125,000 fee. Macho Uno came back to win the Pennsylvania Derby (G3), fell to unheralded horses in the Ohio Derby (G3), and ran fourth in the Breeders' Cup Classic (G1), beaten by 4½ lengths. At season's end, however, Point Given had so dominated his division that he was the unanimous choice as champion three-year-old male by Eclipse Award voters.—*Don Clippinger*

Three-year-old filly

In 2001, the three-year-old filly division played out like "Queen for a Day." Every time a new filly

stepped to the head of the class, one of her rivals soon would take her place, which is why the brilliant sprinter Xtra Heat emerged as the Eclipse Award winner as champion three-year-old filly.

Heiligbrodt Racing Stable's and Team Valor's Golden Ballet reached the divisional lead first, winning the Santa Ynez Stakes (G2), Las Virgenes Stakes (G1), and Santa Anita Oaks (G1) before finishing second to Verne Winchell's Fleet Renee in Keeneland Race Course's Ashland Stakes (G1). Golden Ballet returned to win Hollywood Park's Railbird Stakes (G2) on May 19, but injury forced her to the sidelines for the rest of the year.

Fleet Renee's position at the top of the division was short-lived; after her Ashland victory on April 7, she finished fourth behind Juddmonte Farms' Flute in the Kentucky Oaks (G1). The Kentucky Oaks was Flute's third career start, following a maiden win by a head and a second-place finish by a length to Golden Ballet in the Santa Anita Oaks. After winning the Kentucky Oaks, Flute tacked on an allowance victory and a 4¾-length victory in Saratoga Race Course's Alabama Stakes (G1) over Centaur Farms' Exogenous.

Exogenous avenged the loss by taking the Gazelle Handicap (G1) over Fleet Renee, and the homebred Unbridled filly then beat Flute in the Beldame Stakes (G1) to make her case for the title. Fleet Renee, Flute, and Exogenous were scheduled to settle the three-year-old filly championship in the Breeders' Cup Distaff (G1) at Belmont Park, but the showdown never materialized. Fleet Renee scratched the day before the October 27 race. While walking onto the track for the Distaff, Exogenous flipped and banged her head, an injury that took her life five days later.

As a result of the absences of Fleet Renee and Exogenous, the championship was Flute's to lose, and she indeed lost it, running seventh in the Distaff to Roger Devenport's longshot winner Unbridled Elaine, who gamely defeated 2000 Distaff winner Spain by a head. Unbridled Elaine might have been three-year-old champion had she not subsequently running third to Forest Secrets in Churchill Downs's Falls City Handicap (G3).

None of the five fillies in contention for the championship—Golden Ballet, Fleet Renee, Flute, Exogenous, and Unbridled Elaine—had a clearcut edge over the others, so Eclipse voters went for Xtra Heat, who took the path less traveled to the championship. Trainer John Salzman purchased Xtra Heat for $5,000 for golfing buddies Harry Deitchman and Ken Taylor and himself as a two-year-old in 2000. Xtra Heat won nine of 13 starts in 2001, including Belmont's Prioress Stakes (G1), but she may well have secured a title with two losses. Taking on older males, Xtra Heat finished a game second by a half-length to

Squirtle Squirt in the Breeders' Cup Sprint (G1) and a strong third to Delaware Township in the Frank J. De Francis Memorial Dash Stakes (G1). Her only prior defeats in 2001 had been a second by a nose to Cat Chat in the Nassau County Stakes (G2) and a second by 3¼ lengths to Victory Ride in Saratoga's Test Stakes (G1).

—*Bill Heller*

Two-year-old male

Shortly after Johannesburg's victory in the Breeders' Cup Juvenile (G1), jockey Michael Kinane said he believed the media attention accorded race-favorite Officer had been misplaced. "He's the general," Kinane said of Johannesburg, "and the other one is the Officer." Indeed, the performance of Michael Tabor's and Susan Magnier's Johannesburg in his only North American start was so impressive that he was voted champion two-year-old male and was a candidate (with Point Given and Tiznow) for North America's Horse of the Year. But the unbeaten, globe-trotting Hennessy colt might not have achieved universal acclaim as the year's outstanding juvenile if his American challengers had not stumbled so badly, especially in the Breeders' Cup Juvenile.

Kinane was correct that Americans had overlooked Johannesburg, but The Thoroughbred Corp.'s Officer had earned his media attention with a spotless record on the road to Belmont Park and the Breeders' Cup World Thoroughbred Championships on October 27. Bred in California by Martin and Pam Wygod, the Bertrando colt won his first three races by a total of 24 lengths, including a seven-length score in the Best Pal Stakes (G3) at Del Mar. He so overmatched his competitors that John Toffan and Trudy McCaffery decided to ship their promising colt Came Home far from his California base to avoid meeting Officer in the Del Mar Futurity (G2). Came Home whipped a hapless group of East Coast two-year-olds by two lengths in Saratoga Race Course's Hopeful Stakes (G1) to remain undefeated.

Officer fulfilled expectations by winning the Del Mar Futurity by an easy 1½ lengths at 1-to-10 odds on September 7, and veteran California observers said he was the best California two-year-old they had seen in decades. Trainer Bob Baffert, leaving nothing to chance, then shipped Officer to New York for Belmont's Champagne Stakes (G1) on October 6. Against lightweight competition, he won by 3¾ lengths. While Officer was conquering both coasts, another West Coast colt was coming to hand. Owned by Jerry and John Amerman, Siphonic won his maiden start at Del Mar and then scored a frontrunning, six-length victory in Keeneland Race Course's Lane's End Breeders' Futurity Stakes (G2) on the same afternoon as the Champagne.

Sent off as the 0.75-to-1 favorite in the Breeders' Cup Juvenile, Officer led to the top of the stretch before faltering and finishing fifth, 5¼ lengths behind Johannesburg. Siphonic finished third, and 5-to-1 second choice Came Home, making his first start since the Hopeful, checked in seventh, but only a neck behind Officer. Baffert, believing that Officer had not run up to his potential in the Breeders' Cup, started him a week later in the California Cup Juvenile, but Officer embarrassed himself by finishing second as the 2-to-5 choice in the state-bred restricted race.

Repent, winner of the Kentucky Cup Juvenile Stakes (G3), went off as a 44.25-to-1 longshot in the Breeders' Cup Juvenile, but he was the only horse running at Johannesburg at the end, finishing second by 1¼ lengths. He subsequently won Churchill Downs's Kentucky Jockey Club Stakes (G2) at 4-to-5 odds.—*Don Clippinger*

Two-year-old filly

The 2001 two-year-old filly division mirrored its male counterpart in several ways. Some very promising fillies starred through the summer, but in the end a young horse with overseas connections collected all the marbles at the Breeders' Cup World Thoroughbred Championships. Precocious speed usually is a ticket to prominence early in the season for juvenile fillies, and Cashier's Dream certainly possessed bountiful speed. Owned by Heiligbrodt Racing Stable and Team Valor, she won her maiden-claiming debut by two lengths from off the pace, but she became a front-runner for the remainder of her 2001 starts, running an opening quarter-mile in less than :22 in three of them. She won the Debutante Stakes (G3) at Churchill Downs by 3½ lengths; finished second by a neck to Edmund Gann's You in the Adirondack Stakes (G2) at Saratoga Race Course; won the Spinaway Stakes (G1) at the same track by six lengths at odds of 3-to-10; and finished her season by running second by 6¼ lengths to You in the Frizette Stakes (G1) at Belmont Park.

You, a stalker, also began her career with an easy victory in a maiden claimer and then ran second to Cashier's Dream by three lengths in an allowance race. Both starts were at Churchill Downs, where she was trained by Hal Wiggins. You was then sold by her breeder to Edmund Gann and she went to trainer Bobby Frankel. You then won the Adirondack and Frizette before running a dull fourth as the 0.95-to-1 favorite in the Breeders' Cup Juvenile Fillies (G1). A top East Coast filly, Michael Tabor's Bella Bellucci, was seventh early in her maiden start and then made a spectacular run to win by 5¾ lengths. She rallied from fourth to win the Astarita Stakes (G2) by a half-length before finishing third in the Breeders' Cup.

The West Coast was represented by Habibti, who, like Officer, was owned by The Thoroughbred Corp. and trained by Bob Baffert. She won her first two starts decisively, taking a Del Mar maiden allowance by two lengths before winning the Del Mar Debutante (G1) by the same margin on August 26. Baffert gave her a two-month break before the Breeders' Cup Juvenile Fillies, and she ran a dull seventh after being bumped at the start.

The Breeders' Cup Juvenile Fillies belonged to Godolphin Racing and trainer Eoin Harty, whose Tempera, subsequently voted champion two-year-old filly, and Imperial Gesture finished first and second, respectively. After running third in her debut at Hollywood Park, Tempera won a maiden race there by three lengths and the Sorrento Stakes (G2) at Del Mar by nine lengths before finishing third by four lengths as the 1-to-2 favorite to Habibti in the Del Mar Debutante. Harty backed off on her training, and she won the Breeders' Cup race by 1½ lengths at 11.90-to-1 after a wide trip under jockey David Flores.

Imperial Gesture, sent off at 53.75-to-1 in the Breeders' Cup Juvenile Fillies, also had been beaten by Habibti, finishing fifth by 10½ lengths to Habibti in her debut. Imperial Gesture then won a maiden race at Saratoga by 10¾ lengths and ran second by 4½ lengths to Ronald and Susie Anson's unbeaten Tali'sluckybusride in the Oak Leaf Stakes (G1) at Santa Anita. Tali'sluckybusride did not run in the Breeders' Cup Juvenile Fillies. Imperial Gesture took the lead late in the Breeders' Cup Juvenile Fillies but could not hold off Tempera. Even so, Imperial Gesture beat Bella Bellucci by 3½ lengths for second.

—*Bill Heller*

Older male

Tiznow may not have repeated as Horse of the Year in 2001, but his second victory in the Breeders' Cup Classic (G1) assured him the title as champion older male and settled bragging rights in a division that had several contenders but no dominant player. Owned by Cee's Stable following the death of breeder and co-owner Cecilia Straub-Rubens shortly after the 2000 Breeders' Cup Classic, Tiznow started the year as though he intended to sweep the board again. He won the San Fernando Breeders' Cup Stakes (G2) but was second in the Strub Stakes (G2) before running away to a five-length triumph in the Santa Anita Handicap (G1). Tiznow soon developed a mysterious back ailment, though, that kept him out of action for more than six months, and his attitude soured to the point that he would only train when he wanted.

While Tiznow was causing headaches for trainer Jay Robbins, several horses were making their cases for the 2001 title, and three of the most accomplished challengers resided in trainer Bobby Frankel's barn. The first to reach prominence was

Juddmonte Farms' Skimming, who won Hollywood Park's Californian Stakes (G2), was impeded and placed second in the Hollywood Gold Cup Stakes (G1), and took the San Diego Handicap (G2) before winning the Pacific Classic Stakes (G1) for a second straight year. He finished second in the Goodwood Breeders' Cup Handicap (G2) and fell out of contention for the title.

Taking his place were Juddmonte's Aptitude and Lido Palace (Chi), owned by Jerry and John Amerman. Second to Albert the Great in Belmont Park's Suburban Handicap (G2), Lido Palace dispatched Albert the Great in both Saratoga Race Course's Whitney Handicap (G1) and Belmont's Woodward Stakes (G1). After the Woodward, Frankel and the Amermans decided to point Lido Palace toward the $2-million Japan Cup Dirt, in which the four-year-old colt finished a distant eighth.

Frankel's top prospect for the Breeders' Cup Classic was Aptitude, who had finished second in the 2000 Kentucky Derby (G1) and Belmont Stakes (G1). After finishing sixth to Captain Steve in the Dubai World Cup (UAE-G1), Aptitude ran third in the Californian and was advanced to the winner's circle in the Hollywood Gold Cup when Futural was disqualified for interfering with Skimming. Aptitude made his own good fortune from that July 1 race until the Breeders' Cup, winning the Saratoga Breeders' Cup Handicap (G2) by 4¼ lengths and the Jockey Club Gold Cup (G1) by a commanding ten lengths.

Tiznow recovered sufficiently to finish third in the Woodward and the Goodwood Breeders' Cup, and he consented to train once he reached Belmont Park for the Classic. Aptitude went off as the 2.35-to-1 favorite, with Tiznow at 6.90-to-1. But Aptitude never found his way into the race, and Tiznow was in the bridle at all times. Prix de l'Arc de Triomphe (Fr-G1) winner Sakhee zipped past Tiznow early in the stretch, but the Cee's Tizzy colt fought back relentlessly, gained a nose advantage in the final strides, and locked up the title as North America's outstanding older male.—*Don Clippinger*

Older female

The 2001 older female division was arguably one of the most wide-open and inscrutable in history. In sharp contrast to 2000, when Riboletta (Brz) was a nearly unanimous champion after winning seven graded stakes victories, five of them Grade 1, not one filly or mare in the division managed more than two Grade 1 victories on the main track, and only two managed that feat. For one of the few times in its history, the Breeders' Cup Distaff (G1) played no significant role in determining the division championship. Two candidates, 2000 Distaff victor Spain and Tranquility Lake, ran in the Belmont Park race,

but Spain's second-place finish was not enough to gain her the title after only one Grade 2 victory in 2001.

When the dust settled and all Eclipse Award ballots were counted, championship honors went to Gourmet Girl, a California-bred six-year-old mare who was purchased for $3,500 at a Del Mar yearling sale. Gourmet Girl earned the crown with two impressive Grade 1 victories, in the Apple Blossom Handicap at Oaklawn and the Vanity Handicap at Hollywood Park. The only other older female to win two Grade 1 stakes on the dirt was a second Cal-bred, Lazy Slusan, a six-year-old mare who captured the Santa Margarita Handicap at Santa Anita Park and the Milady Breeders' Cup Handicap at Hollywood Park.

Several other division members had their moments with one Grade 1 victory: Critical Eye won the Hempstead Handicap at Belmont; Miss Linda (Arg) took the Spinster Stakes at Keeneland Race Course; Pompeii captured the Personal Ensign Handicap at Saratoga Race Course; and Serra Lake won the Go for Wand Handicap, also at Saratoga. Spain, upset winner of the 2000 Breeders' Cup Distaff and third-place finisher for divisional honors that year, was relegated to runner-up honors again after finishing second by a head in her Breeders' Cup defense. Her only stakes victory of the year came in the La Canada Stakes (G2) at Santa Anita in February. Tranquility Lake was the only older female to win graded stakes on both dirt and turf, defeating Gourmet Girl in the Clement L. Hirsch Handicap (G2) on the main track and defending Palomar Handicap (G2) honors on grass, both at Del Mar. However, she failed to win a Grade 1 and only raced twice on dirt, the latter a distant ninth in the Breeders' Cup.

Her poor showing at Belmont left the door open for Gourmet Girl to complete her Cinderella story for trainer A. Pico Perdomo, who spotted the bargain yearling, and owner Gary Tanaka, who purchased her privately at the beginning of her four-year-old year. Perdomo credited the addition of blinkers in the second start of 2001 for the mare's banner campaign, highlighted by a 4½-length victory in the Apple Blossom and a five-length romp in the Vanity. At Perdomo's suggestion, she was retired to the breeding shed early in 2002.—*Steve Schuelein*

Turf male

For the third consecutive year, a European-based horse who made only one United States start ruled as the champion turf male in 2001, and the outcome reflected both the brilliance of European champion Fantastic Light and the lack of consistency among America's turf horses. More than a dozen male turf contenders won major stakes in 2001, but not one of them achieved

a preeminent position before Godolphin Racing's Fantastic Light ran away to victory in the Breeders' Cup Turf (G1).

Bienamado, owned by Trudy McCaffery, John Toffan, and Robert Sangster, was the first to score major victories. He won the San Marcos Stakes (G2) at Santa Anita Park on January 20 and, after a failed try on dirt in the Santa Anita Handicap (G1), took two Grade 1 races, the San Juan Capistrano Invitational Handicap and Charles Whittingham Memorial Handicap, in succession. However, he raced only once more in 2001, finishing a distant seventh to Silvano (Ger) in the Arlington Million Stakes (G1) on August 18.

With Bienamado out of the picture, at least five turf specialists made their bid for the title. Perhaps the most interesting was Augustin Stables' With Anticipation, a Relaunch gelding out of Fran's Valentine who was trained by Jonathan Sheppard. Beginning with a Keeneland Race Course allowance race in April, With Anticipation reached the finish line first in five straight turf races, although he was disqualified from a victory in the United Nations Handicap (G1) on July 1. After that misstep, he won the Sword Dancer Handicap (G1) at Saratoga Race Course and Belmont Park's Man o' War Stakes (G1). But he faded badly after setting the early pace under pressure in the Breeders' Cup Turf and finished seventh.

Hap, trained by Bill Mott, also had an opportunity to seize the top prize in the Breeders' Cup Turf. Winner of the Bernard Baruch Handicap (G2) at Saratoga, Hap finished second by three lengths in the Arlington Million and won the Keeneland Turf Mile Stakes (G2). But he posed no serious threat to Fantastic Light in the Breeders' Cup Turf, finishing fifth by more than ten lengths.

Among West Coast-based turf horses, Timboroa (GB) gained some attention when Edmund Gann's turf performer won the Del Mar Handicap (G2) and the Turf Classic Invitational Stakes (G1) by three lengths at Belmont. But he could do no better than third in the Breeders' Cup Turf. David Milch's Val Royal (Fr) certainly did little wrong for trainer Julio Canani, coming back after missing the 2000 season to win the Oak Tree Breeders' Cup Mile Stakes (G2) and the Breeders' Cup Mile (G1). But the Mile now is rarely regarded as a championship race, and Val Royal was overshadowed by Fantastic Light's victory in the Turf. One intriguing candidate receiving little attention after being scratched from the Breeders' Cup Mile was undefeated Numerous Times, who never started until his four-year-old season and won his three 2001 starts, including the Atto Mile Stakes (Can-G1), all at Woodbine.—*Bill Heller*

Turf female

The 2001 season for turf females was framed in sadness. Stronach Stable's defending turf champion Perfect Sting, winner of the Black Helen Handicap (G2) in mid-April, sustained an injury while running sixth against males in the Manhattan Handicap (G1) at Belmont Park on June 9 and was subsequently retired. She had won 13 of 19 grass starts and earned more than $2.1-million. As the season neared a conclusion, Janet and Robert Aron's Spook Express (SAf), a hard-hitting millionaire mare who had been second in the Breeders' Cup Filly and Mare Turf (G1), broke down near the wire in the Matriarch Stakes (G1) at Hollywood Park and was euthanized.

Nine fillies and mares won Grade 1 grass stakes in 2001, none more impressively than Juddmonte Farms' Banks Hill (GB), trained in France by Andre Fabre. A winner of the Prix de Sandringham (Fr-G2) and Coronation Stakes (Eng-G1), Banks Hill dominated the Breeders' Cup Filly and Mare Turf, winning by 5½ lengths, and was named champion. While the division had other candidates for the title, none of them showed the consistency in top-level competition to outweigh Banks Hill's brilliance in her one United States start.

Early in the year, Astra won Santa Anita Park's Santa Barbara Handicap (G2) by three lengths and Hollywood Park's Beverly Hills Handicap (G1) by four. But she finished ninth to Edouard de Rothschild's England's Legend (Fr) as the 7-to-10 favorite in the Beverly D. Stakes (G1) on August 18 at Arlington Park on a yielding course that she failed to handle and did not race again in 2001. England's Legend, who previously had taken the New York Handicap (G2) at Belmont Park, followed her Beverly D. victory with a close second to Sheikh Maktoum bin Rashid al Maktoum's Lailani (GB) in the Flower Bowl Handicap (G1) at Belmont before running 11th as the 2.65-to-1 favorite in the Breeders' Cup Filly and Mare Turf. Lailani's victory in the Flower Bowl made her seven for seven in 2001, but she finished a wide eighth in the Breeders' Cup.

Red Baron's Barn's talented Janet (GB) won Hollywood Park's Ramona Handicap (G1), defeating title contender Tranquility Lake and, after a poor effort in Saratoga Race Course's Diana Handicap (G2), came back to win Santa Anita Park's Yellow Ribbon Stakes (G1). She skipped the Breeders' Cup but had her season go steadily downhill, with a third in the Las Palmas Handicap (G1) and sixth in the Matriarch Stakes (G1).

Other contenders had their moments in the winner's circle but not enough to earn them a title. John Oxley's well-traveled, three-year-old filly Snow Dance won five of six grass starts, but her

third-place finish in Keeneland Race Course's Queen Elizabeth II Challenge Cup Stakes (G1) knocked her out of contention. Starine (Fr), owned and trained by Bobby Frankel, won Saratoga's Diana but was well beaten in the Breeders' Cup Filly and Mare Turf. Tranquility Lake ran well on dirt and grass, but her ninth-place finish in the Breeders' Cup race effectively ended her hopes for a championship.—*Bill Heller*

Sprinter

The 2001 sprint class was one of the deepest in racing history, and heading it through much of the year was Kona Gold, 2000's champion sprinter after winning the Breeders' Cup Sprint (G1) in track-record time. Under adroit handling by trainer Bruce Headley, who co-owned Kona Gold with Irwin and Andrew Molasky, the gelding extended his winning streak to seven in 2001, capturing the San Carlos Handicap (G1), Potrero Grande Breeders' Cup Handicap (G2), and—in a memorable showdown with Carolyn Chapman's and Theresa McArthur's Caller One—the Bing Crosby Handicap (G2) at Del Mar. Kona Gold's three-quarter-length victory over Caller One, who had taken the Dubai Golden Shaheen Stakes (UAE-G3) and Los Angeles Handicap (G3), left the pecking order in the sprint division unchanged.

Then, Kona Gold lost, finishing second by 2½ lengths to Swept Overboard in the Ancient Title Breeders' Cup Handicap (G1) at Santa Anita Park on October 6, three weeks before the Breeders' Cup Sprint at Belmont Park. Suddenly, other sprinters had hope for the title. Kona Gold, despite eight victories and six seconds in his prior 14 starts, was vulnerable, and a strong lineup stood ready to take him on in the Breeders' Cup. David Holloway's nine-year-old warrior Bet On Sunshine tuned up for his third appearance in the Breeders' Cup Sprint—he had been third in both 1997 and 2000—by winning the Aristides Handicap (G3) at Churchill Downs, the Arlington Sprint Handicap, and the Phoenix Breeders' Cup Handicap (G3) at Keeneland Race Course. New Farm's Delaware Township won the Forego Handicap (G1) at Saratoga Race Course and the Forest Hills Handicap (G2) at Belmont Park, his third victory in four starts there. Hal Earnhardt's El Corredor entered the Breeders' Cup Sprint off victories in his only two 2001 starts, the Pat O'Brien (G2) and Del Mar Breeders' Cup (G2) Handicaps at Del Mar. Michael Tabor's Left Bank won the Vosburgh Stakes (G1) by a half-length over David Lanzman's Squirtle Squirt, a three-year-old who previously had won the King's Bishop Stakes (G1) at Saratoga for trainer Bobby Frankel. The wild card in the sprint race was Xtra Heat, a three-year-old filly who was unbeaten in ten starts at six furlongs but had never faced males before the Breeders' Cup Sprint. With undaunted courage, Xtra Heat almost won the Sprint after setting sizzling fractions under pressure. She came up a half-length short to Squirtle Squirt, who gave Racing Hall of Fame trainer Frankel his first Breeders' Cup victory. Delaware Township, who finished sixth in the Sprint, came back to win the Frank J. De Francis Memorial Dash Stakes (G1) by three lengths, with Xtra Heat finishing third. At season's end, Squirtle Squirt was voted champion sprinter, while Xtra Heat garnered the title as champion three-year-old filly.

—*Bill Heller*

Steeplechase

The 2001 steeplechase season was a drama in three acts, with one player dominating in each segment. Sadly, the drama was a tragedy, with a young king dying before reaching his prime.

The early season belonged to Pompeyo (Chi), a 1998 Chilean classic winner purchased by George Strawbridge Jr.'s Augustin Stables. So headstrong that he was virtually uncontrollable when sent to trainer Neil Drysdale in California, Pompeyo found a new career over fences with Sanna Neilson, Strawbridge's stepdaughter who trained all three leading steeplechase candidates in 2001.

The 2000 season's top novice steeplechase horse, Pompeyo, started his 2001 season with a 6½-length victory in the Woodward-Kirkover Cup Novice Hurdle Stakes in Camden, South Carolina. On that same March 31 program, owner-trainer Jennifer Majette's Al Skywalker soared to a 12-length victory in the top-rated Carolina Cup Steeplechase Stakes. However, the Skywalker gelding never would reproduce that victory in top-level competition.

Pompeyo won his second start of the year, taking the Royal Chase for the Sport of Kings at Keeneland Race Course by three lengths over 2000 champion All Gong (NZ) on April 27. That would be Pompeyo's final start of the year. Neilson put him away for a fall season, but fate intervened before he had a chance to show off his full potential.

Three National Steeplechase Association races were held in conjunction with the American Triple Crown races, and Augustin's Praise the Prince (NZ) moved to the fore. Overshadowed by Pompeyo in 2000 and early in the 2001 season, Praise the Prince won the Hard Scuffle Hurdle Stakes at Churchill Downs on May 3 in his first start of the season and finished second by a neck to Flasher in the Joe Aitcheson Hurdle Stakes at Pimlico Race Course two weeks later. At Belmont Park on June 7, Praise the Prince won the Meadowbrook Hurdle Stakes. He took the first of Saratoga Race Course's top jump races, the A. P. Smithwick Memorial Steeplechase Handicap, but finished third in the New York Turf

Writers Steeplechase Handicap to It's a Giggle, who, like Al Skywalker, could not duplicate his winning performance the rest of the year.

As the fall season approached, misfortune struck Neilson's barn in eastern Pennsylvania. During morning work, Pompeyo was kicked by another horse and sustained a fractured left elbow. He was treated at the nearby New Bolton Center of the University of Pennsylvania's School of Veterinary Medicine. With Pompeyo out for the year, the veteran turf gelding Lord Zada moved to the forefront. He finished second to Quel Senor (Fr) in the Breeders' Cup Steeplechase and drew away to a 15½-length triumph in the Marion duPont Scott Colonial Cup Hurdle Stakes at Camden on November 18. When Quel Senor was pulled up in the Colonial Cup, the championship picture was wide open, and Eclipse Award voters went with Pompeyo, who was euthanized in January 2002 as a result of his injury. Praise the Prince, the year's leading earner with $225,742, was crowned as the National Steeplechase Association's champion.

—*Don Clippinger*

Daily Racing Form/NTRA National Handicapping Championship

Herman Miller, 50, a landscaper from Oakland, California, won the third annual $212,000 *Daily Racing Form*/National Thoroughbred Racing Association National Handicapping Championship, held on January 25-26, 2002, in Las Vegas. Miller won the $100,000 first prize and an Eclipse Award as 2001 Handicapper of the Year by defeating 176 other finalists, who had qualified in 88 qualifying tournaments held at 48 racetracks, off-track betting facilities, and horse racing and handicapping Web sites around the country.

In the two-day tournament, contestants had to make 30 $2 win and $2 place bets at eight different racetracks. Miller's winning total was $205.30 and included nine winners.

Year	Winner	Residence	Winning total
2001	Herman Miller	Oakland, CA	$205.30
2000	Judy Wagner	New Orleans, LA	$237.70
1999	Steve Walker	Lincoln, NE	$305.40

European Racing in 2001

Aidan O'Brien, trainer for Coolmore Stud's principals and chief clients, dominated the English and European racing scene in 2001, surpassing even the storied accomplishments of the legendary Vincent O'Brien, his predecessor at Ballydoyle. With Ballingarry's victory in the Criterium de Saint-Cloud (Fr-G1) on November 13, O'Brien notched his 23rd Group 1 or Grade 1 winner, eclipsing the mark of 22 set by Vincent O'Brien—no relation—in 1977 and equaled by D. Wayne Lukas a decade later. Aidan O'Brien's sole Grade 1 victory came in the Breeders' Cup Juvenile with Johannesburg.

But O'Brien and his Coolmore Stud clients were by no means the sole players on the European stage. Sheikh Mohammed bin Rashid al Maktoum's Godolphin operation always is formidable and in 2001 fielded two remarkable runners, Fantastic Light and Sakhee, both of whom were trained by Saeed bin Suroor. Fantastic Light was voted Cartier Horse of the Year in Europe after bringing home a Breeders' Cup Turf (G1) trophy. Sakhee won the Prix de l'Arc de Triomphe (Fr-G1) by six lengths and came within a nose of winning the Breeders' Cup Classic (G1). Sakhee was the leader in the International Classifications, assigned 133 pounds to 129 for Fantastic Light.

O'Brien, who was 32 when he set his Group 1 record, finished the 2001 British campaign with 20 winners from 99 runners and total purses of $4,823,568. He finished more than $1.8-million ahead of Sir Michael Stoute, the Newmarket-based trainer who was second.

O'Brien's leading three-year-old was Michael Tabor's and Susan Magnier's Galileo (Ire) who, after slamming Golan in the Epsom Derby (Eng-G1) in June, looked to be heading for stardom when he added the Irish Derby (Ire-G1). That view was further endorsed when the powerful colt beat Fantastic Light by two lengths after an epic battle with Godolphin's five-year-old in the King George VI and Queen Elizabeth Stakes (Eng-G1) at Ascot in July.

But Galileo, who was being hailed as one of the greatest of all time, came crashing back to earth when Fantastic Light gained dramatic revenge by a head in an equally enthralling battle in the Irish Champion Stakes (Ire-G1) at Leopardstown in September. Fantastic Light finished his career in a blaze of glory with his effortless victory in the Breeders' Cup Turf.

Galileo ended the season on a down note when he never found his stride in the Breeders' Cup Classic and finished sixth to winner Tiznow; he was retired to the Coolmore Stud in County Tipperary. Galileo was rated as Europe's champion three-year-old male at 129 pounds in the International Classifications but was one pound below American champion Point Given.

In addition to the Derby with Galileo, Ballydoyle's youthful trainer took two other British classics, the Epsom Oaks (Eng-G1) with Imagine and the St. Leger Stakes (Eng-G1) with the

highly impressive Milan (GB), who finished second in the Breeders' Cup Turf. O'Brien-trained Black Minnaloushe won the classic Irish Two Thousand Guineas (Ire-G1).

Before O'Brien began his march through England's classics, Stoute had made a brilliant start when Golan, superbly ridden by Kieren Fallon, stormed to victory in the classic Two Thousand Guineas (Eng-G1). The following day, fellow Newmarket trainer Michael Jarvis landed his first British classic when Ameerat took the One Thousand Guineas (Eng-G1).

On the Continent, Andre Fabre maintained a masterful hand. He trained Juddmonte Farms' Banks Hill (GB) to victories in the Coronation Stakes (Eng-G1) and the Breeders' Cup Filly and Mare Turf (G1). At year's end, the three-year-old filly was ranked atop her division in the International Classifications and was voted North America's champion turf female. Fabre backed into victory in the classic Poule d'Essai des Poulains (French Two Thousand Guineas) (Fr-G1) when Jean-Luc Lagardere's Vahorimix was advanced to first upon the disqualification of Godolphin's Noverre for a medication violation. Vahorimix also was elevated to first in the Prix du Haras de Fresnay-le-Buffard Jacques le Marois (Fr-G1) at Deauville when Proudwings was disqualified for impeding Noverre, who was third.

Europe's jockey-trainer alliances always are something of a soap opera, and Fallon—sacked ignominiously by Henry Cecil in the late 1990s—again lost a major client, reportedly because of discontent among owners. Fallon, who had lost his riding title in 2000 after being sidelined with an arm injury sustained in a fall at Royal Ascot in June, returned to top riding form in '01. But he was informed late in the year that Stoute would not retain his services for 2002. Fallon responded by locking up his sixth English title with 166 victories, four more than 2000 champion jockey Kevin Darley.—*Alan Smith*

Richest North American Races of 2001 by Value to Winner

Race (Grade)	Purse	Value to winner	Track	Dist.	Winner
Breeders' Cup Classic (G1)	$4,000,000	$2,080,000	Belmont	1¼m	Tiznow
Breeders' Cup Distaff (G1)	2,360,000	1,227,200	Belmont	1⅛m	Unbridled Elaine
Breeders' Cup Turf (G1)	2,140,000	1,112,800	Belmont	1½m	Fantastic Light
Haskell Invitational H. (G1)	1,500,000	900,000	Monmouth	1⅛m	Point Given
Canadian International S. (Can-G1)	1,500,000	900,000	Woodbine	1½m	Mutamam (GB)
Breeders' Cup Filly & Mare Turf (G1)	1,390,000	722,800	Belmont	1¼m	Banks Hill (GB)
Breeders' Cup Mile (G1)	1,140,000	592,800	Belmont	1m	Val Royal (Fr)
Kentucky Derby (G1)	1,112,000	812,000	Churchill Downs	1¼m	Monarchos
Whitney H. (G1)	1,008,000	540,000	Saratoga	1⅛m	Lido Palace (Chi)
Preakness S. (G1)	1,000,000	650,000	Pimlico	1³⁄₁₆m	Point Given
Atto Mile (Can-G1)	1,000,000	600,000	Woodbine	1m	Numerous Times
Jockey Club Gold Cup S. (G1)	1,000,000	600,000	Belmont	1¼m	Aptitude
Pacific Classic S. (G1)	1,000,000	600,000	Del Mar	1¼m	Skimming
Arlington Million S. (G1)	1,000,000	600,000	Arlington	1¼m	Silvano (Ger)
Belmont S. (G1)	1,000,000	600,000	Belmont	1½m	Point Given
Florida Derby (G1)	1,000,000	600,000	Gulfstream	1⅛m	Monarchos
Queen's Plate S.	1,000,000	600,000	Woodbine	1¼m	Dancethruthedawn
Santa Anita H. (G1)	1,000,000	600,000	Santa Anita	1¼m	Tiznow
Travers S. (G1)	1,000,000	600,000	Saratoga	1¼m	Point Given
Breeders' Cup Juvenile (G1)	1,000,000	520,000	Belmont	1¹⁄₁₆m	Johannesburg
Breeders' Cup Juvenile Fillies (G1)	1,000,000	520,000	Belmont	1¹⁄₁₆m	Tempera
Breeders' Cup Sprint (G1)	1,000,000	520,000	Belmont	6f	Squirtle Squirt
Stephen Foster H. (G2)	831,000	515,220	Churchill Downs	1⅛m	Guided Tour
Blue Grass S. (G1)	750,000	465,000	Keeneland	1⅛m	Millennium Wind
Alabama S. (G1)	750,000	450,000	Saratoga	1¼m	Flute
Beldame S. (G1)	750,000	450,000	Belmont	1⅛m	Exogenous
Flower Bowl Invitational H. (G1)	750,000	450,000	Belmont	1¼m	Lailani (GB)
Hollywood Gold Cup S. (G1)	750,000	450,000	Hollywood	1¼m	Aptitude
Louisiana Derby (G2)	750,000	450,000	Fair Grounds	1¹⁄₁₆m	Fifty Stars
Metropolitan H. (G1)	750,000	450,000	Belmont	1m	Exciting Story
Pimlico Special H. (G1)	750,000	450,000	Pimlico	1³⁄₁₆m	Include
Turf Classic Invitational S. (G1)	750,000	450,000	Belmont	1½m	Timboroa (GB)
Santa Anita Derby (G1)	750,000	450,000	Santa Anita	1⅛m	Point Given
Wood Memorial S. (G2)	750,000	450,000	Aqueduct	1⅛m	Congaree
Beverly D. S. (G1)	700,000	420,000	Arlington	1³⁄₁₆m	England's Legend (Fr)
Kentucky Oaks (G1)	609,200	377,704	Churchill Downs	1⅛m	Flute
Delaware H. (G3)	600,300	360,000	Delaware	1¼m	Irving's Baby
Jim Dandy S. (G1)	600,000	360,000	Saratoga	1⅛m	Scorpion

Race (Grade)	Purse	Value to winner	Track	Dist.	Winner
Oaklawn H. (G1)	600,000	360,000	Oaklawn	$1\frac{1}{8}$m	Traditionally
Explosive Bid H. (G2)	600,000	360,000	Fair Grounds	$1\frac{1}{8}$m	Tijiyr (Ire)
Turfway Spiral S. (G2)	600,000	360,000	Turfway	$1\frac{1}{8}$m	Balto Star
Ashland S. (G1)	576,250	357,275	Keeneland	$1\frac{1}{16}$m	Fleet Renee
WinStar Galaxy S. (G2)	563,500	349,370	Keeneland	$1\frac{3}{16}$m	Spook Express (SAf)
Overbrook Spinster S. (G1)	562,000	348,440	Keeneland	$1\frac{1}{8}$m	Miss Linda (Arg)
Shadwell Keeneland Turf Mile (G2)	558,500	346,270	Keeneland	1m	Hap
Queen Elizabeth II Challenge Cup S. (G1)	500,000	310,000	Keeneland	$1\frac{1}{8}$m	Affluent
Champagne S. (G1)	500,000	300,000	Belmont	$1\frac{1}{16}$m	Officer
Citation H. (G2)	500,000	300,000	Hollywood	$1\frac{1}{16}$m	Good Journey
Diana H. (G2)	500,000	300,000	Saratoga	$1\frac{1}{8}$m	Starine (Fr)
Donn H. (G1)	500,000	300,000	Gulfstream	$1\frac{1}{8}$m	Captain Steve
E. P. Taylor S. (Can-G1)	500,000	300,000	Woodbine	$1\frac{1}{4}$m	Choc Ice (Ire)
Hawthorne Gold Cup H. (G2)	500,000	300,000	Hawthorne	$1\frac{1}{4}$m	Duckhorn
Illinois Derby (G2)	500,000	300,000	Sportsman's	$1\frac{1}{8}$m	Silent Scope
Man o' War S. (G1)	500,000	300,000	Belmont	$1\frac{3}{8}$m	With Anticipation
New Orleans H. (G2)	500,000	300,000	Fair Grounds	$1\frac{1}{8}$m	Include
Suburban H. (G2)	500,000	300,000	Belmont	$1\frac{1}{4}$m	Albert the Great
Swaps S. (G1)	500,000	300,000	Hollywood	$1\frac{1}{8}$m	Congaree
Sword Dancer Invitational H. (G1)	500,000	300,000	Saratoga	$1\frac{1}{2}$m	With Anticipation
United Nations H. (G1)	500,000	300,000	Monmouth	$1\frac{3}{8}$m	Senure
Woodbine Oaks	500,000	300,000	Woodbine	$1\frac{1}{8}$m	Dancethruthedawn
Apple Blossom H. (G1)	500,000	300,000	Oaklawn	$1\frac{1}{16}$m	Gourmet Girl
Arkansas Derby (G2)	500,000	300,000	Oaklawn	$1\frac{1}{8}$m	Balto Star
Breeders S.	500,000	300,000	Woodbine	$1\frac{1}{2}$m	Sweetest Thing
Californian S. (G2)	500,000	300,000	Hollywood	$1\frac{1}{8}$m	Skimming
Frizette S. (G1)	500,000	300,000	Belmont	$1\frac{1}{16}$m	You
Hollywood Derby (G1)	500,000	300,000	Hollywood	$1\frac{1}{8}$m	Denon
Massachusetts H. (G2)	500,000	300,000	Suffolk Downs	$1\frac{1}{8}$m	Include
Matriarch S. (G1)	500,000	300,000	Hollywood	$1\frac{1}{8}$m	Starine (Fr)
Meadowlands Cup H. (G2)	500,000	300,000	The Meadowlands	$1\frac{1}{8}$m	Gander
Pennsylvania Derby (G3)	500,000	300,000	Philadelphia	$1\frac{1}{8}$m	Macho Uno
Strub S. (G2)	500,000	300,000	Santa Anita	$1\frac{1}{8}$m	Wooden Phone
Super Derby (G1)	500,000	300,000	Louisiana Downs	$1\frac{1}{4}$m	Outofthebox
West Virginia Derby	500,000	300,000	Mountaineer	$1\frac{1}{8}$m	Western Pride
Woodward S. (G1)	500,000	300,000	Belmont	$1\frac{1}{8}$m	Lido Palace (Chi)
Yellow Ribbon S. (G1)	500,000	300,000	Santa Anita	$1\frac{1}{4}$m	Janet (GB)
Lone Star Derby	500,000	292,500	Lone Star	$1\frac{1}{8}$m	Percy Hope
Goodwood Breeders' Cup H. (G2)	488,000	300,000	Santa Anita	$1\frac{1}{8}$m	Freedom Crest
Shoemaker Breeders' Cup Mile (G1)	475,000	285,000	Hollywood	1m	Irish Prize
Hollywood Futurity (G1)	456,750	274,050	Hollywood	$1\frac{1}{16}$m	Siphonic
Lane's End Breeders' Futurity (G2)	454,400	281,728	Keeneland	$1\frac{1}{16}$m	Siphonic
Walmac Int'l Alcibiades S. (G2)	452,800	280,736	Keeneland	$1\frac{1}{16}$m	Take Charge Lady
Clark H. (G2)	452,000	280,240	Churchill Downs	$1\frac{1}{8}$m	Ubiquity
Prairie Meadows Cornhusker Breeders' Cup H. (G3)	401,625	240,000	Prairie Meadows	$1\frac{1}{8}$m	Euchre
Kentucky Cup Classic H. (G2)	400,000	254,000	Turfway	$1\frac{1}{8}$m	Guided Tour
In Reality S.	400,000	240,000	Calder	$1\frac{1}{16}$m	Booklet
Personal Ensign H. (G1)	400,000	240,000	Saratoga	$1\frac{1}{4}$m	Pompeii
Ramona H. (G1)	400,000	240,000	Del Mar	$1\frac{1}{8}$m	Janet (GB)
San Juan Capistrano Inv. H. (G1)	400,000	240,000	Santa Anita	$1\frac{3}{4}$m	Bienamado
Secretariat S. (G1)	400,000	240,000	Arlington	$1\frac{1}{4}$m	Startac
Eddie Read H. (G1)	400,000	240,000	Del Mar	$1\frac{1}{8}$m	Redattore (Brz)
Frank E. Kilroe Mile (G2)	400,000	240,000	Santa Anita	1m	Road to Slew
Manhattan H. (G1)	400,000	240,000	Belmont	$1\frac{1}{4}$m	Forbidden Apple
My Dear Girl S.	400,000	240,000	Calder	$1\frac{1}{16}$m	Blissful Kiss
Princess Rooney H. (G3)	400,000	240,000	Calder	6f	Dream Supreme
Washington Park H. (G2)	400,000	240,000	Arlington	$1\frac{1}{4}$m	Guided Tour
Coolmore Lexington S. (G2)	371,475	230,315	Keeneland	$1\frac{1}{16}$m	Keats
Hollywood Starlet S. (G1)	358,000	214,800	Hollywood	$1\frac{1}{16}$m	Habibti
Coaching Club American Oaks (G1)	350,000	210,000	Belmont	$1\frac{1}{2}$m	Tweedside
Philip H. Iselin H. (G2)	350,000	210,000	Monmouth	$1\frac{1}{8}$m	Broken Vow
Prince of Wales S.	350,000	210,000	Fort Erie	$1\frac{3}{16}$m	Win City
Charles Whittingham H. (G1)	350,000	210,000	Hollywood	$1\frac{1}{4}$m	Bienamado
Woodford Reserve Turf Classic (G1)	300,000	216,938	Churchill Downs	$1\frac{1}{8}$m	White Heart (GB)
Hollywood Starlet S. (G1)	200,000	214,800	Hollywood	$1\frac{1}{16}$m	Habibti

2001 North American Stakes Races

Achievement H. (R), Woodbine, April 1, $145,530, 3yo, Canadian-bred, 6f, 1:11.51, MILLENNIUM ALLSTAR, Swamp Line, Win City. 6 started.

ACK ACK H.-G3, Churchill Downs, Oct. 28, $114,300, 3yo & up, 7½f, 1:28.63 (NTR), ILLUSIONED, Strawberry Affair, Fappie's Notebook. 11 started.

Ack Ack S. (R), Hollywood Park, June 6, $90,550, 4yo & up, nonwinners of a graded stake in 2001, 7½f, 1:28.19, GREY MEMO, National Saint, Elaborate. 8 started.

A. C. Kemp H., The Downs at Albuquerque, Sept. 19, $26,750, 2yo, 7f, 1:23.65, PACER, Royal de Hope, Co Twining Niner. 9 started.

ACORN S.-G1, Belmont Park, June 8, $200,000, 3yo, f, 1m, 1:34.92, FOREST SECRETS, Victory Ride, Real Cozzy. 8 started.

Ada H., Remington Park, Nov. 18, $40,175, 3yo & up, f & m, 1⅛m, 1:50.81, DEVOUT SINNER, Gin N Ginger, Runaway Magic. 5 started.

Adena Springs Matchmaker S., Fort Erie, June 12, $79,380, 3yo & up, f & m, 5fT, :58.91, PETE'S FANCY, Ring of Flowers, Mema's Turning Red. 10 started.

Adena Springs Matchmaker Sprint S., Thistledown, Sept. 29, $35,000, 3yo & up, f & m, 6f, 1:10.72, ROSE FRANCES, Athenavega, Free of Charge. 4 started.

Adena Springs Matchmaker Turf Sprint S., Remington Park, Sept. 16, $35,540, 3yo & up, f & m, 5fT, :57.84, GOLDEN HURRICANE, Naturalingredients, Islay Mist (GB). 7 started.

ADIRONDACK S.-G2, Saratoga Race Course, Aug. 13, $150,000, 2yo, f, 6½f, 1:15.16, YOU, Cashier's Dream, Magic Storm. 7 started.

AEGON TURF SPRINT S.-G3, see TURF SPRINT S.-G3.

AFFECTIONATELY H.-G3, Aqueduct, Jan. 13, $110,500, 3yo & up, f & m, 1 1/16m, 1:43.17, PENTATONIC, Strolling Belle, Pompeii. 8 started.

AFFIRMED H.-G3, Hollywood Park, June 17, $100,000, 3yo, 1 1/16m, 1:43.10, UNTIL SUNDOWN, Top Hit, Bayou the Moon. 5 started.

Affirmed S. (1st Div.) (R), Calder Race Course, Sept. 1, $125,000, 2yo, progeny of eligible stallions standing in Florida, 7f, 1:26.52, BOG HUNTER, Thiscannonsloaded, A Major Pleasure. 9 started.

Affirmed S. (2nd Div.) (R), Calder Race Course, Sept. 1, $125,000, 2yo, progeny of eligible stallions standing in Florida, 7f, 1:26.16, CAREY'S GOLD, Mountain Forum, Quick Talker. 9 started.

Affirmed S., Turf Paradise, Feb. 24, $22,800, 4yo & up, 1m, 1:37.84, MAYBE SPECIAL (GB), Expresso Bay, Well Planned. 8 started.

African Prince S. (R), Suffolk Downs, April 14, $25,000, 3yo, Massachusetts-bred, 6f, 1:14.51, WOODSIDE, Cutting Concorde, Sunlit Ridge. 8 started.

Agassiz S. (R), Assiniboia Downs, Sept. 3, $26,950, 3yo & up, c & g, Manitoba-bred, 1m, 1:41, GUS AGAIN, Certified Coin, Sovereignadversary. 8 started.

A GLEAM H.-G2, Hollywood Park, July 1, $200,000, 3yo & up, f & m, 7f, 1:22.19, GO GO, Kitty On the Track, Nany's Sweep. 5 started.

A. G. VANDERBILT H.-G2, Saratoga Race Course, Aug. 5, $200,000, 3yo & up, 6f, 1:08.57, FIVE STAR DAY, Delaware Township, Bonapaw. 7 started.

Ahwatukee Express S., Turf Paradise, Sept. 30, $30,000, 3yo, f, 6f, 1:09.31, KNOLL LAKE, Salty Helen, Cove Point. 11 started.

Airline S., Louisiana Downs, July 21, $40,000, 3yo, 6f, 1:09.13, TRIPLE CARD, Ceviche, Joyful Tune. 7 started.

ALABAMA S.-G1, Saratoga Race Course, Aug. 18, $750,000, 3yo, f, 1¼m, 2:01.88, FLUTE, Exogenous, Two Item Limit. 7 started.

Alameda County Fillies and Mares H., Pleasanton, July 7, $50,600, 3yo & up, f & m, 1 1/16m, 1:42.60, MIMI'S CAFE, J Vivendi, Aloha Mangos. 6 started.

Alamedan H., Pleasanton, July 8, $50,600, 3yo & up, 1 1/16m, 1:40.60, REDS SUPERSTAR, White Cloud, New Advantage. 6 started.

Alamo S., Sam Houston Race Park, Dec. 8, $25,000, 2yo, 7f, 1:25.07, DUSTY SPIKE, De Real Deal, Boston Common. 6 started.

Albany H., Golden Gate Fields, Dec. 1, $69,513, 3yo & up, 6f, 1:08.66, RADAR CONTACT, Rio Oro, Secret Launch. 9 started.

Albany S. (R), Saratoga Race Course, Aug. 22, $198,667, 3yo, New York-bred, 1⅛m, 1:50.49, PERSONAL PRO, Sherpa Guide, Farmer Jake. 12 started.

Alberta Bred S. (R), Lethbridge, Sept. 30, $6,700, 3yo, f, Alberta-bred, abt6f, 1:12.20, RAGTIME MISS, Fighting Song, Recent Ruckus. 7 started.

Alberta-Bred S. (R), Lethbridge, Oct. 28, $6,700, 3yo & up, Alberta-bred, 1 1/16m, 1:47.40, SPECIAL MADE, Rag King, Stage Door Jade. 7 started.

Alberta Bred S. (R), Lethbridge, Sept. 30, $6,700, 3yo, Alberta-bred, abt6f, 1:10.20, NO LAW BREAKER, Jake Gonna Win, Control Office. 7 started.

Alberta Breeders' H. (R), Northlands Park, Sept. 22, $50,000, 3yo & up, Alberta-bred, 1 1/16m, 1:43, HIGHLAND LEADER, Tyko Tycoon, South Side. 7 started.

ALBERTA DERBY-G3, Stampede Park, June 16, $100,000, 3yo, 1 1/16m, 1:46, FANCY AS, Baie Comeau, Sixthirtyjoe. 5 started.

Alberta Oaks (R), Northlands Park, Sept. 22, $40,000, 3yo, f, Alberta-bred, 1m, 1:38.80, BRIGHTON BELLE, Classy Approach, Randi. 10 started.

Alberta Premier's Futurity (R), Northlands Park, Sept. 22, $40,000, 2yo, Alberta-bred, 1m, 1:40.20, EXCLUSIVE BANKER, Crescent Remark, By a Nose. 10 started.

Albuquerque Derby, The Downs at Albuquerque, June 5, $53,300, 3yo, 1 1/16m, 1:45.90, ALYOU, Sharethetime, Silver Matt. 9 started.

Albuquerque Derby H., The Downs at Albuquerque, Sept. 16, $26,100, 3yo, 1 1/16m, 1:45.68, BEEHAY, Sharethetime, Appleton (Mex). 5 started.

Alex M. Robb H. (R), Aqueduct, Jan. 6, $85,525, 3yo & up, New York-bred, 1 1/16m, 1:42.79, TURNOFTHECENTURY, Chasin' Wimmin, Pooska Hill. 10 started.

Alex M. Robb H. (R), Aqueduct, Dec. 30, $84,850, 3yo & up, New York-bred, 1 1/16m, 1:44.30, SWEET RICKY, Mount Intrepid, Spectacularspencer. 10 started.

Algoma S. (R), Woodbine, Sept. 3, $101,700, 3yo & up, f & m, Canadian-bred CTHS Sales yearlings, 1 1/16m, 1:47.56, HEALING KNOWLEDGE, Pete's Fancy, Jovial Blast. 7 started.

Alison K. McClay Memorial S., Penn National Race Course, June 30, $20,000, 3yo, f, 6f, 1:10.92, SUMMER SHENANIGANS, U F Step Sharply, Crissie's Sweet. 9 started.

ALL ALONG BREEDERS' CUP S.-G3, Colonial Downs, July 14, $150,000, 3yo & up, f & m, 1⅛mT, 1:47.53 (ECR), COLSTAR, Lucky Lune (Fr), Crystal Sea. 8 started.

ALL-AMERICAN H.-G3, Bay Meadows, May 28, $150,000, 3yo & up, 1 1/16m, 1:41.69, EUCHRE, Irisheyesareflying, Moonlight Charger. 8 started.

All Brandy S. (R), Pimlico, June 9, $75,000, 3yo & up, f & m, Maryland-bred, 1⅛mT, 1:52.06, JAZZ, Maria's Tiara, Ginger's Proud. 8 started.

Allen Bogan Memorial S. (R), Lone Star Park, June 30, $100,000, 3yo & up, f & m, Texas-bred, 1m, 1:35.88, NANIE'S DINNER, Coastalota, Eccentric Lady. 11 started.

Allen E. Paulson H. (R), Gulfstream Park, Feb. 25, $75,000, 3yo & up, f & m, progeny of eligible stallions standing in Florida, 1mT, 1:34.34, SILVER RAIL, Erin Murphy, Zenith. 9 started.

Alliance H., Louisiana Downs, Oct. 20, $25,000, 3yo & up, 1 1/16m, 1:45.33, BIBLICAL, L. A. Spider Legs, Strappado. 6 started.

All Sold Out S. (R), Fairmount Park, Oct. 16, $36,000, 2yo, f, Illinois-conceived and/or -foaled, 6f, 1:14.20, TEJANO HONEY, Secret Pride, Lil' Mary's Kitty. 10 started.

Alma North S. (R), Timonium, Sept. 1, $40,000, 3yo & up, f & m, Maryland-bred, 1 1/16m, 1:46.27, STEPPEDOUTOFADREAM, Saluteloot, Grand Valley. 5 started.

Almost Heaven S., Charles Town, June 9, $41,400, 3yo & up, f & m, 7f, 1:26.51, VANNA GO, A Lot of Mary, Sweet Annuity. 6 started.

Al Swihart Memorial H., Fonner Park, May 5, $25,200, 3yo & up, f & m, 6½f, 1:19.40, RODEO FAN, Mature Miss, Run Around Sue. 7 started.

Althea S., Oaklawn Park, April 14, $50,000, 3yo, f, 1m, 1:38.05, GOLLY GREELEY, Suzanne's Flying, Minister's Baby. 9 started.

Alydar S., Hollywood Park, May 23, $78,150, 3yo, 1⅛m, 1:48.41, BAYOU THE MOON, Until Sundown, Romanceishope. 5 started.

Alydar S., Arlington Park, July 8, $53,750, 3yo, 1m, 1:35.95, DISCREET HERO, Copper Country, Tub Tosser. 7 started.

Alysheba Breeders' Cup S., Lone Star Park, May 12, $100,000, 3yo, 7f, 1:21.54, TOUCH TONE, Son of Rocket, Kazoo. 7 started.

Alyssa H. (R), Beulah Park, May 5, $25,000, 3yo & up, f & m, starters at Beulah Park in 2001, 6f, 1:10.22, END OF THE HILL, Amature Night, Demitryst. 12 started.

Amadevil H. (R), Lincoln State Fair, July 8, $20,000, 3yo & up, Nebraska-bred, 6f, 1:11.40, DOUG'S SHADOW, Ty Man, Death Trappe.

5 started.

Ambassador of Luck H. (R), Philadelphia Park, Sept. 3, $50,000, 3yo & up, f & m, Pennsylvania-bred, 1 1/16m, 1:47.68, BETTY'S HAT, Debutante's Dream, Another Bird. 9 started.

Amelia Peabody S. (R), Suffolk Downs, Dec. 8, $25,000, 2yo, f, Massachusetts-bred, 6f, 1:15.66, MY HONEYCHILD, Trace the Blush, Proper Gun. 7 started.

Americana H., Calder Race Course, July 4, $50,000, 3yo & up, 1⅛mT, 1:50.72, TAKE CHARGE MEGAN, Special Coach, Mr. Livingston. 10 started.

American Beauty S., Oaklawn Park, Feb. 18, $50,000, 4yo & up, f & m, 6f, 1:10.20, MY BRENT'S DIAMOND, Two Dot Slew, Lady Gin. 5 started.

AMERICAN DERBY-G2, Arlington Park, July 22, $250,000, 3yo, 1 3/16mT, 2:03.27, FAN CLUB'S MISTER, Monsieur Cat, Royal Spy. 7 started.

AMERICAN H.-G2, Hollywood Park, July 4, $150,000, 3yo & up, 1⅛mT, 1:48.19, TAKARIAN (Ire), Fighting Falcon, Fateful Dream. 7 started.

AMERICAN TURF S.-G3, Churchill Downs, May 4, $117,900, 3yo, 1 1/16mT, 1:42.89, STRATEGIC PARTNER, Baptize, Dynameaux. 6 started.

Amos H. (R), Calder Race Course, July 28, $35,230, 3yo & up, non-winners of $25,000 at one mile or over in 2001, 1 1/16m, 1:45.49, DANCING GUY, Western Honors, Golden Concorde. 9 started.

AMSTERDAM S.-G2, Saratoga Race Course, Aug. 3, $135,700, 3yo, 6f, 1:11.03, CITY ZIP, Speightstown, Smile My Lord. 6 started.

Anchor Gaming Allowance S., Sunland Park, Feb. 4, $26,800, 3yo, 6f, 1:11.80, MISS EINSTEIN, Ticketless, Hot On Ice. 5 started.

ANCIENT TITLE BREEDERS' CUP H.-G1, Santa Anita Park, Oct. 6, $207,100, 3yo & up, 6f, 1:07.67, SWEPT OVERBOARD, Kona Gold, I Love Silver. 6 started.

Anderson Fowler S., Monmouth Park, July 22, $50,000, 3yo, 5fT, :55.56, RIDEOUTS PATTON, Rock, Sparkling Number. 6 started.

Angelo Testa S., Hialeah Park, May 12, $27,000, 3yo, 1 1/16mT, 1:42.76, ALTERED BIRDIE, Sea Air, Tv Sports Director. 7 started.

Angenora S. (R), Thistledown, April 21, $40,000, 3yo & up, f & m, Ohio-bred, 6f, 1:12.44, ATHENAVEGA, Easter Butter, Prizes. 11 started.

Angie C. S., Emerald Downs, July 8, $31,500, 2yo, f, 6f, 1:10.40, STRONG CREDENTIALS, Strikes No Spares, Perfect Plan. 5 started.

Angi Go S., Turf Paradise, April 22, $23,800, 3yo, f, 1mT, 1:38.96, MOONLIT MADDIE, The Queen and I, Lucy T. 6 started.

Angi Go. S. (R), Les Bois Park, July 14, $11,618, 3yo, f, Idaho-bred, 7f, 1:26.38, THE QUEEN AND I, Hey She's a Dancer, Todasha. 9 started.

Anka Germania S., Gulfstream Park, March 8, $75,250, 4yo & up, f & m, abt1 1/16mT, 1:44.05, PENNY'S GOLD, Miss Tobacco, Tippity Witch. 6 started.

Ann Arbor S. (R), Great Lakes Downs, July 6, $50,000, 3yo, f, Michigan-bred, 1m, 1:44.45, EMPRESS LIVIA, Little Match Girl, I Match Too. 7 started.

Annie Oakley H. (R), Thistledown, June 23, $50,000, 3yo, f, Ohio-bred, 1 1/16m, 1:45.52, EYE SLEW THE CITY, Ashwood C C, Across the Creek. 9 started.

Ann Owens Distaff H. (R), Turf Paradise, April 7, $30,000, 3yo & up, f & m, Arizona-bred, 6f, 1:09.57, CHUICHUPA, O'Hara, Drag Time Gal. 9 started.

Anoakia S., Santa Anita Park, Oct. 21, $86,800, 2yo, f, 6f, 1:11.07, PONCHE DE LEONA, Asian Adventure, Cinnful Bride. 5 started.

Answer Do S. (R), Hollywood Park, July 16, $75,025, 3yo & up, California-bred, 5½fT, 1:01.23, GIBSON COUNTY, The Morris Monroe, Indiahoma. 5 started.

Answer Do S., Turf Paradise, May 22, $23,900, 3yo & up, 6f, 1:09.30, STORMY AMBITION, Iza Redhead, Doc Art. 5 started.

Anthony DeSpirito S., Suffolk Downs, Nov. 10, $25,000, 2yo, 6f, 1:12.79, LITTLE BILLY, Jeremiah's Judge, Stylish Sultan. 12 started.

Anthony Fair H., Anthony Downs, July 22, $5,000, 3yo & up, 6½f, 1:23.26, CHASERVILLE, Mr. Fools Gold, Candyfortheguest, Overprint. 7 started.

Anthony Thoroughbred Futurity, Anthony Downs, July 22, $10,000, 2yo, 5f, 1:04.48, BEVERLYS GOLD, A. D.'s Dream, Patch Conway. 5 started.

Apache County Thoroughbred Maiden S., Apache County Fair, Sept. 22, $3,428, 3, 4, 5 & 6 yo, 6f, 1:14, JAFFA, Let George Do It, Cry No More. 6 started.

A.P. Indy S., Keeneland, Oct. 6, $83,100, 3yo & up, f & m, 5½fT, 1:04.06, CONFESSIONAL, Thunder Sands, Charm. 8 started.

Appalachian S., Keeneland, April 8, $113,500, 3yo, f, 1mT, 1:35.22, BOLD ANSWER, Voodoo Dancer, Word Puzzle. 9 started.

APPLE BLOSSOM H.-G1, Oaklawn Park, April 8, $500,000, 4yo & up, f & m, 1 1/16m, 1:42.15, GOURMET GIRL, Lu Ravi, Lazy Slusan. 11 started.

APPLETON H.-G2, Gulfstream Park, Jan. 6, $150,000, 3yo & up, 1mT, 1:33.69, ASSOCIATE, Band Is Passing, El Mirasol. 12 started.

Appleton H., Far Hills, Oct. 20, $24,999, 4yo & up, abt2⅜mT, 3:56.36, SPRING SALUTE, Turkish Corner, Iron County Xmas. 11 started.

Appointment H. (R), Delaware Park, May 27, $58,700, 3yo & up, non-winners of a stakes race worth $30,000 to the winner in 2001 or for an optional claiming price of $100,000, 6f, 1:09.66, GRANGEVILLE, Stormin Oedy, Bobby's Buckaroo. 6 started.

April Run S., Pimlico, May 27, $48,500, 3yo & up, f & m, 1¼m, 2:06.40, SALUTELOOT, Polly Jo, Free Vacation. 4 started.

Aprisa H., Fairplex Park, Sept. 12, $49,000, 3yo & up, 6f, 1:10.40, THE MORRIS MONROE, Profound Secret, Lucayan Prince. 6 started.

A. P. Smithwick Memorial Steeplechase H., Saratoga Race Course, Aug. 9, $81,350, 4yo & up, 2 1/16mT, 3:39.36, PRAISE THE PRINCE (NZ), Aggro Crag, Spring Salute. 7 started.

AQUEDUCT H.-G3, Aqueduct, Jan. 20, $110,500, 3yo & up, 1 1/16m, 1:42.20, LIBERTY GOLD, Coyote Lakes, Talk's Cheap. 7 started.

Arapahoe Park H., Arapahoe Park, Aug. 19, $27,800, 3yo & up, 1⅛m, 1:50, OUT 'N ABOUT, Personal Beau, Darn Tootin. 8 started.

Arapahoe Park Sprint H., Arapahoe Park, June 17, $26,700, 3yo & up, 6f, 1:11, MOONLIGHT MAVERICK, Oh Gracie, Formal Feast. 5 started.

ARCADIA H.-G2, Santa Anita Park, April 7, $150,000, 4yo & up, 1⅛mT, 1:49.74, LAZY LODE (Arg), Night Patrol, Wake the Tiger. 5 started.

Arcadia S. (R), Louisiana Downs, June 30, $42,800, 3yo, Louisiana-bred, 6f, 1:10.02, PRINCE SLEW, Toolighttoquittoo, Pink Duck. 6 started.

Arctic Cloud S., Pimlico, June 3, $36,400, 3yo, f, 6f, 1:10.13, XTRA HEAT, Musical Times, Bewixed. 3 started.

Arctic Queen H. (R), Finger Lakes, Aug. 11, $30,000, 3yo & up, f & m, New York-bred, 6f, 1:12.13, END OF THE HILL, Belongs to Mony, Double the Debt. 6 started.

ARISTIDES H.-G3, Churchill Downs, June 30, $108,400, 3yo & up, 6½f, 1:14.79, BET ON SUNSHINE, Alannan, Dash for Daylight. 6 started.

Arizona Breeders' Derby (R), Turf Paradise, April 7, $52,506, 3yo, Arizona-bred, 1 1/16m, 1:42.65, RESOLVE, Blaine County High, Cubbie's Grey. 5 started.

Arizona Breeders' Futurity (R), Turf Paradise, Nov. 24, $41,490, 2yo, f, Arizona-bred, 6f, 1:10.12, CALCE CLUNES, Reatta Pass, Fool's Mate. 11 started.

Arizona Breeders' Futurity (R), Turf Paradise, Nov. 24, $43,764, 2yo, c & g, Arizona-bred, 6f, 1:09.64, JETSON, Willcox, Hollywood Warrior. 11 started.

Arizona Oaks, Turf Paradise, Feb. 3, $75,000, 3yo, f, 1 1/16m, 1:43.36, BLUE SPRINGS, Royal Alliance, Catahoula Rose. 8 started.

Arizona Stallion S. (R), Turf Paradise, May 6, $38,938, 3yo, progeny of eligible stallions standing in Arizona, 7½fT, 1:31.63, RADICAL RAGE, Ryan's Partner, Brian's Shot. 6 started.

ARKANSAS DERBY-G2, Oaklawn Park, April 14, $500,000, 3yo, 1⅛m, 1:49.04, BALTO STAR, Jamaican Rum, Son of Rocket. 11 started.

Ark-La-Tex H., Louisiana Downs, Aug. 4, $75,000, 3yo & up, 1⅛m, 1:48.30, UNRULLAH BULL, L. A. Spider Legs, Rebridled. 6 started.

ARLINGTON CLASSIC S.-G2, Arlington Park, June 30, $200,000, 3yo, 1⅛mT, 1:48.80, BAPTIZE, Indygo Shiner, Cherokee Kim. 6 started.

ARLINGTON H.-G3, Arlington Park, July 28, $250,000, 3yo & up, 1¼mT, 2:02.53, MAKE NO MISTAKE (Ire), Takarian (Ire), El Gran Papa. 7 started.

ARLINGTON MATRON H.-G3, Arlington Park, Oct. 6, $150,000, 3yo & up, f & m, 1⅛m, 1:51.53, HUMBLE CLERK, Maltese Superb, Lakenheath. 7 started.

ARLINGTON MILLION S.-G1, Arlington Park, Aug. 18, $1,000,000, 3yo & up, 1¼mT, 2:02.64, SILVANO (Ger), Hap, Redattore (Brz). 12 started.

Arlington Sprint H., Arlington Park, Aug. 25, $100,000, 3yo & up, 6f, 1:10.06, BET ON SUNSHINE, Tic N Tin, Robin de Nest. 8 started.
ARLINGTON-WASHINGTON FUTURITY-G2, Arlington Park, Sept. 29, $150,000, 2yo, 1m, 1:38.78, PUBLICATION, It'sallinthechase, Dubai Squire. 7 started.
ARLINGTON-WASHINGTON LASSIE S.-G3, Arlington Park, Sept. 22, $100,000, 2yo, f, 1m, 1:39.34, JOANIES BELLA, Brief Bliss, First Again. 9 started.
Ascot Graduation Breeders' Cup H., Hastings Park Racecourse, Oct. 14, $95,485, 2yo, 1 1/16m, 1:46.96, NO TIME FLAT, Woody's Diamond, Potato Lad. 10 started.
ASCOT H.-G3, Bay Meadows, June 10, $100,000, 3yo, 1 1/16mT, 1:44.17, SIR ALFRED, Hoovergetthekeys, Sea to See. 8 started.
ASHLAND S.-G1, Keeneland, April 7, $576,250, 3yo, f, 1 1/16m, 1:43.77, FLEET RENEE, Golden Ballet, Latour. 11 started.
Ashley T. Cole H. (R), Belmont Park, Sept. 22, $85,275, 3yo & up, New York-bred, 1⅛m, 1:48.89, BRAVE ONE, No Bad Habits, Whitmore's Conn. 8 started.
Aspen Cup S., Ruidoso Downs, June 23, $16,800, 3yo, f, 6f, 1:12.20, WAVEBAND, Rampaging Irish, Egotistic. 9 started.
Aspen H. (R), Arapahoe Park, June 24, $28,200, 3yo & up, c & g, Colorado-bred, 6f, 1:09.80, HOT WHEELS, Ex Kay E, Getaway in Style. 9 started.
Aspidistra H., Calder Race Course, June 16, $50,000, 3yo & up, f & m, 1 1/16mT, 1:44.76, QUEEN OF OZ, Silver Bandana, Lady Brook. 12 started.
Aspirant S. (R), Finger Lakes, Aug. 18, $63,300, 2yo, New York-bred, 6f, 1:11.14, SMOKIEISABANDIT, Eye of the Comet, White Ibis. 7 started.
Assault S. (R), Lone Star Park, June 30, $150,000, 3yo & up, Texas-bred, 1 1/16m, 1:42.24, LIGHTS ON BROADWAY, Desert Darby, Captain Countdown. 7 started.
Assiniboia Oaks, Assiniboia Downs, Sept. 9, $29,400, 3yo, f, 1 1/16m, 1:47.60, LITTLE LOLITTA, Frisky Lover, Love Play. 6 started.
ASTARITA S.-G2, Belmont Park, Oct. 8, $103,400, 2yo, f, 6½f, 1:16.67, BELLA BELLUCCI, Forest Heiress, Speed to Burn. 4 started.
Astoria S., Belmont Park, July 1, $108,500, 2yo, f, 5½f, 1:05.65, TOUCH LOVE, Smok'n Frolic, V V S Flawless. 7 started.
ATBA Fall Sales S. (R), Turf Paradise, Oct. 20, $78,655, 2yo, c & g, yearlings consigned to the 2000 ATBA sale, 6f, 1:11.12, JETSON, Mister Party, Charm Attack. 11 started.
ATBA Fall Sales S. (R), Turf Paradise, Oct. 20, $80,660, 2yo, f, yearlings consigned to the 2000 ATBA sale, 6f, 1:11.28, DE SHAY, Calce Clunes, Fancy Prancer. 10 started.
Atchison, Topeka, Santa Fe H., The Woodlands, Oct. 20, $20,000, 3yo & up, 6f, 1:10.80, KIDD CAT, Fun to Run, Pasomonte Paul. 6 started.
ATHENIA H.-G3 (1st Div.), Belmont Park, Oct. 26, $137,875, 3yo & up, f & m, 1 1/16mT, 1:42.09, VERRUMA (Brz), Siringas (Ire), Freefourracing. 8 started.
ATHENIA H.-G3 (2nd Div.), Belmont Park, Oct. 26, $137,875, 3yo & up, f & m, 1 1/16mT, 1:40.53, BABAE (Chi), Batique, Sweet Prospect (GB). 8 started.
Atherton S., Bay Meadows, April 15, $53,275, 3yo, 6f, 1:10.06, BEYOND BRILLIANT, Mango Marquerita, Millennium Song. 4 started.
Atlanta Cup Hurdle S., Atlanta, April 14, $97,000, 4yo & up, abt2⅞mT, ELECTRON, All Gong (GB), Masamadas (GB). 6 started.
ATTO MILE S.-G1, Woodbine, Sept. 9, $1,000,000, 3yo & up, 1mT, 1:32.79 (NCR), NUMEROUS TIMES, Affirmed Success, Quiet Resolve. 14 started.
Auburn S., Emerald Downs, May 5, $35,000, 3yo, c & g, 6f, 1:09, JUMRON WON, Tactical Allusion, Star of Elttaes. 7 started.
Audubon Oaks, Ellis Park, Aug. 4, $50,000, 3yo, f, 1mT, 1:32.93, VALORY, Casual Feat, The Hess Express. 9 started.
Au Revoir H., Les Bois Park, Aug. 12, $6,450, 3yo & up, 1¼m, 2:05.92, ALMOST GOLDEN, Northern Ricky, The Gray Jaklin. 7 started.
Autobot S., Hawthorne Race Course, Oct. 31, $44,500, 3yo, 1 1/16mT, 1:43.92, MYSTERY GIVER, Freeway Ticket, Lord Livermore. 8 started.
Autotote Derby, Lethbridge, Oct. 28, $10,900, 3yo, 1 1/16m, 1:48.60, FLY BESIDE ME, C D Fuse, Minister of Speed. 6 started.
Autumn Classic H. (R), Remington Park, Nov. 23, $27,000, 3yo & up, Oklahoma-bred, 6f, 1:08.91, ABBI'S CHOICE, Medium Rare, Slewmeister. 8 started.
AUTUMN H.-G3, Woodbine, Nov. 10, $163,800, 3yo & up, 1 1/16m, 1:44.83, WIN CITY, Wicklow Highlands, Kiss a Native. 7 started.
Autumn Leaves H., Mountaineer Park, Oct. 2, $57,850, 3yo & up, f & m, 1⅜mT, 2:14.96, AMOURETTE, Cabot Cove, Colonial Ball. 8 started.
Awad S., Pimlico, June 17, $40,000, 3yo & up, 1⅛mT, 1:53.01, TROOPER RED, Holditholditholdit, Dynamic Trick. 5 started.
Awad S., Arlington Park, Aug. 10, $64,000, 3yo, abt1 1/16mT, 1:45.23, MONSIEUR CAT, Rahy's Secret, Altered Birdie. 8 started.
A & W Restaurants S., Lethbridge, Oct. 14, $8,800, 3yo & up, f & m, 7f, 1:25.80, A TEMPTING LIGHT, Flying Jo, Kims Black Lady. 8 started.
AZALEA BREEDERS' CUP S.-G3, Calder Race Course, July 14, $250,000, 3yo, f, 6f, 1:11.81, HATTIESBURG, Southern Tour, Spanish Glitter. 11 started.
Azalea H., Remington Park, Aug. 12, $35,385, 3yo & up, f & m, 1 1/16mT, 1:44.31, VOLADORA, Runaway Magic, Good Timin Brook. 5 started.
Aztec Oaks (R), SunRay Park, Nov. 18, $67,209, 3yo, f, New Mexico-bred, 6½f, 1:17.40, SANDY SAGE, Dancing Capote, Hasty's Looker. 10 started.
Babe Hall S., Rillito Park, Feb. 25, $3,854, 3yo & up, 6f, 1:11.80, DABONA, Terraforming, Manzanola. 8 started.
Baby Doe H., Arapahoe Park, July 15, $27,700, 3yo & up, f & m, 7f, 1:25, PURLS LEDGEND, One Foxy Lady, Bates Again. 9 started.
Bachman S., Fonner Park, March 3, $15,975, 3yo, 4f, :47.80, HARVEY BENGAL, Watch Me Dazzle, De North Branch. 10 started.
Backstretch Chapel S. (R), Emerald Downs, Aug. 25, $25,000, 3yo, c & g, Washington-bred, 6½f, 1:16, ROAD AFLEET, Alfurune, Wagon Wheel. 10 started.
Bahamas S., Hialeah Park, April 1, $50,000, 3yo, 6f, 1:09.23, AMERICAN CENTURY, Rich Coins, Illusioned. 7 started.
Bald Eagle Breeders' Cup H., Pimlico, Sept. 8, $97,000, 3yo & up, 1mT, 1:33.97, LA REINE'S TERMS, Cherokeeinthehills, In Frank's Honor. 9 started.
Baldski H., Calder Race Course, Sept. 23, $33,870, 3yo & up, 1⅛mT, 1:47.73, KASSAR, Saint Joseph, Diablo Reigns. 10 started.
BALDWIN S.-G3, Santa Anita Park, Feb. 25, $110,000, 3yo, 6½f (originally scheduled on the turf), 1:16.29, SKIP TO THE STONE, Trailthefox, Bills Paid. 6 started.
Bal Harbour S., Hialeah Park, April 7, $27,400, 3yo, 1⅛mT, 1:48.74, MOOMTAZZ, Potaro (Ire), Mr Notebook. 9 started.
Ballade S. (R), Woodbine, June 13, $100,800, 3yo & up, f & m, progeny of eligible stallions standing in Ontario, 6f, 1:10.04, MYSTERIOUS AFFAIR, Ruby Park, Sports Flashy. 4 started.
BALLERINA BREEDERS' CUP S.-G3, Hastings Park Racecourse, Oct. 8, $142,677, 3yo & up, f & m, 1⅛m, 1:49.74, GREY TOBE FREE, Fabulous Flight, Make Contact. 9 started.
BALLERINA H.-G1, Saratoga Race Course, Aug. 26, $250,000, 3yo & up, f & m, 7f, 1:22.33, SHINE AGAIN, Country Hideaway, Dream Supreme. 5 started.
BALLSTON SPA BREEDERS' CUP H.-G3, Saratoga Race Course, Aug. 12, $190,200, 3yo & up, f & m, 1 1/16mT, 1:40.69, PENNY'S GOLD, Babae (Chi), Chaste. 6 started.
BALTIMORE RAVENS BREEDERS' CUP H.-G3, Pimlico, June 16, $140,000, 3yo & up, 1⅛m, 1:50.52, LIGHTNING PACES, Milwaukee Brew, Grundlefoot. 5 started.
Bam's Penny S. (R), Bay Meadows, Nov. 3, $60,650, 2yo, f, California-bred, 6f, 1:10.68, CINNFUL BRIDE, Bigboystoy, Courtly Colors. 8 started.
Bangles and Beads S., Fairplex Park, Sept. 18, $50,000, 3yo & up, f & m, 6½f, 1:16.41, CREASEINHERJEANS, Madame Roar, Sea Reel. 8 started.
Bara Lass S. (R), Santa Anita Park, March 16, $74,110, 4yo & up, f & m, non-winners of $3,000 twice other than maiden, claiming, or starter, non-winners of three races, or for a claiming price of $80,000, 6f, 1:10.86, PHAENNA, Miss Grimsby, Candi's Princess. 6 started.
Bara Lass S. (R), Sam Houston Race Park, Dec. 1, $50,000, 2yo, f, Texas-bred, 6f, 1:11.19, SLY KONA, Miss Ritz, Lovely Bonita. 7 started.
BARBARA FRITCHIE H.-G2, Laurel Park, Feb. 17, $200,000, 3yo & up, f & m, 7f, 1:23.74, PRIZED STAMP, Superduper Miss, Tax Affair. 6 started.
Barbara Jo Rubin S., Charles Town, March 1, $42,250, 3yo, f, 7f, 1:31.29, LADY CORDELIA, Bewixed, Holly Jolly. 8 started.
Barbara Shinpoch S., Emerald Downs, Sept. 2, $54,450, 2yo, f, 1m, 1:39, ASHBECCA, Lasting Code, Solmar. 10 started.
Barksdale H., Louisiana Downs, Sept. 1, $50,000, 3yo & up, abt1mT,

1:38, AVIESALLSTAR, Main Street, L. A. Spider Legs. 7 started.

Barretts Debutante S. (R), Fairplex Park, Sept. 15, $95,600, 2yo, f, horses sold by Barretts Equine Sales Ltd., 6½f, 1:19.21, DANCEOFTHEFLAGS, Aglow, French Flare. 8 started.

Barretts Juvenile S. (R), Fairplex Park, Sept. 16, $103,650, 2yo, c & g, horses sold by Barretts Equine Sales Ltd., 6½f, 1:18.01, SWEET STEPPER, Vito Corleone, Delong. 10 started.

BASHFORD MANOR S.-G2, Churchill Downs, July 8, $133,750, 2yo, 6f, 1:09.90, LUNAR BOUNTY, Binyamin, Storm Passage. 5 started.

Bassinet S., River Downs, Sept. 1, $100,000, 2yo, f, 6f, 1:12.20, JOANIES BELLA, Lakeside Cup, Mystery At Sea. 8 started.

Batter Up H. (R), Charles Town, April 21, $40,000, 3yo & up, c & g, starters at Charles Town at least twice since October 21, 2000, excluding stakes, 7f, 1:24.70, BIG BECKER, Proudest Bull, Rebellious Dreamer. 7 started.

Battlefield S., Monmouth Park, June 10, $75,000, 3yo & up, 1⅛mT, 1:47.24, READY TO ROLL (Ire), Indy Vidual, Crash Course. 7 started.

Battle of the Alamo S., Retama Park, Aug. 18, $25,000, 3yo, 6f, 1:11.25, JOYFUL TUNE, Cool Rein, Somethin Brite. 7 started.

Battler Star H. (R), Fair Grounds, March 11, $75,000, 3yo, f, Louisiana-bred, 6f, 1:10.65, LETTUCE LOOSE, Michelle's Crown, Princess Who. 7 started.

Baxter S., Fonner Park, March 24, $15,950, 3yo, 6½f, 1:21.40, TATE'S WAY, Count Basic, My Buba Boy. 10 started.

BAYAKOA H.-G2, Hollywood Park, Dec. 15, $150,000, 3yo & up, f & m, 1 1/16m, 1:42.52, STARRER, Queenie Belle, Tropical Lady (Brz). 7 started.

Bayakoa S., Oaklawn Park, April 14, $50,000, 4yo & up, f & m, 1 1/16m, 1:45.93, DOROTHY ANN, Gobedie, Voladora. 7 started.

BAY MEADOWS BREEDERS' CUP H.-G3, Bay Meadows, Sept. 22, $110,000, 3yo & up, abt1⅛mT, 1:47.50, SUPER QUERCUS (Fr), Most Likely (Arg), Sign of Hope (GB). 6 started.

BAY MEADOWS BREEDERS' CUP SPRINT H.-G3, Bay Meadows, Sept. 8, $142,500, 3yo & up, 6f, 1:07.94, LEXICON, Swept Overboard, You and You Alone. 4 started.

BAY MEADOWS DERBY H.-G3, Bay Meadows, Nov. 4, $100,000, 3yo, abt1⅛mT, 1:46.81, BLUE STELLER (Ire), Sir Alfred, Sea to See. 8 started.

Bay Meadows Oaks, Bay Meadows, May 19, $53,100, 3yo, f, 1 1/16mT, 1:43.34, ALLRIGHT NOW (Fr), Skywriting, Super Tuesday. 8 started.

Bayou Breeders' Cup H., Fair Grounds, March 3, $152,450, 4yo & up, f & m, 1⅛m (originally scheduled on the turf), 1:53.82, ON A SOAPBOX, Always Sure, Lady Tamworth. 6 started.

Bayou City S., Sam Houston Race Park, Jan. 27, $25,000, 3yo, f, 6f, 1:09.69, MY MEGGIE MEG, Sister's Shamrock, Bricketta. 8 started.

Bayouland Sales S. (R), Evangeline Downs, Aug. 4, $36,000, 2yo, horses sold at a Louisiana Thoroughbred Breeders sale, 5f, 1:00.20, COURVOISIER, Doeny Rain, Three Bags Full. 11 started.

BAY SHORE S.-G3, Aqueduct, April 14, $150,000, 3yo, 7f, 1:22.46, SKIP TO THE STONE, Multiple Choice, Friday's a Comin'. 8 started.

BC Lotto H., Kamloops, Aug. 12, $11,050, 3yo & up, 1m, 1:38.20, ADANAC, Diamond Ace, So Cool. 5 started.

Beacon Hill S. (R), Suffolk Downs, May 26, $25,000, 3yo, Massachusetts-bred, abt1mT, 1:43.58, SUNLIT RIDGE, Rita's Partner, Silver and Green. 9 started.

Beau Brummel S., Fairplex Park, Sept. 14, $49,000, 2yo, c & g, 6½f, 1:18.66, DEBONAIR JOE, Meadow Slew, Four Cards Too. 6 started.

Beaufort S. (R), Northlands Park, Sept. 22, $44,000, 3yo, Alberta-bred, 1 1/16m, 1:43.40, THEY CALL ME CODY, Sixthirtyjoe, Miki Bleu Eyes. 8 started.

BEAUGAY H.-G3, Aqueduct, May 6, $109,900, 3yo & up, f & m, 1 1/16mT, 1:41.74, GAVIOLA, Truebreadpudding, Efficient Frontier. 6 started.

Beau Genius H., Great Lakes Downs, Sept. 1, $25,000, 4yo & up, 7f, 1:25.67, ABOVE THE WIND, Mywayistheonlyway, Crashpad. 10 started.

Beautiful Day H., Delaware Park, July 16, $67,400, 3yo & up, f & m, abt1⅛mT, 1:50.36, QUIDNASKRA, Minkie, Rhum. 8 started.

Beaver State S., Portland Meadows, Jan. 27, $8,325, 3yo, 5½f, 1:06.49, PROVO, Viva Lavilla, Danzilation. 6 started.

BED O' ROSES BREEDERS' CUP H.-G3, Aqueduct, April 21, $157,700, 3yo & up, f & m, 1m, 1:34.98, COUNTRY HIDEAWAY, Critical Eye, Jostle. 7 started.

Behave Yourself H. (R), Charles Town, March 10, $40,000, 3yo & up, f & m, starters at Charles Town at least twice since September 10, 2000, excluding stakes, 6½f, 1:21.78, A LOT OF MARY, Bea Minute, Blues Sistah. 10 started.

BEL AIR H.-G2, Hollywood Park, July 7, $100,000, 3yo & up, 1 1/16m, 1:41.74, SMILE AGAIN, Freedom Crest, Dig for It. 6 started.

Belair S., Laurel Park, Jan. 14, $52,671, 3yo, f, 1 1/16m, 1:47.05, ULTRAVASE, Your Out, Erin Moor. 4 started.

BELDAME S.-G1, Belmont Park, Oct. 6, $750,000, 3yo & up, f & m, 1⅛m, 1:49.20, EXOGENOUS, Flute, Spain. 8 started.

Belle Roberts H., Emerald Downs, Sept. 3, $60,000, 3yo & up, f & m, 1⅛m, 1:50, MAKE CONTACT, Latter Day Paula, My Maebasket. 7 started.

Belmont Day H., Eureka Downs, June 9, $5,300, 3yo & up, 7f, 1:28.72, JUST A ECLIPSE, Biggen, Noble Dreamer. 8 started.

BELMONT S.-G1, Belmont Park, June 9, $1,000,000, 3yo, 1½m, 2:26.56, POINT GIVEN, A P Valentine, Monarchos. 9 started.

BEN ALI S.-G3, Keeneland, April 27, $106,800, 4yo & up, 1⅛m, 1:48.47, BROKEN VOW, Perfect Cat, Jadada. 5 started.

Benburb S. (R), Fort Erie, July 22, $55,100, 3yo & up, Canadian-bred, 1 1/16mT, 1:43.72, BEAU GENTLEMAN, Coastal Display, Smoke'n'ashes. 8 started.

Ben Cohen S., Pimlico, May 6, $40,000, 3yo & up, 5fT, :56.56, JUST CALL ME CARL, Dr. Max, Grangeville. 9 started.

Benjamin Harrison S. (R), Hoosier Park, Oct. 27, $42,700, 3yo, c & g, Indiana-bred, 1 1/16m, 1:42.85, RED'S HONOR, Hail to Wild Again, Pelican Beach. 6 started.

Ben Jones H., Charles Town, March 24, $40,000, 3yo & up, c & g, 6½f, 1:19.97, ALL THE MARBLES, Smooth Roller, Confucius Say. 10 started.

Bensalem S., Philadelphia Park, June 9, $50,000, 3yo & up, 1½mT, 2:32.48, DAWN OF THE CONDOR, Arizona Storm, Asking for Luck. 6 started.

Bergen County S., The Meadowlands, Sept. 3, $100,000, 3yo, 6f, 1:08.67, CITY ZIP, San Nicolas, Sea of Green. 5 started.

BERKELEY H.-G3, Golden Gate Fields, March 31, $100,000, 3yo & up, 1m, 1:34.18, BLADE PROSPECTOR (Brz), Dixie Dot Com, Milk Wood (GB). 6 started.

BERNARD BARUCH H.-G2, Saratoga Race Course, July 27, $150,000, 3yo & up, 1⅛mT, 1:47.06, HAP, Royal Strand (Ire), Dr. Kashnikow. 7 started.

Bernie Dowd H. (R), Monmouth Park, July 22, $50,000, 3yo & up, New Jersey-bred, 6f, 1:09.83, SEA OF TRANQUILITY, H. M. S. Jackson, Just Beforemidnite. 10 started.

Bersid S., Turf Paradise, Nov. 11, $21,696, 3yo & up, f & m, 1m, 1:37.18, GLEEFULLY, Miss Pixie, Balboa Park. 5 started.

Bertram F. Bongard S. (R), Belmont Park, Sept. 30, $81,300, 2yo, New York-bred, 7f, 1:25.32, WHITE IBIS, Smokieisabandit, Eye of the Comet. 7 started.

BESSARABIAN H.-G3, Woodbine, Nov. 18, $141,475, 3yo & up, f & m, 7f, 1:22.38, ELEKTRALINE, Feathers, Ahead by a Century. 8 started.

Best of Ohio Distaff Championship S. (R), Beulah Park, Oct. 8, $75,000, 3yo & up, f & m, Ohio-bred, 1⅛m, 1:49.77, ASHWOOD C C, Lady Cherie, Special Appeal. 13 started.

Best of Ohio Endurance Championship S. (R), Beulah Park, Oct. 8, $100,000, 3yo & up, Ohio-bred, 1¼m, 2:00.32, MAJESTIC DINNER, Fax a Freddy, Devil Time. 9 started.

Best of Ohio Juvenile Championship S. (R), Beulah Park, Oct. 8, $75,000, 2yo, Ohio-bred, 1 1/16m, 1:44.57, U S S TINOSA, Watch Me Fire, Eyes for Hannah. 10 started.

Best of Ohio Juvenile Fillies Championship S. (R), Beulah Park, Oct. 8, $75,000, 2yo, f, Ohio-bred, 1 1/16m, 1:44.09, JOANIES BELLA, Crypto's Twinjet, Mercer's Launch. 14 started.

Best of Ohio Sprint Championship S. (R), Beulah Park, Oct. 8, $50,000, 3yo & up, Ohio-bred, 6f, 1:08.63, JOHN Q'S WINNER, Q One for Two, Kels On the Attack. 11 started.

BEST PAL S.-G3, Del Mar, Aug. 15, $138,000, 2yo, 6½f, 1:15.08, OFFICER, Metatron, Essence of Dubai. 3 started.

Best Turn S., Aqueduct, Feb. 24, $80,975, 3yo, 6f, 1:09.09, PUT IT BACK, Stake Runner, My New Love. 6 started.

Bettie Bullock Memorial Derby, Wyoming Downs, Aug. 12, $8,825, 3yo, 5½f, 1:04.63, NICKEL LOU, Colorado City, Righteous Desire. 8 started.

Bettor's Invitational H., Grants Pass, July 7, $5,875, 3yo & up, 6½f, 1:21.46, THEYCALLMECOLONEL, Imus, Whirling Ace. 6 started.

Bet Twice S., Monmouth Park, July 14, $50,000, 3yo & up, 1mT, 1:34.85, SARDAUKAR (GB), I'm Sentimental, Crash Course. 10 started.

Bet Twice S., Arlington Park, Aug. 18, $62,750, 3yo, 6f, 1:11.79, WILD HITS, Tub Tosser, Don Regino. 5 started.

BEVERLY D. S.-G1, Arlington Park, Aug. 18, $700,000, 3yo & up, f & m, 1 3/16mT, 1:56.75, ENGLAND'S LEGEND (Fr), The Seven Seas, Spook Express (SAf). 9 started.

BEVERLY HILLS H.-G1, Hollywood Park, June 24, $200,000, 3yo & up, f & m, 1¼mT, 1:59.61, ASTRA, Happyanunoit (NZ), Kalypso Katie (Ire). 5 started.

BEWITCH S.-G3, Keeneland, April 26, $200,000, 4yo & up, f & m, 1½mT, 2:30.28, KEEMOON (Fr), Playact (Ire), Krisada. 8 started.

Bien Bien S. (R), Hollywood Park, Nov. 7, $72,400, 3yo, non-winners of $60,000 at a mile or over, 1mT, 1:34.15, MIZZEN MAST, Momentum, Lookn East. 6 started.

Bienvenidos S., Turf Paradise, Sept. 28, $22,800, 3yo & up, 1m, 1:38.76, GO BUX, Prince of the Wild, Cascade Casey. 8 started.

Big Red Mile H. (R), Lincoln State Fair, May 28, $12,900, 3yo & up, Nebraska-bred, 1m, 1:37.20, HIGH DICE, Buzz Bar, Seville's Runaway. 5 started.

Bill Callihan H., Columbus, Sept. 2, $8,017, 3yo & up, f & m, 6½f, 1:20.40, CASH CRUISE, Statsie's Charmer, Tizablaze. 10 started.

Bill of Rights H., Calder Race Course, Oct. 14, $38,480, 3yo & up, 5fT, :56.38, SEJM'S MADNESS, Uncle Rocco, True Love's Secret. 8 started.

Bill Thomas Memorial H., Sunland Park, March 10, $42,400, 3yo & up, 6½f, 1:16.60, ODDSONJACK, Overdone, Mr. de Falls. 5 started.

Bill Wineberg S. (R), Portland Meadows, Nov. 25, $14,650, 2yo, c & g, Oregon-bred, 6f, 1:13.64, LETHAL GRANDE, Ransome Road, Big Harry Deal. 9 started.

Billy Powell S., The Downs at Albuquerque, May 27, $37,600, 2yo, 5f, :58.49, SLIM'S SECRET, Pacer, Russian Olive. 7 started.

Billy the Kid S., Ruidoso Downs, Aug. 12, $12,800, 3yo, 1m, 1:44.20, LIVE SHOW, I'm Not Bluffin, Jivey Road. 3 started.

BING CROSBY BREEDERS' CUP H.-G2, Del Mar, July 22, $196,000, 3yo & up, 6f, 1:08.22, KONA GOLD, Caller One, Swept Overboard. 4 started.

Birdcatcher S., Northlands Park, Sept. 1, $50,000, 2yo, c & g, 6½f, 1:18.60, DANCE ME FREE, Silent Shoes, Onastar. 10 started.

Bird of Pay S., Northlands Park, Sept. 3, $50,000, 2yo, f, 6½f, 1:19, BRASS TO DIAMONDS, Sweet Monarch, Symbol's Remark. 8 started.

Bison City S. (R), Fort Erie, July 1, $266,250, 3yo, f, Canadian-bred, 1 1/16m, 1:43.73, QUICK BLUE, Poetically, Penny Perfect. 5 started.

Bit and Bridle H. (R), Charles Town, May 12, $40,000, 3yo & up, f & m, starters at Charles Town at least twice since November 12, 2000, excluding stakes, 1 1/16m, 1:51.13, MY SISTER PEARL, Real Women, Times Awasten Pal. 9 started.

BLACK-EYED SUSAN S.-G2, Pimlico, May 18, $200,000, 3yo, f, 1⅛m, 1:50.84, TWO ITEM LIMIT, Indy Glory, Tap Dance. 5 started.

Black Gold H., Fair Grounds, Jan. 7, $75,000, 3yo, abt7½fT, 1:31.71, RAHY'S SECRET, Mr. Miesque, Dynameaux. 8 started.

BLACK HELEN H.-G2, Hialeah Park, April 14, $200,000, 3yo & up, f & m, 1⅛mT, 1:47.17, PERFECT STING, Clearly a Queen, Spook Express (SAf). 5 started.

Black Mesa H. (R), Remington Park, Sept. 30, $26,000, 3yo & up, f & m, Oklahoma-bred, 7f, 1:22.79, DEVOUT SINNER, Pretty Rocky, Naturalingredients. 10 started.

Black Mountain H., Turf Paradise, March 10, $35,000, 3yo & up, 1 1/16m, 1:43.68, YUKON STRIKE, Our Best Man, March of Kings. 8 started.

Black Swan S., Fairplex Park, Sept. 19, $49,000, 2yo, f, 1 1/16m, 1:46.07, ROARING BLAZE, Happy Michelle, (DH) Queen of Swords, (DH) Wild and Icy. 6 started.

Blair's Cove S. (R), Canterbury Park, July 4, $37,600, 3yo & up, c & g, Minnesota-bred, 1 1/16mT, 1:43.65, ASHAR, Bleu Victoriate, King of Knights. 11 started.

Blaze O'Brien S., Turf Paradise, March 25, $24,200, 3yo & up, 1 1/16mT, 1:42.59, HANGONSLEWPYHANGON, Rainbow Style (Ire), Rub. 10 started.

Blazing Bart H., Calder Race Course, June 3, $33,450, 3yo & up, 1 1/16mT, 1:42.34, BAND IS PASSING, Wertz, Dance the Ballado. 10 started.

Block House Hurdle S., Tryon, April 21, $27,900, 4yo & up, abt2½mT, 4:40.20, BROWN LAD (Fr), Darn Tipalarm, How Goes. 4 started.

Bloomfield H., SunRay Park, Oct. 20, $31,500, 3yo & up, 1m, 1:37, CROONER SLEW, Moro Grande, Mr. de Falls. 10 started.

Blue and Grey S. (R), Charles Town, Oct. 27, $50,000, 3yo & up, West Virginia-bred or Virginia-bred and/or -sired, 7f, 1:27.55, NATIVE HEIR, Turbotaxman, Blazing Colors. 8 started.

Bluegrass H., Lincoln State Fair, June 2, $10,800, 3yo & up, f & m, 6f, 1:11, SWEET FANTASTIC, Sandpit Dancer, Cindy's Doll. 10 started.

BLUE GRASS S.-G1, Keeneland, April 14, $750,000, 3yo, 1⅛m, 1:48.32, MILLENNIUM WIND, Songandaprayer, Dollar Bill. 7 started.

Blue Hen S., Delaware Park, Sept. 15, $75,300, 2yo, f, 1m, 1:39.93, TREASURE COAST GEM, Short Note, Fluid. 6 started.

Blue Mountain Futurity (R), Penn National Race Course, Nov. 16, $71,300, 2yo, f, Pennsylvania-bred, 6f, 1:14.73, SWIFT CASE, Entwining, Concernina. 9 started.

Blue Norther H., Santa Anita Park, Jan. 7, $74,309, 3yo, f, 1mT, 1:36.77, SMART TIMING, Skatesheba (Fr), Haitian Vacation. 4 started.

Blue Sparkler S., Monmouth Park, July 28, $72,750, 3yo & up, f & m, 6f, 1:10.52, SHUTUP AND DANCE, Timely Affair, Cedar Knolls. 4 started.

Bobbie Bricker Memorial H. (R), Beulah Park, Oct. 28, $45,000, 3yo & up, f & m, Ohio-bred, 1 1/16m, 1:45.24, LADY CHERIE, Stormy Wars, Left Lane Lorrain. 9 started.

Bob Bryant S. (R), Prairie Meadows, May 28, $72,300, 3yo, f, Iowa-bred, 6f, 1:10.28, SHARKY'S REVIEW, I'm a City Girl, Seattle Prospector. 10 started.

Bob Feller S., Prairie Meadows, June 2, $51,375, 3yo & up, 6f, 1:09.82, SAND RIDGE, Kings Command, Willowbrook Lane. 7 started.

Bob Harding S., Monmouth Park, Aug. 26, $75,000, 3yo & up, 1mT, 1:34.64, SCAGNELLI, Rudirudy, Crash Course. 7 started.

Bob Johnson Memorial S., Lone Star Park, July 15, $75,000, 3yo & up, 1m, 1:36.33, CAPTAIN COUNTDOWN, T. B. Track Star, Unrullah Bull. 7 started.

Boeing H., Emerald Downs, July 15, $40,000, 3yo & up, f & m, 1 1/16m, 1:42.80, CROSSATYOUROWNRISK, Latter Day Paula, Taste the Passion. 7 started.

Boiling Springs Breeders' Cup H., The Meadowlands, Sept. 21, $194,000, 3yo, f, 1 1/16m (originally scheduled on the turf as a Grade 3), 1:42.63, MYSTIC LADY, Shooting Party, Plunderthepeasants. 4 started.

Boise River Festival Derby, Les Bois Park, June 23, $19,022, 3yo, 1m, 1:40.16, COWBOY JAZZ, L. B. Makin' Money, The Lord Is Eager. 8 started.

Boise River H., Les Bois Park, June 24, $5,750, 3yo & up, 5f, :59.02, ALEYNA'S PLACE, Better Choice, Easter Chief. 5 started.

Bold Ego H., Sunland Park, Jan. 6, $28,200, 3yo & up, f & m, 5½f, 1:03, YULLA YULLA, Malady, Deposit the Cash. 7 started.

Bold Josh H. (R), The Meadowlands, Sept. 26, $50,000, 3yo & up, New Jersey-bred, 6f, 1:09.71, HOLIEST PUNCH, H. M. S. Jackson, Spectacular Slew. 6 started.

Bold Ruckus S. (R), Woodbine, June 6, $107,200, 3yo, progeny of eligible stallions standing in Ontario, 6fT, 1:11.45, SAN MONT ANDREAS, Kings Reception, Fogerty. 9 started.

BOLD RULER H.-G3, Aqueduct, April 14, $109,200, 3yo & up, 6f, 1:08.67, SAY FLORIDA SANDY, Delaware Township, Lake Pontchartrain. 7 started.

Bold Venture H., Woodbine, July 21, $107,600, 3yo & up, 6½f, 1:16.05, TEMPERED APPEAL, Catahoula Parish, Mr. Epperson. 5 started.

Bonnie Heath S. (R), Gulfstream Park, Feb. 25, $64,000, 3yo, progeny of eligible stallions standing in Florida, 6f, 1:10.76, FRIDAY'S A COMIN', Light of Justice, Colebrook Ruckus. 6 started.

BONNIE MISS S.-G2, Gulfstream Park, March 16, $250,000, 3yo, f, 1⅛m, 1:52.05, TAP DANCE, Halo Reality, Unbridled Lassie. 7 started.

Boo La Boo S. (R), Santa Anita Park, Feb. 17, $108,100, 3yo, f, California-bred, 6f, 1:10.58, WARREN'S WHISTLE, Comedy Class, Royally Chosen. 7 started.

Border Cup S. (R), Fort Erie, July 22, $57,050, 3yo & up, f & m, Canadian-bred, 1 1/16mT, 1:44.17, KATSUMI, Lewinsky, Classy Pickup. 12 started.

Borderland Derby, Sunland Park, March 4, $37,900, 3yo & up, 1m, 1:38.60, PARTING GUEST, Golden Tangle, Mecke Monster. 8 started.

Born Famous H., Calder Race Course, June 17, $52,850, 3yo & up, f & m, 6f, 1:12.90, PRECIOUS FEATHER, Valid Forbes, Tour Hostess. 8 started.

Born to Run H. (R), Charles Town, May 19, $40,000, 3yo & up, c & g, starters at Charles Town at least twice since November 19, 2000, excluding stakes, 1 1/16m, 1:47.29, BIG BECKER, Rebellious Dreamer,

Slew's Smile. 8 started.

Bossier City H., Louisiana Downs, Aug. 11, $40,000, 3yo, abt1 1/16mT, 1:43.31, SEATTLE NIGHT, Rare Cure, Virginia Pride. 7 started.

Boston Common S. (R), Suffolk Downs, May 12, $25,000, 3yo, f, Massachusetts-bred, abt1mT, 1:44.07, SUNLIT RIDGE, Classlylilprincess, Viva Concorde. 6 started.

BOUGAINVILLEA H.-G3, Hialeah Park, March 31, $100,000, 3yo & up, 1⅛mT, 1:50.10, MAKE NO MISTAKE (Ire), Aly's Alley, A Little Luck. 11 started.

Bourbonette Breeders' Cup S., Turfway Park, March 24, $117,000, 3yo, f, 1m, 1:37.55, SWEET NANETTE, Upside, Heathers Promise. 7 started.

Bouwerie S. (R), Belmont Park, May 13, $81,950, 3yo, f, New York-bred, 7f, 1:23.77, BON FEARLESS, Look Upon, Beijio. 7 started.

Bowl Game S., Arlington Park, Oct. 21, $55,000, 3yo & up, 1 1/16mT, 1:44.44, LANGSTON, Jake the Flake, Minor Wisdom. 9 started.

BOWLING GREEN H.-G2, Belmont Park, July 7, $150,000, 3yo & up, 1⅜mT, 2:10.62, KING CUGAT, Slew Valley, Man From Wicklow. 7 started.

Brandywine S., Delaware Park, May 26, $75,600, 3yo & up, 1m, 1:37.22, PINE DANCE, Quick Punch, Liberty Gold. 7 started.

Brave Raj S., Calder Race Course, Sept. 22, $100,000, 2yo, f, 1m 70y, 1:47.16, MS BROOKSKI, Redoubled Miss, Ciudad de Carson. 10 started.

BREEDERS' CUP CLASSIC-G1, Belmont Park, Oct. 27, $3,664,000, 3yo & up, 1¼m, 2:00.62, TIZNOW, Sakhee, Albert the Great. 13 started.

BREEDERS' CUP DISTAFF-G1, Belmont Park, Oct. 27, $2,161,760, 3yo & up, f & m, 1⅛m, 1:49.21, UNBRIDLED ELAINE, Spain, Two Item Limit. 11 started.

BREEDERS' CUP FILLY & MARE TURF-G1, Belmont Park, Oct. 27, $1,273,240, 3yo & up, f & m, 1¼mT, 2:00.36, BANKS HILL (GB), Spook Express (SAf), Spring Oak (GB). 12 started.

BREEDERS' CUP JUVENILE-G1, Belmont Park, Oct. 27, $916,000, 2yo, c & g, 1 1/16m, 1:42.27, JOHANNESBURG, Repent, Siphonic. 12 started.

BREEDERS' CUP JUVENILE FILLIES-G1, Belmont Park, Oct. 27, $916,000, 2yo, f, 1 1/16m, 1:41.49, TEMPERA, Imperial Gesture, Bella Bellucci. 9 started.

BREEDERS' CUP MILE-G1, Belmont Park, Oct. 27, $1,044,240, 3yo & up, 1mT, 1:32.05, VAL ROYAL (Fr), Forbidden Apple, Bach (Ire). 12 started.

BREEDERS' CUP SPRINT-G1, Belmont Park, Oct. 27, $916,000, 3yo & up, 6f, 1:08.41, SQUIRTLE SQUIRT, Xtra Heat, Caller One. 14 started.

Breeders' Cup Steeplechase S., Far Hills, Oct. 20, $238,750, 4yo & up, abt2⅝mT, 4:54.36, QUEL SENOR (Fr), Lord Zada, Praise the Prince (NZ). 9 started.

BREEDERS' CUP TURF-G1, Belmont Park, Oct. 27, $2,960,240, 3yo & up, 1½mT, 2:24.36, FANTASTIC LIGHT, Milan (GB), Timboroa (GB). 11 started.

Breeders' S. (R), Woodbine, Aug. 11, $500,000, 3yo, Canadian-bred, 1½mT, 2:29.90, SWEETEST THING, Flaming Sky, Asia. 6 started.

Brent's Princess S. (R), Thistledown, May 26, $40,000, 3yo & up, f & m, Ohio-bred, 6f, 1:11.38, BEATMICHIGANAGAIN, Lady Cherie, Mandy G. 8 started.

Brickyard S. (R), Hoosier Park, Oct. 21, $44,400, 3yo & up, Indiana-bred, 6f, 1:09.53, RED'S HONOR, Fight for Ally, Salutee. 11 started.

Bridgeburg S. (R), Fort Erie, Oct. 8, $61,500, 3yo & up, starters at Fort Erie at least twice in 2001, 1 1/16m, 1:44.54, STORM CRUISER, Dimanno, Right Stop. 9 started.

Brighouse Belles S., Hastings Park Racecourse, June 16, $35,852, 3yo & up, f & m, 1 1/16m, 1:45.08, GROOMS DERBY, Fabulous Flight, Make Contact. 8 started.

BRITISH COLUMBIA BREEDERS' CUP OAKS-G3, Hastings Park Racecourse, Sept. 8, $161,161, 3yo, f, 1⅛m, 1:50.45, COLLECT CALL, Inish Glora, Withoutapproval. 9 started.

British Columbia Cup Classic H. (R), Hastings Park Racecourse, Aug. 6, $70,590, 3yo & up, British Columbia-bred, 1⅛m, 1:52.27, LORD NELSON, Reciever General, Work Visa. 6 started.

British Columbia Cup Debutante S. (R), Hastings Park Racecourse, Aug. 4, $53,370, 2yo, f, British Columbia-bred, 6½f, 1:20.41, LADY VYE, Beautiful Stranger, Neemrana. 8 started.

British Columbia Cup Distaff H. (R), Hastings Park Racecourse, Aug. 6, $54,100, 3yo & up, f & m, British Columbia-bred, 1⅛m, 1:53.53, PRINCESS PREMIER, Full Scream Ahead, Fabulous Flight. 9 started.

British Columbia Cup Nursery S. (R), Hastings Park Racecourse, Aug. 4, $53,240, 2yo, c & g, British Columbia-bred, 6½f, 1:20.54, NO TIME FLAT, Intact, Regal Soldier. 10 started.

British Columbia Cup Sprint H. (R), Hastings Park Racecourse, Aug. 6, $54,400, 3yo & up, British Columbia-bred, 6½f, 1:17.69, MIKE K, Ryson, Spinmeister. 6 started.

British Columbia Cup Stallion H. (R), Hastings Park Racecourse, Aug. 5, $53,950, 3yo, c & g, British Columbia-bred, 1 1/16m, 1:47.54, I'M FREE, Godoliphin Road, Thurston. 9 started.

British Columbia Cup Stallion H. (R), Hastings Park Racecourse, Aug. 5, $54,200, 3yo, f, British Columbia-bred, 1 1/16m, 1:47.43, CATAHOULA ROSE, Lady's Jewel, Magic Dancer. 8 started.

BRITISH COLUMBIA DERBY-G2, Hastings Park Racecourse, Sept. 29, $203,452, 3yo, 1⅛m, 1:50.71, FANCY AS, I'm Free, Diglett. 11 started.

Broad Brush S., The Meadowlands, Oct. 19, $100,000, 3yo & up, 1 1/16m, 1:41.84, TALK'S CHEAP, Runspastum, Rize. 6 started.

Broadway H. (R), Aqueduct, April 7, $81,125, 3yo & up, f & m, New York-bred, 7f, 1:21.06, DAT YOU MIZ BLUE, Bonneville, Pearly White. 6 started.

BROOKLYN H.-G2, Belmont Park, June 10, $250,000, 3yo & up, 1⅛m, 1:47.41, ALBERT THE GREAT, Perfect Cat, Top Official. 7 started.

Brookmeade S. (R), Colonial Downs, July 28, $40,000, 3yo & up, f & m, Virginia-bred or -sired, 1 1/16mT, 1:44.80, CLASS YANKEE, Kim, Berta's Silver. 7 started.

Brooks Fields H., Canterbury Park, June 16, $35,000, 3yo & up, 7½fT, 1:31.15, AMERICAN SPIRIT, Silver Zipper, Diplomatic Corps. 11 started.

Brother Brown S., Remington Park, Oct. 5, $25,900, 3yo & up, 5fT, :55.85, OTRO MAMBO, Big Bay Brite, Gambler's Share. 11 started.

BROWN BESS H.-G3, Golden Gate Fields, Feb. 3, $100,000, 4yo & up, f & m, 1 1/16mT, 1:46.87, OUT OF REACH (GB), Miss of Wales (Chi), Keld (Ire). 12 started.

Bruce G. Smith Memorial S., Suffolk Downs, Sept. 29, $25,000, 3yo & up, abt1 1/16mT, 1:47.81, GEORGIA'S JOEY, Magical Madness, Juan of La Mancha. 8 started.

Brumbeau S., Turf Paradise, April 21, $24,200, 3yo & up, f & m, 6f, 1:09.83, DEZIBELLES FORLI, Little Snake Bit, Jennaly. 9 started.

Bryan Station S., Keeneland, Oct. 19, $84,750, 3yo & up, f & m, 1mT, 1:36.06, GINO'S SPIRITS (GB), Watch, Binalegend. 10 started.

B. Thoughtful S. (R), Hollywood Park, April 28, $150,000, 4yo & up, f & m, California-bred, 7f, 1:21.86, LAZY SLUSAN, Image of Glory, Phaenna. 6 started.

Bubbling Over H. (R), Charles Town, April 14, $40,000, 3yo & up, f & m, starters at Charles Town at least twice since October 14, 2000, excluding stakes, 7f, 1:27.42, A LOT OF MARY, Sudden Sunny, Badger Pocket. 10 started.

Bucharest S., Sam Houston Race Park, Feb. 3, $25,000, 3yo, 6f, 1:10.33, TRIPLE CARD, Kentucky Bay, Glows Codetoo. 10 started.

Buckeye Native S. (R), River Downs, Aug. 12, $45,000, 3yo & up, Ohio-bred, 1 1/16m, 1:48.40, KNIGHT VILLAIN, Brother Darcy, Deadline Dude. 9 started.

Buckpasser S., Arlington Park, Aug. 18, $63,000, 3yo & up, 1⅛m, 1:52.27, NEON SHADOW, Double Affair, A'fire. 5 started.

Budweiser S., Rillito Park, March 11, $3,052, 3yo & up, 1 1/16m, 1:52.40, CEE'S MARFA, Hand Axe, S. S. Tell. 8 started.

BUENA VISTA H.-G2, Santa Anita Park, Feb. 19, $150,000, 4yo & up, f & m, 1mT, 1:36.67, RARE CHARMER, Elegant Ridge (Ire), Uncharted Haven (GB). 11 started.

Bueno S. (R), Turf Paradise, Feb. 24, $22,800, 4yo & up, f & m, Arizona-bred, 6½f, 1:16.64, O'HARA, Nikki's Angel, Drag Time Gal. 8 started.

Buffalo Bayou S., Sam Houston Race Park, Nov. 10, $25,000, 3yo & up, 1 1/16mT, 1:43.60, SCHAUMBURG, L. A. Spider Legs, Coach Rags. 10 started.

Buffalo S. (R), Assiniboia Downs, Sept. 15, $34,300, 2yo, Manitoba-bred, 1m, 1:43.60, RARE DEPUTY, Trebbiano, Goin N Style. 7 started.

Bull Dog S. (R), Fresno, Oct. 14, $49,600, 3yo & up, California-bred, 6f, 1:08.80, TAKIN IT DEEP, The Morris Monroe, Jim's Relaunch. 6 started.

Bull Page S. (R), Woodbine, July 29, $133,500, 2yo, c & g, progeny of eligible stallions standing in Ontario, 6f, 1:12.10, MOLLY'S WISDOM, Mighty Quinn, Young Whiz. 8 started.

Bully Sprint Series S., Lethbridge, Oct. 7, $5,800, 3yo & up, 1¹⁄₁₆m, 2:02.40, ISLAND SLEW, Roll the Stage, Sentosa. 8 started.

Bungalow H. (R), Fairmount Park, Oct. 16, $35,900, 3yo & up, f & m, Illinois-conceived and/or -foaled, 1m, 1:40.20, RAIN BOOTS, Shawnee Vali, Something Wicked. 8 started.

Bunty Lawless S. (R), Woodbine, Oct. 20, $142,625, 3yo & up, progeny of eligible stallions standing in Ontario, 1mT, 1:38.62, STARBEAU, Bristol Pistol, Val de Dash. 13 started.

Burnaby H., Hastings Park Racecourse, June 30, $37,318, 3yo, 1¹⁄₁₆m, 1:44.22, I'M FREE, Diglett, Irish Pleasure. 7 started.

Busanda S., Aqueduct, Jan. 28, $81,125, 3yo, f, 1m 70y, 1:41.55, DIVERSA, Sweep Dreams, Stop for Schnapps. 5 started.

Busher S., Aqueduct, March 3, $80,300, 3yo, f, 1¹⁄₁₆m, 1:45.74, DIVERSA, Sweep Dreams, Stop for Schnapps. 5 started.

Bustles and Bows S., Fairplex Park, Sept. 13, $50,000, 2yo, f, 6¹⁄₂f, 1:16.61, GREEN EYED LADY (GB), Past You, Icantgoforthat. 8 started.

Buttons and Bows H., Sun Downs, April 14, $3,400, 3yo & up, f & m, 4f, :47.40, NIFTY NITE, Casa Toni, O' Gata Yolanda. 5 started.

Caballos del Sol H., Turf Paradise, Oct. 13, $30,000, 3yo & up, 6f, 1:08.77, OH GRACIE, Shot of Gold, Eagleton. 10 started.

Cactus Cup H., Turf Paradise, Feb. 25, $25,000, 3yo, f, 6f, 1:09.65, CHANNING WAY, Sonora Desert, We Love Aleyna. 6 started.

Cactus Flower H., Turf Paradise, March 10, $50,000, 3yo & up, f & m, 6f, 1:10.02, LITTLE SNAKE BIT, Miss Belle O, Ode to Elaine. 5 started.

Cactus Wren H. (R), Turf Paradise, Dec. 8, $30,000, 3yo & up, Arizona-bred, 6¹⁄₂f, 1:16.28, KOMAX, G Malleah, Radical Rate. 8 started.

Cadillacing S., Gulfstream Park, Jan. 11, $53,200, 3yo, f, 6f, 1:10, GOLD MOVER, Thunder Bertie, Look of the Lynx. 5 started.

Caesar Rodney H., Delaware Park, July 8, $145,500, 3yo & up, 1⁷⁄₁₆m (originally scheduled on the turf), 1:43.82, SUMITAS (Ger), Runspastum, Lightning Paces. 4 started.

Caesar's Wish S. (R), Pimlico, April 21, $75,000, 3yo, f, Maryland-bred, 1⁷⁄₁₆m, 1:45.71, HUNKA HUNKA LORI Z, Guillotine, Rico Ends Well. 6 started.

Cajun S. (R), Louisiana Downs, Oct. 13, $38,450, 3yo & up, Louisiana-bred, 6f, 1:10.58, KETTLE MAN, Early Goer, Oak Hall. 11 started.

Calder Breeders' Cup H., Calder Race Course, May 26, $143,250, 3yo & up, f & m, 1¹⁄₁₆mT, 1:44.71, SILVER BANDANA, Platinum Tiara, Clearly a Queen. 12 started.

CALDER DERBY-G3, Calder Race Course, Oct. 20, $200,000, 3yo, 1¹⁄₈m (originally scheduled on the turf), 1:51.12, WESTERN PRIDE, Tour of the Cat, Built Up. 10 started.

Calder Oaks, Calder Race Course, Oct. 13, $200,000, 3yo, f, 1¹⁄₈mT, 1:49.22, SARA'S SUCCESS, Grey Ballet, Sheppard's Watch (GB). 10 started.

Calder Turf Sprint H., Calder Race Course, July 14, $100,000, 3yo & up, 5fT, :56.91, TEXAS GLITTER, Sejm's Madness, Kipperscope. 7 started.

Calgary Sun Marathon S., Lethbridge, Sept. 15, $5,600, 3yo & up, 1⁷⁄₁₆m, 1:54.80, WEEKEND SPECIAL, Mr. I R S, End Zone. 6 started.

Calgary Sun Marathon S., Lethbridge, Sept. 3, $5,700, 3yo & up, 1⁷⁄₁₆m, 1:47.60, WEEKEND SPECIAL, End Zone, Mr. I R S. 7 started.

California Breeders' Champion S. (R), Santa Anita Park, Dec. 28, $150,000, 2yo, f, California-bred, 7f, 1:24.09, LADY GEORGE, Super High, Daddy's Gold. 10 started.

California Breeders' Champion S. (R), Santa Anita Park, Dec. 28, $150,000, 2yo, c & g, California-bred, 7f, 1:23.32, EARL OF DANBY, Gobi Dan, Joey Franco. 10 started.

California Cup Classic H. (R), Santa Anita Park, Nov. 3, $250,000, 3yo & up, California-bred, 1¹⁄₈m, 1:49.14, IRISHEYESAREFLYING, Figlio Mio, Vixen Storm. 9 started.

California Cup Distaff H. (R), Santa Anita Park, Nov. 3, $150,000, 3yo & up, f & m, California-bred, abt6¹⁄₂fT, 1:12.72, JEWELED PIRATE, Warren's Whistle, Storm Kisu. 14 started.

California Cup Distaff Starter H. (R), Santa Anita Park, Nov. 3, $50,000, 3yo & up, f & m, California-bred starters for a claiming price of $40,000 or less in 2001, 1¹⁄₈mT, 1:47.32, LIL SISTER STICH, Super Tuesday, Dazzling Diamonds. 11 started.

California Cup Juvenile Fillies S. (R), Santa Anita Park, Nov. 3, $125,000, 2yo, f, California-bred, 1⁷⁄₁₆m, 1:45.84, LADY GEORGE, Fragrant Cloud, Believe in Slew. 10 started.

California Cup Juvenile S. (R), Santa Anita Park, Nov. 3, $125,000, 2yo, c & g, California-bred, 1⁷⁄₁₆m, 1:43.98, YOUGOTTAWANNA, Officer, Surprized. 12 started.

California Cup Matron H. (R), Santa Anita Park, Nov. 3, $150,000, 3yo & up, f & m, California-bred, 1⁷⁄₁₆m, 1:43.48, CEE DREAMS, Favorite Funtime, Elaine's Angel. 9 started.

California Cup Mile H. (R), Santa Anita Park, Nov. 3, $175,000, 3yo & up, California-bred, 1mT, 1:34.97, NATIVE DESERT, Spinelessjellyfish, Ringaskiddy. 9 started.

California Cup Sprint H. (R), Santa Anita Park, Nov. 3, $150,000, 3yo & up, California-bred, 6f, 1:08.82, CEEBAND, Stormy Jack, Gibson County. 6 started.

California Cup Starter H. (R), Santa Anita Park, Nov. 3, $50,000, 3yo & up, California-bred starters for a claiming price of $40,000 or less in 2001, 1¹⁄₄mT, 2:01, AS WE KNOW IT, White Cloud, Bolchina's Prize. 9 started.

California Cup Starter Sprint H. (R), Santa Anita Park, Nov. 3, $50,000, 3yo & up, California-bred starters for a claiming price of $32,000 or less in 2001, 5¹⁄₂f, 1:02.45, RIO ORO, Jersey Rebel, Simony. 9 started.

California Derby, Bay Meadows, April 14, $200,000, 3yo, 1¹⁄₈m, 1:49.25, TAKIN IT DEEP, Early Flyer, Sirpa. 7 started.

CALIFORNIAN S.-G2, Hollywood Park, June 10, $500,000, 3yo & up, 1¹⁄₈m, 1:48.12, SKIMMING, Futural, Aptitude. 8 started.

California Oaks, Golden Gate Fields, Feb. 19, $100,000, 3yo, f, 1⁷⁄₁₆mT, 1:55.48, ASWHATILLDOIS (Ire), Dawaytogold, Color Me Special. 8 started.

California Sire S. (R), Hollywood Park, July 8, $100,000, 3yo, f, progeny of eligible stallions standing in California, 1⁷⁄₁₆mT, 1:42.74, SUPER TUESDAY, (DH) Dena's Diamond, (DH) Ace's Valentine. 6 started.

California Sire S. (R), Hollywood Park, June 9, $100,000, 3yo, progeny of eligible stallions standing in California, 1⁷⁄₁₆m, 1:41.76, WINSTON CHI, Jamaican Rum, Cherokee Kim. 5 started.

California Sires S. (R), Santa Anita Park, Sept. 27, $100,000, 2yo, f, progeny of eligible stallions standing in California, 7f, 1:25.36, MOOSSA'S GIRL, Mama Mama, Shalini. 6 started.

California Sires S. (R), Santa Anita Park, Sept. 28, $100,000, 2yo, c & g, progeny of eligible stallions standing in California, 7f, 1:24.64, SHARPER TOO, Ima Mile High Guy, Gobi Dan. 7 started.

California Sprint Championship H. (R), Bay Meadows, Oct. 6, $100,000, 3yo & up, California-bred, 6f, 1:08.16, CEEBAND, Gibson County, Reds Superstar. 7 started.

California Thoroughbred Breeders Association S. (R), Del Mar, July 20, $125,000, 2yo, f, California-bred, 5¹⁄₂f, 1:05.75, ASIAN ADVENTURE, Martial's Princess, Believe in Slew. 7 started.

California Turf Championship H. (R), Bay Meadows, Sept. 3, $100,000, 3yo & up, California-bred, 1mT, 1:36.37, (DH) SPINELESSJELLYFISH, (DH) NATIVE DESERT, Flying Rudolph. 5 started.

Camilla Urso H., Golden Gate Fields, Nov. 17, $55,600, 3yo & up, f & m, 6f, 1:07.88, HALL OF GOLD, Creaseinherjeans, Time for Romance. 7 started.

Canada Construction S. (R), Grand Prairie, July 28, $1,600, 2yo & up, c & g, Canadian-bred, 6f, 1:14.80, CLASS CARTER, Minystik Ryder, Charming Sand. 6 started.

Canada Day S., Assiniboia Downs, July 1, $26,950, 3yo & up, f & m, 1m, 1:40.40, OKANAGAN INVADER, Regal Eyre, Kitty Would. 8 started.

CANADIAN DERBY-G3, Northlands Park, Aug. 25, $150,000, 3yo, 1⁷⁄₈m, 2:18, FANCY AS, Stage Classic, Thurston. 7 started.

CANADIAN H.-G2, Woodbine, Sept. 9, $243,000, 3yo & up, f & m, abt1⁷⁄₈mT, 1:43.76 (NCR), DIADELLA, Nymphenburg, Cayman Sunset (Ire). 12 started.

CANADIAN INTERNATIONAL S.-G1, Woodbine, Sept. 30, $1,500,000, 3yo & up, 1¹⁄₂mT, 2:28.46, MUTAMAM (GB), Paolini (Ger), Lodge Hill. 12 started.

Canadian Juvenile S., Northlands Park, Oct. 13, $50,000, 2yo, 1⁷⁄₁₆m, 1:48.20, CRESCENT REMARK, Dance Me Free, Sir Deuces. 9 started.

CANADIAN TURF H.-G3, Gulfstream Park, Feb. 24, $160,000, 3yo & up, 1⁷⁄₁₆mT, 1:39.43, INEXPLICABLE, Band Is Passing, David Copperfield. 8 started.

Candy Eclair H. (R), Delaware Park, June 5, $60,100, 3yo & up, f & m, non-winners of a stake worth $30,000 to the winner in 2001 or for an optional claiming price of $100,000, 6f, 1:11.39, BROOMESSE, Difficult Doll, Rude Coyote. 8 started.

Candy Eclair S. (R), Gulfstream Park, March 10, $100,000, 4yo & up, f & m, non-winners of a race other than maiden, claiming, or starter or non-winners of two races, 6f, 1:10.39, SHUTUP AND

DANCE, Golightly, Silvery Bay. 10 started.

Candy Eclair S., Monmouth Park, Aug. 11, $50,000, 3yo, f, 5fT, :56.58, SPARKLING NUMBER, Carsonality, Glamour Tour. 6 started.

Canterbury Park Breeders' Cup Derby, Canterbury Park, June 2, $100,000, 3yo, 1mT, 1:37.32, FAN CLUB'S MISTER, Rahy's Secret, Rocinante. 8 started.

Canterbury Park Juvenile S., Canterbury Park, July 14, $50,000, 2yo, 5½f, 1:05.28, PURPLE PLEASURE, Bug Hall, Whitegoldndiamonds. 11 started.

Canterbury Park Oaks, Canterbury Park, June 17, $35,000, 3yo, f, 1$\frac{1}{16}$mT, 1:45.12, SAVANNAH CANON, Renaissance Fair, First Mystery. 9 started.

Cape Henlopen H., Delaware Park, July 22, $69,100, 3yo & up, 1½mT, 2:29.48, JOHN'S CALL, Grundlefoot, Dynamic Trick. 9 started.

Capital City H. (R), Penn National Race Course, Aug. 31, $29,828, 3yo & up, Pennsylvania-bred, 1$\frac{1}{16}$m, 1:44.49, WATCHMAN'S WARNING, Sly Ole Buck, Classic Verse. 4 started.

Capitol City Futurity, Lincoln State Fair, July 15, $10,720, 2yo, 4½f, :51.60, BENGAL BOY, Astrickyas, Darrella. 6 started.

Captain Condo S. (R), Emerald Downs, June 16, $35,000, 2yo, c & g, Washington-bred, 5f, :58.60, KENNY HAWK, Briar Knight, Beat the Klok. 12 started.

Captain My Captain S. (R), Philadelphia Park, July 28, $50,000, 3yo & up, Pennsylvania-bred, 5fT, :57.43, GRANGEVILLE, Sir Echo, Pal Joey. 8 started.

Captain Stanley Harrison H., Marquis Downs, Sept. 15, $6,500, 3yo, f, 1⅛m, 1:56.15, RED VIL DO, Sing On Stage, Miss Canuck. 4 started.

Captive Miss S., Monmouth Park, June 16, $50,000, 3yo, f, 1$\frac{1}{16}$mT, 1:41.53, MARQ OF BEAUTY, Diversa, The Goddess Athird. 8 started.

CARDINAL H.-G3, Churchill Downs, Nov. 10, $169,350, 3yo & up, f & m, 1⅛mT, 1:49.12, WATCH, Sitka, Gino's Spirits (GB). 9 started.

Cardinal H. (R), Arlington Park, June 23, $75,000, 3yo & up, Illinois-conceived and/or -foaled, 1$\frac{1}{16}$mT, 1:42.61, RENO RUMBLE, Treat Me Doc, Smilin' Slew. 13 started.

Caribbean S., Hialeah Park, May 5, $32,000, 3yo, 7f, 1:22.89, NORTHEND, Rocket Ryan, Built Up. 10 started.

CARLETON F. BURKE H.-G3, Santa Anita Park, Oct. 28, $150,000, 3yo & up, 1½mT, 2:26.10, CAGNEY (Brz), Kerrygold (Fr), Northern Quest (Fr). 9 started.

Carlos Salazar S. (R), The Downs at Albuquerque, May 20, $32,900, 3yo & up, f & m, New Mexico-bred, 7f, 1:23.43, TRIP'S ECLIPSE, Me a Spirit Too, Gollygot. 9 started.

Carmel H., Bay Meadows, Sept. 15, $50,650, 3yo, f, 1$\frac{1}{16}$mT, 1:44.54, ALINGA (Ire), (DH) Blushing Ballerina, (DH) Walts Wharf. 9 started.

Carolina Cup Hurdle S., Camden, March 31, $93,000, 4yo & up, abt2¼mT, 4:24.80, AL SKYWALKER, Campanile, Assurance. 7 started.

Carolina S., Hawthorne Race Course, Nov. 9, $44,750, 3yo, f, 1$\frac{1}{16}$mT, 1:42.54, AESTHETE APPROVAL, Twilite Tryst, Curious Conundrum. 9 started.

Carotene S., Woodbine, June 16, $107,000, 3yo & up, f & m, 1mT, 1:37.41, BRISTOL PISTOL, Red Satin Slippers, Great Fever (Fr). 9 started.

Carousel H., Oaklawn Park, April 7, $50,000, 4yo & up, f & m, 6f, 1:09.96, THE HAPPY HOPPER, My Brent's Diamond, Midge Too. 5 started.

Carousel S., Laurel Park, Dec. 22, $50,000, 3yo & up, f & m, 1$\frac{1}{16}$m, 1:45.04, BLUE HILLS, Unbridled Lady, Powerful Package. 6 started.

Carris Memorial H., Remington Park, Nov. 2, $25,000, 3yo & up, f & m, 1m, 1:39.10, WESTERN DELIGHT, Darlin Dixie, Islay Mist (GB). 6 started.

Carry Back S., Calder Race Course, July 14, $250,000, 3yo, 6f, 1:11.08, ILLUSIONED, Beyond Brilliant, Gallant Frolic. 10 started.

CARTER H.-G1, Aqueduct, May 6, $300,000, 3yo & up, 7f, 1:21.33, PEEPING TOM, Say Florida Sandy, Hook and Ladder. 7 started.

Carterista H. (1st Div.), Calder Race Course, July 21, $52,000, 3yo & up, 1m, 1:39.38, HAL'S HOPE, Tahkodha Hills, Silver Jet. 5 started.

Carterista H. (2nd Div.), Calder Race Course, July 21, $55,000, 3yo & up, 1m, 1:40.47, OUT OF CHAMPAGNE, Mr. Livingston, On Gossamer Wings. 6 started.

Carter McGregor Jr. Memorial S. (R), Lone Star Park, May 28, $50,000, 3yo & up, Texas-bred, 6f, 1:08.06 (NTR), TRIPLE CARD, Boots On Sunday, Lights On Broadway. 10 started.

Cassidy H. (R), Calder Race Course, Sept. 2, $53,900, 3yo & up, f & m, Florida-bred, 6f, 1:11.81, FLYING BIRDIE, Sugar N Spice, Tour Hostess. 7 started.

Cat's Cradle H. (R), Hollywood Park, Nov. 23, $102,250, 3yo & up, f & m, California-bred, 7½f, 1:28.03, FAVORITE FUNTIME, Feverish, Queenie Belle. 5 started.

Cavalier Cup S. (R), Colonial Downs, Aug. 7, $29,100, 3yo & up, progeny of Virginia-based stallions whose seasons were donated and sold through the 2001 VTA stallion auction, 7f, 1:23.13, ROBBIE'S PRINCE, Over to You, Carrena Rose. 4 started.

C. Edmund O'Brien S., Pimlico, May 26, $45,500, 3yo & up, 5f, :56.96, GOVERNOR'S PRIDE, Dr. Max, Rudirudy. 3 started.

Ceetown S., Turf Paradise, May 12, $24,000, 3yo, f, 6½f, 1:18.15, STORMY SPIRIT, Waveband, Lucy T. 7 started.

Central Iowa S., Prairie Meadows, Sept. 22, $60,000, 3yo & up, f & m, 1$\frac{1}{16}$m, 1:44.49, NUT N BETTER, Lady Tamworth, Livin for Love. 5 started.

Centre Stage Anne S. (R), Fort Erie, July 1, $55,050, 3yo & up, f & m, Canadian-foaled starters at Fort Erie at least twice in 2001, 6f, 1:11.63, TSAKPINA, Perfectlydelicious, Classy Pickup. 8 started.

CERF H. (R), Del Mar, Sept. 5, $84,020, 3yo & up, f & m, non-winners of a race worth $50,000 to the winner other than closed, claiming, or starter in 2001, 6f, 1:09.59, GLOBAL, High Margin, Forward Filly (SAf). 7 started.

Challedon S. (R), Laurel Park, Dec. 30, $60,000, 3yo & up, Maryland-bred, 7f, 1:24.53, MONK'S FALCON, Forty Eight Hours, Jorgie Stover. 11 started.

Challenger S., Tampa Bay Downs, Feb. 10, $50,000, 3yo, 1mT, 1:36.56, FIRST SPEAR, Creek's Shore, A. P. Topper. 12 started.

Chamisa H., The Downs at Albuquerque, May 6, $33,000, 4yo & up, f & m, 7f, 1:22.11, GOOD TIMIN BROOK, Shimmering Sand, Purls Ledgend. 9 started.

CHAMPAGNE S.-G1, Belmont Park, Oct. 6, $500,000, 2yo, 1$\frac{1}{16}$m, 1:43.39, OFFICER, Jump Start, Heavyweight Champ. 5 started.

Chandler H., Turf Paradise, Nov. 10, $30,000, 3yo, f, 7½fT, 1:30.93, SASSY CHIMES, Moonlit Maddie, Bel Serenata. 9 started.

Chantilly S., Assiniboia Downs, June 3, $26,950, 3yo, f, 6f, 1:12, SASSY CHIMES, Mountain Crest, Pettycashyou. 9 started.

Chapel Belle S., Louisiana Downs, Aug. 12, $40,000, 3yo, f, abt1$\frac{1}{16}$mT, 1:43.49, CHAUSSON POIRE, Prado's Trick, Mountain Kitten. 8 started.

Chapel of Dreams H., Calder Race Course, Aug. 26, $32,190, 3yo & up, f & m, 1⅛mT, 1:49.94, SMILIN' N BLUSHING, Jelly Fish, (DH) Cybil, (DH) Grand Veranda. 6 started.

CHAPOSA SPRINGS H.-G3, Calder Race Course, Dec. 29, $100,000, 3yo & up, f & m, 7f, 1:24.15, VAGUE MEMORY, Gold Mover, Platinum Tiara. 10 started.

Chariot Chaser H., Northlands Park, June 30, $35,775, 3yo, f, 6½f, 1:19.80, BRIGHTON BELLE, Sister Brass, Willow. 9 started.

Charles H. Russell H., Bay Meadows, Oct. 20, $50,550, 3yo & up, f & m, 6f, 1:09.25, HALL OF GOLD, Creaseinherjeans, De Goddaughter. 7 started.

Charles Town Dash H., Charles Town, July 4, $75,000, 3yo & up, 4½f, :50.55, GOVERNOR'S PRIDE, Wise Dusty, Desktop. 8 started.

CHARLES WHITTINGHAM H.-G1, Hollywood Park, June 10, $350,000, 3yo & up, 1¼mT, 1:59.34, BIENAMADO, Senure, Timboroa (GB). 9 started.

Charlie Barley H., Woodbine, June 24, $104,000, 3yo, 1$\frac{1}{16}$mT, 1:40.90, STRUT THE STAGE, Legal Heir, Stage Classic. 9 started.

Charlie Iles Thoroughbred Derby, The Downs at Albuquerque, May 12, $39,278, 3yo, 7f, 1:21.68, SILVER MATT, Alyou, A J Dustdevil. 10 started.

Cherokee Frolic S. (R), Calder Race Course, Dec. 30, $37,310, 3yo & up, f & m, non-winners of $25,000 at one mile or over, 1$\frac{1}{16}$m, 1:46.44, BLONDAWAY, Gentille Alouette, Laurel Light. 6 started.

CHICAGO BREEDERS' CUP H.-G3, Arlington Park, June 16, $157,270, 3yo & up, f & m, 7f, 1:22.18, TRIP, Hidden Assets, Rose of Zollern (Ire). 7 started.

Chicagoland H. (R), Sportsman's Park, March 31, $75,000, 3yo & up, Illinois-bred, 6f, 1:11.43, CLASSIC APPEAL, Tic N Tin, Spanish Hall. 8 started.

Chick Lang Jr. Memorial H., Retama Park, Sept. 15, $35,000, 3yo & up, 1m, 1:38.14, LIGHTS ON BROADWAY, Happy Smile, St. Martin's Cloak. 6 started.

Chief Narbona S. (R), The Downs at Albuquerque, May 20, $32,900, 3yo, f, New Mexico-bred, 6f, 1:11.67, LITBIT RECKLESS, Sandy

Sage, Flying Choke. 9 started.

Chief Pennekeck S., The Meadowlands, Nov. 9, $75,000, 3yo & up, 6f, 1:08.64, GOVERNOR'S PRIDE, Loaded Gun, (DH) Ticket to Freedom, (DH) Grangeville. 9 started.

Chip S. (R), Gulfstream Park, March 10, $100,000, 4yo & up, f & m, non-winners of three races other than maiden, claiming, or starter, non-winners of four races, or for a claiming price of $75,000, 6f, 1:10.79, SHINE AGAIN, People's Princess, Penny Blues. 12 started.

Choice S., Monmouth Park, Aug. 26, $75,000, 3yo, 1⅛mT, 1:47.77, ONE EYED JOKER, Szep, First Spear. 8 started.

Chou Croute H., Fair Grounds, Feb. 24, $150,000, 4yo & up, f & m, 1 1/16m, 1:44.17, LU RAVI, Frankly My Dear, Enquiry Woman. 7 started.

Chris Christian Futurity, Les Bois Park, June 27, $19,855, 2yo, 5f, 1:00.57, BABY GO BABY, Fadi, Guns a Blazen. 8 started.

Chriscinca S., Calder Race Course, Dec. 31, $37,461, 3yo & up, f & m, 1 1/16m, 1:47.76, FLAMING LIGHT, Tiffish, Timely Tina. 4 started.

Christiana S., Delaware Park, July 1, $100,300, 3yo, f, abt1⅛mT, 1:52.50, FIDDLE, Ruff, Steiners Baby Girl. 6 started.

Christmas Futurity, Turf Paradise, Dec. 22, $75,000, 2yo, 6½f, 1:15.28, AYANNA, Bug Hall, Bella Cash. 9 started.

Christmas H., Mountaineer Park, Dec. 26, $57,175, 3yo & up, 6f, 1:14.15, NATIVE HEIR, Tonto Gusto, Mort. 5 started.

Chuck Taliaferro Memorial S., Remington Park, Aug. 11, $27,585, 3yo & up, 5½f, 1:03.23, MEDIUM RARE, Custer, Big Bay Brite. 6 started.

CHURCHILL DOWNS DISTAFF H.-G2, Churchill Downs, Nov. 3, $222,200, 3yo & up, f & m, 1m, 1:35.30, NASTY STORM, Forest Secrets, Trip. 8 started.

CICADA S.-G3, Aqueduct, March 25, $103,100, 3yo, f, 7f, 1:23.39, XTRA HEAT, Erin Moor, Chasm. 4 started.

Cicero H., Sportsman's Park, March 11, $50,000, 3yo & up, f & m, 6f, 1:11.68, Q. P. CAT, Capitol View, Lady Louwane. 7 started.

CIGAR MILE H.-G1, Aqueduct, Nov. 24, $350,000, 3yo & up, 1m, 1:33.35, LEFT BANK, Graeme Hall, Red Bullet. 9 started.

Cimarron S., Remington Park, Sept. 23, $25,540, 2yo, f, 6½f, 1:18.74, FLYING GAL, Bayakoa's Image, Talk Too. 7 started.

Cincinnatian S. (R), River Downs, July 14, $50,000, 3yo, f, Ohio-bred, 1 1/16mT, 1:44.80, LEFT LANE LORRAIN, Furious Flight, Palm Canyon. 11 started.

Cincinnati Trophy S., Turfway Park, Jan. 6, $43,500, 3yo, f, 6½f, 1:19.36, CREATIVITY, Rank Her Alexis, Soul Onarazorsedge. 9 started.

Cinderella S., Hollywood Park, June 9, $97,125, 2yo, f, 5½f, 1:04.60, GEORGIA'S STORM, Asian Adventure, Respectful. 8 started.

CINEMA H.-G3, Hollywood Park, May 20, $108,600, 3yo, 1⅛mT, 1:48.40, SLIGO BAY (Ire), Learing At Kathy, Marine (GB). 7 started.

CITATION H.-G2, Hollywood Park, Nov. 24, $500,000, 3yo & up, 1 1/16mT, 1:44.30, GOOD JOURNEY, Decarchy, Irish Prize. 8 started.

Citation S., Hialeah Park, April 22, $51,850, 3yo, 1⅛mT, 1:46.76, SIR BRIAN'S SWORD, Moomtazz, Sea Air. 8 started.

CITGO DISTAFF TURF MILE S.-G3, see DISTAFF TURF MILE S.-G3.

City Centre Bingo H., Marquis Downs, July 22, $6,000, 3yo & up, f & m, 1m, 1:42.74, PRINCESS BRIARTIC, Marfa Magic, Truly Remarkable. 5 started.

City of Anderson S. (R), Hoosier Park, Oct. 5, $34,000, 2yo, f, Indiana-bred, 5½f, 1:05.62, MISS INDIANA, Amanda's Crown, Whoisvendeladente. 10 started.

City of Bridges Sophomore S. (R), Marquis Downs, Sept. 1, $7,475, 3yo, c & g, Canadian-bred, 1 1/16m, 1:47.44, FIRST AFFAIR, Tip the Ring, Mi Pequeno Amigo. 4 started.

City of Edmonton Distaff H., Northlands Park, Aug. 25, $50,000, 3yo & up, f & m, 1 1/16m, 1:45.40, TECATE, Little Lolitta, Slewability. 8 started.

City of Hialeah S., Hialeah Park, March 31, $51,600, 3yo, f, 6f, 1:09.14, DEVILISH ERICA, Hidden Creek, Cheeks Eightyeight. 7 started.

City of Phoenix H., Turf Paradise, Oct. 6, $30,000, 3yo & up, f & m, 6f, 1:09.75, SALTY HELEN, Top Bracket, Kimme a Star. 7 started.

City of Roses H., Portland Meadows, Dec. 16, $8,450, 3yo & up, f & m, 1m, 1:45.06, CONSTANTLY CLASSY, Primadonna Poppy. 5 started.

City of South Miami S., Hialeah Park, March 17, $51,200, 3yo, f, 7f, 1:22.65, VICTORY AT SEA, (DH) Hurry Rafaela, (DH) Perchance to Dream. 5 started.

City of Vancouver S. (R), Hastings Park Racecourse, May 5, $37,039, 3yo, British Columbia-bred, 6½f, 1:17.34, I'M FREE, Irish Pleasure, Jazzy Yacht. 4 started.

CJ's Oilfield Services S., Grand Prairie, Aug. 5, $2,460, 3yo & up, f & m, 6f, 1:15, KLASSY CHASSY, Sweet N Brassy, Nokzcatoffzfence. 8 started.

Claiming Crown Express S. (R), Canterbury Park, Aug. 4, $48,000, 3yo & up, starters for a claiming price of $7,500 or less since July 31, 2000, 6f, 1:09.68, THE MACCABEE, Lord of Time, Hot Affair. 10 started.

Claiming Crown Glass Slipper S. (R), Canterbury Park, Aug. 4, $74,250, 3yo & up, f & m, starters for a claiming price of $12,500 or less since July 31, 2000, 6½f, 1:16.68, FRENCH TEACHER, Beauty's Due, Lost Judgement. 13 started.

Claiming Crown Iron Horse S. (R), Canterbury Park, Aug. 4, $49,500, 3yo & up, starters for a claiming price of $5,000 or less since July 31, 2000, 1 1/16m, 1:45.75, SECRET SQUALL, Home a Winner, Gotthard. 13 started.

Claiming Crown Jewel S. (R), Canterbury Park, Aug. 4, $141,000, 3yo & up, starters for a claiming price of $25,000 or less since July 31, 2000, 1⅛m, 1:50.74, SING BECAUSE, Halo Kris, Banner Salute. 8 started.

Claiming Crown Rapid Transit S. (R), Canterbury Park, Aug. 4, $99,000, 3yo & up, starters for a claiming price of $16,000 or less since July 31, 2000, 6½f, 1:16.18, SASSY HOUND, Crowns Runner, Exert. 13 started.

Clarendon S. (R), Woodbine, June 30, $149,175, 2yo, Canadian-bred, 5½f, 1:04.97, SHAWS CREEK, Molly's Wisdom, Cool Rain Falling. 6 started.

CLARK H.-G2, Churchill Downs, Nov. 23, $452,000, 3yo & up, 1⅛m, 1:48.26, UBIQUITY, Include, Mr Ross. 10 started.

Classic H., Marquis Downs, July 29, $6,000, 3yo, f, 1m, 1:42.36, RED VIL DO, Sing On Stage, Ms. Lady Rose. 6 started.

Classy 'n Smart S. (R), Woodbine, Nov. 21, $108,900, 3yo & up, f & m, progeny of eligible stallions standing in Ontario, 1 1/16m, 1:45.19, MOONLIGHT AFFAIR, Regal Snicker, Niki Nikininedoors. 10 started.

CLEMENT L. HIRSCH H.-G2, Del Mar, Aug. 5, $294,000, 3yo & up, f & m, 1 1/16m, 1:41.78, TRANQUILITY LAKE, Gourmet Girl, Nany's Sweep. 4 started.

CLEMENT L. HIRSCH MEMORIAL TURF CHAMPIONSHIP S.-G1, Santa Anita Park, Sept. 30, $300,000, 3yo & up, 1¼mT, 1:59.47, SENURE, White Heart (GB), Cagney (Brz). 6 started.

Cleveland Gold Cup S. (R), Thistledown, July 4, $100,000, 3yo, Ohio-bred, 1⅛m, 1:50.84, UNBRIDLED TIME, Blame It On Ruby, Start Sooner. 10 started.

Cleveland Kindergarten S. (R), Thistledown, July 7, $40,000, 2yo, Ohio-bred, 5½f, 1:05.38, HARLAN'S HOLIDAY, Truth Matters, All Star Lover. 10 started.

CLIFF HANGER H.-G3, The Meadowlands, Sept. 22, $150,000, 3yo & up, 1 1/16mT, 1:43.14, CRASH COURSE, Solitary Dancer, Union One. 10 started.

Club House Special S., Columbus, Aug. 12, $7,775, 2yo, 6f, 1:17.20, YANKEE FELLA, Secret Banker, Come Home New York. 8 started.

Clyde B. Stephens Memorial S., Delta Downs, Feb. 24, $20,125, 3yo, 7f, 1:25.46, MAGIC KEY, Love Come Quick, Giuseppe's Majesty. 8 started.

COACHING CLUB AMERICAN OAKS-G1, Belmont Park, July 21, $350,000, 3yo, f, 1½m, 2:30.70, TWEEDSIDE, Exogenous, Unbridled Lassie. 8 started.

Coca Cola Classic H., Marquis Downs, July 21, $6,000, 3yo & up, 1m, 1:38.53, ROUGE ROYALE, Beau Ring, Star of the Show. 4 started.

Coca-Cola Sprint H., Fonner Park, March 31, $30,240, 3yo & up, 6½f, 1:19, SHOT OF GOLD, Leaping Plum, Buzz Bar. 9 started.

Coconut Grove S., Hialeah Park, April 29, $26,600, 3yo, f, 1⅛mT, 1:50.31, WANDER MOM, Light Dancer, Free the Magic. 7 started.

Colin S., Woodbine, July 15, $110,800, 2yo, 6f, 1:12.07, RUM SPLASHER, Expected Hour, Square Cut Diamond. 6 started.

Colleen S., Monmouth Park, Aug. 4, $50,000, 2yo, f, 5½f, 1:03.55, FOREST HEIRESS, Al Max Diner, Ghost Wrestling. 6 started.

Collegian S., Suffolk Downs, Feb. 3, $25,000, 3yo, 6f, 1:13.49, CLIFF-DIVER, Yasou Daniel, Pluperfect. 10 started.

Col. E. R. Bradley H., Fair Grounds, Jan. 4, $75,000, 4yo & up, abt1 1/16mT, 1:42.99, CORNISH SNOW, Royal Strand (Ire), Talkmeister. 13 started.

Colonel Power H., Fair Grounds, Jan. 13, $75,000, 4yo & up, 6f, 1:10.67, DISTRICT, Bonapaw, Crucible. 5 started.

Colonel Power S., Hawthorne Race Course, Dec. 2, $43,000, 3yo

& up, 6½f, 1:17.28, TIC N TIN, Willowbrook Lane, Magic Doe. 6 started.

Colonial Cup Hurdle S., Camden, Nov. 18, $100,000, 4yo & up, abt2¾mT, 5:05.60 (NCR), LORD ZADA, All Gong (GB), Al Skywalker. 11 started.

Colorado Derby, Arapahoe Park, Aug. 5, $61,200, 3yo, 1⅟₁₆m, 1:45, BEEHAY, Sharethetime, I've Been Crowned. 9 started.

COL. R. S. MCLAUGHLIN H.-G3, Woodbine, Sept. 15, $107,600, 3yo, 1⅛m, 1:51.54, WIN CITY, Magic Flute, Brushing Bully. 4 started.

Columbiana H., Hialeah Park, May 5, $75,000, 3yo & up, f & m, 1⅛mT, 1:49.19, CLEARLY A QUEEN, My Sweet Westly, Silver Rail. 11 started.

Columbia River S., Portland Meadows, Nov. 4, $8,175, 2yo, 5f, 1:00.63, MANITO GENTLEMAN, White Tie Ole, Brass Halo. 5 started.

Columbia S., Tampa Bay Downs, May 5, $50,000, 3yo & up, abt1⅛mT, 1:47.90, GUARDIANOFTHEGATE, Trooper Red, Special Coach. 10 started.

Columbine H., Arapahoe Park, Aug. 12, $28,100, 3yo & up, f & m, 1⅟₁₆m, 1:45, PURLS LEDGEND, Jennaly, Krisi My Girl. 9 started.

Columbus Day S., Suffolk Downs, Oct. 8, $25,000, 3yo & up, f & m, 6f, 1:13.43, SLICK LADY, Lucky Paws, Shehaz Pazzaz. 8 started.

Columbus Futurity (R), Columbus, Aug. 26, $11,625, 2yo, Nebraska-bred, 6f, 1:14.20, C. C. DIAMOND, Ottis P Coaltrain, Why Knot. 10 started.

COMELY S.-G3, Aqueduct, April 13, $110,100, 3yo, f, 1m, 1:36.17, TWO ITEM LIMIT, Mandy's Gold (DQ from 1st), It All Adds Up. 7 started.

Comet S., The Meadowlands, Sept. 8, $48,500, 2yo, 6f, 1:09.73, FINAL TABLE, Boston Common, Winning Talk. 4 started.

COMMONWEALTH BREEDERS' CUP S.-G2, Keeneland, April 14, $270,750, 3yo & up, 7f, 1:22.39, ALANNAN, Valiant Halory, Liberty Gold. 8 started.

Concord S., Rockingham Park, Sept. 23, $25,000, 2yo, f, 6f, 1:12.64, YACHT TO PAY FOR, Mrscoppolaskitchen, Darby Haven. 11 started.

CONNAUGHT CUP S.-G3 (1st Div.), Woodbine, May 26, $165,150, 4yo & up, 1⅟₁₆mT, 1:47.49, RED SEA (GB), River Boat, Silver Axe. 7 started.

CONNAUGHT CUP S.-G3 (2nd Div.), Woodbine, May 26, $166,650, 4yo & up, 1⅟₁₆mT, 1:48.17, DEL MAR SHOW, Lodge Hill, Kimberlite Pipe. 8 started.

Conniver S. (R), Laurel Park, March 24, $60,000, 4yo & up, f & m, Maryland-bred, 7f, 1:24.57, A LOT OF MARY, Case of the Blues, Silent Valay. 7 started.

Conroe S., Sam Houston Race Park, Dec. 15, $25,000, 3yo, 6f, 1:10.65, KENTUCKY BAY, Run Zeal Run, Wild Again Again. 10 started.

Continental Mile S., Monmouth Park, Sept. 1, $50,000, 2yo, 1mT, 1:36.75, HUNTER CRUISE, Fine and Dandy, Dr Gold. 8 started.

Contrary Rose S. (R), Pimlico, Sept. 6, $40,000, 3yo & up, f & m, non-winners of a $35,000 stake in 2001, 6f, 1:11.26, CLASSIC OLYMPIO, Lip Sing's Affair, Halfway North. 6 started.

Convenience S. (R), Calder Race Course, Sept. 29, $50,000, 3yo, f, progeny of eligible stallions standing in Florida, 1⅟₁₆m, 1:46.72, SARA'S SUCCESS, Halo Reality, Sea Mist. 6 started.

Convenience S. (R), Hollywood Park, June 8, $80,750, 4yo & up, f & m, non-winners of three other than maiden, claiming or starter or four races lifetime, 1⅟₁₆m, 1:43.64, SETAREH, Mind for Gold, Deviletta. 8 started.

Cool Air H. (R), Calder Race Course, Aug. 4, $54,100, 3yo & up, f & m, Florida-bred, 5f, :58.73, FLYING BIRDIE, Penny Blues, Miss Vermont Jet. 6 started.

COOLMORE LEXINGTON S.-G2, Keeneland, April 21, $371,475, 3yo, 1⅟₁₆m, 1:43.54, KEATS, Griffinite, Bay Eagle. 10 started.

Cool Reception S. (R), Fort Erie, Aug. 13, $54,850, 3yo & up, Canadian-bred, 1⅟₁₆m, 1:45.63, INTHEEVENTOFAFIRE, Northernprospector, Smoke'n'ashes. 8 started.

Coors Starter Allowance S. (R), Fonner Park, May 13, $10,755, 3yo & up, starters for a claiming price of $5,000 or less in 2000-01, 1⅛m, 1:53.80, REALLY SOVEREIGN, Summo Sun, Trumpty Dumpty. 7 started.

Copper Top Futurity (R), Sunland Park, April 8, $131,656, 2yo, New Mexico-bred, 4½f, :52.80, DEVON'S PROSPECT, How Bout Now, Gray Ryder. 9 started.

Coral Gables S., Hialeah Park, May 13, $31,450, 3yo & up, 1⅟₁₆m, 1:44.24, TAHKODHA HILLS, General Grant, Select Decor. 7 started.

Coral Springs S., Hialeah Park, April 14, $27,400, 3yo, f, 5½fT, 1:03.42, MY GIRL LISA, Free the Magic, Storm Lass. 11 started.

Cordially S. (R), Delaware Park, Sept. 23, $61,300, 3yo, f, non-winners of three races or for a claiming price of $80,000, 1mT, 1:37.08, SALTY YOU, New Economy, Quppy. 9 started.

Cormorant S. (R), Aqueduct, Nov. 11, $100,000, 3yo & up, progeny of eligible stallions standing in New York, 1mT, 1:36.51, UNION ONE, Jini's Jet, Winloc's Nelson. 11 started.

Corona H., Hollywood Park, Dec. 16, $73,660, 3yo & up, f & m, 6f, 1:09.86, KALOOKAN QUEEN, Salty Helen, Ivory Tower (Arg). 6 started.

Coronation Futurity (R), Woodbine, Oct. 28, $250,000, 2yo, Canadian-bred, 1⅛m, 1:53.63, STREAKIN ROB, Foregone, Affirmed Feeling. 10 started.

Correction H., Aqueduct, Feb. 3, $80,550, 3yo & up, f & m, 6f, 1:10.97, FICKLE FANNY, Slash Cottage, Live Wire Lil. 6 started.

Corte Madera S., Golden Gate Fields, Dec. 29, $55,700, 2yo, f, 1m, 1:39.03, RUNAWAY AB, My Sand Dollar, Unforgettable R N. 7 started.

COTILLION H.-G2, Philadelphia Park, Oct. 6, $250,000, 3yo, f, 1⅟₁₆m, 1:43.86, MYSTIC LADY, Zonk, Celtic Melody. 8 started.

Council Oak S., Fair Meadows at Tulsa, July 28, $27,215, 3yo & up, 6½f, 1:17.60, BIG BAY BRITE, College Dean, Sidoslew. 7 started.

Count Fleet S., Aqueduct, Jan. 6, $82,025, 3yo, 1m 70y, 1:43.30, JUST ALLEN, Personable Pete, Native Heir. 7 started.

COUNT FLEET SPRINT H.-G3, Oaklawn Park, April 12, $125,000, 4yo & up, 6f, 1:08.18, BONAPAW, Chindi, Bidis. 7 started.

Count Lathum H., Northlands Park, Aug. 4, $35,000, 3yo, 1⁵⁄₁₆m, 2:14.40, KID COPPER, Bubblegum Kid, Harbour Ice. 6 started.

Count Turf S., Delaware Park, Aug. 25, $75,300, 2yo, 6f, 1:12.94, SQUARE CUT DIAMOND, Ride the Tiger, Outstander. 6 started.

Courtship S., Bay Meadows, Oct. 7, $57,550, 2yo, f, 6f, 1:10.29, EXCESSIVE PRAYER, Past You, The News' West. 4 started.

Cover Girl H., Hastings Park Racecourse, Sept. 8, $35,000, 3yo & up, f & m, 6½f, 1:16.75, GROOMS DERBY, Bamboo Queen, Miss Pixie. 7 started.

COWDIN S.-G3, Belmont Park, Oct. 7, $106,800, 2yo, 6½f, 1:19.16, SUNRAY SPIRIT, Davids Expectation, Harmony Hall. 5 started.

Coyote H., Turf Paradise, Feb. 17, $50,000, 4yo & up, 6f, 1:09.13, HANGONSLEWPYHANGON, Tavasco, Iza Redhead. 7 started.

Crabapple S., Oaklawn Park, Feb. 4, $50,000, 4yo & up, 1m, 1:38.73, GATEWOOD, Remington Rock, Mr Ross. 10 started.

Cradle S., River Downs, Sept. 3, $206,300, 2yo, 1⅟₁₆m, 1:46.40, HARLAN'S HOLIDAY, Request for Parole, Arctic Sand. 11 started.

Crank It Up S., Monmouth Park, June 3, $50,000, 3yo, 5f, :57.47, FOREST HEIR, Unreal Party, American Century. 6 started.

Credenza S. (R), Penn National Race Course, June 30, $25,000, 3yo, f, Pennsylvania-bred, 1⅟₁₆m, 1:48.35, ONE LUCKY ONE, Singapore Thunder, Fast Lane Terry. 5 started.

Creme Fraiche S., The Meadowlands, Nov. 10, $75,000, 3yo & up, 1³⁄₁₆m, 1:53.95 (ETR), RIZE, Pickupspeed, Banner Headline. 7 started.

Crescent City Derby (R), Fair Grounds, Jan. 20, $75,000, 3yo, Louisiana-bred, 1⅟₁₆m, 1:47.89, MR. SULU, Pink Duck, Bullet Rocket. 9 started.

Crescent S., Lone Star Park, May 5, $100,000, 3yo & up, 6½f, 1:15.90, DR LEWIS, Vinnie's Boy, T. B. Track Star. 7 started.

Criterium S., Calder Race Course, July 7, $100,000, 2yo, 5½f, 1:06.79, JUGGERNAUT, Pure Precision, Bog Hunter. 7 started.

Critical Miss S., Philadelphia Park, Aug. 25, $50,000, 2yo, f, 6f, 1:13.08, FRIONA, Hansel's Annie Gal, Phyxius. 6 started.

CROWN ROYAL AMERICAN TURF S.-G3, see AMERICAN TURF S.-G3.

Crown Royal Hurdle H., Pine Mountain-Calloway Garden, Nov. 3, $33,950, 4yo & up, abt2⅜mT, 3:54.60, TEB'S BEND, Darn Tipalarm, Spring Salute. 6 started.

Cryptoclearance S., Gulfstream Park, Feb. 28, $67,575, 4yo & up, 1⅟₁₆m, 1:43.17, ROCK AND ROLL, Day Trade, Reporter. 6 started.

Crystal Water H. (R), Santa Anita Park, March 24, $150,000, 4yo & up, California-bred, 1mT, 1:33.82, ROAD TO SLEW, Native Desert, Lily's Lad. 7 started.

CTBA Breeders' Oaks (R), Arapahoe Park, Aug. 26, $30,000, 3yo, f, Colorado-bred, 1m, 1:39.80, JUST REACT, Bangle, Black Sea. 8 started.

CTBA Derby (R), Arapahoe Park, Aug. 25, $30,000, 3yo, Colorado-bred, 1⅟₁₆m, 1:44.80, TANGARAE TANGO, Socko, Ex Kay E. 9

started.

CTBA Futurity (R), Arapahoe Park, Aug. 12, $30,000, 2yo, Colorado-bred, 6f, 1:11.20, THIS CHRIS, Gone With the Win, Dancing Doc. 9 started.

CTBA Lassie S. (R), Arapahoe Park, Aug. 18, $30,000, 2yo, f, Colorado-bred, 6f, 1:12.40, MAKE THE DEPOSIT, She's Finding Time, Mybabypicture. 7 started.

CTBA Marian S. (R), Fairplex Park, Sept. 17, $45,500, 3yo, f, California-bred, 1⅟₁₆m, 1:45.70, SPIDERETTE, Thewholebag, Always the Lady. 4 started.

CTHS Sales S. (R), Assiniboia Downs, Sept. 3, $26,950, 2yo, c & g, sold at the CTHS (Manitoba Div.) sale, 6f, 1:15.80, GOIN N STYLE, Crown and Glory, Silver Greek. 6 started.

CTHS Sales S. (R), Assiniboia Downs, Sept. 3, $26,950, 2yo, f, sold at the CTHS (Manitoba Div.) sale, 6f, 1:15.40, WHAT FOUR, Ruanwar, Regal Polka. 7 started.

CTHS Sales S. (R), Hastings Park Racecourse, July 1, $65,280, 2yo, c & g, Canadian-bred sold at a CTHS (British Columbia Div.) sale, 6½f, 1:19.48, EXCITED AT LAST, Regal Courier, Smiles Are Free. 6 started.

CTHS Sales S. (R), Hastings Park Racecourse, July 1, $65,040, 2yo, f, Canadian-bred sold at a CTHS (British Columbia Div.) sale, 6½f, 1:20.11, REGAL HEIR, Haunting You, Ponti Victoria. 8 started.

CTT & Thoroughbred Owners of California H., Del Mar, Aug. 30, $76,050, 3yo & up, f & m, 1⅜mT, 2:13.85, NEPENTHE, Bucarest (Arg), Nuit de Siam (Fr). 7 started.

"Cub" Klahr H., Les Bois Park, June 3, $4,345, 3yo & up, 7f, 1:23.48, ALMOST GOLDEN, J. D. for Shur, Moyamba. 4 started.

Cumberland S. (R), Pimlico, June 24, $40,000, 3yo & up, f & m, non-winners of a $25,000 stake, 6f, 1:11.50, DR MARGARET, Sexual Harrasment, Lovely Amanda. 7 started.

Cup and Saucer S. (R), Woodbine, Oct. 6, $250,000, 2yo, Canadian-bred, 1⅟₁₆mT, 1:50.20, ATLANTIC FURY, El Soprano, Classic Case. 6 started.

Curribot H., Sunland Park, Feb. 10, $32,700, 3yo & up, 1⅟₁₆m, 1:43.20, ACCOMODATOR, Gratteau, Brew. 8 started.

C. W. "Doc" Pardee S. (R), Turf Paradise, April 7, $15,000, 3yo & up, f & m, Arizona-bred, 1m, 1:39.90, CHANGEFORAFIFTY, Pleasant Fawn, Deducted. 7 started.

Cyclones S. (R), Prairie Meadows, July 5, $79,900, 3yo & up, Iowa-bred, 1⅟₁₆m, 1:45.16, ELODARE, Elvis Rocks, My Baby. 6 started.

Cy-Fair S., Sam Houston Race Park, Nov. 17, $25,000, 3yo, f, 6½f, 1:17.19, MISS PHOTOGENIC, Raymond's Dream, Babyexpectations. 9 started.

Czaria H., Sunland Park, Feb. 11, $27,600, 3yo & up, f & m, 6f, 1:12, SHARP EYES, Purls Ledgend, Deposit the Cash. 7 started.

Dade Turf Classic S., Ellis Park, Sept. 1, $43,500, 3yo & up, f & m, 1⅛mT, 1:49.56, STAR QUEEN, Golden Antigua, Fast Delivery. 11 started.

DAHLIA H.-G2, Hollywood Park, Dec. 15, $150,000, 3yo & up, f & m, 1⅟₁₆mT, 1:43.24, VERRUMA (Brz), Vencera (Fr), Heads Will Roll (GB). 8 started.

Da Hoss S., Pimlico, Sept. 29, $100,000, 3yo & up, 1⅛mT, 1:51.32, KEY LORY, Warrant, Grundlefoot. 10 started.

Da Hoss S., Turf Paradise, April 23, $24,100, 3yo, 1mT, 1:36.30, RESOLVE, Ironman Dehere, Our Colors. 8 started.

Daily Courier Inaugural H., Grants Pass, June 16, $2,425, 3yo & up, 5½f, 1:06.16, IMUS, Theycallmecolonel, Lefty McSlew. 6 started.

Daily Racing Form Claiming Crown Emerald S. (R), Canterbury Park, Aug. 4, $121,250, 3yo & up, starters for a claiming price of $20,000 or less since July 31, 2000, 1⅟₁₆mT, 1:42.22, AL'S DEARLY BRED, Metatonia, Concielo. 11 started.

Dallas Turf Cup H., Lone Star Park, June 16, $300,000, 3yo & up, 1⅛mT, 1:49.30, EL GRAN PAPA, Dignitas Dancer, Nat's Big Party. 8 started.

Dame Mysterieuse S., Gulfstream Park, March 16, $73,169, 3yo, f, 7f, 1:22.54, MANDY'S GOLD, Raging Fever, Ilusoria. 4 started.

Damitrius S., Delaware Park, April 28, $72,750, 3yo & up, 6f, 1:11.15, DELAWARE TOWNSHIP, Bobby's Buckaroo, In C C's Honor. 4 started.

Damon Runyon S. (R), Aqueduct, Dec. 16, $81,575, 2yo, New York-bred, 1⅟₁₆m, 1:46.48, EYE OF THE COMET, Netcong, No Parole. 7 started.

Dan and Sue Frost Thoroughbred S., Rillito Park, Feb. 3, $4,184, 3yo & up, 5½f, 1:05.60, BLUE STEEL HIGH, High Riser, Camera Ready. 8 started.

DANCE SMARTLY H.-G3, Woodbine, July 7, $172,500, 3yo & up, f & m, 1⅛mT, 1:47.81, ALEXIS (Ire), Badouizm, Only to You. 10 started.

Dancing Count S., Laurel Park, March 24, $55,350, 3yo, 6f, 1:11.61, SEA OF GREEN, Faah Emiss, My Golden Son. 6 started.

Daniel's Boy H., Calder Race Course, Oct. 29, $32,960, 3yo & up, 7f, 1:24.67, SEA OF TRANQUILITY, Groomstick Stock's, American Halo. 8 started.

Daniel Van Clief S. (R), Colonial Downs, Aug. 4, $40,000, 3yo & up, Virginia-bred and/or -sired, 1⅟₁₆mT, 1:43.33, BLAZING COLORS, Cherokeeinthehills, Oak Level. 9 started.

Danville H., Golden Gate Fields, March 25, $58,575, 3yo & up, 6f, 1:08.05, EL DORADO SHOOTER, Amarillo Pride, Majorbigtimesheet. 4 started.

Danzig S. (R), Penn National Race Course, May 4, $25,450, 3yo, Pennsylvania-bred, 6f, 1:09.73, BEAU'S SURPRISE, Hunt Gold, Take the Bait. 5 started.

David L. "Zeke" Ferguson Memorial Steeplechase H., Colonial Downs, July 14, $50,000, 4yo & up, abt2¼mT, 4:08.51, INDISPENSABLE, Avanico, Al Skywalker. 6 started.

Davie S., Hialeah Park, May 19, $31,850, 3yo & up, f & m, 5½fT, 1:02.47, PENNY BLUES, Elvi Gamble, High Stepper. 9 started.

DAVONA DALE S.-G2, Gulfstream Park, Feb. 25, $103,000, 3yo, f, 1⅟₁₆m, 1:45.51, LATOUR, Gold Mover, Courageous Maiden. 7 started.

Dayjur H., Hollywood Park, Dec. 17, $72,450, 3yo & up, 5½fT, 1:02.52, LAKE WILLIAM, Texas Glitter, Shadow Caster. 6 started.

Dearly Precious S., Aqueduct, Feb. 17, $79,875, 3yo, f, 6f, 1:11.88, XTRA HEAT, Schatzeli, I'm a Little Busy. 5 started.

Dearly Precious S., Monmouth Park, July 21, $50,000, 3yo, f, 6f, 1:09.54, STORMY PICK, Summer Shenanigans, Caty's Quest. 5 started.

DEBUTANTE S.-G3, Churchill Downs, July 7, $110,500, 2yo, f, 5½f, 1:02.52 (NTR), CASHIER'S DREAM, Lakeside Cup, Colonial Glitter. 8 started.

Debutante S., Remington Park, Aug. 24, $20,900, 2yo, f, 5½f, 1:05.58, LEAP FOR JOY, Joe's Baby Ruth, Here Comes Kari. 5 started.

Debutante S., Assiniboia Downs, July 22, $26,950, 2yo, f, 5½f, 1:06.80, SANDS FURY, Torquilla, Swing in Satin. 9 started.

Decoration Day H., Mountaineer Park, May 28, $58,125, 3yo & up, f & m, 1m (originally scheduled at 7½ furlongs on the turf), 1:37.72, CHELSIE'S HOUSE, More Than Half, Elaine's Booboo. 7 started.

Dee Lance S., Hawthorne Race Course, May 19, $43,250, 3yo, 6f, 1:11.41, WINNIE'S POOH BEAR, Brassy Babe, Too Many Bucks. 5 started.

DELAWARE H.-G3, Delaware Park, July 22, $600,300, 3yo & up, f & m, 1¼m, 2:05.21, IRVING'S BABY, Under the Rug, Lazy Slusan. 6 started.

DELAWARE OAKS-G3, Delaware Park, July 21, $261,000, 3yo, f, 1⅟₁₆m, 1:45.27, ZONK, Mystic Lady, Lady Andromeda. 11 started.

Delicada S., Louisiana Downs, Aug. 5, $39,200, 3yo & up, f & m, 1⅟₁₆m, 1:43.92, TAFFY, Nanie's Dinner, Midge Too. 5 started.

DEL MAR BREEDERS' CUP H.-G2, Del Mar, Sept. 2, $250,000, 3yo & up, 1m, 1:35.24, EL CORREDOR, Figlio Mio, Performing Magic. 6 started.

DEL MAR DEBUTANTE S.-G1, Del Mar, Aug. 26, $250,000, 2yo, f, 7f, 1:22.22, HABIBTI, Who Loves Aleyna, Tempera. 5 started.

DEL MAR DERBY-G2, Del Mar, Sept. 3, $300,000, 3yo, 1⅛mT, 1:47.93, ROMANCEISHOPE, Indygo Shiner, Blue Steller (Ire). 10 started.

DEL MAR FUTURITY-G2, Del Mar, Sept. 5, $250,000, 2yo, 7f, 1:22.33, OFFICER, Kamsack, Metatron. 5 started.

DEL MAR H.-G2, Del Mar, Aug. 25, $250,000, 3yo & up, 1⅜mT, 2:12.59 (ECR), TIMBOROA (GB), Northern Quest (Fr), Super Quercus (Fr). 7 started.

DEL MAR OAKS-G1, Del Mar, Aug. 18, $300,000, 3yo, f, 1⅛mT, 1:47.98, GOLDEN APPLES (Ire), Affluent, Reine de Romance (Ire). 8 started.

Delta Colleen H., Hastings Park Racecourse, Sept. 23, $35,411, 3yo & up, f & m, 1⅟₁₆m, 1:44.57, GROOMS DERBY, Make Contact, Princess Premier. 7 started.

Delta Downs H., Delta Downs, March 24, $20,125, 3yo & up, 1m, 1:38.89, DIVIDEND M, Dirty Duke, Super Smart Sam. 10 started.

Delta Love S., Calder Race Course, Aug. 12, $34,940, 3yo, f, 7½fT, 1:31.67, COMPANY STORM, Free the Magic, Happily Unbridled. 7 started.

Delta Miss S., Louisiana Downs, Sept. 9, $40,000, 2yo, f, 6f, 1:12.49, DANCING DREAMS, Queen of the Isle, East Coast Soldier. 6

started.

DEMOISELLE S.-G2, Aqueduct, Nov. 24, $200,000, 2yo, f, 1⅛m, 1:50.57, SMOK'N FROLIC, Lady Shari, Proxy Statement. 7 started.

Denise Rhudy Memorial S., Delaware Park, May 28, $75,300, 3yo, f, 1 1/16m (originally scheduled on the turf), 1:45.21, ANCLOTE, Lil Punkindo, Urban Dancer. 6 started.

Deputed Testamony S. (R), Laurel Park, Feb. 10, $72,750, 3yo, Maryland-bred, 1⅛m, 1:54.73, RONNIE'S HOT ROD, Allans Money, It's a Problem. 4 started.

DEPUTY MINISTER H.-G3, Gulfstream Park, Feb. 4, $118,500, 3yo & up, 6½f, 1:16.08, ISTINTAJ, Fappie's Notebook, Fantastic Finish. 8 started.

Deputy Minister S. (R), Woodbine, Oct. 21, $108,600, 3yo, progeny of eligible stallions standing in Ontario, 7f, 1:22.39, DEVIL VALENTINE, Moonlight Affair, Indian Dan. 8 started.

Derby Day H., Eureka Downs, May 5, $5,300, 3yo & up, 4f, :46.47, JUST A ECLIPSE, Mr. Fools Gold, Biggen. 7 started.

Derby Day H., Blue Ribbon Downs, May 5, $11,850, 3yo & up, 6f, 1:10, FUN TO RUN, Cover Keeper, Hedorunrun. 10 started.

DERBY TRIAL S.-G3, Churchill Downs, April 28, $117,100, 3yo, 1m, 1:36.44, MEETYOUATHEBRIG, Dream Run, One by the Knows. 11 started.

Derby Trial S., Assiniboia Downs, July 15, $26,950, 3yo, 1 1/16m, 1:47, CORPORATE SHUFFLE, G and L Special, Miki Bleu Eyes. 6 started.

Derby Trial S., Fairplex Park, Sept. 10, $50,000, 3yo, 1 1/16m, 1:43.85, HUGGY BOY, Swordfish, Legendary Weave. 8 started.

DESERT STORMER H.-G3, Hollywood Park, June 2, $106,000, 3yo & up, f & m, 6f, 1:08.09, GO GO, Kalookan Queen, Wired to Fly. 5 started.

Desert Vixen S. (R), Calder Race Course, Aug. 11, $75,000, 2yo, f, progeny of eligible stallions standing in Florida, 6f, 1:12.79, PHARMSTAR, Blissful Kiss, Be Silver. 7 started.

Designated Dancer S., Calder Race Course, July 29, $33,770, 3yo, f, 1 1/16m, 1:48.81, VALID FORBES, North Park Legend, Morning Sun. 5 started.

Dessie and Fern Sawyer Futurity (R), The Downs at Albuquerque, Sept. 23, $59,675, 2yo, f, New Mexico-bred, 6f, 1:11.07, DANCING PROMISE, Prairie Fire, Quell. 12 started.

Deutsche Banc Alex Brown Legacy Cup Hurdle S., Shawan Downs, Sept. 29, $30,000, 4yo & up, abt2⅝mT, 4:42.80, DARN TIPALARM, All Gong (GB), Lord Zada. 12 started.

Devil's Honor H. (R), Philadelphia Park, Oct. 6, $50,000, 3yo & up, Pennsylvania-bred, 7f, 1:23.64, CLASSIC VERSE, Iron Punch, Sly Ole Buck. 10 started.

Diamond A-USA S., Lone Star Park, May 28, $200,000, 3yo, 1 1/16mT, 1:48.12, ROYAL SPY, Dr. Park, Baptize. 11 started.

Diamondback H. (R), Yavapai Downs, Aug. 19, $10,350, 3yo & up, Arizona-bred, 6f, 1:10.44, BUZZ'S DANCER, Strip, Sonnyhangover. 9 started.

Diamond Trail S., Prairie Meadows, May 19, $50,000, 3yo & up, f & m, 1m 70y, 1:41.13, ASHER, Due to Win, Croupier. 5 started.

DIANA H.-G2, Saratoga Race Course, Sept. 3, $500,000, 3yo & up, f & m, 1⅛mT, 1:46.17, STARINE (Fr), Babae (Chi), Penny's Gold. 9 started.

Diane Kem H., Portland Meadows, Nov. 11, $8,800, 3yo & up, f & m, 5f, :59.27, MISSY MUFFET, Actxotic, Primadonna Poppy. 9 started.

Dine' Derby (R), SunRay Park, Nov. 17, $65,180, 3yo, c & g, New Mexico-bred, 6½f, 1:16.80, CIENTO, Friskie Feddie, Don the Cookster. 9 started.

Diplomat Way H., Fair Grounds, Jan. 21, $75,000, 4yo & up, 1 1/16m, 1:44.51, VALHOL, Frazee's Folly, Miner's Prize. 6 started.

DISCOVERY H.-G3, Aqueduct, Oct. 31, $109,300, 3yo, 1⅛m, 1:48.62, EVENING ATTIRE, Street Cry (Ire), Free of Love. 7 started.

Display S., Woodbine, Nov. 17, $112,500, 2yo, 1 1/16m, 1:44.62, TAILS OF THE CRYPT, Streakin Rob, Funny Soldier. 9 started.

DISTAFF BREEDERS' CUP H.-G2, Aqueduct, March 24, $181,600, 3yo & up, f & m, 7f, 1:23.66, DREAM SUPREME, Folly Dollar, Country Hideaway. 5 started.

DISTAFF H.-G2, Churchill Downs, May 5, $165,000, 4yo & up, f & m, 7f, 1:20.70, DREAM SUPREME, La Feminn, Nany's Sweep. 5 started.

Distaff S., Lone Star Park, April 28, $100,000, 3yo & up, f & m, 1 1/16m, 1:43.31, DASHING LESLEY, Voladora, Fiesty Countess. 6 started.

Distaff S. (R), Assiniboia Downs, Sept. 3, $26,950, 3yo & up, f & m, Manitoba-bred, 1m, 1:42.60, CON'S NIGHT FLIGHT, Marcy Jo Ann, Polka Tune. 9 started.

DISTAFF TURF MILE S.-G3, Churchill Downs, May 5, $113,600, 3yo & up, f & m, abt1mT, 1:36.69, IFTIRAAS (GB), Gino's Spirits (GB), Solvig. 7 started.

Dixie Belle S., Oaklawn Park, Feb. 2, $50,000, 3yo, f, 6f, 1:10.76, CHERYL P., Babyexpectations, Booter's Nix. 9 started.

Dixie Miss S., Louisiana Downs, July 28, $40,000, 3yo, f, 6f, 1:10.78, MISS PHOTOGENIC, Rail to Seattle, Trickski. 8 started.

Dixie Poker Ace H. (R), Fair Grounds, March 4, $75,000, 4yo & up, Louisiana-bred, 1m, 1:38.58, DOCTOR MIKE, Zarb's Luck, Oak Hall. 7 started.

DIXIE S.-G2, Pimlico, May 19, $200,000, 3yo & up, 1⅛mT, 1:48.56, HAP, Make No Mistake (Ire), Cynics Beware. 8 started.

DOGWOOD S.-G3, Churchill Downs, May 26, $109,700, 3yo, f, 1 1/16m, 1:43.41, NASTY STORM, Love At Noon, Golly Greeley. 7 started.

DOMINION DAY H.-G3, Woodbine, July 1, $166,800, 3yo & up, 1¼m, 2:05.69, A FLEETS DANCER, Tarquinius, Ground Storm. 8 started.

Donald Le Vine Memorial S., Philadelphia Park, Aug. 18, $50,000, 3yo & up, 7f, 1:22.55, MONK'S FALCON, Just Beforemidnite, Holiday Music. 10 started.

Don Bernhardt S., Ellis Park, July 28, $49,500, 3yo & up, 6½f, 1:16.51, DASH FOR DAYLIGHT, Better Road, Proven Cure. 10 started.

Don Juan De Onate S. (R), The Downs at Albuquerque, May 20, $32,900, 3yo, c & g, New Mexico-bred, 6f, 1:10.41, DON'S FERRARI, Lendl's Choke, Don the Cookster. 9 started.

Donna Jensen H., Portland Meadows, April 21, $11,050, 3yo & up, f & m, 1 1/16m, 1:49.64, SMOOZIE, Oh Molly, Lime Springs. 8 started.

Donna Reed S. (R), Prairie Meadows, Sept. 1, $78,600, 4yo & up, f & m, Iowa-bred, 1m 70y, 1:42.08, SUMTHINTOTALKABOUT, Nut N Better, Lady Tamworth. 6 started.

DONN H.-G1, Gulfstream Park, Feb. 3, $500,000, 3yo & up, 1⅛m, 1:48.95, CAPTAIN STEVE, Albert the Great, Gander. 7 started.

Doubledippindebbie H., Calder Race Course, Dec. 10, $39,020, 3yo & up, f & m, 7½f, 1:28.15, BAY STREET GAL, On the Horizon, Raponera. 10 started.

Doubledogdare S., Keeneland, April 19, $108,500, 4yo & up, f & m, 1 1/16m, 1:44.38, DARLING MY DARLING, Frankly My Dear, Fast Delivery. 6 started.

Double Your Flavor S. (R), Sam Houston Race Park, March 31, $25,000, 4yo & up, f & m, Texas-bred, 7f, 1:24.92, COASTALOTA, Nobody's Fool, You're No Dancer. 9 started.

Dover S., Delaware Park, Sept. 22, $75,600, 2yo, 1m, 1:38.65, BOOKLET, Ride the Tiger, Midwatch. 7 started.

Dowager S., Keeneland, Oct. 14, $111,400, 3yo & up, f & m, 1½mT, 2:35.77, ONLY TO YOU, Bowl of Emeralds, Krisada. 7 started.

Dowd Mile H., Fonner Park, April 14, $37,520, 3yo & up, 1m, 1:39.60, HIGH DICE, Buzz Bar, Battle Mountain. 7 started.

Dowling S. (R), Great Lakes Downs, July 7, $50,000, 3yo, c & g, Michigan-bred, 1m, 1:41.88, SECRET ROMEO, Timely Factor, Blackstone Dreamer. 6 started.

Doylestown H., Philadelphia Park, July 7, $50,000, 3yo & up, f & m, 1⅛m, 1:50.43, POMPEII, Gold for My Gal, Powerful Package. 8 started.

Dr. A. B. Leggio Memorial H., Fair Grounds, Dec. 1, $60,000, 3yo & up, f & m, abt5½fT, 1:03.82, HALLOWED DREAMS, Repository, Cheryl P. 9 started.

Draft Card S. (R), Delaware Park, Oct. 15, $59,100, 3yo, non-winners of a stake at a mile or over, 1 1/16m, 1:47.06, GALLANT SNOWMAN, Loaded Brush, Quite Rightly. 7 started.

Dr. Ernest Benner S. (R), Charles Town, Sept. 22, $26,850, 2yo, West Virgina-breds nominated to WVBC, 6½f, 1:21.09, ADAMS TRIBE, Tori's Thunder, Count On Justin. 10 started.

Dr. Fager H., Wyoming Downs, June 30, $3,125, 3yo & up, 7½f, 1:35.03, FADSKI, Hesa Gem, Pickles. 6 started.

Dr. Fager S. (1st Div.) (R), Calder Race Course, Aug. 11, $75,000, 2yo, c & g, progeny of eligible stallions standing in Florida, 6f, 1:13.56, CAREY'S GOLD, Royal Lad, Bog Hunter. 9 started.

Dr. Fager S. (2nd Div.) (R), Calder Race Course, Aug. 11, $75,000, 2yo, progeny of eligible stallions standing in Florida, 6f, 1:13.48, O'ROCKY, Concorde's Appeal, Valid Action. 9 started.

Dr. James Penny Memorial H., Philadelphia Park, June 30, $100,000, 3yo & up, f & m, 1 1/16mT, 1:44.41, IFTIRAAS (GB), Doc's Destiny, Impending Bear. 6 started.

Dr. O. G. Fisher Memorial H., SunRay Park, Oct. 6, $31,400, 3yo & up, f & m, 7f, 1:23.20, PURLS LEDGEND, Good Timin Brook, K J Lucky Seven. 9 started.

D. S. "Shine" Young Memorial Futurity (R), Evangeline Downs,

July 3, $100,000, 2yo, Louisiana-bred, 5f, :59, HAIL TO BAG, Rapide, Abagfullofit. 12 started.

DTHA Owners' Day H. (R), Delaware Park, Sept. 8, $76,200, 3yo & up, starters in a non-stake race at Delaware Park in 2001, 1⅛m, 1:50.31, CONCERNED MINISTER, Scottish Halo, Full Brush. 9 started.

Duchess of York H., Stampede Park, June 9, $40,000, 3yo & up, f & m, 1 1/16m, 1:45, GOLDEN REMARK, Slewability, Tecate. 7 started.

DUCHESS S.-G3, Woodbine, Aug. 11, $142,900, 3yo, f, 7f, 1:22.48, MEADOW GEM, Gold Mover, Poetically. 8 started.

Due Bill S., Hawthorne Race Course, Nov. 24, $43,000, 3yo & up, f & m, 1 1/16m, 1:49.48, ADAM'S TIME, Magic Motel, Twilight Aurora. 6 started.

Duncan Hopeful S., Greenelee County Fair, March 25, $4,308, 3, 4, 5 & 6yo, 5½f, 1:07.80, DESERT GODESS, Hootin Hussie, Midnight Flash. 7 started.

DURHAM CUP H.-G3, Woodbine, Oct. 7, $160,950, 3yo & up, 1⅛m, 1:51.71, A FLEETS DANCER, Kiss a Native, Win City. 5 started.

Dust Commander S., Turfway Park, Feb. 17, $50,000, 4yo & up, 1m, 1:34.96, WILLOWBROOK LANE, Double Affair, Market Mover. 10 started.

Dwight Patterson H. (R), Turf Paradise, April 7, $25,000, 3yo & up, Arizona-bred, 1 1/16mT, 1:44.33, NICS ECLIPSE, G Malleah, Jessica Miss. 11 started.

DWYER S.-G2, Belmont Park, July 8, $145,500, 3yo, 1 1/16m, 1:40.38, E DUBAI, Windsor Castle, Hero's Tribute. 4 started.

Earlene McCabe Derby (R), Sacramento, Aug. 26, $50,050, 3yo, California-bred, 6f, 1:08, LOVE THAT LION, Flylikethewind, Song of the Moment. 6 started.

Early's Top Seeded H., Marquis Downs, June 30, $6,000, 3yo & up, 1m, 1:39.74, ROUGE ROYALE, Star of the Show, Beau Ring. 5 started.

East View S. (R), Aqueduct, Dec. 9, $80,000, 2yo, f, New York-bred, 1 1/16m, 1:44.92, SEEYOUINMYDREAMS, Lucky Sucre, Sunday Driver. 5 started.

EATONTOWN H.-G3, Monmouth Park, Aug. 5, $100,000, 3yo & up, f & m, 1⅛mT, 1:47.50, COUSIN GIGI, Quidnaskra, Crystal Sea. 8 started.

E. B. Johnston S., Fairplex Park, Sept. 9, $49,000, 3yo & up, f & m, 1 1/16m, 1:44.35, CEE DREAMS, Feverish, Cee's Elegance. 6 started.

ECLIPSE H.-G2, Woodbine, May 12, $136,875, 4yo & up, 1 1/16m, 1:44.14, GRAEME HALL, Black Cash, Gandria. 7 started.

EDDIE READ H.-G1, Del Mar, July 28, $400,000, 3yo & up, 1⅛mT, 1:47.16, REDATTORE (Brz), Native Desert, Super Quercus (Fr). 6 started.

Edgewood S., Churchill Downs, May 12, $113,800, 3yo, f, 1mT, 1:37.75, LA VIDA LOCA (Ire), Bold Answer, Heads Will Roll (GB). 10 started.

Edmonton Juvenile S., Northlands Park, Aug. 1, $36,600, 2yo, c & g, 6f, 1:13.40, DANCE ME FREE, Swanee River, Onastar. 10 started.

Edward Babst Memorial H. (R), Beulah Park, April 7, $40,000, 3yo & up, Ohio-bred, 6f, 1:10.58, DOWN THEPIKE MIKE, Mike Reggie Jr, C. L. Rib. 9 started.

Edward J. DeBartolo Sr. Memorial Breeders' Cup H., Remington Park, Sept. 3, $150,000, 3yo & up, 1⅜mT, 2:15.16, BEST OF K C, Esperence, Rebridled. 6 started.

Eel River Sprint S., Ferndale, Aug. 11, $7,550, 3yo & up, 5f, :59.04, CANDELOTTO, Fight for Silver, Hello Senor. 5 started.

Egret S., The Meadowlands, Sept. 28, $50,000, 3yo, f, 5fT, :58.24, POLISH HOSTESS, Sparkling Number, Carsonality. 8 started.

Eight Thirty H., Delaware Park, Oct. 8, $58,500, 3yo & up, 1m, 1:37.55, BALARAT, Lyracist, Stans Dream. 6 started.

Eillo S., Gulfstream Park, Feb. 18, $66,300, 4yo & up, 7f, 1:23.33, ROLLIN WITH NOLAN, Silver Jet, Smokin Pete. 9 started.

E. K. Rolfson Senior Memorial S. (R), Chippewa Downs, June 24, $4,750, 4yo & up, North Dakota-bred, 1m, 1:46.40, BIG DAKOTA KID, Music Time, Energy Plus. 4 started.

EL CAMINO REAL DERBY-G3, Golden Gate Fields, March 10, $200,000, 3yo, 1 1/16m, 1:40.85, HOOVERGETTHEKEYS, Startac, Mo Mon. 8 started.

EL ENCINO S.-G2, Santa Anita Park, Jan. 21, $147,000, 4yo, f, 1 1/16m, 1:42.55, CHILUKKI, Spain, Queenie Belle. 4 started.

Elge Rasberry Memorial S. (R), Fair Grounds, Jan. 4, $28,699, 3yo, f, Louisiana-bred, 6f, 1:12, LETTUCE LOOSE, Mysia Jo, Lil Irish Eyes. 9 started.

Elgin S. (R), Woodbine, Sept. 3, $101,900, 3yo & up, c & g, Canadian-bred yearlings sold at a CTHS (Ontario Div.) sale, 1 1/16m, 1:46.96, BOLD N' FANCY, Prince of Style, Dawn Watcher. 6 started.

Elie Destruel H., Santa Rosa, Aug. 6, $43,320, 3yo & up, f & m, abt6f, 1:08.65, SLEWSBOX, Carson Jen, Phaenna. 8 started.

Eliza S., Arlington Park, Aug. 12, $63,250, 2yo, f, 6f, 1:11.75, HONEST DECEIVER, Typhoon Bertie, Lil' Mary's Kitty. 6 started.

El Joven S., Retama Park, Sept. 1, $100,000, 2yo, c & g, 1m (originally scheduled on the turf), 1:40.62, FRENCH ASSAULT, Premeditation, Front Nine. 12 started.

ELKHORN S.-G3, Keeneland, April 25, $113,400, 4yo & up, 1½mT, 2:29.13, WILLIAMS NEWS, Gritty Sandie, Craigsteel (GB). 9 started.

Elko County Thoroughbred Derby, Elko County Fair, Sept. 3, $9,420, 3yo, 7f, 1:26.60, RIGHTEOUS DESIRE, Capitan Reef, Jac Four Girls. 5 started.

Elko County Thoroughbred Futurity, Elko County Fair, Sept. 3, $16,150, 2yo, 5½f, 1:10.20, NORTHERN REQUEST, Crooked Monkey, Weigh the Coin. 8 started.

Ellis Park Breeders' Cup H., Ellis Park, Aug. 11, $103,300, 3yo & up, f & m, 6f, 1:09.35, MISS SEFFENS, Chumsie, Hattiesburg. 5 started.

Ellis Park Debutante S., Ellis Park, Aug. 18, $98,750, 2yo, f, 7f, 1:25.17, (DH) LAKESIDE CUP, (DH) PLAYING 'N GOLD, Ghost Queen. 11 started.

Ellis Park Juvenile S., Ellis Park, Aug. 18, $100,000, 2yo, 7f, 1:24.37, REQUEST FOR PAROLE, Twin Talk, Classic Hero. 8 started.

El Paso Times H., Sunland Park, March 3, $37,600, 3yo, f, 6f, 1:14, RUFFENA, Wampus Who, Ocean Motion. 8 started.

Emerald Breeders' Cup Distaff H., Emerald Downs, Aug. 19, $78,750, 3yo & up, f & m, 1m, 1:36.40, FLEET PACIFIC, Make Contact, Latter Day Paula. 7 started.

Emerald Downs Breeders' Cup Derby, Emerald Downs, Sept. 9, $120,000, 3yo, 1⅛m, 1:49.80, JUMRON WON, I'm Free, Poker Brad. 8 started.

Emerald Downs H., Hastings Park Racecourse, July 7, $34,778, 3yo, f, 6½f, 1:17.92, IVY LANE, Lady's Jewel, Sabrinas Spirit. 3 started.

Emerald Express S., Emerald Downs, July 14, $31,500, 2yo, c & g, 6f, 1:11.80, MELCAPWALKER, Blameitontherain, Horatio. 9 started.

Emerald H., Emerald Downs, June 17, $75,000, 3yo & up, 1m, 1:35.60, MAKORS MARK, Crowning Meeting, Rub. 9 started.

Emerald Necklace S. (R), Thistledown, Sept. 22, $30,000, 2yo, f, Ohio-bred, 6f, 1:12.74, MERCER'S LAUNCH, Ohio Ann, Little Forest. 6 started.

Emerald S. (R), Philadelphia Park, June 2, $50,000, 3yo & up, starters for a claiming price of $20,000 or less since July 31, 2000, 1 1/16m, 1:43.74, R. ENCOUNTER, Flask, Squeaky Brogan. 5 started.

Emeryville S., Golden Gate Fields, April 1, $52,650, 3yo, f, 6f, 1:09.91, HALL OF GOLD, Gifted Daughter, I'm a Lil Princess. 7 started.

Empire Classic H. (R), Belmont Park, Oct. 21, $250,000, 3yo & up, New York-bred, 1⅛m, 1:49.16, SCOTTISH HALO, Duplicitous, Saratoga Sunrise. 8 started.

Endeavour S., Tampa Bay Downs, Jan. 2, $75,000, 3yo & up, f & m, 1⅛mT, 1:48.48, CYBIL, Megans Bluff, Golden Saint. 6 started.

ENDINE S.-G3, Delaware Park, Sept. 8, $150,000, 3yo & up, f & m, 6f, 1:09.64, XTRA HEAT, Ivy's Jewel, Big Bambu. 5 started.

Endless Surprise S., Laurel Park, March 17, $58,913, 4yo & up, 6f, 1:09.67, DISCO RICO, In C C's Honor, Dr. Max. 3 started.

Enjoy the Silence H., Hialeah Park, April 28, $50,000, 3yo & up, f & m, 7f, 1:22.99, TO MARQUET, Coolbythepool, Sugar N Spice. 9 started.

Ensign Ray H. (R), Calder Race Course, Aug. 18, $30,730, 3yo & up, non-winners of $25,000 at a mile or over since May 1, 1 1/16m, 1:40.77, MR. LIVINGSTON, Special Coach, Just Listen. 10 started.

E. P. TAYLOR S.-G1, Woodbine, Sept. 30, $500,000, 3yo & up, f & m, 1¼mT, 2:03.01, CHOC ICE (Ire), Volga (Ire), Spring Oak (GB). 13 started.

Equalize S. (R), Gulfstream Park, March 10, $117,900, 3yo & up, Florida-bred, 1mT, 1:33.35, HONORABLE PIC, Band Is Passing, El Mirasol. 8 started.

Ernest Finley H., Santa Rosa, July 28, $50,700, 3yo & up, abt6f, 1:09.26, MISTAKENLY SPECIAL, Radar Contact, Today a Star. 7 started.

Escaped H. (R), The Meadowlands, Nov. 7, $100,000, 3yo & up, New Jersey-bred, 1m 70y, 1:40.79, RED WEASEL, Summer Swing, Holiest Punch. 8 started.

Escondido H. (R), Del Mar, Aug. 1, $83,975, 3yo & up, non-winners

of a race worth $50,000 to the winner at a mile or over in 2001, 1⅜mT, 2:14.19, CAGNEY (Brz), Continental Red, Shelter Cove. 7 started.

ESSEX H.-G3, Oaklawn Park, Feb. 24, $75,000, 4yo & up, 1 1/16m, 1:43.59, MR ROSS, Remington Rock, Maysville Slew. 7 started.

Estrapade H., Arlington Park, Oct. 28, $75,000, 3yo & up, f & m, 1 1/16mT, 1:46.62, IOYA TWO, Please Sign In, Lady Angharad (Ire). 7 started.

Estrapade S., Hollywood Park, July 16, $106,500, 3yo & up, f & m, 1½mT, 2:27.20, THE SEVEN SEAS, Nepenthe, Letter of Intent. 5 started.

Eternal Search S. (R), Woodbine, Aug. 1, $100,000, 3yo, f, progeny of eligible stallions standing in Ontario, 1 1/16m, 1:44.71, DEVASTATING, Moonlight Affair, Classy Daniela. 4 started.

E. T. Springer S. (R), The Downs at Albuquerque, Sept. 8, $31,950, 3yo & up, New Mexico-bred, 7f, 1:22.23, CIENTO, Ben Told, Bobby Blurr. 11 started.

Eureka Downs Thoroughbred Derby, Eureka Downs, May 28, $13,960, 3yo, 6f, 1:17, DE NORTH BRANCH, Marlin's Ruler, Moscows Quick Trip. 6 started.

Evangeline Downs Sprint Championship H., Evangeline Downs, June 23, $30,000, 3yo & up, 6f, 1:11, OAK HALL, Early Goer, Kadhaaf. 7 started.

Evangeline Mile H., Evangeline Downs, Aug. 18, $75,000, 3yo & up, 1m, 1:38.80, TWO PUNCH SONNY, Oak Hall, Unrullah Bull. 8 started.

Evan Shipman H. (R), Belmont Park, July 22, $81,725, 3yo & up, New York-bred, 1 1/16m, 1:42.32, FOURTH AND SIX, Duplicitous, Shut Out Time. 7 started.

Evanston Derby, Wyoming Downs, July 14, $3,600, 3yo, 6f, 1:14.02, COLORADO CITY, Capitan Reef, Fragrant Prospect. 6 started.

Evansville S. (R), Hoosier Park, Oct. 26, $43,200, 3yo, f, Indiana-bred, 1 1/16m, 1:45.51, FRIENDLY SPIRIT, Taloa, Winning Glory. 8 started.

Everett Nevin Alameda County Futurity (R), Pleasanton, July 6, $53,400, 2yo, California-bred, 5f, :57.73, SURPRIZED, Green Team, Duddly Doo Run. 9 started.

Everget S., Delaware Park, Aug. 13, $75,000, 2yo, f, 6f, 1:11.55, HAUNTED LASS, Knock Twice, Bronze Abe. 5 started.

EVERGLADES S.-G3, Hialeah Park, March 18, $100,000, 3yo, 1 1/16mT, 1:43.02, PROUD MAN, Baptize, Strategic Partner. 8 started.

EXCELSIOR BREEDERS' CUP H.-G3, Aqueduct, April 28, $190,000, 3yo & up, 1⅛m, 1:48.92, CAT'S AT HOME, Top Official, Boston Party. 8 started.

Excess Energy S., Turf Paradise, Jan. 15, $20,256, 3yo, f, 6f, 1:11.24, SONORA DESERT, Lucy T, Channing Way. 4 started.

Executive Board H., Lincoln State Fair, June 24, $13,500, 3yo & up, 1m 70y, 1:39.40, HIGH DICE, Doug's Shadow, Old Man's Delite. 5 started.

Expedite Plus S., Fort Erie, Aug. 6, $54,900, 3yo & up, 6f, 1:10.39, GOLDEN RETURNS, Tempered Appeal, Doug's Legacy. 6 started.

EXPLOSIVE BID H.-G2, Fair Grounds, March 25, $600,000, 4yo & up, abt1⅛mT, 1:50.72, TIJIYR (Ire), Northcote Road, King Cugat. 13 started.

Express H., The Downs at Albuquerque, April 29, $32,800, 4yo & up, 5½f, 1:03.05, MAJORBIGTIMESHEET, Frederiction, Oddsonjack. 7 started.

Express S. (R), Philadelphia Park, June 2, $25,000, 3yo & up, starters for a claiming price of $7,500 or less since July 31, 2000, 6f, 1:09.22, MAJESTIC IRISH, The Maccabee, Storm Regent. 5 started.

Fabulous Frolic S., Calder Race Course, Nov. 10, $60,000, 2yo, 1mT, 1:39.22, MOUNTAIN FORUM, Breakfast in Maui, Out of Nickles. 12 started.

Fairfield S., Solano County Fair, July 21, $47,520, 3yo, f, 6f, 1:10.50, JOKE, Song of the Moment, Channing Way. 8 started.

Fair Grounds Breeders' Cup H., Fair Grounds, Feb. 3, $154,349, 4yo & up, abt1⅛mT, 1:54.03, CANDID GLEN, Sunspot, Solitary Dancer. 12 started.

FAIR GROUNDS OAKS-G2, Fair Grounds, March 10, $350,000, 3yo, f, 1 1/16m, 1:44.58, REAL COZZY, Mystic Lady, She's a Devil Due. 9 started.

Fair Grounds Sales S. (R), Fair Grounds, Feb. 4, $80,000, 3yo, sold at the Fair Grounds Sales Co. two-year-olds in training sale, 1 1/16m, 1:45.23, SAN PEDRO, Rahy's Secret, Aw Heck. 8 started.

Fair Lady S. (R), Hastings Park Racecourse, April 16, $38,500, 3yo, f, British Columbia-bred, 6½f, 1:17.94, QUEEN OF MY NIGHTS, Catahoula Rose, Addy's Hoedown. 5 started.

Fairlee Wild H., Calder Race Course, Oct. 7, $38,630, 3yo & up, f & m, 1mT, 1:36.62, I NO BEST, Reve Russe, Raponera. 10 started.

Fair Queen H., The Downs at Albuquerque, Sept. 14, $27,000, 3yo, f, 6½f, 1:15.96, SASSY CHIMES, T. C. Lu, Wampus Who. 11 started.

Fairway Fun S., Turfway Park, March 31, $50,000, 4yo & up, f & m, 1 1/16m, 1:42.42, TRIP, Fast Delivery, Wave Me Home. 9 started.

Fall Classic Distaff H. (R), Northlands Park, Sept. 22, $50,000, 3yo & up, f & m, Alberta-bred, 1 1/16m, 1:43.60, NORTHERN NEECHITOO, La Belle Bleu, Tuppence. 8 started.

Fall H., Mountaineer Park, Sept. 25, $57,725, 3yo & up, 1¼m (originally scheduled at 1⅜m on the turf), 2:06.22, NATURE, Mort, Xclusive Imp. 7 started.

FALL HIGHWEIGHT H.-G2, Aqueduct, Nov. 22, $112,200, 3yo & up, 6f, 1:09.60, YONAGUSKA, Big E E, Voodoo. 8 started.

Falls Amiss H. (R), Lincoln State Fair, July 8, $22,500, 3yo & up, f & m, Nebraska-bred, 1m 70y, 1:41, DOUBLE DREAMIN DEB, Sandpit Dancer, Statsie's Charmer. 6 started.

FALLS CITY H.-G3, Churchill Downs, Nov. 22, $273,500, 3yo & up, f & m, 1⅛m, 1:49.49, FOREST SECRETS, Printemps (Chi), Unbridled Elaine. 7 started.

Fanfreluche S. (R), Woodbine, Oct. 21, $148,095, 2yo, f, Canadian-bred, 6f, 1:11, MISS NOIRE, My Valley Girl, Matter of Law. 7 started.

Fantasia S. (R), Louisiana Downs, July 1, $44,200, 3yo, f, Louisiana-bred, 6f, 1:10.59, RAIL TO SEATTLE, Princess Rail, Miss Nitap. 10 started.

Fantastic Girl S. (R), Del Mar, July 23, $77,445, 3yo & up, f & m, non-winners of $35,000 since April 20, 2001, 6½f, 1:16.40, KALOOKAN QUEEN, Kitty On the Track, Filigree. 5 started.

FANTASY S.-G2, Oaklawn Park, April 13, $200,000, 3yo, f, 1 1/16m, 1:43.32, MYSTIC LADY, Collect Call, Mysia Jo. 10 started.

Fantasy S., Hastings Park Racecourse, Sept. 29, $43,337, 2yo, f, 1 1/16m, 1:46.55, SHELBY MADISON, Beautiful Stranger, Lady Vye. 7 started.

Farer Belle Lee H. (R), Great Lakes Downs, Sept. 15, $50,000, 3yo & up, f & m, Michigan-bred, 1 1/16m, 1:49.98, FLYINGHANNAH, Sefas Rose, True Ruby. 8 started.

Fashion S., Belmont Park, June 7, $82,225, 2yo, f, 5f, :57.92, SMOK'N FROLIC, Ghost Wrestling, My Heart's Deelite. 7 started.

FASTNESS H.-G3, Hollywood Park, May 13, $110,400, 3yo & up, 1⅛mT, 1:50.01, IRISH PRIZE, Timboroa (GB), City West (Arg). 8 started.

FAYETTE S.-G3, Keeneland, Oct. 27, $166,950, 3yo & up, 1⅛m, 1:50.05, CONNECTED, Broken Vow, Outofthebox. 9 started.

Federal Way H., Emerald Downs, May 6, $33,378, 3yo, f, 6½f, 1:16.20, SHANDRA SMILES, Aunt Sophie, Best Judgement. 8 started.

Federico Tesio S., Pimlico, April 21, $145,500, 3yo, 1⅛m, 1:49, MARCIANO, Talk Is Money, Burning Roma. 4 started.

Feedbag Special Claiming S., Rillito Park, March 10, $2,298, 3yo & up, 4f, :50, BINGO PRIZE, Cop Out, Sam San. 8 started.

Fern Sawyer H., Ruidoso Downs, July 1, $22,500, 3yo & up, f & m, 1m, 1:44.40, WESTERN KAPER, Chasin'rain, Soaring Ego. 7 started.

Fiesta Mile S. (R), Retama Park, Oct. 6, $35,000, 3yo & up, f & m, Texas-bred, 1mT, 1:35.46, MINNEAPOLIS BABE, Eccentric Lady, Peppy Priscilla. 11 started.

Fifth Avenue S. (R), Aqueduct, Nov. 11, $100,000, 2yo, f, progeny of eligible stallions standing in New York, 6f, 1:11.39, PRINCESS DIXIE, Sunday Driver, Dancing Blues. 9 started.

FIFTH SEASON BREEDERS' CUP S.-G3, Oaklawn Park, April 11, $95,000, 3yo & up, 1 1/16m, 1:43.13, REMINGTON ROCK, Kombat Kat, Da Devil. 7 started.

Finale H., Marquis Downs, Sept. 15, $6,000, 3yo & up, 1 1/16m, 1:44.10, BEAU RING, Rouge Royale, Eviticus. 4 started.

Find H. (R), Laurel Park, Nov. 3, $75,000, 3yo & up, Maryland-bred, 1⅛mT, 1:50.12, LA REINE'S TERMS, My Request, Cynics Beware. 8 started.

Finger Lakes Juvenile S. (R), Finger Lakes, Oct. 13, $30,000, 2yo, New York-bred, 6f, 1:12.13, J'S WILD SLEW, Blue Burn, Hamanjiz. 8 started.

Finlandia Cup H., Del Mar, Aug. 19, $76,425, 3yo, f, 1mT, 1:34.47, TATES CREEK, American Czarina, Dispersed Reward. 8 started.

FIRECRACKER BREEDERS' CUP H.-G2, Churchill Downs, July 4, $276,000, 3yo & up, 1mT, 1:34.68, IRISH PRIZE, Aly's Alley, Where's Taylor (DQ from 2nd). 7 started.

Firecracker H., Mountaineer Park, July 3, $58,575, 3yo & up, f & m,

1mT, 1:34.90, RUTHIAN, Elaine's Booboo, Cabot Cove. 10 started.

Fire Plug S., Pimlico, April 7, $72,750, 3yo & up, 6f, 1:09.63, DISCO RICO, In C C's Honor, Dr. Max. 4 started.

First Episode S. (R), Suffolk Downs, April 7, $25,000, 3yo & up, f & m, Massachusetts-bred, 1 1/16m, 1:48.46, E. J.'S LAURA, Big Miss, Vale of Tears. 7 started.

FIRST FLIGHT H.-G2, Belmont Park, Oct. 26, $150,000, 3yo & up, f & m, 7f, 1:23.21, SHINE AGAIN, Dream Supreme, Kalookan Queen. 6 started.

FIRST LADY H.-G3, Gulfstream Park, Jan. 14, $117,000, 3yo & up, f & m, 6f, 1:10.41, ANOTHER, Curious Treasures, Dynamite Diablo. 11 started.

First Lady H., Ruidoso Downs, June 16, $16,400, 3yo & up, f & m, 6f, 1:11.40, CHASIN'RAIN, Hava Peer, Soaring Ego. 7 started.

First State S., Delaware Park, Oct. 21, $97,000, 2yo, 1 1/16m, 1:49.99, RIDE THE TIGER, Lucky Locomotion, Mazoolian Ghost. 4 started.

Flaman Rentals Open S., Lethbridge, Sept. 22, $6,800, 3yo & up, 7f, 1:25.40, ROYALTEA BEY, High Seas, One Classy Dude. 8 started.

FLAMINGO S.-G3, Hialeah Park, April 7, $250,000, 3yo, 1⅛m, 1:48.23, THUNDER BLITZ, Tour of the Cat, Talk Is Money. 9 started.

Flaming Page H., Woodbine, Sept. 1, $101,000, 3yo & up, f & m, 1½mT, 2:27.24, FREE VACATION, Aiglonne, Red Satin Slippers. 6 started.

Flashaway H., Portland Meadows, April 21, $7,075, 3yo & up, 4½f, :52.47, KNIGHT COVER, Wegota Slewzy, Candelotto. 7 started.

FLASH S.-G3, Belmont Park, June 8, $82,275, 2yo, 5f, :56.93, BUSTER'S DAYDREAM, Harmony Hall, Huber Woods. 8 started.

Flawlessly S., Hollywood Park, May 28, $150,000, 3yo, f, 1⅛mT, 1:48.29, VOODOO DANCER, Innit (Ire), Beefeater Baby. 6 started.

Flawlessly S., Arlington Park, Aug. 26, $63,000, 3yo, f, 1⅛m (originally scheduled on the turf), 1:51.54, SCOOP, Glory Glory, Amybdancing. 5 started.

Fleet Treat S. (R), Del Mar, July 22, $100,000, 3yo, f, California-bred non-winners of a race worth $50,000 to winner twice, 7f, 1:22.93, ABOVE PERFECTION, Lighten Up Tiny, Re Vote. 7 started.

FLEUR DE LIS H.-G3, Churchill Downs, June 16, $333,000, 3yo & up, f & m, 1⅛m, 1:49.27, SAUDI POETRY, Secret Status, Asher. 8 started.

Floor Show H., Delaware Park, Aug. 21, $60,500, 3yo, 1⅛mT, 1:49.63, BARNABUS, Please Me Doc, Star Over the Bay. 8 started.

Floral Fiesta S., Bay Meadows Fair, Aug. 11, $44,200, 3yo, f, 1mT, 1:37.39, PLANONCOMETBEBOPIN, Color Me Special, Song of the Moment. 7 started.

Floral Park H., Belmont Park, Sept. 9, $108,400, 3yo & up, f & m, 6f, 1:10.03, GOLD MOVER, Dat You Miz Blue, Finder's Fee. 6 started.

Florence S., Turfway Park, Jan. 13, $49,000, 3yo, 6½f, 1:17.57, ACCELERANT, X Country, Salutee. 8 started.

Florida Breeders' Distaff S., Ocala Training Center, March 19, $35,000, 3yo & up, f & m, 1 1/16m, 1:47.60, PIC A LIL, Living On the Line, Zamba Canuta. 5 started.

FLORIDA DERBY-G1, Gulfstream Park, March 10, $1,000,000, 3yo, 1⅛m, 1:49.95, MONARCHOS, Outofthebox, Invisible Ink. 13 started.

FLORIDA OAKS-G3, Tampa Bay Downs, March 18, $150,000, 3yo, f, 1 1/16m, 1:45.36, QUICK TIP, Southern Fiction, Emery Board. 9 started.

Florida Thoroughbred Charities S. (R), Ocala Training Center, March 19, $35,000, 3yo & up, sold at an OBS sale, 5f, :59.60, STANDARD SYLVIA, Beau Dancer, Max O Max. 5 started.

FLOWER BOWL INVITATIONAL S.-G1, Belmont Park, Sept. 29, $750,000, 3yo & up, f & m, 1¼mT, 2:01.88, LAILANI (GB), England's Legend (Fr), Starine (Fr). 6 started.

Floyd Duncan Memorial S., Rockingham Park, Sept. 15, $25,000, 2yo, c & g, 6f, 1:14.27, METHOD MAN, Circus Bar, Little Billy. 8 started.

Floyd Duncan S., Suffolk Downs, Jan. 27, $25,000, 4yo & up, f & m, 6f, 1:11.54, DIFFICULT DOLL, Golden Apple, Random Honors. 9 started.

Flying Eagle Marathon S., Lethbridge, Sept. 30, $6,700, 3yo & up, 1 3/16m, 2:03.80, END ZONE, Mr. I R S, Sentosa. 7 started.

Flying Julia S. (R), Santa Anita Park, Jan. 3, $70,501, 4yo & up, f & m, non-winners of $3,000 twice other than maiden, claiming, or starter, or of three races or starters for a claiming price of $62,500, 1m, 1:36.94, POTRIMAGIC (Arg), Excessively Hot, Cee Dreams. 8 started.

Flying Lark S., Portland Meadows, Feb. 9, $8,350, 3yo, 6f, 1:11.22, DANZILATION, Provo, Viva Lavilla. 6 started.

Flying Pidgeon H., Calder Race Course, Oct. 13, $100,000, 3yo & up, 1⅜mT, 2:16.39, MR. PLEASENTFAR (Brz), Just Listen, Kassar. 9 started.

Foggy Road H., Delaware Park, Aug. 22, $59,500, 3yo & up, 6f, 1:10.76, IN C C'S HONOR, Governor's Pride, Normandy Beach. 7 started.

Fonner Park Special S. (R), Fonner Park, April 8, $30,900, 3yo, c & g, Nebraska-bred, 6f, 1:13.40, TATE'S WAY, Tauke, Watch Me Dazzle. 6 started.

Fonner Park Special S. (R), Fonner Park, April 7, $31,200, 3yo, f, Nebraska-bred, 6f, 1:15.60, CLAMATO ROSE, Irish Flyer, Missy's Pride. 9 started.

Foolish Pleasure S., Calder Race Course, Sept. 22, $100,000, 2yo, 1m 70y, 1:45.89, JUGGERNAUT, The Judge Sez Who, Mountain Forum. 10 started.

Foothill S., Fairplex Park, Sept. 7, $50,000, 3yo, 6½f, 1:16.86, PRESIDIO HEIGHTS, Kinston, Bettor Royalty. 8 started.

FOREGO H.-G1, Saratoga Race Course, Sept. 1, $250,000, 3yo & up, 6½f, 1:15.53, DELAWARE TOWNSHIP, Left Bank, Alannan. 9 started.

Forego S., Turfway Park, Jan. 27, $50,000, 4yo & up, 6½f, 1:18.14, SOLD TO WALLSTREET, Willowbrook Lane, Mr. Kody. 5 started.

Forerunner S., Keeneland, April 20, $109,400, 3yo, 1⅛mT, 1:48.73, KALU, Cee Dee, Ye of Little Faith. 7 started.

FOREST HILLS H.-G2, Belmont Park, Oct. 7, $250,000, 3yo & up, 6f, 1:09.49, DELAWARE TOWNSHIP, Hook and Ladder, Yonaguska. 5 started.

FORT MARCY H.-G3, Aqueduct, May 5, $112,900, 3yo & up, 1 1/16mT, 1:41.62, STRATEGIC MISSION, Pine Dance, Legal Jousting (Ire). 9 started.

Fort McHenry H., Pimlico, July 4, $75,000, 3yo & up, 1½mT, 2:30.14, PICKUPSPEED, Blue Goblin, Canta Ke Brave. 8 started.

Fort Springs S., Keeneland, Oct. 18, $77,924, 2yo, 6f, 1:11.44, HANDSOME HUNK, El Malicia, Truman's Raider. 4 started.

Fort Wayne S. (R), Hoosier Park, Oct. 6, $42,850, 3yo, c & g, Indiana-bred, 6f, 1:11.31, RED'S HONOR, Hail to Wild Again, Gravano. 8 started.

Forty-Niner H., Golden Gate Fields, Nov. 23, $100,000, 3yo & up, 1 1/16m, 1:41.71, SAN NICOLAS, Moonlight Meeting, Profound Secret. 9 started.

FORWARD GAL S.-G3, Gulfstream Park, Jan. 28, $113,000, 3yo, f, 7f, 1:22.43, GOLD MOVER, Hazino, Thunder Bertie. 5 started.

Foster City H., Bay Meadows, May 20, $51,438, 3yo & up, 1 1/16mT, 1:42.38, CASINO KING (Ire), Rhapsodist, Shelter Cove. 6 started.

FOUNTAIN OF YOUTH S.-G1, Gulfstream Park, Feb. 17, $200,000, 3yo, 1 1/16m, 1:43.48, SONGANDAPRAYER, Outofthebox, City Zip. 11 started.

FOURSTARDAVE H.-G2, Saratoga Race Course, Aug. 25, $200,000, 3yo & up, 1 1/16mT, 1:39.30, DR. KASHNIKOW, Tubrok, Aly's Alley. 12 started.

Foxbrook Supreme Hurdle S., Far Hills, Oct. 20, $75,000, 4yo & up, abt2½mT, 4:43.63, TRES TOUCHE, P. C. Plod, War Talk. 12 started.

Fox Sports Network H., Emerald Downs, May 20, $35,000, 3yo & up, 6½f, 1:15, HANDY N BOLD, Shake Loose, Crafty Boy. 9 started.

Foxy J. G. S. (R), Philadelphia Park, June 2, $50,000, 3yo, f, Pennsylvania-bred, 7f, 1:24.49, KAILIKI, Als Delight, Golden Lake. 11 started.

Fraise S., Gulfstream Park, March 15, $76,725, 4yo & up, abt1⅛mT, 1:48.47, ALY'S ALLEY, Ivars Big Peaceful, Monarch's Maze. 9 started.

Frances A. Genter S., Calder Race Course, Dec. 15, $100,000, 3yo, f, 7½fT, 1:28.56, AMELIA, Sara's Success, Ing Ing (Fr). 12 started.

Frances Genter S. (R), Canterbury Park, July 8, $42,920, 3yo, f, Minnesota-bred, 6f, 1:12.61, FANCY INJUN, Blumin Bauble, Timbia. 11 started.

Frances Slocum S. (R), Hoosier Park, Nov. 25, $43,100, 3yo & up, f & m, Indiana-bred, 1 1/16m, 1:47.51, MARCIANN, Heresyour Chickey, Lady's Legal Ma Ja. 8 started.

Francis "Jock" LaBelle Memorial S., Delaware Park, May 13, $75,000, 3yo, 1m 70y, 1:42.82, CITIROYAL, American Prince, Cliffdiver. 5 started.

Francis Scott Key S., Laurel Park, Jan. 6, $54,029, 4yo & up, f & m, 5½f, 1:04.50, DOC CALLS HER KATE, Lady Chance, Elektraline. 4 started.

Frank Arnason Sire S. (R), Assiniboia Downs, June 24, $26,950,

2yo, Canadian-bred, 5f, 1:01.20, CROWN AND GLORY, What Four, Bashful Dancer. 9 started.

FRANK E. KILROE MILE H.-G2, Santa Anita Park, March 3, $400,000, 4yo & up, 1mT, 1:35.96, ROAD TO SLEW, Val Royal (Fr), (DH) Exchange Rate, (DH) Hawksley Hill (Ire). 10 started.

Frank Figueroa Memorial Starter S. (R), Santa Cruz County Fair, May 5, $3,191, 3yo & up, starters for a claiming price of $2,500 or less, 6f, 1:12.40, NOSHO, Real Dancer, Duplicate Key. 7 started.

Frank Gall Memorial H. (R), Charles Town, Aug. 11, $41,800, 3yo & up, West Virginia-bred, 7f, 1:26.07, REBELLIOUS DREAMER, Turbotaxman, Virginia Glide. 9 started.

FRANK J. DE FRANCIS MEMORIAL DASH S.-G1, Laurel Park, Nov. 17, $300,000, 3yo & up, 6f, 1:09, DELAWARE TOWNSHIP, Early Flyer, Xtra Heat. 7 started.

Franklin S., Keeneland, Oct. 13, $84,825, 3yo, 1mT, 1:38.39, DEELITEFUL IRVING, Silver Spear, Wudantunoit. 6 started.

Fran's Valentine S. (R), Hollywood Park, April 28, $175,000, 4yo & up, f & m, California-bred, 1 1/16mT, 1:40.53, RARE CHARMER, She's Grand, Kinky Kinky. 6 started.

Fred "Cappy" Capossela S., Aqueduct, Jan. 15, $81,150, 3yo, 6f, 1:10.91, FOREST HEIR, Bianco Appeal, Bay Head King. 7 started.

Fred Mendel Memorial H., Marquis Downs, Aug. 18, $6,000, 3yo & up, 1⅛m, 1:52, BEAU RING, Rouge Royale, Cap in Hand. 5 started.

FRED W. HOOPER H.-G3, Calder Race Course, Dec. 29, $100,000, 3yo & up, 1⅛m, 1:51.05, KISS A NATIVE, Hal's Hope, Groomstick Stock's. 8 started.

Free House S. (R), Hollywood Park, Dec. 5, $50,000, 2yo, California-bred non-winners of $28,500 other than maiden, claiming, or starter, 6½f, 1:17.10, CABLE READY, Main Player, Debonair Joe. 6 started.

Free Press S., Assiniboia Downs, June 17, $26,950, 3yo & up, 6f, 1:11, SMOKY CINDER, Kalfaari, Latter Day Ace. 7 started.

Free Spirits H., Ruidoso Downs, July 21, $16,200, 3yo & up, 6f, 1:11.40, SILVER MATT, Mucho Daniero, Mr. de Falls. 5 started.

Free Vacation H. (R), Hastings Park Racecourse, Aug. 25, $54,300, 3yo, f, Canadian-bred, 1 1/16m, 1:44.92, LADY'S JEWEL, Catahoula Rose, Sabrinas Spirit. 7 started.

Friendship S. (R), Louisiana Downs, Nov. 11, $65,768, 2yo, f, Texas-bred, 6f, 1:11.17, MISS RITZ, Truly Sunlit, Go and Look. 10 started.

Friendship S. (R), Louisiana Downs, Nov. 10, $73,184, 2yo, c & g, Texas-bred, 6f, 1:10.51, FRONT NINE, Balkan, Onlynurimagination. 7 started.

FRIZETTE S.-G1, Belmont Park, Oct. 6, $500,000, 2yo, f, 1 1/16m, 1:43.94, YOU, Cashier's Dream, Riskaverse. 5 started.

Frontier H. (R), Great Lakes Downs, Sept. 17, $50,000, 3yo & up, Michigan-bred, 1⅛m, 1:55.10, ABOVE THE WIND, Q Commercial Jette, That Gift. 9 started.

Front Range H., Arapahoe Park, July 4, $28,100, 3yo & up, 7f, 1:24.60, MUCHO DANIERO, Out 'n About, Oh Gracie. 9 started.

Frost King S. (R), Woodbine, Oct. 10, $103,800, 2yo, progeny of eligible stallions standing in Ontario, 7f, 1:23.76, MIGHTY QUINN, Barbeau Ruckus, Barath. 7 started.

Full Steam Ahead S., Charles Town, May 3, $42,250, 3yo & up, 4½f, :52.54, XORDINARY DANCER, Bright Reward, Last Enchantment. 9 started.

Furl Sail H., Fair Grounds, Dec. 28, $75,000, 3yo & up, f & m, 1m (originally scheduled at abt1m on the turf), 1:39.70, MIMI'S TIZZY, Naturally Wild, Alpine At Clark. 8 started.

Fury S. (R), Woodbine, May 6, $146,205, 3yo, f, Canadian-bred, 7f, 1:24.74, TREASUREINMYHAND, Chamul, Mysteryachievement. 6 started.

F. W. Gaudin Memorial H., Fair Grounds, Dec. 16, $75,000, 3yo & up, 6f, 1:10.03, ROBIN DE NEST, Crucible, Bonapaw. 6 started.

Gaily Gaily S., Gulfstream Park, March 2, $69,050, 3yo, f, 1⅛mT, 1:48.79, O K TO DANCE, Honest Scarlet, Word Puzzle. 11 started.

Gala Lil S., Pimlico, April 1, $66,160, 4yo & up, f & m, 1⅛m, 1:50.64, ZENITH, Proud Owner, Leave No Prints. 7 started.

GALLANT BLOOM H.-G2, Belmont Park, Sept. 29, $129,225, 3yo & up, f & m, 6½f, 1:17.60, FINDER'S FEE, Cedar Knolls, Gold Mover. 4 started.

Gallant Bob H., Philadelphia Park, Oct. 6, $150,000, 3yo, 6f, 1:11.14, SEA OF GREEN, Bay Head King, Beyond Brilliant. 8 started.

GALLANT FOX H.-G3, Aqueduct, Jan. 1, $111,700, 3yo & up, 1⅝m, 2:44.74, COYOTE LAKES, Le Beaucet, K. O.'s Crypto. 9 started.

GALLANT FOX H.-G3, Aqueduct, Dec. 29, $115,400, 3yo & up, 1⅝m, 2:45.77, COYOTE LAKES, Pleasant Divorce, Top Official. 12 started.

Gallant Serenade S. (R), Delaware Park, Aug. 6, $59,100, 3yo, non-winners of a stake since February 1, 2001, 6f, 1:11.60, SHORE BREEZE, Western Shore, Saratoga Broadway. 7 started.

GALLORETTE H.-G3, Pimlico, May 18, $100,000, 3yo & up, f & m, 1 1/16mT, 1:42.81, LICENSE FEE, Starine (Fr), Crystal Sea. 8 started.

GAMELY BREEDERS' CUP H.-G1, Hollywood Park, May 26, $221,350, 3yo & up, f & m, 1⅛mT, 1:47.34, HAPPYANUNOIT (NZ), Tranquility Lake, Beautiful Noise. 7 started.

GARDEN CITY BREEDERS' CUP H.-G1, Belmont Park, Sept. 9, $244,000, 3yo, f, 1⅛mT, 1:47.69, VOODOO DANCER, Shooting Party, Wander Mom. 10 started.

GARDENIA H.-G3, Ellis Park, Aug. 11, $200,000, 3yo & up, f & m, 1⅛m, 1:50.16, ASHER, Zenith, Royal Fair. 8 started.

Garland of Roses H., Aqueduct, Dec. 8, $82,775, 3yo & up, f & m, 6f, 1:10.38, RAGING FEVER, Dat You Miz Blue, Look of the Lynx. 7 started.

Gasparilla S., Tampa Bay Downs, Feb. 3, $50,000, 3yo, f, 7f, 1:28.69, FROZEN DINNER, Bigcuz, Hidden Creek. 9 started.

Gateway to Glory S., Fairplex Park, Sept. 20, $49,000, 2yo, 1 1/16m, 1:45.58, RAINMAN'S REQUEST, Sunkosi, Debonair Joe. 6 started.

GAZELLE H.-G1, Belmont Park, Sept. 8, $250,000, 3yo, f, 1⅛m, 1:47.68, EXOGENOUS, Two Item Limit, Fleet Renee. 8 started.

GCFA Accredited Texas-Bred S. (R), Gillespie County Downs, Aug. 26, $15,500, 3yo & up, Texas-bred, 7f, 1:30.31, TOUCHOVILLE, Cedona Red, Hopeful Arrow. 6 started.

Geisha H. (R), Pimlico, April 21, $100,000, 3yo & up, f & m, Maryland-bred, 1 1/16m, 1:43.71, SHINE AGAIN, Unbridled Lady, Case of the Blues. 7 started.

Gene Francis & Associates S., Anthony Downs, July 21, $5,000, 3yo & up, 1 1/16m, 1:53.13, BOLD SUNDANCE, Jade Soldier, Moscow Gold Bar. 7 started.

General Douglas MacArthur H. (R), Belmont Park, Sept. 7, $81,175, 3yo & up, New York-bred, 7f, 1:23.87, JOHN PAUL TOO, No Bad Habits, Impeachthepro. 6 started.

GENERAL GEORGE H.-G2, Laurel Park, Feb. 19, $200,000, 3yo & up, 7f, 1:22, PEEPING TOM, Delaware Township, Disco Rico. 7 started.

Generous Portion S. (R), Del Mar, Aug. 29, $100,000, 2yo, f, California-bred non-winners of a race worth $35,000 to the winner other than closed or claiming, 6f, 1:10.80, WHITEWINESIPPER, Lady George, Britetonzmyday. 6 started.

GENEROUS S.-G3, Hollywood Park, Nov. 24, $200,000, 2yo, 1mT, 1:40.31, MOUNTAIN RAGE, Miesque's Approval, National Park (GB). 8 started.

Genesee Valley Breeders' H. (R), Finger Lakes, Aug. 4, $40,000, 3yo & up, New York-bred, 1 1/16m, 1:46.22, IMPEACHTHEPRO, Alley Ball, Makem Hagar. 7 started.

Genesee Valley Hunt Cup S., Genesee Valley, Oct. 13, $23,250, 4yo & up, abt3½mT, 7:29.80, MAKE ME A CHAMP, Dr. Ramsey, Holzmann. 6 started.

Gentilly H. (R), Fair Grounds, March 24, $100,000, 3yo, Louisiana-bred, abt1mT, 1:39.91, L'HOMME, Mysia Jo, Mr. Sulu. 13 started.

GENUINE RISK H.-G2, Belmont Park, May 12, $150,000, 3yo & up, f & m, 6f, 1:09.55, KATZ ME IF YOU CAN, Lucky Livi, Shine Again. 10 started.

GEORGE C. HENDRIE H.-G3, Woodbine, May 13, $143,000, 4yo & up, f & m, 6½f, 1:18.17, MYSTERIOUS AFFAIR, Ruby Park, El Prado Essence. 6 started.

George Lewis Memorial S. (R), Thistledown, July 29, $50,000, 3yo & up, Ohio-bred, 1⅛m, 1:51.42, FERVENT AFFAIR, Fax a Freddy, Huw. 13 started.

George Maloof Futurity (R), The Downs at Albuquerque, Sept. 23, $55,696, 2yo, c & g, New Mexico-bred, 6f, 1:09.75, NINETY NINE JACK, How Bout Now, Bulletman Jack. 12 started.

George Rosenberger Memorial S. (R), Delaware Park, Sept. 8, $75,900, 3yo & up, f & m, starters in a non-stake race at Delaware in 2001, 1 1/16mT, 1:42.45, CRYSTAL SEA, Anclote, All Spades. 8 started.

George Royal S., Hastings Park Racecourse, May 6, $35,893, 3yo & up, 6½f, 1:16.72, BALL AND CHAIN, King Jeremy, Digital Dan. 6 started.

George W. Barker S. (R), Finger Lakes, May 28, $30,000, 3yo & up, New York-bred, 6f, 1:11.41, IMPEACHTHEPRO, Makem Hagar, Saigon Lieutenant. 7 started.

Georgia Bragging Rights S. (R), River Downs, June 23, $25,000, 3yo & up, Georgia-bred, 1 1/16m (originally scheduled on the turf),

1:49.60, GROOVY ADD VICE, Shannon's Fame, All We Can Stand. 8 started.

Georgia On My Mind H., Calder Race Course, July 7, $50,000, 3yo & up, f & m, 1mT, 1:38.15, DISPERSED REWARD, I No Best, Rocky North. 11 started.

Georgia Peaches H., Calder Race Course, Nov. 22, $50,000, 3yo & up, f & m, 1 1/16mT, 1:41.82, RAPONERA, Light Dancer, Bay Street Gal. 10 started.

Gilded Time S., Arlington Park, Aug. 16, $60,625, 2yo, 6f, 1:12.58, DOUBLE ZERO SEVEN, Pass Rush, Super Striker. 4 started.

Ginger Welch Memorial S., Les Bois Park, July 15, $7,150, 3yo & up, f & m, 1m, 1:39.17, PERSONAL FLEET, Irish Elms, Taylor Creek. 9 started.

Girl Powder H. (R), The Meadowlands, Sept. 19, $50,000, 3yo & up, f & m, New Jersey-bred, 6f, 1:10.50, ARPEGGIO, She's Jane, Golden Made. 9 started.

Glacial Princess S. (R), Beulah Park, Dec. 1, $40,000, 2yo, f, Ohio-bred, 1 1/16m, 1:47.74, CAROLINE ANN, Brynes Girls, Royally Graced. 6 started.

Gladstone Hurdle S., Far Hills, Oct. 20, $50,000, 3yo, abt2⅛mT, 4:09.69, GEAUX BEAU, North Atlantic, Hobe Sound. 8 started.

Glass Slipper S. (R), Philadelphia Park, June 2, $30,000, 3yo & up, f & m, starters for a claiming price of $12,500 or less since July 31, 2000, 6½f, 1:17.30, LOST JUDGEMENT, Habby's Stuff, Aliso Creek. 8 started.

Glassy Dip S., Hawthorne Race Course, Nov. 17, $44,250, 3yo & up, abt5fT, BEWARE AVALANCHE, Distinctive Mr. B, Jolie's Song. 8 started.

Gleaming S. (R), Delaware Park, July 7, $58,100, 3yo, non-winners of $25,000 twice at a mile or over on the turf in 2001, abt1 1/16mT, 1:45, PLEASE ME DOC, Referral, American Prince. 5 started.

Glendale H., Turf Paradise, Feb. 10, $50,000, 4yo & up, f & m, 1 1/16m, 1:45.58, POLAIRE (Ire), No Malo, Balboa Park. 12 started.

Glens Falls H., Saratoga Race Course, Aug. 10, $106,700, 3yo & up, f & m, 1¼m (originally scheduled at 1⅜m on the turf), 2:07.56, IRVING'S BABY, New Assembly (Ire), Caveat's Shot. 4 started.

Global Television S., Lethbridge, Oct. 14, $8,700, 3yo, f, abt6f, 1:11.40, FIGHTING SONG, Da Good Stuff, Falstaffs's Jewel. 7 started.

Glorious Song S., Woodbine, Nov. 11, $116,700, 2yo, f, 7f, 1:25.04, BOSTON TWIST, Platel, Estrada. 7 started.

GO FOR WAND H.-G1, Saratoga Race Course, July 29, $250,000, 3yo & up, f & m, 1⅛m, 1:49.62, SERRA LAKE, Pompeii, March Magic. 8 started.

Go for Wand S., Delaware Park, May 6, $75,000, 3yo, f, 1m, 1:41.04, EMERY BOARD, Strike It Up, Dark Ending. 5 started.

Go for Wand S. (R), Philadelphia Park, Oct. 6, $50,000, 3yo, f, Pennsylvania-bred, 6f, 1:13.32, GOLDEN LAKE, Foxy Power, First Violin. 7 started.

Goldarama H., Calder Race Course, Oct. 28, $37,340, 3yo & up, f & m, 6f, 1:12.34, SUGAR N SPICE, Not in Order, Platinum Tiara. 7 started.

Gold Beauty H., Hialeah Park, March 17, $50,000, 3yo & up, f & m, 6f, 1:09.22, SUGAR N SPICE, Lucky Livi, Dream for a Moment. 9 started.

Gold Cup S., Assiniboia Downs, Sept. 30, $34,300, 3yo & up, 1⅛m, 1:52, BEAU RING, Kalfaari, Smoky Cinder. 6 started.

Golddigger H., Portland Meadows, March 10, $8,450, 3yo & up, f & m, 6f, 1:12, AMBERRAE, Wegota Slewzy, Oh Molly. 7 started.

Gold Digger S., Pimlico, April 28, $40,000, 3yo & up, f & m, 6f, 1:11.60, PRIZED STAMP, Fickle Fanny, Believe in Prayer. 5 started.

Golden Ballet S. (R), Hollywood Park, Dec. 8, $50,000, 2yo, f, California-bred non-winners of $28,500 other than maiden, claiming, or starter, 6½f, 1:16.59, BELLA BELLA BELLA, Daddy's Gold, Martial's Princess. 7 started.

Golden Bear S., Golden Gate Fields, Nov. 24, $59,263, 2yo, 6f, 1:10.33, CAPPUCHINO, Wild Celebration, Vito Corleone. 7 started.

Golden Boy S., Assiniboia Downs, June 10, $26,950, 3yo, 6f, 1:11.20, CORPORATE SHUFFLE, Kenyawin, Wartock. 6 started.

Golden Circle S., Prairie Meadows, April 27, $50,000, 3yo, 6f, 1:09.80, WISE BLUES, Gold Spun Fun, Vicechairman. 5 started.

GOLDEN GATE BREEDERS' CUP H.-G3, Golden Gate Fields, March 4, $242,500, 3yo & up, 1⅜mT, 1:58.58, NORTHERN QUEST (Fr), Eagleton, Entorchado (Ire). 6 started.

GOLDEN GATE DERBY-G3, Golden Gate Fields, Jan. 13, $150,000, 3yo, 1 1/16m, 1:42.88, HOOVERGETTHEKEYS, High Cascade, Media Mogul (GB). 7 started.

Golden Gull S. (R), Charles Town, Sept. 22, $26,300, 2yo, f, West Virgina-breds nominated to WVBC, 4½f, :53.77, THIRD PROSPECT, Whatacon, Power of Faith. 10 started.

Golden Horseshoe S. (R), Fort Erie, Aug. 21, $56,400, 3yo & up, f & m, Canadian-bred, 6½f, 1:19.76, EVERYTHING, Lewinsky, Love Shy. 10 started.

Golden Poppy H., Golden Gate Fields, Dec. 8, $66,013, 3yo & up, f & m, 1 1/16mT, 1:46.55, LIL SISTER STICH, Slow Down, Elegant Ridge (Ire). 7 started.

GOLDEN ROD S.-G2, Churchill Downs, Nov. 24, $215,200, 2yo, f, 1 1/16m, 1:43.82, BELTERRA, Take Charge Lady, Lotta Rhythm. 5 started.

Golden State Mile S., Golden Gate Fields, Feb. 10, $100,000, 3yo, 1m, 1:35.01, GOLD TRADER, Champagne Day, Lil' Country. 6 started.

Golden Sylvia H., Mountaineer Park, June 19, $58,350, 3yo & up, f & m, 1m, 1:34.77, INSIDE AFFAIR, Prized Ambition, Alma Mater. 10 started.

Goldfinch S., Prairie Meadows, April 28, $51,375, 3yo, f, 6f, 1:09.40, HATTIESBURG, Pretty Rocky, Prairie Smoke. 6 started.

Gold Rush Futurity, Arapahoe Park, Aug. 26, $68,950, 2yo, 6f, 1:11, BUG HALL, Russian Olive, Co Twining Niner. 12 started.

Gold Rush S., Golden Gate Fields, Dec. 15, $56,988, 2yo, 1m, 1:34.69, DANTHEBLUEGRASSMAN, U S S Tinosa, Cappuchino. 9 started.

GOODWOOD BREEDERS' CUP H.-G2, Santa Anita Park, Oct. 7, $488,000, 3yo & up, 1⅛m, 1:48.86, FREEDOM CREST, Skimming, Tiznow. 6 started.

Goss L. Stryker S. (R), Laurel Park, March 11, $60,000, 3yo, Maryland-bred, 7f, 1:25.12, CHARLIE'S CARDS, Ronnie's Hot Rod, Smile My Lord. 7 started.

GOTHAM S.-G3, Aqueduct, March 18, $200,000, 3yo, 1m, 1:35.14, RICHLY BLENDED, Mr. John, Voodoo. 8 started.

Go to Will H., Calder Race Course, Dec. 23, $38,650, 3yo & up, 5fT, :55.39, KIPPERSCOPE, True Love's Secret, Firefighter Rob. 10 started.

Gottstein Futurity, Emerald Downs, Sept. 15, $100,000, 2yo, 1 1/16m, 1:46.40, HORATIO, Melcapwalker, Moloch. 12 started.

Governor's Buckeye Cup S. (R), River Downs, Sept. 2, $75,000, 3yo & up, Ohio-bred, 1¼m, 2:08, MAJESTIC DINNER, Recognize, Unbridled Time. 8 started.

Governor's Cup H., Remington Park, Nov. 24, $75,000, 3yo & up, 1⅛m, 1:49.71, RARE CURE, Secret Session, Maysville Slew. 6 started.

Governor's Cup H., Wyoming Downs, July 14, 3yo & up, 4½f, :54.05, TESTHAVEN, River's Run Deep, Truly A Habit. 6 started.

Governor's Cup H., Les Bois Park, July 18, $5,723, 3yo & up, 1m, 1:36.94, RASHA, Almost Golden, Ive Been There. 4 started.

Governor's Cup H., Fairplex Park, Sept. 24, $49,000, 3yo & up, 6½f, 1:16.86, LOVE THAT LION, The Morris Monroe, Tiz Adaptable. 6 started.

Governor's H., Emerald Downs, Aug. 5, $60,000, 3yo & up, 6½f, 1:15, HANDY N BOLD, April Surprise, Snohomish Loot. 5 started.

Governor's H., Ellis Park, Aug. 25, $73,750, 3yo & up, 1m, 1:36.04, FAJARDO, Dash for Daylight, Storm Day. 8 started.

Governor's H., Ruidoso Downs, June 24, $22,600, 3yo & up, 7½f, 1:32.80, BREW, Bobby Blurr, Slew in the Face. 7 started.

Governor's Lady H. (R), Sportsman's Park, March 31, $75,000, 3yo & up, f & m, Illinois-bred, 6f, 1:12.54, PUNY, Lil Bobbie Too, Sandy's Way. 10 started.

Governor's H., Sacramento, Aug. 25, $75,900, 3yo & up, 1⅛m, 1:47.80, REDS SUPERSTAR, Moonlight Meeting, Radar Contact. 9 started.

Governor's Speed H., Portland Meadows, March 31, $8,700, 3yo & up, 6f, 1:12.01, CHANTILLY LAD, Capable Quest, Bob Stories. 8 started.

Gowell S., Turfway Park, Dec. 22, $48,000, 2yo, f, 6f, 1:11.02, TIMELESS LOVE, Bo's Sister, Iffy. 12 started.

Go With the Times H., Calder Race Course, Sept. 6, $37,640, 3yo & up, 5fT, :55.02, KIPPERSCOPE, Uncle Rocco, Blue Grey. 8 started.

Graceful Klinchit Distaff H., Marquis Downs, July 8, $6,000, 3yo & up, f & m, 1m, 1:42.15, PRINCESS BRIARTIC, Truly Remarkable, Scarey Berry Pie. 5 started.

Graduation S. (R), Del Mar, July 25, $125,000, 2yo, California-bred, 5½f, 1:04.32, OFFICER, Crown the King, Bid N Ask. 6 started.

Graduation S. (R), Delta Downs, Feb. 10, $31,025, 3yo, non-winners of a race as of January 1, 2001, 5f, 1:00.68, TYLER'S PRIORITY, Tracie's Trooper, Upper Class. 10 started.

Graduation S., Assiniboia Downs, July 8, $26,950, 2yo, 5½f, 1:07.40, NESS GADOLL, Yo Mac, Miss Gold Dee. 5 started.

Grand Canyon H. (R), Turf Paradise, April 7, $35,000, 3yo & up, Arizona-bred, 6f, 1:08.40, MISTAKENLY SPECIAL, Los Cabo, Doc Art. 7 started.

Grand National Timber S., Grand National, April 21, $26,400, 5 yo's & up, abt3mT, 7:10, WELTER WEIGHT, Southwoods, Sam Sullivan. 4 started.

Grand Prairie Turf Challenge S., Lone Star Park, July 3, $125,000, 3yo, 1mT, 1:36.06, ROYAL SPY, Rockchalk Jayhawk, Kris Havingfunnow. 7 started.

Grasmick H., Fonner Park, Feb. 17, $15,625, 3yo & up, 4f, :46, LEAPING PLUM, Diplomatic Corps, Loveitorleaveit. 6 started.

GRAVESEND H.-G3, Aqueduct, Dec. 15, $107,900, 3yo & up, 6f, 1:10.37, HERE'S ZEALOUS, Peeping Tom, Say Florida Sandy. 6 started.

Gray's Lake S. (R), Prairie Meadows, May 27, $71,533, 3yo, c & g, Iowa-bred, 6f, 1:09.96, LE NUMEROUS, Weahrushhah, Who Devil Who. 10 started.

Great Falls S., The Meadowlands, Nov. 10, $50,000, 3yo, 6f, 1:09.20, BEAU'S SURPRISE, Dixie Two Thousand, Sea of Green. 7 started.

Great Lady M. H., Hollywood Park, June 10, $85,050, 3yo & up, f & m, 5½fT, 1:02.52, CONNATE (NZ), Dusty Heather, Fair Apache. 6 started.

Great Lakes H., Great Lakes Downs, Sept. 1, $25,000, 4yo & up, f & m, 7f, 1:25.72, FLYINGHANNAH, Sefas Rose, Mugme Again. 8 started.

Great White Way S. (R), Aqueduct, Nov. 11, $100,000, 2yo, c & g, progeny of eligible stallions standing in New York, 6f, 1:10.98, WHITE IBIS, Marine Salute, (DH) Stage Music, (DH) Artistic Awareness. 7 started.

Green Carpet H. (R), River Downs, June 2, $50,000, 3yo, Ohio-bred, 1$\frac{1}{16}$m, 1:46.20, UNBRIDLED TIME, Taylortwofeathers, Blame It On Ruby. 7 started.

Green Power Futurity, Lethbridge, Oct. 21, $8,400, 2yo, abt6f, 1:10.80, POSIDONAS, Temptinglittlemiss, Prosperity Rose. 6 started.

Green River S., Keeneland, Oct. 25, $113,900, 2yo, f, 1$\frac{1}{16}$mT, 1:45.88, STYLELISTICK, Lush Soldier, Atlantic Fury. 10 started.

GREY BREEDERS' CUP S.-G1, Woodbine, Oct. 8, $273,750, 2yo, 1$\frac{1}{16}$m, 1:47.03, CHANGEINTHEWEATHER, Eye for an Eye, Pat's Expectation. 13 started.

Groomstick H., Calder Race Course, Aug. 18, $60,000, 3yo & up, 6f, 1:12.05, FAPPIE'S NOTEBOOK, Alice's Notebook, Callie and Jake. 8 started.

Groovy S. (R), Sam Houston Race Park, Dec. 1, $50,000, 2yo, Texas-bred, 6f, 1:10.74, BALKAN, Onlynurimagination, Front Nine. 10 started.

G. Sydney Halter S., Assiniboia Downs, May 27, $26,950, 3yo & up, 5½f, 1:05, TIMELY RUCKUS, Robnroy, Tejano Ruler. 7 started.

GULFSTREAM PARK BREEDERS' CUP H.-G1, Gulfstream Park, Feb. 10, $140,000, 3yo & up, 1⅜mT, 2:13.50, SUBTLE POWER (Ire), Whata Brainstorm, Stokosky. 9 started.

GULFSTREAM PARK BREEDERS' CUP SPRINT CHAMPIONSHIP H.-G2, Gulfstream Park, March 9, $200,000, 3yo & up, 7f, 1:21.85, HOOK AND LADDER, Trippi, Rollin With Nolan. 6 started.

GULFSTREAM PARK H.-G1, Gulfstream Park, March 3, $200,000, 3yo & up, 1¼m, 2:02.96, SIR BEAR, Pleasant Breeze, Broken Vow. 9 started.

Gus Fonner H., Fonner Park, April 28, $100,000, 3yo & up, 1$\frac{1}{16}$m, 1:44.20, ROCKY ROBYN, Battle Mountain, (DH) Desert Demon, (DH) Moore's Flat. 9 started.

Gus Grissom S. (R), Hoosier Park, Nov. 11, $43,400, 3yo & up, Indiana-bred and/or -sired, 1$\frac{1}{16}$m, 1:48.82, SPECIAL EXPRESS, Augustus McCrae, Big Duffus. 9 started.

Haggin S., Hollywood Park, June 17, $78,400, 2yo, 5½f, 1:04.44, EXPECTED PROGRAM, Tracemark, Square Cut Diamond. 6 started.

H. A. Hindmarsh S. (R), Woodbine, Sept. 22, $61,840, 3yo & up, f & m, sold at a CBS sale, 1$\frac{1}{16}$m, 1:45.77, TIME TO DECIDE, Cafe Dancer, Inspired Kiss. 7 started.

Hail Emperor S., Laurel Park, Nov. 17, $50,000, 3yo & up, 1$\frac{1}{16}$m, 1:43.95, GRUNDLEFOOT, Cowboy Magic, P Day. 10 started.

Hail the Ruckus Dating Game S., Lethbridge, Oct. 28, $6,800, 3yo & up, 7f, 1:26, A TEMPTING LIGHT, Demonite, Special Sweetpea. 7 started.

Half Moon Bay S., Bay Meadows, Sept. 29, $59,375, 3yo, 1$\frac{1}{16}$mT, 1:44.41, SEA TO SEE, Irish Warrior, Sir Alfred. 10 started.

Half Moon S., The Meadowlands, Oct. 20, $100,000, 3yo, f, 6f, 1:08.51, LOOK OF THE LYNX, Arianna's Passion, Gold Mover. 7 started.

Halton S. (R), Woodbine, Sept. 3, $102,100, 3yo & up, Canadian-bred sold at a CTHS yearling sale, 1⅛mT, 1:46.78, STEADY RUCKUS, Bristol Pistol, Wide Release. 7 started.

Hancock County H., Mountaineer Park, May 15, $56,950, 3yo & up, f & m, 5f, :56.26, BIG BAMBU, One to Five, Chelsie's House. 5 started.

Hangover S., Hawthorne Race Course, Jan. 1, $43,000, 4yo & up, 6f, 1:11.47, SWEET BABY JAMES, Magic Doe, Silver Zipper. 6 started.

Hank Mills Sr. Memorial H., Wyoming Downs, July 14, $3,675, 3yo & up, 5½f, 1:05.72, PICKLES, Rush for Glory, Lovehermadly. 7 started.

Hannah Dustin S., Suffolk Downs, Feb. 24, $25,000, 4yo & up, f & m, 1m 70y, 1:49.29, CAJUN SEASON, Keep Refrigirated, Reign Rose. 10 started.

Hansel S., Turfway Park, March 24, $59,000, 3yo, 6f, 1:09.48, ONE BY THE KNOWS, Devil Anse, Kazoo. 8 started.

HANSHIN CUP H.-G3, Arlington Park, July 7, $100,000, 3yo & up, 1m, 1:36.21, BRIGHT VALOUR, Apt to Be, Castlewood. 8 started.

Happy Trails H., Calder Race Course, Jan. 2, $29,440, 4yo & up, 5f, :56.25, ELVI GAMBLE, Sejm's Madness, Lord of the Dance. 12 started.

Hard Scuffle Hurdle S. (R), Churchill Downs, May 3, $106,700, 4yo & up, non-winners over hurdles prior to March 1, 2000, abt2$\frac{1}{16}$mT, 3:49, PRAISE THE PRINCE (NZ), Tres Touche, War Talk. 7 started.

Harham's Sizzler S. (R), Sportsman's Park, April 28, $73,170, 3yo, Illinois-bred, 1m, 1:37.80, MEADOW CHAMP, Crack the Vault, Apple Dapple. 10 started.

Harold C. Ramser Sr. H., Santa Anita Park, Oct. 14, $110,500, 3yo, f, 1mT, 1:33.70, CINDY'S HERO, Gabriellina Giof (GB), Walts Wharf. 8 started.

Harold E. Snowden Memorial S., Hialeah Park, March 24, $53,250, 3yo & up, 5½fT, 1:04.26, GRANGEVILLE, Sejm's Madness, Wertz. 10 started.

Harper County H., Anthony Downs, July 15, $3,500, 3yo & up, abt5f, 1:04.02, MR. FOOLS GOLD, Rhinasti, Over Advantage. 7 started.

Harrison E. Johnson Memorial H., Laurel Park, March 18, $80,700, 4yo & up, 1¼m, 2:00.62, DUCKHORN, Do I Ever, Mercaldo. 6 started.

Harry F. Brubaker H. (R), Del Mar, Aug. 17, $76,350, 3yo & up, non-winners of $45,000 other than closed, claiming, or starter at a mile or over since March 1, 2001, 1$\frac{1}{16}$mT, 1:40.62, SARAFAN, I've Decided, Lonesome Dude. 9 started.

Harry Henson S., Hollywood Park, June 30, $72,250, 3yo, 5½fT, 1:01.81, ROCKY BAR, Bills Paid, Coil N Strike. 5 started.

Harry J. Addison Jr. S. (R), Woodbine, Sept. 22, $60,160, 3yo & up, c & g, sold at a CBS sale, 1$\frac{1}{16}$m, 1:45.54, BOLD N' FANCY, Thank You Sir, Rajab's Dancer. 5 started.

Harry Jeffreys S., Assiniboia Downs, Aug. 26, $26,950, 3yo, 1⅛m, 1:52.60, CORPORATE SHUFFLE, Flying Commander, Command Start. 8 started.

Harry W. Henson H., Sunland Park, April 7, $53,100, 3yo & up, f & m, 1m, 1:37.40, HAVA PEER, Jenizara (Chi), Sunnie Do It. 9 started.

Harvest H., The Downs at Albuquerque, April 7, $31,900, 3yo, 5½f, 1:03.82, SILVER MATT, Beehay, Slim's Boot. 6 started.

Harvey Arneault Memorial H., Mountaineer Park, Aug. 11, $57,500, 3yo & up, 6f, 1:07.81 (NTR), HUSTLER, In C C's Honor, Jeanies Rob. 8 started.

HASKELL INVITATIONAL H.-G1, Monmouth Park, Aug. 5, $1,500,000, 3yo, 1⅛m, 1:49.77, POINT GIVEN, Touch Tone, Burning Roma. 6 started.

Hassayampa S., Yavapai Downs, Aug. 21, $11,600, 3yo, 1$\frac{1}{16}$m, 1:48.29, CONTINENTAL MAN, Trick Conviction, Alltime Blues. 8 started.

Hasta La Vista H., Turf Paradise, May 6, $50,000, 3yo & up, 1⅞mT, 3:16.55, FELON (Ire), Glowing Idea, Lightning Draw. 10 started.

Hasta La Vista S. (R), Hialeah Park, May 20, $30,000, 3yo & up, f & m, Florida-bred, 5½fT, 1:03.96, ACTXQUISITE, Copelia, Natalie's Moment. 7 started.

Hastings Park H., Emerald Downs, May 13, $35,000, 3yo & up, f & m, 6½f, 1:16.40, FLEET PACIFIC, Miss Pixie, Crossatyourownrisk. 7 started.

Hawkeyes S. (R), Prairie Meadows, July 7, $80,600, 3yo & up, f & m, Iowa-bred, 1 1/16m, 1:45.85, SHARKY BONO, Lady Tamworth, Scarlet Glory. 8 started.

HAWTHORNE DERBY-G3, Hawthorne Race Course, May 12, $250,000, 3yo, 1 1/8mT, 1:50.49, KALU, Proud Man, Rahy's Secret. 7 started.

HAWTHORNE GOLD CUP H.-G2, Hawthorne Race Course, May 19, $500,000, 3yo & up, 1 1/4m, 2:01.61, DUCKHORN, Lido Palace (Chi), Guided Tour. 7 started.

HAWTHORNE H.-G2, Hollywood Park, May 6, $147,000, 3yo & up, f & m, 1 1/16m, 1:43.21, PRINTEMPS (Chi), Feverish, Brianda (Ire). 4 started.

Hay Patcher H., Delaware Park, Aug. 27, $60,900, 3yo, f, abt1 1/16mT, 1:44.55, Atrial Flutter, LADY OF THE FUTURE, New Economy. 9 started.

HBPA City of Charles Town H., Charles Town, Oct. 12, $51,625, 3yo & up, f & m, 1 1/8m, 1:54.86, MY SISTER PEARL, Rockin Roy, Real Women. 8 started.

HBPA City of Ranson H., Charles Town, Oct. 12, $51,525, 3yo & up, 7f, 1:25.72, CLEVER GEM, Raire Standard, Profigliano. 7 started.

HBPA Flags Up S. (R), Charles Town, July 22, $41,550, 3yo & up, f & m, starters at Charles Town in 2001, 4 1/2f, :52.10, WILD FASHION, Silent Glory, Lip Sing's Affair. 10 started.

HBPA Governor's Cup H., Charles Town, Oct. 12, $51,300, 3yo & up, 4 1/2f, :50.98, GOVERNOR'S PRIDE, Citiworld, Case It Out. 6 started.

HBPA H., Ellis Park, July 14, $81,250, 3yo & up, f & m, 1m, 1:36.89, ROSE OF ZOLLERN (Ire), Trip, Maltese Superb. 10 started.

HBPA Jefferson County S. (R), Charles Town, July 22, $41,500, 3yo & up, starters at Charles Town in 2001, 1 1/8m, 1:54.82, MONK'S FALCON, Lightnin' Gulch, Rebellious Dreamer. 9 started.

HBPA Kelly Kip S. (R), Charles Town, July 22, $42,000, 3yo & up, starters at Charles Town in 2001, 4 1/2f, :51.38, WISE DUSTY, Citiworld, Basic Trainee. 9 started.

HBPA Lady Di S. (R), Charles Town, July 22, $41,700, 3yo & up, f & m, starters at Charles Town in 2001, 7f, 1:26.71, VANNA GO, Sweet Annuity, My Sister Pearl. 7 started.

HBPA Sagebrush Derby, Kamloops, Aug. 26, $5,250, 3yo, 1m, 1:38.80, VICTOR'S HONOR, He's a Ringer, Dynamic Devil. 5 started.

Heartlight No. One S., Pimlico, June 2, $40,000, 3yo & up, f & m, 1 1/16m, 1:43.60, CASE OF THE BLUES, Inside Affair, April in Calgary. 6 started.

Heavenly Cause S. (R), Laurel Park, Nov. 17, $60,000, 2yo, f, Maryland-bred, 7f, 1:24.75, BRONZE ABE, Runnin Wonder, Phyxius. 5 started.

Helena S., Suffolk Downs, April 21, $25,000, 3yo, f, 1m, 1:41.17, BUZZING B'S, Demaloot's Girl, Sunlit Ridge. 7 started.

Helen B. Anthony Memorial S., Yavapai Downs, June 2, $10,000, 3yo, f, 6f, 1:10.04, LUCY T, Stormy Spirit, Bonus Paid. 5 started.

HEMPSTEAD H.-G1, Belmont Park, June 23, $250,000, 3yo & up, f & m, 1 1/16m, 1:42.18, CRITICAL EYE, Jostle, Apple of Kent. 7 started.

Henry P. Russell H. (R), Santa Anita Park, Oct. 8, $78,450, 3yo & up, non-winners of $50,000 other than closed or claiming at a mile or over in 2001, 1 1/8mT, 1:47.99, DELTA FORM (Aus), Quake, Seinne (Chi). 5 started.

Henry S. Clark S., Pimlico, April 29, $75,000, 3yo & up, 1mT, 1:33.80, PRIVATE SLIP, Inexplicable, Watchman's Warning. 12 started.

Herald Gold Plate H., Stampede Park, June 10, $50,000, 3yo & up, 1 1/16m, 1:44.20, RED EXIT, Code Name Fred, Scotman. 6 started.

Herat S., Laurel Park, Feb. 25, $55,400, 3yo, 1 1/16m, 1:46.47, MARCIANO, Unaccountedlea, Dissident Shah. 6 started.

HERECOMESTHEBRIDE S.-G3, Gulfstream Park, Jan. 21, $111,500, 3yo, f, 1 1/16m (originally scheduled on the turf), 1:46.73, MYSTIC LADY, Open Minded, Ruff. 7 started.

Hialeah Breeders' Cup H., Hialeah Park, March 25, $70,000, 3yo & up, f & m, 1 1/16mT, 1:40.91, GINO'S SPIRITS (GB), Miss Tobacco, Silver Bandana. 10 started.

Hialeah Juvenile S., Hialeah Park, May 22, $52,400, 2yo, 5f, :59.71, TABAC, Barnacle Steve, Cherokee Road. 11 started.

Hialeah Sprint Championship H., Hialeah Park, April 7, $75,000, 3yo & up, 6f, 1:08.91, I'M SENTIMENTAL, Kipperscope, Silver Jet. 6 started.

HIALEAH TURF CUP H.-G2, Hialeah Park, April 21, $200,000, 3yo & up, 1 7/16mT, 1:53.06, DEL MAR SHOW, Honor Glide, Profit Option. 7 started.

Hibiscus S., Hialeah Park, April 8, $32,000, 3yo & up, f & m, 1 1/16m, 1:43.17, PIC A LIL, Meadow Mystery, Castlebrook. 7 started.

Hidden Light S. (R), Santa Anita Park, Oct. 19, $51,700, 2yo, f, non-winners of $30,000 other than closed or claiming at a mile or over, 1mT, 1:35.62, LA MARTINA (GB), Happy Michelle, Film Critic. 9 started.

Higgler H., Calder Race Course, Aug. 20, $34,570, 3yo & up, 1 1/16m, 1:47.26, DANCING GUY, Tahkodha Hills, Puchungo (Per). 7 started.

High Alexander S. (R), Hawthorne Race Course, Dec. 8, $102,060, 3yo & up, Illinois-conceived and/or -foaled, 1 1/16m, 1:47, PADDY'S SPY, Spanish Hall, Cane Ridge. 12 started.

HIGHLANDER H.-G3, Woodbine, Sept. 30, $164,850, 3yo & up, 6f, 1:10.65, MR. EPPERSON, Olympian, Tempered Appeal. 8 started.

Highland Happening S., Suffolk Downs, Oct. 6, $25,000, 3yo & up, f & m, abt1 1/16mT, 1:47.75, SUNLIT RIDGE, Rodeo Springs, Big Miss. 10 started.

Hildene S. (R), Delaware Park, Oct. 28, $42,800, 2yo, f, Virginia-bred, 6f, 1:14.74, SATURDAY'S CHILD, Metal Chimes, Sis Go Kid. 7 started.

HILL PRINCE S.-G3, Belmont Park, June 16, $114,600, 3yo, 1 1/8mT, 1:48.25, PROUD MAN, Package Store, Navesink. 10 started.

Hill Rise H., Santa Anita Park, Jan. 6, $89,475, 3yo, 1mT, 1:35.57, JAMAICAN RUM, Startac, Dim Sums. 6 started.

Hillsborough H., Bay Meadows, Oct. 13, $52,075, 3yo & up, f & m, 1 1/16mT, 1:44.30, SLOW DOWN, Aviate, Shericaine (Ire). 8 started.

Hillsborough S., Tampa Bay Downs, March 18, $100,000, 3yo & up, f & m, 1 1/16mT, 1:41.23, SONG FOR ANNIE, Megans Bluff, Inside Affair. 11 started.

Hillsdale S. (R), Hoosier Park, Oct. 6, $32,300, 2yo, c & g, Indiana-bred, 5 1/2f, 1:05.54, PEMAQUID POINT, Indy Energy, Cowboy's Limelite. 6 started.

Hilltop S., Pimlico, May 16, $60,500, 3yo, f, 1 1/16mT, 1:45.10, GUILLOTINE, Tweedside, Dear Pickles (GB). 3 started.

Hirsch Jacobs S., Pimlico, May 12, $75,000, 3yo, 6f, 1:10.20, CITY ZIP, Sea of Green, Stake Runner. 7 started.

Hi-Way Service Inc. S., Lethbridge, Oct. 14, $8,800, 3yo & up, 5 1/2f, 1:08, WIN FOR JIM, Roman Reality, Bad Toda Bone. 8 started.

Hoist Her Flag S., Canterbury Park, June 9, $35,000, 3yo & up, f & m, 6f, 1:10.76, NUT N BETTER, Atyour Convenience, Quite Spender. 9 started.

Holiday Cheer S., Turfway Park, Dec. 29, $50,000, 3yo & up, 6f, 1:12.46, DANCING MISSILE, Personal First, Sold to Wallstreet. 8 started.

Holiday Inaugural S., Turfway Park, Dec. 1, $50,000, 3yo & up, f & m, 6f, 1:10.57, SPANISH GLITTER, City Fair, Marquesa Jen. 10 started.

Hollie Hughes H. (R), Aqueduct, Feb. 18, $79,650, 3yo & up, New York-bred, 6f, 1:09.43, SAY FLORIDA SANDY, Kashatreya, Entepreneur. 5 started.

Holly Beach S. (R), Laurel Park, Jan. 15, $43,275, 4yo & up, f & m, non-winners of a stake, 1 1/8m, 1:52.71, IRVING'S BABY, Inn Between, Meghan's Joy. 7 started.

Holly S., The Meadowlands, Nov. 3, $100,000, 2yo, f, 6f, 1:09.75, AL MAX DINER, Phyxius, Forum Search. 7 started.

HOLLYWOOD DERBY-G1, Hollywood Park, Nov. 25, $500,000, 3yo, 1 1/8mT, 1:49.28, DENON, Sligo Bay (Ire), Aldebaran. 12 started.

HOLLYWOOD FUTURITY-G1, Hollywood Park, Dec. 15, $456,750, 2yo, 1 1/16m, 1:42.09, SIPHONIC, Fonz's, Officer. 8 started.

HOLLYWOOD GOLD CUP S.-G1, Hollywood Park, July 1, $750,000, 3yo & up, 1 1/4m, 2:01.79, APTITUDE, Skimming, Futural (DQ from 1st). 5 started.

HOLLYWOOD JUVENILE CHAMPIONSHIP S.-G3, Hollywood Park, July 15, $107,400, 2yo, 6f, 1:09.20, CAME HOME, Metatron, A Major Pleasure. 6 started.

HOLLYWOOD OAKS-G2, Hollywood Park, July 14, $150,000, 3yo, f, 1 1/8m, 1:49.20, AFFLUENT, Collect Call, Secret of Mecca. 5 started.

HOLLYWOOD PREVUE S.-G3, Hollywood Park, Nov. 17, $100,000, 2yo, 7f, 1:22.03, FONZ'S, Popular, Labamta Babe. 7 started.

HOLLYWOOD STARLET S.-G1, Hollywood Park, Dec. 16, $358,000, 2yo, f, 1 1/16m, 1:43.12, HABIBTI, You, Tali'sluckybusride. 5 started.

HOLLYWOOD TURF CUP S.-G1, Hollywood Park, Dec. 1, $250,000, 3yo & up, 1 1/2mT, 2:29.86, SUPER QUERCUS (Fr), Bonapartiste (Fr), Blazing Fury. 9 started.

HOLLYWOOD TURF EXPRESS H.-G3, Hollywood Park, Nov. 23, $200,000, 3yo & up, 5 1/2fT, 1:01.86, SWEPT OVERBOARD, Speak in Passing, Blu Air Force (Ire). 10 started.

Hollywood Wildcat S., Calder Race Course, Dec. 1, $100,000, 2yo, f, 1 1/16mT, 1:43.13, AUGUST STORM, Kathy K D, Piano Chimes. 11 started.
HOLY BULL S.-G3, Gulfstream Park, Jan. 20, $100,000, 3yo, 1 1/16m, 1:46.06, RADICAL RILEY, Buckle Down Ben, Cee Dee. 8 started.
HONEY BEE H.-G3, The Meadowlands, Nov. 2, $194,000, 3yo, f, 1 1/16m, 1:42.29, MYSTIC LADY, Latour, Shiny Band. 4 started.
HONEYBEE S.-G3, Oaklawn Park, March 10, $75,000, 3yo, f, 1 1/16m, 1:46.07, XTREME BID, My White Corvette, Pajamas. 7 started.
HONEY FOX H.-G3, Gulfstream Park, Jan. 7, $100,000, 3yo & up, f & m, 1mT, 1:35.60, SPOOK EXPRESS (SAf), Please Sign In, Lady Dora. 12 started.
Honey Fox H., Del Mar, Aug. 3, $76,200, 3yo & up, f & m, 1 3/8mT, 2:13.96, KEEMOON (Fr), Bucarest (Arg), Nepenthe. 8 started.
Honey Jay H. (R), Beulah Park, Sept. 16, $40,000, 3yo & up, Ohio-bred, 6f, 1:08.73, MAJESTIC DINNER, John Q's Winner, Q One for Two. 10 started.
Honey Mark S., Hawthorne Race Course, May 5, $61,250, 4yo & up, 6f, 1:10.05, WILLOWBROOK LANE, Silver Zipper, Chindi. 10 started.
HONEYMOON BREEDERS' CUP INVITATIONAL H.-G2, Hollywood Park, July 1, $217,000, 3yo, f, 1 1/4mT, 2:01.28, INNIT (Ire), Live Your Dreams, Beefeater Baby. 9 started.
Honeymoon S. (R), Retama Park, Oct. 6, $25,000, 2yo, f, Texas-bred, 6f, 1:12.89, LOVELY BONITA, Wayne's Princess, Bonus Bid. 10 started.
Honeymoon S., Louisiana Downs, July 14, $40,000, 3yo & up, f & m, abt1mT, 1:37.21, NANIE'S DINNER, Taffy, Sarah Lane's Oates. 8 started.
Hong Kong Jockey Club H., Hastings Park Racecourse, July 21, $36,719, 3yo & up, 1 1/16m, 1:43.76, LORD NELSON, King Jeremy, Greenbaypacker. 4 started.
HONG KONG JOCKEY CLUB TROPHY S.-G2, Woodbine, July 22, $273,500, 3yo & up, 1 3/8mT, 2:16.98, ALLENDE, Muntej (GB), Quiet Resolve. 7 started.
Honky Star H., Delaware Park, Aug. 20, $59,900, 3yo & up, f & m, 6f, 1:10.19, HONGKONG CHARLEY, Ivy's Jewel, Askara. 7 started.
HONORABLE MISS H.-G3, Saratoga Race Course, Aug. 1, $103,000, 3yo & up, f & m, 6f, 1:09.64, BIG BAMBU, Country Hideaway, Dat You Miz Blue. 4 started.
Honor Guard S., Pimlico, May 28, $70,000, 3yo, 1 1/8m, 1:49.51, SARATOGA GAMES, Ronnie's Hot Rod, Lit de Lace. 5 started.
Honor the Hero S., Turf Paradise, Dec. 15, $22,800, 3yo & up, 6f, 1:08.79, HANGONSLEWPYHANGON, Quinton's Gold, Classy Sheikh. 8 started.
Hoofprint on My Heart H., Stampede Park, May 27, $33,960, 3yo, 1m, 1:37.40, FANCY AS, Sixthirtyjoe, Kid Copper. 6 started.
Hoosier Debutante S., Hoosier Park, Nov. 10, $104,500, 2yo, f, 6f, 1:11.78, GHOST QUEEN, Tejano Honey, Lead Story. 10 started.
Hoosier Juvenile S., Hoosier Park, Nov. 24, $102,650, 2yo, c & g, 6f, 1:10.63, CASHEL CASTLE, Just Le Facts, Handsome Hunk. 5 started.
Hoover S., Laurel Park, Feb. 3, $54,950, 4yo & up, 6f, 1:09.31, DISCO RICO, Dr. Max, Trounce. 5 started.
Hoover S. (R), River Downs, Aug. 4, $40,000, 2yo, Ohio-bred, 6f, 1:13.40, HARLAN'S HOLIDAY, Highland Rim, U S S Tinosa. 13 started.
HOPEFUL S.-G1, Saratoga Race Course, Sept. 1, $200,000, 2yo, 7f, 1:21.94, CAME HOME, Mayakovsky, Thunder Days. 7 started.
Hopemont S., Keeneland, Oct. 26, $111,800, 2yo, 1 1/16mT, 1:45.85, STAGE CALL (Ire), Daisyago, Midwatch. 8 started.
Horatius S., Laurel Park, Feb. 11, $57,500, 3yo, 6f, 1:11.06, MY GOLDEN SON, Native Heir, Danny E. 6 started.
Horizon Computer Solutions H., Marquis Downs, Sept. 7, $6,000, 3yo & up, f & m, 1 1/8m, 1:52.63, WATSHERNAME, Remarkable Ability, Truly Remarkable. 4 started.
Horizon S. (R), River Downs, July 22, $50,000, 3yo, Ohio-bred, 1 1/16m, 1:48.80, TURKOWAR, Foxy Fritzy, Boodles Brown. 8 started.
Horsemen's Park Breeders' Derby (R), Horsemen's Park, July 22, $25,500, 3yo, Nebraska-bred, 1m, 1:37.60, TAUKE, Tate's Way, Cube's Kat. 6 started.
Hot Springs S., Oaklawn Park, March 25, $50,000, 4yo & up, 6f, 1:10.09, BIDIS, Beverly Greedy, Sand Ridge. 7 started.
Howard B. Noonan S. (R), Beulah Park, March 24, $40,000, 3yo, Ohio-bred, 6f, 1:11.91, STORMY HOSTAGE, Taylortwofeathers, Buckeye Bert. 10 started.
Hudson H. (R), Belmont Park, Oct. 21, $125,000, 3yo & up, New York-bred, 6f, 1:10.28, IMPEACHTHEPRO, Say Florida Sandy, Well Fancied. 11 started.
HUMANA DISTAFF H.-G2, see DISTAFF H.-G2.
Humboldt County Marathon H., Ferndale, Aug. 19, $10,270, 3yo & up, 1 5/8m, 2:50.75, IRONMAN DEHERE, Twothousandegrees, Panzeer (GB). 5 started.
Humphrey S. Finney S. (R), Pimlico, June 23, $60,000, 3yo, Maryland-bred, 1 1/8m, 1:51.81, SARATOGA GAMES, Ronnie's Hot Rod, Dissident Shah. 5 started.
Huntington S., Aqueduct, Nov. 25, $82,500, 2yo, 6f, 1:10.34, IRON DEPUTY, Volley Ball, Mr. Kipp. 8 started.
Hurricane Bertie S., Calder Race Course, May 27, $51,800, 3yo, f, 6f, 1:11.61, SILK CONCORDE, Hidden Creek, Lucette. 5 started.
Hurricane Bertie S., Gulfstream Park, March 4, $83,700, 4yo & up, f & m, 6f, 1:09.85, SWEPT AWAY, Sahara Gold, Lily's Affair. 10 started.
Hurricane Viv H., Calder Race Course, June 4, $32,840, 3yo & up, f & m, 1 1/16m, 1:47.80, GOLD FOR MY GAL, Cash's Pride, Jelly Fish. 8 started.
Huskerette S. (R), Horsemen's Park, July 20, $24,250, 3yo, f, Nebraska-bred, 1m, 1:37.60, OGLALA SUE, Clamato Rose, Irish Flyer. 4 started.
HUTCHESON S.-G2, Gulfstream Park, Jan. 27, $150,000, 3yo, 7f, 1:22.63, YONAGUSKA, City Zip, Sparkling Sabre. 11 started.
Idaho Cup Classic S. (R), Les Bois Park, July 28, $32,382, 4yo & up, Idaho-bred, 1m, 1:36.99, RASHA, Rub, J. D. for Shur. 8 started.
Idaho Cup Derby (R), Les Bois Park, July 28, $31,490, 3yo, c & g, Idaho-bred, 1m, 1:37.22, LOOKN EAST, Cowboy Jazz, La Fontaine. 6 started.
Idaho Cup Distaff Derby (R), Les Bois Park, July 28, $30,155, 3yo, f, Idaho-bred, 1m, 1:40.12, THE QUEEN AND I, Hey She's a Dancer, Lovely and Yours. 7 started.
Idaho Cup Distaff Maturity (R), Les Bois Park, July 28, $30,317, 4yo & up, f & m, Idaho-bred, 1m, 1:38.99, SOMER WONDERS, Love and Fun, Irish Elms. 6 started.
Idaho Cup Juvenile Championship S. (R), Les Bois Park, July 28, $38,435, 2yo, Idaho-bred, 5f, 1:00.08, TROPHY EDITION TOO, Mr Motion, Jazzing Jack. 9 started.
Idaho Cup Sprint S. (R), Les Bois Park, July 28, $12,402, 3yo & up, Idaho-bred, 5f, :58.88, SCHUYLER ROAD, Sherri Shine, South Bound n Down. 10 started.
Idaho Cup Thoroughbred Claiming S. (R), Les Bois Park, July 28, $8,897, 3yo & up, Idaho-bred, 7f, 1:24.33, SAN DIEGO PETE, Free Jazz, Bo's Bursting Star. 8 started.
Illini Princess H. (R), Hawthorne Race Course, Nov. 10, $75,000, 3yo & up, f & m, Illinois-conceived and/or -foaled, 1 1/16m, 1:46.65, TAP YOUR FEET, Shemya, Magic Motel. 11 started.
Illinois Breeders' Debutante S. (R), Hawthorne Race Course, Dec. 15, $91,350, 2yo, f, Illinois-conceived and/or -foaled, 1 1/16m, 1:49.75, WHITE O MORN, Summer Mis, Gracility. 7 started.
Illinois Coronet H. (R), Hawthorne Race Course, Nov. 10, $75,000, 3yo & up, Illinois-conceived and/or -foaled, 1 1/16m, 1:44.44, CHICAGO SIX, San Pedro, Not Happening. 6 started.
ILLINOIS DERBY-G2, Sportsman's Park, April 7, $500,000, 3yo, 1 1/8m, 1:51.37, DISTILLED, Saint Damien, Dream Run. 8 started.
Imperial Cup S., Aiken, March 24, $29,100, 4yo & up, abt2 1/8mT, 4:20, DEVIL'S REACH, Commanders Palace, Brown Lad (Fr). 5 started.
I'm Smokin S. (R), Del Mar, Sept. 3, $100,000, 2yo, California-bred non-winners of a race worth $35,000 to the winner other than closed or claiming, 6f, 1:10.80, SHARPER TOO, Yougottawanna, Synergize. 11 started.
Inaugural H., Portland Meadows, Oct. 27, $11,375, 3yo & up, 5f, 1:00.48, TOMTOM TOMMALICE, Star Expresso, Bold Chant. 8 started.
Inaugural H., Evangeline Downs, April 14, $30,000, 3yo, 6f, 1:11.40, MYSTIC NIGHT, Prince Slew, Dr. Frosty. 10 started.
Inaugural H., Wyoming Downs, June 23, $3,975, 3yo & up, 6f, 1:12.82, FADSKI, Rush for Glory, Fire Ball John. 8 started.
Inaugural H., Marquis Downs, June 2, $6,000, 3yo & up, 6f, 1:12.43, STAR OF THE SHOW, Beau Ring, Burlington House. 5 started.
Inaugural H., Les Bois Park, May 5, $6,400, 3yo & up, 6 1/2f, 1:20.20, ALMOST GOLDEN, Moyamba, Rasha. 7 started.
Inaugural H., SunRay Park, Sept. 1, $31,350, 3yo & up, 6 1/2f, 1:17.60, DON'T WALK AT NITE, Rasha, Sky Diver. 9 started.
Inaugural S., Yavapai Downs, May 26, $15,000, 3yo & up, 6f, 1:09.21, MELVILLE, Diablo His Due, Stormy Ambition. 9 started.

Inaugural S., Columbus, July 27, $7,736, 3yo, f, 6f, 1:13.20, IRISH FLYER, I'm a City Girl, St Patti's Charm. 7 started.

Inaugural S., Arapahoe Park, June 9, $27,200, 3yo, 6f, 1:13.20, UNCLE PUNK, Lord Beshara, Tangarae Tango. 5 started.

Inaugural S., Tampa Bay Downs, Dec. 15, $50,000, 2yo, 6f, 1:11.43, BOG HUNTER, Showmeitall, How About My Place. 11 started.

Independence Breeders' Cup H., Louisiana Downs, July 4, $99,000, 3yo & up, 1 1/16mT, 1:41.71, NAT'S BIG PARTY, Candid Glen, Colonial Power. 10 started.

Independence Day H., Emerald Downs, July 4, $40,000, 3yo & up, 6½f, 1:15, MIKE K, Handy N Bold, Kid Katabatic. 5 started.

Independence Day H., Mountaineer Park, July 3, $59,375, 3yo & up, 1mT, 1:33.81 (NCR), DAKOTA PROSPECT, Medievil Hero, Find the Mine. 11 started.

INDIANA BREEDERS' CUP OAKS-G3, Hoosier Park, Oct. 5, $205,800, 3yo, f, 1 1/16m, 1:44.06, SCOOP, Gold Huntress, Caressing. 9 started.

Indiana Derby, Hoosier Park, Oct. 6, $314,100, 3yo, 1 1/16m, 1:42.22, ORIENTATE, Saratoga Games, Trion Georgia. 11 started.

Indiana Futurity (R), Hoosier Park, Nov. 17, $74,600, 2yo, c & g, Indiana-bred, 6f, 1:12.43, PEMAQUID POINT, Wishing Heart, Cowboy's Limelite. 12 started.

Indiana Stallion S. (R), Hoosier Park, Nov. 30, $42,750, 2yo, f, Indiana-bred and/or -sired, 6f, 1:12.90, AMANDA'S CROWN, One Eyed Jackie, Drop of Rain. 6 started.

Indiana Stallion S. (R), Hoosier Park, Dec. 1, $42,900, 2yo, c & g, Indiana-bred and/or -sired, 6f, 1:12.60, RESTITUTION, Indy Energy, Ali Be Warned. 8 started.

Indian Maid S., Hawthorne Race Course, May 27, $59,700, 4yo & up, f & m, 1 1/16m (originally scheduled on the turf), 1:44.94, ALYBGOOD, Adam's Time, Dahlia's Krissy. 5 started.

Indian Summer S., Keeneland, Oct. 17, $80,625, 2yo, f, 6f, 1:11.88, VICKI VALLENCOURT, Purple Princess, Lotta Rhythm. 5 started.

INGLEWOOD H.-G3, Hollywood Park, April 21, $107,100, 3yo & up, 1 1/16mT, 1:41.65, FATEFUL DREAM, National Anthem (GB), Casino King (Ire). 5 started.

Ingrid Knott's H. (R), Arapahoe Park, July 7, $30,000, 3yo & up, f & m, Colorado-bred, 6f, 1:12.40, JENNALY, Summer Aly, Party Girl. 9 started.

In Reality S. (R), Calder Race Course, Oct. 13, $400,000, 2yo, progeny of eligible stallions standing in Florida, 1 1/16m, 1:46.56, BOOKLET, Rulebook, Carey's Gold. 14 started.

Inside Information S., Monmouth Park, July 14, $75,000, 3yo & up, f & m, 1mT, 1:34.44, PIAZZA DI SPAGNA (Chi), Mumtaz (Fr), Arty'svirginiagirl. 7 started.

Interborough H., Aqueduct, Jan. 1, $83,125, 3yo & up, f & m, 6f, 1:10.01, SLASH COTTAGE, My Dear Abby, Live Wire Lil. 8 started.

Interior Futurity, Kamloops, Sept. 9, $2,910, 2yo, 6½f, 1:22, DIG FOR DUG, Colnel R D Duke, Run Devil Run. 4 started.

International Gold Cup Timber S., Great Meadows, Oct. 20, $43,650, 4yo & up, abt3½mT, 7:26.60, THOR THORS, Kanawha, Matchless. 5 started.

Iowa Breeders' Derby (R), Prairie Meadows, Sept. 1, $74,733, 3yo, c & g, Iowa-bred, 1 1/16m, 1:44.89, WHO DEVIL WHO, Take Me Up, Tcs Express Prince. 7 started.

Iowa Breeders' Oaks (R), Prairie Meadows, Sept. 1, $77,500, 3yo, f, Iowa-bred, 1m 70y, 1:43.54, SHARKY'S REVIEW, Sound of Gold, I'm a City Girl. 10 started.

Iowa Cradle S. (R), Prairie Meadows, Sept. 1, $74,430, 2yo, c & g, Iowa-bred, 6f, 1:11.36, WAR GENERAL, First Copy, Medical First. 10 started.

Iowa Derby, Prairie Meadows, July 6, $250,000, 3yo, 1 1/16m, 1:42.67, TOUCH TONE, Buckle Down Ben, Drewman. 7 started.

Iowa Distaff S., Prairie Meadows, July 6, $125,000, 3yo & up, f & m, 1 1/16m, 1:42.43, ROYAL FAIR, Please Sign In, Frankly My Dear. 6 started.

Iowa Oaks, Prairie Meadows, July 5, $155,250, 3yo, f, 1 1/16m, 1:43.88, UNBRIDLED ELAINE, Supreme Song, Sharky's Review. 6 started.

Iowa S., Calder Race Course, July 15, $34,190, 3yo, f, 1 1/16m, 1:48.20, SARA'S SUCCESS, Man I Love Clare, Frozen Dinner. 7 started.

Iowa Sorority S. (R), Prairie Meadows, Sept. 1, $74,000, 2yo, f, Iowa-bred, 6f, 1:11.79, TRUE TEAR DROPS, Orphan Lover, Dazzling Crypto. 7 started.

Iowa Sprint H., Prairie Meadows, July 4, $150,000, 3yo & up, 6f, 1:08.64, BONAPAW, Sand Ridge, Chindi. 6 started.

Iowa Stallion Futurity (R), Prairie Meadows, Sept. 17, $56,194, 2yo, progeny of eligible stallions standing in Iowa, 6f, 1:11.85, SEMPRE BLUMIN, D J Cody, Lady Sundari. 9 started.

Iowa Stallion S. (R), Prairie Meadows, July 28, $98,173, 3yo, progeny of eligible stallions standing in Iowa, 1m 70y, 1:43.62, SHARKY'S REVIEW, (DH) Politicalplayboy, (DH) Tcs Express Prince. 6 started.

Iowa State Fair S., Prairie Meadows, Aug. 11, $51,200, 3yo & up, f & m, 6f, 1:10.19, SUMTHINTOTALKABOUT, Nut N Better, Trickle Down. 7 started.

Irish Day H., Emerald Downs, June 24, $40,000, 3yo, f, 1 1/16m, 1:45.20, GRACEFUL CAT, Aunt Sophie, Silver Echo. 7 started.

Irish O'Brien S. (R), Santa Anita Park, March 17, $107,300, 4yo & up, f & m, California-bred, abt6½fT, 1:11.84, LA FEMINN, Go Go, Fire Sale Queen. 6 started.

Iron Horse S. (R), Philadelphia Park, June 2, $25,000, 3yo & up, starters for a claiming price of $5,000 or less since July 31, 2000, 1 1/16m, 1:43.83, GOTTHARD, Bellwether, Five Tango Charlie. 7 started.

Iroquois H. (R), Philadelphia Park, July 28, $50,000, 3yo & up, Pennsylvania-bred, 1 1/16m, 1:45.24, B FLAT MAJOR, Classic Verse, Cool Robert. 5 started.

Iroquois H. (R), Belmont Park, Oct. 20, $125,000, 3yo & up, f & m, New York-bred, 7f, 1:24.03, MADDIE MAY, Bedside Manner, Beijio. 8 started.

Iroquois Hurdle S., Percy Warner, May 12, $88,000, 4yo & up, abt3mT, 5:35, RAND (NZ), All Gong (GB), Electron. 6 started.

IROQUOIS S.-G3, Churchill Downs, Nov. 4, $113,200, 2yo, 1m, 1:35.01, HARLAN'S HOLIDAY, Request for Parole, Gold Dollar. 10 started.

Irving Distaff S., Lone Star Park, April 14, $75,000, 3yo & up, f & m, 7½fT, 1:30.94, EURYANTHE (Ire), Sarah Lane's Oates, D Gerry Ray. 10 started.

Isaac Murphy H. (R), Arlington Park, June 23, $75,000, 3yo & up, f & m, Illinois-conceived and/or -foaled, 6f, 1:11.20, RAIN BOOTS, Come September, Lil Bobbie Too. 9 started.

Isadorable S. (R), Suffolk Downs, March 17, $25,000, 4yo & up, f & m, Massachusetts-bred, 6f, 1:13.07, DR MARGARET, Big Miss, Land Ahoy. 7 started.

Islander S., Fonner Park, May 12, $16,395, 3yo, f, 6f, 1:14.60, CLAMATO ROSE, Call the Michaels, Burning Memories. 7 started.

Island Whirl H., Louisiana Downs, Oct. 27, $25,000, 3yo & up, 6½f, 1:15.42, KETTLE MAN, Triple Card, Ceviche. 9 started.

Jack Betta Be Rite S. (R), Finger Lakes, Aug. 25, $30,000, 3yo & up, f & m, New York-bred, 1 1/16m, 1:44.36, ALLEY BALL, Watrals Twelvbelow, That Belongs to Me. 6 started.

Jack Diamond Futurity (R), Hastings Park Racecourse, Sept. 9, $99,479, 2yo, c & g, Canadian-bred, 6½f, 1:18.78, LONG RIFLE, Commodore Craig, Intact. 7 started.

Jack Hardy S., Assiniboia Downs, Aug. 6, $26,950, 3yo, f, 1m, 1:39.80, SASSY CHIMES, Brighton Belle, Mountain Crest. 5 started.

Jacques Cartier S., Woodbine, April 8, $109,300, 4yo & up, 6f, 1:09.53, WAKE AT NOON, Exciting Story, Olympian. 7 started.

Jaipur H., Belmont Park, May 27, $100,900, 3yo & up, 7f (originally scheduled as a Grade 3 on the turf), 1:21.69, AFFIRMED SUCCESS, Texas Glitter, Bought in Dixie. 3 started.

JAMAICA H.-G2, Belmont Park, Sept. 23, $200,000, 3yo, 1 1/8mT, 1:51.53, NAVESINK, Strategic Partner, Baptize. 7 started.

Jameela S. (R), Pimlico, March 28, $60,000, 3yo, f, Maryland-bred, 6f, 1:10.33, GIGI'S MAGIC, Your Out, Urban Dancer. 6 started.

James B. Moseley Breeders' Cup H., Suffolk Downs, June 2, $142,500, 3yo & up, 6f, 1:10.03, MAX'S PAL, Makin Progress, Markus. 5 started.

James F. Lyttle Memorial H., Santa Rosa, Aug. 3, $44,750, 3yo, 1 1/16m, 1:42.33, TANNERSMYMAN, Takin It Deep, I'madrifter. 6 started.

James Leakos Sophomore S. (R), Marquis Downs, July 14, $7,865, 3yo, f, Saskatchewan-bred, 1m, 1:39.75, MS. LADY ROSE, Rapadash, Compeer's Bequest. 7 started.

Jammed Lovely S. (R), Woodbine, Nov. 4, $143,370, 3yo, f, Canadian-bred, 7f, 1:23.99, POETICALLY, Beautiful Belle, Noble Strike. 5 started.

Jane Driggers Debutante S. (R), Portland Meadows, Dec. 15, $8,675, 2yo, f, Oregon-bred, 6f, 1:15.24, ABSOLUTISM, Stately's Choice, Jimbos Valentine. 8 started.

Janet Wineberg S. (R), Portland Meadows, Nov. 24, $16,310, 2yo, f, Oregon-bred, 6f, 1:14.25, LAMMY, Absolutism, Stately's Choice. 7 started.

Japan Racing Association S., Laurel Park, Oct. 20, $50,000, 3yo,

1⅛mT, 1:49.44, DIMPLED BALLOT, Jakey D, Bowman Mill. 6 started.

Jasmine S., Hialeah Park, May 6, $31,200, 3yo, f, 7f, 1:23.74, RICH PEACE, Rhubarb Red, Silk Concorde. 6 started.

Jean Lafitte Futurity, Delta Downs, April 13, $102,375, 2yo, 4f, :47.06, TAYLOR'S QUEEN, Bara Lad, Onlynurimagination. 10 started.

JEFFERSON CUP S.-G3, Churchill Downs, June 9, $282,500, 3yo, 1⅛mT, 1:48.81, INDYGO SHINER, Strategic Partner, Fast City. 9 started.

JEH Stallion Station S. (R), Lone Star Park, May 28, $50,000, 3yo & up, f & m, Texas-bred, 6½f, 1:15.30, LITTLE ANGEL, Flyers Legacy, Nobody's Fool. 9 started.

Jennings H. (R), Pimlico, April 21, $100,000, 3yo & up, Maryland-bred, 1⅛m, 1:48.91, INCLUDE, Waited, Carney's Prospect. 6 started.

JENNY WILEY S.-G3, Keeneland, April 12, $113,900, 4yo & up, f & m, 1 1/16mT, 1:40.93, PENNY'S GOLD, License Fee, Solvig. 9 started.

JEROME H.-G2, Belmont Park, Sept. 22, $150,000, 3yo, 1m, 1:34.57, EXPRESS TOUR, Illusioned, Burning Roma. 5 started.

Jersey Breeders' H. (R), Monmouth Park, June 16, $50,000, 3yo & up, New Jersey-bred, 1m, 1:36.76, SEA OF TRANQUILITY, Thistyranthasclass, Joey's Law. 6 started.

JERSEY DERBY-G3, Monmouth Park, May 27, $100,000, 3yo, 1 1/16m (originally scheduled on the turf), 1:44.31, MYSTIC LADY, Sir Brian's Sword, What's Your Wish. 6 started.

Jersey Lilly S., Sam Houston Race Park, Feb. 24, $50,000, 4yo & up, f & m, 1 1/16mT, 1:44.79, EURYANTHE (Ire), Impending Bear, Millie Thane. 11 started.

JERSEY SHORE BREEDERS' CUP S.-G3, Monmouth Park, July 4, $100,000, 3yo, 6f, 1:09.02, CITY ZIP, Sea of Green, Songandaprayer. 5 started.

Jersey Village S. (R), Sam Houston Race Park, Feb. 17, $25,000, 4yo & up, Texas-bred, 1 1/16m, 1:45.63, CAPTAIN COUNTDOWN, J W Jet, Quiet Man. 6 started.

Jessman Cloud Memorial S., Fresno, Oct. 6, $101,800, 2yo, 6f, 1:09.45, SURPRIZED, Debonair Joe, Green Team. 8 started.

Jewel S. (R), Philadelphia Park, June 2, $50,000, 3yo & up, starters for a claiming price of $25,000 or less since July 31, 2000, 1⅛m, 1:51.08, BARRISTER, Kernal K, Yankee Tribe. 5 started.

Jiffy Lube S., Sam Houston Race Park, Nov. 3, $25,000, 3yo & up, f & m, 1 1/16mT, 1:44.80, DUE TO WIN AGAIN, Runaway Magic, Slapstick. 12 started.

Jim Beam H., Marquis Downs, Aug. 24, $6,000, 3yo & up, f & m, 1 1/16m, 1:47.53, REMARKABLE ABILITY, Princess Briartic, Truly Remarkable. 4 started.

Jim Bowie S., Retama Park, Sept. 8, $35,000, 3yo, 1 1/16mT, 1:42.72, KRIS HAVINGFUNNOW, Lost Agenda, Paris Savage. 7 started.

Jim Coleman Province H., Hastings Park Racecourse, July 15, $37,829, 3yo, 1 1/16m, 1:45.93, I'M FREE, El Nino Mi Amor, Irish Pleasure. 7 started.

JIM DANDY S.-G1, Saratoga Race Course, Aug. 4, $600,000, 3yo, 1⅛m, 1:48.90, SCORPION, Free of Love, Congaree. 6 started.

Jim Edgar Illinois Futurity (R), Hawthorne Race Course, Dec. 22, $106,000, 2yo, Illinois-conceived and/or -foaled, 1 1/16m, 1:46.26, COLORFUL TOUR, Mucho Rapido, Riverdance Tour. 10 started.

Jim Murray Memorial H. (R), Hollywood Park, May 12, $74,970, 3yo & up, non-winners of $60,000 at a mile or over in 2001, 1½mT, 2:26.74, KUDOS, Indigo Myth, Piranesi (Ire). 4 started.

J J'sdream S., Calder Race Course, June 30, $100,000, 2yo, f, 5½f, 1:06.55, BLISSFUL KISS, Lacy Lady, Little Miss Echo. 12 started.

J & L Bit Supply S., Grand Prairie, Aug. 4, $3,825, 3yo & up, 6½f, 1:23.40, WIN FOR JIM, Western Glory, Today's Pick. 5 started.

JOCKEY CLUB GOLD CUP S.-G1, Belmont Park, Oct. 6, $1,000,000, 3yo & up, 1¼m, 2:01.49, APTITUDE, Generous Rosi (GB), Country Be Gold. 7 started.

Joe Aitcheson Hurdle S. (R), Pimlico, May 17, $107,250, 4yo & up, non-winners over hurdles prior to March 1, 2000, abt2⅜mT, 3:45.30, FLASHER, Praise the Prince (NZ), Golden Marvel (Fr). 9 started.

Joe Marovich S., Arlington Park, June 17, $54,000, 3yo, 7f, 1:23.29, TUB TOSSER, Winnie's Pooh Bear, Spectacular Cat. 8 started.

John A. Damico S. (R), Gulfstream Park, Feb. 25, $64,450, 3yo, f, progeny of eligible stallions standing in Florida, 6f, 1:10.91, HAZINO, Honey Eyed, Artic Party. 7 started.

John and Kitty Fletcher S. (R), Emerald Downs, Sept. 8, $25,000, 3yo, f, Washington-bred non-winners of $19,000 since April 20, 2001, 6½f, 1:16, WHATDIDSHESAY, From Venus, Knight Weave. 7 started.

John Battaglia Memorial S., Turfway Park, March 3, $99,000, 3yo, 1 1/16m, 1:45.08, BONNIE SCOT, X Country, Daring Pegasus. 7 started.

John B. Campbell H., Laurel Park, Feb. 18, $100,000, 4yo & up, 1 3/16m, 1:55.37, DO I EVER, Tibado, Top Official (DQ from 1st). 10 started.

John B. Connally Breeders' Cup Turf H., Sam Houston Race Park, Feb. 24, $212,000, 3yo & up, 1⅛mT, 1:50.51, CANDID GLEN, Profit Option, Gold Nugget. 9 started.

John Bullit H., Canterbury Park, July 21, $40,000, 3yo & up, 1 1/16mT, 1:44.04, IVARS BIG PEACEFUL, Turk Flyer, Minor Wisdom. 9 started.

John D. Marsh S. (R), Colonial Downs, July 21, $40,000, 3yo, Virginia-bred or -sired, 1 1/16mT, 1:43.76, UNACCOUNTEDLEA, Cobbley's Promise, Mark of Royalty. 5 started.

John Henry H., Evangeline Downs, May 5, $30,000, 3yo & up, 1 1/16m, 1:46.20, OAK HALL, Dividend M, Strike for Richard. 5 started.

John Henry S., Arlington Park, Aug. 17, $66,000, 3yo & up, abt1 1/16mT, 1:43.25, GALIC BOY, Orleans Road, Buff. 12 started.

John Henry S., The Meadowlands, Oct. 19, $100,000, 3yo & up, 1mT, 1:33.88 (NCR), BECKON THE KING, Strategic Mission, Buying Rain. 12 started.

John J. Reilly H. (R), Monmouth Park, May 26, $50,000, 3yo & up, New Jersey-bred, 6f, 1:08.77, THISTYRANTHASCLASS, Just Beforemidnite, Knockout Kid. 9 started.

John J. Shumaker S. (R), Penn National Race Course, July 27, $30,575, 3yo & up, f & m, Pennsylvania-bred, 1 1/16mT, 1:41.94, FINAL ONE, A Real Nor'easter, Lady of the Press. 7 started.

John Longden 6000 H., Hastings Park Racecourse, June 10, $42,272, 3yo & up, 1 1/16m, 1:43.50, RAMPAGING ALF, Ball and Chain, Lord Nelson. 10 started.

John McSorley S., Monmouth Park, July 8, $50,000, 3yo & up, 5f, :56.54, RUDIRUDY, Special Occasion, Riot. 5 started.

John Patrick H., Northlands Park, July 21, $33,000, 3yo & up, f & m, 1m, 1:38, CRIMSON HUE, Uncas Ruckus, Docket Court. 5 started.

John Wayne S. (R), Prairie Meadows, June 23, $64,900, 3yo & up, c & g, Iowa-bred, 6f, 1:08.98, SURE SHOT BISCUIT, Reuben, Grindrock. 7 started.

John W. Galbreath Memorial S. (R), Beulah Park, Nov. 4, $50,000, 2yo, f, Ohio-bred, 1 1/16m, 1:46.68, CRYPTO'S TWINJET, Bates Choice, Mercer's Launch. 8 started.

Joseph A. Gimma S. (R), Belmont Park, Sept. 30, $82,950, 2yo, f, New York-bred, 7f, 1:25.65, SHESASTONECOLDFOX, Princess Dixie, Dancing Blues. 9 started.

Joseph M. O'Farrell S., Hialeah Park, May 20, $61,800, 3yo, 6f, 1:10.09, HANA HIGHWAY, Built Up, Rich Coins. 9 started.

Joseph T. Grace H., Santa Rosa, Aug. 4, $100,600, 3yo & up, 1 1/16m, 1:42.15, RED EYE, Prodigious, Moonlight Meeting. 6 started.

Journal H., Northlands Park, June 23, $33,751, 3yo & up, 6½f, 1:17.20, (DH) RUN JOEY RUN, (DH) TIMELY RUCKUS, Timboruck. 6 started.

Journal Star S., Lincoln State Fair, May 27, $10,480, 3yo, 6f, 1:12.60, HARVEY BENGAL, My Buba Boy, Full Response. 5 started.

J. R. Straus Memorial S., Retama Park, Aug. 3, $35,000, 3yo & up, 6f, 1:10.86, BOOTS ON SUNDAY, Lights On Broadway, Lightening Ball. 6 started.

Juan Gonzalez Memorial S., Pleasanton, July 1, $52,040, 2yo, f, 5f, :57.93, BRITETONZMYDAY, Believe in Slew, The News' West. 9 started.

Judge Faulkner H., Blue Ribbon Downs, July 22, $7,150, 3yo & up, 6f, 1:11.60, FLAGSHIP COUNSELOR, Freely Bend, Cordell. 7 started.

Judy's Red Shoes S., Calder Race Course, Sept. 8, $50,000, 3yo, f, 1 1/16m, 1:46.69, HAPPILY UNBRIDLED, Company Storm, Sea Mist. 8 started.

Junior Champion S., Monmouth Park, Aug. 19, $50,000, 2yo, f, 1mT, 1:37.75, ONCE AROUND, Christmas Party, Multitudinous. 10 started.

JUST A GAME BREEDERS' CUP H.-G3, Belmont Park, June 9, $189,050, 3yo & up, f & m, 1mT, 1:32.62, LICENSE FEE, Shopping for Love, Veil of Avalon. 11 started.

Justakiss H., Delaware Park, Aug. 4, $59,100, 3yo & up, f & m, 1 1/16m, 1:47.87, MUMBO JUMBO, Brig, Sarai's Dancer. 6 started.

Just Smashing S., The Meadowlands, Sept. 3, $75,000, 3yo, f, 1mT, 1:35.43, COZZY CORNER, Nouvelle, The Goddess Athird. 11 started.

Juvenile S., Remington Park, Sept. 14, $21,740, 2yo, 6f, 1:11.50,

COSINEROS, Mighty Beau, Sugar Shaker. 6 started.

Juvenile S., Philadelphia Park, Sept. 1, $50,000, 2yo, 6f, 1:11.91, WOODEN STONE, Incredible Carson, Angelic Hero. 5 started.

Juvenile S. (R), Thistledown, Sept. 8, $75,000, 2yo, Ohio-bred, 1 1/16m, 1:46.50, U S S TINOSA, Watch Me Fire, Truth Matters. 10 started.

Juvenile S. (R), Woodbine, Sept. 23, $60,340, 2yo, c & g, sold at a CBS sale, 6f, 1:12.14, NOWYOUSEEIT, Embattle, Chivas On Ice. 5 started.

Juvenile S. (R), Woodbine, Sept. 23, $63,880, 2yo, f, sold at a CBS sale, 6f, 1:14.13, HAGLEY'S QUEST, Missadryannaatto, Cellular. 8 started.

J. W. Sifton S. (R), Assiniboia Downs, Sept. 22, $34,300, 3yo, Manitoba-bred, 1⅛m, 1:53.80, COMMAND START, G and L Special, Budge. 5 started.

Kachina H., Turf Paradise, Dec. 29, $30,000, 3yo & up, f & m, 1m, 1:35.92, DYNATROL, Gleefully, Balboa Park. 9 started.

Kachina S., Ruidoso Downs, July 29, $68,805, 2yo, f, 6f, 1:12.20, DANCING PROMISE, Scifi Flick, French Flare. 12 started.

Kansas Oaks, The Woodlands, Oct. 28, $25,000, 3yo, f, 1 1/16m, 1:47.60, SPANISH GUITAR, Jade Julia, Crafty Creek. 8 started.

Kansas Thoroughbred Derby (R), The Woodlands, Oct. 13, $20,000, 3yo, f, Kansas-bred, 1m 70y, 1:50.20, JAKOTA MOON, Discreetly Irish, Westmeadow Cowgirl. 5 started.

Kansas Thoroughbred Derby (R), The Woodlands, Oct. 14, $20,000, 3yo, c & g, Kansas-bred, 1m 70y, 1:46.60, DIAMOND ROO, Scarlet Lad, Risen Ruler. 5 started.

Kansas Thoroughbred Futurity (R), The Woodlands, Oct. 5, $20,000, 2yo, f, Kansas-bred, 5½f, 1:09.20, BEVERLYS GOLD, Me N Wendi, Brandy Vee. 7 started.

Kansas Thoroughbred Futurity (R), The Woodlands, Oct. 6, $20,000, 2yo, c & g, Kansas-bred, 5½f, 1:08.40, RAISE A BOOGER, Jacques Swinger, Axtell G R. 5 started.

Katy S. (R), Sam Houston Race Park, Feb. 24, $25,000, 3yo, f, Texas-bred, 7f, 1:25.92, BOLD MARK, Sister's Shamrock, Triple Spin. 9 started.

Keith Brodkin Memorial S., Suffolk Downs, June 2, $25,000, 3yo & up, 5f, :57.79, CONSIDER THE NIGHT, High Above, Cliffdiver. 8 started.

KELSO H.-G2, Belmont Park, Oct. 6, $250,000, 3yo & up, 1mT, 1:36.77, FORBIDDEN APPLE, Sarafan, City Zip. 9 started.

Kelso S., Delaware Park, Oct. 20, $75,300, 3yo & up, 1 3/16m, 2:01.76, GRUNDLEFOOT, Wedlock, Judge's Case. 6 started.

Ken Maddy Sprint H. (R), Golden Gate Fields, Feb. 24, $125,000, 3yo & up, California-bred, 6f, 1:08, EL DORADO SHOOTER, Echo Eddie, Full Moon Madness. 5 started.

Kennedy Road S., Woodbine, Dec. 1, $109,500, 3yo & up, 6f, 1:09.77, OLYMPIAN, Praise From Dixie, Wake At Noon. 8 started.

Kenneth L. Graf Memorial H., Rockingham Park, Sept. 3, $25,000, 3yo & up, f & m, 1 1/16mT, 1:46.61, DANCEROSYDANCE, Big Miss, Reprized Dream. 9 started.

Kenny Noe Jr. H., Calder Race Course, Dec. 15, $100,000, 3yo & up, 7f, 1:23.31, FAPPIE'S NOTEBOOK, Kiss a Native, Dancing Guy. 6 started.

Kenora S. (R), Woodbine, Sept. 3, $102,000, 3yo & up, Canadian-bred CTHS Sales yearlings, 6f, 1:10.76, ESTONIA, Perlong, Tricky Hearts. 5 started.

Ken Pearson Memorial H., Stampede Park, May 21, $34,320, 3yo & up, f & m, 1m, 1:38.80, TECATE, Uncas Ruckus, Regal Eyre. 7 started.

KENT BREEDERS' CUP S.-G3, Delaware Park, July 22, $249,000, 3yo, 1⅛mT, 1:49.98, NAVESINK, Bowman Mill, Harrisand (Fr). 10 started.

Kent H., Emerald Downs, May 27, $35,738, 3yo, f, 1m, 1:38.40, QUE FACIL CORAZON, Silver Echo, Best Judgement. 5 started.

KENTUCKY BREEDERS' CUP S.-G3, Churchill Downs, May 28, $162,600, 2yo, 5½f, 1:03.11 (NTR), LEELANAU, Gygistar, Lakeside Cup. 6 started.

Kentucky Colonel S., Ellis Park, July 21, $50,000, 3yo, 1mT, 1:33.48, WUDANTUNOIT, Trion Georgia, Absterous. 12 started.

KENTUCKY CUP CLASSIC H.-G2, Turfway Park, Sept. 22, $400,000, 3yo & up, 1⅛m, 1:47.90, GUIDED TOUR, Balto Star, A Fleets Dancer. 6 started.

Kentucky Cup Juvenile Fillies S., Turfway Park, Sept. 22, $95,000, 2yo, f, 1m, 1:37.29, PLAYING 'N GOLD, Humble Danzig, Que Bonita. 6 started.

KENTUCKY CUP JUVENILE S.-G3, Turfway Park, Sept. 22, $100,000, 2yo, 1 1/16m, 1:43.78, REPENT, French Assault, Gold Dollar. 7 started.

Kentucky Cup Ladies Turf H., Kentucky Downs, Sept. 23, $100,000, 3yo & up, f & m, 1mT, 1:39.16, GINO'S SPIRITS (GB), Please Sign In, Tabadabado. 5 started.

Kentucky Cup Mile H., Kentucky Downs, Sept. 23, $200,000, 3yo & up, 1mT, 1:37.68, MINOR WISDOM, Cocktails and Lies, Dernier Croise (Fr). 7 started.

KENTUCKY CUP SPRINT S.-G2, Turfway Park, Sept. 22, $147,500, 3yo, 6f, 1:09.22, SNOW RIDGE, City Zip, Dream Run. 5 started.

Kentucky Cup Turf Dash S., Kentucky Downs, Sept. 23, $100,000, 3yo & up, 6fT, 1:11.34, AMAZON RIVER, One by the Knows, El Basque. 7 started.

KENTUCKY CUP TURF H.-G3, Kentucky Downs, Sept. 23, $300,000, 3yo & up, 1½mT, 2:28.68, CHORWON, The Knight Sky, Man From Wicklow. 7 started.

KENTUCKY DERBY-G1, Churchill Downs, May 5, $1,112,000, 3yo, 1¼m, 1:59.97, MONARCHOS, Invisible Ink, Congaree. 17 started.

KENTUCKY JOCKEY CLUB S.-G2, Churchill Downs, Nov. 24, $217,000, 2yo, 1 1/16m, 1:44.42, REPENT, Request for Parole, High Star. 6 started.

KENTUCKY OAKS-G1, Churchill Downs, May 4, $609,200, 3yo, f, 1⅛m, 1:48.85, FLUTE, Real Cozzy, Collect Call. 13 started.

Kevin McHugh Memorial H., Rockingham Park, Aug. 19, $25,000, 3yo, 1 1/16mT, 1:46.92, RAPID RYAN, Tango Kid, Financial Diplomat. 10 started.

Khaled S. (R), Hollywood Park, April 28, $175,000, 4yo & up, California-bred, 1 1/16mT, 1:40.77, SPINELESSJELLYFISH, Lesters Boy, Native Desert. 9 started.

Kimberlite Pipe S., Kentucky Downs, Sept. 22, $45,000, 2yo, 6fT, NTA, PHARAOH'S CAT, Bert's Nicky, Handsome Hunk. 9 started.

Kindergarten S., Portland Meadows, April 29, $7,400, 2yo, 4½f, :55.25, JIMBOS VALENTINE, B J's Black Gold, Anna's Blue Moon. 8 started.

Kingarvie S. (R), Woodbine, Dec. 2, $130,625, 2yo, progeny of eligible stallions standing in Ontario, 1 1/16m, 1:44.78, BARBEAU RUCKUS, Bravely, Streakin Rob. 7 started.

King Cotton S., Oaklawn Park, Feb. 17, $50,000, 4yo & up, 6f, 1:09.91, BIDIS, E J Harley, Sand Ridge. 5 started.

King County H., Emerald Downs, June 23, $40,000, 3yo & up, f & m, 1m, 1:37, LATTER DAY PAULA, Taste the Passion, Run a Copy. 9 started.

KING EDWARD BREEDERS' CUP H.-G2, Woodbine, June 10, $341,400, 3yo & up, 1⅛mT, 1:47.12, QUIET RESOLVE, Kimberlite Pipe, Spindrift (Ire). 10 started.

Kingland S., The Meadowlands, Sept. 29, $100,000, 3yo, 6f, 1:08.77, SAN NICOLAS, Run Kush Run, Sea of Green. 8 started.

King Rex H., Calder Race Course, Nov. 18, $37,130, 3yo & up, 1⅛m, 1:51.84, BEST OF THE REST, Hal's Hope, Watch Your Pennies. 6 started.

KING'S BISHOP S.-G1, Saratoga Race Course, Aug. 25, $200,000, 3yo, 7f, 1:21.97, SQUIRTLE SQUIRT, Illusioned, City Zip. 8 started.

Kings Court S., Louisiana Downs, July 8, $39,200, 3yo & up, 6f, 1:09.80, FUN TO RUN, Overdone, Itsacryingshame. 5 started.

Kings Point H. (R), Aqueduct, April 1, $82,625, 3yo & up, New York-bred, 1⅛m, 1:50.10, TODDLER, John Paul Too, No Bad Habits. 8 started.

Kingston H. (R), Belmont Park, May 20, $86,625, 3yo & up, New York-bred, 1⅛mT, 1:48.22, PEBO'S GUY, John Paul Too, Galactic. 12 started.

KLAQ H., Sunland Park, Nov. 24, $28,100, 3yo & up, 5½f, 1:04.71, TERMINATOR WON, Wild Dan, Gee Wally. 9 started.

Klassy Briefcase S., Monmouth Park, June 17, $50,000, 3yo & up, f & m, 5f, :57.61, TUGGER, Cedar Knolls, Curious Treasures. 6 started.

Klondike H., Northlands Park, July 28, $33,450, 3yo & up, 1 1/16m, 1:45.60, TYKO TYCOON, Code Name Fred, Run Joey Run. 5 started.

Klondike S., Hastings Park Racecourse, May 19, $36,141, 3yo, 6½f, 1:16.86, DIGLETT, I'm Free, Smokin Finish. 6 started.

KNICKERBOCKER H.-G2, Belmont Park, Oct. 26, $150,000, 3yo & up, 1¼mT, 2:02.55, SUMITAS (Ger), Manndar (Ire), Crash Course. 11 started.

Kobuk King S. (R), Del Mar, July 19, $64,750, 3yo & up, non-winners of three races or for a claiming price of $62,500, 1⅜mT, 2:15.14, BEAT ALL, Sestino (Ire), War Declaration (Ire). 6 started.

Kokopelli H., Turf Paradise, Jan. 6, $25,000, 4yo & up, 1mT, 1:38.72,

HANGONSLEWPYHANGON, Maybe Special (GB), Thatsusintheolbean. 6 started.

K'thryn's Doll S., Turf Paradise, April 1, $23,800, 3yo, f, 6f, 1:10.34, CHANNING WAY, The Queen and I, Lucy T. 6 started.

Kudzu Juvenile S. (R), Hoosier Park, Oct. 13, $35,000, 2yo, Alabama-bred, 5½f, 1:07.38, HIT A DOUBLE, Ruben John, Classic Casey. 5 started.

Ky Alta H., Northlands Park, July 14, $32,025, 3yo & up, 1¹⁄₁₆m, 1:46.20, FANCY AS, Sixthirtyjoe, Autumn Weekend. 4 started.

Labor Day H., Mountaineer Park, Sept. 3, $58,025, 3yo & up, 1mT, 1:34.58, RHYTHMEAN, Find the Mine, Confucius Say. 8 started.

Labor Day H., Columbus, Sept. 3, $7,817, 3yo & up, 6½f, 1:18.80, MR ZOOHA, Citibid, Let Me Lead. 6 started.

LA BREA S.-G1, Santa Anita Park, Dec. 29, $200,000, 3yo, f, 7f, 1:21.29, AFFLUENT, Royally Chosen, Love At Noon. 12 started.

LA CANADA S.-G2, Santa Anita Park, Feb. 11, $111,000, 4 yo, f, 1⅛m, 1:49.74, SPAIN, Chilukki, Letter of Intent. 5 started.

LADIES H.-G3, Aqueduct, Dec. 22, $111,100, 3yo & up, f & m, 1¼m, 2:05.80, SUMMER COLONY, Stop for Schnapps, Strolling Belle. 9 started.

Ladnesian S., Hastings Park Racecourse, July 21, $37,617, 2yo, c & g, 6½f, 1:18.72, INTACT, No Time Flat, Magnemite. 8 started.

Lady Angela S. (R), Woodbine, April 22, $137,000, 3yo, f, progeny of eligible stallions standing in Ontario, 7f, 1:26.37, MOONLIGHT AFFAIR, Mysteryachievement, Classical Romance. 10 started.

Lady Baltimore S., Pimlico, July 1, $40,000, 3yo & up, f & m, 1⅛mT, 1:51.91, AMOURETTE, Silver Rail, Proud Owner. 5 started.

Lady Fingers S. (R), Finger Lakes, Aug. 18, $65,350, 2yo, f, New York-bred, 6f, 1:10.78, SHESASTONECOLDFOX, Princess Dixie, Alltappedout. 6 started.

Lady Hallie H., Sportsman's Park, April 8, $97,000, 3yo & up, f & m, 1¹⁄₁₆m, 1:42.86, LADY MELESI, Please Sign In, Adam's Time. 4 started.

Lady Morvich H., Bay Meadows Fair, Aug. 18, $48,150, 3yo & up, f & m, 1¹⁄₁₆mT, 1:44.43, MIMI'S CAFE, Aviate, Palace Royale (Ire). 6 started.

Lady Razorback Futurity (R), Louisiana Downs, Nov. 4, $25,000, 2yo, f, Arkansas-bred, 6f, 1:11.49, HUMBLE DANZIG, Princess Pamela, Magical Miss. 11 started.

Lady Slipper S. (R), Canterbury Park, May 19, $36,900, 3yo & up, f & m, Minnesota-bred, 6f, 1:11.99, NIDARI, Playful Edition, Linens N Lace. 8 started.

LADY'S SECRET BREEDERS' CUP H.-G2, Santa Anita Park, Sept. 29, $209,400, 3yo & up, f & m, 1¹⁄₁₆m, 1:43.64, QUEENIE BELLE, Letter of Intent, Nany's Sweep. 6 started.

Lady's Secret H., Remington Park, Nov. 17, $25,000, 3yo & up, f & m, 6½f, 1:15.94, EAST IS EAST, Darlin Dixie, Spanish Guitar. 7 started.

Lady's Secret S., Monmouth Park, Aug. 5, $75,000, 3yo & up, f & m, 1m 70y, 1:41.15, MISS LINDA (Arg), Steppedoutofadream, Gold for My Gal. 7 started.

Lafayette H., Golden Gate Fields, Jan. 1, $100,000, 4yo & up, 1mT, 1:38.36, EAGLETON, Yaralino (GB), Montemiro (Fr). 10 started.

LAFAYETTE S.-G3, Keeneland, April 11, $111,000, 3yo, 7f, 1:22.61, GRIFFINITE, Sam Lord's Castle, Yonaguska. 7 started.

Lafayette S., Evangeline Downs, Sept. 3, $50,000, 2yo, 6f, 1:11.20, HAIL TO BAG, Rapido, Doeny Rain. 10 started.

La Fiesta H., The Downs at Albuquerque, April 14, $32,400, 3yo, f, 5½f, 1:04.10, RUFFENA, Gimme a Clue, Sassy Chimes. 7 started.

La Habra S., Santa Anita Park, March 2, $115,100, 3yo, f, abt6½fT, 1:14.81, SERENA'S TUNE, Langoureuse, Innit (Ire). 11 started.

LA JOLLA H.-G3, Del Mar, Aug. 11, $150,000, 3yo, 1¹⁄₁₆mT, 1:41.72, MARINE (GB), Romanceishope, Mister Approval. 8 started.

LAKE GEORGE S.-G3 (1st Div.), Saratoga Race Course, July 30, $111,750, 3yo, f, 1¹⁄₁₆mT, 1:41.06, LIGHT DANCER, Owsley, Cozzy Corner. 9 started.

LAKE GEORGE S.-G3 (2nd Div.), Saratoga Race Course, July 30, $112,250, 3yo, f, 1¹⁄₁₆mT, 1:41.45, VOODOO DANCER, Sadler's Sarah, O K to Dance. 9 started.

LAKE PLACID H.-G2, Saratoga Race Course, Aug. 20, $150,000, 3yo, f, 1⅛mT, 1:47.42, SNOW DANCE, Wander Mom, Mystic Lady. 12 started.

Lakeview Thoroughbred Farms S. (R), Hollywood Park, April 28, $70,000, 3yo & up, f & m, California-bred non-winners of $3,000 other than maiden, claiming, or starter or non-winners of two races, 1¹⁄₁₆m, 1:45.33, CEE'S ELEGANCE, The Heebster, Glittering Affair. 11 started.

Lakeway S., Retama Park, Aug. 10, $25,000, 3yo, f, 6f, 1:11.99, SISTER'S SHAMROCK, Madison Grace, Outofnowhere. 6 started.

La Lorgnette S., Woodbine, Oct. 14, $113,400, 3yo, f, 1¹⁄₁₆m, 1:44.82, MADAME RED, Royal Fact, Miss Benny. 10 started.

Lamplighter H., Monmouth Park, July 7, $75,000, 3yo, 1¹⁄₁₆mT, 1:41.94, FIRST SPEAR, Spruce Run, Tremmor. 6 started.

LANDALUCE S.-G3, Hollywood Park, July 7, $108,400, 2yo, f, 6f, 1:10.45, GEORGIA'S STORM, Respectful, Who Loves Aleyna. 7 started.

Landaura S., Laurel Park, Feb. 24, $54,750, 3yo, f, 1¹⁄₁₆m, 1:44.30, FLEET RENEE, Giving Noreen, Sunshine in Paris. 5 started.

Land of Enchantment H. (R), Ruidoso Downs, July 15, $43,000, 3yo & up, New Mexico-bred, 7½f, 1:34.20, BOBBY BLURR, Marks Mark, Pack and Drift. 10 started.

Land of Jazz S., Ferndale, Aug. 17, $7,540, 3yo & up, 7f, 1:27.38, DISCONECT, Candelotto, Science Fiction. 7 started.

Land of Lincoln S. (R), Sportsman's Park, March 31, $75,000, 3yo, Illinois-bred, 6f, 1:12.61, MEADOW CHAMP, Jim's Nasty, Can't Stop James. 8 started.

LANE'S END BREEDERS' FUTURITY-G2, Keeneland, Oct. 6, $454,400, 2yo, 1¹⁄₁₆m, 1:43.79, SIPHONIC, Harlan's Holiday, Metatron. 11 started.

LANE'S END CHURCHILL DOWNS H.-G2, Churchill Downs, May 5, $179,550, 4yo & up, 7f, 1:20.50, ALANNAN, Bonapaw, Exchange Rate. 10 started.

Lansing S. (R), Great Lakes Downs, May 25, $45,000, 3yo, c & g, Michigan-bred, 6f, 1:15.44, SECRET ROMEO, Island N Abreeze, Blackstone Dreamer. 10 started.

LA PREVOYANTE H.-G2, Calder Race Course, Dec. 29, $150,000, 3yo & up, f & m, 1½mT, 2:26.63, KRISADA, Sweetest Thing, Great Fever (Fr). 10 started.

La Prevoyante S. (R), Woodbine, Sept. 16, $129,375, 3yo, f, progeny of eligible stallions standing in Ontario, 1mT, 1:36.77, MOONLIGHT AFFAIR, Classic Ingrid, Bubbi Trap. 6 started.

La Puente S. (R), Santa Anita Park, March 31, $83,475, 3yo, nonwinners of $50,000 at a mile or over in 2001, 1m, 1:35.30, MARINE (GB), (DH) Media Mogul (GB), (DH) River God. 9 started.

Larkspur H. (R), Great Lakes Downs, June 23, $45,000, 3yo & up, f & m, Michigan-bred, 7f, 1:27.58, SEFAS ROSE, Flyinghannah, Prima Gold. 8 started.

Larry Lashyn Futurity, Marquis Downs, Aug. 4, $6,000, 2yo, 6f, 1:15.33, ROYAL BRITTANY, Good Old Sprite, Gatopresson. 7 started.

Larry R. Riviello President's Cup S., Philadelphia Park, Aug. 18, $100,000, 3yo, 1m, 1:38.06, TRION GEORGIA, Beau's Surprise, Repunzel's Knight. 6 started.

LAS CIENEGAS H.-G3, Santa Anita Park, April 8, $109,500, 4yo & up, f & m, abt6½fT, 1:13.54, GO GO, Separata (Chi), Dianehill (Ire). 8 started.

La Senorita S., Retama Park, Sept. 1, $100,000, 2yo, f, 1m (originally scheduled on the turf), 1:44.02, VICTORY ROAD, Mightbeachamp, Humble Dot. 8 started.

LAS FLORES H.-G3, Santa Anita Park, Feb. 24, $134,000, 4yo & up, f & m, 6f, 1:08.83, GO GO, La Feminn, Cover Gal. 6 started.

Las Madrinas H., Fairplex Park, Sept. 21, $100,000, 3yo & up, f & m, 1¹⁄₁₆m, 1:44.52, MIMI'S CAFE, Revillew Slew, Warren's Whistle. 8 started.

LAS PALMAS H.-G2, Santa Anita Park, Nov. 4, $250,000, 3yo & up, f & m, 1⅛mT, 1:46.61, GOLDEN APPLES (Ire), Dancingonice, Janet (GB). 9 started.

Lassie S., Portland Meadows, Oct. 28, $8,400, 2yo, f, 5f, 1:01.23, LAMMY, Aurora Dawn, Jimbos Valentine. 6 started.

Lassie S., Hastings Park Racecourse, Aug. 18, $35,883, 2yo, f, 6½f, 1:17.47, LASTING CODE, Lady Vye, Gabriola. 6 started.

Last Chance Derby, Turf Paradise, Dec. 30, $22,800, 3yo, 1¹⁄₁₆m, 1:42.63, RESOLVE, Komax, Ironman Dehere. 7 started.

Last Don B. S. (R), Turf Paradise, March 18, $23,800, 3yo & up, Arizona-bred, 6f, 1:10.60, JOMAX, Thrice the Vice, G Malleah. 6 started.

LAS VIRGENES S.-G1, Santa Anita Park, Feb. 10, $200,000, 3yo, f, 1m, 1:36.89, GOLDEN BALLET, Two Item Limit, Affluent. 7 started.

Late Bloomer S., Delaware Park, April 21, $58,300, 3yo & up, f & m, 6f, 1:10.14, ELEKTRALINE, Lily's Affair, Memory Work. 6 started.

LA TROIENNE S.-G3, Churchill Downs, May 3, $121,000, 3yo, f, 7f, 1:22.90, CARESSING, Sweet Nanette, Golly Greeley. 9 started.

Laurel Lane S. (R), Louisiana Downs, Oct. 14, $39,700, 2yo, f, Louisiana-bred, 6f, 1:12.59, C J'S STAR, Doc Knows Best, Taylor's Queen. 11 started.

Lauries Dancer S. (R), Fort Erie, Aug. 14, $53,650, 3yo & up, f & m, Canadian-bred that have started at least twice at Fort Erie in 2001, 1 1/16m, 1:43.87, PROSPECTIVE GAL, Orientalspringhope, Is She Real. 6 started.

La Voyageuse H., Woodbine, March 31, $95,750, 4yo & up, f & m, 5f, :57.79, TORRID AFFAIR, Barlee Mist, Julie's Witt. 10 started.

Lawdy Miss Clawdy S. (R), Sportsman's Park, April 28, $73,305, 3yo, f, Illinois-bred, 1m, 1:39.83, EXPLOSIVE ACTION, Mattina, Tenafly. 10 started.

LAWRENCE REALIZATION H.-G3, Belmont Park, Oct. 13, $150,000, 3yo, 1 1/2mT, 2:27.04, SHARP PERFORMANCE, Tiger Trap, Whitmore's Conn. 6 started.

La Zanzara S. (R), Hollywood Park, May 11, $75,000, 4yo & up, f & m, non-winners of a graded stake at a mile or more in 2001, 1 1/4m, 2:04.32, JIG (Ire), The Seven Seas, Dangerous Mind (Ire). 6 started.

LAZARO BARRERA MEMORIAL S.-G3, Hollywood Park, May 28, $108,600, 3yo, 7f, 1:20.42, EARLY FLYER, Squirtle Squirt, Top Hit. 7 started.

Lazer Show S., Arlington Park, Oct. 13, $55,000, 3yo & up, f & m, 5f (originally scheduled on the turf), :59.21, BRITTSKER, Diablos First Lady, Sumthintotalkabout. 8 started.

Leader of the Band H., Delaware Park, May 30, $56,648, 3yo & up, 1 1/16m (originally scheduled on the turf), 1:45.93, BALARAT, Mr. Elway, Mister Business. 4 started.

Lecomte S., Fair Grounds, Jan. 27, $100,000, 3yo, 1m, 1:37.98, SAM LORD'S CASTLE, Wild Hits, Mc Mahon. 10 started.

Lee and Grant S. (R), Colonial Downs, July 4, $30,000, 3yo & up, West Virginia-bred and/or Virginia-bred or -sired, 1mT, 1:37.54, PLEASE RUN, Oak Level, Von Bellinghausen. 10 started.

Legal Justice S., Philadelphia Park, June 23, 3yo & up, 5f, :57.44, COPELAN'S NUMBER, Grangeville, Pal Joey. 7 started.

Legal Light S., Delaware Park, June 2, $72,750, 3yo, 6f, 1:11.05, BEYOND BRILLIANT, Max Jones, Sea of Green. 4 started.

Lenta S., Calder Race Course, Nov. 17, $60,000, 3yo, f, 1 1/16mT, 1:42.62, GREY BALLET, Blondaway, Jennasietta. 11 started.

Leonard Richards S., Delaware Park, June 17, $200,000, 3yo, 1 1/16m, 1:42.41, BURNING ROMA, Marciano, Bay Eagle. 5 started.

Les Mackin H., Yavapai Downs, July 16, $10,500, 3yo & up, 1 1/16m, 1:44.34, LEAVEN, Golden Zodiac, Vaclav (Arg). 8 started.

Les Mademoiselle S., Ferndale, Aug. 18, $8,530, 3yo & up, f & m, 1 1/16m, 1:46.80, ANNUAL RAINFALL, Conezdesertglitter, My American Girl. 5 started.

Lethbridge Light Horse Overnite Sprint S., Lethbridge, Sept. 1, $6,700, 3yo & up, 5 1/2f, 1:07.20, WIN FOR JIM, Bad Toda Bone, Ugly Weekend. 7 started.

Let It Ride.com S. (R), Del Mar, Aug. 16, $65,852, 3yo & up, non-winners of three races or for a claiming price of $62,500, 1 3/8mT, 2:14.12, KIM LOVES BUCKY, War Declaration (Ire), Prairieton. 6 started.

Lewis and Clark S., Great Falls, July 29, $5,700, 3yo, 7f, 1:29.40, HOLLISTER SLEW, Impressive Knight, I've Got a Dream. 6 started.

Lexington Park Claiming S., Pimlico, April 29, $41,300, 4yo & up, 1 1/16m, 1:43.70, JUDGE'S CASE, Notably Frosty, Memory Tap. 5 started.

LEXINGTON S.-G3, Belmont Park, July 15, $150,000, 3yo, 1 1/4mT, 1:58.93, SHARP PERFORMANCE, Package Store, Whitmore's Conn. 8 started.

Liberada H., Calder Race Course, Aug. 5, $54,770, 3yo & up, f & m, 1 1/16m, 1:46.27, RACING FOR PAHM, Coolbythepool, Cash's Pride. 8 started.

Liberation H. (R), Hastings Park Racecourse, June 17, $37,556, 3yo, f, British Columbia-bred and/or -owned, 1 1/16m, 1:45.44, LADY'S JEWEL, Queen of My Nights, Castle Mountain. 6 started.

Liberty Bell S., Philadelphia Park, July 2, $50,000, 3yo, 1 1/16mT, 1:45.26, MOOMTAZZ, Pegylation, Mr. Numbers. 9 started.

LIEUTENANT GOVERNORS' H.-G3, Hastings Park Racecourse, July 1, $80,710, 3yo & up, 1 1/16m, 1:49.95, RAMPAGING ALF, Lord Nelson, King Jeremy. 9 started.

Ligature S. (R), Penn National Race Course, June 30, $25,000, 3yo & up, Pennsylvania-bred, 6f, 1:09.27, TONTO GUSTO, Bohemia Slew, Flask. 8 started.

Light Hearted S., Delaware Park, July 22, $83,000, 3yo & up, f & m, 6f, 1:10.81, SUPERDUPER MISS, Ivy's Jewel, Lorline. 8 started.

Lightning Jet S. (R), Hawthorne Race Course, Nov. 10, $75,000, 3yo & up, Illinois-conceived and/or -foaled, 6f, 1:10.86, MAGIC DOE, Manitowish, Tic N Tin. 6 started.

Likely Exchange S., Turfway Park, Feb. 3, $49,500, 4yo & up, f & m, 1m, 1:39.50, FAST DELIVERY, Blarin Speed, Dashing Lesley. 9 started.

Lilac H., Stampede Park, June 2, $34,501, 3yo, f, 1m, 1:39.60, (DH) LITTLE LOLITTA, (DH) C D COOL, Dana's Remark. 7 started.

Lil E. Tee S. (R), Philadelphia Park, Oct. 6, $50,000, 3yo, Pennsylvania-bred, 6f, 1:11.65, BEAU'S SURPRISE, K Mac, Two Raise Limit. 6 started.

Lincoln Heritage H. (R), Arlington Park, June 23, $75,000, 3yo & up, f & m, Illinois-conceived and/or -foaled, 1 1/16mT, 1:42.45, IOYA TWO, Cozy, Erin Murphy. 12 started.

Lincoln Thoroughbred H. (R), Ruidoso Downs, July 15, $43,400, 3yo & up, f & m, New Mexico-bred, 6f, 1:12, NUPAR, Me a Spirit Too, Festival Legs. 9 started.

Lincroft H. (R), Monmouth Park, Aug. 12, $50,000, 3yo & up, New Jersey-bred, 1m, 1:38.36, BEKNOWN TO ME, Holiest Punch, H. M. S. Jackson. 6 started.

Lineage Day Thoroughbred Claiming S. (R), The Downs at Albuquerque, May 20, $11,400, 3yo & up, New Mexico-bred, 6f, 1:10.25, SPARKLING TAN, Oh Johnny Oh, He's a Bandit. 10 started.

Lineage H. (R), The Downs at Albuquerque, May 20, $32,900, 3yo & up, New Mexico-bred, 1 1/16m, 1:42.99, ODDSONJACK, Ben Told, Piute. 9 started.

Linear H. (R), Calder Race Course, June 9, $55,950, 3yo & up, Florida-bred, 5fT, :55.78, HONORABLE PIC, Sejm's Madness, Sam's Concorde. 8 started.

Lite the Fuse S., Laurel Park, Oct. 27, $75,000, 3yo & up, 6f, 1:09.91, DISCO RICO, In C C's Honor, Sassy Hound. 5 started.

Little Everglades Hurdle S., Little Everglades, March 11, $50,000, 4yo & up, abt2mT, 3:31.80, WAR TALK, Emancipate, Pelagos (Fr). 7 started.

Little Ones S. (R), Great Lakes Downs, Aug. 20, $45,000, 2yo, c & g, Michigan-bred, 5 1/2f, 1:07.65, SPRING WINDS, To Be Springs, Equi Power. 10 started.

Little Silver S., Monmouth Park, June 2, $48,500, 3yo, f, 6f, 1:10, HARMONY LODGE, Appealing Satin, Gigi's Magic. 4 started.

Little Sucker S. (R), Hawthorne Race Course, Dec. 1, $97,920, 3yo & up, f & m, Illinois-conceived and/or -foaled, 1 1/16m, 1:47.97, OUT OF OPTIONS, Q. P. Cat, Cottage Rose. 7 started.

Live the Dream H., Del Mar, Sept. 5, $76,650, 3yo & up, 1mT, 1:33.54, LONESOME DUDE, Speak in Passing, Lord Jim (Arg). 10 started.

Local Thriller H., Delaware Park, July 31, $69,100, 3yo & up, f & m, 5fT, :56.74, ATLANTIC DESTINY (Ire), Lariat, Maypole Dance. 9 started.

LOCUST GROVE H.-G3, Churchill Downs, June 23, $172,800, 3yo & up, f & m, 1 1/8mT, 1:48.79, COLSTAR, Solvig, Megans Bluff. 11 started.

Lone Star Derby, Lone Star Park, April 7, $500,000, 3yo, 1 1/8m, 1:50.27, PERCY HOPE, Fifty Stars, Gift of the Eagle. 8 started.

LONE STAR PARK H.-G3, Lone Star Park, May 28, $300,000, 3yo & up, 1 1/16m, 1:40.53, DIXIE DOT COM, Fan the Flame, Big Numbers. 8 started.

Lone Star Park Turf Sprint H., Lone Star Park, May 28, $100,000, 3yo & up, 5fT, :58.47, VINNIE'S BOY, Wild Hits, Cowboy Ettiquette. 12 started.

LONGACRES MILE H.-G3, Emerald Downs, Aug. 19, $250,000, 3yo & up, 1m, 1:35.40, IRISHEYESAREFLYING, Handy N Bold, Makors Mark. 10 started.

Long Branch Breeders' Cup S., Monmouth Park, July 15, $100,000, 3yo, 1 1/16m, 1:43.28, BURNING ROMA, This Fleet Is Due, Thunder Blitz. 7 started.

Longfellow S., Monmouth Park, June 23, $75,000, 3yo & up, 6f, 1:09.04, MAX'S PAL, I'm Sentimental, Personal First. 6 started.

Longhorn H. (R), Retama Park, Oct. 6, $35,000, 3yo & up, Texas-bred, 6f, 1:10.85, HAPPY SMILE, St. Martin's Cloak, J W Jet. 7 started.

LONG ISLAND H.-G2, Aqueduct, Nov. 10, $150,000, 3yo & up, f & m, 1 1/2mT, 2:29.36, QUEUE, Sweetest Thing, Lady Dora. 13 started.

Long Look S., The Meadowlands, Sept. 28, $75,000, 3yo & up, f & m, 1 1/8m, 1:48.74, PEOPLE'S PRINCESS, Gaelic Bay, Poivre (Chi). 5 started.

Looker Group Fillies & Mares S., Lethbridge, Sept. 15, $6,800, 3yo & up, f & m, abt6f, 1:11.40, A TEMPTING LIGHT, Easy Remark,

Ebony Mystique. 8 started.

LOS ANGELES H.-G3, Hollywood Park, May 27, $107,300, 3yo & up, 6f, 1:08.35, CALLER ONE, Stormy Jack, Rapidough. 6 started.

Los Ninos S., Ruidoso Downs, July 29, $30,083, 2yo, c & g, 6f, 1:11.60, RED AND RARE, Pacer, Super Charge. 9 started.

Lost Code H., Sportsman's Park, March 3, $50,000, 3yo & up, 6f, 1:11.96, TIC N TIN, Willowbrook Lane, Magic Doe. 8 started.

Louise Kimball Distaff Championship S. (R), Suffolk Downs, Dec. 1, $25,000, 3yo & up, f & m, Massachusetts-bred, 1 1/16m, 1:46.98, BIG MISS, Sunlit Ridge, Little Carbon. 6 started.

Louisiana Breeders' Derby (R), Louisiana Downs, Oct. 13, $67,000, 3yo, Louisiana-bred, 1 1/16m, 1:47.29, SKY MART, Prince Slew, Herecomesdafuzz. 14 started.

Louisiana Breeders' Oaks (R), Louisiana Downs, Oct. 14, $67,850, 3yo, f, Louisiana-bred, 1 1/16m, 1:47.77, WILD SQUAW, Autobesarah, Miss Nitap. 12 started.

Louisiana Champions Day Classic S. (R), Fair Grounds, Dec. 8, $150,000, 3yo & up, Louisiana-bred, 1⅛m, 1:50.99, OAK HALL, One Brick Shy, Doctor Mike. 9 started.

Louisiana Champions Day Juvenile S. (R), Fair Grounds, Dec. 8, $100,000, 2yo, c & g, Louisiana-bred, 6f, 1:11.11, HAIL TO BAG, Walk in the Snow, Fine Stormy. 9 started.

Louisiana Champions Day Ladies S. (R), Fair Grounds, Dec. 8, $100,000, 3yo & up, f & m, Louisiana-bred, 1 1/16m, 1:45.61, MIDGE TOO, Eastern Sun, Autobesarah. 10 started.

Louisiana Champions Day Lassie S. (R), Fair Grounds, Dec. 8, $100,000, 2yo, f, Louisiana-bred, 6f, 1:11.13, KWIK KASH, C J's Star, Sunny Scarlett. 12 started.

Louisiana Champions Day Sprint S. (R), Fair Grounds, Dec. 8, $100,000, 3yo & up, Louisiana-bred, 6f, 1:09.94, MY BRENT'S DIAMOND, Kettle Man, Zarb's Luck. 10 started.

Louisiana Champions Day Starter H. (R), Fair Grounds, Dec. 8, $50,000, 3yo & up, Louisiana-bred starters for a claiming price of $20,000 or less in 2001, 1 1/16m, 1:45.05, SUNUP SUNDOWN, Proper Sunday, Pancho Pete. 12 started.

Louisiana Champions Day Turf S. (R), Fair Grounds, Dec. 8, $100,000, 3yo & up, Louisiana-bred, abt1 1/16mT, 1:44.51, MR. SULU, Bourbon Boogie, L'Homme. 11 started.

LOUISIANA DERBY-G2, Fair Grounds, March 11, $750,000, 3yo, 1 1/16m, 1:44.78, FIFTY STARS, Millennium Wind, Hero's Tribute. 9 started.

Louisiana Downs H., Louisiana Downs, Sept. 22, $100,000, 3yo & up, 1 1/16m, 1:44.47, MAYSVILLE SLEW, Northcote Road, Inkatha (Fr). 12 started.

Louisiana Futurity (R), Fair Grounds, Dec. 23, $62,775, 2yo, c & g, Louisiana-bred, 6f, 1:11.06, ZUPPY, Hail to Bag, Abagfullofit. 7 started.

Louisiana Futurity (R), Fair Grounds, Dec. 22, $61,275, 2yo, f, Louisiana-bred, 6f, 1:12.49, SUNNY SCARLETT, Sweet Remiss, Amiera River. 6 started.

Louisiana H., Fair Grounds, Dec. 29, $75,000, 3yo & up, 1 1/16m, 1:44.77, SAN PEDRO, Remington Rock, Valhol. 7 started.

LOUISVILLE BREEDERS' CUP H.-G2, Churchill Downs, May 4, $279,000, 3yo & up, f & m, 1 1/16m, 1:42.53, SAUDI POETRY, Royal Fair, Dreams Gallore. 8 started.

Louisville H., Churchill Downs, June 2, $109,900, 3yo & up, 1⅜mT, 2:16.28, WITH ANTICIPATION, Profit Option, Gritty Sandie. 6 started.

Lou Smith Memorial H., Rockingham Park, July 28, $25,000, 3yo & up, 1 1/16m, 1:44.83, MINER'S TRICK, Personal Moon, Sky Approval. 6 started.

Loyalty S. (R), Thistledown, Aug. 18, $30,000, 2yo, Ohio-bred, 6f, 1:10.86, WATCH ME FIRE, Joanies Bella, Dinkers Millennium. 6 started.

Lucky Lavender Girl H., Calder Race Course, July 14, $33,680, 3yo & up, f & m, 5fT, :57.33, ELVI GAMBLE, Tis Your Country, Shes Like Rio. 7 started.

Lulu's Ransom S., Calder Race Course, Nov. 10, $60,000, 2yo, f, 1mT, 1:38.93, AUGUST STORM, Social Place, Whitewashed. 8 started.

Luther Burbank H., Santa Rosa, July 29, $53,890, 3yo & up, f & m, 1 1/16m, 1:41.35, TWO ON THE AISLE, Mimi's Cafe, Dream of Gifts. 6 started.

Lyman Sprint Championship H. (R), Philadelphia Park, May 5, $50,000, 3yo & up, Pennsylvania-bred, 7f, 1:23.16, BOHEMIA SLEW, Lord Sanford, Sly Ole Buck. 6 started.

Lyphard H. (R), Penn National Race Course, Aug. 10, $30,700, 3yo & up, Pennsylvania-bred, 6f, 1:09.52, TONTO GUSTO, Pal Joey, Carried Away. 6 started.

Lyrique H., Louisiana Downs, Sept. 2, $50,000, 3yo, f, 1 1/16m, 1:47.44, CHAUSSON POIRE, Autobesarah, Lady Virginia. 8 started.

Mackinac H. (R), Great Lakes Downs, Sept. 17, $50,000, 3yo, Michigan-bred, 1 1/16m, 1:47.81, SECRET ROMEO, Island N Abreeze, Native Ruck. 9 started.

Madamoiselle H., Northlands Park, Aug. 10, $31,875, 3yo & up, f & m, 1 1/16m, 1:46, NORTHERN NEECHITOO, Tecate, Crimson Hue. 4 started.

Madison County S. (R), Hoosier Park, Sept. 29, $44,200, 3yo & up, f & m, Indiana-bred and/or -sired, 6f, 1:11.95, WABASH SUE, Lace and Lightning, Hoosier Lover. 11 started.

Mae de Vol Sprint H., Bay Meadows, Sept. 1, $53,250, 3yo & up, f & m, 6f, 1:09.76, SLEWSBOX, Carson Jen, Phaenna. 7 started.

Magic City Classic S. (R), River Downs, June 16, $35,000, 3yo & up, Alabama-bred, 6f, 1:12.20, CHIEF TUDOR, Mr. Tony Z., Owen's Way. 7 started.

Magnolia State H. (R), Fair Grounds, March 26, $13,900, 3yo & up, Mississippi-owned, 6f, 1:10.94, WAVERLY BELL, Irismycase, Princess Suzi. 8 started.

Maiden S. (R), Hollywood Park, April 28, $60,000, 3yo & up, c & g, California-bred, 6½f, 1:15.91, EX FEDERALI, Speedy Pick, Market Cap. 14 started.

Maiden S. (R), Hollywood Park, April 28, $60,000, 3yo & up, f & m, California-bred, 6½f, 1:16.35, LIGHTEN UP TINY, Miss Skagit State, Mahdee's Gold. 14 started.

Maid of the Mist S. (R), Belmont Park, Oct. 21, $100,000, 2yo, f, New York-bred, 1m, 1:39.74, PRINCESS DIXIE, Sunday Driver, Dancing Blues. 9 started.

Majorette H., Louisiana Downs, Oct. 6, $25,000, 3yo & up, f & m, 6½f, 1:18.14, OUTOFNOWHERE, Cinderella Story, Star Engagement. 6 started.

MAKER'S MARK MILE S.-G2, Keeneland, April 13, $226,600, 4yo & up, 1mT, 1:34.44, NORTH EAST BOUND, Brahms, Strategic Mission. 8 started.

MALIBU S.-G1, Santa Anita Park, Dec. 26, $200,000, 3yo, 7f, 1:22.13, MIZZEN MAST, I Love Silver, Giant Gentleman. 13 started.

Mamie Eisenhower S. (R), Prairie Meadows, June 24, $64,200, 3yo & up, f & m, Iowa-bred, 6f, 1:09.36, NUT N BETTER, Lady Tamworth, Sumthintotalkabout. 6 started.

Mamzelle S., Churchill Downs, May 3, $109,700, 3yo & up, f & m, 5fT, :55.92 (NCR), SEPARATA (Chi), Elvi Gamble, Penny Marie. 6 started.

Manatee S., Tampa Bay Downs, Jan. 27, $50,000, 3yo & up, f & m, 7f, 1:24.45, SILVER STOCKINGS, Inside Affair, Little Won. 10 started.

Manayunk S., Philadelphia Park, Sept. 29, $50,000, 2yo, f, 1m, 1:40.97, MARESHA, Avalos, Entwining. 7 started.

Manchester H., Rockingham Park, Sept. 1, $25,000, 3yo & up, 6f, 1:12.05, GOODBAR, First Shot, Cox's Sweep. 7 started.

Manhattan Beach S., Hollywood Park, June 29, $73,045, 3yo, f, 5½fT, 1:02.60, GABRIELLINA GIOF (GB), Brisquette, Pretty 'n Smart. 8 started.

MANHATTAN H.-G1, Belmont Park, June 9, $400,000, 3yo & up, 1¼mT, 2:00.77, FORBIDDEN APPLE, King Cugat, Tijiyr (Ire). 10 started.

Manhattan H. (R), The Woodlands, Oct. 7, $25,000, 3yo & up, f & m, Kansas-bred, 6f, 1:14, DUNHAM'S SOCIAL, Sunnie Do It, Miss Gold Kiss. 6 started.

Manila S., Arlington Park, Oct. 20, $75,000, 2yo, 1mT, 1:39.61, RYLSTONE, U S S Tinosa, Jaha (Fr). 12 started.

Manila S. (R), Hollywood Park, June 23, $75,090, 3yo, non-winners of two races other than maiden, claiming, starter, or California-bred races or non-winners of three races lifetime, 1mT, 1:34.20, ROMANCEISHOPE, Macabe, Winston Chi. 6 started.

Manila S., The Meadowlands, Sept. 28, $75,000, 3yo & up, 1⅜mT, 2:17.94, ELTAWAASUL, Spindrift (Ire), Ready to Roll (Ire). 11 started.

MANITOBA DERBY-G3, Assiniboia Downs, Aug. 6, $98,000, 3yo, 1⅛m, 1:51.80, STAGE CLASSIC, Fancy As, Corporate Shuffle. 5 started.

Manitoba Maturity (R), Assiniboia Downs, July 14, $34,300, 4yo, Manitoba-bred, 1 1/16m, 1:46.60, GUS AGAIN, Dawn of Forever, Base Camp. 5 started.

Manitoba S. (R), Assiniboia Downs, June 30, $26,950, 3yo, c & g, Manitoba-bred, 1m, 1:41.40, G AND L SPECIAL, Command Start, U Otabe Wild. 5 started.

Manor Downs Futurity, Retama Park, May 21, $58,000, 2yo, 4½f, :52.96, WILD GEAR, (DH) Bayakoa's Image, (DH) Runaway Verdict. 10 started.

MAN O' WAR S.-G1, Belmont Park, Sept. 8, $500,000, 3yo & up, 1⅜mT, 2:15.11, WITH ANTICIPATION, Silvano (Ger), Ela Athena (GB). 8 started.

MAPLE LEAF S.-G3, Woodbine, Nov. 3, $226,200, 3yo & up, f & m, 1¼m, 2:03.62, CATCH THE RING, Mountain Angel, Madame Red. 8 started.

Marathon S., Turf Paradise, March 4, $24,400, 4yo & up, 1⅝m, 2:47.67, CALIGRAPHY, El Tinieblas (Mex), Way the Best. 11 started.

Marcellus Frost Hurdle H., Percy Warner, May 12, $50,000, 4yo & up, abt2mT, 3:56.20, CANTA KE BRAVE, Iron County Xmas, Aggro Crag. 7 started.

Mardi Gras H., Fair Grounds, Feb. 27, $75,000, 4yo & up, abt7½fT, 1:31.80, NORTHCOTE ROAD, Inkatha (Fr), Three Wonders. 7 started.

Marfa S., Turfway Park, Sept. 29, $60,750, 3yo & up, 6½f, 1:16.57, LITTLE LEE, Sea of Tranquility, Two Punch Sonny. 5 started.

Margarita Breeders' Cup H., Retama Park, Aug. 4, $33,500, 3yo & up, f & m, 1 1/16mT, 1:43.34, ANTOLOGICA (Chi), Screen Attraction, Caustic Remark. 11 started.

Marie P. DeBartolo Oaks, Louisiana Downs, Sept. 23, $50,000, 3yo, f, 1 1/16mT, 1:44.95, CHAUSSON POIRE, Wild Squaw, La Recherche. 12 started.

MARINE S.-G2, Woodbine, May 19, $136,000, 3yo, 1 1/16m, 1:45.89, WIN CITY, High Commissioner, Lunar Secret. 6 started.

Marluel's Troy S. (R), Fairmount Park, Oct. 16, $36,000, 2yo, c & g, Illinois-conceived and/or -foaled, 6f, 1:14, WRIGHT ON HUSTON, Slew the City, Spanish Charm. 10 started.

Marquis Carousel H., Marquis Downs, Sept. 14, $5,300, 3yo, 1⅛m, 1:55.15, ICE JAMER, Smokin Six Pack, Kelchinko. 5 started.

Marquis Cup H., Marquis Downs, July 15, $6,000, 3yo, 1m, 1:42.10, ICE JAMER, Wendys Choice, Teton Temptor. 5 started.

Marquis Oaks H., Marquis Downs, June 8, $6,000, 3yo, f, 6f, 1:15.37, RAPADASH, Ms. Lady Rose, She's Home Alone. 9 started.

Marshua's River S., Gulfstream Park, March 14, $84,325, 4yo & up, f & m, abt5fT, :55.84 (NCR), ELVI GAMBLE, Gather the Day, Automated. 12 started.

Martanza H. (R), Sam Houston Race Park, Dec. 1, $75,000, 3yo & up, f & m, Texas-bred, 1m, 1:39.08, COASTALOTA, Holly Sue, Crook's Angel. 7 started.

Martha Washington S., Oaklawn Park, Feb. 19, $50,000, 3yo, f, 6f, 1:10.07, CHERYL P., Star Engagement, Cat Out. 5 started.

Mary Goldblatt S. (R), Portland Meadows, March 17, $10,975, 3yo, f, Oregon-bred, 1m, 1:42.42, HURRICANE RYLIE, Moon Pilot, Annie N Will. 7 started.

MARYLAND BREEDERS' CUP H.-G3, Pimlico, May 19, $200,000, 3yo & up, 6f, 1:10.40, DISCO RICO, Flame Thrower, Istintaj. 6 started.

Maryland Hunt Cup S., Glyndon, April 28, $60,450, 5 yo's & up, abt4mT, 8:38.60, SOLO LORD, Welter Weight, Floating Interest. 4 started.

Maryland Juvenile Championship S. (R), Laurel Park, Dec. 31, $100,000, 2yo, Maryland-bred, 1⅛m, 1:54.10, MAGIC WEISNER, Invent, War Native. 7 started.

Maryland Juvenile Filly Championship S. (R), Laurel Park, Dec. 29, $100,000, 2yo, f, Maryland-bred, 1⅛m, 1:53.61, TRUE SENSATION, Dish It to Me, Bronze Abe. 5 started.

Maryland Million Classic S. (R), Pimlico, Oct. 13, $190,000, 3yo & up, progeny of eligible stallions standing in Maryland, 1 3/16m, 1:57.20, SUMERSET, Lightning Paces, P Day. 9 started.

Maryland Million Distaff H. (R), Pimlico, Oct. 13, $47,500, 3yo & up, f & m, Maryland-bred, 1 1/16m, 1:47.34, BELLE VISAGE, Noah's Ark, Roby. 8 started.

Maryland Million Distaff Starter H., Pimlico, Oct. 13, $95,000, 3yo & up, f & m, 6f, 1:11.54, CASE OF THE BLUES, Trueytoo, Summer Shenanigans. 9 started.

Maryland Million Hurdle H. (R), Shawan Downs, Sept. 29, $22,500, 3yo & up, progeny of eligible stallions standing in Maryland, abt2mT, 3:56.40, WICOMICO, Pinkie Swear, Calliope. 5 started.

Maryland Million Ladies S. (R), Pimlico, Oct. 13, $95,000, 3yo & up, f & m, progeny of eligible stallions standing in Maryland, 1⅛mT, 1:48.40, STAL QUEST, Purrfect Punch, Canavakiss. 10 started.

Maryland Million Lassie S. (R), Pimlico, Oct. 13, $95,000, 2yo, f, progeny of eligible stallions standing in Maryland, 6f, 1:11.85, NIGHT BREEZE, (DH) Bronze Abe, (DH) Madame X Ski. 8 started.

Maryland Million Nursery S. (R), Pimlico, Oct. 13, $95,000, 2yo, progeny of eligible stallions standing in Maryland, 6f, 1:11.70, PAL'S PARTNER, Private Opening, Square Cut Diamond. 9 started.

Maryland Million Oaks (R), Pimlico, Oct. 13, $95,000, 3yo, f, progeny of eligible stallions standing in Maryland, 1 1/16m, 1:45.71, ALONG CAME MARY, Magic Stream, Guillotine. 7 started.

Maryland Million Sprint H. (R), Pimlico, Oct. 13, $95,000, 3yo & up, progeny of eligible stallions standing in Maryland, 6f, 1:10.47, JORGIE STOVER, In C C's Honor, Forty Eight Hours. 8 started.

Maryland Million Starter H. (R), Pimlico, Oct. 13, $47,500, 3yo & up, progeny of eligible stallions standing in Maryland, 1⅛m, 1:51.42, BLAZING COLORS, Surviving Princess, Admiral Bo. 8 started.

Maryland Million Sweepstakes S. (R), Pimlico, Oct. 13, $47,500, 3yo, progeny of eligible stallions standing in Maryland, 1 1/16m, 1:43.77, DOCENT, Bada Bam Bada Boom, Deliver Hope. 7 started.

Maryland Million Turf S. (R), Pimlico, Oct. 13, $95,000, 3yo & up, progeny of eligible stallions standing in Maryland, 1⅛mT, 1:48.52, ELBERTON, Watchman's Warning, Cynics Beware. 8 started.

Maryland Racing Media H., Laurel Park, Feb. 10, $68,040, 4yo & up, f & m, 1 3/16m, 1:59.07, IRVING'S BABY, Back in Shape, Unbridled Lady. 8 started.

Mason Hougland Memorial Timber S., Percy Warner, May 12, $50,000, 4yo & up, abt3mT, 6:23.60, THOR THORS, Matchless, High Card. 6 started.

Massachusetts Derby (R), Suffolk Downs, Dec. 3, $25,000, 3yo, Massachusetts-bred, 1 1/16m, 1:48.01, JINI'S JET, Famous Future, Jr. Conquistador. 6 started.

MASSACHUSETTS H.-G2, Suffolk Downs, June 2, $500,000, 3yo & up, 1⅛m, 1:48.61, INCLUDE, Sir Bear, Broken Vow. 7 started.

Massachusetts Oaks (R), Suffolk Downs, Dec. 21, $25,000, 3yo, f, Massachusetts-bred, 1 1/16m, 1:47.96, SUNLIT RIDGE, Oh Sham Baby, Viva Concorde. 7 started.

Massachusetts Thoroughbred Breeders Championship (R), Suffolk Downs, Dec. 15, $24,500, 3yo & up, Massachusetts-bred, 1 1/16m, 1:44.94, JINI'S JET, Papa Ho Ho, African Sundance. 5 started.

Massachusetts Thoroughbred Breeders' S. (R), Suffolk Downs, April 28, $25,000, 3yo & up, Massachusetts-bred, 1 1/16m, 1:46.77, DIGGIN' FOR FUN, Al Bark, Dawn's First Light. 8 started.

Matchmaker H. (R), Lincoln State Fair, June 16, $13,375, 3yo & up, f & m, Nebraska-bred, 1m, 1:36.80, SWEET FANTASTIC, Sandpit Dancer, Mytrump. 10 started.

Matiara S., Hollywood Park, Nov. 10, $100,000, 3yo, f, 1⅛mT, 1:47.75, HEADS WILL ROLL (GB), Live Your Dreams, Waki Music. 7 started.

Matinee Girl H., Portland Meadows, Jan. 6, $6,700, 4yo & up, f & m, 1 1/16m, 1:47.61, AMBERRAE, Cyamaria, Skii N Fashion. 7 started.

MATRIARCH S.-G1, Hollywood Park, Nov. 25, $500,000, 3yo & up, f & m, 1⅛mT, 1:50.16, STARINE (Fr), Lethals Lady (GB), Golden Apples (Ire). 12 started.

Matron H., Marquis Downs, June 9, $6,000, 3yo & up, f & m, 6f, 1:14.37, JUDGE SMILES, Truly Remarkable, Sundowncindy. 7 started.

Matron S., Assiniboia Downs, Sept. 23, $34,300, 3yo & up, f & m, 1⅛m, 1:53.20, MISS SANDY DEE, Love Play, Farrmost. 8 started.

Matt Scudder S., The Meadowlands, Oct. 13, $50,000, 3yo, 5fT, :55.83, TAKE ACHANCE ON ME, Pirate's Gold, Rock. 11 started.

Maxine M. Piggott S. (R), Turf Paradise, April 7, $30,000, 3yo, f, Arizona-bred, 6½f, 1:16.10, SONORA DESERT, Knoll Lake, Stormy Spirit. 8 started.

Maxxam Gold Cup H., Sam Houston Race Park, Jan. 20, $100,000, 4yo & up, 1⅛m, 1:51.19, VILAXY, Allen's Oop, Rebridled. 6 started.

Mayor's Mile S., Fair Meadows at Tulsa, July 14, $27,215, 3yo & up, 1m, 1:39.60, FOURTEEN TEN, College Dean, Cost of Diamonds. 6 started.

MAZARINE BREEDERS' CUP S.-G1, Woodbine, Sept. 22, $275,000, 2yo, f, 1 1/16m, 1:46.99, LADY SHARI, Jealous Forum, Mulrainy. 9 started.

McConnell Springs S. (R), Keeneland, Oct. 24, $73,375, 3yo, non-winners of a stake over a mile, 1 1/16m, 1:44.26, FREON FLIER, On the Game, Trion Georgia. 5 started.

McGee Park Derby, SunRay Park, Oct. 13, $31,200, 3yo, 1m, 1:37, BEEHAY, Sassy Chimes, Silver Set. 8 started.

Meadow Brook Hurdle S. (R), Belmont Park, June 7, $107,100, 4yo

& up, non-winners over hurdles prior to March 1, 2000, 2½mT, 4:49.27, PRAISE THE PRINCE (NZ), Pelagos (Fr), War Talk. 10 started.

MEADOWLANDS CUP H.-G2, The Meadowlands, Sept. 28, $500,000, 3yo & up, 1⅛m, 1:47.11, GANDER, Broken Vow, Include. 5 started.

Meafara S., Arlington Park, Aug. 3, $63,250, 3yo, f, 6f, 1:10.87, SPANISH GLITTER, For Elise, Hazino. 6 started.

Mecke S., Calder Race Course, Dec. 1, $100,000, 2yo, 1$\frac{1}{16}$mT, 1:42.22, POLITICAL ATTACK, Finality, Deeliteful Guy. 12 started.

Megan's Interco S., Turf Paradise, May 22, $24,000, 3yo & up, 1mT, 1:35.98, SNOHOMISH LOOT, Credit Call, Vaclav (Arg). 8 started.

Melair S. (R), Hollywood Park, April 28, $150,000, 3yo, f, California-bred, 6½f, 1:17, CHANNING WAY, Comedy Class, Warren's Whistle. 6 started.

Memorial Day H., Mountaineer Park, May 28, $58,525, 3yo & up, 1m (originally scheduled at 7½f on the turf), 1:36.65, NATURE, Boy Genius, Mister Mud. 8 started.

Memorial Day H., Calder Race Course, May 28, $75,000, 3yo & up, 1$\frac{1}{16}$m, 1:45.81, HAL'S HOPE, American Halo, Tahkodha Hills. 7 started.

Memorial S. (R), Fort Erie, Oct. 8, $57,250, 3yo & up, f & m, starters at Fort Erie at least twice in 2001, 1$\frac{1}{16}$m, 1:45.58, NATIVE WAGER, Melo Note, Signs of Glory. 9 started.

Merial S. (R), Hollywood Park, April 28, $70,000, 3yo & up, California-bred non-winners of $3,000 other than maiden, claiming, or starter or non-winners of two races, 1$\frac{1}{16}$m, 1:43, VALIANT WONDER, Cowboy Ballad, Waingarth. 10 started.

Merrillville S. (R), Hoosier Park, Oct. 13, $42,950, 3yo & up, f & m, Indiana-bred, 6f, 1:12.62, MARCIANN, Heresyour Chickey, Celona's Girl. 8 started.

Merry Time S. (R), Thistledown, June 9, $50,000, 3yo & up, f & m, Ohio-bred, 1$\frac{1}{16}$m, 1:44.98, BEATMICHIGANAGAIN, Belle of Liberty, Ms. Quimet. 11 started.

MERVYN LEROY H.-G2, Hollywood Park, May 5, $150,000, 3yo & up, 1$\frac{1}{16}$m, 1:42.02, FUTURAL, Skimming, Moonlight Charger. 5 started.

Mesa H., Turf Paradise, Oct. 27, $30,000, 3yo & up, f & m, 6½f, 1:15.33, TIME FOR ROMANCE, Top Bracket, Miss Pixie. 8 started.

Mesquite Breeders' Cup Mile S., Lone Star Park, June 9, $100,000, 3yo, f, 1m, 1:36.91, ZETA, Slapstick, Cheryl P. 5 started.

METROPOLITAN H.-G1, Belmont Park, May 28, $750,000, 3yo & up, 1m, 1:37.14, EXCITING STORY, Peeping Tom, Alannan. 10 started.

Miami Mile Breeders' Cup H., Calder Race Course, Sept. 3, $135,000, 3yo & up, 1mT, 1:33.75 (ECR), MR. LIVINGSTON, Honorable Pic, Pisces. 8 started.

Mia's Hope H., Calder Race Course, July 22, $32,100, 3yo & up, f & m, 1$\frac{1}{16}$m, 1:47.05, CASTLEBROOK, Coolbythepool, Tour Hostess. 6 started.

Michael G. Schaefer Mile S., Hoosier Park, Nov. 17, $103,800, 3yo & up, 1m, 1:35.59, FREON FLIER, Snuck In, Tiltam. 7 started.

Michigan Breeders' Governor's Cup H. (R), Great Lakes Downs, Aug. 27, $50,000, 3yo & up, Michigan-bred, 1$\frac{1}{16}$m, 1:47.28, THAT MONETARY, That Gift, Pongo Boy. 8 started.

Michigan Futurity (R), Great Lakes Downs, Oct. 26, $67,000, 2yo, Michigan-bred, 1m 70y, 1:49.84, EQUI POWER, To Be Springs, Match Break. 7 started.

Michigan Juvenile Fillies S. (R), Great Lakes Downs, Oct. 27, $64,750, 2yo, f, Michigan-bred, 1m 70y, 1:49.77, BORN TO DANCE, Part Magic, Salinas Regal Luck. 4 started.

Michigan Oaks (R), Great Lakes Downs, Sept. 15, $50,000, 3yo, f, Michigan-bred, 1$\frac{1}{16}$m, 1:50.21, EMPRESS LIVIA, Foreign Country, I Match Too. 9 started.

Michigan Sire S. (R), Great Lakes Downs, Oct. 5, $120,000, 2yo, c & g, eligible for the Michigan sire stakes program, 6f, 1:15.72, CAPABLE CAPERS, Lite Ruckus, Owens County. 9 started.

Michigan Sire S. (R), Great Lakes Downs, Oct. 5, $120,000, 2yo, f, eligible for the Michigan sire stakes program, 6f, 1:14.23, BORN TO DANCE, Midway Girl, Rock a Lot. 10 started.

Michigan Sire S. (R), Great Lakes Downs, Oct. 5, $120,000, 3yo, c & g, eligible for the Michigan sire stakes program, 1$\frac{1}{16}$m, 1:49.25, LITE UP, Secret Romeo, Blackstone Dreamer. 7 started.

Michigan Sire S. (R), Great Lakes Downs, Oct. 5, $120,000, 3yo, f, eligible for the Michigan sire stakes program, 1$\frac{1}{16}$m, 1:49.28, TANK GRRRL, Just Tricks, Empress Livia. 8 started.

Michigan Sire S. (R), Great Lakes Downs, Oct. 5, $120,000, 4yo & up, c & g, eligible for the Michigan sire stakes program, 1⅛m, 1:56.27, SMOOTH ROLLER, Catch the Dew, That Gift. 8 started.

Michigan Sire S. (R), Great Lakes Downs, Oct. 5, $120,000, 4yo & up, f & m, eligible for the Michigan sire stakes program, 1⅛m, 1:57.63, SEFAS ROSE, Flyinghannah, Destinys Draw. 9 started.

Middleground S., Lone Star Park, July 14, $101,000, 2yo, c & g, 5½f, 1:03.38, EXPLOSIVE TRUTH, Nuclear Assembly, Angela'stoughwater. 8 started.

Mid-Peninsula S. (R), Bay Meadows Fair, Aug. 12, $52,150, 2yo, f, California-bred, 5½f, 1:04.06, BRITETONZMYDAY, Gyrene, Asian Adventure. 6 started.

MIESQUE S.-G3, Hollywood Park, Nov. 23, $200,000, 2yo, f, 1mT, 1:36.38, FORTY ON LINE (GB), Riskaverse, Daisyago. 10 started.

Mike Lee S. (R), Belmont Park, June 30, $140,167, 3yo, New York-bred, 7f, 1:23.79, SOLAR DEPUTY, Sweet Ricky, Bakhoor. 14 started.

MILADY BREEDERS' CUP H.-G1, Hollywood Park, June 3, $254,300, 3yo & up, f & m, 1$\frac{1}{16}$m, 1:42.25, LAZY SLUSAN, Lady Melesi, Feverish. 6 started.

Mile Hi H., Yavapai Downs, Aug. 4, $10,000, 3yo & up, 1$\frac{1}{16}$m, 1:47.83, VACLAV (Arg), Venturesome Beau, Iron Heart. 7 started.

Miles Valentine Memorial Hurdle S., Fair Hill, May 28, $30,000, 4yo & up, abt2¼mT, 4:32.60, QUEL SENOR (Fr), Devil's Reach, Avanico. 7 started.

Millard Harrell S. (R), Charles Town, Sept. 15, $25,700, 3yo, West Virginia-bred nominated to WVBC, 7f, 1:27.55, PAST TENCE, Parisian Lord, Wahama High. 5 started.

Millarville Derby, Millarville, July 1, $3,850, 3yo & up, 1⅛m, 2:00, RUNAWAY DON, End Zone, Notnomde. 7 started.

Miller Lite S., Lone Star Park, June 23, $75,000, 3yo & up, f & m, 5fT, :56.03, HALLOWED DREAMS, Sweet and Firm, Argentina Avenue. 6 started.

Mill Race S., Philadelphia Park, July 28, $50,000, 3yo & up, f & m, 5fT, :57.92, MALIE'S PRINCESS, Merry Princess, Atlanticcitydancer. 10 started.

Milwaukee Avenue H. (R), Sportsman's Park, March 31, $75,000, 3yo & up, Illinois-bred, 1$\frac{1}{16}$m, 1:46.27, CHICAGO SIX, Mr. High Tops, R. Little Redhead. 8 started.

Minneapolis H., Canterbury Park, Sept. 3, $40,000, 3yo & up, f & m, 1$\frac{1}{16}$mT, 1:42.25, BINALEGEND, Be My Friend, Picnic Spread. 11 started.

Minnesota Classic Championship S. (R), Canterbury Park, Aug. 18, $44,750, 3yo & up, Minnesota-bred, 1$\frac{1}{16}$m, 1:45.95, NIX OF TIME, Bleu Victoriate, Bucnasty. 6 started.

Minnesota Derby (R), Canterbury Park, July 28, $51,745, 3yo, c & g, Minnesota-bred, 1m 70y, 1:45.55, NOW PLAYING, Timberwolf Power, Dance Hall Prize. 8 started.

Minnesota Distaff Classic Championship S. (R), Canterbury Park, Aug. 18, $43,800, 3yo & up, f & m, Minnesota-bred, 1$\frac{1}{16}$m, 1:47.98, BLITZ JOI, Shesa Shesa, Playful Edition. 6 started.

Minnesota Distaff Sprint Championship S. (R), Canterbury Park, Aug. 18, $38,550, 3yo & up, f & m, Minnesota-bred, 6f, 1:13.53, NIDARI, Muir Eireann, Blumin Bauble. 7 started.

Minnesota HBPA Classic H., Canterbury Park, July 7, $25,450, 3yo & up, 6½f, 1:16.59, SHOT OF GOLD, Satchmo, Deher's Turn. 6 started.

Minnesota HBPA Turf Classic H., Canterbury Park, July 7, $25,525, 3yo & up, f & m, 1mT, 1:37.56, PICNIC SPREAD, Diablos First Lady, Runaway Magic. 11 started.

Minnesota Juvenile Sprint S. (R), Canterbury Park, July 29, $37,275, 2yo, Minnesota-bred, 5½f, 1:06.46, DOUBLE DUCES, J. P. Jet, Toga Switch. 9 started.

Minnesota Oaks (R), Canterbury Park, July 28, $53,103, 3yo, f, Minnesota-bred, 1m 70y, 1:45.76, BLUMIN BAUBLE, Timbia, Fancy Injun. 9 started.

Minnesota Sprint Championship S. (R), Canterbury Park, Aug. 18, $38,950, 3yo & up, Minnesota-bred, 6f, 1:10.96, CROCROCK, Not So Fast Brutus, Tushar. 7 started.

Minstrel S., Louisiana Downs, Sept. 8, $40,000, 2yo, 6f, 1:11.01, TRICKY STORM, Ruling Star, Chief Black Hawk. 7 started.

MINT JULEP H.-G3, Churchill Downs, May 19, $113,600, 4yo & up, f & m, 1$\frac{1}{16}$mT, 1:42.88, MEGANS BLUFF, Sitka, Good Game. 10 started.

Miracle Wood S., Laurel Park, Jan. 27, $57,150, 3yo, 1$\frac{1}{16}$m, 1:45.96, TALK IS MONEY, Marciano, Bay Eagle. 8 started.

Miss America H., Bay Meadows, April 8, $100,000, 3yo & up, f & m, 1mT, 1:36.13, ALEXINE (Arg), Matiere Grise (Fr), Vapor Trail. 10

started.

Miss California S. (R), Bay Meadows, May 27, $60,400, 3yo, f, California-bred, 6f, 1:09.21, CHANNING WAY, Exquisite Woman, Bafferta. 6 started.

Miss Gibson County S., Turf Paradise, Nov. 17, $22,900, 2yo, f, 6f, 1:10, WINTER MEETING, Whitegoldndiamonds, Bella Cash. 8 started.

Miss Grillo S., Aqueduct, Nov. 4, $86,700, 2yo, f, 1⅛mT, 1:51.61, RISKAVERSE, Lujien Lujien, Kathy K D. 12 started.

Miss Houston S., Sam Houston Race Park, Nov. 24, $25,000, 2yo, f, 7f, 1:25.70, WAYNE'S PRINCESS, Point Gained, French Lass. 8 started.

Miss Indiana S. (R), Hoosier Park, Nov. 16, $74,450, 2yo, f, Indiana-bred, 6f, 1:12.15, AMANDA'S CROWN, Connies Travels, Meladrie. 11 started.

Miss Indy Anna S., Suffolk Downs, May 19, $25,000, 3yo & up, f & m, 6f, 1:12.11, CAJUN SEASON, She Rules, Valid Miss Chain. 6 started.

Mississippi Futurity (R), Fair Grounds, Nov. 30, $26,275, 2yo, Mississippi-owned, 6f, 1:11.40, CLEVER SEVEN, Glitzi's Classic, Little Joe Tubb. 7 started.

Miss Jealski H., Calder Race Course, June 25, $32,760, 3yo & up, f & m, 1m, 1:40.77, CASTLEBROOK, No Mo Strawberries, Raponera. 8 started.

Miss Kansas City H., The Woodlands, Oct. 21, $25,000, 3yo & up, f & m, 1$\frac{1}{16}$m, 1:48.40, CELTIC SMOKE, Dunham's Social, Run Around Sue. 7 started.

Miss Liberty S., The Meadowlands, Oct. 19, $100,000, 3yo, f, 1$\frac{1}{16}$mT, 1:43, MEDIA ACCESS, (DH) Atrial Flutter, (DH) The Goddess Athird. 12 started.

Miss Mommy S., Hawthorne Race Course, Dec. 30, $44,500, 2yo, f, 6½f, 1:19.21, ELEMENTARY, Delicatessa, Tejano Honey. 9 started.

Miss Moneypenny S. (R), Fort Erie, Sept. 3, $63,650, 3yo & up, f & m, starters at Fort Erie at least twice in 2001, 1$\frac{1}{16}$mT, 1:45.59, RING OF FLOWERS, Signs of Glory, Ellesmere. 12 started.

Miss Oceana S., Arlington Park, Sept. 15, $54,000, 3yo, f, 6f, 1:10.87, SPANISH GLITTER, Raintree Lake, Southern Tour. 7 started.

Miss Ohio S. (R), Thistledown, Aug. 25, $40,000, 2yo, f, Ohio-bred, 6f, 1:12.48, BATES CHOICE, Beau's Regal Gal, Cat Crossing. 7 started.

Miss Preakness S., Pimlico, May 17, $100,000, 3yo, f, 6f, 1:11.20, KIMBRALATA, Carafe, Stormy Pick. 5 started.

Miss Spin S., Laurel Park, March 3, $67,260, 4yo & up, f. & m, 6½f, 1:17.43, ELEKTRALINE, Silent Valay, Prized Stamp. 7 started.

Miss Woodford S., Monmouth Park, Sept. 2, $50,000, 3yo, f, 6f, 1:10.84, STORMY PICK, Irish Fantasy, Carafe. 8 started.

Missy Good S. (R), Penn National Race Course, June 30, $25,000, 3yo & up, f. & m, Pennsylvania-bred, 6f, 1:11.15, MALVERN ROSE, Worth Waiting, Reef Club. 6 started.

Mister Diz S. (R), Pimlico, Sept. 15, $50,000, 3yo & up, Maryland-bred, 5fT, :56.11, ELBERTON, Tyaskin, Maypole Dance. 8 started.

Misty Isle S., Arlington Park, Aug. 4, $64,000, 3yo, f, 1$\frac{1}{16}$mT, 1:42.68, SLUICE, Twilite Tryst, Sheikh Away. 7 started.

Mo Bay H., Delaware Park, July 10, $59,300, 3yo & up, abt5fT, :57.08, GRANGEVILLE, Rudirudy, Just Call Me Carl. 7 started.

Moccasin S., Hollywood Park, Nov. 18, $100,000, 2yo, f, 7f, 1:23.45, AYANNA, Ponche de Leona, Unforgettable R N. 12 started.

MODESTY H.-G3, Arlington Park, July 28, $150,000, 3yo & up, f & m, 1$\frac{3}{16}$mT, 1:55.47, IOYA TWO, Megans Bluff, Solvig. 11 started.

Mo Exception H., Calder Race Course, Sept. 22, $37,400, 3yo & up, 6½f, 1:18.02, CALLIE AND JAKE, (DH) Dancing Guy, (DH) Alice's Notebook. 7 started.

Mohawk H. (R), Belmont Park, Oct. 20, $150,000, 3yo & up, New York-bred, 1⅛mT, 1:47.87, I'M ALL YOURS, Statement, Celtic Sky. 12 started.

Molly Brown H., Arapahoe Park, June 24, $27,300, 3yo & up, f & m, 6f, 1:10, ONE FOXY LADY, Gollygot, Ashley Anne's Wish. 7 started.

MOLLY PITCHER BREEDERS' CUP H.-G2, Monmouth Park, June 30, $300,000, 3yo & up, f & m, 1$\frac{1}{16}$m, 1:43.79, MARCH MAGIC, Vivid Sunset, Shine Again. 7 started.

Moment to Buy H., Golden Gate Fields, Dec. 2, $59,050, 3yo, f, 1$\frac{1}{16}$m (originally scheduled on the turf), 1:41.78, LINDSAY JEAN, Super Tuesday, De Goddaughter. 9 started.

Mom's Command S., Suffolk Downs, Oct. 27, $25,000, 2yo, f, 6f, 1:14.52, MRSCOPPOLASKITCHEN, Eternal Reigns, Boardwalk Baby. 9 started.

Mona Lake S., Great Lakes Downs, Aug. 31, $25,000, 3yo, f, 7f, 1:26.62, JUST TRICKS, Ozilda's Karen, Foreign Country. 8 started.

Monique Rene H., Louisiana Downs, Aug. 26, $49,000, 3yo & up, f & m, 6f, 1:09.31, MIDGE TOO, Prized Amberpro, Hallowed Dreams. 5 started.

Monmouth Beach S., Monmouth Park, June 9, $50,000, 3yo & up, f & m, 1m 70y, 1:41.85, WITTENBERG, Powerful Package, Resort. 8 started.

MONMOUTH BREEDERS' CUP OAKS-G2, Monmouth Park, July 28, $250,000, 3yo, f, 1⅛m, 1:51.02, UNBRIDLED ELAINE, Unrestrained, Indy Glory. 7 started.

MONROVIA H.-G3, Santa Anita Park, Dec. 31, $118,150, 3yo & up, f & m, abt6½fT, 1:15.09, PAGA (Arg), Twin Set (Ger), Impeachable. 13 started.

Montauk H. (R), Aqueduct, Dec. 2, $81,000, 3yo & up, f & m, New York-bred, 1⅛m, 1:51.96, LOVELY AMANDA, Too Scarlet, Along Came Mary. 7 started.

Montclair H., Golden Gate Fields, Jan. 20, $62,175, 4yo & up, 6f, 1:07.55 (NTR), EL DORADO SHOOTER, Roaring Red, Highland Gold. 5 started.

Moonbeam H. (R), Great Lakes Downs, Aug. 18, $50,000, 3yo & up, f & m, Michigan-bred, 1$\frac{1}{16}$m, 1:48.41, FLYINGHANNAH, True Ruby, Prima Gold. 9 started.

Moonlight Jig S. (R), Pimlico, Oct. 8, $40,000, 3yo & up, f & m, non-winners of a $35,000 stake in 2001, 1$\frac{1}{16}$m, 1:44.22, BRIG, Unbridled Lady, Powerful Package. 9 started.

Morven S., The Meadowlands, Oct. 5, $50,000, 2yo, 5fT, :57.97, NUMBERS MAN, True Genius, Deeliteful Guy. 10 started.

MORVICH H.-G3, Santa Anita Park, Nov. 5, $107,800, 3yo & up, abt6½fT, 1:11.46 (ECR), EL CIELO, Speak in Passing, Islander. 6 started.

MOTHER GOOSE S.-G1, Belmont Park, June 30, $250,000, 3yo, f, 1⅛m, 1:47.19, FLEET RENEE, Real Cozzy, Exogenous. 10 started.

Mountaineer HBPA H. (R), Mountaineer Park, Oct. 23, $57,350, 3yo & up, f & m, starters at Mountaineer at least three times in 2001, 6f, 1:12.14, DEMITRYST, More d'Amour, Diamond Affair. 9 started.

Mountaineer Mile H., Mountaineer Park, Nov. 3, $73,300, 3yo & up, 1m, 1:37.53, TOUR THE HIVE, Little Lee, Ewer All Wet. 8 started.

Mountain State H., Mountaineer Park, July 3, $57,400, 3yo & up, 6f, 1:09.76, JEANIES ROB, Holiday Music, B. L.'s Ghost. 7 started.

Mountain Valley S., Oaklawn Park, Feb. 10, $50,000, 3yo, 6f, 1:10.33, SON OF ROCKET, Firststatedeposit, Much too Tough. 9 started.

Mount Elbert H. (R), Arapahoe Park, Aug. 4, $30,000, 3yo & up, c & g, Colorado-bred, 1$\frac{1}{16}$m, 1:43.60, DARN TOOTIN, Hot Wheels, Well Planned. 10 started.

Mount Royal H., Stampede Park, May 20, $35,820, 3yo, f, 6f, 1:12.40, BRIGHTON BELLE, Shudabinajumper, Little Lolitta. 9 started.

Mount Vernon H. (R), Belmont Park, June 24, $83,475, 3yo & up, f & m, New York-bred, 1⅛mT, 1:48.05, TRUEBREADPUDDING, Key Oui, Polly Jo. 9 started.

M. R. Jenkins Memorial H., Stampede Park, May 6, $34,980, 4yo & up, f & m, 6f, 1:10.80, CRIMSON HUE, Slewability, Golden Remark. 8 started.

Mr. Nickerson H., Philadelphia Park, May 19, $50,000, 3yo & up, 6f, 1:10.28, HOLIDAY MUSIC, Copelan's Number, Personal First. 5 started.

Mr. Prime Minister H., Hastings Park Racecourse, Aug. 19, $37,975, 3yo, 6½f, 1:16.47, I'M FREE, Kat Dancer, Paladdie. 7 started.

MR. PROSPECTOR H.-G3, Gulfstream Park, Jan. 15, $120,000, 3yo & up, 6f, 1:09.63, ISTINTAJ, Miners Gamble, Smokin Pete. 13 started.

Mrs. Penny S. (R), Philadelphia Park, Oct. 6, $50,000, 3yo & up, f & m, Pennsylvania-bred, 1$\frac{1}{16}$mT, 1:45.66, ARTY'SVIRGINIAGIRL, Debutante's Dream, Final One. 9 started.

MRS. REVERE S.-G2, Churchill Downs, Nov. 17, $172,500, 3yo, f, 1$\frac{1}{16}$mT, 1:42.86, SNOW DANCE, Stylish, Cozy Island. 10 started.

Ms. S., Portland Meadows, Feb. 24, $8,400, 3yo, f, 6f, 1:14.08, DAWSONS LANDING, Abrupt, Nancys Blazen Lady. 7 started.

Ms. Southern Ohio S. (R), River Downs, Aug. 5, $45,000, 3yo & up, f & m, Ohio-bred, 1$\frac{1}{16}$mT, 1:42.80, DOUBLY FUN, Shamrock Slew, Cabot Cove. 10 started.

MTOBA Stallion Service Auction S. (R), Great Lakes Downs, July 27, $18,214, 3yo, progeny of services sold at the MTOBA Stallion Service Auction, 7f, 1:30.11, ISLAND N ABREEZE, I Ain't Talkin, Parisall. 7 started.

Mt. Rainier Breeders' Cup H., Emerald Downs, July 29, $86,250,

3yo & up, 1 1/16m, 1:42, MAKORS MARK, Kittys Link, Crowning Meeting. 6 started.

Mt. St. Helens S., Portland Meadows, April 7, $8,500, 3yo, f, 1m, 1:42.23, HURRICANE RYLIE, Annie N Will, Moon Pilot. 8 started.

M. Tyson Gilpin S. (R), Delaware Park, Oct. 28, $43,200, 2yo, Virginia-bred, 6f, 1:15.57, CHAMBORD LIQUEUR, Cozy Spirit, Kris's Prayer. 7 started.

Muscogee Nation S., Fair Meadows at Tulsa, Aug. 4, $27,965, 3yo & up, f & m, 6½f, 1:18.60, GOLDEN HURRICANE, Snappy Okie, Mrsknowitall. 10 started.

Muskegon Classic H., Great Lakes Downs, Aug. 4, $50,000, 3yo & up, 1m, 1:43.19, Q COMMERCIAL JETTE, Secret Romeo, That Monetary. 10 started.

Muskoka S. (R), Woodbine, Sept. 3, $102,700, 2yo, f, Canadian-bred CTHS Sales yearlings, 7f, 1:25.82, MISS NOIRE, Parisia, Mulrainy. 9 started.

MY CHARMER H.-G3, Calder Race Course, Dec. 8, $100,000, 3yo & up, f & m, 1⅛mT, 1:49.85, BATIQUE, Please Sign In, Wander Mom. 12 started.

My Charmer S., Turfway Park, Dec. 8, $50,000, 3yo & up, f & m, 1 1/16m, 1:45.23, FAST DELIVERY, Miss Pickums, Momentous. 10 started.

My Dear Girl S. (R), Calder Race Course, Oct. 13, $400,000, 2yo, f, progeny of eligible stallions standing in Florida, 1 1/16m, 1:46.08, BLISSFUL KISS, Ms Brookski, Sweep Princess. 9 started.

My Dear S., Woodbine, June 23, $110,300, 2yo, f, 5f, :58.79, JEALOUS FORUM, Bold Kiss, Playing Games. 6 started.

My Fair Lady S., Suffolk Downs, May 5, $25,000, 3yo & up, f & m, 1m 70yT, 1:43.32, STEP WITH STYLE, Buzzing B's, Hurri to the Line. 9 started.

My Friend Russ S. (R), Delaware Park, Sept. 17, $61,800, 3yo, non-winners of three races or for a claiming price of $80,000, 1mT, 1:36.69, STAUCH, Dancing On the Bar, Jakey D. 9 started.

My Juliet S., Philadelphia Park, May 5, $48,500, 3yo & up, f & m, 6f, 1:10.26, ELEKTRALINE, Crescent Coast, Mountain Girl. 4 started.

My Luck Runs North H., Calder Race Course, July 16, $32,040, 3yo & up, 7f, 1:24.30, BUILT UP, Callie and Jake, Puchungo (Per). 6 started.

Mystery Jet S. (R), Suffolk Downs, March 17, $25,000, 3yo, f, Massachusetts-bred, 6f, 1:13.92, OH SHAM BABY, Sunlit Ridge, Misty Isle. 9 started.

Naked Greed S., Calder Race Course, June 10, $50,000, 3yo, 6f, 1:12.85, NORTHEND, Gallant Frolic, Hana Highway. 9 started.

Nanaimo H., Hastings Park Racecourse, July 22, $37,441, 3yo, f, 1 1/16m, 1:45.11, LADY'S JEWEL, Catahoula Rose, Inish Glora. 8 started.

Nancy's Glitter S. (R), Calder Race Course, Aug. 25, $54,000, 3yo & up, f & m, Florida-bred, 1 1/16m, 1:48.16, CASTLEBROOK, Coolbythepool, Racing for Pahm. 7 started.

Nandi S. (R), Woodbine, July 28, $134,625, 2yo, f, progeny of eligible stallions standing in Ontario, 6f, 1:13.50, JADE EYED, Matter of Law, Parisia. 8 started.

Nany H., Calder Race Course, Sept. 24, $32,540, 3yo & up, f & m, 6½f, 1:19.18, TOO MANY, Valid Forbes, Sugar N Spice. 6 started.

NASHUA S.-G3, Belmont Park, Oct. 26, $109,300, 2yo, 1m, 1:37.61, LISTEN HERE, Monthir, Thunder Days. 6 started.

NASSAU COUNTY S.-G2, Belmont Park, May 9, $150,000, 3yo, f, 7f, 1:23.02, CAT CHAT, Xtra Heat, Shooting Party. 6 started.

Nassau H., Belmont Park, Oct. 28, $139,200, 3yo & up, 1mT, 1:33.62, ALDEBARAN, Capsized, Tubrok. 7 started.

NASSAU S.-G3, Woodbine, June 3, $196,175, 3yo & up, f & m, 1 1/16mT, 1:47.31, ONLY TO YOU, Heliotrope, Bristol Pistol. 7 started.

Nastique S., Delaware Park, May 20, $76,800, 3yo & up, f & m, 1 1/16m, 1:46.14, UNDER THE RUG, Weekend Kaper, Zenith. 11 started.

NATALMA S.-G3 (1st Div.), Woodbine, Sept. 8, $163,250, 2yo, f, 1mT, 1:34.66, GINGER GOLD, West Madisyn, Southey. 7 started.

NATALMA S.-G3 (2nd Div.), Woodbine, Sept. 8, $144,850, 2yo, f, 1mT, 1:35.44, LUSH SOLDIER, Strait From Texas, Bala. 9 started.

National Hunt Cup Hurdle H., Malvern, May 19, $46,500, 4yo & up, abt2¼mT, 4:28.80, AL SKYWALKER, Darn Tipalarm, Popular Gigalo. 4 started.

NATIONAL JOCKEY CLUB H.-G3, Sportsman's Park, April 22, $200,000, 4yo & up, 1⅛m, 1:48.28, CHICAGO SIX, Guided Tour, Glacial. 5 started.

National Jockey Club Oaks, Sportsman's Park, April 14, $150,000, 3yo, f, 1 1/16m, 1:43.83, SCOOP, Unbridled Lassie, Giving Noreen. 5 started.

NATIONAL MUSEUM OF RACING HALL OF FAME H.-G2, Saratoga Race Course, Aug. 6, $150,000, 3yo, 1⅛mT, 1:47.94, BAPTIZE, Strategic Partner, Saint Verre. 7 started.

Native Dancer S., Laurel Park, Jan. 27, $56,200, 4yo & up, 1⅛m, 1:52.21, DO I EVER, Ewer All Wet, Tibado. 8 started.

NATIVE DIVER H.-G3, Hollywood Park, Dec. 9, $100,000, 3yo & up, 1⅛m, 1:48.24, MOMENTUM, Euchre, Last Parade (Arg). 7 started.

Navajo Princess S., The Meadowlands, Oct. 19, $100,000, 3yo & up, f & m, 1⅜mT, 2:15.33, CRUISE ALONG, Queue, Chez Cherie (GB). 11 started.

NEARCTIC H.-G2, Woodbine, June 24, $223,400, 3yo & up, 6fT, 1:08.86, MR. EPPERSON, Airbourne Command, Alea Iacta Est. 9 started.

Nebraska Breeders' Debutante S. (R), Columbus, Sept. 9, $14,250, 2yo, f, nominated to the Nebraska Breeders' Sweepstakes, 6f, 1:22.20, BENGAL GAL, Magic Trump, Ginger Moon. 5 started.

Nebraska Breeders' Juvenile S. (R), Columbus, Sept. 9, $14,250, 2yo, c & g, nominated to the Nebraska Breeders' Sweepstakes, 6f, 1:19, DAZZLING J. R., C. C. Diamond, Mr Clearwater. 5 started.

Nebraska Breeders' Sophomore Fillies S. (R), Lincoln State Fair, July 8, $14,250, 3yo, f, Nebraska Breeders Sweepstakes eligible, 1m 70y, 1:42, CLAMATO ROSE, Burning Memories, Missy's Pride. 5 started.

Nebraska Breeders' Sophomore S. (R), Lincoln State Fair, July 8, $13,110, 3yo, Nebraska Breeders Sweepstakes eligible, 1 1/16m, 1:46.20, TAUKE, Watch Me Dazzle, Harvey Bengal. 3 started.

Nebraska Derby, Fonner Park, April 21, $30,960, 3yo, 1m, 1:39.60, COUNT BASIC, Tate's Way, Tauke. 7 started.

Nebraskaland H. (R), Horsemen's Park, July 21, $27,000, 4yo & up, Nebraska-bred, 1m, 1:38.40, LET ME LEAD, Slip and Slide, Doug's Shadow. 9 started.

Needles S., Calder Race Course, Oct. 6, $50,000, 3yo, 1 1/16mT, 1:43.40, TV SPORTS DIRECTOR, Tour of the Cat, Vikadontis. 12 started.

Nellie Morse S., Laurel Park, Jan. 20, $62,200, 4yo & up, f & m, 1 1/16m, 1:46.63, TOO TOO DIVINE, Sheldons Jet, Tookin Down. 8 started.

New Braunfels S., Retama Park, Aug. 25, $25,000, 3yo & up, f & m, 6f, 1:10.37, NOBODY'S FOOL, Secret Spender, Argentina Avenue. 6 started.

New Castle H., Delaware Park, Aug. 19, $101,500, 3yo & up, f & m, 1⅛mT, 1:48.47, QUEUE, Batique, Minkie. 10 started.

NEW HAMPSHIRE SWEEPSTAKES H.-G3, Rockingham Park, June 23, $200,000, 3yo & up, abt1⅛mT, 1:46.32, HAP, Gander, Flash of Joy. 7 started.

New Jersey Futurity (R), The Meadowlands, Nov. 9, $80,000, 2yo, c & g, New Jersey-bred, 6f, 1:09.92, PARFY'S LEGACY, Numbers Man, Our Wildcat. 9 started.

New Jersey Futurity (R), The Meadowlands, Nov. 9, $80,000, 2yo, f, New Jersey-bred, 6f, 1:10.37, OUR COZZETTE, Ambers Smile, Willie's Luv. 8 started.

New Jersey Hunt Cup S., Far Hills, Oct. 20, $22,000, 4yo & up, abt3¾mT, 7:03.45, BREDESEN MOE, Where's Pepo, Charlie's Dewan. 6 started.

New Mexico Breeder's Association H. (R), SunRay Park, Sept. 16, $56,050, 3yo & up, New Mexico-bred, 1m, 1:38.40, SAN FELIPE'S KING, Pack and Drift, Bobby Blurr. 6 started.

New Mexico Distaff H. (R), SunRay Park, Sept. 2, $56,400, 3yo & up, f & m, New Mexico-bred, 6½f, 1:18.20, CHARLOTTE'S EGO, Me a Spirit Too, Nupar. 9 started.

New Mexico Racing Commission H. (R), Sunland Park, Jan. 27, $67,300, 3yo & up, f & m, New Mexico-bred, 6f, 1:09.20, YULLA YULLA, Jewel From Texas, Gollygot. 7 started.

New Mexico Racing Commission H. (R), Sunland Park, Dec. 1, $103,900, 3yo & up, f & m, New Mexico-bred, 6f, 1:10.45, YULLA YULLA, Gollygot, Soaring Ego. 12 started.

New Mexico State Fair Breeders' Derby (R), The Downs at Albuquerque, Sept. 22, $48,781, 3yo, New Mexico-bred, 1 1/16m, 1:40.74, CIENTO, Mia's Lad, Don's Ferrari. 10 started.

New Mexico State Fair H., The Downs at Albuquerque, Sept. 23, $37,300, 3yo & up, 1⅛m, 1:49.63, OUT 'N ABOUT, C. D. Haj, Darn Tootin. 7 started.

NEW ORLEANS H.-G2, Fair Grounds, March 4, $500,000, 4yo & up, 1⅛m, 1:49.18, INCLUDE, Nite Dreamer, Valhol. 5 started.

New Providence S. (R), Woodbine, May 20, $128,875, 3yo & up, progeny of eligible stallions standing in Ontario, 6f, 1:12.01, KRZ RUCKUS, Code Name Louie, Great Defender. 6 started.

New Westminster S., Hastings Park Racecourse, Aug. 19, $38,080, 2yo, 6½f, 1:18.64, FULL GAINER, Colondelivery, Regal Soldier. 6 started.

New Year Maiden Sprint S., Sunland Park, Jan. 27, $25,513, 3yo, 5½f, 1:05.60, GEORGE W., Hadastar, Ebony Express. 9 started.

New Year's Eve H., Mountaineer Park, Dec. 31, $58,300, 3yo & up, f & m, 6f, 1:11.33, KEEPONDEALING, Marciann, Demitryst. 8 started.

New York Breeders' Futurity (R), Finger Lakes, Sept. 3, $137,900, 2yo, New York-bred, 6f, 1:11.51, SHESASTONECOLDFOX, Princess Dixie, White Ibis. 7 started.

New York Derby (R), Finger Lakes, July 28, $148,867, 3yo, New York-bred, 1 1/16m, 1:46.16, SWEET RICKY, Personal Pro, Unwaquoited Love. 8 started.

NEW YORK H.-G2, Belmont Park, July 14, $250,000, 3yo & up, f & m, 1¼mT, 1:59.63, ENGLAND'S LEGEND (Fr), Gaviola, Spook Express (SAf). 7 started.

New York Oaks (R), Finger Lakes, Sept. 3, $60,000, 3yo, f, New York-bred, 1 1/16m, 1:47.20, ALONG CAME MARY, Seeking It All, That Belongs to Me. 10 started.

New York Turf Writers Cup Steeplechase H., Saratoga Race Course, Aug. 30, $107,700, 4yo & up, abt2⅝mT, 4:12.04 (ECR), IT'S A GIGGLE, Canta Ke Brave, Praise the Prince (NZ). 6 started.

NEXT MOVE H.-G3, Aqueduct, March 31, $103,900, 3yo & up, f & m, 1⅛m, 1:50.65, ATELIER, Pompeii, Tax Affair. 4 started.

NIAGARA BREEDERS' CUP H.-G2, Woodbine, Sept. 1, $335,100, 3yo & up, 1½mT, 2:26.52, HONOR GLIDE, Royal Strand (Ire), Strike Smartly. 9 started.

Niagara S. (R), Finger Lakes, July 21, $30,000, 3yo, f, New York-bred, 6f, 1:12.57, WE'LL SEA YA, Aerobee, Mark's Mission. 13 started.

Nick Shuk Memorial S., Delaware Park, June 11, $75,900, 3yo, 1 1/16mT, 1:43.71, POTARO (Ire), Unaccountedlea, Punkin Head. 8 started.

Nicole S., Hawthorne Race Course, May 1, $44,750, 4yo & up, f & m, abt1 1/16mT, 1:43.39, GOLDEN ANTIGUA, Diablos First Lady, Tell It. 8 started.

NOBLE DAMSEL H.-G3, Belmont Park, Sept. 22, $113,800, 3yo & up, f & m, 1m (originally scheduled on the turf), 1:35.18, TUGGER, Shine Again, Tippity Witch. 6 started.

Noble Royalty H., Calder Race Course, Sept. 15, $50,000, 3yo & up, f & m, 1 1/16m, 1:42.55, CASTLEBROOK, Coolbythepool, Diana My Love. 5 started.

Noel Laing S., Montpelier, Nov. 3, $24,250, 4yo & up, abt2½mT, 4:39.40, AL SKYWALKER, Devil's Craft, Nijinsky's Pride (NZ). 5 started.

No Le Hace S., Retama Park, Oct. 27, $25,000, 3yo & up, 7½fT, 1:28.63, KRIS HAVINGFUNNOW, Tin Smithen, Shimmering Bronze. 12 started.

NORFOLK S.-G2, Santa Anita Park, Sept. 29, $250,000, 2yo, 1m, 1:37.16, ESSENCE OF DUBAI, Ibn Al Haitham (GB), Ecstatic. 6 started.

Norgor Derby, Ruidoso Downs, June 3, $16,400, 3yo, 6f, 1:11, LIVE SHOW, Timeless Note, I'm Not Bluffin. 7 started.

Norman Hall S. (R), Suffolk Downs, Dec. 22, $25,000, 2yo, Massachusetts-bred, 6f, 1:11.82, STYLISH SULTAN, Storm Lad, Jeremiah's Judge. 5 started.

Norman S., Remington Park, Oct. 7, $34,000, 3yo, 1mT, 1:34.40, SKIPJACK, Wow, Prideov Fappiano. 10 started.

Norristown H., Philadelphia Park, May 28, $50,000, 3yo & up, 1⅛m, 1:50.37, SICK AS A PARROT (GB), Tibado, Chronicle S. 8 started.

Northampton S. (R), Northampton Fair, Sept. 16, $15,600, 3yo & up, Massachusetts-bred, abt6½f, 1:20.69, ABIT ERATIC, Distinctly Carotic, Papa Ho Ho. 6 started.

North Dakota Derby, Assiniboia Downs, July 1, $19,600, 3yo, 1m, 1:42, NORTHERN CHEYENNE, Marco T, High Storada. 7 started.

North Dakota Futurity, Assiniboia Downs, Sept. 2, $25,480, 2yo, 6f, 1:16.80, BIG R, Winaferd, Twilight Ladd. 6 started.

North Dakota Stallion S. (R), Assiniboia Downs, Aug. 4, $19,600, 3yo, North Dakota-bred, 1 1/16m, 1:51.20, NORTHERN CHEYENNE, High Storada, Airingout. 5 started.

North Dakota Stallion S. (R), Assiniboia Downs, Aug. 19, $25,480, 2yo, eligible through the NDTA, 6f, 1:15, HALO ALO, Valentines Journey, Regal Polka. 8 started.

Northern Dancer S. (R), Laurel Park, Nov. 24, $75,000, 3yo, Maryland-bred, 1⅛m, 1:51.55, SARATOGA GAMES, Bada Bam Bada Boom, Loaded Brush. 6 started.

Northern Lights Debutante S. (R), Canterbury Park, Aug. 18, $56,115, 2yo, f, Minnesota-bred, 6f, 1:13.92, SUSIE BLUES, American Profit, Ashley's Affair. 12 started.

Northern Lights Futurity (R), Canterbury Park, Aug. 18, $55,998, 2yo, c & g, Minnesota-bred, 6f, 1:13.87, J. P. JET, One Trick Ata Time, Speedy Exit. 11 started.

Northern Spur S., Oaklawn Park, April 13, $50,000, 3yo, c & g, 1m, 1:36.88, COMPENDIUM, Gail's Drive, Afternoon Pleasure. 7 started.

Northern Wolf S., Laurel Park, Jan. 13, $55,500, 4yo & up, 5½f, 1:03.41, DR. MAX, Trounce, In C C's Honor. 7 started.

Northlands Oaks, Northlands Park, July 20, $34,351, 3yo, f, 1m, 1:38.80, LITTLE LOLITTA, C D Cool, Chickadee Creek. 7 started.

North Miami Beach S., Hialeah Park, March 18, $50,899, 3yo, 6f, 1:09.53, RICH COINS, Friday's a Comin', Tru Bull. 4 started.

North Randall S. (R), Thistledown, Aug. 11, $40,000, 3yo, Ohio-bred, 6f, 1:11.10, TURKOWAR, Blame It On Ruby, Reggie's Winner. 10 started.

Northwest Stallion S. (R), Emerald Downs, July 28, $36,000, 2yo, f, progeny of eligible stallions, 6½f, 1:18.60, IPPODAMIA, Midnight Margie, Wild Blackberries. 6 started.

Northwest Stallion S. (R), Emerald Downs, Aug. 4, $36,000, 2yo, c & g, progeny of eligible stallions, 6½f, 1:18.20, DEVIL'S ENEMY, Kenny Hawk, Slew of the Night. 11 started.

Not Surprising H., Calder Race Course, Sept. 3, $38,030, 3yo & up, 7f, 1:24.24, ALICE'S NOTEBOOK, Best of the Rest, Silver Jet. 9 started.

Nuit D'Amour H., Delaware Park, May 19, $56,260, 3yo, f, 6f, 1:10.15, KIDSAREFUN, Hunka Hunka Lori Z, Hennie's Honor. 4 started.

Nureyev S., Keeneland, Oct. 5, $83,025, 3yo & up, 5½fT, 1:02.22, MORLUC, Grangeville, Alea Iacta Est. 7 started.

Nursery S., Hollywood Park, May 19, $86,250, 2yo, f, 5f, :57.95, FERTILE, Georgia's Storm, Asian Adventure. 8 started.

Oakland H., Bay Meadows, April 21, $97,500, 3yo & up, 6f, 1:08.46, FREESPOOL, Amarillo Pride, Hopewell Heart. 4 started.

OAKLAWN BREEDERS' CUP S.-G3, Oaklawn Park, March 18, $200,000, 3yo & up, f & m, 1 1/16m, 1:44.30, HERITAGE OF GOLD, Lu Ravi, Ive Gota Bad Liver. 8 started.

OAKLAWN H.-G1, Oaklawn Park, April 7, $600,000, 4yo & up, 1⅛m, 1:48.15, TRADITIONALLY, Mr Ross, Wooden Phone. 7 started.

OAK LEAF S.-G1, Santa Anita Park, Sept. 30, $250,000, 2yo, f, 1m, 1:37.77, TALI'SLUCKYBUSRIDE, Imperial Gesture, Ms Louisett. 6 started.

Oakley S. (R), Colonial Downs, July 15, $40,000, 3yo, f, Virginia-bred or -sired, 1 1/16mT, 1:44.46, CLASS YANKEE, Royal Sting, Blue Hills. 8 started.

OAK TREE BREEDERS' CUP MILE S.-G2, Santa Anita Park, Oct. 7, $219,000, 3yo & up, 1mT, 1:33.21, VAL ROYAL (Fr), Thady Quill, I've Decided. 6 started.

OAK TREE DERBY-G2, Santa Anita Park, Oct. 13, $150,000, 3yo, 1⅛mT, 1:46.56, NO SLIP (Fr), Sligo Bay (Ire), Romanceishope. 9 started.

Obeah S., Delaware Park, June 24, $101,500, 3yo & up, f & m, 1⅛m, 1:51.20, UNDER THE RUG, Zenith, Irving's Baby. 10 started.

OBS Championship S. (R), Ocala Training Center, March 19, $100,000, 3yo, c & g, passed through the ring at an OBS sale, 1 1/16m, 1:47.60, SAINT DAMIEN, Saved by the Sword, A. P. Topper. 6 started.

OBS Championship S. (R), Ocala Training Center, March 19, $100,000, 3yo, f, passed through the ring at an OBS sale, 1 1/16m, 1:48.80, SEA MIST, Miss Annie Bea, Buzzing B's. 7 started.

OBS Sprint S. (R), Ocala Training Center, March 19, $50,000, 3yo, c & g, passed through the ring at an OBS sale, 6f, 1:13.20, ANTSINMYPANTS, Condensed Version, Twin Shooter. 7 started.

OBS Sprint S. (R), Ocala Training Center, March 19, $50,000, 3yo, f, passed through the ring at an OBS sale, 6f, 1:14.60, DARK ENDING, Dream Me, School of Deelites. 8 started.

Ocean Bay S., Turf Paradise, March 4, $22,600, 4yo & up, f & m, 1mT, 1:37.65, BALBOA PARK, Sea Side Queen, Look to Be Proud. 6 started.

Ocean Hotel S., Monmouth Park, June 24, $50,000, 3yo, f, 5fT, :56.38, SPARKLING NUMBER, Always On the Go, Hazino. 10 started.

OCEANPORT H.-G3, Monmouth Park, Aug. 5, $100,000, 3yo & up, 1 1/16mT, 1:40.39, KEY LORY, North East Bound, Crash Course. 13 started.

Oceanside S. (1st Div.) (R), Del Mar, July 18, $87,100, 3yo, nonwinners of a race worth $50,000 to the winner in 2001, 1mT, 1:35.90,

SIGFRETO, Sea to See, Mister Approval. 10 started.

Oceanside S. (2nd Div.) (R), Del Mar, July 18, $87,100, 3yo, non-winners of a race worth $50,000 to the winner in 2001, 1mT, 1:34.47, DR. PARK, Euribor (Ire), Our Main Man. 10 started.

Office Queen S., Calder Race Course, June 23, $50,000, 3yo, f, 1 1/16m, 1:49.59, MULTIPLICITY, Wander Mom, Rich Peace. 9 started.

Ogataul H. (R), Fonner Park, March 17, $18,200, 3yo & up, Nebraska-bred, 6f, 1:13.20, TY MAN, High Dice, Whatta Brave. 8 started.

Ohio Debutante H. (R), Thistledown, Sept. 1, $40,000, 3yo, f, Ohio-bred, 6f, 1:10.50, SCIOTO BOOTSKI, Eye Slew the City, Ashwood C C. 9 started.

OHIO DERBY-G2, Thistledown, Sept. 29, $300,000, 3yo, 1 1/8m, 1:48.66, WESTERN PRIDE, Woodmoon, Macho Uno. 6 started.

Ohio Freshman S. (R), Beulah Park, Nov. 18, $40,000, 2yo, Ohio-bred, 1 1/16m, 1:48.55, COAX ME CODY, Watch Me Fire, Mercer's Launch. 7 started.

Ohio Valley H., Mountaineer Park, May 29, $58,100, 3yo & up, f & m, 6f, 1:10.48, FREE OF CHARGE, Budding Blossom, Alma Mater. 10 started.

Oh Say S. (R), Delaware Park, Oct. 31, $59,900, 3yo & up, non-winners of a stake in 2001 or for an optional claiming price of $100,000, 5 1/2f, 1:04.45, TROUNCE, Jolie's Intention, Desktop. 8 started.

Oklahoma-Bred Thoroughbred Futurity (R), Blue Ribbon Downs, Sept. 3, $30,046, 2yo, Oklahoma-bred, 6f, 1:13.20, BE HE RUNS, Proper Mariner, Tontitown Lady. 8 started.

Oklahoma Classics Day Classic S. (R), Remington Park, Oct. 21, $90,000, 3yo & up, Oklahoma-bred, 1 1/16m, 1:44.09, MR ROSS, Peyvon, Vince. 5 started.

Oklahoma Classics Day Distaff S. (R), Remington Park, Oct. 21, $50,000, 3yo & up, f & m, Oklahoma-bred, 1m 70y, 1:42.91, DEVOUT SINNER, Voladora, Fastybutnasty. 8 started.

Oklahoma Classics Day Lassie S. (R), Remington Park, Oct. 21, $50,000, 2yo, f, Oklahoma-bred, 6f, 1:11.43, BAYAKOA'S IMAGE, Here Comes Kari, Tontitown Lady. 12 started.

Oklahoma Classics Day Sprint S. (R), Remington Park, Oct. 21, $50,000, 3yo & up, Oklahoma-bred, 6f, 1:09.42, MEDIUM RARE, Expert, Big Bay Brite. 9 started.

Oklahoma Classics Day Starter H. (R), Remington Park, Oct. 21, $25,000, 3yo & up, Oklahoma-bred, 7f, 1:23.39, ITCHISLEW PARK, Pop I, Suprise Package. 7 started.

Oklahoma Classics Day Turf S. (R), Remington Park, Oct. 21, $50,000, 3yo & up, Oklahoma-bred, 1mT, 1:36.41, BAJA HARRI, Halo Enclosed, Mahal. 7 started.

Oklahoma Classics Day Juvenile S. (R), Remington Park, Oct. 21, $50,000, 2yo, c & g, Oklahoma-bred, 6f, 1:10.55, APRIL'S LUCKY BOY, Expensive Risk, Mighty Beau. 8 started.

OKLAHOMA DERBY-G3, Remington Park, Aug. 12, $300,000, 3yo, 1 1/8m, 1:49.79, TOP HIT, Unbridled Time, Compendium. 6 started.

Oklahoma Derby (R), Fair Meadows at Tulsa, Aug. 4, $45,000, 3yo, Oklahoma-bred, 4f, :45.60, HERE COMES REBEL, Danlee, Zoyie. 10 started.

Old Hickory S., Fair Grounds, Nov. 24, $60,000, 2yo, c & g, 5 1/2f, 1:05.45, LEAD BY EXAMPLE, Walk in the Snow, Far Away Bell. 10 started.

Old Ironsides S., Suffolk Downs, June 2, $25,000, 3yo & up, 1m 70y, 1:43.70, FLASH OF JOY, Yasou Family, Lujean. 8 started.

Old Line Policy S., Turf Paradise, May 14, $23,900, 3yo, 6 1/2f, 1:17.13, EX KAY E, Old Woody, Look to Luke. 5 started.

Old South H., Louisiana Downs, Oct. 28, $25,000, 3yo & up, f & m, abt1 1/16mT, 1:42.50, MIMI'S TIZZY, Wild Squaw, Due to Win. 8 started.

Omaha H., Horsemen's Park, July 22, $100,000, 3yo & up, 1m, 1:35.80 (NTR), SURE SHOT BISCUIT, Battle Mountain, Fan the Flame. 5 started.

Omnibus S., Monmouth Park, Aug. 26, $75,000, 3yo & up, f & m, 1 1/16mT, 1:41.44, ZEITING (Ire), Cousin Gigi, Ladies Night In. 7 started.

One Dreamer S. (R), Gulfstream Park, March 10, $121,600, 3yo & up, f & m, Florida-bred, 1m, 1:35.13, LAURICA, Siberian Mirage, Silver Bandana. 9 started.

Ontario Colleen H., Woodbine, Aug. 26, $145,600, 3yo, f, 1mT, 1:37.26, SOUNDTRACK, Libretto, Skipping Stone. 10 started.

Ontario County S. (R), Finger Lakes, July 14, $30,000, 3yo, New York-bred, 6f, 1:12.04, CRISPY JET, Unwaquoited Love, Graceful Devil. 9 started.

Ontario Damsel S. (R), Woodbine, July 2, $146,880, 3yo, f, progeny of eligible stallions standing in Ontario, 6 1/2fT, 1:15.78, HIGHLAND MOOD, Bel Serenata, Chopinina. 6 started.

Ontario Debutante S., Woodbine, Aug. 12, $117,800, 2yo, f, 6f, 1:10.91, PLATEL, Jealous Forum, Ginger Gold. 8 started.

Ontario Fashion H., Woodbine, Oct. 27, $115,000, 3yo & up, f & m, 6f, 1:11.11, FEATHERS, El Prado Essence, Dreams Go Bye. 10 started.

Ontario Lassie S. (R), Woodbine, Nov. 25, $144,180, 2yo, f, Canadian-bred, 1 1/16m, 1:46.34, WHAT A BREEZE, Gonetofarr, Halo Alfaari. 5 started.

Ontario Matron H., Woodbine, June 17, $150,500, 3yo & up, f & m, 1 1/16m, 1:44.36, MOUNTAIN ANGEL, Nymphenburg, Gandria. 8 started.

On Trust H. (R), Hollywood Park, Nov. 22, $102,550, 3yo & up, California-bred, 7 1/2f, 1:28.65, STORMY JACK, Waingarth, Ceeband. 7 started.

Open Fire S., Delaware Park, Oct. 6, $75,300, 3yo & up, f & m, 1 1/8m, 1:52.38, SHAG, Vitrina Cat (Arg), Zenith. 6 started.

Open Mind H. (R), Monmouth Park, June 9, $50,000, 3yo & up, f & m, New Jersey-bred, 6f, 1:10.48, ANJIZ SLEW, Eleven North, Arpeggio. 7 started.

ORCHID H.-G2, Gulfstream Park, March 10, $194,000, 3yo & up, f & m, 1 1/2mT, 2:25.24, INNUENDO (Ire), Windsong, Aiglonne. 4 started.

Oregon Derby, Portland Meadows, April 14, $26,900, 3yo, 1 1/8m, 1:52.02, DANZILATION, Viva Lavilla, Fly Buddy Fly. 7 started.

Oregon Distaff Starter H. (R), Portland Meadows, Dec. 15, $4,695, 3yo & up, f & m, Oregon-bred starters for a claiming price of $4,000 or less in 2001, 6f, 1:15.09, BURNING SEA, Left Right Left, Natural Born Lover. 6 started.

Oregon Futurity (R), Portland Meadows, Dec. 15, $28,510, 2yo, Oregon-bred, 1m, 1:44.23, FIT TO BET, Lethal Grande, Maloya's Sun. 10 started.

Oregon Hers S. (R), Portland Meadows, Dec. 15, $8,700, 3yo, f, Oregon-bred, 1m, 1:42.47, TIFFA, Alyssa Lou, Missy Muffet. 8 started.

Oregon His S. (R), Portland Meadows, Dec. 15, $8,675, 3yo, c & g, Oregon-bred, 1 1/16m, 1:49.07, YESSS, Fly Buddy Fly, Viva Lavilla. 9 started.

Oregon Oaks S., Portland Meadows, April 28, $10,775, 3yo, f, 1 1/16m, 1:48.99, HURRICANE RYLIE, Annie N Will, Moon Pilot. 6 started.

Oregon Sprint Championship S. (R), Portland Meadows, Dec. 15, $8,300, 3yo & up, Oregon-bred, 6f, 1:13.40, LOVERS SON, Tomtom Tommalice, Dynamite Whirlwind. 5 started.

Oregon Starter H. (R), Portland Meadows, Dec. 15, $4,620, 3yo & up, Oregon-bred starters for a claiming price of $4,000 or less in 2001, 1m, 1:42.30, OUR C. C., Shy Boots, Neardistracted. 5 started.

Oregon Starter Sprint H. (R), Portland Meadows, Dec. 15, $4,238, 3yo & up, Oregon-bred starters for a claiming price of $3,200 or less in 2001, 5 1/2f, 1:08.19, WHIRLING ACE, Aglo Pilgrim, Breezy Native. 6 started.

Orphan Kist H. (R), Fonner Park, March 10, $18,200, 3yo & up, f & m, Nebraska-bred, 6f, 1:12.80, MISS DISTINCTION, Sandpit Dancer, Sweet Fantastic. 9 started.

Osiris Plate S., Assiniboia Downs, Aug. 6, $26,950, 2yo, 6f, 1:12.60, NESS GADOLL, Torquilla, Holy Bold. 7 started.

Osunitas H. (R), Del Mar, Aug. 8, $81,175, 3yo & up, f & m, non-winners of a race worth $50,000 to the winner at a mile or over in 2001, 1 1/16mT, 1:41.06, PAGA (Arg), La Ronge, Dianehill (Ire). 8 started.

OS West Oregon Futurity (R), Portland Meadows, Dec. 15, $28,510, 2yo, Oregon-bred, 1m, 1:44.23, FIT TO BET, Lethal Grande, Maloya's Sun. 10 started.

OTBA Sales S. (R), Portland Meadows, Nov. 10, $7,200, 2yo, sold at an OTBA sale, 5f, :59.88, LETHAL GRANDE, Gammagoat Kid, Be Still My Heart. 7 started.

OTBA Sophomore S. (R), Portland Meadows, March 3, $12,225, 3yo, Oregon-bred, 1 1/16m, 1:48.41, YESSS, Our Sleep Robber, Tate Man. 9 started.

OTBA Stallion S. (R), Portland Meadows, Jan. 6, $7,825, 3yo, Oregon-bred progeny of eligible stallions, 6f, 1:14.07, YESSS, Poncho Power, Tate Man. 4 started.

Overage S., Hawthorne Race Course, May 5, $44,000, 4yo & up, abt1 1/16mT, 1:41.48, GALIC BOY, Langston, Sean's Sunshine. 6 started.

OVERBROOK SPINSTER S.-G1, Keeneland, Oct. 7, $562,000, 3yo & up, f & m, 1 1/8m, 1:49.79, MISS LINDA (Arg), Starrer, Printemps (Chi). 10 started.

Overlander S., Kamloops, June 10, $2,625, 3yo & up, 6 1/2f, 1:19, AD-

VYCATOR, Bad Toda Bone, Perfect Policy. 5 started.

Overnite Sprint S., Lethbridge, Sept. 1, $6,700, 3yo & up, 5½f, 1:08, IT'S ALL A BLURR, Annulet, Peptide. 7 started.

Overskate S. (R), Woodbine, July 4, $105,700, 3yo & up, progeny of eligible stallions standing in Ontario, 7f, 1:24.27, KRZ RUCKUS, A Genuine Honour, Steady Ruckus. 8 started.

Ozark Hills H., Blue Ribbon Downs, March 4, $7,700, 3yo & up, 4f, :45.86, AVENUE OF STYLE, Voucher, Cover Keeper. 8 started.

Pacifica H., Bay Meadows, Oct. 28, $51,725, 3yo & up, 1 1/16mT, 1:41.35, NIGHT PATROL, Most Likely (Arg), Kittys Link. 6 started.

PACIFIC CLASSIC S.-G1, Del Mar, Aug. 19, $1,000,000, 3yo & up, 1¼m, 1:59.96, SKIMMING, Dixie Dot Com, Dig for It. 6 started.

Pago Hop S., Fair Grounds, Dec. 15, $100,000, 3yo, f, abt1mT, 1:39.90, LA RECHERCHE, Twilite Tryst, Stal Quest. 14 started.

Palisades S., Keeneland, April 22, $109,200, 3yo, f, 1⅛mT, 1:49.33, O K TO DANCE, La Recherche, Langoureuse. 7 started.

PALM BEACH S.-G3, Gulfstream Park, Feb. 19, $134,500, 3yo, 1⅛mT, 1:48.32, PROUD MAN, One Eyed Joker, Strategic Partner. 12 started.

Palo Alto H., Bay Meadows, June 2, $50,850, 3yo & up, f & m, 1 1/16mT, 1:42.97, SHOW ME GENIUS, Sky High Dancer, Matiere Grise (Fr). 10 started.

PALOMAR H.-G2, Del Mar, Sept. 1, $150,000, 3yo & up, f & m, 1 1/16mT, 1:41.94, TRANQUILITY LAKE, La Ronge, Al Desima (GB). 6 started.

PALOS VERDES H.-G2, Santa Anita Park, Jan. 28, $200,000, 4yo & up, 6f, 1:08.33, MEN'S EXCLUSIVE, Big Jag, Freespool. 6 started.

Palo Verde H., Turf Paradise, Feb. 24, $25,000, 3yo, 6½f, 1:16.10, TOP HIT, Sunnys Buddy, Disconect. 6 started.

PAN AMERICAN H.-G2, Gulfstream Park, March 11, $250,000, 3yo & up, 1½mT, 2:23.75, WHATA BRAINSTORM, Subtle Power (Ire), Craigsteel (GB). 7 started.

Panhandle H., Mountaineer Park, May 5, $58,100, 3yo & up, 5f, :56.76, GOVERNOR'S PRIDE, B. L.'s Ghost, Jeanies Rob. 10 started.

Panthers S., Prairie Meadows, June 16, $50,000, 3yo, f, 1m, 1:37.71, KERRY BLUE, Supreme Song, Open Minded. 5 started.

Pan Zareta H., Fair Grounds, Feb. 10, $75,000, 4yo & up, f & m, 6f, 1:09.68, HALLOWED DREAMS, My Alibi, Fiesty Countess. 6 started.

Paradise Mile H., Turf Paradise, Dec. 15, $75,000, 3yo & up, 1mT, 1:38, FIGHTING FALCON, King Slayer (GB), Bristolville. 7 started.

Paradise Valley H., Turf Paradise, Nov. 17, $30,000, 3yo, 7½fT, 1:30.75, R. BAGGIO, Resolve, Ironman Dehere. 9 started.

Paragon H., Emerald Downs, July 21, $40,000, 3yo, f, 1 1/16m, 1:44, AUNT SOPHIE, Neon Queen, Clever Coed. 9 started.

Park Avenue S. (R), Aqueduct, April 22, $100,000, 3yo, f, progeny of eligible stallions standing in New York, 1m, 1:36.28, LADY KATIE, Bon Fearless, Beijio. 5 started.

Park Heights Claiming S., Pimlico, July 7, $43,700, 4yo & up, 1 1/16m, 1:42.73, NOTABLY FROSTY, Memory Tap, Over to You. 7 started.

Parkland Heritage S. (R), Marquis Downs, Aug. 19, $12,100, 3yo, f, Saskatchewan-bred, 1 1/16m, 1:48.87, MS. LADY ROSE, Red Vil Do, Sing On Stage. 7 started.

Parnitha S. (R), Fort Erie, July 1, $55,300, 3yo & up, Canadian-foaled starters at Fort Erie at least twice in 2001, 6f, 1:10.31, EXCITING FLASH, Smart Ascot, Beau Gentleman. 9 started.

Pasco S., Tampa Bay Downs, Jan. 13, $50,000, 3yo, 7f, 1:25.31, ONE SPECIAL JUDGE, Simply Sir, Mute Gingrich. 9 started.

Paseana H., Santa Anita Park, Jan. 18, $92,225, 4yo & up, f & m, 1 1/16m, 1:42.55, FEVERISH, Lovellon (Arg), Cookin Vickie. 7 started.

Paseana S., Oaklawn Park, Feb. 3, $50,000, 4yo & up, f & m, 1m, 1:38.69, ASHER, Embraceable, Gobedie. 11 started.

Passing Mood S. (R), Woodbine, July 18, $104,400, 3yo, f, progeny of eligible stallions standing in Ontario, 7fT, 1:23.46, HIGHLAND MOOD, Moonlight Affair, Marjorie Daw. 6 started.

Pass the Line H. (R), Calder Race Course, Oct. 27, $54,700, 3yo & up, Florida-bred, 1 1/16mT, 1:44.79, SEJM'S MADNESS, Saint Joseph, Band Is Passing. 8 started.

Paterson H., The Meadowlands, Sept. 7, $91,000, 3yo & up, 6f, 1:09.11, SAY FLORIDA SANDY, Disco Rico, Loaded Gun. 3 started.

PAT O'BRIEN H.-G2, Del Mar, Aug. 12, $150,000, 3yo & up, 7f, 1:20.42, EL CORREDOR, Swept Overboard, Ceeband. 7 started.

Patricia S., Hialeah Park, April 8, $75,000, 3yo, f, 1 1/16mT, 1:41.25, PLATINUM TIARA, O K to Dance, Wander Mom. 8 started.

Patrick Wood S. (R), Great Lakes Downs, Sept. 17, $45,000, 2yo, c & g, Michigan-bred, 6½f, 1:21.68, SPRING WINDS, Equi Power, Tiro Fijo. 10 started.

Pat White S., Rillito Park, March 10, $3,802, 3yo & up, f & m, 6f, 1:19.80, BROADWAY'S PET, Whats Reality, Star of Hollywood. 5 started.

Paumonok H., Aqueduct, Jan. 27, $80,925, 3yo & up, 6f, 1:09.17, LEXICON, Say Florida Sandy, Kashatreya. 6 started.

Peach Blossom S., Delaware Park, April 7, $75,000, 3yo, f, 6f, 1:10.22, LIL PUNKINDO, Stormy Pick, Honey Eyed. 5 started.

Peach of It H. (R), Sportsman's Park, March 31, $75,000, 3yo & up, f & m, Illinois-bred, 1m, 1:42.27, FACCIA BELLA, Bugsy Mae, Royal Bandita. 10 started.

Pearl Necklace S. (R), Pimlico, June 30, $60,000, 3yo, f, Maryland-bred, 1 1/16mT, 1:42.52, SADLER'S SARAH, Guillotine, Jewel of the North. 7 started.

PEBBLES H.-G3 (1st Div.), Belmont Park, Oct. 14, $110,100, 3yo, f, 1⅛mT, 1:47.75, HEADS WILL ROLL (GB), New Economy, Salty You. 8 started.

PEBBLES H.-G3 (2nd Div.), Belmont Park, Oct. 14, $110,600, 3yo, f, 1⅛mT, 1:47.50, LOVE N' KISS S., Calista (GB), Shooting Party. 8 started.

PEGASUS H.-G2, The Meadowlands, Oct. 19, $250,000, 3yo, 1⅛m, 1:46.55, VOLPONI, Burning Roma, Giant Gentleman. 6 started.

Pelican S., Tampa Bay Downs, Dec. 29, $50,000, 3yo & up, 6f, 1:11, WINNIE'S POOH BEAR, Distinctive Mr. B, Mountain Top. 12 started.

Pelican State S. (R), Louisiana Downs, Nov. 3, $25,000, 2yo, Louisiana-bred, 6½f, 1:16.83, WALK IN THE SNOW, Won Better, Rapide. 11 started.

Pelleteri Breeders' Cup H., Fair Grounds, March 18, $113,900, 3yo & up, 6f, 1:09.60, BONAPAW, Abajo, Crucible. 6 started.

Penninsula S. (R), Fort Erie, Aug. 20, $55,150, 3yo & up, Canadian-bred, abt7fT, 1:27.09, BOLD ARBITRAGE, Malcoha, Beau Gentleman. 8 started.

PENNSYLVANIA DERBY-G3, Philadelphia Park, Sept. 3, $500,000, 3yo, 1⅛m, 1:49.69, MACHO UNO, Unbridled Elaine, Touch Tone. 6 started.

Pennsylvania Futurity (R), Philadelphia Park, Nov. 17, $50,000, 2yo, c & g, Pennsylvania-bred, 7f, 1:23.63, OSWAYO, Pal's Partner, Volley Ball. 9 started.

Pennsylvania Governor's Cup H., Penn National Race Course, Aug. 3, $100,000, 3yo & up, 1 1/16mT, 1:40.10, BUENOS DIAS, Sir Echo, Holditholditholdit. 11 started.

Pennsylvania Hunt Cup S., Unionville, Oct. 28, $29,100, 5 yo's & up, abt4mT, 8:56.80, BIT OF SCOTCH (GB), Where's Pepo, Stone Buster. 5 started.

Pennsylvania Oaks, Philadelphia Park, Sept. 3, $50,000, 3yo, f, 1m 70y, 1:42.14, INDY BIRD, Urban Dancer, Bernie's Gold. 6 started.

Penny Ridge H., Stampede Park, June 17, $40,000, 3yo, f, 1 1/16m, 1:48.80, WILLOW, Dana's Remark, Randi. 5 started.

Peppy Addy S. (R), Philadelphia Park, May 28, $50,000, 3yo, Pennsylvania-bred, 7f, 1:23.96, BEAU'S SURPRISE, Docent, K Mac. 5 started.

Pepsi-Cola H., Emerald Downs, May 28, $40,802, 3yo, c & g, 6½f, 1:15.60, JUMRON WON, Tactical Allusion, Danzilation. 6 started.

Pepsi Cola H. (R), Sunland Park, Jan. 20, $68,700, 3yo, New Mexico-bred, 6f, 1:11.20, FRISKIE FEDDIE, I'm Not Bluffin, Prospector Nugget. 11 started.

Perfect Arc S. (R), Aqueduct, Nov. 11, $100,000, 3yo & up, f & m, progeny of eligible stallions standing in New York, 1mT, 1:37.12, WAKE UP KISS, Lovely Amanda, Impeachable. 9 started.

Perryville S., Keeneland, Oct. 11, $81,225, 3yo, abt7f, 1:27.25, DREAM RUN, Strawberry Affair, Solingen. 5 started.

PERSONAL ENSIGN H.-G1, Saratoga Race Course, Aug. 24, $400,000, 3yo & up, f & m, 1¼m, 2:04.60, POMPEII, Beautiful Pleasure, Irving's Baby. 7 started.

Personal Ensign S., Monmouth Park, Sept. 2, $75,000, 3yo & up, f & m, 1 1/16m, 1:46.15, STROLLING BELLE, Southern Fiction, Search Party. 5 started.

Pete Axthelm S., Calder Race Course, Dec. 22, $100,000, 3yo, 7½fT, 1:28.15, ONE EYED JOKER, Tour of the Cat, Boastful. 12 started.

Pete Condellone H. (R), Fairmount Park, Oct. 16, $35,900, 3yo & up, Illinois-conceived and/or -foaled, 1m, 1:38.80, TIC N TIN, Shadow Mountain, Multiple Metal. 7 started.

PETER PAN S.-G2, Belmont Park, May 26, $200,000, 3yo, 1⅛m, 1:47.47, HERO'S TRIBUTE, Dayton Flyer, E Dubai. 7 started.

PHILADELPHIA PARK BREEDERS' CUP H.-G3, Philadelphia Park, July 28, $188,000, 3yo & up, 6f, 1:08.51, SAY FLORIDA SANDY, Wake At Noon, Max's Pal. 4 started.

Phil D. Shepherd S., Fairplex Park, Sept. 8, $49,500, 3yo & up, 1 1/16m, 1:44.34, LITERAL PROWLER, Grey Memo, Indiahoma. 8 started.

PHILIP H. ISELIN H.-G2, Monmouth Park, Aug. 26, $350,000, 3yo & up, 1 1/8m, 1:49.55, BROKEN VOW, First Lieutenant, Sir Bear. 5 started.

PHOENIX BREEDERS' CUP S.-G3, Keeneland, Oct. 6, $268,500, 3yo & up, 6f, 1:09.65, BET ON SUNSHINE, Robin de Nest, Erlton. 5 started.

Phoenix Gold Cup H., Turf Paradise, March 10, $100,000, 3yo & up, 6f, 1:09.10, FREESPOOL, No Cal Bread, Tavasco. 8 started.

Phoenix Leisure Thoroughbred Championship H., Wyoming Downs, Aug. 12, $5,250, 3yo & up, 1m, 1:37.23, RASHA, Fadski, Wonroads. 8 started.

Phoenix S., The Meadowlands, Oct. 20, $100,000, 3yo & up, f & m, 5fT, :57.65, SERENA'S TUNE, Maypole Dance, Merry Princess. 11 started.

Piedra Foundation H. (R), Del Mar, Aug. 24, $95,150, 3yo & up, f & m, non-winners of $45,000 other than closed, claiming, or starter at a mile or over since February 1, 2001, 1m, 1:36.28, FAVORITE FUNTIME, Queenie Belle, Red Hot and Blue. 5 started.

Pierce County S. (R), Emerald Downs, June 10, $35,000, 2yo, f, Washington-bred, 5f, PERFECT PLAN, Music to My Heart, Artic Mist. 9 started.

Pilgrim S., Aqueduct, Nov. 6, $83,475, 2yo, 1 1/8mT, 1:50.80, MIESQUE'S APPROVAL, Finality, Regal Sanction. 9 started.

PIMLICO DISTAFF H.-G3, Pimlico, May 19, $200,000, 3yo & up, f & m, 1 1/8m, 1:50.22, SERRA LAKE, Jostle, Prized Stamp. 6 started.

PIMLICO SPECIAL H.-G1, Pimlico, May 12, $750,000, 3yo & up, 1 3/16m, 1:55.61, INCLUDE, Albert the Great, Pleasant Breeze. 6 started.

Pinellas S., Tampa Bay Downs, April 7, $50,000, 3yo, f, 1 1/16mT, 1:43.08, THE GODDESS ATHIRD, Chausson Poire, Across the Creek. 9 started.

Pinjara S. (R), Santa Anita Park, Oct. 12, $61,350, 2yo, non-winners of $30,000 other than closed or claiming at one mile or over, 1mT, 1:34.42, YOUGOTTAWANNA, Mountain Rage, Holdthehelm. 9 started.

Pinon H. (R), The Downs at Albuquerque, April 8, $52,200, 3yo & up, f & m, New Mexico-bred, 6 1/2f, 1:15.91, YULLA YULLA, Gollygot, Tanka Gold. 6 started.

Pioneer S., Louisiana Downs, Aug. 18, $40,000, 2yo, 5 1/2f, 1:06, NUCLEAR ASSEMBLY, Whambam, Abagfullofit. 7 started.

Pio Pico S. (R), Fairplex Park, Sept. 14, $50,000, 3yo & up, f & m, California-bred, 6 1/2f, 1:16.66, WARREN'S WHISTLE, Song of Summer, Storm Kisu. 8 started.

Pippin S., Oaklawn Park, Feb. 25, $50,000, 4yo & up, f & m, 1 1/16m, 1:44.63, ASHER, Due to Win, Ive Gota Bad Liver. 6 started.

Pirate's Bounty H. (R), Del Mar, Sept. 1, $71,150, 3yo & up, non-winners of $50,000 since April 25, 2001, 6f, 1:08.87, FREESPOOL, Tavasco, Capo Di Capo. 8 started.

Pistol Packer H. (R), Philadelphia Park, June 16, $50,000, 3yo & up, f & m, Pennsylvania-bred, 7f, 1:23.87, ARTY'SVIRGINIAGIRL, Lost Judgement, (DH) Betty's Hat, (DH) Run for Joy. 9 started.

Plate Trial S. (R), Woodbine, June 2, $162,750, 3yo, Canadian-bred, 1 1/8m, 1:52.08, WIN CITY, Millennium Allstar, Brushing Bully. 6 started.

PLAY THE KING H.-G3, Woodbine, Aug. 25, $146,000, 3yo & up, 7fT, 1:21.84, MR. EPPERSON, Heliotrope, Alea lacta Est. 12 started.

Pleasanton S., Pleasanton, July 5, $44,120, 3yo, 1 1/16m, 1:43.15, IRONMAN DEHERE, Robaleur, Padirac. 5 started.

Pleasanton Senorita S., Pleasanton, July 4, $41,850, 3yo, f, 1m 70y, 1:40.94, PLANONCOMETBEBOPIN, Gifted Daughter, Color Me Special. 6 started.

Pleasant Temper S., Kentucky Downs, Sept. 16, $45,000, 3yo & up, f & m, 1mT, 1:37.05, SILENT EMOTION, Lapuma, Star Queen. 10 started.

Plymouth S. (R), Great Lakes Downs, June 16, $45,000, 3yo, f, Michigan-bred, 7f, 1:31.45, I MATCH TOO, La Vie Hawk, Let's Improvise. 10 started.

PNE Speed H., Hastings Park Racecourse, Aug. 26, $38,010, 3yo & up, 6 1/2f, 1:16.05, KING JEREMY, Galavant, Ryson. 7 started.

Pocahontas S., Churchill Downs, Nov. 3, $111,500, 2yo, f, 1m, 1:37.96, LOTTA RHYTHM, Cunning Play, Joanies Bella. 8 started.

Poinciana Breeders' Cup H., Hialeah Park, April 7, $90,000, 3yo & up, f & m, 7f, 1:21.91, MARCH MAGIC, Penny Blues, Hidden Assets. 7 started.

POKER H.-G3, Belmont Park, July 4, $110,400, 3yo & up, 1mT, 1:34.60, AFFIRMED SUCCESS, In Frank's Honor, Union One. 6 started.

Politely S., Monmouth Park, May 26, $50,000, 3yo & up, f & m, 1m, 1:36.20, HER HALO, Hemline, Final One. 5 started.

Politely S. (R), Laurel Park, Nov. 10, $60,000, 3yo, f, Maryland-bred, 7f, 1:24.31, URBAN DANCER, Your Out, Winter Leaf. 8 started.

Pollyanna Pixie S., Hawthorne Race Course, June 1, $44,250, 3yo, f, 6 1/2f, 1:17.81, SOUL ONARAZORSEDGE, Abba Gold, Garrettslilnora. 7 started.

Polly Drummond S., Delaware Park, Oct. 14, $100,600, 2yo, f, 1 1/16m, 1:47.36, FIRST AGAIN, Lady Shari, Short Note. 7 started.

Polly's Jet H., Delaware Park, Aug. 29, $60,100, 3yo, f, abt5fT, :57.64, CARSONALITY, Sparkling Number, Twice as Sweet. 8 started.

Polynesian Flyer H., Portland Meadows, April 7, $6,825, 3yo & up, 1m, 1:39.22, CHINQUAPIN CHARLIE, Skeeber, Wapato Wind. 10 started.

Pomona Derby, Fairplex Park, Sept. 22, $100,000, 3yo, abt1 1/8m, 1:50.27, SIGFRETO, Huggy Boy, Swordfish. 11 started.

Ponca City S., Remington Park, Aug. 18, $30,000, 3yo, f, 6f, 1:11.53, CALL ME KRYSTAL, Western Delight, Golden Hurricane. 6 started.

Ponche H., Calder Race Course, May 26, $36,790, 3yo & up, 6 1/2f, 1:17.88, CALLIE AND JAKE, Silver Jet, Thrillin Discovery. 8 started.

Pontalba S., Fair Grounds, Nov. 25, $60,000, 2yo, f, 5 1/2f, 1:05.20, FLICK, Purple Princess, Carson's Baby. 6 started.

Pony Express H. (R), The Downs at Albuquerque, May 20, $32,900, 3yo & up, New Mexico-bred, 5 1/2f, 1:02.78, THATSAKNIFE, Wild Dan, See Ya Cat. 6 started.

Portland Meadows Claiming S., Portland Meadows, April 29, $6,500, 4yo & up, 1 5/8m, 2:52.64, MUTINY BAY, Inaki, Magic Syn. 8 started.

Portland Meadows Mile H., Portland Meadows, April 21, $32,250, 3yo & up, 1m, 1:39.03, CHINQUAPIN CHARLIE, Rub, Skeeber. 8 started.

Potomac S. (R), Laurel Park, Jan. 7, $42,750, 4yo & up, Maryland-bred non-winners of a stake, 1 1/16m, 1:45.53, KEN DOLL, Do I Ever, Clark's Clone. 5 started.

POTRERO GRANDE BREEDERS' CUP H.-G2, Santa Anita Park, April 1, $200,900, 4yo & up, 6 1/2f, 1:15.03, KONA GOLD, (DH) Hollycombe, (DH) Explicit. 4 started.

Powder Break H., Calder Race Course, Nov. 3, $54,560, 3yo & up, f & m, 1mT, 1:39.70, RAPONERA, Golden Saint, Silver Bandana. 10 started.

Powerless S. (R), Hawthorne Race Course, Nov. 10, $75,000, 3yo & up, f & m, Illinois-conceived and/or -foaled, 6f, 1:11.72, CAPITOL VIEW, Lil Bobbie Too, Darling L. 11 started.

Prairie Bayou S., Turfway Park, Dec. 15, $50,000, 3yo & up, 1 1/8m, 1:50.85, CRAFTY SHAW, Double Affair, Glacial. 7 started.

Prairie Express S., Prairie Meadows, May 5, $50,000, 3yo & up, 5f, :56.80, SAND RIDGE, I'm Registered, Riker. 8 started.

Prairie Gold Juvenile S., Prairie Meadows, June 30, $50,000, 2yo, 5f, :58.64, COCKLE BURR MAN, Purple Pleasure, Crazy Deputy. 8 started.

Prairie Gold Lassie S., Prairie Meadows, June 29, $50,000, 2yo, f, 5f, :57.18, FANCY PRANCER, Go and Look, Devil's Rush. 7 started.

Prairieland H., Marquis Downs, Sept. 1, $6,000, 3yo, f, 1 1/16m, 1:47.53, RED VIL DO, Sing On Stage, Rapadash. 5 started.

Prairie Lily Sales S. (R), Marquis Downs, Sept. 2, $32,760, 2yo, sold at the Prairie Lily sale, abt7f, 1:27.74, SWING IN SATIN, Slew Tonic, Gatopresson. 9 started.

PRAIRIE MEADOWS CORNHUSKER BREEDERS' CUP H.-G3, Prairie Meadows, July 7, $401,625, 3yo & up, 1 1/8m, 1:47.72, EUCHRE, Dixie Dot Com, Sure Shot Biscuit. 7 started.

Prairie Meadows Debutante S., Prairie Meadows, Oct. 5, $58,750, 2yo, f, 6f, 1:12.08, ORPHAN LOVER, Iffy, True Tear Drops. 8 started.

Prairie Meadows Derby, Prairie Meadows, Aug. 18, $77,625, 3yo, 1 1/8m, 1:49.57, HORRIBLE EVENING, Quadrophonic Sound, Take Me Up. 6 started.

Prairie Meadows Freshman S., Prairie Meadows, Oct. 6, $60,625, 2yo, 6f, 1:11.06, WAR GENERAL, Medical First, Second Tuesday. 6 started.

Prairie Meadows H., Prairie Meadows, Sept. 3, $100,000, 3yo & up, 1 1/8m, 1:48.60, CHICAGO SIX, Neon Shadow, Da Devil. 6 started.

Prairie Meadows Oaks, Prairie Meadows, Aug. 25, $76,312, 3yo, f, 1 1/16m, 1:44.64, CURIOUS CONUNDRUM, Momentous, Barney's Mistress. 6 started.

Prairie Meadows Sprint S., Prairie Meadows, Sept. 15, $47,000,

3yo & up, 6f, 1:09.72, SURE SHOT BISCUIT, Fun to Run, Boot Hill. 7 started.

Prairie Mile S., Prairie Meadows, May 21, $60,000, 3yo, 1m, 1:36.76, JUNIOR DEPUTY, Compendium, Solingen. 8 started.

Prairie Rose S., Prairie Meadows, May 12, $52,750, 3yo & up, f & m, 6f, 1:10.22, VIA GRAS, Answer to Jordan, Nut N Better. 7 started.

Preakness Day H., Eureka Downs, May 19, $5,300, 3yo & up, 6f, 1:14.81, JUST A ECLIPSE, The Amazing Pirate, Forty Sixer. 6 started.

PREAKNESS S.-G1, Pimlico, May 19, $1,000,000, 3yo, 1 3/16m, 1:55.51, POINT GIVEN, A P Valentine, Congaree. 11 started.

Precisionist H., Prairie Meadows, May 26, $99,750, 3yo & up, 1 1/16m, 1:42.80, SURE SHOT BISCUIT, Battle Mountain, Bravo Bull. 6 started.

Prelude S., Louisiana Downs, Sept. 3, $50,000, 3yo, 1⅛m, 1:51.79, RARE CURE, Quadrophonic Sound, Wow. 7 started.

Premiere S. (R), Lone Star Park, April 5, $50,000, 3yo & up, Texas-bred, 1m, 1:37.56, CAPTAIN COUNTDOWN, Desert Air, Desert Demon. 9 started.

Premier H., Arapahoe Park, July 8, $28,000, 3yo, 7f, 1:24.40, SILVER SET, Sharethetime, Tangarae Tango. 8 started.

PREMIER'S S.-G3, Hastings Park Racecourse, Oct. 14, $101,676, 3yo & up, 1⅜m, 2:20.07, FANCY AS, Lord Nelson, Colonial Secretary. 7 started.

Prescott Valley S., Yavapai Downs, July 15, $10,000, 3yo & up, 6f, 1:08.50, STORMY AMBITION, Hemandan, Trevally (Mex). 8 started.

President's Cup H., Lincoln State Fair, June 9, $10,420, 3yo & up, 6f, 1:11.20, DOUG'S SHADOW, High Dice, Hannah's Hero. 4 started.

President's H., Stampede Park, May 13, $34,620, 3yo, 6f, 1:11.20, FANCY AS, Boldanzar, Wild After Dark. 7 started.

Presidents S., Turfway Park, Feb. 10, $50,000, 3yo, 1m, 1:39.18, BONNIE SCOT, Big Will, X Country. 9 started.

Preview S., Portland Meadows, March 24, $8,725, 3yo, 1m, 1:39.44, DANZILATION, Viva Lavilla, Yesss. 8 started.

Prevue S., Remington Park, Nov. 4, $25,585, 2yo, 7f, 1:24.99, MOONMON, April's Lucky Boy, Princeton Avenue. 8 started.

Primal H., Calder Race Course, June 30, $27,430, 3yo & up, 1 1/16m, 1:46.90, PUCHUNGO (Per), Hal's Hope, Out of Champagne. 7 started.

Primer S., Pimlico, Sept. 22, $43,400, 2yo, 6f, 1:11.17, INCREDIBLE CARSON, Outstander, Square Cut Diamond. 7 started.

Primonetta S., Pimlico, April 8, $75,000, 3yo & up, f & m, 6f, 1:09.81, LILY'S AFFAIR, Sincerely, Lucky Livi. 6 started.

Prince of Wales S. (R), Fort Erie, July 22, $350,000, 3yo, Canadian-bred, 1 3/16m, 1:56.14, WIN CITY, Dancethruthedawn, Brushing Bully. 6 started.

Princess Elaine S. (R), Canterbury Park, July 7, $37,275, 3yo & up, f & m, Minnesota-bred, 1 1/16mT, 1:45.67, PLAYFUL EDITION, Shesa Shesa, Pickin the Pace. 10 started.

Princess Elizabeth S. (R), Woodbine, Oct. 13, $250,000, 2yo, f, Canadian-bred, 1 1/16m, 1:43.48, GINGER GOLD, Mulrainy, Gonetofarr. 8 started.

Princess Futurity, Louisiana Downs, Sept. 30, $71,000, 2yo, f, 6½f, 1:19.34, DANCING DREAMS, Queen of the Isle, Taylor's Queen. 9 started.

Princess Margaret S., Northlands Park, Aug. 5, $36,650, 2yo, f, 6f, 1:12.80, SLY LADY, Code's Decree, Sweet Monarch. 10 started.

Princess of Palms H., Turf Paradise, Jan. 27, $25,000, 4yo & up, f & m, 6f, 1:10.96, ODE TO ELAINE, Little Snake Bit, Emerging Class. 6 started.

PRINCESS ROONEY H.-G3, Calder Race Course, July 14, $400,000, 3yo & up, f & m, 6f, 1:10.48, DREAM SUPREME, Hidden Assets, Sugar N Spice. 9 started.

PRINCESS S.-G2, Hollywood Park, June 16, $100,000, 3yo, f, 1 1/16m, 1:41.90, STARRER, Love At Noon, Affluent. 6 started.

Princess S., Lincoln State Fair, May 26, $10,180, 3yo, f, 6f, 1:12, IRISH FLYER, Con Air Won, Anti Versary. 4 started.

Princeton S., The Meadowlands, Sept. 21, $75,000, 3yo, 1 1/16m (originally scheduled on the turf), 1:42.86, GIANT GENTLEMAN, Rapid Ryan, First Spear. 5 started.

PRIORESS S.-G1, Belmont Park, July 4, $200,000, 3yo, f, 6f, 1:08.26, XTRA HEAT, Above Perfection, Harmony Lodge. 7 started.

Prismatical S., The Meadowlands, Oct. 26, $100,000, 3yo & up, f & m, 1 1/16m, 1:43.71, A. O. L. HAYES, Vitrina Cat (Arg), Steppedoutofadream. 5 started.

Private Terms S., Pimlico, March 31, $60,450, 3yo, 1⅛m, 1:50.51, BAY EAGLE, Marciano, Charlie's Cards. 8 started.

Private Terms S., Suffolk Downs, Jan. 24, $25,000, 4yo & up, 6f, 1:11.58, MAKIN PROGRESS, High Above, Makeyourselfathome. 10 started.

Prom S., The Meadowlands, Oct. 12, $50,000, 2yo, f, 5fT, :56.51, AUGUST STORM, Forum Search, Warm Weather. 12 started.

Pro or Con H. (R), Santa Anita Park, Feb. 3, $150,000, 4yo & up, f & m, California-bred, 1m, 1:35.13, JEWELED PIRATE, Lazy Slusan, Mimi's Cafe. 9 started.

Proud Puppy H., Finger Lakes, July 7, $30,000, 3yo & up, f & m, 6f, 1:11.60, END OF THE HILL, Alley Ball, Belongs to Mony. 8 started.

Providencia S. (R), Santa Anita Park, March 31, $81,975, 3yo, f, nonwinners of $50,000 at a mile or over in 2001, 1⅛mT, 1:50.13, DYNAMOUS, Heads Will Roll (GB), Little Firefly (Ire). 7 started.

P. R. Smith S., Hialeah Park, May 19, $32,400, 3yo & up, 1 3/16mT, 1:54.19, LOUISIANA ALLEN, Trooper Red, Take Charge Megan. 11 started.

PUCKER UP S.-G3, Arlington Park, Sept. 15, $150,000, 3yo, f, 1⅛mT, 1:47.93, SNOW DANCE, Kiss the Devil, Twilite Tryst. 12 started.

Punch Line S. (R), Colonial Downs, Aug. 5, $40,000, 3yo & up, Virginia-bred or sired, 5fT, :57.08, BOP, Polish Vision, Oxford Tea Party. 7 started.

Purple Violet S. (R), Arlington Park, June 23, $75,000, 3yo, f, Illinois-conceived and/or -foaled, 1m, 1:38.27, SHEMYA, Shania's Code, Ballado's Baby. 8 started.

Puss N Boots S. (R), Fort Erie, Sept. 3, $67,400, 3yo & up, starters at Fort Erie at least twice in 2001, 1 1/16mT, 1:44.60, NORTHERNPROSPECTOR, Beau Gentleman, Don't Seven Out. 12 started.

Queen City Oaks (R), River Downs, July 28, $100,000, 3yo, f, Ohio-bred, 1⅛m, 1:53.60, ASHWOOD C C, Eye Slew the City, Runaway Rose. 8 started.

QUEEN ELIZABETH II CHALLENGE CUP S.-G1, Keeneland, Oct. 13, $500,000, 3yo, f, 1⅛mT, 1:50.03, AFFLUENT, Golden Apples (Ire), Snow Dance. 10 started.

Queen of the Desert S., Turf Paradise, April 8, $23,900, 3yo & up, f & m, 1m, 1:37.95, TOP BRACKET, Paige's Sister, Blue Yodel. 7 started.

Queen of the Green H., Turf Paradise, Dec. 1, $75,000, 3yo & up, f & m, 1mT, 1:36.69, ALEXINE (Arg), Miss Pixie, Deliciosa (Arg). 10 started.

Queen S., Turfway Park, March 24, $60,000, 4yo & up, f & m, 6f, 1:11.42, MOUNTAIN GIRL, Katz Me If You Can, Seeyouinseptember. 10 started.

QUEENS COUNTY H.-G3, Aqueduct, Dec. 1, $111,900, 3yo & up, 1 3/16m, 1:55.08, EVENING ATTIRE, Balto Star, Top Official. 8 started.

Queen's Cup Timber S., Charlotte, April 28, $22,000, 5 yo's & up, abt3mT, 6:55, THOR THORS, Fifth Creek, Patrician Power. 7 started.

Queen's H., Horsemen's Park, July 21, $31,200, 3yo & up, f & m, 6f, 1:11, NATURALINGREDIENTS, Double Dreamin Deb, Statsie's Charmer. 8 started.

Queen's Plate S. (R), Woodbine, June 24, $1,000,000, 3yo, Canadian-bred, 1¼m, 2:03.78, DANCETHRUTHEDAWN, Win City, Brushing Bully. 10 started.

Queenston S. (R), Woodbine, May 5, $145,260, 3yo, Canadian-bred, 7f, 1:24.13, WIN CITY, Millennium Allstar, Highland Legacy. 5 started.

Quick Card S. (R), Delaware Park, Oct. 30, $59,700, 3yo & up, nonwinners of 2 races over one mile in 2001 other than maiden, claiming, starter, or closed or for an optional claiming price of $100,000, 1m 70y, 1:43.85, JOHNNY DOLLAR, Cherokeeinthehills, Sumerset. 6 started.

Quicken Tree S. (R), Hollywood Park, April 28, $100,000, 4yo & up, California-bred, 1½mT, 2:26.32, RINGASKIDDY, Adminniestrator, Continental Red. 11 started.

Quick n Cool S., Turf Paradise, May 12, $23,800, 3yo & up, f & m, 5½f, 1:04.66, DEZIBELLES FORLI, Port d'Enfer, The Kinded. 5 started.

Quick Step H. (R), Thistledown, May 12, $40,000, 3yo & up, Ohio-bred, 6f, 1:11.28, DOWN THEPIKE MIKE, Knight Villain, Forty Niner's Rock. 6 started.

Quill S., Delaware Park, Sept. 2, $58,600, 3yo & up, f & m, 1⅛m, 1:51.81, VITRINA CAT (Arg), April in Calgary, Sarai's Dancer. 5 started.

Race Artist S., Calder Race Course, Dec. 2, $37,440, 3yo, f, 6f, 1:10.96, FLY ME CRAZY, Flying Birdie, Gaby G. 6 started.

Racing Star H., Calder Race Course, June 26, $28,290, 3yo & up,

5f, :59.47, SILVER JET, Uncle Rocco, Honorable Pic. 7 started.

Radnor Hunt Cup Timber S., Malvern, May 19, $22,000, 4yo & up, abt3½mT, 7:17.80, SAM SULLIVAN, Bredesen Moe (DQ from 1st), Atomistic. 3 started.

RAILBIRD S.-G2, Hollywood Park, May 19, $150,000, 3yo, f, 7f, 1:21.57, GOLDEN BALLET, Starrer, Pretty 'n Smart. 6 started.

Rainbow Connection S. (R), Fort Erie, July 10, $101,500, 3yo & up, f & m, progeny of eligible stallions standing in Ontario, 5fT, :57.39, SPORTS FLASHY, Ice Tie, Found Treasure. 5 started.

Rainbow Miss S. (R), Oaklawn Park, April 1, $58,000, 3yo, f, Arkansas-bred, 6f, 1:11.40, SUZANNE'S FLYING, Dancing Flo, Tune in Reality. 8 started.

Rainbow S. (R), Oaklawn Park, March 31, $65,500, 3yo, c & g, Arkansas-bred, 6f, 1:12.91, TUB TOSSER, Bound to Blast, Hickory Dick Doc. 12 started.

Raise a Cup H., Delaware Park, June 25, $60,300, 3yo, 5½f, 1:04.14, SMILE MY LORD, Unreal Party, Castle of Sand. 8 started.

Ralph Hayes S. (R), Prairie Meadows, Sept. 1, $78,400, 4yo & up, c & g, Iowa-bred, 1 1/16m, 1:44.63, SURE SHOT BISCUIT, Fruitcake Jim, D. W. Wheels. 5 started.

Ralph M. Hinds Pomona Invitational H., Fairplex Park, Sept. 23, $99,000, 3yo & up, abt1⅛m, 1:50.70, JUST RULER, Grey Memo, L'Effaceur. 7 started.

RAMONA H.-G1, Del Mar, July 21, $400,000, 3yo & up, f & m, 1⅛mT, 1:48.20, JANET (GB), Tranquility Lake, Minor Details. 6 started.

RAMPART H.-G2, Gulfstream Park, March 4, $200,000, 3yo & up, f & m, 1⅛m, 1:50.48, DE BERTIE, Apple of Kent, Scratch Pad. 7 started.

RANCHO BERNARDO H.-G3, Del Mar, Aug. 19, $150,000, 3yo & up, f & m, 6½f, 1:15.52, KALOOKAN QUEEN, Go Go, Warren's Whistle. 6 started.

Rapid Transit S. (R), Philadelphia Park, June 2, $40,000, 3yo & up, starters for a claiming price of $16,000 or less since July 31, 2000, 6½f, 1:16.94, NASTY BILLY RAY, Slaymaster, Sonofaqueen. 7 started.

RARE TREAT H.-G3, Aqueduct, Feb. 19, $110,300, 3yo & up, f & m, 1⅛m, 1:50.71, POMPEII, Biogio's Rose, Back in Shape. 8 started.

Rattlesnake S., Turf Paradise, Jan. 14, $25,000, 3yo, 1m, 1:39.98, PROHIBITIVE, Mecke Monster, Double Time. 7 started.

Raven Run S., Keeneland, Oct. 10, $109,900, 3yo, f, 7f, 1:23.30, NASTY STORM, Hattiesburg, Forest Secrets. 7 started.

Raymond G. Woolfe Memorial Hurdle S., Camden, Nov. 18, $25,000, 3yo, abt2¼mT, 4:33.80, GEAUX BEAU, Buster's Dream, Capeless. 7 started.

Razorback Futurity (R), Louisiana Downs, Nov. 4, $25,000, 2yo, c & g, Arkansas-bred, 6f, 1:12.41, EAST TEXAS SAM, Snowball King, My Good Trick. 14 started.

RAZORBACK H.-G3, Oaklawn Park, March 17, $125,000, 4yo & up, 1 1/16m, 1:42.60, MR ROSS, Graeme Hall, Maysville Slew. 9 started.

R. C. Anderson S. (R), Assiniboia Downs, July 7, $26,950, 3yo, f, Manitoba-bred, 1m, 1:41.40, NASTY MILLIE, Mountain Crest, Cayenne Pepper. 10 started.

Ready Jet Go S., The Meadowlands, Nov. 10, $75,000, 3yo & up, f & m, 6f, 1:08.79, DAT YOU MIZ BLUE, Arianna's Passion, La Galerie (Arg). 6 started.

Real Good Deal S. (R), Del Mar, Aug. 13, $100,000, 3yo, California-bred non-winners of a race worth $50,000 to the winner twice, 7f, 1:22.28, WAINGARTH, Stoney, Bring the Heat. 7 started.

REBEL S.-G3, Oaklawn Park, March 24, $100,000, 3yo, 1 1/16m, 1:43.82, CRAFTY SHAW, Arctic Boy, Strike It Smart. 9 started.

Rebel S., Louisiana Downs, Aug. 19, $40,000, 2yo, f, 5½f, 1:04.64, DANCING DREAMS, Queen of the Isle, Khazi. 9 started.

RED BANK H.-G3, Monmouth Park, May 28, $150,000, 3yo & up, 1mT, 1:36.38, PAVILLON (Brz), Western Summer, Runspastum. 10 started.

Red Bud H., Blue Ribbon Downs, April 29, $7,150, 3yo & up, f & m, 5½f, 1:04.60, MALL HAWK, Blonde Okie, Tulsa Shuttle. 7 started.

Red Camelia H. (R), Fair Grounds, March 26, $100,000, 4yo & up, f & m, Louisiana-bred, abt1m, 1:39.54, SPARKLES OF LUCK, Sarah Lane's Oates, High Hopes Irish. 11 started.

Red Diamond Express H. (R), Northlands Park, Sept. 22, $40,000, 3yo & up, Alberta-bred, 6½f, 1:17.20, ROBNROY, Timely Ruckus, Timboruck. 7 started.

Red Dog H., Delaware Park, Aug. 18, $58,100, 3yo & up, 1 1/16m, 1:45.01, DO I EVER, Mister Business, B Flat Major. 5 started.

Red Earth H., Remington Park, Sept. 21, $21,740, 3yo & up, 1mT, 1:36.84, FOURTEEN TEN, College Dean, Custer. 6 started.

RED SMITH H.-G2, Aqueduct, Nov. 17, $150,000, 3yo & up, 1⅜mT, 2:16.94, MR. PLEASENTFAR (Brz), Eltawaasul, Regal Dynasty. 12 started.

Redwood Empire S., Santa Rosa, Aug. 5, $47,690, 2yo, 5½f, 1:03.59, KISS AN ANGEL, Duddly Doo Run, Surprized. 7 started.

REEVE SCHLEY JR. S.-G3, Monmouth Park, July 7, $100,000, 3yo, f, 1 1/16mT, 1:42.70, SILVER TORNADO, Marq of Beauty, Platinum Tiara. 5 started.

Regal Rumor S., Hawthorne Race Course, May 26, $57,550, 4yo & up, f & m, 6f, 1:12.01, COME SEPTEMBER, Capitol View, Faccia Bella. 7 started.

REGRET S.-G3, Churchill Downs, June 16, $167,250, 3yo, f, 1 1/16mT, 1:42.75, CASUAL FEAT, Amaretta, La Vida Loca (Ire). 8 started.

Regret S., Monmouth Park, July 4, $75,000, 3yo & up, f & m, 6f, 1:08.75, BIG BAMBU, Katz Me If You Can, Superduper Miss. 8 started.

Regret S. (R), Great Lakes Downs, May 26, $45,000, 3yo, f, Michigan-bred, 6f, 1:16.83, I MATCH TOO, Weezy, Joy of Brandy. 9 started.

Reid Brekkas Contracting S., Grand Prairie, July 29, $2,325, 3yo & up, 1m, 1:44.20, DIAMOND EAGLE, Money Belt, Hogan's Hero. 5 started.

Relaunch S. (R), Del Mar, Aug. 10, $64,850, 3yo, non-winners of three races or for a claiming price of $80,000, 1mT, 1:34.85, BRICKS AND IVY, Macabe, Crazy Larrys. 6 started.

Reloy H., Santa Anita Park, Jan. 25, $75,725, 4yo & up, f & m, 1½mT, 2:29.29, KEEMOON (Fr), Juvenia, Ridjouna (Fr). 5 started.

Reluctant Guest S., Arlington Park, Aug. 19, $57,330, 3yo & up, f & m, 1m (originally scheduled at 1 1/16m on the turf), 1:38.19, BINALEGEND, Moonlady (Ger), Alybgood. 3 started.

Remington MEC Mile S., Remington Park, Nov. 24, $75,975, 2yo, 1m, 1:38.95, IT'SALLINTHECHASE, Expensive Risk, April's Lucky Boy. 9 started.

Remington Park Oaks, Remington Park, Sept. 9, $30,000, 3yo, f, 1mT, 1:37.42, WESTERN DELIGHT, Madison Grace, Golden Rhythm. 10 started.

Remington Park Sprint Championship H., Remington Park, Aug. 26, $29,880, 3yo & up, 6f, 1:10.33, HOMEFIELDHIT, Medium Rare, Cowboy Ettiquette. 5 started.

REMSEN S.-G2, Aqueduct, Nov. 24, $200,000, 2yo, 1⅛m, 1:51.28, SAARLAND, Nokoma, Silent Fred. 9 started.

Restoration S., Monmouth Park, Aug. 5, $75,000, 3yo, 1 1/16mT, 1:41.67, SPRUCE RUN, One Eyed Joker, Punkin Head. 13 started.

Retama Park Turf Cup H., Retama Park, Aug. 11, $50,000, 3yo & up, 1 1/16m, 1:42.20, NAT'S BIG PARTY, Gold Nugget, Dynaboy. 7 started.

Revidere S., Monmouth Park, May 27, $50,000, 3yo, f, 1m, 1:39.82, ZONK, Classy Place, Lady Diplomat. 5 started.

Ribbon S., Arlington Park, June 24, $54,000, 3yo, f, 7f, 1:23.60, HATTIESBURG, Sams Tune, Heart of a Chief. 8 started.

Ribbons and Lace S., Sun Downs, May 5, $3,700, 3yo & up, f & m, 7f, 1:28.80, CHARMINGER, Gotta Motion, Lack of Money. 8 started.

Richard King H. (R), Sam Houston Race Park, Dec. 1, $50,000, 3yo & up, Texas-bred, 1⅛mT, 1:51.67, CHAUFFE AU ROUGE, D C Storm, Gold Nugget. 9 started.

Richmond Derby Trial H., Hastings Park Racecourse, Sept. 2, $37,765, 3yo, 1 1/16m, 1:44.68, PALADDIE, Keyron, Godoliphin Road. 9 started.

Richmond H., Golden Gate Fields, Feb. 17, $51,625, 4yo & up, f & m, 6f, 1:08.16, ROLLETTE, Mister Crafty, Box Office Girl. 8 started.

Richmond S. (R), Hoosier Park, Nov. 11, $43,100, 3yo & up, f & m, Indiana-bred, 1 1/16m, 1:47.14, HERESYOUR CHICKEY, Lady's Legal Ma Ja, Nightair. 8 started.

Ricks Memorial H., Remington Park, Sept. 2, $50,000, 3yo & up, f & m, 1mT, 1:35.84, DARLIN DIXIE, Mumtaz (Fr), Runaway Magic. 7 started.

Ridan S. (R), Gulfstream Park, March 10, $100,000, 4yo & up, c & g, non-winners of two races other than maiden, claiming, or starter or non-winners of three races, 6f, 1:09.05, EXPLICIT, Praise From Dixie, Quixote's Prince. 12 started.

Riley Allison Derby, Sunland Park, April 1, $52,300, 3yo, 1 1/16m, 1:43.60, GOLDEN TANGLE, Mecke Monster, La Fontaine. 6 started.

Riley Allison Futurity, Sunland Park, Dec. 30, $148,305, 2yo, 6½f, 1:16.68, INTERMINABLE GOLD, Premeditation, Mr Motion. 9 started.

Rio Grande Thoroughbred Futurity (R), Ruidoso Downs, July 15, $88,045, 2yo, New Mexico-bred, 6f, 1:11.60, STAR SMASHER, How Bout Now, Prairie Fire. 11 started.

Rio Grande Kindergarten Futurity (R), Ruidoso Downs, June 10, $74,967, 2yo, New Mexico-bred, 5f, :59.20, HOW BOUT NOW, Ninety Nine Jack, Prairie Fire. 9 started.

Rise Jim S. (R), Suffolk Downs, March 31, $25,000, 3yo & up, Massachusetts-bred, 6f, 1:12.73, DIGGIN' FOR FUN, Dr Margaret, Al Bark. 8 started.

Risen Star S., Fair Grounds, Feb. 18, $125,000, 3yo, 1¹⁄₁₆m, 1:43.45, DOLLAR BILL, Gracie's Dancer, Rahy's Secret. 10 started.

RIVA RIDGE S.-G2, Belmont Park, June 9, $150,000, 3yo, 7f, 1:21.76, PUT IT BACK, Flame Thrower, Touch Tone. 6 started.

River 107 FM Oaks, Lethbridge, Oct. 27, $8,700, 3yo, f, abt6f, 1:11, RAGTIME MISS, Everetts Codey, Morning Breeze. 8 started.

River Cities Breeders' Cup S., Louisiana Downs, Sept. 15, $144,000, 3yo & up, f & m, abt1¹⁄₁₆mT, 1:42.42, CHAMPS ELYSEES, Euryanthe (Ire), Watch. 7 started.

RIVER CITY H.-G3, Churchill Downs, Nov. 11, $177,300, 3yo & up, 1¹⁄₈mT, 1:47.90, DR. KASHNIKOW, Tijiyr (Ire), Strategic Mission. 8 started.

River Memories S., Woodbine, Nov. 4, $106,000, 3yo & up, f & m, 1mT, 1:39.93, DIADELLA, Bristol Pistol, Ring of Flowers. 9 started.

Riverside S. (R), Retama Park, Oct. 6, $25,000, 2yo, Texas-bred, 6f, 1:10.63, FRONT NINE, Mutch Bigger Boots, Quantum Silver. 7 started.

Rizzi S., Calder Race Course, Sept. 9, $37,660, 3yo, 6⁷⁄₈f, 1:17.21, TOUR OF THE CAT, Built Up, Radical Riley. 7 started.

R. J. Speers S., Assiniboia Downs, Sept. 16, $26,950, 3yo & up, 1⁷⁄₁₆m, 1:46, SMOKY CINDER, Kalfaari, Gus Again. 6 started.

Road Runner H. (R), Ruidoso Downs, July 15, $42,800, 3yo, New Mexico-bred, 5³⁄₄f, 1:03.60, LIVE SHOW, Don's Ferrari, Friskie Feddie. 8 started.

Roamin Rachel S., Philadelphia Park, May 12, $48,500, 3yo, f, 6f, 1:11.61, HONEY EYED, Gigi's Magic, Above the Harbor. 4 started.

ROBERT F. CAREY MEMORIAL H.-G3, Hawthorne Race Course, Nov. 3, $150,000, 3yo & up, 1mT, 1:35.10, GALIC BOY, Where's Taylor, Good Journey. 10 started.

Robert G. Dick Memorial Breeders' Cup S., Delaware Park, July 21, $154,500, 3yo & up, f & m, 1³⁄₈mT, 2:17.20, AMOURETTE, Aiglonne, Krisada. 9 started.

Robert G. Leavitt Memorial H. (R), Charles Town, Aug. 31, $36,600, 3yo, West Virginia-bred, 7f, 1:25.46, PAST TENCE, Minnies Adam Ant, Parisian Lord. 7 started.

Robert K. Kerlan Memorial H., Hollywood Park, June 23, $75,480, 3yo & up, 5⁵⁄₈f, 1:01.53, SWEPT OVERBOARD, King Slayer (GB), Lake William. 6 started.

Robert R. Hilton Memorial S. (R), Charles Town, Sept. 15, $25,000, 3yo & up, West Virginia-bred nominated to the WVBC, 7f, 1:26.75, TURBOTAXMAN, Coolmars, In Front by Two. 7 started.

Robsphere S., Gulfstream Park, March 12, $84,425, 3yo, 1¹⁄₈mT, 1:47.28, PUNKIN HEAD, Act of Reform, Tom the River Rat. 11 started.

Robyn's Tune S., Calder Race Course, Oct. 21, $53,080, 3yo, f, 5f, :58.26, FLYING BIRDIE, Rich Peace, Pageant Baby. 7 started.

Rocket Man S., Calder Race Course, July 14, $50,000, 2yo & up, 2f, :20.98 (NTR), PUMA, Roy's Ruckus, Texas Code. 9 started.

Rockingham Park Breeders' Cup H., Rockingham Park, July 4, $73,250, 3yo & up, f & m, 1¹⁄₁₆mT, 1:45.31, STEP WITH STYLE, Song for Annie, Big Miss. 8 started.

Rockingham Park Derby, Rockingham Park, July 15, $25,000, 3yo, 1¹⁄₁₆m, 1:45.28, LUCKY SAM, Comic Genius, New York's Picc. 9 started.

Rockingham Park Distaff H., Rockingham Park, July 14, $25,000, 3yo & up, f & m, 6f, 1:11.67, PIC A LIL, Lucky Paws, Miss Yiayia. 9 started.

Rockingham Park Oaks, Rockingham Park, June 30, $25,000, 3yo, f, 1¹⁄₁₆mT, 1:46.52, SUNLIT RIDGE, Buzzing B's, Misty Diablo. 9 started.

Rockingham Park Sprint H., Rockingham Park, July 21, $25,000, 3yo & up, 6f, 1:10.08, COX'S SWEEP, Captain Red, Harty Congrats. 6 started.

Rocky Mountain Turf Club S. (R), Lethbridge, June 16, $6,800, 3yo & up, f & m, Alberta-bred, abt6f, 1:13, EBONY MYSTIQUE, Little Wiccan, Special Sweetpea. 8 started.

Rocky Mountain Turf Club S. (R), Lethbridge, June 16, $6,800, 3yo

& up, c & g, Alberta-bred, abt6f, 1:11.80, I DON'T CARE, Cool Mission, Weekend Special. 8 started.

Roger Van Hoozer Memorial S. (R), Charles Town, Sept. 15, $25,650, 3yo & up, f & m, West Virginia-bred nominated to the WVBC, 7f, 1:29.81, SWEET ANNUITY, Longfield Star, Siouxperhoney. 6 started.

Rollicking S. (R), Laurel Park, Nov. 17, $60,000, 2yo, Maryland-bred, 7f, 1:24.41, WAR NATIVE, Private Opening, Ride the Tiger. 7 started.

Rollin On Over S. (R), Beulah Park, April 14, $40,000, 3yo, Ohio-bred, 6f, 1:11.93, L G SWEENY, Boodles Brown, Thirty Corps. 10 started.

Roman Brother S. (R), Calder Race Course, July 28, $50,000, 3yo, progeny of eligible stallions standing in Florida, 1¹⁄₁₆mT, 1:44.58, TV SPORTS DIRECTOR, Sword Chief, Connot. 9 started.

Ropersandwranglers S., Emerald Downs, April 20, $25,000, 4yo & up, f & m, 6f, 1:09, RUN A COPY, One Number Short, Elegant Colors. 8 started.

Rose DeBartolo Memorial S. (R), Thistledown, July 14, $75,000, 3yo & up, f & m, Ohio-bred, 1³⁄₁₆m, 1:52.70, LADY CHERIE, Ms. Quimet, Prizes. 6 started.

Rosenna S., Delaware Park, June 4, $75,900, 3yo & up, f & m, 1⁷⁄₁₆mT, 1:44.21, QUIDNASKRA, Verruma (Brz), Pretty Dutch. 8 started.

Round Table H., Bay Meadows, May 13, $50,925, 3yo, 1mT, 1:36.90, IMPERIAL MEASURE (GB), Times Square (GB), Wa Dancer. 7 started.

ROUND TABLE S.-G3, Arlington Park, July 28, $125,000, 3yo, 1³⁄₈m, 1:49.73, DISCREET HERO, Western Pride, X Country. 6 started.

Royal Chase for the Sport of Kings Hurdle S., Keeneland, April 27, $185,875, 4yo & up, abt2³⁄₈mT, 4:34.56, POMPEYO (Chi), All Gong (GB), Rand (NZ). 10 started.

ROYAL HEROINE S.-G3, Hollywood Park, July 7, $109,900, 3yo & up, f & m, 1mT, 1:34.41, KALATIARA (Aus), Dianehill (Ire), Al Desima (GB). 7 started.

Royal North S. (R), Beulah Park, April 8, $40,000, 3yo, f, Ohio-bred, 6f, 1:10.98, RUNAWAY ROSE, Ashwood C C, Princess Time. 10 started.

ROYAL NORTH H.-G3, Woodbine, Aug. 4, $143,825, 3yo & up, f & m, 6fT, 1:09.10, CONFESSIONAL, Heliotrope, Ahead by a Century. 9 started.

Royal Palm H., Hialeah Park, March 17, $100,000, 3yo & up, 1³⁄₁₆mT, 1:39.83, DEL MAR SHOW, Gateman (GB), Dillonmyboy. 8 started.

Royal Signal S. (R), Delaware Park, Aug. 5, $59,200, 3yo, f, nonwinners of a stake since February 1, 2001, 6f, 1:11.37, URBAN DANCER, Maggie's Mischief, Musical Times. 6 started.

R. R. M. Carpenter Jr. Memorial S., Delaware Park, July 21, $97,000, 3yo & up, 1⁷⁄₁₆m, 1:45.07, BROKEN VOW, Jarf, Connected. 4 started.

Rudy Baez S., Suffolk Downs, March 24, $25,000, 3yo, 1m, 1:41.49, CLIFFDIVER, Yasou Daniel, Lunar Secret. 6 started.

Ruffian S., Arapahoe Park, July 22, $27,300, 3yo, f, 7f, 1:24.40, CHOPPERS PASSION, Illusive Barroness, Crafty Cindy. 7 started.

Ruff/Kirschberg Memorial H. (R), Beulah Park, Nov. 24, $45,000, 3yo & up, Ohio-bred, 1¹⁄₁₆m, 2:02.87, LADY CHERIE, Youdrivemewild, Brother Darcy. 8 started.

Ruidoso Horse Sales Thoroughbred Futurity (R), Sunland Park, Dec. 8, $61,777, 2yo, sold through the Ruidoso sale, 6f, 1:10.14, STAR SMASHER, Ninety Nine Jack, Royal de Hope. 12 started.

Ruidoso Mile H., Ruidoso Downs, Aug. 11, $25,900, 3yo & up, 1m, 1:40.20, MUCHO DANIERO, Marfa's Pirate, Brew. 9 started.

Ruidoso Oaks, Ruidoso Downs, July 28, $22,200, 3yo, f, 6f, 1:10.80, WAMPUS WHO, Waveband, Rampaging Irish. 6 started.

Ruidoso Thoroughbred Championship S., Ruidoso Downs, Sept. 2, $36,900, 3yo & up, 1¹⁄₁₆m, 1:44.20, BREW, Gratteau, Mucho Daniero. 4 started.

Ruidoso Thoroughbred Derby, Ruidoso Downs, Sept. 2, $27,400, 3yo, 1¹⁄₁₆m, 1:43.40, LUCKY BLUFF, Silver Matt, Mystery Years. 7 started.

Ruidoso Thoroughbred Futurity, Ruidoso Downs, Sept. 2, $68,464, 2yo, 6f, 1:10.60, MISS HADLEY, Alvis, Bonita Lake. 9 started.

Rumson S., Monmouth Park, Aug. 4, $75,000, 3yo, 6f, 1:10.29, SEA OF GREEN, Beau's Surprise, Run Kush Run. 6 started.

Runza H., Fonner Park, April 14, $17,130, 3yo & up, f & m, 6f, 1:12.80, MISS DISTINCTION, Run Around Sue, Mature Miss. 8 started.

Rushaway S., Turfway Park, March 24, $100,000, 3yo, 1¹⁄₁₆m, 1:43.35, PERCY HOPE, X Country, High Cascade. 8 started.

Rushing Man S., The Meadowlands, Nov. 3, $100,000, 3yo, 1³⁄₁₆mT, 1:41.64, ONE EYED JOKER, Moomtazz, First Spear. 8 started.

Rutgers S., The Meadowlands, Oct. 12, $75,000, 3yo, 1³⁄₈mT, 2:18.07,

DEPUTY STRIKE, Bicentennial, Jeeves. 8 started.

Ruth C. Funkhouser S. (R), Charles Town, Sept. 22, $25,900, 3yo, f, West Virgina-breds nominated to the WVBC, 7f, 1:28.21, IN DEFIANCE, Sweet Music, Hoity Toity. 9 started.

Ruthless S., Aqueduct, Jan. 7, $80,575, 3yo, f, 6f, 1:11.31, XTRA HEAT, Major Wager, Montana Cat. 5 started.

SABIN H.-G3, Gulfstream Park, Jan. 24, $103,000, 3yo & up, f & m, 1 1/16m, 1:44.74, DE BERTIE, Royal Fair, Frankly My Dear. 8 started.

Sacramento H., Golden Gate Fields, March 3, $58,950, 3yo & up, f & m, 1m, 1:35.78, GOURMET GIRL, Linda Love, Puerto Plata. 9 started.

Sadie Diamond Futurity (R), Hastings Park Racecourse, Sept. 8, $99,626, 2yo, f, Canadian-bred, 6 1/2f, 1:17.65, BEAUTIFUL STRANGER, Grace for You, Shelby Madison. 11 started.

Sadie Hawkins H. (R), Charles Town, Aug. 25, $36,650, 3yo & up, f & m, West Virginia-bred, 7f, 1:27.79, SWEET ANNUITY, Longfield Star, Peacomb Hen. 9 started.

Safely Kept H., Hollywood Park, Nov. 24, $74,980, 3yo & up, f & m, 5 1/2fT, 1:05.06, ROLLY POLLY (Ire), Twin Set (Ger), Salty Helen. 8 started.

Safely Kept S., Arlington Park, Aug. 18, $63,000, 3yo & up, f & m, 6f, 1:10.62, THE HAPPY HOPPER, Sandy's Way, Trip. 5 started.

Saguaro S., Turf Paradise, Sept. 29, $30,000, 3yo, 6f, 1:10.10, EXPERT, (DH) Rocky Bar, (DH) Rah Rah Party. 8 started.

Sail On By S., Turf Paradise, Nov. 18, $22,800, 2yo, 6f, 1:10.04, FOUR CORNERS, Tickle the Ivories, Bug Hall. 8 started.

Salem County S., The Meadowlands, Sept. 7, $50,000, 2yo, f, 1 1/16mT, 1:42.81, MINIMALIST, Piano Chimes, Farewell My Lovely. 7 started.

SALVATOR MILE H.-G3, Monmouth Park, Aug. 5, $150,000, 3yo & up, 1m, 1:36.74, SEA OF TRANQUILITY, Knock Again, Hal's Hope. 7 started.

Sam F. Davis S., Tampa Bay Downs, March 3, $50,000, 3yo, 1 1/16m, 1:45.20, BURNING ROMA, American Prince, Talking Red. 9 started.

Sam Houston Distaff H., Sam Houston Race Park, Jan. 13, $50,000, 4yo & up, f & m, 1 1/16m, 1:45.30, GOBEDIE, Screen Attraction, Precious Cat. 8 started.

Sam Houston Oaks, Sam Houston Race Park, March 10, $25,000, 3yo, f, 1m, 1:38.54, CHERYL P., Boggs Eyes, Spanish Guitar. 11 started.

Sam Houston Sprint H., Sam Houston Race Park, Jan. 6, $50,000, 4yo & up, 7f, 1:22.70, CAPTAIN COUNTDOWN, Oak Hall, Gold Press. 8 started.

Sam Houston Texan Juvenile S., Sam Houston Race Park, Dec. 1, $150,000, 2yo, 1 1/16m, 1:44.16, JEREMIAH JACK, French Assault, Private Emblem. 11 started.

Sam Houston Turf Sprint Cup H., Sam Houston Race Park, Feb. 24, $50,000, 4yo & up, 5fT, :57.45, TESTIFY, Vinnie's Boy, Boots On Sunday. 12 started.

Sam J. Whiting Memorial H., Pleasanton, June 30, $50,600, 3yo & up, 6f, 1:08.80, FLOM'S PROSPECTOR, Roaring Red, Lacey Evitan. 6 started.

Sam McCracken Memorial H., Rockingham Park, Sept. 2, $25,000, 3yo & up, 1 1/16mT, 1:45.14, BEN SPEEDIN, Spoof, Flash of Joy. 8 started.

Samuel H. (R), Beulah Park, Dec. 15, $25,000, 3yo & up, starters at Beulah Park since September 15, 2001, 6f, 1:10.34, MONTANA HOOFER, John Q's Winner, A's an B's. 9 started.

SAN ANTONIO H.-G2, Santa Anita Park, Feb. 4, $300,000, 4yo & up, 1 1/8m, 1:48.26, GUIDED TOUR, Lethal Instrument, Moonlight Charger. 8 started.

San Antonio Oaks, Retama Park, Oct. 20, $35,000, 3yo, f, 1 1/16mT, 1:43.11, DUE TO WIN AGAIN, Madison Grace, Golden Rhythm. 9 started.

SAN BERNARDINO H.-G2, Santa Anita Park, April 7, $150,000, 4yo & up, 1 1/8m, 1:47.87, FUTURAL, Irisheyesareflying, Tribunal. 5 started.

SAN CARLOS H.-G1, Santa Anita Park, March 4, $150,000, 4yo & up, 7f, 1:21.35, KONA GOLD, Blade Prospector (Brz), Grey Memo. 7 started.

San Carlos H., Bay Meadows, April 29, $50,600, 3yo & up, 1m, 1:35.77, JORROCKS, Boss Ego, Mistakenly Special. 6 started.

SAN CLEMENTE H.-G2, Del Mar, July 29, $150,000, 3yo, f, 1mT, 1:34.88, REINE DE ROMANCE (Ire), Gabriellina Giof (GB), La Vida Loca (Ire). 8 started.

Sandhills Cup Hurdle S., Stoneybrook at Five Points, Apr. 7, $30,000, 4yo & up, abt2 1/8mT, 4:25.60, HUNT LANE, Aggro Crag, Indispensable. 8 started.

Sandia H., The Downs at Albuquerque, Sept. 15, $27,000, 3yo & up, 5 1/2f, 1:03.71, DON'T WALK AT NITE, Wild Dan, Crooner Slew. 5 started.

SAN DIEGO H.-G2, Del Mar, July 29, $250,000, 3yo & up, 1 1/16m, 1:41.62, SKIMMING, Futural, Captain Steve. 7 started.

Sandman Hotel S., Lethbridge, May 27, $6,600, 3yo & up, f & m, abt6f, 1:11, WHATS THE RUSH, Flying Jo, Ye Roo. 6 started.

Sandpiper S., Tampa Bay Downs, Jan. 6, $50,000, 3yo, f, 6f, 1:13, POLITICAL WIFE, Quite Spender, Bigcuz. 11 started.

Sands Point S., Belmont Park, June 17, $107,800, 3yo, f, 1 1/8m (originally scheduled on the turf), 1:50.43, TWEEDSIDE, Owsley, Platinum Tiara. 4 started.

Sandy Blue S. (R), Del Mar, July 28, $65,075, 3yo, f, non-winners of three races or for a claiming price of $80,000, 1 1/16mT, 1:44.14, LIVE YOUR DREAMS, Alinga (Ire), Karla June (GB). 5 started.

SAN FELIPE S.-G2, Santa Anita Park, March 17, $250,000, 3yo, 1 1/16m, 1:41.94, POINT GIVEN, I Love Silver, Jamaican Rum. 8 started.

San Felipe S., Sam Houston Race Park, Dec. 22, $25,000, 3yo & up, f & m, 6f, 1:10.14, MIDGE TOO, Fran's Flash, Western Side. 8 started.

SAN FERNANDO BREEDERS' CUP S.-G2, Santa Anita Park, Jan. 13, $190,800, 4 yo, 1 1/16m, 1:42.05, TIZNOW, Walkslikeaduck, Wooden Phone. 6 started.

SANFORD S.-G2, Saratoga Race Course, July 26, $107,800, 2yo, 6f, 1:10.55, BUSTER'S DAYDREAM, Seeking the Money, Heavyweight Champ. 6 started.

SAN FRANCISCO BREEDERS' CUP MILE H.-G2, Bay Meadows, April 28, $263,750, 3yo & up, 1mT, 1:35.14, REDATTORE (Brz), Hawksley Hill (Ire), Kerrygold (Fr). 9 started.

SAN GABRIEL H.-G2, Santa Anita Park, Dec. 30, $150,000, 3yo & up, 1 1/8mT, 1:50.56, IRISH PRIZE, Sligo Bay (Ire), El Gran Papa. 11 started.

SAN GABRIEL H.-G2, Santa Anita Park, Jan. 1, $150,000, 4yo & up, 1 1/8mT, 1:47.88, IRISH PRIZE, Manndar (Ire), Here Comes Big C. 8 started.

SAN GORGONIO H.-G2, Santa Anita Park, Jan. 15, $150,000, 4yo & up, f & m, 1 1/8mT, 1:50.02, UNCHARTED HAVEN (GB), Brianda (Ire), Beautiful Noise. 12 started.

Sangue H., Louisiana Downs, Aug. 25, $50,000, 3yo & up, f & m, 1 1/16mT, 1:42.13, NANIE'S DINNER, Due to Win, Peruvian Waltz. 7 started.

San Jacinto S. (R), Sam Houston Race Park, Dec. 1, $50,000, 3yo & up, f & m, Texas-bred, 1 1/16mT, 1:46.67, PEPPY PRISCILLA, Lampsas County, Princess Liza. 7 started.

San Jose S., Bay Meadows, April 22, $55,700, 3yo, f, 1m, 1:37.47, DE GODDAUGHTER, Super Tuesday, Dawaytogold. 6 started.

SAN JUAN CAPISTRANO INVITATIONAL H.-G1, Santa Anita Park, April 14, $400,000, 4yo & up, abt1 3/4mT, 2:42.96, BIENAMADO, Persianlux (GB), Blueprint (Ire). 11 started.

San Juan County Commissioners H., SunRay Park, Nov. 11, $51,400, 3yo & up, 1 1/8m, 1:50.60, MORO GRANDE, Crooner Slew, Rainbow Parcel. 9 started.

San Juan County Juvenile S., SunRay Park, Nov. 3, $46,551, 2yo, c & g, 6 1/2f, 1:18.40, MR MOTION, Johns Hot Water, Co Twining Niner. 10 started.

San Juan Juvenile S., SunRay Park, Oct. 27, $50,847, 2yo, f, 6 1/2f, 1:19.40, RUSSIAN OLIVE, Bonita Lake, Mynexthorse. 9 started.

SAN LUIS OBISPO H.-G2, Santa Anita Park, Feb. 17, $200,000, 4yo & up, 1 1/2mT, 2:27.70, PERSIANLUX (GB), Devon Deputy, Falcon Flight (Fr). 10 started.

SAN LUIS REY H.-G2, Santa Anita Park, March 11, $250,000, 4yo & up, 1 1/2mT, 2:28.57, BLUEPRINT (Ire), Devon Deputy, Kerrygold (Fr). 8 started.

SAN MARCOS S.-G2, Santa Anita Park, Jan. 20, $150,000, 4yo & up, 1 1/4mT, 2:02.75, BIENAMADO, Kerrygold (Fr), Northern Quest (Fr). 7 started.

San Marino H. (R), Santa Anita Park, Feb. 18, $77,984, 4yo & up, non-winners of $50,000 at a mile or over in 2000-2001, 1 1/4mT, 2:03.03, KERRYGOLD (Fr), Beat All, Groover. 4 started.

SAN MIGUEL S.-G3, Santa Anita Park, Jan. 13, $107,500, 3yo, 6f, 1:08.60, LASERSPORT, Early Flyer, Bills Paid. 6 started.

SAN PASQUAL H.-G2, Santa Anita Park, Jan. 7, $200,000, 4yo & up, 1 1/16m, 1:41.94, FREEDOM CREST, Bosque Redondo, Sultry Substitute. 8 started.

San Pedro S., Santa Anita Park, March 25, $79,650, 3yo, 6 1/2f, 1:15.86, BEYOND BRILLIANT, So Urgent, Pie N Burger. 5 started.

SAN RAFAEL S.-G2, Santa Anita Park, March 3, $200,000, 3yo, 1m,

1:35.79, CRAFTY C. T., Palmeiro, Early Flyer. 9 started.

SAN SIMEON H.-G3, Santa Anita Park, April 16, $133,625, 4yo & up, abt6½fT, 1:12.34, LAKE WILLIAM, Macward, Touch of the Blues (Fr). 6 started.

SANTA ANA H.-G2, Santa Anita Park, March 18, $150,000, 4yo & up, f & m, 1⅛mT, 1:47.27, BEAUTIFUL NOISE, High Walden, Matiere Grise (Fr). 12 started.

SANTA ANITA DERBY-G1, Santa Anita Park, April 7, $750,000, 3yo, 1⅛m, 1:47.77, POINT GIVEN, Crafty C. T., I Love Silver. 6 started.

SANTA ANITA H.-G1, Santa Anita Park, March 3, $1,000,000, 4yo & up, 1¼m, 2:01.55, TIZNOW, Wooden Phone, Tribunal. 12 started.

SANTA ANITA OAKS-G1, Santa Anita Park, March 10, $300,000, 3yo, f, 11/16m, 1:41.83, GOLDEN BALLET, Flute, Affluent. 8 started.

SANTA BARBARA H.-G2, Santa Anita Park, April 14, $250,000, 4yo & up, f & m, 1¼mT, 2:01.33, ASTRA, Beautiful Noise, Uncharted Haven (GB). 7 started.

SANTA CATALINA S.-G2, Santa Anita Park, Jan. 21, $107,700, 3yo, 1 1/16m, 1:42.38, MILLENNIUM WIND, Palmeiro, Denied. 6 started.

Santa Lucia H. (R), Santa Anita Park, April 7, $80,400, 4yo & up, f & m, non-winners of $50,000 at a mile or over other than claiming or starter in 2001, 1 1/16m, 1:43.53, PRINTEMPS (Chi), Saudi Poetry, Win for Us (Ger). 6 started.

SANTA MARGARITA INVITATIONAL H.-G1, Santa Anita Park, March 10, $300,000, 4yo & up, f & m, 1⅛m, 1:48.59, LAZY SLUSAN, Spain, Critikola (Arg). 7 started.

SANTA MARIA H.-G1, Santa Anita Park, Feb. 18, $200,000, 4yo & up, f & m, 1 1/16m, 1:43.37, LOVELLON (Arg), Feverish, Critikola (Arg). 5 started.

SANTA MONICA H.-G1, Santa Anita Park, Jan. 27, $200,000, 4yo & up, f & m, 7f, 1:22.50, NANY'S SWEEP, Serenita (Arg), Surfside. 7 started.

Santa Paula S., Santa Anita Park, April 16, $85,975, 3yo, f, 6½f, 1:16.46, STARRER, Skywriting, Warren's Whistle. 7 started.

Santa Teresa H., Sunland Park, March 11, $43,700, 3yo & up, f & m, 6½f, 1:16.40, MALADY, Jenizara (Chi), Okanagan Invader. 10 started.

SANTA YNEZ S.-G2, Santa Anita Park, Jan. 20, $150,000, 3yo, f, 7f, 1:22.30, GOLDEN BALLET, Affluent, Warren's Whistle. 9 started.

SANTA YSABEL S.-G3, Santa Anita Park, Jan. 6, $109,300, 3yo, f, 1 1/16m, 1:44.69, COLLECT CALL, Irguns Angel, Eminent. 8 started.

SAN VICENTE S.-G2, Santa Anita Park, Feb. 3, $150,000, 3yo, 7f, 1:21.51, EARLY FLYER, Lasersport, D'wildcat. 5 started.

SAPLING S.-G3, Monmouth Park, Aug. 18, $150,000, 2yo, 6f, 1:10.82, PURE PRECISION, Truman's Raider, Wild Navigator. 8 started.

SARANAC H.-G3, Saratoga Race Course, Sept. 2, $112,500, 3yo, 1 3/16mT, 1:54.88, BLAZING FURY, Fast City, Rapid Ryan. 9 started.

SARATOGA BREEDERS' CUP H.-G2, Saratoga Race Course, Aug. 19, $291,000, 3yo & up, 1¼m, 2:01.55, APTITUDE, Perfect Cat, A Fleets Dancer. 7 started.

Saratoga H., Bay Meadows, May 26, $61,300, 3yo & up, 6f, 1:08.66, FLOM'S PROSPECTOR, Five Star Day, El Dorado Shooter. 7 started.

SARATOGA SPECIAL S.-G2, Saratoga Race Course, Aug. 15, $150,000, 2yo, 6½f, 1:17.35, JUMP START, Heavyweight Champ, Booklet. 6 started.

Sardula S., Santa Anita Park, March 22, $87,950, 3yo, f, 5½f, 1:03.66, WARREN'S WHISTLE, Comedy Class, Joke. 6 started.

Saskatchewan Derby, Marquis Downs, Aug. 5, $15,000, 3yo, 1 1/16m, 1:49.35, RED VIL DO, Brass Ruhler, Wendys Choice. 5 started.

Saskatchewan Futurity S. (R), Marquis Downs, July 22, $9,150, 2yo, c & g, Saskatchewan-bred, 6f, 1:18.53, ARCTIC ROCKET, Good Old Sprite, Debonair Blitz. 4 started.

Saskatchewan Futurity S. (R), Marquis Downs, July 22, $9,650, 2yo, f, Saskatchewan-bred, 6f, 1:16.29, ROYAL BRITTANY, Silver Missile, Remarkable Odyssey. 6 started.

Saskatoon H., Marquis Downs, June 15, $6,000, 3yo, 6f, 1:15.25, ICE JAMER, Take Me Dancer, Wendys Choice. 7 started.

Sauce Boat S., Arlington Park, Sept. 30, $53,000, 3yo, 6½f, 1:16.37, MEADOWMINER, Winnie's Pooh Bear, Ballado's Devil. 6 started.

Saylorville S., Prairie Meadows, July 3, $125,000, 3yo & up, f & m, 6f, 1:08.62, MISS SEFFENS, The Happy Hopper, Via Gras. 6 started.

Scarlet and Gray H. (R), Beulah Park, Nov. 11, $40,000, 3yo & up, f & m, Ohio-bred, 6f, 1:10.16, SCIOTO BOOTSKI, Athenavega, Lady Cherie. 12 started.

Schenectady H. (R), Belmont Park, Sept. 23, $83,100, 3yo & up, f & m, New York-bred, 6f, 1:09.49, BEDSIDE MANNER, Maddie May, Boundanddetermined. 8 started.

SCHUYLERVILLE S.-G2, Saratoga Race Course, July 25, $109,100, 2yo, f, 6f, 1:11.12, TOUCH LOVE, Lakeside Cup, Lost Expectations. 6 started.

Scissortail H., Remington Park, Nov. 9, $23,560, 3yo, 6f, 1:10.05, IT'S ROO, Abbi's Choice, That Tat. 10 started.

Scottsdale H., Turf Paradise, March 18, $35,000, 3yo, f, 1mT, 1:37.31, MOONLIT MADDIE, Lucy T, Caught On Video. 7 started.

Seagram Cup S., Woodbine, Aug. 5, $133,625, 3yo & up, 1 1/16m, 1:43.97, TRAJECTORY, Exciting Story, Catch the Ring. 5 started.

Sea O Erin Breeders' Cup Mile S., Arlington Park, Sept. 3, $121,300, 3yo & up, 1mT, 1:35.73, INTERN, Minor Wisdom, Langston. 12 started.

Searching S., Pimlico, April 28, $75,000, 3yo & up, f & m, 1mT, 1:34.51, COLSTAR, Queue, Maria's Tiara. 10 started.

Seattle H., Emerald Downs, April 29, $35,000, 3yo & up, 6f, 1:09, HANDY N BOLD, Rampaging Alf, Ryson. 7 started.

Seattle Slew H., Emerald Downs, July 1, $40,463, 3yo, c & g, 1m, 1:37, JUMRON WON, Jade Green, Tactical Allusion. 5 started.

Seaway S., Woodbine, Sept. 2, $113,000, 3yo & up, f & m, 7f, 1:24.24, EL PRADO ESSENCE, Meadow Gem, Ahead by a Century. 7 started.

SECRETARIAT S.-G1, Arlington Park, Aug. 18, $400,000, 3yo, 1¼mT, 2:04.91, STARTAC, Strut the Stage, Sharp Performance. 11 started.

SELENE S.-G1, Woodbine, May 21, $274,750, 3yo, f, 1 1/16m, 1:48.02, DARK ENDING, Turner's Hall, Royal Fact. 7 started.

Selma S. (R), Retama Park, Oct. 6, $25,000, 3yo, f, Texas-bred, 5fT, :56.60, LITTLE ANGEL, Eagle Lake, Wild Irish. 10 started.

Seminole H., Hialeah Park, April 15, $75,000, 3yo & up, 1⅛m, 1:48.65, FAPPIE'S NOTEBOOK, General Grant, Rize. 9 started.

Senate Appointee H., Hastings Park Racecourse, Aug. 25, $37,352, 3yo & up, f & m, 1 1/16m, 1:44.42, GREY TOBE FREE, Grooms Derby, Pretzel Logic. 8 started.

SENATOR KEN MADDY H.-G3, Santa Anita Park, Sept. 26, $110,400, 3yo & up, f & m, abt6½fT, 1:13.27, A LA REINE, Nanogram, Global. 8 started.

Send More Money S. (R), Penn National Race Course, June 30, $25,000, 3yo, Pennsylvania-bred, 1 1/16m, 1:44.10, BEAU'S SURPRISE, Panther Pond, Brimstone Tough. 6 started.

SENORITA S.-G3, Hollywood Park, April 22, $109,800, 3yo, f, 1mT, 1:35.13, FANTASTIC FILLY (Fr), Innit (Ire), Blushing Bride (GB). 8 started.

Sensational Star H. (R), Santa Anita Park, Jan. 14, $109,600, 4yo & up, California-bred non-winners of $50,000 twice other than closed or claiming since March 1, abt6½fT, 1:14.42, ECHO EDDIE, Unlimited Value, Macward. 8 started.

Sequoyah S., Remington Park, Nov. 11, $21,400, 2yo, f, 6½f, 1:17.08, BEDANKEN, Lucky M, Leap for Joy. 7 started.

Serena's Song S., Monmouth Park, July 4, $50,000, 3yo, f, 1m 70y, 1:42.07, ASTRID, Latour, Strike It Up. 8 started.

SHADWELL KEENELAND TURF MILE S.-G2, Keeneland, Oct. 7, $558,500, 3yo & up, 1mT, 1:35.98, HAP, Where's Taylor, Aly's Alley. 9 started.

Shady Well S. (R), Woodbine, July 8, $146,745, 2yo, f, Canadian-bred, 5½f, 1:07.11, GINGER GOLD, Western Resolve, Irish Line. 7 started.

Shakertown S., Keeneland, April 18, $85,200, 3yo & up, 5½fT, 1:02.71, AIRBOURNE COMMAND, Final Row (GB), Grangeville. 10 started.

Shakopee Turf Express H., Canterbury Park, May 28, $35,000, 3yo & up, 5f, :58.14, JACK'S STORM, Royal Tramp, I'm Registered. 9 started.

Shamrock S., Sportsman's Park, April 21, $50,000, 3yo, 6f, 1:09.84, SECRET ROMEO, Brassy Babe, Island N Abreeze. 6 started.

Sham S. (R), Santa Anita Park, Feb. 9, $96,750, 3yo, non-winners of $50,000 at one mile or over, 1⅛m, 1:50.51, WILD AND WISE, Swordfish, Special Times. 6 started.

Sham Say S. (R), Pimlico, April 14, $40,000, 3yo & up, f & m, non-winners of a stakes, 1 1/16m, 1:43.17, SERELA, Weekend Kaper, Broomesse. 6 started.

Shecky Greene H., Delaware Park, July 3, $58,700, 3yo & up, 1 1/16m, 1:44.14, B FLAT MAJOR, Trajectory, Judge's Case. 6 started.

SHEEPSHEAD BAY H.-G2, Belmont Park, June 2, $150,000, 3yo & up, f & m, 1⅜m (originally scheduled at abt1⅜m on the turf), 2:18.18, CRITICAL EYE, Playact (Ire), Janet (GB). 5 started.

Shenandoah River S., Delaware Park, Sept. 22, $58,800, 3yo & up, 1⅛m (originally scheduled on the turf), 1:51.80, HARBOR OF GRACE, Royal Romp, Johnny Dollar. 5 started.

Shepperton S. (R), Woodbine, Aug. 18, $131,125, 3yo & up, Canadian-bred, 6½f, 1:15.85, HOPEFUL MOMENT, Krz Ruckus, Trailthefox. 5 started.

SHIRLEY JONES H.-G3, Gulfstream Park, Feb. 14, $100,000, 3yo & up, f & m, 7f, 1:22.40, HIDDEN ASSETS, Another, Dream Supreme. 6 started.

Shiskabob S. (R), Louisiana Downs, Oct. 13, $65,000, 3yo & up, Louisiana-bred, 1 1/16m, 1:46.07, WHITE STAR, Doctor Mike, Cyrus. 8 started.

Shocker T. H., Calder Race Course, Oct. 13, $100,000, 3yo & up, f & m, 1 1/16m, 1:43.90, COOLBYTHEPOOL, Happily Unbridled, Vague Memory. 8 started.

SHOEMAKER BREEDERS' CUP MILE S.-G1, Hollywood Park, May 28, $475,000, 3yo & up, 1mT, 1:33.68, IRISH PRIZE, Touch of the Blues (Fr), Brahms. 9 started.

Shortgrass Heritage S. (R), Marquis Downs, Aug. 19, $12,700, 3yo, c & g, Saskatchewan-bred, 1 1/16m, 1:51.10, WENDYS CHOICE, Redlind, Arctic Prospect. 9 started.

Showtime Deb S. (R), Hawthorne Race Course, Nov. 25, $49,590, 2yo, f, Illinois-conceived and/or -foaled, 6f, 1:14.23, LIL' MARY'S KITTY, Dinner in Reno, My Carati. 9 started.

SHUVEE H.-G2, Belmont Park, May 19, $200,000, 3yo & up, f & m, 1m, 1:35.16, APPLE OF KENT, March Magic, Country Hideaway. 5 started.

Sickles Image S. (R), Great Lakes Downs, Sept. 15, $45,000, 2yo, f, Michigan-bred, 6 1/2f, 1:22.94, BORN TO DANCE, Luanne's Gift, Rock a Lot. 6 started.

Sidney Baer Memorial H., Delaware Park, Aug. 26, $58,100, 3yo, abt 5fT, :57.95, ROCK, Appellant, Shoobie. 5 started.

Silky Sullivan H., Golden Gate Fields, March 17, $50,450, 3yo & up, 1 1/16m, 1:45.83, CASINO KING (Ire), Irish Opinion, Bristolville. 6 started.

Silverado H. (R), The Downs at Albuquerque, April 22, $52,000, 3yo & up, New Mexico-bred, 6f, 1:08.88, YULLA YULLA, Wild Dan, Runmore Mema. 6 started.

Silver Bullet Centennial H., Remington Park, Sept. 14, $74,400, 3yo & up, 7f, 1:21.35, MR ROSS, Unrullah Bull, Homefieldhit. 5 started.

SILVERBULLETDAY S.-G3, Fair Grounds, Feb. 17, $125,000, 3yo, f, 1 1/16m, 1:46.09, LAKENHEATH, Morning Sun, Beloved by All. 5 started.

Silver Bullet S., Blue Ribbon Downs, Nov. 25, $7,400, 3yo & up, 6f, 1:13.60, CANROCK, Cordell, Freely Bend. 7 started.

Silver Deputy S., Woodbine, Sept. 2, $92,700, 2yo, 6 1/2f, 1:18.90, NICHOLLE'S DEVIL, Pat's Expectation, Rundle. 6 started.

Silver Maiden S., Arlington Park, Oct. 8, $54,500, 3yo, f, 7f, 1:23.08, SPANISH GLITTER, Emily Ring, Shemya. 9 started.

Silver Spur S., Lone Star Park, July 15, $100,000, 2yo, f, 5 1/2f, 1:04.56, MISS RITZ, Wild Gear, Sea Bag. 8 started.

Simcoe S. (R), Woodbine, Sept. 3, $102,800, 2yo, c & g, Canadian-bred CTHS sales yearlings, 7f, 1:24.12, RARE FRIENDS, Mighty Quinn, Molly's Wisdom. 6 started.

Simply Majestic S., Calder Race Course, June 2, $60,000, 3yo, 1 1/16mT, 1:45.51, BUILT UP, Tv Sports Director, Tour of the Cat. 10 started.

SINGAPORE PLATE S.-G3, Arlington Park, Aug. 11, $125,000, 3yo, f, 1 1/8m, 1:50.74, CARESSING, Gal On the Go, Scoop. 8 started.

Singing Beauty S. (R), Laurel Park, Feb. 19, $44,950, 4yo & up, f & m, non-winners of a stake, 7f, 1:24.55, END SWEEP'S GIRL, Honestly Honey, Broomesse. 10 started.

Sir Barton S., Pimlico, May 19, $100,000, 3yo, 1 1/16m, 1:44.03, BURNING ROMA, Mi Amigo Guelo, It's So Simple. 9 started.

Sir Barton S. (R), Woodbine, Nov. 24, $125,125, 3yo, c & g, progeny of eligible stallions standing in Ontario, 1 1/8m, 1:45.08, DEVIL VALENTINE, Indian Dan, Ruff Tuff Stuff. 4 started.

Sir Beaufort S., Santa Anita Park, Dec. 26, $77,400, 3yo, 1mT, 1:36.39, ORIENTATE, Sigfreto, Blue Steller (Ire). 10 started.

Sir Winston Churchill H., Hastings Park Racecourse, Sept. 22, $36,035, 3yo & up, 1 1/8m, 1:50.87, COLONIAL SECRETARY, Lord Nelson, King Jeremy. 8 started.

SIXTY SAILS H.-G3, Sportsman's Park, April 29, $300,000, 3yo & up, f & m, 1 1/8m, 1:49.11, LICENSE FEE, Lady Melesi, Megans Bluff. 8 started.

Sixty Sails H., Fair Grounds, Jan. 14, $75,000, 4yo & up, f & m, abt 1 1/16mT, 1:42.67, HISTOIRE SAINTE (Fr), Song for Annie, Always Sure. 10 started.

Skipat S., Pimlico, June 9, $75,000, 3yo & up, f & m, 6f, 1:09.95, BIG BAMBU, Superduper Miss, Ivy's Jewel. 9 started.

SKIP AWAY H.-G3, Gulfstream Park, Jan. 13, $103,000, 3yo & up, 1 1/16m, 1:42.31, AMERICAN HALO, Vision and Verse, Pleasant Breeze. 10 started.

Skip Away S., Monmouth Park, June 30, $75,000, 3yo & up, 1 1/16m,

---

1:42.20, BROKEN VOW, Rize, Mercaldo. 6 started.

Skip Trial S., The Meadowlands, Oct. 19, $100,000, 3yo & up, 6f, 1:09.11, RUN KUSH RUN, Oro de Mexico, Istintaj. 9 started.

Ski Roundtop Cup Timber S., Shawan Downs, Sept. 29, $23,250, 4yo & up, abt 3 1/2mT, 8:04, DR. RAMSEY, Charlie's Dewan, Make Me a Champ. 4 started.

SKY CLASSIC H.-G2, Woodbine, Oct. 28, $169,500, 3yo & up, 1 3/8mT, 2:21.79, STAGE CLASSIC, Strike Smartly, Silver Axe. 10 started.

Skywalker H., Santa Anita Park, Nov. 2, $75,300, 3yo & up, 1m, 1:34.97, I LOVE SILVER, Bosque Redondo, So Urgent. 7 started.

Sleepy Hollow S. (R), Belmont Park, Oct. 20, $100,000, 2yo, New York-bred, 1m, 1:38.31, WHITE IBIS, Private Emblem, Never Give In. 8 started.

Slight in the Rear S. (R), Fairmount Park, Oct. 16, $35,800, 3yo, f, Illinois-conceived and/or -foaled, 6f, 1:13.20, DENTONS RUBY, Shania's Code, Twe Twa Two. 7 started.

Slipton Fell H., Mountaineer Park, June 9, $58,275, 3yo & up, 1m 70y, 1:41.05, BOY GENIUS, Hustler, Leave Me Out. 12 started.

Smart Halo S., Pimlico, April 22, $38,800, 3yo, f, 6f, 1:11.35, KIM-BRALATA, Ultravase, Perusha. 4 started.

Smile Sprint H., Calder Race Course, Oct. 13, $200,000, 3yo & up, 6f, 1:09.89, FAPPIE'S NOTEBOOK, Thrillin Discovery, Salty Glance. 12 started.

Snow Chief S. (R), Hollywood Park, April 28, $250,000, 3yo, California-bred, 1 1/8m, 1:50.86, ROMANCEISHOPE, Mr. Joe C, Hoovergetthekeys. 11 started.

Snow Goose H., Laurel Park, March 10, $63,031, 4yo & up, f & m, 1 1/4m, 2:03.53, IRVING'S BABY, Gin Talking, Proud Owner. 4 started.

Snow White S., Charles Town, Dec. 22, $41,800, 2yo, f, 7f, 1:27.19, THE WORLD OWES ME, Afnan, Stealing the Candy. 8 started.

Solana Beach H. (R), Del Mar, Sept. 2, $125,000, 3yo & up, f & m, California-bred, 1mT, 1:35.79, TOP OF OUR GAME, Mimi's Cafe, Thewholebag. 6 started.

Solano County Juvenile Filly S. (R), Solano County Fair, July 22, $51,900, 2yo, f, California-bred, 5 1/2f, 1:04.29, CHARBUKA, Gyrene, Iowna Harley. 5 started.

Solo Haina H., Calder Race Course, Nov. 26, $34,010, 3yo & up, f & m, 1 1/8mT, 1:48.09, VEIL OF AVALON, On the Horizon, Great Fever (Fr). 10 started.

Some Sensation S., Santa Anita Park, March 9, $78,150, 3yo, f, 1mT, 1:37.05, FANTASTIC FILLY (Fr), Heads Will Roll (GB), Little Firefly (Ire). 9 started.

Somethingroyal S. (R), Colonial Downs, July 29, $40,000, 3yo & up, f & m, Virginia-bred or sired, 6f, 1:10.33, SMOCK, Elfin Glen, Silent Glory. 5 started.

Sonny Hine S., Laurel Park, Nov. 22, $68,500, 3yo, 6f, 1:09.17, HE'S A KNOCKOUT, Giant Gentleman, Jorgie Stover. 8 started.

Sonny Hine S., Charles Town, Nov. 8, $42,000, 2yo, f, 7f, 1:29.53, JOLIE'S JULIA, Nasty Sabrina, Atsa Pretty Muffin. 8 started.

Sonoma H., Northlands Park, Aug. 11, $50,000, 3yo, f, 1 1/16m, 1:46, LITTLE LOLITTA, Milton Road, C D Cool. 8 started.

Sophomore Sprint Championship S., Mountaineer Park, Nov. 27, $56,900, 3yo, 6f, 1:09.33, NATIVE HEIR, Gold Star, Freeway Ticket. 4 started.

SORORITY S.-G3, Monmouth Park, Sept. 1, $150,000, 2yo, f, 6f, 1:11.61, FOREST HEIRESS, Haunted Lass, Divine Angel. 6 started.

SORRENTO S.-G2, Del Mar, Aug. 4, $150,000, 2yo, f, 6 1/2f, 1:16.13, TEMPERA, Roepactful, Roaring Blaze. 8 started.

Southampton S., Philadelphia Park, July 21, $50,000, 3yo, f, 1 1/16mT, 1:45.69, THE GODDESS ATHIRD, Proudtobeaprado, Lady Katie. 6 started.

South Bend S. (R), Hoosier Park, Dec. 1, $34,500, 2yo, c & g, Indiana-bred, 1m, 1:40.71, COWBOY'S LIMELITE, Saint Golddigger, Drops of Jupiter. 11 started.

Southern Belle H., Grants Pass, June 30, $2,450, 3yo & up, f & m, 6 1/2f, 1:22.05, MISSY MUFFET, Frosty Bear, Aurora Blue. 7 started.

Southern Belle S. (R), Louisiana Downs, Nov. 3, $25,000, 2yo, f, Louisiana-bred, 6 1/2f, 1:18.02, TAYLOR'S QUEEN, C J's Star, Wish Cashmere. 9 started.

South Mississippi Owners & Breeders S. (R), Fair Grounds, Feb. 9, $25,000, 3yo, Mississippi-owned, 6f, 1:12.34, WAR THREAT, Princess Suzi, One Fast Girl. 9 started.

South Ocean S. (R), Woodbine, Oct. 31, $104,000, 2yo, f, progeny of eligible stallions standing in Ontario, 1 1/16m, 1:46.45, GALADRIEL, Bright Knight, Spanish Decree. 7 started.

Southwest H., Blue Ribbon Downs, March 10, $8,125, 3yo & up, 7f, 1:26.37, NATIVES RAP, Flagship Counselor, Hedorunrun. 10 started.

Southwest S., Oaklawn Park, March 3, $75,000, 3yo, 1m, 1:38.34,

SON OF ROCKET, Arctic Boy, Crafty Shaw. 8 started.

Soviet Problem H., Golden Gate Fields, March 24, $100,000, 3yo & up, f & m, 6f, 1:08.16, IMAGE OF GLORY, Box Office Girl, Cover Gal. 8 started.

Spangled Jimmy H., Northlands Park, July 7, $33,725, 3yo & up, 1m, 1:38.20, RUN JOEY RUN, Tyko Tycoon, Rancour. 5 started.

Spartan H. (R), Great Lakes Downs, June 15, $45,000, 3yo, c & g, Michigan-bred, 7f, 1:28.67, SECRET ROMEO, Magic Spark, Lite Up. 9 started.

SPECTACULAR BID S.-G3, Gulfstream Park, Jan. 3, $100,000, 3yo, 6f, 1:11.04, ICANSEETHERAIN, Diablo's Choice, American Century. 10 started.

Spectacular Bid S., Arlington Park, Sept. 8, $75,000, 2yo, 6f, 1:11.07, DOUBLE ZERO SEVEN, Lunar Bounty, Tinker. 7 started.

Speedboat S., Great Lakes Downs, May 4, $25,000, 3yo & up, 5½f, 1:09.50, TOUCH OF POWER, That Monetary, Crashpad. 6 started.

Speed H., Lincoln State Fair, May 20, $10,320, 3yo & up, 4½f, :54.20, LOVEITORLEAVEIT, Mr Zooha, Letthebigredroll. 8 started.

Speed H., Les Bois Park, May 28, $6,550, 3yo & up, 4½f, :51.56, ALEYNA'S PLACE, Rasha, Easter Chief. 10 started.

Speedster H., Blue Ribbon Downs, May 28, $7,800, 3yo & up, 5f, :57.38, COVER KEEPER, As de Oro, Cordell. 9 started.

SPEED TO SPARE CHAMPIONSHIP S.-G3, Northlands Park, Sept. 8, $100,000, 3yo & up, 1⅞m, 2:17.20, RANCOUR, Scotman, Imprimature. 7 started.

Spend a Buck H., Calder Race Course, Oct. 13, $100,000, 3yo & up, 1 1/16m, 1:42.59 (ETR), BEST OF THE REST, Dancing Guy, Sir Bear. 7 started.

Spend a Buck S., Monmouth Park, June 10, $50,000, 3yo, 1mT, 1:35.68, SPRUCE RUN, American Prince, Davy Jones. 9 started.

Spicy H. (R), Arapahoe Park, July 29, $30,000, 3yo & up, f & m, Colorado-bred, 1 1/16m, 1:49.80, JENNALY, Party Girl, Chantilly Saddle. 9 started.

Spicy Living S. (R), Delaware Park, July 17, $70,200, 3yo, f, non-winners of a stake at a mile or over on the turf in 2001, abt1 1/16mT, 1:44.93, LIGHT DANCER, Waiting Time, Go Baby Go (Ire). 10 started.

Spicy Living Sweepstakes H., Rockingham Park, Aug. 5, $100,000, 3yo & up, f & m, abt1⅛mT, 1:48.56, SHOPPING FOR LOVE, Step With Style, Big Miss. 6 started.

SPINAWAY S.-G1, Saratoga Race Course, Aug. 31, $200,000, 2yo, f, 7f, 1:23.47, CASHIER'S DREAM, Smok'n Frolic, Magic Storm. 7 started.

Spindletop S. (R), Sam Houston Race Park, March 3, $25,000, 3yo, Texas-bred, 7f, 1:24.44, SOLINGEN, B. L.'s Ghost, Kentucky Bay. 9 started.

Spirit of Fighter S., Calder Race Course, May 24, $36,230, 3yo & up, f & m, 6f, 1:12.46, DYNAMITE DIABLO, French Madam, Sugar N Spice. 7 started.

Spirit of Texas S. (R), Sam Houston Race Park, Dec. 1, $50,000, 3yo & up, Texas-bred, 6f, 1:10.23, COWBOY CUMBIA, Wild Again Again, Hey Woody. 12 started.

Sport of Kings Futurity, Louisiana Downs, Sept. 29, $59,780, 2yo, 6½f, 1:18.95, TRICKY STORM, Crazy Deputy, Proud and Steady. 5 started.

SPORT PAGE H.-G3, Belmont Park, Oct. 27, $109,400, 3yo & up, 6½f, 1:15.54, YONAGUSKA, Silky Sweep, Big E E. 6 started.

Sportsman's Park Breeders' Cup H., Sportsman's Park, March 24, $103,500, 3yo & up, 1m, 1:41.02, CHICAGO SIX, Apt to Be, Frazee's Folly. 6 started.

Spring Fever S., Oaklawn Park, March 11, $50,000, 4yo & up, f & m, 5½f, 1:04.36, SECRET SIP, The Happy Hopper, Naturalingredients. 8 started.

Springfield S. (R), Arlington Park, June 23, $75,000, 3yo, Illinois-conceived and/or -foaled, 1m, 1:38.15, ACT OF WAR, Crack the Vault, Lil Mephistopheles. 7 started.

Spring Novice Hurdle S., Atlanta, April 14, $48,500, 4yo & up, abt2mT, 3:47.20, TRES TOUCHE, Devil's Egg, War Talk. 5 started.

Spring Open Sprint S., Lethbridge, June 3, $6,800, 3yo & up, 7f, 1:26.80, S. S. TELL, Weekend Special, Sagreeno. 8 started.

Spring S. (R), Sam Houston Race Park, March 24, $25,000, 4yo & up, Texas-bred, 7f, 1:24.38, I. B. DEONE, Marked Native, J W Jet. 7 started.

Spring Sprint S., Lethbridge, June 2, $6,800, 3yo & up, 5½f, 1:08, SLED, It's All a Blurr, High Seas. 6 started.

Spruce Fir H. (R), Monmouth Park, Sept. 2, $50,000, 3yo & up, f & m, New Jersey-bred, 1mT, 1:36.95, GAELIC BAY, Riviera Grace, Pine Baroness. 8 started.

Squan Song S. (R), Laurel Park, Dec. 26, $50,000, 3yo & up, f & m, Maryland-bred non-winners of a stake, 7f, 1:24.90, WINTER LEAF, Timely Irony, Anything for You. 6 started.

Stage Door Betty H., Calder Race Course, Dec. 22, $100,000, 3yo & up, f & m, 1 1/16m, 1:46.74, EXTEND, Happily Unbridled, Halo Reality. 9 started.

Stampede Park Sprint Championship H., Stampede Park, May 5, $33,720, 4yo & up, 6f, 1:10.80, CASH ON THE RUN, Timboruck, Timely Ruckus. 6 started.

Stanley Panco Maiden Memorial S. (R), Atlantic City Race Course, May 4, $30,000, 3yo & up, New Jersey-bred, abt1mT, 1:40.86, MR. DENIM, She's a Witch, Samba in Rio. 11 started.

Star Ball H., Golden Gate Fields, Nov. 10, $55,750, 3yo & up, f & m, 1 1/16mT, 1:44.14, AVIATE, Shericaine (Ire), Slow Down. 6 started.

Star de Naskra S. (R), Pimlico, April 21, $60,000, 3yo, Maryland-bred, 6f, 1:10.51, JORGIE STOVER, Smile My Lord, Ronnie's Hot Rod. 7 started.

Stardust S. (R), Louisiana Downs, Oct. 13, $37,700, 2yo, Louisiana-bred, 6f, 1:12.06, RAPIDE, Walk in the Snow, Doeny Rain. 9 started.

Star of Texas S. (R), Sam Houston Race Park, Dec. 1, $100,000, 3yo & up, Texas-bred, 1 1/16m, 1:43.66, LIGHTS ON BROADWAY, Captain Countdown, Frankly Tee Riffic. 7 started.

STARS AND STRIPES BREEDERS' CUP H.-G3, Arlington Park, July 1, $190,500, 3yo & up, 1½mT, 2:27.86 (ECR), FALCON FLIGHT (Fr), Langston, Williams News. 11 started.

Stars and Stripes H., Les Bois Park, July 4, $6,500, 3yo & up, 7½f, 1:31.49, RASHA, San Diego Pete, Almost Golden. 7 started.

Star Shoot S., Woodbine, April 7, $110,500, 3yo, f, 6f, 1:12.27, CHAMUL, Gone On Sheila, Dark Ending. 8 started.

State Fair Futurity (R), Lincoln State Fair, July 1, $13,200, 2yo, Nebraska-bred, 4½f, :51.60, OTTIS P COALTRAIN, Bengal Boy, Why Knot. 8 started.

Steady Growth S. (R), Woodbine, May 30, $110,200, 3yo & up, progeny of stallions standing in Ontario, 1 1/16m, 1:44.25, CASINO PRINCE, Prince of Style, Speed River. 10 started.

Stefanita S., Laurel Park, Nov. 17, $51,500, 3yo & up, f & m, 7f, 1:24.10, KIMBRALATA, Ivy's Jewel, Outstanding Info. 6 started.

Steinlen H., Hollywood Park, Nov. 11, $73,500, 3yo & up, 1 1/16mT, 1:40.61, LONESOME DUDE, Kudos, Agol Lack. 8 started.

Steinlen S., Arlington Park, Oct. 7, $53,250, 3yo, abt1⅛mT, 1:52.18, BAHROBA, Mystery Giver, Slough Creek. 6 started.

STEPHEN FOSTER H.-G2, Churchill Downs, June 16, $831,000, 3yo & up, 1⅛m, 1:47.74, GUIDED TOUR, Captain Steve, Brahms. 8 started.

Stevens S. (R), Fonner Park, May 12, $15,550, 3yo, Nebraska-bred, 1m, 1:41.20, TAUKE, Watch Me Dazzle, Scheraboca's Tune. 5 started.

Steve Van Buren H., Philadelphia Park, Sept. 3, $75,000, 3yo & up, f & m, 7f, 1:22.59, VIKKI SLEW, Lorline, Cedar Knolls. 6 started.

St. Nick S., Charles Town, Dec. 8, $40,000, 2yo, 7f, 1:27.54, CLOUDY MIST, Adams Tribe, Cozy Spirit. 9 started.

STONERSIDE BEAUMONT S.-G2, Keeneland, April 22, $250,000, 3yo, f, abt7f, 1:27.86, XTRA HEAT, Mountain Bird, Raging Fever. 5 started.

Stonerside Sprint S. (R), Lone Star Park, June 30, $50,000, 3yo, Texas-bred, 6f, 1:09.20, TRIPLE CARD, Elite Spirit, Some Fortune. 6 started.

Storm Cat S. (R), Philadelphia Park, Oct. 6, $50,000, 2yo, Pennsylvania-bred, 6f, 1:10.81, VOLLEY BALL, Oswayo, Pal's Partner. 7 started.

Storm Cat S., Keeneland, Oct. 7, $77,052, 3yo & up, f & m, 6f, 1:10.48, MISS SEFFENS, Another, Pine for Me. 4 started.

Storm Cat S., The Meadowlands, Oct. 6, $75,000, 2yo, 1m 70y, 1:42.73, VINEMEISTER, Kiss With Caution, Just Le Facts. 8 started.

Stormy Blues Breeders' Cup H., Pimlico, Oct. 6, $88,500, 3yo, f, 6f, 1:10.91, STORMY PICK, Outstanding Info, Skip the Print. 4 started.

St. Patrick's Day S., Charles Town, March 17, $41,950, 3yo & up, 1⅜m, 1:57.36, BIG BECKER, Rebellious Dreamer, Native Son. 9 started.

St. Patrick's Day S., Turf Paradise, March 17, $24,300, 3yo & up, f & m, 7½fT, 1:30.71, LOOK TO BE PROUD, Winsome Merit, Lookn Might Fine. 9 started.

St. Paul S., Canterbury Park, June 23, $35,000, 3yo, 6f, 1:11.06, ADMONITION, Brockton Bogey, Corporate Shuffle. 11 started.

Straight Deal Breeders' Cup H., Pimlico, Aug. 18, $112,000, 3yo & up, f & m, 6f, 1:09.07, XTRA HEAT, Superduper Miss, Shutup and Dance. 5 started.

Straight Deal S. (R), Delaware Park, Oct. 28, $62,100, 3yo & up, f

& m, non-winners of two races over one mile in 2001 other than maiden, claiming, closed, or starter or for an optional claiming price of $100,000, 1m 70y, 1:43.58, SHAG, Avenging Passion, Brig. 10 started.

Stravinsky S., Keeneland, April 21, $84,150, 3yo & up, f & m, 5 1/2fT, 1:02.47, CONFESSIONAL, Crystal Sea, Katz Me If You Can. 9 started.

Strawberry Morn S., Hastings Park Racecourse, May 12, $35,268, 3yo & up, f & m, 6 1/2f, 1:16.97, MAKE CONTACT, Grooms Derby, El Tiare. 7 started.

Strike the Gold H., Charles Town, June 16, $75,000, 3yo & up, c & g, 1 1/8m, 1:53.37, CONFUCIUS SAY, Big Becker, Smooth Roller. 9 started.

STRUB S.-G2, Santa Anita Park, Feb. 3, $500,000, 4yo, 1 1/8m, 1:48.43, WOODEN PHONE, Tiznow, Jimmy Z. 6 started.

Sturgeon River S. (R), Northlands Park, Sept. 22, $40,000, 2yo, f, Alberta-bred, 1m, 1:41.60, REEYRE, Hartney Oak, O Howrude. 8 started.

STUYVESANT H.-G3, Belmont Park, Oct. 27, $107,700, 3yo & up, 1 1/8m, 1:47.95, GRAEME HALL, Country Be Gold, Cat's At Home. 6 started.

STYMIE H.-G3, Aqueduct, March 10, $109,800, 3yo & up, 1 1/8m, 1:48.43, WIND RUSH, Turnofthecentury, Boston Party. 8 started.

SUBURBAN H.-G2, Belmont Park, July 1, $500,000, 3yo & up, 1 1/4m, 2:00.39, ALBERT THE GREAT, Lido Palace (Chi), Include. 6 started.

Subway Sandwiches S., Lethbridge, Oct. 14, $8,600, 3yo, c & g, abt6f, 1:10.80, NO LAW BREAKER, Diamond Crest, Jake Gonna Win. 6 started.

Sugar Bowl S., Fair Grounds, Dec. 31, $75,000, 2yo, 6f, 1:11.51, MAPP HILL, Lead by Example, Cojet. 9 started.

Summer Finale H., Mountaineer Park, Sept. 3, $58,500, 3yo & up, f & m, 1mT, 1:35.23, INSIDE AFFAIR, Cabot Cove, Chelsie's House. 11 started.

Summer King H., Delaware Park, July 14, $67,400, 3yo & up, f & m, 1m 70y, 1:42.68, GOWESTFORGOLD, Saluteloot, Shag. 8 started.

SUMMER S.-G2, Woodbine, Sept. 9, $181,750, 2yo, 1mT, 1:35.14, EL SOPRANO, Miesque's Approval, North Brooklyn. 10 started.

Summing S., The Meadowlands, Sept. 22, $75,000, 3yo, 1 1/16m, 1:42.50, BOWMAN'S BAND, Mongoose, Temple Yard. 6 started.

Summit S., The Meadowlands, Oct. 6, $75,000, 3yo, f, 1m 70y, 1:41.53, UNRESTRAINED, Latour, Miss Kate. 7 started.

Summit Silver Cup H. (R), Thistledown, May 5, $50,000, 3yo, Ohio-bred, 1 1/16m, 1:45.62, TAYLORTWOFEATHERS, Blame It On Ruby, Stormy Hostage. 7 started.

Sun Beau S., Hawthorne Race Course, June 2, $59,850, 4yo & up, 1 1/16mT, 1:44.74, WHERE'S TAYLOR, Treat Me Doc, Galic Boy. 7 started.

Sunbelt S., Remington Park, Oct. 7, $22,000, 3yo, f, 7 1/2fT, 1:28.25, BIEN NICOLE, Spanish Guitar, Repository. 9 started.

Sun City H., Turf Paradise, May 5, $35,000, 3yo & up, f & m, 1mT, 1:36.83, LOOKN MIGHTY FINE, Winsome Merit, Fille Filly Fifi. 11 started.

Suncoast S., Tampa Bay Downs, Feb. 24, $50,000, 3yo, f, 1 1/16m, 1:48.88, CLASSY PLACE, Frozen Dinner, Chinsegut. 6 started.

Sun Devil S., Turf Paradise, Jan. 13, $25,000, 3yo, f, 1m, 1:40.64, SUNSET POINT, Proclaiming, Catahoula Rose. 6 started.

Sun H., Hastings Park Racecourse, July 14, $35,873, 3yo & up, f & m, 1 1/8m, 1:50.79, MAKE CONTACT, Fabulous Flight, Bamboo Queen. 7 started.

Sunland Park H., Sunland Park, April 7, $72,900, 3yo & up, 1 1/16m, 1:42 (ETR), BREW, Gratteau, Hangonslewpyhangon. 7 started.

Sunland Park Oaks, Sunland Park, March 31, $42,300, 3yo & up, f & m, 1m, 1:38.60, GEMS AND GOLD, Miss Einstein, Momaless. 7 started.

Sunland Park Yuletide Derby, Sunland Park, Dec. 2, $28,100, 3yo, 6 1/2f, 1:16.63, BEEHAY, Golden Tangle, Alyou. 10 started.

Sunny Slope S., Santa Anita Park, Oct. 20, $77,900, 2yo, 6f, 1:08.66, ROMAN DANCER, American System, Cappuchino. 5 started.

Sunnyvale H., Bay Meadows, June 3, $56,075, 3yo & up, f & m, 6f, 1:09.63, BRITE GIRL, Selector, Aloha Mangos. 6 started.

Sun Power S. (R), Hawthorne Race Course, Nov. 24, $49,185, 2yo, c & g, Illinois-conceived and/or -foaled, 6f, 1:13.30, CART'S FORTY FOUR, Improviser, Getem Frank. 8 started.

SunRay Park & Casino S., SunRay Park, Sept. 3, $31,000, 3yo, 6 1/2f, 1:17.40, SILVER SET, Appleton (Mex), Zynastry. 6 started.

Sunset Gun S. (R), Suffolk Downs, May 28, $25,000, 3yo & up, f & m, Massachusetts-bred, 1 1/16m, 1:47.93, EXPENSIVE VERDICT, Weepecket, Big Miss. 6 started.

SUNSET H.-G2, Hollywood Park, July 15, $200,000, 3yo & up, 1 1/2mT, 2:26.16, BLUEPRINT (Ire), Kudos, Northern Quest (Fr). 5 started.

Sun Sprint Championship H., Northlands Park, Aug. 6, $49,000, 3yo & up, 6 1/2f, 1:17.40, TIMELY RUCKUS, Run Joey Run, Vying Road. 4 started.

SUPER DERBY-G1, Louisiana Downs, Sept. 23, $500,000, 3yo, 1 1/4m, 2:06.20, OUTOFTHEBOX, E Dubai, Quadrophonic Sound. 9 started.

Supernaturel S., Hastings Park Racecourse, May 20, $32,508, 3yo, f, 6 1/2f, 1:17.72, CASTLE MOUNTAIN, Queen of My Nights, Up to Me. 3 started.

Super S., Tampa Bay Downs, Jan. 20, $50,000, 3yo & up, 7f, 1:24.08, SEA OF TRANQUILITY, Fort Metfield, American Dot Com. 11 started.

Supertrack Racing Series S. (R), Gulfstream Park, March 10, $100,000, 4yo & up, c & g, non-winners of three races other than maiden or claiming, non-winners of four races, or for a claiming price of $75,000, 1 1/16m, 1:44.28, CALL IT OFF, Foxy Sneakers, Capote Sun. 12 started.

Supertrack Racing Series S. (R), Gulfstream Park, March 10, $100,000, 4yo & up, f & m, non-winners of four races other than maiden or claiming or for a claiming price of $100,000, 1 1/16m, 1:44.74, LADY MELESI, Tina Dynamite, Oatsee. 11 started.

Survive S. (R), Santa Anita Park, Jan. 1, $109,100, 4yo & up, f & m, California-bred non-winners of $50,000 twice other than closed or claiming since March 1, 2000, 5 1/2f, 1:03.71, GO GO, Filigree, Pert Laura. 8 started.

Susan B. Anthony H. (R), Finger Lakes, June 23, $40,000, 3yo & up, f & m, New York-bred, 6f, 1:11.41, BELONGS TO MONY, Alley Ball, Mich's Pitch. 9 started.

Susan's Girl S. (R), Calder Race Course, Sept. 1, $125,000, 2yo, f, progeny of eligible stallions standing in Florida, 7f, 1:26.37, BOLD WORLD, Pharmstar, Sweep Princess. 11 started.

Susan's Girl S., Delaware Park, June 9, $75,000, 3yo, f, 1 1/16m, 1:46.14, STRIKE IT UP, Lady Andromeda, Emery Board. 5 started.

Sussex H., Delaware Park, Sept. 1, $100,600, 3yo & up, abt1 1/8mT, 1:49.93, KEY LORY, Warrant, Parade Leader. 7 started.

Suthern Accent S., Louisiana Downs, July 7, $38,800, 3yo & up, f & m, 6f, 1:10.04, MIDGE TOO, Sweet and Firm, Unique Creek. 4 started.

Sutter S., Golden Gate Fields, Dec. 30, $55,500, 2yo, 6f, 1:10.51, STEADY ROLLIN, Mighty David, Arsen. 6 started.

Sutter S., Golden Gate Fields, Feb. 10, $60,337, 3yo, 6f, 1:08.44, HER FIRST MAKI, Beyond Brilliant, (DH) Sempai, (DH) Takin It Deep. 6 started.

SUWANNEE RIVER H.-G3, Gulfstream Park, Feb. 18, $100,000, 3yo & up, f & m, 1 1/8mT, 1:47.28, SPOOK EXPRESS (SAf), Gaviola, Windsong. 8 started.

Svisdahl Pipehandlers S. (R), Grand Prairie, July 22, $2,325, 2yo & up, f & m, Canadian-bred, 6f, 1:16.60, NOKZCATOFFZFENCE, Winning a Go Go, Reign Storm. 5 started.

SWALE S.-G3, Gulfstream Park, March 10, $150,000, 3yo, 7f, 1:22.25, D'WILDCAT, Tarek, Yonaguska. 6 started.

SWAPS S.-G1, Hollywood Park, July 15, $500,000, 3yo, 1 1/8m, 1:48.61, CONGAREE, Until Sundown, Jamaican Rum. 6 started.

Sweet and Sassy S., Delaware Park, Sept. 29, $97,000, 3yo & up, f & m, 6f, 1:10.26, XTRA HEAT, Ivy's Jewel, Superduper Miss. 4 started.

Sweet Briar Too S., Woodbine, June 23, $92,700, 3yo & up, f & m, 6 1/2f, 1:16.19, TORRID AFFAIR, El Prado Essence, Except for Wanda. 6 started.

SWORD DANCER INVITATIONAL H.-G1, Saratoga Race Course, Aug. 11, $500,000, 3yo & up, 1 1/2mT, 2:26.41, WITH ANTICIPATION, King Cugat, Slew Valley. 9 started.

S. W. Randall Plate H., Hastings Park Racecourse, Sept. 3, $36,852, 3yo & up, 1 1/8m, 1:50.03, LORD NELSON, Colonial Secretary, Mt. Ouray. 8 started.

Swynford S., Woodbine, Sept. 23, $109,900, 2yo, 7f, 1:25.83, RARE FRIENDS, Grimer, Pat's Expectation. 6 started.

Sycamore Breeders' Cup S., Keeneland, Oct. 7, $166,200, 3yo & up, 1 1/2mT, 2:31.29, ROCHESTER, Chorwon, Regal Dynasty. 7 started.

Sydney Gendelman H. (R), River Downs, June 24, $50,000, 3yo & up, Ohio-bred, 1 1/16mT, 1:44.80, FAX A FREDDY, Leave Me Out, Huw. 9 started.

Tacoma H., Emerald Downs, July 22, $40,000, 3yo, c & g, 1 1/16m, 1:42.40, JADE GREEN, Sabertooth, Diglett. 8 started.

Tah Dah S. (R), River Downs, July 21, $40,000, 2yo, f, Ohio-bred, 5 1/2f, 1:05.60, JOANIES BELLA, Crypto's Twinjet, Mercer's Launch. 10 started.

Taking Risks S. (R), Timonium, Sept. 3, $40,000, 3yo & up, Maryland-bred, 1¹/₁₆m, 1:45.44, CLARK'S CLONE, Clever Gem, Waited. 5 started.

Tallahassee S., Hialeah Park, May 12, $26,600, 3yo & up, 6f, 1:09.56, SALTY GLANCE, Diamond Studs, Kipperscope. 8 started.

Tall Ben H., Portland Meadows, Jan. 6, $6,750, 4yo & up, 1¹/₁₆m, 1:48.01, POPSICLE PETE, Skeeber, My Constant Star. 7 started.

Tampa Bay Breeders' Cup S., Tampa Bay Downs, March 11, $80,450, 3yo & up, 1¹/₁₆mT, 1:41.91, DELAY OF GAME, Johnny Dollar, An Oscar for Bert. 11 started.

Tampa Bay Derby, Tampa Bay Downs, March 18, $200,000, 3yo, 1¹/₁₆m, 1:44.30, BURNING ROMA, American Prince, Paging. 11 started.

TANFORAN H.-G3, Golden Gate Fields, Feb. 4, $100,000, 4yo & up, 1¹/₁₆mT, 1:45.51, YARALINO (GB), Robynhood, El Cielo. 7 started.

Taylor's Special H., Fair Grounds, Feb. 25, $100,000, 4yo & up, 6f, 1:09.63, ABAJO, Crucible, Fantastic Finish. 5 started.

Taylor's Special S., Arlington Park, Oct. 27, $54,750, 3yo & up, abt5F, 1:01.53, MINERS GAMBLE, Bold Pilot, Final Row (GB). 7 started.

T. C. Clark Memorial S. (R), Rillito Park, March 11, $2,299, 8 yo's & up, starters at Rillito Park in 2001, 7f, 1:29.20, EASTERN COUNT, The Hoosegow, No Ninos. 8 started.

Technology S. (R), Gulfstream Park, March 10, $100,000, 4yo & up, c & g, non-winners of four races other than maiden, claiming, or starter or for a claiming price of $100,000, 6f, 1:10.68, AMARILLO PRIDE, He Be Irish, Valid Lightning. 9 started.

Teddy Drone S., Monmouth Park, Aug. 5, $75,000, 3yo & up, 6f, 1:10.19, NORMANDY BEACH, Night Caller, Loaded Gun. 7 started.

Teeworth Plate H., Stampede Park, May 26, $32,040, 3yo & up, 1m, 1:37, SCOTMAN, Run Joey Run, Three Johns. 4 started.

Tejano Run S., Turfway Park, March 17, $50,000, 4yo & up, 1¹/₈m, 1:50.21, GLACIAL, Castelli Secrets, Hallshill Road. 7 started.

Tejas S. (R), Retama Park, Oct. 6, $25,000, 3yo, Texas-bred, 5fT, :56.29, WILD AGAIN AGAIN, Top Card, Brother Julius. 11 started.

Tempe H., Turf Paradise, March 17, $35,000, 3yo, 1mT, 1:37.69, IRONMAN DEHERE, Resolve, Our Colors. 11 started.

Temple Gwathmey Hurdle H., Middleburg, April 21, $50,000, 4yo & up, abt2¹/₂mT, 5:64, ROWDY IRISHMAN, Aggro Crag, Indispensable. 8 started.

TEMPTED S.-G3, Belmont Park, Oct. 28, $111,500, 2yo, f, 1m, 1:37.77, SMOK'N FROLIC, Saintly Action, Wopping. 8 started.

Temptress S. (R), Great Lakes Downs, Aug. 17, $45,000, 2yo, f, Michigan-bred, 5¹/₂f, 1:07.42, BORN TO DANCE, Midway Girl, Rock a Lot. 5 started.

Tenacious H., Fair Grounds, Dec. 2, $75,000, 3yo & up, 1¹/₁₆m, 1:43.96, VALHOL, Dixieland Diamond, Rebridled. 5 started.

Ten Thousand Lakes S. (R), Canterbury Park, May 20, $37,600, 3yo & up, c & g, Minnesota-bred, 6f, 1:11.20, NOT SO FAST BRUTUS, Crocrock, King of Knights. 11 started.

Terre Haute S. (R), Hoosier Park, Nov. 30, $33,800, 2yo, f, Indiana-bred, 1m, 1:42.59, LOUISE'S LOVE CODE, Thesullivanfive, Connies Travels. 9 started.

Territorial Fair S. (R), The Downs at Albuquerque, May 20, $32,900, 3yo, New Mexico-bred, 1¹/₁₆m, 1:44.80, I'M NOT BLUFFIN, Elysian Elway, Mia's Lad. 7 started.

TEST S.-G1, Saratoga Race Course, July 28, $250,000, 3yo, f, 7f, 1:21.72, VICTORY RIDE, Xtra Heat, Nasty Storm. 8 started.

Testum S. (R), Les Bois Park, July 14, $11,190, 3yo, c & g, Idaho-bred, 7f, 1:23.44, LOOKN EAST, L. B. Makin' Money, Cowboy Jazz. 7 started.

Texas Heritage S., Sam Houston Race Park, March 17, $25,000, 3yo, 1m, 1:38.41, B. L.'S GHOST, Solingen, Triple Card. 10 started.

Texas Horse Racing Hall of Fame S. (R), Retama Park, Oct. 6, $100,000, 3yo & up, Texas-bred, 1¹/₁₆mT, 1:40.90, CHAUFFE AU ROUGE, Gold Nugget, Tin Smithen. 9 started.

TEXAS MILE S.-G3, Lone Star Park, April 28, $300,000, 3yo & up, 1m, 1:34.72, DIXIE DOT COM, Mr Ross, Five Straight. 7 started.

Texas Stallion S. (R), Lone Star Park, May 6, $73,556, 3 & 4yo, Texas-bred, 1m (originally scheduled on turf), 1:40.09, ONE MANZ FORTUNE, W G's Talkin to Me, Just El Nino. 11 started.

Texas Stallion S. (R), Sam Houston Race Park, Dec. 29, $56,488, 2yo, c & g, nominated and eligible for the Texas Stallion Stakes Series, 6¹/₂f, 1:19.05, GONE OFF, Fitzroyal, Onlynurimagination. 8 started.

Texas Stallion S. (R), Lone Star Park, May 6, $65,640, 3 & 4yo, f, Texas-bred, 1m (originally scheduled on turf), 1:42, SECRET BRICK, Eagle Lake, Lady Zotti. 7 started.

Texas Stallion S. (R), Retama Park, Sept. 22, $53,783, 3yo, c & g, nominated to the Texas Stallion Stakes Series, 6f, 1:12.98, HESTHETOPPS, Brother Julius, Marked for Promise. 7 started.

Texas Stallion S. (R), Sam Houston Race Park, Dec. 29, $52,713, 2yo, f, nominated and eligible for the Texas Stallion Stakes Series, 6¹/₂f, 1:20.41, QUANTA, Saucy Viva, Smarten Sunny. 6 started.

Texas Stallion S. (R), Retama Park, Sept. 22, $54,615, 3yo, f, nominated to the Texas Stallion Stakes Series, 6f, 1:10.73, EAGLE LAKE, Only Irish, Bricketta. 9 started.

Tex's Zing S. (R), Fairmount Park, Oct. 16, $35,800, 3yo, c & g, Illinois-conceived and/or -foaled, 6f, 1:12.20, FREEWAY TICKET, Proper Joe, Big Adam J. 7 started.

Thanksgiving H., Portland Meadows, Nov. 23, $8,500, 3yo & up, 1m, 1:42.41, CHINQUAPIN CHARLIE, Silver Sky, Tomtom Tommalice. 7 started.

Thanksgiving H., Fair Grounds, Nov. 22, $75,000, 3yo & up, 6f, 1:08.74, BONAPAW, Robin de Nest, Crucible. 6 started.

The Downs at Alberquerque H., The Downs at Albuquerque, June 3, $68,800, 3yo & up, 1¹/₁₆m, 1:48.47 (NTR), BREW, Darn Tootin, Expensive Ways. 9 started.

Thelma S., Fair Grounds, Jan. 6, $75,000, 3yo, f, 6f, 1:12.06, SWEET NANETTE, Hattiesburg, Cheryl P. 5 started.

THE VERY ONE H.-G3, Gulfstream Park, Feb. 11, $100,000, 3yo & up, f & m, 1³/₈mT, 2:13.62, INNUENDO (Ire), Lucky Lune (Fr), Silver Bandana. 10 started.

The Very One S., Pimlico, May 18, $75,000, 3yo & up, f & m, 5fT, :56.46, CONFESSIONAL, Merry Princess, Dressy Dress. 7 started.

The Vid S., Calder Race Course, Nov. 24, $60,000, 3yo, 1¹/₁₆mT, 1:40.46, TOUR OF THE CAT, Tv Sports Director, Vikadontis. 12 started.

Thirty Eight Go Go S., Laurel Park, Nov. 17, $53,500, 3yo & up, f & m, 1¹/₈m, 1:51.71, GOTTCHA LAST, Powerful Package, Proud Owner. 7 started.

Thomas Edison S., The Meadowlands, Sept. 29, $50,000, 3yo & up, 5fT, :56.95, MANOFGLORY, Governor's Pride, Sejm Boogie. 8 started.

Thomas F. Moran S. (R), Suffolk Downs, June 9, $25,000, 3yo & up, Massachusetts-bred, abt1¹/₁₆mT, 1:46.78, ABIT ERATIC, Ysaye, Ybbs. 9 started.

Thomas J. Malley S., Monmouth Park, Aug. 25, $50,000, 3yo & up, f & m, 5fT, :55.76, MAYPOLE DANCE, Wilma Lee, Go Carolina. 9 started.

Thoroughbred Claiming S., Gila County Fair, Oct. 7, $2,434, 3yo & up, 1¹/₈m, 2:00.80, CLIFF'S BEAT, Across Alaska, Cop Out. 8 started.

Thoroughbred Claiming S., Mohave County Fair, May 13, $2,057, 3yo & up, 1¹/₁₆m, 1:44.20, AVAILABLETOBEAKING, Somfas Dancer, Intimidator Rules. 4 started.

THOROUGHBRED CLUB OF AMERICA S.-G3, Keeneland, Oct. 21, $109,000, 3yo & up, f & m, 6f, 1:09.24, CAT CAY, Spanish Glitter, Another. 7 started.

Three Chimneys Juvenile S., Churchill Downs, May 5, $116,000, 2yo, 5f, :57.28 (NTR), (DH) OPEN STORY, (DH) CITY STREET, Storm Witch. 8 started.

Three Ring S., Calder Race Course, Dec. 8, $100,000, 2yo, f, 1¹/₁₆m, 1:45.65, MS BROOKSKI, Stormy Frolic, Redoubled Miss. 7 started.

Ticonderoga H. (R), Belmont Park, Oct. 21, $150,000, 3yo & up, f & m, New York-bred, 1¹/₁₆mT, 1:48.08, RANSOM'S PRIDE, Eventail, Spectaculaireontap. 12 started.

Tiffany Lass S. (R), Fair Grounds, Jan. 28, $100,000, 3yo, f, 1m, 1:39.30, WOOD SPRITE, Morning Sun, Curve Ahead. 8 started.

Timber Music S. (R), Hastings Park Racecourse, July 21, $35,668, 2yo, f, British Columbia-bred or -owned, 6¹/₂f, 1:19.89, LASTING CODE, Beautiful Stranger, Gabriola. 8 started.

Times Square S., Aqueduct, April 22, 3yo, c & g, progeny of eligible stallions standing in New York, 1m, 1:36.57, TOM'S THUNDER, Deputy Shaker, Redding Woods. 7 started.

Time to Leave S., Bay Meadows, June 9, $57,400, 2yo, f, 5f, :58.61, MISS JEANNE CAT, Fabulous Gamble, Capital Growth. 6 started.

Toboggan H., Aqueduct, March 17, $107,300, 3yo & up, 7f, 1:21.25, PEEPING TOM, Say Florida Sandy, Lake Pontchartrain. 6 started.

Toddler S., Pimlico, Sept. 22, $46,200, 2yo, f, 6f, 1:12.13, NIGHT BREEZE, Chain Blue, Phyxius. 8 started.

Toes Knows S. (R), Laurel Park, Jan. 1, $40,000, 4yo & up, f & m, non-winners of a stake, 5¹/₂f, 1:05.42, IVY'S JEWEL, Wild Fashion, Fickle Fanny. 11 started.

Tokyo City Cup H., Santa Anita Park, March 24, $79,150, 4yo & up,

1m, 1:35.52, FUTURAL, New Advantage, Grey Memo. 8 started.

Tomball S. (R), Sam Houston Race Park, Feb. 10, $25,000, 4yo & up, f & m, Texas-bred, 1¹/₁₆m, 1:46.65, LADY ZOTTI, Eccentric Lady, Minneapolis Babe. 6 started.

Tom Bane S. (R), Turf Paradise, April 7, $15,000, 3yo & up, Arizona-bred, 6f, 1:09.33, RADICAL RATE, Lineman's Gold, Young. 7 started.

Tomboy S. (R), River Downs, May 19, $50,000, 3yo, f, Ohio-bred, 1¹/₁₆m, 1:48.40, ACROSS THE CREEK, Irish Flight, Imaginary Dream. 11 started.

TOM FOOL H.-G2, Belmont Park, July 4, $150,000, 3yo & up, 7f, 1:21.24, EXCHANGE RATE, Say Florida Sandy, Here's Zealous. 5 started.

To Much Coffee S. (R), Hoosier Park, Nov. 25, $43,850, 3yo & up, Indiana-bred, 1¹/₁₆m, 1:44.77, FIGHT FOR ALLY, Joanies No Phony, Hail to Wild Again. 9 started.

Tondi H., Fonner Park, May 6, $25,000, 3yo & up, 6f, 1:12, DIPLO-MATIC CORPS, Leaping Plum, Thatsusintheolbean. 6 started.

Toon's Mile H., Marquis Downs, Sept. 3, $6,000, 3yo & up, 1m, 1:37.33, BEAU RING, Eviticus, Rouge Royale. 4 started.

Top Corsage S., Arlington Park, Sept. 22, $51,895, 3yo & up, f & m, 1m (originally scheduled at 1¹/₁₆m on the turf), 1:37.22, INSTINCT, Golden Antigua, Flinch (GB). 4 started.

TOP FLIGHT H.-G2, Aqueduct, Nov. 23, $150,000, 3yo & up, f & m, 1m, 1:35.45, CAT CAY, Tugger, Atelier. 9 started.

Top Flight S., Arlington Park, Sept. 1, $75,000, 2yo, f, 6f, 1:11.77, VICKI VALLENCOURT, Don't Ruffle Me, Strong Credentials. 8 started.

Topsider S., Suffolk Downs, Oct. 13, $25,000, 3yo & up, 6f, 1:11.96, GOODBAR, Flex Jet, Apache Native. 6 started.

TORONTO CUP H.-G3, Woodbine, July 14, $132,375, 3yo, 1¹/₈mT, 1:47.91, STRUT THE STAGE, Stage Classic, Legal Heir. 4 started.

Torrey Pines S. (R), Del Mar, Aug. 31, $81,400, 3yo, f, non-winners of a race worth $50,000 to winner at a mile or over in 2001, 1m, 1:36.18, Cindy's Hero, TAMARA PRINCESS (Brz), Warren's Whistle. 5 started.

Tougaloo S. (R), Thistledown, April 29, $40,000, 3yo, f, Ohio-bred, 6f, 1:13.42, LEFT LANE LORRAIN, Storm Witness, Blue Electra. 7 started.

Tour's Big Red S., Calder Race Course, Dec. 9, $37,310, 3yo, 1¹/₁₆m, 1:44.58, BUILT UP, Gold Ballad, Sea Leon. 6 started.

Track Robbery S., Turf Paradise, April 3, $23,800, 3yo & up, f & m, 6f, 1:10.71, DEZIBELLES FORLI, Little Snake Bit, Something Classy. 6 started.

Transylvania S., Keeneland, April 6, $113,800, 3yo, 1mT, 1:35.28, BAPTIZE, Dynameaux, Act of Reform. 9 started.

TRAVERS S.-G1, Saratoga Race Course, Aug. 25, $1,000,000, 3yo, 1¹/₄m, 2:01.40, POINT GIVEN, E Dubai, Dollar Bill. 9 started.

TREMONT S.-G3, Belmont Park, June 30, $106,300, 2yo, 5¹/₂f, 1:03.96, BUSTER'S DAYDREAM, Draw Play, Day Trader. 5 started.

TRIPLE BEND BREEDERS' CUP INVITATIONAL H.-G2, Hollywood Park, July 1, $296,000, 3yo & up, 7f, 1:21.17, CEEBAND, Squirtle Squirt, Elaborate. 10 started.

Tri State H., Ellis Park, Sept. 3, $72,500, 3yo & up, 1¹/₁₆mT, 1:46.30, PROMISE OF WAR, Chorwon, Al's Dearly Bred. 9 started.

TROPICAL PARK DERBY-G3, Calder Race Course, Jan. 1, $100,000, 3yo, 1¹/₁₆mT, 1:47.95, PROUD MAN, Mr Notebook, Cee Dee. 11 started.

Tropical Park Oaks, Calder Race Course, Jan. 2, $100,000, 3yo, f, 1¹/₁₆mT, 1:44.52, VOODOO DANCER, Grey Ballet, Open Minded. 8 started.

Tropical Park Steeplechase H., Calder Race Course, Dec. 9, $50,000, 4yo & up, abt2¹/₄mT, 4:19.01, P. C. PLOD, Plumb Bob, Ethical Actions. 7 started.

TROPICAL TURF H.-G3, Calder Race Course, Dec. 8, $100,000, 3yo & up, 1¹/₈mT, 1:46.90, BAND IS PASSING, Crash Course, Groomstick Stock's. 12 started.

TRUE NORTH H.-G2, Belmont Park, June 9, $150,000, 3yo & up, 6f, 1:08.77, SAY FLORIDA SANDY, Wake At Noon, Explicit. 8 started.

Truly Bound H., Fair Grounds, Dec. 30, $75,000, 3yo & up, f & m, 1¹/₁₆m, 1:45.84, GOLD FOR MY GAL, Instinct, Momentous. 8 started.

Truly Bound H., Fair Grounds, Jan. 5, $75,000, 3yo & up, f & m, 1¹/₁₆m, 1:46.09, GOLD FOR MY GAL, Bejoyfulandrejoyce, Knight Woman. 7 started.

TTA Sales Futurity (R), Lone Star Park, June 30, $168,700, 2yo, c & g, sold at a TTA sale, 5f, :57.41 (NTR), NUCLEAR ASSEMBLY, Three Glitter Men, Mr. Campbell Sir. 9 started.

TTA Sales Futurity (R), Lone Star Park, June 30, $147,440, 2yo,

f, sold at a TTA sale, 5f, :57.60, SMOKE BUSTER, She's Rite On Time, Friona. 11 started.

Tulsa County S. (R), Fair Meadows at Tulsa, June 30, $31,525, 3yo & up, Oklahoma-bred, 6¹/₂f, 1:18.20, GOLD SPUN FUN, College Dean, Trickmeister. 8 started.

Tulsa Dash S., Fair Meadows at Tulsa, June 21, $28,690, 3yo & up, 4f, :45.80, HOOKED ON EXPRESSO, Honey Im Charging, Bold Sky Beauty. 10 started.

Tulsa Sprint S. (R), Fair Meadows at Tulsa, July 21, $33,550, 3yo & up, Oklahoma-bred, 4f, :44.60, VALID SUNRISE, Lady J, As de Oro. 10 started.

TURF CLASSIC INVITATIONAL S.-G1, Belmont Park, Sept. 29, $750,000, 3yo & up, 1¹/₂mT, 2:29.43, TIMBOROA (GB), King Cugat, Cetewayo. 6 started.

TURF CLASSIC S.-G1, Churchill Downs, May 5, $349,900, 3yo & up, 1¹/₈mT, 1:48.75, WHITE HEART (GB), King Cugat, Brahms. 8 started.

Turf Distance Series Final S., Turf Paradise, May 5, $40,050, 3yo & up, 1³/₈mT, 2:16.41, CATHEDRAL FRIEND, Moonray, Gondolier's Song. 12 started.

TURF SPRINT S.-G3, Churchill Downs, May 4, $113,700, 3yo & up, 5fT, :56.60, MORLUC, Testify, Texas Glitter. 9 started.

Turf Paradise Breeders' Cup H., Turf Paradise, Feb. 3, $147,000, 3yo & up, 1¹/₁₆mT, 1:43.89, DEVINE WIND, Zanetti (DQ from 1st), Montemiro. 7 started.

Turf Paradise Derby, Turf Paradise, Feb. 3, $100,000, 3yo, 1¹/₁₆m, 1:41.72, STARTAC, Golden Tangle, Learing At Kathy. 11 started.

TURFWAY BREEDERS' CUP S.-G3, Turfway Park, Sept. 22, $200,000, 3yo & up, f & m, 1¹/₁₆m, 1:42.47, TRIP, Precious Feather, Spain. 7 started.

TURFWAY PARK FALL CHAMPIONSHIP S.-G3, Turfway Park, Sept. 8, $82,500, 3yo & up, 1¹/₈m, 1:49.83, GENEROUS ROSI (GB), Storm Day, Jadada. 6 started.

TURFWAY SPIRAL S.-G2, Turfway Park, March 24, $600,000, 3yo, 1¹/₈m, 1:47.23, BALTO STAR, Halo's Stride, Mongoose. 9 started.

TURNBACK THE ALARM H.-G3, Aqueduct, Nov. 3, $108,500, 3yo & up, f & m, 1¹/₈m, 1:51.19, ROCHELLE'S TERMS, Resort, Strolling Belle. 6 started.

Tux and Tails S., Lethbridge, Oct. 14, $8,700, 3yo & up, 7f, 1:25.80, HIGH SEAS, Sagreeno, Weekend Special. 7 started.

Twixt S. (R), Laurel Park, Dec. 1, $75,000, 3yo, f, Maryland-bred, 1¹/₁₆m, 1:52.40, YOUR OUT, Polish Hostess, Winter Leaf. 6 started.

Twixtslusive H., Delaware Park, June 26, $60,300, 3yo & up, f & m, 1¹/₁₆mT, 1:49.94, HIDDEN CAT, Battenkill, Miss Sara Toga. 8 started.

Tyro S., Monmouth Park, July 29, $50,000, 2yo, 5¹/₂f, 1:05.12, PURE PRECISION, Doc Wild, Outstander. 7 started.

U Can Do It H., Calder Race Course, Nov. 24, $60,000, 3yo & up, f & m, 6¹/₂f, 1:18.48, VAGUE MEMORY, Platinum Tiara, Castlebrook. 8 started.

Unbridled S. (R), Calder Race Course, Aug. 19, $53,900, 3yo, Florida-bred, 1¹/₁₆m, 1:46.55, BUILT UP, Radical Riley, Lavender's Lad. 7 started.

UNITED NATIONS H.-G1, Monmouth Park, July 1, $500,000, 3yo & up, 1³/₈mT, 2:13.56, SENURE, With Anticipation (DQ from 1st), Gritty Sandie. 8 started.

Unity Hall H., Delaware Park, June 12, $58,500, 3yo, f, 6f, 1:11.44, SUMMER SHENANIGANS, Hunka Hunka Lori Z, Maggie's Mischief. 6 started.

U. S. Bank S., Emerald Downs, April 22, $35,000, 3yo, f, 6f, 1:09.80, BEST JUDGEMENT, Shandra Smiles, Anita Maria. 6 started.

U. S. Championship Supreme Hurdle S. (R), Pine Mountain, Calloway Garden, Nov. 3, $75,000, 4yo & up, non-winners over hurdles prior to September 1, 2000, abt2³/₈mT, 3:52.80, P. C. PLOD, War Talk, Feeling So Pretty. 8 started.

UtiliCorp Networks Canada S., Lethbridge, Oct. 14, $10,800, 3yo & up, 1¹/₈m, 1:54.80, ROLL THE STAGE, Sentosa, End Zone. 8 started.

Vacaville H., Solano County Fair, July 14, $50,900, 3yo & up, f & m, 6f, 1:10, PHAENNA, One Number Short, Brite Girl. 9 started.

VAGRANCY H.-G3, Belmont Park, June 16, $106,800, 3yo & up, f & m, 6¹/₂f, 1:15.32, DAT YOU MIZ BLUE, Dream Supreme, Katz Me If You Can. 5 started.

Valdale S., Turfway Park, Feb. 24, $50,000, 3yo, f, 1m, 1:39.45, GAL ON THE GO, City Fair, Rank Her Alexis. 12 started.

Valedictory H., Woodbine, Dec. 2, $110,400, 3yo & up, 1³/₄m, 2:57.37, QUEENSGATE, A Fleets Dancer, Winning Skier. 8 started.

Valiant Pete H. (R), Santa Anita Park, April 15, $105,900, 4yo &

up, California-bred, 6f, 1:08.27, ECHO EDDIE, Full Moon Madness, Champ's Star. 5 started.
Valid Expectations S., Lone Star Park, May 28, $100,000, 3yo & up, f & m, 6f, 1:08.34 (ETR), HALLOWED DREAMS, Sweet and Firm, Naturalingredients. 7 started.
Valkyr H. (R), Hollywood Park, July 14, $71,625, 3yo & up, f & m, California-bred, 5$^1/_2$fT, 1:02.05, FAIR APACHE, Global, Warren's Whistle. 5 started.
Vallejo S., Golden Gate Fields, Jan. 27, $50,600, 3yo, f, 6f, 1:09.58, JOKE, Deb's Royal Flush, Gifted Daughter. 7 started.
Valley Forge S., Philadelphia Park, Oct. 8, $50,000, 2yo, 1m, 1:40.08, MAZOOLIAN GHOST, Coach Knight, Up a Notch. 7 started.
VALLEY STREAM S.-G3, Aqueduct, Nov. 18, $80,775, 2yo, f, 6f, 1:08.66, FOREST HEIRESS, A New Twist, On Parade. 6 started.
VALLEY VIEW S.-G3, Keeneland, Oct. 20, $113,600, 3yo, f, 1$^1/_{16}$mT, 1:42.93, (DH) CHAUSSON POIRE, (DH) COZZY CORNER, Quick Tip. 10 started.
Valor Farm S. (R), Lone Star Park, June 30, $50,000, 3yo, f, Texas-bred, 6f, 1:09.42, ROYAL ROUNDABOUT, Miss Photogenic, Little Angel. 8 started.
Van Berg Derby, Columbus, Aug. 19, $7,792, 3yo, 1m 70y, 1:44.40, TAUKE, I'm a City Girl, Clamato Rose. 7 started.
Vandal S. (R), Woodbine, Aug. 19, $149,175, 2yo, Canadian-bred, 6f, 1:11.66, RARE FRIENDS, Shaws Creek, Ajjalah. 7 started.
VANITY H.-G1, Hollywood Park, June 30, $250,000, 3yo & up, f & m, 1$^1/_8$m, 1:49.21, GOURMET GIRL, Lazy Slusan, Setareh. 5 started.
Veiled Look S. (R), Delaware Park, Oct. 29, $60,800, 3yo & up, f & m, non-winners of a stake in 2001 or for an optional claiming price of $100,000, 5$^1/_2$f, 1:06.09, MISS SULLIVAN, Outstanding Info, Elektraline. 8 started.
VERNON O. UNDERWOOD S.-G3, Hollywood Park, Dec. 2, $100,000, 3yo & up, 6f, 1:09.04, MEN'S EXCLUSIVE, Tavasco, Caller One. 7 started.
Via Borghese S., Gulfstream Park, Feb. 9, $58,350, 3yo, f, 1$^1/_{16}$mT, 1:42.87, RUFF, Marq of Beauty, Word Puzzle. 10 started.
Vice Regent S. (R), Woodbine, Aug. 8, $105,600, 3yo, progeny of eligible stallions standing in Ontario, 1mT, 1:36.83, INDIAN DAN, Devil Valentine, Playing With Fire. 8 started.
Victoria Day S., Assiniboia Downs, May 21, $26,950, 3yo & up, f & m, 5$^1/_2$f, 1:07.40, ISPYMYTIE, Miss Sandy Dee, Christmas Lights. 7 started.
Victoria Day S., Hastings Park Racecourse, May 21, $37,649, 3yo & up, 6$^1/_2$f, 1:16.08, KING JEREMY, Lord Nelson, Ball and Chain. 6 started.
Victoria Lass H., Fair Grounds, March 17, $125,000, 4yo & up, f & m, 6f, 1:08.34 (NTR), HALLOWED DREAMS, My Brent's Diamond, My Alibi. 5 started.
Victoriana S. (R), Woodbine, Aug. 6, $133,750, 3yo & up, f & m, progeny of eligible stallions standing in Ontario, 1$^1/_{16}$mT, 1:39.85, NYMPHENBURG, Knight Dancer, Bristol Pistol. 8 started.
Victorian Queen S. (R), Woodbine, Oct. 3, $103,900, 2yo, f, progeny of eligible stallions standing in Ontario, 6f, 1:12.65, PARISIA, Jade Eyed, My Valley Girl. 7 started.
Victoria Park S., Woodbine, June 9, $107,800, 3yo, 1$^1/_8$m, 1:51.67, DREAM LAUNCHER, Slewhome, High Commissioner. 5 started.
Victoria S., Woodbine, June 16, $110,200, 2yo, 5f, :58.80, EXPECTED HOUR, Tepu Sultan, Spy Hill. 6 started.
Victoria S. (R), Louisiana Downs, Oct. 14, $38,750, 3yo & up, f & m, Louisiana-bred, 6f, 1:11.45, MIDGE TOO, Mike's Sister, Joe K's Kathy. 8 started.
Victor S. Myers Jr. S. (R), Canterbury Park, July 8, $39,615, 3yo, c & g, Minnesota-bred, 6f, 1:11.58, BALIN, Now Playing, Timberwolf Power. 7 started.
VIGIL H.-G3, Woodbine, April 28, $137,375, 4yo & up, 7f, 1:23.49, EXCITING STORY, Wake At Noon, Grand End Sweep. 7 started.
Vincennes S. (R), Hoosier Park, Oct. 5, $42,450, 3yo, f, Indiana-bred, 6f, 1:13.11, FRIENDLY SPIRIT, Taloa, Ramona's Rose. 5 started.
Vincent A. Moscarelli Memorial S., Delaware Park, Aug. 11, $75,000, 3yo, 1$^1/_8$m, 1:50.43, WEDLOCK, Confucius Say, Gallant Snowman. 5 started.
VINERY MATCHMAKER H.-G3, Monmouth Park, June 16, $100,000, 3yo & up, f & m, 1$^1/_8$mT, 1:46.19 (NCR), BATIQUE, Melody Queen (GB), Lucky Lune (Fr). 8 started.
VIOLET H.-G3, The Meadowlands, Sept. 28, $150,000, 3yo & up, f & m, 1$^1/_{16}$mT, 1:43.56, CLEARLY A QUEEN, Queue, Paga (Arg). 12 started.
Violet S. (R), Sportsman's Park, March 31, $75,000, 3yo, f, Illinois-bred, 6f, 1:13.64, SHEMYA, Dentons Ruby, Twill. 9 started.
Virginia Derby, Colonial Downs, July 14, $200,000, 3yo, 1$^1/_4$mT, 2:02.17, POTARO (Ire), Bay Eagle, Confucius Say. 9 started.
Virginia Gold Cup Timber S., Great Meadows, May 5, $50,000, 5 yo's & up, abt4mT, 8:29, IRONFIST, Bredesen Moe, Atomistic. 8 started.
Virginia Hunt Cup Timber S., Montpelier, Nov. 3, $22,000, 4yo & up, abt4mT, 8:57, BREDESEN MOE, The Headman (Ire), Fast Steppin Man. 3 started.
Virginia Stallion S. (R), Colonial Downs, July 8, $40,000, 3yo & up, progeny of eligible stallions standing in Virginia, 6f, 1:10.19, NATIVE HEIR, Robbie's Prince, Oxford Tea Party. 6 started.
Vivace H., Calder Race Course, Aug. 17, $34,340, 3yo & up, f & m, 6f, 1:12.76, VAGUE MEMORY, Not in Order, Too Many. 7 started.
Vivacious H. (R), River Downs, Aug. 19, $50,000, 3yo & up, f & m, Ohio-bred, 1$^1/_{16}$m, 1:49.20, LADY CHERIE, Prizes, Ms. Quimet. 9 started.
Viva El Paso H. (R), Sunland Park, Dec. 8, $103,800, 3yo & up, New Mexico-bred, 6$^1/_2$f, 1:16.04, CIENTO, Runmore Mema, Down Hill Racer. 12 started.
VOSBURGH S.-G1, Belmont Park, Sept. 22, $300,000, 3yo & up, 7f, 1:20.73, LEFT BANK, Squirtle Squirt, Big E E. 6 started.
Vulcan S. (R), Fair Grounds, March 9, $35,000, 3yo, Alabama-bred, 6f, 1:13.31, BREKENRICK, Big Daddy Doc, Poker's Pride. 7 started.
Wade Snapp Memorial S., Les Bois Park, May 28, $9,850, 3yo & up, 6$^1/_2$f, 1:19.88, MING LUE, Hope'n to Win, Deli Chef. 8 started.
Wadsworth Memorial H., Finger Lakes, Sept. 4, $30,000, 3yo & up, 1$^1/_8$m, 1:52.91, WOODWORK, Makem Hagar, Saigon Lieutenant. 9 started.
Wafare Farm S., Lone Star Park, May 19, $75,000, 3yo, f, 6f, 1:09.81, HATTIESBURG, Lady Virginia, Cheryl P. 8 started.
Walmac Farm Matchmaker S. (R), Louisiana Downs, Oct. 14, $64,450, 3yo & up, f & m, Louisiana-bred, 1$^1/_{16}$m, 1:46.95, MRS. MAC, Mysia Jo, Go Zippy Go. 5 started.
WALMAC INT'L. ALCIBIADES S.-G2, Keeneland, Oct. 5, $452,800, 2yo, f, 1$^1/_{16}$m, 1:46.23, TAKE CHARGE LADY, Never Out, Cunning Play. 11 started.
Walmac Lone Star Oaks, Lone Star Park, July 4, $125,000, 3yo, f, 1$^1/_{16}$mT, 1:44.32, LA RECHERCHE, Devout Sinner, Smokin N Jokin. 7 started.
Walter Haight H., Laurel Park, Dec. 15, $51,500, 3yo & up, 1$^1/_8$m, 1:50, GRUNDLEFOOT, Cowboy Magic, Sumerset. 6 started.
Walter R. Cluer Memorial H., Turf Paradise, Nov. 3, $30,000, 3yo & up, 7$^1/_2$fT, 1:28.71, BRISTOLVILLE, Eagleton, Snohomish Loot. 10 started.
Waquoit S., Suffolk Downs, Feb. 21, $25,000, 4yo & up, 1$^1/_{16}$m, 1:51.42, CROWN NOBLE, Makeyourselfathome, Why So Quiet. 11 started.
Warfield S. (R), Keeneland, Oct. 12, $80,425, 3yo & up, non-winners of a graded stake at a mile or over, 1$^1/_{16}$m, 1:42.49, CONNECTED, Neon Shadow, Storm Day. 6 started.
Washington Breeders' Cup Oaks, Emerald Downs, Aug. 18, $88,750, 3yo, f, 1$^1/_8$m, 1:49.20, GRACEFUL CAT, Inish Glora, Lady's Jewel. 10 started.
Washington Championship H. (R), Emerald Downs, Sept. 17, $60,000, 3yo & up, Washington-bred, 1$^1/_{16}$m, 1:42.60, MAKORS MARK, Snohomish Loot, Kittys Link. 7 started.
Washington Owners' Breeders' Cup H., Emerald Downs, Aug. 12, $64,375, 3yo, c & g, 1$^1/_{16}$m, 1:41.60, DIGLETT, Poker Brad, Jumron Won. 8 started.
WASHINGTON PARK H.-G2, Arlington Park, July 21, $400,000, 3yo & up, 1$^1/_4$m, 2:00.76, GUIDED TOUR, A Fleets Dancer, Duckhorn. 5 started.
Washington State Legislators H., Emerald Downs, June 3, $35,000, 3yo & up, f & m, 6$^1/_2$f, 1:16, FLEET PACIFIC, Taste the Passion, Crossatyourownrisk. 7 started.
Waterford Park H., Mountaineer Park, May 19, $57,250, 3yo & up, 6f, 1:08.96, BIDIS, Leave Me Out, Nature. 6 started.
Waya H., Hollywood Park, Dec. 8, $72,500, 3yo & up, f & m, 1$^1/_2$mT, 2:30.21, NEPENTHE, Built To Last (Brz), Boismorand (Fr). 6 started.
Waya S., Pimlico, Sept. 15, $75,000, 3yo & up, f & m, 1$^1/_{16}$mT, 1:42.46, LADY OF THE FUTURE, Preseli (Ire), Brazen Bride. 10 started.
Wayward Lass S., Tampa Bay Downs, Feb. 17, $50,000, 3yo & up, f & m, 1$^1/_{16}$m, 1:45.10, INSIDE AFFAIR, Royal Fair, Silver Stockings. 7 started.
Weekend Delight S., Turfway Park, Sept. 15, $75,000, 3yo & up, f & m, 6f, 1:09.94, NASTY STORM, Hidden Assets, City Fair. 6 started.

Wende S., Turf Paradise, May 19, $24,300, 3yo & up, f & m, 1mT, 1:37.51, PAIGE'S SISTER, Alissa Quinn, Grendella. 11 started.

WESTCHESTER H.-G3, Aqueduct, April 7, $108,200, 3yo & up, 1m, 1:33.60, CAT'S AT HOME, Little Hans, Milwaukee Brew. 6 started.

Western Borders H., Calder Race Course, Nov. 17, $60,000, 3yo & up, 6½f, 1:16.86, GROOMSTICK STOCK'S, Dancing Guy, Sea of Tranquility. 8 started.

Western Canada H., Northlands Park, July 1, $33,675, 3yo, 6½f, 1:17.60, SIXTHIRTYJOE, Lucky Prince, Wondrous Zeal. 6 started.

Westerner H., Northlands Park, Aug. 25, $35,000, 3yo & up, 1 5/16m, 2:10.80, RANCOUR, Run Joey Run, Scotman. 8 started.

Western Heritage S. (R), Marquis Downs, Aug. 19, $11,500, 2yo, c & g, Saskatchewan-bred, 6½f, 1:23.15, BRITTS XPRESS, Good Old Sprite, Slew Tonic. 5 started.

West Mesa H., The Downs at Albuquerque, Sept. 21, $26,850, 3yo & up, f & m, 7f, 1:21.68, PURLS LEDGEND, K J Lucky Seven, Okanagan Invader. 12 started.

West Point H. (R), Saratoga Race Course, Aug. 17, $86,800, 3yo & up, New York-bred, 1⅛m, 1:49.11, I'M ALL YOURS, Reluctant Groom, Brave One. 12 started.

West Virginia Breeders' Classic S. (R), Charles Town, Oct. 13, $225,000, 3yo & up, West Virginia-bred, -sired, or -raised, 1⅛m, 1:51.75, CONFUCIUS SAY, Coolmars, Rebellious Dreamer. 8 started.

West Virginia Breeders' Classic S. (R), Charles Town, Oct. 13, $67,500, 2yo, f, West Virginia-bred, -sired, or -raised, 4½f, :53.41, WHATACON, Scalped Ticket, Third Prospect. 9 started.

West Virginia Breeders' Classic S. (R), Charles Town, Oct. 13, $67,500, 3yo & up, West Virginia-bred, -sired, or -raised, 4½f, :52.08, DOUBLEDAR DIAMOND, Red Top's Boy, Diamond Pete. 9 started.

West Virginia Derby, Mountaineer Park, Aug. 11, $500,000, 3yo, 1⅛m, 1:47.20 (NTR), WESTERN PRIDE, Saratoga Games, Thunder Blitz. 9 started.

West Virginia Division of Tourism Breeders' Classic S. (R), Charles Town, Oct. 13, $67,500, 3yo, f, West Virginia-bred, -sired, or -raised, 7f, 1:27.99, IN DEFIANCE, Amazon Adam, Sweet Music. 9 started.

West Virginia Fillies and Mares Breeders' Classic S. (R), Charles Town, Oct. 13, $135,000, 3yo & up, f & m, West Virginia-bred, -sired, or -raised, 7f, 1:26.78, LONGFIELD STAR, Siouxperhoney, Aye Got a Secret. 9 started.

West Virginia Futurity (2nd Div.) (R), Charles Town, Nov. 17, $38,538, 2yo, West Virginia-bred, 7f, 1:30.13, NEAL'S RODEO, Social Mix, Storm Now. 6 started.

West Virginia Futurity (1st Div.) (R), Charles Town, Nov. 17, $37,688, 2yo, West Virginia-bred, 7f, 1:28.45, ADAMS TRIBE, Shark Eye, Count On Justin. 7 started.

West Virginia Governor's H., Mountaineer Park, Aug. 11, $57,750, 3yo & up, 1 1/16m, 1:43.94, WINNING CONNECTION, Nature, Xclusive Imp. 9 started.

West Virginia House of Delegates Speaker's Cup H., Mountaineer Park, Aug. 11, $58,325, 3yo & up, 1mT, 1:36.90, JAKE THE FLAKE, Val de Dash, Morava. 9 started.

West Virginia Legislature Chairman's Cup H., Mountaineer Park, Aug. 11, $57,175, 3yo & up, 4½f, :50.33 (NTR), FINA DUR, Diablos Ordination, Knave. 5 started.

West Virginia Lottery Breeders' Classic S. (R), Charles Town, Oct. 13, $67,500, 3yo, West Virginia-bred, -sired, or -raised, 7f, 1:25.75, PAST TENCE, Parisian Lord, Where's Ralph. 9 started.

West Virginia Oaks, Charles Town, Dec. 22, $41,650, 3yo & up, f & m, 1⅛m, 1:55.83, ELISE'S NOTEBOOK, My Sister Pearl, Real Women. 7 started.

West Virginia "Onion Juice" Breeders' Classic (R), Charles Town, Oct. 13, $67,500, 3yo & up, c & g, West Virginia-bred, -sired, or -raised, 7f, 1:25.32, TURBOTAXMAN, Hot Ziggity, In Front by Two. 9 started.

West Virginia Senate President's Cup H., Mountaineer Park, Aug. 11, $58,100, 3yo & up, f & m, 1mT, 1:37.07, ELAINE'S BOOBOO, Chelsie's House, Cozy Lass. 10 started.

West Virginia Vincent Moscarelli Memorial Breeders' Classic S. (R), Charles Town, Oct. 13, $67,500, 2yo, West Virginia-bred, -sired, or -raised, 6½f, 1:21.02, ADAMS TRIBE, Social Mix, Shark Eye. 9 started.

What a Pleasure S., Calder Race Course, Dec. 8, $100,000, 2yo, 1 1/16m, 1:47.08, O'ROCKY, Speedy Leon, The Judge Sez Who. 8 started.

What a Summer S., Laurel Park, Jan. 28, $57,600, 4yo & up, f & m, 6f, 1:11.53, DOC CALLS HER KATE, Ivy's Jewel, It's a True Ring. 8 started.

Wheat City S., Assiniboia Downs, Aug. 6, $26,950, 3yo & up, 1m, 1:39, KALFAARI, Crooner Slew, Smoky Cinder. 8 started.

Whimsical S., Woodbine, April 13, $145,300, 4yo & up, f & m, 6f, 1:11.78, MYSTERIOUS AFFAIR, Torrid Affair, Ruby Park. 7 started.

Whirlaway H., Fair Grounds, Feb. 11, $125,000, 4yo & up, 1 1/16m, 1:44.01, INCLUDE, Connected, Kombat Kat. 8 started.

Whirlaway S., Aqueduct, Feb. 10, $78,850, 3yo, 1 1/16m, 1:44.52, REGAL SHIVERS, Voodoo, What's Your Wish. 5 started.

White Oak H. (R), Arlington Park, June 23, $75,000, 3yo & up, Illinois-conceived and/or -foaled, 6f, 1:10.35, TIC N TIN, Classic Appeal, Out of My Way. 10 started.

WHITNEY H.-G1, Saratoga Race Course, July 28, $1,008,000, 3yo & up, 1⅛m, 1:47.94, LIDO PALACE (Chi), Albert the Great, Gander. 7 started.

Who Doctor Who H. (R), Lincoln State Fair, July 8, $21,825, 3yo & up, Nebraska-bred, 1 1/16m, 1:42.60, HIGH DICE, Old Man's Delite, Kathryn's Ego. 4 started.

Wickerr H. (R), Del Mar, July 27, $79,050, 3yo & up, non-winners of $40,000 other than closed, claiming, or starter at 1 mile or over since May 1, 2001, 1mT, 1:35.02, THADY QUILL, Touch of the Blues (Fr), Spinelessjellyfish. 8 started.

Wide Country S., Laurel Park, March 25, $56,500, 3yo, f, 1⅛m, 1:50.93, STRIKE IT UP, Sunshine in Paris, Sweep Dreams. 5 started.

WIDENER H.-G3, Hialeah Park, March 24, $200,000, 3yo & up, 1⅛m, 1:45.52 (NTR), ALBERT THE GREAT, U So Bad, High Security (Ven). 7 started.

Wildcat H., Turf Paradise, April 14, $35,000, 3yo & up, 1⅜mT, 2:16.11, TURK FLYER, Glowing Idea, Felon (Ire). 8 started.

Wild Event S. (R), Calder Race Course, Dec. 22, $55,200, 3yo, Florida-bred, 1 1/16mT, 1:41.58, OFFICER'S SWORD, Built Up, Vikadontis. 9 started.

Wild Rose H., Prairie Meadows, June 9, $50,000, 3yo & up, f & m, 1 1/16m, 1:44.73, RODEO FAN, Due to Win, Itsaprincess. 5 started.

Wild Rose H., Northlands Park, June 29, $34,850, 3yo & up, f & m, 6½f, 1:20.20, NORTHERN NEECHITOO, Uncas Ruckus, Tecate. 7 started.

Wiley Post H., Remington Park, Aug. 17, $21,200, 3yo & up, 1m 70y, 1:41.73, BEST OF K C, During the Act, Fourteen Ten. 6 started.

Willard L. Proctor Memorial S., Hollywood Park, May 26, $78,750, 2yo, 5f, :56.81, EXPECTED PROGRAM, Fonz's, Square Cut Diamond. 7 started.

William Almy Jr. S., Suffolk Downs, April 16, $25,000, 3yo & up, 6f, 1:11.12, MARKUS, Makin Progress, Personal Moon. 7 started.

William "Bill" Hartack S., Charles Town, April 5, $41,500, 3yo, 7f, 1:26.28, CONFUCIUS SAY, Not for Sam, Action Request. 7 started.

WILLIAM DONALD SCHAEFER H.-G3, Pimlico, May 19, $100,000, 3yo & up, 1⅛m, 1:49.55, PERFECT CAT, Rize, Judge's Case. 8 started.

William Henry Harrison S. (R), Hoosier Park, Oct. 7, $42,600, 3yo & up, c & g, Indiana-bred, 6f, 1:12.01, J D'S DIAMOND, Special Express, Indiana Royale. 7 started.

William Jefferson Clinton S., Charles Town, May 26, $41,850, 3yo & up, f & m, 4½f, :51.97, WILD FASHION, Quite Revealing, Lip Sing's Affair. 9 started.

William Kyne H., Portland Meadows, Jan. 27, $8,325, 3yo & up, 1⅛m, 1:53.67, SKEEBER, Wapato Wind, My Constant Star. 6 started.

Willow Lake H., Yavapai Downs, Aug. 28, $10,000, 3yo & up, f & m, 1m, 1:38.73, MOONLIT MADDIE, My Kina Bluff, Delightful Time. 8 started.

WILL ROGERS S.-G3, Hollywood Park, April 20, $109,800, 3yo, 1mT, 1:35.10, (DH) MEDIA MOGUL (GB), (DH) DR. PARK, Learing At Kathy. 8 started.

Willy Fiddle Memorial S. (R), Les Bois Park, June 16, $11,640, 3yo & up, c & g, Idaho-bred, 7½f, 1:31.66, RASHA, Fadski, San Diego Pete. 7 started.

Wilmington H., Delaware Park, Sept. 29, $100,300, 3yo & up, 6f, 1:10.69, SASSY HOUND, Monk's Falcon, Max's Pal. 6 started.

WILSHIRE H.-G3, Hollywood Park, April 29, $108,600, 3yo & up, f & m, 1mT, 1:34.69, TRANQUILITY LAKE, Dianehill (Ire), Out of Reach (GB). 7 started.

Wine Country H. (R), Finger Lakes, July 4, $30,000, 3yo & up, New York-bred, 6f, 1:10.69, IMPEACHTHEPRO, Bal Harbour, Kissane. 7 started.

Wink Novotny Memorial S., Great Lakes Downs, Sept. 2, $25,000, 3yo, 7f, 1:24.77, SECRET ROMEO, Native Ruck, Patton Poser. 7 started.

Winning Colors S., Arlington Park, July 21, $64,000, 3yo, f, 1m,

1:36.83, BOGGS EYES, Gal On the Go, Abba Gold. 8 started.

Winning Colors S. (R), Les Bois Park, June 24, $11,010, 3yo & up, f & m, Idaho-bred, 7f, 1:25.46, BABY GOOFHAUF, Love and Fun (DQ from 1st), Irish Elms. 6 started.

Winnipeg Futurity, Assiniboia Downs, Sept. 30, $39,200, 2yo, 1m, 1:40, NESS GADOLL, Holy Bold, Trebbiano. 7 started.

Winnipeg Sun S., Assiniboia Downs, Aug. 5, $26,950, 3yo & up, f & m, 1¹/₁₆m, 1:46.60, MISS SANDY DEE, All in White, Regal Eyre. 8 started.

Winsham Lad H., Sunland Park, Jan. 13, $28,200, 3yo & up, 1m, 1:36.40, BREW, Gratteau, Mr. de Falls. 9 started.

WinStar Distaff H., Lone Star Park, May 28, $200,000, 3yo & up, f & m, 1mT, 1:42.23, VOLADORA, Dyna Likes Bingo, Iftiraas (GB). 10 started.

WINSTAR GALAXY S.-G2, Keeneland, Oct. 5, $563,500, 3yo & up, f & m, 1³/₁₆mT, 1:54.24, SPOOK EXPRESS (SAf), Solvig, Veil of Avalon. 9 started.

Wintergreen S., Turfway Park, March 10, $43,500, 4yo & up & up, f & m, 1m, 1:35.66, MYSTICS BLUE ROSE, Two Dot Slew, Fast Delivery. 10 started.

Winter Solstice S. (R), Santa Anita Park, Feb. 8, $78,700, 4yo & up, f & m, non-winners of $35,000 other than closed or claiming since November 1, abt6¹/₂f, 1:13.98, SEPARATA (Chi), Automated, Fair Apache. 7 started.

Wishing Well S., Turfway Park, Jan. 28, $50,000, 4yo & up, f & m, 6f, 1:12.53, HOLY BLITZ, Two Dot Slew, Fair Margarita. 10 started.

Wistful H. (R), The Meadowlands, Oct. 24, $100,000, 3yo & up, f & m, New Jersey-bred, 1m 70y, 1:41.34, GAELIC BAY, Sea Femma, Firecard. 7 started.

WITHERS S.-G3, Aqueduct, May 5, $150,000, 3yo, 1m, 1:35.66, RICHLY BLENDED, Le Grande Danseur, Telescam. 7 started.

W. L. MCKNIGHT H.-G2, Calder Race Course, Dec. 29, $150,000, 3yo & up, 1¹/₂mT, 2:27.95, PROFIT OPTION, Deeliteful Irving, Eltawaasul. 12 started.

W. Meredith Bailes Memorial S. (R), Colonial Downs, July 22, $40,000, 3yo & up, Virginia-bred or sired, 6f, 1:09.16, NATIVE HEIR, Finn McCool, Holiday Music. 6 started.

WNBC S. (R), Belmont Park, June 9, $65,000, 4yo & up, f & m, non-winners of a stake, 1m, 1:35.12, TAX AFFAIR, Imadeed, Vivid Sunset. 8 started.

Wolf Hill S., Monmouth Park, June 2, $50,000, 3yo & up, 5f, :57.34, RUDIRUDY, Testame, Erlton. 6 started.

Wolverine S. (R), Great Lakes Downs, June 30, $45,000, 3yo & up, Michigan-bred, 7f, 1:26.73, Q COMMERCIAL JETTE, Above the Wind, That Gift. 9 started.

Wonders Delight S. (R), Penn National Race Course, May 11, $24,638, 3yo, f, Pennsylvania-bred, 6f, 1:11.20, GOLDEN LAKE, Moorestown, Foxy Power. 4 started.

Wonder Where S. (R), Woodbine, Sept. 29, $250,000, 3yo, f, Canadian-bred, abt1¹/₄mT, 2:06.08, SWEETEST THING, Noble Strike, Soundtrack. 8 started.

Woodbine Oaks (R), Woodbine, June 9, $500,000, 3yo, f, Canadian-bred, 1¹/₈m, 1:51.74, DANCETHRUTHEDAWN, Dancen in the Sun, Quick Blue. 12 started.

Woodchopper H., Fair Grounds, Dec. 22, $100,000, 3yo, abt1¹/₁₆mT, 1:44.09, FAN CLUB'S MISTER, Mystery Giver, Even the Score. 12 started.

WOODFORD RESERVE TURF CLASSIC S.-G1, see TURF CLASSIC S-G1.

Woodland Heritage S. (R), Marquis Downs, Aug. 19, $12,100, 2yo, f, Saskatchewan-bred, 6¹/₂f, 1:23.18, ROYAL FRACTIONS, Royal Brittany, Remarkable Odyssey. 7 started.

Woodlands Derby, The Woodlands, Oct. 27, $20,000, 3yo, 1¹/₁₆m, 1:48.60, SCARLET LAD, Diamond Roo, American Czar. 5 started.

Woodlands H., The Woodlands, Nov. 4, $20,000, 3yo & up, 1¹/₁₆m, 1:47, GANGSTA RAP, Amazon Ace, Cheryl's Gazelle. 7 started.

Woodlands Juvenile S., The Woodlands, Nov. 3, $15,000, 2yo, 6f, 1:12.80, R NANEE, Proper Mariner, Chief Kickapoo. 9 started.

Woodlawn S., Pimlico, May 5, $75,000, 3yo, 1¹/₁₆mT, 1:42.40, UNACCOUNTEDLEA, Ronnie's Hot Rod, What's Your Wish. 11 started.

WOOD MEMORIAL S.-G2, Aqueduct, April 14, $750,000, 3yo, 1¹/₈m, 1:47.96, CONGAREE, Monarchos, Richly Blended. 6 started.

Woodside H., Bay Meadows, May 5, $51,900, 3yo & up, f & m, 6f, 1:09.24, SLEWSBOX, Miss Grimsby, Onslaught. 6 started.

Woodstock S., Woodbine, April 21, $111,500, 3yo, 6f, 1:11.40, LUNAR SECRET, Dream Launcher, Oye Yoye Yoye. 9 started.

WOODWARD S.-G1, Belmont Park, Sept. 8, $500,000, 3yo & up, 1¹/₈m, 1:47.42, LIDO PALACE (Chi), Albert the Great, Tiznow. 5 started.

Woodward-Kirkover Cup Novice Hurdle S., Camden, Mar. 31, $50,000, 4yo & up, abt2mT, 4:12.20, POMPEYO (Chi), Flasher, Emancipate. 4 started.

Work the Crowd H. (R), Golden Gate Fields, Jan. 6, $100,000, 4yo & up, f & m, California-bred, 1mT, 1:38.91, LAZY SLUSAN, Mind for Gold, Shoe Crazy. 6 started.

World Appeal S., The Meadowlands, Oct. 26, $100,000, 2yo, 1¹/₁₆mT, 1:43.06, EMERGENCY STATUS, Ricky N Chip, Deeliteful Guy. 10 started.

WTBA Lads S., Emerald Downs, Aug. 26, $36,000, 2yo, c & g, 6¹/₂f, 1:17.20, DEVIL'S ENEMY, Star of Rehaan, Melcapwalker. 11 started.

Yaddo H. (R), Saratoga Race Course, Aug. 27, $84,875, 3yo & up, f & m, New York-bred, 1¹/₁₆mT, 1:48.36, RANSOM'S PRIDE, Longingtobeme, Polly Jo. 9 started.

Yankee Affair S., Gulfstream Park, March 16, $84,325, 4yo & up, abt5fT, :56.76, SEJM'S MADNESS, Airbourne Command, Uncle Rocco (DQ from 1st). 11 started.

Yankee Affair S. (R), Philadelphia Park, Oct. 6, $50,000, 3yo & up, Pennsylvania-bred, 1¹/₁₆mT, 1:45.31, SIR ECHO, Royal Romp, Nordagus. 6 started.

Yankee Fashion S., Suffolk Downs, Feb. 12, $25,000, 3yo, f, 6f, 1:13.28, MILLIE'S TUNE, Eternal Optimism, Honey Hawk. 12 started.

Yaqthan S., Kentucky Downs, Sept. 15, $45,000, 3yo & up, 1mT, 1:36.59, KARLY'S HARLEY, Dakota Prospect, Wertz. 7 started.

Yavapai Classic H., Yavapai Downs, June 17, $10,000, 3yo & up, f & m, 6f, 1:09.70, DEZIBELLES FORLI, Stonecreek, American Lady. 6 started.

Yavapai Distance Series Final S., Yavapai Downs, Aug. 19, $11,700, 3yo & up, 1¹/₄m, 2:07.89, PRONTO DINERO, Oil Man, Endowing. 8 started.

Yavapai Downs H., Yavapai Downs, Aug. 25, $16,600, 3yo & up, 6f, 1:08.83, STORMY AMBITION, Vaclav (Arg), Red Seattle. 6 started.

Yavapai Downs Thoroughbred Futurity S., Yavapai Downs, Sept. 3, $23,200, 2yo, 6f, 1:09.47, BELLA CASH, Doctor Dragon, Refunded. 9 started.

Yavapai Sprint Series Final S., Yavapai Downs, Aug. 19, $12,150, 3yo & up, 6f, 1:10.81, TAMS BIG PIE, Debonair Kennedy, Somfas Dancer. 9 started.

Yearling Sales S. (R), Northlands Park, Aug. 19, $49,000, 2yo, c & g, Canadian-bred sold at the CTHS (Alberta Div.) sale, 6¹/₂f, 1:20, DANCE ME FREE, Brass Spike, Onastar. 9 started.

Yearling Filly Sales S. (R), Northlands Park, Aug. 19, $50,000, 2yo, f, Canadian-bred sold at the CTHS (Alberta Div.) sale, 6¹/₂f, 1:19, BRASS TO DIAMONDS, Chapel Lites, Sweet On You Too. 7 started.

Yellow Brick Road H. (R), Charles Town, June 23, $75,000, 3yo & up, f & m, starters at Charles Town at least twice since December 23, 2000, excluding stakes races, 1¹/₁₆m, 1:54.95, VANNA GO, La Belle Danse, Real Women. 9 started.

YELLOW RIBBON S.-G1, Santa Anita Park, Sept. 29, $500,000, 3yo & up, f & m, 1¹/₄mT, 1:58.64, JANET (GB), Tranquility Lake, Al Desima (GB). 8 started.

Yellow Rose S. (R), Sam Houston Race Park, Dec. 1, $50,000, 3yo & up, f & m, Texas-bred, 6f, 1:10, LITTLE ANGEL, Miss Photogenic, Highly Salted. 8 started.

YERBA BUENA BREEDERS' CUP H.-G3, Bay Meadows, May 12, $150,000, 3yo & up, f & m, 1³/₈mT, 2:17.09, JANET (GB), Keemoon (Fr), Alexine (Arg). 4 started.

Yorkton Mile S., Yorkton Exh. Assoc., July 7, $1,323, 3yo & up, 1m, 1:45.20, COSTA NOMORE, Home Town Gal, Pleasure J. 7 started.

Zany Tactics S., Turf Paradise, April 18, $23,800, 3yo & up, 6f, 1:08.42, NO CAL BREAD, Iza Redhead, Stormy Ambition. 6 started.

Zany Tactics S. (R), Santa Anita Park, April 8, $105,800, 3yo, California-bred, 6¹/₂f, 1:16.78, TRAILTHEFOX, Crescendo, Flags At Dawn. 5 started.

Zip Pocket S., Turf Paradise, March 24, $23,800, 3yo & up, 5¹/₂f, 1:03.10, NO CAL BREAD, Kahlo (Mex), Thatsusintheolbean. 5 started.

Zwaanendael S., Delaware Park, April 29, $59,600, 3yo, 6f, 1:11.39, UNREAL PARTY, Shore Breeze, Sea of Green. 6 started.

How American Races Are Graded

At the urging of European racing officials who in 1972 had created the pattern race system to identify and grade the best-quality races in Europe, the Thoroughbred Breeders and Owners Association created the North American Graded Stakes Committee and undertook to create a similar grading system for the '73 racing season. The gradings were principally designed to assist buyers of bloodstock by identifying the North American races that in the recent past had consistently attracted the highest levels of competition. Grade 1 would be the highest level, followed by Grade 2 and Grade 3, the latter being the lowest level of stakes race accorded a grade.

The first North American gradings, totaling 330 races, were announced in January 1974, and the English Jockey Club immediately accepted them. Fasig-Tipton Co. began to publish the gradings in its catalogs in 1975, and Keeneland Association followed in '76. In 1998, Canadian racing authorities began to grade that nation's races, and the name of the TOBA-led organization was changed to the American Graded Stakes Committee and dealt only with United States stakes races.

Grades of all America's best races are reviewed annually by the American Graded Stakes Committee because stakes programs are dynamic and ever-changing products of conditions, and the quality of any race's contestants may differ markedly one year to the next. When a trend in the quality of the field of a race is established, be it improving or deteriorating quality, the race is re-evaluated for grading. Members have said that they take a five-year view of each race when considering the gradings.

Committee

The committee has ten voting members: five TOBA members serving five-year terms and five racing official members elected by the TOBA committee members and serving three-year terms. In addition, the committee's grading sessions have guest observers and invited guests. To be considered for membership on the committee, a candidate must have served as a guest observer for at least one grading session.

Seven votes are required to raise any race's grading, and six votes are needed to downgrade a race.

Members of the committee for the November 27-28, 2001, sessions at which 2002 gradings were determined:

TOBA: Russell B. Jones (chairman), Gary E. Biszantz, C. Steven Duncker, Dell Hancock, and Barry K. Schwartz.

Racing official members: Howard L. Battle, Frank C. Gabriel Jr., Michael S. Lakow, Thomas S. Robbins, and Robert D. Umphrey.

Guest observers: Rollin W. Baugh, Georganne Hale, and Robert T. Manfuso.

Invited guests: Reynolds Bell, Pam Blatz-Murff, Terence R. P. Collier, Hiroshi Ito, Bryan Krantz, F. Jack Liebau, and John Phillips.

Criteria

To be eligible for grading, a race must meet several criteria for being graded and for retaining the graded status. Among the criteria are:

Purse: The race must have a minimum purse: $125,000 for Grade 1, $100,000 for Grade 2, and $75,000 for Grade 3.

Continuity: In general, a race must have two prior runnings under essentially the same conditions to be graded, although in rare circum-

2002 Graded Stakes by Racetrack

Track	G1	G2	G3	Total
Belmont Park	22	23	18	63
Santa Anita Park	14	31	11	56
Hollywood Park	12	14	21	47
Churchill Downs	5	10	19	34
Aqueduct	3	6	24	33
Gulfstream Park	5	8	20	33
Saratoga	12	13	5	30
Arlington Park	11	3	10	24
Keeneland	5	7	10	22
Del Mar	5	11	3	19
Monmouth Park	2	3	10	15
Calder Race Course	0	3	9	12
Oaklawn Park	2	2	7	11
Pimlico	2	2	6	10
Laurel Park	1	2	5	8
Bay Meadows	0	1	6	7
Fair Grounds	0	4	2	6
Hialeah Park	0	2	4	6
Meadowlands	0	2	4	6
Turfway Park	0	2	4	6
Golden Gate Fields	0	0	6	6
Delaware Park	0	0	5	5
Hawthorne	0	1	2	3
Lone Star Park	0	0	3	3
Philadelphia Park	0	1	2	3
Sportsman's Park	0	1	2	3
Hoosier Park	0	0	2	2
Tampa Bay Downs	0	0	2	2
Louisiana Downs	0	1	0	1
Suffolk Downs	0	1	0	1
Thistledown	0	1	0	1
Colonial Downs	0	0	1	1
Ellis Park	0	0	1	1
Emerald Downs	0	0	1	1
Kentucky Downs	0	0	1	1
Mountaineer Park	0	0	1	1
Prairie Meadows	0	0	1	1
Remington Park	0	0	1	1
Rockingham Park	0	0	1	1
Totals	**101**	**155**	**230**	**486**

Purse Comparison

	Grade/Group 1		Grade/Group 2		Grade/Group 3		Total	
	Races	Average 1st money	Races	Average 1st money	Races	Average 1st money	Races	Average 1st money
2000 season								
*Canada	6	$375,000	10	$118,500	26	$75,577	42	$128,571
Ireland	10	228,638	3	59,307	23	36,624	36	91,852
Great Britain	27	283,545	29	88,603	54	43,463	110	114,293
France	26	157,590	26	51,320	55	34,535	107	68,515
Italy	8	106,628	7	53,600	10	35,492	25	63,277
Germany	6	204,231	15	64,654	22	38,328	43	70,660
U.S.	96	353,839	152	141,999	225	87,286	473	158,968
1999 season								
*Canada	6	360,000	11	94,091	24	105,000	41	139,390
Ireland	10	251,170	3	66,600	23	41,073	36	101,560
Great Britain	26	259,006	30	82,257	53	38,885	109	103,328
France	25	172,240	27	58,650	55	39,145	107	75,165
Italy	8	79,246	7	40,662	10	27,429	25	47,716
Germany	6	166,363	15	78,613	21	43,101	42	73,392
U.S.	92	328,714	146	141,382	212	84,577	450	152,920
1998 season								
Ireland	9	195,852	5	52,696	22	28,314	36	73,585
Great Britain	25	254,552	31	82,206	52	39,406	108	101,494
France	25	163,700	27	57,650	54	39,150	106	73,500
Italy	8	93,605	7	43,493	10	29,954	25	54,113
Germany	6	151,943	15	76,108	21	40,645	42	69,210
North America	84	326,911	144	134,695	218	84,171	446	146,202

*Canada listed in Canadian dollars.

stances Grade 1 status has been accorded immediately to races of special note, such as the Breeders' Cup races. Races with restrictions other than sex or age are not eligible to be graded.

In addition, if track management changes a graded race from dirt to grass, or vice versa, or changes the race's distance by more than one-quarter mile or from less than one mile to more than one mile, or vice versa, the race will be considered a new race and ineligible for grading until it has been run twice under the same conditions.

In determining a grading, the committee considers the quality of its field over the prior five years as measured by several statistical yardsticks. Among the considerations are:

• Points based on number of in-the-money finishes in unrestricted black-type races;

• Percentage of graded stakes winners in the field;

• Quality points assigned to the race based on the number of graded stakes winners in the field; and

• Ratings of the North American Rating Committee, a panel of racing secretaries who each week assign a hypothetical weight to every horse running in American black-type races.

Beginning in 1999, graded turf races moved to the main track because of course conditions were automatically downgraded one grade, although the American Graded Stakes Commit-

tee reviews each such race within five days of the running and can restore the original grading. The change in grading affects only that year's running and is not considered in the grading process.

While most changes approved by the American Graded Stakes Committee are effective with the following racing year, downgrades of races run early in the year are effective in the following calendar year. For instance, the downgrading of the Gulfstream Park Handicap from Grade 1 to Grade 2 was approved at the 2001 meeting but becomes effective in 2003 because the race is run within the first months of the year.

The American Graded Stakes Committee notifies racetracks with races in the lowest echelons of their respective gradings that the races may be downgraded. However, the race will not be considered for downgrading until it has been run another time, or twice if the race is scheduled to be run before May 1 of the following year.

For 2002, 486 American stakes races were graded, with 101 Grade 1 races, 155 Grade 2 races, and 230 Grade 3 races. The number of Grade 1 races was unchanged from 2001, while there were two fewer Grade 2 races and ten more Grade 3 races, for a net change of eight additional graded stakes.

More graded stakes are offered in the United States than all group races throughout Europe, which has evoked criticism among some Euro-

peans who contend that American black type is cheapened by the plentiful graded races. For 2002, gradings were assigned to 486 of 751 unrestricted races with purses of at least $75,000. However, less than 1% of all American races are graded, a smaller percentage than Ireland, Great Britain, or France. In 2000, for example, 0.9% of all United States races were graded, while 2.8% of French races were group races, and in Ireland the percentage was slightly more than 5%.

For 2002, four races were raised from Grade 2 to Grade 1 level: the $750,000 Wood Memorial Stakes at Aqueduct, the $500,000 Shadwell Keeneland Turf Mile Stakes at Keeneland Race Course, and the $750,000 Stephen Foster and $150,000 Humana Distaff Handicaps at Churchill Downs. See chart for other changes.

Summary of Grade Changes

	No.	% graded stakes	Change in races from 2001
Grade 1	101	20.8%	No change
Grade 2	155	31.9%	−2
Grade 3	230	47.3%	+10
All graded	486	64.7%	+8
Ungraded	265	35.3%	
All eligible races	751		

2002 Graded Stakes Changes
Upgrades

Grade 2 to Grade 1: Humana Distaff H. (Churchill Downs), Shadwell Keeneland Turf Mile S. (Keeneland Race Course), Stephen Foster H. (Churchill), Wood Memorial S. (Aqueduct)

Grade 3 to Grade 2: Falls City H., Fleur de Lis H. (Churchill), Lazaro S. Barrera Memorial H. (Hollywood Park), Princess Rooney S. (Calder Race Course), Vagrancy H. (Belmont Park)

Ungraded to Grade 3: Floral Park H. (Belmont), Indiana Derby (Hoosier Park), Leonard Richards S. (Delaware Park), Lone Star Derby (Lone Star Park), Long Branch S. (Monmouth Park), Louisville H. (Churchill), Memorial Day H. (Calder), Miami Mile H. (Calder), Miss Preakness S. (Pimlico Race Course), Raven Run S. (Keeneland), Risen Star S. (Fair Grounds), Tampa Bay Derby (Tampa Bay Downs), West Virginia Derby (Mountaineer Park)

2002 Graded Stakes by State

State	G1	G2	G3	Totals
California	31	57	47	135
New York	37	42	47	126
Kentucky	10	19	35	64
Florida	5	13	35	53
Illinois	11	5	14	30
New Jersey	2	5	14	21
Maryland	3	4	11	18
Arkansas	2	2	7	11
Louisiana	0	5	2	7
Delaware	0	0	5	5
Pennsylvania	0	1	2	3
Texas	0	0	3	3
Indiana	0	0	2	2
Iowa	0	0	1	1
Massachusetts	0	1	0	1
New Hampshire	0	0	1	1
Ohio	0	1	0	1
Oklahoma	0	0	1	1
Virginia	0	0	1	1
Washington	0	0	1	1
West Virginia	0	0	1	1
Totals	**101**	**155**	**230**	**486**

Downgrades

Grade 1 to Grade 2: Jim Dandy S. (Saratoga Race Course), Oak Leaf S. (Santa Anita Park), Super Derby (Louisiana Downs), Swaps S. (Hollywood)

Grade 2 to Grade 3: Arlington-Washington Futurity (Arlington Park), Bashford Manor S. (Churchill), Bel Air H. (Hollywood), Fall Highweight H. (Aqueduct), Hawthorne H. (Hollywood), Kentucky Cup Sprint S. (Turfway Park), Railbird S. (Hollywood)

Grade 3 to ungraded: Laurel Turf Cup S. (Laurel Park), Reeve Schley Jr. S. (Monmouth), Round Table S. (Arlington)

Ineligible for grading: William P. Kyne H. (Bay Meadows Race Course), previously Grade 3

Discontinued: Sweetest Chant S. (Gulfstream Park), previously Grade 3

Downgrades Effective in 2003

Grade 1 to Grade 2: Gulfstream Park H. (Gulfstream)
Grade 2 to Grade 3: Illinois Derby (Sportsman's Park), San Bernardino H. (Santa Anita)
Grade 3 to ungraded: Honeybee S. (Oaklawn Park), Stymie H. (Aqueduct)

Graded Stakes History

Ack Ack Handicap

Grade 3, Churchill Downs, three-year-olds and up, 7½ furlongs, dirt. Held October 28, 2001, with a gross value of $114,300. First held in 1991. Graded since 1997. Stakes record 1:28.63 (2001 Illusioned).

Year	Winner	Jockey	Second	Third	Strs	Final Time	1st Purse
2001	Illusioned, 3, 118	P. Day	Strawberry Affair, 3	Fappie's Notebook, 3	11	1:28.63	$70,866
2000	Chindi, 6, 113	T. T. Doocy	Smolderin Heart, 5	Millencolin, 5	10	1:29.30	$70,494
1999	Littlebitlively, 5, 119	C. H. Borel	Run Johnny, 7	Tactical Cat, 7	11	1:28.97	$71,672
1998	Distorted Humor, 5, 120	C. H. Borel	Crafty Friend, 5	Chindi, 5	6	1:29.61	$68,262
1997	Cat's Career, 4, 108	W. Martinez	Rare Rock, 4	Victor Cooley, 4	6	1:32.06	$69,130
1996	Western Trader, 5, 113	C. H. Borel	Top Account, 4	Strategic Intent, 4	8	1:29.84	$70,308
1995	Mystery Storm, 3, 112	C. Gonzalez	I'm Very Irish, 4	Tarzans Blade, 4	10	1:29.10	$75,660
1994	Lost Pan, 4, 114	D. M. Barton	Sir Vixen, 6	Groovy Jett, 6	8	1:30.27	$54,795

1992-'93 not held. 1995 equaled track record; 2001 new track record.

Acorn Stakes

Grade 1, Belmont Park, three-year-old fillies, 1 mile, dirt. Held June 8, 2001, with a gross value of $200,000. First held in 1931. Graded since 1973. Stakes record 1:34.20 (1982 Cupecoy's Joy).

Year	Winner	Jockey	Second	Third	Strs	Final Time	1st Purse
2001	Forest Secrets	C. J. McCarron	Victory Ride	Real Cozzy	8	1:34.92	$120,000
2000	Finder's Fee	J. R. Velazquez	C'Est L' Amour	Roxelana	10	1:37.38	$120,000
1999	Three Ring	J. D. Bailey	Better Than Honour	Madison's Charm	8	1:36.16	$120,000
1998	Jersey Girl	M. E. Smith	Santaria	Brave Deed	10	1:36.32	$90,000
1997	Sharp Cat	G. L. Stevens	Dixie Flag	Ajina	7	1:34.41	$90,000
1996	Star de Lady Ann	M. E. Smith	Yanks Music	Stop Traffic	12	1:34.62	$90,000
1995	Cat's Cradle	C. W. Antley	Country Cat	Lucky Lavender Gal	7	1:37.53	$90,000
1994	Inside Information	M. E. Smith	Cinnamon Sugar (Ire)	Sovereign Kitty	5	1:34.26	$90,000
1993	Sky Beauty	M. E. Smith	Educated Risk	In Her Glory	6	1:35.50	$90,000
1992	Prospectors Delite	P. Day	Pleasant Stage	Turnback the Alarm	12	1:35.10	$113,400

Adirondack Stakes

Grade 2, Saratoga Race Course, two-year-old fillies, 6½ furlongs, dirt. Held August 13, 2001, with a gross value of $150,000. First held in 1901. Graded since 1973. Stakes record 1:15.16 (2001 You).

Year	Winner	Jockey	Second	Third	Strs	Final Time	1st Purse
2001	You	E. S. Prado	Cashier's Dream	Magic Storm	7	**1:15.16**	$90,000
2000	Raging Fever	J. D. Bailey	Two Item Limit	Secret Lover	6	1:17.47	$90,000
1999	Regally Appealing	E. S. Prado	Miss Wineshine	Trump My Heart	6	1:16.86	$90,000
1998	Things Change	J. A. Santos	Extended Applause	Brittons Hill	9	1:18.14	$90,000
1997	Salty Perfume	S. J. Sellers	Brac Drifter	Joustabout	6	1:17.94	$90,000
1996	Storm Song	P. Day	Last Two States	(DH) Exclusive Hold	9	1:17.60	$84,075
				(DH) Larkwhistle			
1995	Flat Fleet Feet	M. E. Smith	Steady Cat	Western Dreamer	7	1:16.74	$65,760
1994	Seeking Regina	J. D. Bailey	Changing Ways	Phone Bird	7	1:18.51	$66,600
1993	Astas Foxy Lady	R. P. Romero	Footing	Casa Eire	6	1:10.11	$68,520
1992	Sky Beauty	E. Maple	Missed the Storm	Distinct Habit	7	1:10.16	$70,560

1992-'93 6 furlongs. 1996 dead heat for third.

Aegon Turf Sprint Stakes (see Turf Sprint Stakes)

Affectionately Handicap

Grade 3, Aqueduct, three-year-olds and up, fillies and mares, 1¹⁄₁₆ miles, dirt. Held January 13, 2001, with a gross value of $110,500. First held in 1976. Graded since 1977. Stakes record 1:41.87 (1998 Sweetzie).

Year	Winner	Jockey	Second	Third	Strs	Final Time	1st Purse
2001	Pentatonic, 6, 117	A. T. Gryder	Strolling Belle, 5	Pompeii, 5	8	1:43.17	$66,300
2000	Theresa the Teacha, 5, 114	H. Castillo Jr.	Roaring Twenties, 4	Two Fer Boston, 4	10	1:46.42	$51,855
1999	Biding Time, 5, 118	A. T. Gryder	Shoop, 8	Daily Reflection, 8	9	1:44.62	$50,220
1998	Sweetzie, 6, 113	J. M. Pezua	Shoop, 7	Gold Colony, 7	10	**1:41.87**	$50,700
1997	Mil Kilates, 4, 113	J. F. Chavez	Whaleneck, 4	Shoop, 4	8	1:44.63	$39,996
1996	Lotta Dancing, 5, 120	H. Castillo Jr.	Winner's Edge, 4	Vinista, 4	6	1:42.43	$39,024
1995	Sea Ditty, 4, 113	A. Madrid Jr.	Beloved Bea, 5	Acting Proud, 5	9	1:46.93	$50,190
1994	Poolesta (Ire), 5, 115	F. Lovato Jr.	Hey Baba Lulu, 6	Groovy Feeling, 6	7	1:44.80	$49,425
1993	Hilbys Brite Flite, 4, 111	J. R. Velazquez	My Treasure, 5	Lady Lear, 6	8	1:44.64	$52,470
1992	Get Lucky, 4, 113	M. E. Smith	My Treasure, 5	Haunting, 5	7	1:46.00	$52,650

Affirmed Handicap

Grade 3, Hollywood Park, three-year-olds, 1¹⁄₁₆ miles, dirt. Held June 17, 2001, with a gross value of $100,000. First held in 1979. Graded since 1979. Stakes record 1:40.83 (1999 General Challenge).

Year	Winner	Jockey	Second	Third	Strs	Final Time	1st Purse
2001	Until Sundown, 117	G. L. Stevens	Top Hit	Bayou the Moon	5	1:43.10	$60,000
2000	Tiznow, 111	V. Espinoza	Dixie Union	Millencolin	6	1:42.35	$80,550
1999	General Challenge, 124	D. R. Flores	Desert Hero	Crowning Storm	5	**1:40.83**	$75,000
1998	Old Trieste, 118	C. J. McCarron	Old Topper	Kraal	4	1:41.84	$62,340
1997	Deputy Commander, 116	C. S. Nakatani	Hello (Ire)	Holzmeister	6	1:42.89	$61,500
1996	Hesabull, 117	E. Delahoussaye	Benton Creek	Semoran	7	1:43.25	$61,050
1995	Mr Purple, 120	C. S. Nakatani	Pumpkin House	Oncefortheroad	6	1:42.37	$77,050
1994	R Friar Tuck, 113	J. D. Bailey	Pollock's Luck	Wild Invader	8	1:49.08	$96,100
1993	Codified, 117	G. L. Stevens	Roman Image	Future Storm	7	1:48.85	$94,100
1992	Natural Nine, 117	L. A. Pincay Jr.	Prospect for Four	Never Round	8	1:49.42	$95,500

1992 Silver Screen H. 1992-'94 1⅛ miles.

A Gleam Handicap

Grade 2, Hollywood Park, three-year-olds and up, fillies and mares, 7 furlongs, dirt. Held July 1, 2001, with a gross value of $200,000. First held in 1941. Graded since 1986. Stakes record 1:20.53 (1998 A. P. Assay).

Year	Winner	Jockey	Second	Third	Strs	Final Time	1st Purse
2001	Go Go, 4, 124	E. Delahoussaye	Kitty On the Track, 4	Nany's Sweep, 4	5	1:22.19	$120,000
2000	Honest Lady, 4, 121	K. J. Desormeaux	Seth's Choice, 4	Hookedonthefeelin, 4	5	1:21.47	$120,000

Year	Winner	Jockey	Second	Third	Strs	Final Time	1st Purse
1999	**Enjoy the Moment**, 4, 117	D. R. Flores	Snowberg, 4	Woodman's Dancer, 4	6	1:21.35	$120,000
1998	**A. P. Assay**, 4, 116	E. Delahoussaye	Exotic Wood, 6	Closed Escrow, 5	5	**1:20.53**	$150,000
1997	**Toga Toga Toga**, 5, 119	G. L. Stevens	Our Summer Bid, 5	Radu Cool, 5	7	1:22.75	$65,040
1996	**Igotrhythm**, 4, 116	E. Delahoussaye	Klassy Kim, 5	Cat's Cradle, 5	5	1:21.54	$63,840
1995	**Angi Go**, 5, 117	G. L. Stevens	Desert Stormer, 5	Dancing Mirage, 5	6	1:21.45	$62,700
1994	**Golden Klair (GB)**, 4, 117	C. J. McCarron	Cargo, 5	Minidar, 5	4	1:22.00	$60,400
1993	**Bold Windy**, 4, 115	G. L. Stevens	La Spia, 4	Bountiful Native, 4	9	1:21.62	$65,700
1992	**Forest Fealty**, 5, 116	M. A. Pedroza	Brought to Mind, 5	Devil's Orchid, 5	8	1:22.13	$64,800

1998 equaled track record.

A. G. Vanderbilt Handicap

Grade 2, Saratoga Race Course, three-year-olds and up, 6 furlongs, dirt. Held August 5, 2001, with a gross value of $200,000. First held in 1985. Graded since 1990. Stakes record 1:08.29 (1996 Prospect Bay).

Year	Winner	Jockey	Second	Third	Strs	Final Time	1st Purse
2001	**Five Star Day**, 5, 117	G. K. Gomez	Delaware Township, 5	Bonapaw, 5	7	1:08.57	$120,000
2000	**Successful Appeal**, 4, 118	E. S. Prado	Intidab, 7	Chasin' Wimmin, 7	8	1:09.21	$120,000
1999	**Intidab**, 6, 113	R. G. Davis	Artax, 4	Yes It's True, 4	7	1:09.03	$90,000
1998	**Kelly Kip**, 4, 122	J-L. Samyn	Trafalger, 4	Receiver, 4	7	1:09.60	$82,545
1997	**Royal Haven**, 5, 116	R. Migliore	Cold Execution, 6	Punch Line, 6	7	1:09.65	$65,220
1996	**Prospect Bay**,4,113	J. D. Bailey	Honour and Glory, 3	Lite the Fuse, 5	7	**1:08.29**	$65,760
1995	**Not Surprising**, 5, 115	R. G. Davis	Chimes Band, 4	Mining Burrah, 4	10	1:09.60	$67,140
1994	**Boundary**, 4, 117	J. R. Velazquez	Cherokee Run, 4	I Can't Believe, 4	7	1:08.61	$65,880
1993	**Gold Spring (Arg)**, 5, 119	P. Day	Friendly Lover, 5	Detox, 5	7	1:09.31	$70,680
1992	**For Really**, 5, 115	P. Day	Burn Fair, 5	Drummond Lane, 5	9	1:08.68	$71,520

1992-'93,1996-'97 A Phenomenon S.; 1994-'95,1998-'99 A Phenomenon H. 1992-'94 Grade 3. 2000 Intidab finished first, DQ to second.

Alabama Stakes

Grade 1, Saratoga Race Course, three-year-old fillies, 1¼ miles, dirt. Held August 18, 2001, with a gross value of $750,000. First held in 1872. Graded since 1973. Stakes record 2:00.80 (1990 Go for Wand).

Year	Winner	Jockey	Second	Third	Strs	Final Time	1st Purse
2001	**Flute**	E. S. Prado	Exogenous	Two Item Limit	7	2:01.88	$450,000
2000	**Jostle**	M. E. Smith	Secret Status	Spain	8	2:04.72	$450,000
1999	**Silverbulletday**	J. D. Bailey	Strolling Belle	Gandria	7	2:02.71	$240,000
1998	**Banshee Breeze**	J. D. Bailey	Lu Ravi	Manistique	6	2:03.41	$150,000
1997	**Runup the Colors**	J. D. Bailey	Ajina	Tomisue's Delight	6	2:02.28	$150,000
1996	**Yanks Music**	J. R. Velazquez	Escena	My Flag	7	2:03.06	$150,000
1995	**Pretty Discreet**	M. E. Smith	Friendly Beauty	Rogues Walk	9	2:02.14	$120,000
1994	**Heavenly Prize**	M. E. Smith	Lakeway	Sovereign Kitty	7	2:03.25	$120,000
1993	**Sky Beauty**	M. E. Smith	Future Pretense	Silky Feather	8	2:03.49	$120,000
1992	**November Snow**	C. W. Antley	Saratoga Dew	Pacific Squall	7	2:02.75	$120,000

All Along Breeders' Cup Stakes

Grade 3, Colonial Downs, three-year-olds and up, fillies and mares, 1⅛ miles, turf. Held July 14, 2001, with a gross value of $150,000. First held in 1988. Graded since 1990. Stakes record 1:47.34 (1994 Alice Springs).

Year	Winner	Jockey	Second	Third	Strs	Final Time	1st Purse
2001	**Colstar**, 5	J. K. Court	Lucky Lune (Fr), 4	Crystal Sea, 4	8	1:47.53	$75,000
2000	**Idle Rich**, 5	A. T. Gryder	Emanating, 4	Orange Sunset (Ire), 4	11	1:55.95	$60,000
1999	**Tampico**, 6	E. S. Prado	Heavenly Advice, 5	Absolutely Queenie, 5	10	1:47.63	$60,000
1998	**Bursting Forth**, 4	E. S. Prado	The Unforgiven, 4	Be Elusive, 4	8	1:48.01	$60,000
1997	**Beyrouth**, 5	D. S. Rice	Hero's Pride (Fr), 4	Palliser Bay, 4	10	1:49.27	$67,830
1996	**Another Legend**, 4	C. O. Klinger	Brushing Gloom, 4	Short Time, 4	7	1:58.80	$60,000
1994	**Alice Springs**, 4	R. R. Douglas	Via Borghese, 5	Mz. Zill Bear, 5	6	**1:47.34**	$150,000
1993	**Lady Blessington (Fr)**, 5	C. A. Black	Via Borghese, 4	Logan's Mist, 4	5	1:51.58	$150,000
1992	**Marble Maiden (GB)**, 3	T. Jarnet	Wedding Ring (Ire), 3	Sheba Dancer (Fr), 3	8	1:49.89	$180,000

1995 not held. 1992-'94,1996-2000 All Along S. 1992-'94,1996 held at Laurel Park; 1997 Delaware Park; 1999 Pimlico. 1992-'94,1996-'97 Grade 2. 2000 1³⁄₁₆ miles. 2001 equaled course record.

All-American Handicap

Grade 3, Bay Meadows, three-year-olds and up, 1¹⁄₁₆ miles, dirt. Held May 28, 2001, with a gross value of $150,000. First held in 1968. Graded since 1985. Stakes record 1:40.62 (1999 Worldly Ways [GB]).

Year	Winner	Jockey	Second	Third	Strs	Final Time	1st Purse
2001	**Euchre**, 5, 118	J. P. Lumpkins	Irisheyesareflying, 5	Moonlight Charger, 5	8	1:41.69	$82,500
2000	**Peach Flat**, 6, 114	J. Valdivia Jr.	Boss Ego, 4	Casey Griffin, 4	5	1:42.48	$75,000
1999	**Worldly Ways (GB)**, 5, 116	R. A. Baze	Barter Town, 4	(DH) Scooter Brown, 4	8	**1:40.62**	$60,000
				(DH) Highland Gold, 4			

Year	Winner	Jockey	Second	Third	Strs	Final Time	1st Purse
1998	Wild Wonder, 4, 121	R. A. Baze	Crypto Star, 4	General Royal, 4	6	1:41.33	$60,000
1997	Mister Fire Eyes (Ire), 5, 115	R. J. Warren Jr.	Region, 8	Tolemeo, 8	6	1:41.28	$60,000
1996	Tzar Rodney (Fr), 4, 114	T. M. Chapman	Joy of Glory, 7	Opera Score, 7	6	1:49.74	$60,000
1995	Bluegrass Prince (Ire), 4, 114	T. M. Chapman	Lord Shirldor (SAf), 6	Kinema Red, 6	7	1:49.01	$68,750
1994	Slew of Damascus, 6, 122	T. M. Chapman	Fast Cure, 5	The Tender Track, 5	6	1:43.75	$55,000
1993	Never Bend, 6, 115	C. S. Nakatani	Stark South, 5	Daros (GB), 5	6	1:42.53	$55,000
1992	Gum, 6, 112	G. Boulanger	Forty Niner Days, 5	Prudent Manner (Ire), 5	7	1:41.73	$55,000

1992-2000 held at Golden Gate Fields. 1995-'96 1⅛ miles. 1992-'96 turf. 1999 dead heat for third.

American Derby

Grade 2, Arlington Park, three-year-olds, 1³⁄₁₆ miles, turf. Held July 22, 2001, with a gross value of $250,000. First held in 1884. Graded since 1973. Stakes record 1:54.60 (1955 Swaps).

Year	Winner	Jockey	Second	Third	Strs	Final Time	1st Purse
2001	Fan Club's Mister	R. A. Meier	Monsieur Cat	Royal Spy	7	2:03.27	$150,000
2000	Pine Dance	E. Ahern	Hymn (Ire)	Del Mar Show	4	1:55.46	$120,000
1997	Honor Glide	G. K. Gomez	Worldly Ways (GB)	Daylight Savings	8	1:55.94	$120,000
1996	Jaunatxo	J. L. Diaz	Trail City	Marlin	12	1:55.82	$180,000
1995	Gold and Steel (Fr)	A. T. Gryder	Torrential	Unanimous Vote (Ire)	7	1:55.02	$180,000
1994	(DH) Vaudeville	A. D. Lopez		Star Campaigner	10	1:55.29	$120,000
	(DH) Overbury (Ire)	S. J. Sellers					
1993	Explosive Red	S. J. Sellers	Earl of Barking (Ire)	Newton's Law (Ire)	9	1:59.92	$180,000
1992	The Name's Jimmy	P. Day	Standiford	May I Inquire	14	1:59.41	$180,000

1998-'99 not held. 1994 dead heat for first. 1996 Trail City finished first, DQ to second.

American Handicap

Grade 2, Hollywood Park, three-year-olds and up, 1⅛ miles, turf. Held July 4, 2001, with a gross value of $150,000. First held in 1938. Graded since 1973. Stakes record 1:45.60 (1987 Clever Song).

Year	Winner	Jockey	Second	Third	Strs	Final Time	1st Purse
2001	Takarian (Ire), 6, 114	G. K. Gomez	Fighting Falcon, 5	Fateful Dream, 5	7	1:48.19	$90,000
2000	Dark Moondancer (GB), 5, 122	C. J. McCarron	Sardaukar (GB), 4	Sunshine Street, 4	6	1:46.74	$90,000
1999	Takarian (Ire), 4, 114	G. K. Gomez	Montemiro (Fr), 5	Special Quest (Fr), 5	6	1:47.37	$90,000
1998	Magellan, 5, 116	G. L. Stevens	Bonapartiste (Fr), 4	Sharekann (Ire), 4	8	1:47.05	$90,000
1997	El Angelo, 5, 118	A. O. Solis	Naninja, 4	Wavy Run (Ire), 4	6	1:46.99	$96,360
1996	Labeeb (GB), 4, 119	E. Delahoussaye	Gold and Steel (Fr), 4	Earl of Barking (Ire), 4	8	1:45.78	$66,120
1995	Silver Wizard, 5, 118	G. L. Stevens	Romarin (Brz), 5	Savinio, 5	5	1:46.02	$91,900
1994	Blues Traveller (Ire), 4, 115	C. W. Antley	Gothland (Fr), 5	Johann Quatz (Fr), 5	7	1:46.50	$128,000
1993	†Toussaud, 4, 114	K. J. Desormeaux	Man From Eldorado, 5	Journalism, 5	6	1:46.87	$126,000
1992	Man From Eldorado, 4, 114	K. J. Desormeaux	Bold Russian (GB), 5	Golden Pheasant, 5	4	1:47.11	$122,000

1995-'96 about 1⅛ miles. † denotes female.

American Turf Stakes

Grade 3, Churchill Downs, three-year-olds, 1¹⁄₁₆ miles, turf. Held May 4, 2001, with a gross value of $117,900. First held in 1992. Graded since 1998. Stakes record 1:40.93 (1997 Royal Strand [Ire]).

Year	Winner	Jockey	Second	Third	Strs	Final Time	1st Purse
2001	Strategic Partner	J. R. Velazquez	Baptize	Dynameaux	6	1:42.89	$73,098
2000	King Cugat	J. D. Bailey	Lendell Ray	Go Lib Go	11	1:41.25	$73,222
1999	Air Rocket	J. D. Bailey	Haus of Dehere	Conserve	10	1:42.65	$71,548
1998	Dernier Croise (Fr)	G. L. Stevens	Tenbyssimo (Ire)	Silver Lord	10	1:44.28	$78,120
1997	Royal Strand (Ire)	P. Day	Rob 'n Gin	Deputy Commander	10	1:40.93	$71,796
1996	Broadway Beau	C. J. McCarron	Trail City	Gotcha	10	1:41.87	$76,375
1995	Unanimous Vote (Ire)	G. L. Stevens	Nostra	Native Regent	12	1:42.07	$76,700
1994	Jaggery John	M. E. Smith	Milt's Overture	Zuno Star	10	1:45.05	$56,453
1993	Desert Waves	S. J. Sellers	Compadre	Super Snazzie	5	1:42.64	$36,628
1992	Senor Tomas	M. E. Smith	Coaxing Matt	Black Question	8	1:43.10	$37,440

1997 equaled course record. 1993 Compadre finished first, DQ to second; 1995-2001 Crown Royal American Turf S.

Amsterdam Stakes

Grade 2, Saratoga Race Course, three-year-olds, 6 furlongs, dirt. Held August 3, 2001, with a gross value of $135,700. First held in 1993. Graded since 1998. Stakes record 1:09.13 (1996 Distorted Humor).

Year	Winner	Jockey	Second	Third	Strs	Final Time	1st Purse
2001	City Zip	J. F. Chavez	Speightstown	Smile My Lord	6	1:11.03	$81,420
2000	Personal First	P. Day	Disco Rico	Trippi	6	1:09.33	$66,000
1999	Successful Appeal	E. S. Prado	Lion Hearted	Silver Season	9	1:10.25	$50,340
1998	(DH) Secret Firm	E. S. Prado		Southern Bostonian	8	1:10.28	$33,060
	(DH) Mint	E. Coa					

Year	Winner	Jockey	Second	Third	Strs	Final Time	1st Purse
1997	Oro de Mexico	C. W. Antley	Trafalger	Kelly Kip	7	1:10.58	$49,275
1996	Distorted Humor	P. Day	Gold Fever	Stu's Choice	7	1:09.13	$32,820
1995	Kings Fiction	P. Day	Lord Carson	Ft. Stockton	5	1:09.75	$32,250
1994	Chimes Band	J. D. Bailey	Ledford	Halo's Image	6	1:09.90	$32,325
	Mr. Shawklit	W. H. McCauley	Scarlet Rage	Groovy Jett	5	1:10.89	$32,325
1993	Evil Bear	J. A. Santos	Punch Line	Digging In	5	1:22.09	$28,800

1993-'97 Screen King S. 1998-2000 Grade 3. 1993 held at Belmont Park. 1993 seven furlongs. 1994 two divisions. 1998 dead heat for first.

Ancient Title Breeders' Cup Handicap

Grade 1, Santa Anita Park, three-year-olds and up, 6 furlongs, dirt. Held October 6, 2001, with a gross value of $207,100. First held in 1985. Graded since 1990. Stakes record 1:07.67 (2001 Swept Overboard).

Year	Winner	Jockey	Second	Third	Strs	Final Time	1st Purse
2001	Swept Overboard, 4, 116	E. Delahoussaye	Kona Gold, 7	I Love Silver, 7	6	1:07.67	$124,260
2000	Kona Gold, 6, 124	A. O. Solis	Regal Thunder, 6	Elaborate, 6	4	1:08.11	$123,060
1999	Lexicon, 4, 116	K. J. Desormeaux	Kona Gold, 5	Regal Thunder, 5	8	1:07.84	$125,400
1998	Gold Land, 7, 117	K. J. Desormeaux	†A. P. Assay, 4	Swiss Yodeler, 4	8	1:08.50	$94,020
1997	Elmhurst, 7, 114	C. S. Nakatani	Swiss Yodeler, 3	Larry the Legend, 3	8	1:08.82	$95,000
1996	Lakota Brave, 7, 117	E. Delahoussaye	Letthebighossroll, 8	Paying Dues, 8	5	1:08.16	$93,700
1995	†Track Gal, 4, 116	G. L. Stevens	Siphon (Brz), 4	Forest Gazelle, 4	6	1:08.32	$59,150
1994	Saratoga Gambler, 6, 113	M. A. Pedroza	Uncaged Fury, 3	Concept Win, 3	8	1:08.87	$62,500
1993	Cardmania, 7, 116	E. Delahoussaye	Music Merci, 7	Bahatur, 7	8	1:08.04	$61,975
1992	Gray Slewpy, 4, 118	K. J. Desormeaux	Trick Me, 4	Light of Morn, 4	9	1:08.48	$59,372

1992-'98 Grade 3; 1999-2000 Grade 2. 1996 Criollito finished third, DQ to fourth. † denotes female.

Anne Arundel Stakes

Grade 3, Laurel Park, three-year-old fillies, 1⅛ miles, dirt. Held November 25, 2000, with a gross value of $100,000. First held in 1974. Graded since 1996. Stakes record 1:49.34 (1999 Undermine).

Year	Winner	Jockey	Second	Third	Strs	Final Time	1st Purse
2000	Gin Talking	R. A. Dominguez	Tax Affair	A. O. L. Hayes	9	1:50.21	$60,000
1999	Undermine	L. Melancon	Gold From the West	Batique	9	1:49.34	$60,000
1998	Merengue	M. T. Johnston	Queen of Oz	Manoa	9	1:51.97	$60,000
1997	G. O'Keefe	M. T. Johnston	Snit	Cotton Carnival	9	1:51.20	$60,000
1996	Hay Let's Dance	S. B. Martinez	Double Stake	Mesabi Maiden	7	1:50.82	$45,000
1995	Blue Sky Princess	M. G. Pino	Substantial	Blonde Actress	11	1:51.46	$45,000
1994	Miss Slewpy	L. C. Reynolds	Cherokee Wonder	Churchbell Chimes	6	1:51.11	$45,000
1993	By Your Leave	M. G. Pino	Tennis Lady	Double Sixes	9	1:52.58	$33,030
1992	Avian Assembly	L. C. Reynolds	Gammy's Alden	Singing Ring	11	1:50.77	$30,000

2001 not held. 1992 Anne Arundel H.

Apple Blossom Handicap

Grade 1, Oaklawn Park, four-year-olds and up, fillies and mares, 1 1/16 miles, dirt. Held April 8, 2001, with a gross value of $500,000. First held in 1958. Graded since 1977. Stakes record 1:40.20 (1984 Heatherten).

Year	Winner	Jockey	Second	Third	Strs	Final Time	1st Purse
2001	Gourmet Girl, 6, 113	C. H. Borel	Lu Ravi, 6	Lazy Slusan, 6	11	1:42.15	$300,000
2000	Heritage of Gold, 5, 118	S. J. Sellers	Lu Ravi, 6	Bordelaise (Arg), 5	7	1:42.22	$300,000
1999	Banshee Breeze, 4, 122	J. D. Bailey	Sister Act, 4	Silent Eskimo, 4	6	1:41.64	$300,000
1998	Escena, 5, 117	J. D. Bailey	Glitter Woman, 4	Toda Una Dama (Arg), 4	7	1:40.95	$300,000
1997	Halo America, 7, 117	C. H. Borel	Jewel Princess, 5	Different (Arg), 5	8	1:41.65	$300,000
1996	Twice the Vice, 5, 117	C. J. McCarron	Halo America, 6	Serena's Song, 6	7	1:41.71	$300,000
1995	Heavenly Prize, 4, 120	P. Day	Halo America, 5	Paseana (Arg), 5	6	1:42.76	$300,000
1994	Nine Keys, 4, 116	M. E. Smith	Mamselle Bebette, 4	Re Toss (Arg), 4	10	1:42.15	$300,000
1993	Paseana (Arg), 6, 124	C. J. McCarron	Looie Capote, 4	Luv Me Luv Me Not, 4	9	1:41.80	$300,000
1992	Paseana (Arg), 5, 124	C. J. McCarron	Fit for a Queen, 6	Slide Out Front, 6	8	1:42.13	$300,000

Appleton Handicap

Grade 2, Gulfstream Park, three-year-olds and up, 1 mile, turf. Held January 6, 2001, with a gross value of $150,000. First held in 1952. Graded since 1973. Stakes record 1:33.69 (2001 Associate).

Year	Winner	Jockey	Second	Third	Strs	Final Time	1st Purse
2001	Associate, 6, 114	J. F. Chavez	Band Is Passing, 5	El Mirasol, 5	12	1:33.69	$90,000
2000	Band Is Passing, 4, 115	E. Coa	Hibernian Rhapsody (Ire), 5	Shamrock City, 5	11	1:40.11	$60,000
1999	Behaviour (GB), 7, 113	S. J. Sellers	Notoriety, 6	Legs Galore, 6	6	1:45.77	$60,000
1998	Sir Cat, 5, 119	J. D. Bailey	Wild Event, 5	Kingcanrunallday, 5	5	1:42.69	$60,000
1997	Montjoy, 5, 116	M. E. Smith	Mighty Forum (GB), 6	Elite Jeblar, 6	12	1:39.88	$60,000
1996	The Vid, 6, 122	W. H. McCauley	Dove Hunt, 5	Montreal Red, 5	11	1:41.79	$60,000
1995	Dusty Screen, 7, 116	W. H. McCauley	The Vid, 5	Dove Hunt, 5	7	1:42.72	$60,000

Year	Winner	Jockey	Second	Third	Strs	Final Time	1st Purse
1994	**Paradise Creek**, 5, 121	M. E. Smith	Fourstars Allstar, 6	Elite Jeblar, 6	8	1:40.57	$60,000
1993	**Cigar Toss (Arg)**, 6, 112	B. G. Moore	Bidding Proud, 4	Archies Laughter, 4	9	1:43.55	$60,000
1992	**Royal Ninja**, 6, 112	J. D. Bailey	Archies Laughter, 4	Native Boundary, 4	12	1:42.49	$60,000

1992-'97,1999 Grade 3. 1992-2000 1¹⁄₁₆ miles. 1993,1995,1998-'99 dirt.

Aqueduct Handicap

Grade 3, Aqueduct, three-year-olds and up, 1¹⁄₁₆ miles, dirt. Held January 20, 2001, with a gross value of $110,500. First held in 1902. Graded since 1985. Stakes record 1:41.13 (1995 Danzig's Dance).

Year	Winner	Jockey	Second	Third	Strs	Final Time	1st Purse
2001	**Liberty Gold**, 7, 115	J. Bravo	Coyote Lakes, 7	Talk's Cheap, 7	7	1:42.20	$66,300
2000	**Sky Approval**, 6, 115	C. H. Velasquez	Parental Pressure, 9	Phone the King, 9	8	1:44.45	$49,770
1999	**Mr. Sinatra**, 5, 118	A. T. Gryder	Brushing Up, 6	Wouldn't We All, 6	5	1:43.11	$49,335
1998	**Star of Valor**, 5, 113	A. T. Gryder	Christian Soldier, 4	Mr. Sinatra, 4	8	1:42.48	$49,725
1997	**Pacific Fleet**, 5, 112	J. F. Chavez	More to Tell, 6	Admiralty, 6	8	1:43.45	$39,924
1996	**Mighty Magee**, 4, 118	M. J. Luzzi	May I Inquire, 7	More to Tell, 7	8	1:43.89	$39,780
1995	**Danzig's Dance**, 6, 111	J. F. Chavez	Key Contender, 7	Golden Larch, 7	8	**1:41.13**	$50,010
1994	**As Indicated**, 4, 121	R. G. Davis	Primitive Hall, 5	Jacksonport, 5	6	1:45.77	$48,690
1993	**Shots Are Ringing**, 6, 118	J. R. Velazquez	A Call to Rise, 5	Federal Funds, 5	6	1:44.44	$52,650
1992	**Formal Dinner**, 4, 112	A. Cordero Jr.	Shots Are Ringing, 5	Island Edition, 5	6	1:43.60	$51,750

1992 Shots Are Ringing finished first, DQ to second. 1995 equaled track record.

Arcadia Handicap

Grade 2, Santa Anita Park, four-year-olds and up, 1¹⁄₈ miles, turf. Held April 7, 2001, with a gross value of $150,000. First held in 1988. Graded since 1990. Stakes record 1:47.88 (2000 Falcon Flight [Fr]).

Year	Winner	Jockey	Second	Third	Strs	Final Time	1st Purse
2001	**Lazy Lode (Arg)**, 7, 121	L. A. Pincay Jr.	Night Patrol, 5	Wake the Tiger, 5	5	1:49.74	$90,000
2000	**Falcon Flight (Fr)**, 4, 114	B. Blanc	Bonapartiste (Fr), 6	Otavalo (Ire), 6	7	**1:47.88**	$97,950
1999	**Commitisize**, 4, 117	D. R. Flores	Majorien (GB), 5	Ladies Din, 5	7	1:48.25	$90,000
1998	**Hawksley Hill (Ire)**, 5, 117	G. L. Stevens	Precious Ring, 5	Kirkwall (GB), 5	8	1:49.96	$100,410
1997	**Labeeb (GB)**, 5, 120	E. Delahoussaye	Talloires, 7	Pinfloron (Fr), 7	6	1:35.96	$80,100
1996	**Tychonic (GB)**, 6, 118	G. L. Stevens	Debutant Trick, 6	Savinio, 6	6	1:35.84	$80,300
1995	**Savinio**, 5, 116	C. J. McCarron	River Flyer, 4	Romarin (Brz), 4	7	1:34.74	$91,800
1994	**Norwich (GB)**, 7, 117	P. A. Valenzuela	Megan's Interco, 5	Gothland (Fr), 5	5	1:34.14	$75,850
1993	**Val des Bois (Fr)**, 7, 118	P. A. Valenzuela	Star of Cozzene, 5	C. Sam Maggio, 5	7	1:35.07	$77,750
1992	**Exbourne**, 6, 122	G. L. Stevens	Repriced, 4	Madjaristan, 4	6	1:33.21	$95,000

1992-2000 El Rincon H. 1992-'97 1 mile.

Aristides Handicap

Grade 3, Churchill Downs, three-year-olds and up, 6¹⁄₂ furlongs, dirt. Held June 30, 2001, with a gross value of $108,400. First held in 1989. Graded since 1999. Stakes record 1:14.79 (2001 Bet On Sunshine).

Year	Winner	Jockey	Second	Third	Strs	Final Time	1st Purse
2001	**Bet On Sunshine**, 9, 120	C. H. Borel	Alannan, 5	Dash for Daylight, 5	6	**1:14.79**	$67,208
2000	**Bet On Sunshine**, 8, 119	F. C. Torres	Proven Cure, 6	Sun Bull, 6	7	1:15.11	$68,014
1999	**Run Johnny**, 7, 116	P. Day	Squall Valley, 4	Neon Shadow, 4	8	1:16.27	$68,572
1998	**Thisnearlywasmine**, 4, 115	S. J. Sellers	Partner's Hero, 4	El Amante, 4	7	1:15.72	$67,518
1997	**High Stakes Player**, 5, 119	S. J. Sellers	Trafalger, 3	Bet On Sunshine, 3	7	1:15.85	$67,580
1996	**Lord Carson**, 4, 115	D. M. Barton	Criollito (Arg), 5	Bet On Sunshine, 5	5	1:15.94	$70,525
1995	**Boone's Mill**, 3, 106	D. M. Barton	Ojai, 6	Hot Jaws, 6	7	1:15.90	$69,924
1994	**Never Wavering**, 5, 116	S. J. Sellers	Demaloot Demashoot, 4	American Chance, 4	8	1:16.55	$53,479
1993	**Gold Spring (Arg)**, 5, 115	F. A. Arguello Jr.	Take Me Out, 5	In the Zone, 5	6	1:16.43	$35,718
1992	**Tricky Fun**, 4, 113	P. Day	Guns of Cielo, 5	Richman, 5	6	1:16.35	$44,720

1992-'95 Aristides Breeders' Cup H. 2000 new track record.

Arkansas Derby

Grade 2, Oaklawn Park, three-year-olds, 1¹⁄₈ miles, dirt. Held April 14, 2001, with a gross value of $500,000. First held in 1936. Graded since 1973. Stakes record 1:46.80 (1984 Althea).

Year	Winner	Jockey	Second	Third	Strs	Final Time	1st Purse
2001	**Balto Star**	M. Guidry	Jamaican Rum	Son of Rocket	11	1:49.04	$300,000
2000	**Graeme Hall**	R. Albarado	Snuck In	Impeachment	14	1:49.08	$300,000
1999	**Certain**	K. J. Desormeaux	Torrid Sand	Ecton Park	7	1:49.30	$300,000
1998	**Victory Gallop**	A. O. Solis	Hanuman Highway (Ire)	Favorite Trick	9	1:49.86	$300,000
1997	**Crypto Star**	P. Day	Phantom On Tour	Pacificbounty	11	1:49.34	$300,000
1996	**Zarb's Magic**	R. D. Ardoin	Grindstone	Halo Sunshine	12	1:49.21	$300,000

Year	Winner	Jockey	Second	Third	Strs	Final Time	1st Purse
1995	Dazzling Falls	G. K. Gomez	Flitch	On Target	8	1:50.60	$300,000
1994	Concern	G. K. Gomez	Blumin Affair	Silver Goblin	9	1:48.16	$300,000
1993	Rockamundo	C. H. Borel	Kissin Kris	Foxtrail	10	1:48.17	$300,000
1992	Pine Bluff	J. D. Bailey	Lil E. Tee	Desert Force	6	1:49.49	$300,000

1999 Valhol finished first, DQ to seventh.

Arlington Classic Stakes

Grade 2, Arlington Park, three-year-olds, 1⅛ miles, turf. Held June 30, 2001, with a gross value of $200,000. First held in 1929. Graded since 1978. Stakes record 1:47.59 (1997 Honor Glide).

Year	Winner	Jockey	Second	Third	Strs	Final Time	1st Purse
2001	Baptize	M. Guidry	Indygo Shiner	Cherokee Kim	6	1:48.80	$120,000
2000	King Cugat	R. Albarado	Boyum	El Ballezano	5	1:48.16	$90,000
1997	Honor Glide	G. K. Gomez	Brave Act (GB)	Daylight Savings	8	1:47.59	$75,000
1996	Trail City	P. Day	More Royal	Winter Quarters	5	1:48.61	$120,000
1995	Hawk Attack	P. Day	Via Lombardia (Ire)	Bryntirion	10	1:48.04	$120,000
1994	Eagle Eyed	C. S. Nakatani	Mr. Angel	Star Campaigner	11	1:48.46	$180,000
1993	Boundlessly	P. Day	Hegar	Williamstown	13	1:49.89	$180,000
1992	Saint Ballado	J. A. Krone	Desert Force	Star Recruit	6	1:46.82	$180,000

1998-'99 not held. 1992-'93 dirt. 1997 equaled course record.

Arlington Handicap

Grade 3, Arlington Park, three-year-olds and up, 1¼ miles, turf. Held July 28, 2001, with a gross value of $250,000. First held in 1929. Graded since 1973. Stakes record 2:00.40 (1985 Pass the Line).

Year	Winner	Jockey	Second	Third	Strs	Final Time	1st Purse
2001	Make No Mistake (Ire), 6, 116	R. Albarado	Takarian (Ire), 6	El Gran Papa, 6	7	2:02.53	$150,000
2000	Northern Quest (Fr), 5, 113	R. Albarado	Profit Option, 5	Where's Taylor, 5	11	2:02.13	$90,000
1997	Wild Event, 4, 114	M. Guidry	Storm Trooper, 4	Chorwon, 4	8	2:01.52	$90,000
1996	Torch Rouge (GB), 5, 116	M. Guidry	Sentimental Moi, 6	Volochine (Ire), 6	6	2:03.32	$120,000
1995	Manilaman, 4, 114	R. P. Romero	Snake Eyes, 5	Bluegrass Prince (Ire), 5	7	2:02.82	$120,000
1994	Fanmore, 6, 119	P. Day	Marastani, 4	Split Run, 4	7	2:01.72	$150,000
1993	Evanescent, 6, 114	A. T. Gryder	Split Run, 5	Magesterial Cheer, 5	9	2:00.93	$150,000
1992	Sky Classic, 5, 125	P. Day	Duckaroo, 6	Glity, 6	9	2:00.62	$150,000

1998-'99 not held. 1992-'97 Grade 2. 1992 Plate Dancer finished second, DQ to fifth.

Arlington Matron Handicap

Grade 3, Arlington Park, three-year-olds and up, fillies and mares, 1⅛ miles, dirt. Held October 6, 2001, with a gross value of $150,000. First held in 1930. Graded since 1973. Stakes record 1:48.40 (1986 Queen Alexandra).

Year	Winner	Jockey	Second	Third	Strs	Final Time	1st Purse
2001	Humble Clerk, 4, 114	L. Melancon	Maltese Superb, 4	Lakenheath, 4	7	1:51.53	$90,000
2000	Megans Bluff, 3, 111	C. R. Woods Jr.	On a Soapbox, 4	Tutorial, 4	8	1:51.41	$90,000
1997	Omi, 4, 114	M. Guidry	Gold Memory, 4	Trick Attack, 4	6	1:51.93	$60,000
1996	Belle of Cozzene, 4, 115	D. R. Pettinger	War Thief, 4	Your Ladyship, 4	9	1:49.34	$75,000
1995	Mariah's Storm, 4, 117	R. N. Lester	Mysteriously, 4	Minority Dater, 4	9	1:50.98	$60,000
1994	Hey Hazel, 4, 115	M. G. Pino	Passing Vice, 4	Pennyhill Park, 4	8	1:49.58	$60,000
1993	Erica's Dream, 5, 115	W. Martinez	Pleasant Jolie, 5	Meafara, 5	6	1:50.09	$60,000
1992	Lemhi Go, 4, 114	E. Fires	Beth Believes, 6	Diamond City, 6	8	1:49.67	$45,000

1998-'99 not held.

Arlington Million Stakes

Grade 1, Arlington Park, three-year-olds and up, 1¼ miles, turf. Held August 18, 2001, with a gross value of $1,000,000. First held in 1981. Graded since 1983. Stakes record 1:58.69 (1995 Awad).

Year	Winner	Jockey	Second	Third	Strs	Final Time	1st Purse
2001	Silvano (Ger), 5	A. Suborics	Hap, 5	Redattore (Brz), 5	12	2:02.64	$600,000
2000	Chester House, 5	J. D. Bailey	Manndar (Ire), 4	Mula Gula, 4	7	2:01.37	$1,200,000
1997	Marlin, 4	G. L. Stevens	Sandpit (Brz), 8	Percutant (GB), 8	8	2:02.54	$600,000
1996	Mecke, 4	R. G. Davis	Awad, 6	Sandpit (Brz), 6	9	2:00.49	$600,000
1995	Awad, 5	E. Maple	Sandpit (Brz), 6	The Vid, 6	11	1:58.69	$600,000
1994	Paradise Creek, 5	P. Day	Fanmore, 6	Muhtarram, 6	14	1:59.78	$600,000
1993	Star of Cozzene, 5	J. A. Santos	Evanescent, 6	Johann Quatz (Fr), 6	8	2:07.50	$600,000
1992	Dear Doctor (Fr), 5	C. B. Asmussen	Sky Classic, 5	Golden Pheasant, 5	12	1:59.84	$600,000

1998-'99 not held. 1995 new course record.

Arlington-Washington Futurity

Grade 2, Arlington Park, two-year-olds, 1 mile, dirt. Held September 29, 2001, with a gross value of $150,000. First held in 1927. Graded since 1973. Stakes record 1:35.80 (1989 Secret Hello).

Year	Winner	Jockey	Second	Third	Strs	Final Time	1st Purse
2001	Publication	R. A. Meier	It'sallinthechase	Dubai Squire	7	1:38.78	$90,000

Year	Winner	Jockey	Second	Third	Strs	Final Time	1st Purse
2000	Trailthefox	S. J. Sellers	Starbury	Blame It On Ruby	11	1:37.25	$90,000
1997	Cowboy Dan	D. Kutz	Captain Maestri	Fiamma	9	1:37.68	$90,000
1996	Night in Reno	M. Guidry	Flying With Eagles	Thisnearlywasmine	8	1:36.67	$120,000
1994	Evansville Slew	P. Compton	Valid Wager	Mr Purple	9	1:37.84	$120,000
1993	Polar Expedition	C. C. Bourque	Gimme Glory	Delicate Cure	6	1:39.28	$120,000
1992	Gilded Time	C. J. McCarron	Boundlessly	Rockamundo	6	1:37.84	$200,580

1995,1998-'99 not held.

Arlington-Washington Lassie Stakes

Grade 3, Arlington Park, two-year-old fillies, 1 mile, dirt. Held September 22, 2001, with a gross value of $100,000. First held in 1929. Graded since 1973. Stakes record 1:36.58 (1991 Speed Dialer).

Year	Winner	Jockey	Second	Third	Strs	Final Time	1st Purse
2001	Joanies Bella	M. St. Julien	Brief Bliss	First Again	9	1:39.34	$60,000
2000	Thunder Bertie	J. Beasley	Caressing	Zahwah	10	1:36.91	$60,000
1997	Silver Maiden	S. Laviolette	Arctic Lady	So Generous	6	1:37.54	$60,000
1996	Southern Playgirl	R. P. Romero	Leo's Gypsy Dancer	Broad Dynamite	7	1:38.27	$90,000
1994	Shining Light	J. L. Diaz	She's a Lively One	Alltheway Bertie	5	1:41.70	$90,000
1993	Mariah's Storm	R. N. Lester	Shapely Scrapper	Minority Dater	14	1:38.95	$90,000
1992	Eliza	P. A. Valenzuela	Banshee Winds	Tourney	6	1:39.58	$134,850

1995,1998-'99 not held. 1992-'94,1996-'97 Grade 2.

Ascot Handicap

Grade 3, Bay Meadows, three-year-olds, 1¹⁄₁₆ miles, turf. Held June 10, 2001, with a gross value of $100,000. First held in 1973. Graded since 1988. Stakes record 1:41.45 (1999 Mr. Broad Blade).

Year	Winner	Jockey	Second	Third	Strs	Final Time	1st Purse
2001	Sir Alfred, 114	J. P. Lumpkins	Hoovergetthekeys	Sea to See	8	1:44.17	$55,000
2000	Designed for Luck, 118	F. T. Alvarado	Tender Offer (Ire)	Peteski's Charm	7	1:43.85	$55,000
1999	Mr. Broad Blade, 118	P. A. Valenzuela	Seayabyebye	Incitatus	8	1:41.45	$55,000
1998	†Sierra Virgen, 116	D. Carr	I. M. Bzy	Casino King (Ire)	9	1:42.86	$28,300
1997	Brave Act (GB), 120	G. F. Almeida	Go	Shellbacks	7	1:42.16	$55,000
1996	Matty G, 115	A. O. Solis	Dombey (GB)	Vieux Moulin (Fr)	7	1:43.00	$55,000
1995	Perfect, 116	A. D. Lopez	Longliner	Awesome Thought	9	1:43.59	$55,000
1994	Pollock's Luck, 116	T. M. Chapman	Carloun (Fr)	Jacques Aboard	8	1:43.31	$55,000
1993	Siebe, 115	R. D. Hansen	Nonproductiveasset	Cigar	11	1:41.66	$55,000
1992	Modernise, 112	C. S. Nakatani	Major Impact	Don's Terry	8	1:43.06	$55,000

1999 not graded. 1999 dirt. † denotes female.

Ashland Stakes

Grade 1, Keeneland, three-year-old fillies, 1¹⁄₁₆ miles, dirt. Held April 7, 2001, with a gross value of $576,250. First held in 1936. Graded since 1973. Stakes record 1:41.72 (1999 Silverbulletday).

Year	Winner	Jockey	Second	Third	Strs	Final Time	1st Purse
2001	Fleet Renee	J. R. Velazquez	Golden Ballet	Latour	11	1:43.77	$357,275
2000	Rings a Chime	S. J. Sellers	Zoftig	Circle of Life	6	1:44.43	$341,155
1999	Silverbulletday	J. D. Bailey	Marley Vale	Gold From the West	6	1:41.72	$337,280
1998	Well Chosen	C. R. Woods Jr.	Let	Banshee Breeze	7	1:43.00	$344,410
1997	Glitter Woman	M. E. Smith	Anklet	Storm Song	6	1:43.98	$337,125
1996	My Flag	J. D. Bailey	Cara Rafaela	Mackie	5	1:42.69	$335,265
1995	Urbane	E. Delahoussaye	Conquistadoress	Post It	6	1:43.41	$207,483
1994	Inside Information	M. E. Smith	Bunting	Private Status	6	1:46.99	$171,198
1993	Lunar Spook	S. J. Sellers	Avie's Shadow	Roamin Rachel	7	1:43.43	$171,973
1992	Prospectors Delite	C. Perret	Spinning Round	Luv Me Luv Me Not	10	1:42.65	$186,063

Astarita Stakes

Grade 2, Belmont Park, two-year-old fillies, 6½ furlongs, dirt. Held October 8, 2001, with a gross value of $103,400. First held in 1946. Graded since 1973. Stakes record 1:16.40 (1974 Stulcer).

Year	Winner	Jockey	Second	Third	Strs	Final Time	1st Purse
2001	Bella Bellucci	G. L. Stevens	Forest Heiress	Speed to Burn	4	1:16.67	$63,955
2000	Xtra Heat	M. T. Johnston	Gold Mover	Major Wager	8	1:16.71	$66,060
1999	Silentlea	R. G. Davis	Valerie's Dream	Lucky Livi	10	1:17.44	$67,620
1998	Paved in Gold	J. F. Chavez	Blushing Deed	Paula's Girl	5	1:18.86	$63,780
1997	Ninth Inning	R. G. Davis	Salty Perfume	Madam Fireplace	5	1:17.44	$64,680
1996	Broad Dynamite	D. W. Cordova	Glitter Woman	Biding Time	4	1:24.02	$63,960
1995	Top Secret	M. E. Smith	Plum Country	Mesabi Maiden	8	1:36.79	$69,480
1994	Miss Golden Circle	J. A. Krone	Golden Bri	Mistress S.	6	1:23.67	$64,740
1993	Shapely Scrapper	J. Bravo	Brighter Course	Fashion Maven	4	1:24.02	$67,560
1992	Missed the Storm	M. E. Smith	Dispute	Statuette	6	1:24.90	$67,920

1992-'94,1996-'97 held at Aqueduct. 1992-'94,1996 7 furlongs; 1995 1 mile.

Athenia Handicap

Grade 3, Belmont Park, three-year-olds and up, fillies and mares, 1¹⁄₁₆ miles, turf. Held October 26, 2001, in two divisions, with a gross value of $137,875 (both divisions). First held in 1978. Graded since 1980. Stakes record 1:40.53 (2001 Babae [Chi] [2nd Div.]).

Year	Winner	Jockey	Second	Third	Strs	Final Time	1st Purse
2001	Verruma (Brz), 5, 114	J. R. Velazquez	Siringas (Ire), 3	Freefourracing, 3	8	1:42.09	$82,725
	Babae (Chi), 5, 116	J. F. Chavez	Batique, 5	Sweet Prospect (GB), 5	8	**1:40.53**	$82,725
2000	Wild Heart Dancing, 4, 115	J. F. Chavez	Fickle Friends, 4	Silken (GB), 4	8	1:43.40	$67,500
1999	Antoniette, 4, 119	J. F. Chavez	Dominique's Joy, 4	Prospectress, 4	8	1:41.89	$66,840
1998	Tampico, 5, 114	J. Bravo	Irish Daisy, 5	Rumpipumpy (GB), 5	10	1:42.90	$51,210
1997	Rapid Selection, 4, 113	J. Bravo	Dynasty, 4	Preachersnightmare, 4	6	1:47.11	$65,940
1996	Sixieme Sens, 4, 116	J. D. Bailey	Rapunzel Runz, 5	Fashion Star, 5	7	1:37.92	$66,660
1995	Caress, 4, 114	R. G. Davis	Manila Lila, 5	Vinista, 5	6	1:54.18	$68,340
1994	Lady Affirmed, 3, 111	J. F. Chavez	Irving's Girl, 4	Cox Orange, 4	11	1:48.66	$52,245
1993	Trampoli, 4, 117	M. E. Smith	Kirov Premiere (GB), 3	Dahlia's Dreamer, 3	8	2:17.16	$54,000
1992	Fairy Garden, 4, 112	J. A. Krone	Passagere du Soir (GB), 5	Seewillo, 5	5	2:13.62	$52,020

1994-'95, 1998-2000 held at Aqueduct. 1992-'93 1³⁄₈ miles; 1994-'95,1997 1¹⁄₈ miles; 1996 1 mile. 1995 dirt. 2001 two divisions.

Azalea Breeders' Cup Stakes

Grade 3, Calder Race Course, three-year-old fillies, 6 furlongs, dirt. Held July 14, 2001, with a gross value of $250,000. First held in 1972. Graded since 1996. Stakes record 1:11.20 (1977 Countless Pruner; 1980 She Can't Miss).

Year	Winner	Jockey	Second	Third	Strs	Final Time	1st Purse
2001	Hattiesburg	M. Guidry	Southern Tour	Spanish Glitter	11	1:11.81	$150,000
2000	Swept Away	P. Day	Precious Feather	Watchfull	8	1:11.53	$120,000
1999	Show Me the Stage	R. J. Courville	Could Be	Exact	9	1:11.91	$75,000
1998	Cassidy	J. A. Rivera II	Holy Capote	Fantasy Angel	8	1:11.93	$75,000
1997	Little Sister	F. Lovato Jr.	Princess Pietrina	Maggie Auxier	7	1:13.08	$120,000
1996	J J'sdream	H. Castillo Jr.	Supah Avalanche	Race Artist	7	1:23.87	$65,100
1995	Lucky Lavender Gal	R. R. Douglas	Chaposa Springs	Dancin Renee	6	1:23.50	$60,000
1994	Cut the Charm	H. Castillo Jr.	Just a Little Kiss	Tasso Bee	11	1:25.51	$60,000
1993	Kimscountrydiamond	J. Vasquez	Nijivision	Hollywood Wildcat	10	1:23.44	$60,000
1992	C. C.'s Return	R. J. Thibeau Jr.	Fortune Forty Four	Subtle Dancer	7	1:25.33	$30,000

1992-'93 Azalea H.; 1994-'95 Azalea S. 1992-'96 7 furlongs.

Baldwin Stakes

Grade 3, Santa Anita Park, three-year-olds, 6½ furlongs, dirt (originally scheduled on the turf). Held February 25, 2001, with a gross value of $110,000. First held in 1968. Graded since 1995. Stakes record 1:12.80 (1968 Royal Fols; 1969 Tell).

Year	Winner	Jockey	Second	Third	Strs	Final Time	1st Purse
2001	Skip to the Stone	C. S. Nakatani	Trailthefox	Bills Paid	6	1:16.29	$66,000
2000	Fortifier	B. Blanc	Performing Magic	Joopy Doopy	8	1:16.79	$66,870
1999	American Spirit	E. Ramsammy	Chomper (Ire)	Impressive Grades	13	1:13.93	$69,300
1998	Wrekin Pilot (GB)	E. Delahoussaye	Commitisize	Tenbyssimo (Ire)	8	1:13.32	$66,240
1997	Latin Dancer	C. A. Black	King of Swing	Swiss Yodeler	11	1:14.48	$67,850
1996	Sandtrap	C. S. Nakatani	Strangelove	Benton Creek	6	1:15.03	$64,300
1995	Sierra Diablo	E. Delahoussaye	Raji	Huge Gator	6	1:15.36	$47,300
1994	Silver Music	C. W. Antley	Eagle Eyed	Makinanhonestbuck	8	1:13.76	$48,375
1993	Future Storm	K. J. Desormeaux	Concept Win	Siebe	11	1:15.02	$51,550
1992	Reckless Ruckus	P. A. Valenzuela	Fabulous Champ	Slerp	8	1:17.28	$49,850

1993-'94,1996-'99 about 6½ furlongs. 1993-'94,1996-'99 turf

Ballerina Handicap

Grade 1, Saratoga Race Course, three-year-olds and up, fillies and mares, 7 furlongs, dirt. Held August 26, 2001, with a gross value of $250,000. First held in 1979. Graded since 1981. Stakes record 1:21.22 (1992 Serape).

Year	Winner	Jockey	Second	Third	Strs	Final Time	1st Purse
2001	Shine Again, 4, 113	J-L. Samyn	Country Hideaway, 5	Dream Supreme, 5	5	1:22.33	$150,000
2000	Dream Supreme, 3, 113	P. Day	Country Hideaway, 4	Bourbon Belle, 4	9	1:22.97	$150,000
1999	Furlough, 5, 114	M. E. Smith	Bourbon Belle, 4	(DH) Hurricane Bertie, 4	10	1:23.04	$120,000
				(DH) Catinca, 4			
1998	Stop Traffic, 5, 118	S. J. Sellers	Runup the Colors, 4	U Can Do It, 4	6	1:22.23	$120,000
1997	Pearl City, 3, 110	J. Bravo	Ashboro, 4	Flashy n Smart, 4	5	1:22.39	$90,000
1996	Chaposa Springs, 4, 120	S. J. Sellers	Capote Belle, 3	Broad Smile, 3	6	1:21.88	$90,000
1995	Classy Mirage, 5, 118	J. A. Krone	Inside Information, 4	Laura's Pistolette, 4	6	1:22.55	$90,000
1994	Roamin Rachel, 4, 118	P. Day	Classy Mirage, 4	Twist Afleet, 4	6	1:21.85	$65,040
1993	Spinning Round, 4, 119	J. F. Chavez	November Snow, 4	Apelia, 4	7	1:21.49	$69,120
1992	Serape, 4, 116	C. W. Antley	Harbour Club, 5	Nannerl, 5	9	**1:21.22**	$71,160

1992-'93 Ballerina S. 1999 dead heat for third.

Ballston Spa Breeders' Cup Handicap

Grade 3, Saratoga Race Course, three-year-olds and up, fillies and mares, 1 1/16 miles, turf. Held August 12, 2001, with a gross value of $190,200. First held in 1989. Graded since 1995. Stakes record 1:39.47 (1997 Valor Lady).

Year	Winner	Jockey	Second	Third	Strs	Final Time	1st Purse
2001	**Penny's Gold**, 4, 118	J. D. Bailey	Babae (Chi), 5	Chaste, 5	6	1:40.69	$126,120
2000	**License Fee**, 5, 116	P. Day	Pico Teneriffe, 4	Hello Soso (Ire), 4	7	1:43.53	$125,700
1999	**Pleasant Temper**, 5, 118	J. D. Bailey	Cuanto Es, 4	Lets Get Cozzy, 4	5	1:41.84	$124,680
1998	**Memories of Silver**, 5, 122	J. D. Bailey	Witchful Thinking, 4	Ashford Castle, 4	7	1:40.93	$126,600
1997	**Valor Lady**, 5, 112	J. R. Velazquez	Antespend, 4	Rumpipumpy (GB), 4	6	**1:39.47**	$130,200
1996	**Danish (Ire)**, 5, 115	J. A. Santos	Apolda, 5	(DH) Upper Noosh, 4 (DH) Caress, 5	8	1:41.50	$126,360
1995	**Weekend Madness (Ire)**, 5, 117	S. J. Sellers	Irish Linnet, 7	Allez Les Trois, 7	7	1:40.34	$93,300
1994	**Weekend Madness (Ire)**, 4, 115	S. J. Sellers	You'd Be Surprised, 5	Heed, 5	8	1:43.77	$93,510
1993	**One Dreamer**, 5, 116	E. Fires	Eenie Meenie Miney, 4	Irish Linnet, 4	10	1:39.38	$94,440
1992	**Aurora**, 4, 114	C. Perret	Olden Rijn, 4	Irish Linnet, 4	7	1:36.94	$93,870

1992-'93 Aqueduct Breeders' Cup H.; 1994-'96 Saratoga Breeders' Cup H. 1992-'93 held at Aqueduct. 1992-'93 1 mile. 1996 dead heat for third.

Baltimore Ravens Breeders' Cup Handicap

Grade 3, Pimlico, three-year-olds and up, 1 1/8 miles, dirt. Held June 16, 2001, with a gross value of $140,000. First held in 1986. Graded since 1988. Stakes record 1:47.63 (1996 Pyramid Peak).

Year	Winner	Jockey	Second	Third	Strs	Final Time	1st Purse
2001	**Lightning Paces**, 4, 114	G. W. Hutton	Milwaukee Brew, 4	Grundlefoot, 4	5	1:50.52	$60,000
2000	**Leave It to Beezer**, 7, 115	T. L. Dunkelberger	Eastern Daydream, 5	Thunder Flash, 5	6	1:49.02	$60,000
1999	**Testafly**, 5, 114	G. W. Hutton	Rod and Staff, 6	Willing, 6	7	1:49.80	$60,000
1998	**Testafly**, 4, 115	G. W. Hutton	Hot Brush, 4	Proud and True, 4	7	1:49.86	$60,000
1997	**Pyramid Peak**, 5, 118	P. Day	Wild Deputy, 4	Tam's Armada, 4	7	1:48.83	$125,520
1996	**Pyramid Peak**, 4, 122	W. H. McCauley	Coup D' Argent, 4	Personal Merit, 4	4	**1:47.63**	$124,350
1995	**Poor But Honest**, 5, 109	D. P. Butler	Mary's Buckaroo, 4	Rugged Bugger, 4	5	1:49.01	$126,120
1994	**Taking Risks**, 4, 117	M. T. Johnston	Conte Di Savoya, 5	Frottage, 5	7	1:49.21	$65,880
1993	**Sunny Sunrise**, 6, 120	M. T. Johnston	Snappy Landing, 4	Baron Mathew, 4	6	1:48.97	$108,750
1992	**Excellent Tipper**, 4, 112	E. S. Prado	Sunny Sunrise, 5	Out of Place, 5	10	1:47.64	$105,000

1992-2000 Baltimore Breeders' Cup H. 1992-'97 held at Laurel Park. 1992 new track record; 1996 equaled track record.

Barbara Fritchie Handicap

Grade 2, Laurel Park, three-year-olds and up, fillies and mares, 7 furlongs, dirt. Held February 17, 2001, with a gross value of $200,000. First held in 1952. Graded since 1973. Stakes record 1:21.40 (1989 Tappiano).

Year	Winner	Jockey	Second	Third	Strs	Final Time	1st Purse
2001	**Prized Stamp**, 4, 113	T. L. Dunkelberger	Superduper Miss, 5	Tax Affair, 5	6	1:23.74	$120,000
2000	**Tap to Music**, 5, 115	J. Bravo	Her She Kisses, 4	Di's Time, 4	13	1:24.75	$120,000
1999	**Passeggiata (Arg)**, 6, 113	M. G. Pino	Catinca, 4	Nothing Special, 4	8	1:23.55	$150,000
1998	**J J'sdream**, 5, 115	L. C. Reynolds	Palette Knife, 5	Stylish Encore, 5	10	1:24.21	$150,000
1997	**Miss Golden Circle**, 5, 118	R. Migliore	Lottsa Talc, 7	Whaleneck, 7	12	1:23.05	$120,000
1996	**Lottsa Talc**, 6, 117	F. T. Alvarado	Up an Eighth, 5	Evil's Pic, 5	14	1:22.61	$120,000
1995	**Smart 'N Noble**, 4, 117	M. G. Pino	Dust Bucket, 4	Gooni Goo Hoo, 4	10	1:24.13	$120,000
1994	**Mixed Appeal**, 6, 111	A. C. Salazar	Known as Nancy, 4	Winka, 4	12	1:23.31	$120,000
1993	**Moon Mist**, 4, 112	T. G. Turner	Ritchie Trail, 5	Femma, 5	9	1:23.50	$120,000
1992	**Wood So**, 5, 113	M. G. Pino	Wide Country, 4	Wait for the Lady, 4	7	1:24.56	$120,000

Bashford Manor Stakes

Grade 2, Churchill Downs, two-year-olds, 6 furlongs, dirt. Held July 8, 2001, with a gross value of $133,750. First held in 1902. Graded since 1991. Stakes record 1:09.90 (2001 Lunar Bounty).

Year	Winner	Jockey	Second	Third	Strs	Final Time	1st Purse
2001	**Lunar Bounty**	F. Lovato Jr.	Binyamin	Storm Passage	5	**1:09.90**	$82,925
2000	**Duality**	C. H. Borel	Strait Cat	Take Arms	9	1:10.09	$86,258
1999	**Dance Master**	B. D. Peck	Sky Dweller	Snuck In	8	1:10.38	$89,280
1998	**Time Bandit**	C. R. Woods Jr.	Yes It's True	Haus of Dehere	8	1:10.78	$68,262
1997	**Favorite Trick**	P. Day	Double Honor	Cowboy Dan	8	1:09.92	$68,696
1996	**Boston Harbor**	M. J. Luzzi	Prairie Junction	Nobel Talent	8	1:09.96	$72,150
1995	**A. V. Eight**	A. J. Trosclair	Aggie Southpaw	Seeker's Reward	8	1:11.40	$71,630
1994	**Hyroglyphic**	G. K. Gomez	Boone's Mill	Hobgoblin	13	1:10.25	$75,660
1993	**†Miss Ra He Ra**	W. Martinez	Ramblin Guy	Riverinn	13	1:12.98	$76,180
1992	**Mountain Cat**	C. R. Woods Jr.	Tempered Halo	Storm Flight	7	1:10.62	$53,869

1992-'98 Grade 3. † denotes female.

Bayakoa Handicap

Grade 2, Hollywood Park, three-year-olds and up, fillies and mares, 1 1/16 miles, dirt. Held December 15, 2001, with a gross value of $150,000. First held in 1981. Graded since 1983. Stakes record 1:41.20 (1993 Golden Klair [GB]).

Year	Winner	Jockey	Second	Third	Strs	Final Time	1st Purse
2001	Starrer, 3, 118	J. D. Bailey	Queenie Belle, 4	Tropical Lady (Brz), 4	7	1:42.52	$90,000
2000	Feverish, 5, 119	E. Delahoussaye	Gourmet Girl, 5	Lazy Slusan, 5	9	1:42.26	$90,000
1999	Manistique, 4, 124	C. S. Nakatani	Snowberg, 4	Riboletta (Brz), 4	7	1:43.16	$90,000
1998	Manistique, 3, 119	G. L. Stevens	India Divina (Chi), 4	Numero Uno, 4	4	1:42.51	$60,000
1997	Sharp Cat, 3, 121	A. O. Solis			1	1:42.68	$60,000
1996	Listening, 3, 120	C. J. McCarron	Cat's Cradle, 4	Belle's Flag, 4	7	1:42.66	$64,920
1995	Pirate's Revenge, 4, 119	C. W. Antley	Urbane, 3	Ashtabula, 3	5	1:41.80	$61,900
1994	Thirst for Peace, 5, 115	A. O. Solis	Glass Ceiling, 4	Dancing Mirage, 4	7	1:42.28	$63,500
1993	Golden Klair (GB), 3, 115	C. J. McCarron	Pacific Squall, 4	Cargo, 4	7	1:41.20	$63,500
1992	Brought to Mind, 5, 120	P. A. Valenzuela	Re Toss (Arg), 5	Interactive, 5	8	1:42.62	$65,200

1992-'93 Silver Belles H. 1997 won in a walkover.

Bay Meadows Breeders' Cup Handicap

Grade 3, Bay Meadows, three-year-olds and up, about 1 1/8 miles, turf. Held September 22, 2001, with a gross value of $110,000. First held in 1934. Graded since 1981. Stakes record 1:45.45 (1995 Caesour).

Year	Winner	Jockey	Second	Third	Strs	Final Time	1st Purse
2001	Super Quercus (Fr), 5, 117	R. A. Baze	Most Likely (Arg), 5	Sign of Hope (GB), 5	6	1:47.50	$55,000
2000	Devine Wind, 4, 114	G. K. Gomez	Irish Prize, 4	Deploy Venture (GB), 4	6	1:47.19	$110,000
1999	Kirkwall (GB), 5, 114	V. Espinoza	Special Quest (Fr), 4	Game Ploy (Pol), 4	8	1:47.13	$110,000
1998	Hawksley Hill (Ire), 5, 120	A. O. Solis	Magellan, 5	Floriselli, 5	5	1:45.49	$110,000
1997	El Angelo, 5, 119	A. O. Solis	Via Lombardia (Ire), 5	Dreamer, 5	5	1:45.47	$110,000
1996	Gentlemen (Arg), 4, 117	C. S. Nakatani	Party Season (GB), 5	Petit Poucet (GB), 5	5	1:45.90	$110,000
1995	Caesour, 5, 115	R. A. Baze	Johann Quatz (Fr), 6	Canaska Dancer (Ire), 6	6	1:45.45	$110,000
1994	Blues Traveller (Ire), 4, 116	G. L. Stevens	Fastness (Ire), 4	Wharf, 4	6	1:46.03	$110,000
1993	Slew of Damascus, 5, 114	T. M. Chapman	Fast Cure, 4	Lissitki (Fr), 4	7	1:45.91	$110,000
1992	Forty Niner Days, 5, 115	C. S. Nakatani	Bistro Garden, 4	Luthier Enchanteur, 4	8	1:46.58	$137,500

1992-2000 Bay Meadows H. 1992-'95 Grade 2. 1993 1 1/8 miles. 1993,1995 new course record.

Bay Meadows Derby

Grade 3, Bay Meadows, three-year-olds, about 1 1/8 miles, turf. Held November 4, 2001, with a gross value of $100,000. First held in 1954. Graded since 1983. Stakes record 1:45.20 (1978 Quip).

Year	Winner	Jockey	Second	Third	Strs	Final Time	1st Purse
2001	Blue Steller (Ire)	A. O. Solis	Sir Alfred	Sea to See	8	1:46.81	$55,000
2000	Walkslikeaduck	E. Delahoussaye	Jokerman	Calamari	5	1:46.57	$82,500
1999	Mula Gula	R. Q. Meza	†Miss Chryss (Ire)	Fighting Falcon	10	1:45.34	$82,500
1998	Takarian (Ire)	C. A. Black	I. M. Bzy	Prevalence (GB)	8	1:46.80	$82,500
1997	Shellbacks	R. Q. Meza	Brave Act (GB)	Zippersup	7	1:49.01	$82,500
1996	†Ocean Queen	J. A. Garcia	Mateo	Mystic Knight (GB)	8	1:47.80	$110,000
1995	Virginia Carnival	R. J. Warren Jr.	Helmsman	Tabor	10	1:46.17	$55,000
1994	Marvin's Faith (Ire)	M. Castaneda	Western Trader	Turbo Fan	8	1:48.88	$55,000
1993	Ranger (Fr)	G. Boulanger	El Atroz	Guide (Fr)	9	1:48.90	$55,000
1992	Star Recruit	R. D. Hansen	Siberian Summer	Fax News	6	1:49.13	$55,000

1996-2000 Bay Meadows Breeders' Cup Derby. 1994-'95,1997-2001 about 1 1/8 miles. 1992 dirt. † denotes female.

Bay Meadows Breeders' Cup Sprint Handicap

Grade 3, Bay Meadows, three-year-olds and up, 6 furlongs, dirt. Held September 8, 2001, with a gross value of $142,500. First held in 1986. Graded since 2000. Stakes record 1:07.94 (2001 Lexicon).

Year	Winner	Jockey	Second	Third	Strs	Final Time	1st Purse
2001	Lexicon, 6, 117	R. A. Baze	Swept Overboard, 4	You and You Alone, 4	4	1:07.94	$82,500
2000	Lexicon, 5, 115	R. A. Baze	Men's Exclusive, 7	Dixie Dot Com, 7	5	1:09.19	$110,000
1999	Big Jag, 6, 118	J. Valdivia Jr.	Men's Exclusive, 6	Lexicon, 6	6	1:08.87	$110,000
1998	Musafi, 4, 116	D. R. Flores	(DH) Mr. Doubledown, 4 (DH) The Barking Shark, 4		7	1:08.59	$110,000
1997	Tres Paraiso, 5, 116	C. S. Nakatani	Mashaka's Pride, 4	Boundless Moment, 4	5	1:07.98	$110,000
1996	Boundless Moment, 4, 116	K. J. Desormeaux	Concept Win, 4	Paying Dues, 8	11	1:08.81	$110,000
1995	Lucky Forever, 6, 116	G. F. Almeida	Wild Gold, 5	Uncaged Fury, 5	8	1:08.71	$117,700
1994	†Soviet Problem, 4, 120	R. A. Baze	Wild Gold, 5	Concept Win, 4	6	1:08.58	$31,200
1993	Lucky Forever, 4, 114	A. L. Castanon	Cardmania, 7	Scherando, 7	9	1:08.98	$87,750
1992	Superstrike (GB), 3, 114	D. Sorenson	Anjiz, 4	Naevus Star, 4	7	1:08.83	$86,950

1992-'95 Bay Meadows Breeders' Cup H. 1998 dead heat for second. † denotes female.

Bay Shore Stakes

Grade 3, Aqueduct, three-year-olds, 7 furlongs, dirt. Held April 14, 2001, with a gross value of $150,000. First held in 1960. Graded since 1973. Stakes record 1:20.54 (1998 Limit Out).

Year	Winner	Jockey	Second	Third	Strs	Final Time	1st Purse
2001	Skip to the Stone	V. Espinoza	Multiple Choice	Friday's a Comin'	8	1:22.46	$90,000
2000	Precise End	J. F. Chavez	Turnofthecentury	Port Herman	7	1:22.27	$66,000
1999	Perfect Score	E. S. Prado	Royal Ruby	Prince Monty	8	1:22.98	$66,120
1998	Limit Out	J-L. Samyn	Good and Tough	Diamond Studs	6	1:20.54	$65,460
1997	Hawks Landing	R. Migliore	Adverse	Standing On Edge	7	1:22.13	$66,480
1996	Jamies First Punch	J. R. Velazquez	Gold Fever	Firey Jennifer	9	1:22.13	$67,200
1995	Blissful State	M. J. Luzzi	Northern Ensign	Pat n Jac	6	1:23.92	$64,680
1994	Prank Call	J. R. Velazquez	Mr. Shawklit	Popol's Gold	7	1:09.84	$65,940
1992	Three Peat	C. W. Antley	Goldwater	Best Decorated	10	1:21.68	$75,600

1993 not held. 1992 Grade 2. 1994 6 furlongs.

Beaugay Handicap

Grade 3, Aqueduct, three-year-olds and up, fillies and mares, 1 1/16 miles, turf. Held May 6, 2001, with a gross value of $109,900. First held in 1978. Graded since 1986. Stakes record 1:40.16 (1991 Summer Secretary).

Year	Winner	Jockey	Second	Third	Strs	Final Time	1st Purse
2001	Gaviola, 4, 120	J. D. Bailey	Truebreadpudding, 6	Efficient Frontier, 6	6	1:41.74	$65,940
2000	Perfect Sting, 4, 119	J. D. Bailey	License Fee, 5	Fictitious (GB), 5	7	1:42.30	$65,820
1999	Tampico, 6, 114	J. R. Velazquez	U R Unforgetable, 5	Shashobegon, 5	7	1:44.32	$67,020
1998	National Treasure, 5, 117	R. Migliore	Aspiring, 5	Dixie Ghost, 5	7	1:37.94	$67,740
1997	Careless Heiress, 4, 116	J. Bravo	Song of Africa, 4	Gastronomical, 4	6	1:46.28	$65,760
1996	Christmas Gift, 4, 118	J. D. Bailey	Caress, 5	Aucilla, 5	9	1:42.89	$50,805
1995	Caress, 4, 113	R. G. Davis	Shir Dar (Fr), 5	Statuette, 5	8	1:42.06	$49,905
1994	Cox Orange, 4, 112	J. D. Bailey	Irish Linnet, 6	Statuette, 6	5	1:43.32	$49,395
1993	McKaymackenna, 4, 113	J. Velasquez	Aurora, 5	Chinese Empress, 5	10	1:44.80	$57,240
1992	Christiecat, 5, 116	J-L. Samyn	Metamorphose, 4	Navarra, 4	10	1:46.84	$56,520

1992 held at Belmont Park. 1998 1 mile. 1998 dirt.

Bed o' Roses Breeders' Cup Handicap

Grade 3, Aqueduct, three-year-olds and up, fillies and mares, 1 mile, dirt. Held April 21, 2001, with a gross value of $157,700. First held in 1957. Graded since 1973. Stakes record 1:34 (1994 Classy Mirage).

Year	Winner	Jockey	Second	Third	Strs	Final Time	1st Purse
2001	Country Hideaway, 5, 117	J. R. Velazquez	Critical Eye, 4	Jostle, 4	7	1:34.98	$95,520
2000	Ruby Rubles, 5, 113	C. C. Lopez	Up We Go, 4	Go to the Ink, 4	7	1:36.96	$65,580
1999	Catinca, 4, 120	R. Migliore	Foil, 4	License Fee, 4	6	1:34.95	$94,620
1998	Dixie Flag, 4, 117	M. J. Luzzi	Hidden Reserve, 4	U Can Do It, 4	9	1:33.60	$96,780
1997	Flat Fleet Feet, 4, 121	M. E. Smith	Mama Dean, 4	Ashboro, 4	6	1:34.07	$95,940
1996	Punkin Pie, 6, 110	J. C. Trejo	Incinerate, 6	Lottsa Talc, 6	6	1:35.13	$65,220
1995	Incinerate, 5, 113	F. Leon	Imah, 5	Beckys Shirt, 5	5	1:35.86	$63,960
1994	Classy Mirage, 4, 117	R. G. Davis	For all Seasons, 4	Dispute, 4	6	1:34.00	$64,680
1993	Lady d'Accord, 6, 111	J. F. Chavez	Missy's Mirage, 5	Buck Some Belle, 5	5	1:36.76	$67,320
1992	Nannerl, 5, 115	J. A. Krone	English Charm, 6	Spy Leader Lady, 6	7	1:37.27	$68,100
	Lady d'Accord, 5, 114	J. F. Chavez	My Treasure, 5	Crystal Vous, 5	7	1:37.86	$68,580

1992-'95 Bed o' Roses H. 1992-'96 Grade 2. 1992 two divisions.

Bel Air Handicap

Grade 2, Hollywood Park, three-year-olds and up, 1 1/16 miles, dirt. Held July 7, 2001, with a gross value of $100,000. First held in 1939. Graded since 1985. Stakes record 1:40.12 (1997 Crafty Friend).

Year	Winner	Jockey	Second	Third	Strs	Final Time	1st Purse
2001	Smile Again, 6, 116	L. A. Pincay Jr.	Freedom Crest, 5	Dig for It, 5	6	1:41.74	$60,000
2000	Euchre, 4, 114	A. O. Solis	Sultry Substitute, 5	River Keen (Ire), 5	7	1:41.76	$90,000
1999	River Keen (Ire), 7, 115	C. W. Antley	Barter Town, 4	Quake, 4	7	1:40.69	$75,000
1998	Free House, 4, 124	C. J. McCarron	Wild Wonder, 4	Albaha, 4	5	1:41.66	$63,660
1997	Crafty Friend, 4, 116	A. O. Solis	Hesabull, 4	Arrivederci Baby, 4	6	1:40.12	$64,380
1996	Cleante (Arg), 7, 115	C. J. McCarron	Dare and Go, 5	Dernier Empereur, 5	4	1:41.01	$62,940
1995	Soul of the Matter, 4, 121	G. L. Stevens	Cleante (Arg), 6	Luthier Fever, 6	5	1:41.10	$76,200
1994	Region, 5, 117	G. L. Stevens	Tinners Way, 4	Williamstown, 4	6	1:40.21	$92,800
1993	Marquetry, 6, 119	K. J. Desormeaux	Memo (Chi), 6	Desert Sun (GB), 6	6	1:40.94	$92,800
1992	Renegotiable, 4, 113	A. O. Solis	Digression, 5	Missionary Ridge (GB), 5	5	1:41.95	$91,900

1997 equaled track record.

Beldame Stakes

Grade 1, Belmont Park, three-year-olds and up, fillies and mares, 1⅛ miles, dirt. Held October 6, 2001, with a gross value of $750,000. First held in 1939. Graded since 1973. Stakes record 1:45.80 (1990 Go for Wand).

Year	Winner	Jockey	Second	Third	Strs	Final Time	1st Purse
2001	Exogenous, 3	J. Castellano	Flute, 3	Spain, 3	8	1:49.20	$450,000
2000	Riboletta (Brz), 5	C. J. McCarron	Beautiful Pleasure, 5	Pentatonic, 5	5	1:46.14	$450,000
1999	Beautiful Pleasure, 4	J. F. Chavez	Silverbulletday, 3	Catinca, 3	5	1:47.74	$300,000
1998	Sharp Cat, 4	C. S. Nakatani	Tomisue's Delight, 4	Pocho's Dream Girl, 4	7	1:46.20	$240,000
1997	Hidden Lake, 4	R. Migliore	Ajina, 3	Jewel Princess, 3	8	1:48.26	$240,000
1996	Yanks Music, 3	J. R. Velazquez	Serena's Song, 4	Clear Mandate, 4	6	1:47.02	$240,000
1995	Serena's Song, 3	G. L. Stevens	Heavenly Prize, 4	Lakeway, 4	5	1:48.75	$150,000
1994	Heavenly Prize, 3	P. Day	Educated Risk, 4	Classy Mirage, 4	4	1:48.86	$150,000
1993	Dispute, 3	J. D. Bailey	Shared Interest, 5	Vivano, 5	6	1:47.22	$150,000
1992	Saratoga Dew, 3	W. H. McCauley	Versailles Treaty, 4	Coxwold, 4	5	1:46.99	$150,000

Belmont Breeders' Cup Handicap

Grade 2, Belmont Park, three-year-olds and up, 1⅛ miles, turf. Held September 16, 2000, with a gross value of $210,000. First held in 1986. Graded since 1988. Stakes record 1:45.90 (1998 Subordination).

Year	Winner	Jockey	Second	Third	Strs	Final Time	1st Purse
2000	Forbidden Apple, 5, 114	J. A. Santos	Val's Prince, 8	Altibr, 8	6	1:51.73	$126,000
1999	With the Flow, 4, 114	J. A. Santos	Comic Strip, 4	Wised Up, 4	9	1:49.39	$127,620
1998	Subordination, 4, 121	D. R. Flores	Yagli, 5	Bomfim, 5	9	**1:45.90**	$127,020
1997	Fortitude, 4, 112	R. G. Davis	Green Means Go, 5	Boyce, 5	8	1:38.53	$126,600
1996	Gentleman Beau, 4, 114	J. A. Santos	Volochine (Ire), 5	Kiri's Clown, 5	7	1:41.18	$127,140
1995	Dove Hunt, 4, 121	P. Day	Fly Cry, 4	Unfinished Symph, 4	6	1:40.18	$92,970
1994	A in Sociology, 4, 116	J-L. Samyn	Fourstars Allstar, 6	Home of the Free, 6	10	1:40.19	$34,290
1993	Fourstars Allstar, 5, 116	J. A. Santos	Lech, 5	Cleone, 5	6	1:39.88	$92,880
1992	Roman Envoy, 4, 113	C. Perret	Lotus Pool, 5	Daarik (Ire), 5	10	1:41.50	$34,800

2001 not held due to World Trade Center attack. 1992-'93 Saratoga Breeders' Cup H. 1992-'97 Grade 3. 1992-'93 held at Saratoga. 1992-'97 1⅟₁₆ miles. 1996 Kiri's Clown finished first, DQ to third.

Belmont Stakes

Grade 1, Belmont Park, three-year-olds, 1½ miles, dirt. Held June 9, 2001, with a gross value of $1,000,000. First held in 1867. Graded since 1973. Stakes record 2:24 (1973 Secretariat [new world record]).

Year	Winner	Jockey	Second	Third	Strs	Final Time	1st Purse
2001	Point Given	G. L. Stevens	A P Valentine	Monarchos	9	2:26.56	$600,000
2000	Commendable	P. Day	Aptitude	Unshaded	11	2:31.19	$600,000
1999	Lemon Drop Kid	J. A. Santos	Vision and Verse	Charismatic	12	2:27.88	$600,000
1998	Victory Gallop	G. L. Stevens	Real Quiet	Thomas Jo	11	2:29.16	$600,000
1997	Touch Gold	C. J. McCarron	Silver Charm	Free House	7	2:28.82	$432,600
1996	Editor's Note	R. R. Douglas	Skip Away	†My Flag	14	2:28.96	$437,880
1995	Thunder Gulch	G. L. Stevens	Star Standard	Citadeel	11	2:32.02	$415,440
1994	Tabasco Cat	P. Day	Go for Gin	Strodes Creek	6	2:26.82	$392,280
1993	Colonial Affair	J. A. Krone	Kissin Kris	Wild Gale	13	2:29.97	$444,540
1992	A.P. Indy	E. Delahoussaye	My Memoirs (GB)	Pine Bluff	11	2:26.13	$458,880

† denotes female.

Ben Ali Stakes

Grade 3, Keeneland, four-year-olds and up, 1⅛ miles, dirt. Held April 27, 2001, with a gross value of $106,800. First held in 1917. Graded since 1973. Stakes record 1:48.16 (1999 Jazz Club).

Year	Winner	Jockey	Second	Third	Strs	Final Time	1st Purse
2001	Broken Vow, 4	E. S. Prado	Perfect Cat, 4	Jadada, 4	5	1:48.47	$66,216
2000	Midway Magistrate, 6	S. J. Sellers	Liberty Gold, 6	Early Warning, 6	7	1:49.15	$67,518
1999	Jazz Club, 4	P. Day	Smile Again, 4	Early Warning, 4	6	**1:48.16**	$67,456
1998	Storm Broker, 4	R. Albarado	Delay of Game, 5	Gator Dancer, 5	5	1:48.23	$67,208
1997	Louis Quatorze, 4	P. Day	Knockadoon, 5	King James, 5	5	1:49.73	$66,526
1996	Knockadoon, 4	J. D. Bailey	Halo's Image, 5	Thorny Crown, 5	4	1:48.92	$66,216
1995	Wildly Joyous, 4	M. Walls	Danville, 4	Powerful Punch, 4	7	1:49.68	$50,406
1994	Pistols and Roses, 5	M. E. Smith	Sunny Sunrise, 7	Compadre, 7	4	1:51.77	$50,251
1993	Sunny Sunrise, 6	R. Wilson	Conte Di Savoya, 4	Prize Fight, 4	8	1:48.90	$50,933
1992	(DH) Profit Key, 5	S. J. Sellers	Out of Place, 4		6	1:49.95	$34,213
	(DH) Loach, 4	P. A. Valenzuela					

1992 dead heat for first.

Berkeley Handicap

Grade 3, Golden Gate Fields, three-year-olds and up, 1 mile, dirt. Held March 31, 2001, with a gross value of $100,000. First held in 1948. Graded since 2000. Stakes record 1:34.18 (2001 Blade Prospector [Brz]).

Year	Winner	Jockey	Second	Third	Strs	Final Time	1st Purse
2001	Blade Prospector (Brz), 6, 116	O. A. Berrio	Dixie Dot Com, 6	Milk Wood (GB), 6	6	**1:34.18**	$55,000

Year	Winner	Jockey	Second	Third	Strs	Final Time	1st Purse
2000	Voice of Destiny, 4, 113	R. Q. Meza	Mr. Doubledown, 6	Twilight Affair, 6	8	1:35.67	$75,000
1999	Hal's Pal (GB), 6, 117	B. Blanc	Wild Wonder, 5	Worldly Ways (GB), 5	7	1:34.96	$75,000
1998	Wild Wonder, 4, 115	R. A. Baze	General Royal, 4	March of Kings, 4	7	1:35.19	$51,450
1996	Houston Fleet M D, 2, 118	D. Carr	Slewp'a Doop, 2	Big Find, 2	5	1:36.67	$26,600
1995	Double Jab, 4, 115	R. A. Baze	Corslew, 5	Cleante (Arg), 5	8	1:35.18	$49,725
1994	River Special, 4, 115	T. M. Chapman	He's Illustrious, 7	Misty Wind (Ire), 7	8	1:34.33	$32,600
1993	Infamous Deed, 5, 115	R. J. Warren Jr.	Misty Wind (Ire), 5	J. F. Williams, 5	7	1:35.67	$25,960
1992	Music Prospector, 5, 118	R. D. Hansen	Michael's Flyer, 6	Flying Continental, 6	5	1:35.29	$31,450

1997 not held. 1996 two-year-olds.

Bernard Baruch Handicap

Grade 2, Saratoga Race Course, three-year-olds and up, 1⅛ miles, turf. Held July 27, 2001, with a gross value of $150,000. First held in 1959. Graded since 1973. Stakes record 1:45.40 (1973 Tentam).

Year	Winner	Jockey	Second	Third	Strs	Final Time	1st Purse
2001	Hap, 5, 121	J. D. Bailey	Royal Strand (Ire), 7	Dr. Kashnikow, 7	7	1:47.06	$90,000
2000	Hap, 4, 115	J. D. Bailey	Inexplicable, 5	Draw Shot, 5	13	1:45.82	$90,000
1999	Middlesex Drive, 4, 117	S. J. Sellers	Tangazi, 4	Comic Strip, 4	8	1:46.55	$90,000
1998	Yagli, 5, 121	J. D. Bailey	Tamhid, 5	Jambalaya Jazz, 5	9	1:46.22	$85,380
1997	Sentimental Moi, 7, 112	C. P. DeCarlo	Jambalaya Jazz, 5	Boyce, 5	8	1:46.11	$66,480
1996	Volochine (Ire), 5, 113	P. Day	Green Means Go, 4	Compadre, 4	10	1:47.58	$68,700
1995	Fourstars Allstar, 7, 120	J. A. Santos	Turk Passer, 5	Compadre, 5	7	1:47.67	$66,240
1994	Lure, 5, 125	M. E. Smith	Paradise Creek, 5	Fourstardave, 5	5	1:46.10	$64,920
1993	Furiously, 4, 119	J. D. Bailey	Star of Cozzene, 5	Royal Mountain Inn, 5	5	1:45.46	$70,320
1992	Fourstars Allstar, 4, 113	M. E. Smith	Lotus Pool, 5	Maxigroom, 5	6	1:46.06	$70,680

1993 equaled course record.

Best Pal Stakes

Grade 3, Del Mar, two-year-olds, 6½ furlongs, dirt. Held August 15, 2001, with a gross value of $138,000. First held in 1972. Graded since 1983. Stakes record 1:15.08 (2001 Officer).

Year	Winner	Jockey	Second	Third	Strs	Final Time	1st Purse
2001	Officer	V. Espinoza	Metatron	Essence of Dubai	3	**1:15.08**	$90,000
2000	Flame Thrower	C. S. Nakatani	Trailthefox	Legendary Weave	7	1:16.51	$90,000
1999	Dixie Union	A. O. Solis	Exchange Rate	Captain Steve	5	1:16.40	$90,000
1998	Worldly Manner	G. L. Stevens	Domination	Waki American	8	1:16.78	$65,580
1997	Old Topper	A. O. Solis	King of the Wild	Souvenir Copy	8	1:16.57	$68,825
1996	Swiss Yodeler	A. O. Solis	Golden Bronze	Deeds Not Words	8	1:16.12	$65,550
1995	Cobra King	R. A. Baze	Northern Afleet	Desert Native	8	1:15.89	$60,350
1994	Timber Country	A. O. Solis	Desert Mirage	Supremo	7	1:16.60	$46,575
1993	Creston	C. A. Black	Troyalty	Flying Sensation	6	1:16.35	$45,900
1992	Devil Diamond	K. J. Desormeaux	Wheeler Oil	Crafty	6	1:22.60	$45,900

1992-'95 Balboa S. 1992 7 furlongs.

Beverly D. Stakes

Grade 1, Arlington Park, three-year-olds and up, fillies and mares, 1³⁄₁₆ miles, turf. Held August 18, 2001, with a gross value of $700,000. First held in 1987. Graded since 1991. Stakes record 1:53.20 (1990 Reluctant Guest).

Year	Winner	Jockey	Second	Third	Strs	Final Time	1st Purse
2001	England's Legend (Fr), 4	C. S. Nakatani	The Seven Seas, 5	Spook Express (SAf), 5	9	1:56.75	$420,000
2000	Snow Polina, 5	J. D. Bailey	Happyanunoit (NZ), 5	Country Garden (GB), 5	10	1:55.87	$300,000
1997	Memories of Silver, 4	J. D. Bailey	Maxzene, 4	Dance Design (Ire), 4	6	1:54.38	$300,000
1996	Timarida (Ire), 4	J. P. Murtagh	Perfect Arc, 4	Alpride (Ire), 4	11	1:54.06	$300,000
1995	Possibly Perfect, 5	C. S. Nakatani	Alice Springs, 5	Alpride (Ire), 5	7	1:54.95	$300,000
1994	Hatoof, 5	W. R. Swinburn	Flawlessly, 6	Potridee (Arg), 6	8	1:55.59	$300,000
1993	Flawlessly, 5	C. J. McCarron	Via Borghese, 4	Let's Elope (NZ), 4	7	1:55.61	$300,000
1992	Kostroma (Ire), 6	K. J. Desormeaux	Ruby Tiger (Ire), 5	Dance Smartly, 5	13	1:54.10	$300,000

1998-'99 not held. 1993 Let's Elope (NZ) finished first, DQ to third.

Beverly Hills Handicap

Grade 1, Hollywood Park, three-year-olds and up, fillies and mares, 1¼ miles, turf. Held June 24, 2001, with a gross value of $200,000. First held in 1938. Graded since 1973. Stakes record 1:59 (1986 Estrapade).

Year	Winner	Jockey	Second	Third	Strs	Final Time	1st Purse
2001	Astra, 5, 121	K. J. Desormeaux	Happyanunoit (NZ), 6	Kalypso Katie (Ire), 6	5	1:59.61	$120,000
2000	Happyanunoit (NZ), 5, 121	B. Blanc	Sweet Life, 4	Polaire (Ire), 4	5	1:59.32	$150,000
1999	Virginie (Brz), 5, 118	L. A. Pincay Jr.	Tranquility Lake, 4	Keeper Hill, 4	6	2:00.21	$150,000
1998	Squeak (GB), 4, 115	G. L. Stevens	Sixy Saint, 4	Freeport Flight, 4	7	2:01.56	$180,000
1997	Windsharp, 6, 122	C. S. Nakatani	Different (Arg), 5	Donna Viola (GB), 5	6	2:00.72	$180,000
1996	Different (Arg), 4, 117	C. J. McCarron	Bail Out Becky, 4	Flagbird, 4	8	2:00.74	$163,800

Year	Winner	Jockey	Second	Third	Strs	Final Time	1st Purse
1995	**Alpride (Ire)**, 4, 115	C. J. McCarron	Possibly Perfect, 5	Wandesta (GB), 5	6	1:46.67	$185,000
1994	**Corrazona**, 4, 119	G. L. Stevens	Hollywood Wildcat, 4	Flawlessly, 4	7	1:47.40	$188,400
1993	**Flawlessly**, 5, 123	C. J. McCarron	Jolypha, 4	Party Cited, 4	4	1:47.00	$180,200
1992	**Flawlessly**, 4, 122	C. J. McCarron	Kostroma (Ire), 6	Alcando (Ire), 6	5	1:47.13	$184,000

1992-'95 1⅛ miles.

Bewitch Stakes

Grade 3, Keeneland, four-year-olds and up, fillies and mares, 1½ miles, turf. Held April 26, 2001, with a gross value of $200,000. First held in 1962. Graded since 1982. Stakes record 2:27.54 (1999 Bursting Forth).

Year	Winner	Jockey	Second	Third	Strs	Final Time	1st Purse
2001	**Keemoon (Fr)**, 5	J. D. Bailey	Playact (Ire), 4	Krisada, 4	8	2:30.28	$124,000
2000	**The Seven Seas**, 4	A. O. Solis	Innuendo (Ire), 5	Hollywood Baldcat, 5	10	2:29.31	$70,122
1999	**Bursting Forth**, 5	J. F. Chavez	Moments of Magic, 4	Pinafore Park, 4	9	**2:27.54**	$68,758
1998	**Maxzene**, 5	J. A. Santos	Cuando, 4	Gastronomical, 4	8	2:30.50	$69,626
1997	**Cymbala (Fr)**, 4	P. Day	Noble Cause, 4	Last Approach, 4	10	2:28.87	$69,130
1996	**Memories (Ire)**, 5	S. J. Sellers	Future Act, 4	Curtain Raiser, 4	5	2:30.14	$66,030
1995	**Market Booster**, 6	P. Day	Memories (Ire), 4	Abigailthewife, 4	7	2:29.33	$50,732
1994	**Freewheel**, 5	P. Day	Key Chance, 5	Amal Hayati, 5	6	1:50.24	$50,871
1993	**Miss Lenora**, 4	J. A. Krone	Hero's Love, 5	Radiant Ring, 5	8	1:50.60	$51,367
1992	**La Gueriere**, 4	B. D. Peck	Indian Fashion, 5	Plenty of Grace, 5	10	1:48.37	$54,438

1992-'94 1⅛ miles.

Bing Crosby Breeders' Cup Handicap

Grade 2, Del Mar, three-year-olds and up, 6 furlongs, dirt. Held July 22, 2001, with a gross value of $196,000. First held in 1947. Graded since 1985. Stakes record 1:07.80 (1962 Crazy Kid; 1968 Pretense; 1969 Kissin' George; 1978 Bad 'n Big).

Year	Winner	Jockey	Second	Third	Strs	Final Time	1st Purse
2001	**Kona Gold**, 7, 126	A. O. Solis	Caller One, 4	Swept Overboard, 4	4	1:08.22	$120,000
2000	**Kona Gold**, 6, 123	A. O. Solis	Love That Red, 4	Lexicon, 4	6	1:08.50	$124,200
1999	**Christmas Boy**, 6, 114	C. S. Nakatani	Son of a Pistol, 7	Expressionist, 7	6	1:08.11	$96,360
1998	**Son of a Pistol**, 6, 120	A. O. Solis	Gold Land, 7	Boundless Moment, 7	7	1:08.10	$97,200
1997	**First Intent**, 8, 115	R. R. Douglas	Boundless Moment, 5	High Stakes Player, 5	7	1:08.80	$102,000
1996	**Lit de Justice**, 6, 121	C. S. Nakatani	Concept Win, 6	Gold Land, 6	6	1:08.19	$126,750
1995	**Gold Land**, 4, 116	E. Delahoussaye	Lucky Forever, 6	G Malleah, 6	6	1:08.07	$89,300
1994	**King's Blade**, 3, 112	C. S. Nakatani	Memo (Chi), 7	Gundaghia, 7	8	1:08.64	$62,400
1993	**The Wicked North**, 4, 116	C. A. Black	Thirty Slews, 6	Black Jack Road, 6	6	1:08.52	$61,200
1992	**Thirty Slews**, 5, 116	E. Delahoussaye	Slerp, 3	Anjiz, 3	10	1:08.20	$64,900

1992-'95 Bing Crosby H. 1992-'98 Grade 3.

Black-Eyed Susan Stakes

Grade 2, Pimlico, three-year-old fillies, 1⅛ miles, dirt. Held May 18, 2001, with a gross value of $200,000. First held in 1919. Graded since 1973. Stakes record 1:47.83 (1999 Silverbulletday).

Year	Winner	Jockey	Second	Third	Strs	Final Time	1st Purse
2001	**Two Item Limit**	R. Migliore	Indy Glory	Tap Dance	5	1:50.84	$120,000
2000	**Jostle**	K. J. Desormeaux	March Magic	Impending Bear	7	1:52.56	$120,000
1999	**Silverbulletday**	G. L. Stevens	Dreams Gallore	Vee Vee Star	7	**1:47.83**	$120,000
1998	**Added Gold**	J. R. Velazquez	Tappin' Ginger	Hansel's Girl	8	1:49.75	$120,000
1997	**Salt It**	C. H. Marquez Jr.	Buckeye Search	Holiday Ball	7	1:50.52	$120,000
1996	**Mesabi Maiden**	M. E. Smith	Cara Rafaela	Ginny Lynn	8	1:51.00	$120,000
1995	**Serena's Song**	G. L. Stevens	Conquistadoress	Rare Opportunity	7	1:48.45	$120,000
1994	**Calipha**	R. Wilson	Bunting	Golden Braids	13	1:51.12	$120,000
1993	**Aztec Hill**	M. E. Smith	Traverse City	Jacody	10	1:49.78	$120,000
1992	**Miss Legality**	C. J. McCarron	Known Feminist	Diamond Duo	8	1:51.11	$150,000

Black Helen Handicap

Grade 2, Hialeah Park, three-year-olds and up, fillies and mares, 1⅛ miles, turf. Held April 14, 2001, with a gross value of $200,000. First held in 1941. Graded since 1973. Stakes record 1:46.71 (1996 Class Kris).

Year	Winner	Jockey	Second	Third	Strs	Final Time	1st Purse
2001	**Perfect Sting**, 5, 122	E. Coa	Clearly a Queen, 4	Spook Express (SAf), 4	5	1:47.17	$120,000
2000	**Snow Polina**, 5, 115	J. Castellano	Neptune's Bride, 4	Circus Charmer, 4	7	1:49.91	$120,000
1999	**Anguilla**, 4, 119	J. A. Krone	Starry Dreamer, 5	Winfama, 5	6	1:47.43	$120,000
1998	**Sopran Mariduff (GB)**, 4, 115	H. Castillo Jr.	Seebe, 4	Auntie Mame, 4	5	1:47.30	$120,000
1997	**Powder Bowl**, 5, 114	W. H. McCauley	Careless Heiress, 4	La Malleret, 4	6	1:48.91	$120,000
1996	**Class Kris**, 4, 121	G. Boulanger	Electric Society (Ire), 4	Chelsey Flower, 5	7	**1:46.71**	$120,000
1995	**Alice Springs**, 5, 120	R. R. Douglas	Apolda, 4	Cox Orange, 4	7	1:48.74	$120,000
1994	**Aquilegia**, 5, 113	W. H. McCauley	Via Borghese, 5	Tribulation, 5	9	1:48.23	$120,000

Year	Winner	Jockey	Second	Third	Strs	Final Time	1st Purse
1993	**Klassy Individual**, 7, 113	R. R. Douglas	Winnie D., 4	Captive Miss, 4	8	1:48.50	$90,000
1992	**Grab the Green**, 4, 117	J. A. Santos	Vigorous Lady, 6	Gaelic Bird (Fr), 6	14	1:48.01	$90,000

1992-'93 not graded; 1994 Grade 3. 2000 held at Gulfstream Park. 1992 about 1⅛ miles. 1994 Dahlia's Dreamer finished third, DQ to fourth.

Blue Grass Stakes

Grade 1, Keeneland, three-year-olds, 1⅛ miles, dirt. Held April 14, 2001, with a gross value of $750,000. First held in 1911. Graded since 1973. Stakes record 1:47.29 (1996 Skip Away).

Year	Winner	Jockey	Second	Third	Strs	Final Time	1st Purse
2001	**Millennium Wind**	L. A. Pincay Jr.	Songandaprayer	Dollar Bill	7	1:48.32	$465,000
2000	**High Yield**	P. Day	More Than Ready	Wheelaway	8	1:48.79	$465,000
1999	**Menifee**	P. Day	Cat Thief	Vicar	8	1:48.66	$465,000
1998	**Halory Hunter**	G. L. Stevens	Lil's Lad	Cape Town	5	1:47.98	$434,000
1997	**Pulpit**	S. J. Sellers	Acceptable	Stolen Gold	7	1:49.91	$434,000
1996	**Skip Away**	S. J. Sellers	Louis Quatorze	Editor's Note	7	**1:47.29**	$434,000
1995	**Wild Syn**	R. P. Romero	Suave Prospect	Tejano Run	6	1:49.31	$310,000
1994	**Holy Bull**	M. E. Smith	Valiant Nature	Mahogany Hall	7	1:50.02	$310,000
1993	**Prairie Bayou**	M. E. Smith	Wallenda	Dixieland Heat	9	1:49.62	$310,000
1992	**Pistols and Roses**	J. Vasquez	Conte Di Savoya	Ecstatic Ride	11	1:49.19	$325,000

1992-'98 Grade 2.

Boiling Springs Breeders' Cup Handicap

Not graded (originally scheduled as a Grade 3), The Meadowlands, three-year-old fillies, 1¹⁄₁₆ miles, dirt (originally scheduled on the turf). Held September 21, 2001, with a gross value of $194,000. First held in 1977. Graded since 1980. Stakes record 1:40.09 (1998 Mysterious Moll).

Year	Winner	Jockey	Second	Third	Strs	Final Time	1st Purse
2001	**Mystic Lady**, 120	E. Coa	Shooting Party	Plunderthepeasants	4	1:42.63	$120,000
2000	**Storm Dream (Ire)**, 116	J-L. Samyn	Watch	Lady Dora	11	1:47.09	$60,000
1999	**Wild Heart Dancing**, 116	J. F. Chavez	Confessional	Petunia	8	1:43.08	$120,000
1998	**Mysterious Moll**, 116	J. L. Espinoza	Who Did It and Run	Thunder Kitten	12	**1:40.09**	$120,000
1997	**Stoneleigh**, 114	J. A. Santos	Majestic Sunlight	Dancing Water	6	1:41.13	$60,000
	Victory Chime, 114	M. E. Smith	Miss Pop Carn	Colonial Play	9	1:41.99	$60,000
1996	**Careless Heiress**, 118	C. Perret	Briarcliff	Dathuil (Ire)	9	1:50.54	$60,000
1995	**Christmas Gift**, 116	W. H. McCauley	Ring by Spring	Transient Trend	7	1:43.49	$48,000
	Class Kris, 118	R. Wilson	Twilight Encounter	Appointed One	7	1:43.27	$48,000
1994	**Avie's Fancy**, 119	J. C. Ferrer	Teasing Charm	Knocknock	7	1:41.41	$45,000
1993	**Tribulation**, 110	J-L. Samyn	Exotic Sea	Bright Penny	11	1:42.70	$45,000
1992	**Captive Miss**, 120	J. Bravo	Logan's Mist	Aquilegia	9	1:40.78	$45,000

1992-'97 Boiling Springs H. 1992-2000 Grade 3. 1992-2000 turf. 1995, 1997 two divisions.

Bold Ruler Handicap

Grade 3, Aqueduct, three-year-olds and up, 6 furlongs, dirt. Held April 14, 2001, with a gross value of $109,200. First held in 1976. Graded since 1982. Stakes record 1:07.54 (1999 Kelly Kip).

Year	Winner	Jockey	Second	Third	Strs	Final Time	1st Purse
2001	**Say Florida Sandy**, 7, 117	J. Bravo	Delaware Township, 5	Lake Pontchartrain, 5	7	1:08.67	$65,520
2000	**Brutally Frank**, 6, 115	S. Bridgmohan	Kelly Kip, 6	Kashatreya, 6	7	1:08.64	$65,880
1999	**Kelly Kip**, 5, 123	J-L. Samyn	Artax, 4	Brushed On, 4	5	**1:07.54**	$64,440
1998	**Kelly Kip**, 4, 117	J-L. Samyn	Say Florida Sandy, 4	Johnny Legit, 4	8	1:07.61	$66,120
1997	**Punch Line**, 7, 122	R. G. Davis	Golden Tent, 8	Blissful State, 8	6	1:08.80	$64,980
1996	**Lite the Fuse**, 5, 119	J. A. Krone	Cold Execution, 5	Splendid Sprinter, 5	5	1:09.51	$64,500
1995	**Rizzi**, 4, 112	D. V. Beckner	Lite the Fuse, 4	Evil Bear, 4	6	1:08.91	$64,560
1994	**Chief Desire**, 4, 117	J. R. Velazquez	Boom Towner, 6	Won Song, 6	8	1:08.76	$66,300
1993	**Slerp**, 4, 119	J. A. Santos	Argyle Lake, 7	Big Jewel, 7	8	1:09.17	$70,200
1992	**Jolies Appeal**, 4, 119	W. H. McCauley	Reappeal, 6	Fiercely, 6	5	1:09.29	$67,560

1992-'93 Bold Ruler S. 1998,1999 new track record.

Bonnie Miss Stakes

Grade 2, Gulfstream Park, three-year-old fillies, 1⅛ miles, dirt. Held March 16, 2001, with a gross value of $250,000. First held in 1971. Graded since 1982. Stakes record 1:52.05 (2001 Tap Dance).

Year	Winner	Jockey	Second	Third	Strs	Final Time	1st Purse
2001	**Tap Dance**	J. D. Bailey	Halo Reality	Unbridled Lassie	7	**1:52.05**	$150,000
2000	**Cash Run**	J. D. Bailey	Deed I Do	Bejoyfulandrejoyce	6	1:44.11	$120,000
1999	**Three Ring**	J. R. Velazquez	Olympic Charmer	Marley Vale	5	1:43.75	$120,000
1998	**Banshee Breeze**	R. P. Romero	Santaria	Cotton House Bay	8	1:46.57	$120,000
1997	**Glitter Woman**	M. E. Smith	Southern Playgirl	Dixie Flag	5	1:43.25	$120,000

Year	Winner	Jockey	Second	Third	Strs	Final Time	1st Purse
1996	**My Flag**	J. D. Bailey	Escena	La Rosa	5	1:45.77	$120,000
1995	**Mia's Hope**	K. L. Chapman	Minister Wife	Incredible Blues	9	1:44.85	$120,000
1994	**Inside Information**	M. E. Smith	Cinnamon Sugar (Ire)	Jade Flush	10	1:42.94	$120,000
1993	**Dispute**	J. D. Bailey	Sky Beauty	Lunar Spook	6	1:43.67	$120,000
1992	**Spectacular Sue**	W. S. Ramos	Spinning Round	Tricky Cinderella	6	1:44.14	$120,000

1992-2000 1¹⁄₁₆ miles.

Bougainvillea Handicap

Grade 3, Hialeah Park, three-year-olds and up, 1⅛ miles, turf. Held March 31, 2001, with a gross value of $100,000. First held in 1946. Graded since 1973. Stakes record 1:46.04 (1996 Signal Tap).

Year	Winner	Jockey	Second	Third	Strs	Final Time	1st Purse
2001	**Make No Mistake (Ire)**, 6, 114	J. A. Santos	Aly's Alley, 5	A Little Luck, 5	11	1:50.10	$60,000
2000	**Down the Aisle**, 7, 113	J. Castellano	Mi Narrow, 6	Honor Glide, 6	11	1:49.46	$60,000
1999	**Parade Ground**, 4, 119	P. Day	Hibernian Rhapsody (Ire), 4	Sharp Appeal, 4	12	1:47.04	$60,000
1998	**Sharp Appeal**, 5, 115	W. H. McCauley	Ok by Me, 5	Yagli, 5	12	1:46.40	$60,000
1997	**Sharp Appeal**, 4, 114	J. A. Santos	Ok by Me, 4	Claudius, 4	14	1:47.95	$60,000
1996	**Signal Tap**, 5, 114	J. R. Velazquez	Copy Editor, 4	Diplomatic Jet, 4	14	**1:46.04**	$60,000
1995	**Lassigny**, 4, 114	J. D. Bailey	Sergeant Hawk, 5	Myrmidon, 5	14	1:47.92	$60,000
1994	**Awad**, 4, 116	E. Maple	Flying American, 5	Summer Ensign, 5	14	1:53.71	$60,000
1993	**Carterista**, 4, 116	C. E. Lopez Sr.	Gary Gumbo, 4	Spectacular Tide, 4	11	1:54.81	$60,000

1992 not held. 1993 not graded. 2000 held at Gulfstream Park. 1993 about 1³⁄₁₆ miles; 1994 1³⁄₁₆ miles. 1996 new course record.

Bowling Green Handicap

Grade 2, Belmont Park, three-year-olds and up, 1⅜ miles, turf. Held July 7, 2001, with a gross value of $150,000. First held in 1958. Graded since 1973. Stakes record 2:10.20 (1990 With Approval).

Year	Winner	Jockey	Second	Third	Strs	Final Time	1st Purse
2001	**King Cugat**, 4, 119	J. D. Bailey	Slew Valley, 4	Man From Wicklow, 4	7	2:10.62	$90,000
2000	**Elhayq (Ire)**, 5, 113	S. Bridgmohan	Yankee Dollar, 4	Carpenter's Halo, 4	9	2:13.81	$90,000
1999	**Honor Glide**, 5, 114	J. A. Santos	Parade Ground, 4	Fahris (Ire), 4	6	2:11.07	$90,000
1998	**Cetewayo**, 4, 112	J. R. Velazquez	Officious, 5	Chief Bearhart, 5	6	2:13.45	$90,000
1997	**Influent**, 6, 120	J-L. Samyn	Flag Down, 7	Notoriety, 7	8	2:11.06	$90,000
1996	**Flag Down**, 6, 118	J. A. Santos	Broadway Flyer, 5	Diplomatic Jet, 5	9	2:13.29	$90,000
1995	**Sentimental Moi**, 5, 111	R. B. Perez	Awad, 5	Proceeded, 5	8	2:15.48	$90,000
1994	**Turk Passer**, 4, 110	J. R. Velazquez	Sea Hero, 4	Fraise, 4	6	2:13.25	$90,000
1993	**Dr. Kiernan**, 4, 114	C. W. Antley	Spectacular Tide, 4	Lomitas (GB), 4	9	2:17.70	$90,000
1992	**Wall Street Dancer**, 4, 114	P. Day	Fraise, 4	Libor, 4	7	2:12.92	$120,000

1999 Federal Trial finished third, DQ to fourth.

Breeders' Cup Classic

Grade 1, three-year-olds and up, 1¼ miles, dirt. Held October 27, 2001, at Belmont Park with a gross value of $3,664,000. First held in 1984. Graded since 1984. Stakes record 1:59.16 (1997 Skip Away).

Year	Winner	Jockey	Second	Third	Strs	Final Time	1st Purse
2001	**Tiznow**, 4	C. J. McCarron	Sakhee, 4	Albert the Great, 4	13	2:00.62	$2,080,000
2000	**Tiznow**, 3	C. J. McCarron	Giant's Causeway, 3	Captain Steve, 3	13	2:00.75	$2,480,400
1999	**Cat Thief**, 3	P. Day	Budroyale, 6	Golden Missile, 6	14	1:59.52	$2,080,000
1998	**Awesome Again**, 4	P. Day	Silver Charm, 4	Swain (Ire), 4	10	2:02.16	$2,662,400
1997	**Skip Away**, 4	M. E. Smith	Deputy Commander, 3	Dowty, 3	9	**1:59.16**	$2,288,000
1996	**Alphabet Soup**, 5	C. J. McCarron	Louis Quatorze, 3	Cigar, 3	13	2:01.00	$2,080,000
1995	**Cigar**, 5	J. D. Bailey	L'Carriere, 4	Unaccounted For, 4	11	1:59.58	$1,560,000
1994	**Concern**, 3	J. D. Bailey	Tabasco Cat, 3	Dramatic Gold, 3	14	2:02.41	$1,560,000
1993	**Arcangues**, 5	J. D. Bailey	Bertrando, 4	Kissin Kris, 4	13	2:00.83	$1,560,000
1992	**A.P. Indy**, 3	E. Delahoussaye	Pleasant Tap, 5	†Jolypha, 5	14	2:00.20	$1,560,000

1992,1999 held at Gulfstream Park; 1993 Santa Anita Park; 1994, 1998, 2000 Churchill Downs; 1996 Woodbine; 1997 Hollywood Park. 1997 Whiskey Wisdom finished third, DQ to fourth. 1996 new track record. † denotes female.

Breeders' Cup Distaff

Grade 1, three-year-olds and up, fillies and mares, 1⅛ miles, dirt. Held October 27, 2001, at Belmont Park with a gross value of $2,161,760. First held in 1984. Graded since 1984. Stakes record 1:46.15 (1995 Inside Information).

Year	Winner	Jockey	Second	Third	Strs	Final Time	1st Purse
2001	**Unbridled Elaine**, 3	P. Day	Spain, 4	Two Item Limit, 4	11	1:49.21	$1,227,200
2000	**Spain**, 3	V. Espinoza	Surfside, 3	Heritage of Gold, 3	9	1:47.66	$1,227,200
1999	**Beautiful Pleasure**, 4	J. F. Chavez	Banshee Breeze, 4	Heritage of Gold, 4	8	1:47.56	$1,040,000
1998	**Escena**, 5	G. L. Stevens	Banshee Breeze, 3	Keeper Hill, 3	8	1:49.89	$1,040,000
1997	**Ajina**, 3	M. E. Smith	Sharp Cat, 3	Escena, 3	8	1:47.30	$520,000
1996	**Jewel Princess**, 4	C. S. Nakatani	Serena's Song, 4	Different (Arg), 4	6	1:48.40	$520,000

Year	Winner	Jockey	Second	Third	Strs	Final Time	1st Purse
1995	**Inside Information**, 4	M. E. Smith	Heavenly Prize, 4	Lakeway, 4	10	**1:46.15**	$520,000
1994	**One Dreamer**, 6	G. L. Stevens	Heavenly Prize, 3	Miss Dominique, 3	9	1:50.70	$520,000
1993	**Hollywood Wildcat**, 3	E. Delahoussaye	Paseana (Arg), 6	Re Toss (Arg), 6	8	1:48.35	$520,000
1992	**Paseana (Arg)**, 5	C. J. McCarron	Versailles Treaty, 4	Magical Maiden, 4	14	1:48.17	$520,000

1992, 1999 held at Gulfstream Park; 1993 Santa Anita Park; 1994, 1998, 2000 Churchill Downs; 1996 Woodbine; 1997 Hollywood Park.

Breeders' Cup Filly & Mare Turf

Grade 1, three-year-olds and up, fillies and mares, 1¼ miles, turf. Held October 27, 2001, at Belmont Park with a gross value of $1,273,240. First held in 1999. Graded since 1999. Stakes record 2:00.36 (2001 Banks Hill [GB]).

Year	Winner	Jockey	Second	Third	Strs	Final Time	1st Purse
2001	**Banks Hill (GB)**, 3	O. Peslier	Spook Express (SAf), 7	Spring Oak (GB), 7	12	**2:00.36**	$722,800
2000	**Perfect Sting**, 4	J. D. Bailey	Tout Charmant, 4	Catella (Ger), 4	14	2:13.07	$629,200
1999	**Soaring Softly**, 4	J. D. Bailey	Coretta (Ire), 4	Zomaradah (GB), 5	14	2:13.89	$556,400

1999 held at Gulfstream Park; 2000 Churchill Downs. 1999-2000 1⅜ miles.

Breeders' Cup Juvenile

Grade 1, two-year-olds, colts and geldings, 1¹⁄₁₆ miles, dirt. Held October 27, 2001, at Belmont Park with a gross value of $916,000. First held in 1984. Graded since 1984. Stakes record 1:41.47 (1997 Favorite Trick).

Year	Winner	Jockey	Second	Third	Strs	Final Time	1st Purse
2001	**Johannesburg**	M. J. Kinane	Repent	Siphonic	12	1:42.27	$520,000
2000	**Macho Uno**	J. D. Bailey	Point Given	Street Cry (Ire)	14	1:42.05	$556,400
1999	**Anees**	G. L. Stevens	Chief Seattle	High Yield	14	1:42.29	$556,400
1998	**Answer Lively**	J. D. Bailey	Aly's Alley	Cat Thief	13	1:44.00	$520,000
1997	**Favorite Trick**	P. Day	Dawson's Legacy	Nationalore	8	**1:41.47**	$520,000
1996	**Boston Harbor**	J. D. Bailey	Acceptable	Ordway	10	1:43.40	$520,000
1995	**Unbridled's Song**	M. E. Smith	Hennessy	Editor's Note	13	1:41.60	$520,000
1994	**Timber Country**	P. Day	Eltish	Tejano Run	13	1:44.55	$520,000
1993	**Brocco**	G. L. Stevens	Blumin Affair	Tabasco Cat	11	1:42.99	$520,000
1992	**Gilded Time**	C. J. McCarron	It'sali'lknownfact	River Special	13	1:43.43	$520,000

1992, 1999 held at Gulfstream Park; 1993 Santa Anita Park; 1994, 1998, 2000 Churchill Downs; 1996 Woodbine; 1997 Hollywood Park.

Breeders' Cup Juvenile Fillies

Grade 1, two-year-old fillies, 1¹⁄₁₆ miles, dirt. Held October 27, 2001, at Belmont Park with a gross value of $916,000. First held in 1984. Graded since 1984. Stakes record 1:41.49 (2001 Tempera).

Year	Winner	Jockey	Second	Third	Strs	Final Time	1st Purse
2001	**Tempera**	D. R. Flores	Imperial Gesture	Bella Bellucci	9	**1:41.49**	$520,000
2000	**Caressing**	J. R. Velazquez	Platinum Tiara	She's a Devil Due	12	1:42.77	$592,800
1999	**Cash Run**	J. D. Bailey	Chilukki	Surfside	9	1:43.31	$520,000
1998	**Silverbulletday**	G. L. Stevens	Excellent Meeting	Three Ring	10	1:43.68	$520,000
1997	**Countess Diana**	S. J. Sellers	Career Collection	Primaly	14	1:42.11	$535,500
1996	**Storm Song**	C. Perret	Love That Jazz	Critical Factor	12	1:43.60	$520,000
1995	**My Flag**	J. D. Bailey	Cara Rafaela	Golden Attraction	8	1:42.55	$520,000
1994	**Flanders**	P. Day	Serena's Song	Stormy Blues	13	1:45.28	$520,000
1993	**Phone Chatter**	L. A. Pincay Jr.	Sardula	Heavenly Prize	8	1:43.08	$520,000
1992	**Eliza**	P. A. Valenzuela	Educated Risk	Boots 'n Jackie	12	1:42.93	$520,000

1992, 1999 held at Gulfstream Park; 1993 Santa Anita Park; 1994, 1998, 2000 Churchill Downs; 1996 Woodbine; 1997 Hollywood Park.

Breeders' Cup Mile

Grade 1, three-year-olds and up, 1 mile, turf. Held October 27, 2001, at Belmont Park with a gross value of $1,044,240. First held in 1984. Graded since 1984. Stakes record 1:32.05 (2001 Val Royal [Fr]).

Year	Winner	Jockey	Second	Third	Strs	Final Time	1st Purse
2001	**Val Royal (Fr)**, 5	J. Valdivia Jr.	Forbidden Apple, 6	Bach (Ire), 6	12	**1:32.05**	$592,800
2000	**War Chant**, 3	G. L. Stevens	North East Bound, 4	Dansili (GB), 4	14	1:34.67	$608,400
1999	**Silic (Fr)**, 4	C. S. Nakatani	†Tuzla (Fr), 5	Docksider, 5	14	1:34.26	$520,000
1998	**Da Hoss**, 6	J. R. Velazquez	Hawksley Hill (Ire), 5	Labeeb (GB), 5	14	1:35.27	$520,000
1997	**Spinning World**, 4	C. B. Asmussen	Geri, 5	Decorated Hero (GB), 5	12	1:32.77	$572,000
1996	**Da Hoss**, 4	G. L. Stevens	Spinning World, 3	Same Old Wish, 3	14	1:35.80	$520,000
1995	**†Ridgewood Pearl (GB)**, 3	J. P. Murtagh	Fastness (Ire), 5	†Sayyedati (GB), 5	13	1:43.65	$520,000
1994	**Barathea (Ire)**, 4	L. Dettori	Johann Quatz (Fr), 5	Unfinished Symph, 5	14	1:34.50	$520,000
1993	**Lure**, 4	M. E. Smith	†Ski Paradise, 5	Fourstars Allstar, 5	13	1:33.58	$520,000
1992	**Lure**, 3	M. E. Smith	Paradise Creek, 3	Brief Truce, 3	14	1:32.90	$520,000

1992, 1999 held at Gulfstream Park; 1993 Santa Anita Park; 1994, 1998, 2000 Churchill Downs; 1996 Woodbine; 1997 Hollywood Park. 1992, 1994 new course record. † denotes female.

Breeders' Cup Sprint

Grade 1, three-year-olds and up, 6 furlongs, dirt. Held October 27, 2001, at Belmont Park with a gross value of $916,000. First held in 1984. Graded since 1984. Stakes record 1:07.77 (2000 Kona Gold).

Year	Winner	Jockey	Second	Third	Strs	Final Time	1st Purse
2001	Squirtle Squirt, 3	J. D. Bailey	†Xtra Heat, 3	Caller One, 4	14	1:08.41	$520,000
2000	Kona Gold, 6	A. O. Solis	†Honest Lady, 4	Bet On Sunshine, 8	14	**1:07.77**	$520,000
1999	Artax, 4	J. F. Chavez	Kona Gold, 5	Big Jag, 6	14	1:07.89	$624,000
1998	Reraise, 3	C. S. Nakatani	Grand Slam, 3	Kona Gold, 4	14	1:09.07	$572,000
1997	Elmhurst, 7	C. S. Nakatani	Hesabull, 4	Bet On Sunshine, 5	14	1:08.01	$613,600
1996	Lit de Justice, 6	C. S. Nakatani	Paying Dues, 4	Honour and Glory, 3	13	1:08.60	$520,000
1995	†Desert Stormer, 5	K. J. Desormeaux	Mr. Greeley, 3	Lit de Justice, 5	13	1:09.14	$520,000
1994	Cherokee Run, 4	M. E. Smith	†Soviet Problem, 4	Cardmania, 8	14	1:09.54	$520,000
1993	Cardmania, 7	E. Delahoussaye	†Meafara, 4	Gilded Time, 3	14	1:08.76	$520,000
1992	Thirty Slews, 5	E. Delahoussaye	†Meafara, 3	Rubiano, 5	14	1:08.21	$520,000

1992, 1999 held at Gulfstream Park; 1993 Santa Anita Park; 1994, 1998, 2000 Churchill Downs; 1996 Woodbine; 1997 Hollywood Park. 1996, 1999 equaled track record; 2000 new track record. † denotes female.

Breeders' Cup Turf

Grade 1, three-year-olds and up, 1½ miles, turf. Held October 27, 2001, at Belmont Park with a gross value of $2,960,240. First held in 1984. Graded since 1984. Stakes record 2:23.92 (1997 Chief Bearhart).

Year	Winner	Jockey	Second	Third	Strs	Final Time	1st Purse
2001	Fantastic Light, 5	L. Dettori	Milan (GB), 3	Timboroa (GB), 3	11	2:24.36	$1,112,800
2000	Kalanisi (Ire), 4	J. P. Murtagh	Quiet Resolve, 5	John's Call, 5	13	2:26.96	$1,289,640
1999	Daylami (Ire), 5	L. Dettori	Royal Anthem, 4	Buck's Boy, 4	14	2:24.73	$2,040,000
1998	Buck's Boy, 5	S. J. Sellers	Yagli, 5	Dushyantor, 5	13	2:28.74	$1,040,000
1997	Chief Bearhart, 4	J. A. Santos	†Borgia (Ger), 3	Flag Down, 3	14	**2:23.92**	$1,040,000
1996	Pilsudski (Ire), 4	W. R. Swinburn	Singspiel (Ire), 4	Swain (Ire), 4	14	2:30.20	$1,040,000
1995	Northern Spur (Ire), 4	C. J. McCarron	Freedom Cry (GB), 4	Carnegie (Ire), 4	13	2:42.07	$1,040,000
1994	Tikkanen, 3	M. E. Smith	†Hatoof, 5	Paradise Creek, 5	14	2:26.50	$1,040,000
1993	Kotashaan (Fr), 5	K. J. Desormeaux	Bien Bien, 4	Luazur (Fr), 4	14	2:25.16	$1,040,000
1992	Fraise, 4	P. A. Valenzuela	Sky Classic, 5	Quest for Fame (GB), 5	10	2:24.08	$1,040,000

1992, 1999 held at Gulfstream Park; 1993 Santa Anita Park; 1994, 1998, 2000 Churchill Downs; 1996 Woodbine; 1997 Hollywood Park. 1992 new course record. † denotes female.

Brooklyn Handicap

Grade 2, Belmont Park, three-year-olds and up, 1⅛ miles, dirt. Held June 10, 2001, with a gross value of $250,000. First held in 1887. Graded since 1973. Stakes record 1:46.21 (1997 Formal Gold).

Year	Winner	Jockey	Second	Third	Strs	Final Time	1st Purse
2001	Albert the Great, 4, 122	J. F. Chavez	Perfect Cat, 4	Top Official, 4	7	1:47.41	$150,000
2000	Lemon Drop Kid, 4, 120	E. S. Prado	Lager, 6	Down the Aisle, 6	7	1:49.93	$150,000
1999	Running Stag, 5, 117	S. J. Sellers	Deputy Diamond, 4	Sir Bear, 4	8	1:46.39	$210,000
1998	Subordination, 4, 114	E. Coa	Sir Bear, 5	Mr. Sinatra, 5	11	1:46.64	$180,000
1997	Formal Gold, 4, 119	J. D. Bailey	Stephanotis, 4	Circle of Light, 4	8	**1:46.21**	$180,000
1996	Wekiva Springs, 5, 120	M. E. Smith	Mahogany Hall, 5	Admiralty, 5	7	1:46.78	$180,000
1995	You and I, 4, 115	J. F. Chavez	Key Contender, 7	Slick Horn, 7	9	1:49.02	$150,000
1994	Devil His Due, 5, 120	M. E. Smith	Wallenda, 4	Sea Hero, 4	7	1:46.71	$150,000
1993	Living Vicariously, 3, 111	R. G. Davis	Michelle Can Pass, 5	Jacksonport, 5	8	2:17.80	$150,000
1992	Chief Honcho, 5, 117	R. P. Romero	Valley Crossing, 4	Lost Mountain, 4	11	2:16.91	$210,000

1992 Grade 1. 1992-'93 held at Aqueduct. 1992-'93 1⅜ miles. 1992 Lost Mountain finished second, DQ to third.

Brown Bess Handicap

Grade 3, Golden Gate Fields, four-year-olds and up, fillies and mares, 1¹⁄₁₆ miles, turf. Held February 3, 2001, with a gross value of $100,000. First held in 1991. Graded since 1998. Stakes record 1:41.50 (1995 Work the Crowd).

Year	Winner	Jockey	Second	Third	Strs	Final Time	1st Purse
2001	Out of Reach (GB), 4, 115	R. A. Baze	Miss of Wales (Chi), 6	Keld (Ire), 6	12	1:46.87	$55,000
2000	Guinevere, 5, 115	J. Matias	Royal Terminal, 5	Blending Element (Ire), 5	12	1:47.75	$55,000
1999	Call Me (GB), 5	R. Q. Meza	Curitiba, 5	Plus (Chi), 5	9	1:49.16	$50,475
1998	Traces of Gold, 6, 118	R. A. Baze	Taurus Forus, 5	La Soberbia (Arg), 5	6	1:43.14	$55,000
1997	Traces of Gold, 5, 115	R. A. Baze	Notagoldbrick, 4	Princess Kali, 4	7	1:44.52	$55,000
1996	Traces of Gold, 4, 115	R. A. Baze	Luzette (Brz), 6	Just a Wish, 6	7	1:42.15	$55,000
1995	Work the Crowd, 4, 118	R. A. Baze	Watch Rachel, 5	Zoonaqua, 5	7	**1:41.50**	$32,450
1994	Watch Rachel, 4, 115	R. J. Warren Jr.	Wendy's Daughter, 4	Wende, 4	7	1:42.21	$29,550
1993	Splashing Wave, 4, 113	R. Q. Meza	Peterhof's Patea, 5	Darling Dame, 5	7	1:44.92	$29,625
1992	La Paz, 4, 113	R. Q. Meza	Peterhof's Patea, 4	Paula Revere, 4	6	1:43.20	$29,475

1992-'95 Brown Bess Breeders' Cup H. 1992-2000 held at Bay Meadows. 1992-'94 three-year-olds and up. 1996, 1998 dirt.

Buena Vista Handicap

Grade 2, Santa Anita Park, four-year-olds and up, fillies and mares, 1 mile, turf. Held February 19, 2001, with a gross value of $150,000. First held in 1988. Graded since 1990. Stakes record 1:33.48 (1992 Gold Fleece [1st Div]; 1997 Media Nox [GB]).

Year	Winner	Jockey	Second	Third	Strs	Final Time	1st Purse
2001	Rare Charmer, 6, 115	L. A. Pincay Jr.	Elegant Ridge (Ire), 6	Uncharted Haven (GB), 6	11	1:36.67	$90,000
2000	Lexa (Fr), 6, 115	B. Blanc	Here's to You, 4	Sierra Virgen, 4	6	1:36.17	$97,290
1999	Tuzla (Fr), 5, 120	C. S. Nakatani	Supercilious, 6	Green Jewel (GB), 6	5	1:35.79	$90,000
1998	Dance Parade, 4, 116	K. J. Desormeaux	Shake the Yoke (GB), 5	Donna Viola (GB), 5	10	1:36.03	$101,520
1997	Media Nox (GB), 4, 116	C. S. Nakatani	Traces of Gold, 5	Grafin, 5	12	**1:33.48**	$85,250
1996	Matiara, 4, 119	G. L. Stevens	Real Connection, 5	Dirca (Ire), 5	8	1:35.74	$81,800
1995	Lyin to the Moon, 6, 116	K. J. Desormeaux	Jacodra's Devil, 4	Exchange, 4	5	1:36.77	$61,700
1994	Skimble, 5, 118	C. S. Nakatani	Hero's Love, 6	Possibly Perfect, 6	9	1:34.85	$66,300
1993	Marble Maiden (GB), 4, 118	K. J. Desormeaux	Suivi, 4	Party Cited, 4	7	1:36.23	$65,000
1992	Gold Fleece, 4, 114	A. O. Solis	Elegance, 5	Danzante, 5	9	**1:33.48**	$52,100
	Appealing Missy, 5, 117	C. J. McCarron	Exchange, 4	Re Toss (Arg), 4	9	1:34.25	$52,100

1992-'94 Grade 3. 1992 two divisions. 1994 Lady Blessington (Fr) finished first, DQ to ninth.

Calder Derby

Grade 3, Calder Race Course, three-year-olds, 1⅛ miles, dirt (originally scheduled on the turf). Held October 20, 2001, with a gross value of $200,000. First held in 1972. Graded since 1996. Stakes record 1:47.70 (1998 Crowd Pleaser).

Year	Winner	Jockey	Second	Third	Strs	Final Time	1st Purse
2001	Western Pride	D. G. Whitney	Tour of the Cat	Built Up	10	1:51.12	$120,000
2000	Whata Brainstorm	R. B. Homeister Jr.	Muntej (GB)	Womble	12	1:47.80	$120,000
1999	Isaypete	J. C. Ferrer	Rhythmean	Phi Beta Doc	12	1:50.01	$120,000
1998	Crowd Pleaser	J-L. Samyn	Stay Sound	The Kaiser	10	**1:47.70**	$120,000
1997	Blazing Sword	G. Boulanger	(DH) Topaz Runner		10	1:53.15	$90,000
			(DH) Royal Tuneup				
1996	Laughing Dan	P. A. Rodriguez	Sea Horse	Flying Concert	11	1:50.75	$66,300
1995	Pineing Patty	L. Melancon	Sea Emperor	Mucha Mosca	7	1:51.40	$60,000
1994	Halo's Image	G. Boulanger	Honest Colors	Rocky's Halo	10	1:52.38	$90,000
1993	Medieval Mac	M. Russ	Raise an Alarm	Fight for Love	9	1:41.79	$30,000
1992	Birdonthewire	M. T. Hunter	Shahpour	Ponche	7	1:44.36	$30,000

1992-'93 Hollywood H.; 1996 Calder Breeders' Cup Derby. 1998-'99 not graded. 1992 1¹⁄₁₆ miles; 1993 1 mile 70 yards. 1998-2000 turf. 1997 dead heat for second. 1993 new track record.

Californian Stakes

Grade 2, Hollywood Park, three-year-olds and up, 1⅛ miles, dirt. Held June 10, 2001, with a gross value of $500,000. First held in 1954. Graded since 1973. Stakes record 1:45.80 (1980 Spectacular Bid).

Year	Winner	Jockey	Second	Third	Strs	Final Time	1st Purse
2001	Skimming, 5	G. K. Gomez	Futural, 5	Aptitude, 5	8	1:48.12	$300,000
2000	Big Ten (Chi), 5	A. O. Solis	Early Pioneer, 5	Mojave Moon, 5	5	1:49.22	$150,000
1999	Old Trieste, 4	C. J. McCarron	Budroyale, 6	Puerto Madero (Chi), 6	7	1:46.55	$180,000
1998	Mud Route, 4	C. J. McCarron	Deputy Commander, 4	Worldly Ways (GB), 4	6	1:48.15	$150,000
1997	River Keen (Ire), 5	K. J. Desormeaux	Hesabull, 4	Benchmark, 4	6	1:47.38	$150,000
1996	Tinners Way, 6	E. Delahoussaye	Helmsman, 4	Mr Purple, 4	4	1:46.60	$151,980
1995	Concern, 4	M. E. Smith	Tossofthecoin, 5	Tinners Way, 5	8	1:47.74	$160,900
1994	The Wicked North, 5	K. J. Desormeaux	Kingdom Found, 4	Slew of Damascus, 4	7	1:46.68	$165,000
1993	Latin American, 5	G. L. Stevens	Missionary Ridge (GB), 6	Memo (Chi), 6	7	1:46.92	$220,000
1992	Another Review, 4	K. J. Desormeaux	Defensive Play, 5	Ibero (Arg), 5	7	1:48.11	$119,400

1992-'96 Grade 1.

Canadian Turf Handicap

Grade 3, Gulfstream Park, three-year-olds and up, 1¹⁄₁₆ miles, turf. Held February 24, 2001, with a gross value of $160,000. First held in 1967. Graded since 1973. Stakes record 1:39.43 (2001 Inexplicable).

Year	Winner	Jockey	Second	Third	Strs	Final Time	1st Purse
2001	Inexplicable, 6, 115	J. A. Santos	Band Is Passing, 5	David Copperfield, 5	8	**1:39.43**	$90,000
2000	Shamrock City, 5, 114	E. S. Prado	Rhythmean, 4	Sharp Appeal, 4	10	1:47.15	$60,000
1999	Federal Trial, 4, 114	R. G. Davis	Deep Dive, 4	Unite's Big Red, 4	11	1:47.90	$60,000
1998	Subordination, 4, 112	J. D. Bailey	Cimarron Secret, 7	Tour's Big Red, 7	7	1:50.87	$60,000
1997	Devil's Cup, 4, 114	R. Wilson	Da Bull, 5	Green Means Go, 5	12	1:47.01	$60,000
1996	The Vid, 6, 124	W. H. McCauley	Gone for Real, 5	Warning Glance, 5	5	1:47.05	$60,000
1995	The Vid, 5, 117	J. D. Bailey	Star of Manila, 4	Country Coy, 4	9	1:47.19	$60,000
1994	Paradise Creek, 5, 123	M. E. Smith	Glenfiddich Lad, 5	Nijinsky's Gold, 5	8	1:47.84	$60,000
1993	Stagecraft (GB), 6, 112	J. D. Bailey	Roman Envoy, 5	Carterista, 4	10	1:47.80	$60,000
1992	Buckhar, 4, 113	J. Cruguet	Tin Can Ali, 4	Archies Laughter, 4	13	1:48.49	$60,000

1992-'97 Grade 2. 1992-2000 1⅛ miles. 1998 dirt. 1992 new course record.

Cardinal Handicap

Grade 3, Churchill Downs, three-year-olds and up, fillies and mares, 1⅛ miles, turf. Held November 10, 2001, with a gross value of $169,350. First held in 1974. Graded since 1995. Stakes record 1:47.81 (1996 Bail Out Becky [DQ to second]).

Year	Winner	Jockey	Second	Third	Strs	Final Time	1st Purse
2001	**Watch**, 4, 114	C. Perret	Sitka, 4	Gino's Spirits (GB), 4	9	1:49.12	$104,997
2000	**Illiquidity**, 4, 115	J. K. Court	License Fee, 5	Miss of Wales (Chi), 5	12	1:49.72	$109,182
1999	**Pratella**, 4, 114	B. D. Peck	Mingling Glances, 5	Uanme, 5	9	1:48.88	$106,299
1998	**B. A. Valentine**, 5, 115	J. F. Chavez	Mingling Glances, 4	Cuando, 4	13	1:48.62	$111,693
1997	**Colcon**, 4, 114	J. D. Bailey	Dance Clear (Ire), 4	Sagar Pride (Ire), 4	12	1:51.89	$108,903
1996	**Miss Caerleona (Fr)**, 4, 114	L. Melancon	Bail Out Becky, 4	Striesen, 4	12	**1:47.81**	$72,850
1995	**Apolda**, 4, 114	P. Day	Alive With Hope, 4	Lady Reiko (Ire), 4	11	1:49.59	$75,530
1994	**Bold Ruritana**, 4, 116	P. Day	Eternal Reve, 3	Monaassabaat, 3	11	1:48.25	$76,375
1993	**River Ball (Arg)**, 7, 109	J. Parsley	Marshua's River, 6	Logan's Mist, 6	9	1:55.79	$74,945
1992	**Auto Dial**, 4, 113	S. J. Sellers	Radiant Ring, 4	Red Journey, 4	5	1:52.04	$71,500

1992 dirt. 1996 Bail Out Becky finished first, DQ to second.

Carleton F. Burke Handicap

Grade 3, Santa Anita Park, three-year-olds and up, 1½ miles, turf. Held October 28, 2001, with a gross value of $150,000. First held in 1969. Graded since 1973. Stakes record 2:24.24 (1996 Dernier Empereur).

Year	Winner	Jockey	Second	Third	Strs	Final Time	1st Purse
2001	**Cagney (Brz)**, 4, 116	M. E. Smith	Kerrygold (Fr), 5	Northern Quest (Fr), 5	9	2:26.10	$90,000
2000	**Timboroa (GB)**, 4, 114	D. R. Flores	(DH) Res Judicata (GB), 5 (DH) Kerrygold (Fr), 4		9	2:27.91	$84,990
1999	**Public Purse**, 5, 119	A. O. Solis	Star Performance, 6	Achilles (GB), 6	8	2:25.83	$90,000
1998	**Perim (Fr)**, 5, 113	B. Blanc	Single Empire (Ire), 4	Rate Cut, 4	9	2:29.29	$75,000
1997	**Prussian Blue**, 5, 117	K. J. Desormeaux	Embraceable You (Fr), 4	Kessem Power (NZ), 4	7	2:31.37	$75,000
1996	**Dernier Empereur**, 6, 118	C. J. McCarron	Bon Point (GB), 6	Party Season (GB), 6	8	**2:24.24**	$98,750
1995	**Varadavour (Ire)**, 6, 115	A. O. Solis	Patio de Naranjos (Chi), 4	Raintrap (GB), 4	7	2:30.27	$90,350
1994	**Savinio**, 4, 116	C. J. McCarron	Square Cut, 5	Sir Mark Sykes (Ire), 5	8	2:02.69	$95,700
1993	**Know Heights (Ire)**, 4, 117	K. J. Desormeaux	Fanmore, 5	Myrakalu (Fr), 5	7	2:00.07	$96,000
1992	**Missionary Ridge (GB)**, 5, 117	K. J. Desormeaux	Carnival Baby, 4	Myrakalu (Fr), 4	9	2:00.89	$98,000

1992-'97 Grade 2. 1992-'94 1¼ miles; 2000 about 1½ miles. 2000 dead heat for second.

Carter Handicap

Grade 1, Aqueduct, three-year-olds and up, 7 furlongs, dirt. Held May 6, 2001, with a gross value of $300,000. First held in 1895. Graded since 1973. Stakes record 1:20.04 (1999 Artax).

Year	Winner	Jockey	Second	Third	Strs	Final Time	1st Purse
2001	**Peeping Tom**, 4, 118	S. Bridgmohan	Say Florida Sandy, 7	Hook and Ladder, 7	7	1:21.33	$180,000
2000	**Brutally Frank**, 6, 116	S. Bridgmohan	Western Expression, 4	Affirmed Success, 4	7	1:21.66	$120,000
1999	**Artax**, 4, 114	J. F. Chavez	Affirmed Success, 5	Western Borders, 5	9	**1:20.04**	$120,000
1998	**Wild Rush**, 4, 117	K. J. Desormeaux	Banker's Gold, 4	Western Borders, 4	10	1:21.16	$120,000
1997	**Langfuhr**, 5, 122	J. F. Chavez	Stalwart Member, 4	Western Winter, 4	9	1:22.99	$90,000
1996	**Lite the Fuse**, 5, 121	J. A. Krone	Flying Chevron, 4	Placid Fund, 4	10	1:20.92	$90,000
1995	**Lite the Fuse**, 4, 111	R. B. Perez	Our Emblem, 4	You and I, 4	9	1:21.48	$90,000
1994	**Virginia Rapids**, 4, 118	J-L. Samyn	Punch Line, 4	Cherokee Run, 4	11	1:21.45	$90,000
1993	**Alydeed**, 4, 122	C. Perret	Loach, 5	Argyle Lake, 5	10	1:22.70	$90,000
1992	**Rubiano**, 5, 118	J. A. Santos	Kid Russell, 6	In Excess (Ire), 6	9	1:21.41	$120,000

1994-'96 held at Belmont Park. 1999 new track record.

Champagne Stakes

Grade 1, Belmont Park, two-year-olds, 1 1/16 miles, dirt. Held October 6, 2001, with a gross value of $500,000. First held in 1867. Graded since 1973. Stakes record 1:40.59 (1997 Grand Slam).

Year	Winner	Jockey	Second	Third	Strs	Final Time	1st Purse
2001	**Officer**	V. Espinoza	Jump Start	Heavyweight Champ	5	1:43.39	$300,000
2000	**A P Valentine**	J. F. Chavez	Point Given	Yonaguska	10	1:41.45	$300,000
1999	**Greenwood Lake**	J-L. Samyn	Chief Seattle	High Yield	7	1:43.70	$240,000
1998	**The Groom Is Red**	C. S. Nakatani	Lemon Drop Kid	Weekend Money	7	1:42.91	$240,000
1997	**Grand Slam**	G. L. Stevens	Lil's Lad	Halory Hunter	8	**1:40.59**	$240,000
1996	**Ordway**	J. R. Velazquez	Traitor	Gold Tribute	12	1:42.09	$240,000
1995	**Maria's Mon**	R. G. Davis	Diligence	Devil's Honor	8	1:42.39	$300,000
1994	**Timber Country**	P. Day	Sierra Diablo	On Target	11	1:44.01	$300,000
1993	**Dehere**	C. J. McCarron	Crary	Amathos	6	1:35.91	$300,000
1992	**Sea Hero**	J. D. Bailey	Secret Odds	Press Card	10	1:34.87	$300,000

1992-'93 1 mile.

Chaposa Springs Handicap

Grade 3, Calder Race Course, three-year-olds and up, fillies and mares, 6 furlongs, dirt. Held December 29, 2001, with a gross value of $100,000. First held in 1983. Graded since 1992. Stakes record 1:23.09 (1994 Educated Risk).

Year	Winner	Jockey	Second	Third	Strs	Final Time	1st Purse
2001	**Vague Memory**, 4, 113	J. A. Garcia	Gold Mover, 3	Platinum Tiara, 3	10	1:24.15	$60,000
2000	**Could Be**, 4, 115	P. Day	Extended Applause, 4	Class On Class, 4	8	1:24.97	$60,000
	England's Rose, 3, 112	J. R. Velazquez	Swept Away, 3	Sugar N Spice, 3	6	1:24.82	$60,000
1998	**Openstock**, 6, 113	J. A. Garcia	Lily O'Gold, 3	U Can Do It, 3	7	1:24.84	$60,000
1997	**Flashy n Smart**, 4, 118	P. Day	U Can Do It, 4	Special Request, 4	11	1:26.67	$60,000
1996	**Race Artist**, 3, 112	G. Boulanger	La Nina de Orumila, 4	Flat Fleet Feet, 4	7	1:25.21	$60,000
1995	**Chaposa Springs**, 3, 119	J. D. Bailey	Investalot, 4	Easter Doll, 4	7	1:25.32	$60,000
1994	**Educated Risk**, 4, 122	M. E. Smith	Goldarama, 4	Floramera, 4	6	**1:23.09**	$60,000
1993	**Maggies Pistol**, 4, 112	J. A. Bracho	My Own True Love, 5	Luv Me Luv Me Not, 5	11	1:23.97	$45,000
	Lady Sonata, 4, 114	R. D. Lopez	Ophidian, 3	Capture the Crown, 3	11	1:24.47	$45,000
1992	**Magal**, 5, 115	R. Hernandez	Gene Propp's Dream, 5	My Own True Love, 5	12	1:24.37	$51,675

1992-'97 Virginia H. 1993, 2000 held in January and December; 1999 not held. 1996 Chaposa Springs finished first, DQ to sixth.

Charles Whittingham Handicap

Grade 1, Hollywood Park, three-year-olds and up, 1¼ miles, turf. Held June 10, 2001, with a gross value of $350,000. First held in 1969. Graded since 1973. Stakes record 1:57.75 (1993 Bien Bien).

Year	Winner	Jockey	Second	Third	Strs	Final Time	1st Purse
2001	**Bienamado**, 5, 124	C. J. McCarron	Senure, 5	Timboroa (GB), 5	9	1:59.34	$210,000
2000	**White Heart (GB)**, 5, 117	K. J. Desormeaux	Self Feeder (Ire), 6	Deploy Venture (GB), 6	6	2:00.83	$180,000
1999	**River Bay**, 6, 119	A. O. Solis	Majorien (GB), 5	Alvo Certo (Brz), 5	9	2:00.06	$240,000
1998	**Storm Trooper**, 5, 117	K. J. Desormeaux	River Bay, 5	Prize Giving (GB), 5	7	2:03.05	$240,000
1997	**Rainbow Dancer (Fr)**, 6, 116	A. O. Solis	Sunshack (GB), 6	Marlin, 6	6	2:00.09	$240,000
1996	**Sandpit (Brz)**, 7, 120	C. S. Nakatani	Northern Spur (Ire), 5	Awad, 5	6	1:59.52	$300,000
1995	**Earl of Barking (Ire)**, 5, 115	G. F. Almeida	Sandpit (Brz), 6	Savinio, 6	10	1:59.78	$275,000
1994	**Grand Flotilla**, 7, 116	G. L. Stevens	Bien Bien, 5	Blues Traveller (Ire), 5	8	1:59.26	$275,000
1993	**Bien Bien**, 4, 119	C. J. McCarron	Best Pal, 5	Leger Cat (Arg), 5	8	**1:57.75**	$275,000
1992	**Quest for Fame (GB)**, 5, 122	G. L. Stevens	Classic Fame, 6	River Traffic, 6	9	1:58.99	$275,000

1992-'98 Hollywood Turf H. 1993 new course record.

Chicago Breeders' Cup Handicap

Grade 3, Arlington Park, three-year-olds and up, fillies and mares, 7 furlongs, dirt. Held June 16, 2001, with a gross value of $157,270. First held in 1986. Graded since 1992. Stakes record 1:21.24 (1992 Withallprobability).

Year	Winner	Jockey	Second	Third	Strs	Final Time	1st Purse
2001	**Trip**, 4, 114	C. Perret	Hidden Assets, 4	Rose of Zollern (Ire), 4	7	1:22.18	$99,312
2000	**Saoirse**, 4, 118	D. Clark	The Happy Hopper, 4	Dif a Dot, 4	7	1:23.09	$102,195
1997	**J J'sdream**, 4, 118	M. Guidry	Capote Belle, 4	Eseni, 4	7	1:22.25	$101,625
1996	**Bunbeg**, 4, 114	M. Walls	Morris Code, 4	Rhapsodic, 4	8	1:23.86	$102,990
1995	**Low Key Affair**, 4, 113	A. T. Gryder	Morning Meadow, 5	Marina Park (GB), 5	9	1:24.64	$93,840
1994	**Minidar**, 4, 116	V. Belvoir	Spinning Round, 5	Traverse City, 5	10	1:22.49	$93,960
1993	**Meafara**, 4, 121	J. L. Diaz	Shared Interest, 5	Real Display, 5	11	1:22.12	$93,870
1992	**Withallprobability**, 4, 115	G. K. Gomez	Fit for a Queen, 6	Madam Bear, 6	9	**1:21.24**	$93,450

1998-'99 not held

Churchill Downs Distaff Handicap

Grade 2, Churchill Downs, three-year-olds and up, fillies and mares, 1 mile, dirt. Held November 3, 2001, with a gross value of $222,200. First held in 1986. Graded since 1988. Stakes record 1:33.57 (2000 Chilukki).

Year	Winner	Jockey	Second	Third	Strs	Final Time	1st Purse
2001	**Nasty Storm**, 3, 115	P. Day	Forest Secrets, 3	Trip, 3	8	1:35.30	$137,764
2000	**Chilukki**, 3, 116	G. L. Stevens	Reciclada (Chi), 5	Rose of Zollern (Ire), 5	10	**1:33.57**	$154,008
1999	**Let**, 4, 113	C. H. Borel	Roza Robata, 4	Dif a Dot, 4	9	1:34.41	$138,880
1998	**Dream Scheme**, 5, 113	C. H. Borel	Sister Act, 3	Beautiful Pleasure, 3	9	1:34.41	$139,624
1997	**Feasibility Study**, 5, 120	R. Albarado	J J'sdream, 4	Mama's Pro, 4	14	1:37.61	$146,196
1996	**Fast Catch**, 4, 109	W. Martinez	Serena's Song, 4	Bedroom Blues, 4	9	1:36.55	$139,624
1995	**Lakeway**, 4, 122	K. J. Desormeaux	Alcovy, 5	Laura's Pistolette, 5	8	1:35.94	$137,280
1994	**Educated Risk**, 4, 118	P. Day	Pennyhill Park, 4	Alcovy, 4	8	1:35.74	$138,125
1993	**Miss Indy Anna**, 3, 111	P. Day	One Dreamer, 5	Deputation, 5	13	1:37.72	$141,960
1992	**Wilderness Song**, 4, 120	C. Perret	Miss Jealski, 3	Dance Colony, 3	11	1:36.22	$102,440

1992-'95 Churchill Downs Breeders' Cup H. 2000 new track record.

Cicada Stakes

Grade 3, Aqueduct, three-year-old fillies, 7 furlongs, dirt. Held March 25, 2001, with a gross value of $103,100. First held in 1993. Graded since 1996. Stakes record 1:22.38 (1994 Our Royal Blue).

Year	Winner	Jockey	Second	Third	Strs	Final Time	1st Purse
2001	**Xtra Heat**	R. Wilson	Erin Moor	Chasm	4	1:23.39	$63,770
2000	**Finder's Fee**	J. D. Bailey	Apollo Cat	Southern Sandra	6	1:23.07	$65,100

Year	Winner	Jockey	Second	Third	Strs	Final Time	1st Purse
1999	**Potomac Bend**	M. T. Johnston	Carleaville	Jane	7	1:23.18	$48,915
1998	**Jersey Girl**	R. Migliore	Vienna Blues	Babai Danzig	9	1:22.95	$50,175
1997	**Vegas Prospector**	M. J. McCarthy	Ormsby County	Valid Affect	6	1:26.23	$48,375
1996	**J J'sdream**	G. Boulanger	Dahl	Mystic Rhythms	9	1:23.44	$50,310
1995	**Lucky Lavender Gal**	R. G. Davis	Stormy Blues	Dancin Renee	7	1:23.45	$48,870
1994	**Our Royal Blue**	R. Wilson	Sovereign Kitty	Princess Joanne	5	**1:22.38**	$48,375
1993	**Personal Bid**	J. A. Santos	Sheila's Revenge	In Excelcis Deo	4	1:23.52	$31,800

1993 held at Belmont Park.

Cigar Mile Handicap

Grade 1, Aqueduct, three-year-olds and up, 1 mile, dirt. Held November 24, 2001, with a gross value of $350,000. First held in 1988. Graded since 1990. Stakes record 1:32.80 (1989 Dispersal; 1990 Quiet American).

Year	Winner	Jockey	Second	Third	Strs	Final Time	1st Purse
2001	**Left Bank**, 4, 120	J. R. Velazquez	Graeme Hall, 4	Red Bullet, 4	9	1:33.35	$210,000
2000	**El Corredor**, 3, 116	J. D. Bailey	Peeping Tom, 3	Affirmed Success, 3	11	1:34.68	$210,000
1999	**Affirmed Success**, 5, 118	J. F. Chavez	Adonis, 3	Honorifico (Arg), 3	9	1:34.18	$210,000
1998	**Sir Bear**, 5, 116	J. D. Bailey	Affirmed Success, 4	Distorted Humor, 4	8	1:34.05	$180,000
1997	**Devious Course**, 5, 112	J. F. Chavez	Lucayan Prince, 4	Basqueian, 4	12	1:34.98	$150,000
1996	**Gold Fever**, 3, 115	M. E. Smith	Diligence, 3	Top Account, 3	14	1:34.98	$150,000
1995	**Flying Chevron**, 3, 112	R. G. Davis	Wekiva Springs, 4	Dramatic Gold, 4	13	1:34.57	$150,000
1994	**Cigar**, 4, 111	J. D. Bailey	Devil His Due, 5	Punch Line, 5	12	1:36.10	$150,000
1992	**Ibero (Arg)**, 5, 117	L. A. Pincay Jr.	Irish Swap, 5	Nines Wild, 5	7	1:33.97	$300,000

1993 not held. 1992,1994-'96 NYRA Mile H.

Cinema Handicap

Grade 3, Hollywood Park, three-year-olds, 1⅛ miles, turf. Held May 20, 2001, with a gross value of $108,600. First held in 1946. Graded since 1973. Stakes record 1:46.56 (1994 Unfinished Symph).

Year	Winner	Jockey	Second	Third	Strs	Final Time	1st Purse
2001	**Sligo Bay (Ire)**, 118	L. A. Pincay Jr.	Learing At Kathy	Marine (GB)	7	1:48.40	$65,160
2000	**David Copperfield**, 116	V. Espinoza	Duke of Green (GB)	Silver Axe	6	1:47.73	$64,560
1999	**Fighting Falcon**, 119	B. Blanc	Eagleton	Major Hero	8	1:48.06	$66,000
1998	**Commitisize**, 118	D. R. Flores	Killer Image	Lord Smith (GB)	7	1:48.03	$65,220
1997	**Worldly Ways (GB)**, 115	C. S. Nakatani	P. T. Indy	Brave Act (GB)	9	1:48.43	$66,180
1996	**Let Bob Do It**, 120	K. J. Desormeaux	Dr. Sardonica	Winter Quarters	8	1:47.58	$81,660
1995	**Via Lombardia (Ire)**, 119	E. Delahoussaye	Bryntirion	Oncefortheroad	9	1:47.22	$65,400
1994	**Unfinished Symph**, 118	G. Baze	Vaudeville	Fumo Di Londra (Ire)	7	**1:46.56**	$63,100
1993	**Earl of Barking (Ire)**, 121	C. J. McCarron	Manny's Prospect	Minks Law	5	1:47.45	$61,100
1992	**Bien Bien**, 113	C. J. McCarron	Fax News	Prospect for Four	8	1:47.10	$65,600

1992-'93 Grade 2.

Citation Handicap

Grade 2, Hollywood Park, three-year-olds and up, 1¹⁄₁₆ miles, turf. Held November 24, 2001, with a gross value of $500,000. First held in 1977. Graded since 1979. Stakes record 1:39.69 (1999 Brave Act [GB]).

Year	Winner	Jockey	Second	Third	Strs	Final Time	1st Purse
2001	**Good Journey**, 5, 115	C. J. McCarron	Decarchy, 4	Irish Prize, 4	8	1:44.30	$300,000
2000	**Charge d'Affaires (GB)**, 5, 116	J. A. Santos	Ladies Din, 5	Native Desert, 5	10	1:40.30	$300,000
1999	**Brave Act (GB)**, 5, 119	A. O. Solis	Native Desert, 6	Bouccaneer (Fr), 6	11	**1:39.69**	$300,000
1998	**Military**, 4, 118	G. K. Gomez	Mr Lightfoot (Ire), 4	Worldly Ways (GB), 4	8	1:50.58	$180,000
1997	**Geri**, 5, 121	J. D. Bailey	Mufattish, 4	Martiniquais (Ire), 4	6	1:48.35	$180,000
1996	**Gentlemen (Arg)**, 4, 119	G. L. Stevens	Smooth Runner, 5	Via Lombardia (Ire), 5	7	1:45.55	$180,000
1995	**Fastness (Ire)**, 5, 120	G. L. Stevens	Earl of Barking (Ire), 5	Silver Wizard, 5	7	1:44.78	$165,000
1994	**Southern Wish**, 5, 115	C. S. Nakatani	Square Cut, 5	Jeune Homme, 5	7	2:00.20	$137,500
1993	**Jeune Homme**, 3, 114	T. Jarnet	Paradise Creek, 4	Johann Quatz (Fr), 4	8	1:45.84	$137,500
1992	**Leger Cat (Arg)**, 6, 114	C. S. Nakatani	†Trishyde, 3	Luthier Enchanteur, 3	8	1:46.48	$137,500

1992-'93,1995-'98 1⅛ miles; 1994 1¼ miles. 1995 new course record. † denotes female.

Citgo Distaff Turf Mile Stakes (see Distaff Turf Mile Stakes)

Clark Handicap

Grade 2, Churchill Downs, three-year-olds and up, 1⅛ miles, dirt. Held November 23, 2001, with a gross value of $452,000. First held in 1875. Graded since 1973. Stakes record 1:48.26 (2001 Ubiquity).

Year	Winner	Jockey	Second	Third	Strs	Final Time	1st Purse
2001	**Ubiquity**, 4, 113	C. Perret	Include, 4	Mr Ross, 4	10	**1:48.26**	$280,240
2000	**†Surfside**, 3, 113	P. Day	Guided Tour, 4	Maysville Slew, 4	9	1:48.75	$276,272
1999	**Littlebitlively**, 5, 118	C. H. Borel	Pleasant Breeze, 4	Nite Dreamer, 4	12	1:50.88	$284,456
1998	**Silver Charm**, 4, 124	G. L. Stevens	Littlebitlively, 4	Wild Rush, 4	8	1:49.07	$275,776

Year	Winner	Jockey	Second	Third	Strs	Final Time	1st Purse
1997	Concerto, 3, 113	J. D. Bailey	Terremoto, 6	Rod and Staff, 6	11	1:49.72	$284,704
1996	Isitingood, 5, 120	D. R. Flores	Savinio, 6	Coup D' Argent, 6	9	1:48.99	$174,220
1995	Judge T C, 4, 115	J. M. Johnson	Tyus, 5	Alphabet Soup, 5	14	1:49.82	$153,140
1994	Sir Vixen, 6, 112	D. Kutz	Danville, 3	Prize Fight, 3	7	1:51.36	$143,130
1993	Mi Cielo, 3, 117	M. E. Smith	Take Me Out, 5	Forry Cow How, 5	13	1:51.43	$150,540
1992	Zeeruler, 4, 113	G. K. Gomez	Flying Continental, 6	Echelon's Ice Man, 6	13	1:50.11	$76,050

1992-'97 Grade 3. † denotes female.

Clement L. Hirsch Handicap

Grade 2, Del Mar, three-year-olds and up, fillies and mares, 1 1/16 miles, dirt. Held August 5, 2001, with a gross value of $294,000. First held in 1937. Graded since 1983. Stakes record 1:40 (1982 Matching).

Year	Winner	Jockey	Second	Third	Strs	Final Time	1st Purse
2001	Tranquility Lake, 6, 120	E. Delahoussaye	Gourmet Girl, 6	Nany's Sweep, 6	4	1:41.78	$180,000
2000	Riboletta (Brz), 5, 125	C. J. McCarron	Bordelaise (Arg), 5	Gourmet Girl, 6	6	1:42.06	$180,000
1999	A Lady From Dixie, 4, 116	C. W. Antley	Manistique, 4	Yolo Lady, 4	5	1:43.58	$180,000
1998	Sharp Cat, 4, 124	C. S. Nakatani	Supercilious, 5	Numero Uno, 5	4	1:42.16	$180,000
1997	Radu Cool, 5, 117	C. J. McCarron	Supercilious, 4	Swoon River, 4	6	1:42.66	$180,000
1996	Different (Arg), 4, 120	C. J. McCarron	Top Rung, 5	Borodislew, 5	5	1:42.48	$189,200
1995	Borodislew, 5, 118	C. J. McCarron	Lakeway, 4	Golden Klair (GB), 4	6	1:41.87	$178,100
1994	Paseana (Arg), 7, 123	C. J. McCarron	Exchange, 6	Magical Maiden, 6	4	1:40.59	$117,100
1993	Magical Maiden, 4, 120	G. L. Stevens	Vieille Vigne (Fr), 6	Party Cited, 6	8	1:42.68	$123,600
1992	Exchange, 4, 120	L. A. Pincay Jr.	Fowda, 4	Brought to Mind, 4	8	1:42.00	$123,100

1992-'99 Chula Vista H.

Clement L. Hirsch Memorial Turf Championship Stakes

Grade 1, Santa Anita Park, three-year-olds and up, 1 1/4 miles, turf. Held September 30, 2001, with a gross value of $300,000. First run in 1969. Graded since 1973. Stakes record 1:58.48 (1996 Bon Point [GB] [DQ to fifth]).

Year	Winner	Jockey	Second	Third	Strs	Final Time	1st Purse
2001	Senure, 5	A. O. Solis	White Heart (GB), 6	Cagney (Brz), 6	6	1:59.47	$180,000
2000	Mash One (Chi), 6	D. R. Flores	Boatman, 5	Asidero (Arg), 4	6	2:00.67	$180,000
1999	Mash One (Chi), 5	D. R. Flores	Lazy Lode (Arg), 5	Bonapartiste (Fr), 5	6	1:59.07	$180,000
1998	Military, 4	C. S. Nakatani	Bonapartiste (Fr), 4	River Bay, 4	5	2:02.04	$180,000
1997	Rainbow Dancer (Fr), 6	A. O. Solis	Lord Jain (Arg), 5	Sandpit (Brz), 5	5	2:01.94	$180,000
1996	†Admise (Fr), 4	K. J. Desormeaux	Khoraz, 6	Golden Post, 6	5	1:58.48	$180,000
1995	Northern Spur (Ire), 4	C. J. McCarron	Sandpit (Brz), 6	Royal Chariot, 6	8	2:02.37	$180,000
1994	Sandpit (Brz), 5	C. S. Nakatani	Grand Flotilla, 7	Approach the Bench (Ire), 7	5	2:25.12	$180,000
1993	Kotashaan (Fr), 5	K. J. Desormeaux	Luazur (Fr), 4	†Let's Elope (NZ), 4	4	2:25.06	$180,000
1992	Navarone, 4	P. A. Valenzuela	Defensive Play, 5	Daros (GB), 5	6	2:24.29	$240,000

1992-'95 Oak Tree Invitational S.; 1996-'99 Oak Tree Turf Championship S.; 2000 Clement L. Hirsch Turf Championship S. 1992-'94 1 1/2 miles. 1996 Bon Point (GB), finished first, DQ to fifth; 1997 Marlin finished second, DQ to fourth. † denotes female.

Cliff Hanger Handicap

Grade 3, The Meadowlands, three-year-olds and up, 1 1/16 miles, turf. Held September 22, 2001, with a gross value of $150,000. First held in 1977. Graded since 1985. Stakes record 1:39.40 (1988 Wanderkin).

Year	Winner	Jockey	Second	Third	Strs	Final Time	1st Purse
2001	Crash Course, 5, 114	R. Wilson	Solitary Dancer, 5	Union One, 5	0	1:43.14	$90,000
2000	North East Bound, 4, 118	J. A. Velez Jr.	Johnny Dollar, 4	Swamp, 4	11	1:41.78	$90,000
1999	Virginia Carnival, 7, 114	J-L. Samyn	Star Connection, 5	Grapeshot, 5	12	1:42.44	$90,000
1998	Mi Narrow, 4, 111	J. Bravo	Treat Me Doc, 4	Boyce, 4	6	1:43.58	$60,000
1997	Dixie Bayou, 4, 114	J. R. Velazquez	Brave Note (Ire), 6	Joker, 6	10	1:39.45	$60,000
1996	Thorny Crown, 5, 115	M. J. Luzzi	Ihtiraz (GB), 6	Winnetou, 6	5	1:44.71	$60,000
1995	Mighty Forum (GB), 4, 114	W. H. McCauley	Joker, 3	Fourstars Allstar, 3	7	1:41.09	$60,000
1994	Binary Light, 5, 112	J-L. Samyn	Brazany, 4	Burst of Applause, 4	5	1:41.41	$45,000
1993	Excellent Tipper, 5, 117	C. Perret	Rinka Das, 5	First and Only, 5	6	1:43.69	$45,000
1992	Roman Envoy, 4, 116	C. Perret	Futurist, 4	Royal Ninja, 4	8	1:39.92	$45,000

1993, 1996, 1998 dirt. 1997 equaled course record. 1995 Joker finished first, DQ to second.

Coaching Club American Oaks

Grade 1, Belmont Park, three-year-old fillies, 1 1/2 miles, dirt. Held July 21, 2001, with a gross value of $350,000. First held in 1917. Graded since 1973. Stakes record 2:27.80 (1973 Magazine; 1975 Ruffian).

Year	Winner	Jockey	Second	Third	Strs	Final Time	1st Purse
2001	Tweedside	J. R. Velazquez	Exogenous	Unbridled Lassie	8	2:30.70	$210,000
2000	Jostle	M. E. Smith	Resort	Secret Status	7	2:29.99	$210,000
1999	On a Soapbox	J. D. Bailey	Dreams Gallore	Strolling Belle	8	2:29.31	$210,000
1998	Banshee Breeze	J. D. Bailey	Keeper Hill	Best Friend Stro	6	2:31.56	$180,000

Year	Winner	Jockey	Second	Third	Strs	Final Time	1st Purse
1997	Ajina	M. E. Smith	Tomisue's Delight	Key Hunter	5	2:00.45	$150,000
1996	My Flag	J. D. Bailey	Gold n Delicious	Weekend in Seattle	7	2:04.64	$150,000
1995	Golden Bri	J. A. Santos	Serena's Song	Change Fora Dollar	6	2:03.86	$150,000
1994	Two Altazano	J. A. Santos	Plenty of Sugar	Sovereign Kitty	7	2:02.88	$150,000
1993	Sky Beauty	M. E. Smith	Future Pretense	Silky Feather	5	2:01.56	$150,000
1992	Turnback the Alarm	C. W. Antley	Easy Now	Pleasant Stage	7	2:03.53	$150,000

1992-'97 1¼ miles.

Comely Stakes

Grade 3, Aqueduct, three-year-old fillies, 1 mile, dirt. Held April 13, 2001, with a gross value of $110,100. First held in 1945. Graded since 1973. Stakes record 1:35.54 (1999 Madison's Charm).

Year	Winner	Jockey	Second	Third	Strs	Final Time	1st Purse
2001	Two Item Limit	R. Migliore	Mandy's Gold	It All Adds Up	7	1:36.17	$66,060
2000	March Magic	R. Migliore	Jostle	Finder's Fee	6	1:36.79	$65,460
1999	Madison's Charm	J-L. Samyn	Better Than Honour	Oh What a Windfall	7	**1:35.54**	$65,520
1998	Fantasy Angel	J. F. Chavez	Hansel's Girl	Best Friend Stro	12	1:37.44	$69,300
1997	Dixie Flag	J-L. Samyn	Global Star	How About Now	7	1:36.96	$66,120
1996	Little Miss Fast	J. F. Chavez	J J'sdream	Stop Traffic	7	1:36.58	$65,940
1995	Nappelon	J. F. Chavez	Stormy Blues	Incredible Blues	6	1:36.26	$64,440
1994	Dixie Luck	F. Leon	Penny's Reshoot	Our Royal Blue	7	1:37.02	$66,240
1993	Private Light	R. G. Davis	Russian Bride	True Affair	4	1:44.19	$68,280
1992	Saratoga Dew	W. H. McCauley	City Dance	Looking for a Win	7	1:37.22	$69,480

1992-'95 Grade 2. 1993 1¹⁄₁₆ miles. 2001 Mandy's Gold finished first, DQ to second.

Commonwealth Breeders' Cup Stakes

Grade 2, Keeneland, three-year-olds and up, 7 furlongs, dirt. Held April 14, 2001, with a gross value of $270,750. First held in 1987. Graded since 1990. Stakes record 1:20.50 (1998 Distorted Humor).

Year	Winner	Jockey	Second	Third	Strs	Final Time	1st Purse
2001	Alannan, 5	E. S. Prado	Valiant Halory, 4	Liberty Gold, 4	8	1:22.39	$170,965
2000	Richter Scale, 6	R. Migliore	Son's Corona, 5	Deep Gold, 5	6	1:21.07	$128,836
1999	Good and Tough, 4	S. J. Sellers	Purple Passion, 5	Crucible, 5	5	1:22.09	$127,906
1998	Distorted Humor, 5	G. L. Stevens	El Amante, 5	Partner's Hero, 5	8	**1:20.50**	$130,820
1997	Victor Cooley, 4	E. M. Martin Jr.	Western Winter, 5	Appealing Skier, 5	7	1:22.46	$129,332
1996	Afternoon Deelites, 4	K. J. Desormeaux	Western Winter, 4	Our Emblem, 4	6	1:21.12	$131,068
1995	Golden Gear, 4	C. Perret	Turkomatic, 4	Lit de Justice, 4	8	1:22.06	$130,758
1994	Memo (Chi), 7	P. Atkinson	American Chance, 5	British Banker, 5	10	1:22.32	$69,378
1993	Alydeed, 4	C. Perret	Binalong, 4	Senor Speedy, 4	5	1:21.43	$113,057
1992	Pleasant Tap, 5	E. Delahoussaye	To Freedom, 4	Run On the Bank, 4	6	1:22.40	$118,138

1992-'93 Grade 3.

Coolmore Lexington Stakes

Grade 2, Keeneland, three-year-olds, 1¹⁄₁₆ miles, dirt. Held April 21, 2001, with a gross value of $371,475. First held in 1936. Graded since 1973. Stakes record 1:41.06 (1999 Charismatic).

Year	Winner	Jockey	Second	Third	Strs	Final Time	1st Purse
2001	Keats	L. Melancon	Griffinite	Bay Eagle	10	1:43.54	$230,315
2000	Unshaded	S. J. Sellers	Globalize	Harlan Traveler	8	1:43.72	$221,588
1999	Charismatic	J. D. Bailey	Yankee Victor	Finder's Gold	12	**1:41.06**	$234,794
1998	Classic Cat	R. Albarado	Voyamerican	Grand Slam	8	1:42.85	$228,300
1997	Touch Gold	G. L. Stevens	Smoke Glacken	Deeds Not Words	5	1:43.27	$116,963
1996	City by Night	S. J. Sellers	Prince of Thieves	Roar	11	1:42.39	$123,473
1995	Star Standard	P. Day	Royal Mitch	Guadalcanal	5	1:45.02	$99,882
1994	Southern Rhythm	G. K. Gomez	Soul of the Matter	Ulises	8	1:15.72	$85,095
1993	Grand Jewel	J. D. Bailey	El Bakan	Truth of It All	9	1:43.61	$87,219
1992	My Luck Runs North	R. D. Lopez	Lure	Agincourt	5	1:44.06	$89,083

1992-'97 Lexington S. 2001 Mr. John finished second, DQ to eighth.

Cotillion Handicap

Grade 2, Philadelphia Park, three-year-old fillies, 1¹⁄₁₆ miles, dirt. Held October 6, 2001, with a gross value of $250,000. First held in 1969. Graded since 1973. Stakes record 1:42.54 (2000 Jostle).

Year	Winner	Jockey	Second	Third	Strs	Final Time	1st Purse
2001	Mystic Lady, 121	E. Coa	Zonk	Celtic Melody	8	1:43.86	$150,000
2000	Jostle, 124	M. E. Smith	Gold for My Gal	Prized Stamp	7	**1:42.54**	$120,000
1999	Skipping Around, 114	M. J. McCarthy	Strolling Belle	Waltz	10	1:43.45	$120,000
1998	Lu Ravi, 121	W. Martinez	Sister Act	Let	8	1:43.55	$90,000
1997	Snit, 114	R. E. Colton	Proud Run	Salt It	9	1:43.91	$90,000
1996	Double Dee's, 111	F. Leon	Ginny Lynn	Princess Eloise	5	1:44.69	$90,000
1995	Clear Mandate, 113	J. C. Ferrer	Blue Sky Princess	Country Cat	11	1:42.87	$98,730
1994	Sovereign Kitty, 118	W. H. McCauley	Cinnamon Sugar (Ire)	Cavada	8	1:43.52	$97,440
1993	Jacody, 118	T. G. Turner	Aztec Hill	Cearas Dancer	6	1:43.22	$95,520
1992	Star Minister, 117	A. J. Seefeldt	Diamond Duo	Squirm	7	1:44.06	$80,760

Count Fleet Sprint Handicap

Grade 3, Oaklawn Park, four-year-olds and up, 6 furlongs, dirt. Held April 12, 2001, with a gross value of $125,000. First held in 1974. Graded since 1986. Stakes record 1:08.18 (2001 Bonapaw).

Year	Winner	Jockey	Second	Third	Strs	Final Time	1st Purse
2001	Bonapaw, 5, 118	G. Melancon	Chindi, 7	Bidis, 7	7	1:08.18	$75,000
2000	†Show Me the Stage, 4, 116	D. R. Flores	Smolderin Heart, 5	Vinnie's Boy, 5	6	1:09.62	$75,000
1999	Reraise, 4, 122	C. S. Nakatani	Run Johnny, 7	E J Harley, 7	6	1:08.59	$75,000
1998	Chindi, 4, 113	D. R. Pettinger	E J Harley, 6	Western Fame, 6	8	1:09.77	$75,000
1997	High Stakes Player, 5, 120	K. J. Desormeaux	†Capote Belle, 4	Victor Avenue, 4	7	1:08.86	$90,000
1996	Concept Win, 6, 116	G. L. Stevens	Roythelittleone, 4	Spiritbound, 4	7	1:09.06	$90,000
1995	Hot Jaws, 5, 113	C. H. Borel	Demaloot Demashoot, 5	Mr. Cooperative, 5	9	1:09.49	$90,000
1994	Demaloot Demashoot, 4, 115	M. E. Smith	Honor the Hero, 6	Sir Hutch, 6	8	1:08.39	$90,000
1993	Approach, 6, 116	P. Day	Ponche, 4	Never Wavering, 4	13	1:09.64	$90,000
1992	Gray Slewpy, 4, 117	K. J. Desormeaux	Potentiality, 6	Hidden Tomahawk, 6	7	1:08.97	$60,000

1992 three-year-olds and up. † denotes female.

Cowdin Stakes

Grade 3, Belmont Park, two-year-olds, 6½ furlongs, dirt. Held October 7, 2001, with a gross value of $106,800. First held in 1923. Graded since 1973. Stakes record 1:14.35 (1997 Coronado's Quest).

Year	Winner	Jockey	Second	Third	Strs	Final Time	1st Purse
2001	Sunray Spirit	E. Coa	Davids Expectation	Harmony Hall	5	1:19.16	$64,080
2000	Fistfite	R. Migliore	Windsor Castle	American Century	6	1:15.63	$65,280
1999	Twilight Time	M. J. Luzzi	Sky Dweller	Precise End	4	1:17.15	$63,960
1998	Successful Appeal	R. Migliore	Noteasybeingreen	Exiled Groom	5	1:17.11	$63,780
1997	Coronado's Quest	M. E. Smith	Not Tricky	Scatmandu	8	1:14.35	$66,540
1996	Just a Cat	J. Bravo	Jules	Oro Bandito	8	1:23.04	$64,980
1995	Gator Dancer	E. Maple	Skip Away	In Contention	8	1:37.09	$69,540
1994	Old Tascosa	C. E. Lopez Sr.	Thunder Gulch	Adams Trail	8	1:24.79	$66,240
1993	You and I	C. Perret	Bermuda Cedar	Gulliviegold	7	1:22.74	$69,480
1992	Wallenda	W. H. McCauley	Wild Zone	Darien Deacon	10	1:24.12	$74,160

1992-'99 Grade 2. 1992-'94, 1996-'97 held at Aqueduct. 1992-'96 7 furlongs; 1995 1 mile.

Creme Fraiche Handicap

Grade 3, Gulfstream Park, three-year-olds and up, 1¹⁄₁₆ miles, dirt. Held March 11, 2000, with a gross value of $75,000. First held in 1990. Graded since 1993. Stakes record 1:41.49 (1996 Geri).

Year	Winner	Jockey	Second	Third	Strs	Final Time	1st Purse
2000	Dancing Guy, 5, 120	J. D. Bailey	Yankee Victor, 4	Midway Magistrate, 4	8	1:44.94	$45,000
1999	Jazz Club, 4, 114	P. Day	Rock and Roll, 4	Hanarsaan, 4	7	1:42.76	$45,000
1998	K. J.'s Appeal, 4, 114	J. R. Velazquez	Powerful Goer, 4	Tour's Big Red, 4	8	1:42.34	$45,000
1997	Louis Quatorze, 4, 121	P. Day	Strawberry Wine, 5	Exalto, 5	5	1:43.43	$45,000
1996	Geri, 4, 114	J. D. Bailey	Halo's Image, 5	Second Childhood, 5	5	1:41.49	$45,000
1995	Warm Wayne, 4, 112	J. D. Bailey	Meadow Monster, 4	Silent Lake, 4	9	1:43.11	$45,000
1994	Forever Whirl, 4, 113	W. H. McCauley	Northern Trend, 6	Royal n Gold, 6	10	1:41.81	$45,000
1993	Classic Seven, 5, 116	C. E. Lopez Sr.	Devil On Ice, 4	Keratoid, 4	10	1:43.49	$60,000
1992	Peanut Butter Onit, 6, 114	J. A. Santos	Sunny Sunrise, 5	Honest Ensign, 5	7	1:43.78	$45,000

2001 not held.

Crown Royal American Turf Stakes (see American Turf Stakes)

Dahlia Handicap

Grade 2, Hollywood Park, three-year-olds and up, fillies and mares, 1¹⁄₁₆ miles, turf. Held December 15, 2001, with a gross value of $150,000. First held in 1982. Graded since 1984. Stakes record 1:40.40 (1989 [DH] Stylish Star/Saros Brig)

Year	Winner	Jockey	Second	Third	Strs	Final Time	1st Purse
2001	Verruma (Brz), 5, 115	G. K. Gomez	Vencera (Fr), 4	Heads Will Roll (GB), 4	8	1:43.24	$90,000
2000	Follow the Money, 4, 115	V. Espinoza	Smooth Player, 4	Beautiful Noise, 4	7	1:40.71	$90,000
1999	Lady At Peace, 3, 113	G. K. Gomez	Cyrillic, 4	Country Garden (GB), 4	5	1:41.50	$90,000
1998	Tuzla (Fr), 4, 119	C. S. Nakatani	Sonja's Faith (Ire), 4	Curitiba, 4	5	1:41.75	$60,000
1997	Golden Arches (Fr), 3, 117	C. J. McCarron	Sonja's Faith (Ire), 3	Traces of Gold, 3	8	1:41.09	$60,000
1996	Sixieme Sens, 4, 116	C. S. Nakatani	Grafin, 5	Admise (Fr), 5	8	1:42.37	$66,600
1995	Didina (GB), 3, 115	E. Delahoussaye	Dirca (Ire), 3	Rapunzel Runz, 3	10	1:45.20	$68,300
1994	Skimble, 5, 118	E. Delahoussaye	Queens Court Queen, 5	Shir Dar (Fr), 5	8	1:42.33	$66,600
1993	Kalita Melody (GB), 5, 115	C. A. Black	Vinista, 3	Gumpher, 3	7	1:44.73	$64,500
1992	Kostroma (Ire), 6, 124	G. L. Stevens	Vijaya, 5	Guiza, 5	8	1:41.40	$66,500

Davona Dale Stakes

Grade 2, Gulfstream Park, three-year-old fillies, 1¹⁄₁₆ miles, dirt. Held February 25, 2001, with a gross value of $103,000. First held in 1988. Graded since 1993. Stakes record 1:45.51 (2001 Latour).

Year	Winner	Jockey	Second	Third	Strs	Final Time	1st Purse
2001	Latour	J. R. Velazquez	Gold Mover	Courageous Maiden	7	1:45.51	$60,000
2000	Cash Run	J. D. Bailey	Regally Appealing	Secret Status	9	1:40.37	$60,000
1999	Three Ring	J. R. Velazquez	Golden Temper	Gold From the West	5	1:41.53	$60,000

Year	Winner	Jockey	Second	Third	Strs	Final Time	1st Purse
1998	Diamond On the Run	P. Day	Uanme	Dixie Melody	10	1:42.65	$60,000
1997	Glitter Woman	M. E. Smith	City Band	Southern Playgirl	6	1:39.31	$60,000
1996	Plum Country	P. Day	My Flag	La Rosa	8	1:42.08	$60,000
1995	Mia's Hope	K. L. Chapman	Minister Wife	Culver City	6	1:43.26	$60,000
1994	Cut the Charm	J. D. Bailey	She Rides Tonite	Delightful Bet	8	1:41.44	$60,000
1993	Lunar Spook	M. Guidry	Boots 'n Jackie	In Her Glory	7	1:42.09	$30,000
1992	Miss Legality	J. A. Krone	November Snow	Spectacular Sue	8	1:42.00	$30,000

1993-'97 Grade 3. 1992-2000 1 mile 70 yards. 1996 Rare Blend finished second, DQ to sixth.

Debutante Stakes

Grade 3, Churchill Downs, two-year-old fillies, 5½ furlongs, dirt. Held July 7, 2001, with a gross value of $110,500. First held in 1895. Graded since 1996. Stakes record 1:02.52 (2001 Cashier's Dream).

Year	Winner	Jockey	Second	Third	Strs	Final Time	1st Purse
2001	Cashier's Dream	D. J. Meche	Lakeside Cup	Colonial Glitter	8	1:02.52	$68,510
2000	Gold Mover	C. Perret	Princess Belle	Tricky Elaine	9	1:03.79	$69,626
1999	Chilukki	W. Martinez	Miss Wineshine	Cecilia's Crown	9	1:03.66	$69,998
1998	Silverbulletday	W. Martinez	The Happy Hopper	Mancari's Rose	9	1:04.70	$69,502
1997	Love Lock	P. Day	Countess Diana	Quick Lap	13	1:03.84	$72,478
1996	Move	P. Day	Sarah's Prospector	Live Your Best	10	1:05.66	$73,840
1995	Golden Attraction	D. M. Barton	Western Dreamer	Tipically Irish	9	1:04.19	$70,948
1994	Chargedupsycamore	P. Day	Phone Bird	Our Gem	9	1:05.24	$54,405
1993	Fly Love	B. E. Bartram	Miss Ra He Ra	Astas Foxy Lady	11	1:05.23	$37,635
1992	Hollywood Wildcat	F. A. Arguello Jr.	Cosmic Speed Queen	Dixie Band	14	1:06.02	$38,480

1997, 1999 equaled track record; 2001 new track record.

De La Rose Handicap

Grade 3, Gulfstream Park, three-year-olds and up, fillies and mares, 1¹⁄₁₆ miles, turf. Held March 12, 2000, with a gross value of $75,000. First held in 1986. Graded since 1990. Stakes record 1:39.50 (1992 Grab the Green).

Year	Winner	Jockey	Second	Third	Strs	Final Time	1st Purse
2000	Fictitious (GB), 4, 113	J. A. Santos	Tres Coronas, 4	Dyna Two, 4	7	1:40.87	$45,000
1999	Lovers Knot (GB), 4, 114	J. D. Bailey	Pleasant Music, 5	Zinfandoll, 5	8	1:42.28	$45,000
1998	Dispersion, 5, 113	E. M. Jurado	Mistress Fletcher, 6	Bursting Forth, 6	5	1:48.28	$45,000
1997	Romy, 6, 115	F. C. Torres	Elusive, 5	Careless Heiress, 5	10	1:43.56	$60,000
1996	Class Kris, 4, 117	P. Day	Danish (Ire), 5	Logan's Mist, 5	12	1:42.51	$60,000
1995	Cox Orange, 5, 118	J. D. Bailey	Weekend Madness (Ire), 5	Ma Guerre, 5	11	1:43.47	$60,000
1994	Marshua's River, 7, 115	J. A. Santos	Sheila's Revenge, 4	Tango Charlie, 4	5	1:39.54	$60,000
1993	Quilma (Chi), 6, 113	J. A. Santos	Lemhi Go, 5	Palomelle (Fr), 5	8	1:43.88	$76,380
1992	Grab the Green, 4, 119	J. A. Santos	Christiecat, 5	Julie La Rousse (Ire), 5	10	1:39.50	$75,930

2001 not held. 1992-'96 Buckram Oak H. 1993, 1998 div. 1992 new course record.

Delaware Handicap

Grade 3, Delaware Park, three-year-olds and up, fillies and mares, 1¼ miles, dirt. Held July 22, 2001, with a gross value of $600,300. First held in 1937. Graded since 1973. Stakes record 1:59.80 (1987 Coup de Fusil).

Year	Winner	Jockey	Second	Third	Strs	Final Time	1st Purse
2001	Irving's Baby, 4, 113	R. A. Dominguez	Under the Rug, 6	Lazy Slusan, 6	6	2:05.21	$360,000
2000	Lu Ravi, 5, 117	P. Day	Tap to Music, 5	Silverbulletday, 5	8	2:02.21	$360,000
1999	Tap to Music, 4, 116	P. Day	Keeper Hill, 4	Unbridled Hope, 4	13	2:02.15	$300,000
1998	Amarillo, 4, 110	J. A. Krone	Tuxedo Junction, 5	Timely Broad, 5	9	2:04.37	$300,000
1997	Power Play, 5, 114	L. C. Reynolds	Gold n Delicious, 4	Effectiveness, 4	11	2:03.53	$210,000
1996	Urbane, 4, 117	A. O. Solis	Alcovy, 6	Shoop, 6	13	2:01.89	$180,000
1995	Night Fax, 4, 108	J. D. Carle	Cavada, 4	It's Personal, 4	8	2:02.98	$95,070
1994	With a Wink, 4, 114	R. Migliore	Passing Vice, 4	Alphabulous, 4	9	2:03.37	$95,130
1993	Green Darlin, 4, 113	M. J. Luzzi	Girl On a Mission, 4	Starry Val, 4	11	2:03.76	$96,300
1992	Brilliant Brass, 5, 117	E. S. Prado	Train Robbery, 5	Risen Colony, 5	6	2:03.11	$93,780

1992-'95 Grade 2.

Delaware Oaks

Grade 3, Delaware Park, three-year-old fillies, 1¹⁄₁₆ miles, dirt. Held July 21, 2001, with a gross value of $261,000. First held in 1938. Graded since 1999. Stakes record 1:42.81 (1998 Nickel Classic).

Year	Winner	Jockey	Second	Third	Strs	Final Time	1st Purse
2001	Zonk	M. J. McCarthy	Mystic Lady	Lady Andromeda	11	1:45.27	$151,000
2000	Sincerely	M. J. McCarthy	Trip	Valleydar	5	1:43.83	$150,000
1999	Brushed Halory	E. M. Martin Jr.	Gold From the West	Queen's Word	5	1:43.42	$150,000
1998	Nickel Classic	C. H. Borel	Lu Ravi	Taffy Davenport	8	1:42.81	$120,000
1997	Runup the Colors	P. Day	Timely Broad	City Band	10	1:44.27	$90,000
1996	Like a Hawk	R. E. Colton	Mercedes Song	Winter Melody	10	1:37.01	$30,000

1992-'95 not held. 1996 1 mile. 1996 turf.

Del Mar Breeders' Cup Handicap

Grade 2, Del Mar, three-year-olds and up, 1 mile, dirt. Held September 2, 2001, with a gross value of $250,000. First held in 1987. Graded since 1989. Stakes record 1:33.40 (1989 On the Line).

Year	Winner	Jockey	Second	Third	Strs	Final Time	1st Purse
2001	El Corredor, 4, 121	V. Espinoza	Figlio Mio, 4	Performing Magic, 4	6	1:35.24	$150,000
2000	El Corredor, 3, 111	V. Espinoza	Cliquot, 4	Literal Prowler, 4	8	1:35.05	$158,160
1999	Hollycombe, 5, 116	G. L. Stevens	Flying With Eagles, 4	Old Trieste, 5	8	1:35.46	$126,060
1998	Old Trieste, 3, 116	C. J. McCarron	Grajagan (Arg), 4	Stalwart Tsu, 4	4	1:35.35	$123,172
1997	Benchmark, 6, 117	E. Delahoussaye	Crafty Friend, 4	Northern Afleet, 4	5	1:35.57	$126,700
1996	Dramatic Gold, 5, 118	K. J. Desormeaux	Alphabet Soup, 5	Savinio, 5	5	1:34.78	$125,650
1995	Alphabet Soup, 4, 115	C. J. McCarron	Lykatill Hil, 5	Luthier Fever, 5	9	1:34.33	$117,150
1994	Lykatill Hil, 4, 118	E. Delahoussaye	D'Hallevant, 4	Stuka, 4	6	1:34.01	$62,200
1993	Region, 4, 115	C. S. Nakatani	Lottery Winner, 4	L'Express (Chi), 4	10	1:34.98	$122,100
1992	Reign Road, 4, 114	D. R. Flores	Sir Beaufort, 5	Charmonnier, 5	10	1:35.29	$122,000

Del Mar Debutante Stakes

Grade 1, Del Mar, two-year-old fillies, 7 furlongs, dirt. Held August 26, 2001, with a gross value of $250,000. First held in 1951. Graded since 1973. Stakes record 1:21.45 (1994 Call Now).

Year	Winner	Jockey	Second	Third	Strs	Final Time	1st Purse
2001	Habibti	V. Espinoza	Who Loves Aleyna	Tempera	5	1:22.22	$150,000
2000	Cindy's Hero	G. K. Gomez	Notable Career	Euro Empire	5	1:22.61	$150,000
1999	Chilukki	D. R. Flores	Spain	She's Classy	7	1:23.54	$150,000
1998	Excellent Meeting	K. J. Desormeaux	Antahkarana	Colorado Song	9	1:22.34	$150,000
1997	Vivid Angel	K. J. Desormeaux	Griselle	Czarina	8	1:24.26	$150,000
1996	Sharp Cat	R. R. Douglas	Desert Digger	Broad Dynamite	10	1:23.98	$150,000
1995	Batroyale	M. A. Pedroza	Proud Dixie	General Idea	12	1:22.55	$137,500
1994	Call Now	A. O. Solis	How So Oiseau	Ski Dancer	9	1:21.45	$137,500
1993	Sardula	E. Delahoussaye	Phone Chatter	Ballerina Gal	8	1:21.61	$137,500
1992	Beal Street Blues	G. L. Stevens	Fit n Fappy	Zoonaqua	10	1:37.17	$137,500

1999 Vinery Del Mar Debutante S. 1992-'98 Grade 2. 1992 1 mile.

Del Mar Derby

Grade 2, Del Mar, three-year-olds, 1⅛ miles, turf. Held September 3, 2001, with a gross value of $300,000. First held in 1945. Graded since 1973. Stakes record 1:46.60 (1968 [DH] Prince Hemp/Glory Hallelujah).

Year	Winner	Jockey	Second	Third	Strs	Final Time	1st Purse
2001	Romanceishope	C. J. McCarron	Indygo Shiner	Blue Steller (Ire)	10	1:47.93	$180,000
2000	Walkslikeaduck	E. Delahoussaye	Purely Cozzene	New Story	10	1:46.66	$180,000
1999	Val Royal (Fr)	C. S. Nakatani	Fighting Falcon	In Frank's Honor	10	1:48.53	$180,000
1998	Ladies Din	K. J. Desormeaux	Expressionist	Scooter Brown	9	1:48.59	$180,000
1997	Anet	G. L. Stevens	Brave Act (GB)	Worldly Ways (GB)	7	1:48.42	$180,000
1996	Rainbow Blues (Ire)	C. S. Nakatani	The Barking Shark	Mateo	9	1:50.01	$180,000
1995	Da Hoss	R. R. Douglas	Lake George	Tabor	9	1:48.08	$165,000
1994	Ocean Crest	L. A. Pincay Jr.	Unfinished Symph	Powis Castle	10	1:48.74	$165,000
1993	Guide (Fr)	K. J. Desormeaux	Future Storm	The Real Vaslav	12	1:49.73	$165,000
1992	Daros (GB)	E. Delahoussaye	Smiling and Dancin	Major Impact	12	1:48.80	$165,000

1992-'96 Del Mar Invitational Derby. 1994 Eagle Eyed finished third, DQ to seventh. 2000 equaled course record.

Del Mar Futurity

Grade 2, Del Mar, two-year-olds, 7 furlongs, dirt. Held September 5, 2001, with a gross value of $250,000. First held in 1948. Graded since 1973. Stakes record 1:21.67 (1999 Forest Camp).

Year	Winner	Jockey	Second	Third	Strs	Final Time	1st Purse
2001	Officer	V. Espinoza	Kamsack	Metatron	5	1:22.33	$150,000
2000	Flame Thrower	J. D. Bailey	Street Cry (Ire)	Arabian Light	8	1:22.00	$150,000
1999	Forest Camp	D. R. Flores	Dixie Union	Captain Steve	5	1:21.67	$150,000
1998	Worldly Manner	K. J. Desormeaux	Daring General	Waki American	7	1:23.05	$150,000
1997	Souvenir Copy	C. J. McCarron	Old Topper	Commitisize	8	1:23.10	$150,000
1996	Silver Charm	D. R. Flores	Gold Tribute	Swiss Yodeler	7	1:22.88	$150,000
1995	Future Quest	K. J. Desormeaux	Othello	Cavonnier	8	1:21.81	$137,500
1994	On Target	A. O. Solis	Supremo	Timber Country	9	1:22.37	$137,500
1993	Winning Pact	C. S. Nakatani	Ramblin Guy	Ferrara	7	1:22.04	$137,500
1992	River Special	C. J. McCarron	Sudden Hush	Seattle Sleet	7	1:36.64	$137,500

1992 1 mile.

Del Mar Handicap

Grade 2, Del Mar, three-year-olds and up, 1⅜ miles, turf. Held August 25, 2001, with a gross value of $250,000. First held in 1937. Graded since 1973. Stakes record 2:12.59 (2001 Timboroa [GB]).

Year	Winner	Jockey	Second	Third	Strs	Final Time	1st Purse
2001	Timboroa (GB), 5, 118	L. A. Pincay Jr.	Northern Quest (Fr), 6	Super Quercus (Fr), 6	7	2:12.59	$150,000
2000	Northern Quest (Fr), 5, 116	C. J. McCarron	Perssonet (Chi), 5	Alvo Certo (Brz), 5	8	2:12.65	$150,000

Year	Winner	Jockey	Second	Third	Strs	Final Time	1st Purse
1999	Sayarshan (Fr), 4, 115	B. Blanc	Dancing Place (Chi), 6	Ladies Din, 6	8	2:14.35	$150,000
1998	Bonapartiste (Fr), 4, 115	C. J. McCarron	River Bay, 5	Military, 5	6	2:14.18	$150,000
1997	Rainbow Dancer (Fr), 6, 118	A. O. Solis	Dowty, 5	Lord Jain (Arg), 5	8	2:13.68	$150,000
1996	Dernier Empereur, 6, 116	P. A. Valenzuela	Talloires, 6	Party Season (GB), 6	7	2:13.89	$150,000
1995	Royal Chariot, 5, 117	L. A. Pincay Jr.	River Rhythm, 8	Party Season (GB), 8	10	2:13.78	$137,500
1994	Navarone, 6, 117	P. A. Valenzuela	Approach the Bench (Ire), 6	Sir Mark Sykes (Ire), 6	8	2:14.37	$137,500
1993	Luazur (Fr), 4, 116	P. Day	Kotashaan (Fr), 5	Myrakalu (Fr), 5	7	2:15.11	$137,500
1992	Navarone, 4, 117	P. A. Valenzuela	Qathif, 5	Stark South, 5	8	2:15.17	$137,500

1992-'96 Del Mar Invitational H. 2000 Alvo Certo (Brz) finished second, DQ to third. 2001 equaled course record.

Del Mar Oaks

Grade 1, Del Mar, three-year-old fillies, 1⅛ miles, turf. Held August 18, 2001, with a gross value of $300,000. First held in 1957. Graded since 1973. Stakes record 1:47.73 (1994 Twice the Vice).

Year	Winner	Jockey	Second	Third	Strs	Final Time	1st Purse
2001	Golden Apples (Ire)	G. K. Gomez	Affluent	Reine de Romance (Ire)	8	1:47.98	$180,000
2000	No Matter What	V. Espinoza	Theoretically	Premiere Creation (Fr)	9	1:50.02	$150,000
1999	Tout Charmant	D. R. Flores	Smooth Player	Sweet Ludy (Ire)	10	1:48.64	$150,000
1998	Sicy d'Alsace (Fr)	C. S. Nakatani	Adel	Tranquility Lake	10	1:48.26	$150,000
1997	Famous Digger	B. Blanc	Golden Arches (Fr)	See You Soon (Fr)	10	1:49.14	$150,000
1996	Antespend	C. W. Antley	Gastronomical	True Flare	8	1:48.93	$150,000
1995	Bail Out Becky	S. J. Sellers	Sleep Easy	Top Ruhl	9	1:49.72	$137,500
1994	Twice the Vice	G. L. Stevens	Malli Star	Pharma	6	1:47.73	$96,250
1993	Hollywood Wildcat	E. Delahoussaye	Possibly Perfect	Miami Sands (Ire)	10	1:48.31	$96,250
1992	Suivi	A. O. Solis	Race the Wild Wind	Alysbelle	8	1:48.60	$96,250

1992-'94,1996 Del Mar Invitational Oaks. 1992-'93 Grade 2. 1998 Tranquility Lake finished second, DQ to third.

Demoiselle Stakes

Grade 2, Aqueduct, two-year-old fillies, 1⅛ miles, dirt. Held November 24, 2001, with a gross value of $200,000. First run in 1908. Graded since 1973. Stakes record 1:50 (1978 Plankton).

Year	Winner	Jockey	Second	Third	Strs	Final Time	1st Purse
2001	Smok'n Frolic	J. R. Velazquez	Lady Shari	Proxy Statement	7	1:50.57	$120,000
2000	Two Item Limit	R. Migliore	Sweep Dreams	Kingsland	8	1:52.25	$120,000
1999	Jostle	S. Elliott	March Magic	Shawnee Country	8	1:51.51	$120,000
1998	Better Than Honour	R. Migliore	Waltz On By	Oh What a Windfall	9	1:52.70	$120,000
1997	Clark Street	M. E. Smith	Soft Senorita	Mercy Me	8	1:53.98	$120,000
1996	Ajina	P. Day	Hidden Reserve	Biding Time	9	1:53.74	$120,000
1995	La Rosa	J. A. Krone	Quiet Dance	Escena	7	1:50.92	$120,000
1994	Minister Wife	J. D. Bailey	Miss Golden Circle	Special Broad	9	1:53.48	$120,000
1993	Strategic Maneuver	J. D. Bailey	Sovereign Kitty	Princess Tru	6	1:53.62	$120,000
1992	Fortunate Faith	A. Madrid Jr.	True Affair	Our Tomboy	8	1:53.59	$120,000

1998 Tutorial finished first, DQ to fifth.

Deputy Minister Handicap

Grade 3, Gulfstream Park, three-year-olds and up, 6½ furlongs, dirt. Held February 4, 2001, with a gross value of $118,500. First held in 1990. Graded since 2000. Stakes record 1:15.89 (2000 Deep Gold).

Year	Winner	Jockey	Second	Third	Strs	Final Time	1st Purse
2001	Istintaj, 5, 118	J. D. Bailey	Fappie's Notebook, 4	Fantastic Finish, 4	8	1:16.08	$60,000
2000	Deep Gold, 4, 112	J. R. Velazquez	Forty One Carats, 4	Klabin's Gold, 4	8	1:15.89	$60,000
1999	Good and Tough, 4, 115	S. J. Sellers	Western Borders, 5	Mint, 5	7	1:21.63	$60,000
1998	Irish Conquest, 5, 113	E. Coa	Frisk Me Now, 4	Oro de Mexico, 4	10	1:22.54	$60,000
1997	Templado (Ven), 4, 113	J. D. Bailey	Sea Emperor, 5	Punch Line, 5	6	1:09.69	$45,000
1996	Jess C's Whirl, 6, 115	J. A. Krone	Buffalo Dan, 5	Patton, 5	6	1:10.67	$30,000
1995	Chimes Band, 4, 120	J. D. Bailey	Distinct Reality, 4	Ponche, 4	6	1:09.16	$30,000
1994	I Can't Believe, 6, 113	E. Maple	Demaloot Demashoot, 4	Devil On Ice, 4	7	1:08.12	$30,000
1993	Loach, 5, 114	J. A. Santos	Hidden Tomahawk, 5	British Banker, 5	6	1:22.51	$30,000
1992	Take Me Out, 4, 118	J. D. Bailey	Drummond Lane, 5	Frozen Runway, 5	9	1:22.78	$30,000

1992-'93, 1998-'99 7 furlongs; 1994-'97 6 furlongs.

Derby Trial Stakes

Grade 3, Churchill Downs, three-year-olds, 1 mile, dirt. Held April 28, 2001, with a gross value of $117,100. First held in 1924. Graded since 1985. Stakes record 1:34.40 (1969 Ack Ack).

Year	Winner	Jockey	Second	Third	Strs	Final Time	1st Purse
2001	Meetyouathebrig	R. Albarado	Dream Run	One by the Knows	11	1:36.44	$72,602
2000	Performing Magic	P. Day	Sun Cat	Valiant Halory	8	1:35.99	$70,680
1999	Patience Game	C. S. Nakatani	Prime Directive	Straight Man	9	1:37.86	$71,176

Year	Winner	Jockey	Second	Third	Strs	Final Time	1st Purse
1998	Souvenir Copy	D. R. Flores	Yarrow Brae	Black Cash	8	1:35.80	$70,246
1997	Richter Scale	S. J. Sellers	Trafalger	Precocity	8	1:36.17	$70,122
1996	Valid Expectations	D. R. Pettinger	Great Southern	Storm Creek	10	1:36.81	$77,025
1995	Peaks and Valleys	P. Day	Our Gatsby	Strategic Intent	7	1:36.53	$73,515
1994	Numerous	C. J. McCarron	Dynamic Asset	Exclusive Praline	6	1:37.34	$72,540
1993	Cherokee Run	P. Day	Darien Deacon	Ground Force	9	1:37.57	$56,355
1992	Alydeed	C. Perret	Binalong	Dignitas	9	1:36.26	$56,209

Desert Stormer Handicap

Grade 3, Hollywood Park, three-year-olds and up, fillies and mares, 6 furlongs, dirt. Held June 2, 2001, with a gross value of $106,000. First held in 1997. Graded since 2001. Stakes record 1:08.09 (2001 Go Go).

Year	Winner	Jockey	Second	Third	Strs	Final Time	1st Purse
2001	Go Go, 4, 122	E. Delahoussaye	Kalookan Queen, 5	Wired to Fly, 5	5	**1:08.09**	$63,600
2000	Theresa's Tizzy, 6, 118	L. A. Pincay Jr.	Hookedonthefeelin, 4	Seth's Choice, 4	7	1:09.30	$64,980
1999	A. P. Assay, 5, 122	E. Delahoussaye	Woodman's Dancer, 5	Corona Lake, 5	5	1:08.69	$63,600
1998	Corona Lake, 4, 118	E. Delahoussaye	Lavender, 4	Grab the Prize, 4	5	1:14.71	$64,020
1997	Advancing Star, 4, 119	K. J. Desormeaux	Stop Traffic, 4	Tiffany Diamond, 4	5	1:14.21	$60,000

1997-'98 6½ furlongs.

Diana Handicap

Grade 2, Saratoga Race Course, three-year-olds and up, fillies and mares, 1⅛ miles, turf. Held September 3, 2001, with a gross value of $500,000. First held in 1939. Graded since 1973. Stakes record 1:45.40 (1978 Waya [Fr]).

Year	Winner	Jockey	Second	Third	Strs	Final Time	1st Purse
2001	Starine (Fr), 4, 114	J. R. Velazquez	Babae (Chi), 5	Penny's Gold, 5	9	1:46.17	$300,000
2000	Perfect Sting, 4, 123	J. D. Bailey	License Fee, 5	Hello Soso (Ire), 5	9	1:47.01	$300,000
1999	Heritage of Gold, 4, 115	S. J. Sellers	Khumba Mela (Ire), 4	Mossflower, 4	9	1:45.93	$180,000
1998	Memories of Silver, 5, 123	J. D. Bailey	B. A. Valentine, 5	Auntie Mame, 5	8	1:46.14	$180,000
1997	Rumpipumpy (GB), 4, 114	J. A. Santos	B. A. Valentine, 4	Antespend, 4	12	1:48.59	$120,000
1996	Electric Society (Ire), 5, 117	M. E. Smith	Powder Bowl, 4	Upper Noosh, 4	9	1:46.56	$120,000
1995	Perfect Arc, 3, 113	J. R. Velazquez	Danish (Ire), 4	Tiffany's Taylor, 4	9	1:46.85	$85,125
1994	Via Borghese, 5, 115	J. A. Santos	Blazing Kadie, 4	Coronation Cup, 4	7	1:52.01	$83,010
1993	Ratings, 5, 110	J. A. Krone	Lady Blessington (Fr), 5	Garendare (GB), 5	8	1:49.80	$72,240
1992	Plenty of Grace, 5, 114	W. H. McCauley	Ratings, 4	Highland Crystal, 4	12	1:46.66	$75,960

Discovery Handicap

Grade 3, Aqueduct, three-year-olds, 1⅛ miles, dirt. Held October 31, 2001, with a gross value of $109,300. First held in 1945. Graded since 1973. Stakes record 1:47.20 (1973 Forego).

Year	Winner	Jockey	Second	Third	Strs	Final Time	1st Purse
2001	Evening Attire, 111	S. Bridgmohan	Street Cry (Ire)	Free of Love	7	1:48.62	$65,580
2000	Left Bank, 119	J. R. Velazquez	Perfect Cat	Open Sesame	4	1:47.30	$64,020
1999	Adonis, 118	J. R. Velazquez	Best of Luck	Waddaan	6	1:50.11	$64,980
1998	Early Warning, 115	J. F. Chavez	Deputy Diamond	Gulliver	8	1:48.94	$50,010
1997	Mr. Sinatra, 116	M. E. Smith	Concerto	Twin Spires	5	1:49.55	$64,626
1996	Gold Fever, 121	M. E. Smith	Crafty Friend	Early Echoes	8	1:49.01	$66,720
1995	Michael's Star, 112	J. A. Krone	Hunting Hard	Reality Road	10	1:50.34	$67,380
1994	Serious Spender, 113	J. F. Chavez	Unaccounted For	Malmo	4	1:51.24	$63,540
1993	Prospector's Flag, 114	J. F. Chavez	Virginia Rapids	Living Vicariously	8	1:52.30	$70,320
1992	New Deal, 111	R. G. Davis	Offbeat	Dodsworth	11	1:48.08	$74,880

Distaff Breeders' Cup Handicap

Grade 2, Aqueduct, three-year-olds and up, fillies and mares, 7 furlongs, dirt. Held March 24, 2001, with a gross value of $181,600. First held in 1954. Graded since 1973. Stakes record 1:21.18 (1991 Devil's Orchid).

Year	Winner	Jockey	Second	Third	Strs	Final Time	1st Purse
2001	Dream Supreme, 4, 119	A. T. Gryder	Folly Dollar, 4	Country Hideaway, 4	5	1:23.66	$108,960
2000	Honest Lady, 4, 117	B. Blanc	Her She Kisses, 4	Tap to Music, 4	8	1:22.10	$111,300
1999	Furlough, 5, 115	H. Castillo Jr.	Catinca, 4	Tomorrows Sunshine, 4	9	1:23.23	$112,260
1998	Parlay, 4, 114	R. Migliore	Lucky Marty, 5	Green Light, 5	9	1:24.10	$67,260
1997	Miss Golden Circle, 5, 120	R. Migliore	Inquisitive Look, 4	Punkin Pie, 4	6	1:24.47	$65,040
1996	Lottsa Talc, 6, 120	F. T. Alvarado	Traverse City, 6	Dust Bucket, 6	7	1:24.04	$75,820
1995	Recognizable, 4, 120	M. E. Smith	Beckys Shirt, 4	Kurofune Mystery, 4	8	1:22.94	$66,540
1994	Classy Mirage, 4, 114	R. G. Davis	Jill Miner, 4	Air Port Won, 4	8	1:11.37	$66,480
1992	Nannerl, 5, 112	M. E. Smith	Missy's Mirage, 4	Withallprobability, 4	6	1:24.68	$68,880

1993 not held. 1992, 1994-'98 Distaff H. 1994 6 furlongs.

(Humana) Distaff Handicap

Grade 2, Churchill Downs, four-year-olds and up, fillies and mares, 7 furlongs, dirt. Held May 5, 2001, with a gross value of $165,000. First held in 1987. Graded since 1990. Stakes record 1:20.70 (2001 Dream Supreme).

Year	Winner	Jockey	Second	Third	Strs	Final Time	1st Purse
2001	Dream Supreme, 4, 120	P. Day	La Feminn, 5	Nany's Sweep, 5	5	1:20.70	$102,300
2000	Ruby Surprise, 5, 114	J. C. Judice	Honest Lady, 4	Cassidy, 4	8	1:21.25	$102,951
1999	Zuppardo Ardo, 5, 114	S. J. Sellers	French Braids, 4	Prospector's Song, 4	9	1:23.40	$105,183
1998	Colonial Minstrel, 4, 115	J. R. Velazquez	Stop Traffic, 5	Meter Maid, 5	11	1:22.12	$71,300
1997	Capote Belle, 4, 118	J. R. Velazquez	Hidden Lake, 4	J J'sdream, 4	8	1:22.38	$70,060
1996	In Conference, 4, 113	M. E. Smith	Supah Jess, 4	Morris Code, 4	8	1:23.30	$72,930
1995	Laura's Pistolette, 4, 114	C. S. Nakatani	Morning Meadow, 5	Traverse City, 5	10	1:22.24	$74,425
1994	Roamin Rachel, 4, 118	M. E. Smith	Arches of Gold, 5	Glory's Ghost, 5	7	1:23.83	$72,345
1993	Court Hostess, 5, 115	C. J. McCarron	Santa Catalina, 5	Ifyoucouldseemenow, 5	12	1:23.18	$56,550
1992	Ifyoucouldseemenow, 4, 120	C. Perret	Madam Bear, 4	Magal, 4	10	1:22.22	$56,599

1992-'94 Brown and Williamson H.; 1995-2001 Humana Distaff H. 1992-'98 Grade 3.

(Citgo) Distaff Turf Mile Stakes

Grade 3, Churchill Downs, three-year-olds and up, fillies and mares, about 1 mile, turf. Held May 5, 2001, with a gross value of $113,600. First held in 1983. Graded since 1997. Stakes record 1:34.64 (1995 Bold Ruritana).

Year	Winner	Jockey	Second	Third	Strs	Final Time	1st Purse
2001	Iftiraas (GB), 4	J. D. Bailey	Gino's Spirits (GB), 5	Solvig, 5	7	1:36.69	$70,432
2000	Don't Be Silly, 5	J. F. Chavez	Really Polish, 5	Pricearose, 5	8	1:34.78	$71,548
1999	Shires Ende, 4	J. R. Velazquez	Ashford Castle, 5	Sophie My Love, 5	9	1:35.43	$74,152
1998	Witchful Thinking, 4	S. J. Sellers	Colcon, 5	Swearingen, 5	10	1:37.23	$74,896
1997	B. A. Valentine, 4	S. J. Sellers	Striesen, 5	Romy, 5	10	1:36.98	$71,796
1996	Apolda, 5	J. D. Bailey	Country Cat, 4	Bold Ruritana, 4	8	1:36.50	$55,283
1995	Bold Ruritana, 5	P. Day	Icy Warning, 5	Rapunzel Runz, 5	10	1:34.64	$56,111
1994	Weekend Madness (Ire), 4	C. R. Woods Jr.	Russian Bride, 4	Suspect Terrain, 4	9	1:38.58	$55,770
1993	Lady Blessington (Fr), 5	P. Day	You'd Be Surprised, 4	Wassifa (GB), 4	9	1:34.96	$37,570
1992	Quilma (Chi), 5	E. Delahoussaye	Behaving Dancer, 5	Radiant Ring, 5	10	1:35.36	$38,285

1992 Capital Holding S.; 1993-'94 Capital Holding Mile S.; 1995-'97 Providian Mile S.; 1998 Aegon Mile S. 1999 Ashland Mile S.; 2000 Churchill Downs Distaff Turf Mile S.; 2001 Citgo Distaff Turf Mile S. 1992 equaled course record; 1993 new course record.

Dixie Stakes

Grade 2, Pimlico, three-year-olds and up, 1⅛ miles, turf. Held May 19, 2001, with a gross value of $200,000. First held in 1870. Graded since 1973. Stakes record 1:47.04 (1991 Double Booked).

Year	Winner	Jockey	Second	Third	Strs	Final Time	1st Purse
2001	Hap, 5	J. D. Bailey	Make No Mistake (Ire), 6	Cynics Beware, 6	8	1:48.56	$120,000
2000	Quiet Resolve, 5	R. Albarado	Haami, 5	Holditholditholdit, 5	9	1:50.42	$120,000
1999	Middlesex Drive, 4	P. Day	Sky Colony, 6	Divide and Conquer, 6	10	1:48.64	$120,000
1998	Yagli, 5	J. D. Bailey	Sky Colony, 5	Blazing Sword, 5	12	1:51.01	$120,000
1997	Ops Smile, 5	E. S. Prado	Brave Note (Ire), 6	Sharp Appeal, 6	8	1:48.20	$120,000
1996	Gold and Steel (Fr), 4	A. O. Solis	Same Old Wish, 6	Comstock Lode, 6	9	1:52.80	$120,000
1995	The Vid, 5	J. D. Bailey	Pennine Ridge, 4	Blues Traveller (Ire), 4	6	1:52.25	$120,000
1994	Paradise Creek, 5	P. Day	Lure, 5	Astudillo (Ire), 5	5	1:48.51	$90,000
1993	Lure, 4	M. E. Smith	Star of Cozzene, 5	Binary Light, 5	5	1:47.60	$90,000
1992	Sky Classic, 5	P. Day	Fourstars Allstar, 4	Social Retiree, 4	10	1:47.83	$90,000

1992-'94,1996 Dixie H. 1992-'93 Grade 3.

Dogwood Stakes

Grade 3, Churchill Downs, three-year-old fillies, 1⅟₁₆ miles, dirt. Held May 26, 2001, with a gross value of $109,700. First held in 1975. Graded since 1998. Stakes record 1:43.22 (1996 Ginny Lynn).

Year	Winner	Jockey	Second	Third	Strs	Final Time	1st Purse
2001	Nasty Storm	L. Meche	Love At Noon	Golly Greeley	7	1:43.41	$68,014
2000	Welcome Surprise	F. C. Torres	Lady Melesi	Vivid Sunset	7	1:46.80	$68,014
1999	Golden Temper	S. J. Sellers	Boom Town Girl	Honey Hill Lil	8	1:43.73	$69,068
1998	Really Polish	P. Day	Beat the Play	Victorica	5	1:44.78	$67,642
1997	Leo's Gypsy Dancer	P. Day	Buckeye Search	Flying Lauren	7	1:44.95	$69,006
1996	Ginny Lynn	L. Melancon	Everhope	Hidden Lake	7	1:43.22	$53,576
1995	Gal in a Ruckus	W. H. McCauley	Country Cat	Naskra Colors	7	1:43.88	$53,528
1994	Briar Road	L. Melancon	Stella Cielo	Shadow Miss	6	1:44.78	$53,186
1993	With a Wink	C. R. Woods Jr.	Lovat's Lady	Unlaced	8	1:44.21	$36,010
1992	Hitch	B. E. Bartram	Bionic Soul	Secretly	8	1:47.68	$36,075

Donn Handicap

Grade 1, Gulfstream Park, three-year-olds and up, 1⅛ miles, dirt. Held February 3, 2001, with a gross value of $500,000. First held in 1959. Graded since 1973. Stakes record 1:46.40 (1979 Jumping Hill).

Year	Winner	Jockey	Second	Third	Strs	Final Time	1st Purse
2001	**Captain Steve**, 4, 120	J. D. Bailey	Albert the Great, 4	Gander, 4	7	1:48.95	$300,000
2000	**Stephen Got Even**, 4, 115	S. J. Sellers	Golden Missile, 5	Behrens, 5	10	1:48.50	$300,000
1999	**Puerto Madero (Chi)**, 5, 120	K. J. Desormeaux	Behrens, 5	Silver Charm, 5	12	1:48.34	$300,000
1998	**Skip Away**, 5, 126	J. D. Bailey	Unruled, 5	Sir Bear, 5	10	1:50.17	$180,000
1997	**Formal Gold**, 4, 113	J. Bravo	Skip Away, 4	Mecke, 4	10	1:47.49	$180,000
1996	**Cigar**, 6, 128	J. D. Bailey	Wekiva Springs, 5	†Heavenly Prize, 5	8	1:49.12	$180,000
1995	**Cigar**, 5, 115	J. D. Bailey	Primitive Hall, 6	Bonus Money (GB), 6	9	1:49.68	$180,000
1994	**Pistols and Roses**, 5, 113	H. Castillo Jr.	Eequalsmcsquared, 5	Wallenda, 5	11	1:50.67	$180,000
1993	**Pistols and Roses**, 4, 112	H. Castillo Jr.	Irish Swap, 6	Missionary Ridge (GB), 6	9	1:50.10	$240,000
1992	**Sea Cadet**, 4, 115	A. O. Solis	Out of Place, 5	Sunny Sunrise, 5	8	1:48.17	$300,000

† denotes female.

Dwyer Stakes

Grade 2, Belmont Park, three-year-olds, 1¹⁄₁₆ miles, dirt. Held July 8, 2001, with a gross value of $145,500. First held in 1918. Graded since 1973. Stakes record 1:40.38 (2001 E Dubai).

Year	Winner	Jockey	Second	Third	Strs	Final Time	1st Purse
2001	**E Dubai**	J. D. Bailey	Windsor Castle	Hero's Tribute	4	**1:40.38**	$90,000
2000	**Albert the Great**	R. Migliore	More Than Ready	Red Bullet	4	1:42.62	$90,000
1999	**Forestry**	J. D. Bailey	Doneraile Court	Successful Appeal	6	1:41.00	$90,000
1998	**Coronado's Quest**	M. E. Smith	Ian's Thunder	Scatmandu	5	1:42.49	$90,000
1997	**Behrens**	J. D. Bailey	Glitman	Banker's Gold	6	1:42.26	$90,000
1996	**Victory Speech**	J. D. Bailey	Gold Fever	Robb	6	1:41.53	$99,000
1995	**Hoolie**	R. G. Davis	Reality Road	Western Larla	6	1:42.74	$90,000
1994	**Holy Bull**	M. E. Smith	Twining	Bay Street Star	4	1:41.15	$90,000
1993	**Cherokee Run**	P. Day	Miner's Mark	Silver of Silver	6	1:47.62	$120,000
1992	**Agincourt**	J. F. Chavez	Three Peat	Windundermywings	6	1:47.84	$120,000

1992-'93 1⅛ miles. 1992 Three Peat finished first, DQ to second.

Eatontown Handicap

Grade 3, Monmouth Park, three-year-olds and up, fillies and mares, 1⅛ miles, turf. Held August 5, 2001, with a gross value of $100,000. First held in 1971. Graded since 1989. Stakes record 1:47.50 (2001 Cousin Gigi).

Year	Winner	Jockey	Second	Third	Strs	Final Time	1st Purse
2001	**Cousin Gigi**, 4, 115	R. Wilson	Quidnaskra, 6	Crystal Sea, 6	8	**1:47.50**	$60,000
2000	**Reciclada (Chi)**, 5, 115	A. O. Solis	Mumtaz (Fr), 4	Dominique's Joy, 4	8	1:44.34	$60,000
1999	**Formal Tango**, 4, 113	J. D. Bailey	Proud Owner, 4	Natalie Too, 4	7	1:42.62	$60,000
1998	**Gastronomical**, 5, 115	G. L. Stevens	Tampico, 5	(DH) Dance Clear (Ire), 5 (DH) Poopsie, 4	10	1:43.39	$41,400
1997	**B. A. Valentine**, 4, 122	C. J. McCarron	Everhope, 4	Vashon, 4	11	1:41.32	$41,460
1996	**Gail's Brush**, 5, 116	G. Boulanger	Plenty of Sugar, 5	Lady Affirmed, 5	7	1:40.40	$45,000
1995	**Symphony Lady**, 5, 119	J. Bravo	Cox Orange, 5	Grafin, 5	6	1:43.64	$30,000
1994	**Verbal Volley**, 5, 119	R. E. Colton	Irving's Girl, 4	Uptown Show, 4	8	1:44.71	$24,000
1993	**Topsa**, 6, 113	L. R. Rivera Jr.	Naked Royalty, 4	Suspect Terrain, 4	7	1:46.39	$21,000
1992	**Red Journey**, 4, 115	N. Santagata	Hot Times Are Here, 4	Flashing Eyes, 4	7	1:45.06	$21,000

1992-'95, 1997-2000 Eatontown S. 1992-'95 not graded. 1992-2000 1¹⁄₁₆ miles. 1998 dead heat for third.

Eddie Read Handicap

Grade 1, Del Mar, three-year-olds and up, 1⅛ miles, turf. Held July 28, 2001, with a gross value of $400,000. First held in 1974. Graded since 1980. Stakes record 1:46.60 (1986 Al Mamoon).

Year	Winner	Jockey	Second	Third	Strs	Final Time	1st Purse
2001	**Redattore (Brz)**, 6, 115	A. O. Solis	Native Desert, 8	Super Quercus (Fr), 8	6	1:47.16	$240,000
2000	**Ladies Din**, 5, 120	K. J. Desormeaux	Chester House, 5	Gold Nugget, 5	8	1:48.64	$240,000
1999	**Joe Who (Brz)**, 6, 116	C. W. Antley	Ladies Din, 4	Bouccaneer (Fr), 4	10	1:48.75	$240,000
1998	**Subordination**, 4, 117	D. R. Flores	Bonapartiste (Fr), 4	Hawksley Hill (Ire), 4	5	1:47.49	$180,000
1997	**Expelled**, 5, 113	J. A. Garcia	El Angelo, 5	Marlin, 5	7	1:48.60	$180,000
1996	**Fastness (Ire)**, 6, 124	C. S. Nakatani	Smooth Runner, 5	Gold and Steel (Fr), 5	6	1:47.05	$193,000
1995	**Fastness (Ire)**, 5, 115	G. L. Stevens	Romarin (Brz), 5	Northern Spur (Ire), 5	8	1:48.42	$182,600
1994	**Approach the Bench (Ire)**, 6, 113	C. S. Nakatani	Fastness (Ire), 4	Johann Quatz (Fr), 4	7	1:48.83	$187,250
1993	**Kotashaan (Fr)**, 5, 122	K. J. Desormeaux	Leger Cat (Arg), 7	Rainbow Corner (GB), 7	6	1:48.45	$183,750
1992	**Marquetry**, 5, 118	D. R. Flores	Luthier Enchanteur, 5	Leger Cat (Arg), 5	7	1:47.20	$187,250

El Camino Real Derby

Grade 3, Golden Gate Fields, three-year-olds, 1¹⁄₁₆ miles, dirt. Held March 10, 2001, with a gross value of $200,000. First held in 1982. Graded since 1985. Stakes record 1:39.40 (1988 Ruhlmann).

Year	Winner	Jockey	Second	Third	Strs	Final Time	1st Purse
2001	**Hoovergetthekeys**	R. J. Warren Jr.	Startac	Mo Mon	8	1:40.85	$110,000

Year	Winner	Jockey	Second	Third	Strs	Final Time	1st Purse
2000	Remember Sheikh	F. T. Alvarado	True Confidence	Country Coast	14	1:43.47	$110,000
1999	Cliquot	D. R. Flores	Charismatic	No Cal Bread	7	1:43.29	$110,000
1998	Event of the Year	R. A. Baze	Post a Note	Clover Hunter	5	1:40.27	$110,000
1997	Pacificbounty	K. J. Desormeaux	Wild Wonder	Carmen's Baby	6	1:41.85	$110,000
1996	Cavonnier	M. A. Pedroza	Sergeant Stroh	E C's Dream	9	1:43.41	$110,000
1995	Jumron (GB)	G. F. Almeida	Snow Kidd'n	American Day	8	1:43.73	$110,000
1994	Tabasco Cat	P. Day	Flying Sensation	Robannier	7	1:42.78	$110,000
1993	El Atroz	R. Q. Meza	Offshore Pirate	Lykatill Hil	9	1:43.77	$110,000
1992	Casual Lies	A. Patterson	Seahawk Gold	Silver Ray	11	1:42.00	$165,000

1992-2000 held at Bay Meadows.

El Conejo Handicap

Grade 3, Santa Anita Park, three-year-olds and up, 5½ furlongs, dirt. Held December 31, 2000, with a gross value of $108,700. First held in 1981. Graded since 2000. Stakes record 1:01.74 (1999 Kona Gold).

Year	Winner	Jockey	Second	Third	Strs	Final Time	1st Purse
2000	Freespool, 4, 115	C. J. McCarron	Men's Exclusive, 7	Lexicon, 7	7	1:02.50	$65,220
	Freespool, 4, 114	C. J. McCarron	Mellow Fellow, 5	Old Topper, 5	6	1:03.33	$64,200
1999	Kona Gold, 5, 119	A. O. Solis	Big Jag, 6	Mr. Doubledown, 6	6	**1:01.74**	$64,380
1998	The Exeter Man, 6, 114	G. K. Gomez	Tower Full, 6	Red, 6	5	1:02.23	$64,020
1997	High Stakes Player, 5, 115	C. S. Nakatani	Kern Ridge, 6	Subtle Trouble, 6	6	1:02.89	$63,850
1996	Lit de Justice, 6, 119	C. S. Nakatani	A. J. Jett, 4	Fu Man Slew, 4	6	1:01.85	$64,250
1995	Phone Roberto, 6, 114	C. J. McCarron	Lost Pan, 5	Rotsaluck, 5	8	1:02.34	$65,000
1994	Gundaghia, 7, 116	E. Delahoussaye	Sir Hutch, 4	Davy Be Good, 5	6	1:02.01	$64,800
1993	Fabulous Champ, 4, 113	C. J. McCarron	Arrowtown, 5	Slerp, 5	7	1:02.66	$63,800
1992	Gray Slewpy, 4, 114	K. J. Desormeaux	Frost Free, 7	Cardmania, 7	5	1:02.01	$61,275

2001 not held. 2000 held in January and December. 1992-2000 four-year-olds and up. 1995 Lit de Justice finished second, DQ to sixth. 1992,1996,1999 new track record.

El Encino Stakes

Grade 2, Santa Anita Park, four-year-old fillies, 1¹⁄₁₆ miles, dirt. Held January 21, 2001, with a gross value of $147,000. First held in 1954. Graded since 1988. Stakes record 1:41.20 (1980 It's In the Air; 1982 Edge; 1983 Beautiful Glass; 1990 Akinemod).

Year	Winner	Jockey	Second	Third	Strs	Final Time	1st Purse
2001	Chilukki	G. L. Stevens	Spain	Queenie Belle	4	1:42.55	$90,000
2000	Olympic Charmer	C. J. McCarron	Her She Kisses	Smooth Player	7	1:42.71	$97,470
1999	Manistique	G. L. Stevens	Gourmet Girl	Magical Allure	3	1:43.10	$90,000
1997	Fleet Lady	G. K. Gomez	Minister's Melody	I Ain't Bluffing	6	1:43.04	$96,840
1997	Belle's Flag	C. S. Nakatani	Housa Dancer (Fr)	Listening	9	1:41.61	$82,650
1996	Jewel Princess	A. O. Solis	Sleep Easy	Urbane	4	1:41.94	$78,800
1995	Klassy Kim	K. J. Desormeaux	Twice the Vice	Crissy Aya	5	1:42.43	$61,400
1994	Supah Gem	C. S. Nakatani	Sensational Eyes	Stalcreek	8	1:41.33	$64,500
1993	Pacific Squall	C. J. McCarron	Avian Assembly	Magical Maiden	7	1:45.67	$63,900
1992	Exchange	L. A. Pincay Jr.	Grand Girlfriend	Damewood	10	1:43.32	$67,000

1998 I Ain't Bluffing finished first, DQ to third.

Elkhorn Stakes

Grade 3, Keeneland, four-year-olds and up, 1½ miles, turf. Held April 25, 2001, with a gross value of $113,400. First held in 1986. Graded since 1988. Stakes record 2:27.84 (1999 African Dancer).

Year	Winner	Jockey	Second	Third	Strs	Final Time	1st Purse
2001	Williams News, 6	R. Albarado	Gritty Sandie, 5	Craigstool (GB), 5	9	2:29.13	$70,308
2000	Drama Critic, 4	J. D. Bailey	Craigsteel (GB), 5	Dixie's Crown, 5	10	2:28.03	$69,750
1999	African Dancer, 7	J. D. Bailey	Magest, 4	Chorwon, 4	8	**2:27.84**	$68,138
1998	African Dancer, 6	J. D. Bailey	Chief Bearhart, 5	Chorwon, 5	5	2:31.71	$66,712
1997	Chief Bearhart, 4	J. A. Santos	Snake Eyes, 7	Lassigny, 7	8	2:28.43	$68,324
1996	Vladivostok, 4	P. Day	Penn Fifty Three, 4	Party Season (GB), 4	7	2:30.83	$68,262
1995	Marvin's Faith (Ire), 4	C. Perret	Hasten To Add, 5	Opera Score, 5	10	1:47.10	$70,680
1994	Lure, 5	M. E. Smith	Buckhar, 6	Pride of Summer, 6	5	1:53.76	$66,526
1993	Coaxing Matt, 4	P. Day	Cleone, 4	Maxigroom, 4	9	1:47.64	$68,603
1992	Fourstars Allstar, 4	J. D. Bailey	Slew the Slewor, 5	Rainbows for Life, 5	10	1:47.66	$72,995

1992-'95 Grade 2. 1992-'95 1⅛ miles. 1995,1999 new course record.

Endine Stakes

Grade 3, Delaware Park, three-year-olds and up, fillies and mares, 6 furlongs, dirt. Held September 8, 2001, with a gross value of $150,000. First held in 1971. Graded since 2001. Stakes record 1:08.75 (1999 Hurricane Bertie).

Year	Winner	Jockey	Second	Third	Strs	Final Time	1st Purse
2001	Xtra Heat, 3	R. Wilson	Ivy's Jewel, 4	Big Bambu, 4	5	1:09.64	$90,000
2000	Superduper Miss, 4	T. G. Turner	Debby d'Or, 5	Cassidy, 5	7	1:10.22	$60,000

Year	Winner	Jockey	Second	Third	Strs	Final Time	1st Purse
1999	Hurricane Bertie, 4	P. Day	Little Sister, 5	Bourbon Belle, 5	4	**1:08.75**	$60,000
1998	Soverign Lady, 4	M. E. Smith	Weather Vane, 4	Little Sister, 4	8	1:09.43	$45,000
1997	Dancin Renee, 5	J. A. Velez Jr.	Two Punch Lil, 5	Ana Belen (Chi), 5	6	1:10.04	$30,000
1996	Hay Hanne, 4	J. A. Velez Jr.	Know B's, 4	Ayrial Delight, 4	8	1:10.30	$22,770

1992-'95 not held.

Essex Handicap

Grade 3, Oaklawn Park, four-year-olds and up, 1¹⁄₁₆ miles, dirt. Held February 24, 2001, with a gross value of $75,000. First held in 1948. Graded since 1983. Stakes record 1:41 (1976 Navajo; 1987 Sun Master).

Year	Winner	Jockey	Second	Third	Strs	Final Time	1st Purse
2001	Mr Ross, 6, 117	D. R. Pettinger	Remington Rock, 7	Maysville Slew, 7	7	1:43.59	$45,000
2000	Maysville Slew, 4, 115	L. S. Quinonez	Sand Ridge, 5	Mr Ross, 5	7	1:44.12	$45,000
1999	Brush With Pride, 7, 116	T. T. Doocy	Littlebitlively, 5	Treat Me Doc, 5	7	1:43.26	$45,000
1998	Relic Reward, 4, 113	C. H. Borel	Phantom On Tour, 4	Brush With Pride, 4	7	1:43.92	$45,000
1997	No Spend No Glow, 5, 113	R. N. Lester	Illesam, 5	Auggie My Dad, 5	8	1:45.94	$45,000
1996	Classic Fit, 6, 114	C. Gonzalez	Judge T C, 5	Juliannus, 5	4	1:42.98	$47,700
1995	Silver Goblin, 4, 122	D. W. Cordova	Prince of the Mt., 4	Golden Gear, 4	7	1:42.10	$33,150
1994	Greatsilverfleet, 4, 116	G. K. Gomez	Prize Fight, 5	All Gone, 5	5	1:42.08	$32,250
1993	Delafield, 4, 113	P. Day	Famed Devil, 5	Yukon Robbery, 5	8	1:42.11	$33,900
1992	Allijeba, 6, 118	P. Day	On the Edge, 5	Bedeviled, 5	10	1:43.95	$34,500

Everglades Stakes

Grade 3, Hialeah Park, three-year-olds, 1¹⁄₁₆ miles, turf. Held March 18, 2001, with a gross value of $100,000. First held in 1946. Graded since 1999. Stakes record 1:42.25 (1999 Swamp).

Year	Winner	Jockey	Second	Third	Strs	Final Time	1st Purse
2001	Proud Man	R. R. Douglas	Baptize	Strategic Partner	8	1:43.02	$60,000
2000	Tubrok	E. S. Prado	Mr. Livingston	Mt. Bellewood	6	1:44.50	$60,000
1999	Swamp	R. Migliore	Monkey Puzzle	Valid Reprized	7	**1:42.25**	$60,000
1998	Cryptic Rascal	J. A. Krone	Clever Actor	Recommended List	8	1:43.21	$45,000
1997	Trample	P. Day	Willing	Keep It Strait	12	1:42.84	$45,000
1996	Rough Opening	E. Maple	Sharp Appeal	Sampras	10	1:44.05	$45,000
1995	Native Regent	D. Penna	Hollywood Flash	Dixie Dynasty	11	1:43.73	$60,000
1994	Mr. Angel	W. H. McCauley	Pad	Ali'lbito'reality	9	1:48.17	$60,000
1993	Hegar	J. C. Ferrer	Mighty Avanti	Pride Prevails	7	1:52.04	$30,000

1992 not held. 2000 held at Gulfstream Park. 1993-'94 1¹⁄₈ miles. 1993, 2000 dirt.

Excelsior Breeders' Cup Handicap

Grade 3, Aqueduct, three-year-olds and up, 1¹⁄₈ miles, dirt. Held April 28, 2001, with a gross value of $190,000. First held in 1903. Graded since 1973. Stakes record 1:47.69 (1997 Ormsby).

Year	Winner	Jockey	Second	Third	Strs	Final Time	1st Purse
2001	Cat's At Home, 4, 115	F. Leon	Top Official, 6	Boston Party, 6	8	1:48.92	$120,000
2000	Lager, 6, 113	H. Castillo Jr.	Best of Luck, 4	Chester House, 4	9	1:49.76	$120,000
1999	Smart Coupons, 6, 114	R. R. Douglas	Archers Bay, 4	Pasay, 4	9	1:49.71	$120,000
1998	Sir Bear, 5, 117	E. M. Jurado	K. J.'s Appeal, 4	Accelerator, 4	8	1:49.24	$120,000
1997	Ormsby, 5, 116	C. C. Lopez	Greatsilverfleet, 7	Circle of Light, 7	9	**1:47.69**	$120,000
1996	May I Inquire, 7, 111	J. Bravo	Personal Merit, 5	Ormsby, 5	8	1:50.67	$120,000
1995	Iron Gavel, 5, 111	J. R. Martinez Jr.	Electrojet, 6	Danzig's Dance, 6	7	1:49.28	$90,000
1994	Colonial Affair, 4, 121	J. A. Santos	Contract Court, 4	West by West, 4	6	1:49.82	$90,000
1993	Devil His Due, 4, 117	M. E. Smith	Exotic Slew, 6	Bill Of Rights, 6	10	2:03.05	$72,120
1992	Defensive Play, 5, 117	D. R. Flores	Alyten, 4	Will to Reign, 4	5	2:01.95	$102,780

1992-'95 Excelsior H. 1992-'97 Grade 2. 1992-'93 1¹⁄₄ miles.

Explosive Bid Handicap

Grade 2, Fair Grounds, four-year-olds and up, 1¹⁄₈ miles, turf. Held March 25, 2001, with a gross value of $600,000. First held in 1992. Graded since 1996. Stakes record 1:48.98 (2000 Brave Act [GB]).

Year	Winner	Jockey	Second	Third	Strs	Final Time	1st Purse
2001	Tijiyr (Ire), 5, 110	R. Albarado	Northcote Road, 6	King Cugat, 6	13	1:50.72	$360,000
2000	Brave Act (GB), 6, 121	C. B. Asmussen	Where's Taylor, 4	Chester House, 4	13	**1:48.98**	$360,000
1999	Lord Smith (GB), 4, 117	G. K. Gomez	Hawksley Hill (Ire), 6	Chorwon, 6	12	1:51.27	$398,160
1998	Joyeux Danseur, 5, 121	R. Albarado	Martiniquais (Ire), 5	Hollie's Chief, 5	9	1:49.30	$223,980
1997	Always a Classic, 4, 114	E. M. Martin Jr.	Rainbow Blues (Ire), 4	Snake Eyes, 4	7	1:54.83	$131,970
1996	Kazabaiyn, 6, 113	K. J. Desormeaux	Party Season (GB), 5	Coaxing Matt, 5	10	1:50.80	$93,195
1995	Earl of Barking (Ire), 5, 115	G. F. Almeida	Kazabaiyn, 5	Coaxing Matt, 5	11	1:52.01	$93,375
1994	Pride of Summer, 6, 113	R. King Jr.	Alpine Choice, 6	Empire Pool (GB), 6	10	1:49.59	$76,425
	Snake Eyes, 4, 115	B. E. Bartram	Yukon Robbery, 5	(DH) Dipotamos, 6 (DH) Cozzene's Prince, 7	8	1:49.41	$76,305
1993	Coaxing Matt, 4, 114	E. M. Martin Jr.	Dixie Poker Ace, 6	Spending Record, 6	12	1:50.80	$47,010
1992	Slick Groom, 4, 112	K. P. LeBlanc	Little Bro Lantis, 4	Brownsboro, 4	10	1:52.60	$31,590

1992-'94 Explosive Bid S. 1996-2000 Grade 3. 1994 two divisions. 1994 dead heat for third (2nd Div.). 1992 City Ballet finished first, DQ to sixth.

Fair Grounds Oaks

Grade 2, Fair Grounds, three-year-old fillies, 1¹⁄₁₆ miles, dirt. Held March 10, 2001, with a gross value of $350,000. First held in 1966. Graded since 1982. Stakes record 1:42.38 (1997 Blushing K. D.).

Year	Winner	Jockey	Second	Third	Strs	Final Time	1st Purse
2001	**Real Cozzy**	E. M. Martin Jr.	Mystic Lady	She's a Devil Due	9	1:44.58	$210,000
2000	**Shawnee Country**	D. J. Meche	Eden Lodge	Zoftig	9	1:44.81	$210,000
1999	**Silverbulletday**	G. L. Stevens	Runaway Venus	Brushed Halory	7	1:44.99	$223,740
1998	**Lu Ravi**	W. Martinez	Well Chosen	Silent Eskimo	6	1:43.70	$180,000
1997	**Blushing K. D.**	L. Meche	Tomisue's Delight	Cozy Blues	5	**1:42.38**	$105,000
1996	**Bright Time**	L. F. Diaz	Mackie	Proper Dance	6	1:45.98	$94,530
1995	**Brushing Gloom**	J. Brown	Kuda	Legendary Priness	9	1:45.12	$90,000
1994	**Two Altazano**	K. P. LeBlanc	Tricky Code	Minority Dater	6	1:42.50	$93,840
1993	**Silky Feather**	E. J. Perrodin	She's a Little Shy	Sum Runner	7	1:44.60	$64,080
1992	**Prospectors Delite**	P. Day	Glitzi Bj	Desert Radiance	7	1:44.20	$63,990

1992-2000 Grade 3. 1994 equaled track record.

Fall Highweight Handicap

Grade 2, Aqueduct, three-year-olds and up, 6 furlongs, dirt. Held November 22, 2001, with a gross value of $112,200. First held in 1914. Graded since 1973. Stakes record 1:08.40 (1944 Ariel Lad; 1952 Hitex).

Year	Winner	Jockey	Second	Third	Strs	Final Time	1st Purse
2001	**Yonaguska**, 3, 131	J. A. Santos	Big E E, 4	Voodoo, 4	8	1:09.60	$67,320
2000	**Kashatreya**, 6, 131	O. Vergara	Exciting Story, 3	Oro de Mexico, 3	8	1:11.03	$67,140
1999	**Richter Scale**, 5, 134	J. F. Chavez	Aristotle, 3	Bought in Dixie, 3	7	1:09.05	$66,060
1998	**Punch Line**, 8, 136	J. F. Chavez	American Champ, 4	Golden Tent, 4	9	1:10.07	$66,840
1997	**Royal Haven**, 5, 136	R. Migliore	King Roller, 6	Kelly Kip, 6	7	1:10.68	$65,820
1996	**Victor Avenue**, 3, 127	J. F. Chavez	Splendid Sprinter, 4	Stalwart Member, 4	10	1:09.24	$67,440
1995	**Jess C's Whirl**, 5, 126	J. F. Chavez	†Classy Mirage, 5	Demaloot Demashoot, 5	8	1:09.87	$66,180
1994	**Chimes Band**, 3, 135	J. D. Bailey	Golden Pro, 4	Boom Towner, 4	6	1:11.37	$65,940
1993	**Fly So Free**, 5, 135	J. D. Bailey	Demaloot Demashoot, 3	Take Me Out, 3	10	1:09.41	$72,360
1992	**Salt Lake**, 3, 128	M. E. Smith	Burn Fair, 5	Belong to Me, 5	6	1:09.07	$68,520

1992-'93 held at Belmont. † denotes female.

Falls City Handicap

Grade 3, Churchill Downs, three-year-olds and up, fillies and mares, 1⅛ miles, dirt. Held November 22, 2001, with a gross value of $273,500. First held in 1875. Graded since 1973. Stakes record 1:48.85 (1998 Silent Eskimo).

Year	Winner	Jockey	Second	Third	Strs	Final Time	1st Purse
2001	**Forest Secrets**, 3, 113	C. Perret	Printemps (Chi), 4	Unbridled Elaine, 4	7	1:49.49	$169,570
2000	**Bordelaise (Arg)**, 5, 117	P. Day	Spain, 3	On a Soapbox, 3	5	1:50.01	$168,020
1999	**Silent Eskimo**, 4, 117	C. H. Borel	Let, 4	Pleasant Temper, 4	8	**1:48.85**	$171,585
1998	**Tomisue's Delight**, 4, 121	S. J. Sellers	Top Secret, 5	Silent Eskimo, 5	8	1:51.05	$171,740
1997	**Feasibility Study**, 5, 122	M. E. Smith	Omi, 4	Naskra Colors, 4	7	1:50.65	$170,345
1996	**Halo America**, 6, 118	C. H. Borel	Bedroom Blues, 5	Debit My Account, 5	8	1:49.08	$171,120
1995	**Mariah's Storm**, 4, 120	R. N. Lester	Alcovy, 5	Heavenliness, 5	7	1:51.37	$143,390
1994	**Alcovy**, 4, 114	S. E. Miller	Pennyhill Park, 4	Hey Hazel, 4	7	1:51.16	$141,440
1993	**Gray Cashmere**, 4, 120	P. Day	Avie's Shadow, 3	Princess Polonia, 3	7	1:50.96	$142,090
1992	**Bungalow**, 5, 118	P. Day	Wilderness Song, 4	Auto Dial, 4	7	1:52.03	$70,915

Fantasy Stakes

Grade 2, Oaklawn Park, three-year-old fillies, 1¹⁄₁₆ miles, dirt. Held April 13, 2001, with a gross value of $200,000. First held in 1973. Graded since 1975. Stakes record 1:41.20 (1984 My Darling One).

Year	Winner	Jockey	Second	Third	Strs	Final Time	1st Purse
2001	**Mystic Lady**	E. Coa	Collect Call	Mysia Jo	10	1:43.32	$120,000
2000	**Classy Cara**	I. Puglisi	Eden Lodge	Gold for My Gal	8	1:43.95	$120,000
1999	**Excellent Meeting**	K. J. Desormeaux	The Happy Hopper	Dreams Gallore	6	1:42.73	$150,000
1998	**Silent Eskimo**	C. Gonzalez	Misty Hour	Came Unwound	8	1:43.84	$150,000
1997	**Blushing K. D.**	L. Meche	Valid Bonnet	Ajina	5	1:42.61	$150,000
1996	**Escena**	P. Day	Antespend	Ski Trail	7	1:43.93	$150,000
1995	**Cat's Cradle**	C. W. Antley	Forever Cherokee	Humble Eight	8	1:44.29	$150,000
1994	**Two Altazano**	K. P. LeBlanc	Slide Show	Flying in the Lane	11	1:43.64	$150,000
1993	**Aztec Hill**	M. E. Smith	Adorydar	Stalcreek	7	1:44.33	$150,000
1992	**Race the Wild Wind**	C. J. McCarron	Golden Treat	Now Dance	8	1:43.74	$150,000

Fastness Handicap

Grade 3, Hollywood Park, three-year-olds and up, 1⅛ miles, turf. Held May 13, 2001, with a gross value of $110,400. First held in 1997. Graded since 2000. Stakes record 1:46.50 (1999 Bonapartiste [Fr]).

Year	Winner	Jockey	Second	Third	Strs	Final Time	1st Purse
2001	**Irish Prize**, 5, 119	G. L. Stevens	Timboroa (GB), 5	City West (Arg), 5	8	1:50.01	$66,240
2000	**Senure**, 4, 114	B. Blanc	Bonapartiste (Fr), 6	Hook Call (Brz), 6	5	1:47.00	$64,020

Year	Winner	Jockey	Second	Third	Strs	Final Time	1st Purse
1999	**Bonapartiste (Fr)**, 5, 121	C. J. McCarron	Alvo Certo (Brz), 6	Native Desert, 6	6	**1:46.50**	$45,990
1998	**Vetheuil**, 6, 113	B. Blanc	Via Lombardia (Ire), 6	Flick (GB), 6	9	1:34.52	$43,620
1997	**Helmsman**, 5, 123	C. J. McCarron	Smooth Runner, 6	Khoraz, 6	4	1:34.69	$42,800

1997-'98 1 mile.

Fayette Stakes

Grade 3, Keeneland, three-year-olds and up, 1⅛ miles, dirt. Held October 27, 2001, with a gross value of $166,950. First held in 1959. Graded since 1979. Stakes record 1:46.80 (1987 Good Command).

Year	Winner	Jockey	Second	Third	Strs	Final Time	1st Purse
2001	**Connected**, 4	M. St. Julien	Broken Vow, 4	Outofthebox, 4	9	1:50.05	$103,509
2000	**Jadada**, 5	S. J. Sellers	Mojave Moon, 4	Get Away With It (Ire), 4	5	1:54.92	$133,176
1999	**Social Charter**, 4	M. St. Julien	Master O Foxhounds, 4	Early Warning, 4	4	1:55.28	$135,904
1998	**Arch**, 3	S. J. Sellers	Touch Gold, 4	Wild Tempest, 4	4	1:53.87	$98,394
1997	**Whiskey Wisdom**, 4	W. Martinez	City by Night, 4	Pyramid Peak, 4	6	1:48.64	$101,184
1996	**Isitingood**, 5	D. R. Flores	Distorted Humor, 3	Strawberry Wine, 3	8	1:50.42	$120,110
1995	**Judge T C**, 4	J. M. Johnson	Powerful Punch, 6	Sir Vixen, 6	9	1:49.05	$104,625
1994	**Sunny Sunrise**, 7	J. D. Carle	Key Contender, 6	Powerful Punch, 6	7	1:50.18	$67,766
1993	**Grand Jewel**, 3	J. D. Bailey	Split Run, 5	Secreto's Hideaway, 5	8	1:46.87	$68,634
1992	**Barkerville**, 4	S. J. Sellers	Medium Cool, 4	Majesterian, 4	11	1:48.43	$70,680

1999-2000 Fayette Breeders' Cup S. 1992-'96 Grade 2. 1998-2000 1³⁄₁₆ miles. 1993 equaled track record; 1998 new track record.

Fifth Season Breeders' Cup Stakes

Grade 3, Oaklawn Park, three-year-olds and up, 1¹⁄₁₆ miles, dirt. Held April 11, 2001, with a gross value of $95,000. First held in 1988. Graded since 1999. Stakes record 1:40.30 (1991 Hang on Slewpy).

Year	Winner	Jockey	Second	Third	Strs	Final Time	1st Purse
2001	**Remington Rock**, 7	D. E. Simington	Kombat Kat, 4	Da Devil, 4	7	1:43.13	$45,000
2000	**Mr Ross**, 5	E. C. Perner	Relic Reward, 6	Crimson Classic, 6	7	1:42.93	$60,000
1999	**Truluck**, 4	L. Melancon	Slide to the Left, 4	Rock and Roll, 4	8	1:42.28	$60,000
1998	**Acceptable**, 4	A. O. Solis	Littlebitlively, 4	Brush With Pride, 4	8	1:42.50	$60,000
1997	**Krigeorj's Gold**, 4	J. M. Johnson	Bucks Nephew, 7	Prince of the Mt., 7	9	1:43.35	$49,050
1996	**No Spend No Glow**, 4	R. N. Lester	Bucks Nephew, 6	Groovy Jett, 6	7	1:42.96	$47,880
1995	**Tyus**, 5	C. H. Borel	Prince of the Mt., 4	Joseph's Robe, 4	7	1:42.98	$26,760
1994	**Nelson**, 7	S. P. Romero	Punch Line, 4	Senor Tomas, 4	6	1:43.16	$41,640
1993	**Delafield**, 4	J. A. Santos	Far Out Wadleigh, 5	Lanyons Star, 5	11	1:42.43	$43,080
1992	**Medium Cool**, 4	C. S. Nakatani	On the Edge, 5	Hayes G., 5	10	1:43.35	$40,500

Firecracker Breeders' Cup Handicap

Grade 2, Churchill Downs, three-year-olds and up, 1 mile, turf. Held July 4, 2001, with a gross value of $276,000. First held in 1993. Graded since 1995. Stakes record 1:33.78 (1995 Jaggery John).

Year	Winner	Jockey	Second	Third	Strs	Final Time	1st Purse
2001	**Irish Prize**, 5, 122	G. L. Stevens	Aly's Alley, 5	Where's Taylor, 5	7	1:34.68	$175,770
2000	**Conserve**, 4, 116	S. J. Sellers	Riviera (Fr), 6	King Slayer (GB), 6	8	1:35.12	$177,940
1999	**Joe Who (Brz)**, 6, 113	R. Albarado	Middlesex Drive, 4	Wild Event, 4	9	1:36.78	$132,680
1998	**Claire's Honor**, 4, 109	A. J. D'Amico	Soviet Line (Ire), 8	Optic Nerve, 8	9	1:35.93	$177,630
1997	**Soviet Line (Ire)**, 7, 114	P. Day	Volochine (Ire), 6	Same Old Wish, 6	10	1:37.67	$126,077
1996	**Rare Reason**, 5, 115	P. A. Johnson	Artema (Ire), 5	Wavy Run (Ire), 5	9	1:33.81	$131,950
1995	**Jaggery John**, 4, 113	D. Kutz	Rare Reason, 4	Fly Cry, 4	10	**1:33.78**	$74,360
1994	**First and Only**, 7, 118	T. J. Hebert	†Weekend Madness (Ire), 4	Avid Affection, 4	8	1:35.33	$73,580
1993	**Cleone**, 4, 115	C. Perret	Magesterial Cheer, 5	Harlan, 5	9	1:35.90	$74,815

1993-'95 Firecracker H. 1995-'99 Grade 3. 2001 Where's Taylor finished second, DQ to third. 1995 new course record. † denotes female.

First Flight Handicap

Grade 2, Belmont Park, three-year-olds and up, fillies and mares, 7 furlongs, dirt. Held October 26, 2001, with a gross value of $150,000. First held in 1978. Graded since 1982. Stakes record 1:20.65 (1992 Shared Interest).

Year	Winner	Jockey	Second	Third	Strs	Final Time	1st Purse
2001	**Shine Again**, 4, 116	J-L. Samyn	Dream Supreme, 4	Kalookan Queen, 4	6	1:23.21	$90,000
2000	**Country Hideaway**, 4, 117	J. L. Espinoza	Go to the Ink, 4	Cat Cay, 4	7	1:22.60	$90,000
1999	**Country Hideaway**, 3, 114	H. Castillo Jr.	Harpia, 5	Anklet, 5	8	1:23.00	$90,000
1998	**Catinca**, 3, 116	R. Migliore	Glitter Woman, 4	Blue Begonia, 4	7	1:22.14	$82,260
1997	**Dixie Flag**, 3, 113	M. J. Luzzi	Silent City, 3	Aldiza, 3	4	1:22.84	$64,800
1996	**Thunder Achiever**, 3, 112	R. G. Davis	Miss Golden Circle, 4	Call Account, 4	10	1:21.59	$81,864
1995	**Twist Afleet**, 4, 121	G. L. Stevens	Igotrhythm, 3	Lottsa Talc, 3	5	1:22.95	$66,780
1994	**Twist Afleet**, 3, 117	J. D. Bailey	Ann Dear, 4	Incinerate, 4	8	1:23.02	$66,120
1993	**Raise Heck**, 5, 114	R. I. Velez	Regal Victress, 6	Shared Interest, 6	6	1:23.51	$69,000
1992	**Shared Interest**, 4, 111	J. D. Bailey	Missy's Mirage, 4	Nannerl, 4	5	**1:20.65**	$120,000

1993-'94, 1996-2000 held at Aqueduct.

First Lady Handicap

Grade 3, Gulfstream Park, three-year-olds and up, fillies and mares, 6 furlongs, dirt. Held January 14, 2001, with a gross value of $117,000. First held in 1981. Graded since 1993. Stakes record 1:09.60 (1999 Scotzanna).

Year	Winner	Jockey	Second	Third	Strs	Final Time	1st Purse
2001	**Another**, 4, 113	E. S. Prado	Curious Treasures, 4	Dynamite Diablo, 4	11	1:10.41	$60,000
2000	**Hurricane Bertie**, 5, 118	P. Day	Marley Vale, 4	Cassidy, 4	7	1:10.22	$45,000
1999	**Scotzanna**, 7, 114	R. Migliore	U Can Do It, 6	Foil, 6	8	**1:09.60**	$45,000
1998	**U Can Do It**, 5, 115	S. J. Sellers	Start At Once, 5	Vivace, 5	10	1:09.86	$45,000
1997	**Chip**, 4, 113	J. Bravo	Phone the Doctor, 5	Surprising Fact, 5	10	1:09.76	$45,000
1996	**Chaposa Springs**, 4, 122	J. D. Bailey	Phone the Doctor, 4	Market Slide, 4	9	1:10.23	$45,000
1995	**Recognizable**, 4, 113	M. E. Smith	Insight to Cope, 5	Maison de Reve, 5	10	1:09.74	$30,000
1994	**Santa Catalina**, 6, 114	J. D. Bailey	Insight to Cope, 4	Capture the Crown, 4	11	1:11.26	$30,000
1993	**Si Si Sezyou**, 5, 112	R. Hernandez	Illeria, 6	Jeano, 6	11	1:10.06	$30,000
1992	**Withallprobability**, 4, 118	C. Perret	Christina Czarina, 4	Spirit of Fighter, 4	14	1:11.14	$30,000

Flamingo Stakes

Grade 3, Hialeah Park, three-year-olds and up, 1⅛ miles, dirt. Held April 7, 2001, with a gross value of $250,000. First held in 1926. Graded since 1973. Stakes record 1:46.80 (1976 Honest Pleasure).

Year	Winner	Jockey	Second	Third	Strs	Final Time	1st Purse
2001	**Thunder Blitz**	E. S. Prado	Tour of the Cat	Talk Is Money	9	1:48.23	$150,000
2000	**Trippi**	E. Coa	Kombat Kat	Skip a Grade	11	1:50.04	$150,000
1999	**First American**	J. A. Velez Jr.	Forty One Carats	Vision and Verse	8	1:48.90	$150,000
1998	**Chilito**	G. Boulanger	Raffie's Majesty	Comic Strip	8	1:49.70	$120,000
1997	**Frisk Me Now**	E. L. King Jr.	Gold Book	Michelle'sallhands	7	1:52.32	$120,000
1996	**El Amante**	R. B. Perez	Bold Lachee	Will's Way	9	1:49.33	$120,000
1995	**Pyramid Peak**	W. H. McCauley	Royal Mitch	Bullet Trained	8	1:48.16	$120,000
1994	**Meadow Flight**	C. Perret	Bay Street Star	Amathos	10	1:49.63	$120,000
1993	**Forever Whirl**	A. Toribio	Bull Inthe Heather	Pride Prevails	9	1:51.38	$120,000
1992	**Pistols and Roses**	H. Castillo Jr.	Pick Up the Phone	Choctaw Ridge	12	1:50.79	$280,000

1992-'93 not graded. 2000 held at Gulfstream Park.

Flash Stakes

Grade 3, Belmont Park, two-year-olds, 5 furlongs, dirt. Held June 8, 2001, with a gross value of $82,275. First held in 1869. Graded since 2001. Stakes record :56.93 (2001 Buster's Daydream).

Year	Winner	Jockey	Second	Third	Strs	Final Time	1st Purse
2001	**Buster's Daydream**	E. S. Prado	Harmony Hall	Huber Woods	8	**:56.93**	$49,365
2000	**Yonaguska**	J. D. Bailey	The Goo	City Zip	7	:57.86	$49,470
1999	**More Than Ready**	J. R. Velazquez	Diablo's Addition	Bevo	6	:57.10	$49,245

1992-'98 not held.

Fleur de Lis Handicap

Grade 3, Churchill Downs, three-year-olds and up, fillies and mares, 1⅛ miles, dirt. Held June 16, 2001, with a gross value of $333,000. First held in 1975. Graded since 1988. Stakes record 1:48.26 (2000 Heritage of Gold).

Year	Winner	Jockey	Second	Third	Strs	Final Time	1st Purse
2001	**Saudi Poetry**, 4, 114	V. Espinoza	Secret Status, 4	Asher, 4	8	1:49.27	$206,460
2000	**Heritage of Gold**, 5, 121	S. J. Sellers	Silverbulletday, 4	Roza Robata, 4	5	**1:48.26**	$201,252
1999	**Banshee Breeze**, 4, 124	R. Albarado	Silent Eskimo, 4	Meadow Vista, 4	4	1:50.02	$197,718
1998	**Escena**, 5, 123	S. J. Sellers	One Rich Lady, 4	Tomisue's Delight, 4	5	1:50.19	$199,020
1997	**Gold n Delicious**, 4, 113	C. H. Borel	Effectiveness, 4	Everhope, 4	10	1:52.87	$104,718
1996	**Serena's Song**, 4, 124	G. L. Stevens	Halo America, 6	Alcovy, 6	9	1:50.30	$109,493
1995	**Fit to Lead**, 5, 117	S. J. Sellers	Pennyhill Park, 5	Low Key Affair, 5	7	1:51.59	$107,055
1994	**Trishyde**, 5, 117	C. J. McCarron	Eskimo's Angel, 5	Ma Guerre, 5	8	1:51.34	$107,315
1993	**Quilma (Chi)**, 6, 117	R. P. Romero	Fappies Cosy Miss, 5	Hitch, 5	6	1:50.80	$71,240
1992	**Bungalow**, 5, 114	F. C. Torres	Til Forbid, 4	Beth Believes, 4	12	1:50.87	$74,815

Floral Park Handicap

Not graded, Belmont Park, three-year-olds and up, fillies and mares, 6 furlongs, dirt. Held September 9, 2001, with a gross value of $108,400. First held in 1995. Grade 3 since 2002. Stakes record 1:09.20 (1995 Twist Afleet).

Year	Winner	Jockey	Second	Third	Strs	Final Time	1st Purse
2001	**Gold Mover**, 3, 114	E. S. Prado	Dat You Miz Blue, 4	Finder's Fee, 4	6	1:10.03	$65,040
2000	**Big Bambu**, 3, 114	R. G. Davis	Tropical Punch, 4	Cash Run, 4	5	1:09.81	$64,620
1999	**Positive Gal**, 3, 113	J. D. Bailey	Final Proposal, 3	Flamingo Way, 3	7	1:09.23	$49,125
1998	**Blue Begonia**, 5, 114	J. F. Chavez	Dixie Flag, 4	Soverign Lady, 4	5	1:10.30	$48,570
1997	**Creamy Dreamy**, 4, 118	R. G. Davis	Silent City, 3	Secret Prospect, 3	5	1:10.56	$47,835
1996	**Lottsa Talc**, 6, 119	F. T. Alvarado	Fresa, 4	Culver City, 4	5	1:09.81	$38,736
1995	**Twist Afleet**, 4, 120	G. L. Stevens	For all Seasons, 5	Regal Solution, 5	6	**1:09.20**	$32,490

Florida Derby

Grade 1, Gulfstream Park, three-year-olds, 1⅛ miles, dirt. Held March 10, 2001, with a gross value of $1,000,000. First held in 1952. Graded since 1973. Stakes record 1:46.80 (1957 Gen. Duke).

Year	Winner	Jockey	Second	Third	Strs	Final Time	1st Purse
2001	Monarchos	J. F. Chavez	Outofthebox	Invisible Ink	13	1:49.95	$600,000
2000	Hal's Hope	R. I. Velez	High Yield	Tahkodha Hills	10	1:51.49	$450,000
1999	Vicar	S. J. Sellers	Wondertross	Cat Thief	10	1:50.83	$450,000
1998	Cape Town	S. J. Sellers	Lil's Lad	Halory Hunter	6	1:49.21	$450,000
1997	Captain Bodgit	A. O. Solis	Pulpit	Frisk Me Now	8	1:50.74	$300,000
1996	Unbridled's Song	M. E. Smith	Editor's Note	Skip Away	9	1:47.85	$300,000
1995	Thunder Gulch	M. E. Smith	Suave Prospect	Mecke	10	1:49.70	$300,000
1994	Holy Bull	M. E. Smith	Ride the Rails	Halo's Image	14	1:47.66	$300,000
1993	Bull Inthe Heather	W. S. Ramos	Storm Tower	Wallenda	13	1:51.38	$300,000
1992	Technology	J. D. Bailey	Dance Floor	Pistols and Roses	12	1:50.72	$300,000

1998 Lil's Lad finished first, DQ to second.

Florida Oaks

Grade 3, Tampa Bay Downs, three-year-old fillies, 1¹⁄₁₆ miles, dirt. Held March 18, 2001, with a gross value of $150,000. First held in 1984. Graded since 1996. Stakes record 1:44.60 (1986 Noranc).

Year	Winner	Jockey	Second	Third	Strs	Final Time	1st Purse
2001	Quick Tip	R. Migliore	Southern Fiction	Emery Board	9	1:45.36	$90,000
2000	Secret Status	P. Day	March Magic	Musical	8	1:45.05	$75,000
1999	Crown Jewel	L. J. Martinez	Madison's Charm	Here I Go	7	1:46.69	$60,000
1998	Pantufla	P. Day	Puddlejump	Try N Sue	7	1:45.40	$60,000
1997	Anklet	S. J. Sellers	Global Star	Screamer	10	1:45.00	$60,000
1996	Mindy Gayle	J. A. Guerra	Plum Country	Weekend in Seattle	7	1:45.80	$60,000
1995	Sneaky Quiet	M. E. Smith	Commando Dancer	Smooth Quest	6	1:45.40	$60,000
1994	Cavada	K. Whitley	Come On Joy	Strategic Maneuver	7	1:46.40	$60,000
1993	Star Jolie	E. O. Nunez	Hollywood Wildcat	Jacody	11	1:45.60	$60,000
1992	Luv Me Luv Me Not	W. Martinez	Now Dance	Foxy Persuasion	8	1:45.60	$60,000

Flower Bowl Invitational Stakes

Grade 1, Belmont Park, three-year-olds and up, fillies and mares, 1¼ miles, turf. Held September 29, 2001, with a gross value of $750,000. First held in 1978. Graded since 1980. Stakes record 1:59.33 (1998 Auntie Mame).

Year	Winner	Jockey	Second	Third	Strs	Final Time	1st Purse
2001	Lailani (GB), 3	J. D. Bailey	England's Legend (Fr), 4	Starine (Fr), 4	6	2:01.88	$450,000
2000	Colstar, 4	J-L. Samyn	Snow Polina, 5	Pico Teneriffe, 5	5	2:01.78	$450,000
1999	Soaring Softly, 4	J. D. Bailey	Coretta (Ire), 5	Mossflower, 5	7	2:01.41	$300,000
1998	Auntie Mame, 4	J. R. Velazquez	B. A. Valentine, 5	Bahr (GB), 5	5	1:59.33	$240,000
1997	Yashmak, 3	C. S. Nakatani	Maxzene, 4	Memories of Silver, 4	8	1:59.73	$240,000
1996	Chelsey Flower, 5	R. G. Davis	Powder Bowl, 4	Electric Society (Ire), 4	10	2:05.96	$210,000
1995	Northern Emerald, 5	R. B. Perez	Danish (Ire), 4	Duda, 4	10	2:06.68	$120,000
1994	Dahlia's Dreamer, 5	J. F. Chavez	Alywow, 3	Danish (Ire), 3	12	2:05.52	$120,000
1993	Far Out Beast, 6	J-L. Samyn	Dahlia's Dreamer, 4	Lady Blessington (Fr), 4	10	2:03.88	$90,000
1992	Christiecat, 5	J-L. Samyn	Ratings, 4	Plenty of Grace, 4	9	2:01.06	$120,000

1992-'93 Flower Bowl H.

Forego Handicap

Grade 1, Saratoga Race Course, three-year-olds and up, 6½ furlongs, dirt. Held September 1, 2001, with a gross value of $250,000. First held in 1980. Graded since 1983. Stakes record 1:15 (2000 Shadow Caster).

Year	Winner	Jockey	Second	Third	Strs	Final Time	1st Purse
2001	Delaware Township, 5, 116	J. D. Bailey	Left Bank, 4	Alannan, 4	9	1:15.53	$150,000
2000	Shadow Caster, 4, 113	J. F. Chavez	Intidab, 7	Successful Appeal, 7	10	1:15.00	$150,000
1999	Crafty Friend, 6, 119	G. L. Stevens	Affirmed Success, 5	Sir Bear, 5	9	1:21.32	$150,000
1998	Affirmed Success, 4, 115	J. F. Chavez	Receiver, 5	Purple Passion, 5	4	1:21.98	$120,000
1997	Score a Birdie, 6, 113	W. H. McCauley	Victor Cooley, 4	Royal Haven, 4	8	1:22.47	$120,000
1996	Langfuhr, 4, 110	J. F. Chavez	Top Account, 4	Lite the Fuse, 4	7	1:21.90	$90,000
1995	Not Surprising, 5, 121	R. G. Davis	Our Emblem, 4	Lite the Fuse, 4	4	1:21.91	$64,200
1994	American Chance, 5, 113	P. Day	Evil Bear, 4	Go for Gin, 4	7	1:22.74	$66,000
1993	Birdonthewire, 4, 117	M. E. Smith	Harlan, 4	Senor Speedy, 4	9	1:21.88	$73,080
1992	Rubiano, 5, 124	J. A. Krone	Drummond Lane, 5	Diablo, 5	8	1:22.54	$70,080

1992-2000 Grade 2. 1992-'99 7 furlongs.

Forest Hills Handicap

Grade 2, Belmont Park, three-year-olds and up, 6 furlongs, dirt. Held October 7, 2001, with a gross value of $250,000. First held in 1975. Graded since 1984. Stakes record 1:07.66 (1999 Artax).

Year	Winner	Jockey	Second	Third	Strs	Final Time	1st Purse
2001	Delaware Township, 5, 118	E. Coa	Hook and Ladder, 4	Yonaguska, 4	5	1:09.49	$150,000
2000	Delaware Township, 4, 114	P. Day	Bevo, 3	Valiant Halory, 3	7	1:08.56	$150,000

Year	Winner	Jockey	Second	Third	Strs	Final Time	1st Purse
1999	**Artax**, 4, 120	J. F. Chavez	Good and Tough, 4	Intidab, 4	7	**1:07.66**	$150,000
1998	**Punch Line**, 8, 118	J. F. Chavez	King Roller, 7	Johnny Legit, 7	7	1:09.67	$120,000
1997	**Kelly Kip**, 3, 111	J-L. Samyn	Crafty Friend, 4	Royal Haven, 4	11	1:08.83	$120,000
1996	**Lord Carson**, 4, 116	S. J. Sellers	Honour and Glory, 3	Splendid Sprinter, 3	9	1:08.72	$105,000
1995	**Friendly Lover**, 7, 118	R. Wilson	Lite the Fuse, 4	Mining Burrah, 4	11	1:10.13	$86,100
1994	**Meritocrat**, 3, 113	M. E. Smith	Birdonthewire, 5	Lite the Fuse, 5	8	1:09.03	$83,025
1993	**Boom Towner**, 5, 113	F. Lovato Jr.	Take Me Out, 5	Thelastcrusade, 5	7	1:09.29	$69,360
1992	**Belong to Me**, 3, 112	M. E. Smith	Diablo, 5	Fast Turn, 5	9	1:10.05	$71,280

1992-'96 Boojum H. 1992-'93 Grade 3. 1992-'93 held at Aqueduct. 1999 new track record.

Fort Lauderdale Handicap

Grade 3, Gulfstream Park, three-year-olds and up, 1¹⁄₁₆ miles, turf. Held March 11, 2000, with a gross value of $100,000. First held in 1947. Graded since 1995. Stakes record 1:39.30 (1994 Paradise Creek).

Year	Winner	Jockey	Second	Third	Strs	Final Time	1st Purse
2000	**Beckon the King**, 4, 114	J. D. Bailey	Kettle Won, 4	Missionary, 4	8	1:40.36	$60,000
1999	**Garbu**, 5, 113	J. D. Bailey	Wild Event, 6	Sharp Appeal, 6	8	1:39.33	$60,000
1998	**Statesmanship**, 4, 114	J. A. Santos	Subordination, 4	Donthelumbertrader, 4	9	1:40.46	$60,000
1997	**Doublethebetwice**, 4, 116	J. D. Bailey	Donthelumbertrader, 4	Volochine (Ire), 4	8	1:42.61	$60,000
1996	**Winged Victory**, 6, 114	J. D. Bailey	Warning Glance, 5	Marcie's Ensign, 5	12	1:41.94	$60,000
1995	**The Vid**, 5, 120	J. D. Bailey	Flying American, 6	D J's Rainbow, 6	12	1:41.12	$60,000
1994	**Paradise Creek**, 5, 125	M. E. Smith	Bidding Proud, 5	Social Retiree, 5	9	**1:39.30**	$60,000
1993	**Archies Laughter**, 5, 114	J. A. Santos	Pidgeon's Promise, 4	May I Inquire, 4	5	1:44.13	$60,000
1992	**Now Listen**, 5, 114	J. A. Santos	Slew the Slewor, 5	Stage Colony, 5	12	1:40.44	$60,000

2001 not held. 1993 dirt. 1994, equaled course record.

Fort Marcy Handicap

Grade 3, Aqueduct, three-year-olds and up, 1¹⁄₁₆ miles, turf. Held May 5, 2001, with a gross value of $112,900. First held in 1975. Graded since 1980. Stakes record 1:40.88 (2000 Spindrift [Ire]).

Year	Winner	Jockey	Second	Third	Strs	Final Time	1st Purse
2001	**Strategic Mission**, 6, 118	R. Migliore	Pine Dance, 4	Legal Jousting (Ire), 4	9	1:41.62	$67,740
2000	**Spindrift (Ire)**, 5, 115	J-L. Samyn	Middlesex Drive, 5	Wised Up, 5	9	**1:40.88**	$67,680
1999	**Wised Up**, 4, 112	M. J. Luzzi	N B Forrest, 7	La-Faah (Ire), 7	11	1:45.03	$69,660
1998	**Subordination**, 4, 118	J. F. Chavez	Fortitude, 5	Crimson Guard, 5	6	1:35.24	$67,620
1997	**Influent**, 6, 117	J-L. Samyn	Slicious (GB), 5	Montjoy, 5	8	1:47.59	$67,440
1996	**Warning Glance**, 5, 119	M. E. Smith	Shahid (GB), 4	Grand Continental, 4	10	1:42.48	$51,450
1995	**Fourstars Allstar**, 7, 118	J. A. Santos	Chief Master, 5	A in Sociology, 5	8	1:41.69	$50,250
1994	**Adam Smith (GB)**, 6, 118	M. E. Smith	Halissee, 4	Nijinsky's Gold, 4	7	1:42.49	$49,650
1993	**Adam Smith (GB)**, 5, 112	J-L. Samyn	Kiri's Clown, 4	Casino Magistrate, 4	11	1:42.30	$55,260
1992	**Maxigroom**, 4, 111	J. A. Krone	Colchis Island (Ire), 7	Buchman, 7	6	1:42.66	$53,460

1998 1 mile. 1998 dirt.

Forward Gal Stakes

Grade 3, Gulfstream Park, three-year-old fillies, 7 furlongs, dirt. Held January 28, 2001, with a gross value of $113,000. First held in 1981. Graded since 1986. Stakes record 1:21.76 (1997 Glitter Woman).

Year	Winner	Jockey	Second	Third	Strs	Final Time	1st Purse
2001	**Gold Mover**	J. D. Bailey	Hazino	Thunder Bertie	5	1:22.43	$60,000
2000	**Miss Inquisitive**	T. G. Turner	Swept Away	Regally Appealing	9	1:22.25	$45,000
1999	**China Storm**	P. Day	Three Ring	Extended Applause	6	1:23.69	$45,000
1998	**Uanme**	S. J. Sellers	Diamond On the Run	Holy Capote	7	1:24.56	$45,000
1997	**Glitter Woman**	M. E. Smith	City Band	Southern Playgirl	6	**1:21.76**	$45,000
1996	**Mindy Gayle**	J. A. Krone	Marfa's Finale	Supah Jen	7	1:24.54	$45,000
1995	**Chaposa Springs**	H. Castillo Jr.	Culver City	Mackenzie Slew	7	1:24.18	$44,580
1994	**Mynameispanama**	M. Castaneda	Frigid Coed	Wonderlan	9	1:22.97	$45,960
1993	**Sum Runner**	R. P. Romero	Boots 'n Jackie	Lunar Spook	9	1:23.67	$45,270
1992	**Spinning Round**	J. A. Santos	Patty's Princess	Super Doer	5	1:24.85	$44,550

1992-'95 Forward Gal Breeders' Cup S. 1992-'96 Grade 2.

Fountain of Youth Stakes

Grade 1, Gulfstream Park, three-year-olds, 1¹⁄₁₆ miles, dirt. Held February 17, 2001, with a gross value of $200,000. First held in 1945. Graded since 1973. Stakes record 1:41 (1978 Sensitive Prince).

Year	Winner	Jockey	Second	Third	Strs	Final Time	1st Purse
2001	**Songandaprayer**	E. S. Prado	Outofthebox	City Zip	11	1:43.48	$120,000
2000	**High Yield**	P. Day	Hal's Hope	Elite Mercedes	11	1:42.56	$120,000
1999	**Vicar**	S. J. Sellers	Cat Thief	Certain	10	1:45.64	$120,000
1998	**Lil's Lad**	J. D. Bailey	Coronado's Quest	Halory Hunter	4	1:42.63	$120,000

Year	Winner	Jockey	Second	Third	Strs	Final Time	1st Purse
1997	**Pulpit**	S. J. Sellers	Blazing Sword	Captain Bodgit	9	1:41.86	$120,000
1996	**Built for Pleasure**	G. Boulanger	Unbridled's Song	Victory Speech	9	1:43.64	$120,000
1995	**Thunder Gulch**	M. E. Smith	Suave Prospect	Jambalaya Jazz	12	1:43.21	$120,000
1994	**Dehere**	C. Perret	Go for Gin	Ride the Rails	6	1:44.70	$120,000
1993	**Duc d'Sligovil**	J. A. Krone	Bull Inthe Heather	Silver of Silver	9	1:45.16	$113,094
	Storm Tower	R. Wilson	Great Navigator	Kissin Kris	9	1:44.98	$113,094
1992	**Dance Floor**	C. W. Antley	Pistols and Roses	Tiger Tiger	11	1:45.32	$150,258

1993 two divisions. 1992-'98 Grade 2. 1992 Careful Gesture finished second, DQ to fifth.

Fourstardave Handicap

Grade 2, Saratoga Race Course, three-year-olds and up, $1\frac{1}{16}$ miles, turf. Held August 25, 2001, with a gross value of $200,000. First held in 1985. Graded since 1988. Stakes record 1:38.91 (1991 Fourstardave).

Year	Winner	Jockey	Second	Third	Strs	Final Time	1st Purse
2001	**Dr. Kashnikow**, 4, 113	J. R. Velazquez	Tubrok, 4	Aly's Alley, 4	12	1:39.30	$120,000
2000	**Hap**, 4, 118	J. D. Bailey	Altibr, 5	Weatherbird, 5	11	1:40.24	$120,000
1999	**Comic Strip**, 4, 115	P. Day	Divide and Conquer, 5	Bomfim, 5	11	1:41.76	$90,000
1998	**Wild Event**, 5, 116	M. Guidry	Bomfim, 5	Rob 'n Gin, 5	11	1:39.25	$68,940
1997	**Soviet Line (Ire)**, 7, 118	P. Day	Val's Prince, 5	Outta My Way Man, 5	7	1:39.99	$67,500
1996	**Da Hoss**, 4, 113	J. R. Velazquez	Green Means Go, 4	Rare Reason, 4	13	1:40.54	$71,100
1995	**Pride of Summer**, 7, 115	E. Maple	Fourstars Allstar, 7	Jaggery John, 7	8	1:40.85	$69,240
1994	**A in Sociology**, 4, 115	J-L. Samyn	Namaqualand, 4	Fourstars Allstar, 4	9	1:41.23	$68,340
1993	**Lure**, 4, 122	M. E. Smith	Fourstardave, 8	Scott the Great, 8	6	1:40.84	$72,120
1992	**Now Listen**, 5, 119	J. R. Velazquez	Crackedbell, 7	Cold Hoist, 7	5	1:36.64	$71,640

1992-'93, 1995 Daryl's Joy S.; 1994 Daryl's Joy H.; 1996-'97 Fourstardave S. 1992-'99 Grade 3. 1992 1 mile. 1992 dirt.

Frank E. Kilroe Mile Handicap

Grade 2, Santa Anita Park, four-year-olds and up, 1 mile, turf. Held March 3, 2001, with a gross value of $400,000. First held in 1960. Graded since 1973. Stakes record 1:31.89 (1997 Atticus).

Year	Winner	Jockey	Second	Third	Strs	Final Time	1st Purse
2001	**Road to Slew**, 6, 117	L. A. Pincay Jr.	Val Royal (Fr), 5	(DH) Exchange Rate, 4 (DH) Hawksley Hill (Ire), 8	10	1:35.96	$240,000
2000	**Committisize**, 5, 112	V. Espinoza	Chullo (Arg), 4	Sultry Substitute, 6	6	1:36.61	$120,000
1999	**Lord Smith (GB)**, 4, 116	G. K. Gomez	Hawksley Hill (Ire), 6	Ladies Din, 6	6	1:34.53	$90,000
1998	**Hawksley Hill (Ire)**, 5, 115	P. Day	Via Lombardia (Ire), 6	A Magicman (Fr), 6	10	1:34.84	$101,190
1997	**Atticus**, 5, 117	C. S. Nakatani	Pinfloron (Fr), 5	Rainbow Blues (Ire), 5	6	**1:31.89**	$97,400
1996	**Tychonic (GB)**, 6, 116	G. L. Stevens	Debutant Trick, 6	Silver Wizard, 6	8	1:35.52	$99,400
1995	**College Town**, 4, 117	L. A. Pincay Jr.	Romarin (Brz), 5	Finder's Fortune, 5	5	1:40.62	$63,800
1994	**Megan's Interco**, 5, 118	C. A. Black	Tinners Way, 4	Ibero (Arg), 4	7	1:33.86	$64,400
1993	**Leger Cat (Arg)**, 7, 114	C. S. Nakatani	Luthier Enchanteur, 6	The Name's Jimmy, 6	12	1:34.19	$70,800
1992	**Fly Till Dawn**, 6, 120	L. A. Pincay Jr.	Itsallgreektome, 5	Qathif, 5	11	1:34.69	$100,200

1992-2000 Arcadia H. 1992-'94, 2000 Grade 3. 1995, 2000 dirt. 2001 dead heat for third. 1997 new course and world record.

Frank J. De Francis Memorial Dash Stakes

Grade 1, Laurel Park, three-year-olds and up, 6 furlongs, dirt. Held November 17, 2001, with a gross value of $300,000. First held in 1990. Graded since 1992. Stakes record 1:07.95 (2000 Richter Scale).

Year	Winner	Jockey	Second	Third	Strs	Final Time	1st Purse
2001	**Delaware Township**, 5	J. D. Bailey	Early Flyer, 3	†Xtra Heat, 3	7	1:09.00	$180,000
2000	**Richter Scale**, 6	R. Migliore	Just Call Me Carl, 5	Falkenburg, 5	4	**1:07.95**	$180,000
1999	**Yes It's True**, 3	J. D. Bailey	Good and Tough, 4	Storm Punch, 4	6	1:08.67	$180,000
1998	**Kelly Kip**, 4	J-L. Samyn	Affirmed Success, 4	Partner's Hero, 4	6	1:08.50	$180,000
1997	**Smoke Glacken**, 3	C. Perret	Wise Dusty, 6	†Capote Belle, 6	7	1:09.54	$180,000
1996	**Lite the Fuse**, 5	J. A. Krone	Meadow Monster, 5	Prospect Bay, 5	7	1:08.81	$180,000
1995	**Lite the Fuse**, 4	J. A. Krone	Crafty Dude, 6	Hot Jaws, 6	7	1:08.89	$180,000
1994	**Cherokee Run**, 4	C. Perret	Boom Towner, 6	Fu Man Slew, 6	11	1:08.92	$180,000
1993	**Montbrook**, 3	C. J. Ladner III	Lion Cavern, 4	Flaming Emperor, 4	9	1:08.71	$180,000
1992	**Superstrike (GB)**, 5	D. Sorenson	†Parisian Flight, 4	King Corrie, 4	12	1:09.90	$180,000

1992-'93 Grade 3; 1994-'98 Grade 2. 2000 new track record. † denotes female.

Fred W. Hooper Handicap

Grade 3, Calder Race Course, three-year-olds and up, $1\frac{1}{8}$ miles, dirt. Held December 29, 2001, with a gross value of $100,000. First held in 1986. Graded since 1991. Stakes record 1:50.83 (1999 Dancing Guy).

Year	Winner	Jockey	Second	Third	Strs	Final Time	1st Purse
2001	**Kiss a Native**, 4, 116	C. H. Velasquez	Hal's Hope, 4	Groomstick Stock's, 4	8	1:51.05	$60,000
2000	**American Halo**, 4, 111	C. Hunt	General Grant, 3	Sir Bear, 3	8	1:51.68	$60,000
1999	**Dancing Guy**, 4, 120	J. C. Ferrer	Wicapi, 7	Loon, 7	8	**1:50.83**	$60,000

Year	Winner	Jockey	Second	Third	Strs	Final Time	1st Purse
1998	**Wicapi**, 6, 113	J. Bravo	Smuggler's Prize, 4	Best of the Rest, 4	5	1:52.15	$60,000
1997	**Shrike**, 4, 113	J. D. Bailey	Wicapi, 5	Sir Bear, 5	11	1:51.50	$60,000
1996	**Cimarron Secret**, 5, 115	J. A. Velez Jr.	Laughing Dan, 3	Wicapi, 3	8	1:52.70	$60,000
1995	**Bound by Honor**, 4, 112	J. A. Krone	Bay Street Star, 4	Halo's Image, 4	10	1:51.81	$60,000
1994	**Take Me Out**, 6, 115	M. E. Smith	Migrating Moon, 4	Meena, 4	11	1:51.80	$60,000
	Halo's Image, 3, 117	G. Boulanger	Fight for Love, 4	Migrating Moon, 4	7	1:51.44	$60,000
1993	**Barkerville**, 5, 114	R. P. Romero	Pistols and Roses, 4	Count the Time, 4	7	1:52.47	$45,000
1992	**Classic Seven**, 4, 110	C. E. Lopez Sr.	Honest Ensign, 4	Le Merle Blanc, 4	13	1:53.01	$102,960

1992-'96 Tropical Park H. 1994 held in January and December. 1992 four-year-olds and up.

Frizette Stakes

Grade 1, Belmont Park, two-year-old fillies, 1 1/16 miles, dirt. Held October 6, 2001, with a gross value of $500,000. First held in 1945. Graded since 1973. Stakes record 1:42.47 (1996 Storm Song).

Year	Winner	Jockey	Second	Third	Strs	Final Time	1st Purse
2001	**You**	E. S. Prado	Cashier's Dream	Riskaverse	5	1:43.94	$300,000
2000	**Raging Fever**	J. D. Bailey	Out of Sync	Western Justice	10	1:43.57	$300,000
1999	**Surfside**	P. Day	Darling My Darling	March Magic	5	1:43.18	$240,000
1998	**Confessional**	J. D. Bailey	Things Change	Pico Teneriffe	5	1:42.88	$240,000
1997	**Silver Maiden**	J. D. Bailey	Diamond On the Run	Brac Drifter	6	1:42.74	$240,000
1996	**Storm Song**	C. Perret	Sharp Cat	Aldiza	7	**1:42.47**	$240,000
1995	**Golden Attraction**	G. L. Stevens	My Flag	Flat Fleet Feet	5	1:42.95	$150,000
1994	**Flanders**	P. Day	Change Fora Dollar	Pretty Discreet	4	1:43.94	$150,000
1993	**Heavenly Prize**	M. E. Smith	Facts of Love	Footing	7	1:35.46	$150,000
1992	**Educated Risk**	J. D. Bailey	Standard Equipment	Beal Street Blues	8	1:36.62	$150,000

1992-'93 1 mile.

Futurity Stakes

Grade 1, Belmont Park, two-year-olds, 1 mile, dirt. Held September 17, 2000, with a gross value of $200,000. First held in 1888. Graded since 1973. Stakes record 1:35.12 (1995 Maria's Mon).

Year	Winner	Jockey	Second	Third	Strs	Final Time	1st Purse
2000	**Burning Roma**	R. Wilson	City Zip	Scorpion	9	1:37.90	$120,000
1999	**Bevo**	J. Bravo	Greenwood Lake	More Than Ready	8	1:36.16	$90,000
1998	**Lemon Drop Kid**	J. R. Velazquez	Yes It's True	Medievil Hero	5	1:37.50	$90,000
1997	**Grand Slam**	G. L. Stevens	K. O. Punch	Devil's Pride	10	1:35.69	$90,000
1996	**Traitor**	J. R. Velazquez	Night in Reno	Harley Tune	9	1:35.29	$90,000
1995	**Maria's Mon**	R. G. Davis	Louis Quatorze	Honour and Glory	7	**1:35.12**	$90,000
1994	**Montreal Red**	J. A. Santos	Northern Ensign	Wild Escapade	6	1:36.22	$66,180
1993	**Holy Bull**	M. E. Smith	Dehere	Prenup	4	1:23.31	$69,360
1992	**Strolling Along**	C. W. Antley	Fight for Love	Caponostro	9	1:23.67	$72,120

2001 not held due to World Trade Center attack. 1992-'93 7 furlongs. 2000 City Zip finished first, DQ to second.

Gallant Bloom Handicap

Grade 2, Belmont Park, three-year-olds and up, fillies and mares, 6 1/2 furlongs, dirt. Held September 29, 2001, with a gross value of $129,225. First held in 1994. Graded since 1997. Stakes record 1:15.60 (1998 Catinca).

Year	Winner	Jockey	Second	Third	Strs	Final Time	1st Purse
2001	**Finder's Fee**, 4, 113	J. R. Velazquez	Cedar Knolls, 4	Gold Mover, 4	4	1:17.60	$79,928
2000	**Dream Supreme**, 3, 118	P. Day	Finder's Fee, 3	Tropical Punch, 3	5	1:15.86	$64,380
1999	**Positive Gal**, 3, 116	J. D. Bailey	Flamingo Way, 5	Torch, 5	6	1:16.86	$65,820
1998	**Catinca**, 3, 114	R. Migliore	Dixie Flag, 4	Crab Grass, 4	9	**1:15.60**	$50,595
1997	**Top Secret**, 4, 120	J. R. Velazquez	Aldiza, 3	Dixie Flag, 3	7	1:16.00	$49,260
1996	**Miss Golden Circle**, 4, 115	R. Migliore	J J'sdream, 3	Nappelon, 3	9	1:16.26	$50,040
1995	**Classy Mirage**, 5, 123	J. D. Bailey	Dust Bucket, 4	Fantastic Women, 4	5	1:17.34	$48,375
1994	**Vivano**, 5, 116	W. H. McCauley	Ann Dear, 4	Strategic Reward, 4	5	1:10.93	$48,255

1997-2000 Grade 3. 1994 6 furlongs.

Gallant Fox Handicap

Grade 3, Aqueduct, three-year-olds and up, 1 5/8 miles, dirt. Held December 29, 2001, with a gross value of $115,400. First held in 1939. Graded since 1973. Stakes record 2:40.40 (1975 Sharp Gary).

Year	Winner	Jockey	Second	Third	Strs	Final Time	1st Purse
2001	**Coyote Lakes**, 7, 116	M. J. Luzzi	Pleasant Divorce, 3	Top Official, 3	12	2:45.77	$69,240
	Coyote Lakes, 7, 116	C. C. Lopez	Le Beaucet, 5	K. O.'s Crypto, 5	9	2:44.74	$67,020
1999	**Early Warning**, 4, 119	J. F. Chavez	Salty Note, 4	Durmiente (Chi), 4	10	2:42.94	$68,820
1998	**Aavelord**, 4, 115	C. C. Lopez	Coyote Lakes, 4	Brushing Up, 4	7	2:46.10	$66,360
1997	**Unreal Turn**, 5, 117	C. C. Lopez	Mr. Sinatra, 3	Draw, 3	12	2:46.76	$70,020
1996	**Ave's Flag**, 4, 114	J. F. Chavez	Colonial Secretary, 4	Beware the Quest, 4	8	2:45.97	$76,180

Year	Winner	Jockey	Second	Third	Strs	Final Time	1st Purse
1995	Yourmissinthepoint, 4, 120	J. R. Velazquez	Malmo, 4	Private Plan, 4	9	2:45.24	$68,040
1994	Serious Spender, 3, 110	J. F. Chavez	Jacksonport, 5	Recoiled, 5	8	2:44.98	$66,840
1993	Michelle Can Pass, 5, 119	M. E. Smith	Hugatag, 4	Jacksonport, 4	10	2:46.14	$90,000
1992	Michelle Can Pass, 4, 113	A. T. Gryder	Jacksonport, 3	Applebred, 3	13	2:45.80	$109,440

2000 not held; 2001 held in January and December. 1997 Draw finished second, DQ to third.

Gallorette Handicap

Grade 3, Pimlico, three-year-olds and up, fillies and mares, 1¹⁄₁₆ miles, turf. Held May 18, 2001, with a gross value of $100,000. First held in 1952. Graded since 1973. Stakes record 1:41.60 (1985 La Reine Elaine).

Year	Winner	Jockey	Second	Third	Strs	Final Time	1st Purse
2001	License Fee, 6, 118	P. Day	Starine (Fr), 4	Crystal Sea, 4	8	1:42.81	$60,000
2000	Colstar, 4, 120	A. Delgado	Melody Queen (GB), 4	Terreavigne, 4	10	1:43.60	$60,000
1999	Winfama, 6, 114	E. S. Prado	Pleasant Temper, 5	Earth to Jackie, 5	8	1:43.31	$60,000
1998	Tresoriere, 4, 113	J. A. Santos	Bursting Forth, 4	Starry Dreamer, 4	7	1:45.35	$60,000
1997	Palliser Bay, 5, 111	C. H. Marquez Jr.	Elusive, 5	Sangria, 5	8	1:43.81	$60,000
1996	Aucilla, 5, 114	M. E. Smith	Julie's Brilliance, 4	Brushing Gloom, 4	4	1:44.96	$60,000
1995	It's Personal, 5, 112	J. A. Krone	Churchbell Chimes, 4	Open Toe, 4	6	1:43.72	$60,000
1994	Tribulation, 4, 117	J-L. Samyn	McKaymackenna, 5	Fleet Broad, 5	6	1:41.66	$60,000
1993	You'd Be Surprised, 4, 113	J. D. Bailey	Captive Miss, 4	Dior's Angel, 4	12	1:43.54	$60,000
1992	Brilliant Brass, 5, 113	E. S. Prado	Spanish Dior, 5	Stem the Tide, 5	6	1:44.81	$60,000

1995-'96 dirt.

Gamely Breeders' Cup Handicap

Grade 1, Hollywood Park, three-year-olds and up, fillies and mares, 1¹⁄₈ miles, turf. Held May 26, 2001, with a gross value of $221,350. First held in 1939. Graded since 1977. Stakes record 1:45.07 (1993 Toussaud).

Year	Winner	Jockey	Second	Third	Strs	Final Time	1st Purse
2001	Happyanunoit (NZ), 6, 121	B. Blanc	Tranquility Lake, 6	Beautiful Noise, 6	7	1:47.34	$115,710
2000	Astra, 4, 117	K. J. Desormeaux	Happyanunoit (NZ), 5	Tout Charmant, 5	5	1:45.81	$157,170
1999	Tranquility Lake, 4, 119	E. Delahoussaye	Midnight Line, 4	Green Jewel (GB), 4	5	1:46.04	$157,800
1998	Fiji (GB), 4, 123	K. J. Desormeaux	Kool Kat Katie (Ire), 4	Squeak (GB), 4	6	1:47.42	$158,880
1997	Donna Viola (GB), 5, 121	G. L. Stevens	Real Connection, 6	Different (Arg), 6	7	1:47.56	$120,000
1996	Auriette (Ire), 4, 118	K. J. Desormeaux	Flagbird, 5	Didina (GB), 5	6	1:46.59	$128,760
1995	Possibly Perfect, 5, 123	K. J. Desormeaux	Lady Affirmed, 4	Don't Read My Lips, 4	6	1:46.99	$92,900
1994	Hollywood Wildcat, 4, 122	E. Delahoussaye	Mz. Zill Bear, 5	Flawlessly, 5	5	1:46.55	$92,900
1993	Toussaud, 4, 116	K. J. Desormeaux	Gold Fleece, 5	Bel's Starlet, 5	9	1:45.07	$97,700
1992	Metamorphose, 4, 114	G. L. Stevens	Guiza, 5	Silvered, 5	6	1:46.56	$93,300

1992-'97 Gamely H.

Garden City Breeders' Cup Handicap

Grade 1, Belmont Park, three-year-old fillies, 1¹⁄₈ miles, turf. Held September 9, 2001, with a gross value of $244,000. First held in 1979. Graded since 1985. Stakes record 1:47.10 (1998 Pharatta [Ire]).

Year	Winner	Jockey	Second	Third	Strs	Final Time	1st Purse
2001	Voodoo Dancer, 120	C. S. Nakatani	Shooting Party	Wander Mom	10	1:47.69	$150,000
2000	Gaviola, 123	J. D. Bailey	Flawly (GB)	Millie's Quest	8	1:48.89	$150,000
1999	Perfect Sting, 120	P. Day	Nordican Inch (GB)	Ronda (GB)	12	1:49.41	$129,900
1998	Pharatta (Ire), 120	C. S. Nakatani	Tenski	Pratella	12	1:47.10	$129,720
1997	Auntie Mame, 122	J. D. Bailey	Parade Queen	Swearingen	9	1:48.49	$128,040
1996	True Flare, 121	G. L. Stevens	Henlopen	Zephyr	9	1:42.58	$128,460
1995	Perfect Arc, 123	J. R. Velazquez	Bail Out Becky	Christmas Gift	8	1:42.35	$101,070
1994	Jade Flush, 111	R. G. Davis	Lady Affirmed	Saxuality	8	1:46.79	$67,140
1993	Sky Beauty, 124	M. E. Smith	Fadetta	For all Seasons	6	1:35.76	$68,400
1992	November Snow, 124	C. W. Antley	Vivano	Easy Now	4	1:35.91	$66,480

1992-'93 Rare Perfume S.; 1994-'95 Rare Perfume H.; 1996-'97 Rare Perfume Breeders' Cup H. 1992-'98 Grade 2. 1992-'93 1 mile; 1994-'96 1¹⁄₁₆ miles. 1992-'93 dirt.

Gardenia Handicap

Grade 3, Ellis Park, three-year-olds and up, fillies and mares, 1¹⁄₈ miles, dirt. Held August 11, 2001, with a gross value of $200,000. First held in 1982. Graded since 1988. Stakes record 1:47.60 (1988 Lt. Lao).

Year	Winner	Jockey	Second	Third	Strs	Final Time	1st Purse
2001	Asher, 4, 115	M. Guidry	Zenith, 4	Royal Fair, 4	8	1:50.16	$120,000
2000	Silent Eskimo, 5, 116	J. Lopez	Roza Robata, 5	Tap to Music, 5	7	1:50.56	$120,000
1999	Lines of Beauty, 4, 112	F. C. Torres	Roza Robata, 4	Castle Blaze, 4	10	1:49.60	$120,000
1998	Meter Maid, 4, 119	P. A. Johnson	Proper Banner, 4	Three Fanfares, 4	7	1:51.00	$120,000
1997	Three Fanfares, 4, 113	F. A. Arguello Jr.	Gold n Delicious, 4	Birr, 4	7	1:49.00	$120,000
1996	Country Cat, 4, 115	D. M. Barton	Bedroom Blues, 5	Alcovy, 5	8	1:49.60	$120,000

Year	Winner	Jockey	Second	Third	Strs	Final Time	1st Purse
1995	**Laura's Pistolette**, 4, 115	E. M. Martin Jr.	Sadie's Dream, 5	Cat Appeal, 5	9	1:50.80	$120,000
1994	**Alphabulous**, 5, 112	O. Thorwarth	Added Asset, 4	Hey Hazel, 4	10	1:50.00	$120,000
1993	**Erica's Dream**, 5, 113	W. Martinez	Fappies Cosy Miss, 5	Hitch, 5	8	1:49.80	$120,000
1992	**Bungalow**, 5, 118	F. C. Torres	Forever Fond, 4	Fappies Cosy Miss, 4	11	1:48.60	$120,000

1997-'98 Gardenia S.

Gazelle Handicap

Grade 1, Belmont Park, three-year-old fillies, 1⅛ miles, dirt. Held September 8, 2001, with a gross value of $250,000. First held in 1887. Graded since 1973. Stakes record 1:46.80 (1974 Maud Muller).

Year	Winner	Jockey	Second	Third	Strs	Final Time	1st Purse
2001	**Exogenous**, 118	J. Castellano	Two Item Limit	Fleet Renee	8	1:47.68	$150,000
2000	**Critical Eye**, 115	M. E. Smith	Plenty of Light	Resort	8	1:48.54	$120,000
1999	**Silverbulletday**, 124	J. D. Bailey	Queen's Word	Awful Smart	6	1:47.71	$120,000
1998	**Tap to Music**, 112	P. Day	Keeper Hill	French Braids	7	1:49.72	$120,000
1997	**Royal Indy**, 113	P. Day	Starry Dreamer	Pearl City	7	1:49.11	$120,000
1996	**My Flag**, 121	J. D. Bailey	Escena	Top Secret	6	1:48.08	$120,000
1995	**Serena's Song**, 124	G. L. Stevens	Miss Golden Circle	Golden Bri	6	1:47.29	$90,000
1994	**Heavenly Prize**, 123	M. E. Smith	Cinnamon Sugar (Ire)	Sovereign Kitty	5	1:47.20	$90,000
1993	**Dispute**, 120	J. D. Bailey	Silky Feather	In Her Glory	8	1:47.20	$90,000
1992	**Saratoga Dew**, 120	W. H. McCauley	Vivano	Tiney Toast	6	1:47.63	$103,140

General George Handicap

Grade 2, Laurel Park, three-year-olds and up, 7 furlongs, dirt. Held February 19, 2001, with a gross value of $200,000. First held in 1973. Graded since 1991. Stakes record 1:21.96 (1992 Senor Speedy).

Year	Winner	Jockey	Second	Third	Strs	Final Time	1st Purse
2001	**Peeping Tom**, 4, 114	S. Bridgmohan	Delaware Township, 5	Disco Rico, 5	7	1:22.00	$120,000
2000	**Affirmed Success**, 6, 121	J. F. Chavez	Young At Heart, 6	Badge, 6	9	1:22.02	$120,000
1999	**Esteemed Friend**, 5, 116	M. J. Luzzi	Star of Valor, 6	Purple Passion, 6	9	1:22.54	$150,000
1998	**Royal Haven**, 6, 122	R. Migliore	Purple Passion, 4	Wire Me Collect, 4	9	1:23.04	$150,000
1997	**Why Change**, 4, 113	M. Guidry	Appealing Skier, 4	Le Grande Pos, 4	10	1:22.41	$120,000
1996	**Meadow Monster**, 5, 120	R. Wilson	Splendid Sprinter, 4	Cat Be Nimble, 4	9	1:22.11	$120,000
1995	**Who Wouldn't**, 4, 119	J. Rocco	Storm Tower, 5	Powis Castle, 5	8	1:22.08	$120,000
1994	**Blushing Julian**, 4, 118	R. E. Colton	Chief Desire, 4	Who Wouldn't, 4	12	1:22.91	$120,000
1993	**Majesty's Turn**, 4, 118	A. Delgado	Senor Speedy, 6	Ameri Valay, 6	7	1:22.66	$120,000
1992	**Senor Speedy**, 5, 126	J. F. Chavez	Sunny Sunrise, 5	Formal Dinner, 5	12	**1:21.96**	$120,000

1992-'94 General George S.

Generous Stakes

Grade 3, Hollywood Park, two-year-olds, 1 mile, turf. Held November 24, 2001, with a gross value of $200,000. First held in 1982. Graded since 1986. Stakes record 1:34.49 (1992 Earl of Barking [Ire]).

Year	Winner	Jockey	Second	Third	Strs	Final Time	1st Purse
2001	**Mountain Rage**	D. R. Flores	Miesque's Approval	National Park (GB)	8	1:40.31	$120,000
2000	**Startac**	A. O. Solis	Broadway Moon	Deeliteful Irving	9	1:34.76	$120,000
1999	**Jokerman**	P. Day	Purely Cozzene	Kleofus	6	1:35.23	$120,000
1998	**Incurable Optimist**	J. R. Velazquez	Company Approval	Brave Gun	8	1:37.72	$150,000
1997	**Mantles Star (GB)**	C. J. McCarron	F J's Pace	Commitisize	8	1:36.73	$150,000
1996	**Hello (Ire)**	C. J. McCarron	Steel Ruhlr	Divine Insight	12	1:34.77	$150,000
1995	**Old Chapel**	G. L. Stevens	Ayrton S	Heza Gone West	10	1:35.11	$137,500
1994	**Native Regent**	D. Penna	Dangerous Scenario	Claudius	9	1:37.15	$137,500
1993	**Delineator**	R. A. Baze	Devon Port (Fr)	Ferrara	8	1:34.73	$137,500
1992	**Earl of Barking (Ire)**	A. O. Solis	Devil's Rock	Corby	8	**1:34.49**	$137,500

1992 Hoist the Flag S.

Genuine Risk Handicap

Grade 2, Belmont Park, three-year-olds and up, fillies and mares, 6 furlongs, dirt. Held May 12, 2001, with a gross value of $150,000. First held in 1984. Graded since 1986. Stakes record 1:08.40 (1996 Exotic Wood).

Year	Winner	Jockey	Second	Third	Strs	Final Time	1st Purse
2001	**Katz Me If You Can**, 4, 113	J. Bravo	Lucky Livi, 4	Shine Again, 4	10	1:09.55	$90,000
2000	**Imperfect World**, 4, 113	R. G. Davis	Gold Princess, 5	Tropical Punch, 5	7	1:10.00	$90,000
1999	**Foil**, 4, 114	J-L. Samyn	Harpia, 5	Gold Princess, 4	9	1:10.43	$90,000
1998	**J J'sdream**, 5, 118	L. C. Reynolds	Tate, 4	Capote Belle, 4	8	1:10.28	$83,310
1997	**Miss Golden Circle**, 5, 120	R. Migliore	Start At Once, 4	Nappelon, 4	6	1:09.49	$65,040
1996	**Exotic Wood**, 4, 119	M. E. Smith	Lottsa Talc, 6	Miss Golden Circle, 6	6	**1:08.40**	$65,100
1995	**Classy Mirage**, 5, 122	J. A. Krone	Through the Door, 5	Lottsa Talc, 5	4	1:11.25	$64,080
1994	**Apelia**, 5, 119	L. Attard	Spinning Round, 5	Ann Dear, 5	6	1:09.01	$64,680
1993	**Apelia**, 4, 119	L. Attard	Santa Catalina, 5	Reach for Clever, 5	7	1:10.18	$69,600
1992	**Parisian Flight**, 4, 117	J. A. Santos	Serape, 4	Devil's Orchid, 4	6	1:09.18	$70,680

1992-'94 Genuine Risk S.

Glens Falls Handicap

Not graded (originally scheduled as Grade 3), Saratoga Race Course, three-year-olds and up, fillies and mares, 1¼ miles, dirt (originally scheduled at 1⅜ miles on the turf). Held August 10, 2001, with a gross value of $106,700. First held in 1996. Graded since 1999. Stakes record 2:07.41 (2000 I'm Indy Mood).

Year	Winner	Jockey	Second	Third	Strs	Final Time	1st Purse
2001	Irving's Baby, 4, 126	J. D. Bailey	New Assembly (Ire), 4	Caveat's Shot, 4	4	2:07.56	$65,995
2000	I'm Indy Mood, 5, 116	H. Castillo Jr.	Idle Rich, 5	Cybil, 5	6	2:07.41	$66,120
1999	Idle Rich, 4, 115	J. D. Bailey	Adrian, 5	Bundling, 5	7	2:12.81	$65,760
1998	Auntie Mame, 4, 120	J. R. Velazquez	Yvecrique (Fr), 4	Makethemostofit, 4	6	2:13.15	$66,000
1997	Shemozzle (Ire), 4, 115	J. D. Bailey	Picture Hat, 5	Last Approach, 5	5	2:12.89	$64,740
1996	Ampulla, 5, 113	S. J. Sellers	Look Daggers, 4	Electric Society (Ire), 4	8	2:16.49	$67,500

1996-'97 Glens Falls S. 1999-2000 Grade 3. 1996-'99 1⅜ miles. 1996-'99 turf.

Go for Wand Handicap

Grade 1, Saratoga Race Course, three-year-olds and up, fillies and mares, 1⅛ miles, dirt. Held July 29, 2001, with a gross value of $250,000. First held in 1954. Graded since 1973. Stakes record 1:49.44 (1996 Exotic Wood).

Year	Winner	Jockey	Second	Third	Strs	Final Time	1st Purse
2001	Serra Lake, 4, 113	E. S. Prado	Pompeii, 4	March Magic, 4	8	1:49.62	$150,000
2000	Heritage of Gold, 5, 123	S. J. Sellers	Beautiful Pleasure, 5	Roza Robata, 5	5	1:49.84	$150,000
1999	Banshee Breeze, 4, 124	J. D. Bailey	Beautiful Pleasure, 4	Heritage of Gold, 4	5	1:49.95	$150,000
1998	Aldiza, 4, 114	M. E. Smith	Escena, 5	Tomisue's Delight, 5	7	1:49.88	$150,000
1997	Hidden Lake, 4, 123	R. Migliore	Flat Fleet Feet, 4	Clear Mandate, 4	7	1:49.64	$150,000
1996	Exotic Wood, 4, 115	C. J. McCarron	Shoop, 5	Frolic, 5	8	1:49.44	$105,000
1995	Heavenly Prize, 4, 123	P. Day	Forcing Bid, 4	Little Buckles, 4	5	1:49.90	$105,000
1994	Sky Beauty, 4, 123	M. E. Smith	Link River, 4	Life Is Delicious, 4	5	1:49.47	$90,000
1993	Turnback the Alarm, 4, 123	C. W. Antley	Nannerl, 6	November Snow, 6	4	1:36.02	$120,000
1992	Easy Now, 3, 111	J. D. Bailey	Train Robbery, 5	Wide Country, 5	5	1:36.13	$120,000

1992-'97 Go for Wand S. 1992-'93 held at Belmont Park. 1992-'93 1 mile. 1992 Nannerl finished second, DQ to fifth.

Golden Gate Breeders' Cup Handicap

Grade 3, Golden Gate Fields, three-year-olds and up, 1⅛ miles, turf. Held March 4, 2001, with a gross value of $242,500. First held in 1947. Graded since 1975. Stakes record 1:48.21 (1993 Val de Bois [Fr]).

Year	Winner	Jockey	Second	Third	Strs	Final Time	1st Purse
2001	Northern Quest (Fr), 6, 118	V. Espinoza	Eagleton, 5	Entorchado (Ire), 5	6	1:58.58	$137,500
2000	Deploy Venture (GB), 4, 115	R. A. Baze	Single Empire (Ire), 6	Bonapartiste (Fr), 6	6	2:19.12	$120,000
1999	Sayarshan (Fr), 4, 112	B. Blanc	Alvo Certo (Brz), 6	Plicck (Ire), 6	8	2:15.56	$120,000
1998	Dushyantor, 5, 118	C. S. Nakatani	Eternity Range, 5	Star Performance, 5	6	2:15.26	$150,000
1997	Irish Wings (Ire), 5, 114	D. Carr	Savinio, 7	Mufattish, 7	7	1:49.68	$120,000
1996	Time Star, 5, 116	C. A. Black	Sand Reef (GB), 5	Bon Point (GB), 5	5	2:16.37	$120,000
1995	Special Price, 6, 122	E. Delahoussaye	Bluegrass Prince (Ire), 4	Sans Ecocide (GB), 4	6	2:15.14	$110,000
1994	Alex the Great (GB), 5, 118	P. A. Valenzuela	Fanmore, 6	Emerald Jig, 6	8	2:15.11	$165,000
1993	Val des Bois (Fr), 7, 119	P. A. Valenzuela	Norwich (GB), 6	Never Black, 6	5	1:48.21	$165,000
1992	Algenib (Arg), 5, 120	L. A. Pincay Jr.	Missionary Ridge (GB), 5	Never Black, 5	7	2:13.96	$220,000

1992-2000 Golden Gate H. 1992-'96 Grade 2. 1994-'96, 1998-2000 1⅜ miles. 1993 equaled course record.

Golden Gate Derby

Grade 3, Golden Gate Fields, three-year-olds, 1¹⁄₁₆ miles, dirt. Held January 13, 2001, with a gross value of $150,000. First held in 1947. Graded since 1999. Stakes record 1:42.20 (1959 Mr. Eiffel).

Year	Winner	Jockey	Second	Third	Strs	Final Time	1st Purse
2001	Hoovergetthekeys	R. J. Warren Jr.	High Cascade	Media Mogul (GB)	7	1:42.88	$82,500
2000	New Advantage	A. D. Lopez	Nurdlinger	Shake Loose	9	1:42.66	$90,000
1999	Epic Honor	L. Meche	Blue Tune	Brave Gun	8	1:43.58	$90,000
1998	Clover Hunter	R. A. Baze	Mantles Star (GB)	Allen's Oop	8	1:43.33	$120,000
1997	Pacificbounty	K. J. Desormeaux	Dancer's Kolo	Esteemed Friend	12	1:43.08	$120,000

1992-'96 not held.

Golden Rod Stakes

Grade 2, Churchill Downs, two-year-old fillies, 1¹⁄₁₆ miles, dirt. Held November 24, 2001, with a gross value of $215,200. First held in 1910. Graded since 1973. Stakes record 1:43.82 (2001 Belterra).

Year	Winner	Jockey	Second	Third	Strs	Final Time	1st Purse
2001	Belterra	J. K. Court	Take Charge Lady	Lotta Rhythm	5	1:43.82	$133,424
2000	Miss Pickums	J. J. Vitek	Nasty Storm	My White Corvette	9	1:48.84	$138,384
1999	Humble Clerk	J. K. Court	Cash Run	Secret Status	9	1:45.26	$138,880
1998	Silverbulletday	G. L. Stevens	Here I Go	Lefty's Dollbaby	6	1:43.87	$134,292
1997	Love Lock	R. Albarado	Barefoot Dyana	Grechelle	9	1:44.49	$139,996
1996	City Band	S. J. Sellers	Glitter Woman	Water Street	10	1:46.82	$139,996

Year	Winner	Jockey	Second	Third	Strs	Final Time	1st Purse
1995	Gold Sunrise	W. Martinez	Birr	Solana	11	1:45.46	$97,500
1994	Lilly Capote	D. M. Barton	Morris Code	Cat Appeal	8	1:46.66	$97,500
1993	At the Half	P. Day	Spiritofpocahontas	Mystic Union	9	1:46.83	$97,500
1992	Boots 'n Jackie	M. A. Lee	Mollie Creek	Dance Account	6	1:47.29	$97,500

1992-'99 Grade 3.

Goodwood Breeders' Cup Handicap

Grade 2, Santa Anita Park, three-year-olds and up, 1⅛ miles, dirt. Held October 7, 2001, with a gross value of $488,000. First held in 1982. Graded since 1985. Stakes record 1:46.72 (1994 Bertrando).

Year	Winner	Jockey	Second	Third	Strs	Final Time	1st Purse
2001	Freedom Crest, 5, 116	K. J. Desormeaux	Skimming, 5	Tiznow, 5	6	1:48.86	$300,000
2000	Tiznow, 3, 116	C. J. McCarron	Captain Steve, 3	Euchre, 3	7	1:47.38	$240,000
1999	Budroyale, 6, 119	G. K. Gomez	General Challenge, 3	Old Trieste, 3	6	1:48.31	$300,000
1998	Silver Charm, 4, 124	G. L. Stevens	Free House, 4	Score Quick, 4	6	1:47.21	$262,800
1997	Benchmark, 6, 118	E. Delahoussaye	Score Quick, 5	Hesabull, 5	5	1:47.60	$158,750
1996	Savinio, 6, 117	C. S. Nakatani	Dare and Go, 5	Alphabet Soup, 5	4	1:47.88	$189,300
1995	Soul of the Matter, 4, 121	K. J. Desormeaux	Tinners Way, 5	Alphabet Soup, 5	5	1:47.54	$144,450
1994	Bertrando, 5, 120	G. L. Stevens	Dramatic Gold, 3	Tossofthecoin, 3	6	1:46.72	$124,400
1993	Lottery Winner, 4, 115	K. J. Desormeaux	Region, 4	Pleasant Tango, 4	7	1:47.71	$127,200
1992	Reign Road, 4, 116	K. J. Desormeaux	Sir Beaufort, 5	Marquetry, 5	6	1:48.36	$125,200

1992-'95 Goodwood H. 1996 Alphabet Soup finished first, DQ to third.

Gotham Stakes

Grade 3, Aqueduct, three-year-olds, 1 mile, dirt. Held March 18, 2001, with a gross value of $200,000. First held in 1953. Graded since 1973. Stakes record 1:32.40 (1989 Easy Goer).

Year	Winner	Jockey	Second	Third	Strs	Final Time	1st Purse
2001	Richly Blended	R. Wilson	Mr. John	Voodoo	8	1:35.14	$120,000
2000	Red Bullet	A. O. Solis	Aptitude	Performing Magic	9	1:34.27	$120,000
1999	Badge	S. Bridgmohan	Apremont	Robin Goodfellow	11	1:34.72	$90,000
1998	Wasatch	J. D. Bailey	Dr J	Late Edition	10	1:36.56	$90,000
1997	Smokin Mel	J. R. Velazquez	Ordway	Wild Wonder	11	1:34.38	$120,000
1996	Romano Gucci	J. A. Krone	Tiger Talk	Feather Box	10	1:34.40	$120,000
1995	Talkin Man	M. E. Smith	Da Hoss	Devious Course	11	1:36.82	$150,000
1994	Irgun	J. D. Bailey	Bit of Puddin	Jesse F	12	1:36.27	$150,000
1993	As Indicated	C. V. Bisono	Itaka	Strolling Along	8	1:36.24	$120,000
1992	(DH) Lure	M. E. Smith		Best Decorated	8	1:35.63	$102,500
	(DH) Devil His Due	W. H. McCauley					

1992-'97 Grade 2. 1992 dead heat for first.

Gravesend Handicap

Grade 3, Aqueduct, three-year-olds and up, 6 furlongs, dirt. Held December 15, 2001, with a gross value of $107,900. First held in 1959. Graded since 1988. Stakes record 1:08.60 (1973 Petrograd).

Year	Winner	Jockey	Second	Third	Strs	Final Time	1st Purse
2001	Here's Zealous, 4, 114	E. S. Prado	Peeping Tom, 4	Say Florida Sandy, 4	6	1:10.37	$64,740
2000	Say Florida Sandy, 6, 116	J. Bravo	Liberty Gold, 6	Lake Pontchartrain, 6	11	1:09.80	$51,450
1999	Cowboy Cop, 5, 115	A. T. Gryder	Brushed On, 4	Power by Far, 4	9	1:09.41	$50,370
1998	Say Florida Sandy, 4, 117	S. Bridgmohan	Esteemed Friend, 4	Home On the Ridge, 4	8	1:11.17	$50,220
1997	(DH) Stalwart Member, 4, 118	A. T. Gryder		Laredo, 5	7	1:10.08	$32,670
	(DH) Royal Haven, 5, 118	R. Migliore					
1996	Victor Avenue, 3, 119	J. F. Chavez	Royal Haven, 4	Stalwart Member, 4	9	1:09.25	$50,325
1995	Cold Execution, 4, 116	J. M. Pezua	Crafty Alfel, 7	Golden Tent, 7	10	1:09.50	$50,820
1994	Mining Burrah, 4, 111	J. R. Velazquez	Golden Pro, 4	Won Song, 4	9	1:10.85	$51,270
1993	Astudillo (Ire), 3, 108	F. A. Arguello Jr.	Fabersham, 5	Ferociously, 5	6	1:11.91	$51,300
1992	Hidden Tomahawk, 4, 111	J. F. Chavez	Smart Alec, 4	Miner's Dream, 4	8	1:08.65	$52,920

1997 dead heat for first. 1999 Unreal Madness finished third, DQ to ninth. 1992 equaled track record.

Gulfstream Park Breeders' Cup Handicap

Grade 1, Gulfstream Park, three-year-olds and up, 1⅜ miles, turf. Held February 10, 2001, with a gross value of $140,000. First held in 1972. Graded since 1990. Stakes record 2:10.73 (1999 Yagli).

Year	Winner	Jockey	Second	Third	Strs	Final Time	1st Purse
2001	Subtle Power (Ire), 4, 113	P. Day	Whata Brainstorm, 4	Stokosky, 4	9	2:13.50	$60,000
2000	Royal Anthem, 5, 121	J. D. Bailey	Thesaurus, 6	Band Is Passing, 6	7	2:11.34	$120,000
1999	Yagli, 6, 121	J. D. Bailey	Wild Event, 6	Unite's Big Red, 6	6	2:10.73	$120,000
1998	Flag Down, 8, 120	J. A. Santos	Buck's Boy, 5	Copy Editor, 5	12	2:12.59	$120,000
1997	Lassigny, 6, 116	J. D. Bailey	Flag Down, 7	Awad, 7	11	2:11.33	$102,840

Year	Winner	Jockey	Second	Third	Strs	Final Time	1st Purse
1996	Celtic Arms (Fr), 5, 114	M. E. Smith	Broadway Flyer, 5	Flag Down, 5	11	2:13.90	$101,880
1995	Misil, 7, 119	J. A. Santos	Myrmidon, 4	Star of Manila, 4	11	2:12.41	$94,200
1994	Strolling Along, 4, 117	J. D. Bailey	Conveyor, 6	Awad, 6	6	2:05.01	$93,150
1993	Stagecraft (GB), 6, 115	J. D. Bailey	Social Retiree, 6	Futurist, 6	8	2:13.24	$93,600
1992	†Passagere du Soir (GB), 5, 114	J. D. Bailey	Colchis Island (Ire), 7	Crystal Moment, 7	14	2:15.71	$95,130

1992-'98 Grade 2. 1994 1¼ miles. 1994 dirt. 1993,1999 new course record; 1997 equaled course record. † denotes female.

Gulfstream Park Breeders' Cup Sprint Championship Handicap

Grade 2, Gulfstream Park, three-year-olds and up, 7 furlongs, dirt. Held March 9, 2001, with a gross value of $200,000. First held in 1972. Graded since 1996. Stakes record 1:21.70 (1995 Cherokee Run).

Year	Winner	Jockey	Second	Third	Strs	Final Time	1st Purse
2001	Hook and Ladder, 4, 115	R. Migliore	Trippi, 4	Rollin With Nolan, 4	6	1:21.85	$120,000
2000	Richter Scale, 6, 118	R. Migliore	Forty One Carats, 4	Kelly Kip, 4	10	1:23.30	$120,000
1999	Frisk Me Now, 5, 117	E. L. King Jr.	Young At Heart, 5	Good and Tough, 5	6	1:22.86	$60,000
1998	Rare Rock, 5, 117	P. Day	Irish Conquest, 5	Frisco View, 5	7	1:22.00	$120,000
1997	Frisco View, 4, 116	J. D. Bailey	El Amante, 4	Templado (Ven), 4	7	1:23.14	$98,160
1996	Patton, 5, 113	R. G. Davis	Forty Won, 5	Our Emblem, 5	10	1:21.81	$100,140
1995	Cherokee Run, 5, 122	M. E. Smith	Waldoboro, 4	Evil Bear, 4	6	1:21.70	$60,000
1994	I Can't Believe, 6, 113	E. Maple	American Chance, 5	British Banker, 5	8	1:22.55	$60,000
1993	Binalong, 4, 112	J. D. Bailey	Loach, 5	Richman, 5	6	1:22.35	$60,000
1992	Groomstick, 6, 112	W. S. Ramos	Ocala Flame, 4	Cold Digger, 4	9	1:23.98	$60,000

1992-'93 Gulfstream Park Sprint Championship H.; 1994-'95 Gulfstream Park Sprint H. 1996-'98 Grade 3.

Gulfstream Park Handicap

Grade 1, Gulfstream Park, three-year-olds and up, 1¼ miles, dirt. Held March 3, 2001, with a gross value of $200,000. First held in 1946. Graded since 1973. Stakes record 1:59 (1984 Mat-Boy [Arg]).

Year	Winner	Jockey	Second	Third	Strs	Final Time	1st Purse
2001	Sir Bear, 8, 116	E. Coa	Pleasant Breeze, 6	Broken Vow, 6	9	2:02.96	$120,000
2000	Behrens, 6, 120	J. F. Chavez	Adonis, 4	With Anticipation, 4	6	2:01.79	$210,000
1999	Behrens, 5, 114	J. F. Chavez	Archers Bay, 4	Sir Bear, 4	8	2:01.91	$210,000
1998	Skip Away, 5, 127	J. D. Bailey	Unruled, 5	Behrens, 5	6	2:03.21	$300,000
1997	Mt. Sassafras, 5, 113	J. D. Bailey	Skip Away, 4	Tejano Run, 4	6	2:02.39	$300,000
1996	Wekiva Springs, 5, 117	J. D. Bailey	Star Standard, 4	Powerful Punch, 4	8	2:03.18	$300,000
1995	Cigar, 5, 118	J. D. Bailey	Pride of Burkaan, 5	Mahogany Hall, 5	11	2:02.95	$300,000
1994	Scuffleburg, 5, 113	C. Perret	Migrating Moon, 4	Wallenda, 4	10	2:00.46	$300,000
1993	Devil His Due, 4, 113	W. H. McCauley	Offbeat, 4	Pistols and Roses, 4	9	2:01.33	$300,000
1992	Sea Cadet, 4, 119	A. O. Solis	Strike the Gold, 4	Sunny Sunrise, 4	6	2:01.79	$180,000

Hanshin Cup Handicap

Grade 3, Arlington Park, three-year-olds and up, 1 mile, dirt. Held July 7, 2001, with a gross value of $100,000. First held in 1941. Graded since 1983. Stakes record 1:33.20 (1965 Pia Star; 1966 Hedevar; 1979 Bask).

Year	Winner	Jockey	Second	Third	Strs	Final Time	1st Purse
2001	Bright Valour, 5, 119	R. Albarado	Apt to Be, 4	Castlewood, 4	8	1:36.21	$60,000
2000	Bright Valour, 4, 114	J. Campbell	Desert Demon, 4	Battle Mountain, 4	5	1:34.97	$60,000
1997	Announce, 5, 116	C. C. Bourque	Victor Cooley, 4	Hunk of Class, 4	7	1:36.95	$60,000
1996	Golden Gear, 5, 122	M. Guidry	Exclusive Garth, 4	Prospect for Love, 4	10	1:36.13	$105,000
1995	Tarzans Blade, 4, 115	P. Day	Swank, 4	Come On Flip, 4	9	1:35.64	$45,000
1994	Slerp, 5, 117	E. Fires	Seattle Morn, 4	Dancing Jon, 4	5	1:35.43	$60,000
1993	Split Run, 5, 114	E. Fires	Gee Can He Dance, 4	Danc'n Jake, 4	11	1:34.46	$60,000
1992	Katahaula County, 4, 114	C. C. Bourque	The Great Carl, 5	Stalwars, 5	9	1:37.27	$45,000

1998-'99 not held. 1992-'97 Equipoise Mile H.; 2000 Hanshin H. 2000 Yankee Victor finished first, DQ to fifth.

Haskell Invitational Handicap

Grade 1, Monmouth Park, three-year-olds, 1⅛ miles, dirt. Held August 5, 2001, with a gross value of $1,500,000. First held in 1968. Graded since 1973. Stakes record 1:47 (1976 Majestic Light; 1987 Bet Twice).

Year	Winner	Jockey	Second	Third	Strs	Final Time	1st Purse
2001	Point Given, 124	G. L. Stevens	Touch Tone	Burning Roma	6	1:49.77	$900,000
2000	Dixie Union, 117	A. O. Solis	Captain Steve	Milwaukee Brew	9	1:50.00	$600,000
1999	Menifee, 124	P. Day	Cat Thief	Forestry	7	1:48.06	$600,000
1998	Coronado's Quest, 124	M. E. Smith	Victory Gallop	Grand Slam	6	1:48.60	$600,000
1997	Touch Gold, 125	C. J. McCarron	Anet	Free House	5	1:47.62	$850,000
1996	Skip Away, 124	J. A. Santos	Dr. Caton	Victory Speech	7	1:47.73	$450,000
1995	†Serena's Song, 118	G. L. Stevens	Pyramid Peak	Citadeed	11	1:48.94	$300,000
1994	Holy Bull, 124	M. E. Smith	Meadow Flight	Concern	6	1:48.36	$300,000
1993	Kissin Kris, 118	J. A. Santos	Storm Tower	Dry Bean	7	1:49.58	$300,000
1992	Technology, 120	J. D. Bailey	Nines Wild	Scudan	9	1:48.78	$300,000

† denotes female.

Hawthorne Derby

Grade 3, Hawthorne Race Course, three-year-olds, 1⅛ miles, turf. Held May 12, 2001, with a gross value of $250,000. First held in 1965. Graded since 1973. Stakes record 1:44.70 (1991 Rainbows for Life).

Year	Winner	Jockey	Second	Third	Strs	Final Time	1st Purse
2001	Kalu	J. A. Santos	Proud Man	Rahy's Secret	7	1:50.49	$150,000
2000	(DH) Hymn (Ire)	L. A. Pincay Jr.		Lonely Place (Ire)	10	1:53.79	$100,000
	(DH) Rumsontheriver	J. Juarez Jr.					
1999	Minor Wisdom	R. Zimmerman	Air Rocket	Fred of Gold	12	1:49.06	$150,000
1998	Stay Sound	A. J. D'Amico	El Mirasol	Yankee Brass	11	1:47.54	$150,000
1997	River Squall	C. Perret	Honor Glide	Blazing Sword	6	1:48.20	$120,000
1996	Jaunatxo	J. L. Diaz	Trail City	Canyon Run	11	1:47.18	$120,000
1995	Cuzzin Jeb	C. C. Lopez	Hawk Attack	Seven n Seven	9	1:48.90	$90,000
1994	Chrysalis House	M. Guidry	Unfinished Symph	Marvin's Faith (Ire)	11	1:51.88	$90,000
1993	Snake Eyes	G. K. Gomez	Lt. Pinkerton	Ft. Bent	12	1:50.28	$90,000
1992	Bantan	C. C. Bourque	†Words of War	Gee Can He Dance	11	1:48.05	$60,000

2000 dead heat for first. † denotes female.

Hawthorne Gold Cup Handicap

Grade 2, Hawthorne Race Course, three-year-olds and up, 1¼ miles, dirt. Held May 19, 2001, with a gross value of $500,000. First held in 1928. Graded since 1973. Stakes record 1:58.80 (1970 Gladwin; 1974 Group Plan).

Year	Winner	Jockey	Second	Third	Strs	Final Time	1st Purse
2001	Duckhorn, 4, 112	R. A. Meier	Lido Palace (Chi), 4	Guided Tour, 4	7	2:01.61	$300,000
2000	Dust On the Bottle, 5, 112	T. T. Doocy	Guided Tour, 4	Golden Missile, 4	8	2:03.09	$300,000
1999	Supreme Sound (GB), 5, 112	R. A. Meier	Golden Missile, 4	Beboppin Baby, 4	8	2:01.19	$300,000
1998	Awesome Again, 4, 123	P. Day	Unruled, 5	Muchacho Fino, 5	8	2:02.71	$240,000
1997	Buck's Boy, 4, 114	M. Guidry	Cairo Express, 5	Beboppin Baby, 5	7	2:00.54	$180,000
1996	Come On Flip, 5, 113	C. A. Emigh	Michael's Star, 4	Mt. Sassafras, 4	10	2:03.40	$180,000
1995	Yourmissinthepoint, 4, 113	M. Guidry	Basquenian, 4	Sky Carr, 4	9	2:01.00	$150,000
1994	Recoup the Cash, 4, 117	J. L. Diaz	Run Softly, 3	Kissin Kris, 3	11	2:01.99	$240,000
1993	Evanescent, 6, 115	A. T. Gryder	Marquetry, 6	Valley Crossing, 6	7	2:02.19	$240,000
1992	Irish Swap, 5, 115	B. E. Poyadou	Sea Cadet, 4	Evanescent, 4	8	2:01.12	$240,000

1997-2000 Grade 3.

Hawthorne Handicap

Grade 2, Hollywood Park, three-year-olds and up, fillies and mares, 1¹⁄₁₆ miles, dirt. Held May 6, 2001, with a gross value of $147,000. First held in 1974. Graded since 1982. Stakes record 1:41.12 (1993 Freedom Cry).

Year	Winner	Jockey	Second	Third	Strs	Final Time	1st Purse
2001	Printemps (Chi), 4, 116	C. J. McCarron	Feverish, 6	Brianda (Ire), 6	4	1:43.21	$90,000
2000	Riboletta (Brz), 5, 117	C. J. McCarron	Excellent Meeting, 4	Speaking of Time, 4	5	1:42.33	$90,000
1999	Victory Stripes (Arg), 5, 115	C. J. McCarron	Magical Allure, 4	Housa Dancer (Fr), 4	4	1:41.73	$90,000
1998	I Ain't Bluffing, 4, 118	C. J. McCarron	Fun in Excess, 4	Tomorrows Sunshine, 4	5	1:41.49	$63,720
1997	Twice the Vice, 6, 120	C. J. McCarron	Chile Chatte, 4	Listening, 4	7	1:42.72	$64,860
1996	Borodislew, 6, 119	C. S. Nakatani	Jewel Princess, 4	Urbane, 4	6	1:41.28	$64,200
1995	Paseana (Arg), 8, 122	C. J. McCarron	Pirate's Revenge, 4	Top Rung, 4	7	1:42.40	$63,300
1994	Golden Klair (GB), 4, 118	K. J. Desormeaux	Likeable Style, 4	Andestine, 4	4	1:41.41	$60,000
1993	Freedom Cry, 5, 117	A. O. Solis	Vieille Vigne (Fr), 6	Miss High Blade, 6	11	**1:41.12**	$67,600
1992	Sacramentada (Chi), 6, 117	K. J. Desormeaux	Brought to Mind, 5	Re Toss (Arg), 5	5	1:43.04	$61,600

Hempstead Handicap

Grade 1, Belmont Park, three-year-olds and up, fillies and mares, 1¹⁄₁₆ miles, dirt. Held June 23, 2001, with a gross value of $250,000. First held in 1961. Graded since 1973. Stakes record 1:38.90 (1998 Mossflower).

Year	Winner	Jockey	Second	Third	Strs	Final Time	1st Purse
2001	Critical Eye, 4, 115	M. J. Luzzi	Jostle, 4	Apple of Kent, 4	7	1:42.18	$150,000
2000	Beautiful Pleasure, 5, 124	J. F. Chavez	Pentatonic, 5	Roza Robata, 5	6	1:41.54	$150,000
1999	Sister Act, 4, 117	P. Day	Beautiful Pleasure, 4	Catinca, 4	6	1:40.79	$150,000
1998	Mossflower, 4, 114	R. G. Davis	Glitter Woman, 4	Colonial Minstrel, 4	6	**1:39.90**	$150,000
1997	Hidden Lake, 4, 122	R. Migliore	Twice the Vice, 6	Jewel Princess, 6	9	1:40.87	$150,000
1996	Serena's Song, 4, 125	J. D. Bailey	Shoop, 5	Restored Hope, 5	8	1:41.63	$120,000
1995	Heavenly Prize, 4, 122	P. Day	Little Buckles, 4	Sky Beauty, 4	4	1:43.37	$90,000
1994	Sky Beauty, 4, 128	M. E. Smith	You'd Be Surprised, 5	Schway Baby Sway, 5	5	1:47.48	$90,000
1993	Turnback the Alarm, 4, 119	C. W. Antley	Deputation, 4	You'd Be Surprised, 4	6	1:48.14	$90,000
1992	Missy's Mirage, 4, 118	E. Maple	Harbour Club, 5	Versailles Treaty, 5	6	1:47.03	$120,000

1992-'94 1⅛ miles.

Herecomesthebride Stakes

Grade 3, Gulfstream Park, three-year-old fillies, 1¹⁄₁₆ miles, dirt (originally scheduled on the turf). Held January 21, 2001, with a gross value of $111,500. First held in 1984. Graded since 1998. Stakes record 1:46.49 (1997 Auntie Mame).

Year	Winner	Jockey	Second	Third	Strs	Final Time	1st Purse
2001	Mystic Lady	J. D. Bailey	Open Minded	Ruff	7	1:46.73	$60,000
2000	Gaviola	J. D. Bailey	Solvig	Are You Up	8	1:47.28	$45,000
1999	Pico Teneriffe	J. D. Bailey	European Rose	Wild Heart Dancing	8	1:48.82	$45,000
1998	Rashas Warning	M. E. Smith	Quick Lap	Runnaway Dream	7	1:51.44	$45,000
1997	Auntie Mame	J. D. Bailey	Witchful Thinking	Classic Approval	7	**1:46.49**	$45,000
1996	Lulu's Ransom	J. D. Bailey	Cymbala (Fr)	Vashon	9	1:47.55	$30,000
1995	Clever Thing	C. Perret	Transient Trend	Palliser Bay	6	1:53.06	$30,000
1994	Cut the Charm	W. S. Ramos	Mynameispanama	Tambien Me Voy	11	1:43.72	$30,000
1993	Sigrun	R. R. Douglas	So Say all of Us	Supah Gem	8	1:45.79	$30,000
1992	Morriston Belle	D. Penna	Snazzle Dazzle	Miss Jealski	11	1:42.23	$30,000

1995-'97, 1999-2000 1¹⁄₁₆ miles; 1998 about 1¹⁄₈ miles. 1992,1996-2000 turf. 1997 equaled course record.

Hialeah Turf Cup Handicap

Grade 2, Hialeah Park, three-year-olds and up, 1³⁄₁₆ miles, turf. Held April 21, 2001, with a gross value of $200,000. First held in 1929. Graded since 1973. Stakes record 1:51.79 (1998 Yagli).

Year	Winner	Jockey	Second	Third	Strs	Final Time	1st Purse
2001	Del Mar Show, 4, 116	R. G. Davis	Honor Glide, 7	Profit Option, 7	7	1:53.06	$120,000
2000	Monkey Puzzle, 4, 114	R. R. Douglas	Honor Glide, 6	Down the Aisle, 6	12	2:13.50	$120,000
1999	Federal Trial, 4, 115	R. G. Davis	Sharp Appeal, 6	Karamiyan, 6	7	1:52.67	$120,000
1998	Yagli, 5, 114	H. Castillo Jr.	Storm Trooper, 5	Blazing Sword, 5	9	**1:51.79**	$120,000
1997	Sharp Appeal, 4, 116	G. Boulanger	Flag Down, 7	Diplomatic Jet, 7	10	1:54.93	$120,000
1996	Signal Tap, 5, 116	J. R. Velazquez	Flag Down, 6	Mecke, 6	7	1:53.15	$120,000
1995	Turk Passer, 5, 113	J. R. Velazquez	The Vid, 5	Flying American, 5	8	1:54.47	$120,000
1994	Awad, 4, 116	E. Maple	Fraise, 6	Flying American, 6	6	2:30.19	$120,000
1993	Spectacular Tide, 4, 113	R. R. Douglas	Gary Gumbo, 4	Carterista, 4	8	2:25.67	$90,000
1992	Crystal Moment, 7, 113	R. Wilson	Itsallgreektome, 5	†Passagere du Soir (GB), 5	13	2:28.22	$120,000

1992-'93 not graded; 1995-'98 Grade 3. 2000 held at Gulfstream Park. 1992 about 1½ miles; 1993-'94 1½ miles; 2000 1³⁄₈ miles. † denotes female.

Hill Prince Stakes

Grade 3, Belmont Park, three-year-olds, 1¹⁄₈ miles, turf. Held June 16, 2001, with a gross value of $114,600. First held in 1975. Graded since 1981. Stakes record 1:45.69 (1997 Subordination).

Year	Winner	Jockey	Second	Third	Strs	Final Time	1st Purse
2001	Proud Man	R. R. Douglas	Package Store	Navesink	10	1:48.25	$68,760
2000	Promontory Gold	E. S. Prado	Rob's Spirit	Avezzano (GB)	7	1:49.15	$66,540
1999	Time Off	J-L. Samyn	Hoyle	Lenny's Ransom	8	1:47.48	$66,720
1998	Recommended List	J. F. Chavez	Daniel My Brother	Availability	5	1:49.28	$67,800
1997	Subordination	J. R. Velazquez	Rob 'n Gin	Tekken (Ire)	8	**1:45.69**	$67,200
1996	Optic Nerve	J. A. Santos	Fortitude	Allied Forces	7	1:39.70	$66,420
1995	Green Means Go	J. D. Bailey	Smells and Bells	Debonair Dan	10	1:40.33	$68,160
1994	Pennine Ridge	J. D. Bailey	Check Ride	Add the Gold	9	1:39.87	$50,925
1993	Halissee	J. A. Krone	Proud Shot	Logroller	5	1:40.91	$52,020
1992	Free At Last	J. D. Bailey	Casino Magistrate	Kiri's Clown	8	1:41.05	$53,190

1992-'96 1¹⁄₁₆ miles. 1998 dirt. 1992 Casino Magistrate finished first, DQ to second. 1997 new course record.

Hollywood Derby

Grade 1, Hollywood Park, three-year-olds, 1¹⁄₈ miles, turf. Held November 25, 2001, with a gross value of $500,000. First held in 1938. Graded since 1973. Stakes record 1:45.82 (1999 Super Quercus [Fr]).

Year	Winner	Jockey	Second	Third	Strs	Final Time	1st Purse
2001	Denon	C. J. McCarron	Sligo Bay (Ire)	Aldebaran	12	1:49.28	$300,000
2000	Brahms	P. Day	David Copperfield	Zentsov Street	12	1:46.73	$300,000
1999	Super Quercus (Fr)	A. O. Solis	Manndar (Ire)	Fighting Falcon	14	**1:45.82**	$300,000
1998	Vergennes	J. R. Velazquez	Dixie Dot Com	Lone Bid (Fr)	10	1:49.44	$300,000
1997	Subordination	J. D. Bailey	Lasting Approval	Blazing Sword	13	1:50.12	$300,000
1996	Marlin	J. R. Velazquez	Rainbow Blues (Ire)	Devil's Cup	14	1:46.08	$300,000
1995	Labeeb (GB)	E. Delahoussaye	Helmsman	Da Hoss	13	1:46.42	$220,000
1994	River Flyer	C. W. Antley	Dare and Go	Fadeyev	13	1:47.48	$220,000
1993	Explosive Red	C. S. Nakatani	Jeune Homme	Earl of Barking (Ire)	14	1:46.88	$220,000
1992	Paradise Creek	P. Day	Bien Bien	Kitwood	12	1:47.36	$220,000

2000 Designed for Luck finished first, DQ to fifth.

Hollywood Futurity

Grade 1, Hollywood Park, two-year-olds, 1¹⁄₁₆ miles, dirt. Held December 15, 2001, with a gross value of $456,750. First held in 1981. Graded since 1983. Stakes record 1:40.74 (1994 Afternoon Deelites).

Year	Winner	Jockey	Second	Third	Strs	Final Time	1st Purse
2001	Siphonic	J. D. Bailey	Fonz's	Officer	8	1:42.09	$274,050
2000	Point Given	G. L. Stevens	Millennium Wind	Golden Ticket	4	1:42.21	$204,300
1999	Captain Steve	R. Albarado	High Yield	Cosine	6	1:43.27	$251,400
1998	Tactical Cat	L. A. Pincay Jr.	Prime Timber	Premier Property	5	1:42.63	$235,800
1997	Real Quiet	K. J. Desormeaux	Artax	Nationalore	11	1:41.34	$282,120
1996	Swiss Yodeler	A. O. Solis	Stolen Gold	In Excessive Bull	13	1:42.70	$348,510
1995	Matty G	A. O. Solis	Odyle	Ayrton S	7	1:41.75	$275,000
1994	Afternoon Deelites	K. J. Desormeaux	Thunder Gulch	A. J. Jett	5	**1:40.74**	$275,000
1993	Valiant Nature	L. A. Pincay Jr.	Brocco	Flying Sensation	6	1:40.78	$275,000
1992	River Special	L. A. Pincay Jr.	Stuka	Earl of Barking (Ire)	6	1:43.27	$275,000

Hollywood Gold Cup Stakes

Grade 1, Hollywood Park, three-year-olds and up, 1¼ miles, dirt. Held July 1, 2001, with a gross value of $750,000. First held in 1938. Graded since 1973. Stakes record 1:58.20 (1972 Quack).

Year	Winner	Jockey	Second	Third	Strs	Final Time	1st Purse
2001	Aptitude, 4	L. A. Pincay Jr.	Skimming, 5	Futural, 5	5	2:01.79	$450,000
2000	Early Pioneer, 5	V. Espinoza	General Challenge, 4	David, 4	9	2:01.40	$600,000
1999	Real Quiet, 4	J. D. Bailey	Budroyale, 6	Malek (Chi), 6	4	1:59.67	$600,000
1998	Skip Away, 5	J. D. Bailey	Puerto Madero (Chi), 4	Gentlemen (Arg), 4	8	2:00.16	$600,000
1997	Gentlemen (Arg), 5	G. L. Stevens	Siphon (Brz), 6	Sandpit (Brz), 6	6	1:59.26	$600,000
1996	Siphon (Brz), 5	D. R. Flores	Geri, 4	Helmsman, 4	8	2:00.50	$600,000
1995	Cigar, 5	J. D. Bailey	Tinners Way, 5	Tossofthecoin, 5	8	1:59.46	$550,000
1994	Slew of Damascus, 6	G. L. Stevens	Fanmore, 6	Del Mar Dennis, 6	5	2:00.76	$412,500
1993	Best Pal, 5	C. A. Black	Bertrando, 4	Major Impact, 4	10	2:00.17	$412,500
1992	Sultry Song, 4	J. D. Bailey	Marquetry, 5	Another Review, 5	6	2:00.23	$550,000

1992-'96 Hollywood Gold Cup H. 2001 Futural finished first, DQ to third.

Hollywood Juvenile Championship Stakes

Grade 3, Hollywood Park, two-year-olds, 6 furlongs, dirt. Held July 15, 2001, with a gross value of $107,400. First held in 1938. Graded since 1973. Stakes record 1:08.60 (1974 Dimaggio).

Year	Winner	Jockey	Second	Third	Strs	Final Time	1st Purse
2001	Came Home	C. J. McCarron	Metatron	A Major Pleasure	6	1:09.20	$64,440
2000	Squirtle Squirt	L. A. Pincay Jr.	Legendary Weave	Drumcliff	5	1:09.98	$63,540
1999	Dixie Union	A. O. Solis	Exchange Rate	High Yield	5	1:09.95	$63,780
1998	Yes It's True	J. D. Bailey	O'Rey Fantasma	Worldly Manner	7	1:09.58	$61,620
1997	K. O. Punch	G. L. Stevens	Old Topper	Majorbigtimesheet	9	1:09.95	$66,120
1996	Swiss Yodeler	A. O. Solis	Red	Vermilion	5	1:09.77	$61,740
1995	Hennessy	G. L. Stevens	Reef Reef	Desert Native	7	1:09.85	$57,400
1994	Mr Purple	C. J. McCarron	†Serena's Song	Cyrano	7	1:10.16	$57,600
1993	Ramblin Guy	E. Delahoussaye	Swift Walker	Individual Style	8	1:10.09	$57,600
1992	Altazarr	E. Delahoussaye	Tatum Canyon	Just Sid	6	1:10.01	$58,700

1992-'96 Grade 2. † denotes female.

Hollywood Oaks

Grade 2, Hollywood Park, three-year-old fillies, 1¹⁄₈ miles, dirt. Held July 14, 2001, with a gross value of $150,000. First held in 1946. Graded since 1973. Stakes record 1:46.93 (1994 Lakeway).

Year	Winner	Jockey	Second	Third	Strs	Final Time	1st Purse
2001	Affluent	E. Delahoussaye	Collect Call	Secret of Mecca	5	1:49.20	$90,000
2000	Kumari Continent	K. J. Desormeaux	Queenie Belle	Saudi Poetry	5	1:49.13	$90,000
1999	Smooth Player	E. Delahoussaye	Excellent Meeting	Nany's Sweep	5	1:48.17	$90,000
1998	Manistique	G. L. Stevens	Sweet and Ready	Yolo Lady	5	1:48.46	$120,000
1997	Sharp Cat	A. O. Solis	Freeport Flight	Really Happy	5	1:49.64	$120,000
1996	Listening	C. J. McCarron	Antespend	Ocean View	4	1:48.70	$110,640
1995	Sleep Easy	C. S. Nakatani	Bello Cielo	Carsona	5	1:50.24	$122,400
1994	Lakeway	K. J. Desormeaux	Sardula	Fancy 'n Fabulous	4	**1:46.93**	$120,000
1993	Hollywood Wildcat	E. Delahoussaye	Fit to Lead	Adorydar	9	1:48.48	$130,400
1992	Pacific Squall	K. J. Desormeaux	Race the Wild Wind	Alysbelle	7	1:48.07	$127,200

1992-'96 Grade 1. 1995 Predicted Glory finished second, DQ to fifth.

Hollywood Prevue Stakes

Grade 3, Hollywood Park, two-year-olds, 7 furlongs, dirt. Held November 17, 2001, with a gross value of $100,000. First held in 1981. Graded since 1985. Stakes record 1:20.98 (1994 Afternoon Deelites).

Year	Winner	Jockey	Second	Third	Strs	Final Time	1st Purse
2001	Fonz's	L. A. Pincay Jr.	Popular	Labamta Babe	7	1:22.03	$60,000
2000	Proud Tower	V. Espinoza	Chinook Cat	Yonaguska	8	1:23.01	$60,000

Year	Winner	Jockey	Second	Third	Strs	Final Time	1st Purse
1999	Grey Memo	M. S. Garcia	Magical Dragon	Cameron Pass	6	1:24.44	$60,000
1998	Premier Property	D. R. Flores	Select Few	American Spirit	7	1:23.29	$60,000
1997	Commitisize	D. R. Flores	Buttons N Moes	Search Me	6	1:21.64	$60,000
1996	In Excessive Bull	C. S. Nakatani	Thisnearlywasmine	Constant Demand	5	1:21.54	$61,020
1995	Cobra King	C. J. McCarron	Hennessy	Exetera	6	1:21.25	$58,800
1994	Afternoon Deelites	K. J. Desormeaux	Valid Wager	Hunt for Missouri	4	1:20.98	$57,500
1993	Individual Style	C. W. Antley	Egayant	Soul of the Matter	6	1:21.17	$46,150
1992	Stuka	P. A. Valenzuela	Codified	Altazarr	8	1:21.94	$62,350

1992-'95 Hollywood Prevue Breeders' Cup S.

Hollywood Starlet Stakes

Grade 1, Hollywood Park, two-year-old fillies, 1¹⁄₁₆ miles, dirt. Held December 16, 2001, with a gross value of $358,000. First held in 1981. Graded since 1983. Stakes record 1:41.96 (1994 Serena's Song).

Year	Winner	Jockey	Second	Third	Strs	Final Time	1st Purse
2001	Habibti	V. Espinoza	You	Tali'sluckybusride	5	1:43.12	$214,800
2000	I Believe in You	A. O. Solis	Jetin Excess	Whoopddoo	6	1:43.57	$205,050
1999	Surfside	P. Day	She's Classy	Abby Girl	5	1:43.51	$228,150
1998	Excellent Meeting	K. J. Desormeaux	Lacquaria	Perfect Six	6	1:42.14	$240,000
1997	Love Lock	K. J. Desormeaux	Career Collection	Snowberg	6	1:42.17	$168,600
1996	Sharp Cat	C. S. Nakatani	City Band	High Heeled Hope	8	1:44.69	$165,600
1995	Cara Rafaela	C. S. Nakatani	Advancing Star	Chile Chatte	5	1:43.10	$137,500
1994	Serena's Song	C. S. Nakatani	Urbane	Ski Dancer	5	1:41.96	$137,500
1993	Sardula	E. Delahoussaye	Princess Mitterand	Viz	5	1:42.34	$139,095
1992	Creaking Board (GB)	C. S. Nakatani	Passing Vice	Madame l'Enjoleur	9	1:43.73	$137,500

Hollywood Turf Cup Stakes

Grade 1, Hollywood Park, three-year-olds and up, 1½ miles, turf. Held December 1, 2001, with a gross value of $250,000. First held in 1981. Graded since 1983. Stakes record 2:24.80 (1990 It'sallgreektome).

Year	Winner	Jockey	Second	Third	Strs	Final Time	1st Purse
2001	Super Quercus (Fr), 5	A. O. Solis	Bonapartiste (Fr), 7	Blazing Fury, 7	9	2:29.86	$150,000
2000	Bienamado, 4	C. J. McCarron	Northern Quest (Fr), 5	Lazy Lode (Arg), 5	8	2:25.98	$240,000
1999	Lazy Lode (Arg), 5	L. A. Pincay Jr.	Public Purse, 5	Single Empire (Ire), 5	7	2:25.85	$240,000
1998	Lazy Lode (Arg), 4	C. S. Nakatani	Yagli, 5	Ferrari (Ger), 5	10	2:28.36	$300,000
1997	River Bay, 4	A. O. Solis	Awad, 7	Flag Down, 7	12	2:26.47	$300,000
1996	Running Flame (Fr), 4	C. J. McCarron	Marlin, 3	Talloires, 3	10	2:28.53	$300,000
1995	Royal Chariot, 5	A. O. Solis	Talloires, 5	Earl of Barking (Ire), 5	14	2:25.18	$275,000
1994	Frenchpark (GB), 4	C. A. Black	Dare and Go, 3	Regency (GB), 3	11	2:25.66	$275,000
1993	Fraise, 5	C. J. McCarron	Know Heights (Ire), 4	Explosive Red, 4	6	2:32.34	$275,000
1992	Bien Bien, 3	C. J. McCarron	Fraise, 4	†Trishyde, 4	6	2:31.28	$275,000

1992 Fraise finished first, DQ to second. † denotes female.

Hollywood Turf Express Handicap

Grade 3, Hollywood Park, three-year-olds and up, 5½ furlongs, turf. Held November 23, 2001, with a gross value of $200,000. First held in 1985. Graded since 1994. Stakes record 1:01.40 (1991 Gundaghia [1st Div.]; 1991 Answer Do [2nd Div.]).

Year	Winner	Jockey	Second	Third	Strs	Final Time	1st Purse
2001	Swept Overboard, 4, 122	E. Delahoussaye	Speak in Passing, 4	Blu Air Force (Ire), 4	10	1:01.86	$120,000
2000	El Cielo, 6, 122	C. S. Nakatani	Texas Glitter, 4	Full Moon Madness, 4	7	1:01.73	$120,000
1999	Mr. Doubledown, 5, 115	V. Espinoza	Howbaddouwantit, 4	Champ's Star, 4	8	1:01.98	$120,000
1998	Soldier Field, 3, 117	R. Wilson	Surachai, 5	Bodyguard (GB), 5	10	1:02.19	$120,000
1997	Advancing Star, 4, 119	K. J. Desormeaux	Latin Dancer, 3	Surachai, 3	9	1:02.68	$120,000
1996	Sandtrap, 3, 114	A. O. Solis	Cyrano Storme (Ire), 6	Suggest, 6	8	1:01.46	$120,000
1995	Cyrano Storme (Ire), 5, 116	R. R. Douglas	Lakota Brave, 6	Pembroke, 6	9	1:01.64	$110,000
1994	Rotsaluck, 3, 118	F. H. Valenzuela	†Marina Park (GB), 4	D'Hallevant, 4	11	1:02.27	$82,500
1993	Wild Harmony, 4, 117	C. J. McCarron	Robin des Pins, 5	Monde Bleu (GB), 5	8	1:01.88	$110,000
1992	Answer Do, 6, 121	E. Delahoussaye	Repriced, 4	Gundaghia, 4	11	1:02.14	$110,000

† denotes female.

Holy Bull Stakes

Grade 3, Gulfstream Park, three-year-olds, 1¹⁄₁₆ miles, dirt. Held January 20, 2001, with a gross value of $100,000. First held in 1990. Graded since 1995. Stakes record 1:41.62 (1994 Go for Gin).

Year	Winner	Jockey	Second	Third	Strs	Final Time	1st Purse
2001	Radical Riley	E. O. Nunez	Buckle Down Ben	Cee Dee	8	1:46.06	$60,000
2000	Hal's Hope	R. I. Velez	Personal First	Megacles	11	1:44.52	$60,000
1999	Grits'n Hard Toast	R. G. Davis	Doneraile Court	Mountain Range	7	1:45.32	$60,000
1998	Cape Town	J. D. Bailey	Comic Strip	Sweetsouthernsaint	7	1:44.15	$60,000
1997	Arthur L.	J. R. Velazquez	Acceptable	Captain Bodgit	9	1:42.93	$60,000

Year	Winner	Jockey	Second	Third	Strs	Final Time	1st Purse
1996	Cobra King	C. J. McCarron	Editor's Note	Tilden	7	1:43.42	$45,000
1995	Suave Prospect	J. D. Bailey	Bullet Trained	Rush Dancer	8	1:44.03	$45,000
1994	Go for Gin	J. D. Bailey	Halo's Image	Senor Conquistador	6	1:41.62	$45,000
1993	Pride of Burkaan	J. D. Bailey	Kassec	Jetting Along	8	1:44.74	$45,000
1992	Waki Warrior	E. Fires	Scream Machine	Careful Gesture	13	1:44.32	$78,258

1992-'95 Preview S.

Honey Bee Handicap

Grade 3, The Meadowlands, three-year-old fillies, 1¹/₁₆ miles, dirt. Held November 2, 2001, with a gross value of $194,000. First held in 1977. Graded since 1985. Stakes record 1:40.60 (1984 Squan Song).

Year	Winner	Jockey	Second	Third	Strs	Final Time	1st Purse
2001	Mystic Lady, 122	E. Coa	Latour	Shiny Band	4	1:42.29	$120,000
2000	Critical Eye, 121	M. E. Smith	Eventail	Rosie Dooley	7	1:41.90	$120,000
1999	Belle Cherie, 115	J. A. Velez Jr.	Gaelic Bay	Boom Town Girl	11	1:42.19	$90,000
1998	Thunder Kitten, 112	S. J. Sellers	Salty Lady	Patty's Positive	7	1:41.24	$60,000
1997	Fancy Freda, 114	W. H. McCauley	Alarming Prospect	Key Hunter	9	1:41.12	$60,000
1996	Proper Angel, 115	M. G. Pino	Gold n Delicious	Plum Country	6	1:44.62	$30,000
1995	Rogues Walk, 120	J. R. Velazquez	Full and Fancy	Transient Trend	7	1:42.77	$30,000
1994	Sterling Pound, 114	M. E. Smith	Footing	Perfect Night	6	1:42.68	$30,000
1993	Nine Keys, 113	M. E. Smith	Aztec Hill	Broad Gains	6	1:43.00	$30,000
1992	Vivano, 121	M. E. Smith	Caged Heart	Dior's Angel	5	1:43.98	$30,000

1996 Meadowlands Honey Bee H.; 1997 Honey Bee Breeders' Cup H.

Honeybee Stakes

Grade 3, Oaklawn Park, three-year-old fillies, 1¹/₁₆ miles, dirt. Held March 10, 2001, with a gross value of $75,000. First held in 1988. Graded since 1990. Stakes record 1:43 (1989 Imaginary Lady).

Year	Winner	Jockey	Second	Third	Strs	Final Time	1st Purse
2001	Xtreme Bid	D. C. Nuesch	My White Corvette	Pajamas	7	1:46.07	$45,000
2000	Fiesty Countess	T. T. Doocy	Asher	Prairie Pioneer	7	1:44.76	$45,000
1999	Dreams Gallore	G. Murphy	The Happy Hopper	Humble Retha	7	1:43.49	$45,000
1998	Roza Robata	F. A. Arguello Jr.	Sweet and Ready	Bucquestor	9	1:45.95	$45,000
1997	Valid Bonnet	T. T. Doocy	Alyssum	Hooten Annie	6	1:43.68	$45,000
1996	Jetto	L. Melancon	Mama's Pro	Wise Action	7	1:46.32	$45,000
1995	Humble Eight	D. Guillory	Lilly Capote	Traces of Gold	6	1:45.26	$45,000
1994	Shadow Miss	W. Martinez	Slide Show	Accountinquestion	8	1:44.74	$45,000
1993	Aztec Hill	A. T. Gryder	Avie's Shadow	Life Is Delicious	8	1:44.50	$45,000
1992	Totemic	D. R. Miller	Take the Cure	Royal Amazon	5	1:43.29	$45,000

Honey Fox Handicap

Grade 3, Gulfstream Park, three-year-olds and up, fillies and mares, 1 mile, turf. Held January 7, 2001, with a gross value of $100,000. First held in 1985. Graded since 1994. Stakes record 1:35.60 (2001 Spook Express [SAf]).

Year	Winner	Jockey	Second	Third	Strs	Final Time	1st Purse
2001	Spook Express (SAf), 7, 115	M. E. Smith	Please Sign In, 5	Lady Dora, 5	12	1:35.60	$60,000
2000	Dominique's Joy, 5, 113	J. D. Bailey	Circus Charmer, 5	Pico Teneriffe, 5	7	1:39.91	$45,000
1999	Colcon, 6, 119	J. D. Bailey	Lovers Knot (GB), 4	Tampico, 4	10	1:41.71	$45,000
1998	Parade Queen, 4, 118	P. Day	Dispersion, 4	Dance Clear (Ire), 5	12	1:42.10	$45,000
1997	Rare Blend, 4, 118	J. D. Bailey	Queen Tutta, 5	Hurricane Viv, 5	6	1:44.28	$45,000
1996	Apolda, 5, 116	J. D. Bailey	Class Kris, 4	Alice Springs, 4	11	1:41.55	$45,000
1995	Regal Joy, 4, 113	D. Penna	Sambacarioca, 6	Sovereign Kitty, 6	6	1:44.79	$36,000
1994	Sambacarioca, 5, 121	J. D. Bailey	Tiney Toast, 5	Marshua's River, 5	6	1:43.41	$36,000
1993	Hero's Love, 5, 113	E. Fires	Quilma (Chi), 6	Lady Blessington (Fr), 6	14	1:42.90	$30,000
1992	Explosive Kate, 5, 113	D. Penna	Indian Fashion, 5	Belleofbasinstreet, 5	14	1:43.37	$30,000

1992-2000 Joe Namath H. 1992-2000 1¹/₁₆ miles. 1994-'95, 1997 dirt.

Honeymoon Breeders' Cup Invitational Handicap

Grade 2, Hollywood Park, three-year-old fillies, 1¹/₈ miles, turf. Held July 1, 2001, with a gross value of $217,000. First held in 1952. Graded since 1976. Stakes record 2:01.28 (2001 Innit [Ire]).

Year	Winner	Jockey	Second	Third	Strs	Final Time	1st Purse
2001	Innit (Ire), 117	C. J. McCarron	Live Your Dreams	Beefeater Baby	9	2:01.28	$120,000
2000	Classy Cara, 122	I. Puglisi	Kumari Continent	Minor Details	9	1:48.05	$90,000
1999	Sweet Ludy (Ire), 116	G. L. Stevens	Tout Charmant	Aviate	7	1:48.05	$65,160
1998	Country Garden (GB), 120	K. J. Desormeaux	Janine Rose	Chenille (Ire)	6	1:48.74	$64,080
1997	Famous Digger, 116	B. Blanc	Freeport Flight	Kentucky Kaper	8	1:47.68	$65,460
1996	Antespend, 122	C. W. Antley	Clamorosa	Najecam	9	1:47.50	$82,410
1995	Auriette (Ire), 117	E. Delahoussaye	Artica	Top Shape (Fr)	6	1:41.68	$62,100
1994	Work the Crowd, 117	C. J. McCarron	Malli Star	Fancy 'n Fabulous	8	1:39.68	$64,700
1993	Likeable Style, 122	E. Delahoussaye	Adorydar	Vinista	5	1:46.29	$62,200
1992	Pacific Squall, 115	K. J. Desormeaux	Miss Turkana	Morriston Belle	10	1:41.02	$67,100

1992-2000 Honeymoon H. 1992-'97 Grade 3. 1992-'95 1¹/₁₆ miles; 1996-2000 1¹/₈ miles. 1993 dirt.

Honorable Miss Handicap

Grade 3, Saratoga Race Course, three-year-olds and up, fillies and mares, 6 furlongs, dirt. Held August 1, 2001, with a gross value of $103,000. First held in 1992. Graded since 1996. Stakes record 1:08.93 (2000 Bourbon Belle [2nd Div.]).

Year	Winner	Jockey	Second	Third	Strs	Final Time	1st Purse
2001	Big Bambu, 4, 118	J. D. Bailey	Country Hideaway, 5	Dat You Miz Blue, 5	4	1:09.64	$63,708
2000	Debby d'Or, 5, 114	S. J. Sellers	Tropical Punch, 4	Katz Me If You Can, 4	9	1:10.11	$66,450
	Bourbon Belle, 5, 116	W. Martinez	Cassidy, 5	Go to the Ink, 5	8	1:08.93	$65,850
1999	Bourbon Belle, 4, 116	P. A. Johnson	Gold Princess, 4	License Fee, 4	10	1:09.53	$67,560
1998	Furlough, 4, 113	M. E. Smith	Angel's Tearlet, 5	Dixie Flag, 5	6	1:11.32	$48,765
1997	Dancin Renee, 5, 116	R. Migliore	Ashboro, 4	Vivace, 4	6	1:09.16	$48,465
1996	Twist Afleet, 5, 119	M. E. Smith	Broad Smile, 4	In Conference, 4	8	1:09.91	$49,005
1995	Low Key Affair, 4, 115	P. Day	Classy Mirage, 5	Twist Afleet, 5	5	1:09.67	$48,195
1994	Classy Mirage, 4, 122	J. A. Krone	Spinning Round, 5	For all Seasons, 5	6	1:09.72	$48,675
1993	Nannerl, 6, 117	J. D. Bailey	Vivano, 4	Via Dei Portici, 4	6	1:15.19	$29,040
1992	Nice Assay, 4, 115	C. J. McCarron	Madam Bear, 4	Real Irish Hope, 4	5	1:08.97	$31,620

1992-'97 Honorable Miss S. 2000 two divisions. 1993 6½ furlongs.

Hopeful Stakes

Grade 1, Saratoga Race Course, two-year-olds, 7 furlongs, dirt. Held September 1, 2001, with a gross value of $200,000. First held in 1903. Graded since 1973. Stakes record 1:21.94 (2001 Came Home).

Year	Winner	Jockey	Second	Third	Strs	Final Time	1st Purse
2001	Came Home	C. J. McCarron	Mayakovsky	Thunder Days	7	1:21.94	$120,000
2000	(DH) City Zip	J. A. Santos		Macho Uno	11	1:24.52	$80,000
	(DH) Yonaguska	J. D. Bailey					
1999	High Yield	J. D. Bailey	Settlement	Exciting Story	9	1:22.85	$120,000
1998	Lucky Roberto	R. G. Davis	Tactical Cat	Time Bandit	7	1:23.81	$120,000
1997	Favorite Trick	P. Day	K. O. Punch	Jess M	7	1:23.87	$120,000
1996	Smoke Glacken	C. Perret	Ordway	Gun Fight	8	1:23.63	$120,000
1995	Hennessy	G. L. Stevens	Louis Quatorze	Maria's Mon	7	1:23.44	$120,000
1994	Wild Escapade	J. F. Chavez	Montreal Red	Law of the Sea	6	1:23.24	$120,000
1993	Dehere	C. J. McCarron	Slew Gin Fizz	Whitney Tower	7	1:15.97	$120,000
1992	Great Navigator	A. T. Gryder	Strolling Along	England Expects	8	1:15.71	$120,000

1992-'93 6½ furlongs. 2000 dead heat for first.

Humana Distaff Handicap (see Distaff Handicap)

Hutcheson Stakes

Grade 2, Gulfstream Park, three-year-olds, 7 furlongs, dirt. Held January 27, 2001, with a gross value of $150,000. First held in 1954. Graded since 1973. Stakes record 1:20.80 (1978 Sensitive Prince).

Year	Winner	Jockey	Second	Third	Strs	Final Time	1st Purse
2001	Yonaguska	J. D. Bailey	City Zip	Sparkling Sabre	11	1:22.63	$90,000
2000	(DH) Summer Note	S. J. Sellers		American Bullet	8	1:21.76	$60,000
	(DH) More Than Ready	J. R. Velazquez					
1999	Bet Me Best	J. D. Bailey	Texas Glitter	Cat Thief	7	1:22.33	$90,000
1998	Time Limit	J. D. Bailey	Coronado's Quest	Zippy Zeal	5	1:22.53	$60,000
1997	Frisk Me Now	E. L. King Jr.	Confide	Crown Ambassador	8	1:22.51	$60,000
1996	Appealing Skier	R. Wilson	Unbridled's Song	Gold Fever	5	1:24.72	$45,000
1995	Valid Wager	M. A. Pedroza	Mr. Greeley	Don Juan A	7	1:23.51	$45,000
1994	Holy Bull	M. E. Smith	Patton	You and I	5	1:21.23	$45,000
1993	Hidden Trick	R. P. Romero	Great Navigator	Forever Whirl	9	1:23.61	$54,108
1992	My Luck Runs North	R. D. Lopez	Sneaky Solicitor	Frosted Spy	9	1:24.95	$55,008

1993 Demaloot Demashoot finished second, DQ to fourth. 2000 dead head for first.

Illinois Derby

Grade 2, Sportsman's Park, three-year-olds, 1⅛ miles, dirt. Held April 7, 2001, with a gross value of $500,000. First held in 1923. Graded since 1973. Stakes record 1:47.51 (1997 Wild Rush).

Year	Winner	Jockey	Second	Third	Strs	Final Time	1st Purse
2001	Distilled	M. E. Smith	Saint Damien	Dream Run	8	1:51.37	$300,000
2000	Performing Magic	S. J. Sellers	Country Only	Country Coast	9	1:50.86	$300,000
1999	Vision and Verse	H. Castillo Jr.	Prime Directive	Pineaff	10	1:48.47	$300,000
1998	Yarrow Brae	W. Martinez	One Bold Stroke	Orville N Wilbur's	10	1:51.21	$300,000
1997	Wild Rush	K. J. Desormeaux	Anet	Saratoga Sunrise	8	1:47.51	$300,000
1996	Natural Selection	R. P. Romero	El Amante	Irish Conquest	13	1:48.60	$300,000
1995	Peaks and Valleys	J. A. Krone	Da Hoss	Western Echo	13	1:48.99	$300,000
1994	Rustic Light	E. Fires	Amathos	Seminole Wind	7	1:51.89	$300,000
1993	Antrim Rd.	A. T. Gryder	Seattle Morn	Secret Negotiator	13	1:48.68	$300,000
1992	Dignitas	J. D. Bailey	American Chance	Straight to Bed	13	1:49.09	$320,100

1999 held at Hawthorne Race Course. 1997 new track record.

Indiana Breeders' Cup Oaks

Grade 3, Hoosier Park, three-year-old fillies, 1¹⁄₁₆ miles, dirt. Held October 5, 2001, with a gross value of $205,800. First held in 1995. Graded since 2001. Stakes record 1:42.40 (2000 Humble Clerk).

Year	Winner	Jockey	Second	Third	Strs	Final Time	1st Purse
2001	Scoop	R. Albarado	Gold Huntress	Caressing	9	1:44.06	$123,480
2000	Humble Clerk	L. Melancon	Megans Bluff	Miss Seffens	5	**1:42.40**	$92,580
1999	Brushed Halory	E. M. Martin Jr.	The Happy Hopper	Chelsie's House	10	1:44.64	$123,330
1998	French Braids	W. Martinez	Remember Ike	Barefoot Dyana	7	1:43.11	$124,080
1997	Cotton Carnival	E. M. Martin Jr.	Sheepscot	Valid Bonnet	9	1:43.30	$64,440
1996	Princess Eloise	S. T. Saito	Talking Tower	Shuffle Again	6	1:37.00	$33,540
1995	Niner's Home	T. J. Hebert	Alltheway Bertie	Graceful Minister	6	1:37.00	$24,480

1995-'97 Indiana Oaks. 1995-'96 1 mile.

Indiana Derby

Not graded, Hoosier Park, three-year-olds, 1¹⁄₁₆ miles, dirt. Held October 6, 2001, with a gross value of $314,100. First held in 1995. Grade 3 since 2002. Stakes record 1:41.40 (1996 Canyon Run).

Year	Winner	Jockey	Second	Third	Strs	Final Time	1st Purse
2001	Orientate	R. Albarado	Saratoga Games	Trion Georgia	11	1:42.22	$188,460
2000	Mister Deville	L. S. Quinonez	Performing Magic	One Call Close	5	1:41.80	$184,500
1999	Forty One Carats	J. F. Chavez	Zanetti	First American	12	1:42.24	$188,100
1998	One Bold Stroke	R. Albarado	Dixie Dot Com	Da Devil	11	1:43.14	$188,700
1997	Dubai Dust	S. P. LeJeune Jr.	Frisk Me Now	Tansit	8	1:44.00	$127,440
1996	Canyon Run	F. C. Torres	Broadway Bit	Hunk of Class	10	**1:41.40**	$64,560
1995	Peruvian	D. Kutz	I Still Believe	Mine Inspector	11	1:43.00	$66,900

Inglewood Handicap

Grade 3, Hollywood Park, three-year-olds and up, 1¹⁄₁₆ miles, turf. Held April 21, 2001, with a gross value of $107,100. First held in 1938. Graded since 1973. Stakes record 1:38.77 (1998 Fantastic Fellow).

Year	Winner	Jockey	Second	Third	Strs	Final Time	1st Purse
2001	Fateful Dream, 4, 114	D. R. Flores	National Anthem (GB), 5	Casino King (Ire), 5	5	1:41.65	$64,260
2000	Montemiro (Fr), 6, 113	V. Espinoza	Bonapartiste (Fr), 6	Takarian (Ire), 6	8	1:40.71	$66,300
1999	Brave Act (GB), 5, 120	G. F. Almeida	Lord Smith (GB), 4	Expressionist, 4	8	1:39.13	$66,420
1998	Fantastic Fellow, 4, 118	C. S. Nakatani	Via Lombardia (Ire), 6	Sharekann (Ire), 6	6	**1:38.77**	$64,740
1997	El Angelo, 5, 115	C. S. Nakatani	Irish Wings (Ire), 5	Tychonic (GB), 5	5	1:40.29	$63,900
1996	Fastness (Ire), 6, 122	C. S. Nakatani	Helmsman, 4	Tychonic (GB), 4	5	1:39.54	$79,470
1995	Blaze O'Brien, 8, 116	C. A. Black	Savinio, 5	Stoller, 5	7	1:39.53	$79,800
1994	Gothland (Fr), 5, 117	C. S. Nakatani	Rapan Boy (Aus), 6	Johann Quatz (Fr), 6	4	1:39.60	$60,700
1993	The Tender Track, 6, 116	E. Delahoussaye	Journalism, 5	Johann Quatz (Fr), 5	6	1:40.00	$62,500
1992	Golden Pheasant, 6, 121	G. L. Stevens	Blaze O'Brien, 5	Native Boundary, 5	7	1:39.86	$64,900

1992-'94 Grade 2. 1998 new course record.

Iroquois Stakes

Grade 3, Churchill Downs, two-year-olds, 1 mile, dirt. Held November 4, 2001, with a gross value of $113,200. First held in 1982. Graded since 1990. Stakes record 1:35.01 (2001 Harlan's Holiday).

Year	Winner	Jockey	Second	Third	Strs	Final Time	1st Purse
2001	Harlan's Holiday	A. J. D'Amico	Request for Parole	Gold Dollar	10	**1:35.01**	$70,184
2000	Meetyouathebrig	G. L. Stevens	Hero's Tribute	Keats	13	1:35.24	$77,066
1999	Mighty	M. St. Julien	Ifitstobeitsuptome	Nature	7	1:35.88	$68,758
1998	Exploit	C. J. McCarron	Crowning Storm	Olympic Journey	8	1:36.26	$71,114
1997	Keene Dancer	P. Day	Yarrow Brae	Dawn Exodus	7	1:37.84	$68,882
1996	Global View	K. Bourque	Partner's Hero	Haint	6	1:36.49	$68,200
1995	Ide	C. Perret	El Amante	City by Night	8	1:36.89	$73,645
1994	Peruvian	J. A. Santos	Our Gatsby	Super Jeblar	11	1:36.68	$77,025
1993	Tarzans Blade	B. E. Bartram	Dove Hunt	Amathos	11	1:37.00	$74,945
1992	Shoal Creek	B. E. Bartram	Saw Mill	Demaloot Demashoot	13	1:37.51	$76,375

Jaipur Handicap

Not graded (originally scheduled as Grade 3), Belmont Park, three-year-olds and up, 7 furlongs, dirt (originally scheduled on the turf). Held May 27, 2001, with a gross value of $100,900. First held in 1984. Graded since 1986. Stakes record 1:20.06 (1994 Nijinsky's Gold).

Year	Winner	Jockey	Second	Third	Strs	Final Time	1st Purse
2001	Affirmed Success, 7, 123	J. D. Bailey	Texas Glitter, 5	Bought in Dixie, 5	3	1:21.69	$65,475
2000	Gone Fishin, 4, 114	J. R. Velazquez	Weatherbird, 5	French Envoy, 5	12	1:21.73	$52,290
1999	Notoriety, 6, 115	J. L. Espinoza	Optic Nerve, 6	Cryptic Rascal, 6	12	1:21.35	$52,335
1998	Elusive Quality, 5, 115	J. D. Bailey	Bristling, 6	Optic Nerve, 6	11	1:20.99	$51,750
1997	Atraf (GB), 4, 116	J. R. Velazquez	Mighty Forum (GB), 6	Play Smart, 6	4	1:23.64	$49,635

Year	Winner	Jockey	Second	Third	Strs	Final Time	1st Purse
1996	**Grand Continental**, 5, 114	R. Migliore	Inside the Beltway, 5	Goldmine (Fr), 5	10	1:23.78	$51,720
1995	**Inside the Beltway**, 4, 114	J. F. Chavez	Gabr (GB), 5	Golden Cloud, 5	5	1:21.23	$49,245
	Mighty Forum (GB), 4, 117	G. L. Stevens	Dominant Prospect, 5	City Nights (Ire), 5	9	1:21.12	$49,995
1994	**Nijinsky's Gold**, 5, 114	J. A. Santos	Dominant Prospect, 4	Home of the Free, 4	7	**1:20.06**	$34,905
	A in Sociology, 4, 119	E. Maple	Roman Envoy, 6	Halissee, 6	7	1:20.38	$34,905
1993	**Home of the Free**, 5, 117	J. D. Bailey	Wind Symbol (GB), 4	Fourstardave, 4	8	1:20.69	$55,080
1992	**To Freedom**, 4, 117	J. A. Krone	Fourstardave, 7	Smart Alec, 7	5	1:22.83	$55,710

1992-'95 Jaipur S. 1992-2000 Grade 3. 1993-'96,1998-2000 turf. 1994, 1995 two divisions. 1993, 1994 (1st Div.) new course record.

Jamaica Handicap

Grade 2, Belmont Park, three-year-olds, 1⅛ miles, turf. Held September 23, 2001, with a gross value of $200,000. First held in 1929. Graded since 1978. Stakes record 1:49 (1997 Subordination).

Year	Winner	Jockey	Second	Third	Strs	Final Time	1st Purse
2001	**Navesink**, 118	E. S. Prado	Strategic Partner	Baptize	7	1:51.53	$120,000
2000	**King Cugat**, 123	J. D. Bailey	Mandarin Marsh	Parade Leader	8	1:49.63	$120,000
1999	**Monarch's Maze**, 117	J. Bravo	Killer Joe	Monkey Puzzle	8	1:51.66	$90,000
1998	**Vergennes**, 115	J. R. Velazquez	Tangazi	Middlesex Drive	10	1:50.42	$90,000
1997	**Subordination**, 120	J. F. Chavez	Premier Krischief	Skybound	12	**1:49.00**	$90,000
1996	**Allied Forces**, 119	R. Migliore	Cliptomania	Lite Approval	11	1:40.91	$86,325
1994	**Pennine Ridge**, 118	J. R. Velazquez	Holy Mountain	I'm Very Irish	7	1:35.13	$66,540
1993	**Mi Cielo**, 116	M. E. Smith	Prospector's Flag	Cherokee Run	8	1:35.20	$70,440
1992	**West by West**, 112	J-L. Samyn	Offbeat	Portroe	7	1:34.27	$70,320

1995 not held. 1992-'94 1 mile; 1996 1¹⁄₁₆ miles. 1992-'93 dirt.

Jefferson Cup Stakes

Grade 3, Churchill Downs, three-year-olds, 1⅛ miles, turf. Held June 9, 2001, with a gross value of $282,500. First held in 1977. Graded since 2001. Stakes record 1:47.27 (2000 King Cugat).

Year	Winner	Jockey	Second	Third	Strs	Final Time	1st Purse
2001	**Indygo Shiner**	L. Meche	Strategic Partner	Fast City	9	1:48.81	$175,150
2000	**King Cugat**	R. Albarado	Four On the Floor	Field Cat	10	**1:47.27**	$177,940
1999	**Special Coach**	C. H. Velasquez	Silver Chadra	Air Rocket	12	1:50.13	$180,110
1998	**Buff**	C. H. Borel	Keene Dancer	Ladies Din	7	1:50.80	$175,770
1997	**Greed Is Good**	W. Martinez	Royal Strand (Ire)	Crimson Classic	5	1:49.47	$69,068
1996	**Unruled**	C. Perret	Broadway Beau	Trail City	6	1:50.07	$54,210
1995	**Ago**	S. J. Sellers	Michael's Star	Lemon Drop	11	1:49.48	$56,550
1994	**Milt's Overture**	P. Day	Jaggery John	Camptown Dancer	6	1:48.21	$53,528
1993	**Lt. Pinkerton**	T. J. Hebert	Snake Eyes	Mi Cielo	6	1:48.27	$35,555
1992	**Senor Tomas**	P. Day	Coaxing Matt	Black Question	7	1:49.80	$35,945

Jenny Wiley Stakes

Grade 3, Keeneland, four-year-olds and up, fillies and mares, 1¹⁄₁₆ miles, turf. Held April 12, 2001, with a gross value of $113,900. First held in 1989. Graded since 1995. Stakes record 1:40.78 (1996 Apolda).

Year	Winner	Jockey	Second	Third	Strs	Final Time	1st Purse
2001	**Penny's Gold**, 4	J. A. Santos	License Fee, 6	Solvig, 6	9	1:40.93	$70,618
2000	**Astra**, 4	C. S. Nakatani	Pratella, 5	Ronda (GB), 5	8	1:42.48	$69,688
1999	**Pleasant Temper**, 5	J. D. Bailey	Mingling Glances, 5	Red Cat, 5	8	1:40.93	$70,246
1998	**Maxzene**, 5	J. A. Santos	Parade Queen, 4	Rumpipumpy (GB), 4	7	1:42.82	$69,192
1997	**Thrilling Day (GB)**, 4	W. Martinez	Romy, 6	Gastronomical, 6	7	1:41.16	$68,634
1996	**Apolda**, 5	J. D. Bailey	Mediation (Ire), 4	Luzette (Brz), 4	5	**1:40.78**	$69,006
1995	**Romy**, 4	F. C. Torres	Weekend Madness (Ire), 5	Bold Ruritana, 5	9	1:43.32	$52,173
1994	**Misspitch**, 4	M. E. Smith	Park Dream (Ire), 5	Sh Bang, 5	10	1:43.83	$34,658
1993	**Lady Blessington (Fr)**, 5	P. Day	Radiant Ring, 5	Super Fan, 5	6	1:42.59	$34,844
1992	**Indian Fashion**, 5	J. A. Santos	Spanish Parade, 4	Radiant Ring, 4	10	1:41.26	$36,514

1992, 1996 new course record.

Jerome Handicap

Grade 2, Belmont Park, three-year-olds, 1 mile, dirt. Held September 22, 2001, with a gross value of $150,000. First held in 1866. Graded since 1973. Stakes record 1:33.20 (1981 Noble Nashua).

Year	Winner	Jockey	Second	Third	Strs	Final Time	1st Purse
2001	**Express Tour**, 115	J. Velazquez	Illusioned	Burning Roma	5	1:34.57	$90,000
2000	**Fusaichi Pegasus**, 124	K. J. Desormeaux	El Corredor	Albert the Great	5	1:34.07	$90,000
1999	**Doneraile Court**, 117	C. W. Antley	Vicar	Badger Gold	7	1:35.63	$90,000
1998	**Limit Out**, 117	J-L. Samyn	Grand Slam	Scatmandu	5	1:36.22	$90,000
1997	**Richter Scale**, 118	S. J. Sellers	Trafalger	Smokin Mel	8	1:35.88	$90,000

Year	Winner	Jockey	Second	Third	Strs	Final Time	1st Purse
1996	**Why Change**, 112	C. C. Lopez	Distorted Humor	Diligence	10	1:34.22	$90,000
1995	**French Deputy**, 113	G. L. Stevens	Mr. Greeley	Top Account	6	1:33.53	$120,000
1994	**Prenup**, 113	J. D. Bailey	Ulises	End Sweep	8	1:34.59	$120,000
1993	**Schossberg**, 113	J. D. Bailey	Williamstown	Mi Cielo	5	1:35.53	$120,000
1992	**Furiously**, 113	J. D. Bailey	Colony Light	Dixie Brass	6	1:34.20	$120,000

1992-'94 Grade 1.

Jersey Derby

Grade 3, Monmouth Park, three-year-olds, 1 1/16 miles, dirt (originally scheduled on the turf). Held May 27, 2001, with a gross value of $100,000. First held in 1864. Graded since 1973. Stakes record 1:40.80 (1997 Rob 'n Gin).

Year	Winner	Jockey	Second	Third	Strs	Final Time	1st Purse
2001	†**Mystic Lady**	F. Leon	Sir Brian's Sword	What's Your Wish	6	1:44.31	$60,000
2000	**Lendell Ray**	A. T. Gryder	Powerful Appeal	Cogburn	8	1:42.96	$60,000
1999	**Swamp**	R. Migliore	Crash Course	Good Skate	7	1:40.94	$90,000
1998	†**Who Did It and Run**	F. L. Ortiz	Essential	Cryptic Rascal	8	1:41.37	$90,000
1997	**Rob 'n Gin**	J. D. Bailey	Tekken (Ire)	Keep It Strait	9	**1:40.80**	$90,000
1996	**More Royal**	J. A. Krone	Optic Nerve	Value Investor	10	1:42.46	$90,000
1995	**Da Hoss**	J. A. Krone	Claudius	Crimson Guard	10	1:43.01	$90,000
1994	**Zuno Star**	M. E. Smith	Seattle Rob	(DH) Warn Me (GB)	10	1:43.86	$90,000
				(DH) Mr. Angel			
1993	**Llandaff**	J. A. Krone	Logroller	Forest Wind	11	1:42.50	$90,000
1992	**American Chance**	P. Day	Majestic Sweep	Palace Line	9	1:50.86	$180,000

1992-'99 Grade 2. 1992-'98 held at Garden State Park. 1992 1 1/8 miles. 1993-2000 turf. 1994 dead heat for third. 1997, 1999 equaled course record. † denotes female.

Jersey Shore Breeders' Cup Stakes

Grade 3, Monmouth Park, three-year-olds, 6 furlongs, dirt. Held July 4, 2001, with a gross value of $95,000. First held in 1992. Graded since 1994. Stakes record 1:08.53 (1997 Smoke Glacken).

Year	Winner	Jockey	Second	Third	Strs	Final Time	1st Purse
2001	**City Zip**	J. C. Ferrer	Sea of Green	Songandaprayer	5	1:09.02	$60,000
2000	**Disco Rico**	J. Bravo	Max's Pal	Stormin Oedy	6	1:09.05	$60,000
1999	**Yes It's True**	J. D. Bailey	Erlton	Flying Griffoni	4	1:08.59	$60,000
1998	**Good and Tough**	W. H. McCauley	Klabin's Gold	El Mirasol	6	1:10.01	$45,000
1997	**Smoke Glacken**	C. Perret	Partner's Hero	King Buck	4	**1:08.53**	$30,000
1996	**Swing and Miss**	T. G. Turner	Seacliff	Dixie Connection	6	1:10.00	$60,000
1995	**Ft. Stockton**	J. Bravo	Jealous Crusader	Gala Knockout	9	1:22.64	$64,050
1994	**End Sweep**	M. E. Smith	Meadow Flight	Foxie G	5	1:21.20	$63,450
1993	**Montbrook**	C. J. Ladnier	Evil Bear	Shu Fellow	7	1:21.04	$63,420
1992	**Surely Six**	R. Wilson	Superstrike (GB)	Salt Lake	8	1:21.94	$64,230

1992-'96 held at Atlantic City Race Course. 1992-'95 7 furlongs.

Jim Dandy Stakes

Grade 1, Saratoga Race Course, three-year-olds, 1 1/8 miles, dirt. Held August 4, 2001, with a gross value of $600,000. First held in 1964. Graded since 1973. Stakes record 1:47.26 (1996 Louis Quatorze).

Year	Winner	Jockey	Second	Third	Strs	Final Time	1st Purse
2001	**Scorpion**	J. D. Bailey	Free of Love	Congaree	6	1:48.90	$360,000
2000	**Graeme Hall**	J. D. Bailey	Curule	Unshaded	7	1:48.95	$240,000
1999	**Ecton Park**	A. O. Solis	Lemon Drop Kid	Badger Gold	7	1:49.52	$180,000
1998	**Favorite Trick**	P. Day	Deputy Diamond	Raffie's Majesty	7	1:50.00	$150,000
1997	**Awesome Again**	M. E. Smith	Glitman	Affirmed Success	9	1:51.16	$150,000
1996	**Louis Quatorze**	P. Day	Will's Way	Secreto de Estado	8	**1:47.26**	$90,000
1995	**Composer**	J. D. Bailey	Malthus	Pat n Jac	7	1:51.13	$82,575
1994	**Unaccounted For**	J. A. Santos	Tabasco Cat	Ulises	5	1:49.69	$80,820
1993	**Miner's Mark**	C. J. McCarron	Virginia Rapids	Colonial Affair	6	1:49.01	$90,000
1992	**Thunder Rumble**	W. H. McCauley	Dixie Brass	Devil His Due	8	1:47.53	$108,000

1992-2000 Grade 2.

Jockey Club Gold Cup

Grade 1, Belmont Park, three-year-olds and up, 1 1/4 miles, dirt. Held October 6, 2001, with a gross value of $1,000,000. First held in 1919. Graded since 1973. Stakes record 1:58.89 (1997 Skip Away).

Year	Winner	Jockey	Second	Third	Strs	Final Time	1st Purse
2001	**Aptitude**, 4	J. D. Bailey	Generous Rosi (GB), 6	Country Be Gold, 6	7	2:01.49	$600,000
2000	**Albert the Great**, 3	J. F. Chavez	Gander, 4	Vision and Verse, 4	7	1:59.24	$600,000
1999	**River Keen (Ire)**, 7	C. W. Antley	Behrens, 5	Almutawakel (GB), 5	8	2:01.40	$600,000
1998	**Wagon Limit**, 4	R. G. Davis	Gentlemen (Arg), 6	Skip Away, 6	6	2:00.62	$600,000

Year	Winner	Jockey	Second	Third	Strs	Final Time	1st Purse
1997	**Skip Away**, 4	J. D. Bailey	Instant Friendship, 4	Wagon Limit, 4	7	**1:58.89**	$600,000
1996	**Skip Away**, 3	S. J. Sellers	Cigar, 6	Louis Quatorze, 6	6	2:00.70	$600,000
1995	**Cigar**, 5	J. D. Bailey	Unaccounted For, 4	Star Standard, 4	7	2:01.29	$450,000
1994	**Colonial Affair**, 4	J. A. Santos	Devil His Due, 5	Flag Down, 5	8	2:02.19	$450,000
1993	**Miner's Mark**, 3	C. J. McCarron	Colonial Affair, 3	Brunswick, 3	5	2:02.79	$510,000
1992	**Pleasant Tap**, 5	G. L. Stevens	Strike the Gold, 4	A.P. Indy, 4	7	1:58.95	$510,000

Just a Game Breeders' Cup Handicap

Grade 3, Belmont Park, three-year-olds and up, fillies and mares, 1 mile, turf. Held June 9, 2001, with a gross value of $189,050. First held in 1994. Graded since 1997. Stakes record 1:32.53 (1995 Caress).

Year	Winner	Jockey	Second	Third	Strs	Final Time	1st Purse
2001	**License Fee**, 6, 118	P. Day	Shopping for Love, 4	Veil of Avalon, 4	11	1:32.62	$114,780
2000	**Perfect Sting**, 4, 121	J. D. Bailey	Ronda (GB), 4	Snow Polina, 4	7	1:34.48	$111,180
1999	**Cozy Blues**, 5, 112	J. F. Chavez	U R Unforgetable, 5	Mysterious Moll, 5	7	1:33.33	$94,620
1998	**Witchful Thinking**, 4, 118	C. J. McCarron	Sopran Mariduff (GB), 4	Dixie Ghost, 4	9	1:33.45	$95,745
1997	**Memories of Silver**, 4, 120	J. D. Bailey	Dynasty, 4	Elusive, 4	7	1:32.90	$95,370
1996	**Caress**, 5, 117	R. G. Davis	Class Kris, 4	Upper Noosh, 4	7	1:33.30	$94,890
1995	**Caress**, 4, 119	R. G. Davis	Coronation Cup, 4	Grafin, 4	5	**1:32.53**	$49,320
1994	**Elizabeth Bay**, 4, 114	M. E. Smith	Tiffany's Taylor, 5	Statuette, 5	5	1:32.85	$33,330

1994-'95 Just a Game II S. 1996 Class Kris finished first, DQ to second. 1995 equaled course record.

Kelso Handicap

Grade 2, Belmont Park, three-year-olds and up, 1 mile, turf. Held October 6, 2001, with a gross value of $250,000. First held in 1980. Graded since 1984. Stakes record 1:32.40 (1990 Expensive Decision).

Year	Winner	Jockey	Second	Third	Strs	Final Time	1st Purse
2001	**Forbidden Apple**, 6, 118	J. A. Santos	Sarafan, 4	City Zip, 4	9	1:36.77	$150,000
2000	**Forbidden Apple**, 5, 116	J-L. Samyn	Affirmed Success, 6	Johnny Dollar, 6	9	1:34.39	$150,000
1999	**Middlesex Drive**, 4, 117	S. J. Sellers	Divide and Conquer, 5	Wised Up, 5	10	1:35.45	$150,000
1998	**Dixie Bayou**, 5, 112	J. F. Chavez	Sahm, 4	Let Goodtimes Roll, 4	6	1:36.21	$120,000
1997	**Lucky Coin**, 4, 119	R. G. Davis	Hawksley Hill (Ire), 4	†Colcon, 4	12	1:33.72	$120,000
1996	**Same Old Wish**, 6, 113	S. J. Sellers	Da Hoss, 4	Volochine (Ire), 4	10	1:34.42	$105,000
1995	**Mighty Forum (GB)**, 4, 115	E. Delahoussaye	Fastness (Ire), 5	Dowty, 5	14	1:39.58	$120,000
1994	**Nijinsky's Gold**, 5, 114	J. A. Santos	Lure, 5	A in Sociology, 5	7	1:34.18	$120,000
1993	**Lure**, 4, 125	M. E. Smith	Paradise Creek, 4	Daarik (Ire), 4	10	1:35.86	$120,000
1992	**Roman Envoy**, 4, 117	C. Perret	Lure, 3	Val des Bois (Fr), 3	9	1:36.39	$120,000

1992-'96 Grade 3. † denotes female.

Kent Breeders' Cup Stakes

Grade 3, Delaware Park, three-year-olds, 1⅛ miles, turf. Held July 22, 2001, with a gross value of $249,000. First held in 1937. Graded since 1999. Stakes record 1:48.01 (1997 Royal Strand [Ire]).

Year	Winner	Jockey	Second	Third	Strs	Final Time	1st Purse
2001	**Navesink**	R. A. Dominguez	Bowman Mill	Harrisand (Fr)	10	1:49.98	$151,000
2000	**Three Wonders**	P. Day	Field Cat	Dawn of the Condor	8	1:48.95	$150,000
1999	**North East Bound**	J. A. Velez Jr.	Courtside	Swamp	8	1:51.93	$150,000
1998	**Keene Dancer**	P. Day	Red Reef	Danielle's Gray	11	1:50.65	$120,000
1997	**Royal Strand (Ire)**	P. Day	Subordination	Broad Choice	7	**1:48.01**	$90,000
1996	**Sir Cat**	J. D. Bailey	Optic Nerve	Fortitude	5	1:52.93	$60,000

1992-'95 not held. 1997 new course record.

Kentucky Breeders' Cup Stakes

Grade 3, Churchill Downs, two-year-olds, 5½ furlongs, dirt. Held May 28, 2001, with a gross value of $162,600. First held in 1988. Graded since 1999. Stakes record 1:03.11 (2001 Leelanau).

Year	Winner	Jockey	Second	Third	Strs	Final Time	1st Purse
2001	**Leelanau**	J. K. Court	Gygistar	†Lakeside Cup	6	**1:03.11**	$100,812
2000	**†Gold Mover**	C. Perret	City Zip	Unbridled Time	6	1:03.67	$101,091
1999	**†Chilukki**	R. Albarado	Barrier	Sky Dweller	7	1:04.01	$106,485
1998	**Yes It's True**	S. J. Sellers	Tactical Cat	Alannan	8	1:03.61	$85,948
1997	**Favorite Trick**	P. Day	Jess M	†Cutie Luttie	8	1:04.80	$68,882
1996	**†Move**	S. J. Sellers	Prairie Junction	†Live Your Best	7	1:05.74	$71,175
1995	**†Miraloma**	D. M. Barton	Great Southern	A. V. Eight	9	1:04.04	$68,933
1994	**My My**	S. J. Sellers	Wise Affair	Hyroglyphic	11	1:05.96	$37,310
1993	**†Astas Foxy Lady**	T. J. Hebert	Dish It Out	Riverinn	9	1:05.51	$68,738
1992	**Tempered Halo**	P. A. Johnson	Mountain Cat	†Secret Bundle	7	1:05.39	$50,326

1992-'98 not graded. 1998, 2001 new track record. † denotes female.

Kentucky Cup Classic Handicap

Grade 2, Turfway Park, three-year-olds and up, 1⅛ miles, dirt. Held September 22, 2001, with a gross value of $400,000. First held in 1994. Graded since 1996. Stakes record 1:47.43 (1996 Atticus).

Year	Winner	Jockey	Second	Third	Strs	Final Time	1st Purse
2001	Guided Tour, 5, 119	L. Melancon	Balto Star, 3	A Fleets Dancer, 3	6	1:47.90	$254,000
2000	Captain Steve, 3, 115	S. J. Sellers	Golden Missile, 5	Early Pioneer, 5	6	1:49.95	$314,500
1999	Da Devil, 4, 112	C. H. Borel	Social Charter, 4	Cat Thief, 4	8	1:50.54	$314,500
1998	(DH) Wild Rush, 4, 117	P. Day		Acceptable, 4	5	1:47.48	$271,000
	(DH) Silver Charm, 4, 123	G. L. Stevens					
1997	Semoran, 4, 116	K. J. Desormeaux	Distorted Humor, 4	Coup D' Argent, 4	8	1:48.08	$217,000
1996	Atticus, 4, 115	C. S. Nakatani	Judge T C, 5	Isitingood, 5	10	1:47.43	$325,000
1995	Thunder Gulch, 3, 121	G. L. Stevens	Judge T C, 4	Bound by Honor, 4	6	1:49.42	$260,000
1994	Tabasco Cat, 3, 120	P. Day	Mighty Avanti, 4	Best Pal, 4	6	1:50.32	$260,000

1994 Kentucky Cup Classic S. 1996-'98 Grade 3. 1998 dead heat for first.

Kentucky Cup Juvenile Stakes

Grade 3, Turfway Park, two-year-olds, 1¹⁄₁₆ miles, dirt. Held September 22, 2001, with a gross value of $100,000. First held in 1986. Graded since 1989. Stakes record 1:42.89 (1996 Boston Harbor).

Year	Winner	Jockey	Second	Third	Strs	Final Time	1st Purse
2001	Repent	A. J. D'Amico	French Assault	Gold Dollar	7	1:43.78	$62,750
2000	Point Given	S. J. Sellers	Holiday Thunder	The Goo	11	1:47.01	$62,600
1999	Millencolin	P. Day	Personal First	Deputy Warlock	10	1:47.02	$62,600
1998	Aly's Alley	P. A. Johnson	Time Bandit	Mac's Rule	9	1:45.63	$62,600
1997	Laydown	M. E. Smith	Time Limit	Da Devil	7	1:43.17	$62,600
1996	Boston Harbor	D. M. Barton	Play Waki for Me	Dr. Spine	8	1:42.89	$65,000
1995	Editor's Note	G. L. Stevens	Devil's Honor	Never to Squander	8	1:45.07	$65,000
1994	Tejano Run	J. D. Bailey	Gold Miner	Bick	7	1:46.10	$65,000
1993	Bibury Court	S. T. Saito	Moving Van	Durham	11	1:47.75	$81,250
1992	Mountain Cat	C. R. Woods Jr.	Saw Mill	Shoal Creek	10	1:43.50	$97,500

1992-'93 Alysheba S.

Kentucky Cup Sprint Stakes

Grade 2, Turfway Park, three-year-olds, 6 furlongs, dirt. Held September 22, 2001, with a gross value of $147,500. First held in 1994. Graded since 1996. Stakes record 1:08.24 (1996 Appealing Skier).

Year	Winner	Jockey	Second	Third	Strs	Final Time	1st Purse
2001	Snow Ridge	P. Day	City Zip	Dream Run	5	1:09.22	$94,500
2000	Caller One	K. J. Desormeaux	Millencolin	Kings Command	6	1:09.46	$93,750
1999	Successful Appeal	E. S. Prado	Five Star Day	American Spirit	6	1:09.42	$74,400
1998	Reraise	C. S. Nakatani	Copelan Too	Mr Bert	7	1:08.50	$93,900
1997	Partner's Hero	P. Day	Oro de Mexico	Prosong	6	1:09.02	$74,400
1996	Appealing Skier	M. E. Smith	†Capote Belle	Delay of Game	9	1:08.24	$97,500
1995	Lord Carson	M. E. Smith	Ft. Stockton	Evansville Slew	10	1:08.60	$97,500
1994	End Sweep	C. J. McCarron	Exclusive Praline	Chimes Band	7	1:09.99	$97,500

1996 track record. 1995 equaled track record. † denotes female.

Kentucky Cup Turf Handicap

Grade 3, Kentucky Downs, three-year-olds and up, 1½ miles, turf. Held September 23, 2001, with a gross value of $300,000. First held in 1998. Graded since 2001. Stakes record 2:27.60 (1998 Yaqthan [Ire]).

Year	Winner	Jockey	Second	Third	Strs	Final Time	1st Purse
2001	Chorwon, 8, 113	J. K. Court	The Knight Sky, 5	Man From Wicklow, 5	7	2:28.68	$186,000
2000	Down the Aisle, 7, 117	R. Albarado	Crowd Pleaser, 5	Royal Strand (Ire), 5	8	2:27.70	$186,000
1999	Fahris (Ire), 5, 116	S. J. Sellers	Yaqthan (Ire), 9	Royal Strand (Ire), 9	12	2:29.60	$186,000
1998	Yaqthan (Ire), 8, 115	B. D. Peck	Perim (Fr), 5	Chorwon, 5	8	2:27.60	$186,000

1998 established course record.

Kentucky Derby

Grade 1, Churchill Downs, three-year-olds, 1¼ miles, dirt. Held May 5, 2001, with a gross value of $1,112,000. First held in 1875. Graded since 1973. Stakes record 1:59.40 (1973 Secretariat).

Year	Winner	Jockey	Second	Third	Strs	Final Time	1st Purse
2001	Monarchos	J. F. Chavez	Invisible Ink	Congaree	17	1:59.97	$812,000
2000	Fusaichi Pegasus	K. J. Desormeaux	Aptitude	Impeachment	19	2:01.12	$1,038,400
1999	Charismatic	C. W. Antley	Menifee	Cat Thief	19	2:03.29	$886,200
1998	Real Quiet	K. J. Desormeaux	Victory Gallop	Indian Charlie	15	2:02.38	$738,800
1997	Silver Charm	G. L. Stevens	Captain Bodgit	Free House	13	2:02.44	$700,000
1996	Grindstone	J. D. Bailey	Cavonnier	Prince of Thieves	19	2:01.06	$869,800
1995	Thunder Gulch	G. L. Stevens	Tejano Run	Timber Country	19	2:01.27	$707,400
1994	Go for Gin	C. J. McCarron	Strodes Creek	Blumin Affair	14	2:03.72	$628,800
1993	Sea Hero	J. D. Bailey	Prairie Bayou	Wild Gale	19	2:02.42	$735,900
1992	Lil E. Tee	P. Day	Casual Lies	Dance Floor	18	2:03.04	$724,800

Kentucky Jockey Club Stakes

Grade 2, Churchill Downs, two-year-olds, 1¹⁄₁₆ miles, dirt. Held November 24, 2001, with a gross value of $217,000. First held in 1920. Graded since 1973. Stakes record 1:43.14 (1999 Captain Steve).

Year	Winner	Jockey	Second	Third	Strs	Final Time	1st Purse
2001	Repent	A. J. D'Amico	Request for Parole	High Star	6	1:44.42	$134,540
2000	Dollar Bill	C. H. Borel	Holiday Thunder	Gift of the Eagle	6	1:47.18	$135,656
1999	Captain Steve	R. Albarado	Mighty	Personal First	12	**1:43.14**	$143,840
1998	Exploit	C. J. McCarron	Vicar	Grits'n Hard Toast	11	1:44.16	$140,740
1997	Cape Town	W. Martinez	Time Limit	Real Quiet	11	1:43.97	$142,228
1996	Concerto	C. H. Marquez Jr.	Celtic Warrior	Carmen's Baby	11	1:46.91	$142,104
1995	Ide	C. Perret	Editor's Note	El Amante	5	1:44.31	$97,500
1994	Jambalaya Jazz	S. Maple	You're the One	Peaks and Valleys	7	1:46.46	$97,500
1993	War Deputy	G. K. Gomez	Tarzans Blade	Rustic Light	11	1:46.75	$97,500
1992	Wild Gale	S. J. Sellers	Mi Cielo	Shoal Creek	11	1:45.64	$105,918

1992-'97 Grade 3.

Kentucky Oaks

Grade 1, Churchill Downs, three-year-old fillies, 1¹⁄₈ miles, dirt. Held May 4, 2001, with a gross value of $609,200. First held in 1875. Graded since 1973. Stakes record 1:48.83 (1991 Lite Light).

Year	Winner	Jockey	Second	Third	Strs	Final Time	1st Purse
2001	Flute	J. D. Bailey	Real Cozzy	Collect Call	13	1:48.85	$377,704
2000	Secret Status	P. Day	Rings a Chime	Classy Cara	14	1:50.30	$378,696
1999	Silverbulletday	G. L. Stevens	Dreams Gallore	Sweeping Story	11	1:49.92	$341,620
1998	Keeper Hill	D. R. Flores	Banshee Breeze	Really Polish	13	1:52.06	$375,410
1997	Blushing K. D.	L. Meche	Tomisue's Delight	Storm Song	9	1:50.29	$362,514
1996	Pike Place Dancer	C. S. Nakatani	Escena	Cara Rafaela	6	1:49.88	$325,000
1995	Gal in a Ruckus	W. H. McCauley	Urbane	Sneaky Quiet	8	1:50.09	$235,040
1994	Sardula	E. Delahoussaye	Lakeway	Dianes Halo	7	1:51.16	$184,340
1993	Dispute	J. D. Bailey	Eliza	Quinpool	11	1:52.47	$191,230
1992	Luv Me Luv Me Not	F. A. Arguello Jr.	Pleasant Stage	Prospectors Delite	6	1:51.41	$182,455

1997 Sharp Cat finished third, DQ to eighth.

King's Bishop Stakes

Grade 1, Saratoga Race Course, three-year-olds, 7 furlongs, dirt. Held August 25, 2001, with a gross value of $200,000. First held in 1984. Graded since 1986. Stakes record 1:21 (1999 Forestry).

Year	Winner	Jockey	Second	Third	Strs	Final Time	1st Purse
2001	Squirtle Squirt	J. D. Bailey	Illusioned	City Zip	8	1:21.97	$120,000
2000	More Than Ready	P. Day	Valiant Halory	Millencolin	6	1:22.49	$120,000
1999	Forestry	C. W. Antley	Five Star Day	Successful Appeal	12	**1:21.00**	$120,000
1998	Secret Firm	E. S. Prado	Mint	Scatmandu	8	1:22.78	$120,000
1997	Tale of the Cat	J. A. Krone	Oro de Mexico	Trafalger	7	1:21.71	$90,000
1996	Honour and Glory	J. A. Santos	Elusive Quality	Distorted Humor	6	1:21.78	$64,920
1995	Top Account	P. Day	Ft. Stockton	Excelerate	10	1:22.50	$68,100
1994	Chimes Band	J. D. Bailey	End Sweep	Halo's Image	7	1:21.82	$65,700
1993	Mi Cielo	M. E. Smith	Williamstown	Schossberg	11	1:21.73	$74,280
1992	Salt Lake	M. E. Smith	Binalong	Agincourt	10	1:21.53	$73,440

1992-'98 Grade 2.

Knickerbocker Handicap

Grade 2, Belmont Park, three-year-olds and up, 1¹⁄₄ miles, turf. Held October 26, 2001, with a gross value of $150,000. First held in 1960. Graded since 1973. Stakes record 2:02.55 (2001 Sumitas [Ger]).

Year	Winner	Jockey	Second	Third	Strs	Final Time	1st Purse
2001	Sumitas (Ger), 5, 115	E. S. Prado	Manndar (Ire), 5	Crash Course, 5	11	**2:02.55**	$90,000
2000	Charge d'Affaires (GB), 5, 115	J. A. Santos	Devine Wind, 4	Understood, 4	7	1:49.01	$90,000
1999	Charge d'Affaires (GB), 4, 114	J. A. Santos	Comic Strip, 4	Nat's Big Party, 4	7	1:49.06	$66,480
1998	Sahm, 4, 116	J. R. Velazquez	Glok, 4	Let Goodtimes Roll, 4	8	1:49.68	$67,440
1997	Sir Cat, 4, 115	M. E. Smith	Tamhid, 4	Outta My Way Man, 4	5	1:50.02	$69,060
1996	Mr. Bluebird, 5, 113	M. E. Smith	Devil's Cup, 3	Ops Smile, 3	12	1:49.21	$69,660
1995	Diplomatic Jet, 3, 113	M. E. Smith	Flag Down, 5	Easy Miner, 5	11	2:04.97	$87,870
1994	Kiri's Clown, 5, 114	M. J. Luzzi	River Majesty, 5	Red Earth, 5	12	1:49.38	$52,335
1993	River Majesty, 4, 115	M. E. Smith	Daarik (Ire), 6	Home of the Free, 6	6	1:54.54	$52,920
1992	Binary Light, 3, 111	J. Cruguet	Share the Glory, 4	Turkey Point, 4	7	1:52.70	$56,160

1992-'97 Grade 3. 1992-'94,1996-2000 held at Aqueduct. 1992-'94,1996-2000 1¹⁄₈ miles. 1992,1997 dirt.

La Brea Stakes

Grade 1, Santa Anita Park, three-year-old fillies, 7 furlongs, dirt. Held December 29, 2001, with a gross value of $200,000. First held in 1974. Graded since 1983. Stakes record 1:20.45 (1993 Mamselle Bebette).

Year	Winner	Jockey	Second	Third	Strs	Final Time	1st Purse
2001	Affluent	E. Delahoussaye	Royally Chosen	Love At Noon	12	1:21.29	$120,000
2000	Spain	V. Espinoza	Cover Gal	Serenita (Arg)	6	1:22.27	$120,000

Year	Winner	Jockey	Second	Third	Strs	Final Time	1st Purse
1999	Hookedonthefeelin	D. R. Flores	Olympic Charmer	Kalookan Queen	8	1:21.84	$120,000
1998	Magical Allure	G. L. Stevens	Gourmet Girl	Tranquility Lake	7	1:22.06	$120,000
1997	I Ain't Bluffing	E. Delahoussaye	Minister's Melody	Praviana (Chi)	9	1:21.23	$99,540
1996	Hidden Lake	C. J. McCarron	Belle's Flag	Tiffany Diamond	7	1:22.00	$80,900
1995	Exotic Wood	C. J. McCarron	Evil's Pic	Jewel Princess	6	1:21.57	$80,250
1994	Top Rung	G. L. Stevens	Klassy Kim	Twice the Vice	7	1:21.84	$63,700
1993	Mamselle Bebette	C. S. Nakatani	Desert Stormer	Island Orchid	9	1:20.45	$65,900
1992	Arches of Gold	E. Delahoussaye	Race the Wild Wind	Terre Haute	8	1:21.28	$64,800

1992-'93 Grade 3; 1994-'96 Grade 2.

La Canada Stakes

Grade 2, Santa Anita Park, four-year-old fillies, 1⅛ miles, dirt. Held February 11, 2001, with a gross value of $111,000. First held in 1975. Graded since 1977. Stakes record 1:47.60 (1980 Glorious Song; 1982 Safe Play).

Year	Winner	Jockey	Second	Third	Strs	Final Time	1st Purse
2001	Spain	V. Espinoza	Chilukki	Letter of Intent	5	1:49.74	$120,000
2000	Scholars Studio	C. S. Nakatani	Smooth Player	The Seven Seas	5	1:49.14	$120,000
1999	Manistique	G. L. Stevens	Magical Allure	Gourmet Girl	7	1:48.81	$120,000
1998	Fleet Lady	G. K. Gomez	Minister's Melody	I Ain't Bluffing	7	1:48.59	$120,000
1997	Belle's Flag	C. S. Nakatani	Chile Chatte	Housa Dancer (Fr)	8	1:48.26	$133,200
1996	Jewel Princess	A. O. Solis	Dixie Pearl	Privity	6	1:49.42	$129,900
1995	Dianes Halo	C. S. Nakatani	Twice the Vice	Klassy Kim	6	1:49.35	$123,800
1994	Stalcreek	G. L. Stevens	Alyshena	Hollywood Wildcat	4	1:48.85	$120,000
1993	Alysbelle	E. Delahoussaye	Pacific Squall	Interactive	9	1:49.85	$130,850
1992	Exchange	L. A. Pincay Jr.	Winglet	Damewood	8	1:49.96	$128,250

Ladies Handicap

Grade 3, Aqueduct, three-year-olds and up, fillies and mares, 1¼ miles, dirt. Held December 22, 2001, with a gross value of $111,100. First held in 1868. Graded since 1973. Stakes record 2:01.40 (1976 *Bastonera II).

Year	Winner	Jockey	Second	Third	Strs	Final Time	1st Purse
2001	Summer Colony, 3, 114	J. R. Velazquez	Stop for Schnapps, 3	Strolling Belle, 3	9	2:05.80	$66,660
2000	Strolling Belle, 4, 120	H. Castillo Jr.	Pentatonic, 5	Reine Amandine (Fr), 5	7	2:06.60	$66,000
1999	Strolling Belle, 3, 116	H. Castillo Jr.	Maiden Fair, 5	Sazarac Jazz, 4	7	2:04.72	$65,640
1998	Unbridled Hope, 4, 114	R. Migliore	Manoa, 3	Sazarac Jazz, 3	11	2:03.44	$51,150
1997	Prophet's Warning, 4, 112	J. F. Chavez	Mil Kilates, 4	Biogio's Rose, 3	10	2:06.25	$67,620
1996	Miss Slewpy, 5, 120	L. C. Reynolds	Hooded Dancer, 6	Very True, 4	9	2:03.31	$66,600
1995	Transient Trend, 3, 110	J-L. Samyn	Lotta Dancing, 4	Manila Lila, 5	10	2:01.53	$67,800
1994	Tara Roma, 4, 114	F. T. Alvarado	Beloved Bea, 4	Dancer's Gate, 4	10	2:06.77	$84,300
1993	Groovy Feeling, 4, 112	W. H. McCauley	Turnback the Alarm, 4	Avie's Daisy, 5	9	2:05.88	$120,000
1992	Brilliant Brass, 5, 120	E. S. Prado	Low Tolerance, 4	Lady Lear, 3	10	2:03.55	$150,000

1992-'97 Grade 2. 2000 Pentatonic finished first, DQ to second.

Lady's Secret Breeders' Cup Handicap

Grade 2, Santa Anita Park, three-year-olds and up, fillies and mares, 1¹⁄₁₆ miles, dirt. Held September 29, 2001, with a gross value of $209,400. First held in 1993. Graded since 1995. Stakes record 1:40.61 (1994 Hollywood Wildcat).

Year	Winner	Jockey	Second	Third	Strs	Final Time	1st Purse
2001	Queenie Belle, 4, 116	B. Blanc	Letter of Intent, 4	Nany's Sweep, 5	6	1:43.64	$126,240
2000	Smooth Player, 4, 116	E. Delahoussaye	Speaking of Time, 4	Bordelaise (Arg), 5	6	1:42.27	$126,360
1999	Manistique, 4, 123	C. S. Nakatani	Cookin Vickie, 4	Kalosca (Fr), 5	6	1:42.39	$125,100
1998	Magical Allure, 3, 116	D. R. Flores	Victory Stripes (Arg), 4	Housa Dancer (Fr), 5	8	1:42.55	$110,280
1997	Sharp Cat, 3, 117	A. O. Solis	Twice the Vice, 6	Minister's Melody, 3	5	1:41.45	$109,400
1996	Top Rung, 5, 116	E. Fires	Jewel Princess, 4	Sleep Easy, 4	5	1:41.84	$109,450
1995	Borodislew, 5, 120	G. L. Stevens	Top Rung, 4	Golden Klair (GB), 5	6	1:41.61	$74,000
1994	Hollywood Wildcat, 4, 124	E. Delahoussaye	Exchange, 6	Dancing Mirage, 3	5	1:40.61	$61,400
1993	Hollywood Wildcat, 3, 117	E. Delahoussaye	Re Toss (Arg), 6	Wedding Ring (Ire), 4	5	1:41.05	$61,700

1993-'95 Lady's Secret H. 1995 Grade 3.

Lafayette Stakes

Grade 3, Keeneland, three-year-olds, 7 furlongs, dirt. Held April 11, 2001, with a gross value of $111,000. First held in 1937. Graded since 1990. Stakes record 1:21.25 (1993 Cherokee Run).

Year	Winner	Jockey	Second	Third	Strs	Final Time	1st Purse
2001	Griffinite	J. A. Santos	Sam Lord's Castle	Yonaguska	7	1:22.61	$68,820
2000	Caller One	R. G. Davis	Sun Cat	Littleexpectations	8	1:21.73	$70,370
1999	Yes It's True	J. D. Bailey	Trickey Crew	Fort La Roca	5	1:22.15	$66,340
1998	Dontlethebigonego	W. Martinez	Flashing Tammany	Swear by Dixie	6	1:23.15	$67,394
1997	Trafalger	J. D. Bailey	Open Forum	Muchacho Fino	6	1:21.68	$67,456
1996	Wire Me Collect	K. L. Chapman	Appealing Skier	Irish Conquest	9	1:21.82	$69,192

Year	Winner	Jockey	Second	Third	Strs	Final Time	1st Purse
1995	**Mr. Greeley**	J. A. Krone	Peaks and Valleys	Tethra	7	1:21.43	$51,429
1994	**Exclusive Praline**	J. A. Santos	Dynamic Asset	End Sweep	5	1:23.82	$49,321
1993	**Cherokee Run**	P. Day	Poverty Slew	Williamstown	8	**1:21.25**	$52,297
1992	**American Chance**	P. Day	Capitalimprovement	Mon Capitan	7	1:22.16	$53,365

1993 equaled track record.

La Jolla Handicap

Grade 3, Del Mar, three-year-olds, 1¹⁄₁₆ miles, turf. Held August 11, 2001, with a gross value of $150,000. First held in 1937. Graded since 1973. Stakes record 1:41.50 (2000 Purely Cozzene).

Year	Winner	Jockey	Second	Third	Strs	Final Time	1st Purse
2001	**Marine (GB)**, 117	C. S. Nakatani	Romanceishope	Mister Approval	8	1:41.72	$90,000
2000	**Purely Cozzene**, 120	D. R. Flores	Duke of Green (GB)	Sign of Hope (GB)	9	**1:41.50**	$90,000
1999	**Eagleton**, 119	I. D. Enriquez	In Frank's Honor	Zanetti	9	1:41.89	$90,000
1998	**Ladies Din**, 120	G. L. Stevens	Success and Glory (Ire)	Lucayan Indian (Ire)	7	1:41.94	$81,810
1997	**Fantastic Fellow**, 118	A. O. Solis	Worldly Ways (GB)	Falkenham (GB)	7	1:43.43	$85,450
1996	**Ambivalent**, 116	R. R. Douglas	The Barking Shark	Caribbean Pirate	10	1:43.34	$82,850
1995	**Petionville**, 120	C. S. Nakatani	Private Interview	Beau Temps (GB)	7	1:44.26	$74,600
1994	**Marvin's Faith (Ire)**, 114	C. W. Antley	Unfinished Symph	Ocean Crest	7	1:42.38	$62,800
1993	**Manny's Prospect**, 115	C. J. McCarron	Golden Slewpy	Hawk Spell	9	1:42.12	$64,700
1992	**Blacksburg**, 119	K. J. Desormeaux	Free At Last	Fax News	9	1:41.60	$64,700

Lake George Stakes

Grade 3, Saratoga Race Course, three-year-old fillies, 1¹⁄₁₆ miles, turf. Held July 30, 2001 in two divisions, with a gross value of $111,750 (1st Div.) and $112,250 (2nd Div.). First held in 1996. Graded since 1998. Stakes record 1:40.11 (1999 Nani Rose).

Year	Winner	Jockey	Second	Third	Strs	Final Time	1st Purse
2001	**Light Dancer**	M. Guidry	Owsley	Cozzy Corner	9	1:41.06	$67,050
	Voodoo Dancer	J. D. Bailey	Sadler's Sarah	O K to Dance	9	1:41.45	$67,350
2000	**Millie's Quest**	J. R. Velazquez	Shopping for Love	Battenkill	9	1:44.52	$70,080
1999	**Nani Rose**	S. J. Sellers	Perfect Sting	Intrigued	8	**1:40.11**	$67,680
1998	**Tenski**	R. Migliore	Pratella	Camella	8	1:40.86	$50,070
	Caveat Competor	J. R. Velazquez	Mysterious Moll	Recording	10	1:41.05	$50,760
1997	**Auntie Mame**	J. D. Bailey	Crab Grass	Innovate	9	1:42.80	$51,120
1996	**Memories of Silver**	J. D. Bailey	Clamorosa	Captive Number	10	1:42.98	$33,780
	Dynasty	J. D. Bailey	River Antoine	Vashon	8	1:42.26	$33,630

1999 Lake George H. 1996,1998, 2001 two divisions.

Lake Placid Handicap

Grade 2, Saratoga Race Course, three-year-old fillies, 1⅛ miles, turf. Held August 20, 2001, with a gross value of $150,000. First held in 1984. Graded since 1986. Stakes record 1:46.33 (1998 Tenski).

Year	Winner	Jockey	Second	Third	Strs	Final Time	1st Purse
2001	**Snow Dance**, 116	R. Migliore	Wander Mom	Mystic Lady	12	1:47.42	$90,000
2000	**Gaviola**, 122	J. D. Bailey	Good Game	Millie's Quest	11	1:48.04	$90,000
1999	**Badouizm**, 113	R. G. Davis	Confessional	Emanating	8	1:46.44	$90,000
1998	**Tenski**, 119	R. Migliore	Naskra's de Light	Caveat Competor	12	**1:46.33**	$90,000
1997	**Witchful Thinking**, 123	S. J. Sellers	Miss Huff n' Puff	Majestic Sunlight	12	1:47.65	$90,000
1996	**Memories of Silver**, 115	J. D. Bailey	Unify	Henlopen	9	1:47.80	$68,640
1995	**Class Kris**, 112	P. Day	In a Daydream	Shocking Pleasure	9	1:40.90	$67,380
	Bail Out Becky, 115	S. J. Sellers	Fashion Star	Grand Charmer	9	1:41.87	$67,680
1994	**Coronation Cup**, 114	J. D. Bailey	Stretch Drive	Golden Tajniak (Ire)	7	1:43.88	$65,760
	Alywow, 121	M. E. Smith	Irish Forever	Knocknock	9	1:43.81	$66,660
1993	**Amal Hayati**, 121	J. D. Bailey	Eloquent Silver	Irving's Girl	10	1:40.97	$56,940
	Statuette, 114	M. E. Smith	Icy Warning	Dispute	8	1:41.58	$55,980
1992	**Shannkara (Ire)**, 114	M. E. Smith	Tiney Toast	Favored Lady	11	1:41.84	$73,380
	Heed, 114	M. E. Smith	Captive Miss	Mystic Hawk	10	1:40.98	$72,420

1992-'97 Nijana S. 1992-'98 Grade 3. 1992-'95 1¹⁄₁₆ miles. 1992-'95 two divisions.

Landaluce Stakes

Grade 3, Hollywood Park, two-year-old fillies, 6 furlongs, dirt. Held July 7, 2001, with a gross value of $108,400. First held in 1945. Graded since 1973. Stakes record 1:08 (1982 Landaluce).

Year	Winner	Jockey	Second	Third	Strs	Final Time	1st Purse
2001	**Georgia's Storm**	C. J. McCarron	Respectful	Who Loves Aleyna	7	1:10.45	$65,040
2000	**Notable Career**	C. S. Nakatani	Sea Reel	Starrer	7	1:11.10	$65,040
1999	**Magicalmysterycat**	C. W. Antley	She's Classy	Princes Melissa	4	1:11.01	$63,120
1998	**Hookedonthefeelin**	G. L. Stevens	Box Office Girl	Excellent Meeting	11	1:09.60	$62,820
1997	**Career Collection**	C. S. Nakatani	Bent Creek City	Unreal Squeal	7	1:10.41	$62,820

Year	Winner	Jockey	Second	Third	Strs	Final Time	1st Purse
1996	Starry Ice	E. Delahoussaye	Trav n' Kris	Montecito	6	1:11.13	$62,160
1995	Raw Gold	A. O. Solis	Wasmi Song	Liberty Nite	10	1:10.64	$59,600
1994	Serena's Song	G. L. Stevens	Embroidered	Cat's Cradle	10	1:10.11	$66,800
1993	Rhapsodic	E. Delahoussaye	Miss Gibson County	Becky's Appeal	9	1:10.59	$59,800
1992	Zealous Connection	M. A. Pedroza	Medici Bells	Sweet Mama	8	1:09.86	$58,500

1992-'99 Grade 2.

Lane's End Breeders' Futurity Stakes

Grade 2, Keeneland, two-year-olds, 1¹⁄₁₆ miles, dirt. Held October 6, 2001, with a gross value of $454,400. First held in 1910. Graded since 1973. Stakes record 1:42.23 (1993 Polar Expedition).

Year	Winner	Jockey	Second	Third	Strs	Final Time	1st Purse
2001	Siphonic	C. J. McCarron	Harlan's Holiday	Metatron	11	1:43.79	$281,728
2000	Arabian Light	S. J. Sellers	Dollar Bill	Holiday Thunder	10	1:43.18	$279,744
1999	Captain Steve	G. K. Gomez	Graeme Hall	Millencolin	8	1:42.59	$274,040
1998	Cat Thief	P. Day	Answer Lively	Yes It's True	8	1:44.17	$272,552
1997	Favorite Trick	P. Day	Time Limit	Laydown	5	1:43.36	$265,112
1996	Boston Harbor	J. D. Bailey	Blazing Sword	Haint	5	1:45.31	$1,166,005
1995	Honour and Glory	P. Day	City by Night	Blushing Jim	10	1:43.33	$139,252
1994	Tejano Run	J. D. Bailey	Cinch	Gold Miner	11	1:44.71	$71,548
1993	Polar Expedition	C. C. Bourque	Goodbye Doeny	Solly's Honor	8	1:42.23	$122,200
1992	Mountain Cat	P. Day	Living Vicariously	Boundlessly	4	1:45.42	$1,122,200

1992-'96 Breeders' Futurity. 1992,1996 winner's purse includes $1,000,000 bonus from the KTDF.

Lane's End Churchill Downs Handicap

Grade 2, Churchill Downs, four-year-olds and up, 7 furlongs, dirt. Held May 5, 2001, with a gross value of $179,550. First held in 1911. Graded since 1992. Stakes record 1:20.50 (2001 Alannan).

Year	Winner	Jockey	Second	Third	Strs	Final Time	1st Purse
2001	Alannan, 5, 116	E. S. Prado	Bonapaw, 5	Exchange Rate, 5	10	1:20.50	$111,321
2000	Straight Man, 4, 112	J. F. Chavez	Mula Gula, 4	Patience Game, 4	7	1:21.53	$104,904
1999	Rock and Roll, 4, 112	P. Day	Liberty Gold, 5	Run Johnny, 5	7	1:22.81	$103,137
1998	Distorted Humor, 5, 119	G. L. Stevens	Gold Land, 7	El Amante, 7	7	1:21.18	$103,509
1997	Diligence, 4, 114	M. E. Smith	Victor Cooley, 4	Criollito (Arg), 4	9	1:22.37	$70,432
1996	Criollito (Arg), 5, 115	C. J. McCarron	Forty Won, 5	Powis Castle, 5	9	1:22.01	$74,620
1995	Goldseeker Bud, 4, 109	W. Martinez	Level Sands, 4	Go for Gin, 4	11	1:21.75	$75,205
1994	Honor the Hero, 6, 116	G. K. Gomez	Memo (Chi), 7	Saratoga Gambler, 7	6	1:23.05	$71,370
1993	Callide Valley, 5, 116	G. L. Stevens	Furiously, 4	Ojai, 4	11	1:22.01	$56,063
1992	Pleasant Tap, 5, 120	E. Delahoussaye	Take Me Out, 4	Cantrell Road, 4	9	1:22.32	$55,526

1992-'99 Churchill Downs H.; 2000 Winnercomm H. 1992-'97 Grade 3. 1998, 2001 new track record.

Lane's End Spiral Stakes

Grade 2, Turfway Park, three-year-olds, 1¹⁄₈ miles, dirt. Held March 24, 2001, with a gross value of $600,000. First held in 1972. Graded since 1984. Stakes record 1:46.70 (1991 Hansel).

Year	Winner	Jockey	Second	Third	Strs	Final Time	1st Purse
2001	Balto Star	M. Guidry	Halo's Stride	Mongoose	9	1:47.23	$360,000
2000	Globalize	F. C. Torres	Elite Mercedes	Rollin With Nolan	10	1:49.16	$360,000
1999	Stephen Got Even	S. J. Sellers	K One King	Epic Honor	8	1:49.03	$450,000
1998	Event of the Year	R. A. Baze	Yarrow Brae	Truluck	10	1:47.12	$360,000
1997	Concerto	C. H. Marquez Jr.	Jack Flash	Shammy Davis	10	1:48.23	$360,000
1996	Roar	M. E. Smith	Ensign Ray	Victory Speech	9	1:49.70	$360,000
1995	†Serena's Song	C. S. Nakatani	Tejano Run	Mecke	8	1:49.65	$360,000
1994	Polar Expedition	C. C. Bourque	Powis Castle	Chimes Band	11	1:49.03	$360,000
1993	Prairie Bayou	C. J. McCarron	Proudest Romeo	Miner's Mark	9	1:50.97	$360,000
1992	Lil E. Tee	P. Day	Vying Victor	Treekster	11	1:53.44	$300,000

1992-'98 Jim Beam S.; 1999 Gallery Furniture.com S.; 2000-'01 Turfway Spiral S. † denotes female.

La Prevoyante Handicap

Grade 2, Calder Race Course, three-year-olds and up, fillies and mares, 1½ miles, turf. Held December 29, 2001, with a gross value of $150,000. First held in 1976. Graded since 1982. Stakes record 2:25.20 (1988 Singular Bequest).

Year	Winner	Jockey	Second	Third	Strs	Final Time	1st Purse
2001	Krisada, 5, 115	P. Day	Sweetest Thing, 3	Great Fever (Fr), 3	10	2:26.63	$90,000
2000	Prospectress, 5, 114	J. D. Bailey	Innuendo (Ire), 5	Orange Sunset (Ire), 5	10	2:26.97	$90,000
1999	Coretta (Ire), 5, 120	J. A. Santos	Idle Rich, 4	St. Bernadette (Per), 4	8	2:27.27	$90,000
1998	Coretta (Ire), 4, 117	J. A. Santos	Starry Dreamer, 4	(DH) Tedarshana (GB), 4 (DH) Cuando, 4	12	2:26.67	$90,000
1997	Last Approach, 5, 110	J. A. Krone	Flying Concert, 4	Grey Way, 4	6	2:39.13	$90,000
1996	Ampulla, 5, 122	S. J. Sellers	Miss Caerleona (Fr), 4	Electric Society (Ire), 4	8	2:27.50	$90,000

Year	Winner	Jockey	Second	Third	Strs	Final Time	1st Purse
1995	Interim (GB), 4, 116	C. S. Nakatani	Northern Emerald, 5	Caromana, 5	10	2:26.38	$90,000
1994	Trampoli, 5, 120	M. E. Smith	Putthepowdertoit, 4	Adoryphar, 4	14	2:28.14	$90,000
	Abigailthewife, 5, 114	J. A. Santos	Trampoli, 5	Market Booster, 5	14	2:28.91	$90,000
1993	Lemhi Go, 5, 112	M. A. Gonzalez	Indian Chris (Brz), 6	Silvered, 6	6	2:37.53	$60,000
1992	Sardaniya (Ire), 4, 113	J. Cruguet	Flaming Torch (Ire), 5	Expensiveness, 5	9	2:29.62	$90,000

1994 held in January and December. 1992-'93 La Prevoyante Invitational H. 1992 about 1½ miles. 1993, 1997 dirt. 1998 dead heat for third.

Las Cienegas Handicap

Grade 3, Santa Anita Park, four-year-olds and up, fillies and mares, about 6½ furlongs, turf. Held April 8, 2001, with a gross value of $109,500. First held in 1974. Graded since 1992. Stakes record 1:12.50 (1997 Advancing Star).

Year	Winner	Jockey	Second	Third	Strs	Final Time	1st Purse
2001	Go Go, 4, 118	E. Delahoussaye	Separata (Chi), 5	Dianehill (Ire), 5	8	1:13.54	$65,700
2000	Evening Promise (GB), 4, 114	D. Sorenson	La Madame (Chi), 5	Reciclada (Chi), 5	5	1:13.66	$63,840
1999	Desert Lady (Ire), 4, 118	C. S. Nakatani	Hula Queen, 5	Bella Chiarra, 5	7	1:13.55	$65,640
1998	Dance Parade, 4, 119	K. J. Desormeaux	Advancing Star, 5	Imroz, 5	6	1:13.60	$64,800
1997	Advancing Star, 4, 116	G. L. Stevens	Ski Dancer, 5	Grab the Prize, 5	6	1:12.50	$96,550
1996	Ski Dancer, 4, 117	G. L. Stevens	Klassy Kim, 5	Igotrhythm, 5	6	1:14.59	$64,300
1995	Marina Park (GB), 5, 119	A. O. Solis	Pirate's Revenge, 4	Rabiadella, 4	9	1:13.77	$63,175
1994	Mamselle Bebette, 4, 120	C. J. McCarron	Cool Air, 4	Bel's Starlet, 4	5	1:13.05	$45,975
1993	Glen Kate (Ire), 6, 121	C. A. Black	Heart of Joy, 6	Worldly Possession, 6	8	1:12.71	$61,225
1992	Heart of Joy, 5, 123	C. J. McCarron	Sheltered View, 4	Crystal Gazing, 4	9	1:12.72	$63,475

1992-'95 Las Cienegas Breeders' Cup H.

Las Flores Handicap

Grade 3, Santa Anita Park, four-year-olds and up, fillies and mares, 6 furlongs, dirt. Held February 24, 2001, with a gross value of $134,000. First held in 1951. Graded since 1973. Stakes record 1:08.20 (1990 Stormy But Valid).

Year	Winner	Jockey	Second	Third	Strs	Final Time	1st Purse
2001	Go Go, 4, 116	E. Delahoussaye	La Feminn, 5	Cover Gal, 5	6	1:08.83	$80,400
2000	Show Me the Stage, 4, 118	K. J. Desormeaux	Theresa's Tizzy, 6	Woodman's Dancer, 6	6	1:08.54	$79,440
1999	Enjoy the Moment, 4, 117	L. A. Pincay Jr.	Tomorrows Sunshine, 5	Closed Escrow, 5	5	1:08.55	$78,720
1998	Funallover, 4, 114	A. O. Solis	Advancing Star, 4	Zenda's Diablo, 5	7	1:09.10	$79,800
1997	Our Summer Bid, 5, 114	J. Silva	Track Gal, 6	Advancing Star, 6	6	1:09.15	$80,100
1996	Igotrhythm, 4, 115	C. S. Nakatani	Miss L Attack, 6	Little Blue Sheep, 6	7	1:08.88	$81,100
1995	Desert Stormer, 5, 117	K. J. Desormeaux	Velvet Tulip, 5	Flying in the Lane, 5	5	1:08.49	$59,725
1994	Mamselle Bebette, 4, 118	C. S. Nakatani	Arches of Gold, 5	Aspasante, 5	7	1:08.32	$47,475
1993	Bountiful Native, 5, 121	P. A. Valenzuela	Freedom Cry, 5	Forest Fealty, 5	6	1:09.42	$60,325
1992	Forest Fealty, 5, 116	M. A. Pedroza	Middlefork Rapids, 4	Phil's Illusion, 4	9	1:08.87	$49,350

1992-'95 Las Flores Breeders' Cup H.

Las Palmas Handicap

Grade 2, Santa Anita Park, three-year-olds and up, fillies and mares, 1⅛ miles, turf. Held November 4, 2001, with a gross value of $250,000. First held in 1969. Graded since 1973. Stakes record 1:43.92 (1991 Kostroma [new world record]).

Year	Winner	Jockey	Second	Third	Strs	Final Time	1st Purse
2001	Golden Apples (Ire), 3, 115	G. K. Gomez	Dancingonice, 5	Janet (GB), 4	9	1:46.61	$150,000
2000	Smooth Player, 4, 117	E. Delahoussaye	Beautiful Noise, 4	Happyanunoit (NZ), 5	10	1:46.99	$105,000
1999	Sapphire Ring (GB), 4, 118	G. L. Stevens	Cyrillic, 4	Country Garden (GB), 4	11	1:48.20	$150,000
1998	Sonja's Faith (Ire), 4, 115	E. Ramsammy	See You Soon (Fr), 4	Idealistic Cause, 4	6	1:48.92	$90,000
1997	Real Connection, 6, 115	G. F. Almeida	Toda Una Dama (Arg), 4	Luna Wells (Ire), 4	9	1:47.76	$75,000
1996	Wandesta (GB), 5, 120	C. S. Nakatani	Real Connection, 5	Alpride (Ire), 5	5	1:46.72	$79,700
1995	Onceinabluemamoon, 4, 116	B. Blanc	Yearly Tour, 4	Don't Read My Lips, 4	9	1:50.34	$76,400
1994	Aube Indienne (Fr), 4, 115	K. J. Desormeaux	Queens Court Queen, 5	Skimble, 5	5	1:49.62	$61,300
1993	Miatuschka, 5, 114	C. A. Black	Skimble, 4	Potridee (Arg), 4	4	1:47.98	$62,600
1992	Super Staff, 4, 116	K. J. Desormeaux	Flawlessly, 4	Re Toss (Arg), 5	7	1:46.89	$77,750

Las Virgenes Stakes

Grade 1, Santa Anita Park, three-year-old fillies, 1 mile, dirt. Held February 10, 2001, with a gross value of $200,000. First held in 1983. Graded since 1985. Stakes record 1:35.14 (1994 Lakeway).

Year	Winner	Jockey	Second	Third	Strs	Final Time	1st Purse
2001	Golden Ballet	C. J. McCarron	Two Item Limit	Affluent	7	1:36.89	$120,000
2000	Surfside	P. Day	Spain	Rings a Chime	4	1:37.00	$120,000
1999	Excellent Meeting	K. J. Desormeaux	Tout Charmant	Weekend Squall	5	1:35.35	$120,000
1998	Keeper Hill	D. R. Flores	Star of Broadway	Occhi Verdi (Ire)	6	1:36.94	$120,000
1997	Sharp Cat	C. S. Nakatani	High Heeled Hope	Demon Acquire	8	1:35.52	$98,800
1996	Antespend	C. W. Antley	Cara Rafaela	Hidden Lake	6	1:36.45	$96,900
1995	Serena's Song	C. S. Nakatani	Cat's Cradle	Urbane	7	1:35.46	$92,700

Year	Winner	Jockey	Second	Third	Strs	Final Time	1st Purse
1994	Lakeway	K. J. Desormeaux	Fancy 'n Fabulous	Princess Mitterand	8	**1:35.14**	$93,600
1993	Likeable Style	G. L. Stevens	Incindress	Blue Moonlight	6	1:36.67	$91,000
1992	Magical Maiden	G. L. Stevens	Golden Treat	Red Bandana	10	1:36.23	$96,800

La Troienne Stakes

Grade 3, Churchill Downs, three-year-old fillies, 7 furlongs, dirt. Held May 3, 2001, with a gross value of $121,000. First held in 1956. Graded since 1998. Stakes record 1:21.97 (2000 Roxelana).

Year	Winner	Jockey	Second	Third	Strs	Final Time	1st Purse
2001	Caressing	P. Day	Sweet Nanette	Golly Greeley	9	1:22.90	$75,020
2000	Roxelana	L. Melancon	Magicalmysterycat	Watchfull	7	**1:21.97**	$70,308
1999	Sapphire n' Silk	P. Day	English Bay	Grand Deed	6	1:23.85	$69,936
1998	Sister Act	C. H. Borel	Bourbon Belle	Marie J	6	1:24.46	$69,874
1997	Star of Goshen	A. O. Solis	Pearl City	Flying Lauren	8	1:22.75	$70,370
1996	Rare Blend	P. Day	Ruby Baby	Prissy One	8	1:23.75	$55,624
1995	Dixieland Gold	D. Penna	Daylight Ridge	Ivorilla	7	1:22.74	$55,088
1994	Packet	J. M. Johnson	Golden Braids	Miss Ra He Ra	10	1:24.14	$55,770
1993	Traverse City	J. A. Krone	Added Asset	Bellewood	10	1:24.38	$38,025
1992	Bell Witch	J. A. Krone	Take the Cure	Meadow Storm	6	1:24.35	$36,497

1992-'97 not graded.

Laurel Dash Stakes

Grade 3, Laurel Park, three-year-olds and up, 6 furlongs, turf. Held October 28, 2000, with a gross value of $100,000. First held in 1988. Graded since 1990. Stakes record 1:08 (2000 Texas Glitter).

Year	Winner	Jockey	Second	Third	Strs	Final Time	1st Purse
2000	Texas Glitter, 4	A. T. Gryder	Alea Iacta Est, 5	Just Call Me Carl, 5	12	**1:08.00**	$60,000
1999	Grapeshot, 5	M. T. Johnston	Clever Response, 4	Swingin Verse, 4	10	1:12.87	$60,000
1998	Howbaddouwantit, 3	D. V. Beckner	Soldier Field, 3	Sport d'Hiver, 6	11	1:08.63	$60,000
1997	Wise Dusty, 6	O. G. Mancilla	Aberfoyle, 5	Star Trace, 5	6	1:11.40	$60,000
1996	Mayoumbe (Fr), 3	E. S. Prado	Cat Be Nimble, 4	Grand Continental, 5	10	1:16.06	$60,000
1994	†Soviet Problem, 4	C. J. McCarron	†Cool Air, 4	Honor the Hero, 6	11	1:09.06	$120,000
1993	Home of the Free, 5	J. Cruguet	Strike a Gold Mine, 5	Tsunami Spangler, 5	6	1:11.20	$120,000
1992	†Glen Kate (Ire), 5	L. A. Pincay Jr.	†Silicon Bavaria (Fr), 5	Cardoun (Fr), 3	13	1:10.41	$150,000

1995, 2001 not held. 1997 dirt. 2000 new course record. † denotes female.

Laurel Futurity

Grade 3, Laurel Park, two-year-olds, 1⅛ miles, dirt. Held November 4, 2000, with a gross value of $100,000. First held in 1921. Graded since 1973. Stakes record 1:49.35 (1999 Scottish Halo).

Year	Winner	Jockey	Second	Third	Strs	Final Time	1st Purse
2000	Buckle Down Ben	M. J. McCarthy	Gift of the Eagle	Niner's Echo	8	1:51.93	$60,000
1999	Scottish Halo	T. G. Turner	Un Fino Vino	Grundlefoot	8	**1:49.35**	$60,000
1998	Millions	E. S. Prado	Raire Standard	More Better	6	1:51.52	$60,000
1997	Fight for M'lady	C. H. Marquez Jr.	Victory Gallop	Essential	6	1:53.63	$60,000
1996	Captain Bodgit	F. G. Douglas	Concerto	Carrolls Favorite	10	1:49.53	$60,000
1995	Appealing Skier	R. Wilson	Liberty Road	Pirate Performer	8	1:30.70	$60,000
1994	Western Echo	E. S. Prado	Old Tascosa	Shimmering Prince	10	1:30.82	$60,000
1993	Dove Hunt	R. G. Davis	Lotsa Chile	Thrilla in Manila	8	1:49.03	$81,000
1992	Lord of the Bay	R. Wilson	Glorieux Dancer (Fr)	Halissee	11	1:45.54	$120,000

2001 not held. 1992-'93 1¹⁄₁₆ miles; 1994-'95 7½ furlongs. 1992-'93 turf. 1993 Linkatariat finished third, DQ to fourth.

Lawrence Realization Handicap

Grade 3, Belmont Park, three-year-olds, 1½ miles, turf. Held October 13, 2001, with a gross value of $150,000. First held in 1889. Graded since 1973. Stakes record 2:25.94 (1998 Parade Ground).

Year	Winner	Jockey	Second	Third	Strs	Final Time	1st Purse
2001	Sharp Performance, 120	J. R. Velazquez	Tiger Trap	Whitmore's Conn	6	2:27.04	$90,000
2000	Ciro, 123	J. A. Santos	Whata Brainstorm	Lodge Hill	10	2:31.48	$90,000
1999	Gritty Sandie, 114	M. E. Smith	Monkey Puzzle	Just Listen	14	2:28.60	$90,000
1998	Parade Ground, 121	P. Day	Pay Zone	Vergennes	8	**2:25.94**	$83,595
1997	Renewed, 112	F. Leon	Devonwood	Belgravia (GB)	10	2:27.21	$67,320
1996	Da Dean, 113	R. Migliore	Senor Senor	Value Investor	12	2:39.06	$68,880
1995	Flitch, 117	M. E. Smith	Look Daggers	Diplomatic Jet	11	2:34.40	$69,300
1994	Personal Merit, 113	J. F. Chavez	Kristen's Baby	Holy Mountain	8	2:29.30	$67,260
1993	Strolling Along, 114	C. J. McCarron	Scattered Steps	Noble Sheba	12	2:32.70	$75,480
1992	Timber Cat, 114	R. G. Davis	Tomorrow's Spirit	Gainzer	13	2:28.87	$76,560

1992-'93 Lawrence Realization S. 1994 dirt.

Lazaro Barrera Memorial Stakes

Grade 3, Hollywood Park, three-year-olds, 7 furlongs, dirt. Held May 28, 2001, with a gross value of $108,600. First held in 1953. Graded since 2001. Stakes record 1:20.42 (2001 Early Flyer).

Year	Winner	Jockey	Second	Third	Strs	Final Time	1st Purse
2001	Early Flyer	C. J. McCarron	Squirtle Squirt	Top Hit	7	**1:20.42**	$65,160

Year	Winner	Jockey	Second	Third	Strs	Final Time	1st Purse
2000	Caller One	C. S. Nakatani	Dixie Union	Swept Overboard	4	1:21.10	$60,960
1999	Love That Red	G. K. Gomez	Apremont	O'Rey Fantasma	4	1:20.81	$56,910
1998	Reraise	E. Delahoussaye	Souvenir Copy	Full Moon Madness	6	1:08.51	$39,930
1996	Future Quest	K. J. Desormeaux	Slews Royal Son	Tiger Talk	8	1:15.17	$35,100
1995	Flying Standby	C. W. Antley	Desert Pirate	Boundless Moment	6	1:09.09	$40,200

1995, 1998 Playa Del Rey S.; 1996 Playa Del Rey H. 1992-'94, 1997 not held.1995-'96, 1998-2000 not graded. 1995, 1998 6 furlongs; 1996 6½ furlongs.

Leonard Richards Stakes

Not graded, Delaware Park, three-year-olds, 1¹⁄₁₆ miles, dirt. Held June 17, 2001, with a gross value of $200,000. First held in 1937. Grade 3 since 2002. Stakes record 1:42.41 (2001 Burning Roma).

Year	Winner	Jockey	Second	Third	Strs	Final Time	1st Purse
2001	Burning Roma	R. Wilson	Marciano	Bay Eagle	5	1:42.41	$120,000
2000	Grundlefoot	T. L. Dunkelberger	Perfect Cat	Mercaldo	8	1:44.04	$120,000
1999	Stellar Brush	M. J. McCarthy	Smart Guy	Successful Appeal	8	1:42.78	$120,000
1998	Scatmandu	R. Migliore	Hot Wells	True Silver	7	1:42.43	$90,000
1997	Leestown	J. A. Velez Jr.	Universe	Bleu Madura	8	1:43.46	$90,000

1992-'96 not held.

Lexington Stakes

Grade 3, Belmont Park, three-year-olds, 1¼ miles, turf. Held July 15, 2001, with a gross value of $150,000. First held in 1961. Graded since 1973. Stakes record 1:58.93 (2001 Sharp Performance).

Year	Winner	Jockey	Second	Third	Strs	Final Time	1st Purse
2001	Sharp Performance	J. R. Velazquez	Package Store	Whitmore's Conn	8	1:58.93	$90,000
2000	Rob's Spirit	J. D. Bailey	Plato	Rumsonontheriver	6	2:02.87	$90,000
1999	Mythical Gem	J. F. Chavez	Monkey Puzzle	Bugatti	11	2:01.21	$90,000
1998	Parade Ground	M. E. Smith	Ay Rouge	La Reine's Terms	8	2:00.55	$84,060
1997	Private Buck Trout	J. F. Chavez	Red Castle	Renewed	10	2:01.29	$90,000
1996	Ok by Me	J. F. Chavez	Value Investor	Alzeus (Ire)	10	2:03.58	$68,160
1995	Green Means Go	J. D. Bailey	Nostra	Flitch	9	2:01.69	$66,960
1994	Holy Mountain	J. R. Velazquez	Islefaxyou	Check Ride	10	1:59.74	$50,850
1993	Llandaff	J. A. Krone	Strolling Along	Eastern Memories (Ire)	7	2:02.93	$52,380
1992	Spectacular Tide	J. A. Krone	Preferences	Casino Magistrate	6	2:02.20	$69,120

Locust Grove Handicap

Grade 3, Churchill Downs, three-year-olds and up, fillies and mares, 1¹⁄₈ miles, turf. Held June 23, 2001, with a gross value of $172,800. First held in 1982. Graded since 1998. Stakes record 1:47.27(1992 Behaving Dancer).

Year	Winner	Jockey	Second	Third	Strs	Final Time	1st Purse
2001	Colstar, 5, 121	J. K. Court	Solvig, 4	Megans Bluff, 4	11	1:48.79	$107,136
2000	Colstar, 4, 121	A. Delgado	Pricearose, 4	Histoire Sainte (Fr), 4	6	1:47.44	$102,300
1999	Shires Ende, 4, 117	W. Martinez	Formal Tango, 4	Uanme, 4	11	1:49.11	$107,508
1998	Colcon, 5, 118	S. J. Sellers	Leo's Gypsy Dancer, 4	Mingling Glances, 4	6	1:48.53	$103,974
1997	Romy, 6, 121	F. C. Torres	Yokama, 4	Cymbala (Fr), 4	6	1:48.89	$68,634
1996	Bail Out Becky, 4, 121	C. Perret	Ms. Isadora, 4	Memories (Ire), 4	6	1:47.38	$72,670
1995	Memories (Ire), 4, 114	S. J. Sellers	Market Booster, 6	Thread, 6	7	1:47.48	$71,760
1994	Life Is Delicious, 4, 113	J. R. Martinez Jr.	Eurostorm, 4	Obtain, 4	4	1:53.87	$70,850
1993	Lady Blessington (Fr), 5, 121	C. A. Black	Gone Seeking, 4	Crusie, 4	8	1:50.16	$74,425
1992	Behaving Dancer, 5, 117	D. L. Howard	Firm Stance, 4	Olden Rijn, 4	10	1:47.27	$74,750

1994 dirt.

Lone Star Derby

Not graded, Lone Star Park, three-year-olds, 1¹⁄₈ miles, dirt. Held April 7, 2001, with a gross value of $500,000. First held in 1997. Grade 3 since 2002. Stakes record 1:50.27 (2001 Percy Hope).

Year	Winner	Jockey	Second	Third	Strs	Final Time	1st Purse
2001	Percy Hope	J. K. Court	Fifty Stars	Gift of the Eagle	8	1:50.27	$292,500
2000	Tahkodha Hills	E. Coa	Jeblar Sez Who	Big Numbers	7	1:44.05	$180,000
1999	T. B. Track Star	E. M. Martin Jr.	Desert Demon	Congratulate	11	1:42.92	$165,000
1998	Smolderin Heart	T. T. Doocy	Shot of Gold	Troy's Play	8	1:46.29	$145,000
1997	Anet	D. R. Flores	Frisk Me Now	Holzmeister	9	1:40.88	$140,000

1997-2000 1¹⁄₁₆ miles.

Lone Star Park Handicap

Grade 3, Lone Star Park, three-year-olds and up, 1¹⁄₁₆ miles, dirt. Held May 28, 2001, with a gross value of $300,000. First held in 1997. Graded since 2000. Stakes record 1:40.53 (2001 Dixie Dot Com).

Year	Winner	Jockey	Second	Third	Strs	Final Time	1st Purse
2001	Dixie Dot Com, 6, 118	D. R. Flores	Fan the Flame, 4	Big Numbers, 4	8	1:40.53	$180,000

Year	Winner	Jockey	Second	Third	Strs	Final Time	1st Purse
2000	Luftikus, 4, 114	D. R. Flores	Nite Dreamer, 5	Sultry Substitute, 5	11	1:40.87	$180,000
1999	Mocha Express, 5, 116	M. St. Julien	Littlebitlively, 5	Nite Dreamer, 5	7	1:43.36	$183,300
1998	Mocha Express, 4, 114	M. St. Julien	Prince of the Mt., 7	Dickey Rickey, 7	5	1:42.17	$123,000
1997	Connecting Terms, 4, 112	L. Melancon	Humble Seven, 5	Isitingood, 5	7	1:41.97	$120,000

2000 equaled track record; 2001 new track record.

Longacres Mile Handicap

Grade 3, Emerald Downs, three-year-olds and up, 1 mile, dirt. Held August 19, 2001, with a gross value of $250,000. First held in 1935. Graded since 1975. Stakes record 1:33.20 (1998 Wild Wonder; 2000 Edneator).

Year	Winner	Jockey	Second	Third	Strs	Final Time	1st Purse
2001	Irisheyesareflying, 5, 117	I. Puglisi	Handy N Bold, 6	Makors Mark, 4	10	1:35.40	$137,500
2000	Edneator, 4, 111	G. V. Mitchell	Big Ten (Chi), 5	Crafty Boy, 5	11	**1:33.20**	$137,500
1999	Budroyale, 6, 119	G. K. Gomez	Mike K, 5	Kid Katabatic, 6	8	1:34.60	$137,500
1998	Wild Wonder, 4, 121	E. Delahoussaye	Mocha Express, 4	Hal's Pal (GB), 5	9	**1:33.20**	$110,000
1997	Kid Katabatic, 4, 113	C. Loseth	Hesabull, 4	Liberty Road, 4	7	1:34.20	$110,000
1996	Isitingood, 5, 117	D. R. Flores	Cleante (Arg), 7	Humpty's Hoedown, 6	10	1:35.60	$110,000
1995	L. J. Express, 5, 119	M. Allen	Funboy, 4	Secret Damascus, 5	10	1:34.60	$50,350
1994	Want a Winner, 4, 119	V. Belvoir	Sneakin Jake, 7	Forgotten Days, 8	8	1:35.20	$48,250
1993	Adventuresome Love, 7, 117	G. Baze	Sneakin Jake, 6	For the Children, 3	8	1:34.60	$48,050
1992	Bolulight, 4, 121	R. D. Hansen	Ibero (Arg), 5	Charmonnier, 4	12	1:34.00	$181,300

1992 Longacres Park Mile H.; 1993,1995 Budweiser Mile H.; 1994 Emerald Mile H. 1992 held at Longacres; 1993-'95 Yakima Meadows. 1996 established track record; 1998 new track record; 2000 equaled track record.

Long Branch Breeders' Cup Stakes

Not graded, Monmouth Park, three-year-olds and up, 1 1/16 miles, dirt. Held July 15, 2001, with a gross value of $100,000. First held in 1878. Grade 3 since 2002. Stakes record 1:41 (1956 Skipper Bill).

Year	Winner	Jockey	Second	Third	Strs	Final Time	1st Purse
2001	Burning Roma	R. Wilson	This Fleet Is Due	Thunder Blitz	7	1:43.28	$60,000
2000	Thistyranthasclass	J. A. Velez Jr.	Graeme Hall	Summinitup	9	1:43.60	$60,000
1999	Ghost Story	R. G. Davis	Unbridled Jet	Clever Gem	6	1:42.64	$60,000
1998	Favorite Trick	P. Day	Tomorrows Cat	Arctic Sweep	6	1:43.10	$60,000
1997	Jules	A. T. Gryder	Leestown	Capture the Gold	4	1:42.48	$60,000
1996	Dr. Caton	J. Bravo	Devil's Honor	Clash by Night	5	1:41.89	$45,000
1995	Pyramid Peak	W. H. McCauley	Suave Prospect	Mighty Magee	5	1:44.09	$47,250
1994	Meadow Flight	J. Bravo	Red Tazz	Don's Sho	5	1:43.92	$47,370
1993	Bert's Bubbleator	E. L. King Jr.	P. J. Higgins	Signoir Valery	5	1:45.92	$32,310
1992	Scudan	N. Santagata	Pistols and Roses	Munch n' Nosh	8	1:42.18	$39,300

1996-'97 Long Branch S.

Long Island Handicap

Grade 2, Aqueduct, three-year-olds and up, fillies and mares, 1 1/2 miles, turf. Held November 10, 2001, with a gross value of $150,000. First held in 1956. Graded since 1973. Stakes record 2:29.04 (1992 Villandry).

Year	Winner	Jockey	Second	Third	Strs	Final Time	1st Purse
2001	Queue, 4, 115	J. L. Espinoza	Sweetest Thing, 3	Lady Dora, 4	13	2:29.36	$90,000
2000	Moonlady (Ger), 3, 114	C. P. DeCarlo	Playact (Ire), 3	La Ville Rouge, 4	11	2:17.94	$90,000
1999	Midnight Line, 4, 120	J. D. Bailey	Win for Us (Ger), 3	Horatia (Ire), 3	10	2:29.67	$90,000
1998	Coretta (Ire), 4, 114	J. A. Santos	Starry Dreamer, 4	Dixie Ghost, 4	11	2:29.73	$60,000
	Yokama, 5, 120	J. D. Bailey	Moments of Magic, 3	Bristol Channel (GB), 3	11	2:31.03	$60,000
1997	Sweetzie, 5, 115	J. F. Chavez	Sweet Sondra, 4	Scenic Point, 4	6	2:16.66	$90,000
1996	Ampulla, 5, 121	S. J. Sellers	Wandering Star, 3	Beyrouth, 4	12	2:30.70	$87,270
1995	Yenda (GB), 4, 114	C. S. Nakatani	Windsharp, 4	Market Booster, 6	10	2:37.15	$86,400
1994	Market Booster, 5, 115	M. J. Luzzi	Tiffany's Taylor, 5	Lady Affirmed, 3	12	2:31.95	$87,495
1993	Trampoli, 4, 119	M. E. Smith	Bright Generation (Ire), 3	Northern Emerald, 3	5	2:31.57	$68,760
1992	Villandry, 4, 115	M. E. Smith	Ratings, 4	Gina Romantica, 4	8	**2:29.04**	$71,160

1992-'93, 1995 held at Belmont. 1997, 2000 1 3/8 miles. 1997, 2000 dirt. 1998 two divisions.

Los Angeles Handicap

Grade 3, Hollywood Park, three-year-olds and up, 6 furlongs, dirt. Held May 27, 2001, with a gross value of $107,300. First held in 1938. Graded since 1973. Stakes record 1:07.90 (1995 Forest Gazelle).

Year	Winner	Jockey	Second	Third	Strs	Final Time	1st Purse
2001	Caller One, 4, 124	C. S. Nakatani	Stormy Jack, 4	Rapidough, 4	6	1:08.35	$64,380
2000	Highland Gold, 5, 115	C. J. McCarron	Mellow Fellow, 5	Your Halo, 5	6	1:09.11	$64,260
1999	Son of a Pistol, 7, 122	A. O. Solis	Men's Exclusive, 6	Ray of Sunshine (Ire), 6	4	1:08.17	$63,300
1998	Gold Land, 7, 116	K. J. Desormeaux	Mr. Doubledown, 4	The Exeter Man, 4	7	1:08.06	$64,800
1997	Men's Exclusive, 4, 117	L. A. Pincay Jr.	First Intent, 8	Gold Land, 8	7	1:08.97	$80,970
1996	(DH) Paying Dues, 4, 115	C. W. Antley		Score Quick, 5	6	1:08.33	$53,480
	(DH) Abaginone, 5, 119	G. L. Stevens					

Year	Winner	Jockey	Second	Third	Strs	Final Time	1st Purse
1995	**Forest Gazelle**, 4, 117	K. J. Desormeaux	Lucky Forever, 6	Cardmania, 9	9	**1:07.90**	$83,650
1994	**J. F. Williams**, 5, 115	C. J. McCarron	Gundaghia, 5	Thirty Slews, 7	6	1:09.03	$61,900
1993	**Star of the Crop**, 4, 119	G. L. Stevens	Fabulous Champ, 4	Wild Harmony, 4	7	1:08.78	$63,300
1992	**Cardmania**, 6, 118	E. Delahoussaye	Gray Slewpy, 4	Robyn Dancer, 4	5	1:08.73	$61,200

1995 new track record. 1996 dead heat for first. 1997 Surachai finished second, DQ to sixth.

Louisiana Derby

Grade 2, Fair Grounds, three-year-olds, 1¹⁄₁₆ miles, dirt. Held March 11, 2001, with a gross value of $750,000. First held in 1894. Graded since 1973. Stakes record 1:42.60 (1997 Crypto Star).

Year	Winner	Jockey	Second	Third	Strs	Final Time	1st Purse
2001	**Fifty Stars**	D. J. Meche	Millennium Wind	Hero's Tribute	9	1:44.78	$450,000
2000	**Mighty**	S. J. Sellers	More Than Ready	Captain Steve	10	1:43.29	$450,000
1999	**Kimberlite Pipe**	R. Albarado	Answer Lively	Ecton Park	8	1:43.56	$384,000
1998	**Comic Strip**	S. J. Sellers	Nite Dreamer	Captain Maestri	10	1:43.36	$300,000
1997	**Crypto Star**	P. Day	Stop Watch	Smoke Glacken	9	**1:42.60**	$240,000
1996	**Grindstone**	J. D. Bailey	Zarb's Magic	Commanders Palace	8	1:42.79	$222,000
1995	**Petionville**	C. W. Antley	In Character (GB)	Moonlight Dancer	11	1:42.96	$210,000
1994	**Kandaly**	C. Perret	Game Coin	Argolid	10	1:42.86	$195,750
1993	**Dixieland Heat**	R. P. Romero	Offshore Pirate	Tossofthecoin	13	1:44.80	$180,000
1992	**Line In The Sand**	P. Day	Hill Pass	Colony Light	9	1:43.40	$120,000

1992-'98 Grade 3. 1992 Colony Light finished first, DQ to third.

Louisville Breeders' Cup Handicap

Grade 2, Churchill Downs, three-year-olds and up, fillies and mares, 1¹⁄₁₆ miles, dirt. Held May 4, 2001, with a gross value of $279,000. First held in 1986. Graded since 1988. Stakes record 1:42.50 (1996 Jewel Princess).

Year	Winner	Jockey	Second	Third	Strs	Final Time	1st Purse
2001	**Saudi Poetry**, 4, 112	V. Espinoza	Royal Fair, 5	Dreams Gallore, 5	8	1:42.53	$172,980
2000	**Heritage of Gold**, 5, 119	S. J. Sellers	Roza Robata, 5	Bella Chiarra, 5	6	1:42.99	$170,655
1999	**Silent Eskimo**, 4, 113	C. H. Borel	Lu Ravi, 4	Leo's Gypsy Dancer, 4	6	1:43.82	$169,415
1998	**Escena**, 5, 123	J. D. Bailey	One Rich Lady, 4	Three Fanfares, 4	10	1:44.84	$178,405
1997	**Halo America**, 7, 120	C. H. Borel	Escena, 4	Rare Blend, 4	7	1:42.78	$138,012
1996	**Jewel Princess**, 4, 118	C. J. McCarron	Serena's Song, 4	Naskra Colors, 4	6	**1:42.50**	$143,000
1995	**Fit to Lead**, 5, 113	K. J. Desormeaux	Jade Flush, 4	Teewinot, 4	9	1:43.46	$138,125
1994	**One Dreamer**, 6, 115	G. L. Stevens	Kalita Melody (GB), 4	Added Asset, 6	7	1:43.73	$136,630
1993	**Quilma (Chi)**, 6, 113	J. A. Santos	Looie Capote, 4	Hitch, 4	12	1:44.61	$37,570
1992	**Fowda**, 4, 117	P. A. Valenzuela	Dance Colony, 5	Fit for a Queen, 5	7	1:44.16	$100,750

Louisville Handicap

Not graded, Churchill Downs, three-year-olds and up, 1⅜ miles, turf. Held June 2, 2001, with a gross value of $109,900. First held in 1895. Grade 3 since 2002. Stakes record 2:14.15 (1999 Chorwon).

Year	Winner	Jockey	Second	Third	Strs	Final Time	1st Purse
2001	**With Anticipation**, 6, 112	J. K. Court	Profit Option, 6	Gritty Sandie, 5	6	2:16.28	$68,138
2000	**Buff**, 5, 113	F. C. Torres	Williams News, 5	Royal Strand (Ire), 6	11	2:14.31	$71,734
1999	**Chorwon**, 6, 114	C. H. Borel	Buff, 4	Keats and Yeats, 5	8	**2:14.15**	$69,812
1998	**Chorwon**, 5, 114	P. Day	African Dancer, 6	Thesaurus, 4	5	2:17.10	$67,890
1997	**Chorwon**, 4, 113	C. H. Borel	Down the Aisle, 4	Snake Eyes, 7	5	2:19.45	$67,952
1996	**Nash Terrace (Ire)**, 4, 105	D. M. Barton	Vladivostok, 6	Hawkeye Bay, 5	6	2:18.82	$71,760
1995	**Lindon Lime**, 5, 114	C. Perret	Caesour, 5	Snake Eyes, 5	8	1:48.12	$72,800
1994	**L'Hermine (GB)**, 5, 110	L. Melancon	Llandaff, 4	Snake Eyes, 4	5	1:48.36	$70,525
1993	**Stark South**, 5, 116	R. P. Romero	Cleone, 4	Coaxing Matt, 4	5	1:48.88	$71,955
1992	**Lotus Pool**, 5, 115	C. R. Woods Jr.	Buchman, 4	Magesterial Cheer, 4	8	1:47.69	$74,230

Mac Diarmida Handicap

Grade 3, Gulfstream Park, three-year-olds and up, 1⅜ miles, turf. Held January 9, 2000, with a gross value of $100,000. First held in 1995. Graded since 1997. Stakes record 2:14.14 (2000 Unite's Big Red).

Year	Winner	Jockey	Second	Third	Strs	Final Time	1st Purse
2000	**Unite's Big Red**, 6, 113	J. F. Chavez	Thesaurus, 6	Carpenter's Halo, 6	8	**2:12.14**	$60,000
1999	**Panama City**, 5, 114	J. D. Bailey	The Kaiser, 4	Notoriety, 4	5	2:20.65	$60,000
1998	**Copy Editor**, 6, 114	J. D. Bailey	Inkatha (Fr), 4	Lafitte the Pirate (GB), 4	12	2:16.72	$60,000
1997	**Mecke**, 5, 123	J. D. Bailey	Fabulous Frolic, 6	Spicilege, 6	4	2:05.80	$45,000
1996	**A Real Zipper**, 3, 114	A. T. Gryder	Tour's Big Red, 3	Shananie's Finale, 3	12	1:42.66	$30,000
1995	**Kings Fiction**, 3, 112	R. G. Davis	Ops Smile, 3	Mecke, 3	10	1:43.12	$30,000

2001 not held. 1995-'96 Mac Diarmida S. 1995-'96 three-year-olds. 1995 1 mile 70 yards; 1996 1¹⁄₁₆ miles; 1997 1¹⁄₄ miles; 1999 about 1⅜ miles. 1995, 1997 dirt.

Maker's Mark Mile Stakes

Grade 2, Keeneland, four-year-olds and up, 1 mile, turf. Held April 13, 2001, with a gross value of $226,600. First held in 1989. Graded since 1991. Stakes record 1:34.44 (2001 North East Bound).

Year	Winner	Jockey	Second	Third	Strs	Final Time	1st Purse
2001	**North East Bound**, 5	J. A. Velez Jr.	Brahms, 4	Strategic Mission, 4	8	**1:34.44**	$140,492
2000	**Conserve**, 4	S. J. Sellers	Marquette, 4	Inkatha (Fr), 4	9	1:35.08	$105,927
1999	**Soviet Line (Ire)**, 9	J. R. Velazquez	Trail City, 6	Rob 'n Gin, 6	8	1:35.37	$68,696
1998	**Lasting Approval**, 4	R. Albarado	Soviet Line (Ire), 8	Same Old Wish, 8	10	1:35.57	$70,060
1997	**Influent**, 6	J-L. Samyn	Chief Bearhart, 4	Foolish Pole, 4	9	1:34.59	$69,936
1996	**Tejano Run**, 4	J. D. Bailey	Sandpit (Brz), 7	Dove Hunt, 7	10	1:35.03	$70,618
1995	**Dove Hunt**, 4	J. A. Santos	Road of War, 5	Night Silence, 5	10	1:35.95	$53,196
1994	**First and Only**, 7	T. J. Hebert	The Name's Jimmy, 5	Pride of Summer, 5	7	1:36.63	$50,685
1993	**Ganges**, 5	J. D. Bailey	Bidding Proud, 4	Rocket Fuel, 4	10	1:35.40	$52,731
1992	**Shudanz**, 4	C. Perret	To Freedom, 4	Cudas, 4	9	1:36.52	$55,283

1992-'96 Fort Harrod S. 1992-'99 Grade 3.

Malibu Stakes

Grade 1, Santa Anita Park, three-year-olds, 7 furlongs, dirt. Held December 26, 2001, with a gross value of $200,000. First held in 1952. Graded since 1973. Stakes record 1:20 (1980 Spectacular Bid).

Year	Winner	Jockey	Second	Third	Strs	Final Time	1st Purse
2001	**Mizzen Mast**	K. J. Desormeaux	Giant Gentleman	I Love Silver	13	1:22.13	$120,000
2000	**Dixie Union**	A. O. Solis	Caller One	Wooden Phone	6	1:21.62	$120,000
1999	**Love That Red**	G. K. Gomez	Straight Man	Cat Thief	7	1:22.06	$120,000
1998	**Run Man Run**	M. J. Luzzi	Artax	Event of the Year	10	1:21.51	$120,000
1997	**Lord Grillo (Arg)**	E. Delahoussaye	Silver Charm	Swiss Yodeler	9	1:21.46	$120,000
1996	**King of the Heap**	K. J. Desormeaux	Hesabull	Northern Afleet	9	1:21.84	$134,300
1995	**Afternoon Deelites**	K. J. Desormeaux	Score Quick	High Stakes Player	9	1:21.73	$100,000
1994	**Powis Castle**	P. A. Valenzuela	Ferrara	Numerous	8	1:20.96	$64,300
1993	**Diazo**	L. A. Pincay Jr.	Concept Win	Mister Jolie	8	1:21.17	$64,700
1992	**Star of the Crop**	G. L. Stevens	The Wicked North	Bertrando	11	1:20.67	$67,850

1992-'94 Grade 2.

Manhattan Handicap

Grade 1, Belmont Park, three-year-olds and up, 1¼ miles, turf. Held June 9, 2001, with a gross value of $400,000. First held in 1896. Graded since 1973. Stakes record 1:57.79 (1994 Paradise Creek).

Year	Winner	Jockey	Second	Third	Strs	Final Time	1st Purse
2001	**Forbidden Apple**, 6, 117	C. S. Nakatani	King Cugat, 4	Tijiyr (Ire), 4	10	2:00.77	$240,000
2000	**Manndar (Ire)**, 4, 117	C. S. Nakatani	Boatman, 4	Spindrift (Ire), 4	8	1:59.61	$240,000
1999	**Yagli**, 6, 122	J. D. Bailey	Federal Trial, 4	Middlesex Drive, 4	10	1:58.48	$180,000
1998	**Chief Bearhart**, 5, 122	J. A. Santos	Devonwood, 4	Buck's Boy, 4	9	1:58.25	$150,000
1997	**Ops Smile**, 5, 116	R. G. Davis	Flag Down, 7	Always a Classic, 7	8	1:59.08	$120,000
1996	**Diplomatic Jet**, 4, 117	J. F. Chavez	Flag Down, 6	Kiri's Clown, 6	12	2:00.14	$120,000
1995	**Awad**, 5, 121	E. Maple	Blues Traveller (Ire), 5	Kiri's Clown, 5	12	1:58.57	$120,000
1994	**Paradise Creek**, 5, 124	P. Day	Solar Splendor, 7	River Majesty, 7	7	**1:57.79**	$275,000
1993	**Star of Cozzene**, 5, 118	J. A. Santos	Lure, 4	Solar Splendor, 4	8	1:58.99	$190,000
1992	**Sky Classic**, 5, 123	P. Day	Roman Envoy, 4	Leger Cat (Arg), 4	11	2:02.42	$252,860

1993-'96 Manhattan S. 1992-'93 Grade 2. 1994 new course record.

Man o' War Stakes

Grade 1, Belmont Park, three-year-olds and up, 1⅜ miles, turf. Held September 8, 2001, with a gross value of $500,000. First held in 1959. Graded since 1973. Stakes record 2:11.69 (1997 Influent).

Year	Winner	Jockey	Second	Third	Strs	Final Time	1st Purse
2001	**With Anticipation**, 6	P. Day	Silvano (Ger), 5	†Ela Athena (GB), 5	8	2:15.11	$300,000
2000	**Fantastic Light**, 4	J. D. Bailey	†Ela Athena (GB), 4	Drama Critic, 4	8	2:17.44	$300,000
1999	**Val's Prince**, 7	J. F. Chavez	Single Empire (Ire), 5	Federal Trial, 4	7	2:16.69	$300,000
1998	**Daylami (Ire)**, 4	J. D. Bailey	Buck's Boy, 5	Indy Vidual, 4	9	2:13.18	$240,000
1997	**Influent**, 6	J. D. Bailey	Val's Prince, 5	Awad, 7	10	**2:11.69**	$240,000
1996	**Diplomatic Jet**, 4	J. F. Chavez	Mecke, 4	Marlin, 3	8	2:14.37	$240,000
1995	**Millkom (GB)**, 4	G. L. Stevens	Kaldounevees (Fr), 4	Signal Tap, 4	12	2:12.80	$240,000
1994	**Royal Mountain Inn**, 5	J. A. Krone	Flag Down, 4	Fraise, 6	9	2:11.75	$240,000
1993	**Star of Cozzene**, 5	J. A. Santos	Serrant, 5	Dr. Kiernan, 4	8	2:23.14	$240,000
1992	**Solar Splendor**, 5	W. H. McCauley	Dear Doctor (Fr), 5	Spinning (Ire), 5	8	2:12.45	$240,000

† denotes female.

Martha Washington Stakes

Grade 3, Laurel Park, three-year-old fillies, 1¹/₁₆ miles, turf. Held October 29, 2000, with a gross value of $100,000. First held in 1988. Graded since 1988. Stakes record 1:42.21 (2000 Tippity Witch).

Year	Winner	Jockey	Second	Third	Strs	Final Time	1st Purse
2000	**Tippity Witch**	J. L. Espinoza	Senza Paura	Windsong	8	**1:42.21**	$60,000
1999	**Colstar**	A. Delgado	Polaire (Ire)	Jazz	9	1:45.64	$60,000

Year	Winner	Jockey	Second	Third	Strs	Final Time	1st Purse
1998	Mysterious Moll	R. Wilson	Wolfer	Proud Owner	9	1:42.31	$90,000
1997	Cotton Carnival	M. G. Pino	Romantic Notions	Bursting Forth	8	1:46.27	$60,000
1996	Silent Greeting	L. C. Reynolds	Rare Blend	Stop That Broad	9	1:43.41	$60,000
1995	Strawberry Reason	E. S. Prado	Blue Sky Princess	Rosebud (GB)	6	1:44.62	$60,000
1994	Tee Kay	R. Wilson	Avie's Fancy	Lady Ellen	8	1:45.37	$60,000
1993	Tennis Lady	A. J. Seefeldt	Putthepowdertoit	Missymooiloveyou	12	1:42.83	$45,000
1992	Mz. Zill Bear	S. D. Hamilton	Star Minister	Toosie	10	1:48.75	$45,000

2001 not held. 1992 Martha Washington H.; 1998 Martha Washington Breeders' Cup S. 1992 1⅛ miles. 1995-'97 dirt.

Maryland Breeders' Cup Handicap

Grade 3, Pimlico, three-year-olds and up, 6 furlongs, dirt. Held May 19, 2001, with a gross value of $200,000. First held in 1966. Graded since 1994. Stakes record 1:09.07 (1996 Forest Wildcat).

Year	Winner	Jockey	Second	Third	Strs	Final Time	1st Purse
2001	Disco Rico, 4, 118	H. Vega	Flame Thrower, 3	Istintaj, 3	6	1:10.40	$120,000
2000	Dr. Max, 4, 113	S. J. Sellers	Moon Over Prospect, 4	Crucible, 4	7	1:10.91	$60,000
1999	Yes It's True, 3, 113	J. D. Bailey	The Trader's Echo, 5	Purple Passion, 5	8	1:09.20	$120,000
1998	Richter Scale, 4, 117	J. D. Bailey	Trafalger, 4	Original Gray, 4	7	1:09.45	$120,000
1997	Cat Be Nimble, 5, 118	J. Rocco	Political Whit, 4	Excelerate, 4	7	1:10.12	$127,560
1996	Forest Wildcat, 5, 109	J. Bravo	Kayrawan, 4	Demaloot Demashoot, 4	9	1:09.07	$129,720
1995	Commanche Trail, 4, 113	M. E. Smith	Goldminer's Dream, 6	Marry Me Do, 6	6	1:09.35	$92,850
1994	Secret Odds, 4, 119	E. S. Prado	Honor the Hero, 6	Linear, 6	10	1:10.38	$93,615
1993	Senor Speedy, 6, 117	J. D. Bailey	He Is Risen, 5	Who Wouldn't, 5	7	1:09.69	$93,390
1992	Potentiality, 6, 117	P. Day	Smart Alec, 4	Boom Towner, 4	9	1:10.25	$93,300

1992-'93 not graded.

Massachusetts Handicap

Grade 2, Suffolk Downs, three-year-olds and up, 1⅛ miles, dirt. Held June 2, 2001, with a gross value of $500,000. First held in 1935. Graded since 1997. Stakes record 1:47.27 (1998 Skip Away).

Year	Winner	Jockey	Second	Third	Strs	Final Time	1st Purse
2001	Include, 4, 118	J. D. Bailey	Sir Bear, 8	Broken Vow, 8	7	1:48.61	$300,000
2000	Running Stag, 6, 116	J. R. Velazquez	Out of Mind (Brz), 4	David, 5	8	1:49.45	$400,000
1999	Behrens, 5, 118	J. F. Chavez	Running Stag, 5	Real Quiet, 5	6	1:49.14	$400,000
1998	Skip Away, 5, 130	J. D. Bailey	Puerto Madero (Chi), 4	K. J's Appeal, 4	5	1:47.27	$500,000
1997	Skip Away, 4, 119	S. J. Sellers	Formal Gold, 4	Will's Way, 4	6	1:47.92	$500,000
1996	Cigar, 6, 130	J. D. Bailey	Personal Merit, 5	Prolanzier, 5	6	1:49.63	$400,000
1995	Cigar, 5, 124	J. D. Bailey	Poor But Honest, 5	Double Calvados, 5	6	1:48.74	$650,000

1992-'94 not held. 1995-'96 not graded; 1997-'98 Grade 3. 1998 new track record.

Matriarch Stakes

Grade 1, Hollywood Park, three-year-olds and up, fillies and mares, 1⅛ miles, turf. Held November 25, 2001, with a gross value of $500,000. First held in 1981. Graded since 1983. Stakes record 1:46.06 (2000 Tout Charmant).

Year	Winner	Jockey	Second	Third	Strs	Final Time	1st Purse
2001	Starine (Fr), 4	J. R. Velazquez	Lethals Lady (GB), 3	Golden Apples (Ire), 3	12	1:50.16	$300,000
2000	Tout Charmant, 4	C. J. McCarron	Tranquility Lake, 5	Happyanunoit (NZ), 5	9	1:46.06	$300,000
1999	Happyanunoit (NZ), 4	B. Blanc	Tuzla (Fr), 5	Spanish Fern, 5	9	1:46.30	$300,000
1998	Squeak (GB), 4	A. O. Solis	Real Connection, 7	Green Jewel (GB), 7	8	2:05.08	$420,000
1997	Ryafan, 3	A. O. Solis	Maxzene, 4	Yokama, 4	8	2:05.90	$420,000
1996	Wandesta (GB), 5	C. S. Nakatani	Windsharp, 5	Memories of Silver, 5	12	2:00.14	$420,000
1995	Duda, 4	J. D. Bailey	Angel in My Heart (Fr), 3	Wandesta (GB), 3	14	2:00.37	$385,000
1994	Exchange, 6	L. A. Pincay Jr.	Aube Indienne (Fr), 4	Wandesta (GB), 4	8	1:49.42	$220,000
1993	Flawlessly, 5	C. J. McCarron	Toussaud, 4	Skimble, 4	7	1:46.78	$220,000
1992	Flawlessly, 4	C. J. McCarron	Super Staff, 4	Kostroma (Ire), 4	9	1:46.14	$220,000

1995-'98 1¼ miles.

Matron Stakes

Grade 1, Belmont Park, two-year-old fillies, 1 mile, dirt. Held September 17, 2000, with a gross value of $200,000. First held in 1892. Graded since 1973. Stakes record 1:35.16 (1994 Stormy Blues).

Year	Winner	Jockey	Second	Third	Strs	Final Time	1st Purse
2000	Raging Fever	J. D. Bailey	Dancinginmydreams	Ilusoria	5	1:38.20	$120,000
1999	Finder's Fee	H. Castillo Jr.	Darling My Darling	Circle of Life	7	1:36.68	$90,000
1998	Oh What a Windfall	S. J. Sellers	Arrested Dreams	Marley Vale	6	1:39.29	$90,000
1997	Beautiful Pleasure	J. D. Bailey	Diamond On the Run	Carrielle	11	1:35.71	$90,000
1996	Sharp Cat	J. D. Bailey	Storm Song	Fabulously Fast	6	1:36.19	$90,000
1995	Golden Attraction	G. L. Stevens	Cara Rafaela	My Flag	8	1:36.33	$90,000
1994	Stormy Blues	J. A. Santos	Pretty Discreet	Phone Caller	6	1:35.16	$64,740
1993	Strategic Maneuver	J. A. Santos	Astas Foxy Lady	Sovereign Kitty	8	1:23.84	$70,680
1992	Sky Beauty	E. Maple	Educated Risk	Family Enterprize	9	1:23.32	$72,480

2001 not held due to World Trade Center attack. 1992-'93 7 furlongs. 1994 Flanders finished first, DQ to sixth.

Meadowlands Cup Handicap

Grade 2, The Meadowlands, three-year-olds and up, 1⅛ miles, dirt. Held September 28, 2001, with a gross value of $500,000. First held in 1977. Graded since 1979. Stakes record 1:46.06 (1998 K. J.'s Appeal).

Year	Winner	Jockey	Second	Third	Strs	Final Time	1st Purse
2001	Gander, 5, 114	J. R. Velazquez	Broken Vow, 4	Include, 4	5	1:47.11	$300,000
2000	North East Bound, 4, 116	J. A. Velez Jr.	Lord Sterling, 4	Where's Taylor, 4	10	1:48.84	$240,000
1999	Pleasant Breeze, 4, 110	J. F. Chavez	Jazz Club, 4	Vision and Verse, 3	8	1:47.17	$300,000
1998	K. J.'s Appeal, 4, 112	J. R. Velazquez	Hal's Pal (GB), 5	Sir Bear, 5	8	1:46.06	$300,000
1996	Dramatic Gold, 5, 119	K. J. Desormeaux	Formal Gold, 3	Mt. Sassafras, 4	11	1:48.02	$450,000
1995	Peaks and Valleys, 3, 116	J. A. Krone	Poor But Honest, 5	Concern, 4	6	1:48.07	$300,000
1994	Conveyor, 6, 113	M. E. Smith	Personal Merit, 3	Bruce's Mill, 3	11	1:47.96	$300,000
1993	Marquetry, 6, 120	K. J. Desormeaux	Michelle Can Pass, 5	Northern Trend, 5	9	1:47.21	$300,000
1992	Sea Cadet, 4, 120	A. O. Solis	Valley Crossing, 4	American Chance, 3	10	1:48.19	$300,000

1997 not held. 1992-'96, 1998 Grade 1. 1998 new track record.

Memorial Day Handicap

Not graded, Calder Race Course, three-year-olds and up, 1¹⁄₁₆ miles, dirt. Held May 28, 2001, with a gross value of $75,000. First held in 1971. Grade 3 since 2002. Stakes record 1:45.20 (1972 Willmar).

Year	Winner	Jockey	Second	Third	Strs	Final Time	1st Purse
2001	Hal's Hope, 4, 115	R. I. Velez	American Halo, 5	Tahkodha Hills, 4	7	1:45.81	$45,000
2000	Dancing Guy, 5, 121	J. C. Ferrer	Reporter, 5	Groomstick Stock's, 4	9	1:46.28	$45,000
1999	Wicapi, 7, 116	E. Coa	Dancing Guy, 4	Golf Game, 4	8	1:46.79	$45,000
1998	Born Mighty, 4, 114	J. A. Rivera II	Hard Rock Ridge, 5	Auroral, 6	7	1:40.96	$30,000
1997	Vilhelm, 5, 114	J. C. Ferrer	Sir Bear, 4	Donthelumbertrader, 4	9	1:40.91	$30,000
1996	Marcie's Ensign, 4, 115	E. Coa	Derivative, 5	Halo Bird (Arg), 5	9	1:50.02	$30,000
1995	Mr. Light Tres (Arg), 6, 113	K. L. Chapman	Fabulous Frolic, 4	Flying American, 6	11	1:47.17	$30,000
1994	Final Sunrise, 4, 113	P. A. Rodriguez	Crucial Trial, 4	Bill Mooney, 4	4	1:51.86	$30,000
1993	Boots 'n Buck, 4, 116	M. Russ	Yankee Axe, 6	Darian's Reason, 5	10	1:53.82	$30,000
1992	Jodi's Sweetie, 4, 114	J. C. Duarte	Scottish Ice, 4	Bidding Proud, 3	9	1:44.21	$30,000

1992 Memorial Day S. 1992 about 1⅛ miles; 1993-'96 1⅛ miles. 1992, 1995, 1997-'98 turf.

Mervyn LeRoy Handicap

Grade 2, Hollywood Park, three-year-olds and up, 1¹⁄₁₆ miles, dirt. Held May 5, 2001, with a gross value of $150,000. First held in 1980. Graded since 1980. Stakes record 1:40.20 (1989 Ruhlmann).

Year	Winner	Jockey	Second	Third	Strs	Final Time	1st Purse
2001	Futural, 5, 117	C. J. McCarron	Skimming, 5	Moonlight Charger, 5	5	1:42.02	$90,000
2000	Out of Mind (Brz), 5, 116	E. Delahoussaye	Early Pioneer, 5	Skimming, 5	7	1:41.82	$90,000
1999	Budroyale, 6, 118	G. K. Gomez	Moore's Flat, 5	Wild Wonder, 5	6	1:42.12	$90,000
1998	Wild Wonder, 4, 116	E. Delahoussaye	Budroyale, 5	Flick (GB), 5	7	1:40.92	$64,320
1997	Hesabull, 4, 116	G. F. Almeida	Region, 8	Kingdom Found, 8	5	1:41.30	$63,720
1996	Siphon (Brz), 5, 117	D. R. Flores	Del Mar Dennis, 6	Dramatic Gold, 6	4	1:40.44	$61,500
1995	Tossofthecoin, 5, 118	C. S. Nakatani	Ferrara, 4	Polar Route, 4	8	1:40.70	$64,600
1994	Del Mar Dennis, 4, 115	S. Gonzalez Jr.	Tinners Way, 4	Hill Pass, 4	6	1:40.48	$93,300
1993	Marquetry, 6, 117	K. J. Desormeaux	Potrillon (Arg), 5	Lottery Winner, 5	6	1:49.10	$92,800
1992	Another Review, 4, 116	K. J. Desormeaux	Sir Beaufort, 5	Marquetry, 5	5	1:41.38	$87,900

1993 1⅛ miles.

Metropolitan Handicap

Grade 1, Belmont Park, three-year-olds and up, 1 mile, dirt. Held May 28, 2001, with a gross value of $750,000. First held in 1891. Graded since 1973. Stakes record 1:32.81 (1996 Honour and Glory).

Year	Winner	Jockey	Second	Third	Strs	Final Time	1st Purse
2001	Exciting Story, 4, 115	P. Husbands	Peeping Tom, 4	Alannan, 4	10	1:37.14	$150,000
2000	Yankee Victor, 4, 117	H. Castillo Jr.	†Honest Lady, 4	Sir Bear, 4	8	1:34.64	$450,000
1999	Sir Bear, 6, 117	J. R. Velazquez	Crafty Friend, 6	Liberty Gold, 6	8	1:34.55	$300,000
1998	Wild Rush, 4, 119	J. D. Bailey	Banker's Gold, 4	Accelerator, 4	9	1:33.50	$300,000
1997	Langfuhr, 5, 122	J. F. Chavez	Western Winter, 5	Northern Afleet, 5	10	1:33.11	$240,000
1996	Honour and Glory, 3, 110	J. R. Velazquez	(DH) Lite the Fuse, 5 (DH) Afternoon Deelites, 4		9	1:32.81	$240,000
1995	You and I, 4, 112	J. F. Chavez	Lite the Fuse, 4	Our Emblem, 4	9	1:34.63	$300,000
1994	Holy Bull, 3, 112	M. E. Smith	Cherokee Run, 4	Devil His Due, 4	10	1:33.98	$300,000
1993	Ibero (Arg), 6, 119	L. A. Pincay Jr.	Bertrando, 4	Alydeed, 4	9	1:34.29	$300,000
1992	Dixie Brass, 3, 107	J. M. Pezua	Pleasant Tap, 5	In Excess (Ire), 5	11	1:33.68	$300,000

1992-'93 Metropolitan Mile H. 1996 dead heat for second. † denotes female.

Miami Mile Breeders' Cup Handicap

Not graded, Calder Race Course, three-year-olds and up, 1 mile, turf. Held September 3, 2001, with a gross value of $135,000. First held in 1987. Graded since 1989. Stakes record 1:33.75 (2001 Mr. Livingston).

Year	Winner	Jockey	Second	Third	Strs	Final Time	1st Purse
2001	Mr. Livingston, 4, 115	A. Castellano Jr.	Honorable Pic, 4	Pisces, 4	8	1:33.75	$90,000
2000	Band Is Passing, 4, 120	E. Coa	Hurrahy, 7	Tiger Shark, 4	9	1:37.28	$90,000

1999	Sharp Appeal, 6, 114	J. Castellano	Shamrock City, 4	Hurrahy, 6	10	1:35.70	$135,000
1998	Unite's Big Red, 4, 115	E. O. Nunez	Fig Fest, 5	Ensign Ray, 5	10	1:36.62	$120,000
1997	Vilhelm, 5, 114	J. C. Ferrer	Marcie's Ensign, 5	Elite Jeblar, 7	11	1:36.67	$120,000
1996	Satellite Nealski, 3, 112	J. C. Ferrer	Marcie's Ensign, 4	Copy Editor, 4	10	1:47.63	$95,805
1995	Elite Jeblar, 5, 113	E. Fires	Myrmidon, 4	Fabulous Frolic, 4	10	1:47.67	$94,200
1994	The Vid, 4, 114	R. R. Douglas	Mr. Angel, 3	Carterista, 5	9	1:48.28	$94,350
1993	Carterista, 4, 117	M. A. Lee	Wild Forest, 4	Mr. Explosive, 5	13	1:47.51	$95,610
1992	Jodi's Sweetie, 4, 115	J. D. Bailey	Walkie Talker, 3	Futurist, 4	10	1:43.94	$94,140

2001 equaled course record.

Miesque Stakes

Grade 3, Hollywood Park, two-year-old fillies, 1 mile, turf. Held November 23, 2001, with a gross value of $200,000. First held in 1991. Graded since 1995. Stakes record 1:34.30 (1995 Antespend).

Year	Winner	Jockey	Second	Third	Strs	Final Time	1st Purse
2001	Forty On Line (GB)	C. S. Nakatani	Riskaverse	Daisyago	10	1:36.38	$120,000
2000	Fantastic Filly (Fr)	G. K. Gomez	Smart Timing	Eminent	11	1:35.11	$120,000
1999	Prairie Princess	A. O. Solis	She's Classy	Mary Kies	6	1:37.30	$120,000
1998	Here's to You	E. Delahoussaye	Sweet Ludy (Ire)	Nausicaa	7	1:36.57	$120,000
1997	Star's Proud Penny	G. K. Gomez	Superlative	Ransom the Dreamer	9	1:37.42	$120,000
1996	Ascutney	E. Delahoussaye	Wealthy	Clever Pilot	8	1:35.16	$120,000
1995	Antespend	C. W. Antley	Wheatly Special	Platinum Blonde	10	1:34.30	$110,000
1994	Bail Out Becky	K. J. Desormeaux	Miss Union Avenue	Makin Whopee (Fr)	10	1:37.26	$110,000
1993	Tricky Code	C. S. Nakatani	Irish Forever	Roget's Fact	6	1:35.15	$137,500
1992	Creaking Board (GB)	K. J. Desormeaux	Ask Anita	Zoonaqua	10	1:35.62	$137,500

Milady Breeders' Cup Handicap

Grade 1, Hollywood Park, three-year-olds and up, fillies and mares, 1 1/16 miles, dirt. Held June 3, 2001, with a gross value of $254,300. First held in 1952. Graded since 1973. Stakes record 1:40.20 (1980 Image of Reality).

Year	Winner	Jockey	Second	Third	Strs	Final Time	1st Purse
2001	Lazy Slusan, 6, 119	V. Espinoza	Lady Melesi, 4	Feverish, 4	6	1:42.25	$157,980
2000	Riboletta (Brz), 5, 120	C. J. McCarron	Bordelaise (Arg), 5	Excellent Meeting, 5	5	1:42.01	$112,860
1999	Gourmet Girl, 4, 115	E. Delahoussaye	Yolo Lady, 4	Victory Stripes (Arg), 4	5	1:40.97	$112,440
1998	I Ain't Bluffing, 4, 120	C. J. McCarron	Fleet Lady, 4	Real Connection, 4	6	1:42.16	$158,640
1997	Listening, 4, 116	A. O. Solis	Chile Chatte, 4	Exotic Wood, 4	5	1:41.37	$95,220
1996	Twice the Vice, 5, 120	C. J. McCarron	Jewel Princess, 4	Urbane, 4	5	1:40.96	$110,100
1995	Pirate's Revenge, 4, 116	C. W. Antley	Paseana (Arg), 4	Private Persuasion, 8	5	1:41.57	$91,000
1994	Andestine, 4, 116	C. J. McCarron	Golden Klair (GB), 4	Zarani Sidi Anna, 4	7	1:41.40	$94,900
1993	Paseana (Arg), 6, 125	C. J. McCarron	Bold Windy, 4	Re Toss (Arg), 4	7	1:41.67	$94,500
1992	Paseana (Arg), 5, 125	C. J. McCarron	Re Toss (Arg), 5	Fowda, 5	7	1:41.46	$94,200

1992-'95 Milady H.

Mint Julep Handicap

Grade 3, Churchill Downs, four-year-olds and up, fillies and mares, 1 1/16 miles, turf. Held May 19, 2001, with a gross value of $113,600. First held in 1977. Graded since 2001. Stakes record 1:40.98 (1994 Words of War).

Year	Winner	Jockey	Second	Third	Strs	Final Time	1st Purse
2001	Megans Bluff, 4, 118	C. Perret	Sitka, 4	Good Game, 4	10	1:42.88	$70,432
2000	Pratella, 5, 118	L. Melancon	Silver Comic, 4	Histoire Sainte (Fr), 4	8	1:43.08	$69,378
1999	Mingling Glances, 5, 113	L. Melancon	Formal Tango, 4	Red Cat, 4	11	1:42.59	$70,928
1998	B. A. Valentine, 5, 116	F. C. Torres	Lordy Lordy, 4	Mingling Glances, 5	9	1:41.42	$70,804
1997	Valor Lady, 5, 114	R. Albarado	My Secret, 5	Everhope, 5	11	1:41.20	$71,238
1996	Bail Out Becky, 4, 118	C. Perret	Country Cat, 4	Fluffkins, 4	8	1:41.86	$54,698
1995	Romy, 4, 118	J. L. Diaz	Olden Lek, 5	Memories (Ire), 5	6	1:42.69	$54,941
1994	Words of War, 5, 117	C. H. Marquez Jr.	Freewheel, 5	Eurostorm, 5	10	1:40.98	$55,673
1993	Classic Reign, 4, 115	F. A. Arguello Jr.	Tap Routine, 4	Liz Cee, 4	10	1:42.84	$37,375
1992	Lady Shirl, 5, 123	P. A. Johnson	Topsa, 5	Behaving Dancer, 5	10	1:41.41	$37,083

1995-'96, 1998 Mint Julep S. 1997 Romy finished first, DQ to fourth. 1992, 1994 new course record.

Miss Preakness Stakes

Not graded, Pimlico, three-year-old fillies, 6 furlongs, dirt. Held May 17, 2001, with a gross value of $100,000. First held in 1986. Grade 3 since 2002. Stakes record 1:10 (2000 Lucky Livi).

Year	Winner	Jockey	Second	Third	Strs	Final Time	1st Purse
2001	Kimbralata	T. L. Dunkelberger	Carafe	Stormy Pick	5	1:11.20	$60,000
2000	Lucky Livi	R. Wilson	Big Bambu	Swept Away	5	1:10.00	$60,000
1999	Hookedonthefeelin	G. L. Stevens	Silent Valay	Paula's Girl	4	1:11.26	$60,000
1998	Storm Beauty	C. R. Woods Jr.	Brac Drifter	Hair Spray	5	1:10.81	$45,000
1997	Weather Vane	M. G. Pino	Move	Cayman Sunset	4	1:11.94	$64,740
1996	Nic's Halo	R. Wilson	Palette Knife	Crafty But Sweet	4	1:11.75	$32,655
1995	Lilly Capote	G. L. Stevens	Broad Smile	Norstep	7	1:10.90	$32,640
1994	Foolish Kisses	E. S. Prado	Aly's Conquest	Platinum Punch	5	1:12.45	$32,730
1993	My Rosa	E. S. Prado	Fighting Jet	Code Blum	5	1:11.33	$32,175
1992	Toots La Mae	J. Bravo	Missy White Oak	Jazzy One	6	1:11.97	$26,505

Modesty Handicap

Grade 3, Arlington Park, three-year-olds and up, fillies and mares, 1$\frac{3}{16}$ miles, turf. Held July 28, 2001, with a gross value of $150,000. First held in 1942. Graded since 1985. Stakes record 1:55.31 (1993 Hero's Love).

Year	Winner	Jockey	Second	Third	Strs	Final Time	1st Purse
2001	**Ioya Two**, 6, 115	M. Guidry	Megans Bluff, 4	Solvig, 4	11	1:55.47	$90,000
2000	**Wade for Me**, 5, 116	C. A. Emigh	Candleinthedark, 5	Wild Heart Dancing, 4	10	1:57.06	$60,000
1997	**War Thief**, 5, 116	S. J. Sellers	My Secret, 5	Bog Wild, 4	8	1:57.47	$60,000
1996	**Belle of Cozzene**, 4, 114	D. R. Pettinger	Trick Attack, 5	Naskra Colors, 4	6	1:58.24	$60,000
1994	**Assert Oneself**, 4, 115	F. H. Valenzuela	One Dreamer, 6	Seventies, 4	9	1:56.01	$60,000
1993	**Hero's Love**, 5, 120	E. Fires	Silvandry, 5	Silvered, 6	10	**1:55.31**	$60,000
1992	**Tango Charlie**, 3, 114	A. G. Sorrows Jr.	Alcando (Ire)	Hero's Love, 4	13	1:58.79	$45,000

1995, 1998-'99 not held. 1992-'93 Modesty S. 1996 dirt. 1994 Aube Indienne (Fr) finished first, DQ to seventh.

Molly Pitcher Breeders' Cup Handicap

Grade 2, Monmouth Park, three-year-olds and up, fillies and mares, 1$\frac{1}{16}$ miles, dirt. Held June 30, 2001, with a gross value of $300,000. First held in 1946. Graded since 1973. Stakes record 1:41.20 (1983 Ambassador of Luck; 1986 Lady's Secret).

Year	Winner	Jockey	Second	Third	Strs	Final Time	1st Purse
2001	**March Magic**, 4, 113	M. J. Luzzi	Vivid Sunset, 4	Shine Again, 4	7	1:43.79	$180,000
2000	**Lu Ravi**, 5, 116	P. Day	Silverbulletday, 4	Bella Chiarra, 4	7	1:43.17	$180,000
1999	**Heritage of Gold**, 4, 114	C. T. Lambert	Harpia, 5	Tap to Music, 5	6	1:41.76	$180,000
1998	**Relaxing Rhythm**, 4, 116	P. Day	Minister's Melody, 4	Glitter Woman, 4	6	1:42.30	$120,000
1997	**Rare Blend**, 4, 116	M. E. Smith	Top Secret, 4	Chip, 4	5	1:43.60	$120,000
1996	**Halo America**, 6, 117	P. Day	Rogues Walk, 4	Why Be Normal, 4	6	1:41.75	$120,000
1995	**Inside Information**, 4, 124	M. E. Smith	Jade Flush, 4	Halo America, 4	5	1:43.81	$90,000
1994	**Hey Hazel**, 4, 114	R. C. Landry	Ann Dear, 4	Future of Gold, 4	6	1:46.41	$120,000
1993	**Wilderness Song**, 5, 119	D. Clark	Quilma (Chi), 4	Looie Capote, 6	6	1:44.79	$90,000
1992	**Versailles Treaty**, 4, 120	M. E. Smith	Quick Mischief, 6	Cozzene's Wish, 6	6	1:43.18	$90,000

1992-'95 Molly Pitcher H.

Monmouth Breeders' Cup Oaks

Grade 2, Monmouth Park, three-year-old fillies, 1$\frac{1}{8}$ miles, dirt. Held July 28, 2001, with a gross value of $250,000. First held in 1871. Graded since 1973. Stakes record 1:48 (1985 Golden Horde; 1987 Without Feathers).

Year	Winner	Jockey	Second	Third	Strs	Final Time	1st Purse
2001	**Unbridled Elaine**	E. Coa	Unrestrained	Indy Glory	7	1:51.02	$150,000
2000	**Spain**	J. A. Velez Jr.	North Lake Jane	Prized Stamp	7	1:42.78	$150,000
1999	**Silverbulletday**	J. D. Bailey	Boom Town Girl	Bag Lady Jane	4	1:43.03	$150,000
1998	**Kirby's Song**	T. Kabel	Santaria	Brave Deed	6	1:43.31	$120,000
1997	**Blushing K. D.**	L. Meche	Holiday Ball	Snowy Apparition	7	1:41.92	$120,000
1996	**Top Secret**	J. Bravo	Yanks Music	Mesabi Maiden	5	1:42.33	$120,000
1995	**Kathie's Colleen**	J. S. McAleney	Gal in a Ruckus	Country Cat	5	1:51.50	$90,000
1994	**Two Altazano**	C. Perret	Stellarina	Cavada	5	1:52.19	$90,000
1993	**Jacody**	T. G. Turner	Deputy Jane West	Sheila's Revenge	5	1:50.77	$90,000
1992	**Diamond Duo**	T. G. Turner	(DH) Secretly		8	1:51.40	$90,000
			(DH) C. C.'s Return				

1992-'95 Monmouth Oaks. 1996-2000 1$\frac{1}{16}$ miles. 1992 dead heat for 2nd.

Monrovia Handicap

Grade 3, Santa Anita Park, three-year-olds and up, fillies and mares, about 6$\frac{1}{2}$ furlongs, turf. Held December 31, 2001, with a gross value of $118,150. First run in 1968. Graded since 1990. Stakes record 1:12.40 (1981 Kilijaro [Ire]).

Year	Winner	Jockey	Second	Third	Strs	Final Time	1st Purse
2001	**Paga (Arg)**, 4, 117	M. E. Smith	Twin Set (Ger), 4	Impeachable, 4	13	1:15.09	$70,890
2000	**Evening Promise (GB)**, 4, 120	K. J. Desormeaux	Squall Linda, 4	New Heaven (Arg), 6	12	1:12.62	$68,640
1999	**Desert Lady (Ire)**, 4, 116	C. S. Nakatani	Sweet Mazarine (Ire), 5	Supercilious, 6	7	1:14.59	$65,100
	Show Me the Stage, 3, 117	K. J. Desormeaux	Chichim, 4	Honest Lady, 3	4	1:15.14	$64,140
1998	**Madame Pandit**, 5, 116	E. Delahoussaye	Ski Dancer, 4	Dixie Pearl, 6	7	1:15.80	$65,700
1997	**Grab the Prize**, 5, 116	A. O. Solis	Finite E. F., 4	Evil's Pic, 5	7	1:16.89	$66,900
1996	**Klassy Kim**, 5, 116	G. F. Almeida	Ski Dancer, 4	Baby Diamonds, 5	8	1:14.48	$65,650
1995	**Rabiadella**, 4, 117	P. A. Valenzuela	Dezibelle's Star, 4	Las Meninas (Ire), 4	5	1:14.92	$47,450
1994	**Mamselle Bebette**, 4, 117	C. S. Nakatani	Shuggleswon, 4	Kalita Melody (GB), 6	6	1:15.35	$49,650
1993	**Glen Kate (Ire)**, 6, 118	C. A. Black	Bel's Starlet, 6	Heart of Joy, 6	7	1:12.89	$48,650
1992	**Middlefork Rapids**, 4, 116	P. A. Valenzuela	Remarkably Easy, 4	Crystal Gazing, 4	11	1:12.55	$51,150

1999 held in January and December.

Morvich Handicap

Grade 3, Santa Anita Park, three-year-olds and up, about 6$\frac{1}{2}$ furlongs, turf. Held November 5, 2001, with a gross value of $107,800. First held in 1974. Graded since 1999. Stakes record 1:11.47 (2001 El Cielo).

Year	Winner	Jockey	Second	Third	Strs	Final Time	1st Purse
2001	**El Cielo**, 7, 123	J. Valdivia Jr.	Speak in Passing, 4	Islander, 6	6	**1:11.46**	$64,680
2000	**El Cielo**, 6, 119	J. Valdivia Jr.	Kahal (GB), 6	Montemiro (Fr), 6	10	1:12.00	$67,020

Year	Winner	Jockey	Second	Third	Strs	Final Time	1st Purse
1999	Riviera (Fr), 5, 118	B. Blanc	Kahal (GB), 5	Howbaddouwantit, 4	10	1:12.99	$66,840
1998	Musafi, 4, 117	G. K. Gomez	Fabulous Guy (Ire), 4	Expelled, 6	8	1:14.54	$60,000
1997	Reality Road, 5, 115	C. S. Nakatani	Latin Dancer, 3	Torch Rouge (GB), 6	7	1:13.60	$60,000
1996	Comininalittlehot, 5, 117	K. J. Desormeaux	Wild Zone, 6	Wavy Run (Ire), 5	7	1:11.57	$65,100
1995	Score Quick, 3, 113	G. F. Almeida	Dramatic Gold, 4	Fu Man Slew, 4	7	1:14.64	$60,700
1994	Rotsaluck, 3, 115	F. H. Valenzuela	D'Hallevant, 4	Didyme, 4	7	1:13.66	$47,925
1993	Western Approach, 4, 115	K. J. Desormeaux	Yousefia, 4	Exemplary Leader, 7	6	1:12.12	$47,025
1992	Regal Groom, 5, 118	M. A. Pedroza	Bailarin, 5	Repriced, 4	4	1:16.88	$45,150

1992 two-year-olds and up. 1992,1995 6½ furlongs. 1992, 1995 dirt. 1996 new course record; 2001 equaled course record. 1999 Kahal (GB) finished first, DQ to second.

Mother Goose Stakes

Grade 1, Belmont Park, three-year-old fillies, 1⅛ miles, dirt. Held June 30, 2001, with a gross value of $250,000. First held in 1957. Graded since 1973. Stakes record 1:46.58 (1994 Lakeway).

Year	Winner	Jockey	Second	Third	Strs	Final Time	1st Purse
2001	Fleet Renee	J. R. Velazquez	Real Cozzy	Exogenous	10	1:47.19	$150,000
2000	Secret Status	P. Day	Jostle	Finder's Fee	7	1:48.03	$150,000
1999	Dreams Gallore	R. Albarado	Oh What a Windfall	Better Than Honour	6	1:48.69	$150,000
1998	Jersey Girl	M. E. Smith	Keeper Hill	Banshee Breeze	11	1:47.77	$120,000
1997	Ajina	M. E. Smith	Sharp Cat	Tomisue's Delight	6	1:48.56	$120,000
1996	Yanks Music	J. R. Velazquez	Escena	Cara Rafaela	7	1:47.90	$120,000
1995	Serena's Song	G. L. Stevens	Golden Bri	Forested	6	1:50.37	$120,000
1994	Lakeway	K. J. Desormeaux	Cinnamon Sugar (Ire)	Inside Information	6	1:46.58	$120,000
1993	Sky Beauty	M. E. Smith	Dispute	Silky Feather	4	1:49.69	$120,000
1992	Turnback the Alarm	C. W. Antley	Easy Now	Queen of Triumph	7	1:48.80	$120,000

Mr. Prospector Handicap

Grade 3, Gulfstream Park, three-year-olds and up, 6 furlongs, dirt. Held January 15, 2001, with a gross value of $120,000. First held in 1946. Graded since 1999. Stakes record 1:08.45 (1997 Punch Line).

Year	Winner	Jockey	Second	Third	Strs	Final Time	1st Purse
2001	Istintaj, 5, 116	J. D. Bailey	Miners Gamble, 5	Smokin Pete, 5	13	1:09.63	$60,000
2000	Mountain Top, 5, 115	J. A. Santos	Lifeisawhirl, 4	Silver Season, 4	6	1:10.80	$45,000
1999	Cowboy Cop, 5, 114	P. Day	Good and Tough, 4	Mint, 4	6	1:08.80	$45,000
1998	Rare Rock, 5, 116	P. Day	Heckofaralph, 5	Banjo, 5	8	1:08.67	$45,000
1997	Punch Line, 7, 116	P. Day	Appealing Skier, 4	Constant Escort, 4	8	1:08.45	$45,000
1996	Meadow Monster, 5, 114	R. Wilson	Lord Carson, 4	Ponche, 4	8	1:09.47	$30,000
1995	Sweet Beast, 5, 118	M. E. Smith	Exclusive Praline, 4	Distinct Reality, 4	5	1:09.36	$30,000
1994	Binalong, 5, 116	J. D. Bailey	I Can't Believe, 6	Golden Pro, 6	12	1:09.68	$30,000
1993	Surely Six, 4, 113	R. Wilson	Groomstick, 7	Poulain d'Or, 7	9	1:21.85	$30,000
1992	Take Me Out, 4, 115	J. D. Bailey	Gizmo's Fortune, 4	Ocala Flame, 4	10	1:23.75	$30,000

1992-2000 Hallandale H. 1992-'98 not graded. 1992-'93 7 furlongs.

Mrs. Revere Stakes

Grade 2, Churchill Downs, three-year-old fillies, 1¹⁄₁₆ miles, turf. Held November 17, 2001, with a gross value of $172,500. First held in 1991. Graded since 1995. Stakes record 1:42.90 (2001 Snow Dance).

Year	Winner	Jockey	Second	Third	Strs	Final Time	1st Purse
2001	Snow Dance	C. Perret	Stylish	Cozy Island	10	1:42.86	$106,950
2000	Megans Bluff	M. Guidry	Uncharted Haven (GB)	Impending Bear	12	1:43.37	$107,973
1999	Silver Comic	L. Melancon	St Clair Ridge (Ire)	Circle of Gold (Ire)	12	1:45.13	$108,345
1998	Anguilla	P. Day	Darling Alice	White Beauty	11	1:45.67	$107,601
1997	Parade Queen	P. Day	Mystery Code	Starry Dreamer	11	1:45.46	$108,624
1996	Maxzene	J. A. Krone	Fasta	Turkappeal	12	1:43.78	$72,354
1995	Petrouchka	D. Penna	Christmas Gift	Ms. Isadora	11	1:44.20	$75,725
1994	Mariah's Storm	R. N. Lester	Avie's Fancy	Bear Truth	10	1:43.99	$75,400
1993	Weekend Madness (Ire)	C. R. Woods Jr.	Flower Circle	Amal Hayati	10	1:46.32	$74,685
1992	McKaymackenna	J. Velasquez	Spinning Round	Aquilegia	10	1:45.04	$56,209

1995-'97 Grade 3.

My Charmer Handicap

Grade 3, Calder Race Course, three-year-olds and up, fillies and mares, 1⅛ miles, turf. Held December 8, 2001, with a gross value of $100,000. First held in 1984. Graded since 1998. Stakes record 1:46.40 (1995 Danish [Ire]).

Year	Winner	Jockey	Second	Third	Strs	Final Time	1st Purse
2001	Batique, 5, 116	J. F. Chavez	Please Sign In, 5	Wander Morn, 3	12	1:49.85	$60,000
2000	Wild Heart Dancing, 4, 116	J. F. Chavez	Megans Bluff, 3	Orange Sunset (Ire), 4	12	1:47.58	$60,000
1999	Crystal Symphony, 3, 114	C. H. Velasquez	Winfama, 6	Khumba Mela (Ire), 4	12	1:47.65	$60,000
1998	Colcon, 5, 118	J. D. Bailey	Cuando, 4	Winfama, 5	12	1:50.51	$60,000
1997	Overcharger, 5, 116	J. A. Rivera II	Dance Clear (Ire), 4	Hero's Pride (Fr), 4	12	1:48.18	$60,000
1996	Romy, 5, 114	F. C. Torres	Delta Love, 3	Ms. Mostly, 3	7	1:47.33	$60,000
1995	Danish (Ire), 4, 116	J. A. Santos	Cox Orange, 5	Alice Springs, 5	11	1:46.40	$60,000

Year	Winner	Jockey	Second	Third	Strs	Final Time	1st Purse
1994	Caress, 3, 114	R. G. Davis	Putthepowdertoit, 4	Cox Orange, 4	12	1:50.63	$60,000
1993	Chickasha, 4, 115	R. D. Lopez	Marshua's River, 6	Always Nettie, 4	14	1:47.36	$30,000
1992	Julie La Rousse (Ire), 4, 120	J. D. Bailey	Marshua's River, 5	Highland Crystal, 4	10	1:45.78	$30,000
1992	Explosive Kate, 5, 118	D. Penna	Mia Bird Too, 3	Kiwi Mint, 4	9	1:46.58	$30,000
1992	Lady Shirl, 5, 120	E. Fires	Ratings, 4	Seaquay, 6	11	1:44.74	$51,150

Nashua Stakes

Grade 3, Belmont Park, two-year-olds, 1 mile, dirt. Held October 26, 2001, with a gross value of $109,300. First held in 1975. Graded since 1982. Stakes record 1:35.40 (1977 Quadratic).

Year	Winner	Jockey	Second	Third	Strs	Final Time	1st Purse
2001	Listen Here	J. D. Bailey	Monthir	Thunder Days	6	1:37.61	$65,580
2000	Ommadon	A. T. Gryder	Windsor Castle	Griffinite	10	1:36.74	$67,920
1999	Mass Market	M. E. Smith	Polish Miner	Parade Leader	9	1:38.60	$67,020
1998	Doneraile Court	J. D. Bailey	Successful Appeal	Exiled Groom	8	1:36.17	$66,600
1997	Coronado's Quest	M. E. Smith	Not Tricky	Dice Dancer	5	1:37.06	$65,100
1996	Jules	J. A. Santos	Shammy Davis	Sal's Driver	9	1:36.89	$68,340
1994	Devious Course	F. T. Alvarado	Mighty Magee	Old Tascosa	7	1:37.50	$65,580
1993	Popol's Gold	W. H. McCauley	Personal Merit	Sonny's Bruno	11	1:46.68	$74,400
1992	Dalhart	M. E. Smith	Rohwer	Peace Baby	11	1:44.60	$74,640

1995 not held. 1992-'94, 1996-2000 held at Aqueduct. 1992-'93 1 1/16 miles.

Nassau County Stakes

Grade 2, Belmont Park, three-year-old fillies, 7 furlongs, dirt. Held May 9, 2001, with a gross value of $150,000. First held in 1996. Graded since 1998. Stakes record 1:22.19 (1996 Star de Lady Ann).

Year	Winner	Jockey	Second	Third	Strs	Final Time	1st Purse
2001	Cat Chat	J. R. Velazquez	Xtra Heat	Shooting Party	6	1:23.02	$90,000
2000	C'Est L' Amour	E. S. Prado	Tugger	Miss Inquistive	6	1:23.46	$90,000
1999	Oh What a Windfall	M. E. Smith	Paved in Gold	Things Change	8	1:23.59	$66,480
1998	Jersey Girl	M. E. Smith	Countess Diana	Foil	4	1:22.63	$48,831
1997	Alyssum	J. A. Santos	Screamer	Sinclara	7	1:22.90	$49,065
1996	Star de Lady Ann	J. F. Chavez	Stop Traffic	J J'sdream	8	**1:22.19**	$49,590

1998-'99 Grade 3.

National Jockey Club Handicap

Grade 3, Sportsman's Park, four-year-olds and up, 1 1/8 miles, dirt. Held April 22, 2001, with a gross value of $200,000. First held in 1956. Graded since 1984. Stakes record 1:47.60 (1999 Baytown).

Year	Winner	Jockey	Second	Third	Strs	Final Time	1st Purse
2001	Chicago Six, 6, 117	A. J. Juarez Jr.	Guided Tour, 5	Glacial, 5	5	1:48.28	$120,000
2000	Take Note of Me, 6, 120	R. Albarado	Glacial, 5	Nite Dreamer, 5	8	1:49.91	$120,000
1999	Baytown, 5, 114	M. Guidry	Precocity, 5	Fred Bear Claw, 5	7	**1:47.60**	$120,000
1998	Polar Expedition, 7, 117	M. Guidry	Bucks Nephew, 8	Shed Some Light, 8	9	1:49.91	$120,000
1997	Bucks Nephew, 7, 118	G. K. Gomez	Natural Selection, 4	Gotha, 4	8	1:49.87	$120,000
1996	Prory, 4, 113	C. H. Silva	Polar Expedition, 5	Shed Some Light, 5	9	1:50.83	$150,000
1995	Dusty Screen, 7, 116	E. Maple	Come On Flip, 4	Adhocracy, 8	8	1:51.57	$150,000
1994	Recoup the Cash, 4, 113	J. L. Diaz	Dread Me Not, 4	Danc'n Jake, 4	7	1:49.03	$150,000
1993	Stalwars, 8, 118	J. L. Diaz	Count the Time, 4	Richman, 4	8	1:49.46	$150,000
1992	Stalwars, 7, 115	M. Guidry	Richman, 4	Sunny Prince, 4	6	1:48.15	$156,300

1999 held at Hawthorne. 1992, 1993 new track record. 1996 Bucks Nephew finished first, DQ to fourth.

National Museum of Racing Hall of Fame Handicap

Grade 2, Saratoga Race Course, three-year-olds, 1 1/8 miles, turf. Held August 6, 2001, with a gross value of $150,000. First held in 1985. Graded since 1987. Stakes record 1:46.65 (1992 Paradise Creek).

Year	Winner	Jockey	Second	Third	Strs	Final Time	1st Purse
2001	Baptize, 122	J. D. Bailey	Strategic Partner	Saint Verre	7	1:47.94	$90,000
2000	Turnofthecentury, 118	A. T. Gryder	Aldo	Polish Miner	5	1:52.35	$90,000
1999	Marquette, 119	J. D. Bailey	Phi Beta Doc	Good Night	13	1:49.33	$90,000
1998	Parade Ground, 120	S. J. Sellers	Vergennes	Stay Sound	8	1:47.82	$90,000
1997	Rob 'n Gin, 120	J. D. Bailey	River Squall	Subordination	6	1:42.09	$66,000
1996	Sir Cat, 113	J. D. Bailey	Fortitude	Optic Nerve	9	1:40.46	$68,340
1995	Flitch, 113	M. E. Smith	Diplomatic Jet	Nostra	8	1:48.08	$83,700
1994	Islefaxyou, 113	E. Maple	Jaggery John	(DH) Lahint	13	1:48.61	$70,200
				(DH) Mr. Impatience			
1993	A in Sociology, 115	C. W. Antley	Strolling Along	Palashall	10	1:48.81	$73,080
1992	Paradise Creek, 115	M. E. Smith	Smiling and Dancin	Spectacular Tide	8	**1:46.65**	$72,600

1992-'97 National Museum of Racing Hall of Fame S. 1996-'97 1 1/16 miles. 2000 dirt. 1994 dead heat for third.

Native Diver Handicap

Grade 3, Hollywood Park, three-year-olds and up, 1⅛ miles, dirt. Held December 9, 2001, with a gross value of $100,000. First held in 1979. Graded since 1979. Stakes record 1:45.35 (1996 Gentlemen [Arg]).

Year	Winner	Jockey	Second	Third	Strs	Final Time	1st Purse
2001	**Momentum**, 3, 117	C. S. Nakatani	Euchre, 5	Last Parade (Arg), 5	7	1:48.24	$60,000
2000	**Sky Jack**, 4, 118	L. A. Pincay Jr.	Lethal Instrument, 4	Grey Memo, 3	8	1:46.81	$60,000
1999	**General Challenge**, 3, 123	C. J. McCarron	Moore's Flat, 5	Koslanin (Arg), 5	6	1:49.07	$60,000
1998	**Puerto Madero (Chi)**, 4, 121	K. J. Desormeaux	Musical Gambler, 4	River Keen (Ire), 6	5	1:48.43	$60,000
1997	**Refinado Tom (Arg)**, 4, 119	G. L. Stevens	Steel Ruhlr, 3	Boggle, 5	8	1:47.84	$60,000
1996	**Gentlemen (Arg)**, 4, 121	G. L. Stevens	Dramatic Gold, 5	Don't Blame Rio, 3	5	**1:45.35**	$63,840
1995	**Alphabet Soup**, 4, 117	C. W. Antley	El Florista (Arg), 5	Regal Rowdy, 6	5	1:47.03	$61,400
1994	**Best Pal**, 6, 121	C. J. McCarron	Tossofthecoin, 4	Royal Chariot, 4	7	1:48.44	$64,000
1993	**Slew of Damascus**, 5, 118	C. S. Nakatani	Lottery Winner, 4	L'Express (Chi), 4	7	1:47.46	$63,300
1992	**Sir Beaufort**, 5, 119	C. J. McCarron	Memo (Chi), 5	Berillon (GB), 5	5	1:47.88	$61,700

New Hampshire Sweepstakes Handicap

Grade 3, Rockingham Park, three-year-olds and up, about 1⅛ miles, turf. Held June 23, 2001, with a gross value of $200,000. First held in 1964. Graded since 1986. Stakes record 1:45.04 (2000 Inexplicable).

Year	Winner	Jockey	Second	Third	Strs	Final Time	1st Purse
2001	**Hap**, 5, 123	J. R. Velazquez	Gander, 5	Flash of Joy, 5	7	1:46.32	$120,000
2000	**Inexplicable**, 5, 114	J. A. Santos	Where's Taylor, 4	Distant Mirage (Ire), 4	10	**1:45.04**	$120,000
1999	**Adcat**, 4, 113	J. F. Hampshire Jr.	Hurrahy, 6	Hibernian Rhapsody (Ire), 6	8	1:46.29	$120,000
1998	**Statesmanship**, 4, 118	J. A. Santos	Long War, 4	Daylight Savings, 4	7	1:48.49	$120,000
1997	**Ok by Me**, 4, 114	J. Bravo	Influent, 5	Diplomatic Jet, 6	8	1:47.14	$120,000
1996	**Brave Note (Ire)**, 5, 112	R. E. Colton	Darnay (GB), 5	My Mogul, 5	9	1:47.64	$120,000
1995	**Kiri's Clown**, 6, 116	M. J. Luzzi	Pennine Ridge, 4	Torch Rouge (GB), 4	12	1:45.70	$120,000
1994	**Kiri's Clown**, 5, 113	M. J. Luzzi	River Majesty, 5	Fourstars Allstar, 5	8	1:46.76	$120,000
1993	**Fourstars Allstar**, 5, 115	J. A. Santos	Futurist, 5	Eternal Orage, 5	10	1:47.17	$120,000
1992	**Rainbows for Life**, 4, 119	D. Penna	Now Listen, 5	Buckhar, 5	12	1:46.83	$150,000

1992, 1994, 1995, 2000 new course record. 1993 dead heat for first. 1993 Idle Son finished first, DQ to sixth.

New Orleans Handicap

Grade 2, Fair Grounds, four-year-olds and up, 1⅛ miles, dirt. Held March 4, 2001, with a gross value of $500,000. First held in 1918. Graded since 1973. Stakes record 1:48.13 (1998 Phantom On Tour).

Year	Winner	Jockey	Second	Third	Strs	Final Time	1st Purse
2001	**Include**, 4, 114	J. D. Bailey	Nite Dreamer, 6	Valhol, 6	5	1:49.18	$300,000
2000	**Allen's Oop**, 5, 112	W. Martinez	Take Note of Me, 6	Ecton Park, 6	8	1:48.80	$300,000
1999	**Precocity**, 5, 118	E. M. Martin Jr.	Real Quiet, 4	Allen's Oop, 4	8	1:49.17	$320,640
1998	**Phantom On Tour**, 4, 114	L. Melancon	Precocity, 4	Lord Cromby (Ire), 4	8	**1:48.13**	$300,000
1997	**Isitingood**, 6, 121	D. R. Flores	Western Trader, 6	Scott's Scoundrel, 6	7	1:48.43	$180,000
1996	**Scott's Scoundrel**, 4, 116	R. Ardoin	Knockadoon, 4	Patio de Naranjos (Chi), 4	9	1:49.97	$162,540
1995	**Concern**, 4, 125	M. E. Smith	Fly Cry, 4	Tossofthecoin, 4	7	1:49.40	$120,000
1994	**Brother Brown**, 4, 118	P. Day	Far Out Wadleigh, 6	Eequalsmcsquared, 6	10	1:48.83	$120,000
1993	**Latin American**, 5, 112	G. K. Gomez	Delafield, 4	West by West, 4	12	1:49.20	$90,000
1992	**Jarraar**, 5, 112	B. J. Walker Jr.	Irish Swap, 5	Bayou Reality, 5	8	1:48.80	$60,000

1992-2000 Grade 3. 1992, 1994 equaled track record; 1997, 1998 new track record.

New York Handicap

Grade 2, Belmont Park, three-year-olds and up, fillies and mares, 1¼ miles, turf. Held July 14, 2001, with a gross value of $250,000. First held in 1940. Graded since 1977. Stakes record 1:58.40 (1990 Capades).

Year	Winner	Jockey	Second	Third	Strs	Final Time	1st Purse
2001	**England's Legend (Fr)**, 4, 115	C. S. Nakatani	Gaviola, 4	Spook Express (SAf), 4	7	1:59.63	$150,000
2000	**Perfect Sting**, 4, 122	J. D. Bailey	Snow Polina, 5	Pico Teneriffe, 5	8	2:05.36	$150,000
1999	**Soaring Softly**, 4, 117	M. E. Smith	Tampico, 6	Anguilla, 6	6	2:02.25	$150,000
1998	**Auntie Mame**, 4, 118	J. R. Velazquez	Tresoriere, 4	Cuando, 4	8	1:59.50	$120,000
1997	**Maxzene**, 4, 120	M. E. Smith	Memories of Silver, 4	Shemozzle (Ire), 4	6	1:59.91	$120,000
1996	**Electric Society (Ire)**, 5, 115	J. F. Chavez	Danish (Ire), 5	Chelsey Flower, 5	7	2:03.79	$90,000
1995	**Irish Linnet**, 7, 118	J. R. Velazquez	Danish (Ire), 4	Market Booster, 4	6	1:59.92	$65,520
1994	**You'd Be Surprised**, 5, 118	J. D. Bailey	Dahlia's Dreamer, 5	Aquilegia, 5	6	1:59.69	$65,340
1993	**Aquilegia**, 4, 114	J. A. Krone	Via Borghese, 4	Ginny Dare, 4	11	1:59.05	$74,760
1992	**Plenty of Grace**, 5, 111	J. A. Krone	Dancing Devlette, 5	Flaming Torch (Ire), 5	9	2:00.74	$72,720

Next Move Handicap

Grade 3, Aqueduct, three-year-olds and up, fillies and mares, 1⅛ miles, dirt. Held March 31, 2001, with a gross value of $103,900. First held in 1975. Graded since 1977. Stakes record 1:48.96 (1999 Diggins).

Year	Winner	Jockey	Second	Third	Strs	Final Time	1st Purse
2001	**Atelier**, 4, 117	E. S. Prado	Pompeii, 4	Tax Affair, 4	4	1:50.65	$64,264
2000	**Biogio's Rose**, 6, 117	N. Arroyo Jr.	Up We Go, 4	Perlinda (Arg), 4	7	1:51.32	$49,875

Year	Winner	Jockey	Second	Third	Strs	Final Time	1st Purse
1999	**Diggins**, 5, 113	J. L. Espinoza	Biogio's Rose, 5	Powerful Nation, 5	7	**1:48.96**	$48,915
1998	**Panama Canal**, 4, 113	S. Bridgmohan	Endowment, 4	Dewars Rocks, 4	8	1:51.37	$49,455
1997	**Full and Fancy**, 5, 115	R. Migliore	Shoop, 6	Prophet's Warning, 6	8	1:51.12	$49,500
1996	**Madame Adolphe**, 4, 110	F. Leon	Shoop, 5	Lotta Dancing, 5	7	1:51.39	$49,080
1995	**Restored Hope**, 4, 118	M. J. Luzzi	Cherokee Wonder, 4	Sterling Pound, 4	6	1:52.26	$48,975
1994	**Groovy Feeling**, 5, 123	M. J. Luzzi	Broad Gains, 4	Megaroux, 4	4	1:59.79	$63,735
1993	**Low Tolerance**, 4, 114	M. E. Smith	Hilbys Brite Flite, 4	Lady Lear, 4	8	1:55.93	$67,470
1992	**Spy Leader Lady**, 4, 112	M. E. Smith	Haunting, 4	Grecian Pass, 4	6	2:00.26	$67,560

1992-'95 Next Move Breeders' Cup H. 1992-'94 1³⁄₁₆ miles.

Noble Damsel Handicap

Grade 3, Belmont Park, three-year-olds and up, fillies and mares, 1 mile, dirt (originally scheduled on the turf). Held September 22, 2001, with a gross value of $113,800. First held in 1988. Graded since 1988. Stakes record 1:32.80 (1997 Colcon; 1998 Oh Nellie).

Year	Winner	Jockey	Second	Third	Strs	Final Time	1st Purse
2001	**Tugger**, 4, 119	J. D. Bailey	Shine Again, 4	Tippity Witch, 4	6	1:35.18	$68,280
2000	**Gino's Spirits (GB)**, 4, 114	E. S. Prado	La Ville Rouge, 4	Solar Bound, 4	8	1:36.61	$66,720
1999	**Khumba Mela (Ire)**, 4, 118	J. A. Santos	Uanme, 4	Cyrillic, 4	8	1:34.50	$67,740
1998	**Oh Nellie**, 4, 116	J. R. Velazquez	Heaven's Command (GB), 4	Irish Daisy, 5	7	**1:32.80**	$50,400
1997	**Colcon**, 4, 113	J. D. Bailey	Antespend, 4	Tiffany's Taylor, 8	11	**1:32.80**	$69,360
1996	**Perfect Arc**, 4, 125	J. R. Velazquez	Fashion Star, 4	Tough Broad, 4	7	1:42.41	$60,160
1995	**Irish Linnet**, 7, 121	J. R. Velazquez	Caress, 4	Weekend Madness (Ire), 5	7	1:40.67	$60,048
1994	**Irish Linnet**, 6, 117	J. R. Velazquez	Statuette, 4	Cox Orange, 4	10	1:39.59	$50,790
1993	**McKaymackenna**, 4, 120	C. W. Antley	La Piaf (Fr), 4	Heed, 4	10	1:43:74	$55,620
1992	**Miss Otis**, 5, 115	A. Madrid Jr.	Big Big Affair, 5	Tiney Toast, 3	4	1:43:64	$53,460

1992-'93 Noble Damsel S. 1992-'96 1¹⁄₁₆ miles. 1993-2000 turf.

Norfolk Stakes

Grade 2, Santa Anita Park, two-year-olds, 1 mile, dirt. Held September 29, 2001, with a gross value of $250,000. First held in 1970. Graded since 1973. Stakes record 1:34.86 (2000 Flame Thrower).

Year	Winner	Jockey	Second	Third	Strs	Final Time	1st Purse
2001	**Essence of Dubai**	A. O. Solis	Ibn Al Haitham (GB)	Ecstatic	6	1:37.16	$150,000
2000	**Flame Thrower**	V. Espinoza	Street Cry (Ire)	Mr Freckles	8	**1:34.86**	$120,000
1999	**Dixie Union**	A. O. Solis	Forest Camp	Anees	6	1:35.79	$120,000
1998	**Buck Trout**	E. Delahoussaye	Eagleton	Daring General	9	1:37.55	$120,000
1997	**Souvenir Copy**	G. L. Stevens	Old Trieste	Double Honor	7	1:36.00	$120,000
1996	**Free House**	K. J. Desormeaux	Zippersup	Swiss Yodeler	7	1:43.54	$120,000
1995	**Future Quest**	K. J. Desormeaux	Odyle	Exetera	7	1:43.31	$120,000
1994	**Supremo**	G. L. Stevens	Desert Mirage	Strong Ally	9	1:43.48	$120,000
1993	**Shepherd's Field**	C. J. McCarron	Ramblin Guy	Ferrara	7	1:43.11	$120,000
1992	**River Special**	K. J. Desormeaux	Imperial Ridge	Devil Diamond	5	1:43.58	$120,000

1992 Grade 1. 1992-'96 1¹⁄₁₆ miles.

Oaklawn Breeders' Cup Stakes

Grade 3, Oaklawn Park, three-year-olds and up, fillies and mares, 1¹⁄₁₆ miles, dirt. Held March 18, 2001, with a gross value of $200,000. First held in 1987. Graded since 1990. Stakes record 1:42.01 (1999 Sister Act).

Year	Winner	Jockey	Second	Third	Strs	Final Time	1st Purse
2001	**Heritage of Gold**, 6	R. Albarado	Lu Ravi, 6	Ive Gota Bad Liver, 6	8	1:44.30	$120,000
2000	**Heritage of Gold**, 5	S. J. Sellers	Lu Ravi, 5	Light Line, 5	4	1:44.15	$120,000
1999	**Sister Act**, 4	C. H. Borel	Glitter Woman, 5	Mil Kilates, 5	7	**1:42.01**	$60,000
1998	**Turn to the Queen**, 5	T. T. Doocy	Danzalert, 4	Leo's Gypsy Dancer, 4	7	1:44.76	$90,000
1997	**Halo America**, 7	C. H. Borel	Gold n Delicious, 4	Capote Belle, 4	6	1:42.18	$90,000
1996	**Belle of Cozzene**, 4	D. R. Pettinger	Halo America, 6	Little May, 6	5	1:43.32	$94,350
1995	**Halo America**, 5	W. T. Cloninger Jr.	Heavenly Prize, 4	Biolage, 4	6	1:42.59	$92,700
1994	**Morning Meadow**, 4	S. P. Romero	Gravette, 4	Her Valentine, 4	10	1:44.60	$94,650
1993	**Guiza**, 6	C. S. Nakatani	Teddy's Top Ten, 4	Fappies Cosy Miss, 4	8	1:44.79	$93,600
1992	**Cuddles**, 4	D. Guillory	Rare Guest, 5	Dixie Splash, 5	10	1:43.82	$94,500

1992-'97 Oaklawn Breeders' Cup H.; 1995-'99 not graded. 1995 four-year-olds and up.

Oaklawn Handicap

Grade 1, Oaklawn Park, four-year-olds and up, 1⅛ miles, dirt. Held April 7, 2001, with a gross value of $600,000. First held in 1946. Graded since 1973. Stakes record 1:46.60 (1987 Snow Chief).

Year	Winner	Jockey	Second	Third	Strs	Final Time	1st Purse
2001	**Traditionally**, 4, 112	P. Day	Mr Ross, 6	Wooden Phone, 6	7	1:48.15	$360,000
2000	**K One King**, 4, 113	C. H. Borel	Almutawakel (GB), 5	Cat Thief, 5	6	1:48.02	$360,000
1999	**Behrens**, 5, 116	J. F. Chavez	Littlebitlively, 5	Precocity, 5	7	1:47.77	$450,000
1998	**Precocity**, 4, 114	C. Gonzalez	Frisk Me Now, 4	Phantom On Tour, 4	7	1:48.28	$450,000

Year	Winner	Jockey	Second	Third	Strs	Final Time	1st Purse
1997	**Atticus**, 5, 114	S. J. Sellers	Isitingood, 6	Tejano Run, 6	8	1:48.22	$450,000
1996	**Geri**, 4, 115	J. D. Bailey	Wekiva Springs, 5	Scott's Scoundrel, 5	7	1:47.52	$450,000
1995	**Cigar**, 5, 120	J. D. Bailey	Silver Goblin, 4	Concern, 4	7	1:47.22	$450,000
1994	**The Wicked North**, 5, 119	K. J. Desormeaux	Devil His Due, 5	Brother Brown, 5	12	1:47.86	$450,000
1993	**Jovial (GB)**, 6, 117	E. Delahoussaye	Lil E. Tee, 4	Best Pal, 4	10	1:48.63	$450,000
1992	**Best Pal**, 4, 125	K. J. Desormeaux	Sea Cadet, 4	Twilight Agenda, 4	7	1:48.10	$300,000

Oak Leaf Stakes

Grade 1, Santa Anita Park, two-year-old fillies, 1 mile, dirt. Held September 30, 2001, with a gross value of $250,000. First held in 1969. Graded since 1973. Stakes record 1:36.12 (1999 Chilukki).

Year	Winner	Jockey	Second	Third	Strs	Final Time	1st Purse
2001	**Tali'sluckybusride**	J. Valdivia Jr.	Imperial Gesture	Ms Louisett	6	1:37.71	$150,000
2000	**Notable Career**	D. R. Flores	Euro Empire	Cindy's Hero	7	1:36.34	$120,000
1999	**Chilukki**	D. R. Flores	Abby Girl	Spain	5	**1:36.12**	$120,000
1998	**Excellent Meeting**	K. J. Desormeaux	Antahkarana	Stylish Talent	7	1:37.71	$120,000
1997	**Vivid Angel**	E. Delahoussaye	Love Lock	Balisian Beauty	9	1:37.33	$120,000
1996	**City Band**	J. A. Garcia	Clever Pilot	Wealthy	8	1:44.57	$120,000
1995	**Tipically Irish**	L. A. Pincay Jr.	Ocean View	Gastronomical	7	1:42.60	$120,000
1994	**Serena's Song**	C. S. Nakatani	Call Now	Mama Mucci	5	1:41.83	$120,000
1993	**Phone Chatter**	L. A. Pincay Jr.	Sardula	Tricky Code	6	1:41.78	$120,000
1992	**Zoonaqua**	C. J. McCarron	Turkstand	Madame l'Enjoleur	10	1:43.91	$120,000

1992-'96 1 1/16 miles.

Oak Tree Breeders' Cup Mile Stakes

Grade 2, Santa Anita Park, three-year-olds and up, 1 mile, turf. Held October 7, 2001, with a gross value of $219,000. First held in 1986. Graded since 1989. Stakes record 1:32.44 (1996 Urgent Request [Ire]).

Year	Winner	Jockey	Second	Third	Strs	Final Time	1st Purse
2001	**Val Royal (Fr)**, 5	J. Valdivia Jr.	Thady Quill, 4	I've Decided, 4	7	1:33.21	$120,000
2000	**War Chant**, 3	G. L. Stevens	Road to Slew, 5	Sharan (GB), 5	8	1:33.75	$150,000
1999	**Silic (Fr)**, 4	C. S. Nakatani	Bouccaneer (Fr), 4	Brave Act (GB), 5	7	1:33.76	$150,000
1998	**Hawksley Hill (Ire)**, 5	A. O. Solis	Mr Lightfoot (Ire), 4	Magellan, 5	5	1:36.72	$166,200
1997	**Fantastic Fellow**, 3	A. O. Solis	Magellan, 4	Taiki Blizzard, 6	8	1:36.23	$165,000
1996	**Urgent Request (Ire)**, 6	C. J. McCarron	Megan's Interco, 7	Felon (Ire), 4	6	**1:32.44**	$110,300
1995	**Ventiquattrofogli (Ire)**, 5	G. F. Almeida	Megan's Interco, 6	Debutant Trick, 5	8	1:35.30	$76,850
1994	**Bon Point (GB)**, 4	E. Delahoussaye	Journalism, 6	Johann Quatz (Fr), 5	5	1:33.86	$62,050
1993	**Johann Quatz (Fr)**, 4	E. Delahoussaye	Myrakalu (Fr), 5	The Tender Track, 6	5	1:36.28	$62,350
1992	**Twilight Agenda**, 6	C. J. McCarron	Luthier Enchanteur, 5	Bourgogne (GB), 4	8	1:33.36	$65,300

1992-'95 Col. F. W. Koester H.; 1996-'98 Oak Tree Breeders' Cup Mile H. 1996-'99 Grade 3. 1996 new course record.

Oak Tree Derby

Grade 2, Santa Anita Park, three-year-olds and up, 1 1/8 miles, turf. Held October 13, 2001, with a gross value of $150,000. First held in 1969. Graded since 1974. Stakes record 1:46.56 (2001 No Slip [Fr]).

Year	Winner	Jockey	Second	Third	Strs	Final Time	1st Purse
2001	**No Slip (Fr)**	K. J. Desormeaux	Sligo Bay (Ire)	Romanceishope	9	**1:46.56**	$90,000
2000	**Sign of Hope (GB)**	A. O. Solis	David Copperfield	El Gran Papa	5	1:47.71	$150,000
1999	**Mula Gula**	G. L. Stevens	Eagleton	Super Quercus (Fr)	9	1:46.67	$150,000
1998	**Ladies Din**	G. L. Stevens	Dr Fong	Bouccaneer (Fr)	7	1:50.24	$150,000
1997	**Lasting Approval**	A. O. Solis	Voyagers Quest	Early Colony	7	1:50.84	$150,000
1996	**Odyle**	C. J. McCarron	Lago	Rainbow Blues (Ire)	6	1:46.83	$80,250
1995	**Helmsman**	C. J. McCarron	Virginia Carnival	Mr Purple	8	1:48.98	$75,650
1994	**Run Softly**	L. A. Pincay Jr.	Alphabet Soup	Powis Castle	8	1:49.96	$64,800
1993	**Eastern Memories (Ire)**	J. D. Bailey	Cigar	Snake Eyes	9	1:48.03	$66,800
1992	**Blacksburg**	A. O. Solis	Siberian Summer	Star Recruit	10	1:48.12	$67,700

1992-'96 Volante H. 1992-'95 Grade 3.

Oceanport Handicap

Grade 3, Monmouth Park, three-year-olds and up, 1 1/16 miles, turf. Held August 5, 2001, with a gross value of $100,000. First held in 1947. Graded since 1973. Stakes record 1:39.40 (1999 Mi Narrow)

Year	Winner	Jockey	Second	Third	Strs	Final Time	1st Purse
2001	**Key Lory**, 7, 111	C. C. Lopez	North East Bound, 5	Crash Course, 5	13	1:40.39	$60,000
2000	**North East Bound**, 4, 114	J. A. Velez Jr.	Rize, 4	Selective, 7	6	1:44.70	$60,000
1999	**Mi Narrow**, 5, 113	J. Bravo	Hurrahy, 6	Forbidden Apple, 4	8	**1:39.40**	$60,000
1998	**Daylight Savings**, 4, 115	H. Castillo Jr.	Mi Narrow, 4	Rob 'n Gin, 4	8	1:42.31	$60,000
1997	**Boyce**, 6, 118	J. A. Krone	Foolish Pole, 4	Jambalaya Jazz, 5	7	1:40.28	$60,000
1995	**Boyce**, 4, 114	A. S. Black	Myrmidon, 4	Rocket City, 4	9	1:40.91	$45,000
1994	**Nijinsky's Gold**, 5, 120	R. G. Davis	Winnetou, 4	Marco Bay, 4	5	1:41.66	$45,000
1993	**Furiously**, 4, 119	J. D. Bailey	Adam Smith (GB), 5	Rocket Fuel, 6	5	1:39.60	$45,000
1992	**Maxigroom**, 4, 113	R. G. Davis	Rocket Fuel, 5	Go Dutch, 5	9	1:41.77	$45,000

1996 not held. 2000 dirt. 1993, 1999 new course record.

Ohio Derby

Grade 2, Thistledown, three-year-olds, 1⅛ miles, dirt. Held September 29, 2001, with a gross value of $300,000. First held in 1876. Graded since 1973. Stakes record 1:47.40 (1979 Smarten).

Year	Winner	Jockey	Second	Third	Strs	Final Time	1st Purse
2001	Western Pride	D. G. Whitney	Woodmoon	Macho Uno	6	1:48.66	$180,000
2000	Milwaukee Brew	M. J. McCarthy	Brave Quest	Kiss a Native	10	1:50.58	$180,000
1999	Stellar Brush	M. J. McCarthy	Ecton Park	Valhol	13	1:49.22	$180,000
1998	Classic Cat	S. J. Sellers	One Bold Stroke	Hot Wells	10	1:49.92	$180,000
1997	Frisk Me Now	E. L. King Jr.	Anet	Mr. Groush	7	1:48.28	$180,000
1996	Skip Away	J. A. Santos	Victory Speech	Clash by Night	10	1:47.86	$180,000
1995	Petionville	P. Day	Dazzling Falls	Is Sveikatas	6	1:48.93	$180,000
1994	Exclusive Praline	W. Martinez	Concern	Smilin Singin Sam	8	1:48.54	$180,000
1993	Forever Whirl	A. Toribio	Boundlessly	Mighty Avanti	10	1:49.44	$180,000
1992	Majestic Sweep	E. Fires	Technology	Always Silver	8	1:50.07	$180,000

Oklahoma Derby

Grade 3, Remington Park, three-year-olds, 1⅛ miles, dirt. Held August 12, 2001, with a gross value of $300,000. First held in 1989. Graded since 1999. Stakes record 1:48 (1998 Classic Cat).

Year	Winner	Jockey	Second	Third	Strs	Final Time	1st Purse
2001	Top Hit	G. K. Gomez	Unbridled Time	Compendium	6	1:49.79	$180,000
2000	Performing Magic	S. J. Sellers	Mister Deville	Del Mar Danny	9	1:50.36	$180,000
1999	Temperence Time	T. T. Doocy	Answer Lively	Stellar Brush	8	1:49.40	$180,000
1998	Classic Cat	S. J. Sellers	Leave a Legacy	Sir Tiff	8	1:48.00	$180,000
1997	Wild Rush	G. L. Stevens	Blazing Sword	Precocity	9	1:53.60	$180,000
1996	Semoran	R. A. Baze	Connecting Terms	Devil's Honor	5	1:46.60	$180,000
1995	Dazzling Falls	G. K. Gomez	Our Gatsby	Capote's Promise	7	1:42.80	$180,000
1994	Smilin Singin Sam	L. Melancon	Blumin Affair	Silver Goblin	8	1:43.20	$180,000
1993	Marked Tree	G. K. Gomez	Brother Brown	Ragtime Rebel	9	1:43.80	$180,000
1992	Vying Victor	R. D. Hansen	Ecstatic Ride	Capitalimprovement	10	1:43.60	$150,000

1992-2000 Remington Park Derby. 1992-'96 1¹/₁₆ miles; 1997 1³/₁₆ miles. 1992,1995,1998 new track record; 1994 equaled track record.

Orchid Handicap

Grade 2, Gulfstream Park, three-year-olds and up, fillies and mares, 1½ miles, turf. Held March 10, 2001, with a gross value of $194,000. First held in 1954. Graded since 1973. Stakes record 2:24.20 (1990 Coolawin).

Year	Winner	Jockey	Second	Third	Strs	Final Time	1st Purse
2001	Innuendo (Ire), 6, 116	J. D. Bailey	Windsong, 4	Aiglonne, 4	4	2:25.24	$120,000
2000	Lisieux Rose (Ire), 5, 114	J. A. Santos	Champagne Royal, 6	Fly for Avie, 6	10	2:25.64	$120,000
1999	Coretta (Ire), 5, 118	J. A. Santos	Delilah (Ire), 5	Almost Skint (Ire), 5	11	2:23.85	$120,000
1998	Colonial Play, 4, 113	R. G. Davis	Almost Skint (Ire), 4	Gastronomical, 4	11	2:24.75	$120,000
1997	Golden Pond (Ire), 4, 116	W. H. McCauley	Tocopilla (Arg), 7	Miss Caerleona (Fr), 7	11	2:26.84	$120,000
1996	Memories (Ire), 5, 114	J. A. Santos	Caromana, 5	Curtain Raiser, 5	11	2:31.51	$120,000
1995	Exchange, 7, 120	L. A. Pincay Jr.	Market Booster, 6	Northern Emerald, 6	10	2:29.02	$120,000
1994	Trampoli, 5	M. E. Smith	Good Morning Smile, 6	Northern Emerald, 6	7	2:25.42	$120,000
1993	Fairy Garden, 5, 115	W. S. Ramos	Rougeur, 4	Trampoli, 4	14	2:25.79	$120,000
1992	Crockadore, 5, 115	M. E. Smith	Indian Fashion, 5	Sardaniya (Ire), 5	10	2:28.32	$120,000

1992 about 1½ miles. 1992 new course record.

Overbrook Spinster Stakes

Grade 1, Keeneland, three-year-olds and up, fillies and mares, 1⅛ miles, dirt. Held October 7, 2001, with a gross value of $562,000. First held in 1956. Graded since 1973. Stakes record 1:47 (1990 Bayakoa [Arg]).

Year	Winner	Jockey	Second	Third	Strs	Final Time	1st Purse
2001	Miss Linda (Arg), 4	R. Migliore	Starrer, 3	Printemps (Chi), 4	10	1:49.79	$348,440
2000	Plenty of Light, 3	G. K. Gomez	Spain, 3	Roza Robata, 5	6	1:48.18	$336,970
1999	Keeper Hill, 4	K. J. Desormeaux	Banshee Breeze, 4	A Lady From Dixie, 4	9	1:47.19	$344,410
1998	Banshee Breeze, 3	R. Albarado	Runup the Colors, 4	Aldiza, 4	8	1:47.04	$341,930
1997	Clear Mandate, 5	P. Day	Feasibility Study, 5	Naskra Colors, 5	7	1:50.47	$336,350
1996	Different (Arg), 4	C. J. McCarron	Top Secret, 3	Belle of Cozzene, 4	6	1:49.74	$336,040
1995	Inside Information, 4	M. E. Smith	Jade Flush, 4	Mariah's Storm, 4	4	1:50.01	$198,276
1994	Dispute, 4	P. Day	Lets Be Alert, 3	Miss Dominique, 5	8	1:48.91	$204,414
1993	Paseana (Arg), 6	C. J. McCarron	Gray Cashmere, 4	Jacody, 3	9	1:48.46	$205,902
1992	Fowda, 4	P. A. Valenzuela	Paseana (Arg), 5	Meadow Star, 4	10	1:49.91	$209,994

1992-'95 Spinster S.; 1996-2000 Three Chimneys Spinster S.

Pacific Classic Stakes

Grade 1, Del Mar, three-year-olds and up, 1¼ miles, dirt. Held August 19, 2001, with a gross value of $1,000,000. First held in 1991. Graded since 1993. Stakes record 1:59.43 (1994 Tinners Way).

Year	Winner	Jockey	Second	Third	Strs	Final Time	1st Purse
2001	Skimming, 5	G. K. Gomez	Dixie Dot Com, 6	Dig for It, 6	6	1:59.96	$600,000

Year	Winner	Jockey	Second	Third	Strs	Final Time	1st Purse
2000	**Skimming**, 4	G. K. Gomez	Tiznow, 3	Ecton Park, 4	7	2:01.22	$600,000
1999	**General Challenge**, 3	D. R. Flores	River Keen (Ire), 7	Barter Town, 4	8	2:00.57	$700,000
1998	**Free House**, 4	C. J. McCarron	Gentlemen (Arg), 6	Pacificbounty, 4	9	2:00.29	$600,000
1997	**Gentlemen (Arg)**, 5	G. L. Stevens	Siphon (Brz), 6	Crafty Friend, 4	5	2:00.56	$850,000
1996	**Dare and Go**, 5	A. O. Solis	Cigar, 6	Siphon (Brz), 5	6	1:59.85	$600,000
1995	**Tinners Way**, 5	E. Delahoussaye	Soul of the Matter, 4	Blumin Affair, 4	6	1:59.63	$550,000
1994	**Tinners Way**, 4	E. Delahoussaye	Best Pal, 6	Dramatic Gold, 3	9	**1:59.43**	$550,000
1993	**Bertrando**, 4	G. L. Stevens	Missionary Ridge (GB), 6	Best Pal, 5	7	1:59.55	$550,000
1992	**Missionary Ridge (GB)**, 5	K. J. Desormeaux	Defensive Play, 5	Claret (Ire), 4	7	2:00.87	$550,000

1993, 1994 new track record.

Palm Beach Stakes

Grade 3, Gulfstream Park, three-year-olds, 1⅛ miles, turf. Held February 19, 2001, with a gross value of $134,500. First held in 1987. Graded since 1990. Stakes record 1:47.32 (1997 Unite's Big Red).

Year	Winner	Jockey	Second	Third	Strs	Final Time	1st Purse
2001	**Proud Man**	R. R. Douglas	One Eyed Joker	Strategic Partner	12	1:48.32	$90,000
2000	**Mr. Livingston**	S. J. Sellers	Powerful Appeal	Gateman (GB)	11	1:48.04	$45,000
1999	**Swamp**	R. Migliore	Marquette	Valid Reprized	12	1:48.38	$45,000
1998	**Cryptic Rascal**	M. E. Smith	The Kaiser	American Odyssey	8	1:55.01	$45,000
1997	**Unite's Big Red**	R. Hernandez	Trample	Tekken (Ire)	7	**1:47.32**	$45,000
1996	**Harrowman**	M. E. Smith	A Real Zipper	Ok by Me	6	1:49.22	$45,000
1995	**Admiralty**	J. A. Krone	Nostra	Smells and Bells	4	1:51.03	$30,000
1994	**Mr. Angel**	W. H. McCauley	Clint Essential	Fabulous Frolic	9	1:44.66	$30,000
1993	**Kissin Kris**	D. Penna	Pride Prevails	Awad	10	1:46.41	$38,760
1992	**Preferences**	J. C. Duarte	Doo You	Stress Buster	12	1:42.64	$38,940

1992-'93 1¹⁄₁₆ miles; 1994 about 1¹⁄₁₆ miles; 1998 about 1⅛ miles. 1993, 1995 dirt.

Palomar Handicap

Grade 2, Del Mar, three-year-olds and up, fillies and mares, 1¹⁄₁₆ miles, turf. Held September 1, 2001, with a gross value of $150,000. First held in 1945. Graded since 1981. Stakes record 1:41.01 (2000 Tranquility Lake).

Year	Winner	Jockey	Second	Third	Strs	Final Time	1st Purse
2001	**Tranquility Lake**, 6, 123	E. Delahoussaye	La Ronge, 4	Al Desima (GB), 4	6	1:41.94	$90,000
2000	**Tranquility Lake**, 5, 121	E. Delahoussaye	Tout Charmant, 4	Miss of Wales (Chi), 5	7	**1:41.01**	$82,170
1999	**Happyanunoit (NZ)**, 4, 113	B. Blanc	Tuzla (Fr), 5	Isle de France, 4	6	1:41.28	$80,520
1998	**Tuzla (Fr)**, 4, 117	C. S. Nakatani	Ecoute, 5	Call Me (GB), 5	7	1:42.28	$80,970
1997	**Blushing Heiress**, 5, 117	C. J. McCarron	Traces of Gold, 5	Listening, 4	6	1:43.32	$83,200
1996	**Yearly Tour**, 5, 116	C. J. McCarron	Slewvera, 4	Real Connection, 5	8	1:42.56	$81,350
1995	**Morgana**, 4, 118	G. L. Stevens	Yearly Tour, 4	Lady Affirmed, 4	7	1:42.41	$74,450
1994	**Shir Dar (Fr)**, 4, 114	C. S. Nakatani	Baby Diamonds, 3	Prying (Arg), 6	7	1:42.95	$63,600
1993	**Heart of Joy**, 6, 119	D. R. Flores	Kalita Melody (GB), 5	Amal Hayati, 3	8	1:42.07	$63,000
1992	**Super Staff**, 4, 114	C. J. McCarron	Odalea (Arg), 6	Only Yours (GB), 4	10	1:42.20	$64,900

1997-2000 Grade 3.

Palos Verdes Handicap

Grade 2, Santa Anita Park, four-year-olds and up, 6 furlongs, dirt. Held January 28, 2001, with a gross value of $200,000. First held in 1951. Graded since 1988. Stakes record 1:07.20 (1989 Sunny Blossom).

Year	Winner	Jockey	Second	Third	Strs	Final Time	1st Purse
2001	**Men's Exclusive**, 8, 116	L. A. Pincay Jr.	Big Jag, 8	Freespool, 8	6	1:08.33	$120,000
2000	**Kona Gold**, 6, 121	A. O. Solis	Big Jag, 7	Freespool, 7	5	1:08.55	$120,000
1999	**Big Jag**, 6, 116	J. Valdivia Jr.	Kona Gold, 5	Swiss Yodeler, 5	5	1:08.05	$120,000
1998	**Funonthurun**, 4, 113	G. F. Almeida	Red, 4	Elmhurst, 4	9	1:08.93	$120,000
1997	**High Stakes Player**, 5, 118	C. S. Nakatani	Rotsaluck, 6	Larry the Legend, 6	7	1:08.44	$131,640
1996	**Lit de Justice**, 6, 122	E. Delahoussaye	Siphon (Brz), 5	Lakota Brave, 5	9	1:08.88	$135,100
1995	**D'Hallevant**, 5, 117	C. S. Nakatani	Cardmania, 9	Subtle Trouble, 9	10	1:08.44	$94,400
1994	**Concept Win**, 4, 115	G. L. Stevens	J. F. Williams, 5	Scherando, 5	6	1:07.71	$62,100
1993	**Music Merci**, 7, 114	D. R. Flores	Star of the Crop, 4	Cardmania, 4	7	1:08.82	$63,700
1992	**Individualist**, 5, 117	L. A. Pincay Jr.	High Energy, 5	Rushmore, 5	9	1:08.66	$65,600

1992-'97 Grade 3.

Pan American Handicap

Grade 2, Gulfstream Park, three-year-olds and up, 1½ miles, turf. Held March 11, 2001, with a gross value of $250,000. First held in 1962. Graded since 1973. Stakes record 2:23.15 (1999 Unite's Big Red).

Year	Winner	Jockey	Second	Third	Strs	Final Time	1st Purse
2001	**Whata Brainstorm**, 4, 114	J. R. Velazquez	Subtle Power (Ire), 4	Craigsteel (GB), 4	7	2:23.75	$150,000
2000	**Buck's Boy**, 7, 120	E. S. Prado	Thesaurus, 6	Epistolaire (Ire), 6	7	2:24.80	$150,000
1999	**Unite's Big Red**, 5, 114	M. E. Smith	African Dancer, 7	Panama City, 7	7	**2:23.15**	$150,000

Year	Winner	Jockey	Second	Third	Strs	Final Time	1st Purse
1998	Buck's Boy, 5, 115	E. Fires	African Dancer, 6	Royal Strand (Ire), 6	9	2:23.43	$150,000
1997	Flag Down, 7, 117	J. A. Santos	Lassigny, 6	Awad, 6	6	2:27.08	$180,000
1996	Celtic Arms (Fr), 5, 115	M. E. Smith	Broadway Flyer, 5	Flag Down, 5	7	2:25.71	$180,000
1995	Awad, 5, 114	E. Maple	Misil, 7	Frenchpark (GB), 7	9	2:29.44	$180,000
1994	Fraise, 6, 124	M. E. Smith	Summer Ensign, 5	†Fairy Garden, 5	10	2:24.65	$180,000
1993	Fraise, 5, 124	P. A. Valenzuela	Stagecraft (GB), 6	Futurist, 6	8	2:32.86	$180,000
1992	Wall Street Dancer, 4, 114	J. Velasquez	†Passagere du Soir (GB), 5	Missionary Ridge (GB), 5	14	2:25.53	$210,000

1993 about 1½ miles. 1999 new course record. 2000 Beautiful Dancer finished third, DQ to sixth. † denotes female.

Pat O'Brien Handicap

Grade 2, Del Mar, three-year-olds and up, 7 furlongs, dirt. Held August 12, 2001, with a gross value of $150,000. First held in 1986. Graded since 1994. Stakes record 1:20.06 (1995 Lit de Justice).

Year	Winner	Jockey	Second	Third	Strs	Final Time	1st Purse
2001	El Corredor, 4, 119	V. Espinoza	Swept Overboard, 4	Ceeband, 4	7	1:20.42	$90,000
2000	Love That Red, 4, 118	C. S. Nakatani	Cliquot, 4	Son of a Pistol, 8	5	1:21.89	$90,000
1999	Regal Thunder, 5, 116	C. W. Antley	Christmas Boy, 6	Bet On Sunshine, 7	9	1:21.13	$90,000
1998	Old Topper, 3, 116	E. Delahoussaye	Son of a Pistol, 6	Uncaged Fury, 7	5	1:21.51	$95,220
1997	Tres Paraiso, 5, 115	G. L. Stevens	High Stakes Player, 5	Gold Land, 6	7	1:21.45	$68,200
1996	Alphabet Soup, 5, 118	C. W. Antley	Boundless Moment, 4	Lit de Justice, 6	8	1:20.79	$65,450
1995	Lit de Justice, 5, 118	C. S. Nakatani	D'Hallevant, 5	Pembroke, 5	7	1:20.06	$60,440
1994	D'Hallevant, 4, 115	C. S. Nakatani	Minjinsky, 4	J. F. Williams, 5	5	1:20.25	$59,725
1993	Slerp, 4, 117	A. D. Lopez	Portoferraio (Arg), 5	Cardmania, 7	7	1:21.36	$47,850
1992	Light of Morn, 6, 116	E. Delahoussaye	Three Peat, 3	Slerp, 3	12	1:20.65	$66,025

1992-'95 Pat O'Brien Breeders' Cup H. 1994-'98 Grade 3. 1995 equaled track record.

Pebbles Handicap

Grade 3, Belmont Park, three-year-old fillies, 1⅛ miles, turf. Held October 14, 2001 in two divisions, with a gross value of $110,100 (1st Div.) and $110,600 (2nd Div.). First held in 1993. Graded since 1999. Stakes record 1:47.50 (2001 Love n' Kiss S. [2nd Div.]).

Year	Winner	Jockey	Second	Third	Strs	Final Time	1st Purse
2001	Heads Will Roll (GB)	E. S. Prado	New Economy	Salty You	8	1:47.75	$66,060
	Love n' Kiss S.	J. A. Santos	Calista (GB)	Shooting Party	8	1:47.50	$66,360
2000	Lady Dora	J. R. Velazquez	De Aar	Tippity Witch	11	1:48.76	$52,245
1999	Eze	R. G. Davis	Colstar	Jazz	6	1:52.96	$49,950
1998	Sophie My Love	J. R. Velazquez	Appealing Kris	Proud Owner	9	1:52.23	$51,150
1997	Heaven's Command (GB)	J. A. Santos	Wollastina	Colonial Minstrel	10	1:42.81	$51,375
1996	Rare Blend	G. L. Stevens	Polish Spring (Ire)	Inner Circle	9	1:44.47	$52,110
1995	Queen Tutta	G. L. Stevens	Transient Trend	Nappelon	10	1:43.27	$53,820
1994	Saxuality	J. A. Krone	Lady Affirmed	Tensie's Pro	11	1:34.13	$41,580
1993	Statuette	M. E. Smith	Tricky Princess (Fr)	Belle Nuit	11	1:40.68	$45,060

Pegasus Handicap

Grade 2, The Meadowlands, three-year-olds, 1⅛ miles, dirt. Held October 19, 2001, with a gross value of $250,000. First held in 1980. Graded since 1983. Stakes record 1:45.50 (1999 Forty One Carats).

Year	Winner	Jockey	Second	Third	Strs	Final Time	1st Purse
2001	Volponi, 114	S. Bridgmohan	Burning Roma	Giant Gentleman	6	1:46.55	$150,000
2000	Kiss a Native, 119	M. Walls	Cool N Collective	Pine Dance	7	1:48.33	$150,000
1999	Forty One Carats, 120	J. F. Chavez	Unbridled Jet	Talk's Cheap	6	1:45.50	$240,000
1998	Tomorrows Cat, 113	J. Bravo	Limit Out	Comic Strip	6	1:46.05	$300,000
1997	Behrens, 117	J. D. Bailey	Anet	Frisk Me Now	4	1:46.61	$600,000
1996	Allied Forces, 116	R. Migliore	Lite Approval	Defacto	9	1:47.19	$120,000
1995	Flying Chevron, 112	R. G. Davis	Da Hoss	Ghostly Moves	4	1:40.27	$120,000
1994	Brass Scale, 114	E. S. Prado	Hello Chicago	Serious Spender	9	1:49.27	$120,000
1993	Diazo, 117	L. A. Pincay Jr.	Press Card	Schossberg	7	1:47.18	$150,000
1992	Scuffleburg, 111	J. A. Krone	Nines Wild	Agincourt	11	1:49.09	$300,000

1996 Pegasus Breeders' Cup H. 1992-'93 Grade 1. 1995-'96 1 1/16 miles. 1996 turf. 1999 new track record.

Pennsylvania Derby

Grade 3, Philadelphia Park, three-year-olds, 1⅛ miles, dirt. Held September 3, 2001, with a gross value of $500,000. First held in 1979. Graded since 1981. Stakes record 1:47.60 (1989 Western Playboy).

Year	Winner	Jockey	Second	Third	Strs	Final Time	1st Purse
2001	Macho Uno	G. L. Stevens	†Unbridled Elaine	Touch Tone	6	1:49.69	$300,000
2000	Pine Dance	M. J. McCarthy	Mass Market	Cherokeeinthehills	10	1:49.03	$180,000
1999	Smart Guy	R. E. Colton	Ghost Ring	Pineaff	10	1:49.40	$180,000
1998	Rock and Roll	H. Castillo Jr.	Tomorrows Cat	Black Blade	11	1:47.69	$150,000
1997	Frisk Me Now	E. L. King Jr.	Envy of the Crown	Christian Soldier	8	1:48.14	$120,000

Year	Winner	Jockey	Second	Third	Strs	Final Time	1st Purse
1996	Devil's Honor	A. S. Black	Formal Gold	Clash by Night	7	1:48.58	$120,000
1995	Pineing Patty	L. Melancon	Royal Haven	Tenants Harbor	12	1:48.05	$120,000
1994	Meadow Flight	J. Bravo	Red Tazz	Kandaly	9	1:49.08	$120,000
1993	Wallenda	W. H. McCauley	Press Card	Saintly Prospector	9	1:49.33	$120,000
1992	Thelastcrusade	V. H. Molina	Ecstatic Ride	Nines Wild	10	1:49.47	$90,000

1992-'95 Grade 2. † denotes female.

Personal Ensign Handicap

Grade 1, Saratoga Race Course, three-year-olds and up, fillies and mares, 1¼ miles, dirt. Held August 24, 2001, with a gross value of $400,000. First held in 1948. Graded since 1973. Stakes record 2:02.57 (1999 Beautiful Pleasure).

Year	Winner	Jockey	Second	Third	Strs	Final Time	1st Purse
2001	Pompeii, 4, 117	R. Migliore	Beautiful Pleasure, 6	Irving's Baby, 4	7	2:04.60	$240,000
2000	Beautiful Pleasure, 5, 124	J. F. Chavez	Heritage of Gold, 5	Pentatonic, 5	5	2:03.77	$240,000
1999	Beautiful Pleasure, 4, 113	J. F. Chavez	Banshee Breeze, 4	Keeper Hill, 4	6	2:02.57	$240,000
1998	Tomisue's Delight, 4, 115	P. Day	Tuzia, 4	One Rich Lady, 4	8	2:04.08	$240,000
1997	Clear Mandate, 5, 115	M. E. Smith	Shoop, 6	Power Play, 5	6	2:03.71	$210,000
1996	Urbane, 4, 119	A. O. Solis	Shoop, 5	Frolic, 4	8	2:03.05	$180,000
1995	Heavenly Prize, 4, 127	P. Day	Forcing Bid, 4	Cinnamon Sugar (Ire), 4	8	2:04.16	$120,000
1994	Link River, 4, 114	J. A. Krone	You'd Be Surprised, 5	Dispute, 4	7	1:50.46	$120,000
1993	You'd Be Surprised, 4, 115	J. D. Bailey	Avian Assembly, 4	Gray Cashmere, 4	8	1:48.59	$90,000
1992	Quick Mischief, 6, 113	C. Perret	Versailles Treaty, 4	Shared Interest, 4	7	1:47.96	$120,000

1992-'97 John A. Morris H. 1992-'94 1⅛ miles. 2000 Back in Shape finished second, DQ to fourth.

Peter Pan Stakes

Grade 2, Belmont Park, three-year-olds, 1⅛ miles, dirt. Held May 26, 2001, with a gross value of $200,000. First held in 1940. Graded since 1978. Stakes record 1:46.80 (1983 Slew o' Gold).

Year	Winner	Jockey	Second	Third	Strs	Final Time	1st Purse
2001	Hero's Tribute	J. F. Chavez	E Dubai	Dayton Flyer	7	1:47.47	$120,000
2000	Postponed	E. S. Prado	Unshaded	Globalize	9	1:49.71	$120,000
1999	Best of Luck	J-L. Samyn	Treasure Island	Lemon Drop Kid	9	1:47.94	$90,000
1998	Grand Slam	J. D. Bailey	Rubiyat	Parade Ground	7	1:49.14	$90,000
1997	Banker's Gold	E. Maple	Zede	Prince Giustino	4	1:48.79	$90,000
1996	Jamies First Punch	J. R. Velazquez	Unbridled's Song	Diligence	5	1:47.32	$90,000
1995	Citadeed	E. Maple	Pat n Jac	Treasurer (GB)	10	1:50.03	$90,000
1994	Twining	J. A. Santos	Lahint	Gash	5	1:49.11	$90,000
1993	Virginia Rapids	E. Maple	Colonial Affair	Itaka	6	1:48.48	$90,000
1992	A.P. Indy	E. Delahoussaye	Colony Light	Berkley Fitz	7	1:47.49	$106,380

Philadelphia Park Breeders' Cup Handicap

Grade 3, Philadelphia Park, three-year-olds and up, 6 furlongs, dirt. Held July 28, 2001, with a gross value of $188,000. First held in 1986. Graded since 1988. Stakes record 1:07.89 (2000 Iron Punch).

Year	Winner	Jockey	Second	Third	Strs	Final Time	1st Purse
2001	Say Florida Sandy, 7, 118	A. T. Gryder	Wake At Noon, 4	Max's Pal, 4	4	1:08.51	$120,000
2000	Iron Punch, 6, 114	C. M. Cruz	Say Florida Sandy, 6	Just Call Me Carl, 5	7	1:07.89	$60,000
1999	Loaded Gun, 4, 114	J. L. Flores	Artax, 4	Power by Far, 4	9	1:08.52	$60,000
1998	Buffalo Dan, 7, 117	S. Elliott	Western Fame, 6	Inajam, 4	9	1:08.82	$120,000
1997	Cat Be Nimble, 5, 122	J. Rocco	Wire Me Collect, 4	Score a Birdie, 6	6	1:09.33	$90,000
1996	Friendly Lover, 8, 118	W. H. McCauley	Elajjud, 4	Goldminer's Dream, 7	10	1:09.51	$90,000
1995	Friendly Lover, 7, 122	R. Wilson	Buffalo Dan, 4	Goldminer's Dream, 6	9	1:08.45	$93,420
1994	King Ruckus, 4, 122	T. Kabel	Friendly Lover, 6	Demaloot Demashoot, 4	6	1:09.07	$92,580
1993	Blushing Julian, 3, 111	R. E. Colton	Thelastcrusade, 4	Brukabookie, 6	7	1:09.77	$92,640
1992	Smart Alec, 4, 113	M. G. Pino	Megas Vukefalos, 4	Arrowtown, 4	7	1:09.69	$92,820

1998 Thunder Breeze finished third, DQ to eighth. 2000 new track record.

Philip H. Iselin H.

Grade 2, Monmouth Park, three-year-olds and up, 1⅛ miles, dirt. Held August 26, 2001, with a gross value of $350,000. First held in 1884. Graded since 1973. Stakes record 1:46.80 (1985 Spend a Buck; 1992 Jolie's Halo).

Year	Winner	Jockey	Second	Third	Strs	Final Time	1st Purse
2001	Broken Vow, 4, 119	R. A. Dominguez	First Lieutenant, 4	Sir Bear, 8	5	1:49.55	$210,000
2000	Rize, 4, 112	J. C. Ferrer	Sir Bear, 7	Talk's Cheap, 4	6	1:48.42	$210,000
1999	Frisk Me Now, 5, 117	E. L. King Jr.	Call Me Mr. Vain, 5	Black Cash, 4	6	1:49.00	$210,000
1998	Skip Away, 5, 131	J. D. Bailey	Stormin Fever, 4	Devil's Fire, 6	7	1:47.33	$300,000
1997	Formal Gold, 4, 121	K. J. Desormeaux	Skip Away, 4	Distorted Humor, 4	4	1:40.20	$250,000
1996	Smart Strike, 4, 115	C. Perret	Eltish, 4	†Serena's Song, 4	7	1:41.59	$180,000
1995	Schossberg, 5, 118	D. Penna	Poor But Honest, 5	Mickeray, 4	10	1:49.22	$180,000
1994	Taking Risks, 4, 115	M. T. Johnston	Valley Crossing, 6	Proud Shot, 4	9	1:48.33	$150,000

Year	Winner	Jockey	Second	Third	Strs	Final Time	1st Purse
1993	**Valley Crossing**, 5, 113	C. W. Antley	Devil His Due, 4	Bertrando, 4	8	1:49.20	$300,000
1992	**Jolie's Halo**, 5, 116	E. S. Prado	Out of Place, 5	Valley Crossing, 4	11	**1:46.80**	$300,000

1992-'96 Grade 1. 1996-'97 1¹⁄₁₆ miles. 1998 Testafly finished third, DQ to seventh. 1992 equaled track record. † denotes female.

Phoenix Breeders' Cup Stakes

Grade 3, Keeneland, three-year-olds and up, 6 furlongs, dirt. Held October 6, 2001, with a gross value of $268,500. First held in 1831. Graded since 2000. Stakes record 1:07.78 (1993 Anjiz)

Year	Winner	Jockey	Second	Third	Strs	Final Time	1st Purse
2001	**Bet On Sunshine**, 9	C. H. Borel	Robin de Nest, 4	Erlton, 5	5	1:09.65	$166,470
2000	**Five Star Day**, 4	G. K. Gomez	Istintaj, 4	Bet On Sunshine, 8	6	1:07.90	$167,245
1999	**Richter Scale**, 5	K. J. Desormeaux	Bet On Sunshine, 7	Vicar, 3	6	1:08.40	$166,780
1998	**Partner's Hero**, 4	C. H. Borel	Pyramid Peak, 6	High Stakes Player, 6	6	1:09.25	$100,533
1997	**Bet On Sunshine**, 5	F. C. Torres	Receiver, 4	Valid Expectations, 4	5	1:08.70	$97,464
1996	**Forest Wildcat**, 5	J. Bravo	Valid Expectations, 3	Bet On Sunshine, 4	10	1:09.57	$101,246
1995	**Golden Gear**, 4	C. Perret	Hello Paradise, 4	Mississippi Chat, 3	6	1:08.96	$67,456
1994	**Lost Pan**, 4	D. M. Barton	Pacific West, 4	Fort Chaffee, 4	5	1:09.45	$33,728
1993	**Anjiz**, 5	D. A. Miller Jr.	Gold Spring (Arg), 5	Friendly Lover, 5	9	**1:07.78**	$50,251
1992	**British Banker**, 4	D. Kutz	Megas Vukefalos, 4	Binalong, 3	6	1:09.20	$49,693

1994-'95 Phoenix S. 1993 new track record.

Pimlico Distaff Handicap

Grade 3, Pimlico, three-year-olds and up, fillies and mares, 1¹⁄₈ miles, dirt. Held May 19, 2001, with a gross value of $200,000. First held in 1992. Graded since 1994. Stakes record 1:48.70 (1998 Ajina).

Year	Winner	Jockey	Second	Third	Strs	Final Time	1st Purse
2001	**Serra Lake**, 4, 112	P. Day	Jostle, 4	Prized Stamp, 4	6	1:50.22	$120,000
2000	**Roza Robata**, 5, 114	P. Day	Bella Chiarra, 5	On a Soapbox, 5	8	1:49.82	$120,000
1999	**Mil Kilates**, 6, 113	S. J. Sellers	Merengue, 4	Unbridled Hope, 4	8	1:49.05	$120,000
1998	**Ajina**, 4, 120	J. D. Bailey	Naskra Colors, 6	Pocho's Dream Girl, 4	8	**1:48.70**	$120,000
1997	**Rare Blend**, 4, 114	J. D. Bailey	Scenic Point, 4	Aileen's Countess, 4	5	1:51.51	$120,000
1996	**Serena's Song**, 4, 123	G. L. Stevens	Shoop, 5	Churchbell Chimes, 5	4	1:49.75	$120,000
1995	**Pennyhill Park**, 5, 115	M. E. Smith	Halo America, 5	Calipha, 5	6	1:49.32	$120,000
1994	**Double Sixes**, 4, 112	E. S. Prado	Broad Gains, 4	Mz. Zill Bear, 4	6	1:51.19	$120,000
1993	**Deputation**, 4, 114	C. W. Antley	D. Theatrical Gal, 4	Low Tolerance, 4	6	1:49.12	$120,000
1992	**Wilderness Song**, 4, 121	C. Perret	Harbour Club, 5	Brilliant Brass, 5	7	1:49.06	$150,000

1992-'93 not graded.

Pimlico Special Handicap

Grade 1, Pimlico, three-year-olds and up, 1³⁄₁₆ miles, dirt. Held May 12, 2001, with a gross value of $750,000. First held in 1937. Graded since 1990. Stakes record 1:53 (1990 Criminal Type).

Year	Winner	Jockey	Second	Third	Strs	Final Time	1st Purse
2001	**Include**, 4, 114	J. D. Bailey	Albert the Great, 4	Pleasant Breeze, 4	6	1:55.61	$500,000
2000	**Golden Missile**, 5, 116	K. J. Desormeaux	Pleasant Breeze, 5	Lemon Drop Kid, 5	8	1:54.65	$450,000
1999	**Real Quiet**, 4, 120	G. L. Stevens	Free House, 5	Fred Bear Claw, 5	5	1:54.31	$300,000
1998	**Skip Away**, 5, 128	J. D. Bailey	Precocity, 4	Hot Brush, 4	5	1:54.26	$450,000
1997	**Gentlemen (Arg)**, 5, 122	G. L. Stevens	Skip Away, 4	Tejano Run, 4	8	1:53.03	$360,000
1996	**Star Standard**, 4, 111	P. Day	Key of Luck, 5	Geri, 5	4	1:54.46	$360,000
1995	**Cigar**, 5, 122	J. D. Bailey	Devil His Due, 6	Concern, 6	6	1:53.72	$360,000
1994	**As Indicated**, 4, 120	R. G. Davis	Devil His Due, 5	Valley Crossing, 5	6	1:55.08	$360,000
1993	**Devil His Due**, 4, 120	W. H. McCauley	Valley Crossing, 5	Pistols and Roses, 5	6	1:55.53	$510,000
1992	**Strike the Gold**, 4, 114	C. Perret	Fly So Free, 4	Twilight Agenda, 4	7	1:54.86	$420,000

1992-'97 four-year-olds and up. 1993 winner's share includes mid-series bonus of $150,000 from the ACRS.

Poker Handicap

Grade 3, Belmont Park, three-year-olds and up, 1 mile, turf. Held July 4, 2001, with a gross value of $110,400. First held in 1985. Graded since 1988. Stakes record 1:31.63 (1998 Elusive Quality).

Year	Winner	Jockey	Second	Third	Strs	Final Time	1st Purse
2001	**Affirmed Success**, 7, 121	J. D. Bailey	In Frank's Honor, 5	Union One, 4	6	1:34.60	$66,240
2000	**Affirmed Success**, 6, 117	J. F. Chavez	Rabi (Ire), 5	Weatherbird, 5	10	1:34.06	$68,280
1999	**Rob 'n Gin**, 5, 118	J. F. Chavez	Bomfim, 6	Wised Up, 4	8	1:32.81	$69,120
1998	**Elusive Quality**, 5, 117	J. D. Bailey	Za-Im (GB), 4	Fortitude, 5	9	**1:31.63**	$51,240
1997	**Draw Shot**, 4, 118	C. W. Antley	Val's Prince, 5	Fortitude, 4	10	1:33.08	$51,345
1996	**Smooth Runner**, 5, 113	J. A. Krone	Mighty Forum (GB), 5	Da Hoss, 4	10	1:33.62	$51,600
1995	**Caress**, 4, 117	R. G. Davis	Fourstars Allstar, 7	Pennine Ridge, 4	9	1:34.35	$51,030
1994	**Dominant Prospect**, 4, 114	J. F. Chavez	Fourstardave, 9	Nijinsky's Gold, 5	8	1:32.69	$49,905
1993	**Fourstardave**, 8, 117	R. Migliore	Adam Smith (GB), 5	Lech, 5	7	1:33.02	$53,190
1992	**Scott the Great**, 6, 117	J-L. Samyn	Kate's Valentine, 7	Cigar Toss (Arg), 5	7	1:33.27	$54,810

1998 new course and world record.

Potrero Grande Breeders' Cup Handicap

Grade 2, Santa Anita Park, four-year-olds and up, 6½ furlongs, dirt. Held April 1, 2001, with a gross value of $200,900. First held in 1983. Graded since 1988. Stakes record 1:13.71 (1998 Son of a Pistol).

Year	Winner	Jockey	Second	Third	Strs	Final Time	1st Purse
2001	Kona Gold, 7, 126	A. O. Solis	(DH) Hollycombe, 7 (DH) Explicit, 4		4	1:15.03	$123,000
2000	Kona Gold, 6, 122	A. O. Solis	Old Topper, 5	Your Halo, 5	4	1:14.75	$123,060
1999	Big Jag, 6, 119	J. Valdivia Jr.	Gold Land, 8	Son of a Pistol, 8	5	1:15.09	$123,720
1998	Son of a Pistol, 6, 114	G. K. Gomez	White Bronco, 4	Gold Land, 4	9	1:13.71	$66,420
1997	First Intent, 8, 114	R. R. Douglas	Hesabull, 4	Northern Afleet, 4	6	1:14.75	$64,250
1996	Abaginone, 5, 115	G. L. Stevens	Dramatic Gold, 5	Kingdom Found, 5	6	1:14.59	$124,400
1995	Lit de Justice, 5, 115	C. S. Nakatani	Cardmania, 5	Phone Roberto, 9	6	1:14.65	$63,000
1994	Sir Hutch, 4, 117	P. A. Valenzuela	Concept Win, 4	Furiously, 4	5	1:14.48	$61,100
1993	Gray Slewpy, 5, 118	K. J. Desormeaux	Cardmania, 7	Star of the Crop, 7	8	1:14.91	$64,700
1992	Cardmania, 6, 117	E. Delahoussaye	Frost Free, 7	Answer Do, 7	4	1:17.16	$60,200

1992-'95 Potrero Grande H. 1992-'96 Grade 3. 1998 new track record. 1999 Early Pioneer finished second, DQ to fourth. 2001 dead heat for second.

Prairie Meadows Cornhusker Breeders' Cup Handicap

Grade 3, Prairie Meadows, three-year-olds and up, 1⅛ miles, dirt. Held July 7, 2001, with a gross value of $401,625. First held in 1966. Graded since 1973. Stakes record 1:46.62 (1998 Beboppin Baby).

Year	Winner	Jockey	Second	Third	Strs	Final Time	1st Purse
2001	Euchre, 5, 116	G. K. Gomez	Dixie Dot Com, 6	Sure Shot Biscuit, 5	7	1:47.72	$240,000
2000	Sir Bear, 7, 116	E. Coa	Skimming, 4	Ecton Park, 4	5	1:48.49	$240,000
1999	Nite Dreamer, 4, 113	R. Albarado	Mocha Express, 5	Worldly Ways (GB), 5	7	1:48.85	$231,000
1998	Beboppin Baby, 5, 114	J. Campbell	Acceptable, 4	Pacificbounty, 4	8	1:46.62	$150,000
1997	Semoran, 4, 117	D. R. Flores	Mister Fire Eyes (Ire), 5	Come On Flip, 6	9	1:48.47	$120,000
1995	Powerful Punch, 6, 115	C. C. Bourque	All Gone, 5	Glaring, 5	8	1:49.80	$90,000
1994	Zeeruler, 6, 116	R. N. Lester	Powerful Punch, 5	Dancing Jon, 6	8	1:50.20	$75,000
1993	Link, 5, 114	R. Ardoin	Rapid World, 5	Flying Continental, 7	9	1:50.40	$75,000
1992	Irish Swap, 5, 117	B. E. Poyadou	Zeeruler, 4	Stalwars, 7	11	1:47.80	$75,000

1992-'95 Cornhusker H.; 1997 Prairie Meadows Cornhusker H.; 1998 Cornhusker Breeders' Cup H. 1996 not held. 1992-'95 held at AKsarben. 1998 new track record.

Preakness Stakes

Grade 1, Pimlico, three-year-olds, 1³⁄₁₆ miles, dirt. Held May 19, 2001, with a gross value of $1,000,000. First held in 1873. Graded since 1973. Stakes record 1:53.40 (1985 Tank's Prospect).

Year	Winner	Jockey	Second	Third	Strs	Final Time	1st Purse
2001	Point Given	G. L. Stevens	A P Valentine	Congaree	11	1:55.51	$650,000
2000	Red Bullet	J. D. Bailey	Fusaichi Pegasus	Impeachment	8	1:56.04	$650,000
1999	Charismatic	C. W. Antley	Menifee	Badge	13	1:55.32	$650,000
1998	Real Quiet	K. J. Desormeaux	Victory Gallop	Classic Cat	10	1:54.75	$650,000
1997	Silver Charm	G. L. Stevens	Free House	Captain Bodgit	10	1:54.84	$488,150
1996	Louis Quatorze	P. Day	Skip Away	Editor's Note	12	1:53.43	$458,520
1995	Timber Country	P. Day	Oliver's Twist	Thunder Gulch	11	1:54.45	$446,810
1994	Tabasco Cat	P. Day	Go for Gin	Concern	10	1:56.47	$447,720
1993	Prairie Bayou	M. E. Smith	Cherokee Run	El Bakan	12	1:56.61	$471,835
1992	Pine Bluff	C. J. McCarron	Alydeed	Casual Lies	14	1:55.60	$484,120

Princess Rooney Handicap

Grade 3, Calder Race Course, three-year-olds and up, fillies and mares, 6 furlongs, dirt. Held July 14, 2001, with a gross value of $400,000. First held in 1985. Graded since 1999. Stakes record 1:10.12 (1998 U Can Do It).

Year	Winner	Jockey	Second	Third	Strs	Final Time	1st Purse
2001	Dream Supreme, 4, 122	P. Day	Hidden Assets, 4	Sugar N Spice, 6	9	1:10.48	$240,000
2000	Hurricane Bertie, 5, 117	P. Day	Bourbon Belle, 5	Cassidy, 5	7	1:11.43	$240,000
1999	Princess Pietrina, 5, 114	R. B. Homeister Jr.	Hurricane Bertie, 4	U Can Do It, 6	8	1:10.49	$180,000
1998	U Can Do It, 5, 118	E. Coa	Closed Escrow, 5	Colonial Minstrel, 4	9	1:10.12	$150,000
1997	Vivace, 4, 117	R. P. Romero	Ashboro, 4	Special Request, 4	9	1:10.94	$150,000
1996	Chaposa Springs, 4, 126	L. A. Pincay Jr.	Reign Dance, 4	Supah Jess, 4	6	1:23.54	$60,000
1995	Miss Gibson County, 4, 115	G. Boulanger	Goldarama, 5	Sigrun, 5	7	1:23.18	$60,000
1994	Roamin Rachel, 4, 119	W. S. Ramos	Sigrun, 4	Goldarama, 4	10	1:24.01	$60,000
1993	Lady Sonata, 4, 115	M. A. Lee	Fortune Forty Four, 4	Treasured, 6	5	1:23.00	$30,000
1992	Magal, 5, 117	R. Hernandez	Fortune Forty Four, 3	My Own True Love, 4	8	1:23.60	$30,000

1992-'96 7 furlongs.

Princess Stakes

Grade 2, Hollywood Park, three-year-old fillies, 1¹⁄₁₆ miles, dirt. Held June 16, 2001, with a gross value of $100,000. First held in 1966. Graded since 1973. Stakes record 1:41.27 (1992 Race the Wild Wind).

Year	Winner	Jockey	Second	Third	Strs	Final Time	1st Purse
2001	Starrer	C. J. McCarron	Love At Noon	Affluent	6	1:41.90	$60,000
2000	Queenie Belle	B. Blanc	Saudi Poetry	Cash Run	6	1:43.57	$90,000
1999	Excellent Meeting	K. J. Desormeaux	Colorado Song	Dianehill (Ire)	6	1:41.73	$75,000
1998	Sweet and Ready	C. J. McCarron	Brulay	Visible Slew	4	1:42.52	$90,000
1997	Freeport Flight	E. Delahoussaye	Really Happy	Desert Digger	6	1:43.99	$64,440
1996	Listening	C. J. McCarron	Najecam	Pike Place Dancer	5	1:42.96	$63,660
1995	Favored One	A. O. Solis	Our Summer Bid	Sleep Easy	8	1:43.98	$64,100
1994	Sardula	E. Delahoussaye	Fancy 'n Fabulous	Pirate's Revenge	4	1:42.57	$60,200
1993	Fit to Lead	E. Delahoussaye	Swazi's Moment	Passing Vice	5	1:42.52	$61,000
1992	Race the Wild Wind	C. J. McCarron	Magical Maiden	Looie Capote	5	1:41.27	$61,800

Prioress Stakes

Grade 1, Belmont Park, three-year-old fillies, 6 furlongs, dirt. Held July 4, 2001, with a gross value of $200,000. First held in 1948. Graded since 1973. Stakes record 1:08.26 (2001 Xtra Heat).

Year	Winner	Jockey	Second	Third	Strs	Final Time	1st Purse
2001	Xtra Heat	R. Wilson	Above Perfection	Harmony Lodge	7	1:08.26	$120,000
2000	I'm Brassy	M. J. Luzzi	Dat You Miz Blue	Lucky Livi	9	1:09.53	$90,000
1999	Sapphire n' Silk	P. Day	Marley Vale	Confessional	8	1:09.55	$90,000
1998	Hurricane Bertie	P. Day	Catinca	Foil	11	1:08.85	$68,220
1997	Pearl City	J. D. Bailey	Alyssum	Vegas Prospector	5	1:09.40	$64,680
1996	Capote Belle	J. R. Velazquez	Flat Fleet Feet	Miss Maggie	10	1:08.81	$67,200
1995	Scotzanna	R. Platts	Culver City	Miss Golden Circle	9	1:10.61	$66,840
1994	Penny's Reshoot	J. R. Velazquez	Heavenly Prize	Beckys Shirt	6	1:09.07	$64,500
1993	Classy Mirage	J. A. Krone	Missed the Storm	Educated Risk	5	1:08.89	$67,680
1992	American Royale	J. A. Santos	Debra's Victory	Preach	6	1:09.36	$68,280

1992-2000 Grade 2.

Pucker Up Stakes

Grade 3, Arlington Park, three-year-old fillies, 1⅛ miles, turf. Held September 15, 2001, with a gross value of $150,000. First held in 1961. Graded since 1973. Stakes record 1:47.58 (1991 Jinski's World).

Year	Winner	Jockey	Second	Third	Strs	Final Time	1st Purse
2001	Snow Dance	C. Perret	Kiss the Devil	Twilite Tryst	12	1:47.93	$90,000
2000	Solvig	P. Day	Zoftig	Impending Bear	6	1:52.40	$90,000
1997	Witchful Thinking	G. K. Gomez	Swearingen	Cozy Blues	8	1:48.88	$75,000
1996	Ms. Mostly	R. P. Romero	Mountain Affair	Clamorosa	9	1:51.18	$90,000
1995	Grand Charmer	P. Day	Upper Noosh	Set Me Straight	,8	1:49.59	$60,000
1994	Work the Crowd	A. T. Gryder	Irish Forever	Looking for Heaven	14	1:49.32	$60,000
1993	Amal Hayati	W. S. Ramos	Warside	Future Starlet	11	1:53.39	$60,000
1992	Ziggy's Act	G. Boulanger	Bernique	Luv Me Luv Me Not	10	1:48.79	$60,000

Queen Elizabeth II Challenge Cup Stakes

Grade 1, Keeneland, three-year-old fillies, 1⅛ miles, turf. Held October 13, 2001, with a gross value of $500,000. First held in 1984. Graded since 1986. Stakes record 1:45.81 (1996 Memories of Silver).

Year	Winner	Jockey	Second	Third	Strs	Final Time	1st Purse
2001	Affluent	E. Delahoussaye	Golden Apples (Ire)	Snow Dance	10	1:50.03	$310,000
2000	Collect the Cash	S. J. Sellers	Blue Moon (Fr)	Theoretically	9	1:47.94	$310,000
1999	Perfect Sting	P. Day	Tout Charmant	Wannabe Grand (Ire)	9	1:50.66	$310,000
1998	Tenski	R. Migliore	Shires Ende	Sierra Virgen	9	1:48.54	$248,000
1997	Ryafan	A. O. Solis	Auntie Mame	Golden Arches (Fr)	8	1:46.64	$248,000
1996	Memories of Silver	R. G. Davis	Shake the Yoke (GB)	Antespend	10	1:45.81	$248,000
1995	Perfect Arc	J. R. Velazquez	Auriette (Ire)	Country Cat	8	1:49.84	$155,000
1994	Danish (Ire)	J. A. Krone	Eternal Reve	Avie's Fancy	10	1:48.89	$124,000
1993	Tribulation	J-L. Samyn	Miami Sands (Ire)	Possibly Perfect	9	1:53.62	$124,000
1992	Captive Miss	J. A. Krone	Suivi	Trampoli	10	1:48.66	$124,000

Queens County Handicap

Grade 3, Aqueduct, three-year-olds and up, 1³⁄₁₆ miles, dirt. Held December 1, 2001, with a gross value of $111,900. First held in 1902. Graded since 1973. Stakes record 1:54.40 (1972 Sunny and Mild).

Year	Winner	Jockey	Second	Third	Strs	Final Time	1st Purse
2001	Evening Attire, 3, 113	S. Bridgmohan	Balto Star, 3	Top Official, 6	8	1:55.08	$67,140
2000	Boston Party, 4, 114	N. Arroyo Jr.	Talk's Cheap, 4	Turnofthecentury, 3	9	1:56.32	$50,340
1999	Early Warning, 4, 116	J. F. Chavez	Doc Martin, 4	Yankee Victor, 3	7	1:55.03	$49,230
1998	Fire King, 5, 113	F. Lovato Jr.	Las Vegas Ernie, 4	Mr. Sinatra, 4	7	1:56.88	$49,140
1997	Mr. Sinatra, 3, 115	R. Migliore	Delay of Game, 4	Draw, 4	8	1:55.68	$49,725

Year	Winner	Jockey	Second	Third	Strs	Final Time	1st Purse
1996	Topsy Robsy, 4, 111	P. Keim-Bruno	More to Tell, 5	Colonial Secretary, 4	5	1:55.30	$48,705
1995	Aztec Empire, 5, 113	J-L. Samyn	Mighty Magee, 3	More to Tell, 4	9	1:55.56	$50,340
1994	Federal Funds, 5, 112	D. Carr	Jacksonport, 5	Contract Court, 4	8	1:56.42	$49,665
1993	Repletion, 4, 111	M. E. Smith	Dibbs n' Dubbs, 5	Primitive Hall, 4	8	1:44.35	$53,010
1992	Shots Are Ringing, 5, 117	J. R. Velazquez	A Call to Rise, 4	Jacksonport, 3	6	1:54.90	$51,120

1993 1¹⁄₁₆ miles.

Railbird Stakes

Grade 2, Hollywood Park, three-year-old fillies, 7 furlongs, dirt. Held May 19, 2001, with a gross value of $150,000. First held in 1963. Graded since 1973. Stakes record 1:20.60 (1979 Eloquent).

Year	Winner	Jockey	Second	Third	Strs	Final Time	1st Purse
2001	Golden Ballet	C. J. McCarron	Starrer	Pretty 'n Smart	6	1:21.57	$90,000
2000	Cover Gal	L. A. Pincay Jr.	Wired to Fly	Classic Olympio	5	1:22.57	$90,000
1999	Olympic Charmer	C. J. McCarron	Dianehill (Ire)	Fee Fi Foe	9	1:21.18	$90,000
1998	Brulay	G. L. Stevens	Gourmet Girl	Unreal Squeal	6	1:20.84	$64,260
1997	I Ain't Bluffing	E. Delahoussaye	Really Happy	Montecito	7	1:22.77	$66,840
1996	Supercilious	C. S. Nakatani	Tiffany Diamond	Raw Gold	6	1:22.55	$64,260
1995	Sleep Easy	C. S. Nakatani	Texinadress	Laguna Seca	8	1:22.42	$64,600
1994	Sportful Snob	P. A. Valenzuela	Pirate's Revenge	Accountable Lady	5	1:21.94	$61,400
1993	Afto	P. Atkinson	Fit to Lead	Nijivision	8	1:22.48	$64,500
1992	She's Tops	K. J. Desormeaux	Race the Wild Wind	Magical Maiden	9	1:22.78	$66,500

2001 Abby Girl finished first, DQ to fifth.

Ramona Handicap

Grade 1, Del Mar, three-year-olds and up, fillies and mares, 1¹⁄₈ miles, turf. Held July 21, 2001, with a gross value of $400,000. First held in 1945. Graded since 1973. Stakes record 1:47 (1969 Greta [2nd Div.]).

Year	Winner	Jockey	Second	Third	Strs	Final Time	1st Purse
2001	Janet (GB), 4, 116	D. R. Flores	Tranquility Lake, 6	Minor Details, 4	6	1:48.20	$240,000
2000	Caffe Latte (Ire), 4, 117	B. Blanc	Tout Charmant, 4	Alexine (Arg), 4	7	1:47.16	$240,000
1999	Tuzla (Fr), 5, 121	D. R. Flores	Happyanunoit (NZ), 4	Spanish Fern, 4	10	1:47.66	$240,000
1998	See You Soon (Fr), 4, 114	C. S. Nakatani	Sonja's Faith (Ire), 4	Fiji (GB), 4	8	1:47.43	$180,000
1997	Escena, 4, 115	P. Day	Real Connection, 6	Different (Arg), 5	7	1:49.80	$180,000
1996	Matiara, 4, 118	C. S. Nakatani	Alpride (Ire), 5	Pourquoi Pas (Ire), 4	6	1:49.28	$193,500
1995	Possibly Perfect, 5, 123	C. S. Nakatani	Morgana, 4	Yearly Tour, 4	7	1:49.98	$180,600
1994	Flawlessly, 6, 124	C. J. McCarron	Hollywood Wildcat, 4	Skimble, 5	5	1:48.25	$181,000
1993	Flawlessly, 5, 125	C. J. McCarron	Heart of Joy, 6	Let's Elope (NZ), 6	7	1:48.38	$186,500
1992	Flawlessly, 4, 123	C. J. McCarron	Re Toss (Arg), 5	Polemic, 4	7	1:50.00	$187,500

Rampart Handicap

Grade 2, Gulfstream Park, three-year-olds and up, fillies and mares, 1¹⁄₈ miles, dirt. Held March 4, 2001, with a gross value of $200,000. First held in 1976. Graded since 1986. Stakes record 1:50.48 (2001 De Bertie).

Year	Winner	Jockey	Second	Third	Strs	Final Time	1st Purse
2001	De Bertie, 4, 116	J. F. Chavez	Apple of Kent, 5	Scratch Pad, 5	7	**1:50.48**	$120,000
2000	Bella Chiarra, 5, 116	S. J. Sellers	Lines of Beauty, 5	Up We Go, 5	8	1:43.27	$120,000
1999	Banshee Breeze, 4, 122	J. D. Bailey	Glitter Woman, 5	Timely Broad, 5	5	1:42.83	$120,000
1998	Dance for Thee, 4, 113	J. Bravo	Escena, 5	Glitter Woman, 5	6	1:44.73	$120,000
1997	Chip, 4, 114	J. Bravo	Rare Blend, 4	Hurricane Viv, 4	9	1:42.51	$120,000
1996	Investalot, 5, 114	S. J. Sellers	Queen Tutta, 4	Alcovy, 4	9	1:43.99	$120,000
1995	Educated Risk, 5, 126	M. E. Smith	Recognizable, 4	Jade Flush, 4	5	1:43.09	$120,000
1994	Nine Keys, 4, 113	M. E. Smith	Educated Risk, 4	Traverse City, 4	6	1:42.12	$120,000
1993	Girl On a Mission, 4, 112	J. D. Bailey	Luv Me Luv Me Not, 4	Haunting, 4	8	1:45.47	$120,000
1992	Fit for a Queen, 6, 119	J. D. Bailey	Firm Stance, 4	Nannerl, 4	12	1:43.66	$120,000

1992-2000 1¹⁄₁₆ miles. 1993 Now Dance finished second, DQ to fifth.

Rancho Bernardo Handicap

Grade 3, Del Mar, three-year-olds and up, fillies and mares, 6¹⁄₂ furlongs, dirt. Held August 19, 2001, with a gross value of $150,000. First held in 1967. Graded since 1988. Stakes record 1:14.28 (1995 Track Gal).

Year	Winner	Jockey	Second	Third	Strs	Final Time	1st Purse
2001	Kalookan Queen, 5, 119	A. O. Solis	Go Go, 4	Warren's Whistle, 3	6	1:15.52	$90,000
2000	Theresa's Tizzy, 6, 117	L. A. Pincay Jr.	Nany's Sweep, 4	Hookedonthefeelin, 4	6	1:16.23	$90,000
1999	Enjoy the Moment, 4, 119	D. R. Flores	Snowberg, 4	Stop Traffic, 6	6	1:15.97	$90,000
1998	Advancing Star, 5, 120	C. J. McCarron	Closed Escrow, 5	Tiffany Diamond, 5	6	1:14.64	$64,140
1997	Track Gal, 6, 120	G. L. Stevens	Madame Pandit, 4	Advancing Star, 4	8	1:15.64	$69,125
1996	Track Gal, 5, 122	C. J. McCarron	Tricky Code, 5	Evil's Pic, 4	5	1:14.64	$63,550
1995	Track Gal, 4, 118	C. J. McCarron	Desert Stormer, 5	Lakeway, 4	5	**1:14.28**	$58,650
1994	Desert Stormer, 4, 116	E. Delahoussaye	Magical Maiden, 5	Booklore, 4	9	1:14.81	$62,800

Year	Winner	Jockey	Second	Third	Strs	Final Time	1st Purse
1993	Knight Prospector, 4, 119	K. J. Desormeaux	Interactive, 4	Bountiful Native, 5	5	1:16.14	$45,675
1992	Bountiful Native, 4, 117	P. A. Valenzuela	Devil's Orchid, 5	She's Tops, 3	9	1:15.30	$63,400

1992-'95 Rancho Bernardo Breeders' Cup H.

Rare Treat Handicap

Grade 3, Aqueduct, three-year-olds and up, fillies and mares, 1⅛ miles, dirt. Held February 19, 2001, with a gross value of $110,300. First held in 1972. Graded since 1986. Stakes record 1:48.89 (2000 Biogio's Rose).

Year	Winner	Jockey	Second	Third	Strs	Final Time	1st Purse
2001	Pompeii, 4, 115	J. Castellano	Biogio's Rose, 7	Back in Shape, 7	8	1:50.71	$66,180
2000	Biogio's Rose, 6, 115	N. Arroyo Jr.	Roaring Twenties, 4	Sazarac Jazz, 4	6	1:48.89	$48,930
1999	Carta de Amor (Arg), 6, 115	V. Diaz	Deb's Honor, 5	Termly, 5	9	1:50.42	$49,815
1998	Dewars Rocks, 4, 112	J. F. Chavez	Termly, 5	See Your Point, 5	10	1:52.59	$50,310
1997	Prophet's Warning, 4, 113	J. F. Chavez	Full and Fancy, 5	Shoop, 5	8	1:48.90	$49,710
1996	Very True, 4, 115	H. Castillo Jr.	Shoop, 5	Spire, 5	8	1:52.34	$49,710
1995	Restored Hope, 4, 112	M. J. Luzzi	Little Buckles, 4	Sea Ditty, 4	9	1:51.98	$49,905
1994	Groovy Feeling, 5, 121	M. J. Luzzi	Hey Baba Lulu, 6	Poolesta (Ire), 6	8	1:51.30	$48,540
1993	Hey Baba Lulu, 5, 116	W. H. McCauley	Low Tolerance, 4	Hilbys Brite Flite, 4	9	1:49.33	$53,370
1992	Grecian Pass, 5, 112	E. Maple	Risen Colony, 4	Twixt Appeal, 4	6	1:52.15	$50,985
	Haunting, 4, 114	C. W. Antley	Embracing, 5	Royal Residence, 5	6	1:52.64	$50,625

1992 two divisions. 1996 Shoop finished first, DQ to second.

Raven Run Stakes

Not graded, Keeneland, three-year-old fillies, 7 furlongs, dirt. Held October 10, 2001, with a gross value of $109,900. First held in 1999. Grade 3 since 2002. Stakes record 1:20.88 (2000 Darling My Darling).

Year	Winner	Jockey	Second	Third	Strs	Final Time	1st Purse
2001	Nasty Storm	P. Day	Hattiesburg	Forest Secrets	7	1:23.30	$68,138
2000	Darling My Darling	M. E. Smith	Surfside	Cat Cay	6	1:20.88	$51,104
1999	Dreamy Maiden	P. Day	Golden Illusion	Cosmic Wing	6	1:22.64	$37,076

Razorback Handicap

Grade 3, Oaklawn Park, four-year-olds and up, 1¹⁄₁₆ miles, dirt. Held March 17, 2001, with a gross value of $125,000. First held in 1960. Graded since 1978. Stakes record 1:40.40 (1988 Lost Code).

Year	Winner	Jockey	Second	Third	Strs	Final Time	1st Purse
2001	Mr Ross, 6, 119	D. R. Pettinger	Graeme Hall, 4	Maysville Slew, 4	9	1:42.60	$75,000
2000	Well Noted, 5, 112	T. T. Doocy	Crimson Classic, 6	Mr Ross, 6	7	1:43.21	$75,000
1999	Desert Air, 4, 113	C. J. Lanerie	Magnify, 6	Black Tie Dinner, 6	7	1:44.75	$75,000
1998	Brush With Pride, 6, 115	T. T. Doocy	Littlebitlively, 4	Krigeorj's Gold, 4	7	1:43.55	$75,000
1997	No Spend No Glow, 5, 115	R. N. Lester	Illesam, 5	Come On Flip, 5	8	1:43.38	$90,000
1996	Juliannus, 7, 113	R. Albarado	Judge T C, 5	Dazzling Falls, 5	5	1:43.37	$90,000
1995	Silver Goblin, 4, 124	D. W. Cordova	Joseph's Robe, 4	Wooden Ticket, 4	6	1:42.79	$120,000
1994	Prize Fight, 5, 113	P. A. Johnson	Brother Brown, 4	Country Store, 4	8	1:43.70	$90,000
1993	Lil E. Tee, 4, 123	P. Day	Zeeruler, 5	Senor Tomas, 5	7	1:41.55	$90,000
1992	Tokatee, 6, 115	G. K. Gomez	On the Edge, 5	Total Assets, 5	9	1:42.87	$90,000

1992-'96 Grade 2.

Rebel Stakes

Grade 3, Oaklawn Park, three-year-olds, 1¹⁄₁₆ miles, dirt. Held March 24, 2001, with a gross value of $100,000. First held in 1961. Graded since 1990. Stakes record 1:40.80 (1967 Betemight).

Year	Winner	Jockey	Second	Third	Strs	Final Time	1st Purse
2001	Crafty Shaw	J. M. Johnson	Arctic Boy	Strike It Smart	9	1:43.82	$60,000
2000	Snuck In	C. B. Asmussen	Big Numbers	Fan the Flame	12	1:42.99	$60,000
1999	Etbauer	M. E. Smith	Desert Demon	Kutsa	11	1:44.02	$75,000
1998	Victory Gallop	E. Coa	Robinwould	Whataflashyactor	10	1:44.72	$75,000
1997	Phantom On Tour	L. Melancon	Direct Hit	River Squall	12	1:42.93	$75,000
1996	Ide	C. Perret	Blow Out	Bunker Hill Road	7	1:44.10	$60,000
1995	Mystery Storm	C. Perret	Rich Man's Gold	Valid Advantage	7	1:44.41	$75,000
1994	Judge T C	J. M. Johnson	Concern	Milt's Overture	11	1:44.14	$75,000
1993	Dalhart	M. E. Smith	Foxtrail	Mi Cielo	8	1:42.31	$75,000
1992	Pine Bluff	J. D. Bailey	Desert Force	Looks Like Money	7	1:42.83	$75,000

Red Bank Handicap

Grade 3, Monmouth Park, three-year-olds and up, 1 mile, turf. Held May 28, 2001, with a gross value of $150,000. First held in 1974. Graded since 1986. Stakes record 1:33.34 (1991 Double Booked).

Year	Winner	Jockey	Second	Third	Strs	Final Time	1st Purse
2001	Pavillon (Brz), 7, 112	J. Bravo	Western Summer, 4	Runspastum, 4	10	1:36.38	$90,000
2000	Mi Narrow, 6, 114	C. H. Velasquez	Deep Gold, 4	Inkatha (Fr), 4	9	1:34.84	$90,000

Year	Winner	Jockey	Second	Third	Strs	Final Time	1st Purse
1999	Inkatha (Fr), 5, 114	H. Castillo Jr.	Rob 'n Gin, 5	Soviet Line (Ire), 5	8	1:33.95	$90,000
1998	Statesmanship, 4, 117	J. A. Santos	Rob 'n Gin, 4	Bomfim, 4	11	1:35.00	$60,000
1997	Basqueian, 6, 118	R. Wilson	Wild Night Out, 5	Jambalaya Jazz, 5	6	1:35.37	$60,000
1996	Joker, 4, 113	J. A. Velez Jr.	Rare Reason, 5	Diplomatic Jet, 5	8	1:35.90	$60,000
1995	Dove Hunt, 4, 118	W. H. McCauley	Rare Reason, 4	Winnetou, 4	9	1:33.95	$45,000
1994	Adam Smith (GB), 6, 120	J. A. Krone	Discernment, 5	Fourstardave, 5	8	1:34.43	$45,000
1993	Adam Smith (GB), 5, 116	J-L. Samyn	Fourstars Allstar, 5	Rinka Das, 5	8	1:34.39	$45,000
1992	Daarik (Ire), 5, 114	L. Saumell	Leger Cat (Arg), 6	Kate's Valentine, 6	8	1:34.07	$45,000

1997 dirt.

Red Smith Handicap

Grade 2, Aqueduct, three-year-olds and up, 1⅜ miles, turf. Held November 17, 2001, with a gross value of $150,000. First held in 1960. Graded since 1973. Stakes record 2:14.44 (1999 Monarch's Maze).

Year	Winner	Jockey	Second	Third	Strs	Final Time	1st Purse
2001	Mr. Pleasentfar (Brz), 4, 115	J. A. Santos	Eltawaasul, 5	Regal Dynasty, 5	12	2:16.94	$90,000
2000	Cetewayo, 6, 114	R. Migliore	Understood, 4	Val's Prince, 8	13	2:17.93	$90,000
1999	Monarch's Maze, 3, 113	J. Bravo	Williams News, 4	Gritty Sandie, 3	14	2:14.44	$90,000
1998	Musical Ghost, 6, 115	J. R. Velazquez	Rice, 6	Plato's Love, 3	12	2:15.53	$90,000
1997	Instant Friendship, 4, 123	J. R. Velazquez	Demi's Bret, 4	Trample, 3	5	2:17.08	$90,000
1996	Mr. Bluebird, 5, 116	M. E. Smith	Ops Smile, 4	Raintrap (GB), 6	13	2:15.35	$87,750
1995	Flag Down, 5, 114	J. A. Santos	Party Season (GB), 4	Proceeded, 4	11	2:22.03	$69,900
1994	Franchise Player, 5, 109	D. V. Beckner	Red Bishop, 6	Same Old Wish, 4	14	2:20.53	$72,120
1993	Royal Mountain Inn, 4, 110	J. A. Krone	Spectacular Tide, 4	Share the Glory, 5	8	1:59.82	$71,760
1992	Montserrat, 4, 118	J. A. Krone	Preferences, 4	First Rate (Ire), 7	7	2:00.32	$70,920

Regret Stakes

Grade 3, Churchill Downs, three-year-old fillies, 1¹⁄₁₆ miles, turf. Held June 16, 2001, with a gross value of $167,250. First held in 1970. Graded since 1999. Stakes record 1:42.06 (1992 Tiney Toast).

Year	Winner	Jockey	Second	Third	Strs	Final Time	1st Purse
2001	Casual Feat	L. Melancon	Amaretta	La Vida Loca (Ire)	8	1:42.75	$103,695
2000	Solvig	P. Day	Trip	Miss Chief	9	1:42.95	$104,439
1999	Nani Rose	S. J. Sellers	Solar Bound	Suffragette	8	1:42.40	$104,439
1998	Formal Tango	C. R. Woods Jr.	Adel	Pratella	10	1:43.73	$105,927
1997	Starry Dreamer	W. Martinez	Cozy Blues	Swearingen	8	1:42.77	$69,378
1996	Daylight Come	C. C. Bourque	Fleur de Nuit	Esquive (GB)	9	1:45.72	$55,526
1995	Christmas Gift	C. R. Woods Jr.	Bail Out Becky	Grand Charmer	7	1:45.00	$54,210
1994	Packet	J. M. Johnson	Thread	Slew Kitty Slew	7	1:42.14	$54,551
1993	Lovat's Lady	B. D. Peck	Warside	Mari's Key	8	1:42.95	$36,595
1992	Tiney Toast	S. P. Payton	Shes Just Super	Riverjinsky	10	1:42.06	$37,440

Remsen Stakes

Grade 2, Aqueduct, two-year-olds, 1⅛ miles, dirt. Held November 24, 2001, with a gross value of $200,000. First held in 1904. Graded since 1973. Stakes record 1:47.80 (1977 Believe It).

Year	Winner	Jockey	Second	Third	Strs	Final Time	1st Purse
2001	Saarland	J. R. Velazquez	Nokoma	Silent Fred	9	1:51.24	$120,000
2000	Windsor Castle	R. G. Davis	Ommadon	Buckle Down Ben	8	1:51.92	$120,000
1999	Greenwood Lake	J-L. Samyn	Un Fino Vino	Polish Miner	8	1:50.63	$120,000
1998	Comeonmom	J. Bravo	Millions	Wondertross	9	1:49.84	$120,000
1997	Coronado's Quest	M. E. Smith	Halory Hunter	Brooklyn Nick	7	1:52.27	$120,000
1996	The Silver Move	R. Migliore	Jules	Accelerator	8	1:53.54	$120,000
1995	Tropicool	J. F. Chavez	Skip Away	Crafty Friend	11	1:50.30	$170,000
1994	Thunder Gulch	G. L. Stevens	Western Echo	Mighty Magee	10	1:53.80	$120,000
1993	Go for Gin	J. D. Bailey	Arrovente	Linkatariat	7	1:52.79	$120,000
1992	Silver of Silver	J. Vasquez	Dalhart	Wild Gale	11	1:50.25	$120,000

Risen Star Stakes

Not graded, Fair Grounds, three-year-olds, 1¹⁄₁₆ miles, dirt. Held February 18, 2001, with a gross value of $125,000. First held in 1973. Grade 3 since 2002. Stakes record 1:42.98 (1996 Zarb's Magic).

Year	Winner	Jockey	Second	Third	Strs	Final Time	1st Purse
2001	Dollar Bill	C. J. McCarron	Gracie's Dancer	Rahy's Secret	10	1:43.45	$75,000
2000	Exchange Rate	C. S. Nakatani	Mighty	Ifitstobeitsuptome	8	1:44.25	$75,000
1999	Ecton Park	S. J. Sellers	Answer Lively	Kimberlite Pipe	12	1:44.83	$75,000
1998	Comic Strip	S. J. Sellers	Captain Maestri	Time Limit	7	1:44.27	$75,000
1997	Open Forum	D. M. Barton	Crypto Star	Cash Deposit	5	1:44.37	$60,000
1996	Zarb's Magic	E. J. Perrodin	Imminent First	Palikar	9	1:42.98	$37,950

Year	Winner	Jockey	Second	Third	Strs	Final Time	1st Purse
1995	Knockadoon	W. Martinez	Key to Malagra	Scott's Scoundrel	9	1:45.44	$31,882
	Beavers Nose	K. Bourque	Moonlight Dancer	Fuzzy Me	8	1:45.22	$31,792
1994	Fly Cry	R. D. Ardoin	Smilin Singin Sam	Little Jazz Boy	7	1:43.02	$31,155
1993	Dixieland Heat	R. P. Romero	O'Star	Gold Angle	7	1:43.20	$16,080
	Dry Bean	A. T. Gryder	Apprentice	Grand Jewel	6	1:43.80	$16,020
1992	Line In The Sand	S. P. Romero	Hill Pass	Sheik to Sheik	11	1:45.00	$19,635

1993, 1995 two divisions.

Riva Ridge Stakes

Grade 2, Belmont Park, three-year-olds, 7 furlongs, dirt. Held June 9, 2001, with a gross value of $150,000. First held in 1985. Graded since 1988. Stakes record 1:20.33 (1994 You and I).

Year	Winner	Jockey	Second	Third	Strs	Final Time	1st Purse
2001	Put It Back	N. A. Wynter	Flame Thrower	Touch Tone	6	1:21.76	$90,000
2000	Trippi	J. D. Bailey	Bevo	Sun Cat	6	1:23.68	$90,000
1999	Yes It's True	J. D. Bailey	Lion Hearted	Silver Season	8	1:22.35	$90,000
1998	Coronado's Quest	M. E. Smith	Mellow Roll	Flashing Tammany	7	1:22.50	$82,050
1997	Smoke Glacken	C. Perret	Trafalger	Wild Wonder	6	1:20.98	$66,060
1996	Gold Fever	M. E. Smith	Gameel	Bright Launch	9	1:23.30	$67,620
1995	Western Larla	G. L. Stevens	Mr. Greeley	Blu Tusmani	8	1:24.24	$66,960
1994	You and I	C. J. McCarron	End Sweep	Slew Gin Fizz	9	1:20.33	$67,080
1993	Montbrook	C. J. Ladner III	As Indicated	Forever Whirl	10	1:23.34	$74,160
1992	Superstrike (GB)	J. A. Santos	Three Peat	Windundermywings	7	1:22.41	$70,560

1992-'97 Grade 3; 1994 new track record.

River City Handicap

Grade 3, Churchill Downs, three-year-olds and up, 1⅛ miles, turf. Held November 11, 2001, with a gross value of $177,300. First held in 1978. Graded since 1996. Stakes record 1:47.90 (2001 Dr. Kashnikow).

Year	Winner	Jockey	Second	Third	Strs	Final Time	1st Purse
2001	Dr. Kashnikow, 4, 116	R. Albarado	Tijiyr (Ire), 5	Strategic Mission, 6	8	1:47.90	$109,926
2000	Brahms, 3, 112	P. Day	Vergennes, 5	Super Quercus (Fr), 4	9	1:48.09	$111,879
1999	Comic Strip, 4, 119	P. Day	Keats and Yeats, 5	Aboriginal Apex, 6	10	1:50.71	$106,113
1998	Wild Event, 5, 116	S. J. Sellers	Buff, 3	Floriselli, 4	13	1:49.18	$116,436
1997	Same Old Wish, 7, 117	S. J. Sellers	Aboriginal Apex, 4	Joyeux Danseur, 4	9	1:50.90	$106,578
1996	Same Old Wish, 6, 119	S. J. Sellers	Jet Freighter, 5	Franchise Player, 7	7	1:49.21	$70,122
1995	Homing Pigeon, 5, 113	R. P. Romero	Hawk Attack, 3	Dusty Asher, 5	8	1:51.00	$73,320
1994	Lindon Lime, 4, 113	S. J. Sellers	Torch Rouge (GB), 3	Jaggery John, 3	11	1:49.30	$75,660
1993	Secreto's Hideaway, 4, 110	W. Martinez	Little Bro Lantis, 5	Ganges, 5	5	1:53.83	$72,670
1992	Cozzene's Prince, 5, 117	D. Penna	Lotus Pool, 5	Stagecraft (GB), 5	8	1:49.31	$73,060

Robert F. Carey Memorial Handicap

Grade 3, Hawthorne Race Course, three-year-olds and up, 1 mile, turf. Held November 3, 2001, with a gross value of $150,000. First held in 1983. Graded since 1998. Stakes record 1:33.40 (1998 Soviet Line [Ire]).

Year	Winner	Jockey	Second	Third	Strs	Final Time	1st Purse
2001	Galic Boy, 6, 115	R. Sibille	Where's Taylor, 5	Good Journey, 5	10	1:35.10	$90,000
2000	Where's Taylor, 4, 117	C. J. Lanerie	Dernier Croise (Fr), 5	Associate, 5	11	1:36.31	$90,000
1999	Ray's Approval, 6, 114	E. Fires	Stay Sound, 4	Inkatha (Fr), 5	9	1:37.01	$90,000
1998	Soviet Line (Ire), 8, 115	S. J. Sellers	Fun to Run, 5	Wild Event, 5	10	1:33.40	$90,000
1997	Trail City, 4, 119	J. D. Bailey	Power of Opinion, 4	Da Bull, 5	8	1:36.04	$90,000
1996	Homing Pigeon, 6, 114	R. Albarado	Joker, 4	Why Change, 3	12	1:36.58	$90,000
1995	Homing Pigeon, 5, 114	R. Albarado	Gilder, 4	Rare Reason, 4	9	1:38.09	$60,000
1994	Recoup the Cash, 4, 119	J. L. Diaz	Road of War, 4	Glenfiddich Lad, 5	7	1:40.91	$60,000
1993	High Habitation, 5, 114	G. C. Rotana	Beau Fasa, 7	Glenfiddich Lad, 4	12	1:35.33	$60,000
1992	Double Booked, 7, 115	J. C. Ferrer	Evanescent, 5	That's Sunny, 7	11	1:39.82	$60,000

Royal Heroine Stakes

Grade 3, Hollywood Park, three-year-olds and up, fillies and mares, 1 mile, turf. Held July 7, 2001, with a gross value of $109,900. First held in 1986. Graded since 2001. Stakes record 1:33.98 (2000 Tranquility Lake).

Year	Winner	Jockey	Second	Third	Strs	Final Time	1st Purse
2001	Kalatiara (Aus), 4	C. J. McCarron	Dianehill (Ire), 5	Al Desima (GB), 4	7	1:34.41	$65,940
2000	Tranquility Lake, 5	E. Delahoussaye	Dianehill (Ire), 4	Reciclada (Chi), 5	6	1:33.98	$46,590
1999	Tuzla (Fr), 5	C. S. Nakatani	Isle de France, 4	Chime After Chime, 4	5	1:34.32	$42,240
1998	Tuzla (Fr), 4	C. S. Nakatani	Sonja's Faith (Ire), 4	Plus (Chi), 5	6	1:34.33	$42,990

Ruffian Handicap

Grade 1, Belmont Park, three-year-olds and up, fillies and mares, 1¹⁄₁₆ miles, dirt. Held September 16, 2000, with a gross value of $250,000. First held in 1976. Graded since 1976. Stakes record 1:40.35 (2000 Riboletta [Brz]).

Year	Winner	Jockey	Second	Third	Strs	Final Time	1st Purse
2000	Riboletta (Brz), 5, 125	C. J. McCarron	Gourmet Girl, 5	Country Hideaway, 4	7	1:40.35	$150,000
1999	Catinca, 4, 119	J. D. Bailey	Furlough, 5	Keeper Hill, 4	5	1:41.94	$150,000

Year	Winner	Jockey	Second	Third	Strs	Final Time	1st Purse
1998	**Sharp Cat**, 4, 124	C. S. Nakatani	Furlough, 4	Stop Traffic, 5	8	1:42.48	$150,000
1997	**Tomisue's Delight**, 3, 113	J. D. Bailey	Clear Mandate, 5	Mil Kilates, 4	9	1:44.43	$150,000
1996	**Yanks Music**, 3, 116	J. R. Velazquez	Serena's Song, 4	Head East, 4	6	1:41.84	$150,000
1995	**Inside Information**, 4, 125	M. E. Smith	Unlawful Behavior, 5	Incinerate, 5	6	1:40.98	$120,000
1994	**Sky Beauty**, 4, 130	M. E. Smith	Dispute, 4	Educated Risk, 4	4	1:41.79	$120,000
1993	**Shared Interest**, 5, 114	R. G. Davis	Dispute, 3	Turnback the Alarm, 4	5	1:41.92	$120,000
1992	**Versailles Treaty**, 4, 120	M. E. Smith	Quick Mischief, 6	Nannerl, 5	5	1:41.41	$120,000

2001 not held due to World Trade Center attack.

Sabin Handicap

Grade 3, Gulfstream Park, three-year-olds and up, fillies and mares, 1¹⁄₁₆ miles, dirt. Held January 24, 2001, with a gross value of $103,000. First held in 1991. Graded since 1994. Stakes record 1:44.74 (2001 De Bertie).

Year	Winner	Jockey	Second	Third	Strs	Final Time	1st Purse
2001	**De Bertie**, 4, 115	J. F. Chavez	Royal Fair, 5	Frankly My Dear, 5	8	**1:44.74**	$60,000
2000	**Brushed Halory**, 4, 115	M. E. Smith	Roza Robata, 5	Mop Squeezer, 5	5	1:41.84	$45,000
1999	**Timely Broad**, 5, 115	N. J. Petro	Highfalutin, 5	Mudslinger, 5	9	1:42.50	$45,000
1998	**Radiant Megan**, 5, 113	J. A. Krone	Escena, 5	Biding Time, 5	7	1:41.25	$45,000
1997	**Rare Blend**, 4, 120	J. D. Bailey	Golden Gale, 4	Termly, 4	7	1:41.28	$45,000
1996	**Lindsay Frolic**, 4, 117	P. Day	Investalot, 5	Queen Tutta, 5	8	1:43.70	$45,000
1995	**Recognizable**, 4, 115	M. E. Smith	Jade Flush, 4	Sambacarioca, 4	8	1:42.50	$45,000
1994	**Hunzinga**, 5, 113	J. E. Felix	Nine Keys, 4	Pleasant Jolie, 4	9	1:39.57	$45,000
1993	**Now Dance**, 4, 113	M. Guidry	Spinning Round, 4	Luv Me Luv Me Not, 4	10	1:41.68	$30,000
1992	**Lemhi Go**, 4, 113	R. N. Lester	Trumpet's Blare, 5	Tappanzee, 5	8	1:44.79	$45,000

1993-2000 1 mile 70 yards.

Safely Kept Stakes

Grade 3, Laurel Park, three-year-old fillies, 6 furlongs, dirt. Held November 18, 2000, with a gross value of $100,000. First held in 1988. Graded since 1990. Stakes record 1:09.21 (1999 Godmother).

Year	Winner	Jockey	Second	Third	Strs	Final Time	1st Purse
2000	**Swept Away**	J. Beasley	Another	Cat Cay	8	1:09.51	$60,000
1999	**Godmother**	M. G. Pino	Superduper Miss	Rills	7	**1:09.21**	$60,000
1998	**Hair Spray**	J. A. Velez Jr.	Expensive Issue	Ninth Inning	8	1:10.67	$66,390
1997	**Weather Vane**	M. G. Pino	Vegas Prospector	Requesting More	7	1:10.21	$64,800
1996	**J J'sdream**	M. G. Pino	Flat Fleet Feet	Rare Blend	5	1:09.45	$60,000
1995	**Broad Smile**	J. Brown	Scotzanna	Shebatim's Trick	7	1:10.30	$60,000
1994	**Twist Afleet**	D. Carr	Penny's Reshoot	Our Royal Blue	7	1:10.88	$60,000
1993	**Miss Indy Anna**	D. B. Thomas	Ann Dear	Lily of the North	7	1:10.12	$60,000
1992	**Meafara**	B. Swatuk	Squirm	Super Doer	6	1:10.55	$60,000

1992-'95 Columbia S. 1992-'96 held at Pimlico; 1997 Colonial Downs.

Salvator Mile Handicap

Grade 3, Monmouth Park, three-year-olds and up, 1 mile, dirt. Held August 5, 2001, with a gross value of $150,000. First held in 1948. Graded since 1973. Stakes record 1:34.46 (1991 Peanut Butter Onit).

Year	Winner	Jockey	Second	Third	Strs	Final Time	1st Purse
2001	**Sea of Tranquility**, 5, 115	J. C. Ferrer	Knock Again, 4	Hal's Hope, 4	7	1:36.74	$90,000
2000	**Leave It to Beezer**, 7, 120	R. Alvarado Jr.	Delaware Township, 4	Prime Directive, 4	5	1:37.29	$90,000
1999	**Truluck**, 4, 115	J. Bravo	Rock and Roll, 4	Siftaway, 4	6	1:35.18	$90,000
1998	**El Amante**, 5, 119	J. A. Krone	Stormin Fever, 4	Gold Token, 5	8	1:34.95	$60,000
1997	**Distorted Humor**, 4, 114	J. A. Krone	Wild Deputy, 4	Smooth the Loot, 4	4	1:36.03	$60,000
1996	**Smart Strike**, 4, 113	S. Hawley	Cozy Drive, 4	November Sunset, 4	10	1:36.28	$60,000
1995	**Schossberg**, 5, 116	D. Penna	Cast Iron, 4	Relentless Star, 5	9	1:35.86	$45,000
1994	**Storm Tower**, 4, 119	R. Wilson	Cold Digger, 7	Koluctoo Jimmy Al, 4	6	1:36.26	$45,000
1993	**Dusty Screen**, 5, 117	E. L. King Jr.	Count New York, 4	Root Boy, 5	8	1:35.86	$45,000
1992	**Peanut Butter Onit**, 6, 120	A. T. Gryder	Root Boy, 4	He Is Risen, 4	7	1:36.21	$45,000

San Antonio Handicap

Grade 2, Santa Anita Park, four-year-olds and up, 1¹⁄₈ miles, dirt. Held February 4, 2001, with a gross value of $300,000. First held in 1935. Graded since 1973. Stakes record 1:46.20 (1978 Vigors).

Year	Winner	Jockey	Second	Third	Strs	Final Time	1st Purse
2001	**Guided Tour**, 5, 115	L. Melancon	Lethal Instrument, 5	Moonlight Charger, 5	8	1:48.26	$180,000
2000	**Budroyale**, 7, 121	G. K. Gomez	Cat Thief, 4	Elaborate, 4	5	1:48.70	$180,000
1999	**Free House**, 5, 123	C. J. McCarron	Malek (Chi), 6	Dramatic Gold, 6	4	1:48.54	$180,000
1998	**Gentlemen (Arg)**, 6, 124	G. L. Stevens	Da Bull, 6	Refinado Tom (Arg), 6	5	1:47.60	$180,000
1997	**Gentlemen (Arg)**, 5, 122	G. L. Stevens	Alphabet Soup, 6	Kingdom Found, 6	5	1:47.38	$180,300
1996	**Alphabet Soup**, 5, 119	C. W. Antley	Soul of the Matter, 5	Dare and Go, 5	5	1:49.96	$184,900
1995	**Best Pal**, 7, 121	C. J. McCarron	Slew of Damascus, 7	Tossofthecoin, 7	10	1:47.43	$148,500

Year	Winner	Jockey	Second	Third	Strs	Final Time	1st Purse
1994	The Wicked North, 5, 116	K. J. Desormeaux	Region, 5	Hill Pass, 5	9	1:47.48	$155,500
1993	Marquetry, 6, 117	E. Delahoussaye	Sir Beaufort, 6	Reign Road, 6	6	1:48.96	$155,500
1992	Ibero (Arg), 5, 115	A. O. Solis	In Excess (Ire), 5	Cobra Classic, 5	8	1:47.05	$189,750

1994 Hill Pass finished second, DQ to third.

San Bernardino Handicap

Grade 2, Santa Anita Park, four-year-olds and up, 1⅛ miles, dirt. Held April 7, 2001, with a gross value of $150,000. First held in 1957. Graded since 1973. Stakes record 1:45.80 (1979 Star Spangled).

Year	Winner	Jockey	Second	Third	Strs	Final Time	1st Purse
2001	Futural, 5, 115	G. K. Gomez	Irisheyesareflying, 5	Tribunal, 5	5	1:47.87	$90,000
2000	Early Pioneer, 5, 113	M. S. Garcia	David, 4	General Challenge, 4	5	1:49.08	$95,490
1999	Classic Cat, 4, 122	G. L. Stevens	Budroyale, 6	Klinsman (Ire), 6	4	1:47.77	$90,000
1998	Budroyale, 5, 112	M. S. Garcia	Don't Blame Rio, 5	Bagshot, 5	10	1:48.48	$100,530
1997	Benchmark, 6, 114	C. J. McCarron	Kingdom Found, 7	Private Song, 7	7	1:48.26	$97,650
1996	Del Mar Dennis, 6, 118	K. J. Desormeaux	Just Java, 5	Regal Rowdy, 5	6	1:48.37	$96,650
1995	Del Mar Dennis, 5, 117	C. W. Antley	Wharf, 5	Stoller, 5	8	1:47.27	$130,000
1994	Del Mar Dennis, 4, 112	S. Gonzalez Jr.	Hill Pass, 5	Tinners Way, 5	8	1:48.36	$129,400
1993	Memo (Chi), 6, 114	P. Atkinson	Charmonnier, 5	Marquetry, 5	7	1:47.49	$125,800
1992	Another Review, 4, 114	K. J. Desormeaux	Defensive Play, 5	Loach, 5	11	1:47.33	$163,100

San Carlos Handicap

Grade 1, Santa Anita Park, four-year-olds and up, 7 furlongs, dirt. Held March 4, 2001, with a gross value of $150,000. First held in 1935. Graded since 1973. Stakes record 1:20.20 (1981 Flying Paster).

Year	Winner	Jockey	Second	Third	Strs	Final Time	1st Purse
2001	Kona Gold, 7, 125	A. O. Solis	Blade Prospector (Brz), 6	Grey Memo, 6	7	1:21.35	$90,000
2000	Son of a Pistol, 8, 117	G. K. Gomez	Kona Gold, 6	Old Topper, 6	6	1:22.11	$96,930
1999	Big Jag, 6, 118	J. Valdivia Jr.	Kona Gold, 5	Dramatic Gold, 5	5	1:21.18	$90,000
1998	Reality Road, 6, 116	C. J. McCarron	Gold Land, 7	Son of a Pistol, 7	10	1:21.62	$100,530
1997	Northern Afleet, 4, 117	C. J. McCarron	Hesabull, 4	High Stakes Player, 4	7	1:21.45	$97,700
1996	Kingdom Found, 6, 116	C. J. McCarron	Lakota Brave, 7	Lit de Justice, 7	8	1:22.23	$98,850
1995	Softshoe Sure Shot, 9, 113	A. O. Solis	Ferrara, 4	Subtle Trouble, 4	7	1:21.46	$91,600
1994	Cardmania, 8, 122	E. Delahoussaye	The Wicked North, 5	Portoferraio (Arg), 5	7	1:21.23	$63,900
1993	Sir Beaufort, 6, 120	C. J. McCarron	Cardmania, 7	Excavate, 7	6	1:22.22	$62,900
1992	Answer Do, 6, 120	G. L. Stevens	Individualist, 5	Media Plan, 5	7	1:21.23	$63,700

1992-2000 Grade 2.

San Clemente Handicap

Grade 2, Del Mar, three-year-old fillies, 1 mile, turf. Held July 29, 2001, with a gross value of $150,000. First held in 1950. Graded since 1994. Stakes record 1:34.88 (1991 Flawlessly; 2001 Reine de Romance [Ire]).

Year	Winner	Jockey	Second	Third	Strs	Final Time	1st Purse
2001	Reine de Romance (Ire), 116	E. Delahoussaye	Gabriellina Giof (GB)	La Vida Loca (Ire)	8	1:34.88	$90,000
2000	Uncharted Haven (GB), 116	A. O. Solis	Automated	Islay Mist (GB)	10	1:35.13	$90,000
1999	Sweet Ludy (Ire), 118	C. S. Nakatani	Caffe Latte (Ire)	Sweet Life	10	1:35.02	$90,000
1998	Sicy d'Alsace (Fr), 115	C. S. Nakatani	Miss Hot Salsa	Tranquility Lake	10	1:34.97	$67,500
1997	Famous Digger, 120	B. Blanc	Cozy Blues	Really Happy	5	1:36.00	$71,725
1996	True Flare, 116	C. S. Nakatani	Gastronomical	Najecam	10	1:35.59	$67,200
1995	Jewel Princess, 115	C. J. McCarron	Auriette (Ire)	Scratch Paper	6	1:36.12	$59,650
1994	Work the Crowd, 120	C. J. McCarron	Pharma	Dancing Mirage	6	1:36.07	$48,550
1993	Hollywood Wildcat, 120	E. Delahoussaye	Miami Sands (Ire)	Beal Street Blues	10	1:34.89	$49,950
1992	Golden Treat, 121	K. J. Desormeaux	Morriston Belle	Alysbelle	8	1:35.20	$49,350

San Diego Handicap

Grade 2, Del Mar, three-year-olds and up, 1¹⁄₁₆ miles, dirt. Held July 29, 2001, with a gross value of $250,000. First held in 1937. Graded since 1983. Stakes record 1:40.20 (1978 Vic's Magic).

Year	Winner	Jockey	Second	Third	Strs	Final Time	1st Purse
2001	Skimming, 5, 120	G. K. Gomez	Futural, 5	Captain Steve, 4	7	1:41.62	$150,000
2000	Skimming, 4, 112	G. K. Gomez	Prime Timber, 4	National Saint, 4	7	1:41.06	$150,000
1999	Mazel Trick, 4, 116	C. J. McCarron	River Keen (Ire), 7	Tibado, 5	4	1:40.68	$150,000
1998	Mud Route, 4, 117	C. J. McCarron	Hal's Pal (GB), 5	Benchmark, 7	5	1:41.11	$150,300
1997	Northern Afleet, 4, 118	C. J. McCarron	Benchmark, 6	New Century, 5	9	1:41.80	$100,300
1996	Savinio, 4, 116	C. W. Antley	Misnomer, 4	Nonproductiveasset, 6	6	1:40.82	$95,350
1995	Blumin Affair, 4, 116	C. J. McCarron	Rapan Boy (Aus), 7	Luthier Fever, 4	6	1:41.29	$87,200
1994	Kingdom Found, 4, 116	C. J. McCarron	Tossofthecoin, 4	Rapan Boy (Aus), 6	6	1:41.21	$75,850
1993	Fanatic Boy (Arg), 6, 115	C. J. McCarron	Memo (Chi), 6	Missionary Ridge (GB), 6	5	1:48.59	$74,450
1992	Another Review, 4, 120	L. A. Pincay Jr.	Claret (Ire), 4	Quintana, 4	6	1:47.00	$76,050

1992-2000 Grade 3. 1992-'93 1⅛ miles.

Sands Point Stakes

Not graded (originally scheduled as a Grade 3), Belmont Park, three-year-old fillies, 1⅛ miles, dirt (originally scheduled on the turf). Held June 17, 2001, with a gross value of $107,800. First held in 1995. Graded since 1998. Stakes record 1:46.65 (1997 Auntie Mame).

Year	Winner	Jockey	Second	Third	Strs	Final Time	1st Purse
2001	Tweedside	R. Migliore	Owsley	Platinum Tiara	4	1:50.43	$66,674
2000	Gaviola	J. D. Bailey	Shopping for Love	Millie's Quest	8	1:47.77	$66,780
1999	Perfect Sting	P. Day	Pico Teneriffe	Illiquidity	6	1:46.99	$65,160
1998	Recording	J. F. Chavez	Royal Ransom	Naskra's de Light	11	1:48.93	$69,600
1997	Auntie Mame	J. D. Bailey	Hoochie Coochie	Sagasious	8	1:46.65	$66,720
1996	Merit Wings	R. G. Davis	Unify	Turkappeal	10	1:45.83	$51,885
1995	Perfect Arc	J. R. Velazquez	Miss Union Avenue	Transient Trend	5	1:43.14	$49,395

1995-'97 Sands Point H. 1998-2000 Grade 3. 1995-'96 1¹⁄₁₆ miles. 1995-2000 turf.

San Felipe Stakes

Grade 2, Santa Anita Park, three-year-olds, 1¹⁄₁₆ miles, dirt. Held March 17, 2001, with a gross value of $250,000. First held in 1935. Graded since 1973. Stakes record 1:41.20 (1979 Pole Position).

Year	Winner	Jockey	Second	Third	Strs	Final Time	1st Purse
2001	Point Given	G. L. Stevens	I Love Silver	Jamaican Rum	8	1:41.94	$150,000
2000	Fusaichi Pegasus	K. J. Desormeaux	The Deputy (Ire)	Anees	7	1:42.66	$150,000
1999	Prime Timber	D. R. Flores	Exploit	High Wire Act	7	1:42.16	$150,000
1998	Artax	C. J. McCarron	Real Quiet	Prosperous Bid	5	1:41.73	$150,000
1997	Free House	D. R. Flores	Silver Charm	King Crimson	9	1:42.49	$152,400
1996	Odyle	C. S. Nakatani	Smithfield	Cavonnier	7	1:42.43	$152,400
1995	Afternoon Deelites	K. J. Desormeaux	Timber Country	Lake George	4	1:42.11	$117,200
1994	Soul of the Matter	K. J. Desormeaux	Brocco	Valiant Nature	5	1:44.68	$118,500
1993	Corby	C. J. McCarron	Personal Hope	Devoted Brass	6	1:42.11	$121,100
1992	Bertrando	A. O. Solis	Arp	Hickman Creek	6	1:42.76	$120,800

San Fernando Breeders' Cup Stakes

Grade 2, Santa Anita Park, four-year-olds, 1¹⁄₁₆ miles, dirt. Held January 13, 2001, with a gross value of $190,800. First held in 1952. Graded since 1973. Stakes record 1:40.80 (1955 *Poona II).

Year	Winner	Jockey	Second	Third	Strs	Final Time	1st Purse
2001	Tiznow	C. J. McCarron	Walkslikeaduck	Wooden Phone	6	1:42.05	$98,880
2000	Saint's Honor	K. J. Desormeaux	Cat Thief	Mr. Broad Blade	7	1:41.94	$190,200
1999	Dixie Dot Com	D. R. Flores	Event of the Year	Old Topper	8	1:41.06	$190,800
1998	Silver Charm	G. L. Stevens	Mud Route	Lord Grillo (Arg)	4	1:41.94	$125,520
1997	Northern Afleet	C. J. McCarron	Ambivalent	Ready to Order	9	1:48.59	$194,400
1996	Helmsman	C. J. McCarron	Gold and Steel (Fr)	The Key Rainbow (Ire)	9	1:48.87	$134,500
1995	Wekiva Springs	K. J. Desormeaux	Dramatic Gold	Dare and Go	7	1:48.59	$126,800
1994	Zignew	C. J. McCarron	Nonproductiveasset	Pleasant Tango	12	1:47.87	$135,400
1993	Bertrando	C. J. McCarron	Star Recruit	The Wicked North	8	1:51.22	$127,800
1992	Best Pal	K. J. Desormeaux	Olympio	Dinard	9	1:48.25	$130,000

1992-'96 San Fernando S. 1992-'97 1⅛ miles.

Sanford Stakes

Grade 2, Saratoga Race Course, two-year-olds, 6 furlongs, dirt. Held July 26, 2001, with a gross value of $107,800. First held in 1913. Graded since 1973. Stakes record 1:09.60 (1977 Affirmed).

Year	Winner	Jockey	Second	Third	Strs	Final Time	1st Purse
2001	Buster's Daydream	J. R. Velazquez	Seeking the Money	Heavyweight Champ	6	1:10.55	$64,680
2000	City Zip	J. A. Santos	Yonaguska	Scorpion	7	1:10.69	$65,220
1999	More Than Ready	J. R. Velazquez	Mighty	Bulling	5	1:09.65	$64,560
1998	Time Bandit	P. Day	Prime Directive	Texas Glitter	9	1:11.59	$66,480
1997	Polished Brass	P. Day	Double Honor	Jigadee	7	1:10.23	$65,520
1996	Kelly Kip	J-L. Samyn	Boston Harbor	Say Florida Sandy	8	1:10.31	$66,840
1995	Maria's Mon	R. G. Davis	Seeker's Reward	Frozen Ice	11	1:10.80	$68,340
1994	Montreal Red	J. A. Santos	Boone's Mill	De Niro	5	1:10.56	$64,620
1993	Dehere	C. J. McCarron	Prenup	Distinct Reality	6	1:10.48	$68,520
1992	Mountain Cat	P. Day	Satellite Signal	Rule Sixteen	10	1:10.62	$73,440

1992-'98 Grade 3. 1992 Thirty Two Slew finished second, DQ to fourth.

San Francisco Breeders' Cup Mile Handicap

Grade 2, Bay Meadows, three-year-olds and up, 1 mile, turf. Held April 28, 2001, with a gross value of $263,750. First held in 1948. Graded since 1987. Stakes record 1:33.40 (1980 Don Alberto).

Year	Winner	Jockey	Second	Third	Strs	Final Time	1st Purse
2001	Redattore (Brz), 6, 115	J. P. Lumpkins	Hawksley Hill (Ire), 8	Kerrygold (Fr), 8	9	1:35.14	$137,500
2000	Ladies Din, 5, 120	K. J. Desormeaux	Fighting Falcon, 4	Self Feeder (Ire), 4	10	1:35.46	$150,000
1999	†Tuzla (Fr), 5, 112	B. Blanc	Poteen, 5	Rob 'n Gin, 5	10	1:35.46	$180,000

Year	Winner	Jockey	Second	Third	Strs	Final Time	1st Purse
1998	Hawksley Hill (Ire), 5, 119	G. L. Stevens	Fantastic Fellow, 4	Uncaged Fury, 4	6	1:34.33	$120,000
1997	Wavy Run (Ire), 6, 116	B. Blanc	Savinio, 7	Romarin (Brz), 7	7	1:37.11	$120,000
1996	Gold and Steel (Fr), 4, 114	A. O. Solis	Savinio, 6	Debutant Trick, 6	7	1:35.07	$120,000
1995	Unfinished Symph, 4, 118	C. W. Antley	Vaudeville, 4	Torch Rouge (GB), 4	9	1:34.14	$110,000
1994	Gothland (Fr), 5, 115	C. S. Nakatani	Emerald Jig, 5	The Tender Track, 5	11	1:35.46	$110,000
1993	Norwich (GB), 6, 114	K. J. Desormeaux	Qathif, 6	Luthier Enchanteur, 6	8	1:35.57	$137,500
1992	Tight Spot, 5, 125	L. A. Pincay Jr.	Notorious Pleasure, 6	Forty Niner Days, 6	9	1:35.57	$110,000

1992-'98 San Francisco Mile H. 1992-'93 Grade 3. 1992-2000 held at Golden Gate Fields. † denotes female.

San Gabriel Handicap

Grade 2, Santa Anita Park, three-year-olds and up, 1⅛ miles, turf. Held December 30, 2001, with a gross value of $150,000. First held in 1935. Graded since 1973. Stakes record 1:46.20 (1989 Wretham).

Year	Winner	Jockey	Second	Third	Strs	Final Time	1st Purse
2001	Irish Prize, 5, 117	K. J. Desormeaux	Manndar (Ire), 5	Here Comes Big C, 5	8	1:47.88	$90,000
2000	Brave Act (GB), 6, 120	A. O. Solis	Native Desert, 7	Manndar (Ire), 7	6	1:49.25	$97,470
1998	Brave Act (GB), 4, 118	G. F. Almeida	Mash One (Chi), 4	Fabulous Guy (Ire), 4	8	1:46.78	$90,000
1997	Rainbow Blues (Ire), 4, 119	G. L. Stevens	River Deep, 6	Via Lombardia (Ire), 6	7	1:46.89	$81,500
	Martiniquais (Ire), 4, 116	C. S. Nakatani	Bienvenido (Arg), 4	Da Bull, 4	8	1:48.42	$99,180
1996	Romarin (Brz), 6, 119	C. S. Nakatani	Virginia Carnival, 4	Silver Wizard, 4	8	1:49.69	$82,050
1995	Romarin (Brz), 5, 119	C. S. Nakatani	Inner City (Ire), 6	Ianomami (Ire), 6	8	1:49.36	$62,900
1994	Earl of Barking (Ire), 4, 118	C. J. McCarron	Fanmore, 6	Navarone, 6	8	1:48.64	$65,300
1993	Star of Cozzene, 5, 118	G. L. Stevens	Bistro Garden, 5	Leger Cat (Arg), 5	9	1:48.33	$66,100
1992	Classic Fame, 6, 118	E. Delahoussaye	Super May, 6	Defensive Play, 6	6	1:46.69	$64,300

1992-'93 Grade 3. 1997 held in January and December; 1999 not held. 1997-'98 three-year-olds and up.

San Gorgonio Handicap

Grade 2, Santa Anita Park, four-year-olds and up, fillies and mares, 1⅛ miles, turf. Held January 15, 2001, with a gross value of $150,000. First held in 1968. Graded since 1983. Stakes record 1:46.40 (1983 Castilla; 1990 Invited Guest).

Year	Winner	Jockey	Second	Third	Strs	Final Time	1st Purse
2001	Uncharted Haven (GB), 4, 115	A. O. Solis	Brianda (Ire), 4	Beautiful Noise, 4	12	1:50.02	$90,000
2000	Lady At Peace, 4, 115	G. K. Gomez	Spanish Fern, 5	Riboletta (Brz), 5	5	1:48.75	$90,000
1999	See You Soon (Fr), 5, 117	K. J. Desormeaux	Sonja's Faith (Ire), 5	Verinha (Brz), 5	6	1:49.14	$90,000
1998	Golden Arches (Fr), 4, 120	C. J. McCarron	Ecoute, 5	Real Connection, 5	6	1:49.42	$96,870
1997	Sixieme Sens, 5, 116	C. S. Nakatani	Alpride (Ire), 6	Grafin, 6	9	1:47.16	$82,950
1996	Wandesta (GB), 5, 119	C. S. Nakatani	Matiara, 4	Yearly Tour, 4	6	1:49.13	$80,550
1995	Queens Court Queen, 6, 117	C. S. Nakatani	Wende, 5	Vinista, 5	5	1:48.70	$62,000
1994	Hero's Love, 6, 119	L. A. Pincay Jr.	Skimble, 5	Miss Turkana, 5	10	1:47.65	$66,800
1993	Southern Truce, 5, 114	C. S. Nakatani	Laura Ly (Arg), 7	Lite Light, 7	5	1:51.28	$67,100
1992	Paseana (Arg), 5, 118	C. J. McCarron	Laura Ly (Arg), 6	Reluctant Guest, 6	4	1:53.88	$77,250

1992-'93, 1995 dirt. 1998 Escabiosa (Arg) finished third, DQ to fourth.

San Juan Capistrano Invitational Handicap

Grade 1, Santa Anita Park, four-year-olds and up, about 1¾ miles, turf. Held April 14, 2001, with a gross value of $400,000. First held in 1935. Graded since 1973. Stakes record 2:42.96 (2001 Bienamado).

Year	Winner	Jockey	Second	Third	Strs	Final Time	1st Purse
2001	Bienamado, 5, 122	C. J. McCarron	Persianlux (GB), 5	Blueprint (Ire), 5	11	**2:42.96**	$240,000
2000	Sunshine Street, 5, 115	J. D. Bailey	Single Empire (Ire), 6	Chelsea Barracks (GB), 6	5	2:49.06	$240,000
1999	Single Empire (Ire), 5, 118	K. J. Desormeaux	Le Paillard (Ire), 5	Lucayan Indian (Ire), 5	9	2:45.93	$240,000
1998	Amerique, 4, 116	E. Delahoussaye	Star Performance, 5	Kessem Power (NZ), 5	10	2:47.08	$240,000
1997	Marlin, 4, 119	E. Delahoussaye	(DH) African Dancer, 5 (DH) Sunshack (GB), 6	Awad, 5	7	2:44.56	$240,000
1996	Raintrap (GB), 6, 115	A. O. Solis	†Windsharp, 5	Awad, 5	7	2:48.40	$240,000
1995	Red Bishop, 7, 119	M. E. Smith	Special Price, 6	Liyoun (Ire), 6	8	2:48.02	$220,000
1994	Bien Bien, 5, 122	C. J. McCarron	Grand Flotilla, 5	Alex the Great (GB), 7	9	2:46.69	$220,000
1993	Kotashaan (Fr), 5, 121	K. J. Desormeaux	Bien Bien, 4	Fraise, 4	5	2:45.00	$220,000
1992	Fly Till Dawn, 6, 121	P. A. Valenzuela	†Miss Alleged, 5	Wall Street Dancer, 5	9	2:46.53	$275,000

1993, 2001 new course record. 1997 dead heat for second. † denotes female.

San Luis Obispo Handicap

Grade 2, Santa Anita Park, four-year-olds and up, 1½ miles, turf. Held February 17, 2001, with a gross value of $200,000. First held in 1952. Graded since 1973. Stakes record 2:23.80 (1974 Captain Cee Jay).

Year	Winner	Jockey	Second	Third	Strs	Final Time	1st Purse
2001	Persianlux (GB), 5, 113	T. Baze	Devon Deputy, 5	Falcon Flight (Fr), 5	10	2:27.70	$120,000
2000	Dark Moondancer (GB), 5, 120	C. J. McCarron	The Fly (GB), 6	Casino King (Ire), 6	5	2:39.61	$120,000
1999	Kessem Power (NZ), 7, 115	G. L. Stevens	Brave Act (GB), 5	Lazy Lode (Arg), 5	7	2:28.02	$120,000
1998	Bienvenido (Arg), 5, 115	C. J. McCarron	Prize Giving (GB), 5	Callisthene (Fr), 5	6	2:29.34	$120,000

Year	Winner	Jockey	Second	Third	Strs	Final Time	1st Purse
1997	**Shanawi (Ire)**, 5, 111	B. Blanc	Rainbow Dancer (Fr), 6	Bon Point (GB), 6	7	2:24.51	$132,100
1996	†**Windsharp**, 5, 115	E. Delahoussaye	†Wandesta (GB), 5	Virginia Carnival, 5	6	2:30.33	$130,800
1995	**Square Cut**, 6, 114	C. W. Antley	Ianomami (Ire), 5	River Rhythm, 5	10	2:26.04	$133,200
1994	**Fanmore**, 6, 116	K. J. Desormeaux	Bien Bien, 5	Navire (Fr), 5	9	2:27.03	$131,400
1993	**Kotashaan (Fr)**, 5, 114	K. J. Desormeaux	Carnival Baby, 5	The Name's Jimmy, 5	8	2:27.64	$129,600
1992	**Quest for Fame (GB)**, 5, 121	G. L. Stevens	Cool Gold Mood, 5	†Miss Alleged, 5	9	2:28.79	$158,500

† denotes female.

San Luis Rey Handicap

Grade 2, Santa Anita Park, four-year-olds and up, 1½ miles, turf. Held March 11, 2001, with a gross value of $250,000. First held in 1952. Graded since 1973. Stakes record 2:23 (1970 Fiddle Isle; 1980 John Henry).

Year	Winner	Jockey	Second	Third	Strs	Final Time	1st Purse
2001	**Blueprint (Ire)**, 6, 116	G. L. Stevens	Devon Deputy, 5	Kerrygold (Fr), 5	8	2:28.57	$150,000
2000	**Dark Moondancer (GB)**, 5, 122	C. J. McCarron	Single Empire (Ire), 6	Bonapartiste (Fr), 6	6	2:26.00	$150,000
1999	**Single Empire (Ire)**, 5, 122	K. J. Desormeaux	Kessem Power (NZ), 7	Alvo Certo (Brz), 7	7	2:27.97	$150,000
1998	**Kessem Power (NZ)**, 6, 122	L. Dettori	Storm Trooper, 5	Star Performance, 5	12	2:28.40	$150,000
1997	**Marlin**, 4, 122	C. J. McCarron	Sunshack (GB), 5	Peckinpah's Soul (Fr), 6	10	2:28.14	$166,660
1996	†**Windsharp**, 5, 117	E. Delahoussaye	†Wandesta (GB), 5	Silver Wizard, 5	7	2:27.91	$161,900
1995	**Sandpit (Brz)**, 6, 124	C. S. Nakatani	River Rhythm, 8	Square Cut, 8	7	2:27.15	$155,000
1994	**Bien Bien**, 5, 124	C. J. McCarron	Navire (Fr), 5	Grand Flotilla, 5	5	2:26.65	$149,500
1993	**Kotashaan (Fr)**, 5, 124	K. J. Desormeaux	Bien Bien, 4	Fast Cure, 4	4	2:23.91	$148,250
1992	**Fly Till Dawn**, 6, 124	L. A. Pincay Jr.	Provins, 4	Quest for Fame (GB), 4	6	2:27.26	$179,000

1992-2000 San Luis Rey S. 1992-'96 Grade 1. † denotes female.

San Marcos Stakes

Grade 2, Santa Anita Park, four-year-olds and up, 1¼ miles, turf. Held January 20, 2001, with a gross value of $150,000. First held in 1952. Graded since 1973. Stakes record 1:58.02 (1992 Classic Fame).

Year	Winner	Jockey	Second	Third	Strs	Final Time	1st Purse
2001	**Bienamado**, 5	C. J. McCarron	Kerrygold (Fr), 5	Northern Quest (Fr), 5	7	2:02.75	$90,000
2000	**Public Purse**, 6	A. O. Solis	Dark Moondancer (GB), 5	The Fly (GB), 5	7	1:59.58	$98,280
1999	**Brave Act (GB)**, 5	G. F. Almeida	Ferrari (Ger), 5	Native Desert, 5	7	2:04.25	$90,000
1998	**Prize Giving (GB)**, 5	A. O. Solis	Bienvenido (Arg), 5	Martiniquais (Ire), 5	6	2:04.41	$97,380
1997	**Sandpit (Brz)**, 8	C. S. Nakatani	River Deep, 6	Shanawi (Ire), 5	8	2:00.61	$99,000
1996	**Urgent Request (Ire)**, 6	C. W. Antley	Bon Point (GB), 6	Virginia Carnival, 6	6	2:02.26	$97,000
1995	**River Flyer**, 4	C. W. Antley	Silver Wizard, 4	Savinio, 5	7	2:05.61	$92,200
1994	**Bien Bien**, 5	L. A. Pincay Jr.	Explosive Red, 4	Myrakalu (Fr), 4	6	2:00.55	$75,850
1993	**Star of Cozzene**, 5	G. L. Stevens	Kotashaan (Fr), 5	Carnival Baby, 5	7	2:01.71	$77,650
1992	**Classic Fame**, 6	E. Delahoussaye	Fly Till Dawn, 6	French Seventyfive, 6	6	**1:58.02**	$90,600

1992-2000 San Marcos H. 1992 Grade 3. 1996 dirt.

San Miguel Stakes

Grade 3, Santa Anita Park, three-year-olds, 6 furlongs, dirt. Held January 13, 2001, with a gross value of $107,500. First held in 1956. Graded since 1999. Stakes record 1:08.22 (1991 Prince Wild).

Year	Winner	Jockey	Second	Third	Strs	Final Time	1st Purse
2001	**Lasersport**	C. S. Nakatani	Early Flyer	Bills Paid	6	1:08.60	$64,500
2000	**Swept Overboard**	E. Delahoussaye	Forest Camp	Joopy Doopy	6	1:08.99	$64,320
1999	**Cape Canaveral**	D. R. Flores	Aristotle	Actin Time	4	1:09.15	$62,760
1998	**Rio Oro**	D. A. Lozoya	Iron Cat	Cat Doctor	9	1:08.60	$66,180
1997	**Thisnearlywasmine**	C. J. McCarron	Smokin Mel	Renteria	6	1:08.55	$64,350
1996	**Honour and Glory**	G. L. Stevens	Afleetaffair	Valid Expectations	6	1:08.93	$64,350
1995	**Petionville**	C. W. Antley	Regal Fighter	Cold n Calculating	4	1:09.16	$45,225
1994	**Mr. Cooperative**	M. A. Pedroza	Subtle Trouble	Ramblin Guy	8	1:09.53	$48,300
1993	**Denmars Dream**	A. O. Solis	Altazarr	Boss Soss	7	1:08.76	$47,475

1992 not held. 1993-'98 not graded.

San Pasqual Handicap

Grade 2, Santa Anita Park, four-year-olds and up, 1¹⁄₁₆ miles, dirt. Held January 7, 2001, with a gross value of $200,000. First held in 1935. Graded since 1973. Stakes record 1:40.20 (1978 Ancient Title; 1980 Valdez).

Year	Winner	Jockey	Second	Third	Strs	Final Time	1st Purse
2001	**Freedom Crest**, 5, 116	G. L. Stevens	Bosque Redondo, 4	Sultry Substitute, 4	8	1:41.94	$120,000
2000	**Dixie Dot Com**, 5, 118	P. A. Valenzuela	Budroyale, 7	Six Below, 7	6	1:40.95	$120,000
1999	**Silver Charm**, 5, 125	G. L. Stevens	Malek (Chi), 6	Crafty Friend, 6	5	1:41.78	$120,000
1998	**Hal's Pal (GB)**, 5, 113	B. Blanc	Malek (Chi), 5	Flick (GB), 5	9	1:41.89	$120,000
1997	**Kingdom Found**, 7, 115	G. L. Stevens	Savinio, 7	Eltish, 7	4	1:40.74	$122,200
1996	**Alphabet Soup**, 5, 118	C. W. Antley	Luthier Fever, 5	Cezind, 5	8	1:41.66	$130,100
1995	**Del Mar Dennis**, 5, 118	A. O. Solis	Slew of Damascus, 7	Tossofthecoin, 7	6	1:41.23	$116,100
1994	**Hill Pass**, 5, 113	C. J. McCarron	Best Pal, 6	Lottery Winner, 6	7	1:41.00	$87,800
1993	**Jovial (GB)**, 6, 115	M. Walls	Marquetry, 6	Provins, 6	7	1:41.94	$91,400
1992	**Twilight Agenda**, 6, 125	K. J. Desormeaux	Ibero (Arg), 5	Answer Do, 5	5	1:42.32	$89,000

1993 Best Pal finished second, DQ to fifth.

San Rafael Stakes

Grade 2, Santa Anita Park, three-year-olds, 1 mile, dirt. Held March 3, 2001, with a gross value of $200,000. First held in 1975. Graded since 1983. Stakes record 1:34.40 (1982 Prince Spellbound).

Year	Winner	Jockey	Second	Third	Strs	Final Time	1st Purse
2001	Crafty C. T.	E. Delahoussaye	Palmeiro	Early Flyer	9	1:35.79	$120,000
2000	War Chant	K. J. Desormeaux	Archer City Slew	Cocky	6	1:36.45	$120,000
1999	Desert Hero	C. S. Nakatani	Prime Timber	Capsized	9	1:36.45	$120,000
1998	Orville N Wilbur's	C. S. Nakatani	Souvenir Copy	Futuristic	6	1:35.96	$120,000
1997	Funontherun	G. F. Almeida	Inexcessivelygood	Hello (Ire)	10	1:36.01	$121,800
1996	Honour and Glory	G. L. Stevens	Halo Sunshine	Matty G	8	1:36.45	$122,000
1995	Larry the Legend	K. J. Desormeaux	Fandarel Dancer	Timber Country	5	1:37.61	$88,600
1994	Tabasco Cat	P. Day	Powis Castle	Shepherd's Field	5	1:36.39	$89,700
1993	Devoted Brass	K. J. Desormeaux	Union City	Stuka	6	1:35.13	$90,000
1992	A.P. Indy	E. Delahoussaye	Treekster	Prince Wild	6	1:35.41	$90,300

San Simeon Handicap

Grade 3, Santa Anita Park, four-year-olds and up, about 6½ furlongs, turf. Held April 16, 2001, with a gross value of $133,625. First held in 1968. Graded since 1973. Stakes record 1:12.20 (1990 Coastal Voyage).

Year	Winner	Jockey	Second	Third	Strs	Final Time	1st Purse
2001	Lake William, 5, 114	V. Espinoza	Macward, 5	Touch of the Blues (Fr), 5	6	1:12.34	$80,175
2000	El Cielo, 6, 117	J. Valdivia Jr.	King Slayer (GB), 5	Scooter Brown, 5	6	1:12.66	$79,440
1999	Naninja, 6, 115	C. J. McCarron	Expressionist, 4	Indian Rocket (GB), 4	7	1:13.32	$65,220
1998	Labeeb (GB), 6, 120	K. J. Desormeaux	Surachai, 5	Captain Collins (Ire), 5	11	1:12.94	$67,860
1997	Sandtrap, 4, 117	A. O. Solis	Daggett Peak, 6	Tychonic (GB), 6	6	1:12.50	$96,850
1996	†Ski Dancer, 4, 114	G. L. Stevens	Daggett Peak, 5	Boulderdash Bay, 5	6	1:13.98	$64,200
1995	Finder's Fortune, 6, 117	P. A. Valenzuela	Rotsaluck, 4	Pembroke, 4	7	1:13.65	$64,550
1994	Rapan Boy (Aus), 6, 114	G. L. Stevens	The Berkeley Man, 4	Artistic Reef (GB), 4	7	1:13.16	$63,100
1993	Exemplary Leader, 7, 113	M. A. Pedroza	Prince Ferdinand (GB), 4	Wild Harmony, 4	8	1:13.98	$64,300
1992	†Heart of Joy, 5, 119	C. J. McCarron	Regal Groom, 5	Time Gentlemen (GB), 5	10	1:12.94	$69,600

1997 Destiny's Venture finished second, DQ to fourth. † denotes female.

Santa Ana Handicap

Grade 2, Santa Anita Park, four-year-olds and up, fillies and mares, 1⅛ miles, turf. Held March 18, 2001, with a gross value of $150,000. First held in 1968. Graded since 1981. Stakes record 1:46.23 (1993 Exchange).

Year	Winner	Jockey	Second	Third	Strs	Final Time	1st Purse
2001	Beautiful Noise, 5, 115	C. J. McCarron	High Walden, 4	Matiere Grise (Fr), 4	12	1:47.27	$90,000
2000	Spanish Fern, 5, 119	V. Espinoza	Virginie (Brz), 6	Country Garden (GB), 6	7	1:49.30	$97,830
1999	See You Soon (Fr), 5, 119	K. J. Desormeaux	Blending Element (Ire), 6	La Madame (Chi), 6	6	1:49.46	$90,000
1998	Fiji (GB), 4, 115	K. J. Desormeaux	Shake the Yoke (GB), 5	Golden Arches (Fr), 5	6	1:49.85	$96,480
1997	Windsharp, 6, 121	E. Delahoussaye	Wheatly Special, 4	Donna Viola (GB), 4	7	1:49.47	$97,750
1996	Pharma, 5, 116	C. J. McCarron	Angel in My Heart (Fr), 4	Matiara, 4	5	1:49.14	$95,650
1995	Wandesta (GB), 4, 115	C. S. Nakatani	Yearly Tour, 4	Aube Indienne (Fr), 4	7	1:50.18	$90,700
1994	Possibly Perfect, 4, 119	K. J. Desormeaux	Hero's Love, 6	Lady Blessington (Fr), 6	7	1:51.05	$91,000
1993	Exchange, 5, 120	L. A. Pincay Jr.	Party Cited, 4	Villandry, 4	5	1:46.23	$89,700
1992	Gravieres (Fr), 4, 116	G. L. Stevens	Appealing Missy, 5	Explosive Ele, 5	7	1:47.75	$94,900

1992-'96 Grade 1. 1994 Waitryst (NZ) finished third, DQ to seventh.

Santa Anita Derby

Grade 1, Santa Anita Park, three-year-olds, 1⅛ miles, dirt. Held April 7, 2001, with a gross value of $750,000. First held in 1935. Graded since 1973. Stakes record 1:47 (1965 Lucky Debonair; 1973 Sham; 1998 Indian Charlie).

Year	Winner	Jockey	Second	Third	Strs	Final Time	1st Purse
2001	Point Given	G. L. Stevens	Crafty C. T.	I Love Silver	6	1:47.77	$450,000
2000	The Deputy (Ire)	C. J. McCarron	War Chant	Captain Steve	6	1:49.08	$600,000
1999	General Challenge	G. L. Stevens	Prime Timber	Desert Hero	8	1:48.92	$450,000
1998	Indian Charlie	G. L. Stevens	Real Quiet	Artax	7	1:47.00	$450,000
1997	Free House	K. J. Desormeaux	Silver Charm	Hello (Ire)	10	1:47.60	$450,000
1996	Cavonnier	C. J. McCarron	Honour and Glory	Corker	8	1:48.81	$600,000
1995	Larry the Legend	G. L. Stevens	Afternoon Deelites	Jumron (GB)	8	1:47.99	$385,000
1994	Brocco	G. L. Stevens	Tabasco Cat	Strodes Creek	6	1:48.33	$275,000
1993	Personal Hope	G. L. Stevens	Union City	†Eliza	7	1:49.03	$275,000
1992	A.P. Indy	E. Delahoussaye	Bertrando	Casual Lies	7	1:49.25	$275,000

1996 Alyrob finished second, DQ to eighth. † denotes female.

Santa Anita Handicap

Grade 1, Santa Anita Park, four-year-olds and up, 1¼ miles, dirt. Held March 3, 2001, with a gross value of $1,000,000. First held in 1935. Graded since 1973. Stakes record 1:58.60 (1979 Affirmed).

Year	Winner	Jockey	Second	Third	Strs	Final Time	1st Purse
2001	Tiznow, 4, 122	C. J. McCarron	Wooden Phone, 4	Tribunal, 4	12	2:01.55	$600,000
2000	General Challenge, 4, 121	C. S. Nakatani	Budroyale, 7	Puerto Madero (Chi), 7	8	2:01.49	$600,000

Year	Winner	Jockey	Second	Third	Strs	Final Time	1st Purse
1999	**Free House**, 5, 123	C. J. McCarron	Event of the Year, 4	Silver Charm, 4	6	2:00.67	$600,000
1998	**Malek (Chi)**, 5, 115	A. O. Solis	Bagshot, 4	Don't Blame Rio, 4	4	2:02.26	$600,000
1997	**Siphon (Brz)**, 6, 120	D. R. Flores	Sandpit (Brz), 8	Gentlemen (Arg), 8	11	2:00.23	$600,000
1996	**Mr Purple**, 4, 116	E. Delahoussaye	Luthier Fever, 5	Just Java, 5	11	2:02.04	$600,000
1995	**Urgent Request (Ire)**, 5, 116	G. L. Stevens	Best Pal, 7	Dare and Go, 7	10	1:59.25	$550,000
1994	**Stuka**, 4, 115	C. W. Antley	Bien Bien, 5	Myrakalu (Fr), 5	8	2:00.17	$550,000
1993	**Sir Beaufort**, 6, 119	P. A. Valenzuela	Star Recruit, 4	Major Impact, 4	11	2:00.55	$550,000
1992	**Best Pal**, 4, 124	K. J. Desormeaux	Twilight Agenda, 6	Defensive Play, 6	7	1:59.08	$550,000

1994 The Wicked North finished first, DQ to fourth.

Santa Anita Oaks

Grade 1, Santa Anita Park, three-year-old fillies, 1¹⁄₁₆ miles, dirt. Held March 10, 2001, with a gross value of $300,000. First held in 1935. Graded since 1973. Stakes record 1:41.20 (1980 Bold 'n Determined).

Year	Winner	Jockey	Second	Third	Strs	Final Time	1st Purse
2001	**Golden Ballet**	C. J. McCarron	Flute	Affluent	8	1:41.83	$180,000
2000	**Surfside**	P. Day	Kumari Continent	Classy Cara	5	1:44.03	$180,000
1999	**Excellent Meeting**	K. J. Desormeaux	Tout Charmant	Gleefully	6	1:43.26	$150,000
1998	**Hedonist**	K. J. Desormeaux	Keeper Hill	Nijinsky's Passion	7	1:44.14	$150,000
1997	**Sharp Cat**	C. S. Nakatani	Queen of Money	Double Park (Fr)	5	1:42.22	$128,800
1996	**Antespend**	C. W. Antley	Cara Rafaela	Hidden Lake	5	1:43.04	$128,600
1995	**Serena's Song**	C. S. Nakatani	Urbane	Mari's Sheba	5	1:42.71	$121,600
1994	**Lakeway**	K. J. Desormeaux	Dianes Halo	Flying in the Lane	6	1:41.66	$122,800
1993	**Eliza**	P. A. Valenzuela	Stalcreek	Dance for Vanny	9	1:42.97	$129,200
1992	**Golden Treat**	K. J. Desormeaux	Magical Maiden	Queens Court Queen	8	1:43.20	$129,300

Santa Barbara Handicap

Grade 2, Santa Anita Park, four-year-olds and up, fillies and mares, 1¼ miles, turf. Held April 14, 2001, with a gross value of $250,000. First held in 1935. Graded since 1973. Stakes record 1:57.50 (1991 Bequest).

Year	Winner	Jockey	Second	Third	Strs	Final Time	1st Purse
2001	**Astra**, 5, 118	K. J. Desormeaux	Beautiful Noise, 5	Uncharted Haven (GB), 5	7	2:01.33	$150,000
2000	**Caffe Latte (Ire)**, 4, 116	C. S. Nakatani	Happyanunoit (NZ), 5	Country Garden (GB), 5	6	2:00.51	$150,000
1999	**Tranquility Lake**, 4, 116	E. Delahoussaye	Virginie (Brz), 5	Midnight Line, 5	7	2:01.06	$150,000
1998	**Fiji (GB)**, 4, 119	K. J. Desormeaux	Pomona (GB), 5	Ecoute, 5	5	2:00.35	$150,000
1997	**Donna Viola (GB)**, 5, 120	G. L. Stevens	Fanjica (Ire), 5	Windsharp, 5	8	1:59.85	$197,200
1996	**Auriette (Ire)**, 4, 116	K. J. Desormeaux	Angel in My Heart (Fr), 4	Wandesta (GB), 4	5	2:02.10	$190,900
1995	**Wandesta (GB)**, 4, 118	C. S. Nakatani	Yearly Tour, 4	Morgana, 4	7	2:01.77	$126,400
1994	**Possibly Perfect**, 4, 121	K. J. Desormeaux	Pracer, 4	Waitryst (NZ), 4	5	2:00.56	$122,800
1993	**Exchange**, 5, 121	L. A. Pincay Jr.	Trishyde, 4	Revasser, 4	4	2:02.26	$120,400
1992	**Kostroma (Ire)**, 6, 121	K. J. Desormeaux	Miss Alleged, 5	Free At Last (GB), 5	4	1:59.63	$152,700

1992-'95 Grade 1.

Santa Catalina Stakes

Grade 2, Santa Anita Park, three-year-olds, 1¹⁄₁₆ miles, dirt. Held January 21, 2001, with a gross value of $107,700. First held in 1935. Graded since 1998. Stakes record 1:41.40 (1981 Stancharry).

Year	Winner	Jockey	Second	Third	Strs	Final Time	1st Purse
2001	**Millennium Wind**	C. J. McCarron	Palmeiro	Denied	6	1:42.38	$64,620
2000	**The Deputy (Ire)**	C. J. McCarron	High Yield	Captain Steve	6	1:43.04	$64,380
1999	**General Challenge**	G. L. Stevens	Buck Trout	Brilliantly	5	1:42.93	$63,900
1998	**Artax**	C. J. McCarron	Souvenir Copy	Allen's Oop	6	1:42.32	$64,320
1997	**Hello (Ire)**	C. J. McCarron	Bagshot	Carmen's Baby	8	1:42.60	$65,950
1996	**Prince of Thieves**	G. L. Stevens	Smithfield	Matty G	6	1:42.94	$64,250
1995	**Larry the Legend**	K. J. Desormeaux	In Character (GB)	Awesome Thought	5	1:42.93	$45,975
1994	**Wekiva Springs**	K. J. Desormeaux	Gracious Ghost	Dream Trapp	5	1:41.94	$45,900
1993	**Art of Living**	G. L. Stevens	Tossofthecoin	Glowing Crown	5	1:43.48	$45,900
1992	**Vying Victor**	C. A. Black	Turbulent Kris	Al Sabin	11	1:44.33	$51,000

1997 Santa Catalina H. 1998 Grade 3.

Santa Margarita Invitational Handicap

Grade 1, Santa Anita Park, four-year-olds and up, fillies and mares, 1⅛ miles, dirt. Held March 10, 2001, with a gross value of $300,000. First held in 1935. Graded since 1973. Stakes record 1:47 (1954 Cerise Reine; 1986 Lady's Secret).

Year	Winner	Jockey	Second	Third	Strs	Final Time	1st Purse
2001	**Lazy Slusan**, 6, 116	D. R. Flores	Spain, 4	Critikola (Arg), 4	7	1:48.59	$180,000
2000	**Riboletta (Brz)**, 5, 115	C. S. Nakatani	Bordelaise (Arg), 5	Snowberg, 5	5	1:50.40	$180,000
1999	**Manistique**, 4, 122	G. L. Stevens	Magical Allure, 4	India Divina (Chi), 4	4	1:48.31	$180,000
1998	**Toda Una Dama (Arg)**, 5, 114	G. F. Almeida	Exotic Wood, 6	Praviana (Chi), 6	10	1:48.87	$180,000

Year	Winner	Jockey	Second	Third	Strs	Final Time	1st Purse
1997	Jewel Princess, 5, 125	C. S. Nakatani	Top Rung, 6	Hidden Lake, 6	6	1:49.30	$180,000
1996	Twice the Vice, 5, 117	C. J. McCarron	Sleep Easy, 4	Jewel Princess, 4	8	1:49.53	$180,000
1995	Queens Court Queen, 6, 120	C. S. Nakatani	Paseana (Arg), 8	Klassy Kim, 8	5	1:48.81	$180,000
1994	Paseana (Arg), 7, 123	C. J. McCarron	Kalita Melody (GB), 6	Stalcreek, 6	9	1:49.12	$180,000
1993	Southern Truce, 5, 115	C. S. Nakatani	Paseana (Arg), 6	Guiza, 6	9	1:49.46	$180,000
1992	Paseana (Arg), 5, 122	C. J. McCarron	Laramie Moon (Arg), 5	Colour Chart, 5	5	1:47.48	$180,000

1999 Santa Margarita H.

Santa Maria Handicap

Grade 1, Santa Anita Park, four-year-olds and up, fillies and mares, 1 1/16 miles, dirt. Held February 18, 2001, with a gross value of $200,000. First held in 1934. Graded since 1973. Stakes record 1:40.95 (1998 Exotic Wood).

Year	Winner	Jockey	Second	Third	Strs	Final Time	1st Purse
2001	Lovellon (Arg), 5, 116	G. L. Stevens	Feverish, 6	Critikola (Arg), 6	5	1:43.37	$120,000
2000	Manistique, 5, 125	C. S. Nakatani	Snowberg, 5	Gourmet Girl, 5	8	1:42.60	$120,000
1999	India Divina (Chi), 5, 114	G. K. Gomez	Victory Stripes (Arg), 5	Belle's Flag, 5	5	1:42.71	$120,000
1998	Exotic Wood, 6, 121	C. J. McCarron	Toda Una Dama (Arg), 5	Tuxedo Junction, 5	5	1:40.95	$120,000
1997	Jewel Princess, 5, 123	C. S. Nakatani	Cat's Cradle, 5	Top Rung, 5	7	1:41.72	$97,900
1996	Serena's Song, 4, 124	G. L. Stevens	Twice the Vice, 5	Real Connection, 5	5	1:42.21	$95,800
1995	Queens Court Queen, 6, 118	C. S. Nakatani	Paseana (Arg), 8	Key Phrase, 8	5	1:41:61	$89,300
1994	Supah Gem, 4, 116	C. S. Nakatani	Paseana (Arg), 7	Alysbelle, 7	7	1:41.83	$90,700
1993	Race the Wild Wind, 4, 117	K. J. Desormeaux	Paseana (Arg), 6	Southern Truce, 6	5	1:41.27	$90,500
1992	Paseana (Arg), 5, 120	C. J. McCarron	Colour Chart, 5	Campagnarde (Arg), 5	5	1:41.94	$89,100

Santa Monica Handicap

Grade 1, Santa Anita Park, four-year-olds and up, fillies and mares, 7 furlongs, dirt. Held January 27, 2001, with a gross value of $200,000. First held in 1957. Graded since 1973. Stakes record 1:20.60 (1982 Past Forgetting).

Year	Winner	Jockey	Second	Third	Strs	Final Time	1st Purse
2001	Nany's Sweep, 5, 117	K. J. Desormeaux	Serenita (Arg), 4	Surfside, 4	7	1:22.50	$120,000
2000	Honest Lady, 4, 114	C. S. Nakatani	Kalookan Queen, 4	Enjoy the Moment, 4	9	1:21.45	$132,840
1999	Stop Traffic, 5, 120	C. A. Black	Belle's Flag, 6	Closed Escrow, 6	8	1:22.17	$120,000
1998	Exotic Wood, 6, 121	C. J. McCarron	Madame Pandit, 5	Advancing Star, 5	8	1:21.07	$120,000
1997	Toga Toga Toga, 5, 114	J. A. Garcia	Ski Dancer, 5	Grab the Prize, 5	6	1:23.27	$96,750
1996	Serena's Song, 4, 123	G. L. Stevens	Exotic Wood, 4	Klassy Kim, 4	6	1:21.56	$96,800
1995	Key Phrase, 4, 116	C. W. Antley	Flying in the Lane, 4	Desert Stormer, 4	6	1:22.82	$93,100
1994	Southern Truce, 6, 116	G. L. Stevens	Arches of Gold, 5	Mamselle Bebette, 5	9	1:21.44	$93,100
1993	Freedom Cry, 5, 114	A. O. Solis	Devil's Orchid, 6	Mama Simba, 6	7	1:21.78	$91,200
1992	Laramie Moon (Arg), 5, 116	E. Delahoussaye	D'Or Ruckus, 4	Ifyoucouldseemenow, 4	10	1:22.66	$94,700

Santa Ynez Stakes

Grade 2, Santa Anita Park, three-year-old fillies, 7 furlongs, dirt. Held January 20, 2001, with a gross value of $150,000. First held in 1952. Graded since 1973. Stakes record 1:21.20 (1979 Terlingua).

Year	Winner	Jockey	Second	Third	Strs	Final Time	1st Purse
2001	Golden Ballet	C. J. McCarron	Affluent	Warren's Whistle	9	1:22.30	$90,000
2000	Penny Blues	E. Delahoussaye	Classic Olympio	Mean Imogene	5	1:23.38	$63,600
1999	Honest Lady	K. J. Desormeaux	Rayelle	Controlled	4	1:21.67	$63,240
1998	Nijinsky's Passion	C. A. Black	Well Chosen	Vivid Angel	7	1:23.15	$64,980
1997	Queen of Money	D. R. Flores	Goodnight Irene	High Heeled Hope	8	1:22.55	$65,650
1996	Raw Gold	C. W. Antley	Pareja	Hidden Lake	6	1:22.66	$64,550
1995	Serena's Song	C. S. Nakatani	Cat's Cradle	Call Now	5	1:21.45	$59,800
1994	Tricky Code	C. S. Nakatani	Fancy 'n Fabulous	Sophisticatedcielo	6	1:22.16	$59,575
1993	Fit to Lead	C. S. Nakatani	Nijivision	Booklore	8	1:22.55	$62,500
1992	Looie Capote	K. J. Desormeaux	Icy Eyes	Soviet Sojourn	7	1:23.42	$61,450

1992-'95 Santa Ynez Breeders' Cup S. 1995-'98 Grade 3.

Santa Ysabel Stakes

Grade 3, Santa Anita Park, three-year-old fillies, 1 1/16 miles, dirt. Held January 6, 2001, with a gross value of $109,300. First run in 1968. Graded since 1998. Stakes record 1:41.34 (1997 Sharp Cat).

Year	Winner	Jockey	Second	Third	Strs	Final Time	1st Purse
2001	Collect Call	A. O. Solis	Irguns Angel	Eminent	8	1:44.69	$65,580
2000	Surfside	P. Day	Rings a Chime	She's Classy	4	1:43.53	$62,880
1999	Holywood Picture	O. Vergara	Exbourne Free	Gleefully	7	1:43.48	$64,860
1998	Nonies Dancer Ali	G. K. Gomez	Mamaison Miss	Continental Lea	5	1:44.14	$63,660
1997	Sharp Cat	C. S. Nakatani	Clever Pilot	Guthrie	6	1:41.34	$64,300
1996	Antespend	C. W. Antley	Dancing Prism	Rumpipumpy (GB)	5	1:43.87	$64,950
1995	Ski Dancer	K. J. Desormeaux	Dixie Pearl	Wilga	5	1:44.24	$45,750
1994	Princess Mitterand	C. J. McCarron	Dianes Halo	Jacodra's Devil	4	1:43.25	$44,925
1993	Likeable Style	G. L. Stevens	Fit to Lead	Amandari	5	1:44.74	$45,900
1992	Crownette	P. A. Valenzuela	Golden Treat	Looie Capote	9	1:44.33	$48,975

1996 Love Lock finished first, DQ to fifth.

San Vicente Stakes

Grade 2, Santa Anita Park, three-year-olds, 7 furlongs, dirt. Held February 3, 2001, with a gross value of $150,000. First held in 1935. Graded since 1973. Stakes record 1:21.07 (1997 Silver Charm).

Year	Winner	Jockey	Second	Third	Strs	Final Time	1st Purse
2001	Early Flyer	C. J. McCarron	Lasersport	D'wildcat	5	1:21.51	$90,000
2000	Archer City Slew	K. J. Desormeaux	Joopy Doopy	Gibson County	6	1:22.18	$90,000
1999	Exploit	C. J. McCarron	Aristotle	Yes It's True	3	1:22.00	$90,000
1998	Sea of Secrets	K. J. Desormeaux	Late Edition	Pleasant Drive	5	1:22.00	$64,080
1997	Silver Charm	C. J. McCarron	Free House	Funontherun	9	**1:21.07**	$66,400
1996	Afleetaffair	C. S. Nakatani	Honour and Glory	Ready to Order	5	1:22.28	$63,850
1995	Afternoon Deelites	K. J. Desormeaux	Mr Purple	Fandarel Dancer	5	1:21.35	$59,725
1994	Fly'n J. Bryan	C. A. Black	Gracious Ghost	Cois Na Tine (Ire)	6	1:22.32	$60,700
1993	Yappy	P. A. Valenzuela	Denmars Dream	Devoted Brass	9	1:22.33	$63,100
1992	Mineral Wells	P. A. Valenzuela	Star of the Crop	Prince Wild	7	1:21.28	$61,450

1992-'95 San Vicente Breeders' Cup S. 1992-'97 Grade 3.

Sapling Stakes

Grade 3, Monmouth Park, two-year-olds, 6 furlongs, dirt. Held August 18, 2001, with a gross value of $150,000. First held in 1883. Graded since 1973. Stakes record 1:07.84 (1992 Gilded Time).

Year	Winner	Jockey	Second	Third	Strs	Final Time	1st Purse
2001	Pure Precision	E. Coa	Truman's Raider	Wild Navigator	8	1:10.82	$90,000
2000	Shooter	J. Bravo	Snow Ridge	T P Louie	7	1:10.63	$120,000
1999	Dont Tell the Kids	J. E. Tejeira	Outrigger	House Burner	6	1:10.18	$120,000
1998	Yes It's True	S. J. Sellers	Erlton	Heroofthegame	7	1:10.09	$120,000
1997	Double Honor	J. Bravo	Jigadee	E Z Line	8	1:09.75	$120,000
1996	Smoke Glacken	C. Perret	Harley Tune	Country Rainbow	10	1:10.16	$120,000
1995	Hennessy	D. M. Barton	Built for Pleasure	Cashier Coyote	7	1:10.84	$120,000
1994	Boone's Mill	P. Day	Enlighten	Western Echo	6	1:10.46	$120,000
1993	Sacred Honour	C. E. Lopez Sr.	Meadow Flight	Solly's Honor	6	1:11.19	$120,000
1992	Gilded Time	C. J. McCarron	Wild Zone	Great Navigator	8	**1:07.84**	$120,000

1992-'96 Grade 2. 1992 new track record.

Saranac Handicap

Grade 3, Saratoga Race Course, three-year-olds, 1 1/16 miles, turf. Held September 2, 2001, with a gross value of $112,500. First held in 1901. Graded since 1973. Stakes record 1:51.61 (1999 Phi Beta Doc).

Year	Winner	Jockey	Second	Third	Strs	Final Time	1st Purse
2001	Blazing Fury, 113	J. Castellano	Fast City	Rapid Ryan	9	1:54.88	$67,500
2000	Rob's Spirit, 120	J. D. Bailey	Whata Brainstorm	Dawn of the Condor	9	1:55.47	$68,280
1999	Phi Beta Doc, 118	R. A. Dominguez	Monarch's Maze	Big Rascal	8	**1:51.61**	$67,020
1998	Crowd Pleaser, 115	J-L. Samyn	Parade Ground	Reformer Rally	7	1:53.42	$66,060
1997	River Squall, 114	C. Perret	Daylight Savings	Inkatha (Fr)	10	1:52.82	$68,460
1996	Harghar, 113	P. Day	Sir Cat	Defacto	11	1:48.58	$69,180
1995	Debonair Dan, 112	J. F. Chavez	Crimson Guard	Treasurer (GB)	7	1:33.65	$50,400
1994	Casa Eire, 114	J. Bravo	Warn Me (GB)	Presently	8	1:34.67	$66,480
1993	Halissee, 114	J. A. Krone	Forest Wind	Compadre	9	1:34.34	$74,280
1992	Casino Magistrate, 120	E. Maple	Restless Doctor	Smiling and Dancin	10	1:39.37	$76,440

Saratoga Breeders' Cup Handicap

Grade 2, Saratoga Race Course, three-year-olds and up, 1 1/4 miles, dirt. Held August 19, 2001, with a gross value of $291,000. First held in 1865. Graded since 1996. Stakes record 2:01.11 (1999 Running Stag).

Year	Winner	Jockey	Second	Third	Strs	Final Time	1st Purse
2001	Aptitude, 4, 122	J. D. Bailey	Perfect Cat, 4	A Fleets Dancer, 6	7	2:01.55	$180,000
2000	Pleasant Breeze, 5, 116	J. F. Chavez	Catienus, 6	Gander, 4	7	2:02.17	$180,000
1999	Running Stag, 5, 122	S. J. Sellers	Catienus, 5	Golden Missile, 4	8	**2:01.11**	$180,000
1998	Awesome Again, 4, 120	P. Day	Concerto, 4	Early Warning, 3	7	2:03.14	$180,000
1997	Cairo Express, 5, 111	J-L. Samyn	Golden Larch, 4	Instant Friendship, 4	9	2:03.99	$180,000
1996	L'Carriere, 5, 114	J. F. Chavez	Peaks and Valleys, 4	Mahogany Hall, 5	8	2:01.67	$130,000
1995	L'Carriere, 4, 113	J. D. Bailey	Yourmissinthepoint, 4	Unaccounted For, 4	6	2:02.87	$120,000
1994	Thunder Rumble, 5, 112	R. Migliore	West by West, 5	Wallenda, 4	8	1:48.52	$150,000

1992-'93 not held. 1994-'96 Saratoga Cup H. 1996-'97 Grade 3. 1994 1 1/8 miles.

Saratoga Special Stakes

Grade 2, Saratoga Race Course, two-year-olds, 6 1/2 furlongs, dirt. Held August 15, 2001, with a gross value of $150,000. First held in 1901. Graded since 1973. Stakes record 1:16.37 (1996 All Chatter).

Year	Winner	Jockey	Second	Third	Strs	Final Time	1st Purse
2001	Jump Start	P. Day	Heavyweight Champ	Booklet	6	1:17.35	$90,000
2000	City Zip	J. A. Santos	Scorpion	Standard Speed	8	1:16.88	$90,000
1999	Bevo	E. S. Prado	Afternoon Affair	Settlement	6	1:17.78	$90,000

Year	Winner	Jockey	Second	Third	Strs	Final Time	1st Purse
1998	Prime Directive	J. F. Chavez	Silk Broker	Tactical Cat	4	1:17.18	$90,000
1997	Favorite Trick	P. Day	Case Dismissed	K. O. Punch	5	1:17.15	$90,000
1996	All Chatter	J. F. Chavez	Gray Raider	Just a Cat	10	1:16.37	$84,375
1995	Bright Launch	J. A. Santos	Devil's Honor	Severe Clear	8	1:17.98	$66,540
1994	Montreal Red	J. A. Santos	Flitch	Law of the Sea	5	1:17.96	$64,800
1993	Dehere	E. Maple	Slew Gin Fizz	Whitney Tower	9	1:09.92	$71,760
1992	Tactical Advantage	J. A. Krone	Strolling Along	Mi Cielo	10	1:10.59	$72,600

1992-'93 6 furlongs.

Schuylerville Stakes

Grade 2, Saratoga Race Course, two-year-old fillies, 6 furlongs, dirt. Held July 25, 2001, with a gross value of $109,100. First held in 1918. Graded since 1973. Stakes record 1:09.80 (1974 Laughing Bridge [2nd Div.]; 1988 Wonders Delight).

Year	Winner	Jockey	Second	Third	Strs	Final Time	1st Purse
2001	Touch Love	J. F. Chavez	Lakeside Cup	Lost Expectations	6	1:11.12	$65,460
2000	Gold Mover	C. Perret	Seeking It All	Miss Doolittle	5	1:10.33	$64,920
1999	Magicalmysterycat	P. Day	Circle of Life	Regally Appealing	7	1:10.91	$65,700
1998	Call Me Up	J. F. Chavez	Brittons Hill	Fantasy Lake	8	1:12.89	$66,060
1997	Countess Diana	S. J. Sellers	Love Lock	Sequence	6	1:10.39	$64,800
1996	How About Now	R. Migliore	Exclusive Hold	City College	11	1:12.37	$68,220
1995	Golden Attraction	D. M. Barton	Daylight Come	Western Dreamer	8	1:10.84	$65,940
1994	Changing Ways	M. E. Smith	Unacceptable	Artic Experience	10	1:12.66	$67,980
1993	Strategic Maneuver	J. A. Santos	Astas Foxy Lady	She Rides Tonite	11	1:11.15	$73,560
1992	Distinct Habit	J. D. Bailey	Tourney	Lily La Belle	9	1:11.03	$72,480

Secretariat Stakes

Grade 1, Arlington Park, three-year-olds, 1¼ miles, turf. Held August 18, 2001, with a gross value of $400,000. First held in 1974. Graded since 1974. Stakes record 2:00.17 (1995 Hawk Attack).

Year	Winner	Jockey	Second	Third	Strs	Final Time	1st Purse
2001	Startac	A. O. Solis	Strut the Stage	Sharp Performance	11	2:04.91	$240,000
2000	Ciro	M. J. Kinane	King Cugat	Guillamou City (Fr)	8	2:01.64	$240,000
1997	Honor Glide	G. K. Gomez	Casey Tibbs (Ire)	Glok	9	2:02.74	$240,000
1996	Marlin	S. J. Sellers	Trail City	Dancing Fred	10	2:01.09	$300,000
1995	Hawk Attack	P. Day	Mecke	Petit Poucet (GB)	10	2:00.17	$240,000
1994	Vaudeville	G. L. Stevens	Dare and Go	Jaggery John	13	2:01.11	$240,000
1993	Awad	J. Velasquez	Explosive Red	Brazany	14	2:08.74	$240,000
1992	Ghazi	R. G. Davis	Paradise Creek	Tango Charlie	10	2:01.18	$180,000

Senator Ken Maddy Handicap

Grade 3, Santa Anita Park, three-year-olds and up, fillies and mares, about 6½ furlongs, turf. Held September 26, 2001, with a gross value of $110,400. First held in 1969. Graded since 1998. Stakes record 1:11.63 (1992 Bel's Starlet).

Year	Winner	Jockey	Second	Third	Strs	Final Time	1st Purse
2001	A La Reine, 4, 115	A. O. Solis	Nanogram, 4	Global, 4	8	1:13.27	$66,240
2000	Evening Promise (GB), 4, 118	K. J. Desormeaux	Strawberry Way, 5	Southern House (Ire), 4	10	1:13.05	$67,020
1999	Hula Queen, 5, 116	A. O. Solis	Desert Lady (Ire), 4	Ecudienne, 5	11	1:13.05	$67,740
1998	Dance Parade, 4, 120	K. J. Desormeaux	Advancing Star, 5	Green Jewel (GB), 4	8	1:13.87	$60,000
1997	Madame Pandit, 4, 118	E. Delahoussaye	Advancing Star, 4	Highest Dream (Ire), 4	10	1:13.82	$60,000
1996	Dixie Pearl, 4, 116	E. Delahoussaye	Ski Dancer, 4	Cat's Cradle, 4	9	1:12.33	$66,400
1995	Denim Yenem, 3, 115	C. J. McCarron	Miss L Attack, 5	Jacodra's Devil, 4	7	1:14.92	$60,400
1994	Starolamo, 5, 117	K. J. Desormeaux	Sophisticatedcielo, 3	Beautiful Gem, 3	6	1:16.07	$47,475
1993	Toussaud, 4, 122	K. J. Desormeaux	Best Dress, 3	Yousefia, 4	6	1:14.32	$46,950
1992	Bel's Starlet, 5, 120	K. J. Desormeaux	Glen Kate (Ire), 5	Brisa de Mar, 4	9	1:11.63	$49,575

Senorita Stakes

Grade 3, Hollywood Park, three-year-old fillies, 1 mile, turf. Held April 22, 2001, with a gross value of $109,800. First held in 1968. Graded since 1990. Stakes record 1:33.66 (1992 Charme a Gendarme).

Year	Winner	Jockey	Second	Third	Strs	Final Time	1st Purse
2001	Fantastic Filly (Fr)	G. K. Gomez	Innit (Ire)	Blushing Bride (GB)	8	1:35.13	$65,880
2000	Islay Mist (GB)	D. R. Flores	Fire Sale Queen	Miss Pixie	10	1:34.16	$67,080
1999	Coracle	K. J. Desormeaux	Aviate	Dianehill (Ire)	11	1:34.04	$67,740
1998	Dancing Rhythm	K. J. Desormeaux	Phone Alex (Ire)	Star's Proud Penny	7	1:35.39	$64,920
1997	Kentucky Kaper	R. R. Douglas	Ascutney	Ava Knowsthecode	10	1:34.74	$66,780
1996	To B. Super	C. W. Antley	Gastronomical	Ribot's Secret (Ire)	13	1:34.36	$68,940
1995	Top Shape (Fr)	C. S. Nakatani	Artica	Auriette (Ire)	10	1:34.79	$63,900
1994	Rabiadella	L. A. Pincay Jr.	Magical Avie	Fancy 'n Fabulous	6	1:34.84	$60,800
1993	Likeable Style	K. J. Desormeaux	Adorydar	Icy Warning	7	1:34.56	$61,250
1992	Charme a Gendarme	R. Q. Meza	Moonlight Elegance	Morriston Belle	13	1:33.66	$67,250

1992-'95 Senorita Breeders' Cup S.

Shadwell Keeneland Turf Mile Stakes

Grade 2, Keeneland, three-year-olds and up, 1 mile, turf. Held October 7, 2001, with a gross value of $558,500. First held in 1986. Graded since 1988. Stakes record 1:33.72 (2000 Altibr).

Year	Winner	Jockey	Second	Third	Strs	Final Time	1st Purse
2001	Hap, 5	J. D. Bailey	Where's Taylor, 5	Aly's Alley, 5	9	1:35.98	$346,270
2000	Altibr, 5	R. Migliore	Strategic Mission, 5	Quiet Resolve, 5	9	1:33.72	$279,744
1999	Kirkwall (GB), 5	V. Espinoza	Delay of Game, 6	Ladies Din, 4	10	1:37.96	$281,232
1998	Favorite Trick, 3	P. Day	Soviet Line (Ire), 8	Wild Event, 5	5	1:35.00	$168,795
1997	Wild Event, 4	M. Guidry	Trail City, 4	Soviet Line (Ire), 7	10	1:34.66	$134,075
1996	Dumaani, 5	J. A. Krone	Desert Waves, 6	Dove Hunt, 5	9	1:35.68	$133,843
1995	Dumaani, 4	J. A. Krone	Holy Mountain, 4	Mr Purple, 3	10	1:38.78	$116,514
1994	†Weekend Madness (Ire), 4	S. J. Sellers	†Words of War, 5	Pennine Ridge, 3	10	1:38.73	$116,328
1993	Coaxing Matt, 4	E. M. Martin Jr.	Adam Smith (GB), 5	Mr. Light Tres (Arg), 4	9	1:53.16	$116,421
1992	Lotus Pool, 5	C. R. Woods Jr.	Thunder Regent, 5	Chenin Blanc, 6	6	1:48.36	$114,902

† denotes female. 1994-'98 Keeneland Breeders' Cup Mile Stakes. 1992-'93 run at 1⅛ miles.

Sheepshead Bay Handicap

Grade 2, Belmont Park, three-year-olds and up, fillies and mares, 1⅜ miles, dirt (originally scheduled at about 1⅜ miles on the turf). Held June 2, 2001, with a gross value of $150,000. First held in 1959. Graded since 1973. Stakes record 2:11.57 (1997 Maxzene).

Year	Winner	Jockey	Second	Third	Strs	Final Time	1st Purse
2001	Critical Eye, 4, 122	M. J. Luzzi	Playact (Ire), 4	Janet (GB), 4	5	2:18.18	$90,000
2000	Lisieux Rose (Ire), 5, 116	J. A. Santos	Melody Queen (GB), 4	La Ville Rouge, 4	7	2:14.16	$90,000
1999	Soaring Softly, 4, 114	M. E. Smith	Starry Dreamer, 5	Pinafore Park, 5	6	2:15.11	$90,000
1998	Maxzene, 5, 121	J. A. Santos	Sweetzie, 6	Colonial Play, 6	6	2:14.17	$90,000
1997	Maxzene, 4, 117	M. E. Smith	Fanjica (Ire), 5	Future Act, 5	8	2:11.57	$90,000
1996	Chelsey Flower, 5, 114	R. G. Davis	Look Daggers, 4	Transient Trend, 4	10	2:12.64	$67,320
1995	Duda, 4, 112	J. D. Bailey	Danish (Ire), 4	Chelsey Flower, 4	7	2:13.69	$65,700
1994	Market Booster, 5, 114	J. A. Santos	Irish Linnet, 6	Fairy Garden, 4	6	2:11.69	$66,960
1993	Trampoli, 4, 116	M. E. Smith	Aquilegia, 4	Revasser, 4	4	2:14.08	$67,680
1992	Ratings, 4, 112	J. Cruguet	Ristna (GB), 4	Dancing Devlette, 4	12	2:15.14	$75,000

1992-'94 Grade 3. 1992-2000 turf. 1997 new course record.

Shirley Jones Handicap

Grade 3, Gulfstream Park, three-year-olds and up, fillies and mares, 7 furlongs, dirt. Held February 14, 2001, with a gross value of $100,000. First held in 1976. Graded since 1988. Stakes record 1:21.94 (1994 Santa Catalina).

Year	Winner	Jockey	Second	Third	Strs	Final Time	1st Purse
2001	Hidden Assets, 4, 114	J. D. Bailey	Another, 4	Dream Supreme, 4	6	1:22.40	$60,000
2000	Marley Vale, 4, 118	J. R. Velazquez	Cassidy, 5	Class On Class, 5	8	1:22.24	$60,000
1999	Harpia, 5, 118	R. Migliore	Scotzanna, 7	Memories of Gold, 7	5	1:22.17	$60,000
1998	U Can Do It, 5, 116	S. J. Sellers	Glitter Woman, 4	Flashy n Smart, 4	5	1:23.33	$60,000
1997	Chip, 4, 114	J. Bravo	Steady Cat, 4	Flat Fleet Feet, 4	7	1:22.24	$60,000
1996	Dust Bucket, 5, 112	R. G. Davis	Russian Flight (Ire), 4	Culver City, 4	5	1:25.97	$60,000
1995	Educated Risk, 5, 125	M. E. Smith	Elizabeth Bay, 5	Clever Act, 5	5	1:22.94	$60,000
1994	Santa Catalina, 6, 115	P. Day	Jeano, 6	Traverse City, 6	11	1:21.94	$60,000
1993	Jeano, 5, 113	S. J. Sellers	Santa Catalina, 5	Miss Jealski, 5	13	1:23.56	$39,060
1992	Nannerl, 5, 111	J. A. Krone	Withallprobability, 4	Fit for a Queen, 4	10	1:23.23	$36,600

Shoemaker Breeders' Cup Mile Stakes

Grade 1, Hollywood Park, three-year-olds and up, 1 mile, turf. Held May 28, 2001, with a gross value of $475,000. First held in 1938. Graded since 1973. Stakes record 1:32.64 (1994 Megan's Interco).

Year	Winner	Jockey	Second	Third	Strs	Final Time	1st Purse
2001	Irish Prize, 5	G. L. Stevens	Touch of the Blues (Fr), 4	Brahms, 4	9	1:33.68	$285,000
2000	Silic (Fr), 5	C. S. Nakatani	Ladies Din, 5	Sharan (GB), 5	11	1:33.36	$304,800
1999	Silic (Fr), 4	C. S. Nakatani	Ladies Din, 4	Hawksley Hill (Ire), 4	8	1:32.95	$280,200
1998	Labeeb (GB), 6	K. J. Desormeaux	Fantastic Fellow, 4	Hawksley Hill (Ire), 4	7	1:33.29	$319,200
1997	Pinfloron (Fr), 5	D. R. Flores	Surachai, 4	Helmsman, 4	14	1:34.46	$353,400
1996	Fastness (Ire), 6	C. S. Nakatani	Romarin (Brz), 6	Atticus, 6	7	1:32.74	$420,000
1995	Unfinished Symph, 4	C. W. Antley	Rapan Boy (Aus), 7	Journalism, 7	9	1:33.14	$98,400
1994	Megan's Interco, 5	C. A. Black	Furiously, 5	Rapan Boy (Aus), 5	6	1:32.64	$63,200
1993	Journalism, 5	A. O. Solis	Lomitas (GB), 5	Brief Truce, 5	7	1:32.89	$63,800

1993-'95 Shoemaker H. 1992 not held. 1993-'99 Grade 2. 1993, equaled course record; 1994 new course record.

Shuvee Handicap

Grade 2, Belmont Park, three-year-olds and up, fillies and mares, 1 mile, dirt. Held May 19, 2001, with a gross value of $200,000. First held in 1976. Graded since 1978. Stakes record 1:34.38 (1999 Catinca).

Year	Winner	Jockey	Second	Third	Strs	Final Time	1st Purse
2001	Apple of Kent, 5, 114	R. Migliore	March Magic, 4	Country Hideaway, 4	5	1:35.16	$120,000
2000	Beautiful Pleasure, 5, 122	J. F. Chavez	Biogio's Rose, 6	Up We Go, 6	5	1:35.65	$120,000

Year	Winner	Jockey	Second	Third	Strs	Final Time	1st Purse
1999	**Catinca**, 4, 121	R. Migliore	Sister Act, 4	Tap to Music, 4	6	**1:34.38**	$90,000
1998	**Colonial Minstrel**, 4, 117	J. R. Velazquez	Dixie Flag, 4	Hidden Reserve, 4	5	1:36.20	$90,000
1997	**Hidden Lake**, 4, 115	R. Migliore	Flat Fleet Feet, 4	Escena, 4	9	1:35.27	$90,000
1996	**Clear Mandate**, 4, 111	J. A. Krone	Smooth Charmer, 4	Restored Hope, 4	7	1:35.01	$90,000
1995	**Inside Information**, 4, 119	J. A. Santos	Sky Beauty, 5	Restored Hope, 5	4	1:35.10	$80,220
1994	**Sky Beauty**, 4, 125	M. E. Smith	For all Seasons, 4	Looie Capote, 4	4	1:40.60	$90,000
1993	**Turnback the Alarm**, 4, 117	C. W. Antley	Shared Interest, 5	Vivano, 5	9	1:43.11	$90,000
1992	**Missy's Mirage**, 4, 116	E. Maple	Harbour Club, 5	Versailles Treaty, 5	6	1:40.74	$102,960

1992-'96 Grade 1. 1992-'94 1 1/16 miles.

Silverbulletday Stakes

Grade 3, Fair Grounds, three-year-old fillies, 1 1/16 miles, dirt. Held February 17, 2001, with a gross value of $125,000. First held in 1982. Graded since 1999. Stakes record 1:42.48 (1997 Blushing K. D.).

Year	Winner	Jockey	Second	Third	Strs	Final Time	1st Purse
2001	**Lakenheath**	C. J. Lanerie	Morning Sun	Beloved by All	5	1:46.09	$75,000
2000	**Shawnee Country**	D. J. Meche	Chilukki	Humble Clerk	9	1:45.11	$75,000
1999	**Silverbulletday**	G. L. Stevens	Brushed Halory	On a Soapbox	8	1:44.36	$75,000
1998	**Cool Dixie**	R. Ardoin	Lu Ravi	Silent Eskimo	9	1:43.38	$75,000
1997	**Blushing K. D.**	L. Meche	Tomisue's Delight	Morelia	6	**1:42.48**	$60,000
1996	**Up Dip**	C. C. Bourque	Brush With Tequila	Not Likely	8	1:44.61	$37,635
1995	**Legendary Priness**	C. A. Emigh	Broad Smile	Hero's Valor	9	1:44.42	$25,875
1994	**Playcaller**	R. Ardoin	Two Altazano	Briar Road	7	1:44.31	$31,095
1993	**Bright Penny**	R. Ardoin	She's a Little Shy	Wakerup	7	1:44.80	$19,095
1992	**Prospectors Delite**	B. J. Walker Jr.	Royal Med	Glitzi Bj	7	1:43.80	$19,020

1992-2000 Davona Dale S.

Singapore Plate Stakes

Grade 3, Arlington Park, three-year-old fillies, 1 1/8 miles, dirt. Held August 11, 2001, with a gross value of $125,000. First held in 1930. Graded since 1982. Stakes record 1:48.20 (1983 Choose a Partner).

Year	Winner	Jockey	Second	Third	Strs	Final Time	1st Purse
2001	**Caressing**	R. R. Douglas	Gal On the Go	Scoop	8	1:50.74	$75,000
2000	**Megans Bluff**	M. Guidry	Instinct	My Turn Kissin	6	1:50.22	$75,000
1997	**Minister's Melody**	G. K. Gomez	Lady of Blue	Dawn's Black Tie	9	1:51.32	$60,000
1996	**Cuando Puede**	R. Albarado	Ginny Lynn	Effectiveness	8	1:51.33	$75,000
1995	**Niner's Home**	T. J. Hebert	A Goodlookin Broad	Strawberry Reason	7	1:52.15	$45,000
1994	**Mariah's Storm**	R. N. Lester	Stellarina	Minority Dater	7	1:49.63	$60,000
1993	**Added Asset**	S. J. Sellers	Dream Mary	Princess Polonia	9	1:50.19	$60,000
1992	**Pleasant Baby**	G. K. Gomez	Low Tolerance	Pleasureconnection	8	1:55.18	$45,000

1998-'99 not held. 1992-'97 Arlington Heights Oaks; 2000 Arlington Oaks.

Sixty Sails Handicap

Grade 3, Sportsman's Park, three-year-olds and up, fillies and mares, 1 1/8 miles, dirt. Held April 29, 2001, with a gross value of $300,000. First held in 1976. Graded since 1984. Stakes record 1:46.69 (1999 Crafty Oak).

Year	Winner	Jockey	Second	Third	Strs	Final Time	1st Purse
2001	**License Fee**, 6, 116	L. Melancon	Lady Melesi, 4	Megans Bluff, 4	8	1:49.11	$180,000
2000	**Lu Ravi**, 5, 116	P. Day	Tap to Music, 5	Batuka, 5	8	1:49.15	$180,000
1999	**Crafty Oak**, 5, 114	R. Sibille	Highfalutin, 5	Lines of Beauty, 5	7	**1:46.69**	$180,000
1998	**Glitter Woman**, 4, 118	G. L. Stevens	Top Secret, 5	(DH) Im Out First, 5 (DH) Tuxedo Junction, 5	7	1:50.49	$180,000
1997	**Top Secret**, 4, 115	C. Perret	Hurricane Viv, 4	Gold n Delicious, 4	9	1:49.71	$180,000
1996	**Alcovy**, 6, 119	W. Martinez	Shoop, 5	Lotta Dancing, 5	13	1:50.70	$180,000
1995	**Eskimo's Angel**, 6, 114	M. Guidry	Little Buckles, 4	Norfolk Lavender, 4	13	1:51.53	$180,000
1994	**Princess Polonia**, 4, 113	W. S. Ramos	Eskimo's Angel, 5	Joyous Melody, 5	8	1:51.88	$180,000
1993	**Pleasant Baby**, 4, 112	J. L. Diaz	Miss Jealski, 4	Steff Graf (Brz), 4	9	1:49.30	$180,000
1992	**Peach of It**, 6, 114	E. T. Baird	Bungalow, 5	Zend to Aiken, 5	13	1:51.28	$162,090

1999 held at Hawthorne. 1993 new track record; 1999 equaled track record. 1998 dead heat for third.

Skip Away Handicap

Grade 3, Gulfstream Park, three-year-olds and up, 1 1/16 miles, dirt. Held January 13, 2001, with a gross value of $103,000. First held in 1960. Graded since 1991. Stakes record 1:42.31 (2001 American Halo).

Year	Winner	Jockey	Second	Third	Strs	Final Time	1st Purse
2001	**American Halo**, 5, 114	R. G. Davis	Vision and Verse, 5	Pleasant Breeze, 5	10	**1:42.31**	$60,000
2000	**Horse Chestnut (SAf)**, 5, 117	M. E. Smith	Isaypete, 4	Rock and Roll, 4	6	1:42.78	$60,000
1999	**Sir Bear**, 6, 119	J. D. Bailey	Behrens, 5	Hanarsaan, 5	8	1:43.66	$60,000
1998	**Sir Bear**, 5, 112	E. M. Jurado	Black Forest, 4	Kiridashi, 4	7	1:43.27	$60,000

Year	Winner	Jockey	Second	Third	Strs	Final Time	1st Purse
1997	Crafty Friend, 4, 114	M. E. Smith	Diligence, 4	Ghostly Moves, 4	8	1:42.27	$45,000
1996	Halo's Image, 5, 119	P. Day	Wekiva Springs, 5	Flying Chevron, 5	7	1:42.71	$45,000
1995	Fight for Love, 5, 113	J. D. Bailey	Danville, 4	Pride of Burkaan, 4	7	1:43.98	$45,000
1994	Devil His Due, 5, 121	M. E. Smith	Migrating Moon, 4	Northern Trend, 4	8	1:43.17	$45,000
1993	Technology, 4, 118	J. D. Bailey	Barkerville, 5	Bidding Proud, 5	8	1:42.47	$45,000
1992	Honest Ensign, 4, 109	J. Cruguet	Peanut Butter Onit, 6	Strike the Gold, 6	7	1:49.41	$45,000

1992-2000 Broward H. 1992 1⅛ miles. 1995 Northern Trend finished second, DQ to fifth.

Sorority Stakes

Grade 3, Monmouth Park, two-year-old fillies, 6 furlongs, dirt. Held September 1, 2001, with a gross value of $150,000. First held in 1956. Graded since 1973. Stakes record 1:09 (1974 Ruffian).

Year	Winner	Jockey	Second	Third	Strs	Final Time	1st Purse
2001	Forest Heiress	D. V. Beckner	Haunted Lass	Divine Angel	6	1:11.61	$90,000
2000	Stormy Pick	J. C. Ferrer	Zonk	With Ability	7	1:10.96	$90,000
1999	Sister Fiona	J. Bravo	Katz Me If You Can	Mycatcandance	5	1:09.66	$90,000
1998	Appealing Phylly	C. C. Lopez	Paved in Gold	Betty's Star	8	1:10.84	$90,000
1997	Unky and Ally	J. R. Martinez Jr.	Tipperary Melody	Love in the Hills	9	1:11.47	$90,000
1996	Annie Cake	W. H. McCauley	Corporate Vision	Little Sister	7	1:11.62	$90,000
1995	Crafty But Sweet	N. Santagata	Golden Attraction	Careless Heiress	6	1:10.98	$120,000
1994	Stormy Blues	J. A. Krone	Cat Appeal	A Real Eye Opener	9	1:11.03	$120,000
1993	Cat Attack	R. G. Davis	Shapely Scrapper	At the Half	10	1:11.41	$120,000
1992	Hollywood Wildcat	F. A. Arguello Jr.	Family Enterprize	D'Accordress	6	1:10.84	$120,000

Sorrento Stakes

Grade 2, Del Mar, two-year-old fillies, 6½ furlongs, dirt. Held August 4, 2001, with a gross value of $150,000. First held in 1967. Graded since 1986. Stakes record 1:15.26 (1995 Batroyale).

Year	Winner	Jockey	Second	Third	Strs	Final Time	1st Purse
2001	Tempera	D. R. Flores	Respectful	Roaring Blaze	8	1:16.13	$90,000
2000	Give Praise	L. A. Pincay Jr.	Sea Reel	Fort Lauderdale	7	1:17.88	$90,000
1999	Chilukki	D. R. Flores	November Slew	She's Classy	6	1:16.40	$90,000
1998	Silverbulletday	G. L. Stevens	Excellent Meeting	Colorado Song	7	1:17.56	$64,980
1997	Career Collection	C. S. Nakatani	Griselle	Bent Creek City	7	1:17.83	$67,825
1996	Desert Digger	E. Delahoussaye	Silken Magic	Montecito	9	1:16.03	$65,950
1995	Batroyale, 119	G. L. Stevens	Cosmic Fire	Waycross	6	1:15.26	$59,200
1994	How So Oiseau	P. A. Valenzuela	Ski Dancer	Serena's Song	8	1:15.89	$47,100
1993	Phone Chatter	L. A. Pincay Jr.	Rhapsodic	Noassemblyrequired	6	1:16.23	$45,900
1992	Zoonaqua	E. Delahoussaye	Eliza	Medici Bells	11	1:22.67	$49,125

1992-'93 Grade 3. 1992 7 furlongs.

Spectacular Bid Stakes

Grade 3, Gulfstream Park, three-year-olds, 6 furlongs, dirt. Held January 3, 2001, with a gross value of $100,000. First held in 1981. Graded since 1995. Stakes record 1:09.40 (1999 Texas Glitter).

Year	Winner	Jockey	Second	Third	Strs	Final Time	1st Purse
2001	Icanseetherain	J. A. Santos	Diablo's Choice	American Century	10	1:11.04	$60,000
2000	B L's Appeal	M. E. Smith	American Bullet	Tour the Hive	8	1:10.68	$45,000
1999	Texas Glitter	J. R. Velazquez	Valid Trefaire	Lifeisawhirl	9	1:09.40	$45,000
1998	Time Limit	J. D. Bailey	Sejm Run	Governor Hicks	8	1:10.56	$45,000
1997	Confide	M. E. Smith	Kelly Kip	Crown Ambassador	9	1:09.87	$45,000
1996	Seacliff	R. R. Douglas	Built for Pleasure	Gomtuu	8	1:11.92	$45,000
1995	Mr. Greeley	J. A. Krone	Make Me	Sea Emperor	7	1:10.76	$44,823
1994	Halo's Image	J. Vasquez	Distinct Reality	Senor Conquistador	7	1:10.39	$44,811
1993	Great Navigator	J. A. Santos	Demaloot Demashoot	Hidden Trick	8	1:09.53	$45,078
1992	Return to Quarters	W. S. Ramos	Scream Machine	Majestic Sweep	8	1:10.10	$45,048

1992-'95 Spectacular Bid Breeders' Cup S.

Spinaway Stakes

Grade 1, Saratoga Race Course, two-year-old fillies, 7 furlongs, dirt. Held August 31, 2001, with a gross value of $200,000. First held in 1881. Graded since 1973. Stakes record 1:23.18 (1994 Flanders).

Year	Winner	Jockey	Second	Third	Strs	Final Time	1st Purse
2001	Cashier's Dream	D. J. Meche	Smok'n Frolic	Magic Storm	7	1:23.47	$120,000
2000	Stormy Pick	J. C. Ferrer	Nasty Storm	Seeking It All	9	1:24.33	$120,000
1999	Circle of Life	J. R. Velazquez	Surfside	Miss Wineshine	6	1:23.25	$120,000
1998	Things Change	J. A. Santos	Extended Applause	Miss Jennifer Lynn	7	1:24.82	$120,000
1997	Countess Diana	S. J. Sellers	Brac Drifter	Aunt Anne	5	1:24.17	$120,000
1996	Oath	S. J. Sellers	Pearl City	Fabulously Fast	9	1:23.71	$120,000
1995	Golden Attraction	G. L. Stevens	Flat Fleet Feet	Western Dreamer	8	1:23.85	$120,000

Year	Winner	Jockey	Second	Third	Strs	Final Time	1st Purse
1994	**Flanders**	P. Day	Sea Breezer	Stormy Blues	6	**1:23.18**	$120,000
1993	**Strategic Maneuver**	J. A. Santos	Astas Foxy Lady	Delta Lady	9	1:10.34	$120,000
1992	**Family Enterprize**	P. Day	Standard Equipment	Sky Beauty	5	1:09.82	$120,000

1992-'93 6 furlongs. 1992 Sky Beauty finished first, DQ to third; Try in the Sky finished third, DQ to fourth.

Sport Page Handicap

Grade 3, Belmont Park, three-year-olds and up, 6½ furlongs, dirt. Held October 27, 2001, with a gross value of $109,400. First held in 1953. Graded since 1984. Stakes record 1:15.54 (2001 Yonaguska).

Year	Winner	Jockey	Second	Third	Strs	Final Time	1st Purse
2001	**Yonaguska**, 3, 116	C. J. McCarron	Silky Sweep, 5	Big E E, 4	6	**1:15.54**	$65,640
2000	**Stalwart Member**, 7, 117	N. Arroyo Jr.	Istintaj, 4	Mister Tricky (GB), 5	6	1:21.97	$48,690
1999	**Scatmandu**, 4, 115	A. T. Gryder	Aristotle, 3	Watchman's Warning, 4	8	1:22.68	$50,250
1998	**Stormin Fever**, 4, 120	R. Migliore	Olympic Cat, 4	Adverse, 4	9	1:21.49	$50,115
1997	**Stalwart Member**, 4, 114	A. T. Gryder	Basqueian, 6	Why Change, 4	10	1:22.15	$68,640
1996	**Valid Expectations**, 3, 117	C. B. Asmussen	Diligence, 3	Blissful State, 4	10	1:21.80	$68,040
1995	**Siphon (Brz)**, 4, 117	K. J. Desormeaux	In Case, 5	Ft. Stockton, 3	13	1:22.08	$71,460
1994	**Man's Hero**, 4, 111	M. J. Luzzi	Itaka, 4	Storm Tower, 4	10	1:22.10	$51,045
1993	**Boom Towner**, 5, 117	F. Lovato Jr.	Raise Heck, 5	Fabersham, 5	9	1:10.62	$53,730
1992	**R. D. Wild Whirl**, 4, 114	R. G. Davis	Senor Speedy, 5	Burn Fair, 5	6	1:09.93	$51,570

1992-'94, 1996-2000 Aqueduct. 1992-'93 6 furlongs; 1994-2000 7 furlongs.

Stars and Stripes Breeders' Cup Handicap

Grade 3, Arlington Park, three-year-olds and up, 1½ miles, turf. Held July 1, 2001, with a gross value of $190,500. First held in 1929. Graded since 1973. Stakes record 2:27.86 (2001 Falcon Flight [Fr]).

Year	Winner	Jockey	Second	Third	Strs	Final Time	1st Purse
2001	**Falcon Flight (Fr)**, 5, 114	R. R. Douglas	Langston, 4	Williams News, 4	11	**2:27.86**	$96,300
2000	**Williams News**, 5, 115	R. Albarado	Profit Option, 5	Buff, 5	12	2:31.22	$148,425
1997	**Lakeshore Road**, 4, 114	C. H. Borel	Chief Bearhart, 4	Awad, 4	9	2:29.57	$140,025
1996	**Vladivostok**, 6, 116	C. Perret	Raintrap (GB), 6	Special Price, 6	8	2:30.23	$138,075
1995	**Snake Eyes**, 5, 116	R. Albarado	Coaxing Matt, 6	Bucks Nephew, 6	7	1:56.46	$45,000
1994	**Marastani**, 4, 113	A. T. Gryder	Snake Eyes, 4	The Vid, 4	12	1:54.64	$60,000
1993	**Little Bro Lantis**, 5, 114	C. C. Bourque	Stark South, 5	Coaxing Matt, 5	12	1:56.92	$60,000
1992	**Plate Dancer**, 7, 113	E. Fires	Little Bro Lantis, 4	Stark South, 4	9	1:55.00	$60,000

1992-'95 Stars and Stripes H.; 1996-'97 Stars and Stripes Breeders' Cup Turf H. 1998-'99 not held. 1992-'95 1³⁄₁₆ miles. 1995 Kazabaiyn finished second, DQ to fifth. 2001 equaled course record.

Stephen Foster Handicap

Grade 2, Churchill Downs, three-year-olds and up, 1⅛ miles, dirt. Held June 16, 2001, with a gross value of $831,000. First held in 1982. Graded since 1988. Stakes record 1:47.28 (1999 Victory Gallop).

Year	Winner	Jockey	Second	Third	Strs	Final Time	1st Purse
2001	**Guided Tour**, 5, 113	L. Melancon	Captain Steve, 4	Brahms, 4	8	1:47.74	$515,220
2000	**Golden Missile**, 5, 118	K. J. Desormeaux	Ecton Park, 4	Cat Thief, 4	6	1:49.56	$502,200
1999	**Victory Gallop**, 4, 120	J. D. Bailey	Nite Dreamer, 4	Littlebitlively, 4	7	**1:47.28**	$512,895
1998	**Awesome Again**, 4, 113	P. Day	Silver Charm, 4	Semoran, 4	7	1:48.61	$495,690
1997	**City by Night**, 4, 113	S. J. Sellers	Victor Cooley, 4	Semoran, 4	6	1:50.52	$101,649
1996	**Tenants Harbor**, 4, 112	F. C. Torres	Pleasant Tango, 6	Mt. Sassafras, 6	8	1:49.94	$107,933
1995	**Recoup the Cash**, 5, 119	A. T. Gryder	Tyus, 5	Powerful Punch, 5	9	1:49.39	$109,298
1994	**Recoup the Cash**, 4, 112	J. L. Diaz	Taking Risks, 4	Dignitas, 4	7	1:49.46	$106,275
1993	**Root Boy**, 5, 113	T. G. Turner	Discover, 5	Flying Continental, 5	11	1:50.80	$74,100
1992	**Discover**, 4, 116	B. E. Bartram	Barkerville, 4	Classic Seven, 4	13	1:50.14	$75,335

1992-'94 Grade 3. 1999 new track record.

Stonerside Beaumont Stakes

Grade 2, Keeneland, three-year-old fillies, about 7 furlongs, dirt. Held April 22, 2001, with a gross value of $250,000. First held in 1986. Graded since 1986. Stakes record 1:25.61 (1999 Swingin On Ice).

Year	Winner	Jockey	Second	Third	Strs	Final Time	1st Purse
2001	**Xtra Heat**	R. Wilson	Mountain Bird	Raging Fever	5	1:27.86	$155,000
2000	**Sahara Gold**	J. D. Bailey	Swept Away	Darling My Darling	6	1:26.58	$84,847
1999	**Swingin On Ice**	R. Albarado	Secret Hills	Appealing Phylly	7	**1:25.61**	$83,917
1998	**Star of Broadway**	P. Day	Santaria	Bourbon Belle	12	1:26.67	$91,140
1997	**(DH) Make Haste**	P. Day	Santaria	Move	7	1:28.08	$57,042
	(DH) Screamer	R. Albarado					
1996	**Golden Gale**	M. E. Smith	Birr	Bright Time	7	1:26.10	$84,398
1995	**Dixieland Gold**	D. Penna	Niner's Home	Conquistadoress	10	1:27.42	$69,874
1994	**Her Temper**	P. Day	Lotta Dancing	Term Limits	6	1:28.41	$67,456
1993	**Roamin Rachel**	C. W. Antley	Added Asset	Fit to Lead	10	1:26.48	$69,998
1992	**Fluttery Danseur**	S. J. Sellers	Miss Iron Smoke	Spinning Round	8	1:27.46	$53,918

1992-'99 Beaumont S. 1992 Grade 3. 1997 dead heat for first.

Strub Stakes

Grade 2, Santa Anita Park, four-year-olds, 1⅛ miles, dirt. Held February 3, 2001, with a gross value of $500,000. First held in 1948. Graded since 1973. Stakes record 1:47.27 (1998 Silver Charm).

Year	Winner	Jockey	Second	Third	Strs	Final Time	1st Purse
2001	**Wooden Phone**, 4	C. S. Nakatani	Tiznow, 4	Jimmy Z, 4	6	1:48.43	$300,000
2000	**General Challenge**, 4	C. S. Nakatani	Luftikus, 4	Saint's Honor, 4	4	1:48.81	$300,000
1999	**Event of the Year**, 4	C. S. Nakatani	Dr Fong, 4	Hanuman Highway (Ire), 4	7	1:47.65	$300,000
1998	**Silver Charm**, 4	G. L. Stevens	Mud Route, 4	Bagshot, 4	6	**1:47.27**	$300,000
1997	**Victory Speech**, 4	J. D. Bailey	The Barking Shark, 4	Ambivalent, 4	9	2:01.50	$300,000
1996	**Helmsman**, 4	C. J. McCarron	Afternoon Deelites, 4	Mr Purple, 4	9	2:02.76	$300,000
1995	**Dare and Go**, 4	A. O. Solis	Dramatic Gold, 4	Wekiva Springs, 4	5	2:00.15	$275,000
1994	**Diazo**, 4	L. A. Pincay Jr.	Nonproductiveasset, 4	Stuka, 4	11	2:00.33	$275,000
1993	**Siberian Summer**, 4	C. S. Nakatani	Bertrando, 4	Major Impact, 4	8	2:00.78	$275,000
1992	**Best Pal**, 4	K. J. Desormeaux	Dinard, 4	Reign Road, 4	8	1:59.95	$275,000

1992-'93 Charles H. Strub S. 1992-'97 Grade 1. 1992-'97 1¼ miles.

Stuyvesant Handicap

Grade 3, Belmont Park, three-year-olds and up, 1⅛ miles, dirt. Held October 27, 2001, with a gross value of $107,700. First held in 1916. Graded since 1973. Stakes record 1:47 (1973 Riva Ridge).

Year	Winner	Jockey	Second	Third	Strs	Final Time	1st Purse
2001	**Graeme Hall**, 4, 119	J. R. Velazquez	Country Be Gold, 4	Cat's At Home, 4	6	1:47.95	$64,620
2000	**Not So Fast**, 6, 114	H. Castillo Jr.	Top Official, 5	Fire King, 7	6	1:50.03	$64,860
1999	**Best of Luck**, 3, 114	M. E. Smith	Wild Imagination, 5	Durmiente (Chi), 5	9	1:49.77	$67,200
1998	**Mr. Sinatra**, 4, 115	A. T. Gryder	Rock and Roll, 3	Accelerator, 4	5	1:48.16	$65,280
1997	**Delay of Game**, 4, 114	J-L. Samyn	Concerto, 3	Mr. Sinatra, 3	8	1:47.72	$66,060
1996	**Poor But Honest**, 6, 116	J. F. Chavez	Flitch, 4	Admiralty, 4	8	1:49.44	$66,480
1995	**Silver Fox**, 4, 113	M. E. Smith	Yourmissinthepoint, 4	Earth Colony, 4	7	1:48.03	$68,940
1994	**Wallenda**, 4, 118	W. H. McCauley	Lost Soldier, 4	Pistols and Roses, 5	6	1:50.69	$64,560
1993	**Michelle Can Pass**, 5, 115	J. R. Velazquez	Key Contender, 5	Primitive Hall, 4	8	1:51.07	$70,200
1992	**Shots Are Ringing**, 5, 114	J. R. Velazquez	Key Contender, 4	Timely Warning, 7	8	1:49.36	$69,120

1992-'94, 1996-2000 held at Aqueduct.

Stymie Handicap

Grade 3, Aqueduct, three-year-olds and up, 1⅛ miles, dirt. Held March 10, 2001, with a gross value of $109,800. First held in 1956. Graded since 1973. Stakes record 1:46.20 (1972 *Canonero II; 1974 Key to the Kingdom).

Year	Winner	Jockey	Second	Third	Strs	Final Time	1st Purse
2001	**Windrush**, 4, 114	J. Bravo	Turnofthecentury, 4	Boston Party, 4	8	1:48.43	$65,880
2000	**Not So Fast**, 6, 114	O. Vergara	Tarquinius, 4	Prince Waquoit, 4	8	1:49.07	$49,920
1999	**Brushing Up**, 6, 112	S. Bridgmohan	Fire King, 6	Chronicle S., 6	7	1:49.22	$49,005
1998	**Unreal Turn**, 6, 118	C. C. Lopez	Star of Valor, 5	More to Tell, 5	7	1:48.68	$49,215
1997	**Iron Gavel**, 7, 110	J. M. Pezua	More to Tell, 6	Opal Moon, 6	5	1:49.83	$48,180
1996	**More to Tell**, 5, 115	J. F. Chavez	Slick Horn, 6	Iron Gavel, 6	6	1:51.40	$58,680
1995	**More to Tell**, 4, 118	F. T. Alvarado	Aztec Empire, 6	Federal Funds, 5	7	1:51.67	$65,220
1994	**Koluctoo Jimmy Al**, 4, 111	J. F. Chavez	Michelle Can Pass, 6	Federal Funds, 6	11	1:50.99	$67,800
1993	**Two the Twist**, 6, 112	R. Migliore	A Call to Rise, 5	Jacksonport, 5	7	1:48.30	$69,840
1992	**Crackedbell**, 7, 115	A. T. Gryder	Conveyor, 4	Nome, 4	5	1:48.94	$67,080

Suburban Handicap

Grade 2, Belmont Park, three-year-olds and up, 1¼ miles, dirt. Held July 1, 2001, with a gross value of $500,000. First held in 1884. Graded since 1973. Stakes record 1:58.33 (1991 In Excess [Ire]).

Year	Winner	Jockey	Second	Third	Strs	Final Time	1st Purse
2001	**Albert the Great**, 4, 123	J. F. Chavez	Lido Palace (Chi), 4	Include, 4	6	2:00.39	$300,000
2000	**Lemon Drop Kid**, 4, 122	E. S. Prado	Behrens, 6	Lager, 6	6	1:58.97	$300,000
1999	**Behrens**, 5, 121	J. F. Chavez	Catienus, 5	Social Charter, 5	8	2:01.06	$240,000
1998	**Frisk Me Now**, 4, 118	E. L. King Jr.	Ordway, 4	Sir Bear, 4	8	2:00.45	$210,000
1997	**Skip Away**, 4, 122	S. J. Sellers	Will's Way, 4	Formal Gold, 4	6	2:02.39	$210,000
1996	**Wekiva Springs**, 5, 122	M. E. Smith	Mahogany Hall, 5	L'Carriere, 5	7	2:02.78	$300,000
1995	**Key Contender**, 7, 115	J. D. Bailey	Kissin Kris, 5	Federal Funds, 5	10	2:02.30	$210,000
1994	**Devil His Due**, 5, 124	M. E. Smith	Valley Crossing, 6	Federal Funds, 6	5	2:02.52	$210,000
1993	**Devil His Due**, 4, 121	W. H. McCauley	Pure Rumor, 4	West by West, 4	8	2:01.25	$180,000
1992	**Pleasant Tap**, 5, 119	E. Delahoussaye	Strike the Gold, 4	Defensive Play, 4	7	2:00.33	$337,500

1992-'96 Grade 1.

Sunset Handicap

Grade 2, Hollywood Park, three-year-olds and up, 1½ miles, turf. Held July 15, 2001, with a gross value of $200,000. First held in 1938. Graded since 1973. Stakes record 2:23.55 (1996 Talloires).

Year	Winner	Jockey	Second	Third	Strs	Final Time	1st Purse
2001	**Blueprint (Ire)**, 6, 116	G. L. Stevens	Kudos, 4	Northern Quest (Fr), 6	5	2:26.16	$120,000
2000	**Bienamado**, 4, 122	C. J. McCarron	Deploy Venture (GB), 4	Single Empire (Ire), 6	5	2:25.06	$150,000

Year	Winner	Jockey	Second	Third	Strs	Final Time	1st Purse
1999	Plicck (Ire), 4, 116	D. R. Flores	River Bay, 6	Lazy Lode (Arg), 5	8	2:26.97	$150,000
1998	River Bay, 5, 121	A. O. Solis	Lazy Lode (Arg), 4	Devonwood, 4	6	2:27.40	$210,000
1997	Marlin, 4, 120	D. R. Flores	Flyway (Fr), 4	Percutant (GB), 6	6	2:25.39	$240,000
1996	Talloires, 6, 116	K. J. Desormeaux	Awad, 6	Sandpit (Brz), 7	7	**2:23.55**	$420,000
1995	Sandpit (Brz), 6, 124	C. S. Nakatani	Special Price, 6	Liyoun (Ire), 7	5	2:25.50	$464,700
1994	Grand Flotilla, 7, 119	G. L. Stevens	Semillon (GB), 4	Emerald Jig, 5	7	2:26.35	$158,000
1993	Bien Bien, 4, 122	C. J. McCarron	Emerald Jig, 4	Beyton, 4	6	2:25.69	$154,300
1992	Qathif, 5, 114	A. O. Solis	Seven Rivers, 6	Stark South, 4	5	2:26.72	$153,600

1995-'96 Caesars Palace Turf Championship H. 1996 new course record.

Super Derby

Grade 1, Louisiana Downs, three-year-olds, 1¼ miles, dirt. Held September 23, 2001, with a gross value of $500,000. First held in 1980. Graded since 1982. Stakes record 1:59.84 (2000 Tiznow).

Year	Winner	Jockey	Second	Third	Strs	Final Time	1st Purse
2001	Outofthebox	L. Meche	E Dubai	Quadrophonic Sound	9	2:06.20	$300,000
2000	Tiznow	C. J. McCarron	Commendable	Mass Market	6	**1:59.84**	$300,000
1999	Ecton Park	A. O. Solis	Menifee	Pineaff	8	2:00.59	$300,000
1998	Arch	C. S. Nakatani	Classic Cat	Sir Tiff	7	2:01.51	$300,000
1997	Deputy Commander	C. J. McCarron	Precocity	Blazing Sword	6	2:00.92	$300,000
1996	Editor's Note	G. L. Stevens	The Barking Shark	Devil's Honor	11	2:02.37	$450,000
1995	Mecke	J. D. Bailey	Pineing Patty	Scott's Scoundrel	12	2:00.34	$450,000
1994	Soul of the Matter	K. J. Desormeaux	Concern	Bay Street Star	6	2:03.57	$450,000
1993	Wallenda	W. H. McCauley	Saintly Prospector	Peteski	12	2:02.71	$450,000
1992	Senor Tomas	A. T. Gryder	Count the Time	Orbit's Revenge	14	2:04.09	$450,000

Suwannee River Handicap

Grade 3, Gulfstream Park, three-year-olds and up, fillies and mares, 1⅛ miles, turf. Held February 18, 2001, with a gross value of $100,000. First held in 1947. Graded since 1973. Stakes record 1:46.68 (1994 Marshua's River).

Year	Winner	Jockey	Second	Third	Strs	Final Time	1st Purse
2001	Spook Express (SAf), 7, 116	M. E. Smith	Gaviola, 4	Windsong, 4	8	1:47.28	$60,000
2000	Pico Teneriffe, 4, 115	J. F. Chavez	Dominique's Joy, 5	Crystal Symphony, 5	8	1:47.83	$45,000
1999	Winfama, 6, 114	R. Migliore	Circus Charmer, 4	Colcon, 4	10	1:52.38	$45,000
1998	Seebe, 4, 114	D. S. Rice	Colcon, 5	Parade Queen, 5	10	1:47.58	$45,000
1997	Golden Pond (Ire), 4, 115	J. D. Bailey	Rumpipumpy (GB), 4	Elusive, 4	11	1:47.87	$45,000
1996	Class Kris, 4, 116	P. Day	Apolda, 5	Majestic Dy, 5	5	1:49.17	$45,000
1995	Cox Orange, 5, 116	J. D. Bailey	Irving's Girl, 5	Alice Springs, 5	7	1:47.43	$45,000
1994	Marshua's River, 7, 114	J. A. Santos	Sheila's Revenge, 4	Icy Warning, 4	12	**1:46.68**	$45,000
1993	Via Borghese, 4, 116	J. D. Bailey	Marshua's River, 6	Blue Daisy, 6	14	1:48.22	$40,230
1992	Julie La Rousse (Ire), 4, 115	J. D. Bailey	Christiecat, 5	Grab the Green, 5	11	1:48.48	$38,670

1999 about 1⅛ miles. 1992 equaled course record.

Swale Stakes

Grade 3, Gulfstream Park, three-year-olds, 7 furlongs, dirt. Held March 10, 2001, with a gross value of $150,000. First held in 1985. Graded since 1990. Stakes record 1:21.60 (1988 Seeking the Gold)

Year	Winner	Jockey	Second	Third	Strs	Final Time	1st Purse
2001	D'wildcat	C. S. Nakatani	Tarek	Yonaguska	6	1:22.25	$90,000
2000	Trippi	J. D. Bailey	Ultimate Warrior	Harlan Traveler	8	1:23.43	$60,000
1999	Yes It's True	J. D. Bailey	Texas Glitter	Lucky Roberto	5	1:22.29	$60,000
1998	Favorite Trick	P. Day	Good and Tough	Dice Dancer	9	1:22.86	$60,000
1997	Confide	M. E. Smith	Country Rainbow	The Silver Move	6	1:23.35	$45,000
1996	Roar	M. E. Smith	Gomtuu	Dixie Connection	6	1:22.46	$45,000
1995	Mr. Greeley	J. A. Krone	Devious Course	Pyramid Peak	6	1:22.18	$45,000
1994	Arrival Time	C. J. McCarron	Senor Conquistador	Meadow Monster	7	1:22.53	$45,000
1993	Premier Explosion	D. Penna	Demaloot Demashoot	Cherokee Run	8	1:23.23	$53,520
1992	D. J. Cat	J. D. Bailey	Binalong	Always Silver	10	1:23.39	$71,250

Swaps Stakes

Grade 1, Hollywood Park, three-year-olds, 1⅛ miles, dirt. Held July 15, 2001, with a gross value of $500,000. First held in 1974. Graded since 1974. Stakes record 1:45.96 (1997 Free House).

Year	Winner	Jockey	Second	Third	Strs	Final Time	1st Purse
2001	Congaree	G. L. Stevens	Until Sundown	Jamaican Rum	6	1:48.61	$300,000
2000	Captain Steve	C. S. Nakatani	Tiznow	Spacelink	6	1:48.01	$300,000
1999	Cat Thief	P. Day	General Challenge	Walk That Walk	4	1:47.87	$300,000
1998	Old Trieste	C. J. McCarron	Grand Slam	Old Topper	6	1:47.06	$300,000
1997	Free House	K. J. Desormeaux	Deputy Commander	Wild Rush	6	**1:45.96**	$300,000
1996	Victory Speech	J. D. Bailey	Prince of Thieves	Hesabull	5	1:48.28	$300,000

Year	Winner	Jockey	Second	Third	Strs	Final Time	1st Purse
1995	Thunder Gulch	G. L. Stevens	Da Hoss	Petionville	7	1:49.09	$275,000
1994	Silver Music	C. W. Antley	Dramatic Gold	Valiant Nature	6	2:00.76	$123,800
1993	Devoted Brass	L. A. Pincay Jr.	Future Storm	Codified	6	2:00.64	$124,000
1992	Bien Bien	C. J. McCarron	Treekster	Sevengreenpairs	5	2:02.91	$123,400

1992-'98 Grade 2. 1992-'94 1¼ miles.

Sword Dancer Invitational Handicap

Grade 1, Saratoga Race Course, three-year-olds and up, 1½ miles, turf. Held August 11, 2001, with a gross value of $500,000. First held in 1975. Graded since 1981. Stakes record 2:23.20 (1997 Awad).

Year	Winner	Jockey	Second	Third	Strs	Final Time	1st Purse
2001	With Anticipation, 6, 114	P. Day	King Cugat, 4	Slew Valley, 4	9	2:26.41	$300,000
2000	John's Call, 9, 114	J-L. Samyn	Aly's Alley, 4	Single Empire (Ire), 6	8	2:32.17	$300,000
1999	Honor Glide, 5, 116	J. A. Santos	Val's Prince, 7	Chorwon, 6	7	2:28.23	$240,000
1998	Cetewayo, 4, 115	J. R. Velazquez	Val's Prince, 6	Dushyantor, 5	6	2:29.56	$180,000
1997	Awad, 7, 117	P. Day	Fahim (GB), 4	Val's Prince, 5	10	2:23.20	$150,000
1996	Broadway Flyer, 5, 118	M. E. Smith	Kiri's Clown, 7	Flag Down, 6	9	2:32.08	$150,000
1995	Kiri's Clown, 6, 114	M. J. Luzzi	Awad, 5	King's Theatre (Ire), 4	13	2:25.45	$150,000
1994	Alex the Great (GB), 5, 118	P. A. Valenzuela	Kiri's Clown, 5	L'Hermine (GB), 5	10	2:28.66	$150,000
1993	Spectacular Tide, 4, 112	J. A. Krone	Square Cut, 4	Dr. Kiernan, 4	9	2:30.39	$120,000
1992	Fraise, 4, 113	J. D. Bailey	Wall Street Dancer, 4	Montserrat, 4	8	2:25.88	$150,000

Tampa Bay Derby

Not graded, Tampa Bay Downs, three-year-olds, 1¹⁄₁₆ miles, dirt. Held March 18, 2001, with a gross value of $200,000. First held in 1981. Grade 3 in 2002. Stakes record 1:43.80 (1987 Phantom Jet; 1989 Storm Predictions; 1996 Thundering Storm).

Year	Winner	Jockey	Second	Third	Strs	Final Time	1st Purse
2001	Burning Roma	R. Migliore	American Prince	Paging	11	1:44.30	$120,000
2000	Wheelaway	R. Migliore	Impeachment	Perfect Cat	10	1:43.90	$90,000
1999	Pineaff	J. A. Santos	Menifee	Doneraile Court	6	1:45.33	$90,000
1998	Parade Ground	P. Day	Middlesex Drive	Rock and Roll	8	1:44.20	$90,000
1997	Zede	J. D. Bailey	Brisco Jack	Favorable Regard	12	1:44.80	$90,000
1996	Thundering Storm	J. A. Guerra	El Amante	Natural Selection	10	1:43.80	$90,000
1995	Gadzook	G. Boulanger	Composer	Bet Your Bucks	10	1:45.20	$90,000
1994	Prix de Crouton	M. Walls	Able Buck	Parental Pressure	7	1:46.60	$90,000
1993	Marco Bay	R. D. Allen Jr.	Thriller Chiller	Tunecke Charlie	12	1:44.40	$90,000
1992	Careful Gesture	R. N. Lester	Chief Speaker	Clipper Won	12	1:45.93	$120,000

Tanforan Handicap

Grade 3, Golden Gate Fields, four-year-olds and up, 1¹⁄₁₆ miles, turf. Held February 4, 2001, with a gross value of $100,000. First held in 1899. Graded since 1980. Stakes record 1:40.60 (1969 *His Boy II; 1974 Finalista).

Year	Winner	Jockey	Second	Third	Strs	Final Time	1st Purse
2001	Yaralino (GB), 5, 115	D. Carr	Robynhood, 7	El Cielo, 7	7	1:45.51	$55,000
2000	High Tech Friend, 5, 115	R. J. Warren Jr.	Wegotohaveharte, 5	Bolchina's Prize, 5	7	1:43.49	$55,000
1999	Kirkwall (GB), 5, 115	B. Blanc	Kraal, 4	Long Drive, 4	8	1:46.49	$49,875
1998	Reality Road, 6, 115	R. Q. Meza	Dreamer, 6	West Coast Warrior, 6	8	1:39.85	$55,000
1997	River Flyer, 6, 115	D. Carr	Arrivederci Baby, 5	Joy of Glory, 5	8	1:43.74	$55,000
1996	Inner City (Ire), 7, 116	A. D. Lopez	Patio de Naranjos (Chi), 5	Joy of Glory, 5	10	1:50.15	$55,000
1994	Firm Pledge, 4, 114	T. M. Chapman	Caesour, 4	Lykatill Hil, 4	7	1:40.91	$55,000
1993	Slew of Damascus, 5, 116	T. M. Chapman	Journalism, 5	Lord Joe, 5	8	1:43.10	$55,000
1992	Double Found, 6, 113	O. A. Berrio	Bourgogne (GB), 4	Lord Joe, 4	8	1:42.32	$55,000

1992-2000 held at Bay Meadows. 1995 not held. 1992-'94 three-year-olds and up. 1998, 2000 dirt.

Tempted Stakes

Grade 3, Belmont Park, two-year-old fillies, 1 mile, dirt. Held October 28, 2001, with a gross value of $111,500. First held in 1975. Graded since 1980. Stakes record 1:35.40 (1975 Secret Lanvin).

Year	Winner	Jockey	Second	Third	Strs	Final Time	1st Purse
2001	Smok'n Frolic	J. R. Velazquez	Saintly Action	Wopping	8	1:37.77	$66,900
2000	Two Item Limit	R. Migliore	Celtic Melody	Twining Star	6	1:38.53	$65,520
1999	Shawnee Country	J. F. Chavez	To Marquet	Marigalante	5	1:38.60	$65,460
1998	Oh What a Windfall	J. D. Bailey	La Ville Rouge	Honour a Bull	8	1:39.84	$66,120
1997	Dancing With Ruth	T. G. Turner	Soft Senorita	Aunt Anne	6	1:37.55	$65,340
1996	Ajina	J. D. Bailey	Glitter Woman	Aldiza	7	1:36.59	$66,240
1994	Special Broad	J. A. Krone	Carson Creek	Golden Bri	7	1:37.20	$66,000
1993	Sovereign Kitty	J. R. Velazquez	Seeking the Circle	Her Temper	8	1:46.84	$69,720
1992	True Affair	J. Bravo	Broad Gains	Touch of Love	6	1:47.48	$68,520

1995 not held. 1992-'94, 1996-2000 held at Aqueduct. 1992-'93 1¹⁄₁₆ miles.

Test Stakes

Grade 1, Saratoga Race Course, three-year-old fillies, 7 furlongs, dirt. Held July 28, 2001, with a gross value of $250,000. First held in 1922. Graded since 1973. Stakes record 1:21.00 (1987 Very Subtle; 1990 Go for Wand).

Year	Winner	Jockey	Second	Third	Strs	Final Time	1st Purse
2001	Victory Ride	E. S. Prado	Xtra Heat	Nasty Storm	8	1:21.72	$150,000
2000	Dream Supreme	P. Day	Big Bambu	Finder's Fee	11	1:22.66	$150,000
1999	Marley Vale	J. R. Velazquez	Awful Smart	Emanating	11	1:22.77	$150,000
1998	Jersey Girl	M. E. Smith	Brave Deed	Catinca	11	1:23.02	$120,000
1997	Fabulously Fast	J. D. Bailey	Aldiza	Pearl City	9	1:21.65	$90,000
1996	Capote Belle	J. R. Velazquez	Flat Fleet Feet	J J'sdream	8	1:21.08	$90,000
1995	Chaposa Springs	J. D. Bailey	Miss Golden Circle	Daijin	9	1:21.81	$90,000
1994	Twist Afleet	J. D. Bailey	Penny's Reshoot	Heavenly Prize	8	1:22.08	$90,000
1993	Missed the Storm	M. E. Smith	Miss Indy Anna	Educated Risk	5	1:22.12	$90,000
1992	November Snow	C. W. Antley	Meafara	Preach	8	1:21.33	$105,480

Texas Mile Stakes

Grade 3, Lone Star Park, three-year-olds and up, 1 mile, dirt. Held April 28, 2001, with a gross value of $300,000. First held in 1997. Graded since 1999. Stakes record 1:34.44 (1997 Isitingood).

Year	Winner	Jockey	Second	Third	Strs	Final Time	1st Purse
2001	Dixie Dot Com, 6	D. R. Flores	Mr Ross, 6	Five Straight, 6	7	1:34.72	$180,000
2000	Sir Bear, 7	E. Coa	Lexington Park, 4	Luftikus, 4	9	1:35.98	$170,000
1999	Littlebitlively, 5	C. Gonzalez	Real Quiet, 4	Allen's Oop, 4	5	1:35.65	$145,000
1998	Littlebitlively, 4	C. Gonzalez	Anet, 4	Scott's Scoundrel, 4	5	1:37.07	$160,000
1997	Isitingood, 6	D. R. Flores	Spiritbound, 5	Skip Away, 5	7	**1:34.44**	$150,000

The Very One Handicap

Grade 3, Gulfstream Park, three-year-olds and up, fillies and mares, 1⅜ miles, turf. Held February 11, 2001, with a gross value of $100,000. First held in 1987. Graded since 1996. Stakes record 2:13.45 (1999 Delilah [Ire]).

Year	Winner	Jockey	Second	Third	Strs	Final Time	1st Purse
2001	Innuendo (Ire), 6, 115	J. D. Bailey	Lucky Lune (Fr), 4	Silver Bandana, 4	10	2:13.62	$60,000
2000	My Sweet Westly, 4, 110	P. Day	I'm Indy Mood, 5	Manoa, 5	6	2:06.79	$45,000
1999	Delilah (Ire), 5, 116	J. D. Bailey	Starry Dreamer, 5	Justenuffheart, 5	8	**2:13.45**	$45,000
1998	Shemozzle (Ire), 5, 114	J. R. Velazquez	Turkappeal, 5	Yokama, 5	6	2:19.06	$45,000
1997	Tocopilla (Arg), 7, 114	B. D. Peck	Ampulla, 6	Beyrouth, 6	6	2:14.35	$45,000
1996	Electric Society (Ire), 5, 113	M. E. Smith	Northern Emerald, 6	Chelsey Flower, 6	13	2:15.23	$30,000
1995	P J Floral, 6, 113	S. J. Sellers	Trampoli, 5	Memories (Ire), 6	6	2:14.44	$30,000
1994	Russian Tango, 4, 112	J. D. Bailey	Maxamount, 6	Camiunch, 6	6	2:02.58	$30,000
1993	Fairy Garden, 5, 113	W. S. Ramos	Trampoli, 4	Tango Charlie, 4	11	2:14.67	$30,000
1992	Bungalow, 5, 112	S. J. Sellers	Raffinierte (Ire), 4	Lover's Quest, 4	7	2:05.79	$30,000

2000 not graded. 1996 four-year-olds and up. 1992, 1994, 2000 dirt. 1992, 1994, 2000 1¼ miles; 1998 about 1⅜ miles.

Thoroughbred Club of America Stakes

Grade 3, Keeneland, three-year-olds and up, fillies and mares, 6 furlongs, dirt. Held October 21, 2001, with a gross value of $109,000. First held in 1981. Graded since 1988. Stakes record 1:08.70 (1998 Bourbon Belle).

Year	Winner	Jockey	Second	Third	Strs	Final Time	1st Purse
2001	Cat Cay, 4	P. Day	Spanish Glitter, 3	Another, 4	7	1:09.24	$67,580
2000	Katz Me If You Can, 3	J. F. Chavez	Hurricane Bertie, 5	My Alibi, 4	6	1:09.42	$67,394
1999	Cinemine, 4	F. M. Martin Jr.	Bourbon Belle, 4	Lucky Again, 3	5	1:08.86	$62,000
1998	Bourbon Belle, 3	W. Martinez	J J'sdream, 5	Meter Maid, 4	8	**1:08.70**	$62,000
1997	Sky Blue Pink, 3	P. Day	Bluffing Girl, 5	Mama's Pro, 4	7	1:10.06	$62,000
1996	Surprising Fact, 3	P. Day	Morris Code, 4	Mama's Pro, 3	9	1:10.14	$62,000
1995	Cat Appeal, 3	D. M. Barton	Russian Flight (Ire), 3	Traverse City, 5	9	1:10.02	$46,500
1994	Tenacious Tiffany, 4	C. Perret	Roamin Rachel, 4	Jeano, 6	7	1:11.00	$46,500
1993	Jeano, 5	P. Day	Apelia, 4	Fluttery Danseur, 4	6	1:09.39	$46,500
1992	Ifyoucouldseemenow, 4	C. Perret	Harbour Club, 5	Madam Bear, 4	8	1:09.67	$48,750

1999 Bourbon Belle finished first, DQ to second.

Tom Fool Handicap

Grade 2, Belmont Park, three-year-olds and up, 7 furlongs, dirt. Held July 4, 2001, with a gross value of $150,000. First held in 1975. Graded since 1981. Stakes record 1:20.62 (1998 Crafty Friend).

Year	Winner	Jockey	Second	Third	Strs	Final Time	1st Purse
2001	Exchange Rate, 4, 114	J. D. Bailey	Say Florida Sandy, 7	Here's Zealous, 7	5	1:21.24	$90,000
2000	Trippi, 3, 112	J. D. Bailey	Cornish Snow, 7	Sailor's Warning, 7	6	1:21.69	$90,000
1999	Crafty Friend, 6, 116	R. Migliore	Affirmed Success, 5	Artax, 5	5	**1:20.62**	$90,000
1998	Banker's Gold, 4, 115	J. F. Chavez	Boundless Moment, 6	Partner's Hero, 6	6	1:21.04	$90,000

Year	Winner	Jockey	Second	Third	Strs	Final Time	1st Purse
1997	Diligence, 4, 116	J. A. Santos	Royal Haven, 5	Elusive Quality, 5	7	1:22.40	$90,000
1996	Kayrawan, 4, 113	R. Migliore	Cold Execution, 5	Lite the Fuse, 5	5	1:22.95	$64,860
1995	Lite the Fuse, 4, 117	J. A. Krone	Our Emblem, 4	Evil Bear, 4	6	1:21.72	$65,220
1994	Virginia Rapids, 4, 124	J-L. Samyn	Cherokee Run, 4	Boundary, 4	5	1:22.27	$64,380
1993	Birdonthewire, 4, 119	C. Perret	Fly So Free, 5	Take Me Out, 5	5	1:20.93	$67,680
1992	Rubiano, 5, 126	J. A. Krone	Take Me Out, 4	Arrowtown, 4	8	1:21.70	$70,920

1992-'95 Tom Fool S.

Top Flight Handicap

Grade 2, Aqueduct, three-year-olds and up, fillies and mares, 1 mile, dirt. Held November 23, 2001, with a gross value of $150,000. First held in 1940. Graded since 1973. Stakes record 1:34.96 (1994 Educated Risk).

Year	Winner	Jockey	Second	Third	Strs	Final Time	1st Purse
2001	Cat Cay, 4, 117	J. R. Velazquez	Tugger, 4	Atelier, 4	9	1:35.45	$90,000
2000	Reciclada (Chi), 5, 116	J. D. Bailey	Country Hideaway, 4	Critical Eye, 4	8	1:35.54	$90,000
1999	Belle Cherie, 3, 113	J. R. Velazquez	(DH) Harpia, 5 (DH) Furlough, 5		7	1:35.46	$90,000
1998	Catinca, 3, 119	R. Migliore	Furlough, 4	Glitter Woman, 4	5	1:35.81	$90,000
1997	Dixie Flag, 3, 117	M. J. Luzzi	Aldiza, 3	Mil Kilates, 3	9	1:35.34	$90,000
1996	Flat Fleet Feet, 3, 116	M. E. Smith	Queen Tutta, 4	Miss Golden Circle, 4	9	1:37.00	$90,000
1995	Twist Afleet, 4, 123	M. E. Smith	Chaposa Springs, 3	Lotta Dancing, 3	8	1:35.26	$90,000
1994	Educated Risk, 4, 120	M. E. Smith	Triumph At Dawn, 4	Imah, 4	8	1:34.96	$90,000
1993	You'd Be Surprised, 4, 112	J. D. Bailey	Looie Capote, 4	Shared Interest, 4	7	1:48.82	$90,000
1992	Firm Stance, 4, 114	P. Day	Haunting, 4	Lady D'Accord, 4	14	1:50.55	$120,000

1992-'96 Grade 1. 1993 held at Belmont. 1992-'93 1⅛ miles. 1999 dead heat for second.

Travers Stakes

Grade 1, Saratoga Race Course, three-year-olds, 1¼ miles, dirt. Held August 25, 2001, with a gross value of $1,000,000. First held in 1864. Graded since 1973. Stakes record 2:00 (1979 General Assembly).

Year	Winner	Jockey	Second	Third	Strs	Final Time	1st Purse
2001	Point Given	G. L. Stevens	E Dubai	Dollar Bill	9	2:01.40	$600,000
2000	Unshaded	S. J. Sellers	Albert the Great	Commendable	9	2:02.59	$600,000
1999	Lemon Drop Kid	J. A. Santos	Vision and Verse	Menifee	8	2:02.19	$600,000
1998	Coronado's Quest	M. E. Smith	Victory Gallop	Raffie's Majesty	7	2:03.40	$450,000
1997	Deputy Commander	C. J. McCarron	Behrens	Awesome Again	8	2:04.08	$450,000
1996	Will's Way	J. F. Chavez	Louis Quatorze	Skip Away	7	2:02.55	$450,000
1995	Thunder Gulch	G. L. Stevens	Pyramid Peak	Malthus	7	2:03.70	$450,000
1994	Holy Bull	M. E. Smith	Concern	Tabasco Cat	5	2:02.03	$450,000
1993	Sea Hero	J. D. Bailey	Kissin Kris	Miner's Mark	11	2:01.95	$600,000
1992	Thunder Rumble	W. H. McCauley	Devil His Due	Dance Floor	10	2:00.99	$600,000

Tremont Stakes

Grade 3, Belmont Park, two-year-olds, 5½ furlongs, dirt. Held June 30, 2001, with a gross value of $106,300. First held in 1887. Graded since 1981. Stakes record 1:02.56 (1999 More Than Ready).

Year	Winner	Jockey	Second	Third	Strs	Final Time	1st Purse
2001	Buster's Daydream	J. R. Velazquez	Draw Play	Day Trader	5	1:03.96	$63,780
2000	City Zip	J. A. Santos	The Goo	Scorpion	5	1:03.81	$64,320
1999	More Than Ready	J. R. Velazquez	Afternoon Affair	King Kokand	6	1:02.56	$65,040
1998	Tactical Cat	J. D. Bailey	Lucky Roberto	King's Crown	6	1:03.33	$50,400
1997	Time Limit	J. Bravo	Torgan	El Mirasol	5	1:06.65	$32,100
1996	Kelly Kip	J-L. Samyn	Say Florida Sandy	Leestown	7	1:04.60	$33,210
1995	†Rosie O'Greta	J. A. Santos	Busheta Buck	Victory Speech	6	1:07.32	$32,400
1994	De Niro	E. Maple	Jump the Shadow	Mane Ingredient	6	1:05.05	$63,240
1993	Distinct Reality	J. D. Bailey	Gusto Z	Slew Gin Fizz	7	1:04.76	$67,470
1992	England Expects	J. D. Bailey	Peace Baby	Linear	10	1:03.20	$69,900

1992-'95 Tremont Breeders' Cup S. 1997-'98 not graded. 1997 Jigadee finished third, DQ to fourth. 1999 new track record. † denotes female.

Triple Bend Breeders' Cup Invitational Handicap

Grade 2, Hollywood Park, three-year-olds and up, 7 furlongs, dirt. Held July 1, 2001, with a gross value of $296,000. First held in 1952. Graded since 1988. Stakes record 1:19.40 (1980 Rich Cream).

Year	Winner	Jockey	Second	Third	Strs	Final Time	1st Purse
2001	Ceeband, 4, 110	M. S. Garcia	Squirtle Squirt, 3	Elaborate, 3	10	1:21.17	$150,000
2000	Elaborate, 5, 114	V. Espinoza	Cliquot, 4	Lexicon, 4	10	1:21.19	$180,000
1999	Mazel Trick, 4, 115	C. J. McCarron	Christmas Boy, 6	Regal Thunder, 6	8	1:19.97	$180,000
1998	Son of a Pistol, 6, 118	A. O. Solis	The Exeter Man, 6	Benchmark, 6	11	1:20.81	$120,000
1997	Score Quick, 5, 113	G. F. Almeida	Elmhurst, 7	First Intent, 7	11	1:21.01	$100,980

Year	Winner	Jockey	Second	Third	Strs	Final Time	1st Purse
1996	Letthebighossroll, 8, 116	C. J. McCarron	Score Quick, 4	Comininalittlehot, 4	7	1:21.43	$125,460
1995	Concept Win, 5, 118	P. A. Valenzuela	Gold Land, 4	Lucky Forever, 4	6	1:21.09	$63,100
1994	Memo (Chi), 7, 120	P. Atkinson	Minjinsky, 4	Slerp, 4	6	1:20.52	$62,400
1993	Now Listen, 6, 116	K. J. Desormeaux	Cardmania, 7	Star of the Crop, 7	10	1:20.83	$66,400
1992	Slew the Surgeon, 4, 111	M. G. Linares	Softshoe Sure Shot, 6	Record Boom, 6	8	1:21.44	$64,600

1992-'95 Triple Bend H.; 1996-'97 Triple Bend Breeders' Cup H.; 1998 Triple Bend Invitational Breeders' Cup H. 1993 equaled track record; 1994, 1999 new track record. 1992-'97 Grade 3.

Tropical Park Derby

Grade 3, Calder Race Course, three-year-olds, 1⅛ miles, turf. Held January 1, 2001, with a gross value of $100,000. First held in 1976. Graded since 1978. Stakes record 1:46.60 (2000 Go Lib Go).

Year	Winner	Jockey	Second	Third	Strs	Final Time	1st Purse
2001	Proud Man	R. R. Douglas	Mr Notebook	Cee Dee	11	1:47.95	$60,000
2000	Go Lib Go	J. A. Santos	Mr. Livingston	Granting	12	1:46.60	$60,000
1999	Valid Reprized	J. Castellano	Mr. Roark	Wertz	12	1:53.58	$60,000
1998	Draw Again	J. Bravo	Buddha's Delight	Daddy's Dream	11	1:51.28	$60,000
1997	Arthur L.	E. Coa	Unite's Big Red	Keep It Strait	12	1:46.93	$60,000
1996	Ok by Me	J. D. Bailey	Darn That Erica	Tour's Big Red	12	1:47.25	$60,000
1995	Mecke	H. Castillo Jr.	Val's Prince	Claudius	14	1:51.12	$60,000
1994	Fabulous Frolic	J. Cruguet	Wake Up Alarm	Gator Back	14	1:46.99	$60,000
1993	Summer Set	M. A. Gonzalez	Duc d'Sligovil	Silver of Silver	10	1:53.87	$60,000
1992	Technology	J. D. Bailey	Majestic Sweep	Always Silver	10	1:53.01	$134,160

1994 about 1⅛ miles. 1992-'93 dirt.

Tropical Turf Handicap

Grade 3, Calder Race Course, three-year-olds and up, 1⅛ miles, turf. Held December 8, 2001, with a gross value of $100,000. First held in 1972. Graded since 1973. Stakes record 1:44.95 (1993 Carterista).

Year	Winner	Jockey	Second	Third	Strs	Final Time	1st Purse
2001	Band Is Passing, 5, 118	C. Gonzalez	Crash Course, 5	Groomstick Stock's, 5	12	1:46.90	$60,000
2000	Stokosky, 4, 114	C. A. Hernandez	(DH) Special Coach, 4 (DH) Band Is Passing, 4		11	1:48.77	$60,000
1999	Hibernian Rhapsody (Ire), 4, 114	R. R. Douglas	Garbu, 5	Shamrock City, 4	12	1:46.17	$60,000
1998	Unite's Big Red, 4, 115	E. O. Nunez	N B Forrest, 6	Glok, 4	8	1:48.96	$60,000
1997	Sir Cat, 4, 116	J. A. Rivera II	Foolish Pole, 4	Written Approval, 5	6	1:54.08	$60,000
1996	Mecke, 4, 124	R. G. Davis	Satellite Nealski, 3	Elite Jeblar, 6	10	1:46.51	$60,000
1995	The Vid, 5, 120	W. H. McCauley	Elite Jeblar, 5	Scannapieco, 5	12	1:44.99	$60,000
1994	The Vid, 4, 116	R. R. Douglas	Country Coy, 4	Gone for Real, 3	10	1:49.06	$60,000
1993	Carterista, 4, 121	W. S. Ramos	Rinka Das, 5	Daarik (Ire), 6	12	1:44.95	$45,000
1992	Bidding Proud, 3, 115	J. A. Santos	Buckhar, 4	Plate Dancer, 7	7	1:46.02	$30,000
	Carterista, 3, 112	M. A. Lee	Rinka Das, 4	Pidgeon's Promise, 3	11	1:46.35	$30,000

1992 two divisions. 2000 dead heat for second.

True North Handicap

Grade 2, Belmont Park, three-year-olds and up, 6 furlongs, dirt. Held June 9, 2001, with a gross value of $150,000. First held in 1979. Graded since 1983. Stakes record 1:07.80 (1987 Groovy).

Year	Winner	Jockey	Second	Third	Strs	Final Time	1st Purse
2001	Say Florida Sandy, 7, 116	A. T. Gryder	Wake At Noon, 4	Explicit, 4	8	1:08.77	$90,000
2000	Intidab, 7, 117	R. G. Davis	Brutally Frank, 6	Oro de Mexico, 6	7	1:10.22	$90,000
1999	Kashatreya, 5, 110	J-L. Samyn	Artax, 4	The Trader's Echo, 4	9	1:09.63	$90,000
1998	Richter Scale, 4, 119	J. D. Bailey	Trafalger, 4	Kelly Kip, 4	8	1:08.83	$83,160
1997	Punch Line, 7, 122	R. G. Davis	Cold Execution, 5	Jamies First Punch, 6	7	1:08.96	$66,180
1996	Not Surprising, 6, 121	R. G. Davis	Prospect Bay, 4	Forest Wildcat, 4	8	1:09.17	$66,720
1995	Waldoboro, 4, 112	E. Maple	Corma Ray, 5	Mining Burrah, 4	8	1:09.62	$66,300
1994	Friendly Lover, 6, 114	R. Wilson	Boundary, 4	Birdonthewire, 4	9	1:09.65	$67,380
1993	Lion Cavern, 4, 116	J. A. Krone	Arrowtown, 5	Codys Key, 5	7	1:10.33	$69,120
1992	Shining Bid, 4, 112	E. Maple	Arrowtown, 4	To Freedom, 4	9	1:08.28	$71,880

Turf Classic Invitational Stakes

Grade 1, Belmont Park, three-year-olds and up, 1½ miles, turf. Held September 29, 2001, with a gross value of $750,000. First held in 1977. Graded since 1979. Stakes record 2:24.50 (1992 Sky Classic).

Year	Winner	Jockey	Second	Third	Strs	Final Time	1st Purse
2001	Timboroa (GB), 5	E. S. Prado	King Cugat, 4	Cetewayo, 7	5	2:29.43	$450,000
2000	John's Call, 9	J-L. Samyn	Craigsteel (GB), 5	†Ela Athena (GB), 4	12	2:28.58	$450,000
1999	Val's Prince, 7	J. F. Chavez	Dream Well (Fr), 4	Fahris (Ire), 5	7	2:28.63	$360,000
1998	Buck's Boy, 5	S. J. Sellers	Cetewayo, 4	Lazy Lode (Arg), 4	6	2:33.25	$300,000
1997	Val's Prince, 5	M. E. Smith	Flag Down, 7	Ops Smile, 5	5	2:28.92	$300,000
1996	Diplomatic Jet, 4	J. F. Chavez	Awad, 6	Marlin, 3	10	2:27.51	$300,000
1995	Turk Passer, 5	J. R. Velazquez	Hernando (Fr), 5	Celtic Arms (Fr), 4	8	2:36.63	$300,000

Year	Winner	Jockey	Second	Third	Strs	Final Time	1st Purse
1994	**Tikkanen**, 3	C. B. Asmussen	Vaudeville, 3	Yenda (GB), 3	6	2:25.88	$300,000
1993	**Apple Tree (Fr)**, 4	M. E. Smith	Solar Splendor, 6	George Augustus, 5	5	2:28.31	$300,000
1992	**Sky Classic**, 5	P. Day	Fraise, 4	Solar Splendor, 5	6	**2:24.50**	$300,000

1992 new course record. † denotes female.

(Woodford Reserve) Turf Classic Stakes

Grade 1, Churchill Downs, three-year-olds and up, 1⅛ miles, turf. Held May 5, 2001, with a gross value of $349,900. First held in 1987. Graded since 1989. Stakes record 1:46.34 (1993 Lure).

Year	Winner	Jockey	Second	Third	Strs	Final Time	1st Purse
2001	**White Heart (GB)**, 6	G. L. Stevens	King Cugat, 4	Brahms, 4	8	1:48.75	$216,938
2000	**Manndar (Ire)**, 4	C. S. Nakatani	Falcon Flight (Fr), 4	Yagli, 4	8	1:47.91	$217,310
1999	**Wild Event**, 6	S. J. Sellers	Garbu, 5	Hawksley Hill (Ire), 5	7	1:47.25	$206,646
1998	**Joyeux Danseur**, 5	R. Albarado	Lasting Approval, 4	Hawksley Hill (Ire), 4	8	1:48.14	$174,282
1997	**Always a Classic**, 4	J. D. Bailey	Labeeb (GB), 5	Down the Aisle, 5	8	1:49.29	$145,328
1996	**Mecke**, 4	P. Day	Petit Poucet (GB), 4	Winged Victory, 4	11	1:49.48	$165,230
1995	**Romarin (Brz)**, 5	C. S. Nakatani	Blues Traveller (Ire), 5	Hasten To Add, 5	12	1:46.86	$160,095
1994	**Paradise Creek**, 5	P. Day	Lure, 5	Yukon Robbery, 5	7	1:48.34	$152,068
1993	**Lure**, 4	M. E. Smith	Star of Cozzene, 5	Cleone, 5	8	**1:46.34**	$117,683
1992	**Cudas**, 4	P. A. Valenzuela	Sky Classic, 5	Fourstars Allstar, 5	12	1:46.56	$124,703

1992-'99 Early Times Turf Classic S.; 2000-'01 Woodford Reserve Turf Classic S.; 1992-'93 Grade 3; 1994-'95 Grade 2. 1992, 1993 new course record.

Turf Sprint Stakes

Grade 3, Churchill Downs, three-year-olds and up, 5 furlongs, turf. Held May 4, 2001, with a gross value of $113,700. Stakes record :56.09 (1996 Danjur).

Year	Winner	Jockey	Second	Third	Strs	Final Time	1st Purse
2001	**Morluc**, 5	R. Albarado	Testify, 4	Texas Glitter, 4	9	:56.60	$70,494
2000	**Bold Fact**, 5	R. Migliore	Howbaddouwantit, 5	Fantastic Finish, 5	12	:56.37	$75,330
1999	**Howbaddouwantit**, 4	M. E. Smith	Mr Festus, 4	Three Card Willie, 4	11	:57.03	$71,486
1998	**Indian Rocket (GB)**, 4	G. L. Stevens	G H's Pleasure, 6	Claire's Honor, 6	12	:57.32	$75,950
1997	**Sandtrap**, 4	A. O. Solis	Appealing Skier, 4	G H's Pleasure, 4	11	:56.51	$71,734
1996	**Danjur**, 4	J. D. Bailey	Hello Paradise, 5	Linear, 5	10	**:56.09**	$57,281
1995	**Long Suit**, 4	W. Martinez	Bold n' Flashy, 6	Scottish Fantasy, 6	11	:56.90	$57,086

1995-'98 Churchill Downs Turf Sprint S.; 1999-2001 Aegon Turf Sprint S.; 1995 course record; 1996 new course record.

Turfway Breeders' Cup Stakes

Grade 3, Turfway Park, three-year-olds and up, fillies and mares, 1¹⁄₁₆ miles, dirt. Held September 22, 2001, with a gross value of $200,000. First held in 1986. Graded since 1990. Stakes record 1:41.67 (1995 Mariah's Storm).

Year	Winner	Jockey	Second	Third	Strs	Final Time	1st Purse
2001	**Trip**, 4	C. Perret	Precious Feather, 4	Spain, 4	7	1:42.47	$125,500
2000	**Spain**, 3	P. Day	Ruby Surprise, 5	Undermine, 4	9	1:44.85	$156,500
1999	**Ruby Surprise**, 4	W. Martinez	Let, 4	French Braids, 4	8	1:44.95	$162,886
1998	**Biding Time**, 4	C. S. Nakatani	Meter Maid, 4	Dancing Gulch, 4	7	1:43.13	$162,266
1997	**Feasibility Study**, 5	M. E. Smith	City Band, 3	Gold n Delicious, 4	5	1:42.50	$161,522
1996	**Golden Attraction**, 3	G. L. Stevens	Bedroom Blues, 5	Betty Van, 4	8	1:42.53	$205,920
1995	**Mariah's Storm**, 4	R. N. Lester	Serena's Song, 3	Alcovy, 5	5	**1:41.67**	$116,415
1994	**Pennyhill Park**, 4	C. J. McCarron	Roamin Rachel, 4	Hey Hazel, 4	10	1:44.20	$118,073
1993	**Gray Cashmere**, 4	D. Kutz	Deputation, 4	November Snow, 4	8	1:43.39	$117,130
1992	**Fit for a Queen**, 6	R. D. Lopez	Auto Dial, 4	Hitch, 3	9	1:43.30	$117,975

1992 Budweiser Breeders' Cup S.; 1995 Turfway Park Breeders' Cup S. 1992-'98 Grade 2.

Turfway Park Fall Championship Stakes

Grade 3, Turfway Park, three-year-olds and up, 1⅛ miles, dirt. Held September 8, 2001, with a gross value of $82,500. First held in 1919. Graded since 1997. Stakes record 1:48.67 (1992 Flying Continental).

Year	Winner	Jockey	Second	Third	Strs	Final Time	1st Purse
2001	**Generous Rosi (GB)**, 6	L. Meche	Storm Day, 4	Jadada, 6	6	1:49.83	$46,500
2000	**Mount Lemon**, 6	R. Albarado	Unloosened, 5	Phil the Grip, 6	7	1:51.14	$62,600
1999	**Phil the Grip**, 5	R. Albarado	Part the Waters, 5	Metatonia, 4	5	1:52.15	$49,600
1998	**Acceptable**, 4	C. Perret	Magnify, 4	Muchacho Fino, 4	4	1:51.95	$62,600
1997	**Tejano Run**, 5	W. Martinez	Short Stay, 5	Thesaurus, 3	7	1:49.44	$46,950
1996	**Strawberry Wine**, 4	B. D. Peck	Kiridashi, 4	Prospect for Love, 4	8	1:50.15	$65,000
1995	**Bound by Honor**, 4	R. P. Romero	Lord Gordon, 5	Lordly Prospect, 6	6	1:51.54	$48,750
1994	**Meena**, 6	W. Martinez	Powerful Punch, 5	It'sali'lknownfact, 4	4	1:52.92	$27,284
1993	**Powerful Punch**, 4	C. C. Bourque	Medium Cool, 5	Benburb, 4	7	1:50.51	$41,048
1992	**Flying Continental**, 6	J. Velasquez	Alyten, 5	Regal Affair, 6	5	**1:48.67**	$27,511

1992-'95, 1997 Turfway Championship H.; 1996, 1998-'99 Kentucky Cup Classic Preview H.; 2000 Turfway Park Fall Championship H.

Turnback the Alarm Handicap

Grade 3, Aqueduct, three-year-olds and up, fillies and mares, 1⅛ miles, dirt. Held November 3, 2001, with a gross value of $108,500. First held in 1995. Graded since 1999. Stakes record 1:48.89 (1995 Incinerate).

Year	Winner	Jockey	Second	Third	Strs	Final Time	1st Purse
2001	Rochelle's Terms, 4, 113	R. G. Davis	Resort, 4	Strolling Belle, 5	6	1:51.19	$65,100
2000	Atelier, 3, 113	E. S. Prado	Tap to Music, 5	Pentatonic, 5	10	1:48.95	$67,920
1999	Belle Cherie, 3, 112	J. R. Velazquez	Brushed Halory, 3	Sweet Misty, 5	8	1:50.03	$66,000
1998	Snit, 4, 117	J. R. Velazquez	Manoa, 3	Shoop, 7	8	1:51.30	$49,740
1997	Mil Kilates, 4, 116	J. Bravo	Radiant Megan, 4	Shoop, 6	5	1:49.40	$48,330
1996	Shoop, 5, 121	J. D. Bailey	Queen Tutta, 4	Madame Adolphe, 4	4	1:51.35	$48,420
1995	Incinerate, 5, 115	F. Leon	Lotta Dancing, 4	Pretty Discreet, 3	7	**1:48.89**	$49,005

United Nations Handicap

Grade 1, Monmouth Park, three-year-olds and up, 1⅜ miles, turf. Held July 1, 2001, with a gross value of $500,000. First held in 1953. Graded since 1973. Stakes record 2:13.56 (2001 With Anticipation).

Year	Winner	Jockey	Second	Third	Strs	Final Time	1st Purse
2001	Senure, 5, 116	R. G. Davis	With Anticipation, 6	Gritty Sandie, 6	8	**2:13.56**	$300,000
2000	Down the Aisle, 7, 114	R. G. Davis	Aly's Alley, 4	Honor Glide, 4	7	2:13.63	$210,000
1999	Yagli, 6, 124	J. D. Bailey	Supreme Sound (GB), 5	Amerique, 5	6	2:16.02	$150,000
1997	Influent, 6, 117	J-L. Samyn	Geri, 5	Flag Down, 5	4	1:53.72	$240,000
1996	Sandpit (Brz), 7, 122	C. S. Nakatani	Diplomatic Jet, 4	Northern Spur (Ire), 4	8	1:55.71	$300,000
1995	Sandpit (Brz), 6, 122	C. S. Nakatani	Celtic Arms (Fr), 4	Alice Springs, 4	9	1:57.25	$300,000
1994	Lure, 5, 123	M. E. Smith	Fourstars Allstar, 6	Star of Cozzene, 6	5	1:52.66	$300,000
1993	Star of Cozzene, 5, 120	J. A. Santos	Lure, 4	Finder's Choice, 4	7	1:53.22	$300,000
1992	Sky Classic, 5, 123	P. Day	Chenin Blanc, 6	Lotus Pool, 6	9	1:52.53	$300,000

1998 not held. 1992-'97 held at Atlantic City Race Course. 1992-'97 Caesars International H. 1992-'93 Grade 2. 1992-'97 1³⁄₁₆ miles. 1999 equaled course record; 2000 new course record. 2001 With Anticipation finished first, DQ to second.

Vagrancy Handicap

Grade 3, Belmont Park, three-year-olds and up, fillies and mares, 6½ furlongs, dirt. Held June 16, 2001, with a gross value of $106,800. First held in 1948. Graded since 1973. Stakes record 1:15.32 (2001 Dat You Miz Blue).

Year	Winner	Jockey	Second	Third	Strs	Final Time	1st Purse
2001	Dat You Miz Blue, 4, 116	J. R. Velazquez	Dream Supreme, 4	Katz Me If You Can, 4	5	**1:15.32**	$64,080
2000	Country Hideaway, 4, 117	J. D. Bailey	Hurricane Bertie, 5	Imperfect World, 5	7	1:17.05	$65,640
1999	Gold Princess, 4, 114	J. R. Velazquez	Hurricane Bertie, 4	Delta Music, 4	5	1:16.57	$63,840
1998	Chip, 5, 115	J. Bravo	Furlough, 4	Parlay, 4	6	1:15.69	$48,945
1997	Inquisitive Look, 4, 111	J. F. Chavez	Flat Fleet Feet, 4	Mama Dean, 4	6	1:22.07	$64,800
1996	Twist Afleet, 5, 122	J. A. Krone	Smooth Charmer, 4	Lottsa Talc, 4	8	1:20.94	$66,300
1995	Sky Beauty, 5, 125	M. E. Smith	Aly's Conquest, 4	Through the Door, 4	4	1:21.56	$47,865
1994	Sky Beauty, 4, 122	M. E. Smith	For all Seasons, 4	Pamzig, 4	6	1:21.67	$48,855
1993	Spinning Round, 4, 112	J. F. Chavez	Reach for Clever, 6	Nannerl, 6	8	1:24.52	$52,740
1992	Nannerl, 5, 116	J. A. Santos	Serape, 4	Makin Faces, 4	6	1:22.55	$51,210

1992-'97 7 furlongs. 1997 held at Aqueduct. 1999 Hurricane Bertie finished first, DQ to second.

Valley Stream Stakes

Grade 3, Aqueduct, two-year-old fillies, 6 furlongs, dirt. Held November 18, 2001, with a gross value of $80,775. First held in 1995. Graded since 2001. Stakes record 1:08.66 (2001 Forest Heiress).

Year	Winner	Jockey	Second	Third	Strs	Final Time	1st Purse
2001	Forest Heiress	R. Migliore	A New Twist	On Parade	6	**1:08.66**	$48,465
2000	Astrapi	D. Nelson	Major Wager	Look of the Lynx	5	1:10.66	$48,570
1999	Magicalmysterycat	M. E. Smith	Sahara Gold	Silentlea	8	1:10.53	$49,815
1998	Paula's Girl	J. R. Velazquez	President's Girl	Godmother	5	1:11.99	$38,700
1997	Cotton House Bay	J. F. Chavez	Foil	Kate Again	10	1:10.11	$33,990
1996	Dixie Flag	J-L. Samyn	Alyssum	Nimble Tread	6	1:10.13	$32,490
1995	Oxford Scholar	J. D. Bailey	Zee Lady	Stormy Krissy	5	1:12.13	$32,430

1995 held at Belmont Park.

Valley View Stakes

Grade 3, Keeneland, three-year-old fillies, 1¹⁄₁₆ miles, turf. Held October 20, 2001, with a gross value of $113,600. First held in 1991. Graded since 1999. Stakes record 1:41.51 (1992 Spinning Round).

Year	Winner	Jockey	Second	Third	Strs	Final Time	1st Purse
2001	(DH) Cozzy Corner	L. Meche		Quick Tip	10	1:42.93	$46,576
	(DH) Chausson Poire						
2000	Good Game	P. Day	Impending Bear	Soccory	10	1:45.69	$71,176
1999	Gimmeakissee	P. J. Cooksey	The Happy Hopper	Celestialbutterfly	9	1:42.05	$70,122
1998	White Beauty	C. H. Borel	Shires Ende	Leaveemlaughing	8	1:43.09	$52,406
1997	Mingling Glances	J. Bravo	Majestic Sunlight	Fluid Move	9	1:44.51	$52,592

Year	Winner	Jockey	Second	Third	Strs	Final Time	1st Purse
1996	Turkappeal	D. M. Barton	Inner Circle	Mariuka	9	1:46.10	$52,126
1995	Country Cat	D. M. Barton	Appointed One	Petrouchka	10	1:44.88	$51,150
1994	Pharma	C. W. Antley	Mariah's Storm	Thread	9	1:42.48	$50,747
1993	Weekend Madness (Ire)	C. R. Woods Jr.	Life Is Delicious	Augusta Springs	10	1:43.06	$23,870
1992	Spinning Round	F. A. Arguello Jr.	Shes Just Super	Enticed	9	1:41.51	$23,870

2001 dead heat for first.

Vanity Handicap

Grade 1, Hollywood Park, three-year-olds and up, fillies and mares, 1⅛ miles, dirt. Held June 30, 2001, with a gross value of $250,000. First held in 1940. Graded since 1973. Stakes record 1:46.20 (1984 Princess Rooney).

Year	Winner	Jockey	Second	Third	Strs	Final Time	1st Purse
2001	Gourmet Girl, 6, 119	G. L. Stevens	Lazy Slusan, 6	Setareh, 6	5	1:49.21	$150,000
2000	Riboletta (Brz), 5, 123	C. J. McCarron	Speaking of Time, 4	Excellent Meeting, 4	6	1:48.54	$180,000
1999	Manistique, 4, 122	C. J. McCarron	Yolo Lady, 4	Bella Chiarra, 4	6	1:48.06	$240,000
1998	Escena, 5, 124	J. D. Bailey	Housa Dancer (Fr), 5	Different (Arg), 5	7	1:48.13	$210,000
1997	Twice the Vice, 6, 121	K. J. Desormeaux	Real Connection, 6	Jewel Princess, 6	5	1:46.41	$240,000
1996	Jewel Princess, 4, 120	C. S. Nakatani	Serena's Song, 4	Top Rung, 4	6	1:47.17	$150,000
1995	Private Persuasion, 4, 114	G. L. Stevens	Top Rung, 4	Wandesta (GB), 4	7	1:48.30	$165,000
1994	Potridee (Arg), 5, 114	A. O. Solis	Exchange, 6	Golden Klair (GB), 6	8	1:48.08	$165,000
1993	Re Toss (Arg), 6, 116	E. Delahoussaye	Paseana (Arg), 6	Guiza, 6	8	1:47.92	$165,000
1992	Paseana (Arg), 5, 127	C. J. McCarron	Fowda, 6	Re Toss (Arg), 4	6	1:48.06	$165,000

1994-'96; 1998 Vanity Invitational H.

Vernon O. Underwood Stakes

Grade 3, Hollywood Park, three-year-olds and up, 6 furlongs, dirt. Held December 2, 2001, with a gross value of $100,000. First held in 1981. Graded since 1984. Stakes record 1:08.17 (1997 Tower Full).

Year	Winner	Jockey	Second	Third	Strs	Final Time	1st Purse
2001	Men's Exclusive, 8	L. A. Pincay Jr.	Tavasco, 4	Caller One, 4	7	1:09.04	$60,000
2000	Men's Exclusive, 7	L. A. Pincay Jr.	Love All the Way, 5	Lexicon, 5	7	1:09.02	$60,000
1999	Five Star Day, 3	A. O. Solis	Your Halo, 4	Son of a Pistol, 7	5	1:09.91	$60,000
1998	Love That Jazz, 4	K. J. Desormeaux	Peyrano (Arg), 6	Swiss Yodeler, 4	8	1:08.79	$60,000
1997	Tower Full, 5	C. S. Nakatani	Trafalger, 3	Swiss Yodeler, 3	4	1:08.17	$60,000
1996	Paying Dues, 4	P. Day	Men's Exclusive, 3	Kern Ridge, 5	7	1:08.24	$64,860
1995	Powis Castle, 4	G. L. Stevens	Lucky Forever, 6	Plenty Zloty, 5	8	1:08.40	$62,300
1994	Wekiva Springs, 3	K. J. Desormeaux	Cardmania, 8	Gundaghia, 7	9	1:08.37	$63,750
1993	†Meafara, 4	G. L. Stevens	†Arches of Gold, 5	Davy Be Good, 5	6	1:10.01	$60,900
1992	Gundaghia, 5	G. L. Stevens	Gray Slewpy, 4	Cardmania, 6	5	1:09.33	$61,300

1993-'95 Vernon O. Underwood Breeders' Cup S. † denotes female.

Vinery Matchmaker Stakes

Grade 3, Monmouth Park, three-year-olds and up, fillies and mares, 1⅛ miles, turf. Held June 16, 2001, with a gross value of $100,000. First held in 1967. Graded since 1973. Stakes record 1:46.19 (2001 Batique).

Year	Winner	Jockey	Second	Third	Strs	Final Time	1st Purse
2001	Batique, 5	J. C. Ferrer	Melody Queen (GB), 5	Lucky Lune (Fr), 5	8	1:46.19	$60,000
2000	Horatia (Ire), 4	J. A. Santos	Camella, 5	Champagne Royal, 5	11	1:47.52	$60,000
1999	Natalie Too, 5	J. Bravo	Saralea (Fr), 4	U R Unforgetable, 4	6	1:46.81	$60,000
1998	Bursting Forth, 4	M. E. Verge	French Buster, 4	Gastronomical, 4	9	1:48.46	$60,000
1997	Fleur de Nuit, 4	J. A. Krone	Flame Valley, 4	Overcharger, 4	7	1:48.91	$60,000
1996	Powder Bowl, 4	D. S. Rice	Class Kris, 4	Turkish Tryst, 4	6	1:54.71	$60,000
1995	Avie's Fancy, 4	W. H. McCauley	Plenty of Sugar, 4	Northern Emerald, 4	8	1:54.19	$60,000
1994	Alice Springs, 4	J. A. Krone	Hero's Love, 6	Cox Orange, 6	8	1:55.21	$60,000
1993	Fairy Garden, 5	M. E. Smith	Saratoga Source, 4	Logan's Mist, 4	8	1:57.81	$60,000
1992	Radiant Ring, 4	R. E. Colton	Highland Crystal, 4	La Gueriere, 4	8	1:55.92	$60,000

1992-'95 Matchmaker S.; 1997 Gainesway Matchmaker S. 1992-'96 Grade 2. 1992-'96 held at Atlantic City Race Course. 1992-'96 1³⁄₁₆ miles. 2001 new course record.

Violet Handicap

Grade 3, The Meadowlands, three-year-olds and up, fillies and mares, 1¹⁄₁₆ miles, turf. Held September 28, 2001, with a gross value of $150,000. First held in 1977. Graded since 1983. Stakes record 1:39.60 (1989 Gather the Clan).

Year	Winner	Jockey	Second	Third	Strs	Final Time	1st Purse
2001	Clearly a Queen, 4, 115	J. F. Chavez	Queue, 4	Paga (Arg), 4	12	1:43.56	$115,000
2000	Follow the Money, 4, 116	C. J. McCarron	Melody Queen (GB), 4	Fickle Friends, 4	7	1:42.65	$90,000
1999	Tookin Down, 4, 113	E. S. Prado	Proud Run, 5	Darling Alice, 4	7	1:42.39	$90,000
1998	Heaven's Command (GB), 4, 115	R. Migliore	Maxzene, 5	Oh Nellie, 4	7	1:40.71	$60,000
1997	Sangria, 4, 114	R. Wilson	Fasta, 4	Shemozzle (Ire), 4	8	1:42.02	$60,000

Year	Winner	Jockey	Second	Third	Strs	Final Time	1st Purse
1996	Plenty of Sugar, 5, 117	R. E. Colton	Brushing Gloom, 4	Hello Mom, 4	6	1:48.62	$60,000
1995	Symphony Lady, 5, 116	J. Bravo	Kira's Dancer, 6	Irish Linnet, 7	8	1:45.48	$60,000
1994	It's Personal, 4, 111	J. R. Velazquez	Carezza, 5	Artful Pleasure, 4	11	1:42.61	$45,000
1993	Mz. Zill Bear, 4, 113	E. S. Prado	Vivano, 4	Topsa, 6	4	1:44.55	$45,000
1992	Highland Crystal, 4, 116	E. S. Prado	Irish Actress, 5	Navarra, 4	7	1:41.26	$45,000

Vosburgh Stakes

Grade 1, Belmont Park, three-year-olds and up, 7 furlongs, dirt. Held September 22, 2001, with a gross value of $300,000. First held in 1940. Graded since 1973. Stakes record 1:20.20 (1968 Dr. Fager).

Year	Winner	Jockey	Second	Third	Strs	Final Time	1st Purse
2001	Left Bank, 4	J. R. Velazquez	Squirtle Squirt, 3	Big E E, 4	6	1:20.73	$180,000
2000	Trippi, 3	J. D. Bailey	More Than Ready, 3	One Way Love, 5	10	1:21.66	$180,000
1999	Artax, 4	J. F. Chavez	Stormin Fever, 5	Mountain Top, 4	6	1:21.65	$150,000
1998	Affirmed Success, 4	J. F. Chavez	Stormin Fever, 4	Tale of the Cat, 4	7	1:21.99	$150,000
1997	Victor Cooley, 4	J. F. Chavez	Score a Birdie, 6	Tale of the Cat, 3	12	1:22.05	$150,000
1996	Langfuhr, 4	J. F. Chavez	Honour and Glory, 3	Lite the Fuse, 5	8	1:21.25	$120,000
1995	Not Surprising, 5	R. G. Davis	You and I, 4	Our Emblem, 4	13	1:22.48	$120,000
1994	Harlan, 5	J. D. Bailey	American Chance, 5	Cherokee Run, 4	10	1:21.82	$120,000
1993	Birdonthewire, 4	M. E. Smith	Take Me Out, 5	Lion Cavern, 4	6	1:22.28	$120,000
1992	Rubiano, 5	J. A. Krone	Sheikh Albadou (GB), 4	Salt Lake, 3	8	1:22.80	$120,000

Walmac Int'l. Alcibiades Stakes

Grade 2, Keeneland, two-year-old fillies, 1 1/16 miles, dirt. Held October 5, 2001, with a gross value of $452,800. First held in 1952. Graded since 1973. Stakes record 1:42.24 (1998 Silverbulletday).

Year	Winner	Jockey	Second	Third	Strs	Final Time	1st Purse
2001	Take Charge Lady	A. J. D'Amico	Never Out	Cunning Play	11	1:46.23	$280,736
2000	She's a Devil Due	M. Guidry	Nasty Storm	Cash Deal	7	1:44.86	$270,320
1999	Scratch Pad	W. Martinez	Rare Beauty	Cash Run	8	1:44.16	$274,288
1998	Silverbulletday	G. L. Stevens	Extended Applause	Grand Deed	11	1:42.24	$281,976
1997	Countess Diana	S. J. Sellers	Lily O'Gold	Beautiful Pleasure	6	1:45.39	$266,600
1996	Southern Playgirl	R. P. Romero	Screamer	Private Pursuit	7	1:46.94	$168,330
1995	Cara Rafaela	P. Day	Birr	Gold Sunrise	10	1:44.43	$139,252
1994	Post It	S. Maple	Morris Code	Cat Appeal	5	1:46.33	$66,650
1993	Stellar Cat	S. J. Sellers	Slew Kitty Slew	Beau Blush	6	1:44.68	$122,200
1992	Eliza	P. A. Valenzuela	Avie's Shadow	True Affair	6	1:43.30	$122,200

1992-'96 Alcibiades S. 1996 Private Pursuit finished second, DQ to third.

Washington Park Handicap

Grade 2, Arlington Park, three-year-olds and up, 1 1/4 miles, dirt. Held July 21, 2001, with a gross value of $400,000. First held in 1926. Graded since 1973. Stakes record 2:00.76 (2001 Guided Tour).

Year	Winner	Jockey	Second	Third	Strs	Final Time	1st Purse
2001	Guided Tour, 5, 116	L. Melancon	A Fleets Dancer, 6	Duckhorn, 4	5	2:00.76	$240,000
2000	Blazing Sword, 6, 113	J. A. Rivera II	Mula Gula, 4	Nite Dreamer, 5	8	1:50.59	$150,000
1997	Beboppin Baby, 4, 112	G. K. Gomez	City by Night, 4	Stephanotis, 4	5	1:49.03	$90,000
1996	Polar Expedition, 5, 115	M. Guidry	Knockadoon, 4	Tejano Run, 4	8	1:49.97	$120,000
1994	Brother Brown, 4, 117	P. Day	Eequalsmcsquared, 5	Antrim Rd., 4	11	1:49.77	$120,000
1993	Powerful Punch, 4, 114	C. C. Bourque	Memo (Chi), 6	Northern Trend, 5	13	1:50.19	$120,000
1992	Irish Swap, 5, 118	B. E. Poyadou	Clever Trevor, 6	Barkerville, 4	7	1:47.83	$90,000

1995, 1998-'99 not held. 1992-2000 1 1/8 miles.

Westchester Handicap

Grade 3, Aqueduct, three-year-olds and up, 1 mile, dirt. Held April 7, 2001, with a gross value of $108,200. First held in 1918. Graded since 1973. Stakes record 1:33.60 (2001 Cat's At Home).

Year	Winner	Jockey	Second	Third	Strs	Final Time	1st Purse
2001	Cat's At Home, 4, 114	F. Leon	Little Hans, 4	Milwaukee Brew, 4	6	1:33.60	$64,920
2000	Yankee Victor, 4, 115	H. Castillo Jr.	Golden Missile, 5	Watchman's Warning, 5	7	1:34.37	$66,000
1999	Mr. Sinatra, 5, 116	C. C. Lopez	Laredo, 6	Brushing Up, 6	4	1:35.04	$64,202
1998	Wagon Limit, 4, 114	J-L. Samyn	Draw, 5	Lucayan Prince, 5	8	1:34.06	$66,420
1997	Pacific Fleet, 5, 114	F. T. Alvarado	Circle of Light, 4	Stalwart Member, 4	7	1:33.88	$65,940
1996	Valid Wager, 4, 115	J. M. Pezua	Pat n Jac, 4	More to Tell, 4	7	1:34.74	$66,240
1995	Mr. Shawklit, 4, 112	M. J. Luzzi	Devil His Due, 6	Our Emblem, 6	6	1:34.66	$65,760
1994	Virginia Rapids, 4, 116	J-L. Samyn	Colonial Affair, 4	Cherokee Run, 4	7	1:34.52	$65,640
1993	Bill Of Rights, 4, 110	J-L. Samyn	Fly So Free, 5	Loach, 5	10	1:34.69	$72,720
1992	Rubiano, 5, 117	J. A. Santos	Out of Place, 5	Wild Away, 5	6	1:34.83	$68,880

West Virginia Derby

Not graded, Mountaineer Park, three-year-olds, 1⅛ miles, dirt. Held August 11, 2001, with a gross value of $500,000. First held in 1958. Grade 3 since 2002. Stakes record 1:47.20 (2001 Western Pride).

Year	Winner	Jockey	Second	Third	Strs	Final Time	1st Purse
2001	**Western Pride**, 113	D. G. Whitney	Saratoga Games	Thunder Blitz	9	**1:47.20**	$300,000
2000	**Mass Market**, 115	R. Wilson	Hal's Hope	Bet On Red	10	1:49.94	$180,000
1999	**Stellar Brush**, 122	J. Stokes	American Spirit	Harry's Halo	11	1:49.02	$150,000
1998	**Da Devil**, 113	J. K. Court	One Bold Stroke	Jess M	12	1:48.84	$120,000

1992-'97 not held. 2001 new track record.

Whitney Handicap

Grade 1, Saratoga Race Course, three-year-olds and up, 1⅛ miles, dirt. Held July 28, 2001, with a gross value of $1,008,000. First held in 1928. Graded since 1973. Stakes record 1:47 (1974 Tri Jet).

Year	Winner	Jockey	Second	Third	Strs	Final Time	1st Purse
2001	**Lido Palace (Chi)**, 4, 115	J. D. Bailey	Albert the Great, 4	Gander, 5	7	1:47.94	$540,000
2000	**Lemon Drop Kid**, 4, 123	E. S. Prado	Cat Thief, 4	Behrens, 6	6	1:48.30	$680,000
1999	**Victory Gallop**, 4, 123	J. D. Bailey	Behrens, 5	Catienus, 5	8	1:48.66	$360,000
1998	**Awesome Again**, 4, 117	P. Day	Tale of the Cat, 4	Crypto Star, 4	8	1:49.71	$240,000
1997	**Will's Way**, 4, 117	J. D. Bailey	Formal Gold, 4	Skip Away, 4	6	1:48.37	$210,000
1996	**Mahogany Hall**, 5, 113	J. A. Santos	†Serena's Song, 4	Peaks and Valleys, 4	9	1:48.65	$210,000
1995	**Unaccounted For**, 4, 114	P. Day	L'Carriere, 4	Silver Fox, 4	9	1:49.29	$210,000
1994	**Colonial Affair**, 4, 117	J. A. Santos	Devil His Due, 5	West by West, 5	7	1:48.61	$210,000
1993	**Brunswick**, 4, 112	M. E. Smith	West by West, 4	Devil His Due, 4	7	1:47.41	$150,000
1992	**Sultry Song**, 4, 115	J. D. Bailey	Out of Place, 5	Chief Honcho, 5	9	1:47.29	$150,000

† denotes female.

Widener Handicap

Grade 3, Hialeah Park, three-year-olds and up, 1⅛ miles, dirt. Held March 24, 2001, with a gross value of $200,000. First held in 1936. Graded since 1973. Stakes record 1:45.52 (2001 Albert the Great).

Year	Winner	Jockey	Second	Third	Strs	Final Time	1st Purse
2001	**Albert the Great**, 4, 120	J. F. Chavez	U So Bad, 4	High Security (Ven), 4	7	**1:45.52**	$120,000
2000	**Blazing Sword**, 6, 112	J. Castellano	With Anticipation, 5	Karly's Harley, 5	4	1:51.73	$120,000
1999	**Golden Missile**, 4, 109	P. Day	Early Warning, 4	Sir Bear, 4	7	1:47.73	$120,000
1998	**Frisk Me Now**, 4, 118	P. Day	Sir Bear, 5	Black Forest, 5	5	1:47.44	$120,000
1997	**Tejano Run**, 5, 115	P. Day	Ghostly Moves, 5	Mt. Sassafras, 5	7	1:48.35	$120,000
1996	**Mecke**, 4, 119	P. Day	Personal Merit, 5	Jelly Roll Jive, 5	8	1:52.03	$120,000
1995	**Party Manners**, 4, 113	S. J. Sellers	Dusty Screen, 7	Pride of Burkaan, 7	14	1:47.33	$120,000
1994	**West by West**, 5, 114	J-L. Samyn	Migrating Moon, 4	Pistols and Roses, 4	8	1:49.98	$120,000
1993	**Honest Ensign**, 5, 112	P. A. Rodriguez	Northern Trend, 5	Boots 'n Buck, 5	10	1:48.80	$60,000

1992 not held. 1993 not graded. 2000 held at Gulfstream Park. 2000 Lemon Drop Kid finished first, DQ to fourth. 2001 new track record.

William Donald Schaefer Handicap

Grade 3, Pimlico, three-year-olds and up, 1⅛ miles, dirt. Held May 19, 2001, with a gross value of $100,000. First held in 1994. Graded since 2001. Stakes record 1:48.19 (1995 Tidal Surge).

Year	Winner	Jockey	Second	Third	Strs	Final Time	1st Purse
2001	**Perfect Cat**, 4, 115	J. D. Bailey	Rize, 5	Judge's Case, 5	8	1:49.55	$60,000
2000	**Ecton Park**, 4, 116	P. Day	The Groom Is Red, 4	Crosspatch, 4	4	1:49.21	$60,000
1999	**Perfect to a Tee**, 7, 112	A. C. Cortez	Allen's Oop, 4	Smile Again, 4	7	1:49.20	$60,000
1998	**Acceptable**, 4, 118	J. D. Bailey	Littlebitlively, 4	Testafly, 4	8	1:48.76	$60,000
1997	**Western Echo**, 5, 116	E. S. Prado	Suave Prospect, 5	Mary's Buckaroo, 5	5	1:49.41	$60,000
1996	**Canaveral**, 5, 115	S. J. Sellers	Michael's Star, 4	Rugged Bugger, 4	7	1:49.03	$45,000
1995	**Tidal Surge**, 5, 112	J. D. Carle	Mary's Buckaroo, 4	Ameri Valay, 4	5	**1:48.19**	$60,000
1994	**Taking Risks**, 4, 117	M. T. Johnston	Frottage, 5	Super Memory, 5	6	1:49.53	$45,000

1994-2000 not graded.

Will Rogers Stakes

Grade 3, Hollywood Park, three-year-olds, 1 mile, turf. Held April 20, 2001, with a gross value of $109,800. First held in 1938. Graded since 1973. Stakes record 1:33.98 (1998 Magical [GB]).

Year	Winner	Jockey	Second	Third	Strs	Final Time	1st Purse
2001	**(DH) Media Mogul (GB)**	A. O. Solis		Learing At Kathy	8	1:35.10	$43,920
	(DH) Dr. Park	T. Baze					
2000	**Purely Cozzene**	V. Espinoza	Duke of Green (GB)	Silver Axe	8	1:34.67	$66,000
1999	**Eagleton**	C. A. Black	Hidden Magic (GB)	Mr. Reignmaker	11	1:34.38	$67,800
1998	**Magical (GB)**	R. R. Douglas	Commitisize	Son's Corona	8	**1:33.98**	$65,820
1997	**Brave Act (GB)**	C. J. McCarron	P. T. Indy	Without Doubt (Ire)	12	1:34.01	$68,520

Year	Winner	Jockey	Second	Third	Strs	Final Time	1st Purse
1996	**Let Bob Do It**	K. J. Desormeaux	Nightcapper	Dr. Sardonica	10	1:34.05	$67,140
1995	**Via Lombardia (Ire)**	E. Delahoussaye	Mr Purple	Bee El Tee	9	1:34.15	$63,650
1994	**Unfinished Symph**	G. Baze	Silver Music	Valiant Nature	8	1:40.60	$64,600
1993	**Future Storm**	K. J. Desormeaux	Lykatill Hil	Earl of Barking (Ire)	12	1:40.01	$68,900
1992	**The Name's Jimmy**	D. Sorenson	Bold Assert	Prospect for Four	7	1:40.99	$63,600

1992-'94, 1996-2000 Will Rogers H.; 1995 Will Rogers Breeders' Cup H. 1992-'94 1 1/16 miles. 2001 dead heat for first.

Wilshire Handicap

Grade 3, Hollywood Park, three-year-olds and up, fillies and mares, 1 mile, turf. Held April 29, 2001, with a gross value of $108,600. First held in 1953. Graded since 1975. Stakes record 1:33.86 (1999 Sapphire Ring [GB], 2000 Tout Charmant).

Year	Winner	Jockey	Second	Third	Strs	Final Time	1st Purse
2001	**Tranquility Lake**, 6, 123	E. Delahoussaye	Dianehill (Ire), 5	Out of Reach (GB), 5	7	1:34.69	$65,160
2000	**Tout Charmant**, 4, 121	C. J. McCarron	Penny Marie, 4	Perfect Copy, 4	6	**1:33.86**	$64,740
1999	**Sapphire Ring (GB)**, 4, 119	G. L. Stevens	Bella Chiarra, 4	Green Jewel (GB), 4	7	**1:33.86**	$65,160
1998	**Shake the Yoke (GB)**, 5, 118	E. Delahoussaye	Traces of Gold, 6	Cozy Blues, 6	9	1:34.10	$66,240
1997	**Blushing Heiress**, 5, 115	C. J. McCarron	Real Connection, 6	De Puntillas (GB), 6	7	1:40.95	$65,040
1996	**Pharma**, 5, 118	C. S. Nakatani	Didina (GB), 4	Matiara, 4	5	1:40.96	$79,770
1995	**Possibly Perfect**, 5, 121	K. J. Desormeaux	Morgana, 4	Aube Indienne (Fr), 4	5	1:40.37	$76,600
1994	**Skimble**, 5, 118	E. Delahoussaye	Bel's Starlet, 7	Miami Sands (Ire), 7	6	1:41.39	$62,800
1993	**Toussaud**, 4, 116	K. J. Desormeaux	Visible Gold, 5	Wedding Ring (Ire), 5	7	1:40.14	$63,500
1992	**Kostroma (Ire)**, 6, 123	K. J. Desormeaux	Danzante, 4	Appealing Missy, 4	6	1:41.35	$62,600

1992-'97 Grade 2. 1992-'97 1 1/16 miles.

WinStar Galaxy Stakes

Grade 2, Keeneland, three-year-olds and up, fillies and mares, 1 3/16 miles, turf. Held October 5, 2001, with a gross value of $563,500. First held in 1998. Graded since 2000. Stakes record 1:53.91 (1999 Happyanunoit [NZ]).

Year	Winner	Jockey	Second	Third	Strs	Final Time	1st Purse
2001	**Spook Express (SAf)**, 7	M. E. Smith	Solvig, 4	Veil of Avalon, 4	9	1:54.24	$349,370
2000	**Tout Charmant**, 4	C. J. McCarron	Perfect Sting, 4	License Fee, 5	7	1:54.74	$343,480
1999	**Happyanunoit (NZ)**, 4	B. Blanc	Pleasant Temper, 5	Fiji (GB), 5	9	**1:53.91**	$346,270
1998	**Witchful Thinking**, 4	C. J. McCarron	Memories of Silver, 5	Starry Dreamer, 4	6	1:54.24	$169,415

Withers Stakes

Grade 3, Aqueduct, three-year-olds, 1 mile, dirt. Held May 5, 2001, with a gross value of $150,000. First held in 1874. Graded since 1973. Stakes record 1:32.79 (1993 Williamstown).

Year	Winner	Jockey	Second	Third	Strs	Final Time	1st Purse
2001	**Richly Blended**	R. Wilson	Le Grande Danseur	Telescam	7	1:35.66	$90,000
2000	**Big E E**	H. Castillo Jr.	Precise End	Port Herman	8	1:35.69	$90,000
1999	**Successful Appeal**	J. L. Espinoza	Best of Luck	Treasure Island	8	1:35.18	$90,000
1998	**Dice Dancer**	J. F. Chavez	Rubiyat	Limit Out	7	1:34.48	$90,000
1997	**Statesmanship**	W. H. McCauley	Cryp Too	Stormin Fever	7	1:35.30	$67,140
1996	**Appealing Skier**	R. Wilson	Jamies First Punch	Roar	5	1:35.02	$66,120
1995	**Blu Tusmani**	J. A. Santos	Pat n Jac	Slice of Reality	9	1:35.19	$67,260
1994	**Twining**	J. A. Santos	Able Buck	Presently	8	1:34.75	$67,140
1993	**Williamstown**	C. Perret	Virginia Rapids	Farmonthetreeway	12	**1:32.79**	$76,800
1992	**Dixie Brass**	J. M. Pezua	Big Sur	Superstrike (GB)	8	1:33.71	$73,080

1992-'99 Grade 2. 1992-'96 held at Belmont Park. 1993 new track record.

W. L. McKnight Handicap

Grade 2, Calder Race Course, three-year-olds and up, 1 1/2 miles, turf. Held December 29, 2001, with a gross value of $150,000. First held in 1973. Graded since 1975. Stakes record 2:24.11 (1995 Flag Down).

Year	Winner	Jockey	Second	Third	Strs	Final Time	1st Purse
2001	**Profit Option**, 6, 115	M. Guidry	Deeliteful Irving, 3	Eltawaasul, 5	12	2:27.95	$90,000
2000	**A Little Luck**, 6, 114	M. E. Smith	Stokosky, 4	Whata Brainstorm, 3	12	2:29.01	$90,000
1999	**Wicapi**, 7, 114	C. H. Velasquez	Special Coach, 3	King's Jewel, 3	12	2:26.28	$90,000
1998	**Wild Event**, 5, 116	S. J. Sellers	N B Forrest, 6	Glok, 4	8	2:26.93	$90,000
1997	**Panama City**, 3, 117	P. Day	Slicious (GB), 5	Skillington, 4	12	2:27.19	$90,000
1996	**Diplomatic Jet**, 4, 123	J. F. Chavez	Marcie's Ensign, 4	(DH) Identity, 4 (DH) Lassigny, 5	12	2:24.20	$90,000
1995	**Flag Down**, 5, 116	J. A. Santos	Mecke, 3	Green Means Go, 3	12	**2:24.11**	$90,000
1994	**Star of Manila**, 3, 116	C. Perret	Spectacular Tide, 5	Kissin Kris, 4	13	2:28.43	$90,000

Year	Winner	Jockey	Second	Third	Strs	Final Time	1st Purse
	Cobblestone Road, 5, 113	J. C. Ferrer	Daarik (Ire), 7	Fraise, 6	12	2:27.89	$90,000
1993	Antartic Wings, 5, 113	R. R. Douglas	Cigar Toss (Arg), 6	Luv U. Jodi, 6	9	2:33.44	$60,000
1992	Bye Union Ave., 6, 113	R. R. Douglas	†Crockadore, 5	Skate On Thin Ice, 5	9	2:27.23	$90,000

1996 dead heat for third. 1994 held in January and December. † denotes female.

Woodford Reserve Turf Classic Stakes (see Turf Classic Stakes)

Wood Memorial Stakes

Grade 2, Aqueduct, three-year-olds, 1⅛ miles, dirt. Held April 14, 2001, with a gross value of $750,000. First held in 1925. Graded since 1973. Stakes record 1:47.20 (1988 Private Terms).

Year	Winner	Jockey	Second	Third	Strs	Final Time	1st Purse
2001	Congaree	V. Espinoza	Monarchos	Richly Blended	6	1:47.96	$450,000
2000	Fusaichi Pegasus	K. J. Desormeaux	Red Bullet	Aptitude	12	1:47.92	$450,000
1999	Adonis	J. F. Chavez	Best of Luck	Cliquot	11	1:47.71	$360,000
1998	Coronado's Quest	R. G. Davis	Dice Dancer	Parade Ground	11	1:47.47	$300,000
1997	Captain Bodgit	A. O. Solis	Accelerator	Smokin Mel	10	1:48.39	$300,000
1996	Unbridled's Song	M. E. Smith	In Contention	Romano Gucci	6	1:49.80	$300,000
1995	Talkin Man	S. J. Sellers	Is Sveikatas	Candy Cone	8	1:49.24	$300,000
1994	Irgun	G. L. Stevens	Go for Gin	Shiprock	9	1:49.07	$300,000
1993	Storm Tower	R. Wilson	Tossofthecoin	Marked Tree	12	1:48.50	$300,000
1992	Devil His Due	M. E. Smith	West by West	Rokeby (GB)	12	1:49.32	$300,000

1992-'93 Wood Memorial Invitational S. 1992-'94, 2002 Grade 1.

Woodward Stakes

Grade 1, Belmont Park, three-year-olds and up, 1⅛ miles, dirt. Held September 8, 2001, with a gross value of $500,000. First held in 1954. Graded since 1973. Stakes record 1:45.80 (1976 Forego; 1990 Dispersal).

Year	Winner	Jockey	Second	Third	Strs	Final Time	1st Purse
2001	Lido Palace (Chi), 4	J. D. Bailey	Albert the Great, 4	Tiznow, 4	5	1:47.42	$300,000
2000	Lemon Drop Kid, 4	E. S. Prado	Behrens, 6	Gander, 4	5	1:50.53	$300,000
1999	River Keen (Ire), 7	C. W. Antley	Almutawakel (GB), 4	Stephen Got Even, 3	7	1:46.85	$300,000
1998	Skip Away, 5	J. D. Bailey	Gentlemen (Arg), 6	Running Stag, 4	5	1:47.80	$300,000
1997	Formal Gold, 4	K. J. Desormeaux	Skip Away, 4	Will's Way, 4	5	1:47.51	$300,000
1996	Cigar, 6	J. D. Bailey	L'Carriere, 5	Golden Larch, 5	5	1:47.06	$300,000
1995	Cigar, 5	J. D. Bailey	Star Standard, 3	Golden Larch, 4	6	1:47.07	$300,000
1994	Holy Bull, 3	M. E. Smith	Devil His Due, 5	Colonial Affair, 4	8	1:46.89	$300,000
1993	Bertrando, 4	G. L. Stevens	Devil His Due, 4	Valley Crossing, 5	6	1:47.00	$525,000
1992	Sultry Song, 4	J. D. Bailey	Pleasant Tap, 5	Out of Place, 5	8	1:47.05	$300,000

Yellow Ribbon Stakes

Grade 1, Santa Anita Park, three-year-olds and up, fillies and mares, 1¼ miles, turf. Held September 29, 2001, with a gross value of $500,000. First held in 1977. Graded since 1979. Stakes record 1:57.60 (1989 Brown Bess).

Year	Winner	Jockey	Second	Third	Strs	Final Time	1st Purse
2001	Janet (GB), 4	D. R. Flores	Tranquility Lake, 6	Al Desima (GB), 4	8	1:58.64	$300,000
2000	Tranquility Lake, 5	E. Delahoussaye	Spanish Fern, 5	Polaire (Ire), 4	6	2:02.98	$300,000
1999	Spanish Fern, 4	C. J. McCarron	Caffe Latte (Ire), 3	Shabby Chic, 3	7	1:59.52	$300,000
1998	Fiji (GB), 4	K. J. Desormeaux	Sonja's Faith (Ire), 4	Pomona (GB), 5	10	2:05.23	$300,000
1997	Ryafan, 3	A. O. Solis	Fanjica (Ire), 5	Memories of Silver, 4	8	2:03.89	$300,000
1996	Donna Viola (GB), 4	G. L. Stevens	Real Connection, 5	Dixie Pearl, 4	8	2:00.62	$360,000
1995	Alpride (Ire), 4	C. J. McCarron	Angel in My Heart (Fr), 3	Bold Ruritana, 5	12	2:01.68	$360,000
1994	Aube Indienne (Fr), 4	K. J. Desormeaux	Fondly Remembered, 4	Zoonaqua, 4	11	2:02.32	$240,000
1993	Possibly Perfect, 3	C. S. Nakatani	Tribulation, 3	Miatuschka, 5	13	2:02.91	$240,000
1992	Super Staff, 4	K. J. Desormeaux	Flawlessly, 4	Campagnarde (Arg), 5	9	1:59.36	$240,000

Yerba Buena Breeders' Cup Handicap

Grade 3, Bay Meadows, three-year-olds and up, fillies and mares, 1⅜ miles, turf. Held May 12, 2001, with a gross value of $150,000. First held in 1973. Graded since 1993. Stakes record 2:13.60 (1978 *Star Ball).

Year	Winner	Jockey	Second	Third	Strs	Final Time	1st Purse
2001	Janet (GB), 4, 115	D. R. Flores	Keemoon (Fr), 5	Alexine (Arg), 5	4	2:17.09	$82,500
2000	Gleefully, 4, 113	R. Q. Meza	Country Garden (GB), 5	Marie de Bayeux (Fr), 5	8	2:15.99	$120,000
1999	Blending Element (Ire), 6, 117	G. K. Gomez	Queen Douna (Fr), 6	Midnight Line, 6	6	2:17.26	$120,000
1998	Miss Universal (Ire), 5, 114	P. Mercado	Proud Fillie (Fr), 4	Squeak (GB), 4	12	2:15.72	$75,000
1997	De Puntillas (GB), 5, 116	V. Espinoza	Dynatar, 5	Tricky Code, 5	11	1:46.71	$60,000
1996	Fanjica (Ire), 4, 114	D. Carr	Nimble Mind, 4	Dynatar, 4	8	2:17.42	$60,000
1995	Work the Crowd, 4, 123	R. A. Baze	Late Sailing, 5	Ask Anita, 5	5	1:49.27	$68,750
1994	Ask Anita, 4, 116	V. Belvoir	Miami Sands (Ire), 4	Oxava (Fr), 4	7	2:15.55	$55,000
1993	Party Cited, 4, 117	R. J. Warren Jr.	Silvered, 6	Rougeur, 6	6	2:15.11	$55,000
1992	Flaming Torch (Ire), 5, 114	R. A. Baze	Indian Chris (Brz), 5	Silvered, 5	8	2:16.26	$82,500

1992-'98 Yerba Buena H. 1992 not graded. 1992-2000 held at Golden Gate Fields. 1995 1⅛ miles; 1997 1¹⁄₁₆ miles.

Oldest Stakes Races

Although horse racing in North America dates from the Colonial period, stakes races did not become popular until the mid-1800s.

The oldest continually run stakes in North America—meaning that it has been run every year since its inception—is the Queen's Plate Stakes at Woodbine. First run in 1860, the race was named for Queen Victoria, then in the 23rd year of her 64-year reign, and was for horses of all ages foaled in the province of Ontario. The winner of that first Queen's Plate was Don Juan, a five-year-old Sir Tatton Sykes gelding. (Another Queen's Plate, restricted to horses foaled in Quebec, dated from 1836 and was discontinued after World War II.) From 1902 through '51, the race was known as the King's Plate, for a succession of English male monarchs.

North America's oldest stakes race still in existence is the Phoenix Breeders' Cup Stakes (G3), first run in 1831 at the Kentucky Association track in Lexington. Known at various times as the Phoenix Hotel S., Phoenix S., Brennan S., Chiles S., Association S., and the Phoenix H., the race was discontinued in 1930. It was revived with the first spring race meeting of Keeneland Race Course in 1937.

Oldest Continually Run Stakes

Race	Track	First running	First winner
Queen's Plate	Woodbine	1860	Don Juan
Kentucky Derby	Churchill	1875	Aristides
Kentucky Oaks	Churchill	1875	Vinaigrette
Clark H.	Churchill	1875	Voltigeur
Bashford Manor S.	Churchill	1902	Von Rouse
Fall Highweight H.	Aqueduct	1914	Comely
Coaching Club American Oaks	Belmont	1917	Wistful
Dwyer S.	Belmont	1918	War Cloud
Schuylerville S.	Saratoga	1918	Tuscaloosa
Jockey Club Gold Cup S.	Belmont	1919	Purchase
Cowdin S.	Belmont	1923	Mr. Mutt
Wood Memorial S.	Aqueduct	1925	Backbone
Selima S.	Laurel	1926	Fair Star
Whitney H.	Saratoga	1928	Black Maria
Canadian Derby	Northlands	1930	Jack Whittier

Oldest Stakes Races

Race — Track — First running — First winner

PHOENIX BREEDERS' CUP S. — Keeneland — 1831 — McDonough
1831-'77, run as a heat race; 1898-1904,1906-'10, 1914-'16, 1929, 1931-'36, not run; before 1937, held at the Kentucky Association track; 1943-'45, held at Churchill Downs; 1972, 1981, run in two divisions; before 1989, held during the spring meeting; inaugurated in 1831 as the Phoenix Hotel S.; has also been run as Brennan S., Chiles S., Phoenix S., Association S., and Phoenix H.

QUEEN'S PLATE S. — Woodbine — 1860 — Don Juan
Before 1887, run at 1½ miles; 1924-'56, run at 1⅛ miles; before 1938, for three-year-olds and up; 1938, for three- and four-year-olds; 1902-'51, run as the King's Plate; before 1956, held at Old Woodbine; before 1959, for three-year-olds bred and owned in Canada

TRAVERS S. — Saratoga — 1864 — Kentucky
1943, 1944, 1945, held at Belmont Park; 1896, 1898, 1899, 1900, 1911, 1912, not run; before 1890, run at 1¾ miles; 1890-'92, run at 1½ miles; 1895, 1901-'03, run at 1⅛ miles; 1927-'32, run as the Travers Midsummer Derby

JEROME H. — Belmont — 1866 — Watson
1866-'89, held at Jerome Park; 1890-1905, held at Morris Park; 1960, 1962-'67, held at Aqueduct; 1910-'13, not run; 1866-'70, run in two divisions; 1871-'77, run at 2 miles; 1878-'89, run at 1¾ miles; 1890, 1891, 1903, run at 1 5/16 miles; 1892, run at 1½ miles; 1893, 1894, 1896-1909, run at 1¼ miles; 1895, run at 1⅛ miles

BELMONT S. — Belmont — 1867 — Ruthless
1867-'89, held at Jerome Park; 1890-1904, held at Morris Park; 1963-'67, held at Aqueduct; 1911-'12, not run; 1867-'73, run at 1⅝ miles; 1890-'92, 1895, 1904-'05, run at 1¼ miles; 1893-'94, run at 1⅛ miles; 1896-1903, 1906-'25, run at 1⅜ miles; 1895, 1913, run as a handicap stakes

CHAMPAGNE S. — Belmont — 1867 — Sarah B.
Before 1890, held at Jerome Park; 1890-1905, held at Morris Park; 1959, 1963-'67, 1984, held at Aqueduct; 1910-'13, 1956, not run; 1871-'80, run at six furlongs; 1891-1904, run at seven furlongs; 1905-'32, run on the Widener course (165 feet less than seven furlongs); 1933-'39, run on the Widener course at 6½ furlongs; 1940-'83, 1985-'93, run at one mile; 1984, run at 1⅛ miles; 1973, run in two divisions

LADIES H. — Aqueduct — 1868 — Bonnie Braes
Before 1913, for three-year-old fillies; 1931-'34, 1940-2001, for fillies and mares all ages, three-year-olds and up; before 1890, held at Jerome Park; 1890-1904, held at Morris Park; 1950-'58, 1960, held at Belmont Park; 1895, 1911, 1912, not run; before 1874, run at 1⅝ miles; 1889, 1892, run at 1⅛ miles; 1890, 1891, run at 1,400 yards; 1893, 1894, run at 1 1/16 miles; 1896-1939, run at one mile; 1961, 1962, run at 1 5/16 miles; 1874-'85, 1940-'58, 1960, 1963, 1964, run at 1½ miles.

FLASH S. — Belmont — 1869 — Remorseless
1869-1942, 1946-'71, held at Saratoga; 1943-'45, held at Belmont Park on the Widener course; 1981, 1982, held at Belmont Park; 1896, 1898-1900, 1911, 1912, 1960, 1972-'80, 1983-'98, not run; before 1901, run at four furlongs; 1901, run at five furlongs; 1969-'71, run at six furlongs; 1981, 1982, run at 5½ furlongs

DIXIE S. — Pimlico — 1870 — Preakness
1870, run as Dinner Party S.; 1871, run as Reunion S.; 1903-'04, held at Benning, Washington, D.C., at 1¾ miles for three-year-olds; 1870-'88, run at two miles for three-year-olds; 1924-'52, run at 1 3/16 miles; 1960-'87, 1989, 1990, run at 1½ miles; 1955-'59, run at 1⅜ miles; 1988, run at 1⅝ miles; before 1955, 1988, run on dirt; 1889-1901, 1905-'23, not run; 1965-'78, run in two divisions

MONMOUTH PARK BREEDERS' CUP OAKS — Monmouth — 1871 — Salina
1871-'77, run at 1½ miles; 1879-'93, run at 1¼ miles; 1946-'52, 1996-2001, run at 1 1/16 miles; 1953-'95, run at 1⅛ miles; 1891, held at Jerome Park; 1878, 1894-1945, not run; 1976, run as Monmouth Bicentennial Oaks

ALABAMA S. — Saratoga — 1872 — Woodbine
1943-'45, held at Belmont Park; 1893-'96, 1898-1900, 1911, 1912, not run; before 1901, 1904, 1906-'16, run at 1⅛ miles; 1901-'03, run at 1 1/16 miles; 1903, run on turf; 1905, run at 1 5/16 miles

CALIFORNIA DERBY Bay Meadows 1873 Camilla Urso
1897-1909, run at 1¼ miles; 1923, run at 1½ miles; 1936-
'48, 1976-'81, run at 1¹/₁₆ miles; 1874, 1891-'96, 1900, 1911-
'22, 1924-'34, 1939, 1940, 1942, 1943, 1945, 1947, 1949-
'53, 1957, not run; 1873-1959, 1962, held at Tanforan;
1961,1964-2000, held at Golden Gate Fields

PREAKNESS S.   Pimlico   1873   Survivor
Before 1894, run at 1½ miles; 1889, run at 1¼ miles;
1894-1900, 1908, run at 1¹/₁₆ miles; 1901-'07, run at one
mile and 70 yards; 1909, 1910, run at one mile; 1911-
'24, run at 1⅛ miles; 1891-'93, not run; 1890, for three-
year-olds and up; 1890, held at Morris Park, New York;
1894-1908, held at Gravesend, New York; 1918, run in
two divisions

WITHERS S.   Aqueduct   1874   Dublin
1847-'89, held at Jerome Park; 1890-1904, held at Morris
Park; 1956, held at Jamaica; 1984-'96, held at Belmont
Park; 1911, 1912, not run; 1956, run at 1¹/₁₆ miles

CLARK H.   Churchill   1875   Voltigeur
1875-1901, run as three-year-old stakes; 1902-2001, run
as a handicap for three-year-olds and up; 1875-'80, run at
two miles; 1881-'95, run at 1¼ miles; 1902-'21, 1925-'54,
run at 1¹/₁₆ miles; 1953, run in two divisions

KENTUCKY DERBY Churchill   1875   Aristides
Before 1896, run at 1½ miles

KENTUCKY OAKS   Churchill   1875   Vinaigrette
1875-'90, run at 1½ miles; 1891-'95, run at 1¼ miles; 1896-
1919, 1942-'81, run at 1¹/₁₆ miles

Fastest Times of 2001

Distance	Time	Winner, age	Track	Date
2f	:20.98	Puma, 4	Calder Race Course	7-14-01
2½f	:27.80	Crafty Number, 5	Ruidoso Downs	8-18-01
3f	:32.16	Cherokee Road, 2	Hialeah Park	4-30-01
3½f	:38.80	Symbol's Remark, 2	Northlands Park	8-15-01
4f	:43.60	Agate Hunter, 11	Mohave County Fair	5-12-01
about 4f	:45.00	Feu Green, 4	Kin Park	7-15-01
4½f	:50.33	Fina Dur, 7	Mountaineer Race Track	8-11-01
4½fT	:50.09	Knight Balloon, 6	Mountaineer Race Track	7-15-01
5f	:56.07	Olympian, 4	Woodbine	3-31-01
about 5f	:56.26	Entrenched, 4	Northampton Fair	8-25-01
5fT	:55.02	Kipperscope, 4	Calder Race Course	9-06-01
about 5fT	:55.84	Elvi Gamble, 6	Gulfstream Park	3-14-01
		Zarb's Echo, 6	Louisiana Downs	8-26-01
5½f	1:01.60	Rio Oro, 6	Bay Meadows Race Course	10-07-01
about 5½f	1:09.00	Lefty McSlew, 7	Bay Meadows Race Course	7-14-01
		Tank's Star, 9	Bay Meadows Race Course	7-12-01
5½fT	1:01.09	General Express, 6	Ellis Park	7-21-01
about 5½fT	1:03.59	Testify, 4	Fair Grounds	12-06-01
6f	1:07.55	El Dorado Shooter, 4	Golden Gate Fields	1-20-01
about 6f	1:07.60	Hello Senor, 5	Santa Rosa	7-25-01
6fT	1:07.63	Spring Barley, 4	Woodbine	9-5-01
6½f	1:14.34	Love At Noon, 3	Churchill Downs	5-5-01
about 6½f	1:17.86	Cheap Charlie, 5	Timonium	9-3-01
6½fT	1:15.16	Silver Spear, 3	Woodbine	7-13-01
about 6½fT	1:11.46	El Cielo, 7	Santa Anita Park	11-5-01
7f	1:20.42	Early Flyer, 3	Hollywood Park	5-28-01
		El Corredor, 4	Del Mar	8-12-01
about 7f	1:23.60	Little Duke, 5	Kin Park	7-22-01
7fT	1:20.30	Scagnelli, 6	Belmont Park	7-21-01
about 7fT	1:23.52	Frank's Selection, 5	Fort Erie	6-18-01
7½f	1:28.03	Favorite Funtime, 4	Hollywood Park	11-23-01
7½fT	1:27.74	Find the Mine, 6	Mountaineer Race Track	7-15-01
about 7½fT	1:29.20	Zarb's Echo, 6	Louisiana Downs	8-11-01
1m	1:33.35	Left Bank, 4	Aqueduct	11-24-01
1mT	1:32.05	Val Royal (Fr), 5	Belmont Park	10-27-01
about 1mT	1:34.61	Bomfim, 8	Gulfstream Park	2-3-01
1m 40yd	1:38.88	Smilin' Slew, 5	Fair Grounds	3-17-01
1m 70yd	1:39.34	Corporate Courier, 6	Mountaineer Race Track	7-22-01
1m 70ydT	1:38.60	Star of Rio, 4	The Meadowlands	10-24-01
about 1m 70ydT	1:42.38	Bostic Hill, 6	Philadelphia Park	8-27-01
1¹/₁₆m	1:40.08	Jarf, 5	Belmont Park	6-28-01
about 1¹/₁₆m	1:44.10	Ashleigh's Jet, 4	Arlington Park	6-14-01
1¹/₁₆mT	1:39.30	Dr. Kashnikow, 4	Saratoga Race Course	8-25-01
about 1¹/₁₆mT	1:40.96	Strategic Mission, 6	Gulfstream Park	3-3-01
1⅛m	1:45.52	Albert the Great, 4	Hialeah Park	3-24-01
about 1⅛m	1:49.56	Nates Colony, 4	Fairplex Park	9-07-01
1⅛mT	1:45.95	Lazy Lode (Arg), 7	Santa Anita Park	3-15-01
about 1⅛mT	1:43.76	Diadella, 4	Woodbine	9-09-01
1³/₁₆m	1:53.95	Rize, 5	The Meadowlands	11-10-01
1³/₁₆mT	1:51.99	Kudos, 4	Hollywood Park	4-25-01
1¼m	1:59.96	Skimming, 5	Del Mar	8-19-01
about 1¼m	2:00.37	After the Run, 4	Santa Rosa	8-04-01
1¼mT	1:58.64	Janet (GB), 4	Santa Anita Park	9-29-01
about 1¼mT	2:03.62	Litunga, 5	Woodbine	7-08-01
1⁵/₁₆m	2:10.80	Rancour, 4	Northlands Park	8-25-01
1⅜m	2:17.17	Nates Colony, 4	Fairplex Park	9-16-01
1⅜mT	2:10.62	King Cugat, 4	Belmont Park	7-07-01
about 1⅜mT	2:16.46	Sweetest Thing, 3	Woodbine	7-26-01
1½m	2:26.56	Point Given, 3	Belmont Park	6-09-01

Distance	Time	Winner, age	Track	Date
about 1½m	2:30.03	Let's Go Rusty, 4	Hastings Park	9-08-01
1½mT	2:23.75	Whata Brainstorm, 4	Gulfstream Park	3-11-01
about 1½mT	2:30.78	Allende, 4	Woodbine	7-8-01
1⁹⁄₁₆m	2:40.22	Code De, 6	Hoosier Park	11-02-01
1⅝m	2:44.74	Coyote Lakes, 7	Aqueduct	1-1-01
1¾m	2:57.37	Queensgate, 5	Woodbine	12-02-01
about 1¾mT	2:42.96	Bienamado, 5	Santa Anita Park	4-14-01
1⅞m	3:13.29	Flying Commander, 3	Woodbine	12-02-01
1⅞mT	3:15.00	Divorce Proceeds, 6	River Downs	9-03-01
2m	3:27.23	A Storm Is Brewing, 4	Churchill Downs	11-24-01
2mT	3:34.60	Maternity Leave, 5	Colonial Downs	8-4-01
about 2mT	3:30.73	Golden Marvel (Fr), 5	Colonial Downs	7-04-01

North American Dirt and Turf Records

Distance	Time	Winner, age	Track	Date
2f	:20.80	Big Racket, 4	Hippodromo, Mexico	2-5-1945
2½f	:26.53	Yes He Will, 4	Lone Star Park	11-7-1997
3f	:31.20	Raisable Adversary, 11	Remington Park	8-29-1999
3½f	:38.00	Primero Del Anno, 5	Flagstaff	7-4-1998
4f	:43.10	Slewofrainbows, 7	Mohave County Fair	5-23-1999
4fT	:46.60	Fine Tassles, 5	Rillito	1-30-1994
4½f	:49.20	Valiant Pete, 4	Los Alamitos	8-11-1990
4½fT	:50.00	Cake n' Steak, 8	Mountaineer Race Track	8-9-1993
5f	:55.20	Chinook Pass, 3	Longacres	9-17-1982
5fT	:54.60	General Express, 5	Monmouth Park	7-8-2000
5½f	1:01.10	Plenty Zloty, 5	Turf Paradise	4-18-1998
5½fT	1:00.46	Pembroke, 5	Hollywood Park	7-15-1995
6f	1:06.60	G Malleah, 4	Turf Paradise	4-8-1995
6fT	1:07.00	Answer Do, 4	Hollywood Park	12-15-1990
6¼f	1:15.80	Montanic, 4	Washington Park	7-20-1901
6½f	1:13.24	Lucky Forever, 6	Hollywood Park	5-20-1995
6½fT	1:14.20	Key Twenty Two, 6	Woodbine	6-4-1992
about 6½fT	1:11.46	El Cielo, 7	Santa Anita Park	11-5-2001
7f	1:19.40	Rich Cream, 5	Hollywood Park	5-28-1980
		Time to Explode, 3	Hollywood Park	6-26-1982
7fT	1:19.88	Officialpermission, 6	Belmont Park	7-23-2000
7½f	1:26.26	Awesome Daze, 5	Hollywood Park	11-23-1997
7½fT	1:26.54	Court Lark, 6	Calder Race Course	7-16-1994
1m	1:32.20	Dr. Fager, 4	Arlington Park	8-24-1968
1mT	1:31.63	Elusive Quality, 5	Belmont Park	7-4-1998
1m 20yd	1:39.00	Froglegs, 4	Churchill Downs	5-13-1913
1m 40yd	1:38.20	Zafarrancho, 5	Rockingham	6-19-1987
1m 40ydT	1:38.08	Castaneto (Arg), 7	Atlantic City	6-28-1991
1m 55yd	1:40.80	Terrain, 3	Bay Meadows Race Course	11-13-1934
1m 60yd	1:41.00	Brush Hook, 5	Tropical Park	3-16-1938
1m 70yd	1:38.20	Majestic Nasr, 6	Pleasanton	7-11-1993
1m 70ydT	1:37.20	Aborigine, 6	Penn National	8-20-1978
1m 100yd	1:43.80	Old Honesty, 3	Empire City	8-20-1907
1¹⁄₁₆m	1:38.40	Hoedown's Day, 5	Bay Meadows Race Course	10-23-1983
1¹⁄₁₆mT	1:38.00	Told, 4	Penn National	9-14-1980
1⅛m	1:45.00	Simply Majestic, 4	Golden Gate Fields	4-2-1988
1⅛mT	1:43.92	Kostroma (Ire), 5	Santa Anita Park	10-20-1991
1³⁄₁₆m	1:52.40	Riva Ridge, 4	Aqueduct	7-4-1973
1³⁄₁₆mT	1:51.40	Toonerville, 4	Hialeah Park	2-7-1976
1¼m	1:57.80	Spectacular Bid, 4	Santa Anita Park	2-3-1980
1¼mT	1:57.40	Double Discount, 4	Santa Anita Park	10-9-1977
1⁵⁄₁₆m	2:07.32	Gold Star Deputy, 5	Aqueduct	4-10-1999
1⁵⁄₁₆mT	2:06.00	Ruff Mack, 5	Mountaineer Race Track	8-25-1962
1⅜m	2:12.31	Demi's Bret, 4	Aqueduct	10-26-1997
1⅜mT	2:10.20	With Approval, 4	Belmont Park	6-17-1990
1⁷⁄₁₆m	2:23.00	Who's In Command, 5	Hastings Park	8-10-1987
1⁷⁄₁₆mT	2:25.00	Dina's Playmate, 11	River Downs	8-30-1969
1½m	2:24.00	Secretariat, 3	Belmont Park	6-9-1973
1½mT	2:22.80	Hawkster, 3	Santa Anita Park	10-14-1989
1⁹⁄₁₆m	2:35.77	Well Lit, 5	Sportsman's Park	4-25-1992
1⁹⁄₁₆mT	2:40.26	To the Floor, 7	Fair Grounds	3-29-1999
1⅝m	2:38.20	Swaps, 4	Hollywood Park	7-25-1956
1⅝mT	2:37.00	Tom Swift, 5	Saratoga Race Course	8-23-1978
1¾m	2:52.60	Major Pots, 5	Woodbine	12-8-1994
1¾mT	2:56.40	Desperado Dan, 4	Woodbine	7-22-1984
1⅞m	3:11.56	Asserche, 6	Laurel Park	3-20-1994
1⅞mT	3:08.23	Code's Best, 6	Mountaineer Race Track	9-4-2000
2m	3:19.20	Kelso, 7	Aqueduct	10-31-1964
2mT	3:18.00	Petrone, 5	Hollywood Park	7-23-1969
2¼m	3:47.00	Fenelon, 4	Belmont Park	10-4-1941
2¼mT	3:48.40	Buteo, 6	River Downs	9-3-1990
2½m	4:14.60	*Miss Grillo, 6	Pimlico Race Course	11-12-1948

Leading Earners of All Time

North America

Because of the paucity and unreliability of published records of Thoroughbred racing before the Civil War, the earliest leading North American earner whose record can be reliably verified is the great American Eclipse, who became an American popular hero in the 1820s. More than 20 years later, the baton was handed on to the giant filly Peytona, who collected the largest purse on the continent to that date, $41,000, for her victory in the Peyton Stakes at Nashville, Tennessee, in 1843. Her owner promptly changed her name from the unwieldy Glumdalclitch and named her after her most famous win.

The pace of change on the leading earner list has quickened since antebellum days. Perhaps the most exciting exchange occurred in 1947, when Racing Hall of Fame members Assault, Armed, and Stymie batted Whirlaway's previous record around like a badminton shuttlecock. Stymie's durability finally outlasted the other two, and he ended his career with earnings of $918,485. Citation, who became the leading earner in 1950, moved the mark above $1-million the following year.

The great two-year-old and epochal sire Domino held the torch for the longest period, 27 years, from 1893 until supplanted by Man o' War in 1920. Assault and Stymie each held the title for the shortest period, seven days, during their duel in 1947. The only stallion to sire two leading North American money earners is Bull Lea. Peytona and Miss Woodford are the only females to hold the title.

International racing has always complicated the issue. Parole's record earnings include about $20,000 earned on his sojourn in England in 1879-'80. Cigar's earnings similarly include the $2.4-million earned in his Dubai World Cup victory.

As the following list shows, the title of leading North American earner has been held by 27 horses, down to current leader Cigar, who took the title from Alysheba during his 16-race win streak in 1996. As shown in the following worldwide list, the earnings of Japanese-based T.M. Opera O have already far surpassed Cigar's total.

Chronology of Leading American Money Winners

1823—American Eclipse, 1814 ch. h., Duroc—Millers Damsel, by Messenger. 8-8-0-0, **$56,700.**

1845—Peytona, 1839 ch. f., *Glencoe—Giantess, by *Leviathan. 8-6-1-0, **$62,400.**

1861—Planet, 1855 ch. h., Revenue—Nina, by Boston. 31-27-4-0, **$69,700.**

1881—Hindoo, 1878 b. h., Virgil—Florence, by Lexington. 35-30-3-2, **$71,875.**

1881—Parole, 1873 br. h., *Leamington—Maiden, by Lexington. 129-59-22-16, **$82,816.**

1885—Miss Woodford, 1880 br. f., *Billet—Fancy Jane, by Neil Robinson. 48-37-7-2, **$118,270.**

1889—Hanover, 1884 ch. h., Hindoo—Bourbon Belle, by *Bonnie Scotland. 50-32-14-2, **$118,887.**

1892—Kingston, 1884 dk. b. or br. h., Spendthrift—*Kapanga, by Victorious. 138-89-33-12, **$138,917.**

1893—Domino, 1891 br. h., Himyar—Mannie Gray, by Enquirer. 25-19-3-1, **$193,550.**

1920—Man o' War, 1917 ch. h., Fair Play—Mahubah, by *Rock Sand. 21-20-1-0, **$249,465.**

1923—Zev, 1920 dk. b. or br. h., The Finn—Miss Kearney, by *Planudes. 43-23-8-5, **$313,639.**

1930—Gallant Fox, 1927 b. h., *Sir Gallahad III—Marguerite, by Celt. 17-11-3-2, **$328,165.**

1931—Sun Beau, 1925 b. h., *Sun Briar—Beautiful Lady, by Fair Play. 74-33-12-10, **$376,744.**

1940—Seabiscuit, 1933 b. h., Hard Tack—Swing On, by Whisk Broom II. 89-33-15-13, **$437,730.**

1942—Whirlaway, 1938 ch. h., *Blenheim II—Dustwhirl, by Sweep. 60-32-15-9, **$561,161.**

1947 (June 21)—Assault, 1943 ch. h., Bold Venture—Igual, by Equipoise. 42-18-6-7, **$576,670.**

1947 (July 5)—Stymie, 1941 ch. h., Equestrian—Stop Watch, by On Watch. 131-35-33-28, **$595,510.**

1947 (July 12)—Assault, $613,370 (career $675,470).

1947 (July 19)—Stymie, $678,510.

1947 (October 9)—Armed, 1941 dk. b. or br. g., Bull Lea—Armful, by Chance Shot. 81-41-20-10, **$761,500 (career $817,475).**

1947 (October 25)—Stymie $816,060 (career $918,485).

1950—Citation, 1945 b. h., Bull Lea—*Hydroplane II, by Hyperion. 45-32-10-2, **$1,085,760.**

1956—Nashua, 1952 b. h., *Nasrullah—Segula, by Johnstown. 30-22-4-1, **$1,288,565.**

1958—Round Table, 1954 b. h., *Princequillo—*Knight's Daughter, by Sir Cosmo. 66-43-8-5, **$1,749,869.**

1965—Kelso, 1957 dk. b. or br. g., Your Host—Maid of Flight, by Count Fleet. 63-39-12-2, **$1,977,896.**

1979—Affirmed, 1975 ch. h., Exclusive Native—Won't Tell You, by Crafty Admiral. 29-22-5-1, **$2,393,818.**

1980—Spectacular Bid, 1976 gr. h., Bold Bidder—Spectacular, by Promised Land. 30-26-2-1, **$2,781,608.**

1981—John Henry, 1975 b. g., Ole Bob Bowers—Once Double, by Double Jay. 83-39-15-9, **$6,591,860.**

1988—Alysheba, 1984 b. h., Alydar—Bel Sheba, by Lt. Stevens. 26-11-8-2, **$6,679,242.**

1996—Cigar, 1990 b. h., Palace Music—Solar Slew, by Seattle Slew. 33-19-4-5, **$9,999,815.**

International

In the 20th century, America became so accustomed to being the home of the world's leading money-winning racehorse that it did not even notice when Japanese-bred and -trained Oguri Cap soared past American leader Alysheba in 1990.

Since organized Thoroughbred racing originated in England in the early 18th century, it is obvious that the earliest leading earners

must have resided there as well. Determining the first world's richest Thoroughbred is all but impossible because early records are nonexistent or unclear on purse awards.

English record-keepers recorded that in 1889 Donovan broke the record previously held by the French-bred Gladiateur. In turn, Gladiateur had broken the previous record of England's The Flying Dutchman.

The earliest horse who can reliably be accorded the palm of world's leading earner is the undefeated Highflyer, who was foaled in 1774. Based on the exchange rate of $5 to £1 that prevailed in the 19th century (America was still a British colony in 1774), Highflyer earned the equivalent of $38,395 by winning all 12 of his races.

By that standard, American Eclipse surpassed Highflyer, but 1830 Epsom Derby winner *Priam earned more money by the same exchange rate. The title remained in Europe until 1923, when Zev's victory over *Papyrus propelled him past Isinglass, who remained England's leading earner for more than 60 years.

Zev began a 67-year reign for American horses

at the same time the American economy began to dominate the world. Only the huge increases in Japanese purses beginning in the 1980s changed that equation. As shown by the accompanying list of the world's current leading earners, the earnings of T.M.Opera O far exceed any American horse.

Chronology of Leading International Money Winners

1780—Highflyer, 1774 b. h., Herod—Rachel, by Blank. 12-12-0-0, **$38,395.**

1823—American Eclipse, 1814 ch. h., Duroc—Miller's Damsel, by *Messenger. 8-8-0-0, **$56,700.**

1830—*Priam, 1827 br. h., Emilius—Cressida, by Whiskey. 16-14-1-1, **$65,100.**

1850—The Flying Dutchman, 1846 b. h., Bay Middleton—Barbelle, by Sandbeck. 15-14-1-0, **$93,900.**

1865—Gladiateur, 1862 b. h., Monarque—Miss Gladiator, by Gladiator. 19-16-0-1, **$236,537.**

1889—Donovan, 1886 b. h., Galopin—Mowerina, by The Scottish Chief. 21-18-2-1, **$275,775.**

1895—Isinglass, 1890 b. h., Isonomy—Dead Lock, by Wenlock. 12-11-1-0, **$287,275.**

1923—Zev, 1920 dk. b. or br. h., The Finn—Miss Kear-

World's Leading Earners

Through December 31, 2001

Rank	Horse	YOB, Pedigree	Country	Earnings (in dollars)
1.	T.M.Opera O	1996 ch. h., Opera House (GB)—Once Wed, by Blushing Groom (Fr)	Jpn	$16,200,337
2.	Cigar	1990 b. h., Palace Music—Solar Slew, by Seattle Slew	USA	9,999,815
3.	Skip Away	1993 gr. h., Skip Trial—Ingot Way, by Diplomat Way	USA	9,616,360
4.	Special Week	1995 dk. b. or br. c, Sunday Silence—Campaign Girl, by Maruzensky	Jpn	9,346,435
5.	Narita Brian	1991 dk. b. or br. c. Brian's Time—Pacificus, by Northern Dancer	Jpn	9,296,552
6.	Hokuto Vega	1990 b. f. Nagurski—Takeno Falcon, by Philip of Spain	Jpn	8,300,301
7.	Meisho Doto	1996 b. h., Bigstone (Ire)—Princess Reema, by Affirmed	Jpn	8,088,202
8.	Stay Gold	1994 dk. b. or br. h., Sunday Silence—Golden Sash, by Dictus	Jpn	7,656,452
9.	Mejiro McQueen	1987 gr. c, Mejiro Titan—Mejiro Aurola, by Remand	Jpn	7,618,803
10.	Biwa Hayahide	1990 gr. h., Sharrood—Pacificus, by Northern Dancer	Jpn	7,555,480
11.	Fantastic Light	1996 b. h., Rahy—Jood, by Nijinsky II	GB	7,486,957
12.	Mayano Top Gun	1992 ch. h., Brian's Time—Alp Me Please, by Blushing Groom (Fr)	Jpn	7,463,557
13.	Hishi Amazon	1991 dk. b. or br. f., Theatrical (Ire)—Katies (Ire), by Nonoalco	Jpn	6,981,102
14.	Silver Charm	1994 gr. h., Silver Buck—Bonnie's Poker, by Poker	USA	6,944,369
15.	Ogurl Cap	1985 gr. h., Dancing Cap—White Narubi, by *Silver Shark	Jpn	6,919,201
16.	Mejiro Bright	1994 b. h., Mejiro Ryan—Reru du Temps, by Maruzensky	Jpn	6,848,423
17.	Air Groove	1993 b. f., Tony Bin—Dyna Carle, by Northern Taste	Jpn	6,832,242
18.	Captain Steve	1997 ch. h., Fly So Free—Sparkling Delite, by Vice Regent	USA	6,828,356
19.	Alysheba	1984 b. h., Alydar—Bel Sheba, by Lt. Stevens	USA	6,679,242
20.	John Henry	1975 b. g., Ole Bob Bowers—Once Double, by Double Jay	USA	6,591,860
21.	Tiznow	1997 b. c, Cee's Tizzy—Cee's Song, by Seattle Song	USA	6,427,830
22.	Wing Arrow	1995 b. h., Assatis—Sanyo Arrow, by Mr. C B	Jpn	6,273,733
23.	Mejiro Dober	1994 b. f., Mejiro Ryan—Mejiro Beauty, by Partholon	Jpn	6,240,681
24.	Rice Shower	1989 dk. b. or br. h., Real Shadai—Lilac Point, by Maruzensky	Jpn	6,070,429
25.	Grass Wonder	1995 ch. h., Silver Hawk—Ameriflora, by Danzig	Jpn	5,987,405
26.	Dance Partner	1992 b. f., Sunday Silence—Dancing Key, by Nijinsky II	Jpn	5,973,652
27.	Singspiel (Ire)	1992 b. h., In the Wings (GB)—Glorious Song, by Halo	GB	5,952,825
28.	Fast Friend	1994 ch. f., Ines Fujin—The Last Word, by Northern Taste	Jpn	5,896,693
29.	Sakura Laurel	1991 b. h., Rainbow Quest—Lola Lola, by Saint Cyrien	Jpn	5,751,390
30.	Black Hawk (GB)	1994 b. h., Nureyev—Silver Lane, by Silver Hawk	Jpn	5,750,386

1930—Gallant Fox, 1927 b. h., *Sir Gallahad III—Marguerite, by Celt. 17-11-3-2, **$328,165.**
1931—Sun Beau, 1925 b. h., *Sun Briar—Beautiful Lady, by Fair Play. 74-33-12-10, **$376,744.**
1940—Seabiscuit, 1933 b. h., Hard Tack—Swing On, by Whisk Broom II. 89-33-15-13, **$437,730.**
1942—Whirlaway, 1938 ch. h., *Blenheim II—Dustwhirl, by Sweep. 60-32-15-9, **$561,161.**
1947 (June 21)—Assault, 1943 ch. h., Bold Venture—Igual, by Equipoise. 42-18-6-7, **$576,670.**
1947 (July 5)—Stymie, 1941 ch. h., Equestrian—Stop Watch, by On Watch. 131-35-33-28, **$595,510.**
1947 (July 12)—Assault, $613,370 (career $675,470).
1947 (July 19)—Stymie, $678,510.
1947 (October 9)—Armed, 1941 dk. b. or br. g., Bull Lea—Armful, by Chance Shot. 81-41-20-10, **$761,500 (career $817,475).**
1947 (October 25)—Stymie $816,060 (career $918,485).
1950—Citation, 1945 b. h., Bull Lea—*Hydroplane II, by Hyperion. 45-32-10-2, **$1,085,760.**
1956—Nashua, 1952 b. h., *Nasrullah—Segula, by Johnstown. 30-22-4-1, **$1,288,565.**

1958—Round Table, 1954 b. h., *Princequillo—*Knight's Daughter, by Sir Cosmo. 66-43-8-5, **$1,749,869.**
1965—Kelso, 1957 dk. b. or br. g., Your Host—Maid of Flight, by Count Fleet. 63-39-12-2, **$1,977,896.**
1979—Affirmed, 1975 ch. h., Exclusive Native—Won't Tell You, by Crafty Admiral. 29-22-5-1, **$2,393,818.**
1980—Spectacular Bid, 1976 gr. h., Bold Bidder—Spectacular, by Promised Land. 30-26-2-1, **$2,781,608.**
1981—John Henry, 1975 b. g., Ole Bob Bowers—Once Double, by Double Jay 83-39-15-9, **$6,591,860.**
1988—Alysheba, 1984 b. h., Alydar—Bel Sheba, by Lt. Stevens 26-11-8-2, **$6,679,242.**
1990—Oguri Cap, 1985 gr. h., Dancing Cap—White Narubi, by *Silver Shark. 32-22-6-1, **$6,919,201.**
1993—Mejiro McQueen, 1987 gr. h., Mejiro Titan—Mejiro Aurola, by Remand. 14-9-3-0, **$7,618,803.**
1995—Narita Brian, 1991 dk b. or br. h., Brian's Time—Pacificus, by Northern Dancer. 21-12-3-1, **$9,296,552.**
1996—Cigar, 1990 b. h., Palace Music—Solar Slew, by Seattle Slew. 33-19-4-5, **$9,999,815.**
2000—T.M.Opera O, 1996 ch. h., Opera House (GB)—Once Wed, by Blushing Groom (Fr). 26-14-6-3, **$16,200,337.**

Leading North American Earners by Year

Year	Horse, YOB Sex, Pedigree	Earnings
2001	Point Given, 1998 c., Thunder Gulch—Turko's Turn, by Turkoman	$3,350,000
2000	Tiznow, 1997 c., Cee's Tizzy—Cee's Song, by Seattle Song	3,445,950
1999	Cat Thief, 1996 c., Storm Cat—Train Robbery, by Alydar	3,020,500
1998	Awesome Again, 1994 c., Deputy Minister—Primal Force, by Blushing Groom (Fr)	3,845,990
1997	Skip Away, 1993 c., Skip Trial—Ingot Way, by Diplomat Way	4,089,000
1996	Skip Away, 1993 c., Skip Trial—Ingot Way, by Diplomat Way	2,699,280
1995	Cigar, 1990 h., Palace Music—Solar Slew, by Seattle Slew	4,819,800
1994	Concern, 1991 c., Broad Brush—Fara's Team, by Tunerup	2,541,670
1993	Sea Hero, 1990 c., Polish Navy—Glowing Tribute, by Graustark	2,484,190
1992	A.P. Indy, 1989 c., Seattle Slew—Weekend Surprise, by Secretariat	2,622,560
1991	Dance Smartly, 1988 f., Danzig—Classy 'n Smart, by Smarten	2,876,821
1990	Unbridled, 1987 c., Fappiano—Gana Facil, by *Le Fabuleux	3,718,149
1989	Sunday Silence, 1986 c., Halo—Wishing Well, by Understanding	4,578,454
1988	Alysheba, 1984 c., Alydar—Bel Sheba, by Lt. Stevens	3,808,600
1987	Alysheba, 1984 c., Alydar—Bel Sheba, by Lt. Stevens	2,511,156
1986	Snow Chief, 1983 c., Reflected Glory—Miss Snowflake, by *Snow Sporting	1,875,200
1985	Spend a Buck, 1982 c., Buckaroo—Belle de Jour, by Speak John	3,552,704
1984	Slew o' Gold, 1980 c., Seattle Slew—Alluvial, by Buckpasser	2,627,944
1983	Sunny's Halo, 1980 c., Halo—Mostly Sunny, by Sunny	1,011,962
1982	Perrault (GB), 1977 h., Djakao—Innocent Air, by *Court Martial	1,197,400
1981	John Henry, 1975 g., Ole Bob Bowers—Once Double, by Double Jay	1,798,030
1980	Temperence Hill, 1977 c., Stop the Music—Sister Shannon, by Etonian	1,130,452
1979	Spectacular Bid, 1976 c., Bold Bidder—Spectacular, by Promised Land	1,279,334
1978	Affirmed, 1975 c., Exclusive Native—Won't Tell You, by Crafty Admiral	901,541
1977	Seattle Slew, 1974 c., Bold Reasoning—My Charmer, by Poker	641,370
1976	Forego, 1970 g., *Forli—Lady Golconda, by Hasty Road	491,701
1975	Foolish Pleasure, 1972 c., What a Pleasure—Fool-Me-Not, by Tom Fool	716,278
1974	Chris Evert, 1971 f., Swoon's Son—Miss Carmie, by T. V. Lark	551,063
1973	Secretariat, 1970 c., Bold Ruler—Somethingroyal, by *Princequillo	860,404
1972	Droll Role, 1968 c., Tom Rolfe—*Pradella, by Preciptic	471,633
1971	Riva Ridge, 1969 c., First Landing—Iberia, by *Heliopolis	503,263
1970	Personality, 1967 c., Hail to Reason—Affectionately, by Swaps	444,049
1969	Arts and Letters, 1966 c., *Ribot—All Beautiful, by Battlefield	555,604
1968	Forward Pass, 1965 c., On-and-On—Princess Turia, by *Heliopolis	546,674
1967	Damascus, 1964 c., Sword Dancer—Kerala, by *My Babu	817,941
1966	Buckpasser, 1963 c., Tom Fool—Busanda, by War Admiral	669,078
1965	Buckpasser, 1963 c., Tom Fool—Busanda, by War Admiral	568,096
1964	Gun Bow, 1960 c., Gun Shot—Ribbons and Bows, by War Admiral	580,100
1963	Candy Spots, 1960 c., *Nigromante—Candy Dish, by *Khaled	604,481

Following are leaders for racing in North America only. The exception is the second list, which includes worldwide earnings for any horse with one North American start.

Leading Earners in North America
Through 2001

Horse, Sex, YOB	Wins	SWs	SWs	Earnings
Skip Away, 1993 h.	18	16	16	$9,616,360
Cigar, 1990 h.	18	11	14	7,599,815
Alysheba, 1984 h.	11	10	10	6,679,242
John Henry, 1975 g.	39	25	30	6,591,860
Tiznow, 1997 h.	8	7	7	6,427,830
Best Pal, 1988 g.	18	12	17	5,668,245
Sunday Silence, 1986 h.	9	7	7	4,968,554
Easy Goer, 1986 h.	14	10	12	4,873,770
Unbridled, 1987 h.	8	3	5	4,489,475
Silver Charm, 1994 h.	11	10	10	4,444,369
Awesome Again, 1994 h.	9	7	7	4,374,590
Spend a Buck, 1982 h.	10	4	7	4,220,689
Creme Fraiche, 1982 h.	17	11	14	4,024,727
Point Given, 1998 c.	9	8	8	3,968,500
Cat Thief, 1996 h.	4	3	3	3,951,012
Devil His Due, 1989 h.	11	9	9	3,920,405
Ferdinand, 1983 h.	8	5	7	3,777,978
Slew o' Gold, 1980 h.	12	8	8	3,533,534
Precisionist, 1981 h.	20	13	17	3,485,398
Strike the Gold, 1988 h.	6	4	4	3,457,026
Snow Chief, 1983 h.	13	9	12	3,383,210
Cryptoclearance, 1984 h.	12	8	9	3,376,327
Gentlemen (Arg), 1992 h.	9	8	8	3,374,890
Black Tie Affair (Ire), 1986 h.	18	11	13	3,370,694
Sky Classic, 1987 h.	15	9	13	3,320,398
Bet Twice, 1984 h.	10	6	7	3,308,599
Serena's Song, 1992 m.	18	17	17	3,283,388
Real Quiet, 1995 h.	6	5	5	3,271,802
Dance Smartly, 1988 m.	12	6	10	3,263,835
Lemon Drop Kid, 1996 h.	10	7	7	3,245,370
Behrens, 1994 h.	9	7	7	3,243,500
Steinlen (GB), 1983 h.	16	12	14	3,229,752
Captain Steve, 1997 h.	8	6	7	3,228,356
Chief Bearhart, 1993 h.	12	6	9	3,219,017
Bertrando, 1989 h.	9	7	8	3,185,610
Free House, 1994 h.	9	8	8	3,178,971
Sandpit (Brz), 1989 h.	9	7	8	3,147,973
Paseana (Arg), 1987 m.	14	14	14	3,111,292
Gulch, 1984 h.	13	11	11	3,095,521
Silverbulletday, 1996 m.	15	13	14	3,093,207
Concern, 1991 h.	7	4	4	3,079,350
Lady's Secret, 1982 m.	25	15	22	3,021,325
Albert the Great, 1997 h.	8	5	5	3,012,490
Victory Gallop, 1995 h.	9	5	7	3,005,895
Alphabet Soup, 1991 h.	10	6	7	2,990,270
A.P. Indy, 1989 h.	8	6	6	2,979,815
Spain, 1997 m.	7	5	5	2,971,040
Escena, 1993 m.	11	7	7	2,962,639
Awad, 1990 h.	14	8	11	2,949,179
Hansel, 1988 h.	7	6	6	2,936,586
Sea Hero, 1990 h.	6	3	3	2,929,869
Great Communicator, 1983 h.	14	8	9	2,922,615
Thunder Gulch, 1992 h.	9	7	8	2,915,086
Budroyale, 1993 g.	18	5	7	2,900,810
Farma Way, 1987 h.	8	5	6	2,897,175
General Challenge, 1996 g.	9	7	8	2,876,018
With Approval, 1986 h.	13	2	9	2,863,540
Marquetry, 1987 h.	9	6	7	2,844,942
Theatrical (Ire), 1982 h.	7	7	7	2,840,500
Bayakoa (Arg), 1984 m.	18	15	16	2,785,259
Banshee Breeze, 1995 m.	10	8	8	2,784,798
Spectacular Bid, 1976 h.	26	21	23	2,781,608
Buck's Boy, 1993 g.	16	5	9	2,750,148
Beautiful Pleasure, 1995 m.	10	7	7	2,734,078
Forty Niner, 1985 h.	11	7	9	2,726,000
Pleasant Tap, 1987 h.	9	5	6	2,721,169

North American Leaders by Worldwide Stakes Earnings
Through 2001

Horse, year of birth, sex, sire	Years raced	Sts	Wns	SWs	Stakes Earnings
Cigar, 1990 h., by Palace Music	4	33	19	15	$9,895,000
Skip Away, 1993 h., by Skip Trial	4	38	18	16	9,586,620
Fantastic Light, 1996 h., by Rahy	4	25	12	8	7,778,895
Silver Charm, 1994 h., by Silver Buck	4	24	12	11	6,916,619
Captain Steve, 1997 h., by Fly So Free	3	25	9	8	6,800,756
Alysheba, 1984 h., by Alydar	3	26	11	10	6,668,167
John Henry, 1975 g., by Ole Bob Bowers	8	83	39	30	6,498,627
Tiznow, 1997 h., by Cee's Tizzy	2	15	8	7	6,382,830
Best Pal, 1988 g., by *Habitony	7	47	18	17	5,652,295
Taiki Blizzard, 1991 h., by Seattle Slew	4	23	6	3	4,972,168
Sunday Silence, 1986 h., by Halo	3	14	9	7	4,929,254
Easy Goer, 1986 h., by Alydar	3	20	14	12	4,837,890
Behrens, 1994 h., by Pleasant Colony	4	27	9	7	4,524,500
Unbridled, 1987 h., by Fappiano	3	24	8	5	4,449,875
Awesome Again, 1994 h., by Deputy Minister	2	12	9	7	4,321,010
Spend a Buck, 1982 h., by Buckaroo	2	15	10	7	4,199,089
Creme Fraiche, 1982 h., by Rich Cream	6	64	17	14	3,974,327
Seeking the Pearl, 1994 m., by Seeking the Gold	4	21	8	7	3,967,058
Point Given, 1998, c, by Thunder Gulch	2	13	9	8	3,930,900
Cat Thief, 1996 h., by Storm Cat	3	30	4	3	3,909,952
Devil His Due, 1989 h., by Devil's Bag	4	41	11	9	3,895,265
Daylami (Ire), 1994 h., by Doyoun	4	21	11	8	3,800,239
Ferdinand, 1983 h., by Nijinsky II	4	29	8	7	3,760,128
Sandpit (Brz), 1989 h., by Baynoun (Ire)	7	40	14	9	3,707,771
Almutawakel (GB), 1995 h., by Machiavellian	4	19	4	2	3,623,182
Gentlemen (Arg), 1992 h., by Robin des Bois	5	24	13	11	3,561,628
Slew o' Gold, 1980 h., by Seattle Slew	3	21	12	8	3,475,934
Victory Gallop, 1995 h., by Cryptoclearance	3	17	9	7	3,467,405
Precisionist, 1981 h., by Crozier	5	46	20	17	3,437,548
Lando (Ger), 1990 h., by Acatenango	4	24	10	10	3,434,931
Strike the Gold, 1988 h., by Alydar	4	31	6	4	3,402,716
Snow Chief, 1983 h., by Reflected Glory	3	24	13	12	3,370,560
Chief Bearhart, 1993 h., by Chief's Crown	4	26	12	9	3,329,869
Cryptoclearance, 1984 h., by Fappiano	4	44	12	9	3,328,327
Paradise Creek, 1989 h., by Irish River (Fr)	4	25	14	10	3,318,016
Sky Classic, 1987 h., by Nijinsky II	4	29	15	13	3,289,010
Black Tie Affair (Ire), 1986 h., by Miswaki	4	45	18	13	3,287,744
Bet Twice, 1984 h., by Sportin' Life	3	26	10	7	3,277,869
Serena's Song, 1992 m., by Rahy	3	38	18	17	3,265,788
Real Quiet, 1995 h., by Quiet American	3	20	6	5	3,240,042
Dance Smartly, 1988 m., by Danzig	3	17	12	10	3,237,915

Leaders by Graded Stakes Earnings in North America
Through 2001

Horse, year of birth, sex, sire	Years Raced	SWs	Graded Stakes Earnings
Skip Away, 1993, h, by Skip Trial	4	16	$9,548,100
Alysheba, 1984, h, by Alydar	3	10	$6,616,417
Tiznow, 1997, h, by Cee's Tizzy	2	7	$6,382,830
Cigar, 1990, h, by Palace Music	4	14	$5,695,000
John Henry, 1975, g, by Ole Bob Bowers	8	30	$4,953,417
Sunday Silence, 1986, h, by Halo	3	7	$4,929,254
Easy Goer, 1986, h, by Alydar	3	12	$4,775,280
Best Pal, 1988, g, by *Habitony	7	17	$4,713,795
Silver Charm, 1994, h, by Silver Buck	4	10	$4,416,619
Awesome Again, 1994, h, by Deputy Minister	2	7	$4,321,010
Unbridled, 1987, h, by Fappiano	3	5	$4,105,529
Point Given, 1998, c, by Thunder Gulch	2	8	$3,930,900
Cat Thief, 1996, h, by Storm Cat	3	3	$3,909,952
Devil His Due, 1989, h, by Devil's Bag	4	9	$3,895,265
Spend a Buck, 1982, h, by Buckaroo	2	7	$3,809,004

Creme Fraiche, 1982, h, by Rich Cream	6	14	$3,689,091
Ferdinand, 1983, h, by Nijinsky II	4	7	$3,619,978
Slew o' Gold, 1980, h, by Seattle Slew	3	8	$3,454,694
Strike the Gold, 1988, h, by Alydar	4	4	$3,391,210
Gentlemen (Arg), 1992, h, by Robin des Bois	5	8	$3,324,140
Serena's Song, 1992, m, by Rahy	3	17	$3,260,353
Behrens, 1994, h, by Pleasant Colony	4	7	$3,204,500
Real Quiet, 1995, h, by Quiet American	3	5	$3,195,740
Lemon Drop Kid, 1996, h, by Kingmambo	3	7	$3,168,900
Cryptoclearance, 1984, h, by Fappiano	4	9	$3,162,157
Snow Chief, 1983, h, by Reflected Glory	3	12	$3,162,110
Free House, 1994, h, by Smokester	4	8	$3,153,021
Precisionist, 1981, h, by Crozier	5	17	$3,136,608
Black Tie Affair (Ire), 1986, h, by Miswaki	4	13	$3,132,547
Bertrando, 1989, h, by Skywalker	5	8	$3,131,320
Paseana (Arg), 1987, m, by Ahmad	6	14	$3,074,292
Sandpit (Brz), 1989, h, by Baynoun (Ire)	7	8	$3,066,480
Captain Steve, 1997, h, by Fly So Free	3	7	$3,050,756
Gulch, 1984, h, by Mr. Prospector	3	11	$3,049,671
Concern, 1991, h, by Broad Brush	3	4	$3,004,530
Silverbulletday, 1996, m, by Silver Deputy	3	14	$2,998,073
Dance Smartly, 1988, m, by Danzig	3	10	$2,966,963
A.P. Indy, 1989, h, by Seattle Slew	2	6	$2,952,340
Sky Classic, 1987, h, by Nijinsky II	4	13	$2,942,152

Leaders by Grade 1 Earnings in North American Stakes
Through 2001

Horse, year of birth, sex, sire	Years raced	SWs	G1 Stakes Earnings
Skip Away, 1993, h, by Skip Trial	4	16	$7,310,920
Tiznow, 1997, h, by Cee's Tizzy	2	7	$5,815,400
Cigar, 1990, h, by Palace Music	4	14	$5,660,000
Point Given, 1998, c, by Thunder Gulch	2	8	$3,718,300
Devil His Due, 1989, h, by Devil's Bag	4	9	$3,466,000
Cat Thief, 1996, h, by Storm Cat	3	3	$3,366,500
Awesome Again, 1994, h, by Deputy Minister	2	7	$3,255,320
Best Pal, 1988, g, by *Habitony	7	17	$3,158,250
Real Quiet, 1995, h, by Quiet American	3	5	$2,920,920
Strike the Gold, 1988, h, by Alydar	4	4	$2,800,876
Paseana (Arg), 1987, m, by Ahmad	6	14	$2,753,942
A.P. Indy, 1989, h, by Seattle Slew	2	6	$2,725,660
Silver Charm, 1994, h, by Silver Buck	4	10	$2,716,350
Sea Hero, 1990, h, by Polish Navy	3	3	$2,635,900
Lemon Drop Kid, 1996, h, by Kingmambo	3	7	$2,630,400
Gentlemen (Arg), 1992, h, by Robin des Bois	5	8	$2,610,000
Bertrando, 1989, h, by Skywalker	5	8	$2,554,820
Chief Bearhart, 1993, h, by Chief's Crown	4	9	$2,517,668
Fantastic Light, 1996, h, by Rahy	4	2	$2,507,400
Beautiful Pleasure, 1995, m, by Maudlin	5	7	$2,467,500
Sandpit (Brz), 1989, h, by Baynoun (Ire)	7	8	$2,396,000
Concern, 1991, h, by Broad Brush	3	4	$2,375,780
Spain, 1997, m, by Thunder Gulch	3	5	$2,373,900
Banshee Breeze, 1995, m, by Unbridled	3	8	$2,311,680
Daylami (Ire), 1994, h, by Doyoun	4	2	$2,280,000
Serena's Song, 1992, m, by Rahy	3	17	$2,244,400
Albert the Great, 1997, h, by Go for Gin	2	5	$2,237,120
Free House, 1994, h, by Smokester	4	8	$2,229,361
Dance Smartly, 1988, m, by Danzig	3	10	$2,224,073
Hansel, 1988, h, by Woodman	2	6	$2,175,250
Escena, 1993, m, by Strawberry Road (Aus)	4	7	$2,172,000
Farma Way, 1987, h, by Marfa	3	6	$2,160,000
General Challenge, 1996, g, by General Meeting	3	8	$2,110,000
Flawlessly, 1988, m, by Affirmed	5	15	$2,096,700
Alphabet Soup, 1991, h, by Cozzene	4	7	$2,080,000
Thunder Gulch, 1992, h, by Gulch	2	8	$2,064,080
Pleasant Tap, 1987, h, by Pleasant Colony	4	6	$2,030,000
Fraise, 1988, h, by Strawberry Road (Aus)	4	6	$1,982,000
Paradise Creek, 1989, h, by Irish River (Fr)	4	10	$1,967,000
Victory Gallop, 1995, h, by Cryptoclearance	3	7	$1,966,720

Leading Male Earners on Turf in North America
Through 2001

Horse, YOB, sex, sire	Years raced	SWs	Turf Earnings
John Henry, 1975 g., by Ole Bob Bowers	8	30	$5,269,212
Steinlen (GB), 1983 h., by Habitat	5	14	3,229,752
Sky Classic, 1987 h., by Nijinsky II	4	13	3,176,638
Chief Bearhart, 1993 h., by Chief's Crown	4	9	3,164,509
Great Communicator, 1983 h., by Key to the Kingdom	6	9	2,908,485
Awad, 1990 h., by Caveat	7	11	2,871,645
Theatrical (Ire), 1982 h., by Nureyev	4	7	2,840,500
Sandpit (Brz), 1989 h., by Baynoun (Ire)	7	9	2,752,973
Manila, 1983 h., by Lyphard	3	10	2,676,299
Paradise Creek, 1989 h., by Irish River (Fr)	4	10	2,675,514
Fraise, 1988 h., by Strawberry Road (Aus)	4	6	2,613,105
Fantastic Light, 1996 h., by Rahy	4	8	2,507,400
Buck's Boy, 1993 g., by Bucksplasher	5	9	2,493,520
Lure, 1989 h., by Danzig	4	10	2,348,839
Daylami (Ire), 1994 h., by Doyoun	4	8	2,280,000
Marlin, 1993 h., by Sword Dance (Ire)	3	6	2,262,255
With Approval, 1986 h., by Caro (Ire)	3	9	2,254,760
Yankee Affair, 1982 h., by Northern Fling	5	15	2,204,524
Sunshine Forever, 1985 h., by Roberto	3	5	2,083,700
Quiet Resolve, 1995 g., by Affirmed	4	4	2,063,121
Kotashaan (Fr), 1988 h., by Darshaan	4	8	2,017,050
Star of Cozzene, 1988 h., by Cozzene	5	9	2,015,039

Leading Female Earners on Turf in North America
Through 2001

Horse, YOB, sex, sire	Years raced	SWs	Turf Earning
Flawlessly, 1988 m., by Affirmed	5	15	$2,459,250
Perfect Sting, 1996 m., by Red Ransom	4	11	2,163,673
Estrapade, 1980 m., by *Vaguely Noble	4	10	1,789,600
Miss Alleged, 1987 m., by Alleged	3	4	1,532,500
Happyanunoit (NZ), 1995 m., by Yachtie	4	5	1,481,892
Tout Charmant, 1996 m., by Sleewvescent	4	5	1,448,219
Memories of Silver, 1993 m., by Silver Hawk	3	8	1,435,140
Tranquility Lake, 1995 m., by Rahy	4	9	1,420,770
Dance Smartly, 1988 m., by Danzig	3	10	1,412,650
Possibly Perfect, 1990 m., by Northern Baby	4	8	1,367,050
All Along (Fr), 1979 m., by Targowice	4	6	1,337,146
Tuzla (Fr), 1994 m., by Panoramic (GB)	4	8	1,266,079
Carotene, 1983 m., by Great Nephew	4	8	1,242,126
Brown Bess, 1982 m., by *Petrone	6	11	1,224,265
Soaring Softly, 1995 m., by Kris S.	3	5	1,193,450
Irish Linnet, 1988 m., by Seattle Song	6	13	1,191,980
Windsharp, 1991 m., by Lear Fan	4	6	1,191,600
Fieldy (Ire), 1983 m., by Northfields	6	14	1,182,530
Wandesta (GB), 1991 m., by Nashwan	4	6	1,170,650
Royal Heroine (Ire), 1980 m., by Lypheor (GB)	3	5	1,110,900
Bold Ruritana, 1990 m., by Bold Ruckus	6	10	1,102,790
Kostroma (Ire), 1986 m., by Caerleon	4	7	1,093,275
Maxzene, 1993 m., by Cozzene	3	7	1,067,587
Colstar, 1996 m., by Opening Verse	4	7	1,053,056
Sabin, 1980 m., by Lyphard	4	14	998,235
Capades, 1986 m., by Overskate	3	8	991,516
Sangue (Ire), 1978 m., by Lyphard	3	12	974,900
Ryafan, 1994 m., by Lear Fan	2	6	968,000
Auntie Mame, 1994 m., by Theatrical (Ire)	3	8	961,480
Real Connection, 1991 m., by Vigors	5	3	956,438
Hatoof, 1989 m., by Irish River (Fr)	4	8	950,960
Spook Express (SAf), 1994 m., by Comic Blush	4	4	932,270
Gaily Gaily (Ire), 1983 m., by Cure the Blues	6	7	914,939
Anka Germania (Ire), 1982 m., by Malinowski	6	10	903,554
Pebbles (GB), 1981 m., by Sharpen Up (GB)	3	1	900,000
Miesque, 1984 m., by Nureyev	3	2	900,000
The Very One, 1975 m., by One for All	5	13	888,523
Fiji (GB), 1994 m., by Rainbow Quest	4	5	871,410
Lady Shirl, 1987 m., by That's a Nice	6	10	863,973

Leading Two-Year-Old Male Earners in North America
Through 2001

Horse, YOB, sex, sire	Sts	Wns	SWs	Stakes Earnings
Boston Harbor, 1994, h, by Capote	7	6	5	$1,928,605
Mountain Cat, 1990, h, by Storm Cat	8	6	5	$1,460,627
Favorite Trick, 1995, h, by Phone Trick	8	8	7	$1,231,998
Tejano, 1985, h, by Caro (Ire)	10	5	4	$1,177,189
Best Pal, 1988, g, by *Habitony	8	6	5	$1,026,195
Grand Canyon, 1987, h, by Fappiano	8	4	3	$1,019,540
Snow Chief, 1983, h, by Reflected Glory	9	5	4	$935,740
Timber Country, 1992, h, by Woodman	7	4	3	$928,590
Chief's Crown, 1982, h, by Danzig	9	6	5	$920,890
Fly So Free, 1988, h, by Time for a Change	6	4	2	$872,580
Gilded Time, 1990, h, by Timeless Moment	4	4	3	$855,980
Regal Classic, 1985, h, by Vice Regent	8	4	4	$812,500
Roving Boy, 1980, h, by Olden Times	7	5	4	$800,425
Macho Uno, 1998, c, by Holy Bull	4	3	2	$768,803
Tasso, 1983, h, by Fappiano	7	5	3	$761,534
Fali Time, 1981, h, by Faliraki (Ire)	7	3	2	$748,829
Captain Steve, 1997, h, by Fly So Free	8	4	3	$744,880
Officer, 1999, c, by Bertrando	8	5	4	$740,010
Success Express, 1985, h, by Hold Your Peace	8	4	3	$737,207
Siphonic, 1999, c, by Siphon (Brz)	4	3	2	$703,978
Easy Goer, 1986, h, by Alydar	6	4	2	$697,500
Answer Lively, 1996, h, by Lively One	7	4	2	$695,296
Bet Twice, 1984, h, by Sportin' Life	7	5	3	$690,565
Spend a Buck, 1982, h, by Buckaroo	8	5	2	$667,985
River Special, 1990, h, by Riverman	6	3	3	$663,900
Capote, 1984, h, by Seattle Slew	4	3	2	$654,680
Brocco, 1991, h, by Kris S.	4	3	1	$653,550
Stephan's Odyssey, 1982, h, by Danzig	4	3	1	$651,100
King Glorious, 1986, h, by Naevus	5	5	4	$646,100
Forty Niner, 1985, h, by Mr. Prospector	6	5	4	$634,908
Point Given, 1998, c, by Thunder Gulch	6	3	2	$618,500
Swiss Yodeler, 1994, h, by Eastern Echo	9	6	5	$617,200
Rhythm, 1987, h, by Mr. Prospector	5	3	1	$612,920
Anees, 1997, h, by Unbridled	4	2	1	$609,200

Leading Two-Year-Old Filly Earners in North America
Through 2001

Horse, YOB, sex, sire	Sts	Wns	SWs	Stakes Earnings
Silverbulletday, 1996, m, by Silver Deputy	7	6	5	$1,114,110
Countess Diana, 1995, m, by Deerhound	6	5	4	$1,019,785
Meadow Star, 1988, m, by Meadowlake	7	7	6	$992,250
Brave Raj, 1984, m, by Rajab	9	6	5	$933,650
Storm Song, 1994, m, by Summer Squall	7	4	3	$898,205
Outstandingly, 1982, m, by Exclusive Native	6	3	2	$867,872
Eliza, 1990, m, by Mt. Livermore	5	4	3	$808,000
Family Style, 1983, m, by State Dinner	10	4	3	$805,809
Flanders, 1992, m, by Seeking the Gold	5	4	3	$805,000
Excellent Meeting, 1996, m, by General Meeting	8	4	3	$773,824
Chilukki, 1997, m, by Cherokee Run	7	6	5	$762,723
Phone Chatter, 1991, m, by Phone Trick	6	4	3	$753,500
Open Mind, 1986, m, by Deputy Minister	6	4	3	$724,064
Althea, 1981, m, by Alydar	9	5	4	$692,625
Caressing, 1998, f, by Honour and Glory	5	3	2	$690,642
Pleasant Stage, 1989, m, by Pleasant Colony	4	2	2	$687,240
Surfside, 1997, m, by Seattle Slew	6	4	2	$677,350
Golden Attraction, 1993, m, by Mr. Prospector	8	6	5	$675,588
Tempera, 1999, f, by A.P. Indy	5	3	2	$670,240
Cash Run, 1997, m, by Seeking the Gold	6	3	1	$653,352
Twilight Ridge, 1983, m, by Cox's Ridge	5	3	2	$617,808
My Flag, 1993, m, by Easy Goer	6	2	1	$614,614
Raging Fever, 1998, f, by Storm Cat	6	5	4	$598,500
Serena's Song, 1992, m, by Rahy	10	4	3	$597,335
Boots 'n Jackie, 1990, m, by Major Moran	12	4	3	$579,820
Tappiano, 1984, m, by Fappiano	5	4	3	$572,820
Sacahuista, 1984, m, by Raja Baba	9	4	3	$564,965
I'm Splendid, 1983, m, by Our Native	7	4	3	$560,857
Go for Wand, 1987, m, by Deputy Minister	4	3	1	$548,390

Leading Three-Year-Old Male Earners in Single Season in North America
Through 2001

Horse, YOB, sex, sire	Sts	Wns	SWs	Stakes Earnings
Sunday Silence, 1986, h, by Halo	9	7	6	$4,578,454
Easy Goer, 1986, h, by Alydar	11	8	8	$3,837,150
Unbridled, 1987, h, by Fappiano	11	4	3	$3,718,149
Spend a Buck, 1982, h, by Buckaroo	7	5	5	$3,552,704
Tiznow, 1997, h, by Cee's Tizzy	9	5	4	$3,445,950
Point Given, 1998, c, by Thunder Gulch	7	6	6	$3,350,000
Cat Thief, 1996, h, by Storm Cat	13	2	2	$3,020,500
Skip Away, 1993, h, by Skip Trial	12	6	5	$2,699,280
Thunder Gulch, 1992, h, by Gulch	10	7	7	$2,644,080
A.P. Indy, 1989, h, by Seattle Slew	7	5	5	$2,622,560
Hansel, 1988, h, by Woodman	9	4	4	$2,565,680
Concern, 1991, h, by Broad Brush	14	3	2	$2,541,670
Alysheba, 1984, h, by Alydar	10	3	3	$2,511,156
Izvestia, 1987, h, by Icecapade	11	8	8	$2,486,667
Sea Hero, 1990, h, by Polish Navy	9	2	2	$2,484,190
Tabasco Cat, 1991, h, by Storm Cat	12	5	5	$2,164,334
Seeking the Gold, 1985, h, by Mr. Prospector	12	6	4	$2,145,620
Holy Bull, 1991, h, by Great Above	10	8	8	$2,095,000
Forty Niner, 1985, h, by Mr. Prospector	13	6	5	$2,091,092
Sunshine Forever, 1985, h, by Roberto	12	8	5	$2,032,636
Charismatic, 1996, h, by Summer Squall	10	4	3	$2,007,404
Fusaichi Pegasus, 1997, h, by Mr. Prospector	8	6	4	$1,987,800
Victory Gallop, 1995, h, by Cryptoclearance	8	3	3	$1,981,720
Pine Bluff, 1989, h, by Danzig	6	3	3	$1,970,896
Risen Star, 1985, h, by Secretariat	8	6	5	$1,958,368
Proud Truth, 1982, h, by Graustark	11	7	5	$1,926,327
Bet Twice, 1984, h, by Sportin' Life	9	3	3	$1,922,642
Prized, 1986, h, by Kris S.	7	4	4	$1,888,705
Captain Steve, 1997, h, by Fly So Free	11	3	3	$1,882,276
Snow Chief, 1983, h, by Reflected Glory	9	6	6	$1,875,200
Louis Quatorze, 1993, h, by Sovereign Dancer	8	4	2	$1,854,908
Deputy Commander, 1994, h, by Deputy Minister	10	4	3	$1,849,440
Manila, 1983, h, by Lyphard	10	8	6	$1,814,729
Real Quiet, 1995, h, by Quiet American	6	2	2	$1,788,800
With Approval, 1986, h, by Caro (Ire)	10	6	5	$1,772,150
Coronado's Quest, 1995, h, by Forty Niner	11	5	5	$1,739,950
Monarchos, 1998, c, by Maria's Mon	7	4	2	$1,711,600
Menifee, 1996, h, by Harlan	9	3	2	$1,695,400
General Challenge, 1996, g, by General Meeting	11	6	6	$1,658,100
Silver Charm, 1994, h, by Silver Buck	7	3	3	$1,638,750
Java Gold, 1984, h, by Key to the Mint	8	6	4	$1,621,300
Touch Gold, 1994, h, by Deputy Minister	7	4	3	$1,522,313
Strike the Gold, 1988, h, by Alydar	12	2	2	$1,443,850
Broad Brush, 1983, h, by Ack Ack	14	7	7	$1,409,778
Prairie Bayou, 1990, g, by Little Missouri	8	5	5	$1,405,521
Cryptoclearance, 1984, h, by Fappiano	15	4	4	$1,367,150
Lemon Drop Kid, 1996, h, by Kingmambo	9	3	2	$1,349,400
Kissin Kris, 1990, h, by Kris S.	12	2	2	$1,341,292
Tikkanen, 1991, h, by Cozzene	2	2	2	$1,340,000
Free House, 1994, h, by Smokester	10	3	3	$1,336,910
Peaks and Valleys, 1992, h, by Mt. Livermore	8	5	4	$1,323,750

Leading Three-Year-Old Filly Earners in Single Season in North America
Through 2001

Horse, YOB, sex, sire	Sts	Wns	SWs	Stakes Earnings
Dance Smartly, 1988, m, by Danzig	8	8	8	$2,876,821
Spain, 1997, m, by Thunder Gulch	13	5	4	$1,979,500
Silverbulletday, 1996, m, by Silver Deputy	11	8	8	$1,707,640
Unbridled Elaine, 1998, f, by Unbridled's Song	8	4	3	$1,663,175
Serena's Song, 1992, m, by Rahy	13	9	9	$1,524,920
Banshee Breeze, 1995, m, by Unbridled	10	6	4	$1,425,980
Winning Colors, 1985, m, by Caro (Ire)	10	4	4	$1,347,746
Surfside, 1997, m, by Seattle Slew	7	4	4	$1,147,637

Horse, YOB, sex, sire	Sts	Wns	SWs	Earnings
Open Mind, 1986, m, by Deputy Minister	11	8	8	$1,120,308
Flute, 1998, f, by Seattle Slew	7	4	2	$1,094,104
Dancethruthedawn, 1998, f, by Mr. Prospector	6	3	2	$1,045,039
Xtra Heat, 1998, f, by Dixieland Heat	13	9	9	$1,012,040
Lady's Secret, 1982, m, by Secretariat	17	10	10	$994,349
Ajina, 1994, m, by Strawberry Road (Aus)	9	3	3	$979,175
Jostle, 1997, m, by Brocco	9	4	4	$975,570
Ryafan, 1994, m, by Lear Fan	3	3	3	$968,000
Keeper Hill, 1995, m, by Deputy Minister	8	3	2	$949,410
Very Subtle, 1984, m, by Hoist the Silver	12	6	6	$947,135
My Flag, 1993, m, by Easy Goer	10	4	4	$933,043
Sharp Cat, 1994, m, by Storm Cat	11	7	7	$911,300
Exogenous, 1998, f, by Unbridled	7	4	2	$901,500
Hollywood Wildcat, 1990, m, by Kris S.	9	5	5	$893,330
Life's Magic, 1981, m, by Cox's Ridge	12	4	4	$873,956
Blushing K. D., 1994, m, by Blushing John	8	6	6	$845,040
Secret Status, 1997, m, by A.P. Indy	9	5	3	$842,796
Go for Wand, 1987, m, by Deputy Minister	9	7	7	$824,948
Life At the Top, 1983, m, by Seattle Slew	18	6	5	$821,349
Lite Light, 1988, m, by Majestic Light	9	5	5	$804,685
Goodbye Halo, 1985, m, by Halo	11	5	5	$789,117
Mystic Lady, 1998, f, by Thunder Gulch	11	6	6	$775,000
Yanks Music, 1993, m, by Air Forbes Won	7	5	4	$751,000
Dispute, 1990, m, by Danzig	11	6	4	$750,226
Affluent, 1998, f, by Affirmed	10	4	3	$725,200
Sacahuista, 1984, m, by Raja Baba	9	2	2	$724,857
Surfside, 1997, m, by Seattle Slew	13	8	6	$1,824,987
Unbridled Elaine, 1998, f, by Unbridled's Song	11	6	4	$1,770,740
My Flag, 1993, m, by Easy Goer	16	6	5	$1,547,657
Banshee Breeze, 1995, m, by Unbridled	11	6	4	$1,425,980
Sharp Cat, 1994, m, by Storm Cat	18	11	10	$1,417,250
Life's Magic, 1981, m, by Cox's Ridge	19	6	5	$1,411,215
Meadow Star, 1988, m, by Meadowlake	15	11	10	$1,406,950
Winning Colors, 1985, m, by Caro (Ire)	12	6	4	$1,379,146
Go for Wand, 1987, m, by Deputy Minister	13	10	8	$1,373,338
Excellent Meeting, 1996, m, by General Meeting	16	8	7	$1,298,824
Sacahuista, 1984, m, by Raja Baba	18	6	5	$1,289,822
Althea, 1981, m, by Alydar	15	8	7	$1,275,255
Very Subtle, 1984, m, by Hoist the Silver	16	10	8	$1,274,860
Xtra Heat, 1998, f, by Dixieland Heat	22	17	16	$1,274,150
Dancethruthedawn, 1998, f, by Mr. Prospector	10	5	3	$1,258,691
Jostle, 1997, m, by Brocco	14	8	7	$1,238,170
Goodbye Halo, 1985, m, by Halo	15	8	7	$1,220,702
Family Style, 1983, m, by State Dinner	23	6	5	$1,203,648
Ajina, 1994, m, by Strawberry Road (Aus)	13	6	5	$1,192,615
Lite Light, 1988, m, by Majestic Light	18	8	7	$1,152,391
Flute, 1998, f, by Seattle Slew	8	4	2	$1,101,504
Hollywood Wildcat, 1990, m, by Kris S.	14	9	8	$1,091,610
Lady's Secret, 1982, m, by Secretariat	25	13	12	$1,087,172
Eliza, 1990, m, by Mt. Livermore	9	5	4	$1,078,540
Chilukki, 1997, m, by Cherokee Run	15	10	8	$1,071,828
Countess Diana, 1995, m, by Deerhound	10	5	4	$1,052,565
Storm Song, 1994, m, by Summer Squall	12	4	3	$1,020,050
Miss Oceana, 1981, m, by Alydar	19	11	9	$1,010,385
Ryafan, 1994, m, by Lear Fan	3	3	3	$968,000
Keeper Hill, 1995, m, by Deputy Minister	11	3	2	$966,370
Outstandingly, 1982, m, by Exclusive Native	13	4	2	$946,076
Exogenous, 1998, f, by Unbridled	12	5	2	$945,560
Cash Run, 1997, m, by Seeking the Gold	17	5	3	$924,201
Blushing K. D., 1994, m, by Blushing John	10	8	7	$918,900

Leading Male Earners at Two and Three in North America

Through 2001

Horse, YOB, sex, sire	Sts	Wns	SWs	Stakes Earnings
Sunday Silence, 1986, h, by Halo	12	8	6	$4,600,154
Easy Goer, 1986, h, by Alydar	17	12	10	$4,534,650
Spend a Buck, 1982, h, by Buckaroo	15	10	7	$4,220,689
Point Given, 1998, c, by Thunder Gulch	13	9	8	$3,968,500
Unbridled, 1987, h, by Fappiano	17	6	4	$3,892,695
Cat Thief, 1996, h, by Storm Cat	20	4	3	$3,454,112
Tiznow, 1997, h, by Cee's Tizzy	9	5	4	$3,445,950
A.P. Indy, 1989, h, by Seattle Slew	11	8	6	$2,979,815
Hansel, 1988, h, by Woodman	14	7	6	$2,936,586
Thunder Gulch, 1992, h, by Gulch	16	9	8	$2,915,086
Alysheba, 1984, h, by Alydar	17	4	3	$2,870,642
Sea Hero, 1990, h, by Polish Navy	16	5	3	$2,823,910
Snow Chief, 1983, h, by Reflected Glory	18	11	10	$2,810,940
Skip Away, 1993, h, by Skip Trial	18	7	5	$2,787,360
Forty Niner, 1985, h, by Mr. Prospector	19	11	9	$2,726,000
Captain Steve, 1997, h, by Fly So Free	19	7	6	$2,627,156
Bet Twice, 1984, h, by Sportin' Life	16	8	6	$2,613,207
Concern, 1991, h, by Broad Brush	21	4	2	$2,567,450
Izvestia, 1987, h, by Icecapade	13	9	8	$2,498,667
Holy Bull, 1991, h, by Great Above	14	12	10	$2,430,760
Tabasco Cat, 1991, h, by Storm Cat	18	8	6	$2,347,671
Pine Bluff, 1989, h, by Danzig	13	6	5	$2,255,884
Chief's Crown, 1982, h, by Danzig	21	12	10	$2,191,168
Real Quiet, 1995, h, by Quiet American	15	4	3	$2,169,922
Seeking the Gold, 1985, h, by Mr. Prospector	13	7	4	$2,152,820
Best Pal, 1988, g, by *Habitony	18	8	7	$2,133,695
Victory Gallop, 1995, h, by Cryptoclearance	13	6	5	$2,106,600
Coronado's Quest, 1995, h, by Forty Niner	17	10	8	$2,046,190
Sunshine Forever, 1985, h, by Roberto	17	5	5	$2,039,456
Charismatic, 1996, h, by Summer Squall	17	5	3	$2,038,064
Risen Star, 1985, h, by Secretariat	11	8	6	$2,029,845

Leading Filly Earners at Two and Three in North America

Through 2001

Horse, YOB, sex, sire	Sts	Wns	SWs	Stakes Earnings
Dance Smartly, 1988, m, by Danzig	13	11	9	$3,083,455
Silverbulletday, 1996, m, by Silver Deputy	18	14	13	$2,821,750
Spain, 1997, m, by Thunder Gulch	19	6	4	$2,133,335
Serena's Song, 1992, m, by Rahy	23	13	12	$2,122,255
Open Mind, 1986, m, by Deputy Minister	17	12	11	$1,844,372

Leading Male Earners in Single Season at Age Four or Older in North America

Through 2001

Horse, YOB, sex, sire	Age	Sts	Wns	SWs	Stakes Earnings
Cigar, 1990, h, by Palace Music	5	10	10	9	$4,819,800
Skip Away, 1993, h, by Skip Trial	4	11	4	4	$4,089,000
Awesome Again, 1994, h, by Deputy Minister	4	6	6	5	$3,845,990
Alysheba, 1984, h, by Alydar	4	9	7	7	$3,808,600
Tiznow, 1997, h, by Cee's Tizzy	4	6	3	3	$2,981,880
Skip Away, 1993, h, by Skip Trial	5	9	7	7	$2,740,000
Slew o' Gold, 1980, h, by Seattle Slew	4	6	5	4	$2,627,944
Farma Way, 1987, h, by Marfa	4	11	5	5	$2,598,350
Alphabet Soup, 1991, h, by Cozzene	5	7	4	4	$2,536,450
Cigar, 1990, h, by Palace Music	6	7	4	4	$2,510,000
Black Tie Affair (Ire), 1986, h, by Miswaki	5	10	7	7	$2,483,540
John Henry, 1975, g, by Ole Bob Bowers	9	9	6	6	$2,336,650
Silver Charm, 1994, h, by Silver Buck	4	8	5	5	$2,296,506
Criminal Type, 1985, h, by Alydar	5	11	7	6	$2,270,290
Theatrical (Ire), 1982, h, by Nureyev	5	9	7	7	$2,235,500
Bertrando, 1989, h, by Skywalker	4	9	3	3	$2,217,800
Ferdinand, 1983, h, by Nijinsky II	4	10	4	4	$2,185,150
Gentlemen (Arg), 1992, h, by Robin des Bois	5	6	4	4	$2,125,300
Fantastic Light, 1996, h, by Rahy	5	5	1	1	$2,112,800
Wild Again, 1980, h, by Icecapade	4	16	6	4	$2,054,409
Daylami (Ire), 1994, h, by Doyoun	5	1	1	1	$2,040,000
Great Communicator, 1983, h, by Key to the Kingdom	5	11	6	6	$2,017,950
Chief Bearhart, 1993, h, by Chief's Crown	4	7	5	5	$2,011,259
Festin (Arg), 1986, h, by Mat-Boy (Arg)	5	11	3	3	$2,003,250
Kotashaan (Fr), 1988, h, by Darshaan	5	9	6	6	$1,984,100
Pleasant Tap, 1987, h, by Pleasant Colony	5	10	4	4	$1,959,914
Devil His Due, 1989, h, by Devil's Bag	4	11	4	4	$1,939,120
Paradise Creek, 1989, h, by Irish River (Fr)	5	10	8	8	$1,920,872
Strike the Gold, 1988, h, by Alydar	4	13	2	2	$1,920,176
Buck's Boy, 1993, g, by Bucksplasher	5	10	6	6	$1,874,020
Skywalker, 1982, h, by Relaunch	4	9	4	4	$1,811,400
John Henry, 1975, g, by Ole Bob Bowers	6	10	8	8	$1,798,030
Albert the Great, 1997, h, by Go for Gin	4	9	3	3	$1,740,000

Leading Female Earners in Single Season at Age Four or Older in North America
Through 2001

Horse, YOB, sex, sire	Age	Sts	Wns	SWs	Stakes Earnings
Escena, 1993, m, by Strawberry Road (Aus)	5	9	5	5	$2,032,425
Lady's Secret, 1982, m, by Secretariat	4	15	10	10	$1,871,053
Beautiful Pleasure, 1995, m, by Maudlin	4	7	4	3	$1,716,404
Paseana (Arg), 1987, m, by Ahmad	5	9	7	7	$1,518,290
Bayakoa (Arg), 1984, m, by Consultant's Bid	5	11	9	8	$1,406,403
Riboletta (Brz), 1995, m, by Roi Normand	5	11	7	7	$1,384,860
Perfect Sting, 1996, m, by Red Ransom	4	6	5	5	$1,367,000
Banshee Breeze, 1995, m, by Unbridled	4	7	4	4	$1,358,818
Miss Alleged, 1987, m, by Alleged	4	3	2	2	$1,345,000
Heritage of Gold, 1995, m, by Gold Legend	5	8	5	5	$1,332,282
Bayakoa (Arg), 1984, m, by Consultant's Bid	6	10	7	7	$1,234,406
Personal Ensign, 1984, m, by Private Account	4	7	7	7	$1,202,640
Soaring Softly, 1995, m, by Kris S.	4	8	7	5	$1,193,450
Estrapade, 1980, m, by *Vaguely Noble	6	9	3	3	$1,184,800
Serena's Song, 1992, m, by Rahy	4	15	5	5	$1,161,133
Inside Information, 1991, m, by Private Account	4	8	7	6	$1,160,408
Jewel Princess, 1992, m, by Key to the Mint	4	9	5	5	$1,150,800
Tout Charmant, 1996, m, by Slewvescent	4	7	3	3	$1,089,044
Royal Heroine (Ire), 1980, m, by Lypheor (GB)	4	8	4	4	$1,023,500
Safely Kept, 1986, m, by Horatius	4	10	8	7	$959,280
Paseana (Arg), 1987, m, by Ahmad	6	8	3	3	$950,402
Manistique, 1995, m, by Unbridled	4	9	6	6	$935,100
Lu Ravi, 1995, m, by A.P. Indy	5	8	3	3	$918,200
Pebbles (GB), 1981, m, by Sharpen Up (GB)	4	1	1	1	$900,000
Heavenly Prize, 1991, m, by Seeking the Gold	4	7	4	4	$895,900
Tuzla (Fr), 1994, m, by Panoramic (GB)	5	8	4	4	$889,080
Flawlessly, 1988, m, by Affirmed	5	5	4	4	$886,700
Spook Express (SAf), 1994, m, by Comic Blush	7	8	3	3	$866,870
Happyanunoit (NZ), 1995, m, by Yachtie	4	8	4	4	$862,792
Princess Rooney, 1980, m, by Verbatim	4	9	6	5	$854,791
Heritage of Gold, 1995, m, by Gold Legend	4	10	6	5	$853,680
North Sider, 1982, m, by Topsider	5	17	7	6	$847,107
Life's Magic, 1981, m, by Cox's Ridge	4	13	2	2	$844,003
Different (Arg), 1992, m, by Candy Stripes	4	5	4	3	$839,290
One Dreamer, 1988, m, by Relaunch	6	8	4	4	$837,730
Spain, 1997, m, by Thunder Gulch	4	9	1	1	$837,705
All Along (Fr), 1979, m, by Targowice	4	3	3	3	$813,631
Fiji (GB), 1994, m, by Rainbow Quest	4	7	6	4	$805,560
Claire Marine (Ire), 1985, m, by What A Guest	4	12	7	6	$801,565
Snow Polina, 1995, m, by Trempolino	5	10	3	2	$772,943

Leading Runners by Most Stakes Placings Without a Stakes Win in North
Through 2001

Horse, year of birth, sex, sire	Years Raced	Sts	Wns	Stakes Placings	Earnings
Stunning Nativo, 1078 m., by Our Nativo	3	35	3	13	$155,312
Gat's Girl, 1975 m., by Lurullah	5	70	6	11	119,242
Mistress Fletcher, 1992 m., by Sovereign Don	6	71	9	11	260,638
Ladies Agreement, 1970 m., by Royal Union	5	68	14	10	295,193
Little Buckles, 1991 m., by Buckley Boy	5	43	9	10	466,755
Sweets, 1985 g., by Mr. Redoy	8	85	8	10	196,524
Lotta Tike, 1974 m., by Skin Head	5	58	10	10	91,760
Hold the Beans, 1977 h., by Northern Fling	10	186	18	10	175,528
Rule by Reason, 1967 h., by Hail to Reason	6	92	15	10	263,547
Dance Play, 1988 m., by Sovereign Dancer	3	42	4	10	168,431
Vaunted Vamp, 1992 m., by Racing Star	6	78	21	10	419,641
Aces Court, 1981 m., by Know Your Aces	6	75	8	10	112,740
Blue Trumpeter, 1949 h., by Thumbs Up	6	106	15	10	120,912
Distinctive Moon, 1979 m., by Distinctive	3	36	4	10	124,086
Rebridled, 1994 g., by Unbridled	6	60	11	10	424,690
Behind the Scenes, 1984 m., by Hurry Up Blue	4	41	7	10	331,095
Patti L., 1987 m., by Lyphard's Wish (Fr)	5	55	9	10	211,995
Beth Believes, 1986 m., by Believe It	5	44	10	9	357,936
Dianehill (Ire), 1996 m., by Danehill	4	21	4	9	344,393

Naskra Colors, 1992 m., by Star de Naskra	5	28	5	9	411,437
Fappies Cosy Miss, 1988 m., by Fappiano	3	35	4	9	304,885
Aggressively, 1967 h., by Decidedly	5	65	7	9	194,286
Cup o' Shine, 1977 m., by Raise a Cup	4	77	9	9	95,556
Dusty Heather, 1996 m., by M. Double M.	4	42	5	9	464,887
Iron Becky, 1977 m., by Iron Anthony	4	61	6	9	85,781
Runaway Magic, 1997 m., by Runaway Groom	3	18	3	9	131,305
Beaupy, 1962 h., by Beau Gar	5	86	19	9	209,681
Ernani (Ire), 1987 h., by Sadler's Wells	5	32	3	9	289,327
Whiz Along, 1985 h., by Cormorant	6	80	9	9	581,115
She's Content, 1983 m., by Restivo	4	47	9	9	225,501
Shuttered, 1993 m., by Wild Again	4	26	7	9	226,918
River Bank Kid, 1989 m., by Eskimo	5	40	6	9	142,865
Dance Card Filled, 1983 h., by Dance Bid	5	71	10	9	398,706
Dewans Mischief, 1984 m., by Dewan	4	55	18	9	256,399
Capi's First, 1977 m., by Purple Pigeon	3	35	6	9	34,351

Leading Winners of Grade 1 Races in North America
Through 2001

Horse, Sex, YOB	Wins	G1 SWs	SWs	Earnings
John Henry, g, 1975	39	16	30	$6,591,860
Forego, g, 1970	34	14	24	1,938,957
Affirmed, h, 1975	22	14	19	2,393,818
Spectacular Bid, h, 1976	26	13	23	2,781,608
Bayakoa (Arg), m, 1984	18	12	16	2,785,259
Lady's Secret, m, 1982	25	11	22	3,021,325
Cigar, h, 1990	18	11	14	7,599,815
Serena's Song, m, 1992	18	11	17	3,283,388
Skip Away, h, 1993	18	10	16	9,616,360
Paseana (Arg), m, 1987	14	10	14	3,111,292
Susan's Girl, m, 1969	29	9	23	1,251,668
Alysheba, h, 1984	11	9	10	6,679,242
Easy Goer, h, 1986	14	9	12	4,873,770
Flawlessly, m, 1988	16	9	15	2,572,536
Sky Beauty, m, 1990	15	9	13	1,336,000
Seattle Slew, h, 1974	14	8	9	1,208,726
Chief's Crown, h, 1982	12	8	10	2,191,168
Personal Ensign, m, 1984	13	8	10	1,679,880
Heavenly Prize, m, 1991	9	8	8	1,825,940
Foolish Pleasure, h, 1972	16	7	12	1,216,705
Honest Pleasure, h, 1973	12	7	9	839,997
Exceller, h, 1973	8	7	8	1,125,772
Slew o' Gold, h, 1980	12	7	8	3,533,534
Creme Fraiche, h, 1982	17	7	14	4,024,727
Gulch, h, 1984	13	7	11	3,095,521
Goodbye Halo, m, 1985	11	7	10	1,706,702
Open Mind, m, 1986	12	7	11	1,844,372
Go for Wand, m, 1987	10	7	8	1,373,338
Sharp Cat, m, 1994	15	7	14	2,032,575

Leading Winners of Graded Stakes in North America
Through 2001

Horse, Sex, YOB	Wins	Graded SWs	SWs	Earnings
John Henry, g, 1975	39	25	30	$6,591,860
Forego, g, 1970	34	23	24	1,938,957
Spectacular Bid, h, 1976	26	21	23	2,781,608
Affirmed, h, 1975	22	18	19	2,393,818
Ancient Title, h, 1970	24	17	20	1,252,791
Serena's Song, m, 1992	18	17	17	3,283,388
Skip Away, h, 1993	18	16	16	9,616,360
Lady's Secret, m, 1982	25	15	22	3,021,325
Bayakoa (Arg), m, 1984	18	15	16	2,785,259
Paseana (Arg), m, 1987	14	14	14	3,111,292
Precisionist, h, 1981	20	13	17	3,485,398
Flawlessly, m, 1988	16	13	15	2,572,536
Sky Beauty, m, 1990	15	13	13	1,336,000
Silverbulletday, m, 1996	15	13	14	3,093,207
Susan's Girl, m, 1969	29	12	23	1,251,668
Sabin, m, 1980	18	12	14	1,098,341
Safely Kept, m, 1986	24	12	22	2,194,206

Best Pal, g, 1988	18	**12**	17	5,668,245
Sharp Cat, m, 1994	15	**12**	14	2,032,575
Steinlen (GB), h, 1983	16	**12**	14	3,229,752
Foolish Pleasure, h, 1972	16	**11**	12	1,216,705
Creme Fraiche, g, 1982	17	**11**	14	4,024,727
Gulch, h, 1984	13	**11**	11	3,095,521
Housebuster, h, 1987	15	**11**	14	1,229,696
Cigar, h, 1990	18	**11**	14	7,599,815
Black Tie Affair (Ire), h, 1986	18	**11**	13	3,370,694
Optimistic Gal, m, 1973	13	**10**	10	686,861
King's Swan, g, 1980	31	**10**	12	1,924,845
Personal Ensign, m, 1984	13	**10**	10	1,679,880
Alysheba, h, 1984	11	**10**	10	6,679,242
Goodbye Halo, m, 1985	11	**10**	10	1,706,702
Easy Goer, h, 1986	14	**10**	12	4,873,770
Lure, h, 1989	14	**10**	10	2,515,289
Silver Charm, h, 1994	11	**10**	10	4,444,369

Leading Winners of Stakes Races in North America

From 1930 through 2001

Horse, Sex, YOB	Wins	Graded SWs	SWs	Earnings
John Henry, g, 1975	39	25	**30**	$6,591,860
Who Doctor Who, g, 1983	33	1	**26**	813,870
Little Bold John, g, 1982	38	5	**25**	1,956,406
Stymie, h, 1941	35	0	**25**	918,485
Forego, g, 1970	34	23	**24**	1,938,957
Susan's Girl, m, 1969	29	12	**23**	1,251,668
Spectacular Bid, h, 1976	26	21	**23**	2,781,608
Round Table, h, 1954	43	0	**22**	1,749,869
Lady's Secret, m, 1982	25	15	**22**	3,021,325
Safely Kept, m, 1986	24	12	**22**	2,194,206
Citation, h, 1945	32	3	**22**	1,085,760
Swoon's Son, h, 1953	30	0	**21**	970,605
Buckpasser, h, 1963	25	0	**21**	1,462,014
Rosy Way, g, 1989	28	0	**21**	97,389
Ancient Title, g, 1970	24	17	**20**	1,252,791
Amadevil, g, 1974	33	0	**20**	653,534
Chilcoton Blaze, h, 1980	31	0	**20**	490,862
Judy's Red Shoes, m, 1983	25	1	**20**	1,085,668
Fast Gas, h, 1967	29	0	**19**	84,288
Affirmed, h, 1975	22	18	**19**	2,393,818
Rapido Dom, h, 1978	25	0	**19**	466,974
Spirit of Fighter, m, 1983	33	0	**19**	847,454
Delta Colleen, m, 1985	23	0	**19**	810,798
Scott's Scoundrel, h, 1992	22	2	**19**	1,270,052
Armed, g, 1941	41	0	**19**	817,475
Nashua, h, 1952	22	2	**19**	1,288,565
Decathlon, h, 1953	25	0	**18**	269,530
In Rem, g, 1975	21	0	**18**	307,742
Overskate, h, 1975	24	3	**18**	791,634
Energetic King, h, 1979	35	0	**18**	765,776
Orphan Kist, m, 1984	28	0	**18**	631,997
Dixie Poker Ace, g, 1987	27	0	**18**	850,126
Arctic Laur, h, 1988	21	0	**18**	634,809
Timely Ruckus, g, 1993	22	0	**18**	534,731
Say Florida Sandy, h, 1994	28	5	**18**	1,772,544
Fantango Lady, m, 1994	22	0	**18**	279,295

Winningest Horses of All Time

Through 2001

Horse, YOB, sex, sire	Sts	Wins	Earnings
Kingston, 1884, h., by Spendthrift	138	89	$140,195
Bankrupt, 1883, g., by Spendthrift	348	86	41,260
King Crab, 1885, g., by Kingfisher	310	85	55,682
Little Minch, 1880, h., by Glenelg	222	85	58,225
Hiblaze, 1935, h., by Blazes	406	79	32,647
Tippity Witchet, 1915, g., by Broomstick	265	78	88,241
Pan Zareta, 1910, m., by Abe Frank	151	76	39,082
Badge, 1885, h., by *Ill-Used	167	70	73,253
Raceland, 1885, g., by *Billet	130	70	116,391
Welsh Lad, 1934, g., by Prince of Wales	329	67	25,317
Care Free, 1918, g., by Colin	227	67	59,873
Shot One, 1941, g., by Shoeless Joe	360	65	29,982
Worthowning, 1935, g., by Longworth	339	63	41,830
Seth's Hope, 1924, h., by Seth	327	62	74,341
Ed R., 1948, g., by Donnay	248	62	63,552
Vantime, 1939, g., by Playtime	295	62	46,290
Back Bay, 1908, g., by Rubicon	289	62	40,377
Banquet, 1887, g., by *Rayon d'Or	166	62	118,872
Imp, 1894, f, by *Wagner	171	62	70,069
Leochares, 1910, g., by Broomstick	175	62	N/A
Vantryst, 1936, h., by Tryster	334	61	31,971
Mucho Gusto, 1932, h., by Marvin May	217	61	101,880
Shuchor, 1936, g., by Haste	261	61	33,607
Molasses Bill, 1933, g., by Challenger II	262	61	50,699
Brandon Prince, 1929, h., by Axenstein	280	61	47,287
Irene's Bob, 1929, h., by The Turk	237	61	58,010
George de Mar, 1922, h., by Colonel Vennie	333	60	69,091
Indiantown, 1930, h., by Trojan	224	60	55,455
Lewis A. D., 1947, h., by Galway	212	60	65,482
Frank Fogarty, 1918, g., by Wrack	270	60	47,651
Parole, 1873, g., by Leamington	127	59	82,111
Strathmeath, 1888, g., by Strathmore	133	59	114,958
Golden Arrow, 1961, h., by Fort Salonga	176	58	167,264
Charlie Boy, 1955, h., by Graphic	241	58	207,642
Flag Bearer, 1926, h., by Porte Drapeau	222	58	37,683
Top o' the Morning, 1912, c., by Peep o'Day	217	58	48,120
El Puma, 1929, h., by Spanish Prince II	242	57	44,807
End of Street, 1963, h., by Bunty's Flight	202	57	67,686
Columcille, 1948, h., by Alaking	182	57	89,665
Noah's Pride, 1929, g., by Noah	293	56	38,682
Bulwark, 1933, h., by Bull Dog	252	56	65,125
Matchup, 1936, h., by Misstep	229	55	58,528
Tommy Whelan, 1936, g., by Enoch	233	55	33,279
Vote Boy, 1932, g., by Torchilla	304	55	39,240
Argos, 1937, g., by Happy Argo	215	54	37,507
Crying for More, 1965, h., by I'm For More	192	53	183,685
Hamburger Jim, 1928, h., by Whiskaway	212	53	24,383
Bee Golly, 1942, m., by Bee Line	183	53	54,544
Onus, 1933, g., by Jack High	344	53	32,039
Door Prize, 1952, g., by Eight Thirty	131	53	109,920
Post War Style, 1941, m., by Burgoo King	179	53	52,600
Port Conway Lane, 1969, h., by Bold Commander	242	52	431,593
My Blaze, 1930, h., by Big Blaze	338	52	32,707
Alviso, 1932, h., by Hand Grenade	193	52	41,898
Billy Brier, 1953, g., by Bunty Lawless	231	52	83,168
Float Away, 1936, g., by Whiskaway	265	52	61,365
Old Kickapoo, 1924, h., by Runnymede	217	52	35,827
Agrarian-U, 1942, g., by Agrarian	236	52	199,345
Fleet Argo, 1947, g., by Happy Argo	243	52	149,000
Cloudy Weather, 1934, g., by Mud	294	52	53,487

Most Consecutive Victories

Camarero, an unfamiliar name to almost all racing fans, holds the record for the most consecutive victories by a Thoroughbred. His 56 straight wins were not registered in the sport's sometimes murky and poorly documented distant past, however. He raced in the 1950s, going undefeated until his 57th career start. All of his races were in Puerto Rico and were against other Puerto Rican-bred horses. Camarero broke the win mark set by undefeated Kincsem, a Hungarian-bred mare who raced in the late 19th century. Boston made the list

Most Consecutive Victories, continued

of most consecutive wins twice, with 19 wins from 1839-'42 and 17 straight wins from 1836-'38.

Citation and Cigar share the modern record for most consecutive victories, 16, along with Louisiana-bred mare Hallowed Dreams, who won many of her races against overmatched state-breds. Citation and Cigar competed at the highest level of the sport in North America while compiling their win skeins.

Cons. Wins	Horse	Year of Birth	Where Raced
56	Camarero	1951	Puerto Rico
54	Kincsem	1874	Europe, England
39	Galgo Jr.	1928	Puerto Rico
23	Leviathan	1793	United States
22	Miss Petty	1981	Australia
	Pooker T.	1957	Puerto Rico
21	Bond's First Consul	1798	United States
	Lottery	1803	United States
	Meteor	1783	England
	Picnic in the Park	1979	Australia
20	Filch	1773	Ireland
	Fashion	1837	United States
	Kentucky	1861	United States
19	Boston	1833	United States
	Skiff	1821	Scotland
18	Hindoo	1878	United States
	Karayel	1970	Turkey
17	Alice Hawthorn	1838	England
	Beeswing	1835	United States
	Boston	1833	United States
	Careless	1751	England
	Dudley	1914	England
	Gradisco	1957	Venezuela
	Harkaway	1834	Ireland
	Hanover	1884	United States
	Mainbrace	1947	New Zealand
	Sir Ken	1947	England
16	Cigar	1990	United States
	Citation	1945	United States
	Hallowed Dreams	1997	United States
	Luke Blackburn	1877	United States
	Master Bagot	1787	Ireland
	Minimo	1968	Turkey
	Miss Woodford	1880	United States
	Mister Frisky	1987	Puerto Rico, United States
	*Ormonde	1883	England
	Prestige	1903	France
	*Ribot	1952	Europe, England
	The Bard	1883	England
15	Bayardo	1906	England
	*Bernborough	1939	Australia
	Brigadier Gerard	1968	England
	Buckpasser	1963	United States
	Carbine	1885	New Zealand, Australia
	Colin	1905	United States
	Macon	1922	Argentina
	Pretty Polly	1901	England, France
	Rattler	1816	United States
	Squanderer	1973	India
	Thebais	1878	England
	Vander Pool	1928	United States
14	Friponnier	1864	England
	Harry Bassett	1868	United States
	Lucifer	1813	Scotland

	Man o' War	1917	United States
	Nearco	1935	Europe
	*Phar Lap	1926	New Zealand, Australia, Mexico
	*Prince Charlie	1869	England
	Springfield	1873	England
13	Bula	1965	England
	Dungannon	1780	England
	Effie Deans	1815	England
	Grano de Oro	1937	Ireland, Venezuela
	Hippolitus	1767	Ireland
	Kingston	1884	United States
	Limerick	1923	New Zealand, Australia
	Personal Ensign	1984	United States
	Phenomenom	1780	England
	Planet	1855	United States
	Polar Star	1904	England
	Rockingham	1781	England
	Sweet Wall	1925	Ireland
	The Flying Dutchman	1846	England
	Timoleon	1814	United States
	Tremont	1884	United States
	Weimar	1968	Italy

Leading Unbeaten Racehorses

A rare breed, indeed, is the racehorse that completes its career without a defeat on its record. No modern horse can ever expect to equal the record of Kincsem, who went unbeaten in 54 starts over five racing seasons in Hungary. Although her pedigree was largely English, she was bred in Hungary; her name derives from the Magyar "kincs," which mean treasure or jewel. The word itself means "my treasure," and she, indeed, was a jewel.

The most recent jewel to rival Kincsem's luminescence was Ogden Phipps's Personal Ensign, who retired with a perfect record in 13 starts after refusing to be beaten by Winning Colors in the 1988 Breeders' Cup Distaff (G1) at Churchill Downs. The 1988 Kentucky Derby (G1) winner appeared to have the race won at the furlong pole, but Personal Ensign closed relentlessly to gain the victory by a nose.

Following are some of the best-known horses who have retired unbeaten after careers at the top levels of their divisions. Eclipse's record, in particular, is worth noting because 18th-century records are unreliable. He is attributed in various sources with anywhere from ten to 18 victories. In this listing, he is assigned the highest number, and the one fact for certain is that he never was beaten. Similarly, Eclipse's broodmare sire, Regulus, won seven royal plate races at age six, and no other records of his racing career exist.

54 Kincsem, 1874 m., Cambuscan—Waternymph, by Cotswold

18 Eclipse, 1864 h., Marske—Spiletta, by Regulus

16 *Ormonde, 1883 h., Bend Or—Lily Agnes, by Macaroni

    *Ribot, 1952 h., Tenerani—Romanella, by El Greco

15 **Colin,** 1905 h., Commando—*Pastorella, by Springfield
14 **Nearco,** 1935 h., Pharos—Nogara, by Havresac II
13 **Personal Ensign,** 1984 m., Private Account—Grecian Banner, by Hoist the Flag
   Tremont, 1884 h., Virgil—Ann Fief, by Alarm
12 **Asteroid,** 1861 h., Lexington—Nebula, by *Glencoe
   Barcaldine, 1878 h., Solon—Ballyroe, by Belladrum
   Crucifix, 1837 m., *Priam—Octaviana, by Octavian
9 ***Bahram,** 1932 h., Blandford—Friar's Daughter, by Friar Marcus
   St. Simon, 1881 h., Galopin—St. Angela, by King Tom
8 **American Eclipse,** 1814 h., Duroc—Millers Damsel, by *Messenger
   Rare Brick, 1983 h., Rare Performer—Windy Brick, by Mr. Brick
   Sensation, 1877, h., *Leamington—Susan Beane, by Lexington
7 **El Rio Rey,** 1887 h., Norfolk—Marian, by Malcolm
   Regulus, 1739 h., Godolphin Arabian—Grey Robinson, by Bald Galloway
   The Tetrarch, 1911 h., Roi Herode—Vahren, by Bona Vista
5 **Ajax,** 1901 h., Flying Fox—Amie, by Clamart
   Bay Middleton, 1833 h., Sultan—Cobweb, by Phantom
   Landaluce, 1980 f., Seattle Slew—Strip Poker, by Bold Bidder
   Norfolk, 1861 h., Lexington—Novice, by *Glencoe
4 **Golden Fleece,** 1979 h., Nijinsky II—Exotic Treat, by *Vaguely Noble
   Lammtarra, 1992 h., Nijinsky II—Snow Bride, by Blushing Groom (Fr)
   Raise a Native, 1961 h., Native Dancer—Raise You, by Case Ace

Losingest Horses of All Time

Zippy Chippy continued his career of futility into 2002, but he remained short of the modern North American record for losses without a win. Thrust, a chestnut gelding by Bold Salute out of Stitching, by Sting, had very little thrust and lost 105 consecutive races before retiring from the field of battle in 1956.

Thrust finished second five times and was third on seven occasions, with career earnings of $8,180. He was virtually useless as a three-year-old in 1953, posting only one third-place finish and $525 in earnings from 23 starts. He started at least 20 times in each of his three remaining racing seasons.

Zippy Chippy, a foal of 1991, for now is notable only for the length of time he has tried and failed. He began his ninth racing season in 2002, a longer career than any other horse with more than 58 defeats. Following is a list of the sport's leading losers since 1930 through February 2002.

Losses	Horse, YOB	Years Raced	Earnings
105	Thrust, 1950	5	$8,180
93	Zippy Chippy, 1991	9	29,467
92	Star Time, 1943	5	7,215
89	Good Get, 1940	5	2,805
86	Fagrace, 1943	5	6,200
85	Maker of Trouble, 1922	4	565
84	Western Holiday, 1929	5	620
83	City Limit, 1934	5	1,105
82	Master Mark, 1941	6	290
	Giant's Heel, 1943	6	1,560
81	Jibberty Bell, 1955	4	4,802
79	Omashane, 1942	5	1,475
	Arvella, 1957	4	2,531
77	Space, 1942	5	3,070
	Fred Whitham, 1925	7	1,100
76	Sure Its Legal, 1988	5	9,772
	Prima Whisk, 1936	4	670
75	War Bull, 1980	4	10,568
73	Gray Leaves, 1961	4	1,424
	*Cafre II, 1951	7	2,339
	Judgaville, 1981	3	12,965
72	Winnie's Pride, 1988	6	6,790
	Lattanzio, 1991	5	19,163
71	Roman Sandal, 1924	4	990
	Lady Jule, 1925	3	1,095
	Stark Mad, 1946	4	2,950
	Ninon, 1923	3	1,360
70	Red Alley Cat, 1990	6	7,610
69	Tuff Nuggets, 1980	4	8,120
	Buddugie, 1920	4	1,865
68	Lucky Change, 1941	4	3,930
	Buck Flares, 1955	4	6,100
	Right Chief, 1961	4	3,689
67	Bengal Dancer, 1954	4	5,240
	Jimmy What, 1987	6	14,036
	Tchadar, 1924	6	480
66	Rosette, 1926	4	243
	Dominate'em, 1978	4	5,860
	Really Rushing, 1995	5	17,184
	Doug's Dame, 1965	4	3,558
	Filly Gumbo, 1970	3	4,667
	Unclebuck, 1939	7	730
65	Tarbucket, 1932	3	945
	Goodyear, 1927	5	20
	Amarushka, 1981	5	24,336
	Brill Lon, 1956	4	1,420
	Icy Ethel, 1948	5	3,215
	Jacinto's Arky, 1980	4	4,536
	Flashy Lark, 1981	5	14,510
	Petulant, 1928	4	690
	Sam's Tip, 1975	4	14,344
	Alpha's Star, 1990	6	12,530
64	Able Archer, 1957	3	1,847
	Clay K., 1965	6	2,570
	Dawn's Debbie, 1982	3	7,292
	Truckin, 1936	5	865
	Junior T., 1948	4	1,160
	Gosport, 1936	5	465
	Pacific Star, 1946	7	1,000
63	Dusky Boy, 1928	5	1,310
	Castle Rock, 1927	4	625
	Bell's Luck, 1961	4	867
	Ruby's Crystal, 1980	5	5,575
	Sweet Bernice, 1935	8	995
	Mail Plane, 1948	3	1,805

All-Time Leading Horses by Number of Starts
1930-2001

Horse, YOB, Sex, Sire	Years Raced	Starts	Wins	2nds	3rds	Stakes Wins	Earnings
Hiblaze, 1935, h., by Blazes	14	406	79	73	52	0	$32,647
*Galley Sweep, 1933, g., by Aga Khan	14	399	19	34	46	0	$10,677
Shot One, 1941, g., by Shoeless Joe	13	360	65	65	68	0	$29,982
Uno, 1939, m., by Boot to Boot	12	348	35	54	50	0	$100
Onus, 1933, g., by Jack High	15	344	53	58	63	0	$32,039
Worthowning, 1935, g., by *Longworth	14	339	63	62	64	0	$41,830
My Blaze, 1930, h., by Big Blaze	11	338	52	35	51	1	$32,707
Agreed, 1950, g., by Revoked	14	338	39	50	49	0	$68,004
Marabou, 1925, h., by *Hourless	10	337	41	61	44	0	$27,458
Vantryst, 1936, h., by Tryster	13	334	61	78	48	0	$31,971
George de Mar, 1922, h., by *Colonel Vennie	13	333	60	54	64	0	$69,091
Welsh Lad, 1934, g., by Prince of Wales	13	329	67	54	49	0	$25,317
Buffoon, 1937, h., by St. Brideaux	10	329	37	36	45	0	$11,538
Panjab, 1937, g., by *Kiev	11	327	21	32	44	0	$17,929
Seth's Hope, 1924, h., by Seth	11	327	62	51	50	4	$74,341
Copin, 1937, h., by Mate	13	323	42	40	53	0	$27,926
Commission, 1935, h., by Banstar	13	319	41	36	39	0	$25,626
Higher Bracket, 1936, h., by *Rolls Royce	11	318	37	50	51	0	$15,661
Golden Sweep, 1923, h., by Flittergold	10	318	46	47	58	0	$32,285
Bee's Little Man, 1961, h., by *Iceberg II	12	315	42	32	31	0	$108,675
Champ Sorter, 1952, h., by Four Freedoms	12	315	35	43	51	0	$62,747
Appease Not, 1946, g., by King Cole	13	314	42	44	46	0	$122,802
Easiest Way, 1931, g., by *Waygood	11	311	27	38	44	0	$24,375
Mister Snow Man, 1959, g., by *Iceberg II	14	310	43	37	36	0	$104,074
Shannon's Hope, 1956, h., by *Shannon II	12	309	29	36	43	0	$39,848
Port o' Play, 1926, h., by The Porter	9	308	44	47	34	1	$39,234
Behavin Jerry, 1964, h., by Ambehaving	14	307	38	25	48	0	$72,259
Star Soldier, 1934, g., by Son o' Battle	11	305	37	22	50	0	$8,307
It's No Use, 1950, h., by *Basileus II	11	304	25	40	52	0	$68,326
Vote Boy, 1932, g., by Torchilla	11	304	55	37	48	1	$39,240
Dr. Jillson, 1930, h., by *Kiev	12	304	27	42	37	0	$12,522
Chronology, 1935, g., by *Donnacona	13	302	44	41	46	0	$14,632
Mr. Minx, 1952, h., by *Mafosta	12	302	36	48	34	0	$87,072
Bull Market, 1932, g., by Happy Time	14	301	28	49	39	0	$19,275
Call Mac, 1965, g., by Loukenmac	13	301	13	61	58	0	$82,664
Mantados, 1932, h., by Rock Man	14	299	32	47	50	0	$19,840
Nine-O-Two, 1936, g., by Sweep	11	298	48	48	40	0	$13,915
Huppy, 1931, g., by *Donnacona	10	297	12	31	34	0	$7,535
Timon, 1927, g., by *Pandion	10	296	24	32	36	0	$16,393
Ole Sarge, 1956, g., by Carrara Marble	12	296	24	33	33	0	$36,373
Bachelor Boy, 1940, g., by Burgoo King	12	296	33	41	26	0	$52,870
Lorraine S., 1929, m., by Messenger	13	295	39	37	37	0	$23,252
Vantime, 1939, g., by Playtime	13	295	62	65	36	0	$46,290
Easy Knight, 1955, g., by Easy Mon	12	294	22	25	48	0	$48,099
Cloudy Weather, 1934, g., by Mud	14	294	52	55	45	0	$53,487
Noah's Pride, 1929, g., by Noah	11	293	56	46	56	1	$38,682
Jeu de Bar, 1927, h., by Spur	12	293	27	58	46	0	$20,447
Whiskora, 1931, h., by Whiskalong	11	293	29	36	36	0	$11,990
Big Fish, 1931, g., by Old Koenig	13	293	44	37	32	0	$26,330
Aurebon, 1930, g., by Flying Ebony	13	292	43	33	25	0	$20,615
Raffles Problem, 1932, g., by Raffles	14	291	17	35	35	0	$9,420
Maebeau, 1935, h., by Sun Beau	12	291	45	48	44	0	$18,250
Hard Chase, 1932, m., by Purchase	12	291	44	27	26	0	$12,590
Lord Dean, 1929, h., by Chilhowee	11	290	38	42	36	0	$14,150
King Pin, 1927, g., by *Negofol	8	288	36	33	31	0	$27,305
Grand Lady, 1937, m., by Haste	13	287	44	47	54	0	$27,406
Asking, 1952, h., by Pry	12	287	27	31	33	0	$46,442
Royal Doctor, 1961, g., by *Royal Vale	12	286	21	25	34	0	$50,793
Bobs Ace, 1947, g., by War Jeep	10	286	31	29	41	0	$56,957
Eagle Speed, 1946, g., by Sun Again	12	284	40	47	41	0	$66,337
*Instead, 1932, g., by Felstead	12	284	33	52	35	0	$14,954
Bayou Teche, 1961, g., by Bryan G.	12	281	48	35	43	0	$107,577
Black Jet, 1957, h., by Lord Boswell	12	281	21	44	39	0	$51,077
Captain Danger, 1929, g., by Captain Alcock	9	280	28	45	35	0	$17,455
Brandon Prince, 1929, h., by *Axenstein	12	280	61	36	47	0	$47,287
R. Pinchot, 1931, h., by Chatterton	13	280	36	27	43	0	$21,556
Shadow Shot, 1944, h., by Chance Shot	11	279	35	19	40	0	$68,585

*Based on Jockey Club records

All-Time Leading Earners by Deflated Dollars

Comparing horses of different eras is always an entertaining exercise. Was Secretariat a better racehorse than Citation? That question will never be answered definitively because they never met on the track, so comparing horses of one era to another is subjective.

Earnings are one measure of performance, though that yardstick also has its drawbacks because the purses of yesteryear do not compare to the purses of today. There is a way to use earnings as a measure of productivity, however, by deflating the earnings; that is, adjusting earnings to account for the effects of inflation.

In the tables presented on this page and the following two pages, are deflated earnings of the all-time leaders in Thoroughbred racing since 1929. Considered for inclusion on the list is any horse that started at least once in North America. Horses that raced at least once in North America and also raced overseas have all their earnings included, all being converted

to United States dollars and then deflated by racing year.

All-time leading money winner adjusted for inflation is two-time Horse of the Year John Henry, who raced 83 times from 1977 through '84. The durable gelding won the first million-dollar race in the U.S., the 1981 Arlington Million Stakes (G1), and his career ended the year in which the Breeders' Cup was inaugurated. Second on the list is two-time Horse of the Year Cigar, the all-time leading earner in North America in current dollars.

The deflator used to convert all earnings is the Gross Domestic Product implicit price deflator published by the U.S. Bureau of Economic Analysis.

On the first two pages are the all-time leaders by deflated dollars regardless of sex. On the third page is a list of the all-time leading female earners by deflated dollars. Statistics are through December 31, 2001.

All-Time Leading Earners by Deflated Dollars

Horse, sex, year of birth, sire	Yrs raced	Starts	1st	2nd	3rd	Nominal earnings	Deflated earnings
John Henry, g, 1975, by Ole Bob Bowers	8	83	39	15	9	$6,591,860	$11,160,283
Cigar, h, 1990, by Palace Music	4	33	19	4	5	9,999,815	11,051,263
Skip Away, h, 1993, by Skip Trial	4	38	18	10	6	9,616,360	10,338,928
Kelso, g, 1957, by Your Host	8	63	39	12	2	1,977,896	9,486,738
Alysheba, h, 1984, by Alydar	3	26	11	8	2	6,679,242	9,253,731
Round Table, h, 1954, by *Princequillo	4	66	43	8	5	1,749,869	8,914,211
Fantastic Light, h, 1996, by Rahy	4	25	12	5	3	8,486,957	8,599,531
Silver Charm, h, 1994, by Silver Buck	4	24	12	7	2	6,944,369	7,379,190
Nashua, h, 1952, by *Nasrullah	3	30	22	4	1	1,288,565	7,080,085
Captain Steve, h, 1997, by Fly So Free	3	25	9	3	7	6,828,356	6,902,431
Citation, h, 1945, by Bull Lea	4	45	32	10	2	1,085,760	6,851,172
Best Pal, g, 1988, by Habitony	7	47	18	11	4	5,668,245	6,768,344
Stymie, h, 1941, by Equestrian	7	131	35	33	28	918,485	6,740,405
Buckpasser, h, 1963, by Tom Fool	3	31	25	4	1	1,462,014	6,578,748
Sunday Silence, h, 1986, by Halo	3	14	9	5	0	4,968,554	6,507,664
Tiznow, h, 1997, by Cee's Tizzy	2	15	8	4	2	6,427,830	6,502,196
Easy Goer, h, 1986, by Alydar	3	20	14	5	1	4,873,770	6,418,490
Spend a Buck, h, 1982, by Buckaroo	2	15	10	3	2	4,220,689	6,294,380
Taiki Blizzard, h, 1991, by Seattle Slew	4	23	6	8	2	5,523,549	6,081,796
Carry Back, h, 1958, by Saggy	4	62	21	11	11	1,241,165	6,035,044
Armed, g, 1941, by Bull Lea	7	81	41	20	10	817,475	5,810,440
Creme Fraiche, g, 1982, by Rich Cream	6	64	17	12	13	4,024,727	5,794,521
Spectacular Bid, h, 1976, by Bold Bidder	3	30	26	2	1	2,781,608	5,692,034
Unbridled, h, 1987, by Fappiano	3	24	8	6	6	4,489,475	5,656,849
Whirlaway, h, 1938, by *Blenheim II	4	60	32	15	9	561,161	5,463,415
Slew o' Gold, h, 1980, by Seattle Slew	3	21	12	5	1	3,533,534	5,461,539
Forego, g, 1970, by *Forli	6	57	34	9	7	1,938,957	5,373,644
Ferdinand, h, 1983, by Nijinsky II	4	29	8	9	6	3,777,978	5,360,120
Affirmed, h, 1975, by Exclusive Native	3	29	22	5	1	2,393,818	5,282,542
Swoon's Son, h, 1953, by The Doge	4	51	30	10	3	970,605	5,136,548
Precisionist, h, 1981, by Crozier	5	46	20	10	4	3,485,398	5,119,252
Jim and Tonic (Fr), g, 1994, by Double Bed (Fr)	6	36	13	12	4	4,959,719	5,090,429
Damascus, h, 1964, by Sword Dancer	3	32	21	7	3	1,176,781	5,047,945
Snow Chief, h, 1983, by Reflected Glory	3	24	13	3	5	3,383,210	4,917,972
Daylami (Ire), h, 1994, by Doyoun	4	21	11	3	4	4,614,762	4,845,457
Assault, h, 1943, by Bold Venture	6	42	18	6	7	675,470	4,830,340

Horse, sex, year of birth, sire	Yrs raced	Starts	1st	2nd	3rd	Nominal earnings	Deflated earnings
Behrens, h, 1994, by Pleasant Colony	4	27	9	8	3	4,563,500	4,754,523
Native Diver, h, 1959, by Imbros	7	81	37	7	12	1,026,500	4,673,654
Bet Twice, h, 1984, by Sportin' Life	3	26	10	6	4	3,308,599	4,660,713
Awesome Again, h, 1994, by Deputy Minister	2	12	9	0	4	4,374,590	4,642,153
Swaps, h, 1952, by *Khaled	3	25	19	2	2	848,900	4,620,858
Cryptoclearance, h, 1984, by Fappiano	4	44	12	10	7	3,376,327	4,615,939
Seabiscuit, h, 1933, by Hard Tack	6	89	33	15	13	437,730	4,598,592
Devil His Due, h, 1989, by Devil's Bag	4	41	11	12	3	3,920,405	4,543,083
Dahlia, m, 1970, by *Vaguely Noble	5	48	15	3	7	1,489,105	4,487,514
Native Dancer, h, 1950, by Polynesian	3	22	21	1	0	785,240	4,475,505
T. V. Lark, h, 1957, by *Indian Hemp	4	72	19	13	6	902,194	4,436,076
Lady's Secret, m, 1982, by Secretariat	4	45	25	9	3	3,021,325	4,423,319
Fort Marcy, g, 1964, by *Amerigo	6	75	21	18	14	1,109,791	4,422,713
Roman Brother, g, 1961, by Third Brother	4	42	16	10	5	943,473	4,411,973
Secretariat, h, 1970, by Bold Ruler	2	21	16	3	1	1,316,808	4,368,595
Steinlen (GB), h, 1983, by Habitat	5	45	20	10	7	3,297,169	4,332,814
Trinycarol (Ven), m, 1979, by Velvet Cap	4	29	18	3	1	2,644,392	4,322,036
Gulch, h, 1984, by Mr. Prospector	3	32	13	8	4	3,095,521	4,318,871
Seeking the Pearl, m, 1994, by Seeking the Gold	4	21	8	2	3	4,021,716	4,298,877
Dr. Fager, h, 1964, by Rough'n Tumble	3	22	18	2	1	1,002,642	4,290,959
Find, g, 1950, by Discovery	8	110	22	27	27	803,615	4,271,444
Sandpit (Brz), h, 1989, by Baynoun (Ire)	7	40	14	11	6	3,812,597	4,199,396
Symboli Rudolf (Jpn), h, 1981, by Partholon	4	16	13	1	1	2,764,980	4,179,928
Theatrical (Ire), h, 1982, by Nureyev	4	22	10	4	2	2,940,036	4,176,513
Black Tie Affair (Ire), h, 1986, by Miswaki	4	45	18	9	6	3,370,694	4,163,153
Strike the Gold, h, 1988, by Alydar	4	31	6	8	5	3,457,026	4,157,096
Sword Dancer, h, 1956, by Sunglow	3	39	15	7	4	829,610	4,133,306
Cat Thief, h, 1996, by Storm Cat	3	30	4	9	8	3,951,012	4,123,231
Swain (Ire), h, 1992, by Nashwan	4	22	10	4	6	3,797,566	4,073,098
*Cougar II, h, 1966, by Tale of Two Cities	6	50	20	7	17	1,172,625	4,056,053
Sky Classic, h, 1987, by Nijinsky II	4	29	15	6	1	3,320,398	4,041,497
Susan's Girl, m, 1969, by Quadrangle	5	63	29	14	11	1,251,668	3,985,563
Dance Smartly, m, 1988, by Danzig	3	17	12	2	3	3,263,835	3,984,552
Point Given, c, 1998, by Thunder Gulch	2	13	9	3	0	3,968,500	3,981,848
Great Communicator, g, 1983, by Key to the Kingdom	6	56	14	10	7	2,922,615	3,975,558
Bold Ruler, h, 1954, by *Nasrullah	3	33	23	4	2	764,204	3,953,154
Exceller, h, 1973, by *Vaguely Noble	5	33	15	5	6	1,674,587	3,950,911
Candy Spots, h, 1960, by *Nigromante	3	22	12	5	1	824,718	3,919,945
Paradise Creek, h, 1989, by Irish River (Fr)	4	25	14	7	1	3,401,416	3,910,625
Paseana (Arg), m, 1987, by Ahmad	6	36	19	10	2	3,317,427	3,905,404
First Landing, h, 1956, by *Turn-to	3	37	19	9	2	779,577	3,898,190
Mongo, h, 1959, by *Royal Charger	4	46	22	10	4	820,766	3,893,014
Lando (Ger), h, 1990, by Acatenango	4	24	10	3	1	3,438,727	3,888,384
Gentlemen (Arg), h, 1992, by Robin des Bois	5	24	13	4	2	3,608,558	3,877,567
Manila, h, 1983, by Lyphard	3	18	12	5	0	2,692,799	3,873,372
Allez France, m, 1970, by *Sea-Bird	4	21	13	3	1	1,262,801	3,870,264
Riva Ridge, h, 1969, by First Landing	3	30	17	3	1	1,111,497	3,854,642
Crimson Satan, h, 1959, by Spy Song	4	58	18	9	9	796,077	3,825,349
Broad Brush, h, 1983, by Ack Ack	3	27	14	5	5	2,656,793	3,807,830
Almutawakel (GB), h, 1995, by Machiavellian	4	19	4	4	1	3,643,021	3,805,148
Cicada, m, 1959, by Bryan G.	4	42	23	8	6	783,674	3,787,684
Gate Dancer, h, 1981, by Sovereign Dancer	4	28	7	8	7	2,501,705	3,765,553
Bally Ache, h, 1957, by *Ballydam	2	31	16	9	4	758,522	3,759,106
Forty Niner, h, 1985, by Mr. Prospector	2	19	11	5	0	2,726,000	3,745,689
Bertrando, h, 1989, by Skywalker	5	24	9	6	2	3,185,610	3,739,113
Gun Bow, h, 1960, by Gun Shot	3	42	17	8	4	798,722	3,729,573
Social Outcast, g, 1950, by Shut Out	5	58	18	9	6	668,300	3,713,623
With Approval, h, 1986, by Caro (Ire)	3	23	13	5	1	2,863,540	3,711,439
Bayakoa (Arg), m, 1984, by Consultant's Bid	6	39	21	9	0	2,861,701	3,702,417
Victory Gallop, h, 1995, by Cryptoclearance	3	17	9	5	1	3,505,895	3,695,901
Serena's Song, m, 1992, by Rahy	3	38	18	11	3	3,283,388	3,649,826
Awad, h, 1990, by Caveat	7	70	14	10	11	3,270,131	3,641,488
Chief Bearhart, h, 1993, by Chief's Crown	4	26	12	5	3	3,381,557	3,624,851
Hansel, h, 1988, by Woodman	2	14	7	2	3	2,936,586	3,597,953
On Trust, h, 1944, by *Alibhai	7	88	23	19	13	554,145	3,597,828
A.P. Indy, h, 1989, by Seattle Slew	2	11	8	0	1	2,979,815	3,558,282

Female All-Time Earners by Deflated Dollars

Horse, sex, year of birth, sire	Yrs raced	Starts	1st	2nd	3rd	Nominal earnings	Deflated earnings
Dahlia, m, 1970, by *Vaguely Noble	5	48	15	3	7	$1,489,105	$4,487,514
Lady's Secret, m, 1982, by Secretariat	4	45	25	9	3	3,021,325	4,423,319
Trinycarol (Ven), m, 1979, by Velvet Cap	4	29	18	3	1	2,644,392	4,322,036
Seeking the Pearl, m, 1994, by Seeking the Gold	4	21	8	2	3	4,021,716	4,298,877
Susan's Girl, m, 1969, by Quadrangle	5	63	29	14	11	1,251,668	3,985,563
Dance Smartly, m, 1988, by Danzig	3	17	12	2	3	3,263,835	3,984,552
Paseana (Arg), m, 1987, by Ahmad	6	36	19	10	2	3,317,427	3,905,404
Allez France, m, 1970, by *Sea-Bird	4	21	13	3	1	1,262,801	3,870,264
Cicada, m, 1959, by Bryan G.	4	42	23	8	6	783,674	3,787,684
Bayakoa (Arg), m, 1984, by Consultant's Bid	6	39	21	9	0	2,861,701	3,702,417
Serena's Song, m, 1992, by Rahy	3	38	18	11	3	3,283,388	3,649,826
Shuvee, m, 1966, by Nashua	4	44	16	10	6	890,445	3,466,144
Life's Magic, m, 1981, by Cox's Ridge	3	32	8	11	6	2,255,218	3,443,079
All Along (Fr), m, 1979, by Targowice	4	21	9	4	2	2,125,809	3,363,600
Triptych, m, 1982, by Riverman	5	41	14	5	11	2,318,946	3,298,311
Silverbulletday, m, 1996, by Silver Deputy	3	23	15	3	1	3,093,207	3,242,151
Straight Deal, m, 1962, by Hail to Reason	6	99	21	21	9	733,020	3,231,013
Gallorette, m, 1942, by *Challenger II	5	72	21	20	13	445,535	3,226,838
Escena, m, 1993, by Strawberry Road (Aus)	4	29	11	9	3	2,962,639	3,163,024
Let's Elope (NZ), m, 1987, by Nassipour	5	26	11	0	5	2,528,902	3,073,877
Flawlessly, m, 1988, by Affirmed	5	28	16	4	3	2,572,536	3,047,092
Spain, m, 1997, by Thunder Gulch	3	28	7	8	5	2,971,040	3,020,668
Bewitch, m, 1945, by Bull Lea	5	55	20	10	11	462,605	2,967,546
Banshee Breeze, m, 1995, by Unbridled	3	18	10	5	2	2,784,798	2,930,804
Miesque, m, 1984, by Nureyev	3	16	12	3	1	2,070,163	2,889,205
Top Flight, m, 1929, by *Dis Donc	2	16	12	0	0	275,900	2,848,523
Estrapade, m, 1980, by *Vaguely Noble	4	30	12	5	5	1,937,142	2,847,467
Tosmah, m, 1961, by Tim Tam	4	39	23	6	2	612,588	2,842,343
Beautiful Pleasure, m, 1995, by Maudlin	5	25	10	5	2	2,734,078	2,840,840
Safely Kept, m, 1986, by Horatius	4	31	24	2	3	2,194,206	2,796,828
Busher, m, 1942, by War Admiral	3	21	15	3	1	334,035	2,787,550
Honeymoon, m, 1943, by *Beau Pere	6	78	20	14	9	387,760	2,739,614
Old Hat, m, 1959, by Boston Doge	6	80	35	18	9	556,401	2,583,977
Affectionately, m, 1960, by Swaps	4	52	28	8	6	546,659	2,573,947
Open Mind, m, 1986, by Deputy Minister	3	19	12	2	2	1,844,372	2,458,300
Heritage of Gold, m, 1995, by Gold Legend	4	28	16	2	4	2,381,762	2,453,371
Next Move, m, 1947, by Bull Lea	4	46	17	11	3	398,550	2,431,505
Sickle's Image, m, 1948, by Sickletoy	5	73	27	13	16	413,275	2,396,779
Gamely, m, 1964, by Bold Ruler	3	41	16	9	6	574,961	2,377,770
Bed o' Roses, m, 1947, by Rosemont	4	46	18	8	6	383,925	2,358,327
Politely, m, 1963, by *Amerigo	4	49	21	9	5	552,972	2,350,288
Goodbye Halo, m, 1985, by Halo	3	24	11	5	4	1,706,702	2,322,339
Personal Ensign, m, 1984, by Private Account	3	13	13	0	0	1,679,880	2,319,649
Perfect Sting, m, 1996, by Red Ransom	4	21	14	3	0	2,202,042	2,264,878
Very Subtle, m, 1984, by Hoist the Silver	4	29	12	6	4	1,608,360	2,260,913
Family Style, m, 1983, by State Dinner	3	35	10	8	7	1,537,118	2,243,447
Convenience, m, 1968, by Fleet Nasrullah	4	35	15	9	4	648,933	2,190,871
Sharp Cat, m, 1994, by Storm Cat	3	22	15	3	0	2,032,575	2,182,696
Odalea (Arg), m, 1986, by Pepenador	5	21	8	7	2	1,674,812	2,178,661
Gallant Bloom, m, 1966, by *Gallant Man	3	22	16	1	1	535,739	2,151,523
Numbered Account, m, 1969, by Buckpasser	3	22	14	3	2	607,048	2,147,023
Miss Alleged, m, 1987, by Alleged	3	15	5	4	3	1,757,342	2,145,111
Hatoof, m, 1989, by Irish River (Fr)	4	21	9	4	1	1,841,070	2,141,932
Trillion, m, 1974, by Hail to Reason	3	32	9	14	3	957,413	2,132,453
The Very One, m, 1975, by One for All	5	71	22	12	9	1,104,623	2,122,110
Pebbles (GB), m, 1981, by Sharpen Up (GB)	3	15	8	4	0	1,419,632	2,120,660
Outstandingly, m, 1982, by Exclusive Native	4	28	10	4	3	1,412,206	2,120,052
Princess Rooney, m, 1980, by Verbatim	3	21	17	2	1	1,343,339	2,098,086
Royal Native, m, 1956, by *Royal Charger	4	49	18	13	3	422,769	2,091,742
User Friendly (GB), m, 1989, by Slip Anchor	3	16	8	1	2	1,764,938	2,090,198
Jewel Princess, m, 1992, by Key to the Mint	4	29	13	4	7	1,904,060	2,077,562
Winning Colors, m, 1985, by Caro (Ire)	3	19	8	3	1	1,526,837	2,075,584
Heavenly Prize, m, 1991, by Seeking the Gold	4	18	9	6	3	1,825,940	2,063,170
Sangue (Ire), m, 1978, by Lyphard	3	30	13	6	3	1,272,086	2,058,451

Performance Rates for 2001

Performance Rates are an objective measurement of racetrack performance developed by Jockey Club Information Systems. Performance Rates were originally developed by the Jockey Club and first published in *The Thoroughbred Record* in the 1960s. Performance Rates assign a rate to horses based on beaten lengths—who beat whom and by how much—with some adjustments made to standardize beaten distances to account for horses that are not pressed or are eased in large fields. Races in which individual horses did not finish are not counted for those horses.

Time is not a factor in Performance Rates, which are based on every start by every horse in North America in 2001. Performance Rates are expressed in lengths around a theoretical mean of zero. The average performance of the best horses in a given year are generally about 30 lengths better than an average performance of the average horse.

Because of the premium that Performance Rates give to large winning margins, Kentucky Derby (G1) victor Monarchos was the leading three-year-old male of 2001, albeit modestly ahead of Point Given, the year's three-year-old male champion.

At Gulfstream Park, Monarchos opened his three-year-old campaign with a six-length win in a maiden special weight race and a 4¾-length score in an allowance race. He then won the Florida Derby (G1) by 4½ lengths before running second in the Wood Memorial Stakes (G2) prior to his 4¾-length victory in the Kentucky Derby.

Monarchos finished sixth in the Preakness Stakes (G1) and third in the Belmont Stakes (G1), both won by Point Given. Point Given, 5½-length winner of the Santa Anita Derby (G1), won the Belmont by 12¼ lengths.

To be included in Performance Rates, a horse must have made a minimum of three starts in North America in 2001. No winner of a 2001 Breeders' Cup race led a division, and only one Eclipse Award finalist topped a category. That distinction went to You, who won the Frizette Stakes (G1) for two-year-old fillies by 6¼ lengths but was fourth in the Breeders' Cup Juvenile Fillies (G1) as the 0.95-to-1 favorite.

Following are the 100 leading Performance Rates runners by category in 2001.

Two-Year-Old Males

Rank	Horse	Starts	Rating
1.	Harlan's Holiday	6	26.27
2.	Siphonic	4	26.24
3.	Saarland	5	23.89
4.	Cashel Castle	3	23.54
5.	Request for Parole	7	23.34
6.	Officer	8	23.09
7.	Repent	5	22.89
8.	Came Home	4	22.67
9.	Booklet	5	22.20
10.	Squire Boone	4	22.19
11.	El Malicia	3	21.83
12.	Crimson Hero	3	21.70
13.	Pure Precision	4	21.31
14.	Heavyweight Champ	6	21.17
15.	Nokoma	3	21.13
16.	Sky Terrace	3	21.07
17.	French Assault	8	20.97
18.	Dubai Squire	5	20.89
19.	Equality	3	20.82
20.	Fonz's	4	20.41
21.	Cool Cash	3	20.18
22.	Expect	3	20.11
23.	Publication	4	20.05
24.	Mucho Rapido	3	20.00
25.	Twin Talk	3	19.90
26.	Hail to Bag	6	19.89
27.	Yoga	5	19.84
28.	War Native	4	19.83
29.	Unbridled Trick	3	19.67
30.	Kamsack	3	19.63
31.	Honor in War	3	19.60
32.	Man of Destiny	3	19.60
33.	Just Le Facts	4	19.60
34.	Metatron	5	19.45
35.	Labamta Babe	5	19.41
36.	Coach Knight	4	19.39
37.	Easyfromthegitgo	5	19.30
38.	Invent	6	19.26
39.	Jump Start	5	19.23
40.	Truman's Raider	5	19.16
41.	Wadsworth	3	19.10
42.	Play Around	3	19.09
43.	Listen Here	4	19.05
44.	Holy Run	3	18.85
45.	Showmeitall	6	18.80
46.	Halo's Tiger	4	18.79
47.	Monthir	5	18.76
48.	Charioteer	3	18.67
49.	Silent Fred	4	18.66
50.	Sip'n	4	18.64
51.	Requesto	3	18.36
52.	Pass Rush	4	18.22
53.	This Chris	3	18.16
54.	No Trouble	6	18.13
55.	Janadel (Ire)	4	18.09
56.	Governor Hickel	5	18.04
57.	Shining Career	3	18.02
58.	Rare Friends	5	17.98
59.	Boston Common	6	17.88
60.	Nuclear Assembly	6	17.88
61.	Sunray Spirit	5	17.77
62.	Magic Weisner	4	17.72
63.	Ride the Tiger	7	17.68
64.	Premeditation	6	17.68
65.	Tricky Storm	4	17.57
66.	Walk in the Snow	8	17.57
67.	Iron Deputy	3	17.47
68.	Maybry's Boy	6	17.45
69.	Flight	4	17.39
70.	Volley Ball	4	17.28
71.	War General	5	17.22
72.	Thunder Days	6	17.06
73.	War Emblem	3	16.99
74.	Aisle	3	16.97
75.	Police Alert	3	16.95
76.	Handsome Hunk	6	16.93
77.	Dell Place	3	16.92
78.	Cojet	6	16.84
79.	Tinker	3	16.84
80.	Neal's Rodeo	3	16.79
81.	Robe	3	16.78
82.	April's Lucky Boy	4	16.72
83.	Stroud	3	16.70
84.	Royal Moro	3	16.64
85.	U S S Tinosa	7	16.62
86.	Mountain Forum	8	16.62
87.	Truth Matters	6	16.60
88.	Ibn Al Haitham (GB)	5	16.60
89.	Private Emblem	4	16.56
90.	Outstander	6	16.52
91.	Roman Dancer	5	16.49
92.	White Ibis	6	16.44
93.	Buster's Daydream	6	16.33
94.	Flo's Bo	5	16.33
95.	Harmony Hall	6	16.32
96.	Star Smasher	8	16.28
97.	Juggernaut	7	16.27
98.	Shaws Creek	4	16.17
99.	Rylstone	5	16.16
100.	Bay Monster	6	16.14

Two-Year-Old Females

Rank	Horse	Starts	Rating
1.	You	6	27.21
2.	Cashier's Dream	6	26.66
3.	Belterra	3	26.51
4.	Pharmstar	3	24.82
5.	Bella Bellucci	3	24.82
6.	Never Out	3	24.75
7.	Shesastonecoldfox	4	24.05
8.	Imperial Gesture	4	23.91
9.	Habibti	4	23.85
10.	Proxy Statement	3	23.33
11.	Tempera	5	23.13
12.	Don't Ruffle Me	4	22.42
13.	Stormy Frolic	7	22.36
14.	Take Charge Lady	5	22.30
15.	Lake Lady	3	22.27

Rank	Horse	Starts	Rating
16.	Forest Heiress	5	22.26
17.	Ayanna	5	21.99
18.	Sweep Princess	3	21.68
19.	The World Owes Me	3	21.67
20.	Blissful Kiss	5	21.58
21.	Tempo West	5	21.27
22.	Vicki Vallencourt	5	21.25
23.	Cunning Play	5	21.16
24.	Bold World	4	20.53
25.	Saintly Action	5	20.32
26.	Smok'n Frolic	9	20.19
27.	A New Twist	3	20.09
28.	My Antonia	3	19.92
29.	Lotta Rhythm	5	19.91
30.	Strong Credentials	3	19.84
31.	Gilded Wings	3	19.73
32.	Ginger Gold	4	19.71
33.	Joanies Bella	9	19.58
34.	Touch Love	3	19.56
35.	French Satin	4	19.46
36.	C J's Star	5	19.43
37.	Dancing Dreams	6	19.31
38.	Night Breeze	3	19.28
39.	Ms Brookski	5	19.00
40.	Hi Tech Honeycomb	5	18.92
41.	Queen of the Isle	5	18.89
42.	Proper Gamble	3	18.64
43.	Riskaverse	6	18.49
44.	Lots of Talent	4	18.46
45.	Tali'sluckybusride	3	18.24
46.	Water Rights	4	18.22
47.	Lakeside Cup	8	18.14
48.	Ponche de Leona	6	18.08
49.	Lights On	3	18.05
50.	Swing Again	4	17.97
51.	Tejano Honey	4	17.96
52.	Spiked Punch	5	17.89
53.	Crypto's Twinjet	6	17.85
54.	Rizzamatic	4	17.79
55.	Speed to Burn	4	17.75
56.	Ghost Queen	8	17.69
57.	Runaway Ab	3	17.60
58.	Wopping	8	17.51
59.	Afnan	4	17.50
60.	Bedanken	3	17.47
61.	Mulrainy	5	17.45
62.	Exotic Wager	3	17.34
63.	Flick	4	17.32
64.	Charmed Gift	4	17.25
65.	Princess Dixie	6	17.20
66.	Taylor's Queen	5	17.16
67.	Rich Assertion	3	17.05
68.	Abundantly Blessed	4	17.00
69.	Smoke Chaser	5	16.95
70.	Atsa Pretty Muffin	6	16.86
71.	Lujien Lujien	4	16.75
72.	Haunted Lass	4	16.74
73.	Vesta	5	16.72
74.	Besige	3	16.71
75.	Wild Kandace	4	16.67
76.	Miss Indiana	5	16.65
77.	Rich Musique	3	16.64
78.	Who Loves Aleyna	4	16.54
79.	Miss Ritz	8	16.51
80.	Smoke Buster	3	16.50
81.	Summer Mis	4	16.41
82.	Dazzling Crypto	4	16.36
83.	Orphan Lover	6	16.36
84.	Redoubled Miss	6	16.32
85.	Treasure Coast Gem	6	16.31
86.	Radcliffe Yard	8	16.30
87.	Alina Alina	4	16.28
88.	Swinging Gate	7	16.28
89.	Purple Princess	6	16.24
90.	Iffy	6	16.21
91.	August Storm	4	16.18
92.	Emeraldforajudge	9	16.17
93.	Born to Dance	8	16.15
94.	Salem Willow	4	16.13
95.	Buck for Par	7	16.12
96.	She's Vested	3	16.08
97.	Quick Fuse	9	16.07
98.	Every Cloud	3	16.06
99.	Delicatessa	3	16.03
100.	Al Max Diner	6	15.90

Three-Year-Old Males

Rank	Horse	Starts	Rating
1.	Monarchos	7	31.75
2.	Point Given	7	31.25
3.	E Dubai	5	30.58
4.	Invisible Ink	6	28.01
5.	Congaree	7	27.84
6.	Thunder Blitz	8	26.21
7.	Distilled	5	25.55
8.	Macho Uno	4	24.21
9.	Dollar Bill	7	23.86
10.	Touch Tone	3	23.86
11.	Burning Roma	9	23.56
12.	Outofthebox	10	23.20
13.	Bonnie Scot	5	23.08
14.	Marciano	8	23.08
15.	Richly Blended	6	22.91
16.	A P Valentine	9	22.76
17.	D'wildcat	3	22.11
18.	Squirtle Squirt	6	21.95
19.	Put It Back	5	21.54
20.	Volponi	10	21.38
21.	Pure Prize	7	21.17
22.	Learned	3	21.13
23.	Fifty Stars	5	21.12
24.	Rock Slide	10	20.96
25.	Voodoo	5	20.95
26.	Bay Eagle	9	20.90
27.	Free of Love	11	20.86
28.	Aloha Bold	4	20.82
29.	This Fleet Is Due	7	20.78
30.	Hero's Tribute	8	20.72
31.	Express Tour	4	20.72
32.	Navesink	7	20.71
33.	The Deputy Is Home	4	20.46
34.	Percy Hope	7	20.39
35.	Bowman's Band	4	20.39
36.	Strut the Stage	5	20.32
37.	Yonaguska	7	20.31
38.	Griffinite	6	20.27
39.	Joyful Tune	6	20.27
40.	Thesis	4	20.21
41.	Songandaprayer	6	20.10
42.	Windsor Castle	3	20.02
43.	Giant Gentleman	6	19.98
44.	Baptize	7	19.98
45.	X Country	13	19.91
46.	It's So Simple	7	19.70
47.	Wild Years	4	19.70
48.	Saratoga Games	10	19.66
49.	Strike It Smart	5	19.63
50.	Talk Is Money	5	19.59
51.	Tannersmyman	3	19.59
52.	Dream Run	10	19.55
53.	Millennium Wind	5	19.53
54.	Equinox	11	19.50
55.	Western Pride	12	19.50
56.	City Zip	12	19.44
57.	Sharp Performance	6	19.43
58.	Win City	9	19.43
59.	Date More Minors	4	19.42
60.	High Commissioner	5	19.33
61.	Drewman	6	19.30
62.	Woodmoon	7	19.27
63.	Early Flyer	7	19.19
64.	Catamaran	3	19.19
65.	Fancy As	9	19.07
66.	L'Homme	4	19.07
67.	Sam Lord's Castle	6	19.01
68.	Off Campus	3	18.98
69.	Cielo City	4	18.90
70.	Wedlock	7	18.89
71.	Arctic Boy	8	18.86
72.	Balto Star	11	18.75
73.	Polar Ray	8	18.74
74.	Dynamix	3	18.73
75.	Dynameaux	6	18.62
76.	Quadrophonic Sound	11	18.59
77.	Bonus Pack	5	18.58
78.	Package Store	8	18.56
79.	Paynes Bay	8	18.51
80.	Potaro (Ire)	4	18.51
81.	Jamaican Rum	9	18.48
82.	Startac	8	18.35
83.	San Pedro	9	18.30
84.	I'm Free	9	18.29
85.	I Love Silver	11	18.29
86.	Strategic Partner	11	18.28
87.	Buckets	5	18.21
88.	Buckle Down Ben	10	18.12
89.	Trion Georgia	8	18.03
90.	Wrangler	7	18.00
91.	Mr. John	4	17.98
92.	Illusioned	8	17.97
93.	Meetyouathebrig	5	17.96
94.	Act of War	4	17.93
95.	Halo's Stride	6	17.92
96.	Son of Rocket	7	17.86
97.	Discreet Hero	11	17.84
98.	Tex's Trick	4	17.81
99.	Sligo Bay (Ire)	6	17.80
100.	Evening Attire	5	17.78

Three-Year-Old Females

Rank	Horse	Starts	Rating
1.	Victory Ride	4	33.94
2.	Exogenous	7	28.95
3.	Golden Ballet	5	28.66
4.	Fleet Renee	6	28.51
5.	Unbridled Elaine	8	27.33
6.	Flute	7	26.19
7.	Summer Colony	8	25.22
8.	Indy Glory	6	24.90
9.	Mystic Lady	11	24.87
10.	Two Item Limit	9	24.50
11.	Forest Secrets	8	24.39
12.	Mila	4	23.97
13.	Mandy's Gold	4	23.96
14.	Xtra Heat	13	23.86
15.	Astrid	6	23.27
16.	Strike It Up	8	23.12
17.	Real Cozzy	9	23.03
18.	Treasureinmyhand	3	22.94
19.	Caressing	8	22.67
20.	Dancethruthedawn	6	22.63
21.	Starrer	8	22.43
22.	Nasty Storm	8	22.40
23.	Love At Noon	5	22.34
24.	Descapate	4	22.29
25.	Collect Call	8	22.29
26.	Affluent	10	21.73
27.	Tweedside	8	21.55
28.	Hit Gold	4	21.47
29.	Unrestrained	11	21.44
30.	Transcendental	9	21.38
31.	Celtic Melody	4	20.92
32.	Above Perfection	5	20.77
33.	Raging Fever	3	20.71
34.	Gold Mover	10	20.69
35.	Sweet Nanette	4	20.68
36.	Quick Tip	12	20.56
37.	Lady Andromeda	3	20.46

No.	Horse	Starts	Rating
38.	Sunshine in Paris	4	20.40
39.	Snow Dance	8	20.23
40.	Quick Blue	8	20.20
41.	Emery Board	9	20.04
42.	Lakenheath	7	19.94
43.	Golden Apples (Ire)	4	19.84
44.	Zonk	8	19.78
45.	Latour	10	19.76
46.	Steiners Baby Girl	7	19.66
47.	Voodoo Dancer	7	19.56
48.	Shiny Band	12	19.45
49.	Tap Dance	9	19.44
50.	Spanish Glitter	15	19.25
51.	Sweetest Thing	8	19.17
52.	Lil Punkindo	4	19.01
53.	Bold Answer	6	18.98
54.	Valley Affair	6	18.87
55.	It All Adds Up	7	18.86
56.	Major Wager	4	18.74
57.	Sheriffs Lap	5	18.64
58.	Golly Greeley	8	18.62
59.	Too Scarlet	7	18.51
60.	Bold Diva	7	18.49
61.	La Recherche	12	18.46
62.	Salty Farma	3	18.44
63.	Ten Flags	8	18.40
64.	Chesapeake Charm	5	18.38
65.	Cat Chat	3	18.34
66.	Indy Pick	4	18.31
67.	Penny Perfect	5	18.28
68.	Owsley	10	18.28
69.	Heathers Promise	5	18.25
70.	Stop for Schnapps	10	18.15
71.	Our Majestic Cat	4	17.94
72.	Emily Ring	10	17.89
73.	Kimbralata	12	17.87
74.	Darling Deputy	5	17.86
75.	Freefourracing	3	17.84
76.	Perfect Sweep	4	17.77
77.	Silk n' Sapphire	3	17.77
78.	Scoop	10	17.76
79.	Unbridled Lassie	7	17.72
80.	Out of Sync	4	17.70
81.	Sadler's Sarah	5	17.70
82.	Premiere Event	3	17.69
83.	Maltese Indy	9	17.56
84.	Ellie's Moment	4	17.49
85.	Orphan Avie	5	17.40
86.	Trackofthecat	3	17.35
87.	Kiss a Miss	15	17.25
88.	Bon Fearless	5	17.24
89.	Cheryl P.	10	17.19
90.	Trial Fighter	5	17.17
91.	Jordy Girl	4	17.15
92.	Ransom's Pride	7	17.11
93.	Lady Diplomat	8	17.10
94.	Your Out	4	17.10
95.	Miss Kate	9	17.09
96.	Madame Roar	5	17.07
97.	Gulch Legacy	11	17.06
98.	Hidden Creek	5	17.04
99.	Minister's Baby	13	17.04
100.	Royal Roundabout	4	17.01

Males, Four-Year-Olds and Older

Rank	Horse	Starts	Rating
1.	Aptitude	8	29.52
2.	Lido Palace (Chi)	4	27.24
3.	Albert the Great	9	26.50
4.	Captain Steve	5	26.24
5.	Skimming	6	25.71
6.	Broken Vow	10	25.18
7.	Include	9	24.68
8.	Vision and Verse	3	24.52
9.	Sea Run	3	24.29
10.	Ubiquity	5	24.26
11.	Tiznow	6	24.00
12.	Guided Tour	8	23.22
13.	Pleasant Breeze	6	22.52
14.	Gander	10	22.35
15.	Kettle Man	5	21.68
16.	Hap	6	21.11
17.	Perfect Cat	10	20.90
18.	Law Review	5	20.84
19.	Mr Ross	8	20.61
20.	Spectacularspencer	8	20.53
21.	Dixie Dot Com	7	20.52
22.	Val Royal (Fr)	3	20.49
23.	Best of the Rest	5	20.46
24.	Connected	9	20.08
25.	Jumbo C D	3	19.95
26.	Peak Dancer	5	19.87
27.	Futural	9	19.62
28.	Here's Zealous	7	19.60
29.	Delaware Township	9	19.46
30.	Scottish Halo	4	19.40
31.	King Cugat	9	19.32
32.	Top Official	10	19.27
33.	Euchre	4	19.20
34.	Graeme Hall	8	19.18
35.	Left Bank	8	18.98
36.	Milwaukee Brew	4	18.86
37.	Sir Bear	7	18.85
38.	Elite Mercedes	3	18.84
39.	Groomstick Stock's	4	18.77
40.	Wooden Phone	6	18.71
41.	Unshaded	4	18.67
42.	Jarf	8	18.65
43.	Hal's Hope	10	18.61
44.	Patent	3	18.54
45.	Forbidden Apple	4	18.51
46.	Grundlefoot	14	18.47
47.	Traditionally	7	18.47
48.	E Z Glory	8	18.45
49.	Band Is Passing	8	18.31
50.	Crafty Man	5	18.27
51.	Chicago Six	9	18.26
52.	Better Road	4	18.23
53.	Casanova Star	5	18.18
54.	Little Hans	4	18.18
55.	Bonapaw	11	18.13
56.	Caller One	5	18.09
57.	John Paul Too	7	18.09
58.	Whata Brainstorm	3	18.03
59.	Del Mar Show	5	18.03
60.	Northcote Road	11	17.98
61.	Good Journey	4	17.97
62.	Cat's At Home	11	17.93
63.	First Lieutenant	6	17.92
64.	Concerned Minister	6	17.92
65.	Rollin With Nolan	5	17.88
66.	Silky Swoop	4	17.76
67.	Peeping Tom	10	17.74
68.	Brahms	7	17.73
69.	Aly's Alley	7	17.72
70.	Bet On Sunshine	6	17.65
71.	Duplicitous	14	17.64
72.	Darn Tootin	8	17.64
73.	Generous Rosi (GB)	8	17.60
74.	Union One	5	17.60
75.	Tibado	11	17.55
76.	Spicy Prospector	4	17.55
77.	Storm Day	11	17.55
78.	Delay of Game	5	17.49
79.	Where's Taylor	7	17.48
80.	Boston Party	7	17.47
81.	Affirmed Success	5	17.43
82.	Five Star Day	3	17.43
83.	Kona Gold	6	17.39
84.	Thady Quill	4	17.39
85.	Handy N Bold	5	17.34
86.	El Corredor	3	17.34
87.	Apt to Be	8	17.34
88.	A Fleets Dancer	11	17.33
89.	Swept Overboard	8	17.31
90.	Syncline	4	17.31
91.	Valhol	4	17.26
92.	Persianlux (GB)	3	17.21
93.	Rampaging Alf	4	17.21
94.	Sassy Hound	11	17.17
95.	In Frank's Honor	9	17.14
96.	Alannan	9	17.12
97.	Ground Storm	8	17.10
98.	Neon Shadow	8	17.08
99.	Timboroa (GB)	6	17.02
100.	Senator Goldwater	3	17.01

Females, Four-Year-Olds and Older

Rank	Horse	Starts	Rating
1.	License Fee	5	23.05
2.	Apple of Kent	5	22.43
3.	Miss Linda (Arg)	8	21.94
4.	Trip	8	21.18
5.	Printemps (Chi)	4	21.14
6.	Colstar	4	20.97
7.	Atelier	6	20.88
8.	Lu Ravi	3	20.84
9.	Dream Supreme	7	20.73
10.	Spain	9	20.62
11.	Royal Fair	8	20.59
12.	Starine (Fr)	7	20.40
13.	De Bertie	6	20.28
14.	Darling My Darling	4	20.16
15.	Dat You Miz Blue	10	19.83
16.	Strolling Belle	9	19.76
17.	Hemline	6	19.73
18.	Bedside Manner	7	19.67
19.	Country Hideaway	6	19.64
20.	Pompeii	8	19.63
21.	Flyinghannah	9	19.56
22.	Mountain Angel	6	19.52
23.	Shine Again	10	19.39
24.	Spook Express (SAf)	7	19.34
25.	Search Party	7	19.25
26.	Veil of Avalon	7	19.17
27.	Solvig	9	19.13
28.	Vivid Sunset	7	19.10
29.	People's Princess	8	19.06
30.	Penny's Gold	6	19.06
31.	Secret Status	6	19.05
32.	Playact (Ire)	5	19.04
33.	Frankly My Dear	7	18.91
34.	March Magic	6	18.86
35.	Serra Lake	8	18.74
36.	Nessa's Dancer	3	18.71
37.	Sound of the West	5	18.66
38.	Imadeed	6	18.63
39.	Cat Cay	8	18.62
40.	Lady Melesi	7	18.50
41.	Ioya Two	7	18.49
42.	England's Legend (Fr)	6	18.49
43.	Critical Eye	9	18.32
44.	Kalookan Queen	6	18.30
45.	Hallowed Dreams	9	18.25
46.	Catch the Ring	7	18.11
47.	Krisada	9	18.04
48.	Creaseinherjeans	5	17.98
49.	Megans Bluff	9	17.96
50.	Hidden Assets	7	17.93
51.	Impending Bear	6	17.88
52.	Ease 'n Grace	5	17.87
53.	Tugger	10	17.86
54.	Bordelaise (Arg)	4	17.84
55.	Queue	12	17.82
56.	Maltese Superb	7	17.75
57.	Beautiful Pleasure	4	17.74

#	Horse	Starts	Rating
58.	Dance Memories	6	17.73
59.	Please Sign In	9	17.69
60.	Another	8	17.62
61.	Step With Style	8	17.42
62.	Ladies Night In	3	17.41
63.	Wittenberg	5	17.36
64.	Sahara Gold	3	17.35
65.	Lady Cherie	13	17.33
66.	Lucky Lune (Fr)	4	17.26
67.	Babae (Chi)	9	17.26
68.	Gino's Spirits (GB)	10	17.23
69.	Teach	8	17.22
70.	Torrid Affair	5	17.20
71.	Miss Seffens	9	17.15
72.	My Only Desire	3	17.15
73.	Only to You	7	17.13
74.	Polly Jo	6	17.13
75.	La Serina (Ire)	3	17.11
76.	Swept Away	3	17.05
77.	Melody Queen (GB)	3	17.04
78.	Naturally Wild	10	17.01
79.	Lazy Slusan	9	16.99
80.	Truebreadpudding	5	16.97
81.	Iftiraas (GB)	8	16.95
82.	Under the Rug	4	16.88
83.	Fast Delivery	10	16.84
84.	Rose of Zollern (Ire)	7	16.83
85.	Diadella	7	16.81
86.	Maddie May	7	16.73
87.	Summer Solstice (Ire)	3	16.71
88.	East Coast Country	11	16.71
89.	Princess Ellen (GB)	6	16.70
90.	Vanna Go	10	16.70
91.	Yulla Yulla	5	16.70
92.	Golden Antigua	10	16.70
93.	Go Go	7	16.69
94.	Precious Feather	8	16.67
95.	Out of Reach (GB)	3	16.66
96.	Dreams	5	16.66
97.	Shutup and Dance	7	16.62
98.	Sefas Rose	8	16.61
99.	Zeiting (Ire)	8	16.59
100.	Nanie's Dinner	7	16.57

Turf Males, Three and Older

Rank	Horse	Starts	Rating
1.	Hap	6	21.11
2.	Navesink	7	20.71
3.	Val Royal (Fr)	7	20.49
4.	Strut the Stage	5	20.32
5.	Baptize	7	19.98
6.	Package Store	4	19.80
7.	Max's Friend	3	19.63
8.	Sharp Performance	6	19.43
9.	Royal Spy	5	19.42
10.	King Cugat	6	19.32
11.	Key Lory	3	19.22
12.	L'Homme	4	19.07
13.	With Anticipation	6	18.93
14.	Dynameaux	5	18.79
15.	Forbidden Apple	4	18.51
16.	Parlour (Ire)	4	18.51
17.	Band Is Passing	8	18.31
18.	Strategic Partner	11	18.28
19.	Del Mar Show	5	18.03
20.	Whata Brainstorm	3	18.03
21.	Good Journey	4	17.97
22.	Sligo Bay (Ire)	6	17.80
23.	Aly's Alley	7	17.72
24.	Northcote Road	10	17.54
25.	Delay of Game	5	17.49
26.	Where's Taylor	7	17.48
27.	Megantic	6	17.43
28.	Stage Classic	3	17.42
29.	Thady Quill	4	17.39
30.	Blue Steller (Ire)	5	17.29
31.	Persianlux (GB)	3	17.21
32.	Bienamado	4	17.21
33.	In Frank's Honor	9	17.14
34.	Volponi	3	17.11
35.	Kalu	6	17.11
36.	Timboroa (GB)	6	17.02
37.	Decarchy	4	16.98
38.	Brahms	6	16.98
39.	Chorwon	8	16.92
40.	Tijiyr (Ire)	6	16.92
41.	Fan Club's Mister	7	16.90
42.	Irish Prize	9	16.85
43.	Langston	8	16.84
44.	Startac	4	16.84
45.	Flamin' Jolie	4	16.79
46.	Strategic Mission	9	16.77
47.	Galic Boy	6	16.76
48.	Blueprint (Ire)	3	16.70
49.	Warrant	7	16.66
50.	Royal Strand (Ire)	6	16.65
51.	Tiger Trap	6	16.57
52.	Aslaaf	4	16.55
53.	Affirmed Success	3	16.49
54.	Subtle Power (Ire)	4	16.42
55.	Romanceishope	4	16.40
56.	Numerous Times	3	16.26
57.	Proud Man	7	16.25
58.	Thesaurus	7	16.20
59.	Slew Valley	6	16.20
60.	French Joseph	3	16.17
61.	Kris's Sleigh	8	16.16
62.	Grifter	5	16.14
63.	Yaralino (GB)	4	16.13
64.	Slough Creek	7	16.11
65.	Grundlefoot	3	16.10
66.	Beckon the King	7	16.09
67.	Broadway Snowman	4	16.03
68.	Dr. Kashnikow	7	16.02
69.	Sharp Face	4	15.88
70.	Craigsteel (GB)	3	15.87
71.	Union One	4	15.86
72.	Krieger	7	15.86
73.	Schaumburg	6	15.83
74.	Redattore (Brz)	7	15.77
75.	I'm All Yours	6	15.72
76.	Saddlespur	3	15.72
77.	Colonial Colony	6	15.61
78.	White Heart (GB)	4	15.59
79.	Testify	7	15.58
80.	Star Over the Bay	13	15.58
81.	Spruce Run	7	15.57
82.	Crash Course	11	15.52
83.	Dernier Croise (Fr)	7	15.44
84.	Honorable Pic	7	15.42
85.	Deputy's Legacy	5	15.42
86.	Exchange Rate	3	15.39
87.	Two Point Two Mill	7	15.37
88.	Full Flow	9	15.35
89.	Whitmore's Conn	7	15.34
90.	Regal Dynasty	7	15.32
91.	Tv Sports Director	11	15.31
92.	Malabar Gold	3	15.29
93.	Mystic Road	3	15.26
94.	The Price Spirit	3	15.26
95.	Kipperscope	6	15.20
96.	Hawksley Hill (Ire)	4	15.16
97.	Silver Spear	5	15.13
98.	Grangeville	6	15.11
99.	Gallant Gesture	3	15.10
100.	Judson Jr.	3	15.05

Turf Females, Three and Older

Rank	Horse	Starts	Rating
1.	License Fee	4	21.87
2.	Colstar	4	20.97
3.	Starine (Fr)	7	20.40
4.	Affluent	3	20.34
5.	Snow Dance	6	20.29
6.	Golden Apples (Ire)	4	19.84
7.	Sadler's Sarah	3	19.82
8.	Voodoo Dancer	7	19.56
9.	Spook Express (SAf)	7	19.34
10.	Veil of Avalon	7	19.17
11.	Sweetest Thing	8	19.17
12.	Solvig	9	19.13
13.	Penny's Gold	6	19.06
14.	Tweedside	4	19.03
15.	Bold Answer	6	18.98
16.	Valory	3	18.93
17.	Naturally Wild	5	18.90
18.	Salty You	5	18.89
19.	Cozy Island	3	18.60
20.	Ioya Two	7	18.49
21.	England's Legend (Fr)	6	18.49
22.	Nymphenburg	5	18.43
23.	Playact (Ire)	4	18.23
24.	Bien Nicole	3	18.08
25.	Krisada	9	18.04
26.	Queue	12	17.82
27.	Dance Memories	6	17.73
28.	Good Game	8	17.72
29.	Please Sign In	9	17.63
30.	Megans Bluff	8	17.58
31.	La Recherche	11	17.42
32.	Ladies Night In	3	17.41
33.	Casual Feat	8	17.31
34.	Step With Style	7	17.30
35.	Ever With You	5	17.30
36.	Word Puzzle	3	17.28
37.	Lucky Lune (Fr)	4	17.26
38.	Babae (Chi)	9	17.26
39.	Gino's Spirits (GB)	10	17.23
40.	Only to You	7	17.13
41.	Sheikh Away	8	17.13
42.	La Serina (Ire)	3	17.11
43.	Impending Bear	7	17.06
44.	Melody Queen (GB)	3	17.04
45.	Twilite Tryst	8	16.99
46.	Truebreadpudding	5	16.97
47.	La Vida Loca (Ire)	5	16.97
48.	Iftiraas (GB)	8	16.95
49.	Polly Jo	4	16.93
50.	Arty'svirginiagirl	3	16.81
51.	Diadella	5	16.81
52.	Heads Will Roll (GB)	6	16.79
53.	Platinum Tiara	7	16.74
54.	Summer Solstice (Ire)	3	16.71
55.	Tiazo	7	16.71
56.	Owsley	5	16.69
57.	Verruma (Brz)	4	16.67
58.	Out of Reach (GB)	3	16.66
59.	Dreams	5	16.66
60.	Sitka	11	16.64
61.	Tranquility Lake	5	16.62
62.	Zeiting (Ire)	8	16.59
63.	Royal Sting	10	16.55
64.	Silver Bandana	12	16.54
65.	Stylish	6	16.53
66.	Watch	7	16.52
67.	Cozzy Corner	9	16.51
68.	O K to Dance	10	16.49
69.	Gaviola	6	16.45
70.	Golden Antigua	9	16.44
71.	Mi Moochie	5	16.42
72.	New Economy	4	16.41
73.	Jazz	3	16.30
74.	My Sweet Westly	11	16.30
75.	Badouizm	5	16.26
76.	Secret River	6	16.21
77.	Batique	6	16.20
78.	Three Threes	3	16.19
79.	Confessional	4	16.17

Rank	Horse	Starts	Rating
80.	Princess Ellen (GB)	3	16.13
81.	Nanie's Dinner	4	16.11
82.	Eventail	3	16.08
83.	Crystal Sea	9	16.07
84.	Amaretta	7	16.05
85.	Sluice	7	16.05
86.	Diamond Bracelet	7	16.02
87.	Lady Dora	8	16.01
88.	Pretty Dutch	5	16.01
89.	Libretto	3	16.01
90.	Chaste	8	15.96
91.	Shopping for Love	6	15.95
92.	Reine de Romance (Ire)	6	15.94
93.	Quidnaskra	8	15.93
94.	Windsong	10	15.93
95.	Cousin Gigi	10	15.91
96.	Sara's Success	10	15.89
97.	Paga (Arg)	3	15.88
98.	Keemoon (Fr)	6	15.86
99.	Bucarest (Arg)	3	15.86
100.	Maltese Indy	5	15.83

Male Sprinters, Three and Older

Rank	Horse	Starts	Rating
1.	D'wildcat	3	22.11
2.	Squirtle Squirt	6	21.95
3.	Kettle Man	5	21.68
4.	Put It Back	5	21.54
5.	Touch Tone	3	21.17
6.	Aloha Bold	4	20.82
7.	Yonaguska	7	20.31
8.	Joyful Tune	6	20.27
9.	City Zip	8	20.13
10.	Dream Run	6	20.02
11.	Giant Gentleman	3	19.87
12.	Sam Lord's Castle	3	19.64
13.	Here's Zealous	7	19.60
14.	Delaware Township	9	19.46
15.	Catamaran	3	19.19
16.	Early Flyer	5	19.08
17.	Left Bank	6	18.92
18.	Tex's Trick	3	18.64
19.	I Love Silver	6	18.47
20.	Spectacularspencer	4	18.29
21.	Better Road	4	18.23
22.	Rollin With Nolan	4	18.21
23.	Bonapaw	11	18.13
24.	Griffinite	3	18.13
25.	Caller One	5	18.09
26.	Wrangler	7	18.00
27.	Orientate	4	17.83
28.	Accelerant	5	17.82
29.	Beau's Surprise	7	17.80
30.	Equinox	4	17.79
31.	Silky Sweep	4	17.76
32.	Exchange Rate	3	17.66
33.	Illusioned	7	17.64
34.	Mountain General	10	17.59
35.	Speightstown	6	17.57
36.	Bet On Joe	7	17.57
37.	Fappie's Notebook	7	17.53
38.	Handy N Bold	4	17.52
39.	Peeping Tom	8	17.49
40.	Snow Ridge	11	17.49
41.	Five Star Day	3	17.43
42.	Kona Gold	6	17.39
43.	Copper Country	3	17.38
44.	Triple Card	6	17.38
45.	Swept Overboard	8	17.31
46.	Sassy Hound	11	17.17
47.	This Fleet Is Due	3	17.15
48.	Package Store	3	17.09
49.	Phone Ruler	4	17.08
50.	Burning Marque	3	17.07
51.	Native Heir	9	17.07
52.	Not Wild	5	17.05
53.	Crafty C. T.	3	17.03
54.	Secret Romeo	6	16.99
55.	I'm Sentimental	7	16.93
56.	Above the Wind	4	16.91
57.	Keats	3	16.86
58.	Say Florida Sandy	15	16.83
59.	Kela	3	16.82
60.	Kazoo	4	16.79
61.	He's a Knockout	6	16.79
62.	Always On Time	5	16.76
63.	Alannan	8	16.74
64.	Alydelta	7	16.66
65.	Double Star	3	16.65
66.	Proudest Bull	6	16.63
67.	Robin de Nest	13	16.62
68.	Disco Rico	9	16.62
69.	Bet On Sunshine	5	16.56
70.	Lake Pontchartrain	5	16.50
71.	Meandmyloveman	7	16.50
72.	Big Talkin Man	4	16.48
73.	Storm Craft	5	16.47
74.	Mo Mon	3	16.42
75.	Strawberry Affair	6	16.42
76.	Tic N Tin	14	16.39
77.	Dash for Daylight	7	16.36
78.	Hickory Switch	7	16.36
79.	Dancing Guy	3	16.34
80.	Turbotaxman	9	16.32
81.	El Dorado Shooter	4	16.31
82.	Classic Verse	3	16.29
83.	Raire Standard	6	16.24
84.	Classic Appeal	8	16.21
85.	Istintaj	6	16.16
86.	Stone Age	3	16.12
87.	Red's Honor	8	16.06
88.	Sea of Green	12	16.01
89.	Exciting Story	3	16.00
90.	Built Up	7	15.95
91.	Level Three	4	15.91
92.	Solingen	7	15.89
93.	Quixote's Prince	7	15.86
94.	One by the Knows	4	15.84
95.	Triple Odyssey	3	15.84
96.	Baileys Edge	6	15.81
97.	Chindi	9	15.80
98.	Twilight Road	4	15.77
99.	Firststatedeposit	3	15.76
100.	Wicked Will	8	15.74

Female Sprinters, Three and Older

Rank	Horse	Starts	Rating
1.	Victory Ride	3	34.26
2.	Nasty Storm	3	25.32
3.	Xtra Heat	13	23.86
4.	Treasureinmyhand	3	22.94
5.	Quick Blue	3	22.15
6.	Forest Secrets	3	21.87
7.	Mandy's Gold	3	21.63
8.	Celtic Melody	3	21.51
9.	Love At Noon	3	21.29
10.	Gold Mover	4	21.16
11.	Above Perfection	5	20.77
12.	Dream Supreme	7	20.73
13.	Dat You Miz Blue	9	20.73
14.	Raging Fever	3	20.71
15.	Bedside Manner	4	20.45
16.	People's Princess	4	20.31
17.	Sweet Nanette	3	19.99
18.	Shiny Band	4	19.88
19.	Shine Again	7	19.37
20.	Spanish Glitter	15	19.25
21.	Starrer	3	19.24
22.	Country Hideaway	4	19.14
23.	Bon Fearless	3	19.06
24.	Too Scarlet	6	18.95
25.	Major Wager	4	18.74
26.	Shooting Party	7	18.62
27.	Salty Farma	3	18.44
28.	Cat Chat	3	18.34
29.	Lil Punkindo	3	18.31
30.	Kalookan Queen	6	18.30
31.	Hallowed Dreams	9	18.25
32.	Devout Sinner	3	18.11
33.	Kimbralata	11	18.04
34.	Cat Cay	6	17.99
35.	Creaseinherjeans	5	17.98
36.	Imadeed	5	17.95
37.	Dove Creek	3	17.94
38.	Hidden Assets	7	17.93
39.	Emily Ring	10	17.89
40.	Arianna's Passion	7	17.85
41.	Miss Seffens	8	17.83
42.	Silk n' Sapphire	3	17.77
43.	Perfect Sweep	4	17.77
44.	Another	8	17.62
45.	Orphan Avie	5	17.40
46.	Sahara Gold	3	17.35
47.	Keepondealing	11	17.29
48.	Darling Deputy	4	17.23
49.	Torrid Affair	5	17.20
50.	Via Gras	6	17.20
51.	Jordy Girl	4	17.15
52.	Jenny Lake	4	17.11
53.	With Ability	3	17.09
54.	Lighten Up Tiny	5	17.09
55.	Madame Roar	5	17.07
56.	Swept Away	3	17.05
57.	Hidden Creek	5	17.04
58.	Cleverly	4	17.03
59.	Honey Eyed	6	17.02
60.	Royal Roundabout	4	17.01
61.	Designer Phone	3	16.98
62.	Tugger	7	16.95
63.	Hattiesburg	11	16.95
64.	Kiss a Miss	8	16.91
65.	Look of the Lynx	7	16.90
66.	City Fair	11	16.90
67.	Jill's Zi Zi	3	16.88
68.	Valley Affair	3	16.78
69.	Steel Shot	3	16.77
70.	Urban Dancer	8	16.74
71.	Raintree Lake	7	16.71
72.	Yulla Yulla	5	16.70
73.	Go Go	7	16.69
74.	Outstanding Info	9	16.64
75.	Shutup and Dance	7	16.62
76.	Meadow Gem	6	16.54
77.	Cheryl P.	7	16.50
78.	Cindy's Hobby	7	16.48
79.	Schatzeli	3	16.48
80.	Vanna Go	8	16.45
81.	Kerry Blue	5	16.44
82.	Maddie May	6	16.37
83.	Finder's Fee	7	16.25
84.	Detonate	4	16.24
85.	Naturalingredients	11	16.23
86.	Hall of Gold	4	16.21
87.	Stormy Pick	8	16.21
88.	The Happy Hopper	8	16.20
89.	Sonora Desert	3	16.20
90.	Ivy's Jewel	10	16.19
91.	Slash Cottage	3	16.18
92.	Confessional	4	16.16
93.	Flying Birdie	7	16.16
94.	Chumsie	4	16.12
95.	Pleasant Scholar	4	16.12
96.	Donnaree	3	16.11
97.	Poivre (Chi)	6	16.08
98.	Carafe	10	16.04
99.	Mysterious Affair	5	16.02
100.	La Feminn	3	15.99

Experimental Free Handicap

The Experimental Free Handicap, published annually by the Jockey Club, is based on a hypothetical 1⅛-mile race for two-year-olds on dirt. Walter S. Vosburgh, the legendary Jockey Club handicapper, compiled the first Experimental Free Handicap in 1933. He placed Sanford Stakes winner First Minstrel atop his list at 126 pounds, although the filly Mata Hari at 122 pounds effectively was the highweight when considering the five-pound sex allowance then in effect. The 126-pound high weight became the standard impost for a champion of average accomplishment.

Vosburgh, who had been the racing secretary at New York tracks since 1894, retired in 1934, and no Experimental Free Handicap was prepared for that year. John B. Campbell assumed the task in 1935 and continued to compile the list until his death in '54.

Campbell, also racing secretary at the New York tracks, wrote in a 1943 letter that his Experimental Free Handicap was intended primarily as a forecast of how the horses would do as three-year-olds. The Experimental, he wrote, "is based mainly upon my opinion of what the two-year-olds will accomplish as three-year-olds and at distances of a mile and a furlong or greater."

Following Campbell's death, Frank E. "Jimmy" Kilroe assigned the weights through 1960. Thomas Trotter, who compiled the list through 1972, followed him.

Starting in 1969, at the behest of the Jockey Club, the thrust of the Experimental was changed from a prediction of future performance to accomplishment during the two-year-old season exclusively.

Kenneth Noe Jr. prepared the Experimental Free Handicap from 1972 through '75, and Trotter resumed the task in 1976. Beginning in 1979, a committee of three racing secretaries was chosen to establish the Experimental weights. In 1985, for the first time, separate lists were compiled for males and fillies. The 2001 Experimental Free Handicap was prepared by Howard Battle of Keeneland, Mike Lakow of the New York Racing Association, and Tom Robbins of Del Mar.

The highest Experimental weight ever assigned was 132 pounds to Count Fleet in 1942; the following year, he won the Triple Crown. However, 1946 Triple Crown winner Assault was not among the Experimental highweights despite winning the '45 Flash Stakes. All Triple Crown winners since Assault have also been Experimental highweights: Citation (126 pounds), Secretariat (129), Seattle Slew (126), and Affirmed (126).

Past Experimental Free Handicap Highweights

Year	Male	Female
2001	Johannesburg (126)	Tempera (123)
2000	Macho Uno (126)	Caressing (123)
1999	Anees (126)	Cash Run (123)
		Chilukki (123)
		Surfside (123)
1998	Answer Lively (126)	Silverbulletday (123)
1997	Favorite Trick (128)	Countess Diana (125)
1996	Boston Harbor (126)	Storm Song (124)
1995	Maria's Mon (126)	My Flag (123)
	Unbridled's Song (126)	
1994	Timber Country (126)	Flanders (124)
1993	Brocco (126)	Phone Chatter (123)
	Dehere (126)	
1992	Gilded Time (126)	Eliza (123)
1991	Arazi (130)	Pleasant Stage (123)
1990	Fly So Free (126)	Meadow Star (123)
1989	Rhythm (126)	Go for Wand (123)
1988	Easy Goer (126)	Open Mind (123)
1987	Forty Niner (126)	Epitome (123)
		Over All (123)
1986	Capote (126)	Brave Raj (123)
1985†	Ogygian (126)	I'm Splendid (123)
	Tasso (126)	
1984	Chief's Crown (126)	Outstandingly (118)
1983	Devil's Bag (128)	Miss Oceana (120)
1982	Copelan (126)	Landaluce (121)
	Roving Boy (126)	Princess Rooney (121)
1981	Deputy Minister (126)	Before Dawn (120)
	Timely Writer (126)	
1980	Lord Avie (126)	Heavenly Cause (120)
1979	Rockhill Native (126)	Smart Angle (120)
1978	Spectacular Bid (126)	Candy Eclair (119)
		It's in the Air (119)
1977	Affirmed (126)	Lakeville Miss (119)
1976	Seattle Slew (126)	Sensational (119)
1975	Honest Pleasure (126)	Dearly Precious (119)
		Optimistic Gal (119)
1974	Foolish Pleasure (127)	Ruffian (122)
1973	Protagonist (126)	Talking Picture (121)
1972	Secretariat (129)	La Prevoyante (121)
1971	Riva Ridge (126)	Numbered Account (119)
1970	Hoist the Flag (126)	Forward Gal (118)
1969	Silent Screen (128)	Fast Attack (116)
1968	Top Knight (126)	Gallant Bloom (118)
		Process Shot (118)
1967	Vitriolic (126)	Queen of the Stage (117)

Year		
1966	Successor (126)	Regal Gleam (116)
1965	Buckpasser (126)	Moccasin (120)
1964	Bold Lad (130)	Queen Empress (118)
1963	Raise a Native (126)	Castle Forbes (115)
		Tosmah (115)
1962	Never Bend (126)	Affectionately (115)
		Smart Deb (115)
1961	Crimson Satan (126)	Cicada (118)
1960	Hail to Reason (126)	Bowl of Flowers (120)
1959	Warfare (126)	My Dear Girl (117)
1958	First Landing (126)	Quill (117)
1957	Jewel's Reward (126)	Idun (120)
1956	Barbizon (126)	Alanesian (117)
1955	Career Boy (126)	Doubledogdare (116)
		Nasrina (116)
1954	Summer Tan (128)	HIgh Voltage (117)
1953	Porterhouse (126)	Evening Out (118)
	*Turn-to (126)	
1952	Native Dancer (130)	Bubbley (116)
		Sweet Patootie (116)
1951	Tom Fool (126)	Rose Jet (115)
1950	Uncle Miltie (126)	Aunt Jinny (115)
		How (115)
1949	Middleground (126)	Bed o' Roses (119)
1948	Blue Peter (126)	Myrtle Charm (121)
1947	Citation (126)	Bewitch (121)
1946	Cosmic Bomb (126)	First Flight (126)
	Double Jay (126)	
1945	Lord Boswell (128)	Beaugay (121)
1944	Free for All (126)	Busher (119)
	Pavot (126)	
1943	Pukka Gin (126)	Durazna (121)
		Miss Keeneland (121)
1942	Count Fleet (132)	Askmenow (119)
		Good Morning (119)
1941	Alsab (130)	Chiquita Mia (115)
		Ficklebush (115)
1940	Whirlaway (126)	Level Best (121)
1939	Bimelech (130)	Now What (119)
1938	El Chico (126)	Inscoelda (116)
1937	Menow (126)	Jacola (116)
1936	Brooklyn (126)	Rifted Clouds (115)
1935	Red Rain (126)	Forever Yours (116)
1933	First Minstrel (126)	Mata Hari (122)

†Starting in 1985, fillies were ranked separately.
No weights assigned in 1934

2001 **Experimental Free Handicap Colts and Geldings**

Wt.	Horse	Sire—Dam, Broodmare sire (State)	Sts	1st	2nd	3rd	Earnings
126	Johannesburg	Hennessy—Myth, by Ogygian (Ky.)	7	7	0	0	$1,002,893
124	Siphonic	Siphon (Brz)—Cherokee Crossing, by Cherokee Colony (Ky.)	4	3	0	1	703,978
123	Repent	Louis Quatorze—Baby Grace (Arg), by Cipayo (Ky.)	5	3	1	1	415,660
121	Officer	Bertrando—St. Helens Shadow, by Septieme Ciel (Ca.)	8	5	1	1	740,010
119	Came Home	Gone West—Nice Assay, by Clever Trick (Ky.)	4	3	0	0	211,440
	Publication	Petionville—Cat News, by Storm Cat (Ky.)	4	2	0	0	170,535
117	Buster's Daydream	Housebuster—Daydream, by Believe It (Ky.)	6	4	0	0	199,625
	Fonz's	Out of Place—Seton's Encounter, by Spring Double (Fl.)	4	2	2	0	193,740
116	Saarland	Unbridled—Versailles Treaty, by Danzig (Ky.)	5	2	0	0	177,660
115	Essence of Dubai	Pulpit—Epitome, by Summing (Ky.)	4	2	0	1	193,200
	French Assault	French Deputy—Carly's Crown, by Wild Again (Ky.)	8	2	3	0	132,090
	Jump Start	A.P. Indy—Steady Cat, by Storm Cat (Ky.)	5	2	1	0	221,265
	Mayakovsky	Matty G—Joy to Raise, by Raise a Man (Fl.)	2	1	1	0	64,600
	Nokoma	Pulpit—Eliza Blue, by Icecapade (Ky.)	3	1	1	0	67,660
	Request for Parole	Judge T C—Madison's Quest, by Deputy Minister (Ky.)	7	2	3	1	199,912
114	Harlan's Holiday	Harlan—Christmas in Aiken, by Affirmed (Oh.)	6	4	2	0	341,564
	Heavyweight Champ	Two Punch—Moments Delight, by General Assembly (Md.)	6	2	1	2	149,258
	Miesque's Approval	Miesque's Son—Win Approval, by With Approval (Fl.)	6	3	2	1	182,545
	Stage Call (Ire)	Sadler's Wells—Humble Eight, by Seattle Battle (Ireland)	4	2	1	1	96,636
113	Jeremiah Jack	Patton—Cidacape, by Procida. (Ky.)	8	3	0	0	154,926
	Listen Here	Gulch—Listen Now, by Storm Bird (Ky.)	4	3	0	0	115,980
	Pure Precision	Montbrook—Al's Helen, by Distinctive (Fl.)	4	3	1	0	156,400
	Sunray Spirit	Hennessy—Basking, by Alydar (Ky.)	5	2	1	0	111,058
112	Kamsack	Crafty Prospector—Gerri n Jo Go, by Top Command (Ky.)	3	1	1	0	78,200
	Labamta Babe	Skywalker—Bambina Linda (Arg), by Liloy (Fr) (Ky.)	5	1	2	1	65,700
	Sky Terrace	Skywalker—I Aim High, by I Enclose (Ky.)	3	2	0	0	59,978
111	Booklet	Notebook—Crafty Bobbie, by Bob's Dusty (Fl.)	5	4	0	1	339,700
	High Star	Private Terms—Polember, by Polish Navy (Ky.)	4	1	0	0	50,700
	Leelanau	Carson City—Kris's Intention, by Kris S. (Ky.)	2	2	0	0	126,077
	Popular	Saint Ballado—Western Lady, by Gone West (Ky.)	4	1	1	0	45,260
	Silent Fred	Louis Quatorze—D'Youville Nurse, by Dr. Blum (Md.)	4	1	0	1	49,720
	Truman's Raider	Capote—Towering Success, by Irish Tower (Ky.)	5	1	1	2	72,602
110	Dubai Squire	Summer Squall—She Rides Tonite, by Stalwart (Ky.)	5	2	0	2	63,160
	Iron Deputy	Silver Deputy—Femme De Fer (Fr), by Iron Duke (Ky.)	3	2	1	0	82,300
	Monthir	Gulch—Caress, by Storm Cat (Ky.)	5	1	2	0	63,120
	Mountain Rage	Mecke—Sweet Silver Star, by Silver Buck (Fl.)	6	2	2	0	154,760
	Political Attack	Hawk Attack—Cope's Light, by Copelan (Ky.)	6	3	0	0	120,666
109	City Street	Carson City—Starz, by Danzatore (Ky.)	2	2	0	0	78,785
	Expected Program	Valid Expectations—Program Pick, by Peterhof (Fl.)	5	3	0	0	120,240
	It'sallinthechase	Take Me Out—Limestone Landing, by Red Ryder (Ky.)	9	2	3	0	94,160
	Wild Navigator	Wild Zone—Meadow Songbird, by Danzig Connection (NJ)	3	1	1	1	50,470
108	Cashel Castle	Silver Ghost—Desviacion, by Unreal Zeal (Ky.)	3	3	0	0	95,190
	Draw Play	End Sweep—Ann Margot, by Gate Dancer (Fl.)	5	1	2	1	65,258
	Emergency Status	Academy Award—Stated, by *Hawaii (Fl.)	3	2	0	0	82,800
	Finality	Dehere—Finally Found, by Lord Durham (NY)	6	1	2	1	70,655
	Handsome Hunk	Hennessy—Lit'l Rose, by Mr. Prospector (Ky.)	8	3	1	2	137,634
	Ibn Al Haitham (GB)	Zafonic—Awaasif, by *Snow Knight (Great Britain)	5	0	3	1	74,840
	Metatron	Silver Ghost—Dancing Ovation, by Northern Jove (Ky.)	5	1	2	2	142,320
	Roman Dancer	Polish Numbers—Phalanopsis, by Cormorant (NY)	5	2	0	0	101,940
	Twin Talk	Twining—Talking Tower, by Irish Tower (Ky.)	3	2	1	0	50,630
107	April's Lucky Boy	Ide—Poppies and Wheat, by Lost Code (Ok.)	4	2	1	1	49,825
	Binyamin	Gilded Time—Christina Czarina, by Czaravich (Ky.)	4	1	2	0	57,425
	Incredible Carson	Lord Carson—Incredible Me, by Mt. Livermore (Ky.)	6	3	2	0	81,051
	Lunar Bounty	Migrating Moon—So Easily, by Superbity (Fl.)	6	2	1	0	119,225
	O'Rocky	Birdonthewire—Loudmouth Time, by Honey Jay (Fl.)	9	4	0	0	171,890
	Robins Beauty	Matty G—Briar Prospector, by Geiger Counter (Fl.)	7	1	2	1	57,150
106	Bog Hunter	Hunting Hard—United Bog, by Linkage (Fl.)	6	3	0	2	139,150
	Bug Hall	Knight in Savannah—Marina Express, by Expressman (Mt.)	8	3	2	1	90,418
	Davids Expectation	Valid Expectations—No Holding David, by Two Davids (Fl.)	6	1	3	0	78,844
	Double Zero Seven	Beau Genius—Call My Agent, by Phone Trick (Ky.)	7	4	2	0	132,300
	El Malicia	Flying Chevron—Cinefila, by Skywalker (Fl.)	3	2	1	0	47,205
	Expensive Risk	Expense Account—A Story Told, by Here We Come (Ok.)	4	1	3	0	36,810
	Explosive Truth	Proudest Romeo—Beauty's Sake, by Lyphard's Ridge (Fl.)	3	2	0	0	77,610
	Gold Dollar	Seattle Slew—Miss Prospector, by Crafty Prospector (Fl.)	9	1	1	2	66,330
	Hail to Bag	Bag—Mother Knows Best, by Marshua's Dancer (La.)	6	5	1	0	175,395
	Hunter Cruise	Capote—Cruisie, by Assert (Ire) (Ky.)	7	3	0	0	83,949
	Juggernaut	Is It True—Mito's Touch, by Gentle King (Ky.)	7	3	1	0	138,180
	Major Storm	Storm Cat—Next Fall, by Alleged (Ky.)	7	1	0	0	41,859
	Moonmon	Maria's Mon—Taylors Promise, by Promised City (Ky.)	6	2	0	1	47,550
	Mountain Forum	Open Forum—Mountain Affair, by Mt. Livermore (Fl.)	8	2	2	1	91,350
	Numbers Man	Polish Numbers—Clayton's Nobility, by Mark of Nobility (NJ)	6	2	1	0	71,990
	Royalton	El Prado (Ire)—Miss Sanmar, by Recitation (Ky.)	5	1	0	0	35,600
	Rylstone	Mecke—Appealing High, by Valid Appeal (Fl.)	5	1	1	0	54,230
	Steady Rollin	Shadeed—Veiled Look, by Cyane (Ky.)	2	2	0	0	39,950
	Surprized	Prized—Miss Light Lady, by Majestic Light (Ca.)	6	3	0	2	127,250
	U S S Tinosa	Foxhound—Angel Puss, by Wolf Power (SAf) (Oh.)	7	2	3	1	122,319

2001 Experimental Free Handicap Fillies

Wt.	Horse	Sire—Dam, Broodmare sire (State)	Sts	1st	2nd	3rd	Earnings
123	Tempera	A.P. Indy—Colour Chart, by Mr. Prospector (Ky.)	5	3	0	2	$670,240
121	Habibti	Tabasco Cat—Miss Sobriety, by Temperence Hill (Ky.)	4	3	0	0	393,000
120	Imperial Gesture	Langfuhr—Honor an Offer, by Hoist the Flag (Ky.)	4	1	2	0	275,540
	You	You and I—Our Dani, by Homebuilder (Ky.)	6	3	2	0	540,440
118	Cashier's Dream	Service Stripe—Jerry's Sister, by Monetary Gift (Mi.)	6	4	2	0	353,230
117	Tali'sluckybusride	Delineator—Springhurst, by Lord At War (Arg) (Wa.)	3	2	0	1	221,160
116	Belterra	Unbridled—Cruising Haven, by Shelter Half (Ky.)	3	3	0	0	192,359
	Smok'n Frolic	Smoke Glacken—Cherokyfrolicflash, by Green Dancer (Fl.)	9	4	2	0	342,744
	Who Loves Aleyna	Out of Place—Aleyna's Love, by Kris S. (Fl.)	4	1	2	1	99,008
115	Bella Bellucci	French Deputy—Blue Avenue, by Classic Go Go (Ky.)	3	2	0	1	208,555
	Forest Heiress	Forest Wildcat—Penniless Heiress, by Pentelicus (Ky.)	5	4	1	0	210,787
	Take Charge Lady	Dehere—Felicita, by Rubiano (Ky.)	5	3	1	0	371,716
114	Lotta Rhythm	Rhythm—Kim's Blues, by Cure the Blues (Ky.)	5	3	0	2	124,758
	Never Out	Take Me Out—Cabinet Post, by Silver Ghost (Ky.)	3	2	1	0	123,963
113	Cunning Play	Defensive Play—Cunning, by Lord At War (Arg) (Ky.)	5	1	3	1	110,045
	Riskaverse	Dynaformer—The Bink, by Seeking the Gold (Ky.)	6	3	1	2	202,750
	Touch Love	Not For Love—Smartenof, by Smarten (Md.)	3	3	0	0	148,560
112	Forty On Line (GB)	Pharly—Charming Bride, by Charmer (Great Britain)	3	2	0	0	144,456
111	Georgia's Storm	Illinois Storm—Fuljan, by Native Tradition (Ca.)	5	3	1	0	185,085
	Joanies Bella	Mercer Mill—Bello Senorita, by Northrop (Oh.)	9	5	1	1	234,265
110	August Storm	Storm Creek—Smellin Salty, by Salt Lake (Fl.)	4	3	0	0	124,230
	Daisyago	Affirmed—Ladyago, by Northern Dancer (Ky.)	6	1	1	1	101,220
	La Martina (GB)	Atraf—Dance Steppe, by Rambo Dancer (Great Britain)	4	2	0	1	54,873
	Lady Shari	Judge T C—Badgering Shari, by Badger Land (Ky.)	7	2	3	1	276,210
109	Ayanna	In Excess (Ire)—Dance Play, by Sovereign Dancer (Az.)	6	3	2	0	145,750
	Lush Soldier	Lost Soldier—Lady Lush, by Nikoli (Ire) (Fl.)	7	2	1	0	148,618
	Stylelistick	Storm Cat—Magnificient Style, by Silver Hawk (Ky.)	6	2	1	1	121,046
108	Brief Bliss	Navarone—Annul, by Conquistador Cielo (Ky.)	7	1	4	0	50,678
	Kathy K D	Saint Ballado—Stella Cielo, by Conquistador Cielo (Ky.)	5	2	1	1	81,309
	Lujien Lujien	Cozzene—Space Warning, by Caveat (Md.)	4	2	1	0	71,940
	Playing 'n Gold	Honour and Glory—Playing Through, by Messenger of Song (Ky.)	9	3	2	1	150,730
	Speed to Burn	Red Ransom—Hidden Light, by Majestic Light (Ky.)	4	1	1	1	48,302
107	Haunted Lass	Meadow Monster—Importantly, by Exclusive Era (Ky.)	4	3	1	0	113,200
	Ms Brookski	Montbrook—Junk Bond Queen, by Baldski (Fl.)	9	4	1	1	248,060
	Ponche de Leona	Ponche—Perfect and Proud, by Nonparrell (Fl.)	6	4	1	0	110,080
	Vicki Vallencourt	Regal Classic—Esquisite Diamond, by Fight Over (Ky.)	5	3	0	0	121,223
106	First Again	Outflanker—Ells Once Again, by Kennedy Road (Fl.)	5	2	0	1	88,790
	Ms Louisett	Siphon (Brz)—Juliac, by Accipiter (Ky.)	4	0	2	1	48,800
	Piano Chimes	Chimes Band—L'Argent Baby, by Fappiano (NY)	11	2	1	3	57,920
	Purple Princess	Carson City—Tapstress, by Desert Wine (Ky.)	6	2	3	0	91,225
105	A New Twist	Storm Cat—Twist Afleet, by Afleet (Ky.)	3	1	2	0	49,355
	Asian Adventure	Far Out East—Chancy Paula, by Beau's Eagle (Ca.)	6	2	2	2	147,285
	Atlantic Fury	Wild Again—Search the Sea, by Seeking the Gold (Canada)	2	1	0	1	161,390
	Blissful Kiss	Kissin Kris—Blissful Union, by John's Choice (Fl.)	6	2	1	1	336,780
	Flick	Dehere—Texas Cinema, by Mt. Livermore (Ky.)	4	2	1	1	82,205
	Ghost Queen	Silver Ghost—Cappucino Queen, by Java Gold (Ky.)	8	3	2	2	146,533
	Lakeside Cup	Salt Lake—Tricki Mae, by Phone Trick (Ky.)	8	2	3	2	151,445
	Minimalist	Dynaformer—Gdansk's Honour, by Danzig (Ky.)	4	2	0	0	45,680
	Private Port	Sea Salute—Pierpont Account, by Private Account (NY)	4	1	0	0	29,802
	Redoubled Miss	Adhocracy—Redoubled, by Prospector's Halo (Fl.)	6	1	1	2	63,330
	Respectful	Honour and Glory—Still Wishing, by Carson City (Ky.)	7	1	3	3	103,199
	Stormy Frolic	Summer Squall—Lindsay Frolic, by Mt. Livermore (Ky.)	7	2	2	0	57,630
104	Dancing Dreams	Hadif—Miss Fire Dancer, by A Run (Tx.)	6	5	0	0	120,420
	Don't Ruffle Me	Pine Bluff—Delivery Day, by Dayjur (Ky.)	4	2	1	0	68,523
	Fertile	Lite the Fuse—Eureka Lass, by Lucky North (Ky.)	3	2	0	0	77,475
	Maresha	Judge T C—North Again, by Northrop (Ky.)	5	2	1	0	63,650
	Night Breeze	Two Punch—Silent Greeting, by Secret Hello (Va.)	3	3	0	0	93,250
	Proxy Statement	A.P. Indy—Deputation, by Deputy Minister (Ky.)	3	2	0	1	73,600
103	Bronze Abe	Two Punch—Buckles and Kinks, by Waquoit (Md.)	9	3	2	3	113,290
	Carson's Baby	Carson City—Baby Feels So Good, by Baldski (Fl.)	4	2	0	1	42,470
	Fancy Prancer	Bertrando—Oh No It's You, by Miswaki (Ca.)	5	3	0	1	45,595
	Knock Twice	Two Punch—Joe's Tammie, by Zoning (Ky.)	4	1	2	0	44,500
	Miss Jeanne Cat	Tabasco Cat—Few Choice Words, by Valid Appeal (Ky.)	3	2	0	0	50,054
	Open Story	Open Forum—Diablo's Story, by Diablo (Fl.)	8	1	1	2	76,090

Scale of Weights

The scale of weights provides a guideline to the weights that horses carry at different ages and over different distances. As in many standards in Thoroughbred racing, the current scale of weights evolved over time.

The earliest Thoroughbred races in the 17th century were run at catch weights—whatever the rider, usually the owner, weighed. As racing became more sophisticated, various methods were tried to make contests more fair as well as more competitive, including assigning different weights according to the height of the horse, known as "give-and-take" weights.

That concept eventually evolved into assigning different weights to horses of differing perceived abilities. The first recorded handicap race was the Subscription Handicap Plate at Newmarket in 1785.

In 1740, the English Parliament established minimum weights for horses of different ages. Those weights were not meant to be assigned to horses of different ages in the same race, however.

In the mid-19th century, Admiral Henry Rous, British racing's de facto dictator, applied and expanded the concept to horses of different ages in the same race. Rous published the world's first weight-for-age scale in his 1850 book *On the Laws and Practice of Horse Racing*. Rous's scale also recognized that Thoroughbreds mature steadily from ages two through four; he assigned different weights at different distances for every month of the year.

All subsequent scales essentially have been refinements of Rous's work. The first official scale of weights was published in the *Racing Calendar* in 1880. In the modern scale of weights, the differences between weights for three-year-olds and older horses are much smaller than in Rous's day due to the increased early maturity of the modern Thoroughbred.

The scale of weights listed below is the official scale used by American racing secretaries.

Distance and Age	Jan.	Feb.	Mar.	Apr.	May	June	July	Aug.	Sept.	Oct.	Nov.	Dec.
Half mile												
2 years	x	x	x	x	x	x	x	105	108	111	114	114
3 years	117	117	119	119	121	123	125	126	127	128	129	129
4 years	130	130	130	130	130	130	130	130	130	130	130	130
5 years & up	130	130	130	130	130	130	130	130	130	130	130	130
6 furlongs												
2 years	x	x	x	x	x	x	x	102	105	108	111	111
3 years	114	114	117	117	119	121	123	125	126	127	128	128
4 years	129	129	130	130	130	130	130	130	130	130	130	130
5 years & up	130	130	130	130	130	130	130	130	130	130	130	130
1 mile												
2 years	x	x	x	x	x	x	x	x	96	99	102	102
3 years	107	107	111	111	113	115	117	119	121	122	123	123
4 years	127	127	128	128	127	126	126	126	126	126	126	126
5 years & up	128	128	128	128	127	126	126	126	126	126	126	126
1¼ miles												
2 years	x	x	x	x	x	x	x	x	x	x	x	x
3 years	101	101	107	107	111	113	116	118	120	121	122	122
4 years	125	125	127	127	127	126	126	126	126	126	126	126
5 years & up	127	127	127	127	127	126	126	126	126	126	126	126
1½ miles												
2 years	x	x	x	x	x	x	x	x	x	x	x	x
3 years	98	98	104	104	108	111	114	117	119	121	122	122
4 years	124	124	126	126	126	126	126	126	126	126	126	126
5 years & up	126	126	126	126	126	126	126	126	126	126	126	126
2 miles												
3 years	96	96	102	102	106	109	112	114	117	119	120	120
4 years	124	124	126	126	126	126	126	125	125	124	124	124
5 years & up	126	126	126	126	126	126	126	125	125	124	124	124

(a) In races of intermediate lengths, the weights for the shorter distance are carried.

(b) In races exclusively for three-year-olds or four-year-olds, the weight is 126 lbs., and in races exclusively for two-year-olds, it is 122 lbs.

(c) In all races except handicaps and races where the conditions expressly state to the contrary, the scale of weights is less, by the following: for two-year-old fillies, 3 lbs.; for three-year-old and up fillies and mares, 5 lbs. before September 1, and 3 lbs. thereafter.

(d) In all handicaps that close more than 72 hours prior to the race the top weight shall not be less than 126 lbs., except in handicaps for fillies and mares, the top weight shall not be less than 126 lbs. less the sex allowance at the time of the race.

American Match Races

Match races, a prominent part of American Thoroughbred racing through the mid-1970s, slowed to a trickle after Ruffian's fatal showdown with Foolish Pleasure at Belmont Park on July 6, 1975. Of 96 match races in North America during the 20th century, only 13 were contested after the undefeated filly shattered her right front ankle and was euthanized the next day. Only nine of those 13 were in the United States, and none of them commanded the national attention given the Ruffian–Foolish Pleasure match and such earlier match races as Seabiscuit–War Admiral and Nashua–Swaps.

Match races in America were mostly winner take all and trace back to the early 1820s, when American Eclipse engaged in and won two matches. Similarly, the great sire Lexington won twice in head-to-head competition in the 1850s. Since Domino defeated Clifford by three-quarters of a length in a one-mile match race at Sheepshead Bay Racetrack in New York on September 6, 1894, 15 match races have contained at least one starter who was recognized officially or unofficially as a champion. (*Daily Racing Form* first designated champions in 1936.) Thirteen of the 15 races offered wagering, and favorites lost nine of them. None was more noteworthy than War Admiral's loss to Seabiscuit in 1938, and none was more one-sided than Miss Musket's 50-length loss to Chris Evert on July 20, 1974, at Hollywood Park.

To appreciate America's greatest match races, it is necessary to understand the hype and expectations heading into them. For more than a year, racing fans had clamored for a match-up of Seabiscuit and War Admiral, the two dominant horses of the late 1930s. When the two finally were the only two entrants in the $1\frac{3}{16}$-mile Pimlico Special Stakes on November 1, 1938, a record crowd of 40,000 turned out to see Seabiscuit, a five-year-old grandson of Man o' War, take on War Admiral, a four-year-old son of Man o' War who had won the 1937 Triple Crown and 16 of 17 starts prior to the Baltimore race.

Seabiscuit, breaking from the second post position, was sent off at 2.20-to-1 under George Woolf; War Admiral, thought to be the quicker from the gate, was 0.25-to-1 under Charley Kurtsinger. War Admiral was expected to lead at the start, but Seabiscuit outbroke him. Seabiscuit had been on the lead in just one of his previous 13 starts.

War Admiral made several moves at his opponent and once drew within a nose, but Seabiscuit had plenty left and won by four lengths in track record time of 1:56.60.

Nearly 17 years later, Kentucky Derby winner Swaps went off as the 3-to-10 favorite against Preakness and Belmont Stakes winner Nashua in the $100,000 Washington Park Match Race at $1\frac{1}{4}$ miles on August 31, 1955. Swaps was undefeated as a three-year-old and owner-breeder Rex Ellsworth had returned him to California after he defeated Nashua by $1\frac{1}{2}$ lengths in the 1955 Derby. Nashua's only loss in 11 starts had been in the Derby. Swaps was the favorite under Bill Shoemaker, while Nashua was 6-to-5 with Eddie Arcaro. Nashua won by $6\frac{1}{2}$ lengths, leading from start to finish.

The race that effectively ended top-level match races pitted Foolish Pleasure, 1995 Kentucky Derby winner, against undefeated Ruffian, a three-year-old filly who never had been headed in ten career starts, all against other fillies. Jacinto Vasquez was the regular rider of both horses and chose to ride Frank Whiteley-trained Ruffian in the nationally televised race. Ruffian went off at 0.40-to-1; Foolish Pleasure was 0.90-to-1.

Ruffian broke from the rail and narrowly led Foolish Pleasure through a blazing first quarter-mile in :$22\frac{1}{5}$ on Belmont's deep $1\frac{1}{4}$-mile chute. Shortly after they entered the main track, however, Ruffian broke down and swerved to the outside. Foolish Pleasure finished the race under Braulio Baeza. Ruffian, who fought her handlers when coming out of anesthetic after surgery, reinjured her leg, and was euthanized early on July 7. Match races since then never have been the same.—*Bill Heller*

Notable Walkovers since 1914

Walkovers are rare in Thoroughbred racing if only because competition is at the heart of the sport. The most recent walkover occurred in 1997 when Sharp Cat's two opponents, Alzora and Toda Una Dama (Arg) were scratched from the Bayakoa Handicap (G2) after December rains turned Hollywood Park's track muddy. Prior to that, champion Spectacular Bid walked over when Winter's Tale, Temperence Hill, and Dr. Patches were scratched from the 1980 Woodward Stakes (G1).

In consecutive years, Calumet Farm champions Coaltown and Citation walked over in Maryland races. Coaltown was unopposed in the 1949 Edward Burke Handicap at Havre de Grace, and Citation had no opponents entered against him in the 1948 Pimlico Special.

Although walkovers usually involve only one horse, two horses with the same owner may walk over if they are entered in a race and no horses oppose them. Here are several of the most important walkovers since 1914.

Horse, age, sex	Race (Grade)	Date	Track	Distance	Time
Sharp Cat, 3, f.	Bayakoa H. (G2)	12-07-1997	Hollywood	$1\frac{1}{16}$m	1:42.68
Spectacular Bid, 4, c.	Woodward S. (G1)	09-20-1980	Belmont	$1\frac{1}{4}$m	2:$02\frac{2}{5}$
Coaltown, 4, c.	Edward Burke H.	04-23-1949	Havre de Grace	$1\frac{1}{16}$m	1:$52\frac{1}{5}$
Citation, 3, c.	Pimlico Special	10-29-1948	Pimlico	$1\frac{3}{16}$m	1:$59\frac{4}{5}$
Casa Camara, 2, f.	Diamond Ring S.	10-26-1946	Long Branch	1m70y	1:$49\frac{1}{5}$
Stymie, 5, h.	Saratoga Cup	08-31-1946	Saratoga	$1\frac{3}{4}$m	3:$07\frac{2}{5}$
Whirlaway, 4, c.	Pimlico Special	10-28-1942	Pimlico	$1\frac{3}{16}$m	2:$05\frac{2}{5}$
Pilate, 5, h.	Waterboy H.	08-14-1933	Saratoga	7f	1:32
Little Nap, 3, c.	West Point H.	10-29-1930	Empire City	1m70y	1:49
Saguenay, 3, g.	King's Plate	08-05-1927	Blue Bonnets	$1\frac{1}{4}$m	2:$28\frac{3}{5}$
Millwick, 5, g.	Hempstead Highweight H.	05-24-1927	Belmont	6f	Untimed
Exterminator, 6, g.	Saratoga Cup	08-31-1921	Saratoga	$1\frac{3}{4}$m	3:$04\frac{3}{5}$
Royce Rools, 6, g.	Gramatan H.	07-15-1921	Empire City	$1\frac{1}{8}$m	2:$13\frac{4}{5}$
Purchase, 3, c.	Jockey Club S.	09-13-1919	Belmont	$1\frac{1}{2}$m	2:$41\frac{3}{5}$
Roamer, 3, g.	Autumn S.	09-19-1914	Belmont	$1\frac{1}{2}$m	3:04

The Claiming Game

Claiming races are the heart of almost every racing meet in America. In 2001, nearly two-thirds of all races (65.5%) were either straight claiming or maiden claiming. The horses that populate those races are an eclectic band of warriors whose common bond is their owners' willingness to lose them for a specified price as soon as the race is over.

The claimers are typified by such horses as Creme de La Fete, a chestnut gelding who went to post with a price on his head in all but 20 of his 151 career starts in the late 1970s and early '80s. His claiming prices ranged from $7,000 to $72,500.

Creme de La Fete was so well known that he was saluted in a ceremony at Aqueduct. The National Horsemen's Benevolent and Protective Association annually selects a claimer of the year, and the Claiming Crown held each summer has given more attention to the sport's foot soldiers.

But publicity for claimers is rare, accorded usually to horses that were claimed early in their careers and developed into champions, as Stymie did in the 1940s. Or, the attention goes to horses that ran in claiming races but were not taken, such as two-time Horse of the Year John Henry or 1999 Horse of the Year Charismatic.

Most claimers toil in anonymity, week after week, start after start, battling their infirmities as much as the competition. Most males are geldings and race well past their prime.

Claiming races have been a part of Thoroughbred racing for more than three centuries, though they began in England in a much different fashion and were called selling races.

In a story in the January 1972 issue of *The Thoroughbred of California*, Barry H. Irwin uncovered the original set of horse racing rules used in England in 1698, '99, and 1700 for races "at Thettford in the Countys of Norfolke and Suffolke" for the last Friday in September of each year. Eight noblemen and 11 commoners wrote 15 conditions for the races. One was that every owner would sell every horse entered for "Thirty Guineys" and that the "Contributors present shall throw dice" and that "the Purchaser will be he who throwes most at three."

More than 300 years later, if more than one claim is entered on a particular horse, the winner is determined by lot by the stewards. Getting to that point took several revisions once racing became established in the United States.

According to the Jockey Club's 1828 *Racing Calendar*, the owner of the second-place finisher in a selling race was entitled to purchase the winner for a specified sum. That rule was modified to allow all losing owners in a race to buy the winner, with the option to purchase determined by the order of finish. If the owner of the second-place horse did not want the winner, the option to buy passed to the third-place finisher.

In the early 1900s, Canadian racetracks introduced the concept of sealed bids for the winner being submitted within 15 minutes after the race. A similar rule was approved by the Kentucky Association on September 1, 1916, and used at the 1917 spring race meeting in Lexington.

On opening day that spring, April 28, the Kentucky Association approved a Claiming Race Rule that allowed all horses in a claiming race to be purchased, and it set down the chilling reality for the person making a claim. The purchaser would become the owner of the horse "whether he be alive or dead, sound or unsound, or injured during the race or after it." To this day, the claim takes effect as soon as the starting gate opens. If a claimed horse dies during the race, the person who claimed it must not only buy the horse but also pay to remove the horse from the track and pay its burial fees.

Claiming races were well received and soon spread to East Coast tracks in the 1920s. However, selling races remained a part of the Jockey Club's rules of racing to the 1950s. By the 1940s, the selling race had become a variation of a claiming race in which only the winner was auctioned off for at the least the offering price. All other horses in the race were eligible to be claimed for the stated claiming price.

Claiming rules today vary modestly from one racing jurisdiction to another, but two basic concepts apply in all of them. First, any licensed trainer or owner who has had at least one starter at a race meeting may claim any horse at that meeting, although an owner or trainer who lost the last horse of his stable on a claim at the previous meeting is eligible to make a claim. Second, for a period of 30 days, the horse must race for at least 25% more than the price for which it was claimed. For example, a horse claimed for $10,000 cannot start in a claiming race for less than $12,500 for 30 days. Under those restrictions, the horse is frequently referred to as being "in jail," ostensibly because the new owner does not have the freedom to place him at any claiming price. Some racing jurisdictions have experimented with eliminating jail time. In addition, the claimed horse cannot be sold privately to another party in the 30-day period, and the horse cannot race at another track until the end of the race meet at which it was claimed.

For every claimer, there is a claiming trainer, and, like their horses, some have risen to prominence. Hirsch Jacobs, who led the nation in victories 11 times between 1933 and '44, may have been the first great claiming trainer. Jacobs

claimed Stymie from a maiden claimer for $1,500 on June 8, 1943, and Stymie rewarded him by winning more than $900,000.

On the West Coast, one of the most prominent claiming trainers was R. H. "Red" McDaniel, who led the nation in victories from 1950 through 1954. In 1955, McDaniel saddled a winner at Golden Gate Fields and a few minutes later jumped to his death from the San Francisco Bay Bridge.

Claimers have been an integral part of the success of father-son Racing Hall of Fame members Marion and Jack Van Berg. Jack Van Berg led the nation's trainers in victories nine times, including a still-record 496 wins in 1976. Only Richard Dutrow (352 in 1975) and Scott Lake (with 407 in 2001) have won more than 350 races in one year.

Frank "Pancho" Martin won 11 New York training titles, the first in 1971 and then ten straight from 1973 through 1982. The Cuban-born Martin explained his training philosophy in a 1972 magazine article: "The most important thing to remember is to treat your cheapest horse as good as your best," Martin said. "Give a claimer the same care you give a stakes horse, and he'll win for you in his own class. If you improve a horse, move him up in company, but never ask him to do the impossible."

Three of Martin's greatest claimers were Manassa Mauler, a $12,800 claim who won the 1959 Wood Memorial Stakes and earned $359,171; Autobiography, a $29,000 claim who won the '72 Jockey Club Gold Cup over Key to the Mint and Riva Ridge; and *Big Shot II, a $25,000 claim who won a $100,000 stakes, the '71 Century Handicap.

Though Bobby Frankel shifted his base of operations to California in 1972, he had considerable success with claimers in his six New York seasons before heading west. In that period, Frankel developed claimers Barometer, Baitman, and Pataha Prince into stakes winners. Barometer, claimed for $15,000, won the 1970 Suburban Handicap and earned $174,584. Baitman, who was seven years old when Frankel claimed him for $15,000, earned more than $150,000 after the claim. In California, Frankel claimed Wickerr for $50,000 and then won the 1981 and '82 Eddie Read Handicaps (G1) with him. Wickerr also won the 1981 Del Mar Handicap (G2).

West Virginia-based Dale Baird led the nation's trainers in victories 15 times from 1971 through '99, almost exclusively with claimers. He was displaced as America's top trainer by victories in 2000 and '01 by Scott Lake, who races simultaneously at several tracks in the Northeast.

Fifty-two years after Stymie was claimed for $1,500, a first-time starter at Hollywood Park named Budroyale was claimed in a maiden race for $32,000 by trainer Dan Hendricks for Decourcy W. Graham. Budroyale was subsequently claimed twice more for $40,000 and for $50,000 before he matured to win several graded stakes, finish second in the 1999 Breeders' Cup Classic (G1), and earn more than $2.8-million, most of it for small-scale owner Jeffrey Sengara. Such horses as Stymie and Budroyale are the exceptions, but the hope of finding a diamond in the rough keeps many owners and trainers in the claiming game.

—Bill Heller

Some of the Best Claimers

Following are some of the most prominent horses who either were claimed prior to outstanding careers on the racetrack or at stud or started in claiming races but went unclaimed:

ASPIDISTRA—1954 b. m., Better Self—Tilly Rose, by Bull Brier. 14-2-2-2, $5,115. Bred by King Ranch, Aspidistra was purchased by William L. McKnight's Minnesota Mining & Manufacturing Co. employees as a 70th birthday gift in 1957. Aspidistra, named for a hardy house plant, then was in the midst of a non-descript racing career that did not improve after her purchase. For McKnight, she raced for a $6,500 claiming tag. Retired after one racing season at age three, she became the foundation of McKnight's Tartan Farms in Florida, producing 1968 Horse of the Year Dr. Fager and champion sprinter Ta Wee.

BOOM TOWNER—1988 b. g., Obligato—Perfect Profile, by Stop the Music. 82-29-16-14, $962,391. Boom Towner began his eight-year career in a $5,000 maiden claimer at Rockingham Park, winning by 10¾ lengths. He won the 1992 Toboggan Handicap (G3) and was claimed the following year for $50,000 by trainer Mike Hushion for Barry Schwartz. In Hushion's care, Boom Towner won the 1993 Boojum (G3) and Sport Page (G3) Handicaps, both at Aqueduct. He won the Toboggan again in 1995.

BROWN BESS—1982 dk. b. or br. m., *Petrone—Chickadee, by Windy Sands. 36-16-8-6, $1,300,920. Brown Bess's owner-breeder, Calbourne Farm, put her at risk only once, for $50,000 in a Bay Meadows Race Course claimer on September 28, 1986. It was her first start on grass, and she finished second by a nose. Brown Bess would thrive on the grass, winning the 1989 Yellow Ribbon Invitational Stakes (G1) and the Ramona Handicap (G1) on her way to an Eclipse Award as champion female grass horse.

BUDROYALE—1993 b. g., Cee's Tizzy—Cee's Song, by Seattle Song. 52-17-12-2, $2,840,810. First-time starter Budroyale was taken for $32,000 by trainer Dan Hendricks from breeder/co-owner Cecilia Straub-Rubens on December 9, 1995, at Hollywood Park. Budroyale was subsequently claimed for $40,000 by trainer Nick Canani on August 17, 1997, and for $50,000 by trainer Ted West for Jeffrey Sengara on February 15, 1998. He won the 1998 San Bernardino Handicap (G2) and in '99 scored victories in the Goodwood Breeders' Cup Handicap (G2), the Mervyn LeRoy Handicap (G2), and the Longacres Mile Handicap (G3).

He was second five times, including the Breeders' Cup Classic (G1). In 2000, Budroyale won the San Antonio Handicap (G2) the same year his full brother Tiznow won the first of his two Breeders' Cup Classics.

CHARISMATIC—1996 ch. h., Summer Squall—Bail Babe, by Drone. 17-5-2-4, $2,038,064. Charismatic won only one of his first 13 starts and only raced four more times in his career. Trained by D. Wayne Lukas and owned by Robert and Beverly Lewis, Charismatic was placed first in a $62,500 claimer at Santa Anita Park on February 11, 1999. After finishing second in the El Camino Real Derby (G3) at Bay Meadows Race Course, Charismatic was a soundly beaten fourth in the Santa Anita Derby (G1). He subsequently won the Coolmore Lexington Stakes (G2), the Kentucky Derby (G1), and the Preakness Stakes (G1) before finishing third in the Belmont Stakes (G1), in which he sustained two fractures of his left foreleg. He was voted 1999 champion three-year-old male and Horse of the Year.

CREME DE LA FETE—1976 ch. g., Creme Dela Creme—Bridge Day, by *Tudor Minstrel. 151-40-27-16, $460,350. After winning his career debut by a nose as a two-year-old at Keeneland Race Course in 1978, Creme de La Fete finished fifth of six in the Bashford Manor Stakes at Churchill Downs. Unlike many two-year-olds that fade from the racing scene, Creme de La Fete would make 149 more starts. His two best years were in 1981, when he won 12 of 26 starts and $123,180, and in '83, when he won nine of 30 starts and earned $127,240. In his final start, Creme de La Fete was second in a $7,000 claimer at Garden State Park, the 12th racetrack at which he had raced, in June 1985.

DEPUTED TESTAMONY—1980 b. h., Traffic Cop—Proof Requested, by Prove It. 20-11-3-0, $674,329. Owned by Francis Sears and trained by J. William Boniface, Deputed Testamony was not competitive in his first start, finishing sixth by 12¾ lengths in a $25,000 maiden claimer at Bowie Race Course on September 21, 1982. In his next start, the colt won a $22,500 maiden claimer at Keystone Race Track, and Boniface put him at risk once more, in a $40,000 open claimer at the Meadowlands. Deputed Testamony won by three lengths and was not claimed. The following year, he won the Preakness Stakes (G1) and Monmouth Park's Haskell Invitational Handicap (G1). He won his two 1984 starts, including a track-record effort in the City of Baltimore Handicap, before retiring to stud at Boniface's Bonita Farm, the place of his birth.

GAIL'S BRUSH—1991 b. m., Broad Brush—Parade of Roses, by Blues Parade. 39-11-5-4, $250,701. Claimed by John E. Salzman Jr. on November 25, 1995, for $25,000, Gail's Brush made only two starts for the Maryland trainer before she was picked up by owner-trainer Edwin T. Broome from a $40,000 claimer on grass at Gulfstream Park in early 1996. Gail's Brush, whose performance had improved dramatically when switched to grass, made only six starts for Broome, but they included consecutive victories in the 1996 Columbiana Handicap, Politely Stakes, Eatontown Handicap (G3), and Rumson Stakes.

GOLDEN TENT—1989 dk. b. or br. g., Shelter Half—Jump for Gold, by Search for Gold. 114-21-27-17, $732,793. By the standards of racing in the new century, Golden Tent is made of iron. He started once at three and then made 113 starts through 2001. Golden Tent was claimed seven times, four within a little more than four months in 1999 at the age of ten. Trainer Mike Hushion claimed Golden Tent three times

for Barry Schwartz, for whom the gelding finished second in the 1998 Bold Ruler Handicap (G3) and third in the Fall Highweight Handicap (G2) that year.

JEWEL PRINCESS—1992 b. m., Key to the Mint—Jewell Ridge, by Melyno (Ire). 29-13-4-7, $1,904,060. An Eclipse Award winner as outstanding older female after winning the 1996 Breeders' Cup Distaff (G1), Jewel Princess began her career with a third-place finish in a $20,000 maiden claimer at Calder Race Course on October 27, 1994. She won her next start in a $30,000 maiden claimer and never looked back. In the care of Wally Dollase, Jewel Princess won the 1996 Vanity Invitational Handicap (G1) in addition to the Distaff, and in '97 she won the Santa Maria (G1) and Santa Margarita Invitational (G1) Handicaps. At the 2000 Keeneland November breeding stock sale, she was sold for $4.9-million to Coolmore Stud principal owner John Magnier.

JOHN HENRY—1975 b. g., Old Bob Bowers—Once Double, by Double Jay. 83-39-15-9, $6,591,860. John Henry raced five times in claiming races in 1978 but was not claimed. Purchased privately for $27,500 by Sam Rubin in 1978, he made his final claiming start for Sam and Dorothy Rubin's Dotsam Stable at $35,000 on June 28, 1978, at Belmont Park and won by 14 lengths. Trained by Robert Donato, Victor "Lefty" Nickerson, and Ron McAnally, he was Horse of the Year in 1981 and '84 as well as a four-time champion turf male and once champion older male. He retired as the richest North American Thoroughbred of all time. After his final claiming start, he compiled a record of 64-36-13-6 with earnings of $6,527,882.

KING COMMANDER—1949 dk. b. or br. g., Brown King—Guinea Egg, by Cohort. 67-17-15-6, $100,295. King Commander made 27 of his first 31 starts in claimers although he was claimed only once, for $5,000 at Aqueduct in 1952. Converted to steeplechasing after winning three of 32 starts on the flat, King Commander won 14 of 35 starts over fences and was voted champion steeplechase horse in 1954.

KING'S SWAN—1980 b. h., King's Bishop—Royal Cygnet, by *Sea-Bird. 107-31-19-18, $1,924,845. King's Swan already had won 11 of 44 starts and $212,350 when he was claimed in 1985 for $80,000 by trainer Richard Dutrow. The following year, King's Swan won eight of 15 starts, including the Vosburgh Stakes (G1) and Boojum Handicap (G3), and earned $451,207. At seven, he won three Grade 3 stakes in 12 starts and earned $477,218. He was even better at eight, winning five graded stakes, including the Bold Ruler (G2) and Tom Fool (G2) Stakes in 14 starts and banking $539,681.

KOBUK KING—1966 dk. b. or br. h., One-Eyed King—Winby, by Crafty Admiral. 68-12-10-11, $173,921. After showing considerable promise as a two-year-old in 1968, winning three of 13 starts and finishing second in the El Camino Stakes at Bay Meadows Race Course, Kobuk King went zero-for-three as a three-year-old and zero-for-19 at four. Claimed for $15,000 in 1971, Kobuk King found himself and scored consecutive victories in the Cabrillo Handicap at Del Mar, the Tanforan Handicap at Bay Meadows, and Santa Anita Park's Carleton F. Burke Invitational Handicap for co-owners Allegre Stable and Ron McAnally, who trained the horse. He won eight of 18 starts in 1971 but only one of 15 races in his final two years, a division of the '73 Arcadia Handicap (G3) at Santa Anita.

LADY MARYLAND—1934 gr. m., Sir Greysteel—Palestra, by Prince Palatine. 82-18-14-14, $31,067. The 1939 champion handicap mare, Lady Maryland

made 19 of her 82 starts in claimers and was taken for $2,500 in her 28th career start by B. B. Archer. Her final start in a claimer was as a four-year-old for $4,500 at Havre de Grace. She was not claimed and quickly improved in her five-year-old season, winning the Carroll and Ritchie Handicaps at Pimlico Race Course.

LAKEVILLE MISS—1975 dk. b. or br. m., Rainy Lake—Hew, by Blue Prince. 14-7-4-1, $371,582. While Affirmed and Alydar slugged it out for two-year-old male honors in 1977, the juvenile filly championship was taken by the strapping Lakeville Miss, who possessed a blue-collar pedigree and started her career as a $25,000 maiden claimer for owner-breeder Randolph Weinsier. She won a 5½-furlong claiming race at Belmont Park by four lengths on June 30 and never started again for a claiming tag. Trained by Jose Martin, Lakeville Miss won the Matron (G1) and Frizette (G1) Stakes at Belmont and the Selima Stakes (G1) at Laurel Race Course. She concluded her career with a four-length win in the 1978 Coaching Club American Oaks (G1).

LEAVE IT TO BEEZER—1993 b. g., Henbane—Blue Shocker, by Copelan. 75-22-11-13, $587,086. Although he had lost ten straight races, six-year-old Leave It to Beezer was claimed for $32,000 by trainer Scott Lake for Leo Gaspari Racing Stable on December 22, 1999. His third-place finish that day extended his losing streak to 11. Lake backed off on the gelding's training regimen, and Leave It to Beezer responded by winning nine of 15 starts, including the Salvator Mile Handicap (G3) at Monmouth Park and the Baltimore Breeders' Cup Handicap (G3) at Pimlico on the way to earning $350,830 in 2000.

McKAYMACKENNA—1989 b. m., Ends Well—Amuse, by Secretariat. 38-15-6-2, $581,322. R Kay Stable claimed McKaymackenna for $35,000 from a Belmont Park race in which she was beaten by more than 35 lengths. Sloppy tracks like the one she encountered at Belmont on May 16, 1992, were not to her liking; turf racing was her game. After trainer Gary Sciacca claimed her, she won seven grass stakes, including the 1993 Beaugay Handicap (G3) and Noble Damsel Stakes (G3).

PARKA—1958 br. g., *Arctic Prince—Manchon, by *Blenheim II. 93-27-14-18, $446,236. Bred by Marion duPont Scott and unraced at two, Parka was claimed for $10,000 in his 11th career start by Warren A. "Jimmy" Croll Jr. for client Rachel Carpenter. Parka won that Atlantic City Race Course race by a head, and Croll entered him in a $13,000 claimer 15 days later. He won that race by eight lengths and never raced in a claimer again. He was 1965 champion grass horse off victories in the Bougainvillea Handicap at Hialeah Park, the Kelly-Olympic and United Nations Handicaps at Atlantic City, and Aqueduct's Long Island Handicap in his final career start.

PEAT MOSS—1975 b. g., *Herbager—Moss, by Round Table. 55-15-7-9, $635,517. A little more than one year after winning a $10,000 claimer, Claiborne Farm-bred Peat Moss came within a head of upsetting John Henry in the 1981 Jockey Club Gold Cup (G1). Owned and trained by Murray Garren, Peat Moss loved to go a distance, winning the 1980 Display Handicap (G3) at 2¼ miles and the 1980 and '81 Kelso Handicap at two miles. In his first 1981 start, he set an Aqueduct track record for 2⅛ miles when winning a handicap by 6½ lengths in 3:40⅗.

PORT CONWAY LANE—1969 gr. h., Bold Commander—*Grey Taffety, by Grey Sovereign. 242-52-39-

36, $431,593. Port Conway Lane spent most of his lengthy career in claimers, although he started his career in allowance and stakes races, including a second-place finish in the 1971 Marlboro Nursery Stakes. He won Pimlico Race Course's City of Baltimore Handicap twice, in 1974 and '75, as well as Bowie Race Course's '74 Bowie Handicap and '75 Terrapin Handicap. By the end of 1976, however, he was racing principally in claimers and continued to do so through '83.

*PRINCEQUILLO—1940 b. h., by Prince Rose—*Cosquilla, by *Papyrus. 33-12-5-7, $96,550. Exported from England in 1941, *Princequillo was offered for a $2,500 claiming price by owner Anthony Pelleteri on August 20, 1942. Taking him for Boone Hall Stable was Horatio Luro, who would develop *Princequillo into a multiple stakes winner during World War II. At Claiborne Farm, he proved to be an outstanding stallion, leading the general sire list in 1957 and '58 and topping the broodmare sire list eight times in North America and once in England.

SEABISCUIT—1933 b. h., Hard Tack—Swing On, by Whisk Broom II. 89-33-15-13, $437,730. Long before he became a top handicap horse, Seabiscuit lost the first 17 races of his career, including three defeats in $2,500 claimers and a loss in a $4,000 claimer at Havre de Grace in April 1935. Nobody took him, and later Wheatley Stable sold him to Charles Howard. Under the care of Racing Hall of Fame trainer Tom Smith, Seabiscuit went on to spectacular success, including a seven-stakes win streak in 1937, when he was champion handicap horse. The following year, he was voted Horse of the Year and handicap champion.

STYMIE—1941 ch. h., Equestrian—Stop Watch, by On Watch. 131-35-33-28, $918,485. Taken in his third lifetime start for $1,500 by Hirsch Jacobs, Stymie became the richest Thoroughbred of all time by his retirement in 1949, a record that only lasted until Citation exceeded $1-million in 1951. In his prime from ages four through seven, he won 28 of 69 starts, including the Saratoga Cup Stakes and the Gallant Fox, Metropolitan, Grey Lag, Aqueduct, and Sussex Handicaps twice each.

TIMELY WRITER—1979 b., c., Staff Writer—Timely Roman, by Sette Bello. 15-9-1-2, $605,491. A $13,000 yearling purchase owned by Peter and Francis Martin and trained by Dominic Imprescia, Timely Writer made his debut with an eight-length victory in a $30,000 maiden claimer at Monmouth Park. He subsequently won Saratoga Race Course's Hopeful Stakes (G1) and the Champagne Stakes (G1) at Belmont Park, earning him co-highweight with Eclipse Award champion Deputy Minister on the 1981 Experimental Free Handicap. At three, he won the Flamingo Stakes (G1) and Florida Derby (G1), but surgery for an intestinal blockage knocked him out of the Triple Crown races. He returned in the fall but sustained a fatal breakdown in the Jockey Club Gold Cup (G1).

VIDEOGENIC—1982 b. m., Caucasus—Video Babe, by T.V. Commercial. 73-20-9-10, $1,154,360. Trainer Gasper Moschera convinced owner Albert Davis to claim Videogenic for $100,000 on May 24, 1985. She was not much to look at, but she could run, winning 11 stakes races after the claim, including the 1985 Ladies Handicap (G1) at Aqueduct and the 1986 Santa Ana Handicap (G1) at Santa Anita Park. She won more than $1-million for Davis on the racetrack and was sold as a broodmare prospect for $625,000 at the 1988 Keeneland November breeding stock sale.

Racetracks of North America

Arizona

Rillito Park

Location: 4502 N. 1st Ave., Tucson, AZ 85718
Phone: (520) 293-5011
Fax: (520) 293-1287

Racing dates
2001: February 3-March 11, 12 days
2002: February 2-March 3

Leaders
Recent meeting, leading jockey: Floyd Campbell, 9, 2001
Recent meeting, leading trainer: Eddie Tellez, 4, 2001; Gene K. Wilson, 4, 2001, Santiago Lowe, 4, 2001

Fastest Times of 2001
4 furlongs: Blushing God, :44.40, February 3
5 1/2 furlongs: Cornino Bay, 1:04.60, February 4
6 furlongs: Tristaff, 1:10.40, February 4
7 furlongs: Burgandy Blue, 1:22.60, February 4
1 1/16 miles: Rough, 1:45.40, February 18

Turf Paradise

A Phoenix tradition for nearly a half-century, Turf Paradise has survived several ownership changes and the dramatic reshaping of Thoroughbred racing to remain a vital part of the winter racing scene.

Turf Paradise was the vision of businessman Walter Cluer, who purchased 1,400 acres of desert land in 1954 and transformed it into a racetrack, which opened its doors on January 7, 1956. Cluer owned the track until 1980. The track's next two owners, Herb Owens and Robert Walker, added a turf course and off-track betting, respectively.

Hollywood Park purchased the track in 1994 and weathered an influx of Indian casino gambling in Arizona before selling the track to Phoenix developer Jerry Simms in June 2000. But Simms's reign as owner was short-lived; in October 2001, the Arizona Department of Racing stripped him of his license, citing his involvement in a California bribery scandal and alleged organized-crime ties.

While the track's ownership situation has been clouded in recent years, on-track results have been positive. Turf Paradise's 2000-'01 meeting, which lasted 163 days, recorded a handle increase of more than $25-million (from $306-million to $331-million), while purses averaged a record $80,000 per day.

Location: 1501 W. Bell Rd., Phoenix, AZ 85023
Phone: (602) 942-1101
Fax: (602) 942-8659
E-mail: webmaster@turfparadise.net
Web site: http://www.turfparadise.com
Year founded: 1955
Inaugural meeting: January 7, 1956
Acreage: 1,400
Number of stalls: 1,700
Seating capacity: 7,284

Officers
President: Randy Fozzard
Vice President: Dave Johnson

General Manager: Randy Fozzard
Director of Racing: Shawn Swartz
Racing Secretary: Shawn Swartz
Director of Marketing: Vince Francia
Director of Mutuels: Dustin Dix
Director of Publicity: Vince Francia
Director of Simulcasting: Jack Mullen
Horsemen's Liaison: Debbie Zimmerman
Steward: Jerry Nicodemus
Track Announcer: Luke Kruytbosch
Track Photographer: Coady Photography

Racing dates
2001: September 30, 2000-May 22, 2001, 163 days
2002: September 28, 2001-May 19, 2002, 164 days

Track Layout
Main circumference: 1 mile
Main track chute: 3 furlongs, 6 1/2 furlongs
Main width: 80 feet
Main turf circumference: 7 furlongs
Main turf chute: 1/8 mile

Attendance
Highest single day record: 16,000 est., March 18, 1984

Track Records, Main Dirt
4 1/2 furlongs: Kathryn's Doll, :50 2/5, April 9, 1967
5 furlongs: Zip Pocket, :55 2/5, April 22, 1967
5 1/2 furlongs: Plenty Zloty, 1:01.10, April 18, 1995
6 furlongs: G Malleah, 1:06.60, April 8, 1995
6 1/2 furlongs: G Malleah, 1:13.80, December 3, 1994
7 furlongs: Free Duty, 1:26 1/5, January 23, 1985
1 mile: Mr. Pappion, 1:33.20, January 30, 1993
1 1/16 miles: Down the Isle, 1:39 1/5, February 11, 1987
1 1/8 miles: Our Forbes, 1:47.60, November 29, 1996
1 1/4 miles: Truly a Pleasure, 2:01.40, March 26, 1995
1 3/8 miles: Bloom n Character, 2:15 2/5, April 12, 1980
1 5/8 miles: Masked Rider, 2:44.40, February 10, 2002
1 3/4 miles: Arsenal, 2:55 2/5, February 7, 1971
2 miles: Vermejo, 3:24, April 20, 1969
Other: 2 furlongs, Wandering Boy, :21 1/5, December 5, 1965; 3 furlongs, Never Shamed, :31.60, April 1, 1996

Course Records, Main Turf
5 furlongs: Honor the Hero, :56.20, February 5, 1995
7 furlongs: Lord Pleasant, 1:22.80, October 12, 1992
7 1/2 furlongs: Bristolville, 1:28.71, November 3, 2001
1 mile: Prose (Ire), 1:34.83, March 27, 2001
1 1/16 miles: Caesour, 1:40.40, February 5, 1995
1 1/8 miles: Narghile, 1:48, February 1, 1987
1 3/8 miles: Turk Flyer, 2:16.11, April 14, 2001
1 1/2 miles: Senator McGuire, 2:29 3/5, May 22, 1988
Other: 1 7/8 miles, Shadows Fall, 3:09 2/5, May 17, 1987

Fastest Times of 2001 (Dirt)
4 1/2 furlongs: Quickkey, :52.15, May 12
5 furlongs: Quinton's Quest, :58.05, October 26
5 1/2 furlongs: Kahlo (Mex), 1:02.73, March 3
6 furlongs: Uncle Punk, 1:08.39, April 28
6 1/2 furlongs: Hangonslewpyhangon, 1:14.91, December 29
1 mile: Slew Can Go, 1:35.08, April 13; Ceetoit, 1:35.08, December 18
1 1/16 miles: Startac, 1:41.72, February 3
1 1/8 miles: Cut the Corner, 1:50.78, December 16
1 1/4 miles: Caligraphy, 2:05.60, February 13
1 5/8 miles: Caligraphy, 2:47.67, March 4

Fastest Times of 2001 (Turf)
7 1/2 furlongs: Bristolville, 1:28.71, November 3
1 mile: Prose (Ire), 1:34.83, March 27
1 1/16 miles: Hangonslewpyhangon, 1:42.59, March 25

1 1/8 miles: Naughty Nacho, 1:50.70, November 24
1 3/8 miles: Turk Flyer, 2:16.11, April 14
Other: 1 7/8 miles, Felon (Ire), 3:16.55, May 6

Yavapai Downs

Yavapai Downs is the story of two tracks, not one. Located in Arizona's Prescott Valley region, Yavapai opened its doors in 2001 and replaced Prescott Downs, a half-mile oval that had been in operation since 1913.

While Prescott was known for its rustic atmosphere and occasionally wild bullring racing, Yavapai quickly established a reputation as a more refined track, with modern amenities and a one-mile oval. The $23-million facility was completed in 13 months, almost one year ahead of schedule, allowing it to open in May 2001.

The physical plant features a three-story clubhouse and grandstand with Arizona's Mingus Mountains as a backdrop. The backstretch offers stabling for 1,200 horses. During its inaugural meeting, daily purses averaged nearly $50,000 per day.

Prescott, Arizona's summer racing home for the better part of nine decades, was the site of Racing Hall of Fame jockey Pat Day's first riding victory.

Location: P.O. Box 26557, Prescott Valley, AZ 86312
Phone: (928) 775-8000
Fax: (928) 445-0408
Web site: http://www.yavapaidownsatpv.com
Number of stalls: 1,500

Officers
General Manager: Jim Grundy
Director of Finance: Sharon Fisher
Director of Marketing: Terri Fergusen
Director of Publicity: Roxanne Vise

Racing dates
2001: May 26-September 4, 56 days
2002: May 27-September 2

Track Layout
Main circumference: 1 mile

Leaders
Recent meeting, leading jockey: Estaban Angel Gomez, 62, 2001
Recent meeting, leading trainer: Bill F. Brashears, 28, 2001

Fastest Times of 2001 (Dirt)
5 furlongs: Highway One O One, :56.67, September 4
5 1/2 furlongs: Buzz's Dancer, 1:02.90, May 29
6 furlongs: Hemandan, 1:08.26, June 5
1 mile: Houston Hero, 1:35.75, June 19
1 1/16 miles: Leaven, 1:44.34, July 16
1 1/8 miles: Endowing, 1:52.25, July 30
1 1/4 miles: Cave Creek King, 2:07.14, July 22

Arkansas

Oaklawn Park

Arkansas's leading tourist attraction is Oaklawn Park in the resort community of Hot Springs. The track first opened in 1905 but closed two years later due to political problems in the state. The track reopened in 1916 under the ownership of Louis Cella, whose great-nephew Charles Cella is the track's current president and board chairman. Oaklawn, which offers live racing from February to mid-April, annually attracts runners from across the United States for its Racing Festival of the South. The festival features one stakes race each day on the final seven days of the meet, ending with the Arkansas Derby (G2), which was first run in 1936. Although a major steppingstone to the Triple Crown, just one winner of the Arkansas Derby (G2), Sunny's Halo in 1983, has gone on to win the Kentucky Derby (G1). Other major races include the Apple Blossom Handicap (G1) for fillies and mares, which has attracted more Eclipse Award winners than any other festival race, and the Oaklawn Handicap (G1), the track's richest race.

Location: 2705 Central Ave., Hot Springs, AR 71902
Phone: (501) 623-4411
Fax: (501) 624-4950
E-mail: winning@oaklawn.com
Web site: http://www.oaklawn.com
Year founded: 1904
Inaugural meeting: February 24, 1905
Acreage: 120
Number of stalls: 1,600
Seating capacity: 26,200

Officers
President: Charles J. Cella
General Manager: R. Eric Jackson
Racing Secretary: Patrick J. Pope
Director of Operations: Craig Holtz
Director of Mutuels: Bobby Geiger
Director of Publicity: Terry Wallace
Director of Simulcasting: Bobby Geiger
Horsemen's Liaison: Jan Kerr
Track Announcer: Terry Wallace
Track Photographer: Steve Abahazy
Track Superintendent: Donnie Ellison
Other Officials: Kim Burge-Baron, Director of Guest Relations; Ray Russell, Director of Maintenance

Racing dates
2001: February 2-April 14, 52 days
2002: January 25-April 13, 54 days

Track Layout
Main circumference: 1 mile
Main track chute: 6 furlongs
Main width: 70 feet
Main length of stretch: 1,155 feet

Attendance
Average daily recent meeting: 11,251, 2001
Highest single day record: 71,203, April 19, 1986
Highest single meet record: 1,419,650, 1984
Record daily average for single meet: 23,271, 1983

Handle
Single day on-track handle: $15,133,537, April 15, 2000
Record daily average for single meet: $5,061,653, 1998
Single day total handle all sources: $15,133,537, 2000
Average all sources recent meeting: $4,632,609, 2001

Mutuel Records
Highest Win: $350.80, Phaltup, March 7, 1950
Highest Exacta: $3,915.20, April 8, 1994
Highest Trifecta: $46,395, March 12, 1998
Highest Daily Double: $6,902, March 30, 1971
Highest Pick 3: $36,686.80, February 17, 1996
Highest Pick 6: $818,693.40, February 15, 1995

Leaders
Recent meeting, leading owner: K. K. Jayaraman and Vilasini Jayaraman, 14, 2001
Career, leading jockey by titles: Pat Day, 12
Career, leading trainer by titles: Henry Forest, 11
Recent meeting, leading trainer: Cole Norman, 43, 2001
Recent meeting, leading jockey: Calvin H. Borel, 70, 2001

Oaklawn, continued

Records
Single meet, leading jockey by wins: Pat Day, 137, 1986
Single meet, leading trainer by wins: David Vance, 50, 1974
Single day jockey wins: Larry Snyder, 6, April 1, 1969; Pat Day, 6, February 17, 1986; Pat Day, 6, March 11, 1993; Pat Day, 6, February 20, 1995

Track Records, Main Dirt
4 furlongs: Crimson Saint, :44 4/5, April 1, 1971
4 1/2 furlongs: Montague, :53, March 29, 1937
5 furlongs: Miss Brendy, :57 3/5, February 22, 1966
5 1/2 furlongs: Sis Pleasure Fager, 1:02 3/5, February 15, 1984
6 furlongs: Karen's Tom, 1:07 4/5, April 16, 1990
1 mile: Whitebrush, 1:34 2/5, March 10, 1984
1m 70 yds: Winstat, 1:38 2/5, March 7, 1984
1 1/16 miles: Heatherten, 1:40 1/5, April 18, 1984
1 1/8 miles: Snow Chief, 1:46 3/5, April 17, 1987
1 3/16 miles: Brassy, 1:57 2/5, March 29, 1952
1 1/4 miles: Out of Fire, 2:04, March 31, 1937
1 3/8 miles: Homeplace, 2:20 3/5, March 29, 1961
1 1/2 miles: Dapper, 2:31 3/5, March 30, 1957
1 3/4 miles: Flag Carrier, 2:58, April 18, 1987
Other: 2 miles 70 yds, Turntable, 3:34, March 27, 1942

Fastest Times of 2001
5 1/2 furlongs: Missy's Whirl, 1:04.23, March 17
6 furlongs: Bonapaw, 1:08.18, April 12
1 mile: Compendium, 1:36.88, April 13
1 1/16 miles: Gourmet Girl, 1:42.15, April 8
1 1/8 miles: Traditionally, 1:48.15, April 7
1 3/4 miles: Room Mate, 3:02.71, April 14

California

Bay Meadows Race Course

Located 20 miles south of San Francisco in San Mateo, Bay Meadows Race Course was founded in 1934 by the innovative William Kyne, who helped to bring about the legalization of pari-mutuel wagering in California that year. At Bay Meadows, Kyne introduced the totalisator system, photo-finish camera, and the still-popular daily double wager. Bay Meadows also was the site of the first all-enclosed starting gate in America in 1939 and, on October 27, 1945, the destination point of the first equine air passenger when El Lobo, a Thoroughbred, was flown from Los Angeles to an airstrip adjacent to Bay Meadows.

Bay Meadows was the only California racetrack allowed to operate during World War II as Kyne pledged all profits to various war relief projects. In 1951, Coaltown captured the Children's Hospital Handicap, another charity fundraiser.

Bay Meadows introduced the El Camino Real Derby (G3) in 1982 as a prep for the Kentucky Derby (G1), and 17 years later Charismatic finished second by a head in the race (to Cliquot) before winning the Derby and Preakness Stakes (G1). The race was shifted to Golden Gate Fields in 2001.

In November 2000, Magna Entertainment Corp. purchased the track's operating license for $24.1-million, and the property is expected to be developed, with Bay Meadows's dates being run at Magna-owned Golden Gate or at a new track to replace both properties.

Location: 2600 S. Delaware St., San Mateo CA 94403
Phone: (650) 574-7223
Fax: (650) 345-6826
E-mail: help@baymeadows.com
Web site: http://www.baymeadows.com
Year founded: 1934
Inaugural meeting: November 3, 1934
Acreage: 100
Seating capacity: 9,500
Number of stalls: 900

Officers
President: F. Jack Liebau
Vice Presidents: Michael A. Scalzo, Michael Ziegler, Richard J. Lewis
Director of Racing: Thomas S. Robbins
Racing Secretary: C. Gregory Brent Jr.
Director of Mutuels: Bernice Thurman
Director of Publicity: Tom Ferrall
Director of Sales: Dyan Grealish
Director of Simulcasting: Kay Webb
Stewards: Darrel McHargue, Dennis Nevin, John Herbuveaux
Track Announcer: Tony Calo
Track Photographer: William Vassar
Track Superintendent: Robert Turman

Racing dates
2001: August 31-November 5, 52 days
2002: April 3-June 16, 55 days; August 30-November 11, 49 days

Track Layout
Main circumference: 1 mile
Main track chute: 1 1/4 miles, 6 furlongs
Main length of stretch: 990 feet
Main turf circumference: 7 furlongs 32 feet
Main turf chute: 1 1/8 miles
Main turf width: 75 feet

Attendance
Highest single day record: 29,300, April 17, 1948

Handle
Single day on-track handle: $8,660,396, November 6, 1999

Mutuel Records
Highest Win: $599.80
Highest Exacta: $2,108
Highest Daily Double: $5,231
Highest Pick 6: $1,132,466
Highest Other Exotics: $1,298.80; Quinella, $347,970.40, Pick Nine

Leaders
Recent meeting, leading jockey: Russell Baze, 89, Fall 2001
Recent meeting, leading trainer: Jerry Hollendorfer, 35, Fall 2001
Career, leading jockey by titles: Russell Baze, 19

Records
Single day jockey wins: John Adams, 6, April 7, 1938; John Longden, 6, November 22, 1947; Bill Shoemaker, 6, October 13, 1950; William Harmatz, 6, September 23, 1954; Ralph Neves, 6, October 24, 1961; Russell Baze, 6, September 1, 1984; Russell Baze, 6, January 31, 1999

Track Records, Main Dirt
4 furlongs: Ima Dear, :46 2/5, April 2, 1935
4 1/2 furlongs: My Jasmine, :50.63, August 13, 1997
5 furlongs: Mr. Doubledown, :56.44, March 9, 2000
5 1/2 furlongs: Arches of Gold, 1:01:69, November 23, 1994
6 furlongs: Black Jack Road, 1:07 1/5, October 28, 1990
7 1/2 furlongs: Lookabout, 1:30 2/5, November 26, 1936
1 mile: Aristocratical, 1:33 3/5, November 10, 1983
1m 70 yds: Redress, 1:41 3/5, December 10, 1934
1 1/16 miles: Hoedown's Day, 1:38 2/5, October 23, 1983
1 1/8 miles: Super Moment, 1:46 1/5, December 13, 1980
1 3/16 miles: Force of Reason, 1:52 4/5, November 5, 1983

1 1/4 miles: Ask Father, 2:00 2/5, November 28, 1968
1 1/2 miles: Cattle Creek, 2:27 3/5, December 8, 1979
1 5/8 miles: Rag King, 2:43 1/5, December 15, 1990
1 3/4 miles: Tornillo, 2:57 3/5, November 21, 1936
Other: 3 1/2 furlongs, Harrogate, :40 4/5, March 16, 1935

Course Records, Main Turf

4 1/2 furlongs: Salta's Pride, :50.41, September 15, 1994
7 furlongs: First Flyer, 1:24.23, September 4, 1994
7 1/2 furlongs: Hegemony (Ire), 1:28 4/5, October 12, 1984
1 mile: Position's Best, 1:34 3/5, September 6, 1987
1 1/16 miles: Dreamer, 1:40.21, August 17, 1997
1 1/8 miles: Ocean Queen, 1:47.80, October 12, 1996
1 3/8 miles: Golden Doc Ray, 2:16 2/5, October 6, 1979
1 1/2 miles: Swiss Conviction, 2:31.46, October 12, 1998
2 miles: Lighting Star, 3:28.39, March 23, 1997

Fastest Times of 2001 (Dirt)

4 1/2 furlongs: Metatron, :50.59, May 24
5 furlongs: Black Eyed Lilly, :57.97, November 2
5 1/2 furlongs: Rio Oro, 1:01.60, October 7
6 furlongs: Lexicon, 1:07.94, September 8
1 mile: I'madrifter, 1:34.15, October 8
1 1/16 miles: Euchre, 1:41.69, May 28, Kolob, 1:41.69, May 26
1 1/8 miles: Takin It Deep, 1:49.25, April 14
Other: 2 furlongs, Black Gear, :21.69, April 11

Fastest Times of 2001 (Turf)

4 1/2 furlongs: Santano, :50.38, May 17
7 1/2 furlongs: Rhapsodist, 1:31.07, April 7
1 mile: Reddatore (Brz), 1:35.14, April 28
1 1/16 miles: Night Patrol, 1:41.35, October 28
1 3/8 miles: Janet (GB), 2:17.09, May 12

Del Mar

Known as the track "where the surf meets the turf," Del Mar is renowned today for its laid-back environment and rich purses. The Del Mar style is a legacy of the film stars who helped to build it, principally Bing Crosby and Pat O'Brien. But the track's beginnings were rocky. In the mid-1930s, the 22nd District Agricultural Association began to build a fair grounds with a one-mile racetrack and grandstand north of San Diego, and Crosby formed the Del Mar Turf Club to lease the facility for ten years. But the agricultural district soon ran out of money, and Crosby and O'Brien borrowed almost $600,000 to complete the project. The track opened on July 3, 1937, with Crosby greeting the first patron through the turnstiles. The following year, the crooner wrote "Where the Surf Meets the Turf" and sang it on opening day; it is played every day at the track today.

Del Mar was closed during World War II, serving as a Marines training center and an assembly center for B-17 wing ribs. It reopened in 1945, and the lease was extended through 1959. In 1970, a group of prominent California owners and breeders formed the Del Mar Thoroughbred Club and leased the facility for 20 years. The lease was extended for another 20 years in 1990. A rebuilt Del Mar grandstand and clubhouse costing $80-million were completed in 1993, two years after the first running of the track's signature event, the Pacific Classic Stakes (G1).

Location: 2260 Jimmy Durante Blvd., Del Mar, CA 92014-0700
Phone: (858) 755-1141
Fax: (858) 792-1477

E-mail: marys@dmtc.com
Web site: http://www.delmarracing.com
Year founded: 1937
Inaugural meeting: July 3-31, 1937
Acreage: 350
Number of stalls: 2,100
Seating capacity: 14,304

Officers

President: Joe Harper
Vice President: Craig R. Fravel
General Manager: Joe Harper
Director of Racing: Tom Robbins
Racing Secretary: Tom Robbins
Director of Operations: Tim Read
Director of Finance: Michael R. Ernst
Director of Marketing: Craig Dado
Director of Mutuels: Bill Navarro
Director of Publicity: Daniel G. Smith
Director of Sales: Josh Rubinstein
Director of Simulcasting: Denise Austin
Horsemen's Liaison: Lisa Iaria
Stewards: David Samuel, George Slender, Ingrid Fermin
Track Announcer: Trevor Denman
Track Photographer: Benoit and Associates
Track Superintendent: Steve Wood

Racing dates

2001: July 18-September 5, 43 days
2002: July 24-September 11, 43 days

Track Layout

Main circumference: 1 mile
Main track chute: 1 1/4 miles, 7 furlongs
Main width: 80 feet
Main length of stretch: 919 feet
Main turf circumference: 7 1/2 furlongs
Main turf chute: 1 1/8 miles diagonal
Main turf width: 63 feet
Main turf length of stretch: 761 feet
Training track: 1/2 mile

Attendance

Highest single meet record: 709,760, 1990
Record daily average for single meet: 19,776, 1985
Total attendance recent meeting: 664,594, 2001
Average daily recent meeting: 15,456, 2001
Highest single day record: 44,181, August 10, 1996

Handle

Single day on-track handle: $5,657,840, August 15, 1998
Single day total handle all sources: $22,857,785, August 15, 1998
Average all sources recent meeting: $12,055,268, 2001
Average on-track recent meeting: $2,319,552, 2001
Record daily average for single meet: $3,861,247, 1987
Total all sources recent meeting: $518.4-million, 2001
Total on-track recent meeting: $99,740,719, 2001

Mutuel Records

Highest Win: $130.70, *Cipria, September 1, 1955
Highest Exacta: $2,383, August 7, 1987
Highest Trifecta: $13,405.50, July 28, 1997
Highest Daily Double: $5,299.30, July 28, 1971
Highest Pick 3: $57,507.90, August 17, 1995
Highest Pick 6: $1,039,259.20, September 7, 1995
Highest Other Exotics: $133,013.40, Superfecta, September 6, 1998

Leaders

Career, leading jockey by stakes wins: Chris McCarron, 132
Career, leading jockey by titles: Bill Shoemaker, 7
Career, leading jockey by wins: Laffit Pincay Jr., 916
Career, leading owner by titles: Golden Eagle Farm, 6
Career, leading trainer by stakes wins: Charles Whittingham, 74

Del Mar, continued

Career, leading trainer by titles: Farrell W. Jones, 11
Career, leading trainer by wins: Ron McAnally, 387
Recent meeting, leading jockey: Alex Solis, 36, 2001
Recent meeting, leading owner: Juddmonte Farms, 11, 2001
Recent meeting, leading trainer: Bob Baffert, 29, 2001

Records

Single meet, leading jockey by wins: Bill Shoemaker, 94, 1954
Single meet, leading trainer by wins: R. H. McDaniel, 47, 1954
Single day jockey wins: Bill Shoemaker, 6, September 4, 1954; Rudy Rosales, 6, September 6, 1969; Laffit Pincay Jr., 6, July 28, 1976; Laffit Pincay Jr., 6, July 29, 1978
Single day trainer wins: R. H. "Red" McDaniel, 4, September 4, 1954; Farrell W. Jones, 4, August 13, 1963; Ron McAnally, 4, August 20, 1989; Jack Van Berg, 4, August 3, 1995

Track Records, Main Dirt

5 furlongs: Soldier Girl, :56 2/5, August 13, 1964
5 1/2 furlongs: Ack Ack, 1:02 1/5, September 12, 1970; Lakeside Trail, 1:02 1/5, August 18, 1974; Little Mustard, 1:02 1/5, September 5, 1974; Brainstorming, 1:02 1/5, August 28, 1991
6 furlongs: King of Cricket, 1:07 3/5, August 22, 1973
6 1/2 furlongs: Native Paster, 1:13 3/5, September 4, 1988
7 furlongs: Solar Launch, 1:20, August 10, 1990
1 mile: Precisionist, 1:33 1/5, August 1, 1988
1 1/16 miles: ; Windy Sands, 1:40, August 4, 1962; Native Diver, 1:40, August 7, 1965; Matching, 1:40, August 18, 1982
1 1/8 miles: Latin Touch, 1:46, September 1, 1979
1 3/16 miles: Four By Five, 1:56 2/5, August 16, 1954
1 1/4 miles: Bertrando, 1:59.55, August 21, 1993
1 1/2 miles: Spring Boy, 2:29 2/5, August 16, 1958
1 5/8 miles: Ormolu, 2:45, August 24, 1957
1 3/4 miles: Lurline B., 2:57 2/5, August 26, 1949
2 miles: Pilot Anne, 3:24 1/5, September 2, 1949

Course Records, Main Turf

7 1/2 furlongs: Syncopate, 1:27 4/5, August 24, 1981
1 mile: Crystal Hearted (GB), 1:33, July 30, 1999
1 1/16 miles: Ice Hot, 1:40, August 13, 1986
1 1/8 miles: Al Mamoon, 1:46 3/5, August 10, 1986
1 3/8 miles: Navarone, 2:12.56, August 14, 1992

Fastest Times of 2001 (Dirt)

5 furlongs: Newport Beach, :57.67, July 22
5 1/2 furlongs: Sunray Spirit, 1:03.10, August 19
6 furlongs: Kona Gold, 1:08.22, July 22
6 1/2 furlongs: Officer, 1:15.08, August 15
7 furlongs: El Corredor, 1:20.42, August 12
1 mile: El Corredor, 1:35.24, September 2
1 1/16 miles: Skimming, 1:41.62, July 29
1 1/8 miles: El Nativo, 1:50.78, August 25
1 1/4 miles: Skimming, 1:59.96, August 19

Fastest Times of 2001 (Turf)

1 mile: High Demand, 1:33.32, August 22
1 1/16 miles: Sarafan, 1:40.62, August 17
1 1/8 miles: Reddatore (Brz), 1:47.16, July 28
1 3/8 miles: Timboroa (GB), 2:12.59, August 25

Fairplex Park

For nearly 80 years, the Los Angeles County Fair Association has offered racing at Fairplex Park. In recent decades, the fair meet has given the major track Southern California circuit a welcome break between the Del Mar and Oak Tree meets in September. The inaugural Los Angeles County Fair was conducted in 1922, a five-day meet over a half-mile track. By the mid-1930s, after pari-mutuel wagering had been legalized in California,

the fair was extended to a 17-day meeting. With minor changes over the years, the meet has remained essentially the same.

The track, with its five-furlong configuration, has been the scene of some wild racing over the years. It also has witnessed tragedy; in 1999, jockey J. C. Gonzalez was killed in a spill at the track. In May 2002, Fairplex agreed to move the dates to Santa Anita Park, but that proposal sparked considerable opposition.

Location: 1101 W. McKinley Ave., Pomona, CA 91769
Phone: (909) 865-4545
Fax: (909) 865-3602
Web site: http://www.fairplex.com
Year founded: 1922
Inaugural meeting: 1922
Acreage: 487
Seating capacity: 10,000
Number of stalls: 1,306

Officers

President: James E. Henwood
General Manager: Michael Seder
Director of Racing: Neil O'Dwyer
Racing Secretary: Richard Wheeler
Director of Communications: Windy Talrico
Director of Finance: Mike Seder
Director of Marketing: Dale Coleman
Stewards: David Samuel, Tom Ward, Will Meyers
Track Announcer: Trevor Denman
Track Superintendent: Steve Wood

Racing dates

2001: September 6-September 24, 18 days
2002: September 13-September 29, 18 days

Track Layout

Main circumference: 5/8 mile
Main track chute: 1 1/8 miles, 1/4 mile
Main width: 75 feet
Main length of stretch: 660 feet

Attendance

Highest single meet record: 337,491, 1998
Record daily average for single meet: 18,749, 1998
Total attendance recent meeting: 121,497 est., 2001
Average daily record recent meeting: 6,750 est., 2001
Highest single day record: 28,300, September 25, 1948

Handle

Average on-track recent meeting: $713,010, 2000
Average all sources recent meeting: $5,750,000, 2001
Single day total handle all sources: $7,842,907, September 27, 1997
Total all sources recent meeting: $104-million, 2001

Mutuel Records

Highest Win: $182.20, Uncle Fox, September 21, 1976
Highest Exacta: $5,645, September 13, 1986
Highest Trifecta: $29,278.80, September 30, 1996
Highest Daily Double: $4,362.40, September 17, 1990
Highest Pick 6: $199,346.60, September 13, 1999
Highest Other Exotics: $30,497, $1 Superfecta, September 19, 2000

Leaders

Career, leading jockey by wins: Martin Pedroza, 293
Recent meeting, leading trainer: Jeff Mullins, 11, 2001
Career, leading jockey by stakes wins: David Flores, 51
Career, leading trainer by stakes wins: Mel Stute, 41
Career, leading trainer by wins: Mel Stute, 164
Recent meeting, leading jockey: Martin Pedroza, 29, 2001

Records

Single day trainer wins: Gordon Campbell, 4, September 30, 1967; Jerry Fanning, 4, September 24, 1984
Single day jockey wins: David Flores, 6, September 20, 1992; David Flores, 6, September 30, 1992

Track Records, Main Dirt

4 furlongs: Birds Nest Soup, :46.41, September 26, 2000
6 furlongs: Drouilly's Boy, 1:09 1/5, September 19, 1989

6 1/2 furlongs: Bundle of Iron, 1:15 1/5, September 23, 1986
7 furlongs: Best of Time, 1:22.66, September 16, 2000
1 1/16 miles: Monte Parnes (Arg), 1:41 3/5, September 29, 1990
1 1/8 miles: Dachi's Folly, 1:48 2/5, September 29, 1990
1 3/8 miles: Mummy's Pleasure, 2:15, September 28, 1986

Fastest Times of 2001
6 furlongs: Shabab, 1:10.33, September 20
6 1/2 furlongs: Creaseinherjeans, 1:16.41, September 18
7 furlongs: Thrillion, 1:23.21, September 23
1 1/16 miles: Taylorman (NZ), 1:43.35, September 8
1 3/8 miles: Nates Colony, 2:17.17, September 16

Ferndale

Location: 1250 Fifth St., Ferndale, CA 95536
Phone: (707) 786-9525
Fax: (707) 786-9450
Web site: http://www.calfairs.com
Number of stalls: 258 permanent, 200 portable
Seating capacity: 2,200

Officers
President: Don Becker
Vice President: Bill Branstetter
Racing Secretary: Charlie Palmer
Director of Mutuels: George Vidak
Director of Publicity: Stuart Titus
Track Announcer: John McGary

Racing dates
2001: August 9-August 19, 10 days
2002: August 8-August 18, 10 days

Track Layout
Main circumference: 1/2 mile
Main track chute: 5 furlongs, 7 furlongs
Main length of stretch: 530 feet

Leaders
Recent meeting, leading jockey: James E. Burns, 12, 2001
Recent meeting, leading trainer: Dennis Hopkins, 6, 2001

Fastest Times of 2001
5 furlongs: Cielo Canosa, :58.88, August 9; King's Honor, :58.88, August 15
6 1/2 furlongs: Sid's Jett, 1:19.81, August 17
7 furlongs: Panzeer (GB), 1:25.12, August 13
1 1/16 miles: My American Girl, 1:46.30, August 11
1 5/8 miles: Ironman Dehere, 2:50.75, August 19

Fresno

Location: 1121 Chance Ave., Fresno, CA 93702
Phone: (559) 650-3331
Fax: (559) 650-3226
Web site: http://www.fresnofair.com

Officers
President: Andriana Majarian
Vice President: Dean Thonesen
Director of Communications: Kristi Brangle
Director of Marketing: Sheri Durham

Racing dates
2001: October 3-October 14, 11 days
2002: October 2-October 14, 12 days

Leaders
Recent meeting, leading jockey: David B. Patton, 8, 2001
Recent meeting, leading trainer: Rene Amescua, 11, 2001

Fastest Times of 2001
5 furlongs: Tougherthantherest, :56.58, October 6
5 1/2 furlongs: Natural Style, 1:02.34, October 6
6 furlongs: Continental Peak, 1:08.55, October 13
1 mile: Lycka, 1:35.59, October 8

Golden Gate Fields

On April 29, 1949, a 19-year-old apprentice jockey from Texas named Bill Shoemaker rode Shafter V. to victory in the second race at Golden Gate Fields in Albany, California. That win marked the first of a then-record 8,833 victories for Shoemaker, a Racing Hall of Fame jockey. Several famous horses have raced at the San Francisco-area track, as well. Citation, the 1948 Triple Crown winner, defeated champion older male *Noor in the '50 Golden Gate Mile Handicap, setting a world record for one mile in the process. Silky Sullivan captured his first stakes victory in the 1957 Golden Gate Futurity and went on to win 12 of 27 career starts and earned more than $150,000.

On February 1941, entrepreneur Edward "Slip" Madigan opened the track, then known as the Albany Turf Club. The track closed after its first five days of racing due to flooding from heavy rains. During World War II, the United States Navy used Golden Gate as a landing base for amphibious craft. Racing resumed in 1947 after the water problem was resolved, and in '71 the track added a turf course. In 1989, Ladbroke Group purchased Golden Gate for $41-million. As it wound down its North American racing operations, Ladbroke sold the facility to Frank Stronach-led Magna Entertainment Corp. in 1999. The track's perennial leaders in recent years have been Racing Hall of Fame jockey Russell Baze and trainer Jerry Hollendorfer.

Location: 1100 Eastshore Hwy., Albany, CA 94710
Phone: (510) 559-7300
Fax: (510) 559-7467
E-mail: help@baymeadows.com
Web site: http://www.ggfields.com
Inaugural meeting: February 1, 1941, 33 days
Acreage: 225
Number of stalls: 1,425
Seating capacity: 14,750

Officers
President: James Nicol
General Manager: Peter W. Tunney
Racing Secretary: Daniel J. Eidson
Director of Operations: Calvin Rainey
Director of Marketing: Jim Rogers
Director of Mutuels: Bernice Thurman
Director of Publicity: Tom Ferrall
Director of Sales: Jim Rogers
Director of Simulcasting: Paul Porter
Stewards: Darrell McHargue, Dennis Nevin, John Herbuveaux
Track Announcer: Tony Calo
Track Photographer: William Vassar
Track Superintendent: Ken Krausch

Racing dates
2001: November 15, 2000 to April 4, 2001, 102 days
2002: November 17, 2001 to March 31, 2002, 101 days

Track Layout
Main circumference: 1 mile
Main width: 78 feet
Main length of stretch: 1,000 feet
Main turf circumference: 9/10 mile
Main turf chute: 3/16 mile
Main turf width: 65 feet

Mutuel Records
Highest Win: $322.60, Pasadena Slim, October 28, 1957
Highest Exacta: $2,270.20, January 18, 1997
Highest Trifecta: $38,689.20, January 18, 1997

Golden Gate Fields, continued

Highest Daily Double: $8,711.40, November 16, 1960
Highest Pick 3: $18,851, December 13, 1998
Highest Pick 6: $1,074,405.80, May 23, 1990
Highest Other Exotics: $15,771.10, Superfecta, November 28, 1998

Leaders

Recent meeting, leading jockey: Russell Baze, 139, 2000/2001
Recent meeting, leading trainer: Jerry Hollendorfer, 106, 2000/2001

Records

Single day jockey wins: Russell Baze, 7, April 16, 1992
Single day trainer wins: Walter Greenman, 5, November 25, 1970; Ace Gibson, 5, February 24, 1971; Jerry Hollendorfer, 5, May 1, 1996; Jerry Hollendorfer, 5, January 23, 1997

Track Records, Main Dirt

4 furlongs: Glenbar, :47, March 12, 1952, Giddy Up, :47, March 25, 1952
4 1/2 furlongs: Victory Found, :50.30, April 30, 1992
5 furlongs: Valley Land, :56 2/5, April 8, 1990
5 1/2 furlongs: Proudest Hour, 1:02, May 30, 1986
6 furlongs: El Dorado Shooter, 1:07.55, January 20, 2001
1 mile: Caros Love, 1:33, February 13, 1988
1 1/16 miles: Restless Con, 1:39.50, June 24, 1991
1 1/8 miles: Simply Majestic, 1:45, April 2, 1988
1 3/16 miles: Fleet Bird, 1:52 3/5, October 24, 1953
1 1/4 miles: *Noor, 1:58 1/5, June 24, 1950
1 3/8 miles: Forin Sea, 2:18 3/5, October 3, 1959
1 1/2 miles: Bo Donna, 2:29 2/5, June 8, 1979
1 3/4 miles: Sirmark, 2:57 1/5, October 16, 1948
2 miles: Mantourist, 3:25 4/5, October 23, 1948
Other: 2 furlongs, The Money Doctor, :21 4/5, February 21, 1975

Course Records, Main Turf

4 1/2 furlongs: Bonne Nuite, :50.58, May 22, 1994
5 furlongs: Black Tornado, :56, May 10, 1975; L'Natural, :56, May 28, 1977; Goldie's Goldian, :46, May 27, 1978
7 1/2 furlongs: Struttin' George, 1:28, May 5, 1979; His Honor, 1:28, April 25, 1981; Clever Song, 1:28, May 25, 1986
1 mile: Don Alberto, 1:33 2/5, March 22, 1980
1 1/16 miles: Announcer, 1:40 2/5, April 16, 1977
1 1/8 miles: Blues Traveller (Ire), 1:47.71, May 14, 1994
1 3/8 miles: John Henry, 2:13, May 6, 1984
1 1/2 miles: Silveyville, 2:27 2/5, June 10, 1984; Kings Island (Ire), 2:27 2/5, June 9, 1985; Val Danseur, 2:27 2/5, June 8, 1986
2 miles: Never-Rust, 3:25 3/5, June 26, 1988
Other: 2 3/8 miles, Situada (Chi), 4:10 4/5, June 25, 1990

Fastest Times of 2001 (Dirt)

5 furlongs: Out of a Dream, :57.07, November 30; The Lord's Tune, :57.07, December 26
5 1/2 furlongs: Booth Bay, 1:02.55, January 18; Barrybrown, 1:02.55, November 18
6 furlongs: El Dorado Shooter, 1:07.55, January 20
1 mile: Blade Prospector (Brz), 1:34.18, March 31
1 1/16 miles: Hoovergotthekeys, 1:40.85, March 10
1 1/8 miles: Kool, 1:50.62, January 13
Other: 2 furlongs, My Aim Is True, :21.64, March 30

Fastest Times of 2001 (Turf)

4 1/2 furlongs: Santano, :50.75, March 24
1 mile: Eagleton, 1:38.36, January 1
1 1/16 miles: Incitatus, 1:43.53, April 1
1 1/8 miles: Kalemberg (Brz), 1:52.03, March 25

Hollywood Park

Hollywood Park sprung to life in 1938 when the Hollywood Turf Club was formed with Warner Brothers executive Jack L. Warner as its chairman. A who's who of Hollywood power brokers, including actors (Ralph Bellamy), singers (Bing Crosby), and studio executives (Walt Disney, Darryl Zanuck) were among the original shareholders in the Inglewood, California, track.

Not everything has had a Hollywood ending at Hollywood Park, however. A fire in 1949 destroyed the club's physical plant and forced racing over to Santa Anita Park for one year. But the track reopened in time for a typical Hollywood fairy-tale finish when Citation won the 1951 Hollywood Gold Cup to become racing's first equine millionaire. Hollywood again was the backdrop of history 28 years later when Affirmed won the Hollywood Gold Cup (G1) to break racing's $2-million barrier. In 1983, John Henry became the first $4-million horse when he won the Hollywood Turf Cup (G1).

The first Breeders' Cup championship day was staged at Hollywood in 1984. The event returned in 1987 and again in '97.

Hollywood has not been immune from controversy. An expensive rebuilding of the track—including an extension of the track to 1⅛ miles and construction of a new clubhouse structure, the Pavilion of the Stars—preceded the first Breeders' Cup, and fans resented the moving of the finish line toward the new facility. A bitter fight for control of the track raged in the late 1980s and early '90s, and the struggle was resolved in February '91 when R. D. Hubbard wrested control from longtime executive Marjorie Lindheimer Everett in a proxy fight. Hubbard immediately launched a multi-million-dollar renovation program that spruced up the track and transformed the clubhouse pavilion into a card-club casino. As a part of that project, the finish line was returned to its original location. Through the 1980s and '90s, the Inglewood neighborhood deteriorated and was touched by the '92 Los Angeles riots.

In 1999, Churchill Downs Inc. bought Hollywood Park for $140-million. On December 10, 1999, Laffit Pincay Jr. became the winningest rider in racing history with a triumph at Hollywood Park, surpassing the record of 8,833 wins long held by Bill Shoemaker. History and dramatic events just have a way of maintaining their grip on the track the film industry built.

Location: 1050 S. Prairie Ave., Inglewood, CA 90306-0369
Phone: (310) 419-1500
Fax: (310) 672-4664
Web site: http://www.hollywoodpark.com
Year founded: 1938
Inaugural meeting: June 10, 1938
Acreage: 240
Seating capacity: 10,000
Number of stalls: 1,958

Officers

President: Rick Baedeker
Vice President: Don R. Richardson
General Manager: Eual Wyatt Jr.
Director of Racing: Martin Panza
Racing Secretary: Martin Panza
Director of Operations: Rick Baedeker
Director of Communications: Michael Mooney
Director of Marketing: Christy Tucker
Director of Publicity: Michael Mooney
Horsemen's Liaison: Diana Hudak
Stewards: George Slender, Pete Pedersen, Thomas Ward
Track Announcer: Vic Stauffer
Track Photographer: Benoit & Associates
Track Superintendent: Dennis Moore

Racing dates

2001: April 20-July 16, 2001, 66 days; November 7-December 17, 2001, 31 days
2002: April 24-July 21, 65 days; November 6-December 22

Track Layout
Main circumference: 1 1/8 miles
Main track chute: 7 1/2 furlongs
Main width: 92 feet
Main length of stretch: 991 feet
Main turf circumference: 1 mile
Main turf width: 64 feet
Main turf length of stretch: 990 feet
Training track: 1/2 mile

Attendance
Average daily recent meeting: 8,345, Spring/Summer-2001; 7,214, Fall 2001
Highest single meet record: 2,398,528, Spring/Summer-1980
Record daily average for single meet: 34,516, Spring/Summer-1965
Highest single day record: 80,348, May 4, 1980

Handle
Record daily average for single meet: $5,486,172, 1985
Average all sources recent meeting: $10,138,472, Spring/Summer-2001; $9,383,251, Fall 2001
Average on-track recent meeting: $2,060,590-Spring/Summer-2001; $1,674,185, Fall 2001
Single day on-track handle: $13,002,176, November 21, 1987
Single day total handle all sources: $67,096,242, November 2, 1997

Mutuel Records
Highest Win: $361.80, Family Flair, June 29, 1989
Highest Exacta: $6,989.40, May 11, 1991
Highest Trifecta: $28,294, July 17, 1997
Highest Daily Double: $6,141.60, July 10, 1962
Highest Pick 3: $137,200.20, December 17, 1993
Highest Pick 6: $774,014, June 27, 1997
Highest Other Exotics: $190,769.80, Superfecta, November 11, 1994

Leaders
Career, leading jockey by wins: Laffit Pincay Jr., 2,970
Career, leading owner by titles: Juddmonte Farms, 6
Career, leading trainer by titles: Robert Frankel, 12
Career, leading trainer by wins: Charlie Whittingham, 859
Recent meeting, leading jockey: Laffit Pincay Jr., 64, Spring/Summer-2001; Alex Solis, 54, Fall 2001
Recent meeting, leading trainer: Jack Carava, 22, Spring/Summer-2001; Bob Baffert, 22, Fall 2001
Career, leading jockey by stakes wins: Chris McCarron, 282
Career, leading jockey by titles: Bill Shoemaker, 18

Records
Single day trainer wins: Allen Drumheller Sr., 5, July 4, 1955
Single meet, leading jockey by wins: Laffit Pincay Jr., 148
Single meet, leading trainer by wins: Robert Frankel, 60
Single day jockey wins: Bill Shoemaker, 6, June 20, 1953; Laffit Pincay Jr., 6, May 27, 1968; Bill Shoemaker, 6, June 24, 1970; Kent Desormeaux, 6, July 3, 1992

Track Records, Main Dirt
4 1/2 furlongs: Bridge of Royalty, :50.59, May 4, 1995
5 furlongs: Magical Mile, :56 2/5, May 18, 1989; Goodtimesinexcess, :56.25, July 3, 1999
5 1/2 furlongs: Crescendo, 1:02.11, December 7, 2001
6 furlongs: Apalachee Ridge, 1:07.52, December 12, 1997
6 1/2 furlongs: Lucky Forever, 1:13.24, May 20, 1995
7 furlongs: Mazel Trick, 1:19.97, June 27, 1999
7 1/2 furlongs: Awesome Daze, 1:26.26, November 23, 1997
1 mile: Greinton (GB), 1:32 3/5, June 9, 1985
1 1/16 miles: Power Forward, 1:40, December 19, 1987; Crafty Friend, 1:40, July 12, 1997; New Journey, 1:40, November 27, 1997
1 1/8 miles: Gentlemen (Arg), 1:45.35, December 22, 1996
1 3/16 miles: Shorten Sail, 1:55.36, June 7, 1998
1 1/4 miles: Greinton (GB), 1:58 2/5, June 23, 1985
1 3/8 miles: Lovely One (Arg), 2:14.42, May 7, 1994
1 5/8 miles: Ol' Henry, 2:42.50, June 27, 1997
1 3/4 miles: Roman Cuzzin, 2:56.77, July 21, 1997

Course Records, Main Turf
5 1/2 furlongs: Pembroke, 1:00.46, July 15, 1995
6 furlongs: Answer Do, 1:07, December 15, 1990
1 mile: Megan's Interco, 1:32.64, May 22, 1994
1 1/16 miles: Fantastic Fellow, 1:38.77, April 26, 1998
1 1/8 miles: Fastness (Ire), 1:44.78, November 25, 1995
1 3/16 miles: Kudos, 1:51.99, April 25, 2001
1 1/4 miles: Bien Bien, 1:57.75, May 31, 1993
1 1/2 miles: Talloires, 2:23.55, July 21, 1996

Fastest Times of 2001 (Dirt)
4 1/2 furlongs: Fonz's, :51.45, May 12
5 furlongs: Expected Program, :56.81, May 26
5 1/2 furlongs: Crescendo, 1:02.11, December 7
6 furlongs: Go Go, 1:08.09, June 2
6 1/2 furlongs: Waki American, 1:14.95, December 8
7 furlongs: Early Flyer, 1:20.42, May 28
7 1/2 furlongs: Favorite Funtime, 1:28.03, November 23
1 1/16 miles: Smile Again, 1:41.74, July 7
1 1/8 miles: Skimming, 1:48.12, June 10
1 3/16 miles: Dig for It, 1:54.85, May 30
1 1/4 miles: Aptitude, 2:01.79, July 1

Fastest Times of 2001 (Turf)
5 1/2 furlongs: Gibson County, 1:01.23, July 16
1 mile: I've Decided, 1:33.67, July 12
1 1/16 miles: Designed for Luck, 1:39.63, June 14
1 1/8 miles: Kalypso Katie (Ire), 1:47.22, May 2
1 3/16 miles: Kudos, 1:51.99, April 25
1 1/4 miles: Bienamado, 1:59.34, June 10
1 1/2 miles: Blueprint (Ire), 2:26.16, July 15

Los Alamitos Race Course

Thoroughbreds have competed at Los Alamitos Race Course in Cypress, California, since 1994, when the track received permission to begin offering races for the breed. Los Alamitos primarily has been known as a Quarter Horse track since 1947 when nonpari-mutuel racing debuted at the track built by Frank Vessels on his ranch. In 1951, Los Alamitos received approval to begin holding pari-mutuel racing. After Vessels's death in 1963, his son Frank Vessels Jr. took over operation of the track, which five years later began offering night racing. After Vessels Jr.'s death in 1974, his wife, Millie, assumed the track's presidency and became one of the first women to hold a leadership position in Thoroughbred racing. In 1984, Los Alamitos was sold to Hollywood Park and entered a period of decline. Five years later, businessmen and harness racing interests Lloyd Arnold and Chris Bardis bought the facility. Edward C. Allred, a physician and the all-time leading breeder of Quarter Horses by earnings, then purchased a majority interest in Los Alamitos and today is sole owner of the track, which also offers Paint, Appaloosa, and Arabian racing.

Location: 4961 Katella Ave., Los Alamitos, CA 90720
Phone: (714) 995-1234
Fax: (714) 995-6276
E-mail: larace@losalamitos.com
Web site: http://www.losalamitos.com
Year founded: 1951
Inaugural meeting: 1951
Number of stalls: 1,400
Seating capacity: 13,000

Officers
President: H. Rick Henson
General Manager: H. Rick Henson
Director of Racing: Ron Church
Racing Secretary: Ron Church

Los Alamitos, continued

Secretary: G. Michael Lyon
Treasurer: Kathleen Chavez
Director of Operations: Howard Knuchell
Director of Marketing: Jeff True
Director of Mutuels: Bob DiGiovanni
Director of Publicity: Orlando Gutieriez
Director of Sales: Vandi Ekins
Director of Simulcasting: Jeff True
Horsemen's Liaison: Vandi Ekins
Stewards: Albert Christensen, Merlin Volske
Track Announcer: Ed Burgart
Track Photographer: Scott Martinez
Track Superintendent: Frank Sabato

Racing dates
2001: April 29-December 16
2002: January 4-December 29

Track Layout
Main circumference: 5 furlongs
Main track chute: 550 yards
Main length of stretch: 1/8 mile
Inner circumference: 5 furlongs
Inner track chute: 550 yards
Training track: 5 furlongs

Attendance
Average daily recent meeting: 5,588, 2000
Highest single day record: 19,970, May 6, 1983
Highest single meet record: 1,046,158, 1994
Lowest single meet record: 33,833, 1951
Record daily average for single meet: 9,492, 1970

Handle
Average all sources recent meeting: $1,276,936, 2000
Average on-track recent meeting: $318,745, 2000
Record daily average for single meet: $1,276,936, 2000
Single day on-track handle: $2,127,758, June 30, 1995

Leaders
Career, leading trainer by wins: Charles S. Treece, 182
Recent meeting, leading jockey: Jorge Bourdieu, 34, 2000
Recent meeting, leading owner: James Mancuso, 4, 2000; Jimmy B. Bright, 4, 2000
Recent meeting, leading trainer: Charles S. Treece, 27, 2000

Track Records, Main Dirt
4 1/2 furlongs: Valiant Pete, :49 2/5, August 11, 1990

Fastest Times of 2001
4 1/2 furlongs: Twilight Career, :50.50, February 23

Oak Tree at Santa Anita

In 1968, Southern California horsemen Clement Hirsch, Jack K. Robbins, and Louis R. Rowan approached Santa Anita Park President Robert P. Strub with a proposal for a brief, high-quality fall meet at the Arcadia track. Except for the brief Fairplex Park meet, the Southern California racing calendar was empty between the close of Del Mar in September and the opening of Santa Anita's winter-spring meet each December 26. (Hollywood Park then had only a spring-summer meet.) Strub initially resisted, but Santa Anita officials finally agreed to try a fall meet under the auspices of the Oak Tree Racing Association, headed by Hirsch, in October 1969. In case the idea flopped, Oak Tree's directors had to guarantee the first day's purses. The initial 20-day fall meet was a success, and Oak Tree has become an important part of the racing scene in Southern California and nationally.

Oak Tree secured rights to stage the third Breeders' Cup championship day in 1986, and the event attracted an on-track crowd of 69,155, the largest crowd to that point. Oak Tree also played host to the championship day in 1993. In addition, Oak Tree's stakes serve as leading prep races for the Breeders' Cup championship events. Oak Tree was scheduled to host the Breeders' Cup championship again in 2000 and '02, but construction projects of the track's new owner, Frank Stronach-controlled Magna Entertainment Corp., forced shifts to other sites. Oak Tree, which now runs a 32-day meet, is scheduled to be the host for the 2003 Breeders' Cup championship. Hirsch died in 2000 and was succeeded as Oak Tree president by Robbins.

Location: 285 W. Huntington St., Arcadia, CA 91007-3439
Phone: (626) 574-6352
Fax: (626) 446-5803
Web site: http://www.santaanita.com
Inaugural meeting: October 7, 1969

Officers
Executive Vice President: Sherwood Chillingworth
General Manager: F. Jack Liebau
Director of Racing: Michael J. Harlow
Racing Secretary: Michael J. Harlow
Director of Marketing: Stuart Zanville
Director of Publicity: Stuart Zanville
Track Photographer: Benoit & Associates

Racing dates
2001: September 26-November 5, 32 days
2002: October 2-November 3

Attendance
Total attendance recent meeting: 337,024, 2001
Record daily average for single meet: 30,469, 1993
Average daily average recent meeting: 10,532, 2001
Highest single day record: 69,155, November 1, 1986
Highest single meet record: 858,652, 1985

Handle
Single day on-track handle: $15,410,409, November 1, 1986
Average all sources recent meeting: $10,111,519, 2001
Average on-track recent meeting: $2,348,877, 2001
Record daily average for single meet: $10,237,220, 1998
Single day total handle all sources: $36,264,799, November 6, 1993
Total all sources recent meeting: $323,568,604, 2001
Total on-track recent meeting: $75,164,079, 2001

Mutuel Records
Highest Win: $269.20, Arcangues, November 6, 1993
Highest Exacta: $1,834.60, October 19, 1997
Highest Trifecta: $15,805.40, October 19, 1997
Highest Daily Double: $5,000, October 13, 1990
Highest Pick 3: $174,331.80, October 18, 1991
Highest Pick 6: $1,010,221.20, October 19, 1994
Highest Other Exotics: $51,713.70, Superfecta, November 6, 1998

Leaders
Career, leading jockey by stakes wins: Chris McCarron, 72
Career, leading jockey by wins: Laffit Pincay Jr., 611
Career, leading trainer by stakes wins: Charles Whittingham, 68
Career, leading trainer by wins: Ronald McAnally, 225
Recent meeting, leading jockey: Laffit Pincay Jr., 31, 2001
Recent meeting, leading owner: Juddmonte Farms, 4, 2001
Recent meeting, leading trainer: William Spawr, 11, 2001

Records
Single day jockey wins: Steve Valdez, 6, October 15, 1973; Darrel McHargue, 6, October 25, 1979; Patrick Valenzuela, 6, October 21, 1988; Martin Pedroza, 6, October 31, 1992

Track Records, Main Dirt
5 furlongs: Zero Henry, :57.78, October 23, 1996
5 1/2 furlongs: Davy Be Good, 1:02.17, November 14, 1993
6 furlongs: Beira, 1:07 4/5, October 13, 1974; Grenzen, 1:07 4/5, October 7, 1978; Hawkin's Special, 1:07 4/5, October 27, 1978
6 1/2 furlongs: Enjoy the Moment, 1:14.15, October 8, 1998
7 furlongs: Ancient Title, 1:20 4/5, October 18, 1972
1 mile: Salud y Pesetas, 1:33 4/5, October 7, 1987
1 1/16 miles: Cajun Prince, 1:40 1/5, October 9, 1982
1 1/8 miles: My Sonny Boy, 1:46, November 3, 1990
1 1/4 miles: King Pellinore, 2:00, November 6, 1976
1 1/2 miles: Whisk Spree, 2:29.17, October 16, 1993

Course Records, Main Turf
6 1/2 furlongs: Comininalittlehot, 1:11.57, October 27, 1996
1 mile: Urgent Request (Ire), 1:32.44, October 5, 1996
1 1/16 miles: Manistique, 1:42.39, October 10, 1999
1 1/8 miles: Kostroma (Ire), 1:43.92, October 20, 1991
1 1/4 miles: Double Discount, 1:57 2/5, October 9, 1977
1 1/2 miles: Hawkster, 2:22 4/5, October 14, 1989

Fastest Times of 2001 (Dirt)
5 1/2 furlongs: Rio Oro, 1:02.45, November 3
6 furlongs: Swept Overboard, 1:07.67, October 6

Fastest Times of 2001 (Turf)
1 mile: Quake, 1:32.55, September 28
1 1/4 miles: Janet (GB), 1:58.64, September 29
1 1/2 miles: Cagney (Brz), 2:26.10, September 28

Pleasanton

Location: 4501 Pleasanton Ave., Pleasanton, CA 94566
Phone: (925) 426-7519
Fax: (925) 426-7599
Web site: http://www.calfairs.com
Number of stalls: 700
Seating capacity: 6,608

Officers
President: Billie Sherwood
Vice President: Tim Koopmann
General Manager: Rick K. Pickering
Director of Racing: Greg Brent
Racing Secretary: Greg Brent
Director of Finance: Ted Holder
Director of Mutuels: Bernice Thurman
Director of Publicity: Kelly Robinson
Director of Simulcasting: Jeanne Wasserman
Track Superintendent: Paul Wayt

Racing dates
2001: June 27-July 8, 12 days
2002: June 26-July 7, 12 days

Track Layout
Main circumference: 1 mile
Main track chute: 2 furlongs, 6 furlongs
Main width: 60 feet
Main length of stretch: 1,085 feet

Handle
Average on-track recent meeting: $3,301,562, 2000

Leaders
Recent meeting, leading jockey: Jason P. Lumpkins, 17, 2001
Recent meeting, leading trainer: Art Sherman, 5, 2001; Brian J. Koriner, 5, 2001; Charles J. Jenda, 5, 2001

Fastest Times of 2001
4 1/2 furlongs: Hurricane Smoke, :52.08, June 28
5 furlongs: Kiss an Angel, :56.68, July 1
5 1/2 furlongs: Georgieinexcess, 1:03.29, July 7
6 furlongs: Flom's Prospector, 1:08.80, June 30; No Wager, 1:08.80, June 27; Tannersmyman, 1:08.80, July 8
1m 70yds: Ingenious (Ire), 1:40.44, July 7
1 1/16 miles: Reds Superstar, 1:40.60, July 8

Sacramento

Location: 1600 Exposition Blvd., Sacramento, CA 95815
Phone: (916) 263-4677
Fax: (916) 263-3198
Web site: http://www.calfairs.com
Seating capacity: 7,100
Number of stalls: 1,000

Officers
General Manager: Norb Bartosik
Director of Racing: David Elliott
Racing Secretary: Grant Baker
Director of Mutuels: George Vidak
Director of Publicity: David Elliott
Track Announcer: Joe Alto
Track Superintendent: Steve Wood

Racing dates
2001: August 22-September 3, 12 days
2002: August 21-September 2, 12 days

Track Layout
Main circumference: 1 mile
Main track chute: 1 1/4 miles, 6 furlongs
Main length of stretch: 990 feet

Leaders
Recent meeting, leading jockey: Miguel Gaeta Hernandez, 13, 2001
Recent meeting, leading trainer: Clay Brinson, 3, 2001; Dan L. Harrell, 3, 2001; Jeff Bonde, 3, 2001; Jelina Pike, 3, 2001; Rene Amescua, 3, 2001; T. J. Stewart, 3, 2001

Fastest Times of 2001
5 furlongs: Crooked Key, :57.20, August 24
5 1/2 furlongs: Answered Prayer, 1:02.80, September 2
6 furlongs: Love That Lion, 1:08.00, August 26
1 mile: Tenny, 1:34.60, August 22
1 1/16 miles: Valuable Resources, 1:43.80, August 26
1 1/8 miles: Reds Superstar, 1:47.80, August 25
1 1/4 miles: New Journey, 2:02.80, September 3

Santa Anita Park

With the San Bernardino Mountains as a backdrop, an undulating downhill turf course, and an abundance of quality racing, Santa Anita Park symbolizes racing's possibilities. On a big race day, with a sizable crowd in the stands and quality Thoroughbreds on the track, the Arcadia, California, track is one of the world's finest facilities.

The story of Santa Anita is told in two parts. The first part is the original track, the dream of early 20th century California entrepreneur E. J. "Lucky" Baldwin. Opened in 1907, the track gave Los Angeles racing fans a tantalizing glimpse of racing as an opulent spectacle. But Baldwin's death two years later and the lack of legal pari-mutuel wagering in California postponed the Santa Anita dream until the 1930s.

When pari-mutuel wagering was legalized in 1933, the Los Angeles Turf Club was organized and built a $1-million facility near the site of Baldwin's track. Opened in 1934, the track's inaugural 1934-'35 racing season featured two races that immediately had an impact on the national racing calendar, the Santa Anita Handicap and the Santa Anita Derby. Now Grade 1 races, they continue to have an important place on the spring schedule.

With a $100,000 purse for its inaugural running, the Big 'Cap immediately became one of America's best-

Santa Anita Park, continued

known races. The race and its $1-million purse today draw some of the best handicap runners from around North America. The Santa Anita Derby is one of the top Kentucky Derby (G1) prep races and has been utilized by recent Derby winners Silver Charm, Real Quiet, and Charismatic.

Legendary jockey Bill Shoemaker rode in his final race at Santa Anita in February 1990. And the track hosts the noted Oak Tree Racing Association meet each fall. Not all of the action has revolved around the track, however. Canadian industrialist Frank Stronach purchased the track in December 1998, the first purchase in what would become Magna Entertainment Corp.'s chain of racetracks. Stronach, Magna's chairman, has undertaken some controversial improvements and has unveiled plans to expand the track to include an entertainment center.

Location: 285 W. Huntington St., Arcadia, CA 91007-3439
Phone: (626) 574-7223
Fax: (626) 446-1456
E-mail: info@santaanita.com
Web site: http://www.santaanita.com
Year founded: 1907
Inaugural meeting: December 25, 1934
Acreage: 323
Number of stalls: 2,000
Seating capacity: 19,249

Officers
President: F. Jack Liebau
Vice Presidents: Craig Dado, Mike Scalzo
General Manager: Brant Latta
Director of Racing: Michael J. Harlow
Racing Secretary: Michael J. Harlow
Director of Marketing: Stuart A. Zanville
Director of Publicity: Stuart A. Zanville
Track Announcer: Trevor Denman

Racing dates
2001: December 26, 2000 to April 16, 2001, 83 days
2002: December 26, 2001 to April 21, 2002, 85 days

Track Layout
Main circumference: 1 mile
Main track chute: 1 1/4 miles, 7 furlongs
Main width: 85 feet
Main length of stretch: 900 feet
Main turf chute: 1 1/2 miles
Main turf length of stretch: 1,408 feet

Attendance
Average daily recent meeting: 10,486, 2000/2001
Highest single day record: 85,527, March 3, 1985
Highest single meet record: 2,936,086, 1983/1984
Record daily average for single meet: 35,247, 1946/1947
Total attendance recent meeting: 870,338, 2000/2001

Handle
Record daily average for single meet: $11,949,188
Total all sources recent meeting: $921,414,831, 2000/2001
Total on-track recent meeting: $203,283,439, 2000/2001
Single day total handle all sources: $36,264,799, November 6, 1993
Single day on-track handle: $15,410,409, November 1, 1986
Average all sources recent meeting: $11,101,384, 2000/2001
Average on-track recent meeting: $2,449,198, 2000/2001

Mutuel Records
Highest Win: $673.40, Playmay, February 4, 1938

Highest Exacta: $5,208.80, December 26, 1995
Highest Trifecta: $80,883.40, December 26, 1995
Highest Daily Double: $5,000, October 3, 1990
Highest Pick 3: $73,527.30, February 16, 1997
Highest Pick 6: $1,020,221.20, October 16, 1994
Highest Other Exotics: $151,713.70, Superfecta, November 6, 1998

Leaders
Career, leading jockey by stakes wins: William Shoemaker, 260
Career, leading jockey by wins: Laffit Pincay Jr., 2,669
Career, leading trainer by stakes wins: Charles Whittingham, 204
Career, leading trainer by wins: Charles Whittingham, 869
Recent meeting, leading jockey: Laffit Pincay Jr., 73, 2000/2001
Recent meeting, leading owner: The Thoroughbred Corp., 12, 2000/2001
Recent meeting, leading trainer: Bob Baffert, 44, 2000/2001

Records
Single day jockey wins: Laffit Pincay Jr., 7, March 14, 1987
Single day trainer wins: Clyde Van Dusen, 4, February 6, 1941; Farrell Jones, 4, January 5, 1962; M. E. "Buster" Millerick, 4, December 29, 1965; Charles Whittingham, 4, February 9, 1967; Bobby Frankel, 4, January 3, 1976; Bobby Frankel, 4, March 26, 1981; Richard Mandella, 4, November 6, 1993 (all stakes); Mike Mitchell, 4, January 13, 1995

Track Records, Main Dirt
4 furlongs: Valiant Pete, :44 1/5, April 20, 1991
4 1/2 furlongs: Willy Float, :51 2/5, March 23, 1972
5 furlongs: Zero Henry, :57.78, October 23, 1996
5 1/2 furlongs: Kona Gold, 1:01.74, January 3, 1999
6 furlongs: Sunny Blossom, 1:07 1/5, December 30, 1989
6 1/2 furlongs: Son of a Pistol, 1:13.71, April 4, 1998
7 furlongs: Spectacular Bid, 1:20, January 5, 1980
1 mile: Ruhlmann, 1:33 2/5, March 5, 1989
1 1/16 miles: Efervescente (Arg), 1:39.18, January 6, 1993
1 1/8 miles: Star Spangled, 1:45 4/5, March 24, 1979
1 1/4 miles: Spectacular Bid, 1:57 4/5, February 8, 1980
1 3/8 miles: Be Faithful, 2:15 1/5, February 9, 1946
1 1/2 miles: Queen's Hustler, 2:27 1/5, February 19, 1973
1 5/8 miles: Ace Admiral, 2:39 4/5, July 23, 1949
1 3/4 miles: *Noor, 2:52 4/5, March 4, 1950
2 miles: Durango, 3:26 1/5, February 2, 1935; Fuego, 3:26 1/5, June 30, 1945; Jimmy John, 3:26 1/5, March 9, 1946
Other: 2 furlongs, Beautiful Moment, :21, April 3, 1996; 3 furlongs, King Rhymer, :32, February 27, 1947; 2 1/4 miles, English Harry, 3:55 3/5, February 16, 1940; 2 1/2 miles, Big Ed, 4:22, February 23, 1940; 3 miles, 5:20 1/5, English Harry, March 1, 1940

Course Records, Main Turf
1 mile: Atticus, 1:31.89, March 1, 1997
1 1/8 miles: Kostroma (Ire), 1:43.92, October 20, 1991
1 1/4 miles: Double Discount, 1:57 2/5, October 9, 1977; Bequest, 1:57.50, March 31, 1991
1 1/2 miles: Hawkster, 2:22 4/5, October 14, 1989
1 3/4 miles: Marlin, 2:44.56, April 20, 1997

Fastest Times of 2001 (Dirt)
6 1/2 furlongs: Weatherbug, 1:14.65, January 12
7 furlongs: Affluent, 1:21.29, December 29
1 mile: Congaree, 1:34.37, February 28
1 1/16 miles: Golden Ballet, 1:41.83, March 10
1 1/8 miles: Point Given, 1:47.77, April 7
1 1/4 miles: Tiznow, 2:01.55, March 3
1 1/2 miles: Clonmany (Ire), 2:31.10, February 24
Other: 2 furlongs, Fast Silver, :21.53, March 22; 2 furlongs, Georgia's Storm, :21.53, April 13

Fastest Times of 2001 (Turf)
1 1/8 miles: Lazy Lode (Arg), 1:45.95, March 15

Santa Rosa

Location: 1350 Bennett Valley Rd., Santa Rosa, CA 95403
Phone: (707) 545-6206
Fax: (707) 573-9342
Web site: http://www.sonomacountyfair.com
Number of stalls: 1,022

Officers
President: Les Perry
General Manager: G. James Moore
Racing Secretary: C. Gregory Brent Jr.
Director of Finance: Roger Hayes
Director of Mutuels: George Vidak
Director of Publicity: Mary Cilley
Track Announcer: Vic Stauffer

Racing dates
2001: July 25-August 6, 12 days
2002: July 24-August 5, 12 days

Track Layout
Main circumference: 1 mile
Main track chute: 1 1/4 miles, 6 furlongs
Main length of stretch: 1,145.8 feet

Leaders
Recent meeting, leading jockey: Russell A. Baze, 14, 2001
Recent meeting, leading trainer: Armando Lage, 6, 2001

Fastest Times of 2001
4 1/2 furlongs: Miss Tralee, :50.57, July 30
5 furlongs: Red Reigning, :57.53, August 2
5 1/2 furlongs: Prized Match, 1:02.59, August 6
6 furlongs: Northern Palisades, 1:10.37, July 25
1 mile: Endymion, 1:35.14, August 2
1 1/16 miles: Two On the Aisle, 1:41.35, July 29

Stockton

Location: 1658 Airport Wy., Sherman, CA 95205
Phone: (209) 466-5041
Fax: (209) 466-5739
Web site: http://www.calfairs.com
Inaugural meeting: August 1934
Number of stalls: 800

Officers
President: Louis Souza
Vice President: Nanette Martin
General Manager: Forrest J. White
Director of Racing: Forrest J. White
Racing Secretary: Robert Moreno
Director of Mutuels: George Vidak
Director of Publicity: Lea Isetti
Track Announcer: John McGary

Racing dates
2001: June 13-June 24, 10 days
2002: June 12-June 23, 10 days

Track Layout
Main circumference: 1 mile
Main track chute: 1 1/4 miles, 6 furlongs
Main width: 80 feet

Handle
Average on-track recent meeting: $1,542,473, 2000

Leaders
Recent meeting, leading jockey: Ricky L. Frazier, 8, 2001
Recent meeting, leading trainer: Terri Eaton, 5, 2001

Fastest Times of 2001
4 1/2 furlongs: Eishin Boss, :51.66, June 17
5 1/2 furlongs: Anniversary Year, 1:03.54, June 15
6 furlongs: In Your Thoughts, 1:09.30, June 17
1 mile: Wing On Wing, 1:36.89, June 20

Vallejo

Location: 900 Fairgrounds Dr., Vallejo, CA 94589
Phone: (707) 644-4455
Fax: (707) 642-7947
Year founded: 1950
Number of stalls: 884

Officers
President: Raymond Simonds
General Manager: Kim Myrman
Director of Racing: Greg Brent
Racing Secretary: Greg Brent
Treasurer: Richard Martinez
Director of Mutuels: George Vidak
Track Announcer: John McGary

Racing dates
2001: July 11-July 23, 12 days
2002: July 10-July 21, 11 days

Track Layout
Main circumference: 7 furlongs
Main track chute: 6 furlongs
Main length of stretch: 1,085 feet

Handle
Average on-track recent meeting: $2,801,219, 2000

Leaders
Recent meeting, leading jockey: Russell A. Baze, 15, 2001
Recent meeting, leading trainer: Jerry Hollendorfer, 6, 2001

Fastest Times of 2001
4 1/2 furlongs: Smokin Johnnie, :52.38, July 23
5 furlongs: O too Kool, :57.78, July 19
5 1/2 furlongs: Phone Prospector, 1:03.79, July 20
6 furlongs: Rio Oro, 1:09.80, July 19
1 mile: The Candi Kid, 1:36.89, July 19
1 1/16 miles: Delightful Reef, 1:44.55, July 16

Colorado

Arapahoe Park

One of racing's quiet survivors, Denver-area Arapahoe Park has survived a disastrous launch, increased gambling competition, and disputes with horsemen to remain a summer racing fixture in the Rocky Mountains region.

The track opened in the mid-1980s, replacing longtime Denver track Centennial Park. But its location southeast of Denver was far from any interstate highways; interest in the track was negligible, and it was closed for several years after its opening.

The track reopened in the early 1990s but has struggled to develop a fan base amid competition from a state lottery and Indian casinos, which were legalized in the early '90s. A dispute between the track's current owner, Wembley USA, and horsemen over racing dates nearly forced the cancellation of the 2000 race meet.

The future may be brighter for Arapahoe, however. In August 2001, new Wembley USA chief executive officer Ty Howard said he planned to develop some of the nonracing real estate around the track to increase revenue and to attract more people to its rural location. He also has lobbied for video lottery terminals.

Location: 26000 E. Quincy Ave., Aurora, CO 80016
Phone: (303) 690-2400

Arapahoe, continued

Fax: (303) 690-6730
E-mail: Arapahoe@Wembleyusa.com
Web site: http://www.wembleyusa.com/arapahoe
Acreage: 297
Number of stalls: 1,495
Seating capacity: 8,400

Officers

President: Skip Sherman
General Manager: Jim Gartland
Director of Racing: Bill Powers
Racing Secretary: Bill Powers
Director of Operations: Frank Borowitz
Director of Marketing: Stacy Dysart
Director of Mutuels: Nancy O'Neal
Director of Simulcasting: Frank Borowitz
Track Superintendent: Paul Guerrieri

Racing dates

2001: June 8-August 26, 37 days
2002: June 7-September 2, 41 days

Track Layout

Main circumference: 1 mile
Main track chute: 1 5/16 miles, 6 furlongs, 7 furlongs
Main width: 90 feet
Main length of stretch: 1,029 feet

Leaders

Recent meeting, leading jockey: Daryl Montoya, 50, 2001
Recent meeting, leading owner: Tangarae Farms LLP, 19, 2000
Recent meeting, leading trainer: Ramon O. Gonzalez, 30, 2001

Track Records, Main Dirt

4 furlongs: Pleasant Harmony, :46.40, June 25, 1995
4 1/2 furlongs: North of Hollywood, :52.20, May 14, 1993
5 furlongs: Axe Age, :56.60, August 2, 1992
5 1/2 furlongs: Polly's Enchantment, 1:02.60, May 8, 1993
6 furlongs: Jumbled Pete, 1:08.80, August 23, 1993
6 1/2 furlongs: Pray for Booger, 1:18.60, August 25, 1995
7 furlongs: Shattuck, 1:22.60, August 20, 1995
1 mile: Honor Bright, 1:35.20, August 7, 1993
1m 70 yds: Naskra's Advocate, 1:38.20, July 23, 1993
1 1/16 miles: I'm A Gene, 1:43, July 25, 1992
1 1/8 miles: Glaring, 1:50.20, August 13, 1995
1 1/4 miles: Builder's Boy, 2:05.40, June 26, 1992
1 1/2 miles: Luedke, 2:35.80, July 30, 1994
2 miles: Little Reeves, 3:28.40, August 27, 1994

Fastest Times of 2001

4 1/2 furlongs: Gone With the Win, :52.20, June 24
5 furlongs: Jomax, :57, August 18
5 1/2 furlongs: Crafty Cindy, 1:03.20, June 22
6 furlongs: Komax, 1:09, June 30
7 furlongs: Debatable, 1:22.00, August 11
1 mile: Out 'n About, 1:37, August 5
1 1/16 miles: Tangarae Tango, 1:43.40, August 10
1 1/8 miles: Out 'n About, 1:50, August 19
1 3/4 miles: Bold Sundance, 3:06.60, August 26

Delaware

Delaware Park

Competition from racetracks in neighboring Pennsylvania and New Jersey forced the closure of historic Delaware Park in Stanton, Delaware, near Wilmington in September 1982. In late 1983, Maryland developer William Rickman Sr. acquired Delaware Park in part-nership with Maryland horseman William Christmas, and the track ran abbreviated meets in the spring and fall of '84. Rickman's son, William Rickman Jr., managed track operations and in 1994 helped to secure state approval for installing slot machines in the track. Delaware's slots facility opened in December 1995, and revenues from the slots have more than tripled purses.

The track, which today also offers Arabian racing, was designed by banker and horseman William duPont Jr. and became a haven for summer racing fans throughout the Mid-Atlantic region. The track's richest race, the Delaware Handicap (G3), debuted in 1937 as the New Castle Handicap and has been won by some of the sport's leading fillies and mares.

Location: 777 Delaware Park Blvd., Stanton, DE 19804
Phone: (302) 994-2521
Fax: (302) 998-1216
E-mail: programs@delpark.com
Web site: http://www.delpark.com
Year founded: 1936
Inaugural meeting: June 26, 1937

Officers

President: William M. Rickman Jr.
General Manager: Andrew Gentile
Director of Racing: Greg Pettciewicz
Racing Secretary: Sam Abbey
Director of Operations: James Hartman
Director of Communications: Mike McGinnis
Director of Finance: Joseph Lofink
Director of Marketing: Pam Cunningham
Director of Mutuels: Richard Sobocinski
Director of Publicity: Chris Sobocinski
Director of Simulcasting: Dave Lermond
Horsemen's Liaison: Sam Abbey
Stewards: Fritz Burkhardt, Jack Houghton, Lisa Comer
Track Announcer: John Curran
Track Photographer: Mary Lyons
Track Superintendent: Ed Lyons
Other Officials: Joe DeFrancesco, CEO and Director of Slots; William Fasy, Chief Operating Officer; William M. Rickman Sr., Chairman

Racing dates

2001: April 7-November 4, 140 days
2002: April 27-November 17, 139 days

Track Layout

Main circumference: 1 mile
Main track chute: 1 1/4 miles, 6 furlongs
Main width: 100 feet
Main length of stretch: 995 feet
Main turf circumference: 7 furlongs
Main turf chute: 1/8 mile

Attendance

Highest single day record: 35,473, July 5, 1954

Handle

Single day total handle all sources: $3,776,048, July 26, 1998
Single day on-track handle: $2,380,166, August 11, 1974

Mutuel Records

Highest Win: $403.20, Gerabon, June 16, 1949
Lowest Win: $2.20, Spectacular Bid, August 26, 1979
Highest Exacta: $4,565.60, July 21, 1972
Lowest Exacta: $3.80, August 7, 1977; $3.80, August 26, 1979
Highest Trifecta: $50,870.80, May 25, 1974
Highest Daily Double: $5,507.80, July 4, 1941
Lowest Daily Double: $6.40, June 11, 1976
Highest Other Exotics: Quinella, $623.40, June 13, 1968
Lowest Other Exotics: Quinella, $5.40, July 1, 1968

Leaders

Career, leading jockey by titles: Mike McCarthy, 5
Career, leading trainer by titles: Grover "Bud" Delp, 11
Recent meeting, leading jockey: Jeremy Rose, 150, 2001
Recent meeting, leading owner: Mike Gill, 70, 2001
Recent meeting, leading trainer: Timothy F. Ritchey, 87, 2001

Records

Single day jockey wins: Eldon Nelson, 6, June 20, 1958; George Cusimano, 6, July 16, 1968; Greg McCarron, 6, July 6, 1974; Jimmy Edwards, 6, May 28, 1984; Michael McCarthy, 6, November 2, 1997; Michael McCarthy, 6, May 20, 1998
Single meet, leading trainer by wins: Tim Ritchey, 76

Track Records, Main Dirt

4 furlongs: Star Event, :47, May 5, 1997
4 1/2 furlongs: Erlton, :51.80, May 5, 1998
5 furlongs: Milky Way Gal, :56.20, July 29, 1989
5 1/2 furlongs: Dontcloseyoureyes, 1:03, October 14, 1990
6 furlongs: Damitrius, 1:08.20, September 2, 1980
1 mile: Ashlar, 1:35.20, June 25, 1960
1m 70 yds: St. Bonaventure, 1:39.40, June 15, 1970
1 1/16 miles: Lies of Omission, 1:41.20, July 4, 1998
1 1/8 miles: Victoria Park, 1:47.40, June 18, 1960
1 3/16 miles: Gold Star Deputy, 1:56.72, October 31, 1999
1 1/4 miles: Coup de Fusil, 1:59.80, July 25, 1987
1 1/2 miles: Bam, 2:31, June 26, 1948
1 5/8 miles: Flying Restina Run, 2:45.40, September 4, 2000
1 3/4 miles: Cer Vantes, 2:56.40, June 27, 1951
2 miles: Dixies Act, 3:29.40, August 10, 1975
Other: 2 furlongs, Glitter River, :21.60, September 5, 2000; 2 miles 70 yds, Wolfe Tone, 3:34, November 7, 1993; 2 1/4 miles, 3:58.60, Sanguine Sword, July 2, 1986

Course Records, Main Turf

5 furlongs: Incredible Revent, :56, September 4, 1996
5 1/2 furlongs: Jumping to Joy, 1:08.21, October 11, 1994
1 mile: Portsmouth, 1:35, June 17, 1965
1 1/16 miles: Charabanc, 1:40 1/5, July 20, 1963
1 1/8 miles: Royal Strand (Ire), 1:48, July 13, 1997
1 3/8 miles: Cool Prince, 2:12 2/5, July 3, 1965
1 1/2 miles: John's Call, 2:28, July 23, 2000
2 miles: Verdance, 3:24 2/5, September 21, 1986
Other: 1 7/8 miles, *El Moro, 3:11 4/5, July 22, 1963; 2 3/8 miles, Lively London, 4:09, July 25, 1986; 2 7/8 miles, Call Louis, 5:08 1/5, August 24, 1986

Fastest Times of 2001 (Dirt)

4 1/2 furlongs: Where There's Fire, :52.09, May 29
5 furlongs: Mayor Steve, :57.57, September 16
5 1/2 furlongs: The Maccabee, 1:03.67, July 15
6 furlongs: Xtra Heat, 1:09.64, September 8
1 mile: Pine Dance, 1:37.22, May 26
1m 70yds: Fly Forever, 1:41.71, September 23
1 1/16 miles: Burning Roma, 1:42.41, June 17
1 1/8 miles: Concerned Minister, 1:50.31, September 8
1 3/16 miles: Bellwether, 1:59.32, April 21
1 1/4 miles: Irving's Baby, 2:05.21, July 22
1 1/2 miles: Confidence, 2:39.04, October 20

Fastest Times of 2001 (Turf)

5 furlongs: Mayor Steve, :56.72, July 22
1 mile: La Reine's Terms, 1:35.52, June 13
1 1/16 miles: Crystal Sea, 1:42.45, September 8
1 1/8 miles: Queue, 1:48.47, August 19
1 3/8 miles: Amourette, 2:17.20, July 21
1 1/2 miles: John's Call, 2:29.48, July 22

Florida

Calder Race Course

Calder Race Course, which offers live racing from May through early January, is located in Miami next to Pro Player Stadium, home of the National Football League's Miami Dolphins. Built by real-estate businessman Stephen A. Calder, the track was granted summer racing dates for 1970. Because the track was under construction, those dates were run at Tropical Park. Calder Race Course officially opened on May 6, 1971, debuting an all-weather synthetic track surface designed by 3M that remained in place until 1992. In 1972, Tropical Park closed and began holding its meet at Calder; the last several weeks of each year's season are known as the Tropical Park meet. From 1980-'84, Calder underwent $10.5-million in improvements. In 1988, Thoroughbred owner-breeder Bertram R. Firestone bought Calder. Three years later, Kawasaki Leasing Inc. assumed control of the track. The track underwent a $1-million renovation of its first floor, and in 1995 it added full-card simulcasting. In 1999, Churchill Downs Inc. bought Calder for approximately $86-million. Today, Calder features three successful racing events: the Florida Stallion Stakes, a series of races for offspring of Florida stallions; Festival of the Sun, seven stakes races highlighted by the finals of the Florida Stallion Stakes series; and Summit of Speed, five sprint stakes races with combined purses exceeding $1-million. The first national pick four was offered on the Summit of Speed in 2000.

Location: 21001 NW 27th Ave., Miami, FL 33055-0808
Phone: (305) 625-1311
Fax: (305) 623-6695
E-mail: marketing@calderracecourse.com
Web site: http://www.calderracecourse.com
Year founded: 1970
Inaugural meeting: May 6, 1971
Acreage: 220
Number of stalls: 1,850
Seating capacity: 15,575

Officers

President: C. Kenneth Dunn
Vice President: Randall E. Soth
General Manager: Randall E. Soth
Racing Secretary: Robert D. Umphrey
Secretary: Rebecca C. Reed
Treasurer: Michael Abes
Director of Operations: Bill Keers
Director of Admissions: Bill Keers
Director of Communications: Michele Blanco
Director of Marketing: Tammy Gantt
Director of Mutuels: Patrick Mahoney
Director of Publicity: Michele Blanco
Director of Simulcasting: Diane Stoess
Horsemen's Liaison: Joanne Roberts
Stewards: Charles Camac, Jeff Noe, Walter Blum
Track Announcer: Phil Saltzman
Track Photographer: Jean Raftery
Track Superintendent: Steve Cross

Racing dates

2001: May 23-November 3, 122 days
2002: April 26-November 3

Track Layout

Main circumference: 1 mile
Main track chute: 1/4 mile, 7 furlongs
Main length of stretch: 990 feet
Main turf circumference: 7 furlongs
Main turf chute: 1/4 mile

Attendance

Average daily recent meeting: 4,967, 2001
Highest single day record: 23,103, May 4, 1985

Calder, continued

Record daily average for single meet: 9,401, 1976
Total attendance recent meeting: 591,039, 2001

Handle
Total all sources recent meeting: $631,641,042, 2001
Single day total handle all sources: $9,461,604, December 29, 2001
Total on-track recent meeting: $50,534,300, 2001
Single day on-track handle: $2,954,162, May 7, 1988
Average all sources recent meeting: $5,307,907, 2001
Average on-track recent meeting: $424,657, 2001
Record daily average for single meet: $1,206,739, 1986

Mutuel Records
Highest Win: $345.40, Lou Glory, September 12, 1991
Lowest Win: $2.10, Isle O'Style, June 12, 1974
Highest Exacta: $31,133.20, November 3, 1972
Lowest Exacta: $3.40, August 16, 1989
Highest Trifecta: $58,432.40, October 25, 1986
Lowest Trifecta: $10.40, July 31, 1994
Highest Daily Double: $2,671, July 2, 1976
Lowest Daily Double: $3.20, September 16, 1992
Highest Pick 3: $16,038.20, September 2, 1992
Lowest Pick 3: $9, September 12, 2000
Highest Other Exotics: $74,622, Superfecta, October 26, 1996
Lowest Other Exotics: $33.40, Superfecta, August 7, 1995

Leaders
Career, leading jockey by wins: Gene St. Leon, 1,310
Recent meeting, leading jockey: Cornelio Vasquez, 144, 2001
Recent meeting, leading owner: Monarch Stables, 30, 2001
Recent meeting, leading trainer: William P. White, 52, 2001
Career, leading jockey by stakes wins: Gene St. Leon, 73
Career, leading trainer by stakes wins: Frank Gomez, 87
Career, leading trainer by wins: Frank Gomez, 852

Records
Single day jockey wins: George Gomez, 6, May 12, 1977; Walter Guerra, 6, October 3, 1979; Rene Douglas, 6, July 15, 1995; Eibar Coa, 6, September 7, 1998
Single day trainer wins: Arnold N. Winick, 5, September 16, 1972; Stanley Hough, 5, May 12, 1977

Track Records, Main Dirt
4 1/2 furlongs: Imperial Action, :52.54, June 3, 1993
5 furlongs: Honest, :57.61, July 1, 1996
5 1/2 furlongs: My Boy Cary, 1:04.67, July 17, 1993
6 furlongs: Forty One Carats, 1:08.95, October 7, 2000
6 1/2 furlongs: Thrillin Discovery, 1:16.39, November 28, 1998
7 furlongs: Constant Escort, 1:21.82, September 28, 1996
1 mile: Cutandthrust, 1:37.47, September 19, 1993
1 mile 70 yds: Halo's Image, 1:41.78, October 31, 1995
1 1/16 miles: King Rex, 1:43.36, June 22, 1996
1 1/8 miles: Jumping Hill, 1:50, December 30, 1978
1 3/16 miles: Arctic Honeymoon, 1:59 3/5, January 3, 1987
1 1/4 miles: Wicapi, 2:05, June 25, 1996
1 1/2 miles: Lead'm Home, 2:32 3/5, December 31, 1977
1 5/8 miles: Timberlea Tune, 2:50 1/5, October 16, 1971
1 3/4 miles: *Detective II, 3:03 1/5, October 23, 1971
2 miles: *Detective II, 3:30 1/5, November 11, 1971
Other: 2 furlongs, Lifeisawhirl, :20.99, July 15, 2000

Course Records, Main Turf
5 furlongs: Heckofaralph, :54.96, August 1, 1998
7 furlongs: Carterista, 1:22.36, June 19, 1993
7 1/2 furlongs: Court Lark, 1:26.54, July 16, 1994
1 mile: Copy Editor, 1:33.68, August 2, 1998
1 1/16 miles: Spendable, 1:39.33, July 30, 1999
1 1/8 miles: The Vid, 1:44.99, November 25, 1995
1 3/8 miles: King's Design, 2:13, July 23, 1999
1 1/2 miles: Flag Down, 2:24, December 16, 1995
2 miles: Skate On Thin Ice, 3:21.89, January 2, 1996

Fastest Times of 2001 (Dirt)
4 1/2 furlongs: Gold Phantom, :51.86, September 16
5 furlongs: Musique d'Or, :57.97, September 17

6 furlongs: Fappie's Notebook, 1:09.89, October 13
1 mile: High Ideal, 1:36.25, September 15
1m 70yds: Juggernaut, 1:45.89, September 22
1 1/16 miles: Castlebrook, 1:42.55, September 15
Other: 2 furlongs, Puma, :20.98, July 14

Fastest Times of 2001 (Turf)
5 furlongs: Kipperscope, :55.02, September 6
1 mile: Mr. Livingston, 1:33.75, September 3
1 1/8 miles: Kassar, 1:46.44, August 25
1 3/8 miles: Mr. Pleasantfar (Brz), 2:16.39, October 13

Gulfstream Park

Since the 1940s, Gulfstream Park, located north of Miami in Hallandale, Florida, has been a favorite winter destination for horsemen and annually offers high-quality winter racing. Gulfstream opened in February 1939 but went bankrupt and closed after four days of racing. In 1944, James Donn Sr., who owned a local floral shop and was a creditor of the track, reopened Gulfstream. In 1952, the Florida Derby (G1) debuted and became a major stop on the road to the Kentucky Derby (G1). Ten winners of the race, including Northern Dancer, Unbridled, Thunder Gulch, and, most recently, Monarchos, went on to win the Kentucky Derby. Gulfstream in 1989 held the first of the track's three Breeders' Cup championship days. In 1999, Frank Stronach-led Magna Entertainment Corp. purchased Gulfstream for $95-million. Stronach has announced plans for significant additions and improvements to the facility, and in October 2001 Magna broke ground on Palm Meadows, a 304-acre training facility located near Boynton Beach.

Location: 901 S. Federal Hwy., Hallandale, FL 33009-7124
Phone: (954) 454-7000
Fax: (954) 457-6357
Web site: http://www.gulfstreampark.com
Year founded: 1938
Inaugural meeting: February 1-4, 1939
Number of stalls: 1,454
Seating capacity: 20,300
Acreage: 256

Officers
Presidents: Jim McAlpine, Scott Savin
Vice Presidents: Don Amos, Graham Orr
General Manager: Scott Savin
Director of Racing: David Bailey
Racing Secretary: David Bailey
Director of Operations: Dennis Testa
Director of Admissions: Phil Dalton
Director of Communications: Joe Tanenbaum
Director of Finance: Robert W. Zambreny Jr.
Director of Marketing: David Rovine
Director of Mutuels: Patrick Mahony
Director of Publicity: Joe Tanenbaum
Director of Simulcasting: Mike Tanner
Horsemen's Liaison: Raina Chingos-Gunderson
Stewards: Charles Camac, Jeffrey Noe, Walter Blum
Track Announcer: Vic Stauffer
Track Superintendent: Dale Henricksen

Racing dates
2001: January 3-March 16, 63 days
2002: January 3-April 24, 90 days

Track Layout
Main circumference: 1 mile
Main track chute: 3 furlongs, 7 furlongs
Main width: 80 feet

Main length of stretch: 952 feet, 2 inches
Main turf circumference: 7 furlongs
Main turf chute: 1 1/8 miles
Main turf width: 70 feet
Main turf length of stretch: 921 feet

Attendance
Highest single day record: 45,124, November 6, 1999
Average daily recent meeting: 10,281, 2001
Record daily average for single meet: 15,528, 1979
Highest single meet record: 1,096,404, 1991

Handle
Average all sources recent meeting: $10,642,046, 2001
Average on-track recent meeting: $2,053,846, 2001
Record daily average for single meet: $2,121,121, 1998
Single day on-track handle: $7,993,485, March 12, 1994
Single day total handle all sources: $21,102,814, March 16, 1996
Total all sources recent meeting: $670,448,898, 2001

Mutuel Records
Highest Win: $404, Concert Grand, February 14, 1993
Lowest Win: $2.10, Honest Pleasure, April 3, 1976; $2.10, Spectacular Bid, February 7, 1979; $2.10, Spectacular Bid, March 6, 1979
Highest Exacta: $8,948.80, March 13, 1987
Lowest Exacta: $3.80, March 6, 1979; $3.80, March 10, 1991
Highest Trifecta: $96,751.80, January 31, 1993
Lowest Trifecta: $9.60, March 6, 1979
Highest Daily Double: $6,683.60, January 28, 1972
Lowest Daily Double: $6, January 14, 1995
Highest Pick 3: $63,737.60, January 26, 1995
Lowest Pick 3: $9.80, February 22, 1994
Highest Pick 6: $301,585.80, February 24, 1996

Leaders
Career, leading jockey by stakes wins: Jerry Bailey
Career, leading jockey by titles: Jorge Chavez, 4
Career, leading trainer by titles: A. N. Winick, 12
Recent meeting, leading jockey: Jorge Chavez, 81, 2001
Recent meeting, leading trainer: William I. Mott, 28, 2001

Records
Single meet, leading jockey by wins: Julio Pezua, 97, 1987; Wigberto Ramos, 97, 1991; Jerry Bailey, 97, 1996
Single meet, leading trainer by wins: William I. Mott, 39, 1996
Single day jockey wins: Jerry Bailey, 7, March 11, 1995

Track Records, Main Dirt
4 furlongs: Growing Up, :46 1/5, March 12, 1949; Piet, :46 1/5, April 3, 1947
4 1/2 furlongs: Iron Rail, :51 2/5, April 6, 1960
5 furlongs: Punch Line, :56.78, March 16, 1997
5 1/2 furlongs: Rare Rock, 1:02.50, January 3, 1998
6 furlongs: Mr. Prospector, 1:07 4/5, March 31, 1973; Artax, 1:07.89, November 6, 1999
6 1/2 furlongs: Alydeed, 1:15, March 6, 1993; Federal Hill, 1:15, March 25, 1957
7 furlongs: Elusive Quality, 1:20, February 21, 1997
1m 70 yds: Blacksburg, 1:39, February 6, 1994
1 1/16 miles: Saxony Warrior, 1:40 1/5, March 6, 1973
1 1/8 miles: Jumping Hill, 1:46 2/5, February 3, 1979
1 3/16 miles: Michael's Choice, 1:56, March 23, 1960; Sal's Boat, 1:56, April 22, 1960
1 1/4 miles: Mat Boy (Arg), 1:59, March 24, 1984
1 3/8 miles: Blacktype, 2:15 2/5, March 17, 1956; Bayluc, 2:15 2/5, April 2, 1960
1 1/2 miles: Buffalo Lark, 2:27 3/5, April 12, 1975
1 5/8 miles: Toulouse, 2:43 2/5, April 7, 1956
1 3/4 miles: Tisbury, 2:57 2/5, April 20, 1953
2 miles: Undue Influence, 3:25.73, March 16, 1997
Other: 2 1/2 furlongs, Rich Coins, :28, March 31, 2000; 2 1/2 furlongs, Sonnyhero, :28, April 5, 2000; 3 furlongs, El Macho, :32 1/5, February 26, 1974; 1 7/8 miles, Pharawell, 3:13 4/5, April 8, 1947; 2 miles 70 yds, Pharawell, 3:53 4/5, April 17, 1947

Course Records, Main Turf
5 furlongs: Heckofaralph, :56.25, April 8, 2000
1 mile: Lure, 1:32.90, October 31, 1992
1 1/16 miles: Garbu, 1:39.33, March 13, 1999
1 1/8 miles: Auntie Mame, 1:46.54, March 5, 1997
1 3/8 miles: Yagli, 2:10.73, February 6, 1999
1 1/2 miles: Unite's Big Red, 2:23, March 6, 1999
2 miles: Sabinus, 3:22 2/5, April 17, 1971

Interesting facts
Trivia: Bill Shoemaker rode the last winner of his career (Beau Genius) in the 1990 Hallandale Handicap. Turf course opened in 1959.

Fastest Times of 2001 (Dirt)
5 furlongs: Polly's Comet, :57.55, January 12
5 1/2 furlongs: Westgate Pub, 1:04.04, February 15
6 furlongs: Hook and Ladder, 1:08.94, February 10
6 1/2 furlongs: Left Bank, 1:15.22, March 11
7 furlongs: Hook and Ladder, 1:21.85, March 9
1m 70yds: Broken Vow, 1:40.90, February 5
1 1/16 miles: Proper Man, 1:41.99, February 9
1 1/8 miles: Captain Steve, 1:48.95, February 3
1 3/16 miles: Dan's Report, 2:00.27, March 9
1 1/4 miles: Sir Bear, 2:02.96, March 3

Fastest Times of 2001 (Turf)
5 furlongs: Big City Dream, :57.48, March 1
1 mile: Honorable Pic, 1:33.35, March 10
1 1/16 miles: Inexplicable, 1:39.43, February 24
1 1/8 miles: Spook Express (SAf), 1:47.28, February 18; Punkin Head, 1:47.28, March 12
1 3/8 miles: Subtle Power (Ire), 2:13.50, February 10
1 1/2 miles: Whata Brainstorm, 2:23.75, March 11

Hialeah Park

The dowager queen of South Florida racetracks, Hialeah Park did not conduct any racing in 2002, the first year of Florida's latest bout of deregulation of Thoroughbred racing, and there is considerable doubt the track will operate in 2003, even though it applied for racing dates.

Holding its inaugural meeting in 1925, Hialeah was the first Thoroughbred racing operation in the Miami area, and it blossomed after Philadelphia industrialist Joseph E. Widener purchased the track in 1931 and with his partners completely remodeled it. Widener gave the track its distinctive Renaissance Revival architecture and in 1931 imported the track's signature flock of flamingos from Cuba.

Into the 1970s, Hialeah Park held the prime midwinter dates and attracted the best stables from the North to its gentle climate and kind racing surface. Under its soaring palms and pines, such legends as Citation, Nashua, Bold Ruler, Never Bend, Northern Dancer, Seattle Slew, Alydar, and Spectacular Bid prepared for the classics with victories in the track's Flamingo Stakes. By 1979, when Spectacular Bid romped to a 12-length victory in that race, Hialeah had already begun its long decline. In 1978, the track lost exclusive control of the prime racing dates, and in the 1990s it lost the key dates to Gulfstream Park.

Location: 105 E. 21st St., Hialeah, FL 33011
Phone: (305) 885-8000
Fax: (305) 887-8006
Web site: http://www.hialeahpark.com
Inaugural meeting: January 25, 1925

Hialeah, continued

Acreage: 220
Year founded: 1924
Inaugural meeting: January 25, 1925
Number of stalls: 1,631
Seating capacity: 20,000

Officers

President: John Brunetti Jr.
General Manager: Richard Sacco
Director of Racing: Stephen Brunetti
Racing Secretary: J. Sam Abbey
Director of Operations: Jon Van Lindt
Director of Finance: Duane T. Cliburn
Director of Marketing: Steve Bovo
Director of Mutuels: Ed Mackie
Director of Publicity: Joe Savage
Director of Simulcasting: Ed Mackie Jr.
Horsemen's Liaison: Rhonda Soth

Racing dates

2001: March 17-May 22, 61 days

Track Layout

Main circumference: 1 1/8 miles
Main track chute: 3 furlongs, 7 furlongs
Main width: 80 feet
Main length of stretch: 1,410 feet
Main turf circumference: 7 1/2 furlongs
Main turf width: 90 feet
Main turf length of stretch: 975 feet

Attendance

Highest single day record: 42,366, February 18, 1956

Handle

Average on-track recent meeting: $972,682, 2001
Single day on-track handle: $4,822,601, February 28, 1987
Single day total handle all sources: $8,421,464, April 1,1995
Total on-track recent meeting: $59,333,594, 2001

Mutuel Records

Highest Win: $325.60, Robber, 1950
Lowest Win: $2.10, Coaltown, 1949; $2.10, Cure the Blues, March 26, 1981
Highest Exacta: $5,583.80, February 4, 1984
Lowest Exacta: $4, February 17, 1982
Highest Trifecta: $67,432, February 15, 1987
Lowest Trifecta: $8.20, April 22, 1995
Highest Daily Double: $5,919,20, January 25, 1987
Lowest Daily Double: $5.80, May 2, 1981
Highest Pick 3: $19,186, December 28, 1991
Lowest Pick3: $16.20, March 20, 1995; $16.20, April 17, 1995
Highest Pick 6: $382,344.80, January 25, 1982

Leaders

Career, leading jockey by titles: Bobby Ussery, 5
Career, leading trainer by titles: H. A. "Jimmy" Jones, 7
Recent meeting, leading jockey: Rosemary B. Homeister Jr., 60, 2001
Recent meeting, leading trainer: Ralph Ziadie, 23, 2001

Records

Single meet, leading trainer by wins: John Tammaro, 71, 1986
Single day jockey wins: Angel Cordero Jr., 6, February 28, 1968; Craig Perret, 6, March 9, 1989
Single day trainer wins: Ben A. Jones, 4, January 17, 1940; Dan Hurtak, 4, May 17, 1996
Single meet, leading jockey by wins: Jorge Chavez, 93, 1989

Track Records, Main Dirt

4 1/2 furlongs: Elvis On Velvet, :53.53, April 29, 2001
5 furlongs: Barnacle Jim, :56.54, May 16, 1997
5 1/2 furlongs: Lover's Trust, 1:02 3/5, May 6, 1989
6 furlongs: Earthmover, 1:08, March 7, 1985
7 furlongs: Seattle Slew, 1:20 3/5, March 9, 1977
1 1/16 miles: A P Valentine, 1:40.39, March 24, 2001
1 1/8 miles: Albert the Great, 1:45.52, March 24, 2001
1 3/16 miles: Swoon's Plume, 1:55 4/5, March 4, 1978
1 1/4 miles: Turkoman, 1:58 3/5, March 29, 1986
Other: 3 furlongs, Cherokee Road, :32, April 30, 2001

Course Records, Main Turf

5 1/2 furlongs: Glitterman, 1:01 3/5, May 20, 1989
1 1/16 miles: Judge Connelly, 1:38.78, April 2, 1995
1 1/8 miles: Signal Tap, 1:46, March 31, 1996
1 3/16 miles: Toonerville, 1:51 2/5, February 7, 1976
1 1/2 miles: Out of the Realm, 2:24.43, March 26, 1995

Fastest Times of 2001 (Dirt)

4 1/2 furlongs: Salt Water Cowboy, :53.02, May 19
5 furlongs: Mahabarat, :57.05, April 14
5 1/2 furlongs: Angela's Tune, 1:03.18, May 2
6 furlongs: I'm Sentimental, 1:08.91, April 7, Joe's Son Joey, 1:08.91, March 27
7 furlongs: Bravo Bull, 1:21.45, March 23
1 1/16 miles: A P Valentine, 1:40.39, March 24
1 1/8 miles: Albert the Great, 1:45.52, March 24
Other: 3 furlongs, Cherokee Road, :32.16, April 30

Fastest Times of 2001 (Turf)

5 1/2 furlongs: Penny Blues, 1:02.47, May 19
1 1/16 miles: Del Mar Show, 1:39.83, March 17
1 1/8 miles: Sir Brian's Sword, 1:46.76, April 22
1 3/16 miles: Del Mar Show, 1:53.06, April 21

Tampa Bay Downs

Tampa Bay Downs, the only Thoroughbred track on Florida's west coast, opened on February 18, 1926, as Tampa Downs. The initial 39-day meet was orchestrated by Harvey Mayers, a businessman from Ohio, and Churchill Downs executive Col. Matt J. Winn.

Renamed Sunshine Park in 1947, it became known as the "Santa Anita of the South" in the '50s, a nickname provided by legendary sportswriters Grantland Rice, Red Smith, and Arthur Daley, who frequented the track while covering baseball spring training.

Following the sale of the track, its name was changed to Florida Downs in 1965 and to Tampa Bay Downs in 1980. On February 12, 1981, jockey Julie Krone scored the first victory of her Racing Hall of Fame career on Lord Farkle. In 1983, Tampa Bay Downs became the first track in the country to regularly schedule races for Arabians.

Tampa Bay Downs was sold again in 1986 and has since added a picnic area, year-round simulcasting, a seven-furlong turf course, a luxurious Sports Gallery featuring an extensive video racing library, an updated grandstand with private work stations, central air conditioning, and a renovated deli, bar, and pizza area. The track's two biggest races, the $200,000 Tampa Bay Derby (G3) and the $150,000 Florida Oaks (G3), are contested in mid-March for three-year-olds.

Location: 11225 Race Track Rd., Oldsmar, FL 34677
Phone: (813) 855-4401
Fax: (813) 854-3539
Web site: http://www.tampadowns.com
Year founded: 1926
Inaugural meeting: 1926 (39 days)
Acreage: 450
Number of stalls: 1,462
Seating capacity: 6,000

Officers

President: Stella F. Thayer
Vice President: Howell Ferguson, John E. Grady Jr., Peter Berube
General Manager: Peter Berube

Director of Racing: Robert Clark
Racing Secretary: Robert Clark
Secretary: Howell Ferguson
Treasurer: Stella F. Thayer
Director of Operations: Robert Cassanese
Director of Admissions: Judy Gittens
Director of Communications: Margo Flynn
Director of Finance: Greg Gelyon
Director of Marketing: Margo Flynn
Director of Mutuels: Lamarr Daughtry
Director of Publicity: Margo Flynn
Director of Sales: Cathy Dwyer
Horsemen's Liaison: Margo Flynn
Stewards: Art Pedregal, Charles Miranda, Dennis Lima
Track Announcer: Richard Grunder
Track Photographer: Tom Cooley
Track Superintendent: Tom McLaughlin
Other Officials: Lorraine King, Vice President of Administration

Racing dates
2001: December 16, 2000 to May 6, 2001, 93 days
2002: December 15, 2001 to May 5, 2002, 93 days

Track Layout
Main circumference: 1 mile
Main track chute: 3 furlongs, 7 furlongs
Main width: 75 feet
Main length of stretch: 976 feet
Main turf circumference: 7 furlongs
Main turf chute: 1/4 mile
Main turf width: 80 feet

Attendance
Average daily recent meeting: 3,203, 2000/2001
Highest single day record: 9,765, April 8, 1990
Highest single meet record: 457,414, 1988/1989

Handle
Single day on-track handle: $1,198,075, May 5, 2001
Average all sources recent meeting: $1,600,685, 2000/2001
Average on-track recent meeting: $243,194, 2000/2001
Record daily average for single meet: $1,788,733
Single day total handle all sources: $3,877,477, March 18, 2001
Total all sources recent meeting: $148,863,699, 2000/2001

Mutuel Records
Highest Win: $249, March 23, 1988
Highest Trifecta: $50,617, January 26, 1999
Highest Daily Double: $3,320, January 17, 1950
Highest Pick 3: $12,913.40, January 9, 2001
Highest Other Exotics: $33,237.50, Superfecta, January 12, 1999; $9,754, Perfecta, February 8, 1973

Leaders
Career, leading jockey by titles: Bill Henry, 4
Career, leading trainer by titles: Don Ria, 5
Recent meeting, leading jockey: Derek Bell, 93, 2000/2001
Recent meeting, leading owner: Christos Gatis, 17, 2000/2001
Recent meeting, leading trainer: Don Rice, 37, 2000/2001

Records
Single day jockey wins: Richard Depass, 7, March 15, 1980
Single day owner wins: Christos Gatis, 3, April 10, 2001
Single day trainer wins: Don Rice, 3, February 13, 1997; Sam Cronk, 3, December 28, 1997; William Mitchell, 3, April 10, 2001; Duane Knipe, 3, April 24, 2001
Single meet, leading jockey by wins: Bill Henry, 123, 1992/1993; Willie Martinez, 123, 1991/1992
Single meet, leading trainer by wins: Fred Warren, 40, 1982/1983

Track Records, Main Dirt
4 furlongs: Camp Izard, :46.80, May 1, 1993
4 1/2 furlongs: Geronimo J., :52 4/5, March 16, 1984
5 furlongs: Arion Fair, :57 1/5, March 20, 1982
5 1/2 furlongs: Schmoopy, 1:03.55, March 17, 2000

6 furlongs: Bootlegger's Pet, 1:09, January 26, 1974
7 furlongs: Oh So Striking, 1:22.60, April 5, 1997
7 1/2 furlongs: Secret Romeo, 1:22.62, January 22, 2002
1 mile: Double Prince, 1:42 3/5, February 8, 1966; Rianan, 1:42 3/5, February 11, 1966
1m 40 yds: Mistum, 1:41 1/5, March 21, 1981
1m 70 yds: Deep Thought, 1:41 4/5, January 21, 1956
1 1/16 miles: Sunny Prospector, 1:43 2/5, March 29, 1989
1 3/16 miles: Warning Flag, 1:59 3/5, January 25, 1986
1 1/4 miles: Finale Puer, 2:07 2/5, March 7, 1959
1 3/8 miles: Rugged Zeal, 2:20.68, April 23, 2002
1 1/2 miles: Royal Jacopo, 2.33, March 12, 1955
1 5/8 miles: Most Valiant, 2:48.20, March 29, 1997
1 3/4 miles: Our Day, 3:00 2/5, March 20, 1957
2 miles: Boss Man Jarett, 3:30.30, April 24, 1999
Other: 2 furlongs, Silver Dollar Boy, :21 4/5, January 18, 1980; 3 furlongs, Hot Star, :33 2/5, February 14, 1980; 1 7/8 miles, Best Hearted, 3:18 3/5, March 22, 1986; 2 miles 70 yds, Turkey Foot Road, 3:39 4/5, March 22, 1969; 2 1/16 miles, Mystic Fox, 3:37 3/5, March 27; 1988

Course Records, Main Turf
5 furlongs: Exclusive Pow Wow, :56.39, May 5, 2001
1 mile: Lucky J J, 1:33.79, February 12, 2000
1 1/16 miles: Legs Galore, 1:39.65, February 20, 1999
1 1/8 miles: Lilys Cousin, 1:46.34, May 6, 2000

Interesting facts
Previous names and dates: Florida Downs, 1965; Sunshine Park, 1947, Tampa Downs, 1926

Fastest Times of 2001 (Dirt)
5 furlongs: One Silver Lady, :57.41, May 6
5 1/2 furlongs: Meaningful, 1:04.09, May 6
6 furlongs: Smart Revenge, 1:10.12, January 16
7 furlongs: Sea of Tranquility, 1:24.08, January 20; Pyrite Angel, 1:24.08, March 3
1 1/16 miles: Burning Roma, 1:44.30, March 18
1 3/8 miles: Captivator, 2:21.22, March 24
1 1/2 miles: Jr's Bonus, 2:37.09, March 10
Other: 3 furlongs, Charming Skier, :35.25, May 3

Fastest Times of 2001 (Turf)
5 furlongs: Exclusive Pow Wow, :56.39, May 5
1 mile: Namequest, 1:35.56, February 27
1 1/16 miles: Song for Annie, 1:41.23, March 18
1 1/8 miles: Bucks Harbor, 1:51.30, February 11

Tropical Park

Tropical Park no longer has a physical presence but remains alive as the late fall-early winter meeting at Calder Race Course in northwest Miami. The Tropical Park meet at Calder Race Course runs from late October until the first days of January, which approximates the traditional Tropical Park spot in the South Florida rotation. Starting in the late 1940s, Tropical operated from late November until mid-January.

Tropical Park first was a greyhound track and opened as a Thoroughbred track on December 26, 1931, in Coral Gables, a suburb southwest of Miami. The track was sold in 1941 and went through two ownership changes in the early 1950s. Tropical was host for the first Calder Race Course meeting in 1970 and for that season used an experimental, synthetic Tartan track, developed by Minnesota Mining and Manufacturing Co., inside the main, one-mile oval. Calder's investors, including 3M Chairman William L. McKnight, bought out Tropical with the intention of moving its dates to the new track. Tropical closed its gates for the last time on January 15, 1972, and was transformed into a municipal park. Several of Calder's graded stakes races

Tropical Park, continued

are held in the Tropical Park meeting.

Tropical Park still maintains separate meet records from Calder for leading jockey, trainer, etc., though all track records are the same for both.

Location: 21001 NW 27th Ave., Miami, FL 33055-0808
Phone: (305) 625-1311
Fax: (305) 620-2569
Seating capacity: 15,000
Number of stalls: 1,800

Officers
President: C. Kenneth Dunn
Vice President: Randall E. Soth
General Manager: Randall E. Soth

Racing dates
2001: November 4, 2000 to January 2, 2001, 52 days
2002: November 3, 2001 to January 2, 2002, 52 days

Track Layout
Main circumference: 1 mile
Main track chute: 1/4 mile, 7 furlongs
Main turf circumference: 7 furlongs
Main turf chute: 1/4 mile

Attendance
Highest single day record: 17,671, January 14, 1978
Highest single meet record: 514,496, 1979/1980
Record daily average for single meet: 10,324, 1975/1976
Total attendance recent meeting: 262,918, 2001/2002
Average daily recent meeting: 5,056, 2001/2002

Handle
Average all sources recent meeting: $5,787,715, 2001/2002
Average on-track recent meeting: $485,404, 2001/2002
Single day on-track handle: $2,793,767, January 1, 1989
Single day total handle all sources: $8,479,712, December 16, 1995
Total all sources recent meeting: $300,961,190, 2001/2002
Total on-track recent meeting: $25,241,002, 2001/2002

Mutuel Records
Highest Win: $447.40, Skyline's Delight, December 23, 1986
Lowest Win: $2.20, Hold Your Peace, December 18, 1972
Highest Exacta: $10,837.20, December 18, 1988
Lowest Exacta: $4.80, December 18, 1972
Highest Trifecta: $52,398, January 6, 1979
Lowest Trifecta: $11.40, December 9, 1993
Highest Daily Double: $7,907.80, December 14, 1973
Lowest Daily Double: $6.40, April 18, 1992
Highest Pick 3: $28,275, December 21, 1993
Lowest Pick 3: $15.80, December 17, 1988
Highest Other Exotics: $68,684.20, Superfecta, November 16, 1996
Lowest Other Exotics: $37.80, Superfecta, November 16, 1995

Leaders
Career, leading jockey by stakes wins: Jacinto Vasquez, 23, Jose Santos, 23
Career, leading jockey by wins: Jacinto Vasquez, 456
Career, leading trainer by stakes wins: Luis Olivares, 18
Career, leading trainer by wins: Frank Gomez, 315
Recent meeting, leading jockey: Cornelio Velasquez, 60, 2001/2002
Recent meeting, leading owner: Michael Sherman, 11, 2001/2002; Monarch Stables, 11, 2001/2002
Recent meeting, leading trainer: Dan Hurtak, 19, 2001/2002

Records
Single day jockey wins: Jacinto Vasquez, 6, December 22, 1990; Rene Douglas, 6, December 8, 1993; Javier Castellano, 6, December 31, 2000

Fastest Times of 2001 (Dirt)
5 1/2 furlongs: Brereton, 1:04.45, December 12

6 1/2 furlongs: Groomstick Stock's, 1:16.86, November 17
7 furlongs: Fappie's Notebook, 1:23.31, December 15
1 1/8 miles: Kiss a Native, 1:51.05, December 29

Fastest Times of 2001 (Turf)
7 1/2 furlongs: Bay Street Gal, 1:28.15, December 10; One Eyed Joker, 1:28.15, December 22
1 1/16 miles: Tour of the Cat, 1:40.46, November 24
1 1/2 miles: Krisada, 2:26.63, December 29

Idaho

Les Bois Park

Located in Boise on the Western Idaho Fairgrounds, Les Bois Park is one of the largest racetracks in the Northwest and annually holds the Idaho Cup for state-bred Thoroughbreds, Quarter Horses, Paints, and Appaloosas. Operating since May 1970, Les Bois, which is French for "the woods," opened six years after pari-mutuel wagering was legalized in Idaho. The track had difficult times in the late 1980s, when a downturn in horse racing caused the track owners, the Ada County Commission, to put the Les Bois lease up for auction. A group of horsemen led by veterinarian Chris Christian won the lease for $100 per month and successfully lobbied for full-card simulcasting, which turned the track around and allowed it to increase its purses. The track races Thoroughbreds, Quarter Horses, Appaloosas, and Paints from early May to mid-August. Les Bois was the launching pad for Racing Hall of Fame jockey Gary Stevens, who scored his first career victory there aboard Little Star in 1979.

Location: 5610 Glenwood Rd., Boise, ID 83714
Phone: (208) 376-3991
Fax: (208) 378-4032
Web site: http://www.lesboisracing.com

Officers
President: Paul K. Girdner
Director of Racing: Duayne Didericksen
Racing Secretary: Roger White
Director of Marketing: Kassie Cerami
Director of Simulcasting: Ron Andreoli

Racing dates
2001: May 5-August 12, 45 days
2002: May 4-August 11, 45 days

Leaders
Recent meeting, leading jockey: Ron W. Keckler, 42, 2001
Recent meeting, leading trainer: Keith Bennett, 28, 2001

Fastest Times of 2001
4 1/2 furlongs: Aleyna's Place, :51.56, May 28
5 furlongs: Ishio, :56.78, August 12
6 1/2 furlongs: Better Hearts, 1:17.66, August 5
7 furlongs: Lookn East, 1:23.44, July 14
7 1/2 furlongs: Northern Ricky, 1:31.40, July 25
1 mile: Rasha, 1:36.94, July 18
1 1/4 miles: Almost Golden, 2:05.92, August 12

Pocatello Downs

Location: 10588 Fairgrounds Rd.; Pocatello, ID 83204
Phone: (208) 238-1721
Fax: (208) 238-1763

Racing dates
2001: May 12-June 3

Rupert Downs

Location: P.O. Box 263, Rupert, ID 83350

Racing dates
2001: June 30-July 8, 5 days

Illinois

Arlington Park

Arlington Park first opened on October 13, 1927, and has been home to many firsts in Thoroughbred racing. Located northwest of Chicago in Arlington Heights, the track became the first in Illinois to offer turf races in 1934. In 1966, Laffit Pincay Jr. recorded his first United States victory there on his way to a place in the Racing Hall of Fame and more than 9,000 victories, a record. In 1981, Arlington became the world's first track to host a million-dollar race for Thoroughbreds when it inaugurated the Arlington Million (G1). The first running was won by John Henry, who returned to win the race in 1984. Today, the Million is part of Arlington's International Festival of Racing, which also includes the Beverly D. (G1) and Secretariat (G1) Stakes. On July 31, 1985, fire destroyed Arlington's clubhouse, causing the track to shift most of its remaining races to Hawthorne Race Course. The exception was the Million, which was held on August 25 at Arlington, and more than 35,000 fans watched the race from tents and temporary facilities. Those efforts led to Arlington becoming the first racetrack to earn an Eclipse Award. Arlington was rebuilt lavishly by Chicago-area industrialist Richard Duchossois, who closed the track for two seasons—1998 and '99—due to unfavorable economic and regulatory conditions. Arlington reopened in 2000 and the Arlington Million was resumed. Also in 2000, Churchill Downs Inc. purchased the track and assumed about $80-million in loans, while Duchossis received close to 4-million shares of common stock in Churchill.

Location: 2200 W. Euclid Ave., Arlington Heights, IL 60004
Phone: (847) 385-7500
Fax: (847) 385-7251
Web site: http://www.arlingtonpark.com
Year founded: 1926
Inaugural meeting: October 13, 1927
Seating capacity: 35,000
Number of stalls: 2,140

Officers
President: Steve Sexton
Director of Racing: William A. Thayer Jr.
Racing Secretary: David Bailey
Director of Operations: Gil Carmichael
Director of Admissions: Bill Adams
Director of Communications: Dan Leary
Director of Finance: Michael Cody
Director of Marketing: Keith Darby
Director of Mutuels: Jack Lisowski
Director of Publicity: Dan Leary
Director of Simulcasting: Marc Anderson
Track Announcer: John G. Dooley
Track Superintendent: Javier Barajas
Other Officials: Frank Gabriel Jr., Vice President of Racing and Operations; Richard Duchossois, Chairman

Racing dates
2001: June 13-October 28, 102 days
2002: June 5-October 27, 107 days

Track Layout
Main circumference: 1 1/8 miles
Main track chute: 1 mile, 6 1/2 furlongs, 7 1/2 furlongs, 7 furlongs
Main width: 90 feet
Main length of stretch: 1,049 feet
Main turf circumference: 1 mile
Main turf width: 150 feet
Training track: 5 furlongs

Attendance
Average daily recent meeting: 5,890, 2001
Total attendance recent meeting: 594,921, 2001

Handle
Average all sources recent meeting: $3,570,520, 2001
Average on-track recent meeting: $562,421, 2001
Single day total handle all sources: $14,519,027, August 18, 2001
Total all sources recent meeting: $360,622,482, 2001
Total on-track recent meeting: $56,804,502, 2001

Leaders
Recent meeting, leading trainer: Jerry Hollendorfer, 41, 2001
Career, leading jockey by titles: Earlie Fires, 6
Career, leading owner by titles: Calumet Farm, 9
Career, leading trainer by titles: Richard Hazelton, 8; William Hal Bishop, 8
Recent meeting, leading jockey: Rene R. Douglas, 134, 2001
Recent meeting, leading owner: Frank C. Calabrese, 39, 2001

Records
Single meet, leading jockey by wins: Shane Sellers, 219, 1991
Single meet, leading trainer by wins: P. Noel Hickey, 62, 1991
Single day jockey wins: Pat Day, 8, September 13, 1989

Track Records, Main Dirt
4 1/2 furlongs: Wheat Penny, :51.64, June 8, 2000
5 furlongs: Staunch Avenger, :57 1/5, June 29, 1970; Heisa-native, :57 1/5, June 12, 1971; Shecky Greene, :57 1/5, June 15, 1972
5 1/2 furlongs: Hey That's Great, 1:02.60, June 27, 1992
6 furlongs: Taylor's Special, 1:08, August 22, 1986
6 1/2 furlongs: Pentelicus, 1:14 1/5, July 14, 1990
7 furlongs: Tumiga, 1:20 2/5, July 13, 1968
7 1/2 furlongs: I'll Raise You One, 1:28 4/5, August 3, 1987
1 mile: Dr. Fager, 1:32 1/5, August 24, 1968
1m 70 yds: Geo. Groom, 1:42 4/5, October 25, 1927
1 1/16 miles: Kindly Manner, 1:41 2/5, August 22, 1977; Mojave, 1:41 2/5, June 30, 1981
1 1/8 miles: Spectacular Bid, 1:46 1/5, July 19, 1980
1 3/16 miles: Royal Glint, 1:55 4/5, August 30, 1975
1 1/4 miles: Private Thoughts, 1:59 2/5, August 20, 1977
1 3/8 miles: Playdale, 2:15 2/5, July 19, 1932
1 1/2 miles: El Misterio, 2:15 2/5, September 5, 1960
1 5/8 miles: Fool's Robbery, 2:45 3/5, July 5, 1973
1 3/4 miles: *Deux-Moulins, 2:59 2/5, July 14, 1955
2 miles: Swede of Norfolk, 3:26 2/5, August 15, 1970
Other: 1 5/16 miles, Evanescent, 2:10, July 18, 1993; 1 5/16 miles, Rush Home, 2:10, August 7, 1971; 2 1/4 miles, *Djem, 4:05 3/5, July 30, 1953

Course Records, Main Turf
5 furlongs: Ghost Power, :56.37, October 8, 1993
5 1/2 furlongs: Chief Sun Dance, 1:02 3/5, July 6, 1970
1 mile: Gee Can He Dance, 1:34 2/5, September 4, 1995
1m 70yds: Pass the Brandy, 1:38 4/5, July 25, 1970
1 1/16 miles: Zeeruler, 1:41, September 7, 1992
1 1/8 miles: Mr. Leader, 1:47 2/5, July 4, 1970; World Class Splash, 1:47.40, July 11, 1992
1 3/16 miles: Reluctant Guest, 1:53 1/5, September 1, 1990
1 1/4 miles: Awad, 1:58.69, August 27, 1995

Arlington Park, continued

1 1/2 miles: Master Dennis, 2:27 4/5, September 7, 1964
1 5/8 miles: Coincident, 2:45, July 26, 1951
1 3/4 miles: *Pennsburg, 3:02 3/5, July 5, 1941
2 miles: Penaway, 3:25 2/5, July 24, 1953
Other: 2 1/16 miles, *Deux-Moulins, 3:30 4/5, July 28, 1955; 2 1/8 miles, English Harry, 3:45, July 30, 1941

Interesting facts

Previous name and dates: Arlington International Racecourse, 1989-2000
Achievements/milestones: July 13, 1985, destroyed by fire; June 28, 1989, reopens

Fastest Times of 2001 (Dirt)

4 1/2 furlongs: Glenbriar Girl, :51.95, June 13
5 furlongs: The Lord's Tune, :57.40, September 8
5 1/2 furlongs: Cowboy Stuff, 1:05.31, July 22
6 furlongs: Getyourbritchesngo, 1:09.28, September 21
6 1/2 furlongs: Magic Doe, 1:15.31, October 20
7 furlongs: Robin de Nest, 1:21.87, June 13
1 mile: San Pedro, 1:35.60, September 2
1 1/16 miles: Langston, 1:42.05, July 29
1 1/8 miles: Discreet Hero, 1:49.73, July 28
1 1/4 miles: Guided Tour, 2:00.76, July 21

Fastest Times of 2001 (Turf)

5 furlongs: Distinctive Mr. B, :56.36, September 15
1 mile: Intern, 1:35.73, September 3
1 1/8 miles: Snow Dance, 1:47.93, September 15
1 3/16 miles: Ioya Two, 1:55.47, July 28
1 1/4 miles: Make No Mistake (Ire), 2:02.53, July 28
1 1/2 miles: Falcon Flight (Fr), 2:27.86, July 1

Fairmount Park

Fairmount Park, located in Collinsville, Illinois, about 30 minutes east of St. Louis, opened on September 26, 1925. The track was built to resemble a small Churchill Downs by Col. E. R. Bradley, who owned four Kentucky Derby winners, and Col. Matt Winn, who made the Kentucky Derby at Churchill a sporting institution. In 1947, Fairmount Park became the first one-mile oval racetrack in the world to provide lighting for night Thoroughbred racing. Fairmount's most famous horseman is jockey Dave Gall, who retired in 1999 with more than 7,000 wins, placing him among Thoroughbred racing's winningest jockeys. Fairmount, which has been owned since 1969 by Ogden Services Corp., has struggled to compete against riverboat gambling casinos throughout the St. Louis area.

Location: 9301 Collinsville Rd., Collinsville, IL 62234
Phone: (618) 345-4303
Fax: (618) 344-8218
E-mail: fmtpark@fairmountpark.com
Web site: http://www.fairmountpark.com
Inaugural meeting: September 26, 1925
Acreage: 190
Number of stalls: 1,080
Seating capacity: 3,420

Officers

General Manager: Brian F. Zander
Racing Secretary: Bobby Pace
Director of Mutuels: Mike Heidemann
Director of Publicity: John Slone
Director of Simulcasting: Greg Graves
Other Officials: Linda Schwaegel, Group Sales Director

Racing dates

2001: March 16-November 24, 137 days
2002: April 12-October 19, 110 days

Track Layout

Main circumference: 1 mile
Main track chute: 1 1/4 miles, 6 furlongs
Main width: 80 feet
Main length of stretch: 1,050 feet

Track Records, Main Dirt

4 furlongs: Aledo, :45.60, June 2, 1994
4 1/2 furlongs: Vague Promise, :51 3/5, May 19, 1978
5 furlongs: Slight in the Rear, :56 4/5, July 25, 1989
5 1/2 furlongs: Sarof Jr., 1:03 2/5, June 5, 1980
6 furlongs: Ye Country, 1:08 3/5, November 26, 1977
1 mile: Dusty Appeal, 1:37.40, June 20, 1992
1m 70 yds: Dusty Appeal, 1:39 4/5, July 30, 1989
1 1/16 miles: Lt. Lao, 1:40 4/5, July 22, 1989
1 1/8 miles: Andover Man, 1:47 3/5, August 26, 1989
1 1/4 miles: Leaddrop, 2:03, July 2, 1989
1 1/2 miles: *Firth of Tay, 2:33, September 21, 1927
1 5/8 miles: Monthazar, 2:48, November 3, 1973
1 3/4 miles: Lightin Bill, 3:02 4/5, October 14, 1939
2 miles: East Royalty, 3:32.60, December 1, 1991
Other: 2 furlongs, Fantan Sam, :21 2/5, November 22, 1989; 2 miles 70 yds, King Boogie, 3:33 3/5, September 1, 1984; 2 1/16 miles, Tim Trefle, 3:38 4/5, September 10, 1983; 2 1/8 miles, Lucrest, 3:46 1/5, September 24, 1983; 2 1/4 miles, Baye Dawn, 4:00, October 8, 1983; 2 1/2 miles, Cat Walk, 4:29, October 22, 1983

Fastest Times of 2001

4 furlongs: Gotabuck, :47, July 27
4 1/2 furlongs: Tic N Tin, :51.40, September 3
5 furlongs: Tri Tower's, :59.40, May 20
5 1/2 furlongs: Tic N Tin, 1:04.20, April 14
6 furlongs: Tic N Tin, 1:09.80, June 1
1 mile: Tindell, 1:38.80, October 13; Tic N Tin, 1:38.80, October 16
1m 70yds: Viale (Uru), 1:43.40, October 6
1 1/16 miles: Shadow Mountain, 1:45.80, November 9
1 1/8 miles: Heaintnosaint, 1:56.40, November 2
1 1/2 miles: American Czar, 2:41.00, November 24
Other: 2 furlongs, Gotabuck, :21.60, June 26

Hawthorne Race Course

For nearly 100 years, members of the Carey family have overseen Hawthorne Race Course in the Chicago suburb of Stickney. In 1909, Thomas Carey bought the track from horseman and noted gambler Ed Corrigan, who had opened the track in 1891. Under Corrigan's ownership, Hawthorne closed when the state Senate banned racing in Chicago in 1905, and new owner Carey attempted over the next several years to revive racing. He finally was successful in 1922. In 1928, the track's most notable race, the Hawthorne Gold Cup (G2), debuted. Among the winners of the Hawthorne Gold Cup are five-time Horse of the Year Kelso, 1968 Horse of the Year Dr. Fager, and 1991 Horse of the Year Black Tie Affair (Ire). In 1977, a fire destroyed Hawthorne's grandstand, and the remainder of its meet was held at Sportsman's Park, located a block away. Racing returned to the track in 1980. Over the years, Hawthorne has conducted harness racing, and a meet for Standardbreds will resume in 2002. Today, Carey's grandson Thomas F. Carey is Hawthorne's president and general manager.

Location: 3501 S. Laramie Ave., Stickney, IL 60804
Phone: (708) 780-3700
Fax: (708) 780-3677
Web site: http://www.hawthorneracecourse.com

Year founded: 1890, by Edward Corrigan
Inaugural meeting: May 20, 1891
Acreage: 119
Number of stalls: 2,400
Seating capacity: 18,000

Officers
President: Thomas F. Carey
General Manager: Thomas F. Carey
Director of Racing: Gary M. Duch
Racing Secretary: Gary M. Duch
Director of Operations: Thomas F. Carey III
Director of Admissions: Mike Harris
Director of Communications: Jim Miller
Director of Marketing: Howie Fagan
Director of Mutuels: Michael P. Hart
Director of Publicity: Jim Miller
Director of Sales: Caryl Meadows
Directors of Simulcasting: Lorene Heninger, Thomas F. Carey III
Horsemen's Liaison: Eric Viox
Stewards: Eddie Arroyo, Joe Lindeman, Larry Hill, Steve Morgan
Track Announcer: Peter Galassi
Track Superintendents: Gregorio Cardenas, Roosevelt Lomax

Racing dates
2001: May 1-June 10, 31 days; October 31-December 31, 47 days
2002: May 5-June 4, 23 days; November 1-December 31, 43 days

Track Layout
Main circumference: 1 mile
Main track chute: 6 1/2 furlongs
Main width: 75 feet
Main length of stretch: 1,320 feet
Main turf circumference: 7 furlongs 148 feet

Attendance
Highest single day record: 37,792, September 6, 1937

Handle
Average all sources recent meeting: $3,719,476, Fall 2001
Average on-track recent meeting: $226,198, Fall 2001
Record daily average for single meet: $3,575,861, 1996
Single day on-track handle: $10,300,640, May 5, 2001

Leaders
Career, leading jockey by wins: Earlie Fires, 1,117
Recent meeting, leading jockey: Zoe Cadman, Spring 2001; Shane Laviolette, 44, Fall 2001
Recent meeting, leading owner: Frank Calabrese, Spring 2001; Irish Acres Farm, Fall 2001
Recent meeting, leading trainer: Mike Reavis, Spring 2001; Thomas F. Tomillo, 23, Fall 2001

Records
Single day jockey wins: Johnny Heckman, 7, October 1, 1956
Single meet, leading trainer by wins: Richard Hazelton, 48, 1976

Track Records, Main Dirt
4 1/2 furlongs: Joanies Bella, :51.80, May 28, 2001
5 furlongs: De La Concorde, :57, November 11, 1992
5 1/2 furlongs: Marluel's Troy, 1:02 2/5, November 2, 1976
6 furlongs: Satan's Poppy, 1:08 1/5, October 21, 1978
6 1/2 furlongs: Dee Lance, 1:14 2/5, August 27, 1988
1 mile: Actuary, 1:37 1/5, July 17, 1923; Hopeless, 1:37 1/5, August 29, 1925
1m 70 yds: Soldat Bleu, 1:39 1/5, July 27, 1988
1 1/16 miles: Sensitive Prince, 1:39 3/5, September 23, 1978
1 1/8 miles: *Zografos, 1:46 3/5, October 9, 1974
1 3/16 miles: Lindy's Lad, 1:59 2/5, November 12, 1980
1 1/4 miles: Gladwin, 1:58 4/5, October 1, 1970; Group Plan, 1:58 4/5, October 19, 1974
1 1/2 miles: David, 2:29 3/5, October 1, 1969
1 5/8 miles: Viale (Uru), 2:47, December 10, 2000
1 3/4 miles: America Fore, 3:02 1/5, October 2, 1943

Other: 2 furlongs, Minty Flavors, :20.88, May 14, 1999; 1 13/16 miles, Stiffelio (Ire), 3:14.60, November 15, 1997; 2 miles 70 yds, Sun N Shine, 3:30 2/5, October 19, 1974

Course Records, Main Turf
5 furlongs: Sulemark, :56, October 25, 1992
7 furlongs: Glassy Dip, 1:22 3/5, May 30, 1977
7 1/2 furlongs: Joey Jr., 1:27 1/5, November 5, 1989
1 mile: Soviet Line (Ire), 1:33.40, July 25, 1998
1 1/16 miles: Bendecida, 1:40.53, September 6, 1999
1 1/8 miles: Rainbows for Life, 1:44 3/5, October 13, 1991
1 3/16 miles: Royal Glint, 1:54 2/5, September 28, 1974, Sari's Baba; 1:54 2/5, September 24, 1985
1 1/4 miles: Pass the Line, 2:00 2/5, August 10, 1985
1 3/8 miles: Shayzari (Ire), 2:15 1/5, September 3, 1988
1 1/2 miles: Lord Comet, 2:26.87, October 27, 1999
1 3/4 miles: Neverest, 2:58 4/5, August 31, 1973

Interesting facts
Trivia: First major U.S. track to use an electric timer (1931). Track announcer Phil Georgeff enters the Guiness Book of World Records when he calls his 85,000th race on August 13, 1988.

Fastest Times of 2001 (Dirt)
4 1/2 furlongs: Joanies Bella, :51.80, May 28
5 furlongs: Beware Avalanche, :57.41, May 25
6 furlongs: Zeal With a Kiss, 1:10.03, December 28
6 1/2 furlongs: Magic Doe, 1:16.41, December 31
1m 70yds: Lil Mephistopheles, 1:42.41, December 22
1 1/16 miles: Chicago Six, 1:44.44, November 10
1 1/8 miles: All in the Book, 1:52.65, May 26
1 1/4 miles: Duckhorn, 2:01.61, May 19
1 5/8 miles: Sure as Shipp, 2:50.09, December 29

Fastest Times of 2001 (Turf)
1 mile: Galic Boy, 1:35.10, November 3
1 1/16 miles: Aesthete Approval, 1:42.54, November 9
1 1/8 miles: Why Not, 1:49.74, November 9

Sportsman's Park

Located in Cicero, Sportsman's Park has a history as rich and raucous as the near-southwest Chicago suburb where it is located. Cicero, known for its bare-knuckles politics and mob connections, was the site of the Hawthorne Kennel Club, an illegal greyhound track controlled by the Al Capone mob in the early 1930s. Sportsman's opened as a horse track property on May 2, 1932, under the banner of the National Jockey Club. The track's first president was Edward J. O'Hare, a lawyer and Capone associate; O'Hare, who informed on Capone, was gunned down in 1939.

Charles Bidwill Sr., owner of the Chicago Cardinals (now Arizona) football team, served as Sportsman's managing director until his death in 1947. His son Charles W. "Stormy" Bidwill Jr. became Sportsman's president in 1967, and the eldest Bidwill's grandson, Charles W. Bidwill III, became the track's president in '95. Sportsman's track, which had been extended to five furlongs in 1956, was further extended to seven furlongs in '92. Sportsman's was closed for the 1999 season while the track was remodeled into a multiple-use facility, primarily to accommodate an auto-racing track known as Chicago Motor Speedway. Sportsman's reopened in 2000 for Thoroughbred racing. The track's principal race is the Illinois Derby (G2) for three-year-olds, which was first run at Sportsman's in 1963. The race was won in 2002 by eventual Kentucky Derby (G1) winner War Emblem.

Sportsman's Park, continued

Location: 3301 S. Laramie Ave., Cicero, IL 60804
Phone: (773) 242-1121
Fax: (773) 242-0775
Web site: http://www.sportsmanspark.com
Year founded: 1932
Number of stalls: 1,900
Seating capacity: 65,000

Officers
President: Charles W. Bidwill III
Vice President: Terry Hart
General Manager: H. Eddie Arroyo
Racing Secretary: Allan Plever
Treasurer: Michael Bidwell
Director of Operations: Bill Duffy
Director of Communications: Christian Polzin, Stakes Co-ordinator, Dan Leary
Director of Finance: Jeff Kras
Director of Mutuels: Michael Hart
Director of Publicity: John Brokopp
Director of Sales: Sandy Reinhart
Director of Simulcasting: Rhonda Sosnowski
Horsemen's Liaison: P. J. Mudro
Stewards: Eddie Arroyo, Joseph Lindeman, Larry Hill, Steve Morgan
Track Announcer: John G. Dooley
Track Photographer: Four-Footed Fotos
Track Superintendent: Albert Jozwiak

Racing dates
2001: March 2-April 30, 43 days
2002: March 1-May 4, 46 days

Track Layout
Main circumference: 7 furlongs
Main length of stretch: 1,463 feet

Leaders
Career, leading jockey by titles: Tony Skoronski, 11
Career, leading jockey by wins: Randall Meier, 1,074
Career, leading trainer by titles: Richard Hazelton, 20
Recent meeting, leading jockey: Randall Meier, 53, 2001
Recent meeting, leading owner: Louis D. O'Brien, 9, 2001
Recent meeting, leading trainer: Mike Reavis, 29, 2001

Records
Single meet, leading jockey by wins: Mark Guidry, 134, 1992
Single meet, leading trainer by wins: Richard Hazelton, 59, 1981
Single day jockey wins: Chris Valovich, 4, March 11, 2001; Randall Meier, 4, April 1, 2001

Track Records, Main Dirt
5 furlongs: Hez Comin Thru, :58.06, March 3, 2001
5 1/2 furlongs: Faultless Appeal, 1:03.78, April 8, 2001
6 furlongs: Linear, 1:08.85, March 26, 1994
6 1/2 furlongs: Bold Favorite, 1:15 2/5, October 2, 1971
1 mile: Tabasco Cid, 1:36, March 30, 1994
1 1/16 miles: Humble Eight, 1:42.29, June 3, 1995
1 1/8 miles: Wild Rush, 1:47.51, May 10, 1997
1 3/8 miles: Skinny C., 2:17 3/5, May 27, 1974
1 5/8 miles: Ball Hawk, 2:48 2/5, October 24, 1956
2 miles: Tri for Charlie, 3:37 3/5, May 8, 1990
Other: 2 furlongs, Nervous Moment, :20.98, June 8, 1998; 1 7/16 miles, Theoretic, 2:24 1/5, October 15, 1973; 1 9/16 miles, Well Lit, 2:35.77, April 25, 1992

Fastest Times of 2001
5 furlongs: Hez Comin Thru, :58.06, March 3
5 1/2 furlongs: Faultless Appeal, 1:03.78, April 8
6 furlongs: Cat Tracks, 1:09.25, April 30
1 mile: Zarb's Magic, 1:36.76, April 22
1 1/16 miles: Lady Melesi, 1:42.86, April 8
1 1/8 miles: Chicago Six, 1:48.28, April 22

Indiana

Hoosier Park

In 1989, Indiana approved pari-mutuel wagering, and the state's first pari-mutuel racetrack, Hoosier Park, opened its inaugural season of Standardbred racing in 1994. Thoroughbred racing debuted at Hoosier in 1995. Located northeast of Indianapolis in Anderson, Indiana, the $10-million track was developed by majority owner Churchill Downs Inc. in the company's first racing interest outside Kentucky. Hoosier annually holds a Thoroughbred meet, which includes a limited number of Quarter Horse races, and a season for Standardbreds. For 2002, Hoosier hosted two graded stakes, the Indiana Breeders' Cup Oaks (G3) and its richest event, the $300,000 Indiana Derby (G3). With a competitor, Indianapolis Downs, scheduled for opening in late 2002 only 40 miles from its facility, Hoosier requested a reduced schedule of 120 racing dates in 2002 but agreed to 90 Standardbred dates and 70 for Thoroughbreds.

Location: 4500 Dan Patch Circle, Anderson, IN 46013
Phone: (765) 642-7223
Fax: (765) 644-0467
E-mail: info@hoosierpark.com
Web site: http://www.hoosierpark.com
Year founded: 1994
Inaugural meeting: September 1-October 28, 1995
Acreage: 105
Seating capacity: 15,000
Number of stalls: 980

Officers
President: Richard B. Moore
Vice President: Don R. Richardson
General Manager: Richard B. Moore
Director of Racing: Warren Groce
Racing Secretary: Warren Croce
Secretary: Rebecca C. Reed
Treasurer: Steven L. Wilkening
Director of Operations: Ron Fairholm
Director of Admissions: Sue Walters
Director of Communications: Thomas F. Bannon
Director of Finance: Steven L. Wilkening
Director of Marketing: Kristina M. Thompson Johns
Director of Mutuels: Randy Westerman
Director of Publicity: Tammy Knox
Director of Simulcasting: Joy Narducci
Horsemen's Liaison: Kitty Bonham
Stewards: Gary Wilfert, Mike Manganello
Track Announcer: Steve Cross
Track Photographer: Jim Linscott
Track Superintendent: John Betts
Other Officials: Jim Garrett, Director of Group/Guest Services

Racing dates
2001: September 7-December 3, 70 days
2002: August 29-December 1, 70 days

Track Layout
Main circumference: 7 furlongs
Main track chute: 6 furlongs
Main width: 90 feet
Main length of stretch: 1,255 feet

Attendance
Average daily recent meeting: 954, 2001
Highest single day record: 10,827, October 7, 2000
Highest single meet record: 95,468, 1995
Lowest single meet record: 65,750, 1996
Record daily average for single meet: 2,273, 1995
Total attendance recent meeting: 66,812, 2001

Handle

Single day on-track handle: $1,085,338, November 17, 1996
Average all sources recent meeting: $1,144,638, 2001
Average on-track recent meeting: $65,869, 2001
Record daily average for single meet: $1,221,931, 2000
Total all sources recent meeting: $80,124,655, 2001
Total on-track recent meeting: $4,610,807, 2001

Mutuel Records

Highest Win: $200, Mandingo, September 26, 1997
Highest Exacta: $3,212.60, September 10, 2000
Highest Trifecta: $24,911.90, December 1, 2000
Highest Daily Double: $1,988.80, September 22, 1998
Highest Pick 3: $4,095.20, November 13, 1999
Highest Other Exotics: $13,584.40, Superfecta, October 15, 1999

Leaders

Career, leading trainer by titles: Stanley Roberts, 2
Career, leading jockey by stakes wins: Jon Court, 9
Career, leading jockey by titles: Jon Court, 3
Career, leading jockey by wins: Jon Court, 386
Career, leading owner by titles: Highway 1 Racing Stable, 2; Michael Bruder, 2
Career, leading owner by wins: Highway 1 Racing Stable, 66
Career, leading trainer by stakes wins: Dale Romans, 13
Career, leading trainer by wins: Stanley Roberts, 86
Recent meeting, leading jockey: Terry Thompson, 122, 2001
Recent meeting, leading owner: Highway 1 Racing Stable, 20, 2001
Recent meeting, leading trainer: Stanley Roberts, 42, 2001

Records

Single day jockey wins: Jon Court, 6, September 24, 1998; Jon Court, 6, November 24, 1998; Mike Morgan, 6, December 5, 1999
Single day trainer wins: David Pate, 3, October 11, 1995; Bernie Flint, 3, November 4, 1995; Kathleen Cooper, 3, September 20, 1996; Stephen Dunn, 3, September 14, 1997; Stanley Roberts, 3, October 2, 1998; Barbara McBride, 3, September 14, 1999; Stanley Roberts, 3, October 29, 1999; Stanley Roberts, 3, September 22, 2000
Single meet, leading jockey by wins: Terry Thompson, 122, 2001
Single meet, leading owner by wins: Highway 1 Racing Stable, 29
Single meet, leading trainer by wins: Ray Stifano, 39, 2000

Track Records, Main Dirt

5 1/2 furlongs: Chukker Creek, 1:02.20, November 24, 1996; Moro Oro, 1:02.20, September 20, 1996
6 furlongs: Moro Oro, 1:07.40, November 16, 1996
1 mile: Vic's Rebel, 1:33.40, October 13, 1998
1 1/16 miles: Alydar's Rib, 1:41, November 1, 1996
1 5/8 miles: Open Space, 2:41.20, November 16, 1996
Other: 1 9/16 miles, Our Forbes, 2:39.20, November 7, 1997; 1 7/8 miles, Raw New, 3:16.20, December 1, 2000

Fastest Times of 2001

5 1/2 furlongs: Jimmy Jones, 1:03.27, October 17
6 furlongs: Two Punch Sonny, 1:08.91, September 8
1 mile: Freon Flier, 1:35.59, November 17
1 1/16 miles: Orientate, 1:42.22, October 6
1 5/8 miles: Pete's Skianno, 2:47.64, November 16
Other: 1 9/16 miles, Code De, 2:40.22, November 2; 1 7/8 miles, Talented Won, 3:19.48, November 30

Iowa

Prairie Meadows Racetrack

The Thoroughbred industry in Iowa received a boost when Prairie Meadows Racetrack in Altoona, not far from Des Moines, opened in 1989. But financial difficulties forced the track to file for bankruptcy in 1991 and to close for live racing in '92. The following year, Prairie Meadows became the property of Polk County, which today leases the facility to the nonprofit Racing Association of Central Iowa. The track's future was secured in 1995 when slot machines were installed, with a portion of revenues significantly increasing race purses. Today, Prairie Meadows's live racing schedule begins with a Thoroughbred meet that is followed by a mixed meet for Thoroughbreds and Quarter Horses, and concludes with a harness racing season. One of the track's most popular events is the Iowa Classic, a ten-race event for state-bred Thoroughbreds and Quarter Horses. Prairie Meadows's lone Thoroughbred graded stakes is the Prairie Meadows Breeders' Cup Handicap (G3), the track's richest race.

Location: 1 Prairie Meadows Dr., Altoona, IA 50009-0901
Phone: (515) 967-1000
Fax: (515) 967-1344
E-mail: racinginfo@prairiemeadows.com
Web site: http://www.prairiemeadows.com
Inaugural meeting: March 1, 1989-March 15, 1989
Acreage: 233
Seating capacity: 7,000
Number of stalls: 1,350

Officers

President: Robert A. Farinella
General Manager: Robert A. Farinella
Director of Racing: Derron Heldt
Racing Secretary: Pat Pope
Director of Operations: Don McGlory, Gary Palmer
Director of Marketing: Tom Manning
Director of Mutuels: Dorine Lawrence
Director of Publicity: Mary Lou Day-Coady
Director of Simulcasting: Matt Kingdon
Horsemen's Liaison: Chuck Schott
Stewards: Dick Garrison, Johnnie Johnson, Ralph D'Amico
Track Announcer: Ken Miller
Track Photographer: Jack Coady Jr.
Other Officials: Ron Morden, Vice President of Finance

Racing dates

2001: April 27-July 7, 53 days; July 21-October 6, 45 days
2002: April 26-July 6, 53 days; July 15-September 28, 45 days

Track Layout

Main circumference: 1 mile
Main track chute: 2 furlongs, 6 furlongs
Main length of stretch: 990 feet

Attendance

Average daily recent meeting: 9,228, Spring 2001; 8,704, Fall 2001
Total attendance recent meeting: 489,105, Spring 2001; 382,975, Fall 2001

Handle

Average all sources recent meeting: $644,288, Spring 2001; $235,474, Fall 2001
Average on-track recent meeting: $84,633, Spring 2001; $40,546, Fall 2001
Single day on-track handle: $488,070, May 5, 1990
Total all sources recent meeting: $34,147,249, Spring 2001; $10,360,870, Fall 2001
Total on-track recent meeting: $4,485,548, Spring 2001; $1,784,002, Fall 2001

Mutuel Records

Highest Win: $254, August 15, 1998
Lowest Win: $2.20, Who Doctor Who, April 22, 1989
Highest Exacta: $2,424.20, May 19, 1997
Lowest Exacta: $3.60, July 28, 1994
Highest Trifecta: $23,499, September 8, 1997

Prairie Meadows, continued

Lowest Trifecta: $11.20, May 4, 1998
Highest Daily Double: $2,216, September 24, 1998
Lowest Daily Double: $3.20, June 30, 1995

Leaders
Recent meeting, leading jockey: Terry Thompson, 68, Spring 2001; Glenn W. Corbett, 44, Fall 2001
Career, leading jockey by titles: Vicki Warhol, 3
Career, leading trainer by titles: Dick Clark, 8
Recent meeting, leading trainer: Stanley Roberts, 31, Spring 2001; Dick R. Clark, 20, Fall 2001
Recent meeting, leading owner: Highway 1 Racing Stable LLC, 21, Spring 2001; River Ridge Ranch, 18, Fall 2001

Track Records, Main Dirt
4 furlongs: Straight Fever, :46.20, July 16, 1993
4 1/2 furlongs: Echar Una Mano, :51 2/5, March 16, 1989
5 furlongs: Dayjob, :56, May 1, 1999
5 1/2 furlongs: Leaping Plum, 1:02.50, August 5, 1997
6 furlongs: Secret Shamrock, 1:08.21, August 13, 1998
1 mile: Apak, 1:35.07, August 11, 1998
1m 70 yds: Hammertime, 1:40, June 2, 1995
1 1/16 miles: Man the Shipp, 1:40.91, September 20, 1997
1 1/8 miles: Beboppin Baby, 1:46.62, July 4, 1998
1 1/4 miles: Famous Event, 2:02.60, June 23, 1995
1 1/2 miles: Famous Event, 2:32, July 9, 1995
1 5/8 miles: Sir Star, 2:44.3, May 12, 1989
2 miles: Gritti Marco, 3:26, July 28, 1995

Fastest Times of 2001
4 1/2 furlongs: Purple Pleasure, :52.80, May 6
5 furlongs: Sand Ridge, :56.80, May 5
5 1/2 furlongs: Outside the War, 1:03.21, May 18
6 furlongs: Miss Seffens, 1:08.62, July 3
1 mile: Sure Shot Biscuit, 1:36.40, May 6
1m 70yds: Asher, 1:41.13, May 19
1 1/16 miles: Royal Fair, 1:42.43, July 6
1 1/8 miles: Euchre, 1:47.72, July 7

Kansas

Anthony Downs

Location: 521 E. Sherman, Anthony, KS 67003-0444
Phone: (316) 842-3796
Fax: (316) 842-3772
Web site: http://www.ohmygosh.com/anthonydowns/

Officers
President: Dan Bird
Vice President: Joe Wilcox
Director of Racing: Frances Snell
Racing Secretary: Norris E. Gwin
Secretary: Terry Allen
Treasurer: Mel Kitts
Director of Publicity: Tommy Morris

Racing dates
2001: July 13-July 22, 6 days
2002: July 12-July 21, 6 days

Track Layout
Main circumference: 4 furlongs

Leaders
Recent meeting, leading jockey: Earl B. Sutton, 4, 2001; Jeremy L. Tabor, 4, 2001
Recent meeting, leading trainer: Zack Ashlock, 3, 2001

Fastest Times of 2001
4 1/2 furlongs: Pee D. Q., :59.93, July 14
5 furlongs: Loki, 1:02.68, July 20

6 furlongs: Chaserville, 1:23.26, July 22
7 furlongs: Moscow Gold Bar, 1:30.55, July 14
1 1/16 miles: Bold Sundance, 1:53.13, July 21

Eureka Downs

Eureka Downs, located 60 miles east of Wichita in Eureka, runs a 20-day mixed horse meet on weekends and holidays from the first week of May through July 4. The five-eighths-mile track, which dates back to 1872, raced Standardbreds in the late 1940s and was the site of Kansas's first pari-mutuel race for Thoroughbreds on September 3, 1988. The track closed in 1991 and reopened in '93 with the Greenwood County Fair Association and the Kansas Quarter Horse Racing Association co-licensed as operators.

Eureka Downs races Thoroughbreds, Quarter Horses, Appaloosas, Paints, and mules. Nonbetting mule contests began in the late 1990s and proved so popular that they were added to the pari-mutuel menu. Simulcasting is conducted during live racing only.

Location: 210 N. Jefferson St., Eureka, KS 67405
Phone: (316) 583-5528
Fax: (316) 583-5381
E-mail: info@eurekadowns.com
Web site: http://www.eurekadowns.com

Racing dates
2001: May 5-July 4, 19 days

Leaders
Recent meeting, leading jockey: Floyd Campbell, 10, 2001; Jeremy L. Tabor, 10, 2001; Melinda J. Walters, 10, 2001
Recent meeting, leading trainer: Joe F. Thomas Sr., 17, 2001

Fastest Times of 2001
4 furlongs: Dash a Coco, :44.72, May 6
6 furlongs: Extra Credit, 1:13.77, July 1
7 furlongs: Ms. River, 1:27.69, June 10
1 mile: Just a Eclipse, 1:45.71, June 30

The Woodlands

Opened in September 1989 for greyhound racing, The Woodlands began Thoroughbred racing on May 24, 1990. The track, located in the northwest corner of Kansas City, offers a 26-day mixed horse racing meet for Thoroughbreds and Quarter Horses in October and year-round greyhound racing on a separate track. The three types of racing have been conducted concurrently since 1990.

A typical day of horse racing at The Woodlands consists of ten races, with three races for Quarter Horses followed by seven for Thoroughbreds, although the mixture of Quarter Horse and Thoroughbred races varies.

The Woodlands set a single-day attendance record of 22,015 in its first year of Thoroughbred operation with a wallet giveaway. The track's then-parent company filed for bankruptcy protection from its creditors in 1996. The track was sold in 1998 to William M. Grace, principal owner of the St. Jo Frontier Casino in St. Joseph, Missouri. While advocating slot machines at the track, Grace received permission to buy the track's debt securities in 1997.

Location: 9700 Leavenworth Rd., Kansas City, KS 66112
Phone: (913) 299-9797
Fax: (913) 299-9804

Officers
General Manager: James Gartland
Racing Secretary: Doug Schoepf
Director of Publicity: Connie Loesback

Racing dates
2001: October 2-November 3, 26 days
2002: October 2-November 3, 26 days

Track Layout
Main circumference: 1 mile
Main length of stretch: 1,030 feet

Leaders
Recent meeting, leading trainer: Kenneth Gleason, 15, 2001
Recent meeting, leading jockey: Ken A. Shino, 38, 2001

Track Records, Main Dirt
4 1/2 furlongs: Lanyons Star, :51 2/5, June 29, 1990
5 furlongs: Jungle Merit, :57.40, October 29, 1993
5 1/2 furlongs: Axe Age, 1:03.20, August 15, 1993
6 furlongs: Great Immunity, 1:08.50, June 30, 1991
1 mile: French Fritter, 1:36, June 1, 1991
1m 70 yds: Holly's Wind, 1:40 2/5, June 24, 1990
1 1/16 miles: Axle Lode, 1:42.80, September 22, 1996
1 1/8 miles: Model Age, 1:49 4/5, July 18, 1990
1 3/16 miles: Lady Taneb, 1:59, September 7, 1994
1 1/4 miles: Midway Mail, 2:03.20, September 10, 1993
1 1/2 miles: He's A Valentine, 2:33.20, October 14, 1994
1 3/4 miles: Mark of Strength, 3:02, November 5, 1993

Fastest Times of 2001
4 furlongs: King of Diamonds, :45.80, October 10
5 furlongs: Classy Number, :59.40, October 27
5 1/2 furlongs: Pasomonte Paul, 1:03.80, October 28
6 furlongs: Kidd Cat, 1:10.80, October 20
1 mile: Redhanded, 1:39.80, October 6
1m 70yds: Personal Beau, 1:44.60, October 20
1 1/16 miles: Gangsta Rap, 1:47, November 4; Star of Mirador, 1:47, November 4

Kentucky

Churchill Downs

Churchill Downs in Louisville is one of the world's best-known racetracks, and its premier event, the Kentucky Derby (G1), is widely recognized as the sport's most famous race. First staged in 1875, the Derby is one of America's oldest continually run races and annually attracts an on-track audience exceeding 140,000, the nation's largest crowd for a Thoroughbred race, as well as worldwide television viewership in the millions. The Derby has been held at Churchill since the track opened on its current site in 1875. Col. M. Lewis Clark, Jr., the track's founder, built the first grandstand on land he secured from uncles John and Henry Churchill. Churchill Downs had financial problems for the first 28 years of its existence, forcing its sale by Clark and subsequent owners until Col. Matt Winn and partners bought the track in 1902.

The track, whose famous Twin Spires date from 1895, today is owned by Churchill Downs Inc., which also owns Hollywood Park near Los Angeles, Arlington Park near Chicago, Calder Race Course in Miami, and Ellis Park in western Kentucky. It also is part-owner of Hoosier Park in Indiana. Churchill has held five runnings of the Breeders' Cup, beginning in 1988 and most recently in

2000. In 2001, the track announced plans to embark on a $27-million renovation and expansion that includes creating premium suites overlooking the track. That work would begin in December 2002. Additionally, the track has proposed a $100-million rebuilding of the clubhouse area.

Location: 700 Central Ave., Louisville, KY 40208-1200
Phone: (502) 636-4400
Fax: (502) 636-4479
Web site: http://www.churchilldowns.com
Year founded: 1937
Inaugural meeting: May 17, 1875
Acreage: 147
Number of stalls: 1,404
Seating capacity: 48,500

Officers
President: Alexander M. Waldrop
Director of Racing: Douglas Bredar
Racing Secretary: Douglas Bredar
Director of Operations: David Sweazy
Director of Communications: John Asher
Director of Marketing: Kevin Marie Nuss
Director of Sales: Tyrone Tubbs
Horsemen's Liaison: J. L. "Buck" Wheat
Stewards: Bernard J. Hettel, Jack Middleton, Richard S. Leigh
Track Announcer: Luke Kruytbosch
Track Superintendent: Raymond "Butch" Lehr Jr.

Racing dates
2001: April 28-July 8, 53 days; October 28-November 24, 24 days
2002: April 27-July 7, 53 days; October 27-November 30, 30 days

Track Layout
Main circumference: 1 mile
Main track chute: 1 mile
Main width: 80 feet
Main length of stretch: 1,234 1/2 feet
Main turf circumference: 7 furlongs
Main turf width: 80 feet

Attendance
Highest single meet record: 811,446, Spring 1988
Record daily average for single meet: 20,066, Spring 1944
Total attendance recent meeting: 708,181, Spring 2001
Average daily recent meeting: 8,494, Fall 2001
Highest single day record: 163,628, May 4, 1974

Handle
Average all sources recent meeting: $7,282,573, Fall 2001
Average on-track recent meeting: $1,167,394, Fall 2001
Record daily average for single meet: $2,054,901, Spring 1997
Total all sources recent meeting: $174,781,741, Fall 2001, $522,416,506, Spring 2001
Total on-track recent meeting: $92,925,680, Spring 2001
Single day on-track handle: $101,515,004, May 6, 2000, $20,026,875, May 6, 2000

Mutuel Records
Highest Win: $495.60, Gold and Rubies, November 21, 1978
Highest Exacta: $8,062.40, November 13,1984
Highest Trifecta: $55,902.40, November 10, 2000
Highest Daily Double: $6,818.20, October 29, 1984
Highest Pick 3: $114,156, November 4, 2000
Highest Pick 6: $417,389.80, May 10, 1995
Highest Other Exotics: $76,063.80, Superfecta, June 27, 1998

Leaders
Career, leading jockey by stakes wins: Pat Day, 135
Career, leading jockey by titles: Pat Day, 30
Recent meeting, leading trainer: Bernie Flint, 22, Spring 2001; Dale Romans, 22, Spring 2001; Steve Asmussen, 13, Fall 2001

Churchill Downs, continued

Recent meeting, leading owner: Kenneth and Sarah Ramsey, 14, Spring 2001; Kenneth and Sarah Ramsey, 9, Fall 2001
Career, leading trainer by stakes wins: D. Wayne Lukas, 57
Career, leading jockey by wins: Pat Day, 2,049
Career, leading owner by stakes wins: Calumet Farm, 32
Career, leading owner by titles: Calumet Farm, 8; T. Alie Grissom, 8
Career, leading trainer by wins: Bill Mott, 486
Recent meeting, leading jockey: Pat Day, 86, Spring 2001; Pat Day, 32, Fall 2001
Career, leading trainer by titles: D. Wayne Lukas, 11

Records
Single day jockey wins: Pat Day, 7, June 20, 1984
Single meet, leading jockey by wins: Pat Day, 169
Single meet, leading trainer by wins: William I. Mott, 54

Track Records, Main Dirt
4 furlongs: Fair Phantom, :46 3/5, May 7, 1921; Casey, :46 3/5, May 9, 1921; Miss Joy, :46 3/5, May 10, 1921
4 1/2 furlongs: Chilukki, :51, April 28, 1999
5 furlongs: Open Story/City Street (dead heat), :57.28, May 5, 2001
5 1/2 furlongs: Yes It's True, 1:03.61, May 25, 1998
6 furlongs: Kona Gold, 1:07.77, November 4, 2000
6 1/2 furlongs: Love At Noon, 1:14.34, May 5, 2001
7 furlongs: Alannan, 1:20.50, May 5, 2001
7 1/2 furlongs: Super Marfalous, 1:28.82, May 23, 1999
1 mile: Chilukki, 1:33.57, November 4, 2000
1m 70 yds: The Porter, 1:41 3/5, May 30, 1919
1 1/16 miles: Yes Sir, 1:41 3/5, November 25, 1970
1 1/8 miles: Victory Gallop, 1:47.28, June 12, 1999
1 3/16 miles: Bonnie Andrew, 1:58 3/5, November 14, 1942
1 1/4 miles: Secretariat, 1:59 2/5, May 5, 1973
1 3/8 miles: Elliott, 2:20 3/5, October 15, 1906
1 1/2 miles: Cascade Peaks, 2:32.04, June 6, 1999
1 5/8 miles: Tupolev (Arg), 2:49 2/5, July 23, 1983
1 3/4 miles: Caslon Bold, 2:59.64, July 4, 1995
2 miles: Libertarian, 3:22.26, November 28, 1942
Other: 1m 20 yds, Frog Legs, 1:39, May 13, 1913; 1m 50 yds, Hodge, 1:41 4/5, October 4, 1916; 1m 100 yds, The Caxton, 1:49 1/5, May 16, 1902; 2 1/16 miles, Hi Neighbor, 3:40 4/5, November 11, 1949; 2 1/4 miles, Raincoat, 3:53, October 7, 1915; 3 miles, Ten Broeck, 5:26 1/2, September 3, 1876; 4 miles, Sotemia, 7:10 4/5, October 7, 1912

Course Records, Main Turf
5 furlongs: Separata (Chi), :55.92, May 3, 2001
1 mile: Jaggery John, 1:33.78, July 4, 1995
1 1/16 miles: Royal Strand (Ire), 1:40.93, May 2, 1997
1 1/8 miles: Lure, 1:46.34, April 30, 1993
1 3/8 miles: Snake Eyes, 2:13, May 22, 1997
1 1/2 miles: Tikkanen, 2:26.50, November 5, 1994

Fastest Times of 2001 (Dirt)
4 1/2 furlongs: Leelanau, :51.36, May 2
5 furlongs: City Street/Open Story (DH), :57.28, May 5
5 1/2 furlongs: Cashier's Dream, 1:02.52, July 7
6 furlongs: Lake Pontchartrain, 1:08.35, May 5
6 1/2 furlongs: Love At Noon, 1:14.34, May 5
7 furlongs: Alannan, 1:20.50, May 5
7 1/2 furlongs: Illusioned, 1:28.63, October 28
1 mile: Compendium, 1:34.78, June 16
1 1/16 miles: Fajardo, 1:41.69, July 5
1 1/8 miles: Guided Tour, 1:47.74, June 16
1 3/16 miles: Sheriffs Lap, 1:59.70, November 21
1 1/4 miles: Monarchos, 1:59.97, May 5
1 1/2 miles: A Storm Is Brewing, 2:32.02, June 17
2 miles: A Storm Is Brewing, 3:27.23, November 24

Fastest Times of 2001 (Turf)
5 furlongs: Separata (Chi), :55.92, May 3
1 mile: Dernier Croise (Fr), 1:34.43, November 7
1 1/16 miles: Ever With You, 1:40.82, November 7
1 1/8 miles: Dr. Kashnikow, 1:47.90, November 11
1 3/8 miles: With Anticipation, 2:16.28, June 2

Ellis Park

Ellis Park near Henderson, Kentucky, holds the distinction of being the only racetrack where soybeans are grown in the infield. Built in 1922 and designed after Saratoga Race Course, the track located on an island in the Ohio River near Evansville, Indiana, was originally named Dade Park and intended for harness racing. Within one month of its opening, the track replaced harness racing with Thoroughbred racing. Ellis was plagued with financial problems and, in 1923 and '24, the only racing held was for race cars on Labor Day weekend. In 1924, James C. Ellis, who owned construction and oil enterprises, purchased the track for $35,100 and reopened it for racing in 1925. In 1954, two years before Ellis's death, the track's name was changed to James C. Ellis Park. In 1998, Churchill Downs Inc. purchased Ellis, and its purses have benefited from full-card simulcasting revenues. Ellis's richest race each year is the $200,000 Gardenia Stakes (G3) for fillies and mares.

Location: 3300 U.S. Hwy. 41 N, Henderson, KY 42419-0033
Phone: (812) 425-1456
Fax: (812) 425-3725
Web site: http://www.ellisparkracing.com
Year founded: 1922
Inaugural meeting: November 8, 1922
Acreage: 214
Number of stalls: 1,142
Seating capacity: 7,750

Officers
President: Alexander M. Waldrop
Vice President: Paul D. Kuerzi
General Manager: Paul D. Kuerzi
Director of Racing: Douglas Bredar
Racing Secretary: Ben Huffman
Director of Operations: Robert A. Jackson
Director of Admissions: Marianne Wagner
Director of Marketing: B. Todd Mosby
Director of Mutuels: Jeff Hall
Director of Publicity: Luke Kruytbosch
Director of Simulcasting: Robert A. Jackson
Horsemen's Liaison: Donna Porter
Stewards: Ronald Herbstreit, Steve Obrekaitis, Warren Croce
Track Announcer: Luke Kruytbosch
Track Superintendent: Glenn Thompson

Racing dates
2002: July 10-September 2, 41 days
2001: July 11-September 3, 41 days

Track Layout
Main circumference: 1 1/8 miles
Main track chute: 1 mile, 7 furlongs
Main width: Homestretch: 100 feet; Backstretch: 85 feet
Main length of stretch: 1,175 feet
Main turf circumference: 1 mile

Attendance
Total attendance recent meeting: 120,008, 2001
Average daily recent meeting: 2,927, 2001
Highest single day record: 15,500 est., September 4, 1967

Handle
Total on-track recent meeting: $16,835,711, 2001
Total all sources recent meeting: $125,608,889, 2001
Average on-track recent meeting: $410,627, 2001
Average all sources recent meeting: $306,363, 2001

Leaders
Recent meeting, leading owner: Gary Patrick, 11, 2001
Recent meeting, leading trainer: Bernard S. Flint, 13, 2001

Recent meeting, leading jockey: Jon Court, 56, 2001
Career, leading jockey by titles: Leroy Tauzin, 7
Career, leading trainer by titles: Bernard S. Flint, 10

Records
Single day trainer wins: Wayne Bearden, 5, August 7, 1997
Single meet, leading jockey by wins: Mike McDowell, 89
Single meet, leading trainer by wins: Angel Montano, 34
Single day jockey wins: Willie Martinez, 8

Track Records, Main Dirt
5 furlongs: White Image, :57 3/5, July 9, 1988
5 1/2 furlongs: Mount Forloon, 1:03 2/5, July 17, 1988
6 furlongs: Stubilem, 1:09, July 1, 1982
6 1/2 furlongs: American Chance, 1:15, July 16, 1994
7 furlongs: Sheena Native, 1:21 3/5, July 23, 1988
1 mile: Still Waving, 1:34 3/5, August 13, 1988
1 1/8 miles: Lt. Lao, 1:47 3/5, August 27, 1988
1 1/4 miles: Won Du Loup, 2:03, September 4, 1988
1 3/8 miles: Ramona Jay, 2:23, August 24, 1985
1 1/2 miles: Unaccountable, 2:29 3/5, July 23, 1988
1 5/8 miles: Sir Lightning, 2:45.80, August 9, 1992
1 3/4 miles: Bondi, 3:00, August 27, 1966
2 miles: Classic Deal, 3:25 3/5, August 21, 1988
Other: 2 1/4 miles, Bondi, 3:54, September 5, 1966

Course Records, Main Turf
5 1/2 furlongs: Hello Paradise, 1:01, August 18, 1996
1 mile: Slewper Imp, 1:32.60, July 16, 1995; Suffragette, 1:32.60, July 24, 1999
1 1/16 miles: Majestic Jove, 1:39.20, August 27, 1997
1 1/8 miles: Yaqthan (Ire), 1:44.60, September 2, 1996
1 1/4 miles: Ye Slew, 1:59.60, August 6, 1994
1 1/2 miles: Our Forbes, 2:25.40, August 10, 1994
2 miles: Irish Harbour, 3:20.20, September 2, 1996

Interesting Facts
Previous name and dates: Dade Park

Fastest Times of 2001 (Dirt)
5 furlongs: Magic Bid, :57.50, September 3
5 1/2 furlongs: Andelegend, 1:03.69, August 24
6 furlongs: Miss Seffens, 1:09.35, August 11
6 1/2 furlongs: Dash for Daylight, 1:16.51, July 28
7 furlongs: Miner's Prize, 1:23.22, July 20
1 mile: Fajardo, 1:36.04, August 25
1 1/8 miles: Asher, 1:50.16, August 11
2 miles: Pete's Skianno, 3:30.30, September 3

Fastest Times of 2001 (Turf)
5 1/2 furlongs: General Express, 1:01.09, July 21
1 mile: Valory, 1:32.93, August 4
1 1/16 miles: Wild Dream, 1:39.79, August 22
1 1/8 miles: Promise of War, 1:46.30, September 3

Keeneland Race Course

Some tracks offer nothing more than an endless procession of live and simulcast races. But a few American tracks offer a sense of history and a state of mind. Keeneland Race Course falls into the latter category.

Since its opening meeting in October 1936, the Lexington track has developed a unique identity. The stately facility offers two short, marquee meetings—including races such as the Blue Grass Stakes (G1) in the spring and Spinster Stakes (G1) in the fall—in a setting near Lexington that screams atmosphere.

But Keeneland offers more than its race meets. Generating the cash for Keeneland's rich purses are the top-drawer sales that take place next to the track at the sales pavilion. Want to see a future Kentucky Derby (G1) winner? Keeneland's July and September yearling sales often provide that opportunity.

The Keeneland Association was incorporated in 1935 and purchased 147½ acres of land, including an ornate training track, from J. O. "Jack" Keene to build the facility. Lexington, bereft of racing after the Kentucky Association track closed earlier in the 1930s, quickly embraced the new facility, and more than 25,000 people attended the inaugural nine-day meeting.

Crowds in excess of 25,000 on a single day now are common at Keeneland. In one of the few areas of the country where the Thoroughbred is truly king, the Keeneland meets have become one of the social events of the season, drawing a wide range of spectators, including veteran racegoers, local business executives, socialites, breeders, and college students.

Location: 4201 Versailles Rd., Lexington, KY 40592-1690
Phone: (859) 254-3412
Fax: (859) 288-4348
E-mail: keeneland@keeneland.com
Web site: http://www.keeneland.com
Year founded: 1935
Inaugural meeting: October 15-24, 1936
Acreage: 907
Number of stalls: 1,845
Seating capacity: 7,000

Officers
President: Nick Nicholson
Vice President: Stanley H. Jones
Director of Racing: W. B. Rogers Beasley
Racing Secretary: Ben Huffman
Director of Operations: James A. Perry
Director of Auctions: Geoffrey Russell
Director of Communications: R. James Williams
Director of Finance: Harvie Wilkinson
Director of Marketing: Fran Taylor
Director of Sales: Geoffrey Russell
Director of Simulcasting: Maggie Johnson
Stewards: Bernard J. Hettel, Jack Middleton III, R. Spencer Leigh III
Track Announcer: Kurt Becker
Other Officials: James E. Bassett III, Chairman of the Board

Racing dates
2001: April 6-April 27, 15 days; October 5-October 27, 17 days
2002: April 5-April 26, 2002, 16 days; October 4-October 26, 2002, 17 days

Track Layout
Main circumference: 1 1/16 miles
Main track chute: 4 1/2 furlongs, 7 furlongs, 184 feet
Main length of stretch: 1,174 ft.
Main turf circumference: 7 1/2 furlongs
Main turf length of stretch: 1,190 ft.
Training track: 5 furlongs

Attendance
Record daily average for single meet: 14,649, Spring 2001
Total attendance recent meeting: 208,143, Fall 2001, 219,739, Spring 2001
Average daily recent meeting: 12,244, Fall 2001
Highest single day record: 29,687, April 15, 2000
Highest single meet record: 232,339, Spring 1988
Lowest single day record: 1,294, October 16, 1936

Handle
Average all sources recent meeting: $5,202,028, Fall 2001
Average on-track recent meeting: $1,515,845, Fall 2001
Record daily average for single meet: $1,695,948, Spring 2001
Single day on-track handle: $3,060,319, April 15, 2000
Single day total handle all sources: $17,076,993, April 14, 2001

Keeneland, continued

Total all sources recent meeting: $129,387,326, Spring 2001, $88,434,474, Fall 2001

Total on-track recent meeting: $18,743,574, Fall 2001, $25,439,213, Spring 2001

Leaders
Career, leading jockey by wins: Pat Day, 751

Career, leading owner by wins: T. A. Grissom and J. E. Grissom, 171

Career, leading trainer by wins: D. Wayne Lukas, 217

Recent meeting, leading jockey: Pat Day, 22, Spring 2001; Pat Day, 25, Fall 2001

Recent meeting, leading owner: Augustin Stable, 6, Spring 2001; McKee Stables, 5, Fall 2001

Recent meeting, leading trainer: Bill Mott, 7, Spring 2001; Dale Romans, 13, Fall 2001

Career, leading jockey by titles: Pat Day, 19

Career, leading trainer by titles: D. Wayne Lukas, 15

Records
Single meet, leading jockey by wins: Pat Day, 45

Single meet, leading trainer by wins: D. Wayne Lukas, 22

Single day trainer wins: 16 different trainers have saddled three winners in one day

Single day jockey wins: Craig Perret, 6, April 18, 1990; Randy Romero, 6, April 7, 1990

Track Records, Main Dirt
4 1/2 furlongs: Quick Swoon, :51, April 20, 1966; Royality Note, :51, April 23, 1968; Bend the Times, :51, April 8, 1980

6 furlongs: Anjiz, 1:07.78, October 9, 1993

6 1/2 furlongs: Number One Sheikh, 1:14.70, October 11, 2000

7 furlongs: Binalong, 1:20.39, October 13, 1993

1 1/16 miles: Din's Dancer, 1:40 4/5, October 9, 1990

1 1/8 miles: Good Command, 1:46 4/5, October 10, 1987

1 3/16 miles: Arch, 1:53.87, October 11, 1998

1 1/4 miles: Political Fact, 2:02.21, October 15, 1993

1 5/8 miles: Put-in-Bay, 2:45, October 13, 1967; Mr. Copy Chief, 2:45, October 20, 1971

Other: 7 furlongs 184 feet, Lamb Chop, 1:24 3/5, October 10, 1963

Course Records, Main Turf
5 1/2 furlongs: Chris's Thunder, 1:01.72, October 8, 2000

1 mile: Altibr, 1:33.72, October 7, 2000

1 1/16 miles: Quiet Resolve, 1:40.30, April 27, 2000

1 1/8 miles: Memories of Silver, 1:45.81, October 5, 1996

1 3/16 miles: Happyanunoit (NZ), 1:53.91, October 15, 1999

1 1/2 miles: Bursting Forth, 2:27.54, April 22, 1999

1 5/8 miles: Royal Strand (Ire), 2:38.68, October 24, 1999

Fastest Times of 2001 (Dirt)
4 1/2 furlongs: City Street, :51.04, April 20

6 furlongs: Cat Cay, 1:09.24, October 21

6 1/2 furlongs: Slider, 1:16.05, October 10

7 furlongs: Victory Ride, 1:22.34, April 13

1 1/16 miles: Connected, 1:42.40, October 12

1 1/8 miles: Millennium Wind, 1:48.32, April 14

1 3/16 miles: Duplicitous, 1:56.28, April 14

1 1/4 miles: Law Review, 2:05.22, October 21

Fastest Times of 2001 (Turf)
5 1/2 furlongs: Morluc, 1:02.22, October 5

1 mile: North East Bound, 1:34.44, April 13

1 1/16 miles: Penny's Gold, 1:40.93, April 12

1 1/8 miles: Thesaurus, 1:47.53, April 22

1 3/16 miles: Spook Express (SAf), 1:54.24, October 5

1 1/2 miles: Williams News, 2:29.13, April 25

Kentucky Downs

Straddling the Kentucky-Tennessee state border adjacent to Interstate 65, Kentucky Downs has enjoyed a short, colorful history. Opened in 1990 as Dueling Grounds Race Course—the track site was reputed to be the scene of several 19th century duels—the turf-only racecourse was conceived as a simulcasting facility with one day of live racing a year.

That one day of racing featured steeplechase racing and was well-received by the steeplechase community. But ownership controversies dogged the facility until the late 1990s, when businessman Brad Kelley, Turfway Park, and Churchill Downs purchased the facility. Kelley owns 52%, and the tracks each hold 24%. Track officials have found ways to make Kentucky Downs's turf-only status pay off. The track now offers a series of turf stakes on the flat to coincide partly with the Kentucky Cup series of dirt-only races at Turfway Park in Florence, Kentucky.

Location: 5629 Nashville Rd., Franklin, KY 42135

Phone: (270) 586-7778

Fax: (270) 586-8080

Web site: http://www.kentuckydowns.com

Year founded: 1990

Inaugural meeting: April 22, 1990

Officers
General Manager: Ryan Driscoll

Racing Secretary: Rick Leigh

Director of Operations: Jon Goodman

Director of Mutuels: Shelley Spears

Simulcasting Director: Mary Troilo

Racing dates
2001: September 15-September 24, 7 days

2002: September 14-September 23, 7 days

Track Layout
Main turf circumference: 1 5/16 miles

Leaders
Recent meeting, leading trainer: Ricky J. Short, 3, 2001; Thomas F. Proctor, 3, 2001

Career, leading jockey by titles: Jon Court, 2

Recent meeting, leading jockey: Jon Court, 6, 2001

Records
Single meet, leading jockey by wins: Jon Court, 8

Course Records, Main Turf
6 furlongs: Morluc, 1:09.66, September 23, 2000

7 furlongs: Slew of Deuces, 1:22.77, September 18, 2000

1 mile: Rob 'n Gin, 1:35.00, September 19, 1998

1 1/2 miles: Yaqthan (Ire), 2:27.60, September 19, 1998

Interesting facts
Previous name and dates: Dueling Grounds 1990-1996

Fastest Times of 2001 (Turf)
6 furlongs: Gamble Les, 1:10.52, September 17

7 furlongs: Dominique's Cat, 1:23.41, September 18

1 mile: Karly's Harley, 1:36.59, September 15

1 1/2 miles: Chorwon, 2:28.68, September 23

Turfway Park

Turfway Park is the Northern Kentucky successor of Old Latonia, a track that opened in the Latonia section of Covington in 1883 and shut down in 1939. In the late 1950s, an investor group built a new Latonia Race Course in Florence, approximately ten miles from the former site, and it opened on August 27, 1959. On April 9, 1986, Nashville real-estate developer Jerry Carroll and partners bought Latonia for $13.5-million and renamed it Turfway Park. Carroll undertook an extensive renovation program and raised the purse of the track's spring race for three-year-old Triple Crown

prospects, the Jim Beam Stakes (G2), to $500,000 in 1987. The race's purse would peak at $750,000 when it lost its initial sponsor and became the Galleryfurniture.com Stakes (G2) in 1999.

During Carroll's tenure, Turfway was a leader in offering intertrack wagering in Kentucky (1988) and in promoting legislation for full-card simulcasting in '94. Also in 1994, Turfway launched its Kentucky Cup Day of Champions, a September event featuring five stakes races. Carroll and partners sold the track to a partnership led by the Keeneland Association for $37-million on January 15, 1999. The track's premier race for three-year-olds reverted to its original name, the Spiral Stakes, in 2000, and Lane's End became its title sponsor for 2001.

Location: 7500 Turfway Rd., Florence, KY 41042
Phone: (859) 371-0200
Fax: (859) 371-0200
E-mail: turfway@turfway.com
Web site: http://www.turfway.com
Inaugural meeting: April 9, 1986 (Turfway), August 27, 1959 (Latonia)
Acreage: 197
Number of stalls: 1,200

Officers
President: Robert N. Elliston
Vice President: Clifford Reed
General Manager: Greg Schmitz
Director of Racing: Richard S. Leigh
Racing Secretary: Richard S. Leigh
Treasurer: Clifford Reed
Director of Operations: Greg Schmitz
Director of Admissions: Kenny Kramer
Director of Marketing: Brian Gardner
Director of Mutuels: Kenny Kramer
Director of Simulcasting: Mary Troilo
Horsemen's Liaison: Randy Wehrman
Stewards: Brooks Becraft III, Jack Middleton, Ron Herbstreit
Track Announcer: Mike Battaglia
Track Photographer: Pat Lang
Track Superintendent: Daniel Chapman
Other Officials: Jennifer Haas, Media Relations Manager, Randy Wehrman, Stakes Coordinator, Robin Rodgers, Controller

Racing dates
2001: November 26, 2000 to April 5, 2001, 83 days, September 5-October 4, 22 days
2002: November 25, 2001 to April 4, 2002, 92 days, September 4-October 4, 22 days

Track Layout
Main circumference: 1 mile
Main track chute: 1/4 mile, 6 1/2 furlongs
Main width: Backstretch: 50 feet; Homestretch: 90 feet
Main length of stretch: 970 feet

Attendance
Average daily recent meeting: 1,968, Winter/Spring 2000/2001; 2,070, Fall 2001
Highest single day record: 22,480, March 25, 2000
Highest single meet record: 354,867, Spring 1988
Total attendance recent meeting: 120,043, Winter/Spring 2000/2001; 43,477, Fall 2001
Record daily average for single meet: 5,377, Spring 1988

Handle
Average all sources recent meeting: $3,839,360, Winter/Spring 2000/2001; $3,382,467, Fall 2001
Total on-track recent meeting: $26,525,408, Winter/Spring 2000/2001; $7,834,519, Fall 2001
Total all sources recent meeting: $234,200,955, Winter/Spring 2000/2001; $71,031,808, Fall 2001

Average on-track recent meeting: $434,843, Winter/Spring 2000/2001; $373,072, Fall 2001
Single day on-track handle: $3,223,778, April 2, 1994

Mutuel Records
Highest Exacta: $6,777.20, January 29, 1988
Lowest Exacta: $3.20, September 26, 1998
Highest Trifecta: $101,694.80, February 21, 1996
Lowest Trifecta: $5.20, September 26, 1998
Highest Daily Double: $4,575.80, December 12, 1986
Lowest Daily Double: $5, September 24, 1994
Highest Pick 3: $24,752.40, December 26, 1993
Lowest Pick 3: $13.80, November 25, 1990
Highest Pick 6: $1,474,380, March 23, 1988
Highest Other Exotics: $56,375.20, Superfecta, January 5, 2000

Leaders
Career, leading jockey by stakes wins: Michael McDowell, 32
Career, leading jockey by titles: Willie Martinez, 9
Career, leading trainer by stakes wins: D. Wayne Lukas, 28
Career, leading trainer by titles: Bernard Flint, 11
Recent meeting, leading jockey: Kris Prather, 109, Winter/Spring 2001; Jon K. Court, 38, Fall 2001; James Lopez, 38, Holiday
Recent meeting, leading owner: David England, 12, Winter/Spring 2001; Julie Sizemore, 12, Winter/Spring 2001; Wayne Bearden, 12, Winter/Spring 2001; Rosendo Parra, 5, Fall 2001; Billy Hays, 5, Fall 2001; Diamond J Ranch, 5, Fall 2001; Brian S. Dance, 3, Holiday 2001; Billy Hays, 3, Holiday 2001; Select Stable, 3, Holiday 2001; Kimberly Beach and Jeanne Sheets, 3, Holiday 2001
Recent meeting, leading trainer: Bernard S. Flint, 26, Winter/Spring 2001; Bernard S. Flint, 9, Fall 2001; Bernard S. Flint, 17, Holiday

Records
Single day jockey wins: Kris Prather, 6, February 11, 2001
Single meet, leading trainer by wins: John Parisella, 40, Winter/Spring 1996
Single day jockey wins: D. Wayne Lukas, 4; Dennis Freking, 4; George Isaacs, 4; Harry Trotsek, 4; V. R. Wright, 4
Single meet, leading jockey by wins: Kris Prather, 109, Winter/Spring 2001

Track Records, Main Dirt
5 furlongs: Salutee, :56.98, February 23, 2002
5 1/2 furlongs: Da' White Judge, 1:03 4/5, September 29, 1979
6 furlongs: Appealing Skier, 1:08.24, September 21, 1996; Partner's Hero, 1:08.24, March 29, 1998
6 1/2 furlongs: Boone's Mill, 1:14.32, December 30, 1995
1 mile: Secreto's Hideaway, 1:34.12, March 5, 1994
1m 70 yds: Venture, 1:40 3/5, September 2, 1963
1 1/16 miles: Anet, 1:40.73, March 29, 1997
1 1/8 miles: Hansel, 1:46.70, March 30, 1991
1 3/16 miles: Roman Justice, 1:58 3/5, December 24, 1966
1 1/4 miles: Executor, 2:03.82, December 29, 2000
1 3/8 miles: Briarwick, 2:21, December 10, 1968
1 1/2 miles: Canive, 2:31 2/5, September 7, 1963
1 5/8 miles: Bluegrass Warrior, 2:46.61, February 23, 1991
1 3/4 miles: Bluegrass Warrior, 2:59, March 10, 1990
2 miles: Bluegrass Warrior, 3:23.90, March 30, 1991
Other: 2 furlongs, Kadabra, :21.25, March 31, 2001; 3 furlongs, Cut Glass, :34 3/5, March 27, 1976; 1 11/16 miles, Sestos, 2:56 1/5, January 1, 1969

Fastest Times of 2001
5 furlongs: Coin Machine, :58.26, December 23
5 1/2 furlongs: World Champion, 1:05.86, September 26
6 furlongs: Flattened, 1:09.12, March 29
6 1/2 furlongs: Davka Devil, 1:16.21, March 10
1 mile: Willowbrook Lane, 1:34.96, February 17
1 1/16 miles: Trip, 1:42.42, March 31
1 1/8 miles: Balto Star, 1:47.23, March 24
1 1/4 miles: Code De, 2:08.13, September 29
1 1/2 miles: Talented Won, 2:36.77, February 10

Turfway, continued

1 3/4 miles: Talented Won, 2:59.83, March 3
2 miles: Runaway Affair, 3:28.32, March 24
Other: 2 furlongs, Kadabra, :21.25, March 31

Louisiana

Delta Downs

Lee Berwick, a prominent Quarter Horse breeder and owner and a former president of the American Quarter Horse Association, opened the first Delta Downs as a nonpari-mutuel match track on his farm at St. Joseph, Louisiana, on the banks of the Mississippi River. He moved the operation to Vinton, Louisiana, two hours northeast of Houston, and opened Delta Downs in 1973. Berwick served as track president until 1997, when his daughter, Kathryn, succeeded him in the position. In 1999, the Berwicks sold Delta Downs for more than $10-million to Shaun Scott and Jinho Cho, who began renovating the facility in hopes of installing slot machines. In 2001, the track was again sold for $125-million to Las Vegas-based Boyd Gaming Corp., which owns casinos in Louisiana, Nevada, Illinois, and Mississippi. In October 2001, Boyd received approval from the Louisiana Gaming Control Board to operate 1,700 slot machines. Delta Downs offers racing for Thoroughbreds as well as a separate season for Quarter Horses and Paints. The track's richest Thoroughbred event is the $100,000 Jean Lafitte Futurity for two-year-olds and is held each April.

Location: 2717 Hwy. 3063, Vinton, LA 70668
Phone: (337) 589-7441
Fax: (337) 589-2399
E-mail: deltadownsalb@aol.com
Web site: http://www.deltadowns.com
Year founded: 1973
Acreage: 240
Number of stalls: 1,200

Officers
President: William S. Boyd
Vice President: Jack Bernsmeier
General Manager: Jack Bernsmeier
Director of Racing: Trent McIntosh
Racing Secretary: Trent McIntosh
Director of Operations: Charles Sonnier (racing), Lenny Brondum
Director of Communications: Wynn Findley
Director of Finance: Kim Etland
Director of Marketing: Amber Van Tronk
Director of Mutuels: Liz Findley
Director of Publicity: Steve Nick
Director of Simulcasting: Dave Wilson
Stewards: Aaron Emigh, Duane Domingue, Judy Dugas
Track Announcer: Steve Nick
Track Photographer: Coady Photography
Track Superintendent: Daryl Wilfer
Other Officials: Susan Ribio, Director of Human Resources

Racing dates
2001: January 4-April 13, 59 days
2002: November 17, 2001 to April 7, 2002, 82 days

Track Layout
Main circumference: 6 furlongs
Main track chute: 1 1/16 mile, 5 furlongs
Main width: 70 feet
Main length of stretch: 660 feet

Leaders
Recent meeting, leading jockey: Brian Hernandez, 41, 2000/2001
Recent meeting, leading trainer: Doris Herbert, 25, 2000/2001

Track Records, Main Dirt
4 furlongs: Rock Afire, :46 1/5, December 10, 1994
4 1/2 furlongs: Road to Seattle, :52, January 15,1998
5 furlongs: Mollie McLash, :57.69, January 31, 2002
6 1/2 furlongs: Chief Okie Dokie, 1:18.76, February 8, 2002
7 furlongs: Norms Promise, 1:24 3/5, March 2, 1975
7 1/2 furlongs: Junior Gent, 1:33 1/5, March 14, 1974
1 mile: Freon Flier, 1:37.52, March 10, 2002
1m 70 yds: Thriller, 1:42 2/5, September 27, 1973
1 1/16 miles: Norms Promise, 1:43 1/5, March 23, 1975
1 1/8 miles: Lucky Silence, 1:55 2/5, February 18, 1994
1 3/16 miles: Ponderosa Lark, 2:03 3/5, October 31, 1975
1 1/4 miles: Shy Bull, 2:10 1/5, November 3, 1974
1 3/8 miles: Ponderosa Lark, 2:27 1/5, December 15, 1974
1 1/2 miles: Art Work, 2:41 1/5, December 11, 1974
2 miles: Can Em, 3:43 4/5, December 10, 1988
Other: 1 5/16 miles, Gentleman Mike, 2:17 3/5, December 1, 1974; 1 9/16 miles, Landing Officer, 2:51 4/5, December 15,1989

Interesting facts
Trivia: Three alligators live in the infield

Fastest Times of 2001
4 furlongs: Taylor's Queen, :47.06, April 13
4 1/2 furlongs: Frosty Coco, :52.89, December 27
5 furlongs: Canyoukeepasecret, :58.16, March 9
6 1/2 furlongs: Hunting Course, 1:19.86, February 23
7 furlongs: Magic Key, 1:25.46, February 24
7 1/2 furlongs: Samlot, 1:34.36, December 8
1 mile: Dividend M, 1:38.89, March 24
1m 70yds: Impatient Michael, 1:46.91, March 24
1 1/16 miles: Audacious Kid, 1:47.40, March 1

Evangeline Downs

Located in Louisiana's colorful Cajun country, Evangeline Downs near Lafayette is known as the cradle of jockeys. Racing Hall of Fame member Eddie Delahoussaye, multiple Eclipse Award winner Kent Desormeaux, and leading jockeys Shane Sellers and Mark Guidry all won their first races at the track. Several nationally known horses also have competed at Evangeline. In 1977, a two-year-old named John Henry won two of three starts at Evangeline and scored his first stakes win in the Lafayette Futurity. From that beginning, John Henry went on to earn more than $6.5-million and was voted Horse of the Year in 1981 and '84. In 1999 and 2000, Louisiana-bred Hallowed Dreams won 16 consecutive races, including six at Evangeline. The track, which also offers some Quarter Horse racing, conducts live racing from mid-April to early September. The track's future could include a new location and slot machines. Plans call for the track to move to nearby Opelousas to take advantage of a state law that permits slot machines at racetracks if authorized by local parishes (counties). Gaming devices were not approved in St. Landry Parish, where Evangeline is located. The new track would have a grandstand that seats nearly 6,000 fans, a one-mile dirt oval—increased from the current seven-furlong track—and a turf course

configured inside the main track. The facility could also eventually include an 18-hole golf course, water park, amusement park, civic center, and agricultural center.

Location: P.O. Box 90270, Lafayette, LA 70509-0270
Phone: (337) 896-7223
Fax: (337) 896-5445
E-mail: evdinfo@evangelinedowns.com
Web site: http://www.evangelinedowns.com
Year founded: 1966
Inaugural meeting: 1966
Acreage: 133.7
Number of stalls: 960
Seating capacity: 4,200

Officers
President: Charles B. Ashy Sr.
Vice President: Charles B. Ashy Jr.
General Manager: Charles B. Ashy Sr.
Director of Racing: Charles B. Ashy Jr.
Racing Secretary: Norris E. Gwin
Director of Finance: Steve Orrbonne
Director of Marketing: Calzone & Associates
Director of Mutuels: Rachael Conway
Director of Publicity: Calzone & Associates
Director of Simulcasting: Charles B. Ashy Jr.
Stewards: Brent Seward, E. J. Fayard, Larry Munster
Track Announcer: Don Allen
Track Photographer: S. C. I. Photography

Racing dates
2001: April 14-September 3, 82 days
2002: April 13-September 2, 82 days

Track Layout
Main circumference: 7 furlongs
Main track chute: 1 3/16 miles, 6 furlongs
Main width: 70 feet
Main length of stretch: 1,020 feet

Attendance
Highest single day record: 8,218, July 4, 1975
Average daily recent meeting: 1,573, 2000

Handle
Single day total handle all sources: $2,052,653, July 1, 1999
Record daily average for single meet: $1,531,758, 2000
Average all sources recent meeting: $1,531,758, 2000
Average on-track recent meeting: $130,002, 2000

Mutuel Records
Highest Win: $412.20, Princely Greek, April 26, 1987
Highest Exacta: $24,213.90, August 1, 1982
Highest Trifecta: $37,995, August 23, 1997

Leaders
Career, leading trainer by titles: Don Cormier Sr., 8 (consecutive 1992-1999)
Recent meeting, leading jockey: Jamie Theriot, 105, 2001
Recent meeting, leading trainer: Keith L. Bourgeois, 88, 2001

Records
Single day jockey wins: Gerard Melancon, 6, 1984; Shane Sellers, 6, 1985; James Avant, 6, 1988; Curt Bourque, 6, 1989; Curt Bourque, 6, 1991; James Avant, 6, 1995; Kirk LeBlanc, 6, 1995
Single meet, leading jockey by wins: Curt Bourque, 141; Randy Romero, 141
Single meet, leading trainer by wins: Don Cormier Sr., 91, 1996

Track Records, Main Dirt
4 furlongs: Rare Trip, :46 3/5, May 20, 1977
4 1/2 furlongs: Bag in Hand, :51.60, August 28, 2000
5 furlongs: Hallowed Dreams, :57.40, July 3, 1999
5 1/2 furlongs: Hot Patriot, 1:04, June 6, 1997
6 furlongs: Rail, 1:09.20, July 22, 1995

7 1/2 furlongs: Top Silk, 1:31.40, June 2, 1991
1 mile: Selma's Boy, 1:36 3/5, July 12, 1981; Winning Connection, 1:36.60, August 19, 2000
1m 40 yds: Mr. D's Prank, 1:43 3/5, July 11, 1983
1m 70 yds: State Commander, 1:42, April 22, 1991
1 1/16 miles: Nin's Pick, 1:43 2/5, June 19, 1977
1 1/8 miles: Report to Glory, 1:50.80, August 9, 1993
1 3/16 miles: Beebe's Fair Eve, 2:00 4/5, September 13, 1968
1 1/4 miles: Nageire, 2:10 4/5, June 3, 1972
1 3/8 miles: Stubzy, 2:22 2/5, September 12, 1970
1 1/2 miles: Just for Charlie, 2:41 2/5, September 15, 1986
1 5/8 miles: Lucky Man, 2:49.60, August 4, 2000
2 miles: Gray Gardner, 3:31 3/5, August 27, 1990
Other: 1 7/16 miles, Red and Bold, 2:30 1/5, July 31, 1988; 1 7/8 miles, Concho County, 3:19.60, August 18, 2000

Fastest Times of 2001
4 1/2 furlongs: Exoctic Irish, :52.20, August 16
5 furlongs: Diamond of Ice, :58.40, June 2, Savvy Connection, :58.40, August 2
5 1/2 furlongs: Above Cause, 1:04.20, August 18, Jay's Nature, 1:04.20, April 20
6 furlongs: Knight in White, 1:09.80, April 25
7 1/2 furlongs: Devils Madwoman, 1:32.60, August 16; Stormscope, 1:32.60, August 30
1 mile: Forest Echoes, 1:38.80, April 26; Two Punch Sonny, 1:38.80, August 18
1m 70yds: Dividend M, 1:43.60, July 18
1 1/16 miles: To the Floor, 1:46.00, July 12

Fair Grounds

Thoroughbred racing has been conducted at the site of Fair Grounds in New Orleans with few interruptions since 1853, when a racetrack named Union Course held its first Thoroughbred meeting. The track, which has been called Fair Grounds since the 1860s, served as a military camp during the Civil and Spanish-American Wars. At times, changing political climates have halted racing, and devastating fires destroyed the facility in 1919 and '93. Fair Grounds survived, and some of the sport's most famous racehorses have run there. Racing Hall of Fame member Lexington raced twice in matches there, defeating Sallie Waters in 1853 and besting rival Lecompte in '55. Legendary distaffer Pan Zareta died of pneumonia at Fair Grounds in 1918 and was buried at the track. Kentucky Derby winner Black Gold, winner of the Louisiana Derby at Fair Grounds in 1924, was fatally injured in the Salome Handicap in '28 and was buried in the track's infield. Other noted horses who have raced at Fair Grounds include 1941 Triple Crown winner Whirlaway, winner of the inaugural Louisiana Handicap in '42; multiple Fair Grounds stakes winner Master Derby, who captured the '75 Preakness Stakes (G1); and Silverbulletday, who won two Fair Grounds stakes during her '99 championship season. Since 1990, Fair Grounds has been owned by the Krantz family members, who have worked to strengthen the track in the face of competition from other forms of gaming. After the 1993 fire destroyed its grandstand, temporary structures were used during construction of a $34.5-million grandstand and clubhouse, which opened on November 27, 1997. Fair Grounds, which offers live racing from late November through late March, plays host to Louisiana Champions Day, a $1-million event for state-bred Thoroughbreds and Quarter Horses, in December. The Louisiana Derby (G2) in March is a prep race for the Kentucky Derby (G1).

Fair Grounds, continued

Location: 1751 Gentilly Blvd., New Orleans, LA 70119
Phone: (504) 944-5515
Fax: (504) 944-2511
E-mail: fgno@accesscom.net
Web site: http://www.fgno.com
Year founded: 1852
Inaugural meeting: April 13, 1872
Acreage: 145
Number of stalls: 1,950

Officers

President: Bryan G. Krantz
General Manager: Bryan G. Krantz
Director of Racing: Mervin Muniz Jr.
Racing Secretary: Mervin Muniz Jr.
Director of Admissions: George Graham
Director of Marketing: Lenny Vangilder
Director of Mutuels: Eddie Fenasci
Director of Publicity: Lenny Vangilder
Director of Simulcasting: Raymond Beard
Stewards: Bill Hartack, Larry Munster, Peter Kosiba
Track Announcer: Frank Mirahmadi, Michael Wrona
Track Photographer: Louis Hodges Jr.
Track Superintendent: Paul Gregoire

Racing dates

2001: November 23, 2000-March 26, 2001, 88 days
2002: November 22, 2001-March 25, 2002, 89 days

Track Layout

Main circumference: 1 mile
Main track chute: 2 furlongs
Main width: 75 feet
Main length of stretch: 1,346 feet
Main turf circumference: 7 furlongs

Attendance

Total attendance recent meeting: 219,853, 2000/2001
Average daily recent meeting: 2,498, 2000/2001
Highest single day record: 23,662, November 27, 1969

Handle

Single day on-track handle: $740,854, March 12, 2000
Single day total handle all sources: $9,080,419, March 12, 2000
Average all sources recent meeting: $4,800,000+, 2000/2001
Average on-track recent meeting: $293,000+, 2000/2001
Total all sources recent meeting: $430.2-million, 2000/2001
Total on-track recent meeting: $25.8-million, 2000/2001

Mutuel Records

Highest Win: $500.60, Grey Hip, March 16, 1933
Highest Exacta: $2,626.20, January 2, 1999
Lowest Exacta: $2.40, December 13, 1997
Highest Daily Double: $2,917, January 5, 1971
Lowest Daily Double: $5.40, December 10, 1998
Highest Pick 3: $23,731.40, December 26, 1999
Lowest Pick 3: $14.60, December 4, 1998
Highest Pick 6: $108,848.20, March 29, 1999
Highest Other Exotics: $91,533, Superfecta, March 29, 1999
Lowest Other Exotics: $61.80, Superfecta, January 24, 1998

Leaders

Recent meeting, leading trainer: Steven M. Asmussen, 54, 2000/2001, Thomas M. Amoss, 54, 2000/2001
Recent meeting, leading jockey: Lonnie Meche, 99, 2000/2001
Career, leading jockey by titles: Ronald Ardoin, 6
Career, leading trainer by titles: Jack Van Berg, 10

Records

Single day trainer wins: Thomas Amoss, 4, January 19, 1995
Single day jockey wins: James P. Bowlds, 6, March 11, 1965; E. J. Perrodin, 6, November 18, 1979; Randy Romero, 6, February 8, 1984; V. L. "Billy" Smith, 6, March 15, 1990; Shane Romero, 6, February 10, 1991; Shane Romero, 6, February 24, 1991
Single meet, leading trainer by wins: Jack Van Berg, 92
Single meet, leading jockey by wins: Randy Romero, 181

Track Records, Main Dirt

4 furlongs: Blue Carbon, :46 1/5, March 18, 1967
4 1/2 furlongs: Debs Mini Bars, :52 1/5, March 8, 1971
5 furlongs: Foreign Pass, :57.50, November 27, 1998
5 1/2 furlongs: Chief Howcome, 1:03.26, February 11, 2000
6 furlongs: Hallowed Dreams, 1:08.34, March 17, 2001
7 furlongs: For Fair, 1:24 2/5, February 8, 1915
7 1/2 furlongs: Begue, 1:33 3/4, March 30, 1896
1 mile: Kitwe, 1:35.94, March 26, 1998
1m 40 yds: Total Rage, 1:38.52, March 23, 1997
1m 70 yds: Zevson, 1:41, November 26, 1936
1 1/16 miles: Pie in Your Eye, 1:42.02, March 19, 1994
1 1/8 miles: Phantom On Tour, 1:48.13, March 8, 1998
1 3/16 miles: Half Magic, 1:56 1/5, March 21, 1977
1 1/4 miles: It's the One, 2:01 4/5, March 21, 1982; Westheimer, 2:01 4/5, March 24, 1985; Herat, 2:01 4/5, March 16, 1986
1 3/8 miles: Carroll Road, 2:18 1/5, January 30, 1965; Tahuna, 2:18 1/5, March 6, 1965
1 1/2 miles: Tahuna, 2:32 2/5, March 13, 1965
1 5/8 miles: From Afar, 2:49 3/5, February 27, 1954, Major Mansir, 2:49 3/5, January 4, 1904
1 3/4 miles: Aladdin Prince, 3:01 2/5, April 5, 1981
2 miles: Bolster, 3:28 1/5, February 7, 1920
Other: 2 furlongs, Baloma, :21 4/5, February 14, 1952; 2 furlongs, Baloma, :21 4/5, January 26, 1952; 3 furlongs, Henry's Baby, :33 4/5, February 15, 1971; 3 furlongs, It's the Law, :33 4/5, February 18, 1976; 3 1/2 furlongs, Silver Finn, :41, February 24, 1925; 1 mile 20 yds, Grumpy, 1:40 3/5, February 5, 1916; 1 mile 20 yds, Lucky R., 1:40 3/5, January 11, 1916; 1 9/16 miles, Retintin, 2:42 4/5, March 28, 1970; 1 7/8 miles, Julius Caesar, 3:19, February 27, 1900; 2 miles 70 yds, Omar, 3:39 1/5, March 3, 1940; 2 1/16 miles, Quib's Bally, 3:47 1/5, March 6, 1948; 2 1/4 miles, Marvin Neal, 3:56, February 23, 1907; 3 miles, Colonist, 5:35, February 17, 1906; 4 miles, Major Mansir, 8:04 3/5, March 21, 1903

Course Records, Main Turf

5 1/2 furlongs: Beware Avalanche, 1:03.37, March 12, 2000
7 1/2 furlongs: Northcote Road, 1:29.26, March 7, 2000
1 mile: Rich and Ready, 1:35 4/5, January 17, 1982
1 1/16 miles: Dixie Poker Ace, 1:42, January 8, 1994
1 1/8 miles: Rich and Ready, 1:46 4/5, February 21, 1982
1 3/8 miles: Present the Colors, 2:17 1/5, April 4, 1982
1 1/2 miles: Palace Panther (Ire), 2:32, April 6, 1986
Other: 1 9/16 miles, To the Floor, 2:40.26, March 29, 1999

Interesting facts

Previous names and dates: Union Race Course 1872-1952

Fastest Times of 2001 (Dirt)

5 furlongs: Hares, :59.71, December 28
5 1/2 furlongs: Aloha Bold, 1:03.52, December 14
6 furlongs: Hallowed Dreams, 1:08.34, March 17
1 mile: Winning Connection, 1:36.93, March 15
1m 40yds: Smilin' Slew, 1:38.88, March 17
1 1/16 miles: Dollar Bill, 1:43.45, February 18
1 1/8 miles: Include, 1:49.18, March 4

Fastest Times of 2001 (Turf)

1 mile: Kolinor, 1:38.27, January 12

Louisiana Downs

Louisiana Downs, located near Shreveport in Bossier City, opened in 1974. Built by the late shopping-center developer Edward DeBartolo Sr., the track introduced the Super Derby (G1) in 1980, and since then, the fall race has attracted leading three-year-olds. The first running was won by Temperence Hill, winner of that year's Belmont Stakes (G1). The 1¼-mile race's purse initially was $500,000, then one of the biggest pots in the sport, and was increased to $1-million in 1987, when Kentucky

Derby (G1) and Preakness Stakes (G1) victor Alysheba defeated Candi's Gold. In the late 1990s, however, it was reduced to its original $500,000 purse. Two three-year-olds—Sunday Silence in 1989 and Tiznow in 2000—used the Super Derby as a stepping stone to victory in the Breeders' Cup Classic (G1) and Horse of the Year honors in their respective years. DeBartolo's racetrack holdings were sold in the years following his death, and Louisiana Downs was acquired by his son-in-law, John York II. In November 2001, a group of investors headed by Shreveport lawyer Jim Davis announced plans to buy Louisiana Downs. The investor group plans $90-million in renovations, including a 300-room hotel. The track has received permission to operate slot machines and expects to open a casino with approximately 1,700 slot machines in 2003.

Location: 8000 E. Texas St., Bossier City, LA 71171-5519
Phone: (318) 742-5555; (800) 551-2361
Fax: (318) 741-2591
E-mail: bburgess@ladowns.com
Web site: http://www.ladowns.com
Year founded: 1974
Inaugural meeting: October 30, 1974, to January 26, 1975
Acreage: 350
Number of stalls: 1,360
Seating capacity: 17,240

Officers
Vice President: Ray A. Tromba
General Manager: Ray A. Tromba
Director of Racing: Patrick J. Pope
Racing Secretary: Patrick J. Pope
Director of Operations: Cliff D. Burge
Director of Admissions: Tom Stedman
Director of Marketing: Jennifer Ray
Director of Mutuels: Holly Romain
Director of Publicity: Scott Jester
Director of Sales: Tom Showalter
Director of Simulcasting: Dick Pollack
Horsemen's Liaison: Patrick J. Pope
Stewards: Coleman Lloyd, Johnnie Johnson, Judy Dugas
Track Announcer: Frank Mirahmadi
Track Photographer: Reed Palmer Photography
Track Superintendent: George McDermott
Other Officials: John C. York II, Chairman

Racing dates
2001: June 30-November 11, 89 days
2002: June 28-September 22, 80 days

Track Layout
Main circumference: 1 mile
Main track chute: 1 1/4 miles, 7 furlongs
Main width: 80 feet
Main length of stretch: 1,010 feet
Main turf circumference: 7 furlongs 50 feet
Main turf width: 70 feet
Main turf length of stretch: 940 feet

Attendance
Average daily recent meeting: 3,355, 2001
Highest single day record: 26,513, May 26, 1986
Total attendance recent meeting: 298,626, 2001

Handle
Total all sources recent meeting: $187,758,904, 2001
Average all sources recent meeting: $2,109,657, 2001
Single day total handle all sources: $6,763,853, October 2, 1999
Single day on-track handle: $4,371,781, September 27, 1987

Mutuel Records
Highest Win: $249, B.J.'s Spruce, June 21, 1996
Lowest Win: $2.20, Appealing Breeze, 1989; $2.20, Richman,

1990; $2.20, Morning Meadow, 1993; $2.20, Runaway Venus, 1999; $2.20, Smart Ring, 1999
Highest Exacta: $2,780.80, May 1, 1994
Lowest Trifecta: $18.90, August 19, 1994
Highest Daily Double: $5,556.20, October 14, 1976
Highest Pick 3: $37,286.20, June 6, 1992
Lowest Pick 3: $11.80, September 12, 1994
Highest Pick 6: $555,287, May 25, 1991
Highest Other Exotics: $52,017.60, Superfecta, June 2, 1996

Leaders
Career, leading owner by stakes wins: John Franks, 144
Recent meeting, leading trainer: Cole Norman, 108, 2001
Career, leading owner by titles: John Franks, 18
Career, leading trainer by stakes wins: Frank Brothers
Career, leading trainer by wins: C. W. Walker, 820
Recent meeting, leading jockey: Kirk LeBlanc, 123, 2001
Recent meeting, leading owner: Kenneth W. Murphy, 19, 2001
Career, leading jockey by wins: Ronald Ardoin, 2,773
Career, leading trainer by titles: Frank Brothers, 7
Career, leading jockey by stakes wins: Ronald Ardoin
Career, leading jockey by titles: Larry Snyder, 6, Ronald Ardoin, 6

Records
Single day jockey wins: Ricky Frazier, 7, October 27, 1984
Single day trainer wins: Frank Brothers, 5, May 16, 1982; Frank Brothers, 5, September 3, 1984; Jack Van Berg, 5, December 5, 1976
Single meet, leading jockey by wins: Ronald Ardoin, 198
Single meet, leading owner by wins: John Franks, 65, 1983
Single meet, leading trainer by wins: Frank Brothers, 99, 1987

Track Records, Main Dirt
4 1/2 furlongs: Sondor, :51 3/5, May 16, 1984
5 furlongs: Oh Mar, :57.21, September 25, 2000
5 1/2 furlongs: Fighting K, 1:02.84, September 11, 1993
6 furlongs: Tangent, 1:08 4/5, April 28, 1984
6 1/2 furlongs: Prince of the Mt., 1:14.98, May 23, 1996
7 furlongs: Carrysport, 1:21 3/5, July 4, 1984
1m 70 yds: Country Jim, 1:39 2/5, July 4, 1982
1 1/16 miles: Nelson, 1:41.44, August 15, 1993
1 1/8 miles: Mocha Express, 1:48.14, July 24, 1999
1 3/16 miles: Jungle Pocket, 1:57 2/5, August 15, 1984
1 1/4 miles: Tiznow, 1:59.84, September 30, 2000
1 1/2 miles: Frankie's Pal, 2:31 4/5, September 3, 1990
1 3/4 miles: Frankie's Pal, 2:58 4/5, October 14, 1990
2 miles: Vain Lass, 3:35 1/5, November 16, 1975
Other: 1 13/16 miles, Stage Door Joey, 3:09 .91, September 20, 1992

Course Records, Main Turf
5 furlongs: Mo Dinero, :55.40, September 26, 1999
7 1/2 furlongs: Chuck N Luck, 1:28 2/5, August 5, 1989
1 mile: Cherokee Circle, 1:34 1/5, July 24, 1983
1 1/16 miles: Clever Song, 1:40 1/5, August 11, 1985; Marastani, 1:40.29, May 28, 1994
1 1/4 miles: Tali Hai, 2:04.19, August 31, 1997
1 3/8 miles: Semillero (Chi), 2:13 1/5, October 21, 1985

Fastest Times of 2001 (Dirt)
4 1/2 furlongs: Dandy Princess, :51.96, July 6
5 furlongs: Leslie's Love, :58.10, July 27
5 1/2 furlongs: Kettle Man, 1:03.38, July 29
6 furlongs: Triple Card, 1:09.13, July 21
6 1/2 furlongs: Kettle Man, 1:15.42, October 27
7 furlongs: Mountain Kitten, 1:23.00, August 3
1m 70yds: Goodtime Rocket, 1:41.36, July 13
1 1/16 miles: Taffy, 1:43.92, August 5
1 1/8 miles: Unrullah Bull, 1:48.30, August 4
1 1/4 miles: Outofthebox, 2:06.20, September 23

Fastest Times of 2001 (Turf)
7 1/2 furlongs: Ski Bum, 1:29.94, August 16
1 mile: Thrive, 1:36.12, November 10
1 1/16 miles: Nat's Big Party, 1:41.71, July 4

Maryland

Laurel Park

Located in Laurel, midway between Baltimore and Washington, D.C., Laurel Park is one of two tracks owned by the Maryland Jockey Club. Racing first began at Laurel in 1911, and, three years later, New York City grocery entrepreneur James Butler acquired the track and hired Col. Matt Winn as the track's general manager. In 1947, the Maryland Jockey Club bought the track from Butler's estate, but the state's racing commission refused to permit Pimlico Race Course's dates to be moved to Laurel. Baltimore industrialist Morris Schapiro purchased the track in 1950 and put his youngest son, John D. Schapiro, in charge of the facility. Two years later, Laurel debuted the Washington, D.C., International, a turf stakes that was the first North American race to become a major annual target of European horses. Among the winners of the race was Racing Hall of Fame member Kelso in 1964. In 1984, Schapiro sold Laurel to a group of investors headed by Frank De Francis. In late 1986, De Francis and partners bought Pimlico, thus consolidating ownership of Maryland's major tracks. With the Breeders' Cup Turf (G1) and Mile (G1) attracting European and American turf horses, the International was suspended after the 1994 running. De Francis died in 1989 and was succeeded as president by his son, Joe.

Location: P.O. Box 130, Laurel, MD 20725
Phone: (301) 725-0400
Fax: (301) 725-4561
E-mail: webmaster@marylandracing.com
Web site: http://www.marylandracing.com
Inaugural meeting: October 2, 1911
Acreage: 360
Number of stalls: 880
Seating capacity: 5,185

Officers
President: Joseph A. De Francis
General Counsel and Treasurer: Martin Jacobs
Senior Vice President of Public Relations and Marketing: Karin De Francis
Chief Operating Officer: Louis J. Raffetto
Executive Vice President: Timothy T. Capps
Chief Administrative Officer: Robert J. Di Pietro
Chief Financial Officer: Douglas J. Illig
Senior Vice President, Facilities and Courses: John Passero
Senior Vice President, Finance and Development: Antonio Cobuzzi
Director of Racing: Michael Gathagan
Racing Secretary: Georganne Hale
Director of Facilities: John Olsen
Director of Communications: Mike Gathagan
Director of Marketing: Carrie L. Everly
Director of Mutuels: Elizabeth Quill
Director of Publicity: Mike Gathagan
Director of Sales: Keith Leacock
Director of Simulcasting: Dennis Smoter
Horsemen's Liaison: Phoebe Hayes
Stewards: Phillip E. Grove, William J. Passmore
Track Announcer: Dave Rodman

Racing dates
2001: January 1-March 25, 62 days
2002: July 25-August 23, 22 days, October 17, 2001-March 30, 2002

Track Layout
Main circumference: 1 1/8 miles
Main track chute: 7 furlongs
Main width: 75 feet
Main length of stretch: 1,344 feet
Main turf circumference: 1 mile
Main turf width: 70 feet
Main turf length of stretch: 990 feet

Attendance
Highest single day record: 40,276, November 11, 1958

Leaders
Career, leading trainer by titles: King T. Leatherbury, 25
Recent meeting, leading jockey: Ramon Dominguez, 70, Winter-2001
Recent meeting, leading trainer: Dale Capuano, 64, Winter-2001

Records
Single meet, leading jockey by wins: Edgar Prado, 197, Winter-1998/1999
Single meet, leading trainer by wins: King T. Leatherbury, 86, Winter-1995

Track Records, Main Dirt
4 1/2 furlongs: Weighmaster, :52 2/5, April 13, 1964
5 furlongs: Dave's Friend, :57, November 21, 1980
5 1/2 furlongs: Wire Me Collect, 1:02.80, January 25, 1998
6 furlongs: Richter Scale, 1:07.95, July 15, 2000
6 1/2 furlongs: Ebonizer, 1:15 2/5, November 23, 1990
7 furlongs: Tappiano, 1:21 2/5, February 12, 1989
7 1/2 furlongs: Tidal Surge, 1:29.52, March 12, 1994
1 mile: Skipper's Friend, 1:34 2/5, December 6, 1980
1 1/16 miles: Willard Scott, 1:41 4/5, November 16, 1985
1 1/8 miles: Excellent Tipper, 1:47.64, July 5, 1992
1 3/16 miles: Testing, 1:54.51, October 21, 2000
1 1/4 miles: Richie the Coach, 1:59.96, November 23, 1996
1 3/8 miles: Amber Wave, 2:17 4/5, November 28, 1968
1 3/4 miles: Asserche, 2:58.51, February 13, 1994

Course Records, Main Turf
5 furlongs: Sikkim, :57 2/5, November 21, 1967
5 1/2 furlongs: Oops I Am, 1:02.20, June 14, 1994
6 furlongs: Texas Glitter, 1:08, October 28, 2000
1 mile: Portsmouth, 1:34, October 30, 1965
1 1/16 miles: Water Moccasin, 1:39 2/5, June 15, 1987
1 1/8 miles: Finder's Choice, 1:46.13, October 24, 1992
1 3/16 miles: Guilded Youth, 1:53.70, June 27, 1998
1 1/4 miles: Dynamic Trick 1:58.42, October 22, 2000
1 1/2 miles: Kelso, 2:23 4/5, November 11, 1964
2 miles: Summer Ensign, 3:23.64, June 15, 1993

Fastest Times of 2001 (Dirt)
5 1/2 furlongs: Dr. Max, 1:03.41, January 13
6 furlongs: Delaware Township, 1:09, November 17
6 1/2 furlongs: Brilliant Deniro, 1:17.31, January 13
7 furlongs: Peeping Tom, 1:22, February 19
1 1/16 miles: Pleasant Divorce, 1:42.50, October 18
1 1/8 miles: Grundlefoot, 1:50, December 15
1 3/16 miles: Do I Ever, 1:55.37, February 18
1 1/4 miles: Duckhorn, 2:00.62, March 18

Fastest Times of 2001 (Turf)
5 1/2 furlongs: Twice as Sweet, 1:03.10, October 24
1 1/16 miles: Ginontherocks, 1:43.77, October 18
1 1/8 miles: Top Floor Suite, 1:48.62, October 24

Pimlico Race Course

The first horse to win a stakes race at Baltimore's Pimlico Race Course during the track's inaugural season in 1870 is the namesake of one of the world's most famous horse races. Preakness, a colt by legendary 19th-century sire Lexington, won the Dinner Party Stakes that year, and in 1873 the Preakness Stakes (G1)

made its debut. The race was not run in 1891, '92, or '93, and then it was held in New York for 15 years before it was returned to Pimlico in 1909. The Preakness now is the middle jewel of the Triple Crown and is run on the third Saturday in May. The day before the Preakness, Pimlico runs the race's three-year-old filly counterpart, the Black-Eyed Susan Stakes (G2). Another of the track's most famous races is the Pimlico Special Handicap (G1), which in 1938 captured the attention of the nation when Seabiscuit defeated War Admiral in a two-horse race. Today, Pimlico and Laurel Park near Washington, D.C., are owned by the Maryland Jockey Club. The two tracks share host duties for the Maryland Million, a day of racing for state-breds. Pimlico long has been called "Old Hilltop," a nickname that dates from the era when a small rise in the infield was a favorite gathering place for trainers and racing fans. The hill was removed in 1938, but the nickname stuck.

Location: 5200 Park Heights Ave., Baltimore, MD 21215
Phone: (410) 542-9400
Fax: (410) 466-2521
E-mail: webmaster@marylandracing.com
Web site: http://www.marylandracing.com
Year founded: 1743 (Maryland Jockey Club)
Inaugural meeting: October 25, 1870
Acreage: 140
Number of stalls: 800
Seating capacity: 13,047

Officers
President: Joseph A. De Francis
General Counsel and Treasurer: Martin Jacobs
Senior Vice President of Public Relations and Marketing: Karin De Francis
Chief Operating Officer: Louis J. Raffetto
Executive Vice President: Timothy T. Capps
Chief Administrative Officer: Robert J. Di Pietro
Chief Financial Officer: Douglas J. Illig
Senior Vice President, Facilities and Courses: John Passero
Senior Vice President, Finance and Development: Antonio Cobuzzi
Racing Secretary: Georganne Hale
Director of Facilities: John Olsen
Director of Communications: Mike Gathagan
Director of Marketing: Carrie L. Everly
Director of Mutuels: Elizabeth Quill
Director of Sales: Keith Leacock
Director of Simulcasting: Dennis Smoter
Horsemen's Liaison: Phoebe Hayes
Stewards: Josette Edwards, Philip E. Grove, William J. Passmore
Track Announcer: Dave Rodman

Racing dates
2001: March 28-July 7, 77 days; September 6-October 13, 24 days
2002: April 3-June 16, 54 days; September 4-October 5, 20 days

Track Layout
Main circumference: 1 mile
Main track chute: 1 1/4 miles, 6 furlongs
Main width: 70 feet
Main length of stretch: 1,152 feet
Main turf circumference: 7 furlongs

Attendance
Highest single day record: 104,454, May 19, 2001
Average daily recent meeting: 2,669, Fall 2001
Total attendance recent meeting: 57,701, Fall 2001

Handle
Average on-track recent meeting: $185,246, Fall 2001
Average all sources recent meeting: $1,415,597, Fall 2001, $4,580,188, Spring 2001

Total on-track recent meeting: $4,260,662, Fall 2001
Total all sources recent meeting: $50,961,481, Fall 2001
Single day total handle all sources: $62,576,000, May 19, 2001

Mutuel Records
Highest Win: $574, Cadeaux, May 7, 1913
Lowest Win: $2.10, War Admiral, November 3, 1937
Highest Exacta: $5,223.60, May 27, 1989
Lowest Exacta: $2.60, March 28, 1981
Highest Daily Double: $5,932.20, December 1, 1955
Highest Other Exotics: $414,243.90, Twin Trifecta

Leaders
Career, leading jockey by titles: Edgar Prado, 11
Career, leading trainer by titles: King T. Leatherbury, 25
Recent meeting, leading jockey: Mark Johnston, 73, Spring 2000, Ramon Dominguez, 108, Spring 2001, Travis L. Dunkelberger, 24, Fall 2001
Recent meeting, leading trainer: Dale Capuano, 15, Fall 2001, Dale Capuano, 47, Spring 2000, Dale Capuano, 61, Spring 2001

Records
Single meet, leading jockey by wins: Kent Desormeaux, 184, Summer-1989
Single meet, leading trainer by wins: King T. Leatherbury, 100, 1976

Track Records, Main Dirt
4 furlongs: Gavotte, :47 2/5, May 4, 1925
4 1/2 furlongs: Countess Diana, :51.50, June 6, 1997
5 furlongs: Goldminer's Dream, :56.80, May 20, 1993
5 1/2 furlongs: Higher Strata, 1:02.46, July 29, 1995
6 furlongs: Northern Wolf, 1:09, August 18, 1990
7 furlongs: Zeus, 1:26, May 3, 1921
1 mile: June Grass, 1:37 3/5, May 2, 1923
1m 70 yds: Sabotage, 1:41 2/5, December 17, 1958
1 1/16 miles: Deputed Testamony, 1:40 4/5, May 19, 1984
1 1/8 miles: Private Terms, 1:47 1/5, May 27, 1989
1 3/16 miles: Farma Way, 1:52.55, May 11, 1991
1 1/4 miles: Manzotti, 2:01 4/5, March 19, 1988
1 3/8 miles: Narwhal, 2:16 2/5, December 15, 1962
1 1/2 miles: War Trophy, 2:29 2/5, November 8, 1948
1 5/8 miles: Market Wise, 2:43 1/5, November 13, 1941
1 3/4 miles: Blue Hills, 2:55 2/5, October 25, 1949
2 miles: Everett, 3:25 3/5, October 31, 1920
Other: 1 11/16 miles, Post Morton, 2:57 4/5, December 7, 1957; 2 miles 70 yds, Filisteo, 3:30 4/5, October 31, 1941; 2 1/16 miles, Beau Diable, 3:35 3/5, December 10, 1960; 2 1/4 miles, Edith Cavell, 3:52 1/5, November 13, 1926; 2 1/2 miles, Miss Grillo, 4:14 3/5, November 12, 1948

Course Records, Main Turf
5 furlongs: Elberton, :56.11, September 15, 2001
7 furlongs: Lofty Peak, 1:23 1/5, May 14, 1956
1 mile: North East Bound, 1:33.42, May 7, 2000
1 1/16 miles: Air Attack, 1:40.33, May 27, 1991
1 1/8 miles: Double Booked, 1:47.04, May 17, 1991
1 3/16 miles: Bayard Park, 2:01, May 7, 1966
1 1/4 miles: Manzotti, 2:01 4/5, March 19, 1988
1 3/8 miles: Dunsinyne, 2:13.74, June 22, 1997
1 1/2 miles: Fort Marcy, 2:27 2/5, May 9, 1970
Other: 1 7/8 miles, Brightly, 3:17, December 1, 1955

Fastest Times of 2001 (Dirt)
4 1/2 furlongs: Get the Doc, :52.91, June 24
5 furlongs: Governor's Pride, :56.96, May 26
6 furlongs: Xtra Heat, 1:09.07, August 18
1 1/16 miles: Grundlefoot, 1:41.50, August 15
1 1/8 miles: Include, 1:48.91, April 21
1 3/16 miles: Point Given, 1:55.51, May 19
1 1/4 miles: Saluteloot, 2:06.40, May 27

Fastest Times of 2001 (Turf)
5 furlongs: Elberton, :56.11, September 15
1 mile: Private Slip, 1:33.80, April 29
1 1/16 miles: Warrant, 1:40.92, May 4
1 1/8 miles: Stal Quest, 1:48.40, October 13
1 1/2 miles: Pickupspeed, 2:30.14, July 4

Timonium

Although Timonium's annual live meeting lasts only ten days through Labor Day, it attracts more than a half-million fans every year to the community located near Baltimore's northern border. In 2001, Timonium lost two dates because of insufficient purses but still had a successful meet.

Timonium, which was struggling in the early 1990s until the addition of simulcasting both into and out of the track, is operated by the not-for-profit Maryland State Fair and Agricultural Society Inc., which directs all profits to the fair, 4-H Club awards, and improvements.

Racing at Timonium began in September 1887. Its five-eighths-mile track has a four-furlong chute and a 6½-furlong chute. A record crowd of 17,306 attended the races on September 4, 1967. Timonium's record handle of $2,452,514 was set on August 29, 1998. In the early 1980s, it raced as many as 42 dates, but its season was sharply reduced in 1985 when Maryland's mile tracks began running year-round.

Location: 2200 York Rd., Timonium, MD 21094
Phone: (410) 252-0200
Fax: (410) 561-5610
E-mail: msfair@msn.com
Web site: http://www.bcpl.lib.md.us/~mdstfair
Year founded: 1887
Acreage: 100
Number of stalls: 600
Seating capacity: 4,850

Officers
President: F. Grove Miller
Vice President: Howard M. Mosner Jr.
General Manager: Howard M. Mosner Jr.
Racing Secretary: Georganne Hale
Secretary: John H. Mosner Jr.
Treasurer: John H. Mosner Jr.
Director of Mutuels: Richard Insley
Track Announcer: Richard Wooley
Track Photographer: Jerry Frutkoff
Track Superintendent: Don Denmyer

Racing dates
2001: August 25-September 3, 10 days
2002: August 24-September 2, 10 days

Track Layout
Main circumference: 5/8 mile
Main track chute: 4 furlongs, 6 1/2 furlongs
Main width: 70 feet
Main length of stretch: 700 feet

Attendance
Average daily recent meeting: 4,334, 2001
Highest single day record: 17,306, September 4, 1967
Total attendance recent meeting: 34,669, 2001

Handle
Single day on-track handle: $2,452,514, August 29, 1998
Total all sources recent meeting: $15,697,441, 2001
Total on-track recent meeting: $3,140,909, 2001
Average all sources recent meeting: $1,569,741, 2001
Average on-track recent meeting: $392,613, 2001

Leaders
Recent meeting, leading jockey: Alex Estrada, 10, 2001
Recent meeting, leading trainer: Hamilton A. Smith, 5, 2001

Fastest Times of 2001
4 furlongs: Get My Glitter, :44.88, September 3
6 1/2 furlongs: Rocaco, 1:17.78, September 3

1 mile: Treasure Coast Gem, 1:42.55, August 29
1 1/16 miles: Clark's Clone, 1:45.44, September 3

Massachusetts

Brockton Fair

Location: P.O. Box 6, Brockton, MA 02303-0006
Phone: (508) 586-8000
Fax: (508) 821-3239
E-mail: sue@brocktonfair.com
Web site: http://www.brocktonfair.com

Racing dates
2001: June 30-July 31, 20 days
2002: June 29-August 17

Northampton Fair

Location: P.O. Box 305 Northampton MA 01061-0305
Phone: (413) 584-2237
Fax: (413) 586-1297
Web site: http://www.3countyfair.com
Year founded: 1818 (fair)
Inaugural meeting: 1942
Acreage: 50+
Seating capacity: 2,400
Number of stalls: 450

Officers
Director of Racing: Sandy Stanisewski
Racing Secretary: Tom Creel
Director of Operations: John Renaud
Director of Marketing: Sandy Stanisewski
Director of Publicity: Sandy Stanisewski
Stewards: Richard Tobin, William Keene
Track Announcer: Peter Kules
Track Photographer: CB Photo
Track Superintendent: Joe Jasinki

Racing dates
2001: August 31-September 16, 10 days
2002: August 23-September 15

Track Layout
Main circumference: 1/2 mile

Attendance
Average daily recent meeting: 2,000

Handle
Single day on-track handle: $351,000
Total all sources recent meeting: $3,117,913, 2001

Leaders
Recent meeting, leading jockey: Miguel D. Santiago, 20, 2001
Recent meeting, leading trainer: John J. Jacavone Jr., 12, 2001

Suffolk Downs

Built in just 62 days for $2-million by the Eastern Racing Association, Suffolk Downs opened before an estimated crowd of 35,000 in East Boston on July 10, 1935, as the nation's only racetrack with a concrete grandstand. Just one month later, 52,726 fans set an attendance record that still stands.

Suffolk Downs's signature race, the Massachusetts Handicap (G2), was inaugurated in 1935, and it has been won by such champions as Seabiscuit in 1937 and

two-time MassCap winners Cigar and Skip Away in the 1990s.

On June 4, 1966, a fan ran onto the homestretch during the Mayflower Stakes and was brushed by three horses but sustained no injuries. Legendary promoter Bill Veeck carded chariot races, livestock giveaways, and mock Indian battles in the infield during his tenure there in 1969 and '70. He also successfully sued the state to allow children to attend the races.

Following a two-year shutdown in 1990 and '91, James B. Moseley's and John Hall's Sterling Suffolk Racecourse Ltd. leased the track, and Thoroughbred racing returned to Boston. In 1997, Suffolk Racecourse LLC bought Suffolk Downs for $40-million. Suffolk received a major boost at the end of 2001 when the state legislature authorized $3-million in tax revenue and uncashed winning tickets to be used for purses.

Location: 111 Waldemar Ave., East Boston, MA 02128
Phone: (617) 567-3900
Fax: (617) 561-5100
E-mail: sufdowns@shore.net
Web site: http://www.suffolkdowns.com
Year founded: 1935
Inaugural meeting: July 10-August 10, 1935, 28 days
Acreage: 190
Number of stalls: 1,380
Seating capacity: 9,505

Officers
President: John L. Hall II
Director of Racing: John H. Morrissey
Racing Secretary: John H. Morrissey
Director of Operations: Joseph Fatalo
Director of Marketing: JoEllen Gradowski
Director of Mutuels: James Alcott
Director of Publicity: Larry Collmus
Stewards: James Gigliotti, Richard DeStasio, William Keen
Track Announcer: Larry Collmus

Racing dates
2001: January 1-June 9, September 29-December 22, 61 days

Track Layout
Main circumference: 1 mile
Main track chute: 1 1/4 miles, 6 furlongs
Main width: 90 feet
Main length of stretch: 1,030 feet
Main turf circumference: 7 furlongs
Main turf width: 65 to 70 feet
Main turf length of stretch: 1,030 feet

Attendance
Average daily recent meeting: 3,398, Fall 2001, 3,768, Winter/Spring 2001
Highest single day record: 52,726, August 10, 1935
Record daily average for single meet: 18,388, 1945
Total attendance recent meeting: 203,894, Fall 2001, 335,327, Winter/Spring 2001

Handle
Average all sources recent meeting: $818,329, Winter/Spring 2001, $856,371, Fall 2001
Average on-track recent meeting: $138,099, Fall 2001, $170,068, Winter/Spring 2001
Record daily average for single meet: $1,164,240, 1946
Single day on-track handle: $2,175,836, May 30, 1960
Single day total handle all sources: $5,867,414, May 31, 1997
Total all sources recent meeting: $51,382,232, Fall 2001,

$72,831,301, Winter/Spring 2001
Total on-track recent meeting: $15,136,048, Winter/Spring 2001, $8,285,963, Fall 2001

Mutuel Records
Highest Win: $445, Sue Harper, June 14, 1940
Highest Exacta: $9,923,80, January 13, 1985
Highest Trifecta: $51,778, January 13, 1985
Lowest Trifecta: $7.40
Highest Daily Double: $16,515, May 25, 1979
Lowest Daily Double: $3.60, May 30, 1998
Highest Pick 3: $10,515.40, December 26, 1992
Lowest Pick 3: $11, April 21, 1993
Highest Pick 6: $25,399, November 28, 1982
Highest Other Exotics: $23,079.40, Superfecta, March 27, 1996, $9,923.90, Perfecta, January 13, 1985
Lowest Other Exotics: $3.60, Perfecta, November 10, 1985

Leaders
Recent meeting, leading owner: Monarch Stable, 22, Winter/Spring 2001; Yasou Stable Trust, 26, Fall 2001
Recent meeting, leading trainer: Ron Dandy, 35, Fall 2001; Ron Dandy, 53, Winter/Spring 2001
Recent meeting, leading jockey: Joe Hampshire, 124, Winter/Spring 2001; Joe Hampshire, 78, Fall 2001

Records
Single day jockey wins: Leroy Moyers, 7, July 4, 1967

Track Records, Main Dirt
4 furlongs: Crimson Streak, :45 2/5, April 6, 1970
4 1/2 furlongs: Lovely Gypsy, :51 4/5, May 7, 1965; Happy Voter, :51 4/5, May 16, 1966
5 furlongs: Rene Depot, :57 2/5, June 25, 1972
5 1/2 furlongs: Cocopet, 1:04 3/5, July 17, 1943
6 furlongs: Canal, 1:08 1/5, May 14, 1966
1 mile: Back Bay Brave, 1:35 1/5, July 12, 1986
1m 70 yds: Half Breed, 1:40, May 23, 1964
1 1/16 miles: Talent Show, 1:41 4/5, May 12, 1962; Bear the Palm, 1:41 4/5, July 3, 1977
1 1/8 miles: Skip Away, 1:47.27, May 30, 1998
1 3/16 miles: Shut Out, 1:55 2/5, July 4, 1942
1 1/4 miles: Helioscope, 2:01, May 19, 1955
1 1/2 miles: Connie Rab, 2:30 3/5, May 15, 1954
1 5/8 miles: Count Fire, 2:45 2/5, June 23, 1962
1 3/4 miles: Toulouse, 2:58 2/5, June 16, 1956
2 miles: Hutch, 3:35 2/5, August 1, 1950
Other: 2 furlongs, Adriano's Girl, :21.94, June 4, 1997; 2 1/16 miles, Bold Special, 3:35 4/5, April 18, 1983; 2 miles 70 yds, On the Square, 3:39 4/5, April 16, 1973; 2 1/4 miles, Fundy Bay, 3:54 1/5, December 9, 1973

Course Records, Main Turf
5 furlongs: Bishop Ridley, :57 1/5, July 19, 1987
7 1/2 furlongs: Times Ahead, 1:32 2/5, September 3, 1988
1 mile: I'ma Handful, 1:39 2/5, September 4, 1983
1m 70yds: Darn Special, 1:42.44, May 31, 1997
1 1/16 miles: Landing Court, 1:44.91, October 26, 1994
1 3/8 miles: Chompion, 2:20 4/5, July 18, 1970, Gaybrook Swan, 2:20 4/5, July 18, 1970
1 1/2 miles: *Akbar Khan, 2:30 3/5, June 17, 1957
2 miles: Jean-Pierre, 3:19 4/5, June 28, 1969
Other: 1 15/16 miles, Jamf, 3:11 1/5, July 4, 1975

Fastest Times of 2001
5 furlongs: Consider the Night, :57.79, June 2
5 1/2 furlongs: Stage Trick, 1:04.74, January 14
6 furlongs: Radica Gal, 1:09.73, January 14
1 mile: Pip's Angel, 1:39.24, December 14
1m 70yds: Starship Seminole (Ven), 1:41.39, January 13
1 1/16 miles: Lost, 1:44.52, January 29
1 1/8 miles: Include, 1:48.61, June 2
1 1/4 miles: Tuxedo Road, 2:07.71, December 11

Michigan

Great Lakes Downs

One of America's newest racetracks, Great Lakes Downs was born in 1999 out of the necessity to preserve live racing in Michigan following the shuttering of Ladbroke-owned Detroit Race Course. Located at the site of a former Standardbred track in Muskegon, Great Lakes Downs came together quickly as a group of horse owners and racing enthusiasts raised the capital to renovate the facility and prepare for live racing.

After an understated first meeting in 1999, the track gained national attention in the winter of 2000 when Frank Stronach-led Magna Entertainment Corp., in the midst of a track-buying spree, added Great Lakes Downs to its holdings. The track's lengthy meet—approximately 130 days annually—made it an attractive facility for Magna's simulcast-wagering roster. And, because the track offers a comparable level of racing to Magna-owned Thistledown in North Randall, Ohio, the two tracks can compete against one another in Magna's Super Track Racing Series.

Location: 4800 S. Harvey St., Muskegon, MI 49444
Phone: (231) 799-2400
Fax: (231) 798-3120
Web site: http://www.greatlakesdowns.com

Officers
General Manager: Richard Wallington
Racing Secretary: Frank Stacks
Director of Publicity: Janie Goddard

Racing dates
2001: April 30-October 30, 128 days
2002: April 29-October 29, 118 days

Track Layout
Main circumference: 5 furlongs
Main track chute: 4 furlongs, 7 furlongs
Main length of stretch: 580 feet

Leaders
Recent meeting, leading trainer: Gerald S. Bennett, 95, 2001
Recent meeting, leading jockey: T. D. Houghton, 239, 2001

Track Records, Main Dirt
4 furlongs: Dinner Band, :45.87, May 15, 2001
5 1/2 furlongs: Scent a Grade, 1:06.66, June 5, 2000
6 furlongs: Timely Factor, 1:13.15, October 16, 2001
6 1/2 furlongs: Touch of Power, 1:19.57, August 13, 2001
7 furlongs: Secret Romeo, 1:24.77, September 2, 2001
1 mile: Override Battle, 1:40.14, October 31, 2000; Secret Romeo, 1:40.14, October 29, 2001
1m 70 yds: Secret Romeo, 1:49.50, November 4, 2000
1 1/16 miles: That Monetary, 1:47.28, August 27, 2001
1 1/8 miles: The Bold Bruiser, 1:54.11, October 28, 2000
Other: 2 furlongs, Skirt in the Wind, :23.52, June 22, 1999

Fastest Times of 2001
4 furlongs: Dinner Band, :45.87, May 15
5 1/2 furlongs: Dinner Band, 1:06.82, August 25
6 furlongs: Timely Factor, 1:13.15, October 16
6 1/2 furlongs: Touch of Power, 1:19.57, August 13
7 furlongs: Secret Romeo, 1:24.77, September 2
1 mile: Secret Romeo, 1:40.14, October 29
1m 70yds: Born to Dance, 1:49.77, October 27
1 1/16 miles: That Monetary, 1:47.28, August 27
1 1/8 miles: Above the Wind, 1:55.10, September 17
Other: 2 furlongs, Sefa's Shadow, :23.60, June 19

Mt. Pleasant Meadows

Location: 500 N. Mission Rd., Mount Pleasant, MI 48804-0220
Phone: (517) 773-0012
Fax: (517) 773-7616

Racing dates
2001: May 5-September 30, 44 days

Leaders
Recent meeting, leading jockey: Dennis Berryhill, 12, 2001
Recent meeting, leading trainer: Nicole Holst, 9, 2001

Fastest Times of 2001
4 furlongs: Bad Boy Eric, :48.35, August 25
4 1/2 furlongs: Air Supply, :55.10, July 21
5 furlongs: Air Supply, 1:01.45, June 16
5 1/2 furlongs: Gary O, 1:08.25, July 14

Minnesota

Canterbury Park

Canterbury Park is located in Shakopee, southwest of Minneapolis and St. Paul. When the track first opened in 1985, three years after Minnesota legalized pari-mutuel wagering, it was known as Canterbury Downs, and its ownership group included the Santa Anita Operating Co. In 1990, the track was purchased by Ladbroke Racing Corp., but, due to declining business, closed in '92. One year later, Irwin Jacobs, a Twin City financier, purchased the track and sold it to businessman and breeder Curtis Sampson, Sampson's son, Randy, and partner Dale Schenian. Four months later, the owners held an initial public offering of the newly created Canterbury Park Holding Corp. The track, which reopened in 1995 as Canterbury Park, offers Thoroughbred racing and some Quarter Horse racing during its live racing season, which runs from mid-May through early September. In 1999, Canterbury held the first of three consecutive runnings of the Claiming Crown, which quickly became recognized as a major sporting event in Minnesota. In 2001, the 11-race event worth more than $550,000 drew claiming-level runners from across the United States. Canterbury is scheduled to host the event in odd-numbered years from 2003-'07. The Canterbury Card Club, Minnesota's first legal card club, opened in 2000 at the track. Revenues from the 24-hour-a-day card club, which offers poker and other games, supplement race purses.

Location: 1100 Canterbury Rd., Shakopee, MN 55379
Phone: (952) 445-7223; (800) 340-6361
Fax: (952) 496-6480
E-mail: cbypark@canterburypark.com
Web site: http://www.canterburypark.com
Year founded: 1984
Inaugural meeting: June 26, 1985
Acreage: 355
Number of stalls: 1,620
Seating capacity: 22,830

Officers
President: Randall Sampson
General Manager: Randall Sampson
Director of Racing: Douglas Schoepf

Racing Secretary: Douglas Schoepf
Director of Operations: Nat Wess
Director of Finance: Judy Dahlke
Director of Marketing: Linda Erickson
Director of Mutuels: Eric Halstrom
Director of Simulcasting: Linda Arnoldi
Horsemen's Liaison: Mary Green
Track Announcer: Paul Allen
Track Photographer: Palmer/Malarkey Photography
Track Superintendent: Tony Caterina

Racing dates
2001: May 18-September 3, 61 days
2002: May 17-September 2, 62 days

Track Layout
Main circumference: 1 mile
Main track chute: 1 1/4 miles, 3 1/2 furlongs, 6 1/2 furlongs
Main turf circumference: 7 furlongs
Main turf chute: 1 1/16 miles

Attendance
Average daily recent meeting: 4,010, 2001
Total attendance recent meeting: 244,590, 2001
Highest single day record: 27,439, April 24, 1987

Handle
Single day on-track handle: $2,265,404, June 28, 1987
Average all sources recent meeting: $448,382, 2001
Total all sources recent meeting: $43-million, 2001

Leaders
Recent meeting, leading jockey: Derek Bell, 65, 2001
Recent meeting, leading trainer: Doug Oliver, 26, 2001
Recent meeting, leading owner: Valene Farms, 12, 2001

Track Records, Main Dirt
4 1/2 furlongs: Gallapiat's Song, :51.27, June 23, 1991
5 furlongs: Feather in My Hat, :57 1/5, August 25, 1990
5 1/2 furlongs: Nickel Slot, 1:02 4/5, May 17, 1989
6 furlongs: So Long Seoul, 1:08 3/5, May 6, 1990; Iwazza Bad Boy, 1:08.60, August 18, 1996
6 1/2 furlongs: Don's Irish Melody, 1:14, June 12, 1988
1 mile: Minneapple, 1:35 1/5, September 27, 1987
1m 70 yds: Come Summer, 1:40 1/5, August 18, 1985
1 1/16 miles: Power Boat, 1:41 4/5, July 30, 1988
1 1/8 miles: Olympio, 1:46.47, July 7, 1991
1 1/4 miles: John Bullit, 2:04 3/5, July 25, 1986
1 1/2 miles: Loustros (GB), 2:32 3/5, August 28, 1987
1 3/4 miles: Luciole (Arg), 2:59 4/5, October 12, 1985
2 miles: My Tulles Free, 3:25 3/5, September 1, 1986
Other: 3 1/2 furlongs, In Moderation, :39.11, May 26, 1997

Course Records, Main Turf
5 furlongs: Thatsusintheolebean, :56.40, May 23, 1998
7 1/2 furlongs: Honor the Hero, 1:28, June 18, 1995
1 mile: Go Go Jack, 1:33.40, June 3, 1995
1m 70yds: Numchuek, 1:39 1/5, July 6, 1988
1 1/16 miles: Little Bro Lantis, 1:40.20, June 17, 1995
1 1/8 miles: Fluffkins, 1:44, July 22, 1995
1 3/8 miles: Treizieme, 2:12 3/5, August 3, 1986
Other: 1 7/8 miles, John Bullit, 3:11 2/5, September 26, 1987

Interesting facts
Previous name and dates: Canterbury Downs 1984-1994

Fastest Times of 2001 (Dirt)
5 furlongs: Jack's Storm, :58.14, May 28
5 1/2 furlongs: Expert, 1:04.04, July 13
6 furlongs: Crooner Slew, 1:09.47, July 14
6 1/2 furlongs: Sassy Hound, 1:16.18, August 4
1 mile: Cleat, 1:38.58, May 28
1m 70yds: Slew City Jay, 1:43.17, May 18
1 1/16 miles: Secret Squall, 1:45.75, August 4
1 1/8 miles: Sing Because, 1:50.74, August 4
Other: 3 1/2 furlongs, Whitegoldndiamonds, :40.65, June 1

Fastest Times of 2001 (Turf)
5 furlongs: Dancin in the Park, :57.47, July 15

7 1/2 furlongs: Easy Mission, 1:29.81, August 25
1 mile: Shesa Shesa, 1:36.57, August 26
1 1/16 miles: Al's Dearly Bred, 1:42.22, August 4
1 3/8 miles: Ashar, 2:16.89, September 3

Montana

Great Falls

Location: P.O. Box 442, Black Eagle, MT 59414
Phone: (406) 453-0080
Fax: (406) 453-0080

Racing dates
2001: June 23-July 29, 11 days
2002: June 8-July 28

Leaders
Recent meeting, leading jockey: Shannon Wippert, 10, 2001
Recent meeting, leading trainer: Janis D. Schoepf, 5, 2001

Fastest Times of 2001
5 furlongs: My Papa, 1:01.20, July 4; King of Adventure, 1:01.20, July 15
7 furlongs: Summer Prince, 1:28.20, July 1

Helena Downs

Location: P.O. Box 9706, Helena, MT 59604
Phone: (406) 457-9492

Yellowstone Downs

Location: P.O. Box 1138, Billings, MT 59103
Phone: (406) 656-1619
Fax: (406) 633-2503

Officers
Director of Publicity: Ben Carlson

Racing dates
2001: August 25-September 16, 10 days
2002: June 15-July 14, 6 days; August 24-September 22, 11 days

Leaders
Recent meeting, leading jockey: Scott Alan Bergsrud, 13, 2001
Recent meeting, leading trainer: Edward Buxbaum, 7, 2001

Fastest Times of 2001
7 furlongs: Miss Walk Tall, 1:26.20, September 16
1m 70yds: Forceful Arts, 1:43.20, August 25
Other: 5 1/4 furlongs, Seattle Cue, 1:01.80, September 16

Nebraska

Horsemen's Atokad Downs

Live Thoroughbred racing in Nebraska did not die when Omaha's Ak-Sar-Ben closed in 1995 after 74 years. Ak-Sar-Ben, which was torn down in 1997, is Nebraska spelled backward. Atokad is Dakota spelled backward, and the track is located in Dakota County, in the state's northwest corner near the South Dakota border. The

Horsemen's Atokad Downs, continued

five-eighths-mile track in South Sioux City opened on September 20, 1956.

Atokad conducted a late-summer meeting in most years, though it did not race from 1998 through 2000. A single-day meet was resurrected in 2001 by Robert E. Lee, president of the Nebraska Horsemen's and Benevolent Protective Association. Tom Harris is now Atokad's general manager. Eight races with total purses of $130,000 were held on September 22, 2001, and the track was to hold a one-day meet in 2002 to qualify for year-round simulcasting. A record crowd of 6,200 attended on October 18, 1958. The record handle of $483,486 was set on November 9, 1980.

Location: P.O. Box 518, South Sioux City, NE 68776
Phone: (402) 494-5869
Year founded: 1951
Inaugural meeting: September 20,1956
Acreage: 50
Seating capacity: 5,000
Number of stalls: 84 (120 overflow)

Officers
President: Bob Lee
Vice President: Bill Vannoy
General Manager: Tom Harris
Director of Racing: Tom Harris
Racing Secretary: Tom Harris
Secretary: Shelly Hosch
Treasurer: Thelma Carver
Director of Operations: Tom Harris
Director of Admissions: Sally Carver
Director of Auctions: Bob Lee
Director of Communications: Mike Fansler
Director of Finance: Sally Carver
Director of Marketing: Mike Fansler
Director of Mutuels: Mike Fansler
Director of Publicity: Mike Fansler
Director of Sales: Sally Carver
Director of Simulcasting: Tom Harris
Horsemen's Liaison: Bob Lee
Track Announcer: Charles Pernnell
Track Photographer: Coady Services
Track Superintendent: John Riney

Racing dates
2001: September 22
2002: September 22

Track Layout
Main circumference: 5 furlongs
Main track chute: 6 furlongs and 50 yds
Main width: 70 feet
Main length of stretch: 660 feet

Attendance
Total attendance recent meeting: 5,000 est., 2001
Highest single day record: 6,200, October 18, 1958

Handle
Total all sources recent meeting: $162,776, 2001
Total on-track recent meeting: $91,499, 2001
Single day on-track handle: $483,486, November 9, 1980

Leaders
Recent meeting, leading jockey: Armando Martinez, 3, 2001
Recent meeting, leading trainer: Donald F. Cheloha, 1, 2001; Eugene E. Warnke, 1, 2001; Herb Riecken, 1, 2001; Larry L. Staroscik, 1, 2001; Mark Esquibel, 1, 2001; Monty Luark, 1, 2001; Phil B. Storms, 1, 2001; Ronald L. Westermann, 1, 2001

Fastest Times of 2001
4 furlongs: Repeatedly, :46.80, September 22
1 mile: Run Around Sue, 1:41.80, September 22
1m 70yds: Honest Speed, 1:46.60, September 22

Columbus Races

Opened in the 1950, Columbus Races in Columbus, 90 miles northwest of Lincoln, is operated on the Platte County Agricultural Society Fairgrounds. It was at Columbus that Racing Hall of Fame trainer Marion H. Van Berg and his son, Jack, also a Racing Hall of Fame member, began their careers. The elder Van Berg operated a sales barn—offering hogs, cattle, and horses—in addition to running his stable. Columbus usually runs a 25-day summer meet from mid-July through mid-September, racing on Fridays, Saturdays, and Sundays. Extensive simulcasting is also offered. The five-eighths-mile oval has a 6½-furlong chute. A record crowd of 8,856 attended on September 3, 1973. The record handle of $719,725 was set exactly 11 years later.

Location: 822 15th St., Columbus, NE 68601
Phone: (402) 564-0133
Fax: (402) 564-0990
Seating capacity: 4,000
Number of stalls: 1,000

Officers
Racing Secretary: Dennis Kochevar
Director of Publicity: Gary Bock

Racing dates
2001: July 27-September 16, 25 days
2002: July 26-September 15, 25 days

Track Layout
Main circumference: 5 furlongs

Attendance
Highest single day record: 8,856, September 3, 1973

Handle
Single day on-track record: $719,725, September 3, 1984

Leaders
Recent meeting, leading jockey: Jerome Carkeek, 49, 2001
Recent meeting, leading trainer: Marvin A. Johnson, 14, 2001

Fastest Times of 2001
6 furlongs: Come a Stridin, 1:12, August 11
6 1/2 furlongs: Won Fancy Dancer, 1:18, August 24
1m 70yds: Gun Runner, 1:44.20, September 1
1 1/16 miles: Wine Time, 1:47, August 18
1 3/8 miles: Xylocoe, 2:23.60, September 3
Other: 3 1/2 furlongs, Dobob, :40.40, August 3, 3 1/2 furlongs, Hopewell Hall, :40.40, August 31

Fonner Park

The collapse of Omaha's Ak-Sar-Ben racecourse in the mid-1990s dealt a serious blow to Nebraska racing. But Fonner Park in Grand Island has been one of the tracks to keep the flame flickering in the Cornhusker State with its down-home brand of racing.

The 280-acre facility staged its first race meet in 1954. Fonner Park is operated by a nonprofit organization, with the track's profits going to charitable and com-

munity activities in the Grand Island region. With the advent of telephone-account wagering in Nebraska in October 2001, Fonner officials hope to reach more of the state's bettors.

The five-furlong facility has never been known as a racing mecca, but some interesting horses have competed at Fonner Park. One of them was sprinter Leaping Plum, who in 2001 won his seventh consecutive renewal of the opening-week Grasmick Handicap. The 11-year-old gelding also won the Coca-Cola Sprint Handicap four consecutive times (1995-'98).

Human athletes have also been in the spotlight at Fonner Park, with jockey Ken Shino winning eight races there on April 1, 2001, including seven straight.

Location: 700 E. Stolley Park Rd., Grand Island, NE 68802
Phone: (308) 382-4515
Fax: (308) 384-2753
E-mail: fonnerpark@aol.com
Web site: http://www.fonnerpark.com
Year founded: 1953
Inaugural meeting: April 29, 1954
Acreage: 240
Number of stalls: 1,100
Seating capacity: 5,766

Officers
President: Vince Dowding
Vice President: Frank Haack, Francis Gauthier, Gary Rosacker
General Manager: Hugh Miner Jr.
Director of Racing: Douglas Schoepf
Racing Secretary: Douglas Schoepf
Secretary: Doyle Hume
Treasurer: Barry Sandstrom
Director of Operations: Bruce A. Swihart
Director of Mutuels: William McConnell
Director of Simulcasting: Todd W. Otto
Track Announcer: Matt Hook
Track Photographer: Coady Photography
Track Superintendent: Rick Danburg

Racing dates
2001: February 16-May 13, 40 days
2002: February 9-May 11, 40 days

Track Layout
Main circumference: 5/8 mile
Main track chute: 4 furlongs, 6 1/2 furlongs
Main width: 70 feet
Main length of stretch: 700 feet
Training track: 1/2 mile

Attendance
Highest single day record: 10,387, April 2, 1977

Handle
Single day on-track handle: $1,204,660, April 16, 1983

Mutuel Records
Highest Win: $520.40, Black Ticket, March 10, 1977
Lowest Win: $2.20, Ben's Whiz, March 30, 1974; $2.20, Real Style, March 30, 1974; I'ma Game Master, April 29, 1995, $2.20
Highest Exacta: $5,421, March 28, 1994
Lowest Exacta: $4, May 6, 2000
Highest Trifecta: $26,474.40, March 30, 1990
Lowest Trifecta: $14.60, March 15, 1998
Highest Daily Double: $5,451.20, March 18, 1977
Lowest Daily Double: $5, March 10, 1994; $5, April 21, 1995
Highest Pick 3: $13,800.80, February 27, 1988
Lowest Pick 3: $3.20, March 18, 2000
Highest Other Exotics: $17,526.60, Superfecta, March 23, 2001
Lowest Other Exotics: $271.40, Superfecta, March 4, 2001

Leaders
Career, leading jockey by titles: R. D. Williams, 9
Recent meeting, leading trainer: M. A. Johnson, 21, 2001
Career, leading trainer by titles: Tim Gleason, 8
Recent meeting, leading jockey: Perry Compton, 61, 2001

Records
Single day jockey wins: Ken Shino, 8, April 2, 2000
Single day trainer wins: Tim Gleason, 5, February 18, 1989; Marvin Johnson, 5, February 26, 2000; Marvin Johnson, 5, April 2, 2000
Single meet, leading jockey by wins: Perry Compton, 85
Single meet, leading trainer by wins: M. A. Johnson, 50

Track Records, Main Dirt
4 furlongs: Leaping Plum, :44.20, February 17, 1996
5 1/2 furlongs: Little L.M., 1:04 2/5, April 12, 1975
6 furlongs: Orphan Kist, 1:10, April 8, 1989
6 1/2 furlongs: Majority of One, 1:17, March 18, 1989
1 mile: Brian's Star, 1:36 3/5, April 9, 1986; High On Laraka, 1:36 3/5, April 19, 1986
1m 70 yds: Advice, 1:40, April 25, 1987; Shamtastic, 1:40, April 26, 1986
1 1/16 miles: Sahara King, 1:43, April 27, 1996
1 1/8 miles: Potro, 1:51.40, April 25, 1993
1 3/8 miles: Meat Loaf, 2:22 2/5, April 29, 1970
Other: 1 7/16 miles, Wenga, 2:30 2/5, May 1, 1968

Fastest Times of 2001
4 furlongs: Leaping Plum, :46, February 17
6 furlongs: Diplomatic Corps, 1:12, May 6
6 1/2 furlongs: Shot of Gold, 1:19, March 31; Hannah's Hero, 1:19, May 11
1 mile: High Dice, 1:39.60, April 14; Count Basic, 1:39.60, April 21
1m 70yds: Demand Deposit, 1:44, April 28
1 1/16 miles: Rocky Robyn, 1:44.20, April 28
1 1/8 miles: Really Sovereign, 1:53.80, May 13

Horsemen's Park

Boasting a fine simulcasting facility that offers wagering on 15 to 18 racetracks daily, Horsemen's Park opened on January 3, 1998, for simulcasting in south-central Omaha, four miles south of the Ak-Sar-Ben site. Two live races were held each day on two consecutive days in July 1998 by the Nebraska Horsemen's Benevolent and Protective Association, which owns and operates the track.

The meet was expanded to three days in 2000 and '01, with more than $100,000 offered in purses each year. Horsemen's Park will again race three days in 2002.

The track is a five-eighths-mile oval with chutes for seven-furlong and 1⅛-mile races. The simulcasting facility offers seating for 2,800 and contains 600 closed-circuit monitors.

Location: 6303 Q St., Omaha, NE 68117
Phone: (402) 731-2900
Fax: (402) 731-5122
Seating capacity: 2,800

Officers
President: Robert E. Lee
General Manager: Dick Moore
Racing Secretary: Greg Hosch
Director of Mutuels: Mary Palais, Mary Snelling
Director of Simulcasting: Patricia Shefland
Track Superintendent: Tim Hurd

Racing dates
2001: July 20-July 22, 3 days
2002: July 19-July 21, 3 days

Horseman's Park, continued

Track Layout
Main circumference: 5 furlongs
Main width: 65 feet
Main length of stretch: 680 feet

Leaders
Recent meeting, leading jockey: Armando Martinez, 1, 2001;
Jerome Carkeek, 1, 2001, Jiri Peterka, 1, 2001
Recent meeting, leading trainer: Herb Riecken, 1, 2001; Phil
Cirian, 1, 2001; William F. Conyers, 1, 2001

Fastest Times of 2001
6 furlongs: Come a Stridin, 1:10.20, July 21; Pretty Boy Pete,
1:10.20, July 20
1 mile: Sure Shot Biscuit, 1:35.80, July 22
1 3/8 miles: Just for Dino, 2:19.20, July 22

Lincoln State Fair

Location: 27th Street, P.O. Box 81223, Lincoln, NE 68501-
1223
Phone: (402) 474-5371
Fax: (402) 473-4114
Web site: http://www.statefair.org

Officers
President: B. J. Meyer
General Manager: John Skold
Racing Secretary: Gregory C. Hosch
Director of Marketing: Mindy Fuelberth
Director of Mutuels: Mark Jensen
Track Superintendent: Scott Yound

Racing dates
2001: May 18-July 15, 34 days
2002: May 17-July 14, 34 days

Leaders
Recent meeting, leading jockey: Dennis M. Collins, 59, 2001
Recent meeting, leading trainer: Herb Riecken, 17, 2001

Fastest Times of 2001
4 furlongs: Dazzling J. R., :48, July 12
4 1/2 furlongs: Luckiestofthelucky, :51, June 23; Bet Brick,
:51, June 30
6 furlongs: Seville's Runaway, 1:10.60, May 19
1 mile: Sweet Fantastic, 1:36.80, June 16; O'Mike's Gotcha,
1:36.80, July 8
1m 70yds: High Dice, 1:39.40, June 24
1 1/16 miles: High Dice, 1:42.60, July 8
1 1/8 miles: Prince Harper, 1:52.40, July 13
1 3/8 miles: Trumpty Dumpty, 2:17.80, June 17
2 miles: Really Sovereign, 3:32.20, July 4

New Jersey

Atlantic City Race Course

When Atlantic City Race Course opened on July 22,
1946, its roster of stockholders read more like the A-
list from a Hollywood party than investors in a racetrack in McKee City, 13 miles from the Jersey Shore
resort. Bob Hope, Frank Sinatra, Harry James, Xavier
Cugat, and Sammy Kaye were among the initial shareholders. John B. Kelly Sr., an Olympic gold-medal rower,
brick magnate, and father of the late Princess Grace of
Monaco, was Atlantic City's first president. Kelly was
succeeded in 1960 by radio and television pioneer Dr.
Leon Levy, whose son Robert succeeded him. An innovator who arranged the nation's first full-card simulcast from the Meadowlands in September 1983, the

younger Levy also raced 1987 Belmont Stakes (G1)
winner Bet Twice and champion sprinter Housebuster.
Crowds of more than 30,000 turned out to see such
races as the United Nations Handicap (G1), first run
in 1953, and such outstanding horses as Dr. Fager,
Round Table, and Mongo. The disruption of the New
Jersey circuit with the 1977 Garden State Park fire and
the opening of Atlantic City's first casinos the following year hurt the track's business and led to a gradual
reduction in its schedule. Atlantic City conducted a six-
day all-turf meet in 1999 and 2000, and it raced ten days
in 2001 to qualify for year-round, full-card simulcasting. Atlantic City was sold to Greenwood Racing for
$13-million in August 2001, and the track was sched-
uled to offer a ten-day, turf-only live meet in May 2002.

Location: 4501 Black Horse Pike, Mays Landing, NJ 08330
Phone: (609) 641-2190
Fax: (609) 645-8309
Acreage: 250

Officers
President: James J. Murphy
Vice President: Kathy D'Orsaneo
Racing Secretary: Sam Abbey
Director of Publicity: Maureen Gallagher-Bugdon
Track Superintendent: William Gatto

Racing dates
2001: May 4-May 15, 10 days
2002: May 3-May 14, 10 days

Track Layout
Main circumference: 1 1/8 miles
Main width: 100 feet
Main length of stretch: 947.29 feet
Main turf circumference: 1 mile
Main turf width: 100 feet

Leaders
Recent meeting, leading trainer: David W. Geist, 3, 2001;
Derek S. Ryan, 3, 2001; Jonathan E. Sheppard, 3, 2001;
Michael W. Dickinson, 3, 2001
Recent meeting, leading jockey: Luis R. Rivera Jr., 7, 2001

Fastest Times of 2001 (Turf)
5 furlongs: Tyaskin, :56.17, May 11
5 1/2 furlongs: Vigorous Factor, 1:02.92, May 11
1 mile: Encounter, 1:34.69, May 12
1 1/16 miles: Landiland, 1:43.33, May 11
1 1/8 miles: Light Up My Dreams, 1:49, May 11
1 3/16 miles: Private Contract, 1:55.40, May 11

The Meadowlands

The Meadowlands, located on former marshland in
East Rutherford, has been the economic engine of the
Meadowlands Sports Complex. Built by the New Jersey Sports and Exposition Authority for $340-million,
the complex includes the Continental Airlines Arena,
home of basketball's New Jersey Nets and hockey's
New Jersey Devils, and Giants Stadium, where the New
York Giants and Jets play football. The Meadowlands,
which held its first Thoroughbred meet in September
1977, has played host to a number of great moments
in racing history. In 1978, Dr. Patches upset Seattle
Slew in the Paterson Handicap. John Henry, once the
all-time leading earner in the sport, closed his career
with a stunning, come-from-behind victory in the Bal-
lantine's Scotch Classic Handicap in 1984. Four years

later, Alysheba set a 1¼-mile track record when he captured the Meadowlands Cup (G1) during his Horse of the Year campaign. The Meadowlands, whose world-renowned Standardbred meet runs from December through August, conducts Thoroughbred racing from early September to November. During its 49-day meet in 2001, the Meadowlands paid a track and state record $418,556 in average daily purses, with purses totaling a record $18.4-million.

Location: 50 Route 120, East Rutherford, NJ 07073
Phone: (201) 935-8500
Fax: (201) 460-4042
Web site: http://www.thebigm.com
Year founded: 1977
Inaugural meeting: September 6, 1977
Acreage: 220
Number of stalls: 1,760
Seating capacity: 4,650

Officers
President: James A. DiEleuterio Jr.
Vice President: Chris McErlean
General Manager: Chris McErlean
Racing Secretary: Sean Greely
Director of Operations: Dorothye Lombardi
Director of Marketing: Glenn Cademartori
Director of Publicity: Steve Schwartz
Director of Simulcasting: Carol Ciarco
Stewards: Joseph Piarulli, Richard Lawrenson, Samuel Boulmetis Sr.
Track Announcers: Dave Johnson, Ken Warkentin, Sam McKee
Track Photographer: Equi-Photo
Track Superintendent: Dave Harrington

Racing dates
2001: September 3-November 10, 49 days
2002: May 15-May 16, 2 days; September 1-November 30, 64 days

Track Layout
Main circumference: 1 mile
Main track chute: 1 1/4 miles, 6 furlongs
Main width: 90 feet
Main length of stretch: 990 feet
Main turf circumference: 7 furlongs

Attendance
Average daily recent meeting: 4,887, 2001
Highest single meet record: 1,772,209, 1977
Lowest single meet record: 260,172, 2000
Record daily average for single meet: 17,901, 1977
Highest single day record: 41,155
Total attendance recent meeting: 201,608, 2001

Handle
Record daily average for single meet: $2,619,909, 1994
Single day total handle all sources: $5,025,645, 1994
Total all sources recent meeting: $99,247,368, 2001
Total on-track recent meeting: $26,603,368, 2001
Average all sources recent meeting: $2,271,592, 2001
Average on-track recent meeting: $612,252, 2001

Mutuel Records
Highest Win: $354.80, Great Normand, 1990
Lowest Win: $2.20, Spectacular Bid, 1979

Leaders
Career, leading jockey by titles: Joe Bravo, 8
Career, leading trainer by titles: John Forbes, 7
Career, leading jockey by stakes wins: Angel Cordero, 27; Jorge Velasquez, 27
Career, leading jockey by wins: Nick Santagata, 961
Career, leading trainer by stakes wins: Philip G. Johnson, 17

Career, leading trainer by wins: John H. Forbes, 590
Recent meeting, leading jockey: Julian Pimentel, 58, 2001
Recent meeting, leading owner: Richard Englander, 12, 2001
Recent meeting, leading trainer: Robert Klesaris, 17, 2001

Records
Single day trainer wins: John Forbes, 4, November 8, 1978
Single meet, leading jockey by wins: Joe Bravo, 142
Single meet, leading owner by wins: William C. Martucci, 34
Single meet, leading trainer by wins: John Forbes, 47; Joseph Pierce Jr., 47
Single day jockey wins: Julie Krone, 6, September 19, 1989

Track Records, Main Dirt
5 furlongs: Stu's Choice, :55.95, September 6, 1996
5 1/2 furlongs: King Bold Reality, 1:04 1/5, September 15, 1983
6 furlongs: Hay Cody, 1:07.81, September 6, 1996
1 mile: On the Tour, 1:34.43, November 10, 1999
1m 70 yds: Colonel Bart, 1:38.09, September 26, 1998
1 1/16 miles: Black Forest, 1:40.39, September 26, 1998
1 1/8 miles: Forty One Carats, 1:45.50, October 29, 1999
1 3/16 miles: Key Lory, 1:53.88, November 20, 1999
1 1/4 miles: Alysheba, 1:58 4/5, October 14, 1988

Course Records, Main Turf
5 furlongs: Special Occasion, :55.17, September 4, 2000
1 mile: True Diplomacy, 1:34, September 8, 1989
1m 70yds: Cape Playhouse, 1:38, October 25, 1978
1 1/16 miles: Wanderkin, 1:39 2/5, September 30, 1988
1 3/8 miles: Rice, 2:12.02, September 25, 1998

Fastest Times of 2001 (Dirt)
5 furlongs: Fetch Dinner, :56.20, October 30
5 1/2 furlongs: Onthedeanslist, 1:02.44, October 3
6 furlongs: Late Carson, 1:08.27, September 28
1 mile: Williamthenchanted, 1:35.09, September 28
1m 70yds: Hitchin' Post, 1:39.73, October 20
1 1/16 miles: Talk's Cheap, 1:41.84, October 19
1 1/8 miles: Volponi, 1:46.55, October 19
1 3/16 miles: Rize, 1:53.95, November 10

Fastest Times of 2001 (Turf)
5 furlongs: Take Achance On Me, :55.83, October 13
1 mile: Beckon the King, 1:33.88, October 19
1m 70yds: Star of Rio, 1:38.60, October 24
1 1/16 miles: Delirio, 1:40.87, October 11
1 3/8 miles: Cruise Along, 2:15.33, October 19

Monmouth Park

The first Monmouth Park opened in July 1870 and was located three miles from Long Branch, New Jersey. The track's early years included performances by some of the era's most famous horses, including Longfellow and Miss Woodford, the first racehorse to earn $100,000. However, Monmouth fell victim to changing times, and it closed in 1893 after New Jersey outlawed wagering. Fifty years later, pari-mutuel wagering was legalized, and a group of investors led by Amory L. Haskell built a new Monmouth in 1946 at its current location in Oceanport, New Jersey. Since then, the track known for its seaside location has been a popular destination for some of the sport's leading Thoroughbreds. The track's richest race is the Haskell Invitational Handicap (G1), a $1-million race for three-year-olds and the first major event after the Triple Crown races. Monmouth also features the Philip H. Iselin Handicap (G2), named in honor of the former Monmouth president who became involved in the racetrack after it was con-

Monmouth Park, continued

structed near his home. Among Iselin winners were two horses named Horse of the Year, Alysheba (1988) and Skip Away ('98). The Iselin formerly was known as the Monmouth Handicap, which was inaugurated in 1884.

Location: Oceanport Avenue, P.O. Box MP, Oceanport, NJ 07757-1298
Phone: (732) 222-5100
Fax: (732) 571-8658
E-mail: mpinfo@njsea.com
Web site: http://www.monmouthpark.com
Year founded: Original: 1870; Current Track: 1946
Inaugural meeting: July 30, 1870
Acreage: 500
Seating capacity: 18,000
Number of stalls: 1,600

Officers
President: James A. DiEleuterio Jr.
General Manager: Robert J. Kulina
Racing Secretary: Sean Greely
Director of Operations: Horace Smith
Director of Admissions: Judi Gittins
Director of Finance: James Jemas
Director of Marketing: Peter Verdee
Director of Publicity: Steve Schwartz
Director of Simulcasting: John S. Grasty
Horsemen's Liaison: Mary Beth Yates
Stewards: Harvey Wardell, Sam Boulmetis, Steve Pagano
Track Announcer: Larry Collmus
Track Photographer: Bill Denver
Track Superintendent: Dave Harrington
Other Officials: Bill Knauf, Director of Media Relations

Racing dates
2001: May 26-September 2, 72 days
2002: May 11-September 1, 76 days

Track Layout
Main circumference: 1 mile
Main track chute: 1 1/4 miles, 6 furlongs
Main width: 100 feet
Main length of stretch: 985 feet
Main turf circumference: 7 furlongs
Main turf chute: 1 1/16 miles, 1 1/8 miles
Main turf width: 90 feet

Attendance
Highest single meet record: 1,150,658, 1981
Record daily average for single meet: 20,907, 1957
Average daily recent meeting: 10,757, 2001
Highest single day record: 43,591, August 4, 1962

Handle
Single day total handle all sources: $11,407,470, 1999
Average all sources recent meeting: $4,648,153, 2001
Average on-track recent meeting: $1,634,235, 2001
Single day on-track handle: $11,407,470, 1999
Record daily average for single meet: $1,997,807, 1970

Mutuel Records
Highest Win: $229.20, July 15, 1951
Lowest Win: Skip Away, August 30, 1998, $2.10; Silverbulletday, July 10, 1999, $2.10
Highest Trifecta: $62,172, June 15, 1978
Lowest Trifecta: $17.60, July 29, 1985
Highest Daily Double: $3,962.50, July 19, 1952
Lowest Daily Double: $2.80, June 3, 1995

Leaders
Career, leading jockey by titles: Joe Bravo, 8
Career, leading trainer by titles: Budd Lepman, 5; John H. Forbes, 5; Juan Serey, 5
Recent meeting, leading jockey: Eibar Coa, 82, 2001
Recent meeting, leading owner: Runnin Horse Farms, 14, 2000
Recent meeting, leading trainer: J. Willard Thompson, 30, 2001

Records
Single day jockey wins: Walter Blum, 6, June 9, 1961; Chris Antley, 6, July 30, 1984; Julie Krone, 6, August 19, 1987; Joe Bravo, 6, August 31, 1994
Single day trainer wins: J. Willard Thompson, 4, November 8, 1975; Robert Klesaris, 4, July 10, 1987; John H. Forbes, 4, August 28, 1989

Track Records, Main Dirt
5 furlongs: Camden Harbor, :56.22, June 18, 1991
5 1/2 furlongs: American Royale, 1:02.96, July 21, 1991
6 furlongs: Gilded Time, 1:07.84, August 8, 1992
1 mile: Forty Niner, 1:33 4/5, July 16, 1988
1m 70 yds: Razzle Dazzle Rey, 1:39 1/5, May 13, 1978; Grecian Flight, 1:39 1/5, June 17, 1989; Back Bay Banquet, 1:39 1/5, July 10, 1989
1 1/16 miles: Formal Gold, 1:40.20, August 23, 1997
1 1/8 miles: Spend a Buck, 1:46 4/5, August 17, 1985; Jolie's Halo, 1:46.80, August 8, 1992
1 3/16 miles: Okamsel, 1:59 3/5, June 20, 1951
1 1/4 miles: Carry Back, 2:00 2/5, July 14, 1962; Majestic Light, 2:00 2/5, August 30, 1977
1 1/2 miles: Chappys Joy, 2:34 1/5, August 5, 1989
1 3/4 miles: *Halconero, 3:04 1/5, August 5, 1950

Course Records, Main Turf
5 furlongs: Klassy Briefcase, :54.97, June 8, 1991
1 mile: Double Booked, 1:33.34, June 2, 1991
1 1/16 miles: Mi Narrow, 1:39.40, July 11, 1999
1 1/8 miles: Horatia (Ire), 1:47.52, July 2, 2000
1 3/16 miles: *Dorienne, 2:01, June 30, 1953
1 1/4 miles: Muzzle, 2:08 2/5, July 10, 1953
1 3/8 miles: Down the Aisle, 2:13.63, July 1, 2000
1 1/2 miles: Agacode, 2:29 2/5, June 14, 1985

Fastest Times of 2001 (Dirt)
5 furlongs: Rudirudy, :56.54, July 8
5 1/2 furlongs: Forest Heiress, 1:03.55, August 4
6 furlongs: Big Bambu, 1:08.75, July 4
1 mile: Rize, 1:35.57, June 3
1m 70yds: Miss Linda (Arg), 1:41.15, August 5
1 1/16 miles: Broken Vow, 1:42.20, June 30
1 1/8 miles: Broken Vow, 1:49.55, August 26

Fastest Times of 2001 (Turf)
5 furlongs: Special Occasion, :55.12, June 10
1 mile: Magical Madness, 1:34.40, June 23
1 1/16 miles: Key Lory, 1:40.39, August 5
1 1/8 miles: Batique, 1:46.19, June 16
1 3/8 miles: Senure, 2:13.56, July 1

New Hampshire

Rockingham Park

A testimony to the appeal of Thoroughbred racing in New England, Rockingham Park has survived a 25-year shutdown, a hurricane, and a horrific fire to continue as New Hampshire's lone Thoroughbred racetrack. Located in Salem, Rockingham Park opened on June 28, 1906, before a crowd of more than 10,000, thanks to the work of John "Bet-A-Million" Gates and August Belmont II. That initial 21-day meet had one fundamental problem: Betting on horses was illegal in New Hampshire. Pinkerton detectives closed the track, and it remained shuttered for 25 years, though it was used as a site for an aviation exposition, the Rockingham Fair, Grand Circuit harness racing—though no betting was allowed—a bivouac during World War I, and auto racing when a wooden track was laid over the dirt track.

With some prodding by famed sportswriter Damon

Runyon, New Hampshire legislators reconsidered the ban on pari-mutuel racing, and "The Rock" reopened in 1933 and subsequently attracted champions Discovery and Seabiscuit. In September 1938, a hurricane whipped across the track and blew track announcer Babe Rubenstein's box off the roof. Dr. Fager raced at Rockingham in 1967, winning the New Hampshire Sweepstakes Classic by 1¼ lengths over In Reality.

An early-morning fire on July 29, 1980, destroyed the grandstand and damaged the clubhouse. Rockingham reopened in 1984 under the current ownership, Rockingham Venture Inc., headed by track President Joseph E. Carney Jr. Two years later, a turf course was added. A plush Sports Club and family picnic pavilion were added in 1991 after full-card, interstate simulcasting was approved.

Location: Rockingham Park Blvd., P.O. Box 47, Salem, NH 03079
Phone: (603) 898-2311
Fax: (603) 898-1424
Web site: http://www.rockinghampark.com
Year founded: 1906
Inaugural meeting: June 28, 1906
Acreage: 325
Number of stalls: 1,400
Seating capacity: 15,000

Officers
President: Joseph E. Carney Jr.
Vice Presidents: Edward J. Keelan, Edward M. Callahan
General Manager: Edward M. Callahan
Director of Racing: Bob DeStasio
Racing Secretary: L. J. Pambianchi Jr.
Secretary: Daniel Callaghan
Treasurer: Thomas F. Carney
Director of Admissions: Larry Murphy
Director of Communications: Lynne Snierson
Director of Marketing: Lynne Snierson
Director of Mutuels: Kathleen Brothers
Director of Publicity: Lynne Snierson
Director of Simulcasting: John Vitale
Stewards: Thomas Smith
Track Announcer: John Vitale
Track Photographer: Louis Hodges Jr.
Track Superintendent: Ray Messina

Racing dates
2001: June 10-September 23, 75 days
2002: June 9-September 22, 75 days

Track Layout
Main circumference: 1 mile
Main track chute: 1 1/4 miles, 6 furlongs
Main width: 83 feet
Main turf circumference: 7 furlongs
Main turf chute: 1 1/8 miles

Attendance
Average daily recent meeting: 2,948, 2001
Highest single day record: 41,509, September 6, 1965

Handle
Average all sources recent meeting: $592,000, 2001
Average on-track recent meeting: $194,000, 2001
Single day on-track handle: $2,669,721, September 2, 1968
Single day total handle all sources: $2,669,721, September 2, 1968

Leaders
Career, leading jockey by titles: Rudy Baez, 10
Recent meeting, leading jockey: Winston A. Thompson, 99, 2001

Recent meeting, leading owner: Michael Gill, 33
Recent meeting, leading trainer: Ron Dandy, 40, 2001

Records
Single day jockey wins: Rudy Baez, 7, September 27, 1991; Willie Turnbull, 7, July 31, 1942
Single meet, leading jockey by wins: Harry Vega, 302, 1989

Track Records, Main Dirt
4 furlongs: Maria's Brown Eyes, :46 1/5, May 28, 1987
4 1/2 furlongs: Kipper Katz, :52.44, June 25, 1997
5 furlongs: Sneaky Pal, :56 4/5, July 8, 1974
5 1/2 furlongs: Bama Redd, 1:03 4/5, May 21, 1987
6 furlongs: Dandy Blitzen, 1:08 4/5, August 29, 1959
1m 40 yds: Zafarrancho (Arg), 1:38 1/5, June 19, 1987
1 1/16 miles: Herbalist, 1:42, August 19, 1972
1 1/8 miles: Dr. Fager, 1:48 1/5, July 15, 1967
1 1/4 miles: Dr. Fager, 1:59 4/5, September 2, 1967
1 1/2 miles: Girder, 2:29 3/5, October 10, 1953
Other: 2 miles 40 yds, Zagora, 3:34 2/5, September 2, 1985; 2 1/4 miles, Usable, 3:58 2/5, September 4, 1978; 2 1/2 miles, Bert Leo B., 4:23 3/5, July 5, 1978

Course Records, Main Turf
1 mile: Rode to Ankara, 1:37.19, June 24, 1993
1 1/16 miles: Simply Majestic, 1:42 3/5, June 18, 1989; Paris Opera, 1:42 3/5, July 4, 1990
1 1/8 miles: Statesmanship, 1:48.49, June 20, 1998
1 3/8 miles: Autonomo, 2:20.80, June 15, 1991
Other: 1 7/8 miles, Hypnotizer, 3:15 3/5, August 19, 1989

Interesting facts
Trivia: Mentioned in the movie, "The Sting"

Fastest Times of 2001 (Dirt)
4 1/2 furlongs: Termination Dust, :52.70, July 15
5 furlongs: Hail Winston, :57.87, June 10
5 1/2 furlongs: Deer Tango, 1:04.55, June 10
6 furlongs: Cox's Sweep, 1:10.08, July 21
1m 40yds: Apache Native, 1:40.65, June 13
1 1/16 miles: Fitstoatee, 1:44.67, August 11
1 1/8 miles: Core Idea, 1:53.03, July 7
1 3/16 miles: Core Idea, 1:59.57, July 21
1 1/4 miles: Bo Barley, 2:06.24, August 4

Fastest Times of 2001 (Turf)
1 mile: Duke Ora, 1:37.29, June 27
1 1/16 miles: Juan of La Mancha, 1:44.46, June 10

New Mexico

The Downs at Albuquerque

The Downs at Albuquerque, located on the New Mexico State Fairgrounds in Albuquerque, features live Thoroughbred and Quarter Horse racing each spring and during the 17-day New Mexico State Fair in September. The fair dates from 1881, while its race meet, which opened October 1938, is the oldest in New Mexico. The New Mexico State Fair Futurity for Quarter Horses debuted in 1946 and is the oldest continuously run stakes race for the breed. One notable Thoroughbred horseman who competed at Albuquerque early in his career is jockey Mike Smith, a New Mexico native who became a multiple Eclipse Award winner. In 1990, the track debuted The Lineage, a day of racing exclusively for state-bred Thoroughbreds and Quarter Horses. With assistance from its slots casino, which opened in 1999, the track has been able to solidify its business and increase purses.

The Downs at Albuquerque, continued
Location: 201 California St. NE, Albuquerque, NM 87198
Phone: (505) 266-5555
Fax: (505) 268-1970
E-mail: downsatalb@aol.com
Web site: http://www.abqdowns.com

Officers
Director of Racing: Don Cook
Racing Secretary: Rick Kloeppel
Director of Publicity: Mark Lezaurs
Year founded: 1938

Racing dates
2001: March 24-June 5, 2001, 44 days; September 8-September 23, 2001, 17 days
2002: March 29-June 17, 48 days; September 6-September 22, 17 days

Leaders
Recent meeting, leading jockey: Miguel Sanchez Fuentes, 13, Fall 2001
Recent meeting, leading trainer: Todd W. Fincher, 8, Fall 2001

Track Records, Main Dirt
4 furlongs: Chipper J., :45.76, May 6, 2001
4 1/2 furlongs: Silver Matt, :51.22, June 17, 2000
5 furlongs: Scout Revolt, :56.35, December 12, 1998
5 1/2 furlongs: Yulla Yulla, 1:01.68, September 23, 2000
6 furlongs: Huggin the Rail, 1:08.44, September 29, 1996
6 1/2 furlongs: Shellerton, 1:14.92, May 18, 2001
1 mile: Dashing Forbes, 1:35.74, September 16, 1994
1 1/16 miles: Ciento, 1:40.60, September 22, 2001
1 1/8 miles: Brew, 1:48.47, June 3, 2001
1 3/16 miles: Savage Wind, 2:05 4/5, September 23, 1981
1 1/4 miles: Luedke, 2:03.69, April 14, 1996
1 1/2 miles: Luedke, 2:33.73, September 25, 1994
1 5/8 miles: Vikings Shield, 2:43 2/5, April 17, 1988
Other: 1 13/16 miles, Vermejo, 3:05 2/5, September 27, 1970

Fastest Times of 2001
4 furlongs: Come On Nifty, :46.80, April 29
4 1/2 furlongs: Prairie Fire, :52.15, May 11
5 furlongs: O Golly Gee, :57.24, April 22
5 1/2 furlongs: Jim Jams, 1:02.26, April 14
6 furlongs: Crooner Slew, 1:08.82, April 30
6 1/2 furlongs: Shellerton, 1:14.92, May 18; Formal Feast, 1:14.92, May 28
7 furlongs: Silver Matt, 1:21.68, May 12; Purls Ledgend, 1:21.68, September 21
1 mile: C. D. Haj, 1:35.90, May 13
1 1/16 miles: Oddsonjack, 1:42.99, May 20
1 1/8 miles: Brew, 1:48.47, June 3

Ruidoso Downs

Located 7,000 feet above sea level in the pine-covered mountains of southeastern New Mexico, Ruidoso Downs long has been a popular destination for Southwestern horsemen and racing fans seeking to escape the summer heat. Since 1959, the track has held Quarter Horse racing's richest and most famous event, the All American Futurity, which in 1978 became the world's first million-dollar horse race. Leading trainers such as D. Wayne Lukas and Bob Baffert raced Quarter Horses at Ruidoso before switching to Thoroughbred racing. Thoroughbred racing also is a fixture at Ruidoso, where purses have increased significantly due to revenues from the Billy the Kid Casino that opened at the track in 1999. Ruidoso has a unique track configuration for the two breeds that compete there. A separate straightaway for Quarter Horses is located on the outside of the seven-furlong Thoroughbred oval.

Location: P.O. Box 449, Ruidoso Downs, NM 88346
Phone: (505) 378-4431
Fax: (505) 378-4631
E-mail: info@ruidownsracing.com
Web site: http://www.ruidownsracing.com
Inaugural meeting: July 1, 1947
Number of stalls: 2,000
Seating capacity: 7,000

Officers
President: Bruce Rimbo
General Manager: Rick Baugh
Racing Secretary: Rob Junk
Treasurer: Edward Burger
Director of Marketing: Frederick Widaman
Director of Mutuels: Robert Chisholm
Director of Publicity: Frederick Widaman
Director of Simulcasting: Chris Warren

Racing dates
2001: May 25-September 3, 61 days
2002: May 24-September 2, 61 days

Track Layout
Main circumference: 7 furlongs
Main track chute: 1 1/8 miles, 6 furlongs
Main length of stretch: 656 feet

Attendance
Highest single day record: 13,526, September 4, 1999
Average daily recent meeting: 3,389, 2001

Handle
Single day on-track handle: $1,318,233, September 4, 1999

Leaders
Recent meeting, leading jockey: Michael Dennis Clark, 48, 2001
Recent meeting, leading trainer: Joel H. Marr, 19, 2001; Ramon O. Gonzalez, 19, 2001

Track Records, Main Dirt
4 1/2 furlongs: Bold Approach, :52 3/5, June 3, 1988
5 furlongs: King of Stars, :57.20, July 30, 1999
5 1/2 furlongs: Jack Wilson, 1:02.80, August 8, 1992
6 furlongs: Jack Wilson, 1:08.80, August 16, 1992
6 1/2 furlongs: Mr. Tattoo, 1:17 3/5, July 4, 1973
7 furlongs: Fill Mackis Cup, 1:24 2/5, July 15, 1984
7 1/2 furlongs: Last Don B., 1:31, May 29, 1993
1 mile: Set Records, 1:37, July 28, 1995
1m 70 yds: Brogander, 1:45 1/5, January 1, 1954
1 1/16 miles: Roythelittleone, 1:45.40, August 13, 1995
1 1/8 miles: Run John, 1:53.40, July 5, 1996
1 1/4 miles: Best Finish (GB), 2:08.20, September 7, 1998
1 3/8 miles: Start Jumpin, 2:24 1/5, August 18, 1990
1 1/2 miles: Decidedly Henry C., 2:37, August 19, 1989
1 5/8 miles: More Than Glory, 2:25.80, August 15, 1992

Fastest Times of 2001
4 1/2 furlongs: Roho, :53.20, July 19
5 furlongs: Kakioc Firo, :58.20, August 30
5 1/2 furlongs: Don's Ferrari, 1:02.80, August 19
6 furlongs: Gold Revolution, 1:10, August 23
7 1/2 furlongs: Strong Arm Robbery, 1:31.40, August 25
1 mile: Strong Arm Robbery, 1:37, September 1
1 1/16 miles: Lucky Bluff, 1:43.40, September 2
1 1/8 miles: Pancho Norte, 1:58.20, August 12
1 1/4 miles: Gotcha Thinking, 2:10, September 3

Sunland Park

Opened in 1959, Sunland Park was built just across the state line from El Paso, Texas, in New Mexico, which unlike its neighbor allowed pari-mutuel wagering. Sunland launched the career of several notable horsemen and horses. Jerry Bailey, one of Thoroughbred racing's all-time leading riders, began his career

at the track in 1974. Bold Ego, who won Sunland's Riley Allison Futurity in 1980, captured the '81 Arkansas Derby (G1) and ran second in the Preakness Stakes (G1). In the mid-1990s, the track nearly closed because of competition from Native American casinos and pari-mutuel racing in Texas and Oklahoma. New Mexico horsemen and racetracks successfully lobbied for legalizing slot machines at tracks, and Sunland's casino opened in February 1999. With a portion of casino revenues earmarked to purses, the quality of racing improved significantly.

Location: P.O. Box 1, Sunland Park, NM 88063
Phone: (505) 874-5200
Fax: (505) 589-1518
E-mail: sunlandinfo@anchorgaming.com
Web site: http://www.sunland-park.com
Year founded: 1959
Inaugural meeting: October 9, 1959
Number of stalls: 1,600
Seating capacity: 5,710

Officers
President: Harold Payne
General Manager: Harold Payne
Director of Racing: Paul Ryneveld
Racing Secretary: Norm Amundson
Director of Operations: Paul Ryneveld
Director of Communications: Paul Ryneveld
Director of Finance: Charlie Casiano
Director of Marketing: Adeline Rogers
Director of Publicity: Eric Alwan
Director of Sales: Connie Blevins
Director of Simulcasting: Charles Chrisman
Stewards: Bruce Brinkly
Track Announcer: Robert Geller
Track Photographer: Bill Pitt
Track Superintendent: Jimmie Jamison

Racing dates
2001: November 14, 2000-April 8, 2001, 84 days
2002: November 20, 2001-April 7, 2002

Track Layout
Main circumference: 1 mile
Main track chute: 1 1/4 miles, 6 1/2 furlongs
Main width: 80 feet
Main length of stretch: 990 feet

Attendance
Average daily recent meeting: 1,738, 2000/2001
Highest single day record: 8,494
Record daily average for single meet: 1,738, 2000/2001

Handle
Total all sources recent meeting: $40,857,532, 2001/2002
Total on-track recent meeting: $7,112,636, 2001/2002
Average all sources recent meeting: $284,538, 2000/2001
Average on-track recent meeting: $75,081, 2000/2001
Record daily average for single meet: $495,093, 1991
Single day on-track handle: $610,572
Single day total handle all sources: $1,252,008

Leaders
Career, leading jockey by titles: Bobby Harmon, 8
Career, leading trainer by titles: Bob E. Arnett, 12
Recent meeting, leading jockey: Daryl Montoya, 65, 2000/2001
Recent meeting, leading owner: Single Tree Ranch, 2000/2001
Recent meeting, leading trainer: Ramon Gonzalez, 57, 2000/2001

Records
Single day jockey wins: Daryl Montoya
Single meet, leading trainer by wins: Ramon Gonzalez, 37

Track Records, Main Dirt
4 furlongs: Tamran's Jet, :44 4/5, March 22, 1968
4 1/2 furlongs: Bold Liz, :50 2/5, March 25, 1972
5 furlongs: Draconic's Loom, :56 2/5, February 13, 1980
5 1/2 furlongs: Bottle A, 1:02 3/5, April 23, 1972; Huggin the Rail, 1:02.60, February 4, 1995
6 furlongs: M. Star, 1:08 2/5, November 8, 1970
6 1/2 furlongs: Rodeo Hand, 1:15, December 8, 1963
1 mile: Dashing Forbes, 1:35.60, April 23, 1994; Out n' About, 1:35.60, March 16, 2001
1 1/16 miles: Winsham Lad, 1:42, April 22, 1962; Native Shuffle, 1:42, April 11, 1971; Brew, 1:42, April 7, 2001
1 1/8 miles: Winsham Lad, 1:48 1/5, January 8, 1961; Prenupcial, 1:48 1/5, April 28, 1962
1 3/16 miles: Mickey J., 1:58 1/5, November 14, 1970
1 1/4 miles: Curribot, 2:01 2/5, May 6, 1984
1 3/8 miles: Hot Deck, 2:19 2/5, January 10, 1970
1 5/8 miles: Rush Line, 2:47 3/5, April 6, 1969

Interesting facts
Achievements/milestones: Casino opened February 2, 1999

Fastest Times of 2001
4 furlongs: Devon's Prospect, :45.60, March 4
4 1/2 furlongs: Star Smasher, :52.20, March 20
5 furlongs: Terminator Won, :56.41, December 29
5 1/2 furlongs: Yulla Yulla, 1:03, January 6
6 furlongs: Boss Owen, 1:08.80, March 24
6 1/2 furlongs: Boss Owen, 1:15.40, March 9, Dos Amigos, 1:15.40, December 26
1 mile: Out 'n About, 1:35.60, March 16
1 1/16 miles: Brew, 1:42, April 7
1 1/8 miles: Exclusive Dancer, 1:52.33, December 23
1 1/4 miles: Ye Ole Leven, 2:04.20, April 8

SunRay Park

SunRay Park in Farmington, New Mexico, is located in an area called the Four Corners region, where northwestern New Mexico, northeastern Arizona, southeastern Utah, and southwestern Colorado meet. The racetrack, which offers Thoroughbred and Quarter Horse racing, originally was known as San Juan Downs; it was built by San Juan County at the county fairgrounds and opened in 1984. But declining business forced the track to close after its 1993 season. SunRay Gaming of New Mexico LLC secured a ten-year option to operate the track, which was renamed SunRay Park and reopened in October 1999. SunRay Gaming's interest in reviving horse racing at the facility largely was based on its ability to operate a casino with slot machines. A portion of revenues from the slots enhances race purses.

Location: 39 Road 5568, Farmington, NM 87401-1466
Phone: (505) 566-1200
Fax: (505) 326-4292
Web site: http://www.sunraygaming.com

Officers
Director of Publicity: Sharron Freelove

Racing dates
2001: September 3-November 12, 41 days
2002: September 21-November 18

Fastest Times of 2001 (Dirt)
4 1/2 furlongs: Martinis On Ice, :50.60, September 30
6 1/2 furlongs: Crooner Slew, 1:16.80, November 5; Ciento, 1:16.80, November 11
7 furlongs: Purls Ledgend, 1:23.20, October 6
1 mile: Slew in the Face, 1:36.20, October 23
1 1/8 miles: Moro Grande, 1:50.60, November 11

New York

Aqueduct

Offering roughly half of the New York Racing Association's year-round schedule, the track known as the Big A approached an exciting crossroads in 2002 after the New York Legislature in 2001 authorized video-lottery terminals to be installed at the track. Also in 2002, the track's principal Kentucky Derby (G1) prep race, the Wood Memorial Stakes, again was elevated to Grade 1 status after seven years as a Grade 2 race. Fusaichi Pegasus, the 2000 Derby winner, completed his preparation with a Wood victory.

Aqueduct opened as a six-furlong track in New York's Queens Borough on September 27, 1894. Site of the only triple dead heat in a stakes race—Brownie, Bossuet, and Wait a Bit hit the wire together in the Carter Handicap on June 10, 1944—Aqueduct was torn down in 1956 and completely rebuilt over three years. For four years, from 1964 through 1967, Aqueduct played host to the Belmont Stakes while Belmont Park was rebuilt. An all-time record crowd of 73,435 watched Gun Bow win the Metropolitan Handicap on Memorial Day, May 31, 1965.

In 1975, the one-mile inner dirt track was completed, allowing racing throughout the winter. Six years later, Aqueduct opened Equestris, a 300-foot-long, $7-million facility for 1,600 diners. A $3-million renovation in 1985 prior to its only Breeders' Cup championship day expanded Aqueduct's paddock, grandstand, and back-yard seating and installed mini-theaters.

Location: 11000 Rockaway Blvd., Jamaica, NY 11417
Phone: (718) 641-4700
Web site: http://www.nyra.com/aqueduct/
Year founded: 1894
Inaugural meeting: September 27, 1894
Acreage: 192
Number of stalls: 547
Seating capacity: 17,000

Officers
Chairman: Barry K. Schwartz
President: Terence J. Meyocks
Vice Presidents: Alexander W. Ingle, William A. Nader
Racing Secretary: Michael S. Lakow
Treasurer: John Giombarrese
Director of Admissions: Jerry A. Davis Jr.
Director of Communications: Glen Mathes
Director of Finance: Alexander W. Ingle
Director of Marketing: William A. Nader
Director of Mutuels: Vincent Hogan
Horsemen's Liaison: Carmen Barrera
Stewards: Carmine Donofrio, David Hicks, Dr. Theodore Hill
Track Announcer: Tom Durkin
Track Photographer: Adam Coglianese, Bob Coglianese
Track Superintendent: Jerry Porcelli

Racing dates
2001: October 25, 2000 to May 6, 2001, 139 days
2002: October 31, 2001 to May 5, 2002, 132 days

Track Layout
Main circumference: 1 1/8 miles
Main width: 100 feet
Main length of stretch: 1,155.6 feet
Main turf circumference: 7 furlongs
Inner circumference: 1 mile

Attendance
Average daily recent meeting: 4,770, Winter/Spring 2000/2001
Highest single day record: 73,435, May 31, 1965
Total attendance recent meeting: 429,293, Winter/Spring 2000/2001

Handle
Single day on-track handle: $8,171,520, November 2, 1985
Total on-track recent meeting: $131,692,010, Winter/Spring 2000/2001
Average all sources recent meeting: $8,534,729, Winter/Spring 2000/2001
Average on-track recent meeting: $1,463,245, Winter/Spring 2000/2001
Total all sources recent meeting: $768,125,565, Winter/Spring 2000/2001

Mutuel Records
Highest Win: $434, Markobob, September 3, 1943
Highest Pick 6: $767,998, April 9, 1990

Records
Single day jockey wins: Michael Venezia, 6, December 7, 1964; Rudy L. Turcotte, 6, December 2, 1969; Angel Cordero Jr., 6, March 12, 1975; Ron Turcotte, 6, March 5, 1976; Steve Cauthen, 6, January 22, 1977; Steve Cauthen, 6, April 7, 1977; Steve Cauthen, 6, November 29, 1977; Mike Smith, 6, January 13, 1992; Mike Smith, 6, January 30, 1992; Jorge Chavez, 6, February 18, 1996; Shaun Bridgmohan, 6, February 15, 1998

Track Records, Main Dirt
4 1/2 furlongs: About to Burst, :51 3/5, August 26, 1984
6 furlongs: Kelly Kip, 1:07.54, April 10, 1999
6 1/2 furlongs: Coronado's Quest, 1:14.35, October 26, 1997
7 furlongs: Artax, 1:20.04, May 2, 1999
1 mile: Easy Goer, 1:32 2/5, April 8, 1989
1 1/8 miles: Riva Ridge, 1:47, October 15, 1973
1 3/16 miles: Riva Ridge, 1:52 2/5, July 4, 1973
1 1/4 miles: Damascus, 1:59 1/5, July 20, 1968
1 3/8 miles: Demi's Bret, 2:12.31, October 26, 1997
1 1/2 miles: Going Abroad, 2:26 1/5, Octboer 12, 1964
1 5/8 miles: Sharp Gary, 2:40 2/5, December 13, 1975
1 3/4 miles: Malmo, 2:53.73, March 30, 1996
2 miles: Kelso, 3:19 1/5, October 31, 1964
Other: 1 5/16 miles, Gold Star Deputy, 2:07.32, April 10, 1999; 1 7/8 miles, Erin Bright, 3:12 4/5, April 18, 1985; 2 1/4 miles, Paraje, 3:47 4/5, December 5, 1973

Course Records, Main Turf
1 mile: Tax Dodge, 1:34 3/5, November 1, 1985
1 1/16 miles: Spindrift (Ire), 1:40.88, May 6, 2000
1 1/8 miles: Slew the Dragon, 1:47, November 3, 1985
1 3/8 miles: Fluorescent Light, 2:14 1/5, November 7, 1978
1 1/2 miles: Pebbles (GB), 2:27, November 2, 1985
2 miles: Putting Green, 3:30 2/5, November 23, 1984

Track records, Inner dirt
4 1/2 furlongs: Call Me Up, :52.29, February 16, 1998
6 furlongs: Whirling Blade, 1:08.57, March 5, 1997
1 mile: Tejano Couture, 1:35.79, March 9, 2000
1m 70yds: Carry My Colors, 1:38.92, February 5, 2000
1 1/16 miles: Autoroute, 1:41, December 19, 1992
1 1/8 miles: Conveyor, 1:47.33, March 6, 1993
1 3/16 miles: Victoriously, 1:54.42, January 25, 1998
1 1/4 miles: Transient Trend, 2:01.53, December 21, 1995
1 1/2 miles: Piling, 2:29 3/5, March 13, 1983
1 5/8 miles: Relaxing, 2:42 2/5, December 13, 1980
1 3/4 miles: Sophie's Friend, 2:56.73, February 10, 1996
2 miles: Charlie Coast, 3:24 4/5, February 5, 1994
Other: 2 1/16 miles, Rollix, 3:38 4/5, February 3, 1983; 2 1/8 miles, Peat Moss, 3:40 3/5, January 31, 1981; 2 1/4 miles, Field Cat, 3:51 4/5, December 31, 1981

Fastest Times of 2001 (Dirt)
4 1/2 furlongs: Scalped Ticket, :53.17, April 4
5 furlongs: Queen of Saratoga, :59.18, May 2
5 1/2 furlongs: Seeking Greatness, 1:03.08, November 15
6 furlongs: Forest Heiress, 1:08.66, November 18
6 1/2 furlongs: Stake Runner, 1:16.01, April 14
7 furlongs: Dat You Miz Blue, 1:12.06, April 7
1 mile: Left Bank, 1:33.35, November 24
1m 70yds: Stellianos, 1:40.26, January 26
1 1/16 miles: Liberty Gold, 1:42.20, January 20
1 1/8 miles: Congaree, 1:47.96, April 14
1 3/16 miles: Evening Attire, 1:55.08, December 1
1 1/4 miles: Banner Headline, 2:02.99, March 17
1 1/2 miles: Coyote Lakes, 2:30.67, December 9
1 5/8 miles: Coyote Lakes, 2:44.74, January 1

Fastest Times of 2001 (Turf)
1 mile: Ballistic, 1:35.41, April 28
1 1/16 miles: Strategic Mission, 1:41.62, May 5
1 1/8 miles: Mel N Dave, 1:48.01, May 5
1 3/8 miles: Mr. Pleasentfar (Brz), 2:16.94, November 17
1 1/2 miles: Queue, 2:29.36, November 10

Belmont Park

With a 1½-mile oval, Belmont Park on Long Island, is the largest racetrack in North America, and its huge grandstand has a 90,000-person capacity. Built for $2.5-million and opened on May 4, 1905, Belmont is host to the third leg of the Triple Crown, the Belmont Stakes (G1), which was named for German-born financier August Belmont. The first Belmont Stakes was run in 1867 at Jerome Park and was moved to Morris Park in 1890. Within a few years of Belmont Park's opening, antigambling legislation shut the track in 1911 and '12. The track reopened in 1913. The grandstand was rebuilt in 1920, raising seating capacity to 17,500. In 1963, deterioration of the grandstand forced a five-year closing while the current facility was constructed for $30.7-million. In those years, the Belmont and most of the track's dates were run at Aqueduct. Belmont has played host to three runnings of the Breeders' Cup World Thoroughbred Championships—in 1990, '95, and 2001. The most recent running of the championship event marked the first international sporting event to be held in the New York City area following the September 11, 2001, terrorist attack on the World Trade Center.

Location: 2150 Hempstead Pike, Elmont, NY 11003
Phone: (516) 488-6000
E-mail: nyra@nyra.com
Web site: http://www.nyra.com/belmont/
Year founded: 1895
Inaugural meeting: May 4, 1905
Acreage: 430
Number of stalls: 2,200
Seating capacity: 32,941

Officers
Chairman: Barry K. Schwartz
President: Terence B. Meyocks
Vice Presidents: Alexander W. Ingle, William A. Nader
Racing Secretary: Michael S. Lakow
Treasurer: John Giombarrese
Director of Admissions: Jerry A. Davis Jr.
Director of Communications: Glen Mathes
Director of Finance: Alexander W. Ingle
Director of Mutuels: Vincent Hogan
Director of Simulcasting: Liz Bracken
Horsemen's Liaison: Carmen Barrera
Track Announcer: Tom Durkin
Track Photographer: Adam Coglianese, Bob Coglianese

Track Superintendent: Jerry Porcelli

Racing dates
2001: May 9-July 22, 55 days; September 7-October 28, 37 days
2002: May 8-July 21, 55 days; September 6-October 20, 33 days

Track Layout
Main circumference: 1 1/2 miles
Main length of stretch: 1,097 feet
Main turf circumference: 1 5/16 miles
Inner turf circumference: 1 3/16 miles
Training track: 7 furlongs

Attendance
Total attendance recent meeting: 441,392, Spring/Summer-2001; 243,769, Fall 2001
Average daily recent meeting: 8,025, Spring/Summer-2001; 7,618, Fall 2001
Highest single day record: 85,818, June 6, 1999

Handle
Total all sources recent meeting: $607,864,143, Spring/Summer-2001; $429,131,994, Fall 2001
Total on-track recent meeting: $106,147,333, Spring/Summer-2001; $78,050,464, Fall 2001
Average on-track recent meeting: $1,929,952, Spring/Summer-2001; $2,109,472, Fall 2001
Single day on-track handle: $13,087,814, October 27, 2001
Average all sources recent meeting: $11,052,075, Spring/Summer-2001; $13,410,375, Fall 2001

Mutuel Records
Highest Exacta: $5,454, June 1, 1985

Leaders
Recent meeting, leading trainer: Todd Pletcher, 17, Fall 2001
Recent meeting, leading jockey: Jerry Bailey, 36, Fall 2001

Records
Single day jockey wins: Jorge Velasquez, 6, July 9, 1981

Track Records, Main Dirt
5 furlongs: Kelly Kip, :55.75, June 21, 1996
5 1/2 furlongs: More Than Ready, 1:02.56, July 4, 1999
6 furlongs: Artax, 1:07.66, October 16, 1999
6 1/2 furlongs: Confide, 1:14.51, October 16, 1997
7 furlongs: You And I, 1:20.33, June 11, 1994
1 mile: Williamstown, 1:32.79, May 5, 1993
1 1/16 miles: Rock and Roll, 1:39.51, June 13, 1998
1 1/8 miles: Secretariat, 1:45 2/5, September 15, 1973
1 3/16 miles: Lueders, 1:56, June 24, 1982
1 1/4 miles: In Excess (Ire), 1:58 1/5, July 4, 1991
1 3/8 miles: Victoriously, 2:14.72, October 16, 1997
1 1/2 miles: Secretariat, 2:24, June 9, 1973

Course Records, Main Turf
6 furlongs: Masterclass, 1:07.31, May 24, 1992
7 furlongs: Officialpermission, 1:19.88, July 23, 2000
1 mile: Elusive Quality, 1:31.63, July 4, 1998
1 1/16 miles: Fortitude, 1:38.53, September 6, 1997
1 3/8 miles: Influent, 2:11.06, July 13, 1997
1 1/2 miles: Sky Classic, 2:24.50, October 3, 1992
2 miles: King's General (GB), 3:20 2/5, July 4, 1983

Course records, Inner turf
1 1/16 miles: Roman Envoy, 1:39.38, May 23, 1992
1 1/8 miles: Subordination, 1:45.69, June 15, 1997
1 1/4 miles: Paradise Creek, 1:57.79, June 11, 1994
1 3/8 miles: With Approval, 2:10 1/5, June 17, 1990

Fastest Times of 2001 (Dirt)
5 furlongs: In High Gear, :56.63, June 10
5 1/2 furlongs: Proud Citizen, 1:02.99, June 28
6 furlongs: Dat You Miz Blue, 1:07.92, May 26
6 1/2 furlongs: Dat You Miz Blue, 1:15.32, June 16
7 furlongs: Left Bank, 1:20.73, September 22
1 mile: Express Tour, 1:34.57, September 22
1 1/16 miles: Jarf, 1:40.08, June 28
1 1/8 miles: Fleet Renee, 1:47.19, June 30

Belmont Park, continued

1 1/4 miles: Albert the Great, 2:00.39, July 1
1 3/8 miles: Summer Colony, 2:17.45, September 23
1 1/2 miles: Point Given, 2:26.56, June 9

Fastest Times of 2001 (Turf)

6 furlongs: Cyclorama, 1:09.02, July 22
7 furlongs: Scagnelli, 1:20.30, July 21
1 mile: Val Royal (Fr), 1:32.05, October 27
1 1/16 miles: Babae (Chi), 1:40.53, October 26
1 1/8 miles: Man From Wicklow, 1:47.19, June 9
1 1/4 miles: Sharp Performance, 1:58.93, July 15
1 3/8 miles: King Cugat, 2:10.62, July 7
1 1/2 miles: Fantastic Light, 2:24.36, October 27

Finger Lakes

In Native American lore, the Finger Lakes region of upstate New York was created when the Great Spirit placed his hand down on the land to create the series of long, thin lakes. Finger Lakes Race Track, which is located 20 miles from Rochester in Farmington, opened May 23, 1962, and offers racing from mid-April to early December. Owned by Finger Lakes Racing Association Inc., the track has featured Eclipse Award-winning sprinters Not Surprising, Groovy, and Safely Kept. Fio Rito shipped out of western New York to win the 1981 Whitney Handicap (G1) at Saratoga Race Course. In 2001, Shesastonecoldfox became the first horse based at Finger Lakes to compete in the Breeders' Cup World Thoroughbred Championships. The $125,000 New York Derby, which has been held at Finger Lakes since 1969, annually is the track's richest race.

Location: 5857 Route 96, Farmington, NY 14425
Phone: (716) 924-3232
Fax: (716) 924-3967
E-mail: smartin@fingerlakesracetrack.com
Web site: http://www.fingerlakesracetrack.com
Year founded: 1962
Inaugural meeting: May 23, 1962
Acreage: 400
Number of stalls: 1,214
Seating capacity: 6,000

Officers

President: Christian Riegle
General Manager: Christian Riegle
Racing Secretary: Daniel Doocy
Director of Admissions: Brenda Tarzia
Director of Finance: Stephen Richardson
Director of Marketing: Steven Martin
Director of Mutuels: Ann Blazey
Director of Publicity: Steven Martin
Director of Sales: Lizette Manickram
Director of Simulcasting: Patrick Placito
Horsemen's Liaison: Paul Steckel
Stewards: Rick Coyne
Track Announcer: Ross Morton
Track Photographer: Tom Cooley
Track Superintendent: Rick Brongo
Other Officials: Arthur Green, Racing Coordinator

Racing dates

2001: April 13-December 9, 169 days
2002: April 12-December 8, 161 days

Track Layout

Main circumference: 1 mile
Main track chute: 1 1/4 miles, 6 furlongs
Main width: 85 feet
Main length of stretch: 960 feet

Attendance

Average daily recent meeting: 1,259, 2001
Highest single meet record: 698,113, 1974
Lowest single meet record: 222,590, 2000
Record daily average for single meet: 5,032, 1962
Total attendance recent meeting: 207,681, 2001

Handle

Average all sources recent meeting: $991,242, 2001
Single day on-track handle: $765,580, September 24, 1978
Average on-track recent meeting: $122,867, 2001
Total all sources recent meeting: $163,554,953, 2001
Record daily average for single meet: $348,608, 1982
Total on-track recent meeting: $20,273,013, 2001

Mutuel Records

Highest Pick 6: $161,490, June 21, 2001

Leaders

Career, leading trainer by titles: Michael S. Ferraro, 17
Career, leading jockey by titles: Kevin Whitley, 9
Recent meeting, leading jockey: John Grabowski, 198, 2001
Recent meeting, leading owner: Charlton A. Baker, 33, 2001
Recent meeting, leading trainer: Michael S. Ferraro, 85, 2001

Records

Single day jockey wins: Robert Messina, 6, November 23, 2001
Single meet, leading jockey by wins: John Grabowski, 233, 2000
Single meet, leading trainer by wins: Michael S. Ferraro, 107, 1977

Track Records, Main Dirt

4 1/2 furlongs: Top End, :50.60, April 8, 1998
5 furlongs: Wonderous Wise, :57 1/5, April 11, 1989; Bobby's Code, :57.20, April 8, 1998
5 1/2 furlongs: Hilary Star, 1:02 4/5, April 16, 1989; With It, 1:02.80, June 12, 1994; What A Rollick, 1:02.80, December 12, 1994
6 furlongs: Kelly Kip, 1:08.20, June 20, 1998
1 mile: Transact, 1:36.20, August 29, 1994; Fling n Roll, 1:36.20, November 28, 1995
1m 70 yds: C B Account, 1:40, July 6, 1997
1 1/16 miles: Fit for Royalty, 1:43, May 19, 1997
1 1/8 miles: Copper Mount, 1:48.80, August 27, 1994
1 3/16 miles: North Warning, 1:58.40, July 10, 1994
1 1/4 miles: Caramba, 2:05 1/5, July 11, 1987
1 1/2 miles: Brave Beast, 2:33.70, September 22, 1991
1 5/8 miles: North Warning, 2:46.60, September 4, 1994
Other: 2 furlongs, Broadway Blondie, :21.80, April 30, 1998

Interesting facts

Achievements/milestones: 2001 marked 40th season of operation

Fastest Times of 2001

4 1/2 furlongs: Jadod Money, :52.02, April 14
5 furlongs: Ammodio, :58.60, August 3
5 1/2 furlongs: Polish Toy, 1:03.15, August 25
6 furlongs: B. Nimble Jak, 1:10.10, June 29
1m 70yds: Juan Valdez, 1:42.64, June 11
1 1/16 miles: Alley Ball, 1:44.36, August 25
1 1/8 miles: Woodwork, 1:52.91, September 4

Saratoga Race Course

An American landmark and one of the world's leading sports venues, Saratoga Race Course operates six weeks each year and draws huge crowds to the foothills of the Adirondack Mountains in historic Saratoga Springs, approximately 25 miles north of Albany. Saratoga again set attendance and wagering records in 2001. For the first time, on-track attendance climbed above one million to 1,011,669, an increase of 3.4% over 2000, and wa-

gering rose 5% to $124.6-million.

Opened August 2, 1864, Saratoga Race Course is the oldest existing track in America. Major renovations of the facility occurred in 1902, 1928, 1940, 1965, 1985, and 2000, when $8-million was spent to remodel the track's three main entrances, construct state-of-the-art jockeys quarters, and restore an elegant 19th-century fountain in front of the clubhouse gate.

Known as the "graveyard of champions," Saratoga has been host to many of Thoroughbred racing's greatest upsets, none more notable than Man o' War's only career loss to Upset in the 1919 Sanford Stakes; Gallant Fox's loss in the 1930 Travers Stakes to 100-to-1 longshot Jim Dandy; Onion's shocking victory over Secretariat in the 1973 Whitney Stakes (G2); and Runaway Groom's 1982 Travers Stakes (G1) upset of Conquistador Cielo. Racing at Saratoga is enhanced annually by the inductions at the National Museum of Racing and Hall of Fame, Fasig-Tipton's yearling sale, and the Jockey Club Round Table Conference.

Location: P.O. Box 564, Saratoga Springs, NY 12866
Phone: (518) 584-6200
Fax: (518) 587-4646
Web site: http://www.nyra.com/saratoga/
Inaugural meeting: August 3-6, 1863
Year founded: 1863
Acreage: 350
Number of stalls: 1,830
Seating capacity: 18,000

Officers
Chairman: Barry K. Schwartz
President: Terence J. Meyocks
Vice Presidents: Alexander W. Ingle, William A. Nader
Racing Secretary: Michael S. Lakow
Treasurer: John Giombarrese
Director of Admissions: Jerry A. Davis Jr.
Director of Communications: Glen Mathes
Director of Finance: Alexander W. Ingle
Director of Marketing: William A. Nader
Director of Mutuels: Vincent Hogan
Horsemen's Liaison: Carmen Barrera
Stewards: Carmine Donofrio, David Hicks, Dr. Theodore Hill
Track Announcer: Tom Durkin
Track Photographer: Adam Coglianese, Bob Coglianese
Track Superintendent: Jerry Porcelli

Racing dates
2002: July 24-September 2, 36 days
2001: July 25-September 3, 36 days

Track Layout
Main circumference: 1 1/8 miles
Main track chute: 7 furlongs
Main length of stretch: 1,144 feet
Main turf circumference: 1 mile
Main turf length of stretch: 1,144 feet
Inner turf circumference: 7 furlongs
Inner turf length of stretch: 1,164 feet
Training track: 1 mile, 7 furlongs turf

Attendance
Average daily recent meeting: 11,001, 2001
Highest single day record: 66,194, August 15, 1999
Highest single meet record: 1,011,669, 2001
Record daily average for single meet: 28,479, 1989

Handle
Average all sources recent meeting: $561,400,000, 2001
Single day on-track handle: $7,887,462, August 19, 1995
Record daily average for single meet: $3,742,773, 1993
Average on-track recent meeting: $124,680,000, 2001

Mutuel Records
Highest Trifecta: $63,624, August 22, 1974
Highest Daily Double: $4,313.90, August 27, 1945

Leaders
Career, leading trainer by titles: Bill Mott, 7
Recent meeting, leading jockey: Jerry Bailey, 55, 2001
Recent meeting, leading owner: Edward P. Evans, 8, 2000
Recent meeting, leading trainer: Bill Mott, 22, 2001
Career, leading jockey by titles: Angel Cordero Jr., 13

Records
Single meet, leading jockey by wins: Jerry Bailey, 55, 2001
Single meet, leading trainer by wins: Bill Mott, 22, 2001
Single day jockey wins: John Velazquez, 6, September 3, 2001

Track Records, Main Dirt
5 furlongs: Fabulous Force, :56.71, August 18, 1993
5 1/2 furlongs: Mayakovsky, 1:03.32, July 25, 2001
6 furlongs: Spanish Riddle, 1:08, August 18, 1972
6 1/2 furlongs: Topsider, 1:14 2/5, August 1, 1979
7 furlongs: Darby Creek Road, 1:20 3/5, August 8, 1978
1 mile: Key Contender, 1:34.72, August 9, 1992
1 1/8 miles: Tri Jet, 1:47, August 3, 1974
1 3/16 miles: Winter's Tale, 1:54 3/5, August 21, 1982
1 1/4 miles: General Assembly, 2:00, August 18, 1979
1 5/8 miles: Green Highlander, 2:43.57, August 15, 1991
2 miles: James Boswell, 3:26, August 11, 1983

Course Records, Main Turf
1 1/16 miles: Fourstardave, 1:38.91, July 29, 1991
1 1/8 miles: Tentam, 1:45 2/5, August 10, 1973
1 3/16 miles: Phi Beta Doc, 1:51.61, September 1, 1999
1 5/8 miles: Tom Swift, 2:37, August 23, 1978

Course records, Inner turf
1 mile: Bomfim, 1:33.78, August 1, 1999
1 1/16 miles: Roman Envoy, 1:39.99, August 3, 1992
1 1/8 miles: Amarettitorun, 1:46.22, July 26, 1997
1 3/8 miles: Babinda (GB), 2:12, July 26, 1997
1 1/2 miles: Awad, 2:23.20, August 9, 1997

Fastest Times of 2001 (Dirt)
5 furlongs: Goodness, :57.84, August 5
5 1/2 furlongs: Mayakovsky, 1:03.32, July 25
6 furlongs: Left Bank, 1:08.53, August 13
6 1/2 furlongs: You, 1:15.16, August 13
7 furlongs: Victory Ride, 1:21.72, July 28
1 1/8 miles: Lido Palace (Chi), 1:47.94, July 28
1 1/4 miles: Point Given, 2:01.40, August 25

Fastest Times of 2001 (Turf)
1 mile: Strategic Mission, 1:34.21, August 8; Veil of Avalon, 1:34.21, August 25
1 1/16 miles: Dr. Kashnikow, 1:39.30, August 25
1 1/8 miles: Starine (Fr), 1:46.17, September 3
1 3/16 miles: Aslaaf, 1:53.33, July 25
1 3/8 miles: Chez Cherie (GB), 2:14.03, August 8
1 1/2 miles: With Anticipation, 2:26.41, August 11

Ohio

Beulah Park

Ohio's oldest racetrack, Beulah Park is located in Grove City, south of Columbus. Operating since 1923, the track offered a spring meet that once was a popular stopping point for horses in transit from Florida to New York. Beulah was started by successful paving contractor Robert J. Deist. After Deist's death, owner-

Beulah Park, continued

ship of the track passed to his son, Robert Y. Deist. In 1983, the younger Deist sold Beulah, which passed through a succession of owners and was known as Darby Downs from 1983 to '86. Present owners Charles Ruma and Jack Ruscilli purchased Beulah in 1986 and restored the track's original name. Beulah, which also offers some Quarter Horse racing, was the first Ohio track to offer simulcasting, phone wagering, and Internet wagering. Along with Thistledown near Cleveland and River Downs near Cincinnati, Beulah shares host duties for the Best of Ohio day, which offers five stakes races for Ohio-breds.

Location: 3664 Grant Ave., Grove City, OH 43123
Phone: (614) 871-9600
Fax: (614) 871-0433
E-mail: mweiss@iwaynet.net
Web site: http://www.beulahpark.com
Seating capacity: 7,200
Number of stalls: 1,200

Officers
President: Charles J. Ruma
General Manager: Michael Weiss
Director of Racing: Ed Vomacka
Racing Secretary: Ed Vomacka
Director of Publicity: Vic Mason
Track Announcer: Nick Capurro

Racing dates
2001: January 12-May 5, 70 days; September 15-December 23, 65 days
2002: January 11-May 4, 66 days; September 14-December 22

Track Layout
Main circumference: 1 mile
Main length of stretch: 1,100 feet
Main turf circumference: 6 furlongs, less 223 feet

Track Records, Main Dirt
5 furlongs: Love Pappa Mucci, :56.75, February 11, 1994
5 1/2 furlongs: Jilsie's Gigalo, 1:03, May 4, 1991
6 furlongs: Whatta Brave, 1:08.50, October 29, 2000
1 mile: Theoddsonchoice, 1:35.71, March 31, 1996
1m 70 yds: King's Wailea, 1:40.15, November 19, 1993
1 1/16 miles: Din's Dancer, 1:40 4/5, November 3, 1990
1 1/8 miles: Lord Try On, 1:48.96, September 26, 1992
1 3/16 miles: World of Magic, 1:55, September 21, 1991
1 1/4 miles: On the Scent, 2:00.22, October 19, 1991
1 1/2 miles: Doctor's Romance, 2:29.50, March 26, 1994
1 5/8 miles: Big Beans, 2:46, October 5, 1957
1 3/4 miles: Dot Your Eye, 2:57 3/5, October 20, 1971
Other: 2 furlongs, Go Chop, :21 3/5, May 7, 1989; 2 miles 70 yds, Benomen, 3:29.81, November 20, 1993; 2 1/16 miles, She Looks Great, 3:41 2/5, November 28, 1983; 2 1/8 miles, Second City, 3:48 4/5, November 25, 1984; 2 1/4 miles, Hallay's Pride, 3:48.90, May 4, 1991

Course Records, Main Turf
1 mile: Gaelic Cross, 1:35 2/5, September 23, 1987
1m 70yds: Twin to Win, 1:41, October 24, 1986
1 3/8 miles: Syncospin, 2:12 3/5, September 25, 1987
1 5/8 miles: Nigilik, 2:48 1/5, October 24, 1986

Fastest Times of 2001
5 furlongs: Northern Tower, :57.08, January 21
5 1/2 furlongs: Jay's Performer, 1:02.78, March 18
6 furlongs: John Q's Winner, 1:08.63, October 8
1 mile: Old Snively, 1:37.61, April 22
1m 70yds: Exclusively Risque, 1:41.52, April 17

1 1/16 miles: Joanies Bella, 1:44.09, October 8
1 1/8 miles: Ashwood C C, 1:49.77, October 8
1 3/16 miles: Motion to Suppress, 1:59.69, March 10
1 1/4 miles: Majestic Dinner, 2:00.32, October 8
1 1/2 miles: Fairway to Heaven, 2:36.79, November 3
1 3/4 miles: Desert Hawk, 3:04.68, November 17
Other: 2 miles 70 yds, Bulacan, 3:39.03, April 21; 2 1/4 miles, Proper Blue, 3:56.57, December 15

River Downs

With the Ohio River serving as an attractive and sometimes destructive backdrop, River Downs has been part of the southern Ohio racing scene for more than 75 years. The track at Cincinnati's eastern edge opened in July 1925 as Coney Island racetrack. A crowd of 10,000 packed the facility for opening day, according to River Downs historians, and the track was off to a fast start.

But the floods of 1937 put a temporary stop to that. The track rebuilt following the flooding and reopened as River Downs. Sixty years later, the track again endured major Ohio River flooding, but again the track was cleaned up and reopened. The track's grandstand had undergone an extensive rebuilding in the 1980s.

River Downs offers a pair of quality two-year-old stakes every year in the Cradle and the Bassinet (for fillies). The 1984 Cradle was won by Spend a Buck, who the next year won the Kentucky Derby (G1) and was named Horse of the Year. River Downs also was one of the first tracks at which Racing Hall of Fame jockey Steve Cauthen competed. In 2002, River was to conduct a limited seven-and-seven program with Beulah Park, with each track running seven live races and taking seven simulcast races from the other track.

Location: 6301 Kellogg Ave., Cincinnati, OH 45230-0286
Phone: (513) 232-8000
Fax: (513) 232-1269
E-mail: turfclub@one.net
Web site: http://www.riverdowns.com
Year founded: 1925
Inaugural meeting: July 6, 1925
Number of stalls: 1,350
Seating capacity: 9,350

Officers
President: Dr. J. David Rutherford
General Manager: Jack Hanessian
Director of Racing: Gary Wilfert
Racing Secretary: Gary Wilfert
Director of Operations: Kathy Ewing
Director of Communications: John Engelhardt
Director of Mutuels: Larry Alexander
Director of Publicity: John Engelhardt
Director of Simulcasting: Steve Heidorn
Stewards: Mike Manganelo, Philip Gour Jr., Tim Day
Track Announcer: Sean Beirne
Track Photographer: Patrick Lang Photography
Other Officials: John C. Hoover, Chairman of the Board

Racing dates
2001: April 13-September 3, 125 days
2002: April 13-September 2

Track Layout

Main circumference: 1 mile
Main track chute: 3/4 mile, 1 1/4 miles
Main width: 80 feet
Main length of stretch: 1,117 feet
Main turf circumference: 7 furlongs

Attendance

Lowest single day record: 13,768, May 30, 1956

Handle

Total on-track recent meeting: $52,048,822, 2001
Total all sources recent meeting: $100,216,523, 2001

Leaders

Recent meeting, leading jockey: Hector L. Rosario Jr., 111, 2001
Recent meeting, leading trainer: Luis Albert Palacios, 32, 2001

Track Records, Main Dirt

4 1/2 furlongs: Sans Terre, :52 2/5, May 24, 1971
5 furlongs: Banker's Forbes, :57.60, June 7, 1994
5 1/2 furlongs: Tazua, 1:03, August 1, 1964
6 furlongs: Francine M., 1:08 3/5, July 4, 1969
1 mile: Alladin Rib, 1:36 1/5, August 8, 1988
1m 70 yds: South Dakota, 1:40, August 4, 1945
1 1/16 miles: Irish Dude, 1:41 4/5, July 5, 1969
1 1/8 miles: Brown Sugar, 1:49, September 2, 1925
1 1/4 miles: Crusader, 2:02, July 24, 1926
1 1/2 miles: South Dakota, 2:30 3/5, July 1, 1950
1 3/4 miles: Brigler, 2:59 3/5, October 19, 1940
2 miles: South Dakota, 3:21 2/5, July 8, 1950
Other: 1 11/16 miles, Distribute, 2:51 3/5, September 7, 1940;1 7/8 miles, Shot Bills, 3:26 3/5, August 19, 1979; 2 miles 70 yds, Omar, 3:33 3/5, September 2, 1940; 2 1/4 miles, Almac, 3:54, October 31, 1936; 2 1/2 miles, Here Come Midge, 4:30 4/5, June 17, 1972; 3 miles 70 yds, Gloria Dream, 5:32 2/5, August 9, 1972

Course Records, Main Turf

4 1/2 furlongs: Adena, :50 4/5, April 26, 1977
5 furlongs: Hobbs, :56.30, September 1, 1991
7 1/2 furlongs: Stormy Deep, 1:28 2/5, August 15, 1990
1 mile: Bad News Blues, 1:34.20, July 23, 1994
1 1/16 miles: Franchise Player, 1:40.60, June 12, 1994
1 3/8 miles: Hi Rise, 2:15.60, August 15, 2000
1 1/2 miles: Rebel Thunder, 2:28, June 28, 1996
Other: 1 7/16 miles, Dina's Pl'ymate, 2:25, August 30, 1969

Interesting facts

Previous name and dates: Coney Island 1925-1937

Fastest Times of 2001 (Dirt)

4 1/2 furlongs: Premier Shot, :52.80, April 24; Real Surge, :52.80, August 26
5 furlongs: Runto the Mountain, :58.80, June 13
5 1/2 furlongs: Sandi's Silverhope, 1:05.20, April 29
6 furlongs: Knight Villain, 1:11.20, May 28; Robby D, 1:11.20, May 31
1 mile: Take Account, 1:38.40, May 19
1m 70yds: Take Account, 1:43.60, June 2
1 1/16 miles: Paris Academy, 1:45.60, May 17
1 1/8 miles: Ashwood C C, 1:53.60, July 28
1 1/4 miles: Majestic Dinner, 2:08, September 2
1 1/2 miles: Heather's Best, 2:39.80, July 24

Fastest Times of 2001 (Turf)

5 furlongs: Jump and Shoot, :58, June 17
7 1/2 furlongs: Bee Eight (GB), 1:29.80, May 5
1 mile: Talented Won, 1:35.60, May 5
1 1/16 miles: Eighties, 1:42.40, June 27
1 3/8 miles: St. Jovi Anne, 2:18, June 30; Talented Won, 2:18.00, June 24
Other: 1 7/8 miles, Divorce Proceeds, 3:15, September 3

Thistledown

Thistledown in suburban Cleveland is the home of Ohio's most important race, the $300,000 Ohio Derby (G2). Opened on July 20, 1925, Thistledown was owned and operated by the DeBartolo Corp. from 1959 through '99, when the track was purchased by Magna Entertainment Corp.

Thistledown has a full-color Diamond Vision infield display board, and inside the grandstand is its interactive Starting Gate educational museum, which features exhibits, weekly handicapping seminars, and information on racing in Ohio. The track also has two state-of-the-art simulcast theaters.

In the summer of 2000, Thistledown reconfigured the outdoor paddock area to allow fans to be closer to the racing experience. The newly landscaped paddock added more than 9,000 square feet and such amenities as picnic tables, television monitors, and mutuel windows. The North Randall track typically races from late March through the end of December. Starting in the 1990s, Thistledown had conducted seven-and-seven programs—seven live races and seven simulcast races—with the state's two other Thoroughbred tracks, However, that arrangement was scrapped for 2002, with the exception of a brief spring overlap of River Downs and Beulah.

Location: 21501 Emery Rd., North Randall, OH 44128
Phone: (216) 662-8600
Fax: (216) 662-5339
Web site: http://www.thistledown.com
Year founded: 1925
Inaugural meeting: July 20, 1925
Acreage: 128
Number of stalls: 1,428
Seating capacity: 3,800

Officers

President: Jim McAlpine
Vice President: William D. Murphy
General Manager: William D. Murphy
Director of Racing: William Couch
Racing Secretary: William Couch
Director of Operations: Dave Ellsworth
Director of Communications: Heather Cvengros
Director of Finance: Ron Marinko
Director of Marketing: Brent Reitz
Director of Mutuels: David Iacona
Director of Publicity: Heather McColloch
Director of Simulcasting: Greg Davis
Horsemen's Liaison: Alan McKee
Stewards: Allen Fairbanks, Joel McCullar, Kim Sawyer
Track Announcer: Charles Pinnell
Track Photographer: Jeff Zamaiko
Track Superintendent: John Bano

Racing dates

2001: April 6-December 31, 187 days
2002: March 28-December 23, 187 days

Track Layout

Main circumference: 1 mile
Main track chute: 1 1/4 miles, 6 furlongs
Main width: 95 feet
Main length of stretch: 978 feet

Attendance

Highest single day record: 19,411, June 18, 1978
Average daily recent meeting: 3,630, 2001

Thistledown, continued

Highest single meet record: 986,095 (191-day meet, 1979)
Record daily average for single meet: 7,049, 1954

Handle
Single day on-track handle: $3,851,575, July 24, 1999
Average all sources recent meeting: $1,269,241, 2001
Average on-track recent meeting: $178,904, 2001

Mutuel Records
Highest Win: $500.20, Nobody's Secret, November 22, 1995
Highest Daily Double: $4,553.40, June 8, 1967
Highest Pick 6: $89,306.20, November 29, 1985

Leaders
Career, leading jockey by stakes wins: Julio Felix, 12
Career, leading jockey by titles: Michael Rowland, 24
Career, leading trainer by titles: Shirley Girten, 21

Records
Single meet, leading jockey by wins: Antonio Graell, 93, Summit Meet-1976
Single meet, leading trainer by wins: Gary Johnson, 40, Thistledown Meet-1998
Single day jockey wins: Buddy Haas, 6, August 28, 1933; John Adams, 6, September 2, 1942; Danny Weiler, 6, August 12, 1961; Anthony Rini, 6, June 12, 1970; Antonio Graell, 6, February 21, 1976; Benny Feliciano, 6, June 18, 1978; Antonio Graell, 6, November 14, 1980; Tom Ford, 6, December 13, 1982; Michael Rowland, 6, March 29, 1991; Brian Mills, 6, August 28, 1993; Michael Rowland, 6, October 19, 1999
Single day trainer wins: Gary Johnson, 6, November 27, 1999

Track Records, Main Dirt
4 furlongs: Deep Sun, :45 4/5, June 10, 1959
4 1/2 furlongs: Onion Roll, :51.57, November 20, 1992
5 furlongs: Great Allegiance, :57.56, May 18, 1997
5 1/2 furlongs: Down Thepike Mike, 1:03.20, August 10, 1998
6 furlongs: Fancy Threat, 1:08 2/5, November 21, 1987
1 mile: Setting Limits, 1:35 3/5, November 17, 1989
1m 40 yds: Ifthisbe Britches, 1:38 3/5, December 8, 1989; North Island, 1:38 3/5, December 9, 1989
1m 70 yds: Wisdom Seeker, 1:40.92, July 22, 1995
1 1/16 miles: Entitled To Star, 1:41.32, November 25, 1995
1 1/8 miles: Smarten, 1:45 2/5, June 17, 1979
1 3/16 miles: Smoke Screen, 1:55 3/5, July 17, 1954
1 1/4 miles: Pert Near, 2:03, December 1, 1979
1 1/2 miles: Martha's Wave, 2:31 4/5, June 18, 1955
1 5/8 miles: Alsang, 2:46, August 8, 1936
1 3/4 miles: Mala Kee, 2:57 3/5, July 19, 1957
2 miles: Likely Advice, 3:27, December 15, 1980
Other: 2 furlongs, Onion Roll, :20.95, September 27, 1993; 1 9/16 miles, Military Girl, 2:44 1/5, June 13, 1942; 2 miles 40 yds, Winning Mark, 3:29 2/5, July 20, 1940; 2 1/16 miles, Bunker, 3:32 4/5, July 13, 1955; 2 1/8 miles, Lonely Cloud, 3:52.65, July 3, 1992; 2 1/4 miles, Son Richard, 3:54 3/5, August 27, 1938; 2 3/16 miles, Current Data, 3:54 3/5, December 5, 1981; 2 11/16 miles, Bea Beauty, 4:47 4/5, September 8, 1973; 3 miles 40 yds, Bea Beauty, 5:31 4/5, September 22, 1973; 3 5/8 miles, Eastern Promise, 6:49 3/5, October 6, 1973

Fastest Times of 2001
4 furlongs: Cumberland Gap, :45.64, November 10
4 1/2 furlongs: French Reality, :53.68, April 7
5 furlongs: Gherminella, :57.90, September 23
5 1/2 furlongs: Snogun, 1:05.02, August 8
6 furlongs: Tour the Hive, 1:09.80, September 29
1 mile: Ashwood C C, 1:36.58, September 23
1m 40yds: Gina's Jack, 1:42.07, September 29
1m 70yds: C B Account, 1:41.66, September 8
1 1/16 miles: Majestic Dinner, 1:44.20, July 8

1 1/8 miles: Western Pride, 1:48.66, September 29
1 3/16 miles: French Joseph, 1:58.22, July 21
Other: 2 furlongs, Tequila's Fortune, :21.52, April 14

Oklahoma

Blue Ribbon Downs

Blue Ribbon Downs, located near Sallisaw, Oklahoma, was developed by Blue Ribbon Ranch owner Bill Hedge on ranch property. It first offered racing in 1960 as a nonpari-mutuel racetrack, with all business operations based in Hedge's house. In 1973, Hedge sold the track to a group of investors. A decade later, Blue Ribbon was the first track to offer pari-mutuel racing in Oklahoma, but fire destroyed its grandstand two weeks before the 1983 meet was to open. Within one week, a new grandstand was erected. The track's richest Thoroughbred race is the Oklahoma-Bred Thoroughbred Futurity, which is for two-year-old Oklahoma-breds. The track races Thoroughbreds, Quarter Horses, Appaloosas, and Paints from mid-February to early December.

Location: 3700 W. Cherokee, Sallisaw, OK 74955
Phone: (918) 775-7771
Fax: (918) 775-5805
E-mail: brd@blueribbondowns.net
Web site: http://www.blueribbondowns.net
Acreage: 165

Officers
General Manager: Don Essary
Racing Secretary: Burt Cheek
Director of Marketing: Pam Vickery
Director of Mutuels: Ladonna Perkins
Director of Publicity: Pam Dickory
Director of Simulcasting: Tonya Maxwell

Racing dates
2001: February 10-December 9, 121 days
2002: February 2-November 24

Track Records, Main Dirt
4 furlongs: Iwontbeback, :44.35, July 3, 1995
4 1/2 furlongs: Rebel's Jon, :50.35, June 29, 1996
5 furlongs: Pow Wow Al, :56.45, May 27, 1996
5 1/2 furlongs: Rebel's Jon, 1:02, October 1, 1995
6 furlongs: Rebel's Jon, 1:08.45, July 9, 1995
7 furlongs: Prententious Chief, 1:23, September 10, 1995
7 1/2 furlongs: Karate Kick, 1:29.35, September 17, 1994
1 mile: Staged Attraction, 1:36.15, June 10, 1989
1 1/16 miles: Just Ask Rudy, 1:43.15, April 6, 1996
1 1/8 miles: Long On Rowdy, 1:49.35, July 17, 1994
1 1/4 miles: Dare More, 2:03.35, August 28, 1994
1 3/8 miles: Say It All, 2:17.15, October 1, 1995
1 1/2 miles: Mr Sanhedrin, 2:32.35, November 14, 1993
1 5/8 miles: Sharp's Caliber, 2:47.15, December 11, 1994

Fastest Times of 2001
4 furlongs: Avenue of Style, :45.86, March 4
4 1/2 furlongs: Fleet American, :50.80, April 21
5 furlongs: Cover Keeper, :57.38, May 28
5 1/2 furlongs: Cordell, 1:04.40, May 5
6 furlongs: Fun to Run, 1:10, May 5
7 furlongs: Natives Rap, 1:26.37, March 10
7 1/2 furlongs: Hedorunrun, 1:31.91, May 19
1 mile: Hedorunrun, 1:38.61, June 9
1 1/16 miles: Goodman, 1:47, April 15
1 1/8 miles: Goodman, 1:53.04, June 9
1 1/4 miles: Idontneedone, 2:08.40, September 3
1 5/8 miles: Drysdale, 2:51.40, November 24

Fair Meadows at Tulsa

Offering nighttime Thoroughbred, Quarter Horse, Paint, and Appaloosa racing on its five-furlong oval, Fair Meadows at Tulsa is one of the entertainment facilities located at Expo Square, which hosts the Tulsa State Fair and some 400 other events each year. Fair Meadows, which has been holding live racing since 1989, is located on a former auto-racing oval and is next to the stadium of the Tulsa Drillers, the Class AA minor-league baseball team of the Texas Rangers. During racing season, a giant net between the stadium and Fair Meadows keeps foul balls from landing on the track's final turn. Expo Square also includes an amusement park, water park, and hotel, and Fair Meadows offers a state-of-the-art simulcast facility that provides year-round racing action.

Location: 4145 E. 21st St., Tulsa, OK 74114
Phone: (918) 744-6999
Fax: (918) 746-3503
Web site: http://www.fairmeadows.com

Officers
Director of Publicity: Richard Linihan

Racing dates
2001: June 22-August 4, 32 days

Leaders
Recent meeting, leading trainer: Mike R. Teel, 12, 2001
Recent meeting, leading jockey: Curtis Kimes, 31, 2001

Track Records, Main Dirt
4 furlongs: Only Cash, :44.40, May 30, 1997
5 1/2 furlongs: Visibility O, 1:04.60, July 5, 1998
6 furlongs: Carsoni, 1:10.80, August 3, 1995
6 1/2 furlongs: Assension Crozier, 1:16.80, August 20, 1994
1 mile: Judge North, 1:37, August 5, 1995
1 1/16 miles: Citation Rock, 1:46, September 11, 1991
1 1/8 miles: Demascus Slew, 1:51.78, May 30, 1998
1 3/8 miles: Second Avie, 2:20, August 5, 1995
1 5/8 miles: Phantom Cottage, 2:51.80, August 1, 1992

Fastest Times of 2001
4 furlongs: Valid Sunrise, :44.60, July 21
5 1/2 furlongs: Double Jack, 1:03.80, August 1
6 furlongs: Baron Von Tom, 1:12.60, June 23; Sovereign Wine, 1:12.60, July 7; Loded Arrow, 1:12.60, August 4
6 1/2 furlongs: Big Bay Brite, 1:17.60, July 28
1 mile: Cadron Creek, 1:39, July 7
1 1/16 miles: Major Mill, 1:46.40, June 21

Remington Park

Built by the late Edward J. DeBartolo, Remington Park opened its doors on September 1, 1988, and was purchased by Magna Entertainment Corp. in October 1999 after average attendance had plummeted from a high of 11,263 in 1989 to 2,517 in 1998.

The track began a new era in 2001 with the addition of lights, thus allowing evening racing. Thoroughbreds race during a summer-fall meet from mid-August to late November, and Quarter Horses are also featured in a spring meet. The track's feature Thoroughbred race is the $300,000 Oklahoma Derby (G3), run for the 13th time in 2001.

Customers have multiple choices for settings, including the Players Sports Bar, Club One with box seats, a nonsmoking section in the clubhouse, the Silks Restaurant, the Eclipse Restaurant, and luxurious private suites. Remington Park's 59-day 2001 fall meet suffered a 4.3% decline in average daily attendance to 2,337, and on-track wagering dipped 11.5% to a daily average of $120,551.

Location: 1 Remington Pl., Oklahoma City, OK 73111
Phone: (405) 424-1000
Fax: (405) 425-3219
Web site: http://www.remingtonpark.com
Inaugural meeting: September 1, 1988
Seating capacity: 2,355
Number of stalls: 1,312

Officers
President: Frank A. Deal
Vice President: Don Amos
General Manager: Frank A. Deal
Director of Racing: Fred Hutton
Racing Secretary: Fred Hutton
Director of Operations: Suzanne Fleming
Director of Admissions: Diane Bynum
Director of Communications: Dale Day
Director of Marketing: Dale Day
Director of Mutuels: Cathy Nelson
Director of Sales: Sharon Lair
Director of Simulcasting: Cathy Nelson
Stewards: Charlie Cox, David Southard, Mike Corey, Norma Calhoun
Track Announcer: Don Stevens
Track Photographer: Reed Palmer
Track Superintendent: Mike Raidt

Racing dates
2001: January 13-February 25, 22 days; August 11-December 24, 68 days
2002: August 10-December 23, 76 days

Track Layout
Main circumference: 1 mile
Main track chute: 1 3/8 miles, 7 furlongs
Main width: 100 feet
Main length of stretch: 990 feet
Main turf circumference: 7 furlongs
Main turf chute: 1 1/8 miles
Main turf width: 80 feet
Main turf length of stretch: 990 feet

Attendance
Highest single day record: 26,411, February 29, 1992
Record daily average for single meet: 11,128, 1988

Handle
Record daily average for single meet: $1,310,542, 1990
Single day on-track handle: $2,808,243, February 24, 1990

Mutuel Records
Highest Win: $242.40, Wishful Woman, December 4, 1992
Highest Exacta: $5,495.80, December 3, 1988
Highest Trifecta: $58,662.40, February 24, 1995
Highest Daily Double: $2,273.20, February 3, 1990
Highest Pick 3: $18,057.60, November 13, 1994
Highest Other Exotics: $38,968.80, Superfecta, December 1, 1996

Leaders
Career, leading jockey by stakes wins: Don Pettinger, 86
Career, leading jockey by titles: Pat Steinberg, 9
Career, leading trainer by titles: Donnie Von Hemel, 8
Career, leading jockey by wins: Don Pettinger, 1,006
Career, leading owner by stakes wins: Barbara Smicklas and John Smicklas, 16
Career, leading trainer by stakes wins: Donnie Von Hemel, 83

Records
Single day trainer wins: Wade White, 5, November 17, 1993
Single day jockey wins: Tim Doocy, 6, December 5, 1993

Remington Park, continued

Track Records, Main Dirt
4 1/2 furlongs: Payday Two, :52.20, February 26, 2000
5 furlongs: Highland Ice, :57.20, December 3, 1999
5 1/2 furlongs: Run Johnny, 1:02, September 26, 1997
6 furlongs: Smoke of Ages, 1:08, September 29, 1991
6 1/2 furlongs: Kangaroo King, 1:14.40, July 26, 1997
7 furlongs: Golden Gear, 1:20.40, March 18, 1995
1 mile: White Wheels, 1:35.40, August 17, 1997
1m 70 yds: Marked Tree, 1:39.60, March 13, 1993
1 1/16 miles: Valid Bonnet, 1:41.20, July 26, 1997
1 1/8 miles: Classic Cat, 1:48, August 30, 1998
1 3/16 miles: Wild Rush, 1:53.60, August 10, 1997
1 1/4 miles: Double Platinum, 2:03.40, October 10, 1999
1 3/8 miles: Bid the Zeal, 2:18.80, October 2, 1998
1 1/2 miles: Bid the Zeal, 2:31.40, October 24, 1998
Other: 3 furlongs, Raisable Adversary, :31.20, August 29, 1999

Course Records, Main Turf
5 furlongs: Wishful Legacy, :56.80, September 28, 1998
7 1/2 furlongs: Finally Tops, 1:27.60, May 1, 1996
1 mile: No More Hard Times, 1:33.80, September 20, 1992
1 1/16 miles: Burbank, 1:39.20, August 30, 1997
1 1/8 miles: Gauntlett Boy, 1:47 4/5, November 5, 1989
1 3/8 miles: Doctor Trotter, 2:13.80, August 9, 1997
2 miles: Big Notice, 3:29, November 20, 1993

Fastest Times of 2001 (Dirt)
5 furlongs: Speedlite, :57.32, February 19
5 1/2 furlongs: Mark U With Class, 1:03.12, September 3
6 furlongs: Abbi's Choice, 1:08.91, November 23
6 1/2 furlongs: Gambler's Share, 1:15.65, February 18
7 furlongs: Mr Ross, 1:21.35, September 14
1 mile: Rare Note, 1:38.26, January 21
1m 70yds: Sprucity, 1:41.04, October 25
1 1/16 miles: Mr Ross, 1:44.09, October 21
1 1/8 miles: Rare Cure, 1:49.71, November 24

Fastest Times of 2001 (Turf)
5 furlongs: Otro Mambo, :55.85, October 5
7 1/2 furlongs: Bien Nicole, 1:28.25, October 7
1 mile: Kipling, 1:34.43, October 5
1 1/16 miles: Twisted Kris, 1:43.94, August 31
1 3/8 miles: Best of K C, 2:15.16, September 3

Will Rogers Downs

Will Rogers Downs is located on 210 acres just east of Claremore and approximately 25 miles from downtown Tulsa. Live racing on Fridays, Saturdays, and Sundays in the spring of 2001 was reduced from 12 days to ten because of a shortage of horses. Subsequently, Will Rogers Downs planned to scrap spring racing in 2002 and hold a 12-day live meet in November. The track is home to rodeos as well as Will Rogers County Jamborees every other Saturday night, presenting a family-oriented country show and concert.

Location: 20900 S. 4200 Rd., Claremore, OK 74018
Phone: (918) 343-5900
Fax: (918) 343-6399
Web site: http://www.willrogersdowns.com

Racing dates
2001: April 13-May 6, 12 days
2002: November 1-November 24

Leaders
Recent meeting, leading jockey: Franklin Turner, 15, 2001
Recent meeting, leading trainer: Dee Keener, 7, 2001

Fastest Times of 2001
4 furlongs: Wicked Thunder, :45.40, April 29

4 1/2 furlongs: Lost Above, :51.60, April 29
5 furlongs: Edgestone, :58.40, April 27
5 1/2 furlongs: Magic World, 1:05.40, April 21; R C Brinker, 1:05.40, April 27
6 furlongs: Josey's Trick, 1:11, May 5
1 mile: Logan Square, 1:40.80, April 29
1m 70yds: Fiddledee, 1:44, April 29
Other: 2 furlongs, Avenue of Style, :21.60, April 15

Oregon

Grants Pass

Location: 1451 Fairgrounds Rd., Grants Pass, OR 97527
Phone: (541) 476-3215
Fax: (541) 476-0127

Officers
Director of Racing: Al Westoff
Racing Secretary: Jerry Kohls
Director of Operations: Wally Starner (backside)
Director of Publicity: Gary Davison

Racing dates
2001: May 28-July 7, 18 days

Leaders
Recent meeting, leading jockey: Ralph J. Garcia Jr., 11, 2001
Recent meeting, leading trainer: John McDevitt, 7, 2001

Fastest Times of 2001
4 1/2 furlongs: Apeak, :52.31, June 17
5 1/2 furlongs: Apeak, 1:05.05, July 7
6 1/2 furlongs: Go Salem By, 1:20.02, June 24
1 1/16 miles: Canadian Magic, 1:49.90, June 23

Portland Meadows

Founded by Bay Meadows Race Course builder William Kyne, Portland Meadows has a rich history dating back to September 14, 1946, when a crowd of 10,000 watched the nation's first evening Thoroughbred racing card. General Electric Co., which devised the lighting system, boasted at the time: "This system, the first of its kind, has enough power to light a four-lane super highway from Portland to Salem (a distance of more than 40 miles)."

But Portland Meadows officials were powerless to fight the Vanport flood, which in 1948 canceled the track's season after just 13 cards and caused $250,000 in damage. The track was hit again in the early morning hours of April 25, 1970, when a fire razed the grandstand. Portland Meadows was rebuilt, opening its 1971 season before a record crowd of 12,635.

Portland Meadows served as an early proving ground for Racing Hall of Fame jockey Gary Stevens, who won two riding titles there in the early 1980s. New Portland Meadows Inc. operated the track from 1991 until it leased the track to Magna Entertainment Corp. in mid-2001. Portland Meadows was forced to delay its 2001 fall meet by one week because the Environmental Protection Agency determined that the track's backstretch storm-water retention plan was not acceptable. The meet opened October 27.

Location: 1001 N. Schmeer Rd., Portland, OR 97217
Phone: (503) 285-9144

Fax: (503) 285-1015
E-mail: tnpm@portlandmeadows.com
Web site: http://www.portlandmeadows.com

Officers
President: Eugene Ferryman
Vice President: Brian Ferryman
General Manager: Eugene Ferryman
Director of Racing: Jerry Kohls
Racing Secretary: Jerry Kohls
Director of Operations: Woodrow Mitchell
Director of Marketing: Rod Whitesmith

Racing dates
2001: October 19, 2000 to April 28, 2001, 80 days

Fastest Times of 2001
4 1/2 furlongs: Knight Cover, :52.47, April 21
5 furlongs: Missy Muffet, :59.27, November 11
5 1/2 furlongs: Amberrae, 1:05.49, February 23
6 furlongs: Danzilation, 1:11.22, February 9
1 mile: Chinquapin Charlie, 1:39.03, April 21
1 1/16 miles: Shy Boots, 1:46.47, March 24
1 1/8 miles: Danzilation, 1:52.02, April 14
1 1/4 miles: Canadian Magic, 2:11.04, March 24
1 5/8 miles: Mutiny Bay, 2:52.64, April 29
Other: 2 furlongs, Jimbos Valentine, :23.44, April 21

Pennsylvania

Penn National Race Course

Built by a group of Central Pennsylvania investors, Penn National Race Course is located 13 miles from the state capital, Harrisburg. It staged its first race meeting on August 30, 1972. The following year, Penn National bought the racing license of defunct Pitt Park and began an essentially year-round racing schedule. In 1978, Penn National built the state's first turf course.

Led by principal owner Peter D. Carlino, Penn National has been an innovator in Pennsylvania's racing industry. Philadelphia-area businessman Carlino bought one of the track's operating licenses in 1974 and the other in '83. With legalization of telephone betting in 1982, Penn National began the commonwealth's first account-wagering system, and the following year it began the first cable-television broadcast of its races. Following legislative approval of off-track wagering in 1989, Penn National built and operated six facilities in Central Pennsylvania.

In 1994, the track's parent company, Penn National Gaming Inc., held an initial public stock offering. With those proceeds and subsequent stock issues, Penn National has financed the acquisitions of Charles Town Races, a Thoroughbred track in West Virginia, and Pocono Downs, a Standardbred track near Williamsport, Pennsylvania, as well as casino properties. Penn National Gaming's chairman is Peter M. Carlino, son of the track's principal investor.

Location: Route 743, Grantville, PA 17028
Phone: (717) 469-2211
Fax: (717) 469-0423
E-mail: pnrc@pennnational.com
Web site: http://www.pnrc.com
Acreage: 600
Number of stalls: 1,200
Seating capacity: 9,570

Officers
President: Peter M. Carlino
Vice President: Richard T. Schnaars, William J. Bork
General Manager: Richard T. Schnaars
Racing Secretary: Paul Jenkins
Director of Marketing: Frederick D. Lipkin
Director of Mutuels: Jon Schuster
Director of Publicity: Frederick D. Lipkin
Director of Simulcasting: Chris Camplese
Track Announcer: John Bogar
Track Photographer: Stuart Leask

Racing dates
2001: January 1-December 31, 210 days
2002: January 1-December 31, 203 days

Track Layout
Main circumference: 1 mile
Main track chute: 1 1/4 miles, 6 furlongs
Main length of stretch: 990 feet
Main turf circumference: 7 furlongs

Leaders
Recent meeting, leading jockey: David Cora, 279, 2001
Recent meeting, leading owner: Danny Chen, 81, 2001
Recent meeting, leading trainer: Jose Martinez, 146, 2001

Track Records, Main Dirt
4 furlongs: Gross, :46 1/5, April 13, 1973
4 1/2 furlongs: Iron Orebid, :53, August 14, 1998
5 furlongs: On The Phone, :56.60, July 13, 1996
5 1/2 furlongs: Cortan, 1:03 1/5, May 29, 1978
6 furlongs: Jiva Coolit, 1:08 4/5, May 22, 1977
1 mile: Vambourine, 1:36 1/5, June 12, 1977
1m 70 yds: Wee Thunder, 1:39.60, July 13, 1996
1 1/16 miles: A Letter to Harry, 1:41 1/5, September 10, 1978
1 1/8 miles: Collection Agent, 1:49 4/5, August 22, 1987
1 3/16 miles: Bar Tab, 1:55 2/5, October 14, 1972
1 1/4 miles: Adda Nickell, 2:03 3/5, October 30, 1976
1 1/2 miles: Holly Holme, 2:31 2/5, September 29, 1973
1 3/4 miles: Chasqui, 3:00, June 21, 1980
2 miles: Finny Flyer, 3:28, May 25, 1974

Course Records, Main Turf
5 furlongs: Admiral Yi, :55.20, June 24, 1994
1 mile: The Very One, 1:33 1/5, July 15, 1979
1m 70yds: Aborigine, 1:37 1/5, August 20, 1978
1 1/16 miles: Told, 1:38, September 14, 1980
1 1/2 miles: Coalitioncandidate, 2:27, May 27, 1991

Fastest Times of 2001 (Dirt)
4 1/2 furlongs: Rita's Best, :50.67, April 27
5 furlongs: Elegantly Wasted, :57.41, August 29
5 1/2 furlongs: Storm Regent, 1:03.32, March 15
6 furlongs: Tonto Gusto, 1:09.17, May 11
1 mile: Tan Bird, 1:37.58, November 2
1m 70yds: Clever Gent, 1:40.66, August 18
1 1/16 miles: Oros, 1:43.92, July 7
1 1/8 miles: Honor Defend, 1:52.33, March 16
1 3/16 miles: Captivator, 1:59.05, November 2
1 1/4 miles: Captivator, 2:03.93, August 15
1 1/2 miles: Captivator, 2:34.54, July 20
1 5/8 miles: New Episode, 2:48.15, May 18

Fastest Times of 2001 (Turf)
5 furlongs: Cherokee Sunshine, :56.10, August 3
1 mile: Hour Man Uncle Sam, 1:34.73, July 14
1m 70yds: Tunis, 1:39.02, July 20
1 1/16 miles: Buenos Dias, 1:40.10, August 3
1 1/2 miles: Frivolous Pleasure, 2:29.83, September 3

Philadelphia Park

Built reluctantly and inexpensively in the early 1970s, the track now known as Philadelphia Park has had a difficult history. But now, it has emerged as a leader in

Philadelphia Park, continued

providing fan amenities and phone wagering in its region. When racing first arrived in Pennsylvania in the late 1960s, both Thoroughbred and Standardbred racing were conducted at Liberty Bell Park in Philadelphia's Northeast section. But with regional lawmakers insisting on a separate Thoroughbred facility, Keystone Race Track was built for $20-million approximately a mile north of Liberty Bell in Bensalem Township, across the city border in Bucks County. It opened in November 1974 with two ownership groups, which often feuded. Keystone inaugurated the track's signature race, the Pennsylvania Derby (G3), in 1979, and phone betting was authorized in 1982.

In 1984, Robert Brennan-controlled International Thoroughbred Breeders Inc. bought Keystone for $37.5-million to avoid competition for its Garden State Park, which opened in April 1985 (and closed in 2001). Brennan's company renamed the track Philadelphia Park and invested several million dollars into the grandstand and the racing surface, including the addition of a turf course. Financially failing International Thoroughbred Breeders sold the track to Greenwood Racing, headed by British bookmaking executives Robert Green and William Hogwood, for $67-million in 1990, the year in which the track opened the first of its five off-track betting facilities. In May 1999, Philadelphia Park completed an acclaimed, $4-million renovation of its first floor.

Location: 3001 Street Rd., Bensalem, PA 19020-2096
Phone: (215) 639-9000
Fax: (215) 639-0337
Web site: http://www.philadelphiapark.com
Year founded: 1969
Inaugural meeting: 1969
Acreage: 417
Number of stalls: 1,700
Seating capacity: 8,700

Officers
President: Robert W. Green
Chief Executive Officer: Harold G. Handel
General Manager: James L. Gagliano
Director of Racing: Salvatore Sinatra
Racing Secretary: Edward Vomacka
Director of Marketing: James Milligan
Director of Mutuels: Bill Barnes
Director of Publicity: Jenny Ornsteen
Director of Simulcasting: Geri Mercer
Track Announcer: W. Keith Jones
Other Officials: Andrew J. Green, Senior Vice President of Administration

Racing dates
2001: January 1-December 31, 220 days
2002: January 1-December 31, 227 days

Track Layout
Main circumference: 1 mile
Main track chute: 1 1/4 miles, 7 furlongs
Main width: 80 feet
Main length of stretch: 974 feet
Main turf circumference: 7 furlongs
Main turf chute: 1 1/8 miles

Leaders
Career, leading jockey by titles: Rick Wilson, 9
Recent meeting, leading jockey: Rodrigo Madrigal Jr., 166, 2000
Recent meeting, leading trainer: Scott A. Lake, 146, 2000
Career, leading trainer by titles: Efrain T. Garcia, 5

Track Records, Main Dirt
4 furlongs: Heres a Tip, :45, June 11, 1982
4 1/2 furlongs: Distinctive Hat, :51.48, May 2, 1994
5 furlongs: My Favorite Grub, :56, September 7, 1998
5 1/2 furlongs: Saint Verre, 1:02.65, July 17, 2000
6 furlongs: Iron Punch, 1:07.89, July 29, 2000
6 1/2 furlongs: Tricky Mister, 1:14.40, June 21, 1998
7 furlongs: Flaming Bridle, 1:20.61, September 28, 1999
1 mile: Regal Count, 1:34 4/5, December 5, 1985
1m 70 yds: Tragedy, 1:38.70, December 12, 1995
1 1/16 miles: Cool Spring Park, 1:40 4/5, November 4, 1974
1 1/8 miles: Selari Spirit, 1:47, November 30, 1974
1 3/16 miles: Southern Shade, 1:56 2/5, October 20, 1984
1 1/4 miles: It's Always Archie, 2:02, November 23, 1974
1 1/2 miles: Laugh a Minute, 2:31, January 4, 1992
1 5/8 miles: River Wolf, 2:46 2/5, October 13, 1990
1 3/4 miles: Johnny's Silencer, 2:57 4/5, December 17, 1988
2 miles: Perfect to a Tee, 3:25.87, September 2, 1996
Other: 2 furlongs, Queen Millie, :21.32, January 30, 1994; 1 9/16 miles, Laugh a Minute, 2:40.85, January 18, 1992; 1 11/16 miles, Laugh a Minute, 2:53.20, December 21, 1991; 1 13/16 miles, Fire North, 3:04.80, March 14, 1992; 1 7/8 miles, Haberdasher, 3:13 3/5, October 17, 1987; 2 1/4 miles, Transfer Ticket, 3:56, December 31, 1988; 2 1/8 miles, Heavy Medal Man, 3:39.59, April 25, 1992; 2 1/2 miles, Half Chance, 4:24.15, May 25, 1992;

Course Records, Main Turf
5 furlongs: Lou's Bucks, :56, September 20, 1998
7 1/2 furlongs: Here Comes Scott, 1:30.85, September 10, 1994
1 mile: Lake Cecebe, 1:35 3/5, June 28, 1986
1m 70yds: Rolfe's Ruby, 1:39 2/5, June 21, 1986; Marlish, 1:39 2/5, August 13, 1986
1 1/16 miles: Whatever For, 1:40 2/5, June 22, 1986
1 1/8 miles: Whatever For, 1:46 1/5, September 1, 1986
1 3/8 miles: Juanca (Arg), 2:16 2/5, September 1, 1986
1 1/2 miles: Lord Zada, 2:28.38, June 10, 2000
2 miles: Chippenham Park, 3:28 4/5, September 1, 1990

Interesting facts
Previous names and dates: Keystone Race Track 1974-1984, Liberty Bell Park Race Track 1969-1974

Fastest Times of 2001 (Dirt)
4 1/2 furlongs: Carouse, :51.60, June 24
5 furlongs: Orage d'Hiver, :57.08, June 17
5 1/2 furlongs: Elfin Glen, 1:02.99, June 24
6 furlongs: Say Florida Sandy, 1:08.51, July 28
6 1/2 furlongs: Cool Robert, 1:16.06, January 7
7 furlongs: Chronicle S., 1:22.05, February 19
1 mile: Christian Soldier, 1:36.19, June 24
1m 70yds: Silver Trophy, 1:41.13, January 5
1 1/16 miles: R. Encounter, 1:43.74, June 2
1 1/8 miles: Macho Uno, 1:49.69, September 3
1 3/16 miles: Another Irish, 2:00.85, February 10
1 1/4 miles: Colonial Mate, 2:05.22, December 28
1 1/2 miles: Kernal K, 2:34.11, January 17
1 5/8 miles: Uneacy, 2:49.01, March 13
2 miles: Willing Consort, 3:29.82, January 15

Fastest Times of 2001 (Turf)
5 furlongs: Trip Charge, :56.74, September 8
1 mile: Slew o' Stars, 1:36.95, July 10
1m 70yds: Junk Yard Jerry, 1:41.53, October 10
1 1/16 miles: Mariah's Spirit, 1:44.27, July 14
1 1/8 miles: Key to Fame, 1:50.63, July 9
1 3/8 miles: Influence, 2:19.77, July 7
1 1/2 miles: Dawn of the Condor, 2:32.48, June 9

Texas

Lone Star Park

One decade after Texas legalized pari-mutuel racing, Lone Star Park at Grand Prairie opened in 1997 and

joined Sam Houston Race Park in Houston and Retama Park near San Antonio as the three major tracks in the state. Located in the Dallas-Fort Worth metropolitan area, Lone Star was built for $96-million by the Lone Star Jockey Club, a group headed by real estate moguls Trammell Crow and his son, Harlan, of Trammell Crow Co. The track, which holds a Thoroughbred meeting in the spring and a Quarter Horse meet in the fall, has numerous events that draw national attention. The Lone Star Derby was raised to Grade 3 status for 2002. The National Thoroughbred Racing Association All-Star Jockey Championship brings the nation's leading riders to the track for a ten-race competition. Texas-bred Thoroughbreds take center stage for the Stars of Texas Day. Lone Star is scheduled to host the Breeders' Cup World Thoroughbred Championships in 2005. The track's sale to Magna Entertainment Corp. for $99-million was pending in 2002.

Location: 1000 Lone Star Pkwy., Grand Prairie, TX 75050
Phone: (972) 263-7223
Fax: (972) 237-1155
E-mail: bartl@lonestarpark.com
Web site: http://www.lonestarpark.com
Inaugural meeting: April 17, 1997
Acreage: 315
Number of stalls: 1,400
Seating capacity: 12,000

Officers
President: Corey S. Johnsen
Vice President: Jeffrey Greco
Director of Racing: Larry A. Craft
Racing Secretary: Larry A. Craft
Director of Marketing: G.W. Hail
Director of Mutuels: Don Fontenot
Director of Publicity: Darren Rogers
Director of Simulcasting: Mindy Hutchison
Track Announcer: Michael Wrona
Track Photographer: Reed Palmer
Track Superintendent: Ron Moore

Racing dates
2001: April 5-July 15, 74 days
2002: April 4-July 14, 70 days

Track Layout
Main circumference: 1 mile
Main track chute: 7 furlongs
Main width: 90 feet
Main length of stretch: 930 feet
Main turf circumference: 7 furlongs
Main turf chute: 1 1/8 miles
Main turf width: 70 feet
Main turf length of stretch: 900 feet

Attendance
Highest single day record: 33,805, July 3, 2000
Average daily recent meeting: 8,892, 2001
Highest single meet record: 675,321, 2000

Handle
Single day on-track handle: $3,130,221, May 1, 1999
Average all sources recent meeting: $3.2 million, 2001
Single day total handle all sources: $7,218,982, May 1, 1999
Average on-track recent meeting: $1.2 million, 2001

Mutuel Records
Highest Win: $201.40, Slightly Slew, June 26, 1997
Highest Exacta: $3,657.20, May 2, 1998
Highest Trifecta: $31,825.50, May 2, 1998
Highest Daily Double: $3,016.80, July 18, 1998
Highest Pick 3: $15,088.40, July 11, 1997
Highest Pick 6: $39,891.80, April 26, 1998
Highest Other Exotics: $35,640.60, Superfecta, June 27, 1998

Leaders
Career, leading owner by wins: Tom Durant, 17
Career, leading trainer by wins: Dallas Keen, 77
Recent meeting, leading jockey: Corey S. Lanerie, 80, 2001
Recent meeting, leading owner: Ken Murphy, 17, 2001
Recent meeting, leading trainer: Steve Asmussen, 90, 2001
Career, leading jockey by wins: Marlon St. Julien, 165

Records
Single day jockey wins: Ronald Ardoin, 6, July 17, 1997
Single day trainer wins: Steve Asmussen, 3, May 6, 1998; Jim Gaston, 3, June 11, 1998; Dallas Keen, 3, July 9, 1998

Track Records, Main Dirt
4 1/2 furlongs: Rayanegra, :51.39, May 22, 1997
5 furlongs: Joyful Tune, :56.25, May 5, 2002
5 1/2 furlongs: Term Sheet, 1:02.78, July 5, 2001
6 furlongs: Triple Card, 1:08.06, May 28, 2001
6 1/2 furlongs: Spiritbound, 1:14.16, May 3, 1997
7 furlongs: Clooney, 1:20.98, June 22, 2001
1 mile: Isitingood, 1:34.44, April 20, 1997
1 1/16 miles: Dixie Dot Com, 1:40.53, May 28, 2001
1 1/8 miles: Moosekabear, 1:49.69, April 19, 1997
1 3/16 miles: Moosekabear, 1:56.21, May 10, 1997
1 1/4 miles: Tali Hai, 2:04.68, June 14, 1997
1 1/2 miles: Tali Hai, 2:32.57, July 5, 1997
1 3/4 miles: Sir Moon Dancer, 3:00.46, July 19, 1998
Other: 2 1/2 furlongs, Yes He Will, :26.53, October 7, 1997

Course Records, Main Turf
5 furlongs: Icy Morn, :55.60, May 26, 1997
7 1/2 furlongs: Special Moments, 1:28.20, May 24, 1998
1 mile: Kiraday, 1:33.56, July 4, 1997
1 1/16 miles: Sharpest Image (Ire), 1:40.05, June 12, 1998
1 1/8 miles: Yaqthan (Ire), 1:45.54, May 25, 1998
1 3/8 miles: Rugged Bugger, 2:13.53, May 10, 1998
1 1/2 miles: Final Val, 2:28.20, July 4, 1998

Fastest Times of 2001 (Dirt)
4 1/2 furlongs: Thats the Problem, :51.92, April 29
5 furlongs: Nuclear Assembly, :57.41, June 30
5 1/2 furlongs: Term Sheet, 1:02.78, July 5
6 furlongs: Triple Card, 1:08.06, May 28
6 1/2 furlongs: Little Angel, 1:15.30, May 28
7 furlongs: Clooney, 1:20.98, June 22
1 mile: Dixie Dot Com, 1:34.72, April 28
1 1/16 miles: Dixie Dot Com, 1:40.53, May 28
1 1/8 miles: Percy Hope, 1:50.27, April 7

Fastest Times of 2001 (Turf)
5 furlongs: Hallowed Dreams, :56.03, June 23
7 1/2 furlongs: Gold Nugget, 1:29.85, July 7
1 mile: River Sass, 1:34.55, July 3
1 1/16 miles: Twisted Kris, 1:42.40, June 2
1 1/8 miles: National Finals, 1:49.22, June 2
1 3/8 miles: Torgan, 2:18.61, June 23
1 1/2 miles: Pancho Villa Coco, 2:34.52, July 15

Manor Downs

Thoroughbred racing was to debut in 2002 at Manor Downs, a small racetrack near Austin, Texas, that long had offered only straightaway Quarter Horse and Paint racing. Ordered by the Texas Racing Commission to improve its racetrack to accommodate Thoroughbred racing, Manor spent more than $4-million to expand its oval to 7½ furlongs and to renovate the barn area and other areas of the facility. Manor, which is owned by Frances Tapp, was among the tracks in Texas's far-flung non-pari-mutuel circuit that flourished before legislation allowing pari-mutuel wagering was passed in 1987. Unlike the other small tracks in that circuit, Manor survived the transition and is Texas's oldest pari-mutuel facility.

Manor Downs, continued

Location: 9211 Hill Lane, Manor, TX 78653
Phone: (512) 272-5581
Fax: (512) 278-1892
E-mail: manordowns@aol.com
Web site: http://www.manordowns.com

Officers
Racing Secretary: Sammy Burton
Director of Publicity: Brian Monshower
Track Superintendent: Allan Key
Other Officials: Howard Phillips, Chief Operating Officer

Racing dates
2002: May 11-June 9, 10 days
2001: April 21-May 20, 10 days

Retama Park

One of the country's newest racing facilities, Retama Park opened in April 1995 in Selma, 15 minutes northeast of San Antonio. The racetrack is both uniquely named—for the green-limbed deciduous tree or shrub native to south and west Texas—and uniquely designed, with its mission-style, five-tiered grandstand featuring arched entranceways, food courts, the Terrace Dining Room, the Race Book and Sports Bar, and the new Player's Club for Turf and Field Club members. Though attendance was down slightly at Retama Park's 50-day 2001 fall meet (August 3 through October 27), total handle increased by 11% and field size increased 4.5%.

The track's original investors hired well-known racing executive Robert J. Quigley to oversee construction of the $79-million plant and the track's opening, but the facility failed to meet even modest wagering projections. After failing to pay its bondholders, the track filed for bankruptcy protection in 1996 and was purchased by William Allen's Call Now Inc. Thomas Johnson took over as president and chief executive of Call Now on November 29, 2001. The track operates as a training center each winter, with horsemen paying stall rent to use the facilities.

Location: 1 Retama Pkwy., Selma, TX 78154
Phone: (210) 651-7000
Fax: (210) 651-7099
E-mail: run@retamapark.com
Web site: http://www.retamapark.com
Year founded: 1989
Inaugural meeting: April 7, 1995
Acreage: 226
Number of stalls: 1,288
Seating capacity: 6,800

Officers
General Manager: Robert W. Pollock
Director of Racing: Larry A. Craft
Racing Secretary: Larry A. Craft, Michael Shamburg
Director of Admissions: Holly S. Brooks
Director of Finance: Lisa L. Medrano
Director of Mutuels: Jackie F. Hart
Director of Publicity: Douglas B. Vair
Director of Simulcasting: Steven M. Ross
Stewards: Chuck Nuber, Donnie Walker, John Ferrara
Track Announcer: Don Alexander
Track Superintendent: Jesse L. Cardenas

Racing dates
2001: August 3-October 28, 50 days
2002: August 2-October 26, 51 days

Track Layout
Main circumference: 1 mile
Main track chute: 7 furlongs
Main width: 110 feet
Main length of stretch: 990 feet
Main turf circumference: 7 furlongs
Main turf chute: 1 1/8 miles
Main turf width: 90 feet
Main turf length of stretch: 990 feet

Mutuel Records
Highest Win: $136.40, Icy's Baba, August 15, 1999

Leaders
Recent meeting, leading jockey: Steve Bourque, 92, Fall 2001
Recent meeting, leading owner: Leland Cook, 16, Fall 2001
Recent meeting, leading trainer: Danny Pish, 35, Fall 2001

Track Records, Main Dirt
4 1/2 furlongs: Raise a Tab, :51.06, August 1, 1998
5 furlongs: Teed Off, :56.20, August 20, 2000
5 1/2 furlongs: Bailando, 1:02.90, May 13, 1995
6 furlongs: Bucharest, 1:08.82, May 10, 1995
6 1/2 furlongs: Heavily Armed, 1:15.30, August 30, 1997
7 furlongs: Bucharest, 1:21.29, May 4, 1996
1 mile: Mr. Pappion, 1:36.90, May 11, 1995
1 1/16 miles: Heavily Armed, 1:43.20, September 20, 1997
1 1/8 miles: Fletcher's Pride, 1:51.43, August 14, 1998
1 1/4 miles: Call Me Wild, 2:04.01, September 3, 1995
1 3/8 miles: Slews Minister, 2:19.95, October 28, 2000
Other: 2 1/2 furlongs, Texas Hope, :28.20, June 28, 1998; 1 5/16 miles, Opening Remark, 2:13.99, September 5, 1996

Course Records, Main Turf
7 1/2 furlongs: Call Me Wild, 1:28.43, September 17, 1995
1 mile: Empire Pool (GB), 1:34.62, May 6, 1995
1 1/16 miles: Gold Nugget, 1:41.13, October 9, 1999
1 1/8 miles: Untraceable, 1:48.13, August 10, 1996
Other: 1 13/16 miles, Misting Rain, 3:13.22, September 28, 1996

Fastest Times of 2001 (Dirt)
4 1/2 furlongs: Shimmering Bronze, :52.19, August 4
5 furlongs: Brother Love, :58.55, September 22
5 1/2 furlongs: Kristi's Purse, 1:04.49, October 3
6 furlongs: Nobody's Fool, 1:10.37, August 25
6 1/2 furlongs: Somethin Brite, 1:17.90, October 27
7 furlongs: Rough Energy, 1:24.21, October 18
1 mile: Lights On Broadway, 1:38.14, September 15
1 1/16 miles: Momentous Drive, 1:47.05, September 19

Fastest Times of 2001 (Turf)
5 furlongs: Fearless Peer, :56, October 10
7 1/2 furlongs: Bourbon N Coke, 1:28.61, September 14
1 mile: Tin Smithen, 1:34.65, September 20
1 1/16 miles: Chauffe Au Rouge, 1:40.90, October 6
1 1/8 miles: Zigfire, 1:50.65, August 26

Sam Houston Race Park

In April 1994, Sam Houston Race Park opened as the first Class I racetrack in Texas, which had outlawed pari-mutuel wagering for more than 50 years. Built for $85-million and named for one of the state's founding fathers, the racetrack in northwest Houston is a part of the Class I Texas racing circuit that also includes Lone Star Park in the Dallas-Fort Worth metroplex and Retama Park near San Antonio. Sam Houston, which conducts nighttime racing, holds two separate Thoroughbred meets and races Quarter Horses in the summer. Although the track initially posted disappointing results, its fortunes have improved under the leadership of Robert Bork, a race-

track professional who joined the track in 1995 as senior vice president and general manager. The track's signature event is Texas Champions Day, which offers nine lucrative stakes races for state-breds. Sam Houston's majority owner is MAXXAM Inc., a Houston-based Fortune 500 company involved in aluminum, forest products, and real estate that is chaired by Texas native Charles Hurwitz. The track is the home of the Houston Equine Research Organization, a not-for-profit group that works to promote the welfare of racehorses through research and also offers a successful racehorse adoption program.

Location: 7575 Sam Houston Pkwy., Houston, TX 77064
Phone: (281) 807-8700
Fax: (281) 807-8701
Web site: http://www.samhoustonracepark.com
Year founded: 1993
Inaugural meeting: April 29, 1994
Acreage: 230
Seating capacity: 18,000
Number of stalls: 1,250

Officers
President: James Noteware
Vice President: Robert L. Bork
General Manager: Robert L. Bork
Racing Secretary: Eric Johnston
Director of Operations: Ann McGovern
Director of Admissions: Todd Duckett
Director of Communications: Martha Claussen
Director of Finance: Michael Vitek
Director of Marketing: Kerry Graves
Director of Mutuels: Kim Pomposelli
Director of Publicity: Martha Claussen
Director of Sales: Kerry Graves
Director of Simulcasting: Steve Hofmann
Horsemen's Liaison: Huw Williams
Stewards: Fred Winch, Pat Powell, Steve O'Malley
Track Announcer: Michael Chamberlain
Track Photographer: Jack Coady
Track Superintendent: Greg Johnson

Racing dates
2001: November 2, 2000-April 1, 2001, 85 days
2002: November 2, 2001-March 30, 2002, 82 days

Track Layout
Main circumference: 1 mile
Main track chute: 1 1/4 miles, 7 furlongs
Main width: 90 feet
Main length of stretch: 966 feet
Main turf circumference: 7 furlongs
Main turf chute: 1 1/8 miles
Main turf width: 80 feet

Attendance
Average daily recent meeting: 2,955, 2000/2001
Highest single day record: 23,324, July 4, 1999

Handle
Average all sources recent meeting: $2,579,833, 1999/2000
Single day on-track handle: $617,783, July 4, 1999, 4,070,715, December 10, 1999
Single day total handle all sources: $4,070,715, July 4, 1999
Average on-track recent meeting: $164,214, 2000/2001

Leaders
Career, leading trainer by titles: Amos Laborde, 3
Career, leading trainer by wins: Amos Laborde, 212
Career, leading jockey by titles: Steve Bourque, 3
Recent meeting, leading jockey: Steve Bourque, 120, 2000/2001
Career, leading jockey by wins: Steve Bourque, 419
Career, leading owner by wins: Charles Hukill, 35
Recent meeting, leading trainer: Todd Meachum, 33, 2000/2001

Recent meeting, leading owner: P & D Racing Stable, 14, 2000/2001

Records
Single meet, leading trainer by wins: Amos Laborde, 45, 1994, H. B. Johnson, 45, 1999
Single day jockey wins: Austin Lovelace, 7, December 10, 1994
Single day trainer wins: Gilbert Ciavaglia, 5, February 23, 1997
Single meet, leading jockey by wins: Steve Bourque, 120, 2000/2001
Single meet, leading owner by wins: Ripesco Inc., 15, 1999/2000

Track Records, Main Dirt
4 1/2 furlongs: Angels Lady, :51.93, May 4, 1997
5 furlongs: Dixieland Gambler, :57.43, November 1, 1996
5 1/2 furlongs: Bucharest, 1:02.92, April 13, 1996
6 furlongs: Bucharest, 1:08.88, May 11, 1994
6 1/2 furlongs: Brass Jacks, 1:15.74, May 21, 1994
7 furlongs: Bucharest, 1:21.27, May 4, 1996
1 mile: Vindictive Silence, 1:36.51, December 26, 1995
1m 70 yds: Capt. Tiff's Beau, 1:40.52, October 24, 1998
1 1/16 miles: Desert Air, 1:42.74, February 13, 1999
1 1/8 miles: Lost Soldier, 1:48.75, May 3, 1997
1 1/4 miles: Sauvage Isn't Home, 2:04.75, December 29, 1995
1 1/2 miles: Final Val, 2:32.99, February 20, 1998
1 3/4 miles: Final Val, 3:01.50, March 13, 1998
2 miles: Final Val, 3:31.29, April 3, 1998

Course Records, Main Turf
5 furlongs: Go Scotty, :56.93, March 6, 1999
1 mile: Solo Attack, 1:36, March 17, 2001
1 1/16 miles: Luna Delight, 1:43.24, December 4, 1998
1 1/8 miles: Chorwon, 1:47.65, March 6, 1999
1 1/2 miles: Commander Calhoun, 2:32.56, October 3, 1996

Interesting facts
Trivia: First Class 1 racetrack in Texas

Fastest Times of 2001 (Dirt)
5 furlongs: Endless Torrential, :57.93, December 27
5 1/2 furlongs: Cowboy Cumbia, 1:03.75, November 2
6 furlongs: My Meggie Meg, 1:09.69, January 27
6 1/2 furlongs: Miss Photogenic, 1:17.19, November 17
7 furlongs: Captain Countdown, 1:22.70, January 6
1 mile: B. L.'s Ghost, 1:38.41, March 17
1m 70yds: Werehere, 1:42.55, December 7
1 1/16 miles: Lights On Broadway, 1:43.66, December 1
1 1/8 miles: Vilaxy, 1:51.19, January 20

Fastest Times of 2001 (Turf)
5 furlongs: Testify, :57.45, February 24
1 mile: Solo Attack, 1:36.16, March 17
1 1/16 miles: Schaumburg, 1:43.60, November 10
1 1/8 miles: Candid Glen, 1:50.51, February 24
1 1/2 miles: Hawk's View, 2:34.98, February 11

Virginia

Colonial Downs

Colonial Downs has featured a high standard of racing since its opening in 1997, but the facility has been unable to build a strong local brand name or national following, and its owner has feuded with the Virginia Racing Commission.

Constructed in New Kent County, Virginia, approximately 24 miles from Richmond, the track is the only facility to open in Virginia since pari-mutuel wagering was legalized in 1993. The track features seating for 6,000 in an attractive setting. Colonial's ten-furlong dirt

Colonial Downs, continued

track is one of North America's largest, and its turf course has drawn praise for its quality.

But the track has suffered its fair share of controversy since opening four years ago. Its operations run by the Maryland Jockey Club, the track endured several disputes over racing dates, an issue that has also drawn in Maryland's horsemen, who supply most of the track's runners. Colonial originally raced in late summer and early fall but switched to a 25-day, early summer meeting in 2001.

The 2001 meeting turned out to be Colonial's strongest to date. On-track daily attendance skyrocketed 61% to 1,940, while handle increased 21%. In mid-2001, Colonial Chief Executive Officer Jeffrey Jacobs made a buyout offer to all shareholders in the track's holding company.

Location: 10515 Colonial Downs Pkwy., New Kent, VA 23124
Phone: (804) 966-7223
Fax: (804) 966-1565
E-mail: cdwn@richmond.infi.net
Web site: http://www.colonialdowns.com
Year founded: 1997
Inaugural meeting: September 1-October 12, 1997
Acreage: 345
Number of stalls: 1,050
Seating capacity: 6,000

Officers
President: Ian Stewart
Vice President: Jerry Monahan
General Manager: John E. Mooney
Director of Racing: John E. Mooney
Racing Secretary: Clayton Beck
Director of Operations: Jack Howard
Director of Marketing: Darrell Wood
Director of Publicity: Darrell Wood
Director of Simulcasting: Darrell Wood
Stewards: Jean Chalk, Stan Bowker, William Passmore
Track Announcer: Dave Rodman
Track Superintendent: Billy Byers

Racing dates
2001: July 3-August 7, 25 days
2002: June 21-July 23, 26 days

Track Layout
Main circumference: 1 1/4 miles
Main track chute: 1 1/8 miles
Main width: 80 feet
Main length of stretch: 1,290.50 feet
Main turf circumference: 7 1/2 furlongs
Main turf width: 180 feet
Main turf length of stretch: 1,123.62 feet

Attendance
Highest single day record: 13,468, September 1, 1997
Highest single meet record: 108,900, 1997
Record daily average for single meet: 3,630, 1997
Average daily recent meeting: 1,940, 2001

Handle
Record daily average for single meet: $183,594, 1997
Single day on-track handle: $508,199, September 1, 1997
Average all sources recent meeting: $1,103,188, 2001
Average on-track recent meeting: $165,829, 2001
Total on-track recent meeting: $4,145,716, 2001
Single day total handle all sources: $2,105,650, October 3, 1998

Leaders
Career, leading jockey by wins: Mario Pino, 184
Recent meeting, leading owner: Richard Englander, 9, 2001
Career, leading trainer by wins: A. Ferris Allen III, 76
Career, leading jockey by titles: Mario Pino, 3

Recent meeting, leading jockey: Mario Pino, 49, 2001
Recent meeting, leading trainer: A. Ferris Allen III, 10, 2001
Career, leading trainer by titles: A. Ferris Allen III, 5

Records
Single day jockey wins: Mario Pino, 6, July 9, 2001
Single meet, leading jockey by wins: Edgar Prado, 59, 1997
Single meet, leading trainer by wins: A. Ferris Allen III, 25, 1997

Track Records, Main Dirt
5 furlongs: Band Performance, :56.66, September 4, 2000
5 1/2 furlongs: Ameri Prospect, 1:02.94, September 1, 1997
6 furlongs: Capture the Gold, 1:08.11, October 4, 1997
6 1/2 furlongs: Cool Ken Jane, 1:16.60, September 7, 1997
7 furlongs: Sky Watch, 1:20.87, September 1, 1997
1 mile: Assault John, 1:35.48, October 8, 1997
1 1/16 miles: Gold Token, 1:41.09, September 13, 1998
1 1/8 miles: Our Toby, 1:48.95, October 4, 1997
1 1/4 miles: Macgyver, 2:03.54, September 1, 1997
1 1/2 miles: Lord Mendelson, 2:30.13, September 4, 2000

Course Records, Main Turf
5 furlongs: Take Achance On Me, :56.56, July 27, 2001
5 1/2 furlongs: Devereux, 1:01.93, September 24, 1999
6 furlongs: Tyaskin, 1:08.11, September 20, 1998
1 1/16 miles: Lonesome Sound, 1:41.28, September 18, 1998
1 1/8 miles: Kerfoot Corner, 1:47.40, September 26, 1998
1 3/16 miles: Jacsonzac, 1:54.41, October 10, 1998
1 1/4 miles: Phi Beta Doc, 1:59.97, October 2, 1999
1 1/2 miles: Attention Mark, 2:31.76, September 11, 1998
1 5/8 miles: Beluga, 2:45.80, September 26, 1998

Course records, Inner Turf
5 furlongs: Smart Sunny, :56.02, September 8, 2000
5 1/2 furlongs: Smart Sunny, 1:02.94, September 13, 1998
1 mile: La Reine's Terms, 1:34.24, September 17, 1998
1 1/16 miles: Grass Roots, 1:41.01, October 8, 1999
1 1/8 miles: Steak Scam, 1:48.71, September 25, 1999
1 1/4 miles: Franc, 2:03.02, September 9, 2000
1 1/2 miles: Winsox, 2:27.04, September 28, 1998
1 5/8 miles: Our Game, 2:44.82, September 24, 1999

Fastest Times of 2001 (Dirt)
5 1/2 furlongs: Beers, 1:04.37, July 29
6 furlongs: Native Heir, 1:09.16, July 22
7 furlongs: Love Happy, 1:22.46, July 10
1 mile: Dixie Hot Rod, 1:36.35, July 29
1 1/16 miles: Prospective Lover, 1:44.80, July 29
1 1/8 miles: Hawk's Feather, 1:49.26, July 29

Fastest Times of 2001 (Turf)
5 furlongs: Bolero Boy (GB), :56.55, July 14
5 1/2 furlongs: Wilma Lee, 1:02.54, July 3
6 furlongs: Carrena Rose, 1:09.48, July 21
1 mile: Fox's Flyjinsky, 1:35.83, July 13
1 1/16 miles: Classic Investment, 1:42.46, July 23
1 1/8 miles: Colstar, 1:47.53, July 14
1 1/4 miles: Potaro (Ire), 2:02.17, July 14
2 miles: Maternity Leave, 3:34.60, August 4

Washington

Emerald Downs

Emerald Downs returned Thoroughbred racing to the Seattle area when it opened in 1996. Since the 1930s, the hub of Northwest racing had been Longacres, which was sold in '90 to aircraft manufacturer Boeing Co. After Longacres held its last season of live racing in 1992, Yakima Meadows in Yakima became its short-term successor. A group of investors headed by Ron Crockett, who formerly was involved in an airline-related company, built Emerald for $83-million.

The track, which offers live racing from mid-April to mid-September, became the new host of the Northwest's most famous race when the Longacres Mile Handicap (G3) was first held at the track during its inaugural season. The Mile, which debuted at Longacres in 1935, was held at Yakima Meadows in 1993, '94, and '95.

Location: 2300 Emerald Downs Dr., Auburn, WA 98071-0617
Phone: (253) 288-7000
Fax: (253) 288-7750
Web site: http://www.emdowns.com
Inaugural meeting: June 20, 1996
Acreage: 167
Number of stalls: 1,276

Officers
President: Ron Crockett
Vice President: Jack E. Hodge Jr.
Director of Racing: Grant Holcomb
Racing Secretary: Grant Holcomb
Director of Operations: Bob Fraser
Director of Marketing: Susie Sourwine
Director of Mutuels: Gary Hallett
Director of Publicity: Susie Sourwine
Director of Sales: Don Campbell
Director of Simulcasting: Chuck Potter
Track Announcer: Robert Geller
Track Photographer: Reed Palmer
Track Superintendent: Wayne Damron
Other Officials: Grant Clark, Media Relations

Racing dates
2001: April 20-September 15, 96 days
2002: April 19-September 16, 91 days

Track Layout
Main circumference: 1 mile
Main track chute: 1 1/4 miles, 6 1/2 furlongs
Main width: 90 feet
Main length of stretch: 1,033 feet

Handle
Single day on-track handle: $2,731,852, August 22, 1999
Average all sources recent meeting: $1,101,016, 2001

Mutuel Records
Highest Win: $142, My Lady Boots, July 27, 1997
Lowest Win: $2.60, Sharp Cajun, October 5, 1996
Highest Exacta: $2,317.80, August 28, 1998
Lowest Exacta: $2.80, June 13, 1999
Highest Trifecta: $23,782,80, August 28, 1998
Lowest Trifecta: $11.80, August 28, 1999
Highest Daily Double: $1,464.80, July 5, 1999
Lowest Daily Double: $4.40, August 24, 1997
Highest Pick 3: $19,219.40, July 27, 1996
Lowest Pick 3: $4.70, May 8, 1997
Highest Pick 6: $217,140, June 8, 1997
Lowest Pick 6: $146.20, August 31, 1997
Highest Other Exotics: $14,423.10, Superfecta, July 25, 1999
Lowest Other Exotics: $75.20, Superfecta, May 22, 1999

Leaders
Career, leading trainer by wins: Tim McCanna, 228
Recent meeting, leading jockey: Ben Russell, 140, 2001
Recent meeting, leading owner: Seawind Stables, 17, 2001
Recent meeting, leading trainer: Tim McCanna, 51, 2001
Career, leading jockey by stakes wins: Gallyn Mitchell, 22
Career, leading jockey by wins: Frank Gonsalves, 478
Career, leading owner by wins: Ron Crockett, 60
Career, leading trainer by stakes wins: Bud Klokstad, 22

Records
Single day jockey wins: Frank Gonsalves, 5, September 26, 1996; Vann Belvoir, 5, October, 20, 1996; Pedro Alvarado, 5, May 22, 1998; Miguel Perez, 5, April 15, 2000
Single day trainer wins: Jim Penney, 5, September 6, 1998

Track Records, Main Dirt
4 1/2 furlongs: I. M. Adevil, :50.60, May 30, 1999; Pacificat, :50.60, May 21, 2000
5 furlongs: Jazzy Mac, :55.40, August 20, 2000
5 1/2 furlongs: Salt Grinder, 1:01.40, April 20, 2002
6 furlongs: Handy N Bold, 1:07.80, April 30, 2000
6 1/2 furlongs: Love All the Way, 1:14.40, July 4, 1999; Edneator, 1:14.40, April 29, 2000
1 mile: Wild Wonder, 1:33.20, August 23, 1998; Edneator, 1:33.20, September 11, 2000
1 1/16 miles: Kid Katabatic, 1:39.60, July 26, 1998
1 1/8 miles: Flirtacious Girl, 1:47.20, August 21, 1999
1 1/4 miles: Rapid Stream, 2:01.80, August 15, 1998
1 1/2 miles: Keen Line, 2:30.60, September 6, 1997
2 miles: Kavil, 3:26.80, November 1, 1996
Other: 2 furlongs, Midnight Cruiser, :21.40, May 4, 2000

Fastest Times of 2001
4 1/2 furlongs: Flying Notes, :51.40, May 28
5 furlongs: April Surprise, :56.80, August 19
5 1/2 furlongs: If Not Why Not, 1:02.60, April 20
6 furlongs: Weekender, 1:08.60, April 22
6 1/2 furlongs: Sabertooth, 1:14.60, June 24
1 mile: Irisheyesareflying, 1:35.40, August 19
1 1/16 miles: Diglett, 1:41.60, August 12
1 1/8 miles: Graceful Cat, 1:49.20, August 18
1 1/4 miles: Super Writer, 2:03.80, August 3
1 1/2 miles: Faithful Gal, 2:32.60, August 17
Other: 2 furlongs, Adventure Man, :21.40, May 10

Playfair Park

An oasis for racing fans in western Washington for many years, the Spokane track has become a mirage. Saddled with inadequate resources and a racing program that was not attractive to simulcast patrons, Playfair was shuttered for three years starting in 1997. The Lilac City Racing Association received a license to operate a three-month race meeting in 2000, but the meet finished with a 30% decline in handle over 1997, and the association finished the year with an $850,000 shortfall.

Playfair intended to run a September-through-December meeting in 2001, but Lilac City officials were unable to raise sufficient capital to run the meeting and the Washington Horse Racing Commission revoked the organization's racing and simulcasting license in July 2001. Lilac City eventually filed for bankruptcy, preventing the commission from allocating its purse money to Emerald Downs for its 2002 meeting.

Location: 202 N. Altamont St., Spokane, WA 99220
Phone: (509) 534-0505
Fax: (509) 534-0101
Year founded: 1901
Number of stalls: 1,000+

Officers
President: Bruce Wagar
Vice President: Amy Haven
General Manager: Ross Yearout
Director of Racing: Ted Martin
Racing Secretary: Mike Pfliger
Director of Marketing: Tom Blaine

Racing dates
2001: September 16-December 16, 43 days

Track Layout
Main circumference: 5 furlongs

Playfair, continued

Leaders
Recent meeting, leading owner: David L. Martin, 8, 2000; Gene Starlin, 8, 2000; Shellie Quillan, 8, 2000
Recent meeting, leading trainer: Mel White, 21, 2000
Recent meeting, leading jockey: Lorenzo Lopez, 63, 2000

Sun Downs
Location: Benton-Franklin County Fairgrounds, Kennewick, WA

Racing dates
2001: April 7-May 6, 10 days

Leaders
Recent meeting, leading jockey: Connie Doll-Carriere, 6, 2001; Vincent Mario Graffagnini, 6, 2001
Recent meeting, leading trainer: Robert L. Lawrence, 4, 2001; Tracy Lebret, 4, 2001

Fastest Times of 2001
4 furlongs: Stateyourposition, :46.20, April 8
6 furlongs: Little Duke, 1:14.20, April 28
7 furlongs: Charminger, 1:28.80, May 5

Waitsburg Race Track
Location: P.O. Box 391, Waitsburg, WA 99361-0391
Phone: (509) 337-6623
Fax: (509) 337-6026

Racing dates
2001: May 19-May 20, 2 days

Walla Walla
Location: Southeastern Washington Fairgrounds, Walla Walla, WA 99362
Phone: (509) 527-3247
Fax: (509) 527-3259

Officers
President: Dick Monahan
Director of Racing: Dick Monahan
Racing Secretary: Dick Monahan
Director of Publicity: Cory Hewitt

Racing dates
2001: May 12-May 13, 2 days, September 1-September 3, 3 days

West Virginia

Charles Town Races

Founded in 1933 by Albert Boyle, Charles Town Races in Charles Town has been wholly owned by Penn National Gaming Inc. since 2000. The company also owns Penn National Race Course and Pocono Downs harness track in Pennsylvania as well as other gaming and resort facilities. Penn National Gaming bought a majority interest in Charles Town after local voters approved slot machines at the track in late 1996. Charles Town Races has seen its fortunes improve dramatically since the slot machines were installed. Purses for horse racing receive 15% of revenues on all slot-machine play at Charles Town, which offered a record of more than $2-million in stakes purses in 2001. The track's marquee event is the West Virginia Breeders' Classic, a series of races that showcase runners bred, sired, or raised in the state, and is highlighted by the $250,000 West Virginia Breeders Classic. Charles Town broke ground on October 31, 2001, on a $45-million expansion project.

Location: U.S. Route 340, Charles Town, WV 25414
Phone: (304) 725-7001
Fax: (304) 724-4326
Web site: http://www.ctownraces.com
Year founded: 1933
Inaugural meeting: December 2, 1933
Number of stalls: 1,500
Seating capacity: 3,550

Officers
President: James Buchanan
Vice President: Fred Burd
General Manager: Fred Burd
Director of Racing: James E. Hammond Jr.
Racing Secretary: James Hammond
Director of Mutuels: Joy Lushbaugh
Director of Publicity: Roger Ramey
Director of Sales: Ann Fortner
Stewards: Danny Wright, J. Frank Utterback Jr., L. Robert Lotts
Track Announcer: Jeff Cernik
Track Photographer: Mike Montgomery
Track Superintendent: Doug Bowling
Other Officials: Frank Carulli, Simulcast Showhost

Racing dates
2001: January 1-December 31, 210 days
2002: January 3-December 31

Track Layout
Main circumference: 6 furlongs
Main track chute: 1 5/16 miles, 4 1/2 furlongs
Main length of stretch: 660 feet

Attendance
Highest single day record: 21,480, September 17, 1981
Average daily recent meeting: 1,650, 2000

Handle
Single day on-track handle: $1,168,055, March 19, 1977
Total all sources recent meeting: $195,834,066, 2001
Total on-track recent meeting: $144,834,066, 2001
Average all sources recent meeting: $1,138,095, 2001
Average on-track recent meeting: $618,949, 2001

Leaders
Recent meeting, leading jockey: Travis Dunkelberger, 184, 2001
Recent meeting, leading trainer: Ronney Brown, 129, 2001

Records
Single day jockey wins: Travis Dunkelberger, 7, March 30, 2000

Track Records, Main Dirt
4 1/2 furlongs: It's Only Money, :50.36, July 4, 1999
6 1/2 furlongs: Jet Appeal, 1:17, January 6, 1976
7 furlongs: Ohmylove, 1:24, January 7, 1976
1 1/16 miles: My Sister Pearl, 1:43.83, January 4, 2001
1 1/8 miles: A Huevo, 1:50.10, October 10, 1999
1 1/4 miles: Belle d'Amour, 2:05 3/5, June 28, 1941
1 1/2 miles: Guasave Breeze, 2:34, June 9, 1972

Fastest Times of 2001
4 1/2 furlongs: Governor's Pride, :50.55, July 4
6 1/2 furlongs: Hot Ziggity, 1:18.31, September 30
7 furlongs: Big Rut, 1:24.24, January 5
1 1/16 miles: My Sister Pearl, 1:43.83, January 4
1 1/8 miles: Confucius Say, 1:51.75, October 13

Mountaineer Race Track

Mountaineer Race Track in Chester, West Virginia, was recognized in 2001 as one of the top small businesses in the United States when *Forbes* magazine ranked MTR Gaming Group Inc., which owns the track, seventh among the top 200 such enterprises. Much of Mountaineer's success resulted from the legalization of slot machines in 1993, which increased revenues and enabled the track to offer higher purses. In 2001, the track received approval for additional slot machines, enabling it to operate a maximum of 2,500 slot machines. MTR Gaming, headed by Edson Arneault, also owns a golf course, hotel, spa, theater, and other entertainment facilities at the track's location. The track was known as Waterford Park when it was opened in 1951 by the Charles Town Jockey Club; the facility was renamed Mountaineer Park in '87 and Mountaineer Race Track in 2001. Mountaineer offers year-round night racing four nights a week. The West Virginia Derby, whose purse was increased to $500,000 in 2001, is the richest race to be run in West Virginia history. It was granted Grade 3 status for its 2002 running.

Location: Route 2, Chester, WV 26034
Phone: (304) 387-2400
Fax: (304) 378-3156
Web site: http://www.mtrgaming.com
E-mail: info@mtrgaming.com
Year founded: 1951
Inaugural meeting: May 16, 1951
Number of stalls: 1,100
Seating capacity: 7,400

Officers
President: Edson Arneault
Director of Racing: Rose Mary Williams
Racing Secretary: Joseph Narcavish
Director of Finance: Mary Jo Needham
Director of Marketing: Dorothy Welsh
Director of Mutuels: Gary Mackey
Director of Publicity: Tanara Petit
Director of Sales: Alan Selip
Director of Simulcasting: Deborah Howells
Horsemens Liaison: Charles Bailey
Stewards: Jim O'Brien, Larry Dupuy, Steve Kourpas
Track Announcer: Jim Dolan
Track Photographer: Ethel Riser
Track Superintendent: Tom Trevor
Other Officials: Ted Arneault, Chief Executive Officer

Racing dates
2001: January 1-December 31, 210 days
2002: January 1-December 31

Track Layout
Main circumference: 1 mile
Main track chute: 1 1/4 miles, 6 furlongs
Main width: 80 feet
Main length of stretch: 905.31 feet
Main turf circumference: 7 furlongs

Attendance
Lowest single day record: 12,825, May 30, 1956

Handle
Single day on-track handle: $966,508, May 8, 1973

Leaders
Recent meeting, leading trainer: Dale Baird, 38, 2001
Recent meeting, leading jockey: Dana Whitney, 83, 2001

Track Records, Main Dirt
2 furlongs: Promised Cruise, :21, June 23,1990

4 1/2 furlongs: Fina Dur, :50.33, August 11, 2001
5 furlongs: Last At the Table, :56.16, April 1, 2000
5 1/2 furlongs: The Dancer, 1:02.24, December 29, 2000
6 furlongs: Hustler, 1:07.81, August 11, 2001
1 mile: Find the Mine, 1:33.86, July 4, 2000
1 mile 40 yds: Ski Sez, 1:39.83, March 9, 1996
1 mile 70 yds: Mort, 1:38.81, April 1, 2000
1 1/16 miles: It's Reality, 1:41.75, December 23, 2000
1 1/8 miles: Western Pride, 1:47.20, August 11, 2001
1 3/16 miles: No Spend No Glow, 1:56.95, May 19, 2001
1 1/4 miles: Georgie Porgie, 2:03.69, August 6, 1995
1 1/2 miles: Pete's Skianno, 2:31.43, June 10, 2000
1 5/8 miles: Prince Swivel, 2:45, September 8, 1973
1 3/4 miles: Chased Again, 2:58.58, July 18, 1959
2 miles: Sovereign M.D., 3:27.66, December 10, 2000
Other: 2 1/16 miles, Sovereign M.D., 3:28.40, December 30, 2000

Course Records, Main Turf
4 1/2 furlongs: Cake n' Steak, :50, August 9, 1993
5 furlongs: Fina Dur, :55.52, September 6, 1999
7 furlongs: Hyper Two, 1:22.34, August 26, 2000
7 1/2 furlongs: Titos Choice, 1:28.19, May 25, 1998
1m 70yds: Fast and Friendly, 1:34, September 7, 1964; Poteau, 1:34, July 25, 1982
1 3/8 miles: Sunset Party, 2:13.23, September 26, 1999
1 1/2 miles: Guild Hall, 2:33.20, June 20, 1969
1 3/4 miles: Just Steady, 2:57.20, August 18, 1996
Other: 1 7/8 miles, Code's Best, 3:08.23, September 4, 2000

Interesting facts
Previous names and dates: Waterford Park

Fastest Times of 2001 (Dirt)
4 1/2 furlongs: Fina Dur, :50.33, August 11
5 furlongs: Big Bambu, :56.26, May 15
5 1/2 furlongs: One to Five, 1:02.67, August 11
6 furlongs: Hustler, 1:07.81, August 11
1 mile: Inside Affair, 1:34.77, June 19
1m 70yds: Corporate Courier, 1:39.34, July 22
1 1/16 miles: Danar, 1:42.49, February 3
1 1/8 miles: Western Pride, 1:47.20, August 11
1 3/16 miles: No Spend No Glow, 1:56.95, May 19
1 1/4 miles: Code's Best, 2:04.36, May 5
1 5/8 miles: Code's Best, 2:47.94, November 6
1 3/4 miles: Proper Blue, 3:05, November 20
Other: 2 1/16 miles, Pete's Skianno, 3:52.90, December 29

Fastest Times of 2001 (Turf)
4 1/2 furlongs: Knight Balloon, :50.09, July 15
5 furlongs: Decorated Drums, :57.19, June 10
7 furlongs: Decorated Drums, 1:21.73, July 17
7 1/2 furlongs: Find the Mine, 1:27.74, July 15
1 mile: Dakota Prospect, 1:33.81, July 3
1 3/8 miles: Amourette, 2:14.96, October 2

Wyoming

Wyoming Downs

Though it is one of North America's least-known Thoroughbred facilities, Wyoming Downs has been providing racing to southwestern Wyoming for nearly 20 years. Located just north of Evanston, Wyoming Downs offers Thoroughbred and Quarter Horse racing. Like Blue Ribbon Downs in Oklahoma, Wyoming Downs places the majority of its emphasis on the Quarter Horse program. The track's top races are Quarter Horse events, the Silver Dollar and Diamond Classic Futurities, each with estimated purses of $100,000.

For Thoroughbreds, the top event is the $5,000-added Rocky Mountain Futurity for two-year-olds and the

Wyoming Downs, continued

$5,000 Bettie Bullock Memorial Derby for three-year-olds.

Wyoming Downs usually races during the summer. The track also operates a system of off-track betting facilities that offer simulcast wagering year-round.

Location: 10180 Hwy. 89 N., WY 82931
Phone: (307) 789-0511
Fax: (307) 789-4614
E-mail: info@wydowns.com
Web site: http://www.wyomingdowns.com

Officers
President: Eric Nelson
General Manager: Dale Parker
Director of Racing: Dale Parker
Director of Publicity: Nina Earll
Director of Simulcasting: Jodi Lopez

Racing dates
2001: June 23-August 5
2002: June 22-August 18

Leaders
Recent meeting, leading jockey: Antonio Escareno, 4, 2001; Antonio Perez, 4, 2001
Recent meeting, leading trainer: Bert H. Argyle, 4, 2001

Fastest Times of 2001
4 1/2 furlongs: Synapse, :52.94, June 30
5 furlongs: Testhaven, :57.95, August 5
5 1/2 furlongs: Nickel Lou, 1:04.63, August 12
6 furlongs: Investor, 1:09.83, August 12
7 1/2 furlongs: Fadski, 1:35.03, June 30
1 mile: Rasha, 1:37.23, August 12

Canada
Alberta

Evergreen Park (Grand Prairie)

Location: Grand Prairie Fairgrounds, Grand Prairie, AB T8V 3A5
Phone: (780) 532-3279
Fax: (780) 539-0373

Racing dates
2001: July 6-August 5, 15 days
2002: July 5-August 4, 15 days

Fastest Times of 2001
4 furlongs: Another Rio, :46.60, July 6
5 1/2 furlongs: S. S. Tell, 1:07.80, July 14
6 furlongs: Don Coronaige, 1:14.20, July 8
6 1/2 furlongs: Carsons Dream, 1:23.20, August 3
7 furlongs: Nalee's Classic, 1:27.20, July 6
1 mile: Nalee's Classic, 1:43, July 15
1 1/8 miles: Regal Plan, 1:55.20, August 5

Lethbridge

Location: 3401 Parkside Dr., S Lethbridge, AB T1J 1G6
Phone: (403) 380-1905
Fax: (403) 380-1903
E-mail: racedot@telusplanet.net
Web site: http://www.countrytimes.com/whoopupdowns/index.htm
Seating capacity: 3,000
Number of stalls: 300

Officers
President: Max Gibb
Racing Secretary: Jim Ralph
Director of Marketing: Rose Rossi

Director of Publicity: Rose Rossi
Stewards: Don Hamilton, Gary Belecki, Peter Sebzda
Track Announcer: Murray Slough
Track Photographer: Coady Photo

Racing dates
2001: May 5- June 17, 14 days; August 18-October 28, 24 days
2002: May 4- June 16, 15 days; August 24-October 27, 25 days

Track Layout
Main circumference: 4 furlongs

Fastest Times of 2001
5 furlongs: Wise Dancer, :59.40, May 6
5 1/2 furlongs: Bad Toda Bone, 1:06.80, October 20; Tricky Attitude, 1:06.80, October 20
7 furlongs: High Seas, 1:25, September 2; Polish Poppa, 1:25, October 28
1 1/16 miles: Cathy's Whisper, 1:47.40, September 9; Special Made, 1:47.40, October 28
1 1/8 miles: Island Slew, 1:54.40, September 23
1 3/16 miles: Island Slew, 2:02.40, October 7

Northlands Park

Like many Canadian racetracks, Northlands Park in Edmonton races both Thoroughbreds and Standardbreds. Both breeds enjoy richer purses due to the arrival of slot machines. In late December 2001, Northlands Park received 250 additional machines to double its original total as part of a $42-million racing rehabilitation project under Alberta Premier Ralph Klein, an amateur harness driver, former TV reporter, and former Calgary mayor who now is in his third term as the province's chief executive. Opened in July 1925 as Edmonton Racetrack, the track was renamed Northlands Park in January 1964. Northlands Park conducts harness racing from early March through mid-June and Thoroughbred racing from late June through late October. The highlight of the Thoroughbred meet is the $320,000 Alberta Fall Classic in September.

Location: Northlands Spectrum, Edmonton, AB T5J 2N5
Phone: (403) 471-7379
Fax: (403) 471-7134
E-mail: racing@northlands.com
Web site: www.northlands.com

Officers
Racing Secretary: Alan Bott
Director of Communications: Jason Douziech
Director of Mutuels: Glen Weir
Director of Publicity: Bonna Chissell

Racing dates
2001: June 22-October 17, 68 days
2002: June 21-October 19

Track Layout
Main circumference: 5/8 mile
Main width: 70 feet
Main length of stretch: 567 feet

Leaders
Recent meeting, leading jockey: Stephan Heiler, 68, 2001
Recent meeting, leading trainer: Ron K. Smith, 29, 2001

Track Records, Main Dirt
5 1/2 furlongs: So Long Fellas, 1:04 2/5, August 16, 1975
6 1/2 furlongs: Timely Ruckus, 1:15.40, June 26, 1999
6 furlongs: Sageata, 1:09.80, July 22, 1984; Lynn's Dream, 1:09.80, July 6, 2000
1 mile: Bagfull, 1:35 4/5, May 16, 1981
1 1/16 miles: Chilcoton Blaze, 1:42 3/5, August 4, 1984

1 3/8 miles: Slyly Gifted, 2:15 4/5, August 30, 1986
1 5/8 miles: Racey Richard, 2:46, September 1, 1986
Other: 3 1/2 furlongs, Steel Penny Black, :38 1/5, June 14, 1984; 1 5/18 miles, Arctic Laur, 2:09, August 20, 1995

Fastest Times of 2001
5 1/2 furlongs: Sly Lady, 1:07.20, July 20
6 furlongs: Breezy Creek, 1:10.60, August 24; Northern Attack, 1:10.60, September 12; Klondike Trail, 1:10.60, September 29
6 1/2 furlongs: Timely Ruckus, 1:17.20, June 23; Robnroy, 1:17.20, September 22
1 mile: Timely Ruckus, 1:36.80, July 2
1 1/16 miles: Highland Leader, 1:43, September 22
1 3/8 miles: Rancour, 2:17.20, September 8
1 5/8 miles: Dancer's Nugget, 2:45.20, September 21
Other: 3 1/2 furlongs, Symbol's Remark, :38.80, August 15; 1 5/16 miles, Rancour, 2:10.80, August 25

Stampede Park

Though it is famous for its annual Calgary Stampede rodeo, Stampede Park is also a longtime part of the Thoroughbred racing scene in Alberta. Thoroughbred racing debuted at Stampede Park in 1974, with the facility offering racing on a five-furlong oval and stabling for 1,400 horses. Though the track's seating of 25,000 is snug during the Calgary Stampede, it has been more than adequate for racing; the track's record attendance is 6,167, set on August 15, 1981.

Stampede Park in recent years has dealt with uncertainty over the future of racing in Alberta. Track officials planned to halt racing after Resortport Development Corp. announced plans in 1998 to build a $100-million racetrack and resort facility in Calgary. But the plans fell apart, and Stampede Park is now looking at ways to upgrade its facility and maintain racing well into the 21st century. Stampede runs a spring Thoroughbred meet from early April through mid-June and a Standardbred meet in the summer and early fall. Its major Thoroughbred race is the $100,000 Alberta Derby (Can-G3) in mid-June.

Location: Box 1060, Station M, Calgary, AB T2P 2K8
Phone: (403) 261-0214
Fax: (403) 261-0526
E-mail: stpracing@calgarystampede.com
Web site: http://www.stampede-park.com/
Seating capacity: 25,000
Number of stalls: 1,400

Officers
Racing Secretary: Barry McGrath
Director of Mutuels: Sheri Holmes
Director of Publicity: Patty Hunt

Racing dates
2001: April 6-June 17, 43 days
2002: April 5-June 16, 43 days

Attendance
Highest single day record: 6,167, August 15, 1981

Leaders
Recent meeting, leading jockey: Richard Harvey Hamel, 49, 2001
Recent meeting, leading trainer: Ron K. Smith, 27, 2001

Fastest Times of 2001
4 furlongs: T J Quigley, :45.60, April 7
5 1/2 furlongs: Sweet Monarch, 1:09.20, June 13
6 furlongs: Northern Neechitoo, 1:10, June 9
1 mile: Rancour, 1:36.60, June 2
1 1/16 miles: Red Exit, 1:44.20, June 10
Other: 3 1/2 furlongs, Sundown Meg, :40, May 9; 3 1/2 furlongs, Code's Girl, :40, May 27

British Columbia

Hastings Park

For more than 80 years, the racing scene in the Canadian province of British Columbia has focused on the tract of land where Hastings Park currently stands.

Since 1994, the nonprofit Pacific Racing Association has managed racing at Hastings Park, which conducts Thoroughbred racing at the five-furlong facility usually from April through November.

First opened in 1920, Hastings Park reached its peak as a racing facility in the early 1980s, when the track sometimes drew crowds of 20,000 or more. In recent years, the association has attempted to revive interest in racing, and in 2001 the track recorded a 3.4% increase in handle. The track has also appealed to Vancouver's expanding Asian population by offering simulcast wagering from Hong Kong.

Despite these efforts, the future of racing at Hastings Park's current location was uncertain at the start of 2002. The Pacific Racing Association and Woodbine Entertainment Group were on the verge of completing an agreement that would see Woodbine take over racing and off-track wagering in the Vancouver area. Plans include building a new Thoroughbred-Standardbred facility to replace Hastings, which is unable to expand at its current location and is hampered by its bullring track.

Location: Hastings Park Racecourse, Vancouver, BC V5K 3N8
Phone: (604) 254-1631
Fax: (604) 251-0428
Web site: http://www.hastingspark.com
Year founded: 1889
Inaugural meeting: 1920
Acreage: 45
Seating capacity: 5,600
Number of stalls: 1,000

Officers
President: Rick Clough
Vice President: Jim Eccott
General Manager: Phil Heard
Director of Racing: Phil Heard
Racing Secretary: Debbie Peebles
Director of Operations: Dalbir Kanig
Director of Admissions: Michael Brown
Director of Communications: Brian Pound
Director of Finance: Steven Keenan
Director of Marketing: Brenda Smith
Director of Mutuels: Colleen MacLeod
Director of Publicity: Brian Pound
Director of Simulcasting: Curtis Linnell
Horsemen's Liaison: Debbie Peebles
Stewards: Keith Smith, Sten Matell, Wayne Russell
Track Announcer: Dan Jukich
Track Photographer: Larry Goulding
Track Superintendent: Ross Mansell

Racing dates
2001: April 16-November 7, 95 days
2002: April 20-November 3, 89 days

Track Layout
Main track chute: 6 1/2 furlongs
Main width: 65 feet
Main length of stretch: 513 feet
Training track: 1/2 mile

Hastings Park, continued

Attendance
Highest single day record: 21,156, July 9, 1982

Handle
Average all sources recent meeting: $1,292,657, 2001
Average on-track recent meeting: $602,627, 2001
Single day on-track handle: $2,612,316, July 9, 1982
Total all sources recent meeting: $120,217,116, 2001
Total on-track recent meeting: $56,044,378, 2001

Mutuel Records
Highest Win: $508.10, 1953
Highest Exacta: $4,092, 1962
Highest Trifecta: $21,806.20, 1982
Highest Daily Double: $4,863.10, 1995
Highest Pick 3: $11,474, 1993
Highest Other Exotics: $39,752, Superfecta, 1999; $63,326.70, Win 4, 1988; $920,411.70, Sweep 6, 1982

Leaders
Recent meeting, leading jockey: Dave Wilson, 123, 2001
Recent meeting, leading trainer: Harold Barroby, 49, 2001
Career, leading trainer by titles: Harold Barroby, 9
Career, leading trainer by wins: Harold Barroby, 454
Career, leading jockey by titles: Chris Loseth, 8
Career, leading jockey by wins: Chris Loseth, 3,441
Career, leading trainer by stakes wins: Harold Barroby, 148
Career, leading jockey by stakes wins: Chris Loseth
Recent meeting, leading owner: Canada West Ranches, 24, 2001

Records
Single day jockey wins: Chris Loseth, 8, 04/09/84
Single day trainer wins: George Cummings, 5, 11/08/92
Single meet, leading jockey by wins: Mark Patzer, 173, 1991
Single meet, leading trainer by wins: Lance Giesbrecht, 76, 1997

Track Records, Main Dirt
6 furlongs: Great Discretion, 1:10 4/5, May 10, 1969; Humphrey Lad, 1:10 4/5, April 13, 1988; Sir Khaled 1:10 4/5, April 15, 1988
6 1/2 furlongs: Torque Converter, 1:15, July 1, 1996
1m 70 yds: Westbury Road, 1:40 4/5, July 29, 1967
1 1/16 miles: Coral Isle, 1:42 2/5, July 28, 1973; No Time Flat, 1:42 2/5, August 12, 1987; Timley Stitch, 1:42.20, July 6, 1996
1 1/8 miles: Artic Son, 1:46.80, August 3, 1998
1 3/8 miles: Irish Bear, 2:14 4/5, October 17, 1987
1 1/2 miles: Lucky Son, 2:29, August 25, 1995
1 3/4 miles: Glen Glower, 2:59, August 25, 1987
Other: 3 1/2 furlongs, Smokin Finish, :39.79, July 2, 2000

Fastest Times of 2001
6 furlongs: Classic Action, 1:11.80, September 2
6 1/2 furlongs: King Jeremy, 1:16.05, August 26
1 1/16 miles: Rampaging Alf, 1:43.50, June 10
1 1/8 miles: Gery Tobe Free, 1:49.74, October 8
1 3/8 miles: Imprimaturo, 2:18.34, August 25
1 3/4 miles: Sensitive Issue, 3:00.37, September 29
Other: 3 1/2 furlongs, Katys Turn to Star, :39.69, October 3

Kamloops

Location: 479 Chilcotin St., Kamloops, BC V2H 1G4
Phone: (250) 314-9645

Officers
Director of Publicity: Lugi Sale

Racing dates
2001: May 20-September 9
2002 Fall: May 19-June 23; August 11-September 8

Leaders
Recent meeting, leading trainer: Earl Blain, 3, 2001
Recent meeting, leading jockey: Brooke Mellish, 5, 2001; Ronald Joseph Bilodeau, 5, 2001

Fastest Times of 2001
6 1/2 furlongs: Facts Related, 1:18.40, August 12
1 mile: Adanac, 1:38.20, August 12; Free At Heart, 1:38.20, August 19

Kin Park

Location: P.O. Box 682, Vernon, BC V1T 6M6
Phone: (250) 542-5759

Racing dates
2001: July 8-August 5, 5 days
2002: July 17-August 4

Leaders
Recent meeting, leading jockey: Brooke Mellish, 5, 2001; Dexter A. Assoon, 5, 2001
Recent meeting, leading trainer: Rosa Lee Burbank, 3, 2001

Fastest Times of 2001
4 furlongs: Soccer King, :45.60, August 5
6 furlongs: Diamond Ace, 1:13.60, July 8
6 1/2 furlongs: Wise Dancer, 1:19, July 8
1 1/16 miles: W. W. Dixie, 1:47, August 5

Sunflower Downs

Location: P.O. Box 584, Princeton, BC V0H 1W0
Phone: (250) 295-6380
Fax: (250) 295-7322

Officers
President: Brad Hope
Vice President: Brad Carter
General Manager: Jack Powell
Director of Racing: Joe Horton
Treasurer: Evelyn Beale
Director of Mutuels: Roberta Baron
Director of Publicity: June Hope
Stewards: Elaine Covert, Merv Nelson, Sten Matell
Track Announcer: Keith Reid

Racing dates
2001: July 1, 1 day
2001: June 30, 1 day

Manitoba

Assiniboia Downs

Assiniboia Downs continues a rich tradition of horse racing in Winnipeg, dating from the last quarter of the 19th century. Racing enthusiast and businessman Jack Hardy built Assiniboia, which opened in 1958 to replace Polo Park, a 30-year-old track located on property that became a shopping center. In 1974, Jim Wright bought the track and racing experienced a boom under his leadership. By the early 1990s, however, competition from other gambling forms made the track unprofitable. In 1993, Assiniboia was sold to its current owners, the Manitoba Jockey Club, a nonprofit organization that solidified its future by pouring profits from video lottery terminals and full-card simulcasting back into the facility. Assiniboia, which offers live racing from early May through September, was the first track in Canada to offer pick-six and telephone-account wagering. The track's richest race, the Manitoba Derby (Can-G3), has been run at Assiniboia since 1960. In 1970, Queen Elizabeth II and Prince Philip attended the race as part of Manitoba's centennial year. The winner was Fanfre-

luche, a daughter of Northern Dancer who was that year's Canadian Horse of the Year as well as an Eclipse Award winner as North America's champion three-year-old filly. Her son L'Enjoleur won the Manitoba Derby in 1975, the year in which he earned his second Canadian Horse of the Year title.

Location: 3975 Portage Ave., Winnipeg, MB R3K 2E9
Phone: (204) 885-3330
Fax: (204) 831-5348
E-mail: info@assiniboiadowns.com
Web site: http://www.assiniboiadowns.com
Inaugural meeting: 1958
Number of stalls: 936
Seating capacity: 6,000

Officers
General Manager: Sharon Gulyas
Racing Secretary: Ray Miller
Director of Operations: Darren Dunn
Director of Finance: Kris Nancoo
Director of Marketing: Susie Sourwine
Director of Publicity: Ernie Nairn
Director of Simulcasting: Donna Pankiw
Track Announcer: Darren Dunn
Track Photographer: Gerry Hart
Track Superintendent: Keith Trenholm

Racing dates
2001: May 5-September 30, 76 days
2002: May 4-September 29, 76 days

Track Layout
Main circumference: 1 3/16 miles
Main width: 80 feet
Main length of stretch: 990 feet
Training track: 1/2 mile

Attendance
Average daily recent meeting: 1,954, 2001
Highest single day record: 13,276, August 6, 1979
Total attendance recent meeting: 146,558, 2001

Handle
Total all sources recent meeting: $10,135,670, 2001
Single day on-track handle: $713,756, September 5, 1988
Average all sources recent meeting: $133,364, 2001
Average on-track recent meeting: $79,701, 2001
Total on-track recent meeting: $6,057,312, 2001

Mutuel Records
Highest Win: $474.20, May 31, 1986
Highest Exacta: $3,514.80, May 16, 1998
Highest Trifecta: $40,026.60, May 18, 1981
Highest Daily Double: $4,235.50, July 23, 1971
Highest Pick 3: $3,269.40, June 28, 1998
Highest Other Exotics: $14,584.95, Pick 4, September 1, 1986

Leaders
Career, leading jockey by titles: Larry Bird, 29
Recent meeting, leading jockey: Rohan Singh, 82, 2001
Recent meeting, leading owner: Ardel Sayler, 47, 2001
Career, leading jockey by wins: Ken Hendricks, 1,501
Career, leading trainer by wins: Don Gray, 879
Recent meeting, leading trainer: Ardell Sayler, 47, 2001

Records
Single day jockey wins: Jim Sorenson, 7, June 23, 1976

Fastest Times of 2001
4 1/2 furlongs: Jetta's Golden Boy, :53.40, August 18
5 furlongs: Burlington House, :59.40, May 6; Kalfaari, :59.40, May 13
5 1/2 furlongs: Timely Ruckus, 1:05, May 27; Champ's War, 1:05, July 22
6 furlongs: Kalfaari, 1:10.80, July 2; Burlington House, 1:10.80, August 3

7 furlongs: Burlington House, 1:26, July 17
1 mile: Constant Star, 1:38.60, June 16; Silver Trooper, 1:38.60, July 21
1 1/16 miles: Smoky Cinder, 1:46, September 16; Western Quitz, 1:46, September 21
1 1/8 miles: Stage Classic, 1:51.80, August 6
1 1/4 miles: Insurgence, 2:08.80, September 23

Ontario

Fort Erie

Founded in 1897, Fort Erie is one of Canada's oldest racetracks. Located in southern Ontario across the border from Buffalo, New York, the track began its premier event, the Prince of Wales Stakes, in 1959 with the help of prominent Ontario horseman E. P. Taylor. The race for three-year-old Canadian-breds now has become the second leg of Canada's Triple Crown. Taylor-bred Northern Dancer made his career debut at Fort Erie in August 1963. The following year, the Nearctic colt became the first Canadian-bred to win the Kentucky Derby. The track now is owned by Nordic Gaming Corp., which consists of three business interests from southern Ontario and two foreign investors. It underwent $30-million in renovations in 1999 to prepare for 1,200 slot machines that help to support the racing operation.

Location: 230 Catherine St., Fort Erie, ON L2A 5N9
Phone: (905) 871-3200
Fax: (905) 994-36229
E-mail: femedia@forterieracetrack.com
Web site: http://www.forterieracing.com
Inaugural meeting: June 16, 1897
Seating capacity: 4,000
Number of stalls: 1,000

Officers
Director of Communications: Brian Blessing, Daryl Wells
Director of Marketing: Herb McGirr
Director of Mutuels: Chad Gates
Director of Publicity: Brian Blessing
Director of Simulcasting: Chad Gates

Racing dates
2001: April 28-November 13, 116 days
2002: April 27-November 25, 118 days

Track Layout
Main circumference: 1 mile
Main width: 75 feet
Main length of stretch: 1,060 feet
Main turf circumference: 7 furlongs

Leaders
Recent meeting, leading jockey: Christopher Griffith, 128, 2001
Recent meeting, leading owner: Bruno Schickedanz, 35, 2001
Recent meeting, leading trainer: Layne S. Gilforte, 73, 2001

Fastest Times of 2001 (Dirt)
5 furlongs: Papa Dan, :57.14, November 12
5 1/2 furlongs: Deputy Carson, 1:04.20, July 30
6 furlongs: Deputy Carson, 1:08.55, September 9
6 1/2 furlongs: Valid Edition, 1:16.86, October 9
1m 70yds: Mannie's Mistake, 1:42.19, October 2
1 1/16 miles: Dimanno, 1:42.34, September 11
1 1/8 miles: Four Star General, 1:52.35, October 20
1 3/16 miles: Win City, 1:56.14, July 22

Fort Erie, continued

1 1/4 miles: Jack of Hearts, 2:06.22, August 4
Other: 2 furlongs, Appealing Allie, :21.65, November 10; 2 miles 70 yds, Winning Skier, 3:38.69, October 23

Fastest Times of 2001 (Turf)
5 furlongs: Hard Case, :57.28, July 24
1 mile: Sir Frederick, 1:37.34, August 26
1 1/16 miles: Storm Cruiser, 1:42.45, September 18
1 3/8 miles: Winning Skier, 2:19.51, July 30

Woodbine

The addition of 1,700 slot machines in March 2000 boosted '00 purses 3.3% and made Canada's best-known racetrack into a financial success after years of operating under a burdensome debt load. Woodbine, located in the Toronto suburb of Rexdale, is home of the Queen's Plate Stakes, first run in 1860 and North America's oldest continually run stakes race. With a unique track arrangement on its 650 acres, Woodbine is the only track in North America to conduct harness and Thoroughbred racing on the same day. Its 1½-mile grass course, the E. P. Taylor Turf Course, features the longest stretch run in North America, 1,440 feet. Inside the turf course is the one-mile dirt track, which was completely rebuilt in 1994. Inside the main dirt track is a seven-eighths-mile, 85-foot-wide harness track.

Woodbine's rich history extends back to 1874, when the track opened on what was then the eastern outskirts of Toronto, which is now Toronto's downtown. That track's name was changed to Old Woodbine in 1956 and then renamed Greenwood Raceway in 1963.

The present Woodbine opened on June 12, 1956. In 1996, Woodbine became the first Canadian track to host the Breeders' Cup, and it drew a record Woodbine crowd of 42,243. Besides the Queen's Plate, Woodbine hosts the $1-million Canadian International (Can-G1) and the Atto Mile (Can-G1), which has evolved into an important stakes for grass horses aiming for the Breeders' Cup Mile (G1).

Location: 555 Rexdale Blvd., Rexdale, ON M9W 5L2
Phone: (416) 675-6110
Fax: (416) 213-2104
Email: csd@woodbineentertainment.com
Web site: http://www.ojc.com
Year founded: 1874
Inaugural meeting: June 12-July 14 1956; October 1-November 17, 1956
Acreage: 650
Number of stalls: 2,060
Seating capacity: 18,996

Officers
President: David S. Willmot
Vice President: Hugh M. Mitchell
Director of Racing: Hugh M. Mitchell
Racing Secretary: Chris Evans
Secretary: Robert Careless
Treasurer: Tom Valiquette
Director of Operations: Al Dymon
Director of Admissions: Steve Mitchell
Director of Communications: David Gorman
Director of Finance: Tom Valiquette
Director of Marketing: Nick Eaves
Director of Mutuels: Sea Pinsonneault
Director of Publicity: Glenn Crouter
Director of Sales: Joseph Araujo
Director of Simulcasting: Debbie Chomiak
Horsemen's Liaison: Tom Cosgrove
Stewards: Nelson Ham, Richard Grubb, William McMahon
Track Announcer: Dan Loiselle
Track Photographer: Michael Burns
Track Superintendent: Ron Aspden
Other Officials: James W. Ormiston, Executive Vice President/CEO

Racing dates
2001: March 31-December 2, 166 days
2002: March 23-December 1, 168 days

Track Layout
Main circumference: 1 mile
Main width: 85 feet
Main length of stretch: 975 feet
Main turf circumference: 1 1/2 miles
Main turf width: 100 feet
Main turf length of stretch: 1,440 feet

Attendance
Highest single day record: 42,243, October 26, 1996

Handle
Average all sources recent meeting: $2,085,756, 2001
Average on-track recent meeting: $498,739, 2001
Total all sources recent meeting: $344,000,000+, 2001
Total on-track recent meeting: $82,292,020, 2001

Leaders
Career, leading jockey by titles: Sandy Hawley, 18
Career, leading trainer by titles: Frank Merrill, 30
Recent meeting, leading jockey: Todd Kabel, 145, 2001
Recent meeting, leading owner: Sam-Son Farms, 2001
Recent meeting, leading trainer: Robet Tiller, 62, 2001

Records
Single day jockey wins: Richard Grubb, 7, May 16, 1967; Sandy Hawley, 7, May 22, 1972; Sandy Hawley, 7, October 10, 1974

Track Records, Main Dirt
4 1/2 furlongs: Hallmarked, :50.40, March 24, 1996; Written Approval, :50.40, March 24, 1996
5 furlongs: Tailor's Thread, :56.20, April 2, 1999
5 1/2 furlongs: Uncle Woger, 1:02.70, April 4, 1999
6 furlongs: Great Defender, 1:08.17, November 27, 1999
6 1/2 furlongs: Fair Juror, 1:14 3/5, October 17, 1961
7 furlongs: Oronero, 1:20.60, December 6, 1995
1m 70 yds: Regal Courser, 1:39 3/5, August 8, 1998
1 1/16 miles: Kiridashi, 1:40.80, August 17, 1996
1 1/8 miles: Glorious Song, 1:48, July 1, 1981
1 3/16 miles: Runnin Roman, 1:55 4/5, September 15, 1974
1 1/4 miles: Alphabet Soup, 2:01, October 26, 1996
1 3/8 miles: Lovely Sunrise, 2:17, October 26, 1974
1 1/2 miles: Norcliffe, 2:29 1/5, October 29, 1977
1 5/8 miles: *Eugenia II, 2:43 2/5, October 27, 1956
1 3/4 miles: Major Pots, 2:52.60, December 8, 1994
Other: 1 7/8 miles, Barneboro, 3:16.80, December 14, 1996

Course Records, Main Turf
6 furlongs: Wild Zone, 1:07.60, July 7, 1996
6 1/2 furlongs: Always a Rainbow, 1:14.80, June 2, 1996
7 furlongs: Wild Zone, 1:20.20, July 30, 1995
1 mile: Lost Soldier, 1:32.80, July 24, 1996
1 1/16 miles: Jet Freighter, 1:39.20, June 4, 1995; Honolulu Gold, 1:39.20, July 11, 1996; Western Express, 1:39.20, July 12, 1998
1 1/8 miles: Bold Ruritana, 1:45.20, June 18, 1995
1 1/4 miles: Arbalest, 2:01, June 15, 1995; Set Ablaze, 2:01, July 5, 1996
1 3/8 miles: Dawson's Legacy, 2:13.05, September 26, 1999
1 1/2 miles: Raintrap (GB), 2:25.60, October 16, 1994

Course records, Inner turf
5 furlongs: Deputy Regent, :58, July 4, 1982
1 mile: Charlie Barley, 1:34 4/5, May 28, 1989; Myrtle Irene, 1:34.80, September 19, 1993
1 1/16 miles: Overskate, 1:40 4/5, June 3, 1979; Seattle Sangue,

1:40 4/5, June 17, 1990
1 1/4 miles: Mill Native, 2:00, June 26, 1983
1 3/8 miles: Wayover, 2:19 1/5, June 26, 1985
1 1/2 miles: Great Stake, 2:34, July 5, 1985

Interesting facts
Previous name and dates: Ontario Jockey Club 1881-2001
Achievements/milestones: hosted Arlington Million in 1988, hosted Breeders' Cup in 1996

Fastest Times of 2001 (Dirt)
4 1/2 furlongs: Jealous Forum, :52.69, May 5
5 furlongs: Olympian, :56.07, March 31
5 1/2 furlongs: Annie's Creek, 1:04.53, May 9
6 furlongs: Praise From Dixie, 1:09.21, October 13
6 1/2 furlongs: Hopeful Moment, 1:15.85, August 18
7 furlongs: Runaway Love, 1:21.54, December 1
1m 70yds: Steady Ruckus, 1:41.93, June 1
1 1/16 miles: On the Game, 1:43.23, November 18
1 1/8 miles: Mountain Angel, 1:49.71, October 13
1 3/16 miles: Parose, 1:58.05, October 21
1 1/4 miles: Catch the Ring, 2:03.62, November 3
1 1/2 miles: Latin Technology, 2:36.51, October 27
1 3/4 miles: Queensgate, 2:57.37, December 2
Other: 1 7/8 miles, Flying Commander, 3:13.29, December 2

Fastest Times of 2001 (Turf)
6 furlongs: Spring Barley, 1:07.63, September 5
6 1/2 furlongs: Silver Spear, 1:15.16, July 13
7 furlongs: Karra Kul, 1:21.38, June 30
1 mile: Numerous Times, 1:32.79, September 9
1 1/16 miles: Nymphenburg, 1:39.85, August 6
1 1/8 miles: Steady Ruckus, 1:46.78, September 3
1 1/4 miles: Free Vacation, 2:02.21, August 8
1 3/8 miles: Allende, 2:16.98, July 22
1 1/2 miles: Honor Glide, 2:26.52, September 1

Saskatchewan

Marquis Downs

Heartbreak, happiness, and heightened expectations marked racing in the Canadian province of Saskatchewan at the end of Marquis Downs's 2001 meeting.

The venerable Saskatoon institution, which has offered live racing since 1969, endured a significant loss on August 19 when leading rider Isiah Sala died of head injuries following a spill. Jockey Tim Moccasin established a North American record by winning 14 consecutive races in a streak that began on August 24 and carried over to September 1. The 2001 meet ended three weeks later with a 6.4% increase in meet handle.

Marquis Downs, a five-furlong track with a capacity of 4,500, is part of the Saskatoon Prairieland Exhibition, a multipurpose facility that includes meeting and exhibition halls and a casino. Racing annually takes place from May through September.

Location: 2326 Herman Ave., Saskatoon, SK S7K 4E4
Phone: (306) 242-6100
Fax: (306) 242-6907
Seating capacity: 4,500

Officers
President: Joe Bloski
General Manager: Mark Regier

Racing dates
2001: May 5-September 22, 42 days
2002: May 18-September 21

Track Layout
Main circumference: 5 furlongs
Main length of stretch: 660 feet

Handle
Average on-track recent meeting: $15,432, 2001
Total on-track recent meeting: $648,147, 2001

Leaders
Recent meeting, leading jockey: Isiah Sala, 53, 2001
Recent meeting, leading trainer: Tom Gardipy Jr., 33, 2001

Interesting facts
Trivia: Jockey Tim Moccasin rode 14 consecutive winners August 24 through September 1, 2001, believed to be a North American record

Fastest Times of 2001
4 furlongs: Star of the Show, :46.75, May 12, Sundowncindy, :46.75, May 19
6 furlongs: Star of the Show, 1:12.43, June 2
6 1/2 furlongs: Britts Xpress, 1:23.15, August 19
1 mile: Beau Ring, 1:37.33, September 3
1 1/16 miles: Beau Ring, 1:44.10, September 15
1 1/8 miles: Beau Ring, 1:52, August 18

Puerto Rico

El Comandante

El Comandante is all but synonymous with Bold Forbes and Mister Frisky, the two best-known horses to race at the Puerto Rico track. A dual-classic winner and 1976 champion three-year-old in the United States, Bold Forbes began his career at El Comandante. So did Mister Frisky, who started his unbeaten string there in 1989 before coming to the United States and going off as the favorite in the 1990 Kentucky Derby (G1), in which he finished eighth.

Located in Canovanas, El Comandante has been the island's racing outlet for many decades, and in recent years it has added a sophisticated network of off-track wagering outlets and a daily television racing report.

The track, owned by holding company El Comandante Credit Corp., has encountered financial problems, however. In early 2002, the corporation, whose parent company is Equus Gaming Co., announced it was in default on its mortgage notes for the third time in a year. The company made payments on the notes during the default period.

Location: P.O. Box 1675, Canovanas, PR 00729
Phone: (787) 641-6060
Fax: (787) 876-5170
E-mail: ecmc@comandantepr.com
Web site: http://www.comandantepr.com
Acreage: 257
Number of stalls: 1,500+

Officers
President: Juan M. Rivera
Vice President/General Manager: Alejandro Fuentes
Director of Operations: Richard C. Voorhies
Director of Marketing: Jessica Salgado
Director of Finance: Stanley J. Pinkerton

Racing dates
2001: January 1-December 31, 260 days
2002: January 1-December 31

Track Layout
Main circumference: 1 mile
Main track chute: 7 furlongs

North American Racetracks:

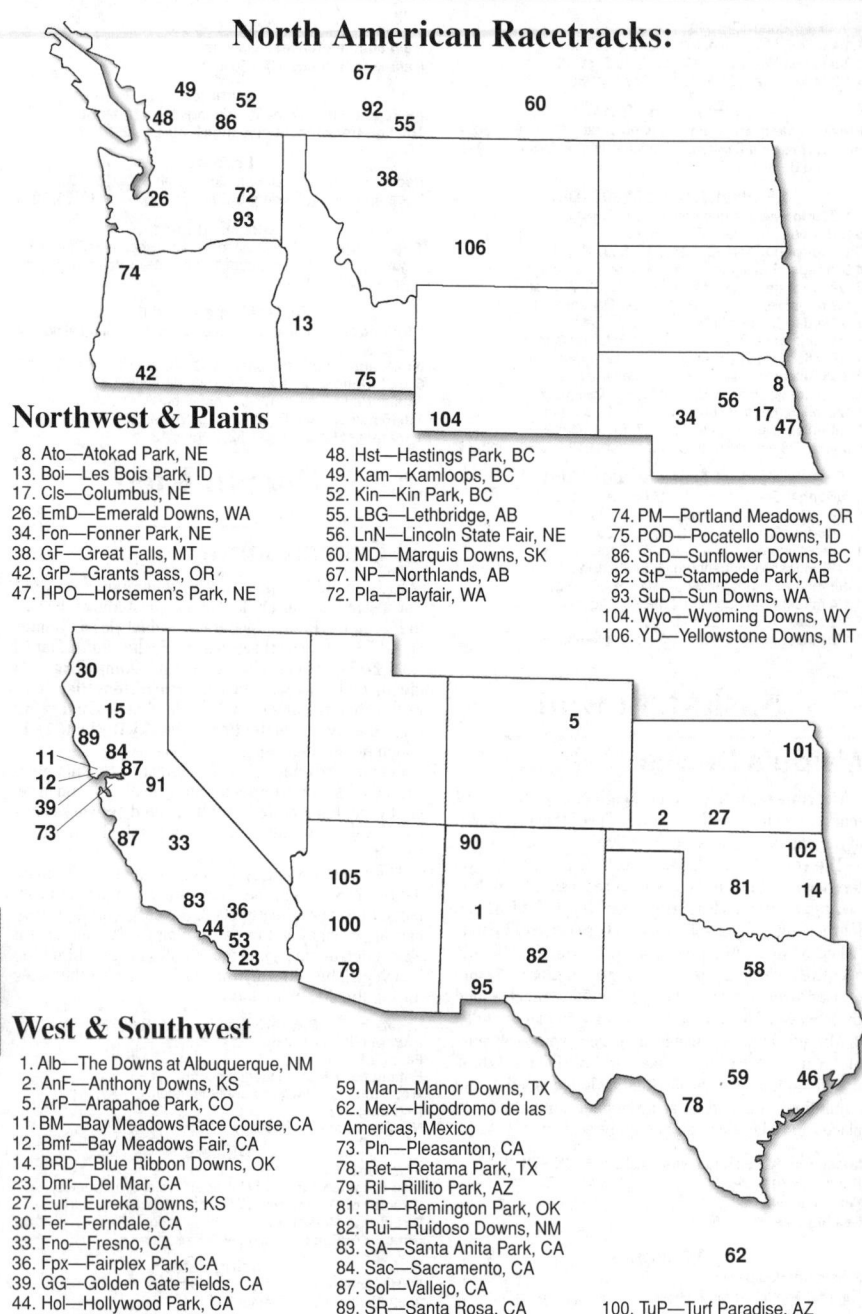

Northwest & Plains

8. Ato—Atokad Park, NE
13. Boi—Les Bois Park, ID
17. Cls—Columbus, NE
26. EmD—Emerald Downs, WA
34. Fon—Fonner Park, NE
38. GF—Great Falls, MT
42. GrP—Grants Pass, OR
47. HPO—Horsemen's Park, NE

48. Hst—Hastings Park, BC
49. Kam—Kamloops, BC
52. Kin—Kin Park, BC
55. LBG—Lethbridge, AB
56. LnN—Lincoln State Fair, NE
60. MD—Marquis Downs, SK
67. NP—Northlands, AB
72. Pla—Playfair, WA

74. PM—Portland Meadows, OR
75. POD—Pocatello Downs, ID
86. SnD—Sunflower Downs, BC
92. StP—Stampede Park, AB
93. SuD—Sun Downs, WA
104. Wyo—Wyoming Downs, WY
106. YD—Yellowstone Downs, MT

West & Southwest

1. Alb—The Downs at Albuquerque, NM
2. AnF—Anthony Downs, KS
5. ArP—Arapahoe Park, CO
11. BM—Bay Meadows Race Course, CA
12. Bmf—Bay Meadows Fair, CA
14. BRD—Blue Ribbon Downs, OK
23. Dmr—Del Mar, CA
27. Eur—Eureka Downs, KS
30. Fer—Ferndale, CA
33. Fno—Fresno, CA
36. Fpx—Fairplex Park, CA
39. GG—Golden Gate Fields, CA
44. Hol—Hollywood Park, CA
46. Hou—Sam Houston, TX
53. LA—Los Alamitos, CA
58. LS—Lone Star Park, TX

59. Man—Manor Downs, TX
62. Mex—Hipodromo de las Americas, Mexico
73. Pln—Pleasanton, CA
78. Ret—Retama Park, TX
79. Ril—Rillito Park, AZ
81. RP—Remington Park, OK
82. Rui—Ruidoso Downs, NM
83. SA—Santa Anita Park, CA
84. Sac—Sacramento, CA
87. Sol—Vallejo, CA
89. SR—Santa Rosa, CA
90. SRP—SunRay Park, NM
91. Stk—Stockton, CA
95. Sun—Sunland Park, NM

100. TuP—Turf Paradise, AZ
101. Wds—The Woodlands, KS
102. WRD—Will Rogers Downs, OK
105. YAV—Yavapai Downs, AZ

Abbreviations and Locations

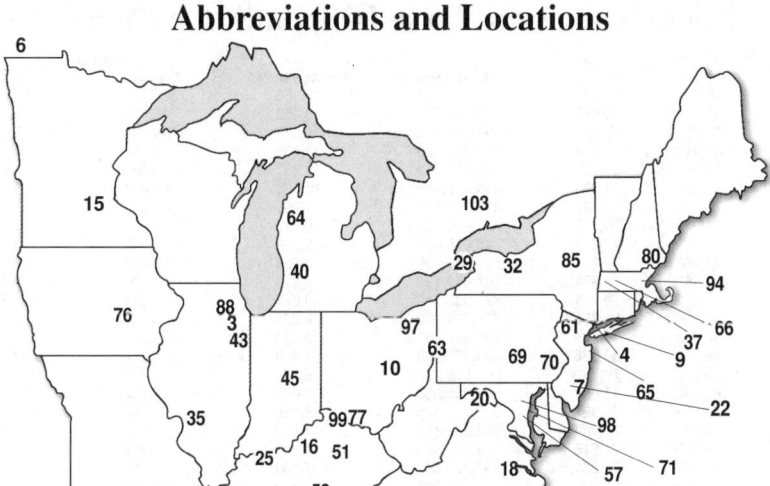

Northeast & Midwest

3. AP—Arlington Park, IL
4. Aqu—Aqueduct, NY
6. AsD—Assiniboia Downs, MB
7. Atl—Atlantic City Race Course, NJ
9. Bel—Belmont Park, NY
10. Beu—Beulah Park, OH
15. Cby—Canterbury Park, MN
16. CD—Churchill Downs, KY
18. Cnl—Colonial Downs, VA
20. CT—Charles Town, WV
22. Del—Delaware Park, DE
25. ElP—Ellis Park, KY
29. FE—Fort Erie, ON
32. FL—Finger Lakes, NY
35. FP—Fairmount Park, IL
37. GBF—Great Barrington, MA
40. GLD—Great Lakes Downs, MI
43. Haw—Hawthorne Race Course, IL
45. Hoo—Hoosier Park, IN
50. KD—Kentucky Downs, KY

51. Kee—Keeneland, KY
57. Lrl—Laurel Park, MD
61. Med—The Meadowlands, NJ
63. Mnr—Mountaineer Park, WV
64. MPM—Mt. Pleasant Meadows, MI
65. Mth—Monmouth Park, NJ
66. Nmp—Northampton Fair, MA
69. Pen—Penn National Race Course, PA
70. Pha—Philadelphia Park, PA
71. Pim—Pimlico, MD
76. PrM—Prairie Meadows, IA
77. RD—River Downs, OH
80. Rkm—Rockingham Park, NH
85. Sar—Saratoga Race Course, NY
88. Spt—Sportsman's Park, IL
94. Suf—Suffolk Downs, MA
97. Tdn—Thistledown, OH
98. Tim—Timonium, MD
99. TP—Turfway Park, KY
103. WO—Woodbine, ON

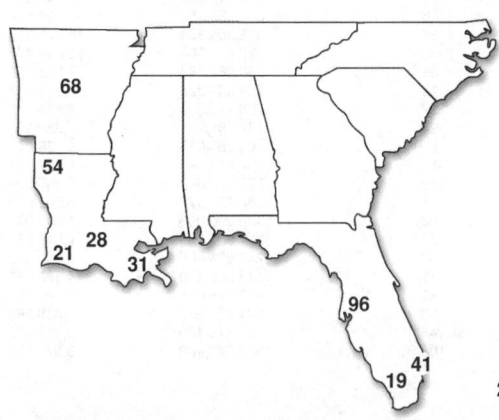

Southeast

19. Crc—Calder Race Course, FL
21. DeD—Delta Downs, LA
24. ElC—El Comandante, PR
28. EvD—Evangeline Downs, LA
31. FG—Fair Grounds, LA
41. GP—Gulfstream Park, FL
54. LaD—Louisiana Downs, LA
68. OP—Oaklawn Park, AK
96. Tam—Tampa Bay Downs, FL

North American Purse Distribution by Year

Year	No. of runners	No. of races	Total purses	Average purse	Per Runner Average	Median
2001	70,942	60,538	$1,146,337,367	$18,936	$16,159	$6,010
2000	69,230	60,579	1,093,661,241	18,053	15,798	5,796
1999	68,435	60,118	1,008,162,608	16,770	14,732	5,310
1998	68,419	61,141	968,366,929	15,838	14,153	4,939
1997	69,067	63,491	888,667,752	13,997	12,867	4,425
1996	70,371	64,263	845,916,706	13,163	12,021	3,937
1995	72,316	68,197	815,987,125	11,965	11,283	3,702
1994	74,939	70,617	770,426,193	10,910	10,280	3,314
1993	78,763	72,224	748,415,925	10,362	9,502	2,850
1992	83,468	77,711	771,136,296	9,989	9,238	2,731
1991	86,483	78,671	761,446,198	9,679	8,805	2,433
1990	89,722	79,971	775,006,519	9,691	8,637	2,376
1989	91,436	82,726	771,421,230	9,325	8,437	2,218
1988	90,482	79,589	736,698,230	9,256	8,142	2,127
1987	89,504	80,376	704,372,435	8,763	7,870	2,101
1986	86,022	77,732	661,826,092	8,514	7,694	2,070
1985	82,548	75,687	641,658,553	8,478	7,773	2,158
1984	78,253	74,396	599,348,425	8,056	7,659	2,345
1983	74,540	71,034	544,260,167	7,662	7,302	2,435
1982	69,505	71,515	526,587,096	7,363	7,576	2,703
1981	65,797	70,881	507,007,953	7,153	7,706	2,865
1980	64,499	68,236	449,631,322	6,589	6,971	2,524
1979	63,728	69,406	414,629,063	5,974	6,506	2,440
1978	62,937	69,498	367,163,242	5,283	5,834	n/a
1977	61,960	68,826	335,720,312	4,878	5,418	2,189
1976	61,084	69,480	318,680,094	4,587	5,217	2,100
1975	58,818	68,203	291,194,571	4,270	4,951	2,058
1974	56,524	65,288	262,942,547	4,027	4,652	1,904
1973	54,812	62,264	233,662,724	3,753	4,263	1,764
1972	52,561	59,417	210,435,265	3,542	4,004	1,647

Data reflect all Thoroughbred purses distributed to racehorses in North America, excluding Mexico and Puerto Rico, from Jockey Club Information Systems data. Steeplechase races are excluded.

Top 25 North American Tracks by Average Handle in 2001

Track	No. of Racing Days	Total Handle	Average Handle
Saratoga Race Course	36	$553,620,155	$15,378,338
Belmont Park (Fall)	37	429,131,994	13,410,375
Del Mar	43	†518,400,000	†12,055,268
Santa Anita Park	83	921,414,831	11,101,384
Belmont Park (Spring)	55	607,864,143	11,052,075
Gulfstream Park	63	670,448,898	10,642,046
Hollywood Park (Spring/Summer)	66	669,139,152	10,138,472
Oak Tree at Santa Anita	32	323,560,604	10,111,519
Churchill Downs (Spring)	53	522,416,506	10,046,471
Hollywood Park (Fall)	31	290,880,783	9,383,251
Keeneland Race Course (Spring)	15	129,387,326	8,625,822
Aqueduct	137	768,125,565	8,534,729
Churchill Downs (Fall)	24	174,781,741	7,282,573
Fairplex Park	17	104,203,615	6,129,624
Tropical Park at Calder	52	300,961,190	5,787,715
Calder Race Course	119	631,641,042	5,307,907
Keeneland Race Course (Fall)	17	88,434,474	5,202,028
Fair Grounds	88	†430,200,000	†4,800,000
Monmouth Park	72	334,667,000	4,648,153
Oaklawn Park	52	240,895,656	4,632,609
Pimlico (Spring/Summer)	77	†343,500,000	†4,580,188
Hialeah Park	61	262,116,875	4,296,998
Turfway Park (Winter/Spring)	83	234,200,955	3,839,360
Hawthorne Race Course (Fall)	45	167,376,420	3,719,476
Arlington Park	103	360,622,482	3,570,520

†Estimated handle

Top 25 Tracks by Average Attendance in 2001

Track	No. of Racing Days	Total Attendance	Average Attendance
Saratoga Race Course	36	1,011,669	28,102
Del Mar	43	664,594	15,456
Keeneland Race Course (Spring)	15	219,739	14,649
Churchill Downs (Spring)	53	708,181	13,619
Keeneland Race Course (Fall)	17	208,143	12,244
Oaklawn Park	52	585,051	11,251
Monmouth Park	72	774,500	10,757
Oak Tree at Santa Anita	32	337,024	10,532
Santa Anita Park	83	870,338	10,486
Gulfstream Park	63	647,732	10,281
Prairie Meadows (Spring/Summer)	53	489,105	9,228
Lone Star Park	74	658,032	8,892
Prairie Meadows (Fall)	45	382,975	8,704
Churchill Downs (Fall)	24	203,858	8,494
Hollywood Park (Spring/Summer)	66	550,770	8,345
Belmont Park (Spring)	55	441,392	8,025
Belmont Park (Fall)	37	243,769	7,618
Hollywood Park (Fall)	31	223,620	7,214
Fairplex Park	17	†121,497	†6,750
Arlington Park	103	594,921	5,890
Tropical Park at Calder	52	262,918	5,056
Calder Race Course	119	591,039	4,967
The Meadowlands	49	239,463	4,887
Aqueduct	137	429,293	4,770
Timonium	8	34,669	4,334

†Estimated attendance

Pari-Mutuel Takeout by State

Pari-mutuel takeout is the amount deducted from wagers before odds are calculated and payments are made to winning bettors. The money taken out from the wagers goes to state taxes, horsemen as purses, the racetrack operators, breed enhancement funds, and other funds. At most tracks, after the state and special allotments are deducted, the track and horsemen split the remainder equally.

ARIZONA—Up to 25% on win-place-show wagers; up to 30% on two-horse wagers; up to 35% on multiple-horse wagers.

ARKANSAS—17% on win-place-show wagers; 21% on multiple wagers.

CALIFORNIA—15.43% on win-place-show wagers; 20.18% on exotic wagers.

COLORADO—18.5% on win-place-show wagers; 25% on exotic wagers.

DELAWARE—17% on win-place-show wagers; 19% on daily doubles and exactas; 27% on all other exotic wagers.

FLORIDA—Individual tracks determine takeout rate.

IDAHO—20% on win-place-show wagers; 20.75% on exotic wagers.

ILLINOIS—17% on total handle; 20.5% on two-horse wagers; 25% on wagers involving three or more horses.

INDIANA—18% on win-place-show wagers; 21.5% on exotic wagers.

IOWA—Up to 18% on win-place-show wagers; up to 24% on two-horse wagers; up to 25% on all other wagers.

KANSAS—18% on win-place-show wagers; up to 22% on multiple wagers.

KENTUCKY—At tracks above $1,200,000 daily average: 16% on win-place-show wagers; 19% on exotic wagers. At tracks below $1,200,000 daily average: 17.5% on win-place-show wagers; 19% on exotic wagers.

LOUISIANA—17% on win-place-show wagers; 20.5% on two-horse wagers; 25% on three-horse wagers.

MARYLAND—17% on win-place-show wagers; 19% on two-horse multiple wagers; 25% on three-horse multiple wagers.

MASSACHUSETTS—19% on win-place-show wagers; 26% on exotic wagers (19% at fairs).

MICHIGAN—17% on win-place-show wagers; 20.5% on multiples; 25% on "special sweepstakes."

MINNESOTA—Up to 17% on win-place-show wagers; 23% on exotic wagers.

MONTANA—20% on win-place-show wagers; up to 26% on exotic wagers.

NEBRASKA—15% to 18% on win-place-show wagers; up to 23% on exotic wagers.

NEW JERSEY—17% on win-place-show wagers; 19% on two-horse wagers; 25% on all other wagers.

NEW HAMPSHIRE—19% on win-place-show wagers; 26% on multiple wagers.

NEW MEXICO—Class A tracks: 19% on win-place-show wagers; 21% to 25% on exotic wagers. Class B tracks: 18.75% to 25% on win-place-show wagers; 21% to 30% on exotic wagers.

NEW YORK—15% on win-place-show wagers; 20% on multiple wagers; 25% on exotics and super exotics.

OHIO—18% on win-place-show wagers; 22.5% on exotic wagers.77

OKLAHOMA—18% on win-place-show wagers; 20% on multiple-horse wagers; 20% on up to three-race wagers (such as Pick Three); 25% on multiple-race wagers (more than three races, such as Pick Six).

OREGON—19% on win-place-show wagers; 22% on multiple wagers. At fairs, up to 22% on all wagers.

PENNSYLVANIA—17% on regular wagering pools; 19% if average daily handle is less than $300,000; 20% on exactas, daily doubles and quinellas; 26% to 35% on trifectas.

SOUTH DAKOTA—4.27% (to special racing funds).

TEXAS—18% on win-place-show wagers; up to 21% on two-horse wagers; up to 25% on three-horse wagers.

VIRGINIA—18% on win-place-show wagers; 22% on all other wagers.

WASHINGTON—16.1% on win-place-show wagers; 22.1% on all other wagers.

WEST VIRGINIA—17.25% on win-place-show wagers; 19% on two-horse wagers; 25% on three horses or more.

WYOMING—20.9% on win-place-show wagers; 25.9% on exotic wagers.

PEOPLE

Leading Owners of 2001

Along with bettors, the primary source of the billions of dollars that make the Thoroughbred industry a living, breathing, wonderful thing is Thoroughbred owners. Owners spend more than $1-billion annually purchasing Thoroughbreds of various descriptions at public auctions and by private contract, thus taking on the privilege and responsibility of paying further untold sums for their training, veterinary care, board, and other expenses. In return, owners in North America get a shot at more than $1-billion annually in purses.

That $1-billion gets divided up among thousands of owners but, in the natural order of things, some do better than others. The following lists rate the accomplishments of owners in 2001 according to various criteria. The annual THOROUGHBRED TIMES leading owners list ranks owners according to four equally weighted criteria: total earnings, average earnings per starter, percent stakes winners from starters, and percent graded

stakes winners from starters. That weighted list purposely favors quality over quantity, rewarding owners with good percentages in the best races.

Other lists included here rank the leading owners of 2001 by each of those criteria individually, as well as by number of wins, giving full credit to quantity as well as quality. It takes both to make a $1-billion game go.

Leading Owners by Purses Won

Year	Name	Wins	Earnings
2001	Richard Englander	406	$9,812,272
2000	Stronach Stable	163	11,198,225
1999	Stronach Stable	124	6,221,147
1998	Stronach Stable	91	7,221,416
1997	Allen Paulson	66	5,259,107
1996	Allen E. Paulson	69	9,086,865
1995	Allen E. Paulson	86	7,232,967
1994	John Franks	193	4,518,088

THOROUGHBRED TIMES Leading Owners of 2001

Rankings based on formula that gives equal weighting to four statistical categories for performance in 2001: 1) total earnings; 2) average earnings per starter; 3) percent stakes winners from starters; and 4) percent graded stakes winners from starters. A minimum of ten starters is required to be considered for inclusion. Statistics are for North America only and for racing in 2001. SWs is stakes winners. GSWs is graded stakes winners.

Rank	Owner	No. strs	No. wnrs	No. SWs	% SWs/ strs	No. GSWs	% GSWs/ strs	Total earnings	Average earnings/ starter	Leading earner	Earnings of leading earner
1	Juddmonte Farms Inc.	32	23	10	31.3%	9	28.1%	$6,806,015	$212,688	Skimming	$1,330,000
2	Amerman Racing Stables	19	10	7	36.8%	7	36.8%	2,885,983	151,894	Lido Palace (Chi)	1,040,000
3	Godolphin Inc.	24	10	5	20.8%	5	20.8%	4,464,084	186,004	Fantastic Light	2,112,800
4	Anstu Stables Inc.	16	10	5	31.3%	3	18.8%	2,192,403	137,025	Balto Star	848,820
5	John C. Oxley	25	11	4	16.0%	3	12.0%	3,164,339	126,574	Monarchos	1,711,600
6	Sheikh Maktoum bin Rashid al Maktoum	14	9	4	28.6%	2	14.3%	1,884,803	134,629	Irish Prize	737,580
7	Gary A. Tanaka	43	18	13	30.2%	8	18.6%	3,567,920	82,975	Gourmet Girl	554,950
8	Sam-Son Farm	41	23	8	19.5%	5	12.2%	4,055,490	98,914	Dancethruthedawn	1,045,039
9	Michael B. Tabor	18	10	4	22.2%	4	22.2%	1,914,019	106,334	Left Bank	524,200
10	Edmund A. Gann	15	7	3	20.0%	3	20.0%	1,835,084	122,339	Timboroa (GB)	944,880
11	Allen E. Paulson Living Trust	20	14	4	20.0%	4	20.0%	2,039,991	102,000	Hap	666,270
12	Ogden Phipps	14	11	4	28.6%	4	28.6%	1,326,470	94,748	Traditionally	420,020
13	Roger J. Devenport	10	4	1	10.0%	1	10.0%	1,784,004	178,400	Unbridled Elaine	1,663,175
14	The Thoroughbred Corp.	87	37	8	9.2%	7	8.1%	8,000,763	91,963	Point Given	3,350,000
15	New Farm	16	13	3	18.8%	2	12.5%	1,494,769	93,423	Delaware Township	635,840
16	Augustin Stables	56	25	9	16.1%	5	8.9%	3,083,544	55,063	With Anticipation	802,393
17	Janis R. Whitham	12	5	2	16.7%	2	16.7%	1,060,887	88,407	Affluent	725,200
18	Stonerside Stable	41	19	5	12.2%	4	9.8%	2,464,171	60,102	Congaree	1,063,400
19	James Cassels and Bob Zollars	11	10	2	18.2%	1	9.1%	1,004,949	91,359	Fifty Stars	552,250
20	Tracy Farmer	21	7	1	4.8%	1	4.8%	2,099,635	99,983	Albert the Great	1,740,000
21	Michael Tabor and Sue Magnier	10	1	1	10.0%	1	10.0%	1,030,097	103,010	Johannesburg	520,000
22	Centaur Farms Inc.	28	18	4	14.3%	1	3.6%	1,874,006	66,929	Exogenous	901,500
23	Select Stable	13	7	2	15.4%	2	15.4%	990,546	76,196	Repent	415,660
24	Pin Oak Stable	47	34	8	17.0%	3	6.4%	2,353,451	50,073	Broken Vow	611,596
25	Raymond Dweck	20	12	5	25.0%	1	5.0%	1,229,827	61,491	Richly Blended	323,280
26	John Rotella	14	9	2	14.3%	1	7.1%	1,057,215	75,515	Say Florida Sandy	615,420
27	Edward P. Evans	56	27	9	16.1%	5	8.9%	2,678,518	47,831	Perfect Cat	335,893
28	Robert E. Meyerhoff	29	18	2	6.9%	1	3.5%	2,152,035	74,208	Include	1,435,400
29	Ackerley Brothers Farm	16	9	2	12.5%	1	6.3%	1,113,033	69,565	Miss Linda (Arg)	455,415

Rank	Owner	No. strs	No. wnrs	No. SWs	% SWs/ strs	No. GSWs	% GSWs/ strs	Total earnings	Average earnings/ starter	Leading earner	Earnings of leading earner
30	David and Jill Heerensperger	16	11	1	6.3%	1	6.3%	1,340,749	83,797	Millennium Wind	679,620
31	Henry E. Pabst	12	4	2	16.7%	2	16.7%	858,961	71,580	Keats	277,248
32	Mr. and Mrs. Jerome S. Moss	33	19	5	15.2%	3	9.1%	1,648,012	49,940	Kudos	221,880
33	Bohemia Stable	11	6	1	9.1%	1	9.1%	900,784	81,889	Shine Again	469,750
34	Cam Allard	18	12	2	11.1%	1	5.6%	1,106,923	61,496	A Fleets Dancer	427,487
35	Richard, Bertram, & Elaine Klein	28	12	4	14.3%	3	10.7%	1,361,385	48,621	Outofthebox	607,995
36	Michael E. Pegram	27	17	3	11.1%	1	3.7%	1,434,588	53,133	Captain Steve	601,200
37	Red Baron's Barn	30	13	2	6.7%	1	3.3%	1,689,016	56,301	Janet (GB)	698,580
38	Gary L. and Mary E. West	38	19	3	7.9%	2	5.3%	1,866,566	49,120	Dollar Bill	415,000
39	Fog City Stable	14	8	2	14.3%	2	14.3%	782,660	55,904	Blueprint (Ire)	318,000
40	WinStar Farm	30	14	6	20.0%	2	6.7%	1,317,348	43,912	License Fee	382,560
41	James F. Edwards	14	8	3	21.4%		0.0%	862,152	61,582	Personal Pro	217,184
42	Shadwell Stable	33	15	2	6.1%	2	6.1%	1,593,698	48,294	Mutamam (GB)	900,000
43	Kinsman Stable	29	13	3	10.3%	2	6.9%	1,268,524	43,742	Dream Supreme	541,120
44	Dominion Bloodstock, D. Ball, and H. Galbraith	17	9	2	11.8%	2	11.8%	839,335	49,373	Lady Shari	236,210
45	Eugene and Laura Melnyk	66	32	5	7.6%	2	3.0%	2,744,076	41,577	Tweedside	347,036
46	Claiborne Farm	24	13	3	12.5%	2	8.3%	1,048,738	43,697	Trip	345,855
47	Jayeff B Stables	42	28	4	9.5%	2	4.8%	1,722,273	41,007	Navesink	368,206
48	Frank DiGiulio Jr.	17	8	1	5.9%	1	5.9%	900,284	52,958	Press Exclusive	187,164
49	Herbert and Carol Schwartz	20	9	2	10.0%	1	5.0%	954,472	47,724	Critical Eye	339,736
50	Gatsas Thoroughbreds	13	6	1	7.7%	1	7.7%	749,710	57,670	Gander	557,060
51	Arthur I. Appleton	35	16	3	8.6%	2	5.7%	1,416,443	40,470	Forbidden Apple	622,500
52	Stronach Stable	168	77	11	6.6%	6	3.6%	6,537,681	38,915	Macho Uno	563,400
53	VHW Stables Inc.	18	9	2	11.1%	2	11.1%	832,955	46,275	Fleet Renee	387,735
54	Jam Jar Racing Stable	11	6	2	18.2%		0.0%	704,447	64,041	Shaws Creek	155,748
55	Centennial Farms	19	8	1	5.3%	1	5.3%	944,038	49,686	King Cugat	555,980
56	Sondra D. Bender	24	14	5	20.8%		0.0%	995,473	41,478	La Reine's Terms	133,950
57	James B. Tafel	24	11	3	12.5%	2	8.3%	935,489	38,979	Scoop	288,270
58	McKee Stables Inc.	27	15	2	7.4%		0.0%	1,144,227	42,379	Sitka	195,382
59	Robert B. and Beverly J. Lewis	37	15	3	8.1%		0.0%	1,459,120	39,436	Orientate	293,700
60	Albert Fried Jr.	10	6	1	10.0%	1	10.0%	564,140	56,414	Affirmed Success	343,215
61	Chester and Mary Broman Sr.	29	16	2	6.9%	1	3.5%	1,121,017	38,656	Hook and Ladder	256,100
62	Fox Ridge Farm Inc.	14	6	2	14.3%	1	7.1%	643,379	45,956	Cozzy Corner	202,899
63	Team Block	17	11	2	11.8%	1	5.9%	705,437	41,496	Ioya Two	234,328
64	Overbrook Farm	68	32	5	7.4%	4	5.9%	2,253,477	33,139	Penny's Gold	316,388
65	Eaglestone Farm	19	7	2	10.5%	1	5.3%	754,079	39,688	Alannan	317,955
66	Tom R. Durant	49	9	4	8.2%	1	2.0%	1,693,773	34,567	Touch Tone	607,850
67	Triple AAA Ranch	22	12	6	27.3%	1	4.6%	793,846	36,084	Top Hit	266,632
68	George Krikorian	17	7	1	5.9%	1	5.9%	730,396	42,964	Starrer	406,265
69	Mr. and Mrs. Martin J. Wygod	49	21	2	4.1%	1	2.0%	1,734,216	35,392	Tranquility Lake	568,730
70	C. T. Grether Inc.	13	7	1	7.7%	1	7.7%	613,601	47,200	Crafty C. T.	309,770
71	Fox Hill Farms Inc.	22	12	2	9.1%	1	4.6%	821,508	37,341	Zonk	271,200
72	Desperado Stables Inc.	12	8	2	16.7%		0.0%	575,024	47,919	Freespool	187,978
73	Joseph V. Shields Jr.	12	7	1	8.3%		0.0%	596,945	49,745	Shooting Party	214,146
74	G. Watts & Louise Humphrey Jr.	12	4	1	8.3%	1	8.3%	559,240	46,603	Victory Ride	247,025
75	Theresa McArthur	29	15	1	3.5%	1	3.5%	1,042,555	35,950	Western Pride	680,244
76	Richard E. Trebat	17	10	1	5.9%	1	5.9%	672,643	39,567	Chicago Six	376,108
77	Nickolas DeToro	17	7		0.0%		0.0%	759,084	44,652	Wager's Joy	138,846
78	William J. Condren	18	14	1	5.6%		0.0%	707,726	39,318	Regal Shivers	119,770
79	Rudlein Stable and William L. Clifton Jr.	11	8	1	9.1%		0.0%	531,483	48,317	Wake Up Kiss	117,340
80	William Sorokolit	15	10	1	6.7%	1	6.7%	598,122	39,875	Prized Stamp	205,978
81	Briardale Stable	14	10		0.0%		0.0%	665,883	47,563	Notforloveormoney	114,140
82	John William Hillier	16	8	1	6.3%		0.0%	646,438	40,402	Casino Prince	125,272
83	K. K. and V. D. Jayaraman	34	24	4	11.8%		0.0%	1,066,502	31,368	Royal Spy	323,095
84	S J B Jr. Stable	25	14	3	12.0%		0.0%	835,999	33,440	Ivy's Jewel	158,780
85	Thunderhead Farms	11	5	2	18.2%		0.0%	490,560	44,596	Rodeo Fan	140,370
86	Ol Memorial Stable	12	5		0.0%		0.0%	601,719	50,143	A P Valentine	296,000
87	Samantha, Mace, & Jan Siegel	49	26	2	4.1%	1	2.0%	1,536,041	31,348	Here's Zealous	186,240
88	Heiligbrodt Racing Stable	46	31	6	13.0%	1	2.2%	1,345,586	29,252	Latour	205,425
89	Philip and Marcia Cohen and Steve Klesaris	26	14	1	3.9%		0.0%	888,296	34,165	Booklet	339,700
90	Richard L. Duchossois	14	5	1	7.1%	1	7.1%	545,464	38,962	Innit (Ire)	185,772
91	Norseman Racing Stable	10	6	1	10.0%		0.0%	471,627	47,163	Madame Red	210,350
92	Glen C. Warren	15	9	1	6.7%		0.0%	590,680	39,379	Candid Glen	279,400
93	Trudy McCaffery & John Toffan	28	12	2	7.1%	1	3.6%	866,308	30,940	Came Home	211,440
94	Molinaro Stable	15	6	2	13.3%		0.0%	563,054	37,537	Platel	163,246
95	Theodore F. Burnett	14	8	2	14.3%		0.0%	539,811	38,558	Parisia	115,335

Leading Owners by Earnings in 2001

Owner	No. strs	No. wnrs	Total earnings
Richard A. Englander	360	219	$9,784,822
The Thoroughbred Corp.	87	37	8,000,763
Juddmonte Farms Inc.	32	23	6,806,015
Stronach Stable	168	77	6,537,681
Godolphin Inc.	24	10	4,464,084
Sam-Son Farm	41	23	4,055,490
John Franks	193	84	3,605,752
Gary A. Tanaka	43	18	3,567,920
John C. Oxley	25	11	3,164,339
Augustin Stables	56	25	3,083,544
Amerman Racing Stables	19	10	2,885,983
Bruno Schickedanz	176	92	2,871,749
Michael J. Gill	190	94	2,835,568
Eugene and Laura Melnyk	66	32	2,744,076
Dale Baird	260	122	2,715,933
Edward P. Evans	56	27	2,678,518
Stonerside Stable	41	19	2,464,171
Pin Oak Stable	47	34	2,353,451
Overbrook Farm	68	32	2,253,477
Golden Eagle Farm	114	42	2,213,230
Anstu Stables Inc.	16	10	2,192,403
Robert E. Meyerhoff	29	18	2,152,035
Tracy Farmer	21	7	2,099,635
Allen E. Paulson Living Trust	20	14	2,039,991
Kenneth & Sarah Ramsey	93	47	1,915,608
Michael B. Tabor	18	10	1,914,019
Sheikh Maktoum bin Rashid al Maktoum	14	9	1,884,803
Centaur Farms Inc.	28	18	1,874,006
Gary and Mary West	38	19	1,866,566
Edmund A. Gann	15	7	1,835,084
Mockingbird Farm Inc.	71	27	1,812,845
Roger J. Devenport	10	4	1,784,004
Mr. and Mrs. Martin J. Wygod	49	21	1,734,216
Rosendo G. Parra	128	53	1,723,182
Jayeff B Stables	42	28	1,722,273

Leading Owners by Average Earnings per Starter in 2001

Ten or more starters in 2001

Owner	No. strs	No. wnrs	Average earnings per starter
Juddmonte Farms Inc.	32	23	$212,688
Godolphin Inc.	24	10	186,004
Roger J. Devenport	10	4	178,400
Amerman Racing Stables	19	10	151,894
Anstu Stables Inc.	16	10	137,025
Sheikh Maktoum bin Rashid al Maktoum	14	9	134,629
John C. Oxley	25	11	126,574
Edmund A. Gann	15	7	122,339
Michael B. Tabor	18	10	106,334
Michael Tabor and Sue Magnier	10	1	103,010
Allen E. Paulson Living Trust	20	14	102,000
Tracy Farmer	21	7	99,983
Sam-Son Farm	41	23	98,914
Ogden Phipps	14	11	94,748
New Farm	16	13	93,423
The Thoroughbred Corp.	87	37	91,963
James Cassels & Bob Zollars	11	10	91,359
Janis R. Whitham	12	5	88,407
David & Jill Heerensperger	16	11	83,797

Owner	No. strs	No. wnrs	Total earnings
Gary A. Tanaka	43	18	82,975
Bohemia Stable	11	6	81,889
Select Stable	13	7	76,196
John Rotella	14	9	75,515
Robert E. Meyerhoff	29	18	74,208
Henry E. Pabst	12	4	71,580
Ackerley Brothers Farm	16	9	69,565
Centaur Farms Inc.	28	18	66,929
Jam Jar Racing Stable	11	6	64,041
James F. Edwards	14	8	61,582
Cam Allard	18	12	61,496
Raymond Dweck	20	12	61,491
Stonerside Stable	41	19	60,102
Gatsas Thoroughbreds	13	6	57,670
Albert Fried Jr.	10	6	56,414
Red Baron's Barn	30	13	56,301
Fog City Stable	14	8	55,904
Augustin Stables	56	25	55,063

Leading Owners by Number of Stakes Winners in 2001

Owner	No. strs	No. wnrs	No. SWs
Richard A. Englander	360	219	16
Gary A. Tanaka	43	18	13
Stronach Stable	168	77	11
Juddmonte Farms Inc.	32	23	10
Edward P. Evans	56	27	9
Augustin Stables	56	25	9
Sam-Son Farm	41	23	8
Pin Oak Stable	47	34	8
The Thoroughbred Corp.	87	37	8
Amerman Racing Stables	19	10	7
Triple AAA Ranch	22	12	6
M. Y. Stables Inc.	41	26	6
WinStar Farm	30	14	6
Heiligbrodt Racing Stable	46	31	6
Dennis E. Weir	47	31	6
Mr. and Mrs. Jerome S. Moss	33	19	5
Anstu Stables Inc.	16	10	5
Sondra D. Bender	24	14	5
Overbrook Farm	68	32	5
Frank Carl Calabrese	91	52	5
Eugene and Laura Melnyk	66	32	5
Raymond Dweck	20	12	5
Stonerside Stable	41	19	5
Godolphin Inc.	24	10	5
Ogden Phipps	14	11	4
John Franks	193	84	4
Centaur Farms Inc.	28	18	4
Francis C. McDonnell	35	22	4
Lazy Lane Farms Inc.	22	11	4
Kalarikkal and Vilasini Jayaraman	34	24	4
Pyrite Stables	48	27	4
G. Watts Humphrey Jr.	58	22	4
Michael B. Tabor	18	10	4
John C. Oxley	25	11	4
Allen E. Paulson Living Trust	20	14	4
K 5 Stables	23	16	4
Jacks or Better Farm Inc.	25	10	4
Richard, Bertram, and Elaine Klein	28	12	4
Sheikh Maktoum bin Rashid al Maktoum	14	9	4
Tom R. Durant	49	29	4
Jayeff B Stables	42	28	4
Marvin Johnson and Charles Salem	13	7	4

Leading Owners by Percent Stakes Winners from Starters

Ten or more starters in 2001

Owner	No. strs	No. wnrs	No. SWs	% SWs/ str
Amerman Racing Stables	19	10	7	36.8%
Anstu Stables Inc.	16	10	5	31.3%
Juddmonte Farms Inc.	32	23	10	31.3%
Marvin A. Johnson and Charles R. Salem	13	7	4	30.8%
Gary A. Tanaka	43	18	13	30.2%
Shady Bend Thoroughbreds	10	5	3	30.0%
Ogden Phipps	14	11	4	28.6%
Sheikh Maktoum bin Rashid al Maktoum	14	9	4	28.6%
Triple AAA Ranch	22	12	6	27.3%
Bayard Sharp	12	6	3	25.0%
Raymond Dweck	20	12	5	25.0%
Michael B. Tabor	18	10	4	22.2%
James F. Edwards	14	8	3	21.4%
William J. Smith	14	12	3	21.4%
Sondra D. Bender	24	14	5	20.8%
Godolphin Inc.	24	10	5	20.8%
Edmund A. Gann	15	7	3	20.0%
Ione and Herbert J. Elkins	10	6	2	20.0%
I.O.U. Atonn Stable	10	6	2	20.0%
Allen E. Paulson Living Trust	20	14	4	20.0%
WinStar Farm	30	14	6	20.0%
Jonathan Nance and Micheal Stafford	10	6	2	20.0%
Leo Gaspari Racing Stable	10	10	2	20.0%
Hunt Stables Inc.	10	4	2	20.0%
Moyglare Stud Farm Ltd.	10	5	2	20.0%
Sam-Son Farm	41	23	8	19.5%
New Farm	16	13	3	18.8%
Alter's Racing Stable Inc.	11	6	2	18.2%
Lazy Lane Farms Inc.	22	11	4	18.2%
Thunderhead Farms	11	5	2	18.2%
Robert A. Canning	11	3	2	18.2%
James H. Stone	11	5	2	18.2%
James Cassels & Bob Zollars	11	10	2	18.2%
Jam Jar Racing Stable	11	6	2	18.2%
John P. Bridwell	11	6	2	18.2%
Robert E. Masterson	11	6	2	18.2%
Darwin Olson	11	3	2	18.2%

Leading Owners by Number of Graded Stakes Winners in 2001

Owner	No. strs	No. wnrs	No. GSWs	% GSWs/ str
Juddmonte Farms Inc.	32	23	9	28.1%
Gary A. Tanaka	43	18	8	18.6%
Amerman Racing Stables	19	10	7	36.8%
The Thoroughbred Corp.	87	37	7	8.1%
Stronach Stable	168	77	6	3.6%
Edward P. Evans	56	27	5	8.9%
Augustin Stables	56	25	5	8.9%
Sam-Son Farm	41	23	5	12.2%
Godolphin Inc.	24	10	5	20.8%
Ogden Phipps	14	11	4	28.6%
Overbrook Farm	68	32	4	5.9%
Michael B. Tabor	18	10	4	22.2%
Allen Paulson Living Trust	20	14	4	20.0%

Owner	No. strs	No. wnrs	No. SWs	% SWs/ str
Stonerside Stable	41	19	4	9.8%
Edmund A. Gann	15	7	3	20.0%
Mr. & Mrs. Jerome Moss	33	19	3	9.1%
John Franks	193	84	3	1.6%
Anstu Stables Inc.	16	10	3	18.8%
Pin Oak Stable	47	34	3	6.4%
John C. Oxley	25	11	3	12.0%
Richard, Bertram, and Elaine Klein	28	12	3	10.7%

Leading Owners by Number of Wins in 2001

Owner	No. strs	No. wnrs	No. wins
Richard A. Englander	360	219	405
Dale Baird	260	122	193
Louis D. O'Brien	88	69	179
Bruno Schickedanz	176	92	145
Michael J. Gill	190	94	133
Stronach Stable	168	77	127
Mark Yagour Inc.	134	81	127
John Franks	193	84	118
Monarch Stables Inc.	91	58	110
Daniel J. Chen	89	57	108
Gumpster Stable	80	41	82
Rosendo G. Parra	128	53	78
Kenneth and Sarah Ramsey	93	47	74
Frank Carl Calabrese	91	52	73
The Thoroughbred Corp.	87	37	66
Jack L. Boggs	47	30	61
Golden Eagle Farm	114	42	60
M. Y. Stables Inc.	41	26	60
Worcester Stable	105	42	59
Pin Oak Stable	47	34	58
Eugene and Laura Melnyk	66	32	58
Nelson Bunker Hunt	65	32	56
Diamond Oak Stable	46	29	56
Valene Farms	36	24	54
Sunshine Hill Farm	36	24	54
Robert L. Cole Jr.	41	25	54
Florence Gemma Siravo	37	22	53
Ramon O. Gonzalez	56	30	53
Dennis E. Weir	47	31	53
Jayeff B Stables	42	28	52
Home Team Stables	51	29	51
Stevark Stable and S. Chronister	64	30	51
Charles Lawson	29	22	51
Overbrook Farm	68	32	48
Edward P. Evans	56	27	47
Augustin Stables	56	25	47
Kenneth W. Murphy	38	25	47
E and G Stables	50	29	47
Heiligbrodt Racing Stable	46	31	47
Yasou Stable Trust	27	21	46
Flying Zee Stable	54	27	46
Tom R. Durant	49	29	44
Samantha, Mace, and Jan Siegel	49	26	43
Francis C. McDonnell	35	22	42
Kalarikkal and Vilasini Jayaraman	34	24	42
Pyrite Stables	48	27	42
John S. Cole	35	23	42
Runnin Horse Farm Inc.	50	29	41
Juddmonte Farms Inc.	32	23	41
Jesse Mack Robinson	43	24	39

Leading Breeders of 2001

In decades past, the private breeder was king. Top-quality racing depended upon the private breeders who developed outstanding broodmare bands and had the wherewithal to breed those mares to the best stallions. And, despite the post-World War II emergence of a large commercial breeding industry in the United States, the private breeder remains a vitally important force in the Thoroughbred industry today. The significance of those individuals who breed to race is apparent in THOROUGHBRED TIMES's list of leading breeders for 2001. Of the top ten breeders, only two can be regarded as breeding for the commercial market.

Atop the 2001 list is the late Cecilia Straub-Rubens, whose Tiznow won the '00 Breeders' Cup Classic (G1) only a few days before her death from cancer. Horse of the Year in 2000, Tiznow became the first horse ever to score back-to-back victories in the Breeders' Cup Classic when he won the race again in 2001, and

he later was voted '01 champion older male. Straub-Rubens led the 2001 list because the rankings emphasize quality over quantity. The four criteria, which are assigned equal weight to determine the leading breeders, are total earnings, average earnings per starter, percentage of stakes winners from starters, and percentage of graded stakes winners from starters.

Breeding on a much larger scale than Straub-Rubens, the Juddmonte Farms of Khalid Abdullah bred winners of more than $7-million in 2001, and among its 57 starters were ten graded winners. In 2001, the stable of Ogden Phipps, who died in April 2002, maintained its historically high standards, with four graded stakes winners from only 16 starters. Next on the list was the Canadian powerhouse Sam-Son Farm, created by the late Ernie Samuel and now carried on by his children.

Other lists in this section contain the leaders by each criterion, as well as by number of wins.

THOROUGHBRED TIMES Leading Breeders of 2001

Rankings based on formula that gives equal weighting to four statistical categories for performance in 2001: 1) total earnings; 2) average earnings per starter; 3) percent stakes winners from starters; and 4) percent graded stakes winners from starters. A minimum of ten starters is required to be considered for inclusion. Statistics are for North America only and for racing in 2001. SWs is stakes winners. GSWs is graded stakes winners.

Rank	Breeder	No. strs	No. wnrs	No. SWs	% SWs/ strs	No. GSWs	% GSWs/ strs	Total earnings	Average earnings/ starter	Leading earner	Earnings of leading earner
1	Cecilia Straub-Rubens	13	7	3	23.1%	2	15.4%	$3,579,121	$275,317	Tiznow	$2,981,880
2	Juddmonte Farms	57	35	11	19.3%	10	17.5%	7,367,674	129,257	Skimming	1,330,000
3	Phipps Stable	16	15	4	25.0%	4	25.0%	1,460,395	91,275	Traditionally	420,020
4	Sam-Son Farm	39	23	6	15.4%	3	7.7%	3,448,461	88,422	Dancethruthedawn	1,045,039
5	The Thoroughbred Corp.	29	15	2	6.9%	2	6.9%	4,677,966	161,309	Point Given	3,350,000
6	Gainsborough Farm Inc.	32	17	3	9.4%	2	6.3%	3,860,474	120,640	Fantastic Light	2,112,680
7	Woodlynn Farm Inc.	21	10	2	9.5%	1	4.8%	1,894,278	90,204	Guided Tour	1,384,220
8	J. D. Squires	16	7	1	6.3%	1	6.3%	1,999,540	124,971	Monarchos	1,711,600
9	Dr. and Mrs. R. Smiser West and Mr. and Mrs. M. Miller	16	9	3	18.8%	2	12.5%	1,140,851	71,303	Tweedside	347,036
10	Janis R. Whitham	15	8	2	13.3%	2	13.3%	1,100,076	73,338	Affluent	725,200
11	George Strawbridge Jr.	44	19	5	11.4%	3	6.8%	2,246,642	51,060	With Anticipation	802,393
12	Centaur Farm Inc.	16	8	1	6.3%	1	6.3%	1,356,146	84,759	Exogenous	901,500
13	Parrish Hill Farm	25	11	4	16.0%	1	4.0%	1,474,240	58,970	Millennium Wind	679,620
14	Flaxman Holdings Ltd.	17	9	4	23.5%	2	11.8%	1,017,746	59,867	Good Journey	338,300
15	The Aga Khan's Studs	15	8	2	13.3%	2	13.3%	947,053	63,137	Tijiyr (Ire)	460,160
16	Gainsborough Stud Mgmt.	14	7	2	14.3%	2	14.3%	915,153	65,368	Lailani (GB)	450,000
17	Arthur B. Hancock III and Stonerside Ltd.	12	8	2	16.7%	1	8.3%	819,460	68,288	E Dubai	457,600
18	Robert H. Walter Family Trust	12	6	1	8.3%	1	8.3%	891,743	74,312	Lazy Slusan	678,980
19	Herbert T. Schwartz	17	12	2	11.8%	1	5.9%	983,062	57,827	Critical Eye	339,736
20	Robert E. Meyeroff	55	28	4	7.3%	1	1.8%	2,669,486	48,536	Include	1,435,400
21	Summerwind Farm	14	9	2	14.3%	1	7.1%	849,057	60,647	Indygo Shiner	373,466
22	Robert E. and Lawana L. Low	10	7	1	10.0%	1	10.0%	791,544	79,154	Real Cozzy	459,340
23	Jaime S. Carrion, Trustee	20	13	5	25.0%	2	10.0%	952,479	47,624	Krisada	185,700
24	W. S. Kilroy	13	7	1	7.7%		0.0%	1,078,529	82,964	A P Valentine	535,060
25	Shadwell Farm Inc.	22	11	1	4.6%	1	4.6%	1,235,440	56,156	Sakhee	800,000
26	Kinsman Farm	42	24	3	7.1%	3	7.1%	1,808,785	43,066	Dream Supreme	541,120
27	Pin Oak Stud	74	52	7	9.5%	3	4.1%	2,973,767	40,186	Broken Vow	611,596
28	Carolyn T. Groves	11	4	1	9.1%	1	9.1%	767,700	69,791	Fifty Stars	552,250
29	Adena Springs	204	108	16	7.8%	7	3.4%	8,048,549	39,454	Macho Uno	563,400
30	Lazy Lane Stables Inc.	37	23	4	10.8%	1	2.7%	1,535,496	41,500	Navesink	368,206
31	Edward P. Evans	121	68	13	10.7%	6	5.0%	4,494,584	37,145	Perfect Cat	335,893
32	Grousemont Farm	10	8	1	10.0%	1	10.0%	678,982	67,898	Nasty Storm	383,338
33	Mrs. Richard C. duPont	22	15	1	4.6%	1	4.6%	1,075,013	48,864	Shine Again	469,750
34	Sondra and Howard M. Bender	31	20	6	19.4%		0.0%	1,269,124	40,939	La Reine's Terms	133,950

Rank	Breeder	No. strs	No. wnrs	No. SWs	% SWs/ strs	No. GSWs	% GSWs/ strs	Total earnings	Average earnings/ starter	Leading earner	Earnings of leading earner
35	Centaur Farms Inc.	24	18	3	12.5%		0.0%	1,062,776	44,282	Pharmstar	110,400
36	K. K. and V. Devi Jayaraman	20	19	3	15.0%		0.0%	921,741	46,087	Royal Spy	323,095
37	Ronald E. McKee	17	11	2	11.8%		0.0%	852,037	50,120	Red's Honor	172,208
38	Rosemont Farm Inc.	34	27	3	8.8%	1	2.9%	1,325,389	38,982	Habibti	393,000
39	North Central Bloodstock	15	6	1	6.7%	1	6.7%	760,580	50,705	Tranquility Lake	568,730
40	Cherokee Farms Inc.	12	10	1	8.3%	1	8.3%	670,884	55,907	Smok'n Frolic	342,744
41	John Toffan & Trudy McCaffrey	51	24	3	5.9%	2	3.9%	1,876,428	36,793	Bienamado	540,000
42	James B. Tafel	23	14	3	13.0%	2	8.7%	895,604	38,939	Scoop	288,270
43	Albert Fried Jr.	11	6	1	9.1%	1	9.1%	622,298	56,573	Affirmed Success	343,215
44	Michael C. Byrne	36	22	4	11.1%		0.0%	1,393,031	38,695	Devastating	147,652
45	La Quebrada	19	12	1	5.3%	1	5.3%	831,596	43,768	Miss Linda (Arg)	455,415
46	Beclawat Stable	15	10	2	13.3%		0.0%	743,222	49,548	Miss Noire	201,711
47	CBF Corporation	28	18	3	10.7%		0.0%	1,090,679	38,953	Personal Pro	217,184
48	Gainesway Thoroughbreds Ltd.	38	20	4	10.5%	2	5.3%	1,278,140	33,635	Orientate	293,700
49	Knob Hill Stable	37	24	2	5.4%		0.0%	1,411,945	38,161	Nymphenburg	261,350
50	Jan, Mace, & Samantha Siegel	20	14	2	10.0%	1	5.0%	783,165	39,158	Here's Zealous	186,240
51	Kinghaven Farms Ltd.	41	28	3	7.3%		0.0%	1,485,782	36,239	Poetically	196,395
52	Ocala Stud Farms	65	37	3	4.6%	1	1.5%	2,323,898	35,752	Outofthebox	607,995
53	Elmendorf Farm Inc.	10	7	1	10.0%	1	10.0%	528,060	52,806	Key Lory	205,500
54	Hermitage Farm, David Jones, and R. G. Smith Partnership	14	9	1	7.1%	1	7.1%	637,595	45,543	Until Sundown	276,600
55	Stonerside Ltd.	62	41	2	3.2%	1	1.6%	2,248,129	36,260	Congaree	1,063,400
56	Verne H. Winchell	48	30	2	4.2%	2	4.2%	1,624,153	33,837	Fleet Renee	624,485
57	Jacks or Better Farm Inc.	33	21	6	18.2%	1	3.0%	1,080,428	32,740	Handsome Hunk	137,634
58	Cardiff Farm Managment Corp.	10	7	3	30.0%		0.0%	538,990	53,899	Spinelessjellyfish	201,556
59	Willmott Stable	12	11	1	8.3%	1	8.3%	560,944	46,745	Williams News	157,610
60	Marshall Naify Revocable Trust	30	18	6	20.0%	1	3.3%	983,049	32,768	Collect Call	338,820
61	Lucy G. Bassett	17	12	1	5.9%	1	5.9%	681,231	40,072	Buster's Daydream	199,625
62	Hill 'N' Dale Farms	18	10	2	11.1%		0.0%	728,324	40,462	Steady Ruckus	208,987
63	Pedigree Farms Inc.	10	5	1	10.0%	1	10.0%	490,081	49,008	License Fee	382,560
64	Marshall Naify	17	9	1	5.9%	1	5.9%	677,263	39,839	Hook and Ladder	256,100
65	William Sorokolit	25	19	2	8.0%	1	4.0%	859,163	34,367	Prized Stamp	205,978
66	Minshall Farms, Div. of Fiesta Barbeques	36	26		0.0%		0.0%	1,351,370	37,538	Sun Tzu	140,016
67	Allen E. Paulson	176	89	7	4.0%	4	2.3%	5,508,996	31,301	Hap	919,070
68	Peter E. Blum	19	13	2	10.5%	2	10.5%	686,178	36,115	Multiple Choice	167,230
69	Carl and Olivia Cannata	30	17	2	6.7%	1	3.3%	987,356	32,912	Gourmet Girl	554,950
70	Mt. Brilliant Farm	24	13	2	8.3%	1	4.2%	817,024	34,043	Snow Ridge	250,899
71	Harry T. Mangurian Jr.	236	152	10	4.2%	4	1.7%	7,259,288	30,760	Exciting Story	596,667
72	Eaton Hall Farm	15	10		0.0%		0.0%	721,969	48,131	Cosa Rara	175,560
73	Prestonwood Farm Inc.	68	35	4	5.9%	1	1.5%	2,093,481	30,786	Strategic Partner	265,885
74	Lance Robinson	33	22	3	9.1%	1	3.0%	1,030,885	31,239	Letter of Intent	161,732
75	Wind Hill Farm	18	9	2	11.1%	1	5.6%	638,841	35,491	Starrer	406,265
76	Fox Ridge Farm Inc.	16	6	2	12.5%	1	6.3%	582,951	36,434	Cozzy Corner	202,899
77	Bonnie Heath Farm	27	13	2	7.4%	2	7.4%	837,592	31,022	Honor Glide	281,770
78	Gardiner Farms Ltd.	32	15	1	3.1%		0.0%	1,060,846	33,151	Rare Friends	247,365
79	Patricia Generazio	31	21	2	6.5%		0.0%	988,969	31,902	Outstanding Info	125,080
80	Mrs. Ronald B. Houghton	15	13	1	6.7%		0.0%	593,687	39,579	Watchman's Warning	125,066
81	Max Hugel	28	18	1	3.6%	1	3.6%	903,827	32,280	Proud Man	335,510
82	Overbrook Farm	111	68	6	5.4%	4	3.6%	3,151,491	28,392	Penny's Gold	316,388
83	Bruno Schickedanz	36	23	1	2.8%		0.0%	1,161,468	32,263	Wake At Noon	235,365
84	Mr. and Mrs. J. S. Moss	22	10	2	9.1%	1	4.6%	708,136	32,188	Kudos	221,880
85	J. V. Shields Jr.	19	11	1	5.3%		0.0%	692,269	36,435	Shooting Party	214,146
86	Chester and Mary R. Broman	28	16	1	3.6%		0.0%	918,679	32,810	Ransom's Pride	201,965
87	C. Oliver Goldsmith	12	5	1	8.3%	1	8.3%	472,495	39,375	Disco Rico	349,644
88	Allan D. Rudzik	10	8	2	20.0%		0.0%	447,694	44,769	La Recherche	261,534
89	Audley Farm Inc.	21	13	3	14.3%		0.0%	684,977	32,618	Blazing Colors	138,097
90	Maple Leaf Farm	10	6	1	10.0%	1	10.0%	419,009	41,901	Top Hit	266,632
91	Joseph M. Imbesi	13	9		0.0%		0.0%	579,172	44,552	Notforloveormoney	124,180
92	Gallagher's Stud	22	12	1	4.6%		0.0%	747,508	33,978	Statement	112,470
93	Mockingbird Farm Inc.	325	196	14	4.3%	2	0.6%	9,156,963	28,175	Richly Blended	323,280
94	Claiborne Farm	51	26	3	5.9%	2	3.9%	1,417,604	27,796	Trip	345,855
95	White Fox Farm	24	13	1	4.2%		0.0%	782,660	32,611	Extend	193,326
96	Mike Pegram	13	8	1	7.7%		0.0%	504,893	38,838	Crescendo	123,400
97	Rutledge Farm	11	6	1	9.1%		0.0%	466,147	42,377	Lady Melesi	263,140
98	Fred Watarida	13	10	2	15.4%		0.0%	487,021	37,463	Native Desert	307,226
99	Palides Investments N.V.	26	15	1	3.9%	1	3.9%	796,770	30,645	Western Summer	132,138
100	Earle Mack	10	4	1	10.0%		0.0%	429,167	42,917	Shutup and Dance	196,520
101	Old English Rancho	26	15	2	7.7%		0.0%	795,525	30,597	Mimi's Cafe	200,371
102	Mrs. Timothy J. Gardner	17	11	2	11.8%	1	5.9%	532,949	31,350	Feathers	149,651

Leading Breeders by Earnings in 2001

Breeder	No. strs	No. wnrs	Total earnings
Mockingbird Farm Inc.	325	196	$9,156,963
Adena Springs	204	108	8,048,549
Juddmonte Farms	57	35	7,367,674
Harry T. Mangurian Jr.	236	152	7,259,288
Farnsworth Farms	358	205	6,953,499
John Franks	345	172	6,760,188
Allen E. Paulson	176	89	5,508,996
Mr. and Mrs. John Mabee	234	111	5,030,171
The Thoroughbred Corp.	29	15	4,677,966
Edward P. Evans	121	68	4,494,584
Brereton C. Jones	229	115	4,150,732
Gainsborough Farm Inc.	32	17	3,860,474
Cecilia Straub Rubens	13	7	3,579,121
Arthur I. Appleton	127	75	3,452,785
Sam-Son Farm	39	23	3,448,461
Overbrook Farm	111	68	3,151,491
Pin Oak Stud	74	52	2,973,767
Mr. and Mrs. Martin J. Wygod	113	51	2,937,036
Robert and Bea Roberts	100	48	2,674,243
Robert E. Meyeroff	55	28	2,669,486
Live Oak Stud	100	56	2,580,502
Gilbert G. Campbell	94	54	2,528,816
Ocala Stud Farms	65	37	2,323,898
Stonerside Ltd.	62	41	2,248,129
George Strawbridge Jr.	44	19	2,246,642
Prestonwood Farm Inc.	68	35	2,093,481
Charles Nuckols Jr. & Sons	104	57	2,023,073
J. D. Squires	16	7	1,999,540
Woodlynn Farm Inc.	21	10	1,894,278
John Toffan and Trudy McCaffrey	51	24	1,876,428
Hargus and Sandra Sexton	73	35	1,844,559
Harris Farms Inc.	74	43	1,810,601
Kinsman Farm	42	24	1,808,785
J D Farm	85	55	1,781,506
Arthur B. Hancock III	69	41	1,746,426
Verne H. Winchell	48	30	1,624,153
Everest Stables Inc.	61	35	1,606,137
Kenneth and Sarah Ramsey	58	27	1,549,342
Lazy Lane Stables Inc.	37	23	1,535,496
Kinghaven Farms Ltd.	41	28	1,485,782
Parrish Hill Farm	25	11	1,474,240
Phipps Stable	16	15	1,460,395
Claiborne Farm	51	26	1,417,604
Knob Hill Stable	37	24	1,411,945
Robert H. Walter Family Trust	12	6	74,312
Janis R. Whitham	15	8	73,338
Dr. and Mrs. R. Smiser West and Mr. and Mrs. M. Miller	16	9	71,303
Carolyn T. Groves	11	4	69,791
Arthur B. Hancock III and Stonerside Ltd.	12	8	68,288
Grousemont Farm	10	8	67,898
Gainsborough Stud Management	14	7	65,368
The Aga Khan's Studs	15	8	63,137
Summerwind Farm	14	9	60,647
Flaxman Holdings Ltd.	17	9	59,867
Parrish Hill Farm	25	11	58,970
Herbert T. Schwartz	17	12	57,827
Albert Fried Jr.	11	6	56,573
Shadwell Farm Inc.	22	11	56,156
Cherokee Farms Inc.	12	10	55,907
Cardiff Farm Management Corp.	10	7	53,899
Elmendorf Farm Inc.	10	7	52,806
George Strawbridge Jr.	44	19	51,060
North Central Bloodstock	15	6	50,705
Ronald E. McKee	17	11	50,120
Beclawat Stable	15	10	49,548
Pedigree Farms Inc.	10	5	49,008
Mrs. Richard C. duPont	22	15	48,864
Robert E. Meyeroff	55	28	48,536
Eaton Hall Farm	15	10	48,131
Jaime S. Carrion, Trustee	20	13	47,624

Leading Breeders by Average Earnings per Starter in 2001

Ten or more starters in 2001

Breeder	No. strs	No. wnrs	Average earnings per starter
Cecilia Straub-Rubens	13	7	$275,317
The Thoroughbred Corp.	29	15	161,309
Juddmonte Farms	57	35	129,257
J. D. Squires	16	7	124,971
Gainsborough Farm Inc.	32	17	120,640
Phipps Stable	16	15	91,275
Woodlynn Farm Inc.	21	10	90,204
Sam-Son Farm	39	23	88,422
Centaur Farm Inc.	16	8	84,759
W. S. Kilroy	13	7	82,964
Robert and Lawana Low	10	7	79,154

Leading Breeders by Number of Stakes Winners in 2001

Breeder	No. strs	No. wnrs	No. SWs
Adena Springs	204	108	16
Mockingbird Farm Inc.	325	196	14
Edward P. Evans	121	68	13
Triple AAA Ranch	57	41	11
Juddmonte Farms	57	35	11
Harry T. Mangurian Jr.	236	152	10
Farnsworth Farms	358	205	9
John Franks	345	172	8
Allen E. Paulson	176	89	7
Billingsley Creek Ranch	43	26	7
Live Oak Stud	100	56	7
Pin Oak Stud	74	52	7
Sam-Son Farm	39	23	6
Sondra and Howard M. Bender	31	20	6
Marshall Naify Revocable Trust	30	18	6
Mr. and Mrs. Martin J. Wygod	113	51	6
Overbrook Farm	111	68	6
Jacks or Better Farm Inc.	33	21	6
South River Ranch Inc.	44	27	5
Mr. and Mrs. John C. Mabee	234	111	5
Jaime S. Carrion, Trustee	20	13	5
George Strawbridge Jr.	44	19	5
Gilbert G. Campbell	94	54	5
Arthur B. Hancock III	69	41	4
Arthur I. Appleton	127	75	4
Brereton C. Jones	229	115	4
Calumet Farm	54	31	4
Robert E. Meyeroff	55	28	4
Robert H. and Bea Roberts	100	48	4
Lazy Lane Stables Inc.	37	23	4
Michael C. Byrne	36	22	4
Parrish Hill Farm	25	11	4
Phipps Stable	16	15	4

Prestonwood Farm Inc.	68	35	4
Harris Farms Inc.	74	43	4
J D Farm	85	55	4
Flaxman Holdings Ltd.	17	9	4
Gainesway Thoroughbreds Ltd.	38	20	4
udley Farm Inc.	21	13	3
Cardiff Farm Managment Corp.	10	7	3
CBF Corporation	28	18	3
Cecilia Straub-Rubens	13	7	3
Centaur Farms Inc.	24	18	3
Claiborne Farm	51	26	3
V. J. Callaway	17	9	3
Willard Burbach	14	10	3
River Ridge Ranch	33	18	3
Rosemont Farm Inc.	34	27	3
Southern Nevada Racing Stable	42	22	3
Vern and Debbie Hrycuik	11	4	3

Cherokee Farms Inc.	12	10	1	8.3%
C. Oliver Goldsmith	12	5	1	8.3%
David E. Hager II	28	18	1	3.6%
William Sorokolit	25	19	1	4.0%
Willmott Stable	12	11	1	8.3%
Wimborne Farm Inc.	41	20	1	2.4%
Wind Hill Farm	18	9	1	5.6%
Winsong Farms	20	11	1	5.0%
Woodlynn Farm Inc.	21	10	1	4.8%
W. S. Farish	44	25	1	2.3%

Leading Breeders by Number of Wins in 2001

Breeder	No. strs	No. wnrs	No. wins
Farnsworth Farms	358	205	371
Mockingbird Farm Inc.	325	196	347
John Franks	345	172	303
Harry T. Mangurian Jr.	236	152	297
Mr. and Mrs. John C. Mabee	234	111	206
Brereton C. Jones	229	115	201
Adena Springs	204	108	184
Arthur I. Appleton	127	75	172
Allen E. Paulson	176	89	171
Edward P. Evans	121	68	137
Gilbert G. Campbell	94	54	116
Charles Nuckols Jr. & Sons	104	57	112
Overbrook Farm	111	68	111
J. Adcock	115	63	111
Live Oak Stud	100	56	101
J D Farm	85	55	97
Mr. and Mrs. Martin J. Wygod	113	51	95
Pin Oak Stud	74	52	89
Robert H. and Bea Roberts	100	48	84
Ocala Stud Farms	65	37	82
Harris Farms Inc.	74	43	81
Triple AAA Ranch	57	41	78
Arthur B. Hancock III	69	41	74
Prestonwood Farm Inc.	68	35	73
Hargus and Sandra Sexton	73	35	73
D. W. Frazier	72	41	69
Fares Farm	75	40	69
Stonerside Ltd.	62	41	66
Foxfield	62	29	66
Frank Stronach	60	33	65
Hart Farm Inc.	73	38	64
Hobeau Farm Ltd.	60	34	63
Mr. and Mrs. Guy C. Roberts	57	36	61
John T. L. Jones Jr.	49	29	61
Everest Stables Inc.	61	35	61
Mrs. Henry D. Paxson	55	31	58
Juddmonte Farms	57	35	58
Mr. and Mrs. R. J. Bennett	61	35	57
Kenneth and Sarah Ramsey	58	27	56
Stanley Ersoff	72	32	54
Glen Hill Farm	48	28	54
Ron E. Gomez	50	29	53
Don Eberts	30	23	53
Billingsley Creek Ranch	43	26	52
Calumet Farm	54	31	52
Rosemont Farm Inc.	34	27	52
Michael C. Byrne	36	22	52
Robert E. Meyeroff	55	28	51
South River Ranch Inc.	44	27	51
Marablue Farm	56	35	51

Leading Breeders by Number Graded Stakes Winners in 2001

Breeder	No. strs	No. wnrs	No. GSWs	% GSWs/ str
Juddmonte Farms	57	35	10	17.5%
Adena Springs	204	108	7	3.4%
Edward P. Evans	121	68	6	5.0%
Allen E. Paulson	176	89	4	2.3%
Overbrook Farm	111	68	4	3.6%
Phipps Stable	16	15	4	25.0%
Harry T. Mangurian Jr.	236	152	4	1.7%
John Franks	345	172	4	1.2%
Sam-Son Farm	39	23	3	7.7%
Pin Oak Stud	74	52	3	4.1%
Kinsman Farm	42	24	3	7.1%
George Strawbridge Jr.	44	19	3	6.8%
Arthur I. Appleton	127	75	2	1.6%
Bonnie Heath Farm	27	13	2	7.4%
Cecilia Straub-Rubens	13	7	2	15.4%
Claiborne Farm	51	26	2	3.9%
The Thoroughbred Corp.	29	15	2	6.9%
Verne H. Winchell	48	30	2	4.2%
Live Oak Stud	100	56	2	2.0%
Mockingbird Farm Inc.	325	196	2	0.6%
Mr. and Mrs. Martin Wygod	113	51	2	1.8%
Peter E. Blum	19	13	2	10.5%
The Aga Khan's Studs	15	8	2	13.3%
Jaime S. Carrion, Trustee	20	13	2	10.0%
James B. Tafel	23	14	2	8.7%
Janis R. Whitham	15	8	2	13.3%
J D Farm	85	55	2	2.4%
John Toffan and Trudy McCaffrey	51	24	2	3.9%
Dr. & Mrs. R. Smiser West and Mr.& Mrs. M. Miller	16	9	2	12.5%
Flaxman Holdings Ltd.	17	9	2	11.8%
Gainesway Thoroughbreds	38	20	2	5.3%
Gainsborough Farm Inc.	32	17	2	6.3%
Gainsborough Stud Mgmt.	14	7	2	14.3%
Albert Fried Jr.	11	6	1	9.1%
Arthur B. Hancock III	69	41	1	1.5%
Arthur B. Hancock III and Stonerside Ltd.	12	8	1	8.3%
Brereton C. Jones	229	115	1	0.4%
Carl and Olivia Cannata	30	17	1	3.3%
Carolyn T. Groves	11	4	1	9.1%
Centaur Farm Inc.	16	8	1	6.3%

Leading Trainers of 2001

Trainer Bobby Frankel's 2001 season undoubtedly will be remembered as the one in which he got the Breeders' Cup monkey off his back when Squirtle Squirt unexpectedly won the Breeders' Cup Sprint (G1). But Frankel still is looking for his first victory in a Triple Crown race. For the season, however, the Racing Hall of Fame member was dominant in many categories by which North American trainers are measured.

Frankel's performance in 2001 placed him at the head of the THOROUGHBRED TIMES rankings. He was the leading trainer by total North American earnings with more than $14.6-million, and he also was the runaway leader by stakes winners (31 of his 102 starters) and graded stakes winners (an impressive 24) with a high-quality stable that included several Juddmonte Farms homebreds.

Saeed bin Suroor, who trains for the Godolphin Racing organization, made selective appearances in 2001 and led all trainers by average earnings per starter at more than $250,000 for his 14 starters. He was second in the rankings, right ahead of Canadian-based trainer Mark Frostad, who again had an excellent year with the Sam-Son Farm stable. By numbers, the year's leader was Scott Lake, who racked up 406 wins from his Philadelphia Park base.

Leading Trainers by Year
(Worldwide Earnings)

Year	Name	Wins	Earnings
2001	Bob Baffert	138	$16,354,996
2000	Bob Baffert	146	11,831,605
1999	Bob Baffert	169	16,934,607
1998	Bob Baffert	139	15,000,870
1997	D. Wayne Lukas	175	10,351,397
1996	D. Wayne Lukas	192	14,967,608
1995	D. Wayne Lukas	194	12,842,865
1994	D. Wayne Lukas	147	9,247,457
1993	Robert Frankel	79	8,933,252
1992	D. Wayne Lukas	230	9,806,436
1991	D. Wayne Lukas	289	15,942,223
1990	D. Wayne Lukas	267	14,511,690
1989	D. Wayne Lukas	305	16,103,998

THOROUGHBRED TIMES Leading Trainers of 2001

Rankings based on formula that gives equal weighting to four statistical categories for performance in 2001: 1) total earnings; 2) average earnings per starter; 3) percent stakes winners from starters; and 4) percent graded stakes winners from starters. A minimum of ten starters is required to be considered for inclusion. Statistics are for North America only and for racing in 2001. SWs is stakes winners and GSWs is graded stakes winners.

Rank	Trainer	No. strs	No. wnrs	No. SWs	% SWs/ strs	No. GSWs	% GSWs/ strs	Total earnings	Average earnings/ starter	Leading earner	Earnings of leading earner
1	Robert J. Frankel	102	60	31	30.4%	24	23.5%	$14,607,446	$143,210	Skimming	$1,330,000
2	Saeed bin Suroor	14	5	3	21.4%	3	21.4%	3,588,740	256,339	Fantastic Light	2,112,800
3	Mark R. Frostad	45	24	8	17.8%	5	11.1%	4,164,434	92,543	Dancethruthedawn	1,045,039
4	John T. Ward Jr.	32	13	5	15.6%	4	12.5%	3,523,740	110,117	Monarchos	1,711,600
5	Claude R. McGaughey III	58	35	9	15.5%	8	13.8%	3,645,674	62,856	Traditionally	420,020
6	Christophe Clement	104	47	14	13.5%	10	9.6%	5,557,669	53,439	England's Legend (Fr)	757,480
7	Craig Dollase	37	23	7	18.9%	6	16.2%	2,561,428	69,228	Futural	478,670
8	Richard E. Mandella	95	48	15	15.8%	7	7.4%	4,603,105	48,454	Redattore (Brz)	555,840
9	Bob Baffert	174	85	17	9.8%	10	5.8%	12,754,996	73,305	Point Given	3,350,000
10	Todd A. Pletcher	145	71	19	13.1%	8	5.5%	7,731,203	53,319	Balto Star	848,820
11	Niall M. O'Callaghan	63	26	7	11.1%	5	7.9%	3,851,810	61,140	Guided Tour	1,384,220
12	Jay M. Robbins	17	8	2	11.8%	1	5.9%	3,323,405	195,494	Tiznow	2,981,880
13	Neil D. Drysdale	72	28	8	11.1%	4	5.6%	4,075,178	56,600	Irish Prize	913,350
14	Ronald L. McAnally	76	31	10	13.2%	8	10.5%	3,515,101	46,251	Affluent	725,200
15	William I. Mott	189	91	19	10.1%	11	5.8%	9,418,657	49,834	Hap	919,070
16	Mark A. Hennig	116	52	13	11.2%	8	6.9%	4,973,124	42,872	Mystic Lady	775,000
17	Jenine Sahadi	52	22	8	15.4%	4	7.7%	2,496,693	48,013	Golden Ballet	595,250
18	David E. Hofmans	40	16	4	10.0%	3	7.5%	2,520,267	63,007	Siphonic	703,978
19	Roger L. Attfield	75	38	8	10.7%	3	4.0%	3,840,755	51,210	Sweetest Thing	578,100
20	Robert P. Tiller	55	31	5	9.1%	2	3.6%	3,702,396	67,316	Win City	876,187
21	John C. Kimmel	127	61	12	9.5%	7	5.5%	5,496,627	43,281	Miss Linda (Arg)	455,415
22	Benjamin W. Perkins Jr.	87	44	11	12.6%	3	3.5%	3,784,639	43,502	Delaware Township	635,840
23	Eoin G. Harty	33	16	3	9.1%	3	9.1%	1,771,064	53,669	Tempera	670,240
24	Darrell Vienna	56	28	5	8.9%	2	3.6%	2,762,949	49,338	Janet (GB)	715,080
25	D. Wayne Lukas	157	66	12	7.6%	7	4.5%	5,947,971	37,885	Spain	837,705
26	Alan E. Goldberg	49	32	6	12.2%	2	4.1%	1,996,803	40,751	Navesink	368,206
27	Anthony W. Dutrow	69	40	10	14.5%	1	1.5%	2,780,900	40,303	Burning Roma	473,000
28	Juan "Paco" Gonzalez	29	13	3	10.3%	2	6.9%	1,453,497	50,121	Bienamado	540,000
29	Joseph F. Orseno	49	17	5	10.2%	3	6.1%	1,922,700	39,239	Macho Uno	563,400
30	W. Elliott Walden	127	54	13	10.2%	3	2.4%	4,470,486	35,201	License Fee	382,560

Rank	Trainer	No. strs	No. wnrs	No. SWs	% SWs/ strs	No. GSWs	% GSWs/ strs	Total earnings	Average earnings/ starter	Leading earner	Earnings of leading earner
31	Grover G. Delp	50	34	3	6.0%	1	2.0%	2,681,810	53,636	Include	1,435,400
32	Sid C. Attard	50	24	2	4.0%	2	4.0%	2,536,380	50,728	Numerous Times	676,320
33	Michael W. Dickinson	56	35	6	10.7%	1	1.8%	2,325,249	41,522	Fleet Renee	624,485
34	Wallace A. Dollase	35	14	4	11.4%	3	8.6%	1,373,490	39,243	Good Journey	338,300
35	Simon Bray	35	17	4	11.4%	2	5.7%	1,396,315	39,895	Startac	370,195
36	Timothy F. Ritchey	89	62	9	10.1%		0.0%	3,414,706	38,367	Governor's Pride	213,020
37	Bruce Headley	34	13	2	5.9%	2	5.9%	1,521,563	44,752	Kona Gold	392,420
38	H. Allen Jerkens	53	27	3	5.7%	2	3.8%	2,116,156	39,927	Shine Again	469,750
39	Nicholas P. Zito	96	45	3	3.1%	1	1.0%	5,124,106	53,376	Albert the Great	1,740,000
40	John K. Dolan	49	19	2	4.1%	2	4.1%	2,081,962	42,489	Lazy Slusan	678,980
41	Ben D. A. Cecil	26	5	3	11.5%	2	7.7%	1,142,175	43,930	Golden Apples (Ire)	490,000
42	George R. Arnold II	69	33	5	7.3%	2	2.9%	2,421,943	35,101	Lady Melesi	263,140
43	Flint S. Schulhofer	35	12	1	2.9%	1	2.9%	2,030,034	58,001	Exogenous	901,500
44	James A. Jerkens	43	23	3	7.0%	1	2.3%	1,814,586	42,200	Dat You Miz Blue	273,865
45	C. Beau Greely	26	12	4	15.4%	3	11.5%	1,056,050	40,617	Sligo Bay (Ire)	246,160
46	Thomas J. Skiffington	22	9	1	4.6%	1	4.6%	1,334,451	60,657	Spook Express (SAf)	866,870
47	H. James Bond	61	29	5	8.2%		0.0%	2,338,170	38,331	Personal Pro	217,184
48	Bernard S. Flint	128	72	9	7.0%	3	2.3%	3,934,763	30,740	Outofthebox	591,300
49	Jonathan E. Sheppard	105	48	6	5.7%	3	2.9%	3,350,704	31,911	With Anticipation	802,393
50	David R. Bell	68	30	2	2.9%	2	2.9%	2,660,053	39,121	Heliotrope	250,124
51	Josie Carroll	52	26	6	11.5%		0.0%	1,849,177	35,561	Magic Flute	146,980
52	Julio C. Canani	70	28	2	2.9%	2	2.9%	2,699,901	38,570	Val Royal (Fr)	792,800
53	Linda Rice	81	32	9	11.1%	2	2.5%	2,370,692	29,268	City Zip	401,920
54	Carl A. Nafzger	67	24	3	4.5%	2	3.0%	2,283,663	34,085	Alannan	413,966
55	Patrick J. Kelly	39	18	3	7.7%	2	5.1%	1,363,392	34,959	Cozzy Corner	202,899
56	John Cardella	34	16	2	5.9%		0.0%	1,603,861	47,172	Olympian	164,165
57	David Cotey	22	10	2	9.1%	2	9.1%	978,333	44,470	Stage Classic	279,643
58	Juan Serey	85	46	3	3.5%	1	1.2%	3,075,312	36,180	Say Florida Sandy	615,420
59	H. Graham Motion	111	55	10	9.0%	2	1.8%	3,162,005	28,487	Broken Vow	611,596
60	Chris M. Block	46	25	5	10.9%	1	2.2%	1,472,926	32,020	Ioya Two	234,328
61	Donnie K. Von Hemel	66	40	11	16.7%	1	1.5%	1,876,880	28,438	Mr Ross	442,400
62	Thomas M. Amoss	130	64	11	8.5%	3	2.3%	3,550,018	27,308	Hattiesburg	369,248
63	Dallas Stewart	119	39	4	3.4%	2	1.7%	3,858,427	32,424	Unbridled Elaine	1,295,075
64	Kenneth G. McPeek	91	37	4	4.4%	3	3.3%	2,673,453	29,379	Repent	415,660
65	Gene A. Cilio	62	29	4	6.5%	2	3.2%	1,860,292	30,005	Scoop	288,270
66	Sanna Neilson	21	14	6	28.6%	4	19.1%	802,627	38,220	Praise the Prince (NZ)	225,742
67	Dale L. Romans	92	38	5	5.4%		0.0%	2,927,293	31,818	Sitka	218,507
68	John A. Ross	27	13	3	11.1%		0.0%	1,142,184	42,303	Shaws Creek	155,748
69	Malcolm Pierce	37	13	2	5.4%	1	2.7%	1,349,611	36,476	Diadella	255,991
70	Lawrehce E. Murray	23	14	5	21.7%		0.0%	991,273	43,099	La Reine's Terms	133,950
71	Macdonald Benson	24	8	3	12.5%	1	4.2%	922,964	38,457	Allende	251,532
72	John P. Terranova II	35	14	1	2.9%	1	2.9%	1,379,117	39,403	Gander	557,060
73	Carl Bowman	26	16	2	7.7%		0.0%	1,143,408	43,977	Lu Ravi	230,000
74	Richard E. Schosberg	57	19	3	5.3%	2	3.5%	1,674,903	29,385	Affirmed Success	343,215
75	Scott M. Schwartz	27	10	2	7.4%	1	3.7%	1,014,561	37,576	Critical Eye	339,736
76	Frank L. Brothers	52	26	4	7.7%	2	3.9%	1,424,756	27,399	Trip	345,885
77	Ronny W. Werner	61	33	4	6.6%	1	1.6%	1,755,378	28,777	Touch Tone	607,850
78	John E. Salzman Sr.	48	24	1	2.1%	1	2.1%	1,686,110	35,127	Xtra Heat	1,012,040
79	Neil J. Howard	42	15	1	2.4%	1	2.4%	1,470,030	35,001	Quick Tip	214,153
80	Abraham R. Katryan	65	37	2	3.1%		0.0%	2,104,279	32,374	Wake At Noon	235,365
81	Vito Armata	49	27	3	6.1%		0.0%	1,531,140	31,248	Platel	163,246
82	Ralph Ziadie	80	50	5	6.3%	1	1.3%	2,181,454	27,268	Sir Bear	313,500
83	Daniel C. Peitz	31	12	2	6.5%	1	3.2%	1,038,329	33,511	Real Cozzy	459,340
84	Martin D. Wolfson	46	19	5	10.9%	2	4.4%	1,201,722	26,124	O K to Dance	177,882
85	William W. Perry	28	10	2	7.1%	1	3.6%	971,018	34,679	One Eyed Joker	240,750
86	Richard E. Dutrow Jr.	132	67	4	3.0%	1	0.8%	3,619,639	27,422	Here's Zealous	186,240
87	Robert E. Holthus	65	33	6	9.2%		0.0%	1,731,136	26,633	The Happy Hopper	160,637
88	Scott H. Fairlie	45	19	1	2.2%	1	2.2%	1,481,527	32,923	Mr. Epperson	430,180
89	Michael Wright Jr.	93	50	2	2.2%	1	1.1%	2,689,681	28,921	Kimberlite Pipe	243,542
90	A. Pico Perdomo	13	5	1	7.7%	1	7.7%	675,290	51,945	Gourmet Girl	554,950
91	Christopher S. Paasch	47	16	4	8.5%	1	2.1%	1,278,278	27,197	Collect Call	338,820
92	David M. Carroll	39	16	3	7.7%	1	2.6%	1,129,241	28,955	Connected	277,083
93	Paul J. McGee	73	38	3	4.1%	1	1.4%	1,925,428	26,376	Bet On Sunshine	331,818
94	Patrick L. Reynolds	43	14	2	4.7%	1	2.3%	1,232,210	28,656	Peeping Tom	586,060
95	Cole Norman	170	118	12	7.1%		0.0%	3,793,060	22,312	Royal Spy	322,900
96	Richard A. Violette Jr.	38	17	1	2.6%	1	2.6%	1,215,173	31,978	March Magic	338,530
97	Edwin Thomas Broome	38	25	3	7.9%		0.0%	1,134,462	29,854	Normandy Beach	115,979
98	Warren Stute	39	13	3	7.7%	1	2.6%	1,086,178	27,851	Go Go	446,620

Leading Trainers by Earnings in 2001

Trainer	No. strs	No. wnrs	Total earnings
Robert J. Frankel	102	60	$14,607,446
Bob Baffert	174	85	12,754,996
William I. Mott	189	91	9,418,657
Steven M. Asmussen	375	197	8,068,409
Scott A. Lake	350	218	7,817,856
Todd A. Pletcher	145	71	7,731,203
D. Wayne Lukas	157	66	5,947,971
Christophe Clement	104	47	5,557,669
Jerry Hollendorfer	284	166	5,497,046
John C. Kimmel	127	61	5,496,627
Nicholas P. Zito	96	45	5,124,106
Mark A. Hennig	116	52	4,973,124
Richard E. Mandella	95	48	4,603,105
W. Elliott Walden	127	54	4,470,486
Dale Capuano	230	137	4,397,048
Mark R. Frostad	45	24	4,164,434
Allen Iwinski	177	100	4,134,297
Neil D. Drysdale	72	28	4,075,178
Mark E. Casse	171	62	4,004,798
Bernard S. Flint	128	72	3,934,763
Dallas Stewart	119	39	3,858,427
Niall M. O'Callaghan	63	26	3,851,810
Roger L. Attfield	75	38	3,840,755
Cole Norman	170	118	3,793,060
Benjamin W. Perkins Jr.	87	44	3,784,639
Robert P. Tiller	55	31	3,702,396
Claude R. McGaughey III	58	35	3,645,674
Richard E. Dutrow Jr.	132	67	3,619,639
Saeed bin Suroor	14	5	3,588,740
Thomas M. Amoss	130	64	3,550,018
John T. Ward Jr.	32	13	3,523,740
Ronald L. McAnally	76	31	3,515,101
Timothy F. Ritchey	89	62	3,414,706
Jonathan E. Sheppard	105	48	3,350,704
Jay M. Robbins	17	8	3,323,405
H. Graham Motion	111	55	3,162,005
Juan Serey	85	46	3,075,312

Leading Trainers by Average Earnings per Starter

Ten or more starters in 2001

Trainer	No. strs	No. wnrs	Average earnings per starter
Saeed bin Suroor	14	5	$256,339
Jay M. Robbins	17	8	195,494
Robert J. Frankel	102	60	143,210
John T. Ward Jr.	32	13	110,117
Mark R. Frostad	45	24	92,543
Bob Baffert	174	85	73,305
Craig Dollase	37	23	69,228
Robert P. Tiller	55	31	67,316
David E. Hofmans	40	16	63,007
Claude R. McGaughey III	58	35	62,856
Niall M. O'Callaghan	63	26	61,140
Thomas J. Skiffington	22	9	60,657
Flint S. Schulhofer	35	12	58,001
Neil D. Drysdale	72	28	56,600
Eoin G. Harty	33	16	53,669
Grover G. Delp	50	34	53,636
Christophe Clement	104	47	53,439

Trainer	No. strs	No. wnrs	Total earnings
Nicholas P. Zito	96	45	53,376
Todd A. Pletcher	145	71	53,319
A. Pico Perdomo	13	5	51,945
James Mort Hardy	11	6	51,633
Roger L. Attfield	75	38	51,210
Sid C. Attard	50	24	50,728
J. Paco Gonzalez	29	13	50,121
William I. Mott	189	91	49,834
Darrell Vienna	56	28	49,338
Richard E. Mandella	95	48	48,454
Jenine Sahadi	52	22	48,013
Emile M Allain	10	5	47,907
John Cardella	34	16	47,172
Ronald L. McAnally	76	31	46,251
Bruce Headley	34	13	44,752
Robert J. King Jr.	10	5	44,671
Richard Baltas	15	7	44,598
David Cotey	22	10	44,470
Wayne M. Bailey	12	9	44,333
Carl Bowman	26	16	43,977
Ben D. A. Cecil	26	5	43,930
Benjamin W. Perkins Jr.	87	44	43,502
John C. Kimmel	127	61	43,281
Lawrence E. Murray	23	14	43,099
Mark A. Hennig	116	52	42,872
Reed M. Combest	14	10	42,670
John K. Dolan	49	19	42,489
John A. Ross	27	13	42,303
Nickolas DeToro	18	7	42,211

Leading Trainers by Number of Stakes Winners in 2001

Trainer	No. strs	No. wnrs	No. SWs
Robert J. Frankel	102	60	31
Steven M. Asmussen	375	197	25
William I. Mott	189	91	19
Todd A. Pletcher	145	71	19
Bob Baffert	174	85	17
Richard E. Mandella	95	48	15
Christophe Clement	104	47	14
W. Elliott Walden	127	54	13
Mark A. Hennig	116	52	13
John C. Kimmel	127	61	12
D. Wayne Lukas	157	66	12
Cole Norman	170	118	12
Donnie K. Von Hemel	66	40	11
Thomas M. Amoss	130	64	11
Benjamin W. Perkins Jr.	87	44	11
Anthony W. Dutrow	69	40	10
H. Graham Motion	111	55	10
Scott A. Lake	350	218	10
Ronald L. McAnally	76	31	10
Bernard S. Flint	128	72	9
Claude R. McGaughey III	58	35	9
Linda Rice	81	32	9
Danny Pish	126	56	9
Timothy F. Ritchey	89	62	9
Neil D. Drysdale	72	28	8
Jeff Bonde	92	40	8
Jenine Sahadi	52	22	8
Mark R. Frostad	45	24	8
Thomas H. Voss	47	22	8
Roger L. Attfield	75	38	8
Craig Dollase	37	23	7

David Forster	57	28	7
R. Kory Owens	31	19	7
Gerald S. Bennett	63	40	7
Dale Capuano	230	137	7
Niall M. O'Callaghan	63	26	7
Alan E. Goldberg	49	32	6
Robert E. Holthus	65	33	6
Michael W. Nance	48	29	6
Josie Carroll	52	26	6
Marvin A. Johnson	86	42	6
Jonathan E. Sheppard	105	48	6
Edward Plesa Jr.	95	34	6
Ramon O. Gonzalez	121	71	6
Michael W. Dickinson	56	35	6
Sanna Neilson	21	14	6
H. James Bond	61	29	5
Wayne M. Catalano	91	49	5
Jerry Hollendorfer	284	166	5
J. Eric Kruljac	68	32	5

James E. Jones	21	8	3	14.3%
Reed M. Combest	14	10	2	14.3%
Paul Brettler	14	8	2	14.3%
Christophe Clement	104	47	14	13.5%
Eugene F. Brajczewski Jr.	15	6	2	13.3%
Ronald L. McAnally	76	31	10	13.2%
Claude R. McGaughey III	58	35	9	15.5%
Mary Jo Lohmeier	13	9	2	15.4%
C. Beau Greely	26	12	4	15.4%
Jenine Sahadi	52	22	8	15.4%
Happy Alter	13	7	2	15.4%

Leading Trainers by Percent Stakes Winners from Starters

Ten or more starters in 2001

Trainer	No. strs	No. wnrs	No. SWs	% SWs/str
Robert J. Frankel	102	60	31	30.4%
Sanna Neilson	21	14	6	28.6%
James M. Day	11	3	3	27.3%
Michael Zwiesler	12	6	3	25.0%
Wayne M. Bailey	12	9	3	25.0%
William J. Smith	12	9	3	25.0%
Fern Zdunick	17	11	4	23.5%
R. Kory Owens	31	19	7	22.6%
Lawrence E. Murray	23	14	5	21.7%
Jim Meyaard	14	9	3	21.4%
Saeed bin Suroor	14	5	3	21.4%
Kevin Knudsen	14	9	3	21.4%
Jennifer L. Pedersen	10	3	2	20.0%
Larry E. Hunt Sr.	10	4	2	20.0%
Mel Berkram	15	6	3	20.0%
Darla S. Singh	21	16	4	19.1%
Craig Dollase	37	23	7	18.9%
Linda K. Osborne	11	5	2	18.2%
Mark R. Frostad	45	24	8	17.8%
Pat Sonnen	17	9	3	17.7%
Thomas H. Voss	47	22	8	17.0%
John K. Hennig	18	7	3	16.7%
Kenneth E. Hoffman	12	4	2	16.7%
Donnie K. Von Hemel	66	40	11	16.7%
Fred Costa	12	6	2	16.7%
Bob Barr	12	7	2	16.7%
William A. Kaplan	18	10	3	16.7%
Keith Bennett	31	21	5	16.1%
Joe Frederick Thomas Sr.	25	12	4	16.0%
Richard E. Mandella	95	48	15	15.8%
Robert Earl Barnett	19	7	3	15.8%
John T. Ward Jr.	32	13	5	15.6%
Johnie L. Jamison	32	20	5	15.6%
Anthony W. Dutrow	69	40	10	14.5%
Alan Sobol	35	22	5	14.3%
Heather A. Giglio	21	12	3	14.3%
Allan Jack	14	6	2	14.3%
Sidney Martin	14	9	2	14.3%
Dennis F. Good	14	7	2	14.3%

Leading Trainers by Wins in 2001

Trainer	No. strs	No. wnrs	No. wins
Scott A. Lake	350	218	406
Steven M. Asmussen	375	197	294
Jerry Hollendorfer	284	166	263
Dale Capuano	230	137	235
Cole Norman	170	118	229
Bruce M. Kravets	214	107	206
Gary L. Johnson	226	133	205
Dale Baird	276	129	197
Ralph Martinez	88	69	179
Harry F. Thompson Jr.	161	92	178
Keith L. Bourgeois	136	82	175
Allen Iwinski	177	100	167
Jose A. Martinez	135	75	160
William I. Mott	189	91	152
Ramon O. Gonzalez	121	71	149
John Charles Zimmerman	90	62	138
Bob Baffert	174	85	137
Bernard S. Flint	128	72	132
Ronney W. Brown	152	75	132
Ronald J. Dandy	162	76	131
Todd A. Pletcher	145	71	128
Timothy F. Ritchey	89	62	128
Flint W. Stites	114	57	113
Jeff C. Runco	199	85	113
Richard E. Dutrow Jr.	132	67	111
Thomas M. Amoss	130	64	106
John C. Kimmel	127	61	105
Gerald S. Bennett	63	40	103
Robert J. Frankel	102	60	101
D. Wayne Lukas	157	66	96
William P. White	141	67	95
Stanley W. Roberts	101	48	95
Barbara I. McBride	104	57	93
M. Anthony Ferraro	68	42	93
Doris Hebert	74	43	93
John W. Baird	94	54	92
David W. Geist	82	47	92
Armando Lage	155	57	90
Juan Serey	85	46	89
John Rigattieri	69	43	86
Danny Pish	126	56	86
H. Graham Motion	111	55	86
Dale Angelle	94	44	86
Art Sherman	127	61	85
Michael S. Ferraro	46	39	85
Mark A. Hennig	116	52	85
W. Elliott Walden	127	54	84
Robert W. Camac	95	50	84
Hamilton A. Smith	104	52	84
Layne S. Giliforte	118	58	83

Leading Jockeys of 2001

From 1998 through 2000, Jerry Bailey and Pat Day occupied the leading spots in THOROUGH-BRED TIMES's ranking of leading jockeys based on their number of wins, percentage of wins from total mounts, and average earnings per mount. In 2001, Bailey occupied the top spot for the seventh consecutive year, but a new player entered the top ranks when John Velazquez moved into the second spot.

Bailey, who won his fifth Eclipse Award in 2001, led North America with earnings of $19-million and 58 stakes victories. Velazquez, a native of Puerto Rico, has blossomed under the guidance of Angel Cordero Jr., the Racing Hall of Fame jockey who is the rider's agent. Both Cordero and Velazquez have excelled at Saratoga Race Course, where Cordero won numerous titles and where Velazquez won a record six races on the final day of the 2001 meet. Velazquez finished second in the earnings category with purses exceeding $15-million.

Day finished third in the THOROUGHBRED TIMES rankings, and fourth was Ramon Dominguez, who led North America by victories in 2001 with 433. Russell Baze again led the continent by percentage of winners with 28.1%, and Gary Stevens topped the lists by average earnings per starter with $22,090 per mount.

Leading Jockeys by Year
(Worldwide Earnings)

Year	Name	Wins	Earnings
2001	Jerry Bailey	227	$22,597,720
2000	Pat Day	267	17,479,838
1999	Pat Day	254	18,092,845
1998	Gary Stevens	178	19,358,840
1997	Jerry Bailey	273	18,320,743
1996	Jerry Bailey	300	19,214,409
1995	Jerry Bailey	287	16,308,230
1994	Mike Smith	317	15,979,820
1993	Mike Smith	343	14,024,815
1992	Kent Desormeaux	361	14,193,006
1991	Chris McCarron	265	14,441,083
1990	Gary Stevens	283	13,881,198
1989	Jose Santos	285	13,838,389

THOROUGHBRED TIMES Leading Jockeys of 2001

Rankings based on a formula that gives equal weighting to three statistical categories for performance in 2001: 1) percent winners from mounts; 2) total number of wins; and 3) average earnings per mount. A minimum of 100 starters is required to be considered for inclusion. Statistics are for North America only and for racing in 2001.

Rank	Trainer	No. mounts	No. wins	% wins/ mounts	No. stakes wins	% SWs/ mounts	No. graded st. wins	Total earnings	Average earnings/ mount	Leading earner	Earnings of leading earner
1	Jerry Bailey	910	227	25.0%	58	6.4%	43	$19,015,720	$20,896	Include	$1,210,000
2	John Velazquez	1,411	305	21.6%	37	2.6%	29	15,073,790	10,683	Starine (Fr)	719,589
3	Pat Day	1,197	249	20.8%	31	2.6%	17	14,497,859	12,112	Unbridled Elaine	1,344,550
4	Ramon Dominguez	1,864	433	23.2%	37	2.0%	4	10,535,087	5,652	Irving's Baby	469,747
5	Russell Baze	1,503	423	28.1%	15	1.0%	3	7,225,600	4,807	Mimi's Cafe	90,125
6	Travis Dunkelberger	1,544	394	25.5%	22	1.4%	1	6,928,243	4,487	Prized Stamp	174,418
7	Eibar Coa	1,396	281	20.1%	39	2.8%	9	9,226,516	6,609	Mystic Lady	510,000
8	Robby Albarado	1,401	273	19.5%	23	1.6%	9	10,651,669	7,603	Touch Tone	547,850
9	Jorge Chavez	1,344	246	18.3%	29	2.2%	14	13,829,699	10,290	Monarchos	1,711,600
10	Alex Solis	1,200	222	18.5%	28	2.3%	14	11,531,521	9,610	Redattore (Brz)	410,840
11	Mario Pino	1,443	297	20.6%	24	1.7%	0	6,427,497	4,454	Saratoga Games	330,940
12	Todd Kabel	723	145	20.1%	11	1.5%	3	7,145,426	9,883	Quiet Resolve	344,925
13	Cornelio Velasquez	1,362	275	20.2%	20	1.5%	1	6,243,236	4,584	Blissful Kiss	240,000
14	Chris McCarron	606	123	20.3%	49	8.1%	28	12,759,692	21,056	Tiznow	2,981,880
15	Rene Douglas	1,244	241	19.4%	24	1.9%	6	7,204,535	5,791	Proud Man	328,760
16	Laffit Pincay Jr.	1,252	226	18.1%	22	1.8%	11	10,080,366	8,051	Millennium Wind	465,000
17	Rick Wilson	515	117	22.7%	25	4.9%	8	4,363,282	8,472	Xtra Heat	779,040
18	Jason Lumpkins	1,139	264	23.2%	11	1.0%	3	4,460,509	3,916	Redattore (Brz)	137,500
19	Jeremy Rose	1,572	312	19.9%	10	0.6%	0	6,662,651	4,238	Balarat	167,080
20	Harry Vega	1,066	203	19.0%	17	1.6%	1	5,473,637	5,135	Disco Rico	346,314
21	Edgar Prado	1,569	259	16.5%	32	2.0%	18	14,134,745	9,009	Timboroa (GB)	706,800
22	Joe Bravo	718	139	19.4%	13	1.8%	5	5,280,143	7,354	Say Florida Sandy	250,801
23	Anthony Black	783	156	19.9%	8	1.0%	0	3,552,127	4,537	Grangeville	116,260
24	Gary Stevens	532	99	18.6%	31	5.8%	22	11,752,131	22,090	Point Given	3,350,000
25	Richard Migliore	1,139	191	16.8%	19	1.7%	10	9,173,843	8,054	Miss Linda (Arg)	404,475
26	Mark T. Johnston	1,578	283	17.9%	16	1.0%	0	6,730,095	4,265	Under the Rug	225,000
27	Anthony Lovato	1,010	208	20.6%	13	1.3%	0	3,332,436	3,299	Royal Spy	322,900
28	Kris Prather	502	130	25.9%	2	0.4%	0	1,855,903	3,697	Sold to Wallstreet	75,655
29	Kent Desormeaux	771	133	17.3%	20	2.6%	7	6,984,443	9,059	Irisheyesareflying	333,600
30	Patrick Husbands	870	145	16.7%	10	1.2%	4	8,004,315	9,200	Numerous Times	676,320
31	Gus Brown	108	30	27.8%	9	8.3%	6	815,457	7,551	Praise the Prince (NZ)	225,742
32	Frank Alvarado	1,042	193	18.5%	8	0.8%	0	3,778,739	3,626	Lil Sister Stich	67,815
33	Martin Pedroza	829	144	17.4%	3	0.4%	0	3,645,043	4,397	Global	189,033
34	Michael McCarthy	979	161	16.5%	8	0.8%	1	4,625,559	4,725	Zonk	232,200
35	Jon Kenton Court	1,380	211	15.3%	14	1.0%	5	7,044,447	5,105	Percy Hope	292,500

36	Donnie Meche	767	124	16.2%	13	1.7%	3	4,935,490	6,435	Fifty Stars	552,250
37	Terry Thompson	1,495	267	17.9%	14	0.9%	0	4,449,386	2,976	Sure Shot Biscuit	365,205
38	Emile Ramsammy	929	143	15.4%	10	1.1%	1	6,850,096	7,374	Quick Blue	222,250
39	Calvin Borel	1,343	211	15.7%	7	0.5%	3	5,958,174	4,436	Gourmet Girl	300,000
40	Corey Lanerie	1,021	168	16.5%	5	0.5%	1	4,122,454	4,038	Nat's Big Party	151,230
41	Mark Patzer	519	114	22.0%	12	2.3%	0	1,524,121	2,937	I'm Free	176,264
42	Jose Luis Flores	1,133	206	18.2%	4	0.4%	0	3,204,497	2,828	Sea of Green	96,000
43	Eddie Delahoussaye	781	117	15.0%	25	3.2%	14	8,190,951	10,488	Affluent	592,000
44	Larry Melancon	561	88	15.7%	16	2.9%	8	5,954,704	10,614	Guided Tour	1,384,220
45	Ronald Warren Jr.	838	142	17.0%	7	0.8%	0	3,260,208	3,890	Hoovergetthekeys	276,260
46	David Romero Flores	928	136	14.7%	13	1.4%	10	8,534,697	9,197	Janet (GB)	715,080
47	Garrett K. Gomez	691	104	15.1%	24	3.5%	12	7,355,680	10,645	Skimming	1,330,000
48	Josiah Hampshire Jr.	1,187	283	23.8%	10	0.8%	0	2,515,520	2,119	Step With Style	65,000
49	Stewart Elliott	1,164	209	18.0%	3	0.3%	0	3,207,008	2,755	Alexandra's Angel	77,280
50	Brent E. Bartram	511	88	17.2%	10	2.0%	0	2,496,104	4,885	Potaro (Ire)	165,000
51	Rosemary Homeister	1,380	226	16.4%	14	1.0%	0	4,433,098	3,212	Ms Brookski	248,060
52	Mark Guidry	973	145	14.9%	16	1.6%	8	6,105,128	6,275	Balto Star	660,000
53	Roberto Alvarado Jr.	982	156	15.9%	9	0.9%	0	4,133,336	4,209	Holiest Punch	105,600
54	Michael F. Rowland	1,092	239	21.9%	3	0.3%	0	2,402,491	2,200	Prizes	76,425
55	Craig Perret	208	35	16.8%	15	7.2%	8	3,039,412	14,613	Ubiquity	280,240
56	John A. Grabowski	871	205	23.5%	11	1.3%	0	1,873,605	2,151	Impeachthepro	184,789
57	Charles C. Lopez	1,058	154	14.7%	10	1.0%	2	5,678,454	5,367	Arromanches	222,000
58	Christopher Griffith	686	129	18.8%	2	0.3%		1,999,826	2,915	Exciting Flash	72,420
59	Tyler Baze	1,350	196	14.5%	8	0.6%	2	6,501,987	4,816	Figlio Mio	216,580
60	Corey S. Nakatani	777	111	14.3%	16	2.1%	12	8,488,585	10,925	England's Legend (Fr)	756,000
61	T. D. Houghton	1,512	307	20.3%	20	1.3%	0	3,124,210	2,066	Secret Romeo	225,095
62	Dennis Carr	954	154	16.1%	7	0.7%	1	3,326,149	3,487	Reds Superstar	111,640
63	David Wilson	690	135	19.6%	7	1.0%	0	1,789,167	2,593	Make Contact	128,400
64	Donald R. Pettinger	528	93	17.6%	11	2.1%	2	1,964,276	3,720	Mr Ross	442,400
65	Randall A. Meier	1,241	185	14.9%	9	0.7%	3	4,956,702	3,994	Duckhorn	300,000
66	Glenn W. Corbett	1,276	244	19.1%	14	1.1%	0	2,799,061	2,194	Hangonslewpyhangon	90,010
67	Lonnie Meche	1,081	154	14.3%	14	1.3%	5	5,512,855	5,100	Outofthebox	316,695
68	Victor Espinoza	1,087	144	13.3%	26	2.4%	15	10,394,906	9,563	Spain	822,705
69	Ben Russell	1,017	194	19.1%	7	0.7%	0	2,301,987	2,264	Jumron Won	68,750
70	James McKnight	286	45	15.7%	3	1.1%	3	2,295,115	8,025	Mr. Epperson	430,180
71	Javier Santiago	227	40	17.6%	1	0.4%	0	964,705	4,250	Mazoolian Ghost	59,000
72	Clinton L. Potts	721	147	20.4%	8	1.1%	0	1,563,936	2,169	Beau's Surprise	104,324
73	Mickey Walls	469	70	14.9%	4	0.9%	2	3,372,508	7,191	Changeintheweather	207,840
74	Monte Clifton Berry	944	167	17.7%	11	1.2%	0	2,257,733	2,392	Voladora	169,675
75	Kirk Paul LeBlanc	997	166	16.7%	12	1.2%	0	2,599,650	2,607	Midge Too	147,150
76	Aaron T. Gryder	1,195	157	13.1%	12	1.0%	4	7,225,530	6,046	Say Florida Sandy	354,869
77	David Clark	632	89	14.1%	13	2.1%	2	5,081,371	8,040	Diadella	250,091
78	Steven J. Bourque	1,319	273	20.7%	12	0.9%	0	2,408,079	1,826	Hail to Bag	159,195
79	Julian Pimentel	1,039	145	14.0%	2	0.2%	0	4,387,978	4,223	El Progreso	102,420
80	Michael D. Pindell	774	128	16.5%	5	0.7%	0	2,116,191	2,734	Past Tence	71,130
81	Scott T. Saito	617	114	18.5%	4	0.7%	0	1,483,652	2,405	Ashwood C C	160,040
82	Pedro V. Alvarado	422	82	19.4%	6	1.4%	0	1,079,556	2,558	Rampaging Alf	74,565
83	Dino Luciani	541	79	14.6%	6	1.1%	0	2,955,618	5,463	Krz Ruckus	306,911
84	Paul Albert Nicol Jr.	989	203	20.5%	5	0.5%	0	1,854,769	1,875	Vanna Go	116,368
85	Derek C. Bell	837	162	19.4%	8	1.0%	0	1,722,548	2,058	Ashar	61,821
86	Dana G. Whitney	1,492	223	15.0%	7	0.5%	2	3,927,216	2,632	Western Pride	645,500
87	Manuel Aguilar	1,257	189	15.0%	7	0.6%	0	3,360,979	2,674	Chow Down	83,592
88	Joseph C. Judice	715	104	14.6%	9	1.3%	0	2,718,178	3,802	Request for Parole	199,912
89	Eddie M. Martin Jr.	1,045	140	13.4%	7	0.7%	1	4,194,453	4,014	Real Cozzy	210,000
90	Anthony J. D'Amico	742	102	13.8%	10	1.4%	4	3,187,707	4,296	Repent	415,660
91	Timothy T. Doocy	600	95	15.8%	6	1.0%	0	1,709,415	2,849	Chindi	56,151
92	Samuel B. Krasner	359	63	17.6%	6	1.7%	0	966,011	2,691	Diglett	81,655
93	Gerard Melancon	1,043	151	14.5%	10	1.0%	1	3,050,652	2,925	Bonapaw	350,290
94	Tom G. Turner	518	74	14.3%	5	1.0%	0	2,285,969	4,413	Superduper Miss	119,083
95	Jason R. Eads	863	146	16.9%	2	0.2%	0	1,902,713	2,205	Demitryst	47,484
96	Abel Castellano Jr.	936	136	14.5%	5	0.5%	0	2,803,887	2,996	Juggernaut	135,900
97	Gary Boulanger	647	82	12.7%	8	1.2%	3	5,438,879	8,406	Dancethruthedawn	970,000
98	Todd Glasser	382	65	17.0%	3	0.8%	0	1,009,037	2,641	Vikki Slew	98,359
99	Victor Carrero	784	111	14.2%	0	0.0%	0	2,692,820	3,435	Groom's Dance	60,860
100	Daryl Montoya	744	153	20.6%	6	0.8%	0	1,313,216	1,765	Oddsonjack	89,570
101	Norberto Arroyo Jr.	1,019	127	12.5%	5	0.5%	0	5,079,357	4,985	Shopping for Love	129,069
102	Miguel S. Fuentes	435	76	17.5%	16	3.7%	0	1,050,068	2,414	Yulla Yulla	182,160
103	Javier Castellano	1,135	135	11.9%	9	0.8%	4	6,752,183	5,949	Exogenous	750,000
104	Stephan Heiler	518	93	18.0%	7	1.4%	0	1,126,325	2,174	Northern Neechitoo	101,865
105	Richard H. Hamel	589	93	15.8%	12	2.0%	4	1,532,476	2,602	Fancy As	431,941
106	Mike E. Smith	771	95	12.3%	12	1.6%	6	5,467,810	7,092	Spook Express (SAf)	866,870
107	Jono C. Jones	464	61	13.2%	1	0.2%	1	2,732,783	5,890	Gonetofarr	128,336
108	Chad K. Murphy	733	115	15.7%	1	0.1%	0	1,736,098	2,368	Danar	75,008
109	Larry J. Sterling Jr.	756	105	13.9%	3	0.4%	0	2,436,927	3,223	Out of Options	121,058
110	James S. McAleney	442	57	12.9%	4	0.9%	1	2,937,741	6,646	Sweetest Thing	518,100

Leading Jockeys by Earnings in 2001

Jockey	No. mounts	No. wins	Total earnings
Jerry D. Bailey	910	227	$19,015,720
John R. Velazquez	1,411	305	15,073,790
Pat Day	1,197	249	14,497,859
Edgar S. Prado	1,569	259	14,134,745
Jorge F. Chavez	1,344	246	13,829,699
Chris J. McCarron	606	123	12,759,692
Gary L. Stevens	532	99	11,752,131
Alex O. Solis	1,200	222	11,531,521
Robby Albarado	1,401	273	10,651,669
Ramon A. Dominguez	1,864	433	10,535,087
Victor Espinoza	1,087	144	10,394,906
Laffit A. Pincay Jr.	1,252	226	10,080,366
Eibar Coa	1,396	281	9,226,516
Richard Migliore	1,139	191	9,173,843
David Romero Flores	928	136	8,534,697
Corey S. Nakatani	777	111	8,488,585
Eddie J. Delahoussaye	781	117	8,190,951
Patrick Husbands	870	145	8,004,315
Garrett K. Gomez	691	104	7,355,680
Russell A. Baze	1,503	423	7,225,600
Aaron T. Gryder	1,195	157	7,225,530
Rene R. Douglas	1,244	241	7,204,535
Todd Kabel	723	145	7,145,426
Jon Kenton Court	1,380	211	7,044,447
Kent J. Desormeaux	771	133	6,984,443
Travis L. Dunkelberger	1,544	394	6,928,243
Emile Ramsammy	929	143	6,850,096
Javier Castellano	1,135	135	6,752,183
Mark T. Johnston	1,578	283	6,730,095
Jeremy Rose	1,572	312	6,662,651
Tyler Baze	1,350	196	6,501,987
Mario G. Pino	1,443	297	6,427,497
Cornelio H. Velasquez	1,362	275	6,243,236
Mark Guidry	973	145	6,105,128
Robert C. Landry	461	57	7,902
Robby Albarado	1,401	273	7,603
Gus M. Brown	108	30	7,551
Constant Montpellier	568	63	7,445
Emile Ramsammy	929	143	7,374
Joe Bravo	718	139	7,354
Mickey Walls	469	70	7,191
Mike E. Smith	771	95	7,092
Jose A. Santos	557	67	6,916
Richard Dos Ramos	442	50	6,670

Leading Jockeys by Number of Stakes Wins in 2001

Jockey	No. mounts	No. wins	No. stakes wins
Jerry D. Bailey	910	227	58
Chris J. McCarron	606	123	49
Eibar Coa	1,396	281	39
John R. Velazquez	1,411	305	37
Ramon A. Dominguez	1,864	433	37
Edgar S. Prado	1,569	259	32
Pat Day	1,197	249	31
Gary L. Stevens	532	99	31
Jorge F. Chavez	1,344	246	29
Alex O. Solis	1,200	222	28
Victor Espinoza	1,087	144	26
Eddie Delahoussaye	781	117	25
Rick Wilson	515	117	25
Rene R. Douglas	1,244	241	24
Garrett K. Gomez	691	104	24
Mario G. Pino	1,443	297	24
Robby Albarado	1,401	273	23
Laffit A. Pincay Jr.	1,252	226	22
Travis L. Dunkelberger	1,544	394	22
Kent J. Desormeaux	771	133	20
T. D. Houghton	1,512	307	20
Cornelio H. Velasquez	1,362	275	20
Richard Migliore	1,139	191	19
Jose A. Santos	557	67	17
Harry Vega	1,066	203	17
Mark Guidry	973	145	16
Mark T. Johnston	1,578	283	16
Larry Melancon	561	88	16
Corey S. Nakatani	777	111	16
Miguel Sanchez Fuentes	435	76	16
Russell A. Baze	1,503	423	15
Jose C. Ferrer	739	89	15
Craig Perret	208	35	15
Glenn W. Corbett	1,276	244	14
Jon Kenton Court	1,380	211	14
Rosemary Homeister Jr.	1,380	226	14
Terry J. Thompson	1,495	267	14
Lonnie Meche	1,081	154	14
Joe Bravo	718	139	13
David Clark	632	89	13
David Romero Flores	928	136	13
Esteban Angel Gomez	1,386	244	13
Donnie J. Meche	767	124	13
Jose A. Velez Jr.	612	75	13
Anthony J. Lovato	1,010	208	13
Robbie G. Davis	741	89	13
Steven Joseph Bourque	1,319	273	12
Aaron T. Gryder	1,195	157	12
Richard Harvey Hamel	589	93	12
Kirk Paul LeBlanc	997	166	12

Leading Jockeys by Average Earnings Per Mount in 2001

Jockey	No. mounts	No. wins	Average earnings per starter
Gary L. Stevens	532	99	$22,090
Chris J. McCarron	606	123	21,056
Jerry D. Bailey	910	227	20,896
Craig Perret	208	35	14,613
Pat Day	1,197	249	12,112
Corey S. Nakatani	777	111	10,925
John R. Velazquez	1,411	305	10,683
Garrett K. Gomez	691	104	10,645
Larry Melancon	561	88	10,614
Eddie Delahoussaye	781	117	10,488
Jorge F. Chavez	1,344	246	10,290
Todd Kabel	723	145	9,883
Alex O. Solis	1,200	222	9,610
Victor Espinoza	1,087	144	9,563
Patrick Husbands	870	145	9,200
David Romero Flores	928	136	9,197
Kent J. Desormeaux	771	133	9,059
Edgar S. Prado	1,569	259	9,009
Rick Wilson	515	117	8,472
Gary Boulanger	647	82	8,406
Richard Migliore	1,139	191	8,054
Laffit A. Pincay Jr.	1,252	226	8,051
David Clark	632	89	8,040
James McKnight	286	45	8,025

Leading Jockeys by Percent Stakes Wins from Mounts in 2001

Jockey	No. mounts	No. wins	No. stakes wins	% stakes wins
Chris J. McCarron	606	123	49	8.1%
Craig Perret	208	35	15	7.2%
Jerry D. Bailey	910	227	58	6.4%
Gary L. Stevens	532	99	31	5.8%
Isiah Sala	156	53	8	5.1%
Rick Wilson	515	117	25	4.9%
David Bentley	105	15	5	4.8%
Hugh Cade Huston	211	46	8	3.8%
Miguel S. Fuentes	435	76	16	3.7%
Garrett K. Gomez	691	104	24	3.5%
Eddie Delahoussaye	781	117	25	3.2%
Jose A. Santos	557	67	17	3.1%
Lance K. Ayers	231	46	7	3.0%
Larry Melancon	561	88	16	2.9%
Eibar Coa	1,396	281	39	2.8%
Rohan R. Singh	401	83	11	2.7%
John R. Velazquez	1,411	305	37	2.6%
Pat Day	1,197	249	31	2.6%
Kent Desormeaux	771	133	20	2.6%
Tom Foley	117	16	3	2.6%

Leading Jockeys by Number of Wins in 2001

Jockey	No. mounts	No. wnrs	No. wins
Ramon A. Dominguez	1,864	341	433
Russell A. Baze	1,503	334	423
Travis L. Dunkelberger	1,544	294	394
Jeremy Rose	1,572	234	312
T. D. Houghton	1,512	217	307
John R. Velazquez	1,411	238	305
David Cora	1,600	208	300
Mario G. Pino	1,443	224	297
Josiah Francis Hampshire Jr.	1,187	191	283
Mark T. Johnston	1,578	216	283
Eibar Coa	1,396	224	281
Cornelio H. Velasquez	1,362	214	275
Steven Joseph Bourque	1,319	210	273
Robby Albarado	1,401	226	273
Terry J. Thompson	1,495	207	267
Jason P. Lumpkins	1,139	220	264
Edgar S. Prado	1,569	213	259
Pat Day	1,197	198	249
Jorge F. Chavez	1,344	206	246
Glenn W. Corbett	1,276	182	244
Esteban Angel Gomez	1,386	174	244
Rene R. Douglas	1,244	215	241
Michael Francis Rowland	1,092	178	239
Emilio Flores	1,427	159	231
Jerry D. Bailey	910	175	227
Laffit A. Pincay Jr.	1,252	176	226
Rosemary B. Homeister Jr.	1,380	164	226
Dana G. Whitney	1,492	164	223
Alex O. Solis	1,200	178	222
Luis Antonio Gonzalez	1,291	166	219
Calvin H. Borel	1,343	179	211
Jon Kenton Court	1,380	168	211
Winston Albert Thompson	1,160	147	209
Stewart Elliott	1,164	165	209
Anthony J. Lovato	1,010	141	208
Jose Luis Flores	1,133	153	206
John A. Grabowski	871	130	205
Perry Wayne Ouzts	1,432	156	204
Paul Albert Nicol Jr.	989	138	203
Harry Vega	1,066	157	203
Rex A. Stokes III	1,119	155	201
Taylor M. Hole	1,019	144	200
Rodney A. Prescott	1,490	168	199
Tyler Baze	1,350	158	196
Larry C. Reynolds	1,411	157	194
Ben Russell	1,017	159	194
Frank T. Alvarado	1,042	155	193
Richard Migliore	1,139	147	191
Manuel Aguilar	1,257	146	189
Randall A. Meier	1,241	137	185

Leading Jockeys by Number of Individual Winners in 2001

Jockey	No. mounts	No. wnrs
Ramon A. Dominguez	1,864	341
Russell A. Baze	1,503	334
Travis L. Dunkelberger	1,544	294
John R. Velazquez	1,411	238
Jeremy Rose	1,572	234
Robby Albarado	1,401	226
Mario G. Pino	1,443	224
Eibar Coa	1,396	224
Jason P. Lumpkins	1,139	220
T. D. Houghton	1,512	217
Mark T. Johnston	1,578	216
Rene R. Douglas	1,244	215
Cornelio H. Velasquez	1,362	214
Edgar S. Prado	1,569	213
Steven Joseph Bourque	1,319	210
David Cora	1,600	208
Terry J. Thompson	1,495	207
Jorge F. Chavez	1,344	206
Pat Day	1,197	198
Josiah Francis Hampshire Jr.	1,187	191
Glenn W. Corbett	1,276	182
Calvin H. Borel	1,343	179
Michael Francis Rowland	1,092	178
Alex O. Solis	1,200	178
Laffit A. Pincay Jr.	1,252	176
Jerry D. Bailey	910	175
Esteban Angel Gomez	1,386	174
Jon Kenton Court	1,380	168
Rodney A. Prescott	1,490	168
Luis Antonio Gonzalez	1,291	166
Stewart Elliott	1,164	165
Rosemary B. Homeister Jr.	1,380	164
Dana G. Whitney	1,492	164
Emilio Flores	1,427	159
Ben Russell	1,017	159
Tyler Baze	1,350	158
Larry C. Reynolds	1,411	157
Harry Vega	1,066	157
Perry Wayne Ouzts	1,432	156
Frank T. Alvarado	1,042	155
Rex A. Stokes III	1,119	155
Jose Luis Flores	1,133	153
Richard Migliore	1,139	147
Winston A. Thompson	1,160	147
Manuel Aguilar	1,257	146
Taylor M. Hole	1,019	144
Jamie Theriot	1,119	144
Anthony J. Lovato	1,010	141
Corey J. Lanerie	1,021	140
Paul Albert Nicol Jr.	989	138

Leading Jockeys by Number of Graded Stakes Wins in 2001

Jockey	No. mounts	No. wins	No. graded stakes wins	% graded stakes wins
Jerry D. Bailey	910	227	43	4.7%
John R. Velazquez	1,411	305	29	2.1%
Chris J. McCarron	606	123	28	4.6%
Gary L. Stevens	532	99	22	4.1%
Edgar S. Prado	1,569	259	18	1.2%
Pat Day	1,197	249	17	1.4%
Victor Espinoza	1,087	144	15	1.4%
Jorge F. Chavez	1,344	246	14	1.0%
Eddie Delahoussaye	781	117	14	1.8%
Alex O. Solis	1,200	222	14	1.2%
Garrett K. Gomez	691	104	12	1.7%
Corey S. Nakatani	777	111	12	1.5%
Laffit A. Pincay Jr.	1,252	226	11	0.9%
David R. Flores	928	136	10	1.1%
Richard Migliore	1,139	191	10	0.9%
Jose A. Santos	557	67	10	1.8%
Robby Albarado	1,401	273	9	0.6%
Eibar Coa	1,396	281	9	0.6%
Mark Guidry	973	145	8	0.8%
Larry Melancon	561	88	8	1.4%
Craig Perret	208	35	8	3.9%
Rick Wilson	515	117	8	1.6%

Leading Jockeys by Career Earnings

Jockey	Career earnings
1. Chris McCarron	$261,792,321†
2. Pat Day	258,247,877†
3. Laffit Pincay Jr.	227,680,059†
4. Jerry Bailey	221,068,678†
5. Gary Stevens	203,407,814†
6. Eddie Delahoussaye	192,083,363†
7. Angel Cordero Jr.	164,561,227
8. Kent Desormeaux	151,919,414†
9. Alex Solis	145,999,364†
10. Jose Santos	144,541,072†
11. Mike Smith	142,913,924†
12. Jorge Velasquez	125,544,379
13. Corey Nakatani	124,756,590†
14. Bill Shoemaker	123,375,524
15. Jorge Chavez	119,342,423†
16. Robbie Davis	113,614,773†
17. Russell Baze	112,738,284†
18. Richard Migliore	110,007,930|
19. Shane Sellers	107,939,094†
20. Craig Perret	107,574,738†
21. Eddie Maple	105,338,573
22. Pat Valenzuela	99,166,979†
23. Edgar Prado	97,466,911†
24. Chris Antley	92,203,341
25. John Velazquez	90,455,716†
26. Sandy Hawley	88,681,292
27. Julie Krone	81,335,971
28. Jean-Luc Samyn	79,879,324†
29. Earlie Fires	78,170,624†
30. David Romero	77,248,497†
31. Randy Romero	75,264,198
32. Rick Wilson	73,335,913†
33. Mario Pino	72,553,955†
34. Herb McCauley	70,700,811
35. Aaron Gryder	70,427,720†
36. Joe Bravo	67,820,212†
37. Mark Guidry	67,326,932†
38. Ray Sibille	66,528,200†
39. Robby Albarado	61,921,444†
40. Nick Santagata	61,730,973†
41. Calvin Borel	57,828,844†
42. Ronnie Ardoin	57,456,281†
43. Garrett Gomez	56,992,922†
44. Fernando Toro	56,299,765
45. Rene Douglas	55,092,006†
46. Mark Castaneda	53,068,587
47. Martin Pedroza	52,999,378†
48. Todd Kabel	52,326,643†
49. Jean Cruguet	51,557,267
50. Mark Johnston	51,354,613†

Leading Jockeys by Career Wins

Jockey	Career wins
1. Laffit Pincay Jr.	9,331†
2. Bill Shoemaker	8,833
3. Pat Day	8,182†
4. Russell Baze	7,741†
5. David Gall	7,396
6. Chris McCarron	7,118†
7. Angel Cordero Jr.	7,057
8. Jorge Velasquez	6,795
9. Sandy Hawley	6,449
10. Larry Snyder	6,388
11. Carl Gambardella	6,349
12. Eddie Delahoussaye	6,342†
13. Earlie Fires	6,181†
14. John Longden	6,032
15. Jerry Bailey	5,196†
16. Ronnie Ardoin	5,139†
17. Rudy Baez	4,875
18. Mario Pino	4,848†
19. Eddie Arcaro	4,779
20. Rick Wilson	4,777†
21. Gary Stevens	4,664†
22. Don Brumfield	4,573
23. Edgar Prado	4,487†
24. Steve Brooks	4,451
25. Anthony Black	4,408†
26. Eddie Maple	4,398
27. Walter Blum	4,382
28. Mark Guidry	4,318†
29. Craig Perret	4,312†
30. Randy Romero	4,294
31. Jeff Lloyd	4,276
32. Bill Hartack	4,272
33. Kent Desormeaux	4,185†
34. Ray Sibillo	4,182†
35. Timothy Doocy	4,155†
36. Perry Ouzts	4,154†
37. Mike Smith	4,082†
38. Avelino Gomez	4,081
39. Hugo Dittrach	4,000
40. Phil Grove	3,991
41. Robert Colton	3,971†
42. Leslie Hulet	3,816
43. Ted Atkinson	3,795
44. Ralph Neves	3,722
45. Leroy Moyers	3,770
46. Robert Baird	3,749
47. Shane Sellers	3,719
48. Dan Weiler	3,694
49. Ron Hansen	3,693
50. Mike Rowland	3,685†

†Active jockeys through March 31, 2002

Great Names in Racing of the Past
(Names of Racing Hall of Fame members are in boldface italics.)

As much as great horses are central to the sport, Thoroughbred racing and breeding would not exist without important individuals of the past who worked to perfect the breed or sport and who performed with distinction within the industry. Here are outstanding individuals from racing's history, with members of the Racing Hall of Fame noted in boldface italics.

Adams, John H., 1914-'95. Jockey, trainer. George Woolf Memorial Jockey Award in 1956; leading jockey '37, '42, '43; inducted into Racing Hall of Fame in '65. Rode 3,270 winners, including *Kayak II, Hasty Road. Trained J. O. Tobin. Won 1954 Preakness Stakes aboard Hasty Road.

Aga Khan III, Sultan Sir Mahomed Shah, 1877-1957. Ismaili Muslim leader. Owner of Gilltown, Sheshoon, Ballymany, Sallymount, and Ongar Studs in Ireland; Haras de la Coquenne, Haras de Marly-la-Ville, Haras de Saint-Crespin in France. Leading owner in England 13 times; leading breeder in England eight times. Bred *Bahram, *Nasrullah, *Tulyar, *Mahmoud, *Alibhai, *Khaled, *Masaka; owned Mumtaz Mahal, *Blenheim II. Grandfather of current Aga Khan.

Alexander, A. J., 1824-1902. Iron works, farming. Owner of Woodburn Stud, Kentucky. Stood leading sire Lexington. Leading breeder. Bred Duke of Magenta, Spendthrift, Tom Bowling, Tom Ochiltree, Harry Bassett, Joe Daniels, Fellowcraft, Fonso, etc. Brother of Robert A. S. Alexander.

Alexander, Robert A. S., 1819-'67. Iron works, farming. Founder of Woodburn Stud, Kentucky. Stood leading sire Lexington. Leading breeder. Bred Norfolk, Asteroid, Maiden, Virgil, Preakness, etc. Brother of A. J. Alexander.

Annenberg, Moses L., 1878-1942. Publisher. Published *Daily Racing Form* 1922-'42, *Morning Telegraph.* Founded Triangle Publications.

Arcaro, Eddie, 1916-'97. Jockey. George Woolf Memorial Jockey Award in 1953; inducted into Racing Hall of Fame in '58. Rode 4,779 winners, including Whirlaway, Citation, Bold Ruler, Nashua. Won two Triple Crowns, five Kentucky Derbys, six Preakness Stakes, and six Belmont Stakes.

Bacon, Mary, 1948-'91. Pioneer female jockey; rode 286 winners.

Baldwin, Elias J. "Lucky", 1828-1909. Mining, investments. Owned Rancho el Santa Anita, California. Bred and owned Emperor of Norfolk, Volante, Rey el Santa Anita, Americus. Built original Santa Anita Park racetrack.

Barbee, George, ca. 1855-1941. Jockey. Inducted into Racing Hall of Fame in 1996. Rode Saxon, Survivor, Shirley, Jacobus. Won the first Preakness Stakes aboard Survivor in 1873; won two other Preakness Stakes and one Belmont Stakes.

Barrera, Lazaro, 1924-'91. Trainer. Leading trainer by money won 1977-'80; Eclipse Award trainer 1976-'79; inducted into Racing Hall of Fame in '79. Trained more than 140 stakes winners and six champions, including Affirmed, Bold Forbes. Only trainer to win four consecutive Eclipse Awards.

Bassett, Carroll K., 1905-'72. Jockey. Inducted into Racing Hall of Fame in 1972. Rode more than 100 steeplechase winners, including Battleship, Peacock,

Night Retired, Passive, Sable Muff. Rode Battleship to victory in the American Grand National and two National Steeplechase Hunt Cups.

Beard, Louis A., 1888-1954. Farm manager, racing executive. Managed Greentree Stud 1927-'48. Co-founder and president, Keeneland Race Course; co-founder, American Thoroughbred Breeders Association; co-founder, Grayson Foundation.

Bedwell, H. Guy, 1876-1951. Trainer. Leading trainer by races won in 1909, '12-'17; leading trainer by money won 1918-'19; inducted into Racing Hall of Fame in '71. Trained 2,160 winners, including Sir Barton, Billy Kelly. First trainer to saddle a horse (Sir Barton) to a Triple Crown (1919); won 16 races in 14 days in 1910.

Belmont, August I, 1816-'90. Banker. President of American Jockey Club (Jerome Park) 1866-'86. Owner of Nursery Stud in New York and later in Kentucky. Leading owner. Bred and owned Woodbine, Potomac, Fides, Prince Royal; also owned Glenelg, Fenian, *The Ill-Used.

Belmont, August II, 1853-1924. Banker. First president of Belmont Park; chairman, the Jockey Club 1895-1924; chairman, Belmont Park. Owned Nursery Stud, Kentucky. Leading breeder. Bred Man o' War, Fair Play, Tracery, Beldame; also owned *Hourless, Henry of Navarre.

Bieber, Isidor, 1887-1974. Restaurateur, gambler. Co-owner of Bieber-Jacobs Stable, Stymie Manor, Maryland. Leading breeder 1964-'67; co-breeder of Hail to Reason, Allez France, Affectionately, Straight Deal; also co-owned Stymie, Searching.

Bostwick, George, 1909-'82. Jockey, trainer. Leading amateur steeplechase jockey 1928-'32, '41; leading steeplechase trainer 1940, '51, '55; inducted into Racing Hall of Fame in '68. Rode 87 winners, including Chenango, Escapade, Sussex, Darkness. Trained Neji and Oedipus. Played on six United States championship polo teams.

Marcel Boussac, 1889-1980. Textile tycoon. Leading French breeder 19 times, winner of the French Derby 12 times. Bred notable racehorses or sires Tourbillon, Pharis, Djebel, *Goya II, and *Ambiorix. In 1950 became first foreign owner to lead English owners list, the year he won the Epsom Derby with Galcador. Also bred two-time Prix de l'Arc de Triomphe winner Corrida.

Bowie, Oden, 1826-'94. Railways, politician. Maryland governor 1869-'72; first president of Pimlico Race Course in 1870. Owner of Fairview Plantation, Maryland. Bred Catesby, Crickmore.

Bradley, Edward R., 1859-1946. Gambler. Owner of Idle Hour Stock Farm, Kentucky. Bred and owned Blue Larkspur, Bimelech, Black Helen, Busher, Bubbling Over. Bred and owned four Kentucky Derby winners and imported foundation mare *La Troienne.

Brady, James Cox Jr., 1908-'71. Investments. Chairman of the Jockey Club 1961-'69; chairman of New York Racing Association 1961-'69. Owner of Dixiana Farm, Kentucky, and Hamilton Stable. Bred Long Look, War Plumage, Jungle Cove. Co-founder of Monmouth Park, American Horse Council; oversaw rebuilding of Belmont Park. Father of Nicholas J. Brady, United States treasury secretary 1988-'93.

Brooks, Steve, 1922-'79. Jockey. George Woolf Memorial Jockey Award in 1962; leading jockey in '49; inducted into Racing Hall of Fame in '63. Rode 4,451

winners, including Two Lea, Citation, Round Table. Rode Ponder in 1949 Kentucky Derby.

Brown, Edward D. "Brown Dick", 1850-1906. Trainer, jockey. Inducted into Racing Hall of Fame in 1984. Trained Ben Brush, Plaudit, Spendthrift, Hindoo. Rode Asteroid to an undefeated 9-9-0-0 record in 1864-'65.

Brown, Harry D. "Curly", 1863-1930. Restaurateur, racetrack executive. Founder and first president of Arlington Park; built Laurel Park, Oriental Park. Owned Brown Shasta Farm, California.

Bruce, Benjamin G., 1827-'91. Publisher. Founder and editor of the *Livestock Record* 1875-'91 (predecessor of *The Thoroughbred Record*). Brother of Sanders D. Bruce.

Bruce, Sanders D., 1825-1902. Hotelier, publisher. Co-editor of *Turf, Field and Farm* 1865-1902. Compiler of first four volumes of *American Stud Book*. Brother of Benjamin G. Bruce.

Burch, Preston, 1884-1978. Trainer, breeder, owner. Leading trainer in 1950; inducted into Racing Hall of Fame in '63. Trained more than 70 stakes winners, including George Smith, Sailor, Flower Bowl, Bold. Bred Gallorette. Trained stakes winners in New York, Canada, Cuba, France, and Italy. Wrote influential book on training, *Training Thoroughbred Horses*. Son of William P. Burch; father of Racing Hall of Fame trainer J. Elliott Burch.

Burch, William P., 1846-1926. Trainer. Inducted into Racing Hall of Fame in 1955. Trained Grey Friar, My Own, Decanter. First of three generations of Hall of Fame trainers. Father of Preston Burch.

Burke, Carleton F., 1882-1962. Banker, farmer. First chairman of California Horse Racing Board 1933-'39.

Burlew, Fred, 1871-1927. Trainer. Inducted into Racing Hall of Fame in 1973. Trained 32 stakes winners and two champions, including Beldame, Morvich, Inchcape.

Burns, Tommy H., 1879-1913. Jockey. Leading jockey by races won in 1898-'99; inducted into Racing Hall of Fame in 1983. Rode 1,333 winners, including Broomstick, Imp, Caughnawaga. Set an American record in the 1¼-mile Brighton Beach Handicap aboard Broomstick.

Butler, James Sr., 1855-1934. Grocery-chain owner. Owner of Empire City racetrack. Owner of East View Farm, New York. Bred Questionnaire, Sting, Pebbles, Spur; owned Comely.

Butler, James II, 1891-1940. Grocery-chain owner. President of Empire City Racing Association. Owner of East View Farm, New York.

Butwell, James, 1896-1956. Jockey, racing official. Leading jockey in 1912; leading jockey by races won in '20; inducted into Racing Hall of Fame in '84. Rode 1,402 winners, including Roamer, Sweep, Hilarious, Maskette. Leading American jockey by number of wins at the time of his retirement.

Byers, J. Dallett "Dolly", 1898-1966. Jockey, trainer. Leading steeplechase jockey 1918, '21, '28; leading jockey by money won in '28; inducted into Racing Hall of Fame in '67. Rode 149 winners, including Jolly Roger, Fairmount. Trained Tea-Maker, Lovely Night, Invader. Won the Temple Gwathmey Steeplechase Handicap five years in a row.

Byrnes, Matthew, 1854-1933. Jockey, trainer. Rode *Glenelg, Kingfisher; trained Racing Hall of Fame members Parole, Salvator, Firenze.

Caldwell, Thomas, 1928-2001. Auctioneer. Auctioneer and director of auctions for the Keeneland Association 1975-2001. Owned Gavel Ranch, Oregon.

Campbell, John B., 1876-1954. Racing executive. Racing secretary and handicapper at New York tracks 1935-'54. Handicapped three-way dead heat in 1944 Carter Handicap.

Capossela, Fred, 1903-'91. Famed race caller at New York racetracks 1943-'71.

Cassidy, Mars, 1862-1929. Racing executive. Legendary starter at New York racetracks 1902-'29. Father of Marshall Cassidy.

Cassidy, Marshall, 1892-1968. Racing executive. Executive secretary of the Jockey Club. Developed first modern starting gate; developed modern photofinish camera; instituted first film patrol and saliva tests; founded Jockey Club Round Table meetings. Son of Mars Cassidy.

Cella, Charles, 1875-1940. Hotelier, theater owner. Founder of Oaklawn Park; co-owner of Fort Erie racetrack.

Chenery, Christopher C., 1886-1973. Utilities. First president of Thoroughbred Owners and Breeders Association. Owner of Meadow Stud, Virginia. Bred Secretariat, Riva Ridge, Hill Prince, Cicada, First Landing, Sir Gaylord. Co-founder of New York Racing Association.

Childs, Frank E., 1886-1973. Trainer. Inducted into Racing Hall of Fame in 1968. Trained 23 stakes winners, including *Tomy Lee, Canina, Dinner Gong. Known for his ability to turn claiming horses into stakes winners.

Chinn, Philip T., 1874-1962. Horse trader. Owner of Himyar Stud, Kentucky. Bred 58 stakes winners, including Miss Merriment, Black Maria, In Memoriam, High Resolve. Leading consignor at Saratoga in 1920s; sold then-record $70,000 yearling in '27.

Clark, Henry S., 1904-'99. Trainer. Inducted into Racing Hall of Fame in 1982. Trained 37 stakes winners and one champion, including Tempted, Cyane, Endine, Obeah. Twice won back-to-back Delaware Handicaps.

Clark, John C., 1891-1974. Advertising executive. President of Hialeah Park 1940-'54; first president of Thoroughbred Racing Associations 1942-'43. Owned Sun Briar Court, New York. Bred Charlie McAdam, Accomplish.

Clark, John H. "Trader", 1919-'96. Horse trader, author. President, Thoroughbred Breeders of Kentucky. Author of *Trader Clark*.

Clark, Meriwether Lewis, 1846-'99. Racing executive. Founder and president of Louisville Jockey Club. Founder of Kentucky Derby in 1875. Established first uniform scale of weights in America.

Clay, Ezekiel F., 1841-1920. Farmer, breeder. President, Kentucky Racing Association. Co-owner of Runnymede Farm, Kentucky. Chairman of Kentucky Racing Commission. Bred Hanover, Sir Dixon, Miss Woodford, Raceland.

Clay, Henry, 1777-1852. Lawyer, politician. Owner of Ashland Stud, Kentucky. Bred Heraldry. Father of John M. Clay.

Clay, John M., 1820-'87. Farmer, breeder. Owner of Ashland Stud, Kentucky. Bred Kentucky, Maggie B. B., Daniel Boone, Simon Kenton, Gilroy, Star Davis, Lodi, Day Star. Son of Henry Clay.

Cocks, W. Burling, 1915-'98. Trainer. Leading steeplechase trainer 1949, '65, '73, '80; F. Ambrose Clark Award

in '73; inducted into Racing Hall of Fame in '85. Trained 49 stakes winners, including six American Grand National winners. Trained Zaccio, Down First.

Coe, William R., 1869-1955. Insurance, financier. Owner of Shoshone Farm, Kentucky. Bred and owned Pompey, Pompoon; owned Ladysman, Cleopatra, Black Maria, Pilate.

Coltiletti, Frank, 1904-'87. Jockey, trainer, racing official. Inducted into Racing Hall of Fame in 1970. Rode 667 winners, including Mars, Crusader, Sun Beau. Won Preakness Stakes at age 17 aboard Broomspun in 1921.

Combs, Leslie II, 1901-'90. Breeder. Chairman of Kentucky Racing Commission. Owner of Spendthrift Farm, Kentucky. Leading breeder in 1972. Bred 247 stakes winners, including Majestic Prince, Myrtle Charm, Idun, Mr. Prospector. Originated modern stallion syndicates in 1950s.

Conway, James P., 1910-'84. Trainer. Inducted into Racing Hall of Fame in 1996. Trained 43 stakes winners and five champions, including Chateaugay, Primonetta, Grecian Queen. Won 1963 Kentucky Derby and Belmont Stakes with three-year-old champion colt Chateaugay.

Corrigan, Edward, 1854-1924. Railway investor. Founded Hawthorne Race Course. Raced *McGee.

Cowdin, John E., 1859-1941. Silk merchant. President of Queens County Jockey Club (Aqueduct).

Crawford, Robert H. "Specs", 1897-1975. Jockey, trainer. Leading steeplechase jockey 1919-'20, '22, '26; inducted into Racing Hall of Fame in '73. Rode 139 winners, including Jolly Roger, Fairmount, Lytle, Erne II. Won four American Grand Nationals.

Croker, Richard "Boss", 1841-1922. Real estate, politician. Owner of Glencairn Stud, Ireland. Bred Orby, Rhodora, Grand Parade.

Cromwell, Thomas B., 1871-1957. Publisher, bloodstock agent. Founded *The Blood-Horse*, Cromwell Bloodstock agency. Credited with refining past performance charts.

Crosby, H. L. "Bing", 1903-'77. Entertainer. First president of Del Mar Turf Club 1936-'46. Co-owner of Binglin Stock Farm, California. Owned *Meadow Court, *Ligaroti, *Don Bingo, *Blackie II.

Daingerfield, Algernon, 1867-1941. Racing executive. Executive secretary of the Jockey Club. Son of Foxhall Daingerfield.

Daingerfield, Elizabeth, 1870-1951. Farm manager. Owner of Haylands Farm. Managed Wickliffe Stud, Faraway Farm. Managed leading sires Man o' War, High Time. Daughter of Foxhall Daingerfield.

Daingerfield, Foxhall A., ca. 1840-1913. Farm manager. Managed stud careers of Domino, Commando, Ben Brush, Kingston at Castleton Stud, Kentucky. Father of Algernon and Elizabeth Daingerfield.

Daingerfield, J. Keene, 1910-'93. Racing executive, author. Kentucky state steward 1973-'85. Eclipse Award of Merit in 1989. Author of *Training for Fun and Profit (Maybe)*. Grandson of Foxhall Daingerfield.

Daly, William C. "Father Bill", 1837-1931. Trainer. Famous mentor of Racing Hall of Fame jockeys James McLaughlin, Snapper Garrison, Winnie O'Connor, Danny Maher.

Daly, Marcus, 1842-1900. Mining. Owner of Bitter Root Stock Farm, Montana. Bred *Ogden, Tammany; owned Hamburg.

De Bartolo, Edward J., 1909-'94. Real estate developer. Owner of Louisiana Downs, Thistledown, Rem-

ington Park. Special Eclipse Award in 1988.

De Francis, Frank, 1927-'89. Lawyer, racing executive. Owner of King of Mardi Gras, Hail Emperor. Led groups to buy Laurel Park in 1984 and Pimlico Race Course in '86, thus consolidating ownership of Maryland racetracks.

DeLancey, James, 1732-1801. Real estate. Owner of Bouwerie Farm, New York. Bred Maria Slamerkin, Bashaw. Imported *DeLancey's Cub mare (great American foundation mare), *Lath, *Wildair.

Donn, James Sr., 1887-1972. Landscaping contractor, nursery owner. Chairman of Gulfstream Park 1944-'72. Grandfather of Gulfstream Park executive Douglas Donn.

Doswell, Thomas W., 1792-1890. Tobacco plantations. Owner of Bullfield Plantation. Bred Planet, Eolus, Algerine, Morello, Fanny Washington; owner of Knight of Ellerslie, Nina, Abd-el-Kader. Mentor and partner of Capt. Richard Hancock, who established Ellerslie Stud.

Duke, William, 1858-1926. Trainer. Inducted into Racing Hall of Fame in 1956. Trained Flying Ebony, Coventry. Won the 1924 French Derby with *Pot Au Feu; won '25 Kentucky Derby with Flying Ebony; won '25 Preakness Stakes with Coventry.

Dunn, Neville, 1904-'57. Publisher, editor. Editor of *The Thoroughbred Record* 1941-'57. Co-founder of Thoroughbred Club of America.

duPont, William Jr., 1897-1966. Banker. Owner of Walnut Hall Farm, Virginia. Bred and owned Parlo, Berlo, Rosemont, Fairy Chant, Ficklebush; owned Fair Star, Dauber. Founder of Delaware Park.

Duryea, Herman B., 1862-1916. Investments. Owner of Haras du Gazon, France. Leading owner in 1904, when leasing W. C. Whitney's horses. Bred and owned *Durbar II, Banshee, *Sweeper; also owned Irish Lad.

Dwyer, Michael F., 1847-1906. Meat processor. Leading owner. Owned or co-owned Hindoo, Hanover, Miss Woodford, Kingston, Luke Blackburn, Bramble, Ben Brush, Tremont, etc. Brother of Philip J. Dwyer.

Dwyer, Philip J., 1843-1917. Meat processor. President of Brooklyn Jockey Club (Gravesend), Queens County Jockey Club (Aqueduct). Leading owner. Co-owned Hindoo, Hanover, Miss Woodford, Kingston, Luke Blackburn, Bramble, Tremont, etc. Brother of Michael F. Dwyer.

Easton, William—ca. 1850-1909. Auctioneer. American representative of Tattersalls; auctioneer for Fasig-Tipton Co. First great American auctioneer.

Ellsworth, Rex, 1907-'97. Rancher. Owner of Ellsworth Farm, California. Leading owner and breeder 1962-'63. Bred and owned Swaps, Candy Spots, Olden Times, Prove It; also owned *Prince Royal II.

Engelhard, Charles W., 1917-'71. Precious metals. Owner of Cragwood Stable. Leading owner in England in 1970. Owned Nijinsky II, *Hawaii, Assagai, Ribocco, Ribero, Halo, Mr. Leader, Indiana.

Ensor, Lavelle "Buddy", 1900-'47. Jockey. Inducted into Racing Hall of Fame in 1962. Rode 411 winners, including Exterminator, Grey Lag, Hannibal. Rode 33 winners in 11 days, including five of six races on one of those days, in 1919.

Estes, Joseph A., 1902-'70. Journalist. Editor of *The Blood-Horse* 1930-'63. Invented Average Earnings Index; established Jockey Club Statistical Bureau.

Evans, Thomas Mellon, 1910-'97. Mergers and acquisitions. Owner of Buckland Farm. Bred and owned Pleasant Colony, Pleasant Tap, Stage Colony.

Fairbarn, Robert A., 1867-1951. Financier. Owner of Fairholme Farm, Kentucky. Bred Gallahadion, Hoop, Jr. Co-owner of *Sir Gallahad III, *Blenheim II.

Fasig, William B., 1846-1902. Auctioneer. Co-founder of Fasig-Tipton Co. in 1898. Conducted first equine auctions in Madison Square Garden.

Fator, Laverne, 1900-'36. Jockey. Leading jockey 1925-'26; inducted into Racing Hall of Fame in '55. Rode 1,075 winners, including Grey Lag, Black Maria, Pompey, Scapa Flow. Won consecutive runnings of Belmont Futurity and Carter and Gazelle Handicaps.

Feustel, Louis, 1884-1970. Trainer. Leading trainer in 1920; inducted into Racing Hall of Fame in '64. Trained two champions and Man o' War, Rock View, Ordinance, Ladkin. Won 20 of 21 races with Man o' War.

Field, Marshall W. III, 1893-1956. Publisher, retailer. Bred High Quest, High Strung, Escutcheon, Clang, Eclair; owned Nimba, Stimulus.

Finney, Humphrey S., 1903-'84. Auctioneer. Chairman of Fasig-Tipton Co. 1952-'84. Founded *Maryland Horse*; author of *A Stud Farm Diary, Fair Exchange*. Father of John M. S. Finney.

Finney, John M. S., 1934-'94. Auctioneer. President Fasig-Tipton Co. 1968-'89. Son of Humphrey Finney.

Fisher, Charles T., 1880-1964. Automobile manufacturer. Owner of Dixiana Farm, Kentucky. Bred Spy Song, Mata Hari, Sweep All, Star Reward.

Fitzsimmons, James E. "Sunny Jim", 1874-1966. Trainer. Leading trainer 1930, '32, '36, '39, '55; inducted into Racing Hall of Fame in '58. Trained 2,275 winners, 155 stakes winners, including Triple Crown winners Gallant Fox and Omaha, and eight champions, including Bold Ruler, Nashua, Granville.

Galbreath, John W., 1897-1988. Real estate developer. Owned Darby Dan Farm, Kentucky and Ohio. Eclipse Award, Man of the Year in 1972. Bred and owned Roberto, Chateaugay, Primonetta, Little Current, Graustark, His Majesty, Proud Truth, Proud Clarion. Instrumental in overseeing rebuilding Belmont Park and Aqueduct.

Garner, J. Mack, 1900-'36. Jockey. Leading jockey by races won in 1915; leading jockey by money won in '29; inducted into Racing Hall of Fame in '69. Rode 1,346 winners, including Cavalcade, Blue Larkspur. Won 1934 kentucky derby on cavalcade.

Garrison, Edward R. "Snapper", 1868-1930. Jockey, stable agent, trainer, racing official. Inducted into Racing Hall of Fame in 1955. By his estimate, rode more than 700 winners, including Firenze, Tammany. His come-from-behind style immortalized as "Garrison finish."

Gaver, John M., 1900-'82. Trainer. Leading trainer 1942, '51; inducted into Racing Hall of Fame in '66. Trained 73 stakes winners and four champions, including Tom Fool, Capot, Stage Door Johnny, Devil Diver. Won the handicap triple crown with Tom Fool in 1953.

Genter, Frances S., 1898-1992. Household appliances manufacturer. Owned Frances S. Genter Stable. Eclipse Award owner in 1990. Bred and owned In Reality, Smile; owned Unbridled, My Dear Girl, Rough'n Tumble.

Gentry, Olin B., 1900-'90. Farm manager. Managed Idle Hour Stock Farm, Darby Dan Farm. Planned matings for 188 stakes winners, 20 champions, five

Kentucky Derby winners. Father of Kentucky breeder Tom Gentry.

Gluck, Maxwell F., 1899-1984. Apparel stores. Owner of Elmendorf Farm. Eclipse Award outstanding owner in 1977; leading owner '77, '81; leading breeder '73, '81. Bred and owned Protagonist, Talking Picture, Big Spruce, Hold Your Peace; owned Prince John. Donation founded Maxwell F. Gluck Equine Research Center at University of Kentucky.

Gomez, Avelino, 1929-'80. Jockey. Leading Canadian jockey seven times; North American leading jockey in 1966; inducted into Racing Hall of Fame in '82. Rode 4,081 winners, including Ridan, Buckpasser, Affectionately.

Graham, Florence N. "Elizabeth Arden", 1885-1966. Cosmetics manufacturer. Owner of Maine Chance Farm, Kentucky. Leading owner in 1945. Bred Gun Bow, Jewel's Reward, Jet Action; owned Jet Pilot, Beaugay, Myrtle Charm, Star Pilot, Mr. Busher, Lord Boswell.

Grayson, Cary T., 1878-1938. Physician. Owner of Blue Ridge Farm, Virginia. Bred Insco, My Own, Happy Argo; also owned High Time. Co-founder of Grayson Foundation.

Griffin, Henry "Harry", 1876-1955. Jockey. Inducted into Racing Hall of Fame in 1956. Rode 569 winners, including The Butterflies, Henry of Navarre. One of the original investors in Hollywood Park.

Guerin, O. Eric, 1924-'93. Jockey. Leading apprentice jockey in 1942; inducted into Racing Hall of Fame in '72. Rode 2,712 winners, including Native Dancer, Bed o' Roses, Jet Pilot. Rode Native Dancer in 20 of his 21 victories (in 22 starts).

Guest, Raymond R., 1907-'91. Investments. Owner of Powhatan Plantation, Virginia; Ballygoran Stud, Ireland. Bred and owned Tom Rolfe, Chieftain; bred Cascapedia; owned Sir Ivor, Larkspur.

Guggenheim, Harry F., 1890-1971. Publisher, mining. Owner of Cain Hoy Stable. Leading breeder in England in 1963. Bred and owned Never Bend, Bald Eagle, Ack Ack, Cherokee Rose, Red God; bred Ragusa, Crafty Admiral; owned Dark Star, *Turn-to. Co-founder of New York Racing Association.

Haggin, James Ben Ali, 1821-1914. Lawyer, mining. Owner of Elmendorf Farm, Kentucky; Rancho del Paso, California. Bred Firenze, Africander, Tyrant, Waterboy, Tournament; owned Salvator, Ben Ali.

Haggin, Louis L. II, 1913-'80. Real estate. Chairman of Keeneland Association 1970-'80; president of Thoroughbred Racing Associations 1967-'68; co-founder of Thoroughbred Breeders of Kentucky. Bred and owned Himalayan, Harbor Springs, Tingle. Great-grandson of James Ben Ali Haggin.

Hagyard, Charles W., 1901-'95. Veterinarian. Owner of Hagyard Farm, Kentucky. Breeder of Rough'n Tumble, Rising Market. Stood Hail to Reason, Promised Land. Co-founder of Hagyard-Davidson-McGee equine clinic.

Hancock, Arthur B. Sr., 1875-1957. Breeder. President of Breeders' Sales Co. Founder and owner of Claiborne Farm, Kentucky; owner of Ellerslie Stud, Virginia. Leading breeder 1935-'37, '39, '43. Breeder of Johnstown, Beaugay, Cleopatra, St. James, Jacola, Nimba, Jet Pilot. Imported and syndicated *Sir Gallahad III, *Blenheim II. Son of Richard J. Hancock, father of Arthur B. "Bull" Hancock Jr.

Hancock, Arthur B. Jr. "Bull", 1910-'72. Breeder. President of American Thoroughbred Breeders Association. Owner of Claiborne Farm, Kentucky, and

Ellerslie Stud, Virginia. Leading breeder 1958-'59, '68-'69. Breeder of Round Table, Gamely, Apalachee, Moccasin, Doubledogdare, Bayou, Lamb Chop. Imported and syndicated *Nasrullah, *Ambiorix, *Herbager; stood Bold Ruler, Nijinsky II, *Princequillo, Round Table, etc. Son of A. B. Hancock Sr.; father of Kentucky breeders Arthur B. Hancock III (Stone Farm) and Seth Hancock (Claiborne Farm).

Hancock, Richard J., 1838-1912. Breeder. Founder of Ellerslie Stud, Virginia. Bred Knight of Ellerslie, Elkwood, Eon, Eole, Eolist. Father of A. B. Hancock Sr.

Hanes, John W., 1892-1988. Textiles, investments. Co-founder and first chairman of New York Racing Association; president of National Museum of Racing Hall of Fame. Bred Idun; owned Bold Bidder.

Harbut, Will, 1885-1947. Groom. Stud groom of Man o' War. Coined well-known phrase, "He was the mostest hoss."

Harding, William G., 1808-'86. Farming, railways. Owner of Belle Meade Stud, Tennessee. Bred Vandalite. Stood leading sires *Priam, Vandal, *Bonnie Scotland.

Harper, John, 1803-'74. Farmer. Owner of Nantura Stock Farm, Kentucky. Bred Longfellow, Ten Broeck, Rhynodyne, Fanny Holton.

Harriman, W. Averell, 1891-1986. Railways, politician. Owner of Arden Farm Stable. Owned Chance Play, Ladkin, Mary Jane. As governor of New York (1955-'59), aided formation of New York Racing Association in 1955.

Haskell, Amory L., 1894-1966. Automobiles, safety glass. President of Monmouth Park 1946-'66; president of Thoroughbred Racing Associations 1954-'55. Owner of Blue Sparkler. Aided campaign to legalize pari-mutuel wagering in New Jersey.

Hatton, Charles W., 1906-'75. Journalist. President, New York Turf Writers Association. Eclipse Special Award in 1974. Popularized concept of American Triple Crown.

Hawkins, Abe, Birthdate unknown-1867. Jockey. A slave when he rode Lecompte to victory over Lexington in an 1854 match race, was perhaps the first African-American professional athlete to gain national and international prominence.

Headley, Duval A., 1910-'87. Horseman. President, Keeneland Race Course; president, Thoroughbred Club of America. Owner of Manchester Farm, Kentucky. Breeder of Tom Fool, Dark Mirage, Aunt Ginny. Trained 23 stakes winners, including champions Menow, Apogee. Nephew of Hal Price Headley.

Headley, Hal Petit, 1856-1921. Timber interests. Founder of Beaumont Farm, Kentucky. Bred and owned Ornament. Father of Hal Price Headley.

Headley, Hal Price, 1888-1962. Timber, burley. First president of Keeneland Race Course. Owner of Beaumont Farm, Kentucky. Bred and owned Menow, Alcibiades, Askmenow, Handy Mandy, Chacolet. Co-founder of Keeneland Association; co-founder of American Thoroughbred Breeders Association. Father of Kentucky breeder Alice Headley Chandler (Mill Ridge Farm).

Healey, Thomas J., 1866-1944. Trainer, racing official. Inducted into Racing Hall of Fame in 1955. Trained three champions, including Equipoise, Top Flight, Campfire. Won five Preakness Stakes.

Helis, William G., 1887-1950. Oil exploration. Co-owner of Fair Grounds. Owner of Helis Stock Farm, New Jersey. Owned Cosmic Bomb, Rippey, Salmagundi.

Hernandez, Joe, 1909-'72. Race caller at Santa Anita Park 1935-'72 and Hollywood Park.

Hertz, John M., 1879-1961 and **Frances**, 1881-1963. Taxis and rental cars. Co-owner of Arlington Park. Owner of Stoner Creek Stud, Kentucky; Leona Farm, Illinois. Bred and owned Count Fleet, Anita Peabody, Prince John, Fleet Nasrullah, Blue Banner, Count of Honor; owned Reigh Count; bred *Princequillo.

Hervey, John L., 1870-1947. Journalist. Racing historian and author under pen name of "Salvator." Author of *Racing in America*, Vol. 1, 2, 4.

Hildreth, Samuel, 1866-1929. Trainer, owner. Leading trainer by money won nine times; leading trainer by races won 1921, '27; leading owner by money won 1909-'10, '11; inducted into Racing Hall of Fame in '55. Trained Grey Lag, Zev. Trained ten champions, seven Belmont Stakes winners.

Hine, Hubert M. "Sonny", 1931-2000. Trainer. Trained Skip Away, Guilty Conscience, Skip Trial, Technology.

Hirsch, Clement L., 1914-2000. Canned foods. Co-founder and president of Oak Tree Racing Association. Eclipse Award for distinguished service in 1999. Owner of *Figonero, June Darling.

Hirsch, Mary (Mrs. Charles McLennan), 1914-'63. Trainer. First licensed woman trainer in 1933. Owner (with Charles McLennan) of Cowpens Farm, Maryland. Trained stakes winner No Sir.

Hirsch, Max, 1880-1969. Trainer, jockey, owner, breeder. Inducted into Racing Hall of Fame in 1959. Trained more than 100 stakes winners and six champions, including Assault, Sarazen, Middleground, Bold Venture, Gallant Bloom. Won 1946 Triple Crown with Assault. Father of William J. "Buddy" Hirsch, Mary Hirsch.

Hirsch, William J. "Buddy", 1909-'97. Trainer. Inducted into Racing Hall of Fame in 1982. Trained 56 stakes winners and one champion, including Gallant Bloom. Owned Columbiana. Son of Max Hirsch.

Hitchcock, Thomas, 1861-1941. Trainer. Inducted into Racing Hall of Fame in 1973. Trained three champions: Good and Plenty, Salvidere, Annibal. Captained America's first international polo team.

Hollingsworth, Kent, 1930-'99. Journalist. Editor of *The Blood-Horse* 1963-'87; president of Thoroughbred Club of America 1974-'75; president of National Museum of Racing Hall of Fame 1982-'86.

Hoomes, John, 1755-1805. Stagecoaches. Founder of Virginia Jockey Club. Imported *Diomed, *Spread Eagle, *Buzzard.

Hooper, Fred W., 1898-2000. Highway construction. Owner of Hooper Farm, Florida. Eclipse Award outstanding breeder 1975, '82; Eclipse Award of Merit in '92. Bred and owned Susan's Girl, Precisionist, Crozier, Tri Jet, Copelan; owned Hoop, Jr., Olympia, Education. Brought Racing Hall of Fame jockeys Braulio Baeza, Laffit Pincay Jr., and Jorge Velasquez to United States.

Howard, Charles S., 1881-1950. Automobile dealer, real estate. Leading owner 1937, '40. Owner of Seabiscuit, *Noor, *Kayak II.

Hughes, Hollie, 1888-1981. Trainer. Inducted into Racing Hall of Fame in 1973. Trained more than 20 stakes winners, including, *Tourist II. Trained 1916 Kentucky Derby winner George Smith.

Hunter, John, 1833-1914. Real estate. First chairman of the Jockey Club 1894-'95; co-founder of Saratoga Race Course. Owner of Annieswood Stud, New

York. Owner of Kentucky, Sultana; bred and owned Alarm, Olitipa, Rhadamanthus.

Hyland, John J., Birthdate unknown-1913. Trainer. Inducted into Racing Hall of Fame in 1956. Trained six champions, including Beldame, Henry of Navarre, His Highness, The Butterflies.

Isaacs, Harry Z., 1904-'90. Clothing manufacturer. Owner of Brookfield Farm, Maryland. Bred and owned Intentionally, Intent, Itsabet.

Iselin, Philip H., 1902-'76. Clothing manufacturer. President of Monmouth Park 1966-'77. Instrumental in consolidation of year-end polls into Eclipse Awards.

Jackson, James, 1782-1840. Merchant. Owner of Forks of Cypress Farm, Alabama. Bred Peytona, Reel. Imported *Glencoe, *Galopade, *Leviathan.

Jacobs, Hirsch, 1904-'70. Owner-breeder, trainer. Leading breeder by money won 1964-'67; leading trainer by money won 1946, '60, '65; leading trainer by races won 1933-'39, '41-'44; inducted into Racing Hall of Fame in '58. Trained 3,596 winners and four champions. Bred Affectionately, Hail to Reason, Straight Deal, Personality. Co-owned and trained Hail to Reason, Stymie, Affectionately, Straight Deal.

Janney, Stuart S. Jr., 1907-'88. Lawyer, financier. Chairman, Maryland Racing Commission in 1947; president of Maryland Horse Breeders Association. Owner of Locust Hill Farm, Maryland. Bred and owned Ruffian, Icecapade, Buckfinder, Private Terms. Father of Maryland breeder Stuart S. Janney III.

Jeffords, Walter M. Sr., 1883-1960. Investments. President of Grayson Foundation; president of National Museum of Racing and Hall of Fame 1954-'60. Owner of Faraway Farm, Kentucky. Bred and owned One Count, Pavot, Bateau, Kiss Me Kate, Scapa Flow, Snow Goose, etc.

Jerome, Leonard W., 1817-'91. Financier. Built Jerome Park in 1866; president of Coney Island Jockey Club (Sheepshead Bay racetrack). Owned Kentucky, Fleetwing, Decoursey.

Johnson, Albert, 1900-'66. Jockey, trainer. Leading jockey by money won in 1922; inducted into Racing Hall of Fame in '71. Rode 503 winners, including Exterminator, American Flag, Crusader. Rode two Kentucky Derby winners.

Johnson, William Ransom, 1782-1849. Trainer. Inducted into Racing Hall of Fame in 1986. Trained more than 20 champions, including Boston, Sir Archy. First great American trainer, called the "Napoleon of the Turf;" won 61 of 63 races during a two-year period.

Jones, Ben A., 1882-1961. Trainer. Leading trainer by money won 1941, '43-'44, '52; inducted into Racing Hall of Fame in '58. Trained 11 champions, including Whirlaway, Lawrin, Bewitch, Twilight Tear, Armed. Won six Kentucky Derbys. Father of Horace A. "Jimmy" Jones.

Jones, Horace A. "Jimmy", 1906-2001. Trainer. Leading trainer by money won 1947-'49, '57, '61; inducted into Racing Hall of Fame in '59. Trained 54 stakes winners and seven champions, including Citation, Armed, Coaltown, Tim Tam. First trainer to win more than $1-million in purses. Son of Ben Jones.

Jones, Warner L., 1916-'94. Distiller, breeder. Chairman of Churchill Downs 1984-'92; president of Thoroughbred Breeders of Kentucky. Owner of Hermitage Farm, Kentucky. Eclipse Award of Merit in 1990. Breeder of Dark Star, Lomond, Is It True, Seattle Dancer, Northern Trick, Woodman, King's Bishop. Sold world-record

$13.1-million yearling in 1984; co-founder of the American Horse Council.

Joyner, Andrew Jackson, 1861-1943. Trainer. Leading trainer by races won in 1908; inducted into Racing Hall of Fame in '55. Trained five champions, including Ethelbert, St. James.

Keck, Howard B., 1913-'96. Oil production. Bred Ferdinand; bred and owned Turkish Trousers, Bagdad, Fiddle Isle, Tell, etc.

Keene, Foxhall P., 1867-1941. Sportsman. Owner of Domino, Cap and Bells. Purchased Domino for $3,000 as a yearling. Son of James R. Keene.

Keene, James R., 1838-1913. Financier. Owner of Castleton Stud, Kentucky. Leading owner 1905-'08; leading breeder. Bred and owned Colin, Commando, Peter Pan, Sweep, Kingston, Sysonby, Cap and Bells; owned Domino, Spendthrift. Prime mover in formation of the Jockey Club in 1893. Father of Foxhall P. Keene.

Kenner, Duncan F., 1813-'87. Sugar planter. President, Louisiana Jockey Club. Owner of Blue Bonnet. Owned slave jockey Abe Hawkins.

Kilmer, Willis Sharpe, 1868-1940. Patent-medicine distributor. Owner of Court Manor Stud, Virginia; Sun Briar Court, New York. Bred and owned Sun Beau, Sally's Alley, Chance Sun; owned Exterminator, *Sun Briar; bred Reigh Count.

Kilroe, Frank E. "Jimmy", 1912-'96. Racing executive. Racing secretary and handicapper at Santa Anita Park 1953-'90 and at New York tracks 1954-'59. Eclipse Award of Merit in 1979.

Kirkpatrick, Haden, 1911-'88. Publisher, journalist. Publisher, editor of *The Thoroughbred Record* 1941-'80.

Kleberg, Robert J., 1896-1974. Rancher, oilman. Owner of King Ranch, Kentucky and Texas. Leading owner in 1954. Bred and owned Assault, Middleground, Gallant Bloom, But Why Not, Bridal Flower, Dawn Play, Stymie, Miss Cavandish; owned High Gun.

Klein, Eugene V., 1921-'90. Automobile dealer. Leading owner 1985, '87; Eclipse Award owner 1985-'87. Owned Lady's Secret, Winning Colors, Capote, Life's Magic, Tank's Prospect, Open Mind, Family Style.

Knapp, Willie, 1888-1972. Jockey, trainer, racing official. Inducted into Racing Hall of Fame in 1969. Rode 649 winners, including Exterminator, Upset. Won 1919 Sanford Stakes aboard Upset, handing Man o' War his only loss.

Knight, Henry H., 1889-'59. Automobile dealer. Owner of Almahurst Farm and Coldstream Stud, Kentucky. Bred Almahmoud, Nail, Cosmah. Stood leading sires *Bull Dog, *Heliopolis.

Kummer, Clarence, 1899-1930. Jockey. Leading jockey by money won in 1920; inducted into Racing Hall of Fame in '72. Rode 464 winners, including Man o' War, Sir Barton, Exterminator, Sarazen. Defeated French champion *Epinard by a head aboard Ladkin in 1924 International Special.

Kurtsinger, Charles F., 1906-'46. Jockey. Leading jockey by money won 1931, '37; inducted into Racing Hall of Fame in '67. Rode 721 winners. Won 1931 Kentucky Derby with Twenty Grand; rode War Admiral to victory in 1937 Triple Crown.

Kyne, William P., 1887-1957. Racing executive. General manager of California Jockey Club (Bay Meadows Race Course) 1934-'57; owner of Portland Meadows racetrack 1946-'57. Promoted passage of California pari-mutuel law in 1933.

Lakeland, William, 1853-1914. Trainer. Trained Domino, Hamburg, *Ogden, Electioneer, Exile. Co-breeder and co-owner of Commando.

Laurin, Lucien, 1912-2000. Trainer, jockey. Eclipse Award trainer in 1972; inducted into Racing Hall of Fame in '77. Trained 36 stakes winners and three champions, including Secretariat, Quill, Riva Ridge. Trained 1972-'73 Horse of the Year Secretariat to Triple Crown.

LeRoy, Mervyn, 1900-'87. Movie producer. President of Hollywood Park 1951-'85. Co-bred and owned Honeymoon, Stepfather, Honey's Alibi.

Lewis, J. Howard, 1862-1947. Trainer. Inducted into Racing Hall of Fame in 1969. Trained 14 steeplechase champions, including Bushranger, Fairmount.

Lindheimer, Benjamin F., 1891-1960. Real-estate developer. Chairman of Arlington Park 1938-'60, Washington Park 1934-'60. Father of Marjorie Everett, former executive of Hollywood Park.

Loftus, Johnny, 1895-1976. Jockey, trainer. Leading jockey by money won in 1919; inducted into Racing Hall of Fame in '59. Rode 580 winners, including Man o' War, Sir Barton, Pan Zareta. First jockey to win the Triple Crown (aboard Sir Barton in 1919).

Lord Derby (Edward Stanley, 12th Earl of Derby), 1752-1834. A pillar of 18th-century British racing, he was responsible for founding the Epsom Oaks (1779) and Epsom Derby (1780), the latter bearing his family name after he won a coin toss with Sir Charles Bunbury. Won 1787 Derby with Sir Peter Teazle.

Lord Derby (Edward Stanley, 17th Earl of Derby), 1865-1948. Bred then-record 19 English classic winners, including Hyperion, Sansovino, Fairway, Swynford, Colorado, and *Watling Street. Also bred influential sires Phalaris and Pharos. Generally acknowledged as one of the most successful owners-breeders in British Turf history.

Lorillard, George, 1843-'86. Tobacco sales. President of Monmouth Park. Owner of Westbrook Stable. Leading owner 1877-'80. Owned Tom Ochiltree, Spinaway, Duke of Magenta, Harold, Saunterer, Grenada.

Lorillard, Pierre, 1832-1901. Tobacco sales. Owner of Rancocas Stud, New Jersey. Bred and owned Wanda, Exile, Sibola, Dewdrop, Hiawasse; owned Iroquois, Parole, Saxon, Democrat. First American to win Epsom Derby, with Iroquois in 1881; inspired formation of the Board of Control (predecessor to the Jockey Club) in 1891.

Luro, Horatio, 1901-'91. Trainer. Inducted into Racing Hall of Fame in 1980. Trained 43 stakes winners, including Northern Dancer, *Kayak II, Decidedly, *Princequillo.

Mabee, John C., 1921-2002. Grocery chain. Chairman, Del Mar Thoroughbred Club. Co-owner with wife Betty of Golden Eagle Farm, California. Eclipse Award breeder 1991, '97, '98. Bred and owned Best Pal, Event of the Year, General Challenge, Jeanne Jones, Worldly Manner. Founding member of the board of directors of Breeders' Cup Ltd.; Del Mar's largest growth occurred under his leadership.

MacBeth, Don, 1949-'87. Jockey. George Woolf Memorial Jockey Award in 1987. Rode Chief's Crown, Temperence Hill, Silver Buck, Half Iced. Inspired formation of injured jockey's fund that bears his name.

Madden, John E., 1856-1929. Trainer, owner, breeder. Owner of Hamburg Place. Leading breeder 1917-'27; leading trainer 1901-'03; inducted into Racing Hall of Fame in '83. Trained 38 stakes winners and eight champions. Bred Grey Lag, Sir Barton, Old Rose-

bud; owned Hamburg; trained Hamburg, Plaudit, Sir Martin. Bred five Kentucky Derby winners.

Maher, Danny, 1881-1916. Jockey. Leading jockey in U.S. in 1898; leading jockey in England 1908, '13; inducted into Racing Hall of Fame in '55. Rode 1,771 winners, including Ethelbert, Rock Sand, Banastar.

Maloney, James W., 1909-'84. Trainer. Inducted into Racing Hall of Fame in 1989. Trained 42 stakes winners and two champions, including Gamely, Lamb Chop, Princessnesian.

Markey, Lucille P. (Wright), 1897-1982. Investments. Owner of Calumet Farm, Kentucky. Leading breeder 1950-'57, '61; leading owner 1952, '56-'58, '61. Bred and owned Alydar, Fabius, Tim Tam, Our Mims, Forward Pass, Davona Dale, Iron Liege, Barbizon, Before Dawn.

Mars, Ethel V., 1884-1945. Confectioner. Owner of Milky Way Farm, Tennessee. Leading owner in 1936. Owned Gallahadion, Forever Yours, Sky Larking, Case Ace, Reaping Reward.

Mayer, Louis B., 1885-1957. Movie producer. Owner of Louis B. Mayer Stock Farm, California. Bred Honeymoon, Your Host, On Trust, Clem, Lurline B.

McAtee, J. Linus "Pony", 1897-1963. Jockey. Leading jockey in 1928; inducted into Racing Hall of Fame in '56. Rode 930 winners, including Exterminator, Twenty Grand, Jack High. Won 1927, '28 Kentucky Derby.

McCarthy, Clem, 1883-1962. Sportscaster. First radio broadcast of Kentucky Derby in 1928; broadcast Derby from 1928-'50.

McCreary, Conn, 1921-'79. Jockey, trainer. Inducted into Racing Hall of Fame in 1975. Rode 1,263 winners, including Racing Hall of Fame members Stymie, Twilight Tear, Armed, Searching. Trained three stakes winners.

McDaniel, Henry, 1867-1948. Trainer. Co-leading trainer by races won in 1922; inducted into Racing Hall of Fame in '56. Trained 1,041 recorded winners and four champions, including Exterminator, Reigh Count, Sun Beau.

McDaniel, Robert H. "Red", 1911-'55. Trainer. Leading trainer by races won 1950-'54. Trained *Poona II, Blue Reading.

McGrath, H. Price, 1814-'81. Tailor, bookmaker. Owner of McGrathiana Stud, Kentucky. Bred Aristides, Thora, Tom Bowling.

McKinney, Rigan, 1908-'85. Jockey, trainer, breeder. Leading amateur steeplechase jockey 1933-'34, '36, '38; inducted into Racing Hall of Fame in '68. Rode 138 winners, including Green Cheese, Beacon Hill, Annibal. Trained Navigate, Drift, The Heir. Won American Grand National aboard Green Cheese in 1931.

McKnight, William L., 1888-1978. Industrialist. Chairman, Minnesota Mining and Manufacturing Co. 1949-'66. Co-founder of Calder Race Course. Owner of Tartan Farms, Florida. Eclipse Award, Man of the Year, in 1974. Leading breeder in 1990. Bred and owned Dr. Fager, Ta Wee, Dr. Patches; bred Unbridled.

McLaughlin, James, 1861-1927. Jockey. Leading jockey 1884-'87; inducted into Racing Hall of Fame in 1955. Rode Hindoo, Tecumseh, Tremont, Firenze. Won 1881 Kentucky Derby on Hindoo; won '85 Preakness Stakes aboard Tecumseh; won six Belmont Stakes.

McLennan, Joseph, 1868-1933. Racing executive. Racing secretary at Hialeah Park, Arlington Park.

Meadors, Joel C. "Skeets", 1896-1967. Photographer.

Mellon, Paul, 1908-'99. Investments. Owner of Rokeby Stud, Virginia. Eclipse Award owner-breeder in 1971; breeder in '86; Award of Merit in '93. Bred and owned Mill Reef, Arts and Letters, Key to the Mint, Fort Marcy, Sea Hero, Quadrangle, Run the Gantlet, Java Gold; owned Fit to Fight, Summer Guest, Blue Banner.

Miller, Walter, 1890-1959. Jockey. Leading jockey 1906-'07; inducted into Racing Hall of Fame in '55. Rode 1,904 winners, including Colin, Ballot, Peter Pan, Whimsical. Won 388 races in 1906 (at age 16), a record that stood until Racing Hall of Fame jockey William Shoemaker tied the mark 44 years later in 1950 and broke it in '52.

Mills, James P., 1909-'87 and **Alice**, 1912-2000. Aviation. Owner of Hickory Tree Farm, Virginia. Bred and owned Committed, Believe It, Terpsichorist, Hagley; owned Devil's Bag, Gone West.

Mills, Ogden, 1884-1937. Investments. Co-owner of Wheatley Stable. Bred Seabiscuit, Edelweiss; owned Dice, Diavolo, Dark Secret.

Molter, William, 1910-'60. Trainer. Leading trainer by races won 1946-'49; leading trainer by money won 1954, '56, '58, '59; inducted into Racing Hall of Fame in '60. Trained 2,158 winners and 48 stakes winners, including Round Table, Determine, T. V. Lark.

Mori, Eugene, 1898-1975. Banker, real-estate developer. Builder and president of Garden State Park 1942-'72; owned Hialeah Park 1954-'72. Owner of East Acres Farm, New Jersey. Bred Tosmah; owned Alma North, Cosmah. Promoted pari-mutuel wagering in New Jersey.

Morris, Francis, 1810-'86. Shipping. Owner of Morris Stud, New York. Bred and owned Ruthless, Relentless, Narragansett. Aided Leonard W. Jerome in founding of American Jockey Club and Jerome Park in 1866.

Morris, Green B., 1837-1920. Owner, trainer. Leading owner in 1902. Trained Apollo, Sir Dixon, Strathmeath, Star Ruby.

Morris, John A., 1892-1985. Financier. President of Thoroughbred Racing Associations, Jamaica Racetrack. Eclipse Award, Man of the Year, in 1975. Bred and owned Missile Belle, Proudest Roman, L'Heureux; owned Missile. Great-grandson of Francis Morris.

Morrissey, John, 1831-'78. Prizefighter, gambler. Co-founder of Saratoga Race Course in 1863.

Mulholland, W. F. "Bert", 1884-1968. Trainer. Inducted into Racing Hall of Fame in 1967. Trained 832 winners, 57 stakes winners, and five champions, including Jaipur, Eight Thirty, Lucky Draw, Battlefield. Trained for George D. Widener for more than 40 years.

Munnings, Sir Alfred, 1878-1959. Painter. Greatest English painter of horses of 20th century.

Murphy, Isaac, 1860-'96. Jockey, trainer, owner. Inducted into Racing Hall of Fame in 1955. Rode 530 recorded winners, including Falsetto, Firenze, Salvator, Emperor of Norfolk. First jockey to win three Kentucky Derbys; first jockey elected to Racing Hall of Fame.

Neloy, Eddie, 1921-'71. Trainer. Leading trainer by money won 1966-'68; inducted into Racing Hall of Fame in '83. Trained 60 stakes winners and five champions, including Buckpasser, Bold Lad, Gun Bow.

Neves, Ralph, 1921-'95. Jockey. George Woolf Memorial Jockey Award in 1954; inducted into Racing Hall of Fame in '60. Rode 3,771 winners, ranked sixth in jockey wins at retirement; rode 173 stakes winners, including Round Table, Native Diver. Rode five winners at Bay Meadows after track announcer declared him "deceased" following an accident the previous day.

Newman, Neil, 1886-1951. Journalist. Wrote under the pen name of "Roamer." Author of *Famous Horses of the American Turf* series 1930-'32.

Niarchos, Stavros, 1909-'96. Shipping. Owner of Haras de Fresnay-le-Buffard, France; Oak Tree Farm, Kentucky. Bred and owned Miesque, Spinning World, Kingmambo, Hernando (Fr), Hector Protector, Machiavellian; owned Nureyev.

Niccolls, Richard, 1624-'72. Soldier, politician. Founded first American racecourse, Newmarket, at Salisbury Plain (near modern Hempstead), Long Island, New York.

Notter, Joe, 1890-1973. Jockey. Leading jockey by money won in 1908; inducted into Racing Hall of Fame in '63. Rode Regret, Whisk Broom II, Colin. First jockey to ride a filly, Regret, to victory in the Kentucky Derby (1915); first jockey to win handicap triple crown (on Whisk Broom II).

O'Connor, Winnie, 1884-1947. Jockey, trainer. Leading jockey in 1901; inducted into Racing Hall of Fame in '56. Rode 1,229 winners in United States and France, including Yankee, Reina. One of "Father Bill" Daly's "Five Aces."

Odom, George M., 1883-1964. Jockey, trainer. Inducted into Racing Hall of Fame in 1955. Rode 527 winners, including Broomstick, Delhi, Banastar. Trained Busher, Pasteurized. Won the Belmont Stakes as a jockey and later as a trainer.

O'Farrell, Joe, 1912-'82. Breeder. President, Florida Breeders' Sales Co. Owner of Ocala Stud, Florida. Bred Roman Brother, Office Queen, My Dear Girl. Stood Rough'n Tumble. Primary founder of Florida breeding industry.

Olin, John M., 1892-1982. Small-arms munitions. Bred and owned Cannonade; owned Bold Bidder, Northfields.

O'Neill, Frank, 1886-1960. Jockey. Inducted into Racing Hall of Fame in 1956. Rode Beldame, Roseben, *Prince Palatine. Also successful jockey in France and England.

Palmer, Joe H., 1904-'52. Journalist. Author of *This Was Racing, American Racehorses* series 1944-'51.

Parke, Burley, 1905-'77. Trainer. Inducted into Racing Hall of Fame in 1986. Trained 37 stakes winners and two champions, including Roman Brother, *Noor, Raise a Native. *Noor beat Citation in four consecutive stakes races. Brother of Ivan Parke.

Parke, Ivan, 1908-'95. Jockey, trainer. Leading jockey by races won in 1923, '24 (his first two years of racing); leading jockey by money won in '24; inducted into Racing Hall of Fame in '78. Rode 419 winners, including Backbone. Trained 27 stakes winners, including Exclusive Native, Hoop, Jr. Brother of Burley Parke.

Patrick, Gilbert "Gilpatrick", 1812-ca. 1880. Jockey. Inducted into Racing Hall of Fame in 1970. Rode Ruthless, Boston, Kentucky, Lexington. Rode first Belmont Stakes winner (Ruthless) in 1867.

Paulson, Allen E., 1922-2000. Aviation. Owner of Brookside Farm, Kentucky. Eclipse Award breeder in 1993; owner '95 and '96. Owned and bred Cigar, Ajina, Escena, Fraise; owned Theatrical (Ire), Strawberry Road (Aus), Blushing John, Arazi, Paradise Creek.

Payson, Mrs. Charles S. (Joan Whitney), 1903-'75. Publisher, investments. Co-owner of Greentree

Stud. Leading owner in 1951. Owned and bred Stage Door Johnny, Capot, Bowl Game, Late Bloomer, The Axe II, Cohoes, Stop the Music; owned Tom Fool. Daughter of Mr. and Mrs. Payne Whitney; sister of John Hay Whitney.

Penna, Angel, 1923-'92. Trainer. Leading trainer in Argentina in 1952; leading trainer in Venezuela in '54; leading trainer in France in '74; inducted into Racing Hall of Fame in '88. Trained more than 250 stakes winners, including Allez France, Relaxing, San San, Private Account.

Perry, William Haggin, 1911-'93. Investments. Owner of Waterford Farm, Virginia. Co-owned and co-bred Gamely, Lure, Revidere, Coastal, Lamb Chop, Boldnesian.

Phipps, Mrs. Henry C. (Gladys Mills), 1883-1970. Investments. Owner of Wheatley Stable. Leading owner in 1966. Bred and owned Bold Ruler, Bold Lad, Seabiscuit, High Voltage, Misty Morn, Queen Empress, Successor, Bold Bidder, Castle Forbes. Mother of leading owner-breeder Ogden Phipps; sister of Ogden Mills.

Phipps, Ogden, 1908-2002. Investments. Chairman, Jockey Club 1964-'74; former chairman New York Racing Association. Leading owner by money won 1988, '89; Eclipse Award breeder in '88; Eclipse Award owner 1988, '89; Mr. Fitz Award in '89. Bred and owned Buckpasser, Easy Goer, Private Account. Bred and raced Personal Ensign, who was unbeaten in 13 starts.

Piatt, Thomas, 1877-1965. Farmer. First president of Thoroughbred Club of America; president, Breeders' Sales Co. Owner of Brookdale Farm, Kentucky. Bred Alsab, Donau. Father of Thomas Carr Piatt.

Piatt, Thomas Carr, 1900-'53. Farmer. President, Breeders' Sales Co. 1949-'53. Owner of Crestwood Farm, Kentucky. Co-breeder of Occupation, Occupy, Errard. Son of Thomas Piatt.

Pincus, Jacob, 1838-1918. Trainer, jockey. Leading trainer in 1869; inducted into Racing Hall of Fame in '88. Trained Glenelg, Eagle, Richmond. Trained Iroquois, first American winner of the Epsom Derby.

Porter, William T., 1809-'58. Publisher. Founded *Spirit of the Times* magazine in 1831.

Purdy, Samuel, 1785-1836. Jockey. Inducted into Racing Hall of Fame in 1970. Semi-retired when pulled from the crowd to replace American Eclipse's jockey at the Union Course, winning the next two heats to win the match over Henry.

Reiff, John, 1885-1974. Jockey. Leading jockey in France in 1902; inducted into Racing Hall of Fame in '56. Rode 1,016 winners, including Orby, Tagalie, Retz, Moia. Among the top ten jockeys for ten seasons in France; won two Epsom Derbys and one French Derby.

Rice, Daniel, 1896-1975 and **Ada L.**, 1899-1977. Stock and grain broker. Co-owner of Arlington Park 1940-'68. Owner of Danada Farm, Kentucky. Bred and owned Lucky Debonair, Pucker Up, Proud Delta, Delta Judge, Advocator.

Richards, A. Keene, 1827-'81. Sugar and cotton planter. Owner of Blue Grass Park Stud, Kentucky. Owned *Australian, Starke, War Dance. Bred Fenian, Target, Eliza Davis, Ulrica.

Richards, Leonard P., Birthdate and date of death unknown. Chemical manufacturer. Second chairman of the Delaware Racing Commission.

Riddle, Samuel D., 1862-1951. Textiles. Owner of Faraway Farm, Kentucky; Glen Riddle Stable. Leading owner in 1925. Owned Man o' War; bred and owned War Admiral, Crusader, American Flag, War Relic.

Robertson, Alfred, 1911-'75. Jockey. New York Turf Writers' Association best jockey in 1942; inducted into Racing Hall of Fame in '71. Rode 1,856 winners, including Top Flight, Whirlaway, Riverland, Sky Larking. Twice rode six winners in a single day.

Robertson, William H. P., 1920-'82. Journalist. Editor of *The Thoroughbred Record* 1962-'70. Author of *History of Thoroughbred Racing in America, Hoofprints of the Century*.

Roebling, Joseph M., 1909-'80. Building contractor. Owner of Harbourton Stud, New Jersey. Bred and owned Blue Peter, Fall Aspen, Rainy Lake.

Rogers, John W., ca. 1850-1908. Trainer. Inducted into Racing Hall of Fame in 1955. Trained 11 champions, including Artful, Modesty. Trained Artful to win the 1904 Belmont Futurity, giving Sysonby the only defeat of his career.

Rolapp, R. Richards, 1941-'93. Lawyer. President of American Horse Council 1978-'93.

Ross, John K. L., 1876-1951. Railways. Leading owner 1918-'19. Owned Sir Barton, Billy Kelly, Cudgel.

Rowe, James Sr., 1857-1929. Trainer, jockey. Leading jockey 1871-'73; inducted into Racing Hall of Fame in '55. Trained 34 horses regarded as champions, more than any other Hall of Fame trainer. Trained Colin, Miss Woodford, Regret, Luke Blackburn, Hindoo.

Salmon, Walter J., ca. 1880-1953. Real estate. Owner of Mereworth Farm. Leading breeder in 1946. Bred Discovery, Display, Dr. Freeland, Battleship (first American-bred and -owned winner of England's Grand National Steeplechase), Free For All; owned Vigil.

Samuel, Ernest, 1930-2000. Steel distribution. Owner of Sam-Son Farm, Ontario and Florida. Eclipse Award owner in 1991; leading owner and breeder in '91. Bred and raced more than 100 stakes winners, including Dance Smartly, Sky Classic, Chief Bearhart.

Sande, Earl, 1898-1968. Jockey, trainer. Leading jockey 1921, '23, '27; leading trainer in '38; inducted into Racing Hall of Fame in '55. Rode 968 winners, including Gallant Fox, Zev, Man o' War. Trained Stagehand, Sceneshifter. Won three Kentucky Derbys, five Belmont Stakes, and five Jockey Club Gold Cups.

Sanford, Stephen, 1826-1913. Carpet mills. Owner of Hurricane Stud, New York. Raced only homebreds, which he gave Indian names, including Caughnawaga, Chuctununda, and Mohawk II. Stood Clifford, *Voter. Father of John Sanford.

Sanford, John, 1851-1939. Carpet mills, politician. Owner of Hurricane Stud, New York. Bred and raced *Affection, *Snob II, Sir John Johnson, *Donnacona; owned George Smith. Son of Stephen Sanford.

Sanford, Milton H., 1812-1883. Cotton mills. Owner of Preakness Stud, New Jersey; North Elkhorn Farm, Kentucky. Bred Vagrant, Vigil; also owned Preakness, Virgil, Monarchist. Stood leading sire Glenelg.

Scott, Marion duPont, 1891-1983. Investments. Owner of Montpelier Farm, Virginia. Bred more than 50 stakes winners, including Mongo, Parka, Neji, Soothsayer; owned Proud Delta, Battleship. Founded Carolina Cup Steeplechase in Camden, South Carolina. Member of syndicate that imported leading sire *Blenheim II.

Seagram, Joseph E., 1841-1919. Distiller. Member of Canadian Parliament. President of Ontario Jockey Club. Bred and raced Inferno, Belle Mahone. Won 15 King's (Queen's) Plates.

Shaffer, Charles B., 1859-1943. Oil production. Owner of Coldstream Stud, Kentucky. Bred Bull Lea,

Occupation, Occupy, Star Pilot, Reaping Reward, Plucky Play. Stood leading sires *Bull Dog, *Heliopolis. Father of E. E. Dale Shaffer.

Shaffer, E. E. Dale, 1917-'74. Oil production. Founder of Detroit Race Course; chairman of Kentucky Racing Commission 1950-'51; president of Michigan Racing Association; president of Thoroughbred Racing Associations 1960-'61. Owner of Coldstream Stud, Kentucky. Leading breeder in 1945. Bred Sweet Patootie, Star Pilot, Johns Joy. Stood leading sires *Bull Dog, *Heliopolis. Son of Charles Shaffer.

Shilling, Carroll, 1882-1950. Jockey. Leading jockey in 1910; inducted into Racing Hall of Fame in '70. Rode 969 winners, including Colin, Sir Martin, Fitz Herbert, King James. Won 1912 Kentucky Derby aboard Worth.

Simms, Edward F., 1870-1938. Oil production. Owner of Xalapa Farm, Kentucky. Bred Coventry; owned Eternal, My Play.

Simms, Willie, 1870-1927. Jockey. Leading jockey in 1894; inducted into Racing Hall of Fame in 1977. Rode 1,125 winners, including Henry of Navarre, Ben Brush, Plaudit, Commanche. Won back-to-back Belmont Stakes (1893-'94) aboard Commanche and Henry of Navarre.

Sinclair, Harry F., 1876-1956. Oil production. Owner of Rancocas Stud, New Jersey. Leading owner 1921-'23. Bred and owned Mad Play, Ariel; owned Zev, Grey Lag, Mad Hatter.

Skinner, John S., 1788-1851. Publisher. Founded *American Turf Register* in 1830.

Sloan, James F. "Tod", 1874-1933. Jockey. Inducted into Racing Hall of Fame in 1955. Rode Hamburg, Clifford. "Monkey on a stick" style; credited with popularizing the use of shortened stirrups in United States and England.

Sloane, Isabel Dodge, 1898-1962. Automobile heiress. Owner of Brookmeade Stud, Virginia. First female leading owner 1934, '50. Bred and owned Sword Dancer, Bowl of Flowers, Bold, Sailor, Greek Ship; owned Cavalcade, High Quest.

Smith, George "Pittsburgh Phil", 1862-1905. Gambler. Most successful gambler of Victorian era, died a millionaire.

Smith, Robert A., 1869-1942. Trainer, owner. Leading trainer 1933-'34; inducted into Racing Hall of Fame in '76. Trained more than 27 stakes winners and three champions, including 1934 Horse of the Year Cavalcade, High Quest. Owned Articulate. Won 1934 Kentucky Derby with Cavalcade.

Smith, Tom "Silent Tom", 1879-1957. Trainer. Leading trainer 1940, '45; inducted into Racing Hall of Fame in 2001. Trained 29 stakes winners and six champions, including Seabiscuit, Jet Pilot, *Kayak II. Trained 1947 Kentucky Derby winner Jet Pilot.

Smithwick, Alfred "Paddy", 1927-'73. Jockey. Leading steeplechase jockey by races won 1956-'58, '62; inducted into Racing Hall of Fame in '73. Rode 398 winners, including Neji, Bon Nouvel, Elkridge. Won two American Grand Nationals aboard Neji. Trained two stakes winners.

Sommer, Sigmund, 1917-'79. Real estate. Leading owner 1971-'72. Owned 29 stakes winners, including Autobiography, Sham, Never Bow.

Spreckels, Adolph, 1857-1924. Sugar merchant. President of Pacific Coast Jockey Club. Owner of Napa Stock Farm, California. Bred Morvich; bred and owned Runstar.

Stephens, Woodford C. "Woody", 1913-'98. Trainer. Eclipse Award trainer in 1983; inducted into Racing Hall of Fame in '76. Trained 131 stakes winners and 11 champions, including Swale, Conquistador Cielo, Never Bend. Won five consecutive Belmont Stakes (1982-'86).

Stout, James, 1914-'76. Jockey, racing official. Inducted into Racing Hall of Fame in 1968. Rode Johnstown, Granville, Assault, Omaha, Stymie. Finished in the first triple win dead heat in a major stakes aboard Bousset in the 1944 Carter Handicap.

Strub, Charles H., 1884-1958. Baseball team owner, real estate, investments. Founder of Santa Anita Park. Father of Robert P. Strub.

Strub, Robert P., 1919-'93. Real estate. President of Los Angeles Turf Club (Santa Anita Park); chairman, Santa Anita Operating Co.; president of Thoroughbred Racing Associations 1963-'64. Eclipse Award of Merit in 1992. Son of Charles H. Strub.

Stull, Henry, 1851-1913. Noted American equine painter. First to accurately portray racehorses at a gallop. Owned Swarthmore.

Sutcliffe, Leonard S., 1880-1937. Photographer. Published photographic volumes *Thoroughbred Sires* and *Famous Mares in America*.

Swigert, Daniel, 1833-1912. Breeder. Founded Elmendorf Farm, Kentucky. Leading breeder. Bred Spendthrift, Hindoo, Salvator, Tremont, Baden-Baden. Managed Woodburn Stud. Father-in-law of Leslie Combs Sr.

Swinebroad, George W., 1901-'75. Auctioneer. Legendary auctioneer at Keeneland and Saratoga. Hammered down first $100,000 yearling in 1961.

Swope, Herbert Bayard, 1882-1958. Journalist, investments. Chairman of New York Racing Commission.

Taral, Fred, 1867-1925. Jockey, trainer. Inducted into Racing Hall of Fame in 1955. Rode 1,437 winners, including Domino, Henry of Navarre, Dr. Rice, Ramapo. Rode Domino to nine consecutive victories in 1893.

Tasker, Col. Benjamin Jr., 1720-'60. Planter. Prominent owner-breeder during Colonial era. Owner of Belair Stud, Maryland. Imported great racemare *Selima from England in 1750, notable sire *Othello; bred Pacolet, Selim.

Tayloe, John II, 1721-'79. Planter. Owner of Mount Airy Stud, Virginia. Bred Yorick, Ariel, Bellair; owned *Selima, Moreton's Traveller. Father of John Tayloe III.

Tayloe, John III, 1771-1828. Planter. Owner of Mount Airy Stud, Virginia. Bred American foundation sire Sir Archy, Lady Lightfoot, Grey Diomed, Calypso. Imported *Castianira, dam of Sir Archy. Son of John Tayloe II.

Taylor, Charles P. B., 1935-'97. Investments. Vice president, Breeders' Cup Inc; chairman, Canadian Jockey Club. Owner of Windfields Farm, Canada and Maryland. Son of Edward P. Taylor.

Taylor, Edward P., 1901-'89. Brewing. President, Ontario Jockey Club and Canadian Thoroughbred Horse Society. Owner of Windfields Farm, Canada and Maryland. Leading breeder 1974-'80. Bred and owned Northern Dancer, Nearctic, Victoria Park; bred Nijinsky II, El Gran Senor, Devil's Bag, The Minstrel, Secreto, Shareef Dancer, Storm Bird, Viceregal. Father of Charles P. B. Taylor.

Ten Broeck, Richard, 1809-'92. Gambler, sportsman. Owner of Metairie Race Course, Louisiana. Bred

Umpire; owned Lexington, Lecompte, Prioress, *Eclipse, Starke. Conducted first successful invasion of England in 1860s with American-breds.

Tenney, Meshach, 1907-'93. Trainer. Leading trainer 1962-'63; inducted into Racing Hall of Fame in '91. Trained 36 stakes winners and one champion, including Swaps, Candy Spots, Olden Times, Prove It. Won 1955 Kentucky Derby with Swaps.

Tesio, Federico, 1869-1954. Breeder. Acclaimed Italian breeder of *Ribot, Nearco, Donatello II, Niccolo Dell'Arca. Bred and owned 20 Italian Derby winners. Author of *Breeding the Racehorse*.

Thomas, Barak G., 1826-1906. Planter, publisher. Noted owner-breeder in post-Civil War America. Founded Dixiana Farm, Kentucky. Bred and owned Himyar; bred Domino, Correction.

Thompson, Henry J. "Derby Dick", 1881-1937. Trainer. Inducted into Racing Hall of Fame in 1969. Trained 373 recorded winners and five champions, including Blue Larkspur, Burgoo King, Bubbling Over. First trainer to saddle four Kentucky Derby winners.

Tipton, Edward A., 1855-1930. Auctioneer. Co-founder of Fasig-Tipton Co. in 1898. Manager of Bitter Root Stud, Montana, 1896-1900. Sold company to E. J. Tranter.

Tranter, Enoch J., 1875-1938. Auctioneer. Owner of Fasig-Tipton Co. 1904-'38. Revolutionized Thoroughbred auction business in America. Launched annual yearling sale at Saratoga.

Travers, William R., 1819-'87. Stockbroker. First president of Saratoga Association. Owned Kentucky, Alarm, Sultana.

Trotsek, Harry, 1912-'97. Trainer. Inducted into Racing Hall of Fame in 1984. Trained 96 stakes winners and two champions, including Moccasin, Hasty Road, *Stan. Expert handler of imported horses; coached young jockeys at his jockey school in the 1940s.

Troye, Edward, 1808-'74. Painter. Prolific equine portraitist, his subjects included Lexington, Boston, and many of America's great mid-19th-century Thoroughbreds.

Tuckerman, Bayard J., 1889-1974. Jockey, breeder, owner. First president of Suffolk Downs. Inducted into Racing Hall of Fame in 1973. Rode Homestead. Bred Lavender Hill. Leading amateur jockey.

Turner, Nash, 1881-1937. Jockey, trainer, owner. Inducted into Racing Hall of Fame in 1955. Rode Imp, Flying Star, Goldsmith, Irish Lad. Rider of Imp, the first filly to win the Suburban in 1899; won 1906 French Derby.

Van Berg, Marion H., 1896-1971. Trainer, owner. Leading owner by money won 1965, '68-'70; leading owner by races won 1952, '54, '56, '60-'70; inducted into Racing Hall of Fame in '70. Trained more than 1,470 winners and six stakes winners, including *Estacion, Rose Bed. Father of Racing Hall of Fame trainer Jack Van Berg.

Vanderbilt, Alfred G., 1912-'99. Investments. Chairman, New York Racing Association; president, Belmont Park and Pimlico Race Course. Owner of Sagamore Farm, Maryland. Eclipse Award of Merit in 1994. Bred and owned Native Dancer, Next Move, Bed o' Roses, Now What, Petrify; owned Discovery; bred Conniver, Miss Disco.

Van Ranst, Cornelius W., Birthdate and date of death unknown. Owner of American Eclipse, *Messenger.

Veitch, Sylvester, 1910-'96. Trainer. Inducted into Racing Hall of Fame in 1977. Trained 44 stakes winners and five champions, including Counterpoint, Career Boy. Trained Horse of the Year Counterpoint, who won the 1951 Belmont Stakes.

Vosburgh, Walter, 1855-1938. Handicapper, author. Racing secretary, Westchester Racing Association (Belmont Park) 1894-1934. Author of *Racing in America 1866-1921;* Turf editor of *Spirit of the Times*. Originated Experimental Free Handicap in 1933.

Waggoner, William T., 1852-1934. Oil production, rancher. Early 20th-century force in Texas racing. Owner of 3D's Stock Farm, Texas. Built Arlington Downs racetrack, Texas, in 1929.

Walden, R. Wyndham, Birthdate unknown-1905. Trainer. Inducted into Racing Hall of Fame in 1970. Trained 101 stakes winners, including Duke of Magenta, Grenada, Saunterer. Trained seven Preakness Stakes winners, five consecutively.

Walsh, Michael G., 1906-'93. Trainer. Leading steeplechase trainer by races won 1953-'55; leading steeplechase trainer by money won 1953-'54, '60; F. Ambrose Clark Award in '75; inducted into Racing Hall of Fame in '97. Trained 31 stakes winners and one champion, including King Commander, Independence, Rhythminhim. Founder of Stoneybrook Races in Southern Pines, North Carolina.

Ward, Sherrill, 1911-'84. Trainer. Eclipse Award trainer in 1974; inducted into Racing Hall of Fame in '78. Trained 20 stakes winners and two champions, including Forego, Summer Tan, Idun. Trained Forego, who won five championships (outstanding sprinter, older male, and Horse of the Year in 1974, and champion older male and Horse of the Year in '75).

Warfield, Elisha, 1781-1859. Physician. Co-founder of the Kentucky Association racetrack, Lexington. Owner of The Meadows Stud, Kentucky. Breeder of Lexington, Berthune, Alice Carneal. Known as the "father of the Kentucky Turf."

Welch, Aristides J., 1811-'90. Owner of Erdenheim Stud, Pennsylvania. Bred Iroquois, Parole, Sensation, Harold, Spinaway. Stood leading sire *Leamington.

Wells, Thomas J., 1803-'62. Sugar planter. President of Metairie Race Course. Bred Lecompte, Prioress; owned Reel.

Werblin, David A. "Sonny", 1910-'91. Entertainment and sports executive. First president of New Jersey Sports and Exposition Authority (originally the Meadowlands and now including Monmouth Park). Owner of Silent Screen, Process Shot.

Westrope, Jack, 1918-'58. Jockey. Leading jockey in 1933 at age 15, when he rode 301 winners.

Whitney, Cornelius V., 1899-1992. Investments. First president of National Museum of Racing Hall of Fame. Owner of C. V. Whitney Farm, Kentucky. Leading breeder 1933, '34, '38, '60; leading owner 1930-'33, '60. Bred more than 175 stakes winners. Bred and owned Counterpoint, Silver Spoon, Career Boy, First Flight; owned Equipoise, Top Flight. Son of Harry Payne Whitney.

Whitney, Harry Payne, 1872-1930. Investments. Owner of Brookdale Stud, New Jersey; Whitney Farm, Kentucky. Leading breeder 1926-'32; leading owner 1913, '20, '24, '26, '27, '29. Bred and owned Regret, Equipoise, Top Flight, Whisk Broom II,

Whichone, Whiskery, Pennant, Upset, John P. Grier, Prudery.

Whitney, Mrs. Payne (Helen Hay), 1876-1944. Investments. "First Lady of the American Turf." Owner of Greentree Stud, Kentucky. Leading owner and breeder in 1942. Bred and owned Twenty Grand, Shut Out, Devil Diver, First Minstrel. Mother of John Hay Whitney and Joan Whitney (Mrs. Charles S.) Payson.

Whitney, John Hay "Jock", 1904-'82. Investments, publisher. Co-founder of American Thoroughbred Breeders' Association. Co-owner of Greentree Stud, Kentucky; owner of Mare's Nest Farm, Kentucky. Leading owner in 1951. Bred and raced Stage Door Johnny, Capot, Late Bloomer, Bowl Game, The Axe II, Cohoes, Stop the Music; owned Tom Fool. Stood leading sire The Porter.

Whitney, W. Payne, 1875-1927. Investments. Owner of Greentree Stud, Kentucky. Son of William C. Whitney; brother of H. P. Whitney; father of John Hay Whitney and Joan Whitney (Mrs. Charles S.) Payson.

Whitney, William C., 1841-1904. Transportation, oil production. President of Saratoga Race Course. Owner of La Belle Stud, Kentucky. Leading owner 1901, '03. Owned Volodyovski, Plaudit, Artful, Endurance By Right, Nasturtium; bred Artful, Tanya.

Whittingham, Charles E., 1913-'99. Trainer. Leading trainer 1970-'73, '75, '81, '82; Eclipse Award trainer 1971, '82, '89; inducted into Racing Hall of Fame in '74. Trained 252 stakes winners and 11 champions, including Ack Ack, Sunday Silence, Ferdinand, Turkish Trousers. All-time leading trainer at Hollywood Park and Santa Anita Park; trained two Kentucky Derby winners.

Wickham, John, 1763-1839. Lawyer. Bred champion and leading sire Boston, Tuckahoe.

Widener, George D., 1889-1971. Investments. Chairman of the Jockey Club 1950-'64; president, National Museum of Racing; president, Belmont Park. Owner of Old Kenney Farm, Kentucky; Erdenheim Stud, Pennsylvania. Bred and owned more than 100 stakes winners, including Jaipur, Eight Thirty, What a Treat, Jamestown, High Fleet, Platter, Stefanita, Jester, Seven Thirty, Rare Treat. Nephew of Joseph E. Widener.

Widener, Joseph E., 1871-1943. Investments. President of Hialeah Park, Belmont Park. Owner of Elmendorf Farm, Kentucky. Leading breeder in 1940. Bred Polynesian, Peace Chance, Osmand; owned Chance Shot. Imported leading sire *Sickle. Father of P. A. B. Widener II; uncle of George D. Widener.

Widener, Peter A. B. II, 1896-1952. Investments. Owner of Elmendorf Farm, Kentucky. Son of Joseph E. Widener.

Williamson, Ansel, ca. 1806-81. Trainer. Inducted into Racing Hall of Fame in 1998. Trained Aristides, Tom Bowling, Brown Dick, Virgil. Trained first Kentucky Derby winner, Aristides.

Willmot, Donald G., 1917-'94. Brewer, investments. Owner of Kinghaven Farm, Ontario. Leading owner in 1990. Bred and owned With Approval, Izvestia, Steady Growth, Candle Bright, Bayford, Play the King, Carotene; co-owner of Deputy Minister.

Winfrey, G. Carey, 1885-1962. Trainer, owner. Inducted into Racing Hall of Fame in 1975. Trained 16 stakes winners and one champion, including Dedicate,

Squared Away, Bulwark, Martyr. Stepfather of William C. Winfrey.

Winfrey, William C., 1916-'94. Trainer. Leading trainer in 1964; inducted into Racing Hall of Fame in '71. Trained 38 stakes winners and seven champions, including Native Dancer, Bed o' Roses, Next Move, Bold Lad. Trained Native Dancer, who retired in 1954 with 21 wins in 22 starts. Stepson of G. Carey Winfrey.

Winn, Col. Matt. G., 1861-1949. Racing executive. President of Louisville Jockey Club. Legendary racetrack promoter, developed Kentucky Derby into world-class event.

Winters, Theodore, 1823-'94. Mining. Owner of Rancho del Rio, California; Rancho del Sierra, Nevada. Bred Emperor of Norfolk, Yo Tambien, El Rio Rey, Rey del Rey, Thad Stevens; owned Norfolk.

Withers, David D., 1821-1972. Banker. President, Monmouth Park. Owner of Brookdale Farm, New Jersey. Bred Requital, Laggard, Kinglike.

Woodford, Catesby, 1849-1923. President of Kentucky Racing Association. Owner of Raceland Farm, Kentucky. Co-owner of Runnymede Stud, Kentucky. Stood Hindoo, *Star Shoot. Co-breeder of Miss Woodford, Hanover, Sir Dixon.

Wood, Eugene D., Birthdate unknown-1924. Racing executive. Treasurer of the Metropolitan Jockey Club (Jamaica). Namesake of Wood Memorial Stakes.

Woodward, William Sr., 1876-1953. Banker. Chairman of the Jockey Club 1930-'50. Owner of Belair Stud, Maryland. Leading owner in 1939. Part of syndicate that imported *Sir Gallahad III. Bred and owned Gallant Fox, Omaha, Nashua, Granville, Vagrancy.

Woodward, William Jr., 1920-'55. Banker, sportsman. Owner of Belair Stud. Owned Nashua.

Woolf, George "The Iceman", 1910-'46. Jockey. Leading jockey by money won 1942, '44; inducted into Racing Hall of Fame in '55. Rode 721 winners, including Seabiscuit, Whirlaway, Challedon. Won the Belmont Futurity three straight years, the first running of the Santa Anita Derby, and the Preakness Stakes.

Workman, Raymond "Sonny", 1909-'66. Jockey. Leading jockey by races won 1930, '33, '35; leading jockey by money won 1930, '32; inducted into Racing Hall of Fame in '56. Rode 1,169 winners, including Equipoise, Top Flight, Discovery. Won two Kentucky Derbys, two Belmont Stakes, and the first three runnings of the Pimlico Futurity.

Wright, Warren, 1875-1950. Baking-powder manufacturer, investments. Owner of Calumet Farm, Kentucky. Leading breeder 1941, '44, '47-'50; leading owner 1941, '43-'44, '46-'49. Bred and owned Citation, Whirlaway, Pensive, Ponder, Coaltown, Bewitch, Hill Gail, Twilight Tear, Real Delight, Armed; owned Nellie Flag, Bull Lea. Stood leading sire Bull Lea, Sun Again, Chance Play.

Yoshida, Zenya, 1921-'93. Breeder. Owner of Shadai Farm, Japan; Fontainebleau Farm, Kentucky. Leading Japanese breeder 20 times. Bred Amber Shadai, Gallop Dyna, Dyna Gulliver, Vega; co-owned Wajima; stood Northern Taste, Sunday Silence.

Young, Col. Milton S., 1851-1918. Retail hardware, real estate. Chairman of Kentucky Racing Commission. Owner of McGrathiana Stud, Kentucky. Leading breeder in 1890. Bred Broomstick, Yankee; stood Hanover.

Contemporary Individuals in Racing and Breeding
(Names of Racing Hall of Fame members are in boldface italics.)

Abdullah, Khalid, 1942-. Investments. Owner of Juddmonte Farms, Kentucky and England. Eclipse Award breeder in 1995, 2001; Eclipse Award owner in '92; P.A.B. Widener Trophy in '93; honorary member of Great Britain's Jockey Club in '83. Bred Ryafan, Wandesta (GB), Commander in Chief, Warning (GB), Banks Hill (GB). Owned Known Fact, Dancing Brave, Rainbow Quest. Member of the ruling family of Saudi Arabia; first Arab owner to win a British classic (Two Thousand Guineas [Eng-G1] with Known Fact in 1980).

Abercrombie, Josephine, 1926-. Oil production, boxing promoter. Owner of Pin Oak Farm, Kentucky. Bred and owned Laugh and Be Merry, Peaks and Valleys. Co-owned Maria's Mon. Bred Elocutionist, Touching Wood.

Adams, Frank D. "Dooley", 1927-. Jockey, trainer. Leading steeplechase jockey 1946, '49-'55; inducted into Racing Hall of Fame in '70. Rode 337 winners, including Neji, Elkridge, Oedipus, Refugio, and Floating Isle. Trained Subversive Chick. Operated Refugio Farm training center in Southern Pines, North Carolina, after retiring as a jockey.

Aga Khan, Karim IV, 1936-. Investments, Ismaili Muslim leader. Owner of Gilltown Stud, Sheshoon Stud in Ireland; Haras de Bonneval in France. Bred Shergar, Sinndar, Kahyasi, Daylami (Ire), Kalanisi (Ire). Built Aiglemont training facility near Chantilly, France, in 1977; continued breeding operations begun by his grandfather, Aga Khan III, and his father, Prince Aly Khan.

Aitcheson, Joe Jr., 1929-. Jockey. Leading steeplechase jockey 1961, '63-'64, '67-'70; inducted into Racing Hall of Fame in '78; first jockey to receive the F. Ambrose Clark Memorial Award, in '77. Rode 478 winners, including Amber Diver, Bon Nouvel, Tuscalee, Top Bid, Soothsayer, Inkslinger. Won eight Virginia Gold Cups, seven Carolina Cups, and two Colonial Cups.

Alexander, Helen, 1951-. Investments. President, Thoroughbred Club of America, 1989-'91. Owner of Middlebrook Farm, Kentucky. Bred Aquilegia, Twining. Bred and owned Althea, Aishah, Auto Dial. Granddaughter of Robert J. Kleberg.

Allbritton, Joseph, 1924-. Publishing, banking, broadcasting, real estate. Owner of Lazy Lane Farms, Kentucky and Virginia. Owned Hansel, Secret Hello, Life At the Top, Kittiwake.

Annenberg, Walter, 1908-. Former publisher, *Daily Racing Form*. Took control of his family's Triangle Publications Inc. in 1940 and built largest private publishing empire in the country; ambassador to Great Britain 1968-'74. Sold publishing enterprises by late 1980s. Son of publisher Moses Annenberg.

Anthony, John Ed, 1939-. Timber. Owner of Shortleaf Farm, Arkansas; president of Loblolly Stable. Bred and owned Temperence Hill, Vanlandingham, Prairie Bayou. Owned Cox's Ridge. Established the Exercise Induced Pulmonary Hemorrhage Fund after Demons Begone bled during the 1987 Kentucky Derby (G1).

Appleton, Arthur, 1915-. Electrical manufacturing. Owner of Bridlewood Farm, Florida. Bred and owned Jolie's Halo, Wild Event. Owned Skip Trial. One of stockholders (along with Florida Equine Publications Inc.) of *The Florida Horse*.

Asmussen, Cash, 1962-. Jockey. Leading jockey by money won in France 1985-'86, '88-'90; Eclipse Award as apprentice jockey in '79. Rode Suave Dancer, Hector Protector, Mill Native, Northern Trick. Won inaugural Japan Cup aboard Mairzy Doates in 1981; three times won five races on a single card in New York.

Atkinson, Ted F., 1916-. Jockey, racing official. Leading jockey by money won 1944, '46; leading jockey by races won 1944, '46; inducted into Racing Hall of Fame in '57; George Woolf Memorial Jockey Award in '57. Rode 3,795 winners, including Tom Fool, Gallorette, Devil Diver. Rode 1953 Horse of the Year Tom Fool to handicap triple crown; first jockey whose mounts earned more than $1-million in one year (1946).

Bacharach, Burt, 1929-. Composer. Co-owner of Country Roads Farm, West Virginia. Thoroughbred Owners and Breeders Association Award for outstanding owner-breeder 1995-'96. Bred and owned Heartlight No. One, Afternoon Deelites, Soul of the Matter.

Baeza, Braulio, 1940-. Jockey, trainer. Leading jockey by money won 1965-'68, '75; Eclipse Award jockey 1972, '75; inducted into Racing Hall of Fame in '76; George Woolf Memorial Jockey Award in '68. Rode 3,140 winners, including Buckpasser, Dr. Fager, Ack Ack, Gallant Bloom, Affectionately, Chateaugay. Trained Double Zeus. Rode Buckpasser to one-mile record in 1966 and then lowered it aboard Dr. Fager in '68; first jockey to win more than $3-million in purses in a single year (1967).

Baffert, Bob, 1953-. Trainer. Leading trainer by money won, 1998-2001; Eclipse Award trainer 1997-'99; United Thoroughbred Trainers of America's Trainer of the Year in '98; Mr. Fitz Award in '97. Trained Chilukki, Real Quiet, Silverbulletday, Silver Charm, Point Given. Won a record 13 stakes at Del Mar in 2000; only trainer to win Kentucky Derby (G1) and Preakness Stakes (G1) in consecutive years (1997-'98). Won 2002 Derby and Preakness with War Emblem.

Bailey, Jerry, 1957-. Jockey. President, Jockeys' Guild, 1990-'97. Leading jockey by money won 1995-'98, 2001; inducted into Racing Hall of Fame in '95; Eclipse Award jockey 1995-'97, 2000-'01; George Woolf Memorial Jockey Award in '92; Mike Venezia Award in '93. Rode Cigar, Fit to Fight, Black Tie Affair (Ire), Sea Hero. In 1996, rode Cigar to his 16th consecutive win; rode seven winners on Florida Derby (G1) day program in '95; successfully lobbied for protective vests to be worn by all jockeys; won handicap triple crown with Fit to Fight in '84.

Bassett, James E. "Ted" III, 1921-. Racing executive. Former chairman, Keeneland Association; former president, Breeders' Cup Ltd.; also served

as chairman, Equibase Co.; president, Thoroughbred Racing Associations; chairman, Kentucky Horse Park; president, Thoroughbred Club of America. Co-owner of Lanark Farm, Kentucky. Eclipse Award of Merit in 1995; John W. Galbreath Award in '91; Turf and Field Club Award in '84; Joe Palmer Award in '86; John A. Morris Award in '97; Lord Derby Award in '98. Owned Falconese.

Baze, Russell, 1958-. Jockey. Leading jockey by races won 1992-'96; inducted into Racing Hall of Fame in '99; Special Eclipse Award in '95; Isaac Murphy Award 1995-2001; George Woolf Memorial Jockey Award in 2002. Rode Hawkster, Both Ends Burning, Itsallgreektome. Won 24 stakes races in 1998; won 400 or more races a record seven consecutive years.

Beck, Graham, 1929-. Mining, investments. Owner of Gainesway Farm, Kentucky; Silvercrest Farm, Kentucky; Midway Farm, Kentucky; Highlands Farm, South Africa; Maine Chance Farm, South Africa; Noreen Stud, South Africa. Bred Pompeii, Real Cozzy, Irish Prize. Co-owned Timber Country.

Bell, John A. III, 1918-. Owner, breeder, bloodstock agent. Director, Thoroughbred Owners and Breeders Association; president, Thoroughbred Club of America in 1954; former president, Farm Manager's Club. Owned Jonabell Farm, Kentucky. Bred Battlefield, Aglimmer, One for All, Never Say Die. Bred and owned Epitome. Former president of *The Blood-Horse* magazine; acquired half interest in Cromwell Bloodstock Agency in 1950.

Bellocq, Pierre "Peb", 1926-. Caricaturist. Special Eclipse Award in 1980; John Hervey Award 1965-'66, '68; Knights of Arts and Letters Award in '90; Golden Horseshoe Award in '91. Achieved international acclaim as *Daily Racing Form*'s caricaturist; has murals at Aqueduct, Oaklawn Park, and Arlington Park; founded the Amateur Riders Club of the Americas with son Remi Bellocq.

Bellocq, Remi, 1961-. Marketing executive, organization executive. Former marketing director at Turf Paradise and Santa Anita Park. Named executive director of the National Horsemen's Benevolent and Protective Association in 2001.

Blum, Walter, 1934-. Jockey, racing official. Former president, Jockeys' Guild. Leading jockey by races won 1963-'64; inducted into Racing Hall of Fame in '87; George Woolf Memorial Jockey Award in '65. Rode 4,382 winners, including Affectionately, Gun Bow, Forego, Mr. Prospector, Pass Catcher, Summer Scandal, Boldnesian, Priceless Gem, Lady Pitt.

Boulmetis, Sam Sr., 1927-. Jockey, racing official. Inducted into Racing Hall of Fame in 1973. Rode 2,783 winners. Rode Tosmah, Helioscope, Dedicate. Longtime steward at New Jersey tracks.

Brady, Nicholas J., 1930-. Financier. Chairman, Jockey Club, 1974-'82; United States treasury secretary 1988-'93; Co-owner of Mill House Stable. Bred and owned Sensational, Furiously, Meritus.

Bramlage, Larry, 1952-. Veterinarian. Vice president, American Association of Equine Practitioners in 2002. Jockey Club Gold Medal in 1994; British Equine Veterinary Association's Special Award of Merit in '98. Developed and improved ways to repair serious bone fractures.

Brumfield, Don, 1938-. Jockey, racing official. Inducted into Racing Hall of Fame in 1996; George Woolf Memorial Jockey Award in '88. Rode 4,573 winners, including Forward Pass, Alysheba, Gold Beauty, Our Mims, Old Hat. Retired in 1989 with the most wins in the history of Churchill Downs (925) and Keeneland Race Course (716).

Burch, J. Elliott, 1922-. Trainer. Leading trainer by money won in 1969; inducted into Racing Hall of Fame in '80. Trained more than 30 stakes winners and six champions, including Sword Dancer, Fort Marcy, Arts and Letters, Bowl of Flowers, Run the Gantlet, Key to the Mint. Son of Racing Hall of Fame trainer Preston Burch; grandson of Racing Hall of Fame trainer William Burch.

Campbell, W. Cothran "Cot", 1927-. Advertising, racing syndicates. General partner of Dogwood Stable, South Carolina. John W. Galbreath Award in 1992. Owned Summer Squall, Storm Song, Dominion (GB). Popularized racing syndicates; wrote *Lightning in a Jar: Catching Racing Fever*.

Carey, Thomas, 1932-. Racing executive. President and general manager, Hawthorne Race Course. Inducted into Chicago Sports Hall of Fame in 1998. Instrumental in rebuilding Hawthorne after fire in 1978.

Cauthen, Steve, 1960-. Jockey, racing executive. Leading jockey by races won in 1977; inducted into Racing Hall of Fame in '94; Eclipse Award apprentice jockey in '77; Eclipse Award jockey in '77; Eclipse Award of Merit in '77; George Woolf Memorial Jockey Award in '84. Rode 2,794 winners, including Affirmed, Oh So Sharp (Ire), Old Vic, Arazi, Johnny D., Diminuendo, Indian Skimmer, Pebbles (GB). Rode Affirmed in his Triple Crown victory in 1978; only jockey to win the Kentucky, Epsom, Irish, French, and Italian Derbys; at 18, was youngest jockey to win Kentucky Derby.

Cella, Charles, 1936-. Real estate, racing executive. President, Oaklawn Park; president, Thoroughbred Racing Associations 1975-'76. Owned Northern Spur (Ire), Out of Hock. Initiated the Racing Festival of the South at Oaklawn; became TRA's youngest president in 1975.

Chandler, Alice Headley, 1927-. Farm owner. Chairman, Maxwell F. Gluck Equine Research Center; former chairman, Kentucky Racing Commission; president, Kentucky Thoroughbred Owners and Breeders Association; former president, Kentucky Thoroughbred Associaton; director, Keeneland Association. Owner of Mill Ridge Farm, Kentucky. Bred and owned Keeper Hill. Bred Sir Ivor, Secret Hello, Ciao, Flemensfirth.

Chavez, Jorge, 1961-. Jockey. Leading jockey in New York 1994-'99; Eclipse Award jockey in '99. Rode Monarchos, Artax, Beautiful Pleasure, A P Valentine, Affirmed Success. Rode six winners on single card at Gulfstream Park in 1999.

Chenery, Helen "Penny", 1931-. Investments. President, Thoroughbred Owners and Breeders Association, 1976-'84. Former owner of Meadow Stud and Meadow Stable, Virginia. Bred Alada. Owned Secretariat, Riva Ridge. First woman to head a major national racing organization; one of the first three women inducted into the Jockey Club, in 1983.

Clay, Robert N., 1946-. Farm owner. President, Thoroughbred Owners and Breeders Association, 1990-'93; president, National Thoroughbred Association; president, Thoroughbred Club of America. Co-owner of Three Chimneys Farm, Kentucky. John W. Galbreath Award in 1995. Bred and owned Hidden Lake, Gorgeous. Bred Seaside Attraction, Subordination.

Cordero, Angel Jr., 1942-. Jockey, trainer, jockey's agent. Leading jockey by money won 1976, '82-'83; leading jockey by races won in '68; inducted into Racing Hall of Fame in '88; Eclipse Award jockey 1982-'83; George Woolf Memorial Jockey Award in '72; Mike Venezia Award in '92. Rode 7,076 winners, including Seattle Slew, Slew o' Gold, All Along (Fr), Bold Forbes, Broad Brush. Won jockey's title at Saratoga 13 times, 11 consecutively.

Craig, Sidney, 1932- and **Craig, Jenny**, 1932-. Diet foods. Owners of Rancho del Rayo training center in California. Owned 1992-'93 champion older female Paseana (Arg), Exchange, Dr Devious (Ire), Alpride (Ire).

Croll, Warren A. "Jimmy" Jr., 1920-. Trainer. Inducted into Racing Hall of Fame in 1994; United Thoroughbred Trainers of America Outstanding Trainer Award in '94; Big Sport of Turfdom Award in '95; Mr. Fitz Award in '95. Owned and trained Holy Bull. Trained Mr. Prospector, Bet Twice, Parka, Forward Gal, Housebuster.

Day, Pat, 1953-. Jockey. President, Jockeys' Guild, 2000-'01. Leading jockey by races won 1982-'84, '86, '90-'91; inducted into Racing Hall of Fame in '91; Eclipse Award jockey in 1984, '86-'87, '91; George Woolf Memorial Jockey Award in '85; Mike Venezia Award in '95; Mr. Fitz Award in 2000. Rode Wild Again, Flanders, Lady's Secret, Easy Goer, Summer Squall, Tank's Prospect, Louis Quatorze, Lil E. Tee, Dance Smartly. Second-highest lifetime earnings among jockeys and third-highest number of winners; set a record for most stakes won (60) in a single season in 1991; rode seven winners in one day at Churchill Downs in '84; won on eight of nine mounts at Arlington Park in '89.

De Francis, Joseph, 1955-. Racing executive, lawyer. President, Maryland Jockey Club; president, Pimlico Race Course and Laurel Park. Began parimutuel wagering on simulcast races at Pimlico and Laurel Park. Son of Frank De Francis.

de Kwiatkowski, Henryk, 1924-. Aviation. Owner of Calumet Farm, Kentucky; Kennelot Stable. Joe Palmer Award in 1993. Owned Conquistador Cielo, De La Rose, Danzig. Bought bankrupt Calumet Farm for $17-million at public auction in 1992.

Delahoussaye, Eddie, 1951-. Jockey. Leading jockey in 1978; inducted into Racing Hall of Fame in '93; George Woolf Memorial Jockey Award in '81. Rode A.P. Indy, Princess Rooney, Prized, Gato Del Sol, Sunny's Halo, Pleasant Stage, Thirty Slews, Gate Dancer. One of four jockeys to win consecutive Kentucky Derbys, in 1982-'83.

Delp, Grover G. "Bud", 1932-. Trainer. Eclipse Award trainer in 1980. Trained Spectacular Bid, Include, Timeless Native, Aspro, Silent King. Inducted into Racing Hall of Fame in 2002.

Desormeaux, Kent, 1970-. Jockey. Leading jockey by races won 1987-'89; leading jockey by money won

in '92; Eclipse Award apprentice jockey in '87; Eclipse Award jockey 1989, '92; George Woolf Memorial Jockey Award in '93. Rode Fusaichi Pegasus, Real Quiet, Kotashaan (Fr), Risen Star. Won record 598 races in 1989; won six races on a single card at Hollywood Park in 1992.

Dickinson, Michael, 1950-. Trainer. Owner of Tapeta Farm, Maryland. Trained Da Hoss, Fleet Renee, Cetewayo. Trained first five finishers in England's Cheltenham Gold Cup in 1983.

DiMauro, Steve Sr., 1932-. Trainer. Owner of Di-Mauro Farm, New York. Eclipse Award trainer in 1975. Bred Flip's Pleasure, Father Don Juan. Trained Wajima, Dearly Precious, Nagurski, Father Don Juan.

Dreyfus, Jack J. Jr., 1913. Financier. Chairman, New York Racing Association, in 1969 and '75. Owner Hobeau Farm, Florida. Leading owner by money won in 1967; Eclipse Award of Merit in '76. Bred and owned Beau Purple, Duck Dance, Never Bow, Step Nicely. Exacta introduced in New York betting under his direction; his Beau Purple upset Kelso three times.

Drysdale, Neil, 1947-. Trainer. Inducted into Racing Hall of Fame in 2000. Trained A.P. Indy, Fusaichi Pegasus, Princess Rooney, Tasso, Hollywood Wildcat, Fiji (GB), Bold 'n Determined.

Duchossois, Richard L., 1921-. Industrialist. Chairman, Arlington International Race Course. Owner of Hill 'N Dale Farm, Illinois. Special Eclipse Award in 1989; Special Sovereign Award in '88; Lord Derby Award in '88; Jockey Club Medal in '86; Jockey Agents' Benevolent Association's Man of the Year in '90. Bred Explosive Darling. Rebuilt Arlington Park after the track was destroyed by fire in 1985; under his leadership, Arlington received a Special Eclipse Award in '85, the first awarded to a racetrack.

du Pont, Allaire (Mrs. Richard C.), 1913-. Investments. Owner of Woodstock Farm, Maryland; Bohemia Stable, Maryland. Thoroughbred Owners and Breeders Association award for Maryland in 1984. Bred and owned Kelso, Politely, Believe the Queen. Bred and raced Kelso, only five-time Horse of the Year (1960-'64); one of the first three women inducted into the Jockey Club, in 1983.

Englander, Richard, 1959-. Investments. Eclipse Award owner in 2001, when he led the nation with stable earnings of $9,784,822.

Evans, Edward P. "Ned", 1942-. Publishing. Owner of Spring Hill Farm, Virginia. Bred and owned Minstrella, Prenup, Raging Fever, Fairy Garden, Colonial Minstrel. Owned Withallprobability. Brother of Robert S. Evans; son of Thomas Mellon Evans.

Evans, Robert S. "Shel", 1944-. Manufacturing. Owner of Winter Haven Farm, Florida; Courtland Farm, Maryland. Bred and owned Sewickley, Shared Interest. Bred Forestry, Cash Run. Brother of Edward P. Evans; son of Thomas Mellon Evans.

Everett, Marjorie, 1921-. Racing executive. Former chairman and chief executive officer, Hollywood Park; former owner, Arlington Park; former owner, Washington Park. Undertook major improvements at Hollywood Park, including expanding the circumference of the track, building the Cary Grant Pavilion, and improving the backstretch; successfully

lobbied for inaugural Breeders' Cup to be held at Hollywood Park in 1984.

Farish, William S., 1939-. Investments. Chairman, Churchill Downs, 1992-2001. President and owner of Lane's End, Kentucky. Eclipse Award breeder in 1992, '99; P.A.B. Widener Trophy in '92. Bred or co-bred A.P. Indy, Law Society, Lemon Drop Kid, Charismatic, Summer Squall, Prospectors Delite. Owned Bee Bee Bee, Miss Brio (Chi), Sweet Revenge. Former chairman of the Breeders' Cup executive committee; United States ambassador to Great Britain and Northern Ireland. Nephew of Martha Gerry.

Fires, Earlie, 1947- Jockey. Leading apprentice jockey in 1965; inducted into Racing Hall of Fame in 2001; George Woolf Memorial Jockey Award in '91. Rode In Reality, War Censor, Dike, Abe's Hope, Pattee Canyon, Woozem, Gallant Romeo. Won seven races from eight mounts in a single day at Arlington Park in 1983; won on all six mounts in one day at Hawthorne Race Course in '89.

Firestone, Bertram S., 1931- and **Firestone, Diana**, 1932-. Real estate, investments. Owner, Calder Race Course and Gulfstream Park 1988-'91. Owner of Catoctin Stud, Virginia. Eclipse Award owner in 1980. Owned Genuine Risk. Bred and owned Theatrical (Ire), Paradise Creek, April Run (Ire), Honest Pleasure. Bred What a Summer.

Fishback, Jerry, 1947-. Jockey, bloodstock agent. Leading steeplechase jockey by races won 1971, '73-'75, '77; leading steeplechase jockey by money won in '85; inducted into Racing Hall of Fame in '92. Rode 301 winners, including Cafe Prince, Flatterer. Won the Temple Gwathmey Steeplechase Handicap six times; won four Carolina Cups and four International Gold Cups.

Foreman, Alan, 1950-. Lawyer. Chairman and chief executive officer, Thoroughbred Horsemen's Association. Creator of Mid-Atlantic Thoroughbred Championship (MATCH) series; general counsel for the Maryland Thoroughbred Horsemen's Association.

Forsythe, John, 1918-. Actor. Director, Hollywood Park. Owner of Big Train Farm. Eclipse Award of Merit in 1988. Owned Targa. Longtime Eclipse Awards dinner host.

Frankel, Robert, 1941-. Trainer. Leading trainer by money won in 1993; inducted into Racing Hall of Fame in '95; Eclipse Award trainer in 1993, 2000-'01. Trained Bertrando, Possibly Perfect, Wandesta (GB), Marquetry, Squirtle Squirt. Once called the king of claimers for his ability to turn claiming horses into winners; won a record 60 races at Hollywood Park during his first year in California (1972).

Franks, John, 1925-. Oil production. Owner of Franks Farms, Louisiana; Louisiana Stallions, Louisiana; Southland Farm, Florida. Co-owner of Heatherten Farm, Maryland. Leading owner by money won 1983-'84, '86, '93; leading owner by races won in 1983-'84, '86-'89; leading breeder by races won 1988-'93; leading owner by races won in '89; leading owner by money won in '93; Eclipse Award owner in 1983-'84, '93-'94. Bred and owned Answer Lively, Derby Wish, Kissin Kris. Bred Sharp Cat, Royal Anthem. Owned Heatherten, Dave's Friend, Top Avenger.

Earned $3.1-million in 1984, then a single-season record for owners.

Fuller, Peter, 1923-. Automobile dealer. John A. Morris Award in 1985. Bred and owned Dancer's Image, Mom's Command, Shananie, Donna's Time.

Gaines, John R., 1928-. Breeder. Former chairman, Breeders' Cup Ltd. Founder of Gainesway Farm, Kentucky. Eclipse Award of Merit in 1984; John W. Galbreath Award in '93. Bred Halo, Silent King, Time Limit. Owned Bold Bidder, Oil Royalty. Founder of Breeders' Cup, Kentucky Horse Park; assisted in developing the Maxwell H. Gluck Center for Equine Research at the University of Kentucky.

Gentry, Tom, 1937-. Bloodstock agent, breeder. Former owner of Tom Gentry Farm, Kentucky. Bred Royal Academy, Brazen, Marfa, Terlingua, Pancho Villa, Artichoke.

Gerry, Martha Farish, 1918-. Investments. Owner of Lazy F Ranch, Texas. Bred and owned Forego, Maid of France, Clef d'Argent, French Colonial. Bred and raced three-time Horse of the Year Forego, who earned nearly $2-million from 1973-'78. Aunt of William S. Farish.

Hancock, Arthur B. III, 1943-. Breeder. Former director, Keeneland Association. Owner of Stone Farm, Kentucky. Mr. Fitz Award in 1990. Bred and owned Sunday Silence, Gato Del Sol, Goodbye Halo. Co-bred Fusaichi Pegasus. Stood leading sire Halo. Brother of Seth Hancock; son of Arthur B. "Bull" Hancock Jr.

Hancock, Seth, 1949-. Breeder. Director, Churchill Downs; director, Keeneland Association. President of Claiborne Farm, Kentucky. Eclipse Award breeder 1979, '84. Bred and owned Swale, Forty Niner, Lure. Bred Wajima, Nureyev, Caerleon. Organized a syndicate to acquire Secretariat for more than $6-million. Stood Mr. Prospector, Danzig, Seeking the Gold, Unbridled. Brother of Arthur B. Hancock III; son of Arthur B. "Bull" Hancock Jr.

Harris, John C., 1943-. Breeder, agricultural products. President, California Thoroughbred Breeders Association; director, Thoroughbred Owners of California. Owner of Harris Farms, California. Bred and owned Soviet Problem.

Hartack, William J., 1932-. Jockey, racing official. Leading jockey by races won in 1955-'57, '60; leading jockey by money won in 1956-'57; inducted into Racing Hall of Fame in '59. Rode 4,272 winners, including Northern Dancer, Tim Tam, Majestic Prince. First jockey to earn $3-million in one year (1957); won five Kentucky Derbys (aboard Iron Liege in 1957, Venetian Way in '60, Decidedly in '62, Northern Dancer in '64, and Majestic Prince in '69).

Hawley, Sandy, 1949-. Jockey. Leading jockey by races won in 1970, '72-'73, '76; leading rider in Canada nine times; inducted into Racing Hall of Fame in '92; inducted into Canada's Hall of Fame in '86; Eclipse Award jockey in '76; George Woolf Memorial Jockey Award in '76; Sovereign Award in 1978, '88; Avelino Gomez Memorial Award in '86; Joe Palmer Award in '98. Rode 6,449 winners, including Youth, Desert Waves, Kiridashi, Smart Strike, Highland Vixen. First jockey to win more than 500 races in one season (1973).

Hettinger, John, 1933-. Investments, real estate. Director, Breeders' Cup Ltd. Owner of Akindale Farm,

New York. Special Eclipse Award in 2000. Bred and owned Warfie, Yestday's Kisses, Chase the Dream, Genuine Regret. Instrumental in founding the Racehorse Adoption Referral Program; chairman of the Grayson-Jockey Club Research Foundation; major shareholder, Fasig-Tipton Co.

Hickey, Jay, 1944-. Lawyer, lobbyist. President, American Horse Council. Represented equine organizations, horse owners, and horse breeders during his time as a practicing lawyer.

Hirsch, Joe, 1929-. Journalist. Co-founder and first president of the National Turf Writers Association 1959-'60. Lord Derby Award in 1985; Jockey Club Medal in '89; Mr. Fitz Award in '98; Walter Haight Award in '84; Joe Palmer Award in '94; Eclipse Award of Merit in '92; Eclipse Award for outstanding newspaper writing in '79. Longtime executive columnist of *Daily Racing Form*.

Hubbard, R. D., 1935-. Glass manufacturing. Former chairman and chief executive officer, Hollywood Park; owner, Ruidoso Downs. Owner of Crystal Springs Farm, Kentucky; Frontera Farm, New Mexico. Owned Gentlemen (Arg), Talloires, Leger Cat (Arg), Fit to Lead, Invited Guest, Mistico (Chi). Co-founded the Shoemaker Foundation in 1990 to help horsemen suffering from catastrophic accidents or illnesses.

Humphrey, G. Watts Jr., 1944-. Investments, manufacturing. Director, Breeders' Cup; director, Keeneland Association. Owner of Shawnee Farm, Kentucky. Bred Creme Fraiche, Sacahuista. Owned Likely Exchange, Amherst Wayside, Noble Damsel, Sorbet.

Hunt, Nelson Bunker, 1926-. Oil production. Owned Bluegrass Farm, Kentucky. Eclipse Award breeder in 1976, '85, '87; P.A.B. Widener Trophy in '85-'87. Bred and owned Dahlia, Youth, Empery, Trillion, Estrapade. Owned *Vaguely Noble, Exceller, Glorious Song. Bred Dahlia, the first mare to earn more than $1-million.

Icahn, Carl, 1936-. Financier. Owner of Foxfield Thoroughbreds, Kentucky. John A. Morris Award in 1990. Bred Blushing K. D., Great Navigator, Vaudeville, Helmsman, Brave Tender. Owned Meadow Star, Rose's Cantina, Colonial Waters.

Janney, Stuart III, 1948-. Financier. Chairman, Thoroughbred Owners and Breeders Association. Bred and owned Coronado's Quest, Warning Glance, Deputation, Mesabi Maiden. Aided in the formation of the National Thoroughbred Racing Association.

Jerkens, H. Allen, 1929-. Trainer. Leading trainer in New York in 1957, '62, '66, '69; inducted into Racing Hall of Fame in '75; Mr. Fitz Award in 2001; Eclipse Award trainer in '73. Trained 157 stakes winners, including Sky Beauty, Onion, Beau Purple, Duck Dance, Prove Out. Known as the "Giant Killer" for training horses who upset champions Secretariat, Forego, Buckpasser, Cicada, and Riva Ridge. Father of trainer Jimmy Jerkens.

Johnsen, Corey, 1955-. Racing executive. General manager, Remington Park; vice president and general manager, Lone Star Park. Created the All-Star Jockey Championship in 1997; played a key role in the development, construction, and opening of Remington Park; produced Eclipse Award-winning television program while at Louisiana Downs.

Johnson, Phil G., 1925-. Trainer. Inducted into Racing Hall of Fame in 1997. Trained Quiet Little Table, *Amen II, Maplejinsky, Match the Hatch, Naskra, Nasty and Bold.

Jolley, LeRoy, 1938-. Trainer. Inducted into Racing Hall of Fame in 1987. Trained Foolish Pleasure, Honest Pleasure, Genuine Risk, What a Summer, Manila, Meadow Star. Won the Kentucky Derby in 1980 with Genuine Risk, the first filly to compete in all three Triple Crown races. Son of trainer Moody Jolley.

Jones, Aaron U., 1921-. and **Jones, Marie**. Timber. Bred and owned Lemhi Gold, Western, Tiffany Lass. Owned Riboletta (Brz), Forestry, Plenty of Light.

Jones, Brereton, 1939-. Breeder, politician. Treasurer, Breeders' Cup Ltd.; president and director, Thoroughbred Club of America. Owner of Airdrie Stud, Kentucky. Bred Desert Wine, Southjet, Formidable Lady, Dansil. Owned By Land by Sea, Imp Society, Silver Medallion. Helped persuade Breeders' Cup to supplement purses at tracks around the country in addition to the Breeders' Cup day events in formative stage of the organization; inaugurated Kentucky Thoroughbred Development Fund while governor of Kentucky.

Jones, John T. L. Jr., 1935-. Breeder. Owner and general manager, Walmac International, Kentucky. One of the founding members of the Breeders' Cup championships; stood Alleged, Nureyev, Phone Trick.

Kelly, Tommy J., 1919-. Trainer. Inducted into Racing Hall of Fame in 1993. Trained Plugged Nickle, Colonel Moran, Droll Role, Pet Bully, Globemaster. Father of trainer Pat Kelly.

Krantz, Bryan, 1960-. Racing executive. President and general manager, Fair Grounds Race Course; owner, Jefferson Downs. Built new grandstand after a fire destroyed Fair Grounds's physical plant in 1993.

Krone, Julie, 1963-. Jockey. Inducted into Racing Hall of Fame in 2000. Rode 3,545 winners, including Colonial Affair, Rubiano, Da Hoss, Maxzene, Clear Mandate. Won the Belmont Stakes (G1) in 1993, becoming the first woman to win a Triple Crown race; became the first female jockey to win 3,500 races (in 1999); twice won five races in one day at Fair Grounds in '99.

Lewis, Robert, 1924- and **Lewis, Beverly**, 1927-. Beer distributor. Eclipse Award of Merit in 1997; Big Sport of Turfdom Award in '95. Owned Silver Charm, Charismatic, Serena's Song, Timber Country, Hennessy. Won two-thirds of the Triple Crown in 1997 and '99 (with Silver Charm and Charismatic, respectively).

Levy, Robert, 1931-. Chemical storage. Former owner, Atlantic City Race Course; former president, Thoroughbred Racing Associations. Owner of Muirfield East, Maryland. Owned Housebuster, Smoke Glacken, Bet Twice. Inaugurated full-card simulcasting in 1983.

Liebau, F. Jack, 1938-. Lawyer, racetrack executive. President, Santa Anita Park; vice president, Magna Entertainment; president, Bay Meadows Operating Co.; president, Bay Meadows Race Course; president, Golden Gate Fields. Owner of Valley Creek Farm, California. Owned Yashgan (GB), Boo La Boo, Forzando (GB), Kadial (Ire). Supervised $7-million

improvements at Bay Meadows Race Course; oversees Magna Entertainment tracks in California.

Little, Donald, 1934-. Financial management. Owner of Centennial Farms, Virginia. Owned Colonial Affair, Rubiano, King Cugat. President of the United States Polo Association; organizes racing syndicates with investors.

Longden, John, 1907-. Jockey, trainer. Leading jockey by races won in 1938, '47-'48; leading jockey by money won in 1943, '45; inducted into Racing Hall of Fame in '58; Special Eclipse Award in '94; George Woolf Memorial Jockey Award in '52; Avelino Gomez Memorial Award in '85. Rode then-record 6,032 winners, including Count Fleet, Busher, *Noor. Trained Majestic Prince, Jungle Savage, Baffle. First jockey to win 6,000 races; won five Santa Anita Derbys, five Hollywood Derbys, four Santa Anita Handicaps, and four Hollywood Gold Cups; founded Jockeys' Guild with Eddie Arcaro and Sam Renick in 1940.

Lukas, D. Wayne, 1935-. Trainer. Leading trainer by money won in 1983-'92, '94-'97; leading trainer by races won in 1987-'90; leading trainer by stakes races won in 1985-'92; inducted into Racing Hall of Fame in '99; Eclipse Award trainer in 1985-'87, '94; John W. Galbreath Award in '98. Leading trainer of Eclipse Award winners. Trained Lady's Secret, Thunder Gulch, Timber Country, Gulch, Flanders, Tabasco Cat, Codex, Charismatic. First trainer to reach both $100-million and $200-million in earnings; first trainer to win two Breeders' Cup races in one day (in 1985) and three races in one day (in '88); transformed modern training with entrepreneurial methods.

Madden, Preston, 1934- and **Madden, Anita**, 1933-. Real estate development. Owner of Hamburg Place, Kentucky. Bred Alysheba, Pink Pigeon, Miss Carmie, Romeo, Kentuckian. Owned T. V. Lark. Stood leading sire T. V. Lark; Anita Madden was the first female member of the Kentucky State Racing Commission.

Magnier, John, 1948-. Farm owner. Owner of Coolmore Stud, Ireland; Coolmore Stud, Australia; Ashford Stud, Kentucky. Bred Galileo (Ire), Sadler's Wells, Dr Devious (Ire). Originated shuttle-stallion concept; expanded mare books; stood Sadler's Wells, Be My Guest, El Gran Senor, Woodman, Danehill.

Maktoum, Sheikh Mohammed bin Rashid al, 1949-. Royal family of Dubai. Owner of Raceland Farm, Kentucky; Darley Stud, Kentucky; Dalham Hall Stud, England; Kildangan Stud, Ireland. Bred and owned Dubai Millennium, Intrepidity (GB), In the Wings (GB), Swain (Ire). Owned Oh So Sharp (GB), Daylami (Ire), Pebbles (GB). Created Godolphin Racing, Dubai World Cup.

Mandella, Richard, 1950-. Trainer. Inducted into Racing Hall of Fame in 2001. Trained Kotashaan (Fr), Phone Chatter, Dare and Go, Dixie Union, Gentlemen (Arg), Wild Rush. Trained Dare and Go, who won the Pacific Classic (G1) in 1996, ending Cigar's 16-race winning streak; won four stakes races on the Breeders' Cup day program in '93.

Martin, Frank "Pancho", 1925-. Trainer. Leading trainer by money won in 1974; leading trainer in New York in 1973-'82; inducted into Racing Hall of Fame in '81. Trained 51 stakes winners and two champions, including Autobiography, Outstandingly,

Sham, Manassa Mauler, Rube the Great.

McAnally, Ron, 1932-. Trainer. Inducted into Racing Hall of Fame in 1990; Eclipse Award trainer in 1981, '91-'92; Mr. Fitz Award in '92. Trained John Henry, Bayakoa (Arg), Tight Spot, Paseana (Arg), Northern Spur (Ire). Trained John Henry to record seven Eclipse Awards.

McCarron, Chris, 1955-. Jockey. Leading jockey by races won in 1974-'75, '80; leading jockey by money won in 1980-'81, '84, '91; inducted into Racing Hall of Fame in '89; Eclipse Award apprentice jockey in '74; Eclipse Award jockey in '80; George Woolf Memorial Jockey Award in '80; Mike Venezia Award in '91. Rode Alysheba, John Henry, Lady's Secret, Sunday Silence, Go for Gin. All-time leading earner among jockeys with $264-million; along with his wife, Judy, and comedian Tim Conway, created the Don MacBeth Memorial Fund for disabled jockeys.

McGaughey, Claude R. "Shug" III, 1951-. Trainer. Eclipse Award trainer in 1988. Trained Easy Goer, Personal Ensign, Rhythm, Inside Information, Heavenly Prize, My Flag. Trained Personal Ensign, unbeaten in 13 races; won five graded stakes at Belmont Park on Breeders' Cup preview day in 1993.

McKathan, J. B., 1966- and **McKathan, Kevin**, 1968-. Bloodstock agents. Owners of McKathan Brothers Training Facility in Ocala; purchased Silver Charm, Real Quiet, Silverbulletday, Captain Steve.

McKay, Jim (Jim McManus), 1921-. Broadcaster. President, Maryland Million Ltd. Eclipse Award of Merit in 2000; Big Sport of Turfdom Award in 1987; Joe Palmer Award in '00. Co-founder of Maryland Million; broadcast Triple Crown in 1975-2000 on ABC.

McNair, Robert, 1937- and **McNair, Janice**, 1936-. Energy production. Owner of Stonerside Farms, Kentucky; Greentree Stables, New York. Co-bred Fusaichi Pegasus. Owned Chilukki, Tuzla (Ire), Angel Fever. Co-owned Coronado's Quest, Touch of Gold.

Meeker, Thomas, 1943-. Racing executive. President, Churchill Downs Inc.; president, Thoroughbred Racing Associations. John W. Galbreath Award in 1999. Beginning in 1984, implemented a $25-million, five-year improvement plan for Churchill, including a $3.6-million turf course and a $2.8-million paddock. Undertook $100-million renovation of Churchill Downs in 2002; oversaw expansion of Churchill Downs Inc. to encompass tracks from coast to coast

Meyerhoff, Robert, 1924-. Real estate development. Owner of Fitzhugh Farm, Maryland. Bred and owned Broad Brush, Concern, Include, Valley Crossing.

Miller, MacKenzie "Mack", 1921-. Trainer, breeder. Inducted into Racing Hall of Fame in 1987; Mr. Fitz Award in '96. Trained 72 stakes winners, including champions Leallah, Assagai, Hawaii, and *Snow Knight. Trained Fit to Fight to New York handicap triple crown in 1984; trained Sea Hero to Kentucky Derby victory in 1993.

Moran, Elizabeth, 1932-. Investments. Owner of Brushwood Stable, Pennsylvania. Bred High Yield. Owned Creme Fraiche, Rich Cream, Family Style. Won American Grand National Steeplechase with McAdam in 1984; won English Grand National Steeple-

chase Handicap with Papillon in 2000.

Mott, William, 1953-. Trainer. Inducted into Racing Hall of Fame in 1998; Eclipse Award trainer in 1995-'96. Trained Cigar, Paradise Creek, Ajina, Theatrical (Ire), Geri, Escena, Wekiva Springs. Trained Cigar, who won 16 consecutive races from 1994-'96, including the inaugural Dubai World Cup in '96.

Nafzger, Carl, 1941-. Trainer. Eclipse Award trainer in 1990; Big Sport of Turfdom Award in '90. Trained Unbridled, Banshee Breeze, Unshaded, Vicar, Solvig. Wrote training book *Traits of a Winner: The Formula for Developing Thoroughbred Racehorses* in '94.

Nerud, John A., 1913-. Trainer, breeder. President of Tartan Farms, Florida, 1959-'89. Inducted into Racing Hall of Fame in 1972. Trained 27 stakes winners and five champions, including Dr. Fager, Ta Wee, Delegate, Intentionally, Dr. Patches, *Gallant Man. Bred and owned Cozzene, Fappiano. Trained Dr. Fager, only horse to win four championships in one year.

Niarchos-Gouaze, Maria, Investments. Director, Breeders' Cup Ltd. Owner of Haras de Fresnay-le-Buffard, France. Breeds under the name Flaxman Holdings Ltd. Bred and owned Dream Well, Sulamani. Daughter of shipping magnate Stavros Niarchos.

Nicholson, George "Nick", 1947-. Racing executive. President and chief executive officer, Keeneland Association; executive director, Jockey Club 1989-2000; former chief operating officer, National Thoroughbred Racing Association; president, Thoroughbred Club of America in '91. Jockey Club Gold Medal in 1998. Involved in the planning and development of the Kentucky Horse Park; played key role in formation of Equibase racing and pedigree database; helped to pull industry together to support the National Thoroughbred Racing Association.

Nuckols, Charles Jr., 1922-. Breeder. Former president, Thoroughbred Club of America; director, Keeneland Association. Owner of Nuckols Farm, Kentucky. Bred Hidden Lake, Habitat, Decathlon, Typecast. Co-bred War Emblem. Co-authored the Kentucky Thoroughbred Development Fund as a member of the Thoroughbred Breeders of Kentucky.

O'Byrne, Dermot "Demi", 1944-. Bloodstock agent, veterinarian. Purchased Thunder Gulch, Honour and Glory, High Yield, Fasliyev, Stravinsky, King of Kings (Ire), Johannesburg. Chief talent spotter for Coolmore Stud.

O'Farrell, Michael, 1948-. Breeder. First vice president, Florida Thoroughbred Owners' and Breeders' Association. Owner of Ocala Stud Farm, Florida. Bred Bolshoi Boy, Proudest Duke, Queen Alexandra. Son of Joe O'Farrell.

Oxley, John C., 1937- and **Oxley, Debbie**, 1951-. Oil production. Owner of Fawn Leap Farm, Kentucky. Bred and owned Pyramid Peak. Owned Monarchos, Beautiful Pleasure.

Pape, William L., 1930-. Auto dealership. Former president, National Steeplechase Association. Co-bred champions Flatterer and Martie's Anger; owned champion Athenian Idol.

Payson, Virginia Kraft, 1930-. Investments. Owner of Payson Stud, Kentucky. Bred and owned St. Jovite, L'Carriere. Owned Carr de Naskra. Owner and op-

erator of Payson Park training center in Florida.

Pegram, Mike, 1952-. Fast food franchises. Owned Real Quiet, Silverbulletday, Isitingood, Thirty Slews, Captain Steve.

Perret, Craig, 1951-. Jockey. Eclipse Award jockey in 1990; George Woolf Memorial Jockey Award in '98. Rode Unbridled, Housebuster, Safely Kept, Eillo, Rhythm, Alydeed, Bet Twice. Won a record-tying 57 stakes in 1990.

Phillips, John W., 1952-. Investments, lawyer. Managing partner of Darby Dan Farm, Kentucky. Bred and owned Memories of Silver, Sunshine Forever, Brian's Time, Soaring Softly. Won inaugural running of the Breeders' Cup Filly and Mare Turf with Soaring Softly in 1999. Grandson of John W. Galbreath.

Phipps, Ogden Mills "Dinny", 1940-. Investments. Chairman, Jockey Club; former chairman, New York Racing Association; director, Grayson-Jockey Club Research Foundation. Eclipse Award of Merit in 1978. Bred and owned Inside Information, Rhythm, Educated Risk. Co-bred and owned Successor. Son of Ogden Phipps.

Pincay, Laffit Jr., 1946-. Jockey. Leading jockey by money won in 1970-'74, '79, '85; leading jockey by races won in '71; inducted into Racing Hall of Fame in '75 ; Eclipse Award jockey in 1971, '73-'74, '79, '85; Special Eclipse Award in '99; George Woolf Memorial Jockey Award in '70. Big Sport of Turfdom Award in '85. Rode Affirmed, John Henry, Gamely, Susan's Girl, Desert Vixen, Genuine Risk. Broke Bill Shoemaker's lifetime win record on December 10, 1999, with his 8,834th victory; first jockey to win seven races on a single card at Santa Anita Park, in '87; first jockey to win more than 9,000 races.

Pollard, Carl, 1938-. Health care executive. Chairman, Churchill Downs Inc.; president, Kentucky Derby Museum. Owner of Hermitage Farm, Kentucky. Owned Caressing, Sheepscot, Duck Trap, Take Me Out.

Rasmussen, Leon, 1915-. Journalist. "Bloodlines" columnist, *Daily Racing Form* 1950-'87. Walter Haight Award in 1987; Engelhard Award in '87. Bred and owned Apollo, Nanetta. Popularized Dr. Steven A. Roman's dosage system in his column.

Robertson, Walter, 1949-. Auctioneer. President, Fasig-Tipton Co.; former president, Thoroughbred Club of America. Auctioneer at the Calumet Farm sale in 1992.

Rotz, John L., 1934-. Jockey, racing official. Leading jockey by stakes winners in 1968-'69; inducted into Racing Hall of Fame in '83; George Woolf Memorial Jockey Award in '73. Rode 2,908 winners. Rode Gallant Bloom, Ta Wee, Carry Back, Dr. Fager, Silent Screen.

Salman, Ahmed bin, 1958-. Publisher, Saudi royal family. Owner of The Thoroughbred Corp. Bred and owned Point Given. Owned Sharp Cat, Jewel Princess, Oath, Anees, Royal Anthem, War Emblem.

Samuel-Balaz, Tammy, Investments. Co-owner of Sam-Son Farm, Canada and Florida. Bred and owned Dancethruthedawn, Scatter the Gold, Catch the Ring, Mountain Angel, Quiet Resolve. Daughter of Ernie Samuel.

Santos, Jose, 1961-. Jockey. Leading jockey by money won in 1986-'89; Eclipse Award jockey in '88;

George Woolf Memorial Jockey Award in '99. Rode Lemon Drop Kid, Skip Away, Colonial Affair, Chief Bearhart. Led all jockeys by money won with a then-record $14.86-million in 1988; rode 13 winners in three days at Aqueduct in '88.

Santulli, Richard, 1944-. Aviation. Co-owner of Jayeff B Stable. Bred and owned Ciro. Owned Safely Kept, Banshee Breeze, Korveya.

Savin, Scott, 1960-. Owner, executive. President, Gulfstream Park; president, Florida Horsemen's Benevolent and Protective Association. Owned Big Bet, Cheshire Kitten. Grandson of A. I. "Butch" Savin, owner of Mr. Prospector.

Schulhofer, Flint W. "Scotty", 1926-. Trainer, jockey. Inducted into Racing Hall of Fame in 1992. Trained 80 stakes, including champions Ta Wee, Mac Diarmida, Smile, Fly So Free, Lemon Drop Kid, Rubiano; also trained Cryptoclearance. Began career as steeplechase jockey.

Schwartz, Barry, 1942-. Clothing. Chairman and chief executive officer, New York Racing Association. Owner of Stonewall Farm, New York. Bred and owned Beru, Patricia J. K. Owned Three Ring. Lowered New York's pari-mutuel takeout; mandated color-coded saddlecloths.

Sheppard, Jonathan, 1940-. Trainer, breeder. Owner of Ashwell Stables, Pennsylvania. Leading steeplechase trainer by money won in 1973-'90, '92-'95; inducted into Racing Hall of Fame in '90. Trained 119 stakes winners, including champions Cafe Prince, Flatterer, Athenian Idol, Martie's Anger, Jimmy Lorenzo (GB), Highland Bud. Also trained Storm Cat. Co-bred Martie's Anger, Flatterer.

Sherman, Michael, 1940-. Breeder. Owner and president of Farnsworth Farms, Florida. Leading breeder by stakes winners in 1994-'95; Eclipse Award breeder in '96. Bred Beautiful Pleasure, Jewel Princess, Mecke, Frisk Me Now, Once Wild.

Shoemaker, William, 1931-. Jockey, trainer. President, Jockeys' Guild in 1975-'90. Leading jockey by money won in 1958-'64; inducted into Racing Hall of Fame in '58; Special Eclipse Award in '76; Eclipse Award jockey in '81; Eclipse Award of Merit in '81; George Woolf Memorial Jockey Award in '90; Mike Venezia Award in '90. Rode then-record 8,833 winners and 1,009 stakes winners, including Swaps, Spectacular Bid, Round Table, Ack Ack, Forego, John Henry, Prove It, Olden Times, Sword Dancer. Trained Fire the Groom, Alcando (Ire). First jockey to reach $100-million in earnings; mounts earned more than $123-million in purses.

Smith, Mike, 1965-. Jockey. Leading jockey by races won in 1994; Eclipse Award jockey in 1993-'94; Mike Venezia Award in '94; George Woolf Memorial Jockey Award in 2000. Rode Holy Bull, Lure, Skip Away, Unbridled's Song, Coronado's Quest. Won record 66 stakes in 1994.

Smith, Tim, 1948-. Racing executive. Commissioner, chief executive officer of National Thoroughbred Racing Association. Helped increase national television exposure for horse racing; formed partnership between NTRA and Television Games Network; initiated merger of NTRA and Breeders' Cup Ltd.

Smithwick, D. M. "Mike", 1929-. Trainer. Inducted into Racing Hall of Fame in 1971. Trained 52 stakes

winners and six champions. Trained Neji, Bon Nouvel, Ancestor, Mako, Top Bid, Straight and True. Trained Neji to three championships in 1955, '57, and '58; trained the first two winners (Top Bid and Inkslinger) of the Colonial Cup. Brother of Racing Hall of Fame jockey Paddy Smithwick.

Sommer, Viola (Mrs. Sigmund), 1921-. Real estate. Leading owner in 1982; Eclipse Award owner in '82. Bred and owned Bottled Water. Owned Sham, Ten Below, Tom Swift.

Steinbrenner, George, 1930-. Shipping. Director, Florida Thoroughbred Breeders' and Owners' Association. Owner of Kinsman Farm, Florida. Bred and owned Concerto, Diligence, Eternal Prince. Purchased major interest in Florida Downs (later Tampa Bay Downs) in 1980. Managing partner, New York Yankees.

Stevens, Gary, 1963-. Jockey. President, Jockeys' Guild, 1995-2000. Leading jockey by money won in 1990; inducted into Racing Hall of Fame in '97; Eclipse Award jockey in '98; George Woolf Memorial Jockey Award in '96. Rode more than 4,500 winners, including Point Given, Silver Charm, Winning Colors, Thunder Gulch, Hennessy, Broad Brush. Youngest rider to earn more than $100-million in purses, in 1993; won inaugural NTRA All-Star Jockey Championship in '97.

Strawbridge, George Jr., 1937-. Investments. President, National Steeplechase Association. Owner of Augustin Stables, Pennsylvania. F. Ambrose Clark Award in 1979. Bred and owned Tikkanen, Selkirk, Silver Fling. Bred Treizieme, Turgeon. Owned Cafe Prince, Mo Bay.

Stronach, Frank, 1932-. Auto parts. Chairman, Magna International Corp., Magna Entertainment Corp. Owner of Adena Springs Farm, Kentucky; Adena Springs North, Ontario; Adena Springs South, Florida. Owner of Stronach Stable. Eclipse Award owner in 1998-2000; Eclipse Award breeder in '00; Sovereign Award 1997-'99. Bred and owned Macho Uno, Perfect Sting. Co-owned Touch Gold, Glorious Song. Also bred and owned Awesome Again, richest Canadian-bred runner of all-time with $4,374,590 in total earnings. Through Magna Entertainment, purchased Santa Anita Park, Gulfstream Park, Thistledown, Golden Gate Fields, Remington Park, Great Lakes Downs; company operates Bay Meadows Race Course (owns license) and Portland Meadows (under loaco).

Suroor, Saeed bin, 1967-. Trainer. Leading trainer in England by money won in 1995. Trained Fantastic Light, Swain (Ire), E Dubai, Lammtarra, Mark of Esteem (Ire). Head trainer for Godolphin Racing; won the Emirates World Series with Daylami (Ire) and Fantastic Light in 1999 and 2000, respectively.

Tabor, Michael, 1941-. Betting shop owner, investments. Owned Thunder Gulch, Montjeu (Ire), Desert King, Honour and Glory, Johannesburg, Galileo (Ire), High Chapparal.

Taylor, Duncan, 1956-. Farm owner. Co-owner (with brothers Frank, Ben, and Mark) of Taylor Made Farm and Sales Agency, Kentucky. Sold approximately $670-million total value of horses at public auctions since 1978.

Taylor, Mickey, 1940- and **Taylor, Karen**, 1940-. Timber. Owned and bred Slew o' Gold, Slewpy. Co-owned Seattle Slew, who won 14 of 17 starts, including the Triple Crown in 1977, and earned $1.2-million.

Turcotte, Ron, 1941-. Jockey. Leading jockey by stakes won in 1972-'73; inducted into Racing Hall of Fame in '79; George Woolf Memorial Jockey Award in '79. Rode 3,032 winners, including Secretariat, Damascus, Northern Dancer, Riva Ridge, Shuvee, Dark Mirage, Fort Marcy. Won Triple Crown in 1973 aboard Secretariat. Paralyzed in 1978 spill.

Ussery, Robert N., 1935-. Jockey. Inducted into Racing Hall of Fame in 1980. Rode 3,611 winners, including Hail to Reason, Bally Ache, Bramalea, Never Bow. Ranked fifth by money won among jockeys at retirement; finished first in two consecutive Kentucky Derbys (1967-'68), aboard Proud Clarion and Dancer's Image.

Van Berg, Jack, 1936-. Trainer. Leading trainer by races won in 1968-'70, '72, '74, '76, '83-'84, '86; leading trainer by money won in '76; inducted into Racing Hall of Fame in '85; Eclipse Award trainer in '84; Big Sport of Turfdom Award in '87; Jockey Club Gold Medal in '87; Mr. Fitz Award in '88. Trained Alysheba, Gate Dancer. Holds record for most races won in a single year (496 in 1976); trained champion Alysheba, who retired with a then-record total earnings of $6,679,242; 6,000th career win in February 1995. Son of Racing Hall of Fame trainer Marion Van Berg.

Van Clief, Daniel G. Jr., 1948-. Racing executive. President, Breeders' Cup Ltd.; chairman, Fasig-Tipton Co.; former president, Thoroughbred Club of America. Co-owner of Nydrie Stud, Virginia. Eclipse Award of Merit in 1998; Jockey Club Medal in '84. Worked to put together Breeders' Cup day of championship races; key figure in development of the National Thoroughbred Racing Association.

Van de Kamp, John, 1936-. Lawyer, association executive. President and general counsel, Thoroughbred Owners of California; director, National Thoroughbred Racing Association. Gathered support in the TOC to pass account wagering bill; lobbied for horse industry tax relief measures in California.

Varola, Francesco, 1922-. Author. Author of *Typology of the Racehorse*; added to the dosage theory by creating aptitudinal classes in which he categorized each *chef-de-race* stallion.

Vasquez, Jacinto, 1944-. Jockey, trainer. Inducted into Racing Hall of Fame in 1998. Rode 5,231 winners, including Ruffian, Genuine Risk, Princess Rooney, Forego. Nation's 15th all-time winning jockey at his retirement in 1996; rode Ruffian to victory in the New York filly triple crown in '75.

Veitch, John, 1945-. Trainer. Trained Davona Dale, Our Mims, Before Dawn, Proud Truth. Trained Alydar, who finished second behind Affirmed in all three Triple Crown races in 1978. Son of Racing Hall of Fame trainer Sylvester Veitch.

Velasquez, Jorge, 1946-. Jockey. Leading jockey by races won in 1967; leading jockey by money won in '69; leading jockey by stakes races won in '85; inducted into Racing Hall of Fame in '90; George Woolf Memorial Jockey Award in '86. Rode 6,795 winners, including Alydar, Chris Evert, Davona Dale, Lady's Secret, Shuvee, Fort Marcy. Won the New York filly triple crown with Chris Evert in 1974 and Davona Dale in '79; first jockey to win six of six races in New York, in '81.

Ward, John T. Jr., 1945-. Trainer. Owner of Sugar Grove Farm, Kentucky; John T. Ward Stables, Kentucky. Trained Monarchos, Beautiful Pleasure, Darling My Darling, Jambalaya Jazz, Pyramid Peak. Nephew of Racing Hall of Fame trainer Sherrill Ward.

Weber, Charlotte, 1942-. Investments. Owner of Live Oak Stud, Florida. Bred and owned Peaceful Union, Gnome Home, Medieval Man, Laser Light, Sultry Sun.

Weisbord, Barry, 1950-. Publisher. Joe Palmer Award in 1992. Co-owned Safely Kept. Created the American Championship Racing Series in 1991; created the Matchmaker Breeders' Exchange, the first centralized market for stallion seasons and shares.

West, R. Smiser, Breeder. Owner of Waterford Farm, Kentucky. Bred Lite Light, De La Rose, Chilukki.

Whiteley, Frank Jr., 1915-. Trainer. Inducted into Racing Hall of Fame in 1978. Trained 35 stakes winners and four champions, including Damascus, Forego, Ruffian, Tom Rolfe.

Whitney, Marylou, 1926-. Investments. Owner of Whitney Farm, Kentucky; Blue Goose Stable, Kentucky. Bred and owned Silver Buck. Bred Silver Creamer, Dawn Mountain, Bird Cage. Long known for her Derby Eve parties held each year before the Kentucky Derby and for her parties at Saratoga Springs, New York. Widow of C. V. Whitney.

Willmot, David, 1950-. Breeder, investments. President, Woodbine Entertainment Group, formerly Ontario Jockey Club. Owner of Kinghaven Farms, Canada. John W. Galbreath Award in 2001; Sovereign Award in 1998. Bred and owned Talkin Man, Poetically, Alywow, Play the King, Summer Mood, With Approval. Brought Ontario Jockey Club out of financial troubles; successfully lobbied for legislation to add slot machines at Woodbine racetrack; Kinghaven became the first Canadian stable to earn more than $2-million, in 1986. Son of Donald Willmot.

Wolfson, Louis, 1912-. and **Wolfson, Patrice**—Investments. Owner of Harbor View Farm, Florida. Leading breeder in 1970-'71. Bred and owned Affirmed, Flawlessly, Exclusive Native, It's In the Air, Outstandingly. Owned Raise a Native. Bred and raced two-time Horse of the Year Affirmed, winner of the Triple Crown in 1978.

Ycaza, Manuel, 1938-. Jockey. Inducted into Racing Hall of Fame in 1977. Rode 2,367 winners, including Ack Ack, Dr. Fager, Damascus, Sword Dancer, Gamely, Dark Mirage, Never Bend. Won first New York filly triple crown with Dark Mirage in 1968.

Young, William T., 1918-. Foods, storage. Owner of Overbrook Farm, Kentucky. Eclipse Award breeder in 1994. Bred and owned Storm Cat, Tabasco Cat, Cat Thief, Boston Harbor, Flanders, Surfside, Golden Attraction. Owned Editor's Note, Grindstone.

Zito, Nick, 1948-. Trainer. Trained Go for Gin, Strike the Gold, Louis Quatorze, A P Valentine, Thirty Six Red.

BREEDING
Evolution of the Breed

In genetic terms, the Thoroughbred is a hybrid, created by crossing two or possibly more breeds of horses to produce an animal with specific characteristics. One of those breeds was the Arabian horse, but the exact identities of other contributors are considerably less clear.

Early records do not identify mares mated to the many Arabian, Barb, and Turk (all are varieties of Arabians) stallions imported to England after the Markham Arabian's acquisition by King James I. Although the Markham Arabian was the first Arabian whose importation was noted by history, no doubt many others, both males and females, were brought back from the Middle East over several centuries, beginning with the Crusades in the 12th and 13th centuries. However, many horses called Arabians or Barbs in the *General Stud Book* were certainly not purebreds.

These imports were crossed with native English stock. By the time the modern Thoroughbred was created, there were two varieties of pony-sized English racehorses known as Hobbies and Galloways. Both certainly carried Arabian blood but no one knows how much. Many of these were part of the broodmare band of the royal stud before the Puritan revolution in 1649.

The surge of importations that began with the restoration of King Charles II in 1660 included both males and females. With King Charles leading the way, the English nobility engaged in fierce competition to produce faster and better racehorses, and they quickly learned that the more Arabian blood their stock could claim, the better chance they had.

Foundation Sires

The arrivals of the Byerly Turk around 1690, the Curwen Bay Barb, the Darley Arabian, and finally the Godolphin Arabian (around 1730) sharply accelerated the development of the breed. The Darley Arabian sired Flying Childers, generally recognized as the first great Thoroughbred, in 1714. Through Flying Childers's full brother Bartlett's Childers, the Darley Arabian established today's dominant male line, leading to Phalaris and his descendants.

The Godolphin Arabian was the most prepotent immediate influence among the three founding male-line sires, establishing the male line that leads to Tiznow, Horse of the Year in 2000. Although the Godolphin Arabian male line is now far less prominent than that of the Darley Arabian, about 13% of the genes of the modern Thoroughbred come from the Godolphin Arabian, according to modern statistical studies.

The male line tracing to the Byerly Turk achieved

dominance in the late 18th century through his great-great-grandson Herod. By 1825, inbreeding to Herod had reached its limit, and his overall influence began to decline. Today, his male line appears headed for extinction, with tendrils hanging on in Europe through Ahonoora and in Australia through Century. Nevertheless, more than 17% of the genes of the modern Thoroughbred come from Herod.

Estimated Relationships of Some Important Horses to Modern Thoroughbreds

Horse (year of birth)	Percentage relationship
Herod (1758)	17.2%
Eclipse (1764)	15.2%
Highflyer (1774)	12.8%
Godolphin Arabian (1724)	12.7%
Partner (1718)	11.4%
Regulus (1739)	9.4%
St. Simon (1881)	8.7%
Stockwell (1849)	8.7%
Curwen Bay Barb mare (1710)	8.4%
Birdcatcher (1833)	7.4%
Pocahontas (1837)	7.0%
Matchem (1748)	6.3%
Flying Childers (1715)	5.7%
Darley Arabian (ca. 1700)	5.3%
*Teddy (1913)	4.9%
Byerley Turk (ca. 1680)	4.6%
Curwen Bay Barb (ca. 1695)	4.4%
Hyperion (1930)	4.2%
*Nasrullah (1940)	4.2%
Bald Galloway (ca. 1700)	4.0%

Figures based on an unpublished statistical study. Percentages of horses born since about 1850 may change slightly over time. The more recent the birthdate, the greater the possible change in influence as the breed evolves.

Beneficiary of the intense early inbreeding to Godolphin Arabian and Herod was the Darley Arabian line. The line from Flying Childers was prominent for approximately 50 years, but descendants of his unraced full brother Bartlett's Childers gained ascendance through his great-grandson Eclipse, foaled in 1764. Greatest of the four-milers, Eclipse had a stud career that encompassed the beginning of the shift from the four-mile heat racing popular since King Charles's era to "dash" racing over shorter distances, exemplified by the Epsom Derby, founded in 1780.

Eclipse and Herod surpassed all other horses of their time in producing the speedier, more brilliant horse necessary for dash racing. Added together, Herod, Godolphin Arabian, and Eclipse account for almost 45% of the genes of the modern Thoroughbred.

In the same time period that surviving male

lines were being whittled down to three, female lines descending from the 100 or so foundation mares listed in Volume 1 of the *General Stud Book* were cut in half. That, of course, does not mean that those foundation mares and stallions had no influence on the development of the breed. Indeed, their names persist, sometimes with great influence, in the nether reaches of pedigrees.

Exportation of the Thoroughbred to other countries, particularly to North America, Australia, and Argentina, inevitably resulted in the introduction of female lines not found in the *General Stud Book*. The chaotic circumstances of Colonial and Revolutionary America meant that records were lost on many legitimate members of the breed and invented for many who doubtless were not.

Such chaos inevitably led to controversy. When American racing collapsed early in the 20th century due to antigambling hysteria, England's Turf authority, the Jockey Club, essentially banned American-bred stock from the hallowed pages of the *General Stud Book* when American exports threatened to flood the market. Fortunately for the future of the breed, the "Jersey Act" of 1913 excluding American-breds had a provision that grandfathered in American-bred stock already included in earlier volumes.

Within 40 years, descendants of those acceptable American-breds—including such horses as Nearco and his son *Nasrullah—and descendants of French-bred Tourbillon (branded as a half-bred by the Jersey Act because of his American antecedents) dominated English racing, forcing recision of the exclusionary rules.

Pattern of Racing

Throughout the 19th century and the first half of the 20th century, the English racing program centered on five classic races inaugurated between 1776 and 1808. The Two Thousand Guineas, Epsom Derby, and St. Leger Stakes became recognized as the Triple Crown, while the One Thousand Guineas and Epsom Oaks provided equivalent races open only to females. Other countries followed the English example, with America being the last to follow suit, abandoning four-mile heat racing only after the Civil War. That stubbornness built a vast reserve of stamina in the American Thoroughbred that served the breed well for more than a century.

In the decades flanking the beginning of the 20th century, the character of racing began to change slowly, and with it the character of the Thoroughbred. When American jockeys invaded England in the 1890s, early speed became far more important, and over the next three decades the male-line descendants of one horse, Phalaris, proved best suited to adapting to the new conditions.

Although considered only a sprinter—albeit a top-class one—Phalaris proved capable of siring winners over every distance, and his sons, grandsons, and later descendants have come to dominate Thoroughbred racing worldwide. In an era increasingly dominated by sheer speed, Phalaris-line horses have proved themselves to be the fastest.

In the 20th century, the breed was shaped by the shift from large private studs producing horses for their own racing stables to commercial establishments that produced racing prospects for sale to other owners. That shift accelerated the trend toward speed because buyers tended to prefer horses that they felt would bring a quicker return—that is, precocious types that could race early over short distances. Few commercial breeders are willing or able to concentrate on producing classic-distance horses as some Victorian private breeders had.

Certainly the modern Thoroughbred is a far faster animal than was Flying Childers, whose reputed time of one minute for one mile, or 60 mph, is only a legend. Contemporary Thoroughbreds are on average larger, shorter-legged, proportionally heavier, and lighter-boned than the foundation stock. All those characteristics produce greater speed, often at the expense of stamina and soundness.—*John P. Sparkman*

The Darley Arabian

Of the Thoroughbred's three male-line foundation sires, only the Darley Arabian was almost certainly a pure-blood Arabian. The Godolphin Arabian was almost certainly a Turcoman-Arabian cross, while the Byerley Turk was probably born in England, sired by another Turcoman-Arabian cross horse whose identity is uncertain.

Probably born in what is now Syria in 1700, the Darley Arabian was purchased in Aleppo, then part of the Ottoman Empire, by English merchant Thomas Darley in 1704 and shipped to his brother Richard Darley at Aldby Park near York, England. The Darley Arabian was said to be of the "keheilan" or "manicca" breed, the subset of Arabians then most prized by Bedouins. Ottoman law forbade the sale of any pure-bred Arabian to a foreigner, but Darley's merchant connections in Aleppo allowed him to spirit the horse out of the country.

The Darley Arabian mostly covered his owner's broodmares, but one of the few outside mares bred to him was Leonard Childers's Betty Leedes, by Careless, who produced Flying Childers in 1714 and his full brother Bartlett's Childers in 1715. Flying Childers was unbeaten and considered by far the fastest horse until that time. Darley Arabian also sired the good racehorses Almanzor, Cupid, and Brisk.

Although Flying Childers was a successful sire, his brother Bartlett's Childers—unraced because he was a bleeder—carried on the line. He sired the good racehorse Squirt, who in turn sired Marske, sire of Eclipse (1764). Eclipse in turn founded the male lines that lead to the modern lines of Phalaris (Northern Dancer, *Nasrullah, Native Dancer), St. Simon (*Ribot and *Princequillo), Hyperion, Domino, and Blandford.

Breeding Theories

Flying Childers was the first great racehorse who clearly could be defined as a Thoroughbred, and undoubtedly his breeder, Leonard Childers, had a theory to explain why his greatest creation was so fast. In the three centuries since Flying Childers first saw daylight in 1714, it is certain that most breeders were equally sure they knew why their latest champion could run a hole in the wind.

Over time, however, breeders' ideas about why one horse runs faster than another have coalesced into a remarkably small set of concepts. These concepts range from vaguely general precepts such as "breed the best to the best and hope for the best" to highly specific constructs such as the many varieties of dosage theory.

Breed the Best to the Best

The logic behind the broadest of these ideas—breed the best to the best—is obvious. If speed in the racehorse is determined to a degree by inheritance, then it is logical to assume that the fastest horses—both male and female—have the best chances to pass on their abilities to their offspring.

The history of the breed has shown irrefutably that this assumption is true. In general, the horses that turn out to be the best sires are almost always high-class racehorses themselves. The correlation between racecourse ability and sire success is, of course, far from perfect but undeniably positive.

The case for the female of the species is less clear but still undeniable. On average, the best racemares become more successful broodmares than those females that showed less ability on the racecourse. Thus, if a high-class racehorse is mated to a high-class racemare, the breeder theoretically increases the probability that another high-class racehorse will result.

Because probability is capricious, the odds are still against the breeder. The most successful stallions in history have sired only about 25% stakes winners. Individual broodmares may achieve higher percentages, but percentages based on the relatively small numbers of foals from those mares are meaningless in the larger picture.

So, breeding the best to the best certainly works, on average. However, it is far too general a precept to satisfy many Thoroughbred breeders—and of no use whatsoever to those who cannot afford to buy the best, most expensive racing and stallion prospects.

Inbreeding

For the first 100 years or so of the Thoroughbred's existence as a distinct, definable breed, the number of horses bred each year was so small that inbreeding was inevitable.

Inbreeding, as most commonly used by Thoroughbred breeders, means the repetition of one or more names at least once on both the sire's and dam's side of a pedigree within the first four or five generations. In genetic terms, inbreeding reduces the number of different and distinct gene alleles available to appear in the genome of the new individual. Thus, it increases the chances that the offspring of that mating will display uniform and specific characteristics.

Inbreeding is therefore used in animal husbandry to fix type—that is, to create a more uniform subspecies, which is exactly what Thoroughbred

Some Famous Inbred Horses

Horse (year of birth)	Inbreeding	Accomplishment
Spanker mare (ca 1690)	2x1 Old Morocco mare	Third dam of Flying Childers
Rachel (1763)	2x3 Godolphin Arabian	Dam of Highflyer, undefeated, 13-time leading sire
Eclipse (1764)	3x4 Snake mare	Unbeaten champion, sire line founder
Prunella (1788)	3x3 Blank	Dam of three classic winners, grandam of 7 others
Sir Archy (1802)	3x4 Herod	American foundation sire
Boston (1833)	3x3 *Diomed	Greatest American 4-miler
Lexington (1850)	3x4 Sir Archy	16-time leading American sire
Galopin (1872)	3x3 Voltaire	Epsom Derby winner, sire of St. Simon
Americus (1892)	3x3 Lexington	Key horse in pedigree of *Nasrullah
Flying Fox (1896)	3x2 Galopin	English Triple Crown, grandsire of *Teddy
Bromus (1905)	2x3 Springfield	Dam of Phalaris
Bayardo (1906)	4x2 Galopin	English champion, sire of two Triple Crown winners
Havresac II (1915)	2x3 St. Simon	Leading Italian sire, broodmare sire of Nearco
*Ksar (1918)	3x2 Omnium II	Prix de l'Arc de Triomphe winner, sire of Tourbillon
Pharos (1920)	4x3 St. Simon	Champion Stakes winner, sire of Nearco, Pharis
Hyperion (1930)	4x3 St. Simon	Epsom Derby winner, six-time leading sire
Coronation (1946)	2x2 Tourbillon	Prix de l'Arc de Triomphe winner
*Turn-to (1951)	3x3 Pharos	Sire of sires Hail to Reason, Sir Gaylord, Cyane, Best Turn
Broad Brush (1983)	3x3 *Turn-to	Leading sire of 1995

breeders were doing in the 18th century.

The process of creating the Thoroughbred was largely one of inbreeding to certain prepotent stallions and mares—often very closely. For example, the third dam of Flying Childers is listed in the *General Stud Book*'s Volume 1—detailing the genesis of the Thoroughbred breed—as being by the excellent 17th-century racehorse and sire Spanker and out of Spanker's own dam, the Old Morocco mare. That's about as close as inbreeding can get.

The best racehorses of the 18th century and early 19th century were almost invariably closely inbred to a succession of great stallions, beginning with the Godolphin Arabian and continuing through Eclipse, Herod, and the latter's son Highflyer. By about 1825, the genes of those four stallions were so highly concentrated in the Thoroughbred that breeders were forced to seek outcrosses. Since that time, inbreeding has gone in and out of fashion, and a few great breeders, notably French breeder Marcel Boussac, have used its principles to create great racehorses, sires, and broodmares.

Inbreeding is described in contemporary industry texts by a shorthand method that denotes the name and location in the five-cross pedigree of the individual or individuals to which the subject horse is inbred. Thus "inbred 3x4 to Northern Dancer" means that the name of Northern Dancer appears in the third generation on the sire's side of the pedigree and in the fourth generation of the dam's side.

A more accurate method would be to calculate the inbreeding coefficient, or percentage of inbreeding, to that individual. By that method, the inbreeding coefficient of a horse inbred 3x4 to Northern Dancer would be 1.56%.

Nicks

Thoroughbred breeding is of necessity both a retrospective and a predictive art. Early Thoroughbred breeders could not help but notice the efficacy of inbreeding to certain stallions and mares, and the repeated success of combining certain sires and broodmares also became apparent. For reasons that are now obscure, this pattern of combining a specific sire and broodmares sired by another stallion became known as a nick.

Perhaps the best early example of a nick was the combination of the immortal racehorse and great sire Eclipse and mares by the even-greater sire Herod. This direct cross produced 1784 Epsom Derby winner Serjeant. The reverse cross of Herod on an Eclipse mare produced 1783 St. Leger Stakes winner Phenomenom, but the real gold mine for breeders was in the innumerable crosses of sons of Eclipse on mares by Herod or his sons, and sons of Herod on mares by

Eclipse or his sons. That more generalized nick was preserved in the breed most notably through 1793 Derby winner Waxy (by Eclipse's son Pot8o's out of a Herod mare), tail-male ancestor of the Phalaris male line.

Phalaris, a foal of 1916, contributed to the most famous 20th-century nick. The four current male lines tracing to Phalaris all descend from sons out of Chaucer mares. *Sickle (Raise a Native) and *Pharamond II (Buckpasser) were both foaled by Selene, by Chaucer, while Pharos (*Nasrullah and Northern Dancer) and Fairway (Lord At War [Arg]) were both sons of Scapa Flow, by Chaucer.

Contemporary advocates of nicking theory have compiled and marketed nicking information that evaluates various crosses according to percentage of stakes winners or graded winners produced by all exemplars of that cross. To accumulate sufficient numbers of exemplars of the cross to be statistically meaningful, these formulations frequently extend the concept to include grandsons or great-grandsons of a particular sire crossed on granddaughters or great-granddaughters of another sire.

At that point, such data are focusing on the hypothetical power of one individual in the third generation of a pedigree and another in the fourth while ignoring the rest of the pedigree. Even at the sire–broodmare sire level, statistical studies of some of the most famous nicks such as the *Nasrullah–*Princequillo cross have not been encouraging.

Still, the fact that certain crosses such as Phalaris-Chaucer have had extraordinary impact on the breed lends some credence to the concept.

Bruce Lowe Numbers

For the first 150 years of the Thoroughbred as a distinct breed, breeding theories focused almost entirely on the influence of stallions. Toward the end of the 19th century, however, an Australian, Bruce Lowe, and a German, Herman Goos, independently began to trace every mare in the *General Stud Book* back to the earliest female ancestor recorded in Volume 1. Both found that every mare traced to one of about 50 of approximately 100 original foundation mares recorded in Volume 1.

Goos published his results in *Family Tables of English Thoroughbred Stock*, a monumental work that was the foundation for the even more monumental *Family Tables of Racehorses* by Kazimierz Bobinski and Stefan Zamoyski in 1953. Goos noted that some female lines had been much more successful than others, but Lowe went several steps further. The Australian numbered each family according to the cumulative number of winners of the Epsom Derby, Epsom Oaks, and St. Leger Stakes each had produced

up to his era. Thus, the female line tracing to Tregonwell's Natural Barb mare was named the Number 1 family, and that tracing to the Burton Barb mare was Number 2. In all, 49 families were numbered.

Based on their success rates, Lowe designated families 1 through 5 as his "running" families. He also designated families 3, 8, 11, 12, and 14 his "sire" families, based on his judgment that the highest number of successful sires occurred in those families. He called those family numbers "figures." He then developed several theories of breeding racehorses based on combinations of those families. His theories were published posthumously in 1895 in *Breeding Race Horses by the Figure System*.

Lowe's system ignored the fact that the primary reason families 1 through 5 produced the most classic winners was that they had produced the most foals in pretty much the same proportions. Numerical superiority, not innate hereditary superiority, accounted for the differences. His theories on breeding also ignored the fact that the original foundation mares were so many generations removed from contemporary horses that their genetic influences were negligible.

Bruce Lowe's theories were promoted assiduously by his editor, English journalist and bloodstock agent William Allison. Lowe's theories were widely influential around the turn of the 20th century, especially in America, where Allison's purchases of broodmares formed the basis for James R. Keene's stud. Genetic science in the 20th century proved Lowe's theories were useless, but his numbering system of female lines has remained a valuable contribution.

Vuillier Dosage

The late 19th century was a remarkably fertile period for pedigree research. At about the same time Lowe and Goos were tracing their female lines, French cavalry officer Col. Jean-Joseph Vuillier overheard two men arguing over whether Eclipse or Herod was the more influential sire and set out to answer the question statistically. To do so, Vuillier compiled complete pedigrees of more than 650 high-class racehorses, mostly winners of the English classics that Lowe used.

Although he apparently had no knowledge of either theory, Vuillier correctly applied a modern Mendelian interpretation of Galton's Law of genetic inheritance, which states that each parent contributes 50% of the genetic material to their offspring. Extending his pedigrees to a minimum of 12 generations, he assigned a value of 1 to a name that appeared in the 12th generation, a value of 2 in the 11th, 4 in the tenth, 8 in the ninth, and on down to a value of 2,048 for first-generation parents.

Vuillier Dosages

First Series		Third Series	
Horse	**Dosage**	**Horse**	**Dosage**
Herod (1758)	750	Stockwell (1849)	340
Eclipse (1764)	568	Newminster (1848)	295
Highflyer (1774)	543		
		Fourth Series	
Second Series		St. Simon (1881)	420
Birdcatcher (1833)	288	Galopin (1872)	405
Touchstone (1831)	351	Isonomy (1875)	280
Pocahontas (1837)	313	Hampton (1872)	260
Voltaire (1826)	186	Hermit (1864)	235
Pantaloon (1824)	140	Bend Or (1877)	210
Melbourne (1834)	184		
Bay Middleton (1833)	127		
Gladiator (1833)	95		

To determine the percentage contribution of Eclipse and Herod, Vuillier added up the numbers for each occurrence in each generation. Vuillier found that when he averaged the results for his 650 pedigrees, Herod's average number was 750 while Eclipse's average was only 568. He also discovered that Herod's son Highflyer was almost as influential as Eclipse with an average of 543.

In pursuing his research over 15 years, Vuillier noticed that other, more recent ancestors also accumulated high numbers, and he compiled figures that he called "dosages" for 11 more stallions and one mare, Pocahontas. Vuillier's dosages are in fact remarkably accurate representations of the percentage of genetic influence on the classic Thoroughbred of the 15 horses in his classification.

Since classic winners were frequently the most successful sires of future generations, Vuillier reasoned that the breed as a whole would and should move in the same direction as the classic pedigree. Thus, he concluded the object of a breeding program should be to produce pedigrees with the same dosages as his classic pedigrees.

To facilitate this process, Vuillier devised the *ecart* system. *Ecart* is a French word that translates loosely to mean mathematical difference. For any potential mating using Vuillier's system, the breeder could calculate the dosages of the prospective foal. The difference between the prospective dosages and the ideal is the *ecart*. The object of Vuillier's system was to reduce the ecart as much as possible.

Vuillier published his findings privately in volumes 1 and 2 of *Les Croisements Rationnels* (Rational Breeding) in 1903 and '27. The Aga Khan hired him to manage his stud in 1925, but Vuillier died shortly thereafter. His widow took over and arranged the Aga Khan's matings for more than 30 years. During that period, the Aga Khan was the most successful and influential breeder in the world, with his stud producing such great racehorses and sires as *Bahram,

*Mahmoud, and *Nasrullah. The Vuillier system, privately modernized and updated, is still in use by the current Aga Khan.

Varola Dosage

Vuillier's method was not widely available and was difficult to execute because it required constructing 12-generation pedigrees and keeping track of mathematical data in an era long before computers. Italian journalist Francesco Varola built on Vuillier's work in his *Typology of the Racehorse,* published in 1974. Since Vuillier's published series of influential stallions extended only through the late 19th century, Varola updated and vastly expanded this list of influential stallions. His initial work identified 120 more horses, all born in the 20th century.

Unlike Vuillier, Varola did not utilize Galton's Law in his formulation, applying equal value to an appearance by a given stallion regardless of the generation of the pedigree in which he appeared. Recognizing that the modern Thoroughbred racehorse is much more specialized than in Vuillier's day, Varola divided his 120 stallions initially into five groups defined by his judgment of the type of influence they exerted on the breed.

His five categories—Brilliant, Intermediate, Classic, Stout, and Professional—were based partly on sociological concepts, partly on physical type and racecourse expression, and partly on inspiration. Varola eventually split the Brilliant group into Brilliant and Transbrilliant and Stout into Solid and Rough, but the original five categories quickly became associated in the public mind with varying degrees of stamina. Varola has consistently disavowed this interpretation.

Varola arranged the names of all his "*chefs-de-race*" in a "dosage diagram," dividing the names of each *chef-de-race* (chief of the breed) that occurs in a given pedigree into the five (or seven) categories and totaling the number of occurrences, regardless of generation. The resulting series of numbers offered breeders a thumbnail picture of the balance in a pedigree among all of Varola's different aptitudes.

Varola's chief contribution may be his insight into the increasing specialization of the Thoroughbred into sprinters, stayers, and middle-distance horses, among others, and his recognition that human sociology plays a role in determining the type of racehorse produced in different countries in different eras.

Roman Dosage

In the 1980s, Steve Roman, an American chemistry professor, developed a system combining some of the aspects of the Vuillier and Varola dosage systems. Considering only the first four generations of a pedigree, Roman assigned a numerical value of 16 to any *chef-de-race* that appeared in the first generation of a pedigree, eight to a second-generation *chef,* four for the third generation, and two for the fourth.

Roman interpreted Varola's five original categories strictly in terms of stamina, with Brilliant horses defined as those contributing extreme speed but little stamina, while Professional *chefs* contributed stamina but little speed. Applying the appropriate value according to generation for each occurrence of a *chef*'s name and adding those values up for each of Varola's five aptitudinal categories, Roman devised a "dosage profile" meant to give breeders insight into the relative stamina inherent in a given pedigree.

Roman invented the "dosage index," a single number that is calculated by dividing the total points in the Brilliant and Intermediate categories plus half the Classic points by the total of the points in the Stout and Professional categories plus the other half of the Classic points. The resultant figure is intended to predict a horse's ability to stay classic distances.

Applying his ideas to the history of the Kentucky Derby (G1), Roman found that almost all Derby winners since the 1930s had dosage indexes of 4.00 or less. Leon Rasmussen of *Daily Racing Form* popularized Roman's ideas in the 1980s and early '90s, and, though several Kentucky Derby winners have subsequently defied their Roman dosage, his theories remain popular.

Modern Genetics

The science of genetics, like the other physical sciences, made enormous strides during the 20th century. Though published earlier, Mendel's laws were virtually unknown at the turn of the 20th century, but early in the 21st century the complete human genome was mapped. Science had progressed from cross-breeding garden peas to cloning sheep and other large mammals.

None of this progress has significantly affected Thoroughbred breeding. An equine genome mapping project is under way, but even that should have no immediate effect on the breed because knowing the location of genes does not reveal the traits or characteristics that they control. Even coat-color genetics, once thought to be a relatively simple dominance series consisting of gray, bay (or brown), and chestnut alleles, is not so simple because white Thoroughbreds began to appear about 30 years ago.

The problem is that the traits that produce a successful racehorse are not governed by single genes. Factors such as speed, stamina, temperament, and soundness are each dependent on thousands of different genes working together with the environment to create outstanding racehorses.—*John P. Sparkman*

Foal Registration

Foal registration for all Thoroughbreds in North America—the United States, Canada, and Puerto Rico—is performed by the Jockey Club, which was founded in 1894 and is a not-for-profit organization dedicated to improving the Thoroughbred breed. To be registered in the *American Stud Book*, which is maintained by the Jockey Club, the parentage of all foals must be verified, a process that today includes DNA typing of all stallions, broodmares, and foals.

Registration of American Thoroughbreds was started by Col. Sanders D. Bruce, a Kentuckian who spent a lifetime researching pedigrees of American Thoroughbreds. He published the first volume of the *American Stud Book* in 1873, and he produced six volumes of the registry. In 1896, the project was taken over by the Jockey Club.

Foal Registration by State in North America in 2000

Alabama	54	Iowa	500	New Hampshire	2	Texas	1,920
Alaska	1	Kansas	113	New Jersey	403	Utah	101
Arizona	317	Kentucky	10,026	New Mexico	454	Vermont	2
Arkansas	359	Louisiana	1,203	New York	1,505	Virginia	502
California	3,485	Maine	6	North Carolina	54	Virgin Islands	2
Colorado	279	Maryland	1,178	North Dakota	41	Washington	942
Connecticut	7	Massachusetts	76	Ohio	614	West Virginia	274
Delaware	1	Michigan	246	Oklahoma	1,055	Wisconsin	27
Florida	4,413	Minnesota	172	Oregon	262	Wyoming	30
Georgia	68	Mississippi	17	Pennsylvania	887	**Total U.S.**	**33,689**
Hawaii	1	Missouri	63	Rhode Island	0	**Total Canada**	**2,371**
Idaho	200	Montana	120	South Carolina	77	**Total Puerto Rico**	**523**
Illinois	896	Nebraska	142	South Dakota	63		
Indiana	492	Nevada	8	Tennessee	29		

Trend of Foal Registration in North America

Year	United States	Change	Canada	Change	Puerto Rico	Change	Total	Change
2001	33,315*	−0.1%	2,695*	4.9%	790*	2.5%	**36,800***	0.3%
2000	33,360*	0.6%	2,570*	2.8%	770*	4.5%	**36,700***	−0.2%
1999	33,686	2.3%	2,420	3.5%	650	−11.4%	**36,756**	2.1%
1998	32,926	2.5%	2,339	2.5%	734	−0.8%	**35,999**	2.5%
1997	32,109	−0.4%	2,283	−4.8%	740	1.9%	**35,132**	−0.6%
1996	32,238	1.1%	2,397	−2.0%	726	11.2%	**35,361**	1.1%
1995	31,879	−0.8%	2,445	−5.6%	653	3.3%	**34,977**	−1.0%
1994	32,117	−5.0%	2,591	−4.5%	632	4.5%	**35,340**	−4.8%
1993	33,818	−3.5%	2,713	−2.3%	605	−0.8%	**37,136**	−3.4%
1992	35,050	−8.1%	2,777	−8.2%	610	−2.9%	**38,437**	−8.0%
1991	38,149	−5.4%	3,024	−5.3%	628	1.8%	**41,801**	−5.3%
1990	40,333	−8.8%	3,193	−4.9%	617	−1.4%	**44,143**	−8.5%

*Estimated

Annual Foal Registration in North America

2002	35,600*	1980	35,679	1958	11,377	1936	5,042	1914	1,702
2001	36,800*	1979	32,904	1957	10,832	1935	5,038	1913	1,722
2000	36,700*	1978	31,510	1956	10,112	1934	4,924	1912	1,900
1999	36,756	1977	30,036	1955	9,610	1933	5,158	1911	2,040
1998	35,999	1976	28,809	1954	9,064	1932	5,256	1910	1,950
1997	35,132	1975	28,271	1953	9,040	1931	5,266	1909	2,340
1996	35,361	1974	27,586	1952	8,811	1930	5,137	1908	3,080
1995	34,977	1973	26,811	1951	8,944	1929	4,903	1907	3,780
1994	35,340	1972	25,726	1950	9,095	1928	4,503	1906	3,840
1993	37,136	1971	24,301	1949	8,770	1927	4,182	1905	3,800
1992	38,437	1970	24,361	1948	8,434	1926	3,632	1904	3,990
1991	41,801	1969	23,848	1947	7,705	1925	3,272	1903	3,440
1990	44,143	1968	22,910	1946	6,579	1924	2,921	1902	3,600
1989	48,235	1967	21,876	1945	5,819	1923	2,763	1901	3,784
1988	49,220	1966	20,228	1944	5,650	1922	2,352	1900	3,476
1987	50,917	1965	18,846	1943	5,923	1921	2,035	1899	3,080
1986	51,296	1964	17,343	1942	6,427	1920	1,833	1898	2,940
1985	50,433	1963	15,917	1941	6,805	1919	1,665	1897	2,992
1984	49,247	1962	14,870	1940	6,003	1918	1,950	1893-'96	5,940*
1983	47,237	1961	13,794	1939	6,316	1917	1,680	1803-'92	3,950*
1982	42,894	1960	12,901	1938	5,696	1916	2,128		
1981	38,669	1959	12,240	1937	5,535	1915	2,120	*Estimated	

Live Foal Report for 2001

The Jockey Club's Live Foal Report for 2001 showed again that large books of mares inevitably result in large foal crops for individual stallions. As of December 31, 2001, Tale of the Cat had 129 foals from the 176 mares to which he was bred in 2000. That year, the Ashford Stud stallion had been the North American leader by number of mares bred. The statistics are incomplete but reflect more than 90% of the live foals of 2001 that will be reported to the Jockey Club.

Tale of the Cat was followed in the live foal count by three other Ashford stallions: Hennessy (119), Stravinsky (117), and Grand Slam (115). Top stallion A.P. Indy, based at Lane's End, ranked

fifth with 108 foals from the 130 mares to which he was bred. Kentucky, where both Ashford and Lane's End are located, maintained its position as the leading source of Thoroughbred foals. The 21,012 mares bred to Kentucky-based stallions produced 14,615 foals.

The 70% live-foal rate was affected in 2001 by mare reproductive loss syndrome, a mysterious killer that struck Central Kentucky in the spring and is estimated to have killed 5.3% of the state's potential foal crop.

On the following pages are state-by-state listings of activity by stallions represented by ten or more live foals in 2001.

Leading Stallions by 2001 Foals

Stallion	Mares bred	Live foals	%	State	Stallion	Mares bred	Live foals	%	State
Tale of the Cat	176	129	73	KY	Cherokee Run	110	80	73	KY
Hennessy	165	119	72	KY	Family Calling	116	80	69	FL
Stravinsky	164	117	71	KY	Rahy	106	80	75	KY
Grand Slam	149	115	77	KY	Honor Grades	107	79	74	KY
A.P. Indy	130	108	83	KY	Real Quiet	102	79	77	KY
Unbridled's Song	133	108	81	KY	Red Ransom	103	79	77	KY
Southern Halo	150	107	71	KY	Silver Charm	104	79	76	KY
Kingmambo	133	104	78	KY	Storm Boot	104	79	76	KY
Saint Ballado	139	104	75	KY	Accelerator	106	78	74	KY
Tomorrows Cat	125	103	82	NY	Doneraile Court	135	78	58	KY
Siphon (Brz)	125	101	81	KY	Louis Quatorze	120	78	65	KY
King of Kings (Ire)	138	100	72	KY	Sir Cat	123	78	63	KY
Souvenir Copy	121	95	79	KY	Smokester	100	78	78	CA
Storm Cat	118	95	81	KY	Coronado's Quest	91	77	85	KY
Bertrando	118	94	80	CA	Forestry	111	77	69	KY
Gold Fever	126	93	74	KY	Slewdledo	104	77	74	WA
Deputy Commander	113	92	81	KY	Awesome Again	107	76	71	KY
Mazel Trick	124	92	74	KY	Defrere	106	76	72	KY
Wekiva Springs	127	92	72	KY	Gone West	90	76	84	KY
Distant View	117	91	78	KY	Kissin Kris	112	76	68	FL
Dance Brightly	131	90	69	KY	Silver Deputy	95	75	79	KY
Honour and Glory	126	90	71	KY	Sky Classic	99	75	76	KY
Skip Away	139	90	65	KY	Cee's Tizzy	100	74	74	CA
Stormy Atlantic	137	90	66	FL	Quiet American	102	74	73	KY
El Prado (Ire)	109	89	82	KY	Bianconi	109	73	67	KY
Maria's Mon	119	89	75	KY	Event of the Year	96	73	76	CA
Wild Rush	116	89	77	KY	In Excess (Ire)	101	73	72	CA
Royal Academy	116	88	76	KY	Notable Cat	116	73	63	OK
Crafty Friend	123	87	71	KY	Roar	98	73	74	KY
Cryptoclearance	119	87	73	KY	Pioneering	102	73	72	KY
Elusive Quality	106	87	82	KY	Stormin Fever	105	73	70	KY
Exploit	120	87	73	KY	Distinctive Cat	110	72	65	CA
Langfuhr	120	87	73	KY	Olympio	114	72	63	CA
Victory Gallop	105	87	83	KY	Scatmandu	94	72	77	KY
Dixieland Band	110	86	78	KY	Tactical Cat	97	72	74	KY
Slew City Slew	113	86	76	KY	With Approval	91	72	79	KY
Alphabet Soup	107	85	79	KY	Lil's Lad	91	71	78	KY
Charismatic	106	84	79	KY	Memo (Chi)	89	71	80	CA
Belong to Me	106	83	78	KY	Rizzi	108	71	66	FL
Deputy Minister	98	83	85	KY	Unbridled	88	71	81	KY
Touch Gold	107	83	78	KY	Artax	93	70	75	NY
Runaway Groom	110	82	75	KY	Count the Time	112	70	63	KY
Woodman	110	82	75	KY	Indian Charlie	99	70	71	KY
Boston Harbor	109	81	74	KY	Line In The Sand	106	70	66	FL
Forest Wildcat	99	81	82	KY	Montbrook	103	70	68	FL
Pleasant Tap	102	81	79	KY	Seeking the Gold	86	70	81	KY

Live Foals by Stallions by State or Province in 2001

State	Stallions	Mares bred	Live foals	%	State	Stallions	Mares bred	Live foals	%
Alabama	23	109	61	56	North Carolina	25	85	54	64
Arizona	91	570	316	55	North Dakota	17	107	46	43
Arkansas	69	637	323	51	Ohio	116	875	477	55
California	419	5,604	3,796	68	Oklahoma	267	1,952	1,069	55
Colorado	73	452	205	45	Oregon	53	339	213	63
Connecticut	1	5	5	100	Pennsylvania	120	1,005	601	60
Delaware	1	32	24	75	South Carolina	27	193	89	46
Florida	287	7,239	4,527	63	South Dakota	16	151	64	42
Georgia	24	106	51	48	Tennessee	27	95	38	40
Hawaii	1	1	0	0	Texas	450	3,638	2,009	55
Idaho	68	394	201	51	Utah	49	290	124	43
Illinois	152	1,314	630	48	Virginia	89	643	373	58
Indiana	100	765	363	47	Washington	137	1,650	987	60
Iowa	71	794	384	48	West Virginia	54	550	295	54
Kansas	35	225	107	48	Wisconsin	17	52	27	52
Kentucky	431	21,012	14,615	70	Wyoming	17	54	20	37
Louisiana	183	2,242	1,309	58					
Maine	2	3	3	100	**Canada**				
Maryland	112	1,860	1,213	65	Alberta	93	839	485	58
Massachusetts	22	92	58	63	British Columbia	83	891	511	57
Michigan	60	413	236	57	Manitoba	26	214	106	50
Minnesota	24	190	90	47	New Brunswick	1	1	1	100
Mississippi	12	48	26	54	Nova Scotia	3	6	3	50
Missouri	38	179	92	51	Ontario	109	1,347	832	62
Montana	60	339	149	44	Quebec	3	14	5	36
Nebraska	38	346	173	50	Saskatchewan	29	184	108	59
Nevada	7	13	5	38					
New Hampshire	3	9	6	67	Puerto Rico	85	917	629	69
New Jersey	54	300	184	61					
New Mexico	137	1,167	580	50	**Totals**	**4,654**	**64,729**	**40,319**	**62**
New York	132	2,146	1,411	66					

Stallions With Ten or More Live Foals in 2001
(as of December 31, 2001)

Stallion	Mares bred	Fls	% Mares	Stallion	Fls	% Mares	Stallion	bred	Fls	%
ALABAMA				Apollo	17	11	65	Emerald Jig	26	16	62

Stallion	Mares bred	Fls	%
ALABAMA			
Royal Empire	27	15	56
ARIZONA			
Barricade	35	24	69
Benton Creek	50	42	84
Chanate	25	19	76
Chopin	21	12	57
I lill Street Jove	12	10	83
Hollywood Reporter	18	10	56
Slew Mood	19	11	58
Tax Collection	22	14	64
ARKANSAS			
Big Pistol	26	14	54
Bold Anthony	57	34	60
Country Store	19	10	53
Etbauer	29	17	59
Idabel	22	13	59
Olympic Prospector	13	10	77
Siberian Pine	44	28	64
This Picture	39	19	49
Unbridled's Risk	18	12	67
CALIFORNIA			
Anziyan	35	18	51

Stallion	Mares	Fls	% Mares
Apollo	17	11	65
Avenue of Flags	60	47	78
Batonnier	15	10	67
Bay Street Star	29	23	79
Benchmark	82	53	65
Bertrando	118	94	80
B. Hoedown	14	10	71
Bold Badgett	41	32	78
Bonus Money (GB)	47	35	74
Born Wild	24	19	79
Built for Pleasure	14	11	79
Candi's Gold	26	21	81
Cee's Tizzy	100	74	74
Cherokee Colony	19	10	53
Comet Shine	23	17	74
Commitment	25	18	72
Compelling Sound	27	17	63
Corslew	34	20	59
Cutlass Reality	18	14	78
Dance Floor	56	39	70
Desert Classic	27	17	63
Din's Dancer	28	22	79
Discover	19	12	63
Distinctive Cat	110	72	65
Dominated Debut	13	10	77
Elegant Ease	18	11	61
Emerald Creme	20	17	85

Stallion	bred	Fls	%
Emerald Jig	26	16	62
Encino	11	10	91
Epic Honor	26	21	81
Event of the Year	96	73	76
Fabulous Champ	53	37	70
Falstaff	22	17	77
Fargo	35	24	69
Flying Continental	24	19	79
Flying Victor	44	27	61
Free House	78	64	82
Fruition	60	41	68
General Meeting	85	58	68
Guarani	16	14	88
Half Term	65	36	55
High Brite	64	46	72
Houston	41	29	71
Iam the Iceman	13	11	85
Illinois Storm	23	16	70
In Excess (Ire)	101	73	72
Iron Cat	19	13	68
Larry the Legend	40	28	70
Last Lion	17	12	71
Latin American	62	42	68
Lil Tyler	23	16	70
Lucayan Prince	21	19	90
Makaleha	17	16	94
Makhraj	36	17	47

Stallion	Mares bred	Fls	% Mares
Memo (Chi)	89	71	80
Mortlock (Fr)	21	15	71
Moscow Ballet	41	25	61
Mr. Procrastinator	20	11	55
Mr Purple	26	17	65
Mud Route	54	40	74
Native Prospector	18	10	56
Native Storm	29	19	66
Newton's Law (Ire)	17	11	65
Northern Devil	22	14	64
Ole'	34	21	62
Olympio	114	72	63
Paranoide (Arg)	21	15	71
Perfect Mandate	45	27	60
Phone Roberto	23	16	70
Phone Saga	20	15	75
Proud Irish	20	19	95
Rainbow Blues (Ire)	25	17	68
Ravenwood	16	13	81
Red	34	26	76
Rhythm	38	25	66
Rio Verde	20	15	75
River Flyer	21	17	81
Rock Band	15	10	67
Royal Regatta (Ire)	14	11	79
Score Quick	15	11	73
Seattle Bound	56	39	70
Seattle Proud	15	11	73
Seven Rivers	18	11	61
Sharp Victor	19	18	95
Siberian Summer	45	32	71
Slew of Angels	19	12	63
Slew's Royalty	20	10	50
Slew the Bride	18	12	67
Smokester	100	78	78
Stage Colony	12	12	100
State Performer	10	10	100
Suggest	40	31	78
Surachai	37	28	76
Swiss Yodeler	74	61	82
Synastry	22	19	86
The Good Life	27	16	59
Tinners Way	46	37	80
Tossofthecoin	35	25	71
Trail City	41	26	63
Tricky Creek	49	38	78
Truckee	39	21	54
Turkoman	60	33	55
Twin Spires	62	48	77
Tychonic (GB)	49	26	53
Unusual Heat	35	30	86
Vaudeville	58	48	83
Ventriloquist	31	14	45
Vermont	27	18	67
Via Lombardia (Ire)	17	13	76
Walter Willy (Ire)	18	14	78
Water Bank	16	11	69
Western Fame	62	43	69
Wheatly Hall	18	11	61
Wild Deputy	37	27	73
Wild Gold	37	28	76

COLORADO

Basic Rate	15	11	73
Coverallbases	29	15	52
Gaelic Padraic	17	12	71

FLORIDA

Absent Russian	22	16	73
All Gone	61	41	67

Stallion	Fls	% Mares	
Aloha Prospector	41	20	49
Appealing Skier	90	61	68
Blue Ensign	24	13	54
Bon Point (GB)	38	26	68
Brief Ruckus	29	16	55
Byars	25	19	76
Candy Stripes	34	20	59
Capture the Gold	20	17	85
Cloud Cover	34	19	56
Colony Light	62	43	69
Concerto	77	40	52
Concorde's Tune	45	22	49
Conveyor	24	13	54
Crafty Dude	23	10	43
Cyberspace	46	27	59
Darn That Alarm	33	21	64
Dawn Quixote	21	12	57
Demaloot Demashoot	47	33	70
Diligence	80	45	56
Diplomatic Jet	27	20	74
Dixie Power	16	10	63
D. J. Cat	31	26	84
Double Honor	101	67	66
Double Niner	23	17	74
Dove Hunt	79	51	65
Dr. Caton	51	34	67
Eltish	50	30	60
Eskimo	22	12	55
Explosive Red	91	60	66
Fabulous Frolic	56	39	70
Family Calling	116	80	69
Faygo	16	14	88
First and Only	23	13	57
Formal Dinner	80	52	65
Fortunate Prospect	61	37	61
Friendly Lover	78	56	72
Future Storm	36	20	56
Gold Alert	20	13	65
Groomstick	20	11	55
Halos and Horns	27	16	59
Halo's Image	102	61	60
Hazaam	53	32	60
Helmsman	49	29	59
Hesabull	22	16	73
Holy Mountain	44	31	70
Hunting Hard	24	14	58
Is It True	43	31	72
Island Whirl	33	20	61
Jeblar	38	26	68
Jules	87	54	62
King of the Heap	18	13	72
Kipper Kelly	73	43	59
Kissin Kris	112	76	68
Limit Out	25	13	52
Line In The Sand	106	70	66
Lite the Fuse	95	61	64
Lost Soldier	85	63	74
Lucky Lionel	84	59	70
Lucky North	36	18	50
Lycius	71	47	66
Marco Bay	18	10	56
Master Bill	47	30	64
Matty G	27	18	67
Meadow Monster	21	14	67
Mecke	70	45	64
Metfield	38	24	63
Migrating Moon	41	25	61
Minister's Mark	16	11	69
Minstrel Dancer	15	12	80

Stallion	bred Fls	%	
Mister Jolie	74	47	64
Montbrook	103	70	68
Montreal Red	95	57	60
Native Regent	34	29	85
Nines Wild	59	22	37
Noactor	27	21	78
Northern Afleet	66	39	59
Notebook	52	39	75
Ocala Slew	21	16	76
Oliver's Twist	35	20	57
Open Forum	74	55	74
Outflanker	44	34	77
Pentelicus	92	63	68
Play Both Ends	15	10	67
Ponche	39	23	59
Precocity	43	35	81
Premiership	53	33	62
Private Talk	16	12	75
Proud and True	73	49	67
Proudest Romeo	14	12	86
Quaker Ridge	48	31	65
Reality Road	16	11	69
Rizzi	108	71	66
Robyn Dancer	36	22	61
Rocky Mountain	26	15	58
Safely's Mark	38	20	53
Seacliff	24	15	63
Semoran	51	30	59
Skip Trial	55	29	53
Stack	29	21	72
Star of Valor	27	12	44
Statesmanship	45	23	51
Storm Creek	106	62	58
Stormy Atlantic	137	90	66
Struggler (GB)	54	32	59
Suave Prospect	67	45	67
Sword Dance (Ire)	81	64	79
Tactical Advantage	103	59	57
Thats Our Buck	80	44	55
The Silver Move	28	13	46
Time Bandit	26	18	69
Toolighttoquit	31	25	81
Top Account	48	29	60
Tour d'Or	60	44	73
Traitor	56	29	52
Valid Wager	51	28	55
Way West (Fr)	66	45	68
West Acre	66	47	71
Western Borders	45	33	73
Western Cat	33	15	45
Wheaton	83	51	61
Whitney Tower	22	15	68
Wild Escapade	43	30	70
Wild Event	72	49	68
Wild Wonder	100	52	52
World Stage (Ire	74	30	41
Zafarrancho (Arg)	18	10	56

GEORGIA

Roaring Camp	21	13	62

IDAHO

Carmen's Baby	17	12	71
Hey Rob	22	17	77
Renteria	23	15	65
Shergar's Best (Ire)	24	20	83

ILLINOIS

Allen Charge	18	11	61
Awesome Cat	31	20	65

Breeding — Live Foal Report

Stallion	Mares bred	Fls	% Mares
Canyon Run	13	11	85
Cartwright	59	33	56
Catastrophic	30	14	47
Category Five	37	23	62
City by Night	22	12	55
Emancipator	33	24	73
Hannibal Cat	17	10	59
North Prospect	11	10	91
Presently	17	11	65
Spanish Drummer	31	18	58
Spy Signal	29	10	34
Treasury	19	11	58
Unite	23	11	48
Unreal Zeal	72	48	67
Western Playboy	31	14	45
Z Z Cat	32	21	66

INDIANA

Stallion	Mares bred	Fls	% Mares
Ago	17	10	59
Ali Gaziba	25	11	44
Classy Prospector	17	11	65
Crown Ambassador	27	15	56
D. C. Tenacious	17	11	65
Indy Mood	41	18	44
Moro Oro	19	15	79
Presidential Order	37	23	62
T. H. Fappiano	33	11	33
Tricon	30	10	33

IOWA

Stallion	Mares bred	Fls	% Mares
Cape Storm	56	25	45
Commemorate	50	29	58
De Guerin	14	10	71
Farragut	33	12	36
Honest Ensign	47	27	57
Mercedes Won	53	28	53
Night Runner	24	13	54
Prospect Feature	22	14	64
Sail Me Again	19	11	58
Sharkey	34	22	65
Temptor	22	11	50
Wild Invader	21	10	48
Yankee Fan	28	12	43

KANSAS

Stallion	Mares bred	Fls	% Mares
Big Splash	13	10	77
Blushing Song	15	12	80
Gold Ruler	29	19	66

KENTUCKY

Stallion	Mares bred	Fls	% Mares
Accelerator	106	78	74
Acceptable	53	35	66
Affirmed	48	38	79
Afternoon Deelites	61	47	77
Aggressive Chief	15	10	67
Allied Forces	50	27	54
Alphabet Soup	107	85	79
American Chance	110	67	61
Anet	57	36	63
Announce	83	63	76
A.P. Indy	130	108	83
Arch	83	63	76
Atticus	78	61	78
Awesome Again	107	76	71
Bahri	37	30	81
Banker's Gold	90	62	69
Barkerville	31	20	65
Bates Motel	32	14	44
Beau Genius	80	51	64
Belong to Me	106	83	78
Benny the Dip	46	32	70
Bianconi	109	73	67
Binalong	16	12	75
Boone's Mill	14	10	71
Boston Harbor	109	81	74
Boundary	71	53	75
Bright Launch	30	22	73
Broad Brush	47	37	79
Brunswick	27	16	59
Caller I. D.	73	52	71
Canaveral	32	23	72
Cape Town	94	69	73
Capote	72	57	79
Captain Bodgit	112	62	55
Carolina Kid	17	10	59
Carr de Naskra	26	16	62
Carson City	90	65	72
Cat's Career	83	60	72
Charismatic	106	84	79
Cherokee Run	110	80	73
Chimes Band	16	10	63
Clever Trick	51	38	75
Cobra King	71	53	75
Comic Strip	54	41	76
Composer	37	14	38
Comstock Lode	63	33	52
Confide	110	69	63
Conquistador Cielo	64	53	83
Constant Demand	18	10	56
Coronado's Quest	91	77	85
Count the Time	112	70	63
Cozzene	74	56	76
Crafty Friend	123	87	71
Crafty Prospector	76	63	83
Cryptoclearance	119	87	73
Dance Brightly	131	90	69
Danjur	28	18	64
Danzig	45	36	80
Dare and Go	64	36	56
Dayjur	53	34	64
Deerhound	29	19	66
Defensive Play	31	14	45
Defrere	106	76	72
Demidoff	78	50	64
De Niro	23	11	48
Deputy Commander	113	92	81
Deputy Minister	98	83	85
Desert Secret (Ire)	16	13	81
Devil His Due	87	55	63
Devil's Bag	62	49	79
Diocio (GB)	79	63	80
Distant View	117	91	78
Distorted Humor	81	64	79
Dixieland Band	110	86	78
Dixieland Heat	45	26	58
Doc's Leader	51	34	67
Doneraile Court	135	78	58
Dumaani	45	27	60
Dusty Screen	25	18	72
Dynaformer	80	59	74
Eastern Echo	43	31	72
Editor's Note	57	44	77
El Amante	42	31	74
El Prado (Ire)	109	89	82
Elusive Quality	106	87	82
En Tete	30	19	63
Evansville Slew	77	40	52
Exetera	23	14	61
Expelled	73	47	64
Exploit	120	87	73
Fantastic Fellow	28	16	57
Fastness (Ire)	34	21	62
Fast Play	54	28	52
Favorite Trick	92	62	67
Fit to Fight	53	34	64
Flying Chevron	21	12	57
Fly So Free	48	35	73
Forestry	111	77	69
Forest Wildcat	99	81	82
Formal Gold	93	62	67
Fort Chaffee	18	13	72
French Deputy	79	64	81
Frisk Me Now	45	30	67
General Royal	63	41	65
Gentlemen (Arg)	92	62	67
Ghazi	62	42	68
Gilded Time	63	46	73
Glitterman	61	50	82
Go for Gin	27	23	85
Gold Case	88	68	77
Golden Gear	50	38	76
Gold Fever	126	93	74
Gold Legend	79	52	66
Gold Tribute	18	12	67
Gone West	90	76	84
Good and Tough	65	46	71
Grand Slam	149	115	77
Green Dancer	34	17	50
Grindstone	72	52	72
Gulch	73	59	81
Halory Hunter	72	47	65
Hennessy	165	119	72
Hold for Gold	18	12	67
Holy Bull	63	50	79
Honor Grades	107	79	74
Honour and Glory	126	90	71
Horse Chestnut (SAf)	60	39	65
Ide	45	30	67
Indian Charlie	99	70	71
In the Zone	20	10	50
Irish River (Fr)	38	20	53
Islefaxyou	58	33	57
Jade Hunter	83	54	65
Jambalaya Jazz	40	26	65
Joyeux Danseur	71	50	70
J P Hamer	24	15	63
Judge T C	43	26	60
Just a Cat	56	22	39
Keos	41	31	76
Kingmambo	133	104	78
King of Kings (Ire)	138	100	72
Kiri's Clown	33	16	48
Known Fact	20	12	60
K. O. Punch	70	48	69
Kris S.	66	48	73
Laabity	35	21	60
Labeeb (GB)	50	39	78
Lac Ouimet	82	55	67
Langfuhr	120	87	73
Lasting Approval	29	17	59
Lear Fan	65	55	85
Level Sands	76	53	70
Lil E. Tee	61	41	67
Lil's Lad	91	71	78
Lion Cavern	52	36	69
Lit de Justice	73	56	77
Lord Avie	52	33	63
Lord Carson	63	46	73
Lost Code	63	37	59

Stallion	Mares bred	Fls	% Mares
Louis Quatorze	120	78	65
Loup Sauvage	46	36	78
Lure	28	11	39
Mahogany Hall	24	14	58
Majestic Light	27	18	67
Major Impact	31	23	74
Maria's Mon	119	89	75
Marlin	62	41	66
Marquetry	95	64	67
Mazel Trick	124	92	74
Meadowlake	66	50	76
Menifee	61	38	62
Miesque's Son	42	28	67
Military	44	35	80
Miner's Mark	28	18	64
Mister Baileys (GB)	53	30	57
Miswaki	70	52	74
Mr. Greeley	69	36	52
Mt. Livermore	86	63	73
Mutakddim	33	26	79
Mystery Storm	54	28	52
Navarone	17	12	71
Nicholas	13	10	77
Northern No Trump	29	14	48
Numerous	56	43	77
Nureyev	73	13	18
Old Trieste	74	51	69
Ordway	37	28	76
Othello	26	11	42
Our Emblem	69	50	72
Out of Place	83	59	71
Parade Ground	80	47	59
Party Manners	36	22	61
Patton	48	36	75
Peaks and Valleys	80	58	73
Pembroke	44	31	70
Perfect Vision	64	35	55
Peruvian	22	13	59
Petionville	76	47	62
Phone Trick	82	47	57
Pine Bluff	33	22	67
Pioneering	102	73	72
Pleasant Tap	102	81	79
Polish Navy	62	39	63
Private Terms	56	42	75
Prized	27	18	67
Prospect Bay	89	51	57
Prospectors Gamble	44	29	66
Prospector's Music	22	13	59
Pulpit	76	59	78
Pyramid Peak	55	37	67
Quiet American	102	74	73
Rahy	106	80	75
Real Quiet	102	79	77
Red Ransom	103	79	77
Regal Classic	54	42	78
Repriced	56	29	52
Roar	98	73	74
Rockamundo	15	10	67
Romanov (Ire)	49	28	57
Roy	42	31	74
Royal Academy	116	88	76
Rubiano	37	26	70
Runaway Groom	110	82	75
Run Softly	59	41	69
Sahm	46	36	78
Saint Ballado	139	104	75
Salt Lake	86	59	69
Sandpit (Brz)	51	36	71
Saratoga Six	30	18	60
Scatmandu	94	72	77
Sea of Secrets	85	56	66
Seattle Sleet	56	29	52
Secreniner	27	16	59
Seeking the Gold	86	70	81
Sefapiano	71	48	68
Senor Speedy	23	16	70
Service Stripe	36	19	53
Shuailaan	44	24	55
Silver Charm	104	79	76
Silver Deputy	95	75	79
Silver Ghost	99	68	69
Silver Hawk	58	47	81
Siphon (Brz)	125	101	81
Sir Cat	123	78	63
Skip Away	139	90	65
Sky Classic	99	75	76
Skywalker	45	34	76
Slew City Slew	113	86	76
Smart Strike	72	50	69
Smoke Glacken	78	58	74
Southern Halo	150	107	71
Souvenir Copy	121	95	79
Squadron Leader	21	11	52
Storm Boot	104	79	76
Storm Cat	118	95	81
Stormin Fever	105	73	70
Stravinsky	164	117	71
Strodes Creek	17	13	76
Subordination	59	43	73
Sultry Song	76	59	78
Summer Squall	71	34	48
Swain (Ire)	85	65	76
Tabasco Cat	48	35	73
Tactical Cat	97	72	74
Tale of the Cat	176	129	73
Talkin Man	15	10	67
Tejano Run	35	21	60
Theatrical (Ire)	91	65	71
The Name's Jimmy	46	23	50
Thunder Gulch	64	49	77
Torrential	56	37	66
Touch Gold	107	83	78
Unaccounted For	88	58	66
Unbridled	88	71	81
Unbridled's Song	133	108	81
Valiant Nature	57	39	68
Victory Gallop	105	87	83
Victory Speech	44	33	75
Wagon Limit	36	29	81
Wallenda	15	10	67
Wavering Monarch	25	20	80
Wekiva Springs	127	92	72
Well Decorated	32	22	69
West by West	63	49	78
Westminster	23	11	48
Wild Again	73	44	60
Wild Rush	116	89	77
Wild Syn	19	12	63
Wild Zone	96	64	67
Will's Way	50	37	74
With Approval	91	72	79
Wolf Power (SAf)	57	41	72
Woodman	110	82	75
You and I	38	21	55

LOUISIANA

Stallion	Mares bred	Fls	% Mares
Autocracy	23	15	65
Bag	40	32	80

Stallion	bred	Fls	%
Belek	20	15	75
Believe It	52	30	58
Beowulf	18	10	56
Change Takes Time	21	16	76
City Nights (Ire)	11	10	91
Combat Ready	11	10	91
Corwyn	25	20	80
Derby Wish	17	11	65
Direct Hit	13	11	85
Excavate	61	44	72
Exceller Vice	18	11	61
Finest Hour	78	53	68
Forty Won	47	30	64
Glaring	36	28	78
Goodbye Doeny	55	39	71
Historic	34	19	56
Homebuilder	24	16	67
Ikari	19	10	53
I'ma Hell Raiser	40	27	68
Imperial Falcon	28	18	64
In a Walk	16	11	69
Leestown	80	65	81
Malagra	43	29	67
Moonlight Dancer	25	21	84
Mr. Shawklit	28	16	57
Nelson	15	11	73
On the Sauce	19	12	63
Placid Fund	24	17	71
Prince of the Mt.	25	15	60
Rail	20	11	55
Reprized	18	14	78
Sanctuary	21	11	52
Savings	16	11	69
Scottsville	28	11	39
Sharp Frosty	43	20	47
Spend a Buck	21	19	90
Sport Hunter	15	12	80
Sutter's Prospect	30	18	60
Tirade	18	14	78
Track Rebel	16	13	81
Trophy Hunter	36	17	47
Zarbyev	33	20	61
Zede	18	12	67
Zuppardo's Prince	32	20	63

MARYLAND

Stallion	bred	Fls	%
Allen's Prospect	91	62	68
Awad	52	37	71
Carnivalay	64	33	52
Citidancer	37	22	59
Concern	36	27	75
Crypto Star	60	44	73
Diamond	74	57	77
Horatius	14	11	79
In Case	58	46	79
Itaka	20	13	65
Larrupin'	63	42	67
Malibu Moon	101	61	60
Not For Love	89	68	76
Oh Say	14	12	86
Ops Smile	40	27	68
Partner's Hero	73	51	70
Polish Numbers	78	47	60
Press Card	36	26	72
Private Key	13	12	92
Rinka Das	44	23	52
Rubiyat	23	11	48
Storm Broker	73	45	62
Swear by Dixie	17	14	82

Stallion	Mares bred		
Tamayaz	58	43	74
Two Punch	79	53	67
Valley Crossing	50	32	64
Waquoit	48	30	63
Wayne County (Ire)	42	30	71
Yarrow Brae	62	40	65

MICHIGAN

Cat in Town	19	15	79
Grand Circus Park	26	12	46
Jacodra	15	11	73
Matchlite	31	19	61
Pauliano	24	13	54
Ulises	19	13	68

MINNESOTA

Lakeshore Road	17	10	59
Quaker Hill	19	11	58
Quick Cut	38	23	61

MISSOURI

American Tribute	17	10	59
Steel Robbing	17	13	76

MONTANA

Black Mackee	27	12	44
Strong Minded	14	10	71

NEBRASKA

Blumin Affair	64	41	64
Hesaluckycat	18	10	56
Miracle Heights	32	24	75
O'Brannigan	17	11	65
Silver Launch	41	18	44
Verzy	17	13	76

NEW JERSEY

Bugatti Reef (Ire)	38	21	55
Heff	18	12	67
My Prince Charming	19	14	74
Perfect	13	10	77
Private Interview	33	24	73

NEW MEXICO

Catillac	20	10	50
Danzatore	41	22	54
Devil Begone	40	21	53
Devon Lane	46	28	61
Fair American	23	13	57
Ghostly Moves	36	15	42
Ghost Ranch	21	12	57
He's a Looker	27	11	41
In Excessive Bull	51	37	73
Prince of Fame	16	11	69
Prospector Jones	25	19	76
Retsina Run	20	15	75
Sunday Minister	14	10	71
Tap N Snap	15	10	67

NEW YORK

Abaginone	41	28	68
American Standard	16	10	63
A. P Jet	87	58	67
Artax	93	70	75
Chequer	35	23	66
Cozy Drive	21	10	48
Crimson Guard	36	15	42
Crusader Sword	41	23	56

	Fls	% Mares	
Danzatame	22	13	59
Daygata	16	11	69
Distinctive Pro	44	35	80
Dixie Brass	47	32	68
Ends Well	22	12	55
Goldminers Gold	29	19	66
Gold Token	64	48	75
Gone for Real	18	12	67
Incurable Optimist	44	28	64
Key Contender	51	32	63
Kingsboro	19	11	58
Lucky Roberto	29	23	79
Odyle	25	17	68
Personal Flag	69	49	71
Polish Pro	19	14	74
Preacherman	22	12	55
Prosper Fager	31	20	65
Raffie's Majesty	24	17	71
Rage	29	20	69
Reign Road	32	22	69
Rodeo	95	64	67
Scarlet Ibis	23	10	43
Sea Salute	42	30	71
Signal Tap	67	44	66
Silver Music	21	13	62
Slice of Reality	13	11	85
Spectacular Bid	29	18	62
Storm of Angels	64	39	61
Take Me Out	94	62	66
Tank's Number	14	11	79
Tomorrows Cat	125	103	82
Trick Me	32	18	56
Williamstown	45	28	62

NORTH CAROLINA

Chelsey Cat	15	15	100

OHIO

Academy Award	45	27	60
Coax Me Chad	38	12	32
Defense Witness	26	14	54
Flight Forty Nine	26	17	65
Forest Gazelle	24	14	58
French Legionaire	14	12	86
Gold Market	15	11	73
Latvia	24	10	42
Mercer Mill	22	10	45
Noble Cat	29	19	66
Noon Prospect	19	13	68
Pacific Waves	12	11	92
Private School	31	18	58
Railway Cat	13	10	77
Winthrop	22	19	86

OKLAHOMA

Alamocitos	29	11	38
Bonus Time Cat	52	25	48
Chief's Reward	31	18	58
Coaxing Matt	24	13	54
Coordinator	44	23	52
Deodar	23	15	65
Dreamfield	14	10	71
Ecstatic Ride	24	11	46
French Parliament	39	17	44
Full of Tricks	16	10	63
Ghost Power	29	11	38
Have Fun	15	10	67
Here We Come	33	26	79
Hickory Ridge	13	10	77

Stallion	bred Fls	%	
Inca Chief	25	13	52
Moment of Crisis	20	11	55
Muldoon	39	29	74
My Liege	28	10	36
New Way	27	20	74
Night Ceremony	22	11	50
Notable Cat	116	73	63
Reel On Reel	25	17	68
Slewacide	44	30	68
Speak	37	22	59
Sunrise Shower	14	12	86
Tarakam	34	18	53
Tricky Fun	20	16	80
Undeniable	17	10	59
Unome	20	13	65

OREGON

Abstract	20	12	60
Airdrie Apache	24	20	83
Baquero	59	48	81
Crowning Season (GB)	22	13	59
Gold Meridian	48	30	63
Tiffany Ice	18	12	67

PENNSYLVANIA

Activist	31	17	55
Alyten	21	13	62
Bankbook	22	14	64
Bombardier	23	16	70
Buck'sinthebank	16	11	69
Cappuccio	21	13	62
Corporate Report	38	24	63
Deposit Ticket	53	33	62
Digamist	28	18	64
Flying Pidgeon	33	21	64
Harry the Hat	17	12	71
Manastash Ridge	21	13	62
Obstructed	16	11	69
Peteski	31	11	35
Pok Ta Pok	28	17	61
Power of Mind	34	19	56
Quarry	33	18	55
Roanoke	72	54	75
Sir Eric	22	12	55
Traffic Zack	21	13	62
Tricky Mister	20	13	65
Western Echo	25	12	48

PUERTO RICO

Avenge	15	12	80
Balcony	37	31	84
Cagey Bidder	23	21	91
Eqtesaad	30	24	80
Fappiano's Star	46	36	78
Fiery Special	12	10	83
Full Day	20	15	75
Goldgalliano (Ire)	32	26	81
Goldwater	15	12	80
Greedy	18	16	89
Hard Charger	22	18	82
Johnny Jones	19	13	68
Kunjar	27	23	85
M.D.'s Relampago	22	11	50
Once Ivor	15	12	80
Royal Merlot	39	27	69
Run Turn	30	19	63
Sejm	38	31	82
Storm God	24	18	75

Stallion	Mares bred	Fls	% Mares
Sunshine Jimmy	20	19	95
Sutters Pond	30	12	40
Virtua Cop	12	11	92
Wonder Bird	21	16	76

SOUTH CAROLINA

Stallion	Mares bred	Fls	% Mares
Kokand	71	35	49

SOUTH DAKOTA

Stallion	Mares bred	Fls	% Mares
Neff Lake	24	13	54

TEXAS

Stallion	Mares bred	Fls	% Mares
American Champ	20	12	60
Capote's Prospect	30	16	53
Captain Codex	13	10	77
Cien Fuegos	35	22	63
Claudius	12	11	92
Commanchero	52	29	56
Crafty	60	44	73
Devious Course	41	26	63
Excellent Secret	18	10	56
Fashion Find	17	11	65
Fire Maker	30	17	57
Glazed	18	10	56
Gold Regent	61	45	74
Grand Jewel	19	14	74
Gringo Pilot	26	18	69
Hadif	66	42	64
Hay Halo	27	16	59
Heather's Prospect	20	11	55
Holzmeister	60	34	57
Irish Open	63	34	54
Leo Castelli	39	21	54
Lightning Leap	14	12	86
Lucky So n' So	30	13	43
Majestic Twoeleven	25	16	64
Manzotti	27	15	56
Marked Tree	54	32	59
Meacham	17	13	76
Moving Shoulder	11	10	91
Naevus	27	17	63
Once a Sailor	20	15	75
Pancho Villa	56	33	59
Pele's Smile	18	12	67
Pollock's Luck	53	36	68
Proper Reality	15	12	80
Raise a Govenor	27	17	63
Raja's Best Boy	12	11	92
Raji	18	17	94
Rare Brick	31	18	58
Ray's Word	14	10	71
River Squall	24	14	58
Secret Claim	25	11	44
Seneca Jones	44	23	52
Stephene Mon Amour	15	10	67
Sunny's Halo	91	55	60
Texas City	31	19	61
The Prime Minister	49	26	53
Totem and Taboo	21	11	52
Twilight Agenda	48	27	56
Under David's Wing	17	14	82
Valid Expectations	84	63	75
Wajir	35	23	66
Wayne's Crane	28	20	71
World Appeal	16	10	63
Zeeruler	33	13	39

Stallion	Fls	% Mares

UTAH

Stallion	Fls	% Mares
Bustopher Jones	66	37	56
Dignitas	23	14	61

VIRGINIA

Stallion	Fls	% Mares
Ball's Bluff	20	14	70
Chenin Blanc	23	13	57
Chief Protocol	23	13	57
Fred Astaire	33	15	45
Prenup	33	13	39
Rock Point	32	19	59
Secret Hello	32	23	72
Slavic	41	26	63
Thunder Rumble	26	18	69
Tom Cobbley	18	13	72
Woodman's Image	32	26	81

WASHINGTON

Stallion	Fls	% Mares
Alnaab	18	15	83
Basket Weave	50	34	68
Beefchopper	21	14	67
Bull Inthe Heather	19	12	63
Cahill Road	70	48	69
Cisco Road	27	19	70
Consigliere (GB)	24	17	71
Delineator	21	18	86
Demons Begone	45	30	67
Desert Wine	33	13	39
Detox	21	13	62
Devil On Ice	25	18	72
Flying With Eagles	15	12	80
Free At Last	36	23	64
Game Plan	51	39	76
He's Tops	52	39	75
Ihtimam	18	12	67
Jazzing Around	31	18	58
Jumron (GB)	18	13	72
Katowice	30	25	83
Key to the Carr	20	10	50
Knight in Savannah	20	12	60
Majesterian	22	11	50
Personable Joe	36	21	58
Peterhof	15	10	67
Petersburg	22	15	68
Russellthemussell	15	12	80
Salty Shoes	22	11	50
Slewdledo	104	77	74
Snowbound	49	26	53
Son of Briartic	38	25	66
Stolen Gold	35	20	57
Storm Blast	22	12	55
Swing and Miss	36	26	72
Tahoe City	44	28	64
Tough Knight	23	13	57

WEST VIRGINIA

Stallion	Fls	% Mares
Citislipper	28	20	71
Enough Reality	19	10	53
Feel the Power	23	12	52
My Boy Adam	50	25	50
Seeking the Crown	28	19	68
Standing On Edge	34	17	50
Storm Center	28	13	46
Truculent Schular	28	23	82
Valid Indy	18	11	61
Weshaam	28	14	50

Stallion	bred	Fls	%

ALBERTA

Stallion	bred	Fls	%
Banjo	37	14	38
Blazing Fire	24	13	54
Brass Minister	21	13	62
Chapel Creek	27	13	48
Ciano Cat	39	23	59
Esteem	20	16	80
Exclusive Era	30	15	50
Fast Account	22	14	64
Highland Ruckus	43	26	60
King's Nest	22	13	59
Lenado Road	19	16	84
Magic Prospect	43	24	56
Parlay Me	15	11	73
Ranger (Fr)	20	12	60
Regal Remark	33	26	79
Silver of Silver	11	10	91
Sir Ap	19	13	68
Vilzak	23	12	52
Weekend Guest	47	37	79

BRITISH COLUMBIA

Stallion	bred	Fls	%
Alfaari	42	28	67
Baron de Vaux	26	20	77
Dixieland Brass	49	26	53
Katahaula County	57	42	74
On Target	66	46	70
Orchid's Devil	20	13	65
Regal Intention	53	29	55
Ringside	14	10	71
Silver Fox	26	12	46
Stephanotis	38	25	66
Turbulent Kris	24	16	67
Vying Victor	56	30	54
Western Trick	33	18	55
Yoonevano	31	16	52

MANITOBA

Stallion	bred	Fls	%
Act Smart	20	11	55
His Excellence	21	14	67
Saratoga Express	21	11	52

ONTARIO

Stallion	bred	Fls	%
Alydeed	49	36	73
Archers Bay	78	57	73
Ascot Knight	43	31	72
Birdonthewire	43	32	74
Bold Executive	76	45	59
Bold n' Flashy	59	31	53
Canyon Creek (Ire)	85	62	73
Compadre	58	30	52
Crown Attorney	52	36	69
Dr. Adagio	28	17	61
Elajjud	32	17	53
Great Gladiator	38	23	61
I Can't Believe	60	42	70
Inspired Prospect	19	12	63
Kiridashi	62	37	60
Nerud	18	15	83
Porto Foricos	18	11	61
Sea Wall	17	10	59
Soaking Smoking	16	10	63
Tethra	64	39	61
War Deputy	14	11	79
Western Gentleman	38	14	37
Whiskey Wisdom	37	31	84

Report of Mares Bred for 2001

The Jockey Club's Report of Mares Bred for 2001 contained for the first time a North American stallion bred to more than 200 mares. Thunder Gulch, sire of top 2000 juvenile and 2001 Horse of the Year Point Given, was bred to 216 mares at Ashford Stud near Versailles, Kentucky. Another Ashford stallion, Honour and Glory, was bred to 192 mares in an unusual breeding season for the bellwether Central Kentucky industry.

With mare reproductive loss syndrome causing nearly 3,000 mares to abort their fetuses within weeks of conception (or 30% of the potential 2002 Kentucky foal crop), many stallions were bred to several more mares than had been originally planned. For instance, Seattle Slew was bred to 63 mares as his book was expanded to accommodate owners whose broodmares had lost their pregnancies.

In all, Kentucky stallions were bred to 20,962 mares, down slightly from 21,012 in 2000. Florida had the second-largest total of mares bred, followed by California, Texas, and New York.

According to the Jockey Club report, which was not complete for the 2001 breeding season, approximately 2,600 fewer mares were bred in 2001 than in the previous year. On the following pages are state-by-state listings of stallions bred to ten or more mares in 2000.

Leading Stallions by Mares Bred
(as of December 31, 2001)

Stallion, location	Mares bred	Stallion, location	Mares bred	Stallion, location	Mares bred	Stallion, location	Mares bred
Thunder Gulch, KY	216	Cryptoclearance, KY	109	Rizzi, FL	96	Souvenir Copy, KY	84
Honour and Glory, KY	192	Captain Bodgit, KY	108	Distorted Humor, KY	95	Spinning World, KY	84
High Yield, KY	170	Charismatic, KY	108	Doneraile Court, KY	95	Gone West, KY	83
Louis Quatorze, KY	162	Bertrando, CA	107	Meadow Monster, MD	95	Boston Harbor, KY	82
Fusaichi Pegasus, KY	151	Tale of the Cat, KY	107	More Than Ready, KY	95	Cape Canaveral, KY	82
Wheaton, FL	140	Unbridled's Song, KY	107	Stephen Got Even, KY	95	Distant View, KY	82
Royal Anthem, KY	134	Valid Expectations, TX	107	Wild Rush, KY	95	Dixieland Band, KY	82
A. P. Jet, NY	133	Sky Classic, KY	106	Dance Brightly, KY	94	Lucky Lionel, KY	82
Crafty Friend, KY	132	Stravinsky, KY	106	Smoke Glacken, KY	94	Silver Deputy, KY	82
Maria's Mon, KY	129	Belong to Me, KY	105	Touch Gold, KY	94	Boundary, KY	81
Stormy Atlantic, FL	128	Cee's Tizzy, CA	105	Cat Thief, KY	93	Memo (Chi), CA	81
A.P. Indy, KY	127	Evansville Slew, KY	105	Meadowlake, KY	93	Seeking the Gold, KY	81
Afternoon Deelites, KY	126	Golden Missile, KY	105	Precise End, NY	93	Southern Halo, KY	81
Allen's Prospect, MD	126	Yes It's True, FL	105	Fly So Free, KY	92	Zamindar, FL	81
Devil His Due, KY	125	Awesome Again, KY	104	Highland Ruckus, ON	92	Formal Gold, KY	80
King of Kings (Ire), KY	125	Gilded Time, KY	104	Lemon Drop Kid, KY	92	Gentlemen (Arg), KY	80
Stormin Fever, KY	124	Halo's Image, FL	104	Rodeo, NY	91	Parade Ground, KY	80
Mr. Greeley, KY	123	Lite the Fuse, KY	104	Cherokee Run, KY	90	Richter Scale, KY	80
Skip Away, KY	121	Mazel Trick, KY	104	Sweetsouthernsaint, FL	90	Slewdledo, WA	80
Grand Slam, KY	120	Unbridled Jet, MD	104	Bold n' Flashy, ON	89	Subordination, KY	80
Royal Academy, KY	120	Storm Creek, KY	103	Crowd Pleaser, MD	89	Sunny's Halo, TX	80
Exploit, KY	119	Tomorrows Cat, NY	103	Olympio, CA	89	Sword Dance (Ire), FL	80
Old Trieste, KY	118	Vicar, KY	103	Best of Luck, KY	88	High Brite, KY	79
Open Forum, FL	117	Bianconi, KY	102	Anees, KY	87	In Excess (IRE), CA	79
Yankee Victor, KY	117	Lion Cavern, KY	102	Chester House, KY	87	In Excessive Bull, NM	79
Slew Gin Fizz, FL	116	Siphon (Brz), KY	102	Montbrook, FL	87	Storm Boot, KY	79
Storm Cat, KY	116	Woodman, KY	102	Red Ransom, KY	87	Thats Our Buck, FL	79
Wild Zone, TX	116	Double Honor, CA	101	Wild Wonder, FL	87	Benchmark, CA	78
Holy Bull, KY	115	Family Calling, FL	101	Deputy Minister, KY	86	Cartwright, IL	78
Robyn Dancer, FL	115	Foxtrail, KY	101	El Prado (Ire), KY	86	Coordinator, OK	78
Lord Carson, KY	114	Line In The Sand, FL	101	Pleasant Tap, KY	86	Crafty Prospector, KY	78
Running Stag, KY	114	Rahy, KY	101	The Deputy (Ire), KY	86	Forest Wildcat, KY	78
Straight Man, FL	114	Marquetry, KY	100	Two Punch, MD	86	Mutakddim, KY	78
Silver Charm, KY	113	Event of the Year, CA	99	Victory Gallop, KY	86	Theatrical (IRE), KY	78
Honor Grades, KY	112	Kingmambo, KY	99	Accelerator, KY	85	Regal Classic, NY	77
Malibu Moon, MD	112	Lost Soldier, FL	99	Cape Town, KY	85	Storm and a Half, AR	77
Notable Cat, OK	112	Real Quiet, KY	99	Friendly Lover, KY	85	Successful Appeal, FL	77
Peaks and Valleys, KY	112	Rubiano, KY	99	Glitterman, KY	85	Tactical Cat, KY	77
Swiss Yodeler, CA	112	Dynaformer, KY	98	Miner's Mark, FL	85	Leestown, LA	77
Carson City, KY	111	Out of Place, KY	98	Mt. Livermore, KY	85	Pulpit, KY	76
Artax, KY	110	Pioneering, KY	98	Unbridled, KY	85	Smart Strike, KY	76
Langfuhr, KY	110	Forestry, KY	97	Diesis (GB), KY	84	War Chant, KY	76
Saint Ballado, KY	110	Alphabet Soup, KY	96	Dixie Union, KY	84	Arch, KY	75
Tiger Ridge, FL	110	Bartok (Ire), CA	96	Horse Chestnut (SAf), KY	84		
Chief Seattle, KY	109	Gold Case, KY	96	Pine Bluff, KY	84		

Stallions and Mares Bred by State or Province
(as of December 31, 2001)

State	Stallions	Mares bred	State	Stallions	Mares bred	State	Stallions	Mares bred
Alabama	16	90	Mississippi	12	68	Vermont	3	39
Arizona	58	402	Missouri	25	139	Virginia	69	505
Arkansas	61	550	Montana	38	219	Washington	105	1,263
California	385	5,720	Nebraska	32	326	West Virginia	47	587
Colorado	66	407	Nevada	4	15	Wisconsin	12	24
Connecticut	1	5	New Hampshire	1	5	Wyoming	14	47
Florida	268	6,813	New Jersey	43	238	Unknown	59	227
Georgia	19	92	New Mexico	133	1,149	Puerto Rico	62	704
Idaho	52	272	New York	121	2,206	Virgin Islands	1	3
Illinois	122	1,211	North Carolina	16	55	**Province**		
Indiana	87	752	North Dakota	12	80	Alberta	74	825
Iowa	63	708	Ohio	95	789	British Columbia	74	790
Kansas	27	177	Oklahoma	217	1,858	Manitoba	22	221
Kentucky	429	20,962	Oregon	44	420	New Brunswick	2	7
Louisiana	172	2,064	Pennsylvania	106	952	Nova Scotia	2	5
Maine	3	3	South Carolina	24	229	Ontario	91	1,276
Maryland	95	1,851	South Dakota	18	166	Quebec	4	7
Massachusetts	21	104	Tennessee	23	83	Saskatchewan	21	149
Michigan	64	526	Texas	363	3,297	**Totals**	**4,067**	**62,119**
Minnesota	27	240	Utah	42	197			

Stallions Bred to Ten or More Mares in 2001
(as of December 31, 2001)

Stallion	Mares bred	Stallion	Mares bred	Stallion	Mares bred	Stallion	Mares bred
ALABAMA		Benchmark	78	Free House	44	Northern Devil	21
Casey On Deck	17	Bertrando	107	Fruition	33	Not Tricky	21
Royal Empire	26	B. Hoedown	10	Future Storm	65	Old Topper	53
		Bold Badgett	54	Game Plan	48	Ole'	23
ARIZONA		Boomerang	11	General Meeting	59	Olympio	89
Barricade	49	Born Wild	39	Haint	21	Paranoide (Arg)	18
Benton Creek	34	Boulder Dam	10	Half Term	16	Perfect Mandate	11
Buck Strider	33	Brave Romane	13	Helmsman	52	Pharisien (Fr)	11
Calumar	11	Cactus Creole	10	High Brite	79	Phone Roberto	25
Chanate	44	Candi's Gold	16	Houston	25	Phone Saga	24
Chopin	25	Candyman Bee	12	Hunter's Glory	13	Phonetics	13
Racey Remarque	10	Category Five	37	Iam the Iceman	15	Proud Irish	46
Relaunch a Tune	17	Cee's Tizzy	105	Illinois Storm	30	Red	31
Tax Collection	14	Cherokee Colony	14	In Excess (Ire)	79	Rhythm	50
Truce Maker	16	Chullo (Arg)	11	Iron Cat	18	Rio Verde	32
		Cold n Calculating	11	Kahuna Jack	49	River Flyer	13
ARKANSAS		Comet Shine	30	Kessem Power (NZ)	21	Robannier	17
American General	12	Commitment	22	King of the Hunt	24	Royal Regatta (Ire)	11
A. V. Eight	31	Corslew	19	Larry the Legend	40	Scherando	22
Bold Anthony	38	Country Light	17	Last Lion	26	Score Quick	14
Caracey	13	Crowning Storm	40	Latin American	74	Seattle Bound	39
Cinnamon Creek	64	Dance Floor	64	Lil Tyler	35	Seven Rivers	18
Country Store	12	Demon's Crown	10	Lindsey's Roberto	17	Siberian Summer	31
Etbauer	22	Desert Secret (Ire)	16	Loyal Double	10	Silver Ray	12
Gremlin Grey	12	Devon Lane	52	Lucayan Prince	26	Simply Majestic	12
Harperstown	12	Din's Dancer	44	Mach One	10	Six Below	47
Idabel	17	Discover	13	Majesterian	17	Slew the Bride	17
Southern Forest	12	Distinctive Cat	41	Makaleha	29	Slewpy	26
Storm and a Half	77	Dominated Debut	17	Makhraj	25	Slewvescent	24
This Picture	34	Double Honor	101	Malek (Chi)	42	Smokester	40
Unbridled's Risk	16	Emerald Creme	18	Mantles Star (GB)	21	Smooth Runner	16
		Emerald Jig	13	Matty G	18	Stage Colony	13
CALIFORNIA		Endow	10	Memo (Chi)	81	State Performer	13
All Thee Power	14	Epic Honor	26	Moscow Ballet	63	Strike Gold	15
American Day	13	Event of the Year	99	Mr Purple	23	Suggest	13
Anziyan	36	Fabulous Champ	30	Mr. Broad Blade	10	Surachai	35
Apollo	23	Falstaff	27	Mr. Procrastinator	17	Swiss Yodeler	112
Avenue of Flags	43	Fargo	33	Mud Route	61	Synastry	15
Bartok (Ire)	96	Fine n' Majestic	21	Muqtarib	25	Tactical Heir	10
Bay Street Star	35	Flying Continental	37	My King (Ger)	14	Tahoe City	17
Beau Genius	40	Flying Victor	44	Native Storm	25	The Good Life	17
		For Really	23	Newton's Law (Ire)	11	Tinners Way	22

Stallion	Mares bred
Town Caper	31
Trail City	52
Tricky Creek	21
Truckee	51
Truly Met	16
Turkoman	74
Twin Spires	57
Tychonic (GB)	56
Unusual Heat	35
Valid Wager	71
Vaudeville	46
Ventriloquist	14
Via Lombardia (Ire)	20
Wanpum	15
Western Fame	38
What a Spell	11
Wild Deputy	33
Wild Gold	41

COLORADO

Stallion	Mares bred
Basic Rate	11
Cash Deposit	36
Coverallbases	26
Crafty Harold	16
Dash Ahead	10
Exploding Rainbow	11
Kennedy Factor	19
San Rafael Pass	13
Sinceilostmybaby	16
Smilin Singin Sam	35
Woody Win	10

FLORIDA

Stallion	Mares bred
Absent Russian	15
Adcat	39
Aloha Prospector	35
Anjiz	24
Appealing Skier	39
Badge	32
Believe It	14
Blue Ensign	12
Bon Point (GB)	29
Brief Ruckus	32
Byars	20
Capture the Gold	49
Carlisle Bay	14
Classic Cat	26
Cloud Cover	28
Cohiba	32
Colony Light	48
Comeonmom	11
Commitisize	27
Concerto	51
Concorde's Tune	65
Conveyor	13
Crown Pleasure	12
Cyberspace	13
Dance Master	32
Darn That Alarm	18
David	13
Dawn Quixote	16
Diligence	43
Dixie Power	10
D. J. Cat	22
Dove Hunt	29
Dr. Caton	52
Eltish	44
Eskimo	15
Fabulous Frolic	61
Family Calling	101
Fast 'n Royal	14

Stallion	Mares bred
Faygo	20
Forever Whirl	13
Formal Dinner	61
Fortunate Move	13
Fortunate Prospect	55
Gold Alert	20
Greenwood Lake	67
Groomstick	22
Halos and Horns	29
Halo's Image	104
Hazaam	41
Hesabull	42
Holy Mountain	38
Hubble	14
Hunting Hard	56
Impeachment	25
Is It True	46
Island Whirl	28
Jeblar	25
Jules	49
Keep Dreaming	11
Kelly Kip	51
Kipper Kelly	43
Kissin Kris	64
Laubali	15
Limit Out	23
Line In The Sand	101
Littlebitlively	70
Lost Soldier	99
Lucky North	20
Lycius	57
Marco Bay	36
Master Bill	44
Meadow Flight	20
Mecke	29
Metfield	35
Migrating Moon	47
Miner's Mark	85
Minstrel Dancer	13
Mister Jolie	52
Montbrook	87
Montreal Red	22
Native Regent	24
Noactor	31
Northern Afleet	70
Northern Trend	15
Notebook	59
Ocala Slew	12
Oliver's Twist	17
Open Forum	117
Outflanker	60
Part the Waters	10
Pentelicus	49
Piccolino	18
Precocity	39
Premiership	20
Proud and True	43
Proudest Romeo	23
Quaker Ridge	42
Reality Road	18
Regal Humor	16
Reparations	25
Reprized	21
Rizzi	96
Robyn Dancer	115
Rocky Mountain	11
Sam's Sunny Hour	10
Sasha's Prospect	42
Seacliff	32
Semoran	52
Skip Trial	28

Stallion	Mares bred
Slew Gin Fizz	116
Stack	13
Star of Valor	29
Statesmanship	11
Stormy Atlantic	128
Straight Man	114
Struggler (GB)	19
Suave Prospect	55
Successful Appeal	77
Sweetsouthernsaint	90
Sword Dance (Ire)	80
Tactical Advantage	61
Thats Our Buck	79
The Silver Move	26
Thisnearlywasmine	13
Tiger Ridge	110
Time Bandit	30
Toolighttoquit	22
Top Account	63
Tour d'Or	73
Traitor	33
Twin Halo	10
Untuttable	31
Way West (Fr)	38
West Acre	43
Western Borders	29
Western Cat	49
Wheaton	140
Whitney Tower	27
Wild Escapade	36
Wild Event	69
Wild Wonder	87
Wind Whipper	61
Wised Up	42
World Stage	68
World Stage (Ire)	68
Worldly Manner	64
Yes It's True	105
Zamindar	81

GEORGIA

Stallion	Mares bred
Roaring Camp	26
Sheikh Adel	11

IDAHO

Stallion	Mares bred
Chisos	11
Firmlin	10
Hey Rob	15
Jestic	19
Kings Blood (Ire)	13
Present Value	18
Pro Chapeau	10
Renteria	21
Shergar's Best (Ire)	11
Thunderah	14

ILLINOIS

Stallion	Mares bred
Alaskan Frost	50
A Lee Rover	11
Allen Charge	21
Awesome Cat	33
Bold Revenue	17
Canyon Run	12
Cartwright	78
Charlie Barley	25
Cherokee Saga	10
City by Night	45
Classic Account	14
Classified Facts	22
Conte Di Savoya	22
Diazo	31

Stallion	Mares bred
Double Niner	19
Electric Blue	18
Emancipator	12
Executive Order	20
Fact Book	15
Gogarty (Ire)	17
Hannibal Cat	16
He's a Tough Cat	11
Jolly Blade	10
Let Him Go	15
Macaso	21
Mt. Magazine	22
Palmister	21
Presently	27
Seattle Morn	34
Shakeel	23
Smokin Mel	10
Spanish Drummer	37
U Folks	11
Unite	19
Unreal Zeal	67
Western Playboy	29
Wild Gambler	11
Zagor	17
Z Z Cat	27

INDIANA

Stallion	Mares bred
Ali Gaziba	21
Assembly Dancer	14
Bidding Proud	15
Bordagaray	10
Bravoure	12
Cat Power	41
Classy Prospector	16
Crown Ambassador	22
D. C. Tenacious	12
Fiscal	20
Gallant Step	13
Guys from Space	12
Hit the Roof	25
Indy Mood	41
Jungle Express	13
Magic Flagship	13
Mexican Bandit	10
Moro Oro	25
Presidential Order	25
Riflery	19
Seattle Rob	12
Sir Riddle	11
Swiss Trick	15
T. H. Fappiano	13
Tricon	24
Waki Warrior	26

IOWA

Stallion	Mares bred
At the Threshold	13
Buzz Saw	11
Cape Storm	29
Cat's Debut	10
Champagneforashley	13
Change Takes Time	21
Commemorate	23
De Guerin	10
Dignitas	20
Farragut	18
H. J. Baker	26
Honest Ensign	31
Humming	13
Kyle's Our Man	55
Lord Pleasant	12
Mercedes Won	32

Stallion	Mares bred	Stallion	Mares bred	Stallion	Mares bred	Stallion	Mares bred
Mocha Express	20	Chester House	87	Ghazi	33	Mongol Warrior	10
Night Runner	20	Chief Seattle	109	Gilded Time	104	More Than Ready	95
Parfaitement	11	Chimes Band	39	Glitterman	85	Mr. Greeley	123
Prospect Feature	13	Clever Trick	45	Go for Gin	68	Mt. Livermore	85
Purdue King	18	Cobra King	19	Gold Case	96	Mutakddim	78
Sharkey	32	Comic Strip	63	Golden Gear	42	Mystery Storm	31
Shotiche	20	Commendable	58	Golden Missile	105	Northern No Trump	28
Temujin	16	Composer	41	Gold Fever	74	Northern Spur (Ire)	16
Tiger Talk	13	Comstock Lode	41	Gold Legend	50	Numerous	23
West Buoyant	20	Confide	47	Gold Tribute	53	Nureyev	44
Wild Invader	30	Conquistador Cielo	69	Gone West	83	Old Trieste	118
Yankee Fan	17	Constant Demand	18	Good and Tough	66	Ordway	18
		Coronado's Quest	74	Grand Slam	120	Our Emblem	31
KANSAS		Count the Time	69	Grindstone	71	Out of Place	98
Gold Ruler	19	Cozzene	65	Gulch	68	Parade Ground	80
Groom's Image	11	Crafty Friend	132	Halory Hunter	17	Party Manners	29
Life Interest	11	Crafty Prospector	78	High Yield	170	Peaks and Valleys	112
Prospect North	17	Crimson Classic	13	Hold for Gold	17	Pembroke	34
So Ever Clever	12	Cryptoclearance	109	Holy Bull	115	Perfect Vision	37
Speedy Nijinsky	12	Dance Brightly	94	Home At Last	16	Peruvian	11
Torey Ridge	15	Danzig	49	Honor Grades	112	Petionville	62
		Dare and Go	48	Honour and Glory	192	Phone Trick	71
KENTUCKY		Dayjur	23	Horse Chestnut (SAf)	84	Pine Bluff	84
Accelerator	85	Deerhound	21	Ide	29	Pioneering	98
Acceptable	34	Defensive Play	15	Indian Charlie	73	Pistols and Roses	26
Afternoon Deelites	126	Defrere	34	In the Zone	14	Pleasant Tap	86
Aggressive Chief	17	Demidoff	36	Intidab	13	Pleasantprospector	10
Aljabr	55	Deputy Commander	73	Irgun	58	Polish Navy	68
Allied Forces	41	Deputy Minister	86	Irish River (Fr)	20	Private Terms	53
Alphabet Soup	96	Devil His Due	125	Islefaxyou	31	Prized	48
American Chance	72	Devil's Bag	64	Jade Hunter	52	Prospect Bay	36
Anees	87	Diesis (GB)	84	Jambalaya Jazz	45	Prospectors Gamble	15
Anet	40	Distant View	82	Joyeux Danseur	49	Puerto Madero (Chi)	28
Announce	43	Distorted Humor	95	Just a Cat	51	Pulpit	76
Answer Lively	36	Dixie Union	84	Kandaly	11	Pyramid Peak	61
A.P. Indy	127	Dixieland Band	82	Kayrawan	20	Quiet American	59
Arch	75	Dixieland Heat	64	Kingmambo	99	Rahy	101
Artax	110	Doneraile Court	95	King of Kings (Ire)	125	Real Quiet	99
Atticus	55	Down the Aisle	57	K One King	46	Red Ransom	87
Awesome Again	104	Dumaani	27	K. O. Punch	43	Repriced	73
Bahri	47	Dusty Screen	19	Kris S.	55	Richter Scale	80
Banker's Gold	63	Dynaformer	98	Laabity	23	Roar	59
Barkerville	19	Eastern Echo	27	Labeeb (GB)	35	Rockamundo	11
Basic	16	Editor's Note	59	Lac Ouimet	45	Rod and Staff	18
Bates Motel	26	El Amante	34	Langfuhr	110	Romanov (Ire)	30
Behrens	52	El Angelo	12	Lasting Approval	32	Royal Academy	120
Belong to Me	105	Elnadim	43	Lear Fan	65	Royal Anthem	134
Bernstein	67	El Prado (Ire)	86	Lemon Drop Kid	92	Rubiano	99
Best of Luck	88	Elusive Quality	56	Level Sands	25	Run Softly	20
Bianconi	102	En Tete	13	Lil E. Tee	36	Runaway Groom	66
Birdonthewire	36	Evansville Slew	105	Lil's Lad	73	Running Stag	114
Boston Harbor	82	Expelled	41	Lion Cavern	102	Sahm	37
Boundary	81	Exploit	119	Lit de Justice	32	Saint Ballado	110
Bright Launch	52	Fast Play	41	Lite the Fuse	104	Salt Lake	68
Broad Brush	47	Fastness (Ire)	13	Lord Avie	66	Sandpit (Brz)	63
Brunswick	11	Favorite Trick	56	Lord Carson	114	Saratoga Six	32
Caller I. D.	30	Fit to Fight	65	Louis Quatorze	162	Scatmandu	74
Canaveral	30	Flying Chevron	22	Lucky Lionel	82	Sea of Secrets	39
Cape Canaveral	82	Fly So Free	92	Luhuk	68	Seattle Sleet	25
Cape Town	85	Fly Till Dawn	11	Lure	52	Seattle Slew	63
Capote	42	Forestry	97	Mahogany Hall	17	Secreniner	26
Captain Bodgit	108	Forest Wildcat	78	Maria's Mon	129	Seeking the Gold	81
Carolina Kid	24	Formal Gold	80	Marquetry	100	Sefapiano	40
Carson City	111	Fort Chaffee	15	Mazel Trick	104	Senor Speedy	26
Cat Creek Slew	15	Foxtrail	101	Meadowlake	93	Service Stripe	57
Cat Thief	93	Friendly Lover	85	Menifee	70	Shadeed	15
Catienus	66	Frisk Me Now	19	Miesque's Son	53	Shawaf	37
Catrail	63	Furiously	14	Mighty	67	Shuailaan	34
Cat's Career	66	Fusaichi Pegasus	151	Military	40	Silic (Fr)	60
Charismatic	108	General Royal	74	Miswaki	71	Silver Charm	113
Cherokee Run	90	Gentlemen (Arg)	80			Silver Deputy	82

Stallion	Mares bred
Silver Ghost	52
Silver Hawk	57
Siphon (Brz)	102
Sir Cat	60
Skip Away	121
Sky Classic	106
Skywalker	62
Slew City Slew	73
Slew o' Gold	23
Smart Strike	76
Smoke Glacken	94
Southern Halo	81
Souvenir Copy	84
Spinning World	84
Squadron Leader	11
Stalwart	31
State Craft	13
Stephen Got Even	95
Storm Boot	79
Storm Brewing	10
Storm Cat	116
Storm Creek	103
Stormin Fever	124
Stravinsky	106
Subordination	80
Sultry Song	34
Summer Squall	50
Swain (Ire)	73
Tactical Cat	77
Tale of the Cat	107
Tejano Run	65
Theatrical (Ire)	78
The Deputy (Ire)	86
The Name's Jimmy	49
Thunder Gulch	216
Torrential	31
Touch Gold	94
Tough Call	14
Unaccounted For	55
Unbridled	85
Unbridled's Song	107
Valiant Nature	25
Vicar	103
Victory Gallop	86
Victory Speech	56
Wagon Limit	35
War Chant	76
Wavering Monarch	53
Wekiva Springs	47
Well Decorated	36
Westminster	14
Wild Again	63
Wild Rush	95
Wild Syn	18
Will's Way	36
With Approval	74
Wolf Power (SAf)	53
Woodman	102
Yankee Victor	117
You and I	65

LOUISIANA

Stallion	Mares bred
A Corking Limerick	18
Autocracy	12
Bag	31
Battle Launch	10
Belek	16
Bermuda Cedar	13
B. J.'s Mark	11
Buddy	16

Stallion	Mares bred
Busterwaggley	13
Cachuma	12
Charlie's Beau	11
City Nights (Ire)	14
Combat Ready	10
Contested Colors	12
Corwyn	49
Dancing Harlan	23
Deputy Diamond	67
Direct Hit	28
Doug's My Doc	10
Emphatic One	10
Esplanade Ridge	18
Excavate	31
Exceller Vice	11
Far Out Wadleigh	14
Finest Hour	71
Forty Won	16
Gebbia	12
Gentle Kent	10
Giuseppe	11
Goodbye Doeny	43
Handkerchief (Arg)	13
Homebuilder	34
I'ma Hell Raiser	30
In a Walk	17
Jersey City	30
Jitterbug Chief	10
King of Tap	10
Lake Holme	29
Leestown	76
Like a Soldier	22
Lot o' Gold	10
Malagra	46
Many a Wish	17
Meena	10
Moonlight Dancer	20
Mr. Sparkles	36
My Friend Max	23
My Mike	13
Northern Niner	18
On the Sauce	26
Placid Fund	23
Prince of the Mt.	35
Pulling Punches	51
Rail	17
Right Jab	13
Scott's Scoundrel	23
Scottsville	14
Secret Odds	17
Sharp Frosty	26
Shelton	10
Slew the Surgeon	36
Smithfield	10
Spend a Buck	29
Spruce Bouquet	11
Stately Slew	22
Trophy Hunter	47
Upping the Ante	20
Winter Halo	25
Wire Me Collect	36
Zarbyev	38
Zede	19
Zuppardo's Prince	25

MARYLAND

Stallion	Mares bred
Aaron's Concorde	10
Allen's Prospect	126
Ameri Valay	10
Another Reef	14
Awad	45

Stallion	Mares bred
Carnivalay	52
Citidancer	55
Concern	40
Crowd Pleaser	89
Crypto Star	53
Deputed Testamony	14
Diamond	57
In Case	19
Larrupin'	42
Lion Hearted	70
Malibu Moon	112
Meadow Monster	95
Not For Love	72
Ops Smile	33
Partner's Hero	56
Polish Numbers	55
Rinka Das	22
Root Boy	12
Rubiyat	25
Secret Firm	24
Storm Broker	47
Swear by Dixie	14
Tamayaz	17
Two Punch	86
Unbridled Jet	104
Valley Crossing	27
Waquoit	33
Wayne County (Ire)	30
Yarrow Brae	65
Zignew	18

MASSACHUSETTS

Stallion	Mares bred
Personal Matter	13
Safely's Mark	13
Sundance Ridge	10
Wee Thunder	16

MICHIGAN

Stallion	Mares bred
Binalong	25
Cat in Town	11
Collateral Attack	17
Demaloot Demashoot	37
Flare Dancer	11
Grand Circus Park	18
Great Allegiance	11
Gulch It	11
Jacodra	11
Matchlite	29
Meadow Prayer	45
Native Factor	18
Pauliano	27
Predecessor	12
Quick and Dirty	16
Quiet Enjoyment	20
Research	20
Speedy Cure	12
Ulises	17

MINNESOTA

Stallion	Mares bred
Charging Through	11
Lakeshore Road	28
North Prospect	24
Olaf	15
Quaker Hill	18
Quick Cut	39
Takur	15
Victor's Gent	10

MISSISSIPPI

Stallion	Mares bred
Golden Omen	17

Stallion	Mares bred
Valid Victorious	14

MISSOURI

Stallion	Mares bred
American Tribute	17
Dark Hyacinth	11
Liginsky	13
Lucky South	17
Steel Robbing	14

MONTANA

Stallion	Mares bred
Autoroute	10
Fatih	13
Knight in Savannah	28
Matthews Keep	17
Nassau Square	10
Ourcurtaincall	10
Perry Road	11
Stop the Fighting (Ire)	10
Strong Minded	15

NEBRASKA

Stallion	Mares bred
Bengal Bay	16
Blumin Affair	52
Buzzer	24
Fighting Fantasy	12
Glenview	13
Hesaluckycat	16
Miracle Heights	33
More to Tell	15
O'Brannigan	14
Shawklit Player	11
Silver Launch	38

NEVADA

Stallion	Mares bred
The Danzig Kid	10

NEW JERSEY

Stallion	Mares bred
Bugatti Reef (Ire)	23
Fort Wayne	13
Jack Livingston	14
Munch n' Nosh	17
My Prince Charming	17
Perfect	13
Private Interview	26
Tree	14

NEW MEXICO

Stallion	Mares bred
Adams Trail	21
Adios Mundo	16
Blind Man's Bluff	11
Con Artist	15
Corwyn Bay (Ire)	25
Danzatore	24
Dee Lance	15
Desert God	16
Devil Begone	54
Devil Diamond	18
Digging In	16
Eishin Storm	15
Fair American	17
Ferrara	17
Ghost Ranch	10
Ghostly Moves	28
Gold Decorum	13
He's a Looker	17
Highland Park	29
Hoedown's Day	11
Hoolie	10
In Excessive Bull	79
Jack Wilson	12

Stallion	Mares bred
Just a Tune	13
Old Chapel	11
Paramour	10
Parting the Sea	19
Patsyprospect	23
Poles Apart	15
Prince of Fame	15
Prospector Jones	31
Retsina Run	15
R. Payday	16
Run Paul Run	11
Sadler Slew	27
Schizoid	11
Someplace Fast	12
Tap N Snap	22
Tricky Fun	15
Waki Bob	11
You Know How It Is	15

NEW YORK

Stallion	Mares bred
Abaginone	58
Adonis	43
Always Fair	14
American Standard	10
A. P Jet	133
Brushed On	38
Carry My Colors	11
Chequer	28
Claramount	18
Cozy Drive	20
Crimson Guard	11
Crusader Sword	25
Danzatame	41
Daygata	15
Distinctive Pro	56
Dixie Brass	55
Financial Matter	24
Gold Token	35
Goldminers Gold	26
Gone for Real	16
Irish Conquest	18
Key Contender	47
Kingsboro	10
Let Goodtimes Roll	11
Malibu Wesley	40
Manlove	17
Mesopotamia	17
Mighty Magee	47
Millions	26
Nines Wild	29
Northernhemisphere	10
Obligato	15
Odyle	14
Optic Nerve	10
Personal Flag	72
Polish Pro	16
Preacherman	16
Precise End	93
Raffie's Majesty	27
Rage	13
Regal Classic	77
Reign Road	15
River Keen (Ire)	46
Rob 'n Gin	14
Rodeo	91
Satellite Sun	13
Scarlet Ibis	24
Sea Salute	30
Signal Tap	21
Silver Music	14
Spectacular Bid	22

Stallion	Mares bred
Storm of Angels	41
Take Me Out	46
Tank's Number	15
The Wicked North	23
Tomorrows Cat	103
Treasure Cove	29
Tri Line	12
Western Expression	70
Williamstown	35

NORTH CAROLINA

Stallion	Mares bred
Chelsey Cat	16

NORTH DAKOTA

Stallion	Mares bred
Codys Key	16
Storada	11
Win Lose Or Draw	20

OHIO

Stallion	Mares bred
Academy Award	63
Al Sabin	19
Camp Izard	11
Canvas	18
Coax Me Chad	22
Defense Witness	20
Devil's Luck	13
Flight Forty Nine	20
Forest Gazelle	13
French Legionaire	17
Gold Market	15
Hard Wire	10
I'll Raise You One	19
King of the Nile	10
Launch a Leader	18
Left Banker	10
Magnificent One	10
Mercer Mill	31
Noble Cat	22
Noon Prospect	13
Northern Symphony	16
Pacific Waves	15
Political Folly	17
Pride of Burkaan	18
Private School	36
Rhodes	12
Swift Crusader	19
Winthrop	18

OKLAHOMA

Stallion	Mares bred
Alamocitos	15
Alleged Risk	24
Alydot	11
Avies Copy	16
Backoff Dude	10
Bonus Time Cat	43
Burbank	33
Chief's Reward	23
Christmas Storm	11
Confederate Hero	10
Coordinator	78
Deodar	21
Dreamfield	16
Ecstatic Ride	15
Expense Account	23
Fashionable Enough	10
French Parliament	24
Full of Tricks	11
Ghost Tension	25
Have Fun	21
Here We Come	35

Stallion	Mares bred
Inca Chief	18
Indy Talent	18
Jungle Blade	10
King of Scat	54
Kipling	44
Lost Opportunity	22
Maddy's Waquoit	10
Magna	20
Mi Selecto	72
Minister's Mark	11
Moro	12
Muldoon	25
My Liege	26
New Way	24
Night Ceremony	11
Notable Cat	112
Officer of Court	17
Peace Prize (Ire)	10
Perdition's Son	17
Proper Reality	17
Reel On Reel	14
Seattle Sun	10
Serves Em Right	12
Soviet State	12
Speak	24
Stauder	12
Storm Ruler	12
Sunrise Shower	10
Tarakam	26
Track Barron	17
Trouble Onthe Line	10
Undeniable	11
Unome	15
Wild Colony	20

OREGON

Stallion	Mares bred
Abstract	43
Airdrie Apache	23
Baquero	52
Cascadian	35
Crowning Season (GB)	51
Danjur	51
Gold Meridian	41
Superior Success	10
Tiffany Ice	12
True Confidence	39

PENNSYLVANIA

Stallion	Mares bred
Activist	23
Alyten	16
Attorney	30
Bankbook	12
Bombardier	16
Buck'sinthebank	13
Corporate Report	17
Count On Steve	10
De Niro	54
Deposit Ticket	41
Digamist	14
Fini Cassette	10
Flying Pidgeon	28
Foligno	15
Harry the Hat	26
Knockadoon	28
Obstructed	14
Patton	46
Pin Stripe	17
Pok Ta Pok	24
Power by Far	27
Power of Mind	22
Quarry	33

Stallion	Mares bred
Roanoke	50
Sir Eric	12
Southern Rhythm	25
Tricky Mister	17
Two Plus	14
Western Echo	16

PUERTO RICO

Stallion	Mares bred
Balcony	27
Be Frank	11
Blustery	11
Cagey Bidder	10
Ceramal	14
Chicago Bound	10
Don Serafin	12
Eqtesaad	50
Fappiano's Star	55
Glitman	18
Goldwater	22
Hard Charger	17
Johnny Jones	23
Laurentide	11
Macavity	30
M.D.'s Relampago	15
Nather	11
Once Ivor	15
Royal Merlot	35
Run Turn	10
Sejm	27
Shining Spring	15
Stake Procpect	10
Storm God	22
Virtua Cop	21
Wonder Bird	27

SOUTH CAROLINA

Stallion	Mares bred
Go West	19
Is Sveikatas	15
Kokand	59
Play Both Ends	12
Ride the Storm	26
Signal	18
Stormville	12

SOUTH DAKOTA

Stallion	Mares bred
Alyone	10
Crafty Ridan	21
Gaelic Padraic	10
Get Me Out	10
Neff Lake	26
Storm of the Night	35

TENNESSEE

Stallion	Mares bred
Doppler	12
Moonlight Guy	10
Wild Hackett To	11

TEXAS

Stallion	Mares bred
Aggie Southpaw	12
Alleged Stardom	15
American Champ	34
Assault Cat	21
Boone's Mill	28
Capote's Prospect	27
Cat Strike	23
Cien Fuegos	26
Classic Look	12
Claudius	15
Clever Return	10
Cold Bid	11

Stallion	Mares bred
Cold Hearted Man	11
Commanchero	33
Conquer	10
Country Side	11
Crafty	28
Devil's Rock	21
Devious Course	21
Diogenes	11
Dmitri	11
Eagle Station	11
Endless Queue	10
Excellent Secret	23
Fashion Find	26
Fire Maker	31
Foreign Holding	18
Gary Gumbo	10
Gold Regent	34
Gringo Pilot	11
Hadif	43
Haymarket (GB)	22
High Energy	12
Holzmeister	26
Hurlingham	10
Imtoocool	16
Irish Open	43
Jan's Kinsman	10
Joe Who (Brz)	31
Karen's Cat	36
Kell's Sea Captain	10
Kentucky Jazz	11
Lacotte (Ire)	13
Lucky So n' So	34
Magic Cat	71
Majestic Twoeleven	20
Major Procida	10
Man From Eldorado	11
Manzotti	15
Marked Tree	45
Miswaki Gold	12
Moving Shoulder	21
Mr. Roberts	12
Myrmidon	14
Naevus	30
Night Beat	25
Olmos	11
Once a Sailor	16
Pancho Villa	74
Pele's Smile	13
Phone Fantasy	20
Political Whit	13
Pollock's Luck	34
Power Storm	18
Raise a Govenor	19
Raja's Best Boy	19
Rare Brick	23
Ray's Word	14
Relagate	10
River Squall	26
Ruhlmann	12
Seattle Pattern	14
Secret Claim	11
Seneca Jones	32
Siebe	10
Six Speed	12
Star Programmer	72
Sudden Storm	15
Sunny's Halo	80
Texas City	43
The Prime Minister	29
Totem and Taboo	13
Trapp Mountain	14

Stallion	Mares bred
Truluck	33
Tuesday's Special	17
Twilight Agenda	44
Under David's Wing	19
Valid Expectations	107
Waco Connection	13
Wajir	32
Wayne's Crane	20
Western Challenge (GB)	14
Western City	23
Western Trader	17
Why Change	16
Wild Zone	116
Zeeruler	14

UTAH

Stallion	Mares bred
Bustopher Jones	35
Isnad	12
Thunder Falcon	10
Wouldn't We All	12

VIRGINIA

Stallion	Mares bred
Ball's Bluff	21
Bring To Light	10
Chenin Blanc	14
Chief Protocol	20
Fred Astaire	19
Hay Halo	45
Husband	11
Musical River	10
Pleasant Dancer	13
Prenup	35
Rock Point	24
Secret Hello	45
Slavic	18
Supremo	27
Tahoe (Fr)	10
Two Smart	19

WASHINGTON

Stallion	Mares bred
Alnaab	11
Basket Weave	45
Beefchopper	22
Bull Inthe Heather	21
Cahill Road	60
Cathedral Bells	12
Cisco Road	20
Delineator	18
Demons Begone	40
Detox	20
Dixieland Glo	18
Flying With Eagles	26
Former	11
Free At Last	44
He's Tops	24
Ihtimam	22
Individual Style	17
Jazzing Around	20
Jumron (GB)	20
Kansas City	14
Katowice	31
Kriskris (Ire)	11
La Saboteur	32
Lord Charmer	10
Matricule	31
Mr. Easy Money	20
Ore Grade	21
Personable Joe	36
Peterhof	13
Petersburg	28
Russellthemussell	11

Stallion	Mares bred
Salty Shoes	10
Slewdledo	80
Snowbound	50
Stolen Gold	22
Storm Blast	24
Swing and Miss	30
Swiss Account	10
Taylor's Special	20
Tough Knight	25
Tropic Lightning	23

WEST VIRGINIA

Stallion	Mares bred
Citislipper	19
Eastover Court	57
Enough Reality	17
Gneiss	16
Jove Stone	14
Loach	11
Makin	55
My Boy Adam	59
Native Slew	12
Northern Wolf	11
Robb	29
Runaway Macho	14
Standing On Edge	25
Storm Center	20
Tank	34
Tidehaven	10
Truculent Schular	30
Valid Indy	18
Weshaam	27

ALBERTA

Stallion	Mares bred
Banjo	31
Bashful Cloud	10
Battle Creek	13
Blazing Fire	20
Brass Minister	25
Cache In	11
Candid Cameron	10
Chapel Creek	25
Ciano Cat	55
Deputy Bodman	13
Desperately	15
Devonwood	44
Esteem	14
Exclusive Era	13
Fast Account	12
Go Gary Go	25
Ground Stroke	28
Hail the Ruckus	16
Incinderator	22
John the Magician	32
King's Nest	18
Lenado Road	13
Magic Prospect	27
Parlay Me	17
Ranger (Fr)	18
Rebmec	29
Rokeby (GB)	13
Royal Rumpus	10
Sir Ap	15
Vilzak	22
Weekend Guest	42
Yaak River	13

BRITISH COLUMBIA

Stallion	Mares bred
Alfaari	19
Alybro	11
Baron de Vaux	23

Stallion	Mares bred
Captain Collins (Ire)	11
Devil On Ice	18
Dixieland Brass	33
Feu d'Enfer	31
Katahaula County	48
King of Cats	12
Malmo	16
Musing	18
On Target	30
Orchid's Devil	18
Regal Intention	62
Regal Remark	18
Ringside	13
Silver Fox	32
Sky White	14
Stephanotis	44
Turbulent Kris	17
Vying Victor	56
Western Trick	22
Yoonevano	35

MANITOBA

Stallion	Mares bred
Act Smart	19
Boanerges	15
Buie	19
Circulating	19
His Excellence	25
Polka	14
Saratoga Express	14
Shrike	10
Sunset Ridge	11

ONTARIO

Stallion	Mares bred
Alydeed	37
Archers Bay	65
Ascot Knight	66
Bold Executive	56
Bold n' Flashy	89
Canyon Creek (Ire)	49
Compadre	51
Crown Attorney	57
Dr. Adagio	14
Elajjud	14
Franc Coeur	14
Great Gladiator	39
Grey Counter	10
Highland Ruckus	92
I Can't Believe	36
Inspired Prospect	18
Kiridashi	55
Matter of Honor	18
My Imperial Slew	11
No Malice	12
Pete's Sake	13
Porto Foricos	42
Randy Regent	13
Regal Discovery	17
Synastry Express	12
Talkin Man	15
Tethra	47
War Deputy	12
Welbred Fred	12
Whiskey Wisdom	55
Wonneberg	26

SASKATCHEWAN

Stallion	Mares bred
Blowin de Turn	10
Clash of Steel	10
Pole Position	14
Royal Quiz	17
Shaheen	19

SIRES AND BROODMARES

Leading General Sires
by 2001 Earnings

Leading sires of North America with a minimum of one starter in North America in 2001.
The sire lists on the following pages do not include steeplechase statistics.

Sire, YOB, Sire	Loc	2001 Stud fee	Strs	Wnrs	SWs/ Stk Wins	Leading Earner (Earnings)	Progeny Earnings
DANEHILL, 86, by Danzig	Ire.	$65,955	419	187	47/83	Fairy King Prawn ($1,676,237)	$13,542,612
THUNDER GULCH, 92, by Gulch	Ky.	75,000	189	84	14/28	Point Given ($3,350,000)	8,364,491
RAHY, 85, by Blushing Groom (Fr)	Ky.	75,000	142	70	10/16	Fantastic Light ($3,634,859)	8,363,634
SADLER'S WELLS, 81, by Northern Dancer	Ire.	175,879	230	86	37/49	Galileo (Ire) ($2,233,580)	8,056,575
A.P. INDY, 89, by Seattle Slew	Ky.	325,000	123	70	8/11	Aptitude ($1,410,000)	6,745,452
DYNAFORMER, 85, by Roberto	Ky.	30,000	167	92	14/19	Starrer ($406,265)	6,191,996
FLY SO FREE, 88, by Time for a Change	Ky.	7,500	115	54	3/4	Captain Steve ($4,201,200)	5,742,141
BROAD BRUSH, 83, by Ack Ack	Ky.	100,000	132	75	7/17	Include ($1,435,400)	5,593,630
DEHERE, 91, by Deputy Minister	Jpn.	N/A	265	136	17/25	Take Charge Lady ($371,716)	5,488,244
CEE'S TIZZY, 87, by Relaunch	Ca.	15,000	77	46	9/15	Tiznow ($2,981,880)	5,263,777
END SWEEP, 91, by Forty Niner	Jpn.	17,738	184	115	7/10	Swept Overboard ($439,140)	5,183,490
UNBRIDLED, 87, by Fappiano	Dead		117	61	7/11	Exogenous ($901,500)	5,137,893
NUREYEV, 77, by Northern Dancer	Dead		90	52	17/24	Skimming ($1,330,000)	5,127,966
MT. LIVERMORE, 81, by Blushing Groom (Fr)	Ky.	50,000	184	101	7/9	Orientate ($293,700)	5,090,753
CARSON CITY, 87, by Mr. Prospector	Ky.	35,000	170	108	12/15	City Zip ($401,920)	5,085,185
ROYAL ACADEMY, 87, by Nijinsky II	Ky.	25,000	329	132	19/26	Val Royal (Fr) ($792,800)	4,976,058
ALLEN'S PROSPECT, 82, by Mr. Prospector	Md.	12,500	223	132	0/10	In C C's Honor ($165,297)	4,943,948
TWINING, 91, by Forty Niner	Ky.	N/A	155	95	9/13	Two Item Limit ($648,760)	4,866,345
PHONE TRICK, 82, by Clever Trick	N.Y.	30,000	190	100	4/6	Caller One ($1,436,380)	4,778,770
GULCH, 84, by Mr. Prospector	Ky.	60,000	166	77	10/21	Garcia Marquez ($614,668)	4,648,821
STORM CAT, 83, by Storm Bird	Ky.	400,000	128	69	14/18	Black Minnaloushe ($454,741)	4,619,840
WILD AGAIN, 80, by Icecapade	Ky.	60,000	146	79	6/13	Shine Again ($469,750)	4,428,830
COZZENE, 80, by Caro (Ire)	Ky.	60,000	138	70	8/11	Real Cozzy ($459,340)	4,417,384
CRAFTY PROSPECTOR, 79, by Mr. Prospector	Ky.	35,000	159	82	5/9	Agnes Digital ($1,307,640)	4,400,156
GILDED TIME, 90, by Timeless Moment	Ky.	20,000	190	99	9/11	Early Flyer ($300,660)	4,368,528
SALT LAKE, 89, by Deputy Minister	Ky.	20,000	202	116	9/14	Big Bambu ($215,129)	4,336,976
EL PRADO (Ire), 89, by Sadler's Wells	Ky.	30,000	161	88	12/16	El Prado Essence ($235,882)	4,277,993
SKY CLASSIC, 87, by Nijinsky II	Ky.	20,000	157	81	5/9	Stage Classic ($279,643)	4,200,023
WOODMAN, 83, by Mr. Prospector	Ky.	45,000	317	125	9/11	Illusioned ($335,726)	4,181,989
SEATTLE SLEW, 74, by Bold Reasoning	Ky.	150,000	80	32	8/12	Flute ($1,094,104)	4,169,330
NOTEBOOK, 85, by Well Decorated	Fl.	15,000	131	76	9/16	Delaware Township ($635,840)	4,164,083
THEATRICAL (Ire), 82, by Nureyev	Ky.	80,000	136	54	6/14	Hap ($919,070)	4,128,805
CURE THE BLUES, 78, by Stop the Music	Dead		158	91	8/10	Dat You Miz Blue ($273,865)	4,097,350
CRYPTOCLEARANCE, 84, by Fappiano	Ky.	20,000	197	98	5/7	Millennium Wind ($679,620)	4,073,461
DIXIE BRASS, 89, by Dixieland Band	N.Y.	10,000	123	75	9/11	Dixie Dot Com ($679,000)	4,051,577
UNBRIDLED'S SONG, 93, by Unbridled	Ky.	40,000	112	46	6/9	Unbridled Elaine ($1,663,175)	4,001,602
KRIS S., 77, by Roberto	Ky.	150,000	138	78	8/10	Sharp Performance ($279,780)	3,965,469
TOUR D'OR, 82, by Medaille d'Or	Fl.	10,000	118	77	6/8	Express Tour ($1,290,000)	3,965,466
BERTRANDO, 89, by Skywalker	Ca.	30,000	121	66	10/13	Officer ($740,010)	3,933,318
REGAL CLASSIC, 85, by Vice Regent	N.Y.	10,000	215	100	4/5	Bristol Pistol ($191,756)	3,926,026
BELONG TO ME, 89, by Danzig	Ky.	40,000	158	84	6/7	Winning Boy ($339,216)	3,878,061
MARIA'S MON, 93, by Wavering Monarch	Ky.	12,500	90	48	7/8	Monarchos ($1,711,600)	3,870,550
BLACK TIE AFFAIR (Ire), 86, by Miswaki	Jpn.	N/A	187	98	5/11	License Fee ($382,560)	3,865,818
HENNESSY, 93, by Storm Cat	Ky.	N/A	151	68	9/14	Johannesburg ($1,002,893)	3,850,177
NUMEROUS, 91, by Mr. Prospector	N.J.	7,500	196	103	10/18	Numerous Times ($676,320)	3,831,672
MACHIAVELLIAN, 87, by Mr. Prospector	Eng.	86,526	128	68	6/9	Medicean ($580,127)	3,811,437
GLITTERMAN, 85, by Dewan	Ky.	15,000	127	74	6/12	Balto Star ($848,820)	3,776,640
HOUSEBUSTER, 87, by Mt. Livermore	Va.	N/A	136	60	7/14	Electronic Unicorn ($841,436)	3,736,319
RUBIANO, 87, by Fappiano	Ky.	10,000	147	63	3/7	Burning Roma ($614,000)	3,731,912
DIXIELAND BAND, 80, by Northern Dancer	Ky.	75,000	161	81	7/8	Hook and Ladder ($256,100)	3,722,089
TABASCO CAT, 91, by Storm Cat	Jpn.	N/A	123	70	9/12	Habibti ($393,000)	3,709,431
GO FOR GIN, 91, by Cormorant	Ky.	12,500	65	36	3/6	Albert the Great ($1,740,000)	3,672,354
LORD AT WAR (Arg), 80, by General (Fr)	Dead		90	52	8/14	Trip ($345,855)	3,651,592
MARQUETRY, 87, by Conquistador Cielo	Ky.	15,000	177	85	5/7	Squirtle Squirt ($817,720)	3,650,197
MR. PROSPECTOR, 70, by Raise a Native	Dead		76	30	6/8	Dancethruthedawn ($1,045,039)	3,622,996
SUNDAY SILENCE, 86, by Halo	Jpn.	N/A	380	181	20/25	Stay Gold ($2,225,600)	3,621,241
NOT FOR LOVE, 90, by Mr. Prospector	Md.	10,000	99	63	5/7	Duckhorn ($453,760)	3,614,809
HOLY BULL, 91, by Great Above	Ky.	25,000	134	60	7/10	Macho Uno ($563,400)	3,604,146
CAERLEON, 80, by Nijinsky II	Dead		187	75	17/23	Bach (Ire) ($449,666)	3,602,449
QUIET AMERICAN, 86, by Fappiano	Ky.	35,000	132	72	3/7	Irving's Baby ($599,262)	3,574,748

Leading North American Sires
by Progeny Earnings in 2001

Earnings in North America only for stallions who stand or last stood in North America or had 25 North American starters in 2001.

Sire, Where stands	Strs	Wnrs	SWs	Leading earner (earnings)	Progeny earnings
Thunder Gulch, Ky.	93	51	7	Point Given ($3,350,000)	$7,700,425
Dynaformer, Ky.	142	84	12	Starrer ($406,265)	5,800,760
A.P. Indy, Ky.	98	53	7	Aptitude ($1,290,000)	5,793,383
Broad Brush, Ky.	127	71	5	Include ($1,435,400)	5,577,384
Rahy, Ky.	92	49	6	Fantastic Light ($2,112,800)	5,296,384
Cee's Tizzy, Ca.	77	46	9	Tiznow ($2,981,880)	5,263,777
End Sweep, Jpn.	173	107	7	Swept Overboard ($439,140)	5,170,966
Unbridled, Dead	107	58	6	Exogenous ($901,500)	4,956,553
Carson City, Ky.	159	104	10	City Zip ($401,920)	4,946,753
Allen's Prospect, Md.	222	132	10	In C C's Honor ($165,297)	4,934,015
Mt. Livermore, Ky.	155	89	7	Orientate ($293,700)	4,836,921
Twining, Ky.	145	91	9	Two Item Limit ($648,760)	4,704,894
Dehere, Jpn.	148	91	9	Take Charge Lady ($371,716)	4,552,809
Wild Again, Ky.	132	73	5	Shine Again ($469,750)	4,319,683
Salt Lake, Ky.	184	107	8	Big Bambu ($215,129)	4,264,125
El Prado (Ire), Ky.	151	85	12	El Prado Essence ($235,882)	4,229,454
Gilded Time, Ky.	178	94	9	Early Flyer ($300,660)	4,217,053
Notebook, Fl.	125	73	9	Delaware Township ($635,840)	4,118,278
Dixie Brass, Dead	123	75	9	Dixie Dot Com ($679,000)	4,095,377
Cozzene, Ky.	98	54	8	Real Cozzy ($459,340)	4,056,929
Cure the Blues, Dead	154	89	8	Dat You Miz Blue ($273,865)	4,016,766
Seattle Slew, Dead	61	27	7	Flute ($1,094,104)	4,015,890
Cryptoclearance, Ky.	188	95	5	Millennium Wind ($679,620)	3,987,107
Sky Classic, Ky.	140	72	4	Stage Classic ($279,643)	3,916,946
Bertrando, Ca.	120	66	10	Officer ($740,010)	3,888,258
Black Tie Affair (Ire), Jpn.	141	87	5	License Fee ($382,560)	3,857,493
Maria's Mon, Ky.	88	46	7	Monarchos ($1,711,600)	3,855,325
Unbridled's Song, Ky.	61	32	5	Unbridled Elaine ($1,663,175)	3,818,984
Storm Cat, Ky.	103	54	11	Saudi Poetry ($418,080)	3,791,105
Glitterman, Ky.	123	72	6	Balto Star ($848,820)	3,774,022
Kris S., Dead	110	63	6	Sharp Performance ($279,780)	3,742,055
Regal Classic, N.Y.	143	74	4	Bristol Pistol ($191,756)	3,703,526
Theatrical (Ire), Ky.	87	34	6	Hap ($919,070)	3,683,712
Not For Love, Md.	98	62	5	Duckhorn ($453,760)	3,616,959
Marquetry, Ky.	172	84	5	Squirtle Squirt ($817,720)	3,592,274
Holy Bull, Ky.	126	58	7	Macho Uno ($563,400)	3,570,914
Tabasco Cat, Jpn.	106	60	8	Habibti ($393,000)	3,531,987
Belong to Me, Ky.	147	81	6	I'm All Yours ($203,810)	3,506,762
Lord At War (Arg), Dead	85	50	8	Trip ($345,855)	3,506,206
Montbrook, Fl.	91	64	10	Outofthebox ($607,995)	3,505,081
Rubiano, Ky.	128	78	3	Burning Roma ($614,000)	3,473,408
Beau Genius, Ca.	145	90	7	Takin It Deep ($197,362)	3,468,058
Go for Gin, Ky.	64	36	3	Albert the Great ($1,740,000)	3,467,779
Personal Flag, N.Y.	128	73	4	Say Florida Sandy ($615,420)	3,421,360
Quiet American, Ky.	124	66	3	Irving's Baby ($599,262)	3,420,572
Runaway Groom, Ky.	176	91	6	Fajardo ($139,174)	3,411,119
Phone Trick, N.Y.	171	92	3	Caller One ($236,380)	3,392,728
Numerous, N.J.	121	67	3	Numerous Times ($676,320)	3,364,739
Two Punch, Md.	158	80	7	Marciano ($208,060)	3,352,808
With Approval, Ky.	147	80	5	Allende ($251,532)	3,335,320
Mr. Greeley, Ky.	134	70	4	Fan Club's Mister ($362,610)	3,306,169
French Deputy, Jpn.	100	63	6	Left Bank ($524,200)	3,299,069
Polish Numbers, Md.	137	79	6	One Eyed Joker ($240,750)	3,294,881
Nureyev, Dead	30	19	8	Skimming ($1,330,000)	3,268,586
Meadowlake, Ky.	139	73	5	Collect Call ($338,820)	3,254,661
Devil His Due, Ky.	147	77	3	This Fleet Is Due ($193,100)	3,233,545
Mr. Prospector, Dead	45	20	6	Dancethruthedawn ($1,045,039)	3,226,776
Dixieland Band, Ky.	131	67	6	Hook and Ladder ($256,100)	3,214,627
In Excess (Ire), Ca.	103	53	8	Romanceishope ($529,410)	3,210,377
Robyn Dancer, Fl.	156	94	4	Superduper Miss ($199,583)	3,199,125
Forest Wildcat, Ky.	78	43	8	Snow Dance ($403,900)	3,115,455
Seeking the Gold, Ky.	72	36	8	Dream Supreme ($541,120)	3,114,371
Gulch, Ky.	97	53	5	Nasty Storm ($383,338)	3,107,398
Diablo, Jpn.	133	89	4	Exciting Story ($596,667)	3,094,785
Crafty Prospector, Ky.	138	74	4	Crafty C. T. ($309,770)	3,085,989

Leading North American Sires
by Average Earnings per Runner in 2001

Sire	Strs	Wnrs	Average
Nureyev	30	19	$108,953
Thunder Gulch	93	51	82,800
Mr. Prospector	45	20	71,706
Cee's Tizzy	77	46	68,361
Seattle Slew	61	27	65,834
Pick Up the Phone	28	19	64,185
Unbridled's Song	61	32	62,606
El Gran Senor	31	18	60,093
A.P. Indy	98	53	59,116
Rahy	92	49	57,569
Go for Gin	64	36	54,184
Hansel	45	20	48,061
Unbridled	107	58	46,323
Caerleon	28	10	46,243
Irish River (Fr)	47	22	46,033
Mutakddim	44	31	45,764
Eagle Eyed	27	19	44,675
Royal Academy	44	22	44,061
Broad Brush	127	71	43,916
Maria's Mon	88	46	43,811
Seeking the Gold	72	36	43,255
Theatrical (Ire)	87	34	42,342

Leading North American Sires
by Median Earnings per Runner in 2001

Sire	Strs	Wnrs	Median
Virginia Rapids	47	33	$26,700
Nureyev	30	19	23,900
Mutakddim	44	31	23,838
Not For Love	98	62	22,648
Henbane	25	16	20,590
Bold Executive	79	42	20,540
Rizzi	77	56	20,461
Danzig	42	26	20,148
French Deputy	100	63	19,745
Lord At War (Arg)	85	50	19,732
Storm Cat	103	54	19,710
Unaccounted For	73	50	19,290
Matter of Honor	48	28	18,988
A.P. Indy	98	53	18,933
Strodes Creek	46	32	18,918
Eastover Court	32	17	18,603
Unbridled	107	58	18,371
Roy	59	37	18,368
Carson City	159	104	18,100
Frosty the Snowman	31	22	18,010
Tethra	26	16	18,001
American Chance	61	40	17,970

Leading North American Sires
by Number of Winners in 2001

Sire	Strs	Wnrs	Wnrs/ Strs %
Allen's Prospect	222	132	59.5%
End Sweep	173	107	61.8%
Salt Lake	184	107	58.2%
Carson City	159	104	65.4%
West by West	156	99	63.5%
Cryptoclearance	188	95	50.5%
Gilded Time	178	94	52.8%
Fortunate Prospect	156	94	60.3%
Robyn Dancer	156	94	60.3%
Phone Trick	171	92	53.8%
Dehere	148	91	61.5%
Twining	145	91	62.8%
Runaway Groom	176	91	51.7%
Beau Genius	145	90	62.1%
Diablo	133	89	66.9%
Cure the Blues	154	89	57.8%
Mt. Livermore	155	89	57.4%
Black Tie Affair (Ire)	141	87	61.7%
Flying Continental	153	87	56.9%
El Prado (Ire)	151	85	56.3%

Leading North American Sires
by Number of Wins in 2001

Sire	Strs	Wnrs	Wins
Allen's Prospect	222	132	256
End Sweep	173	107	209
Carson City	159	104	207
Salt Lake	184	107	196
Cryptoclearance	188	95	182
Beau Genius	145	90	182
Robyn Dancer	156	94	181
Twining	145	91	178
Diablo	133	89	174
Gilded Time	178	94	173
Runaway Groom	176	91	172
Notebook	125	73	171
Fortunate Prospect	156	94	170
West by West	156	99	167
Black Tie Affair (Ire)	141	87	165
El Prado (Ire)	151	85	161
Glitterman	123	72	158
Dynaformer	142	84	157
Mt. Livermore	155	89	156
Press Card	149	78	155
Dehere	148	91	154
Flying Continental	153	87	153
With Approval	147	80	152
Cure the Blues	154	89	152

Leading North American Sires
by Number of Stakes Winners in 2001

Sire	Strs	Wnrs	SWs
Dynaformer	142	84	12
El Prado (Ire)	151	85	12
Storm Cat	103	54	11
Montbrook	91	64	10
Carson City	159	104	10
Allen's Prospect	222	132	10
Bertrando	120	66	10
Dehere	148	91	9
Notebook	125	73	9
Gilded Time	178	94	9
Cee's Tizzy	77	46	9
Twining	145	91	9
Lord At War (Arg)	85	50	8
Forest Wildcat	78	43	8
Tabasco Cat	106	60	8
Nureyev	30	19	8
Dixie Brass	123	75	8
Seeking the Gold	72	36	8
Cure the Blues	154	89	8
Salt Lake	184	107	8
Cozzene	98	54	8
In Excess (Ire)	103	53	8

Leading North American Sires
by Number of Graded Stakes Winners in 2001

Sire	Strs	Wnrs	GSWs
Cozzene	98	54	6
Kris S.	110	63	5
Storm Cat	103	54	5
Seattle Slew	61	27	5
Nureyev	30	19	5
Theatrical (Ire)	87	34	5
Seeking the Gold	72	36	5
Lord At War (Arg)	85	50	4
Forest Wildcat	78	43	4
Tabasco Cat	106	60	4
French Deputy	100	63	4
Dynaformer	142	84	4
Honor Grades	115	67	4
Thunder Gulch	93	51	4
Hennessy	97	46	4
Unbridled	107	58	4
Holy Bull	126	58	4
Wild Again	132	73	4
Twining	145	91	4
A.P. Indy	98	53	4

Leading Worldwide Sires
by Progeny Earnings in 2001

Worldwide earnings for stallions with one North American starter in 2001.

Sire, Where stands	Strs	Wnrs	SWs	Leading earner (earnings)	Progeny earnings
Sunday Silence, Jpn.	381	181	20	Stay Gold ($3,238,753)	$57,449,026
Danehill, Ire.	455	213	48	Air Eminem ($1,759,044)	22,968,174
Afleet, Jpn.	214	100	5	Preeminence ($1,119,761)	17,778,145
French Deputy, Jpn.	110	69	8	Kurofune ($2,801,914)	9,387,761
Rahy, Ky.	142	69	10	Fantastic Light ($3,634,859)	9,282,193
Broad Brush, Ky.	132	75	7	Nobo True ($1,840,750)	8,997,754
Thunder Gulch, Ky.	190	85	14	Point Given ($3,350,000)	8,906,581
Caerleon, Dead	191	82	17	Zenno El Cid ($1,362,724)	8,707,474
Royal Academy, Ky.	367	156	19	Val Royal (Fr) ($792,800)	8,698,029
Forty Niner, Jpn.	128	61	0	Toho Daio ($492,139)	8,471,823
Sadler's Wells, Ire.	231	86	37	Galileo (Ire) ($2,233,580)	8,101,809
Crafty Prospector, Ky.	159	82	5	Agnes Digital ($3,341,517)	7,913,282
Nureyev, Dead	90	52	17	Black Hawk (GB) ($1,412,216)	7,746,336
Woodman, Ky.	346	138	10	Raise Suzuran ($687,842)	7,719,471
A.P. Indy, Ky.	123	70	8	Aptitude ($1,410,000)	7,689,823
Kingmambo, Ky.	126	64	14	American Boss ($1,677,417)	7,597,291
End Sweep, Jpn.	184	115	7	South Vigorous ($752,481)	7,217,663
Last Tycoon (Ire), Jpn.	280	96	10	Sadamu Blue Sky ($347,574)	7,022,070
Dehere, Jpn	269	144	17	Defier ($442,578)	6,981,847
Cozzene, Ky.	138	70	8	God of Chance ($585,893)	6,781,397
Dynaformer, Ky.	167	92	14	Starrer ($406,265)	6,256,811
Fly So Free, Ky.	115	54	3	Captain Steve ($4,201,200)	5,938,893
Unbridled, Dead	117	61	7	Exogenous ($901,500)	5,855,229
Storm Cat, Ky.	128	69	14	Gaily Egret ($719,253)	5,691,300
Gulch, Ky.	166	77	10	Garcia Marquez ($614,668)	5,585,598
Mt. Livermore, Ky.	184	101	7	Orientate ($293,700)	5,551,981
Carson City, Ky.	170	109	12	City Zip ($401,920)	5,313,649
Seeking the Gold, Ky.	111	51	10	Dream Supreme ($541,120)	5,289,524
Cee's Tizzy, Ca.	77	46	9	Tiznow ($2,981,880)	5,263,777
Salt Lake, Ky.	202	115	9	Keiai Cheyenne ($256,835)	5,193,347
Phone Trick, N.Y.	192	102	4	Caller One ($1,436,380)	5,123,829
Hennessy, Ky.	156	70	9	Johannesburg ($1,002,893)	5,005,665
Black Tie Affair (Ire), Jpn.	187	98	5	License Fee ($382,560)	4,998,395
Allen's Prospect, Md.	223	132	10	In C C's Honor ($165,297)	4,944,848
Wild Again, Ky.	146	79	6	Shine Again ($469,750)	4,940,963
Twining, Ky.	155	95	9	Two Item Limit ($648,760)	4,880,105
Theatrical (Ire), Ky.	136	54	6	Hap ($919,070)	4,824,642
Tabasco Cat, Jpn.	123	70	9	Megere ($525,917)	4,777,045
Ogygian, Jpn.	109	34	1	Fujino Condor ($440,210)	4,748,601
Lammtarra, Jpn.	99	34	1	Meisho Ramses ($531,800)	4,721,506
Seattle Slew, Dead	80	32	8	Flute ($1,094,104)	4,699,762
Jolie's Halo, Jpn.	147	57	5	Agnes Storm ($300,772)	4,668,893
Unbridled's Song, Ky.	113	46	6	Unbridled Elaine ($1,663,175)	4,646,251
Dixieland Band, Ky.	161	81	7	Monte Carlo ($499,458)	4,628,656
Gilded Time, Ky.	190	99	9	Early Flyer ($300,660)	4,577,373
Miswaki, Ky.	138	64	6	Taiki Treasure ($1,135,788)	4,445,316
Gone West, Ky.	167	81	12	Scoop ($280,270)	4,436,258
Danzig, Ky.	94	53	12	Magnaten ($930,322)	4,396,581
Cure the Blues, Dead	158	91	8	Soushun ($289,574)	4,386,924
Southern Halo, Ky.	235	124	16	Miss Linda (Arg) ($455,415)	4,327,276
Sky Classic, Ky.	158	82	5	Stage Classic ($279,643)	4,305,462
El Prado (Ire), Ky.	161	88	12	El Prado Essence ($235,882)	4,277,993
Warning (GB), Dead	128	53	7	Calstone Light O ($785,679)	4,254,920
Rubiano, Ky.	147	83	3	Burning Roma ($614,000)	4,235,251
Green Desert, Eng.	118	55	11	Mejiro Darling ($1,111,949)	4,223,582
Conquistador Cielo, Ky.	121	59	5	Neopolis ($525,658)	4,222,146
Kris S., Dead	138	78	8	Sharp Performance ($279,780)	4,208,891
Notebook, Fl.	131	76	9	Delaware Township ($635,840)	4,173,251
Bigstone (Ire), Vic.	165	64	4	Meisho Doto ($2,725,887)	4,169,173
Housebuster, Va.	137	62	7	Electronic Unicorn ($841,436)	4,157,361
Regal Classic, N.Y.	227	116	4	Bristol Pistol ($191,756)	4,147,645
Mr. Prospector, Dead	76	30	6	Dancethruthedawn ($1,045,039)	4,141,524
Dixie Brass, Dead	123	75	10	Dixie Dot Com ($679,000)	4,095,377
Cryptoclearance, Ky.	197	98	5	Millennium Wind ($679,620)	4,074,361
Meadowlake, Ky.	149	77	6	Siberian Meadow ($453,084)	4,052,344

Leading Worldwide Sires by Average Earnings per Runner in 2001

Sire	Strs	Wnrs	Average
Sunday Silence	381	181	$150,785
Nureyev	90	52	86,070
French Deputy	110	69	85,343
Afleet	214	100	83,075
Bahri	38	13	70,547
Cee's Tizzy	77	46	68,361
Broad Brush	132	75	68,165
Forty Niner	128	61	66,186
Rahy	142	69	65,368
Pick Up the Phone	28	19	64,185
A.P. Indy	123	70	62,519
Kingmambo	125	62	60,583
Seattle Slew	80	32	58,747
Go for Gin	65	36	56,498
Mr. Prospector	76	30	54,494
Fly So Free	115	54	51,643
Danehill	453	210	50,284
Unbridled	117	61	50,045
Crafty Prospector	159	82	49,769
Cozzene	138	70	49,141
Lammtarra	99	34	47,692
Seeking the Gold	111	51	47,653

Leading Worldwide Sires by Median Earnings per Runner in 2001

Sire	Strs	Wnrs	Median
Sunday Silence	381	181	$59,822
Afleet	214	100	33,498
Forty Niner	128	61	32,885
Virginia Rapids	48	33	24,889
Not For Love	99	63	22,840
French Deputy	110	69	20,667
Henbane	25	16	20,590
Rizzi	81	58	20,461
Bold Executive	80	42	19,305
Unaccounted For	76	51	19,245
Matter of Honor	48	28	18,988
End Sweep	184	115	18,923
Eastover Court	32	17	18,603
Strodes Creek	47	32	18,600
American Chance	62	41	18,533
Carson City	170	109	18,103
Frosty the Snowman	31	22	18,010
Tethra	26	16	18,001
Valid Appeal	65	40	18,000
Danzig	94	53	17,699
Wheaton	64	40	17,599
Summer Squall	95	53	17,540

Leading Worldwide Sires by Number of Winners in 2001

Sire	Strs	Wnrs	Wnrs/ Strs %
Danehill	453	210	46.4%
Sunday Silence	381	181	47.5%
Royal Academy	367	156	42.5%
Dehere	269	144	53.5%
Night Shift	283	133	47.0%
Allen's Prospect	223	132	59.2%
Woodman	324	127	39.2%
Southern Halo	235	124	52.8%
Brief Truce	274	117	42.7%
End Sweep	184	115	62.5%
Salt Lake	202	115	56.9%
Carson City	170	109	64.1%
Numerous	200	106	53.0%
West by West	161	102	63.4%
Mt. Livermore	184	101	54.9%
Afleet	214	100	46.7%
Regal Classic	215	100	46.5%
Geiger Counter	209	100	47.8%
Gilded Time	190	99	52.1%
Phone Trick	191	99	51.8%
Black Tie Affair (Ire)	187	98	52.4%
Cryptoclearance	197	98	49.7%

Leading Worldwide Sires by Number of Wins in 2001

Sire	Strs	Wnrs	Wins
Danehill	453	210	347
Sunday Silence	381	181	265
Allen's Prospect	223	132	256
Dehere	269	144	226
End Sweep	184	115	225
Royal Academy	367	156	222
Carson City	170	109	214
Salt Lake	202	115	207
Night Shift	283	133	201
Brief Truce	274	117	195
Geiger Counter	209	100	193
Cryptoclearance	197	98	189
Beau Genius	152	94	189
Southern Halo	235	124	186
Twining	155	95	185
Numerous	200	106	184
Woodman	324	127	183
Robyn Dancer	157	94	181
Diablo	137	91	180
Gilded Time	190	99	179
Notebook	131	76	178
Black Tie Affair (Ire)	187	98	176
Runaway Groom	183	92	174

Leading Worldwide Sires by Number of Stakes Winners in 2001

Sire	Strs	Wnrs	SWs
Danehill	453	210	48
Sadler's Wells	231	86	37
Sunday Silence	381	181	20
Royal Academy	367	156	19
Zabeel	136	49	18
Roy	123	73	18
Dehere	269	144	17
Caerleon	191	82	17
Nureyev	90	52	17
Southern Halo	235	124	16
Rainbow Quest	115	52	15
In the Wings (GB)	85	39	14
Thunder Gulch	190	85	14
Kingmambo	125	62	14
Storm Cat	128	69	14
Dynaformer	167	92	14
Barathea (Ire)	233	88	13

Leading Worldwide Sires by Number of Graded/Group Stakes Winners in 2001

Sire	Strs	Wnrs	GSWs
Danehill	453	210	28
Sadler's Wells	231	86	19
Roy	123	73	14
Southern Halo	235	124	13
Zabeel	136	49	12
Nureyev	90	52	10
Darshaan	125	57	9
Royal Academy	367	156	9
Caerleon	191	82	9
Hussonet	8	4	8
Danzig	94	53	8
Thunder Gulch	190	85	7
Fort Wood	1		7
Grand Lodge	239	93	7
Storm Cat	128	69	7
Rainbow Quest	115	52	7
Seattle Slew	80	32	6
Last Tycoon (Ire)	280	96	6
In the Wings (GB)	85	39	6
Numerous	200	106	6
Dehere	269	144	6
Cozzene	138	70	6
Lode	94	49	6
Gone West	167	81	6
Seeking the Gold	111	51	6

Leading Juvenile Sires
by North American Progeny Earnings in 2001

Earnings in North America only for stallions who stand or last stood in North America or had ten North American starters in 2001.

Sire, Where stands	Strs	Wnrs	SWs	Leading earner (earnings)	Progeny earnings
Valid Expectations, Tx.	49	27	3	Expected Program ($120,240)	$1,397,911
Judge T C, Pa.	64	26	3	Lady Shari ($276,210)	1,319,907
Dehere, Jpn.	33	21	4	Take Charge Lady ($371,716)	1,235,550
Hennessy, Ky.	40	16	3	Johannesburg ($520,000)	1,217,337
A.P. Indy, Ky.	20	8	2	Tempera ($670,240)	1,196,281
Open Forum, Tx.	45	20	3	Jealous Forum ($183,865)	1,072,687
Smoke Glacken, Ky.	44	19	3	Smok'n Frolic ($342,744)	1,048,867
End Sweep, Jpn.	59	28	2	Al Max Diner ($104,500)	962,162
Siphon (Brz), Ky.	20	6	1	Siphonic ($703,978)	895,148
Bertrando, Ca.	14	3	2	Officer ($740,010)	834,908
Golden Gear, Fl.	31	14	2	Ginger Gold ($362,339)	832,290
Foxhound, Eng.	34	20	3	Shesastonecoldfox ($196,320)	828,240
Montbrook, Fl.	31	20	2	Ms Brookski ($248,060)	824,765
You and I, Ky.	18	7	3	You ($540,440)	747,070
French Deputy, Jpn.	29	16	2	Bella Bellucci ($208,555)	734,758
Notebook, Fl.	21	12	2	Booklet ($339,700)	721,745
Twining, Ky.	43	19	1	Cloudy Mist ($92,666)	716,435
Out of Place, Ky.	33	17	1	Fonz's ($193,740)	694,943
Capote, Ky.	34	14	2	Hunter Cruise ($83,949)	692,921
Carson City, Ky.	31	14	3	Leelanau ($126,077)	691,308
Louis Quatorze, Ky.	40	9	1	Repent ($415,660)	681,908
Is It True, Fl.	28	16	3	Juggernaut ($138,180)	679,480
Salt Lake, Ky.	39	17	2	Lakeside Cup ($151,445)	677,072
Storm Cat, Ky.	24	12	2	Stylelistick ($121,046)	659,900
Langfuhr, Ky.	36	12	0	Imperial Gesture ($275,540)	635,660
Honour and Glory, Ky.	26	12	1	Playing 'n Gold ($150,730)	625,439
Two Punch, Md.	35	10	2	Heavyweight Champ ($149,258)	619,430
Silver Ghost, Ky.	27	11	2	Ghost Queen ($146,533)	618,370
Gone West, Ky.	11	5	2	Came Home ($211,440)	617,944
Gilded Time, Ky.	30	8	2	Interminable Gold ($120,677)	598,853
Kissin Kris, Fl.	13	8	2	Blissful Kiss ($336,780)	591,442
Phone Trick, N.Y.	39	19	0	Playing Games ($69,745)	587,769
Service Stripe, Ky.	5	3	2	Cashier's Dream ($353,230)	584,067
Tabasco Cat, Jpn.	25	8	2	Habibti ($393,000)	580,247
Bag, Dead	32	15	3	Hail to Bag ($175,395)	561,734
Saint Ballado, Ky.	25	11	0	Kathy K D ($81,309)	560,477
Wild Again, Ky.	25	13	1	Atlantic Fury ($161,390)	553,448
Pulpit, Ky.	21	9	1	Essence of Dubai ($193,200)	550,246
Wild Zone, Tx.	36	13	0	North Brooklyn ($89,779)	538,676
Helmsman, Ca.	23	9	1	Rare Friends ($247,365)	528,317
High Brite, Ca.	27	10	2	Britetonzmyday ($168,890)	527,974
Mecke, Fl.	17	12	2	Mountain Rage ($154,770)	508,965
El Prado (Ire), Ky.	32	11	2	El Soprano ($194,834)	502,534
Fortunate Prospect, Fl.	34	17	1	Bold World ($81,360)	484,807
Allen's Prospect, Md.	29	9	3	Square Cut Diamond ($124,714)	480,187
Forest Wildcat, Ky.	30	8	1	Forest Heiress ($210,787)	472,917
Mutakddim, Ky.	11	6	2	Miss Noire ($201,711)	472,127
Unbridled, Dead	19	5	2	Belterra ($192,359)	469,649
Lost Soldier, Fl.	32	11	1	Lush Soldier ($148,618)	460,983
Mr. Greeley, Ky.	47	13	0	Tepu Sultan ($48,968)	459,099
Devil His Due, Ky.	40	15	2	Pemaquid Point ($87,164)	457,292
Regal Classic, N.Y.	24	8	2	Tails of the Crypt ($145,192)	455,711
Friendly Lover, Fl.	25	10	2	Jade Eyed ($128,255)	444,820
Bold Executive, On.	16	4	1	Streakin Rob ($239,753)	442,909
In Excess (Ire), Ca.	18	10	2	Ayanna ($145,750)	427,134
Tejano Run, Ky.	21	7	2	Shaws Creek ($155,748)	416,033
Dynaformer, Ky.	20	6	2	Riskaverse ($202,750)	415,033
Take Me Out, N.Y.	18	8	2	Never Out ($123,963)	413,015
Birdonthewire, Fl.	20	10	2	O'Rocky ($171,890)	412,800
Matty G, Ky.	26	13	1	Mayakovsky ($64,600)	409,031
Ide, Ky.	29	11	1	Big Ide ($53,010)	406,202
Polish Numbers, Md.	21	8	2	Roman Dancer ($101,940)	404,220
Meadowlake, Ky.	27	12	0	Cottonwood Cowboy ($48,340)	403,488
Williamstown, N.Y.	39	11	1	Vinemeister ($74,900)	402,173
Avenue of Flags, Ca.	24	10	1	Danceoftheflags ($66,820)	399,575

Leading North American Juvenile Sires by Average Earnings per Runner in 2001

Sire	Strs	Wnrs	Average
A.P. Indy	20	8	$59,814
Bertrando	14	3	59,636
Gone West	11	5	56,177
Kissin Kris	13	8	45,496
Siphon (Brz)	20	6	44,757
Mutakddim	11	7	44,542
You and I	18	7	41,504
Dehere	33	21	37,441
Notebook	21	12	34,369
Hennessy	40	16	30,433
Tethra	13	6	30,053
Mecke	17	12	29,939
Valid Expectations	49	27	28,529
Bold Executive	16	4	27,682
Storm Cat	24	12	27,496
Golden Gear	31	14	26,848
Montbrook	31	20	26,605
Pulpit	21	9	26,202
Mercer Mill	13	5	26,134
French Deputy	29	16	25,336
All Gone	13	9	25,059
Unbridled	19	5	24,718

Leading North American Juvenile Sires by Median Earnings per Runner in 2001

Sire	Strs	Wnrs	Median
Storm Cat	24	12	$27,198
Gone West	11	5	25,200
Mutakddim	11	7	23,442
Dehere	33	21	21,500
Mecke	17	12	21,135
Outflanker	19	11	17,575
Matter of Honor	11	5	17,041
Kissin Kris	13	8	16,280
Valid Expectations	49	27	16,230
Rizzi	11	8	15,600
Is It True	28	16	13,320
Meadowlake	27	12	13,230
Notebook	21	12	13,170
Honour and Glory	26	12	12,605
Cherokee Run	20	11	12,522
Valid Wager	23	13	12,496
Montbrook	31	20	12,250
Avenue of Flags	24	10	11,939
Colony Light	11	6	11,909
Foxhound	34	20	11,460
Native Regent	14	7	11,365
Saint Ballado	25	11	11,320

Leading North American Juvenile Sires by Number of Winners in 2001

Sire	Strs	Wnrs	Wnrs/ Strs %
End Sweep	59	28	47.5%
Valid Expectations	49	27	55.1%
Judge T C	64	26	40.6%
Dehere	33	21	63.6%
Open Forum	45	20	44.4%
Montbrook	31	20	64.5%
Foxhound	34	20	58.8%
Phone Trick	39	19	48.7%
Smoke Glacken	44	19	43.2%
Twining	43	19	44.2%
Fortunate Prospect	34	17	50.0%
Salt Lake	39	17	43.6%
Out of Place	33	17	51.5%
Hennessy	40	16	40.0%
French Deputy	29	16	55.2%
Is It True	28	16	57.1%
Jeblar	32	15	46.9%
Devil His Due	40	15	37.5%
Bag	32	15	46.9%
Vying Victor	28	14	50.0%

Leading North American Juvenile Sires by Number of Wins in 2001

Sire	Strs	Wnrs	Wins
Valid Expectations	49	27	40
End Sweep	59	28	40
Judge T C	64	26	38
Twining	43	19	30
Dehere	33	21	29
Open Forum	45	20	28
Montbrook	31	20	28
Foxhound	34	20	28
Salt Lake	39	17	27
Smoke Glacken	44	19	26
Bag	32	15	24
Is It True	28	16	24
Phone Trick	39	19	22
Fortunate Prospect	34	17	21
Devil His Due	40	15	21
Golden Gear	31	14	21
French Deputy	29	16	21
Carson City	31	14	21
Line In The Sand	24	13	20
Wild Zone	36	13	20
Valid Wager	23	13	20
Out of Place	33	17	20

Leading North American Juvenile Sires by Number of Stakes Winners in 2001

Sire	Strs	Wnrs	SWs
Dehere	33	21	4
Allen's Prospect	29	9	3
Hennessy	40	16	3
Valid Expectations	49	27	3
Smoke Glacken	44	19	3
Open Forum	45	20	3
Sepoy (Arg)	5	4	3
Bengal Bay	5	4	3
Bag	32	15	3
You and I	18	7	3
Foxhound	34	20	3
Judge T C	64	26	3
Is It True	28	16	3
Carson City	31	14	3

Leading North American Juvenile Sires by Number of Graded Stakes Winners in 2001

Sire	Strs	Wnrs	GSWs
Gone West	11	5	2
Hennessy	40	16	2
A.P. Indy	20	8	2
Unbridled	19	5	2
Gulch	20	6	1
Louis Quatorze	40	9	1
Illinois Storm	9	1	1
Smoke Glacken	44	19	1
Pulpit	21	9	1
Mercer Mill	13	5	1
El Prado (Ire)	32	11	1
Siphon (Brz)	20	6	1
Harlan	6	4	1
Bertrando	14	3	1
Montbrook	31	20	1
Migrating Moon	15	6	1
Lost Soldier	32	11	1
Not For Love	17	9	1
You and I	18	7	1
Service Stripe	5	3	1
Golden Gear	31	14	1
Dehere	33	21	1
Delineator	5	3	1
Forest Wildcat	30	8	1
Judge T C	64	26	1
Tabasco Cat	25	8	1
French Deputy	29	16	1
Petionville	25	8	1
Mecke	17	12	1
Carson City	31	14	1
Housebuster	26	10	1
Out of Place	33	17	1

Leading Worldwide Juvenile Sires
by Progeny Earnings in 2001

Worldwide earnings for stallions with one two-year-old North American starter in 2001.

Sire, Where stands	Strs	Wnrs	SWs	Leading earner (earnings)	Progeny earnings
Hennessy, Ky.	55	20	4	Johannesburg ($1,002,893)	$1,834,102
Valid Expectations, Tx.	49	27	3	Expected Program ($120,240)	1,397,911
A.P. Indy, Ky.	27	14	2	Tempera ($670,240)	1,341,798
Dehere, Ky.	47	24	8	Take Charge Lady ($371,716)	1,340,477
Sadler's Wells, Ire.	63	17	8	Gossamer ($213,463)	1,325,583
Judge T C, Pa.	64	26	3	Lady Shari ($276,210)	1,319,907
Gone West, Ky.	30	17	4	Came Home ($211,440)	1,138,096
End Sweep, Jpn.	63	31	2	Al Max Diner ($104,500)	1,116,894
Smoke Glacken, Ky.	45	19	3	Smok'n Frolic ($342,744)	1,084,836
Open Forum, Tx.	45	20	3	Jealous Forum ($183,865)	1,072,687
Royal Academy, Ky.	77	16	5	Bel Esprit ($536,130)	1,016,108
Unbridled's Song, Ky.	29	10	1	Agnes Sonic ($519,572)	962,963
Forty Niner, Ky.	19	10	0	Meiner Select ($203,843)	936,040
Honour and Glory, Ky.	36	15	2	Silver Pallet ($158,317)	926,882
Saint Ballado, Ky.	32	14	0	Kite Hill Wind ($136,580)	918,176
Siphon (Brz), Ky.	21	7	1	Siphonic ($703,978)	910,697
Golden Gear, Fl.	32	14	2	Ginger Gold ($362,339)	882,406
Storm Cat, Ky.	29	15	2	Sophisticat ($160,772)	870,028
Meadowlake, Ky.	29	13	1	Siberian Meadow ($453,084)	856,572
Foxhound, Eng.	41	21	3	Shesastonecoldfox ($196,320)	851,006
Bertrando, Ca.	14	3	2	Officer ($740,010)	834,908
Montbrook, Fl.	31	20	2	Ms Brookski ($248,060)	824,765
Boston Harbor, Jpn.	27	12	1	Cafe Bostonian ($183,752)	816,373
Louis Quatorze, Ky.	45	11	1	Repent ($415,660)	813,516
Salt Lake, Ky.	42	18	3	Lakeside Cup ($151,445)	781,771
Silver Ghost, Ky.	29	12	2	Ghost Suzuka ($162,855)	781,225
Carson City, Ky.	34	17	3	Leelanau ($126,077)	768,893
French Deputy, Jpn.	31	17	2	Bella Bellucci ($208,555)	761,862
Pulpit, Ky.	23	10	1	Grandson ($206,172)	756,418
You and I, Ky.	18	7	3	You ($540,440)	747,070
Capote, Ky.	35	15	2	Hunter Cruise ($83,949)	742,295
Notebook, Fl.	22	12	2	Booklet ($339,700)	725,981
Twining, Ky.	45	20	1	Cloudy Mist ($92,666)	722,592
Langfuhr, Ky.	44	13	0	Imperial Gesture ($275,540)	706,397
Phone Trick, N.Y.	45	21	0	Playing Games ($69,745)	695,627
Out of Place, Ky.	34	17	1	Fonz's ($193,740)	694,943
Is It True, Fl.	28	16	3	Juggernaut ($138,180)	679,480
Danzig, Ky.	14	8	1	Star El Dorado ($385,719)	632,609
Tabasco Cat, Jpn.	27	9	2	Habibti ($393,000)	629,711
Two Punch, Md.	35	10	2	Heavyweight Champ ($149,258)	619,430
Gilded Time, Ky.	32	10	2	Interminable Gold ($120,677)	614,634
Woodman, Ky.	62	14	4	Hawk Wing ($272,310)	601,168
Kissin Kris, Fl.	13	8	2	Blissful Kiss ($336,780)	591,442
Service Stripe, Ky.	5	3	2	Cashier's Dream ($353,230)	584,067
Bag, Dead	32	15	3	Hail to Bag ($175,395)	561,734
Wild Again, Ky.	26	13	1	Atlantic Fury ($161,390)	558,568
Forest Wildcat, Ky.	35	12	I	Forest Heiress ($210,787)	555,415
Wild Zone, Tx.	36	13	0	North Brooklyn ($89,779)	538,676
Helmsman, Ca.	25	9	1	Rare Friends ($247,365)	528,317
High Brite, Ca.	28	10	2	Britetonzmyday ($168,890)	527,974
Maria's Mon, Ky.	37	12	1	Grass Volante ($116,230)	514,856
Housebuster, Va.	27	11	1	Buster's Daydream ($199,625)	513,284
Mecke, Fl.	17	12	2	Mountain Rage ($154,770)	508,965
El Prado (Ire), Ky.	35	11	2	El Soprano ($194,834)	503,917
Boundary, Ky.	26	10	2	Saga Novel ($299,891)	503,343
Mutakddim, Ky.	18	9	6	Miss Noire ($201,711)	495,559
Regal Classic, N.Y.	30	9	3	Tails of the Crypt ($145,192)	492,975
Fortunate Prospect, Fl.	35	18	1	Bold World ($81,360)	490,760
Unbridled, Dead	21	6	2	Belterra ($192,359)	488,138
Allen's Prospect, Md.	29	9	3	Square Cut Diamond ($124,714)	480,187
Dynaformer, Ky.	25	9	4	Riskaverse ($202,750)	478,148
Zafonic, Eng.	37	16	1	Zipping ($159,818)	476,974
Deputy Minister, Ky.	27	10	0	Dynamite Kids ($48,438)	476,149
Kingmambo, Ky.	25	8	1	Kitasan Ocean ($130,403)	467,275
Gulch, Ky.	36	12	2	Listen Here ($115,980)	465,635

Leading Worldwide Juvenile Sires by Average Earnings per Runner in 2001

Sire	Strs	Wnrs	Average
Bertrando	14	3	$59,636
A.P. Indy	27	14	49,696
Forty Niner	19	10	49,265
Kissin Kris	13	8	45,496
Danzig	14	8	45,186
Siphon (Brz)	21	7	43,367
You and I	18	7	41,504
Gone West	30	17	37,937
Hennessy	55	20	33,347
Unbridled's Song	29	10	33,206
Notebook	22	12	32,999
Pulpit	23	10	32,888
Boston Harbor	27	12	30,236
General Meeting	13	4	30,081
Tethra	13	6	30,053
Storm Cat	29	15	30,001
Mecke	17	12	29,939
Meadowlake	29	13	29,537
Saint Ballado	32	14	28,693
Valid Expectations	49	27	28,529
Dehere	47	24	28,521
Mutakddim	18	9	28,433
Bold Executive	16	4	27,682
Golden Gear	32	14	27,575

Leading Worldwide Juvenile Sires by Median Earnings per Runner in 2001

Sire	Strs	Wnrs	Median
Forty Niner	19	10	$48,258
Storm Cat	29	15	25,200
Deputy Minister	27	10	23,467
Mecke	17	12	21,135
Matter of Honor	11	5	17,041
Kissin Kris	13	8	16,280
Valid Expectations	49	27	16,230
Danzig	14	8	16,180
Rizzi	11	8	15,600
Outflanker	20	12	14,933
Saint Ballado	32	14	13,425
Is It True	28	16	13,320
Meadowlake	29	13	13,230
Notebook	22	12	12,985
A.P. Indy	27	14	12,917
In Excess (Ire)	19	10	12,840
Cherokee Run	22	12	12,522
Tactical Advantage	29	14	12,280
Montbrook	31	20	12,250
Avenue of Flags	24	10	11,939
Valid Wager	24	13	11,928
Colony Light	11	6	11,909

Leading Worldwide Juvenile Sires by Number of Winners in 2001

Sire	Strs	Wnrs	Wnrs/ Strs %
End Sweep	63	31	49.2%
Valid Expectations	49	27	55.1%
Judge T C	64	26	40.6%
Dehere	47	24	51.1%
Charnwood Forest (Ire)	47	22	46.8%
Phone Trick	45	21	46.7%
Foxhound	41	21	51.2%
Hennessy	55	20	36.4%
Open Forum	45	20	44.4%
Montbrook	31	20	64.5%
Twining	45	20	44.4%
Alzao	48	19	39.6%
Smoke Glacken	45	19	42.2%
Fortunate Prospect	35	18	51.4%
Salt Lake	42	18	42.9%
Sadler's Wells	63	17	27.0%
Gone West	30	17	56.7%
French Deputy	31	17	54.8%
Carson City	34	17	50.0%
Out of Place	34	17	50.0%

Leading Worldwide Juvenile Sires by Number of Wins in 2001

Sire	Strs	Wnrs	Wins
End Sweep	63	31	43
Valid Expectations	49	27	40
Judge T C	64	26	38
Dehere	47	24	32
Twining	45	20	31
Charnwood Forest (Ire)	47	22	30
Hennessy	55	20	29
Salt Lake	42	18	29
Foxhound	41	21	29
Open Forum	45	20	28
Montbrook	31	20	28
Smoke Glacken	45	19	26
Sadler's Wells	63	17	24
Phone Trick	45	21	24
Gone West	30	17	24
Bag	32	15	24
Is It True	28	16	24
Carson City	34	17	24
Alzao	48	19	23
Fortunate Prospect	35	18	23
French Deputy	31	17	23

Leading Worldwide Juvenile Sires by Number of Stakes Winners in 2001

Sire	Strs	Wnrs	SWs
Sadler's Wells	63	17	8
Dehere	47	24	8
Southern Halo	24	10	6
Mutakddim	18	9	6
Roy	21	10	5
Royal Academy	77	16	5
Spend a Buck	12	4	4
Gone West	30	17	4
Hennessy	55	20	4
Dynaformer	25	9	4
Allen's Prospect	29	9	3
Woodman	52	11	3
Thunder Gulch	32	11	3
Valid Expectations	49	27	3
Smoke Glacken	45	19	3
Open Forum	45	20	3
Alhaarth	36	12	3
Desert King	58	12	3
Sepoy (Arg)	5	4	3
Quest for Fame (GB)	22	8	3
Bengal Bay	5	4	3
Salt Lake	42	18	3
Bag	32	15	3
Numerous	25	10	3
You and I	18	7	3
Foxhound	41	21	3
Judge T C	64	26	3
Is It True	28	16	3
Carson City	34	17	3

Leading Worldwide Juvenile Sires by Number of Graded/Group Stakes Winners in 2001

Sire	Strs	Wnrs	GSWs
Sadler's Wells	63	17	6
Roy	21	10	4
Gone West	30	17	4
Royal Academy	77	16	4
Spend a Buck	12	4	3
Southern Halo	24	10	3
Woodman	52	11	3
Mutakddim	18	9	3
Nureyev	11	6	2
Thunder Gulch	32	11	2
Hennessy	55	20	2
A.P. Indy	27	14	2
Stuka	26	8	2
Dehere	47	24	2
Unbridled	21	6	2

Leading Freshman Sires
by North American Progeny Earnings in 2001

Earnings in North America only for stallions who stand or last stood in North America or had ten North American starters in 2001.

Sire, Where stands	Strs	Wnrs	SWs	Leading earner (earnings)	Progeny earnings
Valid Expectations, Tx.	49	27	3	Expected Program ($120,240)	$1,397,911
Open Forum, Tx.	45	20	3	Jealous Forum ($183,865)	1,072,687
Smoke Glacken, Ky.	44	19	3	Smok'n Frolic ($342,744)	1,048,867
Siphon (Brz), Ky.	20	6	1	Siphonic ($703,978)	895,148
Louis Quatorze, Ky.	40	9	1	Repent ($415,660)	681,908
Langfuhr, Ky.	36	12	0	Imperial Gesture ($275,540)	635,660
Pulpit, Ky.	21	9	1	Essence of Dubai ($193,200)	550,246
Helmsman, Ca.	23	9	1	Rare Friends ($247,365)	528,317
Lost Soldier, Fl.	32	11	1	Lush Soldier ($148,618)	460,983
Tejano Run, Ky.	21	7	2	Shaws Creek ($155,748)	416,033
Matty G, Ky.	26	13	1	Mayakovsky ($64,600)	409,031
Outflanker, Fl.	19	11	1	First Again ($88,790)	394,906
Editor's Note, Ky.	33	13	0	Short Note ($68,100)	393,220
Boston Harbor, Jpn.	21	8	1	Boston Twist ($130,884)	360,554
Meadow Monster, Md.	17	8	1	Haunted Lass ($113,200)	349,737
Mercer Mill, Oh.	13	5	2	Joanies Bella ($234,265)	339,739
Sir Cat, Ky.	27	9	1	Pharaoh's Cat ($67,000)	302,999
Captain Bodgit, Ky.	35	12	0	Lazer Hill ($39,271)	302,126
Whiskey Wisdom, On.	15	3	1	Molly's Wisdom ($151,483)	294,416
Cat's Career, Tx.	24	8	0	Cat's Delight ($56,634)	273,284
Sandpit (Brz), Ky.	29	8	1	Ashbecca ($46,731)	267,071
Gold Case, Ky.	18	7	1	Classic Case ($91,172)	261,130
Jules, Fl.	18	8	2	Front Nine ($79,610)	255,071
Crown Ambassador, In.	14	5	2	Amanda's Crown ($96,230)	251,701
Suave Prospect, Fl.	23	9	0	Suave Darling ($44,380)	250,794
Halo's Image, Fl.	26	11	0	Raised Eyebrows ($44,225)	248,413
Illinois Storm, Ca.	9	1	1	Georgia's Storm ($185,085)	237,179
Alphabet Soup, Ky.	24	7	0	Winning Chance ($46,794)	231,833
Balcony, P.R.	5	2	1	Fascinatin Lady ($206,099)	230,004
Adhocracy, Fl.	5	3	1	Pharmstar ($110,400)	218,575
Victory Speech, Jpn	28	7	0	Recite ($71,311)	206,422
Chequer, N.Y.	28	4	0	Extra Check ($45,780)	202,958
Fabulous Frolic, Fl.	11	9	0	Fabulous Fury ($51,280)	199,091
Ormsby, N.Y.	13	5	0	Nypuddles ($49,800)	176,798
Dr. Caton, Fl.	23	6	0	Typhoon Bertie ($40,735)	173,492
Siberian Summer, Ca.	13	4	2	Russian Olive ($52,009)	169,733
Marlin, Tur.	26	4	0	Past You ($67,625)	163,975
Native Regent, Fl.	14	7	0	Swinging Gate ($35,160)	155,173
Wild Escapade, Fl.	17	5	0	Thiscannonsloaded ($74,060)	154,593
Top Account, Fl.	27	5	0	Bjelks ($22,533)	147,810
Just a Cat, Ab.	17	8	0	Scarlet O'Hara ($34,560)	147,557
Devon Lane, Ca.	13	5	1	Devon's Prospect ($77,095)	143,079
Appealing Skier, Md.	11	8	0	Knight Skier ($31,100)	138,168
Always a Classic, Tur.	15	5	0	Classic Runaway ($50,692)	138,021
Abaginone, N.Y.	19	7	0	Totally Selfish ($30,600)	136,089
Devious Course, Tx.	22	9	0	Las Devious ($23,220)	135,516
Atticus, Ky.	18	6	0	Attico ($33,430)	127,472
Canyon Creek (Ire), On.	12	6	0	Norman Vincent ($25,265)	122,493
Hold for Gold, Ky.	13	5	0	Fashion Award ($36,330)	115,565
Eltish, Fl.	6	3	1	Kud'zu Magic ($77,580)	114,835
Urgent Request (Ire), Ca.	16	4	2	Rainman's Request ($39,200)	112,318
Noble Cat, Oh.	10	6	0	Noble Invitation ($33,670)	111,765
Struggler (GB), Fl.	10	6	0	Yakima Canutt ($37,780)	106,816
Proudest Romeo, Fl.	4	3	1	Explosive Truth ($77,610)	103,552
Spinning World, Ire.	11	2	0	Global Vision ($42,985)	101,289
Soft Gold (Brz), Ca.	3	2	2	Bella Bella Bella ($52,800)	98,760
Circus Surprise, Mi.	7	3	0	Midway Girl ($49,742)	93,395
Tamayaz, Md.	20	3	0	Tamayaz's Legend ($22,560)	90,713
Ikari, Tx.	2	1	1	Victory Road ($89,940)	90,578
Wild Gold, Ca.	12	6	0	Natasha's Reno ($26,715)	87,812
K. O. Punch, Ky.	11	3	0	Super Punch ($22,250)	81,793
Presidential Order, In.	10	3	0	Indy Energy ($42,040)	81,778
World Stage (Ire), Fl.	15	4	0	Worldly Victor ($33,740)	78,992
Summer of Storms, Dead	3	1	1	Tricky Storm ($77,600)	78,950
Fort Wayne, N.J.	5	1	0	Big Hearted Wayne ($40,790)	77,265

Leading North American Freshman Sires by Average Earnings per Runner in 2001

Sire	Strs	Wnrs	Average
Siphon (Brz)	20	6	$44,757
Valid Expectations	49	27	28,529
Pulpit	21	9	26,202
Mercer Mill	13	5	26,134
Smoke Glacken	44	19	23,838
Open Forum	45	20	23,837
Helmsman	23	9	22,970
Outflanker	19	11	20,785
Meadow Monster	17	8	20,573
Tejano Run	21	7	19,811
Whiskey Wisdom	15	3	19,628
Fabulous Frolic	11	9	18,099
Crown Ambassador	14	5	17,979
Langfuhr	36	12	17,657
Boston Harbor	21	8	17,169
Louis Quatorze	40	9	17,048
Matty G	26	13	15,732
Gold Case	18	7	14,507
Lost Soldier	32	11	14,406
Jules	18	8	14,171
Ormsby	13	5	13,600
Siberian Summer	13	4	13,056

Leading North American Freshman Sires by Median Earnings per Runner in 2001

Sire	Strs	Wnrs	Median
Outflanker	19	11	$17,575
Valid Expectations	49	27	16,230
Native Regent	14	7	11,365
Smoke Glacken	44	19	10,455
Fabulous Frolic	11	9	10,260
Canyon Creek (Ire)	12	6	9,952
Appealing Skier	11	8	8,818
Open Forum	45	20	8,758
Pulpit	21	9	8,200
Noble Cat	10	6	8,158
Oliver's Twist	10	6	7,900
Siberian Summer	13	4	7,700
Struggler (GB)	10	6	7,655
Wild Gold	12	6	7,145
Crown Ambassador	14	5	7,080
Ormsby	13	5	6,960
Meadow Monster	17	8	6,750
Editor's Note	33	13	6,658
Matty G	26	13	6,648

Leading North American Freshman Sires by Number of Winners in 2001

Sire	Strs	Wnrs	Wnrs/Strs %
Valid Expectations	49	27	55.1%
Open Forum	45	20	44.4%
Smoke Glacken	44	19	43.2%
Matty G	26	13	50.0%
Editor's Note	33	13	39.4%
Langfuhr	36	12	33.3%
Captain Bodgit	35	12	34.3%
Lost Soldier	32	11	34.4%
Halo's Image	26	11	42.3%
Outflanker	19	11	57.9%
Fabulous Frolic	11	9	81.8%
Devious Course	22	9	40.9%
Suave Prospect	23	9	39.1%
Helmsman	23	9	39.1%
Louis Quatorze	40	9	22.5%
Sir Cat	27	9	33.3%
Pulpit	21	9	42.9%
Meadow Monster	17	8	47.1%
Cat's Career	24	8	33.3%
Appealing Skier	11	8	72.7%
Jules	18	8	44.4%
Just a Cat	17	8	47.1%
Boston Harbor	21	8	38.1%
Sandpit (Brz)	29	8	27.6%

Leading North American Freshman Sires by Number of Wins in 2001

Sire	Strs	Wnrs	Wins
Valid Expectations	49	27	40
Open Forum	45	20	28
Smoke Glacken	44	19	26
Outflanker	19	11	18
Editor's Note	33	13	17
Langfuhr	36	12	15
Matty G	26	13	15
Halo's Image	26	11	14
Sir Cat	27	9	14
Captain Bodgit	35	12	14
Lost Soldier	32	11	13
Helmsman	23	9	13
Meadow Monster	17	8	12
Louis Quatorze	40	9	12
Fabulous Frolic	11	9	11
Devious Course	22	9	11
Jules	18	8	11
Pulpit	21	9	11
Boston Harbor	21	8	11
Sandpit (Brz)	29	8	11
Struggler (GB)	10	6	11
Tejano Run	21	7	10
Devon Lane	13	5	10
Mercer Mill	13	5	10
Suave Prospect	23	9	9
Cat's Career	24	8	9
Gold Case	18	7	9
Noble Cat	10	6	9
Alphabet Soup	24	7	8
Wild Escapade	17	5	8
Appealing Skier	11	8	8
Victory Speech	28	7	8
Just a Cat	17	8	8
Crown Ambassador	14	5	8
Balcony	5	2	8
Siphon (Brz)	20	6	8
Siberian Summer	13	4	7
Wild Gold	12	6	7
Abaginone	19	7	7
Eltish	6	3	7
Native Regent	14	7	7
Slew Sangue	11	6	7
Top Account	27	5	7
Dr. Caton	23	6	7
Canyon Creek (Ire)	12	6	7
World Stage (Ire)	15	4	7
Atticus	18	6	6
Oliver's Twist	10	6	6
Grace of Darby	6	4	6
Always a Classic	15	5	6
Hold for Gold	13	5	6

Leading North American Freshman Sires by Number of Stakes Winners in 2001

Sire	Strs	Wnrs	SWs
Valid Expectations	49	27	3
Smoke Glacken	44	19	3
Open Forum	45	20	3
Siberian Summer	13	4	2
Tejano Run	21	7	2
Jules	18	8	2
Mercer Mill	13	5	2
Crown Ambassador	14	5	2
Urgent Request (Ire)	16	4	2
Soft Gold (Brz)	3	2	2

Leading North American Freshman Sires by Number of Graded Stakes Winners in 2001

Sire	Strs	Wnrs	GSWs
Lost Soldier	32	11	1
Louis Quatorze	40	9	1
Illinois Storm	9	1	1
Smoke Glacken	44	19	1
Pulpit	21	9	1
Mercer Mill	13	5	1
Siphon (Brz)	20	6	1

Leading Worldwide Freshman Sires
by Progeny Earnings in 2001

Worldwide earnings for stallions with one two-year-old North American starter in 2001.

Sire, Where stands	Strs	Wnrs	SWs	Leading earner (earnings)	Progeny earnings
Valid Expectations, Tx.	49	27	3	Expected Program ($120,240)	$1,397,911
Smoke Glacken, Ky.	45	19	3	Smok'n Frolic ($342,744)	1,084,836
Open Forum, Tx.	45	20	3	Jealous Forum ($183,865)	1,072,687
Siphon (Brz), Ky.	21	7	1	Siphonic ($703,978)	910,697
Boston Harbor, Jpn.	27	12	1	Cafe Bostonian ($183,752)	816,373
Louis Quatorze, Ky.	45	11	1	Repent ($415,660)	813,516
Pulpit, Ky.	23	10	1	Grandson ($206,172)	756,418
Langfuhr, Ky.	44	13	0	Imperial Gesture ($275,540)	706,397
Helmsman, Ca.	25	9	1	Rare Friends ($247,365)	528,317
Lost Soldier, Fl.	32	11	1	Lush Soldier ($148,618)	460,983
Spinning World, Ire.	42	16	2	Maltese World ($60,811)	447,611
Editor's Note, Ky.	34	13	0	Short Note ($68,100)	427,245
Tejano Run, Ky.	21	7	2	Shaws Creek ($155,748)	416,033
Matty G, Ky.	26	13	1	Mayakovsky ($64,600)	409,031
Outflanker, Fl.	20	12	1	First Again ($88,790)	402,394
Meadow Monster, Md.	17	8	1	Haunted Lass ($113,200)	349,737
Mercer Mill, Oh.	13	5	2	Joanies Bella ($234,265)	339,739
Sir Cat, Ky.	29	9	1	Pharaoh's Cat ($67,000)	313,462
Captain Bodgit, Ky.	35	12	0	Lazer Hill ($39,271)	302,126
Whiskey Wisdom, On.	15	3	1	Molly's Wisdom ($151,483)	294,416
Cat's Career, Tx.	24	8	0	Cat's Delight ($56,634)	273,284
Suave Prospect, Fl.	24	10	0	Suave Darling ($44,380)	268,935
Sandpit (Brz), Ky.	29	8	1	Ashbecca ($46,731)	267,071
Gold Case, Ky.	18	7	1	Classic Case ($91,172)	261,130
Jules, Fl.	19	8	2	Front Nine ($79,610)	255,520
Crown Ambassador, In.	14	5	2	Amanda's Crown ($96,230)	251,701
Halo's Image, Fl.	26	11	0	Raised Eyebrows ($44,225)	248,413
Desert King, Ire.	58	12	3	Red Briar (Ire) ($34,413)	247,810
Alphabet Soup, Ky.	25	8	0	Winning Chance ($46,794)	240,704
Illinois Storm, Ca.	9	1	1	Georgia's Storm ($185,085)	237,179
Alhaarth, Ire.	36	12	3	Dominica ($42,688)	235,202
Balcony, P.R.	5	2	1	Fascinatin Lady ($206,099)	230,004
Adhocracy, Fl.	5	3	1	Pharmstar ($110,400)	218,575
Victory Speech, Jpn.	28	7	0	Recite ($71,311)	206,422
Marlin, Tur.	30	6	0	Past You ($67,625)	204,304
Chequer, N.Y.	28	4	0	Extra Check ($45,780)	202,958
Fabulous Frolic, Fl.	11	9	0	Fabulous Fury ($51,280)	199,091
Atticus, Ky.	26	8	0	Attico ($33,430)	182,562
Ormsby, N.Y.	13	5	0	Nypuddles ($49,800)	176,798
Dr. Caton, Fl.	23	6	0	Typhoon Bertie ($40,735)	173,492
Revoque, Ire.	43	9	0	Meanya ($58,773)	171,182
Siberian Summer, Ca.	13	4	2	Russian Olive ($52,009)	169,733
Native Regent, Fl.	14	7	0	Swinging Gate ($35,160)	155,173
Wild Escapade, Fl.	17	5	0	Thiscannonsloaded ($74,060)	154,593
Entrepreneur, Ire.	35	6	0	Bringontheclowns ($43,443)	154,057
Top Account, Fl.	27	5	0	Bjelks ($22,533)	147,810
Just a Cat, Ab.	17	8	0	Scarlet O'Hara ($34,560)	147,557
Devon Lane, Ca.	13	5	1	Devon's Prospect ($77,095)	143,079
Atraf (GB), Eng.	25	9	1	La Martina (GB) ($54,873)	142,986
Appealing Skier, Md.	11	8	0	Knight Skier ($31,100)	138,168
Always a Classic, Tur.	15	5	0	Classic Runaway ($50,692)	138,021
Abaginone, N.Y.	19	7	0	Totally Selfish ($30,600)	136,089
Devious Course, Tx.	22	9	0	Las Devious ($23,220)	135,516
Canyon Creek (Ire), On.	12	6	0	Norman Vincent ($25,265)	122,493
Hold for Gold, Ky.	13	5	0	Fashion Award ($36,330)	115,565
Urgent Request (Ire), Ca.	17	4	2	Rainman's Request ($39,200)	114,980
Eltish, Fl.	6	3	1	Kud'zu Magic ($77,580)	114,835
Noble Cat, Oh.	10	6	0	Noble Invitation ($33,670)	111,765
Struggler (GB), Fl.	10	6	0	Yakima Canutt ($37,780)	106,816
Proudest Romeo, Fl.	4	3	1	Explosive Truth ($77,610)	103,552
Soft Gold (Brz), Ca.	3	2	2	Bella Bella Bella ($52,800)	98,760
Circus Surprise, Mi.	7	3	0	Midway Girl ($49,742)	93,395
Tamayaz, Md.	20	3	0	Tamayaz's Legend ($22,560)	90,713
Ikari, Tx.	2	1	1	Victory Road ($89,940)	90,578
Wild Gold, Ca.	12	6	0	Natasha's Reno ($26,715)	87,812

Leading Worldwide Freshman Sires
by Average Earnings per Runner in 2001

Sire	Strs	Wnrs	Average
Siphon (Brz)	21	7	$43,367
Pulpit	23	10	32,888
Boston Harbor	27	12	30,236
Valid Expectations	49	27	28,529
Mercer Mill	13	5	26,134
Smoke Glacken	45	19	24,107
Open Forum	45	20	23,837
Helmsman	25	9	21,133
Meadow Monster	17	8	20,573
Outflanker	20	12	20,120
Tejano Run	21	7	19,811
Whiskey Wisdom	15	3	19,628
Fabulous Frolic	11	9	18,099
Louis Quatorze	45	11	18,078
Crown Ambassador	14	5	17,979
Langfuhr	44	13	16,054
Matty G	26	13	15,732
Gold Case	18	7	14,507
Lost Soldier	32	11	14,406
Ormsby	13	5	13,600
Jules	19	8	13,448
Siberian Summer	13	4	13,056

Leading Worldwide Freshman Sires
by Median Earnings per Runner in 2001

Sire	Strs	Wnrs	Median
Valid Expectations	49	27	$16,230
Outflanker	20	12	14,933
Smoke Glacken	45	19	11,420
Native Regent	14	7	11,365
Fabulous Frolic	11	9	10,260
Canyon Creek (Ire)	12	6	9,952
Appealing Skier	11	8	8,818
Open Forum	45	20	8,758
Pulpit	23	10	8,200
Boston Harbor	27	12	8,200
Noble Cat	10	6	8,158
Oliver's Twist	10	6	7,900
Siberian Summer	13	4	7,700
Struggler (GB)	10	6	7,655
Wild Gold	12	6	7,145
Crown Ambassador	14	5	7,080
Editor's Note	34	13	6,973
Ormsby	13	5	6,960
Meadow Monster	17	8	6,750
Matty G	26	13	6,648

Leading Worldwide Freshman Sires
by Number of Winners in 2001

Sire	Strs	Wnrs	Wnrs/ Strs %
Valid Expectations	49	27	55.1%
Open Forum	45	20	44.4%
Smoke Glacken	45	19	42.2%
Spinning World	42	16	38.1%
Langfuhr	44	13	29.5%
Matty G	26	13	50.0%
Editor's Note	34	13	38.2%
Boston Harbor	27	12	44.4%
Outflanker	20	12	60.0%
Captain Bodgit	35	12	34.3%
Alhaarth	36	12	33.3%
Desert King	58	12	20.7%
Lost Soldier	32	11	34.4%
Halo's Image	26	11	42.3%
Louis Quatorze	45	11	24.4%
Suave Prospect	24	10	41.7%
Pulpit	23	10	43.5%
Fabulous Frolic	11	9	81.8%
Devious Course	22	9	40.9%
Helmsman	25	9	36.0%
Sir Cat	29	9	31.0%
Revoque	43	9	20.9%
Atraf (GB)	25	9	36.0%

Leading Worldwide Freshman Sires
by Number of Wins in 2001

Sire	Strs	Wnrs	Wins
Valid Expectations	49	27	40
Open Forum	45	20	28
Smoke Glacken	45	19	26
Outflanker	20	12	19
Spinning World	42	16	18
Editor's Note	34	13	17
Boston Harbor	27	12	17
Langfuhr	44	13	16
Alhaarth	36	12	16
Desert King	58	12	16
Matty G	26	13	15
Halo's Image	26	11	14
Louis Quatorze	45	11	14
Sir Cat	29	9	14
Captain Bodgit	35	12	14
Atraf (GB)	25	9	14
Lost Soldier	32	11	13
Helmsman	25	9	13
Pulpit	23	10	13
Meadow Monster	17	8	12
Fabulous Frolic	11	9	11
Devious Course	22	9	11
Suave Prospect	24	10	11
Jules	19	8	11
Sandpit (Brz)	29	8	11
Struggler (GB)	10	6	11
Tejano Run	21	7	10
Devon Lane	13	5	10
Mercer Mill	13	5	10
Entrepreneur	35	6	10
Revoque	43	9	10
Alphabet Soup	25	8	9
Cat's Career	24	8	9
Gold Case	18	7	9
Noble Cat	10	6	9
Siphon (Brz)	21	7	9
Atticus	26	8	8
Wild Escapade	17	5	8
Appealing Skier	11	8	8
Victory Speech	28	7	8
Just a Cat	17	8	8
Crown Ambassador	14	5	8
Balcony	5	2	8

Leading Worldwide Freshman Sires
by Number of Stakes Winners in 2001

Sire	Strs	Wnrs	SWs
Valid Expectations	49	27	3
Smoke Glacken	45	19	3
Open Forum	45	20	3
Alhaarth	36	12	3
Desert King	58	12	3
Siberian Summer	13	4	2
Tejano Run	21	7	2
Spinning World	42	16	2
Jules	19	8	2
Mercer Mill	13	5	2
Crown Ambassador	14	5	2
Urgent Request (Ire)	17	4	2
Soft Gold (Brz)	3	2	2

Leading Worldwide Freshman Sires
by Number of Graded/Group Stakes Winners in 2001

Sire	Strs	Wnrs	GSWs
Lost Soldier	32	11	1
Spinning World	42	16	1
Louis Quatorze	45	11	1
Illinois Storm	9	1	1
Smoke Glacken	45	19	1
Pulpit	23	10	1
Mercer Mill	13	5	1
Alhaarth	36	12	1
Siphon (Brz)	21	7	1

Leading Broodmare Sires
by North American Progeny Earnings in 2001

Earnings in North America only for stallions who stand or last stood in North America or had 25 North American starters in 2001.

Sire, Where stands	Strs	Wnrs	SWs	Leading earner (earnings)	Progeny earnings
Mr. Prospector, Dead	296	149	19	Tempera ($670,240)	$8,954,133
Dixieland Band, Ky.	251	145	8	Monarchos ($1,711,600)	7,614,244
Deputy Minister, Ky.	229	125	15	Redattore (Brz) ($555,840)	7,355,606
Fappiano, Dead	196	104	14	Albert the Great ($1,740,000)	7,283,594
Vice Regent, Dead	243	142	8	Captain Steve ($601,200)	6,747,741
Valid Appeal, Dead	259	159	18	Exciting Story ($596,667)	6,695,852
Nijinsky II, Dead	174	84	10	Fantastic Light ($2,112,800)	6,578,356
Halo, Dead	266	151	14	Sligo Bay (Ire) ($246,160)	6,300,676
Danzig, Ky.	163	92	10	Dancethruthedawn ($1,045,039)	6,090,059
Relaunch, Dead	269	148	10	Starrer ($406,265)	5,983,312
Topsider, Dead	156	97	8	Guided Tour ($1,384,220)	5,913,388
Lyphard, Pens.	123	57	10	Skimming ($1,330,000)	5,554,926
Private Account, Pens.	241	125	6	Pompeii ($436,621)	5,499,985
Conquistador Cielo, Ky.	207	111	9	Dixie Dot Com ($679,000)	5,459,032
Turkoman, Ca.	99	46	3	Point Given ($3,350,000)	5,395,656
Seattle Slew, Dead	231	124	9	Astra ($270,000)	5,265,633
Green Dancer, Dead	197	99	8	Spook Express (SAf) ($866,870)	5,093,381
Spectacular Bid, N.Y.	184	94	9	Janet (GB) ($715,080)	4,842,384
Bold Ruckus, Dead	199	113	6	Mysterious Affair ($288,789)	4,805,549
Cox's Ridge, Dead	249	125	7	Orientate ($293,700)	4,583,868
Stop the Music, Dead	183	91	5	Include ($1,435,400)	4,452,140
Pleasant Colony, Pens.	154	99	11	Country Hideaway ($236,936)	4,404,399
Seattle Song, Dead	69	29	5	Tiznow ($2,981,880)	4,260,590
Majestic Light, Dead	234	109	4	King Cugat ($555,980)	4,165,735
Crafty Prospector, Ky.	189	112	8	Graeme Hall ($315,923)	4,159,473
Storm Bird, Pens.	162	85	4	Kimberlite Pipe ($250,042)	4,149,193
Our Native, Dead	196	107	11	Sure Shot Biscuit ($368,985)	4,099,497
Mr. Leader, Dead	224	133	6	Fleet Renee ($624,485)	4,044,195
Storm Cat, Ky.	128	74	9	Baptize ($368,136)	3,991,887
Smarten, Pens.	165	88	8	Kimbralata ($203,000)	3,961,767
Miswaki, Ky.	220	114	6	Royal Corona ($118,459)	3,898,992
Flying Paster, Dead	182	92	7	Victory Ride ($247,025)	3,849,025
Clever Trick, Ky.	249	120	5	Came Home ($211,440)	3,846,110
Baldski, Dead	166	90	8	Ms Brookski ($248,060)	3,834,710
Sovereign Dancer, Dead	232	113	3	Ayanna ($145,750)	3,793,545
Phone Trick, N.Y.	131	82	7	Exogenous ($901,500)	3,668,901
Kris S., Dead	158	95	5	Innit (Ire) ($185,772)	3,653,605
His Majesty, Dead	182	100	7	Williams News ($157,610)	3,552,130
Wild Again, Ky.	183	91	7	Dat You Miz Blue ($273,865)	3,537,997
Alleged, Dead	143	74	6	Collect Call ($338,820)	3,475,883
Affirmed, Dead	187	92	2	Harlan's Holiday ($341,564)	3,474,107
The Minstrel, Dead	136	64	7	Navesink ($368,206)	3,399,139
Slew o' Gold, Ky.	121	60	5	Golden Ballet ($595,250)	3,307,798
Devil's Bag, Ky.	141	59	4	Balto Star ($848,820)	3,285,634
Cure the Blues, Dead	139	73	7	Grundlefoot ($215,670)	3,269,390
Lost Code, Dead	100	48	5	Squirtle Squirt ($817,720)	3,228,781
Saratoga Six, Ky.	132	60	5	Dollar Bill ($415,000)	3,209,429
Apalachee, Dead	160	84	6	Disco Rico ($349,644)	3,154,772
Copelan, Dead	151	87	4	On the Game ($188,535)	2,927,374
Temperence Hill, Thi.	152	79	5	Habibti ($393,000)	2,923,263
Caveat, Dead	130	71	2	Two Item Limit ($648,760)	2,918,518
Premiership, Fl.	126	74	5	Songandaprayer ($314,000)	2,917,383
Woodman, Ky.	120	54	6	Distilled ($337,890)	2,908,698
Taylor's Falls, Dead	74	42	4	Unbridled Elaine ($1,663,175)	2,879,830
Fit to Fight, Ky.	140	81	6	Euchre ($351,500)	2,870,336
Star de Naskra, Dead	194	96	2	Do I Ever ($177,492)	2,858,137
Silent Screen, Dead	166	97	1	Screen Happy ($177,294)	2,836,880
Irish Tower, Dead	144	81	1	Affirmed Success ($343,215)	2,804,186
Well Decorated, Ky.	189	93	4	Image of a Cat ($108,240)	2,745,089
Strawberry Road (Aus), Dead	99	55	3	Affluent ($725,200)	2,736,159
Afleet, Jpn	93	56	3	Estrellero ($363,112)	2,735,390
Great Above, Dead	166	90	10	El Cielo ($167,680)	2,723,263
Pirate's Bounty, Pens.	195	94	3	Candid Glen ($279,400)	2,715,722
Believe It, La.	153	77	3	Buster's Daydream ($199,625)	2,681,309
Far North, Dead	130	70	5	Crafty C. T. ($309,770)	2,580,935

Leading North American Broodmare Sires by Average Earnings per Runner in 2001

Sire	Strs	Wnrs	Average
Seattle Song	69	29	$61,748
Caerleon	25	9	61,251
Turkoman	99	46	54,502
Lyphard	123	57	45,162
Seeking the Gold	58	34	42,013
Saros (GB)	36	13	41,331
Compliance	28	13	39,278
Badger Land	38	28	39,188
Theatrical (Ire)	56	31	39,070
Taylor's Falls	74	42	38,917
Topsider	156	97	37,906
Nijinsky II	174	84	37,807
Septieme Ciel	26	14	37,673
Ascot Knight	37	21	37,550
Danzig	163	92	37,362
Fappiano	196	104	37,161
Sadler's Wells	42	14	34,796
Cherokee Colony	35	15	33,578
Silver Deputy	42	23	32,888
El Gran Senor	48	20	32,766
Lord At War (Arg)	62	31	32,664
Red Ransom	44	19	32,485
Shananie	28	19	32,374

Leading North American Broodmare Sires by Median Earnings per Runner in 2001

Sire	Strs	Wnrs	Median
Seeking the Gold	58	34	$18,718
Gulch	65	43	18,000
Afleet	93	56	16,500
Forty Niner	91	54	15,599
Topsider	156	97	15,031
Vice Regent	243	142	14,740
Personal Flag	55	31	14,670
Cojak	45	26	14,522
Danzig	163	92	14,190
Deputy Minister	229	125	14,115
Fast Play	56	35	13,944
Dayjur	28	20	13,906
Proper Reality	39	28	13,874
Fappiano	196	104	13,260
Ogygian	89	52	13,218
Proud Appeal	45	23	13,161
Pleasant Colony	154	99	12,938
Turkoman	99	46	12,825
Strawberry Road (Aus)	99	55	12,800
Shadeed	44	23	12,779
Ascot Knight	37	21	12,673

Leading North American Broodmare Sires by Number of Winners in 2001

Sire	Strs	Wnrs	Wnrs/ Strs %
Valid Appeal	259	159	61.4%
Halo	266	151	56.8%
Mr. Prospector	296	149	50.3%
Relaunch	269	148	55.0%
Dixieland Band	251	145	57.8%
Vice Regent	243	142	58.4%
Mr. Leader	224	133	59.4%
Cox's Ridge	249	125	50.2%
Private Account	241	125	51.9%
Deputy Minister	229	125	54.6%
Seattle Slew	231	124	53.7%
Clever Trick	249	120	48.2%
Miswaki	220	114	51.8%
Sovereign Dancer	232	113	48.7%
Bold Ruckus	199	113	56.8%
Crafty Prospector	189	112	59.3%
Conquistador Cielo	207	111	53.6%
Majestic Light	234	109	46.6%
Our Native	196	107	54.6%
Fappiano	196	104	53.1%

Leading North American Broodmare Sires by Number of Wins in 2001

Sire	Strs	Wnrs	Wins
Relaunch	269	148	286
Valid Appeal	259	159	271
Halo	266	151	263
Mr. Prospector	296	149	257
Vice Regent	243	142	256
Dixieland Band	251	145	249
Mr. Leader	224	133	244
Cox's Ridge	249	125	244
Crafty Prospector	189	112	234
Seattle Slew	231	124	230
Deputy Minister	229	125	229
Private Account	241	125	216
Sovereign Dancer	232	113	203
Topsider	156	97	202
Conquistador Cielo	207	111	201
Fappiano	196	104	199
Miswaki	220	114	197
Bold Ruckus	199	113	194
Clever Trick	249	120	194
Silent Screen	166	97	193
Our Native	196	107	192
Majestic Light	234	109	191

Leading North American Broodmare Sires by Number of Stakes Winners in 2001

Sire	Strs	Wnrs	SWs
Mr. Prospector	296	149	19
Valid Appeal	259	159	18
Deputy Minister	229	125	15
Halo	266	151	14
Fappiano	196	104	14
Our Native	196	107	11
Pleasant Colony	154	99	11
Nijinsky II	174	84	10
Lyphard	123	57	10
Great Above	166	90	10
Relaunch	269	148	10
Danzig	163	92	10
Seattle Slew	231	124	9
Spectacular Bid	184	94	9
Conquistador Cielo	207	111	9
Storm Cat	128	74	9
Vice Regent	243	142	8
Green Dancer	197	99	8
Topsider	156	97	8
Baldski	166	90	8
Smarten	165	88	8
Dixieland Band	251	145	8
Crafty Prospector	189	112	8

Leading North American Broodmare Sires by Number of Graded Stakes Winners in 2001

Sire	Strs	Wnrs	GSWs
Mr. Prospector	296	149	9
Pleasant Colony	154	99	6
Lyphard	123	57	5
Green Dancer	197	99	5
Storm Cat	128	74	5
Halo	266	151	4
Valid Appeal	259	159	4
Private Account	241	125	4
Fappiano	196	104	4
Danzig	163	92	4
Nijinsky II	174	84	3
Our Native	196	107	3
Topsider	156	97	3
The Minstrel	136	64	3
Dixieland Band	251	145	3
Phone Trick	131	82	3
Kris S.	158	95	3
Deputy Minister	229	125	3
Fit to Fight	140	81	3

Leading Worldwide Broodmare Sires by Progeny Earnings in 2001

Worldwide earnings for stallions with one North American starter in 2001.

Sire, Where stands	Strs	Wnrs	SWs	Leading earner (earnings)	Progeny earnings
Danzig, Ky.	353	171	18	Caller One ($1,436,380)	$18,291,970
Mr. Prospector, Dead	487	238	31	Behind the Mask ($954,996)	17,234,871
Nureyev, Dead	302	110	12	Jungle Pocket ($4,487,549)	16,148,153
Nijinsky II, Dead	342	143	19	Fantastic Light ($3,634,859)	15,659,010
Lyphard, Pens.	380	156	19	Skimming ($1,330,000)	13,603,472
Affirmed, Dead	276	136	13	Meisho Doto ($2,725,887)	11,898,977
Vice Regent, Dead	294	158	13	Captain Steve ($4,201,200)	11,795,523
Caerleon, Dead	310	125	17	Preeminence ($1,119,761)	11,691,866
Sadler's Wells, Ire.	363	154	16	Sakhee ($2,039,656)	10,982,397
Dixieland Band, Ky.	285	166	12	Monarchos ($1,711,600)	10,110,347
Fappiano, Dead	269	125	20	Albert the Great ($1,740,000)	10,019,805
Miswaki, Ky.	322	155	12	Galileo (Ire) ($2,233,580)	9,531,508
Halo, Dead	345	178	17	Lady Ballade (Ire) ($685,318)	9,080,637
Seattle Slew, Dead	355	174	16	Ishino Rainbow ($286,581)	8,738,627
Green Dancer, Dead	369	172	15	Spook Express (SAf) ($866,870)	8,711,773
Valid Appeal, Dead	269	164	19	Broad Appeal ($1,461,548)	8,490,732
Storm Bird, Pens.	298	135	12	Garcia Marquez ($614,668)	8,372,421
Conquistador Cielo, Ky.	267	136	13	Dixie Dot Com ($679,000)	8,190,514
Deputy Minister, Ky.	263	139	19	Redattore (Brz) ($555,840)	8,111,187
Topsider, Dead	239	132	12	Guided Tour ($1,384,220)	7,554,745
Chief's Crown, Dead	157	80	8	Agnes Digital ($3,341,517)	7,456,159
Majestic Light, Dead	308	134	9	Tobougg ($830,184)	6,999,168
Spectacular Bid, N.Y.	245	119	13	Janet (GB) ($715,080)	6,979,801
Private Account, Pens.	299	148	8	Pompeii ($436,621)	6,824,308
Relaunch, Dead	289	154	10	Starrer ($406,265)	6,673,675
Riverman, Dead	335	147	12	Anabaa Blue ($620,795)	6,659,676
Alleged, Dead	335	155	12	Collect Call ($338,820)	6,275,587
Woodman, Ky.	276	120	11	Distilled ($337,890)	6,225,238
The Minstrel, Dead	305	125	18	China Visit ($404,642)	6,204,078
Storm Cat, Ky.	169	90	11	Tenzan Desert ($374,596)	5,901,718
Turkoman, Ca.	111	52	5	Point Given ($3,350,000)	5,733,438
Shirley Heights, Dead	277	123	21	Rosebud ($1,770,032)	5,506,386
Alysheba, Sda.	142	78	8	Air Eminem ($1,759,044)	5,337,414
Afleet, Jpn.	111	65	4	Nobo Jack ($2,355,510)	5,315,829
Cox's Ridge, Dead	284	142	10	Republic Lass ($403,463)	5,277,771
Stop the Music, Dead	228	103	6	Include ($1,435,400)	5,249,615
Irish River (Fr), Pens.	296	119	7	Sakura Akane O ($327,493)	5,108,574
Slew o' Gold, Ky.	182	83	9	Golden Ballet ($595,250)	5,084,273
Our Native, Dead	219	116	13	Persian Punch ($390,687)	5,057,143
Pleasant Colony, Pens.	185	110	13	Country Hideaway ($236,936)	5,047,504
Devil's Bag, Ky.	184	80	6	Balto Star ($848,820)	5,040,786
Darshaan, Dead	201	75	17	Milan (GB) ($981,247)	4,917,291
Bold Ruckus, Dead	203	115	7	Mysterious Affair ($288,789)	4,907,344
Saratoga Six, Ky.	168	83	7	Dollar Bill ($415,000)	4,788,941
Cure the Blues, Dead	211	103	10	Road Bakushin ($310,100)	4,781,215
Seattle Song, Dead	100	41	7	Tiznow ($2,981,880)	4,707,683
Wild Again, Ky.	221	107	8	Osumi Slayer ($510,510)	4,689,535
Crafty Prospector, Ky.	206	117	8	Graeme Hall ($315,923)	4,602,125
Clever Trick, Ky.	274	131	6	Elegant Fashion ($430,038)	4,587,948
Smarten, Pens.	180	92	9	Kimbralata ($203,000)	4,433,724
Kris, Pens.	254	94	11	Kris the Brave ($640,031)	4,245,523
Silver Hawk, Ky.	148	73	5	Black Minnaloushe (GB) ($1,412,216)	4,240,351
Baldski, Dead	176	95	8	Pink Papillon ($283,632)	4,229,439
Mr. Leader, Dead	251	143	9	Fleet Renee ($624,485)	4,224,714
Seeking the Gold, Ky.	81	43	10	Lord Platinum ($674,219)	4,110,514
Sovereign Dancer, Dead	264	121	4	Ayanna ($145,750)	4,038,659
Ogygian, Jpn.	108	62	8	Johannesburg ($1,002,893)	4,026,044
Flying Paster, Dead	189	94	7	Victory Ride ($247,025)	3,946,556
Gulch, Ky.	115	61	4	Summer Candle ($337,639)	3,915,699
Diesis (GB), Ky.	199	96	11	Senure ($550,000)	3,904,365
Kris S., Dead	174	100	6	Innit (Ire) ($185,772)	3,899,584
Star de Naskra, Dead	216	105	2	South Vigorous ($752,481)	3,840,399
Forty Niner, Jpn.	124	67	4	Trip ($345,855)	3,810,218
Phone Trick, N.Y.	145	86	8	Exogenous ($901,500)	3,753,679
His Majesty, Dead	204	108	9	Williams News ($157,610)	3,734,369

Leading Worldwide Broodmare Sires
by Average Earnings per Runner in 2001

Sire	Strs	Wnrs	Average
Classic Go Go	32	16	$110,827
Kahyasi	27	12	54,250
Nureyev	302	110	53,471
Danzig	345	168	52,915
Turkoman	111	52	51,653
Seeking the Gold	81	43	50,747
Afleet	110	65	48,629
Chief's Crown	154	77	48,215
Seattle Song	100	41	47,077
Nijinsky II	342	143	45,787
Beau's Eagle	67	35	44,731
Affirmed	276	136	43,112
Saros (GB)	37	13	40,364
Vice Regent	294	158	40,121
Sunday Silence	38	12	40,051
Badger Land	38	28	39,188
Taylor's Falls	74	42	38,917
Compliance	29	13	37,924
Caerleon	310	125	37,716
Alysheba	142	78	37,587
Ogygian	108	62	37,278
Fappiano	269	125	37,248

Leading Worldwide Broodmare Sires
by Median Earnings per Runner in 2001

Sire	Strs	Wnrs	Median
Sunday Silence	38	12	$26,409
Easy Goer	32	20	19,458
Steady Growth	25	15	18,400
Seeking the Gold	81	43	16,800
Gulch	115	61	15,320
Personal Flag	57	32	14,670
Cojak	47	26	13,905
Proper Reality	41	30	13,874
Fast Play	59	36	13,356
Sunshine Forever	34	17	13,189
Proud Appeal	45	23	13,161
Deputy Minister	263	139	13,140
Turkoman	111	52	12,920
Greinton (GB)	71	41	12,816
Strawberry Road (Aus)	107	61	12,800
Broad Brush	89	51	12,750
Bet Big	47	29	12,587
Bold Ruckus	203	115	12,520
Sunny North	34	20	12,472
Forty Niner	124	67	12,463
Zilzal	37	20	12,440
Great Gladiator	52	28	12,412

Leading Worldwide Broodmare Sires
by Number of Winners in 2001

Sire	Strs	Wnrs	Wnrs/ Strs %
Mr. Prospector	487	238	48.9%
Halo	337	174	51.6%
Seattle Slew	355	174	49.0%
Danzig	345	168	48.7%
Dixieland Band	285	166	58.2%
Valid Appeal	269	164	61.0%
Green Dancer	336	160	47.6%
Vice Regent	294	158	53.7%
Lyphard	380	156	41.1%
Alleged	335	155	46.3%
Miswaki	322	155	48.1%
Relaunch	289	154	53.3%
Sadler's Wells	363	154	42.4%
Private Account	299	148	49.5%
Riverman	335	147	43.9%
Mr. Leader	251	143	57.0%
Nijinsky II	342	143	41.8%
Cox's Ridge	284	142	50.0%
Deputy Minister	263	139	52.9%
Affirmed	276	136	49.3%
Storm Bird	298	135	45.3%

Leading Worldwide Broodmare Sires
by Number of Wins in 2001

Sire	Strs	Wnrs	Wins
Mr. Prospector	487	238	391
Seattle Slew	355	174	306
Halo	337	174	298
Relaunch	289	154	296
Danzig	345	168	295
Dixieland Band	285	166	283
Vice Regent	294	158	281
Valid Appeal	269	164	278
Cox's Ridge	284	142	270
Miswaki	322	155	268
Alleged	335	155	263
Lyphard	380	156	258
Mr. Leader	251	143	257
Riverman	335	147	255
Private Account	299	148	255
Nijinsky II	342	143	254
Topsider	236	129	247
Deputy Minister	263	139	245
Green Dancer	336	160	243
Crafty Prospector	206	117	240
Conquistador Cielo	261	134	237
Storm Bird	298	135	235
Affirmed	276	136	233
Fappiano	269	125	232
Majestic Light	308	134	228

Leading Worldwide Broodmare Sires
by Number of Stakes Winners in 2001

Sire	Strs	Wnrs	SWs
Mr. Prospector	487	238	31
Shirley Heights	277	123	21
Fappiano	269	125	20
Nijinsky II	342	143	19
Lyphard	380	156	19
Valid Appeal	269	164	19
Deputy Minister	263	139	19
The Minstrel	305	125	18
Danzig	345	168	18
Halo	337	174	17
Darshaan	201	75	17
Caerleon	310	125	17
Seattle Slew	355	174	16
Sadler's Wells	363	154	16
Green Dancer	336	160	15
Marscay	198	72	14
Vice Regent	294	158	13
Our Native	219	116	13
Affirmed	276	136	13
Spectacular Bid	236	114	13
Rainbow Quest	183	71	13
Pleasant Colony	185	110	13

Leading Worldwide Broodmare Sires
by Number of Graded/Group Stakes Winners in 2001

Sire	Strs	Wnrs	GSWs
Mr. Prospector	487	238	15
Marscay	198	72	10
Green Dancer	336	160	9
Riverman	335	147	8
The Minstrel	305	125	8
Southern Halo	94	48	8
Nijinsky II	342	143	7
Lyphard	380	156	7
Danzig	345	168	7
Pleasant Colony	185	110	7
Caerleon	310	125	7
Fappiano	269	125	6
Shirley Heights	277	123	6
Darshaan	201	75	6
Storm Cat	169	90	6
Deputy Minister	263	139	6

Leading General Sire by Year

Year	General sire	Earnings	Year	General sire	Earnings	Year	General sire	Earnings
2001	Danehill	$13,542,612	1953	Bull Lea	1,155,846	1905	Hamburg	153,160
2000	Storm Cat	9,269,521	1952	Bull Lea	1,630,847	1904	*Meddler	222,555
1999	Storm Cat	10,383,259	1951	Count Fleet	1,160,847	1903	*Ben Strome	106,965
1998	Deputy Minister	8,526,094	1950	*Heliopolis	852,292	1902	Hastings	113,865
1997	Deputy Minister	8,581,511	1949	Bull Lea	991,842	1901	Sir Dixon	165,682
1996	Palace Music	5,231,734	1948	Bull Lea	1,334,027	1900	Kingston	116,368
1995	Sadler's Wells	5,862,410	1947	Bull Lea	1,259,718	1899	*Albert	95,975
1994	Broad Brush	5,397,181	1946	*Mahmoud	638,025	1898	Hanover	118,590
1993	Danzig	5,082,552	1945	War Admiral	591,352	1897	Hanover	122,374
1992	Danzig	6,932,569	1944	Chance Play	431,100	1896	Hanover	86,853
1991	Danzig	6,997,402	1943	*Bull Dog	372,706	1895	Hanover	106,908
1990	Alydar	6,661,455	1942	Equipoise	437,141	1894	*Sir Modred	134,318
1989	Halo	7,525,638	1941	*Blenheim II	378,981	1893	Himyar	249,502
1988	Mr. Prospector	9,575,605	1940	*Sir Gallahad III	305,610	1892	Iroquois	183,026
1987	Mr. Prospector	5,877,385	1939	*Challenger II	316,281	1891	Longfellow	189,334
1986	Lyphard	4,045,447	1938	*Sickle	327,822	1890	*St. Blaise	189,005
1985	Buckaroo	4,145,272	1937	The Porter	292,262	1889	*Rayon d'Or	175,877
1984	Seattle Slew	5,361,259	1936	*Sickle	209,800	1888	*Glenelg	130,746
1983	Halo	2,773,637	1935	Chance Play	191,465	1887	*Glenelg	120,031
1982	His Majesty	2,675,823	1934	*Sir Gallahad III	180,165	1886	*Glenelg	114,088
1981	Nodouble	2,499,946	1933	*Sir Gallahad III	136,428	1885	Virgil	73,235
1980	Raja Baba	2,483,352	1932	Chatterton	210,040	1884	*Glenelg	98,862
1979	Exclusive Native	2,872,605	1931	*St. Germans	315,585	1883	*Billet	89,998
1978	Exclusive Native	1,969,867	1930	*Sir Gallahad III	422,200	1882	*Bonnie Scotland	103,475
1977	Dr. Fager	1,593,079	1929	*Chicle	289,123	1881	*Leamington	139,219
1976	What a Pleasure	1,622,159	1928	High Time	307,631	1880	*Bonnie Scotland	135,700
1975	What a Pleasure	2,011,878	1927	Fair Play	361,518	1879	*Leamington	70,837
1974	T. V. Lark	1,242,000	1926	Man o' War	408,137	1878	Lexington	50,198
1973	Bold Ruler	1,488,622	1925	Sweep	237,564	1877	*Leamington	41,700
1972	Round Table	1,199,933	1924	Fair Play	296,102	1876	Lexington	90,570
1971	Northern Dancer	1,288,580	1923	The Finn	285,759	1875	*Leamington	64,518
1970	Hail to Reason	1,400,839	1922	*McGee	222,491	1874	Lexington	51,889
1969	Bold Ruler	1,357,144	1921	Celt	206,167	1873	Lexington	71,565
1968	Bold Ruler	1,988,427	1920	Fair Play	269,102	1872	Lexington	71,515
1967	Bold Ruler	2,249,272	1919	*Star Shoot	197,233	1871	Lexington	109,095
1966	Bold Ruler	2,306,523	1918	Sweep	139,057	1870	Lexington	120,360
1965	Bold Ruler	1,091,924	1917	*Star Shoot	131,674	1869	Lexington	56,375
1964	Bold Ruler	1,457,156	1916	*Star Shoot	138,163	1868	Lexington	68,340
1963	Bold Ruler	917,531	1915	Broomstick	94,387	1867	Lexington	54,030
1962	*Nasrullah	1,474,831	1914	Broomstick	99,043	1866	Lexington	92,725
1961	*Ambiorix	936,976	1913	Broomstick	76,009	1865	Lexington	58,750
1960	*Nasrullah	1,419,683	1912	*Star Shoot	79,973	1864	Lexington	28,440
1959	*Nasrullah	1,434,543	1911	*Star Shoot	53,895	1863	Lexington	14,235
1958	*Princequillo	1,394,540	1910	Kingston	85,220	1862	Lexington	9,700
1957	*Princequillo	1,698,427	1909	Ben Brush	75,143	1861	Lexington	22,425
1956	*Nasrullah	1,462,413	1908	Hastings	154,061	1860	Revenue	49,450
1955	*Nasrullah	1,433,660	1907	Commando	270,345			
1954	*Heliopolis	1,406,638	1906	*Meddler	151,243			

Leading Juvenile Sire by Year

Year	Juvenile sire	Earnings	Year	Juvenile sire	Earnings	Year	Juvenile sire	Earnings
2001	Hennessy	$1,766,695	1981	Hoist the Flag	680,753	1961	Bryan G.	428,810
2000	Honour and Glory	1,436,584	1980	Raja Baba	807,335	1960	*My Babu	437,240
1999	Storm Cat	1,570,026	1979	Mr. Prospector	529,665	1959	Determine	413,765
1998	Storm Cat	1,686,995	1978	Secretariat	600,617	1958	*Turn-to	463,280
1997	Phone Trick	1,737,764	1977	In Reality	432,596	1957	Jet Jewel	360,402
1996	Capote	2,756,558	1976	Raja Baba	419,872	1956	*Nasrullah	422,573
1995	Storm Cat	1,281,030	1975	What a Pleasure	611,071	1955	*Nirgal	293,800
1994	Woodman	1,303,362	1974	What a Pleasure	387,748	1954	*Nasrullah	625,692
1993	Storm Cat	1,567,979	1973	Raise a Native	311,002	1953	Roman	550,966
1992	Storm Cat	1,729,366	1972	Bold Ruler	541,990	1952	Polynesian	341,730
1991	Blushing Groom (Fr)	1,295,629	1971	First Landing	551,120	1951	Menow	274,700
1990	Woodman	1,310,633	1970	Hail to Reason	473,244	1950	War Relic	272,182
1989	Mr. Prospector	1,514,223	1969	Prince John	418,183	1949	Roman	227,604
1988	Caerleon	953,353	1968	Bold Ruler	609,243	1948	War Admiral	346,260
1987	Mr. Prospector	1,566,919	1967	Bold Ruler	1,126,844	1947	Bull Lea	420,940
1986	Rajab	950,335	1966	Bold Ruler	941,493	1946	*Mahmoud	283,983
1985	Fappiano	1,232,408	1965	Tom Fool	592,871	1945	*Sickle	183,510
1984	Danzig	2,146,530	1964	Bold Ruler	967,814	1944	Case Ace	230,525
1983	Alydar	1,136,063	1963	Bold Ruler	343,585	1943	*Bull Dog	178,344
1982	Olden Times	948,900	1962	*Nasrullah	574,231	1942	*Bull Dog	221,332

Leading Freshman Sire by Year

Year	Freshman sire	Earnings	Year	Freshman sire	Earnings	Year	Freshman sire	Earnings
2001	Valid Expectations	$1,397,911	1992	Forty Niner	578,567	1983	Alydar	1,136,063
2000	Honour and Glory	1,436,584	1991	Capote	1,185,886	1982	Seattle Slew	666,755
1999	Cherokee Run	1,369,126	1990	Woodman	1,310,633	1981	Turn and Count	283,279
1998	End Sweep	947,013	1989	Secreto	584,023	1980	Foolish Pleasure	536,783
1997	Gilded Time	730,106	1988	Chief's Crown	760,842	1979	L'Enjoleur	201,116
1996	Salt Lake	850,954	1987	Crafty Prospector	349,405	1978	Mr. Prospector	309,168
1995	Farma Way	818,043	1986	Sportin' Life	781,754	1977	Roberto	359,285
1994	Red Ransom	817,550	1985	Fappiano	1,232,408	1976	Raja Baba	419,872
1993	Seeking the Gold	939,642	1984	Danzig	2,146,530	1975	Al Hattab	217,630

Leading Broodmare Sire by Year

Year	Broodmare sire	Earnings	Year	Broodmare sire	Earnings	Year	Broodmare sire	Earnings
2001	Mr. Prospector	$11,430,437	1981	Double Jay	3,453,131	1961	Bull Lea	1,632,559
2000	Mr. Prospector	10,390,642	1980	Prince John	3,423,135	1960	Bull Lea	1,915,881
1999	Mr. Prospector	11,124,523	1979	Prince John	2,856,004	1959	Bull Lea	1,481,291
1998	Mr. Prospector	9,364,191	1978	Crafty Admiral	2,298,048	1958	Bull Lea	1,646,812
1997	Mr. Prospector	9,829,817	1977	Double Jay	2,696,490	1957	*Mahmoud	1,593,782
1996	Seattle Slew	9,105,905	1976	*Princequillo	2,763,189	1956	*Bull Dog	1,683,908
1995	Seattle Slew	8,291,630	1975	Double Jay	2,233,642	1955	*Sir Gallahad III	1,499,162
1994	Nijinsky II	7,606,160	1974	Olympia	2,292,178	1954	*Bull Dog	1,780,267
1993	Nijinsky II	7,179,266	1973	*Princequillo	3,079,810	1953	*Bull Dog	1,941,345
1992	Secretariat	7,345,089	1972	*Princequillo	2,717,859	1952	*Sir Gallahad III	1,656,221
1991	Northern Dancer	6,030,243	1971	Double Jay	2,053,235	1951	*Sir Gallahad III	1,707,823
1990	*Grey Dawn II	6,211,259	1970	*Princequillo	2,451,785	1950	*Sir Gallahad III	1,376,629
1989	Buckpasser	10,111,605	1969	*Princequillo	2,189,583	1949	*Sir Gallahad III	1,393,104
1988	Buckpasser	7,593,450	1968	*Princequillo	2,104,439	1948	*Sir Gallahad III	1,468,648
1987	Hoist the Flag	5,516,181	1967	*Princequillo	2,302,065	1947	*Sir Gallahad III	1,458,309
1986	Prince John	4,468,468	1966	*Princequillo	2,007,184	1946	*Sir Gallahad III	1,529,393
1985	Speak John	5,187,865	1965	Roman	2,394,944	1945	*Sir Gallahad III	1,020,235
1984	Buckpasser	5,111,391	1964	War Admiral	2,028,459	1944	*Sir Gallahad III	1,024,290
1983	Buckpasser	3,479,749	1963	Count Fleet	1,866,809	1943	*Sir Gallahad III	703,301
1982	Prince John	3,072,150	1962	War Admiral	1,654,396	1942	*Chicle	533,572

All-Time Leading Sires

The sire lists on the following pages do not include steeplechase statistics.

By Progeny Earnings

Through December 31, 2001

Name, YOB, Sire	Where Stood	Earnings
Sunday Silence, 1986, by Halo	Jpn.	$285,114,225
Danehill, 1986, by Danzig	Ire., Jpn., Aus.	108,478,640
Mr. Prospector, 1970, by Raise a Native	U.S.	91,443,571
Danzig, 1977, by Northern Dancer	U.S.	88,617,152
Caerleon, 1980, by Nijinsky II	Ire.	84,532,633
Sadler's Wells, 1981, by Northern Dancer	Ire.	76,167,883
Seattle Slew, 1974, by Bold Reasoning	U.S.	74,438,525
Afleet, 1984, by Mr. Prospector	U.S., Jpn.	73,409,122
Nureyev, 1977, by Northern Dancer	Fr., U.S.	70,283,093
Woodman, 1983, by Mr. Prospector	U.S., Aus.	66,940,948
Storm Cat, 1983, by Storm Bird	U.S.	66,489,070
Crafty Prospector, 1979, by Mr. Prospector	U.S.	64,683,994
Alydar, 1975, by Raise a Native	U.S.	60,556,180
Last Tycoon (Ire), 1983, by Try My Best	Ire., Aus.,Jpn.	58,777,998
Wild Again, 1980, by Icecapade	U.S.	58,696,570
Deputy Minister, 1979, by Vice Regent	U.S.	58,520,837
Miswaki, 1978, by Mr. Prospector	U.S.	58,111,761
Crystal Glitters, 1980, by Blushing Groom (Fr)	Fr., Jpn.	56,047,992
Nijinsky II, 1967, by Northern Dancer	U.S.	55,220,808
Dancing Brave, 1983, by Lyphard	Eng., Jpn.	52,585,432
Dixieland Band, 1980, by Northern Dancer	U.S.	52,424,354
Relaunch, 1976, by In Reality	U.S.	51,922,360
Seeking the Gold, 1985, by Mr. Prospector	U.S.	50,843,867
Bravest Roman, 1972, by Never Bend	Jpn.	50,815,695
Conquistador Cielo, 1979, by Mr. Prospector	U.S.	50,313,521
Lyphard, 1969, by Northern Dancer	Fr., U.S.	49,819,471
Cozzene, 1980, by Caro (Ire)	U.S.	49,755,400
Theatrical (Ire), 1982, by Nureyev	U.S.	49,687,654
Cure the Blues, 1978, by Stop the Music	U.S.	49,375,060
Pleasant Colony, 1978, by His Majesty	U.S.	48,167,498
Kris S., 1977, by Roberto	U.S.	47,101,562
Vice Regent, 1967, by Northern Dancer	Can.	46,597,100
Forty Niner, 1985, by Mr. Prospector	U.S., Jpn.	46,586,924
Rahy, 1985, by Blushing Groom (Fr)	U.S.	46,298,309
Broad Brush, 1983, by Ack Ack	U.S.	45,884,016
Mogami, 1976, by Lyphard	Jpn.	45,642,678
Valid Appeal, 1972, by In Reality	U.S.	45,433,477
Green Dancer, 1972, by Nijinsky II	Fr., U.S.	44,617,379
Halo, 1969, by Hail to Reason	U.S.	44,186,178
Bold Ruckus, 1976, by Boldnesian	Can.	43,996,882
Private Account, 1976, by Damascus	U.S.	43,773,812
Riverman, 1969, by Never Bend	Fr., U.S.	43,414,107
Affirmed, 1975, by Exclusive Native	U.S.	43,355,704
Gulch, 1984, by Mr. Prospector	U.S.	42,645,178
Mr. Leader, 1966, by Hail to Reason	U.S.	42,503,722
Mt. Livermore, 1981, by Blushing Groom (Fr)	U.S.	42,413,392
Cox's Ridge, 1974, by Best Turn	U.S.	41,228,701
Gone West, 1984, by Mr. Prospector	U.S.	41,041,646
Silver Hawk, 1979, by Roberto	U.S.	40,583,440
Irish River (Fr), 1976, by Riverman	Fr., U.S.	40,394,599
Devil's Bag, 1981, by Halo	U.S.	40,190,537
Sovereign Dancer, 1975, by Northern Dancer	U.S.	40,009,001

All-Time Leading Sires by Number of Winners
Through 2001

Name, YOB, Sire	Where Stood	Wnrs
Danehill, 1986, by Danzig	Ire., Jpn., Aus.	791
Mr. Prospector, 1970, by Raise a Native	U.S.	709
Mr. Leader, 1966, by Hail to Reason	U.S.	667
Woodman, 1983, by Mr. Prospector	U.S., Aus.	620
Sadler's Wells, 1981, by Northern Dancer	Ire.	581
Miswaki, 1978, by Mr. Prospector	U.S.	579
Caerleon, 1980, by Nijinsky II	Ire.	572
Last Tycoon (Ire), 1983, by Try My Best	Ire., Jpn., Aus., NZ	571
Danzig, 1977, by Northern Dancer	U.S.	559
Valid Appeal, 1972, by In Reality	U.S.	558
Clever Trick, 1976, by Icecapade	U.S.	558
Green Dancer, 1972, by Nijinsky II	Fr., U.S.	557
Night Shift, 1980, by Northern Dancer	Eng., U.S., Ire.	552
Riverman, 1969, by Never Bend	Fr., U.S.	536
Be My Guest, 1974, by Northern Dancer	Ire.	536
Alzao, 1980, by Lyphard	Ire., Aus.	534
Crafty Prospector, 1979, by Mr. Prospector	U.S.	518
Cure the Blues, 1978, by Stop the Music	U.S.	517
Bluebird, 1984, by Storm Bird	Ire., Aus.	517
Pirate's Bounty, 1975, by Hoist the Flag	U.S.	516
Dixieland Band, 1980, by Northern Dancer	U.S.	515
Nijinsky II, 1967, by Northern Dancer	U.S.	505
Wild Again, 1980, by Icecapade	U.S.	499
Lyphard, 1969, by Northern Dancer	Fr., U.S.	497
Geiger Counter, 1982, by Mr. Prospector	Can., U.S., Aus.	495
Allen's Prospect, 1982, by Mr. Prospector	U.S.	489
Irish River (Fr), 1976, by Riverman	Fr., U.S.	486
Runaway Groom, 1979, by Blushing Groom (Fr)	U.S.	484
*Grey Dawn II, 1962, by *Herbager	U.S.	484
Star de Naskra, 1975, by Naskra	U.S.	480
Explodent, 1969, by Nearctic	U.S.	478
Sunday Silence, 1986, by Halo	Jpn.	477
Apalachee, 1971, by Round Table	U.S.	477
Royal Academy, 1987, by Nijinsky II	Ire., U.S., Aus.	476
Phone Trick, 1982, by Clever Trick	U.S.	475
Relaunch, 1976, by In Reality	U.S.	473
Alleged, 1974, by Hoist the Flag	U.S.	473
Persian Bold, 1975, by Bold Lad	Ire.	471
Vice Regent, 1967, by Northern Dancer	Can.	466
Conquistador Cielo, 1979, by Mr. Prospector	U.S.	465
Halo, 1969, by Hail to Reason	U.S.	460
Olden Times, 1958, by Relic	U.S.	459
Nureyev, 1977, by Northern Dancer	Fr., U.S.	454
Seattle Slew, 1974, by Bold Reasoning	U.S.	452
Kris S., 1977, by Roberto	U.S.	452
Cox's Ridge, 1974, by Best Turn	U.S.	452
Raise a Bid, 1968, by Raise a Native	U.S.	451
Marshua's Dancer, 1968, by Raise a Native	U.S.	451
Sir Ivor, 1965, by Sir Gaylord	Ire., U.S.	450

All-Time Leading Sires by Stakes Winners
Through 2001

Name, YOB, Sire	Where Stood	SWs
Sadler's Wells, 1981, by Northern Dancer	Ire.	184
Mr. Prospector, 1970, by Raise a Native	U.S.	177
Danehill, 1986, by Danzig	Ire., Jpn., Aus.	175
Danzig, 1977, by Northern Dancer	U.S.	165
Nijinsky II, 1967, by Northern Dancer	U.S.	153
Northern Dancer, 1961, by Nearctic	Can., U.S.	146
Nureyev, 1977, by Northern Dancer	Fr., U.S.	131
Riverman, 1969, by Never Bend	Fr., U.S.	127
*Sir Tristram, 1971, by Sir Ivor	N.Z.	124
Caerleon, 1980, by Nijinsky II	Ire.	120
Lyphard, 1969, by Northern Dancer	Fr., U.S.	114
Vice Regent, 1967, by Northern Dancer	Can.	104
Seattle Slew, 1974, by Bold Reasoning	U.S.	100

Name, YOB, Sire	Where Stood	Wnrs
Southern Halo, 1983, by Halo	Arg., U.S.	98
Alleged, 1974, by Hoist the Flag	U.S.	94
*Nasrullah, 1940, by Nearco	Ire., U.S.	93
Storm Cat, 1983, by Storm Bird	U.S.	92
Sir Ivor, 1965, by Sir Gaylord	Ire., U.S.	92
Blushing Groom (Fr), 1974, by Red God	U.S.	91
Nodouble, 1965, by *Noholme II	U.S.	89
Nearco, 1935, by Pharos	Eng.	89
Habitat, 1966, by Sir Gaylord	Ire.	89
Dixieland Band, 1980, by Northern Dancer	U.S.	88
Relaunch, 1976, by In Reality	U.S.	87
Valid Appeal, 1972, by In Reality	U.S.	86
Miswaki, 1978, by Mr. Prospector	U.S.	85
Hyperion, 1930, by Gainsborough	Eng.	85
Green Dancer, 1972, by Nijinsky II	Fr., U.S.	84
Round Table, 1954, by *Princequillo	U.S.	83
Mr. Leader, 1966, by Hail to Reason	U.S.	83
Sharpen Up (GB), 1969, by Atan	Eng., U.S.	82
Roberto, 1969, by Hail to Reason	U.S.	82
Bold Ruler, 1954, by *Nasrullah	U.S.	82
Woodman, 1983, by Mr. Prospector	U.S., Aus.	81
In Reality, 1964, by Intentionally	U.S.	81
Irish River (Fr), 1976, by Riverman	Fr., U.S.	79
Cure the Blues, 1978, by Stop the Music	U.S.	79
Crafty Prospector, 1979, by Mr. Prospector	U.S.	79
Alzao, 1980, by Lyphard	Ire., Aus.	79
*Court Martial, 1942, by Fair Trial	Eng., U.S.	79
Roy, 1983, by Fappiano	Chi., Arg., U.S.	78
Raise a Native, 1961, by Native Dancer	U.S.	78
Nashua, 1952, by *Nasrullah	U.S.	77
Caro (Ire), 1967, by Fortino II	Fr., U.S.	77
Alydar, 1975, by Raise a Native	U.S.	77
Affirmed, 1975, by Exclusive Native	U.S.	77
Rainbow Quest, 1981, by Blushing Groom (Fr)	Eng.	76
Icecapade, 1969, by Nearctic	U.S.	72
Lord Avie, 1978, by Lord Gaylord	U.S.	71
Ghadeer, 1978, by Lyphard	Brz.	71
Fairy King, 1982, by Northern Dancer	Ire.	71
Diesis (GB), 1980, by Sharpen Up (GB)	U.S.	71
Damascus, 1964, by Sword Dancer	U.S.	71
*Grey Dawn II, 1962, by *Herbager	U.S.	71

Steeplechase races excluded.

All-Time Leading Sires by Percentage of Stakes Winners
Through 2001

Name, YOB, Sire	Where Stood	%SWs
Northern Dancer, 1961, by Nearctic	Can., U.S.	22.6%
Bold Ruler, 1954, by *Nasrullah	U.S.	22.4%
*Nasrullah, 1940, by Nearco	Ire., U.S.	21.8%
Round Table, 1954, by *Princequillo	U.S.	20.5%
Hoist the Flag, 1968, by Tom Rolfe	U.S.	19.9%
*Sea-Bird, 1962, by Dan Cupid	U.S.	18.9%
Nearco, 1935, by Pharos	Eng.	18.4%
Nijinsky II, 1967, by Northern Dancer	U.S.	17.7%
Blushing Groom (Fr), 1974, by Red God	U.S.	17.4%
Kalamoun, 1970, by Zeddaan	Ire., Fr.	17.1%
Hyperion, 1930, by Gainsborough	Eng.	17.1%
Danzig, 1977, by Northern Dancer	U.S.	16.7%
*Mahmoud, 1933, by *Blenheim II	Eng., U.S.	16.6%
Never Bend, 1960, by *Nasrullah	U.S.	16.5%
Nureyev, 1977, by Northern Dancer	Fr., U.S.	16.3%
Tentam, 1969, by Intentionally	U.S.	16.1%
Roberto, 1969, by Hail to Reason	U.S.	16.0%
Philately, 1962, by *Princequillo	U.S.	16.0%
*Court Martial, 1942, by Fair Trial	Eng., U.S.	15.8%
*Amerigo, 1955, by Nearco	U.S.	15.7%
Mill Reef, 1968, by Never Bend	Eng.	15.7%
Sea Aglo, 1971, by *Sea-Bird	Eng.	15.6%
Alycidon, 1945, by Donatello II	Eng.	15.5%
*Heliopolis, 1936, by Hyperion	U.S.	15.3%
*Ribot, 1952, by Tenerani	Ity., Eng., U.S.	15.2%

Nedayr, 1935, by Neddie	U.S.	15.1%
Vice Regent, 1967, by Northern Dancer	Can.	15.1%
Bull Lea, 1935, by *Bull Dog	U.S.	14.9%
Tanerko, 1953, by Tantieme	Fr.	14.8%
Mr. Prospector, 1970, by Raise a Native	U.S.	14.8%
Eight Thirty, 1936, by Pilate	U.S.	14.7%
*Herbager, 1956, by Vandale	Fr., U.S.	14.5%
*Royal Charger, 1942, by Nearco	Ire., U.S.	14.5%
Pelouse, 1951, by Pavot	U.S.	14.4%
Native Dancer, 1950, by Polynesian	U.S.	14.4%
In Reality, 1964, by Intentionally	U.S.	14.4%
Chop Chop, 1940, by Flares	Can.	14.4%
Dante, 1942, by Nearco	Eng.	14.3%

All-Time Leading Sires by Number of Graded/Group Stakes Winners
Through 2001

Name, YOB, Sire	Where Stood	GSWs
Danehill, 1986, by Danzig	Ire., Jpn., Aus.	113
Sadler's Wells, 1981, by Northern Dancer	Ire.	107
Mr. Prospector, 1970, by Raise a Native	U.S.	107
Nijinsky II, 1967, by Northern Dancer	U.S.	99
Danzig, 1977, by Northern Dancer	U.S.	92
*Sir Tristram, 1971, by Sir Ivor	NZ	83
Northern Dancer, 1961, by Nearctic	Can., U.S.	78
Nureyev, 1977, by Northern Dancer	Fr., U.S.	75
Southern Halo, 1983, by Halo	Arg., U.S.	74
Caerleon, 1980, by Nijinsky II	Ire.	71
Riverman, 1969, by Never Bend	Fr., U.S.	67
Lyphard, 1969, by Northern Dancer	Fr., U.S.	64
Roy, 1983, by Fappiano	Chi., Arg., U.S.	61
Blushing Groom (Fr), 1974, by Red God	U.S.	60
Seattle Slew, 1974, by Bold Reasoning	U.S.	59
Storm Cat, 1983, by Storm Bird	U.S.	58
Alleged, 1974, by Hoist the Flag	U.S.	58
Habitat, 1966, by Sir Gaylord	Ire.	56
Ghadeer, 1978, by Lyphard	Brz.	55
Rainbow Quest, 1981, by Blushing Groom (Fr)	Eng.	51
Cipayo, 1974, by Lacydon	Arg.	48
Alydar, 1975, by Raise a Native	U.S.	47
Sir Ivor, 1965, by Sir Gaylord	Ire., U.S.	45
*Vaguely Noble, 1965, by Vienna	U.S.	44
Roberto, 1969, by Hail to Reason	U.S.	42
Fitzcarraldo, 1981, by Cipayo	Arg.	42
Last Tycoon (Ire), 1983, by Try My Best	Ire., Jpn., Aus., NZ	41
Green Dancer, 1972, by Nijinsky II	Fr., U.S.	41
Egg Toss, 1977, by Buckpasser	Arg.	41
Damascus, 1964, by Sword Dancer	U.S.	41
Irish River (Fr), 1976, by Riverman	Fr., U.S.	40
Mill Reef, 1968, by Never Bend	Eng.	39
Foveros, 1976, by Averof	SAf	39
Fairy King, 1982, by Northern Dancer	Ire., Aus.	39
Diesis (GB), 1980, by Sharpen Up (GB)	U.S.	39
Caro (Ire), 1967, by Fortino II	Fr., U.S.	39
Affirmed, 1975, by Exclusive Native	U.S.	39
Zamazaan, 1965, by Exbury	NZ	38
Zabeel, 1986, by *Sir Tristram	NZ	38
Majestic Light, 1973, by Majestic Prince	U.S.	38
Bluebird, 1984, by Storm Bird	Ire., Aus.	38

All-Time Leading Broodmare Sires by Progeny Earnings
Through 2001

Name, YOB, Sire	Stood	Earnings
Northern Taste, 1971, by Northern Dancer	Jpn.	$334,684,225
Nijinsky II, 1967, by Northern Dancer	U.S.	157,933,508
Mr. Prospector, 1970, by Raise a Native	U.S.	157,217,562
Northern Dancer, 1961, by Nearctic	Can., U.S.	141,836,512

Tosho Boy, 1973, by Tesco Boy	Jpn.	136,551,132
Lyphard, 1969, by Northern Dancer	Fr., U.S.	128,875,262
Secretariat, 1970, by Bold Ruler	U.S.	113,242,403
Blushing Groom (Fr), 1974, by Red God	U.S.	109,869,896
Alydar, 1975, by Raise a Native	U.S.	104,616,672
Danzig, 1977, by Northern Dancer	U.S.	104,346,887
Seattle Slew, 1974, by Bold Reasoning	U.S.	99,240,265
Tesco Boy, 1963, by Princely Gift	Jpn.	96,527,088
Damascus, 1964, by Sword Dancer	U.S.	91,397,204
Vice Regent, 1967, by Northern Dancer	Can.	90,990,931
Bravest Roman, 1972, by Never Bend	Jpn.	87,720,413
Halo, 1969, by Hail to Reason	U.S.	86,584,032
Raise a Native, 1961, by Native Dancer	U.S.	85,842,067
Riverman, 1969, by Never Bend	Fr., U.S.	84,928,658
Partholon, 1960, by Milesian	Jpn.	83,587,592
In Reality, 1964, by Intentionally	U.S.	82,109,573
Nureyev, 1977, by Northern Dancer	Fr., U.S.	81,727,597

All-Time Leading Broodmare Sires by Graded/Group Stakes Winners
Through 2001

Name, YOB, Sire	Where Stood	Graded SWs
Nijinsky II, 1967, by Northern Dancer	U.S.	112
Northern Dancer, 1961, by Nearctic	Can., U.S.	112
Habitat, 1966, by Sir Gaylord	Ire.	111
Mr. Prospector, 1970, by Raise a Native	U.S.	108
Northfields, 1968, by Northern Dancer	Ire., Aus., SAf	99
Riverman, 1969, by Never Bend	Fr., U.S.	86
Lyphard, 1969, by Northern Dancer	Fr., U.S.	85
*Vaguely Noble, 1965, by Vienna	U.S.	79
*Sir Tristram, 1971, by Sir Ivor	NZ	75
Prince John, 1953, by *Princequillo	U.S.	69
Sir Ivor, 1965, by Sir Gaylord	Ire., U.S.	68
Graustark, 1963, by *Ribot	U.S.	67
Buckpasser, 1963, by Tom Fool	U.S.	66
Nureyev, 1977, by Northern Dancer	Fr., U.S.	64
Roberto, 1969, by Hail to Reason	U.S.	63
Secretariat, 1970, by Bold Ruler	U.S.	62
Alydar, 1975, by Raise a Native	U.S.	61
Mill Reef, 1968, by Never Bend	Eng.	61
Blushing Groom (Fr), 1974, by Red God	U.S.	60
Damascus, 1964, by Sword Dancer	U.S.	59
Green Dancer, 1972, by Nijinsky II	Fr., U.S.	59
Sovereign Edition, 1962, by Sovereign Path	NZ	59

All-Time Leading Broodmare Sires by Stakes Winners
Through 2001

Name, YOB, Sire	Where Stood	SWs
Northern Dancer, 1961, by Nearctic	Can., U.S.	223
Mr. Prospector, 1970, by Raise a Native	U.S.	222
Nijinsky II, 1967, by Northern Dancer	U.S.	213
Habitat, 1966, by Sir Gaylord	Ire.	207
Hyperion, 1930, by Gainsborough	Eng.	176
Lyphard, 1969, by Northern Dancer	Fr., U.S.	175
Raise a Native, 1961, by Native Dancer	U.S.	174
*Princequillo, 1940, by Prince Rose	U.S.	170
Prince John, 1953, by *Princequillo	U.S.	169
*Nasrullah, 1940, by Nearco	Ire., U.S.	159
Nearco, 1935, by Pharos	Eng.	156
*Vaguely Noble, 1965, by Vienna	U.S.	151
Damascus, 1964, by Sword Dancer	U.S.	150
Secretariat, 1970, by Bold Ruler	U.S.	149
*Sir Gallahad III, 1920, by *Teddy	Fr., U.S.	147
Riverman, 1969, by Never Bend	Fr., U.S.	147
Fleet Nasrullah, 1955, by *Nasrullah	U.S.	145
Sir Ivor, 1965, by Sir Gaylord	Ire., U.S.	144
Northfields, 1968, by Northern Dancer	Ire., Aus., SAf	143
Graustark, 1963, by *Ribot	U.S.	141

Biographies of Leading Sires

2001—DANEHILL, 1986 b. h., Danzig—Razyana, by His Majesty. Bred in Kentucky by Juddmonte Farms. 9-4-1-2, $321,064. Highweighted sprinter at three on European Free Handicap. Retired to Coolmore Stud, Ireland, in 1990. Since 1991, shuttled annually to Coolmore Australia. Stood in Japan for 1996 Northern Hemisphere season. Leading sire in Australia five times. Through 2001, sire of 175 stakes winners (11%) and ten champions. Best runners: European highweights Banks Hill (GB), Desert King, Mozart (Ire), Tiger Hill; Hong Kong Horse of the Year Fairy King Prawn; and Australian champions Dane Ripper, Danewin, Catbird, and Merlene. In 2001, set a single-season record with 48 stakes winners.

2000, 1999—STORM CAT, 1983 dk. b. or br. h., Storm Bird—Terlingua, by Secretariat. Bred in Pennsylvania by W. T. Young Storage Inc., raced for W. T. Young. 8-4-3-0, $570,610. Won Young America Stakes (G1) and finished second by a nose to champion Tasso in 1985 Breeders' Cup Juvenile (G1). Entered stud in 1988 at Overbrook Farm in Kentucky for initial fee of $25,000; by 2002, stood for American-high of $500,000. Through 2001, sire of 92 stakes winners (13% of foals) from first 11 crops to race, including European highweight Giant's Causeway and major American winners Tabasco Cat, Cat Thief, and Sharp Cat.

1998, 1997—DEPUTY MINISTER, 1979 dk. b. or br. h., Vice Regent—Mint Copy, by Bunty's Flight. Bred in Canada by Mr. and Mrs. Morton Levy's Centurion Farms. 22-12-2-2, $696,964. Canadian Horse of the Year in 1981; Eclipse- and Sovereign Award-winning two-year-old colt. Half-interest purchased by Kinghaven Farm midway through two-year-old season; purchased by Robert Brennan of Due Process Stable prior to 1982 season. Entered stud in 1984 at Windfields Farm Maryland; relocated in '88 to Brookdale Farm in Kentucky. Sire of 69 stakes winners through 2001, including 11 millionaires. Best include Racing Hall of Fame member Go for Wand; two-time champion and filly triple crown winner Open Mind; 1993 champion juvenile male Dehere; 1998 Breeders' Cup Classic (G1) winner Awesome Again. Broodmare sire of more than 60 stakes winners.

1996—PALACE MUSIC, 1981 ch. h., The Minstrel—Come My Prince, by Prince John. Bred in Kentucky by Mereworth Farm. Sold for $130,000 to Nelson Bunker Hunt at 1982 Keeneland July and raced for partnership of Hunt and Allen Paulson. 21-7-5-3, $918,700. Group/Grade 1 turf stakes winner in England and North America. Stood one season at Hunt's Bluegrass Farm in Kentucky, then moved in 1988 to Paulson's Brookside Farm. Shuttled between Kentucky and New Zealand for several years before relocating permanently in 1991 to Australia, where he stands at Rangal Park Stud. Was 1996 leading U.S. sire due to one horse—Cigar, a two-time Horse of the Year and leading American money winner ($9,999,815). Also sire of several important Australasian runners, including 1992 champion stayer Naturalism.

1995—SADLER'S WELLS, 1981 b. h., Northern Dancer—Fairy Bridge, by Bold Reason. Bred in Kentucky by Swettenham Stud and Partners. 11-6-3-0, $713,690. Winner of 1984 Irish Two Thousand Guineas (Ire-G1) and Eclipse Stakes (Eng-G1). Leading sire in England in 1990, 1992-2001; leading sire in France in '93. Through 2001, sire of 12 champions and 194 stakes winners (14%), including 110 group or graded winners. Best include champions: Montjeu, 1999 Prix de l'Arc de Triomphe (Fr-G1), etc., $3,178,177; Galileo (Ire), 2001 Epsom Derby (Eng-G1), Irish Derby (Ire-G1), etc., $2,245,373; Northern Spur (Ire), Breeders' Cup Turf (G1), etc., $1,614,425; Old Vic, Irish Derby, etc., $1,273,350; Barathea (Ire), Breeders' Cup Mile (G1), etc., $1,189,181.

1994—BROAD BRUSH, 1983 b. h., Ack Ack—Hay Patcher, by Hoist the Flag. Bred in Maryland by Robert E. Meyerhoff and raced three seasons for Meyerhoff. 27-14-5-5, $2,656,793. Winner of Santa Anita Handicap (G1), Suburban Handicap (G1), etc. Syndicated and entered stud in 1988 at Gainesway Farm in Kentucky. Through 2001, sire of 70 stakes winners (14%), including 1994 Breeders' Cup Classic (G1) winner Concern, $4-million-earner Broad Appeal (in Japan), and 2001 North American Grade 1 winners Include and Pompeii.

1993, 1991-'92—DANZIG, 1977 b. h., Northern Dancer—Pas de Nom, by Admiral's Voyage. Bred in Pennsylvania by Derry Meeting Farm and William S. Farish. Sold for $310,000 to Henryk de Kwiatkowski at the 1978 Saratoga yearling sale. 3-3-0-0, $32,400. Undefeated New York allowance winner before injury ended his career. Entered stud in 1981 at Claiborne Farm. Through 2001, sire of 165 stakes winners (19%), including champions in U.S., Canada, Japan, England, France, Ireland, Spain, and United Arab Emirates. Best runners: 1984 two-year-old male champion Chief's Crown, two-time Breeders' Cup Mile (G1) winner Lure, and 1991 Canadian Triple Crown winner Dance Smartly. Through 2001, broodmare sire of 87 stakes winners, including 2000 Kentucky Derby (G1) winner Fusaichi Pegasus.

1990—ALYDAR, 1975 ch. h, Raise a Native—Sweet Tooth, by On-and-On. Bred in Kentucky by Calumet Farm. 26-14-9-1, $957,195. Won 1978 Blue Grass Stakes (G1), Florida Derby (G1), etc.; second to Affirmed in all three 1978 Triple Crown races. Entered stud in 1980 at Calumet Farm and became leading American freshman sire of 1983. Sired 77 stakes winners (11%) in 11 crops, with career progeny earnings of $60,604,510. Best runners include Horses of the Year Alysheba (1988) and Criminal Type ('90), North American champions Easy Goer, Turkoman, and Althea, and 1991 Kentucky Derby (G1) winner Strike the Gold. Broodmare sire of more than 100 stakes winners of $105-million through 2001. Died at age 15 at Calumet on November 15, 1990, following a leg injury of suspicious origin.

1989, 1983—HALO, 1969 dk. b. or br. h., Hail to Reason—Cosmah, by Cosmic Bomb. Bred in Kentucky by John R. Gaines. Purchased for $100,000 by Charles Engelhard at 1970 Keeneland July yearling sale. 31-9-8-5, $259,553. Won 1974 United Nations Handicap (G1). Sold for $600,000 to stand in England, but sale fell through upon discovery he was a cribber. Syndicated for $30,000 per share and retired in 1974 to Windfields Farm Maryland. In 1984, was sold based on $36-million valuation and moved to Stone Farm in Kentucky. Sire of more than 60 stakes winners, including champion and Racing Hall of Fame member Sunday Silence, a seven-time leading sire in Japan; 1983 Kentucky Derby winner Sunny's Halo; and champions Glorious Song and Devil's Bag. Broodmare sire of more than 100 stakes winners. Pensioned in 1997 and died at Stone Farm on November 28, 2000, at age 31.

1988, 1987—MR. PROSPECTOR, 1970 b. h., Raise a Native—Gold Digger, by Nashua. Bred in Kentucky by Leslie Combs II. Sold for a sale-topping $220,000 at 1971 Keeneland July sale to Abraham I. "Butch" Savin, for whom he won the Gravesend and Whirlaway Handicaps

and set a Gulfstream Park track record: six furlongs in 1:07⅗, in 1973. 14-7-4-2, $112,171. Retired in 1975 to Savin's Aisco Farm in Florida and was top freshman sire of '78. Moved to Claiborne Farm in Kentucky in 1981. Sired 177 stakes winners (15% of foals) and 15 champions through 2001, including Gulch, Forty Niner, Conquistador Cielo, and Woodman. Broodmare sire of more than 225 stakes winners. Leading broodmare sire five times. Died of peritonitis at Claiborne Farm on June 1, 1999, at age 29.

1986—LYPHARD, 1969 b. h., Northern Dancer—Goofed, by *Court Martial. Bred in Pennsylvania by Mrs. J. O. Burgwin. Sold for $35,000 as a weanling at 1969 Keeneland November sale; resold as a yearling in Ireland for $38,000. 12-6-1-0, $195,427. Became one of Europe's top milers, winning 1972 Prix de la Foret and Prix Jacques le Marois while racing for Mrs. Pierre Wertheimer. Retired in 1973 and stood five seasons in France, where he was twice leading sire and subsequently was twice leading broodmare sire. For 1978 season, moved to Gainesway Farm in Kentucky and syndicated. Sired 115 stakes winners (14%) and eight champions, including Manila, Dancing Brave, and Three Troikas (Fr). Broodmare sire of 179 stakes winners through 2001. Pensioned at Gainesway in 1996.

1985—BUCKAROO, 1975 b. h., Buckpasser—Stepping High, by No Robbery. Bred in Kentucky by Greentree Stud. 18-5-5-1, $138,604. Won 1978 Saranac (G2) and Peter Pan (G3) Stakes. Retired to Greentree in 1980. Sold privately in 1985 to Gary and Stephen Wolfson and moved to Happy Valley Farm in Florida. Relocated in 1991 to Florida Stallion Station and again in '92 to Bridlewood Farm near Ocala. Leading sire of 1985 due largely to Horse of the Year and Kentucky Derby (G1) winner Spend a Buck, who received a $2-million bonus for winning the Jersey Derby (G3). Also sired millionaires Roo Art and Lite the Fuse among 29 stakes winners from 17 crops. Died of kidney failure on July 30, 1996, at the University of Florida School of Veterinary Medicine at age 21.

1984—SEATTLE SLEW, 1974 dk. b. or br. h., Bold Reasoning—My Charmer, by Poker. Bred in Kentucky by Ben Castleman. Sold at 1975 Fasig-Tipton Kentucky July sale for $17,500 to partnership of Mickey and Karen Taylor and Jim and Sally Hill. 17-14-2-0, $1,208,726. Champion at two, three, and four, Horse of the Year at three; in 1977, became first to win American Triple Crown while undefeated. Retired in 1979 to Spendthrift Farm in Kentucky but later relocated to Three Chimneys Farm. Sired more than 100 stakes winners through 2001, including Horse of the Year and top sire A.P. Indy, champions Slew o' Gold, Surfside, Swale, Capote, and Landaluce. First to sire winners of $5-million in a single season (1984). Noted sire of sires. Broodmare sire of Cigar; twice leading broodmare sire. Died on May 7, 2002, at Hill 'n' Dale Farm in Kentucky, at age 28.

1982—HIS MAJESTY, 1968 b. h., *Ribot—Flower Bowl, by *Alibhai. Bred in Kentucky by Mr. and Mrs. John W. Galbreath. Full brother to Graustark. 22-5-6-3, $99,430. Only stakes victory was 1971 Everglades Stakes. Syndicated for $2-million valuation and retired in 1974 to his birthplace, Darby Dan Farm, where he remained throughout a 23-season stud career. Sired 59 stakes winners and champions in U.S., Italy, Canada, Panama, and Mexico. Best includes 1981 champion and dual-classic winner Pleasant Colony, 1991 grass champion Tight Spot, and $2-million earner Majesty's Prince. Maternal grandsire of leading international sire Danehill and 85 other stakes winners. Died at Darby Dan on September 21, 1995, at age 27.

1981—NODOUBLE, 1965 ch. h., *Noholme II—Abla-Jay, by Double Jay. Bred in Arkansas by Gene Goff. 42-13-11-5, $846,749. Two-time champion handicap horse, 1969-'70; known as "Arkansas Traveler" because he won stakes in seven states. Winner of 1969 Santa Anita Handicap, '70 Metropolitan Handicap, etc. Retired in 1971 and stood at four different farms from California to Florida before moving in '86 to Three Chimneys Farm in Kentucky. Sired 91 stakes winners, including two-time Canadian Horse of the Year Overskate, Japan Cup (Jpn-G1) winner Mairzy Doates, and world record-setter Double Discount. Broodmare sire of 90 stakes winners through 2001. Pensioned in 1988. Died of colic at Three Chimneys on April 26, 1990, at age 25.

1980—RAJA BABA, 1968 b. h., Bold Ruler—Missy Baba, by *My Babu. Bred in Kentucky by Michael G. Phipps. 41-7-12-9, $123,287. Modest stakes winner retired in 1974 to Hermitage Farm in Kentucky and sired 62 stakes winners, including 1987 champion and Breeders' Cup Distaff (G1) winner Sacahuista, two-time Mexican Horse of the Year Gran Zar (Mex), and Canadian champion sprinter Summer Mood. Broodmare sire of more than 75 stakes winners of $60-million to date. Pensioned at Hermitage in 1987 and lived well into his 30s.

1979, 1978—EXCLUSIVE NATIVE, 1965 ch. h., Raise a Native—Exclusive, by Shut Out. Bred in Florida by Harbor View Farm. 13-4-4-3, $169,013. Won 1968 Arlington Classic Stakes but far better sire than racehorse. Entered stud in 1969 at Spendthrift Farm in Kentucky for a fee of $1,500. Eventually sired 66 stakes winners, including Racing Hall of Fame members Affirmed and Genuine Risk—the former an American Triple Crown winner, the latter only the second filly to win the Kentucky Derby (G1). Syndicated in 1972 for $1.8-million. Broodmare sire of 96 stakes winners. Died of cancer at Spendthrift Farm on April 21, 1983, at age 18.

1977—DR. FAGER, 1964 b. h., Rough'n Tumble—Aspidistra, by Better Self. Bred in Florida by William L. McKnight's Tartan Farms. 22-18-2-1, $1,002,642. Horse of the Year in 1968. Set world record mile of 1:32⅕ at Arlington Park carrying 134 pounds. Syndicated for $3.2-million in 1968 and entered stud the next year at Tartan Farms in Florida, where he sired nine crops. His 35 stakes winners include 1978 champion sprinter Dr. Patches, '75 champion juvenile filly Dearly Precious, and '77 Canadian Horse of the Year L'Alezane. Broodmare sire of 98 stakes winners, including notable sires Fappiano and Quiet American. Inducted into the Racing Hall of Fame in 1971. Died at Tartan Farms on August 5, 1976, at age 12, from torsion of the large colon.

1976, 1975—WHAT A PLEASURE, 1965 ch. h., Bold Ruler—Grey Flight, by *Mahmoud. Bred in Kentucky by Wheatley Stable. 18-6-5-2, $164,935. Won Hopeful Stakes and ranked fourth on 1967 Experimental Free Handicap. Sold in 1968 to Howard Sams. Entered stud the following year at Sams's Waldemar Farm in Florida. Sired 50 stakes winners, including Foolish Pleasure and Honest Pleasure, juvenile champions in 1974 and '75, respectively. Syndicated in 1976 for $8-million. Ranked twice as top juvenile sire by money won. Broodmare sire of 81 stakes winners, including champion juveniles Gilded Time and Tasso. Died of a heart attack at Waldemar Farm on March 13, 1983, at age 18.

1974—T. V. LARK, 1957 b. h., *Indian Hemp—Miss Larksfly, by Heelfly. Bred in California by Dr. Walter D. Lucas and raised in a half-acre paddock. Sold for $10,000 to Chase McCoy at 1958 Del Mar yearling sale. 72-19-13-6, $902,194. Champion grass horse of 1961 with victory

over Kelso in Washington, D.C., International. Sold for $600,000 to syndicate headed by Preston Madden and retired in 1963 to Hamburg Place in Kentucky. First crop included world record-setter Pink Pigeon. Sired 53 stakes winners and 35% stakes horses from winners. Did not establish an enduring male line but became broodmare sire of Racing Hall of Fame filly Chris Evert. Died at Hamburg on March 6, 1975, at age 18.

1973, 1963-'69—BOLD RULER, 1954 dk. b. h., *Nasrullah—Miss Disco, by Discovery. Bred in Kentucky by Wheatley Stable. 33-23-4-2, $764,204. Racing Hall of Fame member, 1957 Horse of the Year. Retired to Claiborne Farm in 1959 and began his reign as perennial leading sire four years later. Became the dominant force in American breeding throughout the 1960s and '70s, leading by progeny earnings seven times in succession, eight times overall—more than any other 20th-century stallion. Also six times leading juvenile sire. Sired 43% stakes horses from starters, 82 stakes winners, and 11 champions, among them Secretariat, Gamely, Wajima, and Bold Bidder. Broodmare sire of 119 stakes winners, although he never led in that category. Died of cancer at Claiborne on July 12, 1971, at age 17.

1972—ROUND TABLE, 1954 b. h., *Princequillo—*Knight's Daughter, by Sir Cosmo. Bred in Kentucky by Claiborne Farm. Sold privately in 1957 to Travis Kerr. 66-43-8-5, $1,749,869. Set or equaled 16 track, American, and world records. Horse of the Year in 1958, three-time champion grass horse. Entered stud in 1960 at Claiborne Farm. Made international impact, siring 83 stakes winners from 19 crops, including champions in England, Ireland, France, and Canada. Did not establish powerful male line, although several sons proved useful stallions. Broodmare sire of 125 stakes winners, including champions Outstandingly, De La Rose, and Bowl Game. Inducted into Racing Hall of Fame in 1972. Pensioned in 1978 and died at Claiborne on June 13, 1987, at age 33.

1971—NORTHERN DANCER, 1961 b. h., Nearctic—Natalma, by Native Dancer. Bred in Canada by E. P. Taylor. 18-14-2-2, $580,647. Champion in Canada and U.S., won 1964 Kentucky Derby, Preakness Stakes. Entered stud in 1965 at Windfields Farm in Canada but later relocated to Windfields's Maryland division. Syndicated in 1970 for $2.4-million. Became one of the most sought-after commercial stallions of all time, with numerous offspring selling at auction for $1-million and more. Leading sire in England four times. Leading U.S. broodmare sire in 1991. Former international leader by stakes winners, with 146—including 23 champions and noted sires Sadler's Wells, Nijinsky II, Danzig, Lyphard, Nureyev, and Storm Bird. Daughters produced more than 225 stakes winners (19 champions) through 2001. Inducted into the Racing Hall of Fame in 1976. Died of colic at Windfields in Maryland on November 16, 1990, at age 29. Buried at Windfields, Canada.

1970—HAIL TO REASON, 1958 br. h., *Turn-to—Nothirdchance, by Blue Swords. Bred in Kentucky by Bieber-Jacobs Stable. 18-9-2-2, $328,434. Champion at two. Sesamoid injury forced retirement in 1961 to Hagyard Farm in Kentucky. Syndicated for $1,085,000. Leading sire and juvenile sire of 1970, and also among leading sires in England and France. Sired 43 stakes winners, including 1970 co-Horse of the Year Personality and fillies Trillion, Straight Deal, and Regal Gleam. Several sons became top sires, including two-time American leader Halo and 1972 Epsom Derby winner Roberto, both of whom kept this male line alive. Daughters produced millionaires Allez France, Triptych, Royal Glint,

Colonial Waters, and 109 additional stakes winners. Died at Hagyard on February 24, 1976, at age 18.

1962, 1959-'60, 1955-'56—*NASRULLAH, 1940 b. h., Nearco—Mumtaz Begum, by *Blenheim II. Bred in Ireland by the Aga Khan. 10-5-1-2, $15,259. Champion at two in England and classic-placed at three but generally a disappointment due to tendency to sulk before and during races. Entered stud in 1944 at Great Barton Stud in England; sold and relocated the next year to Brownstown Stud in Ireland. Purchased in 1950 for approximately $400,000 by A. B. Hancock on behalf of an American syndicate and sent to Claiborne Farm in Kentucky for '51 breeding season. Sired 93 international stakes winners and established an enduring male line through Racing Hall of Fame son Bold Ruler and English-raced sons Red God and Grey Sovereign. Reigned five times as leading sire in America and once in England. Broodmare sire of 159 stakes winners. Suffered fatal heart attack at Claiborne on May 26, 1959, at age 19.

1961—*AMBIORIX, 1946 dk. b. h., Tourbillon—Lavendula, by Pharos. Bred in France by Marcel Boussac. 7-4-2-0, $25,165. Champion at two in France, winning Grand Criterium, and added the Prix Lupin at three before being narrowly beaten in the Prix du Jockey-Club (French Derby). Three-quarter brother to champion *My Babu. After failing to acquire *My Babu, A. B. Hancock purchased *Ambiorix in 1949 for syndication in America. Entered stud at Claiborne Farm in Kentucky the following year and ultimately sired 51 stakes winners, including champion two- and three-year-old filly High Voltage. Leading sire of 1961 when runners included major winners Ambiopoise, Hitting Away, Make Sail, and Sarcastic. Also a successful broodmare sire, leading the list in England in 1963. Pensioned in 1972 and died at Claiborne in January 1975 at age 29.

1958, 1957—*PRINCEQUILLO, 1940 b. h., Prince Rose—*Cosquilla, by *Papyrus. Bred in England by American Laudy Lawrence. 33-12-5-7, $96,550. Imported to U.S. as a yearling, leased to Anthony Pelleteri at two, and claimed for $2,500 by future Racing Hall of Fame trainer Horatio Luro for Dimitri Djordjaze. Became a top stayer, with victories including the 1943 Jockey Club Gold Cup. Retired in 1945 to A. B. Hancock's Ellerslie Farm in Virginia for $250 fee. Moved two years later to Claiborne Farm in Kentucky. Racing Hall of Fame members Round Table and Hill Prince were among his 65 stakes winners, and *Princequillo arguably was one of America's two greatest broodmare sires (along with *Sir Gallahad III) of the 20th century. Ranked eight times atop that list as daughters produced 170 stakes winners, including champions Secretariat, Mill Reef, Fort Marcy, Key to the Mint, and Bold Lad. Died at Claiborne on July 18, 1964, at age 24.

1954, 1950—*HELIOPOLIS, 1936 b. h., Hyperion—Drift, by Swynford. Bred in England by Lord Derby. 15-5-2-1, $71,216, stakes winner at two and three in England, third in 1939 Epsom Derby. Imported to America the following year by Charles B. Shaffer and finished last after sulking in his only U.S. start, an allowance race at Hialeah Park. Retired in 1941 to Shaffer's Coldstream Stud in Kentucky. Sold in 1951 to Henry Knight and relocated to Almahurst Farm. Among his 53 stakes winners were 1954 Belmont Stakes victor and champion High Gun, and champion fillies Grecian Queen, Parlo, Berlo, and Aunt Jinny. Died at Almahurst on April 2, 1959, at age 23.

1953, 1952, 1947-'49—BULL LEA, 1935 br. h., *Bull Dog—Rose Leaves, by Ballot. Bred in Kentucky by Coldstream Stud. 27-10-7-3, $94,825. Sold as a yearling for $14,000

to Calumet Farm. A moderately good racehorse, he won the Widener Handicap and Blue Grass Stakes. Retired to Calumet in 1940 for a $750 fee and became one of the greatest American sires of all time. Sired 57 stakes winners, including a record seven Racing Hall of Fame members—Citation, Armed, Coaltown, Bewitch, Two Lea, Real Delight, and Twilight Tear. In 1947, became first stallion with single-season progeny earnings of $1-million. Four-time leading broodmare sire of 100-plus stakes winners. Died and buried at Calumet on June 16, 1964, at age 29.

1951—COUNT FLEET, 1940 br. h., Reigh Count—Quickly, by Haste. Bred in Kentucky by Mrs. John D. Hertz. 21-16-4-1, $250,300. In the Hertz colors, won 1943 Triple Crown, taking Belmont Stakes by 25 lengths. Retired in 1944 to Stoner Creek Farm near Paris, Kentucky, where he remained for the next 30 years. Outstanding sire and even better broodmare sire, leading in the latter category in 1963 and ranking in the top five ten times. Among his 39 stakes winners were back-to-back Horses of the Year and Belmont Stakes winners Counterpoint (1951) and One Count ('52). Daughters produced 118 stakes winners and seven champions, including Racing Hall of Fame member Kelso. Pensioned in 1966. Count Fleet was inducted into the Racing Hall of Fame in 1961. He died at Stoner Creek on December 3, 1973, at age 33.

1946—*MAHMOUD, 1933 gr. h., *Blenheim II—Mah Mahal, by Gainsborough. Bred in France by the Aga Khan. 11-4-2-3, $86,439. Champion at three in England in 1936 when he won the Epsom Derby in record time. Entered stud at Newmarket in 1937. Purchased in 1940 by C. V. Whitney and imported to stand at his Kentucky farm. Prior to his arrival, gray Thoroughbreds were spurned by many prominent American breeders, but *Mahmoud made the color acceptable. Sired 66 stakes winners, including U.S. champions Oil Capitol, The Axe II, and First Flight, and European champions *Majideh and Donatella. Leading broodmare sire of 1957 and among leaders throughout the 1960s. Daughters produced 139 stakes winners, including Racing Hall of Fame members *Gallant Man and Silver Spoon. Died at C. V. Whitney Farm on September 18, 1962, at age 29.

1945—WAR ADMIRAL, 1934 br. h., Man o' War—Brushup, by Sweep. Bred in Kentucky by Samuel D. Riddle and raced for Glen Riddle Stable. 26-21-3-1, $273,240. Racing Hall of Fame runner is generally acknowledged as Man o' War's best son, both on the track and in the stud. Won 1937 Triple Crown and stood alongside Man o' War at Faraway Farm in Kentucky. Sire of 40 stakes winners, including 1945 Horse of the Year Busher, champion Blue Peter, and the great racemares-broodmares Searching and Busanda. Twice leading broodmare sire of 113 stakes winners, including champions Buckpasser, Hoist the Flag, and Affectionately. Died on October 30, 1959, at age 25 and buried next to Man o' War at Faraway. Remains were exhumed, along with his sire's in the 1970s, and reinterred at the Kentucky Horse Park.

1944, 1935—CHANCE PLAY, 1923 ch. h., Fair Play—*Quelle Chance, by Ethelbert. Bred in Kentucky by August Belmont II. 39-16-9-2, $137,946. A handsome horse who resembled his sire, he raced for W. Averell Harriman's Log Cabin Stable and was considered best horse of the year in 1927. Retired in 1929, stood at farms from Kentucky to New York until purchased by Warren Wright, who made him one of first stallions to stand at Calumet Farm in Lexington. Sired 23 stakes winners, including 1939 champion juvenile filly Now What and '45 Jockey Club Gold Cup winner Pot o' Luck. Pensioned in 1947

following heart attack. Euthanized at Calumet on July 6, 1950, at age 27 and buried in the farm's cemetery.

1943—*BULL DOG, 1927 b. or br. h., *Teddy—Plucky Liege, by Spearmint. Bred in France by Jefferson Davis Cohn. 8-2-1-0, $7,802. Stakes winner at three in France. Full brother to leading sire *Sir Gallahad III and half brother to top European sires Bois Roussel and Admiral Drake. Imported by C. B. Shaffer in 1930 to stand at his Coldstream Stud in Kentucky. Top runners include champion two-year-olds Occupy and Our Boots and five-time leading American sire Bull Lea. Sired 52 stakes winners in 18 crops, and 27% of his starters were of stakes class. In 1953, he supplanted *Sir Gallahad III atop broodmare sire list and subsequently led that list three times. His daughters produced 89 stakes winners and four champions. Pensioned in 1948. Died at Coldstream on October 10, 1954, at age 27.

1942—EQUIPOISE, 1928 ch. h., Pennant—Swinging, by Broomstick. Bred in Kentucky by Harry Payne Whitney. 51-29-10-4, $338,610. First great racehorse to carry colors of Whitney's son, Cornelius Vanderbilt Whitney. Nicknamed the "Chocolate Soldier" because of his dark chestnut color and combative spirit, he was an American champion at ages two, four, and five. Entered stud at C. V. Whitney Farm in 1935. Sired just four crops and 74 foals, nine of whom won stakes, including 1940 champion juvenile filly Level Best and 1942 Kentucky Derby and Belmont Stakes winner Shut Out. Broodmare sire of 1946 Triple Crown winner Assault. First foals were two-year-olds when he died of enteritis at age ten on August 4, 1938. Inducted into Racing Hall of Fame in 1957.

1941—*BLENHEIM II, 1927 br. h., Blandford—Malva, by Charles O'Malley. Bred in England by Lord Carnarvon. Sold as yearling to the Aga Khan for about $20,000. 10-5-3-0, $73,060. Injury forced retirement following victory in 1930 Epsom Derby. Stood in Europe for six seasons, siring 1936 Epsom Derby winner *Mahmoud, Italian champion Donatello II. Sold in 1936 for reported $250,000 to an American syndicate and sent to Claiborne Farm in Kentucky. Sire of more than 45 stakes winners, including 1941 American Triple Crown winner Whirlaway and 1943 champion handicap mare Mar-Kell. Broodmare sire of more than 120 stakes winners, including *Nasrullah and Kentucky Derby winners Ponder, Hill Gail, and Kauai King. Died at Claiborne on May 26, 1958, at age 31.

1940, 1933-'34, 1930—*SIR GALLAHAD III, 1920 b. h., *Teddy—Plucky Liege, by Spearmint. Bred in France by Jefferson Davis Cohn. 24-11-3-3, $17,009, Poule d'Essai des Poulains (French Two Thousand Guineas), match with *Epinard, etc. Full brother to leading sire *Bull Dog, half brother to top European sires Bois Roussel and Admiral Drake. Stood 1925 season in France, then sold for $125,000 to U.S. syndicate headed by A. B. Hancock. First important American stallion syndication. Stood at Claiborne Farm in Kentucky for remainder of career. First U.S. crop included 1930 Triple Crown winner Gallant Fox, and with two crops racing he led general sire list for the first of four times. Sired 56 stakes winners, including three Kentucky Derby victors and several champions. Not a notable sire of sires but an all-time great broodmare sire, leading in that category 12 times. Died and buried at Claiborne on July 8, 1949, at age 29.

1939—*CHALLENGER II, 1927 b. h., Swynford—Sword Play, by Great Sport. Bred in England by the National Stud. 2-2-0-0 $10,930, Richmond S., Clearwell S., ranked third on English Free Handicap, one pound above future leading American sire *Blenheim II. Classic engagements canceled upon death of owner Lord Dewar under the

rules then in force. Sold for reported $100,000 to William L. Brann and Robert Castle and imported to U.S. but injured in paddock accident before he could race again. Stood 17 seasons at Brann's Glade Valley Farm in Maryland, the first leading sire to spend his entire career outside Kentucky since *Sir Modred in 1894. Sired 34 stakes winners (11% of foals), including future Racing Hall of Fame members Challedon and Gallorette. Died at Glade Valley on December 23, 1948, at age 21.

1938, 1936—*SICKLE, 1924 br. h., Phalaris—Selene, by Chaucer. Bred in England by Lord Derby. 10-3-4-2, $23,629, stakes winner at two, third in the 1927 Two Thousand Guineas. Half brother to the great racehorse and sire Hyperion, full brother to *Pharamond II. Stood one season in England before being imported under a lease agreement in 1930 by Joseph E. Widener, who eventually purchased him for a reported $100,000. Sent to Widener's Elmendorf Farm in Kentucky, where he replaced deceased Fair Play as head of the stud. Sired 22% stakes horses from foals, with 41 stakes winners, including champions Stagehand, Star Pilot, and *Gossip II. Broodmare sire of 57 stakes winners, including 1951 Horse of the Year Counterpoint. Died on December 26, 1943, at Elmendorf at age 19.

1937—THE PORTER, 1915 b. h., Sweep—Ballet Girl, by St. Leonards. Bred in Kentucky by David Stevenson. Raced for Samuel Ross and later Edward McLean. 52-26-10-8, $89,249, Annapolis Handicap, etc. Stood barely 15 hands. From 1922-'31 stood at McLean Stud in Virginia. At age 16, purchased for $27,000 at McLean's 1931 dispersal by Mrs. John Hay Whitney and sent to Kentucky. Sired 11% stakes winners from foals, with the best of his 34 stakes winners being 1937 Santa Anita Handicap winner Rosemont, '37 Suburban Handicap winner Aneroid, and the top juvenile Porter's Mite. Died at Mare's Nest Farm in Kentucky on October 23, 1944, at age 29.

1932—CHATTERTON, 1919 ch. h., Fair Play—Chit Chat, by *Rock Sand. Bred in Kentucky by August Belmont II. 32-15-5-4, $26,565. Bred like Man o' War, by Fair Play out of *Rock Sand mare. Sold privately and raced for Frank J. Kelley. Multiple stakes winner in Midwest, though not a top runner. Stood 1924 in California but after Kelley's death sent to Claiborne Farm in Kentucky. Remained there except for 1932 season when leased to Arrowbrook Farm in Illinois. His position atop list was due almost entirely to 1932 champion and Belmont Stakes winner Faireno. Also sired 1928 champion juvenile filly Current and nine other stakes winners. Died at Claiborne of kidney ailment on July 14, 1933, at age 14.

1931—*ST. GERMANS, 1921 b. h., Swynford—Hamoaze, by Torpoint. Bred in England by Lord Astor. 20-9-4-4, $44,793, Coronation Cup, Doncaster Cup, etc., second in Epsom Derby. Imported by Payne Whitney to stand at his Greentree Stud. Advertised "for private use only" in early years. He suffered from low fertility and averaged fewer than ten foals per crop, but those highly successful. Best of 23 stakes winners (13% of foals) was 1931 Horse of the Year Twenty Grand, winner of the Kentucky Derby and Belmont Stakes; two-time handicap champion Devil Diver; and 1936 Kentucky Derby-Preakness Stakes winner Bold Venture. Twenty Grand was sterile, and several prominent male-line descendants experienced fertility problems. Died at Greentree Stud on May 18, 1929, at age 18 following attack of enteritis.

1929—*CHICLE, 1913 b. h., Spearmint—Lady Hamburg II, by Hamburg. Bred in France by Harry Payne Whitney but raced in U.S. 10-3-0-2, $4,765. Had soundness problems but nonetheless won Champagne Stakes and Brook-

lyn Derby (now Dwyer Stakes). Entered stud in Kentucky at H. P. Whitney Farm for fee of $500. Fee later raised as high as $1,500. Bad tempered, kept muzzled as a stallion for safety of farm workers. Sired six stakes winners from first 13-foal crop and about 40 overall—including champion juveniles Whichone and Mother Goose. Leading broodmare sire of 1942. Died on May 20, 1939, at age 26, at C. V. Whitney Farm near Lexington.

1928—HIGH TIME, 1916 ch. h., Ultimus—Noonday, by Domino. Bred in Kentucky by Wickliffe Stud of Corrigan and McKinney. 7-1-0-1, $3,950, Hudson S., 3rd Great American S. Highly inbred to Domino, with three crosses in first three generations. Beautiful physical specimen, sold at auction as two-year-old for $8,500. Career limited by throat problems. Won Aqueduct's Hudson Stakes in track-record time for five furlongs. Retired at three to Haylands Stud in 1919 but was not well received by Kentucky breeders. In later years, changed ownership several times before settling at Dixiana Farm in Kentucky. Sired about 40 stakes winners, including Racing Hall of Fame champion gelding Sarazen and 1928 champion juvenile colt High Strung. Leading broodmare sire of 1940. Died at Dixiana on November 20, 1937, at age 21.

1927, 1924, 1920—FAIR PLAY, 1905 ch. h., Hastings—*Fairy Gold, by Bend Or. Bred in Kentucky by August Belmont II. 32-10-11-3, $86,950. Racing Hall of Fame runner had misfortune to come along in same crop as unbeatable Colin. Won 1908 Lawrence Realization. When betting was outlawed in New York, shipped to England, where heavy weight assignments and a deteriorating attitude led to a 6-0-0-0 record. Retired to Nursery Stud in 1910. When Belmont died in 1924, sold at age 20 on $100,000 bid to Joseph Widener. Renowned for producing stamina, the three-time leading sire got champions Chance Play and Mad Hatter but was immortalized as sire of Man o' War, through whom his male line survives today. Leading broodmare sire in 1931, '34, and '38. Died at age 24 in paddock at Elmendorf Farm in Kentucky on December 16, 1929.

1926—MAN O' WAR, 1917 ch. h., Fair Play—Mahubah, by *Rock Sand. Bred in Kentucky by August Belmont II. 21-20-1-0, $249,465. Sold at auction as yearling for $5,000 to Samuel Riddle. Became one of the greatest racehorses of all time, winning Preakness and Belmont Stakes. Retired in 1921 to Hinata Stock Farm but soon moved to Faraway Farm, both in Kentucky. Instant success, led general sire list with only three crops racing. Top runners include future Racing Hall of Fame members War Admiral and Crusader, as well as six other American champions. Also a great broodmare sire. As Riddle's private stallion, did not receive the best mares yet sired 64 stakes winners, 17% of foals. Died at age 30 at Faraway on November 1, 1947. Thousands attended funeral, which was nationally broadcast by radio and filmed for newsreels. Grave and larger-than-life bronze statue relocated in late 1970s to Kentucky Horse Park.

1925, 1918—SWEEP, 1907 br. h., Ben Brush—Pink Domino, by Domino. Bred in Kentucky by James R. Keene. 13-9-2-2, $59,998, champion at two in 1909 when he won the Futurity Stakes and added Belmont Stakes at three. Sold at 1913 Keene estate dispersal at Madison Square Garden for $17,500 to partnership of John Barbee, J. C. Carrick, and Andrew Stone. Led broodmare sire list twice and twice was leader by number of two-year-old winners. Sired more than 40 stakes winners. Top runners include 1918 champion juvenile Eternal and handicap star The Porter, leading sire of 1937. Died at age 24 from "indigestion" on August 15, 1931, at Glen-Helen Stud in Kentucky.

1923—THE FINN, 1912 bl. h., *Ogden—Livonia, by *Star Shoot. Bred in Kentucky by John E. Madden. 50-19-10-6, $38,965. Raced initially for Madden before being sold to H. C. Hallenbeck. Victories included Belmont and Withers Stakes, as well as Metropolitan, Manhattan, and Havre de Grace Handicaps. Generally regarded as champion three-year-old colt of 1915. Madden later bought him back and in 1923 he was sold again, for $100,000 to W. R. Coe. Stood thereafter at Hinata Stock Farm in Kentucky. Sired Kentucky Derby winners Flying Ebony and Zev, the latter America's first racehorse to top $300,000 in earnings (1924). Died at Hinata on September 4, 1925, from "inflammation of the bowels," at age 13.

1922—*McGEE, 1900 b. h., White Knight—Remorse, by Hermit. Bred in England by Lord Bradford. 53-24-14-5, $18,391, Fleetfoot H., etc. Only foal by an unraced stallion. Sold cheaply as yearling to Ed Corrigan for $125 to $500 and imported to U.S. Raced in Midwest, a minor stakes winner of 24 races. Primarily a sprinter—set American 5½-furlong record in 1903. Retired to Corrigan's Freeland Stud near Lexington, then sold in 1908 for $1,300 to Charles Moore. Relocated to nearby Mere Hill Stud where his 1909 fee was $50. Sired 20 stakes winners, most notably the great gelding Exterminator and Donerail, winner of 1913 Kentucky Derby at 91.45-to-1. His last foal was conceived in 1930 when *McGee was 30 years old. Prior to his death at Mere Hill on September 18, 1931, he was believed to be the oldest stallion in Kentucky.

1921—CELT, 1905 ch. h., Commando—*Maid Of Erin, by Amphion. Bred in Kentucky by James R. Keene. 6-4-1-1, $29,975. Lightly raced winner of 1908 Brooklyn Handicap, overshadowed by unbeaten stablemate Colin, another son of Commando. Stood initially at Castleton Stud, then leased for 1912 to stand at Hancock family's Ellerslie Stud in Virginia. Though lease expired in 1913, A. B. Hancock acquired him that fall for $20,000 at Keene's estate dispersal. Returned to Ellerslie to sire a total 29 stakes winners (15% of foals). In 1930, was top broodmare sire when Gallant Fox swept the Triple Crown. Died at age 14 in 1919.

1919, 1916-'17, 1911-'12—*STAR SHOOT, 1898 ch. h., Isinglass—Astrology, by Hermit. Bred in England by Maj. Eustace Loder. 10-3-1-3, $34,747, National Breeders' Produce S., etc. A good two-year-old, developed wind problems at three and was unplaced in two starts that season. Because he was from a family not noted for producing good sires, he was sold to America and entered stud in 1902 at Runnymede Farm in Kentucky, where he was an immediate success. Purchased privately by John Madden in 1912 and relocated to Hamburg Place. One of the most influential American-based stallions of his time, his sons include future Racing Hall of Fame members Grey Lag and Sir Barton. In 1916, had record 27 juvenile winners. Died of pneumonia at Hamburg on November 19, 1919, at age 21.

1915, 1913-'14—BROOMSTICK, 1901 b. h., Ben Brush—*Elf, by Galliard. Bred in Kentucky by Col. Milton Young. 39-14-11-5, $74,730, Travers S., etc. Young acquired *Elf for $250 in foal with Broomstick. Colt was sold privately to race for coal millionaire Samuel Brown. Racing Hall of Fame runner raced through age four. Retired in 1906 to Brown's Senorita Stud in Kentucky. Sold for $7,250 two years later at estate sale of his owner to H. P. Whitney. Eventually sired 25% stakes winners from foals—nearly 60 in all—including the first New York handicap triple crown winner, Whisk Broom II; the first filly Ken-

tucky Derby winner, Regret; 1911 Derby winner Meridian; and '12 Two Thousand Guineas winner *Sweeper. Died at C. V. Whitney Farm in Kentucky, on March 24, 1931, at age 30.

1910, 1900—KINGSTON, 1884 br. h., Spendthrift—*Kapanga, by Victorious. Bred in Kentucky by James R. Keene. 138-89-33-12, $140,195, First Special S., etc. Raced through age ten, primarily for Phil and Mike Dwyer. His 89 career victories remains an all-time record, and for about one year (1892-'93) he reigned as America's leading money earner. Entered stud in 1895 at Eugene Leigh's La Belle Farm in Kentucky for a $150 fee. Moved in a few years to Keene's Castleton Farm near Lexington, where he stood privately with leading sires Ben Brush and Commando. Represented by Futurity Stakes winners Ballyhoo Bey (1900) and Novelty ('10), as well as 1900 Belmont Stakes winner Ildrim. Died at Castleton on December 4, 1912, at age 28.

1909—BEN BRUSH, 1893 b. h., Bramble—Roseville, by Reform. Bred in Kentucky by Catesby Woodford and Ezekiel Clay. 40-25-5-5, $65,208. Small, plain, and tough, a superb racehorse, and Racing Hall of Fame member. Sold as yearling for $1,200 to Eugene Leigh and Ed Brown, and again at three for reported $25,000 to Mike Dwyer. Won 1896 Kentucky Derby and '97 Suburban Handicap. Sold to James R. Keene for stud duty at Castleton Farm in Kentucky. Following Keene's death in 1913, acquired for $10,000 by Kentucky Senator Johnson Camden and lived out his days at Camden's Hartland Stud near Versailles. Established noted male line that endured for decades. Best offspring include three-time leading American sire Broomstick and two-time leader Sweep. Died at age 25 on June 8, 1918.

1908, 1902—HASTINGS, 1893 br. h., Spendthrift—*Cinderella, by Tomahawk or Blue Ruin. Bred in Kentucky by Dr. J. D. Neet. 21-10-8-0, $16,340. Raced at two for Gideon and Daly. Upon dispersal of that stable in 1895, acquired for $37,000 by August Belmont II. Won 1896 Belmont Stakes, although generally not regarded as a top racehorse. Entered stud in 1898 at Belmont's Nursery Stud in Kentucky and was known for his savage disposition. By far his best was the 1905 colt Fair Play, the future sire of Man o' War. Died at Nursery Stud in 1917 at age 24 following an attack of paralysis.

1907—COMMANDO, 1898 b. h., Domino—Emma C., by *Darebin. Bred in Kentucky by James R. Keene. 9-7-2-0, $58,196. Coarse and heavily muscled, he did not resemble his handsome sire but was at least his equal on the racecourse. In the James R. Keene colors, won 1901 Belmont Stakes. The Racing Hall of Fame member retired to Keene's Castleton Stud in 1902 to take the place of Domino, who died at age six in 1897. Immediate success at stud but, like his sire, he died young. From three crops and 27 foals, sired ten stakes winners, among them Racing Hall of Fame members Peter Pan and Colin, and influential sires Celt and Ultimus. Died of tetanus at Castleton in early March 1905 at age seven.

1906, 1904—*MEDDLER, 1890 b. h., *St Gatien—Busybody, by Petrarch. Bred in England by George Abington Baird. 3-3-0-0, $16,689, Dewhurst S., etc. By an Epsom Derby winner and out of an Epsom Oaks winner. Unraced after two-year-old season after the death of his owner, which, under rules in force at the time, voided his nominations to the three-year-old classics. Sold in 1893 for $76,000 to American William Forbes who stood him initially at Neponset Stud in Massachusetts. Upon Forbes's death in 1897, sold to W. C. Whitney for $49,000 and moved to La Belle Stud in Kentucky. Sold at 1904 Whitney es-

tate dispersal for $51,000. Represented by champion fillies Trigger, Tangle, and Tanya (winner of 1905 Belmont Stakes). When American racing was decimated by 1909 antiwagering legislation, relocated to France, where he died on April 17, 1916, at Haras de Fresnay-le-Buffard in Normandy at age 26.

1905—HAMBURG, 1895 b. h., Hanover—Lady Reel, by Fellowcraft. Bred in Kentucky by C. J. Enright. Sold for $1,250 as yearling to John E. Madden, who later named his famous breeding farm, Hamburg Place, for the Racing Hall of Fame member. 21-16-3-2, $60,380, Lawrence Realization, etc. Sold privately for $40,001 to Marcus Daly in 1898. Stood two seasons at Daly's Bitter Root Stud in Montana. After Daly's death in 1900, sold for $60,000 to W. C. Whitney, who sent him to La Belle Stud in Kentucky. At 1904 Whitney dispersal, sold for $70,000 to Whitney's son Harry Payne Whitney, who took him to Brookdale Stud in New Jersey. Sired Racing Hall of Fame filly Artful, champions Borrow, Hamburg Belle, Burgomaster, and Rosie O'Grady, and foundation mare Frizette. Died at Brookdale on September 15, 1915, at age 20.

1903—*BEN STROME, 1886 b. h., Bend Or—Strathfleet, by The Scottish Chief. Bred in England by the Duke of Westminster. 35-3-6-6, $2,975. Big, 16.2 hands tall, good-looking, and beautifully bred, but a poor racehorse in England. Entered stud in 1894 at Thomas J. Carson's Dixiana Farm in Kentucky. When his first foals were yearlings, Dixiana advertised that a limited number of approved mares would be accepted by special contract, which meant at no cost. By 1904, his fee had jumped to $300, one of the highest in the country. Most noted as sire of Racing Hall of Fame member Roseben, but offspring also included juvenile champions Eugenia Burch and Highball. Died at Dixiana in 1909 at age 23.

1901—SIR DIXON, 1885 br. h., *Billet—Jaconet, by *Leamington. Bred in Kentucky by Col. Ezekiel Clay. 29-10-7-7, $54,915. Sold for $1,125 as yearling to Green B. Morris, who resold him at three for $20,000 to Mike and Phil Dwyer. A high-strung, delicate type, he was unable to endure the tough campaigns required by the Dwyers but nevertheless scored victories in the 1888 Belmont, Withers, and Travers Stakes. Stood his entire career at Clay's Runnymede Stud in Kentucky. Sired champions Butterflies, Blue Girl, Kilmarnock, and Running Water, and 1905 Kentucky Derby winner Agile. Died on March 23, 1909, at age 14 after breaking his right hip in a paddock accident.

1899—*ALBERT, 1882 b. h., Albert Victor—Hawthorn Bloom, by Kettledrum. Bred in England by Sir Richard Jardine. 6-1-1-0, $2,547. A racehorse of modest talents, won a minor stakes at Newcastle as a two-year-old. Imported as a stallion by Alfred Withers. Later spent most of his breeding career at the Adelbert Stud of Williams and Radford near Hopkinsville, Kentucky. Advertised at a $100 fee in 1896, with a reference to him as "the most uniform sire of winners in America—they mature early and make great campaigners." Not an outstanding sire, his best was probably 1899 juvenile champion Mesmerist and the good filly Hatasoo, an ancestress of many top racehorses. Believed to have died in 1907, because his last five foals arrived the following spring.

1898, 1895-'97—HANOVER, 1884 ch. h., Hindoo—Bourbon Belle, by *Bonnie Scotland. Bred in Kentucky at Col. Ezekiel Clay's Runnymede Farm. 50-32-14-2, $118,887, champion three-year-old, 1887 Belmont Stakes, etc. Sold as a yearling for $1,350 to Phil and Mike Dwyer. Won 17 consecutive races at two and three and ultimately retired with American earnings record. One of America's better all-time stallions, his best by far was Racing Hall of Fame

member and leading sire Hamburg. Hanover was valued at $100,000 when he died on March 23, 1899, at McGrathiana Stud in Kentucky at age 15. Cause of death was said to be blood poisoning caused by a leg injury. He was originally buried at McGrathiana, but his skeleton was later exhumed for research and display.

1894—*SIR MODRED, 1877 b. h., Traducer—Idalia, by Cambuscan. Bred in New Zealand by Middle Park Stud. Among the foremost racehorses of his day in New Zealand, with victories in the Canterbury Derby, Canterbury Cup, and Metropolitan Stakes. Imported to California in 1885 by James Ben Ali Haggin. In 1894, became the first California-based stallion to lead the American sire list when his offspring won 137 races and $134,318. Notable offspring include champion Tournament, 1893 Belmont Stakes winner Comanche, 1890 Travers Stakes winner Sir John, and the outstanding fillies Gloaming and Lucania. Stood at Haggin's 44,000-acre Rancho del Paso near Sacramento, where he was pensioned for several seasons prior to his death due to infirmities of old age in June 1904 at age 27.

1893—HIMYAR, 1875 b. h., Alarm—Hira, by Lexington. Bred in Kentucky by Maj. Barak Thomas. 27-14-6-4, $11,650, Phoenix Hotel Stakes, etc. Finished second in 1878 as one of the heaviest favorites ever for the Kentucky Derby. High-strung, nervous, and hard to train, considered primarily a speed horse. Entered stud in 1882 at Thomas's Dixiana Farm near Lexington and got, among others, immortal racehorse and sire Domino and '98 Kentucky Derby winner Plaudit. In 1893, due largely to Domino, he established a single-season progeny earnings record of $259,252 that would stand for 24 years. Died at age 30 on December 30, 1905, and was buried at Dixiana under a tombstone that reads: "Speed springs eternal from his ashes."

1892—IROQUOIS, 1878 br. h., *Leamington—Maggie B.B., by *Australian. Bred by Aristides Welch at Erdenheim Stud in Pennsylvania. 26-12-4-3, $99,707. Sold as a yearling to tobacco magnate Pierre Lorillard, who exported him to race in England. First American-bred winner of Epsom Derby and St. Leger Stakes; finished second in the Two Thousand Guineas. Wall Street briefly halted trading to celebrate news of his Derby triumph. Returned to U.S., he raced three times without success, probably because of pulmonary bleeding. Retired to stud at W. H. Johnson's Belle Meade Farm, where he died in 1899 at age 11. His offspring included champion Tammany.

1891—LONGFELLOW, 1867 br. h., *Leamington—Nantura, by Brawner's Eclipse. Bred, owned, and trained by John Harper. 16-13-2-0, $11,200. Standing a towering 17 hands, he was named for his long legs and not for the noted poet. One of the great racehorses of the 1870s, an injury forced his retirement to Harper's Nantura Stud near Midway, Kentucky. Sired more than 40 stakes winners, including Kentucky Derby winners Leonatus and Riley, 1886 Preakness winner The Bard, and champions Thora and Freeland. A dominant bay, it was said that all of his foals but one were bay or brown. Died at Nantura on November 5, 1893, and was buried with a marker that reads: "King of Racers and King of Stallions."

1890—*ST. BLAISE, 1880 ch. h., Hermit—Fusee, by Marsyas. Bred in England by Lord Alington. 16-7-2-1, $41,066. Won 1883 Epsom Derby. Imported for $30,000 in 1885 by August Belmont to stand at his Nursery Stud in Kentucky. Following Belmont's death, sold at auction in 1891 by Tattersalls of New York for a then-world record $100,000. Purchased on a solitary bid by Charles Reed of Tennessee. Not successful for Reed, sold at auction again

in 1902 for $8,300 to James B. A. Haggin of Elmendorf Farm, Kentucky, but subsequently purchased privately by August Belmont II. At age 22, he returned to Nursery Stud to live out his days. Best runners include 1890 Futurity Stakes winner Potomac and '96 Preakness Stakes winner Margrave. Died in October 1909 at age 29.

1889—*RAYON D'OR, 1876 ch. h., Flageolet—Araucaria, by Ambrose. Bred in France by Haras de Dangu. 28-15-7-4, $110,207. Won from five to 18 furlongs, including 1879 St. Leger, and carried up to 132 pounds to victory. Imported in 1883 by W. L. Scott, who paid nearly $40,000 for him and stood him initially at his Algeria Stud in Pennsylvania. When Algeria dispersed in 1892, purchased by August Belmont II and moved to Nursery Stud in Kentucky. Sired many top runners, including Brooklyn Handicap winner Tenny, Futurity Stakes winner Chaos, and Banquet, winner of 62 races and $118,872. Died from "fever" on July 15, 1896, at Nursery Stud at age 20.

1888, 1886-'87, 1884—GLENELG, 1866 b. h., Citadel—*Babta, by Kingston. Imported *in utero* by R. W. Cameron, who earlier had imported four-time leading sire *Leamington. Foaled at Cameron's Clifton Farm in New York. 18-10-5-2, $23,340. Purchased as a yearling by August Belmont I for $2,000. Big, bad-tempered, and prone to colic, he nonetheless won the 1869 Travers Stakes and other important races. After his racing days, he was sold to Milton H. Sanford for $10,000. His many outstanding runners include Racing Hall of Fame mare Firenze. Died on October 23, 1897, at age 31 at the farm of Tyree Bate in Castalian Springs, Tennessee.

1885—VIRGIL, 1864 dk. b. h., Vandal—Hymenia, by *Yorkshire. Bred in Woodford County, Kentucky, by Harmony H. C. Gratz. 10-7-2-1, $2,950, Sequel S. three times, etc. A beautiful, nearly black horse, owned during his racing days by Milton Sanford, primarily a sprinter in an era that prized stamina (although he won once at two miles). Initially had few opportunities as a stallion and was even broken to harness and used to pull a carriage. Sold cheaply in 1874. When his son Vagrant won the 1876 Kentucky Derby, Virgil was repurchased by Sanford. He subsequently sired Racing Hall of Fame member Hindoo (also a great sire) and unbeaten Tremont. Died at Quindaro Stud in Kentucky in 1893 at age 29.

1883—*BILLET, 1865 br. h., Voltigeur—Calcutta, by Flatcatcher. Bred in England by James Smith. 18-5-3-1, $3,983. Insignificant racehorse in England, racing most often in selling races. Imported to America in 1869 and stood several seasons in Illinois. After son Elias Lawrence established a Saratoga three-mile record in 1878, was moved to Runnymede Stud in Paris, Kentucky, where he remained until his death on January 17, 1889, at age 24. Top runners include Racing Hall of Fame member Miss Woodford, the first American Thoroughbred to top $100,000 in earnings, and 1901 leading sire Sir Dixon.

1882, 1880—*BONNIE SCOTLAND, 1853 b. h., Iago—Queen Mary, by Gladiator. Bred in England by William l'Anson. 4-2-1-0, $6,308. Lightly raced and never truly sound because of an injury as a foal, won Liverpool St. Leger and Doncaster Stakes. Imported to America in 1857, believed to have stood originally in Ohio before relocating to Gen. W. G. Harding's famous Belle Meade Stud near Nashville, Tennessee. Offspring include Racing Hall of Fame member Luke Blackburn, 1883 Belmont Stakes winner George Kinney, and champion Bramble. Died in his paddock at Belle Meade on February 2, 1880, at age 27.

1881, 1879, 1877, 1875—*LEAMINGTON, 1853 br. h., Faugh-a-Ballagh—Mare by Pantaloon. Bred in England. 24-8-3-3, $33,446, Goodwood S., Tradesmen's Plate twice,

etc. Imported in 1865 by R. W. Cameron of New York after standing six seasons in England. In U.S., stood first at Bosque Bonita Stud in Kentucky, later at Cameron's Clifton Stud on Staten Island, and finally at Aristides Welch's Erdenheim Stud near Philadelphia. Sire of Racing Hall of Fame members Longfellow and Parole, inaugural Kentucky Derby winner Aristides, and Iroquois, first American-bred winner of the Epsom Derby. Many of his best offspring were out of Lexington mares and were raced by the Lorillard brothers, George and Pierre, who dominated American racing during the 1870s and '80s. Died at Erdenheim on May 6, 1878, at age 25.

1878, 1876, 1861-'74—LEXINGTON, 1850 b. h., Boston—Alice Carneal, by *Sarpedon. Bred in Kentucky by Dr. Elisha Warfield. 7-6-1-0, $56,600, Great Post S., etc. Sold to Richard Ten Broeck as a three-year-old and in 1855 set an American four-mile record of 7:19¾. By then, he was going blind and was sold for $15,000 to R. A. Alexander of Woodburn Stud, Kentucky. He stood at that Midway farm his entire career except for an interlude in Illinois for his own safety during the Civil War. As with *Glencoe, a number of his offspring were utilized as Civil War mounts. His many outstanding runners include champions Kentucky, Asteroid, Norfolk, Duke of Magenta, Harry Bassett, Sultana, and Tom Bowling. Lexington's post-Civil War fee of $500 was unprecedented. His male-line survived into the 20th century, and numerous crosses of his name are still present in far branches of modern pedigrees. The unprecedented 16-time leading sire died on July 1, 1875, at age 25. His skeleton is in the possession of the Smithsonian Institution in Washington, D.C.

1860—REVENUE, 1843 b. h., *Trustee—Rosalie Somers, by Sir Charles. Bred in Virginia by statesman John M. Botts. 21-16-5-0. Son of a leading sire and champion racemare. Stood at Botts's farm in Virginia, where he sired the great Planet, widely viewed as the best American racehorse in the era preceding the Civil War, compiling a 31-27-4-0 record and surpassing Peytona as America's top earner with $69,700, a mark that stood for 20 years. In 1860, Revenue became the first stallion to lead an American sire list based on earnings ($49,450) rather than races won (the previously recognized standard), although he led by wins as well. He died in Virginia in September 1868 at age 25.

1859—*ALBION, 1837 bl. h., Cain or Actaeon—Panthea, by Comus or Blacklock. Bred in England; reportedly was a successful racehorse in America during the early 1840s. A reliable sire of winners during pre-Civil War years and later an outstanding broodmare sire. Died in 1859 at age 22 in Sumner County, Tennessee.

1858, 1854-'57, 1849-'50, 1847—*GLENCOE, 1831 ch. h., Sultan—Trampoline, by Tramp. Bred in England by Lord Jersey. 10-8-1-1, $33,459. Winner of 1834 Two Thousand Guineas, third in Epsom Derby. Stood one season in England, getting legendary broodmare Pocahontas. Imported in 1836 by James Jackson, who reportedly paid $10,000 for him. Swaybacked but otherwise handsome, he was much admired by breeders of the day. Stood from 1837-'44 in Alabama; 1845-'48 in Tennessee; and 1849-'57 in Kentucky as property of A. Keene Richards, an ardent secessionist who allegedly turned over many of his offspring for use as Confederate mounts during the Civil War. Sired the great mares Reel and Peytona, the latter America's leading money winner from 1845-'61 ($62,400), as well as top sons Star Davis and Vandal. Died of "lung fever" on August 25, 1857, at Blue Grass Park in Georgetown, Kentucky.

1853, 1851-'52—BOSTON, 1833 b. h., Timoleon—Sister to Tuckahoe, by Ball's Florizel. Bred in Virginia by John Wickham. 45-40-2-1, $51,700. Sold at two for $800 to Nathaniel Rives to satisfy a gaming debt. Racing Hall of Fame member won 30 four-mile heat races. Nicknamed "Old White Nose" for his distinctively blazed face, his vicious temper struck fear into the hearts of his handlers. Sire of Racing Hall of Fame member Lexington and his great rival, Lecompte, as well as the great racemare Nina, dam of Planet. Died in 1850 at age 17 at Col. E. M. Blackburn's farm in Woodford County, Kentucky.

1848 (co-leader), 1843, 1837-'39—*LEVIATHAN, 1823 ch. h., Muley—Coxcomb's dam, by Windle. Bred in England. 19-15-3-0, $11,096, Dee S., etc. At 16 hands, large for his time. Imported in 1830 by James Jackson of Alabama. Not well received at first because of his enormous size. In 1838, became America's first $100,000 sire when his progeny won 92 races. At one time, his $75 fee was the highest in America. Stood in Tennessee, managed by Col. George Elliott. Died in Gallatin, Tennessee, in 1846, at age 23 from "inflammation of the bowels."

1848 (co-leader)—*TRUSTEE, 1829 ch. h., Catton—Emma, by Whisker. 11-4-3-3, $7,446, Claret S., etc. Third in 1832 Epsom Derby in first career start. Brother to 1835 Epsom Derby winner Mundig, half brother to 1843 Derby winner Cotherstone. Imported in 1835 by Commodore Robert Stockton, later senator from New Jersey. Not well received by American breeders and moved often during his stud career. Stood in New York between 1836-'41; Virginia in 1842; Kentucky in 1843-'44; Virginia in 1845-'46; and back to New York in 1847, where he remained until his death at age 27. Sire of Racing Hall of Fame filly Fashion, the great mare Levity, and leading 1860 American sire Revenue. Died in 1856 at West Farms, Westchester County, New York.

1846, 1844-'45, 1842—*PRIAM, 1827 b. h., Emilius—Cressida, by Whisker. Bred in England by Sir John Shelley. 16-14-1-1, $65,100. Winner of the 1830 Epsom Derby, Goodwood Cup. Considered the greatest English racehorse of his era. Imported in 1837 by Merritt and Co., for $15,000, then believed to be a record. Leading American sire four times. Sire of Epsom Oaks winners Crucifix, Miss Letty, and Industry before his importation. Sire in America of Margaret Wood, Little Trick, Lucy Long.

Died in Tennessee in 1847 at age 20.

1841, 1840—MEDOC, 1829 ch. h., American Eclipse—Young Maid of the Oaks, by *Expedition. Bred in New York by James Bathgate. 5-4-1-0, $5,300. Greatest son of American Eclipse. Entered stud in Kentucky in 1835. His offspring won 61 races in 1840 and 51 races the following year. Sire of top four-miler Grey Medoc, Bob Letcher, Mary Morris, Picayune. Broke his near foreleg when he stepped in a hole during exercise in 1839 and died at age ten from the injury at Col. William Buford's farm in Woodford County, Kentucky.

1836, 1830-'33—SIR CHARLES, 1816 ch. h., Sir Archy—*Citizen mare, by *Citizen. Won 20 of 25 starts. Believed to have been bred in Virginia by W. R. Johnson. Ancestry of his dam questioned; some referred to her as a "cart mare" whose pedigree had been fabricated. Dominant in long heat races throughout the South. Beaten while lame in final start, 1822 match with American Eclipse for the national championship in Washington, D.C. Died on June 7, 1833, at age 17 at George Johnson's Earnscliffe Plantation, Virginia. Sired the great racemares Trifle, Bonnets o' Blue, and Rosalie Somers, and notable racehorse and sire Wagner.

1835—BERTRAND, 1821 b. h., Sir Archy—Eliza, by *Bedford. Bred in South Carolina by Col. John R. Spann. Won 13 of 15 starts. In 1826, he was sold to Hutchcraft and Co. and sent to Kentucky, where he stood his entire 12-season career, and was said to have covered between 175 and 200 mares per season. He is credited with vastly improving the Thoroughbred of the Bluegrass region. His best include John Bascombe, Richard Singleton, and Queen Mary, dam of Longfellow. Died in Hopkinsville, Kentucky, in 1838 at age 17.

1834—MONSIEUR TONSON, 1822 b. h., Pacolet—Madam Tonson, by Top Gallant. Bred in Tennessee by Thomas Foxhall. Won 11 of 12 starts; only defeat was his first start as a two-year-old. William R. Johnson, the "Napoleon of the Turf" in America, bought him for $10,000. Stood initially in Virginia, later in North Carolina, and finally was sent to Kentucky where he died. Sire of South Carolina champion Argyle and many other winners.

Note: *Prior to 1860, leading sires were based on races won rather than progeny earnings.*

Stallion Syndications

In part because the definition of stallion syndication has changed over the decades, pinpointing the first syndication contract is difficult, if not impossible. However, the earliest syndication agreement comparable in form and intent to modern syndicates was that of Tracery in 1923. That agreement between the syndicators, the International Horse Agency and Exchange, and a group of 30 subscribers placed a value of $219,840 on the 1912 St. Leger winner, who was the sire of '23 Epsom Derby victor *Papyrus.

The principal idea behind that syndicate and all subsequent ones was to spread the risk of purchasing a very expensive breeding horse (and, in Tracery's case, returning him from Argentina). From the beginning of the Thoroughbred breeding industry in the late 17th century

right up to the 20th century, Thoroughbred breeding was essentially a private affair, with rich aristocrats wholly owning stallions and breeding mostly their own mares to those sires.

As Thoroughbred breeding slowly became more commercial in the late 19th and early 20th centuries, a new method of financing was required, both to spread the risk of failure and to ensure that a stallion received an appropriate number and quality of mares. Syndication was the answer. In Tracery's case, spreading the risk was a wise strategy because the stallion died after only one season at stud in England.

In a modern syndicate agreement, individuals agree to purchase a specific percentage of ownership in a stallion—the percentage ownership is determined by the number of shares—

with payment for that percentage interest usually spread in installments over several years. In return, the buyer of a syndicate share gains the right to breed one or more mares to that stallion each year without additional payments (except for agreed maintenance fees). The syndicate manager normally receives a specified number of free nominations each year as compensation.

The similarity to buying stock market shares is evident. The syndicate manager receives capital to pay for a major capital asset, and shareholders gain the possibility of dividends from the share through sale of the nomination or value of the produce. Shares also may be sold later to other investors at a profit (or loss), just as in the stock market, although syndication agreements may place restrictions on the marketability of the shares.

Although the first clearly identifiable syndicate was English, Americans soon became active syndicators. Arthur B. Hancock Sr. of Claiborne Farm formed a four-man partnership in 1926 to purchase the high-class French miler *Sir Gallahad III for $125,000. When *Sir Gallahad III sired Triple Crown winner Gallant Fox in his first crop, making him leading sire for the first of four times, the syndication process gained impetus in America. In 1936, Hancock syndicated another leading

sire, *Blenheim II, for a record price. In his first crop, *Blenheim II sired Triple Crown winner Whirlaway.

The record returned to England in 1945 when the good young sires Stardust and Tehran were syndicated in rapid succession, but the record price returned to America in '48 when Leslie Combs II purchased *Alibhai from Louis B. Mayer as a replacement for Combs's first syndicated horse, *Beau Pere, who died before covering a mare.

Combs also syndicated Nashua, the first $1-million stallion, as a four-year-old in 1956. The record price remained in America until 1983 (except for a brief period in '79) when Sheikh Mohammed bin Rashid al Maktoum syndicated his Irish Derby (Ire-G1) winner, Shareef Dancer, for a reported $40-million.

That reported price signifies one of the problems with modern syndications. With values soaring to astronomical figures, stallion managers now often decline to publish the exact price per share or contact terms. Thus, the $60-million to $70-million figure for current record holder Fusaichi Pegasus is based on approximate figures released by the syndicate manager and private communications from syndicate members.

Chronology of Record Stallion Syndications

Stallion	Year	Chronology of Syndication price	Farm	Seller	Share price	No. shares
Tracery	1923	$219,400	Cobham Stud (Eng.)	Senor Unzue	$5,485	40
*Blenheim II	1936	$240,000	Claiborne Farm (Ky.)	H. H. Aga Khan	$30,000	8
Tehran	1945	$403,000	Barton Stud (Eng.)	Prince Aly Khan	$10,075	40
Stardust	1945	$451,360	Gilltown Stud (Ire.)	H. H. Aga Khan	$11,284	40
Alibhai*	1948	$500,000	Spendthrift Farm (Ky.)	Louis B. Mayer	$16,667	30
The Phoenix	1948	$619,920	Ballykisteen Stud (Ire.)	Fred Myerscough	$15,498	40
Nashua	1955	$1,251,200	Spendthrift (Ky.)	Estate of William Woodward Jr.	$39,200	32
Graustark	1966	$2,400,000	Darby Dan Farm (Ky.)	John W. Galbreath	$60,000	40
Raise a Native	1967	$2,625,000	Spendthrift Farm (Ky.)	Louis Wolfson and Leslie Combs	$75,000	35
Buckpasser	1967	$4,800,000	Claiborne Farm (Ky.)	Ogden Phipps (retained 16 shares)	$150,000	32
*Vaguely Noble	1969	$5,000,000	Gainesway Farm (Ky.)	Nelson Bunker Hunt and Dr. Robert Franklyn	$125,000	40
Nijinsky II	1970	$5,440,000	Claiborne Farm (Ky.)	Charles W. Englehard (retained 10 shares)	$170,000	32
Secretariat	1973	$6,080,000	Claiborne Farm (Ky.)	Meadow Stable	$190,000	32
Wajima	1975	$7,200,000	Spendthrift Farm (Ky.)	East-West Stable (retained 20 shares)	$200,000	36
What a Pleasure	1976	$8,000,000	Waldemar Farm (Ky.)	Waldemar (retained 16 shares)	$250,000	32
The Minstrel	1977	$9,000,000	Windfields Farm (Md.)	Robert Sangster, et al.	$250,000	36
Seattle Slew	1978	$12,000,000	Spendthrift Farm (Ky.)	Wooden Horse Investments (retained 20 shares)	$300,000	40
Alleged	1978	$16,000,000	Walmac-Warnerton Int'l. (Ky.)	Robert Sangster, et.al.	$400,000	40
Troy	1979	$16,500,000	Highclere Stud (Eng.)	Sir Michael Sobell and Arnold Weinstock	$412,500	40
Spectacular Bid	1980	$22,000,000	Claiborne Farm (Ky.)	Hawksworth Farm (retained 20 shares)	$550,000	40
Storm Bird	1981	$30,000,000	Ashford Stud (Ky.)	Robert Sangster, et.al.	$750,000	40
Conquistador Cielo	1982	$36,400,000	Claiborne Farm (Ky.)	Henryk de Kwiatkowski (retained 10 shares)	$910,000	40
Shareef Dancer	1983	$40,000,000	Dalham Hall Stud (Eng.)	Ashton Upthorpe Stud	$1,000,000	40
Lammtarra	1996	$42,000,000	Arrow Stud (Jpn.)	Dalham Hall Stud	$1,050,000	40
Fusaichi Pegasus	2000	†$60,000,000	Ashford Stud (Ky.)	Fusao Sekiguchi	$1,500,000	40

†Estimated value

Leading Stud Farms by Stallion Progeny Earnings

Minimum of 200 starters for a farm's stallions in 2001

Rank	Name (State)	Earnings	Avg. earnings	% SWs	% GSWs
1	Lane's End (KY)	$46,361,721	$26,861	4.75%	1.45%
2	Claiborne Farm (KY)	29,458,528	27,026	4.59%	2.20%
3	Three Chimneys Farm (KY)	29,401,244	33,717	5.28%	2.41%
4	Gainesway (KY)	28,379,878	27,769	3.82%	1.66%
5	Ashford Stud (KY)	23,040,020	25,487	3.76%	2.10%
6	Vinery Kentucky (KY)	20,774,126	20,984	3.64%	0.81%
7	Walmac Int'l (KY)	18,865,307	25,425	5.39%	2.56%
8	Brookdale Farm (KY)	17,478,496	27,015	4.17%	1.55%
9	Harris Farms (CA)	14,790,484	23,255	4.56%	0.63%
10	Ocala Stud Farm (FL)	14,270,408	24,647	5.18%	1.04%
11	Northview Stallion Station (MD)	13,432,785	22,767	4.07%	0.34%
12	Wafare Farm (KY)	12,982,692	19,036	2.64%	0.29%
13	Pin Oak Stud (KY)	12,632,787	24,722	3.33%	0.59%
14	Airdrie Stud (KY)	12,564,523	24,492	4.68%	1.56%
15	Overbrook Farm (KY)	12,124,987	27,494	6.58%	2.27%
16	Farnsworth Farms (FL)	11,502,181	18,552	1.77%	0.32%
17	Spendthrift Farm (KY)	10,418,385	20,269	2.72%	0.58%
18	Darby Dan Farm (KY)	10,359,240	21,855	4.43%	2.32%
19	Country Life Farm (MD)	9,130,010	22,323	4.65%	0.24%
20	Taylor Made Farm (KY)	8,767,643	31,538	4.32%	1.08%
21	Sez Who Thoroughbreds (FL)	8,586,645	24,120	4.78%	1.12%
22	Franks Farms, Southland division (FL)	8,515,073	17,378	2.45%	0.82%
23	Margaux Farm (KY)	8,271,703	18,630	2.25%	0.45%
24	Crestwood Farm (KY)	7,919,770	19,949	4.28%	1.01%
25	Adena Springs Kentucky (KY)	7,847,043	22,549	5.46%	1.15%
26	McMahon of Saratoga Thoroughbreds (NY)	7,832,550	21,577	2.48%	0.55%
27	Windfields Farm (KY)	7,686,060	20,387	2.92%	0.27%
28	Mill Ridge Farm (KY)	7,549,935	20,080	5.32%	2.66%
29	Jonabell Farm (KY)	7,295,762	25,780	5.65%	2.47%
30	Hill 'n' Dale Farms (KY)	7,246,287	22,859	5.36%	2.84%
31	Bridlewood Farm (FL)	6,822,365	19,164	3.65%	0.56%
32	Brookside Stallions at Diamond A Farm (KY)	5,488,756	26,137	3.81%	2.38%
33	El Dorado Farms (WA)	5,235,416	12,525	2.87%	0.24%
34	Pin Oak Lane Farm, Pa. division (PA)	5,092,472	15,339	2.11%	0.00%
35	Golden Eagle Farm (CA)	5,043,150	19,103	1.89%	0.00%
36	Reigle Heir Farms (PA)	5,036,551	18,052	2.51%	0.36%
37	Red River Farms (LA)	4,978,490	11,063	1.56%	0.00%
38	J Z Stock Farm (CA)	4,898,806	17,622	2.88%	0.00%
39	T-Square Stud (FL)	4,684,009	17,543	2.25%	0.00%
40	Gainsborough Farm (KY)	4,609,530	20,396	1.77%	0.89%
41	Payson Stud (KY)	4,116,313	15,246	1.48%	0.74%
42	Highcliff Farm (NY)	4,102,713	16,281	0.79%	0.00%
43	Hidden Point Farm (FL)	4,061,569	17,357	2.99%	0.00%
44	Blooming Hills Farm (CA)	3,999,105	13,112	0.66%	0.00%
45	Huisache Farm (TX)	3,747,633	16,365	3.49%	0.00%
46	Glencrest Farm (KY)	3,464,674	16,040	4.17%	0.00%
47	Double S Thoroughbreds (TX)	3,459,545	13,674	1.19%	0.79%
48	Clear Creek Stud (LA)	3,228,222	13,796	4.27%	0.00%
49	Ternes Farm (BC)	2,838,532	13,779	3.40%	0.00%
50	Valor Farm (TX)	2,684,605	11,424	2.55%	0.00%
51	Woodstead Farm (WA)	2,584,359	11,589	0.90%	0.45%
52	Circle H Ranch (CA)	2,561,597	11,186	0.44%	0.00%

Leading Stud Farms of 2001

LANE'S END—Location: Versailles, Kentucky. **Founded:** 1979. **Principals:** William S. Farish and Bill Farish. **Acreage:** 1,600. **Stallions for 2002:** A.P. Indy, Belong to Me, Charismatic, Dixieland Band, Dixie Union, Eastern Echo, Fit to Fight, Gold Fever, Gulch, Kingmambo, Lemon Drop Kid, Lil's Lad, Lord Avie, Parade Ground, Pine Bluff, Pleasant Tap, Roar, Rubiano, Silver Ghost, Smart Strike, Stephen Got Even, Summer Squall. **Graded stakes winners of 2001 by Lane's End stallions:** Adilabad, Aptitude, Dubai Destination, Egyptband, Forty Mechuda, Gold Mover, Hook and Ladder, Indygo Shiner, Jump Start, King Cugat, Listen Here, Megans Bluff, Nasty Storm, Nayef, P. C. Plod, Penny's Gold, Quick Tip, Saranac Lake, Summer Colony, Tap Dance, Tempera, Until Sundown, Voodoo Dancer, War Talk.

CLAIBORNE FARM—Location: Paris, Kentucky. **Founded:** 1910. **President:** Seth Hancock. **Acreage:** 2,764. **Stallions for 2002:** Arch, Boundary, Conquistador Cielo, Coronado's Quest, Danzig, Devil's

Bag, Go for Gin, Horse Chestnut (SAf), Ordway, Out of Place, Private Terms, Pulpit, Seeking the Gold, Sultry Song. **Graded stakes winners of 2001 by Claiborne stallions:** Alannan, Albert the Great, Belterra, Broken Vow, Catch the Ring, Chimes At Midnight, Country Hideaway, Dream Supreme, Essence of Dubai, Exchange Rate, Exogenous, Fath, Fonz's, Golden Snake, Ishiguru, Lexicon, Masterful, Meetyouathebrig, Modigliani, Rochelle's Terms, Saarland, Shibboleth, Victory Ride, Wind Rush.

THREE CHIMNEYS FARM—Location: Midway, Kentucky. **Founded:** 1973. **Principal:** Robert N. Clay. **Acreage:** 1,500. **Stallions for 2002:** Albert the Great, Atticus, Capote, Dynaformer, Fly So Free, Joyeus Danseur, Miesque's Son, Point Given, Rahy, Seattle Slew, Silver Charm, Slew o' Gold, War Chant, Wild Again. **Graded stakes winners of 2001 by Three Chimneys stallions:** Another, Baptize, Blazing Fury, Bright Valour, Captain Steve, Chicago Six, Critical Eye, Dearly, Deep Sleep, Electron, Fantastic Light, Fleet Renee, Flute, Noverre, Sahara Slew, Scorpion, Serra Lake, Shine Again, Smile Again, Starrer, Tranquility Lake.

GAINESWAY—Location: Lexington. **Founded:** 1979. **Principal:** Graham Beck. **Acreage:** 1,680. **Stallions for 2002:** Bates Motel, Broad Brush, Cozzene, Fastness (Ire), Formal Gold, K One King, Lear Fan, Luhuk, Mt. Livermore, Sir Cat, Smoke Glacken, Strategic Mission, Subordination, Wolf Power (SAf). **Graded stakes winners of 2001 by Gainesway stallions:** Blondine, Casual Feat, Chorwon, Cozzy Corner, Galic Boy, Gaviola, Hidden Assets, Hoovergetthekeys, Include, Irish Prize, Mizzen Mast, Navesink, Nobo True, Pompeii, Real Cozzy, Smok'n Frolic.

ASHFORD STUD—Location: Versailles, Kentucky. **Founded:** 1910. **Principals:** John Magnier and partners. **Acreage:** 1,500. **Stallions for 2002:** A P Valentine, Bianconi, Black Minnaloushe, Fusaichi Pegasus, Giant's Causeway, Grand Slam, Hennessy, High Yield, Honour and Glory, King of Kings (Ire), Louis Quatorze, Lure, Royal Academy, Southern Halo, Spinning World, Stravinsky, Tale of the Cat, Thunder Gulch, Victory Speech, Woodman. **Graded stakes winners of 2001 by Ashford stallions:** Bon Vivant, Caressing, Discreet Hero, England's Legend (Fr), Hawk Wing, Illusioned, Ivory Tower, Lucido, Miss Gazon (Ire), Miss Linda (Arg), Mystic Lady, Petit Club, Point Given, Put It Back, Quad's Melody, Repent, Spain, Tweedside, Val Royal (Fr).

VINERY KENTUCKY—Location: Lexington. **Founded:** 1987. **Principal:** Thomas Simon. **Acreage:** 462. **Stallions for 2002:** Brahms, Gilded Time, Indian Charlie, Langfuhr, Lord Carson, Marquetry, More Than Ready, Real Quiet, Red Ransom, Runaway Groom, Sandpit (Brz). **Graded stakes winners of 2001 by Vinery Kentucky stallions:** American Halo, China Visit, Early Flyer, Fort La Roca, Lasersport, Perfect Sting, Squirtle Squirt, Slew the Red.

WALMAC INTERNATIONAL—Location: Lexington. **Founded:** 1936. **Principal:** John T. L. Jones Jr. **Acreage:** 1,097. **Stallions for 2002:** Confide, Evansville Slew, Favorite Trick, Gentlemen (Arg), Irgun, Lasting Approval, Mighty, Miswaki, Puerto Madero (Chi), Romanov (Ire), Salt Lake, Saratoga Six, Scatmandu, Sea of Secrets. **Graded stakes winners of 2001 by Walmac stallions:** Big Bambu, Black Hawk, Caller One, Good Journey, Inexplicable, Istintaj, King Charlemagne, Lake William, March Magic, Mesha-

heer, Momentum, Panis, Rancour, Senure, Skimming, Stonemason, Tertullian, Toroca, Tough Speed.

BROOKDALE FARM—Location: Versailles, Kentucky. **Founded:** 1983. **Principal:** Fred Seitz. **Acreage:** 375. **Stallions for 2002:** Crafty Prospector, Deputy Minister, Forest Wildcat, Silver Deputy, Will's Way, With Approval. **Graded stakes winners of 2001 by Brookdale stallions:** Agnes Digital, Allende, Atelier, Crafty C. T., Crafty Shaw, D'wildcat, Forest Heiress, Forest Secrets, Liberty Gold, Snow Dance.

HARRIS FARMS—Location: Coalinga, California. **Founded:** 1937. **Chairman:** John C. Harris. **Acreage:** 440. **Stallions for 2002:** Cee's Tizzy, Cutlass Reality, Downtown Seattle, Flying Continental, High Brite, Huddle Up, Lake George, Moscow Ballet, Paranoide (Arg), Soft Gold (Brz), Tinners Way. **Graded stakes winners of 2001 by Harris Farms stallions:** Golden Ballet, Gourmet Girl, Irisheyesareflying, Tiznow.

OCALA STUD FARM—Location: Ocala. **Founded:** 1956. **Principal:** J. Michael O'Farrell Jr. **Acreage:** 500. **Stallions for 2002:** Concerto, Concorde's Tune, Mecke, Montbrook, Montreal Red, Notebook, Pentelicus, Ponche, Slew Gin Fizz, Sweetsouthernsaint, Trippi. **Graded stakes winners of 2001 by Ocala Stud Farm stallions:** Delaware Township, Dusty's Lil Book, Monteration, Mountain Rage, Outofthebox, Pure Precision.

NORTHVIEW STALLION STATION—Location: Chesapeake City, Maryland. **Founded:** 1989. **Principals:** Richard Golden, Allaire duPont, and Tom Bowman. **Acreage:** 400. **Stallions for 2002:** Awad, Concern, Crowd Pleaser, Diamond, Lion Hearted, Not For Love, Partner's Hero, Polish Numbers, Tamayaz, Two Punch, Waquoit. **Graded stakes winners of 2001 by Northview stallions:** Duckhorn, Touch Love.

WAFARE FARM—Location: Midway, Kentucky. **Founded:** 1984. **Principals:** Nathan Fox and Richard Kaster. **Acreage:** 325. **Stallions for 2002:** Acceptable, Barkerville, Canaveral, Catrail, Deerhound, Fast Play, Glitterman, Laabity, Polish Navy, Prospectors Gamble, Richter Scale. **Graded stakes winners of 2001 by Wafare stallions:** Babae (Chi), Balto Star.

PIN OAK STUD—Location: Versailles, Kentucky. **Founded:** 1952. **Principal:** Josephine Abercrombie. **Acreage:** 750. **Stallions for 2002:** Broken Vow, Maria's Mon, Peaks and Valleys, Sky Classic, Wekiva Springs. **Graded stakes winners of 2001 by Pin Oak Stud stallions:** Monarchos, Silver Tornado, Stage Classic.

AIRDRIE STUD—Location: Midway, Kentucky. **Founded:** 1972. **Principals:** Brereton C. and Libby Jones. **Acreage:** 2,500. **Stallions for 2002:** Afternoon Deelites, Banker's Gold, Deputy Commander, Mazel Trick, Silver Hawk, Siphon (Brz), Slew City Slew, Stormin Fever, Yankee Victor, You and I. **Graded stakes winners of 2001 by Airdrie stallions:** Albarahin, And That's That, Lady Shari, Mutafaweq, Narooma, Siphonic, Win City, You.

OVERBROOK FARM—Location: Lexington. **Founded:** 1972. **Principal:** William T. Young. **Acreage:** 2,000. **Stallions for 2002:** Boston Harbor, Cape Canaveral, Cape Town, Carson City, Cat Thief, Editor's Note, Grindstone, Pioneering, Storm Cat, Tactical Cat. **Graded stakes winners of 2001 by Overbrook stallions:** Batique, Black Minnaloushe, Cat Chat, City Zip, Dietrich, Finder's Fee, Five Star Day, Katz Me If You Can, Leelanau, Saudi Poetry.

Broodmares of the Year
As awarded by the Kentucky Thoroughbred Owners and Breeders Association

2001—TURKO'S TURN
Ch. m. 1992, by Turkoman—Turbo Launch, by Relaunch
Dam of 3 foals, all winners, including **POINT GIVEN**, 9 wins, $3,968,500, 2001 Horse of the Year, 2001 champion three-year-old male, 2001 Preakness S. (G1), etc.

2000—PRIMAL FORCE
B. m. 1987, by Blushing Groom (Fr)—
Prime Prospect, by Mr. Prospector
Dam of 6 foals, 3 starters, all winners, including **MACHO UNO**, 5 wins, $1,359,803, 2000 champion two-year-old male, 2000 Breeders' Cup Juvenile (G1), etc.; **AWESOME AGAIN**, 9 wins, $4,374,590, 1998 Breeders' Cup Classic (G1), etc.

1999—ANNE CAMPBELL
B. m. 1973, by Never Bend—Repercussion, by *Tatan
Dam of 13 foals, 10 starters, 7 winners, including **MENIFEE**, 5 wins, $1,732,000, 1999 Haskell Invitational H. (G1), etc.; **DESERT WINE**, 8 wins, $1,618,043, 1984 Californian S. (G1), etc.

1998—IN NEON
B. m. 1982, by Ack Ack—Shamara, by Dewan
Dam of 7 foals, all starters, 6 winners, including **SHARP CAT**, 15 wins, $2,032,575, 1998 Beldame S. (G1), etc.; **ROYAL ANTHEM**, 9 wins, $1,876,876, 1998 Canadian International S. (Can-G1), etc.; **STAR RECRUIT**, 5 wins, $807,200, 1991 Alysheba S. (G3), etc.

1997—SLIGHTLY DANGEROUS
B. m. 1979, by Roberto—Where You Lead,
by Raise a Native
Dam of 13 foals, 11 starters, 10 winners, including **COMMANDER IN CHIEF**, 5 wins, $1,311,514, 1993 champion three-year-old male in Eur, 1993 Epsom Derby (Eng-G1), etc.; **WARNING (GB)**, 8 wins, $937,280, 1987 champion two-year-old male in Eng, 1988 champion three-year-old in Eng, 1988 Queen Elizabeth II S. (Eng-G1), etc.; **YASHMAK**, 4 wins, $529,382, 1997 Flower Bowl Invitational H. (G1), etc.; **DUSHYANTOR**, 5 wins, $1,197,570, 1996 Great Voltigeur S. (Eng-G2), etc.; **JIBE**, 2 wins, $98,912.

1996—PERSONAL ENSIGN
B. m. 1984, by Private Account—
Grecian Banner, by Hoist the Flag
Dam of 7 foals, 6 starters, all winners, including **MY FLAG**, 6 wins, $1,557,057, 1995 Breeders' Cup Juvenile Fillies (G1), etc.; **MINER'S MARK**, 6 wins, $967,170, 1993 Jockey Club Gold Cup (G1), etc.; **TRADITIONALLY**, 5 wins, $495,660, 2001 Oaklawn H. (G1).

1995—NORTHERN SUNSET (Ire)
Ch. m. 1977, by Northfields—
=Moss Greine (GB), by *Ballymoss
Dam of 13 foals, 12 starters, 11 winners, including **ST. JOVITE**, 6 wins, $1,604,439, 1992 Horse of the Year in Eur, 1991 champion two-year-old in Ire, 1992 Irish Derby (Ire-G1), etc.; **SALEM DRIVE**, 8 wins, $1,046,065, 1987 Bougainvillea H. (G2), etc.; **LAC OUIMET**, 12 wins, $817,863, 1986 Jim Dandy S. (G2), etc.; **L'CARRIERE**, 8 wins, $1,726,175, 1996 Saratoga Cup H. (G3).

1994—FALL ASPEN
Ch. m. 1976, by Pretense—Change Water, by Swaps
Dam of 14 foals, 13 starters, 12 winners, including **TIMBER COUNTRY**, 5 wins, $1,560,400, 1994 champion two-year-old male, 1995 Preakness S. (G1), etc.; **BIANCONI**, 3 wins, $134,520, 1998 Diadem S. (Eng-G2); **FORT WOOD**, 3 wins, $359,995, 1993 Grand Prix de Paris (Fr-G1), etc.; **NORTHERN ASPEN**, 5 wins, $253,678, 1987 Gamely H. (G1), etc.; **HAMAS (Ire)**, 5 wins, $237,814, 1993 July Cup S. (Eng-G1), etc.; **COLORADO DANCER (Ire)**, 3 wins, $203,389, 1989 Prix de Pomone (Fr-G2), etc.; **ELLE SEULE**, 3 wins, $101,478, 1986 Prix d'Astarte (Fr-G2); **MAZZACANO (GB)**, 3 wins,

$153,421, 1989 Goodwood Cup (Eng-G3); **PRINCE OF THIEVES**, 2 wins, $368,474.

1993—GLOWING TRIBUTE
B. m. 1973, by Graustark—Admiring, by Hail to Reason
Dam of 11 foals, 10 starters, 9 winners, including **SEA HERO**, 6 wins, $2,929,869, 1993 Kentucky Derby (G1), etc.; **HERO'S HONOR**, 8 wins, $499,025, 1984 Bowling Green H. (G1), etc.; **GLOWING HONOR**, 6 wins, $296,450, 1988, 1989 Diana H. (G2), etc.; **WILD APPLAUSE**, 5 wins, $240,136, 1984 Diana H. (G2), etc.; **CORONATION CUP**, 3 wins, $172,181, 1994 Nijana S. (G3); **MACKIE**, 3 wins, $164,579, 1996 Busher S. (G3); **SEATTLE GLOW**, 4 wins, $69,023.

1992—WEEKEND SURPRISE
B. m. 1980, by Secretariat—Lassie Dear, by Buckpasser
Dam of 13 foals, 11 starters, 7 winners, including **A.P. INDY**, 8 wins, $2,979,815, 1992 Horse of the Year, 1992 champion three-year-old male, 1992 Belmont S. (G1), etc.; **SUMMER SQUALL**, 13 wins, $1,844,282, 1990 Preakness S. (G1), etc.; **WELCOME SURPRISE**, 2 wins, $143,574, 2000 Dogwood S. (G3).

1991—TOLL BOOTH
B. m. 1971, by Buckpasser—Missy Baba, by *My Babu
Dam of 12 foals, all starters, 11 winners, including **PLUGGED NICKLE**, 11 wins, $647,206, 1980 champion sprinter, 1980 Florida Derby (G1), etc.; **CHRISTIECAT**, 11 wins, $799,745, 1992 Flower Bowl H. (G1), etc.; **KEY TO THE BRIDGE**, 7 wins, $289,747, 1988 Beaugay H. (G3); **TOLL FEE**, 7 wins, $333,917; **TOLL KEY**, 9 wins, $290,218; **IDLE GOSSIP**, 5 wins, $101,721; **TOKENS ONLY**, 4 wins, $50,455.

1990—KAMAR
B. m. 1976, by Key to the Mint—
Square Angel, by Quadrangle
Dam of 9 foals, 8 starters, 7 winners, including **KEY TO THE MOON**, 13 wins, $714,536, 1984 champion three-year-old male in Can, 1984 Discovery H. (G3), etc.; **GORGEOUS**, 8 wins, $1,171,370, 1989 Ashland S. (G1), etc.; **SEASIDE ATTRACTION**, 4 wins, $272,541, 1990 Kentucky Oaks (G1); **HIAAM**, 3 wins, $48,081, 1986 Princess Margaret S. (Eng-G3).

1989—RELAXING
B. m. 1976, by Buckpasser—Marking Time, by To Market
Dam of 12 foals, 9 starters, all winners, including **EASY GOER**, 14 wins, $4,873,770, 1988 champion two-year-old male, 1989 Belmont S. (G1), etc.; **EASY NOW**, 4 wins, $359,466, 1992 Go for Wand S. (G1), etc.; **CADILLACING**, 7 wins, $268,137, 1988 Ballerina S. (G1), etc.

1988—GRECIAN BANNER
Dkbbr. m., 1974, by Hoist the Flag—*Dorine,
by =Aristophanes (GB)
Dam of 7 foals, 5 starters, all winners, including **PERSONAL ENSIGN**, 13 wins, $1,679,880, 1988 champion older female, 1996 Broodmare of the Year, 1988 Breeders' Cup Distaff (G1), etc.; **PERSONAL FLAG**, 8 wins, $1,258,924, 1988 Suburban H. (G1), etc.

1987—BANJA LUKA
B. m. 1968, by Double Jay—Legato, by Dark Star
Dam of 9 foals, all starters, 7 winners, including **FERDINAND**, 8 wins, $3,777,978, 1987 Horse of the Year, 1987 champion older male, 1986 Kentucky Derby (G1), etc.; **DONNA INEZ**, 4 wins, $101,275; **JAYSTON**, 7 wins, $92,143; **DANCING**, 4 wins, $77,925; **ANCIENT ART**, 4 wins, $74,250; **PLINTH**, 3 wins, $65,980.

1986—TOO BALD
Dk. b. br. m. 1964, by Bald Eagle—Hidden Talent, by Dark Star
Dam of 12 foals, 11 starters, all winners, including **CAPOTE**, 3 wins, $714,470, 1986 champion two-year-old male, 1986

Breeders' Cup Juvenile S. (G1), etc.; **EXCELLER**, 15 wins, $1,674,587, 1978 Jockey Club Gold Cup (G1), etc.; **VAGUELY HIDDEN**, 8 wins, $239,313, 1990 New Jersey Turf Classic S. (G3); **AMERICAN STANDARD**, 5 wins, $180,120; **BALDSKI**, 7 wins, $103,214.

1985—DUNCE CAP II
Dk. b. br. m. 1960, by Tom Fool—Bright Coronet, by Bull Lea
Dam of 10 foals, 8 starters, all winners, including **LATE BLOOMER**, 11 wins, $512,040, 1978 champion older female, 1978 Beldame S. (G1), etc.; **JOHNNY APPLESEED**, 4 wins, $91,910, 1976 Louisiana Derby (G2); **LATE ACT**, 9 wins, $661,089, 1985 Cliff Hanger H. (G3), etc.

1984—HASTY QUEEN II
Dk. b. br. m. 1963, by One Count—Queen Hopeful, by Roman
Dam of 16 foals, 14 starters, 12 winners, including **FIT TO FIGHT**, 14 wins, $1,042,075, 1984 Brooklyn H. (G1), etc.; **HASTY FLYER**, 10 wins, $293,663, 1974 Round Table H. (G3), etc.; **HASTY TAM**, 16 wins, $211,738; **PLAYFUL QUEEN**, 5 wins, $101,837; **MICHAEL NAVONOD**, 6 wins, $86,380; **HASTY CUTIE**, 8 wins, $63,639.

1983—COURTLY DEE
Dk. b. br. m. 1968, by Never Bend—Tulle, by War Admiral
Dam of 18 foals, 17 starters, 15 winners, including **ALTHEA**, 8 wins, $1,275,255, 1983 champion two-year-old filly, 1984 Arkansas Derby (G1), etc.; **ALI OOP**, 7 wins, $174,020, 1976 Sapling S. (G1); **KETOH**, 3 wins, $173,550, 1985 Cowdin S. (G1); **AQUILEGIA**, 8 wins, $446,081, 1993 New York H. (G2), etc.; **TWINING**, 5 wins, $238,140, 1994 Peter Pan S. (G2), etc.; **AISHAH**, 6 wins, $169,340, 1990 Rare Perfume S. (G2); **NATIVE COURIER**, 14 wins, $522,635, 1981 Bernard Baruch H. (G3), etc.; **PRINCESS OOLA**, 5 wins, $108,291.

1982—BEST IN SHOW
Ch. m. 1965, by Traffic Judge—Stolen Hour, by Mr. Busher
Dam of 17 foals, 12 starters, 9 winners, including **MALINOWSKI**, 2 wins, 1975 champion two-year-old in Ire, 1976 Ladbroke Craven S. (Eng-G3); **BLUSH WITH PRIDE**, 6 wins, $536,807, 1982 Kentucky Oaks (G1), etc.; **GIELGUD**, 1 win, $56,635, 1980 Champagne S. (Eng-G2); **MONROE**, 3 wins, $34,422, 1980 Ballyogan S. (Ire-G3).

1981—NATASHKA
Dk. b. br. m. 1963, by Dedicate—Natasha, by *Nasrullah
Dam of 9 foals, 7 starters, all winners, including **GREGORIAN**, 4 wins, $194,912, 1980 Joe McGrath Memorial S. (Ire-G1), etc.; **TRULY BOUND**, 9 wins, $382,449, 1980 Arlington-Washington Lassie S. (G2), etc.; **IVORY WAND**, 5 wins, $97,452, 1976 Test S. (G3); **BLOOD ROYAL**, 4 wins, $28,870, 1975 Jockey Club Cup (Eng-G3), etc.; **ARKADINA**, 2 wins, $79,830, Athasi S. (Ire-G3).

1980—KEY BRIDGE
B. m. 1959, by *Princequillo—Blue Banner, by War Admiral
Dam of 11 foals, 8 starters, 7 winners, including **FORT MARCY**, 21 wins, $1,109,791, 1970 Horse of the Year, 1967, 1968, 1970 champion turf male, 1970 champion older male, 1967, 1970 Washington D.C. International S., etc.; **KEY TO THE MINT**, 14 wins, $576,015, 1972 champion three-year-old male, 1973 Suburban H. (G1), etc.; **KEY TO CONTENT**, 7 wins, $354,772, 1981 United Nations H. (G1), etc.; **KEY TO THE KINGDOM**, 7 wins, $109,590, 1974 Stymie H. (G3).

1979—SMARTAIRE
Dk. b. br. m. 1962, by *Quibu—Art Teacher, by Olympia
Dam of 12 foals, all starters, 10 winners, including **SMART ANGLE**, 7 wins, $414,217, 1979 champion two-year-old filly, 1979 Frizette S. (G1), etc.; **SMARTEN**, 11 wins, $716,426, 1979 American Derby (G2), etc.; **QUADRATIC**, 6 wins, $233,941, 1977 Cowdin S. (G2); **SMART HEIRESS**, 6 wins, $154,999.

1978—PRIMONETTA
Ch. m. 1958, by Swaps—Banquet Bell, by Polynesian
Dam of 7 foals, 6 starters, all winners, including **CUM LAUDE LAURIE**, 8 wins, $405,207, 1977 Beldame S. (G1), etc.;

PRINCE THOU ART, 3 wins, $167,902, 1975 Florida Derby (G1); **MAUD MULLER**, 3 wins, $138,383, 1974 Gazelle H. (G2), etc.; **GRENFALL**, 4 wins, $19,467, 1971 Gallinule S. (Ire-G2), etc.

1977—SWEET TOOTH
B. m. 1965, by On-and-On—Plum Cake, by Ponder
Dam of 13 foals, 10 starters, 8 winners, including **OUR MIMS**, 6 wins, $368,034, 1977 champion three-year-old filly, 1977 Coaching Club American Oaks (G1), etc.; **ALYDAR**, 14 wins, $957,195, 1978 Blue Grass S. (G1), etc.; **SUGAR AND SPICE**, 5 wins, $257,046, 1980 Mother Goose S. (G1), etc.

1976—*GAZALA II
Dk. b. br. m. 1964, by Dark Star—*Belle Angevine, by =L'Amiral (Fr)
Dam of 10 foals, 8 starters, 6 winners, including **YOUTH**, 8 wins, $716,146, 1976 champion three-year-old in Fr, 1976 champion turf male, 1976 Prix du Jockey Club (Fr-G1), etc.; **MISSISSIPIAN**, 3 wins, $248,520, 1973 champion two-year-old in Fr, 1973 Grand Criterium (Fr-G1), etc.; **GONZALES**, 4 wins, $103,968, 1980 Irish St. Leger (Ire-G1), etc.; **SILKY BABY**, 2 wins, $51,351, 1981 Prix de Guiche (Fr-G3); **BEST OF BOTH**, 6 wins, $242,150.

1975—SHENANIGANS
Gr. m. 1963, by Native Dancer—Bold Irish, by Fighting Fox
Dam of 6 foals, all winners, including **RUFFIAN**, 10 wins, $313,428, 1974 champion two-year-old filly, 1975 champion three-year-old filly, 1975 Filly Triple Crown, 1975 Coaching Club American Oaks (G1), etc.; **ICECAPADE**, 13 wins, $256,646, 1973 William duPont Jr. H. (G2), etc.; **BUCKFINDER**, 9 wins, $230,513, 1978 William duPont Jr. H. (G2).

1974—COSMAH
B. m. 1953, by Cosmic Bomb—Almahmoud, by *Mahmoud
Dam of 15 foals, 10 starters, 9 winners, including **TOSMAH**, 23 wins, $612,588, 1963 champion two-year-old filly, 1964 champion three-year-old filly, 1964 champion handicap female, 1964 Beldame S., etc.; **HALO**, 9 wins, $259,553, 1974 United Nations H. (G1), etc.; **FATHERS IMAGE**, 7 wins, $173,318; **MARIBEAU**, 4 wins, $20,925.

1973—SOMETHINGROYAL
B. m. 1952, by *Princequillo—Imperatrice, by Caruso
Dam of 18 foals, 15 starters, 11 winners, including **SECRETARIAT**, 16 wins, $1,316,808, 1972, 1973 Horse of the Year, 1972 champion two-year-old male, 1973 champion three-year-old male, 1973 champion turf male, 1973 Triple Crown, 1973 Kentucky Derby (G1), etc.; **SIR GAYLORD**, 10 wins, $237,404, 1961 Sapling S. (G1), etc.; **FIRST FAMILY**, 7 wins, $188,040, 1966 Gulfstream Park H., etc.; **SYRIAN SEA**, 6 wins, $178,245, 1967 Selima S., etc.

1972—*MOMENT OF TRUTH II
Ch. m. 1959, by =Matador (GB)—=Kingsworthy (Ire), by =Kingstone (GB)
Dam of 9 foals, all winners, including **CONVENIENCE**, 15 wins, $648,933, 1973 Vanity H. (G1), etc.; **NIGHT ALERT**, 3 wins, $121,268, 1980 Prix Jean Prat (Fr-G2), etc.; **INDULTO**, 27 wins, $466,789, 1966 Withers S., etc.; **PROLIFERATION**, 7 wins, $66,680; **PUNTILLA**, 3 wins, $64,255.

1971—IBERIA
Ch. m. 1954, by *Heliopolis—War East, by *Easton
Dam of 10 foals, all starters, 8 winners, including **RIVA RIDGE**, 17 wins, $1,111,497, 1971 champion two-year-old male, 1973 champion older male, 1972 Kentucky Derby, etc.; **HYDROLOGIST**, 10 wins, $277,958, 1970 Excelsior H., etc.; **POTOMAC**, 3 wins, $37,361.

1970—LEVEE
Ch. m. 1953, by Hill Prince—Bourtai, by Stimulus
Dam of 11 foals, 9 starters, 7 winners, including **SHUVEE**, 16 wins, $890,445, 1970, 1971 champion handicap mare, 1969 Filly Triple Crown, 1969 Coaching Club American Oaks, etc.; **ROYAL GUNNER**, 6 wins, $334,650; **NALEE**, 8 wins, $141,631, 1963 Black-Eyed Susan S., etc.; **A. T'S OLIE**, 6 wins, $82,211.

1969—ALL BEAUTIFUL
Ch. m. 1959, by Battlefield—Parlo, by *Heliopolis
Dam of 12 foals, 11 starters, 9 winners, including **ARTS AND LETTERS**, 11 wins, $632,404, 1969 Horse of the Year, 1969 champion three-year-old male, 1969 champion handicap horse, 1969 Belmont S., etc.

1968—DELTA
B. m. 1952, by *Nasrullah—Bourtai, by Stimulus
Dam of 10 foals, all starters, 9 winners, including **OKAVANGO**, 6 wins, $153,802, 1975 San Pasqual H. (G2), etc.; **DIKE**, 7 wins, $351,274, 1969 Wood Memorial S., etc.; **CANAL**, 33 wins, $280,358; **CABILDO**, 22 wins, $267,265; **SHORE**, 6 wins, $62,357.

1967—KERALA
B. m. 1958, by *My Babu—Blade of Time, by *Sickle
Dam of 12 foals, 5 starters, all winners, including **DAMASCUS**, 21 wins, $1,176,781, 1967 Horse of the Year, 1967 champion three-year-old male, 1967 champion handicap male, 1967 Preakness S., etc.

1966—JULIETS NURSE
Dk. b. br. m. 1948, by Count Fleet—Nursemaid, by Luke McLuke
Dam of 13 foals, all starters, 11 winners, including **RUN FOR NURSE**, 22 wins, $253,145; **GALLANT ROMEO**, 15 wins, $202,401, 1966 Vosburgh H., etc.; **WOOZEM**, 7 wins, $163,083, 1966 Demoiselle S., etc.; **DUTIFUL**, 5 wins, $80,780.

1965—POCAHONTAS
Dk. b. br. m. 1955, by Roman—How, by *Princequillo
Dam of 9 foals, 5 starters, all winners, including **TOM ROLFE**, 16 wins, $671,297, 1965 champion three-year-old male, 1965 Preakness S., etc.; **LADY REBECCA**, 2 wins, $26,434, 1974 Prix Vanteaux (Fr-G3); **CHIEFTAIN**, 13 wins, $405,256, 1964 Governor's Gold Cup, etc.; *WENONA, 3 wins, Blandford S. (Ire), etc.

1964—MAID OF FLIGHT
Dk. b. br. m. 1951, by Count Fleet—Maidoduntreath, by Man o' War
Dam of 11 foals, 10 starters, 9 winners, including **KELSO**, 39 wins, $1,977,896, 1960, 1961, 1962, 1963, 1964 Horse of the Year, 1960 champion three-year-old male, 1961, 1962, 1963, 1964 champion handicap horse, 1960, 1961, 1962, 1963 1964 Jockey Club Gold Cup, etc.

1963—MISTY MORN
B. m. 1952, by *Princequillo—Grey Flight, by *Mahmoud
Dam of 10 foals, 8 starters, 7 winners, including **SUCCESSOR**, 7 wins, $532,254, 1966 champion two-year-old, 1966 Champagne S., etc.; **BOLD LAD**, 14 wins, $516,465, 1964 champion two-year-old, 1964 Champagne S., etc.; **SUNRISE FLIGHT**, 11 wins, $380,995, 1963 Gallant Fox H., etc.; **BEAUTIFUL DAY**, 7 wins, $160,007; **BOLD CONSORT**, 6 wins, $38,147.

1962—TRACK MEDAL
Dk. b. br. m. 1950, by *Khaled—Iron Reward, by *Beau Pere
Dam of 10 foals, 8 starters, 6 winners, including **OUTING CLASS**, 6 wins, $229,759, 1962 Hopeful S., etc.; *O'HARA, 8 wins, $202,180, 1966 Sunset H.; **TUTANKHAMEN**, 12 wins, $157,530, 1962 Manhattan H.; **FOOL'S GOLD II**, 1 win, 1962 Musidora S. (Eng).

1961—STRIKING
B. m. 1947, by War Admiral—Baby League, by Bubbling Over
Dam of 15 foals, 12 starters, 11 winners, including **HITTING AWAY**, 13 wins, $309,079, 1961 Dwyer H., etc.; **BATTER UP**, 7 wins, $166,504, 1962 Black-Eyed Susan S., etc.; **MY BOSS LADY**, 4 wins, $64,174; **GLAMOUR**, 6 wins, $60,775; **BASES FULL**, 3 wins, $17,627.

1960—SIAMA
B. m. 1947, by Tiger—China Face, by Display
Dam of 9 foals, 5 starters, all winners, including **BALD EAGLE**, 12 wins, $692,946, 1960 champion handicap male, 1959, 1960 Washington D.C. International, etc.; **ONE-EYED KING**, 15 wins, $266,281, 1960 Arlington H., etc.; **DEAD AHEAD**, 8 wins, $73,645.

1959—*KNIGHT'S DAUGHTER
B. m. 1941, by =Sir Cosmo (Ire)—=Feola (GB), by =Friar Marcus (GB)
Dam of 7 foals, all starters, 6 winners, including **ROUND TABLE**, 43 wins, $1,749,869, 1958 Horse of the Year, 1957, 1958, 1959 champion turf male, 1958, 1959 champion older male, 1957 Hollywood Gold Cup, etc.; **MONARCHY**, 7 wins, $85,737; *LOVE GAME, 1 win.

1958—MISS DISCO
B. m. 1944, by Discovery—Outdone, by Pompey
Dam of 11 foals, 7 starters, all winners, including **BOLD RULER**, 23 wins, $764,204, 1957 Horse of the Year, 1957 champion three-year-old male, 1957 champion sprinter, 1957 Preakness S., etc.; **INDEPENDENCE**, 12 wins, $132,088; **NASCO**, 7 wins, $71,930.

1957—BELLE JEEP
B. m. 1949, by War Jeep—Model Beauty, by *Blenheim II
Dam of 14 foals, 12 starters, all winners, including **JEWEL'S REWARD**, 7 wins, $448,592, 1957 champion two-year-old male, 1957 Champagne S., etc.; **TRIPLE CROWN**, 4 wins, $128,874, 1974 San Jacinto S. (G2), etc.; **LORD JEEP**, 11 wins, $64,504; **EVASIVE ACTION**, 3 wins, $47,004.

1956—SWOON
Ch. m. 1942, by Sweep Like—Sadie Greenock, by Greenock
Dam of 10 foals, all starters, 8 winners, including **SWOON'S SON**, 30 wins, $970,605, 1956 American Derby, etc.; **DO-GOON**, 28 wins, $220,360, 1954 Hawthorne Juvenile H., etc.

1955—IRON REWARD
B. m. 1946, by *Beau Pere—Iron Maiden, by War Admiral
Dam of 11 foals, 9 starters, 5 winners, including **SWAPS**, 19 wins, $848,900, 1956 Horse of the Year, 1956 champion handicap horse, 1955 Kentucky Derby, etc.; **THE SHOE**, 10 wins, $105,000, 1958 Cinema H., etc.; **LIKE MAGIC**, 10 wins, $87,872.

1954—TRAFFIC COURT
Dk. b. br. m. 1938, by Discovery—Traffic, by Broomstick
Dam of 3 foals, all winners, including **HASTY ROAD**, 14 wins, $541,402, 1953 champion two-year-old male, 1954 Preakness S., etc.; **TRAFFIC JUDGE**, 13 wins, $432,450, 1957 Suburban H., etc.

1953—GAGA
B. m. 1942, by *Bull Dog—Alpoise, by Equipoise
Dam of 5 foals, all winners, including **TOM FOOL**, 21 wins, $570,165, 1953 Horse of the Year, 1951 champion two-year-old male, 1953 champion sprinter, 1953 champion older male, 1953 Surburban H., etc.; **AUNT JINNY**, 5 wins, $106,020, 1950 Demoiselle S., etc.

1952—ACE CARD
B. m. 1942, by Case Ace—Furlough, by Man o' War
Dam of 12 foals, all starters, 11 winners, including **ONE COUNT**, 9 wins, $245,625, 1952 Horse of the Year, 1952 champion three-year-old male, 1952 Belmont S., etc.; **POST CARD**, 14 wins, $170,525; **MY CARD**, 7 wins, $98,404, 1963 Selima S.; **YILDIZ**, 7 wins, $90,475, 1951 Flamingo S., etc.

1951—*ALPENSTOCK III
Dk. b. br. m. 1936, by =Apelle (Ity)—=Plymstock (GB), by =Polymelus (GB)
Dam of 13 foals, 10 starters, 8 winners, including **RUHE**, 11 wins, $294,490, 1951 Blue Grass S., etc.; **STURDY ONE**, 13 wins, $202,970, 1951 Tanforan H., etc.; **ALLADIER**, 9 wins, $61,712, 1951 Breeders' Futurity.

1950—HILDENE
B. m. 1938, by Bubbling Over—Fancy Racket, by *Wrack
Dam of 13 foals, 12 starters, 9 winners, including **HILL PRINCE**,
17 wins, $422,140, 1950 Horse of the Year, 1949 champion
two-year-old male, 1950 champion three-year-old male, 1951
champion older male, 1950 Preakness S., etc.; **FIRST LAND-
ING**, 19 wins, $779,577, 1958 champion two-year-old male,
1958 Champagne S., etc.; **THIRD BROTHER**, 9 wins,
$310,787; **MANGOHICK**, 23 wins, $115,115; **PRINCE HILL**,
8 wins, $98,300.

1949—EASY LASS
Bl. m. 1940, by *Blenheim II—Slow and Easy, by Colin
Dam of 7 foals, all starters, 6 winners, including **COALTOWN**,
23 wins, $415,675, 1949 Horse of the Year, the 1948 champion
sprinter, 1949 champion older male, 1949 Washington Park
H., etc.; **WISTFUL**, 13 wins, $213,060, 1949 champion three-
year-old filly, 1949 Coaching Club of America Oaks, etc.;
ROSEWOOD, 9 wins, $92,950; **FANFARE**, 9 wins, $46,140.

1948—OUR PAGE
B. m. 1940, by Blue Larkspur—Occult, by *Dis Donc

Dam of 5 foals, all winners, **BULL PAGE**, 9 wins, $25,730,
1951 Horse of the Year in Canada, 1951 champion older
horse in Canada, 1951 Canadian Championship S.; **NAVY
PAGE**, 21 wins, $127,322, 1953 Jerome H., etc.; **SPORT
PAGE**, 4 wins, $79,175; **BROTHER TEX**, 8 wins, $77,633;
PAGE BOOTS, 3 wins, $51,635.

1947—POTHEEN
Dk. b. br. m. 1928, by Wildair—Rosie O'Grady, by Hamburg
Dam of 12 foals, 11 starters, 9 winners, including **BEWITCH**,
20 wins, $462,605, 1947 champion two-year-old filly, 1949
champion older female, 1947 Washington Park Futurity, etc.;
POT O' LUCK, 14 wins, $239,150, 1945 Jockey Club Gold
Cup, etc.; **LOT O LUCK**, 9 wins, $46,950.

1946—BLOODROOT
B. m. 1932, by Blue Larkspur—*Knockany Bridge,
by =Bridge of Earn (GB)
Dam of 13 foals, 11 starters, 8 winners, including **ANCESTOR**,
26 wins, $237,956, 1959 champion steeplechaser, 1952 Dis-
covery H., etc.; **BE FAITHFUL**, 14 wins, $189,040, 1947
Hawthorne Gold Cup H., etc.; **BRIC A BAC**, 13 wins, $103,225,
1945 San Juan Capistrano H., etc.; **BIMLETTE**, 4 wins,

Leading Broodmares by Progeny Earnings
Worldwide leaders 1930-2001

Broodmare, YOB, Sire—Dam	Fls.	Strs.	Wnrs.	SWs	Progeny Earnings	Leading earner (earnings)
Once Wed, 1984, Blushing Groom (Fr)—Noura	10	9	7	1	$18,363,013	T.M.Opera O ($16,200,337)
Pacificus, 1981, Northern Dancer—Pacific Princess	10	9	7	3	18,128,908	Narita Brian ($9,296,552)
Dancing Key, 1983, Nijinsky II—Key Partner	10	10	7	3	14,199,565	Dance Partner ($5,973,652)
Katies (Ire), 1981, Nonoalco—Mortefontaine	13	10	9	5	11,158,708	Hishi Amazon ($6,981,102)
Solar Slew, 1982, Seattle Slew—Gold Sun (Arg)	11	6	6	2	10,323,580	Cigar ($9,999,815)
Ingot Way, 1981, Diplomat Way—Ingot	14	8	7	1	9,974,079	Skip Away ($9,616,360)
Campaign Girl, 1987, Maruzensky—Lady Shiraoki	3	2	2	1	9,519,113	Special Week ($9,346,435)
Cee's Song, 1986, Seattle Song—Lonely Dancer	10	7	4	2	9,332,382	Tiznow ($6,427,830)
Golden Sash, 1988, Dictus—Dyna Sash	7	6	3	1	9,189,417	Stay Gold ($8,682,142)
Mejiro Aurola, 1978, Remand—Mejiro Iris	10	6	5	2	9,135,636	Mejiro Mc Queen ($7,618,803)
Takeno Falcon, 1982, Philip of Spain—Cool Fair	8	7	5	1	9,125,589	Hokuto Vega ($8,300,301)
Tree of Knowledge (Ire), 1977, Sassafras (Fr)—Sensibility	10	7	5	2	9,019,381	Taiki Blizzard ($5,523,549)
Princess Reema, 1984, Affirmed—First Fling	12	9	9	2	9,009,934	Meisho Doto ($8,088,202)
Tokai Natural, 1982, Nice Dancer—Tokai Midori	11	11	9	2	8,932,717	Tokai Teio ($4,698,139)
Reru du Temps, 1982, Maruzensky—Kei Tsunami	7	5	4	2	8,833,507	Mejiro Bright ($6,848,423)
Happy Trails, 1984, Posse—Roycon (GB)	9	8	7	2	8,801,069	Shinko Lovely ($4,596,546)
Dyna Carle, 1980, Northern Taste—Shadai Feather	9	9	8	1	8,772,234	Air Groove ($6,832,242)
Jood, 1989, Nijinsky II—Kamar	7	5	4	1	8,589,330	Fantastic Light ($8,486,957)
Sakura Clare, 1982, Northern Taste—Clare Bridge	11	7	5	2	8,543,641	Sakura Chitose O ($5,178,760)
Powerful Lady, 1981, Maruzensky—Roch Tesco	14	9	8	2	8,185,910	Winning Ticket ($3,359,368)
Legacy of Strength, 1982, Affirmed—Katonka	10	9	7	2	8,022,612	Stinger ($3,468,418)
Tenzan Otome, 1983, Maruzensky—Mombetsu Kachidoki	8	7	5	2	8,020,189	Osumi Jet ($4,915,054)
Mejiro Beauty, 1982, Partholon—Mejiro Nagasaki	7	7	7	1	7,996,641	Mejiro Dober ($6,240,681)
Floral Magic, 1985, Affirmed—Rare Lady	7	7	7	1	7,829,990	Narita Top Road ($7,205,830)
Croupier Lady, 1983, What Luck—Question d'Argent	8	8	6	1	7,641,695	Genuine ($5,455,575)
Never Ichiban, 1971, Never Beat—Miss Nanba Ichiban	14	9	6	1	7,636,765	Daitaku Helios ($4,629,341)
Bel Sheba, 1970, Lt. Stevens—Belthazar	13	13	11	5	7,594,619	Alysheba ($6,679,242)
Urakawa Miyuki, 1981, *Habitony—Kemmaru Midori	8	7	5	1	7,594,173	Nice Nature ($5,232,135)
Sakura Hagoromo, 1984, Northern Taste—Clear Amber	8	7	7	1	7,574,929	Sakura Bakushin O ($4,800,631)
Alp Me Please, 1981, Blushing Groom (Fr)—Swiss	7	6	2	1	7,567,701	Mayano Top Gun ($7,463,557)
Mountain Queen, 1982, Nizon—Yamaka Queen	11	7	6	1	7,308,160	Kyoto City ($5,622,437)
Bonnie's Poker, 1982, Poker—What a Surprise	11	9	6	1	7,086,460	Silver Charm ($6,944,369)
Lilac Point, 1979, Maruzensky—Kuri Katsura	10	7	4	1	7,049,963	Rice Shower ($6,070,429)
Sparkling Delite, 1985, Vice Regent—Sparkling Topaz	6	4	3	1	6,895,204	Captain Steve ($6,828,356)
Mysteries, 1986, Seattle Slew—Phydilla (Fr)	10	6	4	3	6,816,984	Agnes World ($3,365,680)
Once Double, 1967, Double Jay—Intent One	10	9	8	2	6,770,102	John Henry ($6,591,860)
Wakia, 1987, Miswaki—Rascal Rascal	4	4	4	1	6,693,685	Silence Suzuka ($3,523,898)
Chancey Squaw, 1991, Chief's Crown—Allicance	4	2	1	1	6,690,366	Agnes Digital ($7,068,806)
Lola Lola, 1985, Saint Cyrien—Bold Lady	7	7	4	1	6,629,651	Sakura Laurel ($5,751,390)
Glorious Song, 1976, Halo—Ballade	13	9	8	3	6,575,951	Singspiel (Ire) ($5,952,825)
Duplicit, 1985, Danzig—Fabulous Fraud	10	10	9	1	6,506,240	Nishino Flower ($3,441,504)
Crafty Wife, 1985, Crafty Prospector—Wife Mistress	9	8	7	1	6,497,687	Big Short ($2,984,808)
Sanyo Arrow, 1988, Mr C B—Taniichi Power	5	4	2	1	6,473,824	Wing Arrow ($6,273,733)
Dyna Fairy, 1983, Northern Taste—Fancy Dyna	10	8	6	2	6,462,706	Rosen Kavalier ($4,137,973)

Leading Broodmares by Progeny Earnings, continued

Broodmare, YOB, Sire—Dam	Fls.	Strtrs.	Wnrs.	SWS	Progeny Earnings	Leading earner (earnings)
Songline, 1987, Western Symphony—Mcangus	5	2	1	1	6,443,180	Sunline ($6,443,017)
No Class, 1974, Nodouble—Classy Quillo	8	7	7	6	6,408,741	Sky Classic ($3,320,398)
The Last Word, 1987, Northern Taste—Gloria Wave	7	7	5	1	6,355,767	Fast Friend ($5,896,693)
Antique Value, 1979, Northern Dancer—Moonscape	11	10	9	3	6,284,249	Vega ($2,105,918)
Silver Lane, 1985, Silver Hawk—Strait Lane	9	4	3	2	6,250,207	Black Hawk (GB) ($5,750,386)
Dyna Actress, 1983, Northern Taste—Model Sport	8	8	5	2	6,241,595	Stage Champ ($4,077,863)
Doff the Derby, 1981, Master Derby—Margarethen	12	10	9	6	6,185,617	Osumi Tycoon ($2,842,458)
Buper Dance, 1983, Lyphard—My Bupers	9	8	6	1	6,147,747	Irish Dance ($2,355,600)
Ameriflora, 1989, Danzig—Graceful Touch	5	3	3	1	6,128,233	Grass Wonder ($5,987,405)
Ubetshedid, 1980, King Pellinore—Ubetido	11	9	6	1	6,067,705	Best Pal ($5,668,245)
Kuri Pussy, 1975, Arrow Express—Montaroch	13	8	6	1	5,988,123	Matikanetannhauser ($4,522,666)
North Of Eden (Ire), 1983, Northfields—Tree of Knowledge (Ire)	13	9	7	4	5,952,176	Paradise Creek ($3,401,416)
Yamanin Policy, 1981, Blushing Groom (Fr)—Yamahouyuu (Jpn)	12	10	4	1	5,945,152	Yamanin Zephyr ($4,957,983)
I Dreamed a Dream, 1987, Well Decorated—Hidden Trail	5	5	4	2	5,937,885	Air Shakur ($4,405,675)
Dominus Rose, 1981, Tosho Boy—Oferu	11	9	5	1	5,919,242	Fujino Makken O ($3,735,159)
Welsh Muffin (Ire), 1987, Caerleon—Muffitys	8	5	4	1	5,853,277	Taiki Shuttle ($4,997,744)
Primal Force, 1987, Blushing Groom (Fr)—Prime Prospect	9	3	3	2	5,789,369	Awesome Again ($4,374,590)
Beautiful Bid, 1984, Baldski—Biddy Big	13	6	5	3	5,783,425	Beautiful Pleasure ($2,734,078)
Northern Sunset (Ire), 1977, Northfields—Moss Greine	14	12	11	4	5,693,824	L'Carriere ($1,726,175)
Momiji Dancer, 1980, Viceregal—Momigi	11	8	3	1	5,688,363	Marvelous Sunday ($5,305,340)
Relaxing, 1976, Buckpasser—Marking Time	12	9	9	3	5,653,704	Easy Goer ($4,873,770)
Maurita (NZ), 1978, Harbor Prince—Cathmoi	8	8	6	2	5,642,770	Marvelous Crown ($4,421,958)
Magaro, 1980, Caro (Ire)—Magic	11	11	9	2	5,562,140	Tayasu Tsuyoshi ($3,392,998)
Waka Suzuran, 1982, Contrite—Okiwaka	8	5	3	1	5,561,759	Fujiyama Kenzan ($4,809,453)
Bubble Company (Fr), 1977, Lyphard—Prodice (Fr)	11	8	6	3	5,540,136	Bubble Gum Fellow ($4,887,021)
Line of Thunder, 1987, Storm Bird—Shoot a Line (GB)	9	7	5	2	5,510,009	Thunder Gulch ($2,915,086)
Madonna Bamboo, 1978, Moubariz—Nimbus Bamboo	12	9	5	2	5,491,217	Bamboo Memory ($2,982,696)
Millracer, 1983, *Le Fabuleux—Marston's Mill	11	9	7	2	5,442,873	Shinin' Racer ($1,915,140)
City Fortress, 1983, Troy—Queen's Castle	8	6	4	2	5,442,152	Desert Boy ($3,825,146)
Dyna Landing, 1980, Northern Taste—Nice Landing	11	5	4	1	5,438,290	Ikuno Dictus ($3,910,417)
Dance Charmer, 1990, Nureyev—Skillful Joy	4	4	2	1	5,424,788	Jungle Pocket ($5,584,623)
Sour Bamboo, 1983, Gentilhombre—Orange Nimbus	8	8	6	2	5,404,572	Spring Bamboo ($2,493,658)
Weekend Surprise, 1980, Secretariat—Lassie Dear	14	11	8	3	5,394,814	A.P. Indy ($2,979,815)
Jimka, 1978, Jim French—Kastueuse	13	11	8	1	5,346,380	Jim and Tonic (Fr) ($4,959,719)
Fairy Doll, 1991, Nureyev—Dream Deal	3	3	1	1	5,333,743	To the Victory ($5,303,281)
Eight Carat, 1975, *Pieces of Eight II—Klairessa (GB)	10	5	5	5	5,291,038	Octagonal ($4,535,801)
Passing Mood, 1978, Buckpasser—Cool Mood	9	7	6	5	5,263,274	With Approval ($2,863,540)
Subtle Change, 1988, Law Society—Santa Luciana	6	6	3	2	5,211,430	Manhattan Cafe ($4,164,517)
Robe Decollete, 1988, No Attention—Kai Murasaki	4	3	1	1	5,200,877	Daiwa Texas ($5,200,877)
Twiglet, 1987, Twig Moss—Extradite	8	4	3	2	5,165,331	Fairy King Prawn ($4,601,520)
Wishing Well, 1975, Understanding—Mountain Flower	6	4	4	1	5,155,797	Sunday Silence ($4,968,554)
Infinie, 1982, Maruzensky—Lucky Jo O	9	9	6	1	5,148,591	Maillot Jaune ($2,902,598)
Thunderdome, 1983, Lyphard—Mr. P's Girl	11	9	9	2	5,110,448	Toyo Lyphard ($3,438,006)
Sister Mill, 1990, Mill George—Sweet Angelet	4	3	2	1	5,108,206	Seiun Sky ($5,032,543)
National Flag, 1986, Dictus—Dyna World	5	4	4	2	5,050,386	Inter Flag ($2,498,883)
Nihon Pillow Clear, 1984, Bravest Roman—Nihon Pillow Aster	9	6	4	2	5,025,006	Nihon Pillow Prince ($2,556,470)
Agnes Flora, 1987, Royal Ski—Agnes Lady	6	5	4	2	5,018,400	Agnes Flight ($2,770,206)
Sea Port, 1980, Averof—Anchor	13	8	7	1	5,002,606	Indigenous ($4,946,060)
Gana Facil, 1981, *Le Fabuleux—Charedi	8	6	5	2	4,982,479	Unbridled ($4,489,475)
Donna Lydia, 1983, Jim French—Daigo Hamaisami	8	6	6	1	4,969,665	Legacy World ($3,600,710)
Brave Woman (Jpn), 1985, Bravest Roman—Chiyoda Fuji	7	6	6	2	4,922,953	Kokuto Julian ($2,369,206)
Dyna Saloon, 1981, Northern Taste—Shadai Clear	10	7	3	2	4,914,413	Tunante ($2,687,203)
Vain Gold, 1979, Mr. Prospector—Chancy Dance	11	11	9	2	4,886,964	Behind the Mask ($2,762,686)
Chance, 1980, Dandy Lute—Star Moon	11	11	5	1	4,872,443	Shako Grade ($2,558,293)

Most Graded or Group Stakes Winners for a Broodmare
(1930-2001)

8 Fall Aspen 1976, Pretense—Change Water, by Swaps. 14 foals, 13 starters, 12 winners, 9 stakes winners, 8 graded/group stakes winners (Fort Wood [Fr-G1], Hamas [Ire] [Eng-G1], Timber Country [G1], Northern Aspen [G1], Colorado Dancer [Ire] [Fr-G2], Bianconi [Eng-G2], Elle Seule [Fr-G2], Mazzacano [GB] [Eng-G3])

7 Courtly Dee 1968, Never Bend—Tulle, by War Admiral. 18 foals, 17 starters, 15 winners, 8 stakes winners, 7 graded/group stakes winners (Ali Oop [G1], Althea [G1], Ketoh [G1], Aishah [G2], Aquilegia [G2], Twining [G2], Native Courier [G3])

6 Dahlia 1970, *Vaguely Noble—Charming Alibi, by Honeys Alibi. 13 foals, 11 starters, 8 winners, 6 stakes winners, 6 graded/group stakes winners (Dahar [Fr-G1], Dahlia's Dreamer [G1], Rivlia [G1]), Delegant [G1], Wajd [Fr-G2], Llandaff [G2],

Glowing Tribute 1973, Graustark—Admiring, by Hail to Reason. 12 foals, 10 starters, 9 winners, 7 stakes winners, 6 graded/group stakes winners (Hero's Honor [G1], Sea Hero [G1], Glowing Honor [G2], Wild Applause [G2], Coronation Cup [G3], Mackie [G3])

5 **Blessings (Fr)** 1971, Floribunda—*Marabelle, by Miralgo. 17 foals, 11 starters, 8 winners, 6 stakes winners, 5 graded/group stakes winners (Bleding [Arg] [Arg-G1], Sings [Arg-G1], Blue Bles [Arg-G3], Blue Boss [Aus-G3], Flibless [Arg-G3])

Chaldee 1978, Banner Sport—Gevar, by Right of Way. 13 foals, 7 starters, 6 winners, 5 stakes winners, 5 graded/group stakes winners (Potrichal [Arg] [Arg-G1], Potrinner [Arg] [Arg-G1], Potrizaris [Arg] [Arg-G1], Potridee [Arg] [G1], Sun Banner [Arg-G3])

Coup de Folie 1982, Halo—Raise the Standard, by Hoist the Flag. 12 foals, 10 starters, 6 winners, 5 stakes winners, 5 graded/group stakes winners (Machiavellian [Fr-G1], Coup de Genie [Fr-G1], Exit to Nowhere [Fr-G1], Hydro Calido [Fr-G2], Ocean of Wisdom [Fr-G3])

Eight Carat 1975, *Pieces of Eight II—Klairessa [GB], by *Klairon. 10 foals, 5 starters, 5 winners, 5 stakes winners, 5 graded/group stakes winners (Marquise [NZ-G1], Mouawad [Aus-G1], Octagonal [Aus-G1], Our Diamond Lover [NZ-G1], Kaapstad [Aus-G1])

*Lupe II 1967, Primera—Alcoa, by Alycidon. 10 foals, 9 starters, 8 winners, 5 stakes winners, 5 graded/group stakes winners (Lascaux [Fr-G2], Louveterie [Fr-G3], Legend of France [Eng-G3], Leonardo Da Vinci [Fr] [Eng-G3], L'Ile Du Reve [Eng-G3])

Princess Tracy (Ire) 1981, Ahonoora—Princess Ru, by Princely Gift. 10 foals, 9 starters, 7 winners, 5 stakes winners, 5 graded/group stakes winners (Tracy's Element [Aus] [SAf-G1], Danasinga [Aus-G1], Topasannah [SAf-G2], Cullen [Aus-G3], Towkay [Aus-G3])

Summoned 1978, Crowned Prince—Sweet Life, by *Pardao. 16 foals, 13 starters, 9 winners, 5 stakes winners, 5 graded/group stakes winners (Zeditavo [Aus-G2], Square Deal [Aus-G3], Alannon [Aus-G3], Pampas Fire [Aus-G3], Zedagal [Aus-G3])

Most Stakes Winners for a Broodmare
(1930-2001)

9 **Fall Aspen** 1976, Pretense—Change Water, by Swaps. 14 foals, 13 starters, 12 winners, 9 stakes winners (Bianconi, Colorado Dancer [Ire], Elle Seule, Fort Wood, Hamas [Ire], Mazzacano [GB], Northern Aspen, Prince of Thieves, Timber Country)

Fallow 1957, *Worden—Galloway Queene, by Colombo. 16 foals, 11 starters, 12 winners, 9 stakes winners (Fact [Arg], Factory, Fairly [Arg], Fallowed, Far, *Farm, Farmer, Fazenda [Arg], *Fizz)

Grey Flight 1945, *Mahmoud—Planetoid, by Ariel. 15 foals, 15 starters, 14 winners, 9 stakes winners (Bold Princess, Bold Queen, Full Flight, Gray Phantom, Misty Day, Misty Flight, Misty Morn, Signore, What a Pleasure)

8 **Astronomie** 1932, Asterus—Likka, by Sardanapale. 10 foals, 9 starters, 8 winners, 8 stakes winners (Arbar, Arbele, *Asmena, Caracalla, Estremadur, Floriados, Marsyas II, Pharas)

Courtly Dee 1968, Never Bend—Tulle, by War Admiral. 18 foals, 17 starters, 15 winners, 8 stakes winners (Aishah, Ali Oop, Althea, Aquilegia, Ketoh, Native Courier, Princess Oola, Twining)

Retorica 1955, Snob—Rochelle, by Selim Hassan. 12 foals, 9 starters, 8 winners, 8 stakes winners (*Legent II, Leon II, Lioness, *Lirio, Llegador [Arg], Locomotor, *Lostalo, Ruizero [Arg])

7 **Bold Pat** 1975, Bold Destroyer—Bolerita, by Bolero. 14 foals, 13 starters, 11 winners, 7 stakes winners (A Bold Embrace, Arctic Pat, Bay Is O. K., Bold Fawn, Elegant Black, Milden's Girl, Pat's Bold Brat)

Dan's Dream 1961, Your Host—Rosella, by War Relic. 15 foals, 15 starters, 12 winners, 7 stakes winners (Costly Dream, Dream 'n Be Lucky, El Corazon, Go On Dreaming, Jesta Dream Away, Once Upon a Star, Royal Knightmare)

Donatella 1939, *Mahmoud—Delleana, by Clarissimus. 13 foals, 12 starters, 10 winners, 7 stakes winners (*Daumier, De Dreux, Delaroche, *Dominate II, *Donatellina II, Donna Lydia, Duccio)

Flying B. G. 1978, Barachois—Up Alone, by Solo Landing. 16 foals, 12 starters, 11 winners, 7 stakes winners (B. G.'s Drone, Burnone Gimmetwo, Draconic's B. G., Flying Drone, Soiree, Talent Connection, Texas Holdem)

Glowing Tribute 1973, Graustark—Admiring, by Hail to Reason. 12 foals, 10 starters, 9 winners, 7 stakes winners (Coronation Cup, Glowing Honor, Hero's Honor, Mackie, Sea Hero, Seattle Glow, Wild Applause)

7 **Here's Lookn Adder** 1983, Superbity—Sarah Blue Eyes, by Explodent. 12 foals, 9 starters, 9 winners, 7 stakes winners (Drumm Valley, Jessen, Just Lookn, Lookn At a Blurr, Lookn At Another, Peak Out, Takin It Deep)

Moccasin 1963, Nantallah—*Rough Shod II, by Gold Bridge. 9 foals, 8 starters, 7 winners, 7 stakes winners (Apalachee, Belted Earl, Brahms, Flippers, Indian, Nantequos, Scuff)

My Dear Girl 1957, Rough'n Tumble—Iltis, by War Relic. 15 foals, 14 starters, 13 winners, 7 stakes winners (Gentle Touch, In Reality, My Dear Lady, Really and Truly, Return to Reality, Superbity, Watchfulness)

Qui Royalty 1977, Native Royalty—Qui Blink, by Francis S. 14 foals, 12 starters, 10 winners, 7 stakes winners (Appointed One, Bakharoff, Demonry, Emperor Jones, Majlood, Sum, Thyer)

Roar n' Honey 1965, Hezahoney—Rip 'n Roar, by Rippey. 14 foals, 12 starters, 11 winners, 7 stakes winners (Bar Tender, Dandy Man, My Favorite Gal, One That Got Away, Singh Honey, Sonny Says, St. Aubin)

Soumida 1953, Tehran—*Sou'wester, by Blue Peter. 10 foals, 8 starters, 8 winners, 7 stakes winners (Sarcelle, Senechal, Siska, Solidor, Solon, Sorana, *Soudard)

Toll Booth 1971, Buckpasser—Missy Baba, by *My Babu. 13 foals, 12 starters, 11 winners, 7 stakes winners (Christiecat, Idle Gossip, Key to the Bridge, Plugged Nickle, Tokens Only, Toll Fee, Toll Key)

Up the Flagpole 1978, Hoist the Flag—The Garden Club, by *Herbager. 11 foals, 10 starters, 10 winners, 7 stakes winners (Allied Flag, Flagbird, Fold the Flag, Long View, Prospectors Delite, Runup the Colors, Top Account)

6 **Accra** 1941, Annapolis—Ladala, by Ladkin. 11 foals, 11 starters, 10 winners, 6 stakes winners (Mandingo, Mongo, Nahodah, Nala, Neji, Songai)

Adriana 1944, Arjaman—Adriatica, by Janitor. 15 foals, 14 starters, 11 winners, 6 stakes winners (Ametta, Anatol, Andrea II, Appell, Aspiration, *Ataturk II)

Alta Mira 1948, *Don Bingo—Music Hall, by Snark. 9 foals, 9 starters, 9 winners, 6 stakes winners (Collin Baykey, Craig D., Donn Baykey, Ky. Miracle, Ky. Music, Son of Donn)

Apostille 1944, Astrophel—Polititia, by Comedy King. 8 foals, 6 starters, 6 winners, 6 stakes winners (Apostol, Bingo, Poisson Volant, Postboy, Postman, Virgule)

Banja Luka 1968, Double Jay—Legato, by Dark Star. 9 foals, 9 starters, 7 winners, 6 stakes winners (Ancient Art, Dancing, Donna Inez, Ferdinand, Jayston, Plinth)

Most Stakes Winners for a Broodmare, continued

Bargain 1943, Millero—Bonne Fille, by Bermejo. 7 foals, 7 starters, 6 winners, 6 stakes winners (Corbar, Dadiva, Moon Shine, Postwar, *Propina, Shilling)

6 Battle Creek Girl 1977, His Majesty—Far Beyond, by Nijinsky II. 19 foals, 17 starters, 15 winners, 6 stakes winners (Everhope, Parade Ground, Parade Leader, Speed Dialer, Tricky Creek, Wavering Girl)

Blessings (Fr) 1971, Floribunda—*Marabelle, by Miralgo. 17 foals, 11 starters, 8 winners, 6 stakes winners (Bleding [Arg], Blue Bles, Blue Boss, Flibless, Fritz, Sings)

Blue Denim 1940, Blue Larkspur—Judy O'Grady, by Man o' War. 15 foals, 14 starters, 11 winners, 6 stakes winners (Blue Prince, Green Baize, Piano Jim, Policeman Day, Suleiman, Tahiti)

Confirm 1977, Proudest Roman—Spanked, by Cornish Prince. 17 foals, 15 starters, 11 winners, 6 stakes winners (Autumn Glitter, Confirmed Dancer, Hollycombe, Ron Bon, Saratoga Sizzle, Yolanda)

Dahlia 1970, *Vaguely Noble—Charming Alibi, by Honeys Alibi. 13 foals, 11 starters, 8 winners, 6 stakes winners (Dahar, Dahlia's Dreamer, Delegant, Llandaff, Rivlia, Wajd)

Doff the Derby 1981, Master Derby—Margarethen, by *Tulyar. 12 foals, 10 starters, 9 winners, 6 stakes winners (Generous, Imagine, Osumi Tycoon, Strawberry Roan [Ire], Wedding Bouquet [Ire], Windy Triple K.)

Dumka 1971, Kashmir II—Faizebad [Fr], by *Prince Taj. 8 foals, 8 starters, 7 winners, 6 stakes winners (Dafayna, Dalsaan, Dayzaan, Dolka [Ire], Dolpour, Doyoun)

Eterna 1954, Atabor—Eme, by Lord Wembley. 9 foals, 7 starters, 7 winners, 6 stakes winners (El Califa, *El Fakir, El Faraon, Envidiada [Arg], Esporazo, Eternelle)

Floral Victory 1962, Victoria Park—La Belle Rose, by Le Lavandou. 17 foals, 15 starters, 13 winners, 6 stakes winners (Floral Dancer, Happy Victory, Nonparrell, Northern Ballerina, Snow Blossom, Victego)

Fun House 1958, The Doge—Recess, by Count Fleet. 9 foals, 9 starters, 9 winners, 6 stakes winners (Court Ruling, Funny Cat, Fun Palace, Good Manners, King's Palace, Yes Sir)

Gran Corrida 1961, Prince d'Or—Gay Ega, by Gay Boy. 13 foals, 7 starters, 6 winners, 6 stakes winners (A Esperar, Galopon, Grandeza Real, Grandor Real, Gran Real, Real Corrida)

*Green Valley II 1967, *Val de Loir—Sly Pola, by Spy Song. 15 foals, 14 starters, 13 winners, 6 stakes winners (Ercolano, Green Dancer, Pink Valley, Sir Raleigh, Soviet Lad, Val Danseur)

Hasty Queen II 1963, One Count—Queen Hopeful, by Roman. 16 foals, 14 starters, 12 winners, 6 stakes winners (Fit to Fight, Hasty Cutie, Hasty Flyer, Hasty Tam, Michael Navonod, Playful Queen)

Height of Fashion (Fr) 1979, Bustino—Highclere [GB], by Queen's Hussar. 12 foals, 10 starters, 8 winners, 6 stakes winners (Alwasmi, Mukddaam, Naohwan, Nayef, Sarayir, Unfuwain)

Il Mondo 1968, Promised Land—Nunzi Nunzi, by *Endeavour II. 13 foals, 13 starters, 8 winners, 6 stakes winners (Balimondo, Craftysmypapa, Mondanza, Mondo Lea, Mondolu, Turnin Doe)

Imperatrice 1938, Caruso—Cinquepace, by Brown Bud. 16 foals, 13 starters, 10 winners, 6 stakes winners (Imperial Hill, Imperium, Scattered, Speedwell, Squared Away, Yemen)

Kazanlik 1960, Ommeyad—Rose Supreme, by Supreme Court. 13 foals, 10 starters, 8 winners, 6 stakes winners (Boabdil, Darling Bud, Frances Jordan, Gay George, *Lark Rise II, Orient Rose)

Lapel 1935, Apelle—Lampeto, by Tetratema. 9 foals, 9 starters, 9 winners, 6 stakes winners (Carlist, Cassock, Durante, Golden Spur, Red Carnation, Val d'Assa)

Loudrangle 1974, Quadrangle—Lady Known as Lou, by Nearctic. 9 foals, 7 starters, 7 winners, 6 stakes winners

(Dancing With Wings, No Louder, Ruling Angel, Slew of Angels, Tiffany Tam, Tilt My Halo)

6 Missy Baba 1958, *My Babu—*Uvira II, by Umidwar. 14 foals, 12 starters, 12 winners, 6 stakes winners (Chokri, Dromba, Gay Missile, Master Bold, Raja Baba, Sauce Boat)

Nas-Mahal 1959, *Nasrullah—*Love Game, by Big Game. 12 foals, 11 starters, 9 winners, 6 stakes winners (Beja, Celine, Craelius, Epidaurus, Tell, Turkish Trousers)

No Class 1974, Nodouble—Classy Quillo, by Outing Class. 8 foals, 7 starters, 7 winners, 6 stakes winners (Always a Classic, Classic Reign, Classy 'n Smart, Grey Classic, Regal Classic, Sky Classic)

Patsy Dru 1959, Alorter—Patsy, by Escadru. 17 foals, 17 starters, 15 winners, 6 stakes winners (Astaconda, Great Commander, Levant, Patsy's Reign, Prom Crasher, Shotgun Pat)

Phase 1939, Windsor Lad—Lost Soul, by Solario. 14 foals, 12 starters, 9 winners, 6 stakes winners (Narrator, Neasham Belle, Netherton Maid, None Nicer, No Pretender, Setting Star)

Picture Light 1954, *Court Martial—Queen of Light, by Borealis. 13 foals, 11 starters, 9 winners, 6 stakes winners (Dazzling Light, Father Christmas, Illuminous, Miss Pinkie, Photo Flash, Welsh Pageant)

Polite Society 1952, War Admiral—Doggin' It, by *Bull Dog. 12 foals, 12 starters, 12 winners, 6 stakes winners (Big Brigade, Blue Society, La Gentillesse, Long Position, Montjuich, Rising Market)

*Queen's Statute 1954, Le Lavandou—Statute, by Son-in-Law. 14 foals, 13 starters, 13 winners, 6 stakes winners (Court Royal, Dance Act, Down North, Epic Queen, Menedict, North of the Law)

Radiant Light 1953, Sayajirao—Wakening Light, by Eight Thirty. 13 foals, 7 starters, 7 winners, 6 stakes winners (Grand Slam, Mairona [Chi], Mediatore, Metapio, Morgan, *Morgana II)

Ripeck 1959, *Ribot—Kyak, by Big Game. 10 foals, 10 starters, 8 winners, 6 stakes winners (Anchor, Balinger, Bireme, Buoy, Fluke, *Kedge)

Stafaralla 1935, Solario—Mirawala, by Phalaris. 14 foals, 8 starters, 7 winners, 6 stakes winners (Anwar, Inshalla, Iran, Kerman, *Norooz, Tehran)

Sun Princess 1937, Solario—Mumtaz Begum, by *Blenheim II. 13 foals, 11 starters, 9 winners, 6 stakes winners (Alassio, *Flaneur II, Lucky Bag, *Royal Charger, Royal Justice, Tessa Gillian)

Tata 1938, Tresiete—Tacana, by Leteo. 6 foals, 6 starters, 6 winners, 6 stakes winners (Taia, Taimado, Taitao, Talon, Tatai, Tolpan)

Theresina 1927, Diophon—Teresina, by Tracery. 13 foals, 10 starters, 8 winners, 6 stakes winners (*Benane, Byculla, Eboo, *Nemrod, Tambara, Turkhan)

Tokamura 1940, Navarro—Tofanella, by Apelle. 16 foals, 3 starters, 12 winners, 6 stakes winners (Tanaka, Theodorica, Titano, Tommaso Da Modena, *Tommaso Guidi, *Toulouse Lautrec)

Vera Me 1979, Polar Night—Vera Jae, by Gaylord's Feather. 13 foals, 13 starters, 11 winners, 6 stakes winners (Amazonpassage, Heatherforyou, Jessica Jae, Mebazaar, Polar Barron, Steaksonme)

Verdura 1948, *Court Martial—Bura, by *Bahram. 12 foals, 11 starters, 11 winners, 6 stakes winners (Avon's Pride, Gratitude, Heathen, Highest Hopes, Patroness, Pharsalia)

Yakima Swinger 1974, Canadian Gil—Eternal Heeler, by Heeler. 12 foals, 11 starters, 11 winners, 6 stakes winners (Bucks for Bob, Hat Rock, Lyon Swinger, Rock On Merit, Sarajevo Merit, Slightly Sinister)

Zanzara 1951, Fairey Fulmar—Sunright, by Solario. 17 foals, 15 starters, 14 winners, 6 stakes winners (Duke Ellington, Enrico, Enticement, Farfalla, Matatina, Showdown)

Most Foals for a Broodmare
(1930-2001)

Broodmare, YOB, Pedigree	Foals	Starters	Winners	Wins	Earnings
*Betsy Ross II 1939, *Mahmoud—*Celerina, by *Teddy	23	19	13	44	$152,943
Day Line 1963, *Day Court—Fast Line, by Mr. Busher	21	17	14	42	421,940
Cequillo 1956, *Princequillo—Boldness, by *Mahmoud	20	18	14	81	1,031,646
Feather Bed 1961, Johns Joy—Silly Sara, by *Rustom Sirdar	20	17	13	60	305,357
Alanette 1962, Alarullah—Jaconet, by *Jacopo	20	18	9	33	128,897
Wisp O'Will 1964, New Policy—Miss Willow, by Oil Capitol	20	16	14	70	894,640
Bold Bikini 1969, Boldnesian—Ran-Tan, by Summer Tan	20	14	12	37	974,619
Wind in Her Sails 1972, Mr. Leader—Bunch of Daisies, by Sir Gaylord	20	13	12	44	375,991
Such 'n Such 1974, Ack Ack—Long Stemmed Rose, by Jacinto	20	16	11	46	733,795
Wayward Miss 1936, Brumeux—Miss Contrary, by Cannobie	20	16	4	26	12,805
Ingenuity 1956, My Request—Resourceful, by Shut Out	19	13	8	40	205,902
Mid Evening 1957, Billings—Mideau, by *Bull Dog	19	17	12	100	572,999
Brown Berry 1960, Mount Marcy—Brown Baby, by Phalanx	19	17	13	48	1,861,434
Saygood 1967, Royal Ascot—Saybrook, by Brookfield	19	13	10	44	644,686
Kadesh 1970, Lucky Mel—News Release, by Fleet Nasrullah	19	15	14	45	879,370
Heat of Holme 1970, *Noholme II—Heat Lamp, by Better Self	19	16	12	49	1,062,475
Gold Idol 1972, Don B.—Suzi Juris, by Imbros	19	18	13	54	382,085
Queen's Turf 1972, Round Table—Good Queen Bess, by Bold Ruler	19	14	10	28	316,412
My Room 1972, Bold Lad—Extra Place, by Round Table	19	16	12	50	520,454
Gaelic Logic 1975, Bold Reason—Irish Party, by Irish Lancer	19	14	12	31	493,852
Nobile Decretum 1975, Noble Decree—Mid Evening, by Billings	19	13	5	16	292,887
Shocking Moment 1976, Info—Reneged's Belle, by Reneged	19	16	14	60	701,401
First Paula 1976, First Dawn—First Color, by Black Mountain	19	13	5	41	254,929
Battle Creek Girl 1977, His Majesty—Far Beyond, by Nijinsky II	19	17	15	80	4,108,911
Capulet 1977, Gallant Romeo—Indaba, by Sir Gaylord	19	16	10	52	571,097
Blinking Owl 1938, *Pharamond II—Baba Kenny, by Black Servant	19	16	15	66	195,196
Miss Sandman 1974, Manacle—Sandby, by *Klairon	19	18	8	15	123,164
Akino Mairie 1973, Arrow Express—Tetsuno Arc, by Arctic Vale	19	7	2	4	527,746
Delagoa (Fr) 1975, Targowice—Derna, by Sunny Boy	19	12	9	20	138,506
Extremadura 1954, British Empire—Lesina, by Pont l'Eveque	19	8	8	21	12,269
Miss Maverick 1960, Vilmorin—Top Table, by Big Game	19	19	9	12	51,573
Port Margaret 1951, Gustator—Port Beam, by Portlaw	19	16	5	11	15,986
Sarasail 1966, Hitting Away—*Sail Riona, by *Royal Charger	19	9	1	1	3,394
Photo Flash 1965, *Match II—Picture Light, by *Court Martial	19	16	8	20	78,798
Avra 1957, Vulgan—Golden Flight, by Gold Bridge	19	11	3	5	3,457
Indian Nurse 1955, *Mahmoud—Gallant Nurse, by War Admiral	18	16	9	61	302,530
Sun Rondeau 1956, Bull Brier—M. Louise, by Sun Teddy	18	16	14	75	484,084
Miss Velocity 1957, Spy Song—Fairy Dancer, by Blenheim	18	17	17	140	560,219
Sweet Error 1957, Errard King—Sweet Afton, by Balladier	18	13	12	71	270,726
Fast Line 1958, Mr. Busher—Throttle Wide, by Flying Heels	18	11	8	41	505,961
Winter Garden 1958, Windfields—Rustic Charm, by Reaping Reward	18	16	11	69	429,783
Eyeshadow 1959, *My Babu—Pretty One, by *Bull Dog	18	13	9	43	487,662
Gay Tribute 1960, Citation—Be Happy, by *Beau Pere	18	14	9	20	142,685
Ivory Tower 1960, Hill Prince—Rosy Prospect, by Rosemont	18	16	10	69	1,115,730
Tattooed Miss 1960, Mark-Ye-Well—Mossy Number, by Eight Thirty	18	18	15	66	375,182
Maid to Measure 1960, Mark-Ye-Well—Bushleaguer, by War Admiral	18	16	11	92	403,140
Tite Boat 1961, Fleet Feet—Rippina, by Rippey	18	16	13	81	365,100
Nevada Princess 1961, Prince Khaled—Nevada Bond, by Bymeabond	18	12	8	49	186,675
Gorgeous Gay 1962, Blue Gay—*Felicitate, by Genetout	18	15	10	70	465,565
Arizona Jubilee 1964, Spotted Moon—The Frog Hook, by Kilmallock	18	17	16	54	271,893
Cheeveetah 1964, Prince John—Wise Intentions, by Intent	18	15	13	82	392,221
Sweeping Beauty 1964, Eddie Schmidt—Gold Crest, by King Cole	18	17	13	72	1,337,295
Best in Show 1965, Traffic Judge—Stolen Hour, by Mr. Busher	18	12	9	29	782,311
Sword Fish 1965, New Policy—Pez Vela, by *Windy City II	18	12	11	66	596,473
Hurricane Helen 1966, Etonian—Case Goods, by Case Ace	18	16	11	53	270,626
Ask No Questions 1966, Nearctic—Questage, by Sun Again	18	16	14	93	600,586
Durga 1966, *Tatan—Durani, by Bold Ruler	18	18	12	59	956,320
Duchess Rae 1966, Hitting Away—His Duchess, by *Blenheim II	18	14	9	59	416,895
Bee for Me 1966, Cyane—Tempted, by *Half Crown	18	12	9	35	360,734
Fanfreluche 1967, Northern Dancer—Ciboulette, by Chop Chop	18	16	14	76	2,189,751
Lighted Lamp 1967, Sir Gaylord—*Chandelier, by Goyama	18	17	10	19	328,113
Carry Me Home 1967, Coursing—Market Basket, by *Radiotherapy	18	16	14	62	515,860
Antigua Anthem 1968, Nashua—English Harbor, by War Admiral	18	15	9	34	534,860
Pia Mia 1968, Pia Star—Surprise Lady, by Discovery	18	18	16	58	933,832
Courtly Dee 1968, Never Bend—Tulle, by War Admiral	18	17	15	71	3,446,275
Set Me Free 1969, Octopus—*Justly, by Fair Trial	18	12	11	34	266,961

Most Foals for a Broodmare, continued

Broodmare, YOB, Pedigree	Foals	Starters	Winners	Wins	Earnings
Courtesan 1969, *Gallant Man—La Dauphine, by *Princequillo	**18**	13	8	40	392,257
Cozumel 1969, T. V. Lark—Tipopick, by Tipoquill	**18**	17	11	59	650,274
Hail Proudly 1969, Francis S.—Spanglet, by *Alibhai	**18**	16	12	74	1,078,798
Fading Image 1970, Crozier—Fading Wave, by *Quibu	**18**	14	13	67	488,716
Make Plans 1971, Go Marching—Sister Antoine, by *Royal Serenade	**18**	15	10	36	730,992
Heroine 1971, Vitriolic—Classify, by Piet	**18**	17	11	49	474,698
Tamara Alain 1972, Judge Kilday—Lil's Intent, by Swoon's Son	**18**	17	14	69	870,193
Day and a Half 1972, Time Tested—Jolly, by Jovial Jove	**18**	16	15	90	942,371
Fashion Dancer 1972, Dancer's Image—Fashion Plate, by Cohoes	**18**	14	11	30	N/A
Mlle. Liebe 1972, Bupers—*Lorgnette II, by High Hat	**18**	10	6	30	573,471
Turn Capp 1972, Turn to Reason—Capped, by Thinking Cap	**18**	16	14	70	1,316,043
Starlet O'Hara 1973, Silent Screen—Perfect Gem, by *Royal Gem II	**18**	15	12	51	554,689
Strait Lane 1974, Chieftain—Level Sands, by *Mahmoud	**18**	16	12	39	3,255,001
Poker's Errand 1974, Poker—Gallant Lesina, by *Gallant Man	**18**	17	15	79	621,568
Troubles Trouble 1974, Advocator—Grinand Bearit, by Olympia	**18**	17	12	44	1,127,287
Saxon's Secret 1974, Royal Saxon—Secret Verdict, by Clandestine	**18**	16	10	50	809,809
Hollyhock 1974, Olden Times—Nasturtium, by *Nasrullah	**18**	16	12	56	500,216
Rare Lady 1974, Never Bend—Double Agent, by Double Jay	**18**	14	13	66	1,428,566
Tea At Five 1975, Olden Times—Lady Attica, by Spy Song	**18**	12	9	57	1,811,656
Liberally Laced 1975, Silent Screen—Miss Glamour Gal, by *Ambiorix	**18**	13	7	32	411,908
Bold Pythian 1975, Bold Reason—Pythian, by Warfare	**18**	18	15	76	589,322
Say What You Mean 1976, Judger—Call the Queen, by Hail to Reason	**18**	15	12	44	746,083
Tweak 1976, Secretariat—Ta Wee, by Intentionally	**18**	16	13	30	723,872
All's Well 1976, Well Mannered—Rhubarb, by Barbizon	**18**	12	9	31	341,154
Morning Games 1976, *Grey Dawn II—Major Play, by B. Major	**18**	17	8	37	1,770,188
Five Star's Sister 1976, Lt. Stevens—Whileaway, by Summer Tan	**18**	14	9	20	455,726
Monroe 1977, Sir Ivor—Best in Show, by Traffic Judge	**18**	14	12	34	1,379,084
Alaki Miss 1977, Olden Times—Calaki, by T. V. Lark	**18**	16	11	65	736,623
So Smooth 1977, Third Martini—Theonia, by Fleet Nasrullah	**18**	14	9	33	713,350
Dear Guinevere 1977, Fearless Knight—Brave and Free, by Warfare	**18**	16	15	59	1,386,132
Full Reign 1979, Secretariat—Hill River, by Hill Rise	**18**	12	8	27	389,289
Tie a Bow 1979, Dance Spell—Bold Bikini, by Boldnesian	**18**	12	7	33	444,055
Bachelor's Catch 1939, Interlace—Bachelor's Toi, by Bachelor's Double	**18**	10	5	10	9,145

Most Consecutive Foals for a Broodmare
(1930-2001)

Broodmare, Year of Birth, Pedigree	Foals	Consecutive Foals
Bold Bikini 1969, Boldnesian—Ran-Tan, by Summer Tan	20	**19**
Photo Flash 1965, *Match II—Picture Light, by *Court Martial	19	**19**
Sarasail 1966, Hitting Away—*Sail Riona, by *Royal Charger	19	**19**
Such 'n Such 1974, Ack Ack—Long Stemmed Rose, by Jacinto	20	**19**
Gallant Lady 1930, *Sir Gallahad III—*Peroration, by Clarissimus	18	**18**
Maxencia (Fr) 1977, Tennyson—Matuschka, by *Orsini II	18	**18**
So What 1978, Iron Ruler—Merry Mama, by Prince John	17	**18**
Whitewood 1960, *Worden—Solarist, by Supreme Court	18	**18**
***Ankole** 1960, Crepello—Sun Path, by Hyperion	17	**17**
***Danae II** 1947, *The Solicitor II—Justitia, by Birthright	17	**17**
Aroh Miss 1977, Mississipian—Marble Arch, by Bold Lad	17	**17**
Ayano Chanel 1975, Eastern Fleet—Erimo Chanel, by Tamanar	18	**17**
Baroness Elsie 1925, Stedfast—Madame Esmond, by Radium	15	**17**
Bee for Me 1966, Cyane—Tempted, by *Half Crown	18	**17**
Duchess Rae 1966, Hitting Away—His Duchess, by *Blenheim II	18	**17**
Extra Alarm 1973, Blazing Count—Deedee O., by Roman Bout	17	**17**
Five Star's Sister 1976, Lt. Stevens—Whileaway, by Summer Tan	18	**17**
Full Reign 1979, Secretariat—Hill River, by Hill Rise	18	**17**
Jesster's Lady 1955, Cosmic Bomb—Elementary, by Count Fleet	17	**17**
Joyce Grove 1946, Bois Roussel—Samovar, by Caerleon	17	**17**
Maid to Measure 1960, Mark-Ye-Well—Bushleaguer, by War Admiral	18	**17**
Orama 1932, Diophon—Cantelupe, by Amadis	17	**17**
Queen Ambra 1977, Alhambra—King's Quote, by Bold Monarch	17	**17**
Red Haste 1971, Red Monk—Plumed, by Alsab	17	**17**
Ritas Gray 1968, Reneged—Close Play, by Shut Out	17	**17**
Trinity 1978, Logical—Trinidad, by Make Tracks	17	**17**
Vali 1954, Sunny Boy—Her Slipper, by Tetratema	18	**17**
Vital Match 1966, *Match II—Vitality Plus, by Never Say Die	17	**17**
Wild Sketch 1966, Rambunctious—Sketch Artist, by Roman Artist	17	**17**

Broodmare, Year of Birth, Pedigree	Foals	Consecutive Foals
Winter Garden 1958, Windfields—Rustic Charm, by Reaping Reward	18	17
Wisp O'Will 1964, New Policy—Miss Willow, by Oil Capitol	20	17
***Betsy Ross II** 1939, *Mahmoud—*Celerina, by *Teddy	23	16
***Mary Ellard** 1951, *Tudor Minstrel—Anacapri, by Tiberius	18	16
***Take a Chance II** 1968, Baldric—Never Too Late, by Never Say Die	16	16
Amtare 1970, *Petare—Trollius, by *Ambiorix	17	16
Auntie May 1975, *Siliconn II—Aunt Anna, by Great Nephew	17	16
Ballymaginathy 1945, Ballyogan—Ins An Mala, by Apron	18	16
Beausite 1938, Bold Archer—Orama, by Diophon	16	16
Best in Show 1965, Traffic Judge—Stolen Hour, by Mr. Busher	18	16
Carose 1974, Caro (Ire)—Pomme Rose, by *Carvin II	16	16
Chambord 1955, Chamossaire—Life Hill, by Solario	17	16
Dog Show 1940, *Bull Dog—Pomp and Glory, by Man o' War	16	16
Donna 1956, Donore—Bashful, by Precipitation	16	16
Edabull 1936, *Bull Dog—Lady Emmeline, by King James	18	16
Elizabeth C. G. 1967, Windy Sea—Fleet Judy, by Fleet Nasrullah	16	16
Esencia 1977, El Virtuoso—Emboscada, by Gran Atleta	16	16
Evening Y'all 1971, Double Hitch—Evening Relic, by Iamarelic	17	16
Fibber 1981, No Robbery—Little True, by *Western Sky II	16	16
Homespun 1969, Round Table—Gal I Love, by *Nasrullah	17	16
Joy Rider 1969, Prince John—Ride Free, by Hasty Road	16	16
Jungle Princess 1964, Make Tracks—Jungle Queen, by Claro	17	16
Light of Day 1939, Hyperion—Leger Day, by Winalot	17	16
Lightfoot Lassie 1969, *Sensitivo—Goomah, by Bolero	17	16
Luckie to Knight 1978, Key to the Kingdom—Kerry Bay, by *Ambiorix	15	16
Luxury 1972, Jaipur—*Decor II, by *Court Martial	15	16
Mirra-Mirra 1977, Vain—Lady Sita, by *Landau	18	16
Morgane 1957, Popof—Morcote, by Chateau Bouscaut	16	16
My Bupers 1967, Bupers—Princess Revoked, by Revoked	17	16
Nangela Dear 1978, Lord Durham—Nangela, by Nearctic	16	16
Nimble Folly 1977, Cyane—Instant Sin, by Restless Native	16	16
Norska 1982, Northfields—Gwendolyn, by Bagdad	16	16
Once for All 1964, Quorum—Little Honey, by Sayajirao	17	16
Pemba 1948, Phidias—Tentatrice, by Corn Belt	17	16
Proudest Moment 1974, Proudest Roman—First Moment, by First Landing	16	16
Quick Verdict 1952, Be Sure Now—*Juristic, by Fairway	18	16
Seductive Lady 1970, Maribeau—Genoa Jib, by Sailor	16	16
Snowshill Rose 1947, Pay Up—Spring Sown, by Ethnarch	16	16
Star Face 1977, African Sky (GB)—Suemette, by Danseur	17	16
Sun Rondeau 1956, Bull Brier—M. Louise, by Sun Teddy	18	16
Supper Show 1969, Knightly Manner—Rosie Redmond, by Royal Coinage	17	16
Sweet Surcease 1963, War Trouble—Patricia R., by Count Turf	16	16
Vampiress 1980, Amberbee—Praktikly Purfect, by *Gallant Man	16	16
Vaucouleurs 1976, Kashmir II—Hillana, by Nasram	17	16
Yankee Miss 1974, Bold Bidder—Single Line, by Rash Prince	16	16

Most Wins by Broodmare's Offspring
(1930-2001)

Broodmare, YOB, Sire—Dam	Foals	Starters	Winners	Starts	Wins	Earnings
Slow and Easy 1922, Colin—*Shyness	15	14	11	962	182	$287,417
***Adorable II** 1925, Sardanapale—Incredule	15	13	12	1,175	181	164,936
Cotton Candy 1945, Stimulus—Sugar Bird	13	12	12	1,109	178	359,502
Transit 1926, *Chicle—*Traverse	10	10	10	1,169	178	308,632
***Clonaslee** 1922, Orpiment—Bullet Proof	18	17	16	1,170	176	258,219
Sag Rock 1930, Rock Man—Atomin	13	12	11	981	170	237,689
Dame Mariechen 1931, High Time—Carrie Hogan	14	14	14	1,149	167	254,771
Pevensea 1935, Enoch—Truly Movin	13	13	13	1,177	166	167,298
Lady Excellent 1932, Nocturnal—Falco	14	13	12	1,180	165	185,899
Ginogret 1941, *Gino—Sunlygret	12	12	12	982	164	223,038
Alondra 1947, War Admiral—Lady Lark	17	17	15	1,173	163	496,993
Doggerel 1935, *Bull Dog—Shenanigan	10	9	9	1,113	163	200,484
Jemima Lee 1929, General Lee—Miss Jemima	15	15	14	860	163	219,609
Sassaby 1931, Broomstick—Saucy Sue	9	9	9	1,112	163	321,217
Agnes Ayres 1923, King James—Sweet Mary	15	14	12	1,201	161	364,151
Lady Floyd 1924, Sir Martin—Fruit Cake	13	11	10	1,015	159	151,435
Much Ado 1921, Ed Crump—*Teetotal	14	13	13	1,026	159	93,168
Vanrose 1920, Vandergrift—Lucille Morois	13	10	9	993	159	123,744
Blame 1921, *Wrack—Censure	11	10	9	1,153	157	132,321
Balking 1935, Balko—Bodega	11	11	10	853	156	426,263
***Miss Turley** 1924, Bachelor's Jap—Raftonia	12	12	11	967	154	74,273

Most Wins by Broodmare's Offspring, continued

Broodmare, YOB, Sire—Dam	Foals	Starters	Winners	Starts	Wins	Earnings
New Melody 1952, Bimelech—Melodious	13	13	13	961	154	688,387
Mary Kelly 1926, Ormondale—Starina	14	14	13	1,097	153	136,548
Kind Annie 1938, Brilliant—*Chaucer Girl	12	11	10	992	152	273,962
Daunt 1925, Lucullite—Dauntless	13	13	13	817	151	230,505
Knightess 1929, *Bright Knight—Markiluna	13	13	10	1,005	151	175,222
Lucy T. 1933, Whichone—*Refugee III	13	11	9	1,092	151	254,071
Cariboo Lass 1928, *Marcus—Mary Fuller	13	12	11	1,115	150	126,034
Softie 1943, Flares—Sicklefeather	16	15	13	1,073	150	338,172
*Flamante 1926, Flamboyant—*Flaminia	11	10	10	960	149	210,627
Maradadi 1930, Stimulus—Virginia L.	18	18	13	1,065	148	428,469
Vinnie 1948, Vincentive—Glorious Time	15	14	11	851	148	422,519
Accra 1941, Annapolis—Ladala	11	11	10	646	146	1,632,463
Happy Factor 1941, Benefactor—Miss Jemima	13	10	10	940	146	337,080
Lady Gallivant 1922, *Hourless—*Lady's Gauntlet	11	10	10	1,049	146	148,508
Hastily Yours 1936, John P. Grier—*Hastily	14	12	11	1,080	145	692,799
Mintairy 1927, Mint Briar—*Airy Fairy	10	10	10	776	145	195,913
Pennant Girl 1929, *Rire Aux Larmes—Flying Pennant	14	14	10	848	144	254,551
Royalite 1922, Lucullite—Royal Ensign	9	8	8	853	144	122,635
Panoramic 1932, Chance Shot—Dustwhirl	11	11	11	975	144	686,387
*Valdina Spirea 1940, Canon Law—*Spiraea II	14	14	13	1,157	143	413,361
Predicament 1929, *Waygood—Precipitate	15	13	13	1,024	142	184,201
Cushion 1917, Nonpareil—Hassock	12	9	9	617	142	140,109
Miss Velocity 1957, Spy Song—Fairy Dancer	18	17	17	1,174	140	560,219
Scuttle 1928, Whiskaway—Sea Tale	11	11	11	927	140	199,437
Brown Maiden 1933, Brown Bud—Tailor Maid	10	10	10	1,165	140	202,886
Sis Tartan 1947, Port au Prince—Tartan Betsy	10	10	9	824	139	343,586
Sly Marie 1962, Neptune—*Marie Lou	12	12	11	911	139	523,325
Glacial 1926, *Hourless—*Snowcapt	15	15	13	1,093	139	199,418
Greedy Girl 1926, *Vulcain—Grasp	12	10	10	817	137	196,899
*Legend of the Lake 1929, Dark Legend—Narrow Water	10	10	7	766	137	105,120
Nancy Clay 1923, *Wrack—Nancy Lee	14	12	11	854	137	163,667
Baffling Miss 1927, Baffling—Miss Merle	4	4	4	764	136	86,250
Dog Show 1940, *Bull Dog—Pomp and Glory	16	15	15	892	136	361,952
May Morning 1935, Pompey—Howdy	9	9	9	1,087	135	227,415
Nortell 1955, El Mono—Control Board	12	12	12	864	135	477,660
Annabell Lee 1926, *Volta—Compose	12	11	11	774	135	288,719
Cinema 1923, Sweep—*Magic Lantern II	13	12	10	957	134	144,407
Dark Victory 1929, *Traumer—Sun Vive	11	11	10	1,179	134	213,242
Pelota 1924, *War Cloud—Muriel	15	13	12	949	134	152,597
Riva 1930, *Wrack—Celiva	15	13	13	1,101	134	195,657
Admittance 1946, Maeda—Stitches	15	15	15	1,217	133	208,098
Montecito 1936, Bewithus—Crescent	12	10	9	770	133	263,555
Pretty Pol 1925, *Wormleighton—Polly Connelly	9	8	6	704	133	92,968
Mrs. Burke 1923, *Berrilldon—Pinkie	12	11	11	1,248	133	104,588
Paradox 1923, *Omar Khayyam—*Silent Queen	13	12	11	1,092	133	151,734
Cash Book 1933, *Bull Dog—Saleslady	15	13	10	932	132	456,643
Neltone 1953, *Two Ton Tony—Nellie Vee	14	14	10	768	131	290,809
Petite 1927, *Colonel Vennie—Victoire	11	10	10	796	131	134,275
Wildwood 1923, Master Robert—Crestwood Girl	12	12	10	724	131	146,222
Burgoo Ann 1942, Burgoo King—Step Quick	12	12	11	907	131	209,364
Hurry Home 1921, *Omar Khayyam—*Breathing Spell	14	13	10	1,128	131	105,900
High Tea 1949, Challedon—Eight O'Clock	16	16	13	990	130	234,932
Rock Mart 1941, Sunador—Rock Haven	13	10	9	741	130	317,635
Sovietta 1928, *Stefan the Great—Last Straw	12	12	12	759	130	225,515
Beauty Slave 1922, Black Toney—*Padula	14	13	10	1,081	129	188,659
Escalade 1936, *Sir Gallahad III—Escadrille	13	12	12	986	129	701,376
Hazel Spears 1925, Drastic—Impressive	14	12	11	948	129	211,059
Jamesville 1934, Pompey—Moonlit	12	12	11	876	129	327,172
Parley 1923, *Under Fire—Colloquy	11	11	8	784	129	95,782
Binary Star 1924, *North Star III—*Padula	12	11	9	817	129	154,735
Drystone 1929, Man o' War—*Keystone	12	12	11	1,107	129	189,932
Knight's Fancy 1933, *Sir Gallahad III—Fancy Light	13	13	13	956	129	212,783
Yellow Blossom 1918, Luke McLuke—Micaela	14	14	10	871	129	102,033
*Samoa 1923, Cylgad—*Theresa II	14	13	11	790	128	101,576
Stitches 1925, *Polymelian—*Lacework	15	14	13	910	128	178,410
Mary Gardner 1926, Whisk Broom II—Voterina	10	10	10	882	128	97,494
Alley 1938, Rolled Stocking—Gossip Avenue	13	10	9	857	127	430,216
Lotus 1923, *Light Brigade—*Humanity	13	12	10	898	127	143,644
Midi's Mom 1945, Arabs Arrow—Brown Street	11	10	9	764	127	448,183
Dorothy Dean 1909, *Marchmont II—Dont Ask Me	6	5	5	936	127	83,906
Fib 1928, Westy Hogan—Hyperbole	10	10	9	856	127	316,096
Miss Dora 1918, Jack Atkin—Dorval	14	10	9	1,112	127	83,443
*Sun Maiden 1921, Sundridge—*First Attempt II	11	11	11	918	127	167,542
Aero Wave 1960, Sailor—Flight	12	11	8	653	126	636,696
Canuck Priority 1965, Canadian Champ—Priority Miss	14	14	13	712	126	953,351
Sistova 1933, *Blue Pete—Silistria	8	8	8	570	126	84,823
Top Lady 1923, Ormondale—Play Toy	10	8	8	870	126	121,595

Most Winners for a Broodmare
(1930-2001)

Broodmare, YOB, Sire—Dam	Foals	Starters	Winners	SWs	Earnings
Miss Velocity 1957, Spy Song—Fairy Dancer	18	17	17	0	$560,219
*Mindrum Maid 1939, *Mahmoud—Imp	17	17	17	0	$149,615
Lady Ambassador 1959, Hill Prince—Your Hostess	17	17	16	1	$880,817
Pia Mia 1968, Pia Star—Surprise Lady	18	18	16	3	$933,832
Northern Beauty 1955, Borealis—Fleeting Beauty	19	15	16	2	$237,330
Arizona Jubilee 1964, Spotted Moon—The Frog Hook	19	17	16	1	$271,893
*Clonaslee 1922, Orpiment—Bullet Proof	18	17	16	1	$258,219
Sable Lady 1927, *Waygood—Kolinsky	17	17	16	0	$180,004
Tattooed Miss 1960, Mark-Ye-Well—Mossy Number	18	18	15	2	$375,182
Miss Cotton 1962, Swoon's Son—Always Movin	16	15	15	4	$959,195
Pines Lady 1966, Pinebloom—Lady Peabody	15	15	15	0	$497,559
Courtly Dee 1968, Never Bend—Tulle	18	17	15	8	$3,446,275
Proof Enough 1969, Prove It—Theonia	16	16	15	3	$910,495
Day and a Half 1972, Time Tested—Jolly	18	16	15	2	$942,371
Cherry Lady 1973, Bold Lad—Cherry Fool	16	15	15	1	$773,746
Newsun 1973, Penowa Rullah—Sunshine Bright	16	16	15	2	$1,273,538
Bold Pythian 1975, Bold Reason—Pythian	18	18	15	0	$589,322
Bonnie Blade 1976, Blade—Promised Princess	16	16	15	1	$1,037,485
Dear Guinevere 1977, Fearless Knight—Brave and Free	19	16	15	1	$1,386,132
Sweet Tulle 1978, Tom Tulle—Little Divy	17	16	15	0	$265,600
Admittance 1946, Maeda—Stitches	15	15	15	0	$208,098
Alondra 1947, War Admiral—Lady Lark	17	17	15	2	$496,993
Blinking Owl 1938, *Pharamond II—Baba Kenny	19	16	15	0	$195,196
Dog Show 1940, *Bull Dog—Pomp and Glory	16	15	15	1	$361,952
Our Patty 1933, Brown Bud—Perjury	17	15	15	0	$141,309
Amazer 1967, Mincio—*Alzara	17	17	15	2	$1,916,353
Godzilla 1972, Gyr—Gently	15	15	15	2	$4,353,027
Patsy Dru 1959, Alorter—Patsy	17	17	15	6	$459,604
Grecian Coin 1960, Royal Coinage—Greek Pillar	17	15	15	0	$787,886
Wolf Hands 1963, All Hands—Wolf Bait	16	16	15	3	$462,595
Tweentzel Pie 1966, Four-and-Twenty—Peachywillow	16	16	15	2	$633,905
Stepping High 1969, No Robbery—*Bebop II	17	17	15	2	$1,377,143
Dancing Liz 1972, Northern Dancer—Crimson Queen	16	16	15	1	$1,193,174
Ribbon Duster 1973, Dust Commander—First Ribbon	17	16	15	1	$588,113
Poker's Errand 1974, Poker—Gallant Lesina	18	17	15	1	$621,568
Battle Creek Girl 1977, His Majesty—Far Beyond	19	17	15	6	$4,108,911
Mideau 1942, *Bull Dog—Wild Waters	18	18	15	1	$509,729
Maxencia (Fr) 1977, Tennyson—Matuschka	18	15	15	2	$389,796
First Formal 1953, Rippey—Evening Blue	15	15	14	4	$673,769
Smart Woman 1953, *Djeddah—Wood Spirit	16	15	14	1	$233,226
Lovita H. 1955, Take Away—Miss Fiddle	17	17	14	2	$538,215
Shy Dancer 1955, Bolero—Shy Bim	16	16	14	4	$1,268,439
Cequillo 1956, *Princequillo—Boldness	20	17	14	4	$1,031,646
Pinecrest Miss 1956, *Royal Serenade—Bully Babe	15	14	14	0	$397,371
Alamo Maid 1958, Brookfield—*Memsahib II	16	16	14	0	$263,482
Hot Road 1963, Road House—Fay Destiny	16	14	14	2	$534,491
Day Line 1963, *Day Court—Fast Line	21	17	14	1	$421,940
Via Satellite 1963, *Empire Link—High Hurry	16	15	14	1	$358,660
Polly N. 1965, *Quibu—Poliniss	17	15	14	1	$911,456
Miss Debbie Lee 1966, Accomplish—Lucky Gay	17	17	14	4	$614,903
Carry Me Home 1967, Coursing—Market Basket	18	16	14	3	$515,860
Bambar 1968, Ambehaving—*Barra II	17	16	14	2	$1,115,201
Kadesh 1970, Lucky Mel—News Release	19	15	14	3	$879,370
Seductive Lady 1970, Maribeau—Genoa Jib	16	15	14	1	$715,283
Tamara Alain 1972, Judge Kilday—Lil's Intent	18	17	14	2	$870,193
Turn Capp 1972, Turn to Reason—Capped)	18	16	14	3	$1,316,043
Perceptive Lady 1973, Damascus—Aesthetic	15	15	14	0	$502,793
Peace Please 1978, Hold Your Peace—Please Say Yes	16	15	14	1	$771,254
Audacious Lady 1936, Sun Beau—Dark Edwina	17	16	14	1	$195,034
Best by Test 1931, Black Toney—Better Judgment	16	15	14	4	$421,125
Dame Mariechen 1931, High Time—Carrie Hogan	14	14	14	2	$254,771
Gayee 1929, Bostonian—*Lucky Flight	14	14	14	0	$190,097
Grey Flight 1945, *Mahmoud—Planetoid	15	15	14	9	$1,194,159
Twotimer 1940, Double Scotch—Candy May	15	15	14	0	$188,023
Zanzara 1951, Fairey Fulmar—Sunright	17	15	14	6	$55,106
Come On Honey 1956, Free America—Sweet as Honey	16	16	14	2	$185,762
Ask the Prince 1956, *Princequillo—Blue Case	15	14	14	2	$499,993
Sun Rondeau 1956, Bull Brier—M. Louise	18	16	14	3	$484,084
Little Johns Joy 1962, Johns Joy—Little Tihee	17	16	14	0	$228,387

Most Winners for a Broodmare, continued

Broodmare, YOB, Sire—Dam	Foals	Starters	Winners	SWs	Earnings
Colour Her Fleet 1962, Fleet Path—Dijon	14	14	**14**	1	$477,039
Say Yore Mine 1962, *Cavan—Saygosh	17	17	**14**	0	$384,371
Wee Ticky 1962, Alarullah—Irish Story	14	14	**14**	0	$173,966
Flou-Wolf 1963, Francis S.—Sparkle	16	14	**14**	1	$445,860
Song Song 1964, Middle Brother—Fan Song	16	16	**14**	2	$419,916
La Chunga 1964, Bolero—Lady's Delight	16	16	**14**	1	$511,459
Wisp O'Will 1964, New Policy—Miss Willow	20	16	**14**	4	$894,640
Twolympia 1964, Olympia—Toluene	17	16	**14**	2	$577,829
Peace Movement 1966, Admiral's Voyage—Deep Blue Sea	16	15	**14**	1	$622,814
Ask No Questions 1966, Nearctic—Questage	18	16	**14**	2	$600,586
Misty Bride 1967, Hethersett—*Sister Grey	16	16	**14**	2	$1,403,809
Fanfreluche 1967, Northern Dancer—Ciboulette	18	16	**14**	5	$2,189,751
Lucy Malarkey 1969, Coursing—Mother Wit	15	14	**14**	0	$200,031
Supper Show 1969, Knightly Manner—Rosie Redmond	17	14	**14**	2	$647,971
Lovely Lance 1970, Assagai—Hurry On Gal	14	14	**14**	1	$689,263
Marching Margy 1971, Go Marching—*Cancelada	16	14	**14**	2	$886,295
Brave and Free 1971, Warfare—Donna Armona	17	14	**14**	2	$961,050
Lovely Pond 1975, Duck Dance—Golpey	15	14	**14**	1	$1,360,652
Shocking Moment 1976, Info—Reneged's Belle	21	16	**14**	1	$701,401
Bold Essence 1977, Native Charger—Cologne	16	15	**14**	1	$962,389
Amaranth 1936, Blue Larkspur—*Lespedeza II	15	14	**14**	1	$234,243
Blue Tack 1937, Hard Tack—Blue Eagle	14	14	**14**	0	$220,827
End Play 1946, Jack High—Blue Black	16	15	**14**	1	$213,704
Escutcheon 1927, *Sir Gallahad III—*Affection	16	15	**14**	1	$223,518
***Honeysuckle II** 1948, Full Bloom—Fair Honey	17	17	**14**	0	$75,903
Jacinth 1936, *Jacopo—Calycanthus	14	14	**14**	0	$146,483
Jemima Lee 1929, General Lee—Miss Jemima	15	15	**14**	0	$219,609
Lady Hamilton 1944, War Admiral—Apogee	16	15	**14**	0	$129,650
Light of Day 1939, Hyperion—Leger Day	17	17	**14**	5	$235,020
Owena 1925, The Porter—My My	14	14	**14**	1	$265,339
Pabilera 1949, Embrujo—Parlera	17	12	**14**	0	$54,121
Sky Susan 1940, Hadagal—Wise Susan	17	16	**14**	0	$241,219
Sun Tigress 1946, Tiger—Sun Agnes	18	16	**14**	2	$326,404
Ballymaginathy 1945, Ballyogan—Ins An Mala	18	17	**14**	3	$46,306

Most Starts by Broodmare's Offspring
(1930-2001)

Broodmare, YOB, Sire—Dam	Foals	Starters	Winners	Starts	Earnings
Our Patty 1933, Brown Bud—Perjury	17	15	15	1,275	$141,309
Mrs. Burke 1923, *Berrilldon—Pinkie	12	11	11	1,248	104,588
Admittance 1946, Maeda—Stitches	15	15	15	1,217	208,098
Mica 1924, Fair Play—Malachite	9	8	8	1,215	106,918
Tabset 1938, Upset Lad—McTab	12	12	12	1,212	194,434
Agnes Ayres 1923, King James—Sweet Mary	15	14	12	1,201	364,151
Lina Clark 1919, Delhi—Prism	13	13	11	1,187	115,562
Lady Excellent 1932, Nocturnal—Falco	14	13	12	1,180	185,899
Dark Victory 1929, *Traumer—Sun Vive	11	11	10	1,179	213,242
Pevensea 1935, Enoch—Truly Movin	13	13	13	1,177	167,298
***Adorable II** 1925, Sardanapale—Incredule	15	13	12	1,175	164,936
Miss Velocity 1957, Spy Song—Fairy Dancer	18	17	17	1,174	560,219
Alondra 194?, War Admiral—Lady Lark	17	17	15	1,173	496,993
***Clonaslee** 1922, Orpiment—Bullet Proof	18	17	16	1,170	258,219
Transit 1926, *Chicle—*Traverse	10	10	10	1,169	308,632
Brown Maiden 1933, Brown Bud—Tailor Maid	10	10	10	1,165	202,886
***Valdina Spirea** 1940, Canon Law—*Spiraea II	14	14	13	1,157	413,361
Blame 1921, *Wrack—Censure	11	10	9	1,153	132,321
Respite 1922, Hilarious—Lucinda	13	12	9	1,151	134,844
Dame Mariechen 1931, High Time—Carrie Hogan	14	14	14	1,149	254,771
Galful 1940, Hadagal—Armful	16	16	13	1,136	183,184
Hurry Home 1921, *Omar Khayyam—*Breathing Spell	14	13	10	1,128	105,900
Happy Seas 1939, *Happy Argo—Golden Billows	12	10	9	1,120	188,979
Cariboo Lass 1928, *Marcus—Mary Fuller	13	12	11	1,115	126,034
Doggerel 1935, *Bull Dog—Shenanigan	10	9	9	1,113	200,484
Asianna 1935, Wise Counsellor—Asia	13	11	10	1,112	185,443
Miss Dora 1918, Jack Atkin—Dorval	14	10	9	1,112	83,443
Sassaby 1931, Broomstick—Saucy Sue	9	9	9	1,112	321,217
Cotton Candy 1945, Stimulus—Sugar Bird	13	12	12	1,109	359,502
Drystone 1929, Man o' War—*Keystone	12	12	11	1,107	189,932

Broodmare, YOB, Sire—Dam	Foals	Starters	Winners	Starts	Earnings
Riva 1930, *Wrack—Celiva	15	13	13	1,101	195,657
Mary Kelly 1926, Ormondale—Starina	14	14	13	1,097	136,548
Glacial 1926, *Hourless—*Snowcapt	15	15	13	1,093	199,418
Lucy T. 1933, Whichone—*Refugee III	13	11	9	1,092	254,071
Paradox 1923, *Omar Khayyam—*Silent Queen	13	12	11	1,092	151,734
*Play Polly 1934, Chance Play—Hasten Polly	14	14	10	1,091	177,356
May Morning 1935, Pompey—Howdy	9	9	9	1,087	227,415
Beauty Slave 1922, Black Toney—*Padula	14	13	10	1,081	188,659
Hastily Yours 1936, John P. Grier—*Hastily	14	12	11	1,080	692,799
Softie 1943, Flares—Sicklefeather	16	15	13	1,073	338,172
*Soul Mate 1920, Argos—Affinity	14	12	12	1,070	110,177
Devil's Garden 1922, Colin—Garden of Allah	15	14	11	1,065	118,561
Maradadi 1930, Stimulus—Virginia L.	18	18	13	1,065	428,469
Fairy Day 1934, Man o' War—Ides	12	12	11	1,064	307,853
Audley Girl 1935, *Bright Knight—Princess Doreen	13	12	11	1,061	221,924
Blue Tack 1937, Hard Tack—Blue Eagle	14	14	14	1,059	220,827
Lady Gallivant 1922, *Hourless—*Lady's Gauntlet	11	10	10	1,049	148,508
Sky Susan 1940, Hadagal—Wise Susan	17	16	14	1,048	241,219
Sly Glance 1927, Fair Play—*Love-Blink	13	13	9	1,048	115,799
May Mack 1932, *Epinard—Mary Belle	15	13	11	1,047	152,980
Nony G. 1937, Easter Bells—Mildred Hamburg	13	13	12	1,046	198,423
Question 1923, Fair Play—*Qu'elle Est Belle II	11	10	8	1,043	181,255
Colour Her Fleet 1962, Fleet Path—Dijon	14	14	14	1,037	477,039
O Play 1937, Okapi—Playwell	10	10	9	1,034	221,566
Last Trial 1946, Heather Broom—Trial	16	16	11	1,030	310,019
Much Ado 1921, Ed Crump—*Teetotal	14	13	13	1,026	93,168
Predicament 1929, *Waygood—Precipitate	15	13	13	1,024	184,201
Whiskey Sour 1947, Double Scotch—Dream Belle	11	10	10	1,023	228,842
Lady Floyd 1924, Sir Martin—Fruit Cake	13	11	10	1,015	151,435
Moving Star 1928, *North Star III—Cinema	9	9	8	1,015	217,174
Madfinis 1929, Mad Hatter—Finis	11	11	10	1,012	140,885
Plaid 1921, *Wrack—Kilts	12	12	12	1,011	194,600
Silver Dime 1931, Vandergrift—Louvain	14	14	11	1,010	139,998
Edabull 1936, *Bull Dog—Lady Emmeline	18	17	10	1,008	386,305
True Trick 1942, Chance Play—True Flier	15	14	13	1,007	575,637
Antidote 1925, Bachelor's Double—*Prescription	15	13	11	1,005	163,887
Betty Vic 1934, Victorian—Black Betty	15	15	10	1,005	189,738
Knightess 1929, *Bright Knight—Markiluna	13	13	10	1,005	175,222
Chiz 1926, *Wrack—The Marchioness	10	10	9	1,001	73,029
Off Gold 1932, Polydor—*Silva Plana	16	13	9	999	204,792
Ampersand 1933, *Diapason—Miss Montgomery	12	12	9	997	232,099
Doreena 1941, *Quatre Bras II—Princess Doreen	9	9	9	995	205,639
Stell 1939, Good Goods—Squall	10	10	10	994	179,309
Vanrose 1920, Vandergrift—Lucille Morois	13	10	9	993	123,744
Kind Annie 1938, Brilliant—*Chaucer Girl	12	11	10	992	273,962
Coffee Spot 1955, Eight Thirty—Cheesecloth	14	13	12	991	333,822
Princella 1929, *Spanish Prince II—Miss Marcella	12	12	11	991	141,804
Bay Queen 1951, Alaking—Brine	11	11	9	990	167,407
High Tea 1949, Challedon—Eight O'Clock	16	16	13	990	234,932
La Rica 1943, *Don Mike—Maybeth	13	11	11	989	213,857
Sun Tigress 1946, Tiger—Sun Agnes	18	16	14	988	326,404
Imperial Play 1933, Chance Play—Pond Lily	17	15	12	987	181,473
Escalade 1936, *Sir Gallahad III—Escadrille	13	12	12	986	701,376
Mad Kiss 1927, Mad Hatter—Tabouche	11	11	11	986	98,263
Parabola 1932, Infinite—Jane Frances	14	12	12	985	247,707
Phantom Fairy 1924, *Negofol—Phantom Maid	13	13	11	984	107,475
Flavia 1922, *Under Fire—Mary Orr	10	10	8	982	121,027
Ginogret 1941, *Gino—Sunlygret	12	12	12	982	223,038
Pious 1927, Dominion—*Annarella	9	9	8	982	167,257
Io 1924, *Omond—Simona	14	14	12	981	96,607
Sag Rock 1930, Rock Man—Atomin	13	12	11	981	237,689
Mideau 1942, *Bull Dog—Wild Waters	18	18	15	981	509,729
The Beasel 1927, Sunspot—*Antipodes	13	12	9	980	287,879
Forget 1934, Transmute—Watchola	12	11	10	978	132,631
Fair Moneta 1925, Fair Play—*Moneta III	14	13	13	976	89,172
Rita Jane 1941, Charing Cross—Sing Low	9	9	9	976	236,564
*Cairn 1929, Colorado—*Bessema	12	12	10	975	154,371
Panoramic 1932, Chance Shot—Dustwhirl	11	11	11	975	686,387
Tesuque 1922, *Troutbeck—Micaela	12	12	11	973	104,186
Gloria Monk 1930, *Monk's Way—Gloria Quayle	11	11	11	972	139,191

AUCTIONS
Auction Review of 2001

In 2001, the Thoroughbred marketplace was buffeted by financial and psychological shocks from the real world, and only the yearling segment managed to maintain an average price per horse close to the record levels of 2000. As a result, the market retreated somewhat from the $1-billion in total sales achieved in 2000 to total receipts of $846-million, a 22.5% decline but still the third-highest total in history. In general, prices declined across the board, but the lower echelons were hardest hit as buyer selectivity again increased, as evidenced by the increase in overall buy-back rate to 28.7%. No individual price records were set, but Keeneland July once again broke the world record for average price for one sale.

Yearlings

Although the terrorist attacks of September 11, 2001, occurred on the scheduled second day of the year's largest yearling sale, Keeneland September, the combination of a significantly fewer yearlings offered in the select arena and the extraordinary selectivity of buyers kept average price for the year from falling more than 3.6% below the 2000 average.

Still, the negative factors that plagued other market segments were visible even in the most global figures that describe the yearling market in 2001:

- 12,702 horses offered, up 0.1%.
- 9,032 horses sold, down 5.5%.
- Average declined 3.6% to $52,402.
- Median dropped 21.7% to $9,000.
- Total receipts dipped 8.9% to $473,295,356.
- Buy-backs soared 17% to 28.9%.

While average price remained above $50,000, that gaudy mean provided little consolation for anyone whose horses did not match the highly selective criteria for conformation and radiograph results that buyers almost universally employ now in choosing yearlings.

The top 10% of the market remained essentially level with the top 10% of the market in 2000, but the rest of the market declined markedly, as highlighted by the sharply lower median price, with half above $9,000 and half below that level.

The strength at the market's top was further illustrated by the fact that 52 yearlings sold for $1-million or more in North America, only five fewer than the record 57 sold in 2000. Seven more sold at that level in England, Ireland, or France in 2001, compared with ten in 2000.

The highest-priced horse of the year in any category, Stonerside Stable's Storm Cat colt out of Halory, by Halo, elicited a $6.4-million bid from agent Demi O'Byrne on the delayed second day of the Keeneland September sale. Lane's End was the agent selling the colt. Amid predictions of impending doom, average at Keeneland's July sale once again soared to a world record, topping out at $710,247.

Despite the 8.9% drop in total receipts from North American yearling sales in 2001, the yearling segment of the market actually gained market share from the other three main segments. The $473,295,356 in total receipts represented 55.9% of the total North American Thoroughbred auction marketplace, compared with 47.4% of the North American total in 2000. Only the yearling market kept the Thoroughbred marketplace from sliding into disastrous territory in 2001.

Weanlings

The weanling market was the most difficult of the four major market segments to analyze in 2001. The Keeneland November auction, the largest collection of foals of 2001 offered anywhere, was hit by an inharmonious convergence of four negative factors, any one of which by itself could have accounted for a market downturn. Whatever the joint effects of the worldwide economic slump, the September 11 terrorist attacks, mare reproductive loss syndrome (MRLS), and the absence of a consignment from perennial market leader Gaines-Gentry Thoroughbreds, the weanling market suffered more than any segment except broodmares.

The bare figures from the 2001 weanling market tell much of the story:

- Number offered declined 18.1% to 2,654.
- Number sold dipped 18% to 1,926.
- Average dropped 23.6% to $27,285.
- Total receipts plummeted 37.3% to $52,551,239.
- Median declined 30% to $7,000.

The absence of the Gaines-Gentry consignment, leading seller of weanlings for much of the 1990s, was most apparent at the top of the market, where only one North American weanling managed a seven-figure price, compared with four in 2000. The most expensive American weanling was Hill 'n' Dale Farm's Storm Cat filly out of Better Than Honour, by Deputy Minister, who will be partly owned by her breeder after Canadian Ted Burnett bid $1.5-million for her at Keeneland November, with Hill 'n' Dale owner John Sikura retaining an interest.

Just how much of the decline in the weanling market in 2001 was due to the four major negative factors and how much to a decline in buyer demand was impossible to decipher. The weanling segment of the marketplace has long been the most volatile—and it was likely to be even more unpredictable in 2002, with the absence of 30% of the Kentucky foal crop due to MRLS.

Two-Year-Olds

Like every other segment of the Thoroughbred trade, the market for two-year-olds in training registered declines in practically every statistic in 2001 from year-earlier levels. Fewer horses sold for less money at a lower average price. But, because the juvenile sale season was over well before the terrorist attacks, the declines were not as large as in some other segments. On the other hand, the market for two-year-olds is clearly the segment of the industry where buyer selectivity was applied most stringently.

Global statistics for the 2001 juvenile market include:

- 2,676 horses sold, down 11.6%.
- $126,973,553 in total receipts, down 18%.
- Average declined 7.2% to $47,449.
- Median remained steady at $20,000.
- Top price declined from $2-million to $1.05-million.

The only important statistic that did not decline was the specific one both buyers and sellers would like to see improved: buy-back rate. The percentage of horses not reaching their minimum sale prices increased from 32.7% in 2000 to a record 34.7% in '01, confirming that selectivity is the hallmark and bane of the juvenile marketplace.

After a disastrous year for juvenile pinhookers in 2000, the resellers decreased their investment at yearling sales later that year. Equally inevitable was the pullback that resulted in smaller catalogs at virtually every sale of two-year-olds in training and a perceptible drop in catalog quality in 2001. That reduction in investment helped the bottom line somewhat but failed to return pinhooking operations as a whole to profitability. In 2000, the nation's pinhookers lost a disastrous $23-million on paper. Their change in tactics reduced the apparent loss in 2001 to $14.6-million, far below the profitability levels of the mid- to late 1990s.

The highest-priced horse of the year came at Ocala Breeders' Sales Co.'s March sale, where Eugene Melnyk paid $1.05-million for a colt by Dehere out of Sweet Gold, by Gilded Time. Hartley/De Renzo Thoroughbreds had purchased the colt for $50,000 at the 2000 Keeneland September yearling sale. The highest-priced filly, Bella Bellucci, purchased for $925,000 by

agent Demi O'Byrne from Crupi's New Castle Farm, agent, at the Fasig-Tipton Calder sale, won the Astarita Stakes (G2) and ran third in the Breeders' Cup Juvenile Fillies (G1).

Consignors at juvenile sales still appear to be caught in an unenviable vise. Prices for yearlings remain so high that resellers have very little room to make a profit. Furthermore, buyers who purchase yearlings to race are now applying many of the same stringent conformational evaluations that have long served pinhookers well, leaving them very few affordable horses of the type they must have to attract buyers the following year.

Broodmares

The market for broodmares suffered most from each of the negative factors attacking the Thoroughbred marketplace in 2001. Because most broodmares sell in the autumn, those sales occurred after the September 11 terrorist attacks, which added another negative influence to the effects of the worldwide economic slowdown. In addition, MRLS was largely responsible for the 9.1% decline in number of broodmares offered for sale during the year because most breeders prefer not to sell barren mares.

The following figures summarize the difficulties of the marketplace:

- Number sold declined 13.4% to 4,952.
- Total receipts plummeted 40.8% to $187,490,811.
- Average declined 31.7% to $37,862.
- Median fell 27.8% to $6,500.
- Buy-back rate rose from 22.4% in 2000 to 26.1%.

As in other segments of the marketplace, prices at the top of the market remained strong for the few offerings that met the requirements of breeding establishments operating in the upper echelons. This included the year's most expensive mare, Twenty Eight Carat, then an 11-year-old mare in foal to Fusaichi Pegasus, who was purchased for $4-million by Betty Moran of Brushwood Stable. Consigned by Lane's End as agent, Twenty Eight Carat has already produced Grade 1 winner A P Valentine.

Twenty Eight Carat was one of 18 broodmares sold in North America for seven-figure prices, compared with 43 in 2000. Four more sold at that level in England at the Tattersalls December sale.

The paucity of high-quality stock available is partly responsible for 30%-plus declines in average for the top 30% of the market.

Although demand for Thoroughbred stock was clearly down in general in 2001, the combination of negative factors in the last four months of the year exacerbated the effects of that decline on the market for broodmares.

—*John P. Sparkman*

Chronological Review of Major 2001 Sales

	No. sold	Total	(% Chg)	Average	(% Chg)	Highest price
January						
Keeneland January horses of all ages	1,207	$39,657,700	(−34.9%)	$32,856	(−33.1%)	$1,700,000
Ocala Breeders' Sales Co. winter mixed	684	5,394,400	(−27.9%)	7,887	(−22.7%)	105,000
Keeneland January horses of all ages Internet auction	11	72,700		6,609		30,900
Heritage Place winter mixed	56	183,300	(+2.2%)	3,273	(+0.4%)	20,000
Barretts Equine Ltd. winter mixed	429	6,026,200	(+192.0%)	14,047	(+149.8%)	185,000
February						
Fasig-Tipton Texas winter mixed	142	568,100	(−18.9%)	4,001	(−1.2%)	20,000
Fasig-Tipton Midlantic winter mixed	145	896,800	(−48.0%)	6,185	(−32.3%)	67,000
Ocala Breeders' Sales Co. selected two-year-olds in training	136	14,124,000	(−9.5%)	103,853	(−5.5%)	900,000
Fasig-Tipton Kentucky winter mixed	319	2,806,200	(+2.9%)	8,797	(−13.5%)	65,000
Thomas Sales Co. Horseman's Racing Bred winter mixed	71	133,875	(−26.8%)	1,886	(+0.1%)	10,500
Arkansas Thoroughbred Sales Co. winter mixed	146	617,600	(+2.7%)	4,230	(−21.9%)	47,000
Fasig-Tipton Florida selected two-year-olds in training	136	28,186,000	(−16.3%)	207,250	(−4.0%)	1,000,000
March						
Barretts Equine Ltd. March selected two-year-olds in training	71	10,085,000	(−41.7%)	142,042	(−21.1%)	750,000
Fair Grounds Sales Co. selected two-year-olds in training	25	388,400	(−13.9%)	15,536	(+10.2%)	50,000
Ocala Breeders' Sales March selected two-year-olds in training	216	15,166,000	(−13.4%)	70,213	(+0.2%)	1,050,000
Fasig-Tipton Texas two-year-olds in training	193	4,494,900	(−23.5%)	23,290	(+3.8%)	250,000
April						
Keeneland April two-year-olds in training	91	14,898,000	(−19.5%)	163,714	(+8.8%)	775,000
Louisiana Thoroughbred Breeders Sales Co. spring mixed	114	399,300	(+4.2%)	3,503	(−15.0%)	16,000
Ocala Breeders' Sales Co. spring two-year-olds in training	685	18,058,600	(+4.2%)	26,363	(+2.4%)	550,000
May						
Barretts Equine Ltd. spring two-year-olds in training	163	4,437,400	(−10.6%)	27,223	(−9.0%)	215,000
Fasig-Tipton Midlantic two-year-olds in training	268	8,529,400	(+5.9%)	31,826	(−5.6%)	270,000
June						
American Equine Sales two-year-olds in training	30	298,800		9,960		27,500
CTHS (Ontario division) two-year-olds in training	33	697,638	(−13.0%)	21,141	(+10.8%)	71,753
San Antonio Rose classic mixed horse	80	158,150	(+118.7%)	1,977	(+20.3%)	24,700
Ocala Breeders' Sales Co. June two-year-olds in training and horses of racing age	230	3,842,200	(+19.3%)	16,705	(+11.5%)	110,000
Heritage Place spring mixed	14	38,300	(+28.3%)	2,736	(−26.7%)	5,200
Illinois Thoroughbred Breeders two-year-olds in training and horses of racing age	42	704,700	(−32.8%)	16,779	(+8.8%)	100,000
July						
Fasig-Tipton Midlantic two-year-olds in training and horses of racing age	91	1,701,500	(+29.3%)	18,698	(+30.7%)	240,000
Keeneland July selected yearling	89	63,212,000	(−21.7%)	710,247	(+14.4%)	4,000,000
Fasig-Tipton Kentucky selected yearling	237	23,148,000	(−11.6%)	97,671	(+25.7%)	625,000
August						
Minnesota Thoroughbred Association horses of all ages	46	92,900	(+3.8%)	2,020	(−27.8%)	12,500
Louisiana Thoroughbred Breeders Sales Co. summer mixed	100	319,500	(−44.8%)	3,195	(−25.4%)	20,000
Fasig-Tipton Saratoga selected yearling	162	62,412,000	(+49.0%)	385,259	(+26.0%)	3,300,000
Fasig-Tipton New York Saratoga preferred yearling	82	3,557,000	(+4.0%)	43,378	(+4.0%)	180,000
California Thoroughbred Breeders Del Mar August yearling	104	4,541,000	(+9.9%)	43,663	(+36.3%)	200,000
Ruidoso Annual Thoroughbred yearling	152	1,065,500	(+26.7%)	7,010	(+0.1%)	110,000
Michigan Thoroughbred Owners and Breeders Association yearling	20	145,800	(+37.4%)	7,290	(+37.4%)	46,000
Ocala Breeders' Sales Co. selected and open yearling	814	12,208,200	(−22.0%)	14,998	(−7.5%)	305,000
CTHS (Alberta division) summer yearling	145	758,238	(+53.1%)	5,229	(+26.7%)	22,764
Indiana Thoroughbred Owners and Breeders Association horses of all ages	42	107,350	(+23.5%)	2,556	(+8.8%)	7,400
Fasig-Tipton Texas summer yearling	258	2,906,200	(+0.3%)	11,264	(+8.1%)	95,000
American Equine Sales wine country yearling	79	608,000	(+3.6%)	7,696	(+1.0%)	40,000
September						
CTHS (Saskatchewan division) yearling	23	59,641	(+68.7%)	2,593	(+10.0%)	6,504
Canadian Breeders Sales autumn yearling	182	4,200,281	(−17.0%)	23,078	(−21.1%)	97,560
CTHS (Manitoba division) yearling	30	98,080	(+32.8%)	3,269	(+15.1%)	10,211
Washington Thoroughbred Breeders summer yearling	140	2,442,400	(−48.0%)	17,446	(−28.3%)	105,000
Keeneland September yearling	2,895	254,190,600	(−12.9%)	87,803	(−0.3%)	6,400,000
Iowa Thoroughbred Breeders and Owners Association fall mixed	75	289,375	(+23.8%)	3,858	(+28.7%)	28,000
Oregon Thoroughbred Breeders' Association mixed	75	165,400	(+86.2%)	2,205	(+34.0%)	9,500
CTHS (British Columbia division) fall mixed	108	433,555	(−33.0%)	4,014	(−30.5%)	26,016
Canadian Breeders Sales open yearling sale and breeding stock	272	1,489,221	(−29.8%)	5,475	(−25.9%)	29,268

	No. sold	Total	(% Chg)	Average	(% Chg)	Highest price
Genesee Valley Breeders Association Finger Lakes horses of all ages	35	51,000	(−41.9%)	1,457	(−0.3%)	8,500
Keeneland September yearling internet RNA auction sale	5	27,800	(−94.4%)	5,560	(−85.5%)	15,400
October						
Fasig-Tipton Midlantic Eastern fall yearling	541	9,153,000	(−18.9%)	16,919	(−15.2%)	180,000
Barretts Equine Ltd. October preferred yearling	222	2,228,300	(−17.6%)	10,037	(+17.0%)	120,000
Breeders Sales Co. of Louisiana yearling and mixed	147	696,750	(+49.6%)	4,740	(−23.7%)	40,000
Midwest Regional mixed	99	292,700	(+14.3%)	2,957	(+7.4%)	30,000
Ocala Breeders' Sales Co. fall mixed	838	6,210,700	(−56.3%)	7,411	(−42.2%)	63,000
Illinois Thoroughbred Breeders fall mixed sale	71	217,900		3,069		21,500
CTHS (Alberta division) fall mixed	48	85,017	(+119.0%)	1,771	(+0.3%)	12,358
Alamo Classic fall mixed	115	311,450	(+60.4%)	2,708	(+60.3%)	52,000
Keeneland October yearling	338	5,092,900		15,068		400,000
Fasig-Tipton Kentucky fall preferred and open yearling	323	4,144,800	(−38.8%)	12,832	(−4.8%)	360,000
Arizona Thoroughbred Breeders Association fall mixed	113	809,300	(+8.0%)	7,162	(+4.2%)	60,000
Heritage Place fall mixed	128	276,750	(+37.6%)	2,162	(−6.0%)	7,600
Barretts Equine Ltd. fall mixed	350	1,833,800	(−10.7%)	5,239	(−13.8%)	57,000
Fasig-Tipton New York horses of racing age	95	1,038,400	(+120.2%)	10,931	(+71.5%)	70,000
November						
Fasig-Tipton Kentucky fall selected mixed	110	6,491,500	(−42.4%)	59,014	(−36.7%)	700,000
Keeneland November breeding stock	2,506	179,568,600	(−41.0%)	71,655	(−22.9%)	4,000,000
Stallion Access fall selected seasons and shares	40	932,000	(−50.8%)	23,300	(−54.5%)	260,000
Keeneland November breeding stock internet RNA auction	7	31,900	(+20.8%)	4,557	(−48.2%)	7,000
December						
Washington Thoroughbred Breeders Assoc. winter mixed	236	908,200	(−19.6%)	3,848	(−12.4%)	37,000
Fasig-Tipton Midlantic December mixed	448	3,530,500	(−18.2%)	7,881	(+3.4%)	100,000
Arkansas Thoroughbred Sales Co. fall mixed	148	457,200	(−53.9%)	3,089	(−59.5%)	30,000
Fasig-Tipton Texas mixed	143	534,300		3,736		60,000
Fasig-Tipton Kentucky December mixed	121	531,400	(−55.1%)	4,392	(−26.8%)	50,000

Histories of Major Sales

Following are the ten-year histories of several prominent Thoroughbred auctions in North America. The sales are listed by type of sale, with the order within each category determined by total sales.

Keeneland September yearlings

Year	Offered	Sold	Gross	(% Chg)	Average	(% Chg)	High Price
2001	4,003	2,895	$254,190,600	(−12.9%)	$87,803	(−0.3%)	$6,400,000
2000	4,302	3,313	291,827,100	(+25.2%)	88,085	(+13.8%)	6,800,000
1999	3,788	3,011	233,020,800	(+37.2%)	77,390	(+30.3%)	3,900,000
1998	3,528	2,860	169,811,800	(+9.8%)	59,375	(+9.2%)	2,100,000
1997	3,396	2,844	154,666,800	(+12.7%)	54,384	(+16.3%)	2,300,000
1996	3,649	2,936	137,233,800	(+5.5%)	46,742	(+6.2%)	1,400,000
1995	3,495	2,955	130,085,300	(+24.4%)	44,022	(+18.4%)	1,200,000
1994	3,264	2,812	104,552,900	(+19.8%)	37,181	(+6.1%)	625,000
1993	2,862	2,492	87,308,100	(+11.3%)	35,035	(+23.0%)	775,000
1992	3,188	2,754	78,427,400	(+1.2%)	28,478	(−4.0%)	400,000

Keeneland July selected yearlings

Year	Offered	Sold	Gross	(% Chg)	Average	(% Chg)	High Price
2001	132	89	$63,212,000	(−21.7%)	$710,247	(+14.4%)	$4,000,000
2000	180	130	80,732,000	(+5.1%)	621,015	(+6.7%)	3,600,000
1999	181	132	76,815,000	(+6.8%)	581,932	(+20.5%)	3,000,000
1998	201	149	71,932,000	(+15.0%)	482,765	(+35.0%)	4,000,000
1997	236	175	62,565,000	(+7.1%)	357,514	(+2.2%)	1,500,000
1996	204	167	58,430,000	(+25.8%)	349,880	(+41.6%)	1,700,000
1995	225	188	46,450,000	(+2.6%)	247,074	(+5.9%)	1,250,000
1994	257	194	45,265,000	(−8.3%)	233,325	(−1.2%)	1,050,000
1993	251	209	49,350,000	(+4.7%)	236,124	(−9.3%)	1,050,000
1992	266	181	47,120,000	(−35.8%)	260,331	(−18.8%)	1,700,000

Fasig-Tipton Saratoga selected yearlings

Year	Offered	Sold	Gross	(% Chg)	Average	(% Chg)	High Price
2001	201	162	$62,412,000	(+49.0%)	$385,259	(+26.0%)	$3,300,000
2000	173	137	41,901,000	(+7.6%)	305,847	(+17.0%)	4,200,000

Fasig-Tipton Saratoga, continued

Year	Offered	Sold	Gross	(% Chg)	Average	(% Chg)	High Price
1999	201	149	38,957,000	(+13.8%)	261,456	(+23.7%)	3,000,000
1998	220	162	34,246,000	(+23.7%)	211,395	(+15.3%)	1,700,000
1997	205	151	27,691,000	(+1.4%)	183,384	(+13.5%)	1,400,000
1996	220	169	27,311,000	(+21.1%)	161,604	(+26.2%)	630,000
1995	207	176	22,545,000	(+21.4%)	128,097	(+32.5%)	440,000
1994	241	192	18,566,000	(+53.4%)	96,698	(+3.9%)	520,000
1993	162	130	12,101,000	(+0.5%)	93,085	(−4.2%)	350,000
1992	152	124	12,046,000	(−20.0%)	97,145	(−19.4%)	525,000

Fasig-Tipton Kentucky July selected yearlings

Year	Offered	Sold	Gross	(% Chg)	Average	(% Chg)	High Price
2001	381	237	$23,148,000	(−11.6%)	$97,671	(+25.7%)	$625,000
2000	517	337	26,186,500	(+17.9%)	77,705	(+3.6%)	525,000
1999	361	296	22,211,000	(+58.2%)	75,037	(+35.3%)	525,000
1998	340	253	14,036,500	(+43.9%)	55,480	(+5.3%)	220,000
1997	238	185	9,751,000	(−2.6%)	52,708	(+36.3%)	290,000
1996	393	259	10,013,500	(+52.2%)	38,662	(+4.0%)	300,000
1995	227	177	6,580,500	(+16.6%)	37,178	(+18.5%)	200,000
1994	245	180	5,645,000	(+24.1%)	31,361	(−0.8%)	170,000
1993	173	144	4,550,500	(+95.2%)	31,601	(−6.5%)	147,000
1992	97	69	2,331,000	(−35.0%)	33,783	(−0.1%)	115,000

Fasig-Tipton Calder selected two-year-olds in training

Year	Offered	Sold	Gross	(% Chg)	Average	(% Chg)	High Price
2001	237	136	$28,186,000	(−16.3%)	$207,250	(−4.0%)	$1,000,000
2000	264	156	33,690,000	(+0.9%)	215,962	(+17.1%)	1,950,000
1999	296	181	33,386,000	(+26.9%)	184,453	(+33.9%)	1,100,000
1998	302	191	26,303,000	(+13.6%)	137,712	(+14.2%)	1,000,000
1997	297	192	23,162,000	(+1.7%)	120,635	(+16.1%)	780,000
1996	309	219	22,765,000	(+22.2%)	103,950	(+11.1%)	875,000
1995	306	199	18,624,000	(+39.0%)	93,588	(+31.3%)	550,000
1994	276	188	13,403,000	(+17.7%)	71,293	(+25.2%)	390,000
1993	318	200	11,386,000	(−8.0%)	56,930	(−3.9%)	450,000
1992	292	209	12,376,000	(+14.1%)	59,215	(−5.5%)	350,000

Barretts selected two-year-olds in training

Year	Offered	Sold	Gross	(% Chg)	Average	(% Chg)	High Price
2001	130	71	$10,085,000	(−41.7%)	$142,042	(−21.1%)	$750,000
2000	170	96	17,287,000	(−21.4%)	180,073	(−20.6%)	2,000,000
1999	172	97	21,995,000	(−3.2%)	226,753	(+30.8%)	2,000,000
1998	200	131	22,711,000	(−28.9%)	173,366	(−21.8%)	1,000,000
1997	255	144	31,926,000	(−3.3%)	221,708	(+7.4%)	1,100,000
1996	233	160	33,016,000	(+56.1%)	206,350	(+56.1%)	900,000
1995	274	160	21,148,000	(+57.4%)	132,175	(+61.3%)	900,000
1994	240	164	13,440,000	(+51.6%)	81,951	(+39.6%)	700,000
1993	237	151	8,863,400	(−7.5%)	58,698	(−5.1%)	430,000
1992	280	155	9,584,000	(−33.0%)	61,832	(−20.1%)	370,000

Keeneland November breeding stock

Year	Offered	Sold	Gross	(% Chg)	Average	(% Chg)	High Price
2001	3,383	2,506	$179,568,600	(−41.0%)	$71,655	(−22.9%)	$4,000,000
2000	4,367	3,277	304,549,800	(−4.1%)	92,936	(+1.3%)	4,900,000
1999	4,227	3,461	317,666,000	(+20.0%)	91,784	(+17.2%)	4,700,000
1998	4,312	3,379	264,657,700	(+23.7%)	78,324	(+10.3%)	7,000,000
1997	3,673	3,013	213,979,800	(+25.4%)	71,019	(+17.6%)	1,400,000
1996	3,451	2,826	170,691,800	(+21.2%)	60,400	(+22.5%)	2,600,000
1995	3,505	2,855	140,822,300	(+16.3%)	49,325	(+1.6%)	2,500,000
1994	2,932	2,494	121,056,900	(+32.5%)	48,539	(+10.3%)	2,700,000
1993	2,300	2,075	91,342,900	(+24.6%)	44,021	(+16.6%)	1,150,000
1992	2,324	1,942	73,337,200	(−11.6%)	37,764	(−9.7%)	1,100,000

Highest-Priced Horses of All Time
North American Top-Priced Yearlings
(With subsequent race record)

Key—SW: stakes winner. spl: stakes placed.

$13,100,000 Seattle Dancer, 1984 c., Nijinsky II-My Charmer, by Poker. Consignor: Warner L. Jones Jr.; Buyer: BBA (England), agent for Robert Sangster and partners. 1985 Keeneland July. 5 starts, 2 wins, $152,413, SW, Ire-G2.

$10,200,000 Snaafi Dancer, 1982 c., Northern Dancer-My Bupers, by Bupers. Consignor: Crescent Farm; Buyer: Aston Upthorpe Stud, agent for Sheikh Mohammed bin Rashid al Maktoum. 1983 Keeneland July. Unraced.

$8,250,000 Imperial Falcon, 1983 c., Northern Dancer-Ballade, by *Herbager. Consignor: Windfields Farm; Buyer: BBA (England), agent for Robert Sangster and partners. 1984 Keeneland July. 3 starts, 2 wins, $13,395.

$7,100,000 Jareer, 1983 c., Northern Dancer-Fabuleux Jane, by *Le Fabuleux. Consignor: Bruce Hundley, agent for Ralph C. Wilson Jr.; Buyer: Darley Stud Management. 1984 Keeneland July. 9 starts, 1 win, $5,591.

$7,000,000 Laa Etaab, 1984 c., Nijinsky II-Crimson Saint, by Crimson Satan. Consignor: Tom Gentry; Buyer: Gainsborough Farm. 1985 Keeneland July. Unraced.

$6,800,000 Tasmanian Tiger, 1999 c., Storm Cat-Hum Along, by Fappiano. Consignor: Lane's End, agent; Buyer: Demi O'Byrne. 2000 Keeneland September. 2 starts, placed in Ireland.

$6,500,000 Amjaad, 1983 c., Seattle Slew-Desiree, by Raise a Native. Consignor: Spendthrift Farm, agent for Mr. and Mrs. Louis E. Wolfson and Mrs. Ethel D. Jacobs; Buyer: Darley Stud Management. 1984 Keeneland July. 4 starts, unplaced.

$6,400,000 Van Nistelrooy, 2000 c., Storm Cat-Halory, by Halo. Consignor: Lane's End, agent for Stonerside Stable; Buyer: Demi O'Byrne. 2001 Keeneland September. Unraced.

$5,500,000 Alajwad, 2000, c., Storm Cat-La Affirmed, by Affirmed. Consignor: Eaton Sales, agent; Buyer: John Ferguson Bloodstock. 2001 Keeneland September. Unraced.

$5,400,000 Obligato, 1983 c., Northern Dancer-Truly Bound, by In Reality. Consignor: Windfields Farm; Buyer: BBA (Ireland), agent for Robert Sangster and partners. 1984 Keeneland July. 2 starts, unplaced.

$5,300,000 King's Consul, 1999 c., Kingmambo-Battle Creek Girl, by His Majesty. Consignor: Lane's End, agent; Buyer: John Ferguson Bloodstock. 2000 Keeneland September. 1 start, 1 win, $24,600.

$5,100,000 Wassl Touch, 1983 c., Northern Dancer-Queen Sucree, by *Ribot. Consignor: North Ridge Farm; Buyer: Darley Stud Management. 1984 Keeneland July. 6 starts, 3 wins, $30,168, SW.

$4,600,000 Parlando, 1983 c., Northern Dancer-Bubbling, by Stage Door Johnny. Consignor: Wild Oak Plantation; Buyer: BBA (Ireland), agent for Robert Sangster and partners. 1984 Fasig-Tipton Saratoga. Unraced.

$4,600,000 Professor Blue, 1983 c., Northern Dancer-Mississippi Mud, by Delta Judge. Consignor: Lane's End; Buyer: BBA (England), agent for Stavros Niarchos. 1984 Keeneland July. 7 starts, placed, $5,171.

$4,400,000 Moon's Whisper, 1999 f., Storm Cat-East of the Moon, by Private Account. Consignor: Lane's End; Buyer: Shadwell Estate Co. Ltd. 2000 Keeneland September. Unraced.

$4,400,000 Shah Jehan, 1999 c., Mr. Prospector-Voodoo Lily, by Baldski. Consignor: Lane's End, agent; Buyer: Demi O'Byrne. 2000 Keeneland September. 7 starts, 2 wins, $72,022 in U.S., Ireland, England, and France.

$4,250,000 Empire Glory, 1981 c., Nijinsky II-Spearfish, by Fleet Nasrullah. Consignor: Glencoe Farm; Buyer: BBA (Ireland). 1982 Keeneland July. 6 starts, 2 wins, $35,420, SW, Ire-G3.

$4,250,000 Foxboro, 1982 c., Northern Dancer-Desert Vixen, by In Reality. Consignor: North Ridge Farm; Buyer: BBA (England), agent for Robert Sangster and partners. 1983 Keeneland July. 1 start, unplaced.

$4,200,000 Distinction, 1999 c., Seattle Slew-Omi, by Wild Again. Consignor: Double Diamond Farm; Buyer: David J. Shimmon. 2000 Fasig-Tipton Saratoga. 7 starts, placed, $8,758.

$4,100,000 Gallant Archer, 1982 c., Nijinsky II-Belle of Dodge Me, by Creme dela Creme. Consignor: E A. Seltzer and Parlina; Buyer: Aston Upthorpe Stud, agent for Sheikh Mohammed bin Rashid al Maktoum. 1983 Keeneland July. 16 starts, 5 wins, $294,477, SW, G3.

$4,000,000 Elnawaagi, 1983 c., Roberto-Gurkhas Band, by Lurullah. Consignor: Keswick Stables; Buyer: Darley Stud Management. 1984 Fasig-Tipton Saratoga. 11 starts, 4 wins, $23,607, SW.

$4,000,000 Fusaichi Pegasus, 1997 c., Mr. Prospector-Angel Fever, by Danzig. Consignor: Stone Farm, agent; Buyer: Fusao Sekiguchi. 1998 Keeneland July. 9 starts, 6 wins, $1,994,400, SW, G1.

$4,000,000 Showlady, 1999 f., Theatrical (Ire)-Claxton's Slew, by Seattle Slew. Consignor: Brookside Farms; Buyer: John Ferguson Bloodstock. 2000 Keeneland September. Unraced.

$4,000,000 Warhol, 2000 c., Saint Ballado-Charm a Gendarme, by Batonnier. Consignor: Taylor Made Sales Agency, agent; Buyer: Demi O'Byrne. 2000 Keeneland July. Unraced.

$3,900,000 Dubai to Dubai, 1998 c., Kris S.-Mr. P's Princess, by Mr. Prospector. Consignor: Harold Harrison; Buyer: John Ferguson Bloodstock. 1999 Keeneland September. 10 starts, 2 wins, $95,157 in U.S. and UAE.

$3,800,000 Hoyer, 2000 c., Mr. Prospector-Destination Mir, by Cherokee Colony. Consignor: Lazy E Ranch; Buyer: John Ferguson Bloodstock. 2000 Keeneland September. Unraced.

$3,750,000 Alchaasibiyeh, 1983 f., Seattle Slew-Fine Prospect, by Mr. Prospector. Consignor: Spendthrift Farm; Buyer: Darley Stud Management. 1984 Keeneland July. 6 starts, placed, $2,098.

$3,700,000 Warrshan, 1986 c., Northern Dancer-Secret Asset, by Graustark. Consignor: Hermitage Farm; Buyer: Darley Stud Management. 1987 Keeneland July. 11 starts, 4 wins, $125,928, SW, Eng-G3.

$3,700,000 Scene Seeker, 2000 f., Seeking the Gold-Escena, by Strawberry Road (Aus). Consignor: Denali Stud, agent for Falls Creek Farm; Buyer: Reynolds Bell, agent. 2000 Keeneland July. Unraced.

$3,600,000 Northern State, 1985 c., Northern Dancer-South Ocean, by New Providence. Consignor: Windfields Farm; Buyer: Darley Stud Management. 1986 Keeneland July. 4 starts, 1 win, $2,137.

$3,600,000 America's Storm, 1999 c., Storm Cat-Lilly Capote, by Capote. Consignor: Hartwell Farm, agent; Buyer: Padua Stables and Gaines-Gentry. 2000 Keeneland September. 3 starts, placed, $12,090.

$3,600,000 Born Perfect, 1999 f., Mr. Prospector-Molly Girl, by Seattle Slew. Consignor: Mr. and Mrs. John C. Mabee; Buyer: Padua Stables. 2000 Keeneland July. Unraced.

$3,600,000 Act of Duty, 2000 c., Mr. Prospector-Nuryette, by Nureyev. Consignor: Three Chimneys Sales, agent for Warner L. Jones Farm; Buyer: John Ferguson Bloodstock. 2000 Keeneland July. Unraced.

North American Top-Priced Weanlings

$2,500,000   **Magic of Life**, 1985 f., Seattle Slew—Larida, by Northern Dancer. Consignor: Newstead Farm Trust. Buyer: British Bloodstock Agency (England). 1985 Newstead Farm Trust Dispersal. 9 starts, 4 wins, $254,841, SW, Eng-G1.

$2,300,000   **Ghashtah**, 1987 f., Nijinsky II—My Charmer, by Poker. Consignor: Hermitage Farm. Buyer: Shadwell Estate Co. Ltd. 1987 Warner L. Jones Jr. Dispersal. Unraced.

$1,500,000   **King Charlemagne**, 1998 c., Nureyev—Race the Wild Wind, by Sunny's Halo. Consignor: Ashford Stud, agent. Buyer: Demi O'Byrne. 1998 Keeneland November. 6 starts, 3 wins, $200,211, SW, Fr-G1, Eng-G3, Ire-G3.

$1,450,000   **Juniper**, 1998 c., Danzig—Montage, by Alydar. Consignor: Taylor Made Sales Agency, agent. Buyer: Demi O'Byrne. 1998 Keeneland November. 5 starts, 1 win, $37,214, spl, Eng-G2, Ire-G3.

$1,400,000   **Winthrop**, 1996 c., Storm Cat—Tinnitus, by Restless Wind. Consignor: John R. Gaines Thoroughbreds, agent. Buyer: Demi O'Byrne. 1996 Keeneland November. Unraced.

$1,400,000   **Restoration**, 1999 c., Sadler's Wells—Madame Est Sortie (Fr), by Longleat. Consignor: Eaton Sales, agent for Padua Stables. Buyer: M. W. Miller III, agent. 1999 Keeneland November. Unraced.

$1,300,000   **New Trieste**, 1999 c., A.P. Indy—Lovlier Linda, by Vigors. Consignor: John R. Gaines Thoroughbreds, agent. Buyer: Paul Shanahan. 1999 Keeneland November. Unraced.

$1,200,000   **Net Dancer**, 1989 f., Nureyev—Doubles Partner, by Damascus. Consignor: Bruce Hundley, agent for Ralph C. Wilson Jr. and Oxford Stable. Buyer: E. Hudson. 1989 Keeneland November. 13 starts, 2 wins, $46,225, spl.

$1,200,000   **Tide Cat**, 1998 f., Storm Cat—Maytide, by Naskra. Consignor: John R. Gaines Thoroughbreds, agent. Buyer: Brad Martin, agent for 505 Farms. 1998 Keeneland November. Unraced.

$1,200,000   **She's a Beauty**, 2000 f., Storm Cat—Now That's Funny, by Saratoga Six. Consignor: Gaines-Gentry Thoroughbreds. Buyer: Timothy Hyde. 2000 Keeneland November. Unraced.

$1,175,000   **Razeen**, 1987 c., Northern Dancer—Secret Asset, by Graustark. Consignor: Hermitage Farm. Buyer: Darley Stud Management. 1987 Warner L. Jones Jr. Dispersal. 9 starts, 3 wins, $106,665, SW, spl, G2.

$1,150,000   **A. P. Petal**, 2000 f., A.P. Indy—Golden Petal, by Mr. Prospector. Consignor: Taylor Made Sales Agency, agent. Buyer: B. Wayne Hughes. 2000 Keeneland November. Unraced.

$1,100,000   **Worood**, 1985 f., *Vaguely Noble—Farouche, by Northern Dancer. Consignor: Newstead Farm Trust. Buyer: British Bloodstock Agency (England). 1985 Newstead Farm Trust Dispersal. 16 starts, 3 wins, $82,067, SW, Fr.

$1,100,000   **Hold That Tiger**, 2000 c., Storm Cat—Beware of the Cat, by Caveat. Consignor: Lane's End, agent for Ten Broeck Farm. Buyer: Demi O'Byrne. 2000 Keeneland November. Unraced.

$1,050,000   **Seaside Attraction**, 1987 f., Seattle Slew—Kamar, by Key to the Mint. Consignor: Hermitage Farm. Buyer: Monty Hinton. 1987 Warner L. Jones Jr. Dispersal. 12 starts, 4 wins, $272,541, SW, G1.

$1,050,000   **Unnamed**, 2000 f., Storm Cat—Jetapat, by Tri Jet. Consignor: Brereton C. Jones, agent. Buyer: Bradley and Bowden, agent. 2000 Keeneland November.

$1,000,000   **Swiss Desert**, 1989 c., Danzig—Strictly Raised, by Raise a Native. Consignor: Bruce Hundley, agent for Kentucky Select Bloodstock and Kentucky Heritage Thoroughbred Breeding Partners. Buyer: Gainsborough Farm. 1989 Keeneland November. Unraced.

$1,000,000   **Blissful**, 1996 f., Mr. Prospector—Angel Fever, by Danzig. Consignor: Stone Farm, agent. Buyer: J. B. & B. Stables. 1996 Keeneland November. 3 starts, unplaced, $3,240.

$1,000,000   **Lemon Tart**, 1998 f., Deputy Minister—Lemon Dove, by Forty Niner. Consignor: Hill 'n' Dale Sales Agency, agent. Buyer: Brushwood Stable. 1998 Keeneland November. 4 starts, unplaced, $2,460.

$1,000,000   **Malibu Karen**, 1998 f., Seeking the Gold—Regent's Walk, by Vice Regent. Consignor: Claiborne Farm, agent for Edward A. Cox Jr. Buyer: B. Wayne Hughes. 1998 Keeneland November. 5 starts, placed twice, $18,490.

$1,000,000   **Princess Atoosa**, 1998 f., Gone West—Kooyonga (Ire), by Persian Bold. Consignor: Eaton Sales, agent. Buyer: Brushwood Stable. 1998 Keeneland November. Unraced.

North American Top-Priced Two-Year-Olds

$2,000,000 La Salle Street, 1997 c., Not for Love—Three Grand, by Assert (Ire). Consignor: H. T. Stables, agent, for Cam Allard. Buyer: Demi O'Byrne. 1999 Keeneland April. 3 starts, placed, $3,420.

$2,000,000 Morocco, 1997 c., Brocco—Roll Over Baby, by Rollin On Over. Consignor: Sequel Bloodstock, agent. Buyer: The Thoroughbred Corp. 1999 Barretts March. 13 starts, 4 wins, $129,740.

$2,000,000 Gotham City, 1998 c., Saint Ballado—What a Reality, by In Reality. Consignor: Jerry Bailey Sales Agency. Buyer: David J. Shimmon. 2000 Barretts March. 2 starts, unplaced, $2,880.

$1,950,000 Yonaguska, 1998 c., Cherokee Run—Marital Spook, by Silver Ghost. Consignor: Niall Brennan Stables, agent. Buyer: Demi O'Byrne. 2000 Fasig-Tipton Florida February. 15 starts, 6 wins, $521,355, SW, G1.

$1,650,000 Harmony Lodge, 1998 f., Hennessy—Win Crafty Lady, by Crafty Prospector. Consignor: Eddie Woods, agent. Buyer: Eugene Melnyk. 2000 Fasig-Tipton Florida February. 7 starts, 3 wins, $116,220, SW.

$1,300,000 Minstress, 1983 f., The Minstrel—Fleet Victress, by *King of the Tudors. Consignor: Newstead Farm Trust. Buyer: W. S. Farish. 1985 Newstead Farm Trust Dispersal. 19 starts, 5 wins, $147,399, SW.

$1,250,000 Lochlin Slew, 1997 f., Seattle Slew—Lochlin, by Screen King. Consignor: M. W. Miller III, agent. Buyer: B. Wayne Hughes. 1999 Keeneland April.

$1,250,000 Le Chat, 1998 c., Storm Cat—Adorable Micol, by Riverman. Consignor: Hartley/De Renzo Thoroughbreds, agent. Buyer: John Moynihan, agent. 2000 Fasig-Tipton Florida February. 3 starts, 1 win, $28,470.

$1,200,000 Task, 1996 f., Mr. Prospector—Department, by Secretariat. Consignor: Claiborne Farm and Nicole Perry Gorman. Buyer: Course Investment. 1998 Keeneland January. 3 starts, unplaced, $405.

$1,200,000 Dance Master, 1997 c., Gone West—Nijinsky's Lover, by Nijinsky II. Consignor: Jerry Bailey Sales Agency.

Buyer: Padua Stables. 1999 Barretts March. 19 starts, 4 wins, $196,455, SW, G2.

$1,100,000 Scatmandu, 1995 c., Storm Cat—Princess Alydar, by Alydar. Consignor: Jerry Bailey Sales Agency, agent, for Bailey-Ellenberg Select. Buyer: John C. Kimmel, agent. 1997 Barretts March. 16 starts, 6 wins, $330,789, SW, G3.

$1,100,000 I'm Persuaded, 1997 c., Deputy Minister—The Way We Were, by Avatar. Consignor: The Kindergarten Farm, agent. Buyer: Narvick International. 1999 Keeneland April. 7 starts, 1 win, $38,900.

$1,100,000 Prather, 1997 c., Brocco—Dazzling Dixie, by Dixieland Band. Consignor: Welcome Gate Farm, agent. Buyer: Aaron and Marie Jones. 1999 Fasig-Tipton Florida February. Unraced.

$1,050,000 Warners, 1999 c., Dehere—Sweet Gold, by Gilded Time. Consignor: Hartley/De Renzo Thoroughbreds, agent. Buyer: Eugene N. Melnyk. 2001 Ocala Breeders' Sales Co's March. 4 starts, 1 win, $72,800, spl G3.

$1,000,000 Marie J, 1995 f., Mr. Prospector—In My Cap, by Vice Regent. Consignor: M. W. Miller III, agent. Buyer: John Ferguson Bloodstock. 1997 Barretts March. 11 starts, 2 wins, $139,800, spl (G3).

$1,000,000 Something Else, 1995 f., Seeking the Gold—Rythmical, by Fappiano. Consignor: Kirkwood Stables, agent. Buyer: The Thoroughbred Corp. 1997 Barretts March. 3 starts, placed, $18,144.

$1,000,000 Awesome Cat, 1996 c., Storm Cat—Pookette, by Miswaki. Consignor: M. W. Miller III, agent. Buyer: Chester Broman. 1998 Fasig-Tipton Florida February. Unraced.

$1,000,000 Measure, 1996 f., Seeking the Gold—Number, by Nijinsky II. Consignor: Claiborne Farm and Nicole Perry Gorman. Buyer: Demi O'Byrne. 1998 Keeneland January. 1 start, placed, $4,868.

$1,000,000 Public Figure, 1996 c., Clever Trick—Belle of Killarney, by Little Current. Consignor: Jerry Bailey Sales Agency, agent, for Bailey-Ellenberg Select. Buyer: The Thoroughbred Corp. 1998 Barretts March. Unraced.

$1,000,000 Satin Cat (name changed after sale; sold as Unchain My Heart), 1997 f., Storm Cat—Mended Heart, by *Le Fabuleux. Consignor: Jerry Bailey Sales Agency, agent, for Bailey-Ellenberg Select. Buyer: The Thoroughbred Corp. 1999 Barretts March. 9 starts, 2 wins, $78,864.

$1,000,000 Songandaprayer, 1998 c., Unbridled's Song—Alizea, by Premiership. Consignor: Robert N. Scanlon, agent. Buyer: Robert and Leslie Hurley. 2000 Fasig-Tipton Florida February. 8 starts, 3 wins, $380,480, SW, G1.

$1,000,000 Rosetti, 1999 c., Seattle Slew—Chic Shirine, by Mr. Prospector. Consignor: M. W. Miller, agent. Buyer: Demi O'Byrne. 2001 Fasig-Tipton Florida February. Unraced.

North American Top-Priced Broodmares

$7,000,000 Miss Oceana, 1981, Alydar—Kittiwake, by *Sea-Bird. (Northern Dancer). Consignor: Newstead Farm Trust. Buyer: Foxfield. 1985 Newstead Farm Trust mixed sale.

$7,000,000 Korveya, 1982, Riverman—Konafa, by Damascus. (Woodman). Consignor: Claiborne Farm, agent. Buyer: Reynolds Bell Jr., agent. 1998 Keeneland November.

$6,000,000 Priceless Fame, 1975, Irish Castle—Comely Nell, by Commodore M. (Seattle Slew). Consignor: Highclere, agent for Joseph O. Morrissey. Buyer: Darley Stud Management. 1984 Fasig-Tipton Kentucky November.

$5,500,000 Princess Rooney, 1980, Verbatim—Parrish Princess, by Drone. (Danzig). Consignor: Stone Farm agent. Buyer: Wichita Equine. 1985 Keeneland November.

$5,400,000 Life's Magic, 1981, Cox's Ridge—Fire Water, by Tom Rolfe. (Mr. Prospector). Consignor: Mel Hatley Racing Stables, agent. Buyer: Eugene V. Klein. 1986 Keeneland November.

$5,400,000 Lady's Secret, 1982, Secretariat—Great Lady M., by Icecapade. Consignor: D. Wayne Lukas, agent for Eugene V. Klein. Buyer: Fasig-Tipton Bloodstock, agent. 1987 Night of the Stars, Fasig-Tipton Kentucky November.

$5,250,000 Producer, 1976, Nashua—*Marion, by =Tantieme (Fr). (Northern Dancer). Consignor: Walnut Green, agent for Carelaine Stable. Buyer: BBA (England). 1983 Keeneland November

$5,000,000 Mackie, 1993, Summer Squall—Glowing Tribute, by Graustark. (Mr. Prospector). Consignor: Eaton Sales, agent. Buyer: Britton House Stud. 2000 Keeneland January.

$4,900,000 Jewel Princess, 1992, Key to the Mint—Jewell Ridge, by Melyno (Ire). (Storm Cat). Consignor: Lane's End, agent. Buyer: John Magnier. 2000 Keeneland November.

$4,700,000 Dance Design (Ire), 1993, Sadler's Well—Elegance in Design (Ire), by Habitat. (A.P. Indy). Consignor: Eaton Sales, agent. Buyer: Hugo Lascelles, agent. 1999 Keeneland November.

$4,700,000 Catchascatchcan (GB), 1995, =Pursuit of Love (GB)—=Catawba (GB), by Mill Reef. (Danzig). Consignor: Claiborne Farm, agent. Buyer: Lyons Demesne. 2000 Keeneland November.

$4,600,000 It's in the Air, 1976, Mr. Prospector—A Wind Is Rising, by Francis S. (Seattle Slew). Consignor: Hill 'n' Dale Sales Agency. Buyer: Darley Stud Management. 1984 Keeneland November.

$4,600,000 Winglet, 1988, Alydar—Highest Trump, by Bold Bidder. (Storm Cat). Consignor: Lane's End, agent for Brookside Farms. Buyer: John Magnier. 1999 Keeneland November.

$4,600,000 Myhrr, 1997, Mr. Prospector—Miesque, by Nureyev. Consignor: Lane's End, agent. Buyer: Reynolds Bell Jr., agent. 2000 Keeneland November.

$4,500,000 Two Rings, 1970, Round Table—Allofthem, by Bagdad. (Nijinsky II). Consignor: Mint Lane Farm, agent for Kinghaven Farms. Buyer: Due Process Stable. 1983 Keeneland November.

$4,500,000 Estrapade, 1980, *Vaguely Noble—Klepto, by No Robbery. Consignor: Blue Grass Farm, agent. Buyer: Allen E. Paulson. 1985 Keeneland November.

$4,400,000 Life's Magic, 1981, Cox's Ridge—Fire Water, by Tom Rolfe. (Alydar). Consignor: D. Wayne Lukas, agent for Eugene V. Klein. Buyer: Shadwell Estate Co. Ltd. 1987 Night of the Stars, Fasig-Tipton Kentucky November.

$4,200,000 Magical Allure, 1995, General Meeting—Rare Lady, by Never Bend. (Storm Cat). Consignor: Eaton Sales, agent for Mr. and Mrs. John C. Mabee. Buyer: Shadwell Estate Co. Ltd. 2000 Keeneland November.

$4,100,000 Sangue (Ire), 1978, Lyphard—Prodice (Fr), by =Prominer (GB). (Seattle Slew). Consignor: Henry Moreno, agent for R. Charlene Parks. Buyer: Nelson Bunker Hunt. 1984 Keeneland November.

$4,100,000 Love Sign, 1977, Spanish Riddle—Native Nurse, by Graustark (Seattle Slew). Consignor: Three Chimneys Farm. Buyer: Arthur I. Appleton. 1984 Keeneland November.

DIRECTORY
National Industry Organizations

American Academy of Equine Art
2516 Versailles Rd.
Lexington, KY 40504
Ph: (859) 243-0948
Fax: (859) 243-0998
E-mail: julieb@aaea.net
Web site: *http://www.aaea.net*
President: Werner Rentsch

American Association of Equine Practioners
4075 Iron Works Pkwy.
Lexington, KY 40511
Ph: (859) 233-0147
Fax: (859) 233-1968
E-mail: aeepoffice@aol.com
Web site: *http://www.aaep.org/*
President: Jerry B. Black, D.V.M.

American Farriers Assn.
4059 Iron Works Pkwy., Ste. 1
Lexington, KY 40511
Ph: (859) 233-7411
Fax: (859) 231-7862
E-mail: farriers@americanfarriers.org
Web site: *http://www.americanfarriers.org*
President: Emil Carre

American Horse Council
1700 K St. NW, Ste. 300
Washington, D.C. 20006
Ph: (202) 296-4031
Fax: (202) 296-1970
E-mail: ahc@horsecouncil.org
Web site: *http://www.horsecouncil.org*
President: James J. Hickey Jr.

American Horse Protection Assn.
1000 29th St. NW., Ste. T-100
Washington, D.C. 20007
Ph: (202) 965-0500
Fax: (202) 965-9621
Web site: *http://www.americanhorseprotection.org*

Animal Transportation Assn.
10700 Richmond Ave., Ste. 201
Houston, TX 77042
Ph: (281) 443-4595
Fax: (281) 443-4596
E-mail: aata@npscmgmt.com
Web site: *http://www.npscmgmt.com/aata*

Association for Equine Sports Medicine
3579 E. Foothill Blvd. #288
Pasadena, CA 91107-3119
Ph: (909) 869-4859
Fax: (909) 869-6788
E-mail: aesm@relaypoint.net
Web site: *http://www.aesm.org*
President: Michael A. Foss, D.V.M.

Association of Racing Commissioners Int'l
2343 Alexandria Dr., Ste. 200
Lexington, KY 40504-3276
Ph: (859) 224-7070

Fax: (859) 224-7071
E-mail: lpowell@arci.com
Web site: *http://www.arci.com*
President: Lonny T. Powell

Breeders' Cup Ltd.
P.O. Box 4230
Lexington, KY 40544-4230
Ph: (859) 223-5444
Fax: (859) 223-3945
E-mail: breederscup@breederscup.com
Web site: *http://www.breederscup.com*
President: D. G. Van Clief Jr.

Canadian Thoroughbred Horse Assn.
17687 56A Ave.
Surrey BC V3S 1G4 Canada
Ph: (614) 246-5783
Fax: (703) 349-3172

Canadian Veterinary Medical Assn.
339 Booth St.
Ottawa, ON K1R 7K1 Canada
Ph: (613) 236-1162
Fax: (613) 236-9681
E-mail: admin@cvma-acmv.org
Web site: *http://www.canadianveterinarians.net*

Grayson-Jockey Club Research Foundation
821 Corporate Dr.
Lexington, KY 40503
Ph: (859) 224-2850
Fax: (859) 224-2853
E-mail: ebowen@jockeyclub.com
Web site: *http://www.jockeyclub.com*
President: Edward L. Bowen

Horsemen's Benevolent and Protective Assn.
(National)
4063 Iron Works Pkwy., Bldg. B, Ste. 2
Lexington, KY 40511-8905
Ph: (859) 259-0451
Fax: (859) 259-0452
E-mail: racing@hbpa.org
Web site: *http://www.hbpa.org*
Executive Director: Remi Bellocq
President: John Roark

Jockey Club Information Systems
821 Corporate Dr.
Lexington, KY 40503-2794
Ph: (859) 224-2800
Fax: (859) 224-2810
E-mail: tjcis@tjcis.com
Web sites: *http://www.tjcis.com*
        http://www.equineline.com
President: Carl Hamilton

Jockey Club of Canada
P.O. Box 156
Rexdale, ON M9W 5L2 Canada
Ph: (416) 675-7756
Fax: (416) 675-6378
E-mail: tjcc@ftn.net
Web site: *http://www.jockeyclubcanada.com*

Jockeys' Benefit Assn. of Canada
9 Hernshaw Crescent
Etobicoke, ON M9C 3M3 Canada
Ph: (416) 620-6860
Fax: (416) 620-6983
E-mail: jockey@netcom.ca
President: Chris Loseth

Jockeys' Guild
P.O. Box 250
Lexington, KY 40588-0250
Ph: (859) 259-3211
Fax: (859) 252-0938
Web site: *http://www.jockeysguild.com*
President: L. Wayne Gertmenian

National Horse Carriers Assn.
2053 Buck Ln.
Lexington KY 40511
Ph: (859) 255-9406
Web site: *http://www.nationalhorsecarriers.com*
President: Robert D. Maxwell

National Steeplechase Assn.
400 Fair Hill Dr.
Elkton, MD 21921-2573
Ph: (410) 392-0700
Fax: (410) 392-0706
E-mail: steeplechs@aol.com
Web site: *http://www.nationalsteeplechase.com*
President: George Strawbridge Jr.

National Thoroughbred Racing Assn.
2525 Harrodsburg Rd., 5th Fl.
Lexington, KY 40504-3359
Ph: (859) 223-5444
Fax: (859) 245-6868
E-mail: ntra@ntra.com
Web site: *http://www.ntra.com*
Commissioner: Tim Smith

National Turf Writers Assn.
1244 Meadow Ln.
Frankfort, KY 40601
Ph: (502) 875-4864
E-mail: dliebman@bloodhorse.com
President: Jennie Rees

North American Pari-Mutuel Regulators Assn.
P.O. Box 446
Cheyenne, WY 82003
Ph: (888) 627-7250
Fax: (307) 777-3681
E-mail: flamb@state.wy.us
Web site: *http://www.napraonline.com*
President: Sherry Strebel

Puerto Rico Thoroughbred Breeders Assn.
P.O. Box 270281
San Juan, PR 00928-3081
Ph: (787) 725-8715
Fax: (787) 725-8606
E-mail: criadores@icepr.com

The Jockey Club
40 E. 52nd St.
New York, NY 10022
Ph: (212) 371-5970
Fax: (212) 371-6123
E-mail: comments@jockeyclub.com
Web site: *http://www.jockeyclub.com*
Chairman: Ogden Mills Phipps

Thoroughbred Club of America
P.O. Box 8098
Lexington, KY 40533-8098
Ph: (859) 254-4282
Fax: (859) 231-6131
President: Dell Hancock

Thoroughbred Owners and Breeders Assn.
P.O. Box 4367
Lexington, KY 40544-4367
Ph: (859) 276-2291
Fax: (859) 276-2462
E-mail: TOBA@iglou.com
Web site: *http://www.TOBA.org*
President: Dan Metzger

Thoroughbred Racing Assns. of North America
420 Fair Hill Dr., Ste. 1
Elkton, MD 21921-2573
Ph: (410) 392-9200
Fax: (410) 398-1366
E-mail: traoffice@dpnet.net
Web site: *http://www.tra-online.com*
President: Bryan G. Krantz
Executive Vice President: Chris Scherf

Thoroughbred Racing Protective Bureau
420 Fair Hill Dr., Ste. 2
Elkton, MD 21921
Ph: (410) 398-2261
Fax: (410) 398-1499
E-mail: trpbinfo@trpb.com
Web site: *http://www.trpb.com*
President: Paul W. Berube

Triple Crown Productions
700 Central Ave.
Louisville, KY 40208-1200
Ph: (502) 636-4405
Fax: (502) 636-4554
E-mail: TripleCrown@KentuckyDerby.com
Web site: *http://www.visatriplecrown.com*
President: Thomas H. Meeker

Turf Publicists of America
P.O. Box 90
Jamaica, NY 11417
Ph: (718) 641-4700
Fax: (718) 843-7673
E-mail: bzalubil@nyrainc.com
Web site: *http://www.turfpublicists.com*
President: Bob Curran Jr.

United Thoroughbred Trainers of America
P.O. Box 7065
Louisville, KY 40257-0065
Ph: (502) 893-0025
Fax: (502) 893-0026
E-mail: uttainc@aol.com
Web site: *http://www.thebackstretch.com/index.html*

Racing Commissions

Arizona
3877 N. 7th St., Ste. 201
Phoenix, AZ 85014
Ph: (602) 277-1704
Fax: (602) 277-1165
E-mail: ador@racing.state.az.us
Executive Director: Wade W. Turner
Chairman: A. Melvin McDonald

Arkansas
P.O. Box 3076
Little Rock, AR 72203
Ph: (501) 682-1467
Fax: (501) 682-5273
E-mail: bob.cohee@dfa.state.ar.us
Executive Director: Bob Cohee
Chairman: Cecil Alexander

Birmingham
2102 6th Ave. N.
Birmingham, AL 35203
Ph: (205) 328-7223
Chairman: Michael G. Kendrick

British Columbia
4720 Kingsway #2003
Burnaby, BC V5H 4N2 Canada
Ph: (604) 660-7400
Fax: (604) 660-7414
Chairman: Lorna Romilly

California
California Horse Racing Board
1010 Hurley Wy., Ste. 300
Sacramento, CA 95825
Ph: (916) 263-6000
Fax: (916) 263-6042
Executive Director: Roy C. Wood Jr.
Chairman: Alan Landsburg

Canada
Canadian Pari-Mutuel Agency
6 Antares Dr., Ste. 12, Phase II
Nepean, ON K2E 2A9 Canada
Ph: (613) 946-1700
Fax: (613) 952-7466
E-mail: emassey@em.agr.ca
Executive Director: Elizabeth Massey

Colorado
1881 Pierce St., Ste. 108
Lakewood, CO 80214
Ph: (303) 205-2990
Fax: (303) 205-2950
E-mail: dhartman@spike.dor.state.co.us
Executive Director: David C. Reitz
Chairman: W. Gale Davey

Delaware
2320 S. DuPont Hwy.
Dover, DE 19901
Ph: (302) 698-4599
Fax: (302) 697-4748
E-mail: johnwayne@dda.state.de.us
Executive Director: John F. Wayne
Chairman: Bernard J. Daney

Florida
Division of Pari-Mutuel Wagering
1940 N. Monroe St.
Tallahassee, FL 32399-1035
Ph: (850) 488-9130
Fax: (850) 488-0550

Idaho
P.O. Box 700
Meridian, ID 83642
Ph: (208) 884-7080
E-mail: ardie.noyes@isp.state.id.us
Executive Director: Eugene O. Baker
Chairman: Dr. Michael Lineberry

Illinois
Illinois Racing Board
100 W. Randolph St., Ste. 1
Chicago, IL 60601
Ph: (312) 814-2600
Fax: (312) 814-5062
Chairman: Ralph M. Gonzalez

Indiana
150 W. Market St., ISTA Center, Ste. 530
Indianapolis, IN 46204
Ph: (317) 233-3119
Fax: (317) 233-4470
Executive Director: Joe Gorajec
Chairman: Richard Beck

Iowa
717 E. Court Ave., Ste. B
Des Moines, IA 50309
Ph: (515) 281-7352
Fax: (515) 242-6560
E-mail: irgc@irgc.state.ia
Chairman: Rita Sealock

Kansas
3400 SW. Van Buren St.
Topeka, KS 66611-2228
Ph: (785) 296-5800
Fax: (785) 296-0900
E-mail: kracing@cjnetworks.com
Executive Director: Tracy T. Diel
Chairman: Gene Olander

Kentucky
4063 Iron Works Pkwy., Bldg B
Lexington, KY 40511-8462
Ph: (859) 246-2040
Fax: (859) 246-2039
E-mail: bernard.hettel@mail.state.ky.us
Executive Director: Bernard J. Hettel
Chairman: C. Frank Shoop

Louisiana
320 N Carrollton Ave., Ste. 2-B
New Orleans, LA 70119
Ph: (504) 483-4000
Fax: (504) 483-4898
Executive Director: Charles Gardiner
Chairman: Albert M. Stall

Manitoba
P.O. Box 46086 RPO Westdale
Winnipeg, MB R3R 3S3 Canada
Ph: (204) 885-7770
Fax: (204) 831-0942
E-mail: dwilliams@manitobahorsecomm.org
Executive Director: D. F. Williams QC
Chairman: David Miles

Maryland
500 N. Calvert St., Rm. 201
Baltimore, MD 21202-3651
Ph: (410) 230-6330
Fax: (410) 333-8308
E-mail: mhopkins@dllr.state.md.us
Chairman: John B. Franzone

Massachusetts
1 Ashburton Pl., Rm. 1313
Boston, MA 02108
Ph: (617) 727-2581
Fax: (617) 227-6062
Chairman: Robert M. Hutchinson Jr.

Mexico
Apartado Postal 34050, Hipodromo de las Americas
Lomas de Sotelo, C.P 11619 Mexico
Ph: 011-52-5-557-1042
Fax: 011-52-5-557-1042

Michigan
Office of Racing Commissioner
37650 Professional Center Dr., Ste. 105-A
Livonia, MI 48154-1100
Ph: (734) 462-2400
Fax: (734) 462-2429
E-mail: christopherk@state.mi.us
Commissioner: Annette M. Bacola

Minnesota
P.O. Box 630
Shakopee, MN 55379
Ph: (612) 496-7950
Fax: (612) 496-7954
E-mail: nlchgrd.Krueger@state.mn.us
Executive Director: Richard Krueger
Chairman: Cindy Piper

Missouri
P.O. Box 1847
Jefferson City, MO 65102-1847
Ph: (573) 526-4080
Fax: (573) 526-1999
E-mail: kmullall@mail.state.mo.us
Executive Director: Kevin Mullally

Montana
1424 9th Ave.
Helena, MT 59620-0512
Ph: (406) 444-4287
Fax: (406) 444-4305
Executive Director: Sam Murfitt

Nebraska
P.O. Box 95014
Lincoln, NE 68509-5014
Ph: (402) 471-4155

Fax: (402) 471-2339
Chairman: Dennis Lee

New Hampshire
244 N. Main St.
Concord, NH 03301-5041
Ph: (603) 271-2158
Fax: (603) 271-3381
E-mail: pkelley@nhpmc.state.nh.us
Executive Director: Paul M. Kelley
Chairman: Timothy J. Connors

New Jersey
P.O. Box 088
Trenton, NJ 08625
Ph: (609) 292-0613
Fax: (609) 599-1785
Executive Director: Francesco Zanzuccki
Chairman: Noel Gross

New Mexico
300 San Mateo Blvd. NE., Ste. 110
Albuquerque, NM 87108-1519
Ph: (505) 841-6000
Fax: (505) 841-6413
E-mail: nmrc@state.nm.us
Executive Director: Julian Luna
Chairman: Greg Drake

New York
New York State Racing and Wagering Board
1 Watervliet Avenue Ext., Ste. 2
Albany, NY 12206-1668
Ph: (518) 453-8460
Fax: (518) 453-8490
E-mail: info@racing.state.ny.us
Chairman: Michael Hoblock Jr.

North Dakota
900 E. Boulevard Ave.
Bismarck, ND 85805-0400
Ph: (701) 328-4290
Fax: (701) 328-4300
Chairman: G. Roy Gilbreath

Ohio
77 S. High St., 18th Fl.
Columbus, OH 43266-0416
Ph: (614) 466-2757
Fax: (614) 466-1900
Executive Director: Clifford A. Nelson II
Chairman: C. Luther Heckman

Oklahoma
2614 Villa Prom
Oklahoma City, OK 73107-2421
Ph: (405) 943-6472
Fax: (405) 943-6474
E-mail: ohrc@socket.net
Executive Director: Gordon L. Hare
Chairman: Sherry Strebel

Oregon
800 NE. Oregon St. #11-310
Portland, OR 97232
Ph: (503) 731-4052
Fax: (503) 731-4053

E-mail: sbarham@oregonvos.net
Executive Director: Steven W. Barham
Chairman: Stephen S. Walters

Pennsylvania
2310 N. Cameron St., Rm. 304
Harrisburg, PA 17110
Ph: (717) 787-1942
Executive Director: Benjamin H. Nolt Jr.
Chairman: Cayler H. Walker

South Dakota
South Dakota Commission on Gaming
118 W. Capitol Ave.
Pierre, SD 57501
Ph: (605) 773-6050
Fax: (605) 773-6053
E-mail: craig.sparrow@state.sd.us
Executive Director: Larry Eliason
Chairman: John Wiles

Texas
P.O. Box 12080
Austin, TX 78711-2080
Ph: (512) 833-6699
Fax: (512) 833-6907
E-mail: paula@txrc.state.tx.us
Executive Director: Paula C. Flowerday
Chairman: Terry Lacy

Virginia
10700 Horsemen's Rd.
New Kent, VA 23124
Ph: (804) 966-7400
Fax: (804) 966-7418
E-mail: bowker@vrc.state.va.us
Chairman: Robin Traywick Williams

Washington
6326 Martin Way, Ste. 209
Lacey, WA 98516
Ph: (360) 459-6462
Fax: (360) 459-6461
E-mail: whrc@whrc.state.wa.us
Chairman: Patrick LePley

West Virginia
106 Dee Dr.
Charleston, WV 25311
Ph: (304) 558-2150
Fax: (304) 558-6319
Chairman: Robert J. Burke

Wyoming
2515 Warren Ave., Ste. 301
Cheyenne, WY 82002
Ph: (307) 777-5887
Fax: (307) 777-6005
E-mail: flamb@state.wy.us
Executive Director: Frank R. Lamb

State and Provincial Racing Organizations

Alabama Horsemen's Benevolent and Protective Assn.
1523 Indian Hills
Hartsdale, AL 35640
Ph: (256) 773-3592
Fax: (256) 773-3592
President: Skip Drinkard

Alberta Division Canadian Thoroughbred Horse Society
225 17th Ave. SW. #401
Calgary, AB T2S 2T8 Canada
Ph: (403) 229-3609
Fax: (403) 244-6909
E-mail: cthalta@cadvision.com
Web site: *http://www.cthsalta.com*
President: Jim Thomson

Alberta Racing Corp.
9707 110th St., #720
Edmonton, AB T5K 2L9 Canada
Ph: (780) 415-5432
Fax: (780) 488-5105
Web site: *http://www.thehorses.com*

Arizona Horsemen's Benevolent and Protective Assn.
P.O. Box 43636
Phoenix, AZ 85080
Ph: (602) 942-3336
Fax: (602) 866-3790
E-mail: azhbpa@uswest.net
President: Dale V. Ray

Arizona Thoroughbred Breeders Assn.
P.O. Box 41774
Phoenix, AZ 85080
Ph: (602) 942-1310
Fax: (602) 942-8225
E-mail: atba@worldnet.att.net
Web site: *http://www.atba.net*
President: Frank W. Covello

Arkansas Horsemen's Benevolent and Protective Assn.
P.O. Box 1670
Hot Springs, AR 71902
Ph: (501) 623-7641
Fax: (501) 623-1350
President: Bill Walmsley

Arkansas Thoroughbred Breeders and Horsemen's Assn.
P.O. Box 21641
Hot Springs, AR 71903-1641
Ph: (501) 624-6328
Fax: (501) 623-5722
E-mail: atbha@direclynx.net
President: Cynthia Baker

British Columbia Division Canadian Thoroughbred Horse Society
17687 56A Ave.
Surrey, BC V3S 1G4 Canada
Ph: (604) 574-0145
Fax: (604) 574-5868
E-mail: cths@axionet.com

British Columbia Horsemen's Benevolent and Protective Assn.
609 W. Hastings St. #888
Vancouver, BC V6B 4W4 Canada
Ph: (604) 984-4311
Fax: (604) 984-0749
President: Russ Edwards

California Assn. of Thoroughbred Racetracks
980 9th St., Ste. 1550
Sacramento, CA 95814-2735
Ph: (916) 449-6820
Fax: (916) 449-6830

California Equine Council
P.O. Box 40000
Studio City, CA 91604
Ph: (818) 771-0702
Fax: (818) 768-7752

California Thoroughbred Breeders Assn.
P.O. Box 60018
Arcadia, CA 91066-6018
Ph: (626) 445-7800
Fax: (626) 574-0852
E-mail: info@ctba.com
Web site: http://www.ctba.com
President: Weston L. Fitzpatrick

California Thoroughbred Farm Managers Assn.
P.O. Box 321
Murrieta, CA 92564
Ph: (909) 677-6571
Fax: (909) 677-6446
E-mail: cboots@webtv.net
Web site: http://www.thoroughbredinfo.com/show case/ctfma.htm
President: Dennis O'Neill

California Thoroughbred Horsemen's Foundation
P.O. Box 660129
Arcadia, CA 91066-6251
Ph: (626) 446-0169
Fax: (626) 447-6251

California Thoroughbred Trainers
P.O. Box 660039
Arcadia, CA 91066-0039
Ph: (626) 447-2145
Fax: (626) 446-0270
E-mail: caltrnrs@pacbell.net
Web site: http://www.thoroughbredinfo.com/show case/CTT.htm
President: Leigh Ann Howard

Colorado Horsemen's Assn.
P.O. Box 460635
Aurora, CO 80046-0635
Ph: (303) 690-5919
Fax: (303) 766-5268

Colorado Horsemen's Benevolent and Protective Assn.
4898 Jackson Creek Rd.
Sedalia, CO 81035
Ph: (303) 688-9020
President: Jack Rosenquist

Colorado Thoroughbred Breeders Assn.
4701 Marion St., Ste. 203
Denver, CO 80216
Ph: (303) 294-0260
Fax: (303) 292-0957
E-mail: info@colo-ctba.com
Web site: http://www.colo-ctba.com
President: F. A. Heckendorf

Eastern Canadian Thoroughbred Assn.
Longview Farm, RR 4
Ashton, ON K0A 1B0 Canada
Ph: (613) 257-5837
Fax: (613) 257-5837
E-mail: info@ecta-equine.ca
Web site: http://www.ecta-equine.ca
President: Mary Pappone

Florida Horsemen's Assn.
2140 Miracle Ln.
Chuluota, FL 32766
Ph: (407) 365-3810

Florida Horsemen's Benevolent and Protective Assn.
P.O. Box 1808, Carol City Branch
Opa Locka, FL 33055
Ph: (305) 625-4591
Fax: (305) 625-5259
E-mail: fhbpa@bellsouth.net
President: Linda Mills

Florida Thoroughbred Breeders' and Owners' Assn.
801 SW. 60th Ave.
Ocala, FL 34474-1827
Ph: (352) 629-2160
Fax: (352) 629-3603
E-mail: ftboa@aol.com
Web site: http://www.ftboa.com
President: Harold J. Plumley

Florida Thoroughbred Farm Managers
6998 NW. Highway 27, Ste. 106B
Ocala, FL 34482
Ph: (352) 401-3535
Fax: (352) 401-3533
E-mail: ftfm@atlantic.net
Web site: http://www.flfarmmanagers.com
President: Bobby Jones

Florida Turf Writers/Media Assn.
P.O. Box 374
Hallandale, FL 33008
Ph: (954) 434-3737
Fax: (954) 457-6497
E-mail: kingbaker4@aol.com

**Georgia Thoroughbred Owners and
  Breeders Assn.**
P.O. Box 895
Buford, GA 30515
Ph: (770) 649-2793
Fax: (770) 649-2793
E-mail: gtoba@mindspring.com
Web site: http://www.gtoba.com
President: Jack Damico

Horse Council of British Columbia
2669 Deacon St.
Abbotsford, BC V2T 6H3 Canada
Ph: (604) 504-0245
Fax: (604) 504-0248
E-mail: hcbc@uniserve.com
Web site: http://www.horsecouncilbc.com
President: Ken Huber

Horse Protection Assn. of Florida
20690 NW. 130th Ave.
Micanopy, FL 32667
Ph: (352) 466-4366
Fax: (305) 245-0688
E-mail: director@hpaf.org
Web site: http://www.hpaf.org

**Idaho Horsemen's Benevolent and
  Protective Assn.**
P.O. Box 878
Eagle, ID 83616
Ph: (208) 939-0650

Idaho Thoroughbred Assn.
5000 Chinden Blvd.
Boise, ID 83714
Ph: 208-375-5930
Fax: 208-375-5959
Web site: http://www.cyberhighway.net/~ita

Idaho Thoroughbred Breeders Assn.
3085 N. Cole Rd., Ste. 113
Boise, ID 83704
Ph: (208) 375-5930
Fax: (208) 375-5959
E-mail: ita@micron.net

**Illinois Horsemen's Benevolent and
  Protective Assn.**
P.O. Box 429
Caseyville, IL 62232-0429
Ph: (618) 345-7724
Fax: (618) 344-9049
President: Lou O'Brien

**Illinois Thoroughbred Breeders and
  Owners Foundation**
P.O. Box 336
Caseyville, IL 62232
Ph: (618) 344-3427
Fax: (618) 346-1051
E-mail: itboffp@apci.net
Web site: http://www.illinoisracingnews.com/itbof.htm
President: John D. Bauman

Illinois Thoroughbred Horsemen's Assn.
P.O. Box 50366
Cicero, IL 60804
Ph: (708) 652-2201
Fax: (708) 652-2259
E-mail: office@itha.org
Web site: http://www.itha.org/
President: Joe Kasperski Jr.

Indiana Horse Council
225 S. East St. #738
Indianapolis, IN 46202
Ph: (317) 692-7115
Fax: (317) 692-7350
E-mail: indequine@aol.com
Web site: http://www.indianahorsecouncil.org

**Indiana Horsemen's Benevolent and
  Protective Assn.**
4500 Dan Patch Cir.
Anderson, IN 46013
Ph: (317) 894-1520
Fax: (317) 894-1530
E-mail: inhbpa@aol.com
President: Dan Horrell

**Indiana Thoroughbred Owners and
  Breeders Assn.**
P.O. Box 3753
Carmel, IN 46082-3753
Ph: (317) 462-0046
Fax: (317) 467-0396
E-mail: mail@itoba.com
Web site: http://www.itoba.com
President: Jerry C. Walker

**Iowa Horsemen's Benevolent and
  Protective Assn.**
7289 W. 100th St. N.
Mingo, IA 50168
Ph: (515) 363-4280
Fax: (515) 967-4963
E-mail: iahbpa@aol.com
President: Dick Clark

**Iowa Thoroughbred Breeders and
  Owners Assn.**
1 Prairie Meadows Dr.
Altoona, IA 50009
Ph: (515) 957-3002
Fax: (515) 957-1368
E-mail: ITBOA@PrairieMeadows.com
Web site: http://www.iowathoroughbred.com
President: Scott Pope

Kansas Horse Council
P.O. Box 1612
Manhattan, KS 66505-1612
Ph: (785) 776-0662
Fax: (785) 770-8558
E-mail: kansashorsecouncil@yahoo.com
Web site: http://www.kansashorsecouncil.com
President: Steve Lindsey

**Kansas Horsemen's Benevolent and
Protective Assn.**
16585 SW. 90th Ave.
Zenda, KS 67159
Ph: (620) 243-6641
Fax: (509) 479-7127
E-mail: liljavan@socencom.net
President: Ralph Lilja

Kansas Thoroughbred Assn.
215 Monroe Dr.
Fredonia, KS 66736-1262
Ph: (316) 378-4772
Fax: (316) 378-4772
E-mail: gejo@twinmounds.com
President: Dwight Daniels

Kentucky Horse Council
P.O. Box 11706
Lexington, KY 40577-1706
Ph: (800) 459-4677
Fax: (859) 299-9849
E-mail: kyhorse.council@verizon.net
Web site: http://www.kentuckyhorse.org
President: Darryl Hacker

**Kentucky Horsemen's Benevolent and
Protective Assn.**
3733 S. 4th St.
Louisville, KY 40214-1712
Ph: (502) 363-1077
Fax: (502) 367-6800
E-mail: kyhbpalou@ntr.net
Web site: http://www.hbpa.org
President: Alex Harthill, D.V.M.

Kentucky Thoroughbred Assn.
4079 Iron Works Pkwy.
Lexington, KY 40511
Ph: (859) 381-1414
Fax: (859) 233-9737
E-mail: contact@kta-ktob.com
Web site: http://www.kta-ktob.com
President: R. Alex Rankin

Kentucky Thoroughbred Farm Managers Club
P.O. Box 4688
Lexington, KY 40544-4688
Ph: (859) 296-4279
E-mail: kyfarmclub@aol.com
Web site: http://www.ktfmc.org
President: Steven Johnson

Kentucky Thoroughbred Owners and Breeders
4079 Iron Works Pkwy.
Lexington, KY 40511
Ph: (859) 259-1643
Fax: (859) 233-9737
E-mail: contact@kta-ktob.com
Web site: http://www.kta-ktob.com
President: R. Alex Rankin

**Louisiana Horsemen's Benevolent and
Protective Assn.**
1535 Gentilly Blvd.
New Orleans, LA 70119
Ph: (504) 945-1555
Fax: (504) 945-1579
E-mail: lahbpa@aol.com
President: Oran Trahan

Louisiana Thoroughbred Breeders Assn.
P.O. Box 24650
New Orleans, LA 70184
Ph: (504) 947-4676
Fax: (504) 943-2149
E-mail: ltba@iamerica.net
President: Neal McFadden

**Manitoba Division Canadian Thoroughbred
Horse Society**
Westdale Postal Outlet Box 46152
Winnipeg, MB R3R 3S3 Canada
Ph: (204) 832-1702
Fax: (204) 831-6735
E-mail: cthsmb@escape.ca
President: Brent Hrymak

Manitoba Horse Council
200 Main St., Ste. 207
Winnipeg, MB R3C 4M2 Canada
Ph: (204) 925-5718
Fax: (204) 925-5737
E-mail: admin1.mhc@sport.mb.ca
Web site: http://www.escape.ca/~mhc

Manitoba Jockey Club
3975 Portage Ave.
Winnipeg MB R3K 2E9 Canada
Ph: (204) 885-3330
Fax: (204) 831-5348
E-mail: info@assiniboiadowns.com
Web site: http://www.assiniboiadowns.com

Maryland Horse Breeders Assn.
P.O. Box 427
Timonium, MD 21094
Ph: (410) 252-2100
Fax: (410) 560-0503
E-mail: mdhobr@erols.com
Web site: http://www.mdhorsebreeders.com
President: Michael Pons

Maryland Horse Council
P.O. Box 233
Lisbon, MD 21765
Ph: (410) 489-7826
Fax: (410) 489-7828
E-mail: equiery@erols.com
Web site: http://www.mdhorsecouncil.org
President: Lu Anne Levens

Maryland Million Ltd.
P.O. Box 365
Timonium, MD 21094
Ph: (410) 252-2100
Fax: (410) 252-0503
E-mail: info@mdhorsebreeders.com
Web site: http://www.mdhorsebreeders.com/Million/
Default.cfm
President: Richard F. Blue Jr.

Maryland Thoroughbred Horsemen's Assn.
6314 Windsor Mill Rd.
Baltimore, MD 21207
Ph: (410) 265-6842
Fax: (410) 265-6841
E-mail: mdhorsemen@erols.com
Web site: http://www.mdhorsebreeders.com/MTHA/
Index.cfm
President: Werner Rentsch

Mid-Atlantic Thoroughbred Championships (MATCH)
10500 Little Patuxent Pkwy., Ste. 420
Columbia, MD 21044
Ph: (410) 740-4901
Fax: (410) 740-0800
E-mail: aforeman@matchseries.com
Web site: http://www.matchseries.com

Michigan Horsemen's Benevolent and Protective Assn.
28001 Schoolcraft Rd.
Livonia, MI 48150
Ph: (313) 261-5700
Fax: (313) 261-5703

Minnesota Horsemen's Benevolent and Protective Assn.
1100 Canterbury Rd.
Shakopee, MN 55379
Ph: (612) 496-6442
Fax: (612) 496-6443
E-mail: mnhbpa@pclink.com
Web site: http://www.pclink.com/mnhbpa
President: Tom Metzen Sr.

Minnesota Thoroughbred Assn.
1100 Canterbury Rd.
Shakopee, MN 55379
Ph: (952) 496-3770
Fax: (952) 296-3672
E-mail: mtassoc@voyager.net
President: Chuck Yahnke

Mississippi Thoroughbred Owners and Breeders Assn.
107 Sundown Rd.
Madison, MS 39110
Ph: (601) 856-8293
President: Bruns Myers Jr.

Missouri Equine Council
P.O. Box 681
Republic, MO 65738-0681
Ph: (417) 732-4062
E-mail: info@mo-equine.org
Web site: http://www.mo-equine.org
President: Harriet Francis

Montana Horsemen's Benevolent and Protective Assn.
139 New Dracut Hill Rd.
Vaughn, MT 59487
Ph: (406) 467-2904

Nebraska Thoroughbred Breeders Assn.
P.O. Box 2215
Grand Island, NE 68802
Ph: (308) 384-4683
Fax: (308) 384-9172
E-mail: NTBAI@KDSI.net
President: Jim Cranwell

Newfoundland Equestrian Assn.
P.O. Box 372, Station C
Saint John's, NF A1C 5J9 Canada
Ph: (709) 576-1317
Fax: (709) 754-2411
E-mail: nea@webpage.ca
Web site: http://www.webpage.ca/nea
President: Will Small

New Hampshire Horse Council
273 Poor Farm Rd.
New Ipswich, NH 03071
Ph: (603) 456-3230
E-mail: brookee171@hotmail.com
Web site: http://www.nhhorsecouncil.com
President: James S. Clark-Dawe

New Mexico Horse Breeders' Assn.
P.O. Box 36869
Albuquerque, NM 87176-6869
Ph: (505) 262-0224
Fax: (505) 265-8009
E-mail: donnamartin@zianet.com
Web site: http://www.nmhorsebreeders.com
President: Lonnie Barber

New Mexico Horse Council
P.O. Box 10206
Albuquerque, NM 87184-0206
Ph: (505) 345-8959
Fax: (505) 877-7285
E-mail: valcole@flash.net
Web site: http://www.nmhorsecouncil.org
President: Rob Atchley

New York Horsemen's Benevolent and Protective Assn.
P.O. Box 25250
Farmington, NY 14425
Ph: (716) 924-3004
Fax: (716) 924-1433
E-mail: flhbpa@frontiernet.net
President: Paul Steckel

New York State Horse Council
760 Webster Rd.
Webster, NY 14580-9559
Ph: (716) 872-3178
E-mail: questions@nyshc.org
Web site: http://www.nyshc.org
President: Diane K. Jones

New York Thoroughbred Breeders
57 Phila St., 2nd Fl.
Saratoga Springs, NY 12866
Ph: (518) 587-0777
Fax: (518) 587-1551
E-mail: nytb@nybreds.com
Web site: http://www.nybreds.com
President: Gerald Nielsen

New York State Thoroughbred Breeding and Development
1 Penn Plaza, Ste. 725
New York, NY 10119
Ph: (212) 465-0660
Fax: (212) 465-8205
E-mail: nybreds@nybreds.com
Web site: http://www.nybreds.com

New York Thoroughbred Horsemen's Assn.
P.O. Box 170070
Jamaica, NY 11417
Ph: (718) 848-5045
Fax: (718) 848-9269
Web site: http://www.nytha.com
President: Richard Bomze

North Carolina Horse Council
P.O. Box 12999
Raleigh, NC 27605
Ph: (919) 821-1030
Fax: (919) 821-1415
E-mail: cindy@nchorsecouncil.com
Web site: http://www.nchorsecouncil.com
President: Glenn Petty

North Carolina Thoroughbred Breeders Assn.
2103 Orange Factory Rd.
Bahama, NC 27503
Ph: (919) 471-0131
Fax: (919) 286-9421
President: Reggie Beeson

Ohio Horsemen's Benevolent and Protective Assn.
P.O. Box 400
Grove City, OH 43123-0400
Ph: (614) 875-1269
Fax: (614) 875-0786
E-mail: ohio-hbpa@iwaynet.net
Web site: http://www.ohio-hbpa.com
President: Gus George

Ohio Thoroughbred Breeders and Owners Assn.
6024 Harrison Ave., Ste. 13
Cincinnati, OH 45248-1621
Ph: (513) 574-0440
Fax: (513) 574-2313
E-mail: gb.otbo@fuse.net
Web site: http://www.otbo.com
President: Thomas McCann

Oklahoma Horsemen's Benevolent and Protective Assn.
1 Remington Pl.
Oklahoma City, OK 73111
Ph: (405) 427-8753
Fax: (405) 427-7099
E-mail: canron1@go.com
President: Blaine Story

Oklahoma Thoroughbred Assn.
2000 SE. 15th St., Bldg. 450, Ste. A
Edmond, OK 73013
Ph: (405) 330-1006
Fax: (405) 330-6206
E-mail: info@otawins.com

Web site: http://www.otawins.com
President: David Brookins

Oklahoma Thoroughbred Breeders Assn.
R.R. 6, Box 164
Blanchard, OK 73010-9236
Ph: (405) 485-3030

Ontario Division Canadian Thoroughbred Horse Society
P.O. Box 172
Rexdale, ON M9W 5L1 Canada
Ph: (416) 675-3602
Fax: (416) 675-9405
E-mail: cthsont@idirect.com
Web site: http://www.cthsont.com

Ontario Equestrian Federation
1185 Eglinton Ave. E., Ste. 103
North York, ON M3C 3C6 Canada
Ph: (416) 426-7232
Fax: (416) 426-7355
E-mail: horse@horse.on.ca
Web site: http:www.horse.on.ca

Ontario Horse Breeders Assn.
15925 Keele St.
King City, ON L7B 1A3 Canada
Ph: (905) 727-4491

Ontario Horsemen's Benevolent and Protective Assn.
135 Queens Plate Dr., Ste. 370
Toronto, ON M9W 6V1 Canada
Ph: (416) 747-5252
Fax: (416) 747-9606
President: Lawrence D. Regan

Oregon Horsemen's Benevolent and Protective Assn.
11919 N. Jantzen Ave.
Portland, OR 97217
Ph: (503) 285-4941
Fax: (503) 285-4942
E-mail: ohbpa@aol.com
President: Dave Benson

Oregon Thoroughbred Breeders Assn.
P.O. Box 17248
Portland, OR 97217
Ph: (503) 285-0658
Fax: (503) 285-0659
E-mail: otba@mindspring.com
Web site: http://www.thoroughbredinfo.com/show case/otba.htm
President: Bruce Loudon

Pennsylvania Equine Council
P.O. Box 21
Dallas, PA 18612
Ph: (888) 304-0281
E-mail: siforstr@epix.net
Web site: http://www.pastatehorsecouncil.homestead. com
President: Bruce Rappoport

Pennsylvania Horse Breeders Assn.
701 E. Baltimore Pike, Ste. C-1
Kennet Square, PA 19348
Ph: (610) 444-1050
Fax: (610) 444-1051
E-mail: exsec@pabred.com
Web site: *http://www.pabred.com*
President: Robert A. Szeyller

Pennsylvania Horsemen's Benevolent and Protective Assn.
P.O. Box 88
Grantville, PA 17028
Ph: (717) 469-2790
Fax: (717) 469-7714
E-mail: PAHBPA@paonline.com
President: John Wames

Pennsylvania Thoroughbred Horsemen's Assn.
P.O. Box 300
Bensalem, PA 19020-0300
Ph: (215) 638-2012
Fax: (215) 638-2919
President: Lawrence Riviello

Quebec Division Canadian Thoroughbred Horse Society
1684 McCullough
Dunham QC J0E 1M0 Canada
Ph: (514) 538-8172
Fax: (514) 538-8170

Saskatchewan Division Canadian Thoroughbred Horse Society
1229 Spadina Crescent W.
Saskatoon, SK S7M 1P4 Canada
Ph: (306) 242-9128
Fax: (306) 665-5829
E-mail: dturner@sk.sympatico.ca

Saskatchewan Horse Federation
2205 Victoria Ave.
Regina, SK S4P 0S4 Canada
Ph: (306) 780-9244
Fax: (306) 525-4009
E-mail: sk.horse@sk.sympatico.ca
Web site: *http://www.saskhorsefed.com*
President: Connie Dorsch

South Carolina Thoroughbred Owners and Breeders
Route 1, Box 19-A
Wando, SC 29492
Ph: (803) 432-3388
Fax: (803) 432-5777
President: Ted Hoover

Sunshine State Horse Council
P.O. Box 4158
North Fort Myers, FL 33918-4158
Ph: (727) 731-2999
E-mail: jean1sshc@aol.com
Web site: *http://www.sshc.org*
President: Dan Coffman

Texas Horsemen's Benevolent and Protective Assn.
P.O. Box 142533
Austin, TX 78714
Ph: (512) 467-9799
Fax: (512) 467-9790
E-mail: azopardi@aol.com
Web site: *http://www.texashorsemen.com*
President: Jim Helzer

Texas Thoroughbred Breeders Assn.
P.O. Box 14967
Austin, TX 78761
Ph: (512) 458-6133
Fax: (512) 453-5919
E-mail: info@texasthoroughbred.com
Web site: *http://www.validinteractive.com/tta/*
President: Michael Barnett

Thoroughbred Breeders Cooperative
15 Hutchinson Rd.
Allentown, NJ 08501
Ph: (201) 488-4446
Fax: (201) 488-4213

Thoroughbred Breeders' Assn. of New Jersey
4444 N. Ocean Blvd.
Long Branch, NJ 07740
Ph: (732) 870-9718
Fax: (732) 870-9719
E-mail: duartej@njbreds.com
Web site: *http://www.njbreds.com*
President: John Perrotta

Thoroughbred Owners of California
285 W. Huntington Dr.
Arcadia, CA 91007
Ph: (626) 574-6620
Fax: (626) 821-1515
E-mail: santaanita@toconline.com
Web site: *http://www.toconline.com*
Chairman: Jack B. Owens
President: John K. Van de Kamp

Thoroughbred Owners of Florida
P.O. Box 2148
Hobe Sound, FL 33475
Ph: (800) 382-3892
Fax: (800) 382-6563

Vermont Horse Council
P.O. Box 105
Montpelier, VT 05601-0105
Ph: (800) 722-1419
Fax: (802) 229-1150
E-mail: newsilk@together.net

Virginia Gold Cup Assn.
P.O. Box 840
Warrenton, VA 20188
Ph: (540) 347-2612

Fax: (540) 349-1829
E-mail: diane@vagoldcup.com
Web site: http://www.vagoldcup.com

Virginia Horsemen's Benevolent and Protective Assn.
38 Garrett St.
Warrenton, VA 20186
Ph: (540) 347-0033
Fax: (540) 347-0034
E-mail: race@vhbpa.org
Web site: http://www.vhbpa.org
President: Robin Richards

Virginia Thoroughbred Assn.
38-C Garrett St.
Warrenton, VA 20186-3107
Ph: (540) 347-4313
Fax: (540) 347-7314
E-mail: vta@vabred.org
Web site: http://www.vabred.org
President: Deborah A. Easter

Washington Horsemen's Benevolent and Protective Assn.
3702 W. Valley Hwy., Ste. 210
Auburn, WA 98001
Ph: (206) 804-6822
Fax: (206) 804-6899
President: Larry Hills

Washington Thoroughbred Breeders Assn.
P.O. Box 1499
Auburn, WA 98071-1499
Ph: (253) 288-7878
Fax: (253) 288-7890
E-mail: maindesk@washingtonthoroughbred.com

Web site: http://www.washingtonthoroughbred.com
President: Jerry Woods

Washington Thoroughbred Farm Managers Assn.
P.O. Box 857
Enumclaw, WA 98022
Ph: (253) 288-7897
Fax: (253) 288-7890
E-mail: nancy@washingtonthoroughbred.com
Web site: http://www.washingtonthoroughbred.com/IndAddrs/WTFMA.htm

West Virginia Breeders Classics Ltd.
P.O. Box 1251
Charles Town, WV 25414
Ph: (304) 725-0709
Fax: (540) 687-6927
E-mail: wvbcmbn@erols.com
Web site: http://www.wvbc.com
President: Sam Huff

West Virginia Horsemen's Benevolent and Protective Assn.
P.O. Box 358
Chester, WV 26034
Ph: (304) 387-9772
Fax: (304) 387-1925
E-mail: hbpa@raex.com
President: Charles E. Bailey

West Virginia Thoroughbred Breeders Assn.
P.O. Box 626
Charles Town, WV 25414
Ph: (304) 728-6868
Fax: (304) 724-7870
President: Cynthia O'Bannon

Charitable Organizations

Bright Futures Farm
44793 Harrison Rd.
Spartansburg, PA 16434
Ph: (814) 827-8270
Fax: (814) 827-8278
E-mail: bdee@brightfuturesfarm.org
Web site: http://www.brightfuturesfarm.org

California Equine Retirement Foundation
34033 Kooden Rd.
Winchester, CA 92596
Ph: (909) 926-4190
Fax: (909) 926-4181
E-mail: cerf@pe.net
Web site: http://www.cerfhorses.org

Citizens for Animal Protection
P.O. Box 1496
Litchfield, CT 06759
Ph: (203) 699-8447

Fax: (203) 699-8447
E-mail: capinc1496@aol.com
Web site: http://www.geocities.com/Petsburgh/Zoo/7966

Community Association for Riding for the Disabled
4777 Dufferin St.
North York, ON M3H 5T3 Canada
Ph: (416) 667-8600
Fax: (416) 739-7520
E-mail: card.info@sympatico.ca
Web site: http://www.card.ca

Days End Farm Horse Rescue
15856 Frederick Rd.
Lisbon, MD 21765
Ph: (301) 854-5037
Fax: (301) 854-5146
E-mail: defhr@erols.com
Web site: http://www.defhr.org

Don MacBeth Memorial Jockey Fund
P.O. Box 18470
Encino, CA 91416
Ph: (310) 550-4542
Fax: (818) 981-6914
E-mail: info@macbethfund.org
Web site: http://www.macbethfund.org

Equine Rescue League
P.O. Box 4366
Leesburg, VA 20177
Ph: (703) 771-1240
E-mail: smithmc@citizen.infi.net
Web site: http://www.equinerescueleague.org

Exceller Fund to Rescue Horses
4701 Spruce St.
Flower Mound, TX 75028
Ph: (972) 874-7486
E-mail: excellerfund@earthlink.net
Web site: http://www.excellerfund.org

Grayson-Jockey Club Research Foundation
821 Corporate Dr.
Lexington, KY 40503
Ph: (859) 224-2850
Fax: (859) 224-2853
E-mail: ebowen@jockeyclub.com
Web site: http://www.jockeyclub.com

Horses' Haven
P.O. Box 519
South Lyon, MI 48178
Ph: (248) 486-3312
Fax: (248) 486-3418
E-mail: horsesmail@ismi.net; barbarabaker14@gte.net
Web site: http://www.ismi.net/horseshaven

Indiana Hooved Animal Humane Society
102 Spring Grove Ave.
Salem, IN 47167
Ph: (812) 883-8012
Fax: (812) 883-8175
E-mail: ihahs@earthlink.net
Web site: http://www.ihahs.org

Jockeys' Guild Disabled Riders Fund
250 W. Main St., Ste. 1820
Lexington, KY 40507
Ph: (859) 259-3211

Kentucky Horse Park Foundation
4089 Iron Works Pike
Lexington, KY 40511
Ph: (859) 255-5727
Fax: (859) 254-7121
E-mail: khpf@mis.net
Web site: http://www.kyhorsepark.com/khp/foundation

Lone Star Equine Rescue
P.O. Box 5103
College Station, TX 77844-5103

Ph: (409) 776-9396
Fax: (413) 803-0282
E-mail: info@lser.org
Web site: http://www.lser.org

Maryland Horsemen's Assistance Fund
6314 Windsor Mill Rd.
Baltimore, MD 21207
Ph: (410) 265-6843
Fax: (410) 265-6841
E-mail: mdassistance@erols.com
Web site: http://www.mdhorsemen.com

New Hampshire Equine Humane Assn.
27 Main St.
Goffstown, NH 03045
Ph: (603) 497-5900
E-mail: nehharescue@aol.com
Web site: http://nheha.homestead.com/main.html

New Vocations Racehorse Adoption Program
3293 Wright Rd.
Laura, OH 45337-9706
Ph: (937) 947-4020
Fax: (937) 947-3201
E-mail: DMorgan513@aol.com
Web site: http://www.horseadoption.com

Piedra Foundation
4211 Holly Ln.
Bonsall, CA 92003
Ph: (760) 726-9206
Fax: (760) 726-9342
E-mail: tpf@piedra.org
Web site: http://www.piedra.org

Project Equus
P.O. Box 18030
Boulder, CO 80308-1030
Ph: (303) 545-6800
Fax: (303) 545-6800
E-mail: equus@projectequus.org
Web site: http://www.projectequus.org

Racetrack Chaplaincy of America
P.O. Box 91640
Los Angeles, CA 90009
Ph: (310) 419-1640
Fax: (310) 419-1642
E-mail: etorres@racetrackchaplaincy.org
Web site: http://www.racetrackchaplaincy.org

Recycle Racehorses
853 Raughley Hill Rd.
Harrington, DE 19952
Ph: (302) 398-4682
Fax: (302) 398-5196
E-mail: delahorse@aol.com
Web site: http://www.delawarehorse.com

ReRun
P.O. Box 96
Carlisle, KY 40311-0096

Ph: (859) 289-7786
Fax: (859) 289-7786
E-mail: rerunhorse@kih.net
Web site: *http://www.rerun.org*

Second Career Racehorses
25 S. Division
Grand Rapids, MI 49503
Ph: (616) 913-2790
Fax: (616) 913-2801
E-mail: scr@cybernet-usa.com
Web site: *http://www.secondcareerracehorses.org*

Shoemaker Foundation
P.O. Box 17026
Ingelwood, CA 90308-7026
Ph: (310) 419-1503
Fax: (310) 672-3899

Thoroughbred Charities of America
1341 Bohemia Mill Rd.
Middletown, DE 19709
Ph: (302) 378-7192
Fax: (302) 378-0535

E-mail: moonscrape@dmv.com
Web site: *http://www.thoroughbredcharities.com*

Thoroughbred Retirement Foundation
450 Shrewsbury Plaza, Ste. 351
Shrewsbury, NJ 07702
Ph: (800) 728-1660
Fax: (802) 496-3276
E-mail: trfinc@msn.com
Web site: *http://www.trfinc.org*

United Pegasus Foundation
120 S. 1st Ave.
Arcadia, CA 91006
Ph: (626) 279-1306
Fax: (626) 452-8620
E-mail: unitedpegasus@yahoo.com
Web site: *http://www.unitedpegasus.com*

Winner's Circle Foundation
285 W. Huntington Dr.
Arcadia, CA 91007
Ph: (626) 574-6498
Fax: (626) 821-9091

Sales Companies

Agence Francaise de Vente du Pur-Sang
32 Avenue Hocquart de Turtot #51
Deauville, 14800 France
Ph: 02 31 81 81 00
Fax: 02 31 81 81 01
E-mail: af@deauville-sales.com
Web site: *http://www.deauville-sales.com*

American Equine Sales
4061 E. Castro Valley Blvd., Ste. 276
Castro Valley, CA 94552
Ph: (925) 600-8060
Fax: (925) 600-8061
E-mail: aes@mciworld.com
Web site: *http://www.thoroughbredinfo.com/show case/aes.htm*

Arizona Thoroughbred Breeders Assn.
P.O. Box 41774
Phoenix, AZ 85080
Ph: (602) 942-1310
Fax: (602) 942-8225
E-mail: atba@worldnet.att.net
Web site: *http://www.atba.net*
Executive Director: Yvonne Kunz

Arkansas Breeders' Sales Co.
P.O. Box 1665
Hot Springs, AR 71902
Ph: (501) 624-6336
Fax: (501) 623-5722

Arkansas Thoroughbred Sales Co.
P.O. Box 180159
Fort Smith, AR 72918-0159
Ph: (800) 752-8034
Fax: (501) 648-3980

Barretts Equine Ltd.
P.O. Box 2010
Pomona, CA 91769
Ph: (909) 629-3099
Fax: (909) 629-2155
E-mail: BarrettsEq@aol.com
Web site: *http://www.barretts.com*

Breeders Sales Co. of Louisiana
P.O. Box 24650
New Orleans, LA 70184
Ph: (504) 947-4676
Fax: (504) 943-2149
E-mail: ltba@iamerica.net

California Thoroughbred Breeders Sales
P.O. Box 60018
Arcadia, CA 91066-6018
Ph: (626) 445-7800
Fax: (626) 574-0852
E-mail: info@ctba.com
Web site: *http://www.ctba.com*

Canadian Breeders Sales
P.O. Box 10 Station B
Etobicoke, ON M9W 5K9 Canada
Ph: (416) 674-1460
Fax: (416) 675-6430
Web site: *http://www.canadiansales.com*

Doncaster Bloodstock Sales Ltd.
Auction Mart Offices Hawick
Roxburghshire, TD9 9NN England
Ph: (01450) 372222
Fax: (01450) 378017
E-mail: winners@dbsauctions.com
Web site: *http://www.dbsauctions.com*
Executive Director: Henry G. Beeby
Chairman: G. H. Beeby

Fair Grounds Sales Co.
1751 Gentilly Blvd. N.
New Orleans, LA 70152
Ph: (504) 944-5515
Fax: (504) 944-2511

Fasig-Tipton Co.
2400 Newtown Pike
Lexington, KY 40583
Ph: (859) 255-1555
Fax: (859) 254-0794
E-mail: info@fasigtipton.com
Web site: *http://www.fasigtipton.com*
Chairman: D. G. Van Clief Jr.
President: Walt Robertson

Fasig-Tipton Florida
21001 NW. 27th Ave.
Miami, FL 33056
Ph: (305) 626-3947
Fax: (305) 625-9242
E-mail: fasigtip@aol.com
Web site: *http://www.fasigtipton.com*

Fasig-Tipton Midlantic
356 Fair Hill Dr., Ste. C
Elkton, MD 21921
Ph: (410) 392-5555
Fax: (410) 392-5556
Web site: *http://www.fasigtipton.com*

Fasig-Tipton New York
40 Elmont Rd.
Elmont, NY 11003-0036
Ph: (516) 328-1800
Fax: (516) 328-1808
Web site: *http://www.fasigtipton.com*

Finger Lakes Thoroughbred Sales
P.O. Box 301
Shortsville, NY 14548-0301
Ph: (716) 289-8524
Fax: (716) 289-8524
E-mail: GVBA@nybreds.com
Web site: *http://www.nybreds.com/GVBA/flsale.html*

Goffs Bloodstock Sales Ltd.
Kildare Paddocks Kill
County Kildare, Ireland
Ph: 01135345877211
Fax: 01135345877119
E-mail: powell@goffs.ie
Web site: *http://www.goffs.com*
Chairman: Michael Osborne

Heritage Place Sales Co.
2829 S. MacArthur Blvd.
Oklahoma City, OK 73128
Ph: (405) 682-4551
Fax: (405) 686-1267
E-mail: info@heritageplace.com
Web site: *http://www.heritageplace.com*

Illinois Breeders' Sales Co.
P.O. Box 50031
Cicero, IL 60804
Ph: (847) 663-0890
Fax: (847) 663-0891
E-mail: grdi@aol.com

**Illinois Thoroughbred Breeders and Owners
Foundation**
P.O. Box 336
Caseyville, IL 62232
Ph: (618) 344-3427
Fax: (618) 346-1051
E-mail: itboffp@apci.net
Web site: *http://www.illinoisracingnews.com/itbof.htm*

**Iowa Thoroughbred Breeders and Owners
Assn.**
1 Prairie Meadows Dr.
Altoona, IA 50009
Ph: (515) 957-3002
Fax: (515) 957-1368
E-mail: ITBOA@PrairieMeadows.com
Web site: *http://www.iowathoroughbred.com*
Executive Director: Judy Grett

Keeneland Association
4201 Versailles Rd.
Lexington, KY 40592-1690
Ph: (859) 254-3412
Fax: (859) 288-4348
E-mail: keeneland@keeneland.com
Web site: *http://www.keeneland.com*
President: Nick Nicholson
Director of Sales: Geoffrey G. Russell

Louisiana Thoroughbred Breeders Sales Co.
P.O. Box 789
Carencro, LA 70520
Ph: (318) 896-6152
Fax: (318) 896-6153
E-mail: ltbscl1@aol.com
Web site: *http://www.evangelinedowns.com/ltbsc.html*

Magic Millions Sales
28 Ascot Ct.
Bundall, QLD 9726 Australia
Ph: + 61 7 5538 8933
Fax: +61 7 5531 7082
E-mail: info@magicmillions.com.au
Web site: *http://www.magicmillions.com.au*
Executive Director: John Singleton
Chairman: Gerry Harvey

Nor-Cal Sales Co.
12514 Plum Ln.
Wilton, CA 95693
Ph: (916) 687-6331
Fax: (916) 687-8249
E-mail: seaorbit@aol.com

Ocala Breeders' Sales Co.
P.O. Box 99
Ocala, FL 34478
Ph: (352) 237-2154
Fax: (352) 237-3566
E-mail: obs@obssales.com
Web site: *http://www.obssales.com*
Director of Sales: Tom Ventura

Ohio Thoroughbred Breeders and Owners Assn.
6024 Harrison Ave., Ste. 13
Cincinnati, OH 45248-1621
Ph: (513) 574-0440
Fax: (513) 574-2313
E-mail: gb.otbo@fuse.net
Web site: *http://www.otbo.com*

Ontario Division Canadian Thoroughbred Horse Society
P.O. Box 172
Rexdale, ON M9W 5L1 Canada
Ph: (416) 675-3602
Fax: (416) 675-9405
E-mail: cthsont@idirect.com
Web site: *http://www.cthsont.com*

Oregon Thoroughbred Breeders Assn.
P.O. Box 17248
Portland, OR 97217
Ph: (503) 285-0658
Fax: (503) 285-0659
E-mail: otba@mindspring.com
Web site: *http://www.thoroughbredinfo.com/show case/otba.htm*
Executive Director: Ursula V. Gibbons

Puerto Rico Breeders Sales Co.
Mercantil Plaza Bldg., Ste. 417, Ave. Ponce de Leon
Hato Rey, PR 00918
Ph: (787) 250-6168

Fax: (787) 274-0547
Web site: *http://www.x1nariz.com/noticias3.html*

Ruidoso Horse Sales Co.
P.O. Box 909
Ruidoso Downs, NM 88346
Ph: (505) 378-4474
Fax: (505) 378-4788

San Antonio Horse Sale Co.
6514 N. New Braunfels Ave.
San Antonio, TX 78209-3828
Ph: (210) 824-7552
Fax: (210) 824-7562
Executive Director: Patti Ann Sherwood

Tattersalls Ltd.
Terrace House Newmarket
Suffolk, CB8 9BT Great Britain
Ph: +44 (0) 1638 665931
Fax: +44 (0) 1638 660850
E-mail: sales@tattersalls.com
Web site: *http://www.tattersalls.com*
Chairman: Edmond Mahony

Tattersalls (Ireland) Ltd.
Fairyhouse Ratoath
County Meath, Ireland
Ph: 353-1-8864300
Fax: 353-1-8864303
E-mail: info@tattersalls.ie
Web site: *http://www.tattersalls.ie*
Chairman: Edmond Mahony

Tennessee Breeders Sales Co.
2474 Old Natchez Trace Rd.
Franklin, TN 37069-6302
Ph: (615) 373-8197

Thomas Sales Co.
10310 N. Yale Ave.
Sperry, OK 74073
Ph: (918) 288-7308
Fax: (918) 288-7330
E-mail: thomas.sales@worldnet.att.net

Washington Thoroughbred Breeders Assn.
P.O. Box 1499
Auburn, WA 98071-1499
Ph: (253) 288-7878
Fax: (253) 288-7890
E-mail: maindesk@washingtonthoroughbred.com
Web site: *http://www.washingtonthoroughbred.com*

Woodbine Sales
P.O. Box 156
Rexdale, ON M92 5L2 Canada
Ph: (416) 674-1460
Fax: (416) 675-6430

REFERENCE
Rules of Racing

The following model rules were developed by the Association of Racing Commissioners International. Although individual states implement their own regulations for how racing is conducted in their jurisdictions, the model rules combine both time-tested concepts and new developments in the Thoroughbred sport. The following rules encompass the running of the race. Other Association of Racing Commissioners International model rules cover such matters as racing officials, medications, and pari-mutuel wagering, among others.

I. Entries and nominations
A. Entering
No horse shall be qualified to start unless it has been and continues to be entered.

B. Procedure
1. Entries and nominations shall be made with the racing secretary and shall not be considered until received by the racing secretary, who shall maintain a record of time of receipt of them for a period of one year.

2. An entry shall be in the name of the horse's licensed owner and made by the owner, trainer, or a licensed designee of the owner or trainer.

3. Races printed in the condition book shall have preference over substitute and extra races.

4. An entry must be in writing, by telephone, or facsimile machine to the racing secretary. The entry must be confirmed in writing should the stewards or the racing secretary so request.

5. The person making an entry shall clearly designate the horse so entered.

6. No alteration may be made in any entry after the closing of entries, but an error may be corrected with permission of the stewards.

7. No horse may be entered in more than one race (with the exception of stakes races) to be run on the same day on which pari-mutuel wagering is conducted.

8. Any permitted medication or approved change of equipment must be declared at time of entry.

C. Limitation as to spouses
No entry in any race shall be accepted for a horse owned wholly or in part by, or trained by, a person whose husband or wife is under license suspension at time of such entry; except that, if the license of a jockey has been suspended for a routine riding offense, the stewards may waive this rule.

D. Coupled entries
1. Two or more horses entered in a race shall be joined as a mutuel entry and single betting interest if they are owned or leased in whole or in part by the same owner or are trained by a trainer who owns or leases any interest in any of the other horses in the race.

2. No more than two horses having common ties through ownership or training may be entered in an overnight race. Under no circumstances may both horses of a coupled entry start to the exclusion of a single entry. When making a coupled entry, a preference for one of the horses must be made.

3. No entry shall be coupled in any race in which the gross purse is $1-million or more.

4. In all races in which paragraph D. 3. applies, the racing secretary shall have the authority to establish a mutuel field and coupled entries in any race with more than 14 starters.

E. Nominations
1. Any nominator to a stakes race may transfer or declare such nomination prior to closing.

2. Joint nominations and entries may be made by any one of joint owners of a horse, and each such owner shall be jointly and severally liable for all payments due.

3. Death of a horse, or a mistake in its entry when such horse is eligible, does not release the nominator or transferee from liability for all stakes fees due. No fees paid in connection with a nomination to a stakes race that is run shall be refunded, except as otherwise stated in the conditions of a stakes race.

4. Death of a nominator to a stakes race shall not render void any subscription, entry, or right of entry. All rights, privileges, and obligations shall be attached to the legal heirs of the decedent or the successor owner of the horse.

5. When a horse is sold privately or at public auction or claimed, stakes engagements shall be transferred automatically to its new owner; except when the horse is transferred to a person whose license is suspended or who is otherwise disqualified to race or enter the horse, then such nomination shall be void as of the date of such transfer.

6. All stakes fees paid toward a stakes race shall be allocated to the winner unless otherwise provided by the conditions for the race. If a stakes race is not run for any reason, all such nomination fees paid shall be refunded.

F. Closings
1. Entries for purse races and nominations to stakes races shall close at the time designated by the association in previously published conditions for such races. No entry, nomination, or declaration shall be accepted after such closing time; except in the event of an emergency or if an overnight

race fails to fill, the racing secretary may, with the approval of a steward, extend such closing time.

2. Except as otherwise provided in the conditions for a stakes race, the deadline for accepting nominations and declarations is midnight of the day of closing, provided they are received in time for compliance with every other condition of the race.

G. Number of starters in a race

The maximum number of starters in any race shall be limited to the number of starting positions afforded by the association starting gate and its extensions. The number of starters may be further limited by the number of horses that, in the opinion of the stewards, can be afforded a safe, fair, and equal start.

H. Split or divided races

1. In the event a race is canceled or declared off, the association may split any overnight race for which post positions have not been drawn.

2. Where an overnight race is split, forming two or more separate races, the racing secretary shall give notice of not less than 15 minutes before such races are closed to grant time for making additional entries to such split races.

I. Post positions

Post positions for all races shall be determined by lot and shall be publicly drawn in the presence of a steward or steward designee.

J. Also-eligible list

1. If the number of entries for a race exceeds the number of horses permitted to start, the racing secretary may create and post an also-eligible list.

2. If any horse is scratched from a race for which an also-eligible list was created, a replacement horse shall be drawn from the also-eligible list into the race in order of preference. If none is preferred, a horse shall be drawn into the race from the also-eligible list by public lot.

3. Any owner or trainer of a horse on the also-eligible list who does not wish to start the horse in such race shall so notify the racing secretary prior to scratch time for the race, thereby forfeiting any preference to which the horse may have been entitled.

4. A horse that draws into a straightaway race from the also-eligible list shall start from the post position vacated by the scratched horse. In the event more than one horse is scratched, post positions of horses drawing in from the also-eligible list shall be determined by public lot.

5. A horse that draws into a non-straightaway race from the also-eligible list shall start from the outermost post position. In the event more than one horse is scratched, post positions of horses drawing in from the also-eligible list shall be determined by public lot.

K. Preferred list

The racing secretary shall maintain a list of entered horses eliminated from starting by a surplus of entries, and these horses shall constitute a preferred list and have preference. The manner in which the preferred list shall be maintained and all rules governing such list shall be the responsibility of the racing secretary. Such rules must be submitted to the racing commission 30 days prior to the commencement of the race meeting and are subject to the approval of the commission.

II. Declarations and scratches

Declarations and scratches are irrevocable.

A. Declarations

1. A "declaration" is the act of withdrawing an entered horse from a race prior to the closing of entries.

2. The declaration of a horse before closing shall be made by the owner, trainer, or their licensed designee in the form and manner prescribed in these rules.

B. Scratches

1. A "scratch" is the act of withdrawing an entered horse from a contest after the closing of entries.

2. The scratch of a horse after closing shall be made by the owner, trainer, or their licensed designee, with permission from the stewards.

3. A horse may be scratched from a stakes race for any reason at any time up until 45 minutes prior to post time for that race.

4. No horse may be scratched from an overnight race without approval of the stewards.

5. In overnight races, horses that are physically disabled or sick shall be permitted to be scratched first. Should horses representing more than ten betting interests in the daily double or exotic wagering races, or horses representing more than eight betting interests in any other overnight race, remain in after horses with physical excuses have been scratched, then owners or trainers may be permitted at scratch time to scratch horses without physical excuses down to such respective minimum numbers for such races. This privilege shall be determined by lot if an excessive number of owners or trainers wish to scratch their horses.

6. Entry of any horse that has been scratched or excused from starting by the stewards because of a physical disability or sickness shall not be accepted until the expiration of three racing days after such horse was scratched or excused and the horse has been removed from the Veterinarian's List by the official veterinarian.

III. Weights

A. Allowances

1. Weight allowance must be claimed at time of entry and shall not be waived after the posting of entries, except by consent of the stewards.

2. A horse shall start with only the allowance of weight to which it is entitled at time of starting, regardless of its allowance at time of entry.

3. Horses not entitled to the first weight allowance in a race shall not be entitled to any subsequent allowance specified in the conditions.

4. Claim of weight allowance to which a horse is not entitled shall not disqualify it unless protest is made in writing and lodged with the stewards at least one hour before post time for that race.

5. A horse shall not be given a weight allowance for failure to finish second or lower in any race.

6. No horse shall receive allowance of weight nor be relieved extra weight for having been beaten in one or more races, but this rule shall not prohibit maiden allowances or allowances to horses that have not won a race within a specified period or a race of a specified value.

7. Except in handicap races that expressly provide otherwise, two-year-old fillies shall be allowed three pounds, and fillies and mares three years old and upward shall be allowed five pounds before September 1 and three pounds thereafter in races where competing against male horses.

B. Penalties

1. Weight penalties are obligatory.

2. Horses incurring weight penalties for a race shall not be entitled to any weight allowance for that race.

3. No horse shall incur a weight penalty or be barred from any race for having been placed second or lower in any race.

4. Penalties incurred and allowances due in steeplechase or hurdle races shall not apply to races on the flat, and vice versa.

5. The reports, records, and statistics as published by *Daily Racing Form*, Equibase, or other recognized publications shall be considered official in determining eligibility, allowances, and penalties, but may be corrected.

IV. Workouts
A. Requirements

A horse shall not start unless it has participated in an official race or has an approved timed workout satisfactory to the stewards. The workout must have occurred at a pari-mutuel or commission-recognized facility within the previous 30 days. A horse that has not started for a period of 60 days or more shall be ineligible to race until it has completed a timed workout approved by the stewards prior to the day of the race in which the horse is entered. The association may impose more stringent workout requirements.

B. Identification

1. Unless otherwise prescribed by the stewards or the commission, the official lip tattoo must have been affixed to a horse's upper lip or other identification method approved by the appropriate breed registry and the commission applied prior to its participation in workouts from the gate, schooling races, or workouts required for removal from the Stewards' List, Starter's List, Veterinarian's List, or Bleeder List.

2. The trainer or exercise rider shall take each horse scheduled for an official workout to be identified by the clocker or clocker's assistant immediately prior to the workout.

3. A horse shall be properly identified by its lip tattoo or other identification method approved by the appropriate breed registry and the commission immediately prior to participating in an official timed workout.

4. The trainer or trainer's designee shall be required to identify the distance the horse is to be worked and the point on the track where the workout will start.

C. Information dissemination

Information regarding a horse's approved timed workout or workouts shall be furnished to the public prior to the start of the race for which the horse has been entered.

D. Restrictions

A horse shall not be taken onto the track for training or a workout except during hours designated by the association.

V. Ineligible horses

A horse is ineligible to start in a race when:

1. It is not stabled on the grounds of the association or present by the time established by the commission;

2. Its breed registration certificate is not on file with the racing secretary or horse identifier, unless the racing secretary has submitted the certificate to the appropriate breed registry for correction;

3. It is not fully identified and tattooed on the inside of the upper lip or identified by any other method approved by the appropriate breed registry and the commission;

4. It has been fraudulently entered or raced in any jurisdiction under a different name, with an altered registration certificate or altered lip tattoo or other identification method approved by the appropriate breed registry and the commission;

5. It is wholly or partially owned by a disqualified person or a horse is under the direct or indirect training or management of a disqualified person;

6. It is wholly or partially owned by the spouse of a disqualified person or a horse is under the direct or indirect management of the spouse of a disqualified person, in such cases, it being presumed that the disqualified person and spouse constitute a single financial entity with respect to the horse, which presumption may be rebutted;

7. The stakes or entry money for the horse has not been paid in accordance with the conditions of the race;

8. The losing jockey mount fee is not on deposit with the horsemen's bookkeeper;

9. Its name appears on the Starter's List, Stewards' List, or Veterinarian's List;

10. It is a first-time starter and has not been approved to start by the starter;

11. It is owned in whole or in part by an undisclosed person or interest;

12. It lacks sufficient official published workouts or race past performance(s);

13. It has been entered in a stakes race and has subsequently been transferred with its engagements, unless the racing secretary has been notified of such prior to the start;

14. It is subject to a lien that has not been approved by the stewards and filed with the horsemen's bookkeeper;

15. It is subject to a lease not filed with the stewards;

16. It is not in sound racing condition;

17. It has had a surgical neurectomy performed on a heel nerve that has not been approved by the official veterinarian;

18. It has been trachea tubed to artificially assist breathing;

19. It has been blocked with alcohol or otherwise drugged or surgically denerved to desensitize the nerves above the ankle;

20. It has impaired eyesight in both eyes;

21. It is barred or suspended in any recognized jurisdiction;

22. It does not meet the eligibility conditions of the race;

23. Its owner or lessor is in arrears for any stakes fees, except with approval of the racing secretary;

24. Its owner(s), lessor(s), and/or trainer have not completed the licensing procedures required by the commission;

25. It is by an unknown sire or out of an unknown mare; or

26. There is no current negative test certificate for Equine Infectious Anemia attached to its breed registration certificate, as required by statute.

VI. Running of the race
A. Equipment

1. No whip shall be used unless it has affixed to the end of it a looped leather "popper" not less than 1¼" in width and not over 3" in length, and is "feathered" above the "popper" with not less than three rows of leather "feathers," each "feather" not less than 1" in length. No whip shall exceed 31" in length. All whips are subject to inspection and approval by the stewards.

2. No bridle shall exceed two pounds.

3. A horse's tongue may be tied down with clean bandages, gauze, or tongue strap.

4. No licensee may add blinkers to a horse's equipment or discontinue their use without the prior approval of the starter, the paddock judge, and the stewards.

5. No licensee may change any equipment used on a horse in its last race in this jurisdiction without approval of the paddock judge.

B. Racing numbers

1. Each horse shall carry a conspicuous saddlecloth number corresponding to the official number given that horse on the official program.

2. In the case of a coupled entry that includes more than one horse, each horse in the entry shall carry the same number, with a different distinguishing letter following the number. As an example, two horses in the same entry shall appear in the official program as 1 and 1A.

3. Each horse in the mutuel field shall carry a separate number or may carry the same number with a distinguishing letter following the number.

C. Jockey requirements

1. Jockeys shall report to the jockeys' quarters at the time designated by the association. Jockeys shall report their engagements and any overweight to the clerk of scales. Jockeys shall not leave the jockeys' quarters except to ride in scheduled races until all of their riding engagements of the day have been fulfilled, except as approved by the stewards.

2. A jockey who has not fulfilled all riding engagements who desires to leave the jockeys' quarters must first receive the permission of the stewards and must be accompanied by an association security guard.

3. While in the jockeys' quarters, jockeys shall have no contact or communication with any person outside the jockeys' quarters other than commission personnel and officials, an owner or trainer for whom the jockey is riding, or a representative of the regular news media, except with the permission of the stewards. Any communication permitted by the stewards may be conducted only in the presence of the clerk of scales or other person designated by the stewards.

4. Jockeys shall be weighed out for their respective mounts by the clerk of scales not more than 30 minutes before post time for each race.

5. Only valets employed by the association shall assist jockeys in weighing out.

6. A jockey must wear a safety vest when riding in any official race. The safety vest shall weigh no more than two pounds and be designed to provide shock-absorbing protection to the upper body of at least a rating of five as defined by the British Equestrian Trade Association (BETA).

7. A jockey's weight shall include his or her clothing, boots, saddle and its attachments, and any other equipment except the whip, bridle, bit or reins, safety helmet, safety vest, blinkers, goggles, and number cloth.

8. Seven pounds is the limit of overweight any horse is permitted to carry.

9. Once jockeys have fulfilled their riding engagements for the day and have left the jockeys' quarters, they shall not be readmitted to the jockeys' quarters until after the entire racing program for that day has been completed, except with permission of the stewards.

D. Paddock to post

1. Each horse shall carry the full weight assigned for that race from the paddock to the starting post, and shall parade past the stewards' stand, unless excused by the stewards. The post parade shall not exceed 12 minutes, unless otherwise ordered by the stewards. It shall be the duty of the stewards to ensure that the horses arrive at the starting gate as near to post time as possible.

2. After the horses enter the track, no jockey may dismount nor entrust his horse to the care of an attendant unless, because of accident occurring to the jockey, the horse, or the equipment, and with the prior consent of the starter. During any delay during which a jockey is permitted to dismount, all other jockeys may dismount and their horses may be attended by others. After the horses enter the track, only the jockey, an assistant starter, the official veterinarian, the racing veterinarian, or an outrider or pony rider may touch the horse before the start of the race.

3. If a jockey is injured on the way to the post, the horse shall be returned to the paddock or any other area designated by the stewards, resaddled with the appropriate weight, and remounted with a replacement jockey.

4. After passing the stewards' stand in parade, the horses may break formation and proceed to the post in any manner unless otherwise directed by the stewards. Once at the post, the horses shall be started without unnecessary delay.

5. Horses shall arrive at the starting post in post-position order.

6. In case of accident to a jockey or his or her mount or equipment, the stewards or the starter may permit the jockey to dismount and the horse to be cared for during the delay, and may permit all jockeys to dismount and all horses to be attended to during the delay.

7. If a horse throws its jockey on the way from the paddock to the post, the horse must be returned to the point where the jockey was thrown, where it shall be remounted and then proceed over the route of the parade to the post.

The horse must carry its assigned weight from paddock to post and from post to finish.

8. If a horse leaves the course while moving from paddock to post, the horse shall be returned to the course at the nearest practical point to that at which it left the course, and shall complete its parade to the post from the point at which it left the course unless ordered scratched by the stewards.

9. No person shall willfully delay the arrival of a horse at the post.

10. The starter shall load horses into the starting gate in any order deemed necessary to ensure a safe and fair start. Only the jockey, the racing veterinarian, the starter, or an assistant starter shall handle a horse at the post.

E. Post to finish

1. The start

a. The starter is responsible for assuring that each participant receives a fair start.

b. If, when the starter dispatches the field, any door at the front of the starting-gate stalls should not open properly due to a mechanical failure or malfunction or should any action by any starting personnel directly cause a horse to receive an unfair start, the stewards may declare such a horse a nonstarter.

c. Should a horse, not scratched prior to the start, not be in the starting-gate stall, thereby causing it to be left when the field is dispatched by the starter, the horse shall be declared a nonstarter by the stewards.

d. Should an accident or malfunction of the starting gate or other unforeseeable event compromise the fairness of the race or the safety of race participants, the stewards may declare individual horses to be nonstarters, exclude individual horses from one or more pari-mutuel pools, or declare a "no contest" and refund all wagers except as otherwise provided in the rules involving multirace wagers.

2. Interference, jostling, or striking

a. A jockey shall not ride carelessly or willfully so as to permit his or her mount to interfere with, impede, or intimidate any other horse in the race.

b. No jockey shall carelessly or willfully jostle, strike, or touch another jockey or another jockey's horse or equipment.

c. No jockey shall unnecessarily cause his or her horse to shorten its stride so as to give the appearance of having suffered a foul.

3. Maintaining a straight course

a. When the way is clear in a race, a horse may be ridden to any part of the course, but if any horse swerves or is ridden to either side so as to interfere with, impede, or intimidate any other horse, it is a foul.

b. The offending horse may be disqualified if,

in the opinion of the stewards, the foul altered the finish of the race, regardless of whether the foul was accidental, willful, or the result of careless riding.

c. If the stewards determine the foul was intentional or due to careless riding, the jockey may be held responsible.

d. In a straightaway race, every horse must maintain position as nearly as possible in the lane in which it starts. If a horse is ridden, drifts, or swerves out of its lane in such a manner that it interferes with, impedes, or intimidates another horse, it is a foul and may result in the disqualification of the offending horse.

4. Disqualification

a. When the stewards determine that a horse shall be disqualified for interference, they may place the offending horse behind such horses as in their judgment it interfered with, or they may place it last.

b. If a horse is disqualified for a foul, any horse or horses with which it is coupled as an entry may also be disqualified.

c. When a horse is disqualified for interference in a time-trial race, for the purposes of qualifying only, it shall receive the time of the horse it is placed behind plus one-hundredth of a second penalty or more exact measurement if photo-finish equipment permits, and shall be eligible to qualify for the finals or consolations of the race on the basis of the assigned time.

d. Possession of any electrical or mechanical stimulating or shocking device by a jockey, horse owner, trainer, or other person authorized to handle or attend to a horse shall be prima-facie evidence of a violation of these rules and is sufficient grounds for the stewards to scratch or disqualify the horse.

e. The stewards may determine that a horse shall be unplaced for the purpose of purse distribution and time-trial qualification.

5. Horses shall be ridden out

All horses shall be ridden out in every race. A jockey shall not ease up or coast to the finish without reasonable cause, even if the horse has no apparent chance to win prize money. A jockey shall give a best effort during a race, and each horse shall be ridden to win.

6. Use of whips

a. Although the use of a whip is not required, any jockey who uses a whip during a race shall do so only in a manner consistent with exerting his or her best efforts to win.

b. In all races where a jockey will ride without a whip, an announcement of such fact shall be made over the public address system.

c. No electrical or mechanical device or other expedient designed to increase or retard the speed of a horse, other than the whip approved

by the stewards, shall be possessed by anyone or applied by anyone to the horse at any time on the grounds of the association during the meeting, whether in a race or otherwise.

d. Whips shall not be used on two-year-old horses before April 1 of each year.

e. Prohibited use of the whip includes whipping a horse:

i. On the head, flanks, or on any other part of its body other than the shoulders or hindquarters except when necessary to control a horse;

ii. During the post parade or after the finish of the race except when necessary to control the horse;

iii. Excessively or brutally, causing welts or breaks in the skin;

iv. When the horse is clearly out of the race or has obtained its maximum placing;

v. Persistently even though the horse is showing no response under the whip; or

vi. Striking another rider or horse.

7. Horse leaving the racecourse

If a horse leaves the racecourse during a race, it must turn back and resume the race from the point at which it originally left the course.

8. Order of finish

a. The official order of finish shall be decided by the stewards with the aid of the photo-finish camera, and in the absence of the photo-finish film strip, the video replay. The photo finish and video replay are only aids in the stewards' decision. The decision of the stewards shall be final in all cases.

b. The nose of the horse shall determine the placement of the horse in relationship to other horses in the race.

9. Returning after the finish

a. After a race has been run, the jockey shall ride promptly to the place designated by the stewards, dismount, and report to the clerk of scales to be weighed in. Jockeys shall weigh in with all pieces of equipment with which they weighed out.

b. If a jockey is prevented from riding to the designated unsaddling area because of an accident or illness to the jockey or the horse, the jockey may walk or be transported to the scales or may be excused from weighing in by the stewards.

10. Unsaddling

a. Only persons authorized by the stewards may assist the jockey with unsaddling the horse after the race.

b. No one shall place a covering over a horse before it is unsaddled.

11. Weighing in

a. A jockey shall weigh in at least at the same weight at which he or she weighed out, and if under that weight by more than two pounds, his or her mount shall be disqualified from any

portion of the purse money.

b. In the event of such disqualification, all money wagered on the horse shall be refunded unless the race has been declared official.

c. No jockey shall weigh in at more than two pounds over the proper or declared weight, excluding the weight attributed to inclement weather conditions and/or of health and safety equipment approved by the stewards.

12. Dead heats

a. When two horses run a dead heat for first place, all purses or prizes to which first and second horses would have been entitled shall be divided equally between them; and this principle applies in dividing all purses or prizes whatever the number of horses running a dead heat and whatever places for which the dead heat is run.

b. In a dead heat for first place, each horse involved shall be deemed a winner and liable to penalty for the amount it shall receive.

c. When a dead heat is run for second place and an objection is made to the winner of the race and sustained, the horses that ran a dead heat shall be deemed to have run a dead heat for first place.

d. If the dividing owners cannot agree as to which of them is to have a cup or other prize that cannot be divided, the question shall be determined by lot by the stewards.

VII. Protests, objections, and inquiries
A. Stewards to inquire

1. The stewards shall take cognizance of foul riding and, upon their own motion or that of any racing official or person empowered by this chapter to object or complain, shall make diligent inquiry or investigation into such objection or complaint when properly received.

2. In determining the extent of disqualification, the stewards in their discretion may:

a. Declare null and void a track record set or equaled by a disqualified horse or any horses coupled with it as an entry;

b. Affirm the placing judges' order of finish and hold the jockey responsible if, in the stewards' opinion, the foul riding did not affect the order of finish; or

c. Disqualify the offending horse and hold the jockey blameless if in the stewards' opinion the interference to another horse in a race was not the result of an intentional foul or careless riding on the part of a jockey.

B. Race objections

1. An objection to an incident alleged to have occurred during the running of a race shall be received only when lodged with the clerk of scales, the stewards, or their designees, by the owner, the authorized agent of the owner, the trainer, or the jockey of a horse engaged in the same race.

2. An objection following the running of any race must be filed before the race is declared official, whether all or some riders are required to weigh in or the use of a "fast official" procedure is permitted.

3. The stewards shall make all findings of fact as to all matters occurring during and incident to the running of a race, shall determine all objections and inquiries, and shall determine the extent of disqualification, if any, of horses in the race. Such findings of fact and determinations shall be final.

C. Prior objections

1. Objections to the participation of a horse entered in any race shall be made to the stewards in writing, signed by the objector, and filed not later than one hour prior to post time for the first race on the day that the questioned horse is entered. Any such objection shall set forth the specific reason or grounds for the objection in such detail so as to establish probable cause for the objection. The stewards upon their own motion may consider an objection until such time as the horse becomes a starter.

2. An objection to a horse entered in a race may be made on, but not limited to, the following grounds or reasons:

a. A misstatement, error, or omission in the entry under which a horse is to run;

b. The horse entered to run is not the horse it is represented to be at the time of entry, or the age was erroneously given;

c. The horse is not qualified to enter under the conditions specified for the race, or the allowances are improperly claimed or not entitled the horse, or the weight to be carried is incorrect under the conditions of the race;

d. The horse is owned in whole or in part, or leased or trained by a person ineligible to participate in racing or otherwise ineligible to own a racehorse as provided in these rules; or

e. The horse was entered without regard to a lien filed previously with the racing secretary.

3. The stewards may scratch from the race any horse that is the subject of an objection if they have reasonable cause to believe that the objection is valid.

D. Protests

1. A protest against any horse that has started in a race shall be made to the stewards in writing, signed by the protestor, within 72 hours of the race exclusive of nonracing days. If the incident upon which the protest is based occurs within the last two days of the meeting, such protest may be filed with the commission within 72 hours exclusive of Saturdays, Sundays, or official holidays. Any such protest shall set forth the specific reason or reasons for the protest in such

detail as to establish probable cause for the protest.

2. A protest may be made on any of the following grounds:

a. Any grounds for objection as set forth in this chapter;

b. The order of finish as officially determined by the stewards was incorrect due to oversight or errors in the numbers of the horses that started the race;

c. A jockey, trainer, owner, or lessor was ineligible to participate in racing as provided in this chapter;

d. The weight carried by a horse was improper by reason of fraud or willful misconduct; or

e. An unfair advantage was gained in violation of the rules.

3. Notwithstanding any other provision in this article, time limitation on the filing of protests shall not apply in any case in which fraud or willful misconduct is alleged, provided the stewards are satisfied that the allegations are bona fide and verifiable.

4. No person shall file any objection or protest knowing the same to be inaccurate, false, untruthful, or frivolous.

5. The stewards may order any purse, award, or prize for any race withheld from distribution pending the determination of any protest. In the event any purse, award, or prize has been distributed to an owner or for a horse that by reason of a protest or other reason is disqualified or determined to be not entitled to such purse, award, or prize, the stewards or the commission may order such purse, award, or prize returned and redistributed to the rightful owner or horse. Any person who fails to comply with an order to return any purse, award, or prize erroneously distributed shall be subject to fines and suspension.

Registration Rules for Breeding

History of registration

The Jockey Club, an organization dedicated to improving Thoroughbred breeding and racing, registers more than 30,000 Thoroughbred foals each year, introducing them to the *American Stud Book* following a disciplined process of initiation that began more than 300 years ago.

Early in the 17th century, three stallions brought to England—the Darley Arabian, the Godolphin Arabian, and the Byerly Turk—became the foundation sires of the Thoroughbred industry. In 1791, James Weatherby published the first stud book, the *General Stud Book*. It listed the pedigrees of 387 mares that could each be traced to one of three descendants of the foundation sires: Eclipse, a direct descendant of the Darley Arabian; Matchem, a grandson of the Godolphin Arabian; and Herod, a great-great-grandson of the Byerly Turk.

In America, Patrick Edgar attempted to publish a national stud registry in 1833 but was unsuccessful. One year later, John Skinner reprinted the entire *General Stud Book* and added the existing pedigrees of American horses at the end. Following Skinner's effort, the pedigree section of *Mason's Farrier* was the only available resource until 1867, when John H. Wallace published *Wallace's American Stud Book*. Wallace soon abandoned the enterprise, which was a fiscal failure, and turned his attention to compiling the American Trotting Registry.

One year later, Col. Sanders D. Bruce published the *American Stud Book*. In 1896, the Jockey Club acquired the rights to Bruce's work. Now, more than 100 years later, the Jockey Club continues to maintain the *American Stud Book* to ensure the integrity of the breed.

Today, registering a Thoroughbred is as simple as logging onto the Internet. Through the Jockey Club Interactive™ (*http://www.registry. jockeyclub.com*), owners and breeders can complete registration forms, submit digital photos, review a database of active names, and check the status of a registration. A goal of the Jockey Club is to provide a virtual foal certificate that will eliminate paper, which can be lost, destroyed, or illegally altered, while at the same time providing real-time access to all registry-related information.

How to register

All requirements of the Principal Rules and Requirements of the *American Stud Book* must be met within one year of a foal's originally reported foaling date.

Step 1

For foals of 2001 and after, the foal's sire and dam must be DNA-typed. For foals of 2000 and earlier, the foal's sire and dam must be blood-typed.

Step 2

Report of Mares Bred (Deadline: August 1 each year)

Stallion owners must file a report of all Thoroughbred mares bred to a stallion in a breeding season (February-July).

Step 3

Live Foal/No Foal Report (Deadline: Within

30 days after foaling)

1. The owner of record in the Jockey Club files will receive a preprinted Live Foal/No Foal Report. Note: All changes of mare ownership should be reported to the Jockey Club immediately.

2. The Live Foal/No Foal Report must be filed within 30 days of the birth of a foal, or when it is determined that a mare will not have a foal. Note: The registration services department at the Jockey Club should be contacted if a preprinted Live Foal/No Foal Report is not received by the time the foal is born.

Step 4

DNA/Blood-Typing (Deadline: Within 45 days of receipt of DNA/blood kit)

1. Between four to seven months after the reported foaling date, a Registration DNA/Blood-typing Kit will be mailed to the address shown on the Live Foal/No Foal Report. Note: If DNA/blood kit is not used within 45 days, the DNA/blood-typing process may have to be restarted at an additional fee.

2. Mane hairs pulled/blood drawn from the foal must be mailed to the laboratory shown on the preprinted mailer.

Notes:

Helpful hints for taking a DNA sample:

• Clean the mane comb thoroughly before pulling the mane.

• Grasp the mane close to the neck to help ensure you get roots.

• Do not try to pull a sample if the mane is wet.

Helpful hints for drawing blood:

• If, for some reason, a syringe must be used to draw blood, insert needle through stopper and depress plunger on syringe slowly.

• Do not remove stoppers or chemicals from tubes.

• Do not shake tubes; turn them end over end.

• Refrigerate blood if not mailing the same day. (Do not put tubes in Styrofoam container during refrigeration, and do not freeze the sample).

• Do not mail samples on the weekend or immediately before a holiday. (If samples are untestable on receipt by laboratory, another kit will be mailed and the process must be repeated).

Step 5

Registration/DNA-Typing/Blood-Typing Form (Deadline: Send to the Jockey Club when DNA/blood sample is mailed to lab. Before sending to the Jockey Club, be certain that):

1. Both sides of form are completed, including:

i) Written description of markings, indicating:

• All white markings.

• All flesh-colored markings.

• All dark and chestnut markings on coronet.

• All head and neck cowlicks (except cowlick at the very top of forehead).

• Any other distinguishing characteristics.

ii) Signature by foal's owner or authorized agent.

iii) One to six name choices. (This could avoid additional naming fees).

2. A set of four color photos is enclosed, clearly showing color and all markings from the front, back, and both sides. Note: Do not take photographs until the foal has shed its "baby hair."

3. The Stallion Service Certificate (acquired from the stallion owner) is attached.

4. Fee payment is enclosed.

How to name a horse

A. A name may be claimed on the Registration Form, on a Name Claiming Form, or through Jockey Club Interactive™. Name selections should be listed in order of preference. Names will be assigned based upon availability and compliance with the naming rules as stated herein. Names may not be claimed or reserved by telephone. When a foreign language name is submitted, an English translation must be furnished to the Jockey Club. An explanation must accompany "coined" or "made-up" names that have no apparent meaning. Horses born in the United States, Puerto Rico, or Canada and currently residing in another country must be named by the Jockey Club through the Stud Book Authority of their country of residence.

B. If a valid attempt to name a foal is submitted to the Jockey Club by February 1 of the foal's two-year-old year and such a name is determined not eligible for use, no additional fee is required for a subsequent claim of name for that foal. If a valid attempt to name a foal is not submitted to the Jockey Club by February 1 of the foal's two-year-old year, a fee is required to claim a name for such a foal.

C. A reserved name must be used within one year (365 days) from the day it was reserved. Reserved names cannot be used until written notification requesting the assignment of the name to a specific horse is received by the Registry Office. If the reserved name is not used within one year (365 days) from its reservation, it will thereafter be available for any horse. A fee is required to reserve a name for a foal.

D. A foal's name may be changed at any time prior to starting in its first race. Ordinarily, no name change will be permitted after a horse has started in its first race or has been used for breeding purposes. However, in the event a name must be changed after a horse has started in its first race, both the old and new names must be used until the horse has raced three times following the name change. The prescribed fee and the Certificate of Foal Registration must

accompany any request to the Registry Office for a change of name.

E. Names of horses more than ten years old may be eligible if they are not excluded under Rule F and have not been used during the preceding five years either in the stud or on the turf.

Names of both geldings and horses that never raced or were not used in the stud may be available five years from the date of their death as reported.

F. The following classes of names are not eligible for use:

1. Names consisting of more than 18 letters (spaces and punctuation marks count as letters).

2. Initials such as C.O.D., F.O.B., etc.

3. Names ending in "filly," "colt," "stud," "mare," "stallion," or any similar horse-related term.

4. Names consisting entirely of numbers, except numbers above 30 may be used if they are spelled out.

5. Names ending with a numerical designation such as "2nd" or "3rd," whether or not such a designation is spelled out.

6. Names of persons unless written permission to use their name is on file with the Jockey Club.

7. Names of "famous" people no longer living unless approval is granted by the Board of Stewards of the Jockey Club.

8. Names of "notorious" people.

9. Names of racetracks or graded stakes races.

10. Recorded names such as assumed names or stable names.

11. Names clearly having commercial significance, such as trade names.

12. Copyrighted material, titles of books, plays, motion pictures, popular songs, etc., unless the applicant furnishes the Jockey Club with proof that the copyright has been abandoned or that such material has not been used within the past five years.

13. Names that are suggestive or have a vulgar or obscene meaning.

14. Names that are currently active either in the stud or on the turf, and names similar in spelling or pronunciation to such names.

15. Permanent names and names similar in spelling or pronunciation to permanent names. The list of criteria to establish a permanent name is as follows:

a. Horses in the Racing Hall of Fame;

b. Horses that have been voted Horse of the Year;

c. Horses that have won an Eclipse Award;

d. Horses that have won a Sovereign Award (Canadian championship);

e. Annual leading sire and broodmare sire by progeny earnings;

f. Cumulative money winners of $2-million or more;

g. Horses that have won the Kentucky Derby (G1), Preakness Stakes (G1), Belmont Stakes (G1), Jockey Club Gold Cup (G1), Breeders' Cup Classic (G1), or Breeders' Cup Turf (G1);

h. Horses included in the International List of Protected Names.

G. In addition, the Registrar of the Jockey Club reserves the right of approval on all name-claiming requests.

Age definitions

Foal: A young horse of either sex in its first year of life.

Suckling: A foal of any sex in its first year of life while it is still nursing.

Weanling: A foal of any sex in its first year of life after being separated from its dam.

Yearling: A colt, filly, or gelding in its second calendar year of life (beginning January 1 of the year following its birth).

Two-Year-Old: A colt, filly, or gelding in its third calendar year of life (beginning January 1 of the year following its yearling year).

Color definitions

The following colors are recognized by the Jockey Club:

Bay: The entire coat of the horse may vary from a yellow-tan to a bright auburn. The mane, tail, and lower portion of the legs are always black, unless white markings are present.

Black: The entire coat of the horse is black, including the muzzle, the flanks, the mane, tail, and legs, unless white markings are present.

Chestnut: The entire coat of the horse may vary from a red-yellow to a golden-yellow. The mane, tail, and legs are usually variations of coat color, unless white markings are present.

Dark Bay/Brown: The entire coat of the horse will vary from a brown, with areas of tan on the shoulders, head, and flanks, to a dark brown, with tan areas seen only in the flanks and/or muzzle. The mane, tail, and lower portion of the legs are always black, unless white markings are present.

Gray/Roan: In order to reduce the number of corrections involving the colors gray and roan, the Jockey Club has combined these colors into one color category. This does not change the individual definitions of the colors for gray and roan and in no way impacts on the two-coat color inheritance principle as stated in (a previous rule).

Gray: The majority of the coat of the horse is a mixture of black and white hairs. The mane, tail, and legs may be either black or gray, unless white markings are present.

Roan: The majority of the coat of the horse is a mixture of red and white hairs or brown and white hairs. The mane, tail, and legs may be

black, chestnut, or roan, unless white markings are present.

Breeding terminology

Bred (Mated): Any filly or mare that has undergone the physical act of breeding (mating).

Bred (Area Foaled): The term "bred" is sometimes used to describe the location where a foal was born; i.e., Kentucky-bred, New York-bred, etc.

Breeder: The breeder of a foal is the owner of the dam at the time of foaling, unless the dam was under a lease or foal-sharing agreement at the time of foaling. In that case, the person(s) specified by the terms of the agreement is (are) the breeder of the foal.

Stallion: A male horse that is used to produce foals.

Sire: A male horse that has produced, or is producing, foals.

Broodmare: A filly or mare that has been bred (mated) and is used to produce foals.

Dam: A female horse that has produced, or is producing, foals.

Maiden: A filly or mare that has never been bred (mated).

In Foal (Pregnant) Broodmare: A filly or mare that was bred (mated), conceived, and is currently in foal (pregnant).

Aborted: A term used to describe a broodmare that has been pronounced in foal (pregnant) based on an examination of 42 days or more post breeding (mating) and lost her foal prematurely; or a broodmare from whom an aborted fetus has been observed.

Barren (Not Pregnant): A term used to describe a filly or mare, other than a maiden mare, that was bred (mated) and did not conceive during the last breeding season.

Breeding (Mating): The physical act of a stallion mounting a filly or mare with intromission and ejaculation of semen into the reproductive tract.

Sex terminology

Colt: An entire male horse four years old or younger.

Horse: When reference is made to sex, a "horse" is an entire male five years old or older.

Ridgling ("rig"): A lay term used to describe either a monorchid or cryptorchid.

Cryptorchid: A male horse of any age that has no testes in his scrotum but was never gelded (the testes are undescended).

Monorchid: A male horse of any age that has only one testicle in his scrotum—the other testicle was either removed or is undescended.

Gelding: A male horse of any age that is unsexed—had both testicles removed.

Filly: A female horse four years old or younger.
Mare: A female horse five years old or older.

Deadlines

Report of Mares Bred (Stallion Reports): This report must be filed by August 1 of the breeding year.

Live Foal/No Foal Report (Mare Reports):
• Reporting live foal information. This report must be filed no later than 30 days after the foaling date.
• Reporting no foal information. This report must be filed no later than 30 days after the intended foaling date or in January if the mare was "not bred."

Foal registration: All requirements must be completed by one year from the foaling date, including blood typing.

Naming: Must be named by February 1 of two-year-old year to avoid paying a fee.

Death: Must be reported within 30 days of the death.

Foreign registration: Requirements must be met within 60 days of the horse's arrival to avoid paying an additional fee.

Export: Requirements must be met within 90 days of the horse's departure to avoid paying an additional fee.

Geldings and spayed females: Must be reported immediately.

Fees

Foal registration fees: If all requirements are completed within the one-year deadline (includes DNA/blood-typing of the foal and parentage verifications, as well as ownership transfers and corrections):

Foals of 2000 or later: $200

If DNA/blood kit is used and foal is not registered: $80

By December 31 of yearling year: $525

By December 31 of two-year-old year: $775

Beyond December 31 of two-year-old year: $2,000

Reserved names: $50

Foal-naming fee: After February 1 of the foal's two-year-old year. (Before this date, no fee is required): $50

Name-change fee: $100

DNA/blood-typing fees:
DNA/blood-typing, entry into the Ownership Registry: $80
Restart/Reactivate DNA/blood-typing case: $80

Duplicate certificate fee: $150

Corrected certificate fee (six months after original certificates issued): $50

Certificate of exportation fees:
If all requirements are completed within 60

days of the horse's departure from the United States, Canada, or Puerto Rico: $150

If all requirements are completed after 60 days of the horse's departure from the United States, Canada, or Puerto Rico: $400

Certificate of foreign registration fees:
If all requirements are completed within 60 days of the horse's arrival in the United States, Canada, or Puerto Rico: $150

If all requirements are completed after 60 days and up until one year of the horse's arrival in the United States, Canada, or Puerto Rico: $400

If all requirements are not completed within one year of the horse's arrival in the United States, Canada, or Puerto Rico, and the horse is eligible for late registration: $750

American horses returning to the U.S.:
$150
Thirty-day (foreign) racing permit fee:
If applied for within 30 days of the horse's arrival in the United States, Canada, or Puerto Rico: $150
Express handling fee: $50

How to contact the Jockey Club:
Address: The Jockey Club, 821 Corporate Drive, Lexington, KY 40503-2794
Telephone: (859) 224-2700
Registration Services: (800) 444-8521
Fax: (859) 224-2710
Web site: *http://home.jockeyclub.com*
Jockey Club Interactive™ Web site: *http://www.registry.jockeyclub.com*

How to Handicap a Race

Handicapping a horse race is fun and intellectually challenging, and it also can be profitable. This does not mean you are destined to retire to a life of luxury if you learn how to handicap, but you can have winning afternoons and even winning years at the racetrack.

There is no feeling in the world quite like the one when you have correctly handicapped a race, a feeling that is tangibly rewarded if you bet your selection. Picking a winner evokes a feeling of pride as well as bragging rights with your friends. Handicapping is an intellectual exercise, a skill that should improve as you become more experienced—as long as you are realistic.

Wagering at racetracks is pari-mutuel, which means bettors are competing against other bettors in every single race. (See following section on pari-mutuel wagering and odds.) There is no single right way to handicap. But a good start is setting up a realistic framework.

Framework of reality
You are not going to win every race. Nobody does. No person has the magic answer to crank out winner after winner—not public handicappers, the expensive daily sheets, speed handicappers, system players, or your Aunt Tillie betting her favorite colors.

The reality of horse racing is that, year after year, at every track in North America, favorites in Thoroughbred racing win 25% to 35% of the time. This means the betting public is wrong two out of three times. If you can correctly handicap vulnerable favorites, you will be able to identify overlays, which simply means horses whose odds are higher than they should be. Locating one or two overlays can allow you to have a successful afternoon. An underlay is a horse whose odds are shorter than justified by past performances

Track condition abbreviations

Thoroughbred racing is contested on dirt and turf, the latter also called grass. The abbreviations for track conditions:

Dirt	Turf
ft: fast	**hd:** hard
gd: good	**fm:** firm
sy: sloppy	**gd:** good
my: muddy	**yl:** yielding
	sf: soft

or physical condition.

A fundamental point here is that there is a difference between handicapping and wagering. Money management, which is deciding which races to bet and how to bet them with a myriad of options available, is a whole different ballgame. But money management also is a skill you can hone. For now, remember: There are no rules that state you have to bet every race or even any race.

Reading past performance lines
The raw materials for handicapping any race are past performances, statistical pictures of the horses' previous starts. Past performances are contained in either *Daily Racing Form* or a program published by the track. In general, the *Racing Form*, a tabloid newspaper, provides slightly more information than the magazine-size track past-performance programs.

Before you tackle the past-performance lines, you will want to understand the abbreviations and terms in the accompanying boxes. You will run into them both in past performances and in news accounts of races. You cannot handicap

Orange

7

2-1

MONARCHOS (L)

Gr/Rn.c 98 Maria s Mon-Regal Band by Dixieland Band

Breeder: J. D. Squires (KY) (February 9, 1998)

GOLD, light blue blocks, white stripes on sleeves, gold cap

Owner: John C. Oxley

Trainer: John T. Ward Jr (1-0-0-0)

Jorge F. Chavez (2-1-1-0)

126

Turf:	0	0	0	0	$0	**2001:** 5 4 1 0		**$1,601,600**
Off Track:	0	0	0	0	$0	**2000:** 2 0 0 1		**$4,030**
						Life: 7 4 1 1		**$1,605,630**

05May01	8CD	1¼	ft	:44^{86}	1:35^{00}	1:59^{97}	3 Ky Derby G1-1000K	16	13^{16}	10^{7½}	6^{2¼}	2^{½}	1^{4¾}	Chavez,J	L	126	10.50	**94**	Mnrchos 4¾ ,InvsbleInk ^{ns} ,Cngre 4	bmp start,rally 6wide	17
14Apr01	10Aqu	1⅛	ft	:46^{12}	1:10^{11}	1:47^{96}	3 WoodMenG2-750k	2	5^{7}	5^{7¼}	5^{5¼}	2^{5}	2^{2¾}	Chavez,J	L	123	*.90	**94**	Cngare 2¾ ,Narchos 7 ,RchlyBlended 4	inside run, gamely	6
10Mar01	11GP	1⅛	ft	:46^{82}	1:11^{47}	1:49^{95}	3 FlaDerbyG1-1000k	7	11^{7¾}	11^{7¾}	7^{1½}	1^{2}	1^{4½}	Chavez,J	L	122	*1.40^{e}	**94**	Mnrchs 4½ ,Otfthbox 2½ ,Invsblink ½	strong 6 wide move	13
03Feb01	10GP	1$\frac{1}{16}$	ft	:47^{99}	1:12^{42}	1:43^{31}	3 Alw35000nw1/x	3	3^{2}	2^{2½}	2^{1½}	1^{½}	1^{4¾}	Chavez,J	L	120	*2.00	**88**	Monarchos 4¾ ,Dstiled 3¾ ,ThnderBlitz 7	drew away,driving	11
13Jan01	8GP	7f	ft	:22^{56}	:45^{58}	1:22^{37}	3 Msw	3	8	3^{2}	1^{1}	1^{3}	1^{6}	Chavez,J	L	122	5.50	**90**	Monarchos 6 ,Tampa 3¼ ,JudgeSilver ½	inside, drew away	12
24Nov00	7CD	6½f	ft	:21^{88}	:45^{82}	1:18^{13}	2 Msw	6	10	11^{13¼}	11^{13½}	7^{11½}	3^{5¼}	Martinez, W	L	120	13.50	**72**	Dream Run ^{hd} ,BigTalkinMan 5¾ , Monarchos ½	no space late threat	12
07Oct00	4Kee	7f	ft	:22^{02}	:45^{83}	1:22^{20}	2 Msw	11	7	7^{3½}	6^{4}	10^{9¼}	8^{12½}	Cooksey, P	L	120	9.80	**70**	DvilsDomain 4 ,PrvateSon 1¾ ,MandThe ^{hd}	tired after 1/2	12

Workouts: **14May Pim 1m ft 1:52.80 b 1/1** **27Apr CD 4f ft :48.80 b 6/26** **08Apr CD 5f ft 1:00.20 b 4/21** **01Apr CD 5f sy 1:02.40 b 3/10**

without reading and comprehending past-performance lines, and doing so is surprisingly easy—no matter how intimidating *Daily Racing Form* or track programs appear to beginners.

Let's start with the big picture and examine one past-performance line, that of 2001 Kentucky Derby (G1) winner Monarchos when he ran in the Preakness Stakes (G1) at Pimlico Race Course. Beneath the race number and the conditions for that race—for example, whether it is restricted to fillies or three-year-olds or claiming horses running for a specified price—are the horses in that race. The names are listed in post position order in the *Racing Form*. A racetrack program will list the horses by the numbers they will be wearing on their saddlecloths in the race. This is the number you will use when placing a bet.

In cases of betting entries, which are usually two or more horses owned by the same person or under the care of the same trainer, those horses will be listed first as program number 1. The horse closest to the rail will be 1, and the other horse will be 1A. Beneath the program numbers are the betting odds—set by a track employee—and the post position in cases of entries.

Let's continue with the past-performance lines of Monarchos (courtesy of Equibase LLC, which provides past-performance information to both *Daily Racing Form* and track programs).

Each horse's name will have with it specific information about the horse: color, age with date of birth, sire, dam, the sire of the dam, state where foaled, and the breeder. Also in the header are the colors of the owner's silks, the weight to be carried (126 pounds in this case), names of the owner, trainer, and jockey with the records of the trainer and jockey at that track. The capital letter L in parentheses after the horse's name indicates it was treated with the antibleeding medication furosemide. The horse's race record is at the far right. It contains the racing record for this year and last (the number of starts, followed by wins, seconds, thirds, and earnings), a lifetime record, and the horse's record on wet tracks, at the same distance as this race, and at Pimlico. To that point, Monarchos had never run on a wet track, at 1$\frac{3}{16}$ miles, or at Pimlico.

Beneath all that information are the horse's past performances. Each past-performance line is a compilation of that horse's performance in a race, starting with the most recent race on top.

Types of bets

Win Your horse must finish first to collect.

Place Your horse must finish first or second.

Show Your horse must finish first, second, or third.

Quinella You bet two horses and they must finish first and second in either order.

Exacta You bet two horses and they must finish first and second in exact order.

Exacta box A multiple bet in which you select two or more horses and bet all combinations of them finishing first and second.

Exacta wheel You bet one horse to win and every other horse in the field to finish second.

Triple or trifecta You bet three horses and they must finish first, second, and third in exact order.

Triple or trifecta box A multiple bet in which you select three horses and they must finish first, second, and third in any order.

Superfecta You bet four horses and they must finish first, second, third, and fourth in exact order.

Superfecta box You bet four horses and they must finish first, second, third, and fourth in any order.

Daily (or instant, late, or middle) double You must pick the winners of two consecutive races.

Pick three or four You must pick the winners of three or four consecutive races.

Pick six You must pick the winners of six consecutive races. There is usually a consolation payoff if you select five.

The past-performance line can be split into thirds. Let's start with the left one-third of the past performance:

05May01-CD8 1¼m   ft   Stk   Kentucky DerbyG1

This identifies Monarchos's most recent race: on May 5, 2001, it was the eighth race at Churchill Downs (CD8), the distance was 1¼ miles, the track was fast, the type of race was a stakes, the name of the race was the Kentucky Derby, and it was a Grade 1 race—one of 101 highest-ranked stakes races in the United States. (See section on graded stakes.)

The next set of numbers reveals how the race was run and gives additional information on Monarchos:

78 :44⁸⁶ 1:59⁹⁷ 16 13¹⁶ 2¹ 1⁴³⁴ ChavezJF 11-1 **94**

The first boldface number is Monarchos's early pace number, which is more useful in sprint- and middle-distance races. Monarchos did not have any early speed, and he had a relatively low number. The next two numbers are the times in which the leader completed the first half-mile and the complete race distance.

Because of its tight format, the Equibase past-performance line lists only the half-mile time. *Daily Racing Form* past performances contain more fractional times and therefore provide a better picture of a race's pace, which is an important consideration when handicapping.

The next numbers describe where Monarchos was in the race. The first number, 16, is his post position. He was the 16th horse out from the rail in the 2001 Kentucky Derby. The next numbers with superscript figures tell how Monarchos ran his race. The first number, 13¹⁶, indicates that Monarchos was in 13th position after a half-mile and 16 lengths behind the leader.

The next number, 2¹, is Monarchos's position at the furlong pole, which is one-eighth mile from the finish line. This number is not totally accurate. Race charts—more on those later—provide a complete picture of the race, and the Derby chart has Monarchos second by a half-length. The number was adjusted to a whole number for space considerations.

Racing terms and comments

Here are some terms commonly used in racing news stories and chart footnotes. Additional terms can by found in the following chapter, Glossary of Terms.

Apprentice An inexperienced jockey. Horses with apprentice jockeys carry five, seven, or ten pounds less than their rivals.

Bolted The horse made a sharp, sudden move to the extreme outside.

Bore in or bore out Instead of racing in a straight line, the horse veered inside or outside.

Boxed in The horse was trapped with nowhere to move.

Brushed The horse made light contact with another horse.

Dogs Pylons or traffic cones put around a course to protect the area on the inside near the rail. Horses that work around dogs cover more distance on turns. The symbol is (d) in a workout.

Driving The horse was all out to win.

Entry Two or more horses are coupled in the wagering because of common ownership or, in some jurisdictions, the same trainer. You bet on one and collect if either member of the entry wins.

Field Two or more horses coupled as one betting entity. Just as in an entry, you get more than one horse and collect if any horse in the field wins.

Furlong One-eighth of a mile.

Furosemide A diuretic commonly used in American Thoroughbred racing to prevent or limit pulmonary bleeding. Trade name is Salix (formerly Lasix).

Gamely The horse showed courage.

Greenly The horse showed inexperience by racing erratically.

Handily The horse won comfortably.

Hung The horse made an apparent winning move but then failed to sustain it.

Ridden out The jockey continued to ride the winning horse to the wire.

Route A race of one mile or longer.

Saved ground The horse raced on the inside, thereby taking a shorter route around the track than its opponents.

Sprint A race shorter than one mile.

Steadied The jockey had to physically stop his riding motion because of traffic problems.

Taken up The jockey had to restrain his horse severely, usually because of traffic problems or interference.

Unruly The horse acted up before the start.

Used up The horse expended all its energy by contesting the pace early in the race.

Willingly The horse continued to run its best without undo urging.

The last number, $1^{43/4}$, is his finish position, which means he won by $4\frac{3}{4}$ lengths. Again, Equibase's data are skeletal, revealing little of what occurred in the intervening five-eighths of a mile. *Daily Racing Form* past performances have more points of call, as the position figures are known. In a $1\frac{1}{4}$-mile race such as the Derby, the *Form*'s points of call are at each quarter-mile, the furlong pole (also known as the stretch call), and the finish.

Next in the past-performance line is the jockey, the approximate betting odds at post time (actually 10.50-to-1 rather than 11-to-1), and Monarchos's speed rating. The higher the speed rating, the better. Speed ratings adjust for different conditions and other factors. His 94 figure was good but not great, even though Monarchos was the second-fastest Derby winner in history—behind only the great Secretariat. So what happened? The Churchill Downs track was freaky fast that day, with three track records falling, and Monarchos's speed figure was adjusted to take into account the very fast track.

Here is the righthand one-third of the past-performance line:

Monarchos$^{4\,3/4}$ InvisibleInk^{no} Congaree^4 bmp start, rally 6wide

This part of the past-performance line lists the top three finishers and the distances separating them. Invisible Ink closed late to take second, a nose in front of Congaree, who was four lengths ahead of the fourth finisher. The comments at the end reveal a bit about how the race was run. Monarchos was bumped at the start (bmp start) and rallied six horse widths off the rail (rally 6wide) to gain the victory.

Underneath the horse's past-performance lines are its workouts with the date, the track or training track where he worked, the time, whether the horse was breezing, which means not at full speed, or if it worked handily (under urging from his rider), and how that workout compared to all the horses that worked the same distance that morning on that track. Workouts can be very important, particularly when they are coming back after a layoff, but Monarchos's was not. He was galloping fast enough that Pimlico's clockers—the individuals who time workouts—caught him going a mile in 1:52^{80} and classified it as breezing.

Both program and *Daily Racing Form* past performances provide a bare outline of a race. The full details of a race are found in the charts, which are compiled by Equibase at North American tracks. The charts provide detailed information on how the race was run and footnotes that detail each horse's trip in that race. Serious handicappers often will save all charts from the track they attend most often to provide details unavailable in the past-performance lines because of space restrictions.

Three Schools of Handicapping

There are three main schools of handicapping—form, class, and speed—each taking different approaches. Class asks: How much ability has this horse shown and what has been the quality of its competition? Form asks: How has this horse performed most recently and how is it most likely to race today? Speed simply asks: How fast is this horse?

Handicappers have been arguing for decades over which one of the three schools is most important. A healthy understanding of each will aid your handicapping.

Class

One way class can be measured is by the level of competition the horse has faced in its past. That is why it is so important to read past-performance lines from the bottom line (least recent) up to see how a horse is coming into today's race and whether or not it has previously faced other horses in this race. (See box, How to improve your handicapping.) Let's say we're handicapping a race for $10,000 claimers. Horse A's last race was in an $8,000 claimer, which he won. So he is now moving up to $10,000. But previously in his past-performance lines, he may have already raced in $10,000 claimers or for an even higher claiming price. How he previously performed at that level could be vital information in evaluating his chances when moving up to the $10,000 level today.

A second way class can be gauged is by a horse's average earnings per start. Horse B has made $50,000 in his career from ten starts. Horse C has made $55,000 in his career from 25 starts. Horse B's average earnings per start, $5,000, are considerably higher than Horse C, whose average per start is $2,200. Be aware, though, that money does not mean everything. Earnings in races restricted to horses bred in one state—for example, for California-breds only—can inflate a horse's earnings and present a distorted picture of its ability to compete in the race you are handicapping.

A third way to measure class is by the number of wins a horse has or does not have. Chronic losers should be avoided at all costs. If a maiden has had ten or more starts without a win, stay away. If an allowance horse has had 15 starts or more with only one win, stay away. This strategy may not work every time, but in the long run you will save yourself a bundle of money by avoiding horses that find a way to lose and frequently get overbet because they always come close to winning.

Form

Horses are athletes, not machines. Even the best horses cannot maintain their highest level of performance for an extended period of time, which is why Cigar's 16-race winning streak in the mid-1990s was so remarkable.

Experienced horses tend to run in form cycles. They are either moving forward or backward. Many times, horses tip off which direction they are headed in a previous race. If a horse had been performing very poorly for several races and then shows a sign of life by perhaps rallying from ninth to fourth, it may very well improve again in its next start.

If a horse who had been racing well throws in a clinker, was there a legitimate excuse? Did it get overextended in a speed duel, get forced wide, or run into traffic? Did that problem cause its poor performance or simply masquerade it? Again, going through all of a horse's past-performance lines will frequently give clues. If a horse races wide in four of five starts, there is a great chance it will do it again if it draws an outside post position.

You should expect young horses to improve. Monarchos is an example. In his first career start as a two-year-old in 2000, Monarchos had the 11 post position, advanced to sixth, fell back to tenth, and rallied to finish eighth, losing a seven-furlong race by 12½ lengths at odds of 9.80-to-1 at Keeneland Race Course. In his second start, a 6½-furlong race at Churchill Downs in November 2000, he fell back to 11th in the field of 12 before rallying strongly to finish third by 5½ lengths at 13.50-to-1, closing 7½ lengths in the final 2½ furlongs. Though the comment in the *Daily Racing Form* of his run in the race said, "No late threat," Monarchos had definitely improved and showed that he wanted to beat horses. His third start was at Gulfstream Park in a seven-furlong race on January 13, 2001. The extra half-furlong could only help his running style. He went off at 5.50-to-1 in the field of 12 and won by six lengths. He subsequently won a Gulfstream allowance race and the Florida Derby (G1) before finishing second in the Wood Memorial Stakes (G2) at Aqueduct.

Another example is 2001 Arkansas Derby (G2) winner Balto Star. In his first start, a six-furlong sprint at Belmont in 2000, he was bet down to 6-to-5 (1.20-to-1) but tired badly to finish eighth in a race that was not run especially fast. Treated with the medication furosemide to limit pulmonary bleeding (a condition common to many race-horses), he went off at 4.60-to-1, was prominent early, and faded late to finish fifth. Trainer Todd Pletcher then took an unorthodox step, taking a horse that had tired in two sprint races and entering him in a 1⅛-mile race. Although tiring late, Balto Star finished fourth, beaten 6¾ lengths.

Five Ways to Improve Your Handicapping

1. Always handicap past performance lines from the bottom (least recent) to the top. This strategy will definitely give you an edge on other bettors who only handicap a horse's most recent few races. This process helps you to find potentially important information. Maybe two or more of the horses in this race competed against each other previously, and perhaps more than once.

2. Get and use as much pertinent information as you can. Read the analysis boxes in *Daily Racing Form* next to a horse's past-performance lines. Use the significant statistics that the *Form* provides underneath each horse's past-performance lines, such as a trainer's record with two-year-olds or with layoff horses or switching a horse from dirt to grass. Subscribe to THOROUGHBRED TIMES and peruse the sire statistics, especially for grass horses and two-year-olds. The more you learn, the better handicapper you become.

3. Improve your knowledge of odds, wet-track horses, and horses' ability to race on grass based on their breeding. When you study a race, write down what you think the final odds will be and then see how they compare with the actual final odds. For a turf race or a race on a wet track, write down who you think will perform well. Do the same thing with two-year-olds. Then see how they do. These are exercises that will only take you a couple minutes, and in time you will develop a better sense of the game.

4. Watch as many races as you can. Watch the replays of the prior day's races shown before the first race every day, or videotape the late-night recap shows on television that some tracks offer. If your track or off-track betting facility has a replay center, where you can look up most horses' last race or several recent races, make use of it. You are allowed to take notes.

5. Cross out a horse's irrelevant past performance lines, such as grass races when handicapping a dirt race. With a stroke of pen or pencil, you can wipe out starts that are immaterial to today's race and concentrate on the pertinent starts.

The trainer then shortened the distance to $1\frac{1}{16}$ miles for his next race on January 1, 2001, and the gelding continued his improvement, winning by 11 lengths. He subsequently won an Aqueduct allowance race and Turfway Park's Spiral Stakes (G2) by more than 12 lengths before his Arkansas Derby victory.

A final note on form: When a horse follows a good performance with a fast workout, expect him to maintain his edge.

Speed

If every race went to the horse with the highest speed figure, racing would become quite boring and not much fun to bet on. Speed is part of the equation, but it is not the complete answer. Speed must always be considered in context. If a horse is a front-runner with good early speed, is it the lone speed in the race? Or will it be pressured? And, if so, how hard will it be pressed?

There is a world of difference between a horse running loose on the lead—running freely without pressure from other horses—and being pressed hard on the lead by one or two others. If there are three speed horses in the race, has any one of them ever rated from just off the pace? And, if so, has that horse won when doing so? Maybe the horse has a past-performance line four races back that had a similar scenario.

This is another reason to go over a horse's past-performance lines from the bottom up. For example, a race might contain three speed horses—they usually break sharply from the gate and dictate the early pace of the race. Examine the three speed horses' opening quarter-mile and half-mile times in each of their races. If one of them routinely runs a quarter-mile in :22 and a half in :45 while the other two show :23 and :46 splits, it is reasonable to assume the other two horses will not make the lead and therefore should be discarded.

If a horse has shown speed and tired under early pressure, make sure it will be pressured again in today's race. If not, it may be able to go gate to wire, which means leading from start to finish. Also, some speed horses must be on the lead to win, and watch out for those that will not extend themselves when they do not make the lead.

Always be sure to differentiate speed in sprints from speed in races at one mile or longer, which are known as route races. A front-runner in a longer race may be able to dictate the early pace while running the first half-mile in 48 seconds. If entered in a sprint, the same horse might be required to run a :46 half-mile to be on the lead.

What is good speed?

Almost any Thoroughbred can go one furlong (one-eighth mile) in 12 seconds (:12) and two furlongs in :24. Maintaining or exceeding that rate an additional furlong or furlongs constitutes a sharp workout, be it three furlongs in :36, or four furlongs in :48. The farther the workout, the more impressive the move. *Daily Racing Form* will tell you how each horse's workout compared with other horses that worked the same morning at the same distance. The best of the day is marked with a bullet in front of the date of the workout. Factor in that training tracks are slower than main tracks, so a good workout on a training track should be given greater consideration.

Changes

Change is good, sometimes. They are worth noting all the time, be it equipment, the use of furosemide (Salix), track surface, or a change in jockey, trainer, or both. The most common equipment change is the addition or removal of blinkers. Blinkers tend to keep a horse more focused because its field of sight has been narrowed. Subsequently, most horses adding blinkers show more early speed. Conversely, horses that have blinkers removed may show less speed. Again, it is important to check a horse's past-performance lines to see whether it ever raced with (or without) blinkers and how it performed.

Horses using furosemide for the first time frequently improve greatly. Other horses improve the second time they use furosemide, presumably because they become accustomed to its diuretic effects. Past performances in *Daily Racing Form* and some past-performance programs reveal how much of a difference furosemide can make. For example, Live Doppler finished fourth by 18½ lengths in a one-mile, $25,000 maiden claimer at Aqueduct without furosemide in late April 2001. Treated with furosemide a few hours before his next race under the same conditions and at the same distance, he finished second by 2½ lengths. It was the same track, same distance, and same level of competition, but a vastly different result.

A change from dirt to grass or vice versa can be a defining moment for many horses. Many times, there is absolutely no connection between a horse's form on dirt and grass. We need only think of Cigar, a superstar on dirt and just another horse on turf. When a horse has raced on dirt and is making his first grass start, check *Daily Racing Form* statistics for the trainer's record with first-time turf horses and read the *Form*'s analysis of the race, which frequently discusses that horse's grass breeding.

Jockey changes can be important if there is a significant difference in the two riders' abilities.

When a horse switches riders from a Chris McCarron to a Gary Stevens, the impact is minimal because they are both Racing Hall of Fame jockeys. A switch from a jockey with a poor record to McCarron or vice versa is significant. When there is a rider switch, check the two riders' records in the *Racing Form*.

Jockeys, just like horses, can perform at different levels on dirt and grass. Jerry Bailey is one of the top jockeys on dirt, but on grass he's in a class by himself. Other jockeys win less frequently in turf races. Usually, apprentices do better on dirt than on grass.

Layoffs

No Thoroughbred races 12 months a year. They need time off. But once they have resumed racing, there should not be long gaps between their races or in their workouts. These absences often are a sign of unsoundness. If a horse races well, shows no workouts for a month, and then races again, be wary. If there is a gap of more than a month between workouts, something happened to stop this horse's training.

Use the statistics in the *Form* to see a trainer's percentage of winners with horses off significant layoffs. And go through the horse's past-performance lines from the bottom up to see if it has ever raced off similar layoffs. If they have, how did they perform?

Post positions

Post positions are extremely important in turf racing because the turns are much tighter with the grass course on the inside of the dirt course. You can check out how many winners are coming from each post position on the dirt track and grass course in the *Form* or daily program. Invariably, you will find that horses from the extreme outside posts have not done well on grass. For example, at the Pimlico 2001 spring meet from March 28 through May 6, post position eight was zero for 13, post nine one for 11 and post positions 10 through 12 had produced no winners. You should factor that information into your handicapping. If a horse breaks from the 12 post, races wide, and rallies for fourth, it may do much better in its next start with a better post position.

On some dirt courses, races at seven furlongs and one mile may be more difficult for horses breaking from the first post position, immediately next to the rail. If a horse is devoid of early speed, it most likely will get caught behind faster pacesetters and will be trapped behind horses when ready to make a run at the leaders.

Trainer patterns

Trainers have patterns and proclivities, and you should be aware of them. Some are more adept with older horses while others excel with two-year-olds. Some do equally well on grass and dirt; others definitely do not. Some train their horses hard, and others do the exact opposite. Some can have their horses fit to race off long layoffs, but others never do.

Thanks to the innovations of the *Racing Form* over the past few years, much of that information is readily available to all handicappers by the trainer statistics at the bottom of each horse's past performance lines. They will show each trainer's percentage of winners with horses coming off layoffs, first time on grass, first-time starters, first start after claiming a horse, stretching out from sprint to route, and other significant statistics. Trainers also can have winning and losing streaks. If a trainer has been struggling but does well with a couple horses, other horses in his barn may be ready to perform better, too.

Handicapping two-year-olds

Handicapping horses with established form is difficult enough. Handicapping a two-year-old maiden race loaded with first-time starters is even more daunting. Here are some clues. First-timer starters with several good workouts— for example, four furlongs in :48 or :49 and five furlongs in 1:00 or 1:01—do as well as those with one blazing bullet workout at three furlongs, in :35⅗ or :36. Some trainers' horses usually improve dramatically in their second or third starts. Some stallions are extremely proficient at siring precocious two-year-olds. Other sires' progeny do well in distance races or on turf. Again, going through available statistics can only help your handicapping.

Weight

In general, the longer the race, the more important the weight assignment. If trainers regarded weight as unimportant, they would not rush to use every hot apprentice that shows up with a five-pound weight allowance.

Weight can be overrated, but the significant factor is how a horse's weight in today's race relates to the assignments of the other horses. If two horses had been close to each other in their previous start at equal weights and now one of them carries three pounds more and the other five pounds less, that eight-pound swing could mean a lot.

Final thought

In many ways, handicapping is comparable to a chess match. Many factors must be considered to forecast how a race will unfold and how those factors will affect the race's outcome. The process can be mind-twisting at first, but in time your handicapping will become more skillful and more fun. Good luck and good racing.—*Bill Heller*

Handicapping a Sample Race

Six three-year-olds started in the eighth race at Aqueduct on April 20, 2001, a $48,000 allowance at one mile run on a fast track. By post position order, they were:

1. Dash 'n Dance. He had been extremely impressive winning his first two career starts, a maiden race by 2¾ lengths at 9-to-2 odds and an allowance race by a neck with a furious late rally at 8-to-1. Moved up to stakes company, he finished a distant fourth at 6-to-1 in the field of six. In his previous start, his first on a sloppy track, he was second by three lengths to Late Extra, who also was entered for this April 20 race. Since that start, Dash 'n Dance had had two workouts, both on the Belmont Park training track: four furlongs in :48⅕, the third-fastest of 30 horses at that distance on April 9, and a bullet workout of four furlongs in :48, the fastest of 45 horses at that distance on April 15.

2. Late Extra. Until his victory in the slop, he had compiled a record of one win in a $40,000 maiden claimer, three seconds, and three thirds in nine dirt starts. His sixth in his lone turf race was irrelevant for this race on dirt. In his victory on a sloppy track, he pressed the pace in :22⅘ for the first quarter-mile and then edged clear by 1½ lengths after a half-mile in :46⅕. He opened a 5½-length lead in the stretch and won by three lengths. The comment in the *Racing Form* was, "When asked, cruised." He had not worked since. What's important to note is that in all three of his route tries, he had lost ground in the stretch. It's also worth noting that he had carried four pounds less than Dash 'n Dance in their last race. Today, they carried equal weight.

3. Cliffdiver. The New England shipper had won three straight starts dating back to the previous November: an allowance race, a $25,000 stakes by a neck at six furlongs, and, in his prior start, a one-length, gate-to-wire victory in a $25,000 Suffolk Downs stakes at 9-to-2. How that stakes race compared to an allowance race at Aqueduct was difficult to gauge. The quality of racing at Suffolk is significantly lower than racing in New York and this purse is almost twice the size of his two stakes wins, but one of Cliffdiver's stakes races was at this distance. His two workouts after his stakes race were slow ones at Suffolk Downs—five furlongs in 1:05 (ninth-fastest of ten) and four furlongs in :50 (third-fastest of ten).

4. Welcome Matt. This shipper had two wins and two seconds in his first four starts, all at Philadelphia Park. After running sixth of seven in the Count Fleet Stakes at Aqueduct, he was fourth of eight in a stakes at Laurel Park. Given nearly two months off, he returned to win an allowance race at a mile and 70 yards at Philadelphia Park, prevailing by a head as the 9-to-10 favorite. His workout for this race was five furlongs in 1:02⅕ at Philadelphia (13th-fastest of 38).

5. Mercenary. Though it took a while for him to get going—he required seven starts to score his maiden victory—he had followed with an allowance victory on a sloppy track, a sixth in the Best Turn Stakes (in which he finished 1½ lengths behind Dash 'n Dance), and a third in a tougher allowance race at this distance of one mile behind Ommadon, a top two-year-old the previous year. His two workouts since were slow.

6. Rapid Ryan. He had won three of his first five starts but then had run a distant fourth in an allowance race at this distance. Given more than six weeks off, he had returned with blinkers for the first time. Sent off at 6-to-1, he was a strong second in a quickly run sprint, 1:10⅗. He followed that good effort with three good workouts, the first two on the Belmont training track: four furlongs in :49 (11th-fastest of 60), and five furlongs in 1:02⅖, which was second-fastest of eight. His final workout on the main track at Belmont was five furlongs in 1:00⅖, eighth-fastest of 36.

Analysis: In an obviously well-balanced race, Late Extra figured to be overbet off his victory in a sprint on a sloppy track. He had tired in all his route races. Dash 'n Dance had done little wrong in his career. Finishing second by three lengths while making his first start on a sloppy track was hardly a disgrace, and his two sharp workouts since suggested he was at the top of his game. He had rallied in all four of his starts, all at six furlongs, and figured to be able to stretch out to one mile (eight furlongs) without a problem. Of the others, Cliffdiver and Welcome Matt were the unknowns, but each had won a route race in his most recent start. Mercenary was certainly a factor, and Rapid Ryan's return race with blinkers was sharp. The top selection was Dash 'n Dance, who went off at 3.65-to-1. Late Extra was favored at 4-to-5, Mercenary 4-to-1, Rapid Ryan 10-to-1, Cliffdiver 12-to-1, and Welcome Matt 13-to-1.

The result? Cliffdiver, the Suffolk shipper, dueled Late Extra into defeat but could not hold off Dash 'n Dance, who won by a nose and paid $9.30. Welcome Matt was third, followed by Rapid Ryan, Mercenary, and Late Extra.

How Pari-Mutuel Wagering Began

Virtually all betting on horse races in North America, as in most countries, is conducted using the pari-mutuel wagering system. Unlike a casino, where bettors play against the house, racehorse bettors bet against each other, with the track holding the bets and, after taking out money for the track, purses, state taxes, etc., returning the money bet to the winning patrons after each race is run.

Unlike most traditions in North American horse racing, pari-mutuel wagering came from France rather than England. The system was devised in the mid-1860s by Pierre Oller, a Paris perfume merchant who had become disenchanted with the city's bookmakers.

Oller developed a variation of the auction pool, in which betting interests in individual horses were sold. Because fairly large sums of money were required to buy the winning interest in a favorite in the auction pools, they were not widely used by small-scale bettors. Oller's system allowed small wagers on all horses and quickly came into wide use in France. He called his wagering system perier mutuel, which means to wager among ourselves. Adopted in England, it became known as Paris mutuals, and finally pari-mutuel.

New York tracks used the pari-mutuel system (known then as Paris pools) in the early 1870s. Col. M. Lewis Clark, the founder of Churchill Downs, observed the pari-mutuels in operation during a sojourn in Europe in the early 1870s and introduced the devices at his track in 1878. (Auction pools were used in 1875, 1876, and 1877, the first three years of Churchill's existence.)

Bookmakers soon made their appearance in both New York and Louisville, and the popularity of betting with bookmakers supplanted the pari-mutuel machines. Clark abandoned pari-mutuels in 1889 at the demand of bookmakers.

In 1908, however, anti-Churchill forces took over City Hall and banned bookmaking. Col. Matt Winn, then the track's general manager, rounded up six of the old pari-mutuel machines, refurbished them, and used them for betting on the 1908 Kentucky Derby. Pari-mutuel wagering on the Derby day program that year was $67,570 ($18,300 of that total on the Derby, won by Stone Street at 23.72-to-1 odds), with another $12,669 in auction pools.

The first machines sold only one denomination of ticket, $5 for the 1908 Derby program, but by 1911 Winn had commissioned new machines that offered $2, $5, and $10 tickets. By 1914, most American tracks had switched to the pari-mutuel system as antigambling sentiment led to bans against bookmaking.

Betting Odds and Payouts

Pari-mutuel betting odds are based on the percentage of the net wagering pool placed on each horse. For instance, a horse sent off at even money, or 1-to-1 odds, has attracted 50% of the net wagering pool.

The net wagering pool on which the odds are based is total wagering minus deductions broadly known as takeout—money taken out for state tax, horsemen's purses, the track's share, and other deductions. Total wagering is known as handle, which the track holds until after each race is run and then returns the net balance to winning bettors.

When devising a program betting line, also known as the morning line, a line maker generally will assign odds based on 125% of handle to account for takeout.

All tracks in North America show payouts after each race on their tote boards based on a $2 wager. To figure the exact odds, for instance, at which a horse went off in the win pool, subtract the $2 bet and divide by two. If a horse paid $4.70 to win, its winning odds were 1.35-to-1 ([$4.70-$2]/2=1.35).

Exact betting odds usually are rounded down to the nearest 10 cents, although some jurisdictions round to the next lowest 5 cents. Rounding is used so pennies and nickels are not used in paying off winning bettors. The money left over from rounding is known as breakage. Individual state laws determine how this breakage money is distributed at the end of the year.

Odds	Percentage of handle	Pari-mutuel payout
1-to-20	95.23%	$2.10
1-to-10	90.91	2.20
1-to-5	83.33	2.40
2-to-5	71.42	2.80
1-to-2	66.66	3.00
4-to-5	55.55	3.60
Even (1-to-1)	50.00	4.00
7-to-5	41.67	4.80
9-to-5	35.71	5.60
2-to-1	33.33	6.00
5-to-2	28.57	7.00
3-to-1	25.00	8.00
7-to-2	22.23	9.00
4-to-1	20.00	10.00
9-to-2	18.19	11.00
5-to-1	16.67	12.00
10-to-1	9.09	22.00
15-to-1	6.25	32.00
20-to-1	4.76	42.00
30-to-1	3.23	62.00
50-to-1	1.96	102.00
100-to-1	0.99	202.00

Distance equivalents

Distances of races have been directly or indirectly derived from distances conventionally run in England, the cradle of Thoroughbred racing. Distances of English races are measured in the traditional English system of furlongs and miles. A furlong is 660 feet, or one-eighth of a mile, and a mile is comprised of eight furlongs.

France used the metric system instituted by Napoleon for its racing since the inception of racing in that country. As racing countries around the world have adopted the metric system of measurement, racing distances often have been changed to metric equivalents.

The following table includes equivalent distances for both systems.

Furlongs to Meters

Furlongs	Miles	Approx. meters	Exact meters
1.00	1/8	200	201.168
2.00	1/4	400	402.336
3.00	3/8	600	603.504
4.00	1/2	800	804.672
4.50	9/16	900	905.256
5.00	5/8	1,000	1,005.840
5.50	1 1/16	1,100	1,106.424
6.00	3/4	1,200	1,207.008
6.50	1 3/16	1,300	1,307.592
7.00	7/8	1,400	1,408.176
7.50	1 5/16	1,500	1,508.760
8.00	1	1,600	1,609.344
8.32	1&70 yds.	1,670	1,673.717
8.50	1 1/16	1,700	1,709.928
9.00	1 1/8	1,800	1,810.512
9.50	1 3/16	1,900	1,911.096
10.00	1 1/4	2,000	2,011.680
10.50	1 5/16	2,100	2,112.264
11.00	1 3/8	2,200	2,212.848
11.50	1 7/16	2,300	2,313.432
12.00	1 1/2	2,400	2,414.016
12.50	1 9/16	2,500	2,514.600
13.00	1 5/8	2,600	2,615.184
13.50	1 11/16	2,700	2,715.768
14.00	1 3/4	2,800	2,816.352
14.50	1 13/16	2,900	2,916.936
15.00	1 7/8	3,000	3,017.520
15.50	1 15/16	3,100	3,118.104
16.00	2	3,200	3,218.688
16.50	2 1/16	3,300	3,319.272
17.00	2 1/8	3,400	3,419.856
18.00	2 1/4	3,600	3,621.024
19.00	2 3/8	3,800	3,822.192
20.00	2 1/2	4,000	4,023.360
21.00	2 5/8	4,200	4,224.528
22.00	2 3/4	4,400	4,425.696
23.00	2 7/8	4,600	4,626.864
24.00	3	4,800	4,828.032

Meters to Furlongs

Meters	Approx. furlongs	Approx. miles	Exact furlongs	Exact miles
200	1.00	1/8	0.9942	.1243
400	2.00	1/4	1.9884	.2485
600	3.00	3/8	2.9826	.3728
800	4.00	1/2	3.9768	.4971
900	4.50	9/16	4.4739	.5592
1,000	5.00	5/8	4.9710	.6214
1,100	5.50	11/16	5.4681	.6835
1,200	6.00	3/4	5.9652	.7456
1,300	6.50	13/16	6.4623	.8078
1,400	7.00	7/8	6.9594	.8699
1,500	7.50	15/16	7.4565	.9321
1,600	8.00	1	7.9536	.9942
1,670	8.32	1&70 yds.	7.9784	.9973
1,700	8.50	1 1/16	8.4506	1.0563
1,800	9.00	1 1/8	8.9477	1.1185
1,900	9.50	1 3/16	9.4448	1.1806
2,000	10.00	1 1/4	9.9419	1.2427
2,100	10.50	1 5/16	10.4390	1.3049
2,200	11.00	1 3/8	10.9361	1.3670
2,300	11.50	1 7/16	11.4332	1.4292
2,400	12.00	1 1/2	11.9303	1.4913
2,500	12.50	1 9/16	12.4274	1.5534
2,600	13.00	1 5/8	12.9245	1.6156
2,700	13.50	1 11/16	13.4216	1.6777
2,800	14.00	1 3/4	13.9187	1.7398
2,900	14.50	1 13/16	14.4158	1.8020
3,000	15.00	1 7/8	14.9129	1.8641
3100	15.50	1 15/16	15.4100	1.9263
3200	16.00	2	15.9071	1.9884
3300	16.50	2 1/16	16.4042	2.0505
3400	17.00	2 1/8	16.9013	2.1127
3500	17.50	2 3/16	17.3984	2.1748
3600	18.00	2 1/4	17.8955	2.2369
3700	18.50	2 5/16	18.3926	2.2991
3800	19.00	2 3/8	18.8897	2.3612
3900	19.50	2 7/16	19.3868	2.4233
4000	20.00	2 1/2	19.8839	2.4855
4100	20.50	2 9/16	20.3810	2.5476
4200	21.00	2 5/8	20.8781	2.6098
4300	21.50	2 11/16	21.3752	2.6719
4400	22.00	2 3/4	21.8723	2.7340
4500	22.50	2 13/16	22.3694	2.7962
4600	23.00	2 7/8	22.8665	2.8583
4700	23.50	2 15/16	23.3636	2.9204
4800	24.00	3	23.8607	2.9826

Countries and Measurements Used

Argentina....................................furlongs and meters
Australia ....meters
Brazil...meters
Canada ....furlongs
Chile...meters
England ....furlongs
France...meters
Germany ....meters
Hong Kong ....meters
Ireland ....furlongs
Italy ....meters
Japan...meters
New Zealand....................................meters
United Arab Emirates.................meters
United States ....furlongs

Glossary of Common Racing and Breeding Terms

account wagering Betting by phone, in which a bettor must open an account with a track or an off-track agency. A synonym: phone betting.

acey-deucy Uneven stirrups, popularized by Racing Hall of Fame jockey Eddie Arcaro, who rode with his left (inside) iron lower than his right to achieve better balance on turns.

across the board A bet on a horse to win, place, and show. If the horse wins, the player collects three ways; if second, two ways (place and show); and if third, one way (show).

action 1) A horse's manner of moving. 2) A term meaning wagering.

added money Money added to the purse of a race by the racing association, a breeding fund, or other source. The association's money is added to the amount paid by owners in nomination, eligibility, entry, and starting fees. Added-money stakes became less common in the 1990s as more tracks went to guaranteed purses.

agent A person empowered to transact business for a stable owner or a jockey, or one empowered to sell or buy horses for an owner or a breeder.

airing Not running at best speed in a race; usually used in reference to a horse in an easy winning effort.

all-age race A race for two-year-olds and up.

all out When a horse extends itself to the utmost.

allowance race A race for which the racing secretary drafts certain conditions to determine weights to be carried based on the horse's age, sex, past performance, or a combination of all three.

allowances Reductions in weights to be carried, with the adjustments based on the conditions of the race or because an apprentice jockey is on a horse. Also, a weight reduction that female horses are entitled to when racing against males or that three-year-olds receive against older horses.

also-eligible A horse officially entered for a race but not permitted to start unless the field is reduced by scratches below a specified number.

also-ran A horse that does not finish first, second, or third.

American Horse Council A national association of individuals, organizations, and companies formed as a lobbying group to represent all breeds of the horse industry. Based in Washington, D.C., the AHC works on tax regulations, import and export rules, disease prevention and control, trails and recreation enhancement, and humane concerns. Founded in 1969, AHC was formed as an advocate of the entire American horse industry though started principally by Thoroughbred interests concerned about legislation that was being discussed in Congress that would have negatively affected racing and breeding.

American Stud Book Official book of foal registrations in North America maintained by the Jockey Club.

apprentice jockey Rider at the beginning of his career who has not ridden a certain number of winners within a specified period of time. Also known as a bug rider, from the asterisk used in racing programs and past performances to denote the weight allowance such riders receive.

apprentice allowance Weight concession given to an apprentice rider: usually ten pounds until the fifth winner, seven pounds until the 35th winner, and five pounds for one calendar year from the 35th winner. More rarely, a three-pound allowance is allowed to a rider under contract to a specific stable or owner for two years from his or her first win. This rule varies from state to state. Apprentices do not receive an allowance when riding in a stakes race. All jockeys going from track to track must have a receipt from the clerk of scales from their track verifying the jockey's most recent total number of wins.

apron The (usually) paved area between the grandstand and the racing surface.

Association of Racing Commissioners International (RCI) Formerly the National Association of State Racing Commissioners (NASRC). Its office is based in Lexington.

asterisk Used with names of horses to denote they were imported into the United States. Practice preceded the use of country codes starting January 1, 1977.

auxiliary starting gate A second starting gate used when the number of horses in a race exceeds the capacity of the main starting gate.

average earnings index (AEI) A breeding statistic that compares racing earnings of a stallion's or mare's foals to those of all other foals racing at that time. An AEI of 1.00 is considered average, 2.00 is twice the average, 0.50 half the average, etc.

baby race A race for two-year-olds.

backstretch 1) Straight portion of the far side of the racing surface between the turns. 2) Generally, a racetrack's stable area, which often contains dormitories, a track kitchen, chapel, and recreation area for stable employees. It gained its name because most stable areas are located along the racetrack's backstretch.

bad doer A horse with a poor appetite, a condition that may be due to nervousness or other causes.

bandage Wrappings used on a horse's legs are three to six inches wide and are made of a variety of materials. In a race, they are used for support or protection against injury. Rundown bandages are used during a race to affix a pad under the fetlock to avoid injury due to abrasion when the fetlocks sink toward the ground during the weight-bearing portion of the canter. A horse may also wear standing bandages, thick cotton wraps used during shipping and while in the stall to prevent swelling, injury, or both, or to apply medication.

bar shoe A horseshoe closed at the back to help support the frog and heel of the hoof. It is often worn by horses with quarter cracks or bruised feet.

base The portion of the track that lies under the thick top layer, or cushion. The base provides support and drainage.

bat A jockey's whip.

battery A term for an illegal electrical device used by a jockey to stimulate a horse by electrical

shock during a race. Also known as a machine or a joint.

bay A horse color that varies from a yellow tan to a bright auburn. The mane, tail, and lower portion of the legs are always black, except where white markings are present.

bearing in (or out) Deviating from a straight course. May be due to weariness, infirmity, inexperience, or the rider overusing the whip or reins to make a horse alter its course.

bell Signal sounded when the starter opens the gates or, at some tracks, to mark the close of betting.

Beyer number A handicapping tool, popularized by author Andrew Beyer, assigning a numerical value (speed figure) to each race run by a horse based on final time and track condition. This enables different horses running at different racetracks to be objectively compared.

bid in The act of buying back a horse that does not meet a minimum price at public auction. Synonym for buy-back, reserve not attained (RNA).

Big Red Refers to either of two famous chestnut-colored horses: Man o' War or Secretariat.

Bill Daly (on the) Taking a horse to the front at the start of a race and remaining there to the finish. Term stems from "Father Bill" Daly, a famous old-time horseman who developed many great jockeys.

birthdays All Thoroughbreds born in the Northern Hemisphere celebrate their birthday on January 1. In the Southern Hemisphere, all Thoroughbred birthdays are as follows: South America, July 1; South Africa, Australia, and New Zealand, August 1.

bit A stainless steel, rubber, or aluminum bar attached to the bridle; it is placed in the bar, the space between front and back teeth in the horse's mouth, and is one of the means by which a jockey exerts guidance and control. The most common racing bit is the D-bit, named because the rings extending from the bar are shaped like the letter D. Most racing bits are snaffled (snaffle bit), which means the metal bar is made up of two pieces, connected in the middle, which leaves it free to swivel. Other bits may be used to correct specific problems, such as bearing in or out.

black A horse color that includes the hair and the skin of the muzzle, flanks, mane, tail, and legs, unless white markings are present.

black type Boldface type, used in sales catalogs and stakes results, to distinguish horses that have won or placed in a stakes race. Sales companies today have eliminated the use of black type for stakes below a certain monetary level—$15,000 in 1985; $20,000 from 1986-'89; $25,000 beginning in 1990; and $30,000 beginning in 2002. If a horse's name appears in boldface capital letters in a catalog or stakes results, the horse has won at least one black-type event. If the name appears in boldface type with capital and lower-case letters, the horse was second or third in at least one black-type event.

blaze A generic term describing a large, white vertical marking on a horse's face.

bleeder A horse that bleeds within its lungs when small capillaries that surround the lungs' air sacs (alveoli) rupture. The veterinary term is exercise-induced pulmonary hemorrhage. Blood may be seen coming out of the horse's nostrils, known as epistaxis, although it is typically discovered by an examination using a fiber-optic endoscope after exercise or racing. Hot, humid weather and cold conditions are known to exacerbate the problem. The most common preventive treatment currently available is the use of the diuretic furosemide (Salix). Less than one bleeder in 20 shows signs of epistaxis.

blind switch A circumstance in which a rider's actions cause him to be impeded during a race by moving into a space in which he finds himself blocked.

blinkers A cup-shaped device to limit a horse's vision and thus prevent it from swerving from objects or other horses on either side while racing. Blinker cups come in a variety of sizes and shapes to allow as little or as much vision as the trainer feels is necessary.

blister Counterirritant causing acute inflammation used to increase blood supply and blood flow and to promote healing in the leg.

bloodstock Horses of Thoroughbred breeding, especially such horses used for or considered in relation to racing.

bloodstock agent A person who advises or represents a buyer or a seller of Thoroughbreds at a public auction or a private sale. A bloodstock agent usually works on commission, often 5% of the purchase or sale price, and can also prepare a horse for sale.

blood typing A way to verify a horse's parentage. Blood typing was usually completed within the first year of a horse's life and was necessary before registration papers were issued by the Jockey Club. Beginning in 2001, the Jockey Club adopted DNA technology to verify horse's parentage.

blowout A short, timed workout, usually a day or two before a race, designed to sharpen a horse's speed. Usually three-eighths or one-half mile in distance.

blue hen Used to describe a great broodmare, the producer of a number of stakes winners and whose daughters, granddaughters, and great-granddaughters in turn produced important winners.

board Short for tote board, on which odds, betting pools, and other information are displayed.

boat race Slang for a fixed race.

bobble A bad step away from the starting gate, usually caused by the track surface breaking away from under a horse's hooves, causing it to duck its head or nearly go to his knees.

bolt Sudden veering from a straight course, usually to the outside rail.

bomb(er) A winning horse sent off at extremely high odds.

book 1) The group of mares being bred to a stallion in a given year. If a stallion attracts the maximum number of mares allowed by the farm manager, he has a full book. 2) A term used to describe a jockey's riding commitments with his agent.

bookie Short for bookmaker.

bookmaker A person who books bets.

bottom 1) Stamina in a horse developed over a long period of time. 2) Subsurface of a racing strip.

bottom line A Thoroughbred's breeding on the female side. It is the lower half of an extended pedigree diagram.

bounce A poor race run immediately after a career-best or near-best performance.

box 1) A wagering term denoting a combination bet whereby all possible numeric combinations are covered for certain horses. 2) A disadvantageous position in a race, behind and between horses.

boxed (in) To be trapped between, behind, or inside of other horses.

brace (or bracer) Rubdown liniment used on a horse after a race or workout.

break 1) To train a young horse to wear a bridle and saddle, carry a rider, and respond to a rider's commands. Most often done when the horse is a yearling. 2) To leave from the starting gate.

breakage In pari-mutuel payoffs, which are rounded down to a nickel or dime, the pennies that are left over. Breakage may be used for any of a number of purposes. Depending upon a state's rules of racing, the money goes to the state, the track, purses, or benevolence programs.

breakdown When a horse suffers a potentially career-ending injury, usually to a leg.

breather Easing off on a horse for a short distance in a race to permit it to conserve or renew its strength.

bred A horse is considered to have been bred in the state or country where it was foaled.

breeder Owner of the dam at time of foaling unless the dam was under a lease or foal-sharing arrangement at the time of foaling. In that case, the person(s) specified by the terms of the agreement is (are) the breeder(s) of the foal.

breed-back rule Restriction imposed in some jurisdictions that for a mare's offspring to be eligible for state-bred bonuses, the mare, after foaling, must be bred to a stallion standing in that state.

Breeders' Cup Thoroughbred racing's year-end championship. Known as Breeders' Cup day, Breeders' Cup championship day, or beginning in 2001 as World Thoroughbred Championships, it consists of races conducted on one day at one of several major North American racetracks each year. The Breeders' Cup concept was developed by Lexington breeder John R. Gaines. The first Breeders' Cup races were run in 1984 at Hollywood Park in Inglewood, California. Breeders' Cup day now comprises eight races totaling $13-million in purses: $1-million Breeders' Cup Sprint, for three-year-olds and older at six furlongs; $1-million Breeders' Cup Juvenile Fillies, for two-year-old fillies at 1$\frac{1}{16}$ miles; $2-million Breeders' Cup Distaff, for three-year-olds and older, fillies and mares, at 1$\frac{1}{8}$ miles; $1-million Breeders' Cup Mile, for three-year-olds and older at one mile on turf; $1-million Breeders' Cup Juvenile, for two-year-olds at 1$\frac{1}{16}$ miles; $1-million Filly and Mare Turf, for fillies and mares at 1$\frac{3}{8}$ miles on turf; $2-million Breeders' Cup Turf, for three-year-olds and older at 1$\frac{1}{2}$ miles on turf; $4-million Breeders' Cup Classic, for three-year-olds and older at 1$\frac{1}{4}$ miles. The Classic was raised to $4-million from $3-million beginning with the 1996 running at Woodbine; the Distaff was increased from $1-million to $2-million in '98. The Filly and Mare Turf was added for 1999. The distances of some of the races have been changed over the years. The Distaff started as a 1$\frac{1}{4}$-mile race before being shortened to 1$\frac{1}{8}$ miles for the 1988 running. Both the Juvenile and Juveniles Fillies were held at one mile the first three years until changed to 1$\frac{1}{16}$ miles in 1986. The $250,000 Breeders' Cup Steeplechase was run from 1986 through '93 and resumed in 2000. Breeders' Cup Ltd. also contributes funds to existing races, and each of those races has Breeders' Cup as part of its name, such as the Gamely Breeders' Cup Handicap (G1).

Breeders' Cup Ltd. Corporate entity that oversees the Breeders' Cup program. It is a not-for-profit organization based in Lexington.

breeding fund A state fund set up to provide bonuses for state-breds.

breeding right The right to breed one mare per year to a specific stallion. Breeding rights, as opposed to stallion shares, do not usually come with bonuses (money derived from extra seasons sold), nor are they assessed expenses.

breeze (breezing) Working a horse at a moderate speed, less effort than handily.

bridge jumper A person who wagers large amounts of money, usually on short-priced horses to show, hoping to realize a small but almost certain profit. The term comes from the structure these bettors may seek if they lose.

bridle A piece of equipment, usually made of leather or nylon, that fits on a horse's head; other equipment, such as a bit and the reins, are attached to it.

broken wind Abnormality of the upper or lower respiratory tract causing loss of normal air exchange, generally resulting in reduced performance.

broodmare A mare that has been bred and is used to produce foals.

broodmare sire The maternal sire; the sire of the dam.

Broodmare Sire Index The Broodmare Sire Index is an average of the Racing Index (RI) of all foals out of the sire's daughters that started at least three times. For BSI to be calculated, a broodmare sire must be represented by a minimum of 75 starters lifetime.

brush 1) During a race when two horses slightly touch each other. 2) Injury that occurs when one hoof strikes the inside of the opposite limb. 3) A type of obstacle used in steeplechase racing.

bucked shins Inflammation of the covering of the bone (periosteum) of the front surface of the cannon bone to which young horses are particularly susceptible. This is primarily a condition of the front legs.

bullet work The best workout time for a particular distance on a given day at a track. Derived from the printer's bullet that precedes the time of the workout in listings. Also known as a black-letter work in some parts of the country.

bullring A small racetrack, usually less than one mile in circumference.

Bute Short for generic phenylbutazone, a nonsteroidal anti-inflammatory medication that is legal in many racing jurisdictions. Often known by the trade names Butazolidin and Butazone.

buy-back A horse put through a public auction that fails to reach a minimum (reserve) price set by the

consignor and so is retained. The consignor must pay a fee to the auction company based on a percentage of the reserve to cover the auction company's marketing, advertising, and other costs. A synonym for reserve not attained (RNA).

calk A projection on the heels of a horseshoe, similar to a cleat, on the rear shoes of a horse to prevent slipping, especially on a wet track. Also known as a sticker.

(race) call Running position of horses in a race at various points.

cast A horse positioned on its side or back and wedged against a wall in such a way that it cannot get up.

chalk Wagering favorite in a race. Term dates from the days when on-track bookmakers would write current odds on a chalkboard and the horse that was bet the most used the most chalk.

chalk player Bettor who wagers on favorites.

champion Horse or individual determined to be the outstanding performer in his or her division in a specific year. In the United States, champions are determined by voting in the Eclipse Awards balloting.

chart A statistical picture of a race (from which past performances are compiled) showing the position and margin of each horse at designated points of call (depending on the distance of the race), as well as the horse's age, weight carried, owner, trainer, jockey, and the race's purse, conditions, payoff prices, odds, time, and other data. Before 1991, all charts were compiled by *Daily Racing Form*. From 1991 to '98, charts were compiled by both *Daily Racing Form* and Equibase; since mid-1998, charts have been compiled exclusively by Equibase.

check(ed) When a jockey slows a horse due to other horses impeding its progress.

chestnut 1) A horse color that may vary from a red-yellow to golden-yellow. The mane, tail, and legs are usually variations of coat color, except where white markings are present. 2) Horny, irregular growths found on the inside of the legs. On the forelegs, they are just above the knees. On the hind legs, they are just below the hocks. No two horses have been found to have the same chestnuts, and so chestnuts may be used for identification. Also called night eyes.

chiropractic The use of bone alignment to treat specific or general health problems.

chute Extension of backstretch or homestretch to permit a straight start in a race as opposed to starting on or near a turn.

claiming Process by which a licensed person may purchase a horse entered in a designated race for a predetermined price. When a horse has been claimed, its new owner assumes title after the starting gate opens although the former owner is entitled to all purse money earned in that race. Sometimes called halter or haltered, for the act of putting a new halter on a claimed horse so that it can be led back to its new barn.

claiming box, claims box Box in which claims are deposited before the race.

claiming race A race in which each horse entered is eligible to be purchased at a set price. Claims must be made before the race and only by licensed owners or their agents who have a horse registered to race at that meeting or who have received a claim certificate from the stewards. A claiming race in which there is an option to have horses entered to be claimed for a stated price or not eligible to be claimed is an optional claiming race.

classic 1) A race of traditional importance. 2) Used to describe a distance. The American classic distance is 1¼ miles on dirt. The European classic distance is 1½ miles on turf.

clerk of scales An official whose chief duty is to weigh the riders before and after a race to ensure proper weight is or was carried.

climbing When a horse lifts its front legs abnormally high as it gallops, causing it to run inefficiently.

clocker Individual who times workouts and races.

closer A horse that runs best in the latter part of the race, coming from off the pace.

clubhouse turn Generally, the turn on a racing oval that is closest to the clubhouse facility; usually the first turn after the finish line.

colors (horse) Colors accepted by the Jockey Club are bay, black, chestnut, dark bay or brown, gray/roan, and white. In 1996, the Jockey Club started combining gray and roan, which had been separate colors previously.

colt An ungelded (entire) male horse four years old or younger.

commingle Combining mutuel pools from off-track sites with the host track.

company Class of horses in a race or the class of horses a runner usually keeps.

comparable index (CI) Indicates the average earnings of progeny produced from mares bred to one sire when these same mares are bred to other sires. A CI of 1.00 is considered average, 2.00 is twice the average, and 0.50 half the average.

condition book(s) A series of booklets issued by a track's racing secretary setting forth conditions of races to be run at that track.

conditioner 1) A trainer. 2) A workout or race to enable a horse to attain fitness.

conditions The requirements for being able to enter a horse in a particular race as written by the track's racing secretary. Conditions may include age, sex, money or races won, weight carried, and the distance of the race.

conformation The physical makeup and bodily proportions of a horse.

connections Persons identified with a horse, such as owner, trainer, rider, and stable employees.

consolation double A payoff to holders of daily double tickets combining the winning horse in the first race of the double with a scratched horse in the second.

cooling out Restoring a horse to normal body temperature, usually by walking, after it has become overheated during exercise or racing. All horses that are exercised and raced are cooled out.

coupled (entry) Two or more horses running as an entry in a single betting unit.

cover A single breeding of a stallion to a mare.

crop 1) The number of foals by a sire in a given year. 2) All horses collectively born in the same year. 3) A jockey's whip.

cup horse A term once used to describe horses

competing at the highest level of the sport in races at a distance.

cuppy (track) A drying and loose racing surface that breaks away under a horse's hooves.

cushion Top portion of a racetrack.

cut down Horse suffering injuries from being struck by the shoes of another horse. Or, due to a faulty stride, a horse may cut itself down.

daily double Type of wager calling for the selection of winners of two consecutive races, usually the first and second.

Daily Racing Form A daily newspaper containing news, past performance data, and handicapping information. Founded in 1895, it is the successor of the *Morning Telegraph*. The *Morning Telegraph* was founded in 1833 and was closed during a strike by printers in 1972.

dam The female parent of a foal.

dam's sire (broodmare sire) The sire of a broodmare. Used in reference to the maternal grandsire of a foal.

dark A day when there is no racing at the track.

dark bay or brown A horse color that ranges from brown with areas of tan on the shoulders, head, and flanks, to a dark brown, with tan areas seen only in the flanks, muzzle, or both. The mane, tail, and lower portions of the legs are always black unless white markings are present.

dark horse Probably a good horse whose full potential is unknown before a race.

dead heat Two or more horses finishing a race in a tie.

dead track Racing surface lacking resiliency.

declared In the United States, a horse withdrawn from a stakes race in advance of scratch time. In Europe, a horse confirmed to start in a race.

deep stretch A position very close to the finish line in race.

Derby A stakes event for three-year-olds, deriving its name from Lord Derby.

disqualification Change in order of finish by officials for an infraction of the rules.

distaffer A female horse.

distaff race A race for female horses.

distanced Horse so far behind the rest of the field of runners that it is out of contact and unable to regain a position of contention. A horse beaten more than 40 lengths.

dogs Rubber traffic cones (or a barrier) placed at certain distances out from the inner rail when the track is wet, muddy, soft, yielding, or heavy to prevent horses during the workout period from churning the footing along the rail.

dope 1) Any illegal drug. 2) Slang term for past performances: Readers of past performances are said to dope out a race.

dosage Although other dosage theories exist, the term is most commonly associated with the one interpreted by Dr. Steven Roman. A variation of Dr. Franco Varola's work on pedigree analysis, the system identifies patterns of ability in horses based on a list of prepotent sires, each of whom is designated a *chef-de-race*. The dosage system puts these sires into one of five categories: brilliant, intermediate, classic, solid, or professional, which are subjective judgments of speed and stamina. Sires can be listed in up to two *chef-de-race* categories. Each generation of sires is worth 16 points, divided by the amount of sires; i.e., the immediate sire is worth 16 points while the four sires four generations back are worth four points apiece.

dosage index (DI) A mathematical reduction of the dosage profile to a number reflecting a horse's potential for speed or stamina. The higher the number, the more likely the horse is suited to be a sprinter. The average dosage index of all horses is about 4.00. The dosage index (DI) is derived from the dosage profile to reflect the ratio of speed to stamina in a pedigree. This is calculated by adding points from the two speed categories (brilliant and intermediate), plus half of those from the classic (middle) category, and dividing that total by the points from the two stamina categories (solid and professional), plus the other half of the classic points. The higher the DI, the more speed is supposedly present in the pedigree. A 4.00 DI is generally the cutoff where a horse is considered not likely to be competitive at the American classic distance of 1¼ miles.

driving A horse that is all out to win and under strong urging from its jockey.

drop down A horse meeting a lower class of rival than it had been running against previously.

dwelt Extremely late in breaking from the gate.

earmuffs A piece of equipment that covers a horse's ears to prevent it from hearing distracting sounds.

eased A horse that is gently pulled up during a race.

easily Running or winning without being pressed by rider or opposition.

Eclipse Award Thoroughbred racing's year-end awards, honoring the top horses and people in several categories. Named for the great 18th-century racehorse and sire Eclipse, who was undefeated in 18 career starts and sired the winners of 344 races. The Eclipse Awards are sponsored by the National Thoroughbred Racing Association, *Daily Racing Form*, and National Turf Writers Association. They were first given out in 1971; previously, separate year-end champions were named by *Daily Racing Form* (beginning in 1936) and the Thoroughbred Racing Associations (beginning in 1950).

eligible Qualified to start in a race, according to conditions.

engagement 1) Stakes nomination. 2) Riding commitment.

entire An ungelded horse. In Europe, where geldings are not permitted to enter certain races, the race conditions might read: Entire colts and fillies.

entry Two or more horses with common ownership (in some cases, trained by the same trainer) that are paired as a single betting unit in one race or are placed together by the racing secretary as part of a mutuel field. Rules on entries vary from state to state. Also known as a coupled entry.

entry fee Money paid by an owner to enter a horse in a stakes race—and is what usually defines a race as a stakes. Entry fees are not required for overnight races and some invitational stakes races.

epistaxis Blood coming out of the horse's nostrils. See bleeder.

Equibase Co. A partnership between the Jockey Club

and the Thoroughbred Racing Associations to establish and maintain an industry-owned, central database of racing records. Equibase past-performance information is used in track programs across North America. Formed in 1990, Equibase first collected data in '91. In 1998, it began supplying past performance information to *Daily Racing Form* and became the sole collector of racing data.

estrus (heat) Associated with ovulation; a mare usually is receptive to breeding during estrus. Referred to as horsing.

euthanize To end a horse's life because of a catastrophic injury or critical illness and to prevent further pain and suffering.

evenly Neither gaining nor losing position during a race.

exacta (or perfecta) A wager in which the first two finishers in a race, in exact order of finish, must be picked. Called an exactor in Canada.

exacta box A wager in which all possible combinations using a given number of horses are bet on.

exercise rider Individual who is licensed to exercise a horse during morning training hours.

exotic (wager) Any wager other than win, place, or show that requires multiple combinations. Examples of exotic wagers: trifecta, pick six, pick three.

Experimental Free Handicap A year-end assessment of the best North American two-year-olds of the season. It is put together by a panel of racing secretaries under the auspices of the Jockey Club and is based on performances in unrestricted races. Two lists are drawn up, one for males and one for females. Only the handicap for two-year-olds is called the Experimental Free Handicap; lists for older horses are free handicaps. First started by Walter Vosburgh in 1933. Race based on Experimental was run at Aqueduct from 1940 to '56 at six furlongs (Experimental Free Handicap No. 1) and another from 1946 to '52 at 1¹⁄₁₆ miles (Experimental Free Handicap No. 2).

extended Running at top speed.

farrier Horseshoer, blacksmith.

fast (track) Footing that is dry, even, and resilient.

fault Weak points of a horse's conformation or character as a racehorse.

feather Light weight. Usually refers to the weight a horse is assigned to carry in a race.

fee 1) Amount paid to a jockey for riding in a race. 2) The cost of nominating, entering, or starting a horse in a stakes race.

field The horses in a race.

field horse (or mutuel field) Two or more starters running as a single betting unit (entry), when there are more starters in a race than positions on the totalizator board.

filly Female horse four years old or younger.

firm (track) A condition of a turf course corresponding to fast on a dirt track. A firm, resilient surface.

flag Signal manually held a short distance in front of the gate at the exact starting point of a race. In some jurisdictions, official timing starts when flag is dropped by the flagman to denote proper start.

flagman Person who drops the flag to signal the start of a race.

flak jacket Similar to a jacket worn by football quarterbacks, the jockey's flak jacket protects the chest, ribs, kidneys, and back from injury.

flat race Contested on level ground as opposed to a steeplechase race. Often used in the term, on the flat.

flatten out A very tired horse that slows considerably, dropping its head on a straight line with its body. Some horses, however, like to run with their heads lowered.

float 1) An equine dental procedure in which sharp points on the teeth are filed down. 2) The instrument with which the above procedure is performed.

floating Flat plate or wooden implement (float) dragged over the surface of a wet track to aid in draining water.

foal(ed) 1) A horse of either sex in its first year of life. 2) Can also denote the offspring of either a male or female parent. 3) To give birth.

Fontana safety rail An aluminum rail, in use since 1981, designed to help reduce injuries to horse and rider. It has more of an offset (slant) to provide greater clearance between the rail and the vertical posts as well as a protective cover to keep horse and rider from striking the posts.

founding sires The Darley Arabian, Byerly Turk, and Godolphin Barb. Every Thoroughbred must trace its parentage to one of the three founding sires.

fractional time Intermediate times recorded in a race, as at the quarter-mile, half-mile, three-quarters, etc.

free handicap A race in which no nomination fees are required. More recently, and more commonly, a ranking of horses three years old and up by weight for a theoretical race or as an intellectual challenge.

frog The V-shaped, pliable support structure on the bottom of the foot.

front-runner A horse whose running style is to attempt to get on or near the lead at the start of the race and to continue there as long as possible.

frozen (track) The condition of a racetrack where any moisture present is frozen.

full brother, full sister Horses that share the same sire and dam.

furlong One-eighth of a mile, which is equal to 220 yards or 660 feet.

furosemide A medication used in the treatment of bleeders, commonly known by the trade name Salix, a diuretic. Although research has not determined definitively how furosemide reduces bleeding, it is widely believed that the diuretic effect reduces pressure within capillaries in the lungs.

futurity A race for two-year-olds in which the owners make a scheduled series of payments over a period of time to keep their horses eligible. Purses for these races vary but can be considerable.

gait The characteristic footfall pattern of a horse in motion. Thoroughbreds have four natural gaits: walk, trot, canter, and gallop. Thoroughbreds compete at a gallop.

gap An opening in the rail where horses enter and leave the course.

Garrison finish A close victory, usually from off the pace. Derived from Ed "Snapper" Garrison, a 19th-century rider known for his close finishes.

gate card A card, issued by the starter, stating that a

horse is properly schooled in starting-gate procedures.

gelding A male horse of any age that has been neutered by having both testicles removed (gelded).

gentleman jockey Amateur rider, generally in steeplechases.

get Progeny of sire.

girth An elastic and leather band, sometimes covered with sheepskin, that passes under a horse's belly and is connected to both sides of the saddle.

good (track) A dirt track that is almost fast or a turf course slightly softer than firm.

grab a quarter Injury to the back of the hoof or foot caused by a horse stepping on itself (usually affects the front foot). Being stepped on from behind in the same manner usually affects the back foot. Very common in racing, the injury is usually minor.

graded race Established in 1973 to classify select stakes races in North America, at the request of European racing authorities, who had set up group races two years earlier. Grading of races is performed by a committee under the direction of the Thoroughbred Owners and Breeders Association. See graded stakes section elsewhere in this book.

grandsire The grandfather of a horse; father (sire) of the horse's dam or sire.

grass slip Used in some areas, permission to exercise a horse on the turf course. Also known as a turf card.

gray A horse color in which the majority of the coat is a mixture of black and white hairs. The mane, tail, and legs may be either black or gray unless white markings are present. Starting with foals of 1993, the color classifications gray and roan were combined as roan or gray.

Grayson-Jockey Club Research Foundation A privately financed charitable organization established in 1989, which combined the Grayson Foundation Inc. (begun in 1940) and the Jockey Club Research Foundation.

group race Designation of best races in countries outside North America. European authorities began designating races as Group 1, Group 2, and Group 3 in 1971. North American officials, under the direction of the Thoroughbred Owners and Breeders Association, began grading races in 1973.

guineas By definition, a guinea is 21 shillings, or in current usage a pound and a shilling. Thus, the guinea is equal to 1.05 pounds. Used by sales companies in England and Ireland to report sales since it includes the sales company's commission.

half brother, half sister Horses out of the same dam but by different sires. Horses with the same sire and different dams are not considered half siblings in Thoroughbred racing.

halter Like a bridle, but lacking a bit and reins. Used to handle horses around the stable and when they are not being ridden.

hand Four inches. A horse's height is measured in hands and inches from the top of the shoulder (withers) to the ground; that is, 15.2 hands is 15 hands, 2 inches, or a total of 62 inches. Thoroughbreds typically range from 15 to 17 hands.

handicap 1) Race for which the track handicapper assigns the weights to be carried. 2) To make selections on the basis of past performances.

handicap horse A horse that competes in handicap races.

handicapper 1) A person, usually the racing secretary, who assigns weights to horses. 2) A bettor that is making selections based on information of horses' performances from previous starts.

handily 1) Working in the morning with maximum effort. 2) A horse racing well within itself, with little exertion from the jockey.

handle Amount of money wagered in the pari-mutuels on a race, a program, during a meeting, or for a year.

hand ride Urging a horse with the hands and not using the whip.

hard (track) A condition of a turf course where there is no resiliency to the surface.

hardboot A Kentucky horseman.

hard-knocker A tough horse who makes a lot of starts.

harrow Implement or unit with pulling teeth, or tines, used to rake and loosen the upper surface of a track.

head A margin between horses. One horse leading another by the length of its head.

head of the stretch Beginning of the straight run to the finish line.

head to head Running on even terms.

heat 1) A race in which more then one running is required to decide the winner. Not used in flat racing today, though it was common in the 19th century. Still used in harness racing. 2) A breeding term for estrus in a mare.

heavy (track) Wettest possible condition of a turf course; not usually found in North America.

helmet A lightweight fiberglass cap worn by riders to prevent head injuries. It is required equipment and is not considered part of a jockey's riding weight.

high weight Refers to highest weight assigned or carried in a race.

homebred A horse bred by its owner.

homestretch Long section of racetrack closest to the stands.

hood A covering, usually nylon, that goes over a horse's head; blinkers or earmuffs may be attached to it.

hoof The foot of the horse. Consists of several parts that play an integral role in supporting the weight of the horse.

hopped A horse that has been illegally stimulated with a drug.

horse When reference is made to sex, an ungelded male five years old or older.

Horsemen's Benevolent and Protective Association A national organization of horsemen, largely composed of owners, that has divisions at a majority of tracks in North America to help owners and trainers negotiate purses and other issues with track management.

hotwalker A person or automatic machine that walks horses to cool them out after workout or races.

hung A horse that does not advance its position in a race when called upon by its jockey.

icing 1) A physical therapy procedure, properly known

as cryotherapy. 2) When a horse's leg or legs are placed in a tub of ice or ice packs are applied to the legs to reduce inflammation or swelling.

impost Weight carried by a horse or assigned to a horse.

inbreeding Denotes same parents appearing more than once relatively close up in a pedigree, though definition of what constitutes inbreeding remains hotly debated.

infield Area enclosed by the inner rail of the racetrack.

in hand Running under moderate control, at less than top speed.

inquiry A review of the running of the race to check into a possible infraction of the rules, called by the stewards. Also, a sign flashed by officials on the tote board on such occasions. If lodged by a jockey, it is called an objection.

in the money A horse that finishes first, second, or third in a race.

Irish rail Movable rail.

isolation barn A facility used to separate horses to ensure that disease is not carried into the area.

jail Requirement that a claimed horse when it next runs in a claiming race must run for a claiming price 25% higher over the next 30 days.

Jockey Club Organization dedicated to the improvement of Thoroughbred breeding and racing. Incorporated February 10, 1894, in New York City, the Jockey Club serves as North America's Thoroughbred registry, responsible for the maintenance of the *American Stud Book*, a register of all Thoroughbreds foaled in the United States, Puerto Rico, and Canada; and of all Thoroughbreds imported into those countries from jurisdictions that have a registry recognized by the Jockey Club and the International Stud Book Committee.

jockey fee Sum paid to rider for competing in a race.

Jockeys' Guild National organization of professional riders.

jockey's race A race whose outcome will hinge mostly on strategic thinking by the riders; one in which riders must pay close attention to pace to keep their horses fresh for a strong finish.

jog Slow, easy gait.

joint 1) Point of juncture of two bones and usually composed of fibrous connective tissue and cartilage. 2) Slang for an illegal electrical stimulation device.

jumper Steeplechase or hurdle horse.

juvenile Two-year-old horse.

key horse A single horse used in multiple combinations in an exotic wager.

kilometer One thousand meters and equal to .62 of a mile.

lame A deviation from a normal gait due to pain in a limb or its supporting structures.

Lasix See Salix.

late double A second daily double offered during the latter part of the program.

lead Refers to the leading leg when a horse is racing in full stride. The lead leg is the one that reaches out the farthest and bears the full weight of the horse's impact. Horses usually race on the left, or inside, lead on the turn, and on the right, or outside, lead on straightaways. Changing leads refers to the horse's ability to switch leads at the proper time.

leaky-roof circuit Minor tracks.

leg up To help a jockey mount a horse.

length A measurement approximating the length of a horse and used to describe the distances between horses in a race. A length is approximately eight feet.

listed race A stakes race just below a group race or graded race in quality.

lock Slang for a sure winner.

longe 1) A long rope fastened to a horse's head and held by a trainer, who causes the horse to move around in a circle. 2) A method of exercising a horse on a tether (longe line).

lug (bearing in or lugging out) Deviating from a straight course. May be due to weariness, infirmity, inexperience, or the rider overusing the whip or reins to make a horse alter its course.

maiden 1) A horse or rider that has not won a race. 2) A female that has never been bred.

maiden race A race for nonwinners.

mare Female horse five years old or older. Also, any female that has been bred regardless of age.

mare's month September. In theory, mares that have not run well during the summer often perform better in September.

mash Soft, moist mixture, hot or cold, of grain and other feed that is easily digested by horses.

massage Rubbing of various parts of the anatomy to stimulate healing.

match race A race between two horses.

medication list A list kept by the track veterinarian and published by the track showing which horses have been treated with legally prescribed medications.

meter The basic unit of length in the metric system. It is equal to approximately 39.37 inches. It takes 100 centimeters to make a meter and 1,000 meters to make a kilometer. To convert to inches, multiply by 39.37 (5 meters x 39.37 inches = 196.85 inches). To convert to yards, multiply by 1.1 (5 meters x 1.1 = 5.5 yards). Most European races are expressed in meters. A mile is approximately 1,600 meters, the distance at which the classic Poule d'Essai des Pouliches (Fr-G1) and the Poule d'Essai des Poulains (Fr-G1) are run. The Prix de l'Arc de Triomphe (Fr-G1) is 2,400 meters, or approximately 1½ miles; the Prix Eugene Adam (Fr-G2) is 2,000 meters, or approximately 1¼ miles. See Distance Conversion Table elsewhere in this book.

middle distance Broadly, from one mile to 1¼ miles.

minus pool A negative mutuel pool created when a horse is so heavily played that, after deductions of state tax and commission, not enough money remains to pay the legally prescribed minimum on each winning bet. The racing association usually makes up the difference.

money rider A rider who excels in rich races.

monkey on a stick Type of riding with short stirrups popularized by riding great Todhunter Sloan shortly before 1900.

morning glory Horse that performs well in morning workouts but fails to reproduce that form in races.

morning line Probable odds on each horse in a race, as determined by a mathematical formula used by the track odds maker, who tries to gauge both the ability of the horse and the most likely final odds as determined by the bettors. Those odds now are

known as the program-line odds because they appear in the track's official program.

mud calks Special cleats that help a horse gain traction on a muddy track.

muddy (track) Condition of a racetrack that is wet but has no standing water.

mudder Horse that races well on muddy tracks. Also known as a mudlark.

mutuel pool Short for pari-mutuel pool. Sum of the wagers on a race or event, such as the win pool, daily double pool, exacta pool, etc.

muzzle 1) Nose and lips of a horse. 2) A guard placed over a horse's mouth to prevent it from biting or eating.

name (of a Thoroughbred) Names of North American Thoroughbreds are registered by the Jockey Club. They can be no longer than 18 characters, including punctuation and spaces.

National Thoroughbred Association Started as concept of advertising agency executive Fred Pope in early 1990s, with backing from owner-breeder John R. Gaines. The NTA was based on the concept that owners possess rights to their horses' images for simulcasting purposes, with the owners banding together to form a major league of racing through the pooling of simulcasting rights. Hamilton Jordan and Tim Smith were brought in to help sell the concept in 1997, and the NTA initiative eventually led to a broader industry coalition, the formation of the National Thoroughbred Racing Association. NTA officially was folded into the NTRA in August 1998.

National Thoroughbred Racing Association A not-for-profit association created by a consensus of industry factions to market the sport. Founding members were Breeders' Cup Ltd., the Jockey Club, Keeneland Association, and Oak Tree Racing Association, with each putting up $1-million in seed money. Before officially launching the office, the National Thoroughbred Association became a founding member when it ceased its existence and was rolled into the NTRA. In 2000, the Thoroughbred Owners and Breeders Association retroactively became a founding member. The NTRA first proposed a business plan to the industry in August 1997. The NTRA officially opened for business on April 1, 1998. Its first commissioner was Tim Smith. D. G. Van Clief Jr. of Breeders' Cup Ltd. acted as interim chief executive officer of the NTRA in its formative stages. The NTRA formally merged many of its administrative functions with Breeders' Cup Ltd. on January 1, 2001.

National Museum of Racing and Hall of Fame Building in Saratoga Springs, New York, that houses a museum and a Racing Hall of Fame. The National Museum of Racing was founded in 1950. It had its first home in the old Canfield Casino, Congress Park, Saratoga Springs. It moved to its present site in 1955, the same year the Racing Hall of Fame was created.

near side Left side of a horse. Side on which a horse is mounted.

neck Unit of measurement. About the length of a horse's neck; a little less than a quarter of a length.

nod Lowering of head. To win by a nod, a horse extends its head with its nose touching the finish line ahead of a close competitor.

nominator One who owns a horse at the time it is named to compete in a stakes race or makes it eligible to a stakes program such as the Breeders' Cup.

North American Pari-Mutuel Regulators Association Organization founded in 1997 as a splinter group from the Association of Racing Commissioners International due to philosophical differences in practices and policies. NAPRA's original members were Alabama, Arizona, Florida, Idaho, Kansas, Minnesota, Oklahoma, Oregon, Saskatchewan, South Dakota, Wisconsin, and Wyoming. Joining the organization by January 2002 were the Alberta Racing Corp., British Columbia, Canadian Pari-Mutuel Agency, Colorado, Florida Division of Pari-Mutuel Wagering, Kentucky, Manitoba, Maryland, Montana, New Mexico, North Dakota, Pennsylvania, and Virginia.

nose Smallest advantage a horse can win by. Called a short head in Britain.

nose band A leather strap that goes over the bridge of a horse's nose to help secure the bridle. A figure-eight nose band goes over the bridge of the nose and under the rings of the bit to help keep the horse's mouth closed. The figure-eight nose band keeps the tongue from sliding up over the bit and is used on horses that do not like having a tongue tie used.

Oaks A stakes event for three-year-old fillies.

objection Claim of foul lodged by rider, patrol judge, or other official after the running of a race. If lodged by an official, it is called an inquiry.

odds-on Odds of less than even money.

odds maker The individual who prepares the program line for a track.

official 1) Notice displayed when a race result is confirmed. 2) Used to denote a racing official.

off side Right side of horse.

off-track betting Wagering at legalized betting outlets usually run by the tracks, management companies specializing in pari-mutuel wagering, or, in New York, by independent corporations chartered by the state. Wagers at OTB sites are usually commingled with on-track betting pools.

on the bit When a horse is eager to run. Also known as in the bridle.

on the board Finishing among the first three.

on the muscle Denotes a fit horse.

on the nose Betting a horse to win only.

optional claiming A claiming race in which there is an option to have horses entered to be claimed for a stated price or not eligible to be claimed.

outcross When a horse has no inbreeding, especially within the first five generations.

out of the money A horse that finishes worse than third.

over at the knee A leg that looks like it has a forward arc with its center at the knee when viewed from the side.

overcheck A strap that holds the bit in place.

overgirth An elastic band that goes completely around a horse and over the saddle, to keep the saddle from slipping.

over-reaching Toe of hind shoe striking the forefoot or foreleg.

overland, overland route Racing wide throughout,

outside other horses.

overlay A horse going off at higher odds than it appears to warrant based on its past performances.

overnight A sheet published by the racing secretary's office listing the entries for an upcoming racing card.

overnight race A race in which entries close in a specific number of hours before running (such as 48 hours) and do not require an entry fee, as opposed to a stakes race for which nominations close weeks and sometimes months in advance and usually require a monetary payment for a horse to be eligible.

overweight Excess weight carried by a horse when the rider exceeds the required weight.

pacesetter The horse that is running in front (on the lead).

paddock Area where horses are saddled and paraded before being taken onto the track.

paddock judge Official in charge of paddock and saddling routine.

panel A slang term for a furlong.

pari-mutuel A form of wagering originated in 1865 by Frenchman Pierre Oller in which all money bet is divided and distributed to those who have winning tickets after taxes, takeout, and other deductions are made. Oller called his system perier mutuel, meaning mutual stake or betting among ourselves. As this wagering method was adopted in England, it became known as Paris mutuals, and soon after pari-mutuels.

parlay A multirace bet in which all winnings are subsequently wagered on a succeeding race.

parrot mouth A horse with an extreme overbite.

part wheel Using a key horse or horses in different, but not all possible, exotic wagering combinations.

pasteboard track A lightning-fast racing surface.

past performances A horse's racing record, earnings, bloodlines, and other data, presented in composite form.

patrol judges Officials who observe the progress of a race from various vantage points around the track.

pattern race Synonym for a group race in Europe.

photo finish A result so close it is necessary to use the finish-line camera to determine the order of finish.

pick (number) A type of multirace wager in which the winners of all the included races must be selected. Pick three (sometimes called the daily triple), pick six, and pick nine are commonly used by tracks in the United States.

pill Small numbered ball used in a blind draw to decide post positions.

pinched back A horse forced back when racing in close quarters, particularly on turns.

pin firing Thermocautery used to increase blood flow to the leg and intended to promote healing.

pinhooker A person who buys a racehorse prospect with the intention of reselling it at a profit. Examples are weanling-to-yearling pinhookers and yearling-to-juvenile pinhookers.

pipe-opener Exercise at a brisk speed.

place Second position at finish.

place bet Wager on a horse to finish first or second.

placing judge Official who posts the order of finish in a race.

plate(s) 1) A prize for a winner. Usually less valuable than a cup. 2) Generic term for lightweight horseshoes, usually made of aluminum, that are used during a race.

plater Vernacular for a claiming horse.

pocket A position in a race with horses in front and alongside.

pole(s) Markers at measured distances around the track designating the distance from the finish. The quarter pole, for instance, is one-quarter mile from the finish line, not from the start.

pony Any horse or pony that leads the parade of the field from paddock to starting gate. A horse or pony that accompanies a horse to the starting gate. Also known as a lead pony.

post 1) Starting point for a race. 2) An abbreviated version of post position.

post parade Horses going from paddock to starting gate past the stands.

post position Position of stall in starting gate from which a horse starts.

preferred list Horses with prior rights to starting, usually because they have previously been entered in races that have not filled with the minimum number of starters or they have been excluded from races that drew an excess of entries.

prep (race) A workout (or race) used to prepare a horse for a future engagement.

program line Probable odds on each horse in a race, as determined by a mathematical formula used by the track odds maker, who tries to gauge both the ability of the horse and the likely final odds as determined by the bettors. These odds are published in the track's official program and formerly were known as the morning line.

prop When a horse suddenly stops moving by digging its front feet into the ground.

public trainer One whose services are not exclusively engaged by a single stable and who accepts horses from a number of owners.

pull up To stop or slow a horse during or after a race or workout.

purse The total monetary amount distributed after a race to the owners of the entrants finishing in the top positions, usually five. Some racing jurisdictions may pay purse money through other places.

quarantine barn 1) A United States Department of Agriculture structure used to isolate foreign horses for a short period of time to ensure they are not carrying a disease. The structure may be at a racetrack, an airport, or a specially designated facility. Horses must be cleared by a federal veterinarian before being released from quarantine. 2) Any facility used to keep infected horses away from the general equine population.

quarter crack A vertical crack between the toe and heel, usually extending into the coronary band.

quinella Wager in which the first two finishers must be picked in either order.

rabbit A speed horse running as an entry with another, who is usually a come-from-behind horse.

Racing Index Racing Index (RI) is based on the average earnings per start for all runners in the United States, Canada, England, Ireland, France, Italy, Germany, Puerto Rico, and the United Arab Emirates. RI is determined by calculating the average earnings

per start, divided into males and females, of all starters in each individual country, and the average for each individual year is by definition 1.00. Median RI is much lower.

racing secretary Official who drafts conditions of races and assigns weights for handicap events.

rail The barrier on either side of the racing strip. Sometimes referred to as the fence.

rail runner Horse that prefers to run next to the inside rail.

rank A horse that refuses to settle under a jockey's handling in a race, running in a headstrong manner without respect to pace.

receiving barn Structure used to house horses shipping in for a race on a specific day. Horses trained on farms or at training centers often will be placed in the receiving barn until their races.

redboard 1) Old-time method of declaring a race official by posting a red flag or board on the tote board. 2) A mildly derogatory phrase used to describe someone who claims to have selected the winner, but always after the race.

refuse 1) When a horse will not break from the gate. 2) In jumping races, balking at a jump.

reins Long straps, usually made of leather, that are connected to the bit and used by the jockey to control the horse.

reserve A minimum price, set by the consignor, for a horse in a public auction.

reserve not attained A minimum price, or reserve, set by the consignor for a horse at a public auction that is not met by those who are bidding. RNA.

reserved 1) Held for a particular engagement or race. 2) Held off the pace.

ridden out A horse that finishes a race under mild urging; not as severe as driving.

ride short Using short stirrups.

ridgling (rig) A term describing either a cryptorchid or a monorchid.

roan A horse color in which the majority of the coat is a mixture of red and white hairs or brown and white hairs. The mane, tail, and legs may be black, chestnut, or roan unless white markings are present. Starting with foals of 1993, the color classifications of gray and roan were combined as roan or gray.

rogue Ill-tempered horse.

route A race of long distance; broadly, a race at a distance farther than 1⅛ miles in North America.

router Horse that performs well at longer distances.

run down Abrasions of the heel.

run-out bit A special type of bit to prevent a horse from bearing out (or in).

saddle A Thoroughbred racing saddle is the lightest saddle used, weighing less than two pounds.

saddlecloth A cotton cloth that goes under the saddle to absorb sweat. It usually has the horse's program number on it and, often in major races, the horse's name.

saddlepad A piece of felt, sheepskin, or more usually, foam rubber, used as a base for the saddle.

Salix An antibleeder medication that had been named Lasix until the medication's manufacturer, Intervet, changed the name in 2001. Its generic name is furosemide, and it was first used in veterinary practice in 1967.

savage When a horse bites another horse or a person.

scale of weights Fixed weights to be carried by horses according to their age, sex, race distance, and time of year. See scale of weights table elsewhere in this book.

schooling Process of familiarizing a horse with the starting gate and teaching it racing practices. A horse also may be schooled in the paddock. In steeplechasing, to teach a horse to jump.

schooling list List of horses eligible to school at the starting gate before being permitted to race.

scratch To be taken out of a race before a horse starts. Trainers usually scratch horses due to adverse track conditions or a horse's health. A veterinarian can scratch a horse at any time.

second call A secondary mount of a jockey in a race in case his primary mount is scratched.

second dam Grandmother of a horse. Also known as a grandam.

set A group of horses being exercised together.

set down 1) To be suspended, usually referring to a jockey. 2) When a jockey assumes a lower crouch in the saddle while urging the horse to pick up speed.

sex allowance Female horses (fillies and mares), according to their age and the time of year, are allowed to carry three to five pounds less when racing against males.

shadow roll A bulky piece of material, usually sheepskin or synthetic fabric, that is secured over the bridge of a horse's nose to keep it from seeing shadows on the track. Often used with horses that shy away from shadows on the track or jump them.

shank Rope or strap attached to a halter or bridle by which a horse is led.

shedrow Stable area; walking path within a barn.

sheets A handicapping tool assigning a numerical value to each race run by a horse to enable different horses running at different racetracks to be objectively compared. Two principal companies in this field are operated by Len Ragozin, the originator, and Jerry Brown.

short A horse in need of more workouts or racing to reach winning form.

show Third position at the finish.

show bet Wager on a horse to finish in the money; third or better.

shut off Unable to improve position due to being surrounded by other horses.

silks Jacket and cap worn by riders to designate owner of the horse, or at some smaller tracks, to designate post positions (e.g., yellow for post position one, blue for two, etc.).

Silky Sullivan A term sometimes used for a horse that makes a big run from far back. Named for the horse Silky Sullivan, who once made up 41 lengths to win a six-furlong race.

simulcast A simultaneous live television transmission of a race to other tracks, off-track betting offices, or other outlets for the purpose of wagering.

sire 1) The male parent. 2) To beget foals. According to cataloging standards and standard usage, a stallion must sire a winner to be called a sire; he is a stallion until that time.

Sire Index (SI) Sire Index is an average of the Racing Index (RI) of all foals by a sire that have started at

least three times. For SI to be calculated, a sire must be represented by a minimum of three crops and 25 starters lifetime.

slipped A breeding term meaning spontaneous abortion.

sloppy (track) A racing strip that is saturated with water and has standing water visible.

slow (track) A racing strip that is wet on both the surface and base.

snip Small patch of white hairs on the nose or lips of a horse.

socks Solid white markings extending from the top of the hoof to the ankles. Also called stockings.

soft (track) Condition of a turf course with a large amount of moisture. Horses' hooves sink deeply into the surface.

sophomores Three-year-old horses.

speed figure A handicapping tool in which a numerical value is assigned to a horse's performance.

speedy cut Injury to the inside of the knee or hock caused by a strike from another foot.

spit box A generic term describing a barn or area to which horses are taken for post-race testing. Tests may include saliva, urine, or blood.

spit the bit Or spit out the bit. A term referring to a tired horse that begins to run less aggressively.

split(s) Fractional times in a race in increments of one-eighth of a mile.

sprint Short race, less than one mile.

stakes A race for which the owner usually must pay a fee to run a horse. The fees can be for nominating, maintaining eligibility, entering, and starting; the track adds additional money to make up the total purse. Some stakes races are by invitation and require no payment or fee.

stakes-placed Finished second or third in a stakes race.

stakes horse A horse whose level of competition includes mostly stakes races.

stallion A male horse used for breeding.

stallion season The right to breed one mare to a specific stallion during one breeding season.

stallion share A lifetime right to breed one mare to a specific stallion each breeding season. Although generally limited to one mare per season per share, larger stallion books have in some cases allowed share owners to breed more than one mare each year. Stallion share owners are usually assessed a proportionate share of expenses and will also share in any bonuses.

stall walker Horse that moves about its stall constantly and frets rather than resting.

star 1) Any of a number of white markings on the forehead. (The forehead is defined as being above an imaginary line connecting the tops of the eyes.) 2) A type of credit a horse receives from the racing secretary if it is excluded from an overfilled race, giving it priority in entering future races.

starter 1) An official responsible for ensuring a fair start to the race. The starter supervises the loading of horses into the starting gate by assistant starters who collectively are known as a gate crew. The starter also has control of opening the gate. 2) A horse that is in the starting gate when the race begins, whether he runs or not.

starter race An allowance or handicap race restricted to horses that have started for a specific claiming price or less.

starting gate Partitioned mechanical device having stalls in which the horses are confined until the starter releases the stalls' front doors to begin the race.

stayer A horse that can race long distances successfully.

steadied A horse being taken in hand by its rider, usually when in close quarters.

step up A horse moving up in class to meet better competition.

steward Official of the race meeting responsible for enforcing the rules of racing.

steeplechase A race in which horses are required to jump a series of obstacles on the course. Steeplechase races in the United States are run over National Fences (artificial brush fences), natural brush fences, and timber fences. In England and Ireland, jump races are over hurdles and steeplechase fences.

stick A jockey's whip.

stirrups Metal D-shaped rings into which a jockey places his or her feet. They can be raised or lowered by shortening or lengthening the leather straps that connect the stirrups to the saddle. Also known as irons.

stockings Solid white markings extending from the top of the hoof to the knee or hock. Also called socks.

stone English system of weights is based on stones. A stone is equal to 14 pounds; thus, 126 pounds is nine stone.

(home) stretch Final straight; portion of the racetrack from the end of the final turn to the finish line.

stretch call Position of horses at the eighth pole, or one-eighth mile from the finish.

stretch runner Horse that runs fastest nearing the finish of a race.

stretch turn Bend of track into the final straightaway.

stride Manner of going. Also, distance covered between successive imprints of the same hoof.

stripe A white marking running down a horse's face, starting under an imaginary line connecting the tops of the eyes.

stud 1) Male horse used for breeding. 2) A breeding farm.

stud book Registry and genealogical record of Thoroughbreds, maintained by the Jockey Club of the country in question.

subscription Fee paid by owner to nominate a horse for a stakes race or to maintain eligibility for a stakes.

substitute race Alternate race used on overnight sheets to replace a regularly scheduled race that does not fill or is canceled.

suckling A foal in its first year of life, while it is still nursing.

sulk When a horse refuses to extend itself.

swayback Horse with a prominent concave shape of the backbone, usually just behind the withers (saddle area). Lordosis.

tack Rider's racing equipment. Also applied to stable gear.

tail off Used to describe a fit horse losing its competitive edge.

takeout Commission deducted from mutuel pools that is shared by the track, horsemen (in the form of purses), and local and state governing bodies in

the form of tax. Also called take.

taken up A horse pulled up sharply by its rider due to being in close quarters.

tattoo A permanent, indelible mark on the inside of the upper lip used to identify the horse.

teaser A male horse used at breeding farms to determine whether a mare is ready to receive a stallion.

teletimer Electronic means to time races, including fractional times at various points of call. The lead horse trips an electronic beam of light and the clockings are transmitted instantly to the tote board.

Thoroughbred A Thoroughbred is a horse whose parentage traces to any of the three founding sires—the Darley Arabian, Byerly Turk, and Godolphin Barb. The horse also must have satisfied the rules and requirements of the Jockey Club for inclusion in the *American Stud Book*, or it is registered in a foreign stud book recognized by the Jockey Club and the International Stud Book Committee.

Thoroughbred Horsemen's Association A representative group organized on local levels primarily in Mid-Atlantic states to represent the interests of owners in negotiations with tracks on purses and other issues. Started as an alternative to the Horsemen's Benevolent and Protective Association.

Thoroughbred Racing Associations An industry group founded in 1942 and comprising about 50 racetracks in North America.

tight Vernacular for fit and ready to race.

tightener 1) A race used to give a horse a level of fitness that cannot be obtained through morning exercise alone. 2) A leg brace.

timber topper Steeplechase horse racing over post-and-rail fences.

tongue tie Strip of cloth or cloth-like material used to stabilize a horse's tongue to prevent it from choking down in a race or workout or to keep the tongue from sliding up over the bit, rendering the horse uncontrollable. Also known as a tongue strap.

top line 1) A Thoroughbred's breeding on its sire's side. 2) The visual line presented by the horse's back.

totalizator An automated pari-mutuel system that dispenses and records betting tickets, calculates and displays odds and payoffs, and provides the mechanism for cashing winning tickets. Often shortened to tote.

tote board Structure in the racetrack infield where up-to-the-minute odds and other information are listed. It may also show the amounts wagered in each mutuel pool as well as information such as jockey and equipment changes. Also known as the board.

tout Person who professes to have, and sells, advance information on a race.

track bias A racing surface that favors a particular running style or position.

track condition Condition of the racetrack surface.

trial In Thoroughbred racing, a preparatory race created in tandem with a subsequent, more important stakes race to be run a few days or weeks hence. In Europe, a trial can refer to a vigorous morning workout with other horses.

trifecta A wager in which the first three finishers must be selected in exact order. Called a triactor in Canada and a triple in some parts of the United States.

trifecta box A trifecta wager in which all possible combinations using a given number of horses are bet upon.

trip An individual horse's race, with specific reference to the difficulty (or lack of difficulty) the horse had during competition, such as whether the horse was repeatedly blocked or had an unobstructed run.

Triple Crown Used generically to denote a series of three important races. In the United States, the Kentucky Derby, Preakness Stakes, and Belmont Stakes make up the Triple Crown. In England, the Two Thousand Guineas, Epsom Derby, and St. Leger Stakes. In Canada, the Queen's Plate, Prince of Wales Stakes, and Breeders' Stakes.

turn down(s) Rear shoe that is turned down—from a half-inch to one inch at the ends—to provide better traction on an off-track. Illegal in most jurisdictions.

twitch A restraining device usually consisting of a stick with a loop of rope or chain at one end, which is placed around a horse's upper lip and twisted, releasing endorphins that relax a horse and curb its fractiousness while it is being handled.

underlay A horse at shorter odds than seem warranted by its past performances.

under wraps Horse under stout restraint in a race or workout to keep it from pulling away from the competition by too large a margin.

untried 1) Not raced or tested for speed. 2) A stallion that has not been bred.

unwind Gradually withdrawing a horse from intensive training.

valet A person employed by a racing association to clean and care for a jockey's tack and other riding equipment.

walkover A race in which only one horse competes.

washed out A horse that becomes so nervous that it sweats profusely. Also known as washy or lathered (up).

weanling A foal less than one-year-old that has been separated (weaned) from its dam.

weigh in (out) The certification by the clerk of scales of a rider's weight before (after) a race. A jockey weighs in fully dressed with all equipment except for his or her helmet, whip, and (in many jurisdictions) flak jacket.

weight for age An allowance condition in which each entrant is assigned a weight according to its age. Females usually receive a sex allowance as well.

wheel Betting all possible combinations in an exotic wager using at least one horse as the key.

white A horse color, extremely rare, in which all the hairs are white. The horse's eyes are brown, not pink, as would be the case for an albino.

wire The finish line of a race.

withers Area above the shoulder, where the neck meets the back.

workout A fast gallop at a predetermined distance.

yearling A horse in its second calendar year of life, beginning January 1 of the year following its birth for horses born in the Northern Hemisphere.

yielding Condition of a turf course with considerable moisture. Horses sink into it noticeably.

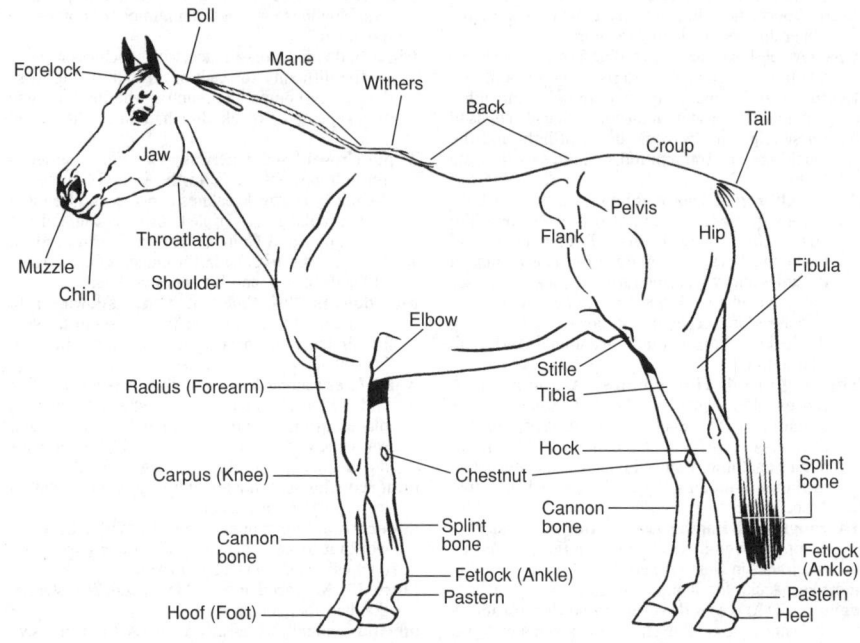

Conformation and Anatomy Terms

The following are words and expressions commonly used to describe Thoroughbred anatomy and conformation. This glossary contains many terms and definitions found in *The Media Guide to Equine Sport*, published by the American Association of Equine Practitioners.

angular limb deformity A limb that does not have correct conformation because of developmental problems in the angles of the joints.

anterior Toward the front.

back at the knee A leg that looks as though it has a backward arc, with its apex at the knee when viewed from the side.

cannon bone The third metacarpal (front leg) or metatarsal (rear leg), also referred to as the shin bone. The largest bone between the knee and ankle joints.

carpus A joint in the horse's front leg, more commonly referred to as the knee.

caudal Toward the tail.

coffin bone The third phalanx (P3). The major bone within the confines of the hoof. Also called the pedal bone.

conformation The physical makeup and bodily proportions of a horse: How the horse is put together.

coronary band Where the hair meets the hoof. Also called the coronet.

cow hocks Abnormal conformation in which the points of the hocks turn in.

cranial Toward the head.

curb A thickening of the plantar ligament of the hock.

deep flexor tendon Present in all four legs, but injuries most commonly affect the front legs. Located on the back (posterior) of the front leg between the knee and the foot and between the hock and the foot on the rear leg. The function is to flex the digit (pastern) and knee (carpus) and to extend the elbow on the front leg and extend the hock on the rear leg. Functions in tandem with the superficial flexor tendon.

digital The part of the limb below the ankle (fetlock) joint. Includes the long and short pastern bones and the coffin bone.

digital cushion The area beneath the coffin bone in the back of the foot that separates it from the frog. The digital cushion serves as a shock absorber for the foot.

distal Away from a reference point. Usually refers to the limbs.

distal sesamoidean ligaments Attach to the bottom of the sesamoid bones, passing down and attaching to the long and short pastern bones.

dorsal Up; toward the back or spine. Also used to describe the front of the lower limb below the knee (front) or hock (rear).

extensor tendon Extends the knee (carpus) joint, ankle joint, pastern, and foot and flexes the elbow.

The muscles begin above the knee and attach to the coffin and pastern bones.

fault Weak points of a horse's conformation or character as a racehorse.

fetlock (joint) Joint located between the cannon bone and the long pastern bone, also referred to as the ankle.

frog The V-shaped, pliable support structure on the bottom of the foot.

hock A large joint just above the shin bone in the rear legs. Corresponds to the level of the knee of the front leg.

hoof The foot of the horse. Consists of several parts that play an integral role in supporting the weight of the horse.

inferior check ligament A direct continuation of the posterior (back) ligaments of the knee (carpus), located below the knee. Function is in support of the deep flexor tendon.

insensitive laminae The layer just under the wall of the hoof; similar to the human fingernail. It is an integral structure that helps attach the hoof wall to the underlying coffin bone.

joint Point of juncture of two bones and usually composed of fibrous connective tissue and cartilage.

joint capsule The saclike structure that encloses the ends of bones in certain joints; contains synovial fluid.

ligament A band of fibrous tissue that connects bones, supports and strengthens joints, and limits the range of motion. Some ligaments support certain organs.

medial Pertaining to the middle in anatomy, nearer the median plane (the vertical plane that bisects the body into right and left halves).

metacarpal The cannon bone, located between the knee and the fetlock joint in the front leg. The cannon bone of the front leg is the third metacarpal.

metatarsal Cannon bone in the hind leg.

musculoskeletal system Consisting of the bones, muscles, ligaments, tendons, and joints of the head, vertebral column, and limbs, together with the associated muscles, tendons, ligaments, and joints.

muzzle Nose and lips of a horse.

navicular bone A small, flat bone within the confines of the hoof that helps—along with the short pastern bone and the coffin bone—to make up the coffin joint.

open knee A condition of young horses in which the physis of the knee has not closed, an immature knee. Often used to describe the status of the physis immediately above the knee and is an indicator of long bone growth in two-year-olds.

palmer Back of the front limb from the knee down.

parrot mouth A horse with an extreme overbite.

pastern (bones) The area between the fetlock joint and the hoof. The joint between the long and short pastern bones is called the pastern joint. Can also be used to describe the area of the limb or to describe a specific bone: long pastern bone. Technically known as the P1 (long) and the P2 (short).

physis The growth plate at the end of the long bones (such as the cannon bone) that lets the bone grow in length.

plantar Pertaining to the sole of the foot or back of the hind limb from the hock down.

plantar ligament The large ligament that is below and behind the hock joint.

poll The top of the head between the ears.

posterior Situated behind or toward the rear.

proximal Toward the body; the proximal cannon region is the upper portion of the cannon bone.

respiratory system Organ system responsible for gas exchange from nostrils to lungs.

sensitive laminae The area of the hoof that contains nerves and vessels.

sesamoid bones Two small bones (medial and lateral sesamoids) located above and at the back of the fetlock joint. Four common fractures of the sesamoids are apical (along the top of the bone), abaxial (the side of the sesamoid away from the ankle joint), midbody (sesamoid broken in half), and basilar (through the bottom) fractures.

sesamoid (fracture) Fracture of the sesamoid bone. Fractures can be small chips or involve the entire bone. Surgical repair is often done by arthroscopy.

splint Either of the two small bones that lie along the sides of the cannon bone.

stifle The large joint above the hock is made up of femur, patella, and tibia.

superficial flexor tendon Present in all four legs, but injuries most commonly affect the front legs. Located on the back (posterior) of the front leg between the knee and the foot and between the hock and the foot in the rear leg. Functions are to flex the digit (pastern) and knee (carpus), to extend the elbow on the front leg, and to extend the hock on the rear leg. Functions in tandem with the deep flexor tendon.

superior check ligament Fibrous band of tissue that originates above the knee and attaches to the superficial flexor tendon. Primary function is support of this tendon. Accessory ligament of the superficial flexor tendon.

suspensory ligament Originates at the back of the knee (front leg) and the back of the top part of the cannon bone (hind leg), attaching to the sesamoid bones. The lower portion of the ligament attaches the lower part of the sesamoid bones to the pastern bones. Its function is to support the fetlock. The lower ligaments that attach the sesamoid bone to the pastern bones are the distal sesamoidean ligaments.

synovial joint A movable joint that consists of articulating bone ends covered by articular cartilage held together with a joint capsule and ligaments and containing synovial fluid in the joint cavity.

synovial sheath The inner lining of a tendon sheath that produces synovial fluid. Allows ease of motion for the tendons as they cross joints.

tendon Cords of strong, white (collagen) elastic fibers that connect a muscle to a bone or other structure and transmit the forces generated by muscular contraction to the bones.

toe-in A conformation flaw in which the front of the foot angles inward and looks pigeon-toed, often causing the leg to swing outward during locomotion (paddling).

toe-out A conformation flaw in which the front of the foot faces out, often causing the leg to swing inward during locomotion (winging).

ventral Down; toward the belly.

vocal folds The membranes attached to the arytenoid cartilages in the larynx. Vibration produces vocalization.

white line When looking at the sole of the foot, the thin area between the insensitive outer hoof wall (insensitive laminae) and the inner sensitive laminae.

withers Area above the shoulder, where the neck meets the back.

Common Veterinary Terms

The following are commonly used veterinary terms. This glossary contains many terms and definitions found in the *Media Guide to Equine Sport*, published by the American Association of Equine Practitioners.

acupressure Utilizing stimulation on acupuncture points to treat an animal.

acupuncture A centuries-old therapy for treating an animal or human through the use of needles, electrical current, or moxibustion (heat and herbs) to stimulate or realign the body's electrical fields.

anhydrosis Inability to sweat in response to work output or increases in body temperature. A horse with this condition is also known as a nonsweater. Most are athletic horses, though frequently the condition appears in pastured horses not being ridden. Most commonly occurs when both the temperature and humidity are high. Horses raised in temperate regions and then transported to hot climates are most prone to develop the condition, but even acclimated horses can be at risk. Clinical signs include inability to sweat, increased respiratory rate, elevated body temperature, and decreased exercise tolerance. The condition sometimes can be reversed if the horse is moved to a more temperate climate.

anterior enteritis Acute inflammation of the small intestine producing signs of abdominal distress, such as colic and diarrhea.

arthritis Inflammation of a joint. An increase in the amount of synovial fluid in the joint is a result of this inflammation. Accumulation of synovial fluid in the fetlock joint is called a wind puff or wind gall. In young horses, a swelling in the fetlock joint, particularly on the front of the joint where the cannon and long pastern bones meet, is called a green osselet. This swelling is a result of inflammation and reactive changes of the front edges of these two bones and adjacent cartilage. If the green osselet does not heal, a chronic osselet might develop with a permanent buildup of synovial fluid in the joint and inflammation and thickening of the joint capsule over the damaged area with secondary bone changes following the initial inflammation.

arthroscope A tiny tube containing a lens that is used for viewing areas inside a joint. Usually attached to a small video camera.

arthroscopic surgery Utilizing an arthroscope to perform surgery, eliminating the need to open the joint with a large incision to view the damaged area.

articular cartilage Cartilage that covers the ends of bones where they meet in a joint.

arytenoid cartilages Triangular cartilages in the upper part of the entrance to the larynx. Movements of the arytenoid cartilages control the diameter of the laryngeal opening.

ataxia Loss or failure of muscular coordination.

atrophy To waste away; usually used in describing muscles.

bleeder A horse that bleeds within its lungs when small capillaries that surround the lungs' air sacs (alveoli) rupture. The veterinary term is exercise-induced pulmonary hemorrhage. Blood may be seen coming out of the horse's nostrils, known as epistaxis, although it is typically discovered by an examination using a fiber optic endoscope after exercise or racing. Hot, humid weather and cold conditions are known to exacerbate the problem. The most common preventive treatment currently available is the use of the diuretic furosemide (Salix). Less than one bleeder in 20 shows signs of epistaxis.

blister Counterirritant causing acute inflammation used to increase blood supply and blood flow to promote healing in the leg.

bog spavin A filling with excess synovial fluid of the largest joint of the hock, called the tibial tarsal joint.

bone graft Utilizing bone taken from one part of the body to promote formation of bone in another region.

bone spavin Arthritis of the hock joint. A bone spavin that has progressed to the point that the arthritis can be seen externally is called a jack spavin.

bowed tendon A type of tendinitis. The most common injury to the tendon is a strain or bowed tendon, so named because of the appearance of a bow shape due to swelling. The most common site of injury is in the superficial flexor tendon between the knee and the ankle. Despite aggressive treatment with anti-inflammatory drugs, physical therapy, and rest, horses commonly reinjure the tendon when they return to strenuous training. Two surgeries are felt to aid horses to come back to racing: tendon splitting at the lesion site to release accumulated fluid and blood, and superior check ligament desmotomy. The latter surgery is designed to reduce forces on the tendon when the horse returns to training and racing.

breakdown When a horse suffers a potentially career-ending injury, usually to the leg.

broken wind Abnormality of the upper or lower respiratory tract causing loss of normal air exchange, generally resulting in reduced performance.

bronchodilator A drug that widens the airways in the lungs to improve breathing and to relieve muscle contraction or buildup of mucus.

bucked shins Inflammation of the covering of the bone (periosteum) of the front surface of the cannon bone to which young horses are particularly susceptible. Usually a condition of the front legs.

bursa A sac containing synovial fluid (a natural lubricant). The purpose is to pad or cushion and thus facilitate motion between soft tissue and bone, most commonly where tendons pass over bones.

bursitis Inflammation in a bursa that results in swelling due to accumulation of synovial fluid. Capped elbow is inflammation of the bursa over the point of elbow (olecranon process of the ulna). Capped hock is inflammation of the bursa over the point of the hock (tuber calcis).

Bute Short for generic phenylbutazone, a nonsteroidal anti-inflammatory medication that is legal in many racing jurisdictions. Often known by the trade names Butazolidin and Butazone.

capillary refill time The amount of time it takes for blood to return to capillaries after it has been forced out, normally two seconds; usually assessed by pressing the thumb against the horse's gums. When the pressure is removed, the gum looks white but the normal pink color returns as blood flows into the capillaries.

capped elbow Inflammation of the bursa over the point of the elbow. Also known as a shoe boil.

capped hock Inflammation of the bursa over the point of the hock.

chiropractic The use of bone alignment to treat specific or general health problems.

chronic obstructive pulmonary disease Commonly known as COPD, a hyperallergenic response of the respiratory system that involves damage to the lung tissue, similar in many ways to human asthma. Affected horses may cough, develop a nasal discharge, and have a reduced tolerance for exercise. Respiratory rate is increased and lung elasticity is diminished.

chronic osselet Permanent buildup of synovial fluid in a joint, characterized by inflammation and thickening of the joint capsule over the damaged area. Usually accompanied by changes in the bone and cartilage.

clenbuterol A bronchodilator used for respiratory ailments. It is not permissible for use on race day.

closed knees A condition when the cartilaginous growth plate above the knee (distal radial physis) has turned to bone. Indicates completion of long bone growth and is one sign of maturity.

Coggins test A test for a horse used for identifying antigens or antibodies for a viral disease, specifically equine infectious anemia.

colic Often used broadly to describe abdominal pain, it is the leading cause of death among horses. Its causes include obstruction in the large colon; a twist in the intestine that shuts off the food passageway and blocks the blood supply; or gastric ulcers.

comminuted (fracture) A fracture with more than two fragments.

compound (fracture) A fracture in which the damaged bone breaks through the skin. Also known as an open fracture.

condylar (fracture) A fracture in the lower knobby end (condyle) of the lower (distal) end of a long bone such as the cannon bone or humerus (upper front limb).

congenital Present at birth.

contagious equine metritis (CEM) A venereal disease. Mares may have a profuse vaginal discharge. No symptoms may be obvious in stallions.

corticosteroids Hormones (class of steroid) that are either naturally produced by the adrenal gland or man-made. They function as anti-inflammatory hormones or as hormones that regulate the chemical stability (homeostasis) of the body. One common misconception is that a horse receiving corticosteroids experiences an increase in its natural abilities and therefore has an unfair advantage.

cough To expel air from the lungs in a spasmodic manner. Can be a result of inflammation or irritation to the upper airways (pharynx, larynx, or trachea) or may involve the lower airways of the lungs (deep cough).

cracked hoof A vertical split of the hoof wall. Cracks may extend upward from the bearing surface of the wall or downward from the coronary band, as the result of a defect in the band. Varying in degrees of severity, cracks can result from injuries or concussion. Hooves that are dry or thin (shelly) or improperly shod are susceptible to cracking upon concussion. Corrective trimming and shoeing may remedy mild cracks, but in severe cases, when the

crack extends inward to the sensitive laminae, more extensive treatment is required, such as using screws and wires to stabilize the sides of the crack.

cribber A horse that clings to objects with its teeth and sucks air into its stomach. Also known as a wind sucker.

cryptorchid A unilateral cryptorchid is a male horse of any age that has one testicle undescended. A bilateral cryptorchid is a male horse of any age that has both testicles undescended. The Jockey Club defines cryptorchid as a male horse of any age that has both testicles undescended.

cup Refers to the irregular occlusal surface of the tooth (the surfaces that meet when a horse closes its mouth) and is used as a visual method of determining age in a horse.

curb A thickening of the plantar ligament of the hock.

degenerative joint disease (DJD) Any joint problem that has progressive degeneration of joint cartilage and the underlying (subchondral) bone. Occurs most frequently in the joints below the radius in the foreleg and femur in the hind leg. Some of the more common causes include repeated trauma, conformation faults, blood disease, traumatic joint injury, subchondral bone defects osteochondritis dissecans (OCD) lesions, and excessive intra-articular corticosteroid injections. Also known as osteoarthritis or as developmental orthopedic disease (DOD).

desmitis Inflammation of a ligament. Often a result of tearing of any number of ligament fibrils.

deworming The use of drugs (anthelmintics) to kill internal parasites, often performed by administration of oral paste or liquid or by passing a nasogastric tube into the horse's stomach.

digestible energy The amount of energy a horse is able to digest from its feed.

DMSO Dimethyl sulfoxide, a topical anti-inflammatory. Its chief characteristic is its ability to penetrate the skin and therefore act as a vehicle for medications.

dorsal displacement of the soft palate A condition in which the soft palate, located on the floor of the airway near the larynx, moves up into the airway. A minor displacement causes a gurgling sound during exercise, while in more serious cases the palate can block the airway. This is sometimes known as choking down, but the tongue does not actually block the airway. The base of the tongue is connected to the larynx, of which the epiglottis is a part. When the epiglottis is retracted, the soft palate can move up into the airway (dorsal displacement). This condition can sometimes be managed with equipment such as a figure-eight noseband or a tongue tie. In more extreme cases, surgery might be required, most commonly a myectomy.

drench Liquid administered through mouth.

EEE (Eastern equine encephalomyelitis) One of several different types of encephalomyelitis that are extremely contagious, causing sickness and death in horses by affecting the central nervous system. EEE is spread by mosquitoes and can affect humans. Can be prevented by annual vaccination.

endoscope An instrument used for direct visual inspection of a hollow organ or body cavity such as the upper airway or stomach. A fiber optic endoscope comprises a long, flexible tube that has a series of

lenses and a light at the end to allow the veterinarian to view and photograph the respiratory system through the airway. Other internal organs may be viewed through a tiny surgical opening. A video endoscope has a small camera at its tip.

entrapped epiglottis A condition in which the thin membrane lying below the epiglottis moves up and covers the epiglottis. The abnormality may obstruct breathing. It is usually corrected by surgery to cut the membrane if it impairs respiratory function.

enzyme-linked immunosorbant assay A test, commonly referred to as the ELISA test, that is used post-race to detect the presence of drugs in racehorses. Developed in the early 1990s by the University of Kentucky.

epiphysitis An inflammation in the growth plate (physis) at the ends of the long bones (such as the cannon bone). Symptoms include swelling, tenderness, and heat. Although the exact cause is unknown, contributing factors seem to be high caloric intake (either from grain or a heavily lactating mare) and a fast growth rate.

equine protozoal myeloencephalitis Commonly called EPM. A neurological condition in a horse caused by a parasite that infects the horse's central nervous system. The cause of EPM is *Sarcocystis neurona*, a small protozoan organism that is slightly larger than a bacterium. One of the hosts necessary to complete the organism's life cycle is the opossum.

equine viral arteritis (EVA) A highly contagious disease that is characterized by swelling in the legs of all horses and swelling in the scrotum of stallions. Can cause abortion in mares and can be shed in the semen of stallions for years after infection.

exercise-induced pulmonary hemorrhage (EIPH) See bleeder.

fissure (fracture) Longitudinal crack through only one surface of a bone.

float An equine dental procedure in which sharp points on the teeth are filed down.

founder See laminitis.

fracture A break in a bone.

furosemide A medication used in the treatment of bleeders, commonly known by the trade name Salix, a diuretic. Although research has not determined definitively how furosemide reduces bleeding, it is widely believed that the diuretic effect reduces pressure within capillaries in the lungs.

gastric ulcers Ulceration of a horse's stomach. Often causes symptoms of abdominal distress (colic) and general unthriftiness.

gravel Infection of the hoof resulting from a crack in the white line (the border between the insensitive and sensitive laminae). An abscess usually forms in the sensitive structures and eventually breaks at the coronet as the result of the infection.

heaves Emphysema.

heel crack A crack on the heel of the hoof. Also called a sand crack.

hematoma A blood-filled area resulting from injury.

hyaluronic acid A normal component of joint fluid. Also can be a man-made intra-articular medication used to relieve joint inflammation.

IM Abbreviation for intramuscular.

impaction A type of colic caused by a blockage of the intestines by ingested materials (constipation).

intra-articular Within a joint.

intramuscular An injection given in a muscle.

intravenous An injection given in a vein.

ischemia Deficiency of blood supply, which may be temporary or permanent. Caused by the shutting down of blood vessels.

IV Abbreviation for intravenous.

lactic acid Organic acid normally present in muscle tissue, produced by anaerobic muscle metabolism as a byproduct of exercise. An increase in lactic acid causes muscle fatigue, inflammation, and pain.

lame A deviation from a normal gait due to pain in a limb or its supporting structures.

laminitis An inflammation of the sensitive laminae of the foot. There are many factors involved, including changes in the blood flow through the capillaries of the foot. Many events can cause laminitis, including ingesting toxic levels of grain, eating lush grass, systemic disease problems, high temperature, toxemia, retained placenta, excessive weight-bearing as occurs when the opposite limb is injured, and the administration of some drugs. Laminitis usually manifests itself in the front feet, develops rapidly, and is life-threatening. In mild cases, however, a horse can resume a certain amount of athletic activity. Also known as founder.

magnetic therapy Physical therapy technique using magnetic fields. The low-energy electrical field created by the magnetic field causes dilation of the blood vessels (vasodilation) and tissue stimulation. Magnetic therapy may be used on soft tissue to treat such injuries as tendinitis or bony (skeletal) injuries such as bucked shins.

metacarpal (fracture) Usually refers to a fracture of the cannon bone, located between the knee and the fetlock joint in the front leg. Also may refer to a fracture of the splint bone. The cannon bone of the front leg is the third metacarpal.

monorchid A male horse of any age that has only one testicle in his scrotum; the other testicle was either removed or is undescended.

nasogastric tube A long tube that is capable of reaching from the nose to the stomach.

navicular disease A degenerative disease that affects the navicular bone (small bone in the back of the foot), navicular bursa, and deep flexor tendon. Generally considered a disease of the front feet. Both front feet are often affected, but one will usually be more noticeable than the other.

neurectomy A surgical procedure in which the nerve supply to the navicular area is removed. The toe and remainder of the foot retain feeling. Also referred to as *posterior digital neurectomy* or *heel nerve*. Also known as nerving.

oblique (fracture) Fracture at an angle.

OCD lesion (osteochondritis dissecans) A cartilaginous or bony lesion that is the result of a fragment of cartilage and its underlying bone becoming detached from an articular surface. The lesions occur commonly in the knee joint and are associated with a failure in bone development.

oiled (oiling) Administration of mineral oil via nasogastric tube to relieve gas or to break a blockage. Preventative procedure commonly used in long van rides to prevent impaction with subsequent colics.

open knee A condition of young horses in which the

physis of the knee has not closed; an immature knee. Often used to describe the status of the physis immediately above the knee and is an indicator of long bone growth in two-year-olds.

osteoarthritis A permanent form of arthritis with progressive loss of the articular cartilage in a joint.

pastern (bones) The area between the fetlock joint and the hoof. The joint between the long and short pastern bones is called the pastern joint. Can also be used to describe the area of the limb or to describe a specific bone: long pastern bone. Technically known as the P1 (long) and P2 (short).

periostitis Inflammation of the tissue (periosteum) that overlies bone. Periostitis of the cannon bone is referred to as bucked shins, while periostitis of the splint bone is called a splint, which may be expressed as popped a splint.

phenylbutazone A nonsteroidal anti-inflammatory medication that is legal in many racing jurisdictions. Trade names are Butazolidin and Butazone.

physis The growth plate at the end of the long bones (such as the cannon bone) that lets the bone grow in length.

pin firing Thermocautery used to increase blood flow to the leg and intended to promote healing.

pulled suspensory Suspensory ligament injury (suspensory desmitis) in which some portion of the fibers of the ligament have been disrupted and some loss of support of the distal limb may have occurred.

quarter crack A crack between the toe and heel, usually extending into the coronary band.

radiograph The picture or image on film generated by X rays.

ring bone Osteoarthritis of joints between the pastern bones (high ring bone) or just above the coronet (low ring bone).

roaring (laryngeal hemiplegia) A whistling sound made by a horse during inhalation while exercising. The condition is caused by a partial or total paralysis of the nerves controlling the muscles that elevate the arytenoid cartilages and thereby open the larynx. In severe cases, a surgical procedure known as tie-back surgery (laryngoplasty) is performed, in which a suture is inserted through the cartilage to hold it out of the airway permanently. Paralysis almost exclusively occurs on the left side and most frequently in horses over 16 hands tall.

run down Abrasions of the heel.

saucer (fracture) Stress fracture of the front of the cannon bone; the fracture can be straight or curved.

screw fixation A procedure in which steel-alloy screws are surgically inserted to hold together a fractured bone.

sesamoid (fracture) Fracture of the sesamoid bone. Fractures can be small chips or involve the entire bone. Surgical repair is often done by arthroscopy.

sesamoiditis Inflammation of the sesamoid bones.

simple (fracture) A fracture along a single line that does not penetrate the skin.

slab (fracture) A bone fracture in a joint that extends from one articular surface to another. Most often seen in the third carpal bone of the knee.

slipped Spontaneous abortion.

splint A condition in which calcification occurs on the splint bone and causes a bump. This condition can occur in response to a fracture or other irritation to the splint bone. A common injury is a popped splint.

stress (fracture) A fracture created by the repetitive stress placed on a bone, most often in athletic training. Usually seen in the front of the cannon bone as a severe form of bucked shins. Also seen in the tibia and causes a hard-to-diagnose hind-limb lameness.

synchronous diaphragmatic flutter A contraction of the diaphragm in synchrony with the heartbeat after strenuous exercise. Affected horses have a noticeable twitch or spasm in the flank area that may cause an audible sound, hence the term thumps. Most commonly seen in electrolyte-depleted or exhausted horses. The condition resolves spontaneously with rest.

synovitis Inflammation of a synovial structure, typically a synovial sheath.

tendinitis Inflammation of a tendon.

thermography Diagnostic technique utilizing instrumentation that measures temperature differences. Records the surface temperature of a horse. Unusually hot or cold areas may be indicative of some underlying pathology (deviation from the normal).

thoroughpin Swelling of the synovial sheath of the deep flexor tendon above the hock.

tie-back surgery A procedure (laryngoplasty) used to suture the arytenoid cartilage out of the airway.

toe crack A crack near the front of the hoof.

torsion A twist in the intestine.

toxemia Poisoning sometimes caused by the absorption of bacterial products (endotoxins) formed at a local source of infection.

tubing Inserting a nasogastric tube through a horse's nostril into its stomach for the purpose of providing oral medication.

twitch A restraining device usually consisting of a stick with a loop of rope or chain at one end, which is placed around a horse's upper lip and twisted, releasing endorphins that relax a horse and curb its fractiousness while it is being handled.

tying up (acute rhabdomyolysis) A form of muscle cramps that ranges in severity from mild stiffness to a life-threatening disease. A generalized condition of muscle-fiber breakdown usually associated with exercise. The cause of the muscle-fiber breakdown is uncertain. Signs include sweating, reluctance to move, stiffness, and general distress.

ultrasound 1) Diagnostic ultrasound: A technique that uses ultrasonic waves to image internal structures. 2) Therapeutic ultrasound: A therapy to create heat and stimulate healing.

Venezuelan equine encephalomyelitis (VEE) A highly contagious disease affecting the central nervous system that can cause illness or death in horses and humans.

wobbler syndrome Neurological disease clinically associated with general incoordination and muscle weakness. Can be caused by an injury to the spinal cord in the area of the cervical (neck) vertebrae or is associated with malformation of the cervical vertebrae.

Xeroradiography: A costly type of x-ray procedure using specially sensitized screens that give higher resolution on the edges of bone and better visualization of soft tissue structures.

INTERNATIONAL
Major Stakes Races
Canada
Atto Mile Stakes

Grade 1, Woodbine, Ontario, three-year-olds and up, 1 mile, turf. Held September 9, 2001, with a gross value of $1,000,000. First held in 1997.

Year	Winner	Jockey	Second	Third	Strs	Final Time	1st Purse
2001	Numerous Times, 4	P. Husbands	Affirmed Success, 7	Quiet Resolve, 6	14	1:32.79	$600,000
2000	Riviera (Fr), 6	J. R. Velazquez	Arkadian Hero, 5	Affirmed Success, 6	13	1:33.18	$600,000
1999	Quiet Resolve, 4	R. C. Landry	Rob 'n Gin, 5	Jim and Tonic (Fr), 5	15	1:33.19	$630,000
1998	Labeeb (GB), 6	K. J. Desormeaux	Jim and Tonic (Fr), 4	Poteen, 4	11	1:33.00	$450,000
1997	Geri, 5	C. W. Antley	Helmsman, 5	Crown Attorney, 4	12	1:36.20	$300,000

1997-'98 Woodbine Mile S. 1999 Hawksley Hill (Ire) finished first, disqualified to fourth.

Breeders' Stakes

Not graded, Woodbine, Ontario, three-year-olds, foaled in Canada, 1½ miles, turf. Held August 11, 2001, with a gross value of $500,000. First held in 1889.

Year	Winner	Jockey	Second	Third	Strs	Final Time	1st Purse
2001	†Sweetest Thing	J. S. McAleney	Flaming Sky	†Asia	6	2:29.90	$300,000
2000	Lodge Hill	M. E. Smith	Master Stuart	Scatter the Gold	7	2:28.97	$300,000
1999	†Free Vacation	L. L. Gulas	John the Drummer	American Falcon	13	2:28.45	$195,000
1998	†Pinafore Park	R. C. Landry	Patriot Love	Comet Kris	9	2:30.20	$180,000
1997	John the Magician	S. R. Bahen	†One Emotion	†Heaven to Earth	12	2:35.60	$175,860
1996	Chief Bearhart	M. Walls	Firm Dancer	Sealaunch	9	2:28.60	$171,120
1995	Charlie's Dewan	C. Perret	Mt. Sassafras	Dagda	13	2:26.40	$182,700
1994	Basqueian	J. M. Lauzon	Pagagar	Testalino	5	2:47.80	$149,739
1993	Peteski	C. Perret	Flashy Regent	English Toff	4	2:30.40	$237,549
1992	Blitzer	D. J. Seymour	†Classic Reign	Rodin	11	2:35.60	$180,000

1994 held at Fort Erie. † denotes female.

Canadian International Stakes

Grade 1, Woodbine, Ontario, three-year-olds and up, 1½ miles, turf. Held September 30, 2001, with a gross value of $1,500,000. First held in 1938.

Year	Winner	Jockey	Second	Third	Strs	Final Time	1st Purse
2001	Mutamam (GB), 6	R. Hills	Paolini (Ger), 4	Lodge Hill, 4	12	2:28.46	$900,000
2000	Mutafaweq, 4	L. Dettori	Williams News, 5	Daliapour (Ire), 4	12	2:27.62	$900,000
1999	Thornfield, 5	R. A. Dos Ramos	Fruits of Love, 4	Courteous (GB), 4	9	2:32.39	$936,000
1998	Royal Anthem, 3	G. L. Stevens	Chief Bearhart, 5	Parade Ground, 3	8	2:29.60	$630,000
1997	Chief Bearhart, 4	J. A. Santos	Down the Aisle, 4	Romanov (Ire), 3	6	2:29.00	$600,000
1996	Singspiel (Ire), 4	G. L. Stevens	Chief Bearhart, 3	Mecke, 4	7	2:33.20	$600,000
1995	Lassigny, 4	P. Day	Mecke, 3	Hasten To Add, 5	15	2:29.80	$653,250
1994	Raintrap (GB), 4	R. G. Davis	†Alywow, 3	Volochine (Ire), 3	9	2:25.60	$606,900
1993	Husband, 3	C. B. Asmussen	Cozzene's Prince, 6	Regency (GB), 3	11	2:36.40	$623,100
1992	Snurge (Ire), 5	R. T. Quinn	Ghazi, 3	Wiorno (GB), 4	14	2:39.00	$636,000

1992-'95 Rothmans Ltd. International S. 1992 Wiorno (GB) finished first, disqualified to third; 2002 Zindabad (Fr) finished third, DQ to sixth. † denotes female.

E. P. Taylor Stakes

Grade 1, Woodbine, Ontario, three-year-olds and up, fillies and mares, 1¼ miles, turf. Held September 30, 2001, with a gross value of $500,000. First held in 1956.

Year	Winner	Jockey	Second	Third	Strs	Final Time	1st Purse
2001	Choc Ice (Ire), 3	J. P. Murtagh	Volga (Ire), 3	Spring Oak (GB), 3	13	2:03.01	$300,000
2000	Fly for Avie, 5	T. Kabel	Lady Upstage (Ire), 3	Innuendo (Ire), 5	9	2:02.78	$300,000
1999	Insight (Fr), 4	M. E. Smith	Cerulean Sky (Ire), 3	Midnight Line, 4	7	2:05.34	$300,000
1998	Zomaradah (GB), 3	G. L. Stevens	Tresoriere, 4	Griselda, 3	8	2:02.40	$273,600
1997	Kool Kat Katie (Ire), 3	O. Peslier	Mousse Glacee (Fr), 3	L'Annee Folle (Fr), 4	9	2:02.00	$206,460
1996	Wandering Star, 3	W. H. McCauley	Flame Valley, 3	Carling (Fr), 4	8	2:04.60	$204,120
1995	Timarida (Ire), 3	L. Dettori	Matiara, 3	Bold Ruritana, 3	13	2:03.60	$213,120
1994	Truly a Dream (Ire), 3	C. J. McCarron	Bold Ruritana, 4	Hero's Love, 6	9	2:01.60	$207,180
1993	Hero's Love, 5	E. Fires	Dance for Donna, 4	Lady Shirl, 6	7	2:14.40	$204,300
1992	Hatoof, 3	W. R. Swinburn	Urban Sea, 3	Hero's Love, 4	12	2:07.80	$210,960

Prince of Wales Stakes

Not graded, Fort Erie, Ontario, three-year-olds, foaled in Canada, 1³/₁₆ miles, dirt. Held July 22, 2001, with a gross value of $350,000. First held in 1929.

Year	Winner	Jockey	Second	Third	Strs	Final Time	1st Purse
2001	Win City	C. Montpellier	†Dancethruthedawn	Brushing Bully	6	1:56.14	$210,000
2000	Scatter the Gold	T. Kabel	For Our Sake	Cool N Collective	7	1:56.01	$170,280
1999	†Gandria	C. Montpellier	Woodcarver	Euchre	8	1:56.23	$155,700
1998	Archers Bay	R. C. Landry	Nite Dreamer	One Way Love	6	1:55.20	$118,500
1997	Cryptocloser	W. Martinez	C. C. On Ice	Rabbit in a Hat	7	1:56.00	$117,660
1996	Stephanotis	M. Walls	Firm Dancer	Kristy Krunch	7	1:55.20	$121,620
1995	Kiridashi	L. Attard	Regal Discovery	Mt. Sassafras	6	1:55.00	$121,800
1994	Bruce's Mill	C. Perret	Basqueian	Parental Pressure	4	1:53.20	$87,296
1993	Peteski	D. Penna	Flashy Regent	Cheery Knight	8	1:54.40	$72,203
1992	Benburb	L. Attard	Alydeed	Judge Carson	6	1:57.40	$107,700

† denotes female.

Queen's Plate Stakes

Not graded, Woodbine, Ontario, three-year-olds, foaled in Canada, 1¼ miles, dirt. Held June 24, 2001, with a gross value of $1,000,000. First held in 1860.

Year	Winner	Jockey	Second	Third	Strs	Final Time	1st Purse
2001	†Dancethruthedawn	G. Boulanger	Win City	Brushing Bully	10	2:03.78	$600,000
2000	Scatter the Gold	T. Kabel	I and I	For Our Sake	16	2:05.53	$600,000
1999	Woodcarver	M. Walls	†Gandria	Euchre	17	2:03.13	$300,000
1998	Archers Bay	K. J. Desormeaux	Brite Adam	Kinkennie	13	2:02.20	$300,000
1997	Awesome Again	M. E. Smith	Cryptocloser	Sovereign Storm	14	2:04.20	$255,420
1996	Victor Cooley	E. Ramsammy	Stephanotis	Kristy Krunch	13	2:03.80	$255,480
1995	Regal Discovery	T. Kabel	Freedom Fleet	Mt. Sassafras	14	2:03.80	$261,660
1994	Basqueian	J. M. Lauzon	Bruce's Mill	Parental Pressure	11	2:03.40	$276,420
1993	Peteski	C. Perret	Cheery Knight	Janraffole	11	2:04.20	$218,600
1992	Alydeed	C. Perret	Grand Hooley	Benburb	12	2:04.60	$228,900

† denotes female.

England

Derby S.

Group 1, Epsom, three-year-olds, colts and fillies, about 1½ miles, turf. Held June 9, 2001, with a gross value of $1,379,900. First held in 1780.

Year	Winner	Jockey	Second	Third	Strs	Final Time	1st Purse
2001	Galileo (Ire)	M. J. Kinane	Golan	Tobougg	12	2:33.20	$800,342
2000	Sinndar	J. Murtagh	Sakhee	Beat Hollow (GB)	15	2:36.75	$918,981
1999	Oath	K. Fallon	Daliapour	Beat All	16	2:37.43	$990,671
1998	High-Rise (Ire)	O. Peslier	City Honours	Border Arrow	15	2:33.88	$978,679
1997	Benny the Dip	W. Ryan	Silver Patriarch	Romanov (Ire)	13	2:34.77	$971,448
1996	Shaamit	M. Hills	Dushyantor	Shantou	20	2:35.05	$804,894
1995	Lammtarra	W. Swinburn	Tamure (Ire)	Presenting	15	2:32.31	$805,687
1994	Erhaab	W. Carson	King's Theatre (Ire)	Colonel Collins	25	2:34.16	$717,662
1993	Commander in Chief	M. J. Kinane	Blue Judge	Blues Traveller (Ire)	16	2:34.51	$693,078
1992	Dr Devious (Ire)	J. Reid	St. Jovite	Silver Wisp	18	2:36.19	$649,473

Gold Cup

Group 1, Ascot Racecourse, four-year-olds and up, about 2½ miles, turf. Held June 21, 2001, with a gross value of $297,297. First held in 1807.

Year	Winner	Jockey	Second	Third	Strs	Final Time	1st Purse
2001	Royal Rebel, 5	J. Murtagh	Persian Punch, 8	Jardines Lookout, 4	12	4:18.90	$172,432
2000	Kayf Tara, 6	M. J. Kinane	Far Cry, 5	Compton Ace, 4	11	4:24.53	$184,308
1999	Enzeli, 4	J. Murtagh	Invermark, 5	Kayf Tara, 5	17	4:18.85	$191,662
1998	Kayf Tara, 4	L. Dettori	Double Trigger, 7	Three Cheers, 4	16	4:32.36	$198,132
1997	Celeric, 5	P. Eddery	Classic Cliche, 5	Election Day, 5	13	4:26.19	$187,197
1996	Classic Cliche, 4	M. Kinane	Double Trigger, 5	Nononito, 5	7	4:23.20	$182,980
1995	Double Trigger, 4	J. Weaver	Moonax, 4	Admiral's Well, 5	7	4:20.25	$178,465
1994	Arcadian Heights, 6	M. Hills	Vintage Crop, 7	Sonus, 5	9	4:27.67	$169,666
1993	Drum Taps, 7	L. Dettori	Assessor, 4	Turgeon, 7	10	4:32.57	$166,410
1992	Drum Taps, 6	L. Dettori	Arcadian Heights, 4	Turgeon, 6	6	4:18.20	$198,590

King George VI and Queen Elizabeth Stakes

Group 1, Ascot Racecourse, three-year-olds and up, 1½ miles, turf. Held July 28, 2001, with a gross value of $1,068,525. First held in 1951.

Year	Winner	Jockey	Second	Third	Strs	Final Time	1st Purse
2001	Galileo (Ire), 3	M. J. Kinane	Fantastic Light, 5	Hightori, 4	12	2:27.71	$619,745
2000	Montjeu (Ire), 4	M. J. Kinane	Fantastic Light, 4	Daliapour, 4	7	2:29.98	$654,023
1999	Daylami (Ire), 5	L. Dettori	Nedawi, 4	Fruits of Love, 4	8	2:29.35	$539,676
1998	Swain (Ire), 6	L. Dettori	High-Rise (Ire), 3	Royal Anthem, 3	8	2:29.60	$587,463
1997	Swain (Ire), 5	J. Reid	Pilsudski (Ire), 5	Helissio, 4	8	2:36.45	$490,509
1996	Pentire, 4	M. Hills	Classic Cliche, 4	Shaamit, 3	8	2:28.11	$457,867
1995	Lammtarra, 3	L. Dettori	Pentire, 3	Strategic Choice, 4	7	2:31.01	$445,877
1994	King's Theatre (Ire), 3	M. Kinane	White Muzzle (GB), 4	Wagon Master, 4	12	2:28.92	$408,813
1993	Opera House (GB), 5	M. Roberts	White Muzzle (GB), 3	Commander in Chief, 3	10	2:33.94	$409,307
1992	St. Jovite, 3	S. Craine	Saddlers' Hall (Ire), 4	Opera House (GB), 4	8	2:30.85	$497,878

Oaks S.

Group 1, Epsom, three-year-old fillies, about 1½ miles, turf. Held June 8, 2001, with a gross value of $503,663. First held in 1779.

Year	Winner	Jockey	Second	Third	Strs	Final Time	1st Purse
2001	Imagine	M. J. Kinane	Flight of Fancy	Relish The Thought	14	2:36.70	$292,125
2000	Love Divine	T. Quinn	Kalypso Katie (Ire)	Melikah (Ire)	16	2:43.11	$288,823
1999	Ramruma	K. Fallon	Noushkey	Zahrat Dubai	10	2:38.72	$286,775
1998	Shahtoush	M. J. Kinane	Bahr (GB)	Midnight Line	8	2:38.23	$289,342
1997	Reams of Verse	K. Fallon	Gazelle Royale	Crown of Light	12	2:35.59	$297,432
1996	Lady Carla (GB)	P. Eddery	Pricket	Mezzogiorno	11	2:35.55	$309,279
1995	Moonshell (Ire)	L. Dettori	Dance a Dream (GB)	Pure Grain (GB)	10	2:35.44	$236,037
1994	Balanchine	L. Dettori	Wind in Her Hair (Ire)	Hawajiss	10	2:40.37	$223,758
1993	Intrepidity (GB)	M. Roberts	Royal Ballerina (Ire)	Oakmead (Ire)	14	2:34.19	$228,404
1992	User Friendly (GB)	G. Duffield	All At Sea	Pearl Angel (GB)	7	2:39.77	$269,851

One Thousand Guineas

Group 1, Newmarket, three-year-old fillies, 1 mile, turf. Held May 6, 2001, with a gross value of $431,850. First held in 1814.

Year	Winner	Jockey	Second	Third	Strs	Final Time	1st Purse
2001	Ameerat	P. Robinson	Muwakleh	Toroca	15	1:38.30	$250,473
2000	Lahan (GB)	R. Hills	Princess Ellen (GB)	Petrushka (Ire)	18	1:36.38	$221,517
1999	Wince	K. Fallon	Wannabe Grand (Ire)	Valentine Waltz (Ire)	22	1:37.91	$206,757
1998	Cape Verdi	L. Dettori	Shahtoush	Exclusive	16	1:37.86	$214,081
1997	Sleepytime	K. Fallon	Oh Nellie	Dazzle	15	1:37.66	$169,872
1996	Bosra Sham	P. Eddery	Matiya (Ire)	Bint Shadayid	13	1:37.75	$151,461
1995	Harayir	R. Hills	Aqaarid	Moonshell (Ire)	14	1:36.72	$178,983
1994	Las Meninas (Ire)	J. Reid	Balanchine	Coup de Genie	15	1:36.71	$166,127
1993	Sayyedati (GB)	W. R. Swinburn	Niche	Ajfan	12	1:37.34	$163,969
1992	Hatoof	W. R. Swinburn	Marling (Ire)	Kenbu (Fr)	14	1:39.45	$192,254

St. Leger S.

Group 1, Doncaster, three-year-olds, colts and fillies, about 1¾ miles and 127 yards, turf. Held September 15, 2001, with a gross value of $544,381. First held in 1776.

Year	Winner	Jockey	Second	Third	Strs	Final Time	1st Purse
2001	Milan (GB)	M. J. Kinane	Demophilos	Mr Combustible	10	3:05.10	$326,629
2000	Millenary	T. Quinn	Air Marshall	Chimes At Midnight	11	3:02.58	$315,018
1999	Mutafaweq	R. Hills	†Ramruma	Adair	9	3:02.75	$353,664
1998	Nedawi	J. Reid	†High and Low	Sunshine Street	9	3:05.61	$335,898
1997	Silver Patriarch	P. Eddery	Vertical Speed	The Fly (GB)	10	3:06.92	$295,420
1996	Shantou	L. Dettori	Dushyantor	Samraan	11	3:05.10	$271,692
1995	Classic Cliche	L. Dettori	Minds Music	Istidaad	10	3:09.74	$259,794
1994	Moonax	P. Eddery	Broadway Flyer	Double Trigger	8	3:04.19	$236,950
1993	Bob's Return	P. Robinson	Armiger	Edbaysaan	9	3:07.85	$292,567
1992	†User Friendly (GB)	G. Duffield	Sonus	Bonny Scot	7	3:05.48	$323,139

† denotes female.

Two Thousand Guineas

Group 1, Newmarket, three-year-olds, colts and fillies, 1 mile, turf. Held May 5, 2001, with a gross value of $431,850. First held in 1809.

Year	Winner	Jockey	Second	Third	Strs	Final Time	1st Purse
2001	Golan	K. Fallon	Tamburlaine	Frenchmans Bay	18	1:37.40	$250,473
2000	King's Best	K. Fallon	Giant's Causeway	Barathea Guest	27	1:37.77	$265,820
1999	Island Sands	L. Dettori	Enrique	Mujahid	16	1:37.14	$276,426
1998	King of Kings (Ire)	M. Kinane	Lend a Hand	Border Arrow	18	1:39.25	$286,219
1997	Entrepreneur	M. Kinane	Revoque	Poteen	16	1:35.64	$213,832
1996	Mark of Esteem (Ire)	L. Dettori	Even Top (Ire)	Bijou d'Inde	13	1:37.59	$184,212
1995	Pennekamp	T. Jarnet	Celtic Swing	Bahri	11	1:35.16	$190,487
1994	Mister Baileys (GB)	J. Weaver	Grand Lodge	Colonel Collins	23	1:35.08	$194,491
1993	Zafonic	P. Eddery	Barathea (Ire)	Bin Ajwaad	14	1:35.32	$173,569
1992	Rodrigo de Triano	L. Piggott	Lucky Lindy	Pursuit of Love	16	1:38.37	$203,189

France

Poule d'Essai des Poulains (French Two Thousand Guineas)

Group 1, Longchamp, three-year-old colts, about 1 mile, turf. Held May 13, 2001, with a gross value of $233,800. First run in 1883.

Year	Winner	Jockey	Second	Third	Strs	Final Time	1st Purse
2001	Vahorimix	C. Soumillon	Clearing	Denon	12	1:35.40	$133,600
2000	Bachir	L. Dettori	Berine's Son	Valentino	7	1:39.40	$140,100
1999	Sendawar	G. Mosse	Dansili (GB)	Kingsalsa	15	1:36.20	$162,600
1998	Victory Note	J. A. Reid	Muhtathir (GB)	Desert Prince (Ire)	12	1:34.50	$168,500
1997	Daylami (Ire)	G. Mosse	Loup Sauvage	Visionary	6	1:42.60	$175,700
1996	Ashkalani	G. Mosse	Spinning World	Tagula	10	1:37.60	$193,200
1995	Vettori	L. Dettori	Atticus	Petit Poucet (GB)	8	1:40.40	$210,920
1994	Green Tune	O. Doleuze	Turtle Island	Psychobabble (Ire)	7	1:37.40	$177,230
1993	Kingmambo	C. Asmussen	Bin Ajwaad	Hudo	10	1:39.10	$187,740
1992	Shanghai	F. Head	Rainbow Corner (GB)	Lion Cavern	9	1:38.20	$180,800

2002 Noverre finished first, DQ to 12th.

Poule d'Essai des Pouliches (French One Thousand Guineas)

Group 1, Longchamp, three-year-old fillies, about 1 mile, turf. Held May 13, 2001, with a gross value of $233,800. First held in 1883.

Year	Winner	Jockey	Second	Third	Strs	Final Time	1st Purse
2001	Rose Gypsy	M. J. Kinane	Banks Hill (GB)	Lethals Lady (GB)	15	1:36.70	$133,600
2000	Bluemamba	T. Jarnet	Peony	Alshakr	11	1:40.20	$140,100
1999	Valentine Waltz (Ire)	R. Cochrane	Karmifira (Fr)	Calando	14	1:36.00	$162,600
1998	Zalaiyka	G. Mosse	Cortona	La Nuit Rose	14	1:35.70	$168,500
1997	Always Loyal	F. Head	Seebe	Red Camellia	7	1:40.20	$175,700
1996	Ta Rib	W. Carson	Shake the Yoke (GB)	Sagar Pride (Ire)	9	1:38.70	$193,200
1995	Matiara	F. Head	Carling (Fr)	Shaanxi	16	1:42.40	$210,920
1994	East of the Moon	C. Asmussen	Agathe	Belle Argentine	8	1:37.10	$177,230
1993	Madeleine's Dream	C. Asmussen	Ski Paradise	Gold Splash	8	1:36.40	$187,740
1992	Culture Vulture	T. R. Quinn	Hydro Calido	Guislaine (Fr)	9	1:37.00	$180,800

Prix de Diane (French Oaks)

Group 1, Chantilly, three-year-old fillies, about 1⁵⁄₁₆ miles, turf. Held June 10, 2001, with a gross value of $385,858. First held in 1843.

Year	Winner	Jockey	Second	Third	Strs	Final Time	1st Purse
2001	Aquarelliste	D. Boeuf	Nadia	Time Away	12	2:09.50	$220,490
2000	Egyptband	O. Doleuze	Volvoreta	Goldamix (Ire)	14	2:08.50	$203,420
1999	Daryaba	G. Mosse	Star of Akkar	Visionnaire (Fr)	14	2:16.10	$224,700
1998	Zainta	G. Mosse	Abbatiale	Insight (Fr)	11	2:11.20	$235,340
1997	Vereva	G. Mosse	Mousse Glacee (Fr)	Brilliance (Fr)	12	2:08.20	$240,520
1996	Sil Sila	C. Asmussen	Miss Tahiti	Matiya (Ire)	12	2:07.30	$269,080
1995	Carling (Fr)	T. Thulliez	Matiara	Tryphosa	12	2:07.70	$282,240
1994	East of the Moon	C. Asmussen	Her Ladyship	Agathe	9	2:07.90	$248,850
1993	Shemaka	G. Mosse	Baya	Dancienne	14	2:16.00	$260,582
1992	Jolypha	P. Eddery	Sheba Dancer (Fr)	Verveine	12	2:09.50	$259,770

Prix de l'Arc de Triomphe

Group 1, Longchamp, three-year-olds and up, about 1½ miles, turf. Held October 7, 2001, with a gross value of $1,470,000. First held in 1920.

Year	Winner	Jockey	Second	Third	Strs	Final Time	1st Purse
2001	Sakhee, 4	L. Dettori	†Aquarellliste, 3	Sagacity, 3	17	2:36.10	$840,000
2000	Sinndar, 3	J. P. Murtagh	†Egyptband, 3	†Volvoreta, 3	10	2:25.80	$806,400
1999	Montjeu (Ire), 3	M. J. Kinane	El Condor Pasa, 4	Croco Rouge, 4	14	2:38.50	$654,000
1998	Sagamix, 3	O. Peslier	†Leggera (Ire), 3	Tiger Hill, 3	14	2:34.50	$724,000
1997	Peintre Celebre, 3	O. Peslier	Pilsudski (Ire), 5	†Borgia (Ger), 3	18	2:24.60	$677,600
1996	Helissio, 3	O. Peslier	Pilsudski (Ire), 4	Oscar Schindler, 4	16	2:29.90	$771,600
1995	Lammtarra, 3	L. Dettori	Freedom Cry (GB), 4	Swain (Ire), 3	16	2:31.80	$811,600
1994	Carnegie (Ire), 3	T. Jarnet	Hernando (Fr), 4	Apple Tree (Fr), 5	20	2:31.10	$754,440
1993	†Urban Sea, 4	E. Saint-Martin	White Muzzle (GB), 3	Opera House (GB), 5	23	2:37.90	$879,050
1992	Subotica (Fr), 4	T. Jarnet	†User Friendly (GB), 3	Vert Amande, 4	18	2:39.00	$1,039,500

† denotes female.

Prix du Jockey-Club (French Derby)

Group 1, Chantilly, three-year-olds, colts and fillies, about 1½ miles, turf. Held June 3, 2001, with a gross value of $905,100. First held in 1836.

Year	Winner	Jockey	Second	Third	Strs	Final Time	1st Purse
2001	Anabaa Blue	C. Soumillon	Chichicastenango	Grandera	14	2:27.90	$517,200
2000	Holding Court	P. Robinson	Lord Flasheart	Circus Dance	14	2:31.80	$359,750
1999	Montjeu (Ire)	C. Asmussen	Nowhere to Exit	Rhagaas	8	2:33.50	$395,500
1998	Dream Well (Fr)	C. Asmussen	Croco Rouge	Sestino (Ire)	13	2:29.30	$417,250
1997	Peintre Celebre	O. Peslier	Oscar	Astarabad	14	2:29.60	$433,500
1996	Ragmar	G. Mosse	Polaris Flight	Le Destin	15	2:27.20	$484,250
1995	Celtic Swing	K. Darley	Poliglote (GB)	Winged Love	11	2:32.80	$504,000
1994	Celtic Arms (Fr)	G. Mosse	Solid Illusion	Alriffa	15	2:31.30	$444,375
1993	Hernando (Fr)	C. Asmussen	Dernier Empereur	Hunting Hawk	11	2:27.20	$465,325
1992	Polytain	L. Dettori	Marignan	Contested Bid	17	2:30.30	$463,875

Prix Royal-Oak (French St. Leger)

Group 1, Longchamp, three-year-olds and up, about 1¹⁵⁄₁₆ miles, turf. Held October 28, 2001, with a gross value of $95,270.

Year	Winner	Jockey	Second	Third	Strs	Final Time	1st Purse
2001	Vinnie Roe, 3	P. J. Smullen	Generic, 6	Germinis, 7	13	3:37.60	$54,440
2000	Amilynx, 4	O. Peslier	San Sebastian, 6	Tajoun, 6	11	3:33.40	$51,280
1999	Amilynx, 3	O. Peslier	Tajoun, 5	Northerntown, 3	7	3:40.60	$65,200
1998	Tiraaz, 4	G. Mosse	†Erudite, 3	Asolo, 4	7	3:58.40	$72,840
1997	†Ebadiyla, 3	G. Mosse	†Snow Princess, 5	Oscar Schindler, 5	11	3:26.50	$67,160
1996	†Red Roses Story (Fr), 4	V. Vion	Moonax, 5	†Helen of Spain, 4	5	3:38.40	$77,840
1995	Sunshack (GB), 4	T. Jarnet	Shrewd Idea (GB), 5	†Sunrise Song, 4	7	3:16.20	$81,160
1994	Moonax, 3	P. Eddery	Always Earnest, 6	†Dalara, 3	7	3:28.90	$75,444
1993	Raintrap (GB), 3	P. Eddery	Mashaallah, 5	Sonus, 4	8	3:45.80	$70,324
1992	Assessor, 3	T. Quinn	†Always Friendly, 4	†Sought Out, 4	12	3:35.80	$83,160

† denotes female.

Ireland

Irish Derby

Group 1, the Curragh, three-year-olds, colts and fillies, 1½ miles, turf. Held July 1, 2001, with a gross value of $971,712. First held in 1866.

Year	Winner	Jockey	Second	Third	Strs	Final Time	1st Purse
2001	Galileo (Ire)	M. J. Kinane	Morshdi	Golan	12	2:27.10	$551,571
2000	Sinndar	J. P. Murtagh	Glyndebourne (Ire)	Ciro	11	2:33.90	$584,814
1999	Montjeu (Ire)	C. Asmussen	Daliapour	Tchaikovsky	10	2:30.10	$583,427
1998	Dream Well (Fr)	C. Asmussen	City Honours	Desert Fox	10	2:44.30	$592,554
1997	Desert King	C. Roche	Dr Johnson	Loup Sauvage	10	2:32.50	$601,322
1996	Zagreb	P. Shanahan	Polaris Flight	His Excellence	13	2:30.60	$546,276
1995	Winged Love	O. Peslier	Definite Article (GB)	Annus Mirabilis (Fr)	13	2:30.10	$556,247
1994	†Balanchine	L. Dettori	King's Theatre (Ire)	Colonel Collins	9	2:32.70	$515,040
1993	Commander in Chief	P. Eddery	Hernando (Fr)	Foresee	11	2:31.20	$524,676
1992	St. Jovite	C. Roche	Dr Devious (Ire)	Contested Bid	10	2:25.10	$591,093

† denotes female.

Irish One Thousand Guineas

Group 1, the Curragh, three-year-old fillies, 1 mile, turf. Held May 27, 2001, with a gross value of $245,903. First held in 1922.

Year	Winner	Jockey	Second	Third	Strs	Final Time	1st Purse
2001	Imagine	J. A. Heffernan	Crystal Music	Toroca	16	1:41.10	$138,443
2000	Crimplene (Ire)	P. Robinson	Amethyst (Ire)	Storm Dream (Ire)	13	1:39.80	$133,195
1999	Hula Angel	M. Hills	Golden Silca	Dazzling Park	17	1:38.80	$151,446
1998	Tarascon	J. P. Spencer	Kitza (Ire)	La Nuit Rose	13	1:38.40	$120,461
1997	Classic Park	S. Craine	Strawberry Roan (Ire)	Caiseal Ros (Ire)	10	1:42.20	$128,119
1996	Matiya (Ire)	W. Carson	Dance Design (Ire)	My Branch	12	1:39.80	$131,497
1995	Ridgewood Pearl (GB)	C. Roche	Warning Shadows	Khaytada	10	1:43.90	$137,791
1994	Mehthaaf	W. Carson	Las Meninas (Ire)	Relatively Special	10	1:49.00	$127,067
1993	Nicer (Ire)	M. Hills	Goodnight Kiss	Danse Royale (Ire)	14	1:44.20	$174,235
1992	Marling (Ire)	W. Swinburn	Market Booster	Tarwiya	9	1:41.10	$196,988

Irish St. Leger S.

Group 1, the Curragh, three-year-olds and up, 1¾ miles, turf. Held September 15, 2001, with a gross value of $263,160. First held in 1915.

Year	Winner	Jockey	Second	Third	Strs	Final Time	1st Purse
2001	Vinnie Roe, 3	P. J. Smullen	Millenary, 4	Marienbard, 4	8	2:58.40	$153,159
2000	Arctic Owl, 6	D. Harrison	Yavana's Pace, 8	Mutafaweq, 4	8	3:02.20	$110,412
1999	Kayf Tara, 5	L. Dettori	Yavana's Pace, 7	Silver Patriarch, 5	5	3:12.50	$143,953
1998	Kayf Tara, 4	J. Reid	Silver Patriarch, 4	†Delilah (Ire), 4	7	3:05.70	$131,690
1997	Oscar Schindler, 5	S. Craine	Persian Punch, 4	†Whitewater Affair, 4	7	3:06.40	$132,223
1996	Oscar Schindler, 4	S. Craine	†Key Change, 3	Sacrament, 5	9	2:59.10	$137,349
1995	Strategic Choice, 4	T. R. Quinn	Moonax, 4	Oscar Schindler, 3	7	3:00.90	$141,290
1994	Vintage Crop, 7	M. J. Kinane	†Rayseka, 4	†Kithanga, 4	8	3:07.30	$133,045
1993	Vintage Crop, 6	M. J. Kinane	Assessor, 4	Foresee, 3	8	3:06.70	$123,262
1992	Mashaallah, 4	S. Cauthen	Snurge (Ire), 5	Drum Taps, 6	9	3:02.01	$163,314

† denotes female.

Irish Two Thousand Guineas

Group 1, the Curragh, three-year-olds, colts and fillies, 1 mile, turf. Held May 26, 2001, with a gross value of $245,903. First held in 1921.

Year	Winner	Jockey	Second	Third	Strs	Final Time	1st Purse
2001	Black Minnaloushe	J. P. Murtagh	Mozart (Ire)	Minardi	12	1:41.40	$138,443
2000	Bachir	L. Dettori	Giant's Causeway	Cape Town	8	1:39.80	$137,926
1999	Saffron Walden	O. Peslier	Enrique	Orpen	10	1:38.10	$151,379
1998	Desert Prince (Ire)	O. Peslier	Fa-Eq	Second Empire (Ire)	7	1:35.80	$169,717
1997	Desert King	C. Roche	Verglas (Ire)	Romanov (Ire)	12	1:38.30	$171,383
1996	Spinning World	C. Asmussen	Rainbow Blues (Ire)	Beauchamp King	10	1:38.80	$175,902
1995	Spectrum	J. Reid	Adjareli	Bahri	9	1:40.30	$187,592
1994	Turtle Island	J. Reid	Guided Tour	Ridgewood Ben	9	1:50.10	$169,989
1993	Barathea (Ire)	M. Roberts	Fatherland (Ire)	Massyar (Ire)	11	1:43.00	$175,777
1992	Rodrigo de Triano	L. Piggott	Ezzoud (Ire)	Brief Truce	6	1:41.00	$198,616

Kildangan Stud Irish Oaks

Group 1, the Curragh, three-year-old fillies, 1½ miles, turf. Held July 15, 2001, with a gross value of $244,168. First run in 1895.

Year	Winner	Jockey	Second	Third	Strs	Final Time	1st Purse
2001	Lailani (GB)	L. Dettori	Mot Juste (GB)	Karsavina (Ire)	12	2:30.50	$137,466
2000	Petrushka (Ire)	J. Murtagh	Melikah (Ire)	Inforapenny	10	2:31.20	$133,775
1999	Ramruma	K. Fallon	Sunspangled	Sister Bella (Ire)	7	2:33.00	$153,443
1998	Winona (Ire)	J. Murtagh	Kitza (Ire)	Bahr (GB)	9	2:39.80	$157,965
1997	Ebadiyla	J. Murtagh	Yashmak	Brilliance (Fr)	11	2:33.70	$170,988
1996	Dance Design (Ire)	M. Kinane	Shamadara	Key Change	6	2:29.70	$192,348
1995	Pure Grain (GB)	J. Reid	Russian Snows	Valley of Gold	10	2:33.60	$185,279
1994	Bolas (GB)	P. Eddery	Hawajiss	Gothic Dream	10	2:37.60	$171,295
1993	Wemyss Bight (GB)	P. Eddery	Royal Ballerina (Ire)	Oakmead (Ire)	11	2:35.00	$162,573
1992	User Friendly (GB)	G. Duffield	Market Booster	Arrikala	9	2:33.10	$212,040

Richest Foreign Races of 2001

Race (Grade)	Value to Winner	Total Purse	Track, Country	Distance	Date	Winner
Dubai World Cup (UAE-G1)	$3,600,000	$6,000,000	Nad al Sheba, United Arab Emirates	abt. 1¼m	3/24/2001	Captain Steve
Japan Cup (Jpn-G1)	2,105,291	3,995,856	Tokyo, Japan	abt. 1½mT	11/25/2001	Jungle Pocket
Tokyo Yushun	1,229,250	2,343,770	Tokyo, Japan	abt. 1½mT	5/27/2001	Jungle Pocket
Hong Kong Cup (HK-G1)	1,307,726	2,307,751	Sha-Tin, Hong Kong	abt. 1¼mT	12/16/2001	Agnes Digital
Takarazuka Kinen	1,107,480	2,107,568	Hanshin, Japan	abt. 1⅜mT	6/24/2001	Meisho Doto
Tenno Sho	1,090,973	2,065,824	Kyoto, Japan	abt. 2mT	4/29/2001	T.M. Opera O
UAE Derby (UAE-G3)	1,200,000	2,000,000	Nad al Sheba, United Arab Emirates	abt. 1⅛m	3/24/2001	Express Tour
Dubai Sheema Classic (UAE-G2)	1,200,000	2,000,000	Nad al Sheba, United Arab Emirates	abt. 1½mT	3/24/2001	Stay Gold
Dubai Duty Free (UAE-G2)	1,200,000	2,000,000	Nad al Sheba, United Arab Emirates	abt. 1⅛mT	3/24/2001	Jim and Tonic (Fr)
Melbourne Cup (Aus-G1)	1,204,574	1,998,132	Flemington, Australia	abt. 2mT	11/6/2001	Ethereal
Satsuki Sho	1,097,883	1,961,235	Nakayama, Japan	abt. 1¼mT	4/15/2001	Agnes Tachyon
Hong Kong Mile (HK-G1)	1,025,667	1,794,918	Sha-Tin, Hong Kong	abt. 1mT	12/16/2001	Eishin Preston
Hong Kong Vase (HK-G1)	1,025,667	1,794,918	Sha-Tin, Hong Kong	abt. 1½mT	12/16/2001	Stay Gold
Kikuka Sho	931,280	1,772,758	Kyoto, Japan	abt. 1⅞mT	10/21/2001	Manhattan Cafe
February S.	876,874	1,658,300	Tokyo, Japan	abt. 1m	2/18/2001	Nobo True
Takamatsunomiya Kinen	834,125	1,575,801	Chukyo, Japan	abt. 6fT	3/25/2001	Trot Star
Sprinters S.	781,610	1,491,711	Nakayama, Japan	abt. 6fT	9/30/2001	Trot Star
Yasuda Kinen	770,330	1,470,183	Tokyo, Japan	abt. 1mT	6/3/2001	Black Hawk
Derby S. (Eng-G1)	832,242	1,434,900	Epsom, England	abt. 1½mT	6/9/2001	Galileo (Ire)
Prix de l'Arc de Triomphe (Fr-G1)	805,800	1,410,150	Longchamp, France	abt. 1½mT	10/7/2001	Sakhee
Shuka Sho	740,035	1,404,403	Kyoto, Japan	abt. 1¼mT	10/14/2001	T.M. Ocean
Queen Elizabeth II Cup (Eng-G1)	710,669	1,246,788	Sha-Tin, Hong Kong	abt. 1¼mT	4/22/2001	Silvano (Ger)
W. S. Cox Plate (Aus-G1)	668,520	1,124,104	Moonee Valley, Australia	abt. 1¼mT	10/27/2001	Northerly
Caulfield Cup (Aus-G1)	621,476	1,116,676	Caulfield, Australia	abt. 1½mT	10/20/2001	Ethereal
Kyoto Kinen	584,739	1,110,209	Kyoto, Japan	abt. 1⅜mT	2/17/2001	Maquereau
Nakayama Kinen	584,487	1,109,849	Nakayama, Japan	abt. 1⅛mT	2/25/2001	American Boss
American Jockey Club Cup	584,109	1,109,310	Nakayama, Japan	abt. 1⅜mT	1/21/2001	American Boss
Nikkei Shinsun Hai	582,725	1,107,332	Kyoto, Japan	abt. 1½mT	1/14/2001	Stay Gold
Derby Italiano (Ity-G1)	537,347	1,086,274	Rome, Italy	abt. 1½mT	5/27/2001	Morshdi
King George VI and Queen Elizabeth S. (Eng-G1)	618,352	1,066,125	Ascot, England	1½mT	7/28/2001	Galileo (Ire)
Sankei Osaka Hai	553,966	1,051,726	Hanshin, Japan	abt. 1¼mT	4/1/2001	Toho Dream
Nikkei Sho	551,462	1,048,149	Nakayama, Japan	abt. 1$\frac{9}{16}$mT	3/24/2001	Meisho Doto
Hong Kong Sprint (HK-G3)	576,938	1,025,667	Sha-Tin, Hong Kong	abt. 5fT	12/16/2001	Falvelon
Godolphin Mile (UAE-G3)	600,000	1,000,000	Nad al Sheba, United Arab Emirates	abt. 1m	3/24/2001	Festival of Light
Atto Mile S. (Can-G1)	600,000	1,000,000	Woodbine, Canada	1mT	9/9/2001	Numerous Times
Yomiuri Milers Cup	521,809	986,323	Hanshin, Japan	abt. 1mT	4/14/2001	Joten Brave
Sankei-Sho All Comers	513,984	979,782	Nakayama, Japan	abt. 1⅜mT	9/23/2001	Air Smap
Mainichi Okan	513,984	979,782	Tokyo, Japan	abt. 1⅛mT	10/7/2001	Eishin Preston
Kyoto Daishoten	513,984	979,782	Kyoto, Japan	abt. 1½mT	10/7/2001	T.M. Opera O
Irish Derby (Ire-G1)	580,084	966,794	The Curragh, Ireland	1½mT	7/1/2001	Galileo (Ire)
Prix du Jockey-Club (Fr-G1)	544,400	952,700	Chantilly, France	abt. 1½mT	6/3/2001	Anabaa Blue
Hochi Hai Yayoi Sho	473,264	904,134	Nakayama, Japan	abt. 1¼mT	3/4/2001	Agnes Tachyon
Hochi Hai Yonsai Himba Tokubetsu	460,806	872,122	Hanshin, Japan	abt. 7fT	3/11/2001	Rosebud
Sho Flora S.	452,966	857,561	Tokyo, Japan	abt. 1¼mT	4/22/2001	Oiwake Hikari
T. V. Tokyo Hai Aoba Sho	447,833	853,254	Tokyo, Japan	abt. 1½mT	4/20/2001	Le Zele
Irish Champion S. (Ire-G1)	533,388	837,422	Leopardstown, Ireland	abt. 1¼mT	9/8/2001	Fantastic Light
Nippon Sho St. Lite Kinen	433,674	831,209	Nakayama, Japan	abt. 1⅜mT	9/16/2001	Shinko Calido
Kobe Shimbun Hai	433,674	831,209	Hanshin, Japan	abt. 1¼mT	9/23/2001	Air Eminem
Sho Rose S.	417,612	795,069	Hanshin, Japan	abt. 1¼mT	9/16/2001	Diamond Biko
Grosser Preis von Baden (Ger-G1)	450,500	765,850	Baden-Baden, Germany	abt. 1½mT	9/2/2001	Morshdi
Kokura Daishoten	391,963	743,106	Kokura, Japan	abt. 1⅛mT	2/4/2001	Misuzu Chardon
Tokyo Shimbun Hai	391,837	742,926	Tokyo, Japan	abt. 1mT	1/30/2001	Checkmate
Silk Road S.	391,522	742,477	Kyoto, Japan	abt. 6fT	2/4/2001	Trot Star
Hankyu Hai	391,396	742,297	Hanshin, Japan	abt. 6fT	2/25/2001	Daitaku Yamato
Negishi S.	383,035	731,508	Tokyo, Japan	abt. 7f	1/29/2001	Nobo True
Kyoto Himba S.	382,909	731,328	Kyoto, Japan	abt. 1mT	1/28/2001	Grace Namura
Heian S.	382,846	731,238	Kyoto, Japan	abt. 1⅛m	1/21/2001	Mambo Twist
Lord Derby Challenge Trophy	327,398	703,422	Nakayama, Japan	abt. 1mT	4/1/2001	Checkmate
Laurel R. C. Sho Nakayama Himba S.	368,229	703,408	Nakayama, Japan	abt. 1⅛mT	3/10/2001	Eishin Rudens (Jpn)
March S.	362,620	692,606	Nakayama, Japan	abt. 1⅛m	3/25/2001	Island Oja
Mainichi Hai	361,547	691,073	Hanshin, Japan	abt. 1¼mT	3/24/2001	Kurofune
Arlington Cup	364,738	690,599	Hanshin, Japan	abt. 1mT	2/24/2001	Dantsu Flame

English Triple Crown

Over its long history, the English Triple Crown has proved to be as elusive as its younger American cousin, or even more so. Approaching its third century, the English Triple Crown has been won only 15 times, four times more than the American Triple Crown in less than a century and a half. The American Triple Crown has not had a winner since Affirmed in 1978, and the English drought extends slightly longer. Since Gainsborough became the 13th winner in 1918, only two more have followed: unbeaten *Bahram in '35 and the brilliant Nijinsky II in '70.

The English Triple Crown for three-year-olds, dating from 1809, consists of the one-mile Two Thousand Guineas at Newmarket in May, the 1½-mile Epsom Derby at Epsom Downs in June, and the St. Leger Stakes at 1¾ miles and 127 yards at Doncaster Race Course in September. Over the years, there has been some variance in the distances of the three races, and alternative races were used during war years.

The St. Leger Stakes was named for the popular local sportsman Lt. Col. Anthony St. Leger. Alabaculia was the first winner of the St. Leger Stakes in 1776. Four years later, *Diomed, later imported to the United States, won the initial running of the Epsom Derby. The first Two Thousand Guineas was taken by Wizard in 1809, nine years after Champion became the first three-year-old to win both the Epsom Derby and the St. Leger Stakes. In 1813, Sir Charles Bunbury's Smolensko became the first Thoroughbred to win the Two Thousand Guineas and the Epsom Derby.

Forty years later in 1853, West Australian became the first to win all three stakes. He was followed by Gladiateur (1865), Lord Lyon (1866), *Ormonde (1886), Common (1891), Isinglass (1893), Galtee More (1897), Flying Fox (1899), Diamond Jubilee (1900), *Rock Sand (1903), Pommern (1915), Gay Crusader (1917), Gainsborough (1918), *Bahram (1935), and Nijinsky II (1970).

In today's racing world, the English Triple Crown is a prize not pursued. The most recent horse with a chance to seize the crown, 1989 Two Thousand Guineas (Eng-G1) and Epsom Derby (Eng-G1) victor Nashwan, was withheld from the St. Leger Stakes (Eng-G1) by owner Sheikh Hamdan bin Rashid al Maktoum to point for the Prix de l'Arc de Triomphe (Fr-G1), in which he did not start because of injury.

Here are the 15 English Triple Crown winners:

WEST AUSTRALIAN—1850 b. h., Melbourne—Mowerina, by Touchstone. 10-9-1-0, $68,615. Known popularly as "the West," West Australian gave owner-breeder John Bowes his fourth and final Epsom Derby victory. Trained by John Scott, West Australian ran second in the Criterion Stakes to Speed the Plough and then beat his rival in the Glasgow Stakes as a two-year-old. At three, West Australian won the Two Thousand Guineas by a half-length over the Duke of Bedford's Sittingbourne and the Epsom Derby by a desperate neck over the same opponent. West Australian won the St. Leger easily, and at four won the Triennial Stakes and the Ascot Gold Cup. Though not widely regarded as a success at stud, he sired The Wizard, the 1860 Two Thousand Guineas winner, and his son *Australian sired Spendthrift, tail-male ancestor of the Man o' War male line that leads to Tiznow.

GLADIATEUR—1862 b. h., Monarque—Miss Gladiator, by Gladiator. 19-16-0-1, $236,537. French-bred and -owned Gladiateur shattered the notion that England's Thoroughbreds were superior when he won the 1865 Two Thousand Guineas, earning the gleeful nickname "Avenger of Waterloo" among the French. Trained at Newmarket by Tom Jennings, he added the Epsom Derby "in a canter" and the St. Leger. In between, he traveled to his native France and captured that country's greatest race at the time, the Grand Prix de Paris. At four, Gladiateur won the Gold Cup at Ascot by 40 lengths after reputedly trailing by 300 yards at one point. He was not a success at stud.

LORD LYON—1863 b. h., Stockwell—Paradigm, by Paragone. 19-15-3-1, $180,497. Leased to Richard Sutton, the second son of Sir Richard Sutton, and trained by James Dover, Lord Lyon dead-heated with Redan in the Champagne Stakes for two-year-olds at Doncaster and then won the Criterion and Troy Stakes at Newmarket. After winning the Two Thousand Guineas by one length over Monarch of the Glen, Lord Lyon completed the Triple Crown by beating Savernake by a head in the Epsom Derby and the same rival by inches in the St. Leger. The following year, Lord Lyon won the Ascot Biennial and the Stockbridge Cup. His most famous offspring were *Ormonde's rival Minting, winner of the 1886 Grand Prix de Paris, and 1877 Oaks winner Placida.

*ORMONDE—1883 b. h., Bend Or—Lily Agnes, by Macaroni. 16-16-0-0, $138,340. Considered by many as the finest Thoroughbred of the 19th century, the Duke of Westminster's *Ormonde was unbeaten in his 16-race career despite developing a wind infirmity. At four in the Hardwicke Stakes, he bested Grand Prix de Paris winner Minting. *Ormonde sired just seven foals in his first season at stud in England, but that crop included Orme, a multiple major stakes winner and sire of 1899 Triple Crown winner Flying Fox. After a stint in Argentina, William O'Brien Macdonough, an American, bought *Ormonde for $150,000 in 1893 and stood him in California. From 1894 through 1905, *Ormonde sired just 17 foals, but 12 started and five, including Ormondale, won stakes races.

COMMON—1888 br. h., Isonomy—Thistle, by Scottish Chief. 5-4-0-1, $77,567. Owned by his breeder, Lord Allington, and Sir Frederick Johnstone, Common was a colt with dubious joints and thus was not raced at two by trainer John Porter. Common made his debut in the 1891 Two Thousand Guineas, and his profuse sweating prompted Prince Soltykoff to remark, "He's very well named." Uncommon on the Newmarket course, Common won easily. He won the Epsom Derby by two lengths in a downpour and subsequently won the St. James's Palace Stakes before finishing third in the Eclipse Stakes. In the final start of his only racing season, Common completed the Triple Crown by winning the St. Leger by one length. Common's prog-

eny included 1898 One Thousand Guineas winner Nun Nicer and Mushroom, who became a successful stallion in Belgium.

ISINGLASS—1890 b. h., Isonomy—Deadlock, by Wenlock. 12-11-1-0, $279,231. Despite soundness problems that he passed on to his progeny, Isinglass lost only once for his owner, Col. Harry McCalmont, in a four-year career. Isinglass suffered the only loss in his three-year-old campaign when he was defeated by Raeburn in the Lancashire Plate at Manchester, giving the winner ten pounds over an inadequate distance. At four, Isinglass captured the Princess of Wales's Stakes, Eclipse Stakes, and Jockey Club Stakes. As a five-year-old, he won the 1895 Ascot Gold Cup and retired as the sport's all-time money winner. Isinglass stood at his owner's Cheveley Park Stud near Newmarket and sired three British classic winners as well as *Star Shoot, who was North America's leading sire five times and also was leading broodmare sire five times.

GALTEE MORE—1894 b. h., Kendal—Morganette, by Springfield. 13-11-1-0, $131,312. Galtee More, named after a peak in the Galtee Mountains, was owned by John Gubbins, who used his considerable inheritance from an uncle to open two stud farms, one of which housed Galtee More's sire, Kendal. Trained by Sam Darling, Galtee More won the Molecomb Stakes, the Rous Plate, and the Middle Park Plate as a two-year-old. At three in 1897, Galtee More completed the Triple Crown by taking the St. Leger by three-quarters of a length over the filly Chelandry. At the end of his racing career, Galtee More was sold by Gubbins to the Russian government, and the stallion subsequently was purchased by German interests. His most noteworthy progeny was Orchidee II, dam of Oleander, leading German sire in the 1930s and '40s. Galtee More's half brother Ard Patrick won the Epsom Derby in 1902.

FLYING FOX—1896 b. h., Orme—Vampire, by Galopin. 11-9-2-0, $194,867. A large colt with beautiful shoulders, Flying Fox became the Duke of Westminster's second Triple Crown winner despite a difficult temperament that most likely came from his dam. At two in 1898, Flying Fox won the New, Stockbridge Foal, and Criterion Stakes, and he finished second in both the Imperial Produce Stakes and in the Middle Park Plate. Flying Fox was unbeaten at three and ended his career with a four-length victory in the Jockey Club Stakes. Flying Fox sired French classic winner Val d'Or, and his grandson *Teddy (by French Derby winner Ajax) became an important influence on North American bloodlines through full brothers *Sir Gallahad III and *Bull Dog.

DIAMOND JUBILEE—1897 b. h., St. Simon—Perdita, by Hampton. 16-6-5-1, $142,131. Owned by the Prince of Wales, Diamond Jubilee was described as "ferocious, with a nature more befitting the bullring than the racecourse." He was found to be a cryptorchid (and thus spared from gelding) after finishing unplaced in his first two starts at two. Diamond Jubilee's trainer, Richard Marsh, gave Diamond Jubilee's groom, 18-year-old Herbert Jones, a chance to ride the ridgling, and Diamond Jubilee won the Two Thousand Guineas by four lengths. He won the Epsom Derby by a half-length and the St. Leger by one length. After standing at stud in England, he was sold in 1906 to Las Ortegas Stud in Argentina, where he was the leading sire from 1914 through '16. Diamond Jubilee was a full brother to the outstanding racehorse Persimmon, winner of the Epsom Derby and the St. Leger in 1896.

*ROCK SAND—1900 br. h., Sainfoin—Roquebrune, by St. Simon. 20-16-1-3, $221,703. Although he hobbled along at a trot and canter, once warmed up *Rock Sand would fully extend himself at a gallop and never finished unplaced in his career. He won six stakes races as a two-year-old in 1902, and at three he won the St. James's Palace Stakes and Bennington Stakes in addition to the Triple Crown contests. He won the Hardwicke, Princess of Wales's, Lingfield Park Plate, First Foal, and the Jockey Club Stakes at four. Best known for his success as a broodmare sire, *Rock Sand sired Mahubah, dam of Man o' War. *Rock Sand's other leading daughters included Hour Glass, dam of Blue Glass and *Hourless, and Tea Biscuit, dam of Hard Tack. *Rock Sand's most accomplished sons were Tracery, winner of the St. James's Palace and the Eclipse Stakes and one of the leading sires in England for many years in the 1920s; Friar Rock, who won the 1916 Belmont Stakes and Suburban Handicap in the United States; and 1916 Preakness Stakes winner Damrosch.

POMMERN—1912 b. h., Polymelus—Merry Agnes, by St. Hilaire. A homebred of Solomon B. Joel, at two Pommern won the Richmond Stakes at Goodwood and the Imperial Produce Stakes at Kempton. Steve Donoghue was engaged to ride Pommern in his unusual three-year-old season. Pommern won the 1915 Two Thousand Guineas comfortably at Newmarket. With World War I raging across the English Channel in France, Epsom Downs was requisitioned by the military, and Pommern scored a two-length victory in the substitute for the Epsom Derby, the New Derby at 1½ miles on Newmarket's July Course. He then won the substitute for the St. Leger, the 1¾-mile September Stakes at Newmarket. In his only start at four, Pommern won the June Stakes at Newmarket. His best offspring were Adam's Apple, who won the 1927 Two Thousand Guineas; Pondoland, second in the 1922 Two Thousand Guineas; and Glommen, who won the Goodwood Cup.

GAY CRUSADER—1914 b. c., Bayardo—Gay Laura, by Beppo. 10-8-2-0, $53,530. Bred and owned by A. W. "Fairie" Cox, Gay Crusader was the first foal of his dam and from his sire's first crop. Trained by Alec Taylor, Gay Crusader was a small colt who developed sore shins in June of his two-year-old season. He made a late start that year, losing his debut before winning the Criterion Stakes. After finishing second in his three-year-old debut in the Column Produce Stakes, Gay Crusader won the 1917 Two Thousand Guineas by a head over Magpie, who was also trained by Taylor. With Magpie exported to Australia, Gay Crusader won the Epsom Derby, which was delayed until July 31 because of World War I, by four lengths. He then won the September Stakes, the St. Leger substitute. Gay Crusader also won the Newmarket Gold Cup, Champion Stakes, and Lowther Stakes. A tendon injury ended his career before his first start as a four-year-old. At stud, his best were Hot Night, second in the 1927 Epsom Derby, and Hurstwood, third in the 1924 Derby.

GAINSBOROUGH—1915 b. h., Bayardo—Rosedrop, by St. Frusquin. 9-5-2-1, $67,021. Lady Jane Douglas bred Gainsborough and became the first woman to own an Epsom Derby winner when the colt took the 1918 classic. Gainsborough gave his sire, Bayardo, a second straight Triple Crown winner. Gainsborough, who was twice champion sire, sired Hyperion, the 1933 Epsom Derby winner who went on to be England's leading sire six times. Gainsborough also sired 1932 Two Thousand Guineas winner Orwell and Solario, who was

England's leading sire in 1937 and its leading brood-mare sire in 1949 and 1950. Gainsborough died in 1945 at the age of 30 and was buried at Gainsborough Stud, which was originally named Harwood Stud.

*BAHRAM—1932 br. h., Blandford—Friar's Daughter, by Friar Marcus. 9-9-0-0, $212,816. A large colt who grew to 16.2 hands, *Bahram was bred and raced in England by the Aga Khan. Unbeaten in nine career starts through his three-year-old season, *Bahram won the National Produce, Rous Memorial, Gimcrack, and Middle Park Stakes at two. In addition to sweeping the Triple Crown at three, he won the St. James's Palace Stakes. England's second-leading sire in 1940, he was sold for $160,000 to an American syndicate that included Alfred G. Vanderbilt, Walter P. Chrysler, James Cox Brady, and S. W. Labrot. *Bahram stood in Maryland and Virginia before being sold in 1945 to stand in Argentina. *Bahram's 25 stakes winners included 1940 St. Leger and Irish Derby winner Turkhan, 1940 Irish Oaks winner Queen of Shiraz, and 1942 Two Thousand Guineas winner Big Game, who became the leading sire in England in 1948, and the excellent sire Persian Gulf, winner of the 1944 Coronation Cup.

NIJINSKY II—1967 b. h., Northern Dancer—Flaming Page, by Bull Page. 13-11-2-0, $677,220. Bred in Canada by E. P. Taylor and owned by Charles W. Engelhard, Nijinsky II was Northern Dancer's first international champion. He was a powerful, sickle-hocked colt who more closely resembled his dam than his diminutive sire. Trained by Vincent O'Brien, Nijinsky II was a champion in England and Ireland at two in 1969. He won the Two Thousand Guineas at odds of 4-to-7, the Epsom Derby at 11-to-8 odds, and the St. Leger at 2-to-7 odds, all under Lester Piggott. That year, Nijinsky II won the Irish Sweeps Derby and the King George VI and Queen Elizabeth Stakes. His only defeats were in his final two starts, the Prix de l'Arc de Triomphe and Champion Stakes. At stud at Claiborne Farm in Kentucky, he was England's leading sire in 1986 and North America's leading broodmare sire in '93 and '94. Nijinsky II at one time was the all-time leading sire of stakes winners with 155, surpassing the record of his sire. Nijinsky II sired 11 champions, including 1987 North American Horse of the Year Ferdinand, '83 French champion Caerleon, two-time English champion Ile de Bourbon, and two undefeated winners of the Epsom Derby, Golden Fleece and Lammtarra.—*Bill Heller*

The Influence of England's Triple Crown Worldwide

Although England's Triple Crown is the original and perhaps most difficult Triple Crown to win in the world, historically it has served as a model for racing programs around the globe. Virtually every major racing country has its set of Guineas, Derbys, and St. Legers, or their equivalents. As in most aspects of Thoroughbred racing, England, the birthplace of the Thoroughbred, established the pattern that the rest of the world adapted for its own local purposes, and the idea of a series of classic tests for three-year-olds is universal.

The Triple Crown in the United States evolved into the familiar Kentucky Derby (G1), Preakness Stakes (G1), and Belmont Stakes (G1) early in the 20th century, but several American racing jurisdictions in the 19th century attempted to establish Triple Crown series more closely modeled on the English pattern. For example, the Withers, Belmont, and Lawrence Realization Stakes were originally intended to be New York's version of the English series.

Other former English colonies such as Australia and New Zealand likewise established Guineas-Derby-St. Leger series, and those races still exist in Antipodean lands, though it has been many years since there has been a serious objective as a series for owners and trainers. As racing throughout the world has become more specialized, winning a Triple Crown over a variety of distances as wide as that in England has become increasingly difficult.

Argentina, historically the most important South American racing country, established its own series, the Polla de Potrillos (Arg-G1), Gran Premio Jockey Club (Arg-G1), and Gran Premio Nacional (Arg-G1) over 1,600 meters, 2,000 meters, and 2,500 meters, respectively, but went one better than the English. The Argentines also required their best

three-year-olds to beat older horses in the 2,400-meter Gran Premio Carlos Pellegrini (Arg-G1) to win their Quadruple Crown. Twenty three-year-olds have captured the Argentine Triple Crown since 1902, with Refinado Tom (Arg) in '96 the most recent winner. Only ten horses, the last being the great *Forli in 1966, have completed the Quadruple Crown.

English fillies have an opportunity to win their version of the Triple Crown, though no filly has ever completed the Two Thousand Guineas (Eng-G1), Epsom Derby (Eng-G1), St. Leger (Eng-G1) triple. Two fillies, however, have won four of the five English classics, failing only to capture the Derby. Formosa in 1868 dead-heated in the Two Thousand and won the One Thousand Guineas, Epsom Oaks, and St. Leger. Sceptre won the One Thousand, Two Thousand, Oaks, and St. Leger in 1902 but was beaten into fourth place in the Derby by Ard Patrick.

Nine fillies have won a "fillies Triple Crown" consisting of the One Thousand Guineas, Oaks, and St. Leger:

1868 Formosa, ch. f., Buccaneer—Eller, by Chanticleer
1871 Hannah, b. f., King Tom—Mentmore Lass, by Melbourne
1874 Apology, ch. f., Adventurer—Mandragora, by Rataplan
1892 La Fleche, br. f., St. Simon—Quiver, by Toxophilite
1902 Sceptre, b. f., Persimmon—Ornament, by Bend Or
1904 Pretty Polly, ch. f., Gallinule—Admiration, by Saraband
1942 Sun Chariot, b. f., Hyperion—Clarence, by Diligence
1955 Meld, b. f., Alycidon—Daily Double, by Fair Trial
1985 Oh So Sharp (GB), ch. f., Kris—Oh So Fair, by Graustark

2001 International Classifications

Two-Year-Olds

Wt.	Horse	Sire–Dam, Broodmare sire	Trained	Sts	1st	2nd	3rd	Earnings
126	Johannesburg	Hennessy–Myth, by Ogygian	Ire	7	7	0	0	$1,002,893
122	Hawk Wing	Woodman–La Lorgnette, by Val de l'Orne (Fr)	Ire	4	3	1	0	272,310
	Queen's Logic (f)	Grand Lodge–Lagrion, by Diesis (GB)	GB	4	4	0	0	254,526
119	Captain Rio	Pivotal–Beloved Visitor, by Miswaki	GB	6	3	0	2	305,630
	Dubai Destination	Kingmambo–Mysterial, by Alleged	GB	3	2	1	0	98,039
	Rock of Gibraltar	Danehill–Offshore Boom, by Be My Guest	Ire	7	5	1	0	534,128
117	Act One	In the Wings (GB)–Summer Sonnet, by Baillamont	Fr	3	3	0	0	147,170
	High Chaparral	Sadler's Wells–Kasora, by Darshaan	Ire	3	2	1	0	177,697
116	Zipping	Zafonic–Zelda, by Caerleon	Fr	6	2	3	1	159,818
115	Ballingarry	Sadler's Wells–Flamenco Wave, by Desert Wine	Ire	4	2	0	1	66,631
	Castle Gandolfo	Gone West–Golden Oriole, by Northern Dancer	Ire	4	2	2	0	141,160
	Landseer	Danehill–Sabria, by Miswaki	Ire	6	2	3	0	315,840
	Naheef	Marju–Golden Digger, by Mr. Prospector	GB	3	2	1	0	105,139
114	Firebreak	Charnwood Forest–Breakaway, by Song	GB	6	4	1	0	122,037
	Gossamer (f)	Sadler's Wells–Brocade, by Habitat	GB	3	3	0	0	213,463
	Guys and Dolls	Efisio–Dime Bag, by High Line	GB	4	2	1	1	61,871
	Redback	Mark of Esteem (Ire)–Patsy Western, by Precocious	GB	10	3	2	1	101,390
	Tendulkar	Spinning World–Romanette, by Alleged	Ire	2	1	0	1	41,281
113	Meshaheer	Nureyev–Race the Wild Wind, by Sunny's Halo	GB	4	2	0	2	71,866
	Saddad	Gone West–Lite Light, by Majestic Light	GB	3	2	0	0	53,800
112	Black Sam Bellamy	Sadler's Wells–Urban Sea, by Miswaki	Ire	3	0	0	2	12,025
	Leggy Lou (f)	Mujadil–Alzeam, by Alzao	GB	5	2	0	1	44,084
	Mutinyonthebounty	Sadler's Wells–Threatening, by Warning (GB)	Ire	4	2	0	1	129,247
	Rashbag	Reprimand–Pleasuring, by Good Times	Fr	5	4	1	0	80,892
	Sholokhov	Sadler's Wells–La Meilleure, by Lord Gayle	Ire	4	2	1	1	177,274
111	Fight Your Corner	Muhtarram–Dame Ashfield, by Grundy	GB	5	3	0	1	39,168
	Hothaifah	Green Desert–Hyabella, by Shirley Heights	Fr	5	2	1	0	43,264
	Silent Honor (f)	Sunday Silence–Wood Vine, by Woodman	GB	3	2	0	1	61,124
	Sulk (f)	Selkirk–Masskana, by Darshaan	GB	4	2	0	0	120,739
	War Zone	Danzig–Proflare, by Mr. Prospector	Fr	6	3	1	1	91,276
	Where Or When	Danehill Dancer–Future Past, by Super Concorde	GB	6	3	0	0	62,475
110	Bandari	Alhaarth–Miss Audimar, by Mr. Leader	GB	4	3	0	0	36,106
	Bernebeau	Green Tune–Princesse Bilbao, by Highest Honor (Fr)	Fr	4	2	2	0	111,804
	Caesarion	Danehill–Carelaine, by Woodman	Fr	3	0	3	0	26,663
	Danseuse d'Etoile (f)	Highest Honor (Fr)–Latifolia, by Dancing Brave	Fr	3	1	1	1	62,566
	Mister Cosmi	Royal Applause (GB)–Degree, by Warning (GB)	GB	7	2	1	1	101,045
	Peppershot	Big Shuffle–Pasca, by Lagunas	Ger	4	1	3	0	90,090
	Prism	Spectrum–Seal Indigo, by Glenstal	GB	7	4	1	0	57,245
	Quarter Moon (f)	Sadler's Wells–Jude, by Darshaan	Ire	2	1	1	0	159,561

Three-Year-Olds (Turf)

14 furlongs +

Wt.	Horse	Sire–Dam, Broodmare sire	Trained	Sts	1st	2nd	3rd	Earnings
122	Milan (GB)	Sadler's Wells–Kithanga, by Darshaan	Ire	8	2	2	1	981,247
120	Vinnie Roe	Definite Article (GB)–Kayu, by Tap On Wood	Ire	8	4	0	1	328,298
114	Demophilos	Dr Devious (Ire)–Graecia Magna, by Private Account	GB	7	1	0	2	115,205
	Double Honour	Highest Honor (Fr)–Silver Cobra, by Silver Hawk	GB	8	3	2	0	64,050
113	Wareed	Sadler's Wells–Truly Special, by Caerleon	GB	4	1	1	0	53,066
111	Alleluia (f)	Caerleon–Alruccaba, by Crystal Palace	GB	8	6	1	0	68,355
110	Fair Question	Rainbow Quest–Fair of the Furze, by Ela-Mana-Mou	GB	6	1	2	0	73,181

11 furlongs +

Wt.	Horse	Sire–Dam, Broodmare sire	Trained	Sts	1st	2nd	3rd	Earnings
129	Galileo (Ire)	Sadler's Wells–Urban Sea, by Miswaki	Ire	7	5	1	0	2,233,580
125	Milan (GB)	Sadler's Wells–Kithanga, by Darshaan	Ire	8	2	2	1	981,247
124	Storming Home	Machiavellian–Try To Catch Me, by Shareef Dancer	GB	7	2	1	1	290,950
123	Jungle Pocket	Tony Bin–Dance Charmer, by Nureyev	Jpn	6	3	0	2	4,487,549
121	Golan	Spectrum–Highland Gift, by Generous	GB	6	2	1	1	785,298
	Sagacity	Highest Honor (Fr)–Saganeca, by Sagace	Fr	6	0	2	2	211,732
120	Aquarelliste (f)	Danehill–Agathe, by Manila	Fr	5	4	1	0	700,022
	Morshdi	Slip Anchor–Reem Albaraari, by Sadler's Wells	GB	5	2	1	1	1,058,652
119	Anabaa Blue	Anabaa–Allez Les Trois, by Riverman	Fr	7	3	2	0	620,795
	Grandera	Grand Lodge–Bordighera, by Alysheba	GB	5	1	3	1	412,603
117	Blazing Fury	Dynaformer–Blazing Kadie, by Our Native	USA	7	2	1	1	296,690
	Boreal	Java Gold–Britannia, by Tarim	Ger	8	2	3	2	415,669
116	Diamilina (f)	Linamix–Diamonaka, by Akarad	Fr	7	4	2	0	142,109
	Maille Pistol	Pistolet Bleu (Fr)–Bric Mamaille, by Bricassar	Fr	6	3	0	0	112,414
116	Mr Combustible	Hernando (Fr)–Warg, by Dancing Brave	GB	6	2	2	1	249,748
115	Alexius	Rainbow Quest–Alexandrine, by Val de l'Orne (Fr)	GB	2	2	0	0	48,999
	Dantsu Flame	Brian's Time–Inter Pyrenees, by Sanquirico	Jpn	7	1	3	0	1,717,628

Wt.	Horse	Sire–Dam, Broodmare sire	Trained	Sts	1st	2nd	3rd	Earnings
	Okawango	Kingmambo–Krissante, by Kris	Fr	4	0	1	1	85,054
	Sabiango	Acatenango–Spirit of Eagles, by Beau's Eagle	Ger	6	3	1	1	268,108
	Sharp Performance	Kris S.–Theatre Flight, by Theatrical (Ire)	USA	6	4	0	2	279,780
114	Asian Heights	Hernando (Fr)–Miss Rinjani, by Shirley Heights	GB	2	1	1	0	52,272
	Demophilos	Dr Devious (Ire)–Graecia Magna, by Private Account	GB	7	1	0	2	115,205
	High Pitched	Indian Ridge–Place de l'Opera, by Sadler's Wells	GB	6	4	1	1	71,158
	Perfect Sunday	Quest for Fame (GB)–Sunday Bazaar, by Nureyev	GB	6	2	2	0	150,812
113	Falbrav	Fairy King–Gift of the Night, by Slewpy	Ity	6	3	2	1	299,797
	Hill Country	Danehill–Rose of Jericho, by Alleged	GB	5	1	1	0	20,073
112	Flight of Fancy (f)	Sadler's Wells–Phantom Gold, by Machiavellian	GB	2	0	1	0	114,366
	Foundation Spirit	Hernando (Fr)–Fanny's Cove, by Mill Reef	Fr	9	1	1	3	141,363
	Head in the Clouds (f)	Rainbow Quest–Ballerina, by Dancing Brave	GB	7	2	2	0	81,198
	Mare Nostrum (f)	Caerleon–Salvora, by Spectacular Bid	Fr	5	1	1	1	90,225
	Pugin	Darshaan–Gothic Dream, by Nashwan	Ire	6	2	2	0	80,003
	Sweetest Thing	Candy Stripes–Escape Reality, by Lear Fan	Can	8	4	2	0	11,000
111	Beekeeper	Rainbow Quest–Chief Bee, by Chief's Crown	GB	3	2	0	0	67,760
	Monos	Kornado–Mama Leone, by Northern Baby	Ger	8	0	4	1	140,286
	Mot Juste (GB) (f)	Mtoto–Bunting, by Shaadi	GB	7	1	2	0	144,697
	Relish The Thought (f)	Sadler's Wells–Viz, by Kris S.	GB	4	0	1	1	72,764
	Snowstorm	Environment Friend–Choral Sundown, by Night Shift	GB	7	0	2	2	77,583
110	Lady Pastel (f)	Tony Bin–Pink Turtle, by Blushing Groom (Fr)	Jpn	10	4	3	2	1,870,043
	Lierac	Kornado–Last Love Forever, by Sunshine Forever	Ger	4	1	2	0	73,334
	Moon Queen (Ire) (f)	Sadler's Wells–Infamy, by Shirley Heights	Fr	8	3	4	0	108,121
	Noroit	Monsun–Noble Princesse, by Windwurf (Ger)	Ger	7	2	0	2	90,861
	Rosebud	Sunday Silence–Rose Colour, by Shirley Heights	Jpn	7	1	3	1	770,032
	Sangreal	Celtic Swing–Grosvenor Gardens, by Grosvenor	Fr	4	2	1	0	38,752
	Sydenham	A.P. Indy–Crystal Shard, by Mr. Prospector	GB	6	1	1	0	11,296
	Theatre Script	Theatrical (Ire)–Gossiping, by Chati	GB	3	0	0	1	21,935
	Walking Around	Linamix–Walk On Air, by Cure the Blues	Fr	4	1	1	0	29,445

9½ furlongs +

Wt.	Horse	Sire–Dam, Broodmare sire	Trained	Sts	1st	2nd	3rd	Earnings
128	Galileo (Ire)	Sadler's Wells–Urban Sea, by Miswaki	Ire	7	5	1	0	2,233,580
123	Banks Hill (GB) (f)	Danehill–Hasili, by Kahyasi	Fr	7	3	3	0	1,145,276
121	Nayef	Gulch–Height of Fashion (Fr), by Bustino	GB	7	4	0	2	506,730
120	Viscount	Quest for Fame (GB)–Antwerp, by *Sir Tristram	Aus	8	4	1	1	394,247
119	Grandera	Grand Lodge–Bordighera, by Alysheba	GB	5	1	3	1	412,603
	Tobougg	Barathea (Ire)–Lacovia, by Majestic Light	GB	5	0	2	1	830,184
118	Black Minnaloushe	Storm Cat–Coral Dance (Fr), by Green Dancer	Ire	9	2	1	1	454,741
	Lailani (GB) (f)	Unfuwain–Lailati, by Mr. Prospector	GB	8	7	0	0	747,740
117	Chichicastenango	Smadoun–Smala, by Antheus	Fr	7	2	1	2	547,123
	Hawkeye	Danehill–Tea House, by Sassafras (Fr)	GB	8	3	0	2	306,036
115	Carnival Dancer	Sadler's Wells–Red Carnival, by Mr. Prospector	GB	4	2	1	0	58,384
	Strut the Stage	Theatrical (Ire)–Ruby Ransom, by Red Ransom	Can	5	3	1	0	328,268
114	Dilshaan	Darshaan–Avila, by Ajdal	GB	2	1	0	0	120,246
	Masterful	Danzig–Moonlight Serenade (Fr), by Dictus	GB	7	3	4	0	84,043
	Nadia (f)	Nashwan–Nazoo, by Nijinsky II	Fr	5	1	2	0	175,970
	Startac	Theatrical (Ire)–Tenga, by Mr. Prospector	USA	8	2	2	0	370,195
	Zoellner	Dashing Blade–Zypern, by Acatenango	Ger	5	1	2	0	49,804
113	Celtic Silence	Celtic Swing–Smart 'n Noble, by Smarten	GB	2	0	1	0	145,611
	Chancellor	Halling–Isticanna, by Far North	GB	6	1	2	0	86,921
	Equerry	St. Jovite–Colour Chart, by Mr. Prospector	Fr	1	1	0	0	30,646
	Time Away	Darshaan–Not Before Time, by Polish Precedent	GB	7	1	0	3	113,947
112	Choc Ice	Kahyasi–Sherkiya, by Goldneyev	Fr	10	2	1	1	335,657
	Mare Nostrum (f)	Caerleon–Salvora, by Spectacular Bid	Fr	5	1	1	1	90,225
	Najah (f)	Nashwan–Mehthaaf, by Nureyev	GB	5	2	1	0	72,695
	T. M. Ocean	Dancing Brave–River Girl, by Rivlia	Jpn	6	3	0	1	2,361,518
111	Monos	Kornado–Mama Leone, by Northern Baby	Ger	8	0	4	1	140,286
	Mot Juste (GB) (f)	Mtoto–Bunting, by Shaadi	GB	7	1	2	0	144,697
	Pryor	Kornado–Peninsula, by Elegant Air	Ger	6	3	0	0	74,822
	Saint Damien	Saint Ballado–Wife Begone, by Demons Begone	USA	9	1	3	0	223,470
	Spring Oak (GB) (f)	Mark of Esteem (Ire)–English Spring, by *Grey Dawn II	Fr	5	1	0	3	281,921
110	Amiwain	Unfuwain–Amen, by Alydar	Fr	3	0	1	0	19,649
	Fan Club's Mister	Mr. Greeley–Exciting Fandance, by Lear Fan	USA	13	5	2	1	362,610
	Indian Creek	Indian Ridge–Blue Water, by Bering (GB)	GB	8	3	0	2	120,164
	Innit (Ire) (f)	Distinctly North–Tidal Reach, by Kris S.	USA	5	1	2	1	185,772
	Krombacher	Lando (Ger)–Kallista, by Zeddaan	Ger	7	2	1	1	53,348
	Lagudin	Eagle Eyed–Liaison, by Blushing Groom (Fr)	Ire	7	2	1	3	66,037
	Limerick Boy	Alwuhush–Limoges, by Koenigsstuhl	Ger	6	2	1	0	64,404
	Marhoob	Mr. Prospector–Flagbird, by Nureyev	GB	5	2	1	0	24,970
	Rosebud	Sunday Silence–Rose Colour, by Shirley Heights	Jpn	7	1	4	1	1,770,032
	Sensible	Sadler's Wells–Raisonnable, by Common Grounds	Fr	4	2	1	0	38,157
	Volga (f)	Caerleon–Verveine, by Lear Fan	Fr	6	2	2	0	192,031

7 furlongs +

Wt.	Horse	Sire–Dam, Broodmare sire	Trained	Sts	1st	2nd	3rd	Earnings
123	Noverre	Rahy–Danseur Fabuleux, by Northern Dancer	GB	7	1	3	1	495,369
119	No Excuse Needed	Machiavellian–Nawaiet, by Zilzal	GB	4	1	1	0	163,216
118	Black Minnaloushe	Storm Cat–Coral Dance (Fr), by Green Dancer	Ire	9	2	1	1	454,741
117	Affluent (f)	Affirmed–Trinity Place, by Strawberry Road (Aus)	USA	10	4	2	3	725,200
	Clearing	Zafonic–Bright Spells, by Alleged	GB	2	1	1	0	78,280
	Imagine (f)	Sadler's Wells–Doff the Derby, by Master Derby	Ire	4	2	1	1	443,702
	Olden Times	Darshaan–Garah, by Ajdal	GB	6	2	0	1	159,846
	Vahorimix	Linamix–Vadsa Honor, by Highest Honor (Fr)	Fr	6	3	0	0	323,648
116	Golden Apples (Ire) (f)	Pivotal–Loon, by Kaldoun	USA	8	3	2	2	510,237
	Navesink	Irish River (Fr)–Sailing Minstrel, by The Minstrel	USA	7	4	0	1	368,206
115	Denon	Pleasant Colony–Aviance, by Northfields	USA	5	2	0	2	375,028
	Munir	Indian Ridge–Al Bahathri, by Blushing Groom (Fr)	GB	7	2	1	0	148,271
	Royal Dragon	Danehill–Carmelized, by Key to the Mint	Ger	5	4	0	0	199,724
	Sligo Bay (Ire)	Sadler's Wells–Angelic Song, by Halo	USA	6	1	3	0	246,160
	Tamburlaine	Royal Academy–Well Bought, by Auction Ring	GB	8	0	3	0	150,512
	Voodoo Dancer (f)	Kingmambo–Zuri, by Danzig	USA	7	4	1	0	408,050
114	Baptize	Dynaformer–Screening Room, by Storm Cat	USA	7	3	2	0	368,136
	Frenchman's Bay	Polar Falcon–River Fantasy, by Irish River (Fr)	GB	2	0	1	2	60,196
	Keltos	Kendor–Loxandra, by Last Tycoon (Ire)	Fr	6	4	0	0	84,763
	King of Tara	Fairy King–La Bella Fontana, by Lafontaine	Fr	8	4	1	1	121,854
	Lethals Lady (f)	Rudimentary–Madiyla, by Darshaan	Fr	11	1	2	2	188,141
	Proud Man	Manlove–Proud Entrance, by At the Threshold	USA	8	4	1	0	335,510
	Rose Gypsy (f)	Green Desert–Krisalya, by Kris	Ire	5	1	2	0	148,352
	Snow Dance (f)	Forest Wildcat–Northern Pageant, by Spectacular Bid	USA	8	5	1	2	403,900
113	Ameerat (f)	Mark of Esteem (Ire)–Walimu, by Top Ville	GB	4	1	0	0	260,010
	Bonnard	Nureyev–Utr, by Mr. Prospector	Ire	8	1	2	3	82,568
	Crystal Music	Nureyev–Crystal Spray (GB), by Beldale Flutter	GB	6	0	2	0	182,778
	Kalu	Honor Grades–Barely Rarely, by Rare Performer	USA	6	3	1	0	255,333
	Lonhro	Octagonal–Shadea, by Straight Strike	Aus	7	7	0	0	641,454
	Lurina (f)	Lure–Alligatrix, by Alleged	GB	3	1	0	1	18,004
112	Giovane Imperatore	Halling–Siddharta, by Chief's Crown	Ity	7	4	0	1	179,772
	Momentum	Nureyev–Imprudent Love, by Foolish Pleasure	USA	9	4	3	1	137,929
	Muwakleh (f)	Machiavellian–Elfaslah, by Green Dancer	GB	3	2	1	0	365,017
	Priors Lodge	Grand Lodge–Addaya, by Persian Bold	GB	6	2	1	1	58,294
	Reine de Romance (Ire) (f)	Vettori–Romanche, by Galetto	USA	9	3	2	2	210,840
	Romanceishope	In Excess (Ire)–Romantic Fibs, by Prized	USA	11	5	1	4	529,410
	Tempting Fate (f)	Persian Bold–West of Eden, by Crofter	GB	4	0	0	2	75,323
111	Aghnoyoh	Local Suitor–Aghniyah, by Lyphard	Ger	11	5	1	3	145,235
	Amonita (f)	Anabaa–Spectacular Joke, by Spectacular Bid	Fr	6	1	1	0	43,188
	Ascension (f)	Night Shift–Outeniqua, by Bold Lad	GB	1	1	0	0	40,410
	Dandoun	Halling–Moneefa, by Darshaan	GB	5	3	0	0	50,145
	Grass Eiko O	French Deputy–Explosive Girl, by Explodent	Jpn	8	1	1	2	634,568
	Independence (f)	Selkirk–Yukon Hope, by Forty Niner	GB	9	4	1	1	136,076
	Khaliyna	Danehill–Khalisa (Ire), by Persian Bold	Fr	4	0	1	0	14,532
	Minardi	Boundary–Yarn, by Mr. Prospector	Ire	5	0	0	1	44,462
110	Beckett	Fairy King–Groom Order, by Groom Dancer	Ire	3	1	1	0	36,034
	Blue Steller (Ire)	Barathea (Ire)–Banque Privee, by Private Account	USA	8	2	1	3	145,517
	Calista (GB) (f)	Caerleon–Proskona, by Mr. Prospector	Fr	6	2	2	0	73,772
	Dash For Cash	Secret Savings–Gulistan, by Rubiton	Aus	13	4	4	2	577,069
	Fantastic Filly (Fr) (f)	Myrakalu (Fr)–River Sans Retour, by Vacarme	USA	2	2	0	0	111,960
	Indygo Shiner	A.P. Indy–Navarra, by El Gran Senor	USA	8	3	2	0	372,466
	Limerick Boy	Alwuhush–Limoges, by Koenigsstuhl	Ger	6	2	1	0	64,404
	Malhub	Kingmambo–Arjuzah (Ire), by Ahonoora	GB	4	1	0	0	20,978
	Marine (GB)	Marju–Ivorine, by Blushing Groom (Fr)	USA	7	2	0	1	159,957
	Monnavanna (Ire) (f)	Machiavellian–Mezzogiorno, by Unfuwain	GB	9	3	2	1	80,220
	No Slip (Fr)	Exit to Nowhere–Slipstream Queen, by Conquistador Cielo	USA	7	3	0	1	158,243
	Reel Buddy	Mr. Greeley–Rosebud (GB), by Indian Ridge	GB	9	2	1	2	77,204

5 furlongs +

Wt.	Horse	Sire–Dam, Broodmare sire	Trained	Sts	1st	2nd	3rd	Earnings
125	Mozart (Ire)	Danehill–Victoria Cross, by Spectacular Bid	Ire	7	3	1	2	460,426
117	King Charlemagne	Nureyev–Race the Wild Wind, by Sunny's Halo	Ire	3	3	0	0	152,778
115	Do The Honours (f)	Highest Honor (Fr)–Persian Secret, by Persain Heights	Fr	7	4	0	1	68,004
113	Iron Mask	Danzig–Raise a Beauty, by Alydar	Fr	4	1	0	0	330,960
	Ishiguru	Danzig–Strategic Maneuver, by Cryptoclearance	Ire	7	2	2	0	101,371
	Orientor	Inchinor (GB)–Orient, by Bay Express	GB	14	3	3	3	205,811
112	Pan Jammer	Piccolo–Ingerence, by Akarad	GB	8	0	1	2	38,723
111	Call Me Big	Big Shuffle–Call Me Alice, by Alzao	Ger	8	1	3	1	52,282
	Mugharreb	Gone West–Marling (Ire), by Lomond	GB	7	2	1	1	45,177
	Pomfret Lad	Cyrano de Bergerac–Lucky Flinders, by Free State	GB	2	0	0	1	2,581
110	Danehurst (f)	Danehill–Miswaki Belle, by Miswaki	GB	6	3	0	0	74,349
	Freud	Storm Cat–Mariah's Storm, by Rahy	Ire	7	1	1	1	34,273
	Misty Eyed (f)	Paris House–Bold as Love, by Lomond	GB	6	0	1	3	65,663
	The Trader	Selkirk–Snowing, by Tate Gallery	GB	14	3	1	2	103,015
	Volata	Flying Spur–Musianica, by Music Boy	GB	5	2	0	0	56,309

Older Horses (Turf)

14 furlongs +

Wt.	Horse	Sire–Dam, Broodmare sire	Trained	Sts	1st	2nd	3rd	Earnings
123	Bienamado	Bien Bien–Nakterjal (GB), by Vitiges	USA	5	3	0	0	$540,000
119	Persian Punch	Persian Heights–Rum Cay, by Our Native	GB	7	2	1	2	390,681
116	Give the Slip	Slip Anchor–Falafil, by Fabulous Dancer	GB	7	1	1	0	492,791
	Royal Rebel	Robellino–Greenvera, by Riverman	GB	8	1	0	1	192,150
115	Germinis	Vaguely Pleasant–Grey Valley, by Vigors	Fr	8	1	0	1	152,454
114	Ethereal (f)	Rhythm–Romanee Conti, by *Sir Tristram	Aus	6	2	0	3	1,931,308
	Maquereau	Tony Bin–Antique Value, by Northern Dancer	Jpn	7	1	3	0	1,012,062
	Persianlux (GB)	Persian Bold–Luxurious, by Lyphard	USA	3	1	1	0	200,000
	San Sebastian	Niniski–Top of the League, by High Top	GB	8	0	1	1	52,866
	Solo Mio	Sadler's Wells–Marie de Flandre, by Crystal Palace	GB	5	2	1	0	72,885
113	Admire Boss	Sunday Silence–Vega, by Tony Bin	Jpn	5	0	1	1	342,488
	Generic	Hero's Honor–Tweed Girl, by Windwurf (Ger)	Fr	13	7	2	2	231,021
	Marienbard	Caerleon–Marienbad, by Darshaan	GB	5	1	1	1	171,671
	Rainbow High	Rainbow Quest–Imaginary, by Dancing Brave	GB	8	1	1	1	25,625
112	King's Boy	Platini–King's Blade, by Sure Blade	Ger	7	3	0	1	170,599
111	Jardine's Lookout	Fourstars Allstar–Foolish Flight, by Fools Holme	GB	6	0	1	1	69,490
110	Akbar	Doyoun–Akishka, by Nishapour	GB	8	2	1	3	105,762
	London Bank	Bigstone (Ire)–Bourbon Queen, by Ile de Bourbon	Ity	7	3	2	0	150,299
	Romantic Affair	Persian Bold–Broken Romance, by Ela-Mana-Mou	GB	5	0	2	1	37,318
	Samsaam	Sadler's Wells–Azyaa, by Kris	GB	6	0	2	0	59,753

11 furlongs +

Wt.	Horse	Sire–Dam, Broodmare sire	Trained	Sts	1st	2nd	3rd	Earnings
133	Sakhee	Bahri–Thawakib (Ire), by Sadler's Wells	GB	4	3	1	0	2,039,656
124	Hightori	Vettori–High Mecene, by Highest Honor (Fr)	Fr	8	2	1	3	896,189
122	T M Opera O	Opera House (GB)–Once Wed, by Blushing Groom (Fr)	Jpn	7	2	3	0	3,523,028
120	King Cugat	Kingmambo–Tricky Game, by Majestic Light	USA	6	1	4	1	555,980
	Meisho Doto	Bigstone (Ire)–Princess Reema, by Affirmed	Jpn	6	2	1	1	2,725,887
	Millenary	Rainbow Quest–Ballerina, by Dancing Brave	GB	5	1	2	1	186,101
	Stay Gold	Sunday Silence–Golden Sash, by Dictus	Jpn	7	3	0	0	3,238,753
	Timboroa (GB)	Salse–Kisumu, by Damister	USA	7	2	1	2	944,880
	With Anticipation	Relaunch–Fran's Valentine, by Saros (GB)	USA	9	4	1	0	802,393
119	Kutub	In the Wings (GB)–Minnie Habit, by Habitat	GB	8	5	1	0	848,375
118	Ekraar	Red Ransom–Sacahuista, by Raja Baba	GB	7	1	1	1	450,305
	Holding Court	Hernando (Fr)–Indian Love Song, by Be My Guest	GB	5	1	0	2	91,616
	Mutafaweq	Silver Hawk–The Caretaker (Ire), by Caerleon	GB	6	1	0	1	228,920
	Mutamam (GB)	Darshaan–Petal Girl, by Caerleon	GB	5	3	0	0	979,807
	Sky Heights	Zabeel–Moet Heights, by Engagement	Aus	7	1	1	0	347,626
117	American Boss	Kingmambo–Redeemer, by Dixieland Band	Jpn	9	2	1	0	1,677,417
	Hot Secret	Hunting Hawk–Suda Nadeshiko, by Tai Tehm	Jpn	6	1	0	2	905,872
	Little Rock	Warning (GB)–Much Too Risky, by Bustino	GB	6	0	1	1	55,188
	Mirio	Priolo–Mira Monte, by Baillamont	Fr	4	3	0	1	194,092
	Narita Top Road	Soccer Boy–Floral Magic, by Affirmed	Jpn	6	1	0	3	1,448,023
	Paolini	Lando (Ger)–Prairie Darling, by Stanford	Ger	6	2	1	1	722,257
	Samum	Monsun–Sacarina, by Old Vic	Ger	2	0	1	0	28,607
	Senure	Nureyev–Diese, by Diesis (GB)	USA	4	2	1	0	550,000
	Wellbeing	Sadler's Wells–Charming Life, by *Sir Tristram	GB	3	0	1	0	83,663
116	Give the Slip	Slip Anchor–Falafil, by Fabulous Dancer	GB	7	1	1	0	492,791
	Royal Rebel	Robellino–Greenvera, by Riverman	GB	8	1	0	1	192,150
115	Germinis	Vaguely Pleasant–Grey Valley, by Vigors	Fr	8	4	1	1	152,454
114	Ethereal (f)	Rhythm–Romanee Conti, by *Sir Tristram	Aus	6	2	0	3	1,931,308
	Maquereau	Tony Bin–Antique Value, by Northern Dancer	Jpn	7	1	3	0	1,012,062
	Persianlux (GB)	Persian Bold–Luxurious, by Lyphard	USA	3	1	1	0	200,000
	San Sebastian	Niniski–Top of The League, by High Top	GB	8	0	1	1	52,866
	Solo Mio	Sadler's Wells–Marie de Flandre, by Crystal Palace	(NZ)	5	2	1	0	72,885
113	Admire Boss	Sunday Silence–Vega, by Tony Bin	Jpn	5	0	1	1	342,488
	Blueprint (Ire)	Generous–Highbrow, by Shirley Heights	USA	3	2	0	1	318,000
	Bonapartiste (Fr)	Kendor–Fab's Melody, by Devil's Bag	USA	2	0	0	1	24,000
	Cetewayo	His Majesty–Aletta Maria, by Diesis (GB)	USA	1	1	0	0	120,000
	Ela Athena (GB) (f)	Ezzoud (Ire)–Crodelle, by Formidable	GB	4	0	2	1	121,372
	Fusaichi Zenon	Sunday Silence–Elizabeth Rose, by Northern Taste	Jpn	4	0	1	0	63,750
	Idaho Quest	Rainbow Quest–Javandra, by Lyphard	Fr	9	1	2	2	54,690
	Krisada (f)	Kris S.–Funistrada, by Fappiano	USA	9	2	1	3	185,700
	Marienbard	Caerleon–Marienbad, by Darshaan	GB	5	1	1	1	171,671
	Northern Quest (Fr)	Rainbow Quest–Northern Goddess, by Night Shift	USA	9	1	1	3	259,500
	St. Expedit	Sadler's Wells–Miss Rinjani, by Shirley Heights	GB	4	1	1	0	84,695
	Super Tassa (f)	Lahib–Center Moriches, by Magical Wonder	Ity	7	2	2	2	356,822
	Yavana's Pace	Accordion–Lady in Pace, by Burslem	GB	10	3	1	1	163,843
112	Agnes Flight	Sunday Silence–Agnes Flora, by Royal Ski	Jpn	2	0	1	0	227,250
	Compton Bolter	Red Sunset–Milk and Honey, by So Blessed	GB	11	2	1	2	99,089
	Daiwa Texas	Tolomeo (Ire)–Robe Decollete, by No Attention	Jpn	11	0	1	1	595,749
	Egyptband (f)	Dixieland Band–Egyptown (Fr), by Top Ville	Fr	4	1	1	1	103,659

Wt.	Horse	Sire–Dam, Broodmare sire	Trained	Sts	1st	2nd	3rd	Earnings
112	Falcon Flight (Fr)	Persian Bold–Flying Circus, by Gay Mecene	USA	8	1	0	1	231,850
	Keemoon (Fr) (f)	Goldneyev–Mahonie, by Kenmare	USA	6	3	1	0	245,155
	Lodge Hill	Cozzene–L'Insatiable, by Caveat	Can	9	0	2	1	232,070
	Lucido	Royal Academy–Lady Ambassador, by General Assembly	GB	4	2	0	0	46,251
	Profit Option	Alleged–Miss Angel T., by Talc	USA	2	0	0	1	28,000
	Sacred Song (f)	Diesis (GB)–Ruby Ransom, by Red Ransom	GB	4	1	1	2	121,007
	Slew Valley	Valley Crossing–Slewway, by Slewpy	USA	1	0	0	0	1,700
	Subtle Power (Ire)	Sadler's Wells–Mosaique Bleue, by Shirley Heights	USA	4	2	1	0	139,000
	To the Victory	Sunday Silence–Fairy Doll, by Nureyev	Jpn	1	0	0	0	105,602
	Williams News	Alleged–Wooden Crown, by His Majesty	USA	8	1	1	1	157,610
111	Gritty Sandie	Manila–Madam Sandie, by Our Native	USA	8	0	0	2	112,670
	Matikane Kinnohosi	Seattle Slew–Alysbelle, by Alydar	Jpn	2	0	1	0	246,739
	Mont Rocher	Caerleon–Cuixmala, by Highest Honor (Fr)	Fr	7	3	1	1	72,140
	Passimo	Lomitas–Partida, by Acatenango	Ger	6	0	0	1	30,409
	Sagittarius	Sadler's Wells–Ste Nitouche, by Riverman	Nor	7	4	3	0	81,681
110	Abitara (f)	Rainbow Quest–Arastou, by Surumu	Ger	5	2	0	1	77,791
	Aeskulap	Acatenango–Aerope, by Celestial Storm	GB	8	1	1	1	120,815
	Bonvivant	Sternkoenig–Bonne Chance, by Surumu	Ger	6	1	0	0	72,644
	Boreas	In the Wings (GB)–Reamur, by Top Ville	GB	5	1	0	2	36,692
	Craigsteel (GB)	Suave Dancer–Applecross, by Glint of Gold	USA	3	0	0	2	38,840
	Dano-Mast	Unfuwain–Camera Girl, by Kalaglow	Den	5	2	0	2	77,041
	Desert Boy	Green Desert–City Fortress, by Troy	HK	10	1	0	0	433,829
	Epitre	Common Grounds–Epistolienne, by Law Society	Fr	5	0	1	1	21,257
	Kerrygold (Fr)	Tel Quel (Fr)–Star System, by Northern Treat	USA	10	1	2	2	176,814
	Lear Spear	Lear Fan–Golden Gorse, by His Majesty	GB	1	0	0	1	3,643
	Mr. Pleasentfar (Brz)	Emmson–Pleasant Tale, by Pleasant Colony	USA	7	3	0	1	168,350
	Muntej (GB)	Muhtarram–El Rabab, by Roberto	Fr	6	0	1	1	75,590
	Queue (f)	French Deputy–P J Floral, by Baldski	USA	1	0	0	0	6,000
	Stokosky	Stack–Fama, by Forever Sparkle	USA	2	1	0	0	27,600
	Tico Tico Tac	Soccer Boy–One-Eyed Bamboo, by Brian's Time	Jpn	6	0	1	1	459,272
	Valley Chapel	Selkirk–Valley Springs, by Saratoga Six	Nor	9	4	2	1	266,901

9½ furlongs +

Wt.	Horse	Sire–Dam, Broodmare sire	Trained	Sts	1st	2nd	3rd	Earnings
133	Sakhee	Bahri–Thawakib (Ire), by Sadler's Wells	GB	4	3	1	0	2,039,656
129	Fantastic Light	Rahy–Jood, by Nijinsky II	GB	6	4	2	0	3,634,859
124	Bienamado	Bien Bien–Nakterjal (GB), by Vitiges	USA	5	3	0	0	540,000
123	Silvano (Ger)	Lomitas–Spirit of Eagles, by Beau's Eagle	Ger	8	3	1	1	2,066,359
122	Kalanisi (Ire)	Doyoun–Kalamba, by Green Dancer	GB	2	0	1	1	96,568
	Northerly	Serheed–North Bell, by Bellwether	Aus	8	5	2	0	1,028,387
120	Agnes Digital	Crafty Prospector–Chancey Squaw, by Chief's Crown	Jpn	7	4	0	1	3,341,517
	Astra (f)	Theatrical (Ire)–Savannah Slew, by Seattle Slew	USA	3	2	0	0	270,000
	Golden Snake	Danzig–Dubian (GB), by High Line	GB	3	1	1	0	125,458
118	England's Legend (Fr) (f)	Lure–Mystery Tune, by Commanche Run	USA	6	3	1	0	757,480
	Hap	Theatrical (Ire)–Committed, by Hagley	USA	6	4	1	0	919,000
117	Endless Hall	Saddler's Hall (Ire)–Endless Joy, by Law Society	GB	5	1	0	0	1,098,123
	Senure	Nureyev–Diese, by Diesis (GB)	USA	4	2	1	0	550,000
116	Janet (GB) (f)	Emperor Jones–Bid Dancer, by Spectacular Bid	USA	11	4	0	3	715,080
	Shogun Lodge	Grand Lodge–Pride of Tahnee, by Best Western	Aus	6	1	2	1	206,405
	Universal Prince	Scenic–Biscay Bird, by Bluebird	Aus	7	0	2	2	89,866
	White Heart (GB)	Green Desert–Barari, by Blushing Groom (Fr)	USA	6	1	1	0	327,938
115	Cagney (Brz)	Roy–Donnegalle, by Campero	USA	8	2	1	1	192,965
	Indigenous	Marju–Sea Port, by Averof	HK	10	0	0	4	477,881
	Terre A Terre	Kaldounevees (Fr)–Toujours Juste, by Always Fair	Fr	8	4	0	2	421,406
	With the Flow	Irish River (Fr)–Principle, by Viceregal	Fr	7	0	0	2	243,210
114	Air Shakur	Sunday Silence–I Dreamed a Dream, by Well Decorated	Jpn	3	0	1	0	314,437
	Albarahin	Silver Hawk–My Dear Lady, by Mr. Prospector	GB	8	3	3	0	104,199
	Gaviola (f)	Cozzene–Forest Key, by Green Forest	USA	6	1	2	0	148,552
	Island House	Grand Lodge–Fortitude, by Last Tycoon	GB	7	1	1	2	56,178
	King Keitel	Keitel–Paula's Glory, by All Glory	Aus	7	0	1	0	99,235
	Manndar (Ire)	Doyoun–Madiriya (Ire), by Diesis (GB)	USA	4	0	2	0	60,000
	Muakaad (GB)	Muhtarram–Forest Lair, by Habitat	Ire	6	3	1	0	143,403
	Saddle Up	Bold Russian–Queen's Rule, by Riyahi	Ind	8	3	1	1	458,865
	Shibuni's Falcon	Polar Falcon–Shibuni, by Damister	Ity	9	3	0	0	148,965
	Slew the Red	Red Ransom–Great Lady Slew, by Seattle Slew	Fr	7	3	0	1	88,764
	Spook Express (SAf) (f)	Comic Blush–Park Walk, by Green Dancer	USA	8	3	1	3	866,870
	Sumitas (Ger)	Lomitas (GB)–Subia, by Koenigsstuhl	USA	7	2	0	0	204,000
113	Adilabad	Gulch–Adaiyka (Ire), by Doyoun	GB	6	2	0	1	73,907
	Kudos	Kris S.–Souq, by Damascus	USA	11	4	2	0	221,880
	Northern Quest (Fr)	Rainbow Quest–Northen Goddess, by Night Shift	USA	9	1	1	3	259,500
112	Bocelli	Lord Ballina–Sweet Vienna, by Dahar	Sing	13	6	1	2	587,273
	Crash Course	Holy Bull–Track Gossip, by Shahrastani	USA	11	3	1	5	213,880
	Daiwa Texas	Tolomeo (Ire)–Robe Decollete, by No Attention	Jpn	11	0	1	1	595,749
	Ibuki Government	Commander In Chief–Rosita, by Mill George	Jpn	14	4	2	1	1,178,340

Wt.	Horse	Sire–Dam, Broodmare sire	Trained	Sts	1st	2nd	3rd	Earnings
	Jammaal	Robellino–Navajo Love Song, by Dancing Brave	Ire	7	2	2	3	124,093
	Kaapstad Way	Kaapstad–Crysell Way, by Star Way	Aus	7	0	0	1	21,865
	Meisho Odo	Sunny's Halo–Altadena, by Lyphard	Jpn	8	1	1	1	832,698
	Passage West	Be My Native–Nordicolini, by Nordico	HK	10	1	1	1	227,177
	Sobriety	Namaqualand–Scanno's Choice, by Pennine Walk	HK	9	2	0	3	1,092,684
	Toho Dream	Mejiro Ryan–Sakura Sasayaki, by No Attention	Jpn	9	3	0	0	891,331
111	Al Desima (GB) (f)	Emperor Jones–Miss Up n Go, by Gorytus	USA	12	1	3	4	175,678
	Beautiful Noise (f)	Sunny's Halo–Listen Well, by Secretariat	USA	5	1	1	2	214,142
	Make No Mistake (Ire)	Darshaan–Respectfully, by The Minstrel	USA	6	2	1	0	250,000
	Mont Rocher	Caerleon–Cuixmala (GB), by Highest Honor	Fr	7	3	1	1	72,140
	Pawn Broker	Selkirk–Dime Bag, by High Line	GB	4	0	1	3	21,572
	Solvig (f)	Caerleon–Incha (GB), by Nashwan	USA	9	1	2	3	320,490
	Uncharted Haven (GB) (f)	Turtle Island–Tochar Ban, by Assert (Ire)	USA	3	1	0	2	138,000
110	Del Mar Show	Theatrical (Ire)–Prankstress, by Foolish Pleasure	USA	5	4	0	0	320,190
	Idol	Masterclass–Venetian Court, by Pompeii Court	HK	8	1	0	0	450,720
	Megans Bluff	Pine Bluff–Cozzena, by Cozzene	USA	9	1	3	2	202,617
	Takarian (Ire)	Doyoun–Takarouna, by Green Dancer	USA	6	1	1	0	164,000
	The Whistling Teal	Rudimentary–Lonely Shore, by Blakeney	GB	6	3	1	0	72,844

7 furlongs +

Wt.	Horse	Sire–Dam, Broodmare sire	Trained	Sts	1st	2nd	3rd	Earnings
125	Slickly (Fr)	Linamix–Slipstream Queen, by Conquistador Cielo	GB	4	3	0	0	255,896
124	Val Royal (Fr)	Royal Academy–Vadlava, by Bikala	USA	3	2	1	0	792,800
123	Eishin Preston	Green Dancer–Warranty Applied, by Monteverdi (Ire)	Jpn	12	4	2	1	2,704,835
	Jim and Tonic (Fr)	Double Bed (Fr)–Jimka, by Jim French	Fr	6	2	3	0	788,743
122	Fairy King Prawn	Danehill–Twiglet, by Twig Moss	HK	7	4	1	0	1,676,237
	Summoner	Inchinor (GB)–Sumoto, by Mtoto	GB	3	2	1	0	297,176
121	Medicean	Machiavellian–Mystic Goddess, by Storm Bird	GB	4	3	0	1	580,127
	Observatory	Distant View–Stellaria, by Roberto	GB	2	1	0	0	84,626
120	Forbidden Apple	Pleasant Colony–North Of Eden (Ire), by Northfields	USA	5	2	1	0	725,060
	Perfect Sting (f)	Red Ransom–Valid Victress, by Valid Appeal	USA	2	1	0	0	120,000
119	Bach (Ire)	Caerleon–Producer, by Nashua	Ire	12	2	2	3	449,666
	Mount Abu	Foxhound–Twany Angel, by Double Form	GB	8	2	1	1	157,235
	Starine (Fr) (f)	Mendocino–Grisonnante, by Kaldoun	USA	11	4	3	1	752,305
118	Hap	Theatrical (Ire)–Committed, by Hagley	USA	6	4	1	0	919,070
	Irish Prize	Irish River (Fr)–Cadeaux d'Amie, by Lyphard	USA	9	5	0	1	913,350
117	Brahms	Danzig–Queena, by Mr. Prospector	USA	7	0	1	3	248,335
	Happyanunoit (NZ) (f)	Yachtie–Easter Queen, by Rajah	USA	2	1	1	0	155,710
	Sunline (f)	Desert Sun (GB)–Songline, by Western Symphony	NZ	7	3	3	1	634,705
	Tough Speed	Miswaki–Nature's Magic, by Nijinsky II	GB	6	2	1	0	96,233
116	Black Hawk (GB)	Nureyev–Silver Lane, by Silver Hawk	Jpn	4	1	2	1	1,412,216
	China Visit	Red Ransom–Furajet, by The Minstrel	GB	7	2	3	1	404,642
	Distant Music	Distant View–Musicanti, by Nijinsky II	GB	6	1	0	0	113,208
	Electronic Unicorn	Housebuster–Lilac Garden, by Roberto	HK	8	2	1	1	841,436
	Quiet Resolve	Affirmed–Quiet Cleo, by No Louder	Can	8	1	0	2	385,010
115	Cape Town	Desert Style–Rossaldene, by Mummy's Pet	GB	3	2	0	0	66,227
	Hawksley Hill (Ire)	Rahy–Gaijin (Ire), by Caerleon	USA	4	1	2	1	153,600
	Nicobar (GB)	Indian Ridge–Duchess of Alba, by Belmez	GB	6	2	0	1	133,347
	Proudwings	Dashing Blade–Peraja, by Kaiseradler	Ger	8	3	0	1	288,969
	Redattore (Brz)	Roi Normande–Political Intrigue, by Deputy Minister	USA	8	3	0	2	555,840
	Right Wing	In the Wings (GB)–Nekhbet (Ire), by Artaius	GB	6	3	0	0	75,745
	Touch of the Blues (Fr)	Cadeaux Genereux–Silabteni, by Nureyev	USA	4	0	2	1	129,305
	Warningford	Warning (GB)–Barford Lady, by Stanford	GB	7	1	1	3	117,078
	Zenno El Cid	Caerleon–Embla, by Dominion (GB)	Jpn	8	3	1	0	1,362,724
114	Affirmed Success	Affirmed–Towering Success, by Irish Tower	USA	5	2	1	0	343,215
	Arkadian Hero	Trempolino–Careless Kitten, by Caro (Ire)	GB	5	0	1	1	93,679
	Breaktime	Danehill–Homareno Princess, by Prince of Birds	Jpn	4	0	2	1	497,147
	Daitaku Riva	Fuji Kiseki–Spring Never, by Sakura Yutaka O	Jpn	5	1	2	1	791,912
	Manndar (Ire)	Doyoun–Madiriya, by Diesis (GB)	USA	4	0	2	0	60,000
	Road to Slew	Slewpy–Plumeria Lei, by Bold Tropic (SAf)	USA	2	2	0	0	330,000
	Swallow Flight	Bluebird–Mirage, by Red Sunset	GB	7	4	3	1	118,280
	Tout Charmant (f)	Slewvescent–Charm a Gendarme, by Batonnier	USA	3	0	0	0	46,175
113	Banyumanik	Perugino–Bennetta, by Top Ville	Ger	6	2	0	0	64,127
	Colstar (f)	Opening Verse–Ascend, by Risen Star	USA	4	3	0	0	230,136
	Dr. Kashnikow	El Gran Senor–One More Breeze, by Mythical Ruler	USA	8	5	0	1	335,706
	Fath	Danzig–Desirable (Ire), by Lord Gayle	GB	9	2	3	0	104,444
	Island Sands	Turtle Island–Tiavanita, by J. O. Tobin	GB	4	1	11	1	30,369
	License Fee (f)	Black Tie Affair (Ire)–Star Deputy, by Deputy Minister	USA	6	3	1	0	382,560
	Numerous Times	Numerous–Dramatical, by Theatrical (Ire)	Can	3	3	0	0	676,320
	Penny's Gold (f)	Kingmambo–Penny's Valentine, by Storm Cat	USA	6	4	0	1	316,388
	Shibboleth	Danzig–Razyana, by His Majesty	GB	4	2	0	0	47,514
	Tijiyr (Ire)	Primo Dominie–Tijara, by Darshaan	USA	6	2	1	1	460,160
112	Aly's Alley	Alwuhush–Aly Capri, by Alydar	USA	7	2	2	2	244,072

Wt.	Horse	Sire–Dam, Broodmare sire	Trained	Sts	1st	2nd	3rd	Earnings
112	Band is Passing	Pass the Line–Fairforband, by Fairway Fortune	USA	8	2	3	1	204,842
	Bocelli	Lord Ballina–Sweet Vienna, by Dahar	Sing	13	6	1	2	587,273
	Golden Silca (f)	Inchinor (GB)–Silca-Cisa, by Hallgate	GB	5	0	2	0	128,208
	Kaapstad Way	Kaapstad–Crysell Way, by Star Way	Aus	7	0	0	1	21,865
	Late Night Out	Lahib–Chain Dance, by Shareef Dancer	GB	9	3	2	3	142,561
	Lazy Lode (Arg)	Lode–Lazy Fables, by Babas Fables	USA	3	2	0	0	133,200
	Meisho Odo	Sunday Silence–Altadena, by Lyphard	Jpn	8	1	1	1	832,698
	Native Desert	Desert Classic–Miss C. Native, by Princely Native	USA	8	2	2	1	307,226
	Nice One Clare	Mukaddamah–Sarah-Clare, by Reach	GB	9	3	1	1	273,974
	North East Bound	D'Accord–North East Dancer, by Far North	USA	8	1	1	0	215,668
	Peppercorn	Big Shuffle–Pasca, by Lagunas	Ger	10	2	3	1	88,547
	Show a Heart	Brave Warrior–Miss Sandman, by Regal Advice	Aus	6	1	1	0	120,185
	Sir Nicholas	Cadeaux Genereux–Final Shot, by Dalsaan	HK	16	1	3	2	642,353
	Taiki Treasure	Miswaki–Royal Bride, by Blushing Groom (Fr)	Jpn	8	2	3	1	1,135,788
	Where's Taylor	Absent Russian–Ms. K. L. Taylor, by Taylor's Falls	USA	7	2	2	1	223,510
111	Beautiful Noise (f)	Sunny's Halo–Listen Well, by Secretariat	USA	5	1	1	2	214,142
	Charm Scene Park	Chief's Crown–Quarantieme, by Bletchingly	HK	9	1	0	1	423,824
	Kimberlite Pipe	Take Me Out–Rajas Secret, by Storm Bird	USA	11	3	1	2	250,042
	Make No Mistake (Ire)	Darshaan–Respectfully, by The Minstrel	USA	6	2	1	0	250,000
	Mr. Murphy	Danehill–Marscay's Dream, by Marscay	Aus	7	1	0	0	111,608
	Sky and Ryu	Polish Patriot–Energy Tosho, by Tosho Boy	Jpn	4	2	1	1	505,012
	Testa Rossa	Perugino–Bo Dapper, by Sir Dapper	Aus	2	0	0	0	48,966
	Umistim	Inchinor (GB)–Simply Sooty, by Absalom	GB	7	2	0	0	40,997
	Umrum	Umatilla–Rhum Dancer, by Command Module	Aus	10	0	0	2	31,879
	Valentino	Nureyev–Divine Danse (Fr), by Kris	GB	5	1	0	2	34,263
110	Atavus	Distant Relative (Ire)–Elysian, by Northfields	GB	10	4	1	0	230,161
	Dane Friendly	Danehill–Always Friendly, by High Line	Ity	7	0	4	1	87,604
	Eagle Cafe	Gulch–Net Dancer, by Nureyev	Jpn	9	0	1	1	285,043
	El Lute	Scenic (Ire)–Easily, by Swing Easy	Ger	4	1	0	0	33,773
	Faberger	Dashing Blade–Friedrichslust, by Caerleon	Ger	6	0	1	1	40,557
	Fateful Dream	Distant View–Fitnah, by Fit to Fight	USA	5	1	0	1	101,621
	Joten Brave	Dancing Brave–Takuno Gal, by Royal Ski	Jpn	6	1	1	0	723,237
	Mull of Kintyre	Danzig–Retrospective, by Easy Goer	Ire	5	0	1	1	32,575
	Prolix	Kris–Ajuga, by The Minstrel	SA	8	4	1	0	13,516
	Shinko Edward	Lear Fan–Powder Storm, by Storm Bird	Jpn	4	0	2	0	347,206
	Social Harmony	Polish Precedent–Latest Chapter, by Ahonoora	Ire	10	0	2	2	34,671
	Stinger (f)	Sunday Silence–Legacy of Strength, by Affirmed	Jpn	6	1	0	2	750,478
	Sugarfoot	Thatching–Norpella, by Northfields	GB	5	0	1	0	14,266
	Thady Quill	Nureyev–Alleged Devotion, by Alleged	USA	4	3	1	0	170,210
	Tillerman	In the Wings (GB)–Autumn Tint, by Roberto	GB	4	0	0	1	35,383
	Up And Away (GB)	Le Glorieux (GB)–Ultima Ratio, by Viceregal	Ger	10	4	2	2	115,697
	Yaralino	Caerleon–Wemyss Bight (GB), by Dancing Brave	USA	4	1	1	0	93,000

5 furlongs +

Wt.	Horse	Sire–Dam, Broodmare sire	Trained	Sts	1st	2nd	3rd	Earnings
119	Nuclear Debate	Geiger Counter–I'm an Issue, by Cox's Ridge	Fr	9	1	2	1	310,756
117	Bahamian Pirate	Housebuster–Shining Through, by Deputy Minister	GB	12	1	2	3	106,352
	Harmonic Way	Lion Cavern–Pineapple, by Superlative	GB	8	2	0	0	132,025
	Pipalong (f)	Pips Pride–Limpopo, by Green Desert	GB	9	1	0	1	73,687
	Trot Star	Damister–Carmancita, by Wise Counsellor	Jpn	5	3	0	0	1,982,702
116	Black Hawk (GB)	Nureyev–Silver Lane, by Silver Hawk	Jpn	4	1	2	1	1,412,216
	Superior Premium	Forzando (GB)–Devils Dirge, by Song	GB	5	0	0	1	4,877
	Three Points	Bering (GB)–Trazi, by Zalazl	GB	7	0	3	0	95,705
115	Danger Over	Warning–Danilova, by Lyphard	Fr	5	0	1	0	19,304
	Falvelon	Alannon–Devil's Zephyr, by Zephyr Zing	Aus	4	1	2	1	634,979
	Imperial Beauty	Imperial Ballet (Ire)–Multimara, by Arctic Tern	Fr	5	1	0	1	89,000
114	Bishops Court	Clantime–Indigo, by Primo Dominie	GB	7	1	0	2	115,205
	Daitaku Yamato	Daitaku Helios–Daitaku Brains, by Tesco Boy	Jpn	6	1	1	1	722,332
	Misraah	Lure–Dwell, by Habitat	GB	8	1	1	1	82,882
	Morluc	Housebuster–Flashing Eyes, by Time to Explode	USA	6	2	1	0	358,730
113	All Thrills Too	St. Covet–Red Slippers, by Citidancer	Aus	9	4	1	2	565,938
	Cassandra Go (f)	Indian Ridge–Rahaam, by Secreto	GB	4	2	2	0	248,542
	Confessional (f)	Holy Bull–Whisper Who Dares, by Green Dancer	USA	4	4	0	0	234,270
	Dananeyev	Goldneyev–Danagroom, by Groom Dancer	Fr	8	3	0	1	90,716
	Rushcutter Bay	Mon Tresor–Llwy Bren, by Lidhame	GB	6	1	0	0	33,396
	Shibboleth	Danzig–Razyana, by His Majesty	GB	4	2	0	0	47,514
	Symboli Sword	Green Desert–Kenbu (Fr), by Kenmare	Jpn	8	0	2	0	387,999
	Vision of Night (GB)	Night Shift–Dreamawhile, by Known Fact	GB	7	2	1	0	100,310
112	Century Kid	Centaine–Zeffi, by Pompeii Court	Aus	7	0	1	1	76,430
	El Cielo	El Prado (Ire)–Only Above, by Great Above	USA	5	3	0	1	167,680
	Invincible Spirit	Green Desert–Rafha (GB), by Kris	GB	6	3	1	0	93,429
	Kier Park	Foxhound–Merlannah, by Shy Groom	GB	8	0	1	1	28,775
	Repertory	Anshan (GB)–Susie's Baby, by Balidar	GB	10	2	0	3	133,648
	Sartorial	Elbio (GB)–Madam Slaney, by Prince Tenderfoot	GB	6	2	1	1	69,054

Wt.	Horse	Sire–Dam, Broodmare sire	Trained	Sts	1st	2nd	3rd	Earnings
	Trillion Win	American Standard–Scarletts Revenge, by Marshua's Dancer	Sing	7	2	2	0	183,530
111	Deep Sleep	Rahy–Night and Dreams, by Fappiano	Fr	7	1	2	0	46,629
	Primo Valentino	Primo Dominie–Dorothea Brooke, by Dancing Brave	GB	3	1	0	0	21,098
	Tedburrow	Dowsing–Gwiffina, by Welsh Saint	GB	13	1	1	1	39,489
	Waltz in the Park	Bletchley Park–Corporate Dancer, by Corporate Raider	Aus	2	2	0	0	192,182
110	Cameron	Indian Ridge–Casolana, by Zeddaan	Ity	5	3	0	0	81,994
	Daiwa Caerleon	Caerleon–J'Ai Deux Amours, by Top Ville	Jpn	10	0	0	0	321,126
	Indian Spark	Indian Ridge–Ammes Gift, by *Ballymoss	GB	13	1	1	1	51,917
	King of Danes	Danehill–Impulsive Rhythm, by Rubiton	HK	8	1	0	0	338,040
	Mejiro Darling (f)	Green Desert–Isle of Glass, by Affirmed	Jpn	8	2	1	0	1,111,949
	Monkston Point	Fayruz–Doon Belle, by Ardoon	GB	9	2	0	2	60,337
	Mull of Kintyre	Danzig–Retrospective, by Easy Goer	Ire	5	0	1	1	32,575
	Social Harmony	Polish Precedent–Latest Chapter, by Ahonoora	Ire	10	0	2	2	34,671
	Summer Beau	Sky Filou–Long Summer, by Long Row	Sing	10	2	5	1	234,363

Three-Year-Olds (Dirt)
11 furlongs +

Wt.	Horse	Sire–Dam, Broodmare sire	Trained	Sts	1st	2nd	3rd	Earnings
130	Point Given	Thunder Gulch–Turko's Turn, by Turkoman	USA	7	6	0	0	$3,350,000
115	Tweedside (f)	Thunder Gulch–Twitchet, by Roberto	USA	9	4	2	0	347,036

9½ furlongs +

Wt.	Horse	Sire–Dam, Broodmare sire	Trained	Sts	1st	2nd	3rd	Earnings
125	Kurofune	French Deputy–Blue Avenue, by Classic Go Go	Jpn	6	4	0	1	2,801,914
	Monarchos	Maria's Mon–Regal Band, by Dixieland Band	USA	7	4	1	1	1,711,600
121	A P Valentine	A.P. Indy–Twenty Eight Carat, by Alydar	USA	9	1	2	1	535,060
	E Dubai	Mr. Prospector–Words of War, by Lord at War (Arg)	USA	6	3	3	0	577,600
	Flute (f)	Seattle Slew–Rougeur, by Blushing Groom (Fr)	USA	7	4	2	0	1,094,104
120	Macho Uno	Holy Bull–Primal Force, by Blushing Groom (Fr)	USA	4	1	1	1	563,400
119	Dollar Bill	Peaks and Valleys–Saratoga Dame, by Saratoga Six	USA	7	1	0	2	415,000
118	Invisible Ink	Thunder Gulch–Conquistress, by Conquistador Cielo	USA	6	2	1	1	379,500
115	Griffinite	Unbridled's Song–Copious, by In Reality	USA	6	1	1	0	157,935
	Outofthebox	Montbrook–Cricket Box, by Notebook	USA	10	3	2	2	607,995
114	Free of Love	Meadow Flight–Love Spanish, by Spanish Drums	USA	11	2	3	1	234,353
113	Win City	Slew City Slew–Winsfordan, by Domasca Dan	Can	9	6	1	2	876,187
112	Thunder Blitz	Holy Bull–Rasant, by Assert (Ire)	USA	8	1	2	3	273,370

7 furlongs +

Wt.	Horse	Sire–Dam, Broodmare sire	Trained	Sts	1st	2nd	3rd	Earnings
125	Kurofune	French Deputy–Blue Avenue, by Classic Go Go	Jpn	6	4	0	1	2,801,914
123	Congaree	Arazi–Mari's Sheba, by Mari's Book	USA	7	4	0	3	1,063,400
121	Flute (f)	Seattle Slew–Rougeur, by Blushing Groom (Fr)	USA	7	4	2	0	1,094,104
120	Exogenous (f)	Unbridled–Tangled up in Blue, by Phone Trick	USA	7	4	2	1	901,500
	Fleet Renee (f)	Seattle Slew–Darien Miss, by Mr. Leader	USA	6	4	0	1	624,485
	Golden Ballet (f)	Moscow Ballet–Golden Jewel Box, by Slew o' Gold	USA	6	4	1	0	595,250
	Unbridled Elaine (f)	Unbridled's Song–Carols Folly, by Taylor's Falls	USA	8	4	1	1	1,663,175
118	Millennium Wind	Cryptoclearance–Bali Babe, by Drone	USA	5	2	1	0	679,620
117	Express Tour	Tour d'Or–Express Fashion, by Private Express	USA	5	2	0	0	1,290,000
	Forest Secrets	Forest Wildcat–Garden Secrets, by Time for a Change	USA	8	3	2	1	400,035
	Two Item Limit (f)	Twining–Spa Warning, by Caveat	USA	9	2	2	2	648,760
116	Burning Roma	Rubiano–While Rome Burns, by Overskate	USA	9	5	1	3	614,000
	Real Cozzy (f)	Cozzene–Mining My Business, by Mining	USA	9	3	2	1	459,340
	Street Cry (Ire)	Machiavellian–Helen Street (GB), by Troy	USA	3	1	2	0	571,860
115	Fifty Stars	Quiet American–My Bubbling Belle, by Tsunami Slew	USA	5	1	1	0	552,250
	Mystic Lady (f)	Thunder Gulch–Diane Suzanne, by Compliance	USA	11	6	2	1	775,000
114	Balto Star	Glitterman–Miss Livi, by Devil's Bag	USA	11	5	2	1	848,820
	Crafty C. T.	Crafty Prospector–Andriana B., by Far North	USA	6	2	2	0	309,770
	Songandaprayer	Unbridled's Song–Alizea, by Premiership	USA	6	1	1	1	314,000
	Starrer (f)	Dynaformer–To the Hunt, by Relaunch	USA	9	3	3	0	406,265
113	Nasty Storm (f)	Gulch–A Stark Is Born, by Graustark	USA	8	5	0	1	383,338
	Palmeiro	Pleasant Tap–Fortune Pending, by Fortunate Prospect	USA	9	1	5	1	179,540
	She's a Devil Due (f)	Devil His Due–Fabulous Star, by Fappiano	USA	2	0	0	1	38,500
	Western Pride	Way West (Fr)–Strongerthanpride, by Proud Birdie	USA	12	7	1	0	718,199
112	Hero's Tribute	Sea Hero–Eastern Dawn, by Damascus	USA	8	2	0	2	265,362
	Richly Blended	Rizzi–Valid Blend, by Valid Appeal	USA	6	4	0	1	323,280
	Scorpion	Seattle Slew–Petiteness, by Chief's Crown	USA	10	3	0	0	455,400
	Touch Tone	Pick Up the Phone–Super Seniorita, by El Baba	USA	6	3	1	2	607,850
111	Collect Call (f)	Meadowlake–Negative Pledge, by Alleged	USA	8	2	2	2	338,820
	Volponi	Cryptoclearance–Prom Knight, by Sir Harry Lewis	USA	10	3	2	0	266,176
110	Evening Attire	Black Tie Affair (Ire)–Concolour, by Our Native	USA	5	2	0	1	140,090
	Hoovergetthekeys	Mt. Livermore–Desert Orchid, by Saros (GB)	USA	10	3	1	1	276,260
	Meetyouatthebrig	Out of Place–Always Be Mine, by Kris S.	USA	5	1	1	0	98,602
	Percy Hope	Ide–Ridinghood, by Red Ransom	USA	7	2	2	0	370,200
	Tap Dance (f)	Pleasant Tap–Lyrical Prayer, by The Minstrel	USA	9	2	1	1	222,556

5 furlongs +

Wt.	Horse	Sire–Dam, Broodmare sire	Trained	Sts	1st	2nd	3rd	Earnings
126	Squirtle Squirt	Marquetry–Lost the Code, by Lost Code	USA	6	3	3	0	817,720
122	Xtra Heat (f)	Dixieland Heat–Begin, by Hatchet Man	USA	13	9	3	1	1,012,040
119	Victory Ride (f)	Seeking the Gold–Young Flyer, by Flying Paster	USA	4	3	1	0	247,025
117	Lasersport	Gilded Time–Beamy, by Forty Niner	USA	2	1	1	0	94,500
116	City Zip	Carson City–Baby Zip, by Relaunch	USA	12	4	2	3	401,920
115	Above Perfection (f)	In Excess (Ire)–Something Perfect, by Somethingfabulous	USA	5	3	1	0	170,270
	Mizzen Mast	Cozzene–Kinema, by Graustark	USA	7	3	1	0	291,106
114	Early Flyer	Gilded Time–Bistra, by Classic Go Go	USA	7	2	3	1	300,660
	Gold Mover (f)	Gold Fever–Intentional Move, by Tentam	USA	10	3	3	2	257,316
	Yonaguska	Cherokee Run–Marital Spook, by Silver Ghost	USA	7	3	0	3	278,060
113	D'Wildcat	Forest Wildcat–D'Enough, by D'Accord	USA	3	2	0	1	135,600
	Illusioned	Woodman–Undeniably, by In Reality	USA	9	5	2	1	335,726
	Put it Back	Honour and Glory–Miss Shoplifter, by Exuberant	USA	5	5	0	0	220,185
	Raging Fever (f)	Storm Cat–Pennant Fever, by Seattle Slew	USA	3	1	1	1	88,205
112	Flame Thrower	Saint Ballado–Metromane, by Metrogrand	USA	2	0	2	0	70,000
111	Cat Chat (f)	Storm Cat–Phone Chatter, by Phone Trick	USA	3	2	0	0	115,800
	I Love Silver	Silver Ghost–Lost Love, by Lost Code	USA	11	3	3	3	321,532
	Mandy's Gold (f)	Gilded Time–Manduria, by Aloma's Ruler	USA	4	3	1	0	105,240
110	Sam Lord's Castle	Carson City–Private Treasure, by Explodent	USA	6	2	1	0	131,700
	Skip to the Stone	Skip Trial–Winner's Ticket, by Jolie's Halo	USA	7	3	0	0	190,116

Older Horses (Dirt)

9½ furlongs +

Wt.	Horse	Sire–Dam, Broodmare sire	Trained	Sts	1st	2nd	3rd	Earnings
128	Tiznow	Cee's Tizzy–Cee's Song, by Seattle Song	USA	6	3	1	2	2,981,880
125	Albert the Great	Go for Gin–Bright Feather, by Fappiano	USA	9	3	4	1	1,740,000
124	Aptitude	A.P. Indy–Dokki, by Northern Dancer	USA	6	3	0	1	1,410,000
121	Captain Steve	Fly So Free–Sparkling Delite, by Vice Regent	USA	6	2	1	1	4,201,200
	Skimming	Nureyev–Skimble, by Lyphard	USA	6	3	3	0	1,330,000
120	Futural	Future Storm–Twigazuri, by Dixieland Band	USA	9	3	3	1	478,670
118	Guided Tour	Hansel–Dancing Mahmoud, by Topsider	USA	8	4	1	1	1,384,220
	Include	Broad Brush–Illeria, by Stop the Music	USA	9	5	1	2	1,435,400
116	Pompeii (f)	Broad Brush–Flying Heat, by Private Account	USA	8	3	2	1	436,621
115	State Shinto	Pleasant Colony–Sha Tha, by Mr. Prospector	USA	5	1	0	0	325,338
114	Beautiful Pleasure (f)	Maudlin–Beautiful Bid, by Baldski	USA	4	0	1	0	87,500
	Regular Member	Commander in Chief–Sister Moon, by Nasr El Arab	Jpn	6	2	0	2	1,460,330
	Sir Bear	Sir Leon–Spicy Pearl, by Bet Big	USA	7	1	1	2	313,500
113	Dixie Dot Com	Dixie Brass–Sky Meadows, by Conquistador Cielo	USA	7	2	3	0	679,000
	Regent Bluff	Park Regent–Sally Belle, by Goodly	Jpn	9	2	3	0	1,144,411
112	Dig For It	Digamist–Switch Point, by Personality	USA	13	3	1	3	294,638
	Pleasant Breeze	Pleasant Tap–Sleepy Time, by Turkoman	USA	6	0	1	2	148,500
	Sei Mi	Potrillazo–Seine, by Logical	SA	6	1	3	0	194,876
	To the Victory (f)	Sunday Silence–Fairy Doll, by Nureyev	Jpn	5	1	1	2	2,620,684
	Wing Arrow	Assatis–Sanyo Arrow, by Mr. C B	Jpn	5	1	2	0	1,229,953
111	Irving's Baby	Quiet American–Irving's Girl, by Badger Land	USA	12	5	0	3	559,262
	Miracle Opera	Opera House (GB)–Max Fleet, by Dancer's Image	Jpn	7	4	1	1	1,296,799
110	Broche	Summer Squall–Ribbonwood, by Diesis	UAE	6	1	2	0	50,916
	Generous Rosi (GB)	Generous–Come On Rosi, by Valiyar	USA	9	2	2	2	291,025

7 furlongs +

Wt.	Horse	Sire–Dam, Broodmare sire	Trained	Sts	1st	2nd	3rd	Earnings
124	Lido Palace (Chi)	Rich Man's Gold–Sonada, by Quick Decision	USA	6	2	2	1	1,240,000
121	Captain Steve	Fly So Free–Sparkling Delite, by Vice Regent	USA	6	2	1	1	4,201,200
120	Left Bank	French Deputy–Marshesseaux, by Dr. Blum	USA	8	4	1	0	524,200
119	Gourmet Girl (f)	Cee's Tizzy–Rhondaling (GB), by Welsh Pageant	USA	6	3	1	0	554,950
	Spain (f)	Thunder Gulch–Drina, by Regal and Royal	USA	9	1	3	2	837,705
118	Broken Vow	Unbridled–Wedding Vow, by Nijinsky II	USA	10	5	2	2	611,596
	Include	Broad Brush–Illeria, by Stop the Music	USA	9	5	1	2	1,435,400
117	Chilukki (f)	Cherokee Run–Song of Syria, by Damascus	USA	2	1	1	0	130,000
116	Atelier (f)	Deputy Minister–Aishah, by Alydar	USA	6	3	0	1	282,524
	Miss Linda (Arg) (f)	Southern Halo–Miss Peggy, by Fitzcarraldo	USA	8	3	0	1	455,415
	Peeping Tom	Eagle Eyed–Artful Pleasure, by Nasty and Bold	USA	10	4	2	0	586,060
115	Best of the Bests	Machiavellian–Sueboog, by Darshaan	UAE	3	1	0	0	57,183
	Lazy Slusan (f)	Slewvescent–Three Flights Up, by Topsider	USA	9	4	2	2	678,980
	Nobo True	Broad Brush–Nastique, by Naskra	Jpn	10	3	1	1	1,840,750
	Printemps (Chi) (f)	Hussonet–Wrist, by Worldwatch	USA	4	2	1	1	249,140
	Traditionally	Mr. Prospector–Personal Ensign, by Private Account	USA	7	3	1	0	420,020
	Walkslikeaduck	Blushing John–Nabla, by Theatrical (Ire)	USA	1	0	1	0	52,960
114	Exciting Story	Diablo–Appealing Story, by Valid Appeal	USA	6	2	3	0	596,667
	Feverish (f)	Pirate's Bounty–Blonde Fever, by Flying Paster	USA	10	1	4	1	209,661
	Freedom Crest	To Freedom–Crestothetrail, by Gold Crest	USA	6	2	1	0	440,000
	Jostle (f)	Brocco–Moon Drone, by Drone	USA	5	0	2	1	143,512
	Wooden Phone	Pick Up the Phone–Teaksberry Road, by High Honors	USA	6	2	1	2	623,876

Wt.	Horse	Sire–Dam, Broodmare sire	Trained	Sts	1st	2nd	3rd	Earnings
113	Apple of Kent (f)	Kris S.–Proflare, by Mr. Prospector	USA	5	2	4	1	214,317
	Critical Eye (f)	Dynaformer–Critical Crew, by Dr. Blum	USA	9	2	1	0	339,736
	Dixie Dot Com	Dixie Brass–Sky Meadows, by Conquistador Cielo	USA	7	2	3	0	679,000
	Euchre	Personal Flag–Solid Eight, by Fit to Fight	USA	4	2	1	0	351,500
	Festival of Light	A.P. Indy–Aurora, by Danzig	UAE	3	3	0	0	623,146
	Gander	Cormorant–Lovely Nurse, by Sawbones	USA	10	2	1	2	557,060
	Heritage of Gold (f)	Gold Legend–Lyphard Gal, by Lyphard	USA	2	1	0	0	120,000
	Serra Lake (f)	Seattle Slew–Tara Roma, by Lyphard	USA	8	4	0	0	393,140
112	Connected	Twining–Auto Dial, by Phone Trick	USA	9	4	1	1	277,083
	Graeme Hall	Dehere–Win Crafty Lady, by Crafty Prospector	USA	8	3	2	0	315,923
	Lovellon (Arg) (f)	Potrillon–Helen D., by Sham	USA	3	1	1	0	135,205
112	Red Bullet	Unbridled–Cargo, by Caro (Ire)	USA	3	1	0	1	86,500
	Secret Status (f)	A.P. Indy–Private Status, by Alydar	USA	6	2	2	0	154,042
	Ubiquity	Colonial Affair–Racing Queen, by Alysheba	USA	5	2	2	1	331,500
	Wing Arrow	Assatis–Sanyo Arrow, by Mr. C B	Jpn	5	1	2	0	1,229,953
111	Cat Cay (f)	Pleasant Colony–Cadillacing, by Alydar	USA	8	3	1	2	217,990
	Critikola (Arg) (f)	Tough Critic–Hola Keats, by *Keats	USA	4	0	0	0	60,000
	Curule	Go for Gin–Reservation, by Cryptoclearance	USA	5	0	2	1	215,215
	Lu Ravi (f)	A.P. Indy–At the Half, by Seeking the Gold	USA	3	1	2	0	230,000
	Queenie Belle (f)	Bertrando–Lady Argyle, by Don B.	USA	6	1	2	2	206,170
110	Chicago Six	Wild Again–Secretaridge, by Secretariat	USA	9	5	0	0	376,108
	Conflict (Fr)	Warning (GB)–La Dama Bonita, by El Gran Senor	UAE	6	1	1	1	169,927
	De Bertie	De Niro–Pigeon Pea, by Topsider	USA	6	3	1	0	228,290
	Irisheyesareflying	Flying Continental–Sharon's Barron, by Track Barron	USA	9	4	2	0	507,100
	Lethal Instrument	Gulch–Running Redhead, by Storm Bird	USA	2	0	1	0	60,000
	March Magic (f)	Evansville Slew–Bay Magic, by Ack Ack	USA	8	3	2	1	338,530
	Mr. Ross	Slewacide–Dusty Donna, by Dust Commander	USA	8	4	2	2	442,400
	Perfect Cat	Tabasco Cat–Perfect Probe, by Mr. Prospector	USA	10	3	4	0	335,893
	Royal Fair (f)	Deputy Minister–Barkerville Belle, by Ruthie's Native	USA	8	1	4	1	219,450
	Saudi Poetry (f)	Storm Cat–Gone to Venus, by Gone West	USA	6	2	1	0	418,080
	Trip (f)	Lord At War (Arg)–Tour, by Forty Niner	USA	8	4	1	2	345,855

5 furlongs +

Wt.	Horse	Sire–Dam, Broodmare sire	Trained	Sts	1st	2nd	3rd	Earnings
127	Delaware Township	Notebook–Sunny Mimosa, by Sunny North	USA	9	4	3	0	635,840
	Kona Gold	Java Gold–Double Sunrise, by Slew o' Gold	USA	6	3	1	0	392,420
124	Caller One	Phone Trick–Baltic Sea, by Danzig	USA	6	2	1	2	1,436,380
123	Swept Overboard	End Sweep–Sheer Ice, by Cutlass	USA	8	3	3	1	439,140
120	El Corredor	Mr. Greeley–Silvery Swan, by Silver Deputy	USA	3	2	0	0	240,000
	Left Bank	French Deputy–Marshesseaux, by Dr. Blum	USA	8	4	1	0	524,200
118	Alannan	Conquistador Cielo–Dame Sybil, by Elocutionist	USA	9	2	1	2	427,955
	Bet On Sunshine	Bet Big–My Own Sunshine, by In Reality	USA	6	4	1	0	331,818
	Dream Supreme (f)	Seeking the Gold–Spinning Round, by Dixieland Band	USA	7	3	2	2	541,120
	Go Go (f)	Falstaff–Key Mist, by Plugged Nickle	USA	7	5	2	0	446,620
116	Big Jag	Kleven–In Hopes, by Affirmed	USA	1	0	1	0	40,000
	Country Hideaway (f)	Seeking the Gold–Our Country Place, by Pleasant Colony	USA	6	2	2	2	236,936
	Dat You Miz Blue (f)	Cure the Blues–Emma Loves Marie, by Wild Again	USA	10	5	2	1	273,865
	Five Star Day	Carson City–Reggie V, by Vanlandingham	USA	3	1	1	0	130,000
	Peeping Tom	Eagle Eyed–Artful Pleasure, by Nasty and Bold	USA	10	4	2	0	586,060
115	Say Florida Sandy	Personal Flag–Lolli Lucka Lolli, by Sweet Candy (Ven)	USA	16	6	5	1	615,420
114	Big Bambu (f)	Salt Lake–Meadowlake Mist, by Meadowlake	USA	7	4	0	1	215,129
	Hallowed Dreams (f)	Malagra–Pacific's Dream, by Brother Machree	USA	9	7	0	1	286,700
	Men's Exclusive	Exclusive Ribot–Men's Number, by Meneval	USA	6	2	1	0	589,000
	Shine Again (f)	Wild Again–Shiner, by Two Punch	USA	10	5	1	3	469,750
	Trippi	End Sweep–Jealous Appeal, by Valid Appeal	USA	4	0	1	1	45,720
113	Bonapaw	Sabona–Pawlova, by Nijinsky II	USA	11	5	2	2	386,200
	Wake At Noon	Cure the Blues–Sermon Time, by Silver Deputy	USA	9	2	3	1	235,365
112	Elaborate	Gilded Time–Jeanie's Gift, by Gulch	USA	6	1	0	3	91,032
	Exchange Rate	Danzig–Sterling Pound, by Seeking the Gold	USA	6	2	0	2	190,953
	Explicit	Distant View–Elegant Victress, by Sir Ivor	USA	7	1	1	2	119,380
	Lexicon	Conquistador Cielo–Felidia (Ire), by Golden Fleece	USA	8	2	1	0	147,235
111	Bertolini	Danzig–Aquilegia, by Alydar	UAE	3	0	0	1	204,728
	Disco Rico	Citidancer–Round It Off, by Apalachee	USA	9	5	1	1	349,644
	Hook and Ladder	Dixieland Band–Taianna, by Cox's Ridge	USA	8	3	1	1	256,100
	Kalookan Queen (f)	Lost Code–Regal Realm, by Majestic Prince	USA	6	3	1	1	225,575
	La Feminn (f)	Memo (Chi)–Lila Finn, by Mamaison	USA	3	1	2	0	124,180
110	Ceeband	Chimes Band–Miss Sonrisa (Chi), by Domineau	USA	11	4	0	2	373,766
	Freespool	Geiger Counter–Broadtail, by Olden Times	USA	6	3	0	1	187,978
	Hidden Assets	Mt. Livermore–Silken Ripples, by Roberto	USA	7	2	3	1	221,304
	Hollycombe	Capote–Confirm, by Proudest Roman	USA	6	0	3	0	73,200
	Istintaj	Nureyev–Mathkurh, by Riverman	USA	7	2	0	2	193,000
	Nany's Sweep (f)	End Sweep–Nany's Appeal, by Valid Appeal	USA	7	1	0	4	233,748

Major Racetracks of the World

Argentina

Hipodromo Argentino

Located in the Palermo district close to downtown Buenos Aires and familiarly known as Palermo, Hipodromo Argentino opened on May 7, 1876. Originally a harness racing facility offering just one Thoroughbred flat race daily, the track changed to full-time Thoroughbred racing on August 18, 1883, and was the first racetrack in Argentina to feature a totalizator. A sales pavilion, veterinary hospital and laboratory, equine institute, and museum complement the racetrack, which is home of the Gran Premio Nacional (Arg-G1), Argentina's equivalent of the Kentucky Derby (G1) and third race of the Argentine Triple Crown. Two of its most famous winners were *Yatasto in 1951 and *Forli in '66. Another major stakes race is the Polla de Potrillos (Argentine Two Thousand Guineas) (Arg-G1), the first race of the Triple Crown, in September. Racing is held over a 2,410-meter,* left-handed track with three chutes. (*See conversion table from metric to English distances in Reference section.)

San Isidro

Located 14 miles north of Buenos Aires on the edge of the Pampas, San Isidro Racecourse was founded on December 8, 1935, by the Jockey Club Argentino. San Isidro hosts the Gran Premio Carlos Pellegrini–Internacional (Arg-G1), the country's most important race, which is the final leg of the San Isidro Quadruple Crown. *Yatasto won the Carlos Pellegrini in 1952 before a record crowd of 104,810. *Forli accomplished the feat in 1966 and was then imported to the United States. A daily card consists of as many as 14 races, which begin in midafternoon and conclude at night under lights. Two overlapping, left-handed turf courses—the main one is 2,738 meters—have three different chutes.

Australia

Eagle Farm

Located on the northern side of Brisbane in Ascot, Eagle Farm boasts a long history and excellent equine facilities. Its racing started on August 14, 1865, under the Queensland Turf Club, which was founded in 1863 by a group of 53 sportsmen. The training facilities include two turf tracks, a wood-fiber track, a sand track, two exercise rings, and an equine swimming pool. The main turf track is approximately 2,026 meters with a single chute. Horses race clockwise and must navigate a slight uphill climb heading for the finish line. During World War II, Eagle Farm was used as a military base by both Australian and United States troops. For those five years, the Queensland Turf Club held race meetings at Albion Park.

Flemington

A breathtaking course with Melbourne's skyline as a backdrop, Flemington has been hosting racing since 1840, and the Melbourne Cup (Aus-G1), its famed stakes race at about two miles on the first Tuesday of November, is treated as a national holiday. On the morning of the Melbourne Cup, a service held at St. Francis's Church is followed by a carnival on Burke Street, Melbourne's central thoroughfare. Up to 100,000 spectators fill Flemington on Melbourne Cup day to celebrate the stakes first run in 1861. The winner of the first Melbourne Cup, Archer, was reported to have walked more than 500 miles from his stable in New South Wales to enter the race. In 1930, *Phar Lap won the race after surviving an attempt on his life while training at Flemington. He was hidden in the ensuing days, arrived at the track just minutes before post time, and won the race in a canter. The legendary runner is honored by a bronze statue outside an entrance into the track. Flemington also holds the Victoria Derby (Aus-G1), first run in 1855 and the oldest established race in Australia. The left-handed, 2,300-meter turf course has a 1,200-meter straight chute.

Moonee Valley

Located less than four miles from central Melbourne, Moonee Valley was founded by William Samuel Cox in 1883. The Cox Plate (Aus-G1), Australia's most important weight-for-age race, is run at Moonee Valley one week before the Melbourne Cup at Flemington. First run in 1922, the Cox Plate was won by *Phar Lap in '30 and '31. In a historic running of the Cox Plate in 1986, Bonecrusher edged fellow New Zealand champion Our Waverley Star by a neck. Moonee Valley offers a wide range of amenities, including a 1,000-seat dining room, glass-enclosed dining boxes, 20 bars, and electronic gaming machines, which were added in 1992. The 1,800-meter, left-handed course is more rectangular than oval, with very sharp turns and short straights, putting a high premium on agility and speed. It is intersected by a diagonal straight course. Inside the main course are hurdle and steeplechase courses.

Randwick

Home of the Australian Jockey Club, Randwick has held racing since 1860, when the club relocated from Homebush. The inaugural running of the Australian Jockey Club St. Leger (Aus-G2) was held in 1841 at Homebush but was moved to Randwick when the track opened. The first AJC Derby (Aus-G1) was run in 1861. The Sydney Cup (Aus-G1) was first contested in April 1865. Randwick,

which is close to Sydney, holds racing festivals in both the spring at the start of October and in the fall in April. The major stakes in the spring is the Metropolitan (Aus-G1) at 2,600 meters. The AJC Derby, Doncaster Handicap (Aus-G1), and Queen Elizabeth Stakes (Aus-G1) are contested in the fall. Randwick's 2,218-meter course with four chutes circles an infield lake and is considered one of the most demanding in Australia.

Rosehill

Located about 14 miles west of Sydney, Rosehill frequently is called Sydney's garden course and is home to Australia's premier race for two-year-olds, the 1,200-meter Golden Slipper Stakes (Aus-G1), first contested in 1957. The beautifully landscaped track was constructed on the land of Australia's most historic agricultural property, Elizabeth Farm, and major festivals are held in both the spring and autumn. The about 2,000-meter course features a 400-meter straight. Races of 1,200 meters (approximately six furlongs) start in the center of the course and traverse a long bend into the straight. Training facilities include Equitrack, grass, sand, and cinder training tracks with stabling available adjacent to the track.

Brazil

Cidade Jardim

Just minutes from downtown São Paulo, Cidade Jardim offers year-round turf and dirt racing on left-handed courses. Cidade Jardim opened January 25, 1941, after Brazilian racing officials deemed Mooca, the track in the center of São Paulo, too small and too crowded. Today, Cidade Jardim is a sprawling facility that houses many important Brazilian racing authorities, including the *Stud-Book Brazileiro*. Cidade Jardim's main turf course is an about 2,000-meter oval with a dirt course of about 1,800 meters. Cidade Jardim also encompasses a training center with two dirt training tracks, a stud farm, and an exhibition center for cultural and scientific activities.

La Gávea

With the Statue of Christ the Redeemer atop Corcovado Mountain in Rio de Janeiro serving as a dramatic backdrop, La Gávea is located adjacent to Lake Rodrigo de Freitas. An outer, 2,120-meter turf course rings a 2,036-meter dirt track with two separate turns out of the home straight. Though racing was conducted in Brazil as early as 1825, betting was not allowed until '72. In that year, the Jockey Club Brazileiro was formed, which led to the opening of La Gavea. La Gavea's spring season in October and November features the Gran Premio Linneo de Paula Machado (Brz-G1), among other stakes. Racing is held year-round on Saturdays and Sundays.

England
Aintree

Located a short distance from Liverpool, Aintree is home to the world's best-known steeplechase race, the Grand National, a 4½-mile marathon over 30 tall, testing fences in early April. The Grand National was first run at Aintree in 1839, when the striking bay Lottery won the third running of a race known then as the Grand Liverpool Steeplechase, which was held at another site in its first two years.

In the 1990s, animal-rights protests forced the taming of the 2¼-mile Grand National Course's more terrifying fences. Most notable was the filling of Becher's Brook, named for Captain Martin Becher, who fell at its tall fence and tumbled into the creek after his mount allegedly was impeded by Lottery. The Chair, one of two obstacles on the 16-fence course that are jumped only once, stands 5' 2" tall, and its landing side is higher than the takeoff side. As many as 40 horses can start in the Grand National, but in 2001 heavy rains, deep ground, and numerous mishaps led to only four horses finishing the course. Two of them, including 2000 winner Papillon, were remounted after losing their riders.

Ascot

Host of the traditional, four-day Royal Meeting in June as well as racing throughout the year in both National Hunt and flat divisions, Ascot is owned by Queen Elizabeth II. Queen Anne marked the course out in Windsor Park, and racing began there in August 1711. The National Hunt course was added in 1965. The Royal Meeting begins with the queen and her royal party driving down the straight mile in horse-drawn carriages to the applause of the crowd, with the men sporting top hats and morning suits and the women wearing elegant hats. Traditionally, the first race is the Queen Anne Stakes (Eng-G2), and the 23 races that follow offer a wide variety of competition from sprinters to stayers. No Ascot race is more demanding than the 2½-mile Ascot Gold Cup (Eng-G1), first run in 1807. The St. James's Palace Stakes (Eng-G1), the King George VI and Queen Elizabeth Stakes (Eng-G1), the King Edward VII Stakes (Eng-G2), the Queen Elizabeth II Stakes (Eng-G1), the Coronation Stakes (Eng-G1) for fillies, and the Meon Valley Stud Fillies' Mile (Eng-G1) are among Ascot's most definitive events. The flat course at Ascot is a right-handed triangular oval of 1¾ miles with two mile chutes. Ascot, which was previously held in a private trust, underwent a $140-million renovation in 2002.

Cheltenham

Located in the Cotswolds in west-central England, Cheltenham is a stunning racecourse that is host each March to the National Hunt Festival, which features the Cheltenham Gold Cup and Champion Hurdle Stakes, championship races for their

respective divisions. The 2001 Cheltenham festival was canceled because of the foot-and-mouth disease outbreak that winter, but in most years the festival is standing room only. The first Gold Cup was held in 1819 as a three-mile flat race on Cleeve Hill, which overlooks the current course. When crowds grew to 50,000, a grandstand was constructed, but it was torn down when an antigambling sentiment swept the area in the 1820s. Racing was re-established at the current site in Prestbury Park in 1831, but there was no racing in Cheltenham from the 1840s through the '90s. Barry Bingham purchased the course, refurbished it, built a new grandstand and running rails, and launched the festival in 1902 as a two-day event. A third day was added in 1923. The Gold Cup was reinstituted the next year, and three years later the Champion Hurdle was added. Cheltenham has separate, left-handed steeplechase and hurdle courses, with a testing, uphill run to the finish post. Among the heroes of Cheltenham are Dorothy Paget's Golden Miller, who won five consecutive runnings of the Gold Cup (1932-'36), and trainer Michael Dickinson, who saddled the first five finishers in the 1983 Gold Cup.

Doncaster

Home of the final leg of the English Triple Crown, the St. Leger Stakes (Eng-G1) in September, Doncaster has hosted racing since 1778. Doncaster runs flat and jump races on separate courses. The pear-shaped, left-handed main course is nearly two miles in circumference. The St. Leger meeting begins with the filly version of the St. Leger Stakes, the Park Hill Stakes (Eng-G3). The Doncaster Cup (Eng-G3), first run in 1766 and the oldest race still run by the Jockey Club, the Champagne Stakes (Eng-G2), May Hill Stakes (Eng-G3), and the Flying Childers Stakes (Eng-G2) for two-year-olds precede the St. Leger, the oldest of the English classics and named for popular local sportsman Lt. Col. Anthony St. Leger. Winners of the St. Leger Stakes include Hambletonian in 1795, Champion (the first horse to win the Epsom Derby and St. Leger Stakes) in 1800, and West Australian, who became the first Triple Crown winner 53 years later. Nijinsky II became the most recent English Triple Crown winner in 1970. The Racing Post Trophy (Eng-G1) is Doncaster's most significant juvenile race.

Epsom

Thoroughbreds have been racing at Epsom, 15 miles south of London in Surrey, for more than 350 years. In 1648, a party of Royalists held races there, and the first recorded race meet was in 1661 on Banstead Downs, which is part of Epsom Downs. The jewel of the racing year is the Epsom Derby (Eng-G1), which traditionally had been run on the first Wednesday in June but now has been moved successfully to the Saturday five weeks after the Two Thousand Guineas (Eng-G1) at Newmarket

on the first Saturday of May. First run in 1780, one year after the initial running of the Epsom Oaks (Eng-G1), the 1½-mile Derby is the middle leg of the English Triple Crown. Epsom has other important stakes during its season, with meets beginning in April and concluding in September of each year. The major races include the Coronation Cup (Eng-G1) and the Diomed Stakes (Eng-G3). The course features a downhill run to the final turn, the world-famous Tattenham Corner, and an uphill pull to the finish.

Goodwood

Located amid rolling countryside on Sussex Downs 60 miles southwest of London, Goodwood traces its history to the Duke of Richmond, who first hosted racing on his estate in 1802. The fifth Duke of Richmond improved the quality of racing at Goodwood by making it part of the English social circuit, a task made easier by the development of a railroad network to transport horses and racegoers to the estate. The about one-mile Sussex Stakes (Eng-G1), the about two-mile Goodwood Cup (Eng-G2), the six-furlong Richmond Stakes (Eng-G2), and the 1¼-mile Nassau Stakes (Eng-G1) for fillies and mares are the major races of the annual July meeting, though racing is also held in May, June, August, and October. Goodwood also is host of the Celebration Mile Stakes (Eng-G2) at the end of August. Goodwood has a skewered figure-eight, right-handed course with a six-furlong straight that allows horses to finish in front of Goodwood's restaurant atop the grandstand.

Newbury

Located west of London, Newbury has its own railway station just yards from the attractive left-handed racecourse. The course measures more than 1¾ miles with a slightly undulating straight mile ideal for galloping.

Fifteen days of flat racing extend from April through October, and steeplechase meets are run there during the colder months. Its major flat races include the one-mile Juddmonte Lockinge Stakes (Eng-G1), and its premier race over fences is the Hennessy Cognac Gold Cup.

Newbury, which opened in 1905, resulted from a chance meeting between well-known trainer John Porter and King Edward VII. It quickly became known as one of the country's best courses, but the course has been pressed into other duties during wartime. Newbury was requisitioned during World War I and was used for troops, supplies, tank testing and repair, and as a prisoner of war camp. In World War II, the track became a major American base and prisoner of war camp.

Racing resumed on April 1, 1949, and now features elegant surroundings, including a sky-lighted "Long Bar" overlooking the track on the first floor and 41 private boxes. The New Grandstand, which

opened to the public in November 2000, features several exhibition spaces as well as conference rooms for up to 1,000 delegates. The course also features an 18-hole, par 71 golf course and a 20-bay driving range. A leisure center with a swimming pool and gymnasium also are on the property.

Newmarket

Newmarket is the headquarters of British racing, and its racecourse is a fitting complement to the training gallops to the east of the course. An observer once said: "Newmarket is one of the only places where a man can go racing; elsewhere he merely goes to the races, which isn't the same thing at all." Racing has been held at Newmarket, a Suffolk town 60 miles northeast of London, for more than 350 years. Newmarket's racing spans the entire British flat season, with the spring season featuring the year's first classics, the Two Thousand Guineas (Eng-G1) and One Thousand Guineas (Eng-G1), down its one-mile Rowley Mile Course on the first weekend in May. In the fall, the Champion Stakes (Eng-G1), Cheveley Park Stakes (Eng-G1), Middle Park Stakes (Eng-G1), and Dewhurst Stakes (Eng-G1) are contested across the flat, a ten-furlong straight that includes the Rowley course. Longer races, such as the rich Cesarewitch Handicap over 2¼ miles, require the use of a ten-furlong extension of the Rowley Mile in a backward, L-shape configuration that extends through the ancient "Devil's Dike." Between those spring and fall events, racing is conducted on the July Course, a straight that connects to the Rowley course. The July Cup (Eng-G1) is the major July stakes. Though Charles I decided Newmarket would be an ideal place to race his horses, his son, Charles II, created the course and named the straight mile after his horse. In 1665, he founded the Newmarket Town Plate, a race that is still contested in a different form. With its uphill finish and no turns, Newmarket is a severe test of stamina.

Sandown Park

Only 14 miles south of central London, Sandown Park opened in 1875 and was the first totally enclosed racecourse in the country. The course was the brainchild of Lt. Col. Owen Williams, and his brother, Hwfa (pronounced "Hoofer"), was instrumental in Sandown Park's development, serving as chairman and clerk of the course for 50 years. The grandstand, rebuilt in 1973 for approximately $5-million, sits on a hill overlooking the racecourse. The right-handed, 1⅜-mile course includes a downhill run to the back straight and a substantial uphill pull to the homestretch. A five-furlong, uphill straight course runs through the main course. Sandown Park's major stakes race is the about 1¼-mile Eclipse Stakes (Eng-G1) in July. It was first run in 1886 and, at the time, was

the country's richest stakes race. In the spring, Sandown features the Whitbread Gold Cup, the National Hunt season's final major race over steeplechase fences. Flat racing is held in short meets from late April through the beginning of October. A $33.4-million renovation of the grandstand was completed in early 2002.

York

Referred to by many as England's Ascot of the North, York is home to the popular Ebor Festival in mid-August at the Knavesmire, common land 20 minutes from the city of York that has featured racing since 1731. The wide horseshoe-shaped, two-mile, unenclosed course has a 4½-furlong straight after a left-handed turn. Two separate chutes are used for sprints of six and seven furlongs. York came to prominence in 1767 when the Gimcrack Club was founded to honor the champion Gimcrack, who won 26 races between 1764 and '71. The club members organized the York meeting to attract the best horses to the North, and by the 1840s the August meeting featured the Ebor Handicap, Yorkshire Oaks (Eng-G1), and the Gimcrack Stakes (Eng-G2). The Nunthorpe Stakes (Eng-G1) was added in 1903. In 1851, one of the most famous match races in Turf history pitted Epsom Derby winners The Flying Dutchman and Voltigeur, who had inflicted the former's only loss the previous year in the Doncaster Cup. More than 100,000 fans turned out to see the rematch, won by The Flying Dutchman. More than a century later, the Benson & Hedges Gold Cup (Eng-G1), now known as the Juddmonte International Stakes, was created to match two champions of the 1970s, Mill Reef and Brigadier Gerard. Mill Reef broke down before the race, but John Galbreath's Epsom Derby (Eng-G1) victor, Roberto, handed Brigadier Gerard his only career defeat and set a course record.

France
Chantilly

Racing at Chantilly, a village approximately 20 miles north of Paris, is held every June in front of the palatial Les Grandes Ecuries (literally, "the big stables") and the Chateau de Chantilly. The palatial stables were built by the Prince de Condé, who believed he would be reincarnated as a horse. The estate includes a lavish stable that can house 250 horses. Chantilly, surrounded by woods, lakes, and 250 acres of greenery, also serves as France's principal training center, with as many as 100 trainers and 3,000 horses using its sand, all-weather, and turf training tracks. Chantilly's premier races are the 2,400-meter Prix du Jockey-Club (Fr-G1), first run in 1836 and popularly known as the French Derby, for three-year-olds, and the 2,100-meter (1⅝-mile) Prix de Diane (French Oaks) (Fr-G1) for three-year-old fillies, begun in 1841.

Deauville

Deauville, sometimes referred to as the Saratoga of France, held its first meet in 1864, the same year as Saratoga Race Course's first meet. It runs a short meeting in August, as Saratoga did for decades, and also features a major sale of yearlings, as does Saratoga. Deauville was founded by the Duke of Morny to cater to Parisian society vacationing on the Normandy coast. The setting allows horses to gallop on the beach or in the surf. There is also polo in the afternoons and the casino in the evenings for entertainment, as well as innumerable first-rate restaurants. Deauville offers a top-class, about one-mile stakes, the Prix du Haras de Fresnay-le-Buffard Jacques Le Marois (Fr-G1), and the about six-furlong Prix Morny (Fr-G1) for two-year-olds. Deauville is a right-handed course of 2,200 meters with a 1,600-meter chute on one end and a short chute on the other. Another stakes, the Grand Prix de Deauville (Fr-G2), is held on the last Sunday of the meeting.

Longchamp

Emperor Napoleon III traveled by boat on the Seine River to attend Longchamp's first day of racing on April 27, 1857, and he was joined at the Paris track by nearly 10,000 countrymen. Finishing second in the first of five races that afternoon was Miss Gladiateur, the dam of Gladiateur, who became a legend as the first French-bred horse to win the Epsom Derby. For Gladiateur's first start after the English classic, 150,000 racegoers turned out to watch him win the Grand Prix de Paris (now a Group 1 race) at Longchamp.

But the race for which Longchamp is best known is the Prix de l'Arc de Triomphe (Fr-G1), first contested in 1920. Horses from both England and Italy took on France's best, and the first winner was Comrade, owned and bred by Frenchman Evremond de Saint-Alary, trained in England by Peter Gilpin, and ridden by Australian jockey Frank Bullock. The 2,400-meter race on the first Sunday in October was an instant international success and has become Europe's championship race.

Other Longchamp stakes have longer histories. The Grand Prix de Paris was inaugurated in 1863 and for a century was France's most important race for three-year-olds. Following the modern trend, its distance was reduced from 3,000 meters to 2,000 meters in 1987. The first classics of each year, the about one-mile Poule d'Essai des Poulains (French Two Thousand Guineas) (Fr-G1) and Poule d'Essai des Pouliches (French One Thousand Guineas) (Fr-G1) for three-year-olds and three-year-old fillies, respectively, are run in May. The Poule d'Essai des Poulains was first run in 1840, while the Poule d'Essai des Pouliches debuted in 1883. Longchamp's right-handed course has a long and testing homestretch with a slightly uphill finish.

Maisons-Laffitte

Secluded near the Saint-Germain forest just west of Paris and home to some 1,800 Thoroughbreds conditioned by more than 80 trainers, Maisons-Laffitte offers one of Europe's most pleasant settings for Thoroughbred racing. Its 2,000-meter straight course, rivaled only by the Rowley Mile at Newmarket in England, is complemented by both right- and left-handed courses to accommodate 35 racing dates from the end of March until the end of July and from early September through early December.

The Prix Robert Papin (Fr-G2) is the first major stakes for two-year-olds each year, while other juvenile stakes, such as the Criterium de Maisons-Laffitte (Fr-G2), are run later in the meet. Among the course's races for two-year-old fillies is the Prix Miesque (Fr-G3), named for the outstanding filly who won two North American championships with her triumphs in the 1987 and '88 Breeders' Cup Mile (G1).

Miesque won the Prix Imprudence at Maisons-Laffitte immediately before her victory in the 1987 One Thousand Guineas (Eng-G1). Among the other champions who have raced at Maisons-Laffitte are *Sea-Bird, Nureyev, Arctic Tern, *Match II, Exbury, and Relko.

Set on more than 120 acres, Maisons-Laffitte is home to the Museum of the Racecourse, which was opened in 1990 and allows fans to review the history of racing by walking through magnificent rooms of an ancient castle.

Saint-Cloud

The most frequently used Parisian track, Saint-Cloud hosts racing from February through July and then from September through December. Its history extends to 1901 when the Societe du Demi-Sang was thrown out of Vincennes by the army and retreated to a strip of land owned by Edmond Blanc to continue racing. After World War I, the course was given to the Societe Sportive d'Encouragement, which supervised Thoroughbred racing at Maisons-Laffitte. The major stakes at Saint-Cloud is the Grand Prix de Saint-Cloud (Fr-G1), which began in 1904 under the name Prix du President de la Republique. *Sea-Bird, fellow Arc winners Rheingold and Sagace (Fr), and Epsom Derby winners Relko and Teenoso all won races at Saint-Cloud, which also was the site of *Vaguely Noble's lone three-year-old defeat.

The inaugural running of the Criterium International (Fr-G1) was won by Act One in 2001. The new stakes was introduced after the distance of the Grand Criterium (Fr-G1) at Longchamp was changed from 1,600 meters to 1,400 meters. Saint-Cloud's left-handed, 2,200-meter course is dissected by a 600-meter straight.

Germany
Baden-Baden

Set among the foothills of the Black Forest nine miles northwest of Baden-Baden, Baden-Baden Racecourse was the idea of Edouard Bénazet, who offered visitors to the world-famous spa not only Thoroughbred racing but also a casino. When the casino closed in 1872, racing was taken over by the Internationale Club, which today supervises racing in short meets from May through June and from August through September. The nearby attractions include a casino, the vineyards of Rebland, Old Town, theaters, concerts and elegant boutiques. Baden-Baden hosts the Grosser Preis von Baden (Ger-G1) and the Grosser Mercedes-Benz Preis (Ger-G2). The three overlapping, left-handed courses at Baden-Baden are named Old Course, New Course, and Straight Course.

Hamburg

Hamburg is the home of the Deutsches Derby (Ger-G1), a 2,400-meter race for three-year-olds first contested in 1869 under the management of the Hamburger Renn-Club. Hamburg's other major stakes include the Hansa-Preis (Ger-G2) at 2,100 meters, the Deutscher Herold-Preis (Ger-G3) at the same distance, and the 1,200-meter Holsten-Trophy (Ger-G3). The racetrack is about six miles from Hamburg and is accessible by the motorway to Berlin, the subway, and the bus. Racing is conducted from the end of June through early July over a right-handed turf course of approximately 2,000 meters.

Hong Kong
Happy Valley

Surrounded today by Hong Kong's towering buildings, Happy Valley was built on reclaimed marshland and has held racing since 1846. Training horses is not easy on the 31-square-mile island, now under the control of the People's Republic of China, but the rich purses attract horsemen whose runners are housed in high-rise stables. Overshadowed by Sha Tin, Happy Valley conducts a 60-day racing season that lasts from September through June.

Sha Tin

In 1959, Sir John Saunders, then chairman of the Royal Hong Kong Jockey Club, proposed creating a racetrack in Sha Tin Bay to alleviate overcrowding at Happy Valley. After three years of planning, the project of reclaiming 250 acres from the bay was begun. The 14,000 cubic feet of soil needed was taken from the top of one of the nearby mountains, allowing development of that property and financing the cost of the track.

Working round the clock on a tight, three-year schedule, Sha Tin opened as planned on October 7, 1978, with an expansive grandstand that encompasses 16½ acres. A 1,900-meter turf course encircles an all-weather dirt track. Sha Tin's major races are the Hong Kong Derby for four-year-olds, run every February at the start of the Chinese New Year since 1990, the Hong Kong Cup (HK-G1), the Hong Kong Vase (HK-G1), the Hong Kong Mile (HK-G1), and the Hong Kong Sprint (HK-G2).

Ireland
The Curragh

According to legend, St. Bridget was offered as much of the Curragh plain as she could cover with her cloak. Unfurling the cloak from her shoulder, she threw it to cover the whole plain of Kildare. When she gathered her cloak up, the land was covered in the richest and deepest grass imaginable—ideal for training and racing Thoroughbreds. Match races have been held there for centuries. The first recorded one was in 1634 when the Earl of Ormond beat Lord Digby in a four-mile race. The first race recorded at the Curragh was in 1741, and the first Irish Derby (Ire-G1) was held in 1866. By 1921, all five Irish classic stakes were contested at the Curragh. Joining the race were the Irish Oaks (Ire-G1), the Irish St. Leger (Ire-G1), the Irish Two Thousand Guineas (Ire-G1), and the Irish One Thousand Guineas (Ire-G1). Located 30 miles west of Dublin, the Curragh offers race meets from mid-March to the beginning of November. The horseshoe-shaped, right-handed course is two miles in length with an uphill, straight run-in of three furlongs to the finish line.

Leopardstown

Roughly six miles from Dublin, Leopardstown overcame a troubled past. Nine years after its opening in 1888, the five-furlong course was found to be only 4½ furlongs long. Capt. George Quin, who headed a syndicate that had purchased the course, constructed a new five-furlong course that was not well received. Finally, Richard "Boss" Croker, owner of 1907 Irish Derby and Epsom Derby winner Orby, purchased additional land and a larger course was constructed. Leopardstown was owned by Fred Clarke until he sold the track to the Irish Racing Board in 1967. Two years later, Leopardstown received an extensive facelift, reopening in 1971 with a new grandstand, an enclosed betting hall, new dining and bar facilities, and a new stable area. Another renovation in 1988 extended the grandstand and added 16 private boxes. Race meets are held at Leopardstown from mid-March through mid-November over a left-handed turf course of about 2,800 meters. Leopardstown's premier race is the Irish Champion Stakes (Ire-G1). Because of construction on an adjacent motorway, Leopardstown could not con-

duct five-furlong races in 2002. As a result, the Phoenix Stakes (Ire-G1), Phoenix Sprint Stakes (Ire-G3), and Flying Five Stakes (Ire-G3) were moved to the Curragh, and the Matron (Ire-G3) and Desmond Stakes (Ire-G3) were moved from the Curragh to Leopardstown.

Italy
Capannelle
Less than eight miles from the Colosseum in Rome, Capannelle opened in 1926. The grandstand, turf course, and interior dirt course are close to an ancient Roman aqueduct and are not far from St. Peter's Basilica in the Vatican. Race meets are held from March to mid-June and from September through November over right-handed turf and sand courses that are slightly uphill near the start and slightly downhill near the finish. National Hunt races also are contested here. Top stakes include the Premio Presidente della Repubblica (Ity-G1) for four-year-olds and up, the Derby Italiano (Ity-G1) for three-year-olds, and the Premio Roma (Ity-G1) for three-year-olds and older. Capannelle's training facilities include 2,600-meter turf and dirt tracks, another turf course inside them, and a 1,200-meter sand track around the stabling area.

San Siro
Racing began at San Siro in 1888 on a racecourse designed by architect Giulio Valerio. In 1909, a training center was added to the facility located just north of downtown Milan. Today, some 200 acres of training grounds include two turf tracks, two sand tracks, and a nearby all-weather track. San Siro's racecourse consists of three right-handed, overlapping turf courses of 2,800, 2,000, and 1,800 meters. Race meets are held from mid-March through July and from September to mid-November. Its premier races are the Oaks d'Italia (Ity-G1) for three-year-old fillies, the Gran Criterium (Ity-G1) for two-year-olds, and the Gran Premio di Milano (Ity-G1) and the Premio del Jockey Club (Ity-G1) for three-year-olds and up.

Japan
Hanshin
The newest of the Japan Racing Association's four major tracks, Hanshin opened in 1949 and is about 12 miles from Osaka. Hanshin completed an extensive modernization in 1991 and races from March through June and in September and December. A lush, wide, right-handed turf course—slightly downhill in the backstretch and slightly uphill in the homestretch—encircles a dirt track.

On the second Sunday in April, Hanshin stages the 1,600-meter Oka Sho (Japan's equivalent of the one-mile One Thousand Guineas [Eng-G1]), named for the cherry blossom in bloom at that time each year. Other major stakes include the all-age Grand

Prix Takarazuka Kinen in mid-June and the Hanshin Sansai Himba Stakes in early December for two-year-old fillies.

Kyoto
Another of the major Japan Racing Association tracks, Kyoto Racecourse is located six miles south of Kyoto and stages racing in January, February, April, May, October, and November over a 1,900-meter, right-handed turf course that is uphill in the backstretch. Enclosed within the main course is a dirt course, an inner turf course, and a huge lake. A mammoth walking ring allows thousands of fans to see horses prepare for their race. The Spring Tenno Sho (Emperor's Cup) is a 3,200-meter endurance stakes for four-year-olds and older held on the last Sunday in April. In November, three major stakes are held on successive Sundays: the 3,000-meter Kikuka Sho (Japanese St. Leger) for three-year-olds, the final leg of the Japanese Triple Crown; the 2,400-meter Queen Elizabeth Cup, which is the concluding race of the Japanese filly triple crown; and the 1,600-meter Mile Championship.

Tokyo
Home of Japan's premier race, the Japan Cup (Jpn-G1), Tokyo Racecourse at Fuchu, 15 miles west of Tokyo, was built in 1933. The 1,878-meter interior dirt course is based on the design of American courses but is uniquely fine-tuned to handle Japan's heavier precipitation. The track is packed firmly with a layer of mountain sand and covered with loose river sand, giving horses a strong bottom underneath and a surface on top to absorb impact and ease stress on their legs. The undulating turf course is 2,116 meters. The Japan Cup, which is run left-handed on turf at 2,400 meters, begins on a 400-meter straight run that minimizes the impact of poor post position. Horses either bred in Japan or imported there prior to racing took the top seven spots in the 2001 $2-million Japan Cup Dirt, while Japanese horses finished first through fifth in the '01 Japan Cup. Kurofune, a three-year-old Kentucky-bred son of French Deputy, won the second running of the Japan Cup Dirt before a crowd of 92,599 on November 24, 2001, defeating Lido Palace (Chi), winner of the 2001 Whitney Handicap (G1) and Woodward Stakes (G1), who finished eighth. The next day, another Japanese three-year-old, Jungle Pocket, edged defending champion T.M. Opera O, the world's richest Thoroughbred, by a neck in the 21st running of the Japan Cup before 115,196 fans. Attendance for both races was up despite a major renovation of the grandstand that will force the two stakes to be held at Nakayama in 2002. The Japan Racing Association operates both Tokyo Racecourse and Nakayama, 12 miles east of Tokyo.

New Zealand
Ellerslie

Several of New Zealand's 21 Group 1 races are held at Ellerslie, including the New Zealand Derby (NZ-G1) and the Easter Handicap (NZ-G1). The track, approximately five miles from New Zealand's largest city, Auckland, boasts an elegant grandstand and beautifully maintained grounds. Racing was first conducted about one mile from Ellerslie on January 5, 1842, but the present site was not used until May 25, 1874, a national holiday to observe Queen Victoria's birthday. Ellerslie's major stakes are held from December 26 through January 2 and during the first week in June. The main track is a 1,870-meter, right-handed turf course with a finishing straight of 380 meters that is slightly downhill.

Trentham

Located about 20 miles north of New Zealand's capital city, Wellington, Trentham was founded in 1870, not long after the city itself was built. Trentham's figure-eight steeplechase course is ringed by a wide, 2,000-meter turf course with a 450-meter home straight. Its major races include the Wellington Cup Handicap (NZ-G1), the Telegraph Handicap (NZ-G1), and the New Zealand Oaks (NZ-G1). Trentham was home of the country's top yearling sale for more than six decades. In its second year in 1928, the sale included a chestnut colt bought for 160 guineas. Named *Phar Lap, he was sent to Australia and made racing history. In 1988, the sale was shifted north, closer to the major breeding operations in the country.

South Africa
Gosforth Park

Just three miles from downtown Johannesburg, Gosforth Park races from late February to early May. The track, which began racing at the start of the 20th century, is named for the English birthplace of one of its founders, John Wilson, the clerk of the course who was born in Gosforth, a town in Lancashire. Two features of the right-handed, pear-shaped track are its aluminum rail, first installed in 1964, and alternative bends in its turf course. When one of the bends becomes worn, the other one is used while the first one is repaired. Gosforth Park also has an all-weather training track, the Jockey's Academy for aspiring riders, and the National Yearling Sales. Gosforth is home to the South Africa Classic (SAf-G1).

Greyville

Located in a complex that includes a championship golf course, Greyville has conducted racing just outside the city of Durban since 1844. In 1897, the Durban Turf Club took over the track's administration. The 2,000-meter Rothmans July Handicap, the country's most prestigious race, is held on the first Saturday of the month and attracts crowds of up to 60,000. Other major stakes are the South African Guineas (SAf-G1) in May, the South African Fillies Guineas (SAf-G1), and the Daily News Two Thousand (SAf-G1). The right-handed, pear-shaped turf course of about 2,800 meters features tight turns and a straight of nearly 500 meters.

Turffontein

Only two miles south of Johannesburg, Turffontein has been home to racing since 1889, just one year after the first Thoroughbred race was held in the city. While maintaining its traditions, including a Royal Box, Turffontein has been thoroughly modernized. The grandstand, rebuilt in the 1970s, allows a panoramic view of the course, and the Ascot Bar and Lounge, Caradoc Room, and Lawn Enclosure give fans many alternatives for enjoying their day at the races. The course has its own water source, which allows for beautiful lawns, numerous flower gardens, meticulously maintained trees and shrubs, and a bird sanctuary. Racing is conducted mostly on Saturdays on a testing, uphill, right-handed turf course of 2,658 meters. Its single chute allows for a 1,200-meter straight. Turffontein also has a 2,000-meter grass training track and four sand training tracks. The South Africa Derby (SAf-G1), Champion Stakes (SAf-G1), and Horse Chestnut 1600 Stakes (SAf-G1), formerly the President's Cup, are three of Turffontein's biggest races.

United Arab Emirates
Nad al Sheba

Offering the world's richest race, the $6-million Dubai World Cup (UAE-G1), and no betting on any of its races, Nad al Sheba Racecourse is located within the tiny sheikhdom of Dubai in the United Arab Emirates. First laid out in 1986 and resurfaced in 1997 before the third running of the World Cup, the 2,200-meter (1⅜-mile), left-handed dirt course has three chutes. A left-handed turf course inside the dirt course is composed of Bermuda hybrid grass, which thrives in hot and humid climates. Two-time North American Horse of the Year Cigar won the inaugural Dubai World Cup in 1996 to give the stakes instant credibility. Buttressing the 2002 Dubai World Cup on March 23 were the Dubai Duty Free Stakes (UAE-G1), the Dubai Golden Shaheen (UAE-G1), the Dubai Sheema Classic (UAE-G1), the UAE Derby (UAE-G3), and the Godolphin Mile (UAE-G2). The Dubai World Cup Committee pays a wide array of costs for visiting horses competing in Dubai, including roundtrip airfare, feed, bedding, and veterinary treatment.

*See table of conversions from metric to English distances in Reference section on page 586.

International Sire Lists
Earnings by Country for Calendar Year 2001
Argentina

Sire	Strs	Wnrs	SWs	Leading Earner (Earnings)	Total Earnings
Roy	73	42	12	Ice Point ($126,942)	$746,960
Southern Halo	121	68	9	Flirteador ($39,295)	$685,167
Numerous	90	55	7	Miss Cursi ($40,702)	$521,649
Ride the Rails	105	54	2	Kitur ($24,882)	$461,772
Lode	84	43	5	Decencia (Arg) ($62,416)	$459,083
Candy Stripes	101	51	1	Persky ($26,861)	$409,146
Equalize	115	52	0	Maximal ($17,123)	$392,330
Hidden Prize	36	18	2	Second Reality ($213,729)	$370,906
Shy Tom	105	46	4	Renombrado Tom ($30,270)	$362,575
Interprete	79	37	2	Insociable ($48,393)	$345,324

Australia

Sire	Strs	Wnrs	SWs	Leading Earner (Earnings)	Total Earnings
Danehill	187	90	22	Ha Ha ($629,818)	$3,649,808
Rhythm	29	14	3	Ethereal ($2,299,352)	$2,584,127
Zabeel	140	53	6	Don Eduardo ($818,431)	$2,541,254
Royal Academy	149	67	8	Bel Esprit ($536,130)	$1,795,146
Scenic (Ire)	147	66	6	Universal Prince ($335,148)	$1,754,746
Serheed	73	24	1	Northerly ($1,226,956)	$1,594,885
Grand Lodge	110	48	4	Shogun Lodge ($453,432)	$1,387,838
Strategic	87	37	5	Mistegic ($666,039)	$1,382,467
Dehere	113	61	5	Defier ($442,578)	$1,341,109
Canny Lad	131	45	4	Republic Lass ($403,463)	$1,244,143

Brazil

Sire	Strs	Wnrs	SWs	Leading Earner (Earnings)	Total Earnings
Choctaw Ridge	140	61	7	Gregoriano ($53,192)	$471,745
Minstrel Glory	168	77	2	Jukaha ($16,909)	$328,177
Ghadeer	135	62	4	Instant Killer ($16,059)	$303,629
Clackson	111	47	4	Lord Marcos ($28,440)	$274,515
Dodge	78	42	3	Lost Love ($68,983)	$260,916
Roi Normand	89	39	5	Rizzolini ($29,830)	$260,745
Midnight Tiger	116	51	4	Cartoon ($12,285)	$244,036
Irish Fighter	141	60	1	Cachito Mio ($8,594)	$243,125
Fast Gold	140	61	0	House Of Lords ($11,706)	$241,719
Tsunami Slew	96	42	3	Trancaferro ($43,083)	$221,119

Canada

Sire	Strs	Wnrs	SWs	Leading Earner (Earnings)	Total Earnings
Regal Classic	72	39	2	Bristol Pistol ($191,756)	$2,662,826
Bold Executive	68	34	4	Streakin Rob ($239,753)	$2,126,332
Ascot Knight	63	33	3	Queensgate ($138,098)	$1,737,006
Bold Ruckus	28	14	2	Krz Ruckus ($306,911)	$1,536,336
Numerous	22	15	1	Numerous Times ($676,320)	$1,525,632
Matter of Honor	45	27	0	Nikie Your Honor ($181,766)	$1,331,311
War Deputy	62	31	2	Cruel Dawn ($159,774)	$1,290,326
Highland Ruckus	54	28	3	Highland Mood ($212,688)	$1,192,807
Mr. Prospector	6	3	1	Dancethruthedawn ($970,000)	$1,186,319
Friendly Lover	40	21	3	Moonlight Affair ($303,293)	$1,157,779

England

Sire	Strs	Wnrs	SWs	Leading Earner (Earnings)	Total Earnings
Sadler's Wells	105	35	12	Galileo (Ire) ($1,420,087)	$3,977,732
Danehill	85	38	7	Mozart (Ire) ($401,794)	$1,959,878
Machiavellian	55	26	4	Medicean ($580,127)	$1,725,943
Indian Ridge	90	43	6	Cassandra Go ($248,542)	$1,446,730
Grand Lodge	56	23	5	Grandera ($309,163)	$1,061,004

Sire	Strs	Wnrs	SWs	Leading Earner (Earnings)	Total Earnings
Inchinor (GB)	70	26	2	Summoner ($297,176)	$919,886
Rahy	11	5	2	Fantastic Light ($437,800)	$889,280
Selkirk	73	34	5	Independence ($87,163)	$855,615
Rainbow Quest	56	27	5	Millenary ($135,574)	$838,701
Caerleon	50	19	5	Marienbard ($119,620)	$798,865
Darshaan	60	24	5	Dilshaan ($120,246)	$752,553
Spectrum	57	14	2	Golan ($554,051)	$749,456
Polar Falcon	81	38	3	Smart Predator ($83,210)	$747,748
Hernando (Fr)	38	16	2	Mr Combustible ($236,398)	$710,901
Efisio	85	37	2	Riberac ($192,475)	$707,146

France

Sire	Strs	Wnrs	SWs	Leading Earner (Earnings)	Total Earnings
Danehill	46	17	8	Aquarelliste ($700,022)	$1,630,128
Linamix	69	44	5	Vahorimix ($292,764)	$1,412,691
Anabaa	42	22	5	Anabaa Blue ($620,795)	$1,173,894
Exit to Nowhere	89	47	0	Malacca ($49,304)	$1,041,772
Bering (GB)	81	36	4	Baryton ($66,661)	$991,695
Sadler's Wells	56	17	9	Moon Queen (Ire) ($103,621)	$905,069
Kendor	81	37	2	Keltos ($79,090)	$857,170
Bahri	3	1	1	Sakhee ($840,000)	$843,540
Pistolet Bleu (Ire)	65	25	4	Maille Pistol ($112,414)	$797,771
Kaldoun	61	27	1	Victory Sovereign ($84,144)	$749,048

Germany

Sire	Strs	Wnrs	SWs	Leading Earner (Earnings)	Total Earnings
Big Shuffle	110	62	7	Peppershot ($90,090)	$917,838
Dashing Blade	136	62	4	Flying Dash (Ger) ($71,838)	$917,554
Acatenango	64	27	7	Sabiango ($268,108)	$783,197
Monsun	61	34	6	Subiaco ($109,180)	$601,229
Java Gold	27	16	3	Boreal ($415,669)	$548,594
Slip Anchor	12	8	2	Morshdi ($466,100)	$520,496
Platini	106	41	2	Adare Manor ($31,043)	$448,473
Law Society	82	31	2	Anzillero ($135,564)	$446,959
Lando (Ger)	42	24	2	Paolini ($62,427)	$435,326
Lomitas (GB)	71	31	2	Stingray ($30,561)	$403,216

Hong Kong

Sire	Strs	Wnrs	SWs	Leading Earner (Earnings)	Total Earnings
Danehill	44	24	3	Fairy King Prawn ($1,276,237)	$5,549,309
Snippets	16	8	1	Solid Contact ($505,172)	$2,062,013
Housebuster	11	5	0	Electronic Unicorn ($841,436)	$1,667,564
Last Tycoon (Ire)	30	11	0	All The Best ($211,723)	$1,661,729
Marju	16	4	1	Indigenous ($477,881)	$1,552,552
Crafty Prospector	1	1	1	Agnes Digital ($1,307,640)	$1,307,640
Marscay	17	7	1	Smytzer's Da Hall ($350,614)	$1,294,209
Royal Academy	16	5	0	Kenwood Melody ($403,916)	$1,104,418
Chief's Crown	12	6	1	Charming City ($423,824)	$1,096,936
Namaqualand	2	1	1	Sobriety ($1,092,684)	$1,092,684

Ireland

Sire	Strs	Wnrs	SWs	Leading Earner (Earnings)	Total Earnings
Sadler's Wells	71	29	7	Galileo (Ire) ($813,493)	$1,760,633
Rahy	5	2	2	Fantastic Light ($684,259)	$790,211
Danehill	35	16	4	Dress To Thrill ($82,460)	$534,341
Caerleon	18	7	1	Bach (Ire) ($235,390)	$381,875
Indian Ridge	31	10	1	Caumshinaun ($103,863)	$347,220
Woodman	13	4	1	Hawk Wing ($272,310)	$333,786
Spectrum	28	9	1	Marionnaud ($96,906)	$330,763
Erins Isle (Ire)	51	12	0	Affianced (Ire) ($56,083)	$318,505
Definite Article (GB)	6	5	1	Vinnie Roe ($225,852)	$316,276
Danzig	10	6	3	Ishiguru ($101,371)	$312,340

Italy

Sire	Strs	Wnrs	SWs	Leading Earner (Earnings)	Total Earnings
Roi Danzig	82	38	1	Tenero Giacomo ($120,546)	$908,189
Love the Groom	97	45	0	Sweet Groom ($62,963)	$833,537
In the Wings (GB)	29	13	3	Kutub ($238,772)	$815,382
Sikeston	64	30	1	Czar ($86,491)	$719,552
Sri Pekan	27	18	3	Clefairy ($112,461)	$640,601
Slip Anchor	29	15	1	Morshdi ($400,050)	$569,209
Night Shift	47	28	0	Fluxus ($55,213)	$558,629
Danehill	20	12	2	Nil ($100,473)	$536,148
Lycius	41	19	1	Slap Shot ($92,593)	$528,359
Brief Truce	34	22	0	L Erede ($48,907)	$518,556

Japan

Sire	Strs	Wnrs	SWs	Leading Earner (Earnings)	Total Earnings
Sunday Silence	373	177	18	Manhattan Cafe ($3,112,302)	$53,809,008
Tony Bin	207	86	10	Jungle Pocket ($4,487,549)	$26,835,078
Brian's Time	169	72	3	Dantsu Flame ($1,717,628)	$17,041,867
Afleet	181	83	4	Preeminence ($1,119,761)	$16,876,447
Commander in Chief	146	35	4	Regular Member ($1,460,330)	$12,763,700
Fuji Kiseki	159	70	3	Daitaku Riva ($791,912)	$12,727,704
Opera House (GB)	65	18	3	T.M.Opera O ($3,523,028)	$9,714,751
Jade Robbery	163	56	1	Yamakatsu Suzuran ($483,666)	$8,932,471
Forty Niner	103	51	0	Toho Daio ($492,139)	$8,007,081
Danehill	52	21	2	Air Eminem ($1,759,044)	$7,859,057

Puerto Rico

Sire	Strs	Wnrs	SWs	Leading Earner (Earnings)	Total Earnings
Eqtesaad	30	18	2	Estrellero ($363,112)	$864,615
Goldgalliano (Ire)	44	32	1	Wandy's Pride ($85,420)	$729,917
Once Ivor	41	19	1	Borinquen ($98,650)	$491,555
Lord Cardinal	37	24	1	El Siboney ($72,148)	$465,189
Fappiano's Star	26	19	1	Bricola ($92,732)	$443,484

Saudi Arabia

Sire	Strs	Wnrs	SWs	Leading Earner (Earnings)	Total Earnings
Another Review	38	13	7	Msarreb ($52,839)	$268,828
Mirror Black	27	9	5	Najmat Alsaaed ($105,574)	$228,792
Polar Run	21	6	3	Mahari ($38,496)	$147,888
Thoughtless	28	7	2	Mojazif ($31,726)	$112,612
Night Shift	6	1	1	Alaessam ($71,715)	$86,900

United Arab Emirates

Sire	Strs	Wnrs	SWs	Leading Earner (Earnings)	Total Earnings
Fly So Free	1	1	1	Captain Steve ($3,600,000)	$3,600,000
Sunday Silence	2	1	1	Stay Gold ($1,200,000)	$2,400,000
Phone Trick	1	1	1	Caller One ($1,200,000)	$1,200,000
Tour d'Or	1	1	1	Express Tour ($1,200,000)	$1,200,000
Double Bed (Fr)	1	1	1	Jim and Tonic (Fr) ($1,200,000)	$1,200,000
Machiavellian	20	14	1	Street Cry (Ire) ($550,000)	$1,150,829
A.P. Indy	3	2	1	Festival of Light ($623,146)	$749,954
Vettori	1	1	1	Hightori ($657,183)	$657,183
Rahy	7	0	0	Fantastic Light ($400,000)	$593,446
Danehill	3	0	0	Fairy King Prawn ($400,000)	$405,553

Sovereign Awards

Inaugurated in 1975, four years after the Eclipse Awards were instituted, the Sovereign Awards honor the best horses and outstanding individuals in Canadian racing. Administered by the Jockey Club of Canada, Sovereign Awards are presented in ten horse categories, and a Canadian Horse of the Year is selected from the nine racing categories. In addition, a Broodmare of the Year award is presented annually.

Sovereign Awards are awarded to individuals in five categories: owner, breeder, trainer, jockey, and apprentice jockey. In addition, the E. P. Taylor Award of Merit, formerly known as the Man of the Year, is presented in most years. Sovereign Awards are presented in four media categories.

Unlike the Eclipse Awards, for which a horse must make only one start in North America, the Sovereign Awards require a horse to start at least three times in Canada in the current racing year to be eligible.

With Canada's highest-quality racing concentrated in Ontario, the Sovereign Awards commonly go to horses that have raced in that province.

The best of Canada have been honored with Eclipse Awards in the past. Most recently, 1997 Canadian Horse of the Year Chief Bearhart was voted an Eclipse Award as champion turf male. In 1991, Canadian Triple Crown winner Dance

Smartly was honored with an Eclipse Award as champion three-year-old filly, and 1981 Canadian Horse of the Year Deputy Minister was voted champion juvenile male in Eclipse Award voting for that season.

2001 Sovereign Awards

Robert P. Tiller, a trainer who regards himself as a hands-on horseman, walked away with four Sovereign Awards in 2001. In addition to the title as outstanding trainer, Tiller trained Win City, who collected honors as Horse of the Year and outstanding three-year-old male, and Rare Friends, champion two-year-old male.

Win City, a Slew City Slew gelding, won six 2001 stakes, including the Prince of Wales Stakes, middle jewel of the Canadian Triple Crown. He also finished second in the Queen's Plate to Dancethruthedawn, recipient of a Sovereign Award as outstanding three-year-old filly.

In the Horse of the Year balloting, Win City received 99 votes to 71 for Numerous Times, undefeated champion grass male, and 70 for Dancethruthedawn. Sovereign recipients are selected by a panel of sportswriters, broadcasters, and racing officials from across Canada. Horses need not be bred in Canada but must have made at least three starts at Canadian tracks during the year to be eligible.

Tiller, a native of the Netherlands and a 30-

History of the Sovereign Awards

Year	E. P. Taylor Award of Merit†	Owner	Breeder	Trainer	Jockey	Apprentice Jockey
2001	Not awarded	Sam-Son Farms	Sam-Son Farms	Bob Tiller	Patrick Husbands	Chantal Sutherland
2000	Mike Harris	Sam-Son Farms	Sam-Son Farms	Mark Frostad	Patrick Husbands	Cory Clark
1999	George Hendrie	Stronach Stables	Frank Stronach	Mark Frostad	Patrick Husbands	Ben Russell
1998	David Willmot	Stronach Stables	Frank Stronach	Michael Wright Jr.	David Clark	Helen Vanek
1997	Not awarded	Frank Stronach	Frank Stronach	Mark Frostad	Emile Ramsammy	Rui Pimentel
1996	Not awarded	Minshall Farms	Minshall Farms	Barbara Minshall	Emile Ramsammy	Neil Poznansky
1995	Charles Taylor	Frank Stronach	Kinghaven Farms	Danny Vella	Todd Kabel	Dave Wilson
1994	Jack Kenney	Frank Stronach	Kinghaven Farms	Danny Vella	Robert Landry	Dave Wilson
1993	Not awarded	Frank Stronach	Kinghaven Farms	Roger Attfield	Robert Landry	Constant Montpellier
1992	Col. Charles Baker	Knob Hill Stable	Knob Hill Stable	Philip England	Todd Kabel	Stanley Bethley
1991	Ernest Samuel	Sam-Son Farms	Sam-Son Farms	Jim Day	Mickey Walls	Mickey Walls
1990	James Wright	Kinghaven Farms	Kinghaven Farms	Roger Attfield	Don Seymour	Mickey Walls
1989	George C. Frostad	Kinghaven Farms	Kinghaven Farms	Roger Attfield	Don Seymour	Maree Richards
1988	Sandy Hawley	Sam-Son Farms	Sam-Son Farms	Jim Day	Sandy Hawley	Jim McAleney
1987	Larry Regan	Kinghaven Farms	Kinghaven Farms	Roger Attfield	Don Seymour	Jim McAleney
1986	D. G. Willmot	D. G. Willmot	D. G. Willmot	Roger Attfield	Larry Attard	Todd Kabel
1985	George Gardiner	Ernest Samuel	E. P. Taylor	Jim Day	Don Seymour	Nancy Jumpsen
1984	Jim Coleman	Ernest Samuel	Frank Stronach	Mike Doyle	Chris Loseth	Robert King
1983	Joe Thomas	B. K. Yousif	Mr. and Mrs. Russell Bennett	Bill Marko	Larry Attard	Robert King
1982	Jean-Louis Levesque	D. G. Willmot	D. G. Willmot	Bill Marko	Lloyd Duffy	Richard Dos Ramos
1981	Jim Bentley	Dave Kapchinsky	Tom Webb	Ron Brock	Erwin Driedger	Richard Dos Ramos
1980	Jack Stafford	Ernest Samuel	Mr. and Mrs. Marvin Hamilton	Gerry Belanger	Gary Stahlbaum	Valerie Thompson
1979	George C. Hendrie	James Shields	D. G. Willmot	Jim Day	Robin Platts	Ray Creighton
1978	Ron Turcotte	Conn Smythe	Jean-Louis Levesque	F. H. Merrill	Sandy Hawley	Ron Hansen
1977	E. P. Taylor	Bory Margolus	Conn Smythe	Red Smith	Avelino Gomez	Brad Smythe
1976	Jack Diamond	George Gardiner	E. P. Taylor	Lou Cavalaris	Chris Rogers	Chris Loseth
1975	E. P. Taylor	Jack Stafford	Bory Margolus	Gil Rowntree	Hugo Dittfach	Jeff Fell

†Formerly known as Man of the Year

year veteran of the Woodbine backstretch, encouraged owners-breeders Frank DiGiulio and Frank DiGiulio Jr. to change course five years ago and develop their own horses. Win City, bred by the DiGiulios, was a result of that initiative. The elder DiGiulio died early in 2001.

The E. P. Taylor Award of Merit, named for the legendary Canadian breeder and racing-association leader, was not awarded in 2001.

Other award recipients, in addition to Tiller, were:

Sam-Son Farms, outstanding breeder and outstanding owner. The racing and breeding operation begun by the late Ernest Samuel took both titles for the second straight year. With Mark Frostad as its trainer, Sam-Son also collected Sovereign Awards for Dancethruthedawn; Mountain Angel, older female; and Dance Smartly, broodmare of the year.

Patrick Husbands, outstanding jockey. He won the Sovereign Award for the third consecutive year. Through the end of the 2001 Canadian racing season, he had won 145 races from 871 starts and had purse earnings exceeding $8-million.

Chantal Sutherland, outstanding apprentice jockey. She galloped horses at Woodbine while attending Toronto's York University and began riding full time after graduation. She ended the Canadian season with 59 victories from 448 mounts and earnings of $1,966,252.

Horses honored with 2001 Sovereign Awards were:

Horse of the Year
Three-year-old male
WIN CITY, 1998 b. g., Slew City Slew—Winsfordan, by Domasca Dan. 2001 record: 9-6-1-2, $876,187. Career: 11-7-1-2, $909,451. Breeders: Frank DiGiulio and Frank DiGiulio Jr. Owner: Frank DiGiulio Jr. Trainer: Robert P. Tiller. In 2001, won Prince of Wales S., Marine S. (Can-G2), Autumn H. (Can-G3), Col. R. S. McLaughlin H. (Can-G3), Plate Trial S., Queenston S.; 2nd, Queen's Plate S.

Three-year-old filly
DANCETHRUTHEDAWN, 1998 dk. b. br. f., Mr. Prospector—Dance Smartly, by Danzig. Owner and breeder: Sam-Son Farms. Trainer: Mark Frostad. 2001 record: 6-3-1-0, $1,045,039. Career: 10-5-1-1, $1,258,691. In 2001, won Queen's Plate S., Woodbine Oaks; 2nd, Prince of Wales S.

Two-year-old male
RARE FRIENDS, 1999 ch. g., Helmsman—Legion Etrangere, by Carson City. Career: 5-4-0-0, $247,365. Breeder: Gardiner Farms. Owner: Frank DiGiulio Jr. and Robert Tiller. Trainer: Robert Tiller. In 2001, won Swynford S., Vandal S., Simcoe S.

Two-year-old filly
GINGER GOLD, 1999 gr. ro. f., Golden Gear—Gleaming Glory, by Vigors. Career: 4-3-0-1, $362,339. Breeder: Mel Lawson. Owner: Jim Dandy Stable. Trainer: Sid C. Attard. In 2001,

History of the Sovereign Awards

Year	Broodmare of the Year	Two-Year-Old Filly	Two-Year-Old Male	Three-Year-Old Filly	Three-Year-Old Male
2001	Dance Smartly	Ginger Gold	Rare Friends	Dancethruthedawn	Win City
2000	Primarily	Poetically	Highland Legacy	Catch the Ring	Kiss a Native
1999	Sharpening Up	Hello Seattle	Exciting Story	Gandria	Woodcarver
1998	Fleet Courage	Fantasy Lake	Riddell's Creek	Kirby's Song	Archers Bay
1997	Charming Sassafras	Primaly	Dawson's Legacy	Cotton Carnival	Cryptocloser
1996	Amelia Bearhart	Larkwhistle	Cash Deposit	Silent Fleet	Victor Cooley
1995	Sea Regent	Silken Cat	Gomtuu	Scotzanna	Peaks and Valleys
1994	Rainbow Connection	Honky Tonk Tune	Talkin Man	Alywow	Bruce's Mill
1993	Bold Debra	Term Limits	Comet Shine	Deputy Jane West	Peteski
1992	Ballado	Doputy Jano Woot	Truth of It All	Hope for a Breeze	Denburb
1991	Classy 'n Smart	Buckys Solution	Free At Last	Dance Smartly	Bolulight
1990	Shy Spirit	Dance Smartly	Rainbows for Life	Lubicon	Izvestia
1989	Passing Mood	Wavering Girl	Sky Classic	Blushing Katy	With Approval
1988	Polite Lady	Legarto	Mercedes Won	Tilt My Halo	Regal Intention
1987	Arctic Vixen	Phoenix Factor	Regal Classic	One From Heaven	Afleet
1986	Loudrangle	Ruling Angel	Blue Finn	Carotene	Golden Choice
1985	No Class	Stage Flite	Grey Classic	La Lorgnette	Imperial Choice
1984	Friendly Ways	Deceit Dancer	Dauphin Fabuleux	Classy 'n Smart	Key to the Moon
1983	Two Rings	Ada Prospect	Prince Avatar	Northern Blossom	Bompago
1982	Yonnie Girl	Candle Bright	Sunny's Halo	Avowal	Runaway Groom
1981	Native Flower	Choral Group	Deputy Minister	Rainbow Connection	Frost King
1980	Hangin Round	Rainbow Connection	Bayford	Par Excellance	Ben Fab
1979	Fitz's Fancy	Par Excellance	Allan Blue	Kamar	Steady Growth
1978	Fanfreluche	Liz's Pride	Medaille d'Or	La Voyageuse	Overskate
1977	Doris White	L'Alezane	Overskate	Northernette	Dance in Time
1976	Northern Minx	Northernette	Sound Reason	Bye Bye Paris	Norcliffe
1975	Reasonable Wife	Seraphic	Proud Tobin	Momigi	L'Enjoleur

won Natalma S. (Can-G3), Princess Elizabeth S., Shady Well S.

Older male
A FLEETS DANCER, 1995 ch. h., Afleet—My Dream Come True, by Vice Regent. Breeder: OWD Inc. Owner: Cam Allard. Trainer: Roger L. Attfield. 2001 record: 11-3-2-2, $427,487. Career: 38-12-3-6, $936,739. In 2001, won Dominion Day H. (Can-G3), Durham Cup H. (Can-G3); 2nd Washington Park H. (G2).

Older female
MOUNTAIN ANGEL, 1997 ch. f., Mt. Livermore—All An Angel, by Alydar. Owner-breeder: Sam-Son Farms. Trainer: Mark Frostad. 2001 record: 6-4-1-0, $259,977. Career: 11-6-2-0, $418,977. In 2001, won Ontario Matron H.; 2nd Maple Leaf S. (Can-G3).

Turf male
NUMEROUS TIMES, 1997 b. c., Numerous—Dramatical, by Theatrical (Ire). Breeder: Patrick B. Ballentine Estate. Owner: Committee Stable. Trainer: Sid C. Attard. 2001 record: 3-3-0-0, $676,320. Career: 6-6-0-0, $771,960. In 2001, won Atto Mile S. (Can-G1) in course-record 1:32.79.

Turf female
SWEETEST THING, 1998 b. f., Candy Stripes—Escape Reality, by Lear Fan. Breeder: Kingview

Farms. Owners: Michael Canino, William Werner, and P. Canino. Trainer: Roger Attfield. Career: 8-4-2-0, $578,100. In 2001, won Breeders' S.; Wonder Where S.; 2nd Long Island H. (G2).

Sprinter
MR. EPPERSON, 1995 b. g., Cabrini Green—Cut the Twinkle, by The Axe II. Breeder: Hal Snowden Jr. Owners: Richard and Scott Fairlie, Brian Brolley, and Ronald Marlow. Trainer: Scott Fairlie. 2001 record: 9-5-0-1, $430,180. Career: 43-16-5-7, $796,024. In 2001, won Nearctic H. (Can-G2), Highlander H. (Can-G3), Play the King H. (Can-G3).

Broodmare of the Year
DANCE SMARTLY, 1988 dk. b. br. m., Danzig—Classy 'n Smart, by Smarten. Race record: 17-12-2-3, $3,263,835. Bred and owned by Sam-Son Farms. 1991 Canadian Horse of the Year and Canadian Triple Crown winner, Eclipse Award recipient as champion three-year-old filly. Won Breeders' Cup Distaff (G1), Queen's Plate S., Prince of Wales S., Breeders' S., etc. Through 2001, dam of 5 foals, 5 starters, 4 winners, 2 stakes winners, 1 champion. Dam of Scatter the Gold (Mr. Prospector), winner of 2000 Queen's Plate S., Prince of Wales S.; Dancethruthedawn (Mr. Prospector), 2001 champion three-year-old filly, winner of 2001 Queen's Plate, Woodbine Oaks, etc.

History of the Sovereign Awards

Year	Older Female	Older Male	Turf Female†	Turf Male	Sprinter	Horse of the Year
2001	Mountain Angel	A Fleets Dancer	Sweetest Thing	Numerous Times	Mr. Epperson	Win City
2000	Saoirse	One Way Love	Heliotrope	Quiet Resolve	One Way Love	Quiet Resolve
1999	Magic Code	Deputy Inxs	Free Vacation	Thornfield	Deputy Inxs	Thornfield
1998	Santa Amelia	Terremoto	Colorful Vices	Chief Bearhart	Deputy Inxs	Chief Bearhart
1997	Woolloomooloo	Chief Bearhart	Woolloomooloo	Chief Bearhart	Glanmire	Chief Bearhart
1996	Windsharp	Mt. Sassafras	Windsharp	Chief Bearhart	Langfuhr	Mt. Sassafras
1995	Bold Ruritana	Basqueian	Bold Ruritana	Hasten To Add	Scotzanna	Peaks and Valleys
1994	Pennyhill Park	King Ruckus		Alywow	King Ruckus	Alywow
1993	Dance for Donna	Cozzene's Prince		Hero's Love	Apelia	Peteski
1992	Wilderness Song	Rainbows for Life		Rainbows for Life	King Corrie	Benburb
1991	Avant's Gold	Sky Classic		Sky Classic	King Corrie	Dance Smartly
1990	Diva's Debut	Twist the Snow		Izvestia	Twist the Snow	Izvestia
1989	Proper Evidence	Steady Power		Charlie Barley	Mr. Hot Shot	With Approval
1988	Carotene	Play the King		Carotene	Play the King	Play the King
1987	Carotene	Play the King		Carotene	Play the King	Afleet
1986	Bessarabian	Let's Go Blue		Carotene	New Connection	Ruling Angel
1985	Lake Country	Ten Gold Pots		Imperial Choice	Summer Mood	Imperial Choice
1984	Sintrillium	Canadian Factor		Bounding Away	Diapason	Dauphin Fabuleux
1983	Eternal Search	Travelling Victor		Kingsbridge	Fraud Squad	Travelling Victor
1982	Eternal Search	Frost King		Frost King	Avowal	Frost King
1981	Glorious Song	Driving Home		Ben Fab	Eternal Search	Deputy Minister
1980	Glorious Song	Overskate		Overskate	La Voyageuse	Glorious Song
1979	La Voyageuse	Overskate		Overskate		Overskate
1978	Christy's Mount	Giboulee		Overskate		Overskate
1977	Reasonable Win	Norcliffe		Momigi		L'Alezane
1976	Momigi	Victorian Prince		Victorian Prince		Norcliffe
1975	Victorian Queen	Rash Move		Victorian Queen		L'Enjoleur

†1995 marks the first year the award for turf horse to be divided into male and female categories.

Quick Reference Index